American Literature

The Makers and the Making

VOLUME I

American Literature

The Makers and the Making

VOLUME I

Cleanth Brooks R. W. B. Lewis Robert Penn Warren

St. Martin's Press   New York

DOUBLEDAY & COMPANY, INC.: Excerpt from "A True Sight of Sin" by Thomas Hooker, excerpt from "Magnalia Christi Americana" by Cotton Mather, "The Covenant of Grace" by Thomas Shepard, and excerpt from "A Model of Christian Charity" by John Winthrop from *The American Puritans: Their Prose and Poetry.* Copyright © 1956 by Perry Miller. Used by permission of Doubleday & Company, Inc.

DOVER PUBLICATIONS, INC.: Excerpt from "Ornithological Biography (1839)" by John Audubon, from *Audubon the Naturalist* by Francis Hobart Herrick.

FARRAR, STRAUS & GIROUX, INC.: Excerpt from *Homage to Mistress Bradstreet* by John Berryman, copyright © 1956 by John Berryman. Reprinted with the permission of Farrar, Straus & Giroux.

J. FISCHER, BROTHERS: Lyrics for "Bonny Barbara Allen" and "The Hangsman's Tree," from *American Anthology of Old World Ballads,* ed. by Reed Smith, 1937.

GROVE PRESS: George Washington Harris's "Mrs. Yardley's Quilting Party," in *Selected Works,* edited by Brom Weber, Grove Press, 1954.

HARCOURT BRACE JOVANOVICH, INC.: Excerpts from "Mr. Edwards and the Spider" and "After the Surprising Conversions," from *Lord Weary's Castle,* copyright 1944, 1946, by Robert Lowell. Reprinted by permission of Harcourt Brace Jovanovich, Inc. Excerpt from "The Life of William Bradford" by Cotton Mather in *Selections from Cotton Mather,* edited by Kenneth B. Murdock. Copyright © 1960. Reprinted by permission of Harcourt Brace Jovanovich, Inc. and the editor.

HARPER & ROW, PUBLISHERS, INC.: Excerpts from "The Diary of Samuel Sewall (1878–1882)" by Samuel Sewall, "The Day of Doom" by Michael Wigglesworth, and "The Bloudy Tenent of Persecution" by Roger Williams. From *The Puritans: A Sourcebook* of *Their Writings,* Volume I, edited by Perry Miller and Thomas H. Johnson, Harper Torchbook edition. Reprinted by permission.

HARVARD UNIVERSITY PRESS: "To My Dear Children," "The Prologue," "Contemplations," "The Author to Her Book," "Before the Birth of One of Her Children," "To My Dear and Loving Husband," "A Letter to Her Husband," and "Upon the Burning of Our House." Reprinted by permission of the publishers from *The Works of Anne Bradstreet,* edited by Jeannine Hensley. Cambridge, Mass., The Belknap Press of Harvard University Press, Copyright, 1967, by the President and Fellows of Harvard College. Excerpts from "The Secret History of the Line" and "History of the Dividing Line Betwixt Virginia and North Carolina Run in the Year of Our Lord 1728." Reprinted by permission of the publishers from Louis B. Wright, ed., *The Prose Works of William Byrd of Westover.* Cambridge, Mass., The Belknap Press of Harvard University Press, Copyright, 1966, by the President and Fellows of Harvard College.

HILL & WANG, INC.: Excerpts from "Personal Narrative" and "Sinners in the Hands of an Angry God" by Jonathan Edwards, from *Jonathan Edwards: Representative Selections* edited by Clarence H. Faust and Thomas H. Johnson, Copyright 1962. Reprinted by permission.

HOLT, RINEHART AND WINSTON, INC.: Excerpts from "New Hampshire" and "The Gift Outright," from *The Poetry of Robert Frost* edited by Edward Connery Lathem. Copyright 1923, © 1969 by Holt, Rinehart and Winston, Inc. Copyright 1951 by Robert Frost. Reprinted by permission of Holt, Rinehart and Winston, Inc. Excerpt from "The Soveraignty of Goodness and God" by Mary Rowlandson, from *Colonial American Writing,* edited by Roy Harvey Pearce.

Letter to the Reader

A number of years ago the three of us, friends of long standing, came together to plan a textbook on American literature. We set out to read the body of our literature, no small part of it by some of us for the first time, and to try to divest ourselves of preconceptions about it. As we read and reread it and discussed it among ourselves, we constantly discovered new ranges of meaning, new relationships, and new dimensions of interest. In fact, as we worked and talked, our notion of the book kept changing and expanding, and what the book now is we could not have remotely envisaged in our early discussions.

How we began work on this book

We were aware that we represented divergent personalities, interests, and degrees of specialization, but we hoped to make a virtue of these very differences. Different perspectives on an author might produce a portrait more nearly in the round. Somewhat contradictory judgments might not result in mere anemic compromises but might, in fact, stimulate further explorations and new insights. At the very least, our divergences could be mutually corrective: we could hope to eliminate the more obvious errors and the more shallow oversimplifications. But allowing for differences, it was plain that we shared a community of interests within which our occasional disagreements could be contained and might even prove to have positive value.

How shall we describe that community of interests? In the first place, we were not concerned to perpetuate any previously established pattern— nor to set up a new orthodoxy. Our method was inductive, and our mode of working was social; that is, we read and we talked. There was a certain liberation in realizing that we could discover the nature and scale of our book only in the open-ended process of our own explorations.

What we chose and why

From the beginning we had to ask ourselves, in what way was material to justify itself to us for inclusion and discussion? Literary quality would obviously be the primary consideration, but early on we agreed that our book was not to be simply a treasury of masterpieces. It would also concern itself with the origin and development of masterpieces and with the circumstances that might account for the failure, or partial failure, of other works. Thus on occasion we might include a work that we thought was, by absolute literary standards, second or third rate, provided it told us something about the background of some first-rate achievement or about the taste of a period, or had proved politically significant, or illustrated a temptation to which this or that author was peculiarly susceptible.

In addition to the distinction between good and bad work, or significant and insignificant, we were forced, in choosing our materials, to recognize a more radical distinction—the distinction between what one may call "primary" and "secondary" literature. By primary literature we mean writing that was printed and transmitted as formal literary art—in this book mainly fiction and poetry, though we do include three plays. By secondary literature we mean writing that, however "artful," was regarded by the author as an instrument for achieving some extrinsic and nonliterary purpose—works such as essays, letters, travel writing, nature writing, diaries, philosophy, and history; or compositions that have basically survived by oral transmission or at least by reason of something like "folk consciousness."

Though it does seem sensible in a book on American literature to put stress on works that make the formal claim to be literature, we have included a large amount of secondary literature as well, and perhaps we ought to say something about what may strike some readers as an unusual hospitality toward such work. In the first place, it is not always easy to draw a hard and fast line between primary and secondary literature. Works written to serve a nonliterary purpose may also have genuine literary qualities and may even embody a powerful imaginative vision. Jonathan Edwards' "terror sermon" at Enfield, in 1740, was presumably delivered with the aim of bringing his listeners to religious conversion, but present-day readers—whether Christians or not—recognize it as a magnificent artistic creation: and in this book, in fact, we regard it chiefly, though not exclusively, at this level. There are, however, other types of composition, folk materials especially, which, though clearly secondary by reason of origin and transmission, spring basically or in considerable part from the artistic impulse and, as in the case of Appalachian ballads or Negro spirituals and the blues, may achieve great charm or power.

But there is a reason beyond intrinsic value for drawing heavily on secondary literature. It can often throw light on the creation of primary literature and may, in fact, have inspired or nourished it. For example, the muckraking literature of the 1890's can illuminate aspects of Stephen Crane's *Maggie: A Girl of the Streets*; Theodore Dreiser's autobiography can tell us much about the impulse behind his fiction and the personal experiences that he incorporated into it; and behind Mark Twain lies a vast body of folk creation. Secondary literature often represents the raw experience on which the artist worked.

Literature, clearly, does not exist in a vacuum. It feeds on life and life feeds on it. Without a deep awareness of the complex relationship between the two, the reader cannot understand nor, in the full sense, appreciate literature—even literature rigorously contemplated as art. The keenest enjoyment of literature—and the most fruitful study of it—derives from a sense of the continuing dialectic between the formal aspects of art and the raw, undefined, and finally perhaps undefinable reality that is the stuff of art. By "dialectic" we here mean the interplay between the artist's drive toward his special conception of form and meaning and the resistance set up by the qualities, and even by the competing "meanings," of his materials. In one sense, the interplay is a contest between two sets of forces. Even the truly great artist never, perhaps, wins absolutely—or if he does win a particular battle, he never wins the war. The conflict, fought next year and on fresh terrain, will go on and on, for reality is in some sense incorrigible, perhaps never to be fully conquered—fully encompassed and understood. Yet a *Moby-Dick* or *Scarlet Letter* is an individual victory. In our selections of primary literature we have meant to take account of such victories, great and small; but we have also tried to keep alive in the reader's mind—through our selections of secondary literature and through our own critical commentaries, many of which have to do with the writer's background and problems—a sense of the stubborn, cross-grained, and ultimately mysterious reality with which the artist is forced to wrestle.

As we have said, this book has come to be very different from our original notion of it. Though we began by thinking of an anthology with relatively brief introductions and headnotes, we found, as the work proceeded, that this plan would not accommodate a discussion of the urgent issues that kept arising. Eventually we found that we were being driven to write a history, though a history of a very special kind. To begin with, we always remembered that a work of literature is written by an individual, marked by his special personality and personal past, and that the literary work represents in a deep way the writer's attempt to confront and find meaning in his experience. But the individual writer, we also wanted to emphasize, exists in a certain milieu—the political and economic context, the social institu-

How we came to see our book as a "history"

tions, the emotional and intellectual climate; and literature, as we have suggested, represents a continuing dialectic between the individual and his world. Thus, in one perspective at least, our book developed into a history of the American sensibility. But it remains peculiarly a *literary* history in that it characteristically takes into account aesthetic considerations and theories, the growth of literary modes, techniques, and forms, and the changes in literary tastes and fashions. Nor could such a history fail to recall, if only occasionally and sparingly, literary and intellectual currents emanating from Great Britain and Europe.

Yet our concern remained focused, naturally, on the American scene, and we became more and more urgently aware of what may be called thematic continuities in American history, which, in turn, become the basic and recurring themes of American literature. Here is a very informal list: America vs. Europe, relation of the past and the future to the present; East vs. West; the American "mission," the American Eden, and millennialism; apocalypse—the coming horror; the self vs. society, secession vs. unity, private intuition vs. collective wisdom; materialism vs. idealism; technology vs. nature (including human nature); poetry vs. science.

All of this sounds very ambitious and pretentious—even, perhaps, schematic and abstract. But our history is in fact informal and essayistic. It reflects the inductive process of reading, discussing, and working outward from the individual works of literature. Our historical commentary is constantly interrupted by a contemplation of particular poems and pieces of fiction. The reader is thus forced to return again and again, as we were, to the concrete literary documents. These are never merely "illustrations" of historical generalizations. If a literary work has any artistic value it will always reveal itself to be in excess of the historical comment, speaking to the reader in its own mode and living its own life. Though we trust that our commentaries will throw some light on the literature presented here, we are never allowed to forget that the literature presented is also lighting up history—is even changing history. In dealing with literature we have sought, above all, to give a sense of the "thingness" rather than the "aboutness"— we want the sense of "aboutness" in the end to return the reader to a richer experience of the literature itself.

Some critical approaches

In this book we have engaged in several kinds of literary criticism, and they can be best distinguished by referring to the "three R's" of criticism— the writer, the writing, and the reader. In a certain sense, a piece of writing can, indeed, be said to exist in itself, and can be examined more or less in its own terms. But it also exists in a shifting complex of relationships, each of which contributes in a subtle and sometimes mysterious way to the actuality—even the aesthetic actuality—of the work. A work, of course, is created by an individual in his particular evolving world, but it is responded to variously, by readers of widely different backgrounds, and over successive generations. It has, too, its own literary ancestry, but it may, in its turn, exert influence on later work and, even, on general attitudes toward life.

We feel such relationships to be complex rather than simple, dynamic rather than static. As with the biographer's help we learn more about Hemingway's personal life, and with the historian's help more about the epoch he lived through, we may find ourselves perceiving more artistry and more richness of experience in, say, *A Farewell to Arms*. Melville was a good deal ahead of his time, imaginatively and as a literary technician; today *Moby-Dick* is understood so much more fully than it was a century ago that in some real sense it has become a different book. When Emily Dickinson's poems were first published in the 1890's, critical theory and literary taste were simply not ready to cope with them; but developments in criticism in the twenties and thirties of this century, the resulting return to favor of seventeenth-century English metaphysical verse, and a clearer grasp of the American romantic tradition prepared a generation of readers for whom it could almost be said that Dickinson's poetry had at last been born.

To such aspects as these we have tried to do some justice, but they do not exhaust the critical possibilities. There is, for instance, what is known as genre criticism, a mode much in fashion today and in certain quarters brilliantly practiced. In some respects, this approach develops out of formal criticism (which stresses the work, the writing), but genre criticism aims to identify and to define the literary work as a member of a special class rather than to evaluate it for itself. With genre study as a self-enclosed system we ourselves have here little to do; but some discrimination among literary forms has, of course, been an indispensable part of our job. We have pursued the distinction, somewhat anxiously debated in the early nineteenth century, between the "novel" and the "romance"; later, we have traced the ascendancy of romance fiction in the work of Hawthorne and Melville; and we have had a good deal to say about the realistic novel in its various states from Howells through Stephen Crane to Dreiser and beyond. In poetry, "imagism" and "symbolism" demanded discussion, and long ambitious poems, like Eliot's *The Waste Land*, Hart Crane's *The Bridge*, and Archibald MacLeish's *Conquistador*, required some reflection on the traditional epic and its availability as a genre to poets in our time.

As an example of the flexibility of critical treatment we have tried to maintain, take the case of Henry James's "The Jolly Corner." It is a kind of ghost story of 1909 in which a man (after half a lifetime's absence) returns to this country to inspect his property on a "jolly corner" in New York City, and, as he wanders through the house at night, finds that he is stalking a phantom figure who oddly and menacingly seems to resemble him. Immediately preceding the story is an editorial headnote that very briefly combines three different critical perspectives: first, with James's help it identifies the genre of the story—a ghost story of the kind James liked as being akin to the fairy tale; second, it relates the work to James's visit to the United States in 1904–5, his first view of his native country in more than two decades; and third, it offers a few analytic remarks and raises a question or two about the inner movement of the tale.

But the headnote, especially under the second and third topics, simply brings to focus certain issues treated in more detail elsewhere in the section on James. For the second topic, there is considerable biographical material in the general introduction to James, material that will allow the student to locate the story in the larger frame of James's life. He will find there a discussion of James's slowly worked out and fateful decision to expatriate himself and to pursue the life of art in England and on the Continent—an act whose consequences reverberated through the writing of "The Jolly Corner" and beyond it. The biographical account can also help the student to perceive the story as one moment in the unending process by which James sought to understand his own nature. One of the creative motives behind the story is, we suggest, James's deep suspicion that had he remained in America instead of becoming an expatriate he might have succumbed, in some degree at least, to the demoralizing materialism by which, as he saw it, the country was being consumed; and, as the headnote to "The Jolly Corner" indicates, we have provided, in a selection from *The American Scene*, a glimpse of the New York that the returning James found under the spell of rampant and disorderly greed. Furthermore, we have given a broader context to the world of New York by a discussion, in the preliminary note to the period 1861–1914, of the dominant values in America during the Gilded Age and the decades following.

James was an extraordinarily fascinating individual, and the relation of his work to his period is fascinating and complex; and in our space we have been able to do little more than suggest the biographical and social origins of "The Jolly Corner"; even so we have had to push on beyond those concerns, for, after all, the story itself is central to our interest. So we have tried to offer in the introduction a sufficient amount of analysis and commentary on style to allow the student to grasp the rich implications of the story and to arrive at some estimate of James as a literary craftsman.

We do not mean to suggest by this anatomy of the critical context of "The Jolly Corner" that there is a set pattern which we have followed in every case. There is, obviously, considerable difference in the scale of various treatments, in procedure and emphasis. In one case, we may have felt that the most useful thing we can say about a work in the headnote is to mention the historical event that inspired it; in another—say, a poem by Emily Dickinson—it might have seemed appropriate to limit comment to analysis of her unusual manner of punctuation or to point out the alternative verbal possibilities she can be shown to have contemplated; in still a third, the point worth making may be the work's place in some particularly American literary tradition.

The introductions to authors vary in much the same way as do those to individual works. Whittier, for instance, requires us to look more closely at the politics of his time (in particular, the antislavery movement) than does Edwin Arlington Robinson or Hart Crane. Henry James was, in his own phrase, "that obstinate finality," an artist: the growth of his art and of James himself as a personage in the world of letters occupies much of the James section. William Faulkner has clearly emerged as one of the towering figures in American literary history and would undoubtedly warrant the elaborate separate treatment accorded to Hawthorne, Melville, Mark Twain, and Dreiser; yet, in our view, Faulkner can best be understood and appreciated within the long and mixed tradition of southern writing, and he appears accordingly as the climax of two related sections, the first of which goes back as early as 1861. By the time we come to his work in the second of these sections, so much has been said about "the southern imagination" and southern culture and society that relatively few words are needed to introduce Faulkner himself, before getting on into the riches of his fiction.

How to handle the novel was one of our most vexing problems, and one for which, at various times, we considered different solutions. Of the American novels written before the Second World War, there are, we decided, nine necessary to a basic knowledge of American literature—though this is not to say that all nine can always be read in a single course. The novels are:

A special topic: the novel

The Scarlet Letter, by Hawthorne
Moby-Dick, by Melville
One of the several masterpieces by Henry James (*Portrait of a Lady*, *The Ambassadors*, *The Wings of the Dove*, *The Golden Bowl*)
The Adventures of Huckleberry Finn, by Twain
The Red Badge of Courage, by Crane
An American Tragedy, by Dreiser
The Great Gatsby, by Fitzgerald
The Sun Also Rises or *A Farewell to Arms*, by Hemingway
One of the several masterpieces by Faulkner (*The Sound and the Fury*, *Light in August, Absalom, Absalom!*)

The nine basic novels could not, of course, be accommodated in this work; they would run to more than 1,500,000 words—that is, to three-quarters of the available space in our volumes. In addition to these nine items, there are also other novels with which, for a variety of reasons, we think the student should have more than a passing acquaintance:

The Leatherstocking cycle, by Cooper
Uncle Tom's Cabin, by Stowe
The Rise of Silas Lapham or *A Hazard of New Fortunes*, by Howells
Main Street or *Babbitt*, by Lewis
Look Homeward, Angel or *Of Time and the River*, by Wolfe
U.S.A., by Dos Passos
Miss Lonelyhearts or *The Day of the Locust*, by West
Studs Lonigan, by Farrell
The Grapes of Wrath, by Steinbeck
Native Son, by Wright

We realize, of course, that America has no more persuasive claim to literary eminence than its novelists. Yet to include even three or four novels (but which three or four?) would have severely restricted our use of other material that we felt to be of the utmost importance and that was readily adapted for our use and not always readily available elsewhere. So for complete texts of novels we are depending on the many available soft-cover editions, from among which the teacher can make his own selections. We have, however, provided here elaborate discussions and analyses of the nine novels we have named as basic, and somewhat more limited treatments of the novels on our second list, plus a few others besides.

In spite of the fact that a part of a novel cannot stand for the whole, we have sometimes, nevertheless, printed particular sections of a number of novels. We have done so for special reasons, trying to consider each case on its own merits. For instance, the Leatherstocking cycle is, we think, basic; but, clearly, the whole cycle could not be used in a course, nor does any one novel suggest the impact of the whole. So we have used key parts of each of the items in the cycle to give a sense of the structure and meaning of the whole. A teacher may wish, of course, to use one complete novel (and that, if time permits, would be highly desirable), but even so, he could scarcely expect one novel to stand for the cycle.

To take another kind of example, we have used a sequence from *An American Tragedy* that we regard not only as central to an understanding of that novel and of Dreiser's method, but as central to Dreiser's work in general. Even if a teacher should agree with us that *An American Tragedy* is basic, he might not, because of its length, want to require that his students read it; in which case, our selection, in conjunction with the critical discussion, would give the student some feeling at least for Dreiser's characteristic qualities.

Just as we have varied our methods and emphases in our critical treatment of different authors, the teacher, we assume, will want to do the same. In fact, in all our discussions, we three have always envisaged a fourth editor: the teacher. He will have his own methods, opinions, and interpretations and may sometimes find ours downright wrong-headed. We expect this. We have had our own critical disputes. What we do hope, however, is that we have stated our views clearly enough, have developed them cogently enough, and have drawn issues sharply enough to enable the teacher or student more positively and dramatically to frame and present his own convictions.

Some ways to use this book

Since this book is, among other things, a history, it is only natural that its organization should be, in the main, chronological. But it is not strictly so; other considerations inevitably cross-hatch pure chronology. We have mentioned the two sections on southern writing, which overlap periods treated elsewhere. Similarly, the two sections on black literature together span many decades, for like Faulkner and other white southern writers, black writers in America, whether of the North or the South, have worked in terms of a special tradition and cultural context. Again, as another example, we have a broad section on "Literature of the Nonliterary World," with such subsections as "Political Writing" and "Tale and Character." Any one of these subsections may overlap periods covered earlier or later in the book. One teacher may choose to follow our arrangement only partially and, having covered the writers in the "main stream" of, say, Volume Two, may then, preferring to treat southern literature as an entity in itself, cut back in time to the Reconstruction period by taking up the first of the two southern sections and follow that immediately with the second. A similar procedure could be followed by the teacher who wished to pursue, without a break in the continuity, the development of black literature from 1861 to 1945.

Or the teacher may prefer to devise other groupings. For instance, for that period between the Civil War and the Second World War he might make a chronological study of a category such as "realism," including poetry and fiction written by black and by white writers. Having done this, he might then return to the Civil War period and follow through with another category of his choice and devising—for instance, the literature of the expatriates. Either of these procedures would afford special values and insights. Again, a teacher might find it useful to follow poetry, fiction, or the literature of ideas through, as independent units. Or one can imagine a course organized around recurrent themes of American literature—or at least with them as a basis for continuing discussion.

To return to the crucial matter of critical judgments: Are they ever to be settled once and for all? The vitality of a literary work is attested to by the fact that it continues to provoke new explorations and new assessments, to provide new perspectives of meaning and invite new insights. This is not to say that anything goes, that pure impressionism or pure relativism is to be accepted, but it is to say that one should be wary of dogmatism; and that, even while driving as hard as possible to make distinctions, perform analyses, and clarify formulations, one should realize that absolute and total "truth" is certainly not possible in such matters and, if it were, perhaps not wholly desirable. We do not delude ourselves that our book is in any sense "definitive." Nor do we offer a precise prescription for its use. There are many ways to cut the cake. We have baked it; the teacher must cut it to suit himself. What we hope for is that what we have written will be regarded as a serious, thoughtful, and reasonably well-informed effort to make sense of a rich and various body of literature.

Cleanth Brooks
R. W. B. Lewis
Robert Penn Warren

New Haven, Connecticut
January 15, 1973

Acknowledgments

We are deeply and obviously indebted to many critics and scholars in the field of American literature, but there are a few individuals to whom we wish to make more particular acknowledgment: Daniel Aaron, June Guicharnaud, Daniel Hoffman, Mary Pitlick, Louis Popp, David Rosen, and C. Vann Woodward. We would also like to thank Sylvia Newman, who edited the manuscript. And special gratitude is owed to David Milch for long, devoted, and invaluable assistance.

C. B.
R. W. B. L.
R. P. W.

Contents

1

"Before We Were the Land's": Pre-National Literature 1620–1743

Literature existed in America before America existed. The *name* "America" had of course been given to the New World early in the sixteenth century, in honor of its alleged discoverer, the Florentine merchant Amerigo Vespucci.[1] But another century had passed before the first permanent settlements on this continent were made, and America as a political and cultural reality would not be born for more than 170 years after that. During this long latter period, a great deal of literature was composed, some of it of a very high order. But it was not in any meaningful sense *American* literature. It did not arise out of an imaginative response to America itself—as a scene, a society, a historical event, a cluster of possibilities; for America, so understood, had not yet come into being.

The mind and imagination of the inhabitants of the New World did not yet—to put the case differently—belong to that world. They still belonged for the most part to England. Robert Frost expressed the paradox perfectly in "The Gift Outright," the poem he read at the inauguration ceremonies in January, 1961, at the invitation of the President-elect, John F. Kennedy:

---

[1] The designation would outrage Ralph Waldo Emerson, who, like many others, felt that the country should have been named after Christopher Columbus rather than, in Emerson's uncharitable words, "a pickle dealer who managed in this lying world to supplant Columbus and to baptize half the earth with his own dishonest name."

> The land was ours before we were the land's.
> She was our land more than a hundred years
> Before we were her people. She was ours
> In Massachusetts, in Virginia;
> But we were England's, still colonials,
> Possessing what we still were unpossessed by,
> Possessed by what we now no more possessed.
> Something we were withholding made us weak
> Until we found out that it was ourselves
> We were withholding from our land of living,
> And forthwith found salvation in surrender.
> Such as we were we gave ourselves outright
> (The deed of gift was many deeds of war)
> To the land vaguely realizing westward,
> But still unstoried, artless, unenhanced,
> Such as she was, such as she would become.

The development of a recognizably native literature required, as Frost suggests, an imaginative submission to the natural, the social, the intellectual environment, and this could not occur until that environment was at last perceived as a distinct and challenging phenomenon.

The colonization of the eastern American seaboard was as much the end of a long process as the beginning of a new chapter in history. There had been the voyages of Columbus—starting in October, 1492, and with the belated patronage of the Queen of Spain—to the Bahamas, Cuba, Haiti, and other islands, each of which he went to his grave believing to be either Japan or the Asia mainland. Soon afterward, Vespucci sailed down the coast of South America and possibly (historians are divided on the point) up that of North America as well; unlike Columbus, Vespucci eventually realized that what he had hit upon was not the orient but a new land mass which he was the first to call *Mundus Novus*, or "New World." There followed, in the course of the sixteenth century, explorers from several nations—Spain, France, Holland, Portugal; by mid-century, English fishermen were cruising the banks of Newfoundland. And behind these expeditions there lay legends of Irish monks and Buddhist missionaries making their way, a millennium earlier, to this or that portion of the North American continent, and the actual voyage of the Norseman Leif Erikson about the year 1000, from Greenland to (so it is generally believed) Cape Cod. Historians have argued that many other sea-going adventurers must have touched accidentally on these shores: the American land mass was simply too big to miss over the centuries. Or, as Mark Twain's Pudd'nhead Wilson put it in his acerbic way: "It was wonderful to find America, but it would have been more wonderful to miss it."

The idea of "colonizing" in the New World, of establishing permanent settlements there, was slow in forming.[2] The early visitors were just that. They set up short-term posts and garrisons for protection while carrying on trade with the Indians and gathering raw materials to carry back to the parent country. It was the English who were first seized by the epochal idea of colonization, and for several suggestively diverse reasons they were the first successful colonizers. One reason was the shrewd business sense of English merchants: there were, so they realized, riches to be extracted from the New World soil by those willing to stay and work it. The discovery of the tobacco crop in Virginia, for example (about 1613), made it worthwhile for the bedeviled fortune hunters who had come to Jamestown to hang on; by 1617, they were shipping 500,000 pounds of tobacco to England each year. Another reason was the attraction of America as an asylum. Many convicted criminals who signed on with one or another of the London shipping companies, and came to this country as able-bodied laborers, did so as the only alternative to the gallows. And, particularly among those who founded or joined the colonies in New England, there was a powerful religious motive: the determination to plant a model community of the faithful in the new hemisphere, to advance the gospel of Jesus, and to expand the ranks of Christians by converting the heathen. Business drive, the pursuit of liberty, religious zeal—one begins already to make out, very faintly, the American profile.

We have come to think of the Puritans as the first white settlers of America—perhaps, as we shall soon observe, because it is they who dominate the written record of the period. But there had been earlier visitors to the region: the Spanish had established the settlement of St. Augustine in 1565; a small group of Englishmen, at the behest of Walter Raleigh, tried to found a colony on Roanoke Island, off the coast of North Carolina, in 1594; they and those who were sent to replace them disappeared; too, an outpost had been briefly set up on the Maine coast in 1607, only to give way before the severities of the weather; in 1614, Captain John Smith had surveyed and mapped the entire New England coastline. And before that there had been the hazardous settlement at Jamestown, Virginia, in 1607, a colony which managed

---

[2] See "The Colony as an Idea," in *The American Republic* (1959), edited by Daniel Aaron, Richard Hofstadter, and William Miller. The word "colonize" seems to have been coined as late as 1622, by Francis Bacon.

to stay alive despite disease, lack of food, and Indian forays (all of which reduced its members, during the first winter, from five hundred to sixty).[3]

The first Puritan "plantation" (or settlement) was founded in Plymouth, Massachusetts, by those determined souls who arrived at the northernmost tip of Cape Cod just before Christmas, 1620, on the *Mayflower*, after going wildly off course on a voyage which was intended to land them at a point many hundreds of miles south. The more stable and enduring Massachusetts Bay Colony was established in and around Boston in 1630, by the company that came over on the *Arbella* under the leadership of John Winthrop.

Additional colonies sprang up quickly in the wake of Virginia and Massachusetts. In 1634 Maryland, named after Henrietta Marie, the queen of Charles I, and founded as a refuge for Catholics, was carved out of northern Virginia and granted to an English nobleman named Baltimore; it too prospered on tobacco. Thirty years later New Netherland was wrested from the Dutch by the English (the Dutch had been there half a century and had purchased the island of Manhattan for twenty-four dollars worth of supplies) and renamed New York; in the same year, 1664, New Jersey came into existence through a grant from the Duke of York. William Penn's splendid experiment got under way. Back in England, Penn, to the fury of his aristocratic father, had espoused the Quaker doctrines and was seeking a New World refuge for his persecuted coreligionists. In 1681, he was ceded a large tract of land by Charles II in payment for a royal debt owed the older Penn, now dead. William named the area "Sylvania" for its ranging forests (the king added "Penn" for the father) and promptly set up an elective parliament, wide suffrage, and the most liberal government of all the colonies. New England, meanwhile, was expanding from Massachusetts into Rhode Island, Connecticut, New Hampshire, and Maine; the Carolinas were settled in 1670, and Georgia in 1733. A good deal of land was ours by this time, but we were still far from being the land's.

The most important phase of what we are calling "pre-national literature" consists in the writings of an array of New Englanders, known as "Puritans," between the second quarter of the seventeenth century and an indeterminate moment—we have chosen the date 1743—in the century which followed. It behooves us now to ask who the Puritans were, what they were like, what

---

[3] When Sir Thomas Gates arrived as governor in 1610, he found Jamestown a scene of almost total devastation: "The church ruined and unfrequented, empty howses . . . rent up and burnt, the living not hable, as they pretended, to step into the woodes to gather other fire-wood; and, it is true, the Indians as fast killing without as the famine and pestilence within."

they believed—and, eventually, in what ways they can speak to us today. The hundred-odd persons who came to Plymouth on the *Mayflower*, and the six hundred-odd who crossed the Atlantic a decade later on the fleet whose flagship was the *Arbella*, were for the most part decidedly godly folk—English Protestants who had struggled for some years to make "the churches of God" (in the words of William Bradford) "revert to their ancient purity and recover their primitive order, liberty and beauty." It was their concern for primitive ecclesiastical purity that had won them the name of Puritans and earned them the special hostility of the Stuart kings. The founders of Plymouth represented an extremist faction: they wanted to break away entirely from the Church of England, and they were known (and widely distrusted) as "Separatists," though they thought of themselves (and the name has come down to us) as "Pilgrims." The *Arbella* constituency sought more moderately to work within the system. They earnestly professed their friendship for the mother church; but after the accession of Charles I in 1625, it became clear that this might best be maintained at a considerable distance. Both sects dispensed with bishops and church courts, and both insisted on simplicity in church rituals, practices, vestments.

By 1640, some twenty thousand Puritans were spread across the New England landscape. Most of these—like most other settlers south of them—lived on farms of perhaps several hundred acres, often separated by many miles. These were the first Americans to gain a consciousness of an exceedingly influential phenomenon in American experience—sheer *space*, space of a sort unimaginable in England or on the European continent. But no few gathered in the rapidly growing cities. What it felt and looked like for the farmer paying a visit, say, to Boston, has been vividly suggested by Edmund S. Morgan:

> The colonial farmer riding into a city for the first time left a road that was only a ribbon of stumps and mud and came upon streets of gravel or cobblestones, where a bewildering activity surrounded him. Swine roamed everywhere, feeding on the refuse; drovers herded sheep and cattle to the butchers. Elegant carriages rolled impatiently behind lumbering wagons as great packs of barking dogs worried the horses. Sailors reeled out of taverns, and over the roofs of the houses could be seen the swaying masts and spars of their ships. The farmer had been told that the city was a nursery of vice and prodigality. He now saw that it was so. Every shop had wares to catch his eye: exquisite fabrics, delicate chinaware, silver buckles, looking glasses, and other imported luxuries that never reached the cross-roads store. Putting up at the tavern, he found himself drinking too much rum. And there were willing girls, he heard, who

had lost their virtue and would be glad to help him lose his. Usually he returned to the farm to warn his children as he had been warned. He seldom understood that the vice of the city, if not its prodigality, was mainly for transients like himself. Permanent residents had work to do. (*The National Experience*, 1968, p. 61)[4]

There was, indeed, work to do, in the city and on the farm alike, and the Puritans were a tough and hard-working people. But as the description above indicates, they were by no means the austere, ascetic, humorless, prudish people they have too often been taken to be. It was the constant task of the minister not to forbid the church members any physical pleasures, but to caution severely against excess. The Puritans, for example, liked good drink and often lots of it. On this score they were characteristically instructed by Increase Mather in a sermon of 1637: "Drink is in itself a good creature of God, and to be received with thankfulness; but the abuse of drink is from Satan; the wine is from God, but the Drunkard is from the devil." The Puritans also liked good food. A typical dinner might consist of corn meal and boiled meat, with vegetables, but there were festive occasions, too, featuring giant lobsters weighing up to twenty-five pounds, and perhaps bass, sturgeon, eels, and oysters, or game from the forest—deer, turkey, partridge, wild geese, ducks. There were athletic contests at suited intervals, for physical well-being or for pure entertainment: wrestling matches, bouts at quarter-staff, robust duels with buckler and broadsword.

Nor was the sexual aspect of life something to be repressed or denied. Courting couples, for example, could indulge in the modestly erotic game known as bundling, during which, on a cold New England evening, a young maiden might entertain her male companion by inviting him into her bed, there to lie "bundling" with him, separated only by a long, narrow, wooden bar. And while adultery was of course a very serious affair, no marriage was considered to *be* a marriage until sexual union took place. In New Haven, for example, it was a matter of written law that a husband's impotence was cause for annulment; and several marriage contracts in Massachusetts were declared broken for the same reason. In this regard, the Puritan attitude simply followed traditional and orthodox Christian doctrine, but it is of interest that it did.

There were always, too, the minor and ever-continuing offenses against established propriety. A law forbade smoking in public and even with a friend in the privacy of one's home; but everyone did smoke, even the

[4] Hawthorne, in "My Kinsman, Major Molyneux," offers a brilliantly hallucinatory image of just such a young farmer entering Boston at night and being weirdly confronted by a prostitute, tavern-brawlers, and general turbulence. (See the Hawthorne section.)

kitchen maids. Men were supposed to keep their hair closely cropped, but the young liked to display their hair down nearly to their shoulders, and one irate minister disinherited his nephew for doing so. And despite sternest warnings about simplicity of dress, young men and women adopted an astonishing variety of colorful and bizarre clothing—periwigs and straw hats, satin doublets and assorted trousers, silk stockings, fancy shoes and golden topped gloves for the men; masks and stomachers, mantles and muffs, gowns with pewter buttons, tortoise-shell combs and silver-buckled shoes for the women.

Thus, as Edmund S. Morgan has said, the Puritans "knew how to laugh, and they knew how to love." Yet it is also true, as Morgan observes, "that they did not spend their best hours in either love or laughter. They had fixed their eyes on a heavenly goal, which directed and informed their lives." Even before they arrived in the New World, they had begun to think through and to articulate the relation between that heavenly goal and their lives on earth—to describe, as best they could, the nature and purpose of human life in the light of God's plans and promises, or of so much of the latter as man was able to grasp. The coordinates of that description had their source in the thinking of the two greatest European theologians of the previous century, Martin Luther and John Calvin. From Luther the Puritans took the idea that men were essentially wicked, and God all-powerful, with the corollary that no human actions—no "good works"—were of the slightest value in gaining redemption. But it was Calvin who was even more important for the development of Puritan thought, and his *Institutes of the Christian Religion*, first published in 1536, was the major text from which they drew doctrinal speculation.

In addition to solidifying and giving intellectual structure to Luther's theses, Calvin advanced in particular the doctrine of "predestination"—the theory that God quite arbitrarily (in the humanly rational perspective) and from the beginning of time had chosen some, probably only a few, for salvation; and others, probably the great mass of mankind, for eternal damnation. The Puritans were not appalled by this theory. Not all, perhaps, felt as Jonathan Edwards did: in his *Personal Narrative* (1740), Edwards declared that the doctrine of God's sovereignty "in choosing whom he would to eternal life, and rejecting whom he pleased" was "exceedingly pleasant, bright and sweet." But most Puritans did find the idea of predestination oddly invigorating; they saw themselves caught up in an extraordinary divine enterprise. Far from taking predestination as an argument against hard work and virtuous conduct (on the grounds that none of this would do any good), the Puritans undoubtedly found the doctrine a tremendous spur to moral and practical achievement.

This paradox may show with special force in the Puritans' increasing addiction to commercial activity, eventually to strong economic individualism. It has been famously argued—in Max Weber's *The Protestant Ethic and the Spirit of Capitalism* (1920) and Roger H. Tawney's *Religion and the Rise of Capitalism* (1926)—that there was something inherent in Puritan doctrine to impel Puritans to energetic moneymaking. This is, in effect, alleged to be the belief that the acquisition of wealth (always of course through "godly discipline"), if not a step toward salvation, may just possibly be a sign that one has been saved. In Tawney's words:

> Since conduct and action, though availing nothing to attain the free gift of salvation, are a proof that the gift has been accorded, what is rejected as a means is resumed as a consequence, and the Puritan flings himself into practical activities with the daemonic energy of one who, all doubts allayed, is conscious that he is a sealed and chosen vessel. . . . Convinced that character is all and circumstances nothing, he sees in the poverty of those who fall by the way, not a misfortune to be pitied and relieved, but a moral failing to be condemned, and in riches, not an object of suspicion—though like other gifts they may be abused—but the blessing which rewards the triumph of energy and will. Tempered by self-examination, self-discipline, self-control, he is the practical ascetic, whose victories are won not in the cloister, but on the battlefield, in the counting-house, and in the market.

This interpretation has been challenged of late, and the Puritan commercial vigor has been related to the general economic upsurge of the age, the expansionist financial spirit observable everywhere in the Western world—and to the fact that the New Englanders, however pious, were also English, and therefore (allegedly) business-minded. Whatever the mixture of causes, the Puritans undeniably worked the marketplace as hard as they could; and it was indeed a series of parliamentary acts which brought economic discomfort to the colonies—from the Navigation Acts of 1650 and 1651 through the Stamp Act of 1756, and the so-called Intolerable Acts following the Boston Tea Party in 1773—which helped bring on the Revolution.

The influence of the Calvinist doctrines on other areas of Puritan life is not so problematic. To begin with, what had brought them to America was the desire to establish in a new land the community of God's will, and what sustained them was the ennobling sense of the historic drama they were enacting. When William Bradford, in his *Of Plymouth Plantation*, depicts the Puritan adventure as part of a "great design," and a "great and honorable action," his referent is the Calvinist conviction that man's conduct does not determine but reveals his place in God's scheme. And when John Winthrop, in his sermon on board the *Arbella*, speaking of the New World settlement, emphasized the necessity of its establishment as "a model of Christian charity," it is because in the absence of such conduct the settlers will see that their souls are lost.

If life was thus the process of discovering whether or not one was saved, and conduct and consequence were the indices, then every event (and every thought) partook of a heightened significance. We need not wonder, then, at the Puritans' extreme sensitivity to threats to the established order. For the order so established, they were convinced, was a reflection of God's will, and the toleration of its compromise would reveal the tolerant as damned. The dissenter, of course, believed with equal conviction that concession would mark the taint of his own soul, and the conflict of convictions on the most practical matters of governance had the deepest religious implications. The paradigm of such a conflict, and one which demonstrates the blending of political with religious concern, is the one-man fight waged by Roger Williams against the colony at Massachusetts Bay.

Williams was a remarkably sweet-tempered and engaging but also utterly intransigent man who came from England in 1631. He stirred up the Boston community with charge after public charge: that the churches in America had not separated absolutely enough from the English church, not even the austere Plymouth congregation; that the English king was "a public liar," who had no authority to grant New World lands to the first settlers; that God did not desire any organized church of any kind; that, finally, individual conscience has primacy over all laws and institutions, ecclesiastical and civil, this last point being the main burden of his diatribe "The Bloudy Tenent of Persecution." Williams was banished to Rhode Island in 1636; but his chief contention became imbedded in the American—especially, though by no means exclusively, the New England—consciousness. The supremacy of the individual conscience was appealed to—in the name of "the higher law" —by members of the abolitionist contingent in the years before the Civil War. Thoreau introduced the phrase "civil disobedience" to describe the kind of opposition one might peacefully exert against laws and policies one might openly abhor. And behind those persons who in recent years have preached and practiced civil disobedience, we can see not only the figure of Thoreau but also the attractive, unmanageable shadow of Roger Williams.

The case of Roger Williams illustrates the conflicting tendencies of Calvinism in its New World environment. On the one hand, there was the profound belief in the importance of social order and stability—and exactly because the newly founded order was a grand design with what would later be called a "manifest destiny": to serve as a beacon for all of Christian man-kind. But on the other hand, the colony was established as, in effect, an act of dissent, and its manner of origin inevitably encouraged fresh acts of dissent on the part of some of its members; man's final responsibility, it could be argued, was not to any earthly authority, but to God.[5]

When we come to consider John Greenleaf Whittier and his abolitionist activities in association with Garrison and others, as well as in our introductory essay to the period 1826–61, we shall reflect further on the dilemmas arising from the conflict between the assertion of private conscience and the rule of law. Here we may observe that the conflict could be much more easily handled in a theocracy—like that of seventeenth-century Boston—than in a democracy like that of nineteenth- and twentieth-century America. Within the Puritan community, indeed, the real struggle appears not to have been between the orthodox and the heretics, but between those religious fanatics who wanted to exterminate every vestige of "heresy" and those, like Winthrop, who were more concerned with an orderly and to some limited degree a tolerant conduct of human affairs.

From their own point of view the Puritans had a good deal more trouble with people outside the community than within: with Anabaptists and Anglicans, but most especially with the Quakers. If here, as in their response to "witches"[6] and the Indians, the fanatics among the Puritans did hold sway, it must be admitted that the peace-loving Quakers of New England did, at times, disturb the peace. They might come, individually, to public worship and at the end of it feel called upon to bear witness to the workings of the "Inner Light" within them, often adding a rebuke to the practices and beliefs

---

[5] The case of Anne Hutchinson, who was also banished to Rhode Island (in 1637) and eventually died there in an Indian raid, is somewhat different from that of Williams. Mistress Hutchinson's claim was that of having received direct revelation from God rather than true doctrine from the Bible. This rather allied her with the detested Quakers (see below, and also the section on John Woolman later in this volume), as well as placing her in a tradition which would be continued by such groups as the Millerites (see introduction, 1826–61). She was a brilliant and appealing woman; and although she may have lost her case through an imprudent outburst, her trial before the General Court was one of the shabbiest episodes in Puritan history. At the end, when banishment was voted, she asked quietly enough: "I desire to know wherefore I am banished." To this, Governor Winthrop, in an unhappy moment in an otherwise honorable career, replied ignobly: "Say no more, the court knows wherefore and is satisfied."

[6] As did just about everyone else in the Christian world at the time, the Puritans really did believe in witches; and between February, 1692, and January, 1693, twenty "witches" were executed at Salem, Massachusetts. Beyond its irreducible hideousness the episode reflects again something of that same tension between authority and nonconformist conduct we have noted in the case of Williams and of the Quakers, and of the extremity of response being a function of the setting of the conflict in religious terms.

of the orthodox. Cotton Mather may have been exaggerating, but he claimed to be quoting verbatim when he reported the denunciation of a certain Puritan divine by a Quaker named Fisher: "Thou hedgehog and grinning dog; thou bastard that tumbled out of the mouth of the Babilonish bawd; thou mole; thou tinker," and so on. Too, the Quakers might scandalize the decorous by refusing to take off their hats in church. Some few might even come to church naked.[7]

For a short while the Puritans tried to ignore the Quakers. Then they moved against them. Quakers were not only imprisoned, and banished: some were whipped through the streets, or had their ears and tongues cut off. In the familiar and unhappy cycle, force only prompted further intransigence. Several Quakers were finally hanged, one of them a woman.

In "The Gentle Boy" Hawthorne accurately discloses the failings, the bigotry, and the partial justifications of both parties—Puritans and Quakers alike—in this chapter of American history and the extent to which the hostility was as much a matter of social class, of belonging and not belonging, as it was of religious belief. But it is also true that these conflicts found their expression in religious terms, and as religious beliefs were strong, their being so expressed absorbed and transformed and deepened every conflict into one of the first extremity.

It is in this perspective that we must view the Puritans' treatment of the Indians and, to a certain extent, the Indians' treatment by the colonials at large. Though motives as common as mistrust of the stranger and as secular as greed undoubtedly informed the conduct of many settlers, and though in many instances no motive beyond bestial impulse may be made out, it seems clear that the framing of the inevitable tensions between the two races in religious terms inspired in the settlers a peculiarly ferocious response. The black man aroused no correspondingly angry zeal in the colonial heart, for while his nature had not yet been determined (the question being whether he was simply property or a lower animal form) it was clear that he was not human. The Indian *was* human, had once been declared so by papal decree, yet by his color, by his conduct, in his heathen, naturalistic religious rites, the Indian persistently betrayed the humanity he allegedly possessed. At least this was a way of looking at it. It may have afforded some comfort to that New

---

[7] The Quakers' behavior can be partly explained by the fact that in New England they found themselves an oppressed minority, as they had been in the mother country, and felt impelled to assert both themselves and their religious cause against an intolerant majority. The Quaker communities of Pennsylvania and New Jersey, as we shall see, had an altogether different time of it by virtue of their greater proportion in the population and were able to practice the peaceful and friendly creed they preached.

England force which in 1637 set fire to a village belonging to the Pequot tribe
and shot down the villagers as they tried to escape the flames, or to those who in
1674 took after the Wampanoags, led by King Philip, and eventually wiped
them out, to believe that they were doing God's work, that they were destroying, as the Indians were often called, the "red devils," the emissaries of Satan.
Such a thought would certainly be of more comfort to the high-minded than
that of being engaged in a land-grab. Of course some individuals, not so high-
minded, invoke no such lofty motives. The Virginia militiamen who in the
last part of the seventeenth century wantonly murdered a number of Susque-
hannock chiefs who had come to negotiate peace were not moved by theological considerations.[8]

It is not surprising, in the light of the preceding and necessarily brief discussion of their character and experience, that it was the Puritans' religious
vision which gave rise to their literary achievement. But before proceeding to a
discussion of that achievement, a number of reminders are in order. We have
been concentrating on the life and thought of Puritan New England, but it is
well to recall, first, that the Puritan culture flourished, across the seventeenth
century, alongside of the very different and larger and more complex cultural
developments in England and on the continent. As to the latter, the names
alone can evoke the European age: Bacon and Newton, Milton and Dryden,
Rembrandt and Vermeer, Descartes and Spinoza. But the Puritans drew
little from the achievements of those men of genius; they had no time for
secular philosophy and little interest in the plastic arts. When the "new
thought" did make its way from Europe to America, it did so through other
channels—for example, the liberal arts colleges which were founded seriatim,
beginning with Harvard (1636), Yale (1701), Princeton (1746), Columbia
(1754), and Pennsylvania (1755). It was here that the new physics of Newton and the psychology and social philosophy of John Locke first made their
impact, and it was the colleges that helped usher in the next distinguishable
phase of American cultural history—that known variously as the Enlightenment or the Age of Reason (see the introduction to the next section and to
Franklin). The new thought introduced a view of the universe more secular
and scientific, more humanistic and earthly—yet also, as someone plaintively
remarked, less sublime—than that of the Puritans.

[8] In this instance the Indians retaliated by killing several dozen white men. Subsequently, in an episode known as Bacon's Rebellion, a revenge party, in defiance of
William Berkeley, the governor of Virginia, managed to massacre a large number of
Indians and gain temporary control of most of the colony before their leader, Nathaniel
Bacon, died of fever. Though satirized by the Maryland poet Ebenezer Cook, Bacon
was later nominated for the pantheon of American heroes of "independence" by no
less a personage than Thomas Jefferson.

We may also remind ourselves again that the New England Puritans formed only one of a number of groups of settlers in the New World. But what sets them apart for the purposes of this book is that virtually alone among these groups, at least until well into the eighteenth century, the Puritans contributed a substantial body of intellectual and literary work. Virtually no non-Puritan writing on this continent has survived from the seventeenth century.[9] We may now observe that this literary preeminence of the Puritans as against the other colonizers was not an accident, but was rather the result of the fact that they, uniquely, brought with them to these shores the requisite for any literature: a solid cultural framework within which to think and to articulate.

That framework controlled the Puritan literary achievement, determined its subject, and dictated its various forms. The subject would be no less (and no more) than man's relation to God and the way he might best serve as His vessel and the instrument of His glory. The forms would be such as might best reflect, enact, and dramatize that subject: the sermon, the diary, the allegory, the tract, the meditational and devotional poem, the apocalyptic pronouncement. We will identify these forms and comment upon their most effective practitioners in the pages that follow.

Here, as a matter of historical overview, we should point out that it was exactly because the culture of Puritan New England *was* an import—because it preceded and hence conditioned the energies of response to the actual New World environment—that as a culture it was not destined to survive. The cultural framework gave way slowly, here and there, bit by bit, to visions and literary efforts that sprang out of the primary experience of the New World. What has survived from Puritanism is not a coherent culture but a *tradition* —a habit of self-inquiry, a view of human nature, an attitude to history. We shall have innumerable occasions, throughout these volumes, to observe the ineradicable vestiges and continuing resonance of that tradition for the ages which followed.

Puritan writing, then, however impressive and compelling, was composed by individuals who did not, in Frost's phrase, belong to and were not possessed by "the land." Yet within it, even during its heyday but most strikingly during its decline, we make out the first signs of that other and more native kind of writing: work emerging from the author's original and direct response to the world immediately around him. This is to be marked

[9] Among the first stirrings from southerly directions was Ebenezer Cook's sprightly satire of misadventures in Maryland, *The Sot-Weed Factor* of 1708, and, in 1729, William Byrd's gossipy report on the "dividing line" between Virginia and North Carolina (see selections in our text). John Woolman's remarkable investigations into Negro slavery and his account of his many travels fall just outside our period (see selection in our text).

in several poems by Anne Bradstreet and in the writings of Samuel Sewall, and most clearly (if surprisingly) in some of the ruminations of Jonathan Edwards. In these and other works America begins, for the first time, to enter into the literature of its occupants.

FURTHER READINGS

Daniel Aaron, Richard Hofstadter, and William Miller, eds., *The American Republic* (1959; 2 vols.), Chaps. 1–4

C. M. Andrews, *The Colonial Period of American History* (1934–38; 4 vols.)

John M. Blum *et al.*, eds., *The National Experience* (3rd ed.; 1973), Chaps. 1–3

J. B. Brebner, *The Explorers of North America, 1492–1806* (1933)

Samuel Eliot Morison, *The European Discovery of America* (1971)

C. P. Nettels, *The Roots of American Civilisation* (1938)

Jeannine Hensley, ed., with an introd. by Adrienne Rich, *The Works of Anne Bradstreet* (1967)

George Langdon, *Pilgrim Colony: A History of New Plymouth, 1620–1691* (1966)

Robert Middlekauf, *The Mathers: Three Generations of Puritan Intellectuals* (1971)

Perry Miller, *The New England Mind: The Seventeenth Century* (1939)

———, *The New England Mind: From Colony to Province* (1953)

———, *Errand into the Wilderness* (1952; a collection of essays)

——— and Thomas H. Johnson, eds., *The Puritans* (1938; an anthology)

———, *The American Puritans* (1956; a paperback abridgment of the preceding anthology)

Edmund S. Morgan, *The Puritan Family* (1944)

———, *The Puritan Dilemma: The Story of John Winthrop* (1958)

———, *Roger Williams: The Church and the State* (1967)

Samuel Eliot Morison, *Builders of the Bay Colony* (1930)

———, *The Intellectual Life of Colonial New England* (1956)

Kenneth B. Murdock, *Cotton Mather* (1926; selections and commentary)

H. R. Niebuhr, *The Kingdom of God in America* (1956)

———, *The Social Sources of Denominationalism* (1929; 1954)

Roy Harvey Pearce, *Colonial American Writing* (1959; a paperback anthology)

———, "The Significance of the Captivity Narrative," *American Literature*, 19 (1947)

(Note: the definitive edition of Mary Rowlandson's *The Captivity* is being prepared by Robert Diebold of Talladega College.)

Arthur M. Schlesinger, Jr., and Morton White, eds., *Paths of American Thought* (1963)

Herbert W. Schneider, *The Puritan Mind* (1930; paperback, 1958)

Donald E. Stanford, ed., *The Poems of Edward Taylor* (1960)

William R. Taylor, *Cavalier and Yankee* (1961)

Elizabeth White, *Anne Bradstreet* (1971)

The Puritan

Sense of History

The first four writers represented in these selections—William Bradford, John Winthrop, Cotton Mather, and Thomas Shepard—address themselves to questions of history: to a record of concrete historical fact, to a meditation on the unique nature of the present historical moment, to the ultimate meaning of the historical process. If the Puritan mind was much exercised by these matters, it was because, to begin with, every earthly event, however seemingly casual, was a part of God's timeless and all-encompassing plan; and, as such, it had to be scrupulously reported and carefully interpreted by men. But the Puritans, as we have remarked, looked into history with a special intensity and excitement; for the role they had been chosen to play in the universal drama was, as they felt, altogether exceptional. On them rested the enormous and stirring burden of planting in the New World wilderness a community of godliness wherein man's destiny might meet its ultimate test. Such a community, in Winthrop's words, would be as nakedly visible to the rest of the Christian world as a city perched high upon a hill.

A major reason for the Puritans' confidence in this historic mission was their belief that history was overwhelmingly meaningful—because God, the governor of history, had willed that it should be so. According to the theory worked out by New England Protestants, God had of his own volition entered into an agreement—a "covenant"—with man, by the terms of which God's purposes could be rationally discerned amid the vicissitudes of human history, within the play of large and small human experiences. It was an extraordinary thing for God to have done, the Puritans acknowledged. Thomas Shepard observed in the 1640's that God "might have done good to man without binding Himself in the bonds of Covenant." God, nonetheless, had taken on just those bonds, and the intellect of man was thus empowered to seek out and to give a written account of the grand pattern made up of the myriad individual incidents and persons.

Written history was, finally and by the same token, a highly important mode of instruction. The facts had to be faithfully set down; but each of them bristled with dramatic significance, and in pointing to that significance, the historian was delivering a lesson on the learning of which a man's salvation might depend.

WILLIAM BRADFORD (1590–1657)

In his history *Of Plymouth Plantation*—the story of the founding, the development, and the decline of that colony between 1620 and 1650— William Bradford, its governor for more than thirty years, gave the first expression to the idea that America was the scene of a unique experiment. It was an epic theme, and Bradford's account, which is at once heroic and humane in spirit, is cast to some extent in an epic and specifically a Virgilian mold.

After leaving England and trying unsuccessfully to make a life for themselves in Holland, the Pilgrims determined with extraordinary courage to make a second start in America. Their great belief in the venture helped them survive the various calamities, miseries and terrors of the voyage, and the worse ones that awaited them in the Cape Cod winter. "They that know the winters of that country," Bradford tells us, "know them to be sharp and violent, and subject to cruel and fierce storms." But it was all in the greatest of causes; and despite Indian attacks and wild beasts, despite near starvation and conditions that led the governor's own wife to drown herself in the icy Atlantic,[1] the Pilgrims endured.

The motivating idea of the Plymouth settlement endured much longer than the colony itself. The idea we find reformulated in the minister Dimmesdale's election day sermon at the climax of *The Scarlet Letter*. The minister's subject, Hawthorne writes, "had been the relation between the Deity and the communities of mankind, with a special reference to the New England which they were here planting in the wilderness"; as he spoke, "a spirit as of prophecy had come upon him," and he began "to foretell a high and glorious destiny for the newly gathered people of the Lord." In the course of time, that sense of high destiny expanded beyond New England and was applied to an entire nation as, in Frost's words, it was "vaguely realizing westward." Two centuries after the dissolution of Plymouth, Americans were still obsessed with what they called even then, with remarkable self-assurance, a "manifest destiny" to be the moral and practical leader of the world. Nor has this conviction—at times beneficent, more frequently disastrous—yet been eradicated from the American mind.

What was missing from the nineteenth- and twentieth-century versions of the old idea was the Puritans' briskly tragic view of human nature and its effect on their estimate of the chances of success in their mission. They knew that the darkness of men's hearts could bring all to ruin. And, indeed, Bradford's tone saddens

[1] Such is the conjecture of Samuel Eliot Morison, in his introduction to *Of Plymouth Plantation* (1952). Cotton Mather speaks only of the governor's "dearest consort accidentally falling overboard." Bradford does not mention his wife's death.

and darkens as the years pass and as his narrative keeps pace with events. He tells of abandoning the effort to have property kept communally; and, later, of how "some kind of wickedness did grow and break forth here, in a land where the same was so much witnessed and so narrowly looked into," and he puzzles and worries over it. He records, finally, how, in 1642, it was proposed by many that the plantation be moved to Nauset—not "for want or necessity so much . . . as for the enriching of themselves." Both moral restiveness and a desire for worldly goods, it appears, motivated the proposed changes. Several new independent churches, in fact, came "out of the bowels" of Plymouth. "And thus," Bradford concludes, "was this poor church left, like an ancient mother grown old and forsaken of her children. . . . She that had made many rich became herself poor." And thus, too, there comes to an end Bradford's archetypal story of the origins, the initial successes, the strains and tensions, and the ultimate dissolution of the great design. That story is emblematic, to a certain extent, of the Puritan experience. The City of God was not to be founded on American shores. More generally, we may see in Bradford's account the first announcement in an American setting of one of the richest themes in literature: the testing of the ideal by the actual, of the idea by experience. To cite but a few examples, the theme is present in Henry Adams' account of Thomas Jefferson's sacrifice of his exalted sense of America's purpose to his recognition of the exigencies of political reality in the decision to purchase Louisiana (see the section on Henry Adams). We may see it, too, in all the work of William Faulkner, and especially in *The Bear*, where Faulkner describes the great community of hunters in the nineteenth-century Mississippi wilderness: a community "of men, not white nor black nor red, but men, hunters,

with the will and hardiness to endure and the humility and skill to survive"; a community dedicated to the great virtues of courage and humility and pride and the rest, but one which likewise went down and disappeared before the encroachment of men impatient with these virtues and bent on "the enriching of themselves." And behind both Bradford and Faulkner, and other narratives like theirs, one makes out the ancient legend of the Round Table at Camelot —of the rise, triumphs, troubles, and dissolution of that model community.

Cotton Mather's sketch of Bradford's life, which appears later in this section, remains a chief source of information and was, indeed, the only biography of Bradford until 1955. Bradford was born in Austerfield, Yorkshire, in 1590, the son of a yeoman farmer. He was himself to be trained as a farmer; but at a very early age, he became a devoted reader of the Bible and joined a group in nearby Scrooby which was forming a separate Congregational church. He went with this group—the Pilgrims, as they were later called—to Leyden in Holland, and then in 1620 to Massachusetts. In 1621, he was elected governor of Plymouth, and he was reelected thirty times. As Mather says, Bradford was a man of "more than ordinary piety, wisdom and courage"; and he was the foremost member of the "plantation" until his death.

Bradford's first wife, Dorothy May, drowned in Provincetown Bay in December, 1620, very possibly a suicide. A few years later, he married the widow Alice Southworth, who bore him three children. Bradford read widely—he left behind a library of four hundred volumes; and his history shows that he was anything but an artless writer. But what most comes through to us in his writing is a personality of natural authority who was yet almost wholly free of personal ambition.

From Of Plymouth Plantation (1630–51)

The history *Of Plimmoth Plantation* (its original spelling) was compiled between 1630 and 1651, but it was not published until 1856,

after the manuscript—which had apparently been made off with by a British soldier during the Revolution—was discovered in the library of the Bishop of London. The text we use here is as established by Samuel Eliot Morison, in *Of Plymouth Plantation: A New Edition* (1963). Where chapter titles appear in brackets they are Morison's. Other titles are Bradford's.

And first of the occasion and inducements thereunto; the which, that I may truly unfold, I must begin at the very root and rise of the same. The which I shall endeavour to manifest in a plain style, with singular regard unto the simple truth in all things; at least as near as my slender judgment can attain the same.

CHAPTER 1

[The Separatist Interpretation of the Reformation in England, 1550-1667]

It is well known unto the godly and judicious, how ever since the first breaking out of the light of the gospel in our honourable nation of England, (which was the first of nations whom the Lord adorned therewith after the gross darkness of popery which had covered and overspread the Christian world), what wars and oppositions ever since, Satan hath raised, maintained and continued against the Saints, from time to time, in one sort or other. Sometimes by bloody death and cruel torments; other whiles imprisonments, banishments and other hard usages; as being loath his kingdom should go down, the truth prevail and the churches of God revert to their ancient purity and recover their primitive order, liberty and beauty.

. . .

CHAPTER 4

Showing the Reasons and Causes of Their Removal

. . .

Lastly (and which was not least), a great hope and inward zeal they had of laying some good foundation, or at least to make some way thereunto, for the propagating and advancing the gospel of the kingdom of Christ in those remote parts of the world; yea, though they should be but even as stepping-stones unto others for the performing of so great a work.

These and some other like reasons moved them to undertake this resolution of their removal; the which they afterward prosecuted with so great difficulties, as by the sequel will appear.

The place they had thoughts on was some of those vast and unpeopled countries of America, which are fruitful and fit for habitation, being devoid of all civil inhabitants, where there are only savage and brutish men which range up and down, little otherwise than the wild beasts of the same. This proposition being made public and coming to the scanning of all, it raised many variable opinions amongst men and caused many fears and doubts amongst themselves. Some, from their reasons and hopes conceived, laboured to stir up and encourage the rest to undertake and prosecute the same; others again, out of their fears, objected against it and sought to divert from it; alleging many things, and those neither unreasonable nor unprobable; as that it was a great design and subject to many unconceivable perils and dangers; as, besides the casualties of the sea (which none can be freed from), the length of the voyage was such as the weak bodies of women and other persons worn out with age and travail (as many of them were) could never be able to endure. And yet if they should, the miseries of the land which they should be exposed unto, would be too hard to be borne and likely, some or all of them together, to consume and utterly to ruinate them. For there they should be liable to famine and nakedness and the want, in a manner of all things. The change of air, diet and drinking of water would infect their bodies with sore sicknesses and grievous diseases. And also those which should escape or overcome these difficulties should yet be in continual danger of the savage people, who are cruel, barbarous and most treacherous, being most furious in their rage and merciless where they overcome; not being content only to kill and take away life, but delight to torment men in the most bloody manner that may be; flaying some alive with the shells of fishes, cutting off the members and joints of others by piecemeal and broiling on the coals, eat the collops [pieces] of their flesh in their sight whilst they live, with other cruelties horrible to be related.

And surely it could not be thought but the very

hearing of these things could not but move the very bowels of men to grate within them and make the weak to quake and tremble. It was further objected that it would require greater sums of money to furnish such a voyage and to fit them with necessaries, than their consumed estates would amount to; and yet they must as well look to be seconded with supplies as presently to be transported. Also many precedents of ill success and lamentable miseries befallen others in the like designs were easy to be found, and not forgotten to be alleged; besides their own experience, in their former troubles and hardships in their removal into Holland, and how hard a thing it was for them to live in that strange place, though it was a neighbour country and a civil and rich commonwealth.

It was answered, that all great and honourable actions are accompanied with great difficulties and must be both enterprised and overcome with answerable courages. It was granted the dangers were great, but not desperate. The difficulties were many, but not invincible. For though there were many of them likely, yet they were not certain. It might be sundry of the things feared might never befall; others by provident care and the use of good means might in a great measure be prevented; and all of them, through the help of God, by fortitude and patience, might either be borne or overcome. True it was that such attempts were not to be made and undertaken without good ground and reason, not rashly or lightly as many have done for curiosity or hope of gain, etc. But their condition was not ordinary, their ends were good and honourable, their calling lawful and urgent; and therefore they might expect the blessing of God in their proceeding. Yea, though they should lose their lives in this action, yet might they have comfort in the same and their endeavours would be honourable. They lived here but as men in exile and in a poor condition, and as great miseries might possibly befall them in this place; for the twelve years of truce were now out and there was nothing but beating of drums and preparing for war, the events whereof are always uncertain. The Spaniard might prove as cruel as the savages of America, and the famine and pestilence as sore here as there, and their liberty less to look out for remedy.

After many other particular things answered and alleged on both sides, it was fully concluded by the major part to put this design in execution and to prosecute it by the best means they could.

CHAPTER 9

Of Their Voyage, and How They Passed the Sea; and of Their Safe Arrival at Cape Cod

September 6. These troubles being blown over, and now all being compact together in one ship, they put to sea again with a prosperous wind, which continued divers days together, which was some encouragement unto them; yet, according to the usual manner, many were afflicted with seasickness. And I may not omit here a special work of God's providence. There was a proud and very profane young man, one of the seamen, of a lusty, able body, which made him the more haughty; he would alway be contemning the poor people in their sickness and cursing them daily with grievous execrations; and did not let to tell them that he hoped to help to cast half of them overboard before they came to their journey's end, and to make merry with what they had; and if he were by any gently reproved, he would curse and swear most bitterly. But it pleased God before they came half seas over, to smite this young man with a grievous disease, of which he died in a desperate manner, and so was himself the first that was thrown overboard. Thus his curses light on his own head, and it was an astonishment to all his fellows for they noted it to be the just hand of God upon him.

After they had enjoyed fair winds and weather for a season, they were encountered many times with cross winds and met with many fierce storms with which the ship was shroudly [wickedly] shaken, and her upper works made very leaky; and one of the main beams in the midships was bowed and cracked, which put them in some fear that the ship could not be able to perform the voyage. So some of the chief of the company, perceiving the mariners to fear the sufficiency of the ship as appeared by their mutterings, they entered into serious consultation with the master and other officers of the ship, to consider in time of the danger, and rather to return than to cast themselves into a desperate and inevitable peril. And truly there was great distraction and difference of opinion amongst the mariners themselves; fain would they do what could be done for their wages' sake (being now near half the seas over) and on the other hand they were loath to hazard their lives too desperately. But in examining of all opinions, the master and others affirmed they knew the ship to be strong and firm under water; and for the buckling of the main beam, there was a great iron screw the passengers brought out of Holland, which would raise the beam into his place; the which being done, the carpenter and master affirmed that with a post put under it, set firm in the lower deck and otherways bound, he would make it sufficient. And as for the decks and upper works, they would caulk them as well as they could, and though with the working of the ship they would not long keep staunch, yet there would otherwise be no great danger, if they did not overpress her with sails. So they committed themselves to the will of God and resolved to proceed.

In sundry of these storms the winds were so fierce and the seas so high, as they could not bear a knot of sail, but were forced to hull [heave to and drift with the wind] for divers days together. And in one of them, as they thus lay at hull in a mighty storm, a lusty young man called John Howland, coming upon some occasion above the gratings was, with a seele [pitch] of the ship, thrown into sea; but it pleased God that he caught hold of the topsail halyards which hung overboard and ran out at length. Yet he held his hold (though he was sundry fathoms under water) till he was hauled up by the same rope to the brim of the water, and then with a boat hook and other means got into the ship again and his life saved. And though he was something ill with it, yet he lived many years after and became a profitable member both in church and commonwealth. In all this voyage there died but one of the passengers, which was William Butten, a youth, servant to Samuel Fuller, when they drew near the coast.

But to omit other things (that I may be brief) after long beating at sea they fell with that land which is called Cape Cod; the which being made and certainly known to be it, they were not a little joyful. After some deliberation had amongst themselves and with the master of the ship, they tacked about and resolved to stand for the southward (the wind and weather being fair) to find some place about Hudson's River for their habitation. But after they had sailed that course about half the day, they fell amongst dangerous shoals and roaring breakers, and they were so far entangled therewith as they conceived themselves in great danger; and the wind shrinking upon them withal, they resolved to bear up again for the Cape and thought themselves happy to get out of those dangers before night overtook them, as by God's good providence they did. And the next day they got into the Cape Harbor where they rid in safety.

A word or two by the way of this cape. It was thus first named by Captain Gosnold and his company,[1] Anno 1602, and after by Captain Smith was called Cape James; but it retains the former name amongst seamen. Also, that point which first showed those dangerous shoals unto them they called Point Care, and Tucker's Terrour; but the French and Dutch to this day call it Malabar by reason of those perilous shoals and the losses they have suffered there.

Being thus arrived in a good harbor, and brought safe to land, they fell upon their knees and blessed the God of Heaven who had brought them over the vast and furious ocean, and delivered them from all the perils and miseries thereof, again to set their feet on the firm and stable earth, their proper element. And no marvel if they were thus joyful, seeing wise Seneca was so affected with sailing a few miles on the coast of his own Italy, as he affirmed, that he had rather remain twenty years on his way by land than pass by sea to any place in a short time, so tedious and dreadful was the same unto him.[2]

But here I cannot but stay and make a pause, and stand half amazed at this poor people's present condition; and so I think will the reader, too, when he well considers the same. Being thus passed the vast ocean, and a sea of troubles before in their preparation (as may be remembered by that which went before), they had now no friends to welcome them nor inns to entertain or refresh their weather-beaten bodies; no houses or much less towns to repair to, to seek for succour. It is recorded in Scripture as a mercy to the Apostle and his ship-wrecked company, that the barbarians showed them no small kindness in refreshing them, but these savage barbarians, when they met with them (as after will appear) were readier to fill their sides full of arrows than otherwise. And for the season it was winter, and they that know the winters of that country know them to be sharp and violent, and subject to cruel and fierce storms, dangerous to travel to known places, much more to search an unknown coast. Besides, what could they see but a hideous and desolate wilderness, full of wild

---

[1] Because they took much of that fish there [Bradford].

[2] Epistle 53 [Bradford].

beasts and wild men—and what multitudes there might be of them they knew not. Neither could they, as it were, go up to the top of Pisgah to view from this wilderness a more goodly country to feed their hopes; for which way soever they turned their eyes (save upward to the heavens) they could have little solace or content in respect of any outward objects. For summer being done, all things stand upon them with a weather-beaten face, and the whole country, full of woods and thickets, represented a wild and savage hue. If they looked behind them, there was the mighty ocean which they had passed and was now as a main bar and gulf to separate them from all the civil parts of the world. If it be said they had a ship to succour them, it is true; but what heard they daily from the master and company? But that with speed they should look out a place (with their shallop [dinghy]) where they would be, at some near distance; for the season was such as he would not stir from thence till a safe harbor was discovered by them, where they would be, and he might go without danger; and that victuals consumed apace but he must and would keep sufficient for themselves and their return. Yea, it was muttered by some that if they got not a place in time, they would turn them and their goods ashore and leave them. Let it also be considered what weak hopes of supply and succour they left behind them, that might bear up their minds in this sad condition and trials they were under; and they could not but be very small. It is true, indeed, the affections and love of their brethren at Leyden was cordial and entire towards them, but they had little power to help them or themselves; and how the case stood between them and the merchants at their coming away hath already been declared.

What could now sustain them but the Spirit of God and His grace? May not and ought not the children of these fathers rightly say: "Our fathers were Englishmen which came over this great ocean, and were ready to perish in this wilderness; but they cried unto the Lord, and He heard their voice and looked on their adversity," etc. "Let them therefore praise the Lord, because He is good: and His mercies endure forever." "Yea, let them which have been redeemed of the Lord, shew how He hath delivered them from the hand of the oppressor. When they wandered in the desert wilderness out of the way, and found no city to dwell in, both hungry and thirsty, their soul was overwhelmed in them. Let them confess before the Lord His lovingkindness and His wonderful works before the sons of men."[3]

CHAPTER 10

Showing How They Sought Out a Place of Habitation; and What Befell Them Thereabout

Being thus arrived at Cape Cod the 11th of November, and necessity calling them to look out a place for habitation (as well as the master's and mariners' importunity); they having brought a large shallop with them out of England, stowed in quarters in the ship, they now got her out and set their carpenters to work to trim her up; but being much bruised and shattered in the ship with foul weather, they saw she would be long in mending. Whereupon a few of them tendered themselves to go by land and discover those nearest places, whilst the shallop was in mending; and the rather because as they went into that harbor there seemed to be an opening some two or three leagues off, which the master judged to be a river. It was conceived there might be some danger in the attempt, yet seeing them resolute, they were permitted to go, being sixteen of them well armed under the conduct of Captain Standish, having such instructions given them as was thought meet.

They set forth the 15th of November; and when they had marched about the space of a mile by the seaside, they espied five or six persons with a dog coming towards them, who were savages; but they fled from them and ran up into the woods, and the English followed them, partly to see if they could speak with them, and partly to discover if there might not be more of them lying in ambush. But the Indians seeing themselves thus followed, they again forsook the woods and ran away on the sands as hard as they could, so as they could not come near them but followed them by the track of their feet sundry miles and saw that they had come the same way. So, night coming on, they made their rendezvous and set out their sentinels, and rested in quiet that night; and the next morning followed their track till they had headed a great creek and so left the sands, and turned another way into the woods. But they still followed them by guess, hoping to find their dwellings; but they soon lost both them and themselves, falling

[3] Psalms 107:1–8 [Bradford].

into such thickets as were ready to tear their clothes and armor in pieces; but were most distressed for want of drink. But at length they found water and refreshed themselves, being the first New England water they drunk of, and was now in great thirst as pleasant unto them as wine or beer had been in foretimes.

Afterwards they directed their course to come to the other shore, for they knew it was a neck of land they were to cross over, and so at length got to the seaside and marched to this supposed river, and by the way found a pond of clear, fresh water, and shortly after a good quantity of clear ground where the Indians had formerly set corn, and some of their graves. And proceeding further they saw new stubble where corn had been set the same year; also they found where lately a house had been, where some planks and a great kettle was remaining, and heaps of sand newly paddled with their hands. Which, they digging up, found in them divers fair Indian baskets filled with corn, and some in ears, fair and good, of divers colours, which seemed to them a very goodly sight (having never seen any such before). This was near the place of that supposed river they came to seek, unto which they went and found it to open itself into two arms with a high cliff of sand in the entrance but more like to be creeks of salt water than any fresh, for aught they saw; and that there was good harborage for their shallop, leaving it further to be discovered by their shallop, when she was ready. So, their time limited them being expired, they returned to the ship lest they should be in fear of their safety; and took with them part of the corn and buried up the rest. And so, like the men from Eshcol, carried with them of the fruits of the land and showed their brethren; of which, and their return, they were marvelously glad and their hearts encouraged.

After this, the shallop being got ready, they set out again for the better discovery of this place, and the master of the ship desired to go himself. So there went some thirty men but found it to be no harbor for ships but only for boats. There was also found two of their houses covered with mats, and sundry of their implements in them, but the people were run away and could not be seen. Also there was found more of their corn and of their beans of various colours; the corn and beans they brought away, purposing to give them full satisfaction when they should meet with any of them as, about some six months afterward they did, to their good content.

And here is to be noted a special providence of God, and a great mercy to this poor people, that here they got seed to plant them corn the next year, or else they might have starved, for they had none nor any likelihood to get any till the season had been past, as the sequel did manifest. Neither is it likely they had had this, if the first voyage had not been made, for the ground was now all covered with snow and hard frozen; but the Lord is never wanting unto His in their greatest needs; let His holy name have all the praise.

· · ·

CHAPTER 11

The Remainder of Anno 1620 [The May-flower Compact]

I shall a little return back, and begin with a combination made by them before they came ashore; being the first foundation of their government in this place. Occasioned partly by the discontented and mutinous speeches that some of the strangers amongst them had let fall from them in the ship: That when they came ashore they would use their own liberty, for none had power to command them, the patent they had being for Virginia and not for New England, which belonged to another government, with which the Virginia Company had nothing to do. And partly that such an act by them done, this their condition considered, might be as firm as any patent, and in some respects more sure.

The form was as followeth:

IN THE NAME OF GOD, AMEN.

We whose names are underwritten, the loyal subjects of our dread Sovereign Lord King James, by the Grace of God of Great Britain, France, and Ireland King, Defender of the Faith, etc.

Having undertaken, for the Glory of God and advancement of the Christian Faith and Honour of our King and Country, a Voyage to plant the First Colony in the Northern Parts of Virginia, do by these presents solemnly and mutually in the presence of God and one of another, Covenant and Combine ourselves together into a Civil Body Politic, for our better ordering and preservation and furtherance of the ends aforesaid; and by virtue hereof to enact, constitute and frame such just and equal

Laws, Ordinances, Acts, Constitutions and Offices, from time to time, as shall be thought most meet and convenient for the general good of the Colony, unto which we promise all due submission and obedience. In witness whereof we have hereunder subscribed our names at Cape Cod, the 11th of November, in the year of the reign of our Sovereign Lord King James, of England, France and Ireland the eighteenth, and of Scotland the fifty-fourth. Anno Domini 1620.

. . .

CHAPTER 32

Anno Dom: 1642 [Wickedness Breaks Forth]

Marvelous it may be to see and consider how some kind of wickedness did grow and break forth here, in a land where the same was so much witnessed against and so narrowly looked unto, and severely punished when it was known, as in no place more, or so much, that I have known or heard of; insomuch that they have been somewhat censured even by moderate and good men for their severity in punishments. And yet all this could not suppress the breaking out of sundry notorious sins (as this year, besides other, gives us too many sad precedents and instances), especially drunkenness and uncleanness. Not only incontinency between persons unmarried, for which many both men and women have been punished sharply enough, but some married persons also. But that which is worse, even sodomy and buggery (things fearful to name) have broke forth in this land oftener than once.

I say it may justly be marveled at and cause us to fear and tremble at the consideration of our corrupt natures, which are so hardly bridled, subdued and mortified; nay, cannot by any other means but the powerful work and grace of God's Spirit. But (besides this) one reason may be that the Devil may carry a greater spite against the churches of Christ and the gospel here, by how much the more they endeavour to preserve holiness and purity amongst them and strictly punisheth the contrary when it ariseth either in church or commonwealth; that he might cast a blemish and stain upon them in the eyes of [the] world, who use to be rash in judgment. I would rather think thus, than that Satan hath more power in these heathen lands, as some have thought, than in more Christian nations, especially over God's servants in them.

2. Another reason may be, that it may be in this case as it is with waters when their streams are stopped or dammed up. When they get passage they flow with more violence and make more noise and disturbance than when they are suffered to run quietly in their own channels; so wickedness being here more stopped by strict laws, and the same more nearly looked unto so as it cannot run in a common road of liberty as it would and is inclined, it searches everywhere and at last breaks out where it gets vent.

3. A third reason may be, here (as I am verily persuaded) is not more evils in this kind, nor nothing near so many by proportion as in other places; but they are here more discovered and seen and made public by due search, inquisition and due punishment; for the churches look narrowly to their members, and the magistrates over all, more strictly than in other places. Besides, here the people are but few in comparison of other places which are full and populous and lie hid, as it were, in a wood or thicket and many horrible evils by that means are never seen nor known; whereas here they are, as it were, brought into the light and set in the plain field, or rather on a hill, made conspicuous to the view of all.

. . .

CHAPTER 34

Anno Dom: 1644 [Proposal to Remove to Nauset]

Mr. Edward Winslow was chosen Governor this year.

Many having left this place (as is before noted) by reason of the straitness and barrenness of the same and their finding of better accommodations elsewhere more suitable to their ends and minds; and sundry others still upon every occasion desiring their dismissions, the church began seriously to think whether it were not better jointly to remove to some other place than to be thus weakened and as it were insensibly dissolved. Many meetings and much consultation was held hereabout, and divers were men's minds and opinions. Some were still for staying together in this place, alleging men might here live if they would be content with their condition, and that it was not for want or necessity so much that they removed as for the enriching of themselves. Others were resolute upon removal and so signified that here they could not stay; but if the church did not remove, they must. Insomuch as many were swayed rather than there should be a dissolution, to condescend to a removal if a fit place could be found that might more conveniently and comfortably receive the whole, with such accession of others as might come to them for their better strength and subsistence; and some such-like cautions and limitations.

So as, with the aforesaid provisos, the greater part consented to a removal to a place called Nauset, which had been superficially viewed and the good will of the purchasers to whom it belonged obtained, with some addition thereto from the Court. But now they began to see their errour, that they had given away already the best and most commodious places to others, and now wanted themselves. For this place was about 50 miles from hence, and at an outside of the country remote from all society; also that it would prove

so strait as it would not be competent to receive the whole body, much less be capable of any addition or increase; so as, at least in a short time, they should be worse there than they are now here. The which with sundry other like considerations and inconveniences made them change their resolutions. But such as were before resolved upon removal took advantage of this agreement and went on, notwithstanding; neither could the rest hinder them, they having made some beginning.

And thus was this poor church left, like an ancient mother grown old and forsaken of her children, though not in their affections yet in regard of their bodily presence and personal helpfulness; her ancient members being most of them worn away by death, and these of later time being like children translated into other families, and she like a widow left only to trust in God. Thus, she that had made many rich became herself poor.

JOHN WINTHROP (1588–1649)

If William Bradford was the key figure in the plantation at Plymouth, his counterpart in the Massachusetts Bay Colony was undoubtedly John Winthrop. Winthrop, who was born in England in 1588, came from a wealthy and influential Sussex family. He spent two years at Cambridge, married at seventeen (and was thereafter a most devoted husband), and entered upon a distinguished career as justice of the peace and attorney at the Inner Temple. When the Massachusetts Bay Colony was founded in 1629, however, with an eye to the New World settlement, Winthrop joined the group, accepted the position of governor, and supervised the journey to Charlestown, Massa-

chusetts, on board the *Arbella* in 1630. Like Bradford, Winthrop was governor of his colony almost uninterruptedly until his death in 1649.

Winthrop's great quality was a sort of genius for creating and maintaining order in the theocratic society of Boston. He quickly sensed a threat to that order and (except perhaps in the case of Anne Hutchinson) met that threat with calmness and foresight. He strongly opposed the divisive opinions of Roger Williams, but he retained his real fondness for that incorrigible but extremely winning disturber of the peace; and it was Winthrop who sent secret word to Williams of his impending arrest in 1636, giving Williams time to escape to Rhode Island.

From A Model of Christian Charity (1630)

The following sermon was preached on board the *Arbella*, en route to the New World, in the spring of 1630. It is the most forthright statement of that world's "great design." The Bay

Colony, Winthrop says, is to be "a model of Christian charity." If the settlers will follow the counsel of Micah—"to do justly, to love mercy, to walk humbly with our God"—then God "shall make us a praise and a glory, that men shall say of succeeding plantations: 'The Lord make it like that of New England!' "

The Puritans, Winthrop told them, would be in a situation of extreme visibility: "For we must consider that we shall be as a city upon a hill, the eyes of all people are upon us."

———

God Almighty in His most holy and wise providence hath so disposed of the condition of mankind as in all times some must be rich, some poor; some high and eminent in power and dignity, others mean and in subjection.

The reason hereof:

First, to hold conformity with the rest of His works, being delighted to show forth the glory of His wisdom in the variety and difference of the creatures and the glory of His power, in ordering all these differences for the preservation and good of the whole, and the glory of His greatness: that as it is the glory of princes to have many officers, so this great King will have many stewards, counting Himself more honored in dispensing His gifts to man by man than if He did it by His own immediate hand.

Secondly, that He might have the more occasion to manifest the work of His Spirit: first, upon the wicked in moderating and restraining them, so that the rich and mighty should not eat up the poor, nor the poor and despised rise up against their superiors and shake off their yoke; secondly, in the regenerate, in exercising His graces in them—as in the great ones, their love, mercy, gentleness, temperance, etc., in the poor and inferior sort, their faith, patience, obedience, etc.

Thirdly, that every man might have need of other, and from hence they might be all knit more nearly together in the bond of brotherly affection. From hence it appears plainly that no man is made more honorable than another or more wealthy, etc., out of any particular and singular respect to himself, but for the glory of his creator and the common good of the creature, man. Therefore God still reserves the property of these gifts to Himself (Ezek. 16. 17). He there calls wealth His gold and His silver, etc. (Prov. 3. 9). He claims their service as His due: "Honor the Lord with thy riches." All men being thus (by divine providence) ranked into two sorts, rich and poor, under the first are comprehended all such as are able to live comfortably by their own means duly improved, and all others are poor, according to the former distribution.

There are two rules whereby we are to walk, one towards another: justice and mercy. These are always distinguished in their act and in their object, yet may they both concur in the same subject in each respect: as sometimes there may be an occasion of showing mercy to a rich man in some sudden danger of distress, and also doing of mere justice to a poor man in regard of some particular contract.

There is likewise a double law by which we are regulated in our conversation, one towards another: in both the former respects, the law of nature and the law of grace, or the moral law or the law of the Gospel—to omit the rule of justice as not properly belonging to this purpose, otherwise than it may fall into consideration in some particular cases. By the first of these laws, man, as he was enabled so, withal [is] commanded to love his neighbor as himself; upon this ground stand all the precepts of the moral law, which concerns our dealings with men. To apply this to the works of mercy, this law requires two things: first, that every man afford his help to another in every want or distress; secondly, that he perform this out of the same affection which makes him careful of his own good according to that of our savior (Matt. 7. 12): "Whatsoever ye would that men should do to you." This was practiced by Abraham and Lot in entertaining the angels and the old man of Gibea.

The law of grace or the Gospel hath some difference from the former, as in these respects: first, the law of nature was given to man in the estate of innocency, this of the Gospel in the estate of regeneracy. Secondly, the former propounds one man to another as the same flesh and image of God, this as a brother in Christ also, and in the communion of the same spirit, and so teacheth us to put a difference between Christians and others. "Do good to all, especially to the household of faith." Upon this ground the Israelites were to put a difference between the brethren of such as were strangers though not of the Canaanites. Thirdly, the law of nature could give no rules for dealing with enemies, for all are to be considered as friends in the estate of innocency; but the Gospel commands love to an enemy. Proof: "If thine enemy hunger, feed him; love your enemies, do good to them that hate you" (Matt. 5. 44).

This law of the Gospel propounds likewise a difference of seasons and occasions. There is a time when a Christian must sell all and give to the poor as they did in the apostles' times; there is a time also when a Christian, though they give not all yet, must give beyond their ability, as they of Macedonia (II Cor. 8). Likewise, community of perils calls for extraordinary liberality, and so doth community in some special service for the church. Lastly, when there is no other means whereby our Christian brother may be relieved in this distress, we must help him beyond our ability, rather than tempt God in putting him upon help by miraculous or extraordinary means. . . .

1. For the persons, we are a company professing ourselves fellow members of Christ, in which respect only, though we were absent from each other many miles, and had our employments as far distant, yet we ought to account ourselves knit together by this bond of love, and live in the exercise of it, if we would have comfort of our being in Christ. This was notorious in the practice of the Christians in former times, as is testified of the Waldenses from the mouth of one of the adversaries, Aeneas Sylvius: *Mutuo solent amare penè antequam norint*—they used to love any of their own religion even before they were acquainted with them.

2. For the work we have in hand, it is by mutual consent, through a special overruling providence and a more than an ordinary approbation of the churches of Christ, to seek out a place of cohabitation and consortship, under a due form of government both civil and ecclesiastical. In such cases as this, the care of the public must oversway all private respects by which not only conscience but mere civil policy doth bind us; for it is a true rule that particular estates cannot subsist in the ruin of the public.

3. The end is to improve our lives to do more service to the Lord, the comfort and increase of the body of Christ whereof we are members, that ourselves and posterity may be the better preserved from the common corruptions of this evil world, to serve the Lord and work out our salvation under the power and purity of His holy ordinances.

4. For the means whereby this must be effected, they are twofold: a conformity with the work and the end we aim at; these we see are extraordinary, therefore we must not content ourselves with usual ordinary means. Whatsoever we did or ought to have done when we lived in England, the same must we do, and more also where we go. That which the most in their churches maintain as a truth in profession only, we must bring into fa-

miliar and constant practice: as in this duty of love we must love brotherly without dissumulation, we must love one another with a pure heart fervently, we must bear one another's burdens, we must not look only on our own things but also on the things of our brethren. Neither must we think that the Lord will bear with such failings at our hands as He doth from those among whom we have lived. . . .

Thus stands the cause between God and us: we are entered into covenant with Him for this work; we have taken out a commission, the Lord hath given us leave to draw our own articles. We have professed to enterprise these actions upon these and these ends; we have hereupon besought Him of favor and blessing. Now if the Lord shall please to hear us and bring us in peace to the place we desire, then hath He ratified this covenant and sealed our Commission, [and] will expect a strict performance of the articles contained in it. But if we shall neglect the observation of these articles which are the ends we have propounded, and dissembling with our God, shall fall to embrace this present world and prosecute our carnal intentions, seeking great things for ourselves and our posterity, the Lord will surely break out in wrath against us, be revenged of such a perjured people, and make us know the price of the breach of such a covenant.

Now the only way to avoid this shipwreck and to provide for our posterity is to follow the counsel of Micah: to do justly, to love mercy, to walk humbly with our God. For this end, we must be knit together in this work as one man. We must entertain each other in brotherly affection; we must be willing to abridge ourselves of our superfluities, for the supply of others' necessities; we must uphold a familiar commerce together in all meekness, gentleness, patience and liberality. We must delight in each other, make others' conditions our own, rejoice together, mourn together, labor and suffer together: always having before our eyes our commission and community in the work, our community as members of the same body. So shall we keep the unity of the spirit in the bond of peace, the Lord will be our God and delight to dwell among us, as His own people, and will command a blessing upon us in all our ways, so that we shall see much more of His wisdom, power, goodness, and truth than formerly we have been acquainted with. We shall find that the God of Israel is among us, when ten of us shall be able to resist a thousand of our enemies, when He shall make us a praise and glory, that men shall say of succeeding plantations: "The Lord make it like that of New England." For we must consider that we shall be as a city upon a hill, the eyes of all people are upon us. So that if we shall deal falsely with our God in this work we have undertaken, and so cause Him to withdraw His present help from us, we shall be made a story and a by-word through the world: we shall open the mouths of enemies to speak evil of the ways of God and all professors for God's sake; we shall shame the faces of many of God's worthy servants, and cause their prayers to be turned into curses upon us, till we be consumed out of the good land whither we are going.

And to shut up this discourse with that exhortation of Moses, that faithful servant of the Lord, in his last farewell to Israel (Deut. 30): Beloved, there is now set before us life and good, death and evil, in that we are commanded this day to love the Lord our God, and to love one another, to walk in His ways and to keep His commandments and His ordinance and His laws and the articles of our covenant with Him, that we may live and be multiplied, and that the Lord our God may bless us in the land whither we go to possess it: but if our hearts shall turn away so that we will not obey, but shall be seduced and worship . . . other gods, our pleasures and profits, and serve them, it is propounded unto us this day, we shall surely perish out of the good land whither we pass over this vast sea to possess it.

Therefore, let us choose life,
that we, and our seed,
may live; by obeying His
voice and cleaving to Him,
for He is our life and
our prosperity.

COTTON MATHER (1663–1728)

Cotton Mather's great strengths and great weaknesses derived from his justified pride of family. He was the grandson of John Cotton, perhaps the most eminent and certainly the most admired minister in the first generation of New England Puritans. His paternal grandfather, Richard Mather, had been driven from his pulpit in England because of his excessively Puritan views and had come to this country, eventually to become the first minister of Dorchester, and one of the first to work out the special nature of the church in New England (or "the New England way") as distinguished from the Church of England. A younger son of this grave, kindly, and learned man, Increase Mather, married Maria Cotton, who by this time was also the young man's step-sister.[1] Increase was a more complex figure than his father, though like him he was an invaluable and devoted public servant, sparing no effort to secure a charter

from the British Crown (in 1688) which gave Massachusetts for the time a larger degree of self-government than was enjoyed by any other among the American Crown colonies. In 1685, he became the head of Harvard College and worked equally hard to ensure its own relative freedom of action; in the course of time, however, he ran up against the prejudices of the Corporation and after a good many quarrels and recriminations was forced to resign in 1701.

But Increase Mather, brilliant, impassioned, and deeply prejudiced in his own way, seems not to have been an easy man to deal with. He had a loathing for the ungodly and an extraordinary concern for the spiritual state both of himself and of others, among the latter particularly his children. His life was a series of inner crises, the most serious being those which followed the deaths of his father and mother, and he went to his grave tormented by the possibility that he was not regenerate.

In his earlier years, when he was convinced that New England was in very fact the New Jerusalem and the last best hope for redemp-

[1] After the death of John Cotton and that of Richard Mather's first wife Katharine, Richard married Cotton's widow.

tion in the history of mankind, he thundered against the temporal authorities, sternly summoning them to reform their ways, and warning them—to borrow the title of a "jeremiad"[2] of 1674—that *The Day of Trouble Is Near.* Later, he lost faith in the future of New England, turned mystical, and began to discourse upon the utterly mysterious nature of God's relationship to the world rather than the reasonableness thereof as allegedly guaranteed by the covenant.[3]

If Cotton Mather inherited his grandfathers' scholarly aptitude and rhetorical eloquence, he also inherited something of his father's disturbed, vehement, and self-punishing nature. These qualities combined with an inevitable consciousness of the family's remarkable accomplishments —the Mathers comprised the first of those American families which, like the Adamses two centuries later, handed down to successive generations an almost intolerable burden of achievement. Cotton Mather had both the gifts and the energy not only to respond to this legacy but to add a prodigious chapter to it; it was rather *his* son Increase, or "Cresy," who violated the family tradition by consorting with harlots (begetting a bastard son by one of them), rioting in the streets of Boston, and refusing to study. Mather was only dimly and intermittently aware that these were acts of rebellion against an overpowering father.

Cotton Mather was overpowering in other ways. He entered Harvard at twelve (in 1675) and performed with a brilliance that even surprised his demanding father. He was a voracious reader and accumulated a library that was one of the wonders of the New World. He was an inexhaustible writer, turning out more than five hundred books on an incredible variety of subjects. He had a passionate interest in history and biography and the grand sweep of events which disclosed the working out of God's plans; but he

also kept a wary eye on the new sciences and experimented a little on his own. He inveighed with a kind of violent splendor against every kind of heretic and deviationist, thereby, among other things, earning a reputation as the vigorously bigoted leader in the condemnation and killing of the alleged witches in Salem in 1692. Time has not been able to dispel this image, but the case is in fact not a simple one. Cotton Mather did not, of course, take any part in the actual trials, and he came to believe that the judges had been terribly wrong in admitting some of the evidence (that involving the apparition of witches' specters). But he clung to the idea that at least some of the accused might well have been witches—though, if so, they represented God's punishment for New England's sinfulness.

Sinfulness was never very far from Cotton Mather's mind, or his imagination. He had at times a sense of his own vileness, both of body and of spirit, beyond anything that Puritan doctrine really required. This seems to have been connected in part with his pronounced sexuality. He could say, in a tone that coincided with doctrine, "I do not apprehend, that Heaven requires me utterlie to lay aside my fondness for my lovelie Consort," but he could also express a genuine horror at bodily actions. The latter feeling did not prevent him from marrying three times and begetting no less than fifteen children; but it did contribute to the tremendous tension under which he lived his entire life and to the hysterical fervor that often discolors his writing style.

That life was increasingly beset with difficulties. His third wife, Lydia, showed signs of derangement soon after their marriage in 1715, took to hiding his papers or spilling ink on them, exploded in "prodigious Paroxyms" of rage, and finally went insane. "Cresy," a savage disappointment and the family disgrace, was lost at sea in 1724; eleven other children had already died young, and another died in 1724. Mather bore bravely on, writing, preaching, and quarreling until his death in 1728.

Despite his sometimes violently reactionary views (as they must be called in the context of

---

[2] On the preaching of jeremiads, or prophetic warnings, and on the apocalyptic temper of the Puritans, see the introduction to Michael Wigglesworth.

[3] On the conflict between the Puritan belief that God's governance could be rationally understood and the belief that it was wholly inaccessible to human reason, see the introduction to Thomas Shepard.

his age), Mather is in some ways a queerly attractive figure. In *Grandfather's Chair*, Nathaniel Hawthorne would give an engrossing and well-balanced account of this emotionally unbalanced man and would testify to the extraordinary power of his mind.

From Magnalia Christi Americana (1702)

A GENERAL INTRODUCTION

The Annals of Christ in America is a sort of loose prose epic of the history of New England to 1700. The first of its seven books tells of the early settlers; the next of the lives of the colony's governors, and then of the leading ministers. Later books deal with the history of Harvard College, and of some of its graduates; the history of the Congregational church; and related matters. It remains a treasury of information about seventeenth-century New England.

Above all, perhaps, its opening pages reflect once more the Puritan sense of a divine mission; and the first lines, no doubt deliberately, echo the beginning of the *Aeneid*.

---

1. I write the wonders of the Christian religion, flying from the depravations of Europe to the American strand; and, assisted by the holy author of that religion, I do, with all conscience of truth, required therein by Him who is the truth itself, report the wonderful displays of His infinite power, wisdom, goodness, and faithfulness, wherewith His divine providence hath irradiated an Indian wilderness.

I relate the considerable matters that produced and attended the first settlement of colonies which have been renowned for the degree of reformation professed and attained by evangelical churches, erected in those ends of the earth; and a field being thus prepared, I proceed unto a relation of the considerable matters which have been acted thereupon.

I first introduce the actors that have in a more exemplary manner served those colonies, and give remarkable occurrences in the exemplary lives of many magistrates, and of more ministers, who so lived as to leave unto posterity examples worthy of everlasting remembrance.

I add hereunto the notables of the only Protestant university that ever shone in that hemisphere of the New World, with particular instances of Criolians in our biography provoking the whole world with virtuous objects of emulation.

I introduce then the actions of a more eminent importance that have signalized those colonies, whether the establishments, directed by their synods, with a rich variety of synodical and ecclesiastical determinations, or the disturbances with which they have been from all sorts of temptations and enemies tempestuated, and the methods by which they have still weathered out each horrible tempest.

And into the midst of these actions, I interpose an entire book wherein there is, with all possible veracity, a collection made of memorable occurrences and amazing judgments and mercies befalling many particular persons among the people of New England.

Let my readers expect all that I have promised them in this bill of fare; and it may be they will find themselves entertained with yet many other passages, above and beyond their expectation, deserving likewise a room in history; in all which there will be nothing but the author's too mean way of preparing so great entertainments to reproach the invitation.

2. The reader will doubtless desire to know what it was that

> . . . *tot volvere casus*
> *Insignes pietate viros, tot adire labores,*
> *Impulerit.*

[". . . drove men eminent in piety to endure so many calamities and to undertake so many hardships" (*Aeneid*, I, 9–11).] And our history shall, on many fit occasions which will be therein offered, endeavor with all historical fidelity and simplicity, and with as little offense as may be, to satisfy him. The sum of the matter is that from the beginning of the Reformation in the English nation there hath always been a generation of godly men, desirous to pursue the reformation of religion, according to the word of God and the example of the best reformed churches, and answering the character of good men given by Josephus in his paraphrase on the words of Samuel to Saul, μηδὲν ἄλλο πραχθήσεσθαι καλῶς ὑφ' ἑαυτῶν νομίζοντες ἢ ὅτι ἄν ποιήσωσι τοῦ θεοῦ κεκελευκότος ["They think they do nothing right in the service of God but what they do according to the command of God"]. And there hath been another generation of men, who have still employed the power which they have generally still had in their hands, not only to stop the progress of the desired reformation but also, with innumerable vexations, to persecute those that most heartily wish well unto it. There were many of the reformers who joined with the Rev. John Fox in the complaints, which he then entered in his *Martyrology*, about the baits of Popery yet left in the church, and in his wishes: God take them away or ease us from them, for God knows they be the cause of much blindness and strife amongst men! They zealously decried the policy of complying always with the ignorance and vanity of the people, and cried out earnestly for purer administrations in the House of God, and more conformity to the law of Christ and primitive Christianity, while others would not hear of going any further than the first essay of reformation. 'Tis very certain that the first reformers never intended that what they did should be the absolute boundary of reformation, so that it should be a sin to proceed any further; as, by their own going beyond Wiclif, and changing and growing in their own models also, and the confessions of Cranmer, with the *Scripta Anglicana* of Bucer, and a thousand other things was abundantly demonstrated. But after a fruitless expectation, wherein the truest friends of the Reformation long waited, for to have that which Heylin himself owns to have been the design of the first reformers, followed as it should have been, a party very unjustly arrogated to themselves the venerable name of "The Church of England," by numberless oppressions grievously smote those their fellow servants. Then 'twas that, as our great Owen hath expressed it: "Multitudes of pious, peaceable Protestants were driven, by their severities, to leave their native country, and seek a refuge for their lives and liberties, with freedom for the worship of God, in the wilderness in the ends of the earth."

3. It is the history of these Protestants that is here attempted—Protestants that highly honored and affected the Church of England, and humbly petition to be a part of it; but by the mistake of a few powerful brethren driven to seek a place for the exercise of the Protestant religion, according to the light of their consciences, in the deserts of America. And in this attempt I have proposed not only to preserve and secure the interest of religion in the churches of that little country, New England, so far as the Lord Jesus Christ may please to bless it for that end, but also to offer unto the churches of the Reformation, abroad in the world, some small memorials that may be serviceable unto the designs of reformation, whereto, I believe, they are quickly to be awakened. I am far from any such boast concerning these churches, that they have need of nothing; I wish their works were more perfect before God. Indeed, that which Austin called "the perfection of Christians" is like to be, until the term for the Antichristian apostasy be expired, "the perfection of churches" too. *Ut agnoscant se nunquam esse perfectas* ["That they acknowledge themselves never to be perfect"]. Nevertheless, I persuade myself that, so far as they have attained, they have given great examples of the methods and measures wherein an evangelical reformation is to be prosecuted, and of the qualifications requisite in the instruments that are to prosecute it, and of the difficulties which may be most likely to obstruct it, and the most likely directions and remedies for those obstructions.

It may be 'tis not possible for me to do a greater service unto the churches on the best island of the universe than to give a distinct relation of those great examples which have been occurring among churches of exiles, that were driven out of that island into an horrible wilderness, merely for their being well-willers unto the Reformation. When that blessed martyr, Constantine, was carried, with other martyrs, in a dungcart, unto the place of execution, he pleasantly said, "Well, yet we are a precious odor to God in Christ." Though the reformed churches in the American regions have, by very injurious representations of their brethren (all which they desire to forget and forgive!), been many times thrown into a dungcart, yet as they have been a precious odor to God in Christ, so, I hope, they will be a precious odor unto His people —and not only precious, but useful also, when the history of them shall come to be considered. A reformation of the church is coming on, and I cannot but thereupon say, with the dying Cyrus to his children in Xenophon, Ἐκ τῶν προγεγεννημένων μανθάνετε, αὐτὴ γὰρ ἀρίστη διδασκαλία ["Learn from the things that have been done already, for this is the best way of learning"].

The reader hath here an account of the things that have been done already. Bernard upon that clause in the Canticles—"O thou fairest among women"—has this ingenious gloss: *Pulchram, non omnimode quidem, sed pulchram inter mulieres eam docet, videlicet cum distinctione, quatenus ex hoc amplius reprimatur, et sciat quid desit sibi* ["He calls her fair, not absolutely, but fair among women, that is to say with a distinction, so that she may thereby be more restrained, and may know her deficiencies"]. Thus I do not say that the churches of New England are the most regular that can be, yet I do say, and am sure, that they are very like unto those that were in the first ages of Christianity. And if I assert that in the reformation of the church, the state of it in those ages is not a little to be considered, the great Peter Ramus, among others, has emboldened me. For when the Cardinal of Lorrain, the Maecenas of that great man, was offended at him for turning Protestant, he replied, *Inter opes illas, quibus me ditasti, has etiam in aeternam recordabor, quod beneficio, Poessiacae responsionis tuae didici, de quindecim a Christo saeculis, primum vere esse aureum reliqua, quo longius abscederent esse nequiora, atque deteriora: Tum igitur cum fieret optio, aurem saeculum delegi* ["Among those riches with which you enriched me, this I was mindful of always, which I learned from your reply at Poissy —that of the fifteen centuries since Christ, the first is truly golden. The rest, the farther they are removed from the first, are the more worthless and degenerate. Therefore when choice was to be made, I chose the golden age"]. In short, the first age was the golden one; to return unto that will make a man a Protestant, and I may add, a Puritan. 'Tis possible that our Lord Jesus Christ carried some thousands of reformers into the retirements of an American desert on purpose that, with an opportunity granted unto many of his faithful servants, to enjoy the precious liberty of their ministry, tho' in the midst of many temptations all their days, he might there, to them first, and then by them, give a specimen of many good things which he would have his churches elsewhere aspire and arise unto. And this being done, he knows whether there be not all done that New England was planted for, and whether the plantation may not, soon after this, come to nothing. Upon that expression in the sacred scriptures, "Cast the unprofitable Servant into Outer Darkness," it hath been imagined by some that the *Regiones Exterae* of America are the *Tenebrae Exteriores* which the unprofitable are condemned unto. No doubt the authors of those ecclesiastical impositions and severities which drove the English Christians into the dark regions of America esteemed those Chris-

tians to be a very unprofitable sort of creatures. But behold, ye European churches, there are golden candlesticks (more than twice seven times seven!) in the midst of this outer darkness; unto the upright children of Abraham, here hath arisen light in darkness. And let us humbly speak it, it shall be profitable for you to consider the light, which from the midst of this outer darkness is now to be darted over unto the other side of the Atlantic ocean. But we must therewithal ask your prayers that these golden candlesticks may not quickly be removed out of their place!

4. But whether New England may live anywhere else or no, it must live in our history!

THE LIFE OF WILLIAM BRADFORD

Mather's style was more learnedly allusive, nervous, and exclamatory than the modernized version of "A General Introduction" would suggest, and to indicate some of its queer flavor we present here Mather's life of Bradford as it appeared in Book 2 of the first edition of the *Magnalia.*

---

2. Among those Devout People was our *William Bradford,* who was Born *Anno* 1588 [1590]. in an obscure Village call'd *Ansterfield* [Austerfield], where the People were as unacquainted with the *Bible,* as the *Jews* do seem to have been with *part* of it in the Days of *Josiah;* a most Ignorant and Licentious *People,* and *like unto their Priest.* Here, and in some other Places, he had a Comfortable *Inheritance* left him of his Honest Parents, who died while he was yet a Child, and cast him on the Education, first of his *Grand Parents,* and then of his *Uncles,* who devoted him, like his Ancestors, unto the Affairs of *Husbandry.* Soon and long Sickness kept him, as he would afterwards thankfully say, from the *Vanities of Youth,* and made him the fitter for what he was afterwards to undergo. When he was about a Dozen Years Old, the Reading of the *Scriptures* began to cause great Impressions upon him; and those Impressions were much assisted and improved, when he came to enjoy Mr. *Richard Clifton*'s Illuminating Ministry, not far from his Abode; he was then also further befriended, by being brought into the Company and Fellowship of such as were then called *Pro-*

fessors; though the Young Man that brought him into it, did after become a Prophane and Wicked *Apostate*. Nor could the *Wrath* of his *Uncles*, nor the *Scoff* of his *Neighbours* now turn'd upon him, as one of the *Puritans*, divert him from his Pious Inclinations.

3. At last beholding how fearfully the Evangelical and Apostolical *Church-Form*, whereinto the Churches of the *Primitive Times* were cast by the good Spirit of God, had been *Deformed* by the *Apostacy* of the *Succeeding Times*; and what little Progress the *Reformation* had yet made in many Parts of *Christendom* towards its Recovery, he set himself by Reading, by Discourse, by Prayer, to learn whether it was not his Duty to *withdraw* from the Communion of the *Parish-Assemblies*, and *engage* with some *Society* of the Faithful, that should keep close unto the *Written Word* of God, as the *Rule* of their *Worship*. And after many Distresses of Mind concerning it, he took up a very Deliberate and Understanding *Resolution* of doing so; which *Resolution* he chearfully Prosecuted, although the provoked *Rage* of his Friends tried all the ways imaginable to reclaim him from it, unto all whom his Answer was, *Were I like to endanger my Life, or consume my Estate by any ungodly Courses, your Counsels to me were very seasonable: But you know that I have been Diligent and Provident in my Calling, and not only desirous to augment what I have, but also to enjoy it in your Company; to part from which will be as great a Cross as can befal me. Nevertheless, to keep a good Conscience, and walk in such a Way as God has prescribed in his Word, is a thing which I must prefer before you all, and above Life it self. Wherefore, since 'tis for a good Cause that I am like to suffer the Disasters which you lay before me, you have no Cause to be either angry with me, or sorry for me; yea, I am not only willing to part with every thing that is dear to me in this World for this Cause, but I am also thankful that God has given me an Heart so to do, and will accept me so to suffer for him. Some* lamented him, *some* derided him, *all* disswaded him: Nevertheless the more they did it, the more fixed he was in his Purpose to seek the Ordinances of the Gospel, where they should be dispensed with most of the *Commanded Purity*; and the *sudden Deaths* of the chief Relations which thus lay at him, quickly after convinced him what a Folly it had been to have quitted his *Profession*, in Expectation of any Satisfaction from them. So to *Holland* he attempted a removal.

4. Having with a great Company of Christians Hired a Ship to Transport them for *Holland*, the Master perfidiously betrayed them into the Hands of those *Persecutors*, who Rifled and Ransack'd their Goods, and clapp'd their Persons into Prison at *Boston*, where they lay for a Month together. But Mr. *Bradford* being a Young Man of about *Eighteen*, was dismissed sooner than the rest, so that within a while he had Opportunity with some others to get over to *Zealand*, through *Perils* both by *Land* and *Sea* not inconsiderable; where he was not long Ashore e're a *Viper* seized on his Hand, that is, an Officer, who carried him unto the Magistrates, unto whom an envious Passenger had accused him as having *fled* out of *England*. When the Magistrates understood the True Cause of his coming thither, they were well satisfied with him; and so he repaired joyfully unto his Brethren at *Amsterdam*, where the Difficulties to which he afterwards stooped in Learning and Serving of a *Frenchman* at the Working of *Silks*, were abundantly Compensated by the *Delight* wherewith he sat under the *Shadow* of our Lord in his purely dispensed Ordinances. At the end of Two Years, he did, being of Age to do it, convert his Estate in *England* into Money; but Setting up for himself, he found some of his Designs by the *Providence* of God frowned upon, which he judged a *Correction* bestowed by God upon him for certain Decays of *Internal Piety*, whereinto he had fallen; the *Consumption* of his *Estate* he thought came to prevent a *Consumption* in his *Virtue*. But after he had resided in *Holland* about half a Score Years, he was one of those who bore a part in that Hazardous and Generous Enterprize of removing into *New-England*, with part of the *English* Church at *Leyden*, where at their first Landing, his dearest Consort accidentally falling Overboard, was drowned in the *Harbour*; and the rest of his Days were spent in the Services, and the Temptations, of that *American Wilderness*.

5. Here was Mr. *Bradford* in the Year 1621. Unanimously chosen the *Governor* of the Plantation: The Difficulties whereof were such, that if he had not been a Person of more than Ordinary Piety, Wisdom and Courage, he must have sunk under them. He had with a Laudable Industry been laying up a Treasure of *Experiences*, and he had now occasion to use it: Indeed nothing but an *Experienced* Man could have been suitable to the Necessities of the People. The Potent Nations of the *Indians*, into whose Country they were come, would have cut them off, if the Blessing of God

upon *his* Conduct had not quell'd them; and if his Prudence, Justice and Moderation had not over-ruled them, they had been ruined by their own *Distempers.* One *Specimen* of his Demeanour is to this Day particularly spoken of. A Company of Young Fellows that were newly arrived, were very unwilling to comply with the Governour's Order for *Working* abroad on the Publick Account; and therefore on *Christmass-Day,* when he had called upon them, they excused themselves, with a pretence that it was against their *Conscience* to *Work* such a Day. The Governour gave them no Answer, only that he would spare them till they were better informed; but by and by he found them all at *Play* in the Street, sporting themselves with various Diversions; whereupon Commanding the Instruments of their Games to be taken from them, he effectually gave them to understand, *That it was against his Conscience that they should play whilst others were at Work; and that if they had any Devotion to the Day, they should show it at Home in the Exercises of Religion, and not in the Streets with Pastime and Frolicks;* and this gentle Reproof put a final stop to all such Disorders for the future.

6. For Two Years together after the beginning of the Colony, whereof he was now Governour, the poor People had a great Experiment of *Man's not living by Bread alone;* for when they were left all together without one Morsel of *Bread* for many Months one after another, still the good Providence of God relieved them, and supplied them, and this for the most part out of the *Sea.* In this low Condition of Affairs, there was no little Exercise for the *Prudence* and *Patience* of the Governour, who chearfully bore his part in all: And that *Industry* might not flag, he quickly set himself to settle *Propriety* [property] among the New-Planters; foreseeing that while the whole Country labour'd upon a *Common Stock,* the *Husbandry* and *Business* of the Plantation could not *flourish,* as *Plato* and others long since dream'd that it would, if a *Community* were established. Certainly, if the Spirit which dwelt in the *Old Puritans,* had not inspired these *New-Planters,* they had sunk under the Burden of these Difficulties; but our *Bradford* had a *double Portion* of that Spirit.

7. The Plantation was quickly thrown into a *Storm* that almost overwhelmed it, by the unhappy Actions of a Minister sent over from *England* by the *Adventurers* concerned for the Plantation; but by the Blessing of Heaven on the Conduct of the Governour, they Weathered out that *Storm.* Only the *Adventurers* hereupon breaking to pieces, threw up all their Concernments with the *Infant Colony;* whereof they gave this as one Reason, *That the Planters dissembled with His Majesty, and their Friends in their Petition, wherein they declared for a Church-Discipline, agreeing with the* French *and others of the Reforming Churches in* Europe. Whereas 'twas now urged, that they had admitted into their Communion a Person, who at his Admission utterly *renounced* the Churches of *England,* (which Person by the way, was *that* very Man who had made the Complaints against them) and therefore though they denied the *Name* of Brownists yet they were the *Thing.* In Answer hereunto, the very Words written by the Governour were these; *Whereas you Tax us with dissembling about the* French Discipline, *you do us wrong, for we both hold and practice the* Discipline *of the* French *and other* Reformed Churches (*as they have published the same in the* Harmony of Confessions) *according to our Means, in Effect and Substance. But whereas you would tie us up to the* French Discipline *in every Circumstance, you derogate from the* Liberty *we have in Christ Jesus. The Apostle* Paul *would have none to* follow him *in any thing, but wherein he* follows Christ; *much less ought any Christian or Church in the World to do it. The* French *may err, we may err, and other Churches may err, and doubtless do in many* Circumstances. *That Honour therefore belongs only to the* Infallible Word of God, *and pure Testament of Christ, to be propounded and followed as the* only *Rule and Pattern for Direction herein to all Churches and Christians. And it is too great Arrogancy for any Men or Church to think, that he or they have so sounded the Word of God unto the bottom, as precisely to set down the Churches Discipline without Error in Substance or Circumstance, that no other without blame may digress or differ in any thing from the same. And it is not difficult to shew that the* Reformed Churches *differ in many* Circumstances *among themselves.* By which Words it appears how far he was free from that *Rigid Spirit* of *Separation,* which broke to pieces the *Separatists* themselves in the *Low Countries,* unto the great Scandal of the *Reforming Churches.* He was indeed a Person of a *well-temper'd Spirit,* or else it had been scarce possible for him to have kept the Affairs of *Plymouth* in so good a *Temper* for *Thirty Seven* Years together; in every one of which he was chosen their Governour, except the *Three Years,* wherein Mr. *Winslow,* and the *Two Years,* wherein Mr. *Prince,* at the choice of the People, took a *turn* with him.

8. The *Leader* of a People in a *Wilderness* had need be a *Moses*; and if a *Moses* had not led the People of *Plymouth-Colony*, when this Worthy Person was their Governour, the People had never with so much Unanimity and Importunity still called *him* to lead them. Among many Instances thereof, let this one piece of *Self denial be told for a Memorial of him, wheresoever this History shall be considered.* The Patent of the Colony was taken in *his* Name, running in these Terms, *To William Bradford, his Heirs, Associates and Assigns:* But when the number of the *Freemen* was much Increased, and many New *Townships* Erected, the *General Court* there desired of Mr. *Bradford*, that he would make a Surrender of the same into *their Hands*, which *he* willingly and presently assented unto, and confirmed it according to their Desire by his *Hand* and *Seal*, reserving no more for himself than was his *Proportion*, with others, by *Agreement*. But as he found the Providence of Heaven many ways *Recompencing* his many Acts of *Self-denial*, so he gave this Testimony to the Faithfulness of the Divine Promises; *That he had forsaken Friends, Houses and Lands for the sake of the Gospel, and the Lord gave them him again. Here* he prospered in his *Estate*; and besides a Worthy *Son* which he had by a former Wife, he had also Two Sons and a Daughter by another, whom he Married in this Land.

9. He was a Person for *Study* as well as *Action*; and hence, notwithstanding the Difficulties through which he passed in his Youth, he attained unto a notable Skill in *Languages*; the *Dutch* Tongue was become almost as Vernacular to him as the *English*; the *French* Tongue he could also manage; the *Latin* and the *Greek* he had Mastered; but the *Hebrew* he most of all studied, *Because,* he said, *he would see with his own Eyes the Ancient Oracles of God in their Native Beauty.* He was also well skill'd in *History,* in *Antiquity,* and in *Philosophy*; and for *Theology* he became so versed in it, that he was an *Irrefragable Disputant* against the *Errors*, especially those of *Anabaptism*, which with Trouble he saw rising in his Colony; wherefore he wrote some Significant things for the Confutation of those Errors. But the *Crown* of all was his Holy, Prayerful, Watchful and Fruitful *Walk with God*, wherein he was very Exemplary.

10. At length he fell into an Indisposition of Body, which rendred him unhealthy for a whole *Winter*; and as the *Spring* advanced, his Health yet more declined; yet he felt himself not what he counted *Sick*, till one *Day*; in the *Night* after which, the God of Heaven so fill'd his Mind with *Ineffable Consolations*, that he seemed little short of *Paul*, rapt up unto the *Unutterable* Entertainments of *Paradise*. The next Morning he told his Friends, *That the good Spirit of God had given him a Pledge of his Happiness in another World, and the First-fruits of his Eternal Glory:* And on the Day following he died, *May* 9. 1657. in the 69th Year of his Age. Lamented by all the Colonies of *New-England*, as a Common Blessing and Father to them all.

THOMAS SHEPARD (1605–1649)

Thomas Shepard was born in England, studied at Cambridge, and was for a time lecturer at the University of Essex. He came to America in 1635, became the minister of the church in Cambridge, Massachusetts, and developed into one of the most powerful and popular preachers in the first generation of the Massachusetts Bay Colony.

Shepard's sermon on "the covenant of grace" is perhaps the most succinct statement of the covenant theory to have come out of early New England. This theory, as we have said, declared among other things that God had entered into an agreement whereby his plans and actions, otherwise utterly beyond the grasp of finite human reason, could be perceived and understood within the operations of history. The covenant, as Shepard puts it, "is the midst between both God's purposes and performances"; and in an intricate but decipherable rhetorical pattern, he adds: "For in God's Covenant we see with open face God's secret purpose for time past—God's purposes toward His people being, as it were, nothing else but promises concealed, and God's promises in the Covenant being nothing else but His purposes revealed." That revelation of purpose was, in effect, the discoverable meaning of history. This was not at all to say that the interpretation of history was easy, only that it was not impossible. The covenant theory was, in fact, a remarkable instrument for asserting at one and the same time the absolute and utterly immeasurable power of God *and* the divinely granted good fortune of man in being permitted to inhabit a rational universe. And one great thing the Puritans believed they could rationally affirm was the destiny of their city upon the hill.

To get the full force of the covenant theory, it should be contrasted with its opposite, which appealed simultaneously to certain Puritans. This might be called the "Job principle," since it was first and most magnificently expressed in the Old Testament Book of Job. There, one recalls, it is the majestic *in*comprehensibility of God's action—in visiting upon his faithful servant Job a series of dreadful sufferings—which is insisted upon. It is the unbridgeable distance between God's plan and man's puny capacity to understand it which becomes evident; and those, like Bildad and other counselors of Job, who argue for rational cause and effect in the crises of human life are guilty of the worst of blasphemies. Their sin is to attempt to subjugate the will of God to mortal reason; and God's voice, speaking to devastating effect out of the whirlwind, proclaims the fact. During the Puritan epoch, it was Jonathan Edwards who most vigorously articulated the Job principle—though his highly dialectical mind embraced, as we shall see, both of the major alternatives we have been discussing.

Much of the most distinguished American writing in the nineteenth and twentieth centuries can be gauged by noticing which of these two alternatives—the covenant theory or the Job principle—any given writer espouses, or to what extent a writer may (like Edwards) artfully shift between them. Emerson, for example, seems in his first essay *Nature* (1836) to be wholly covenant-minded, to be altogether certain of the accessibility of meaning to the human mind; "spiritual facts," he suggests, can be read almost without effort by the observation of natural objects. In the later essay, "Experience," he sounds sadly skeptical. "Sleep lingers all our lifetime about our eyes," he says there. "All things swim and glitter," and our capacity for perception is threatened. Hawthorne hedges, sometimes struggling without success to wrest meaning from experience, sometimes making it rather heavy-handedly explicit, sometimes leaving open a choice among several possibilities. And one way to understand Captain Ahab in *Moby-Dick* is to see him as an outraged New England Puritan, challenging God for having violated the covenant. "In each event," Ahab tells the crew assembled on the *Pequod*'s quarter-deck, "in the living act, the undoubted deed—there, some unknown but still reasoning thing puts forth the mouldings of its features from behind the unreasoning mask." There is reason, there *must* be reason, behind the unreason of human life and history; but what has enraged Ahab is that the white whale, the symbol or incarnation of that hidden "reasoning thing," has struck at him with "*inscrutable* malice," and "that inscrutable thing is chiefly what I hate."

The Covenant of Grace (1651)

The blessed God hath evermore delighted to reveal and communicate Himself by way of Covenant. He might have done good to man before his fall, as also since his fall, without binding Himself in the bond of Covenant; Noah, Abraham, and David, Jews, Gentiles, might have had the blessings intended, without any promise or Covenant. But the Lord's heart is so full of love (especially to His own) that it cannot be contained so long within the bounds of secrecy—*viz.* from God's eternal purpose to the actual accomplishment of good things intended—but it must aforehand overflow and break out into the many streams of a blessed Covenant. The Lord can never get near enough to His people, and thinks He can never get them near enough unto Himself, and therefore unites and binds and fastens them close to Himself, and Himself unto them, by the bonds of a Covenant. And therefore when we break our Covenant, and that will not hold us, He takes a faster bond and makes a sure and everlasting Covenant, according to Grace, not according to Works; and that shall hold His people firm unto Himself, and hold Himself close and fast unto them, that He may never depart from us.

Oh! the depth of God's grace herein: that when sinful man deserves never to have the least good word from Him, that He should open His whole heart and purpose to him in a Covenant; that when he deserves nothing else but separation from God, and to be driven up and down the world as a vagabond, or as dried leaves fallen from our God, that yet the Almighty God cannot be content with it, but must make Himself to us, and us to Himself, more sure and near than ever before! And is not this Covenant then (Christian reader) worth thy looking into and searching after? Surely never was there a time wherein the Lord calls His people to more serious searching into the nature of the Covenant than in these days.

For are there not some who cut off the entail to children of those in Covenant, and so lessen and shorten the riches of grace in the Lord's free Covenant, and that in the time of more grace under the Gospel than He was wont to dispense under the Law? Are there not others who preach a new, or rather another Gospel or Covenant—*viz.* that actual remission of sins and reconciliation with God (purchased indeed in redemption by Christ's death) is without, nay, before faith . . . ? Is it not time for the people of God now to pry into the secret of God's Covenant—which He reveals to them that fear Him (Psal. 25. 14)—when, by clipping of it and distinguishing about it, the beautiful countenance of it begins to be changed and transformed by those angels of "new light" [from that] which once it had when it began to be published in the simplicity of it by the Apostles of Christ (II Cor. 11. 3)? Nay, is not the time come wherein the Lord of hosts seems to have a quarrel against all the world, and especially His churches and people, whom He goes on to waste by the sharpest sword that (almost) was ever drawn out? And is it not the duty of all that have the least spark of holy fear and trembling to ask and search diligently what should be the reason of

this sore anger and hot displeasure, before they and theirs be consumed in the burning flames of it?

Search the scriptures, and there we shall find the cause, and see God Himself laying His finger upon that which is the sore and the wound of such times: for so it is said (Isa. 24. 1–5), "Behold, the Lord maketh the earth empty and waste, and turns it upside down, and scattereth abroad the inhabitants thereof; and it shall be as with the people, so with the priest; and the land shall be utterly spoiled." Why? "For the earth is defiled under the inhabitants thereof." Why so? "Because they have transgressed the laws, changed the ordinance, and broken the everlasting Covenant." And therefore when the Lord shall have wasted His church, and hath made it as Adnah and Zeboim, when heathen nations shall ask, "Wherefore hath the Lord done all this against this land? What meaneth the heat of His great anger?", the answer is made by the Lord Himself expressly (Deut. 29. 25): *viz.* "Because they have forsaken the Covenant of the Lord God of their fathers." And no wonder, for they that reject the Covenant of Grace, they break the league of peace between God and themselves. And hence, if acts of hostility in desolating kingdoms, churches, families and persons break out from a long-suffering God, they may easily see the cause, and that the cause and quarrel of God herein is just.

As all good things are conveyed to God's people not barely by common providence but by special Covenant (Isa. 16, 8, 9), so all the evils they meet with in this world (if in them the face of God's anger appears), upon narrow search, will be found to arise from breach of Covenant, more or less. So that if it be the great cause of all the public calamities of the church and people of God, and those calamities are already begun, and God's hand is stretched out still—was there then ever a more seasonable time and hour to study the Covenant, and so see the sin, repent of it, and at last to lay hold of God's rich grace and bowels in it, lest the Lord go on and fulfill the word of His servants, and expose most pleasant lands to the doleful lamentation of a very little remnant, reserved as a few coals in the ashes, when all else is consumed?

As particular persons, when they break their Covenant, the Lord therefore breaks out against them: so, when whole churches forsake their Covenant, the Lord therefore doth sorely visit them. Sins of ignorance the Lord Jesus pities (Heb. 5. 2) and many times winks at, but sins against light He cannot endure (II Pet. 2. 21). Sins against light are great, but sins against the purpose and Covenant, nay God's Covenant, are by many degrees worse, for the soul of man rusheth most violently and strongly against God when it breaks through all the light of the mind and purposes of the will that stand in his way to keep him from sin. And is not this done by breach of Covenant? And therefore no wonder if the Lord makes His people's chain heavy by sore affliction, until they come to consider and behold this sin, and learn more fear (after they are bound to their good behavior) of breaking Covenant with God again.

It is true, the Covenant effectually made can never be really broke, yet externally it may. But suppose God's churches were in greatest peace, and had a blessed rest from all their labors round about them: yet what is the child's position, but his legacy left him, written with the finger of God his father, in the New Covenant, and the blood of Jesus Christ his redeemer, in His last will and testament? What is a Christian's comfort, and where doth it chiefly lie, but in this: that the Lord hath made with him an everlasting Covenant, in all things stablished and sure? Which were the last breathing of the sweet singer of Israel, and the last bubblings up of the joy of his heart (II Sam. 23. 5).

God the Father's eternal purposes are sealed secrets, not immediately seen, and the full and blessed accomplishments of those purposes are not yet experimentally felt. The Covenant is the midst between both God's purposes and performances, by which and in which we come to see the one before the world began, and by a blessed faith (which makes things absent, present) to enjoy the other, which shall be our glory when this world shall be burned up and all things in it shall have an end. For in God's Covenant we see with open face God's secret purpose for time past—God's purposes toward His people being, as it were, nothing else but promises concealed, and God's promises in the Covenant being nothing else but His purposes revealed. As also, in the same Covenant and promises we see performances for [the] future, as if they were accomplishments at present. Where then is a Christian's comfort but in that Covenant, wherein two eternities (as it were) meet together, and whereby he may see accomplishments (made sure to him) of eternal glory, arising from blessed purposes of eternal grace? In a word, wherein he fastens upon God, and hath Him from everlasting to everlasting, comprehended at hand near and obvious in His words of a gracious Covenant?

The Church of God is therefore bound to bless God much for this food in season, and for the holy judicious and learned labors of this aged, experienced and precious servant of Christ Jesus, who hath taken much pains to discover—and that not in words and allegories but in the demonstration and evidence of the Spirit—the great mystery of godliness wrapped up in the Covenant, and hath now fully opened sundry knotty questions concerning the same, which happily have not been brought so fully to light until now. Which cannot but be of singular and seasonable use, to prevent apostasies from the simplicity of the Covenant and Gospel of Christ. The sermons were preached in the remote ends of the earth and, as it were, set under a bushel, a church more remote from the numerous society of others of the saints; if now, therefore, the light be set upon a hill, 'tis where it should stand, and where Christ surely would have it put. The good Lord enlighten the minds of all those who seek for the truth by this and such like helps; and the Lord enlighten the whole world with His glory, even with the glory of His Covenant, grace and love, that His people hereby may be sealed up daily until all fulness of assurance and peace, in these evil times.

The Puritan

Sense of the Self

While the Puritans were intent upon large questions about God's purposes and the processes of history, each was no less preoccupied with the condition of his own soul. They were given, and were so enjoined by their ministers, to the most unflinching exploration of their inmost selves. The three writers we now come to—Thomas Hooker, Mary Rowlandson, and Samuel Sewall— reflect this habit of strenuous self-searching and the compelling reasons that led to it. It is sometimes suggested that the phenomenon of "the inward journey"—of the self's descent *into* the self—was a primary Romantic convention and largely invoked in the nineteenth century. Undoubtedly it was, as the stories and poems of Poe testify, and as Whitman makes apparent in almost all his major poems (for instance, in the "night journey" wonderfully sketched out in "The Sleepers"). But if it was a Romantic convention, it was so in part because it had been a Puritan imperative.

It had always, of course, been a basic tenet of Protestant doctrine (a view that has its origins in St. Augustine, particularly his *Confessions*) that an individual must find out what sins he has been guilty of by self-examination, rather than by checking his conduct against a list of sins in some prescribed book. But for the Puritan, self-examination was a truly demanding exercise. A true sight of sin, Thomas Hooker declared in a representative sermon of 1659, meant nothing less than what the phrase implied: a man must not simply think about his sinfulness; he must *see* it and feel its ugly power to the quick. "We must look wisely and steadily upon our distempers, look sin in the face and discern it to the full." We must, in short, experience it. In elaborating on this cardinal point, Hooker brilliantly exploits the figure of the journey—an external as analogue to an inward journey.

There is a great odds betwixt the knowledge of a traveler, that in his own person hath taken a view of many coasts, passed through many countries and hath there taken upon his abode for some time, and by experience hath been an eyewitness of the extreme cold and scorching heats . . . and another that sits by his fireside and happily reads the story of these in a book. . . . The like difference is there in the right discerning of sin. The one hath surveyed the compass of his whole course, searched the frame of his own heart, and examined the windings and turnings of his own ways. . . . Another happily hears the like preached or repeated, reads them writ or recorded.

Hooker's exceedingly impressive sermon is a good example of what is meant by speaking of the Puritans as tough and bold; contemporary urgings by psychologists and sociologists that we should "face up to ourselves" seem, by comparison, to lack strength and conviction. Not that all Puritans acted upon the call to moral self-inspection; but an array of diaries and letters testify to their acceptance as a firm principle of life of the constant need to do so.

In American Romantic writing, as we have said, the inward journey reappears as a predominantly *psychological* event; and to the examples of Poe and Whitman, already mentioned, we may add several of Melville's writings—*Typee* and *Clarel*, and shorter pieces like "The Encantadas" and "I and My Chimney." We shall even argue that Francis Parkman's first and best-known work, *The Oregon Trail*, may be taken on one level as a searching out of the self's hidden territories. But meanwhile, the older and more recognizable Puritan idea of *moral* self-exploration, with all its hazards and terrors, continued to be sounded. Hawthorne, as usual, gave the theme his own special twist when he wrote in his notebook the following possibility for a little fable:

The human Heart to be allegorized as a cavern; at the entrance there is sunshine, and flowers growing about it. You step within, but a short distance and begin to find yourself surrounded with a terrible gloom, and monsters of divers kinds; it seems like Hell itself. You are bewildered, and wander long without hope. At last a light strikes upon you. You peep towards it, and find yourself in a region that seems, in some sort, to reproduce the flowers and sunny beauty of the entrance, but all perfect. These are the depths of the human heart, or of human nature.

Beyond Hawthorne, there are those key moments in the novels of Henry James—Isabel Archer's night-long vigil before the fire in *The Portrait of a Lady* comes first to mind—when the main character communes with himself or herself, searching out the personal qualities and relationships that have brought matters to some intense moral crisis. And in one dimension Henry Adams, in his *Education,* and in another T. S. Eliot, in "Ash Wednesday," have provided fresh models of Puritanic self-examination. In more recent years Robert Lowell, especially in *Life Studies,* has offered another such model, while Theodore Roethke has produced superb instances of the Romantic inward journey.

There is, finally the nature of the sinfulness truly taken sight of. Hooker, speaking for his fellow Puritans generally, makes out two aspects: first, that sin expresses a radical hatred of God, indeed a desire to annihilate Him (one thinks again of Captain Ahab, and others who engage in what existentialists call a quarrel with God); second, that it separates man *from* God. "It's that which makes a separation between God and the soul," Hooker says; which "breaks that union and communion with God for which we were made, and in the enjoyment of which we should be blessed and happy." It is a familiar enough idea; but nothing better illustrates both the continuity of the old Puritan conviction and the crucial transformation of it by later writers than the revelation—by Hawthorne and James in particular—that the worst consequence of human sin, indeed the worst *kind* of human sin, is the separation of man from *man,* the loss of union and communion between human beings. In Hawthorne's tale "Ethan Brand," the "unpardonable sin" is precisely Ethan's loss of what Hawthorne calls "his hold on the magnetic chain of humanity," his inability to be any longer "a brother-man." This is John Marcher's sin, too, in James's strange and brilliantly murky *The Beast in the Jungle,* which might be thought of as a subtle companion-piece to "Ethan Brand" and as sharing in its Puritan ancestry.

THOMAS HOOKER (1586–1647)

Thomas Hooker, who was born in England, had already earned a wide reputation there as a preacher and teacher when his Puritan sentiments got him into severe difficulties with the Anglican authorities. He fled to Holland in 1630 and was minister of an English church at Delft for two years. Then some of his English friends invited him to come to America—to Newtown, Massachusetts—to become their pastor. He did so, but after a few years both he and his congregation felt the impulse to "separate" still further. Against the express orders of the magistrates in Massachusetts, they removed to Hartford, Connecticut. Hooker was the dominant figure in the new colony until his death; his eloquence, indeed, made him influential throughout the Puritan world. His popularity rested on a style—as "A True Sight of Sin" shows—more figurative and elaborate than stylistic purists could approve.

From A True Sight of Sin

Wherein this true sight and apprehension of sin properly discovers itself:

I answer, a true sight of sin hath two conditions attending upon it, or it appears in two things: we must see sin (1) clearly; (2) convictingly—what it is in itself and what it is to us, not in the appearance and paint of it, but in the power of it; not to fathom it in the notion and conceit only, but to see it with application.

We must see it clearly in its own nature, its native color and proper hue. It's not every slight conceit, not every general and cursory, confused thought or careless consideration that will serve the turn or do the work here. We are all sinners: it is my infirmity, I cannot help it; my weakness, I cannot be rid of it. No man lives without faults and follies, the best have their failings, "In many things we offend all." But alas! all this wind shakes no corn, it costs more to see sin aright than a few words of course. It's one thing to say sin is thus and thus, another thing to see it to be such; we must look wisely and steadily upon our distempers, look sin in the face and discern it to the full. The want whereof is the cause of our mistaking our estates and not redressing of our hearts and ways: (Gal. 6, 4) "Let a man prove his own work." Before the goldsmith can sever and see the dross asunder from the gold, he must search the very bowels of the metal, and try it by touch, by taste, by hammer and by fire; and then he will be able to speak by proof what it is. So here: we perceive sin in the crowd and by hearsay, when we attend some common and customary expressions taken up by persons in their common converse, and so report what others speak, and yet never knew the truth, what either others or we say; but we do not single out our corruptions and survey the loathsomeness of them, as they come naked in their own natures.

This we ought to do. There is great odds betwixt the knowledge of a traveler, that in his own person hath taken a view of many coasts, passed through many countries and hath there taken up his abode some time, and by experience hath been an eyewitness of the extreme cold and scorching heats, hath surveyed the glory and beauty of the one, the barrenness and meanness of the other—he hath been in the wars, and seen the ruin and desolation wrought there—and another that sits by his fireside and happily reads the story of these in a book, or views the proportion of these in a map. The odds is great, and the difference of their knowledge more than a little: the one saw the country really, the other only in the story; the one hath seen the very place, the other only in the paint of the map drawn. The like difference is there in the right discerning of sin. The one hath surveyed the compass of his whole course, searched the frame of his own heart, and examined the windings and turnings of his own ways. He hath seen what sin is and what it hath done, how it hath made havoc of his peace and comfort, ruinated and laid waste the very principles of reason and nature and morality, and made him a terror to himself. When he hath looked over the loathsome abominations that lie in his bosom, that he is afraid to approach the presence of the Lord to bewail his sins and to crave pardon, lest he could be confounded for them while he is but confessing of them—afraid and ashamed lest any man living should know but the least part of that which he knows by himself, and could count it happy that himself was not, that the remembrance of those hideous evils of his might be no more. Another happily hears the like preached or repeated, reads them writ or recorded in some authors, and is able to remember and relate them. The odds is marvelous great! The one sees the history of sin, the other the nature of it; the one knows the relation of sin as it is mapped out and recorded, the other the poison, as by experience he hath found and proved it. It's one thing to see a disease in the book or in a man's body, another thing to find and feel it in a man's self. There is the report of it, here the malignity and venom of it.

But how shall we see clearly the nature of sin in his naked hue?

This will be discovered, and may be conceived in the particulars following. Look we at it: first, as it respects God; secondly, as it concerns ourselves.

As it hath reference to God, the vileness of the nature of sin may thus appear:

It would dispossess God of that absolute supremacy which is indeed His prerogative royal, and doth in a peculiar manner appertain to Him, as the diamond of His crown and diadem of His deity; so the Apostle, "He is God over all blessed for ever" (Rom. 9. 5). All from Him and all for Him, He is the absolute first being, the absolute last end, and herein is the crown of His glory. All those attributes of wisdom, goodness, holiness, power, justice, mercy, the shine and concurrency of all these meeting together, is to set out the inconceivable excellency of His glorious name, which exceeds all praise: "Thine is the kingdom, the power and the glory," the right of all and so the rule of all and the glory of all belongs to Him.

Now herein lies the inconceivable heinousness of the hellish nature of sin: it would jostle the Almighty out of the throne of His glorious sovereignty, and indeed be above Him. For the will of man being the chiefest of all His workmanship, all for his body, the body of the soul, the mind to attend upon the will, the will to attend upon God and to make choice of Him and His will, that is next to Him and He only above that: and that should have been His throne and temple or chair of state in which He would have set his sovereignty forever. He did in a special manner intend to meet with man, and to communicate Himself to man in His righteous law, as the rule of His holy and righteous will, by which the will of Adam should have been ruled and guided to Him and made happy in Him; and all creatures should have served God in man, and been happy by or through him, serving of God being happy in him. But when the will went from under the government of his rule, by sin, it would be above God and be happy without Him, for the rule of the law, in each command of it, holds forth a threefold expression of sovereignty from the Lord, and therein the sovereignty of all the rest of His attributes.

. . .

In regard of ourselves, see we and consider nakedly the nature of sin, in four particulars:

It's that which makes a separation between God and the soul, breaks that union and communion with God for which we were made, and in the enjoyment of which we should be blessed and happy: (Isa. 59. 1, 2) "God's ear is not heavy that it cannot hear nor His hand that it cannot help, but your iniquities have separated betwixt God and you and your sins have hid His face that He will not hear." For He professeth, (Psal. 5. 4) that He is a God that wills not wickedness, neither shall iniquity dwell with him. "Into the new Jerusalem shall no unclean thing enter, but without shall be dogs" (Rev. 21. 27). The dogs to their kennel, and hogs to their sty and mire; but if an impenitent wretch should come into heaven, the Lord would go out of heaven: Iniquity shall not dwell with sin. That then that deprives me of my greatest good for which I came into the world, and for which I live and labor in the world, and without which I had better never to have been born—nay, that which deprives me of an universal good, a good that hath all good in it—that must needs be an evil, but have all evil in it. But so doth sin deprive me of God as the object of my will, and that wills all good, and therefore it must bring in truth all evil with it. Shame takes away my honor, poverty my wealth, persecution my peace, prison my liberty, death my life, yet a man may still be a happy man, lose his life, and live eternally. But sin takes away my God, and with Him all good goes: prosperity without God will be my poison, honor without Him my bane; nay, the word without God hardens me, my endeavor without Him profits nothing at all for my good. A natural man hath no God in anything, and therefore hath no good.

. . .

Hence then it follows that sin is the greatest evil in the world, or indeed that can be. For, that which separates the soul from God, that which brings all evils of punishment and makes all evils truly evil, and spoils all good things to us, that must needs be the greatest evil. But this is the nature of sin, as hath already appeared.

But that which I will mainly press is, sin is only opposite to God, and cross as much as can be to that infinite goodness and holiness which is in His blessed majesty. It's not the miseries or distresses that men undergo that the Lord distastes them for, or estrangeth Himself from them; He is with Joseph in the prison, with the three children in the furnace, with Lazarus when he lies among the dogs and gathers the crumbs from the rich man's table, yea, with Job upon the dunghill, but He is not able to bear the presence of sin. Yea, of this temper are His dearest servants: the more of God is in them, the more opposite they are to sin wherever they find it. It was that He commended in the church of Ephesus, "That she could not bear those that were wicked" (Rev. 2. 3). As when the stomach is of a pure temper and good strength, the least surfeit or distemper that befalls, it presently distastes and disburdens itself with speed. So David noted to be "a man after God's own heart." He professeth: (Psal. 101. 3, 7) "I hate the work of them that turn aside, he that worketh deceit shall not dwell in my house; he that telleth lies, shall not tarry in my sight." But when the heart becomes like the stomach, so weak it cannot help itself nor be helped by physic, desperate diseases and dissolution of the whole follows, and in reason must be expected. Hence see how God looks at the least connivance or a faint and feeble kind of opposition against sin as that in which He is most highly dishonored; and He follows it with most hideous plagues, as that indulgent carriage of Eli towards the vile behavior of his sons for their grosser evils: (I Sam. 2. 23, 24) "Why do you such things? It's not well, my sons, that I hear such things." It is not well, and is that all? Why, had they either out of ignorance not known their duty or out of some sudden surprisal of a temptation neglected it, it had not been well; but for them so purposely to proceed on in the practice of such gross evils, and for him so faintly to reprove, the Lord looks at it as a great sin thus feebly to oppose sin. And therefore (verse 29) He tells him that he honored his sons above God, and therefore He professeth, "Far be it from me to maintain thy house and comfort, for he that honors me I will honor, and he that despiseth me shall be lightly esteemed" (verse 30). Hence it is the Lord Himself is called "the holy one of Israel," (Hab. 1. 12) "who is of purer eyes than to behold evil, and cannot look upon iniquity"—no, not in such as profess themselves saints, though most dear unto Him; no, nor in His son the Lord Jesus, not in his saints. (Amos 8. 7). The Lord hath sworn by Himself, "I abhor the excellency of Jacob"; whatever their excellencies, their privileges are, if they do not abhor sin, God will abhor them: (Jer. 22. 24) "Though Coniah was as the signet of my right hand, thence would I pluck Him." Nay, He could not endure the appearance of it in the Lord Christ, for when but the reflection of sin (as I may so say) fell upon our savior, even the imputation of our transgressions to him, though none iniquity was

ever committed by him, the Father withdrew His comforting presence from him, and let loose His infinite displeasure against him, forcing him to cry out, "My God, my God, why hast thou forsaken me?"

Yea, sin is so evil (that though it be in nature, which is the good creation of God) that there is no good in it, nothing that God will own; but in the evil of punishment it is otherwise, for the torments of the devils, and punishments of the damned in hell, and all the plagues inflicted upon the wicked upon earth, issue from the righteous and revenging justice of the Lord, and He doth own such execution as His proper work: (Isa. 45. 7) "Is there any evil in the city," *viz.* of punishment, "and the Lord hath not done it? I make peace, I create evil, I the Lord do all these things." It issues from the justice of God that He cannot but reward everyone according to His own ways and works; those are a man's own, the holy one of Israel hath no hand in them. But he is the just executioner of the plagues that are inflicted and suffered for these; and hence our blessed savior becoming our surety, and standing in our room, he endured the pains of the second death, even the fierceness of the fury of an offended God, and yet it was impossible he could commit the least sin, or be tainted with the least corrupt distemper. And it's certain it's better to suffer all plagues without any one sin than to commit the least sin and to be freed from all plagues. Suppose that all miseries and sorrows that ever befell all the wicked in earth and hell should meet together in one soul, as all waters gathered together in one sea; suppose thou heardest the devil's roaring, and sawest hell gaping, and flames of everlasting burnings flashing before thine eyes? It's certain it were better for thee to be cast into those inconceivable torments than to commit the least sin against the Lord. Thou dost not think so now, but thou wilt find it so one day.

MARY ROWLANDSON (c. 1635–c. 1678)

It is a commonplace that the Puritan mind tended to allegorize experience—to interpret human life in terms of a perpetual struggle between God and the devil for the soul of each

individual man, with the Bible and Biblical commentary providing the chief aids to interpretation. What is not always understood is that the allegorizing habit did not diminish the interest and importance of everyday life. On the contrary, it made daily life much more dramatic and exciting. One can to some extent envy a society for which every action was freighted with such grand and terrible possibilities. One can envy it no less from a more purely literary point of view. The allegorizing habit was related, of course, to the covenant idea, which guaranteed that all of experience could be understood and explained. But it gave to any *narrative* of human events a ready-made pattern wherewith to expose the larger meanings inherent in them.

The Puritan imagination, when it addressed itself to narrative, was supplied with something like what twentieth-century writers and critics have called a "myth" or a "mythic pattern"—a large-scale design by means of which particular experiences can, in the telling of them, be invested with large-scale meaning. Stress should be placed on the phrase "something like." The Puritan "myth" was a rather narrow and inflexible one; it permitted few surprises and allowed little free play for the imagination. But that was just the point. The Puritan "myth"—involving essentially, as we have said, the ever-renewed struggle between God and the devil for the souls of men—was not created, nor was it adapted and then reshaped, by a freely playing imagination. For the Puritans, it was real in the fullest sense of the word; it was, quite simply, true. If it was, indeed, the sort of thing contemporary writers have lamented the absence of, what is lamented of course is the loss of that communally shared faith which could accept the vision of universal conflict and constantly reinterpret human experience by reference to it. A contemporary novelist has reason to envy the unself-conscious confidence with which Mrs. Mary Rowlandson, wife of the pastor of Northampton, Massachusetts, finds and makes clear the spiritual meanings of her horrendous adventure as a captive of the Sagamore and Narragansett Indians during the eleven weeks and five days she spent among them in 1675.

Mrs. Rowlandson's ordeal was dramatic and dreadful enough in its own right, and it is told with a wealth of realistic detail both shocking and touching—from the sudden attack at dawn through the shooting and scalping and disemboweling, the hoots and screams; the capture itself, the removals from this place to that, with Mrs. Rowlandson forced to stagger through the winter countryside, wounded in the breast and with a six-year-old child shot through the groin and dying in her arms; to the later terrors and trials, and the final release and return to what remained of her family. But throughout we are made aware of the author's grasp of the ulterior significance of the adventure—her steady sense of taking part in an allegory of the Christian life. *Her* captivity is also *the* captivity of the Christian soul in the snares of worldly sin and of the devil; it is one with those other captivities which, as recorded in the Bible, likewise typify the Christian's enslavement—that of the children of Israel, of Jonah in the belly of the whale, and so on.

That meaning is disclosed both in the author's rhetoric—her choice of phrases and images—and in her carefully chosen quotations from the Old Testament. When Mrs. Rowlandson says that "Now is the dreadful hour come," when she speaks of the Indians as "hell-hounds" and of the spectacle at night of the Indians "roaring and singing and dancing" as "a resemblance of hell," she is not only telling about her private emotions. She is identifying the event. The Indians are not only devilish, in the casual meaning of that word; they are in very fact the agents of the devil himself; and what she is undergoing is a foretaste of the Day of Doom. The long journey across a "vast desolate wilderness," and then across a dismal swamp which "was as it were a deep dungeon," thence across a river—this is the profoundly perilous Christian journey through the wilderness and swamps of the devil-infested mortal life. Her final release is not merely a merciful and unexpected thing. It is the miraculous rescue of the enslaved Christian soul by an inexplicably merciful God. The Christian soul is rescued, Mrs. Rowlandson affirms by means of a closing quotation from Exodus, even as the Israelites were rescued from the pursuing Egyptians by God's miraculous parting of the Red Sea. In that great Biblical episode and in her personal story, Mrs. Rowlandson is able to "see the salvation of the Lord." And doing so, she can find total coherence and reassurance in her appalling experience.

From The Soveraignty and Goodness of God, Together with the Faithfulness of His Promises Displayed: Being a Narrative of the Captivity and Restauration of Mrs. Mary Rowlandson (1682)

Mrs. Rowlandson was the daughter of a wealthy landowner in Lancaster, Massachusetts, and (in 1656) the wife of the local Congregational minister, Joseph Rowlandson. Most of what we know about her is contained in her account of almost three-months captivity, in the late winter and spring of 1675, by the Narragansett Indians. Her story was published in 1682, apparently after her death. It was immensely popular and in fact continues to be reprinted; it was perhaps the best-written contribution to the developing genre of "captivity literature"—a genre which persisted into the next century, when, however, it declined into a form of conventional and sensational fiction. If Mrs. Rowlandson died, as it is believed, in 1678, then despite the heroism both of her conduct and her narrative, she survived the horrendous experience by only two years.

On the tenth of February 1675, Came the Indians with great numbers upon Lancaster: Their first coming was about Sunrising; hearing the noise of some Guns, we looked out; several Houses were burning, and the Smoke ascending to Heaven. There were five persons taken in one house, the Father, and the Mother and a sucking Child, they knockt on the head; the other two they took and carried away alive. Their were two others, who being out of their Garison upon some occasion were set upon; one was knockt on the head, the other escaped: Another their was who running along was shot and wounded, and fell down; he begged of them his life, promising them Money (as they told me) but they would not hearken to him but knockt him in head, and stript him naked,

and split open his Bowels. Another seeing many of the Indians about his Barn, ventured and went out, but was quickly shot down. There were three others belonging to the same Garison who were killed; the Indians getting up upon the roof of the Barn, had advantage to shoot down upon them over their Fortification. Thus these murtherous wretches went on, burning, and destroying before them.

At length they came and beset our own house, and quickly it was the dolefullest day that ever mine eyes saw. The House stood upon the edg of a hill; some of the Indians got behind the hill, others into the Barn, and others behind any thing that could shelter them; from all which places they shot against the House, so that the Bullets seemed to fly like hail; and quickly they wounded one man among us, then another, and then a third, About two hours (according to my observation, in that amazing time) they had been about the house before they prevailed to fire it (which they did with Flax and Hemp, which they brought out of the Barn, and there being no defence about the House, only two Flankers at two opposite corners and one of them not finished) they fired it once and one ventured out and quenched it, but they quickly fired it again, and that took. Now is the dreadful hour come, that I have often heard of (in time of War, as it was the case of others) but now mine eyes see it. Some in our house were fighting for their lives, others wallowing in their blood, the House on fire over our heads, and the bloody Heathen ready to knock us on the head, if we stirred out. Now might we hear Mothers and Children crying out for themselves, and one another, Lord, What shall we do? Then I took my Children (and one of my sisters, hers) to go forth and leave the house: but as soon as we came to the dore and appeared, the Indians shot so thick that the bulletts rattled against the House, as if one had taken a handfull of stones and threw them, so that we were fain to give back. We had six stout Dogs belonging to our Garrison, but none of them would stir, though another time, if any Indian had come to the door, they were ready to fly upon him and tear him down. The Lord hereby would make us the more to acknowledge his hand, and to see that our help is always in him. But out we must go, the fire increasing, and coming along behind us, roaring, and the Indians gaping before us with their Guns, Spears and Hatchets to devour us. No sooner were we out of the House, but my Brother in Law (being before wounded, in defending the house, in or near the throat) fell down dead, wherat the Indians scornfully shouted, and hallowed, and were presently upon him, stripping off his cloaths, the bulletts flying thick, one went through my side, and the same (as would seem) through the bowels and hand of my dear Child in my arms. One of my elder Sisters Children, named William, had then his Leg broken, which the Indians perceiving, they knockt him on head. Thus were we butchered by those merciless Heathen, standing amazed, with the blood running down to our heels. My eldest Sister being yet in the House, and seeing those wofull sights, the Infidels haling Mothers one way, and Children another, and some wallowing in their blood: and her elder Son telling her that her Son William was dead, and my self was wounded, she said, And, Lord, let me dy with them; which was no sooner said, but she was struck with a Bullet, and fell down dead over the threshold. I hope she is reaping the fruit of her good labours, being faithful to the service of God in her place. In her younger years she lay under much trouble upon spiritual accounts, till it pleased God to make that precious Scripture take hold of her heart, 2 Cor. 12. 9. *And he said unto me, my Grace is sufficient for thee.* More then twenty years after I have heard her tell how sweet and comfortable that place was to her. But to return: The Indians laid hold of us, pulling me one way, and the Children another, and said, Come go along with us; I told them they would kill me: they answered, If I were willing to go along with them, they would not hurt me.

Oh the dolefull sight that now was to behold at this House! *Come, behold the works of the Lord, what dissolations he has made in the Earth.* Of thirty seven persons who were in this one House, none escaped either present death, or a bitter captivity, save only one, who might say as he, Job 1.

15, *And I only am escaped alone to tell the News.* There were twelve killed, some shot, some stab'd with their Spears, some knock'd down with their Hatchets. When we are in prosperity, Oh the little that we think of such dreadfull sights, and to see our dear Friends, and Relations ly bleeding out their heart-blood upon the ground. There was one who was chopt into the head with a Hatchet, and stript naked, and yet was crawling up and down. It is a solemn right to see so many Christians lying in their blood, some here, and some there, like a company of Sheep torn by Wolves, All of them stript naked by a company of hell-hounds, roaring, singing, ranting and insulting, as if they would have torn our very hearts out; yet the Lord by his Almighty power preserved a number of us from death, for there were twenty-four of us taken alive and carried Captive.

I had often before this said, that if the Indians should come, I should chuse rather to be killed by them then taken alive but when it came to the tryal my mind changed; their glittering weapons so daunted my spirit, that I chose rather to go along with those (as I may say) ravenous Beasts, then that moment to end my dayes; and that I may the better declare what happened to me during that grievous Captivity, I shall particularly speak of the severall Removes we had up and down the Wilderness.

The First Remove

Now away we must go with those Barbarous Creatures, with our bodies wounded and bleeding, and our hearts no less than our bodies. About a mile we went that night, up upon a hill within sight of the Town, where they intended to lodge. There was hard by a vacant house (deserted by the English before, for fear of the Indians). I asked them whither I might not lodge in the house that night to which they answered, what will you love English men still? this was the dolefullest night that ever my eyes saw. Oh the roaring, and singing and danceing, and yelling of those black creatures in the night, which made the place a lively resemblance of hell. And as miserable was the wast that was there made, of Horses, Cattle, Sheep, Swine, Calves, Lambs, Roasting Pigs, and Fowl (which they had plundered in the Town) some roasting, some lying and burning, and some boyling to feed our merciless Enemies; who were joyful enough though we were disconsolate. To add to the dolefulness of the former day, and the dismalness of the present night: my thoughts ran upon my losses and sad bereaved condition. All was gone, my Husband gone (at least separated from me, he being in the Bay; and to add to my grief, the Indians told me they would kill him as he came homeward) my Children gone, my Relations and Friends gone, our house and home and all our comforts within door, and without all was gone, (except my life) and I knew not but the next moment that might go too. There remained nothing to me but one poor wounded Babe, and it seemed at present worse than death that it was in such a pitiful condition, bespeaking Compassion, and I had no refreshing for it, nor suitable things to revive it. Little do many think what is the savageness and brutishness of this barbarous Enemy, I even those that seem to profess more than others among them, when the English have fallen into their hands.

Those seven that were killed at Lancaster the summer before upon a Sabbath day, and the one that was afterward killed upon a week day, were slain and mangled in a barbarous manner, by one-ey'd John, and Marlborough's Praying Indians, which Capt. Mosely brought to Boston, as the Indians told me.

The Second Remove

But now, the next morning, I must turn my back upon the Town, and travel with them into the vast and desolate Wilderness, I knew not whither. It is not my tongue, or pen can express the sorrows of my heart, and bitterness of my spirit, that I had at this departure: but God was with me, in a wonderfull manner, carrying me along, and bearing up my spirit, that it did not quite fail. One of the Indians carried my poor wounded Babe upon a horse, it went moaning all along, I shall dy, I shall dy. I went on foot after it, with sorrow that cannot be exprest. At length I took it off the horse, and carried it in my arms till my strength failed, and I fell down with it: Then they set me upon a horse with my wounded Child in my lap, and there being no furniture upon the horse back, as we were going down a steep hill, we both fell over the horses head, at which they like inhumane creatures laught, and rejoyced to see it, though I thought we should there have ended our dayes, as overcome with so many difficulties. But the Lord renewed my strength still,

and carried me along, that I might see more of his Power; yea, so much that I could never have thought of, had I not experienced it.

After this it quickly began to snow, and when night came on, they stopt: and now down I must sit in the snow, by a little fire, and a few boughs behind me, with my sick Child in my lap; and calling much for water, being now (through the wound) fallen into a violent Fever. My own wound also growing so stiff, that I could scarce sit down or rise up, yet so it must be, that I must sit all this cold winter night upon the cold snowy ground, with my sick Child in my armes, looking that every hour would be the last of its life; and having no Christian friend near me, either to comfort or help me. Oh, I may see the wonderfull power of God, that my Spirit did not utterly sink under my affliction: still the Lord upheld me with his gracious and mercifull Spirit, and we were both alive to see the light of the next morning.

The Third Remove

The morning being come, they prepared to go on their way. One of the Indians got up upon a horse, and they set me up behind him, with my poor sick Babe in my lap. A very wearisome and tedious day I had of it; what with my own wound, and my Childs being so exceeding sick, and in a lamentable condition with her wound. It may be easily judged what a poor feeble condition we were in, there being not the least crumb of refreshing that came within either of our mouths, from Wednesday night to Saturday night, except only a little cold water. This day in the afternoon, about an hour by Sun, we came to the place where they intended, *viz.* an Indian Town, called Wenimesset, Norward of Quabaug. When we were come, Oh the number of Pagans (now merciless enemies) that there came about me, that I may say as David, Psal. 27. 13, *I had fainted, unless I had believed,* etc.[1] The next day was the Sabbath: I then remembered how careless I had been of Gods holy time, how many Sabbaths I had lost and mispent, and how evily I had walked in Gods sight; which lay so close unto my spirit, that it was easie for me to see how righteous it was with God to cut off the thread of my life, and cast me out of his presence for ever. Yet the Lord still shewed mercy to me,

---

[1] "Unless I had believed to see the goodness of the Lord in the land of the living." [1682 edition]

and upheld me; and as he wounded me with one hand, so he healed me with the other. This day there came to me one Robbert Pepper (a man belonging to Roxbury) who was taken in Captain Beers his Fight, and had been now a considerable time with the Indians; and up with them almost as far as Albany, to see king Philip, as he told me, and was now very lately come into these parts. Hearing, I say, that I was in this Indian Town, he obtained leave to come and see me. He told me, he himself was wounded in the leg at Captain Beers his fight; and was not able some time to go, but as they carried him, and as he took Oaken leaves and laid to his wound, and through the blessing of God he was able to travel again. Then I took Oaken leaves and laid to my side, and with the blessing of God it cured me also; yet before the cure was wrought, I may say, as it is in Psal. 38. 5, 6. *My wounds stink and are corrupt, I am troubled, I am bowed down greatly, I go mourning all the day long.* I sat much alone with a poor wounded Child in my lap, which moaned night and day, having nothing to revive the body, or cheer the spirits of her, but in stead of that, sometimes one Indian would come and tell me one hour, that your Master will knock your Child in the head, and then a second, and then a third, your Master will quickly knock your Child in the head.

This was the comfort I had from them, miserable comforters are ye all, as he said. Thus nine dayes I sat upon my knees, with my Babe in my lap, till my flesh was raw again; my Child being even ready to depart this sorrowfull world, they bade me carry it out to another Wigwam (I suppose because they would not be troubled with such spectacles) Whither I went with a very heavy heart, and down I sat with the picture of death in my lap. About two houres in the night, my sweet Babe like a Lambe departed this life, on Feb. 18, 1675. It being about six yeares, and five months old. It was nine dayes from the first wounding, in this miserable condition, without any refreshing of one nature or other, except a little cold water. I cannot, but take notice, how at another time I could not bear to be in the room where any dead person was, but now the case is changed; I must and could ly down by my dead Babe, side by side all the night after. I have thought since of the wonderfull goodness of God to me, in preserving me in the use of my reason and senses, in that distressed time, that I did not use wicked and violent means to end my own miserable life. In the morn-

ing, when they understood that my child was dead they sent for me home to my Masters Wigwam: (by my Master in this writing, must be understood Quanopin, who was a Saggamore, and married King Phillips wives Sister; not that he first took me, but I was sold to him by another Narrhaganset Indian, who took me when first I came out of the Garison). I went to take up my dead child in my arms to carry it with me, but they bid me let it alone: there was no resisting, but goe I must and leave it. When I had been at my masters wigwam, I took the first opportunity I could get, to go look after my dead child: when I came I askt them what they had done with it? then they told me it was upon the hill: then they went and shewed me where it was, where I saw the ground was newly digged, and there they told me they had buried it: There I left that Child in the Wilderness, and must commit it, and my self also in this Wilderness-condition, to him who is above all.

But before I go any further, I would take leave to mention a few remarkable passages of providence, which I took special notice of in my afflicted time.

1. Of the fair opportunity lost in the long March, a little after the Fort-fight, when our English Army was so numerous, and in pursuit of the Enemy, and so near as to take several and destroy them: and the Enemy in such distress for food, that our men might track them by their rooting in the earth for Ground-nuts, whilest they were flying for their lives. I say, that then our Army should want Provision, and be forced to leave their pursuit and return homeward: and the very next week the Enemy came upon our Town, like Bears bereft of their whelps, or so many ravenous Wolves, rending us and our Lambs to death. But what shall I say? God seemed to leave his People to themselves, and order all things for his own holy ends. *Shal there be evil in the City and the Lord hath not done it? They are not grieved for the affliction of Joseph, therefore shal they go Captive, with the first that go Captive.* It is the Lords doing, and it should be marvelous in our eyes.

2. I cannot but remember how the Indians derided the slowness, and dulness of the English Army, in its setting out. For after the desolations at Lancaster and Medfield, as I went along with them, they asked me when I thought the English Army would come after them? I told them I could not tell: It may be they will come in May, said

they. Thus did they scoffe at us, as if the English would be a quarter of a year getting ready.

3. Which also I have hinted before, when the English Army with new supplies were sent forth to pursue after the enemy, and they understanding it, fled before them till they came to Baquaug River, where they forthwith went over safely: that that River should be impassable to the English. I can but admire to see the wonderful providence of God in preserving the heathen for farther affliction to our poor Countrey. They could go in great numbers over, but the English must stop: God had an over-ruling hand in all those things.

4. It was thought, if their Corn were cut down, they would starve and dy with hunger: and all their Corn that could be found, was destroyed, and they driven from that little they had in store, into the Woods in the midst of Winter; and yet how to admiration did the Lord preserve them for his holy ends, and the destruction of many still amongst the English! strangely did the Lord provide for them; that I did not see (all the time I was among them) one Man, Woman, or Child, die with hunger.

Though many times they would eat that, that a Hog or a Dog would hardly touch; yet by that God strengthened them to be a scourge to his People.

The chief and commonest food was Groundnuts: They eat also Nuts and Acorns, Harty-choaks, Lilly roots, Ground-beans, and several other weeds and roots, that I know not.

They would pick up old bones, and cut them to pieces at the joynts, and if they were full of wormes and magots, they would scald them over the fire to make the vermine come out, and then boile them, and drink up the Liquor, and then beat the great ends of them in a Morter, and so eat them. They would eat Horses guts, and ears, and all sorts of wild Birds which they could catch: also Bear, Vennison, Beaver, Tortois, Frogs, Squirrels, Dogs, Skunks, Rattle-snakes; yea, the very Bark of Trees; besides all sorts of creatures, and provision which they plundered from the English. I can but stand in admiration to see the wonderful power of God, in providing for such a vast number of our Enemies in the Wilderness, where there was nothing to be seen, but from hand to mouth. Many times in a morning, the generality of them would eat up all they had, and yet have some forther supply against they wanted. It is said, Psal. 81. 13, 14. *Oh, that my People had hearkned*

to me, and Israel had walked in my wayes, I should soon have subdued their Enemies, and turned my hand against their Adversaries. But now our perverse and evil carriages in the sight of the Lord, have so offended him, that instead of turning his hand against them, the Lord feeds and nourishes them up to be a scourge to the whole Land.

5. Another thing that I would observe is, the strange providence of God, in turning things about when the Indians was at the highest, and the English at the lowest. I was with the Enemy eleven weeks and five dayes, and not one Week passed without the fury of the Enemy, and some desolation by fire and sword upon one place or other. They mourned (with their black faces) for their own lossess, yet triumphed and rejoyced in their inhumane, and many times devilish cruelty to the English. They would boast much of their Victories; saying, that in two hours time they had destroyed such a Captain, and his Company at such a place; and such a Captain and his Company in such a place; and such a Captain and his Company in such a place: and boast how many Towns they had destroyed, and then scoffe, and say They had done them a good turn, to send them to Heaven so soon. Again, they would say, This Summer that they would knock all the Rogues in the head, or drive them into the Sea, or make them flie the Countrey: thinking surely, Agag-like, *The bitterness of Death is past.*[2] Now the Heathen begins to think all is their own, and the poor Christians hopes to fail (as to man) and now their eyes are more to God, and their hearts sigh heavenward: and to say in good earnest, *Help Lord, or we perish:* When the Lord had brought his people to this, that they saw no help in any thing but himself: then he takes the quarrel into his own hand: and though they had made a pit, in their own imaginations, as deep as hell for the Christians that Summer, yet the Lord hurll'd them selves into it. And the Lord had not so many wayes before to preserve them, but now he hath as many to destroy them.

But to return again to my going home, where we may see a remarkable change of Providence: At first they were all against it, except my Husband would come for me; but afterwards they assented to it, and seemed much to rejoyce in it; some askt me to send them some Bread, others some Tobacco, others shaking me by the hand, offering me a Hood and Scarfe to ride in; not one moving

---

[2] I Samuel xv. 32. [1682 edition]

hand or tongue against it. Thus hath the Lord answered my poor desire, and the many earnest requests of others put up unto God for me. In my travels an Indian came to me, and told me, if I were willing, he and his Squaw would run away, and go home along with me: I told him No: I was not willing to run away, but desired to wait Gods time, that I might go home quietly, and without fear. And now God hath granted me my desire. O the wonderfull power of God that I have seen, and the experience that I have had: I have been in the midst of those roaring Lyons, and Salvage Bears, that feared neither God, nor Man, nor the Devil, by night and day, alone and in company: sleeping all sorts together, and yet not one of them ever offered me the least abuse of unchastity to me, in word or action. Though some are ready to say, I speak it for my own credit; But I speak it in the presence of God, and to his Glory. Gods Power is as great now, and as sufficient to save, as when he preserved Daniel in the Lions Den; or the three Children in the fiery Furnace. I may well say as his Psal. 107. 12, *Oh give thanks unto the Lord for he is good, for his mercy endureth for ever.* Let the Redeemed of the Lord say so, whom he hath redeemed from the hand of the Enemy, especially that I should come away in the midst of so many hundreds of Enemies quietly and peaceably, and not a Dog moving his tongue. So I took my leave of them, and in coming along my heart melted into tears, more then all the while I was with them, and I was almost swallowed up with the thoughts that ever I should go home again.

. . .

I can remember the time, when I used to sleep quietly without workings in my thoughts, whole nights together, but now it is other wayes with me. When all are fast about me, and no eye open, but his who ever waketh, my thoughts are upon things past, upon the awfull dispensation of the Lord towards us; upon his wonderfull power and might, in carrying of us through so many difficulties, in returning us in safety, and suffering none to hurt us. I remember in the night season, how the other day I was in the midst of thousands of enemies, and nothing but death before me: It is then hard work to perswade my self, that ever I should be satisfied with bread again. But now we are fed with the finest of the Wheat, and, as I may say, With honey out of the rock: In stead of the Husk, we have the fatted Calf: The thoughts of these things in the particulars of them, and of the love and goodness of God towards us, make it true of me, what David said of himself, Psal. 6. 5. *I watered my Couch with my tears.* Oh! the wonderfull power of God that mine eyes have seen, affording matter enough for my thoughts to run in, that when others are sleeping mine eyes are weeping.

I have seen the extreme vanity of this World: One hour I have been in health, and wealth, wanting nothing: But the next hour in sickness and wounds, and death, having nothing but sorrow and affliction.

Before I knew what affliction meant, I was ready sometimes to wish for it. When I lived in prosperity, having the comforts of the World about me, my relations by me, my Heart chearfull and taking little care for any thing; and yet seeing many, whom I preferred before my self, under many tryals and afflictions, in sickness, weakness, poverty, losses, crosses, and cares of the World. I should be sometimes jealous least I should have my portion in this life, and that Scripture would come to my mind, Heb. 12. 6. *For whom the Lord loveth he chasteneth, and scourgeth every Son whom he receiveth.* But now I see the Lord had his time to scourge and chasten me. The portion of some is to have their afflictions by drops, now one drop and then another; but the dregs of the Cup, the Wine of astonishment, like a sweeping rain that leaveth no food, did the Lord prepare to be my portion. Affliction I wanted, and affliction I had, full measure (I thought) pressed down and running over; yet I see, when God calls a Person to any thing, and through never so many difficulties, yet he is fully able to carry them through and make them see, and say they have been gainers thereby. And I hope I can say in some measure, As David did, *It is good for me that I have been afflicted.* The Lord hath shewed me the vanity of these outward things. That they are the Vanity of vanities, and vexation of spirit; that they are but a shadow, a blast, a bubble, and things of no continuance. That we must rely on God himself, and our whole dependance must be upon him. If trouble from smaller matters begin to arise in me, I have something at hand to check my self with, and say, why am I troubled? It was but the other day that if I had had the world, I would have given it for my freedom, or to have been a Servant to a Christian. I have learned to look beyond present and smaller troubles, and to be quieted under them, as Moses said, Exod. 14. 13. *Stand still and see the salvation of the Lord.*

SAMUEL SEWALL (1652–1730)

The most familiar and trifling domestic incidents, as well as more strenuous ordeals like that of Mrs. Rowlandson, were subjected to allegorical interpretation. The private diary kept by Samuel Sewall, a judge in the special court at Salem and the most attractive of Puritans, between 1673 and 1729, gives ample and pleasing evidence of the fact. When his son Joseph hit sister Betty on the forehead with a knob of brass and Sewall—as he tells us in the entry of November 6, 1692—went to the boy's room to spank him, Joseph "sought to shadow and hide himself from me behind the head of the cradle; which gave me sorrowful remembrance of Adam's carriage"— that is, of Adam hiding in the garden when God called out to him chidingly in Eden. Sewall also testifies to the sometimes dire effect upon the sensitive young of Puritan allegorizing, with its warning references to sin and the devil. The same Betty begins to "show signs of dejection and sorrow," and one night burst out "into an amazing cry," declaring that she shall go to hell, that her sins will not be pardoned. Betty had been reading from Cotton Mather, among other things, and that deliberately terrifying writer had so distressed her that when the minister, Mr. Willard, comes to soothe her and pray over her, she "could not give a distinct account, but was confused as his phrase was."

Almost every Puritan kept a diary, and many also wrote autobiographies or "personal narratives," usually narratives of their conversion to true faith in God. The reason, to quote Professor Miller, was "not so much because [the Puritan] was infatuated with himself, but because he needed a strict account of God's dealings with him, so that at any moment and above all at the moment of death, he could review the long transaction."[1] Diary-keeping was, in short, another instance of the Puritan's concern with the state of his individual soul and its relation

with God. No account of God's dealings with the individual in Puritan literature is more engrossing or richer in sheer humanity than that of Samuel Sewall. But we notice that Sewall spends as much time reviewing his transactions with other human beings—most enjoyably, those with the evasive and so femininely inconsistent Mrs. Winthrop—as he does his transactions with God. There is, as well, a relatively purer humanism, or human element, in Sewall's anecdotes and meditations than in the account by Mrs. Rowlandson a generation before. The point should not be exaggerated. But it can be said that for Mrs. Rowlandson the quotations from Scripture and the Biblical imagery were organic to her narrative; they were what gave her narrative its real and final meaning. For Sewall, the Biblical references rather suggest parallels and analogies to the human incident with which he is dealing. At a given moment, Sewall is, so to say, *reminded* of some portion of Biblical narrative (certainly Sewall did not mean to imply, in his allusion to Adam, that he, Sewall, was a type of God); and the human event exists more fully in its own right. In the phase beyond this—as the allegorizing habit loses its authority—we encounter Hawthorne, a writer no longer convinced about the Biblically grounded interpretation of life and making literature of great dramatic tension out of a sort of imaginative indecision.

Although Samuel Sewall is best known today for his *Diary*—first published between 1878 and 1882, and one of the great diaries in English—he was famous in his lifetime as one of New England's most eminent men of political, judicial, and financial affairs. He was born in England, but at the age of nine came to America on his family's second journey. He graduated from Harvard in 1671 and soon after graduation entered upon an illustrious and many-sided career which led, in 1718, to the position of chief justice of the colony's superior court of judicature.

[1] *The American Puritans* (1956), edited by Perry Miller, p. 226.

Sewall's unhappiest performance was as special commissioner in the Salem witchcraft trials of 1692–93. But that affair, as we have already said, should be placed in historical context. For one thing, we have pointed out that there was nothing in the slightest peculiar to Puritanism in a belief in witches. George Lyman Kittredge, in his massive *Witchcraft in Old New England*, has demonstrated beyond question that a belief in witches—and in their dire capacity to inflict grievous physical harm upon human beings and cattle, to ruin crops, set hayricks on fire, spoil dairy products, fly through the air, change into animals, and consort with the devil—goes far back into the mists of the early European Middle Ages. It was thoroughly established Christian doctrine; and it might almost be said to be a component of Western man; it survives here and there in our time.

In the whole of New England history, some thirty-odd witches were executed: most by hanging; none by burning; one at least (a certain Giles Corey) by being pressed to death beneath a weight of stones. Of these, twenty were executed as a result of Salem trials. By comparison, over two hundred were hanged in England between 1645 and 1647 alone; and eighteen were dispatched in a single day in a village in Sussex. The continental figures were far greater.

The Salem outburst, in fact, represented rather a short-lived loss of sanity and judicial good sense on the part of the Puritan authorities than a typically harsh application of policy. In less than four years and in his finest hour (see the diary entry for January 14, 1697), Sewall solemnly and humbly recanted his part in the episode, his statement being read aloud while he stood up silently in the Boston North Church. The jury also recanted. It was an unheard-of action, and it had important repercussions—toward moderation—in England.

Witches continued to be put through ordeals in New England, to be tried, fined, imprisoned, and variously punished. But not a single witch was executed after January, 1693, though hangings continued in England until 1710 and in Germany (for example) until 1775.

Sewall published several books on broadly different subjects during his lifetime. The most interesting of these is *Phaenomena quaedam apocalyptica ad aspectum novi orbis configurata*, translated into English as *The New Heaven and the New Earth* (1697). The book is an eloquent prophecy that New England, if its citizens remain faithful, will become the new heaven on earth foreseen in the New Testament Book of Apocalypse, or Revelation. The treatise contains Sewall's poetical salute to Plum Island: "As long as *Plum Island* shall faithfully keep the commanded Post; Notwithstanding all the hectoring words and hard Blows of the proud and boisterous Ocean; As long as any Salmon, or Sturgeon shall swim in the streams of *Merrimack*. . . . So long shall Christians be born there; and being first made meet, shall from thence be Translated, to be made partakers of the Inheritance of the Saints in Light."

This is one of the earliest instances in American literary history of an imaginative response to the New World as a significant physical environment—a sign of things to come. John Greenleaf Whittier, 150 years later, recognizing Sewall's pioneering artistic impulse, drew upon *The New Heaven and the New Earth* and especially upon the Plum Island passage, in his poem "The Prophecy of Samuel Sewall."

As long as Plum Island, to guard the coast
As God appointed, shall keep its post;
As long as salmon shall haunt the deep
Of Merrimack River, or sturgeons leap. . . .
So long shall Christians here be born,
Grow up and ripen as God's sweet corn. . . .

From The Diary of Samuel Sewall (1878–82)

After the death of the first Mrs. Sewall in October, 1717, Sewall paid court to a Mrs. Denison, but to no avail. In October, 1719, he married a widow named Abigail Tilly. Seven months later, the second Mrs. Sewall fell suddenly ill and died. "About midnight," Sewall recorded, "my dear wife expired to our great astonishment, especially mine." After waiting a decent interval, the sixty-year-old Sewall then made his addresses to Mrs. Winthrop. For all his ardor, this too came to nothing.

———————

Jan. 13, 1677. Giving my chickens meat, it came to my mind that I gave them nothing save Indian corn and water, and yet they eat it and thrived very well, and that that food was necessary for them, how mean soever, which much affected me and convinced what need I stood in of spiritual food, and that I should not nauseat daily duties of Prayer, &c.

Nov. 6, 1692. Joseph threw a knop of Brass and hit his Sister Betty on the forhead so as to make it bleed and swell; upon which, and for his playing at Prayer-Time, and eating when Return Thanks, I whipd him pretty smartly. When I first went in (call'd by his Grandmother) he sought to shadow and hide himself from me behind the head of the Cradle: which gave me the sorrowfull remembrance of Adam's carriage.

April 29, 1695. The morning is very warm and Sunshiny; in the Afternoon there is Thunder and Lightening, and about 2. P.M. a very extraordinary Storm of Hail, so that the ground was made white with it, as with the blossoms when fallen; 'twas as bigg as pistoll and Musquet Bullets; It broke of the Glass of the new House about 480 Quarrels [squares] of the Front; of Mr. Sergeant's about as much; Col. Shrimpton, Major General, Gov\. Bradstreet, New Meetinghouse, Mr. Willard, &c. Mr. Cotton Mather dined with us, and was with me in the new Kitchen when this was; He had just been mentioning that more Ministers Houses than others proportionably had been smitten with Lightening; enquiring what the meaning of God should be in it. Many Hail-Stones broke throw the Glass and flew to the middle of the Room, or farther: People afterward Gazed upon the House to see its Ruins. I got Mr. Mather to pray with us after this awfull Providence; He told God He had broken the brittle part of our house, and prayd that we might be ready for the time when our Clay-Tabernacles should be broken. Twas a sorrowfull thing to me to see the house so far undon again before twas finish'd.

Jan. 13, 1696. When I came in, past 7. at night, my wife met me in the Entry and told me Betty had surprised them. I was surprised with the abruptness of the Relation. It seems Betty Sewall

had given some signs of dejection and sorrow; but a little after dinner she burst out into an amazing cry, which caus'd all the family to cry too; Her Mother ask'd the reason; she gave none; at last said she was afraid she should goe to Hell, her Sins were not pardon'd. She was first wounded by my reading a Sermon of Mr. Norton's, about the 5th of Jan. Text Jnº 7. 34. Ye shall seek me and shall not find me. And those words in the Sermon, Jnº 8. 21. Ye shall seek me and shall die in your sins, ran in her mind, and terrified her greatly. And staying at home Jan. 12. she read out of Mr. Cotton Mather—Why hath Satan filled thy heart, which increas'd her Fear. Her Mother ask'd her whether she pray'd. She answer'd, Yes; but feared her prayers were not heard because her Sins not pardon'd. Mr. Willard though sent for timelyer, yet not being told of the message, . . . He came not till after I came home. He discoursed with Betty who could not give a distinct account, but was confused as his phrase was, and as had experienced in himself. Mr. Willard pray'd excellently. The Lord bring Light and Comfort out of this dark and dreadful Cloud, and Grant that Christ's being formed in my dear child, may be the issue of these painfull pangs.

Dec. 25, 1696. We bury our little daughter. In the chamber, Joseph in course reads Ecclesiastes 3ᵈ a time to be born and a time to die—Elisabeth, Rev. 22. Hanah, the 38th Psalm. I speak to each, as God helped, to our mutual comfort I hope. I order'd Sam. to read the 102. Psalm. Elisha Cooke, Edw. Hutchinson, John Baily, and Josia Willard bear my little daughter to the Tomb.

Note. Twas wholly dry, and I went at noon to see in what order things were set; and there I was entertain'd with a view of, and converse with, the Coffins of my dear Father Hull, Mother Hull, Cousin Quinsey, and my Six Children: for the little posthumous was now took up and set in upon that that-stands on John's: so are three, one upon another twice, on the bench at the end. My Mother ly's on a lower bench, at the end, with head to her Husband's head: and I order'd little Sarah to be set on her Grandmother's feet. 'Twas an awfull yet pleasing Treat; Having said, The Lord knows who shall be brought hether next, I came away.

Jan. 14, 1697. Copy of the Bill I put up on the Fast day; giving it to Mr. Willard as he pass'd by, and standing up at the reading of it, and bowing when finished; in the Afternoon.

Samuel Sewall, sensible of the reiterated strokes

of God upon himself and family; and being sensible, that as to the Guilt contracted upon the opening of the late commission of Oyer and Terminer at Salem (to which the order for this Day relates) he is, upon many accounts, more concerned than any that he knows of, Desires to take the Blame and shame of it, Asking pardon of men, And especially desiring prayers that God, who has an Unlimited Authority, would pardon that sin and all other his sins; personal and Relative: And according to his infinite Benignity, and Sovereignty, Not Visit the sin of him, or of any other, upon himself or any of his, nor upon the Land: But that He would powerfully defend him against all Temptations to Sin, for the future; and vouchsafe him the efficacious, saving Conduct of his Word and Spirit.

Jan. 26, 1697. I lodged at Charlestown, at Mrs. Shepards, who tells me Mr. Harvard built that house. I lay in the chamber next the street. As I lay awake past midnight, In my Meditation, I was affected to consider how long agoe God had made provision for my comfortable Lodging that night; seeing that was Mr. Harvards house: And that led me to think of Heaven the House not made with hands, which God for many Thousands of years has been storing with the richest furniture (saints that are from time to time placed there), and that I had some hopes of being entertain'd in that Magnificent Convenient Palace, every way fitted and furnished. These thoughts were very refreshing to me.

Dec. 23, 1714. Dr. C. Mather preaches excellently from Ps. 37. Trust in the Lord &c. only spake of the Sun being in the centre of our System. I think it inconvenient to assert such Problems.

Oct. 15, 1717. My Wife got some Relapse by a new Cold and grew very bad; Sent for Mr. Oakes, and he sat up with me all night.

Oct. 16. The Distemper increases; yet my Wife speaks to me to goe to Bed.

Oct. 17. Thursday, I asked my wife whether twere best for me to go to Lecture: She said, I can't tell; so I staid at home. put up a Note. It being my Son's Lecture, and I absent, twas taken much notice of. Major Gen¹ Winthrop and his Lady visit us. I thank her that she would visit my poor Wife.

Oct. 18. My wife grows worse and exceedingly Restless. Pray'd God to look upon her. Ask'd not after my going to bed. Had the advice of Mr. Williams and Dr. Cutler.

Oct. 19. Call'd Dr. C. Mather to pray, which he did excellently in the Dining Room, having Suggested good Thoughts to my wife before he went down. After, Mr. Wadsworth pray'd in the Chamber when 'twas suppos'd my wife took little notice. About a quarter of an hour past four, my dear Wife expired in the Afternoon, whereby the Chamber was fill'd with a Flood of Tears. God is teaching me a new Lesson; to live a Widower's Life. Lord help me to Learn; and be a Sun and Shield to me, now so much of my Comfort and Defense are taken away.

Oct. 20. I goe to the publick Worship forenoon and Afternoon. My Son has much adoe to read the Note I put up, being overwhelm'd with tears.

Feb. 6, 1718. This morning wandering in my mind whether to live a Single or a Married Life; I had a sweet and very affectionat Meditation Concerning the Lord Jesus; Nothing was to be objected against his Person, Parentage, Relations, Estate, House, Home! Why did I not resolutely, presently close with Him! And I cry'd mightily to God that He would help me so to doe!

March 14, 1718. Deacon Marion comes to me, sits with me a great while in the evening; after a great deal of Discourse about his Courtship—He told [me] the Olivers said they wish'd I would Court their Aunt [Mrs. Winthrop]. I said little, but said twas not five Moneths since I buried my dear Wife. Had said before 'twas hard to know whether best to marry again or no; whom to marry.

June 9, 1718. . . . Mrs. D[eniso]n came in the morning about 9 aclock, and I took her up into my Chamber and discoursed thorowly with her; She desired me to provide another and better Nurse. I gave her the two last News-Letters—told her I intended to visit her at her own house next Lecture-day. She said, 'twould be talked of. I answer'd, In such Cases, persons must run the Gantlet. Gave her Mr. Whiting's Oration for Abijah Walter, who brought her on horseback to Town. I think little or no Notice was taken of it.

June 17, 1718. Went to Roxbury Lecture, visited Mr. Walter. Mr. Webb preach'd. Visited Govʳ Dudley, Mrs. Denison, gave her Dr. Mather's Sermons very well bound; told her we were in it invited to a Wedding. She gave me very good Curds.

July 25, 1718. I go in the Hackny Coach to Roxbury. Call at Mr. Walter's who is not at home; nor Govʳ Dudley, nor his Lady. Visit Mrs. Denison: she invites me to eat. I give her two Cases with a knife and fork in each; one Turtle shell tackling; the other long, with Ivory handles, Squar'd, cost 4^s 6^d; Pound of Raisins with proportionable Almonds.

Oct. 15, 1718. Visit Mrs. Denison on Horseback; present her with a pair of Shoe-buckles, cost 5^s 3^d.

Nov. 1, 1718. My Son from Brooklin being here I took his Horse, and visited Mrs. Denison. Sat in the Chamber next Maj^r Bowls. I told her 'twas time now to finish our Business: Ask'd her what I should allow her; she not speaking; I told her I was willing to give her Two [Hundred] and Fifty pounds per annum during her life, it it should please God to take me out of the world before her. She answer'd she had better keep as she was, than give a Certainty for an uncertainty; She should pay dear for dwelling at Boston. I desired her to make proposals, but she made none. I had Thoughts of Publishment next Thorsday the 6th. But I now seem to be far from it. May God, who has the pity of a Father, Direct and help me!

Nov. 28, 1718. I went this day in the Coach; had a fire made in the Chamber where I spake with her before, 9^r the first: I enquired how she had done these 3 or 4 weeks; Afterwards I told her our Conversation had been such when I was with her last, that it seem'd to be a direction in Providence, not to proceed any further; She said, It must be what I pleas'd, or to that purpose. Afterward she seem'd to blame that I had not told her so 9^r 1 . . . I repeated her words of 9^r 1. She seem'd at first to start at the words of her paying dear, as if she had not spoken them. But she said she thought twas Hard to part with *All*, and have nothing to bestow on her Kindred. I said, I did not intend any thing of the Movables, I intended all the personal Estate to be to her. She said I seem'd to be in a hurry on Satterday, 9^r 1., which was the reason she gave me no proposals. Whereas I had ask'd her long before to give me proposals in Writing; and she upbraided me, That I who had never written her a Letter, should ask her to write. She asked me if I would drink, I told her Yes. She gave me Cider, Apples and a Glass of Wine: gathered together the little things I had given her, and offer'd them to me; but I would take none of them. Told her I wish'd her well, should be glad to hear of her welfare. She seem'd to say she should not again take in hand a thing of this nature. Thank'd me for what I had given her and Desired my Prayers. I gave Abijah Weld an Angel. Mr. Stoddard and his wife came in their Coach to see their Sister which broke off my Visit. Upon their asking me, I dismiss'd my Coach, and went with

them to see Mr. Danforth, and came home by Moon-shine. Got home about 9. at night. *Laus Deo*.

My bowels yern towards Mrs. Denison: but I think God directs me in his Providence to desist. . . .

Oct. 1, 1720. Satterday, I dine at Mr. Stoddard's: from thence I went to Madam Winthrop's just at 3. Spake to her, saying, my loving wife died so soon and suddenly, 'twas hardly convenient for me to think of Marrying again; however I came to this Resolution, that I would not make my Court to any person without first Consulting with her. Had a pleasant discourse about 7 Single persons sitting in the Fore-seat 7^r 29th, viz. Mad^m Rebekah Dudley, Catharine Winthrop, Bridget Usher, Deliverance Legg, Rebekah Loyd, Lydia Colman, Elizabeth Bellingham. She propounded one and another for me; but none would do, said Mrs. Loyd was about her Age.

Oct. 3, 1720. Waited on Madam Winthrop again; 'twas a little while before she came in. Her daughter Noyes being there alone with me, I said, I hoped my Waiting on her Mother would not be disagreeable to her. She answer'd she should not be against that that might be for her Comfort. I Saluted her, and told her I perceiv'd I must shortly wish her a good Time; (her mother had told me, she was with Child, and within a Moneth or two of her Time). By and by in came Mr. Airs, Chaplain of the Castle, and hang'd up his Hat, which I was a little startled at, it seeming as if he was to lodge there. At last Madam Winthrop came too. After a considerable time, I went up to her and said, if it might not be inconvenient I desired to speak with her. She assented, and spake of going into another Room; but Mr. Airs and Mrs. Noyes presently rose up, and went out, leaving us there alone. Then I usher'd in Discourse from the names in the Fore-seat; at last I pray'd that Katharine [Mrs. Winthrop] might be the person assign'd for me. She instantly took it up in the way of Denyal, as if she had catch'd at an Opportunity to do it, saying she could not do it before she was asked. Said that was her mind unless she should Change it, which she believed she should not; could not leave her Children. I express'd my Sorrow that she should do it so Speedily, pray'd her Consideration, and ask'd her when I should wait on her agen. She setting no time, I mention'd that day Sennight [a week hence]. Gave her Mr. Willard's Fountain open'd with the little print and verses; saying, I hop'd if we did well read that book, we should meet together hereafter, if we did not now. She took the Book, and put it in her Pocket. Took Leave.

Oct. 6, 1720. . . . A little after 6. p.m. I went to Madam Winthrop's. She was not within. I gave Sarah Chickering the Maid 2ˢ, Juno, who brought in wood, 1ˢ. Afterward the Nurse came in, I gave her 18ᵈ, having no other small Bill. After awhile Dr. Noyes came in with his Mother; and quickly after his wife came in: They sat talking, I think, till eight a-clock. I said I fear'd I might be some Interruption to their Business: Dr. Noyes reply'd pleasantly: He fear'd they might be an Interruption to me, and went away. Madam seem'd to harp upon the same string. Must take care of her Children; could not leave that House and Neighbourhood where she had dwelt so long. I told her she might doe her children as much or more good by bestowing what she laid out in Hous-keeping, upon them. Said her Son would be of Age the 7ᵗʰ of August. I said it might be inconvenient for her to dwell with her Daughter-in-Law, who must be Mistress of the House. I gave her a piece of Mr. Belcher's Cake and Ginger-Bread wrapped up in a clean sheet of Paper; told her of her Father's kindness to me when Treasurer, and I Constable. My Daughter Judith was gon from me and I was more lonesom—might help to forward one another in our Journey to Canaan.—Mr. Eyre came within the door; I saluted him, ask'd how Mr. Clark did, and he went away. I took leave about 9 aclock. I told [her] I came now to refresh her Memory as to Monday-night; said she had not forgot it. In discourse with her, I ask'd leave to speak with her Sister; I meant to gain Madᵐ Mico's favour to persuade her Sister. She seem'd surpris'd and displeas'd, and said she was in the same condition!

Oct. 10, 1720. In the Evening I visited Madam Winthrop, who treated me with a great deal of Curtesy; Wine, Marmalade. I gave her a News-Letter about the Thanksgiving Proposals, for sake of the verses for David Jeffries. She tells me Dr. Increase Mather visited her this day, in Mr. Hutchinson's Coach.

Oct. 11, 1720. I writ a few Lines to Madam Winthrop to this purpose: "Madam, These wait on you with Mr. Mayhew's Sermon, and Account of the state of the Indians on Martha's Vineyard. I thank you for your Unmerited Favours of yesterday; and hope to have the Happiness of Waiting on you to-morrow before Eight a-clock after Noon. I pray God to keep you, and give you a joyfull entrance upon the Two Hundred and twenty ninth year of Christopher Columbus his Discovery;

and take Leave, who am, Madam, your humble Servᵗ. S:S.

Oct. 12, 1720. Mrs. Anne Cotton came to door (twas before 8.) said Madam Winthrop was within, directed me into the little Room, where she was full of work behind a Stand; Mrs. Cotton came in and stood. Madam Winthrop pointed to her to set me a Chair. Madam Winthrop's Countenance was much changed from what 'twas on Monday, look'd dark and lowering. At last, the work, (black stuff or Silk) was taken away, I got my Chair in place, had some Converse, but very Cold and indifferent to what 'twas before. Ask'd her to acquit me of Rudeness if I drew off her Glove. Enquiring the reason, I told her twas great odds between handling a dead Goat, and a living Lady. Got it off. I told her I had one Petition to ask of her, that was, that she would take off the Negative she laid on me the third of October; She readily answer'd she could not, and enlarg'd upon it; She told me of it so soon as she could; could not leave her house, children, neighbours, business. I told her she might do som Good to help and support me. Mentioning Mrs. Gookin, Nath, the widow Weld was spoken of; said I had visited Mrs. Denison. I told her Yes! Afterward I said, If after a first and second Vagary she would Accept of me returning, Her Victorious Kindness and Good Will would be very Obliging. She thank'd me for my Book, (Mr. Mayhew's Sermon), But said not a word of the Letter. When she insisted on the Negative, I pray'd there might be no more Thunder and Lightening, I should not sleep all night. I gave her Dr. Preston, The Church's Marriage and the Church's Carriage, which cost me 6ˢ at the Sale. The door standing open, Mr. Airs came in, hung up his Hat, and sat down. After awhile, Madam Winthrop moving, he went out. Jnᵒ Eyre look'd in, I said How do ye, or, your servant Mr. Eyre: but heard no word from him. Sarah fill'd a Glass of Wine, she drank to me, I to her, She sent Juno home with me with a good Lantern, I gave her 6ᵈ and bid her thank her Mistress. In some of our Discourse, I told her I had rather go to the Stone-House adjoining to her, than to come to her against her mind. Told her the reason why I came every other night was lest I should drink too deep draughts of Pleasure. She had talk'd of Canary, her Kisses were to me better than the best Canary. Explain'd the expression Concerning Columbus.

Oct. 13. I tell my Son and daughter Sewall, that the Weather was not so fair as I apprehended.

Oct. 17. In the Evening I visited Madam Winthrop, who Treated me Courteously, but not in Clean Linen as somtimes. She said, she did not know whether I would come again, or no. I ask'd her how she could so impute inconstancy to me. (I had not visited her since Wednesday night being unable to get over the Indisposition received by the Treatment received that night, and *I must* in it seem'd to sound like a made piece of Formality.) Gave her this day's Gazett. Heard David Jeffries say the Lord's Prayer, and some other portions of the Scriptures. He came to the door, and ask'd me to go into Chamber, where his Grandmother was tending Little Katee, to whom she had given Physick; but I chose to sit below. Dr. Noyes and his wife came in, and sat a Considerable time; had been visiting Son and dâter Cooper. Juno came home with me.

Oct. 18, 1720. Visited Madam Mico, who came to me in a splendid Dress. I said, It may be you have heard of my Visiting Madam Winthrop, her Sister. She answered, Her Sister had told her of it. I ask'd her good Will in the Affair. She answer'd, If her Sister were for it, she should not hinder it. I gave her Mr. Homes's Sermon. She gave me a Glass of Canary, entertain'd me with good Discourse, and a Respectfull Remembrance of my first Wife. I took Leave.

Oct. 19, 1720. Midweek, Visited Madam Winthrop; Sarah told me she was at Mr. Walley's, would not come home till late. I gave her Hannah 3 oranges with her Duty, not knowing whether I should find her or no. Was ready to go home: but said if I knew she was there, I would go thither. Sarah seem'd to speak with pretty good Courage, She would be there. I went and found her there, with Mr. Walley and his wife in the little Room below. At 7 a-clock I mentioned going home; at 8. I put on my Coat, and quickly waited on her home. She found occasion to speak loud to the servant, as if she had a mind to be known. Was Courteous to me; but took occasion to speak pretty earnestly about my keeping a Coach: I said 'twould cost £100. per annum: she said twould cost but £40. . . . Exit. Came away somewhat late.

Oct. 20, 1720. . . . Madam Winthrop not being at Lecture, I went thither first; found her very Serene with her dâter Noyes, Mrs. Dering, and the widow Shipreev sitting at a little Table, she in her arm'd Chair. She drank to me, and I to Mrs. Noyes. After awhile pray'd the favour to speak with her. She took one of the Candles, and went into the best Room, clos'd the shutters, sat down upon the Couch. She told me Madam Usher had been there, and said the Coach must be set on Wheels, and not by Rusting. She spake something of my needing a Wigg. Ask'd me what her Sister said to me. I told her, She said, If her Sister were for it, She would not hinder it. But I told her, she did not say she would be glad to have me for her Brother. Said, I shall keep you in the Cold, and asked her if she would be within to morrow night, for we had had but a running Feat. She said she could not tell whether she should, or no. I took Leave. As were drinking at the Governour's, he said: In England the Ladies minded little more than that they might have Money, and Coaches to ride in. I said, And New-England brooks its Name. At which Mr. Dudley smiled. Govr said they were not quite so bad here.

Oct. 21, 1720. Friday, My Son, the Minister, came to me p.m by appointment and we pray one for another in the Old Chamber; more especially respecting my Courtship. About 6. a-clock I go to Madam Winthrop's; Sarah told me her Mistress was gon out, but did not tell me whither she went. She presently order'd me a Fire; so I went in, having Dr. Sibb's Bowels with me to read. I read the two first Sermons, still no body came in: at last about 9. a-clock Mr. Jn° Eyre came in; I took the opportunity to say to him as I had done to Mrs. Noyes before, that I hoped my Visiting his Mother would not be disagreeable to him; He answered me with much Respect. When twas after 9. a-clock He of himself said he would go and call her, she was but at one of his Brothers: A while after I heard Madam Winthrop's voice, enquiring something about John. After a good while and Clapping the Garden door twice or thrice, she came in. I mentioned something of the lateness; she banter'd me, and said I was later. She receiv'd me Courteously. I ask'd when our proceedings should be made publick: She said They were like to be no more publick than they were already. Offer'd me no Wine that I remember. I rose up at 11 a-clock to come away, saying I would put on my Coat, She offer'd not to help me. I pray'd her that Juno might light me home, she open'd the Shutter, and said twas pretty light abroad; Juno was weary and gon to bed. So I came hôm by Star-light as well as I could. At my first coming in, I gave Sarah five Shillings. I writ Mr. Eyre his Name in his book with the date Octob^r 21, 1720. It cost me 8^s. Jehovah jireh! Madam told me she had visited M. Mico, Wendell, and Wm Clark of the South [Church].

Oct. 22, 1720. Dâter Cooper visited me before going out of Town, staid till about Sun set. I brought her going near as far as the Orange Tree. Coming back, near Leg's Corner, Little David Jeffries saw me, and looking upon me very lovingly, ask'd me if I was going to see his Grandmother? I said, Not to-night. Gave him a peny, and bid him present my Service to his Grandmother.

Oct. 24, 1720. I went in the Hackny Coach through the Common, stop'd at Madam Winthrop's (had told her I would take my departure from thence). Sarah came to the door with Katee in her Arms: but I did not think to take notice of the Child. Call'd her Mistress. I told her, being encourag'd by David Jeffries loving eyes, and sweet Words, I was come to enquire whether she could find in her heart to leave that House and Neighbourhood, and go and dwell with me at the Southend; I think she said softly, Not yet. I told her It did not ly in my Lands to keep a Coach. If I should, I should be in danger to be brought to keep company with her Neighbour Brooker, (he was a little before sent to prison for Debt). Told her I had an Antipathy against those who would pretend to give themselves; but nothing of their Estate. I would a proportion of my Estate with my self. And I suppos'd she would do so. As to a Perriwig, My best and greatest Friend, I could not possibly have a greater, began to find me with Hair before I was born, and had continued to do so ever since; and I could not find in my heart to go to another. She commended the book I gave her, Dr. Preston, the Church Marriage; quoted him saying 'twas inconvenient keeping out of a Fashion commonly used. I said the Time and Tide did circumscribe my Visit. She gave me a Dram of Black-Cherry Brandy, and gave me a lump of the Sugar that was in it. She wish'd me a good Journy. I pray'd God to keep her, and came away. Had a very pleasant Journy to Salem.

Oct. 31, 1720. At night I visited Madam Winthrop about 6 p.m. They told me she was gon to Madam Mico's. I went thither and found she was gon; so return'd to her house, read the Epistles to the Galatians, Ephesians in Mr. Eyre's Latin Bible. After the Clock struck 8. I began to read the 103. Psalm. Mr. Wendell came in from his Warehouse. Ask'd me if I were alone? Spake very kindly to me, offer'd me to call Madam Winthrop. I told him, She would be angry, had been at Mrs. Mico's; he help'd me on with my Coat and I came home: left the Gazett in the Bible, which told Sarah of, bid her present my Service to Mrs. Winthrop, and tell her I had been to wait on her if she had been at home.

Nov. 1, 1720. I was so taken up that I could not go if I would.

Nov. 2, 1720. Midweek, went again, and found Mrs. Alden there, who quickly went out. Gave her about ½ pound of Sugar Almonds, cost 3ˢ per £. Carried them on Monday. She seem'd pleas'd with them, ask'd what they cost. Spake of giving her a Hundred pounds per anum if I dy'd before her. Ask'd her what sum she would give me, if she should dy first? Said I would give her time to Consider of it. She said she heard as if I had given all to my Children by Deeds of Gift. I told her 'twas a mistake, Point-Judith was mine &c. That in England, I own'd, my Father's desire was that it should go to my eldest Son; 'twas 20£ per anum; she thought 'twas forty. I think when I seem'd to excuse pressing this, she seem'd to think twas best to speak of it; a long winter was coming on. Gave me a Glass or two of Canary.

Nov. 4, 1720. Friday, Went again about 7. a-clock; found there Mr. John Walley and his wife: sat discoursing pleasantly. I shew'd them Isaac Moses's [an Indian] Writing. Madam W. serv'd Comfeits to us. After awhile a Table was spread, and Supper was set. I urg'd Mr. Walley to Crave a Blessing; but he put it upon me. About 9. they went away. I ask'd Madam what fashioned Necklace I should present her with, She said, None at all. I ask'd her Whereabout we left off last time; mention'd what I had offer'd to give her; Ask'd her what she would give me; She said she could not Change her Condition: She had said so from the beginning; could not be so far from her Children, the Lecture. Quoted the Apostle Paul affirming that a single Life was better than a Married. I answer'd That was for the present Distress. Said she had not pleasure in things of that nature as formerly: I said, you are the fitter to make me a Wife. If she hald in that mind, I must go home and bewail my Rashness in making more haste than good Speed. However, considering the Supper, I desired her to be within next Monday night, if we liv'd so long. Assented. She charg'd me with saying, that she must put away Juno, if she came to me: I utterly deny'd it, it never came in my heart; yet she insisted upon it; saying it came in upon discourse about the Indian woman that obtained her Freedom this Court. About 10. I said I would not disturb the good orders of her House, and came away. She not seeming pleas'd with my Coming away. Spake to her about David Jeffries, had not seen him.

ROGER WILLIAMS (1603?–1683)

Williams, the son of a London tailor, graduated from Cambridge in 1627 and came to New England in 1631. For several years, he ministered at Salem, agitating ever more strenuously for complete separation from the Church of England and other "radical" causes. Banishment was pronounced, and in January, 1635, an officer was sent to arrest him. Governor Winthrop sent him a warning just in time, and Williams fled to Rhode Island. Years later, Williams recalled the event: "When I was unkindly and unchristianly, as I believe, driven from my house and land and wife and children (in the midst of a New England winter, now about thirty-five years past), at Salem, that ever honored Governor, Mr. Winthrop, privately wrote to me to steer my course to Narragansett Bay and Indians, for many high and heavenly and public ends, encouraging me, from the freeness of the place from any English claims or patents."

Williams was the founder of Providence, Rhode Island, and went twice to England to procure a charter for the colony—which, under his leadership, became the chief New England refuge for free thinkers (including Anne Hutchinson). It was in England that Williams published *The Bloudy Tenent of Persecution, for Cause of Conscience, Discussed* and, after John Cotton had made a reasoned public response, a second diatribe called *The Bloudy Tenent Yet More Bloudy: by Mr. Cottons Endeavour to Wash It White in the Blood of the Lambe.*

A part of the original document and of Cotton's reply follow here. Williams was not much of a stylist: his impact came rather from his personality, which was an odd combination of intensity and sweet innocence. *The Bloudy Tenent* is, nonetheless, the first vigorous appeal in the New World to the rights of individual conscience.

From The Bloudy Tenent of Persecution (1644)

To every Courteous Reader.

While I plead the Cause of *Truth* and *Innocencie* against the bloody *Doctrine* of *Persecution* for cause of *conscience*, I judge it not unfit to give *alarme* to my selfe, and all men to prepare to be *persecuted* or hunted for cause of *conscience.*

Whether thou standest charged with 10 or but 2 *Talents,* if thou huntest any for cause of *conscience,* how canst thou say thou followest the *Lambe* of *God* who so abhorr'd that practice? . . .

Who can now but expect that after so many scores of yeares *preaching* and *professing* of more *Truth,* and amongst so many great *contentions* amongst the very best of *Protestants,* a fierie furnace should be heat, and who sees not now the *fires* kindling?

I confesse I have little hopes till those flames are over, that this Discourse against the *doctrine* of *persecution* for cause of *conscience* should passe currant (I say not amongst the *Wolves* and *Lions,* but even amongst the *Sheep* of *Christ* themselves)

yet *liberavi animam meam,* I have not hid within my *breast* my *souls* belief: And although sleeping on the bed either of the pleasures or profits of sinne thou thinkest thy conscience bound to smite at him that dares to waken thee? Yet in the middest of all these *civill* and *spirituall* Wars (I hope we shall agree in these particulars).

First, how ever the proud (upon the advantage of an higher earth or ground) or'elooke the poore and cry out *Schismatickes, Hereticks,* &c. shall *blasphemers* and *seducers* scape unpunished? &c. Yet there is a sorer punishment in the *Gospel* for despising of *Christ* then *Moses,* even when the despiser of *Moses* was put to death without mercie, *Heb.* 10. 28, 29. He that beleeveth not shall bee damned, *Marke* 16. 16.

Secondly, what ever Worship, Ministry, Ministration, the best and purest are practised without *faith* and true perswasion that they are the true institutions of God, they are sin, sinful worships, Ministries, &c. And however in Civill things we may be servants unto men, yet in Divine and Spirituall things the poorest *pesant* must disdaine the service of the highest *Prince*: Be ye not the servants of men, I Cor. 14.

Thirdly, without search and triall no man attaines this faith and right perswasion, I *Thes.* 5. Try all things.

In vaine have *English Parliaments* permitted *English Bibles* in the poorest *English* houses, and the simplest man or woman to search the Scriptures, if yet against their soules perswasion from the Scripture, they should be forced (as if they lived in *Spaine* or *Rome* it selfe without the sight of a *Bible*) to beleeve as the Church beleeves.

Fourthly, having tried, we must hold fast, I *Thessal.* 5. upon the losse of a Crowne, *Revel.* 13. we must not let goe for all the flea bitings of the present afflictions, &c. having bought Truth deare, we must not sell it cheape, not the least graine of it for the whole World, no not for the saving of Soules, though our owne most precious; least of all for the bitter sweetning of a little vanishing pleasure.

For a little puffe of credit and reputation from the changeable breath of uncertaine sons of men.

For the broken bagges of Riches on Eagles wings: For a dreame of these, any or all of these which on our death-bed vanish and leave tormenting stings behinde them: Oh how much better is it from the love of Truth, from the love of the Father of lights, from whence it comes, from the love of the Sonne of God, who is the way and the Truth, to say as he, *John* 18. 37. For this end was I borne, and for this end came I into the World that I might beare witnesse to the Truth.

The ANSWER Of Mr. Iohn Cotton of Boston in New-England, . . . Professedly mainteining Persecution for Cause of Conscience.

The *Question* which you put, is, Whether *Persecution* for cause of *Conscience*, be not against the *Doctrine* of *Jesus Christ* the *King of Kings*.

Now by *Persecution* for Cause of *Conscience*, I conceive you meane, either for professing some point of *Doctrine* which you believe in Conscience to be the Truth, or for practising some *Worke* which in *Conscience* you believe to be a *Religious Duty*.

Now in Points of *Doctrine* some are *fundamentall*, without right beliefe whereof a Man cannot be *saved*: Others are *circumstantiall* or lesse principall, wherein Men may differ in judgement, without prejudice of *salvation* on either part.

In like sort, in Points of *Practice*, some concerne the waightier Duties of the *Law*, as, What *God* we worship, and with what kinde of *Worship*; whether such, as if it be *Right*, fellowship with *God* is held; if *Corrupt*, fellowship with Him is lost.

Againe, in Points of *Doctrine* and *Worship* lesse Principall: either they are held forth in a meeke and *peaceable* way, though the Things be *Erroneous* or unlawfull: Or they are held forth with such *Arrogance* and *Impetuousnesse*, as tendeth and reacheth (even of it selfe) to the disturbance of *Civill Peace*.

Finally, let me adde this one distinction more: When we are persecuted for *Conscience* sake, It is either for *Conscience* rightly informed, or for erronious and blind *Conscience*.

These things premised, I would lay down mine Answer to the Question in certaine *Conclusions*.

First, it is not lawfull to persecute any for *Conscience* sake *Rightly informed*; for in *persecuting* such, *Christ* himselfe is persecuted in them. *Acts* 9. 4.

Secondly, for an *Erronious* and *blind Conscience*, (even in fundamentall and weighty Points) It is not lawfull to persecute any, till after *Admonition* once or twice: and so the Apostle directeth, *Tit.* 3. 10. and giveth the Reason, that in *fundamentall* and principall points of Doctrine or Worship, the Word of *God* in such things is so cleare, that hee cannot but bee convinced in *Conscience* of the dangerous Errour of his way, after once or twice *Admonition*, wisely and faithfully dispensed. And then if any one persist, it is not out of *Conscience*, but against *his Conscience*, as the Apostle saith, vers. 11. He is subverted and sinneth, being condemned of Himselfe, that is, of his owne *Conscience*. So that if such a Man after such Admonition shall still *persist* in the Errour of his way, and be therefore punished; He is not *persecuted* for Cause of *Conscience*, but for sinning *against* his Owne *Conscience*.

The Puritan

Theory of Style

Before moving on to the three poets represented in this section—Michael Wigglesworth, Anne Bradstreet, and Edward Taylor—we should remind ourselves of the Puritan notions about the proper quality and the purpose of the written word. One of the aspects of human activity that the Puritans were determined to purify was that of literary style, and if they were mainly concerned with prose style, particular the style of church sermons, what they had to say bore no less on the writing of poetry. Here as elsewhere, the Puritans were much at odds with the Anglicans, because it seemed to them that the Anglican method of expression (in the sermons of John Donne, for example, or of Lancelot Andrewes) was far too ornate, too allusive and learned, and so failed badly in its only conceivable purpose, which was to reveal and justify God's ways to man. Thomas Hooker marveled, in 1632, over the fact that some ministers drew upon Latin, Greek, and Hebrew in their sermons, even though no one in the congregation might understand a word. It was deplorable, Hooker said, "because all this stings not, they may sit and sleep in their sins, and go to hell hoodwinked, never awakened." That last sentence, with what may be called its vital simplicity, indicates at once the two stylistic qualities most desired by the Puritans. Verbal expression should be plain, but it should sting the sinner into spiritual wakefulness.

The phrase most often invoked by Puritans when writing about rhetoric was "plain style." Bradford begins his history of Plymouth by assuring his readers that the events he is about to narrate he will seek to "manifest in a plain style; with singular regard unto the simple truth in all things." But "plain" in this context did not at all mean rude or rustic, much less artless. **61**

It meant, first, unadorned—by elaborate figures of speech and learned references; just as the church buildings and services and the ministers themselves must be unadorned. It also meant directness and clarity. "Plainness and perspicuity, both for matter and manner of expression, are the things that I have conscientiously endeavored in the whole debate," Hooker insisted in another of his polemical writings. Literary conceits and classical allusions were signs of human vanity, and came between the reader or listener and his God; and Puritans, as one of them observed, "esteemed that preaching best wherein was most of God, least of man, when vain flourishes of wit, and words were declined." At the same time, the writer continued, the Puritan must distinguish between "studied plainness and negligent rudeness."

Long after the ultimate Puritan rhetorical aim—to develop sermons wherein would be "most of God" and "least of man"—had been forgotten, the need for some sort of plain style in American writing continued to be voiced, often in opposition to current literary styles in England. "Studied plainness" is, for example, an apt phrase to describe the highly conscious simplicity of style in the fiction of Ernest Hemingway; and when Hemingway declared (in *The Green Hills of Africa*) that the first genuinely American novel was *The Adventures of Huckleberry Finn*, he argued that Mark Twain was the first American fiction writer to break with the conventions of English prose, as, he said, Emerson and Thoreau had failed to do. But it was in fact Emerson's fondest rhetorical desire to shake up the English language by a large infusion of Yankee colloquialism. And Thoreau, pursuing the same end, achieved an even greater success—as in the key passage in *Walden*:

> I went to the woods because I wished to live deliberately, to front only the essential facts of life. . . . I wanted to live deep and suck out all the marrow of life, to live so sturdily and Spartan-like as to put to rout all that was not life, to cut a broad swath and shave close, to drive life into a corner. . . .

Perhaps the most important motive behind the Puritan plain style was that human discourse should aim not chiefly at the mind, but rather at that cluster of emotions and sensations they called "the heart." The rhetorical target was not the unenlightened mind, but the unconverted and corrupted heart. "Men are to be pricked to the quick," wrote William Ames in his standard textbook on theology (1643),

> that they may feel in every one of them that the Apostle sayeth, namely that the Word of the Lord is a two edged sword, that pierceth into the inward thoughts and affections, and goeth through into the joining together of the bones and marrow.

And spokesmen from Thomas Hooker to Jonathan Edwards asserted that men must not be led simply to think about the mortal issues, but to *experience* the awful peril of their situation on the one hand, and on the other the majesty and beauty of God. To this end, a modest amount of rhetorical flourish might be permitted—since "the way to come to the heart," as one Puritan observed, "is often to pass through the fancy"—but not much. Puritan writing at its best is skimpy in metaphor and largely bereft of far-ranging allusions; but it can be pungent, immediate, energetic, and, with a genius like Edwards, it can be shattering.

After almost a century of relatively mild stylistic debate, Cotton Mather seemed to have brought things to an end by a defense of his own style, which was weird, nervous, and learnedly exclamatory, anything but plain. "After all," he pointed out, "every man will have his own style."

MICHAEL WIGGLESWORTH (1631–1705)

Wigglesworth was born in England and came to America as a child. He graduated from Harvard in 1651 and soon after that became minister of the Congregational church in Malden, Massachusetts, where he remained until his death. He was constantly in poor health—and he was increasingly less active as a preacher and in other public functions; in 1684, he turned down an invitation to become president of Harvard.

But his poetic output was sizable, and much of it is crowded with dire warnings. During the second Puritan generation, a number of ministers, observing the moral backsliding and symptoms of materialism among the faithful, preached what were known as "jeremiads"—exhorting the congregation, on pain of terrible punishment, to return to the ways of righteousness; an example is Wigglesworth's "God's Controversy with New England" (written and circulated in 1662, though not published until two centuries later). The very future of the Christian world, as it seemed, was at stake; and at times, the ministerial mood deepened from the jeremiad into the apocalyptic, in descriptions of the actual and physical end of the world and God's obliteration of most of mankind (the "sheep" or "chosen remnant" excepted) because of man's incurable sinfulness. By far the most popular of these was Wigglesworth's *The Day of Doom,* a long-standing best-seller here and in England.

From The Day of Doom (1662)

The success of this lengthy didactic poem was due to its enjoyably alarming content and its childlike, almost nursery-rhyme manner of expression. Poetically speaking, the work has little to commend it, though the moment of the apocalypse is rendered with a certain vividness, and the catalogues of sinners are offered with a kind of virtuous zest. Wigglesworth was at pains to keep his language "plain" and straightforward, but he lacked Anne Bradstreet's talent for deriving beauty from carefully focused simplicity.

1

Still was the night, Serene and Bright, when all Men sleeping lay;
Calm was the season, and carnal reason thought so 'twould last for ay.
Soul, take thine ease, let sorrow cease, much good thou hast in store:
This was their Song, their Cups among, the Evening before.

The Security of the World before Christ's coming to Judgment. Luk. 12: 19.

2

Wallowing in all kind of sin, vile wretches lay secure:
The best of men had scarcely then their Lamps kept in good ure.
Virgins unwise, who through disguise amongst the best were number'd,
Had clos'd their eyes; yea, and the wise through sloth and frailty slumber'd.

Mat. 25:5.

3

Like as of old, when Men grow bold Gods' threatnings to contemn,
Who stopt their Ear, and would not hear, when Mercy warned them:
But took their course, without remorse, till God began to powre
Destruction the World upon in a tempestuous showre

Mat. 24:37, 38.

4

They put away the evil day, And drown'd their care and fears,
Till drown'd were they, and swept away by vengeance unawares:
So at the last, whilst Men sleep fast in their security,
Surpriz'd they are in such a snare as cometh suddenly.

1 Thes. 5:3.

5

For at midnight brake forth a Light, which turn'd the night to day,
And speedily an hideous cry did all the world dismay.
Sinners awake, their hearts do ake, trembling their loynes surprizeth;
Amaz'd with fear, by what they hear, each one of them ariseth.

The Suddenness, Majesty, & Terror of Christ's appearing.Mat. 25:6. 2 Pet. 3:10.

6

They rush from Beds with giddy heads, and to their windows run,
Viewing this light, which shines more bright then doth the Noon-day Sun.
Straightway appears (they see't with tears) the Son of God most dread;
Who with his Train comes on amain to Judge both Quick and Dead.

Mat. 24:29, 30.

7

Before his face the Heav'ns gave place, and Skies are rent asunder,
With mighty voice, and hideous noise, more terrible than Thunder.
His brightness damps heav'ns glorious lamps and makes them hide their heads,
As if afraid and quite dismay'd, they quit their wonted steads.

8

Ye sons of men that durst contemn the Threatnings of Gods Word.
How cheer you now? your hearts, I trow, are thrill'd as with a sword.
Now Atheist blind, whose brutish mind a God could never see,
Dost thou perceive, dost now believe that Christ thy Judge shall be?

9

Stout Courages, (whose hardiness could Death and Hell out-face)
Are you as bold now you behold your Judge draw near apace?
They cry, no, no: Alas! and wo! our Courage all is gone:
Our hardiness (fool hardiness) hath us undone, undone.

10

No heart so bold, but now grows cold and almost dead with fear:
No eye so dry, but now can cry, and pour out many a tear.
Earths Potentates and pow'rful States, Captains and Men of Might
Are quite abasht, their courage dasht at this most dreadful sight.

Rev. 6:16.

11

Mean men lament, great men do rent their Robes, and tear their hair:
They do not spare their flesh to tear through horrible despair.
All Kindreds wail: all hearts do fail: horror the world doth fill
With weeping eyes, and loud out-cries, yet knows not how to kill.

Mat. 24:30.

12

Some hide themselves in Caves and Delves, in places under ground:
Some rashly leap into the Deap, to scape by being drown'd;
Some to the Rocks (O sensless blocks!) and woody Mountains run,
That there they might this fearful sight, and dreaded Presence shun.

Rev. 6:15, 16.

13

In vain do they to Mountains say, Fall on us, and us hide
From Judges ire, more hot than fire, for who may it abide?
No hiding place can from his Face sinners at all conceal,
Whose flaming Eyes hid things doth 'spy, and darkest things reveal.

14

The Judge draws nigh, exalted high upon a lofty Throne,
Amidst the throng of Angels strong, lo, Israel's Holy One!
The excellence of whose presence and awful Majesty,
Amazeth Nature, and every Creature, doth more than terrify.

Mat. 25:31.

15

The Mountains smoak, the Hills are shook, the Earth is rent and torn,
As if she should be clean dissolv'd, or from the Center born.
The Sea doth roar, forsakes the shore, and shrinks away for fear;
The wild Beasts flee into the Sea, so soon as he draws near.

Rev. 6:14.

16

Whose Glory bright, whose wondrous might, whose Power Imperial,
So far surpass whatever was in Realms Terrestrial;
That tongues of men (nor Angels pen) cannot the same express,
And therefore I must pass it by, lest speaking should transgress.

201

Ye sinful wights, and cursed sprights, that work Iniquity,
Depart together from me for ever to endless Misery;
Your portion take in yonder Lake, where Fire and Brimstone flameth:
Suffer the smart, which your desert as it's due wages claimeth.

The Judge pro-
nounceth the
Sentence of con-
demnation.
Mat. 25:41.

202

Oh piercing words more sharp than swords! what, to depart from *Thee,*
Whose face before for evermore the best of Pleasures be!
What? to depart (unto our smart) from thee *Eternally:*
To be for aye banish'd away, with *Devils* company!

The terrour of
it.

203

What? to be sent to *Punishment,* and flames of *Burning Fire,*
To be surrounded, and eke confounded with Gods *Revengeful ire.*

What? to abide, not for a tide these Torments, but for *Ever*:
To be released, or to be eased, not after years, but *Never*.

204

Oh, *fearful Doom!* now there's no room for hope or help at all:
Sentence is past which aye shall last, Christ will not it recall.
There might you hear them rent and tear the Air with their out-cries:
The hideous noise of their sad voice ascendeth to the Skies.

205

They wring their hands, their caitiff-hands and gnash their teeth for terrour;   *Luk.* 13:28.
They cry, they roar for anguish sore, and gnaw their tongues for horrour.
But get away without delay, Christ pitties not your cry:
Depart to Hell, there may you yell, and roar Eternally.   *Prov.* 1:26.

206

That word, *Depart*, maugre their heart, drives every wicked one,   *It is put in Execution.*
With mighty pow'r, the self-same hour, far from the Judge's Throne.
Away they're chased by the strong blast of his Death-threatning mouth: *Mat.* 25:46.
They flee full fast, as if in haste, although they be full loath.

207

As chaff that's dry, and dust doth fly before the Northern wind:
Right so are they chased away, and can no Refuge find.
They hasten to the Pit of Wo, guarded by Angels stout;   *Matt.* 13:41, 42.
Who to fulfil Christ's holy will, attend this wicked Rout.

208

Whom having brought, as they are taught, unto the brink of Hell   *Hell.*
(That dismal place far from Christ's face, where Death and Darkness dwell: *Mat.* 25:30.
Where Gods fierce Ire kindleth the fire, and vengeance feeds the flame   *Mark.* 9:43.
With piles of Wood, and Brimstone Flood, that none can quench the same,)   *Isa.* 30:33.
     Rev. 21:8.

209

With Iron bands they bind their hands, and cursed feet together,   *Wicked Men.*
And cast them all, both great and small, into that Lake for ever.   *and Devils cast into it for ever.*
Where day and night, without respite, they wail, and cry, and howl   *Mat.* 22:13. &
For tort'ring pain, which they sustain in Body and in Soul.   25:46.

210

For day and night, in their despight, their torments smoak ascendeth.   *Rev.* 14:10, 11.
Their pain and grief have no relief, their anguish never endeth.
There must they ly, and never dy, though dying every day:
There must they dying ever ly, and not consume away.

211

Dy fain they would, if dy they could, but Death will not be had;
God's direful wrath their bodies hath for ev'r Immortal made.
They live to ly in misery, and bear eternal wo;
And live they must whilst God is just, that he may plague them so.

212

But who can tell the plagues of Hell, and torments exquisite?   *The unsufferable torments of*
Who can relate their dismal state, and terrours infinite?   *the damned.*
Who fare the best, and feel the least, yet feel that punishment   *Luk.* 16:24.
Whereby to nought they should be brought, if God did not prevent.   *Jude* 7.

213
The least degree of miserie there felt's incomparable,
The lightest pain they there sustain more than intolerable.
But God's great pow'r from hour to hour upholds them in the fire,
That they shall not consume a jot, nor by it's force expire.

Isa. 33:14.
Mark 9:43, 44.

214
But ah, the wo they undergo (they more than all besides)
Who had the light, and knew the right, yet would not it abide.
The sev'n-fold smart, which to their part, and portion doth fall,
Who Christ his Grace would not imbrace, nor hearken to his call.

Luk. 12:47.

215
The *Amorites* and *Sodomites* although their plagues be sore,
Yet find some ease, compar'd to these, who feel a great deal more.
Almighty God, whose Iron Rod, to smite them never lins.
Doth most declare his Justice rare in plaguing these mens sins.

Mat. 11:24.

216
The pain of loss their Souls doth toss, and wond'rously distress,
To think what they have cast away by wilful wickedness.
We might have been redeem'd from sin, think they, and liv'd above,
Being possest of heav'nly rest, and joying in God's love.

Luk. 16:23, 25.
Luk. 13:28.

217
But wo, wo, wo our Souls unto! we would not happy be;
And therefore bear Gods Vengeance here to all Eternitee.
Experience and woful sense must be our painful teachers
Who n'ould believe, nor credit give, unto our faithful Preachers.

Luk. 13:34.

218
Thus shall they ly, and wail, and cry, tormented, and tormenting
Their galled hearts with pois'ned darts but now too late repenting.
There let them dwell i'th' Flames of Hell; there leave we them to burn,
And back agen unto the men whom Christ acquits, return.

Mark 9:44.
Rom. 2:15.

219
The Saints behold with courage bold, and thankful wonderment,
To see all those that were their foes thus sent to punishment:
Then do they sing unto their King a Song of endless Praise:
They praise his Name, and do proclaim that just are all his ways.

The Saints rejoyce to see Judgment executed upon the wicked World. Ps. 58:10. *Rev.* 19:1, 2, 3.

220
Thus with great joy and melody to Heav'n they all ascend,
Him there to praise with sweetest layes, and Hymns that never end,
Where with long Rest they shall be blest, and nought shall them annoy:
Where they shall see as seen they be, and whom they love enjoy.

They ascend with Christ into Heaven triumphing. Mat. 25:46. 1 *Joh.* 3: 2. 1 *Cor.* 13:12.

221
O glorious Place! where face to face Jehovah may be seen,
By such as were sinners whilere and no dark vail between.
Where the Sun shine, and light Divine, of Gods bright Countenance,
Doth rest upon them every one, with sweetest influence.

Their Eternal happiness and incomparable Glory there.

222

O blessed state of the Renate [reborn]! O wondrous Happiness,
To which they're brought, beyond what thought can reach, or words express!
Griefs water-course, and sorrows sourse, are turn'd to joyful streams.   *Rev.* 21:4.
Their old distress and heaviness are vanished like dreams.

223

For God above in arms of love doth dearly them embrace,
And fills their sprights with such delights, and pleasures in his grace;   *Psal.* 16:11.
As shall not fail, nor yet grow stale through frequency of use:
Nor do they fear Gods favour there, to forfeit by abuse.

224

For there the Saints are perfect Saints, and holy ones indeed,   *Heb.* 12:23.
From all the sin that dwelt within their mortal bodies freed:
Made Kings and Priests to God through Christs dear loves transcendency,   *Rev.* 1:6.
There to remain, and there to reign with him Eternally.   & 22:5.

ANNE BRADSTREET (1612?–1672)

Cotton Mather's comment that "every man will have his own style" had, by the time he made it, already been demonstrated by the only two poets to have survived *as poets* from the Puritan age: Anne Bradstreet and Edward Taylor. The mid-seventeenth-century poems of "Mistress Bradstreet" that continue to move us are written in a kind of poetical plain style, clear, direct, and unadorned, with only an occasional trace of the conventional artificiality shown in so much of the verse then being written in England. The poetry of Edward Taylor, a generation later, is quite another thing: ornate, stuffed with literary conceits, baroque poetry tending to disarray, but with a number of stunning passages.

For the Puritan, writing poetry, like all other human activities, could have only one purpose: to reveal the sovereignty of God and His inexplicable mercy toward sinful man. Neither Anne Bradstreet nor Edward Taylor had the slightest intention of deviating from this solemn goal, and it would be a disservice to their devout souls to suggest that they did. Yet so much of their poetry as can still speak to us does so because of a personal urgency in it, along with the in-

extinguishable love it seems to express for poetry itself and its resources.

Anne Bradstreet was born in England about 1612. Her father, Thomas Dudley, was steward to an earl, and her mother was a gentlewoman whose "estates" (Cotton Mather reported) were "considerable." She grew up in an atmosphere of comfort and cultivation. At sixteen, she was stricken with smallpox, but recovered—apparently completely: her brother-in-law's later tribute to her "comely face" could hardly have been a cruel joke. The same year, she married Simon Bradstreet, an older friend of long-standing; and in 1630, she came with her husband and parents on the *Arbella* to Boston. On board, no doubt she listened to John Winthrop's sermon about the grand potential for New England, but her first response to the actuality was one of dismay. "I found a new world and new manners," she wrote in a letter to her children in her sixtieth year, "at which my heart rose." Eventually, however, she grew "convinced it was the way of God," and she "submitted to it and joined the church at Boston."

Thereafter, despite heavy domestic duties in Cambridge (or Newtown), then in Andover and Ipswich, and despite recurring bouts of sickness, she devoted herself to writing poetry. Hers was a distinguished family in the New World: her father was the second governor of the Bay Colony, a harshly practical man to whom his daughter was devoted; her husband, always active in public affairs, became governor after Anne's death. Not surprisingly, perhaps, her earlier poetry—in fact, about two thirds of her entire work—dealt with historical and public matters and is today not very readable; it is philosophical in the manner of her favorite poet, the hefty but long-winded French Protestant writer, Guillaume du Bartas.

But it is in the later poems, where we can see her heart rising in grief or beating with love, that she survives—poems about her husband, Simon Bradstreet, passionately loving and with a strong, attractive erotic element; about the death of a loved one; about the loss of the family house by fire. These verses, as Adrienne Rich has remarked, "have at every point a transparency which precludes the metaphysical image; her eye is on the realities before her, or on images from the Bible. Her individualism lies in her choice of material rather than in her style." Yet it was the courage of her creative effort, amid the crudities of the New World and a people which distrusted poetry, that drew her to the distinguished contemporary American poet, John Berryman. "I did not choose her," Berryman has said, speaking of his remarkable poem of 1956, "Homage to Mistress Bradstreet"; "somehow she chose me—one point of connection being the almost insuperable difficulty of writing high verse at all in a land that cared and cares so little for it." Thus, in his homage, Berryman addresses his imaginative ancestor:

Outside the New World winters in grand dark
white air lashing high thro' the virgin stands
foxes down foxholes sigh,
surely the English heart quails, stunned. . . .
         We are on each other's hands
who care. Both of our worlds unhanded us. Lie
  stark,
thy eyes look to me mild.

In 1650, her brother-in-law, John Woodbridge, took a bundle of Anne Bradstreet's poems to London, where they were printed as *The Tenth Muse, Lately Sprung Up in America.* The volume was widely admired and received with sometimes hyperbolic praise. The author herself, who had not known about the plan for publication, was not entirely pleased, as she makes clear in "The Author to Her Book." She made various corrections in the first edition; and in 1678, six years after her death, a second edition was brought out in Massachusetts, a dozen-odd new poems being added. But it was not until 1867 that something like a complete edition (based on a then recently discovered manuscript, and edited by John Harvard Ellis) was published.

In the library of the poet Edward Taylor, there was only one volume of poetry: that of Anne Bradstreet.

The texts we use for Anne Bradstreet's writings are as established by Jeannine Hensley in *The Works of Anne Bradstreet* (1967).

To My Dear Children (1672)

This book by any yet unread,
I leave for you when I am dead,
That being gone, here you may find
What was your living mother's mind.
Make use of what I leave in love,
And God shall bless you from above.

My dear children,
  I, knowing by experience that the exhortations of parents take most effect when the speakers leave to speak, and those especially sink deepest which are spoke latest, and being ignorant whether on my death bed I shall have opportunity to speak to any of you, much less to all, thought it the best, whilst I was able, to compose some short matters (for what else to call them I know not) and bequeath to you, that when I am no more with you, yet I may be daily in your remembrance (although

that is the least in my aim in what I now do), but that you may gain some spiritual advantage by my experience. I have not studied in this you read to show my skill, but to declare the truth, not to set forth myself, but the glory of God. If I had minded the former, it had been perhaps better pleasing to you, but seeing the last is the best, let it be best pleasing to you.

The method I will observe shall be this: I will begin with God's dealing with me from my childhood to this day.

In my young years, about 6 or 7 as I take it, I began to make conscience of my ways, and what I knew was sinful, as lying, disobedience to parents, etc., I avoided it. If at any time I was overtaken with the like evils, it was as a great trouble, and I could not be at rest 'till by prayer I had confessed it unto God. I was also troubled at the neglect of private duties though too often tardy that way. I also found much comfort in reading the Scriptures, especially those places I thought most concerned my condition, and as I grew to have more understanding, so the more solace I took in them.

In a long fit of sickness which I had on my bed I often communed with my heart and made my supplication to the most High who set me free from that affliction.

But as I grew up to be about 14 or 15, I found my heart more carnal, and sitting loose from God, vanity and the follies of youth take hold of me.

About 16, the Lord laid His hand sore upon me and smote me with the smallpox. When I was in my affliction, I besought the Lord and confessed my pride and vanity, and He was entreated of me and again restored me. But I rendered not to Him according to the benefit received.

After a short time I changed my condition and was married, and came into this country, where I found a new world and new manners, at which my heart rose. But after I was convinced it was the way of God, I submitted to it and joined to the church at Boston.

After some time I fell into a lingering sickness like a consumption together with a lameness, which correction I saw the Lord sent to humble and try me and do me good, and it was not altogether ineffectual.

It pleased God to keep me a long time without a child, which was a great grief to me and cost me many prayers and tears before I obtained one, and after him gave me many more of whom I now take the care, that as I have brought you into the world, and with great pains, weakness, cares, and fears

brought you to this, I now travail in birth again of you till Christ be formed in you.

Among all my experiences of God's gracious dealings with me, I have constantly observed this, that He hath never suffered me long to sit loose from Him, but by one affliction or other hath made me look home, and search what was amiss; so usually thus it hath been with me that I have no sooner felt my heart out of order, but I have expected correction for it, which most commonly hath been upon my own person in sickness, weakness, pains, sometimes on my soul, in doubts and fears of God's displeasure and my sincerity towards Him; sometimes He hath smote a child with a sickness, sometimes chastened by losses in estate, and these times (through His great mercy) have been the times of my greatest getting and advantage; yea, I have found them the times when the Lord hath manifested the most love to me. Then have I gone to searching and have said with David, "Lord, search me and try me, see what ways of wickedness are in me, and lead me in the way everlasting," and seldom or never but I have found either some sin I lay under which God would have reformed, or some duty neglected which He would have performed, and by His help I have laid vows and bonds upon my soul to perform His righteous commands.

If at any time you are chastened of God, take it as thankfully and joyfully as in greatest mercies, for if ye be His, ye shall reap the greatest benefit by it. It hath been no small support to me in times of darkness when the Almighty hath hid His face from me that yet I have had abundance of sweetness and refreshment after affliction and more circumspection in my walking after I have been afflicted. I have been with God like an untoward child, that no longer than the rod has been on my back (or at least in sight) but I have been apt to forget Him and myself, too. Before I was afflicted, I went astray, but now I keep Thy statutes.

I have had great experience of God's hearing my prayers and returning comfortable answers to me, either in granting the thing I prayed for, or else in satisfying my mind without it, and I have been confident it hath been from Him, because I have found my heart through His goodness enlarged in thankfulness to Him.

I have often been perplexed that I have not found that constant joy in my pilgrimage and refreshing which I supposed most of the servants of God have, although He hath not left me altogether without the witness of His holy spirit, who hath oft given me His word and set to His seal that it shall be well with me. I have sometimes tasted of that hidden manna that the world knows not, and have set up my Ebenezer, and have resolved with myself that against such a promise, such tastes of sweetness, the gates of hell shall never prevail; yet have I many times sinkings and droopings, and not enjoyed that felicity that sometimes I have done. But when I have been in darkness and seen no light, yet have I desired to stay myself upon the Lord, and when I have been in sickness and pain, I have thought if the Lord would but lift up the light of His countenance upon me, although He ground me to powder, it would be but light to me; yea, oft have I thought were I in hell itself and could there find the love of God toward me, it would be a heaven. And could I have been in heaven without the love of God, it would have been a hell to me, for in truth it is the absence and presence of God that makes heaven or hell.

Many times hath Satan troubled me concerning the verity of the Scriptures, many times by atheism how I could know whether there was a God; I never saw any miracles to confirm me, and those which I read of, how did I know but they were feigned? That there is a God my reason would soon tell me by the wondrous works that I see, the vast frame of the heaven and the earth, the order of all things, night and day, summer and winter, spring and autumn, the daily providing for this great household upon the earth, the preserving and directing of all to its proper end. The consideration of these things would with amazement certainly resolve me that there is an Eternal Being. But how should I know He is such a God as I worship in Trinity, and such a Saviour as I rely upon? Though this hath thousands of times been suggested to me, yet God hath helped me over. I have argued thus with myself. That there is a God, I see. If ever this God hath revealed himself, it must be in His word, and this must be it or none. Have I not found that operation by it that no human invention can work upon the soul, hath not judgments befallen divers who have scorned and contemned it, hath it not been preserved through all ages maugre all the heathen tyrants and all of the enemies who have opposed it? Is there any story but that which shows the beginnings of times, and how the world came to be as we see? Do we not know the prophecies in it fulfilled which could not have been so long foretold by any but God Himself?

When I have got over this block, then have I another put in my way, that admit this be the true God whom we worship, and that be his word, yet why may not the Popish religion be the right? They have the same God, the same Christ, the same word. They only enterpret it one way, we another.

This hath sometimes stuck with me, and more it would, but the vain fooleries that are in their religion together with their lying miracles and cruel persecutions of the saints, which admit were they as they term them, yet not so to be dealt withal.

The consideration of these things and many the like would soon turn me to my own religion again.

But some new troubles I have had since the world has been filled with blasphemy and sectaries, and some who have been accounted sincere Christians have been carried away with them, that sometimes I have said, "Is there faith upon the earth?" and I have not known what to think; but then I have remembered the works of Christ that so it must be, and if it were possible, the very elect should be deceived. "Behold," saith our Saviour, "I have told you before." That hath stayed my heart, and I can now say, "Return, O my Soul, to thy rest, upon this rock Christ Jesus will I build my faith, and if I perish, I perish"; but I know all the Powers of Hell shall never prevail against it. I know whom I have trusted, and whom I have believed, and that He is able to keep that I have committed to His charge.

Now to the King, immortal, eternal and invisible, the only wise God, be honour, and glory for ever and ever, Amen.

This was written in much sickness and weakness, and is very weakly and imperfectly done, but if you can pick any benefit out of it, it is the mark which I aimed at.

The Prologue (1650)

The chances are that it was the editor of *The Tenth Muse* rather than Anne Bradstreet who gave this poem its title, and who placed it *as* a prologue near the head of the volume.

"Sweet Bartas" in stanza 2 is Guillaume du Bartas, the sixteenth-century French Protestant and member of the Pléiade, that galaxy of poets presided over by Ronsard. Anne Bradstreet had in fact been following the example of Bartas for some years; it was only at this moment that she abandoned it.

The charming feminism of stanza 5—against all those who will say she should, literally, stick to her knitting—is due in part to the misadventures of Anne Hutchinson, whose very eloquence and wit were the chief cause of her trouble.

1

To sing of wars, of captains, and of kings,
Of cities founded, commonwealths begun,
For my mean pen are too superior things:
Or how they all, or each their dates have run
Let poets and historians set these forth,
My obscure lines shall not so dim their worth.

2

But when my wond'ring eyes and envious heart
Great Bartas' sugared lines do but read o'er,
Fool I do grudge the Muses did not part
'Twixt him and me that overfluent store;
A Bartas can do what a Bartas will
But simple I according to my skill.

3

From schoolboy's tongue no rhet'ric we expect,
Nor yet a sweet consort from broken strings,
Nor perfect beauty where's a main defect:
My foolish, broken, blemished Muse so sings,
And this to mend, alas, no art is able,
'Cause nature made it so irreparable.

4

Nor can I, like that fluent sweet tongued Greek,

Who lisped at first, in future times speak plain.
By art he gladly found what he did seek,
A full requital of his striving pain.
Art can do much, but this maxim's most sure:
A weak or wounded brain admits no cure.

5

I am obnoxious to each carping tongue
Who says my hand a needle better fits,
A poet's pen all scorn I should thus wrong,
For such despite they cast on female wits:
If what I do prove well, it won't advance,
They'll say it's stol'n, or else it was by chance.

6

But sure the antique Greeks were far more mild
Else of our sex, why feigned they those nine
And poesy made Calliope's own child;
So 'mongst the rest they placed the arts divine:
But this weak knot they will full soon untie,
The Greeks did nought, but play the fools and lie.

7

Let Greeks be Greeks, and women what they are
Men have precedency and still excel,
It is but vain unjustly to wage war;
Men can do best, and women know it well.
Preeminence in all and each is yours;
Yet grant some small acknowledgement of ours.

8

And oh ye high flown quills that soar the skies,
And ever with your prey still catch your praise,
If e'er you deign these lowly lines your eyes,
Give thyme or parsley wreath, I ask no bays;
This mean and unrefined ore of mine
Will make your glist'ring gold but more to shine.

From Contemplations (1666?)

What is perhaps most striking about this lengthy poem is its refusal to dissolve the vivid and extremely concrete beauties of nature into some vision of divine glory or of the life after death. There is no doubting Anne Bradstreet's ultimate allegiance. When she says in stanza 2

If so much excellence abide below,
How excellent is He that dwells on high,
Whose power and beauty by His works we know?

she means every word of it. But there is little if any "tension," in modern parlance, between the

excellence of God and the excellence of nature—of the "stately elm," "goodly river," and "gliding streams" so luminously invoked, for example, in stanza 21. They coexist within a wider poetic vision, somehow emblems of each other. Equally coexisting, but in a subtler relation, are the inhabitants of nature and the race of man.

1

Some time now past in the autumnal tide,
When Phoebus wanted but one hour to bed,

The trees all richly clad, yet void of pride,
Where gilded o'er by his rich golden head.
Their leaves and fruits seemed painted, but was true,
Of green, of red, of yellow, mixed hue;
Rapt were my senses at this delectable view.

2

I wist not what to wish, yet sure thought I,
If so much excellence abide below,
How excellent is He that dwells on high,
Whose power and beauty by His works we know?
Sure He is goodness, wisdom, glory, light,
That hath this under world so richly dight;
More heaven than earth was here, no winter and
no night.

3

Then on a stately oak I cast mine eye,
Whose ruffling top the clouds seemed to aspire;
How long since thou wast in thine infancy?
Thy strength, and stature, more thy years admire,
Hath hundred winters past since thou wast born?
Or thousand since thou brakest thy shell of horn?
If so, all these as nought, eternity doth scorn.

4

Then higher on the glistering Sun I gazed,
Whose beams was shaded by the leavie tree;
The more I looked, the more I grew amazed,
And softly said, "What glory's like to thee?"
Soul of this world, this universe's eye,
No wonder some made thee a deity;
Had I not better known, alas, the same had I.

5

Thou as a bridegroom from thy chamber rushes,
And as a strong man, joys to run a race;
The morn doth usher thee with smiles and blushes;
The Earth reflects her glances in thy face.
Birds, insects, animals with vegative,
Thy heat from death and dullness doth revive,
And in the darksome womb of fruitful nature dive.

6

Thy swift annual and diurnal course,
Thy daily straight and yearly oblique path,
Thy pleasing fervor and thy scorching force,
All mortals here the feeling knowledge hath.
Thy presence makes it day, thy absence night,
Quaternal seasons caused by thy might:
Hail creature, full of sweetness, beauty, and delight.

7

Art thou so full of glory that no eye
Hath strength thy shining rays once to behold?

And is thy splendid throne erect so high,
As to approach it, can no earthly mould?
How full of glory then must thy Creator be,
Who gave this bright light luster unto thee?
Admired, adored for ever, be that Majesty.

20

Shall I then praise the heavens, the trees, the earth
Because their beauty and their strength last longer?
Shall I wish there, or never to had birth,
Because they're bigger, and their bodies stronger?
Nay, they shall darken, perish, fade and die,
And when unmade, so ever shall they lie,
But man was made for endless immortality.

21

Under the cooling shadow of a stately elm
Close sat I by a goodly river's side,
Where gliding streams the rocks did overwhelm,
A lonely place, with pleasures dignified.
I once that loved the shady woods so well,
Now thought the rivers did the trees excel,
And if the sun would ever shine, there would I
dwell.

22

While on the stealing stream I fixt mine eye,
Which to the longed-for ocean held its course,
I marked, nor crooks, nor rubs that there did lie
Could hinder ought, but still augment its force.
"O happy flood," quoth I, "that holds thy race
Till thou arrive at thy beloved place,
Nor is it rocks or shoals than can obstruct thy pace,

23

Nor is't enough, that thou alone mayst slide,
But hundred brooks in thy clear waves do meet,
So hand in hand along with thee they glide
To Thetis' house, where all embrace and greet.
Thou emblem true of what I count the best,
O could I lead my rivulets to rest,
So may we press to that vast mansion, ever blest."

24

Ye fish, which in this liquid region 'bide,
That for each season have your habitation,
Now salt, now fresh where you think best to glide
To unknown coasts to give a visitation,
In lakes and ponds you leave your numerous fry;
So nature taught, and yet you know not why,
You wat'ry folk that know not your felicity.

25

Look how the wantons frisk to taste the air,
Then to the colder bottom straight they dive;

Eftsoon to Neptune's glassy hall repair
To see what trade they great ones there do drive,
Who forage o'er the spacious sea-green field,

And take the trembling prey before it yield,
Whose armour is their scales, their spreading fins
    their shield.

The Author to Her Book (1678)

This was evidently written after the publication
in 1650 of *The Tenth Muse*. Its pungent effectiveness and simple excellence of form derive
from the controlling metaphor, which Mistress
Bradstreet drew from something she knew best
and best wrote about—the care, nurture, clothing, and upbringing of children.

Thou ill-formed offspring of my feeble brain,
Who after birth didst by my side remain,
Till snatched from thence by friends, less
    wise than true,
Who thee abroad, exposed to public view,
Made thee in rags, halting to th' press to
    trudge,
Where errors were not lessened (all may
    judge).
At thy return my blushing was not small,
My rambling brat (in print) should
    mother call,

I cast thee by as one unfit for light,
Thy visage was so irksome in my sight;   10
Yet being mine own, at length affection would
Thy blemishes amend, if so I could:
I washed thy face, but more defects I saw,
And rubbing off a spot still made a flaw.
I stretched thy joints to make thee even feet,
Yet still thou run'st more hobbling than
    is meet;
In better dress to trim thee was my mind,
But nought save homespun cloth i' th'
    house I find.
In this array 'mongst vulgars may'st thou
    roam.
In critic's hands beware thou dost not come,   20
And take thy way where yet thou art
    not known;
If for thy father asked, say thou hadst none;
And for thy mother, she alas is poor,
Which caused her thus to send thee out
    of door.

Before the Birth of One of Her Children (1678)

The courage of this poem—the sense it gives of
"grace under pressure," in the modern phrase—
does not conceal Anne Bradstreet's very practical fear of dying during childbirth. (She had,
in fact, seven healthy children.) But perhaps
her chief and most pressing fear is expressed in
lines 25–26: the apprehension that Simon Bradstreet will, after her death, take to himself a
second wife, and her beloved children will acquire a perhaps hostile stepmother.

All things within this fading world hath end,
Adversity doth still our joys attend;
No ties so strong, no friends so dear and sweet,
But with death's parting blow is sure to meet.
The sentence past is most irrevocable,
A common thing, yet oh, inevitable.

How soon, my Dear, death may my steps
    attend,
How soon't may be thy lot to lose thy friend,
We both are ignorant, yet love bids me
These farewell lines to recommend to thee,   10
That when that knot's untied that made us one,
I may seem thine, who in effect am none.
And if I see not half my days that's due,
What nature would, God grant to yours
    and you;
The many faults that well you know I have
Let be interred in my oblivious grave;
If any worth or virtue were in me,
Let that live freshly in thy memory
And when thou feel'st no grief, as I no harms,
Yet love thy dead, who long lay in thine arms.   20
And when thy loss shall be repaid with gains
Look to my little babes, my dear remains.
And if thou love thyself, or loved'st me,

These O protect from step-dame's injury.
And if chance to thine eyes shall bring this
  verse,

With some sad sighs honour my absent hearse;
And kiss this paper for thy love's dear sake,
Who with salt tears this last farewell did take.

To My Dear and Loving Husband (1678)

If ever two were one, then surely we.
If ever man were loved by wife, then thee;
If ever wife was happy in a man,
Compare with me, ye women, if you can.
I prize thy love more than whole mines of gold
Or all the riches that the East doth hold.
My love is such that rivers cannot quench,
Nor ought but love from thee, give recompense.

Thy love is such I can no way repay.
The heavens reward thee manifold, I pray.   10
Then while we live, in love let's so persever[1]
That when we live no more, we may live ever.

[1] The last word of line 11 should presumably be pronounced "persever."

A Letter to Her Husband, Absent upon Public Employment (1678)

The expanding metaphor in this poem of her husband as the sun and herself as the earth is worth exploration. And it is in fact not a static, but a developing metaphor—which leads to imagery of the dead or the winter season and the longed-for spring rebirth, together with a faint hint of the God-man relation in that of sun-earth and husband-wife. It is a deeply personal poem, with an erotic vitality, but manages to bring in a remarkably broad range of reality.

My head, my heart, mine eyes, my life,
  nay, more,
My joy, my magazine of earthly store,
If two be one, as surely thou and I,
How stayest thou there, whilst I at Ipswich lie?
So many steps, head from the heart to sever,
If but a neck, soon should we be together.
I, like the Earth this season, mourn in black,

My Sun is gone so far in's zodiac,
Whom whilst I 'joyed, nor storms, nor frost
  I felt,
His warmth such frigid colds did cause to melt.   10
My chilled limbs now numbed lie forlorn;
Return, return, sweet Sol, from Capricorn;
In this dead time, alas, what can I more
Than view those fruits which through thy
  heat I bore?
Which sweet contentment yield me for a
  space,
True living pictures of their father's face.
O strange effect! now thou art southward gone,
I weary grow the tedious day so long;
But when thou northward to me shalt return,
I wish my Sun may never set, but burn   20
Within the Cancer of my glowing breast,
The welcome house of him my dearest guest.
Where ever, ever stay, and go not thence,
Till nature's sad decree shall call thee hence;
Flesh of thy flesh, bone of thy bone,
I here, thou there, yet both but one.

Here Follows Some Verses upon the Burning of Our House July 10th, 1666. Copied Out of a Loose Paper (1678)

In silent night when rest I took
For sorrow near I did not look
I wakened was with thund'ring noise
And piteous shrieks of dreadful voice.

That fearful sound of "Fire!" and "Fire!"
Let no man know is my desire.
I, starting up, the light did spy,
And to my God my heart did cry

To strengthen me in my distress
And not to leave me succorless.   10
Then, coming out, beheld a space
The flame consume my dwelling place.
And when I could no longer look,
I blest His name that gave and took,
That laid my goods now in the dust.
Yea, so it was, and so 'twas just.
It was His own, it was not mine,
Far be it that I should repine;
He might of all justly bereft
But yet sufficient for us left.   20
When by the ruins oft I past
My sorrowing eyes aside did cast,
And here and there the places spy
Where oft I sat and long did lie:
Here stood that trunk, and there that chest,
There lay that store I counted best.
My pleasant things in ashes lie,
And them behold no more shall I.
Under thy roof no guest shall sit,
Nor at thy table eat a bit.   30
No pleasant tale shall e'er be told,

Nor things recounted done of old.
No candle e'er shall shine in thee,
Nor bridegroom's voice e'er heard shall be.
In silence ever shall thou lie,
Adieu, Adieu, all's vanity.
Then straight I 'gin my heart to chide,
And did thy wealth on earth abide?
Didst fix thy hope on mold'ring dust?
The arm of flesh didst make thy trust?   40
Raise up thy thoughts above the sky
That dunghill mists away may fly.
Thou hast an house on high erect,
Framed by that mighty Architect,
With glory richly furnished,
Stands permanent though this be fled.
It's purchased and paid for too
By Him who hath enough to do.
A price so vast as is unknown
Yet by His gift is made thine own;   50
There's wealth enough, I need no more,
Farewell, my pelf, farewell my store.
The world no longer let me love,
My hope and treasure lies above.

EDWARD TAYLOR (1645?–1729)

Taylor was born in Leicestershire, England. He was the son of a reasonably well-to-do yeoman farmer; but his character and religious beliefs were formed under the inspiration of Oliver Cromwell. When Charles II returned to the English throne, Taylor and his Puritan friends received the expected harassment; and in 1668, he came to New England. He was well received there, by Increase Mather and Charles Chauncey, president of Harvard, among others. He spent some years at Harvard, as both a student and a "scholar of the house." In 1671, he accepted a call to become minister of the Congregational church in Westfield, Massachusetts, and here he stayed for more than fifty years. He was married twice and was the father of fourteen children. One of his grandchildren was Ezra Stiles, the distinguished president of Yale

during the revolutionary years. There is a good deal of information about Taylor in the diary of his life-long friend, Samuel Sewall.

None of Taylor's poems were printed while he was alive; indeed, there is a legend that he forbade their ever being published, and virtually nothing was known about them until 1937, when a large manuscript was discovered in the Yale Library (deposited there probably by Ezra Stiles). And only more recently yet has the full body of his work been published.

Taylor, as his editor Donald E. Stanford, rightly remarks, was "the last important representative of the metaphysical school founded by John Donne and continued by George Herbert, Richard Crashaw, and Henry Vaughan." Taylor's work is an index of the poetic taste of that period, with its strong addiction to Rome; from the most orthodox Puritan point of view, Taylor broke all the rules; it is doubtful if his poetry would have been widely approved, for it bristles with learned conceits and elaborate figures, just as his sermons (against stylistic doctrine) were loaded with a sort of lively pedantry far beyond his congregation's understanding.

Taylor wrote three kinds of poems, in all of which the supreme actor is explicitly or implicitly God. There is *God's Determinations Touching His Elect*, a long apocalyptic poem influenced by Wigglesworth's *The Day of Doom*. There are the "miscellaneous poems," little "happenings" for the most part: reports of curious incidents or aspects of personal life. And there are his two series of *Preparatory Meditations*, 195 of them in all—what Stanford astutely calls Taylor's "secret diary," a poetic personal narrative, each meditation being part of the process of preparing himself to achieve the sacrament of communion and to receive it.

Preface to God's Determinations Touching His Elect

Taylor's best passages reflect a strong affection for the bold figure of speech, a love sometimes amounting to an intoxication with verbal histrionics. The surprising and witty image, here, of God as a Master Bowler launching the sun into its orbit suggests a writer whose imagination leaped to its own stirrings. It never leaped, however, except in praise of God.

Taylor's language, here and elsewhere, is often as startlingly out of the way as that of the early Wallace Stevens. To offer a series of explanatory footnotes, however—for words like "riggalld," "Smaragdine," and "Selvedge"—would run the danger of converting fine and living poetry into a document of philological scholarship. By contrast, for example, exhaustive annotation of Ezra Pound's *Hugh Selwyn Mauberley* (included in our text) does help identify the kind of learned, culture-soaked poetry that Pound was writing in programmatic opposition to what he regarded as the vapid and empty late-Romantic verse of his time. Meanwhile, there is a certain pleasure to be derived from intuiting the meaning of Taylor's language from context, or from rooting around in dictionaries.

Infinity, when all things it beheld
In Nothing, and of Nothing all did build,
Upon what Base was fixt the Lath, wherein
He turn'd this Globe, and riggalld it so trim?
Who blew the Bellows of his Furnace Vast?
Or held the Mould wherein the world was
    Cast?
Who laid its Corner Stone? Or whose
    Command?
Where stand the Pillars upon which it stands?
Who Lac'de and Fillitted the earth so fine,
With Rivers like green Ribbons Smaragdine?   10
Who made the Sea's its Selvedge, and it locks
Like a Quilt Ball within a Silver Box?
Who Spread its Canopy? Or Curtains Spun?
Who in this Bowling Alley bowld the Sun?
Who made it always when it rises set
To go at once both down, and up to get?
Who th'Curtain rods made for this Tapistry?
Who hung the twinckling Lanthorns in
    the Sky?
Who? who did this? or who is he? Why, know
Its Onely Might Almighty this did doe.   20
His hand hath made this noble worke which
    Stands
His Glorious Handywork not made by hands.
Who spake all things from nothing; and
    with ease
Can speake all things to nothing, if he please.
Whose Little finger at his pleasure Can
Out mete ten thousand worlds with halfe
    a Span:
Whose Might Almighty can by half a looks
Root up the rocks and rock the hills by
    th'roots.
Can take this mighty World up in his hande,
And shake it like a Squitchen or a Wand.   30
Whose single Frown will make the Heavens
    shake

Like as an aspen leafe the Winde makes
    quake.
Oh! what a might is this Whose single frown
Doth shake the world as it would shake it
    down?
Which All from Nothing fet, from Nothing,
    All:
Hath All on Nothing set, lets Nothing fall.
Gave All to nothing Man indeed, whereby
Through nothing man all might him Glorify.
In Nothing then imbosst the brightest Gem
More pretious than all pretiousness in them.   40
But Nothing man did throw down all by Sin:
And darkened that lightsom Gem in him.
        That now his Brightest Diamond is grown
        Darker by far than any Coalpit Stone.

Taylor's writing was directed even more resolutely than Anne Bradstreet's to the relation
between God and man—particularly God and
Taylor himself. Even a modest poem like
"Huswifery" invokes humble domestic items as
metaphors for that relationship. It is the more
remarkable that Taylor invests this central motif
with such vigorously earthy imagery: for example, that of the heavens vomiting and flinging
excrement upon carnal sinners in "Upon the
Sweeping Flood." Far from tacking on a spiritual
comment or spiritual appeal to an observed
human or natural event, Taylor *works* the event
with a nervous intensity until it can release an
explosion of religious feeling.

Upon the Sweeping Flood Aug: 13.14. 1683

Oh! that Id had a tear to've quencht that
                flame
        Which did dissolve the Heavens above
Into those liquid drops that Came
        To drown our Carnall love.
Our cheeks were dry and eyes refusde to weep.
Tears bursting out ran down the skies darke
                Cheek.

Were th'Heavens sick? must wee their
                Doctors bee
        And physick them with pills, our sin?
        To make them purg and Vomit, see,
                And Excrements out fling?   10
We've griev'd them by such Physick that
                they shed
Their Excrements upon our lofty heads.

Upon a Spider Catching a Fly

Thou sorrow, venom Elfe.
        Is this thy play,
To spin a web out of thyselfe
        To Catch a Fly?
                For Why?

I saw a pettish wasp
        Fall foule therein.
Whom yet thy Whorle pins did not clasp
        Lest he should fling
                His sting.   10

But as affraid, remote
        Didst stand hereat
And with thy little fingers stroke
        And gently tap
                His back.
Thus gently him didst treate
        Lest he should pet,

And in a froppish, waspish heate
        Should greatly fret
                Thy net.   20

Whereas the silly Fly,
        Caught by its leg
Thou by the throate tookst hastily
        And 'hinde the head
                Bite Dead.

This goes to pot, that not
        Nature doth call.
Strive not above what strength hath got
        Lest in the brawle
                Thou fall.   30

This Frey seems thus to us.
        Hells Spider gets
His intrails spun to whip Cords thus

And wove to nets
  And sets.

To tangle Adams race
  In's stratigems
To their Destructions, spoil'd, made base
  By venom things
    Damn'd Sins.   40
But mighty, Gracious Lord
  Communicate

Thy Grace to breake the Cord, afford
  Us Glorys Gate
  And State.

We'l Nightingaile sing like
  When pearcht on high
In Glories Cage, thy glory, bright,
  And thankfully,
    For joy.   50

Upon a Wasp Child with Cold

The Bare that breaths the Northern blast
Did numb, Torpedo like, a Wasp
Whose stiffend limbs encrampt, lay bathing
In Sol's warm breath and shine as saving,
Which with her hands she chafes and stands
Rubbing her Legs, Shanks, Thighs, and hands.
Her petty toes, and fingers ends
Nipt with this breath, she out extends
Unto the Sun, in greate desire
To warm her digits at that fire.   10
Doth hold her Temples in this state
Where pulse doth beate, and head doth ake.
Doth turn, and stretch her body small,
Doth Comb her velvet Capitall.
As if her little brain pan were
A Volume of Choice precepts cleare.
As if her sattin jacket hot
Contained Apothecaries Shop
Of Natures recepts, that prevails
To remedy all her sad ailes,   20
As if her velvet helmet high
Did turret rationality.
She fans her wing up to the Winde

As if her Pettycoate were lin'de,
With reasons fleece, and hoises sails
And hu'ming flies in thankfull gails
Unto her dun Curld palace Hall
Her warm thanks offering for all.

    Lord cleare my misted sight that I
May hence view thy Divinity.   30
Some sparkes whereof thou up dost hasp
Within this little downy Wasp
In whose small Corporation wee
A school and a schoolmaster see
Where we may learn, and easily finde
A nimble Spirit bravely minde
Her worke in e'ry limb: and lace
It up neate with a vitall grace,
Acting each part though ne'er so small
Here of this Fustian animall.   40
Till I enravisht Climb into
The Godhead on this Lather doe.
Where all my pipes inspir'de upraise
An Heavenly musick furrd with praise.

Huswifery

Make me, O Lord, thy Spining Wheele compleate.
  Thy Holy Worde my Distaff make for mee.
Make mine Affections thy Swift Flyers neate
  And make my Soule thy holy Spoole to bee.
  My Conversation make to be thy Reele
  And reele the yarn thereon spun of thy
    Wheele.

Make me thy Loome then, knit therein this
    Twine:
  And make thy Holy Spirit, Lord, winde
    quills:
Then weave the Web thyselfe. The yarn is fine.

Thine Ordinances make my Fulling Mills.   10
Then dy the same in Heavenly Colours
    Choice,
  All pinkt with Varnisht Flowers of Paradise.

Then cloath therewith mine Understanding,
    Will,
  Affections, Judgment, Conscience, Memory
My Words, and Actions, that their shine
    may fill
  My wayes with glory and thee glorify.
  Then mine apparell shall display before yee
  That I am Cloathd in Holy robes for glory.

From Preparatory Meditations

Taylor's full title for this sequence of poems was *Preparatory Meditations before my Approach to the Lords Supper. Chiefly upon the Doctrin preached upon the Day of administration.* Donald E. Stanford, in *The Poems of Edward Taylor,* observes that the Puritans stressed the crucial need for preparatory meditation prior to receiving and administering the sacrament and quotes one Puritan divine as saying: "No preparation, no participation." Taylor himself, speaking of the Lord's supper as a "wedding supper," declared in a sermon that "Not to prepare is a contempt of the Invitation; and of the Wedden. . . . It is therefore to abide graceless, and Damnable. And what Shame is this? Oh! to strive to avoid this Shame by preparing for this Wedden Supper." "The poetry of meditation," as Louis Martz has demonstrated in several volumes, had a solid tradition in England before Taylor and has continued in this country after Taylor through the poetry of Emily Dickinson in the nineteenth century and Wallace Stevens ("The World as Meditation") and Hart Crane in the twentieth century.

Meditation 1 (1682)

What Love is this of thine, that Cannot bee
    In thine Infinity, O Lord, Confinde,
Unless it in thy very Person see,
    Infinity, and Finity Conjoyn'd?
    What hath thy Godhead, as not satisfide
    Marri'de our Manhood, making it its Bride?

Oh, Matchless Love! filling Heaven to the brim!
    O're running it: all running o're beside
This World! Nay Overflowing Hell; wherein
    For thine Elect, there rose a mighty Tide!   10
    That there our Veans might through thy
        Person bleed,

To quench those flames, that else would
    on us feed.

Oh! that thy Love might overflow my Heart!
    To fire the same with Love: for Love
    I would.
But oh! my streight'ned Breast! my Lifeless
    Sparke!
    My Fireless Flame! What Chilly Love,
    and Cold?
    In measure small! In Manner Chilly! See.
    Lord blow the Coal: Thy Love Enflame
    in mee.

The Experience

Oh! that I alwayes breath'd in such an aire,
    As I suckt in, feeding on sweet Content!
Disht up unto my Soul ev'n in that pray're
    Pour'de out to God over last Sacrament.
    What Beam of Light wrapt up my sight
    to finde
    Me neerer God than ere Came in my
    minde?

Most strange it was! But yet more strange
    that shine
    Which filld my Soul then to the brim
    to spy
My Nature with thy Nature all Divine
    Together joyn'd in Him thats Thou, and I.   10
    Flesh of my Flesh, Bone of my Bone.
      There's run

Thy Godhead, and my Manhood in
    thy Son.

Oh! that that Flame which thou didst on me
    Cast
    Might me enflame, and Lighten ery
    where.
Then Heaven to me would be less at last
    So much of heaven I should have while
    here.
    Oh! Sweet though Short! Ile not forget
    the same.
    My neerness, Lord, to thee did me
    Enflame.

I'le Claim my Right: Give place, ye Angells
    Bright.

Ye further from the Godhead stande
    than I.   20
My Nature is your Lord; and doth Unite
    Better than Yours unto the Deity.
    Gods Throne is first and mine is next:
        to you
    Onely the place of Waiting-men is due.

Oh! that my Heart, thy Golden Harp

    might bee
    Well tun'd by Glorious Grace, that
        e'ry string
Screw'd to the highest pitch, might unto thee
    All Praises wrapt in sweetest Musick bring.
    I praise thee, Lord, and better praise
        thee would
    If what I had, my heart might ever hold.   30

Meditation 8. John 6.51. I Am the Living Bread (1684)

I kening through Astronomy Divine
    The Worlds bright Battlement, wherein
        I spy
A Golden Path my Pensill cannot line,
    From that bright Throne unto my
        Threshold ly.
    And while my puzzled thoughts about
        it pore
    I finde the Bread of Life in't at my doore.

When that this Bird of Paradise put in
    This Wicker Cage (my Corps) to
        tweedle praise
Had peckt the Fruite forbad: and so did fling
    Away its Food; and lost its golden dayes;   10
    It fell into Celestiall Famine sore:
    And never could attain a morsell more.

Alas! alas! Poore Bird, what wilt thou doe?
    The Creatures field no food for Souls
        e're gave.
And if thou knock at Angells dores they show
    An Empty Barrell: they no soul bread have.
    Alas! Poore Bird, the Worlds White Loafe
        is done.
    And cannot yield thee here the smallest
        Crumb.

In this sad state, Gods Tender Bowells run
    Out streams of Grace: And he to end
        all strife   20

The Purest Wheate in Heaven, his deare-dear
    Son
    Grinds, and kneads up into this Bread
        of Life.
    Which Bread of Life from Heaven down
        came and stands
    Disht on thy Table up by Angells Hands.

Did God mould up this Bread in Heaven,
    and bake,
    Which from his Table came, and to
        thine goeth?
Doth he bespeake thee thus, This Soule Bread
    take.
    Come Eate thy fill of this thy Gods
        White Loafe?
    Its Food too fine for Angells, yet come,
        take
    And Eate thy fill. Its Heavens Sugar
        Cake.   30

What Grace is this knead in this Loafe?
    This thing
    Souls are but petty things it to admire.
Yee Angells, help: This fill would to the brim
    Heav'ns whelm'd-down Chrystall meele
        Bowle, yea and higher.
    This Bread of Life dropt in thy mouth,
        doth Cry.
    Eate, Eate me, Soul, and thou shalt
        never dy.

Meditation 56. John 15.24. Had I Not Done Amongst Them the Works, That None Other Man Hath Done, etc. (1703)

Should I with silver tooles delve through the Hill
    Of Cordilera for rich thoughts, that I
My Lord, might weave with an angelick skill
    A Damask Web of Velvet Verse thereby
    To deck thy Works up, all my Web
        would run

To rags, and jags: so snicksnarld to the
    thrum.
Thine are so rich: Within, Without, Refin'd.
    No workes like thine. No Fruits so sweete
        that grow
On th'trees of righteousness, of Angell kinde

And Saints, whose limbs reev'd with them
    bow down low.   10
Should I search ore the Nutmeg Gardens
    shine
Its fruits in flourish are but skegs to thine.

The Clove, when in its White-green'd
    blossoms shoots,
    Some Call the pleasentst sent the World
    doth show.
None Eye e're saw, nor nose e're smelt such
    Fruits
    My Lord, as thine, Thou Tree of Life
    in'ts blow.
Thou Rose of Sharon, Vallies Lilly true
    Thy Fruits most sweet and Glorious
    ever grew.

Thou art a Tree of Perfect nature trim
    Whose golden lining is of perfect Grace   20
Perfum'de with Deity unto the brim,
    Whose fruits, of the perfection, grow,
    of Grace.
    Thy Buds, thy Blossoms, and thy fruits
    adorne
    Thyselfe, and Works, more shining than
    the morn.

Art, natures Ape, hath many brave things done
    As th'Pyramids, the Lake of Meris vast
The Pensile Orchards built in Babylon,
    Psammitich's Labyrinth. (arts Cramping
    task)
    Archimedes his Engins made for war.
    Romes Golden House. Titus his Theater.   30

The Clock at Strasburgh, Dresdens Table-Sight
    Regiamonts Fly of Steele about that flew.
Turrian's Wooden Sparrows in a flight.
    And th'Artificiall man Aquinas slew.
    Mark Scaliota's Lock, and Key and Chain

Drawn by a Flea, in our Queen Betties
    reign.

Might but my pen in natures Inventory
    Its progress make, 't might make such
    things to jump
All which are but Inventions Vents or glory
    Wits Wantonings, and Fancies frollicks
    plump.   40
    Within whose maws lies buried Times,
    and Treasures
    Embalmed up in thick dawbd sinfull
    pleasures.

Nature doth better work than Art: yet thine
    Out vie both works of nature and of Art.
Natures Perfection and the perfect shine
    Of Grace attend thy deed in ev'ry part.
    A Thought, a Word, and Worke of thine,
    will kill
    Sin, Satan, and the Curse: and Law fulfill.

Thou art the Tree of Life in Paradise,
    Whose lively branches are with Clusters
    hung   50
Of Lovely fruits, and Flowers more sweet
    than spice
    Bende down to us: and doe out shine
    the sun,
    Delightfull unto God, doe man rejoyce
    The pleasentst fruits in all Gods Paradise.

Lord feed mine eyes then with thy Doings
    rare,
    And fat my heart with these ripe fruites
    thou bearst.
Adorn my Life well with thy works, make faire
    My Person with apparrell thou prepar'st.
    My Boughs shall loaded bee with fruits
    that spring
    Up from thy Works, while to thy praise
    I sing.   60

JONATHAN EDWARDS (1703–1758) AND THE GREAT AWAKENING

Edwards, born in 1703 at East Windsor, Connecticut, was the grandson of Solomon Stoddard —"Pope" Stoddard as he was called, pastor of the Congregational church in Northampton, Massachusetts, and presiding figure in a sort of ecclesiastical empire which extended down to the Long Island Sound. Edwards went to Yale College, graduating at the age of seventeen, and a few years later became senior tutor (in effect, president) at Yale. In 1726, he became his grandfather's colleague pastor at Northampton, and in 1729, on Stoddard's death, succeeded him. This was rapid promotion even for a young man as talented and eloquent as Edwards; but Edwards' real fame, both national and international, began a few years later, in 1734, with the first wave of that immense religious upheaval known as the Great Awakening.

That remarkable and complex episode consisted primarily in a series of highly emotional, sometimes indeed hysterical, professions of religious belief, of ecstatic or terrified "conversion" to Christian faith. Its sources no doubt lay deep in the psychology and even the sociology of New England, and they involved intricate, and now mostly forgotten, questions of church membership (and hence of salvation). But similar episodes had occurred in various parts of Europe, and they seem everywhere to have reflected above all a severe emotional reaction to the growing theological rationalism— almost, one might say, the commonsense Christianity—of the time.

It should be remembered that Edwards, the strictest and most uncompromising Calvinist New England ever produced, was born only three years before Benjamin Franklin, the quintessential American Deist, or representative of the Enlightenment. Edwards shared many of the intellectual commitments of what would be known as the Age of Reason; he was indeed a good deal ahead of his time, in this country, in his grasp of Newtonian physics and Lockeian psychology and in his extraordinary capacity to press both into the service of a revitalized Christian vision. But Edwards applied both the new sciences and his formidable intellect (the latter has probably not been equaled since on this continent) to the stimulation of emotions—to draw his listeners into a sometimes devastating emotional experience. Conversion to the God Edwards envisaged could, he believed, be nothing less than overpowering.

The Great Awakening had its start, or better perhaps its prologue, in Northampton in late 1734 and continued through the following spring. In that township alone and in a matter of months, more than three hundred men, women, and children—stirred to frenzy by Edwards' sermons—underwent conversion, some of them in a manner so distraught as to make one suspect a deflected sexual element in the experience.

The religious revival began to subside when, in May, 1734, Edwards' uncle-by-marriage, Joseph Hawley, cut his throat. Edwards wrote an account of the whole business to a fellow minister in Boston and then a second account which appeared the next year as *A Faithful Narrative of the Surprising Work of God in the Conversion of Many Hundred Souls in Northampton, and the Neighboring Towns and Villages.* It was an enormously influential work throughout the New World and in Great Britain, serving to create a cult of religious emotionalism comparable, as Perry Miller remarks, to the cult of sensibility (itself leading to a wave of suicides) later stimulated by Goethe's *The Sorrows of Werther.* Edwards took his uncle's suicide as the work of Satan—Satan being "in a Great Rage," while for the moment "the spirit of God was gradually withdrawing from us." Joseph Hawley, lying sleepless in the night, heard voices (Edwards wrote) crying to him: *"Cut your own throat, now is a good opportunity. Now! Now!"* Robert Lowell has drawn very effectively upon Edwards' narrative, modifying it for his imaginative purposes, in his poem "After the Surprising Conversions" (*Lord Weary's Castle*). He speaks in Edwards' voice and refers to Hawley:

I preached one Sabbath on a text from Kings;
He showed concernment for his soul . . .
He meditated terror, and he seemed
Beyond advice or reason. . . .
                    In the latter part of May
He cut his throat. . . .
Satan seemed more let loose among us; God
Abandoned us to Satan, and he pressed
Us hard. . . .
         "My friend,

Cut your own throat. Cut your own throat. Now! Now!"

The Northampton "awakening" came to a temporary halt, as though the population had been shocked out of its ecstasy by Hawley's act. A few years later, however, the atmosphere was again ripe for another campaign for converts. This time the scene had been prepared by a visiting English preacher named George Whitefield,[1] who toured the colonies acting out with very considerable dramatic talent God's damnation of the sinners and the torments of the damned in hell. It was Whitefield who set going the Great Awakening proper and who, with his fellow preachers and imitators, horrified, excited, and "converted" thousands of persons in the course of a year or two. In July, 1741, Jonathan Edwards, to a congregation in Enfield, Massachusetts, already worked up by Whitefield, delivered the sermon known as "Sinners in the Hands of an Angry God." Edwards' chief intellectual adversary, the rationalistic and theologically liberal Charles Chauncey of the First Church in Boston, had deplored what he called "the preaching of terror," and Edwards was never more relentlessly terrifying than at Enfield. The sermon was based on the unsettling text from Deuteronomy, "Their feet shall slide in due time," and it had an immediate and stunning impact. The church was filled with an upswelling of sighs and moans, which turned, as Edwards' relentless discourse went forward, into such "amazing" shrieks that Edwards had to pause till he could again be heard.

The Enfield sermon is an important moment in New England religious history; but it is a no less important moment in the history of American literature. Its rhetoric, for one thing, is a direct assault upon the senses and feelings of its listeners, upon all the faculties that Edwards grouped under the word "heart." Like Thomas Hooker and others, Edwards distinguished between speculative knowledge about the great religious issues and direct and personal experience of the same. "There is a difference

[1] Whitefield, or Whitfield, with John Wesley, was one of the principal founders of Methodism.

between having an opinion, that God is holy and gracious," he wrote elsewhere ("A Divine and Supernatural Light"), "and having a sense of the loveliness and beauty of holiness and grace. . . . The former rests only in the head, speculation only is concerned with it; but the heart is concerned in the latter." It is the heart that is made to shake with fear when Edwards launches into his famous simile: "The God that holds you over the pit of hell, much as one holds a spider, or some loathsome insect over the fire, abhors you, and is dreadfully provoked." How close this is to poetry may be suggested by another of Robert Lowell's poems, "Mr. Edwards and the Spider" (the text of which appears later in these volumes), where, again speaking in Edwards' voice and idiom, Lowell draws upon the Enfield sermon.

> It's well
> If God who holds you to the pit of hell,
> Much as one holds a spider, will destroy,
> Baffle and dissipate your soul.

Elaborating on his text, Edwards drove home again and again the traditional Puritan conviction: namely, that each individual soul is in deadly peril of eternal and agonizing damnation every second of his life. He may lose his moral footing, irredeemably, at any instant. Human life is a constant condition of crisis. "It is no security to wicked men for one moment," Edwards intoned, "that there are no visible means of death at hand. . . . The arrows of death fly unseen at noon-day; the sharpest sight cannot discern them." And for those whose feet do slide fatally, for the damned, the suffering is unspeakable and it is everlasting. "When you look forward"—this is Edwards at his most eloquent—"you shall see a long for ever."

The Enfield sermon, finally, gains much of its pulverizing force from its seemingly absolute rejection of the covenant theory, from its battering insistence that God's treatment of sinful man is simply not bound by the laws of human reason. "There is no other reason to be given. . . . There is no other reason to be given. . . . Yes, there is nothing else to be given as a reason why you do not this very moment drop down into hell." Edwards achieves there a rhetorical power not remote from that in the Book of Job. But it is also worth observing, as others have done, that Edwards' rolling declaration of the utterly nonrational precariousness of the human condition, and the radical anxiety a man may and ought to feel, is exceedingly close to the sense of experience in a good deal of twentieth-century writing—from the disturbing fables of Franz Kafka to the most recent American novel of the terrifying absurd.

It remains true, nonetheless, that Edwards quite genuinely found his image of God to be, in his own word, delightful. In the short "Personal Narrative" Edwards wrote a few years before the Enfield sermon, he recalls that as a youth he regarded the doctrine of God's absolute sovereignty—"in choosing whom he would to eternal life, and rejecting whom he pleased" —as "a horrible doctrine." Now, after his conversion and in his maturity, it seemed to him "exceedingly pleasant, bright and sweet." The "Personal Narrative" is, among other things, Edwards' own exercise in attaining what Hooker called a true sight of his personal sinfulness. When he looks deep into his heart and takes a view of himself, he tells us, "it looks like an abyss deeper than hell." He notes with psychological acuteness that he now has "a vastly greater sense" of his wickedness than he had before his conversion, since now he measures his own nature against the revealed majesty of God. And it is, after all, the majesty of God that his narrative emphasizes; it is with God's majesty that Edwards, heart and mind, is hopelessly in love.

Majesty *and* gentleness, he insists: "I seemed to see them both in a sweet conjunction; majesty and meekness joined together; it was a sweet, and gentle, and holy majesty; and also a majestic meekness; an awful sweetness; a high, and great, and holy gentleness." Not until Herman Melville would there be another American writer whose consciousness was so imbued with the play of contradiction—indeed, with the "conjunction" of major opposites; and Edwards' contradictory image of God would be rivaled by

Melville's image of the godlike whale (as Ishmael remembers it) during the great chase in *Moby-Dick:* "A gentle joyfulness—a mighty mildness of repose in swiftness, invested the gliding whale. . . . Not Jove, not that great majesty supreme! did surpass the glorified White Whale as he so divinely swam."

In 1751, after a long dissension with his congregation, Edwards was expelled from Northampton and went into a kind of exile in the then remote parish at Stockbridge, Massachusetts. He remained there until 1758 and during this time composed most of the treatises on which his towering reputation as a theologian rests, and which comprise the large blocks in a sort of unfinished *summa theologica.* Among these was "The Nature of True Virtue," wherein Edwards argues characteristically that *true* virtue (as against "secondary virtue") is entirely a gift from God, a pure and inexplicable legacy of divine grace; it is a superbly constructed statement which applies intellectual genius and unstinting logic to matters which are declared to be quite beyond intellect and logic. In 1758, Edwards reluctantly accepted a call to be president of the College of New Jersey, later Princeton University. "I have a constitution, in many respects peculiarly unhappy," he wrote the trustees; "attended with . . . a low tide of spirits . . . [and] a disagreeable dulness and stiffness, much unfitting me for conversation, but more especially for the government of a college." He went, however, and died of smallpox in Princeton soon after his arrival.

Part of Edwards' intellectual confidence—in treatises like "The Nature of True Virtue"— came from his belief that, although the mind of God was of course quite out of reach of human understanding, something could indeed be known about God's *domain*, or the world of spirit. For the latter was reflected in the natural world. "The system of created being," Edwards wrote, "may be divided into two parts, the typical world, and the antitypical world." The realm of "types" was "the material and natural world"—the physical earth and the visible heavens, trees and flowers and stars, men and women, children and animals in their bodily existence. The realm of "antitypes," of those divine things shadowed or represented by the physical types, was "the moral, spiritual, and intelligent world, or the city of God." This was the principle worked out in considerable detail by Edwards in the notations gathered together (by Perry Miller in 1948) under the general title *Images or Shadows of Divine Things*.

Edwards' special achievement, in this major contribution to the Puritan theory of allegory, was to restore dignity and significance, as it were, to the physical world and to external human experience (Edwards, that is, legitimizes theoretically, as well as radically extends, the process begun by Samuel Sewall)—by finding *there*, in his immediate and visible surroundings, types of the spiritual world. The more common Christian practice over the centuries had been rather to seek among characters and episodes of the Old Testament for pro-figurings of Christ, the condition of the blessed after death, and so on. To be sure, writers in seventeenth-century England like John Donne and George Herbert and Jeremy Taylor had regularly turned to the world about them, often to quite homely things, for types of the spiritual world; Edmund Spenser, more than a century earlier, had turned to "the world" as well, though the loftier one of the Elizabethan age; while in seventeenth-century Massachusetts, Anne Bradstreet discovered religious significance in the stresses and joys of intimate married life, as well as in the trees and rivers of her husband's estate, and Edward Taylor saw evidences of the relation between God and man in the routines of household work. But Taylor's poetry was unpublished and unknown; Anne Bradstreet had no successor; and by Edwards' time, the type-seeking Puritan mind looked almost exclusively to the Bible.

It was, therefore, a bold intellectual stroke on Edwards' part to go instead to natural phenomena for "shadows" and foreshadowings of divine things. Doing so, he reinvested these phenomena with a kind of spare beauty. "Thus," he says in the thirteenth notation,

I believe the grass and other vegetables growing and flourishing, looking green and pleasant as it were, ripening, blossoming, and bearing fruit from the influences of the heavens, the rain and wind and light and heat of the sun, to be on purpose to represent the dependence of our spiritual welfare upon God's gracious influences and the effusions of His holy spirit. I am sure there are none of the types of the Old Testament are more lively images of spiritual things.

Though the natural scene exists primarily to represent something about the spiritual scene, nature is also observed (and as the passage shows, observed very well) in and of itself. Edwards had learned from Locke to trust the evidence of the senses and from Newton to believe in certain discernible laws governing natural phenomena; and if he found human beings hopelessly corrupt, he also found both nature and man worth the closest possible study.

So Edwards discoursed, by no means unpoetically, about the world of spirit by drawing attention to blossoms, tree-pruning, hills and mountains and rivers, the political triumphs of ancient Rome, the invention of the telescope, spiders, and the lowly hog, as well as the physical messiness of the newborn baby and the ugly spasms of a dying man. It is not too much to say that Edwards, by rooting the Christian vision in such solidly concrete instances, did a good deal to make imaginative literature possible in America. The particular *kind* of literature he made possible is suggested again by *Moby-Dick*, and by Ahab's meditation in a rare moment of mental assurance: "O Nature, and O soul of man! how far beyond all utterance are your linked analogies! not the smallest atom stirs or lives on matter, but has its cunning duplicate in mind." But the point is that with Edwards (and of course with Franklin and other contemporaries), the American mind and imagination were responding further to the natural and human world actually around them. Soon the American mind would belong to that world, and a native literature would be in the making.

BIOGRAPHICAL CHART

1703 Born, October 5, in East Windsor, Connecticut

1716–20 Attends Yale College

1726 Becomes colleague of his grandfather, Solomon Stoddard, in the Congregational church in Northampton, Massachusetts

1727 Marries Sarah Pierrepont

1729 Succeeds Stoddard as pastor, upon the latter's death

1734 Participates in the first wave of "the Great Awakening"

1736 A *Faithful Account of the Surprising Work of God*

c. 1740 "Personal Narrative"

1741 Edwards' sermon "Sinners in the Hands of an Angry God" helps spur the second phase of the Awakening

1751 Dismissed from the pulpit at Northampton and preaches "Farewell Sermon"

1751–58 At Stockbridge, Massachusetts, as pastor of the local church and missionary to the Housatonic Indians; during these years writes his greatest theological studies, including *Freedom of Will, The Nature of True Virtue*, and *The Great Christian Doctrine of Original Sin Defended*

1758 From January until his death on March 22, president of the College of New Jersey (later Princeton College)

FURTHER READINGS

An edition of Edwards' writings is going forward at Yale University and is to be completed in 1977.

Clarence H. Faust and Thomas H. Johnson, eds., *Jonathan Edwards* (1935; selections and commentary)

E. S. Gaustad, *The Great Awakening in New England* (1957)

Perry Miller, *Jonathan Edwards* (1949; an interpretation of his thought)

Ola E. Winslow, *Jonathan Edwards* (1941; a biography)

From Narrative of Surprising Conversions (1736)

After a general account of the churches in Northampton and the neighboring villages, Edwards has described the outbreak of religious excitement in 1734 and later. He then comes to the astonishing story of the child Phebe Bartlet and to the suicide of Joseph Hawley.

───────

But I now proceed to the other instance that I would give an account of, which is of the little child forementioned. Her name is Phebe Bartlet, daughter of William Bartlet. I shall give the account as I took it from the mouths of her parents, whose veracity, none that know them doubt of.

She was born in March, in the year 1731. About the latter end of April, or beginning of May, 1735, she was greatly affected by the talk of her brother, who had been hopefully converted a little before, at about eleven years of age, and then seriously talked to her about the great things of religion. Her parents did not know of it at that time, and were not wont, in the counsels they gave to their children, particularly to direct themselves to her, by reason of her being so young, and, as they supposed not capable of understanding; but after her brother had talked to her, they observed her very earnestly to listen to the advice they gave to the other children, and she was observed very constantly to retire, several times in a day, as was concluded, for secret prayer, and grew more and more engaged in religion, and was more frequently in her closet, till at last she was wont to visit it five or six times in a day, and was so engaged in it, that nothing would, at any time divert her from her stated closet exercises. Her mother often observed and watched her, when such things occurred, as she thought most likely to divert her, either by putting it out of her thoughts, or otherwise engaging her inclinations, but never could observe her to fail. She mentioned some very remarkable instances.

She once, of her own accord, spake of her unsuccessfulness, in that she could not find God, or to that purpose. But on Thursday, the last day of July, about the middle of the day, the child being in the closet, where it used to retire, its mother heard it speaking aloud, which was unusual, and never had been observed before; and her voice seemed to be as of one exceeding importunate and engaged, but her mother could distinctly hear only these words (spoken in her childish manner, but seemed to be spoken with extraordinary earnestness, and out of distress of soul), Pray BESSED LORD give me salvation! I PRAY, BEG pardon all my sins! When the child had done prayer, she came out of the closet, and came and sat down by her mother, and cried out aloud. Her mother very earnestly asked her several times, what the matter was, before she would make any answer, but she continued exceedingly crying, and wreathing her body to and fro, like one in anguish of spirit. Her mother then asked her whether she was afraid that God would not give her salvation. She then answered yes, I am afraid I shall go to hell! Her mother then endeavored to quiet her, and told her she would not have her cry —she must be a good girl, and pray every day, and she hoped God would give her salvation. But this did not quiet her at all—but she continued thus earnestly crying and taking on for some time, till at length she suddenly ceased crying and began to smile, and presently said with a smiling countenance—Mother, the kingdom of heaven is come to me! Her mother was surprised at the sudden alteration, and at the speech, and knew not what to make of it, but at first said nothing to her. The child presently spake again, and said, there is another come to me, and there is another—there is three; and being asked what she meant, she answered—One is, thy will be done, and there is another—enjoy him forever; by which it seems that when the child said, there is three come to me, she meant three passages of its catechism that came to her mind.

After the child had said this, she retired again into her closet; and her mother went over to her brother's, who was next neighbor; and when she came back, the child being come out of the closet, meets her mother with this cheerful speech—I can find God now! Referring to what she had before complained of, that she could not find God. Then the child spoke again, and said—I love God! Her mother asked her how well she loved God, whether she loved God better than her father and mother, she said yes. Then she asked her whether she loved God better than her little sister Rachel, she answered yes, better than any thing! Then her eldest sister, referring to her saying she could find God now, asked her where she could find God; she answered, in heaven. Why, said she, have you been in heaven? No, said the child. By this it seems not

to have been any imagination of any thing seen with bodily eyes that she called God, when she said I can find God now. Her mother asked her whether she was afraid of going to hell, and that had made her cry. She answered, yes, I was; but now I shall not. Her mother asked her whether she thought that God had given her salvation: she answered yes. Her mother asked her, when; she answered to-day. She appeared all that afternoon exceeding cheerful and joyful. One of the neighbors asked her how she felt herself? She answered, I feel better than I did. The neighbor asked her what made her feel better; she answered, God makes me. That evening as she lay abed, she called one of her little cousins to her, that was present in the room, as having something to say to him; and when he came, she told him that heaven was better than earth. The next day being Friday, her mother asking her her catechism, asked her what God made her for; she answered, to serve him; and added, every body should serve God, and get an interest in Christ.

The same day the elder children, when they came home from school, seemed much affected with the extraordinary change that seemed to be made in Phebe; and her sister Abigail standing by, her mother took occasion to counsel her, now to improve her time, to prepare for another world; on which Phebe burst out in tears, and cried out poor Nabby! Her mother told her, she would not have her cry, she hoped that God would give Nabby salvation; but that did not quiet her, but she continued earnestly crying for some time; and when she had in a measure ceased, her sister Eunice being by her, she burst out again, and cried poor Eunice! and cried exceedingly; and when she had almost done, she went into another room, and there looked upon her sister Naomi, and burst out again, crying poor Amy! Her mother was greatly affected at such a behavior in the child, and knew not what to say to her. One of the neighbors coming in a little after, asked her what she had cried for. She seemed, at first, backward to tell the reason: her mother told her she might tell that person, for he had given her an apple; upon which she said, she cried because she was afraid they would go to hell.

At night a certain minister, that was occasionally in the town, was at the house, and talked considerably with her of the things of religion; and after he was gone, she sat leaning on the table, with tears running out of her eyes; and being asked what made her cry, she said it was thinking about God.

The next day being Saturday, she seemed a great part of the day to be in a very affectionate frame, had four turns of crying, and seemed to endeavor to curb herself, and hide her tears, and was very backward to talk of the occasion of it. On the Sabbath day she was asked whether she believed in God; she answered yes; and being told that Christ was the Son of God, she made ready answer, and said, I know it.

From this time there has appeared a very remarkable abiding change in the child: she has been very strict upon the Sabbath, and seems to long for the Sabbath day before it comes, and will often in the week time be inquiring how long it is to the Sabbath day, and must have the days particularly counted over that are between, before she will be contented. And she seems to love God's house—is very eager to go thither. Her mother once asked her why she had such a mind to go? Whether it was not to see fine folks? She said no, it was to hear Mr. Edwards preach. When she is in the place of worship, she is very far from spending her time there as children at her age usually do, but appears with an attention that is very extraordinary for such a child. She also appears very desirous at all opportunities, to go to private religious meetings, and is very still and attentive at home, in prayer time, and has appeared affected in time of family prayer. She seems to delight much in hearing religious conversation. When I once was there with some others that were strangers, and talked to her something of religion, she seemed more than ordinarily attentive; and when we were gone, she looked out very wistly after us, and said—I wish they would come again! Her mother asked her why: says she, I love to hear them talk!

She seems to have very much of the fear of God before her eyes, and an extraordinary dread of sin against him; of which her mother mentioned the following remarkable instance. Some time in August, the last year, she went with some bigger children, to get some plums, in a neighbor's lot, knowing nothing of any harm in what she did; but when she brought some of the plums into the house, her mother mildly reproved her, and told her that she must not get plums without leave, because it was sin: God had commanded her not to steal. The child seemed greatly surprised and burst out into tears, and cried out—I will not have these plums! And turning to her sister Eunice, very earnestly said to her—Why did you ask me to go to that plum tree? I should not have gone if you had not asked me. The other children did not seem to be much affected or concerned; but there was no pacifying Phebe. Her mother told her she might go and ask leave, and then it would not be sin for her to eat them, and sent one of the children to that end; and when she returned, her mother told her that the owner had given leave, now she might eat them, and it would not be stealing. This stilled her a little while, but presently she broke out again into an exceeding fit of crying: her mother asked her what made her cry again? Why she cried now, since they had asked leave? What it was that troubled her now? And asked her several times very earnestly, before she made any answer; but at last, said it was because—BECAUSE IT WAS SIN. She continued a considerable time crying; and said she would not go again if Eunice asked her a hundred times; and she retained her aversion to that fruit for a considerable time, under the remembrance of her former sin.

. . .

She has often manifested a great concern for the good of other souls; and has been wont many times, affectionately to counsel the other children. Once about the latter end of September, the last year, when she and some others of the children were in a room by themselves a husking Indian corn, the child, after a while, came out and sat by the fire. Her mother took notice that she appeared with a more than ordinary serious and pensive countenance, but at last she broke silence, and said I have been talking to Nabby and Eunice. Her mother asked her what she had said to them. Why, said she, I told them they must pray, and prepare to die, that they had but a little while to live in this world, and they must be always ready. When Nabby came out, her mother asked her whether she had said that to them. Yes, said she, she said that and a great deal more. At other times the child took her opportunities to talk to the other children about the great concern of their souls; sometimes so as much to affect them, and set them into tears. She was once exceeding importunate with her mother to go with her sister Naomi to pray: her mother endeavored to put her off, but she pulled her by the sleeve, and seemed as if she would by no means be denied. At last her mother told her, that Amy must go and pray herself; but, said the child, she will not go, and persisted earnestly to beg of her mother to go with her.

She has discovered an uncommon degree of a spirit of charity, particularly on the following occasion: a poor man that lives in the woods, had lately lost a cow that the family much depended on, and being at the house, he was relating his misfortune, and telling of the straits and difficulties they were reduced to by it. She took much notice of it, and it wrought exceedingly on her compassions; and after she had attentively heard him a while, she went away to her father, who was in the shop, and entreated him to give that man a cow; and told him that the poor man had no cow! That the hunters or something else had killed his cow! And entreated him to give him one of theirs. Her father told her that they could not spare one. Then she entreated him to let him and his family come and live at his house; and had much talk of the same nature, whereby she manifested bowels of compassion to the poor.

She has manifested great love to her minister; particularly when I returned from my long journey for my health, last fall, when she heard of it, she appeared very joyful at the news, and told the children of it with an elevated voice, as the most joyful tidings, repeating it over and over. Mr. Edwards is come home! Mr. Edwards is come home! She still continues very constant in secret prayer, so far as can be observed (for she seems to have no desire that others should observe her when she retires, but seems to be a child of a reserved temper), and every night before she goes to bed will say her catechism, and will by no means miss of it: she never forgot it but once, and then after she was abed, thought of it and cried out in tears—I have not said my catechism! And would not be quieted till her mother asked her the catechism as she lay in bed. She sometimes appears to be in doubt about the condition of her soul, and when asked whether she thinks that she is prepared for death, speaks something doubtfully about it: at other times seems to have no doubt, but when asked, replies yes, without hesitation.

In the former part of this great work of God amongst us, till it got to its height, we seemed to be wonderfully smiled upon and blessed in all respects. Satan (as has been already observed) seemed to be unusually restrained; persons that before had been involved in melancholy, seemed to be as it were waked up out of it, and those that had been entangled with extraordinary temptations seemed wonderfully to be set at liberty, and not only so, but it was the most remarkable time of health that ever I knew since I have been in the town. We ordinarily have several bills put up, every Sabbath, for persons that are sick, but now we have not so much as one for many Sabbaths together. But after this it seemed to be otherwise, when this work of God appeared to be at its greatest height. A poor weak man that belongs to the town, being in great spiritual trouble, was hurried with violent temptations to cut his own throat, and made an attempt, but did not do it effectually. He after this continued a considerable time exceedingly overwhelmed with melancholy, but has now, of a long time, been very greatly delivered, by the light of God's countenance lifted up upon him, and has expressed a great sense of his sin in so far yielding to temptation, and there are in him all hopeful evidences of his having been made a subject of saving mercy.

In the latter part of May, it began to be very sensible that the Spirit of God was gradually withdrawing from us, and after this time Satan seemed to be more let loose, and raged in a dreadful manner. The first instance wherein it appeared, was a person's putting an end to his own life, by cutting his throat. He was a gentleman of more than common understanding, of strict morals, religious in his behavior, and a useful, honorable person in the town; but was of a family that are exceeding prone to the disease of melancholy, and his mother was killed with it. He had, from the beginning of this extraordinary time, been exceedingly concerned about the state of his soul, and there were some things in his experience, that appeared very hopefully, but he durst entertain no hope concerning his own good estate. Towards the latter part of his time, he grew much discouraged, and melancholy grew amain upon him, till he was wholly overpowered by it, and was, in great measure, past a capacity of receiving advice, or being reasoned with to any purpose: the devil took the advantage, and drove him into despairing thoughts. He was kept awake nights meditating terror, so that he had scarce any sleep at all, for a long time together. And it was observable at last, that he was scarcely well capable of managing his ordinary business, and was judged delirious by the coroner's inquest. The news of this, extraordinarily affected the minds of people here, and struck them as it were with astonishment. After this, multitudes in this and other towns seemed to have it strongly suggested to them, and pressed upon them, to do as this person had done. And many that seemed to be under no melancholy, some pious persons, that had no special darkness or doubts about the goodness of their state, nor were under any special trouble or concern of mind about any thing spiritual or temporal, yet had it urged upon them, as if somebody had spoken to them, *Cut your own throat, now is a good opportunity.* Now! Now! So that they were obliged to fight with all their might to resist it, and yet no reason suggested to them why they should do it.

Personal Narrative (1740)

I had a variety of concerns and exercises about my soul from my childhood; but had two more remarkable seasons of awakening, before I met with that change by which I was brought to those new dispositions, and that new sense of things, that I have since had. The first time was when I was a boy, some years before I went to college, at a time of remarkable awakening in my father's congregation, I was then very much affected for many months, and concerned about the things of religion, and my soul's salvation; and was abundant in duties. I used to pray five times a day in secret, and to spend much time in religious talk with other boys; and used to meet with them to pray together. I experienced I know not what kind of delight in religion. My mind was much engaged in it, and had much selfrighteous pleasure; and it was my delight to abound in religious duties. I with some of my schoolmates joined together, and built a booth in a swamp, in a very retired spot, for a place of prayer. And besides I had particular secret places of my own in the woods, where I used to retire by myself; and was from time to time much affected. My affections seemed to be lively and easily moved, and I seemed to be in my element when engaged in religious duties. And I am ready to think, many are deceived with such affections, and such a kind of delight as I then had in religion, and mistake it for grace.

But in process of time, my convictions and affections were off; and I entirely lost all those affections and delights and left off secret prayer, at least as to any constant performance of it; and returned like a dog to his vomit, and went on in the ways of sin. Indeed I was at times very uneasy, especially towards the latter part of my time at college; when it pleased God, to seize me with a pleurisy; in which he brought me nigh to the grave, and shook me over the pit of hell. And yet, it was not long after my recovery, before I fell again into my old ways of sin. But God would not suffer me to go on with any quietness; I had great and violent inward struggles, till, after many conflicts with wicked inclinations, repeated resolutions, and bonds that I laid myself under by a kind of vows to God, I was brought wholly to break off all former wicked ways, and all ways of known outward sin; and to apply myself to seek salvation, and practice many religious duties; but without that kind of affection and delight which I had formerly experienced. My concern now wrought more by inward struggles and conflicts, and selfreflections. I made seeking my salvation the main business of my life. But yet, it seems to me, I sought after a miserable manner; which has made me sometimes since to question, whether ever it issued in that which was saving; being ready to doubt, whether such miserable seeking ever succeeded. I was indeed brought to seek salvation in a manner that I never was before; I felt a spirit to part with all things in the world, for an interest in Christ. My concern continued and prevailed, with many exercising thoughts and inward struggles; but yet it never seemed to be proper to express that concern by the name of terror.

From my childhood up, my mind had been full of objections against the doctrine of God's sovereignty, in choosing whom he would to eternal life, and rejecting whom he pleased; leaving them eternally to perish, and be everlastingly tormented in hell. It used to appear like a horrible doctrine to me. But I remember the time very well, when I seemed to be convinced, and fully satisfied, as to this sovereignty of God, and his justice in thus eternally disposing of men, according to his sovereign pleasure. But never could give an account, how, or by what means, I was thus convinced, not in the least imagining at the time, nor a long time after, that there was any extraordinary influence of God's Spirit in it; but only that now I saw further, and my reason apprehended the justice and reasonableness of it. However, my mind rested in it; and it put an end to all those cavils and objections. And there has been a wonderful alteration in my mind, in respect to the doctrine of God's sovereignty, from that day to this; so that I scarce ever have found so much as the rising of an objection against it, in the most absolute sense, in God's shewing mercy to whom he will shew mercy, and hardening whom he will. God's absolute sovereignty and justice, with respect to salvation and damnation, is what my mind seems to rest assured of, as much as of any thing that I see with my eyes; at least it is so at times. But I have often, since that first conviction, had quite another kind of sense of God's sovereignty than I had then. I have often since had not only a conviction, but a delightful conviction. The doctrine has very often appeared exceeding pleasant, bright, and sweet. Absolute sovereignty is what I love to ascribe to God. But my first conviction was not so.

The first instance that I remember of that sort of inward, sweet delight in God and divine things that I have lived much in since, was on reading those words, I Tim. i. 17. *Now unto the King eternal, immortal, invisible, the only wise God, be honor and glory for ever and ever, Amen.* As I read the words, there came into my soul, and was as it were diffused through it, a sense of the glory of the Divine Being; a new sense, quite different from any thing I ever experienced before. Never any words of scripture seemed to me as these words did. I thought with myself, how excellent a Being that was, and how happy I should be, if I might enjoy that God, and be rapt up to him in heaven, and be as it were swallowed up in him for ever! I kept saying, and as it were singing over these words of scripture to myself; and went to pray to God that I might enjoy him, and prayed in a manner quite different from what I used to do; with a new sort of affection. But it never came into my thought, that there was any thing spiritual, or of a saving nature in this.

From about that time, I began to have a new kind of apprehensions and ideas of Christ, and the work of redemption, and the glorious way of salvation by him. An inward, sweet sense of these things, at times, came into my heart; and my soul was led away in pleasant views and contemplations of them. And my mind was greatly engaged to spend my time in reading and meditating on Christ, on the beauty and excellency of his person, and the lovely way of salvation by free grace in him. I found no books so delightful to me, as those that treated of these subjects. Those words Cant. ii. 1, used to be abundantly with me, *I am the Rose of Sharon, and the Lilly of the valleys.* The words seemed to me, sweetly to represent the loveliness and beauty of Jesus Christ. The whole book of Canticles used to be pleasant to me, and I used to be much in reading it, about that time; and found, from time to time, an inward sweetness, that would carry me away, in my contemplations.

This I know not how to express otherwise, than by a calm, sweet abstraction of soul from all the concerns of this world; and sometimes a kind of vision, or fixed ideas and imaginations, of being alone in the mountains, or some solitary wilderness, far from all mankind, sweetly conversing with Christ, and wrapt and swallowed up in God. The sense I had of divine things, would often of a sudden kindle up, as it were, a sweet burning in my heart; an ardor of soul, that I know not how to express.

Not long after I first began to experience these things, I gave an account to my father of some things that had passed in my mind. I was pretty much affected by the discourse we had together; and when the discourse was ended, I walked abroad alone, in a solitary place in my father's pasture, for contemplation. And as I was walking there, and looking up on the sky and clouds, there came into my mind so sweet a sense of the glorious *majesty* and *grace* of God, that I know not how to express. I seemed to see them both in a sweet conjunction; majesty and meekness joined together; it was a sweet, and gentle, and holy majesty; and also a majestic meekness; an awful sweetness; a high, and great, and holy gentleness.

After this my sense of divine things gradually increased, and became more and more lively, and had more of that inward sweetness. The appearance of every thing was altered; there seemed to be, as it were, a calm, sweet cast, or appearance of divine glory, in almost every thing. God's excellency, his wisdom, his purity and love, seemed to appear in every thing; in the sun, moon, and stars; in the clouds, and blue sky; in the grass, flowers, trees; in the water, and all nature; which used greatly to fix my mind. I often used to sit and view the moon for continuance; and in the day, spent much time in viewing the clouds and sky, to behold the sweet glory of God in these things; in the mean time, singing forth, with a low voice my contemplations of the Creator and Redeemer. And scarce any thing, among all the works of nature, was so sweet to me as thunder and lightning; formerly, nothing had been so terrible to me. Before, I used to be uncommonly terrified with thunder, and to be struck with terror when I saw a thunder storm rising; but now, on the contrary, it rejoiced me. I felt God, so to speak, at the first appearance of a thunder storm; and used to take the opportunity, at such times, to fix myself in order to view the clouds, and see the lightnings play, and hear the majestic and awful voice of God's thunder, which oftentimes was exceedingly entertaining, leading me to sweet contemplations of my great and glorious God. While thus engaged, it always seemed natural to me to sing, or chant for my meditations; or, to speak my thoughts in soliloquies with a singing voice.

I felt then great satisfaction, as to my good state; but that did not content me. I had vehement longings of soul after God and Christ, and after more holiness, wherewith my heart seemed to be full, and ready to break; which often brought to my mind the words of the Psalmist, Psal. cxix. 28. *My soul breaketh for the longing it hath.* I often felt a mourning and lamenting in my heart, that I had not turned to God sooner, that I might have had more time to grow in grace. My mind was greatly fixed on divine things; almost perpetually in the contemplation of them. I spent most of my time in thinking of divine things, year after year; often walking alone in the woods, and solitary places, for meditation, soliloquy, and prayer, and converse with God; and it was always my manner, at such times, to sing forth my contemplations. I was almost constantly in ejaculatory prayer, wherever I was. Prayer seemed to be natural to me, as the breath by which the inward burnings of my heart had vent. The delights which I now felt in the things of religion, were of an exceeding different kind from those before mentioned, that I had when a boy; and what I then had no more notion of, than one born blind has of pleasant and beautiful colors. They were of a more inward, pure, soul animating and refreshing nature. Those former delights never reached the heart; and did not arise from any sight of the divine excellency of the things of God; or any taste of the soul satisfying and life-giving good there is in them.

My sense of divine things seemed gradually to increase, until I went to preach at Newyork, which was about a year and a half after they began; and while I was there, I felt them, very sensibly, in a much higher degree than I had done before. My longings after God and holiness, were much increased. Pure and humble, holy and heavenly Christianity, appeared exceeding amiable to me. I felt a burning desire to be in every thing a complete Christian; and conformed to the blessed image of Christ; and that I might live, in all things, according to the pure, sweet and blessed rules of the gospel. I had an eager thirsting after progress in these things; which put me upon pursuing and pressing after them. It was my continual strife day and night, and constant inquiry, how I should *be* more holy, and *live* more holily, and more becoming a child of God, and a disciple of Christ. I now sought an increase of grace and holiness, and a holy life, with much more earnestness, than ever I sought grace before I had it. I used to be continually examining myself, and studying and contriving for likely ways and means, how I should live holily, with far greater diligence and earnestness, than ever I pursued any thing in my life; but yet with too great a dependence on my own strength; which afterwards proved a great damage to me. My experience had not then taught me, as it has done since, my extreme feebleness and impotence, every manner of way; and the bottomless depths of secret corruption and deceit there was in my heart. However, I went on with my eager pursuit after more holiness, and conformity to Christ.

The heaven I desired was a heaven of holiness; to be with God, and to spend my eternity in divine love, and holy communion with Christ. My mind was very much taken up with contemplations on heaven, and the enjoyments there; and living there in perfect holiness, humility and love: And it used at that time to appear a great part of the happiness of heaven, that there the saints could express their love to Christ. It appeared to me a great clog and burden, that what I felt within, I could not express as I desired. The inward ardor of my soul, seemed to be hindered and pent up, and could not freely flame out as it would. I used often to think, how in heaven this principle should freely and fully vent and express itself. Heaven appeared exceedingly delightful, as a world of love; and that all happiness consisted in living in pure, humble, heavenly, divine love.

I remember the thoughts I used then to have of holiness; and said sometimes to myself, "I do certainly know that I love holiness, such as the gospel prescribes." It appeared to me, that there was nothing in it but what was ravishingly lovely; the highest beauty and amiableness . . . a *divine* beauty; far purer than any thing here upon earth; and that every thing else was like mire and defilement, in comparison of it.

Holiness, as I then wrote down some of my contemplations on it, appeared to me to be of a sweet, pleasant, charming, serene, calm nature; which brought an inexpressible purity, brightness, peacefulness and ravishment to the soul. In other words, that it made the soul like a field or garden of God, with all manner of pleasant flowers; all pleasant, delightful, and undisturbed; enjoying a sweet calm, and the gently vivifying beams of the sun. The soul of a true Christian, as I then wrote my meditations, appeared like such a little white flower as we see in the spring of the year; low and humble on the ground, opening its bosom to receive the pleasant beams of the sun's glory; rejoicing as it were in a calm rapture; diffusing around a sweet fragrancy; standing peacefully and lovingly, in the midst of other flowers round about; all in like manner opening their bosoms, to drink in the light of the sun. There was no part of creature holiness, that I had so great a sense of its loveliness, as humility, brokenness of heart and poverty of spirit; and there was nothing that I so earnestly longed for. My heart panted after this, to lie low before God, as in the dust; that I might be nothing, and that God might be ALL, that I might become as a little child.

While at Newyork, I was sometimes much affected with reflections of my past life, considering how late it was before I began to be truly religious; and how wickedly I had lived till then; and once so as to weep abundantly, and for a considerable time together.

On *January* 12, 1723. I made a solemn dedication of myself to God, and wrote it down; giving up myself, and all that I had to God; to be for the future, in no respect, my own; to act as one that had no right to himself, in any respect. And solemnly vowed, to take God for my whole portion and felicity; looking on nothing else, as any part of my happiness, nor acting as if it were; and his law for the constant rule of my obedience: engaging to fight, with all my might, against the world, the flesh, and the devil, to the end of my life. But I have reason to be infinitely humbled, when I consider, how much I have failed, of answering my obligation.

I had, then, abundance of sweet, religious conversation, in the family where I lived, with Mr. John Smith, and his pious mother. My heart was knit in affection, to those, in whom were appearances of true piety; and I could bear the thoughts of no other companions, but such as were holy, and the disciples of the blessed Jesus. I had great longings, for the advancement of Christ's kingdom in the world; and my secret prayer used to be, in great part, taken up in praying for it. If I heard the least hint, of any thing that happened, in any part of the world, that appeared, in some respect or other, to have a favourable aspect, on the interests of Christ's kingdom, my soul eagerly catched at it; and it would much animate and refresh me. I used to be eager to read public news-letters, mainly for that end; to see if I could not find some

news, favourable to the interest of religion in the world.

I very frequently used to retire into a solitary place, on the banks of Hudson's River, at some distance from the city, for contemplation on divine things and secret converse with God: and had many sweet hours there. Sometimes Mr. Smith and I walked there together, to converse on the things of God; and our conversation used to turn much on the advancement of Christ's kingdom in the world, and the glorious things that God would accomplish for his church in the latter days. I had then, and at other times, the greatest delight in the holy scriptures, of any book whatsoever. Oftentimes in reading it, every word seemed to touch my heart. I felt a harmony between something in my heart, and those sweet and powerful words. I seemed often to see so much light exhibited by every sentence, and such a refreshing food communicated, that I could not get along in reading; often dwelling long on one sentence, to see the wonders contained in it; and yet almost every sentence seemed to be full of wonders.

I came away from Newyork in the month of April, 1723, and had a most bitter parting with Madam Smith and her son. My heart seemed to sink within me, at leaving the family and city, where I had enjoyed so many sweet and pleasant days. I went from New York to Wethersfield, by water; and as I sailed away, I kept sight of the city as long as I could. However, that night after this sorrowful parting, I was greatly comforted in God at Westchester, where we went ashore to lodge: and had a pleasant time of it all the voyage to Saybrook. It was sweet to me to think of meeting dear christians in heaven, where we should never part more. At Saybrook we went ashore to lodge on Saturday, and there kept the Sabbath; where I had a sweet and refreshing season, walking alone in the fields.

After I came home to Windsor, I remained much in a like frame of mind, as when at Newyork; only sometimes I felt my heart ready to sink, with the thoughts of my friends at Newyork. My support was in contemplations on the heavenly state; as I find in my Diary of May 1, 1723. It was a comfort to think of that state, where there is fulness of joy; where reigns heavenly, calm, and delightful love, without alloy; where there are continually the dearest expressions of this love; where is the enjoyment of the persons loved, without ever parting; where those persons who appear so lovely in this world, will really be inexpressibly more lovely, and full of love to us. And how sweetly will the mutual lover join together, to sing the praises of God and the Lamb! How will it fill us with joy to think, that this enjoyment, these sweet exercises, will never cease, but will last to all eternity. . . . I continued much in the same frame, in the general, as when at Newyork, till I went to Newhaven, as Tutor of the College: particularly, once at Bolton, on a journey from Boston, while walking out alone in the fields. After I went to Newhaven, I sunk in religion; my mind being diverted from my eager pursuits after holiness, by some affairs, that greatly perplexed and distracted my thoughts.

In September, 1725, I was taken ill at Newhaven, and while endeavouring to go home to Windsor, was so ill at the North Village, that I could go no farther; where I lay sick, for about a quarter of a year. In this sickness, God was pleased to visit me again, with the sweet influences of his Spirit. My mind was greatly engaged there, on divine and pleasant contemplations, and longings of soul. I observed, that those who watched with me, would often be looking out wishfully for the morning; which brought to my mind those words of the Psalmist, and which my soul with delight made its own language, *My soul waiteth for the Lord, more than they that watch for the morning; I say, more than they that watch for the morning;* and when the light of day came in at the window, it refreshed my soul, from one morning to another. It seemed to be some image of the light of God's glory.

I remember, about that time, I used greatly to long for the conversion of some, that I was concerned with; I could gladly honour them, and with delight be a servant to them, and lie at their feet, if they were but truly holy. But some time after this, I was again greatly diverted with some temporal concerns, that exceedingly took up my thoughts, greatly to the wounding of my soul; and went on, through various exercises, that it would be tedious to relate, which gave me much more experience of my own heart, than I ever had before.

Since I came to this town, I have often had sweet complacency in God, in views of his glorious perfections and the excellency of Jesus Christ. God has appeared to me a glorious and lovely Being, chiefly on account of his holiness. The holiness of God has always appeared to me the most lovely of all his attributes. The doctrines of God's absolute sovereignty, and free grace, in shewing mercy to whom he would shew mercy; and man's absolute dependence on the operations of God's Holy Spirit, have very often appeared to me as sweet and glorious doctrines. These doctrines have been much my delight. God's sovereignty has ever appeared to me, great part of his glory. It has often been my delight to approach God, and adore him as a sovereign God, and ask sovereign mercy of him.

I have loved the doctrines of the gospel; they have been to my soul like green pastures. The gospel has seemed to me the richest treasure; the treasure that I have most desired, and longed that it might dwell richly in me. The way of salvation by Christ has appeared, in a general way, glorious and excellent, most pleasant and most beautiful. It has often seemed to me, that it would in a great measure spoil heaven, to receive it in any other way. That text has often been affecting and delightful to me, Isa. xxxii. 2. A *man shall be an hiding place from the wind, and a covert from the tempest, &c.*

It has often appeared to me delightful, to be united to Christ; to have him for my head, and to be a member of his body; also to have Christ for my teacher and prophet. I very often think with sweetness, and longings, and pantings of soul, of being a little child, taking hold of Christ, to be led by him through the wilderness of this world. That text, Math. xviii. 3, has often been sweet to me, *except ye be converted and become as little children, &c.* I love to think of coming to Christ, to receive salvation of him, poor in spirit, and quite empty of self, humbly exalting him alone; cut off entirely from my own root, in order to grow into, and out of Christ; to have God in Christ to be all in all; and to live by faith in the son of God, a life of humble, unfeigned confidence in him. That scripture has often been sweet to me, Psal. cxv. 1. *Not unto us, O Lord, not unto us, but unto thy name give glory, for thy mercy, and for thy truth's sake.* And those words of Christ, Luke x. 21. *In that hour Jesus rejoiced in spirit, and said, I thank thee, O Father, Lord of heaven and earth, that thou hast hid these things from the wise and prudent, and hast revealed them unto babes: Even so, Father, for so it seemed good in thy sight.* That sovereignty of God which Christ rejoiced in, seemed to me worthy of such joy; and that rejoicing seemed to shew the excellency of Christ, and of what spirit he was.

Sometimes, only mentioning a single word caused my heart to burn within me; or only seeing the name of Christ, or the name of some attribute of God. And God has appeared glorious to me, on account of the Trinity. It has made me have exalting thoughts of God, that he subsists in three persons; Father, Son and Holy Ghost. The sweetest joys and delights I have experienced, have not been those that have arisen from a hope of my own good estate; but in a direct view of the glorious things of the gospel. When I enjoy this sweetness, it seems to carry me above the thoughts of my own estate; it seems at such times a loss that I cannot bear, to take off my eye from the glorious, pleasant object I behold without me, to turn my eye in upon myself, and my own good estate.

My heart has been much on the advancement of Christ's kingdom in the world. The histories of the past advancement of Christ's kingdom have been sweet to me. When I have read histories of past ages, the pleasantest thing in all my reading has been, to read of the kingdom of Christ being promoted. And when I have expected, in my reading, to come to any such thing, I have rejoiced in the prospect, all the way as I read. And my mind has been much entertained and delighted with the scripture promises and prophecies, which relate to the future glorious advancement of Christ's kingdom upon earth.

I have sometimes had a sense of the excellent fulness of Christ, and his meetness and suitableness as a Saviour; whereby he has appeared to me, far above all, the chief of ten thousands. His blood and atonement have appeared sweet, and his righteousness sweet; which was always accompanied with ardency of spirit; and inward strugglings and breathings, and groanings that cannot be uttered, to be emptied of myself, and swallowed up in Christ.

Once, as I rode out into the woods for my health, in 1737, having alighted from my horse in a retired place, as my manner commonly has been, to walk for divine contemplation and prayer, I had a view that for me was extraordinary, of the glory of the Son of God, as Mediator between God and man, and his wonderful, great, full, pure and sweet grace and love, and meek and gentle condescension. This grace that appeared so calm and sweet, appeared also great above the heavens. The person of Christ appeared ineffably excellent with an excellency great enough to swallow up all thought and conception . . . which continued as near as I can judge, about an hour; which kept me the greater part of the time in a flood of tears, and weeping aloud. I felt an ardency of soul to be, what

I know not otherwise how to express, emptied and annihilated; to lie in the dust, and to be full of Christ alone; to love him with a holy and pure love; to trust in him; to live upon him; to serve and follow him; and to be perfectly sanctified and made pure, with a divine and heavenly purity. I have, several other times, had views very much of the same nature, and which have had the same effects.

I have many times had a sense of the glory of the third person in the Trinity, in his office of Sanctifier; in his holy operations, communicating divine light and life to the soul. God, in the communications of his Holy Spirit, has appeared as an infinite fountain of divine glory and sweetness; being full, and sufficient to fill and satisfy the soul; pouring forth itself in sweet communications; like the sun in its glory, sweetly and pleasantly diffusing light and life. And I have sometimes had an affecting sense of the exelency of the word of God, as a word of life; as the light of life; a sweet, excellent lifegiving word; accompanied with a thirsting after that word, that it might dwell richly in my heart.

Often, since I lived in this town, I have had very affecting views of my own sinfulness and vileness; very frequently to such a degree as to hold me in a kind of loud weeping, sometimes for a considerable time together; so that I have often been forced to shut myself up. I have had a vastly greater sense of my own wickedness, and the badness of my heart, than ever I had before my conversion. It has often appeared to me, that if God should mark iniquity against me, I should appear the very worst of all mankind; of all that have been, since the beginning of the world to this time; and that I should have by far the lowest place in hell. When others, that have come to talk with me about their soul concerns, have expressed the sense they have had of their own wickedness, by saying that it seemed to them, that they were as bad as the devil himself; I thought their expressions seemed exceeding faint and feeble, to represent my wickedness.

My wickedness, as I am in myself, has long appeared to me perfectly ineffable, and swallowing up all thought and imagination; like an infinite deluge, or mountain over my head. I know not how to express better what my sins appear to me to be, than by heaping infinite upon infinite, and multiplying infinite by infinite. Very often, for these many years, these expressions are in my mind, and in my mouth, "Infinite upon infinite

. . . Infinite upon infinite!" When I look into my heart, and take a view of my wickedness, it looks like an abyss infinitely deeper than hell. And it appears to me, that were it not for free grace, exalted and raised up to the infinite height of all the fulness and glory of the great Jehovah, and the arm of his power and grace stretched forth in all the majesty of his power, and in all the glory of his sovereignty, I should appear sunk down in my sins below hell itself; far beyond the sight of every thing, but the eye of sovereign grace, that can pierce even down to such a depth. And yet it seems to me, that my conviction of sin is exceeding small, and faint; it is enough to amaze me, that I have no more sense of my sin. I know certainly, that I have very little sense of my sinfulness. When I have had turns of weeping and crying for my sins I thought I knew at the time, that my repentance was nothing to my sin.

I have greatly longed of late, for a broken heart, and to lie low before God; and, when I ask for humility, I cannot bear the thoughts of being no more humble than other Christians. It seems to me, that though their degrees of humility may be suitable for them, yet it would be a vile selfexaltation in me, not to be the lowest in humility of all mankind. Others speak of their longing to be "humbled to the dust;" that may be a proper expression for them, but I always think of myself, that I ought, and it is an expression that has long been natural for me to use in prayer, "to lie infinitely low before God." And it is affecting to think, how ignorant I was, when a young Christian, of the bottomless, infinite depths of wickedness, pride, hypocrisy and deceit, left in my heart.

I have a much greater sense of my universal, exceeding dependence on God's grace and strength, and mere good pleasure, of late, than I used formerly to have; and have experienced more of an abhorrence of my own righteousness. The very thought of any joy arising in me, on any consideration of my own amiableness, performances, or experiences, or any goodness of heart or life, is nauseous and detestable to me. And yet I am greatly afflicted with a proud and selfrighteous spirit, much more sensibly than I used to be formerly. I see that serpent rising and putting forth its head continually, every where, all around me.

Though it seems to me, that, in some respects, I was a far better Christian, for two or three years after my first conversion than I am now; and lived in a more constant delight and pleasure; yet, of late years, I have had a more full and constant sense of the absolute sovereignty of God, and a delight in that sovereignty; and have had more of a sense of the glory of Christ, as a Mediator revealed in the gospel. On one Saturday night, in particular, I had such a discovery of the excellency of the gospel above all other doctrines, that I could not but say to myself, "This is my chosen light, my chosen doctrine;" and of Christ, "This is my chosen Prophet." It appeared sweet, beyond all expression, to follow Christ, and to be taught, and enlightened, and instructed by him; to learn of him, and live to him. Another Saturday night, (*January* 1739) I had such a sense, how sweet and blessed a thing it was to walk in the way of duty; to do that which was right and meet to be done, and agreeable to the holy mind of God; that it caused me to break forth into a kind of loud weeping, which held me some time, so that I was forced to shut myself up, and fasten the doors. I could not but, as it were, cry out, "How happy are they which do that which is right in the sight of God! They are blessed indeed, they are the happy ones!" I had, at the same time, a very affecting sense, how meet and suitable it was that God should govern the world, and order all things according to his own pleasure; and I rejoiced in it, that God reigned, and that his will was done.

Sinners in the Hands of an Angry God (1741)

Their foot shall slide in due time.
(DEUT. XXXII. 35)

In this verse is threatened the vengeance of God on the wicked unbelieving Israelites, who were God's visible people, and who lived under the means of grace; but who, notwithstanding all God's wonderful works towards them, remained (as ver. 28.) void of counsel, having no understanding in them. Under all the cultivations of heaven, they brought forth bitter and poisonous fruit; as in the two verses next preceding the text.—The expression I have chosen for my text, *Their foot shall slide in due time*, seems to imply the

[Handwritten annotations:]

Pessimistic philosophy - He believes people perish in Hell. He stresses the precariousness of the human situation. We never know when we will perish. Man is a sinner by nature - Naturally wicked. Adam and Eve were wicked. With Adam's fall we all fell.

God is an angry God and everyone will perish.

Pride is ultimate of all deadly sins.

Evil is in the human nature. INNATE DEPRAVITY

very ominous — sinners will meet their time eventually.

heavy reliance on sternness of the Old Test, instead of the mercy in the N.T.

uses physical world to depict spiritual things. you have to accept the Bible as the word of God

He accuses everyone of lust

Pride is the source of INNATE DEPRAVITY

following things, relating to the punishment and destruction to which these wicked Israelites were exposed.

1. That they were always exposed to *destruction*; as one that stands or walks in slippery places is always exposed to fall. This is implied in the manner of their destruction coming upon them, being represented by their foot sliding. The same is expressed. Psalm lxxiii. 18. "Surely thou didst set them in slippery places; thou castedst them down into destruction."

2. It implies, that they were always exposed to sudden unexpected destruction. As he that walks in slippery places is every moment liable to fall, he cannot foresee one moment whether he shall stand or fall the next; and when he does fall, he falls at once without warning: Which is also expressed in Psalm lxxiii. 18, 19. "Surely thou didst set them in slippery places; thou castedst them down into destruction: How are they brought into desolation as in a moment!"

3. Another thing implied is, that they are liable to fall *of themselves*, without being thrown down by the hand of another; as he that stands or walks on slippery ground needs nothing but his own weight to throw him down.

4. That the reason why they are not fallen already, and do not fall now, is only that God's appointed time is not come. For it is said, that when that due time, or appointed times comes, *their foot shall slide*. Then they shall be left to fall, as they are inclined by their own weight. God will not hold them up in these slippery places any longer, but will let them go; and then, at that very instant, they shall fall into destruction; as he that stands on such slippery declining ground, on the edge of a pit, he cannot stand alone, when he is let go he immediately falls and is lost.

The observation from the words that I would now insist upon is this.—"There is nothing that keeps wicked men at any one moment out of hell, but the mere pleasure of God"—By the *mere* pleasure of God, I mean his *sovereign* pleasure, his arbitrary will, restrained by no obligation, hindered by no manner of difficulty, any more than if nothing else but God's mere will had in the least degree, or in any respect whatsoever, any hand in the preservation of wicked men one moment.—The truth of this observation may appear by the following considerations.

1. There is no want of *power* in God to cast wicked men into hell at any moment. Men's hands cannot be strong when God rises up. The strongest

have no power to resist him, nor can any deliver out of his hands.—He is not only able to cast wicked men into hell, but he can most easily do it. Sometimes an earthly prince meets with a great deal of difficulty to subdue a rebel, who has found means to fortify himself, and has made himself strong by the numbers of his followers. But it is not so with God. There is no fortress that is any defence from the power of God. Though hand join in hand, and vast multitudes of God's enemies combine and associate themselves, they are easily broken in pieces. They are as great heaps of light chaff before the whirlwind; or large quantities of dry stubble before devouring flames. We find it easy to tread on and crush a worm that we see crawling on the earth; so it is easy for us to cut or singe a slender thread that any thing hangs by: thus easy is it for God, when he pleases, to cast his enemies down to hell. What are we, that we should think to stand before him, at whose rebuke the earth trembles, and before whom the rocks are thrown down?

2. They *deserve* to be cast into hell; so that divine justice never stands in the way, it makes no objection against God's using his power at any moment to destroy them. Yea, on the contrary, justice calls aloud for an infinite punishment of their sins. Divine justice says of the tree that brings forth such grapes of Sodom, "Cut it down, why cumbereth it the ground?" Luke xiii. 7. The sword of divine justice is every moment brandished over their heads, and it is nothing but the hand of arbitrary mercy, and God's mere will, that holds it back.

3. They are already under a sentence of *condemnation* to hell. They do not only justly deserve to be cast down thither, but the sentence of the law of God, that eternal and immutable rule of righteousness that God has fixed between him and mankind, is gone out against them, and stands against them; so that they are bound over already to hell. John iii. 18. "He that believeth not is condemned already." So that every unconverted man properly belongs to hell; that is his place; from thence he is, John viii. 23. "Ye are from beneath:" And thither he is bound; it is the place that justice, and God's word, and the sentence of his unchangeable law assign to him.

4. They are now the objects of that very same *anger* and wrath of God, that is expressed in the torments of hell. And the reason why they do not go down to hell at each moment, is not because God, in whose power they are, is not then very

angry with them; as he is with many miserable creatures now tormented in hell, who there feel and bear the fierceness of his wrath. Yea, God is a great deal more angry with great numbers that are now on earth: yea, doubtless, with many that are now in this congregation, who it may be are at ease, than he is with many of those who are now in the flames of hell.

So that it is not because God is unmindful of their wickedness and does not resent it, that he does not let loose his hand and cut them off. God is not altogether such an one as themselves though they may imagine him to be so. The wrath of God burns against them, their damnation does not slumber; the pit is prepared, the fire is made ready, the furnace is now hot, ready to receive them; the flames do now rage and glow. The glittering sword is whet, and held over them, and the pit hath opened its mouth under them.

5. The *devil* stands ready to fall upon them, and seize them as his own, at what moment God shall permit him. They belong to him; he has their souls in his possession, and under his dominion. The scripture represents them as his goods, Luke xi. 12. The devils watch them; they are ever by them at their right hand; they stand waiting for them, like greedy hungry lions that see their prey, and expect to have it, but are for the present kept back. If God should withdraw his hand, by which they are restrained, they would in one moment fly upon their poor souls. The old serpent is gaping for them; hell opens its mouth wide to receive them; and if God should permit it, they would be hastily swallowed up and lost.

6. There are in the souls of wicked men those hellish *principles* reigning, that would presently kindle and flame out into hell fire, if it were not for God's restraints. There is laid in the very nature of carnal men, a foundation for the torments of hell. There are those corrupt principles, in reigning power in them, and in full possession of them, that are seeds of hell fire. These principles are active and powerful, exceeding violent in their nature, and if it were not for the restraining hand of God upon them, they would soon break out, they would flame out after the same manner as the same corruptions, the same enmity does in the hearts of damned souls, and would beget the same torments as they do in them. The souls of the wicked are in scripture compared to the troubled sea, Isa. lvii. 20. For the present, God restrains their wickedness by his mighty power, as he does the raging waves of the troubled sea, saying, "Hith-

erto shalt thou come, but no further;" but if God should withdraw that restraining power, it would soon carry all before it. Sin is the ruin and misery of the soul; it is destructive in its nature; and if God should leave it without restraint, there would need nothing else to make the soul perfectly miserable. The corruption of the heart of man is immoderate and boundless in its fury; and while wicked men live here, it is like fire pent up by God's restraints, whereas if it were let loose, it would set on fire the course of nature; and as the heart is now a 'sink of sin, so if sin was not restrained, it would immediately turn the soul into a fiery oven, or a furnace of fire and brimstone.

7. It is no security to wicked men for one moment, that there are no visible means of death at hand. It is no security to a natural man, that he is now in health, and that he does not see which way he should now immediately go out of the world by any accident, and that there is no visible danger in any respect in his circumstances. The manifold and continual experience of the world in all ages, shows this is no evidence, that a man is not on the very brink of eternity, and that the next step will not be into another world. The unseen, unthought-of ways and means of persons going suddenly out of the world are innumerable and inconceivable. Unconverted men walk over the pit of hell on a rotten covering, and there are innumerable places in this covering so weak that they will not bear their weight, and these places are not seen. The arrows of death fly unseen at noonday; the sharpest sight cannot discern them. God has so many different unsearchable ways of taking wicked men out of the world and sending them to hell, that there is nothing to make it appear, that God had need to be at the expence of a miracle, or go out of the ordinary course of his providence, to destroy any wicked man, at any moment. All the means that there are of sinners going out of the world, are so in God's hands, and so universally and absolutely subject to his power and determination, that it does not depend at all the less on the mere will of God, whether sinners shall at any moment go to hell, than if means were never made use of, or at all concerned in the case.

8. Natural men's prudence and care to preserve their own lives, or the care of others to preserve them, do not secure them a moment. To this, divine providence and universal experience do also bear testimony. There is this clear evidence that men's own wisdom is no security to them from death; that if it were otherwise we should see

some difference between the wise and politic men of the world, and others, with regard to their liableness to early and unexpected death: but how is it in fact? Eccles. ii. 16. "How dieth the wise man? even as the fool."

9. All wicked men's pains and *contrivance* which they use to escape hell, while they continue to reject Christ, and so remain wicked men, do not secure them from hell one moment. Almost every natural man that hears of hell, flatters himself that he shall escape it; he depends upon himself for his own security; he flatters himself in what he has done, in what he is now doing, or what he intends to do. Every one lays out matters in his own mind how he shall avoid damnation, and flatters himself that he contrives well for himself, and that his schemes will not fail. They hear indeed that there are but few saved, and that the greater part of men that have died heretofore are gone to hell; but each one imagines that he lays out matters better for his own escape than others have done. He does not intend to come to that place of torment; he says within himself, that he intends to take effectual care, and to order matters so for himself as not to fail.

But the foolish children of men miserably delude themselves in their own schemes, and in confidence in their own strength and wisdom; they trust to nothing but a shadow. The greater part of those who heretofore have lived under the same means of grace, and are now dead, are undoubtedly gone to hell; and it was not because they were not as wise as those who are now alive: it was not because they did not lay out matters as well for themselves to secure their own escape. If we could speak with them, and inquire of them, one by one, whether they expected, when alive, and when they used to hear about hell, ever to be the subjects of that misery: we doubtless, should hear one and another reply, "No, I never intended to come here: I had laid out matters otherwise in my mind; I thought I should contrive well for myself: I thought my scheme good. I intended to take effectual care; but it came upon me unexpected; I did not look for it at that time, and in that manner; it came as a thief: Death outwitted me: God's wrath was too quick for me. Oh, my cursed foolishness! I was flattering myself, and pleasing myself with vain dreams of what I would do hereafter; and when I was sayin, Peace and safety, then suddenly destruction came upon me."

10. God has laid himself under *no obligation,* by any promise to keep any natural man out of

hell one moment. God certainly has made no promises either of eternal life, or of any deliverance or preservation from eternal death, but what are contained in the covenant of grace, the promises that are given in Christ, in whom all the promises are yea and amen. But surely they have no interest in the promises of the covenant of grace who are not the children of the covenant, who do not believe in any of the promises, and have no interest in the Mediator of the covenant.

So that, whatever some have imagined and pretended about promises made to natural men's earnest seeking and knocking, it is plain and manifest, that whatever pains a natural man takes in religion, whatever prayers he makes, till he believes in Christ, God is under no manner of obligation to keep him a moment from eternal destruction.

So that, thus it is that natural men are held in the hand of God, over the pit of hell; they have deserved the fiery pit, and are already sentenced to it; and God is dreadfully provoked, his anger is as great towards them as to those that are actually suffering the executions of the fierceness of his wrath in hell, and they have done nothing in the least to appease or abate that anger, neither is God in the least bound by any promise to hold them up one moment; the devil is waiting for them, hell is gaping for them, the flames gather and flash about them, and would fain lay hold on them, and swallow them up; the fire pent up in their own hearts is struggling to break out: and they have no interest in any Mediator, there are no means within reach that can be any security to them. In short, they have no refuge, nothing to take hold of; all that preserves them every moment is the mere arbitrary will, and uncovenanted, unobliged forbearance of an incensed God.

Application

The use of this awful subject may be for awakening unconverted persons in this congregation. This that you have heard is the case of every one of you that are out of Christ.—That world of misery, that lake of burning brimstone, is extended abroad under you. There is the dreadful pit of the glowing flames of the wrath of God; there is hell's wide gaping mouth open; and you have nothing to stand upon, nor any thing to take hold of; there is nothing between you and hell but the air; it is only the power and mere pleasure of God that holds you up.

You probably are not sensible of this; you find you are kept out of hell, but do not see the hand of God in it; but look at other things, as the good state of your bodily constitution, your care of your own life, and the means you use for your own preservation. But indeed these things are nothing; if God should withdraw his hand, they would avail no more to keep you from falling, than the thin air to hold up a person that is suspended in it.

Your wickedness makes you as it were heavy as lead, and to tend downwards with great weight and pressure towards hell; and if God should let you go, you would immediately sink and swiftly descend and plunge into the bottomless gulf, and your healthy constitution, and your own care and prudence, and best contrivance, and all your righteousness, would have no more influence to uphold you and keep you out of hell, than a spider's web would have to stop a fallen rock. Were it not for the sovereign pleasure of God, the earth would not bear you one moment; for you are a burden to it; the creation groans with you; the creature is made subject to the bondage of your corruption, not willingly; the sun does not willingly shine upon you to give you light to serve sin and Satan; the earth does not willingly yield her increase to satisfy your lusts; nor is it willingly a stage for your wickedness to be acted upon; the air does not willingly serve you for breath to maintain the flame of life in your vitals, while you spend your life in the service of God's enemies. God's creatures are good, and were made for men to serve God with, and do not willingly subserve to any other purpose, and groan when they are abused to purposes so directly contrary to their nature and end. And the world would spew you out, were it not for the sovereign hand of him who hath subjected it in hope. There are black clouds of God's wrath now hanging directly over your heads, full of the dreadful storm, and big with thunder; and were it not for the restraining hand of God, it would immediately burst forth upon you. The sovereign pleasure of God, for the present, stays his rough wind; otherwise it would come with fury, and your destruction would come like a whirlwind, and you would be like the chaff of the summer threshing floor.

The wrath of God is like great waters that are damned for the present; they increase more and more, and rise higher and higher, till an outlet is given; and the longer the stream is stopped, the more rapid and mighty is its course, when once it is let loose. It is true, that judgment against your evil works has not been executed hitherto; the floods of God's vengeance have been withheld; but your guilt in the mean time is constantly increasing, and you are every day treasuring up more wrath; the waters are constantly rising, and waxing more and more mighty; and there is nothing but the mere pleasure of God, that holds the waters back, that are unwilling to be stopped, and press hard to go forward. If God should only withdraw his hand from the flood-gate, it would immediately fly open, and the fiery floods of the fierceness and wrath of God, would rush forth with inconceivable fury, and would come upon you with omnipotent power; and if your strength were ten thousand times greater than it is, yea, ten thousand times greater than the strength of the stoutest, sturdiest devil in hell, it would be nothing to withstand or endure it.

The bow of God's wrath is bent, and the arrow made ready on the string, and justice bends the arrow at your heart, and strains the bow, and it is nothing but the mere pleasure of God, and that of an angry God, without any promise or obligation at all, that keeps the arrow one moment from being made drunk with your blood. Thus all you that never passed under a great change of heart, by the mighty power of the Spirit of God upon your souls; all you that were never born again, and made new creatures, and raised from being dead in sin, to a state of new, and before altogether unexperienced light and life, are in the hands of an angry God. However you may have reformed your life in many things, and may have had religious affections, and may keep up a form of religion in your families and closets, and in the house of God, it is nothing but his mere pleasure that keeps you from being this moment swallowed up in everlasting destruction. However unconvinced you may now be of the truth of what you hear, by and by you will be fully convinced of it. Those that are gone from being in the like circumstances with you, see that it was so with them; for destruction came suddenly upon most of them; when they expected nothing of it, and while they were saying, Peace and safety: now they see, that those things on which they depended for peace and safety, were nothing but thin air and empty shadows.

The God that holds you over the pit of hell, much as one holds a spider, or some loathsome insect over the first, abhors you, and is dreadfully provoked: his wrath towards you burns like fire; he looks upon you as worthy of nothing else, but to be cast into the fire; he is of purer eyes than to bear to have you in his sight; you are ten thousand times more abominable in his eyes, than the most hateful venomous serpent is in ours. You have offended him infinitely more than ever a stubborn rebel did his prince; and yet it is nothing but his hand that holds you from falling into the fire every moment. It is to be ascribed to nothing else, that you did not go to hell the last night; that you was suffered to awake again in this world, after you closed your eyes to sleep. And there is no other reason to be given, why you have not dropped into hell since you arose in the morning, but that God's hand has held you up. There is no other reason to be given why you have not gone to hell, since you have sat here in the house of God, provoking his pure eyes by your sinful wicked manner of attending his solemn worship. Yea, there is nothing else that is to be given as a reason why you do not this very moment drop down into hell.

O sinner! Consider the fearful danger you are in: it is a great furnace of wrath, a wide and bottomless pit, full of the fire of wrath, that you are held over in the hand of that God, whose wrath is provoked and incensed as much against you, as against many of the damned in hell. You hang by a slender thread, with the flames of divine wrath flashing about it, and ready every moment to singe it, and burn it asunder; and you have no interest in any Mediator, and nothing to lay hold of to save yourself, nothing to keep off the flames of wrath, nothing of your own, nothing that you ever have done, nothing that you can do, to induce God to spare you one moment.—And consider here more particularly,

1. *Whose* wrath it is: it is the wrath of the infinite God. If it were only the wrath of man, though it were of the most potent prince, it would be comparatively little to be regarded. The wrath of kings is very much dreaded, especially of absolute monarchs, who have the possessions and lives of their subjects wholly in their power, to be disposed of at their mere will. Prov. xx. 2. "The fear of a king is as the roaring of a lion: Whoso provoketh him to anger, sinneth against his own soul." The subject that very much enrages an arbitrary prince, is liable to suffer the most extreme torments that human art can invent, or human power can inflict. But the greatest earthly potentates in their greatest majesty and strength, and when clothed in their greatest terrors, are but feeble, despicable worms of the dust, in comparison of the great and

almighty Creator and King of heaven and earth. It is but little that they can do, when most enraged, and when they have exerted the utmost of their fury. All the kings of the earth, before God, are as grasshoppers; they are nothing, and less than nothing: both their love and their hatred is to be despised. The wrath of the great King of kings, is as much more terrible than theirs, as his majesty is greater. Luke xii. 4, 5. "And I say unto you, my friends, Be not afraid of them that kill the body, and after that, have no more that they can do. But I will forewarn you whom you shall fear: fear him, which after he hath killed, hath power to cast into hell: yea, I say unto you, Fear him."

2. It is the *fierceness* of his wrath that you are exposed to. We often read of the fury of God; as in Isaiah lix. 18. "According to their deeds, accordingly he will repay fury to his adversaries." So Isaiah lxvi. 15. "For behold, the Lord will come with fire, and with his chariots like a whirlwind, to render his anger with fury, and his rebuke with flames of fire." And in many other places. So, Rev. xix. 15. we read of "the wine press of the fierceness and wrath of Almighty God." The words are exceeding terrible. If it had only been said, "the wrath of God," the words would have implied that which is infinitely dreadful: but it is "the fierceness and wrath of God." The fury of God! the fierceness of Jehovah! Oh, how dreadful must that be! Who can utter or conceive what such expressions carry in them! But it is also "the fierceness and wrath of *Almighty* God." As though there would be a very great manifestation of his almighty power in what the fierceness of his wrath should inflict, as though omnipotence should be as it were enraged, and exerted, as men are wont to exert their strength in the fierceness of their wrath. Oh! then, what will be the consequence. What will become of the poor worms that shall suffer it! Whose hands can be strong? And whose heart can endure? To what a dreadful, inexpressible, inconceivable depth of misery must the poor creature be sunk who shall be the subject of this!

Consider this, you that are here present, that yet remain in an unregenerate state. That God will execute the fierceness of his anger, implies, that he will inflict wrath without any pity. When God beholds the ineffable extremity of your case, and sees your torment to be so vastly disproportioned to your strength, and sees how your poor soul is crushed, and sinks down, as it were, into an infinite gloom; he will have no compassion upon you, he will not forbear the executions of his wrath, or in the least lighten his hand; there shall be no moderation or mercy, nor will God then at all stay his rough wind; he will have no regard to your welfare, nor be at all careful lest you should suffer too much in any other sense, than only that you shall *not suffer beyond what strict justice requires.* Nothing shall be withheld, because it is so hard for you to bear. Ezek. viii. 18. "Therefore will I also deal in fury: mine eye shall not spare, neither will I have pity; and though they cry in mine ears with a loud voice, yet I will not hear them." Now God stands ready to pity you; this is a day of mercy; you may cry now with some encouragement of obtaining mercy. But when once the day of mercy is past, your most lamentable and dolorous cries and shrieks will be in vain; you will be wholly lost and thrown away of God, as to any regard to your welfare. God will have no other use to put you to, but to suffer misery; you shall be continued in being to no other end; for you will be a vessel of wrath fitted to destruction; and there will be no other use of this vessel, but to be filled full of wrath. God will be so far from pitying you when you cry to him, that it is said he will only "laugh and mock," Prov. i. 25, 26, &c.

How awful are those words, Isa. lxiii. 3, which are the words of the great God. "I will tread them in mine anger, and will trample them in my fury, and their blood shall be sprinkled upon my garments, and I will stain all my raiment." It is perhaps impossible to conceive of words that carry in them greater manifestations of these three things, *viz.* contempt, and hatred, and fierceness of indignation. If you cry to God to pity you, he will be so far from pitying you in your doleful case, or showing you the least regard or favour, that instead of that, he will only tread you under foot. And though he will know that you cannot bear the weight of omnipotence treading upon you, yet he will not regard that, but he will crush you under his feet without mercy: he will crush out your blood, and make it fly, and it shall be sprinkled on his garments, so as to stain all his raiment. He will not only hate you, but he will have you, in the utmost contempt: no place shall be thought fit for you, but under his feet to be trodden down as the mire of the streets.

3. The *misery* you are exposed to is that which God will inflict to that end, that he might show what that wrath of Jehovah is. God hath had it on his heart to show to angels and men, both how

excellent his love is, and also how terrible his wrath is. Sometimes earthly kings have a mind to show how terrible their wrath is, by the extreme punishments they would execute on those that would provoke them. Nebuchadnezzar, that mighty and haughty monarch of the Chaldean empire, was willing to show his wrath when enraged with Shadrach, Meshech, and Abednego: and accordingly gave orders that the burning fiery furnace should be heated seven times hotter than it was before; doubtless, it was raised to the utmost degree of fierceness that human art could raise it. But the great God is also willing to show his wrath, and magnify his awful majesty and mighty power in the extreme sufferings of his enemies. Rom. ix. 22. "What if God, willing to show his wrath, and to make his power known, endure with much long-suffering the vessels of wrath fitted to destruction?" And seeing this is his design, and what he has determined, even to show how terrible the unrestrained wrath, the fury and fierceness of Jehovah is, he will do it to effect. There will be something accomplished and brought to pass that will be dreadful with a witness. When the great and angry God hath risen up and executed his awful vengeance on the poor sinner, and the wretch is actually suffering the infinite weight and power of his indignation, then will God call upon the whole universe to behold that awful majesty and mighty power that is to be seen in it. Isa. xxxiii. 12–14. "And the people shall be as the burnings of lime, as thorns cut up shall they be burnt in the fire. Hear ye that are far off, what I have done; and ye that are near, acknowledge my might. The sinners in Zion are afraid; fearfulness hath surprised the hypocrites," &c.

Thus it will be with you that are in an unconverted state, if you continue in it; the infinite might, and majesty, and terribleness of the omnipotent God shall be magnified upon you, in the ineffable strength of your torments. You shall be tormented in the presence of the holy angels, and in the presence of the Lamb; and when you shall be in this state of suffering, the glorious inhabitants of heaven shall go forth and look on the awful spectacle, that they may see what the wrath and fierceness of the Almighty is; and when they have seen it, they will fall down and adore that great power and majesty. Isa. lxvi. 23, 24. "And it shall come to pass, that from one new moon to another, and from one sabbath to another, shall all flesh come to worship before me, saith the Lord.

And they shall go forth and look upon the carcasses of the men that have transgressed against me; for their worm shall not die, neither shall their fire be quenched, and they shall be an abhorring unto all flesh." *Length of eternity*

4. It is *everlasting* wrath. It would be dreadful to suffer this fierceness and wrath of Almighty God one moment; but you must suffer it to all eternity. There will be no end to this exquisite horrible misery. When you look forward, you shall see a long for ever, a boundless duration before you, which will swallow up your thoughts, and amaze your soul; and you will absolutely despair of ever having any deliverance, any end, any mitigation, any rest at all. You will know certainly that you must wear out long ages, millions of millions of ages, in wrestling and conflicting with this almighty merciless vengeance; and then when you have so done, when so many ages have actually been spent by you in this manner, you will know that all is but a point to what remains. So that your punishment will indeed be infinite. Oh, who can express what the state of a soul in such circumstances is! All that we can possibly say about it, gives but a very feeble, faint representation of it; it is inexpressible and inconceivable: For "who knows the power of God's anger?"

cannot grasp it.

no end

How dreadful is the state of those that are daily and hourly in the danger of this great wrath and infinite misery! But this is the dismal case of every soul in this congregation that has not been born again, however moral and strict, sober and religious, they may otherwise be. Oh that you would consider it, whether you be young or old! There is reason to think, that there are many in this congregation now hearing this discourse, that will actually be the subjects of this very misery to all eternity. We know not who they are, or in what seats they sit, or what thoughts they now have. It may be they are now at ease, and hear all these things without much disturbance, and are now flattering themselves that they are not the persons, promising themselves that they shall escape. If we knew that there was one person, and but one, in the whole congregation, that was to be the subject of this misery, what an awful thing would it be to think of! If we knew who it was, what an awful sight would it be to see such a person! How might all the rest of the congregation lift up a lamentable and bitter cry over him! But, alas! instead of one, how many is it likely will remember this discourse in hell? And it would be a wonder, if some that are now present should not be in hell in a very

short time, even before this year is out. And it would be no wonder if some persons, that now sit here, in some seats of this meeting-house, in health, quiet and secure, should be there before to-morrow morning. Those of you that finally continue in a natural condition, that shall keep out of hell longest will be there in a little time! your damnation does not slumber; it will come swiftly, and, in all probability, very suddenly upon many of you. You have reason to wonder that you are not already in hell. It is doubtless the case of some whom you have seen and known, that never deserved hell more than you, and that heretofore appeared as likely to have been now alive as you. Their case is past all hope; they are crying in extreme misery and perfect despair; but here you are in the land of the living and in the house of God, and have an opportunity to obtain salvation. What would not those poor damned hopeless souls give for one day's opportunity such as you now enjoy!

And now you have an extraordinary opportunity, a day wherein Christ has thrown the door of mercy wide open, and stands in calling and crying with a loud voice to poor sinners; a day wherein many are flocking to him, and pressing into the kingdom of God. Many are daily coming from the east, west, north and south; many that were very lately in the same miserable condition that you are in, are now in a happy state, with their hearts filled with love to him who has loved them, and washed them from their sins in his own blood, and rejoicing in hope of the glory of God. How awful is it to be left behind at such a day! To see so many others feasting, while you are pining and perishing! To see so many rejoicing and singing for joy of heart, while you have cause to mourn for sorrow of heart, and howl for vexation of spirit! How can you rest one moment in such a condition? Are not your souls as precious as the souls of the people at Suffield,[1] where they are flocking from day to day to Christ?

Are there not many here who have lived long in the world, and are not to this day born again? and so are aliens from the commonwealth of Israel, and have done nothing ever since they have lived, but treasure up wrath against the day of wrath? Oh, sirs, your case, in an especial manner, is extremely dangerous. Your guilt and hardness of heart is extremely great. Do you not see how generally persons of your years are passed over and left, in the present remarkable and wonderful dispensation

---

[1] A town in the neighbourhood [Edwards].

of God's mercy? You had need to consider yourselves, and awake thoroughly out of sleep. You cannot bear the fierceness and wrath of the infinite God.—And you, young men, and young women, will you neglect this precious season which you now enjoy, when so many others of your age are renouncing all youthful vanities, and flocking to Christ? You especially have now an extraordinary opportunity; but if you neglect it, it will soon be with you as with those persons who spent all the precious days of youth in sin, and are now come to such a dreadful pass in blindness and hardness.—And you, children, who are unconverted, do not you know that you are going down to hell, to bear the dreadful wrath of that God, who is now angry with you every day and every night? Will you be content to be the children of the devil, when so many other children in the land are converted, and are become the holy and happy children of the King of kings?

And let every one that is yet of Christ, and hanging over the pit of hell, whether they be old men and women, or middle aged, or young people, or little children, now hearken to the loud calls of God's word and providence. This acceptable year of the Lord, a day of such great favours to some, will doubtless be a day of as remarkable vengeance to others. Men's hearts harden, and their guilt increases apace at such a day as this, if they neglect their souls; and never was there so great danger of such persons being given up to hardness of heart and blindness of mind. God seems now to be hastily gathering in his elect in all parts of the land: and probably the greater part of adult persons that ever shall be saved, will be brought in now in a little time, and that it will be as it was on the great out-pouring of the Spirit upon the Jews in the apostles' days; the election will obtain, and the rest will be blinded. If this should be the case with you, you will eternally curse this day, and will curse the day that ever you was born, to see such a season of the pouring out of God's Spirit, and will wish that you had died and gone to hell before you had seen it. Now undoubtedly it is, as it was in the days of John the Baptist, the axe is in an extraordinary manner laid at the root of the trees, that every tree which brings not forth good fruit, may be hewn down and cast into the fire.

Therefore, let every one that is out of Christ, now awake and fly from the wrath to come. The wrath of Almighty God is now undoubtedly hanging over a great part of this congregation: Let every one fly out of Sodom: "Haste and escape for your lives, look not behind you, escape to the mountain, lest you be consumed."

From Images or Shadows of Divine Things

1. Death temporal is a shadow of eternal death. The agonies, the pains, the groans and gasps of death, the pale, horrid, ghastly appearance of the corps, its being laid in the dark and silent grave, there putrifying and rotting and become exceeding loathsome and being eaten with worms (Isa. 66.24), is an image of the misery of hell. And the body's continuing in the grave, and never rising more in this world, is to shadow forth the eternity of the misery of hell.

3. Roses grow upon briars, which is to signify that all temporal sweets are mixt with bitter. But what seems more especially to be meant by it is that pure happiness, the crown of glory, is to be come at in no other way than by bearing Christ's cross, by a life of mortification, self-denial, and labour, and bearing all things for Christ. The rose, that is chief of all flowers, is the last thing that comes out. The briary, prickly bush grows before that; the end and crown of all is the beautiful and fragrant rose.

4. The heavens' being filled with glorious, luminous bodies is to signify the glory and happiness of the heavenly inhabitants, and amongst these the sun signifies Christ and the moon the church.

5. Marriage signifies the spiritual union and communion of Christ and the church, and especially the glorification of the church in the perfection of this union and communion forever.

6. The blood comes from the heart, to intimate that out of the heart are the issues of life. (Prov. 4.23.)

8. Again it is apparent and allowed that there is a great and remarkeable analogy in God's works. There is a wonderfull resemblance in the effects which God produces, and consentaneity in His

manner of working in one thing and another throughout all nature. It is very observable in the visible world; therefore it is allowed that God does purposely make and order one thing to be in agreeableness and harmony with another. And if so, why should not we suppose that He makes the inferiour in imitation of the superiour, the material of the spiritual, on purpose to have a resemblance and shadow of them? We see that even in the material world, God makes one part of it strangely to agree with another, and why is it not reasonable to suppose He makes the whole as a shadow of the spiritual world?

10. Children's coming into the world naked and filthy and in their blood, and crying and impotent, is to signify the spiritual nakedness and pollution of nature and wretchedness of condition with which they are born.

11. The serpent's charming of birds and other animals into their mouths, and the spider's taking and sucking the blood of the fly in his snare are lively representations of the Devil's catching our souls by his temptations.

13. Thus I believe the grass and other vegetables growing and flourishing, looking green and pleasant as it were, ripening, blossoming, and bearing fruit from the influences of the heavens, the rain and wind and light and heat of the sun, to be on purpose to represent the dependence of our spiritual wellfare upon God's gracious influences and the effusions of His holy spirit. I am sure there are none of the types of the Old Testament are more lively images of spiritual things. And we find spiritual things very often compared to them in Scripture.

14. The sun's so perpetually, for so many ages, sending forth his rays in such vast profusion, without any diminution of his light and heat, is a bright image of the all-sufficiency and everlastingness of God's bounty and goodness.

15. And so likewise are rivers, which are ever flowing, that empty vast quantities of water every day and yet there is never the less to come. The spirit communicated and shed abroad, that is to say, the goodness of God, is in Scripture compared to a river, and the trees that grow and flourish by the river's side through the benefit of the water represent the saints who live upon Christ and flourish through the influences of his spirit. (Jer. 17.8; Ps. 1.3; Num. 24.6.)

21. The purity, beauty, sublimity, and glory of the visible heavens as one views it in a calm and temperate air, when one is made more sensible of the height of them and of the beauty of their colour, when there are here and [there] interposed little clouds, livelily denotes the exaltedness and purity of the blessedness of the heavenly inhabitants. How different is the idea from that which we have in the consideration of the dark and dire caverns and abyss down in the depths of the earth! This teaches us the vast difference between the state of the departed saints and of damned souls; it shows the ineffable glory of the happiness of the one and the unspeakeable dolefullness and terrours of the state of the other.

60. That of so vast and innumerable a multitude of blossoms that appear on a tree, so few come to ripe fruit, and that so few of so vast a multitude of seeds as are yearly produced, so few come to be a plant, and that there is so great a waste of the seed of both plants and animals, but one in a great multitude ever bringing forth anything, seem to be lively types how few are saved out of the mass of mankind, and particularly how few are sincere, of professing Christians, that never wither away but endure to the end, and how of the many that are called few are chosen.

61. Ravens, that with delight feed on carrion, seem to be remarkeable types of devils, who with delight prey upon the souls of the dead. A dead, filthy, rotten carcass is a lively image of the soul of a wicked man, that is spiritually and exceeding filthy and abominable. Their spiritual corruption is of a far more loathsome savour than the stench of a putrefying carcass. Such souls the Devil delights in; they are his proper food. Again, dead corpses are types of the departed souls of the dead and are so used. (Isa. 66.24.) Ravens don't prey on the bodies of animals till they are dead; so the Devil has not the souls of wicked men delivered into his tormenting hands and devouring jaws till they are dead. Again, the body in such circumstances being dead and in loathsome putrefaction is a lively image of a soul in the dismal state it is in under eternal death. Ravens are birds of the air that are expressly used by Christ as types of the Devil in the parable of the sower and the seed. The Devil is the prince of the power of the air, as he is called; devils are spirits of the air. The raven by its blackness represents the prince of darkness. Sin and sorrow and death are all in

Scripture represented by darkness or the colour black, but the Devil is the father of sin, a most foul and wicked spirit, and the prince of death and misery.

64. Hills and mountains are types of heaven, and often made use of as such in Scripture. These are difficultly ascended. To ascend them, one must go against the natural tendency of the flesh; this must be contradicted in all the ascent, in every step of it, and the ascent is attended with labour, sweat and hardship. There are commonly many hideous rocks in the way. It is a great deal easier descending into valleys. This is a representation of the difficulty, labour, and self-denial of the way to heaven, and how agreeable it is, to the inclination of the flesh, to descend into hell. At the bottom of valleys, especially deep valleys, there is water, with a lake or other waters, but water, as has been shown else-where in notes on Scripture, commonly signifies misery, especially that which is occasioned by the wrath of God. So in hell is a lake or gulf of misery and wrath.

146. The late invention of telescopes, whereby heavenly objects are brought so much nearer and made so much plainer to sight and such wonderfull discoveries have been made in the heavens, is a type and forerunner of the great increase in the knowledge of heavenly things that shall be in the approaching glorious times of the Christian church.

147. The changing of the course of trade and the supplying of the world with its treasures from America is a type and forerunner of what is approaching in spiritual things, when the world shall be supplied with spiritual treasures from America.

2

An Emergent National Literature
1743–1826

In 1743, Benjamin Franklin proposed to some of his fellow countrymen the establishment of a learned society, modeled generally on the Royal Society in Great Britain. In a letter addressed to some of his friends in the colonies he wrote:

> The first Drudgery of Settling new Colonies, which confines the Attention of People to mere Necessaries, is now pretty well over and there are many in every Province in Circumstances that set them at Ease, and afford Leisure to cultivate the finer Arts, and improve the common Stock of Knowledge.

Franklin had a perceptive eye. There were now prosperous, thriving cities up and down the eastern seaboard, including Boston, Providence, New York, Philadelphia, Baltimore, and Charleston. The colonies had gained economic strength and were relatively secure.[1] Now that the worst drudgery of settlement was past, the time had come to nurture the arts and sciences.

Franklin's proposal bore fruit, and in time the institution he founded came to be known as the American Philosophical Society of Philadelphia, still in proud existence. Franklin described the proper concerns of such a society as follows:

[1] By 1760 the last of the French and Indian wars would be over, the western frontiers of the colonies would be safe from the peril of massive attacks, and the first and most celebrated of the pioneers, Daniel Boone, would be making his way across the mountains into what would become the state of Tennessee and thence into the Kentucky country.

All new-discovered Plants, Herbs, Trees, Roots, their Virtues, Uses, &c.; Methods of Propagating them, and making such as are useful, but particular to some Plantations, more general. Improvements of vegetable Juices, as Cyders, Wines, &c.; New Methods of Curing or Preventing Diseases. All new-discovered Fossils in different Countries, as Mines, Minerals, Quarries; &c. New and useful Improvements in any Branch of Mathematicks; New Discoveries in Chemistry, such as Improvements in Distillation, Brewing, Assaying of ores; &c. New Mechanical Inventions for Saving labour; as Mills and Carriages, &c., and for Raising and Conveying of Water, Draining of Meadows, &c.; All new Arts, Trades, Manufactures, &c. that may be proposed or thought of; Surveys, Maps and Charts of particular Parts of the Sea-coasts, or Inland Countries; Course and Junction of Rivers and great Roads, Situation of Lakes and Mountains, Nature of the Soil and Productions; &c. New Methods of Improving the Breed of useful Animals; Introducing other Sorts from foreign Countries. New Improvements in Planting, Gardening, Clearing Land, &c.

The relevance of such a program to the American colonists is self-evident. The very practical Franklin stressed applied science and new inventions and techniques. But to the student of American literature, the creation of such a society has another kind of relevance: it speaks volumes about the intellectuals of this period, American and European, and about the prevailing climate of ideas.

The era is usually called the Age of Reason or, more briefly still, the Enlightenment. Men set a high value on free inquiry, scientific experiment, and the application of the test of reason. Such was the dominant spirit of the age, and the intellectuals in the American colonies were affected by it no less than those living in the Old World. Franklin's proposals for a "philosophical society" breathe the spirit of the age, and the activities of Thomas Jefferson, who in due time became a president of the American Philosophical Society as well as of the United States, manifest the same spirit.

Since the intellectual leaders of the colonies were largely responsible for bringing on the War of Independence, the temper of their minds and their basic ideas are of the greatest importance. For in spite of the developing conflict of interests between the colonies and the government of Great Britain and specific grievances such as the passage of the Stamp Act and taxes on tea, the Revolution would not have occurred if the climate of ideas had not been what it was. It is a truism that revolutions come when the actual conditions that provoked them are improving, not when they are at their worst. People numbed by the hard conditions under which they live are apathetic. To rebel, one must be *aware* that he has grievances—offenses against the proper order of things—and must also believe that his resistance is not foredoomed to failure.

The colonists, as they became stronger, had begun to see their own particular interests as not necessarily the same as those of the inhabitants of Britain. They gradually came to think of themselves as a people of a special character who, in spite of their derivation from Great Britain, had an identity that was specifically American. But the ultimate appeal of the revolutionary leaders was to principles which were not parochial and special, but universal— the principle that taxes should not be levied without representation, that men had a right to choose their rulers, and that many other important rights were God-given and inalienable.

Thus, though the War of Independence was triggered by specific American problems, the ideas that nourished the revolutionary spirit were ultimately imported from Europe. They had been propagated largely by British and French intellectuals and they were held by many British and French citizens, a matter that played its part in determining the successful outcome of the Revolution. For the cause of American independence was popular among European political thinkers, and even in England there was widespread support for the Americans. Men like the Marquis de Lafayette, a Frenchman, and Baron von Steuben, a German, actually fought on the American side, and Thomas Paine, an Englishman, proved to be one of the most brilliant and effective propagandists for the revolutionary cause. Franklin had met Paine on a visit to England and persuaded him to come to Philadelphia in 1774. Another such British intellectual was the scientist Joseph Priestley, who wrote pamphlets supporting the cause of the American colonists but did not come to America until after the Revolution. It was his continuing passion for liberty, manifested in his avowed sympathy for the French Revolution, that made him seek refuge in America after a mob in Birmingham, England, had burned his library and all his personal belongings.

The Age of Reason is not, of course, synonymous with the Age of Revolt, and a rationalistic turn of mind does not necessarily imply revolutionary zeal. But rationalism was an acid that tended to dissolve certain hitherto unquestioned values and unchallenged relationships. In the period of the Enlightenment men's notions about man and nature and God were radically altered, and the consequences of those alterations deeply affected men's political and social views.

If we think of religion as having to do with men's ultimate values, then the matter of what the founding fathers believed becomes very important. What, for example, was the real religion of Thomas Jefferson, the author of the Declaration of Independence? It was certainly not that of the seventeenth-century Puritans, which we have discussed in earlier pages. Nor was such the religion of Benjamin Franklin, though Franklin, unlike Jefferson, came from a New England background.

The religion of Franklin, Jefferson, and many of the other founding fathers, including George Washington and James Madison, might most accurately be described as Deism. Here is a concise summary of Deism as provided by Basil Willey:

> [The] phase of religious thought with which the term "Deism" is often associated was rendered possible largely by the completeness with which the findings of seventeenth-century science, up to that date, could be made to fuse with the inherited religious certainties. [Isaac] Newton's Great Machine needed a Mechanic, and religion was prepared ahead with that which could serve this purpose. Everywhere what science had so far disclosed was nothing but "order, harmony, and beauty"; and finally the incomparable Newton had linked the infinitely great and the infinitely little in one inspired synthesis. The mighty maze [of the universe] was not without a plan, and Locke could declare with perfect candour that "the works of nature in every part of them sufficiently evidence a Deity." (*The Seventeenth-Century Background*, 1942, p. 279)

Not only did science and religion seem to come together and to reinforce each other; their conjunction eliminated what had for some time seemed to intellectuals a kind of scandal. It was not "reasonable" that God should have "revealed" Himself only at a particular place and in a particular time to a small and obscure people like the Jews. Surely an infinite God, claiming universal worship, must have revealed Himself to all men. The Deist solved the problem by claiming that he could infer the existence and nature of God by contemplating the world He had created. Such a revelation was open to anyone who cast aside superstition and looked thoughtfully at the universe.

Deism removed another "scandal" that had worried the eighteenth-century rationalist: the notion that the Creator of the universe would interfere with its workings from time to time to produce a miracle. Eighteenth-century science had made it plain that God had bound Himself by His own laws. He had fashioned cunningly this marvelous universe, had set it running, and left it to run according to its own inherent laws. It was up to men to take heed of those laws; if they did so, their lives would be wholesome and happy and virtuous.

What the Deists were attempting to do was to slit the Christian envelope, extract the Christian virtues (which they admired), and discard what they regarded as the mere outer wrappings of worthless fable. (It was an action that corresponds rather closely to the present-day attempt to "demythologize" Christianity.)

Since the discerning eye of the scientist found everywhere "order, harmony, and beauty," the great virtues of Deism were reasonableness, toleration, and sympathy. If men could only understand themselves and other men, if they would only see that the order of nature is beautiful and harmonious, if they could but realize that breaking the laws of nature automatically brought penalities, then they would restrain their immoderate desires and any wish to do harm to their neighbors.

The Deists thus held a flattering notion of man; for if one believes that nature is essentially good, and if one conceives of man as grounded firmly in nature, it is not "unreasonable" to suppose that he too is "good," a being who needs only to discern the truth in order to act virtuously. It was no accident that in this climate of ideas sympathy became the great virtue, and what poets called the "social tear" was deemed to be the universal solvent.

How seriously Jefferson himself was involved in Deism is suggested by the fact that he worked out his own revision of the Book of Common Prayer and made a compilation of the Gospels, purging them of what he considered superstitious accretions and significantly entitling it *The Life and Morals of Jesus of Nazareth.*

What may seem surprising to us is how much the Deists, and the deistically inclined, still continued to believe. For example, Jefferson's friend Thomas Paine, author of one of the sharpest attacks upon superstition and priestcraft (*The Age of Reason,* 1794–96), writes that though he doesn't believe the creed professed by the Jewish church or the Roman church or the Greek church or the Turkish church or the Protestant church or "any church that I know of," he does believe "in one God, and no more; and I hope for happiness beyond this life." Yet if reason revealed to Tom Paine the existence of God and the immortality of the soul, it certainly failed to reveal these truths to all men, everywhere. The nub of the matter was well put by Blaise Pascal: nature proves God only to those who already believe in Him on other grounds. Thus, one is inclined to suppose that the Christian nurturing that such Deists as Locke, Jefferson, Paine, and Freneau had received accounts for their ability to find by "mere reason" their way to doctrines which reason did not reveal to latter-day rationalists.

Yet there is not the slightest reason to doubt the sincerity of Paine's declaration of faith or of Jefferson's confidence that the Christian ethic would be more powerful once the orthodox creeds had been quietly dropped. Moreover, even a person to whom deistic rationalism seems naively optimistic has to concede that it produced sound and liberating effects. W. H. Auden is not a person by nature sympathetic with Deism, and he has remarked on the rather "cheap sneers" at Christianity uttered by Gibbon and Voltaire. But Auden writes that one can forgive those sneers if he will but

remember the actual horrors of persecution, witch-hunting, and provincial superstition from which [Gibbon and Voltaire] were trying to deliver mankind. Further, the reaction of the Romantics against them is a proof that up to a point they had succeeded. If the final result of their labors was a desert, they had at least drained some very putrid marshes.

This is the remark of a poet, one who is particularly sensitive to the parching effects of rationalism on poetry. But, as Auden makes plain, the draining of certain bogs was necessary and overdue.

Most of the Virginia Deists came from a background of rather tepid Anglicanism, but there were also deistical (and Unitarian) tendencies in the older Calvinism of New England, such as, for example, constituted Franklin's religious background. As the eighteenth century wore on and New England's daring theocratic experiment receded into the past, and as the strict Calvinist doctrine of predestination came to seem intolerably harsh, more and more intellectuals sought what they regarded as a more reasonable and kindly version of Christianity. In 1785 King's Chapel in Boston, an Episcopal church, declared itself to be Unitarian. By 1815, fourteen of the sixteen pre-Revolutionary Congregational churches in Boston had adopted Unitarian principles. Late in his life, Jefferson called himself a Unitarian, owning to a position that does not appreciably differ from a Deism that retains a good deal of respect for the practical ethics associated with Christianity.

Such developments in Massachusetts and in Virginia were consonant with corresponding tendencies in Great Britain. Franklin and Jefferson were familiar with the writings of Locke and the British empirical philosophers, and both were well acquainted with the related philosophies of the period in France, particularly the ideas of the French *philosophes*.

This group, under the leadership of Denis Diderot, wrote and published the first *Encyclopedia*. Though differing somewhat in purpose and method from a modern encyclopedia, it contained articles on all sorts of subjects. In the treatment of such topics as the Bible, Consecrated Bread, Fanaticism, and Intolerance, the writers called in question orthodox assumptions and poked fun at what they considered to be superstitious and erroneous beliefs. Voltaire was a contributor to the *Encyclopedia*, with articles on Fornication, History, Idolatry, and other subjects. The Encyclopedists had much to do with establishing the climate of opinion out of which the French Revolution came: an insistence on the natural equality of man, on man's inalienable rights, and on society as a compact entered into freely by its members. The relation of these ideas to those held by the founding fathers of the American Republic does not require further comment.

In attempting to describe the climate of opinion of the Enlightenment, we may have implied a consensus among the American intellectuals that in fact did not obtain. It would be a mistake to conclude that the rational temper expressed itself in the same particulars in every intellectual, or that the intellectuals constituted more than a rather small fraction of the population. We must not, that is, assume that most of the colonists shared all or even many of the opinions of men like Jefferson. The New England craftsman or shopkeeper accepted some of the new ideas, as did the Virginia farmer; on the backwoods frontier, we may be sure, Jefferson's concepts of liberty and democratic equality were heartily endorsed. But one would not expect to find everywhere Jefferson's rationalism or Franklin's rather benignant skepticism.

To speak more specifically: when the seventeenth-century New England Puritanism began to break up—and we might make the same observation of the orthodox Church of England doctrines in Virginia—the movement away from orthodoxy did not take simply one direction, that toward Deism or Unitarianism. A more powerful movement numerically was toward a fervent and highly emotional evangelical Christianity, one aimed at the plain people, that stressed a literal understanding of the Scriptures and that expressed itself in revivalistic movements. The most famous of these, called the Great Awakening, was, as we have already remarked, set in motion by the preaching of Jonathan Edwards. In the 1740's it swept through New England and the Middle Atlantic states and on into the South. Edwards was a deeply learned man, but most of the preachers in the frontier settlements were not. At any rate, it would be an emotional and evangelical kind of Christianity that would come to dominate the upland country and the still newer settlements on the western side of the mountains.

In the political life of the young nation, as in religion, opposing tendencies made their appearance at once.[2] They showed themselves almost immediately in Washington's first cabinet. Though Washington had won a unanimous election as our first President, Jefferson, his Secretary of State, and Alexander Hamilton, his Secretary of the Treasury, held sharply divergent views of what the central government ought to be, and out of their differences promptly arose the first two American parties, the Federalist, headed by Hamilton, and the Republican-Democratic, headed by Jefferson.

One of Jefferson's beliefs about nature and natural rights had special political consequences. He believed that nature was so nearly self-regulating

[2] The War of Independence had bred its own internal tensions. Not all the colonists wished to sever the ties with Great Britain. It has been estimated that about a third of them remained loyal to the British Crown or were at least no more than lukewarm toward the Revolution. Many of these Loyalists, or "Tories" as they were called by the "Patriots," lost their homes and property on this account and many of them moved to Canada.

that one ought to interfere with it as little as possible and that though a government was necessary, it was at best a necessary evil: the best government was one that governed least.[3]

Hamilton wished to strengthen the central government and in particular to establish and maintain a sound fiscal condition. He lacked Jefferson's confidence in the people and held suspect Jefferson's radical French ideas.

Jefferson's role as one of the founding fathers of the American Republic is well known. Every school child is aware that he was the author of the Declaration of Independence, and later we shall be giving a good deal of attention to that document and to Jefferson's career as statesman and as author. Hamilton's importance as a founding father is less well known and deserves at least brief comment here.

After the Revolution had been won, the American states worked for a time under a loose confederation which proved to be unsatisfactory, and so in 1787 a convention was called to draft a constitution. To this body Hamilton had been elected as one of the three delegates from New York. But once a constitution was agreed upon by a majority of the delegates, there remained the all-important business of getting it ratified by the individual states. The other two delegates to the convention from New York were opposed to the constitution as drafted and George Clinton, the governor of that crucially important state, had let it be known that he was withholding his support.

To the end of winning the assent of New York and other reluctant states, Hamilton, James Madison of Virginia, and John Jay of New York clubbed together to write *The Federalist* papers, which appeared in the New York newspapers as letters under the signature of "Publius." They set forth clearly and cogently the provisions of the proposed constitution and the compelling reasons for adopting it. All told, there were eighty-five letters,[4] running through the years 1787 and 1788. In 1788 *The Federalist* papers were published as a volume.

The Federalist papers have drawn high praise. They undoubtedly had an influence—some scholars would say a decisive influence—in insuring the adoption of the Constitution. Jefferson declared them the "best commentary on the principles of government which ever was written." They have been used by constitutional authorities down to the present day as testimony indi-

---

[3] Jefferson has for a long time been invoked as the patron saint of states rights. Yet, on occasion, under the pressure of events, Jefferson had to enlarge the power of the federal government, as when, though without any real constitutional precedent, he purchased the Louisiana Territory from France.

[4] Jay contributed only five letters. Modern scholars have had difficulty working out the precise authorship of the rest. The consensus today would give the following distribution: fifty-one written by Hamilton, twenty-six by Madison, with three representing a collaboration by Madison and Hamilton.

cating what the founding fathers really held the Constitution to mean. But they have also had a broader appeal, in part because of the hard clarity of the prose, in part because of the constant appeal to experience—experience as recorded history, especially Roman history, and experience as something common to mankind. The argument of the papers is in fact pragmatic, an early exercise in this recognizably American mode of thought.

The fact that Hamilton and Madison, Jefferson's protégé, joined forces to produce *The Federalist* is a reminder that the architects of the American Republic, in spite of their later differences, could work together. Yet the rather temporary nature of the association of the New Yorker and the Virginian also suggests the kinds of tensions present even at the earliest period. This latter point comes out amusingly in the difficulties scholars have had in deciding which men wrote which letters. As Benjamin Wright points out in the introduction to his edition of *The Federalist*, Hamilton, now Secretary of the Treasury, and Madison, a leader in the House of Representatives, were reluctant to sponsor "an exact assignment of authorship, since each had expressed views on the respective scope of state and national powers [in *The Federalist*] that differed from those they now defended." Madison, for example, did not wish to be saddled with the authorship of the forty-fourth paper, which expounded a "broad interpretation of the 'necessary and proper' clause of Article 1 of the Constitution," an interpretation "that he and Jefferson now denied."

Rather early, then, the young nation was beginning to suffer all the normal growing pains of a newly established state. It is true that our fifth President, James Monroe, in his second term was elected without opposition and that the period is often referred to as the Era of Good Feeling. But the preceding years had not been free of stress and strain. Jefferson's Embargo Act was very unpopular in parts of the country, and the War of 1812 with Great Britain provoked a violent reaction against him, especially in New England.

In any federal system there are bound to be problems with reference to the powers to be exercised by the central government. Jefferson penned the Kentucky Resolutions in protest of the powers assumed by the federal government in passing the Sedition Act of 1790, and his friend James Madison prepared the Virginia Resolutions, which embodied a similar protest. The assertion of the rights of the states was by no means limited to the South. Delegates from the New England states met in the Hartford Convention in 1814 and 1815 to discuss means for forcing the federal government to end the War of 1812. A substantial minority actually advocated secession. Any serious secessionist movement was still a good long way off in the future, but intimations of sectional conflict were already evident and the permanence of the Union had been called in question.

Such were some of the particular problems that troubled the Republic in the period between its founding and Jefferson's death in 1826. But the prevailing tone was hopeful. The feeling was that democracy could be made to work. In fact, the basic tension of which American men of intellect and feeling were most often conscious arose from the difference between men's new and high ideals for America and the realities of life as actually lived on the American continent.

In one area in particular this tension made itself acutely felt. As the middle and northern states gave up slavery because it was morally reprehensible and economically unprofitable, this glaring discrepancy between what Americans professed to believe about human freedom and what they actually practiced began to take on a sectional emphasis, but the abolition of slavery was not to become a burning issue for another twenty years—though men like Franklin were gravely concerned and for the Quaker John Woolman it was of primary importance. Too, as we shall see, southerners like Jefferson were acutely aware of the problem, but during Jefferson's lifetime and that of his New England friend, John Adams, the second President, the principal problem of the young Republic was to realize, develop, and, where necessary, modify the constitutional procedures as the old colonies learned to live together and the settlers moving out from the seaboard colonies pushed through the mountains to the western lands.

What aspects of the American experience were reflected in the emerging American literature? On the more superficial level, a good deal—American flora and fauna, the American landscape, the outward circumstances of American life. Of some of the tensions and conflicts mentioned above, again a good deal, though usually on a polemical and even political level (for example, William Cullen Bryant's "The Embargo," an anti-Jeffersonian satire). But of tensions within the author himself, those inward conflicts out of which the greatest literature is made, very little is to be seen in the poetry and the fiction of the time.

The reasons for this paucity are easily stated: the rationalist temper of the times did not encourage a literature that attempted to explore the depths of the individual psyche. The dominant literary modes of the mother country, particularly in poetry, were poorly adapted to express a radical inwardness in which a man struggles with himself.[5] In any case, the established literary modes and conventions of the motherland were a distraction. The colonial writer felt a compulsion to prove that he too could use them elegantly and effectively. Yet precisely because he was a colonial he lacked the confident

---

[5] Such a struggle was beginning to show itself in Europe toward the end of the eighteenth century: for example, in Denis Diderot's *Rameau's Nephew*, which Lionel Trilling has called the first example of "the opposing self."

sense of possession of the language and its literary tradition that might have allowed him to reshape them to his own purposes. On the other hand, he could not reject the tradition—besides it was his language and tradition too—without reducing himself to a kind of half-articulate primitivism.

Whatever the reasons, the writers of the first quarter of the century show themselves in fact preoccupied with imitations of British models, including even those writers who asked for the creation of a specifically American literature.[6] For what constitutes a truly American literature, as distinguished from the use of inherited literary forms filled with American "content" and singing the praises of the young Republic, was precisely what had to be discovered. Most of the poets and writers of fiction represented in this section were only fumbling toward a true definition.

---

[6] The cry for such a literature was vociferous if often rather brainless: thus, "We have conquered them with the sword, now we will with the pen." The editor of a magazine (the *Portico*, c. 1816) deposed: "Dependence is a state of degradation fraught with disgrace, and to be dependent on a foreign mind for what we can ourselves produce is to add to the crime of indolence the weakness of stupidity." Cornelius Matthews (in the *Broadway Journal*, 1845) wrote: "In behalf of this young America of ours, I insist on nationality and true Americanism in the books this country furnishes to itself and to the world."

The Social Setting: Philosophical, Political, and Occasional Writing

Poets and writers of fiction, however, were not the only writers in the period. Before the need for a native literature entered fully into the American consciousness (see the introduction to our section "Toward an Indigenous Poetry") other concerns pressed more immediately upon mind and imagination. Among these was the need to take stock of the changing conditions of life in the emerging society. The contours of experience, so to say, had to be studied afresh as the effort of Puritan New England to articulate the City of God gave way—amid the growing secularism of the eighteenth century—to a survey of something more like the City of Man.

It may reinforce the point just made to observe that none of the writers in this section are New Englanders. Though Benjamin Franklin was born in Boston, and spent his first years there, he is more properly considered a Philadelphian, while John Woolman was an itinerant Quaker from New Jersey, and Thomas Jefferson was from Virginia. Between them, in their very different .ways, they announced not only the spirit of a new age but the diffusion of cultural energy from New England down along the Atlantic seaboard, a process we will note in our discussions of developments in poetry and prose during the same period. This is not to say, however, that the process was as tidy or as single as the formulation might suggest. It might be remarked, for example, that at roughly the same time that Franklin was writing his *Autobiography*, Jonathan Edwards, in western Massachusetts, was composing the largest and most powerful statement of the Calvinist world view ever issued on the continent.

Franklin and the others, in the pages which follow, address themselves to subjects as various as air pollution and the creation of a new national entity by a declaration of independence. We may note, too, that among the issues confronted by the men of the Enlightenment, as represented here, was that of race: particularly the plight of the American Indian and the curse of Negro slavery. In the means which they choose to discuss such wide-ranging subjects these writers indicate that they are obviously not primarily literary figures. In the sense that their writings serve essentially nonliterary ends they are like the Puritan writers we have discussed. And, like that of the Puritans, their work may be thought of as belonging to the nonliterary world, though we have felt it inappropriate to invoke that phrase until much later in this volume.[1]

[1] See the section called "Literature of the Nonliterary World." The point here is that America could not, logically or historically, be said to possess a *non*literary world until its poets and prose writers had developed a world recognizably and genuinely literary.

BENJAMIN FRANKLIN (1706–1790)

Franklin was thirty-seven when, in 1743, he first conceived of the learned society referred to in the general introduction above. He was already one of Philadelphia's leading citizens and men of business affairs; it would not be long before he would feel wealthy enough to retire from business and devote himself to public service. The story of Franklin's life is indeed the American success story *par excellence*—an almost uninterrupted rise literally from rags to riches, and from obscurity to local and then national and finally world fame and power. For one who, as a Deist, did not believe in miracles, Franklin's career is little short of miraculous. There is something extraordinarily American about it: it is a simple observation and not a boast to say that it could not have happened anywhere else on earth in the eighteenth century; and as we watch it evolve, we have the marked impression of seeing an archetypal American come into being.

Benjamin Franklin's life has been emulated ever since by success-driven Americans; it has been the model for popular fiction of the Horatio Alger variety and has been reenacted in different guises in films and television serials. This has not always endeared Franklin to later generations, and it is unlikely to be an immediate source of appeal to those many members of the present generation who regard success—at least in external and material terms—with mounting skepticism, and whose taste in fiction is for the "anti-hero" rather than the winner. Yet Franklin is a figure very much to be reckoned with, and today as much as ever. He had a many-faceted genius virtually unparalleled in our history; and he practiced the deistic virtues as well as any man of his time—no one more reasonable than Franklin; no one more tolerant not only of others but more importantly of himself; no one more sympathetic to those in trouble. He was the author of one literary masterpiece, his *Autobiography*. If he was a decidedly "representative" American, he was so in Emerson's meaning of the adjective, as a supreme example of his species; and it was altogether fitting that he should crown his career as America's representative in France. He was an eminently practical man, as most Americans like to think of themselves as being; and, intellectually, he was a pragmatist—with Hamilton and the other authors of *The Federalist* papers, one of the first adherents of that peculiarly American brand of philosophy, the basic tenet of which (as developed much later by William James and John Dewey) is that truth is something to be tested by concrete experience and with regard to the benefit of society. Those who have imitated Franklin's pursuit of money, fame, and power have all too often overlooked the fundamental motive behind it all—which was the welfare of mankind.

Born in Boston, in 1706, of yeoman stock, Franklin was, after relatively little schooling, apprenticed to his older brother as a printer's assistant; but at the age of seventeen, he broke free and made his way south to Philadelphia. Arriving there as a ragamuffin, he managed—chiefly by printing (to the end of his days he signed himself with simplicity: "B. Franklin, printer"), but also by selling a great variety of commodities—to amass a fortune sufficient to enable him to retire from business by the time he was forty-one. We should notice that in fact Franklin's several careers—business, municipal, and national—overlapped and intermingled. It was his strategy in the *Autobiography* to suggest that these careers and these roles were successive phases in the happy dream of his life, and it will do no harm to follow his lead.

As a municipal leader in Philadelphia, then, he helped found the American Philosophical Society and the University of Pennsylvania; helped establish a fire company and a police force; looked into the matter of street-paving and dust accumulation; invented the still-sought-after Franklin stove as well as bifocal spectacle lenses; made some remarkable experiments in electricity (for which he was decorated in 1753 by the Royal Society of London); became Deputy General for the colonies and clerk of the General Assembly; and, while doing these

and many other things, wrote endlessly on a vast assortment of subjects—offering many of his thoughts in *Poor Richard's Almanack*, which he began in 1732. Then, at a time (nearing sixty) when most men would be ready to retire altogether, Franklin embarked on more than two decades of increasingly lofty national service—among other things, as the agent of the Province of Pennsylvania in London, where he lobbied against the Stamp Act; as a delegate to the Second Continental Congress and a member of the committee to draft the Declaration of Independence (which was written, except for a few small emendations, by Thomas Jefferson); as a commissioner and then United States Minister Plenipotentiary to France; and finally as delegate to the Constitutional Convention in 1787. It is hardly surprising that upon his death in 1790, there gathered for his funeral the largest crowd the country had ever seen.

With all this—and the list of Franklin's activities and accomplishments is here much foreshortened—he is also an imposing figure in American *literary* history. No few of his letters, his speeches (for example, his speech to the Constitutional Convention), and his articles retain a certain vitality and hefty charm. But his one authentic masterpiece is his *Autobiography*, which was written as it were at three sittings—in 1771, 1784, and 1788. Contemplating this curious and disorderly work today, with its notorious check list of practical virtues to be all so relentlessly pursued (the famous "project" for moral improvement), how are we to respond?

We are likely to respond at first according to our general response to the age Franklin has come to stand for and over which in so many respects he presided. The chief features of that age have been described in the general introduction. What can be added here is that despite its continental origins, and its detestation of the theocratic mind, the Age of Reason did draw from the Puritan epoch which preceded it a commitment to reason. It was as though the old covenant idea had carried the day, and with important consequences for all elements on the intellectual and religious horizon. The Puritan idea of the covenant, it will be recalled, declared that God, miraculously enough, had entered into an agreement whereby his government of the world and man, his plans and promises, could be largely understood by human reason. The Puritans tended to waver between that idea and its opposite: namely, the conviction that God's activity and man's experience were altogether beyond the capacity of man's puny mind to take in and interpret. The most vigorous of Puritan thinkers, as we have said, were able to entertain both beliefs simultaneously, and even, by subtle argumentation, to render them compatible with one another. But as the eighteenth century went forward, the power of man's rational intellect came to be seen as exalted—and not so much, any longer, because God had so covenanted, but rather because man was now regarded as an enlightened and rational being inhabiting a rational universe created by a thoroughly reasonable God, and in tune with a rational physical nature.

It is the absence, generally speaking, from the rational, scientific, and deistic mind of any sense of the *irrational*, the mentally wayward, the incomprehensible, even the terrifying, that makes it so difficult in our own time, with its near cult of the irrational, to come to grips with the Enlightenment. And it was precisely the impulse to recover those qualities—in reaction against the congealing rationalism of unitarian thought—which moved the American Romantics in the Age of Emerson. Thus the Romantics found little in Franklin's personality or the *Autobiography* to inspire them.

It may well be that Franklin's autobiographical narrative, in its good-humored and even-tempered way, makes his rise to wealth, authority, and influence sound much easier than it must have been. One forgets that in his Philadelphia days he had to contend with mediocrity, provincialism, and incompetence, with hostility, envy, and broken promises. He had to forge his remarkable career out of the least encouraging ingredients, as later he had to contend with representatives of the world's strongest political powers. What is even more to be stressed is the personal motive behind all this: that is,

Franklin's concept of the purpose of the life worth living. In 1748, as he was on the verge of retiring from business, he wrote Cadwallader Colden (a fellow scientist):

> I am in a fair way of having no other tasks than such as I shall like to give myself, and of enjoying what I look upon as a great happiness, leisure to read, study, make experiments, and converse at large with such ingenious and worthy men as are pleased to honor me with their friendship or acquaintance, on such points as may produce something for the common benefit of mankind, uninterrupted by the little cares and fatigues of business.

The happy life thus consisted in leisure to read—he had, Franklin tells us, always read voraciously—and to think; to investigate the physical universe. It consisted above all in sharing with other men of high intellectual ability ideas and plans for the improvement of the human lot. Franklin was by no means a "do-gooder," in the sense of being a self-righteous meddler; among his first writings, indeed, were a series of satirical articles signed by a certain "Mrs. Silence Dogood" (a frolicsome rebuttal to Cotton Mather's then recently published *Essays to Do Good*, and sufficiently outrageous to have the journal in which the articles appeared closed down). Rather, he was honestly concerned about the bettering of man's physical condition (as by stoves and bifocal lenses), his mental condition (as by universities and learned societies), and his social condition. Regarding the latter, we may simply take as one major example Franklin's vehement opposition to racial prejudice in general, and to Negro slavery in particular.

Following the massacre of some peaceable Pennsylvania Indians, Franklin published a controlledly angry pamphlet exposing the absurdity of all racial animosity.

> If an *Indian* injures me, does it follow that I may revenge that injury on all *Indians?* It is well known that *Indians* are of different Tribes, Nations and Languages, as well as the White People. In Europe, if the *French*, who

are White People, should injure the *Dutch*, are they to revenge it on the *English* because they too are White People? The only Crime to these poor Wretches seems to have been, that they had reddish-brown Skin, and black Hair; and some people of that Sort, it seems, had murdered some of our Relations.

As to the Negroes, Franklin was among those who argued staunchly against the widely held belief that Negroes were mentally inferior to whites—they were, Franklin insisted, quite the equal of whites in "natural understanding." And it was Franklin who, by helping to found a number of effective reform organizations, made Philadelphia an early spearhead in the anti-slavery movement. The chief of these bore a title (formulated perhaps by Franklin) which speaks eloquently for itself: "The Pennsylvania Society for Promoting the Abolition of Slavery, for the Relief of Free Negroes Unlawfully Held in Bondage, and for Improving the Condition of the African Race." The last act of Franklin's life was to write a satirical defense of slavery—as by an Algerian pirate!—in response to a racist speech by a convention delegate from Georgia.[1]

It is not too much to say that a devotion to human welfare was for Franklin what strict obedience to God's will had been for the Puritans. This was in fact the burden of one of his most characteristic statements:

> The worship of God is a duty; the hearing and reading of sermons may be useful; but, if men rest in hearing and praying, it is as if a tree should value itself on being watered and putting forth leaves, tho' it never produced any fruit.

Franklin thought through his religious beliefs with great care, and he was fully conscious of what he had rejected and what he retained from the old Puritan orthodoxy. Summarizing this for us in the *Autobiography*, he also gives a capsule definition of the Deist creed:

> I had been religiously educated as a Presbyterian; and tho' some of the dogmas of that persuasion, such as the eternal decrees of God, election, reprobation, etc., appeared to me unintelligible, others doubtful, and I early absented myself from the public assemblies of the sect, Sunday being my studying day, I never was without some religious principles. I never doubted, for instance, the existence of the Deity, that he made the world and governed it by his providence, that the most acceptable service of God was the doing of good to man, that our souls are immortal, and that all crimes will be punished and virtue rewarded either here or hereafter.

A critical analysis of that paragraph would be nicely rewarding. One notices that the harshest of the orthodox doctrines are rejected on the grounds that they seem meaningless to human reason. One notices too the sly interjections: "Sunday being my studying day"; one almost sees Franklin peering through his bifocals as he says it, to study our response. The key assertion, of course, is that "the most acceptable service of God was the doing of good to man"; but one can only admire Franklin's hedging about the final recompense for human actions—they will be punished or rewarded "here or hereafter."

Implicit in our discussion at this stage is a comparison and contrast between Franklin's views and those of his contemporary Jonathan Edwards. We can get still closer to Franklin and his *Autobiography* by a further instance of that relation. For Franklin's most important work may be taken as elaborate counterpart to Edwards' "Personal Narrative" (which we have commented on earlier). And like Edwards' brief piece of autobiography, and in the tradition from which it also derives, Franklin's personal narrative can be identified as the story of his conversion—or of a series of conversions, each strictly humanistic and secular in kind: from penniless youth to wealthy and mature entrepreneur; from businessman to municipal leader;

---

[1] It is also true, however, that on one or two occasions Franklin—like his humanistic and strongly antislavery predecessor Samuel Sewall—rather wished that black men had never come to the New World. "Why increase the Sons of Africa," he once wrote, "by Planting them in America?" But he concluded mildly enough: "But perhaps I am partial to the Complexion of My Country, for such kind of Partiality is natural to Mankind."

from his city's first citizen to minister for national and international affairs.

What is at issue here, finally, is Franklin's particular consciousness of self. We recall the Puritan insistence on self-inquiry, the need of each man to make scrupulous examination of his own spiritual nature, to confront its portion of sinfulness and the state of its relation—at any given moment—to God. Edwards' "Personal Narrative" is all compact of such self-inquiry, both by way of reminiscence and as to his soul's condition at the time of writing. Franklin, in his autobiographical account of his several careers, is not precisely looking into his spiritual condition at various stages. Like his fellow Deists, Franklin had entirely discarded the notion of original sin; he had, indeed, little if any notion of sin itself. He was not concerned, as Edwards had been, with periodic backsliding into a sinful condition, or with God's mysterious work of salvation. He took note of certain errors of judgment, as he did of successful strategies. But he saw himself—in the Lockeian and deistic manner—as a creature advancing into the world and (as it were) making himself up as he went. His story is the story of the growth and development of a self. But what gives the *Autobiography* its special quality and what most sharply distinguishes it from Edwards' narrative is that Franklin envisaged the process of what might be called self-creation as the conscious playing of a series of calculated roles.

The personal life—or Franklin's personal life, anyhow—thus assumed the character of a game; and Franklin is perhaps the first master of what is now known as gamesmanship. The game was a serious one, to be sure; and it was double in nature. We can be certain, that is, that in the actual life, the various "Franklins"—the adolescent and the young Franklin, the maturing and middle-aged and elderly Franklin—all quite consciously assumed one role after another; each one, in Franklin's view, representative; each, one might almost say, a standard eighteenth-century "character" or type. But we can be equally sure that the Franklin who was writing the *Autobiography* in 1771, 1784, and 1788 was similarly *re*creating himself in a succession of roles, cast-

ing himself at every step into a representative figure. It is the role-playing, the posing—it is, in short, Franklin's histrionic genius that gives the *Autobiography* its originality. It is this, indeed, which makes the book a sort of model even for fictional autobiography.

The presiding figure in the first section, as Robert F. Sayre has pointed out in his excellent study *The Examined Self* (1964), is the cultivated elderly gentleman "expecting a week's uninterrupted leisure in my present country retirement," in the English countryside. Gazing backward, this leisurely and knowing old gentleman brings himself into focus in representative roles at key moments. There is the seventeen-year-old ragamuffin who arrives in Philadelphia, to whom Franklin carefully draws the attention of the reader (and of his son William to whom the reminiscences are addressed).

> I have been the more particular in this description of my journey; and shall be so of my first entry into that city, that you may in your mind compare such unlikely beginnings with the figure I have since made there. I was in my working dress. . . . I was dirty from my journey. . . . I knew no soul, nor where to look for lodging. . . . My whole stock of cash consisted of a Dutch dollar and about a shilling in proper coin.

And so on, through his famous purchase of "three great puffy rolls," two of which the boy carried under his arms while he walked down the street munching on the other. Later, there is the young man whose energy and industry began to be the talk of the town—the youth who was careful to be seen working late at night in the printer's shop, and who, in Franklin's utterly self-aware recollection, "in order to secure my credit and character as a tradesman . . . took care not only to be in *reality* industrious and frugal, but to avoid all *appearances* of the contrary."

> I dressed plain and was seen at no place of idle diversion. I never went out a fishing or a shooting; a book, indeed, sometimes debauched me from my work, but that was sel-

dom, snug, and gave no scandal; and to show that I was not above my business, I sometimes brought home the paper I purchased at the stores, thro' the streets on a wheelbarrow.

Robert Sayre is right to refer to the items there listed as "props," as though for a stage character: the plain dress, the debauching book, the wheelbarrow. But the charm in the account derives from the elderly author's amusement at his histrionic success and, by implication, at the nature of the narrow urban society in which it took place.

Still later, in the second section, there appears the maturing person dedicated to the project of moral perfection—dedicated, that is, to assuming the part of a strenuously moral individual; and in the third section, we meet the ever-industrious civic leader. So the process continues, as the aging world citizen plays like a comic dramatist in narrative with his own successive self-dramatizations. Of all the writers who have commented on Franklin, it was Herman Melville who first—and best—discerned Franklin's histrionic genius, in his portrait of Franklin in *Israel Potter* (Melville's least-known work of fiction, but like everything that Melville wrote a book of compelling interest). The Franklin who is encountered, in Paris, by the wandering young soldier, Israel Potter, is superbly if irreverently characterized.

> Having carefully weighed the world, Franklin could act any part in it. By nature turned to knowledge, his mind was often grave, but never serious. . . . This philosophical levity of tranquillity, so to speak, is shown in his easy variety of pursuits. Printer, postmaster, almanac maker, essayist, chemist, orator, tinker, statesman, humorist, philosopher, parlor man, political economist, professor of housewifery, ambassador, projector, maxim-monger, herb-doctor, wit:—Jack of all trades, master of each and mastered by none—the type and genius of his land, Franklin was everything but a poet.

"The type and genius of his land" and "every-

thing but a poet"—Melville manages in those juxtaposed phrases not only to identify Franklin as the embodiment of his culture, but to raise, lightly but troublingly, a question about America's hospitality to the creative imagination.[2]

In calling Franklin a "projector," Melville was referring to the elaborate program, or project, for moral improvement, outlined in the second section of the *Autobiography*. It called for daily exercise in such virtues as temperance, frugality, and chastity ("Use venery only for health and offspring"); and it does not make very exciting reading today.[3] D. H. Lawrence articulated the Romantic recoil from Franklin's ethical pragmatism when, speaking of what he called the "barbed wire moral enclosure" of *Poor Richard's Almanack*, he said that "although I still believe that honesty is the best policy, I dislike policy altogether." But Franklin, the utterly politic man, really did believe that virtue was rewarded and vice punished. This was by no means the same as claiming—as many vulgarized emulators of Franklin have done—that honesty is good for business or that humility pays off. It is saying, rather, that other things being equal it is better and more sensible to be virtuous than vicious, and that if one practices virtue and avoids vice the profits and

---

[2] In the light of the portrait of Franklin in *Israel Potter*, it is fascinating to speculate whether Melville may not have had Franklin in mind—that is, his own view of Franklin—in creating the Confidence Man, especially in that changeable figure's most imposing avatar as the Cosmopolitan.

[3] Though Franklin is the most famous exemplar of the disciplined and carefully scheduled life, as represented by his "project," the whole conception is deeply rooted in the American character. We find traces of it in the Puritan belief that every moment of life must be rigorously accounted for, and in the diaries of early Americans as different as Samuel Sewall and William Byrd, each giving a careful listing of the routines of the day. The idea that success depends in good part on meticulous planning persisted through the nineteenth century into our own age, both in the actual lives of men of affairs and in literary narrative. In *The Great Gatsby* the author, F. Scott Fitzgerald, has his hero follow a project for self-advancement which may well have been modeled after Franklin's; and there is a kind of strenuous parody of Franklin in the dedicatedly predatory career of Flem Snopes in Faulkner's *The Hamlet*.

prizes will take care of themselves; they will follow later.

Franklin, as Melville observed, was not a poet—he was a diplomat, something that during his lifetime his country had a more immediate need of and a role for which his histrionic skills beautifully equipped him. Let us watch him in action on a few occasions.

In February, 1764, in the wake of the uprising known as the conspiracy of Pontiac (see the introduction to Francis Parkman), passions between whites and Indians were enflamed throughout the Pennsylvania colony. A large mob of infuriated whites, led by a gang of Indian-killers called the Paxton boys, marched into Philadelphia to protest the government's protection of Indian refugees. The governor, John Penn, fled to Franklin's house at midnight, "his councillors at his heels." Franklin, with a few others, was sent to talk with the invaders, and by firmness and calm reasoning he succeeded in dispersing the crowd and restoring quiet to the city. For twenty-four hours, Franklin wrote a friend, he had been "an ambassador to a country mob"; but Penn, the bloodthirsty grandson of the pacific William, only hated Franklin for his success.

Two years later, Franklin could be found in England debating the Stamp Act before the House of Commons. He had been a leading opponent of this most unpopular piece of legislation and had allied himself behind the scenes with several liberal English statesmen in plans to defeat it. The parliamentary debate was an entirely staged affair, a comedy of sorts, wherein Franklin was fed carefully prepared questions by his secret ally, to each of which he gave a measured and well-briefed reply. A month after this lengthy and fully rehearsed interrogation of America's Deputy Postmaster General, the Stamp Act was repealed.

For as long as it was humanly possible, Franklin clung to his belief in the empire and to the conviction that the interests of both the colonies and the mother country were best served by maintaining the Union. He worked for years with Englishmen of like persuasion—again, behind the scenes and often during long evenings of chess. Franklin was wholly opposed to mob violence, and after the Boston Tea Party in 1774 he made it the first of a series of points for negotiation that reparation be made for the fifteen thousand pounds worth of destruction, and even offered to guarantee the payment. If any American diplomat could have held things together, it was Franklin; but even Franklin's diplomatic adroitness and patience were not enough. The English king and the leading faction in Parliament declared the colonists guilty of criminal disobedience, and they so misread the situation as to call Franklin to his face "one of the bitterest and most mischievous enemies this country [has] ever known" ("I was treated," Franklin recalled, "as the cause of the mischief I was labouring to prevent"). After every effort, public and private, had failed, Franklin gave up and returned to America torn between disgust and despair at the irrevocable end of the imperialist vision, but ready to throw his energies into the huge work of political, financial, and military organization that lay ahead. The battles of Lexington and Concord took place while he was still at sea.

If England was the scene of Franklin's greatest diplomatic defeat, France was the scene of his most brilliant triumphs. He was sent there in 1776 as one of three American "commissioners," to arrange a treaty of alliance with the French. During the previous two years, Franklin had taken part in the Continental Congress in Philadelphia—never speaking, as Jefferson noticed, for more than ten minutes at a time and always speaking to the point. He had helped Jefferson draft the Declaration of Independence. During a secret parley with Lord Howe about putting an end to the hostilities, Howe, according to John Adams, professed his anxiety lest America, which he loved like a brother, should be brought down with British arms: "My lord," said Franklin with an ingenuous air, "we will use our utmost endeavors to save your lordship that mortification."

In France, Franklin was an unqualified success from the start. The French wanted him to be at once a sophisticated statesman and a rustic philosopher, and Franklin played that complex role to the hilt. Wise and learned, a gourmet and lover of good wines, and a gallant with the French ladies, several of them less than half his age, Franklin nonetheless regularly appeared in an unembroidered brown coat and a fur hat, wearing the bifocals he had recently invented, and carrying a crab-tree stick instead of a sword. He set up headquarters in Passy, a mile out of Paris, and here he received an endless throng of diplomatic, intellectual, and social visitors and went about his business unperturbed by the extraordinary network of English spies which surrounded him. When the military news was bad, as it was for long months after his arrival, Franklin kept up a public face of unshaken confidence; and he never lost his assurance, as he told his colleague Arthur Lee:

> The greatest revolution the world ever saw is likely to be effected in a few years; and the power that has for centuries made all Europe tremble, assisted by twenty thousand German mercenaries and favoured by the universal concurrence of Europe to prohibit the sale of warlike stores, the sale of prizes, or the admission of the armed vessels of America, will be effectually humbled by those whom she insulted and injured, because she conceived they had neither spirit nor power to resist or revenge it.

The surrender of General Burgoyne and his entire army at Saratoga, in December, 1777, marked the great turn in America's military fortunes; but with the treaty "of amity and commerce" that Franklin concluded only a few weeks later, he had (in the words of the best of his biographers, Carl Van Doren) "won a diplomatic campaign equal in results to Saratoga."

In 1781, soon after his seventy-fifth birthday, Franklin—now Minister Plenipotentiary to France—asked Congress to be relieved of his duties; he had been engaged in public affairs, he said, for fifty years and had no further ambition "but that of repose." Congress's reply was to appoint him, with John Adams and John Jay, to a committee to seek terms for peace with England. Knowing that peace treaties are usually condemned later as inadequate or even corrupt, Franklin wrote Adams ruefully: "'Blessed are the peacemakers' is, I suppose, to be understood in the other world; for in this they are frequently cursed." But again after many months of patient and tireless effort, and after a prolonged and superbly managed duel with the French foreign minister, Vergennes (who was of course determined that French interests should not be damaged by an entente between England and America), Franklin, as the most influential of the peacemaking threesome, saw the articles of peace signed in Paris in September, 1783.

The former imperialist was now the staunchest advocate of American independence—that is, of America as a politically and culturally independent reality. If Franklin was not a poet, he did perhaps more than any other single American to help create a nation-state in which literature and the arts could take seed. The old actor had performed his last and finest role; the new country was born; an American literature was about to begin.

BIOGRAPHICAL CHART

1706　Born January 17, in Boston, tenth son of Josiah Franklin, a tallow-chandler and soap-boiler

1718　Apprenticed to his half-brother James, a printer; writes a poem, "The Lighthouse Tragedy," a popular success

1722　Publishes the "Silence Dogood" series of articles in James's *New England Courant*

1723　Quarrels with James, leaves Boston for New York, then travels to Philadelphia, where he is hired by printer Samuel Keimer

1724　Goes to London; works as a printer

1726　Returns to Philadelphia as merchant's clerk

1728　Establishes a printing house with Hugh Meredith; becomes public printer for Pennsylvania

1729　Purchases the *Pennsylvania Gazette*

1730　Takes Deborah Reed in common-law marriage

1732　Begins issuing *Poor Richard's Almanack*

1742　Invents the "Franklin stove"

1743	Founds the American Philosophical Society
1749	Writes *Proposals Relating to the Education of Youth in Pennsylvania,* which leads to the founding of the Academy of Philadelphia, later to become the University of Pennsylvania
1751	Experiments in field of electricity culminate with publication of *Experiments and Observations in Electricity*
1753	Receives honorary degrees from Harvard and Yale, and the Copley medal from the Royal Society
1756	Elected to membership in the Royal Society
1757	Elected agent of the Pennsylvania Assembly, presenting claims against the Proprietors, thus moves to London (until 1762)
1765–70	Lobbies against the Stamp Act in London
1774	Deborah Reed Franklin dies
1775	Returns to Philadelphia; participates in Second Continental Congress; advises Washington; meets Thomas Paine
1776	Assists in drafting the Declaration of Independence; goes to Paris to help negotiate treaty of alliance (until 1785); meets La Rochefoucauld, Lavoisier, Diderot, Voltaire; frequents literary salons
1781	Goes to England with Adams *et al.* to negotiate peace settlement
1785	Returns to Philadelphia; elected president of the Executive Council of Pennsylvania
1790	Signs memorial to Congress petitioning the abolition of slavery; dies, April 17, in Philadelphia; buried on the grounds of Christ Church

FURTHER READINGS

Leonard W. Labaree, ed., *The Papers of Benjamin Franklin* (1959–70; 14 vols.)

Alfred O. Aldridge, *Benjamin Franklin, Philosopher and Man* (1965)
————, *Franklin and His French Contemporaries* (1957)
Carl L. Becker, *Benjamin Franklin: A Biographical Sketch* (1946)
I. Bernard Cohen, *Benjamin Franklin: His Contribution to the American Tradition* (1953)
Bruce I. Granger, *Benjamin Franklin: An American Man of Letters* (1964)

Ralph X. Hornberger, *Benjamin Franklin* (1962)
Adrienne Koch, *Power, Morals, and the Founding Fathers: Essays in the Interpretation of the American Enlightenment* (1961)
Frank L. Mott and Chester E. Jorgenson, *Benjamin Franklin: Representative Selections* (1936), Introduction
Charles L. Sanford, ed., *Benjamin Franklin and the American Character* (1955)
Robert F. Sayre, *The Examined Self* (1964)
Carl C. Van Doren, *Benjamin Franklin* (1938)

From the Autobiography (1771, 1788)

TO HIS SON

Twyford, at the Bishop
of St. Asaph's, 1771

Dear Son,

I have ever had a pleasure in obtaining any little anecdotes of my ancestors. You may remember the enquiries I made among the remains of my relations when you were with me in England and the journey I undertook for that purpose. Imagining it may be equally agreeable to you to know the circumstances of *my* life—many of which you are yet unacquainted with—and expecting a week's uninterrupted leisure in my present country retirement, I sit down to write them for you. Besides, there are some other inducements that excite me to this undertaking. From the poverty and obscurity in which I was born and in which I passed my earliest years, I have raised myself to a state of affluence and some degree of celebrity in the world. As constant good fortune has accompanied me even to an advanced period of life, my posterity will perhaps be desirous of learning the means, which I employed, and which, thanks to Providence, so well succeeded with me. They may also deem them fit to be imitated, should any of them find themselves in similar circumstances. That good fortune, when I reflected on it, which is frequently the case, has induced me sometimes to say that were it left to my choice, I should have no objection to go over the same life from its beginning to the end, only asking the advantage authors have of correcting in a second edition some faults of the first. So would I also wish to change some incidents of it for others more favourable. Notwithstanding, if this condition were denied, I should still accept the offer. But as this repetition is not to be expected, that which resembles most living one's life over again, seems to be to recall all the circumstances of it; and, to render this remembrance more durable, to record them in writing. In thus employing myself I shall yield to the inclination so natural to old men of talking of themselves and their own actions, and I shall indulge it, without being tiresome to those who, from respect to my age, might conceive themselves obliged to listen to me, since they will be always free to read me or not. And lastly (I may as well confess it, as the denial of it would be believed by nobody) I shall perhaps not a little gratify my own vanity. Indeed, I never heard or saw the introductory words, "Without Vanity I may say," etc., but some vain thing immediately followed. Most people dislike vanity in others whatever share they have of it themselves, but I give it fair quarter wherever I meet with it, being persuaded that it is often productive of good to the possessor and to others who are within his sphere of action. And therefore, in many cases it would not be altogether absurd if a man were to thank God for his vanity among the other comforts of life.

And now I speak of thanking God, I desire with all humility to acknowledge that I owe the mentioned happiness of my past life to his divine providence, which led me to the means I used and gave them success. My belief of this induces me to *hope*, though I must not *presume*, that the same goodness will still be exercised towards me in continuing that happiness or in enabling me to bear a fatal reverse, which I may experience as others have done—the complexion of my future fortune being known to him only, and in whose power it is to bless to us even our afflictions.

THE ARRIVAL IN PHILADELPHIA

Following an altercation with his older brother, to whom Franklin had been apprenticed (and whose oppressive treatment of Franklin, the latter says, gave him "that aversion to arbitrary power that has stuck to me through my whole life"), and after a brush with the law, the seventeen-year-old lad leaves Boston and comes to Philadelphia, the city whose first citizen he would eventually become.

This might be one occasion of the differences we began to have about this time. Though a brother, he considered himself as my master and me as his apprentice, and accordingly expected the same services from me as he would from another; while I thought he degraded me too much in some he required of me, who from a brother expected more indulgence. Our disputes were often brought before our father, and I fancy I was either generally in the right or else a better pleader, because the judgment was generally in my favour. But my brother was passionate and had often beaten me, which I took extremely amiss. I fancy his harsh and tyrannical treatment of me might be a means of impressing me with that aversion to arbitrary power that has stuck to me through my whole life. Thinking my apprenticeship very tedious, I was continually wishing for some opportunity of shortening it, which at length offered in a manner unexpected.

One of the pieces in our newspaper on some political point which I have now forgotten, gave offence to the Assembly. He was taken up, censured, and imprisoned for a month by the Speaker's warrant, I suppose because he would not discover the author. I, too, was taken up and examined before the Council; but though I did not give them any satisfaction, they contented themselves with admonishing me and dismissed me, considering me, perhaps, as an apprentice who was bound to keep his master's secrets. During my brother's confinement, which I resented a good deal notwithstanding our private differences, I had the management of the paper, and I made bold to give our rulers some rubs in it, which my brother took very kindly, while others began to consider me in an unfavourable light as a young genius that had a turn for libelling and satire. My brother's discharge was accompanied with an order from the House (a very odd one) that "James Franklin should no longer print the paper called the *New England Courant.*" There was a consultation held in our printing house amongst his friends in this conjuncture. Some proposed to elude the order by changing the name of the paper; but my brother seeing inconveniences in that, it was finally concluded on as a better way to let it be printed for the future under the name of "Benjamin Franklin"; and to avoid the censure of the Assembly that might fall on him as still printing it by his apprentice, the contrivance was that my old indenture should be returned to me with a full discharge on the back of it, to show in case of necessity; but to secure to him the benefit of my service, I should sign new indentures for the remainder of the term, which were to be kept private. A very flimsy scheme it was, but, however, it was immediately executed, and the paper went on accordingly under my name for several months. At length a fresh difference arising between my brother and me, I took upon me to assert my freedom, presuming that he would not venture to produce the new indentures. It was not fair in me to take this advantage, and this I therefore reckon one of the first errata of my life. But the unfairness of it weighed little with me, when under the impressions of resentment for the blows his passion too often urged him to bestow upon me, though he was otherwise not an ill-natured man. Perhaps I was too saucy and provoking.

When he found I would leave him, he took care to prevent my getting employment in any other printing house of the town by going round and speaking to every master, who accordingly refused to give me work. I then thought of going to New York as the nearest place where there was a printer; and I was the rather inclined to leave Boston when I reflected that I had already made myself a little obnoxious to the governing party; and from the arbitrary proceedings of the Assembly in my brother's case, it was likely I might if I stayed soon bring myself into scrapes, and further that my indiscreet disputations about religion began to make me pointed at with horror by good people as an infidel or atheist. I determined on the point, but my father now siding with my brother, I was sensible that if I attempted to go openly, means would be used to prevent me. My friend Collins therefore undertook to manage my flight. He agreed with the captain of a New York sloop for my passage, under pretence of my being a young man of his acquaintance that had had an intrigue with a girl of bad character, whose parents would compel me to marry her and therefore I could not appear or come away publicly. I sold some of my books to raise a little money, was taken on board the sloop privately, had a fair wind, and in three days found myself at New York, near three hundred miles from my home, at the age of seventeen, without the least recommendation to or knowledge of any person in the place, and with very little money in my pocket.

The inclination I had had for the sea was by this time done away, or I might now have gratified it. But having another profession and conceiving myself a pretty good workman, I offered my services to the printer of the place, old Mr. Wm. Bradford (who had been the first printer in Pennsylvania, but had removed thence in consequence of a quarrel with the Governor, Geo. Keith). He could give me no employment, having little to do and hands enough already. "But," says he, "my son at Philadelphia has lately lost his principal hand, Aquila Rose, by death. If you go thither I believe he may employ you."

Philadelphia was a hundred miles farther. I set out, however, in a boat for Amboy, leaving my chest and things to follow me round by sea. In crossing the bay we met with a squall that tore our rotten sails to pieces, prevented our getting into the kill, and drove us upon Long Island. In our way a drunken Dutchman, who was a passenger, too, fell overboard; when he was sinking, I reached through the water to his shock pate and drew him up so that we got him in again. His ducking sobered him a little, and he went to sleep, taking first out of his pocket a book which he desired I would dry for him. It proved to be my old favourite author Bunyan's *Pilgrim's Progress* in Dutch, finely printed on good paper with copper cuts, a dress better than I had ever seen it wear in its own language. I have since found that it has been translated into most of the languages of Europe, and suppose it has been more generally read than any other book except, perhaps, the Bible. Honest John was the first that I know of who mixes narration and dialogue, a method of writing very engaging to the reader, who in the most interesting parts finds himself, as it were, admitted into the company and present at the conversation. Defoe has imitated him successfully in his *Robinson Crusoe*, in his *Moll Flanders*, and other pieces; and Richardson has done the same in his *Pamela*, etc.

On approaching the island, we found it was in a place where there could be no landing, there being a great surf on the stony beach. So we dropped anchor and swung out our cable towards the shore. Some people came down to the water edge and hallooed to us, as we did to them, but the wind was so high and the surf so loud that we could not understand each other. There were some canoes on the shore, and we made signs and called to them to fetch us, but they either did not comprehend us or thought it impracticable so they went off. Night approaching, we had no remedy but to have patience till the wind abated, and in the meantime the boatman and I concluded to sleep if we could, and so we crowded into the scuttle with the Dutchman who was still wet, and the spray breaking over the head of our boat leaked through to us, so that we were soon almost as wet as he. In this manner we lay all night with very little rest; but the wind abating the next day, we made a shift to reach Amboy before night, having been thirty hours on the water without victuals or any drink but a bottle of filthy rum, the water we sailed on being salt.

In the evening I found myself very feverish and went to bed; but having read somewhere that cold water drank plentifully was good for a fever, I followed the prescription, sweat plentifully most of the night, my fever left me, and in the morning crossing the ferry, I proceeded on my journey on foot, having fifty miles to Burlington, where I was told I should find boats that would carry me the rest of the way to Philadelphia.

It rained very hard all the day, I was thoroughly soaked and by noon a good deal tired, so I stopped at a poor inn, where I stayed all night, beginning now to wish I had never left home. I made so miserable a figure, too, that I found by the questions asked me I was suspected to be some runaway servant, and in danger of being taken up on that suspicion. However, I proceeded the next day, and got in the evening to an inn within eight or ten miles of Burlington, kept by one Dr. Brown.

He entered into conversation with me while I took some refreshment and, finding I had read a little, became very sociable and friendly. Our acquaintance continued all the rest of his life. He had been, I imagine, an itinerant doctor, for there was no town in England or any country in Europe of which he could not give a very particular account. He had some letters and was ingenious, but he was an infidel and wickedly undertook some years after to travesty the Bible in doggerel verse as Cotton had done with Virgil. By this means he set many of the facts in a very ridiculous light and might have done mischief with weak minds if his work had been published, but it never was. At his house I lay that night, and the next morning reached Burlington, but had the mortification to find that the regular boats were gone a little before and no other expected to go before Tuesday, this being Saturday. Wherefore, I returned to an old woman in the town of whom I had bought some gingerbread to eat on the water and asked her advice; she invited me to lodge at her house till a passage by water should offer; and being tired with my foot travelling, I accepted the invitation. Understanding I was a printer, she would have had

me remain in that town and follow my business, being ignorant of the stock necessary to begin with. She was very hospitable, gave me a dinner of ox cheek with great goodwill, accepting only of a pot of ale in return. And I thought myself fixed till Tuesday should come. However, walking in the evening by the side of the river, a boat came by, which I found was going towards Philadelphia with several people in her. They took me in, and as there was no wind, we rowed all the way; and about midnight, not having yet seen the city, some of the company were confident we must have passed it and would row no farther; the others knew not where we were, so we put towards the shore, got into a creek, landed near an old fence, with the rails of which we made a fire, the night being cold in October, and there we remained till daylight. Then one of the company knew the place to be Cooper's Creek, a little above Philadelphia, which we saw as soon as we got out of the creek, and arrived there about eight or nine o'clock, on the Sunday morning and landed at the Market Street wharf.

I have been the more particular in this description of my journey, and shall be so of my first entry into that city, that you may in your mind compare such unlikely beginnings with the figure I have since made there. I was in my working dress, my best clothes being to come round by sea. I was dirty from my journey; my pockets were stuffed out with shirts and stockings; I knew no soul, nor where to look for lodging. Fatigued with walking, rowing, and want of sleep, I was very hungry, and my whole stock of cash consisted of a Dutch dollar and about a shilling in copper coin, which I gave to the boatmen for my passage. At first they refused it on account of my having rowed, but I insisted on their taking it. A man is sometimes more generous when he has little money than when he has plenty, perhaps through fear of being thought to have but little. I walked towards the top of the street, gazing about till near Market Street, where I met a boy with bread. I have often made a meal of dry bread, and inquiring where he had bought it, I went immediately to the baker's he directed me to. I asked for biscuit, meaning such as we had in Boston, but that sort, it seems, was not made in Philadelphia. I then asked for a threepenny loaf and was told they had none such. Not knowing the different prices nor the names of the different sorts of any bread, I told him to give me three pennyworth of any sort. He gave me accordingly three great puffy rolls. I was surprized at the quantity but took it, and having no room in my pockets, walked off with a roll under each arm and eating the other. Thus I went up Market Street as far as Fourth Street, passing by the door of Mr. Read, my future wife's father, when she, standing at the door, saw me, and thought I made—as I certainly did—a most awkward, ridiculous appearance. Then I turned and went down Chestnut Street and part of Walnut Street, eating my roll all the way, and coming round, found myself again at Market Street wharf near the boat I came in, to which I went for a draught of the river water, and being filled with one of my rolls, gave the other two to a woman and her child that came down the river in the boat with us and were waiting to go farther. Thus refreshed, I walked again up the street, which by this time had many clean dressed people in it who were all walking the same way; I joined them, and thereby was led into the great meetinghouse of the Quakers near the market. I sat down among them, and after looking round awhile and hearing nothing said, being very drowsy through labour and want of rest the preceding night, I fell fast asleep and continued so till the meeting broke up, when someone was kind enough to rouse me. This was therefore the first house I was in or slept in, in Philadelphia.

INVENTIONS AND PUBLIC SERVICE

Here are recalled, among other things, the invention of the Franklin stove, the founding of the University of Philadelphia (the present University of Pennsylvania), and the fight against what has become known as "air pollution"—in this case, caused by the dust rising from the unpaved, uncleaned streets.

The Mr. Whitfield mentioned once or twice is the George Whitefield whose histrionic oratory helped stir the Great Awakening in the 1740's.

———————

In order of time, I should have mentioned before that, having in 1742 invented an open stove for the better warming of rooms and at the same time saving fuel, as the fresh air admitted was warmed in entering, I made a present of the model to Mr.

Robert Grace, one of my early friends, who having an iron furnace, found the casting of the plates for these stoves a profitable thing, as they were growing in demand. To promote that demand, I wrote and published a pamphlet entitled, *An Account of the New-Invented Pennsylvania Fireplaces: Wherein Their Construction and Manner of Operation is Particularly Explained, Their Advantages above Every Other Method of Warming Rooms Demonstrated; and All Objections That Have Been Raised against the Use of Them Answered and Obviated, etc.* This pamphlet had a good effect. Governor Thomas was so pleased with the construction of this stove as described in it that he offered to give me a patent for the sole vending of them for a term of years; but I declined it from a principle which has ever weighed with me on such occasions; viz., *that as we enjoy great advantages from the inventions of others, we should be glad of an opportunity to serve others by any invention of ours, and this we should do freely and generously.* An ironmonger in London, however, after assuming a good deal of my pamphlet, and working up into his own, and making some small changes in the machine, which rather hurt its operation, got a patent for it there, and made, as I was told, a little fortune by it. And this is not the only instance of patents taken out for my inventions by others, tho' not always with the same success, which I never contested, as having no desire of profiting by patents myself and hating disputes. The use of these fireplaces in very many houses both of this and the neighbouring colonies, has been and is a great saving of wood to the inhabitants.

Peace being concluded and the association business therefore at an end, I turned my thoughts again to the affair of establishing an academy. The first step I took was to associate in the design a number of active friends, of whom the Junto furnished a good part, the next was to write and publish a pamphlet entitled *Proposals Relating to the Education of Youth in Pennsylvania.* This I distributed among the principal inhabitants gratis; and as soon as I could suppose their minds a little prepared by the perusal of it, I set on foot a subscription for opening and supporting an academy; it was to be paid in quotas yearly for five years; by so dividing it I judged the subscription might be larger, and I believe it was so, amounting to no less, if I remember right, than five thousand pounds.

In the introduction to these proposals, I stated

their publication not as an act of mine, but of some "public-spirited gentlemen"; avoiding as much as I could, according to my usual rule, the presenting myself to the public as the author of any scheme for their benefit.

The subscribers, to carry the project into immediate execution, chose out of their number twenty-four trustees and appointed Mr. Francis, then Attorney-General, and myself to draw up constitutions for the government of the academy, which being done and signed, a house was hired, masters engaged, and the schools opened, I think, in the same year, 1749.

The scholars encreasing fast, the house was soon found too small, and we were looking out for a piece of ground properly situated, with intention to build, when Providence threw into our way a large house ready built, which with a few alterations might well serve our purpose. This was the building before-mentioned, erected by the hearers of Mr. Whitfield, and was obtained for us in the following manner.

It is to be noted that the contributions to this building being made by people of different sects, care was taken in the nomination of trustees, in whom the building and ground were to be vested, that a predominancy should not be given to any sect, lest in time that predominancy might be a means of appropriating the whole to the use of such sect contrary to the original intention; it was for this reason that one of each sect was appointed, viz., one Church of England man, one Presbyterian, one Baptist, one Moravian, etc.; those in case of vacancy by death were to fill it by election from among the contributors. The Moravian happened not to please his colleagues, and on his death they resolved to have no other of that sect. The difficulty then was, how to avoid having two of some other sect by means of the new choice. Several persons were named and for that reason not agreed to. At length one mentioned me, with the observation that I was merely an honest man, and of *no sect* at all—which prevailed with them to choose me. The enthusiasm which existed when the house was built had long since abated, and its trustees had not been able to procure fresh contributions for paying the ground rent and discharging some other debts the building had occasioned, which embarrassed them greatly. Being now a member of both boards of trustees, that for the building and that for the academy, I had a good opportunity of negotiating with both, and brought them finally to an agreement by which the trustees

for the building were to cede it to those of the academy, the latter undertaking to discharge the debt, to keep forever open in the building a large hall for occasional preachers according to the original intention, and maintain a free school for the instruction of poor children. Writings were accordingly drawn, and on paying the debts the trustees of the academy were put in possession of the premises, and by dividing the great and lofty hall into stories, and different rooms above and below for the several schools, and purchasing some additional ground, the whole was soon made fit for our purpose, and the scholars removed into the building. The care and trouble of agreeing with the workmen, purchasing materials, and superintending the work fell upon me, and I went thro' it the more cheerfully, as it did not then interfere with my private business, having the year before taken a very able, industrious, and honest partner, Mr. David Hall, with whose character I was well acquainted as he had worked for me four years. He took off my hands all care of the printing office, paying me punctually my share of the profits. This partnership continued eighteen years, successfully for us both.

The trustees of the academy after a while were incorporated by a charter from the Governor; their funds were increased by contributions in Britain and grants of land from the Proprietaries, to which the Assembly has since made considerable addition, and thus was established the present University of Philadelphia. I have been continued one of its trustees from the beginning, now near forty years, and have had the very great pleasure of seeing a number of the youth who have received their education in it distinguished by their improved abilities, serviceable in public stations, and ornaments to their country.

. . .

Our city, though laid out with a beautiful regularity, the streets large, straight, and crossing each other at right angles, had the disgrace of suffering those streets to remain long unpaved; and in wet weather the wheels of heavy carriages ploughed them into a quagmire so that it was difficult to cross them. And in dry weather the dust was offensive. I had lived near what was called the Jersey Market and saw with pain the inhabitants wading in mud while purchasing their provisions. A strip of ground down the middle of that market was at length paved with brick so that being once in the market they had firm footing, but were often over shoes in dirt to get there. By talking and writing on the subject, I was at length instrumental in getting the street paved with stone between the market and the bricked foot pavement that was on each side next the houses. This for some time gave an easy access to the market, dry-shod. But the rest of the street not being paved, whenever a carriage came out of the mud upon this pavement, it shook off and left its dirt upon it, and it was soon covered with mire, which was not removed, the city as yet having no scavengers. After some inquiry I found a poor, industrious man who was willing to undertake keeping the pavement clean by sweeping it twice a week and carrying off the dirt from before all the neighbors' doors, for the sum of sixpence per month, to be paid by each house. I then wrote and printed a paper, setting forth the advantages to the neighborhood that might be obtained by this small expense: the greater ease in keeping our houses clean, so much dirt not being brought in by people's feet; the benefit to the shops by more custom, as buyers could more easily get at them, and by not having in windy weather the dust blown in upon their goods, etc., etc. I sent one of these papers to each house and in a day or two went round to see who would subscribe an agreement to pay these sixpences. It was unanimously signed and for a time well executed. All the inhabitants of the city were delighted with the cleanliness of the pavement that surrounded the market, it being a convenience to all; and this raised a general desire to have all the streets paved, and made the people more willing to submit to a tax for that purpose. After some time I drew a bill for paving the city and brought it into the Assembly. It was just before I went to England in 1757 and did not pass till I was gone, and then with an alteration in the mode of assessment, which I thought not for the

better, but with an additional provision for lighting as well as paving the streets, which was a great improvement. It was by a private person, the late Mr. John Clifton, giving a sample of the utility of lamps by placing one at his door that the people were first impressed with the idea of lighting all the city. The honor of this public benefit has also been ascribed to me, but it belongs truly to that gentleman. I did but follow his example and have only some merit to claim respecting the form of our lamps as differing from the globe lamps we at first were supplied with from London. Those we found inconvenient in these respects: They admitted no air below; the smoke therefore did not readily go out above, but circulated in the globe, lodged on its inside, and soon obstructed the light they were intended to afford, giving, besides, the daily trouble of wiping them clean; and an accidental stroke on one of them would demolish it and render it totally useless. I therefore suggested the composing them of four flat panes, with a long funnel above, to draw up the smoke, and crevices admitting air below, to facilitate the ascent of the smoke. By this means they were kept clean, and did now grow dark in a few hours as the London lamps do, but continued bright till morning; and an accidental stroke would generally break but a single pane, easily repaired. I have sometimes wondered that the Londoners did not, from the effect holes in the bottom of the globe lamps used at Vauxhall have in keeping them clean, learn to have such holes in their street lamps. But those holes being made for another purpose, viz., to communicate flame more suddenly to the wick by a little flax hanging down through them, the other use of letting in air seems not to have been thought of. And therefore, after the lamps have been lit a few hours, the streets of London are very poorly illuminated.

Letter to Madame Brillon

Madame d'Hardancourt Brillon, a neighbor of Franklin's in Passy, was the most remarkable of the women whom the elderly statesman came to know during the years in France. She was married to a prosaic, if good-natured, French official some two dozen years her senior; and she found in Franklin at once a gallant and stimulating companion, and an ambiguous figure who could

serve as foster father (she called him "papa," and herself his "daughter") and a replacement for her "older-generation" husband.

Franklin was presumably not the lover of this passionate, lovely, and gifted woman. But here, as elsewhere, he remarks candidly and tenderly how much he would like to be. It should be noticed, however, that Madame Brillon called herself Franklin's "confessor," and Franklin takes the occasion to confess to the commandments he would most enjoy obeying *and* violating.

Passy, March 10, 1778

I am charm'd with the Goodness of my Spiritual Guide, and resign myself implicitly to her Conduct, as she promises to lead me to Heaven in a Road so delicious, when I could be content to travel thither even in the roughest of all the Ways with the Pleasure of her Company.

How kindly partial to her Penitent, in finding him, on examining his Conscience, guilty of only one capital Sin, and to call that by the gentle Name of a *Foible!*

I lay fast hold of your Promise to absolve me of all Sins past, present, and *future*, on the easy and pleasing Condition of loving God, America, and my Guide above all things. I am in Raptures when I thing of being absolv'd of the *future*.

People commonly speak of *Ten* Commandments. I have been taught that there are *twelve*. The *first* was, *Increase and multiply* and replenish the Earth. The *twelfth* is, A new Commandment I give unto you, *that ye love one another*. It seems to me that they are a little misplac'd, and that the last should have been the first. However, I never made any Difficulty about that, but was always willing to obey them both whenever I had an Opportunity. Pray tell me, my dear Casuist, whether my keeping religiously these two Commandments, tho' not in the Decalogue, may not be accepted in Compensation for my breaking so often one of the Ten, I mean that which forbids Coveting my Neighbor's Wife, and which I *confess* I break constantly, God forgive me, as often as I see or think of my lovely Confessor: And I am afraid I should never be able to repent of the Sin, even if I had the full Possession of her.

And now I am consulting you upon a Case of Conscience, I will mention the Opinion of a certain Father of the Church, which I find myself willing to adopt, tho' I am not sure it is orthodox. It is this, That the most effectual Way to get rid of a certain Temptation, is, as often as it returns, to comply with and satisfy it. Pray instruct me how far I may venture to practise upon this Principle?

But why should I be so scrupulous, when you have promised to absolve me of the *future!*

Adieu, my charming Conductress, and believe me ever, with the sincerest Esteem and Affection,

Your most obedient and humble Servant

Remarks on the Politeness of the Savages of North America (1784)

Soon after Franklin, as American commissioner, established himself in Passy—diplomatically halfway between Paris and his enthusiastic admirers there and the uncommitted court at Versailles—he set up a private printing press. Once a printer, always a printer: but Franklin had need of a press to get out the many documents his complicated mission required. He also used the press for more relaxed items and for occasional essays.

Franklin called them his "bagatelles"—light-hearted throwaways, as it were. Yet each of them contained a portion of himself. One of the most expressive is the following, where Franklin's deep antiracism shows to wittiest effect.

Franklin wrote this and the other pieces in French as a language exercise (the French,

most of whom liked everything about him, even liked his faulty French grammar), then translated them into English.

———

Savages we call them, because their manners differ from ours, which we think the Perfection of Civility; they think the same of theirs.

Perhaps if we could examine the manners of different Nations with Impartiality, we should find no People so rude as to be without any Rules of Politeness; nor any so polite as not to have some remains of Rudeness.

The Indian Men, when young, are Hunters and Warriors; when old, Counsellors; for all their Government is by the Counsel or Advice of the Sages; there is no Force, there are no Prisons, no Officers to compel Obedience, or inflict Punishment. Hence they generally study Oratory; the best Speaker having the most Influence. The Indian Women till the Ground, dress the Food, nurse and bring up the Children, and preserve and hand down to Posterity the Memory of Public Transactions. These Employments of Men and Women are accounted natural and honorable. Having few Artificial Wants, they have abundance of Leisure for Improvement by Conversation. Our laborious manner of Life compared with theirs, they esteem slavish and base; and the Learning on which we value ourselves; they regard as frivolous and useless. An Instance of this occurred at the Treaty of Lancaster in Pennsylvania, Anno 1744, between the Government of Virginia & the Six Nations. After the principal Business was settled, the Commissioners from Virginia acquainted the Indians by a Speech, that there was at Williamsburg a College with a Fund for Educating Indian Youth, and that if the Chiefs of the Six-Nations would send down half a dozen of their Sons to that College, the Government would take Care that they should be well provided for, and instructed in all the Learning of the white People. It is one of the Indian Rules of Politeness not to answer a public Proposition the same day that it is made; they think it would be treating it as a light Matter; and that they show it Respect by taking time to consider it, as of a Matter important. They therefore deferred their Answer till the day following; when their Speaker began by expressing their deep Sense of the Kindness of the Virginia Government, in making them that Offer; for we know, says he, that you highly esteem the kind of Learning taught in those Colleges, and that the Maintenance of our Young Men while with you, would be very expensive to you. We are convinced therefore that you mean to do us good by your Proposal, and we thank you heartily. But you who are wise must know, that different Nations have different Conceptions of things; and you will therefore not take it amiss, if our Ideas of this Kind of Education happen not to be the same with yours. We have had some Experience of it: Several of our Young People were formerly brought up at the Colleges of the Northern Provinces; they were instructed in all your Sciences; but when they came back to us, they were bad Runners, ignorant of every means of living in the Woods, unable to bear either Cold or Hunger, knew neither how to build a Cabin, take a Deer, or kill an Enemy, spoke our Language imperfectly; were therefore neither fit for Hunters, Warriors, or Counsellors; they were totally good for nothing. We are however not the less obliged by your kind Offer, tho' we decline accepting it; and to show our grateful Sense of it, if the Gentlemen of Virginia will send us a dozen of their Sons, we will take great Care of their Education, instruct them in all we know, and make *Men* of them.

Having frequent Occasions to hold public Councils, they have acquired great Order and Decency in conducting them. The old Men sit in the foremost Ranks, the Warriors in the next, and the Women and Children in the hindmost. The Business of the Women is to take exact notice of what passes, imprint it in their Memories, for they have no Writing, and communicate it to their Children. They are the Records of the Council, and they preserve Tradition of the Stipulations in Treaties a hundred Years back, which when we compare with our Writings we always find exact. He that would speak, rises. The rest observe a profound Silence. When he has finished and sits down, they leave him five or six Minutes to recollect, that if he has omitted any thing he intended to say, or has any thing to add, he may rise again and deliver it. To interrupt another, even in common Conversation, is reckoned highly indecent. How different this is from the Conduct of a polite British House of Commons, where scarce a Day passes without some Confusion that makes the Speaker hoarse in calling *to order*; and how different from the mode of Conversation in many polite Companies of Europe, where if you do not deliver your Sentence with great Rapidity, you are cut off in the middle of it by the impatient Loquacity of those you converse with, & never suffer'd to finish it.

The Politeness of these Savages in Conversation is indeed carried to excess, since it does not permit them to contradict, or deny the Truth of what is asserted in their Presence. By this means they indeed avoid Disputes, but then it becomes difficult to know their Minds, or what Impression you make upon them. The Missionaries who have attempted to convert them to Christianity, all complain of this as one of the great Difficulties of their Mission. The Indians hear with Patience the Truths of the Gospel explained to them, and give their usual Tokens of Assent and Approbation: you would think they were convinced. No such Matter. It is mere Civility.

A Suedish Minister having assembled the Chiefs of the Sasquehanah Indians, made a Sermon to them, acquainting them with the principal historical Facts on which our Religion is founded, such as the Fall of our first Parents by Eating an Apple, the Coming of Christ to repair the Mischief, his Miracles and Suffering, &c. When he had finished, an Indian Orator stood up to thank him. What you have told us, says he, is all very good. It is indeed bad to eat Apples. It is better to make them all into Cyder. We are much obliged by your Kindness in coming so far to tell us those things which you have heard from your Mothers. In Return I will tell you some of those we have heard from ours.

In the Beginning our Fathers had only the Flesh of Animals to subsist on, and if their Hunting was unsuccessful, they were starving. Two of our young Hunters having killed a Deer, made a Fire in the Woods to broil some Parts of it. When they were about to satisfy their Hunger, they beheld a beautiful young Woman descend from the Clouds, and seat herself on that Hill which you see yonder among the blue Mountains. They said to each other, it is a Spirit that perhaps has smelt our broiling Venison, & wishes to eat of it: let us offer some to her. They presented her with the Tongue: She was pleased with the Taste of it, & said, your Kindness shall be rewarded. Come to this Place after thirteen Moons, and you shall find something that will be of great Benefit in nourishing you and your Children to the latest Generations. They did so, and to their Surprise found Plants they had never seen before, but which from that ancient time have been constantly cultivated among us to our great Advantage. Where her right Hand had touch'd the Ground, they found Maize; where her left Hand touch'd it, they found Kidney-beans; and where her Backside had sat on it, they found Tobacco. The good Missionary, disgusted with this idle Tale, said, what I delivered to you were sacred Truths: but what you tell me is mere Fable, Fiction & Falsehood. The Indian offended, reply'd, my Brother, it seems your Friends have not done you Justice in your Education; they have not well instructed you in the Rules of common Civility. You saw that we who understand and practise those Rules, believed all your Stories; why do you refuse to believe ours?

When any of them come into our Towns, our People are apt to croud round them, gaze upon them, and incommode them where they desire to be private; this they esteem great Rudeness, and the Effect of want of Instruction in the Rules of Civility and good Manners. We have, say they, as much curiosity as you, and when you come into our Towns we wish for Opportunities of looking

at you; but for this purpose we hide ourselves behind Bushes where you are to pass, and never intrude ourselves into your Company.

Their Manner of entring one anothers Villages has likewise its Rules. It is reckon'd uncivil in travelling Strangers to enter a Village abruptly, without giving Notice of their Approach. Therefore as soon as they arrive within hearing, they stop and hollow, remaining there till invited to enter. Two old Men usually come out to them, and lead them in. There is in every Village a vacant Dwelling, called the Strangers House. Here they are placed, while the old Men go round from Hut to Hut acquainting the Inhabitants that Strangers are arrived, who are probably hungry and weary; and every one sends them what he can spare of Victuals and Skins to repose on. When the Strangers are refresh'd, Pipes & Tobacco are brought; and then, but not before, Conversation begins, with Enquiries who they are, whither bound, what News, &c. and it usually ends with Offers of Service, if the Strangers have Occasion of Guides or any Necessaries for continuing their Journey; and nothing is exacted for the Entertainment.

The same Hospitality, esteemed among them as a principal Virtue, is practised by private Persons; of which *Conrad Weiser*, our Interpreter, gave me the following Instance. He had been naturaliz'd among the Six-Nations, and spoke well the Mohock Language. In going thro' the Indian Country, to carry a Message from our Governor to the Council at *Onondaga*, he called at the Habitation of *Canassetego*, an old Acquaintance, who embraced him, spread Furs for him to sit on, placed before him some boiled Beans and Venison, and mixed some Rum and Water for his Drink. When he was well refresh'd, and had lit his Pipe, Canassetego began to converse with him, ask'd how he had fared the many Years since they had seen each other, whence he then came, what occasioned the Journey, &c. &c. Conrad answered all his Questions; and when the Discourse began to flag, the Indian, to continue it, said, Conrad, you have liv'd long among the white People, and know something of their Customs; I have been sometimes at Albany, and have observed that once in seven Days, they shut up their Shops and assemble all in the great House; tell me, what it is for? what do they do there? They meet there, says Conrad, to hear & learn *good things*. I do not doubt, says the Indian, that they tell you so; they have told me the same; but I doubt the Truth of what they say, & I will tell you my Reasons. I went lately to Albany to sell my Skins, & buy Blankets, Knives, Powder, Rum, &c. You know I used generally to deal with Hans Hanson; but I was a little inclined this time to try some other Merchants. However I called first upon Hans, and ask'd him what he would give for Beaver; He said he could not give more than four Shillings a Pound; but, says he, I cannot talk on Business now; this is the Day when we meet together to learn *good things*, and I am going to the Meeting. So I thought to myself since I cannot do any Business to day, I may as well go to the Meeting too; and I went with him. There stood up a Man in black, and began to talk to the People very angrily. I did not understand what he said; but perceiving that he looked much at me, & at Hanson, I imagined he was angry at seeing me there; so I went out, sat down near the House, struck Fire & lit my Pipe; waiting till the Meeting should break up. I thought too, that the Man had mentioned something of Beaver, and I suspected it might be the Subject of their Meeting. So when they came out I accosted my Merchant; well Hans, says I, I hope you have agreed to give more than four Shillings a Pound. No, says he, I cannot give so much. I cannot give more than three Shillings and six Pence. I then spoke to several other Dealers, but they all sung the same Song, three & six Pence, three & six Pence. This made it clear to me that my Suspicion was right; and that whatever they pretended of Meeting to learn *good things*, the real Purpose was to consult, how to cheat Indians in the Price of Beaver. Consider but a little, Conrad, and you must be of my Opinion. If they met so often to learn *good things*, they would certainly have learnt some before this time. But they are still ignorant. You know our Practice. If a white Man in travelling thro' our Country, enters one of our Cabins, we all treat him as I treat you; we dry him if he is wet, we warm him if he is cold, and give him Meat & Drink that he may allay his Thirst and Hunger, & we spread soft Furs for him to rest & sleep on: We demand nothing in return.[1] But if I go into a white Man's House at Albany, and ask for Victuals & Drink, they say, where is your Money? and if I have none, they say, get out, you Indian Dog. You see they have not yet learnt those little *good things*, that we need no Meetings to be instructed in, because our Mothers taught them to us when we were Children. And therefore it is impossible their Meetings should be as they say for any such purpose, or have any such Effect; they are only to contrive *the Cheating of Indians in the Price of Beaver*.

---

[1] *It is remarkable that in all Ages and Countries, Hospitality has been allowed as the Virtue of those, whom the civiliz'd were pleased to call Barbarians; the Greeks celebrated the Scythians for it. The Saracens possess'd it eminently; and it is to this day the reigning Virtue of the wild Arabs. S. Paul too, in the Relation of his Voyage & Shipwreck, on the Island of Melita, says,* The Barbarous People shew'd us no little Kindness; for they kindled a Fire, and received us every one, because of the present Rain & because of the Cold [Franklin].

Letter to George Washington

Lafayette came back to Paris from America in 1779, bearing a letter of recommendation to Franklin from Washington but was so modest as to withhold it for a year. This is Franklin's reply. The praise Franklin quite nobly bestows upon Washington gains further point from Franklin's expressed awareness that the general, like himself, had had to struggle against malice and envy while carrying on the great task.

Passy, March 5, 1780

I have received but lately the Letter your Excellency did me the honour of writing to me in Recommendation of the Marquis de la Fayette. His modesty detained it long in his own Hands. We became acquainted, however, from the time of his Arrival at Paris; and his Zeal for the Honour of our Country, his Activity in our Affairs here, and his firm Attachment to our Cause and to you, impress'd me with the same Regard and Esteem for him that your Excellency's Letter would have done, had it been immediately delivered to me.

Should peace arrive after another Campaign or two, and afford us a little Leisure, I should be happy to see your Excellency in Europe, and to accompany you, if my Age and Strength would permit, in visiting some of its ancient and most famous Kingdoms. You would, on this side of the Sea, enjoy the great Reputation you have acquir'd, pure and free from those little Shades that the Jealousy and Envy of a Man's Countrymen and Cotemporaries are ever endeavouring to cast over living Merit. Here you would know, and enjoy, what Posterity will say of Washington. For 1000 Leagues have nearly the same Effect with 1000 Years. The feeble Voice of those grovelling Passions cannot extend so far either in Time or Distance. At present I enjoy that Pleasure for you, as I frequently hear the old Generals of this martial Country, (who study the Maps of America, and mark upon them all your Operations), speak with sincere Approbation and great Applause of your conduct; and join in giving you the Character of one of the greatest Captains of the Age.

I must soon quit the Scene, but you may live to see our Country flourish, as it will amazingly and rapidly after the War is over. Like a Field of young Indian Corn, which long Fair weather and Sunshine had enfeebled and discolored, and which in that weak State, by a Thunder Gust, of violent Wind, Hail, and Rain, seem'd to be threaten'd with absolute Destruction; yet the Storm being past, it recovers fresh Verdure, shoots up with double Vigour, and delights the Eye, not of its Owner only, but of every observing Traveller.

The best Wishes that can be form'd for your Health, Honour, and Happiness, ever attend you from your Excellency's most obedient and most humble servant.

JOHN WOOLMAN (1720–1772)

The fact that Benjamin Franklin of Philadelphia and Jonathan Edwards of Massachusetts were contemporaries says much about the varieties and contrasts that have shaped American cultural history. The fact that John Woolman of New Jersey was a younger contemporary of both men perhaps says even more. If Franklin was the archetypal pragmatist, man of the world, and insatiably curious experimenter; and Edwards the quintessential Calvinist and most darkly rigorous of theologians; then Woolman may be taken as the exemplary Quaker—that is, as a man for whom all other human beings were quite literally "friends," a man utterly committed (to use the title of one of his writings) to "the true harmony of mankind." Given the circumstances of his time, his place, and his temperament, the gravest obstacle to true harmony in American society, for Woolman, was Negro slavery. He was our first whole-souled abolitionist: the great philosopher Alfred North Whitehead was right to say (in *Adventures in Ideas*, 1933) that the honor of working out the first serious case against slavery "belongs to the Quakers, and in particular to that Apostle of Freedom, John Woolman." Woolman, indeed, explored the relationship between black Amer-

icans and white Americans, discussed it, and—very quietly—took action about it to a degree beyond that of any writer until recent years. Few men of his age speak so directly to the conditions of our own day; one of the several studies of him is called *John Woolman: His Life and Our Times*, by W. Teignmouth Shore, and though that book was written in 1913, the subtitle still applies.

Woolman was born on his father's farm in Rancocas, a village on the river of that name in the province of West Jersey, about eighteen miles from Philadelphia. His parents were people of some means, and though Woolman was the fourth of thirteen children he was brought up in rather more comfort than he later liked to remember. After attending a Quaker school for some years, he set up a tailoring shop in Mount Holly. He also performed services as a sort of legal consultant and notary public, drawing up wills and executing deeds of sale (for example, the sale of a Negro slave described in one of our selections). The two trades combined brought him an income he regarded as excessive; and in 1743 he gave them up to become a Quaker minister. He spent the rest of his life in the ministry, traveling up and down the eastern seaboard, as far north as New Hampshire and as far south as South Carolina, attending Quaker "meetings," spreading the word, conversing with friends, studying social conditions. In 1770, he journied to England; there, while visiting friends in York, he came down with smallpox, and he died in October, 1772, composed and considerate to the end.

Woolman's major work was his *Journal of the Life and Travels of John Woolman in the Service of the Gospel*, first published two years after his death. There have been scores of editions of this remarkable document, including one (in 1871) with an introduction by Woolman's most obvious spiritual descendant, the New England Quaker abolitionist and poet, John Greenleaf Whittier. The English essayist Charles Lamb once remarked—in London, to a visiting American journalist, N. P. Willis—that Woolman's *Journal* was "the only American book I ever read twice." Woolman's character, Lamb added, "is one of the finest I ever met with. He tells a story or two about Negro slaves, that brought the tears into my eyes."[1] The discussion of slavery in the *Journal* is anecdotal, sporadically meditative, and self-searching. Woolman's organized argument in favor of abolition, and against all the proslavery convictions and prejudices, was contained in *Some Considerations on the Keeping of Negroes*, which he wrote in his late twenties, submitted to his dying father for approval and minor corrections, and had published in 1754. Our selections are taken from these two writings.

Woolman came to his abolitionist beliefs out of a Quaker training modified by his personal religious nature. The West Jersey community he grew up and resided in, when not on his travels, was predominantly Quaker. George Fox (1624–1691), the weaver's son from Leicestershire who had founded the Society of Friends, and who left his own journal account of the persecution he and his fellow Quakers had suf-

[1] The easygoing poetaster Willis, in his report on this conversation in the New York *Mirror*, got the name wrong and referred to *Edward* Woolman; Willis would have had no taste for the book if he had ever heard of it.

fered, visited the region in 1672; three years later, the first Quaker immigrants from London arrived at the mouth of the Delaware River, fleeing the savage intolerance Fox described. Their numbers were swelled not only by further clusters of English refugees, but equally by Quakers coming down from New England, after giving up the struggle against Puritan oppression (see pp. 10–11). The New Jersey Quakers, like those in nearby Pennsylvania, were thus able to live out their lives free from the psychological, physical, and legal pressures exerted against their fellows in Massachusetts and England. They could practice their religion in the peaceful and amicable way originally intended, without recourse to the sometimes antic disruptive tactics observable elsewhere.

The essence, indeed almost the whole, of Quaker belief was the principle of the Inner Light—an interior radiation through which God spoke immediately to every individual human spirit, directing the individual with perfect clarity to true understanding and proper action. There was nothing particularly new about this doctrine: it can be traced back to the origins of Christian theory, and behind it. What was new was the Quaker application of it, in a kind of burning assurance that the Inner Light would not merely guide the believer's personal life, but would eventually revolutionize the social order —put it on an altogether different footing of love and trust—and bring about the Kingdom of God on earth.

The Quakers, accordingly, never "did" things; they were "moved" to do things by the welling up of God's light in their souls; and this was nowhere more evident than at the "meetings" (weekly, monthly, quarterly, and yearly) at which the present and future of the Quaker faith were thought about. Commonly, at such meetings, silence would reign throughout the assembly for an hour or more; then a minister might be moved to utter three or four words, before falling silent for a period of reflection; then another few words, and further silence. In this way was God's future kingdom in America haltingly and unheatedly contemplated.

As a minister, John Woolman had little to

say about the coming millennium or the religious experiment in which the Quakers were engaged: he was, so to speak, an exceedingly levelheaded mystic and concerned himself with the conditions and tendencies that most closely surrounded him. It was, nonetheless, his peculiar sense of the Inner Light that led him to the positions he adopted on a number of issues—positions all the harder both to arrive at and to maintain since they ran counter to the actual practices of most of his coreligionists. In the 1750's, for instance, when General Braddock's English troops were skirmishing locally with French and Indian forces, a number of young Quakers with patriotic zeal joined the English; others paid without demur the taxes Braddock imposed to support the militia. Woolman thought and worried his way—guided, as he was sure, by God—to what appeared to him the only possible stance for a Quaker Christian: that of unequivocal pacifism. He faced, resolutely enough, what is sometimes taken as the ultimate test by those inquiring into the sincerity of persons who claim to object to violence of any kind on the grounds of conscience: what would you do if your own country, or neighborhood, were invaded by an enemy bent on conquest? Woolman did not pretend the question was easy, but he had no doubt of his answer: "It requires great self-denial and resignation of ourselves to God, to attain that state wherein we can freely cease from fighting when wrongfully invaded, if, by our fighting, there were a possibility of overcoming the invaders." But the choice once made brings the individual closer to the martyred Christ: "Whoever rightly attains to it, does, in some degree, feel that spirit in which our Redeemer gave his life for us" (*Journal*, Chap. 5).

A century before Thoreau made the gesture of going to jail rather than pay a governmental tax to carry on what he took to be an unjust war, Woolman unobtrusively withheld his own tax payment. Once again, it was a painful decision, and Woolman found himself alone in his action:

> To refuse the active payment of a Tax which our Society generally paid, was exceedingly

disagreeable; but to do a thing contrary to my conscience appeared yet more dreadfull. When this exercise came upon me I knew of none under the like difficulty, and in my distress I besought the Lord to give up all, that so I might follow him wheresoever he pleased to lead me. (*Journal*, Chap. 5)

It should be said here that, while Woolman has certain clear affinities with Thoreau—and perhaps even more with Emerson's doctrine of self-reliance and the individual's nearly total dependence on the urgings of his personal spirit—there is a marked difference in tone and in psychic attitude between Woolman's characteristic writing and that of the nineteenth-century idealists. There is, to put it most simply, much less of the *self* in Woolman's utterances: because there is so much more of God. However admirable, even noble, the attitudes espoused by Thoreau and Emerson may often have been, one cannot but feel that they are basically assertions of a particular ego (Thoreau, the elder Henry James would conclude, was "literally the most childlike, unconscious and unblushing egotist it has ever been my fortune to encounter"). The personality we meet in Woolman's *Journal* is not only unfailingly sweet-tempered and charitable; *in* itself it is at once self-effacing and mentally unsure—every firm conviction it reaches and all the strength to hang onto it come, Woolman makes us feel, from God's illumination of his soul.

Another fruitful comparison: like Roger Williams (see pp. 59–60), Woolman was a singularly attractive person who nonetheless carried a belief, mildly operative with others, to its extreme of significance; yet Woolman had none of Williams' argumentativeness. The danger of any principle like that of the Inner Light is that the believer is tempted to impose upon his community his private, idiosyncratic, and perhaps aggressive opinions. No American believed more deeply in the Inner Light than Woolman; and, so believing, no one pronounced his individual views more softly.

An instance of Woolman's habitual manner occurred in the late 1750's, in Lemon Grove,

Pennsylvania. Woolman and several others had gone to take supper at the home of a prosperous farmer. At the afternoon meeting, Woolman had spoken in favor of abolition; now, arriving at the farmhouse, he discovered there were Negro slaves on the premises, and at once inconspicuously departed, not to return. The next morning, the farmer abruptly informed his wife that he was going to free their slaves, including his wife's favorite slavewoman and companion, Beth—lest Woolman never visit them again.

As the *Journal* candidly reveals, though Woolman was uneasy about slavery from the outset, he did not at first oppose it altogether. He tells us in the opening chapter how he had once reluctantly executed the deed of sale of his employer's woman slave. The passage follows closely upon the account of his remonstrating with an acquaintance whose house had been the scene of disorderly conduct during the Christmas season. By and large, the *Journal* is quite artless as to construction and style; but here it is possible that Woolman intended to suggest, by the juxtaposition, that as he had been somewhat priggish in the one instance so he had been weak in the other. In any event, when the occasion next arose to handle a slave sale, Woolman courteously refused, offering his reasons; and a good deal later (in Chap. 9), he shows how he finally made reparation of a sort for the sale he did help complete.

By this time, Woolman was evincing the greatest scruple against being contaminated in any way by association with slavery: on his trip to Virginia, for example (Chap. 4), he devised a little scheme whereby he could avoid being given free entertainment by the slaveholders whose homes he stayed in—such entertainment, as he knew, being made economically possible only by "the gain of oppression." He was, meanwhile, encountering at every turn the going attitudes toward the blacks and slavery: attitudes which, with the terms changed only a trifle, sound familiar enough in postslavery America. Slaves didn't work nearly as hard as white laborers (this and the next two contentions are found in Chap. 4): Why on earth should they? Woolman asked—slaves, with only

a life of slavery to look forward to, were forced to work "to support others who claim them as their property." It was a kindness to remove the blacks from Africa, where they were unhappy. This, Woolman replied gently, was hypocritical nonsense: slaves were taken from Africa purely for material profit; and if by any chance some *had* been seized out of kindness, why then were they not treated in this country with the same kindness? Why were they not set free? The Negro race descended from the murderous Cain and bore his mark: at this stage, Woolman patiently went over the Biblical and historical evidence to refute the absurd charge.[2]

But it was in *Some Considerations on the Keeping of Negroes* that Woolman marshaled his full resources to indict slavery, to urge instant abolition, and to demolish the arguments in favor of the institution. God, he said again and again, is no respecter of persons—*or of colors.* "All nations are of one blood," and we are all subject to the same frailties, temptations, death, and judgment; all men are brothers, not just some or most, and it is profoundly wrong to suppose that one nation or one race is by nature superior or inferior to any other. As to color, Woolman meets head on the deeply buried prejudice of whites about blackness as such (with some hinted awareness of the fear and hatred involved). The bias against blackness had become so ingrained in the white men's mentality—"the deceivableness of unrighteousness gets so rooted in their intellects"—that they are not even able to examine the question. But "the colour of a man avails nothing," and it is imperative for white men to make the most strenuous effort to escape this bigoted fixation.

Against the claim that Negroes were abject, coarse, dirty, shifty, and so on, Woolman asks that their circumstances be calmly considered. Suppose whites were in a like situation: servile, destitute, ignorant, seeing the fruit of their labor enjoyed by others; suppose white men

---

[2] It may be remembered that for the Quaker the Bible was not the absolute and unequivocal word of God, as it was for the Puritans. The Bible was the great record of religious experience and history; it could support but could not supplant the working of the light within.

"had generally been treated as a contemptible ignorant part of mankind: should we, in that case, be less abject than they now are?" But, Woolman hears it being said, surely the slaveholder deserves some recompense for the risks he has taken in the slave trade, and the money he has invested. That would be true, Woolman replies, if the enterprise were just and reasonable; but since in fact it had been wrong to begin with, that argument has no force at all. He then confronts the kind of allegation one is used rather to hearing from (as it were) the other side: the notion of inherited guilt, and specifically that the Negroes of Woolman's day should be held accountable for the sins and crimes, whatever they may have been, of their black ancestors. This supposition, Woolman says in a moment of unusual warmth, is "too gross to be admitted into the mind of any person, who sincerely desires to be governed by solid principles."

Perhaps Woolman's most penetrating insight, or so it may seem from our vantage point, was that slaveholding, in addition to being monstrously unjust to the Negroes (and counter to every tenet of Christianity), also worked to the severe moral detriment of the slaveholder. The principle invoked here is as old as that of Socrates in Plato's *Republic*, when he maintained at some length that it was much more damaging to the individual character to do injustice than to receive it; but a long chapter of American social history bears ample witness to the truth of Woolman's observation. Woolman put the case largely in terms of human greed— that is, the overweening desire of white Americans for the life of luxury that caused them to exploit and uphold slavery; whereas, he insisted on the basis of reason, illumination, and experience, luxury is rather the enemy of virtue and human contentment than the reverse.

Woolman himself grew more austere as the years passed. He refused to eat sugar, because Negro slaves had taken part in producing it. He took an aversion to wearing clothes that had been dyed even the simplest color, and his "peculiar" manner of dress became a subject for perplexed comment among his friends. Just before he died in England, while arranging for his burial, he asked that his clothes be given to the gravedigger as payment for his work; the gravedigger, having done the job, found none of Woolman's clothes worth taking and made off only with his boots.

Woolman had little traceable impact upon the social conditions of his time. In 1769, the provincial New Jersey government, moving in a recognizably practical American fashion, imposed a high tariff on imported slaves (many years earlier, a similar tax had been passed by the Pennsylvania legislature, only to have it vetoed by the British queen); and this challenge to the pocketbook may have somewhat reduced the slave business. In 1776, at the annual meeting of Friends in Philadelphia (which Woolman had often attended and addressed), it was voted to bar any members who had not freed their slaves. But Woolman's influence worked quietly and almost surreptitiously through his writings, reaching one kind of peak in the antislavery agitation before the Civil War, when it was felt in particular by Whittier (who later wrote a poem in honor of "meek-hearted Woolman").

When we come to the nineteenth-century abolitionists later in this volume (in the introductory note to Part 3), we shall make the point that northern abolitionism did not by and large mean antiracism; that it was shot through with vituperation, as much or more against northern deviationists from the strict line as against southern slaveholders; and that, in its self-righteousness, it tended to give absolute authority to the individual conscience as against the collective opinion of society. Woolman, by contrast, really was antiracist; black men and black women were his brothers and sisters as closely as any other persons on earth. It can be doubted, moreover, that Woolman ever in his lifetime indulged in vituperation: he argued, he debated, he questioned, he insisted; but he never scolded and never vilified. And if his constant appeal for divine guidance may to some appear very remotely similar to the abolitionists' appeal to "the higher law" (and thus perhaps a mask of the assertive ego), it can only be said that the tone and texture of his characteristic expression are utterly different from the characteristic abolitionist oration. No man can say whether God did or did not light up Woolman's heart; but no reader can fail to sense the compassion, the charity, and the humility that sound so gently in his pages.

FURTHER READINGS

Amelia M. Gummere, ed., *The Journal and Essays* (1922)

Rufus Jones, *Quakers in the American Colonies* (1911)

W. Teignmouth Shore, *John Woolman: His Life and Our Times* (1913)

F. B. Tolles, *Quakers in the Atlantic Culture* (1960; a collection of essays)

From *the* Journal of the Life and Travels of John Woolman in the Service of the Gospel (1774)

Instead of offering one or two long passages intact from Woolman's writings, it has seemed to us more useful to present what is in effect a little anthology of his remarks on Negro slavery: actual slaves and slaveholders, and the unjust and unchristian nature of the institution itself. Most of these shorter passages have been commented upon in the introduction.

FROM CHAPTER 1

About the time called Christmas, I observed many people from the country, and dwellers in town, who, resorting to public-houses, spent their time in drinking and vain sports, tending to corrupt one another; on which account I was much troubled. At one house in particular there was much disorder; and I believed it was a duty incumbent on me to go and speak to the master of that house. I considered I was young, and that several elderly Friends in town had opportunity to see these things; but though I would gladly have been excused, yet I could not feel my mind clear.

The exercise was heavy: and as I was reading what the Almighty said to Ezekiel, respecting his duty as a watchman, the matter was set home more clearly; and then, with prayers and tears, I besought the Lord for his assistance, who, in loving kindness, gave me a resigned heart: then, at a suitable opportunity, I went to the public house; and seeing the man amongst much company, I went to him, and told him, I wanted to speak with him; so we went aside, and there, in the fear and dread of the Almighty, I exprest to him what rested on my mind; which he took kindly, and afterwards shewed more regard to me than before. In a few years afterwards he died, middle-aged; and I often thought, that had I neglected my duty in that case, it would have given me great trouble; and I was humbly thankful to my gracious Father, who had supported me herein.

My employer having a Negro woman, sold her, and desired me to write a bill of sale, the man being waiting who bought her: the thing was sudden; and though the thoughts of writing an instrument of slavery for one of my fellow-creatures felt uneasy, yet I remembered I was hired by the year, that it was my master who directed me to do it, and that it was an elderly man, a member of our society who bought her; so, through weakness I gave way, and wrote it; but at the executing of it, I was so afflicted in my mind, that I said before my master and the Friend, that I believed slave-keeping to be a practice inconsistent with the christian religion: this in some degree abated my uneasiness; yet, as often as I reflected seriously upon it, I thought I should have been clearer, if I had desired to be excused from it, as a thing against my conscience; for such it was. And some time after this, a young man, of our society, spoke to me to write a conveyance of a slave to him; he having lately taken a Negro into his house: I told him, I was not easy to write it; for, though many of our meeting and in other places kept slaves, I still believed the practice was not right; and desired to be excused from the writing: I spoke to him in good will; and he told me, that keeping slaves was not altogether agreeable to his mind; but that the slave being a gift made to his wife, he had accepted of her.

FROM CHAPTER 3

About this time believing it good for me to settle, and thinking seriously about a companion, my heart was turned to the Lord with desires that he would give me wisdom to proceed therein agreeable to his will; and He was pleased to give me a well-inclined damsel, Sarah Ellis; to whom I was married the eighteenth day of the eighth month, in the year 1749.

In the fall of the year 1750 died my father, Samuel Woolman, with a fever, aged about sixty years.

In his life-time he manifested much care for us his children, that in our youth we might learn to fear the Lord; often endeavouring to imprint in our minds the true principles of virtue, and particularly to cherish in us a spirit of tenderness, not only towards poor people, but also towards all creatures of which we had the command.

After my return from Carolina in the year 1746, I made some observations on keeping slaves, which some time before his decease I shewed him; and he perused the manuscript, proposed a few alterations, and appeared well satisfied that I found a concern on that account: and in his last sickness, as I was watching with him one night, he being so far spent that there was no expectation of his recovery, but had the perfect use of his understanding, he asked me concerning the manuscript, whether I expected soon to proceed to take the advice of Friends in publishing it? and after some conversation thereon said, I have all along been deeply affected with the oppression of the poor negroes; and now, at last, my concern for them is as great as ever.

. . .

About this time, a person at some distance lying sick, his brother came to me to write his will. I knew he had slaves; and asking his brother, was told he intended to leave them as slaves to his children. As writing is a profitable employ, and

offending sober people was disagreeable to my inclination, I was straitened in my mind; but as I looked to the Lord, he inclined my heart to his testimony: and I told the man, that I believed the practice of continuing slavery to this people was not right; and had a scruple in my mind against doing writings of that kind: that though many in our society kept them as slaves, still I was not easy to be concerned in it; and desired to be excused from going to write the will. I spake to him in the fear of the Lord: and he made no reply to what I said, but went away: he also had some concerns in the practice, and I thought he was displeased with me. In this case I had a fresh confirmation, that acting contrary to present outward interest, from a motive of Divine love, and in regard to truth and righteousness, and thereby incurring the resentments of people, opens the way to a treasure better than silver, and to a friendship exceeding the friendship of men.

The manuscript before mentioned having laid by me several years, the publication of it rested weightily upon me; and this year I offered it to the revisal of Friends; who having examined and made some small alterations in it, directed a number of copies thereof to be published and dispersed amongst Friends.

FROM CHAPTER 4

Feeling the exercise in relation to a visit to the southern provinces to increase upon me, I acquainted our monthly-meeting therewith, and obtained their certificate: expecting to go alone, one of my brothers, who lived in Philadelphia, having some business in North-Carolina, proposed going with me part of the way; but as he had a view of some outward affairs, to accept of him as a companion seemed some difficulty with me, whereupon I had conversation with him at sundry times: and at length, feeling easy in my mind, I had conversation with several elderly Friends of Philadelphia on the subject; and he obtaining a certificate suitable to the occasion, we set off in the fifth month of the year 1757: and coming to Nottingham week-day meeting, lodged at John Churchman's; and here I met with our friend Benjamin Buffington, from New-England, who was returning from a visit to the southern provinces. Thence we crossed the river Susquehannah, and lodged at William Cox's in Maryland; and soon after I entered this province a deep and painful exercise came upon me, which I often had some feeling of since my mind was drawn toward these parts, and with which I had acquainted my brother before we agreed to join as companions.

As the people in this and the southern provinces live much on the labour of slaves, many of whom are used hardly, my concern was, that I might attend with singleness of heart to the voice of the true Shepherd, and be so supported as to remain unmoved at the faces of men.

As it is common for Friends on such a visit to have entertainment free of cost, a difficulty arose in my mind with respect to saving my money by kindness received, which to me appeared to be the gain of oppression.

Receiving a gift, considered as a gift, brings the receiver under obligations to the benefactor, and has a natural tendency to draw the obliged into a party with the giver. To prevent difficulties of this kind, and to preserve the minds of judges from any bias, was that divine prohibition; "Thou shalt not receive any gift: for a gift blindeth the wise, and perverteth the words of the righteous." Exod. xxiii.8. As the disciples were sent forth without any provision for their journey, and our Lord said, The workman is worthy of his meat, their labour in the gospel was considered as a reward for their entertainment, and therefore not received as a gift; yet, in regard to my present journey, I could not see my way clear in that respect. The difference appeared thus: The entertainment the disciples met with, was from such whose hearts God had opened to receive them, from a love to them, and the Truth they published: but we, considered as members of the same religious society, look upon it as a piece of civility to receive each other in such visits; and such reception, at times, is partly in regard to reputation, and not from an inward unity of heart and spirit. Conduct is more convincing than language; and where people, by their actions, manifest that the slave-trade is not so disagreeable to their principles but that it may be encouraged, there is not a sound uniting with some friends who visit them.

The prospect of so weighty a work, and being so distinguished from many who I esteemed before myself, brought me very low; and such were the conflicts of my soul, that I had a near sympathy with the prophet, in the time of his weakness, when he said, "If thou deal thus with me, kill me, I pray thee, if I have found favour in thy sight;" Numb. xi. 15. but I soon saw that this proceeded from the want of a full resignation to the divine will. Many were the afflictions which attended me; and in great abasement, with many tears, my cries were to the Almighty for his gracious and fatherly assistance: and then, after a time of deep trial, I was favoured to understand the state mentioned by the psalmist more clearly than ever I had before; to wit: "My soul is even as a weaned child." Psalm cxxxi. 2. Being thus helped to sink down into resignation, I felt a deliverance from that tempest in which I had been sorely exercised, and in calmness of mind went forward, trusting that the Lord Jesus Christ, as I faithfully attended to him, would be a counsellor to me in all difficulties; and that by his strength I should be enabled even to leave money with the members of society where I had entertainment, when I found that omitting of it would obstruct that work to which I believed he had called me: and as I copy this after my return, I may here add, that oftentimes I did so, under a sense of duty; the way in which I did it was thus: when I expected soon to leave a friend's house where I had entertainment, if I believed that I should not keep clear from the gain of oppression without leaving money, I spoke to one of the heads of the family privately, and desired them to accept of them pieces of silver, and give them to such of their negroes as they believed would make the best use of them; and at other times I gave them to the negroes myself, as the way looked clearest to me: as I expected this before I came out, I had provided a large number of small pieces; and thus offering them to some who appeared to be wealthy people was a trial both to me and them: but the fear of the Lord so covered me at times, that my way was made easier than I expected; and few, if any, manifested any resentment at the offer, and most of them, after some talk, accepted of them.

The seventh day of the fifth month, in the year 1757, lodged at a friend's house; and the next day, being the first of the week, was at Potapsco meeting; then crossed Patuxent river, and lodged at a public house.

On the ninth breakfasted at a friend's house; who afterward, putting us a little on our way, I had conversation with him, in the fear of the Lord, concerning his slaves; in which my heart was tender, and I used much plainness of speech with him, which he appeared to take kindly. We pursued our journey without appointing meetings, being pressed in my mind to be at the yearly-meeting in Virginia; and in my travelling on the road, I often felt a cry rise from the centre of my mind, thus: O Lord, I am a stranger on the earth, hide not thy face from me. On the eleventh day of the fifth month, we crossed the rivers Potowmac and Rappahannock, and lodged at Port-Royal: and on the way we happening in company with a colonel of the militia, who appeared to be a thoughtful man, I took occasion to remark on the difference in general betwixt a people used to labour moderately for their living, training up their children in frugality and business, and those who live on the labour of slaves; the former, in my view, being the most happy life; with which he concurred, and mentioned the trouble arising from the untoward, slothful disposition of the negroes; adding, that one of our labourers would do as much in a day as two of their slaves. I replied, that free men, whose minds were properly on their business, found a satisfaction in improving, cultivating, and providing for their families; but negroes, labouring to support others who claim them as their property, and expecting nothing but slavery during life, had not the like inducement to be industrious.

After some further conversation, I said, that men having power, too often misapplied it; that though we made slaves of the negroes, and the Turks made slaves of the christians, I however believed that liberty was the natural right of all men equally: which he did not deny; but said, the lives of the negroes were so wretched in their own country, that many of them lived better here than there: I only said, there is great odds in regard to us, on what principle we act; and so the conversation on that subject ended; and I may here add, that another person, some time afterward, mentioned the wretchedness of the negroes, occasioned by their intestine wars, as an argument in favour of our fetching them away for slaves: to which I then replied; if compassion on the Africans, in regard to their domestic troubles, were the real motives of our purchasing them, that spirit of tenderness being attended to, would incite us to use them kindly; that as strangers brought out of affliction, their lives might be happy among us; and as they are human creatures, whose souls are as precious as ours, and who may receive the same help and comfort from the holy scriptures as we do, we could not omit suitable endeavours to instruct them therein: but while we manifest by our conduct, that our views in purchasing them are to

advance ourselves; and while our buying captives taken in war, animates those parties to push on that war, and increase desolation amongst them, to say they live unhappy in Africa, is far from being an argument in our favour: and I further said, the present circumstances of these provinces to me appear difficult; that the slaves look like a burthensome stone to such who burthen themselves with them; and that if the white people retain a resolution to prefer their outward prospects of gain to all other considerations, and do not act conscientiously toward them as fellow-creatures, I believe that burthen will grow heavier and heavier, till times change in a way disagreeable to us: at which the person appeared very serious; and owned, that in considering their condition, and the manner of their treatment in these provinces, he had sometimes thought it might be just in the Almighty so to order it.

Having thus travelled through Maryland, we came amongst Friends at Cedar-Creek in Virginia, on the twelfth day of the fifth month; and the next day rode in company with several friends, a day's journey to Camp-Creek: and as I was riding along in the morning, my mind was deeply affected in a sense I had of the want of Divine aid to support me in the various difficulties which attended me; and in an uncommon distress of mind, I cried in secret to the Most High, O Lord! be merciful, I beseech thee, to thy poor afflicted creature. After some time, I felt inward relief: and soon after, a friend in company began to talk in support of the slave-trade, and said, the negroes were understood to be the offspring of Cain, their blackness being the mark God set upon him after he murdered Abel his brother; that it was the design of Providence they should be slaves, as a condition proper to the race of so wicked a man as Cain was: then another spake in support of what had been said. To all which, I replied in substance as follows: That Noah and his family were all who survived the flood, according to scripture; and as Noah was of Seth's race, the family of Cain was wholly destroyed. One of them said, that after the flood Ham went to the land of Nod, and took a wife; that Nod was a land far distant, inhabited by Cain's race; and that the flood did not reach it; and as Ham was sentenced to be a servant of servants to his brethren, these two families being thus joined, were undoubtedly fit only for slaves. I replied, the flood was a judgment upon the world for their abominations; and it was granted, that

Cain's stock was the most wicked, and therefore unreasonable to suppose they were spared. As to Ham's going to the land of Nod for a wife, no time being fixed, Nod might be inhabited by some of Noah's family, before Ham married a second time; moreover the text saith, "That all flesh died that moved upon the earth." Gen. vii. 21. I further reminded them, how the prophets repeatedly declare, "that the son shall not suffer for the iniquity of the father; but every one be answerable for his own sins." I was troubled to perceive the darkness of their imaginations; and in some pressure of spirit, said, the love of ease and gain are the motives in general of keeping slaves, and men are wont to take hold of weak arguments to support a cause which is unreasonable; and added, I have no interest on either side, save only the interest which I desire to have in the Truth: and as I believe liberty is their right, and see they are not only deprived of it, but treated in other respects with inhumanity in many places—I believe He, who is a refuge for the oppressed, will, in his own time plead their cause: and happy will it be for such who walk in uprightness before him: and thus our conversation ended.

FROM CHAPTER 8

The eleventh day of the sixth month, 1769. Sundry cases have happened of late years, within the limits of our monthly-meeting, respecting that of exercising pure righteousness toward the negroes; in which I have lived under a labour of heart, that equity might be steadily kept to. On this account, I have had some close exercise amongst friends; in which, I may thankfully say, I find peace; and as my meditations have been on universal love, my own conduct, in time past, became of late very grievous to me.

As persons setting negroes free in our province, are bound by law to maintain them, in case they have need of relief; some who scrupled keeping slaves for term of life, in the time of my youth, were wont to detain their young negroes in their service till thirty years of age, without wages, on that account: and with this custom I so far agreed that I, being joined to another friend, in executing the will of a deceased friend, once sold a negro lad till he might attain the age of thirty years, and applied the money to the use of the estate.

With abasement of heart I may now say, that sometimes, as I have set in a meeting, with my heart exercised toward that awful Being, who respecteth not persons nor colours, and have looked upon this lad, I have felt that all was not clear in my mind respecting him: and as I have attended to this exercise, and fervently sought the Lord, it hath appeared to me, that I should make some restitution, but in what way I saw not till lately; when being under some concern, that I may be resigned to go on a visit to some part of the West-Indies; and was under close engagement of spirit, seeking to the Lord for counsel herein: that of my joining in the sale aforesaid, came heavily upon me; and my mind, for a time, was covered with darkness and sorrow; and under this sore affliction, my heart was softened to receive instruction: and here I first saw, that as I had been one of the two executors, who had sold this lad nine years longer than is common for our own children to serve, so I should now offer a part of my substance to redeem the last half of that nine years; but as the time was not yet come, I executed a bond, binding me, and my executors, to pay to the man he was sold to, what to candid men might appear equitable, for the last four years and a half of his time, in case the said youth should be living, and in a condition likely to provide comfortably for himself.

Ninth day of the tenth month, 1769. My heart hath often been deeply afflicted under a feeling I have had, that the standard of pure righteousness is not lifted up to the people by us, as a society, in that clearness which it might have been, had we been so faithful to the teachings of Christ, as we ought to have been: and as my mind hath been inward to the Lord, the purity of Christ's government hath been opened in my understanding; and under this exercise, that friends being active in civil society, in putting laws in force which are not agreeable to the purity of righteousness, hath, for several years, been an increasing burthen upon me; having felt, in the openings of universal love, that where a people, convinced of the truth of the inward teachings of Christ, are active in putting laws in execution, which are not consistent with pure wisdom, it hath a necessary tendency to bring dimness over their minds: and as my heart hath been thus exercised, and a tender sympathy in me toward my fellow members, I have, within a few months past, in several meetings for discipline, expressed my concern on this subject.

From Some Considerations on the Keeping of Negroes (1754)

Forasmuch as ye did it to the least of these my brethren, ye did it unto me.
(MATT. xxv. 40)

As many times there are different motives to the same actions; and one does that from a generous heart, which another does for selfish ends.—The like may be said in this case.

There are various circumstances amongst them that keep negroes, and different ways by which they fall under their care; and, I doubt not, there are many well-disposed persons amongst them, who desire rather to manage wisely and justly in this difficult matter, than to make gain of it.

But the general disadvantage which these poor Africans lie under in an enlightened christian country, having often filled me with real sadness, and been like undigested matter on my mind, I now think it my duty, through Divine aid, to offer some thoughts thereon to the consideration of others.

When we remember that all nations are of one blood, Gen. iii. 20. that in this world we are but sojourners; that we are subject to the like afflictions and infirmities of body, the like disorders and frailties in mind, the like temptations, the same death, and the same judgment; and, that the all-wise Being is judge and Lord over us all, it seems to raise an idea of a general brotherhood, and a disposition easy to be touched with a feeling of each other's afflictions: but when we forget those things, and look chiefly at our outward circumstances, in this and some ages past, constantly retaining in our minds the distinction betwixt us and them, with respect to our knowledge and improvement in things divine, natural and artificial, our breasts being apt to be filled with fond notions of superiority, there is danger of erring in our conduct toward them.

We allow them to be of the same species with ourselves; the odds is, we are in a higher station, and enjoy greater favours than they. And when it is thus, that our heavenly Father endoweth some of his children with distinguished gifts, they are intended for good ends; but if those thus gifted are thereby lifted up above their brethren, not considering themselves as debtors to the weak, nor behaving themselves as faithful stewards, none who judge impartially can suppose them free from ingratitude.

When a people dwell under the liberal distribution of favours from heaven, it behoves them carefully to inspect their ways, and consider the purposes for which those favours were bestowed; lest, through forgetfulness of God, and misusing his gifts, they incur his heavy displeasure, whose judgments are just and equal, who exalteth and humbleth to the dust as he seeth meet.

It appears by Holy Record, that men under high favours have been apt to err in their opinions concerning others. Thus Israel, according to the description of the prophet, Isa. lxv. 5. when exceedingly corrupted and degenerated, yet remembered they were the chosen people of God: and could say, "stand by thyself, come not near me, for I am holier than thou." That this was no chance language, but their common opinion of other people, more fully appears, by considering the circumstances which attended when God was beginning to fulfil his precious promises concerning the gathering of the Gentiles.

The Most-High, in a vision, undeceived Peter, first prepared his heart to believe; and, at the house of Cornelius, shewed him of a certainty that God was no respecter of persons.

The effusion of the Holy Ghost upon a people, with whom they, the Jewish christians, would not so much as eat, was strange to them. All they of the circumcision were astonished to see it; and the apostles and brethren of Judea contended with Peter about it, till he, having rehearsed the whole matter, and fully shewn that the Father's love was unlimited, they are thereat struck with admiration, and cry out, "Then hath God also to the Gentiles granted repentance unto life!"

The opinion of peculiar favours being confined to them, was deeply rooted, or else the above instance had been less strange to them for these reasons:—First, They were generally acquainted with the writings of the prophets, by whom this time was repeatedly spoken of, and pointed at. Secondly, Our blessed Lord shortly before expressly said, "I have other sheep, not of this fold, them also must I bring," &c. Lastly, His words to them after his resurrection, at the very time of his ascension, "Ye shall be witnesses unto me, not only in Jerusalem, Judea, and Samaria, but to the uttermost parts of the earth."

Those concurring circumstances, one would think, might have raised a strong expectation of seeing such a time; yet, when it came, it proved matter of offence and astonishment.

To consider mankind otherwise than brethren, to think favours are peculiar to one nation, and exclude others, plainly supposes a darkness in the understanding: for as God's love is universal, so, where the mind is sufficiently influenced by it, it begets a likeness of itself, and the heart is enlarged towards all men. Again, to conclude a people froward, perverse, and worse, by nature, than others, (who ungratefully receive favours, and apply them to bad ends) this will excite a behaviour toward them unbecoming the excellence of true religion.

To prevent such error, let us calmly consider their circumstance; and, the better to do it, make their case ours. Suppose, then, that our ancestors and we had been exposed to constant servitude, in the more servile and inferior employments of life; that we had been destitute of the help of reading and good company; that amongst ourselves we had few wise and pious instructors; that the religious amongst our superiors seldom took notice of us; that while others, in ease, have plentifully heaped up the fruit of our labour, we had received barely enough to relieve nature; and, being wholly at the command of others, had generally been treated as a contemptible, ignorant part of mankind: should we, in that case, be less abject than they now are? Again, if oppression be so hard to bear, that a wise man is made mad by it, Eccl. vii. 7. then a series of those things altering the behaviour and manners of a people, is what may reasonably be expected.

When our property is taken contrary to our mind, by means, appearing to us unjust, it is only through Divine influence, and the enlargement of heart from thence proceeding, that we can love our reputed oppressors: if the negroes fall short in this, an uneasy, if not a disconsolate disposition, will be awakened, and remain like seeds in their minds, producing sloth and many other habits appearing odious to us; with which, being free men, they, perhaps, had not been chargeable. These, and other circumstances, rightly considered, will lessen that too great disparity which some make between us and them.

Integrity of heart hath appeared in some of them; so that, if we continue in the word of Christ (previous to discipleship, John, viii. 31.) and our conduct toward them be seasoned with his love, we may hope to see the good effect of it: the which, in a good degree, is the case with some

into whose hands they have fallen: but that too many treat them otherwise, not seeming conscious of any neglect, is, alas! too evident.

When self-love presides in our minds, our opinions are biassed in our own favour; in this condition, being concerned with a people so situated that they have no voice to plead their own cause, there is danger of using ourselves to an undisturbed partiality; till, by long custom, the mind becomes reconciled with it, and the judgment itself infected.

To humbly apply to God for wisdom, that we may thereby be enabled to see things as they are, and ought to be, is very needful; hereby the hidden things of darkness may be brought to light, and the judgment made clear: we shall then consider mankind as brethren. Though different degrees and a variety of qualifications and abilities, one dependant on another, be admitted, yet high thoughts will be laid aside, and all men treated as becometh the sons of one father, agreeable to the doctrine of Christ Jesus.

He hath laid down the best criterion, by which mankind ought to judge of their own conduct, and others judge for them of their's, one towards another, viz. "Whatsoever ye would that men should do unto you, do ye even so to them." I take it, that all men, by nature, are equally entitled to the equity of this rule, and under the indispensable obligations of it. One man ought not to look upon another man, or society of men, as so far beneath him, but that he should put himself in their place, in all his actions towards them, and bring all to this test, viz. "How should I approve of this conduct, were I in their circumstances, and they in mine?" A. Arscot's Considerations, p. III. fol. 107.

This doctrine being of a moral, unchangeable nature, hath been likewise inculcated in the former dispensation; "If a stranger sojourn with thee in your land, ye shall not vex him; but the stranger that dwelleth with you shall be as one born amongst you, and thou shalt love him as thyself." Lev. xix. 33, 34. Had these people come voluntarily and dwelt amongst us, to have called them strangers would be proper; and their being brought by force, with regret and a languishing mind, may well raise compassion in a heart rightly disposed: but there is nothing in such treatment, which, upon a wise and judicious consideration, will any ways lessen their right of being treated as strangers. If the treatment which many of them meet with be rightly examined, and compared with those precepts, "Thou shalt not vex him, nor oppress him; he shall be as one born amongst you, and thou shalt love him as thyself," Lev. xix. 33. Deut. xxvii. 19. there will appear an important difference betwixt them.

It may be objected, there is cost of purchase, and risque of their lives to them who possess them, and therefore needful that they make the best use of their time. In a practice just and reasonable, such objections may have weight; but if the work be wrong from the beginning, there is little or no force in them. If I purchase a man who hath never forfeited his liberty, the natural right of freedom is in him; and shall I keep him and his posterity in servitude and ignorance? "How should I approve of this conduct, were I in his circumstances, and he in mine?" It may be thought, that to treat them as we would willingly be treated, our gain by them would be inconsiderable: and it were, in divers respects, better that there were none in our country.

We may further consider, that they are now amongst us, and those of our nation the cause of their being here; that whatsoever difficulty accrues thereon, we are justly chargeable with; and to bear all inconveniences attending it, with a serious and weighty concern of mind to do our duty by them, is the best we can do. To seek a remedy by continuing the oppression, because we have power to do it, and see others do it, will, I apprehend, not be doing as we would be done by.

How deeply soever men are involved in the most exquisite difficulties, sincerity of heart, and upright walking before God, freely submitting to his providence, is the most sure remedy: he only is able to relieve, not only persons, but nations, in their greatest calamities.

. . .

As some in most religious societies, amongst the English, are concerned in importing or purchasing the inhabitants of Africa as slaves; and as the professors of christianity of several other nations do the like; these circumstances tend to make people less apt to examine the practice so closely as they would, if such a thing had not been, but was now proposed to be entered upon. It is, however, our duty, and what concerns us individually, as creatures accountable to our Creator, to employ rightly the understanding which he hath given us, in humbly endeavouring to be acquainted with his will concerning us, and with the nature and

tendency of those things which we practise: for as justice remains to be justice, so many people, of reputation in the world, joining with wrong things, do not excuse others in joining with them, nor make the consequence of their proceedings less dreadful in the final issue, than it would be otherwise.

Where unrighteousness is justified from one age to another, it is like dark matter gathering into clouds over us. We may know that this gloom will remain till the cause be removed by a reformation, or change of times; and may feel a desire, from a love of equity, to speak on the occasion; yet, where error is so strong, that it may not be spoken against, without some prospect of inconvenience to the speaker, this difficulty is likely to operate on our weakness, and quench the good desires in us; except we dwell so steadily under the weight of it, as to be made willing to "endure hardness" on that account.

Where men exert their talents against vices generally accounted such, the ill effects whereof are presently perceived in a government, all men who regard their own temporal good, are likely to approve the work. But when that which is inconsistent with perfect equity hath the law, or countenance of the great in its favour, though the tendency thereof be quite contrary to the true happiness of mankind, in an equal, if not greater degree, than many things accounted reproachful to christians; yet, as these ill effects are not generally perceived, they who labour to dissuade from such things, which people believe accord with their interest, have many difficulties to encounter.

The repeated charges which God gave to his prophets, imply the danger they were in of erring on this hand. "Be not afraid of their faces; for I am with thee, to deliver thee, saith the Lord." Jer. i. 8. "Speak all the words that I command thee to speak to them, diminish not a word." Jer. xxvi. 2. "And thou, son of man, be not afraid of them, nor dismayed at their looks. Speak my words to them, whether they will hear or forbear." Ezek. ii. 6, 7.

Under an apprehension of duty, I offer some further considerations on this subject, having endeavoured some years to consider it candidly. I have observed people of our own colour, whose abilities have been inferior to the affairs which relate to their convenient subsistence, who have been taken care of by others, and the profit of such work as they could do, applied toward their support.—I believe there are such amongst negroes;

and that some people in whose hands they are, keep them with no view of outward profit; do not consider them as black men, who, as such, ought to serve white men; but account them persons who have need of guardians, and, as such, take care of them; yet, where equal care is taken in all parts of education, I do not apprehend cases of this kind are likely to occur more frequently amongst one sort of people than another.

It looks to me that the slave-trade was founded, and hath generally been carried on, in a wrong spirit; that the effects of it are detrimental to the real prosperity of our country; and will be more so, except we cease from the common motives of keeping them, and treat them in future agreeable to Truth and pure justice.

Negroes may be imported, who, for their cruelty to their countrymen, and the evil disposition of their minds, may be unfit to be at liberty; and if we, as lovers of righteousness, undertake the management of them, we should have a full and clear knowledge of their crimes, and of those circumstances which might operate in their favour; but the difficulty of obtaining this is so great, that we have great reason to be cautious therein. But, should it plainly appear that absolute subjection was a condition the most proper for the person who is purchased, yet the innocent children ought not to be made slaves, because their parents sinned.

We have account in holy scripture of some families suffering, where mention is only made of the heads of the family committing wickedness; and it is likely that the degenerate Jews, misunderstanding some occurrences of this kind, took occasion to charge God with being unequal; so that a saying became common, "The fathers have eaten sour grapes, and the children's teeth are set on edge." Jeremiah and Ezekiel, two of the inspired prophets, who lived near the same time, were concerned to correct this error. Ezekiel is large on the subject. First, he reproves them for their error. "What mean ye, that ye do so," chap. xviii. verse 2. "As I live, saith the Lord God, ye shall not have occasion any more to use this proverb in Israel." The words, "any more," have reference to time past; intimating, that though they had not rightly understood some things they had heard or seen, and thence supposed the proverb to be well grounded; yet, henceforth, they might know of a certainty, that the ways of God are all equal; that as sure as the Most High liveth, so sure men are only answerable for their own sins.—He thus sums up the matter, ver. 20. "The soul that sinneth, it shall die.

The son shall not bear the iniquity of the father; neither shall the father bear the iniquity of the son. The righteousness of the righteous shall be upon him; and the wickedness of the wicked shall be upon him."

Where men are wicked, they commonly are a means of corrupting the succeeding age; and thereby hasten those outward calamities, which fall on nations when their iniquities are full.

Men may pursue means which are not agreeable to perfect purity, with a view to increase the wealth and happiness of their offspring, and thereby make the way of virtue more difficult to them. And though the ill example of a parent, or a multitude, does not excuse a man in doing evil, yet the mind being early impressed with vicious notions and practices, and nurtured up in ways of getting treasure which are not the ways of Truth; this wrong spirit getting first possession, and being thus strengthened, frequently prevents due attention to the true spirit of wisdom, so that they exceed in wickedness those who lived before them. And, in this channel, though parents labour, as they think, to forward the happiness of their children, it proves a means of forwarding their calamity. This being the case in the age next before the grievous calamity in the seige of Jerusalem, and carrying Judah captive to Babylon, they might say with propriety, This came upon us because our fathers forsook God, and because we did worse than our fathers. See Jer. vii. 26.

As the generation next before them inwardly turned away from God, who yet waited to be gracious; and as they, in that age, continued in those things which necessarily separated from perfect goodness, growing more stubborn, till the judgments of God were poured out upon them, they might properly say, "Our fathers have sinned, and we have borne their iniquities:" Lam. v. 7. And yet, wicked as their fathers were, had they not succeeded them in their wickedness, they had not borne their iniquities.

To suppose it right, that an innocent man shall at this day be excluded from the common rules of justice; be deprived of that liberty, which is the natural right of human creatures; and be a slave to others during life, on account of a sin committed by his immediate parents, or a sin committed by Ham, the son of Noah, is a supposition too gross to be admitted into the mind of any person, who sincerely desires to be governed solid principles.

THOMAS JEFFERSON (1743–1826)

Thomas Jefferson epitomized in his thought, and strove to embody in his actions, the belief then current among intellectuals on both sides of the Atlantic: man and his society were perfectible, and America offered the best setting for the realization of man's happiness in an ideal society. We have already shown how the doctrine of human perfectibility arose out of the new doctrines of the Age of Reason. But perhaps the best way to explain Jefferson's vision of America as the "last, best hope of man," and by way of explanation to approach an understanding of the man himself, is through a brief presentation of that vision as it was expounded by two of Jefferson's contemporaries: Jean de Crèvecoeur and Thomas Paine.

Jean de Crèvecoeur

Crèvecoeur (1735–1813) was born in France, emigrated to Canada during the last of the French and Indian Wars, then later spent a year in exploration around the Great Lakes and in the Ohio River Valley. In 1759 he came to New York, where he settled on a farm with his American wife. During the decade prior to the Revolution Crèvecoeur wrote his celebrated book modestly entitled *Letters from an American Farmer* (1782), in which he points out, among other things, that America is a land of almost limitless natural resources, and that it is occupied by a people upon whom the bonds of political and ecclesiastical authority sit very lightly. The selection by which we have chosen to represent Crèvecoeur emphasizes the importance of the colonists' separation from Europe, the opportunities that separation affords for the great democratic experiment.

What attachment can a poor European emigrant have for a country where he had nothing? The knowledge of the language, the love of a few kindred as poor as himself, were the only cords that tied him: his country is now that which gives him land, bread, protection, and consequence. *Ubi panis ibi patria* [Where one's bread is, there is his country] is the motto of all emigrants. What then *is* the American, this new man? He is either an European, or the descendant of an European, hence that strange mixture of blood, which you will find in no other country. I could point out to you a family whose grandfather was an Englishman, whose wife was Dutch, whose son married a French woman, and whose present four sons have now four wives of different nations. *He* is an American, who, leaving behind him all his ancient prejudices and manners, receives new ones from the new mode of life he has embraced, the new government he obeys, and the new rank he holds. He becomes an American by being received in the broad lap of our great *Alma Mater*. Here individuals of all nations are melted into a new race of men, whose labors and posterity will one day cause great changes in the world. Americans are the western pilgrims, who are carrying along with them that great mass of arts, sciences, vigor, and industry which began long since in the east; they will finish the great circle. The Americans were once scattered all over Europe; here they are incorporated into one of the finest systems of population which has ever appeared, and which will hereafter become distinct by the power of the different climates they inhabit. The American ought therefore to love this country much better than that wherein either he or his forefathers were born. Here the rewards of his industry follow with equal steps the progress of his labor; his labor is founded on the basis of nature, *self-interest*; can it want a stronger allurement? Wives and children, who before in vain demanded of him a morsel of bread, now, fat and frolicsome, gladly help their father to clear those fields whence exuberant crops are to arise to feed and to clothe them all; without any part being claimed, either by a despotic prince, a rich abbot, or a mighty lord. Here religion demands but little of him; a small voluntary salary to the minister, and gratitude to God; can he refuse these? The American is a new man, who acts upon new principles; he must therefore entertain new ideas, and form new opinions. From involuntary idleness, servile dependence, penury, and useless labor, he has passed to toils of a very different nature, rewarded by ample subsistence.—This is an American. (*Letters from an American Farmer*)

Thomas Paine

The intellectual climate of the period and the promise that the New World held out for reformers and revolutionists are also well illustrated by the writings of Thomas Paine (1737–1809). He had been invited to come to this country by Franklin and arrived in Philadelphia in 1774. When the quarrel between the colonists and the mother country intensified, Paine threw himself energetically into the American cause as a propagandist and later as a soldier. His *Common Sense*, published January 10, 1776, had a tremendous sale and proved powerfully influential. Its opening paragraphs furnish an excellent example of the clarity and vigor of Paine's style.

Of the Origin and Design of Government in General with Concise Remarks on the English Constitution

Some writers have so confounded society with government as to leave little or no distinction between them, whereas they are not only different but have different origins. Society is produced by our wants, and government by our wickedness; the former promotes our happiness *positively* by uniting our affections, the latter *negatively* by restraining our vices. The one encourages intercourse, the other creates distinctions. The first is a patron, the last a punisher.

Society in every state is a blessing, but government even in its best state is but a necessary evil, in its worst state an intolerable one; for when we suffer or are exposed to the same miseries *by a government* which we might expect in a country *without government*, our calamity is heightened by reflecting that we furnish the means by which we suffer. Government, like dress, is the badge of lost innocence; the palaces of kings are built on the ruins of the bowers of paradise. For were the impulses of conscience clear, uniform, and irresistibly obeyed, man would need no other lawgiver; but that not being the case, he finds it necessary to surrender up a part of his property to furnish means for the protection of the rest, and this he is induced to do by the same prudence which in every other case advises him out of two evils to choose the least. Wherefore, security being the true design and end of government, it unanswerably follows that whatever form thereof appears most likely to ensure it to us, with the least expense and greatest benefit, is preferable to all others.

The intellectual climate into which Jefferson was born obviously powerfully conditioned but cannot be supposed to explain his character and career. Only very special gifts of mind and personality can account for the way in which he responded to the pressures and challenges of history. He was, in fact, as has been noted earlier, one of the most remarkable men of the colonial era. At one time or another he held all the high posts that his state or his country had to offer: member of the Virginia legislature, Governor of Virginia, delegate to the Continental Congress, our first Secretary of State, our Minister Plenipotentiary to France during a crucial period for the infant American Republic, our second Vice President, our third President. But his political career, brilliant though it was, displays only a portion of his talents and engaged only a fraction of his energies. Jefferson was a scientist, a historian, an authority on education, an amateur architect, and, in brief, a man who took, as did Francis Bacon, all human learning to be his province. He was clearly one of the most articulate men of his generation, and it was no accident that his compatriots chose him to draft the Declaration of Independence.

It is typical of the man that when, as Vice President–Elect, he set out on his journey to Philadelphia, the temporary capitol, he brought with him in his luggage "certain Bones of an Unknown Quadruped," fossil remains of an animal which, after examination and classification by the experts of the day, was named "Megalonyx Jeffersonii" in his honor. Moreover, Jefferson's scientific interests were not merely theoretical. He invented a plow that revolutionized agriculture. Monticello, the house that he built for himself, is not only a charming Palladian edifice, the elegance and delightful proportions of which reflect its builder's knowledge of architecture and his refined taste, but is filled with all sorts of gadgets and labor-saving and comfort-making devices. Next to reading Jefferson's letters, one can perhaps best sense the quality of his mind and personality by visiting Monticello and, nearby, the campus of the University of Virginia, the original buildings of which Jefferson designed.

To return to Jefferson the political philosopher and his career as a statesman: we have thus far stressed the mood of optimism which characterizes his whole earlier career, including his work in drafting the Declaration of Independence. Like the young Wordsworth in England, he rejoiced in talk of "rational liberty, and hope in Man," and in looking back on the years in which he was engaged in the revolutionary cause, he must have said with the poet: "Bliss was it in that dawn to be alive."

Later on, after the cause had been won, Jefferson encountered the day-by-day vicissitudes of a cabinet officer, and there discovered clashes of personalities and conflicts of factional interest much like those associated with government in the Old World. Presumably he had too much in him of the realist to expect miracles from any

political system. At any rate, he continued to believe that the new nation was, on balance, far better than the most advanced societies of Europe, and his primary concern was to secure it against deterioration and corruption. He believed that if it could remain basically agricultural, it might be less vulnerable to such corruption. In 1785 he wrote to John Jay:

> Cultivators of the earth are the most valuable citizens. They are the most vigorous, the most independent, the most virtuous, and they are tied to their country, and wedded to its liberty, by the most lasting bonds. . . . I would not convert them into mariners, artisans, or anything else.

Jefferson replied to the query of another friend:

> You ask me what I think on the expediency of encouraging our States to be commercial? Were I to indulge my own theory, I should wish them to practice neither commerce nor navigation, but to stand, with respect to Europe, precisely on the footing of China.

Did Jefferson really believe it would be desirable to build a Chinese wall around the United States? Not quite: his very way of putting matters hints that he was aware of a certain extravagance in what he was saying. Yet there is no reason to doubt his real distrust of the commercial spirit or his preference for agriculture as the proper base for a democratic society.

A free society required an independent citizenry whose votes were not subject to pressure, including economic pressure, from other men. Significantly, in the constitution that Jefferson drafted for the state of Virginia, he included the following clause: "Every landless citizen is entitled to fifty acres of unappropriated land." A citizen needed property in order to discharge his responsibilities as a citizen.

A good citizen needed also to be informed. Hence it was that Jefferson insisted on public support for education. He proposed that Virginia should set up school districts to provide three years of free schooling in reading, writing, and arithmetic for all children of the state. His scheme also provided state scholarships to enable students of high promise to pursue their studies in secondary schools and colleges.

Jefferson's confidence in the ultimate integrity and good judgment of the people rested upon his belief that man was by nature "endowed with a sense of right and wrong." This natural moral sense, he maintained, was "as much a part of man as his leg or arm." Jefferson conceded that this moral sense needed to be submitted to reason and to be strengthened by exercise, but no human being, he insisted, was without it.

Jefferson's belief in man was not, however, "enthusiastic," that is, an emotional response based on a mystical intuition but, as he was firmly convinced, on reason itself. So also was his belief in man's natural rights. In the Declaration of Independence, he wrote that certain truths were "self-evident," namely, "that all men are created equal, that they are endowed by their Creator with certain inalienable rights; that among these are life, liberty, and the pursuit of happiness."

Yet, as has been remarked over and over, it is by no means self-evident that all men are created equal. Some men are born to grow tall and others to be short; some strong, but others weak; some highly intelligent, and others morons. That men are created equal will seem self-evident only to a man who is the heir of a particular philosophical tradition, for the statement is neither a matter of natural fact nor of scientific law. It is a metaphysical proposition. (To call it a metaphysical proposition is not, of course, to suggest that it is untrue, but simply to put it beyond the range of the measuring sticks of biology and sociology. The proposition is not of that order of truth.)

Like other children of the eighteenth-century Enlightenment, Jefferson was never sufficiently aware of how much his belief in man's rights was the culmination of a long cultural tradition, one in which even the schoolmen of the Middle Ages had a part—though Jefferson loathed the Middle Ages and could not even read Sir Walter Scott's novels because they reeked so much of the medieval world. The very success

of the American experiment seemed to suggest that once the noxious vapors of the Dark Ages had been dispelled, the public virtues that Jefferson espoused would spring up of themselves and flourish. In America, the sun of reason was shining as it had shone in the best days of Greece and Rome. Jefferson could feel its revivifying ray in a very immediate sense. Monarchy, the hereditary nobility, and an authoritarian church had disappeared. Jefferson himself had abolished in Virginia primogeniture and entail and so insured a wider religious freedom and better disposition of landed property. His bill to provide religious freedom in Virginia had disposed of the threat of priestcraft of the medieval sort and lessened the dangers of the fanaticism of local Protestant cults. In Virginia, Jefferson and his compatriots had fashioned, he hoped, a republic like that of Rome when Rome was Rome.

If Jefferson rejoiced in American provincialism, happy that the American people had thus far been protected from the contamination of European decadence and luxury, he was nevertheless well aware of the deficiencies of a provincial society. American cooking was not as good as French, and the French could certainly instruct Americans in civilized drinking. Jefferson writes to a friend that the French "in their pleasures of the table . . . are far before us, because, with good taste they unite temperance. They do not terminate the most sociable meals by transforming themselves into brutes." Jefferson would also like to see his countrymen come nearer to European standards in architecture, sculpture, painting, and music. In one of his letters he observes that music is "an enjoyment, the deprivation of which with us, cannot be calculated." And there is the general matter of manners. He would like to see his "countrymen . . . adopt so much of politeness, as to be ready to make all those little sacrifices of self, which really render European manners amiable. . . ."

Jefferson was also aware that there was in his society something worse than a deficiency: it was the palpable evil of black chattel slavery. Slavery was an injustice that obviously violated his convictions about the natural rights of man. It was not only cruelly unjust to the Negro; it tended to corrupt the whole society, including the owners of the slaves. In his *Notes on the State of Virginia* Jefferson comments specifically on the subversive effects of slavery by asking whether "the liberties of a nation [can] be thought secure when we have removed their only firm bases, a conviction in the minds of the people that their liberties are of the gift of God? That they are not to be violated but with His wrath? Indeed I tremble for my country when I reflect that God is just. . . ."[1]

In 1769 Jefferson's first action as a member of Virginia's House of Burgesses was to propose a bill allowing owners to free their slaves. In 1783, as a delegate to Congress, he proposed action to forbid slavery in the western territories. But it was not only difficult to get such legislation passed: once the slaves were emancipated, what was to be done with them? In his *Notes on the State of Virginia* Jefferson put on record his deep-seated fear that "deep-rooted prejudices entertained by the whites" and "ten thousand recollections, by the blacks, of the injuries they have sustained" would make it impossible for them to live happily in this country. Hence he proposed—as did a number of other men of his time—recolonization to "such place as the circumstances of the time should render most proper." (Compare the solution proposed by Harriet Beecher Stowe, p. 665.) It may be significant that Jefferson never did free his own slaves.[2]

Earlier in this introduction we have suggested that Jefferson admirably sums up the talents, virtues, and intellectual interests of the leaders of the young nation. But it ought to be added that he also beautifully illustrates its tensions and growing pains. Thus, Jefferson opposed industrialization, centralization, and the growth of cities, and yet his purchase of the Louisiana Territory did much to strengthen the federal power and the forces working toward centralization. This was but one of many situations in which practical needs—the infant nation simply had to control the lower Mississippi River— overcame theoretical objections. Jefferson, as we have seen, set great store by rationality and the civilized virtues, yet his native state was one of the foremost in sending out settlers to the frontier where life was primitive and even barbaric. Jefferson was committed to that democracy and to the worth of the frontiersman as well as to those Virginians who knew their classical literature and the works of Voltaire and Volney. Cross-grained reality was constantly testing Jefferson's idealism and his confidence in reason. The fact of slavery in a democratic society—itself a contradiction—might also perilously test the very unity of the American Republic. Jefferson early foresaw that possibility. In 1820, when the issue of slavery began to take a sectional form, the beginnings of that debate alarmed him "like a fire bell in the night": such an alarm, he realized, might well prove to be "the knell of the Union."

When Jefferson was asked what he wished to have recorded on his funerary monument, he passed over such honors as the presidency of his country in favor of three items which he embodied in the following epitaph: "Here was buried/Thomas Jefferson/Author of the Declaration of American Independence/of the Statute of Virginia for religious freedom/And Father of the University of Virginia." Since such were Jefferson's own priorities, we shall probably do well to respect them in making selections of his writings for this text. We print here the Declaration of Independence, selections from his *Notes on the State of Virginia,* and some of his

---

[1] Though Jefferson, as we have seen, believed passionately in man's natural and inalienable rights to life, liberty, and the pursuit of happiness, he was himself a slaveholder. This conflict of interests and beliefs put him into a particularly vulnerable position. Indeed, Winthrop D. Jordan, in his recently published discussion of the white man's attitudes toward the Negro (*White over Black,* 1968), devotes a whole chapter to Thomas Jefferson because he finds in Jefferson a unique battleground of forces in conflict with each other. Jefferson becomes thus a very significant personal instance of a fundamental intellectual contradiction within southern colonial society.

[2] He did free a few house slaves. For the circumstances see Jordon, pp. 464 ff.

letters. The letters will perhaps best of all give a vivid notion of his ideas on education, religion, politics, and American civilization generally. They are good letters, and this means that they not only reflect his ideas but also something of the personality of the man who held them.

BIOGRAPHICAL CHART

1743   Born, April 13, in Shadwell, Albemarle County, Virginia
1760–62   Attends College of William and Mary
1769–74   Serves in Virginia House of Burgesses
1772   Marries Martha Wyles Skelton, January 1
1774   Writes pamphlet *A Summary View of the Rights of British America*
1775–76   Serves in the Continental Congress in Philadelphia; drafts the Declaration of Independence
1779–81   Serves as Governor of Virginia
1781–83   In temporary retirement; *Notes on the State of Virginia* (published in 1784)
1784   Appointed by Congress to aid Benjamin Franklin and John Adams in negotiating commercial treaties with European countries

1785–89   Succeeds Franklin as Ambassador to France
1790–93   Serves as first Secretary of State, under Washington
1797–1801   Serves as Vice President under John Adams
1797   Becomes president of the American Philosophical Society
1801–09   Serves as President of the United States
1803   Purchases the Louisiana Territory from France
1809   Retires to Monticello
1819   University of Virginia, a favorite Jeffersonian cause, is chartered
1826   Dies, July 4, at Monticello, fifty years after the Declaration of Independence

FURTHER READINGS

Julian P. Boyd, ed., *The Papers of Thomas Jefferson* (1950–   ; when completed this will be the definitive edition)
Paul Ford, ed., *The Writings of Thomas Jefferson* (1892–99; 10 vols.)
Adrienne Koch and William Peden, eds., *The Life and Selected Writings of Thomas Jefferson* (1944)

Daniel J. Boorstin, *The Lost World of Thomas Jefferson* (1948; paperback, 1961)
Gilbert Chinard, *Thomas Jefferson: The Apostle of Americanism* (1939)
R. J. Honeywell, *The Educational Work of Thomas Jefferson* (1931)

Adrienne Koch, *The Philosophy of Thomas Jefferson* (1943)
Dumas Malone, *Jefferson and His Time* (a projected five-part biography):
    Jefferson the Virginian; vol 1 (1948)
    Jefferson and the Rights of Man; vol 2 (1951)
    Jefferson and the Ordeal of Liberty; vol 3 (1962)
    Jefferson the President, First Term, 1801–1805; vol. 4 (1970)
E. T. Martin, *Thomas Jefferson, Scientist* (1952)
Merril D. Peterson, *Thomas Jefferson and the New Nation* (1970)

The Declaration of Independence (1776)

In 1774 Jefferson drew up arguments against British tyranny in his "Resolves for Albemarle County." Some months later, he wrote a tract entitled "A Summary View of the Rights of British America." This summary was read at the Virginia Convention held in Williamsburg in August, 1774. Thus, Jefferson had already had some experience in drafting documents asserting American rights when he was asked by the Second Continental Congress, in the summer of 1776, to prepare the draft for a formal declaration of independence from Great Britain. In fact, this request was made of a five-man committee, which included Benjamin Franklin, John Adams, Roger Sherman, and Robert R. Livingston. The other four members of the committee asked Jefferson to do the actual drafting, though they suggested some changes and additions. Further cuts and alterations were later made by the Congress itself, but the Declaration is almost completely Jefferson's own. It was approved by the Congress on July 4, 1776. Jefferson in his *Autobiography* provides us with a vivid account of the circumstances leading up to the final vote of approval and the signing of this document.

When,[1] in the course of human events, it becomes necessary for one people to dissolve the political bands which have connected them with another, and to assume among the powers of the earth the separate and equal station to which the laws of nature and of nature's God entitle them, a decent respect to the opinions of mankind requires that they should declare the causes which impel them to the separation.

We hold these truths to be self evident: that all men are created equal; that they are endowed by their Creator with *certain* [inherent and] inalienable rights; that among these are life, liberty, and the pursuit of happiness; that to secure these rights, governments are instituted among men, deriving their just powers from the consent of the governed; that whenever any form of government becomes destructive of these ends, it is the right of the people to alter or to abolish it, and to institute new government, laying its foundation on such principles, and organizing its powers in such form, as to them shall seem most likely to effect their safety and happiness. Prudence, indeed, will dictate that governments long established should not be changed for light and transient causes; and accordingly all experience hath shown that mankind are more disposed to suffer while evils are sufferable, than to right themselves by abolishing the forms to which they are accustomed. But when a long train of abuses and usurpations, [begun at a distinguished period and] pursuing invariably the same object, evinces a design to reduce them under absolute despotism, it is their right, it is their duty to throw off such government, and to provide new guards for their future security. Such has been the patient sufferance of these colonies; and such is

now the necessity which constrains them to *alter* [expunge] their former systems of government. The history of the present king of Great Britain is a history of *repeated* [unremitting] injuries and usurpations, *all having* [among which appears no solitary fact to contradict the uniform tenor of the rest, but all have] in direct object the establishment of an absolute tyranny over these states. To prove this, let facts be submitted to a candid world [for the truth of which we pledge a faith yet unsullied by falsehood].

He has refused his assent to laws the most wholesome and necessary for the public good.

He has forbidden his governors to pass laws of immediate and pressing importance, unless suspended in their operation till his assent should be obtained; and, when so suspended, he has utterly neglected to attend to them.

He has refused to pass other laws for the accommodation of large districts of people, unless those people would relinquish the right of representation in the legislature, a right inestimable to them, and formidable to tyrants only.

He has called together legislative bodies at places unusual, uncomfortable, and distant from the depository of their public records, for the sole purpose of fatiguing them into compliance with his measures.

He has dissolved representative houses repeatedly [and continually] for opposing with manly firmness his invasions on the rights of the people.

He has refused for a long time after such dissolutions to cause others to be elected, whereby the legislative powers, incapable of annihilation, have returned to the people at large for their exercise, the state remaining, in the meantime, exposed to all the dangers of invasion from without and convulsions within.

He has endeavored to prevent the population of these states; for that purpose obstructing the laws for naturalization of foreigners, refusing to pass others to encourage their migrations hither, and raising the conditions of new appropriations of lands.

He has *obstructed* [suffered] the administration of justice *by* [totally to cease in some of these states] refusing his assent to laws for establishing judiciary powers.

He has made [our] judges dependent on his will alone for the tenure of their offices, and the amount and payment of their salaries.

He has erected a multitude of new offices, [by a self-assumed power] and sent hither swarms of new

[1] The text printed here represents Jefferson's original draft. Words and passages in brackets were struck out by the Congress; words and passages in italics were inserted by the Congress.

officers to harass our people and eat out their substance.

He has kept among us in times of peace standing armies [and ships of war] without the consent of our legislatures.

He has affected to render the military independent of, and superior to, the civil power.

He has combined with others to subject us to a jurisdiction foreign to our constitutions and unacknowledged by our laws, giving his assent to their acts of pretended legislation for quartering large bodies of armed troops among us; for protecting them by a mock trial from punishment for any murders which they should commit on the inhabitants of these states; for cutting off our trade with all parts of the world; for imposing taxes on us without our consent; for depriving us *in many cases* of the benefits of trial by jury; for transporting us beyond seas to be tried for pretended offences; for abolishing the free system of English laws in a neighboring province, establishing therein an arbitrary government, and enlarging its boundaries, so as to render it at once an example and fit instrument for introducing the same absolute rule into these *colonies* [states]; for taking away our charters, abolishing our most valuable laws, and altering fundamentally the forms of our governments; for suspending our own legislatures, and declaring themselves invested with power to legislate for us in all cases whatsoever.

He has abdicated government here *by declaring us out of his protection, and waging war against us* [withdrawing his governors, and declaring us out of his allegiance and protection].

He has plundered our seas, ravaged our coasts, burnt our towns, and destroyed the lives of our people.

He is at this time transporting large armies of foreign mercenaries to complete the works of death, desolation and tyranny already begun with circumstances of cruelty and perfidy *scarcely paralleled in the most barbarous ages, and totally* unworthy the head of a civilized nation.

He has constrained our fellow citizens taken captive on the high seas, to bear arms against their country, to become the executioners of their friends and brethren, or to fall themselves by their hands.

He has *excited domestic insurrection among us, and has* endeavored to bring on the inhabitants of our frontiers, the merciless Indian savages, whose known rule of warfare is an undistinguished destruction of all ages, sexes and conditions [of existence].

[He has incited treasonable insurrections of our fellow citizens, with the allurements of forfeiture and confiscation of our property.

He has waged cruel war against human nature itself, violating its most sacred rights of life and liberty in the persons of a distant people who never offended him, captivating and carrying them into slavery in another hemisphere, or to incur miserable death in their transportation hither. This piratical warfare, the opprobrium of *infidel* powers, is the warfare of the *Christian* king of Great Britain. Determined to keep open a market where *men* should be bought and sold, he has prostituted his negative for suppressing every legislative attempt to prohibit or to restrain this execrable commerce. And that this assemblage of horrors might want no fact of distinguished die, he is now exciting those very people to rise in arms among us, and to purchase that liberty of which he has deprived them, by murdering the people on whom he also obtruded them: thus paying off former crimes committed against the *liberties* of one people, with crimes which he urges them to commit against the *lives* of another.]

In every stage of these oppressions we have petitioned for redress in the most humble terms: our repeated petitions have been answered only by repeated injuries.

A prince whose character is thus marked by every act which may define a tyrant is unfit to be the ruler of a *free* people [who mean to be free. Future ages will scarcely believe that the hardiness of one man adventured, within the short compass of twelve years only, to lay a foundation so broad and so undisguised for tyranny over a people fostered and fixed in principles of freedom.]

Nor have we been wanting in attentions to our British brethren. We have warned them from time to time of attempts by their legislature to extend *an unwarrantable* [a] jurisdiction over *us* [these our states]. We have reminded them of the circumstances of our emigration and settlement ·here, [no one of which could warrant so strange a pretension: that these were effected at the expense of our own blood and treasure, unassisted by the wealth or the strength of Great Britain: that in constituting indeed our several forms of government, we had adopted one common king, thereby laying a foundation for perpetual league and amity with them: but that submission to their parliament was no part of our constitution, nor ever in idea, if history may be credited: and,] we *have* appealed to their native justice and magnanimity *and we have conjured them by* [as well as to] the ties of our common kindred to disavow these usurpations which *would inevitably* [were likely to] interrupt our connection and correspondence. They too have been deaf to the voice of justice and of consanguinity. *We must therefore* [and when occasions have been given them, by the regular course of their laws, of removing from their councils the disturbers of our harmony, they have, by their free election, re-established them in power. At this very time too, they are permitting their chief magistrate to send over not only soldiers of our common blood, but Scotch and foreign mercenaries to invade and destroy us. These facts have given the last stab to agonizing affection, and manly spirit bids us to renounce forever these unfeeling brethren. We must endeavor to forget our former love for them, and hold them as we hold the rest of mankind, enemies in war, in peace friends. We might have a free and a great people together; but a communication of grandeur and of freedom, it seems, is below their dignity. Be it so, since they will have it. The road to happiness and to glory is open to us, too. We will tread it apart from them, and] acquiesce in the necessity which denounces our [eternal] separation *and hold them as we hold the rest of mankind, enemies in war, in peace friends!*

We[2] therefore the representatives of the

United States of America in General Congress assembled, do in the name, and by the authority of the good people of these [states reject and renounce all allegiance and subjection to the kings of Great Britain and all others who may hereafter claim by, through or under them; we utterly dissolve all political connection which may heretofore have subsisted between us and the people or parliament of Great Britain: and finally we do assert and declare these colonies to be free and independent states,] and that as free and independent states, they have full power to levy war, conclude peace, contract alliances, establish commerce, and to do all other acts and things which independent states may of right do.

And for the support of this declaration, we mutually pledge to each other our lives, our fortunes, and our sacred honor.

We, therefore, the representatives of the United States of America in General Congress assembled, appealing to the supreme judge of the world for the rectitude of our intentions, do in the name, and by the authority of the good people of these colonies, solemnly publish and declare, that these united colonies are, and of right ought to be free and independent states; that they are absolved from all allegiance to the British crown, and that all political connection between them and the state of Great Britain is, and ought to be, totally dissolved; and that as free and independent states, they have full power.

[2] The left column represents Jefferson's original drafts; the right column represents the text as altered by the Congress.

From a Letter to Marquis de Chastellux

Chastellux had visited Jefferson at Monticello some months before. The "event" to which Jefferson refers was the death of his wife in the preceding September.

Ampthill, Nov. 26, 1782

It [your letter] found me a little emerging from the stupor of mind which had rendered me as dead to the world as she whose loss occasioned it. Your letter recalled to my memory that there were persons still living of much value to me. If you should have thought me remiss in not testifying

to you sooner how deeply I had been impressed with your worth in the little time I had the happiness of being with you, you will I am sure ascribe it to it's true cause, the state of the dreadful suspense in which I had been kept all the summer & the catastrophe which closed it. Before that event my scheme of life had been determined. I had folded myself in the arms of retirement, and rested all prospects of future happiness on domestic & literary objects. A single event wiped away all my plans and left me a blank which I had not the spirits to fill up. In this state of mind an appointment from Congress found me, requiring me to cross the Atlantic.

From a Letter to George Wythe

It was under Wythe that Jefferson studied law after his graduation from the College of William and Mary.

Paris, August 13, 1786

If all the sovereigns of Europe were to set themselves to work, to emancipate the minds of their subjects from their present ignorance and prejudices, and that, as zealously as they now endeavor the contrary, a thousand years would not place them on that high ground, on which our common people are now setting out. Ours could not have been so fairly placed under the control of the common sense of the people, had they not been separated from their parent stock, and kept from contamination, either from them, or the other people of the old world, by the intervention of so wide an ocean. To know the worth of this, one must see the want of it here. I think by far the most important bill in our whole code, is that for the diffusion of knowledge among the people. No other sure foundation can be devised, for the preservation of freedom and happiness. If anybody thinks that kings, nobles, or priests are good conservators of the public happiness, send him here. It is the best school in the universe to cure him of that folly. He will see here, with his own eyes, that these descriptions of men are an abandoned confederacy against the happiness of the mass of the people. The omnipotence of their effect cannot be better proved, than in this country particularly, where, notwithstanding the finest soil upon earth, the finest climate under heaven, and a people of the most benevolent, the most gay and amiable character of which the human form is susceptible; where such a people, I say, surrounded by so many blessings from nature, are loaded with misery, by kings, nobles, and priests, and by them alone. Preach, my dear Sir, a crusade against ignorance; establish and improve the law for educating the common people. Let our countrymen know, that the people alone can protect us against these evils, and that the tax which will be paid for this purpose, is not more than the thousandth part of what will be paid to kings, priests and nobles, who will rise up among us if we leave the people in ignorance. The people of England, I think, are less oppressed than here. But it needs but half an eye to see, when among them, that the foundation is laid in their dispositions for the establishment of a despotism. Nobility, wealth, and pomp are the objects of their admiration. They are by no means the free-minded people we suppose them in America. Their learned men, too, are few in number, and are less learned, and infinitely less emancipated from prejudice, than those of this country.

Letter to Martha Jefferson

Martha was Jefferson's eldest daughter. At this time she was fifteen years old.

Aix-en-Provence, March 28, 1787

I was happy, my dear Patsy, to receive, on my arrival here, your letter, informing me of your good health and occupations. I have not written you sooner because I have been almost constantly on the road. My journey hitherto has been a very pleasing one. It was undertaken with the hope that the mineral waters of this place might restore strength to my wrist. Other considerations also concurred, instruction, amusement, and abstraction from business, of which I had too much at Paris.

I am glad to learn that you are employed in things new and good, in your music and drawing. You know what have been my fears for some time past —that you do not employ yourself so closely as I could wish. You have promised me a more assiduous attention, and I have great confidence in what you promise. It is your future happiness which interests me, and nothing can contribute more to it (moral rectitude always excepted) than the contracting a habit of industry and activity. Of all the cankers of human happiness none corrodes with so silent, yet so baneful a tooth, as indolence. Body and mind both unemployed, our being becomes a burthen, and every object about us loathsome, even the dearest. Idleness begets ennui, ennui the hypochondria, and that a diseased body.

No laborious person was ever yet hysterical. Exercise and application produce order in our affairs, health of body, cheerfulness of mind, and these make us precious to our friends. It is while we are young that the habit of industry is formed. If not then, it never is afterwards. The fortune of our lives, therefore, depends on employing well the short period of youth. If at any moment, my dear, you catch yourself in idleness, start from it as you would from the precipice of a gulf. You are not, however, to consider yourself as unemployed while taking exercise. That is necessary for your health, and health is the first of all objects. For this reason, if you leave your dancing-master for the summer, you must increase your other exercise.

I do not like your saying that you are unable to read the ancient print of your Livy, but with the aid of your master. We are always equal to what we undertake with resolution. A little degree of this will enable you to decipher your Livy. If you always lean on your master, you will never be able to proceed without him. It is a part of the American character to consider nothing as desperate—to surmount every difficulty by resolution and contrivance. In Europe there are shops for every want: its inhabitants therefore have no idea that their wants can be furnished otherwise. Remote from all other aid, we are obliged to invent and to execute; to find means within ourselves, and not to lean on others. Consider, therefore, the conquering your Livy as an exercise in the habit of surmounting difficulties; a habit which will be necessary to you in the country where you are to live, and without which you will be thought a very helpless animal, and less esteemed. Music, drawing, books, invention, and exercise, will be so many resources to you against ennui. But there are others which, to this object, add that of utility. These are the needle and domestic economy. The latter you cannot learn here, but the former you may. In the country life of America there are many moments when a woman can have recourse to nothing but her needle for employment. In a dull company and in dull weather, for instance, it is ill manners to read; it is ill manners to leave them; no card-playing there among genteel people—that is abandoned to blackguards. The needle is then a valuable resource. Besides, without knowing how to use it herself, how can the mistress of a family direct the works of her servants?

You ask me to write you long letters. I will do it, my dear, on condition you will read them from time to time, and practice what they will inculcate. Their precepts will be dictated by experience, by a perfect knowledge of the situation in which you will be placed, and by the fondest love for you. This it is which makes me wish to see you more qualified than common. My expectations from you are high—yet not higher than you may attain. Industry and resolution are all that are wanting. Nobody in this world can make me so happy, or so miserable, as you. Retirement from public life will ere long become necessary for me. To your sister and yourself I look to render the evening of my life serene and contented. Its morning has been clouded by loss after loss, till I have nothing left but you. I do not doubt either your affection or dispositions. But great exertions are necessary, and you have little time left to make them. Be industrious, then, my dear child. Think nothing unsurmountable by resolution and application and you will be all that I wish you to be.

. . . . Continue to love me with all the warmth with which you are beloved. . . . . . my dear Patsy.

Letter to Marquis de Lafayette

Lafayette had come to America during the American Revolution and fought in Washington's armies. His acquaintance with Jefferson was, therefore, a long-standing one and was to continue to the end of Jefferson's life.

Nice, April 11, 1787

Your head, my dear friend, is full of notable things; and being better employed, therefore, I do not expect letters from you. I am constantly roving about, to see what I have never seen before, and shall never see again. In the great cities, I go to see what travellers think alone worthy of being seen; but I make a job of it, and generally gulp it all down in a day. On the other hand, I am never satiated with rambling through the fields and farms, examining the culture and cultivators, with a degree of curiosity which makes some take me to be a fool, and others to be much wiser than I am. I have been pleased to find among the people a less degree of physical misery than I had expected. They are generally well clothed, and have a plenty of food, not animal indeed, but vegetable, which is as wholesome. Perhaps they are overworked, the excess of the rent required by the landlord obliging them to too many hours of labor in order to produce that, and wherewith to feed and clothe themselves. The soil of Champagne and Burgundy I have found more universally good than I had expected, and as I could not help making a comparison with England, I found that comparison more unfavorable to the latter than is generally admitted. The soil, the climate, and the productions are superior to those of England, and the husbandry as good, except in one point; that of manure. In England, long leases for twenty-one years, or three lives, to wit, that of the farmer, his wife, and son, renewed by the son as soon as he comes to the possession, for his own life, his wife's and eldest child's, and so on, render the farms there almost hereditary, make it worth the farmer's while to manure the lands highly, and give the landlord an opportunity of occasionally making his rent keep pace with the improved state of the lands. Here the leases are either during pleasure, or for three, six, or nine years, which does not give the farmer time to repay himself for the expensive operation of well manuring, and, therefore, he manures ill, or not at all. I suppose, that could the practice of leasing for three lives be introduced in the whole kingdom, it would, within the term of your life, increase agricultural productions fifty per cent.; or were any one proprietor to do it with his own lands, it would increase his rents fifty per cent., in the course of twenty-five years. But I am told the laws do not permit it. The laws then, in this particular, are unwise and unjust, and ought to give that permission. In the southern provinces, where the soil is poor, the climate hot and dry, and there are few animals, they would learn the art, found so precious in England, of making vegetable manure, and thus improving these provinces in the article in which nature has been least kind to them. Indeed, these provinces afford a singular spectacle. Calculating on the poverty of

their soil, and their climate by its latitude only, they should have been the poorest in France. On the contrary, they are the richest, from one fortuitous circumstance. Spurs or ramifications of high mountains, making down from the Alps, and, as it were, reticulating these provinces, give to the valleys the protection of a particular inclosure to each, and the benefit of a general stagnation of the northern winds produced by the whole of them, and thus countervail the advantage of several degrees of latitude. From the first olive fields of Pierrelatte, to the orangeries of Hieres, has been continued rapture to me. I have often wished for you. I think you have not made this journey. It is a pleasure you have to come, and an improvement to be added to the many you have already made. It will be a great comfort to you, to know, from your own inspection, the condition of all the provinces of your own country, and it will be interesting to them at some future day, to be known to you. This is, perhaps, the only moment of your life in which you can acquire that knowledge. And to do it most effectually, you must be absolutely incognito, you must ferret the people out of their hovels as I have done, look into their kettles, eat their bread, loll on their beds under pretence of resting yourself, but in fact, to find if they are soft. You will feel a sublime pleasure in the course of this investigation, and a sublimer one hereafter, when you shall be able to apply your knowledge to the softening of their beds, or the throwing a morsel of meat into their kettle of vegetables.

You will not wonder at the subjects of my letters; they are the only ones which have been presented to my mind for some time past; and the waters must always be what are the fountains from which they flow. According to this, indeed, I should have intermixed, from beginning to end, warm expressions of friendship to you. But according to the ideas of our country, we do not permit ourselves to speak even truths, when they may have the air of flattery. I content myself, therefore, with saying once for all, that I love you, your wife and children. Tell them so, and adieu. Yours affectionately.

From a Letter to Dr. Joseph Priestley

Joseph Priestley was one of the celebrated British intellectuals of the latter eighteenth century. This letter is particularly interesting for its plans for the University of Virginia, an institution which was not set up until twenty-five years later.

Philadelphia, January 18, 1800

We have . . . in Virginia a College [William and Mary] just well enough endowed to draw out the miserable existence to which a miserable constitution has doomed it. It is moreover eccentric in its position, exposed to all bilious diseases as all the lower country is, and therefore abandoned by the public care, as that part of the country itself is in a considerable degree by its inhabitants. We wish to establish in the upper country, and more centrally for the State, an University on a plan so broad and liberal and *modern*, as to be worth patronizing with the public support, and be a temptation to the youth of other States to come and drink of the cup of knowledge and fraternize with us. The first step is to obtain a good plan; that is, a judicious selection of the sciences, and a practicable grouping of some of them together, and ramifying of others, so as to adopt the professorships to our uses and our means. In an institution meant chiefly for use, some branches of science, formerly esteemed, may be now omitted; so may others now valued in Europe, but useless to us for ages to come. As an example of the former, the Oriental learning, and of the latter, almost the whole of the institution proposed to Congress by the Secretary of War's report of the 5th instant. Now there is no one to whom this subject is so familiar as yourself. There is no one in the world who, equally with yourself, unites this full pos-

session of the subject with such a knowledge of the state of our existence, as enables you to fit the garment to him who is to *pay* for it and to *wear* it. To you therefore we address our solicitations, and to lessen to you as much as possible the ambiguities of our object, I will venture even to sketch the sciences which seem useful and practicable for us, as they occur to me while holding my pen. Botany, chemistry, zoology, anatomy, surgery, medicine, natural philosophy, agriculture, mathematics, astronomy, geography, politics, commerce, history, ethics, law, arts, fine arts. This list is imperfect because I make it hastily, and because I am unequal to the subject. It is evident that some of these articles are too much for one professor and must therefore be ramified; others may be ascribed in groups to a single professor. This is the difficult part of the work, and requires a head perfectly knowing the extent of each branch, and the limits within which it may be circumscribed, so as to bring the whole within the powers of the fewest professors possible, and consequently within the degree of expense practicable for us. We should propose that the professors follow no other calling, so that their whole time may be given to their academical functions; and we should propose to draw from Europe the first characters in science, by considerable temptations, which would not need to be repeated after the first set should have prepared fit successors and given reputation to the institution.

From a Letter to John Adams

John Adams, of Massachusetts, was our second President. Jefferson had been his Vice President. Differences arose between them during Adams's administration, but in 1812, through the good offices of Benjamin Rush, a reconciliation and a renewal of friendship were effected. The fine fruit of this was a voluminous and warm correspondence, which lasted until their deaths, both of which occurred, as it happened, on Independence Day, July 4, 1826.

Monticello, June 27, 1813

Men have differed in opinion, and been divided into parties by these opinions, from the first origin of societies, and in all governments where they

have been permitted freely to think and to speak. The same political parties which now agitate the United States, have existed through all time. Whether the power of the people or that of the aristoi ["best" in Greek] should prevail, were questions which kept the States of Greece and Rome in eternal convulsions, as they now schismatize every people whose minds and mouths are not shut up by the gag of a despot. And in fact, the terms of whig and tory belong to natural as well as to civil history. They denote the temper and constitution of mind of different individuals. To come to our own country, and to the times when you and I became first acquainted, we well remember the violent parties which agitated the old Congress, and their bitter contests. There you and I were together, and the Jays, and the Dickinsons, and other anti-independents, were arrayed against us. They cherished the monarchy of England, and we the rights of our countrymen. When our present government was in the mew, passing from Confederation to Union, how bitter was the schism between the Feds and Antis! Here you and I were together again. For although, for a moment, separated by the Atlantic from the scene of action, I favored the opinion that nine States should confirm the constitution, in order to secure it, and the others hold off until certain amendments, deemed favorable to freedom, should be made. I rallied in the first instant to the wiser proposition of Massachusetts, that all should confirm, and then all instruct their delegates to urge these amendments. The amendments were made, and all were reconciled to the government. But as soon as it was put into motion, the line of division was again drawn. We broke into two parties, each wishing to give the government a different direction; the one to strengthen the most popular branch, the other the more permanent branches, and to extend their permanence. Here you and I separated for the first time, and as we had been longer than most others on the public theatre, and our names therefore were more familiar to our countrymen, the party which considered you as thinking with them, placed your name at their head; the other, for the same reason, selected mine. But neither decency nor inclination permitted us to become the advocates of ourselves, or to take part personally in the violent contest which followed. We suffered ourselves, as you so well expressed it, to be passive subjects of public discussion.

From a Letter to John Adams

Monticello, October 28, 1813

I agree with you that there is a natural aristocracy among men. The grounds of this are virtue and talents. Formerly, bodily powers gave place among the aristoi. But since the invention of gunpowder has armed the weak as well as the strong with missile death, bodily strength, like beauty, good humor, politeness and other accomplishments, has become but an auxiliary ground of distinction. There is also an artificial aristocracy, founded on wealth and birth, without either virtue or talents; for with these it would belong to the first class. The natural aristocracy I consider as the most precious gift of nature, for the instruction, the trusts, and government of society. And indeed, it would have been inconsistent in creation to have formed man for the social state, and not to have provided virtue and wisdom enough to manage the concerns of the society. May we not even say, that that form of government is the best, which provides the most effectually for a pure selection of these natural aristoi into the offices of government? The artificial aristocracy is a mischievous ingredient in government, and provision should be made to prevent its ascendency. . . .

With respect to aristocracy, we should further consider, that before the establishment of the American States, nothing was known to history but the man of the old world, crowded within limits either small or overcharged, and steeped in the vices which that situation generates. A government adapted to such men would be one thing; but a very different one, that for the man of these States. Here every one may have land to labor for himself, if he chooses; or, preferring the exercise of any other industry, may exact for it such compensation as not only to afford a comfortable subsistence, but wherewith to provide for a cessation from labor in old age. Every one, by his property, or by his satisfactory situation, is interested in the support of law and order. And such men may safely and advantageously reserve to themselves a wholesome control over their public affairs, and a degree of freedom, which, in the hands of the *canaille* of the cities of Europe, would be instantly perverted to the demolition and destruction of everything public and private. The history of the last twenty-five years of France, and of the last forty years in America, nay of its last two hundred years, proves the truth of both parts of this observation.

But even in Europe a change has sensibly taken place in the mind of man. Science had liberated the ideas of those who read and reflect, and the American example had kindled feelings of right in the people. An insurrection has consequently begun, of science, talents, and courage, against rank and birth, which have fallen into contempt. It has failed in its first effort, because the mobs of the cities, the instrument used for its accomplishment, debased by ignorance, poverty, and vice, could not be restrained to rational action. But the world will recover from the panic of this first catastrophe. Science is progressive, and talents and enterprise on the alert. Resort may be had to the people of the country, a more governable power from their principles and subordination; and rank, and birth, and tinsel-aristocracy will finally shrink into insignificance, even there. This, however, we have no right to meddle with. It suffices for us, if the moral and physical condition of our own citizens qualifies them to select the able and good for the direction of their government, with a recurrence of elections at such short periods as will enable them to displace an unfaithful servant, before the mischief he meditates may be irremediable.

Letter to Mrs. Abigail Adams

Jefferson's differences with her husband never really affected his relations with Mrs. Adams.

Monticello, January 11, 1817

I owe you, dear Madam, a thousand thanks for the letters communicated in your favor of December 15th, and now returned. They give me more information than I possessed before, of the family of Mr. Tracy. But what is infinitely interesting, is the scene of the exchange of Louis XVIII. for Bonaparte. What lessons of wisdom Mr. Adams must have read in that short space of time! More than fall to the lot of others in the course of a long life. Man, and the man of Paris, under those circumstances, must have been a subject of profound speculation! It would be a singular addition to that spectacle, to see the same beast in the cage of St. Helena, like a lion in the tower. That is probably the closing verse of the chapter of his crimes. But not so with Louis. He has other vicissitudes to go through.

I communicated the letters, according to your permission, to my grand-daughter, Ellen Randolph, who read them with pleasure and edification. She is justly sensible of, and flattered by your kind notice of her; and additionally so, by the favorable recollections of our northern visiting friends. If Monticello has anything which has merited their remembrance, it gives it a value the more in our estimation; and could I, in the spirit of your wish, count backwards a score of years, it would not be long before Ellen and myself would pay our homage personally to Quincy. But those twenty years! Alas! where are they? With those beyond the flood. Our next meeting must then be in the country to which they have flown,—a country for us not now very distant. For this journey we shall need neither gold nor silver in our purse, nor scrip, nor coats, nor staves. Nor is the provision for it more easy than the preparation has been kind. Nothing proves more than this that the Being who presides over the world is essentially benevolent. Stealing from us, one by one, the faculties of enjoyment, searing our sensibilities, leading us, like the horse in his mill, round and round the same beaten circle,

　　　——To see what we have seen,
To taste the tasted, and at each return
Less tasteful; o'er our palates to decant
Another vintage—

Until satiated and fatigued with this leaden iteration, we ask our own *congé*. I heard once a very old friend, who had troubled himself with neither poets nor philosophers, say the same thing in plain prose, that he was tired of pulling off his shoes and stockings at night, and putting them on again in the morning. The wish to stay here is thus gradually extinguished; but not so easily that of returning once, in awhile, to see how things have gone on. Perhaps, however, one of the elements of future felicity is to be a constant and unimpassioned view of what is passing here. If so, this may well supply the wish of occasional visits. Mercier has given us a vision of the year 2440; but prophecy is one thing, and history another. On the whole, however, perhaps it is wise and well to be contented with the good things which the master of the feast places before us, and to be thankful for what we have, rather than thoughtful about what we have not. You and I, dear Madam, have already had more than an ordinary portion of life, and more, too, of health than the general measure. On this score I owe boundless thankfulness. Your health was, some time ago, not so good as it has been; and I perceive in the letters communicated some complaints still. I hope it is restored; and that life and health may be continued to you as many years as yourself shall wish, is the sincere prayer of your affectionate and respectful friend.

Letter to Nathaniel Burwell

Burwell was a Virginia friend. This letter on "female education" reflects Jefferson's experience in the education of his own daughters and also his attitude toward fiction and poetry.

Monticello, March 14, 1818

Your letter of February 17th found me suffering under an attack of rheumatism, which has but now left me at sufficient ease to attend to the letters I have received. A plan of female education has never been a subject of systematic contemplation with me. It has occupied my attention so far only as the education of my own daughters occasionally required. Considering that they would be placed in a country situation, where little aid could be obtained from abroad, I thought it essential to give them a solid education, which might enable them, when become mothers, to educate their own daughters, and even to direct the course for sons, should their fathers be lost, or incapable, or inattentive. My surviving daughter accordingly, the mother of many daughters as well as sons, has made their education the object of her life, and being a better judge of the practical part than myself, it is with her aid and that of one of her élèves, that I shall subjoin a catalogue of the books for such a course of reading as we have practiced.

A great obstacle to good education is the inordinate passion prevalent for novels, and the time lost in that reading which should be instructively employed. When this poison infects the mind, it destroys its tone and revolts it against wholesome reading. Reason and fact, plain and unadorned, are rejected. Nothing can engage attention unless dressed in all the figments of fancy, and nothing so bedecked comes amiss. The result is a bloated imagination, sickly judgment, and disgust towards all the real businesses of life. This mass of trash, however, is not without some distinction; some few modelling their narratives, although fictitious, on the incidents of real life, have been able to make them interesting and useful vehicles of a sound morality. Such, I think, are Marmontel's new moral tales, but not his old ones, which are really immoral. Such are the writings of Miss Edgeworth, and some of those of Madame Genlis. For a like reason, too, much poetry should not be indulged. Some is useful for forming style and taste. Pope, Dryden, Thompson, Shakespeare, and of the French, Molière, Racine, the Corneilles, may be read with pleasure and improvement.

The French language, become that of the general intercourse of nations, and from their extraordinary advances, now the depository of all science, is an indispensable part of education for both sexes. In the subjoined catalogue, therefore, I have placed the books of both languages indifferently, according as the one or the other offers what is best.

The ornaments too, and the amusements of life, are entitled to their portion of attention. These, for a female, are dancing, drawing, and music. The first is a healthy exercise, elegant and very attractive for young people. Every affectionate parent would be pleased to see his daughter qualified to participate with her companions, and without awkwardness at least, in the circles of festivity, of which she occasionally becomes a part. It is a necessary accomplishment, therefore, although of short use; for the French rule is wise, that no lady dances after marriage. This is founded in solid physical reasons, gestation and nursing leaving little time to a married lady when this exercise can be either safe or innocent. Drawing is thought less of in this country than in Europe. It is an innocent and engaging amusement, often useful, and a qualification not to be neglected in one who is to become a mother and an instructor. Music is invaluable where a person has an ear. Where they have not, it should not be attempted. It furnishes a delightful recreation for the hours of respite from the cares of the day, and lasts us through life. The taste of this country, too, calls for this accomplishment more strongly than for either of the others.

I need say nothing of household economy, in which the mothers of our country are generally skilled, and generally careful to instruct their daughters. We all know its value, and that diligence and dexterity in all its processes are inestimable treasures. The order and economy of a house are as honorable to the mistress as those of the farm to the master, and if either be neglected, ruin follows, and children destitute of the means of living.

This, Sir, is offered as a summary sketch on a subject on which I have not thought much. It probably contains nothing but what has already occurred to yourself, and claims your acceptance on no other ground than as a testimony of my respect for your wishes, and of my great esteem and respect.

Letter to John Holmes

Holmes was a member of the Massachusetts senate. This letter is particularly interesting in view of the forebodings of what was to come in the sectional conflict that culminated in the Civil War.

Monticello, April 22, 1820

I thank you, dear Sir, for the copy you have been so kind as to send me of the letter to your constituents on the Missouri question. It is a perfect justification to them. I had for a long time ceased to read newspapers, or pay any attention to public affairs, confident they were in good hands, and content to be a passenger in our bark to the shore from which I am not distant. But this momentous question, like a fire-bell in the night, awakened and filled me with terror. I considered it at once as the knell of the Union. It is hushed, indeed, for the moment. But this is a reprieve only, not a final sentence. A geographical line, coinciding with a marked principle, moral and political, once conceived and held up to the angry passions of men, will never be obliterated; and every new irritation will mark it deeper and deeper. I can say, with conscious truth, that there is not a man on earth who would sacrifice more than I would to relieve us from this heavy reproach, in any *practicable* way. The cession of that kind of property, for so it is misnamed, is a bagatelle which would not cost me a second thought, if, in that way, a general emancipation and *expatriation* could be effected; and, gradually, and with due sacrifices, I think it might be. But as it is, we have the wolf by the ears, and we can neither hold him, nor safely let him go. Justice is in one scale, and self-preservation in the other. Of one thing I am certain, that as the passage of slaves from one State to another, would not make a slave of a single human being who would not be so without it, so their diffusion over a greater surface would make them individually happier, and proportionally facilitate the accomplishment of their emancipation, by dividing the burden on a greater number of coadjutors. An abstinence too, from this act of power, would remove the jealousy excited by the undertaking of Congress to regulate the condition of the different descriptions of men composing a State. This certainly is the exclusive right of every State, which nothing in the Constitution has taken from them and given to the General Government. Could Congress, for example, say, that the non-freemen of Connecticut shall be freemen, or that they shall not emigrate into any other State?

I regret that I am now to die in the belief, that the useless sacrifice of themselves by the generation of 1776, to acquire self-government and happiness to their country, is to be thrown away by the unwise and unworthy passions of their sons, and that my only consolation is to be, that I live not to weep over it. If they would but dispassionately weigh the blessings they will throw away, against an abstract principle more likely to be effected by union than by scission, they would pause before they would perpetrate this act of suicide on themselves, and of treason against the hopes of the world. To yourself, as the faithful advocate of the Union, I tender the offering of my high esteem and respect.

Letter to Benjamin Waterhouse

The following letter to one of his friends gives a concise account of Jefferson's matured reflections on religion. Of special interest here is the way in which his own Deism, largely inspired by the achievement of Newtonian science, comes close to merging with the Unitarianism which had begun to catch on in the New England states.

Monticello, June 26, 1822

I have received and read with thankfulness and pleasure your denunciation of the abuses of tobacco and wine. Yet, however sound in its principles, I expect it will be but a sermon to the wind. You will find it is as difficult to inculcate these sanative precepts on the sensualities of the present day, as to convince an Athanasian that there is but one God. I wish success to both attempts, and am happy to learn from you that the latter, at least, is making progress, and the more rapidly in proportion as our Platonizing Christians make more stir and noise about it. The doctrines of Jesus are simple, and tend all to the happiness of man.

1. That there is one only God, and He all perfect.

2. That there is a future state of rewards and punishments.

3. That to love God with all thy heart and thy neighbor as thyself is the sum of religion. These are the great points on which He endeavored to reform the religion of the Jews. But compare with these the demoralizing dogmas of Calvin.

1. That there are three Gods.

2. That good works, or the love of our neighbor, are nothing.

3. That faith is everything, and the more incomprehensible the proposition, the more merit in its faith.

4. That reason in religion is of unlawful use.

5. That God, from the beginning, elected certain individuals to be saved, and certain others to be damned; and that no crimes of the former can damn them; no virtues of the latter save.

Now, which of these is the true and charitable Christian? He who believes and acts on the simple doctrines of Jesus? Or the impious dogmatists, as Athanasius and Calvin? Verily I say these are the false shepherds foretold as to enter not by the door into the sheepfold, but to climb up some other way. They are mere usurpers of the Christian name, teaching a counter-religion made up of the *deliria* of crazy imaginations, as foreign from Christianity as is that of Mahomet. Their blasphemies have driven thinking men into infidelity, who have too hastily rejected the supposed Author himself, with the horrors so falsely imputed to Him. Had the doctrines of Jesus been preached always as pure as they came from his lips, the whole civilized world would now have been Christian. I rejoice that in this blessed country of free inquiry and belief, which has surrendered its creed and conscience to neither kings nor priests, the genuine doctrine of one only God is reviving, and I trust that there is not a *young man* now living in the United States who will not die an Unitarian.

But much I fear, that when this great truth shall be re-established, its votaries will fall into the fatal error of fabricating formulas of creed and confessions of faith, the engines which so soon destroyed the religion of Jesus, and made of Christendom a mere Aceldama; that they will give up morals for mysteries, and Jesus for Plato. How much wiser are the Quakers, who, agreeing in the fundamental doctrines of the gospel, schismatize about no mysteries, and, keeping within the pale of common sense, suffer no speculative differences of opinion, any more than of feature, to impair the love of their brethren. Be this the wisdom of Unitarians, this the holy mantle which shall cover within its charitable circumference all who believe in one God, and who love their neighbor! I conclude my sermon with sincere assurances of my friendly esteem and respect.

From a Letter to John Adams

Jefferson was now eighty-two, but, as this letter indicates, his interest in science and in the intellectual world generally was undiminished.

Monticello, January 8, 1825

I have lately been reading the most extraordinary of all books, and at the same time the most demonstrative by numerous and unequivocal facts. It is Flourend's experiments on the functions of the nervous system, in vertebrated animals. He takes out the cerebrum completely, leaving the cerebellum and other parts of the system uninjured. The animal loses all its senses of hearing, seeing, feeling, smelling, tasting, is totally deprived of will, intelligence, memory, perception, etc., yet lives for months in perfect health, with all its powers of motion, but without moving but on external excitement, starving even on a pile of grain, unless crammed down its throat; in short, in a state of the most absolute stupidity. He takes the cerebellum out of others, leaving the cerebrum untouched. The animal retains all its senses, faculties, and understanding, but loses the power of regulated motion, and exhibits all the symptoms of drunkenness. While he makes incisions in the cerebrum and cerebellum, lengthwise and crosswise, which heal and get well, a puncture in the medulla elongata is instant death; and many other most interesting things too long for a letter. Cabanis has proved by the anatomical structure of certain portions of the human frame, that they might be capable of receiving from the hand of the Creator the faculty of thinking; Flourend proves that they have received it; that the cerebrum is the thinking organ; and that life and health may continue, and the animal be entirely without thought, if deprived of that organ. I wish to see what the spiritualists will say to this. Whether in this state the soul remains in the body, deprived of its essence of thought? or whether it leaves it, as in death, and where it goes? His memoirs and experiments have been reported on with approbation by a committee of the Institute, composed of Cuvier, Bertholet, Dumaril, Portal and Pinel. But all this, you and I shall know better when we meet again, in another place, and at no distant period. In the meantime, that the revived powers of your frame, and the anodyne of philosophy may preserve you from all suffering, is my sincere and affectionate prayer.

From Notes on the State of Virginia (1784)

Jefferson's *Notes on the State of Virginia*, the only book that he published in his lifetime, was written in the winter of 1781–82 and intended as a private communication to the Marquis de Barbé-Marbois, the Secretary of the French Legation in Philadelphia. Many of the questions he put to Jefferson were factual, and Jefferson often answered them in a very matter-of-fact and even statistical way. But his manifold interests in Virginia and his rich knowledge of it sometimes set him off on longer discussions and expressions of opinion. The excerpts printed below represent such discursive passages. Though the *Notes* were not intended for publication, they were too interesting to be withheld from a wider circulation and soon were printed in France (1784). Interest in the *Notes* was very great, and the book was widely reprinted in pirated editions in both France and England.

THE AMERICAN INDIAN

The Indian of North America being more within our reach, I can speak of him somewhat from my own knowledge, but more from the information of others better acquainted with him, and on whose truth and judgment I can rely. From these sources I am able to say, in contradiction to this representation, that he is neither more defective in ardor, nor more impotent with his female, than the white reduced to the same diet and exercise; that he is brave, when an enterprise depends on bravery; education with him making the point of honor consist in the destruction of an enemy by stratagem, and in the preservation of his own person free from injury; or, perhaps, this is nature, while it is education which teaches us to[1] honor force more than finesse; that he will defend himself against a host of enemies, always choosing to be killed, rather than to surrender,[2] though it be to the

---

[1] *Sol Rodomonte sprezza di venire*
   Se non, dove la via meno è sicura. (Ariosto, 14, 117–T. J.)
   [In Ariosto's *Orlando Furioso*, Rodomont was the most valiant and the most boastful of the Saracen warriors. The lines quoted by Jefferson may be translated: "Rodomonte alone scorns to come except by the least safe path."]

[2] In so judicious an author as Don Ulloa [Antonio de Ulloa (1716–1795)], and one to whom we are indebted for the most precise information we have of South America, I did not expect to find such assertions as the following: [here Jefferson quotes in the original Spanish a long statement describing the Indian people as cowardly and pusillanimous. Jefferson gives as his reference Ulloa's *Noticias Americanas*, 1772, a report commissioned by the King of Spain.] Don Ulloa here admits, that the authors who have described the Indians of South America, before they were enslaved, had represented them as a brave people, and therefore seems to have suspected that the cowardice which he had observed in those of the present race might be the effect of subjugation. But supposing the Indians of North America to be cowards also, he concludes the ancestors of those of South America to have been so too, and therefore, that those authors have given fictions for truth. He was probably not acquainted himself with the Indians of North America and had formed his opinion from hear-say. Great numbers of French, of English, and of Americans, are perfectly acquainted with these people. Had he had an

whites, who he knows will treat him well; that in other situations, also, he meets death with more deliberation, and endures tortures with a firmness unknown almost to religious enthusiasm with us; that he is affectionate to his children, careful of them, and indulgent in the extreme; that his affections comprehend his other connections, weakening, as with us, from circle to circle, as they recede from the centre; that his friendships are strong and faithful to the uttermost[3] extremity; that his sensibility is keen, even the warriors weeping most bitterly on the loss of their children, though in general they endeavor to appear superior to human events; that his vivacity and activity of mind is equal to ours in the same situation; hence his eagerness for hunting, and for games of chance. The women are submitted to unjust drudgery. This I believe is the case with every barbarous people. With such, force is law. The stronger sex imposes on the weaker. It is civilization alone which re-

places women in the enjoyment of their natural equality. That first teaches us to subdue the selfish passions, and to respect those rights in others which we value in ourselves. Were we in equal barbarism, our females would be equal drudges. The man with them is less strong than with us, but their women stronger than ours; and both for the same obvious reason; because our man and their woman is habituated to labor, and formed by it. With both races the sex which is indulged with ease is the least athletic. An Indian man is small in the hand and wrist, for the same reason for which a sailor is large and strong in the arms and shoulders, and a porter in the legs and thighs. They raise fewer children than we do. The causes of this are to be found, not in a difference of nature, but of circumstance. The women very frequently attending the men in their parties of war and of hunting, child-bearing becomes extremely inconvenient to them. It is said, therefore, that they have learned the practice of procuring abortion by the use of some vegetable; and that it even extends to prevent conception for a considerable time after. During these parties they are exposed to numerous hazards, to excessive exertions, to the greatest extremities of hunger. Even at their homes the nation depends for food, through a certain part of every year, on the gleanings of the forest; that is, they experience a famine once in every year. With all animals, if the female be badly fed, or not fed at all, her young perish; and if both male and female be reduced to like want, generation becomes less active, less productive. To the obstacles, then, of want and hazard, which nature has opposed to the multiplication of wild animals, for the purpose of restraining their numbers within certain bounds, those of labor and of voluntary abortion are added with the Indian. No wonder, then, if they multiply less than we do. Where food is regularly supplied, a single farm will show more of cattle, than a whole country of forests can of buffaloes. The same Indian women, when married to white traders, who feed them and their children plentifully and regularly, who exempt them from excessive drudgery, who keep them stationary and unexposed to accident, produce and raise as many children as the white women. Instances are known, under these circumstances, of their rearing a dozen children. An inhuman practice once prevailed in this country, of making slaves of the Indians. It is a fact well known with us, that the Indian women so enslaved produced and raised as numerous families as either the whites or blacks among whom

---

opportunity of inquiring of any of these, they would have told him, that there never was an instance known of an Indian begging his life when in the power of his enemies; on the contrary, that he courts death by every possible insult and provocation. His reasoning, then, would have been reversed thus: "Since the present Indian of North America is brave, and authors tell us that the ancestors of those of South America were brave also, it must follow that the cowardice of their descendants is the effect of subjugation and ill treatment." For he observes, ib. § 27, that *los obrages los aniquillan por la inhumanidad con que les trata.*—T. J. [The passage may be freely translated. "Their work is declining because of the inhumanity with which they are being treated."]

[3] A remarkable instance of this appeared in the case of the late Colonel Byrd [William Byrd], who was sent to the Cherokee nation to transact some business with them. It happened that some of our disorderly people had just killed one or two of that nation. It was therefore proposed at the council of the Cherokees that Colonel Byrd should be put to death, in revenge for the loss of their countrymen. Among them was a chief named Silòuee, who, on some former occasion, had contracted an acquaintance and friendship with Colonel Byrd. He came to him every night in his tent, and told him not to be afraid, they should not kill him. After many days deliberation, however, the determination was, contrary to Silòuee's expectation, that Byrd should be put to death, and some warriors were despatched as executioners. Silòuee attended them, and when they entered the tent, he threw himself between them and Byrd, and said to the warriors, "This man is my friend; before you get at him, you must kill me." On which they returned, and the council respected the principle so much as to recede from their determination.—T. J.

they lived. It has been said that Indians have less hair than the whites, except on the head. But this is a fact of which fair proof can scarcely be had. With them it is disgraceful to be hairy on the body. They say it likens them to hogs. They therefore pluck the hair as fast as it appears. But the traders who marry their women, and prevail on them to discontinue this practice, say, that nature is the same with them as with the whites. Nor, if the fact be true, is the consequence necessary which has been drawn from it. Negroes have notoriously less hair than the whites; yet they are more ardent. But if cold and moisture be the agents of nature for diminishing the races of animals, how comes she all at once to suspend their operation as to the physical man of the new world, whom the Count acknowledges to be *"à peu près de même statures que l'homme de notre monde"* ["almost exactly the same height as the man of our world"], and to let loose their influence on his moral faculties? How has this "combination of the elements and other physical causes, so contrary to the enlargement of animal nature in this new world, these obstacles to the development and formation of great germs," been arrested and suspended, so as to permit the human body to acquire its just dimensions, and by what inconceivable process has their action been directed on his mind alone? To judge of the truth of this, to form a just estimate of their genius and mental powers, more facts are wanting, and great allowance to be made for those circumstances of their situation which call for a display of particular talents only. This done, we shall probably find that they are formed in mind as well as in body, on the same module with the[4] *"Homo sapiens Europæus."* The principles of their society forbidding all compulsion, they are to be led to duty and to enterprise by personal influence and persuasion. Hence eloquence in council, bravery and address in war, become the foundations of all consequence with them. To these acquirements all their faculties are directed. Of their bravery and address in war we have multiplied proofs, because we have been the subjects on which they were exercised. Of their eminence in oratory we have fewer examples, because it is displayed chiefly in their own councils. Some, however, we have, of very superior lustre. I may challenge the whole orations of Demosthenes

and Cicero, and of any more eminent orator, if Europe has furnished more eminent, to produce a single passage, superior to the speech of Logan, a Mingo chief, to Lord Dunmore, then governor of this State. And as a testimony of their talents in this line, I beg leave to introduce it, first stating the incidents necessary for understanding it.[5]

NEGRO SLAVERY

There must doubtless be an unhappy influence on the manners of our people produced by the existence of slavery among us. The whole commerce between master and slave is a perpetual exercise of the most boisterous passions, the most unremitting despotism on the one part, and degrading submissions on the other. Our children see this, and learn to imitate it; for man is an imitative animal. This quality is the germ of all education in him. From his cradle to his grave he is learning to do what he sees others do. If a parent could find no motive either in his philanthropy or his self-love, for restraining the intemperance of passion towards his slave, it should always be a sufficient one that his child is present. But generally it is not sufficient. The parent storms, the child looks on, catches the lineaments of wrath, puts on the same airs in the circle of smaller slaves, gives a loose to the worst of passions, and thus nursed, educated, and daily exercised in tyranny, cannot but be stamped by it with odious peculiarities. The man must be a prodigy who can retain his manners and morals undepraved by such circumstances. And with what execration should the statesman be loaded, who, permitting one-half the citizens thus to trample on the rights of the other, transforms those into despots, and these into enemies, destroys the morals of the one part, and the *amor patriæ* of the other. For if a slave can have a country in this world, it must be any other in preference to that in which he is born to live and labor for another; in which he must lock up the faculties of his nature, contribute as far as depends on his individual endeavors to the evanishment of the human race, or entails his own miserable condition on the endless generations proceeding from him. With the morals of the people, their indus-

---

[4] Linn. Syst. Definitions of a Man—T. J. [The reference is to the system of classification of the great Swedish scientist Carl Linnaeus.]

[5] [Jefferson goes on to give an account of the circumstances that occasioned Logan's speech and an excerpt from the speech itself. The speech itself is included in our text in the section on Indian oratory.]

try also is destroyed. For in a warm climate, no man will labor for himself who can make another labor for him. This is so true, that of the proprietors of slaves a very small proportion indeed are ever seen to labor. And can the liberties of a nation be thought secure when we have removed their only firm basis, a conviction in the minds of the people that these liberties are of the gift of God? That they are not to be violated but with His wrath? Indeed I tremble for my country when I reflect that God is just; that his justice cannot sleep forever: that considering numbers, nature and natural means only, a revolution of the wheel of fortune, an exchange of situation is among possible events; that it may become probable by supernatural interference! The Almighty has no attribute which can take side with us in such a contest. But it is impossible to be temperate and to pursue this subject through the various considerations of policy, of morals, of history natural and civil. We must be contented to hope they will force their way into every one's mind. I think a change already perceptible, since the origin of the present revolution. The spirit of the master is abating, that of the slave rising from the dust, his condition mollifying, the way I hope preparing, under the auspices of heaven, for a total emancipation, and that this is disposed, in the order of events, to be with the consent of the masters, rather than by their extirpation.

THE NATURAL BRIDGE

Jefferson was fascinated with this great work of nature and eventually purchased it from the Crown for twenty-five shillings.

The *Natural Bridge*, the most sublime of nature's works, though not comprehended under the present head, must not be pretermitted. It is on the ascent of a hill, which seems to have been cloven through its length by some great convulsion. The fissure, just at the bridge, is, by some admeasurements, two hundred and seventy feet deep, by others only two hundred and five. It is about forty-five feet wide at the bottom and ninety feet at the top; this of course determines the length of the bridge, and its height from the water. Its breadth in the middle is about sixty feet, but more at the ends, and the thickness of the mass, at the summit of the arch, about forty feet. A part of this thickness is constituted by a coat of earth, which gives growth to many large trees. The residue, with the hill on both sides, is one solid rock of lime-stone. The arch approaches the semi-elliptical form; but the larger axis of the ellipsis, which would be the cord of the arch, is many times longer than the transverse. Though the sides of this bridge are provided in some parts with a parapet of fixed rocks, yet few men have resolution to walk to them, and look over into the abyss. You involuntarily fall on your hands and feet, creep to the parapet, and peep over it. Looking down from this height about a minute, gave me a violent headache. If the view from the top be painful and intolerable, that from below is delightful in an equal extreme. It is impossible for the emotions arising from the sublime to be felt beyond what they are here; so beautiful an arch, so elevated, so light, and springing as it were up to heaven! the rapture of the spectator is really indescribable! The fissure continuing narrow, deep, and straight, for a considerable distance above and below the bridge, opens a short but very pleasing view of the North mountain on one side and the Blue Ridge on the other, at the distance each of them of about five miles. This bridge is in the county of Rockbridge, to which it has given name, and affords a public and commodious passage over a valley which cannot be crossed elsewhere for a considerable distance. The stream passing under it is called Cedar-creek. It is a water of James' river, and sufficient in the driest seasons to turn a grist-mill, though its fountain is not more than two miles above.

The Natural Setting:

Travel Writing

While men like Franklin, Jefferson, and Woolman were exploring ideas that were to exfoliate in a new nation and a new culture, others were probing into the wild continent to the west. Some were poor and simple men seeking land, or hunters restless in the encroaching settlements, but others were quite conscious of the meaning of their mission and saw the continent as an arena for the development of a great people.

The basic motivation for westward exploration was of course eminently practical. Economic and military considerations demanded that the settlers know what lay behind them and what resources were there to be exploited. But men like Jefferson, as we have just seen, and Bartram also reveal scientific curiosity, and all of the explorers, including even the trappers and those who traded with the Indians, were impelled, to some degree at least, by a sense of adventure and discovery. James Fenimore Cooper surely touched upon something genuine in his descriptions of the effect of the wilderness on characters like his Natty Bumppo.

The style of travel writing that we sample here is basically plain and utilitarian. Yet from time to time it rises to eloquence as when Bartram first looks on the Mississippi or Lewis describes the "fertile and delightful country" along the Columbia River or Jefferson describes "the most sublime of nature's works," the Natural Bridge of Virginia. (See preceding selection.) The strength of prose of this sort is its unaffected directness. The writer is not trying to write a style: it is usually not "literary" at all, but the writer's imagination is often stirred by what he sees and his prose rises to the occasion.

176 At the beginning of this volume we quoted Robert Frost's poem with its

opening line, "The land was ours before we were the land's." In their response to the wonders of their continent, one sees the writers' imaginations becoming possessed by the land. In fact, the geographical exploration, the scientific investigation, and the inflamed imagination of the early travelers were often found in the records they left.

WILLIAM BYRD (1674–1744)

If William Byrd of Westover had been born in England and had remained there to write at the same level of literary excellence as that for which he is known today, his name would be completely forgotten. The works on which his present fame depends, *The Secret History of the Line* and *The History of the Dividing Line*, the first a personal account, and the second a public one, of the surveying of the boundary between the colonies of Virginia and North Carolina in 1728,[1] do exhibit considerable wit, a shrewd sense of character, and a brisk idiomatic prose, but in England, in a society where a cultivated taste in literature and an easy style were regarded as the natural ornaments of a gentleman, a similar performance would scarcely have merited mention in history.

But Byrd was born in America, and wrote of American subjects, in a world on the edge of a vast wilderness, where such tastes and graces as he cultivated were an anomaly and thus remain worthy of remark. He is, modestly, one of the founders of our literature, not merely because he wrote well, but because, in his person and in the great library he accumulated at his seat of Westover, he represented the civilizing influence of letters and general learning. Byrd also remains, in a way beyond literary consideration, of interest to us: he was, quite literally, in the flesh, a type that history, romance, and mythology have made much of—the gallant and cultivated Cavalier of Virginia.

[1] Byrd had been appointed as one of the government commissioners entrusted with making an accurate survey of the boundary line.

The grandfather of Byrd was, however, a tradesman, a prosperous goldsmith in London. But that grandfather's brother-in-law had early emigrated to America, had made his fortune there, and, childless, had invited his young nephew, William Byrd, to join him as his heir. That first William inherited the estate and business, prospered greatly, and in 1671 sent his own son, at the age of seven, back to England to be educated as befitted his condition.

The young Byrd was an apt pupil. Under a famous schoolmaster (the one chosen by Oliver Cromwell for his sons), he acquired Latin, Greek, Hebrew, French, and Italian. In Holland, unwillingly, he spent time learning the secrets of the tobacco export business and commerce in general—that being one of the family concerns. Again in London, he studied law at the aristocratic Middle Temple, and in due season was called to the bar.

The pupil Byrd was apt in other ways, too. He entered enthusiastically into the literary and dramatic interests of the Temple, in a period when Dryden was the reigning poet, and the wit and sexuality of the Restoration dramatists dominated the stage; and he sought acquaintance with famous writers like William Congreve, William Wycherley, and Nicholas Rowe. He cultivated, too, the young men who were born to great names or whose gifts would make them great. He got himself elected, by influence rather than achievement, to the Royal Society and associated with the savants. He cultivated the vices appropriate to a young blade about town, in low life as well as high, and the years did little to change his tastes. A few years before his death, he could write to one of his old companions in dissipation at the Temple, now a learned judge in Massachusetts:

> If I could persuade our captain of the guard ship to take a cruise to Boston at a proper season, I would come and beat up your quarters at Salem. I want to see what alteration forty years have wrought in you since we used to intrigue together in the Temple. But matrimony has atoned sufficiently for such backslidings, and now I suppose you have so little fellow feeling left for the naughty jades that you can order them a good whipping without any relenting. But though I should be mistaken, yet at least I hope your conscience with the aid of three-score-and-ten has gained a complete victory over your constitution, which is almost the case of, sir, your, ETC.

On his return to America, in 1705, at the death of his father, Byrd took over the family affairs and, in accordance with his station, entered vigorously into public life. Among other distinctions, he became receiver general of his Majesty's revenues in the colony, served thirty-seven years as a member of the Council, being at the end president of that body, and served, in London, as an agent for various affairs of Virginia. In fact, he spent, in middle life, a long period in London, there led an even gayer life than had the young student of law, lost money at the gambling tables, was treated for gonorrhea, cultivated the great, frequented book sellers, and eventually acquired his second wife; and when, in 1721, he came back to America for good, he continued to yearn for a return, which he could not now afford, to the lost world of elegance and pleasure.

Even though remaining in Virginia against his will, Byrd acquited himself well, raised a family, accumulated land (some 179,000 acres at his death), built a great house, entertained learned men in his library, and strove, in spite of distractions of business and pleasure, to keep alive, in this dark place, the light of humane letters. The library was rivaled only by that of Cotton Mather, in far-off New England, that land for which the somewhat synthetic Cavalier had only contempt, though a contempt rather more indulgent than that he held, as we shall see, for his neighbors just to the south, in Carolina.

FURTHER READINGS

Louis B. Wright, ed., *Prose Works* (1966)
———— and Marion Tinling, *The London Diary and Other Writings* (1958)

Richard Croom Beatty, *William Byrd of Westover* (1932)

From The Secret Diary of William Byrd of Westover (1719–20)

Byrd's diaries forcibly remind us that the early settlers of America were not all of them Puritans. They also remind the reader that the colonists at the beginning were not "Americans" at all. Most of them were Englishmen, and those who could readily revisit England were, like Byrd, very much at home there. Byrd's "secret diaries," from which the excerpts printed below are taken, were written in shorthand and were never meant to be published. But their highly private character makes them the more useful for our purposes: the diaries give us all the more nakedly Byrd's temperament and values, including his religious concerns, which apparently were genuine enough though they have nothing to do with Puritanism, evangelical Christianity, or middle-class morality.

IN LONDON (May, 1719)

25. I rose about 7 o'clock and read a chapter in Hebrew and some Greek in Lucian. I said no prayers but had milk for breakfast. The weather continued very warm and clear, the wind southeast. I wrote abundance of Hebrew till 2 o'clock and then read some English till three when I ate some roast chicken. After dinner I put several things in order and took a nap till four. Then I read English till five and then went into the City to Mr. Dick Perry's where was Mrs. C-r-d-k and we played at cards and I lost ten shillings. About nine we went to supper and I ate some ham and cold chicken and drank some rack punch. About eleven we took leave and I walked home where I said my prayers.

26. I rose about 7 o'clock and read a chapter in Hebrew and some Greek in Lucian. I said no prayers, but had milk for breakfast. The weather was clear and very hot, the wind still southeast. I wrote some Hebrew till 11 o'clock and then went to Mr. J-n-n but he was from home. Then to my Lord Islay's but he was from home. Then to my Lord Orrery's, but he was from home; then to Mrs. Southwell's and sat with her about an hour and then went to the Cockpit and saw Mr. Beake and then went home and ate some battered eggs. After dinner I put several things in order and read some French till 5 o'clock and then went to visit Mrs. Pierson; then I went to Will's Coffeehouse and saw my Lord Orrery and then took a walk to Mrs. S-t-r-d but she was from home. Then I picked up a woman and carried her to the tavern and ate some roast lamb. I was very wanton till 12 o'clock and then walked home and said my prayers. This was the hottest day I ever felt at the time of year.

28. I rose about 7 o'clock and read a chapter in Hebrew and some Greek. I neglected my prayers, but had milk for breakfast. The weather was still warm and clear and very dry, the wind north. About eleven came Annie Wilkinson but I would not speak with her. I was disappointed in the coming of Mrs. B-s who wrote me word she would come and breakfast with me, so I read some English and ate some bread and butter because I was to dine late and about 3 o'clock went to dine with Sir Wilfred Lawson and ate some mutton. After dinner we talked a little and about 6 o'clock went to Kensington in Sir Wilfred's coach where there was a ball in the gardens and several ladies and among the rest Miss Perry whom I stuck most to and she complained I squeezed her hand. Here

I stayed till 1 o'clock and then came home and neglected my prayers.

29. I rose about 8 o'clock and read a chapter in Hebrew and some Greek in Lucian. I said my prayers, and had milk for breakfast. The weather continued hot but was a little cloudy. I read some English till 11 o'clock and then came Colonel Blakiston and stayed about half an hour and then I went to Mrs. S-t-r-d-x to inquire after my little daughter and found she was better. Then I went into the City to Garraway's Coffeehouse where I read the news and then went to Mr. Lindsay's to dinner and ate some fish. After dinner we played at faro and I won forty shillings. About 6 o'clock I went to Will's Coffeehouse, and from thence to Lady Guise's and then returned to Will's where Margaret G-t-n called on me and I went with her to the bagnio [brothel] where I rogered her three times with vigor, twice at night and once in the morning. I neglected my prayers.

IN VIRGINIA (June, 1720)

20. I rose about 5 o'clock and read a chapter in Hebrew and some Greek. I said my prayers, and had boiled milk for breakfast. The weather continued very hot. However, about 8 o'clock I went to Mrs. Harrison's in a boat and ate some milk there. We played at piquet and shot with bows and I won five bits. Sometimes we romped and sometimes talked and complained of the heat till dinner and then I ate some hashed lamb. After dinner we romped again and drank abundance of water. We played at piquet again and I stayed till 8 o'clock and then took leave and walked home and found everything well, thank God. I talked with my people and said my prayers and then retired and slept but indifferently because of the exceedingly great heat.

21. I rose about 5 o'clock and read a chapter in Hebrew and some Greek. I neglected to say my prayers, but had milk for breakfast. The weather continued very hot and we began to cut down our wheat. About 9 o'clock came Frank Lightfoot and we played at billiards and then at piquet and I won two bits. Then we sat and talked till dinner when I ate some beans and bacon. After dinner we agreed to take a nap and slept about an hour and then I received a letter from New Kent that told me Willam R-s-t-n was run away. Then Mr. Lightfoot and I played again at piquet till the evening and then walked about the garden till night and then he went away and I gave my people a bowl of punch and they had a fiddle and

danced and I walked in the garden till ten and then committed uncleanness with Annie. I said my prayers.

22. I rose about 5 o'clock and wrote a letter to New Kent. Then I read a chapter in Hebrew and some Greek. I said my prayers and had milk for breakfast. The weather continued hot. I wrote a comic letter to Mr. Lightfoot to invite him and the ladies to dinner, but he wrote me word the ladies could not come for want of a horse. My people made an end of reaping about 12 o'clock, and I sent away the sloop to fetch [sh-l][1] and sent Will with them. I ate some mutton pie. After dinner I took a nap and then read some Latin and lolled about till the evening and then I took a walk in the orchard and ate cherries and then took a walk about the plantation. At night I had my feet washed and walked about in the garden till late. I said my prayers.

[1] Perhaps "shingles" from the sawmill at the Falls. "Shells" or "shale" are other possibilities [Wright and Tinling].

From The Secret History of the Line (1728)

20. . . . My landlord had unluckily sold our men some brandy, which produced much disorder, making some too choleric and others too loving, so that a damsel who came to assist in the kitchen would certainly have been ravished if her timely consent had not prevented the violence. Nor did my landlady think herself safe in the hands of such furious lovers and therefore fortified her bedchamber and defended it with a chamber pot charged to the brim with female ammunition. I never could learn who the ravisher was, because the girl had walked off in the morning early, but Firebrand and his servant were the most suspected, having been engaged in those kind of assaults once before.

21. In the morning Meanwell joined us. We sent away the surveyors about nine, who could carry the line no more than three and a half miles, because the low grounds were covered with thickets. As soon as we had paid a very exorbitant bill and the Carolina men had loaded their vehicle and disposed of their lumber, we mounted and conducted our baggage about ten miles. We took up our quarters at the plantation of John Hill, where we pitched our tent with design to rest there till Monday. This man's house was so poorly furnished that Firebrand and his Carolina train could not find in their hearts to lodge in it, so we had the pleasure of their company in the camp. They perfumed the tent with their rum punch and hunted the poor parson with their unseemly jokes, which turned my stomach as much as their fragrant liquor. I was grave and speechless the whole evening and retired early; by all which I gave them to understand I was not fond of the conversation of those whose wit, like the commons at the university and Inns of Court, is eternally the same.

From History of the Dividing Line Betwixt Virginia and North Carolina Run in the Year of Our Lord (1728)

25. . . . Surely there is no place in the world where the inhabitants live with less labor than in North Carolina. It approaches nearer to the description of Lubberland than any other, by the great felicity of the climate, the easiness of raising provisions, and the slothfulness of the people. Indian corn is of so great increase that a little pains will subsist a very large family with bread, and then they may have meat without any pains at all, by the help of the low grounds and the great variety of mast that grows on the high land. The men, for their parts, just like the Indians, impose all the work upon the poor women. They make their wives rise out of their beds early in the morning, at the same time that they lie and snore till the sun has risen one-third of his course and dispersed all the unwholesome damps. Then, after stretching and yawning for half an hour, they light their pipes, and, under the protection of a cloud of smoke, venture out into the open air;

though if it happen to be ever so little cold they quickly return shivering into the chimney corner. When the weather is mild, they stand leaning with both their arms upon the cornfield fence and gravely consider whether they had best go and take a small heat at the hoe but generally find reasons to put it off till another time. Thus they loiter away their lives, like Solomon's sluggard, with their arms across, and at the winding up of the year scarcely have bread to eat. To speak the truth, 'tis a thorough aversion to labor that makes people file off to North Carolina, where plenty and a warm sun confirm them in their disposition to laziness for their whole lives.

26. Since we were like to be confined to this place till the people returned out of the Dismal [the great Dismal Swamp], 'twas agreed that our chaplain might safely take a turn to Edenton to preach the Gospel to the infidels there and christen their children. He was accompanied thither by Mr. Little, one of the Carolina commissioners, who, to show his regard for the church, offered to treat him on the road with a fricassee of rum. They fried half a dozen rashers of very fat bacon in a pint of rum, both which being dished up together served the company at once both for meat and drink.

Most of the rum they get in this country comes from New England and is so bad and unwholesome that it is not improperly called "killdevil." It is distilled there from foreign molasses, which, if skillfully managed, yields near gallon for gallon. Their molasses comes from the same country and has the name of "long sugar" in Carolina, I suppose from the ropiness of it, and serves all the purposes of sugar, both in their eating and drinking. When they entertain their friends bountifully, they fail not to set before them a capacious bowl of bombo, so called from the admiral of that name. This is a compound of rum and water in equal parts, made palatable with the said long sugar. As good humor begins to flow and the bowl to ebb they take care to replenish it with sheer rum, of which there always is a reserve under the table.

But such generous doings happen only when that balsam of life is plenty; for they have often such melancholy times that neither landgraves nor caciques can procure one drop for their wives when they lie in or are troubled with the colic or vapors. Very few in this country have the industry to plant orchards, which, in a dearth of rum, might supply them with much better liquor. The truth is, there is one inconvenience that easily discourages

lazy people from making this improvement: very often, in autumn, when the apples begin to ripen, they are visited with numerous flights of parakeets, that bite all the fruit to pieces in a moment for the sake of the kernels. The havoc they make is sometimes so great that whole orchards are laid waste, in spite of all the noises that can be made or mawkins [malkin, a scarecrow] that can be dressed up to fright 'em away. These ravenous birds visit North Carolina only during the warm season and so soon as the cold begins to come on retire back toward the sun. They rarely venture so far north as Virginia, except in a very hot summer, when they visit the most southern parts of it. They are very beautiful but, like some other pretty creatures, are apt to be loud and mischievous.

27. Betwixt this [plantation] and Edenton there are many huckleberry slashes, which afford a convenient harbor for wolves and foxes. The first of these wild beasts is not so large and fierce as they are in other countries more northerly. He will not attack a man in the keenest of his hunger but run away from him, as from an animal more mischievous than himself. The foxes are much bolder and will sometimes not only make a stand but likewise assault anyone that would balk them of their prey. The inhabitants hereabouts take the trouble to dig abundance of wolf pits, so deep and perpendicular that when a wolf is once tempted into them he can no more scramble out again than a husband who has taken the leap can scramble out of matrimony.

. . .

Provisions here are extremely cheap and extremely good, so that people may live plentifully at a trifling expense. Nothing is dear but law, physic, and strong drink, which are all bad in their kind, and the last they get with so much difficulty that they are never guilty of the sin of suffering it to sour upon their hands. Their vanity generally lies not so much in having a handsome dining room as a handsome house of office: in this kind of structure they are really extravagant. They are rarely guilty of flattering or making any court to their governors but treat them with all the excesses of freedom and familiarity.

. . .

. . . In the morning we dispatched a runner to

the Nottoway town to let the Indians know we intended them a visit that evening, and our honest landlord was so kind as to be our pilot thither, being about four miles from his house. Accordingly, in the afternoon we marched in good order to the town, where the female scouts, stationed on an eminence for that purpose, had no sooner spied us but they gave notice of our approach to their fellow citizens by continual whoops and cries, which could not possibly have been more dismal at the sight of their most implacable enemies. This signal assembled all their great men, who received us in a body and conducted us into the fort.

This fort was a square piece of ground, enclosed with substantial puncheons or strong palisades about ten feet high and leaning a little outwards to make a scalade more difficult. Each side of the square might be about a hundred yards long, with loopholes at proper distances through which they may fire upon the enemy. Within this enclosure we found bark cabins sufficient to lodge all their people in case they should be obliged to retire thither. These cabins are no other but close arbors made of saplings, arched at the top and covered so well with bark as to be proof against all weather. The fire is made in the middle, according to the Hibernian fashion, the smoke whereof finds no other vent but at the door and so keeps the whole family warm, at the expense both of their eyes and complexion. The Indians have no standing furniture in their cabins but hurdles to repose their persons upon which they cover with mats or deerskins. We were conducted to the best apartments in the fort, which just before had been made ready for our reception and adorned with new mats that were very sweet and clean.

The young men had painted themselves in a hideous manner, not so much for ornament as terror. In that frightful equipage they entertained us with sundry war dances, wherein they endeavored to look as formidable as possible. The instrument they danced to was an Indian drum, that is, a large gourd with a skin braced taut over the mouth of it. The dancers all sang to this music, keeping exact time with their feet while their head and arms were screwed into a thousand menacing postures.

Upon this occasion the ladies had arrayed themselves in all their finery. They were wrapped in their red and blue matchcoats, thrown so negligently about them that their mahogany skins appeared in several parts, like the Lacedaemonian damsels of old. Their hair was braided with white

and blue peak and hung gracefully in a large roll upon their shoulders.

This peak consists of small cylinders cut out of a conch shell, drilled through and strung like beads. It serves them both for money and jewels, the blue being of much greater value than the white for the same reason that Ethiopian mistresses in France are dearer than French, because they are more scarce. The women wear necklaces and bracelets of these precious materials when they have a mind to appear lovely. Though their complexions be a little sad-colored, yet their shapes are very straight and well proportioned. Their faces are seldom handsome, yet they have an air of innocence and bashfulness that with a little less dirt would not fail to make them desirable. Such charms might have had their full effect upon men who had been so long deprived of female conversation but that the whole winter's soil was so crusted on the skins of those dark angels that it required a very strong appetite to approach them. The bear's oil with which they anoint their persons all over makes their skins soft and at the same time protects them from every species of vermin that use to be troublesome to other uncleanly people.

We were unluckily so many that they could not well make us the compliment of bedfellows according to the Indian rules of hospitality, though a grave matron whispered one of the commissioners very civilly in the ear that if her daughter had been but one year older she should have been at his devotion. It is by no means a loss of reputation among the Indians for damsels that are single to have intrigues with the men; on the contrary, they account it an argument of superior merit to be liked by a great number of gallants. However, like the ladies that game [engage in prostitution], they are a little mercenary in their amours and seldom bestow their favors out of stark love and kindness. But after these women have once appropriated their charms by marriage, they are from thenceforth faithful to their vows and will hardly ever be tempted by an agreeable gallant or be provoked by a brutal or even by a fumbling husband to go astray.

The little work that is done among the Indians is done by the poor women, while the men are quite idle or at most employed only in the gentlemanly diversions of hunting and fishing. In this, as well as in their wars, they now use nothing but firearms, which they purchase of the English for skins. Bows and arrows are grown into disuse, except only amongst their boys. Nor is it ill policy, but on the contrary very prudent, thus to furnish the Indians with firearms, because it makes them depend entirely upon the English, not only for their trade but even for their subsistence. Besides, they were really able to do more mischief while they made use of arrows, of which they would let silently fly several in a minute with wonderful dexterity, whereas now they hardly ever discharge their firelocks more than once, which they insidiously do from behind a tree and then retire as nimbly as the Dutch horse used to do now and then formerly in Flanders.

We put the Indians to no expense but only of a little corn for our horses, for which in gratitude we cheered their hearts with what rum we had left, which they love better than they do their wives and children. Though these Indians dwell among the English and see in what plenty a little industry enables them to live, yet they choose to continue in their stupid idleness and to suffer all the inconveniences of dirt, cold, and want rather than disturb their heads with care or defile their hands with labor.

WILLIAM BARTRAM (1739–1823)

William Bartram, like his father, John, was a botanist. The father published in 1751 a book of his travels in upstate New York and in 1769 his *Description of East Florida*. The younger Bartram also traveled in the southern colonies and in the adjacent Spanish possessions. He published his account of these explorations in 1791 as *Travels Through North and South Carolina, Georgia, East and West Florida*. His special interests are described in the subtitle of this work: *An account of the soil and natural productions of these regions; together with observations of the manners of the Indians.*

In the excerpt that follows, Bartram describes his visit to the banks of the Mississippi River in August, 1777. The place names refer to rivers and towns in what is now the eastern part of the state of Louisiana. At the time of Bartram's journey, New Orleans and the vast Louisiana Territory were under Spanish rule (having been ceded by France to Spain in 1762) and Florida, including "West Florida," the strip of the Gulf Coast including Pensacola, Florida, Mobile, Alabama, and the eastern parishes (counties) of Louisiana, were under British rule, having been ceded to England by Spain in the Treaty of Paris in 1763. (These Louisiana parishes are still called the "Florida Parishes.") The British settlements extended below Baton Rouge (which the British had renamed New Richmond). The Spanish fort referred to by Bartram as just below the Iberville River was a frontier outpost of Spanish-held Louisiana. In 1800 Napoleon forced Spain to yield the Louisiana Territory to France, and three years later Jefferson was able to buy it for the United States.

From Travels Through North and South Carolina, Georgia, East and West Florida (1791)

Now having advanced near thirty miles up the Amite, we arrived at a very large plantation, the property of a Scotch gentleman, who received me with civility, entreating me to reside with him; but being impatient to get to the river, and pleading the necessity of prosecuting my travels with alacrity, on account of the season being so far advanced, I was permitted to proceed, and set off next morning. Still ascending the Amite about twenty miles farther, arrived at the forks, where the Iberville comes in on the left hand, ascending which a little way, we soon came to the landing, where are warehouses for depositing merchandize, this being the extremity of navigation up this canal, and here small vessels load and unload. From this place to Manchac, on the banks of the Mississippi just above the mouth of the canal, is nine miles by land; the road straight, spacious, and perfectly level, under the shadow of a grand forest; the trees of the first order in magnitude and beauty, as Magnolia grandiflora, Liriodendron tulipfera, Platanus, Juglans nigra, Fraxinus excelsior, Morus rubra, Laurus sassafras, Laurus Borbonia, Tilea, Liquidambar, styraciflua, &c.

At evening arrived at Manchac, when I directed my steps to the banks of the Mississippi, where I stood for a time as it were fascinated by the magnificence of the great sire[1] of rivers.

The depth of the river here, even in this season, at its lowest ebb, is astonishing, not less than forty fathoms; and the width about a mile or somewhat less: but it is not expansion of surface alone that strikes us with ideas of magnificence; the altitude and theatrical accents of its pensile banks, the steady course of the mighty flood, the trees, high forests, even every particular object, as well as societies, bear the stamp of superiority and excellence; all unite or combine in exhibiting a prospect of the grand sublime. The banks of the river at Manchac, though frequently overflowed by the vernal inundations, are about fifty feet perpendicular height above the surface of the water (by which the channel at those times must be about two hundred and ninety feet deep); and these precipices being an accumulation of the sediment of muddy waters, annually brought down with the floods, of a light loamy consistence, continually cracking and parting, present to view deep yawning chasms, in time split off, as the active perpetual current undermines, and the mighty masses of earth tumble headlong into the river, whose impetuous current sweeps away and

lodges them elsewhere. There are yet visible some remains of a high artificial bank, in front of the buildings of the town, formerly cast up by the French, to resist the inundations, but found to be ineffectual, and now in part tumbled down the precipice: as the river daily encroaches on the bluff, some of the habitations are in danger, and must be very soon removed or swallowed up in the deep gulph of waters. A few of the buildings that have been established by the English, since taking possession of the colony, are large and commodious, particularly the warehouses of Messrs. Swanson & Co. Indian traders and merchants.

The Spaniards have a small fortress and garrison on the point of land below the Iberville, close by the banks of the river, which has a communication with Manchac, by a slender narrow wooden bridge across the channel of Iberville, supported on Wooden pillars, and not a bow shot from the habitations of Manchac. The Iberville in the summer season is dry, and its bed twelve or fifteen feet above the surface of the Mississippi; but in the winter and spring has a great depth of water, and a very rapid stream which flows into the Amite, thence down through the lakes into the bay of Pearls to the ocean.

Having recommendations to the inhabitants of Batonrouge, now called New-Richmond, more than forty miles higher up the river, one of these gentlemen being present at Manchac, gave me a friendly and polite invitation to accompany him on his return home. A pleasant morning; we set off after breakfast, well accommodated in a handsome convenient boat, rowed by three blacks. Two miles above Manchac we put into shore at Alabama: this Indian village is delightfully situated on several swelling green hills, gradually ascending from the verge of the river: the people are a remnant of the ancient Alabama nation, who inhabited the East arm of the great Mobile river, which bears their name to this day, now possessed by the Creeks or Muscogulges, who conquered the former.

[1] Which is the meaning of the word Mississippi [Bartram].

MERIWETHER LEWIS (1774–1809)

Meriwether Lewis, of aristocratic Virginia stock, was a kinsman and neighbor of Jefferson, to whom, for two years during his first term as

President, he served as private secretary. For years Jefferson had dreamed of an expedition to the Pacific, and almost from boyhood Lewis had

had the same project in his head; so it was only natural that, when Jefferson began actual plans for the project (an innocent "scientific expedition," for the Louisiana Territory was then still in the control of Spain), Lewis, a soldier with experience in the recent Indian campaign, should be considered as a leader. (See also the introduction to Zebulon Pike.)

After an intensive instruction in map-making, astronomy, and other scientific matters, Lewis, with William Clark as co-commander, set out in 1804—by which time Jefferson had purchased the Louisiana country from Napoleon. On November 7, 1805, they first saw the Pacific, at the mouth of the Columbia River, and on September 23, 1806, were back in Saint Louis.

The expedition, undertaken in the face of great hazards, was conducted with consummate skill (only one man was lost and that by illness) and ended with success.

Lewis became governor of the newly acquired territory of Louisiana, but was soon caught in a political crossfire which led to the refusal of payment in Washington of vouchers he had issued. He set out to the capital to clear his name, but died on the way in a frontier inn, in Tennessee. Jefferson, who wrote a biographical note on his protégé, assumed that the death was by suicide. Recently, historians have been inclined to accept the idea of murder, with a motive of robbery.

FURTHER READINGS

Elliott Coues, ed., *History of the Expedition under the Command of Lewis and Clark* (1965)
Bernard De Voto, ed., *The Travels of Lewis and Clark* (1953)
Archibald Hanna, ed., *The Lewis and Clark Expedition* (1961)

John E. Bakeless, *Lewis and Clark, Partners in Discovery* (1947)
Richard Dillon, *Meriwether Lewis* (1965)
Vardis Fisher, *Suicide or Murder* (1962)
Charles Morrow Wilson, *Meriwether Lewis of Lewis and Clark* (1934)

From Lewis and Clark's Expedition (1814)

Note that the joint diary of Lewis and Clark was not published until 1814, *after* Pike's journals, though the Lewis and Clark expedition preceded his. Two twentieth-century poems have drawn heavily on the joint diary, Archibald MacLeish's *Frescoes for Mr. Rockefeller's City* (1933) and Robert Penn Warren's *Brother to Dragons* (1953). (For a relevant passage from the former poem, see our text.)

FROM CHAPTER 20

Saturday, November 2. We now examined the rapid below more particularly, and the danger appearing to be too great for the loaded canoes, all those who could not swim were sent with the baggage by land. The canoes then passed safely, and were reloaded; at the foot of the rapid we took a meridian altitude of 59° 45′ 45″. Just as we were setting out seven squaws arrived across the portage loaded with dried fish and bear-grass, neatly packed in bundles, and soon after four Indians came down the rapid in a large canoe. After breakfasting we left our camp at one o'clock, passed the upper point of an island which is separated from the right shore by a narrow channel, through which in high tides the water passes. But at present it contains no running water, and a creek which falls into it from the mountains on the right, is in the same dry condition, though it has the marks of discharging immense torrents at some seasons. The island thus made is three miles in length and about one in width; its situation is high and open, the land rich, and at this time covered with grass and a great number of strawberry vines, from which we gave it the name of Strawberry island. In several places we observed that the Indians had been digging for roots, and indeed the whole island bears every appearance of having been at some period in a state of cultivation. On the left side of the river the low ground is narrow and open: the rapid which we have just passed is the last of all the descents of the Columbia. At this place the first tide-water commences, and the river in consequence widened immediately below the rapid. As we descended, we reached at the distance of one mile from the rapid a creek under a bluff on the left, at three miles is the lower point of Strawberry island. To this immediately succeed three small islands covered with wood; in the meadow to the right, and at some distance from the hills, stands a high perpendicular rock, about eight hundred feet high, and four hundred yards round the base; this we called the Beacon rock. Just below is an Indian village of nine houses, situated between two small creeks.

At this village the river widens to nearly a mile in extent, the low grounds too become wider, and they as well as the mountains on each side are covered with pine, spruce-pine, cottonwood, a species of ash, and some alder. After being so long accustomed to the dreary nakedness of the country above, the change is as grateful to the eye, as it is useful in supplying us with fuel. Four miles from the village is a point of land on the right, where the hills become lower, but are still thickly timbered. The river is now about two miles wide, the current smooth and gentle, and the effect of the tide has been sensible since leaving the rapid. Six miles lower is a rock rising from the middle of the river to the height of one hundred feet, and about eighty yards at its base. We continued six miles further, and halted for the night under a high projecting rock on the left side of the river opposite the point of a large meadow. The mountains, which from the great shoot to this place are high, rugged, and thickly covered with timber chiefly of the pine species, here leave the river on each side; the river becomes two and a half miles in width, and the low grounds are extensive and well supplied with wood. The Indians whom we left at the portage passed us, on their way down the river, and seven others who were descending in a canoe for the purpose of trading below, encamped with us. We had made from the foot of the great shoot twenty-nine miles to-day. The ebb-tide rose at our camp about nine inches, the flood must rise much higher. We saw great numbers of water-fowl, such as swan, geese, ducks of various kinds, gulls, plover, and the white and gray brant, of which last we killed eighteen.

. . . .

Monday 4. The weather was cloudy and cool,

and the wind from the west. During the night, the tide rose eighteen inches near our camp. We set out about eight o'clock, and at the distance of three miles came to the lower end of Diamond island. It is six miles long, nearly three in width, and like the other islands, thinly covered with timber, and has a number of ponds or small lakes scattered over its surface. Besides the animals already mentioned we shot a deer on it this morning. Near the end of Diamond island are two others, separated by a narrow channel filled at high tides only, which continue on the right for the distance of three miles, and like the adjacent low grounds, are thickly covered with pine. Just below the last, we landed on the left bank of the river, at a village of twenty-five houses; all of these were thatched with straw, and built of bark, except one which was about fifty feet long, built of boards in the form of those higher up the river, from which it differed however, in being completely above ground, and covered with broad split boards; this village contains about two hundred men of the Skilloot nation, who seem well provided with canoes, of which there were at least fifty-two, and some of them very large, drawn up in front of the village. On landing we found the Indian from above, who had left us this morning, and who now invited us into a lodge of which he appeared to own a part. Here he treated us with a root, round in shape, and about the size of a small Irish potatoe, which they call wappatoo, it is the common arrowhead or sagittifolia, so much cultivated by the Chinese, and when roasted in the embers till it becomes soft, has an agreeable taste, and is a very good substitute for bread. After purchasing some more of this root, we resumed our journey, and at seven miles distance came to the head of a large island near the left. On the right shore is a fine open prairie for about a mile, back of which the country rises, and is supplied with timber, such as white oak, pine of different kinds, wild crab, and several species of undergrowth, while along the borders of the river, there are only a few cottonwood and ash trees. In this prairie were also signs of deer and elk. When we landed for dinner, a number of Indians from the last village, came down for the purpose, as we supposed, of paying us a friendly visit, as they had put on their favourite dresses. In addition to their usual covering they had scarlet and blue blankets, sailors' jackets and trowsers, shirts and hats. They had all of them either war axes, spears and bow arrows, or muskets and pistols, with tin powder flasks. We smoked with them and endeavoured to show them every attention, but we soon found them very assuming and disagreeable companions. While we were eating they stole the pipe with which they were smoking, and the great coat of one of the men. We immediately searched them all, and discovered the coat stuffed under the root of a tree near where they were sitting; but the pipe we could not recover. Finding us determined not to suffer any imposition, and discontented with them, they showed their displeasure in the only way which they dared, by returning in an ill humour to their village. We then proceeded and soon met two canoes with twelve men of the same Skilloot nation, who were on their way from below. The larger of the canoes was ornamented with the figure of a bear in the bow, and a man in the stern, both nearly as large as life, both made of painted wood, and very neatly fixed to the boat. In the same canoe were two Indians finely dressed and with round hats. This circumstance induced us to give the name of Image canoe to the large island, the lower end of which we now passed at the distance of nine miles from its head. We had seen two smaller islands to the right, and three more near its lower extremity. The Indians in the canoe here made signs that there was a village behind those islands, and indeed we presumed there was a channel on that side of the river, for one of the canoes passed in that direction between the small islands, but we were anxious to press forward, and therefore did not stop to examine more minutely. The river was now about a mile and a half in width, with a gentle current, the bottoms extensive and low, but not subject to be overflowed. Three miles below the Image canoe island we came to four large houses on the left side, at which place we had a full view of the mountain which we first saw on the 19th of October, from the Muscleshell rapid, and which we now find to be the mount St. Helen of Vancouver. It bears north 25° east, about ninety miles distant; it rises in the form of a sugar-loaf to a very great height, and is covered with snow. A mile lower we passed a single house on the left, and another on the right. The Indians had now learnt so much of us, that their curiosity was without any mixture of fear, and their visits became very frequent and troublesome. We therefore continued on till after night, in hopes of getting rid of them; but after passing a village on each side, which on account of the lateness of the hour we saw indistinctly, we found there was no escaping from their importu-

nities. We therefore landed at the distance of seven miles below Image canoe island, and encamped near a single house on the right, having made during the day twenty-nine miles.

The Skilloots whom we passed to-day, speak a language somewhat different from that of the Echeloots or Chilluckittequaws near the long narrows. Their dress is similar, except that the Skilloots possess more articles procured from the white traders; and there is further difference between them, inasmuch as the Skilloots, both males and females, have the head flattened. Their principal food is fish, and wappatoo roots, and some elk and deer, in killing which with their arrows, they seem very expert, for during the short time we remained at the village three deer were brought in. We also observed there a tame brairo.

As soon as we landed we were visited by two canoes loaded with Indians, from whom we purchased a few roots. The grounds along the river continue low and rich, and among the shrubs which cover them is a large quantity of vines resembling the raspberry. On the right the low grounds are terminated at the distance of five miles by a range of high hills covered with tall timber, and running southeast and northwest. The game as usual very abundant, and among other birds we observe some white geese with a part of their wings black.

Tuesday, 5. Our choice of a camp had been very unfortunate; for on a sand island opposite to us were immense numbers of geese, swan-ducks, and other wild fowl, who, during the whole night, serenaded us with a confusion of noises which completely prevented our sleeping. During the latter part of the night it rained, and we therefore willingly left our encampment at an early hour. We passed at three miles a small prairie, where the river is only three quarters of a mile in width, and soon after two houses on the left, half a mile distant from each other; from one of which three men came in a canoe merely to look at us, and having done so returned home. At eight miles we came to the lower point of an island, separated from the right side by a narrow channel, on which, a short distance above the end of the island, is situated a large village: it is built more compactly than the generality of the Indian villages, and the front has fourteen houses, which are ranged for a quarter of a mile along the channel. As soon as were discovered seven canoes came out to see us, and after some traffic, during which they seemed well-disposed and orderly, accompanied us a short distance below. The river here again widens to the space of a mile and a half. As we descended we soon observed, behind a sharp point of rocks, a channel a quarter of a mile wide, which we suppose must be the one taken by the canoes yesterday on leaving Image-canoe island. A mile below the channel are some low cliffs of rocks, near which is a large island on the right side, and two small islands a little further on. Here we met two canoes ascending the river. At this place the shore on the right becomes bold and rocky, and the bank is bordered by a range of high hills covered with a thick growth of pine: on the other side is an extensive low island, separated from the left side by a narrow channel. Here we stopped to dine, and found the island open, with an abundant growth of grass, and a number of ponds well supplied with fowls; and at the lower extremity are the remains of an old village. We procured a swan, several ducks, and a brant, and saw some deer on the island. Besides this island, the lower extremity of which is seventeen miles from the channel just mentioned, we passed two or three smaller ones in the same distance. Here the hills on the right retire from the river, leaving a high plain, between which, on the left bank, a range of high hills running southeast and covered with pine, forms a bold and rocky shore. At the distance of six miles, however, these hills again return and close the river on both sides. We proceeded on, and at four miles reached a creek on the right, about twenty yards in width, immediately below which is an old village. Three miles further, and at the distance of thirty-two miles from our camp of last night, we halted under a point of highland, with thick pine trees on the left bank of the river. Before landing we met two canoes, the largest of which had at the bow the image of a bear, and that of a man on the stern: there were twenty-six Indians on board, but they all proceeded upwards, and we were left, for the first time since we reached the waters of the Columbia, without any of the natives with us during the night. Besides the game already mentioned, we killed a grouse much larger than the common size, and observed along the shore a number of striped snakes. The river is here deep, and about a mile and a half in width. Here too the ridge of low mountains running northwest and southeast, cross the river, and form the western boundary of the plain through which we have just passed. This great plain or valley begins above the mouth of Quicksand river, and is about sixty miles wide in a straight line, while on the right and left it extends to a great distance:

it is a fertile and delightful country, shaded by thick groves of tall timber, watered by small ponds, and running on both sides of the river. The soil is rich, and capable of any species of culture; but in the present condition of the Indians, its chief production is the wappatoo root, which grows spontaneously and exclusively in this region. Sheltered as it is on both sides, the temperature is much milder than that of the surrounding country; for even at this season of the year we observe very little appearance of frost. During its whole extent it is inhabited by numerous tribes of Indians, who either reside in it permanently, or visit its waters in quest of fish and wappatoo roots: we gave it the name of the Columbia valley.

. . .

Thursday 7. The morning was rainy and the fog so thick that we could not see across the river. We observed however, opposite to our camp, the upper point of an island, between which and the steep hills on the right we proceeded for five miles. Three miles lower is the beginning of an island separated from the right shore by a narrow channel; down this we proceeded under the direction of some Indians whom we had just met going up the river, and who returned in order to show us their village. It consists of four houses only, situated on this channel behind several marshy islands formed by two small creeks. On our arrival they gave us some fish, and we afterwards purchased wappatoo roots, fish, three dogs, and two otter skins, for which we gave fishhooks chiefly, that being an article of which they are very fond.

These people seem to be of a different nation from those we have just passed: they are low in stature, ill shaped, and all have their heads flattened. They call themselves Wahkiacum, and their language differs from that of the tribes above, with whom they trade for wappatoo roots. The houses too are built in a different style, being raised entirely above ground, with the eaves about five feet high, and the door at the corner. Near the end opposite to this door is a single fireplace, round which are the beds, raised four feet from the floor of earth; over the fire are hung the fresh fish, and when dried they are stowed away with the wappatoo roots under the beds. The dress of the men is like that of the people above, but the women are clad in a peculiar manner, the robe not reaching lower than the hip, and the body being covered in cold weather by a sort of corset of fur, curiously plaited, and reaching from the arms to the hip; added to this is a sort of petticoat, or rather tissue of white cedar bark, bruised or broken into small strands, and woven into a girdle by several cords of the same material. Being tied round the middle, these strands hang down as low as the knee in front, and to midleg behind, and are of sufficient thickness to answer the purpose of concealment whilst the female stands in an erect position, but in any other attitude is but a very ineffectual defence. Sometimes the tissue is strings of silk grass, twisted and knotted at the end.

After remaining with them about an hour, we proceeded down the channel with an Indian dressed in a sailor's jacket for our pilot, and on reaching the main channel were visited by some Indians who have a temporary residence on a marshy island in the middle of the river, where is a great abundance of water fowl. Here the mountainous country again approaches the river on the left, and a higher mountain is distinguished towards the southwest. At a distance of twenty miles from our camp we halted at a village of Wahkiacums, consisting of seven ill-looking houses, built in the same form with those above, and situated at the foot of the high hills on the right, behind two small marshy islands. We merely stopped to purchase some food and two beaver skins, and then proceeded. Opposite to these islands the hills on the left retire, and the river widens into a kind of bay crowded with low islands, subject to be overflowed occasionally by the tide. We had not gone far from this village when the fog cleared off, and we enjoyed the delightful prospect of the ocean; that ocean, the object of all our labours, the reward of all our anxieties. This cheering view exhilarated the spirits of all the party, who were still more delighted on hearing the distant roar of the breakers.

ZEBULON MONTGOMERY PIKE (1779–1813)

Zebulon Pike was a career officer in the American army. In 1806, then a lieutenant, he was put in charge of an expedition to explore the headwaters of the Arkansas and Red rivers and to reconnoiter the Spanish settlements of New Mexico, which at this time reached up into the present state of Colorado.

After exploring the headwaters of the Arkansas, Pike took his expedition south to one of the upper branches of the Rio Grande and set up a log fort there. The Spaniards of New Mexico, learning of his presence, sent troops to bring him to Santa Fe. Pike decided not to make any resistance but to go peaceably with them, for he wanted to learn something about the geography and resources of the Spanish possessions.

Pike was well treated by the Spaniards, but some of his papers were taken from him and remained in the Mexican archives until they were discovered by an American scholar in 1908. They have since been returned to the United States.

In 1810 Pike published his personal journals under the lengthy title *An Account of the Expeditions to the Sources of the Mississippi, and through the Western Parts of Louisiana . . . And a Tour through the Interior Parts of New Spain, etc.* Jefferson gave his blessing to the publication as a means of acquainting the public with parts of the recently accomplished Louisiana Purchase. The excerpt printed below describes Pike's discovery of the peak in Colorado which was later named for him.

Pike served in the War of 1812 and met his death in 1813 in the invasion of Canada.

From The Expeditions of Zebulon Montgomery Pike (1810)

Nov. 15th [1806]. Marched early. Passed two creeks and many high points of rocks; also, large herds of buffalo.

At two o'clock in the afternoon I thought I could distinguish a mountain to our right, which appeared like a small blue cloud; viewed it with the spy glass, and was still more confirmed in my conjecture, yet only communicated it to Dr. Robinson, who was in front with me; but in half an hour they [the mountains] appeared in full view before us. When our small party arrived on the hill they with one accord gave three cheers to the Mexican mountains. Their appearance can easily be imagined by those who have crossed the Alleghenies; but their sides were whiter, as if covered with snow, or a white stone. Those were a spur of the grand western chain of mountains which divide the waters of the Pacific from those of the Atlantic ocean; and it [the spur] divides the waters which empty into the Bay of the Holy Spirit from those of the Mississippi, as the Alleghenies do those which discharge themselves into the latter river and the Atlantic. They appear to present a natural boundary between the province of Louisiana and New Mexico, and would be a defined and natural boundary.

Before evening we discovered a fork [Purgatory river] on the south side bearing S. 25° W.; and as the Spanish troops appeared to have borne up it, we encamped on its banks, about one mile from its confluence, that we might make further discoveries on the morrow. Killed three buffalo. Distance 24 miles.

Sunday, Nov. 16th. After ascertaining that the Spanish troops had ascended the right branch or main river, we marched at two o'clock. The Arkansaw appeared at this place to be much more navigable than below, where we first struck it; and for any impediment I have yet discovered in the river, I would not hesitate to embark in February at its mouth and ascend to the Mexican mountains, with crafts properly constructed. Distance 11½ miles.

Nov. 17th. Marched at our usual hour; pushed on with an idea of arriving at the mountains, but found at night no visible difference from what we did yesterday. One of our horses gave out and was left in a ravine, not being able to ascend the hill; but I sent back for him and had him brought to the camp. Distance 23½ miles.

Nov. 18th. As we discovered fresh signs of the savages, we concluded it best to stop and kill some meat, for fear we should get into a country where we could not kill game. Sent out the hunters; walked myself to an eminence whence I took the courses to the different mountains, and a small sketch of their appearance. In the evening, found the hunters had killed without mercy, having slain 17 buffalo and wounded at least 20 more.

Having several buffalo brought in, gave out sufficient to last this month. I found it expedient to remain and dry the meat, as our horses were getting very weak, and the one died which was brought up on the 17th. Had a general feast of marrowbones, 136 of them furnishing the repast.

Nov. 20th. Marched at our usual hour; but as our horses' loads were considerably augmented by the death of one horse and the addition of 900 lbs. of meat, we moved slowly and made only 18 miles. Killed two buffalo and took some choice pieces.

Nov. 21st. Marched at our usual hour; passed two Spanish camps, within three miles of each other. We again discovered the tracks of two men, who had ascended the river yesterday. This caused us to move with caution; but at the same time increased our anxiety to discover them. The river was certainly as navigable here, and I think much more so, than some hundred miles below; which I suppose arises from its flowing through a long course of sandy oil, which must absorb much of the water, and render it shoaler below than above, near the mountains. Distance 21 miles.

Nov. 22d. Marched at our usual hour, and with rather more caution than usual. After having marched about five miles on the prairie, we descended into the bottom—the front only ["front only" refers to the vanguard, probably consisting of Pike, Robinson, and Vasquez. The Indians were Pawnees.]; when Baroney cried out *Voila un Savage!* We observed a number running from the woods toward us; we advanced to them, and on turning my head to the left I observed several running on the hill, as it were to surround us; one with a stand of colors. This caused a momentary halt; but perceiving those in front reaching out their hands, and without arms, we again advanced; they met us with open arms, crowding round to touch and embrace us. They appeared so anxious that I dismounted from my horse; in a moment a fellow had mounted him and was off. I then observed that the doctor and Baroney were in the same predicament. The Indians were embracing the soldiers. After some time tranquillity was so far restored, they having returned our horses all safe, as to enable us to learn that they were a war-party from the Grand Pawnees, who had been in search of the Tetaus; but not finding them, were now on their return. An unsuccessful war-party, on their return home, are always ready to embrace an opportunity of gratifying their disappointed vengeance on the first persons whom they meet.

Made for the woods and unloaded our horses, when the two partisans endeavored to arrange the party; it was with great difficulty that they got them tranquil, and not until there had been a bow or two bent on the occasion. When in some order, we found them to be 60 warriors, half with fire-arms, and half with bows, arrows, and lances. Our party was 16 total. In a short time they were ar-ranged in a ring, and I took my seat between the two partisans; our colors were placed opposite each other; the utensils for smoking were paraded on a small seat before us; thus far all was well. I then ordered half a carrot of tabacco, one dozen knives, 60 fire steels, and 60 flints to be presented them. They demanded ammunition, corn, blankets, kettles, etc, all of which they were refused, not-withstanding the pressing instances of my inter-preter to accord some points. The pipes yet lay unmoved, as if they were undetermined whether to treat us as friends or enemies; but after some time we were presented with a kettle of water, drank, smoked, and ate together. During this time Dr. Robinson was standing up to observe their actions, in order that we might be ready to commence hostilities as soon as they. They now took their presents and commenced distributing them, but some malcontents threw them away, by way of contempt.

We began to load our horses, when they en-circled us and commenced stealing everything they could. Finding it was difficult to preserve my pis-tols, I mounted my horse, when I found myself frequently surrounded; during which some were endeavoring to steal the pistols. The doctor was equally engaged in another quarter, and all the soldiers in their positions, in taking things from them. One having stolen my tomahawk, I informed the chief; but he paid no respect, except to reply that "they were pitiful." Finding this, I deter-mined to protect ourselves, as far as was in my power, and the affair began to take a serious as-pect. I ordered my men to take their arms and separate themselves from the savages; at the same time declaring to them that I would kill the first man who touched our baggage. On which they commenced filing off immediately; we marched about the same time, and found they had made out to steal one sword, tomahawk, broad-ax, five canteens, and sundry other small articles. After leaving them, when I reflected on the subject, I felt myself sincerely mortified, that the smallness of my number obliged me thus to submit to the insults of lawless banditti, it being the first time a savage ever took anything from me with the least appearance of force.

After encamping at night the doctor and myself went about one mile back, and waylaid the road,

determined in case we discovered any of the rascals pursuing us to steal our horses, to kill two at least; but after waiting behind some logs until some time in the night, and discovering no person, we returned to camp. Killed two buffalo and one deer. Distance 17 miles.

Sunday, Nov. 23d. Marched at ten o'clock; at one o'clock came to the third fork [St. Charles River], on the south side, and encamped at night in the point of the grand forks [confluence of Fountain river]. As the river appeared to be divid-ing itself into many small branches, and of course must be near its extreme source, I concluded to put the party in a defensible situation, and ascend the north fork [Fountain river] to the high point [Pike's Peak] of the blue mountain [Front range], which we conceived would be one day's march, in order to be enabled, from its pinical [pinnacle], to lay down the various branches and positions of the country. Killed five buffalo. Distance 19 miles.

Nov. 24th. Early in the morning we cut down 14 logs, and put up a breast work, five feet high in three sides and the other thrown on the river. After giving the necessary orders for their govern-ment during my absence, in case of our not re-turning, we marched at one o'clock, with an idea of arriving at the foot of the mountain; but found ourselves obliged to take up our night's lodging under a single cedar which we found in the prairie, without water and extremely cold. Our party be-sides myself consisted of Dr. Robinson, and Pri-vates Miller and Brown. Distance 12 miles.

Nov. 25th. Marched early, with an expectation of ascending the mountain, but was only able to encamp at its base, after passing over small hills covered with cedars and pitch-pines. Our encamp-ment was on a [Turkey] creek, where we found no water for several miles from the mountain; but near its base, found springs sufficient. Took a meridional observation, and the altitude of the mountain. Killed two buffalo. Distance 22 miles.

Nov. 26th. Expecting to return to our camp the same evening, we left all our blankets and pro-visions at the foot of the [Cheyenne] mountain. Killed a deer of a new species (Cariacus macrotis), and hung his skin on a tree with some meat. We commenced ascending; found it very difficult, being obliged to climb up rocks, sometimes almost per-pendicular; and after marching all day we en-camped in a cave, without blankets, victuals, or water. We had a fine clear sky, while it was snowing at the bottom. On the side of the moun-tain we found only yellow and pitch-pine. Some distance up we found buffalo; higher still the new species of deer, and pheasants.

Nov. 27th. Arose hungry, dry, and extremely sore, from the inequality of the rocks on which we had lain all night, but were amply compensated for toil by the sublimity of the prospect below. The unbounded prairie was overhung with clouds, which appeared like the ocean in a storm, wave piled on wave and foaming, while the sky was perfectly clear where we were. Commenced our march up the mountain, and in about one hour arrived at the summit of this chain. Here we found the snow middle-deep; no sign of beast or bird inhabiting this region. The thermometer, which stood at 9° above zero at the foot of the mountain, here fell to 4° below zero. The summit of the Grand Peak, which was entirely bare of vegetation and covered with snow, now appeared at the distance of 15 or 16 miles from us. It was as high again as what we had ascended, and it would have taken a whole day's march to arrive at its base, when I believe no human being could have ascended to its pinical. This, with the conditions of my soldiers, who had only light coveralls on, no stockings, and were in every way ill provided to endure the inclemency of the region; the bad prospect of killing anything to subsist upon, with the further detention of two or three days which it must occasion, determined us to return. The clouds from below had now ascended the mountain and entirely enveloped the summit, on which rest eternal snows. We descended by a long, deep ravine, with much less difficulty than contemplated. Found all our baggage safe, but the provisions all destroyed. It began to snow, and we sought shelter under the side of a projecting rock, where we all four made a meal of one partridge and a piece of deer's ribs the ravens had left us, being the first we had eaten in that 48 hours.

Toward an Indigenous Poetry:
The Beginnings Through Bryant

The early Puritan poets of New England constitute a special case. They belonged to a peculiar community, and they had come to the New World in order to build a society that would embody the values and beliefs of that community. Moreover, those that we have discussed earlier were all transplanted Englishmen. But as generations of homebred Americans began to appear and the first settlements developed into well-established societies, wider literary interests began to develop; and, as the eighteenth century went on, there gradually emerged a consciousness that America needed—and lacked —a literature of her own and a literature that would, among other things, satisfy humanistic and secular interests. In this matter one can discern at least two strains: the gradual fading in New England of the attempt to establish the City of God and the increasing intellectual influence of the colonies to the south and, in particular, of the cities of New York and Philadelphia, where the prosperous merchant and not the Puritan divine was the acknowledged leader. The emerging literature could not only be self-consciously American but less other-worldly in its concerns.

What kind of poetry did Americans write in the eighteenth century? What were its modes and models? In what sense, if any, can it be regarded as distinctively American?

One of the most prominent and interesting groups of eighteenth-century colonial poets were the so-called Connecticut, or Hartford, Wits. The more important of these were Timothy Dwight (1752–1817), John Trumbull (1750–1831), and Joel Barlow (1754–1812). As might be expected, they imi-

Timothy Dwight

193

tated the reigning forms of English verse, often achieving real competence in managing them. Timothy Dwight's long poem *Greenfield Hill* (first published in 1794) is an account of the Connecticut village of Fairfield as seen in a time of peace and in a time of trouble. The poem describes, among other things, the burning of Fairfield by the British in 1779 and an attack on it by Indians; but it also, as in the brief selection quoted below, describes the village as an abode of rural peace, wholesome life, and happiness. Dwight's obvious model was Oliver Goldsmith's *The Deserted Village*. Here are the opening lines of Goldsmith's poem:

> Sweet Auburn, loveliest village of the plain,
> Where health and plenty cheered the labouring swain,
> Where smiling spring its earliest visit paid,
> And parting summer's lingering blooms delayed,
> Dear lovely bowers of innocence and ease,
> Seats of my youth, when every sport could please,
> How often have I loitered o'er thy green,
> Where humble happiness endeared each scene!

And here is a corresponding passage from Dwight's *Greenfield Hill*:

> Fair Verna! loveliest village of the west;
> Of every joy, and every charm, possess'd;
> How pleas'd amid thy varied walks I rove,
> Sweet, cheerful walks of innocence, and love,
> And o'er thy smiling prospects cast my eyes,
> And see the seats of peace, and pleasure, rise,
> And hear the voice of Industry resound,
> And mark the smile of competence, around!
> Hail, happy village! O'er thy cheerful lawns,
> With earliest beauty, spring delighted dawns;   10
> The northward sun begins his vernal smile;
> The spring-bird carols o'er the cressy rill:
> The shower, that patters in the ruffled stream,
> The ploughboy's voice, that chides the lingering team,
> The bee, industrious, with his busy song,
> The woodman's axe, the distant groves among,
> The waggon, rattling down the rugged steep,
> The light wind, lulling every care to sleep,
> All these, with mingled music, from below,
> Deceive intruding sorrow, as I go.   20
>   How pleas'd, fond Recollection, with a smile,

Surveys the varied round of wintery toil!
How pleas'd, amid the flowers, that scent the plain,
Recalls the vanish'd frost, and sleeted rain;
The chilling damp, the ice-endangering street,
And treacherous earth that slump'd beneath the feet.
   Yet even stern winter's glooms could joy inspire:
Then social circles grac'd the nutwood fire;
The axe resounded, at the sunny door;
The swain, industrious, trimm'd his flaxen store;   30
Or thresh'd, with vigorous flail, the bounding wheat,
His poultry round him pilfering for their meat;
Or slid his firewood on the creaking snow;
Or bore his produce to the main below;
Or o'er his rich returns exulting laugh'd;
Or pledg'd the healthful orchard's sparkling draught:
While, on his board, for friends and neighbours spread,
The turkey smoak'd, his busy housewife fed;
And Hospitality look'd smiling round,
And Leisure told his tale, with gleeful sound.   40

Trumbull published two long satires, *The Progress of Dulness* (1772–73), *John Trumbull* a take-off on academic life and various undergraduate attitudes toward it, and *M'Fingal* (1782), a poem that satirizes a Tory squire (to whom the author gives the name M'Fingal) who refuses to join the rest of the inhabitants of his Massachusetts village when the conflict with Great Britain begins.

In choosing *M'Fingal* for his title, Trumbull may well have had in mind John Dryden's *MacFlecknoe*. But in the meter and generally in the spirit of his verse, he is following the example of that other great English satirist of the seventeenth century, Samuel Butler, whose *Hudibras* employs a characteristic meter (sometimes called "Hudibrastic") and affects a rough-and-tumble style.

Here follow the first few lines of *Hudibras*:

When civil dudgeon first grew high,
And men fell out, they knew not why;
When hard words, jealousies, and fears
Set folks together by the ears
And made them fight, like mad or drunk,
For Dame Religion as for punk,
Whose honesty they all durst swear for,
Though not a man of them knew wherefore;
When gospel-trumpeter, surrounded

With long-eared rout, to battle sounded,   10
And pulpit, drum ecclesiastic,
Was beat with fist instead of a stick;—
Then did Sir Knight abandon dwelling,
And out he rode a-colonelling.

With the preceding lines compare, as a sample of Trumbull's satiric style, part of the third canto of *M'Fingal*, entitled "The Liberty Pole." In the passage that follows the Tory squire finds, to his consternation, that the patriots are raising a flagstaff to the top of which they have run up the flag of independence.

Now warm with ministerial ire,
Fierce sallied forth our loyal 'Squire,
And on his striding steps attends
His desperate clan of Tory friends.
When sudden met his wrathful eye
A pole ascending through the sky,
Which numerous throngs of whiggish race
Were raising in the market-place.
Not higher school-boy's kites aspire,
Or royal mast, or country spire;   10
Like spears at Brobdignagian tilting,
Or Satan's walking-staff in Milton.
And on its top, the flag unfurl'd
Waved triumph o'er the gazing world,
Inscribed with inconsistent types
Of Liberty and thirteen stripes.
Beneath, the crowd without delay
The dedication-rites essay,
And gladly pay, in antient fashion,
The ceremonies of libation;   20
While briskly to each patriot, lip
Walks eager round the inspiring flip:
Delicious draught! whose powers inherit
The quintessence of public spirit;
Which whoso tastes, perceives his mind
To nobler politics refined;
Or roused to martial controversy,
As from transforming cups of Circe;
Or warm'd with Homer's nectar'd liquor,
That fill'd the veins of gods with ichor.   30

At hand for new supplies in store,
The tavern opes its friendly door,
Whence to and fro the waiters run,
Like bucket-men at fires in town.
Then with three shouts that tore the sky,
'Tis consecrate to Liberty.

Barlow served in the American army during the Revolution. In later years   *Joel*
he frequently lived abroad, as consul in Algiers (1795) and as a diplomat   *Barlow*
commissioned to negotiate a treaty (1811) with Napoleon. In 1812 he was
caught up in Napoleon's retreat from Moscow, suffered great hardships, died,
and was buried in Poland.

Barlow's most ambitious work and his poetic showpiece is an epic poem,
The Columbiad (1807), written in the heroic couplet (iambic pentameter)
and extending through twelve books. The poem begins with Columbus and
takes us by stages through the American War of Independence. Its theme,
to borrow the words of Roy Harvey Pearce, is "the inexorable progress of
free institutions in the Americas. . . . The final vision, the final book is
charged with an unabashed utopianism—a vision of the brave new world, at
last unified through a universal language, so that all is caught up in one grand
political harmony." The spirit of this early American epic, then, is upward
and onward, but the poem remains firmly on the ground. It is heavy-footedly
pedestrian.

The poets of England during the latter part of the seventeenth and eighteenth centuries, admiring the epic ideal, diligently imitated Virgil and
Milton but failed to produce epics of their own. Their most successful efforts
were in *mock* epics of one sort and another, and so it is with their American
imitator, Joel Barlow. He is now best remembered for his more playful verse,
a mock-pastoral, *The Hasty-Pudding* (1796), written out of his homesickness
for a favorite American dish which he missed and longed for while he lived
abroad. Barlow chooses for his metrical form the Popeian heroic couplet,
though he is probably remembering also the mock pomposity of such eighteenth-century English blank-verse poems as John Philips' *The Splendid
Shilling* or John Dyer's celebration of the British wool trade in *The Fleece.*
Here are the opening lines of Canto 1:

Ye Alps audacious, thro' the heav'ns that rise,
To cramp the day and hide me from the skies;
Ye Gallic flags, that o'er their heights unfurl'd,
Bear death to kings, and freedom to the world,
I sing not you. A softer theme I chuse,

A virgin theme, unconscious of the Muse,
But fruitful, rich, well suited to inspire
The purest frenzy of poetic fire.
  Despise it not, ye Bards to terror steel'd,
Who hurl your thunders round the epic field;   10
Nor ye who strain your midnight throats to sing
Joys that the vineyard and the still-house bring;
Or on some distant fair your notes employ,
And speak of raptures that you ne'er enjoy.
I sing the sweets I know, the charms I feel,
My morning incense, and my evening meal,
The sweets of Hasty-Pudding. Come, dear bowl,
Glide o'er my palate, and inspire my soul.
The milk beside thee, smoking from the kine,
Its substance mingled, married in with thine,   20
Shall cool and temper thy superior heat,
And save the pains of blowing while I eat.
  Oh! could the smooth, the emblematic song
Flow like thy genial juices o'er my tongue,
Could those mild morsels in my numbers chime,
And, as they roll in substance, roll in rhyme,
No more thy aukward unpoetic name
Should shun the muse, or prejudice thy fame;
But rising grateful to th' accustom'd ear,
All Bards should catch it, and all realms revere!   30
  Assist me first with pious toil to trace
Thro' wrecks of time thy lineage and thy race;
Declare what lovely squaw, in days of yore,
(Ere great Columbus sought thy native shore)
First gave thee to the world; her works of fame
Have liv'd indeed, but liv'd without a name.
Some tawny Ceres, goddess of her days,
First learn'd with stones to crack the well-dry'd maize,
Thro' the rough seive to shake the golden show'r,
In boiling water stir the yellow flour: 40
The yellow flour, bestrew'd and stir'd with haste,
Swells in the flood and thickens to a paste,
Then puffs and wallops, rises to the brim,
Drinks the dry knobs that on the surface swim;
The knobs at last the busy ladle breaks,
And the whole mass its true consistence takes.

> Could but her sacred name, unknown so long,
> Rise like her labors, to the son of song,
> To her, to them, I'd consecrate my lays,
> And blow her pudding with the breath of praise.   50

The content of these poems is American—sometimes self-consciously so. But the forms, as we have noted, are borrowed from the reigning English models of the eighteenth century, from the poetry of Alexander Pope or Oliver Goldsmith or Thomas Gray, or from earlier, seventeenth-century poems like *Hudibras*. How could it have been otherwise? The colonists had come from Great Britain and Ireland. They spoke English and they brought their native language with them. But the possession of a language always carries with it more than a mere vocabulary and grammatical system. A language involves also a way of looking at the world, attitudes, and implicit judgments about the nature of reality.

The inevitably imitative character of early American poetry is also illustrated by the work of Phillis Wheatley (1753?–1784), who was brought to Boston from Africa as a child of seven and sold as a slave to John Wheatley. (The Wheatleys made her a member of the family and later gave her her freedom.) She was precocious and learned the English language in sixteen months. How fluent her English became is evident from her poetry. (Her *Poems on Various Subjects, Religious and Moral* was published in London in 1773.) She also mastered the metrical forms and the rhetorical conventions of English neoclassical verse. Thus, in one of her poems she addresses her master and patron as Maecenas, the name of the patron of the Latin poets Horace and Virgil. She invokes the classical gods and goddesses and she employs the elegant circumlocutions beloved of Pope and the other English neoclassical writers. As an example, consider her "Ode to Neptune," a poem written on Mrs. Wheatley's voyage to England. It begins as follows:

Phillis Wheatley

> While raging tempests shake the shore,
> While Æ'lus' thunders round us roar,
> And sweep impetuous o'er the plain
> Be still, O tyrant of the main;
> Nor let thy brow contracted frowns betray,
> While my Susannah skims the wat'ry way.

Compare Pope's

> But when loud surges lash the sounding shore,
> The hoarse, rough verse should like the torrent roar.
> When Ajax strives, some rock's vast weight to throw,
> The line too labours, and the words move slow;

Not so, when swift Camilla scours the plain,
Flies o'er th' unbending corn, and skims along the main.

On a superficial level, Phillis Wheatley's is easy and accomplished verse. Indeed, her poems are quite as good as many of the poems in *Dodsley's Collection,* that popular anthology of mid-eighteenth-century English verse. But hers is hardly authentic *poetry.* Phillis Wheatley's accomplishment was extraordinary, but essentially as a piece of remarkable adaptation.

Ebenezer Cook

If one looks to the colonies south of New England, one sees little to require modification of the general observations already made about early American poetry. A poem with a Maryland setting, published in London in 1708, satirizes the rawness, crudity, and rascality of the people of the American frontier. Like Trumbull's *M'Fingal,* it makes use of Hudibrastic verse. The author is believed to have been Ebenezer Cook (*c.* 1672–1732).

Cook calls his poem "The Sot-Weed Factor." The sot weed is the tobacco plant, and Cook's poem recounts the adventures of an Englishman who came to Maryland to make his fortune as a dealer in tobacco. (John Barth's novel, *The Sot-Weed Factor,* 1960, takes its rise from this poem. See the selection in our text.)

Here follows a short but representative section of the poem in the eighteenth-century spelling and punctuation of the first edition.

Encountring soon the smoaky Seat,
The Planter old did thus me greet:
"Whether you come from Goal[1] or Colledge,
"You're welcome to my certain Knowledge;
"And if you please all Night to stay,
"My Son shall put you in the way.
Which offer I most kindly took,
And for a Seat did round me look;
When presently amongst the rest,
He plac'd his unknown *English* Guest,
Who found them drinking for a whet,
A Cask of Syder on the Fret,[2]
Till Supper came upon the Table,
On which I fed whilst I was able.
So after hearty Entertainment,
Of Drink and Victuals without Payment;
For Planters Tables, you must know,
Are free for all that come and go.

10

[1] Misprint for "gaol," that is, "jail."
[2] Beginning to sour: "on the fret" means in a secondary fermentation.

> While Pon and Milk, with Mush well stoar'd,
> In Wooden Dishes grac'd the Board;   20
> With Homine and Syder-pap,
> (Which scarce a hungry dog wou'd lap)
> Well stuff'd, with Fat from Bacon fry'd,
> Or with Mollossus dulcify'd.

With the help of Cook's own notes, we can make out the menu described in the last six lines: it consisted of corn pone and milk, mush (see Barlow's *Hasty-Pudding*), hominy, cider-pap, "a food made of Syder and small homine, like our oatmeal (Cook's note)" flavored with bacon grease or molasses. This is food of the country indeed, with American cornmeal as the principal cereal. It was obviously not much relished by the stranger from England.

The two ablest poets of New York early in the nineteenth century were Joseph Rodman Drake (1795–1820) and his close friend Fitz-Greene Halleck (1790–1867). They are deft craftsmen, they show a certain sophistication, and they are facile in their handling of meter. But their very skillfulness points up the general emptiness of American verse of this period.

Joseph Rodman Drake and Fitz-Greene Halleck

Drake's most ambitious work is his poem entitled "The Culprit Fay," in which he attempts to transplant the supernatural beings of British fairy lore to the American strand:

> Ouphe and goblin! imp and sprite
> Elf of eve! and starry fay

are set down on the banks of the Hudson River. Drake's fairies have their immediate source in "Anster Fair" (1812) by the Scottish poet William Tennant; ultimately, of course, they go back to Shakespeare's *Midsummer Night's Dream* and Michael Drayton's *Nymphidia*. Drake tries hard to accommodate them to the American scene by making references to American insects like the katydid, to American birds like the whippoorwill, and to American trees like the sassafras. But the grafting of English folklore onto an American stock cannot be said to take.

Halleck, who outlived his friend by many years, did not thereby become a much more thoughtful or mature poet. His work achieves little beyond a certain topicality of reference and a technical dexterity. His best-remembered lines are probably those from a poem celebrating Marco Bozzaris, one of the heroes of the Greek war of independence. This poem (1825) is, of course, "Byronic" in inspiration and to a certain degree in style as well.

> At midnight, in his guarded tent,
> The Turk was dreaming of the hour

When Greece, her knee in suppliance bent,
  Should tremble at his power:
In dreams, through camp and court, he bore
The trophies of a conqueror;
  In dreams his song of triumph heard;
Then wore his monarch's signet ring:
Then pressed that monarch's throne—a king;
As wild his thoughts, and gay of wing,   10
  As Eden's garden bird.

At midnight, in the forest shades,
  Bozzaris ranged his Suliote band,
True as the steel of their tried blades,
  Heroes in heart and hand.
There had the Persian's thousands stood,
There had the glad earth drunk their blood
  On old Platæa's day;
And now there breathed that haunted air
The sons of sires who conquered there,   20
With arm to strike, and soul to dare,
  As quick, as far as they.

An hour passed on—the Turk awoke;
  That bright dream was his last;
He woke—to hear his sentries shriek,
"To arms! they come! the Greek: the Greek!"
He woke—to die midst flame, and smoke,
And shout, and groan, and sabre stroke,
  And death shots falling thick and fast
As lightnings from the mountain cloud;   30
And heard, with voice as trumpet loud,
  Bozzaris cheer his band:
"Strike—till the last armed foe expires;
Strike—for your altars and your fires;
Strike—for the green graves of your sires;
  God—and your native land!"

They fought—like brave men, long and well;
  They piled that ground with Moslem slain,
They conquered—but Bozzaris fell,
  Bleeding at every vein.   40
His few surviving comrades saw

His smile when rang their proud hurrah,
   And the red field was won;
Then saw in death his eyelids close
Calmly, as to a night's repose,
   Like flowers at set of sun. . . .

Bozzaris! with the storied brave
   Greece nurtured in her glory's time,
Rest thee—there is no prouder grave,
   Even in her own proud clime.   50
She wore no funeral weeds for thee,
   Nor bade the dark hearse wave its plume
Like torn branch from death's leafless tree
In sorrow's pomp and pageantry,
   The heartless luxury of the tomb:
But she remembers thee as one
Long loved, and for a season gone;
For thee her poet's lyre is wreathed,
Her marble wrought, her music breathed;
For thee she rings the birthday bells;   60
Of thee her babes' first lisping tells;
For thine her evening prayer is said
At palace couch and cottage bed;
Her soldier, closing with the foe,
Gives for thy sake a deadlier blow;
His plighted maiden, when she fears
For him, the joy of her young years,
Thinks of thy fate, and checks her tears:
   And she, the mother of thy boys,
Though in her eye and faded cheek   70
Is read the grief she will not speak,
   The memory of her buried joys,
And even she who gave thee birth,
Will, by their pilgrim-circled hearth,
   Talk of thy doom without a sigh:
For thou art Freedom's now, and Fame's;
One of the few, the immortal names,
   That were not born to die.

Halleck's "Alnwick Castle" (1827) imitates Sir Walter Scott. The castle
of the Percies recalls the age of chivalry and romance, but even as the visiting

American gazes on the castle walls, he realizes that "these are not romantic times/ . . . Ours are the days of fact, not fable." Alnwick itself is now "but a market town," itself a part of what the poet ruefully concedes is a "banknote world." Halleck's native land is, of course, doubly so: America lacks even the relics of the old heroic days. Thus Halleck honestly faces the issue as he sees it, but if the issue is put in such terms as these, the prospect for an American poetry becomes bleak indeed.

Philip Freneau

One of the most interesting of the poets of this period was Philip Freneau (1752–1832), a close friend and political associate of Thomas Jefferson. He was not only a poet but a newspaper editor, propagandist, and pamphleteer.[1] Drake and Halleck could afford to regard literature as a gentleman's amusement. Drake came of well-to-do merchant stock and was trained for the medical profession; Halleck was a banker and was the secretary of John Jacob Astor, who was at this time laying the foundations of the great Astor fortune. Freneau, on the other hand, had to make his living from his writing, and since verse certainly would not provide one, much of his labor went into political writing and journalism.

Freneau's bitter antipathy toward England—he had been captured and confined on a British prison ship—makes his dependence on English models all the more striking. One is not surprised that his early poem *The House of Night* (1770) should draw heavily on English poets of the "graveyard school" (Edward Young, the author of *Night Thoughts* and Robert Blair, the author of "The Grave"), but even the later poetry of Freneau still walks in shackles to the reigning British modes.

For example, "God Save the Rights of Man" is simply an adaptation of the British national anthem, "God Save the King." If it be objected that this is not a fair illustration since Freneau in this instance wants us to be conscious of the British model for which he is offering an alternative, then consider a quatrain from one of his best-known poems, "To the Memory of the Brave Americans." The Americans in question had fallen at the battle of Ewtaw Springs. Freneau writes:

[1] His Deism and his sharply anti-Federalist sentiments endeared him to Jefferson, who, when he became Secretary of State, secured for Freneau the post of translator in the state department. At this time, Freneau established in Philadelphia the *National Gazette*, a newspaper that became a mouthpiece for the Jeffersonian faction and was vigorous in its attacks on Alexander Hamilton. As Hamilton and Jefferson clashed more and more openly and the political parties gradually came to take form around them, Freneau became a violently partisan writer and editor. President Washington was once so irritated that at a cabinet meeting he referred to "that rascal Freneau." Though committed to a belief in the natural goodness and perfectability of man, Freneau found in his day-to-day experience personal devils enough to excoriate. Even in the eyes of his friend Jefferson, his vehement attacks sometimes went much too far.

> They saw their injured country's woe;
>   The flaming town, the wasted field;
> Then rushed to meet the insulting foe;
>   They took the spear—but left the shield.

Freneau is here using the old-fashioned neoclassical poetical terminology in which soldiers fight with the weapons of the Greeks and Romans. Though he knew that the American riflemen at Ewtaw Springs did not carry spears and had no shields to lay aside, flintlocks were too realistic and unpoetic to be allowed to appear in neoclassical verse.

What Freneau means to say in the last two lines, of course, is that the American patriots were so eager to close with the British that they snatched up only offensive weapons (spears) and did not even bother with defensive armor (shields). But the awkward neoclassical figure of speech used here fails to stress the American soldiers' ardor and in fact fails to make sense.

A more successful poem is "The Indian Burying Ground" (1788). In a note that he supplied for this poem, Freneau observed that the "North American Indians bury their dead in a sitting posture, decorating the corpse with wampum, images of birds, quadrupeds, etc., and (if that of a warrior) with bows, arrows, tomahawks, and other military weapons." Though the life history of the red man soon came to be thought of as "romantic" subject matter, Freneau's poem has a sturdy eighteenth-century logic as he works out the symbolic implications of this choice of posture so different from the Christian custom of placing the dead in a recumbent position, as if asleep.

> In spite of all the learned have said,
>   I still my old opinion keep;
> The posture, that we give the dead,
>   Points out the soul's eternal sleep.
>
> Not so the ancients of these lands—
>   The Indian, when from life released,
> Again is seated with his friends,
>   And shares again the joyous feast.
>
> His imaged birds, and painted bowl,
>   And venison, for a journey dressed,   10
> Bespeak the nature of the soul,
>   Activity, that knows no rest.
>
> His bow, for action ready bent,
>   And arrows, with a head of stone,

Can only mean that life is spent,
 And not the old ideas gone.

Thou, stranger, that shalt come this way,
 No fraud upon the dead commit—
Observe the swelling turf, and say
 They do not lie, but here they sit.   20

Here still a lofty rock remains,
 On which the curious eye may trace
(Now wasted, half, by wearing rains)
 The fancies of a ruder race.

Here still an aged elm aspires,
 Beneath whose far-projecting shade
(And which the shepherd still admires)
 The children of the forest played!

There oft a restless Indian queen
 (Pale Shebah, with her braided hair) 30
And many a barbarous form is seen
 To chide the man that lingers there.

By midnight moons, o'er moistening dews;
 In habit for the chase arrayed,
The hunter still the deer pursues,
 The hunter and the deer, a shade!

And long shall timorous fancy see
 The painted chief, and pointed spear,
And Reason's self shall bow the knee
 To shadows and delusions here.   40

  The influence of neoclassical British models on Freneau was not always so happy. From them he derives his tendency toward direct statement, moralizing illustration, and frank didacticism. If one is to be an American poet, it is first necessary for him to be a poet, and Freneau's penchant for deistic rationality and his argumentative disposition had the effect of flattening a great deal of his poetry into versified prose. The flattening reveals itself not only in such poems as "On the Universality and Other Attributes of the God of Nature," where it might be expected, but also in some of his nature poems. Consider, for example, a poem usually thought to be Freneau's masterpiece, "The Wild Honey Suckle" (1786):

Fair flower, that dost so comely grow,
Hid in this silent, dull retreat,

Untouched thy honied blossoms blow,
Unseen thy little branches greet:
   No roving foot shall crush thee here,
   No busy hand provoke a tear.

By Nature's self in white arrayed,
She bade thee shun the vulgar eye.
And planted here the guardian shade,
And sent soft waters murmuring by;   10
   Thus quietly thy summer goes,
   Thy days declining to repose.

Smit with those charms, that must decay,
I grieve to see your future doom;
They died—nor were those flowers more gay,
The flowers that did in Eden bloom;
   Unpitying frosts, and Autumn's power
   Shall leave no vestige of this flower.

From morning suns and evening dews
At first thy little being came: 20
If nothing once, you nothing lose,
For when you die you are the same;
   The space between, is but an hour,
   The frail duration of a flower.

The poem has some mildly pleasant touches, but the basic method is to present an image and then comment upon it. Worse still, the comments often do not make full "poetic sense": that is to say, the thinking does not provide a justification for the emotions that Freneau means for his reader to feel. For this reason one has to regard the poem as sentimental; it exhibits a superficial reaction rather than presenting a profound insight.

The justification of this last statement is worth spelling out in some detail —not to insure a disparaging dismissal of the poem and certainly not to pull to pieces a slight poetic fabric for the perverse pleasure to be had from un-weaving it. Quite the contrary: a close examination of "The Wild Honey Suckle" may lead us to something positive. It can provide a means for defin-ing the characteristic themes of the great Romantic poets who succeeded those poets of sentiment and gentle melancholy who dominated the latter half of the eighteenth century in England and whom Freneau is imitating here.

The first stanza treats of the advantages as well as the disadvantages of the flower's modest retirement. Its beauty can be admired by few—Freneau is perhaps remembering Thomas Gray's flower "born to blush unseen,/And waste its fragrance on the desert air"—but then the honeysuckle is also less likely to be crushed by someone's foot. The second stanza suggests that the honeysuckle bears a special relationship to nature, which has counseled it to shun the "vulgar eye" and arrayed it in white (because white is the emblem of simplicity and purity?). But, in spite of nature's solicitude, the flower cannot escape its doom. "Unpitying" frosts will destroy it. In actual fact, Nature is indifferent—the "Unpitying" frosts are as much a part of nature as are her "soft waters." The notion that nature has provided a "guardian shade" for the protection of the honeysuckle is a sentimental fancy.

Nor does the poet, in the consolation he offers the flower in the last stanza, meet the real issue. He tells the plant that since it came from nothing in the beginning, its reduction to nothing in the days ahead constitutes no real loss. But the real point, which he ignores, is that the flower lacks the kind of consciousness that the poet possesses. It cannot foresee its death and will not be aware of it when it comes. To have made this point would have involved facing the crucial difference between nature and man: though man is, like the flower, part of nature, he is also somehow "outside" nature. He can see his fate mirrored in that of the other creatures such as a bird or a flower, but the very fact that he can "see" it makes him different from any bird or flower. The human being may at times envy the flower its happy ignorance, or may yearn for its kind of innocence, or may dream of an Eden in which he feels himself in complete harmony with nature; but the human being will always find it impossible to disavow his knowledge—his consciousness of his difference. Out of that very knowledge issues his poetry. Such is the grand theme of the great Romantic poets. Their poetry is emotional, sometimes passionately so, but it is not characteristically sentimental, for it does not evade the real issues through a conscious or unconscious cheat.

At this point it may be worth considering why the grand theme of the Romantics emerged just when it did. The intellectual synthesis achieved in the Middle Ages described man as having a special relationship to nature and to God—who had created the universe. Man was a part of nature, to be sure, but he was markedly different from the other natural creatures, for God had created man in his own image. Man had been given "reason," which meant that he had been bequeathed a godlike knowledge—memory of the past and a prevision of the future, including his own fate as a natural creature.

The conception of man's place in the universe as given by Christian orthodoxy began to alter the impact of the Renaissance and the Reformation; during the eighteenth-century Enlightenment, as we have earlier remarked, the sun of reason had withered those aspects of Christianity which the rationalist had come to consider merely superstition and fable.

As the old synthesis broke up, man's place in the universe became problematical. The absentee God of the Deists had retired from any active intervention in his universe. How could one pray to Him? Nature was a marvelous machine, but how could one enter into a relationship with a machine? Descartes had "cut the throat of poetry" by separating man's reason from nature's body: man's consciousness was absolutely incommensurable with nature; it could not be measured or otherwise described mathematically, whereas nature could be completely described in these terms, and the scientist was invited to get on with the quantitative description. Man thus became an "angel shut up in a machine," that is, sheer reason imprisoned in a mechanical body.

This dualism became increasingly uncomfortable, and in the reaction against rationalism various attempts were made to close the gap separating man from nature.[2] At one extreme one could try to divinize man and make him the soul of nature, or at least see in his imagination a sovereign, reconciling, almost godlike power; at the other extreme one could divinize nature, finding it much more than any machine, alive and pulsing with godhead (pantheism). Between these two positions, one can find in the early nineteenth century a whole spectrum of subtle variations. But whatever the mode of reconciliation, the more sensitive spirits of the age agreed in their location and definition of the problem. Men felt the need to recover the wholeness of life, and with it faith and vitality. In England, poets like Wordsworth and Coleridge, after breaking away from Christianity, later came to some kind of accommodation with it. For other poets like Shelley and Keats, however, and still later, in America, for men like Emerson and Thoreau, and for the transcendentalists in general (see pp. 338–51), there could be no simple return to the orthodoxy of an earlier day, even though they had become convinced of the sterility of the merely rational.

Sources of spiritual vitality had to be sought elsewhere, in the realm of the instinctive, the spontaneous, the deeply emotional. This realm of deep, unstated convictions, of introspection,[3] of powerful though unsystematized insights, of the presuppositions of the spirit—in short, of the recesses of *human* nature—corresponded in a sense to the depths of *physical* nature, especially the wilder and more mysterious aspects of physical nature. Thus, in the mind of the Romantic poet, "nature" and human nature were intimately associ-

---

[2] The reaction occasionally took the form of an attack on science and scientific method. Edgar Allan Poe's "Sonnet—To Science" (included in our text) is rather typical. The real culprit, of course, was not science: science and poetry do not compete with but complement each other. On the other hand, it requires a rather clear-eyed view of both if one is not to see them as opposed and hostile.

[3] The Puritan habit of self-examination might be thought to constitute a great resource for the Romantic writer and so it was, though fully realized only by the later Romantics like Hawthorne, Emerson, and Thoreau.

ated: the early experiences of Wordsworth the child, living among the hills and lakes of Cumberland, stimulated in Wordsworth the poet the insights and intuitions of value which his poetry was written to celebrate. But the world of field and rock and stream also provided Wordsworth with the best vehicle for setting forth, in their fullness, what these intuitions of value were.

That this should be so is not in the least strange when we remember that the Romantics' fundamental article of faith was that man must not divorce himself from a nature of which he was obviously a part and to which he was impelled to return as to a source of strength and vitality. Yet there could be no full return. Man's very anxiety to reestablish rapport with nature—his very consciousness of his separation from it—was, as we have seen, a great part of the difficulty. Keats' nightingale and Wordsworth's green linnet were obviously fully absorbed into the fabric of nature. As instinctive, unself-conscious creatures, not haunted by the passage of time, they lived in a kind of timeless present and were thus "immortal." To the poetic consciousness, at least, nature throbbed through them without let or hindrance; yet the human observer's very ability to note this fact constituted in itself a proof of his own detachment and testified to his own separation from nature.

To sum up these general observations, we may say that the great Romantic poet uses nature in order to come to an understanding of *human* nature[4] and that his interest in natural beauty cannot be separated from his interest in human consciousness and especially in the imaginative power which allows man to enter into some kind of relationship to the world of natural forces about him. Freneau's wild honeysuckle, as we have already noted, reminds the poet of the human situation, but we cannot take the suggested analogies very seriously. They hardly raise the question of man's peculiar status as a being who is rooted in nature and yet who also stands outside nature, with his moral being, his power of choice, his sense of the past, and his vision—joyful or foreboding—of what the future may bring. In his last stanza, Freneau does perhaps hint at man's special plight, but he does not come to grips with it as Keats does in his "Ode to a Nightingale," where, in a fashion similar to that of other great Romantic poems, the "Ode" shows itself to be not finally about a nightingale but about man's consciousness, at once his burden and his glory.

To say this is not, of course, to insist that the typical eighteenth-century poet's concern for picturesque landscape or for the exotic, barbaric, or remote scene, or even for one of Gothic gloom, was always, or merely, a frivolous interest. In any case, we must remember that the poets of the Age of Reason had emotions and did not spend their days being merely "reason-

---

[4] Thoreau frankly said that he went to the woods to learn about himself.

able." In fact, it was in the Age of Reason that the sentimental novel and the Gothic horror story were born. A strict diet of rationalism had made men hunger for the childlike, the primitive, the superstitious, and even the morbidly gloomy. Besides, such aspects of unreason had by now become more titillating than terrifying. Now that men lived under a rational system, the irrational could be indulged for the sake of an aesthetic thrill. Thus, Drake's interest in English fairy lore and Halleck's regret for the disappearance of the medieval world of tournament and border warfare are not fully serious. For them, Romanticism is a kind of game: they do not challenge the assumptions of the Age of Reason.

The later Romantics, however, went on to challenge those assumptions. Indeed, the growing interest in the extrarational (the primitive, the barbarous, even the mad) testifies to an increasing suspicion that rationalism told not quite the whole story about man.

FURTHER READINGS

Nelson F. Adkins, *Fitz-Greene Halleck: An Early Knickerbocker Wit and Poet* (1930)
Leon Howard, *The Connecticut Wits* (1943)

Frank L. Pleadwell, *The Life and Works of Joseph Rodman Drake* (1935)

WILLIAM CULLEN BRYANT (1794–1878)

When we approach William Cullen Bryant, who was soon to become recognized as the best poet that America up to his time had produced, we shall have to ask in what sense we can properly call him a Romantic. But this was not, of course, the kind of question that Bryant's fellow countrymen asked about him. (In their day the term "Romanticism" was not even current.) They were looking for an authentic poet, a man who in his technical proficiency and in the authority with which he voiced his insights could challenge the best of English poetry. They found it very early in Bryant. When in 1815 the editor Charles Dana was shown the manuscript of Bryant's poem "Thanatopsis," he expressed skepticism that verses so accomplished as these could possibly have been composed by any American poet.[1]

Bryant's first published poem, a satire entitled "The Embargo," was printed as a pamphlet in 1808 while he was still a boy of thirteen. It deals with the Embargo Act, a law sponsored by Thomas Jefferson and very unpopular in Bryant's New England. But the mode of satire, as one might guess, is that of the British satirists of the Augustan period.

Bryant's early masterpiece, "Thanatopsis" (1817), also looks back to British eighteenth-century models. In fact it is not very accurate

[1] We have remarked that the poetry of Drake and Halleck is proficient, but it did not appear until after Bryant's "Thanatopsis."

to refer to it as a Romantic poem, if we mean to use the term as it is applied to the mature poems of a Wordsworth or a Coleridge or to the odes of Keats. "Thanatopsis," in fact, may be regarded as a kind of throwback to the English graveyard school, to Thomas Gray's "Elegy Written in a Country Churchyard" (1750), to Robert Blair's "The Grave" (1743), and to the poetry of Henry Kirke White (1785–1806). The tonality is of an austere and carefully controlled melancholy. The speaker has come to terms with himself and eventually finds repose in an almost elegant stoicism.

Yet "Thanatopsis" is more than a pastiche of influences: it is an original compound and has its own individual character. Nature is, of course, prominent in the poem, just as it is in the English graveyard school and in an American poet like Freneau. But though nature provides the background and offers the poet her somber consolation, the nature portrayed is primarily that of the eighteenth-century pre-Romantics. In this regard, Bryant by 1817 had hardly advanced beyond Freneau. Within a few years, to be sure, Bryant would discover Wordsworth and write poems that would reflect Wordsworth's themes, diction, and something of his manner. But to the end, Bryant's remains essentially an old-fashioned eighteenth-century sensibility.

The difference between the sensibility of the young American poet and that of the great English poet shows itself in the difference between their characteristic *poetic methods*. Bryant tends, even in his best nature poetry, to *describe* a flower like the fringed gentian or the yellow violet, or to trace the course of a water bird against the sky, and then to find in the picture or event an application to his own moral life. In such poems, he sometimes gives us touches of description that redeem or almost redeem the rather pat moralistic conclusion. For example, in "To a Waterfowl," the lines

All day thy wings have fanned,
At that far height, the cold, thin atmosphere,

realize powerfully the sense of the bird's solitary flight. When he makes an application of some

aspect of a flower to the moral life of man, he often does this gracefully, as in "The Yellow Violet" (see below). But rarely in his nature poetry does Bryant fuse the thing described with its meaning. That is, the poet is rarely able to make his meaning rise, apparently without effort, from the description of a natural object or from his account of an incident.

Wordsworth, too, sometimes after describing a flower or bird, will go on to make appropriate comments and draw out the implications, but Wordsworth quite properly places among what he called his "Poems of Fancy" these poems in which he draws specific parallels or makes particular contrasts with the human situation. Such poems are lighter in tone than most of his other poetry and they are often consciously playful. In Wordsworth's truly *imaginative* treatment of nature—he called one group of his poems "Poems of the Imagination"—there is an almost complete identification of natural object and human significance. What he accomplishes at his best is a miraculous fusion in which objects or events glow with implicit meanings that require no overt statement.

A telltale sign of the essentially derivative and borrowed character of Bryant's art is the fact that his poetry tends to be so "meter-bound" that a reader can readily beat time as he recites aloud. For those Americans who doubted that poets on this side of the Atlantic could ever achieve strict meter and exact rhyme, Bryant's performance supplied a convincing answer. But vital poetry is distinguished from merely competent versifying by the poet's ability to play off against the metronomic beat of the meter the rhythms of natural speech. (See the discussion of Whitman's poetry on pp. 935–43.) In such poetry one feels a constant slight strain of the sense against the mechanical measure, and it is this that gives to such verse richness and expressive power. The reader may test for himself the relative lack of this quality in Bryant. Let him read aloud some of Bryant's poems and note how little they resist the monotony of the regular beat of the meter. Let him, for instance, read "Thanatopsis" and then read some of, say, Robert Frost's blank verse. Both

Bryant and Frost are New England poets and both poets are ostensibly using the same measure, but the living voice speaks through the very rhythms of Frost's blank verse. In Bryant's it is somewhat deadened and mechanized.[2]

[2] The comparison proposed is not unfair. It is true that the language spoken in New England presumably altered between 1820 and 1930, but the existing evidence would suggest that, at least in rural districts, the alteration in pronunciation, syntax, and even vocabulary was not very great. What was of importance was men's altered view of the proper relation of the rhythms of poetry to the cadences of the language as spoken.

Although in a book about American literature we are bound to be primarily interested in Bryant as a poet, most of his writing was in fact of another kind. Like Freneau, Bryant earned his living as a journalist and newspaper editor. In 1827, at the age of thirty-three, he joined the editorial staff of the New York *Evening Post* and enjoyed a long and successful career as editor and part owner of the newspaper. At his death in 1878, he left an estate worth a million dollars, probably a record for any American poet, past or present.

BIOGRAPHICAL CHART

1794   Born, November 3, in Cummington, Massachusetts
1808   *The Embargo*
1810–11   Attends Williams College for a brief time
1815   Begins work on "Thanatopsis"
1817   An early version of "Thanatopsis" first published in *North American Review*
1821   *Poems* (including final, expanded version of "Thanatopsis"); marries Fanny Fairchild

1825   Goes to New York City
1827   Joins the staff of the New York *Evening Post;* becomes its editor
1834   Travels to Europe for the first time
1850   *Letters of a Traveller*
1869   Wife dies
1870–71   Translates Homer into blank verse
1878   Dies, June 12, in New York

FURTHER READINGS

Parke Godwin, ed., *The Poetical Works of William Cullen Bryant* (1883; 2 vols.)
————, ed., *The Prose Writings of William Cullen Bryant* (1884; 2 vols.)

Parke Godwin, *A Biography of William Cullen Bryant, with Extracts from his Private Correspondence* (1883; 2 vols.)
H. H. Peckham, *Gotham Yankee: A Biography of William Cullen Bryant* (1950)

Thanatopsis (1817, 1821)

Since the title is taken from the Greek words *thanatos* (meaning *death*) and *opsis* (meaning *seeing*), it may be translated as "a view of death." Bryant began work on this poem in 1815, but he kept the poem by him, revised it carefully, and its publication in 1817 came about almost by accident. When Bryant's father found the manuscript of "Thanatopsis" in his son's desk, he discovered along with it the manuscript of a poem entitled "Inscription for the Entrance to a Wood." The elder Bryant did not tell his son that he was turning over the manuscript to the editor of the *North American Review,* and therefore there was no opportunity for William Cullen Bryant to point out that the manuscript leaves comprised two poems and not one, and so curiously the two were initially printed together as a single poem.

Bryant included "Thanatopsis" in his collection of *Poems* in 1821. In the 1821 version, the poet made numerous revisions. Among the most important of these was the insertion of a passage of sixteen-and-a-half lines at the beginning of the poem, a passage which (as the student will see) tells the reader that he is to conceive of all the rest of the poem as having been spoken by nature itself.

One important source of comfort for the speaker of this poem derives from the long view taken of human life and death. Nature counsels him to remember that from the beginning of time men have died and that they will continue to do so as long as the race endures. Death is no respecter of persons: it claims the prince as well as the peasant. Looked at in this long perspective, one is not allowed to feel that he is singled out for a special horror. Instead, he is simply being asked to take his place in the "innumerable caravan, which moves" to "that mysterious realm" to which all men go.

The mood of the poem is one of Stoicism, not of Christian hope. (Curiously enough, other and later poems by Bryant do express a Christian hope. For example, some of his hymns written for the Unitarian hymnal assume the doctrine of immortal life.) That "Thanatopsis" fails to stress any sense of a joyful reunion with nature and instead insists upon manly fortitude in the face of death does not in itself make the poem something less than "romantic." As we have earlier remarked, Wordsworth had his Stoical side and John Keats, who had behind him training in medicine and surgery, was well aware of all the facts about the body and the ultimate decay into which it was bound to fall.

Thus Keats faces in his "Ode to a Nightingale" what Bryant envisions in his lines about every man's going

> To mix forever with the elements,
> To be a brother to the insensible rock,
> And to the sluggish clod

But Keats, one feels, has thought the matter through more thoroughly than Bryant has. In "Ode to a Nightingale," the listener feels a poignant urge to throw off the doubts and anx-ieties and fears that bedevil the human being and to join the nightingale. The nightingale seems not to be cut off from nature as man is, but dwells in, and sings out of, nature's harmonious realm. The listener realizes, however, that his only way to join the nightingale will be through a loss of his consciousness—that is, through death. And yet dead, he would become merely a lump of inert matter, "to thy high requiem, a sod." Thus he will be, as Bryant puts it, mixed "forever with the elements [and] . . . brother to . . . the sluggish clod"—part of nature, to be sure, but unable to hear any more the nightingale's song. This is the human being's dilemma. The very consciousness which renders the world of nature so attractive to him is the thing that bars him out of nature; yet to break through the bar is to lose all awareness of nature.

"Thanatopsis" is usually regarded as Bryant's masterpiece. It does indeed show fine command of language and a powerful resonance, remarkable in a poet so young. For many readers of the twentieth century, however, the grandiloquence of the poem is somewhat faded, and its resounding rhetoric will seem the somewhat mannered vaunt of a talented young man. Yet the poem continues to receive praise and the modern critic Yvor Winters frankly calls it a great poem.

> To him who in the love of Nature holds
> Communion with her visible forms, she speaks
> A various language; for his gayer hours
> She has a voice of gladness, and a smile
> And eloquence of beauty, and she glides
> Into his darker musings with a mild
> And healing sympathy that steals away
> Their sharpness ere he is aware. When thoughts
> Of the last bitter hour come like a blight
> Over thy spirit, and sad images   10
> Of the stern agony, and shroud, and pall,
> And breathless darkness, and the narrow house
> Make thee to shudder and grow sick at heart,
> Go forth, under the open sky, and list
> To Nature's teachings, while from all around,—
> Earth and her waters, and the depths of air,—
> Comes a still voice:—
>
>   Yet a few days, and thee

The all-beholding sun shall see no more
In all his course; nor yet in the cold ground,
Where thy pale form was laid, with many
    tears, 20
Nor in the embrace of ocean, shall exist
Thy image. Earth, that nourished thee, shall claim
Thy growth, to be resolved to earth again,
And, lost each human trace, surrendering up
Thine individual being, shalt thou go
To mix forever with the elements,
To be a brother to the insensible rock,
And to the sluggish clod, which the rude swain
Turns with his share and treads upon. The oak
Shall send his roots abroad and pierce thy mold. 30

Yet not to thine eternal resting-place
Shalt thou retire alone; nor couldst thou wish
Couch more magnificent. Thou shalt lie down
With patriarchs of the infant world—with
    kings,
The powerful of the earth—the wise, the good;
Fair forms, and hoary seers of ages past,
All in one mighty sepulchre. The hills,—
Rock-ribbed and ancient as the sun,—the vales
Stretching in pensive quietness between;
The venerable woods, rivers that move 40
In majesty, and the complaining brooks
That make the meadows green; and, poured
    round all,
Old ocean's gray and melancholy waste,—
Are but the solemn decorations all
Of the great tomb of man. The golden sun,
The planets, all the infinite host of heaven,
Are shining on the sad abodes of death
Through the still lapse of ages. All that tread

The globe are but a handful to the tribes
That slumber in its bosom.—Take the wings 50
Of morning, pierce the Barcan wilderness,
Or lose thyself in the continuous woods
Where rolls the Oregon, and hears no sound
Save his own dashings—yet the dead are there;
And millions in those solitudes, since first
The flight of years began, have laid them down
In their last sleep—the dead reign there alone.
So shalt thou rest—and what if thou withdraw
Unheeded by the living, and no friend
Take note of thy departure? All that breathe 60
Will share thy destiny. The gay will laugh
When thou art gone, the solemn brood of care
Plod on, and each one as before will chase
His favorite phantom; yet all these shall leave
Their mirth and their employments, and
    shall come
And make their bed with thee. As the long train
Of ages glide away, the sons of men,—
The youth in life's green spring, and he who goes
In the full strength of years,—matron and maid,
And the sweet babe, and the gray-headed man,—70
Shall one by one be gathered to thy side
By those who in their turn shall follow them.

So live, that when thy summons comes to join
The innumerable caravan which moves
To that mysterious realm where each shall take
His chamber in the silent halls of death,
Thou go not like the quarry-slave at night,
Scourged to his dungeon, but sustained and
    soothed
By an unfaltering trust, approach thy grave
Like one who wraps the drapery of his couch 80
About him and lies down to pleasant dreams.

The Yellow Violet (1814)

The flower in question is the dogtooth yellow
violet, probably better known today as adder's
tongue. Bryant's description of it is botanically
accurate as well as charming. The reader may,
however, want to ask whether the poet "uses"
the flower didactically to make a moral point,
namely, that we ought not forget our humbler
friends when we arrive in a gayer and richer
world; or whether the reference to human society is justified and necessary in order to define
with precision the poet's present attitude. In
short, the reader ought to ask himself what is
the "tone" of the ending.

When beechen buds begin to swell,
    And woods the blue-bird's warble know,
The yellow violet's modest bell
    Peeps from the last year's leaves below.

Ere russet fields their green resume,
    Sweet flower, I love, in forest bare,
To meet thee, when thy faint perfume
    Alone is in the virgin air.

Of all her train, the hands of Spring
    First plants thee in the watery mould, 10
And I have seen thee blossoming
    Beside the snow-bank's edges cold.

Thy parent sun, who bade thee view
  Pale skies, and chilling moisture sip,
Has bathed thee in his own bright hue,
  And streaked with jet thy glowing lip,

Yet slight thy form, and low thy seat,
  And earthward bent thy gentle eye,
Unapt the passing view to meet,
  When loftier flowers are flaunting nigh.   20

Oft, in the sunless April day,
  Thy early smile has stayed my walk;

But midst the gorgeous blooms of May,
  I passed thee on thy humble stalk.

So they, who climb to wealth, forget
  The friends in darker fortunes tried.
I copied them—but I regret
  That I should ape the ways of pride.

And when again the genial hour
  Awakes the painted tribes of light,   30
I'll not o'erlook the modest flower
  That made the woods of April bright.

To a Waterfowl (1815)

Bryant composed this poem in December, 1815. He told someone later that on a journey to Plainfield, Massachusetts, he felt "very forlorn and desolate indeed, not knowing what was to become of him in the big world," and suddenly saw the bird flying across the sky and took comfort from the realization that the same providence that guided the bird would guide him in choosing what vocation to adopt. The experience is rather movingly presented and the life of the waterfowl is vividly imagined. But some readers may feel that the last two stanzas are a shade too explicit in spelling out the moral of the experience. In any case, this poem is thoroughly typical of Bryant's general poetical strategy and of his excellences and of his faults.

Whither, midst falling dew,
  While glow the heavens with the last steps
    of day,
Far, through their rosy depths, dost thou pursue
  Thy solitary way?

  Vainly the fowler's eye
Might mark thy distant flight to do thee wrong,
As, darkly painted on the crimson sky,
  Thy figure floats along.

Seek'st thou the plashy brink
Of weedy lake, or marge of river wide,   10
Or where the rocking billows rise and sink
  On the chafed ocean-side?

There is a Power whose care
Teaches thy way along that pathless coast—
The desert and illimitable air—
  Lone wandering, but not lost.

All day thy wings have fanned,
At that far height, the cold, thin atmosphere,
Yet stoop not, weary, to the welcome land,
  Though the dark night is near.   20

And soon that toil shall end;
Soon shalt thou find a summer home, and rest,
And scream among thy fellows; reeds shall bend,
  Soon, o'er thy sheltered nest.

Thou'rt gone, the abyss of heaven
Hath swallowed up thy form; yet, on my heart
Deeply has sunk the lesson thou hast given,
  And shall not soon depart.

He who, from zone to zone,
Guides through the boundless sky thy certain
    flight,   30
In the long way that I must tread alone,
  Will lead my steps aright.

To the Fringed Gentian (1829)

This poem is a kind of companion piece to "The Yellow Violet." If the violet is special because it is the earliest New England flower, the fringed gentian has its special place, too, because it blooms after the other flowers are gone.

Thou blossom bright with autumn dew,
And colored with the heaven's own blue,

That openest when the quiet light
Succeeds the keen and frosty night.

Thou comest not when violets lean
O'er wandering brooks and springs unseen,
Or columbines, in purple dressed,
Nod o'er the ground-bird's hidden nest.

Thou waitest late and com'st alone,
When woods are bare and birds are flown,   10
And frosts and shortening days portend

The aged year is near his end.

Then doth thy sweet and quiet eye
Look through its fringes to the sky,
Blue—blue—as if that sky let fall
A flower from its cerulean wall.

I would that thus, when I shall see
The hour of death draw near to me,
Hope, blossoming within my heart,
May look to heaven as I depart.   20

The Death of the Flowers (1825)

The young girl whose death is lamented was Bryant's favorite sister, Sarah. She died at an early age of consumption.

The melancholy days are come, the saddest of
the year,
Of wailing winds, and naked woods, and meadows
brown and sere.
Heaped in the hollows of the grove, the
autumn leaves lie dead;
They rustle to the eddying gust, and to the
rabbit's tread;
The robin and the wren are flown, and from
the shrubs the jay,
And from the wood-top calls the crow through
all the gloomy day.

Where are the flowers, the fair young flowers,
that lately sprang and stood
In brighter light and softer airs, a beauteous
sisterhood?
Alas! they all are in their graves, the gentle race
of flowers
Are lying in their lowly beds, with the fair
and good of ours.   10
The rain is falling where they lie, but the
cold November rain
Calls not from out the gloomy earth the lovely
ones again.

The wind-flower and the violet, they perished
long ago,
And the brier-rose and the orchid died amid
the summer glow;

But on the hills the golden-rod, and the aster
in the wood,
And the yellow sun-flower by the brook,
in autumn beauty stood,
Till fell the frost from the clear cold heaven,
as falls the plague on men,
And the brightness of their smile was gone,
from upland, glade, and glen.

And now, when comes the calm mild day, as
still such days will come,
To call the squirrel and the bee from out
their winter home;   20
When the sound of dropping nuts is heard, though
all the trees are still,
And twinkle in the smoky light the waters of
the rill,
The south wind searches for the flowers whose
fragrance late he bore,
And sighs to find them in the wood and by
the stream no more.

And then I think of one who in her youthful
beauty died,
The fair meek blossom that grew up and faded
by my side.
In the cold moist earth we laid her, when the
forests cast the leaf,
And we wept that one so lovely should have a
life so brief:
Yet not unmeet it was that one, like that young
friend of ours,
So gentle and so beautiful, should perish
with the flowers.   30

O Fairest of the Rural Maids (1821)

This is one of Bryant's very few love poems. The reader may find it interesting to compare this poem with one of Wordsworth's "Lucy" poems, that entitled "Three Years She Grew," first published in 1800. Stanza 5 (in which is heard the voice of nature) reads as follows:

> The stars of midnight shall be dear
> To her; and she shall lean her ear
> In many a secret place
> Where rivulets dance their wayward round,
> And beauty born of murmuring sound
> Shall pass into her face.

The poem was addressed to Frances Fairchild, the girl whom Bryant was to marry in the next year.

> O fairest of the rural maids!
> Thy birth was in the forest shades;
> Green boughs, and glimpses of the sky,
> Were all that met thine infant eye.

> Thy sports, thy wanderings, when a child,
> Were ever in the sylvan wild;
> And all the beauty of the place
> Is in thy heart and on thy face.

> The twilight of the trees and rocks
> Is in the light shade of thy looks;   10
> Thy step is as the wind, that weaves
> Its playful way among the leaves.

> Thine eyes are springs, in whose serene
> And silent waters heaven is seen;
> Their lashes are the herbs that look
> On their young figures in the brook.

> The forest depths, by foot unpressed,
> Are not more sinless than thy breast;
> The holy peace, that fills the air
> Of those calm solitudes, is there.   20

Hymn of the City (1830)

This poem was written in New York, probably in 1830, the year of its first publication. A comparison of it with one of Wordsworth's sonnets on London, "Composed upon Westminster Bridge," will reveal some of the significant differences between the two poets. Both make the point that the city, though man-made, is also a part of nature and that the beauty and peace associated with nature may be found in the city too. Bryant spells out his point.

Wordsworth, on the other hand, as he looks in the dawnlight at the still-sleeping city, exclaims in genuine surprise at the beauty of the morning. The city now seems to lie

> Open unto the fields, the sky;
> All bright and glittering in the smokeless air.

That is, now that the usual pall of smoke that hangs over the workaday city is absent, the pinnacles of its buildings glitter like rocks and crags in some mountainous landscape. Again, since no boats or barges now disturb the river, the poet evidently realizes with a shock that the traffic-soiled Thames is indeed a river, gliding like any other stream "at his own sweet will." In both poems, the city has to go to sleep—has to lose its characteristic bustle and activity and to die away into quietude—before the poet

is able to perceive that it is after all a part of nature too and can be thought of as something organic, beating like a heart, or simply at its proper season going to sleep like an animal.

> Dear God! the very houses seem asleep;
> And all that mighty heart is lying still!

Wordsworth allows his insight to be implied through his description of the city and through a dramatization of his spontaneous reaction to what he sees in this morning's light. He gains thus a unity of effect and a dramatic power that is lacking in Bryant's poem.

The point to be insisted upon here is not that Bryant is a lesser poet than Wordsworth. That fact scarcely calls for argument. The point at issue is rather that in spite of the influence of Wordsworth and the other English Romantics and in spite of Bryant's superficial resemblance to them, Bryant is, in his basic attitudes and poetic strategies, essentially a poet of eighteenth-century temper. This is not to say that he does not have his charm or that his best poems do not have their own merit, but it is useful to define that merit quite specifically. It consists in accurate descriptions of natural scenes from which he makes—often gracefully—appropriate applications to the human situation. We rarely find in his work flashes of imaginative insight. What we more often find is a competent treatment of analogies and a sound application of poetic rhetoric.

Not in the solitude
　Alone may man commune with Heaven, or see,
　Only in savage wood
And sunny vale, the present Deity;
　Or only hear his voice
Where the winds whisper and the waves rejoice.

　Even here do I behold
Thy steps, Almighty!—here, amidst the crowd
　Through the great city rolled,
With everlasting murmur deep and loud—　　10
　Choking the ways that wind
'Mongst the proud piles, the work of human kind.

Thy golden sunshine comes
From the round heaven, and on their dwellings lies
　And lights their inner homes;
For them thou fill'st with air the unbounded skies,
　And givest them the stores
Of ocean, and the harvests of its shores.

　Thy Spirit is around,
Quickening the restless mass that sweeps
　　along;　　20
　And this eternal sound—
Voices and footfalls of the numberless throng—
　Like the resounding sea,
Or like the rainy tempest, speaks of Thee.

　And when the hour of rest
Comes, like a calm upon the mid-sea brine,
　Hushing its billowy breast—
The quiet of that moment too is thine;
　It breathes of Him who keeps
The vast and helpless city while it sleeps.　　30

The Two Graves (1826)

Near Bryant's home at Cummington, Massachusetts, there were in a secluded spot two graves which interested Bryant very much, even from childhood. It is rewarding to compare this poem with "Thanatopsis." The last line of this poem, for example, assumes the resurrection of the body, even though the poem states that a less "cruel creed" would be to believe that the souls of the couple will remain with the body and not depart from this natural resting place until the resurrection day. Other poems on death, such as the "Hymn to Death," "An Indian at the Burial-Place of his Fathers," "The Disinterred Warrior," "The Future Life"—and many others—indicate how powerfully the theme of death held the poet's imagination.

'Tis a bleak wild hill, but green and bright
In the summer warmth and the mid-day light;
There's the hum of the bee and the chirp of
　the wren
And the dash of the brook from the alder-glen.
There's the sound of a bell from the scattered
　flock,

And the shade of the beech lies cool on the rock,
And fresh from the west is the free wind's breath;—
There is nothing here that speaks of death.

　Far yonder, where orchards and gardens lie,
And dwellings cluster, 'tis there men die,　　10
They are born, they die, and are buried near,
Where the populous graveyard lightens the bier.
For strict and close are the ties that bind
In death the children of human-kind;
Yea, stricter and closer than those of life,—
'Tis a neighborhood that knows no strife.
They are noiselessly gathered—friend and foe—
To the still and dark assemblies below.
Without a frown or a smile they meet,
Each pale and calm in his winding-sheet;　　20
In that sullen home of peace and gloom,
Crowded, like guests in a banquet-room.

　Yet there are graves in this lonely spot,
Two humble graves,—but I meet them not.
I have seen them,—eighteen years are past
Since I found their place in the brambles last,—
The place where, fifty winters ago
An aged man in his locks of snow,
And an aged matron, withered with years,
Were solemnly laid!—but not with tears,　　30

For none, who sat by the light of their hearth,
Beheld their coffins covered with earth;
Their kindred were far, and their children dead,
When the funeral-prayer was coldly said.

Two low green hillocks, two small gray stones,
Rose over the place that held their bones;
But the grassy hillocks are levelled again,
And the keenest eye might search in vain,
'Mong briers, and ferns, and paths of sheep,
For the spot where the aged couple sleep.   40

Yet well might they lay, beneath the soil
Of this lonely spot, that man of toil,
And trench the strong hard mould with the spade,
Where never before a grave was made;
For he hewed the dark old woods away,
And gave the virgin fields to the day;
And the gourd and the bean, beside his door,
Bloomed where their flowers ne'er opened before;
And the maize stood up, and the bearded rye
Bent low in the breath of an unknown sky.   50

'Tis said that when life is ended here,
The spirit is borne to a distant sphere;
That it visits its earthly home no more,

Nor looks on the haunts it loved before.
But why should the bodiless soul be sent
Far off, to a long, long banishment?
Talk not of the light and the living green!
It will pine for the dear familiar scene;
It will yearn, in that strange bright world, to
     behold
The rock and the stream in knew of old.   60

'Tis a cruel creed, believe it not!
Death to the good is a milder lot.
They are here,—they are here,—that harmless pair,
In the yellow sunshine and flowing air,
In the light cloud-shadows that slowly pass,
In the sounds that rise from the murmuring grass.
They sit where their humble cottage stood,
They walk by the waving edge of the wood,
And list to the long-accustomed flow
Of the brook that wets the rocks below,   70
Patient, and peaceful, and passionless,
As seasons on seasons swiftly press,
They watch, and wait, and linger around,
Till the day when their bodies shall leave the
     ground.

The Death of Abraham Lincoln (1865)

This poem was written very shortly after Lincoln's assassination.

Oh, slow to smite and swift to spare,
   Gentle and merciful and just!
Who, in the fear of God, didst bear
   The sword of power, a nation's trust!

In sorrow by thy bier we stand,
   Amid the awe that hushes all,

And speak the anguish of a land
   That shook with horror at thy fall.

Thy task is done; the bond are free:
   We bear thee to an honored grave,   10
Whose proudest monument shall be
   The broken fetters of the slave.

Pure was thy life; its bloody close
   Hath placed thee with the sons of light,
Among the noble host of those
   Who perished in the cause of Right.

From The Right of Workmen to Strike (1836)

In May, 1836, twenty-one tailors, because they tried to form a labor union, were indicted for conspiracy injurious to trade and commerce. Judge Edwards instructed the jury to find the men guilty. Bryant, in the editorial of which a portion is printed below, defended the workers' right to strike.[1]

[1] Though labor unions had begun to form toward the end of the eighteenth century, their legal right to strike had not yet been conceded when Bryant published this editorial.

Sentence was passed on Saturday on the twenty "men who had determined not to work." The punishment selected, on due consideration, by the judge, was that officers appointed for the purpose should immediately demand from each of the delinquents a sum of money which was named in the sentence of the court. The amount demanded would not have fallen short of the savings of many years. Either the offenders had not parted with these savings, or their brother workmen raised the ransom money for them on the spot. The fine was paid over as required. All is now well; justice has been satisfied. But if the expenses of their families had anticipated the law, and left nothing in their hands, or if friends had not been ready to buy the freedom of their comrades, they would have been sent to prison, and there they would have staid, until their wives and children, besides earning their own bread, had saved enough to redeem the captives from their cells. Such has been their punishment. What was their offence? They had committed the crime of unanimously declining to go to work at the wages offered to them by their masters. They had said to one another, "Let us come out from the meanness and misery of our caste. Let us begin to do what every order more privileged and more honoured is doing everyday. By the means which we believe to be the best let us raise ourselves and our families above the humbleness of our condition. We may be wrong, but we cannot help believing that we might do much if we were true brothers to each other, and would resolve not to sell the only thing which is our own, the cunning of our hands, for less than it is worth." What other things they may have done is nothing to the purpose: it was for this they were condemned; it is for this they are to endure the penalty of the law.

We call upon a candid and generous community to mark that the punishment inflicted upon these twenty "men who had determined not to work" is not directed against the offence of conspiring to prevent others by force from working at low wages, but expressly against the offence of settling by pre-concert the compensation which they thought they were entitled to obtain. It is certainly superfluous to repeat, that this journal would be the very last to oppose a law levelled at any attempt to molest the labourer who chooses to work for less than the prices settled by the union. We have said, and to cut off cavil, we say it now again, that a conspiracy to deter, by threats of violence, a fellow workman from arranging his own

terms with his employers, is a conspiracy to commit a felony—a conspiracy which, being a crime against liberty, we should be the first to condemn —a conspiracy which no strike should, for its own sake, countenance for a moment—a conspiracy already punishable by the statute, and far easier to reach than the one of which "the twenty" stood accused; but a conspiracy, we must add, that has not a single feature in common with the base and barbarous prohibition under which the offenders were indicted and condemned.

They were condemned because they had determined not to work for the wages that were offered them! Can any thing be imagined more abhorrent to every sentiment of generosity or justice, than the law which arms the rich with the legal right to fix, by assize, the wages of the poor? If this is not SLAVERY, we have forgotten its definition. Strike the right of associating for the sale of labour from the privileges of a freeman, and you may as well at once bind him to a master, or ascribe him to the soil. If it be not in the colour of his skin, and in the poor franchise of naming his own terms in a contract for his work, what advantage has the labourer of the north over the bondman of the south? Punish by human laws a "determination not to work," make it penal by any other penalty than idleness inflicts, and it matters little whether the task-masters be one or many, an individual or an order, the hateful scheme of slavery will have gained a foothold in the land. And then the meanness of this law, which visits with its malice those who cling to it for protection, and shelters with all its fences those who are raised above its threats. A late solicitation for its aid against employers, is treated with derision and contempt, but the moment the "masters" invoked its intervention, it came down from its high place with most indecent haste, and has now discharged its fury upon the naked heads of wretches so forlorn, that their worst faults multiply their titles to a liberty which they must learn to win from livelier sensibilities than the barren benevolence of Wealth, or the tardy magnanimity of Power. . . .

"Self-created societies," says Judge Edwards, "are unknown to the constitution and laws, and will not be permitted to rear their crest and extend their baneful influence over any portion of the community." If there is any sense in this passage it means that self-created societies are unlawful, and must be put down by the courts. Down then with every literary, every religious, and every charitable association not incorporated! What nonsense is this! Self-created societies *are* known to the constitution and laws, for they are not prohibited, and the laws which allow them will, if justly administered, protect them. But suppose in charity that the reporter has put this absurdity into the mouth of Judge Edwards, and that he meant only those self-created societies which have an effect upon trade and commerce. Gather up then and sweep to the penitentiary all those who are confederated to carry on any business or trade in concert, by fixed rules, and see how many men you would leave at large in this city. The members of every partnership in the place will come under the penalties of the law, and not only these, but every person pursuing any occupation whatever, who governs himself by a mutual understanding with others that follow the same occupation.

The Death of Lovejoy (1837)

The Reverend Elijah P. Lovejoy (1802–1837) was an abolitionist editor. On four occasions mobs in Alton, Illinois, attempted to destroy the presses on which his newspaper, the Alton *Observer*, was printed. On the fourth occasion, shots were exchanged between Lovejoy and members of the mob and Lovejoy was killed (November 1). It was this incident that prompted Bryant to write the editorial that follows.

———

We have received by this morning's mail a slip from the Missouri Argus, printed at St. Louis, containing intelligence which has filled us with surprise and horror. A mob, in making an attack upon an abolition press established at Alton, in Illinois, murdered two persons, wounded several others, and triumphing over the objects of their fury by this atrocious violence, destroyed the press which these men had defended at the cost of their blood and their lives.

We give the slip from the Missouri Argus as we received it, but we cannot forbear expressing in the strongest language our condemnation of the manner in which it speaks of this bloody event. The right to discuss freely and openly, by speech, by the pen, by the press, all political questions, and to examine and animadvert upon all political institutions, is a right so clear and certain, so interwoven with our other liberties, so necessary, in fact, to their existence, that without it we must fall at once into despotism or anarchy. To say that he who holds unpopular opinions must hold them at the peril of his life, and that, if he expresses them in public, he has only himself to blame if they who disagree with him should rise and put him to death, is to strike at all rights, all liberties, all protection of law, and to justify or extenuate all crimes.

We regard not this as a question connected with the abolition of slavery in the South, but as a question vital to the liberties of the entire Union. We may have different opinions concerning the propriety of the measures which the abolitionists desire to recommend, but we marvel and we deplore that any difference can exist as to the freedom of discussion. We are astonished that even a single journal can be found, so forgetful of its own rights, to say nothing of its duties to the community, as to countenance, even indirectly, the idea of muzzling the press by the fear of violence.

For our own part we approve, we applaud, we would consecrate, if we could, to universal honor, the conduct of those who bled in this gallant defense of the freedom of the press. Whether they erred or not in their opinions, they did not err in the conviction of their right as citizens of a democratic government, to express them, nor did they err in defending this right with an obstinacy which yielded only to death and the uttermost violence. With these remarks we lay before our readers the brief narrative with which we are furnished of this bloody outrage.

Office of the Missouri Argus,
St. Louis, Nov. 9, 1837
Mob at Alton, Illinois—The Rev. E. P. Lovejoy killed, and his Abolition press destroyed!!
The infatuated editor of the Alton Observer has at length fallen a victim to his obstinacy in the cause of the Abolitionists. Disregarding the known and expressed sentiments of a large portion of the citizens of Alton, in relation to his incendiary publications, and, as it would seem, bent upon his own destruction, he formed the determination to establish another press for the propagation of the

odious and disorganizing principles of Tappan and his eastern confederates. But his temerity has received an awful retribution from the hands of an infuriated and lawless mob.—The following particulars of the tragical outrage is [sic] contained in a postscript to the Alton Telegraph of the 8th inst.:

Lamentable Occurrence.—It is with the deepest regret that we stop the press in order to state that, at a late hour last night, an attack was made by a large number of persons on the warehouse of Messrs. Godfrey, Gilman & Co., for the purpose of destroying a press intended for the revival of the Alton Observer, which, shocking to relate, resulted in the death of two individuals—the Rev. E. P. Lovejoy, late editor of the Observer, and a man named —— Bishop. Seven others were wounded, two severely, and the others slightly. We can add no more at this time, than that the assailants succeeded in effecting their object.

The stress in the foregoing editorial is on the right to express "unpopular" opinions; it is not on the wickedness of slavery as such. Curiously enough, though Bryant in his writings from the 1830's onward makes his attitude toward slavery perfectly clear, he seems to have written only one poem that attacks slavery specifically. It is entitled "The Death of Slavery," written in May, 1866, and published in the following July in the *Atlantic Monthly*. From the first dozen lines (printed below) it can be seen that it is a rather perfunctory set piece, a bundle of stock phrases and epithets, quite without any individual character.

The contrast between "The Death of Slavery" and the two hard-hitting editorials that we have just read underlines the fact that Bryant's poetry was incapable of dealing with the issues of the workaday world and the harsher aspects of life. His best poetry is limited to a very special subject matter: to scenes of pathos and sentiment, to a celebration of the gentler aspects of nature, and to the peaceful rest of death.

> O Thou great Wrong, that, through the slow-
>   paced years,
> Didst hold thy millions fettered, and didst
>   wield
> The scourge that drove the laborer to the
>   field,
> And turn a stony gaze on human tears,
>   Thy cruel reign is o'er;
>   Thy bondmen crouch no more
> In terror at the menace of thine eye;
>   For He who marks the bounds of guilty
>   power,
> Long-suffering, hath heard the captive's cry,
>   And touched his shackles at the appointed
>   hour,
> And lo! they fall, and he whose limbs they
>   galled
> Stand in his native manhood, disenthralled.

The Novel: The Beginnings
Through Irving and Cooper

English settlers had been in America almost a century before the novel, in anything like the form which we now know, developed in England; and in the eighteenth century, even though great novelists, such as Daniel Defoe, Samuel Richardson, Henry Fielding, Tobias Smollett, and Laurence Sterne, had appeared in England, their work was scarcely known in this country. Benjamin Franklin had, it is true, published Richardson's *Pamela* as early as 1744, but, for reasons which we shall discuss, the work of Richardson had a special sufferance.

Two factors in American life worked against the acceptance of fiction. One was the hard, practical demand on energy in a new country, and the other was Puritanism. The effects of Puritanism in this respect are complex and interesting. From the time of Plato on, there had been two deep-seated objections to the arts, objections which the English Puritans simply adapted. First, the arts tell "lies"—give imitations of things, not reality. Second, the arts stimulate unhealthy emotionalism, particularly sexual emotions. English Puritanism had especially attacked the drama, and under the Puritan regime theaters had been forbidden, for in drama the imitation of life and the rendering of emotional states, enacted by actual persons directly before the eyes of an audience, is most vivid. Prose fiction, at one remove, was open to the same charges.

The development of the novel is associated with the rise of the middle class;[1] in eighteenth-century England, the middle class inherited, though in

[1] See Jefferson's letter to Nathaniel Burwell advising that Burwell's daughters not read fiction.

somewhat less rigorous forms, many of the attitudes of Puritanism. The question, then, is how the English novelist circumvented, for the new audience, the inherited objections. The first objection—that of telling "lies"—was gotten around by the claim, justified or not, of a relation to fact. Defoe's *Journal of the Plague Year* is based on fact, as is *Robinson Crusoe*. When the story is based on historical background, the writer suggests that the manuscript has been found in a bottle or an old chest. Or the author, in his role as a fictional character, claims to be a real person sitting down to tell his real story. Even more importantly, the stories the novelists tell are set in a world the middle-class reader may recognize—with the dress, houses, furniture, streets, attitudes, language that he knows from daily life.

But the more the novel developed a realism that avoided the attack of being a "lie," the more, by the very reason of its realism, it ran the risk of being emotionally stimulating. The counter to this attack was obviously to claim that the deplorable conduct presented was there as a moral warning—certainly not as a stimulus to the reader's emotions. So we find the type of novel, stemming from Richardson's *Pamela* and *Clarissa Harlowe*, in which, for example, the frightful risks of seduction and betrayal run by the charmingly defenseless heroine are rendered with full emotional impact and sexual provocations not far short of that in the obvious pornography of the period, such as *The Memoirs of a Woman of Pleasure*—all in the guise of a cautionary tale. Thus the rising, prosperous middle class, prudent, prim, intensely concerned with propriety of manners and respectability of reputation, the class to which the novel was addressed, could have things both ways—emotional titillation and moral justification in one package.

It was only natural that when, in 1744, the canny Benjamin Franklin published a novel for his Philadelphia readers, it should be of this order—*Pamela*, the archetype of what is called the "sentimental novel." It is equally natural that what is known as the first American novel, *The Power of Sympathy*, presumably by Luther William Hill Brown, published in Boston in 1789, is an erotic but tearfully cautionary tale of how a lovely lady stoops to folly; and natural, too, that *The Power of Sympathy* should be based on a real scandal and thus avoid the charge of being a "lie" or the work of an unhealthy imagination. This novel was followed by a host of others, the most famous being *Charlotte Temple*, by Susanna Haswell Rowson, and *The Coquette*, by Hannah Walker Foster, in which the morality was merely the salt to the stew of sometimes distorted sexual titillations not much less provocative and probably even less healthy than that found in the fiction of our century.

The strain of morbidity, violence, and perversion appearing in this early fiction has a relation, not only to the tradition of the sentimental novel, but to the general literature of the Romantic period, on the continent as well as in England, even to the work of such masters as Keats, Byron, and Shelley. Shelley, for instance, was not only the poet of ethereal sentiments and high ideals but also the author of the morbid play *The Cenci*, and a writer who could assert that incest is the most poetical of subjects. But to look at novels like *The Power of Sympathy* in another perspective, we can see that a line runs from these tales of seduction and betrayal straight to Hawthorne's *The Scarlet Letter*. In one sense, we can say that Hawthorne merely took the conventional tale and deepened it morally and psychologically.

CHARLES BROCKDEN BROWN (1771–1810)

In this early fiction we find another strain that was to prove of great importance in later work, the influence of the Gothic romance, a type of novel that developed in England in the eighteenth century dealing with mysteries, supernatural horrors, and villainies in the setting of medieval ruins (best exemplified in *The Castle of Otranto*, by Horace Walpole, *The Mysteries of Udolpho*, by Ann Radcliffe, and *Ambrosio, or the Monk*, by Matthew Gregory Lewis, known, after the fame of his novel, as "Monk" Lewis). The American who developed the genre was Charles Brockden Brown, born in Philadelphia of a Quaker background. Against the wishes of his family, he abandoned the study of law and undertook a career in letters—an idea that for more than another half century would be almost enough to mark a young man as certifiably insane. In spite of ill health and poverty never relieved by his ventures as a merchant, Brown worked feverishly at his literary projects, editing various magazines, translating, writing criticism and fiction. In 1810, he died from tuberculosis.

Though the English Gothic novelists and the German Romantics stood behind Brown's work, other elements appear there too. He was a libertarian and a reformer. He was influenced by Voltaire and Rousseau, and especially by *Political Justice*, written by the English reformer William Godwin. In fact, Brown's first book, *Alcuin*, was a tract on the rights of women; and in fiction it was a novel by Godwin, *Caleb Williams*, that provided his model.

Beyond Brown's interest in reform, however, it was his theory of the use of American materials that distinguishes him from the ordinary imitators of the Gothic novel. In the preface to his *Edgar Huntly*, he boasts that he affected "the passions and engaged the sympathy of the reader" by means other than the "superstitious and exploded manners, Gothic castles and chimeras" usually found in fiction, and proclaimed that "incidents of Indian hostility and perils of the Western wilderness are far more suitable" and that "for an American to overlook them would admit of no apology." Brown's best example of his theory is in the episode of the killing of the Indian (Chap. 17). Though Brown's work lacks any of the realistic detail that Cooper strove to give, this episode does have similarity to the famous chapter in *The Deerslayer* in which Cooper's hero Natty Bumppo is forced to kill his first Indian, and it is possible that Cooper's scene was suggested by this. (In connection with the reluctance of the two heroes to kill, it may be remarked that both Brown and Cooper were of Quaker background—as was the unbloodthirsty Daniel Boone.) Here the hero, after wandering in a great cavern (an episode thought to have given a suggestion for Poe's story "The Pit and the Pendulum"), approaches a light which he dis-covers to be the campfire of Indians at the mouth of the cave.

From Edgar Huntly (1799)

I went forward, but my eyes were fixed upon the fire; presently, in consequence of changing my station, I perceived several feet, and the skirts of blankets. I was somewhat startled at these ap-pearances. The legs were naked, and scored into uncouth figures. The *moccasins* which lay beside them, and which were adorned in a grotesque manner, in addition to other incidents, imme-diately suggested the suspicion that they were Indians. No spectacle was more adapted than this to excite wonder and alarm. Had some mysterious power snatched me from the earth, and cast me, in a moment, into the heart of the wilderness? Was I still in the vicinity of my parental habita-tion, or was I thousands of miles distant?

Were these the permanent inhabitants of this region, or were they wanderers and robbers? While in the heart of the mountain, I had entertained a vague belief that I was still within the precincts of Norwalk. This opinion was shaken for a moment by the objects which I now beheld, but it insen-sibly returned; yet how was this opinion to be reconciled to appearances so strange and uncouth, and what measure did a due regard to my safety enjoin me to take?

I now gained a view of four brawny and terrific figures, stretched upon the ground. They lay paral-lel to each other, on their left sides; in consequence of which their faces were turned from me. Be-tween each was an interval where lay a musket. Their right hands seemed placed upon the stocks of their guns, as if to seize them on the first mo-ment of alarm.

The aperture through which these objects were seen was at the back of the cave, and some feet from the ground. It was merely large enough to suffer a human body to pass. It was involved in profound darkness, and there was no danger of being suspected or discovered as long as I main-tained silence and kept out of view. . . .

Meanwhile my thoughts were busy in accounting for this spectacle. I need not tell thee that Nor-walk is the termination of a sterile and narrow tract which begins in the Indian country. It forms a sort of rugged and rocky vein, and continues upwards of fifty miles. It is crossed in a few places by narrow and intricate paths, by which a com-munication is maintained between the farms and settlements on the opposite sides of the ridge.

During former Indian wars, this rude surface was sometimes traversed by the Red-men, and they made, by means of it, frequent and destructive in-roads into the heart of the English settlements. During the last war, notwithstanding the progress of population, and the multiplied perils of such an expedition, a band of them had once penetrated into Norwalk, and lingered long enough to pillage and murder some of the neighbouring inhabitants.

I have reason to remember that event. My father's house was placed on the verge of this solitude. Eight of these assassins assailed at the dead of night. My parents and an infant child were murdered in their beds; the house was pillaged, and then burnt to the ground. Happily, myself and my two sisters were abroad upon a visit. The pre-ceding day had been fixed for our return to our father's house; but a storm occurred, which made it dangerous to cross the river, and, by obliging us to defer our journey, rescued us from captivity or death.

Most men are haunted by some species of terror or antipathy, which they are, for the most part, able to trace to some incident which befell them in their early years. You will not be surprised that the fate of my parents, and the sight of the body of one of this savage band, who, in the pur-suit that was made after them, was overtaken and killed, should produce lasting and terrific images in my fancy. I never looked upon or called up the image of a savage without shuddering.

I knew that, at this time, some hostilities had been committed on the frontier; that a long course of injuries and encroachments had lately exasper-ated the Indian tribes; that an implacable and exterminating war was generally expected. We imagined ourselves at an inaccessible distance from the danger, but I could not but remember that this persuasion was formerly as strong as at present, and that an expedition which had once succeeded might possibly be attempted again. Here was every token of enmity and bloodshed. Each prostrate figure was furnished with a rifled musket, and a leathern bag tied round his waist, which was, probably, stored with powder and ball.

From these reflections, the sense of my own danger was revived and enforced, but I likewise ruminated on the evils which might impend over others. I should, no doubt, be safe by remaining in this nook; but might not some means be pursued to warn others of their danger? Should they leave this spot without notice of their approach being given to the fearless and pacific tenants of the neighbouring district, they might commit, in a few hours, the most horrid and irreparable devastation.

The alarm could only be diffused in one way. Could I not escape, unperceived, and without alarming the sleepers, from this cavern? The slumber of an Indian is broken by the slightest noise; but, if all noise be precluded, it is commonly profound. It was possible, I conceived, to leave my present post, to descend into the cave, and issue forth without the smallest signal. Their supine posture assured me that they were asleep. Sleep usually comes at their bidding, and, if perchance, they should be wakeful at an unseasonable moment, they always sit upon their haunches, and, leaning their elbows on their knees, consume the tedious hours in smoking. My peril would be great. Accidents which I could not foresee, and over which I had no command, might occur to awaken some one at the moment I was passing the fire. Should I pass in safety, I might issue forth into a wilderness, of which I had no knowledge, where I might wander till I perished with famine, or where my footsteps might be noted and pursued and overtaken by these implacable foes. These perils were enormous and imminent; but I likewise considered that I might be at no great distance from the habitations of men, and that my escape might rescue them from the most dreadful calamities. I determined to make this dangerous experiment without delay.

I came nearer to the aperture, and had, consequently, a larger view of this recess. To my unspeakable dismay, I now caught a glimpse of one seated at the fire. His back was turned towards me, so that I could distinctly survey his gigantic form and fantastic ornaments.

My project was frustrated. This one was probably commissioned to watch and to awaken his companions when a due portion of sleep had been taken. That he would not be unfaithful or remiss in the performance of the part assigned to him was easily predicted. To pass him without exciting his notice (and the entrance could not otherwise be reached) was impossible. Once more I shrunk back, and revolved with hopelessness and anguish the necessity to which I was reduced.

This interval of dreary foreboding did not last long. Some motion in him that was seated by the fire attracted my notice. I looked, and beheld him rise from his place and go forth from the cavern. This unexpected incident led my thoughts into a new channel. Could not some advantage be taken of his absence? Could not this opportunity be seized for making my escape? He had left his gun and hatchet on the ground. It was likely, therefore, that he had not gone far, and would speedily return. Might not these weapons be seized, and some provision be thus made against the danger of meeting him without, or of being pursued?

Before a resolution could be formed, a new sound saluted my ear. It was a deep groan, succeeded by sobs that seemed struggling for utterance but were vehemently counteracted by the sufferer. This low and bitter lamentation apparently proceeded from some one within the cave. It could not be from one of this swarthy band. It must, then, proceed from a captive, whom they had reserved for torment or servitude, and who had seized the opportunity afforded by the absence of him that watched to give vent to his despair.

I again thrust my head forward, and beheld, lying on the ground, apart from the rest, and bound hand and foot, a young girl. Her dress was the coarse russet garb of the country, and bespoke her to be some farmer's daughter. Her features denoted the last degree of fear and anguish, and she moved her limbs in such a manner as showed that the ligatures by which she was confined produced, by their tightness, the utmost degree of pain.

My wishes were now bent not only to preserve myself and to frustrate the future attempts of these savages, but likewise to relieve this miserable victim. This could only be done by escaping from the cavern and returning with seasonable aid. The sobs of the girl were likely to rouse the sleepers. My appearance before her would prompt her to testify her surprise by some exclamation or shriek. What could hence be predicted but that the band would start on their feet and level their unerring pieces at my head!

I know not why I was insensible to these dangers. My thirst was rendered by these delays intolerable. It took from me, in some degree, the power of deliberation. The murmurs which had drawn me hither continued still to be heard. Some torrent or cascade could not be far distant from the entrance of the cavern, and it seemed as if one draught of clear water was a luxury cheaply purchased by death itself. This, in addition to considerations more disinterested, and which I have already mentioned, impelled me forward.

The girl's cheek rested on the hard rock, and her eyes were dim with tears. As they were turned towards me, however, I hoped that my movements would be noticed by her gradually and without abruptness. This expectation was fulfilled. I had not advanced many steps before she discovered me. This moment was critical beyond all others in the course of my existence. My life was suspended, as it were, by a spider's thread. All rested on the effect which this discovery should make upon this feeble victim.

I was watchful of the first movement of her eye which should indicate a consciousness of my presence. I laboured, by gestures and looks, to deter her from betraying her emotion. My attention was, at the same time, fixed upon the sleepers, and an anxious glance was cast towards the quarter whence the watchful savage might appear.

I stooped and seized the musket and hatchet. The space beyond the fire was, as I expected, open to the air. I issued forth with trembling steps. The sensations inspired by the dangers which environed me, added to my recent horrors, and the influence of the moon, which had now gained the zenith, and whose lustre dazzled my long-benighted senses, cannot be adequately described.

For a minute, I was unable to distinguish objects. This confusion was speedily corrected, and I found myself on the verge of a steep. Craggy eminences arose on all sides. On the left hand was a space that offered some footing, and hither I turned. A torrent was below me, and this path appeared to lead to it. It quickly appeared in sight, and all foreign cares were, for a time, suspended.

This water fell from the upper regions of the hill, upon a flat projecture which was continued on either side, and on part of which I was now standing. The path was bounded on the left by an inaccessible wall, and on the right terminated at the distance of two or three feet from the wall in a precipice. The water was eight or ten paces distant, and no impediment seemed likely to rise between us. I rushed forward with speed.

My progress was quickly checked. Close to the falling water, seated on the edge, his back supported by the rock, and his legs hanging over the precipice, I now beheld the savage who left the cave before me. The noise of the cascade and the improbability of interruption, at least from this quarter, had made him inattentive to my motions.

I paused. Along this verge lay the only road by which I could reach the water, and by which I could escape. The passage was completely occupied by this antagonist. To advance towards him, or to remain where I was, would produce the same effect. I should, in either case, be detected. He was unarmed; but his outcries would instantly summon his companions to his aid. I could not hope to overpower him, and pass him in defiance of his opposition. But, if this were effected, pursuit would be instantly commenced. I was unacquainted with the way. The way was unquestionably difficult. My strength was nearly annihilated; I should be overtaken in a moment, or their deficiency in speed would be supplied by the accuracy of their aim. Their bullets, at least, would reach me.

There was one method of removing this impediment. The piece which I held in my hand was cocked. There could be no doubt that it was loaded. A precaution of this kind would never be omitted by a warrior of this hue. At a greater distance than this, I should not fear to reach the mark. Should I not discharge it, and, at the same moment, rush forward to secure the road which my adversary's death would open to me?

Perhaps you will conceive a purpose like this to have argued a sanguinary and murderous disposition. Let it be remembered, however, that I entertained no doubts about the hostile designs of these men. This was sufficiently indicated by their arms, their guise, and the captive who attended them. Let the fate of my parents be, likewise, remembered. I was not certain but that these very men were the assassins of my family, and were those who had reduced me and my sisters to the condition of orphans and dependents. No words can describe the torments of my thirst. Relief to these torments, and safety to my life, were within view. How could I hesitate?

Yet I did hesitate. My aversion to bloodshed was not to be subdued but by the direst necessity. I knew, indeed, that the discharge of a musket would only alarm the enemies who remained behind; but I had another and a better weapon in my grasp. I could rive the head of my adversary, and cast him headlong, without any noise which should be heard, into the cavern.

Still I was willing to withdraw, to re-enter the

cave, and take shelter in the darksome recesses from which I had emerged. Here I might remain, unsuspected, till these detested guests should depart. The hazards attending my re-entrance were to be boldly encountered, and the torments of unsatisfied thirst were to be patiently endured, rather than imbrue my hands in the blood of my fellowmen. But this expedient would be ineffectual if my retreat should be observed by this savage. Of that I was bound to be incontestably assured. I retreated, therefore, but kept my eyes fixed at the same time upon the enemy.

Some ill fate decreed that I should not retreat unobserved. Scarcely had I withdrawn three paces when he started from his seat, and turning towards me, walked with a quick pace. The shadow of the rock, and the improbability of meeting an enemy here, concealed me for a moment from observation. I stood still. The slightest motion would have attracted his notice. At present, the narrow space engaged all his vigilance. Cautious footsteps, and attention to the path, were indispensable to his safety. The respite was momentary, and I employed it in my own defence.

How otherwise could I act? The danger that impended aimed at nothing less than my life. To take the life of another was the only method of averting it. The means were in my hand, and they were used. In an extremity like this, my muscles would have acted almost in defiance of my will.

The stroke was quick as lightning, and the wound mortal and deep. He had not time to descry the author of his fate, but, sinking on the path, expired without a groan. The hatchet buried itself in his breast, and rolled with him to the bottom of the precipice.

———

Though the scene of *Edgar Huntly* is western Pennsylvania and though, with his Indian marauders, Brown is using native American materials, his general effect and atmosphere point forward less toward Cooper than toward Poe. Brown's stories are often concerned with psychical aberrations, and his heroes are marked by grandiose self-assertiveness. He also shares with Poe the impulse to philosophical and psychological analysis and to "scientific" explanation for mysteries. At the same time Brown's interest in obsessed characters points forward to such stories of Hawthorne as "Ethan Brand" and to Captain Ahab of Melville's *Moby-Dick*.

Brown did get a certain fame, if not a living, from his work. He was reviewed and extravagantly praised in England. Shelley admired him, and Keats said of him: "A strange American scion of the German trunk. Powerful genius—accomplish'd horror." Brown was translated and known in Germany and France. At home his reputation long survived him, and Hawthorne remembers him in the story "The Hall of Fantasy."

HUGH HENRY BRACKENRIDGE (1748–1818)

If what the critic Malcolm Cowley has called the "haunted, nocturnal" strain in American literature first appears in Charles Brockden Brown, the realistic, satirical objective bent is first developed by Hugh Henry Brackenridge, the only other of the early novelists whose work has proved durable. Brackenridge, born in Scotland, was raised in western Pennsylvania, on the frontier, but managed to get an education and attended Princeton, where he was a close friend of two young men who were to achieve distinc-

tion, Philip Freneau the poet and James Madison the President. He himself ran through a number of careers—schoolmaster, chaplain in the revolutionary army, journalist, book seller, dramatist, poet, novelist, lawyer, politician, judge of the Pennsylvania Supreme Court.

His mammoth novel *Modern Chivalry* was composed over a period of years, the first two volumes appearing in 1792, with four more volumes over subsequent years. When he died in 1818, he was planning a new section. The novel, which owes much to the great picaresque novels *Don Quixote*, by Cervantes, *Tristram Shandy*, by Laurence Sterne, and *Tom Jones*, by Henry Fielding, is the wandering account of the adventures of Captain Farrago, a land-owner, one-time officer in the Continental army, bumbling but not unintelligent, comfort-loving but humane, and of his servant, a bog-trotting Irish immigrant, Teague O'Regan. Teague is the important character in the novel, brutal and lecherous and cowardly but somehow likable, ignorant and stupid but cunning, the first of a long line of rogues and wanderers in American fiction, with a humor that we shall find repeated in the Jack Downing of Seba Smith, the Sut Lovingood of George Washington Harris, and, at a considerable remove, in the Huck Finn of Mark Twain.

The fundamental motive of *Modern Chivalry* is the satirical investigation of American society, of the pretensions of an unlicked, bumbling democracy, full of absurdities, illogicalities, and confusions of values, where stupidity is as apt to triumph as intelligence, and venality as virtue. In such a society a Teague O'Regan is as good as the next man, and after six volumes of ridiculous adventures, he was to become, according to the plan of the unfinished work, Ambassador to the Court of Saint James—the official representative of America. So, as *Modern Chivalry* looks forward to the fiction of the picaresque rogue, it also looks forward to a fiction of social criticism, specifically a criticism of democracy in action, and in this perspective Brackenridge is the immediate forerunner of Cooper.

Here the unwashed, newly made American begins his genteel education with a dancing lesson (Chap. 7):

From Modern Chivalry (1792–1815)

"Monsieur Patrick," said Monsieur Douperie, for understanding that he was an Irishman, and thinking that all Irishmen were named Patrick, he gave him this appellation: "Monsieur Patrick," said he, "il faut commencer, par les principes; must begin by de principle.

"La primiere principe, de first lessong est placer les pieds; place de foot. Voyez; dis foot, cy; comme cela, (showing him how to place his foot) and ce luy, dat foot, la; comme dis foot. (Showing him by his own foot how to place it) Tournez les pieds; open de foot, quoi! vous ouvrez la bouche; vous open de mout, and not de foot. Vous keep vos foot in de same position, et vous baillez: you open de mout. La secon principe, is to keep de body droit; trait. Must sit firm sur ses membres, on de limb. Tenez votre body as dis (showing him in what manner to keep his body) assieyez vous, sur vos membres, comme ce la; dis way, Monsieur. Quoi! encore la bouche ouverte, you open de mout again, Monsieur Patrick. Fermez la bouche, shut de mout."

I stop here to observe, that the opening of the mouth when an exertion of the mind or body is required, is a habit very common with uninformed men, and not at all peculiar to Teague: you will observe, that men, who have not been long, or at least much in the habit of writing, when they put pen to paper, open the mouth, and protrude the tongue, moving it, as the pen turns to the right hand or to the left; or draws the stroke long or short; and, you will see a cordwainer of good skill in his trade, from mere habit, and not any defect of art, put out his tongue, and move it, as if it could guide his hand, when he is paring nicely the margin of the sole of a shoe or boot: Having made this observation in justice to the bog-trotter, I return to my narration.

The Captain coming in at this point of the business, made enquiry of Monsieur Douperie, what success he appeared to have with his pupil. "Bien tolerable, Monsieur Capitaine," said Monsieur Douperie, "ver tolerable: Monsieur es d'une tres bonne naturel; ver good disposition. A la commencement il ne faut pas nous flatter, must not flatter, wid de plus haut degre, du succes; at de first of de lessong."

The Captain, not so much from the words of the dancing master, as from his countenance, and the tone of his voice, saw, that he was not so sanguine with regard to the proficiency of the bog-trotter as he had been at first: Nevertheless, he was not discouraged in suffering Monsieur Douperie to go on with his lessons; because he expected little more, as has been said, than some improvement of step and gait. Nor did he draw any conclusion unfavorable with respect to the attainments of the bog-trotter in a political career; because he well [knew] that awkwardness of manner is not at all inconsistent with the highest literary and political abilities; and that some of the greatest geniuses that the world has produced have never been able to attain the graces of behavior. . . .

With these reflections withdrawing, he left the Frenchman to go on with his lesson.

"La troiseme principe; de tird lessong," said Monsieur Douperie, "is to lift de foot; you lift de foot, Monsieur Patrick, le pied droit, de right foot furs." Here Teague raised the left. "O! mon dieu," said the dancing master, "le pied droit, et non pas le gauche; de right foot, and not de left. Est il possible, you no disting de right foot from de left. Il faut lever le gauche: a la bonne heure, you lift de left foot.

"Now, Monsieur Patrick; un pas avec le pied gauche; lift de left foot." Here Teague lifted the right foot, thinking of the former lesson, and willing to please the dancing master by giving him that foot which had seemed to be so much in request with him. "O! mon dieu, par blieu," said Monsieur Douperie, "est il possible you no disting de right foot from de left?" . . .

However, composing his temper, and resuming his instructions; he continued, "Now, Monsieur Patrick," said he, "le pied droit, lift de right foot." Here Teague, as he had not pleased his instructor by what he had done last, *viz.* lifting the right foot, now lifted the left, being always at cross purposes, as it were, or still too far forward, or too far back in his motions, to correspond with the directions given.

"O! diable, diable," said the Frenchman, raising his voice, and almost vociferating; "quoi ferai je? il est impossible d'instruire cet garcon: no possible make you understand fat I say, you do. Attendez vous, Monsieur Patrick; you look at me, and lift de foot dat I lift; now I lift de right foot; lift de right foot."

Teague standing opposite the master, and lifting that foot which was on the same side with that of the instructor made the same blunder as before, and lifted the left foot.

Monsieur Douperie enraged beyond all bearing, ran out of the room, and left his scholar for the present.

The day after this, Monsieur Douperie, having composed his temper and attending, the Captain made enquiry, as usual, of the progress of his pupil. The Frenchman endeavoring to put the best face on the matter, said some things of course and complimentary; but could not help intimating that it was "une grand difficulty en le commencement, in de beginning, to make Monsieur disting de difference of de right foot, and de left."

"As to that," said the Captain, "it is a national incapacity; for which, as also for their propensity to make what they call bulls, it is difficult to account. There are not a people more brave than the aborigines of Ireland, and are far from being destitute of talents, and yet there is a certain liability to blunders, both in their words and actions, that is singular. Whether it is that a mind strong and vigorous and of extensive range cannot attend to small things; or that a great flow and hurry of animal spirits, carries them too fast for reflection; or that there is a transposition of the brain, so that things present themselves by contraries to the imagination; I cannot tell: but the fact is so that in their own country, as I have been told, when they are taught to dance, which, by the bye, is a hint which I forgot to give you, they bind on the right and left foot different badges, on the one, a twisted wisp of straw, which they call a *sugan* and on the other a band of ozier twisted in like manner, which they call a *gad:* so that when the word is given to raise the one foot, and depress the other, it is *rise upon sugan, and sink upon gad;* so, that though the tyro may not all at once, and on the word given, be able to distinguish the right foot from the left, he may easily tell gad from sugan, as his eye can assist his ear in this case; the object being simple; whereas right and left are relative terms, and that which is on the right in one position, will be on the left in the contrary."

Monsieur Douperie was willing to avail himself of this hint, for understanding that the bog-trotter was a candidate for state affairs, he was greatly anxious to have the honor of giving him some proficiency. Accordingly, though he did not procure a straw sugan, and an ozier gad, yet he made use of what he thought might be equivalent, *viz.* a red rag, and a blue; so that instead of bidding him move the right foot or the left, he could desire him to move the red rag or the blue.

Having tied these upon his ankles next morning, he began his lesson. "Now, Monsieur Patrick," said he, "lift de foot dat hab de red ribbon." Teague obeyed with exactness and promptitude, and raised that foot. "Now," said Monsieur Douperie, "de foot dat hab de blue ribbon." Teague hit the direction, and raised the foot with the blue rag upon it.

"A la bonne heure, vous y voila," said the dancing master, "ver glad, Monsieur Patrick, you make so good proficiance; en peu de tems, je vous presentera a l'assemble. You danse ver well, short time."

WASHINGTON IRVING (1783–1859)

The youngest of the eleven children of William Irving, Presbyterian deacon and prosperous merchant, was born in New York City on April 8, 1783, within a few days of the official end of the Revolution (Congress ratified the preliminary peace treaty on April 19), and was named in honor of the victor of Yorktown. When Washington Irving was six, his nurse, with her charge in tow, accosted the President in a shop, and the great man patted the head of the namesake thus unceremoniously presented to him.

With independence had come a patriotic clamor for a literature to celebrate the new nation, and the new ideals. But it was only the next generation of fiction writers that could move toward an awareness of what it meant to be an American—as much an awareness, it should be emphasized from the first, of the tensions and centrifugal forces within the society as of those making for unity and uniformity. This we shall find to be true even with the first significant exemplars of that generation after the Revolution, Irving and James Fenimore Cooper.

Irving was only six years older than Cooper, but even a few years in that generation seem to have made a difference: both began working straight from English models, but Cooper moved decisively from those models toward an American sensibility. Irving, even though George Washington had patted him on the head, remains a transitional figure.

Attractive, rather self-indulgent and pleasure-loving, shrewdly observant but without any clear-cut ambition, the young Irving improvised a very agreeable life for himself in New York, then a booming little city of sixty thousand inhabitants. He had no inclination for business and, though he was reading law, and would even be admitted to the bar, regarded the profession with a jaundiced eye. His preference was for theater-going and the gay companionship of a group of young men of literary taste, which included two of his brothers. One of them, Peter, owned a newspaper called the *Morning Chronicle*, to which, by the age of twenty, Irving had begun to contribute articles under the name of "Jonathan Oldstyle, Gent." These attracted a certain amount of flattering attention, even from the great Aaron Burr. Too, while touring Europe (1804–6), Irving developed an interest in music (he would be a passionate opera-goer all his life), and, under the influence of the eminent American artist Washington Allston, in painting. But he continued to devote the major portion of his energies to the social life, and on his return to America was no closer to choosing a serious career than he had been when he had left three years before.

The literary venture that now involved him, the *Salmagundi* papers, was anything but serious, even if the authors—Irving, his brother William, and James Kirke Paulding[1]—spoke of "serious truths conveyed in every paper" and in the first issue professed the purpose "to instruct the young, reform the old, correct the town, and castigate the age." This was to be accomplished by presenting a "striking picture of the town,"

---

[1] Later a novelist, poet, and historian, now chiefly remembered for the play *The Lion of the West*, which launched the legend of Davy Crockett. (See p. 1095.)

and the first issue added: "as everybody is anxious to see his own phiz on canvas, however stupid or ugly it may be, we have no doubt but the whole town will flock to our exhibition." The satire was of an ungentle sort, and the general tone was that of farce and slapstick, with outrageous caricature, exaggeration, and burlesque.

The *Salmagundi* papers came directly out of the eighteenth-century tradition of satire, whose masters were Swift, Pope, Fielding, and Addison and Steele of the *Spectator*; but critics have pointed out an important difference between such examples and the kind of satire we find in the project of Irving and his friends. In the eighteenth-century English satirists, we sense the point of view from which the satire was directed; ordinarily we recognize the set of values by which the author would judge the world he satirizes. The randomness of the satire in the *Salmagundi* papers, the striking out on whimsical impulse, even at the authors themselves as "critics, dilettantes, and cognoscenti," make it impossible to find a center. The authors, in the first issue, remark: "Neither will we puzzle our heads to give an account of ourselves," and later add that though they might be able to do so, "very few men *can* give a tolerable account of themselves." In other words, it is hard, the young authors admit, to know what the responsible center of a man really is; and life is rather a random business—like a "salmagundi," which is a chopped salad of veal and chicken, with onions, pickled herring, and an oil and lemon dressing.

This willingness to regard life as random mixture, to strike out on impulse with little concern beyond the immediate effect—this creating of a kind of satire which is almost a satire on satire itself—can be taken, so some critics argue, as the mark of a society uncertain of its own values and of itself; and such was the society of New York, and America, as it strove to free itself from the colonial mentality. What does give the *Salmagundi* papers unity is not, then, a central attitude, or a point of view; it is simply an energy which rejoices in random exercise, in the high-spirited fun of striking out. This, it may be added, is also the mark of a young society, and with this in mind, we can see some affinity, even in stylistic extravagance, the love of violent exaggeration, and the lack of centrality, between things as different as the tall tales of the frontier (see pp. 1087–90) and this lark of a group of pampered young men in New York.

For the modern reader of the *Salmagundi* papers, something of the high spirits of the lark survives, and even some of the humor—that commodity most vulnerable to changes in space and time. Here, too, he finds the social record, for instance, in "Style, at Balston," an account of life at a fashionable watering place; and here appears for the first time a portrait of that type of southerner who would later come to be known as a "cotton snob."

From Style, at Balston (1807)

The worthy, fashionable, dashing, good-for-nothing people of every state, who had rather suffer the martyrdom of a crowd than endure the monotony of their own homes, and the stupid company of their own thoughts, flock to the Springs; not to enjoy the pleasures of society, or benefit by the qualities of the waters, but to exhibit their equipages and wardrobes, and to excite the admiration, or, what is much more satisfactory, the envy of their fashionable competitors. This, of course, awakens a spirit of noble emulation between the eastern, middle, and southern States; and every lady hereupon finding herself charged in a manner with the whole weight of her country's dignity and style, dresses and dashes, and sparkles, without mercy, at her competitors from other parts of the Union. This kind of rivalship naturally requires a vast deal of preparation and prodigious quantities of supplies. A sober citizen's wife will break half a dozen milliners' shops, and sometimes starve her family a whole season, to enable herself to make the Springs campaign in style. She repairs to the seat of war with a mighty force of trunks and bandboxes, like so many ammunition chests, filled with caps, hats, gowns, ribbons, shawls, and all the various artillery of fashionable warfare. The lady of a Southern planter will lay out the whole annual produce of a rice plantation in silver and gold muslins, lace veils, and new liveries; carry a hogshead of tobacco on her head, and trail a bale of sea-island cotton at her heels; while a lady of Boston or Salem will wrap herself up in the net proceeds of a cargo of whale oil, and tie on her hat with a quintal of codfish.

The planters' ladies, however, have generally the advantage in this contest; for, as it is an incontestable fact, that whoever comes from the West or East Indies, or Georgia, or the Carolinas, or in fact any warm climate, is immensely rich, it cannot be expected that a simple cit of the North can cope with them in style. The planter, therefore, who drives four horses abroad, and a thousand negroes at home, and who flourishes up to the Springs, followed by half a score of black-a-moors, in gorgeous liveries, is unquestionably superior to the northern merchant, who plods on in a carriage and pair; which, being nothing more than is quite necessary, has no claim whatever to style. He, however, has his consolation in feeling superior to the honest cit, who dashes about in a simple gig; he, in return, sneers at the country squire, who jogs along with his scrubby, long-eared pony and saddlebags; and the squire, by way of taking satisfaction, would make no scruple to run over the unobtrusive pedestrian, were it not that the last, being the most independent of the whole, might chance to break his head by way of retort.

The great misfortune is, that this style is supported at such an expense as sometimes to encroach on the rights and privileges of the pocket; and occasions very awkward embarrassments to the tyro of fashion. Among a number of instances, Evergreen mentions the fate of a dashing blade from the South, who made his *entrée* with a tandem and two outriders, by the aid of which he attracted the attention of all the ladies, and caused a coolness between several young couples who, it was thought before his arrival, had a considerable kindness for each other. In the course of a fortnight his tandem disappeared;—the class of good folk who seem to have nothing to do in this world but pry into other people's affairs, began to stare. In a little time longer an outrider was missing!—this increased the alarm, and it was consequently whispered that he had eaten the horses and drank the negro. N. B. Southern gentlemen are very apt to do this on an emergency. Serious apprehensions were entertained about the fate of the remaining servant, which were soon verified by his actually vanishing; and in "one little month" the dashing Carolinian modestly took his departure in the stage-coach!—universally regretted by the friends who had generously released him from his cumbrous load of style.

———————

The lark that Irving and his friends indulged in was rather protracted, running in fact to sixty-five issues. The end came in 1808, by which time Irving was in love with the charming and sickly seventeen-year-old daughter of Judge Hoffman, in whose office he studied law. With the prospect of matrimony, and a good berth in the Judge's office, Irving went more seriously to work, but the girl's death, within a year, freed him of an obligation that he remained very wary of for the rest of his life.[2] Even before the death of Matilda Hoffman, however, Irving had drifted back into a literary project, and with the bereavement, he drove at it with furious energy. Ironically enough, this work in which he sought refuge from grief, was, like the *Salmagundi* venture, comic.

A History of New York from the Beginning of the World to the End of the Dutch Dynasty by Diedrich Knickerbocker was not only comic, but was offered as an elaborate hoax. In October, 1809, the public press carried the notice that a certain Knickerbocker, "a small elderly gentleman, dressed in an old black coat and a cocked hat," and probably not "entirely in his right mind," had disappeared from his lodgings, and three weeks later Knickerbocker's landlord gave notice that, to settle his account, he would sell the manuscript of a book left in the room of the tenant. On December 7, the work appeared. It was an immediate success; Sir Walter Scott roared with laughter at it and Dickens was to wear out his copy.

Several aspects of the *History* are noteworthy,

---

[2] Irving, many years later, undertook one other courtship (or perhaps that is too strong a word for the event), this time being saved, not by the lady's death, but by her good judgment.

the most obvious being that Irving has here found a way of treating American materials in a truly "literary" perspective—a thing that no other writer up to that time had succeeded in doing. When Joel Barlow wrote *The Columbiad* he merely celebrated America in terms as appropriate for a sermon, or a Fourth of July oration, as for a poem. (See p. 197.) The treatment is direct and abstract, with merely a dressing of rhymed couplets and rhetorical flourishes. In the simplest terms, we can say that what Irving now does is to regard the treatment itself as the embodiment of the ultimate

meaning of the thing treated.

To develop this difference between Barlow and Irving, we may say that the former aims directly at the heroic, and that the latter aims at the mock-heroic. Put over against Barlow's rhetoric, we may remember the mere title of the chapter (Bk. 6, Chap. 7) of the *History* recording the battle of Fort Christina: "Containing the Most Horrible Battle Ever Recorded in Poetry or Prose; with the Admirable Exploits of Peter the Headstrong." With that title who could take the battle seriously?

From A History of New York (1809)

The immortal deities, who whilome had seen service at the "affair" of Troy—now mounted their feather-bed clouds, and sailed over the plain, or mingled among the combatants in different disguises, all itching to have a finger in the pie. Jupiter sent off his thunderbolt to a noted coppersmiths, to have it furbished up for the direful occasion. Venus, swore by her chastity she'd patronize the Swedes, and in semblance of a blear eyed trull, paraded the battlements of Fort Christina, accompanied by Diana, as a serjeant's widow, of cracked reputation—The noted bully Mars, stuck two horse pistols into his belt, shouldered a rusty firelock, and gallantly swaggered at their elbow, as a drunken corporal—while Apollo trudged in their rear, as a bandy-legged fifer, playing most villainously out of tune.

On the other side, the ox-eyed Juno, who had won a pair of black eyes over night, in one of her curtain lectures with old Jupiter, displayed her haughty beauties on a baggage waggon—Minerva, as a brawny gin suttler, tucked up her skirts, brandished her fists, and swore most heroically, in exceeding bad dutch, (having but lately studied the language) by way of keeping up the spirits of the soldiers; while Vulcan halted as a club-footed blacksmith, lately promoted to be a captain of militia. All was silent horror, or bustling preparation; war reared his horrid front, gnashed loud his iron fangs, and shook his direful crest of bristling bayonets. . . .

The battle is a frantic and unbloody farce:

And now commenced the horrid din, the desperate struggle, the maddening ferocity, the frantic desperation, the confusion and self abandonment of war. Dutchman and Swede commingled, tugged, panted and blowed. The heavens were darkened with a tempest of missives. Carcasses, fire balls, smoke balls, stink balls and hand grenades, jostling each other, in the air. Bang! went the guns—whack! struck the broad swords—thump! went the cudgels—crash! went the musket stocks—blows—kicks—cuffs—scratches—black eyes and bloody noses swelling the horrors of the scene! Thick-thwack, cut and hack, helter-skelter, higgledy-piggledy, hurley-burley, head over heels, klip-klap, slag op slag, hob over bol, rough and tumble! —— ——
Dunder and blixum! swore the dutchmen, splitter and splutter! cried the Swedes—Storm the works! shouted Hard-koppig Piet—fire the mine! roared stout Risingh—Tantara-ra-ra! twang'd the trumpet of Antony Van Corlear—until all voice and sound became unintelligible—grunts of pain, yells of fury, and shouts of triumph commingling in one hideous clamour. The earth shook as if struck with a paralytic stroke—The trees shrunk aghast, and wilted at the sight—The rocks burrowed in the ground like rabbits, and even Christina creek turned from its course, and ran up a mountain in breathless terror!

Nothing, save the dullness of their weapons, the damaged condition of their powder, and the singular accident of one and all striking with the flat instead of the edge of their swords, could have prevented a most horrible carnage—As it was, the sweat prodigiously streaming, ran in rivers on the field, fortunately without drowning a soul, the combatants being to a man, expert swimmers, and furnished with cork jackets for the occasion—but many a valiant head was broken, many a stubborn rib belaboured, and many a broken winded hero drew short breath that day!

The climax comes when the two commanders, the Swede Risingh and the Dutch Peter Stuyvesant—Peter the Thick-Headed—engage in mortal combat:

No sooner did these two rival heroes come face to face, than they each made a prodigious start of fifty feet (flemish measure), such as is made by your most experienced stage champions. Then did they regard each other for a moment, with bitter aspect, like two furious ram cats, on the very point of a clapper clawing. Then did they throw themselves in one attitude, then in another, striking their swords on the ground, first on the right side, then on the left, at last at it they went, like five hundred houses on fire! Words cannot tell the prodigies of strength and valour, displayed in this direful encounter—an encounter, compared to which the far famed battles of Ajax with Hector, of Eneas with Turnus, Orlando with Rodomont, Guy of Warwick with Colbrand the Dane, or of that renowned Welsh Knight Sir Owen of the mountains with the giant Guylon, were all gentle sports and holliday recreations. At length the valiant Peter watching his opportunity, aimed a fearful blow with the full intention of cleaving his adversary to the very chine; but Risingh nimbly raising his sword, warded it off so narrowly, that glancing on one side, it shaved away a huge canteen full of fourth proof brandy, that he always carried swung on one side; thence pursuing its tranchant course, it severed off a deep coat pocket, stored with bread and cheese—all which dainties rolling among the armies, occasioned a fearful scrambling between the Swedes and Dutchmen, and made the general battle to wax ten times more furious than ever.

Enraged to see his military stores thus woefully laid waste, the stout Risingh collecting all his forces, aimed a mighty blow, full at the hero's crest. In vain did his fierce little cocked hat oppose its course; the biting steel clove through the stubborn ram beaver, and would infallibly have cracked his gallant crown, but that the scull was of such adamantine hardness that the brittle weapon shivered into five and twenty pieces, shedding a thousand sparks, like beams of glory, round his grizly visage.

Stunned with the blow the valiant Peter reeled, turned up his eyes and beheld fifty thousand suns, besides moons and stars, dancing Scotch reels about the firmament—at length, missing his footing, by reason of his wooden leg, down he came, on his seat of honour, with a crash that shook the surrounding hills, and would infallibly have wracked his anatomical system, had he not been received into a cushion softer than velvet, which providence, or Minerva, or St. Nicholas, or some kindly cow, had benevolently prepared for his reception.

The furious Risingh, in despight of that noble maxim, cherished by all true knights, that "fair play is a jewel," hastened to take advantage of the hero's fall; but just as he was stooping to give the fatal blow, the ever vigilant Peter bestowed him a sturdy thwack over the sconce, with his wooden leg, that set some dozen chimes of bells ringing triple bob-majors in his cerebellum. The bewildered Swede staggered with the blow, and in the mean time the wary Peter, espying a pocket pistol lying hard by (which had dropped from the wallet of his faithful squire and trumpeter Van Corlear during his furious encounter with the drummer) discharged it full at the head of the reeling Risingh—Let not my reader mistake—it was not a murderous weapon loaded with powder and ball, but a little sturdy stone pottle, charged to the muzzle with a double dram of true dutch courage, which the knowing Van Corlear always carried about him by way of replenishing his valour. The hideous missive sung through the air, and true to its course, as was the mighty fragment of a rock, discharged at Hector by bully Ajax, encountered the huge head of the gigantic Swede with matchless violence.

This heaven directed blow decided the eventful battle. The ponderous pericranium of general Jan Risingh sunk upon his breast; his knees tottered under him; a deathlike torpor seized upon his Titan frame, and he tumbled to the earth with such tremendous violence, that old Pluto started with affright, lest he should have broken through the roof of his infernal palace.

The comedy in the *History* is compounded, and refined, by the fact that the narrative is presumably written by Diedrich Knickerbocker, who, as a fictional narrator, is not intending mock-heroic burlesque but a serious history in the heroic strain. In fact, the invented narrator is what gives the *History* its main point and comic effect. Knickerbocker, setting up as a historian, is befuddled and befuddling, and what he gives is not history but, unconsciously, a parody of history and of the pomposities and pedantries of historians. For example, to justify the seizure of the New World by European explorers, he begins by saying that nothing is necessary "but to prove that it was totally uninhabited by man." He then proceeds to parody the various arguments of self-justification offered by the Christian white man vis-à-vis the colored races (Bk. 5, Chap. 5). Or, when Knickerbocker discusses the nature of treaties, the crazy logic he offers is irrefutable, and the final comedy is that he is *not* offering this logic as comedy (Bk. 5, Chap. 4).

The basic comedy of the *History* is, to sum up, in the character of Knickerbocker as historian. He isn't certain that we can know what happened in the past, and by his own account of what he thinks *did* happen, we are left uncertain that, if human behavior is largely folly and self-deception and unconscious slapstick, what did happen in the past is worth knowing. Knickerbocker himself indicates that civilization and all values are relative, and he says that if the advanced men in the moon should visit earth in their aircraft, they would consider the civilized white man no different from a savage (Bk. 1, Chap. 5).[3]

So here the random skepticism of *Salmagundi* has been deepened and made more philosophical; and one aspect of that process is represented by certain implied criticisms of American life. For instance, there are criticisms of unimaginative materialism (as here embodied in the Dutch), a suspicion of the democratic process, of the intelligence and decency of ordinary men, of the "new vision" of life in the New World, and of the wisdom of Thomas Jefferson, discernible under the mask of the character William Kieft (Bk. 5, Chap. 1).

In spite of the serious implications of the *History*, it must be remembered that the tone is comic, and that if the comedy is satirical, it is not savage, but good-humored, with the tone of Laurence Sterne rather than Jonathan Swift. Knickerbocker himself, in all his befuddlement, is very much like us all, and even befuddlement can be enjoyed. If Peter Stuyvesant is the almost doltish butt of satire, he is also a vividly created character, with the complications of reality about him, and the most complicated fact is that he somehow has worth and dignity.

Two more remarks should be added about the *History*. If it is, in one sense, a spoof of history, that fact in itself is another comment on the American situation at the time. Americans were concerned to have a "history," to explore their past and celebrate their achievements; but the spoof would imply that if history is ultimately indeterminate and, insofar as it is determinable, often a narrative of folly and delusion, then why bother about it? Why not look to the future? So in this perspective, Irving would be a precursor of the practical Henry Ford, who was to say, "History is bunk." At a deeper level would begin a literary mode, the philosophical spoof of history, which would include *A Connecticut Yankee in King Arthur's Court*, of Mark Twain, and most recently, in another key, *The Sot-Weed Factor*, the brilliant novel by John Barth.

Even the good reception of the *History* did not lead Irving to embrace a literary career. In America, in fact, literature was not yet a profession. There was certainly no encouragement to be drawn from the lives of those few men, like Charles Brockden Brown, who had attempted to live by the pen; and now, though Irving had escaped the law, he was drawn into business, becoming, in 1810, a partner in the family concern, and by 1815, shortly after the treaty of peace with England, finding himself in Liverpool, in the English branch. But he was continuing his literary interests, making notes, reading, seeking out literary company, including Sir Walter Scott, who hospitably received him

---

[3] This passage may well have suggested the Man in the Moon passage in Hawthorne's famous story "My Kinsman, Major Molineux." (The story appears in our text.)

at Abbottsford, in Scotland, and who helped arrange the publication, in England, of Irving's next important work, *The Sketch Book*, by "Geoffrey Crayon, Gent.," which appeared in 1819. By that time the failure of the family business had set Irving finally free for literature.

The ten years between the *History* and *The Sketch Book* mark the difference between the young writer finding his way and the writer asserting his mature subject and his polished style. For one thing, the *History*, as a spoof on history, repudiates the past, while *The Sketch Book* exploits the interests the past holds. The stay in England lies behind this difference, for by this time the Romantic movement was in full flower, and writers such as the Gothic novelists (see p. 226), Keats, Coleridge, and Scott had popularized the poetical, picturesque, and melancholy aspects of the past. But Irving was, after all, American, and in him there remained an American ambivalence toward the past, sharpened and made more dramatic by his new awareness of its attractions.[4]

[4] The lack of a "past" in America was to be bewailed by many writers, including Hawthorne and Henry James. Literally, there was, by the time of the Revolution, a century and a half of past, full of vigorous and romantic activity—even if there were no hoary castles. But what was meant, in one perspective at least, by those who found no past was that the colonial past was not relevant to the national past, which had begun with the Declaration of Independence. In one sense, a colonial people does not, in fact, have a past; its past is the past of the mother country, and it took a long time for the new nation to claim as its own the colonial past. For example, Nathaniel Bacon, of the rebellion that bears his name, which occurred in Virginia in 1676 against the Royal Governor of Virginia, was not redeemed from the infamy of being a rebel until 1804. In that year Thomas Jefferson, then President, proclaimed him a "patriot." But of what *patria* did Jefferson regard Bacon as a "patriot"? Bacon had, in fact, scarcely set foot on Virginia's soil, fresh from England, when he was embroiled in the troubles of the colony, and was dead, by fever or poison, within the year. Jefferson was, clearly, regarding Bacon as the patriot of a *patria* that did not come into existence until a century after his death and would have been unimaginable in his time. In other words, Jefferson's issuing naturalization papers—and a certificate of patriotism—to Bacon was the first important step toward the new nation's claiming of a past. Irving, as we shall see, made a modest but significant gesture with "Rip

In a way, the charm of the past involved for Irving a strongly continuing tradition. Though American, he was only one generation removed from the Old World, and his social and political bias was conservative, that is, Federalist. The sense of continuity was important for him, and what he admired even in English scenery was "the moral feeling that seems to pervade it." He declared that the land was "associated in the mind with ideas of order, of quiet, of sober well-established principles, of hoary usage and reverend custom." He reflected sadly that America could not "boast of a single ruin," in contrast to the "shadowy grandeurs of the past" that bemused him in England. The fact that, as Stanley Williams, his biographer, puts it, he had only a "slender knowledge of the past" is not relevant; attitude, not information, is what is at stake here.

It was, ironically enough, the raw American's openness to this appeal which gave Irving the role of the interpreter of the charm of the English scene to the English—to those Englishmen who, romantically in love with the past, had been more apt to gratify their taste by pondering the antiquities of the continent than by seeing England first. At the same time, in spite of its official subject, *The Sketch Book* exploits the American ambivalences toward England, even as it recognizes and celebrates the appeal of the mother country, and in doing so, sets one of the continuing themes of American literature.

There is, however, one very significant feature shared by the *History* and *The Sketch Book*. As the final appeal of the former depends on the fictionalized narrator, so in the latter it depends on Geoffrey Crayon, Gent. In him we have more than an observer and narrator who serves as a device to give unity to a collection of more or less random sketches and tales. Instead, he is a fully rendered character—much more so than

Van Winkle" and "The Legend of Sleepy Hollow," but the towering literary figures in the story of the redeeming of the colonial past are Cooper and Hawthorne, with the historian Parkman as a staunch collaborator in the project.

Diedrich Knickerbocker. The character is individualized enough to give the author the distance and dramatic irony of anonymity, but is close enough to Irving to serve, without too much distortion, as a mask or mouthpiece for him, as a kind of *persona*. At the very center of Crayon's soul, we find the tensions, ambivalences, and ambiguities which Irving experienced. Crayon, a sensitive gentleman, somewhat uncertain of his own place in the world and in history, is torn between England and America, between the past and the future. At the same time, he is aware of the humor of the situation, and humorous self-deprecation flickers over the whole work.

There is, too, another kind of tension in Crayon's nature, that between his need for sentiment, his penchant for the sweetness of melancholy, and, on the other side of his nature, his ironical, comic, or merely humorous repudiation of these impulses. It is a matter of personal identity and role, as well as of American identity and role, that is here at stake, and the force of Crayon as a dramatization lies in the fact that he is, in an effective ratio, a projection of Irving himself, the middle-aged bachelor of no fixed address and no certain occupation, a perceptive person of warm friendships but with no hearth of his own by which to toast his shins.

Except for Rip Van Winkle and Ichabod Crane, Crayon is Irving's most telling fictional creation, and with him, some critics argue, Irving invents the involved narrator which was to have so important a part, technical and philosophical, in the development of fictional method. In *The Sketch Book*, Irving was, in fact, moving toward the short story, most nearly in "Rip Van Winkle" and "The Legend of Sleepy Hollow." Even if both works are, in a sense, merely extended anecdotes, Irving does have a brisk sense of narrative and a sure eye for social and natural settings, a shrewd sense of how to develop individualized characters from types, and a knack of hitting on key conflicts— Rip against his wife and the world's values; Ichabod Crane, the cadaverous outsider, against the round-bosomed, pink-cheeked Katrina and the thick-thewed, full-blooded Brom, who are so clearly made for each other's lusty delights and stand at the very center of the life process.

By the technical developments in "Rip Van Winkle" and "The Legend of Sleepy Hollow" Irving clearly earns a place in the history of American fiction, but his great contribution lies in the fact that here, as in the *History*, he finds a new way to use American materials. It does not matter that both these tales are adaptations from German sources; that fact merely emphasizes the solidity of the imaginative grounding that Irving managed to give them in America.

The success of *The Sketch Book* was immediate, and Irving became one of the most admired authors in England. With *Bracebridge Hall* (1822), a collection of sketches of English country life centered on Christmas, he attempted to repeat the performance of *The Sketch Book*. Some of the items and incidental effects are charming, but what at the deeper level had made the previous work interesting is here lacking: that is, the dramatic ambivalences in the character of Crayon. Nor do we find a Rip or an Ichabod. Two years later, Irving issued a third collection, the fruit of a stay in Germany, *Tales of a Traveller*, a mixture of almost slapstick humor and the shocks and horrors of the Gothic tales.

The rest of Irving's long life is a story of both anticlimax and increasing popular recognition; his best work had been done, but his fame continued to wax. By 1826, he went to the American legation in Madrid, and out of this period came *The Life and Voyages of Christopher Columbus* (1828), followed by *The Conquest of Granada* (1829), and three years later *The Alhambra*. When in 1832 he returned to America, after seventeen years abroad, he found himself a great public figure.

Back home, Irving tried to reenter American life. He took a rather adventurous trip in the then Southwest and published his *Tour of the Prairies*. At the suggestion of John Jacob Astor, he wrote an account of the fur trade, which had made the Astor fortune, and later a book on the western explorer Benjamin Bonneville. But Irving could not really grasp the importance of the West, certainly not the inward significance which Cooper had already intuited and was making into the legend of Leatherstocking. Irving was too old, nothing in his background fitted him for the effort, and his talent for the charming, the small, and the picturesque was lost against the vast background of forest, prairie, and mountains.

From 1842 until 1846, he was back in Spain, now as ambassador, having become enough of a Democrat, though a rather ambiguous one with the taint of Federalism still about him, to satisfy the administration of President Tyler. After a successful career as a diplomat, he again returned home, now permanently to his estate Sunnyside, at Tarrytown on the Hudson, and settled down to work, struggling valiantly against ill health, depression, and dreams of his mother, from which he would wake with tears running down his cheeks. His monumental, and monumentally dull, *Life of George Washington*, to which he seems to have been mystically committed, was finally completed, the fifth and last volume being published in 1859, the year of his death.

Irving discovered, as we have said, the importance of "treatment" in literature as contrasted with subject. What he was interested in, as he put it in *Bracebridge Hall*, was the "looking at things poetically, rather than politically." He would regard literature as more than, and different from, a work of edification, instruction, propaganda, or patriotism—in short, as an art. As an art, we may say, literature is fundamentally related to the concerns and passions of actual life, but it treats them in dimensions not ordinarily found in actual life: on the one hand, as a vision of significantly generalized human experience and, on the other, as a form expressively created.

The "experience" that Irving treated was neither soaring nor profound; he was temperamentally inclined, as he said, "to see the world in as pleasant a light as circumstances will permit," and though in later years he was subject to nocturnal horrors and neurotic agitations, he carefully steered clear, in his work, of the darker aspects of the human story. The "feeling and fancy" which he said he addressed himself to in *The Sketch Book* and which would provide the continuity of appeal beyond his particular moment in time, involved sympathy and gentle affection, humor, modest self-ironies, amiable regrets, and celebrations of good health and the comforts of life, and if there are occasional morbidities, as in "The Adventure of the German Student," the preposterousness redeems the horror. The point is that Irving looked to the appeal to "feeling and fancy," however superficial, as the basis of the generalized response he would seek beyond the world of "philosopher and politician."

As for the dimension of what we have termed the expressively created, Irving is even more explicit. He abjured, he says of *The Sketch Book*, "lofty themes" and even, as he says in a letter to Henry Brevoort, the emphasis on narrative. He does not seek readers "who are intent more upon the story than the way in which it is told." For him, as for some more recent and famous theorists and practitioners of fiction, including Henry James and the English novelist E. M. Forster, the story is merely "a frame on which to stretch . . . materials." What he values is "the play of thought, of sentiment, and language; the weaving in of characters lightly, yet expressively, delineated; the familiar and faithful exhibition of scenes in common life; and the half-concealed vein of humor that is often playing through the whole. . . ." For a moment it would seem that he is talking merely about the content of his work, but then we realize that he refers to the way items of content are to be treated—not the "thought" and "sentiment" as such but their "play"; not merely "characters" but characters "lightly, yet expressively, delineated" and woven in; not merely "scenes in common life" but such scenes lighted by humor "playing over the whole." He is talking about relations and effects, not about content as such; that is, he is stressing form.

The fact that Irving regards form as expressively created comes out quite clearly when he says that the process of writing is dominated by a single basic feeling for the thing to be done: "I feel how a thing ought to be done, and how I can render it effectively, and if I go counter to this feeling I am likely to come off lamely; yet I cannot reduce the feeling to any rule or maxim. . . ." It is the whole "treatment" that makes for the survival of a work: he wished to write "in such a manner that my productions may have something more than the mere interest of narrative"; and something more, he might have added, than the mere interest of "opinion or idea to recommend them, which is very evanescent; something, if I dare use the phrase, of classic merit, i.e. depending upon style, etc. which gives a production some chance of duration beyond the mere whim and fashion of the day."

Irving's great insight was that to have a national literature the emphasis must be placed on the word "literature" and not on the word "national." He was our first theoretician of literature, albeit a modest one, but his role is significant in that his theorizing came out of his own slow and painful effort to develop a style and general method appropriate for his own feelings for the world.

That style and feeling were of their moment, and that fact meant that both were doomed soon to appear as merely polite imitations of the English tradition. Herman Melville, writing, in 1850, on Hawthorne's *Mosses from an Old Manse*, would say of Irving:

> But that graceful writer, who perhaps of all Americans has received the most plaudits from his own country for his productions— that very popular and amiable writer, however good and self-reliant in many things, perhaps owes his chief reputation to the self-acknowledged imitations of a foreign model, and to the studious avoidance of all topics but smooth ones.

Not only, we notice, is the imitation of a foreign model held against poor Irving, but even more damagingly, the "smooth" subject. How could Melville, at that very moment caught up in the horrors and glories of *Moby-Dick*, find much interest in the polite dubieties and ambivalences of Geoffrey Crayon, Gent.? For what we are to learn is that, by the time of Hawthorne and Melville, the discovery of America was coming to mean the discovery of a dark depth of experience, one which the "amiable" Irving could not, or chose not to, recognize.

BIOGRAPHICAL CHART

1783   Born, April 8, in New York City, eleventh child of William Irving, prosperous merchant; named for George Washington

1799   Studies law

1802   Contributes under name of "Jonathan Oldstyle, Gent." to the *Morning Chronicle*, owned by brother Peter

1804–6   First travels in Europe; admitted to bar

1807   *Salmagundi* papers begin

1809   Love affair with Matilda Hoffman; death of Matilda; *A History of New York*

1815–18   First period abroad; meets Scott; develops interest in folklore and legends

1819   *The Sketch Book*

1820–22   Socially active in London and Paris; *Bracebridge Hall*

1824   *Tales of a Traveller*

1826   Becomes attaché to American legation in Madrid, to translate collection of materials on Columbus

1828   *The Life and Voyages of Christopher Columbus*, in England

1829   *The Conquest of Granada*; appointed by Jackson administration as secretary to Embassy in London

1831   Receives honorary LL.D. from Oxford

1832   *Alhambra*; returns to America, after absence of seventeen years; journeys to the West

1835   *A Tour on the Prairies*; purchases Sunnyside, at Tarrytown

1842   Appointed minister to Spain

1846   Returns to America

1855–57   Works on *Life of George Washington*; four volumes published

1859   Last volume of *Washington* published; dies, November 28, at Sunnyside

FURTHER READINGS

Henry A. Pochmann, ed., *The Complete Works of Washington Irving* (to be completed in the late 1970's; 28 vols.)

Ralph M. Aderman, ed., *Washington Irving Reconsidered* (1969)

Claude G. Bowers, *The Spanish Adventures of Washington Irving* (1940)

John Clendenning, "Irving and the Gothic Tradition," *Bucknell Review*, 12 (1964)

Allen Guttmann, "Washington Irving and the Conservative Imagination," *American Literature*, 36 (May, 1964)

William L. Hedges, *Washington Irving: An American Study, 1802–1932* (1965)

Marcel M. D. Heiman, "Rip Van Winkle: A Psychoanalytic Note on the Story and Its Author," *American Imago*, 16 (1959)

Daniel G. Hoffman, *Form and Fable in American Fiction* (1961)

Pierre M. Irving, *The Life and Letters of Washington Irving* (1863–64)

Lewis Leary, *Washington Irving* (1963)

Donald A. Ringe, "New York and New England: Irving's Criticism of American Society," *American Literature*, 38 (January, 1967)

Edward C. Wagenknecht, *Washington Irving: Moderation Displayed* (1962)

Stanley T. Williams, *The Life of Washington Irving* (1936)

Philip Young, *Three Bags Full: Essays in American Fiction* (1972).

Rip Van Winkle (1819)

The story has been enormously popular, both in the form in which Irving wrote it and in a number of dramatic versions, some five plays, the first by John Kerr (1829), and three operas. The famous actor Joseph Jefferson played the role of Rip for forty-five years, and one of the best of the American poets of this century, Hart Crane, devotes a section to Rip in his most ambitious production, *The Bridge*. At the same time, the figure of Rip has almost detached itself from literature and assumed the status of a folk figure.

Irving did draw the story from a German folk tale, and this fact may have something to do with the sense of a deep but teasingly unresolved meaning, or cluster of meanings, which, in part at least, may account for the abiding popularity. The story has something to do with Time, with both the escape from Time and the victimization by Time. It has something to do with sleep and with waking, and the ambiguous relation of those two realms of being. It has something to do with youth and age, and attitudes toward growth, including a refusal to grow up.

All of these considerations lie at the very heart of our life sense, as the innumerable myths, legends, and folk tales, in many cultures, would testify. We find the Christian legend of the Seven Ephesian Sleepers, and those of good kings like Arthur, Charlemagne, and Frederick Barbarossa (the Rothbart whom Irving refers to in his note as a kind of whimsical distraction from his true source), who sleep for years but will come again, and similar stories of heroes and gods, like the German Siegfried and the Norse Woden (mysteriously referred to in the fragment of verse Irving quotes as an epigraph). Even the account of the Crucifixion and the Resurrection carries the same theme. And we find variants in the tale of Sleeping Beauty and the ballad of "Thomas Rhymer." In some of these versions, certain ideas and certain attitudes are indicated. But not so with Rip's story. There remains the teasing quality at center, which stirs us as an echo of some paradoxical yearning and fear in our own experience. There is also, more specifically, a theory that this tale represents the author's long and fruitless effort to resolve an Oedipal conflict.

The image Irving set in the American landscape has, too, its own indigenous dimension of meaning, its own relation to the developing history of the country which has been repeated in many variations and avatars, from Cooper's

Leatherstocking, Melville's Ishmael and Mark Twain's Huck Finn (none of whom wanted to grow up any more than did Rip, and all of whom escape out of Time), and on to certain characters of Hemingway and F. Scott Fitzgerald.

> By Woden, God of Saxons,
> From whence comes Wensday, that is
>   Wodensday,
> Truth is a thing that ever I will keep
> Unto thylke day in which I creep into
> My sepulchre—

> CARTWRIGHT

[The following Tale was found among the papers of the late Diedrich Knickerbocker, an old gentleman of New York, who was very curious in the Dutch history of the province, and the manners of the descendants from its primitive settlers. His historical researches, however, did not lie so much among books as among men; for the former are lamentably scanty on his favorite topics; whereas he found the old burghers, and still more their wives, rich in that legendary lore, so invaluable to true history. Whenever, therefore, he happened upon a genuine Dutch family, snugly shut up in its low-roofed farmhouse, under a spreading sycamore, he looked upon it as a little clasped volume of black-letter, and studied it with the zeal of a book-worm.

The result of all these researches was a history of the province during the reign of the Dutch governors, which he published some years since. There have been various opinions as to the literary character of his work, and, to tell the truth, it is not a whit better than it should be. Its chief merit is its scrupulous accuracy, which indeed was a little questioned on its first appearance, but has since been completely established; and it is now admitted into all historical collections, as a book of unquestionable authority.

The old gentleman died shortly after the publication of his work, and now that he is dead and gone, it cannot do much harm to his memory to say that his time might have been much better employed in weightier labors. He, however, was apt to ride his hobby his own way; and though it did now and then kick up the dust a little in the eyes of his neighbors, and grieve the spirit of some friends, for whom he felt the truest deference and affection; yet his errors and follies are remembered "more in sorrow than in anger," and it begins to be suspected, that he never intended to injure or offend. But however his memory may be appreciated by critics, it is still held dear by many folks, whose good opinion is well worth having; particularly by certain biscuit-bakers, who have gone so far as to imprint his likeness on their new-year cakes; and have thus given him a chance for immortality, almost equal to the being stamped on a Waterloo Medal, or a Queen Anne's Farthing.]

Whoever has made a voyage up the Hudson must remember the Kaatskill mountains. They are a dismembered branch of the great Appalachian family, and are seen away to the west of the river, swelling up to a noble height, and lording it over the surrounding country. Every change of season, every change of weather, indeed, every hour of the day, produces some change in the magical hues and shapes of these mountains, and they are regarded by all the good wives, far and near, as perfect barometers. When the weather is fair and settled, they are clothed in blue and purple, and print their bold outlines on the clear evening sky; but, sometimes, when the rest of the landscape is cloudless, they will gather a hood of gray vapors about their summits, which, in the last rays of the setting sun, will glow and light up like a crown of glory.

At the foot of these fairy mountains, the voyager may have descried the light smoke curling up from a village, whose shingle-roofs gleam among the trees, just where the blue tints of the upland melt away into the fresh green of the nearer landscape. It is a little village of great antiquity, having been founded by some of the Dutch colonists, in the early times of the province, just about the beginning of the government of the good Peter Stuyvesant, (may he rest in peace!) and there were some of the houses of the original settlers standing within a few years, built of small yellow bricks brought from Holland, having latticed windows and gable fronts, surmounted with weather-cocks.

In that same village, and in one of these very houses (which, to tell the precise truth, was sadly time-worn and weather-beaten), there lived many years since, while the country was yet a province of Great Britain, a simple good-natured fellow of the name of Rip Van Winkle. He was a descendant of the Van Winkles who figured so gallantly in the chivalrous days of Peter Stuyvesant, and accompanied him to the siege of Fort Christina. He inherited, however, but little of the martial character of his ancestors. I have observed that he was a simple good-natured man; he was, moreover, a kind neighbor, and an obedient hen-pecked husband. Indeed, to the latter circumstance might be owing that meekness of spirit which gained him such universal popularity; for those men are most apt to be obsequious and conciliating abroad, who are under the discipline of shrews at home. Their tempers, doubtless, are rendered pliant and malleable in the fiery furnace of domestic tribulation; and a curtain lecture is worth all the sermons in the world for teaching the virtues of patience and long-suffering. A termagant wife may, therefore, in some respects, be considered a tolerable blessing; and if so, Rip Van Winkle was thrice blessed.

Certain it is, that he was a great favorite among all the good wives of the village, who, as usual, with the amiable sex, took his part in all family squabbles; and never failed, whenever they talked those matters over in their evening gossipings, to lay all the blame on Dame Van Winkle. The children of the village, too, would shout with joy whenever he approached. He assisted at their sports, made their playthings, taught them to fly kites and shoot marbles, and told them long stories of ghosts, witches, and Indians. Whenever he went dodging about the village, he was surrounded by a troop of them, hanging on his skirts, clambering on his back, and playing a thousand tricks on him with impunity; and not a dog would bark at him throughout the neighborhood.

The great error in Rip's composition was an insuperable aversion to all kinds of profitable labor. It could not be from the want of assiduity or perseverance; for he would sit on a wet rock, with a rod as long and heavy as a Tartar's lance, and fish all day without a murmur, even though he should not be encouraged by a single nibble. He would carry a fowling-piece on his shoulder for hours together, trudging through woods and swamps, and up hill and down dale, to shoot a few squirrels or wild pigeons. He would never refuse to assist a neighbor even in the roughest toil, and was a foremost man at all country frolics for husking Indian corn, or building stonefences; the women of the village, too, used to employ him to run their errands, and to do such little odd jobs as their less obliging husbands would not do for them. In a word Rip was ready to attend to anybody's business but his own; but as to doing family duty, and keeping his farm in order, he found it impossible.

In fact, he declared it was of no use to work on his farm; it was the most pestilent little piece of ground in the whole country; every thing about it went wrong, and would go wrong, in spite of him. His fences were continually falling to pieces; his cow would either go astray, or get among the cabbages; weeds were sure to grow quicker in his fields than anywhere else; the rain always made a point of setting in just as he had some out-door work to do; so that though his patrimonial estate had dwindled away under his management, acre by acre, until there was little more left than a mere patch of Indian corn and potatoes, yet it was the worst conditioned farm in the neighborhood.

His children, too, were as ragged and wild as if they belonged to nobody. His son Rip, an urchin begotten in his own likeness, promised to inherit the habits, with the old clothes of his father. He was generally seen trooping like a colt at his mother's heels, equipped in a pair of his father's cast-off galligaskins, which he had much ado to hold up with one hand, as a fine lady does her train in bad weather.

Rip Van Winkle, however, was one of those happy mortals, of foolish, well-oiled dispositions, who take the world easy, eat white bread or brown, whichever can be got with least thought or trouble, and would rather starve on a penny than work for a pound. If left to himself, he would have whistled life away in perfect contentment; but his wife kept continually dinning in his ears about his idleness, his carelessness, and the ruin he was bringing on his family. Morning, noon, and night, her tongue was incessantly going, and everything he said or did was sure to produce a torrent of household eloquence. Rip had but one way of replying to all lectures of the kind, and that, by frequent use, had grown into a habit. He shrugged his shoulders, shook his head, cast up his eyes, but said nothing. This, however, always provoked a fresh volley from his wife; so that he was fain to draw off his forces, and take to the outside of the house—the only side which, in truth, belongs to a hen-pecked husband.

Rip's sole domestic adherent was his dog Wolf, who was as much hen-pecked as his master; for Dame Van Winkle regarded them as companions in idleness, and even looked upon Wolf with an evil eye, as the cause of his master's going so often astray. True it is, in all points of spirit befitting an honorable dog, he was as courageous an animal as ever scoured the woods—but what courage can withstand the ever-during and all-besetting terrors of a woman's tongue? The moment Wolf entered the house his crest fell, his tail drooped to the ground, or curled between his legs, he sneaked about with a gallows air, casting many a sidelong glance at Dame Van Winkle, and at the least flourish of a broomstick or ladle, he would fly to the door with yelping precipitation.

Times grew worse and worse with Rip Van Winkle as years of matrimony rolled on; a tart temper never mellows with age, and a sharp tongue is the only edged tool that grows keener with constant use. For a long while he used to console himself, when driven from home, by frequenting a kind of perpetual club of the sages, philosophers, and other idle personages of the village; which held its sessions on a bench before a small inn, designated by a rubicund portrait of His Majesty George the Third. Here they used to sit in the shade through a long lazy summer's day, talking listlessly over village gossip, or telling endless sleepy stories about nothing. But it would have been worth any statesman's money to have heard the profound discussions that sometimes took place, when by chance an old newspaper fell into their hands from some passing traveller. How solemnly they would listen to the contents, as drawled out by Derrick Van Bummel, the schoolmaster, a dapper learned little man, who was not to be daunted by the most gigantic word in the dictionary; and how sagely they would deliberate upon public events some months after they had taken place.

The opinions of this junto were completely controlled by Nicholas Vedder, a patriarch of the village, and landlord of the inn, at the door of which he took his seat from morning till night, just moving sufficiently to avoid the sun and keep in the shade of a large tree; so that the neighbors could tell the hour by his movements as accurately as by a sun-dial. It is true he was rarely heard to speak, but smoked his pipe incessantly. His adherents, however (for every great man has his adherents), perfectly understood him, and knew how to gather his opinions. When any thing that was read or related displeased him, he was observed to smoke his pipe vehemently, and to send forth short, frequent and angry puffs; but when pleased, he would inhale the smoke slowly and tranquilly, and emit it in light and placid clouds; and sometimes, taking the pipe from his mouth, and letting the fragrant vapor curl about his nose, would gravely nod his head in token of perfect approbation.

From even this stronghold the unlucky Rip was at length routed by his termagant wife, who would suddenly break in upon the tranquillity of the assemblage and call the members all to naught; nor was that august personage, Nicholas Vedder himself, sacred from the daring tongue of this terrible virago, who charged him outright with encouraging her husband in habits of idleness.

Poor Rip was at last reduced almost to despair; and his only alternative, to escape from the labor of the farm and clamor of his wife, was to take gun in hand and stroll away into the woods. Here he would sometimes seat himself at the foot of a tree, and share the contents of his wallet with Wolf, with whom he sympathized as a fellow-sufferer in persecution. "Poor Wolf," he would say, "thy mistress leads thee a dog's life of it; but never mind, my lad, whilst I live thou shalt never want a friend to stand by thee!" Wolf would wag his tail, look wistfully in his master's face, and if dogs can feel pity I verily believe he reciprocated the sentiment with all his heart.

In a long ramble of the kind on a fine autumnal day, Rip had unconsciously scrambled to one of the highest parts of the Kaatskill mountains. He was after his favorite sport of squirrel shooting, and the still solitudes had echoed and re-echoed with the reports of his gun. Panting and fatigued, he threw himself, late in the afternoon, on a green knoll, covered with mountain herbage, that crowned the brow of a precipice. From an opening between the trees he could overlook all the lower country for many a mile of rich woodland. He saw at a distance the lordly Hudson, far, far below him, moving on its silent but majestic course, with the reflection of a purple cloud, or the sail of a lagging bark, here and there sleeping on its glassy bosom, and at last losing itself in the blue highlands.

On the other side he looked down into a deep mountain glen, wild, lonely, and shagged, the bottom filled with fragments from the impending cliffs, and scarcely lighted by the reflected rays of the setting sun. For some time Rip lay musing on this scene; evening was gradually advancing; the mountains began to throw their long blue shadows over the valleys; he saw that it would be dark long before he could reach the village, and he heaved a heavy sigh when he thought of encountering the terrors of Dame Van Winkle.

As he was about to descend, he heard a voice from a distance, hallooing, "Rip Van Winkle! Rip Van Winkle!" He looked round, but could see nothing but a crow winging its solitary flight across the mountain. He thought his fancy must have deceived him, and turned again to descend, when he heard the same cry ring through the still evening air; "Rip Van Winkle! Rip Van Winkle!"—at the same time Wolf bristled up his back, and giving a low growl, skulked to his master's side, looking fearfully down into the glen. Rip now felt a vague apprehension stealing over him; he looked anxiously in the same direction, and perceived a strange figure slowly toiling up the rocks, and bending under the weight of something he carried on his back. He was surprised to see any human being in this lonely and unfrequented place, but supposing it to be some one of the neighborhood in need of his assistance, he hastened down to yield it.

On nearer approach he was still more surprised at the singularity of the stranger's appearance. He was a short square-built old fellow, with thick bushy hair, and a grizzled beard. His dress was of the antique Dutch fashion—a cloth jerkin strapped round the waist—several pair of breeches, the outer one of ample volume, decorated with rows of buttons down the sides, and bunches at the knees. He bore on his shoulder a stout keg, that seemed full of liquor, and made signs for Rip to approach and assist him with the load. Though rather shy and distrustful of this new acquaintance, Rip complied with his usual alacrity; and mutually relieving one another, they clambered up a narrow gully, apparently the dry bed of a mountain torrent. As they ascended, Rip every now and then heard long rolling peals, like distant thunder, that seemed to issue out of a deep ravine, or rather cleft, between lofty rocks, toward which their rugged path conducted. He paused for an instant, but supposing it to be the muttering of one of those transient thunder-showers which often take place in mountain heights, he proceeded. Passing through the ravine, they came to a hollow, like a small amphitheatre, surrounded by perpendicular precipices, over the brinks of which impending trees shot their branches, so that you only caught glimpses of the azure sky and the bright evening cloud. During the whole time Rip and his companion had labored on in silence; for though the former marvelled greatly what could be the object of carrying a keg of liquor up this wild mountain, yet there was something strange and incomprehensible about the unknown, that inspired awe and checked familiarity.

On entering the amphitheatre, new objects of wonder presented themselves. On a level spot in the centre was a company of odd-looking personages playing at nine-pins. They were dressed in a quaint outlandish fashion; some wore short doublets, others jerkins, with long knives in their belts, and most of them had enormous breeches, of similar style with that of the guide's. Their visages, too, were peculiar: one had a large beard, broad face, and small piggish eyes: the face of another seemed to consist entirely of nose, and was surmounted by a white sugar-loaf hat set off with a little red cock's tail. They all had beards, of various shapes and colors. There was one who seemed to be the commander. He was a stout old gentleman, with a weather-beaten countenance; he wore a laced doublet, broad belt and hanger, high-crowned hat and feather, red stockings, and high-heeled shoes, with roses in them. The whole group reminded Rip of the figures in an old Flemish painting, in the parlor of Dominie Van Shaick, the village par-

son, and which had been brought over from Holland at the time of the settlement.

What seemed particularly odd to Rip was, that though these folks were evidently amusing themselves, yet they maintained the gravest faces, the most mysterious silence, and were, withal, the most melancholy party of pleasure he had ever witnessed. Nothing interrupted the stillness of the scene but the noise of the balls, which, whenever they were rolled, echoed along the mountains like rumbling peals of thunder.

As Rip and his companion approached them, they suddenly desisted from their play, and stared at him with such fixed statue-like gaze, and such strange, uncouth, lack-lustre countenances, that his heart turned within him, and his knees smote together. His companion now emptied the contents of the keg into large flagons, and made signs to him to wait upon the company. He obeyed with fear and trembling; they quaffed the liquor in profound silence, and then returned to their game.

By degrees Rip's awe and apprehension subsided. He even ventured, when no eye was fixed upon him, to taste the beverage, which he found had much of the flavor of excellent Hollands. He was naturally a thirsty soul, and was soon tempted to repeat the draught. One taste provoked another; and he reiterated his visits to the flagon so often that at length his senses were overpowered, his eyes swam in his head, his head gradually declined, and he fell into a deep sleep.

On waking, he found himself on the green knoll whence he had first seen the old man of the glen. He rubbed his eyes—it was a bright sunny morning. The birds were hopping and twittering among the bushes, and the eagle was wheeling aloft, and breasting the pure mountain breeze. "Surely," thought Rip, "I have not slept here all night." He recalled the occurrences before he fell asleep. The strange man with a keg of liquor—the mountain ravine—the wild retreat among the rocks—the woe-begone party at nine-pins—the flagon—"Oh! that flagon! that wicked flagon!" thought Rip—"what excuse shall I make to Dame Van Winkle!"

He looked round for his gun, but in place of the clean well-oiled fowling-piece, he found an old firelock lying by him, the barrel incrusted with rust, the lock falling off, and the stock worm-eaten. He now suspected that the grave roysters of the mountain had put a trick upon him, and, having dosed him with liquor, had robbed him of his gun. Wolf, too, had disappeared, but he might have strayed away after a squirrel or partridge. He whistled after him and shouted his name, but all in vain; the echoes repeated his whistle and shout, but no dog was to be seen.

He determined to revisit the scene of the last evening's gambol, and if he met with any of the party, to demand his dog and gun. As he rose to walk, he found himself stiff in the joints, and wanting in his usual activity. "These mountain beds do not agree with me," thought Rip, "and if this frolic should lay me up with a fit of the rheumatism, I shall have a blessed time with Dame Van Winkle." With some difficulty he got down into the glen: he found the gully up which he and his companion had ascended the preceding evening; but to his astonishment a mountain stream was now foaming down it, leaping from rock to rock, and filling the glen with babbling murmurs. He, however, made shift to scramble up its sides, working his toilsome way through thickets of birch, sassafras, and witch-hazel, and sometimes tripped up or entangled by the wild grapevines that twisted their coils or tendrils from tree to tree, and spread a kind of network in his path.

At length he reached to where the ravine had opened through the cliffs to the amphitheatre; but no traces of such opening remained. The rocks presented a high impenetrable wall over which the torrent came tumbling in a sheet of feathery foam, and fell into a broad deep basin, black from the shadows of the surrounding forest. Here, then, poor Rip was brought to a stand. He again called and whistled after his dog; he was only answered by the cawing of a flock of idle crows, sporting high in air about a dry tree that overhung a sunny precipice; and who, secure in their elevation, seemed to look down and scoff at the poor man's perplexities. What was to be done? the morning was passing away, and Rip felt famished for want of his breakfast. He grieved to give up his dog and gun; he dreaded to meet his wife; but it would not do to starve among the mountains. He shook his head, shouldered the rusty firelock, and, with a heart full of trouble and anxiety, turned his steps homeward.

As he approached the village he met a number of people, but none whom he knew, which somewhat surprised him, for he had thought himself acquainted with every one in the country round. Their dress, too, was of a different fashion from that to which he was accustomed. They all stared at him with equal marks of surprise, and whenever they cast their eyes upon him, invariably stroked their chins. The constant recurrence of this gesture induced Rip, involuntarily, to do the same, when,

to his astonishment, he found his beard had grown a foot long!

He had now entered the skirts of the village. A troop of strange children ran at his heels, hooting after him, and pointing at his gray beard. The dogs, too, not one of which he recognized for an old acquaintance, barked at him as he passed. The very village was altered; it was larger and more populous. There were rows of houses which he had never seen before, and those which had been his familiar haunts had disappeared. Strange names were over the doors—strange faces at the windows—every thing was strange. His mind now misgave him; he began to doubt whether both he and the world around him were not bewitched. Surely this was his native village, which he had left but the day before. There stood the Kaatskill mountains—there ran the silver Hudson at a distance—there was every hill and dale precisely as it had always been—Rip was sorely perplexed—"That flagon last night," thought he, "has addled my poor head sadly!"

It was with some difficulty that he found the way to his own house, which he approached with silent awe, expecting every moment to hear the shrill voice of Dame Van Winkle. He found the house gone to decay—the roof fallen in, the windows shattered, and the doors off the hinges. A half-starved dog that looked like Wolf was skulking about it. Rip called him by name, but the cur snarled, showed his teeth, and passed on. This was an unkind cut indeed—"My very dog," sighed poor Rip, "has forgotten me!"

He entered the house, which, to tell the truth, Dame Van Winkle had always kept in neat order. It was empty, forlorn, and apparently abandoned. This desolateness overcame all his connubial fears—he called loudly for his wife and children—the lonely chambers rang for a moment with his voice, and then all again was silence.

He now hurried forth, and hastened to his old resort, the village inn—but it too was gone. A large rickety wooden building stood in its place, with great gaping windows, some of them broken and mended with old hats and petticoats, and over the door was painted, "the Union Hotel, by Jonathan Doolittle." Instead of the great tree that used to shelter the quiet little Dutch inn of yore, there now was reared a tall naked pole, with something on the top that looked like a red night-cap, and from it was fluttering a flag, on which was a singular assemblage of stars and stripes—all this was strange and incomprehensible. He recognized on the sign, however, the ruby face of King George, under which he had smoked so many a peaceful pipe; but even this was singularly metamorphosed. The red coat was changed for one of blue and buff, a sword was held in the hand instead of a sceptre, the head was decorated with a cocked hat, and underneath was painted in large characters, General Washington.

There was, as usual, a crowd of folk about the door, but none that Rip recollected. The very character of the people seemed changed. There was a busy, bustling, disputatious tone about it, instead of the accustomed phlegm and drowsy tranquillity. He looked in vain for the sage Nicholas Vedder, with his broad face, double chin, and fair long pipe, uttering clouds of tobacco-smoke instead of idle speeches; or Van Bummel, the schoolmaster, doling forth the contents of an ancient newspaper. In place of these, a lean, bilious-looking fellow, with his pockets full of handbills, was haranguing vehemently about rights of citizens—elections—members of congress—liberty—Bunker's Hill—heroes of seventy-six—and other words, which were a perfect Babylonish jargon to the bewildered Van Winkle.

The appearance of Rip, with his long grizzled beard, his rusty fowling-piece, his uncouth dress, and an army of women and children at his heels, soon attracted the attention of the tavern politicians. They crowded round him, eyeing him from head to foot with great curiosity. The orator bustled up to him, and, drawing him partly aside, inquired "on which side he voted?" Rip stared in vacant stupidity. Another short but busy little fellow pulled him by the arm, and, rising on tiptoe, inquired in his ear, "Whether he was Federal or Democrat?" Rip was equally at a loss to comprehend the question; when a knowing, self-important old gentleman, in a sharp cocked hat, made his way through the crowd, putting them to the right and left with his elbows as he passed, and planting himself before Van Winkle, with one arm akimbo, the other resting on his cane, his keen eyes and sharp hat penetrating, as it were, into his very soul, demanded in an austere tone, "what brought him to the election with a gun on his shoulder, and a mob at his heels, and whether he meant to breed a riot in the village?"—"Alas! gentlemen," cried Rip, somewhat dismayed, "I am a poor quiet man, a native of the place, and a loyal subject of the king, God bless him!"

Here a general shout burst from the by-standers —"A tory! a tory! a spy! a refugee! hustle him! away with him!" It was with great difficulty that the self-important man in the cocked hat restored order; and, having assumed a tenfold austerity of brow, demanded again of the unknown culprit, what he came there for, and whom he was seeking? The poor man humbly assured him that he meant no harm, but merely came there in search of some of his neighbors, who used to keep about the tavern.

"Well—who are they?—name them."

Rip bethought himself a moment, and inquired, "Where's Nicholas Vedder?"

There was a silence for a little while, when an old man replied, in a thin piping voice, "Nicholas Vedder! why, he is dead and gone these eighteen years! There was a wooden tombstone in the church-yard that used to tell all about him, but that's rotten and gone too."

"Where's Brom Dutcher?"

"Oh, he went off to the army in the beginning of the war; some say he was killed at the storming of Stony Point—others say he was drowned in a squall at the foot of Antony's Nose. I don't know —he never came back again."

"Where's Van Bummel, the schoolmaster?"

"He went off to the wars too, was a great militia general, and is now in congress."

Rip's heart died away at hearing of these sad changes in his home and friends, and finding himself thus alone in the world. Every answer puzzled him too, by treating of such enormous lapses of time, and of matters which he could not understand: war—congress—Stony Point;—he had no courage to ask after any more friends, but cried out in despair, "Does nobody here know Rip Van Winkle?"

"Oh, Rip Van Winkle!" exclaimed two or three, "Oh, to be sure! that's Rip Van Winkle yonder, leaning against the tree."

Rip looked, and beheld a precise counterpart of himself, as he went up the mountain: apparently as lazy, and certainly as ragged. The poor fellow was now completely confounded. He doubted his own identity, and whether he was himself or another man. In the midst of his bewilderment, the man in the cocked hat demanded who he was, and what was his name?

"God knows," exclaimed he, at his wit's end; "I'm not myself—I'm somebody else—that's me yonder—no—that's somebody else got into my shoes —I was myself last night, but I fell asleep on the mountain, and they've changed my gun, and every thing's changed, and I'm changed, and I can't tell what's my name, or who I am!"

The by-standers began now to look at each other, nod, wink significantly, and tap their fingers against their foreheads. There was a whisper, also, about securing the gun, and keeping the old fellow from doing mischief, at the very suggestion of which the self-important man in the cocked hat retired with some precipitation. At this critical moment a fresh comely woman pressed through the throng to get a peep at the gray-bearded man. She had a chubby child in her arms, which, frightened at his looks, began to cry. "Hush, Rip," cried she, "hush, you little fool; the old man won't hurt you." The name of the child, the air of the mother, the tone of her voice, all awakened a train of recollections in his mind. "What is your name, my good woman?" asked he.

"Judith Gardenier."

"And your father's name?"

"Ah, poor man, Rip Van Winkle was his name, but it's twenty years since he went away from home with his gun, and never has been heard of since—his dog came home without him; but whether he shot himself, or was carried away by the Indians, nobody can tell. I was then but a little girl."

Rip had but one question more to ask; but he put it with a faltering voice:

"Where's your mother?"

"Oh, she too had died but a short time since; she broke a blood-vessel in a fit of passion at a New-England peddler."

There was a drop of comfort, at least, in this intelligence. The honest man could contain himself no longer. He caught his daughter and her child in his arms. "I am your father!" cried he—"Young Rip Van Winkle once—old Rip Van Winkle now! —Does nobody know poor Rip Van Winkle?"

All stood amazed, until an old woman, tottering out from among the crowd, put her hand to her brow, and peering under it in his face for a moment, exclaimed, "Sure enough! it is Rip Van Winkle—it is himself! Welcome home again, old neighbor—Why, where have you been these twenty long years?"

Rip's story was soon told, for the whole twenty years had been to him but as one night. The neighbors stared when they heard it; some were seen to wink at each other, and put their tongues in their cheeks: and the self-important man in the cocked hat, who, when the alarm was over, had returned to the field, screwed down the corners of his mouth, and shook his head—upon which there was a general shaking of the head throughout the assemblage.

It was determined, however, to take the opinion of old Peter Vanderdonk, who was seen slowly advancing up the road. He was a descendant of the historian of that name, who wrote one of the earliest accounts of the province. Peter was the most ancient inhabitant of the village, and well versed in all the wonderful events and traditions of the neighborhood. He recollected Rip at once, and corroborated his story in the most satisfactory manner. He assured the company that it was a fact, handed down from his ancestor the historian, that the Kaatskill mountains had always been haunted by strange beings. That it was affirmed that the great Hendrick Hudson, the first discoverer of the river and country, kept a kind of vigil there every twenty years, with his crew of the Half-moon; being permitted in this way to revisit the scenes of his enterprise, and keep a guardian eye upon the river, and the great city called by his name. That his father had once seen them in their old Dutch dresses playing at nine-pins in a hollow of the mountain; and that he himself had heard, one summer afternoon, the sound of their balls, like distant peals of thunder.

To make a long story short, the company broke up, and returned to the more important concerns of the election. Rip's daughter took him home to live with her; she had a snug, well-furnished house, and a stout cheery farmer for a husband, whom Rip recollected for one of the urchins that used to climb upon his back. As to Rip's son and heir, who was the ditto of himself, seen leaning against the tree, he was employed to work on the farm; but evinced an hereditary disposition to attend to any thing else but his business.

Rip now resumed his old walks and habits; he soon found many of his former cronies, though all rather the worse for the wear and tear of time; and preferred making friends among the rising generation, with whom he soon grew into great favor.

Having nothing to do at home, and being arrived at that happy age when a man can be idle with impunity, he took his place once more on the bench at the inn door, and was reverenced as one of the patriarchs of the village, and a chronicle of the old times "before the war." It was some time before he could get into the regular track of gossip, or could be made to comprehend the strange events that had taken place during his torpor. How that there had been a revolutionary war—that the country had thrown off the yoke of old England—and that, instead of being a subject of his Majesty

George the Third, he was now a free citizen of the United States. Rip, in fact, was no politician; the changes of states and empires made but little impression on him; but there was one species of despotism under which he had long groaned, and that was—petticoat government. Happily that was at an end; he had got his neck out of the yoke of matrimony, and could go in and out whenever he pleased, without dreading the tyranny of Dame Van Winkle. Whenever her name was mentioned, however, he shook his head, shrugged his shoulders, and cast up his eyes; which might pass either for an expression of resignation to his fate, or joy at his deliverance.

He used to tell his story to every stranger that arrived at Mr. Doolittle's hotel. He was observed, at first, to vary on some points every time he told it, which was, doubtless, owing to his having so recently awaked. It at last settled down precisely to the tale I have related, and not a man, woman, or child in the neighborhood, but knew it by heart. Some always pretended to doubt the reality of it, and insisted that Rip had been out of his head, and that this was one point on which he always remained flighty. The old Dutch inhabitants, however, almost universally gave it full credit. Even to this day they never hear a thunderstorm of a summer afternoon about the Kaatskill, but they say Hendrick Hudson and his crew are at their game of nine-pins; and it is a common wish of all henpecked husbands in the neighborhood, when life hangs heavy on their hands, that they might have a quieting draught out of Rip Van Winkle's flagon.

NOTE

The foregoing Tale, one would suspect, had been suggested to Mr. Knickerbocker by a little German superstition about the Emperor Frederick *der Rothbart*, and the Kypphaüser mountain: the subjoined note, however, which he had appended to the tale, shows that it is an absolute fact, narrated with his usual fidelity:

"The story of Rip Van Winkle may seem incredible to many, but nevertheless I give it my full belief, for I know the vicinity of our old Dutch settlements to have been very subject to marvellous events and appearances. Indeed, I have heard many stranger stories than this, in the villages along the Hudson; all of which were too well authenticated to admit of a doubt. I have even talked with Rip Van Winkle myself, who, when last I saw him, was a very venerable old man, and so perfectly rational and consistent on every other point, that I think no conscientious person could refuse to take this into the bargain; nay, I have seen a certificate on the subject taken before a country justice and signed with a cross,

in the justice's own handwriting. The story, therefore, is beyond the possibility of doubt.

D.K."

POSTSCRIPT

The following are travelling notes from a memorandum-book of Mr. Knickerbocker:

The Kaatsberg, or Catskill mountains, have always been a region full of fable. The Indians considered them the abode of spirits, who influenced the weather, spreading sunshine or clouds over the landscape, and sending good or bad hunting seasons. They were ruled by an old squaw spirit, said to be their mother. She dwelt on the highest peak of the Catskills, and had charge of the doors of day and night to open and shut them at the proper hour. She hung up the new moons in the skies, and cut up the old ones into stars. In times of drought, if properly propitiated, she would spin light summer clouds out of cobwebs and morning dew, and send them off from the crest of the mountain, flake after flake, like flakes of carded cotton, to float in the air; until, dissolved by the heat of the sun, they would fall in gentle showers, causing the grass to spring, the fruits to ripen, and the corn to grow an inch an hour. If displeased, however, she would brew up clouds black as ink, sitting in the midst of them like a bottle-bellied spider in the midst of its web; and when these clouds broke, woe betide the valleys!

In old times, say the Indian traditions, there was a kind of Manitou or Spirit, who kept about the wildest recesses of the Catskill Mountains, and took a mischievous pleasure in wreaking all kinds of evils and vexations upon the red men. Sometimes he would assume the form of a bear, a panther, or a deer, lead the bewildered hunter a weary chase through tangled forests and among ragged rocks; and then spring off with a loud ho! ho! leaving him aghast on the brink of a beetling precipice or raging torrent.

The favorite abode of this Manitou is still shown. It is a great rock or cliff on the loneliest part of the mountains, and, from the flowering vines which clamber about it, and the wild flowers which abound in its neighborhood, is known by the name of the Garden Rock. Near the foot of it is a small lake, the haunt of the solitary bittern, with water-snakes basking in the sun on the leaves of the pond-lilies which lie on the surface. This place was held in great awe by the Indians, insomuch that the boldest hunter would not pursue his game within its precincts. Once upon a time, however, a hunter who had lost his way, penetrated to the garden rock, where he beheld a number of gourds placed in the crotches of trees. One of these he seized and made off with it, but in the hurry of his retreat he let it fall among the rocks, when a great stream gushed forth, which washed him away and swept him down precipices, where he was dashed to pieces, and the stream made its way to the Hudson, and continues to flow to the present day; being the identical stream known by the name of the Kaaters-kill.

The Legend of Sleepy Hollow (1820)

There is an irony in the fact that "Rip Van Winkle" and "The Legend of Sleepy Hollow," which seem so deeply embedded in our national consciousness and which have long since achieved something of the status of indigenous folk tales, are the work of a writer who had so little first-hand contact with folk life, who lived for so many years cut off from all American life, and who, confessing sadly that America had no past and no ruins, immersed himself in the lore of the European past. In general, when Irving wrote out of the European lore, he was, at best, politely dull, and the big question about his work is how he managed, still using the lore as a starting point, to domesticate and dramatize such material in "Rip Van Winkle" and "The Legend of Sleepy Hollow" and, in doing so, to create their haunting resonance.

To begin with, we may point out that the charm of the folk tale is, simply, that it is *not* sophisticated, not advanced, not modern, but, at the same time, affords a sense of continuity—continuity of place, blood, and ineffable meaning—to be set against the striking differences. To gain this effect, Irving had to pull the wool over the eyes of his American reader—to cheat. But in "The Legend of Sleepy Hollow" a teasing paradox enters, for he notifies his reader that he is going to cheat. America has no "past" —at least not in any significantly available sense —but Irving blandly, and humorously, assumes one to exist: we are told that the events to be narrated occurred "in a remote period of American history," and they learn, some four words later, that the period was only "some thirty years ago." Irving is promising to cheat you by making thirty years ago seem like a remote period, and something of puzzle, of tension, of mystery lingers about the exercise of this honest cheating.

How does Irving go about making thirty years ago seem remote? Most obviously by implying that American time is a special kind of time. When Rip wakes up, there has been a "revolution"—and a thousand years had passed overnight; all has been made new. Rip's long sleep is simply a "sleepy hollow"—a place where American time does not prevail; and the real Sleepy Hollow of Ichabod's fate is "like those little brooks of still water which border a rapid stream," the rapid stream, in this case, of American "time." Rip stumbles upon an enchanted spot, outside of time, and enters upon his sleep; and we stumble upon Sleepy Hollow, and the epigraph of the tale, a quotation from James Thomson's *Castle of Indolence*, tells us that it is a "pleasing land of drowsy head." Definitely not the pushing, energetic, practical land of America on the make.

The "land of drowsy head" offers not only the enchantment of dream, but the enchantment of childhood, for, in both tales, the hero is, in one sense, a child. Rip has an "insuperable aversion to all kinds of profitable labor," that is, he wants to "play" all the time, off by himself in the woods or, literally, with children. As for Ichabod, he, the adult teacher, is actually, we are told, the "playmate" of his older students. And both Rip and Ichabod are favorites among tale-telling and gossipy old wives, especially Ichabod with his appetite for marvels. Both Rip and Ichabod have refused to grow up, and if there are differences between them on this point, the differences only emphasize the point. Rip finds matrimony a burden and the wife's insistence that he grow up—that is, go to work—a torment; but if Ichabod wants to get married and even dreams of going west as a well-equipped pioneer, that is only a dream, and if we are told that he has an eye for the fair sex, his fantasies are not full of Katrina's charms but of roast pig. The adult's dream of sex is replaced by the child's dream of food.

Irving's land of enchantment must be set in America, and, technically, he fulfills that requirement. But the inhabitants are not, in the ordinary sense, Americans. They are Dutch—or rather, they are creatures that Irving calls Dutch. Their Dutchness sets their world off from America—insists on a difference and a

distance even as we are told that there is a continuity, with the land of Rip and Brom Bones
only a stone's throw from New York City, after
all.

In "The Legend of Sleepy Hollow," in fact,
Irving gives a mooring in American life more
specific than that afforded by geography. According to Daniel G. Hoffman, Irving has
adapted for literary purposes, for the first time,
a theme that had already appeared in folk tradition—the conflict between the Yankee and the
backwoodsman. Ichabod, allowing for the differences of his infantilism, is the prototype of the
Yankee, he is the "slick" one who knows how to
make his way; and Brom, though more amiable
than the ring-tailed rouser and stomp-and-gouge
artist of frontier and keelboat, is still their
literary prototype who, in the end, outsmarts
the "slicker." Furthermore, it has been suggested by Terence Martin that in these tales,
and elsewhere, Irving is treating the conflict
between the world of imagination (that of art
and literature) and the world of practicality, a
conflict that was central in the young nation,
with its need to occupy, subdue, and organize a
continent. Both Rip and Ichabod are defeated
in life and are defeated by their imagination. In
this connection, there is no problem with the
clearly infantile Rip. But with Ichabod there
seems, at first glance, to be a contradiction between his being a "slicker" and being a victim
of imagination. In his role as "slicker," Ichabod,
the shrewd fellow from Connecticut, is planning
to beat the yokel Brom out of his girl, but he is
the imperfect "slicker"; his imagination, his
belief in the supernatural tales which is an aspect of his already emphasized childishness, undoes all his ambitious scheme. Imagination, that
is, undoes practicality, and poor Ichabod will
never set forth, the well-equipped pioneer with
the blooming Katrina in tow, to go to Kentucky—to occupy, subdue, and organize a continent. So, with this theme of a conflict in
American life, the tale is, in another way,
domesticated.

There is another dimension, however, in
which we may regard the tales of Rip and
Ichabod. They both are shadow images of

Irving. They can't grow up. Rip cannot accept
the role demanded by matrimony or that demanded by America. He cannot even be sure of
his identity—for identity means responsibility,
action. All that is left to him is to sit on the
village bench, telling tales—as Irving does—of a
bygone time, while the practical world of grown
men indulges his childishness. Ichabod is somewhat more complex. He is the yearner, but his
yearning is that of a child. It is subsexual—for
the larder. The bouncing Katrinas of this world,
so beautifully designed for the rambunctious delights of a roarer like Brom Bones, are not for
Ichabod. In the tale Ichabod is afraid of ghosts
because he is a child, but we can invert this and
get a deeper insight; he has remained a child
because he is afraid of ghosts. In creating
Ichabod, Irving was, consciously or unconsciously, diagnosing himself. But little good it
did him in those long nights of depression, when
he dreamed of his long-dead mother and woke
to find his pillow wet with tears.

Perhaps here we find the answer to the question of how Irving, in these two tales, discovered
an enduring folk romance.

> *A pleasing land of drowsy head it was,*
> *Of dreams that wave before the half-*
> *shut eye;*
> *And of gay castles in the clouds that pass,*
> *For ever flushing round a summer sky.*
> CASTLE OF INDOLENCE

In the bosom of one of those spacious coves
which indent the eastern shore of the Hudson, at
that broad expansion of the river denominated by
the ancient Dutch navigators the Tappan Zee, and
where they always prudently shortened sail, and
implored the protection of St. Nicholas when they
crossed, there lies a small market-town or rural
port, which by some is called Greensburgh, but
which is more generally and properly known by
the name of Tarry Town. This name was given,
we are told, in former days, by the good housewives of the adjacent country, from the inveterate
propensity of their husbands to linger about the
village tavern on market days. Be that as it may,
I do not vouch for the fact, but merely advert to
it, for the sake of being precise and authentic. Not
far from this village, perhaps about two miles,

there is a little valley, or rather lap of land, among high hills, which is one of the quietest places in the whole world. A small brook glides through it, with just murmur enough to lull one to repose; and the occasional whistle of a quail, or tapping of a woodpecker, is almost the only sound that ever breaks in upon the uniform tranquillity.

I recollect that, when a stripling, my first exploit in squirrel-shooting was in a grove of tall walnut-trees that shades one side of the valley. I had wandered into it at noon time, when all nature is peculiarly quiet, and was startled by the roar of my own gun, as it broke the Sabbath stillness around, and was prolonged and reverberated by the angry echoes. If ever I should wish for a retreat, whither I might steal from the world and its distractions, and dream quietly away the remnant of a troubled life, I know of none more promising than this little valley.

From the listless repose of the place, and the peculiar character of its inhabitants, who are descendants from the original Dutch settlers, this sequestered glen has long been known by the name of Sleepy Hollow, and its rustic lads are called the Sleepy Hollow Boys throughout all the neighboring country. A drowsy, dreamy influence seems to hang over the land, and to pervade the very atmosphere. Some say that the place was bewitched by a high German doctor, during the early days of the settlement; others, that an old Indian chief, the prophet or wizard of his tribe, held his powwows there before the country was discovered by Master Hendrick Hudson. Certain it is, the place still continues under the sway of some witching power, that holds a spell over the minds of the good people, causing them to walk in a continual reverie. They are given to all kinds of marvellous beliefs; are subject to trances and visions; and frequently see strange sights, and hear music and voices in the air. The whole neighborhood abounds with local tales, haunted spots, and twilight superstitions; stars shoot and meteors glare oftener across the valley than in any other part of the country, and the nightmare, with her whole nine fold, seems to make it the favorite scene of her gambols.

The dominant spirit, however, that haunts this enchanted region, and seems to be commander-in-chief of all the powers of the air, is the apparition of a figure on horseback without a head. It is said by some to be the ghost of a Hessian trooper, whose head had been carried away by a cannon-ball, in some nameless battle during the revolutionary war; and who is ever and anon seen by the country folk, hurrying along in the gloom of night, as if on the wings of the wind. His haunts are not confined to the valley, but extend at times to the adjacent roads, and especially to the vicinity of a church at no great distance. Indeed, certain of the most authentic historians of those parts, who have been careful in collecting and collating the floating facts concerning this spectre, allege that the body of the trooper, having been buried in the churchyard, the ghost rides forth to the scene of battle in nightly quest of his head; and that the rushing speed with which he sometimes passes along the Hollow, like a midnight blast, is owing to his being belated, and in a hurry to get back to the churchyard before daybreak.

Such is the general purport of this legendary superstition, which has furnished materials for many a wild story in that region of shadows; and the spectre is known, at all the country firesides, by the name of the Headless Horseman of Sleepy Hollow.

It is remarkable that the visionary propensity I have mentioned is not confined to the native inhabitants of the valley, but is unconsciously imbibed by every one who resides there for a time. However wide awake they may have been before they entered that sleepy region, they are sure, in a little time, to inhale the witching influence of the air, and begin to grow imaginative—to dream dreams, and see apparitions.

I mention this peaceful spot with all possible laud; for it is in such little retired Dutch valleys, found here and there embosomed in the great State of New-York, that population, manners, and customs, remain fixed; while the great torrent of migration and improvement, which is making such incessant changes in other parts of this restless country, sweeps by them unobserved. They are like those little nooks of still water which border a rapid stream; where we may see the straw and bubble riding quietly at anchor, or slowly revolving in their mimic harbor, undisturbed by the rush of the passing current. Though many years have elapsed since I trod the drowsy shades of Sleepy Hollow, yet I question whether I should not still find the same trees and the same families vegetating in its sheltered bosom.

In this by-place of nature, there abode, in a remote period of American history, that is to say, some thirty years since, a worthy wight of the name of Ichabod Crane; who sojourned, or, as he expressed it, "tarried," in Sleepy Hollow, for the purpose of instructing the children of the vicinity.

He was a native of Connecticut; a State which supplies the Union with pioneers for the mind as well as for the forest, and sends forth yearly its legions of frontier woodsmen and country schoolmasters. The cognomen of Crane was not inapplicable to his person. He was tall, but exceedingly lank, with narrow shoulders, long arms and legs, hands that dangled a mile out of his sleeves, feet that might have served for shovels, and his whole frame most loosely hung together. His head was small, and flat at top, with huge ears, large green glassy eyes, and a long snipe nose, so that it looked like a weather-cock, perched upon his spindle neck, to tell which way the wind blew. To see him striding along the profile of a hill on a windy day, with his clothes bagging and fluttering about him, one might have mistaken him for the genius of famine descending upon the earth, or some scarecrow eloped from a cornfield.

His school-house was a low building of one large room, rudely constructed of logs; the windows partly glazed, and partly patched with leaves of old copy-books. It was most ingeniously secured at vacant hours, by a withe twisted in the handle of the door, and stakes set against the window shutters; so that, though a thief might get in with perfect ease, he would find some embarrassment in getting out; an idea most probably borrowed by the architect, Yost Van Houten, from the mystery of an eel-pot. The school-house stood in a rather lonely but pleasant situation, just at the foot of a woody hill, with a brook running close by, and a formidable birch tree growing at one end of it. From hence the low murmur of his pupils' voices, conning over their lessons, might be heard in a drowsy summer's day, like the hum of a beehive; interrupted now and then by the authoritative voice of the master, in the tone of menace or command; or, peradventure, by the appalling sound of the birch, as he urged some tardy loiterer along the flowery path of knowledge. Truth to say, he was a conscientious man, and ever bore in mind the golden maxim, "Spare the rod and spoil the child."—Ichabod Crane's scholars certainly were not spoiled.

I would not have it imagined, however, that he was one of those cruel potentates of the school, who joy in the smart of their subjects; on the contrary, he administered justice with discrimination rather than severity; taking the burthen off the backs of the weak, and laying it on those of the strong. Your mere puny stripling, that winced at the least flourish of the rod, was passed by with indulgence; but the claims of justice were satisfied by inflicting a double portion on some little, tough, wrong-headed, broad-skirted Dutch urchin, who sulked and swelled and grew dogged and sullen beneath the birch. All this he called "doing his duty by their parents"; and he never inflicted a chastisement without following it by the assurance, so consolatory to the smarting urchin, that "he would remember it, and thank him for it the longest day he had to live."

When school hours were over, he was even the companion and playmate of the larger boys; and on holiday afternoons would convoy some of the smaller ones home, who happened to have pretty sisters, or good housewives for mothers, noted for the comforts of the cupboard. Indeed it behooved him to keep on good terms with his pupils. The revenue arising from his school was small, and would have been scarcely sufficient to furnish him with daily bread, for he was a huge feeder, and though lank, had the dilating powers of an anaconda; but to help out his maintenance, he was, according to country custom in those parts, boarded and lodged at the houses of the farmers, whose children he instructed. With these he lived successively a week at a time; thus going the rounds of the neighborhood, with all his worldly effects tied up in a cotton handkerchief.

That all this might not be too onerous on the purses of his rustic patrons, who are apt to consider the costs of schooling a grievous burden, and schoolmasters as mere drones, he had various ways of rendering himself both useful and agreeable. He assisted the farmers occasionally in the lighter labors of their farms; helped to make hay; mended the fences; took the horses to water; drove the cows from pasture; and cut wood for the winter fire. He laid aside, too, all the dominant dignity and absolute sway with which he lorded it in his little empire, the school, and became wonderfully gentle and ingratiating. He found favor in the eyes of the mothers, by petting the children, particularly the youngest; and like the lion bold, which whilom so magnanimously the lamb did hold, he would sit with a child on one knee, and rock a cradle with his foot for whole hours together.

In addition to his other vocations, he was the singing-master of the neighborhood, and picked up many bright shillings by instructing the young folks in psalmody. It was a matter of no little vanity to him, on Sundays, to take his station in front of the church gallery, with a band of chosen singers; where, in his own mind, he completely carried away the palm from the parson. Certain it is, his voice resounded far above all the rest of the congregation; and there are peculiar quavers still to be heard in that church, and which may even be heard half a mile off, quite to the opposite side of the mill-pond, on a still Sunday morning, which are said to be legitimately descended from the nose of Ichabod Crane. Thus, by divers little makeshifts in that ingenious way which is commonly denominated "by hook and by crook," the worthy pedagogue got on tolerably enough, and was thought, by all who understood nothing of the labor of headwork, to have a wonderfully easy life of it.

The schoolmaster is generally a man of some importance in the female circle of a rural neighborhood; being considered a kind of idle gentlemanlike personage, of vastly superior taste and accomplishments to the rough country swains, and, indeed, inferior in learning only to the parson. His appearance, therefore, is apt to occasion some little stir at the tea-table of a farmhouse, and the addition of a supernumerary dish of cakes or sweetmeats, or, peradventure, the parade of a silver teapot. Our man of letters, therefore, was peculiarly happy in the smiles of all the country damsels. How he would figure among them in the church-yard, between services on Sundays! gathering grapes for them from the wild vines that overrun the surrounding trees; reciting for their amusement all the epitaphs on the tombstones; or sauntering, with a whole bevy of them, along the banks of the adjacent mill-pond; while the more bashful country bumpkins hung sheepishly back, envying his superior elegance and address.

From his half itinerant life, also, he was a kind of travelling gazette, carrying the whole budget of local gossip from house to house; so that his appearance was always greeted with satisfaction. He was, moreover, esteemed by the women as a man of great erudition, for he had read several books quite through, and was a perfect master of Cotton Mather's history of New England Witchcraft, in which, by the way, he most firmly and potently believed.

He was, in fact, an odd mixture of small shrewdness and simple credulity. His appetite for the marvellous, and his powers of digesting it, were equally extraordinary; and both had been increased by his residence in this spellbound region. No tale was too gross or monstrous for his capacious swallow. It was often his delight, after his school was dismissed in the afternoon, to stretch himself on the rich bed of clover, bordering the little brook that whimpered by his school-house, and there con over old Mather's direful tales, until the gathering dusk of the evening made the printed page a mere mist before his eyes. Then, as he wended his way, by swamp and stream and awful woodland, to the farmhouse where he happened to be quartered, every sound of nature, at that witching hour, fluttered his excited imagination: the moan of the whip-poor-will from the hill-side; the boding cry of the tree-toad, that harbinger of storm; the dreary hooting of the screech-owl, or the sudden rustling in the thicket of birds frightened from their roost. The fire-flies, too, which sparkled most vividly in the darkest places, now and then startled him, as one of uncommon brightness would stream across his path; and if, by chance, a huge blockhead of a beetle came winging his blundering flight against him, the poor varlet was ready to give up the ghost, with the idea that he was struck with a witch's token. His only resource on such occasions, either to drown thought, or drive away evil spirits, was to sing psalm tunes;—and the good people of Sleepy Hollow, as they sat by their doors of an evening, were often filled with awe, at hearing his nasal melody, "in linked sweetness long drawn out," floating from the distant hill, or along the dusky road.

Another of his sources of fearful pleasure was, to pass long winter evenings with the old Dutch wives, as they sat spinning by the fire, with a row of apples roasting and spluttering along the hearth, and listen to their marvellous tales of ghosts and goblins, and haunted fields, and haunted brooks, and haunted bridges, and haunted houses, and particularly of the headless horseman, or galloping Hessian of the Hollow, as they sometimes called him. He would delight them equally by his anecdotes of witchcraft, and of the direful omens and portentous sights and sounds in the air, which prevailed in the earlier times of Connecticut; and would frighten them wofully with speculations upon comets and shooting stars; and with the alarming fact that the world did absolutely turn round, and that they were half the time topsy-turvy!

But if there was a pleasure in all this, while snugly cuddling in the chimney corner of a chamber that was all of a ruddy glow from the crackling wood fire, and where, of course, no spectre dared to show his face, it was dearly purchased by the terrors of his subsequent walk homewards. What fearful shapes and shadows beset his path amidst the dim and ghastly glare of a snowy night!—With what wistful look did he eye every trembling ray of light streaming across the waste fields from some distant window!—How often was he appalled by some shrub covered with snow, which, like a sheeted spectre, beset his very path!—How often did he shrink with curdling awe at the sound of his own steps on the frosty crust beneath his foot; and dread to look over his shoulder, lest he should behold some uncouth being tramping close behind him!—and how often was he thrown into complete dismay by some rushing blast, howling among the trees, in the idea that it was the Galloping Hessian on one of his nightly scourings!

All these, however, were mere terrors of the night, phantoms of the mind that walk in darkness; and though he had seen many spectres in his time, and been more than once beset by Satan in divers shapes, in his lonely perambulations, yet daylight put an end to all these evils; and he would have passed a pleasant life of it, in despite of the devil and all his works, if his path had not been crossed by a being that causes more perplexity to mortal man than ghosts, goblins, and the whole race of witches put together, and that was—a woman.

Among the musical disciples who assembled, one evening in each week, to receive his instructions in psalmody, was Katrina Van Tassel, the daughter and only child of a substantial Dutch farmer. She was a blooming lass of fresh eighteen; plump as a partridge; ripe and melting and rosy cheeked as one of her father's peaches, and universally famed, not merely for her beauty, but her vast expectations. She was withal a little of a coquette, as might be perceived even in her dress, which was a mixture of ancient and modern fashions, as most suited to set off her charms. She wore the ornaments of pure yellow gold, which her great-great-grandmother had brought over from Saardam; the tempting stomacher of the olden time; and withal a provokingly short petticoat, to display the prettiest foot and ankle in the country round.

Ichabod Crane had a soft and foolish heart towards the sex; and it is not to be wondered at, that so tempting a morsel soon found favor in his eyes; more especially after he had visited her in her paternal mansion. Old Baltus Van Tassel was a perfect picture of a thriving, contented, liberal-hearted farmer. He seldom, it is true, sent either his eyes or his thoughts beyond the boundaries of his own farm; but within those every thing was snug, happy, and well-conditioned. He was satisfied with his wealth, but not proud of it; and piqued himself upon the hearty abundance, rather than the style in which he lived. His stronghold was situated on the banks of the Hudson, in one of those green, sheltered, fertile nooks, in which the Dutch farmers are so fond of nestling. A great elm-tree spread its broad branches over it; at the foot of which bubbled up a spring of the softest and sweetest water, in a little well, formed of a barrel; and then stole sparkling away through the grass, to a neighboring brook, that bubbled along among alders and dwarf willows. Hard by the farmhouse was a vast barn, that might have served for a church; every window and crevice of which seemed bursting forth with the treasures of the farm; the flail was busily resounding within it from morning to night; swallows and martins skimmed twittering about the caves; and rows of pigeons, some with one eye turned up, as if watching the weather, some with their heads under their wings, or buried in their bosoms, and others swelling, and cooing, and bowing about their dames, were enjoying the sunshine on the roof. Sleek unwieldy porkers were grunting in the repose and abundance of their pens; whence sallied forth, now and then, troops of sucking pigs, as if to snuff the air. A stately squadron of snowy geese were riding in an adjoining pond, convoying whole fleets of ducks; regiments of turkeys were gobbling through the farmyard, and guinea fowls fretting about it, like ill-tempered housewives, with their peevish discontented cry. Before the barn door strutted the gallant cock, that pattern of a husband, a warrior, and a fine gentleman, clapping his burnished wings, and crowing in the pride and gladness of his heart—sometimes tearing up the earth with his feet, and then generously calling his ever-hungry family of wives and children to enjoy the rich morsel which he had discovered.

The pedagogue's mouth watered, as he looked upon this sumptuous promise of luxurious winter fare. In his devouring mind's eye, he pictured to himself every roasting-pig running about with a pudding in his belly, and an apple in his mouth; the pigeons were snugly put to bed in a comfortable pie, and tucked in with a coverlet of crust; the geese were swimming in their own gravy; and the ducks pairing cosily in dishes, like snug married couples, with a decent competency of onion sauce. In the porkers he saw carved out the future sleek side of bacon, and juicy relishing ham; not a turkey but he beheld daintily trussed up, with its gizzard under its wing, and, peradventure, a necklace of savory sausages; and even bright chanticleer himself lay sprawling on his back, in a side-dish, with uplifted claws, as if craving that quarter which his chivalrous spirit disdained to ask while living.

As the enraptured Ichabod fancied all this, and as he rolled his great green eyes over the fat meadow-lands, the rich fields of wheat, of rye, of buckwheat, and Indian corn, and the orchards burthened with ruddy fruit, which surrounded the warm tenement of Van Tassel, his heart yearned after the damsel who was to inherit these domains, and his imagination expanded with the idea, how they might be readily turned into cash, and the money invested in immense tracts of wild land, and shingle palaces in the wilderness. Nay, his busy fancy already realized his hopes, and presented to him the blooming Katrina, with a whole family of children, mounted on the top of a wagon loaded with household trumpery, with pots and kettles dangling beneath; and he beheld himself bestriding a pacing mare, with a colt at her heels, setting out for Kentucky, Tennessee, or the Lord knows where.

When he entered the house the conquest of his heart was complete. It was one of those spacious farmhouses, with high-ridged, but lowly-sloping roofs, built in the style handed down from the first Dutch settlers; the low projecting eaves forming a piazza along the front, capable of being closed up in bad weather. Under this were hung flails, harness, various utensils of husbandry, and nets for fishing in the neighboring river. Benches were built along the sides for summer use; and a great spinning-wheel at one end, and a churn at the other, showed the various uses to which this important porch might be devoted. From this piazza the wondering Ichabod entered the hall, which formed the centre of the mansion and the place of usual residence. Here, rows of resplendent pewter, ranged on a long dresser, dazzled his eyes. In one corner stood a huge bag of wool ready to be spun; in another a quantity of linsey-woolsey just from the loom; ears of Indian corn, and strings of dried apples and peaches, hung in gay festoons along the walls, mingled with the gaud of red peppers; and a door left ajar gave him a peep into the best parlor, where the claw-footed chairs, and dark mahogany tables, shone like mirrors; and irons, with their accompanying shovel and tongs, glistened from their covert of asparagus tops; mock-oranges and conch-shells decorated the mantel-piece; strings of various colored birds' eggs were suspended above it: a great ostrich egg was hung from the centre of the room, and a corner cup-

board, knowingly left open, displayed immense treasures of old silver and well-mended china.

From the moment Ichabod laid his eyes upon these regions of delight, the peace of his mind was at an end, and his only study was how to gain the affections of the peerless daughter of Van Tassel. In this enterprise, however, he had more real difficulties than generally fell to the lot of a knight-errant of yore, who seldom had any thing but giants, enchanters, fiery dragons, and such like easily-conquered adversaries, to contend with; and had to make his way merely through gates of iron and brass, and walls of adamant, to the castle keep, where the lady of his heart was confined; all which he achieved as easily as a man would carve his way to the centre of a Christmas pie; and then the lady gave him her hand as a matter of course. Ichabod, on the contrary, had to win his way to the heart of a country coquette, beset with a labyrinth of whims and caprices, which were for ever presenting new difficulties and impediments; and he had to encounter a host of fearful adversaries of real flesh and blood, the numerous rustic admirers, who beset every portal to her heart; keeping a watchful and angry eye upon each other, but ready to fly out in the common cause against any new competitor.

Among these the most formidable was a burly, roaring, roystering blade, of the name of Abraham, or, according to the Dutch abbreviation, Brom Van Brunt, the hero of the country round, which rang with his feats of strength and hardihood. He was broad-shouldered and double-jointed, with short curly black hair, and a bluff, but not unpleasant countenance, having a mingled air of fun and arrogance. From his Herculean frame and great powers of limb, he had received the nickname of Brom Bones, by which he was universally known. He was famed for great knowledge and skill in horsemanship, being as dexterous on horseback as a Tartar. He was foremost at all races and cock-fights; and, with the ascendency which bodily strength acquires in rustic life, was the umpire in all disputes, setting his hat on one side, and giving his decisions with an air and tone admitting of no gainsay or appeal. He was always ready for either a fight or a frolic; but had more mischief than ill-will in his composition; and, with all his overbearing roughness, there was a strong dash of waggish good humor at bottom. He had three or four boon companions, who regarded him as their model, and at the head of whom he scoured the country, attending every scene of feud or merriment for miles round. In cold weather he was distinguished by a fur cap, surmounted with a flaunting fox's tail; and when the folks at a country gathering descried this well-known crest at a distance, whisking about among a squad of hard riders, they always stood by for a squall. Sometimes his crew would be heard dashing along past the farmhouses at midnight, with whoop and halloo, like a troop of Don Cossacks; and the old dames, startled out of their sleep, would listen for a moment till the hurry-scurry had clattered by, and then exclaim, "Ay, there goes Brom Bones and his gang!" The neighbors looked upon him with a mixture of awe, admiration, and good will; and when any madcap prank, or rustic brawl, occurred in the vicinity, always shook their heads, and warranted Brom Bones was at the bottom of it.

This rantipole [wild, ill-behaved] hero had for some time singled out the blooming Katrina for the object of his uncouth gallantries, and though his amorous toyings were something like the gentle caresses and endearments of a bear, yet it was whispered that she did not altogether discourage his hopes. Certain it is, his advances were signals for rival candidates to retire, who felt no inclination to cross a lion in his amours; insomuch, that when his horse was seen tied to Van Tassel's paling, on a Sunday night, a sure sign that his master was courting, or, as it is termed, "sparking," within, all other suitors passed by in despair, and carried the war into other quarters.

Such was the formidable rival with whom Ichabod Crane had to contend, and, considering all things, a stouter man than he would have shrunk from the competition, and a wiser man would have despaired. He had, however, a happy mixture of pliability and perseverance in his nature; he was in form and spirit like a supple-jack—yielding, but tough; though he bent, he never broke; and though he bowed beneath the slightest pressure, yet, the moment it was away—jerk! he was as erect, and carried his head as high as ever.

To have taken the field openly against his rival would have been madness; for he was not a man to be thwarted in his amours, any more than that stormy lover, Achilles. Ichabod, therefore, made his advances in a quiet and gently-insinuating manner. Under cover of his character of singing-master, he made frequent visits at the farmhouse; not that he had any thing to apprehend from the meddlesome interference of parents, which is so often a stumbling-block in the path of lovers. Balt Van Tassel was an easy indulgent soul; he loved his daughter better even than his pipe, and, like a reasonable man and an excellent father, let her have her way in every thing. His notable little wife, too, had enough to do to attend to her housekeeping and manage her poultry; for, as she sagely observed, ducks and geese are foolish things, and must be looked after, but girls can take care of themselves. Thus while the busy dame bustled about the house, or plied her spinning-wheel at one end of the piazza, honest Balt would sit smoking his evening pipe at the other, watching the achievements of a little wooden warrior, who, armed with a sword in each hand, was most valiantly fighting the wind on the pinnacle of the barn. In the mean time, Ichabod would carry on his suit with the daughter by the side of the spring under the great elm, or sauntering along in the twilight, that hour so favorable to the lover's eloquence.

I profess not to know how women's hearts are wooed and won. To me they have always been matters of riddle and admiration. Some seem to have but one vulnerable point, or door of access; while others have a thousand avenues, and may be captured in a thousand different ways. It is a great triumph of skill to gain the former, but a still greater proof of generalship to maintain possession of the latter, for the man must battle for his fortress at every door and window. He who wins a thousand common hearts is therefore entitled to some renown; but he who keeps undisputed sway over the heart of a coquette, is indeed a hero. Certain it is, this was not the case with the redoubtable Brom Bones; and from the moment Ichabod Crane made his advances, the interests of the former evidently declined; his horse was no longer seen tied at the palings on Sunday nights, and a deadly feud gradually arose between him and the preceptor of Sleepy Hollow.

Brom, who had a degree of rough chivalry in his nature, would fain have carried matters to open warfare, and have settled their pretensions to the lady, according to the mode of those most concise and simple reasoners, the knights-errant of yore—by single combat; but Ichabod was too conscious of the superior might of his adversary to enter the lists against him: he had overheard a boast of Bones, that he would "double the schoolmaster up, and lay him on a shelf of his own school-house"; and he was too wary to give him an opportunity. There was something extremely provoking in this obstinately pacific system; it left Brom no alternative but to draw upon the funds of rustic waggery in his disposition, and to play off boorish practical jokes upon his rival. Ichabod became the object of whimsical persecution to Bones, and his gang of rough riders. They harried his hitherto peaceful domains; smoked out his singing school, by stopping up the chimney; broke into the school-house at night, in spite of its formidable fastenings of withe and window stakes, and turned every thing topsy-turvy: so that the poor schoolmaster began to think all the witches in the country held their meetings there. But what was still more annoying, Brom took all opportunities of turning him into ridicule in presence of his mistress, and had a scoundrel dog whom he taught to whine in the most ludicrous manner, and introduced as a rival of Ichabod's to instruct her in psalmody.

In this way matters went on for some time, without producing any material effect on the relative situation of the contending powers. On a fine autumnal afternoon, Ichabod, in pensive mood, sat enthroned on the lofty stool whence he usually watched all the concerns of his little literary realm. In his hand he swayed a ferule, that sceptre of despotic power; the birch of justice reposed on three nails, behind the throne, a constant terror to evil doers; while on the desk before him might be seen sundry contraband articles and prohibited weapons, detected upon the persons of idle urchins; such as half-munched apples, popguns, whirligigs, fly-cages, and whole legions of rampant little paper game-cocks. Apparently there had been some appalling act of justice recently inflicted, for his scholars were all busily intent upon their books, or slyly whispering behind them with one eye kept upon the master; and a kind of buzzing stillness reigned throughout the school-room. It was suddenly interrupted by the appearance of a negro, in tow-cloth jacket and trowsers, a round-crowned fragment of a hat, like the cap of Mercury, and mounted on the back of a ragged, wild, half-broken colt, which he managed with a rope by way of halter. He came clattering up to the school door with an invitation to Ichabod to attend a merry-making or "quilting frolic," to be held that evening at Mynheer Van Tassel's; and having delivered his message with that air of importance, and effort at fine language, which a negro is apt to display on petty embassies of the kind, he dashed over the brook, and was seen scampering away up the hollow, full of the importance and hurry of his mission.

All was now bustle and hubbub in the late quiet school-room. The scholars were hurried through their lessons, without stopping at trifles; those were nimble skipped over half with impunity, and those who were tardy, had a smart application now and then in the rear, to quicken their speed, or help them over a tall word. Books were flung aside without being put away on the shelves, inkstands were overturned, benches thrown down, and the whole school was turned loose an hour before the usual time, bursting forth like a legion of young imps, yelping and racketing about the green, in joy at their early emancipation.

The gallant Ichabod now spent at least an extra half hour at his toilet, brushing and furbishing up his best, and indeed only suit of rusty black, and arranging his looks by a bit of broken looking-glass, that hung up in the school-house. That he might make his appearance before his mistress in the true style of a cavalier, he borrowed a horse from the farmer with whom he was domiciliated, a choleric old Dutchman, of the name of Hans Van Ripper, and, thus gallantly mounted, issued forth, like a knight-errant in quest of adventures. But it is meet I should, in the true spirit of romantic story, give some account of the looks and equipments of my hero and his steed. The animal he bestrode was a broken-down plough-horse, that had outlived almost every thing but his viciousness. He was gaunt and shagged, with a ewe neck and a head like a hammer; his rusty mane and tail were tangled and knotted with burrs; one eye had lost its pupil, and was glaring and spectral; but the other had the gleam of a genuine devil in it. Still he must have had fire and mettle in his day, if we may judge from the name he bore of Gunpowder. He had, in fact, been a favorite steed of his master's, the choleric Van Ripper, who was a furious rider, and had infused, very probably, some of his own spirit into the animal; for, old and broken-down as he looked, there was more of the lurking devil in him than in any young filly in the country.

Ichabod was a suitable figure for such a steed. He rode with short stirrups, which brought his knees nearly up to the pommel of the saddle; his sharp elbows stuck out like grasshoppers'; he carried his whip perpendicularly in his hand, like a sceptre, and, as his horse jogged on, the motion of his arms was not unlike the flapping of a pair of wings. A small wool hat rested on the top of his nose, for so his scanty strip of forehead might be called; and the skirts of his black coat fluttered out almost to the horse's tail. Such was the appearance of Ichabod and his steed, as they shambled out of the gate of Hans Van Ripper, and it was altogether such an apparition as is seldom to be met with in broad daylight.

It was, as I have said, a fine autumnal day, the sky was clear and serene, and nature wore that rich and golden livery which we always associate with the idea of abundance. The forests had put on their sober brown and yellow, while some trees of the tenderer kind had been nipped by the frosts into brilliant dyes of orange, purple, and scarlet. Streaming files of wild ducks began to make their appearance high in the air; the bark of the squirrel might be heard from the groves of beech and hickory nuts, and the pensive whistle of the quail at intervals from the neighboring stubble-field.

The small birds were taking their farewell banquets. In the fulness of their revelry, they fluttered, chirping and frolicking, from bush to bush, and tree to tree, capricious from the very profusion and variety around them. There was the honest cock-robin, the favorite game of stripling sportsmen, with its loud querulous note; and the twittering blackbirds flying in sable clouds; and the golden-winged woodpecker, with his crimson crest, his broad black gorget, and splendid plumage; and the cedar bird, with its red-tipt wings and yellow-tipt tail, and its little monteiro cap of feathers; and the blue-jay, that noisy coxcomb, in his gay light-blue coat and white under-clothes; screaming and chattering, nodding and bobbing and bowing, and pretending to be on good terms with every songster of the grove.

As Ichabod jogged slowly on his way, his eye, ever open to every symptom of culinary abundance, ranged with delight over the treasures of jolly autumn. On all sides he beheld vast store of apples; some hanging in oppressive opulence on the trees; some gathered into baskets and barrels for the market; others heaped up in rich piles for the cider-press. Farther on he beheld great fields of Indian corn, with its golden ears peeping from their leafy coverts, and holding out the promise of cakes and hasty pudding; and the yellow pumpkins lying beneath them, turning up their fair round bellies to the sun, and giving ample prospects of the most luxurious of pies; and anon he passed the fragrant buckwheat fields, breathing the odor of the bee-hive, and as he beheld them, soft anticipations stole over his mind of dainty slapjacks, well buttered, and garnished with honey or treacle, by the delicate little dimpled hand of Katrina Van Tassel.

Thus feeding his mind with many sweet thoughts and "sugared suppositions," he journeyed along the sides of a range of hills which look out upon some of the goodliest scenes of the mighty Hudson. The sun gradually wheeled his broad disk down into the west. The wide bosom of the Tappan Zee lay motionless and glassy, excepting that here and there a gentle undulation waved and prolonged the blue shadow of the distant mountain. A few amber clouds floated in the sky, without a breath of air to move them. The horizon was of a fine golden tint, changing gradually into a pure apple green, and from that into the deep blue of the mid-heaven. A slanting ray lingered on the woody crests of the precipices that overhung some parts of the river, giving greater depth to the dark-gray and purple of their rocky sides. A sloop was loitering in the distance, dropping slowly down with the tide, her sail hanging uselessly against the mast; and as the reflection of the sky gleamed along the still water, it seemed as if toward evening that Ichabod arrived at the castle of the Heer Van Tassel, which he found thronged with the pride and flower of the adjacent country. Old farmers, a spare leathern-faced race, in homespun coats and breeches, blue stockings, huge shoes, and magnificent pewter buckles. Their brisk withered little dames, in close crimped caps, long-wasted short-gowns, homespun petticoats, with scissors and pincushions, and gay calico pockets hanging on the outside. Buxom lasses, almost as antiquated as their mothers, excepting where a straw hat, a fine ribbon, or perhaps a white frock, gave symptoms of city innovation. The sons, in short square-skirted coats with rows of stupendous brass buttons, and their hair generally queued in the fashion of the times, especially if they could procure an eel-skin for the purpose, it being esteemed, throughout the country, as a potent nourisher and strengthener of the hair.

Brom Bones, however, was the hero of the scene, having come to the gathering on his favorite steed Daredevil, a creature, like himself, full of mettle and mischief, and which no one but himself could manage. He was, in fact, noted for preferring vicious animals, given to all kinds of tricks, which kept the rider in constant risk of his neck, for he held a tractable well-broken horse as unworthy of a lad of spirit.

Fain would I pause to dwell upon the world of charms that burst upon the enraptured gaze of my hero, as he entered the state parlor of Van Tassel's mansion. Not those of the bevy of buxom lasses, with their luxurious display of red and white; but the ample charms of a genuine Dutch country tea-table, in the sumptuous time of autumn. Such heaped-up platters of cakes of various and almost indescribable kinds, known only to experienced Dutch housewives! There was the doughty dough-nut, the tenderer oly koek [a cake fried in deep fat], and the crisp and crumbling cruller; sweet cakes and short cakes, ginger cakes and honey cakes, and the whole family of cakes. And then there were apple pies and peach pies and pumpkin pies; besides slices of ham and smoked beef; and moreover delectable dishes of preserved plums, and peaches, and pears, and quinces; not to mention broiled shad and roasted chickens; together with bowls of milk and cream, all mingled higgledy-piggledy, pretty much as I have enumerated them, with the motherly tea-pot sending up its clouds of vapor from the midst—Heaven bless the mark! I want breath and time to discuss this banquet as it deserves, and am too eager to get on with my story. Happily, Ichabod Crane was not in so great a hurry as his historian, but did ample justice to every dainty.

He was a kind and thankful creature, whose heart dilated in proportion as his skin was filled with good cheer; and whose spirits rose with eating as some men's do with drink. He could not help, too, rolling his large eyes round him as he ate, and chuckling with the possibility that he might one day be lord of all this scene of almost unimaginable luxury and splendor. Then, he thought, how soon he'd turn his back upon the old school-house; snap his fingers in the face of Hans Van Ripper, and every other niggardly patron, and kick any itinerant pedagogue out of doors that should dare to call him comrade!

Old Baltus Van Tassel moved about among his guests with a face dilated with content and good humor, round and jolly as the harvest moon. His hospitable attentions were brief, but expressive, being confined to a shake of the hand, a slap on the shoulder, a loud laugh, and a pressing invitation to "fall to, and help themselves."

And now the sound of the music from the common room, or hall, summoned to the dance. The musician was an old grayheaded negro, who had been the itinerant orchestra of the neighborhood for more than half a century. His instrument was as old and battered as himself. The greater part of the time he scraped on two or three strings, accompanying every movement of the bow with a motion of the head; bowing almost to the ground, and stamping with his foot whenever a fresh couple were to start.

Ichabod prided himself upon his dancing as much as upon his vocal powers. Not a limb, not a fibre about him was idle; and to have seen his loosely hung frame in full motion, and clattering about the room, you would have thought Saint Vitus himself, that blessed patron of the dance, was figuring before you in person. He was the admiration of all the negroes; who, having gathered, of all ages and sizes, from the farm and the neighborhood, stood forming a pyramid of shining black faces at every door and window, gazing with delight at the scene, rolling their white eye-balls, and showing grinning rows of ivory from ear to ear. How could the flogger of urchins be otherwise than animated and joyous? the lady of his heart was his partner in the dance, and smiling graciously in reply to all his amorous oglings; while Brom Bones, sorely smitten with love and jealousy, sat brooding by himself in one corner.

When the dance was at an end, Ichabod was attracted to a knot of the sager folks, who, with old Van Tassel, sat smoking at one end of the piazza, gossiping over former times, and drawing out long stories about the war.

This neighborhood, at the time of which I am speaking, was one of those highly-favored places which abound with chronicle and great men. The British and American line had run near it during the war; it had, therefore, been the scene of marauding, and infested with refugees, cow-boys, and all kinds of border chivalry. Just sufficient time had elapsed to enable each storyteller to dress up his tale with a little becoming fiction, and, in the indistinctness of his recollection, to make himself the hero of every exploit.

There was the story of Doffue Martling, a large blue-bearded Dutchman, who had nearly taken a British frigate with an old iron nine-pounder from a mud breast-work, only that his gun burst at the sixth discharge. And there was an old gentleman who shall be nameless, being too rich a mynheer to be lightly mentioned, who, in the battle of White-plains, being an excellent master of defence, parried a musket ball with a small sword, insomuch that he absolutely felt it whiz round the blade, and glance off at the hilt: in proof of which, he was ready at any time to show the sword, with the hilt a little bent. There were several more that had been equally great in the field, not one of whom but was persuaded that he had a considerable hand in bringing the war to a happy termination.

But all these were nothing to the tales of ghosts

and apparitions that succeeded. The neighborhood is rich in legendary treasures of the kind. Local tales and superstitions thrive best in these sheltered long-settled retreats; but are trampled under foot by the shifting throng that forms the population of most of our country places. Besides, there is no encouragement for ghosts in most of our villages, for they have scarcely had time to finish their first nap, and turn themselves in their graves, before their surviving friends have travelled away from the neighborhood; so that when they turn out at night to walk their rounds, they have no acquaintance left to call upon. This is perhaps the reason why we so seldom hear of ghosts except in our long-established Dutch communities.

The immediate cause, however, of the prevalence of supernatural stories in these parts, was doubtless owing to the vicinity of Sleepy Hollow. There was a contagion in the very air that blew from that haunted region; it breathed forth an atmosphere of dreams and fancies infecting all the land. Several of the Sleepy Hollow people were present at Van Tassel's and, as usual, were doling out their wild and wonderful legends. Many dismal tales were told about funeral trains, and mourning cries and wailings heard and seen about the great tree where the unfortunate Major André was taken, and which stood in the neighborhood. Some mention was made also of the woman in white, that haunted the dark glen at Raven Rock, and was often heard to shriek on winter nights before a storm, having perished there in the snow. The chief part of the stories, however, turned upon the favorite spectre of Sleepy Hollow, the headless horseman, who had been heard several times of late, patrolling the country; and, it was said, tethered his horse nightly among the graves in the churchyard.

The sequestered situation of this church seems always to have made it a favorite haunt of troubled spirits. It stands on a knoll, surrounded by locust-trees and lofty elms, from among which its decent whitewashed walls shine modestly forth, like Christian purity beaming through the shades of retirement. A gentle slope descends from it to a silver sheet of water, bordered by high trees, between which, peeps may be caught at the blue hills of the Hudson. To look upon its grass-grown yard, where the sunbeams seem to sleep so quietly, one would think that there at least the dead might rest in peace. On one side of the church extends a wide woody dell, along which raves a large brook among broken rocks and trunks of fallen trees.

Over a deep black part of the stream, not far from the church, was formerly thrown a wooden bridge; the road that led to it, and the bridge itself, were thickly shaded by overhanging trees, which cast a gloom about it, even in the daytime; but occasioned a fearful darkness at night. This was one of the favorite haunts of the headless horseman; and the place where he was most frequently encountered. The tale was told of old Brouwer, a most heretical disbeliever in ghosts, how he met the horseman returning from his foray into Sleepy Hollow, and was obliged to get up behind him; how they galloped over bush and brake, over hill and swamp, until they reached the bridge; when the horseman suddenly turned into a skeleton, threw old Brouwer into the brook, and sprang away over the tree-tops with a clap of thunder.

This story was immediately matched by a thrice marvellous adventure of Brom Bones, who made light of the galloping Hessian as an arrant jockey. He affirmed that, on returning one night from the neighboring village of Sing Sing, he had been overtaken by this midnight trooper; that he had offered to race with him for a bowl of punch, and should have won it too, for Daredevil beat the goblin horse all hollow, but, just as they came to the church bridge, the Hessian bolted, and vanished in a flash of fire.

All these tales, told in that drowsy undertone with which men talk in the dark, the countenances of the listeners only now and then receiving a casual gleam from the glare of a pipe, sank deep in the mind of Ichabod. He repaid them in kind with large extracts from his invaluable author, Cotton Mather, and added many marvellous events that had taken place in his native State of Connecticut, and fearful sights which he had seen in his nightly walks about Sleepy Hollow.

The revel now gradually broke up. The old farmers gathered together their families in their wagons, and were heard for some time rattling along the hollow roads, and over the distant hills. Some of the damsels mounted on pillions behind their favorite swains, and their light-hearted laughter, mingling with the clatter of hoofs, echoed along the silent woodlands, sounding fainter and fainter until they gradually died away —and the late scene of noise and frolic was all silent and deserted. Ichabod only lingered behind, according to the custom of country lovers, to have a tête-à-tête with the heiress, fully convinced that he was now on the high road to success. What passed at this interview I will not pretend to say, for in fact I do not know. Something, however, I fear me, must have gone wrong, for he certainly sallied forth, after no very great interval, with an air quite desolate and chop-fallen.—Oh these women! these women! Could that girl have been playing off any of her coquettish tricks?—Was her encouragement of the poor pedagogue all a mere sham to secure her conquest of his rival?—Heaven only knows, not I!—Let it suffice to say, Ichabod stole forth with the air of one who had been sacking a hen-roost, rather than a fair lady's heart. Without looking to the right or left to notice the scene of rural wealth, on which he had so often gloated, he went straight to the stable, and with several hearty cuffs and kicks, roused his steed most uncourteously from the comfortable quarters in which he was soundly sleeping, dreaming of mountains of corn and oats, and whole valleys of timothy and clover.

It was the very witching time of night that Ichabod, heavy-hearted and crest-fallen, pursued his travel homewards, along the sides of the lofty hills which rise above Tarry Town, and which he had traversed so cheerily in the afternoon. The hour was as dismal as himself. Far below him, the Tappan Zee spread its dusky and indistinct waste of waters, with here and there the tall mast of a sloop, riding quietly at anchor under the land. In the dead hush of midnight, he could even hear the barking of the watch dog from the opposite shore of the Hudson; but it was so vague and faint as only to give an idea of his distance from this faithful companion of man. Now and then, too, the long-drawn crowing of a cock, accidentally awakened, would sound far, far off, from some farmhouse away among the hills—but it was like a dreaming sound in his ear. No signs of life occurred near him, but occasionally the melancholy chirp of a cricket, or perhaps the guttural twang of a bull-frog, from a neighboring marsh, as if sleeping uncomfortably, and turning suddenly in his bed.

All the stories of ghosts and goblins that he had heard in the afternoon, now came crowding upon his recollection. The night grew darker and darker; the stars seemed to sink deeper in the sky, and driving clouds occasionally hid them from his sight. He had never felt so lonely and dismal. He was, moreover, approaching the very place where many of the scenes of the ghost stories had been laid. In the centre of the road stood an enormous tulip-tree, which towered like a giant above all the other trees of the neighborhood, and formed a kind of landmark. Its limbs were gnarled, and fantastic, large enough to form trunks for ordinary trees, twisting down almost to the earth, and rising again into the air. It was connected with the tragical story of the unfortunate André, who had been taken prisoner hard by; and was universally known by the name of Major André's tree. The common people regarded it with a mixture of respect and superstition, partly out of sympathy for the fate of its ill-starred namesake, and partly from the tales of strange sights and doleful lamentations told concerning it.

As Ichabod approached this fearful tree, he began to whistle: he thought his whistle was answered—it was but a blast sweeping sharply through the dry branches. As he approached a little nearer, he thought he saw something white, hanging in the midst of the tree—he paused and ceased whistling; but on looking more narrowly, perceived that it was a place where the tree had been scathed by lightning, and the white wood laid bare. Suddenly he heard a groan—his teeth chattered and his knees smote against the saddle: it was but the rubbing of one huge bough upon another, as they were swayed about by the breeze. He passed the tree in safety, but new perils lay before him.

About two hundred yards from the tree a small brook crossed the road, and ran into a marshy and thickly-wooded glen, known by the name of Wiley's swamp. A few rough logs, laid side by side, served for a bridge over this stream. On that side of the road where the brook entered the wood, a group of oaks and chestnuts, matted thick with wild grapevines, threw a cavernous gloom over it. To pass this bridge was the severest trial. It was at this identical spot that the unfortunate André was captured, and under the covert of those chestnuts and vines were the sturdy yeomen concealed who surprised him. This has ever since been considered a haunted stream, and fearful are the feelings of the schoolboy who has to pass it alone after dark.

As he approached the stream his heart began to thump; he summoned up, however, all his resolution, gave his horse half a score of kicks in the ribs, and attempted to dash briskly across the bridge; but instead of starting forward, the perverse old animal made a lateral movement, and ran broadside against the fence. Ichabod, whose fears increased with the delay, jerked the reins on the other side, and kicked lustily with the contrary foot: it was all in vain; his steed started, it is true, but it was only to plunge to the opposite side of the road into a thicket of brambles and alder bushes. The schoolmaster now bestowed both whip and heel upon the starveling ribs of old Gunpowder, who dashed forward, snuffling and snorting, but came to a stand just by the bridge, with a suddenness that had nearly sent his rider sprawling over his head. Just at this moment a plashy tramp by the side of the bridge caught the sensitive ear of Ichabod. In the dark shadow of the grove, on the margin of the brook, he beheld something huge, misshapen, black and towering. It stirred not, but seemed gathered up in the gloom, like some gigantic monster ready to spring upon the traveller.

The hair of the affrighted pedagogue rose upon his head with terror. What was to be done? To turn and fly was now too late; and besides, what chance was there of escaping ghost or goblin, if such it was, which could ride upon the wings of the wind? Summoning up, therefore, a show of courage, he demanded in stammering accents—"Who are you?" He received no reply. He repeated his demand in a still more agitated voice. Still there was no answer. Once more he cudgelled the sides of the inflexible Gunpowder, and, shutting his eyes, broke forth with involuntary fervor into a psalm tune. Just then the shadowy object of alarm put itself in motion, and, with a scramble and a bound, stood at once in the middle of the road. Though the night was dark and dismal, yet the form of the unknown might now in some degree be ascertained. He appeared to be a horseman of large dimensions, and mounted on a black horse of powerful frame. He made no offer of molestation or sociability, but kept aloof on one side of the road, jogging along on the blind side of old Gunpowder, who had now got over his fright and waywardness.

Ichabod, who had no relish for this strange midnight companion, and bethought himself of the adventure of Brom Bones with the Galloping Hessian, now quickened his steed, in hopes of leaving him behind. The stranger, however, quickened his horse to an equal pace. Ichabod pulled up, and fell into a walk, thinking to lag behind—the other did the same. His heart began to sink within him; he endeavored to resume his psalm tune, but his parched tongue clove to the roof of his mouth, and he could not utter a stave. There was something in the moody and dogged silence of this pertinacious companion, that was mysterious and appalling. It was soon fearfully accounted for. On mounting a rising ground, which

brought the figure of his fellow-traveller in relief against the sky, gigantic in height, and muffled in a cloak, Ichabod was horror-struck, on perceiving that he was headless!—but his horror was still more increased, on observing that the head, which should have rested on his shoulders, was carried before him on the pommel of the saddle: his terror rose to desperation; he rained a shower of kicks and blows upon Gunpowder, hoping, by a sudden movement, to give his companion the slip—but the spectre started full jump with him. Away then they dashed, through thick and thin; stones flying, and sparks flashing at every bound. Ichabod's flimsy garments fluttered in the air, as he stretched his long lank body away over his horse's head, in the eagerness of his flight.

They had now reached the road which turns off to Sleepy Hollow; but Gunpowder, who seemed possessed with a demon, instead of keeping up it, made an opposite turn, and plunged headlong down hill to the left. This road leads through a sandy hollow, shaded by trees for about a quarter of a mile, where it crosses the bridge famous in goblin story, and just beyond swells the green knoll on which stands the whitewashed church.

As yet the panic of the steed had given his unskilful rider an apparent advantage in the chase; but just as he had got half way through the hollow, the girths of the saddle gave way, and he felt it slipping from under him. He seized it by the pommel, and endeavored to hold it firm, but in vain; and had just time to save himself by clasping old Gunpowder round the neck, when the saddle fell to the earth, and he heard it trampled under foot by his pursuer. For a moment the terror of Hans Van Ripper's wrath passed across his mind—for it was his Sunday saddle; but this was no time for petty fears; the goblin was hard on his haunches; and (unskilful rider that he was!) he had much ado to maintain his seat; sometimes slipping on one side, sometimes on another, and sometimes jolted on the high ridge of his horse's back-bone, with a violence that he verily feared would cleave him asunder.

An opening in the trees now cheered him with the hopes that the church bridge was at hand. The wavering reflection of a silver star in the bosom of the brook told him that he was not mistaken. He saw the walls of the church dimly glaring under the trees beyond. He recollected the place where Brom Bones's ghostly competitor had disappeared. "If I can but reach that bridge," thought Ichabod,

"I am safe." Just then he heard the black steed panting and blowing close behind him; he even fancied that he felt his hot breath. Another convulsive kick in the ribs, and old Gunpowder sprang upon the bridge; he thundered over the resounding planks; he gained the opposite side; and now Ichabod cast a look behind to see if his pursuer should vanish, according to rule, in a flash of fire and brimstone. Just then he saw the goblin rising in his stirrups, and in the very act of hurling his head at him. Ichabod endeavored to dodge the horrible missile, but too late. It encountered his cranium with a tremendous crash—he was tumbled headlong into the dust, and Gunpowder, the black steed, and the goblin rider, passed by like a whirlwind.

The next morning the old horse was found without his saddle, and with the bridle under his feet, soberly cropping the grass at his master's gate. Ichabod did not make his appearance at breakfast—dinner-hour came, but no Ichabod. The boys assembled at the school-house, and strolled idly about the banks of the brook; but no schoolmaster. Hans Van Ripper now began to feel some uneasiness about the fate of poor Ichabod, and his saddle. An inquiry was set on foot, and after diligent investigation they came upon his traces. In one part of the road leading to the church was found the saddle trampled in the dirt; the tracks of horses' hoofs deeply dented in the road, and evidently at furious speed, were traced to the bridge, beyond which, on the bank of a broad part of the brook, where the water ran deep and black, was found the hat of the unfortunate Ichabod, and close beside it a shattered pumpkin.

The brook was searched, but the body of the school-master was not to be discovered. Hans Van Ripper, as executor of his estate, examined the bundle which contained all his worldly effects. They consisted of two shirts and a half; two stocks for the neck; a pair or two of worsted stockings; an old pair of corduroy small-clothes; a rusty razor; a book of psalm tunes, full of dogs' ears; and a broken pitchpipe. As to the books and furniture of the school-house, they belonged to the community, excepting Cotton Mather's History of Witchcraft, a New England Almanac, and a book of dreams and fortune-telling; in which last was a sheet of foolscap much scribbled and blotted in several fruitless attempts to make a copy of verses in honor of the heiress of Van Tassel. These magic books and the poetic scrawl were forthwith consigned to the flames by Hans Van Ripper; who from that

time forward determined to send his children no more to school; observing, that he never knew any good come of this same reading and writing. Whatever money the schoolmaster possessed, and he had received his quarter's pay but a day or two before, he must have had about his person at the time of his disappearance.

The mysterious event caused much speculation at the church on the following Sunday. Knots of gazers and gossips were collected in the churchyard, at the bridge, and at the spot where the hat and pumpkin had been found. The stories of Brouwer, of Bones, and a whole budget of others, were called to mind; and when they had diligently considered them all, and compared them with the symptoms of the present case, they shook their heads, and came to the conclusion that Ichabod had been carried off by the galloping Hessian. As he was a bachelor, and in nobody's debt, nobody troubled his head any more about him. The school was removed to a different quarter of the hollow, and another pedagogue reigned in his stead.

It is true, an old farmer, who had been down to New York on a visit several years after, and from whom this account of the ghostly adventure was received, brought home the intelligence that Ichabod Crane was still alive; that he had left the neighborhood, partly through fear of the goblin and Hans Van Ripper, and partly in mortification at having been suddenly dismissed by the heiress; that he had changed his quarters to a distant part of the country; had kept school and studied law at the same time, had been admitted to the bar, turned politician, electioneered, written for the newspapers, and finally had been made a justice of the Ten Pound Court. Brom Bones too, who shortly after his rival's disappearance conducted the blooming Katrina in triumph to the altar, was observed to look exceedingly knowing whenever the story of Ichabod was related, and always burst into a hearty laugh at the mention of the pumpkin; which led some to suspect that he knew more about the matter than he chose to tell.

The old country wives, however, who are the best judges of these matters, maintain to this day that Ichabod was spirited away by supernatural means; and it is a favorite story often told about the neighborhood round the winter evening fire. The bridge became more than ever an object of superstitious awe, and that may be the reason why the road has been altered of late years, so as to approach the church by the border of the millpond. The school-house being deserted, soon fell to decay, and was reported to be haunted by the ghost of the unfortunate pedagogue; and the ploughboy, loitering homeward of a still summer evening, has often fancied his voice at a distance, chanting a melancholy psalm tune among the tranquil solitudes of Sleepy Hollow.

Postscript, Found in the Handwriting of Mr. Knickerbocker

The preceding Tale is given, almost in the precise words in which I heard it related at a Corporation meeting of the ancient city of Manhattoes, at which were present many of its sagest and most illustrious burghers. The narrator was a pleasant, shabby, gentlemanly old fellow, in pepper-and-salt clothes, with a sadly humorous face; and one whom I strongly suspected of being poor,—he made such efforts to be entertaining. When his story was concluded, there was much laughter and approbation, particularly from two or three deputy aldermen, who had been asleep the greater part of the time. There was, however, one tall, dry-looking old gentleman, with beetling eyebrows, who maintained a grave and rather severe face throughout: now and then folding his arms, inclining his head, and looking down upon the floor, as if turning a doubt over in his mind. He was one of your wary men, who never laugh, but upon good grounds— when they have reason and the law on their side. When the mirth of the rest of the company had subsided, and silence was restored, he leaned one arm on the elbow of his chair, and sticking the other akimbo, demanded, with a slight, but exceedingly sage motion of the head, and contraction of the brow, what was the moral of the story, and what it went to prove?

The story-teller, who was just putting a glass of wine to his lips, as a refreshment after his toils, paused for a moment, looked at his inquirer with an air of infinite deference, and, lowering the glass slowly to the table, observed, that the story was intended most logically to prove:—

"That there is no situation in life but has its advantages and pleasures—provided we will but take a joke as we find it:

"That, therefore, he that runs races with goblin troopers is likely to have rough riding of it.

"Ergo, for a country schoolmaster to be refused the hand of a Dutch heiress, is a certain step to high preferment, in the state."

The cautious old gentleman knit his brows tenfold closer after this explanation, being sorely puzzled by the ratiocination of the syllogism; while, methought, the one in pepper-and-salt eyed him with something of a triumphant leer. At length he observed, that all this was very well, but still he thought the story a little on the extravagant—there were one or two points on which he had his doubts.

"Faith, sir," replied the story-teller, "as to that matter, I don't believe one-half of it myself."

D. K.　1818, 1820

JOHN PENDLETON KENNEDY (1795–1870)

There were many imitators of the kind of essayistic fiction which Irving had popularized in *The Sketch Book* and *Bracebridge Hall*, but only one of these imitations, *Swallow Barn*, by John Pendleton Kennedy, is still read with enjoyment.

The father of that writer had come to America at the end of the Revolution from the Protestant north of Ireland, had become a prominent merchant in Baltimore, and had taken a wife from the Shenandoah Valley branch of the Pendleton family of Virginia, long a power in the Old Dominion. The son, though born and raised in the atmosphere of the new seaport town of Baltimore, then the third largest city in the country, spent his boyhood summers back in the Shenandoah on the several plantations of the family connection. As a young lawyer in Baltimore, nursing literary as well as political ambitions, he early turned his mind to the enchanted summers in Virginia for material for a book. *Swallow Barn* was published in 1832, in Philadelphia.

Though modeled on Irving's *Bracebridge Hall*, *Swallow Barn* provides satisfactions of its own. Kennedy had a shrewd eye, a witty turn of mind, a humorous appreciation of human diversity, and, in a period of prolixity and verbal posturings, some sense of economy and precision in language. Kennedy's work lacks the inner drive of fully developed fiction; it is largely static, a matter of sketches, vignettes, and more or less self-enclosed episodes, but some of the scenes are, taken in themselves, pointed and effective. We have, in fact, a strange work here. What had been conceived as a static composition, "originally intended," as he later said, "for a series of detached sketches of the customs, opinions, and habits of the tidewater region of Virginia," became a sort of hybrid work, the product of the uncertain literary situation of the moment, for, as he says in the first sentence of the preface, "I had great difficulty to prevent myself from writing a novel." And a kind of novel it is, a novel of manners, the earliest example of that genre to appear in America.

It is also the earliest example of a class that has exfoliated almost infinitely in our literary history: the novel of the southern plantation. The romance of the plantation, like that of the old frontier of the East, or that of the western ranch, provides one of the stock legends of American life. In its stereotyped form, as a kind of compensatory daydream, it did not emerge until after the Civil War, but then ran from the work of Thomas Nelson Page to Margaret Mitchell's *Gone with the Wind*, the image of a never-never land populated by belles in crinoline, goatee-ed colonels with impeccable if florid manners and a lethal sense of honor, and faithful darkies singing before the little cabin door.[1] But there is another kind of plantation novel, the kind in which the world is viewed with varying degrees of critical detachment, and it is worth observing that the first example is, in its genial fashion, of this order.

Kennedy, as we have said, had one foot in the world of the Virginia plantation and one in that of the bustling, commercial Baltimore. If he was ravished by the charms of Adam's Bower, the plantation of his uncle and aunt

---

[1] To be completely accurate, we should point out that Margaret Mitchell does set a hard-bitten, tough little bitch, Scarlett O'Hara, in the very middle of her never-never land, and this contrast between realism and romanticism is the key to what virtues the novel does possess.

back in the Shenandoah and the prototype of *Swallow Barn,* he always knew that his active life lay elsewhere and could regard Virginia with a double vision. In the book itself he accentuates his own detachment by presenting the whole as the work of a fictional New Yorker, Mark Littleton, who, on a visit to Virginia, writes to instruct a friend at home in the particulars of that exotic and antiquated life.

In the 1820's, Kennedy already regarded that life as antiquated and wished to record it, for he feared that "the old states" were "losing their original and distinctive habits and modes of life, and in the same degree . . . their exclusive American character," and predicted that a new world of "comfortable insipidity of character" would not compensate for the "loss of that rough but pleasant flavor" of the past. So Kennedy set out to "represent an old decayed place with odd and crotchety people inhabiting it."

Odd and crotchety some of them are, but they are also human and often charming, and if Bel, a dashing young woman, is so much in thrall to Sir Walter Scott that she is trying to train a hawk to sit on her wrist when she rides forth, and would have a minstrel—a local oaf given to thievery—dressed in "a long gown of Kendall green, gathered at the neck with a narrow gorget," she is also, in the midst of her delusions, a delightfully human and healthy young female. Beneath such comic charades and romantic pretensions, Kennedy can catch the feel of life and, at the same time, sense the serious tensions building up beneath it.

Thus in his muted, humorous way, Mark Littleton—or Kennedy—is also the forerunner of other outsiders who, visiting the plantation world, have been struck by the numberless paradoxes in it. For example, how put together in the same package the absurd and sad pretensions to the chivalric ideal, which could mask brutality and express itself in bombast, with the reality of J. E. B. Stuart's lethal gaiety or Lee's magnanimity? Henry Adams, in his *Education of Henry Adams* (see the selection in our text), says that it is hard to remember that in Virginia a rutted red clay road between the ruined fields leads to Mt. Vernon and the figure of Washington. And the paradoxicalities so lightly touched on in *Swallow Barn* lead, on the one hand, to Harriet Beecher Stowe's *Uncle Tom's Cabin* and, on the other, to Faulkner's *Absalom, Absalom!* For both of these are "plantation novels."

And, in the episode of the Grangerfords, so is *The Adventures of Huckleberry Finn.*[2]

[2] As a footnote to *Swallow Barn* as a plantation novel, we may remember that in 1861, though the family was divided, Kennedy went with the Union.

FURTHER READINGS

Charles Bohner, *John Pendleton Kennedy: Gentleman from Baltimore* (1961)
Edward M. Gwathmey, *John Pendleton Kennedy* (1931)

J. V. Ridgely, *John Pendleton Kennedy* (1966)
H. T. Tuckerman, *The Life of John Pendleton Kennedy* (1871)

From Swallow Barn (1832)

The master of this lordly domain is Frank Meriwether. He is now in the meridian of life—somewhere about forty-five. Good cheer and an easy temper tell well upon him. The first has given him a comfortable, portly figure, and the latter a contemplative turn of mind, which inclines him to be lazy and philosophical.

He has some right to pride himself on his personal appearance, for he has a handsome face, with a dark blue eye and a fine intellectual brow. His head is growing scant of hair on the crown, which induces him to be somewhat particular· in the management of his locks in that locality, and these are assuming a decided silvery hue.

It is pleasant to see him ·when he is going to ride to the Court House on business occasions. He is then apt to make his appearance in a coat of blue broadcloth, astonishingly glossy, and with an unusual amount of plaited ruffle strutting through the folds of a Marseilles waistcoat. A worshipful finish is given to this costume by a large straw hat, lined with green silk. There is a magisterial fulness in his garments which betokens condition in the world, and a heavy bunch of seals, suspended by a chain of gold, jingles as he moves, pronouncing him a man of superfluities.

It is considered rather extraordinary that he has never set up for Congress: but the truth is, he is an unambitious man, and has a great dislike to currying favor—as he calls it. And, besides, he is thoroughly convinced that there will always be men enough in Virginia willing to serve the people, and therefore does not see why he should trouble his head about it. Some years ago, however, there

was really an impression that he meant to come out. By some sudden whim, he took it into his head to visit Washington during the session of Congress, and returned, after a fortnight, very seriously distempered with politics. He told curious anecdotes of certain secret intrigues which had been discovered in the affairs of the capital, gave a clear insight into the views of some deep-laid combinations, and became, all at once, painfully florid in his discourse, and dogmatical to a degree that made his wife stare. Fortunately, this orgasm soon subsided, and Frank relapsed into an indolent gentleman of the opposition; but it had the effect to give a much more decided cast to his studies, for he forthwith discarded the "Richmond Whig" from his newspaper subscription, and took to "The Enquirer," like a man who was not to be disturbed by doubts. And as it was morally impossible to believe all that was written on both sides, to prevent his mind from being abused, he from this time forward took a stand against the re-election of Mr. Adams to the Presidency, and resolved to give an implicit faith to all alleged facts which set against his administration. The consequence of this straight-forward and confiding deportment was an unexpected complimentary notice of him by the Executive of the State. He was put into the commission of the peace, and having thus become a public man against his will, his opinions were observed to undergo some essential changes. He now thinks that a good citizen ought neither to solicit nor decline office; that· the magistracy of Virginia is the sturdiest pillar which supports the fabric of the Constitution; and that the people, "though in their opinions they may be mistaken, in their sentiments they are never wrong";—with some such other dogmas as, a few years ago, he did not hold in very good repute. In this temper, he has of late embarked on the millpond of county affairs, and notwithstanding his amiable character and his doctrinary republicanism, I am told he keeps the peace as if he commanded a garrison, and administers justice like a Cadi.

He has some claim to supremacy in this last department; for during three years he smoked segars in a lawyer's office in Richmond, which enabled him to obtain a bird's-eye view of Blackstone and the Revised Code. Besides this, he was a member of a Law Debating Society, which ate oysters once a week in a cellar; and he wore, in accordance with the usage of the most promising law students of that day, six cravats, one over the other, and yellow-topped boots, by which he was recognized as a blood of the metropolis. Having in this way qualified himself to assert and maintain his rights, he came to his estate, upon his arrival at age, a very model of landed gentlemen. Since that time his avocations have had a certain literary tincture; for having settled himself down as a married man, and got rid of his superfluous foppery, he rambled with wonderful assiduity through a wilderness of romances, poems, and dissertations, which are now collected in his library, and, with their battered blue covers, present a lively type of an army of continentals at the close of the war, or a hospital of invalids. These have all, at last, given way to the newspapers—a miscellaneous study very attractive and engrossing to country gentlemen. This line of study has rendered Meriwether a most perilous antagonist in the matter of legislative proceedings.

A landed proprietor, with a good house and a host of servants, is naturally a hospitable man. A guest is one of his daily wants. A friendly face is a necessary of life, without which the heart is apt to starve, or a luxury without which it grows parsimonious. Men who are isolated from society by distance, feel these wants by an instinct, and are grateful for the opportunity to relieve them. In Meriwether, the sentiment goes beyond this. It has, besides, something dialectic in it. His house is open to every body, as freely almost as an inn. But to see him when he has had the good fortune to pick up an intelligent, educated gentleman,—and particularly one who listens well!—a respectable, assentatious stranger!—All the better if he has been in the Legislature, or better still, if in Congress. Such a person caught within the purlieus of Swal-

low Barn, may set down one week's entertainment as certain—inevitable, and as many more as he likes—the more the merrier. He will know something of the quality of Meriwether's rhetoric before he is gone.

Then again, it is very pleasant to see Frank's kind and considerate bearing towards his servants and dependents. His slaves appreciate this, and hold him in most affectionate reverence, and, therefore, are not only contented, but happy under his dominion.

Meriwether is not much of a traveller. He has never been in New England, and very seldom beyond the cofines of Virginia. He makes now and then a winter excursion to Richmond, which, I rather think, he considers as the centre of civilization; and towards autumn, it is his custom to journey over the mountain to the Springs, which he is obliged to do to avoid the unhealthy season in the tide-water region. But the upper country is not much to his taste, and would not be endured by him if it were not for the crowds that resort there for the same reason which operates upon him; and I may add,—though he would not confess it— for the opportunity this concourse affords him for discussion of opinions.

He thinks lightly of the mercantile interest, and, in fact, undervalues the manners of the large cities generally. He believes that those who live in them are hollow-hearted and insincere, and wanting in that substantial intelligence and virtue, which he affirms to be characteristic of the country. He is an ardent admirer of the genius of Virginia, and is frequent in his commendation of a toast in which the state is compared to the mother of the Gracchi: —indeed, it is a familiar thing with him to speak of the aristocracy of talent as only inferior to that of the landed interest,—the idea of a freeholder inferring to his mind a certain constitutional preeminence in all the virtues of citizenship, as a matter of course.

The solitary elevation of a country gentleman, well to do in the world, begets some magnificent notions. He becomes as infallible as the Pope; gradually acquires a habit of making long speeches; is apt to be impatient of contradiction, and is always very touchy on the point of honor. There is nothing more conclusive than a rich man's logic any where, but in the country, amongst his dependents, it flows with the smooth and unresisted course of a full stream irrigating a meadow, and depositing its mud in fertilizing luxuriance. Meriwether's saying, about Swallow Barn, import absolute verity. But I have discovered that they are not so current out of his jurisdiction. Indeed, every now and then, we have quite obstinate discussions when some of the neighboring potentates, who stand in the same sphere with Frank, come to the house; for these worthies have opinions of their own, and nothing can be more dogged than the conflict between them. They sometimes fire away at each other with a most amiable and unconvinceable hardihood for the whole evening, bandying interjections, and making bows, and saying shrewd things with all the courtesy imaginable. But for unextinguishable pertinacity in argument, and utter impregnability of belief, there is no disputant like your country-gentleman who reads the newspapers. When one of these discussions fairly gets under weigh, it never comes to an anchor again of its own accord;—it is either blown out so far to sea as to be given up for lost, or puts into port in distress for want of documents,—or is upset by a call for the boot-jack and slippers—which is something like the previous question in Congress.

If my worthy cousin is somewhat over-argumentative as a politician, he restores the equilibrium of his character by a considerate coolness in religious matters. He piques himself upon being a high-churchman, but is not the most diligent frequenter of places of worship, and very seldom permits himself to get into a dispute upon points of faith. If Mr. Chub, the Presbyterian tutor in the family, ever succeeds in drawing him into this field, as he occasionally has the address to do, Meriwether is sure to fly the course; he gets puzzled with scripture names, and makes some odd mistakes between Peter and Paul, and then generally turns the parson over to his wife, who, he says, has an astonishing memory.

He is somewhat distinguished as a breeder of blooded horses; and, ever since the celebrated race between Eclipse and Henry, has taken to this oc-cupation with a renewed zeal, as a matter affecting the reputation of the state. It is delightful to hear him expatiate upon the value, importance, and patriotic bearing of this employment, and to listen to all his technical lore touching the mystery of horse-craft. He has some fine colts in training, which are committed to the care of a pragmatical old negro, named Carey, who, in his reverence for the occupation, is the perfect shadow of his master. He and Frank hold grave and momentous consultations upon the affairs of the stable, in such a sagacious strain of equal debate, that it would puzzle a spectator to tell which was the leading member in the council. Carey thinks he knows a great deal more upon the subject than his master, and their frequent intercourse has begot a familiarity in the old negro which is almost fatal to Meriwether's supremacy. The old man feels himself authorized to maintain his positions according to the freest parliamentary form, and sometimes with a violence of asseveration that compels his master to abandon his ground, purely out of faint-heartedness. Meriwether gets a little nettled by Carey's doggedness, but generally turns it off in a laugh. I was in the stable with him, a few mornings after my arrival, when he ventured to expostulate with the venerable groom upon a professional point, but the controversy terminated in its customary way. "Who set you up, Master Frank, to tell me how to fodder that 'ere cretur, when I as good as nursed you on my knee?"

"Well, tie up your tongue, you old mastiff," replied Frank, as he walked out of the stable, "and cease growling, since you will have it your own way";—and then, as we left the old man's presence, he added, with an affectionate chuckle—"a faithful old cur, too, that snaps at me out of pure honesty; he has not many years left, and it does no harm to humor him!"

WILLIAM GILMORE SIMMS (1806–1870)

As we have remarked above, John Pendleton Kennedy, in writing *Swallow Barn*, managed to produce the first southern plantation novel. William Gilmore Simms had an important role in the further development of this and other modes of southern fiction. Simms grew up in Charleston, South Carolina, and from his earliest years was very much interested in the nature of southern culture. In his fiction he traced its beginnings in the colonial period, on through the long struggle with the mother country in the War of Independence, and finally its push westward into the frontier country of Alabama and Mississippi.

Simms accepted the fact that the southern way of life was based on agriculture and on black chattel slavery and believed that it found its mature expression in the great plantations. In his fiction, however, he treats not only the planter, but the merchant, the frontiersman, the Indian, the yeoman white, and the black slave as well.

Simms was acquainted with Kennedy and there are hints that he later felt something of a conscious rivalry with him, but in important respects his view of the southern plantation was very different from Kennedy's. As we have noted above, Kennedy believed that the southern plantation, even in his own time, had become an anachronism. Though for him it possessed a certain nostalgic charm, it was done for. Not so in Simms's view: hence his interest in its development and its expansion, a process that he believed had not yet completed itself. Hence, too, as the Civil War approached, Simms attempted to justify and defend the southern plantation establishment, including the South's "peculiar institution" of slavery.

Simms was not by birth a member of the Charleston merchant-planter society. His early life was impoverished and difficult. His mother died in 1808, while he was still an infant, and his Irish immigrant father promptly moved out to Mississippi, leaving his son to be brought up by his grandmother in Charleston. The grandmother apprenticed him to a druggist, but Simms aspired to another kind of life. He acquired a knowledge of the law, was admitted to the bar in 1825, and later edited a Charleston newspaper. But from the beginning his passion was literature. He was a voracious reader and began to write early—at first mostly verse. He was only nineteen when he published his first volume of poetry. At twenty-seven, he had produced *Martin Faber*, his first extended work of fiction.

Because of the difficulties in making his way

to notice and esteem, one might have expected that Simms would look at the landed society of his native state with something comparable to Kennedy's "double vision." Simms was not blind to what he regarded as that society's limitations. It showed too little interest in the arts and in ideas; it had grave economic weaknesses; and, because of its specialized staple crops, it hardly provided sufficient food for its own population. Yet Simms was genuinely committed to what he believed it was on the way to becoming—an ideal society, a kind of "Greek democracy" which, like that of Periclean Athens, was grounded on slavery but which provided order and well-being for all its people in accordance with their capabilities and needs, and in which even the black slaves—so Simms argued—could count on security and kindly treatment.

After the death of his first wife, Simms married again, this time into a land-owning family, so that he now lived on his own plantation, Woodlands, and had found a proper niche in the society that he admired. But there is no reason to think that his second marriage altered his basic notions about the social order of the South, and certainly his position as master of Woodlands and, later, a member of the South Carolina legislature did not cause him to subside into a life of ease and luxury.

He pressed himself hard. Indeed, the number of his literary works is formidable. By 1860 he had published some eighteen volumes of poetry and over thirty volumes of fiction. Besides these works, he somehow found time to write histories, biographies, and many essays, articles, and miscellaneous works. He wrote too much and he wrote too rapidly, as his own friends were frank to tell him. Yet much of what he wrote is lively, and his novels and romances provide a vivid circumstantial account of southern life through a long historical span.

There is, however, very little inner drama in the lives of the characters in his fiction. As Joseph V. Ridgely, in *William Gilmore Simms*, has aptly put it, "most of [his] characters are extroverted actors in a public drama." Simms was no Hawthorne. He presumably had no concern to examine what Melville called the "isolato." He almost never gives us what Faulkner, a century later, in his treatment of what is basically the same kind of material, was to provide: characters that reveal "the problems of the human heart in conflict with itself." The drama that Simms presents is indeed "public." His impulse is to celebrate a way of life. He adheres quite strictly to a decorum of caste and class: men and women of a certain rank are not allowed to descend below a respectable level of conduct. Consequently, his "low" and raffish characters are more interesting than his heroes and heroines. Yet, in fairness to Simms, we should remind ourselves that such are the common failings of nineteenth-century historical romances even when written by Cooper and Sir Walter Scott, Simms's acknowledged masters.

As the Civil War approached, Simms's portrayal of the southern way of life became more and more defensive. His novel *Woodcraft* (1854), originally entitled *The Sword and the Distaff* in its 1852 edition, was intended, it has been plausibly argued, as an answer to Harriet Beecher Stowe's *Uncle Tom's Cabin.*

Simms was active in urging his state to secede and was present to witness the first shots fired at Fort Sumter. He had been sanguine about the prospects for a southern victory, and the war years were thus a bitter period for him, but not only because of the loss of his cause. He suffered deep personal losses as well. During the war his wife and one of his sons died—two other sons had died of yellow fever just before the war began—and in the year in which the war ended, his house was burned by stragglers from General Sherman's army. With it Simms's art gallery and fine library of ten thousand volumes went up in smoke. Simms accepted his fate without whining. He began to attempt to recoup his fortunes by resuming his writing and published three more romances before his death in 1870.

To the reader of our day, some of Simms's most interesting works will be those about the Indian. The best of his colonial romances, *The Yemassee* (1835), has to do with an Indian uprising. The collection of tales entitled *The Wigwam and the Cabin* (1845) contains, as its title suggests, stories about the Indian and the frontiersman. Edgar Allan Poe reviewed this

volume and praised it highly, citing the first tale in it, "Grayling, or, 'Murder Will Out,'" as the "best ghost story we have ever read." More interesting to the modern reader, however, will be such a story as "Oakatibbé, or, The Choctaw Sampson."

The scene of this tale is laid in Mississippi in the 1820's, and it undoubtedly reflects memories of a visit that the young Simms paid to his father in Mississippi. The story begins with the arrival of the narrator at Colonel Harris's plantation. Harris had moved out from one of the coastal states, bought land on the frontier, and begun to farm it with slave labor. The virgin soil has yielded a large crop of cotton and, rather than buy more slaves to harvest it, Colonel Harris has made the experiment of hiring the Choctaw Indians, who live all about him. The first two chapters of the story are largely devoted to a long conversation between Colonel Harris and his visitor on such topics as the difference between the black man and the Indian, the possibility of civilizing an aboriginal people, how this might best be accomplished, and so on.

Like Jefferson, these two southern whites see the black man and the Indian in quite different terms. As against those seventeenth-century white Americans who, we recall, regarded the red men as a disgrace to humanity, Simms's visitor in this story bespeaks the continuing opposite viewpoint, saying flatly that the American Indians are "decidedly the noblest race of aborigines that the world has ever known," and he goes on to say that he thinks that they are capable of attaining a high degree of civilization. In fact he estimates their "natural genius [as] superior to that of the ancient Britons, at the time of the Roman invasion under Julius Caesar."

Yet both men are quite realistic in their calculation of the difficulties involved in getting the red man to accept the white man's culture. The narrator is certain that it is a mistake, for example, to take an Indian boy away from his own people and bring him up in a white civilization, send him to college, and then expect him to settle down as a member of the white community. He will almost certainly become interested in the history of his own people, touched by their plight, inspired by stories of their romantic life, and will finally go back to them. Instead of this procedure, the whole race will have to be "civilized"—just as, according to the narrator, the Hebrews were, and the Britons and the Saxons. But because of the way in which the white settlements in America were established—piecemeal and poorly equipped to become speedily dominant—such an opportunity to civilize the Indians *en masse* has probably been lost forever.

This long discussion is interrupted by the Indians coming up to have their cotton sacks weighed, preliminary to getting their pay. The narrator notices that most of the Indians who have been persuaded to work are old men, young boys, or squaws. Only two or three able-bodied men of the warrior class are there, and Harris's visitor wonders whether the finest looking of the lot, Oakatibbé, has not, by working in the fields, degraded himself in the eyes of his tribe. Colonel Harris, however, insists that this is not true and that Oakatibbé[1] is "a fellow of good sense, and very far from being a coward."

---

[1] Some of Faulkner's stories about the Mississippi of this period have to do with the Indians, and the names of some of Faulkner's Chickasaw chiefs, such as Moketubbe and Ikkemotubbe, are reminiscent of the Choctaw Oakatibbé, for the Chickasaws and the Choctaws belonged to the same language group. Faulkner had in fact originally described the Indians of his stories as Choctaws.

Oakatibbé is challenged by another of the Indians, Loblolly Jack, who is not working but is present to collect his wife's pay, and who is obviously spoiling for a fight. But Colonel Harris quiets the argument.

In the last two chapters of the story, which we print below, we learn that later that evening the two Indians had come to blows and that Oakatibbé has killed Jack. Yet the crucial action with which the story is concerned is not between Oakatibbé and Loblolly Jack, but within Oakatibbé's own breast. The value system of the white man and that of the Indian come into conflict. Much that Colonel Harris and his visitor had discussed earlier bears on this incident and provides a context for it. The Indians' values are not simply dismissed by the white men, but are recognized as having their own worth and dignity. (In this connection, the reader may want to compare Cooper's handling of similar themes; see pp. 286–89).

Simms's story of Oakatibbé has a certain clumsiness: Chapters 3 and 4 amount to not much more than an anecdote used to illustrate the general issues discussed abstractly in Chapters 1 and 2. Yet Oakatibbé's difficult choice is rendered with force and Simms achieves a sharp focus on an interior drama. This story probably represents Simms's nearest approach to a presentation of "the problems of the human heart in conflict with itself."

FURTHER READINGS

J. C. Guilds and J. B. Meriwether, eds., *The Centennial Edition of the Writings of William Gilmore Simms* (1969–　　; to be issued in 15 vols.)
Mary C. Simms Oliphant *et al.*, eds., *The Letters of William Gilmore Simms* (1952–56; 5 vols.)

Jay B. Hubbell, *The South in American Literature* (1954)
Joseph V. Ridgely, *William Gilmore Simms* (1962)
William P. Trent, *William Gilmore Simms* (1892; out of date, but still the only full-length biography)

From Oakatibbé, or, The Choctaw Sampson (1845)

CHAPTER 3

It was probably about ten o'clock that evening. We had finished supper, and Col. H. and myself had resumed the subject upon which we had been previously engaged. But the discussion was languid, and both of us were unquestionably lapsing into that state, when each readily receives an apology for retiring for the night, when we were startled from our drowsy tendencies by a wild and terrible cry, such as made me thrill instinctively with the conviction that something terrible had taken place. We started instantly to our feet, and threw open the door. The cry was more distinct and piercing, and its painful character could not be mistaken. It was a cry of death—of sudden terror, and great and angry excitement. Many voices were mingled together—some expressive of fury, some of fear, and many of lamentation. The tones which finally prevailed over, and continued long after all others had subsided, were those of women.

"These sounds come from the shop of that trader. Those rascally Choctaws are drunk and fighting, and ten to one but somebody is killed among them!" was the exclamation of Col. H. "These sounds are familiar to me. I have heard them once before. They signify murder. It is a peculiar whoop which the Indians have, to denote the shedding of blood—to show that a crime has been committed."

The words had scarcely been uttered, before Slim Sampson came suddenly out into the road, and joined us at the door. Col. H. instantly asked him to enter, which he did. When he came fully into the light, we discovered that he had been drinking. His eyes bore sufficient testimony to the fact, though his drunkenness seemed to have subsided into something like stupor. His looks were heavy, rather than calm. He said nothing, but drew nigh to the fireplace, and seated himself upon one corner of the hearth. I now discovered that his hands and hunting shirt were stained with blood. His eyes beheld the bloody tokens at the same time, and he turned his hand curiously over, and examined it by the fire-light.

"Kurnel," said he, in broken English, "me is one dog fool!"

"How, Sampson?"

"Me drunk—me fight—me kill Loblolly Jack! Look ya! Dis blood 'pon my hands. 'Tis Loblolly Jack blood! He dead! I stick him wid de knife!"

"Impossible! What made you do it?"

"Me drunk! Me dog fool!—Drink whiskey at liquor shop—hab money—buy whiskey—drunk come, and Loblolly Jack dead!"

This was the substance of the story, which was confirmed a few moments after, by the appearance of several other Indians, the friends of the two parties. From these it appeared that all of them had been drinking, at the shop of Ligon, the white man; that, when heated with liquor, both Loblolly Jack and Slim Sampson had, as with one accord, resumed the strife which had been arrested by the prompt interference of Col. H.; that, from words they had got to blows, and the former had fallen, fatally hurt, by a single stroke from the other's hand and knife.

The Indian law, like that of the Hebrews, is eye for eye, tooth for tooth, life for life. The fate of Slim Sampson was ordained. He was to die on the morrow. This was well understood by himself as by all the rest. The wound of Loblolly Jack had proved mortal. He was already dead; and it was arranged among the parties that Slim Sampson was to remain that night, if permitted, at the house of Col. H., and to come forth at early sunrise to execution. Col. H. declared his willingness that the criminal should remain in his house; but, at the same time, disclaimed all responsibility in the business; and assured the old chief, whose name was "Rising Smoke," that he would not be answerable for his appearance.

"He won't run," said the other, indifferently.

"But you will not put a watch over him—I will not suffer more than the one to sleep in my house."

The old chief repeated his assurance that Slim Sampson would not seek to fly. No guard was to be placed over him. He was expected to remain quiet, and come forth to execution at the hour appointed.

"He got for dead," continued Rising Smoke—"he know the law. He will come and dead like a man. Oakatibbé got big heart." Every word which the old fellow uttered went to mine.

What an eulogy was this upon Indian inflexibility! What confidence in the passive obedience of the warrior! After a little farther dialogue, they departed,—friends and enemies—and the unfortunate criminal was left with us alone. He still maintained his seat upon the hearth. His muscles were composed and calm—not rigid. His thoughts, however, were evidently busy; and, once or twice, I could see that his head was moved slowly from side to side, with an expression of mournful self-abandonment. I watched every movement and look with the deepest interest, while Col. H. with a concern necessarily deeper than my own, spoke with him freely, on the subject of his crime. It was, in fact, because of the affair of Col. H. that the unlucky deed was committed. It was true, that, for this, the latter gentleman was in no wise responsible; but that did not lessen, materially, the pain which he felt at having, however unwittingly, occasioned it. He spoke with the Indian in such terms of condolence as conventional usage among us has determined to be the most proper. He proffered to buy off the friends and relatives of the deceased, if the offence could be commuted for money. The poor fellow was very grateful, but, at the same time, told him that the attempt was useless.—The tribe had never been known to permit such a thing, and the friends of Loblolly Jack were too much his enemies, to consent to any commutation of the penalty.

Col. H., however, was unsatisfied, and determined to try the experiment. The notion had only suggested itself to him after the departure of the Indians. He readily conjectured where he should find them, and we immediately set off for the grogshop of Ligon. This was little more than a quarter of a mile from the plantation. When we reached it, we found the Indians, generally, in the worst possible condition to be treated with. They were, most of them, in the last stages of intoxication. The dead body of the murdered man was stretched out in the piazza, or gallery, half covered with a bear-skin. The breast was bare—a broad, bold, manly bosom —and the wound, a deep narrow gash, around which the blood stood, clotted, in thick, frothy masses. The nearer relations of the deceased, were perhaps the most drunk of the assembly. Their grief necessarily entitled them to the greatest share of consolation, and this took the form of whiskey. Their love of excess, and the means of indulgence, encouraged us with the hope that their vengeance might be bought off without much difficulty, but we soon found ourselves very much deceived. Every effort, every offer, proved fruitless; and after vainly exhausting every art and argument, old Rising Smoke drew us aside to tell us that the thing was impossible.

"Oakatibbé hab for die, and no use for talk. De law is make for Oakatibbé, and Loblolly Jack, and me, Rising Smoke, and all, just the same. Oakatibbé will dead to-morrow."

With sad hearts, we left the maudlin and miserable assembly. When we returned, we found Slim Sampson employed in carving with his knife upon the handle of his tomahawk. In the space thus made, he introduced a small bit of flattened silver, which seemed to have been used for a like purpose on some previous occasion. It was rudely shaped like a bird, and was probably one of those trifling ornaments which usually decorate the stocks of rifle and shotgun. I looked with increasing concern upon his countenance. What could a spectator—one unacquainted with the circumstances—have met with

there? Nothing, surely, of that awful event which had just taken place, and of that doom which now seemed so certainly to await him. He betrayed no sort of interest in our mission. His look and manner denoted his own perfect conviction of its inutility; and when we told him what had taken place, he neither answered nor looked up.

It would be difficult to describe my feelings and those of my companion. The more we reflected upon the affair, the more painful and oppressive did our thoughts become. A pain, little short of horror, coupled itself with every emotion. We left the Indian still beside the fire. He had begun a low chanting song just before we retired, in his own language, which was meant as a narrative of the chief events of his life. The death song—for such it was—is neither more nor less than a recital of those deeds which it will be creditable to a son or a relative to remember. In this way the valor of their great men, and the leading events in their history, are transmitted through successive ages. He was evidently refreshing his own memory in preparation for the morrow. He was arranging the narrative of the past, in proper form for the acceptance of the future.

We did not choose to disturb him in this vocation, and retired. When we had got to our chamber, H. who already had one boot off, exclaimed suddenly—"Look you, S., this fellow ought not to perish in this manner. We should make an effort to save him. We must save him!"

"What will you do?"

"Come—let us go back and try and urge him to flight. He can escape easily while all these fellows are drunk. He shall have my best horse for the purpose."

We returned to the apartment.

"Slim Sampson."

"Kurnel!" was the calm reply.

"There's no sense in your staying here to be shot."

"Ugh!" was the only answer, but in an assenting tone.

"You're not a bad fellow—you didn't mean to kill Loblolly Jack—it's very hard that you should die for what you didn't wish to do. You're too young to die. You've got a great many years to live. You ought to live to be an old man and have sons like yourself; and there's a great deal of happiness in this world, if a man only knows where to look for it. But a man that's dead is of no use to himself, or to his friends, or his enemies. Why should you die—why should you be shot?"

"Eh?"

"Hear me; your people are all drunk at Ligon's —blind drunk—deaf drunk—they can neither see nor hear. They won't get sober till morning—perhaps not then. You've been across the Mississippi, hav'nt you? You know the way?"

The reply was affirmative.

"Many Choctaws live over the Mississippi now —on the Red River, and far beyond, to the Red Hills. Go to them—they will take you by the hand —they will give you one of their daughters to wife—they will love you—they will make you a chief. Fly, Sampson, fly to them—you shall have one of my horses, and before daylight you will be down the country, among the white people, and far from your enemies—Go, my good fellow, it would be a great pity that so brave a man should die."

This was the substance of my friend's exhortation. It was put into every shape, and addressed to every fear, hope, or passion which might possibly have influence over the human bosom. A strong conflict took place in the mind of the Indian, the outward signs of which were not wholly suppressible. He started to his feet, trod the floor hurriedly, and there was a tremulous quickness in the movement of his eyes, and a dilation of their orbs, which amply denoted the extent of his emotion. He turned suddenly upon us, when H. had finished speaking, and replied in language very nearly like the following.

"I love the whites—I was always a friend to the whites. I believe I love their laws better than my own. Loblolly Jack laughed at me because I loved the whites, and wanted our people to live like them. But I am of no use now. I can love them no more. My people say that I must die. How can I live?"

Such was the purport of his answer. The meaning of it was simple. He was not unwilling to avail himself of the suggestions of my friend—to fly—to live—but he could not divest himself of that habitual deference to those laws to which he had given implicit reverence from the beginning. Custom is the superior tyrant of all savage nations.

To embolden him on this subject, was now the joint object of Col. H. and myself. We spared no argument to convince him that he ought to fly. It was something in favour of our object, that the Indian regards the white man as so infinitely his superior; and, in the case of Slim Sampson, we were assisted by his own inclinations in favour of those customs of the whites, which he had already in part begun to adopt. We discussed for his benefit that which may be considered one of the leading elements in civilization—the duty of saving and keeping life as long as we can—insisted upon the morality of flying from any punishment which would deprive us of it; and at length had the satisfaction of seeing him convinced. He yielded to our arguments and solicitations, accepted the horse, which he promised voluntarily to find some early means to return, and, with a sigh—perhaps one of the first proofs of that change of feeling and of principle which he had just shown, he declared his intention to take the road instantly.

"Go to bed, Kurnel. Your horse will come back." We retired, and a few moments after heard him leave the house. I am sure that both of us felt a degree of light-heartedness which scarcely any other event could have produced. We could not sleep, however. For myself I answer—it was almost dawn before I fell into an uncertain slumber, filled with visions of scuffling Indians—the stark corpse of Loblolly Jack, being the conspicuous object, and Slim Sampson standing up for execution.

CHAPTER 4

Neither Col. H. nor myself arose at a very early hour. Our first thoughts and feelings at waking were those of exultation. We rejoiced that we had been instrumental in saving from an ignominious death, a fellow creature, and one who seemed so worthy, in so many respects. Our exultation was not a little increased, as we reflected on the disappointment of his enemies; and we enjoyed a hearty laugh together, as we talked over the matter while putting on our clothes. When we looked from the window the area in front of the house was covered with Indians. They sat, or stood, or walked, all around the dwelling. The hour appointed for the delivery of Slim Sampson had passed, yet they betrayed no emotion. We fancied, however, that we could discern in the countenances of most among them, the sentiment of friendship or hostility for the criminal, by which they were severally governed. A dark, fiery look of exultation—a grim anticipation of delight—was evident in the faces of his enemies; while, among his friends, men and women, a subdued concern and humbling sadness, were the prevailing traits of expression.

But when we went below to meet them—when it became known that the murderer had fled, taking with him the best horse of the proprietor, the outbreak was tremendous. A terrible yell went up from the party devoted to Loblolly Jack; while the friends and relatives of Slim Sampson at once sprang to their weapons, and put themselves in an attitude of defence. We had not foreseen the effect of our interposition and advice. We did not know, or recollect, that the nearest connection of the criminal, among the Indian tribes, in the event of his escape, would be required to suffer in his place; and this, by the way, is the grand source of that security which they felt the night before, that flight would not be attempted by the destined victim. The aspect of affairs looked squally. Already was the bow bent and the tomahawk lifted. Already had the parties separated, each going to his own side, and ranging himself in front of some one opponent. The women sunk rapidly into the rear, and provided themselves with billets or fence-rails, as they occurred to their hands; while little brats of boys, ten and twelve years old, kept up a continual shrill clamour, brandishing aloft their tiny bows and *blow-guns*, which were only powerful against the lapwing and the sparrow. In political phrase, "a great crisis was at hand." The stealthier chiefs and leaders of both sides, had sunk from sight, behind the trees or houses, in order to avail themselves of all the arts of Indian strategy. Every thing promised a sudden and stern conflict. At the first show of commotion, Col. H. had armed himself. I had been well provided with pistols and bowie knife, before leaving home; and, apprehending the worst, we yet took our places as peace-makers, between the contending parties.

It is highly probable that all our interposition would have been fruitless to prevent their collision; and, though our position certainly delayed the progress of the quarrel, yet all we could have helped to effect by our interference would have been the removal of the combatants to a more remote battle ground. But a circumstance that surprised and disappointed us all, took place, to settle the strife forever, and to reconcile the parties without any resort to blows. While the turmoil was at the highest, and we had despaired of doing any thing to prevent bloodshed, the tramp of a fast galloping horse was heard in the woods, and the next moment the steed of Col. H. made his appearance, covered with foam, Slim Sampson on his back, and still driven by the lash of his rider at the top of his speed. He leaped the enclosure, and was drawn up still quivering in every limb, in the area between the opposing Indians. The countenance of the noble fellow told his story. His heart

had smitten him by continual reproaches, at the adoption of a conduct unknown in his nation; and which all its hereditary opinions had made cowardly and infamous. Besides, he remembered the penalties which, in consequence of his flight, must fall heavily upon his people. Life was sweet to him —very sweet! He had the promise of many bright years before him. His mind was full of honourable and—speaking in comparative phrase—lofty purposes, for the improvement of himself and nation. We have already sought to show that, by his conduct, he had taken one large step in resistance to the tyrannous usages of custom, in order to introduce the elements of civilization among his people. But he could not withstand the reproaches of a conscience formed upon principles which his own genius was not equal to overthrow. His thoughts, during his flight, must have been of a very humbling character; but his features now denoted only pride, exultation and a spirit strengthened by resignation against the worst. By his flight and subsequent return, he had, in fact, exhibited a more lively spectacle of moral firmness, than would have been displayed by his simple submission in remaining. He seemed to feel this. It looked out from his soul in every movement of his body. He leaped from his horse, exclaiming, while he slapped his breast with his open palm:

"Oakatibbé heard the voice of a chief, that said he must die. Let the chief look here—Oakatibbé is come!"

A shout went up from both parties. The signs of strife disappeared. The language of the crowd was no longer that of threatening and violence. It was understood that there would be no resistance in behalf of the condemned. Col. H. and myself, were both mortified and disappointed. Though the return of Slim Sampson, had obviously prevented a combat *à outrance*, in which a dozen or more might have been slain, still we could not but regret the event. The life of such a fellow seemed to both of us, to be worth the lives of any hundred of his people.

Never did man carry with himself more simple nobleness. He was at once surrounded by his friends and relatives. The hostile party, from whom the executioners were to be drawn, stood looking on at some little distance, the very pictures of patience. There was no sort of disposition manifested among them, to hurry the proceedings. Though exulting in the prospect of soon shedding the blood of one whom they esteemed an enemy, yet all was dignified composure and forbearance. The signs of exultation were no where to be seen. Meanwhile, a conversation was carried on in low, soft accents, unmarked by physical action of any kind, between the condemned and two other Indians. One of these was the unhappy mother of the criminal— the other was his uncle. They rather listened to his remarks, than made any of their own. The dialogue was conducted in their own language. After a while this ceased, and he made a signal which seemed to be felt, rather than understood, by all the Indians, friends and enemies. All of them started into instant intelligence. It was a sign that he was ready for the final proceedings. He rose to his feet and they surrounded him. The groans of the old woman, his mother, were now distinctly audible, and she was led away by the uncle, who, placing her among the other women, returned to the condemned, beside whom he now took his place. Col. H. and myself, also drew nigh. Seeing us, Oakatibbé simply said, with a smile:

"Ah, kurnel, you see, Injun man ain't strong like white man!"

Col. H. answered with emotion.

"I would have saved you, Sampson."

"Oakatibbé hab for dead!" said the worthy fellow, with another, but a very wretched smile.

His firmness was unabated. A procession was formed, which was headed by three sturdy fellows, carrying their rifles conspicuously upon their shoulders. These were the appointed executioners, and were all near relatives of the man who had been slain. There was no mercy in their looks. Oakatibbé followed immediately after these. He seemed pleased that we should accompany him to the place of execution. Our way lay through a long avenue of stunted pines, which conducted us to a spot where an elevated ridge on either hand produced a broad and very prettily defined valley. My eyes, in all this progress, were scarcely ever drawn off from the person of him who was to be the principal actor in the approaching scene. Never, on any occasion, did I behold a man with a step more firm—a head so unbent—a countenance so sweetly calm, though grave—and of such quiet unconcern, at the obvious fate in view. Yet there was nothing in his deportment of that effort which would be the case with most white men on a similar occasion, who seek to wear the aspect of heroism. He walked as to a victory, but he walked with a staid, even dignity, calmly, and without the flush of any excitement on his cheek. In his eye there was none of that feverish curiosity, which seeks for the presence of his executioner, and cannot be

averted from the contemplation of the mournful paraphernalia of death. His look was like that of the strong man, conscious of his inevitable doom, and prepared, as it is inevitable, to meet it with corresponding indifference.

The grave was now before us. It must have been prepared at the first dawn of the morning. The executioners paused, when they had reached a spot within thirty steps of it. But the condemned passed on, and stopped only on the edge of its open jaws. The last trial was at hand with all its terrors. The curtain was about to drop, and the scene of life, with all its hopes and promises and golden joys—even to an Indian golden—was to be shut forever. I felt a painful and numbing chill pas through my frame, but I could behold no sign of change in him. He now beckoned his friends around him. His enemies drew nigh also, but in a remoter circle. He was about to commence his song of death—the narrative of his performances, his purposes, all his living experience. He began a low chant, slow, measured and composed, the words seeming to consist of monosyllables only. As he proceeded, his eyes kindled, and his arms were extended. His action became impassioned, his utterance more rapid, and the tones were distinguished by increasing warmth. I could not understand a single word which he uttered, but the cadences were true and full of significance. The rise and fall of his voice, truly proportioned to the links of sound by which they were connected, would have yielded a fine lesson to the European teacher of school eloquence. His action was as graceful as that of a mighty tree yielding to and gradually rising from the pressure of a sudden gust. I felt the eloquence which I could not understand. I fancied, from his tones and gestures, the play of the muscles of his mouth, and the dilation of his eyes, that I could detect the instances of daring valour, or good conduct, which his narrative comprised. One portion of it, as he approached the close, I certainly could not fail to comprehend. He evidently spoke of his last unhappy affray with the man whom he had slain. His head was bowed—the light passed from his eyes, his hands were folded upon his heart, and his voice grew thick and husky. Then came the narrative of his flight. His glance was turned upon Col. H. and myself, and, at the close, he extended his hand to us both. We grasped it earnestly, and with a degree of emotion which I would not now seek to describe. He paused. The catastrophe was at hand. I saw him step back, so as to place himself at the very verge of the grave—he then threw open his breast—a broad, manly, muscular bosom, that would have sufficed for a Hercules—one hand he struck upon the spot above the heart, where it remained—the other was raised above his head. This was the signal. I turned away with a strange sickness. I could look no longer. In the next instant I heard the simultaneous report, as one, of the three rifles, and when I again looked, they were shoveling in the fresh mould, upon the noble form of one, who, under other more favouring circumstances, might have been a father to his nation.

JAMES FENIMORE COOPER (1789–1851)

William Cooper, the father of the novelist, came of English blood and Quaker stock, and his wife, Elizabeth Fenimore, of the same background. He was a man of strong character, shrewd at business, twice a member of Congress, a judge, a staunch Federalist, and a friend of Aaron Burr. Of great vigor and courage, he prided himself on being a doughty wrestler. When, for instance, he was selling off farms from an enormous colonial land grant that he had bought in upper New York, such was his confidence in his physical prowess that he announced that he would give a free title to one hundred acres to any man who could throw him. His sportsmanship was equal to his vainglory, and when he was, in fact, thrown, and was still lying on his back, he ordered the title drawn. He died from a blow on the head, received in a dispute over politics. This truculence and independence of spirit, keenness of mind and toughness of body were inherited by the son James (the name Fenimore was later added to his name), as were the father's political principles and a sense of patriotic responsibility.

In 1790 when, at the age of fourteen months, James was brought to Cooperstown, the new settlement his father had founded on Otsego Lake, the region was safe enough from Indian forays, but the memories of the famous massacre of Cherry Valley[1] still lingered, and the mysterious forest was still in plain sight. When in 1806 the boy, a junior at Yale, was expelled for what seems to have amounted to little more than high spirits, his father put him to sea in a merchantman, in training for the career of an officer in the then minuscule navy of the United States. So, early in life, the novelist got some acquaintance with the two worlds in which he was to make his fame, the wilderness and the sea.

In 1811, at the age of twenty-two, Cooper resigned his commission and married Susan De Lancey, the Tory history of whose family now seemed romantic rather than treasonable, and who was, as Cooper wrote his brother Richard, the heiress to "a handsome fortune and who would also inherit from an aunt, aetat 72—so you see, Squire, the old woman can't weather it long." For all the emphasis on blood and money, the marriage was a love match, and Cooper was soon happily settled as a gentleman farmer, with, for novelty, a two thirds interest in a whaler out of the famous port of Sag Harbor, Long Island.

There is nothing in this picture of Cooper— not in heredity, education, experience of the sea, the rich marriage, the farming, the genteel society of Federalist politics—to connect him with the morbid and emotionally strained fiction that had been popular in America up to this point any more than with the *Salmagundi* papers or *The Sketch Book*. Or for that matter with literature of any kind. He even detested writing a letter. But all at once, at the age of thirty, he became a writer. He had been reading a novel[2] to his wife, found it unbearably tedious,

[1] During the Revolutionary War, Tories under the command of a Captain Butler, together with the great Mohawk chief Joseph Brant, had massacred thirty-two settlers, many of them women and children, in the process of capturing the frontier fort which guarded the valley.

and flung it down, saying he could do better himself. In that case, she demanded, why didn't he? His novel, called *Precaution,* was published in 1820. As a faithful but inept imitation of Jane Austen's work, particularly her *Persuasion* and *Pride and Prejudice,* it was well received in a quiet way, in both America and England.

No writer ever began with a model more cross-grained to his own talents than Cooper with Jane Austen, with her precise and witty style and her power of subtle psychological observation. But with *The Spy,* of 1821, Cooper found his proper model, Sir Walter Scott, and his proper world. The world was American, even if Cooper had a well-grounded fear that nobody would read a novel about American life, and even if, unlike most novels in fashion, it was thoroughly masculine, a story of the savage guerrilla warfare in Westchester County, in the Revolution, between the Tory bands, called Cowboys, and those of the colonies, called Skinners. By 1823, in *The Pioneers,* Cooper found, too, his theme and found the character that was to make his fame, Natty Bumppo.

In *The Pioneers,* Cooper does not trouble to disguise the scene, saying in the introduction that "New York having but one County of Otsego, and the Susquehanna but one proper source, there can be no mistake as to the site of the tale"—that is, his father's old domain of Cooperstown, a world which later D. H. Lawrence, a great and very different kind of novelist, was to find "marvellously beautiful"—"the raw village street, with wood fires blinking through the unglazed window-chinks, on a winter's night . . . the rough woodsmen and the drunken Indian John. . . . the turkey shooting in the snow . . . night-fishing in the teeming, virgin lake. . . ." And though Cooper himself denies any "real intention to describe" particular characters, Judge Temple is at least parallel to Judge Cooper, who in bringing civilization is, in that process, the destroyer of the wilderness. This is dramatized by the collision of Judge Temple with Natty Bumppo, the old, truculent, independent child of the forest, who is jailed by

Judge Temple for breaking the new-fangled game laws. In this collision, the basic situation of Cooper's fiction emerges, the necessary but tragic destruction of that wilderness which many early explorers had described as a New Eden.

Already in Cooper's time, that world, with the frontiersman as well as the Indian, was doomed, and Cooper's work is their memorial, with at the same time the melancholy recognition of the fact that certain virtues—for instance, those of Judge Temple and those of Natty—are always incompatible, that man must sometimes tragically choose one kind of good over another, that, in the turn of time, gains mean losses, and that every victory, as the philosopher William James was to point out, "leaves something drastic and bitter in the cup."

It is not only Judge Temple's gratitude to Natty for having saved his daughter from a panther that prompts him, when Natty is brought up for poaching, to seek to spare Natty as much distress and humiliation as possible; it is also his appreciation of the man himself and his awareness of the tragic irreconcilability of Natty's virtues with those of the coming civilization, the very civilization for which men like Natty had opened the way. It is to Cooper's credit as a novelist that, after Natty is again free and has again saved the Judge's daughter, this time from a forest fire, he does not contrive a happy ending for the story. Judge Temple now wants to take Natty under his protection, but for Natty to accept this would falsify his character and falsify the theme of the novel. So Natty, an old man now, heads west—as Boone had done. And Indian John has died in the fire.

It would seem doubtful that, at this point in his career, Cooper had more than a general idea of any overall story of Indian John and Natty to be continued in other novels. He had probably conceived them to fill out his story of the contrast between the early days of Cooperstown, with its closeness to nature and the communion in hardship, and the more complicated society that was to come. But the moment in American history was ready for Natty. The citizens of the eastern seaboard, now that the dangers of the Indian raid were gone, could indulge themselves

² Sometimes said to be *Discipline,* by a certain Mrs. Mary Balfour Brunton, published in 1814.

in the vision of beauty and freedom, of the red man at peace with nature, fulfilling himself in the role destined to him in that world. But, in another dimension, the theme lay, uninterpreted and ungeneralized, in Cooper's own boyhood experience. A personal nostalgia and a romantic yearning gave tone to *The Pioneers*. The interpreting and the generalizing of this tone into a complex theme were to come later, in the novels that develop the epic and myth of Natty Bumppo.

Meanwhile, Cooper, again by a kind of accident, discovered another new type of novel. Hearing Scott praised for a technical knowledge of the sea shown in his novel *The Pirate*, Cooper, the ex-naval officer, denied that Scott had such knowledge and set about writing a novel that would be sailorly. The result was *The Pilot*, a novel of the Revolution, with the background of war at sea and with John Paul Jones,[3] the first American naval hero, as the central character. There was, of course, a romantic love story, for Cooper, like the general public of his time, equated the idea of a novel with a love story; but what in *The Pilot* is fresh and strong is the sense of the sea, the atmosphere created by the authenticity of the technical details of seamanship, and the special language of that world.[4] *The Pilot* is the first of several novels of the sea that Cooper was to write, such as *The Two Admirals*, *The Red Rover*, and *Wing-and-Wing*, but *The Pilot* also stands behind a long line of novels of the sea by other hands. *Moby-Dick*, by Melville, with its elaborate technical account of whales and whaling, is, of course, the most famous example of the type, but even Joseph Conrad, almost a century later than Cooper, was to acknowledge him as master. The method of using technical detail that Cooper invented has been adopted by many nonmaritime novelists in developing the setting of a story in some special craft or profession and exploiting the technique and language of that world: for example, the world of war, sport, or the bullring in Hemingway's work.

After *The Pilot* (and *Lionel Lincoln*, a kind of Gothic romance set in revolutionary times) Cooper was, however, to return to the forest, producing in 1826 his most popular work of the Natty Bumppo series, *The Last of the Mohicans*. This is primarily an adventure story, with Cooper's favorite situation of pursuit or wilderness flight and with Natty, now in the prime of life, as Hawkeye, in his characteristic role of protector of civilized whites who are out of their element. Here the characteristic love story involves the rivalry for the hand of Cora between two Indians, a "bad" Indian, Magua, and a "good" Indian, Uncas, the son of the great chief and companion of Natty, the Delaware Chingachgook—who first appeared as the old and whisky-soaked Indian John of *The Pioneers*. But now Cooper has begun his idealization of the frontiersman and the Indian, and he gives them their heroic roles of protectors of beauty in the forest. But over them hangs already the pathos of defeat, age, and death, for *The Pioneers* already exists, and *The Prairie*, to appear in 1827, presents the death of Natty, a death noble and, in a way, triumphant, but even so the end of a world.

Cooper now stood at the peak of his popularity. By now he had left the life of a squire, had moved to New York, had founded a club known as The Lunch, to which various other notables belonged, and had, by vigor of personality and range of conversation, made his presence felt. But in 1826, he sailed for Europe, for a long stay, to spend periods in London, Paris, Switzerland, Italy, Germany, Belgium. He was world-famous—the "American Scott"—and he associated with the great, including Scott himself, with whom no friendship developed, and Lafayette, with whom an intimate one did and who instructed him in French political life. Cooper did not return to America for seven years, until 1833.

During this period Cooper wrote several books with European settings, most notably *The Bravo*,

---

[3] Who appears again in American literature in Melville's novel *Israel Potter* and in a marvelous narrative section of Whitman's *Song of Myself*.

[4] Richard Henry Dana, the author of *Two Years Before the Mast*, would claim, as we shall see, to be the first American to describe life aboard ship from the point of view of the common sailor. See pp. 1080–82.

but he continued his interest in specifically American subjects. In fact, during this period, the contrast with Europe led him to reinspect his own attitudes toward the homeland. For one thing, his patriotism was affronted by European ignorance of, and prejudice against, things American, and as a result of a suggestion by Lafayette he wrote *Notions of the Americans,* which, in spite of much sober sense and some criticism of America, often indulges in excessive praise. The book pleased no one, not Europeans, who by and large ignored it, nor Americans, who regarded his long absence as a betrayal and, because of his consorting with foreign aristocracy, suspected him of being a toady and a snob. By 1833, when he came home, he had lost much of his original following.

This was, however, merely the beginning of Cooper's unpopularity. While in Europe, even if he had been stirred to the defense of America, Cooper had begun to reassess his country. He was prepared to say that Americans were too much under the "influence of foreign themes" to receive a writer who dealt with "American *principles,*" and not "American *things,*" that is, American scenes and characters. Therefore, he declared, he was renouncing his literary career in "polite literature"—by which he meant the novel. Tracts, satire, and his works of travel occupied him for several years. By 1837, a quarrel about trespass on his land at Cooperstown, where he was now settled in the manor of his father, became a widely publicized affair, confirming many in the opinion that Cooper was trying to set himself up as an English lord. A long series of lawsuits for libel (most of which Cooper won) further exacerbated opinion. The novels *Homeward Bound* and *Home As Found,* a slightly disguised account of his experiences in coming back to America which were early examples here of the novel of manners, added to his unpopularity by their critical attitude toward much of American life. His *Naval History* (1839) provoked new controversy and legal action.

Such difficulties had scarcely subsided before Cooper involved himself, on the side of the landlords, in the struggle between tenant farmers and the great "patroon" estates in New York, a struggle that led to violence and terrorism and inspired Cooper's historical trilogy *Satanstoe* (1845), *The Chainbearer* (1845), and *The Redskins* (1846). The strange thing is that, even in this agitated period, Cooper could also write two more novels for the Leatherstocking cycle, *The Pathfinder* (1840), which gives us Natty in love, and *The Deerslayer* (1841), which gives us young Natty being initiated into the tragic aspects of the wilderness.

In the last few years of his life Cooper continued his prolific output, but in work notable only for an occasional scene and for showing the independent and combative old man moving toward religious faith as a solution to the practical difficulties of the world. Cooper died on September 14, 1851, in Otsego Hall. On September 25, in the City Hall of New York, a small memorial meeting was held. Washington Irving presided, Daniel Webster pronounced an address tepid in its praise of the deceased, and William Cullen Bryant offered remarks somewhat more appreciative.

In a sense, Cooper is the founder of American literature. There had, of course, been writers before him, but he is the first to create a massive body of work—an *oeuvre*—the first to be a professional writer (who would declare that "a good, wholesome, profitable and continued pecuniary support, is the applause talent most craves"), the first to regard literature as, in itself, a commentary on, and corrective of, culture, and at the same time the first to create a complex and enduring myth of American life. Furthermore, he was the inventor of three genres, the novel of the frontier, the novel of the sea, and the international novel, that in which cultures collide; and, if we do not regard Kennedy's *Swallow Barn* as a real novel, he was, too, the first American novelist of manners. Washington Irving had had reputation abroad, but Cooper as we have said was the first American writer to achieve truly international fame, a fame which survived the decline of his fortunes in America.

That decline had two phases. There was the

short-range decline, attributable to his specific criticisms of American life and to his difficult, combative personality. The long-range decline may be traced to his deeper attitudes, social, moral, and religious, which affront some of the most cherished beliefs of our century, especially those that cluster about the mystique of democracy and that of progress. But there are, too, more specific causes. Cooper's conception of the novel as a conventional love story, the mechanical nature of much of his plotting, the woodenness of much of the characterization, the verbosity and flatness of style, and the fact that he has been regarded for almost a century as a writer for boys and boys only—all these things have worked against him.

Cooper's defects are indeed real and great, and his work is of an order peculiarly vulnerable to the change in taste following the work of Flaubert, Henry James, and James Joyce. In recent years, however, Cooper has been reassessed. The books once thought only for boys are seen as serious and even profound commentaries on the American experience and a powerful imaginative embodiment of it, his role as a social critic has been recognized, and the relation between his novels of adventure and the works of social criticism has been explored.

The works of social criticism, even if they belong to the second half of Cooper's active career, may provide the best approach to his overall achievement. Cooper was born a Federalist and held that the leveling and centrifugal force of democracy would, if untempered, lead to the destruction of social order and all the values of civilization, and that the only effective check was an elite who, as men of property, would have a stake in order, and who, as cultivated and responsible gentlemen, would envisage the good of all society. Some Federalists had, in fact, conceived of a hereditary aristocracy, based on the English model, as the proper balance to the democratic impulse; but Cooper, however much he may have been pleased, as was maliciously suggested, to find his knees under the table with those of counts, barons, and dukes, did not consider such a class appropriate for America. What he did consider as the ideal

balance against the disintegrative possibilities in a democracy was the American gentleman, educated, responsible, and devoted to the public weal. In Judge Temple of *The Pioneers* and in Edward Effingham in *Home As Found* he attempted to delineate examples of this social type, and in *The American Democrat* (a nonfictional presentation of Cooper's ideas) there is an analysis of what Cooper considers to be the nature and role of the gentleman:

> The social duties of a gentleman are of a high order. The class to which he belongs is the natural repository of the manners, tastes, tone, and, to a certain extent, of the principles of a country. . . . The democratic gentleman must differ in many essential particulars from the aristocratic gentleman, though in their ordinary habits and tastes they may be virtually identical. . . . The democrat recognizing the right of all to participate in power, will be more liberal in his general sentiments . . . but in conceding much to his fellowman, he will proudly maintain his own independence of vulgar domination as indispensable to his personal habits. The same principles and manliness that would induce him to depose a royal despot would induce him to resist a vulgar tyrant.

If Cooper would distinguish the gentleman from the European aristocrat, he would also distinguish him from the plutocrat, from that class for which money is the measure of all things and whom Cooper saw as the corrupter of democracy. What Cooper most feared was the development of a plutocratic tyranny, operating through the disguised manipulation of public opinion and the electorate by demagogues who would pervert the language of true democracy, and by a press which, "as soon as the money principle is applied to it," would convert facts into "articles for the market." It was this fear of plutocracy that prompted Cooper's distrust of the Whig party, which he saw as the political manifestation of plutocracy; and it accounts for his support of Andrew Jackson in his withdrawal of government funds from the Bank of the United States. In *A Let-*

ter to His Countrymen (1834), Cooper wrote of Jackson, "Here the democrat is the best conservative," but in regard to the apparent inconsistency of a Federalist such as himself supporting Jackson, he might well have said, with perfect logic, that the conservative was the best democrat.

One might argue that if the idea of the worth and dignity of the individual man is the basis of the democratic ideal, then Cooper's conservatism was, as he maintained, fundamentally democratic: and that his concern was, ultimately, to protect the essence of democracy from the abuses implicit in a democratic system. This protection was required, not only because demagoguery, plutocracy, and the press might pervert the spirit while maintaining the forms of democracy, but because the institutions might, as he puts it, "create so much community-power as almost to annihilate individuality." Cooper opposed the view, so comforting in a democracy, that the opinion of the majority is necessarily just, and he insisted, in a manuscript left unpublished at his death, upon the "bitterness of the wrongs that are so frequently inflicted by the many on the few"—especially bitter because "though wanting in that apparent violence and sternness that marks the course of law in the hands of narrower governments," there is, in a democracy, no appeal even to "the sympathies of the masses."

Such were the basic social criticisms that Cooper leveled against democracy in America, but there was another type of criticism, a corollary of the social, which we may call the cultural or the aesthetic, a type of criticism to be found in Hawthorne and Henry James and to become common as the years passed. Though Cooper was not unaware that one cause of the cultural barrenness of America was the exigencies of life in a raw world that had to be tamed to man's use, and that another was the colonial mentality that still survived after 1776, he also felt that, in principle, the leveling process of democracy, if unmodified and without models, would tend to debase standards of excellence. As early as *Notions*, Cooper could find the general texture of American life monotonous:

There are no annals for the historian; no follies (beyond the most vulgar and commonplace) for the satirist; no manners for the dramatist; no obscure fictions for the writer of romance; no gross and hardy offences against decorum for the moralist; nor any of the rich artificial auxiliaries of poetry . . . . I have never seen a nation so much alike in all my life, as the people of the United States, and what is more, they are not only like each other, but they are remarkably like that which common sense tells them they ought to resemble.

And by the time he wrote *Home As Found*, he had forgotten the Cooperstown which D. H. Lawrence found so charming in *The Pioneers*; in the later stage of development depicted a nature as ravaged and human society as mean and graceless. *Home As Found* anticipated Sinclair Lewis's *Main Street* by almost a century.

Some of Cooper's social views are open to objections. For one thing, they were, in a sense, anachronistic—of the eighteenth century and not of the nineteenth. True, in New York state, in Virginia, and more spottily elsewhere in the South and in New England, the notion that a landed gentry would give guidance to society continued up to the Civil War, but Cooper, like the planter class of the South and, strangely, certain New England intellectuals (see the introductory essay for the period 1826–61), did not understand the dynamic of the new industrial and financial revolution. Power was passing from the land to the factory and the counting house. We might even hazard that the truculence of Cooper, his hatred of plutocracy, and perhaps the otherworldliness in which he found refuge in his late years have some roots in a sense of being rejected by history. We should remember, however, that no matter what conditioned Cooper, his criticism of the American society is not necessarily invalidated by its origins and that he recognized the central problems of a democratic society. First, how may a democratic society develop responsible leadership? Second, how may it maintain standards of excellence, cultural, political, and moral? Third, how may it afford freedom to the individual and protect itself from the unbridled exploiter, the demagogue, or a plutocratic oligarchy? Fourth, how may it afford justice to the individual or minority against the tyranny of the majority?

These problems are still central to American life, and in defining them Cooper is the first of a long line of social critics. But we should emphasize that in spite of his astringent criticism of democracy, his desire was to save democracy from itself. In his last remarks on the subject, already referred to, he says:

> . . . the community will live on, suffer, and be deluded; it may even fancy itself almost within reach of perfection, but it will live on to be disappointed. There is no such thing on earth—and the only real question for the American statesman is, to measure the results of different defective systems for the government of the human race. We are far from saying that our own, with all its flagrant and obvious defects, will be the worst. . . .

That is, the ultimate issue lies in the nature of man, and the problem is to lead men to act morally. Democracy seems to be, Cooper decides, the best system for inducing men to act morally, but it is deeply imperfect and demands constant vigilance if it is not to degenerate. Cooper would probably have accepted the estimate given much later by the poet James Russell Lowell: "Democracy is nothing more than an experiment in government . . . which must stand or fall on its own merits as others have done before it."

At first glance, the five novels dealing with Natty Bumppo seem very far from the work of Cooper as a social critic, even when such criticism appears in fictional form—for instance, in the historical trilogy. But if we regard Natty as related to the whole of Cooper's work, he acquires a new depth of meaning.

In *The Pioneers*, as we have seen, there is a conflict between Natty and society. Natty is presented as doomed by his virtues as well as by his limitations—doomed, as Cooper, in *The Prairie*, says of Daniel Boone, by the civilization "his own success has drawn around him." There is, then, a paradox in his doom and also in the way he is regarded by Judge Temple, When Elizabeth Temple rebukes her father by pointing out Natty's natural goodness, the Judge says: "Thou hast reason, Bess, and much of it, too." But he also admonishes her to remember that, though natural goodness exists, it is not adequate to establish social order, and that "the laws alone remove us from the condition of the savages." In other words, the ambivalence of Judge Temple illustrates, as Marius Bewley has said in *The Eccentric Design*, the fundamental tensions of the American experience between freedom and law, between nature and civilization, between the individual and society, between the religion of the personal intuition and that of theology. The trial of Natty prefigures the trial of Billy Budd and the inner struggle to be undergone by Huck on his raft.

In looking at such a list of polar opposites, one is tempted to see Natty as standing for one set of extremes against the other—totally opposite to Temple and the settlers. But we must remember that Temple can also appreciate Natty's values, and we must ask what values of Temple and of civilization Natty may, in turn, appreciate. We have *not* said that Natty represents one set of poles in the tension of the American experience; rather, he embodies the tension itself, is subject to the force of both poles of experience, and is, as Balzac called him, a "magnificent moral hermaphrodite, born between the savage and the civilized states of man."

We may best understand this if we think of Natty set against various types who appear in the Leatherstocking series. The Indians, to take them first, are truly children of nature, and Natty, who has all the skills of the forest and who has such rapport with the great Chingachgook and Uncas, seems to have entered their world. But we soon see that there are many "bad" Indians, such as Magua in *The Last of the Mohicans*. Natty is not to be identified with their values, and even for the "good" Indians he states flatly that the "gifts" of the

Indians are different from those of the white man. He can appreciate certain of those "gifts," certain skills and ways of conduct, but remains detached from them. He can even condone the taking of scalps by Indians, or their cruelties, for such things belong to the Indian's world and are consistent with his "gifts." But for Natty, who, as a child, had been trained by Moravian missionaries and thus has the white man's "gifts," such acts are unthinkable. Natty can accept nature, be a child of nature, but only insofar as that is consistent with the white man's civilization and religion. For instance, in the splendid episode in *The Deerslayer* when, on the lake shore, he is attacked by an Indian, he cannot bring himself to kill him when he is unsuspecting and defenseless, even though he knows that the Indian would kill a white man under similar circumstances. Similarly, when his white companions, Hutter and Harry, set out to kill for scalps the women and children of the Indian camp, Natty protests and then dissociates himself from them, even though they are acting in accordance not only with Indian practice but with the white law, which gives bounty money for Indian scalps.

As Natty, in *The Deerslayer*, is in contrast with Hutter and Harry, so, in *The Prairie*, as an old man approaching death, he is in contrast with Ishmael Bush, the rampant individualist, the squatter, who is a law unto himself, and a despoiler of nature; but Natty is also in contrast with the scientist Dr. Obed Bat, who, in his way, is also a despoiler.[5] Both the squatter and the scientist lack the reverence and humility with which man should regard nature even as he uses it. At this point, Natty would, strangely enough, agree with Judge Temple that man, whether the ignorant Ishmael Bush or the educated Dr. Bat, cannot be kept from the rape of nature except by force—presumably by the law imposed by civilization.

As we have said, Natty embodies the tensions that have characterized American experience,

but he embodies them not in the sense of being torn between the opposite poles of that experience but by resolving them. If he yearns for freedom and would avoid the restraints of civilization, he does not yearn for the kind of freedom represented by Ishmael Bush in *The Prairie*, the freedom of the arrogant depredator. The freedom of Natty is the freedom of a man who respects life (even that of the Indian who would kill him), reverences nature, and has morally disciplined himself to a point where the check of law is irrelevant to him. Thus he mediates between the pole of freedom and that of law.

Likewise, he *mediates* between the pole of nature and that of civilization. For example, he can bring his white "gifts" into the wilderness and yet not be destroyed by the wilderness, and in *The Last of the Mohicans*, as elsewhere, we find Natty the protector of the civilized whites lost in the wilderness. And he mediates between the Indian, whose "gifts" he respects, and the white man, whose "gifts" he himself exemplifies in their purest form. There is not too imperfect a parallel, as we shall see later in more detail, between Natty and certain characters of William Faulkner, such as Isaac McCaslin in *The Bear*, who are in tune with nature because they have approached it reverently, who embody the virtues of humility, strength, pride, and endurance, and who stand as a rebuke to the cold-blooded exploitation of nature or of other men which can be found in civilization. Isaac McCaslin, like Natty, stands as a criticism of the civilization from which he derives.

We may note another parallel between Cooper and Faulkner. As we shall learn, Faulkner sets what might be called the "traditional man" over against the abuses of modern civilization. Some critics have held that Faulkner equates that traditional man with an upper class or aristocracy, but in his work the virtues of the traditional man may be as well exemplified by a black cook or a poor white farmer as by a member of the old plantation aristocracy.

Unlike Faulkner, Cooper did take the gentleman as the norm of virtue for society, and it is clear that, as a Federalist and a child of the

---

[5] Obed Bat may be compared to certain "scientists" in American literature, for instance, Aylmer in Hawthorne's "The Birthmark" and Margoth in Melville's epic poem *Clarel*.

eighteenth century, he did believe in a fairly rigid social structure. For instance, he is very careful in his novels to make his love stories between members of the upper class, and when, in *The Pathfinder*, he finally undertakes to show Natty in love, he is careful to devise a young woman who is socially appropriate. And Cora, who, in *The Last of the Mohicans*, is beloved by Uncas, is given a trace of Negro blood to make her appropriate for the Indian.

Granting Cooper's preference for a hierarchical society, we must note that Natty, though of a low social order, embodies the basic virtues of the gentleman and, outside society, serves as a rebuke to it. So far so good, but it is hard to say exactly how much confusion or incoherence may be involved in Cooper's treatment of Natty as "gentleman"—or how much recognized tension. How much does Cooper, looking at Natty's career, correspond to Judge Temple speaking to Bess? Or can we, while allowing for the literal difficulty of fitting a man like Natty into society, suggest that at least part of the urge to idealize Natty, to raise him into the sky as a mythic constellation (or merely to keep him safely isolated in the woods), came from the impulse to get him and his virtues into a sphere where they would not be socially inconvenient? Cooper does not even let him marry and settle down into prosperity and become a senator—as happens to Ben Boden, at the end of *The Oak Openings*,[6] whose success, Cooper patriotically remarks, "shows the power of man when left free to make his own exertions."

In his own time and since, certain critics have attacked Cooper by saying that Natty is not a convincing picture of the frontiersman. Even then, however, Cooper found defenders who claimed to know certain frontiersmen with skills

and virtues approaching those of Natty. Boone himself had the frontiersman's skills attributed to Natty, loved freedom, moved west (like Natty in *The Prairie*), and lived into the role of a mythic demigod. Boone's history, in fact, provided Cooper with certain specific episodes, as in the pursuit of Cora in *The Last of the Mohicans*, which echoes the real-life rescue of Jemima Boone and two other girls captured by Indians at Boonesboro. But most important of all, perhaps, is the fact that Boone, for all his reputation as an Indian fighter, was, like Natty, peculiarly lacking in the bloodthirstiness common on the frontier, and was, occasion permitting, beloved by the Indians, even being adopted into a tribe. And if tradition can be believed, he took an innocent joy in nature, something unknown among the Ishmael Bushes of the frontier; he was, in fact, once discovered toward sunset lying in a glade singing to the wilderness, out of pure delight—in a shockingly unmelodious voice. Henry Nash Smith, in *Virgin Land*, points out other instances of real frontiersmen of gentle spirit and delicate sensibilities. But even with such factual justifications for Natty, Cooper was prepared to defend him, in the preface to *The Deerslayer*, as an idealization— a human possibility raised to mythic proportions.

Cooper's Indians, like Natty, were subject to attack, the most famous coming, in 1828, from Lewis Cass, an Indian agent and governor of the Michigan Territory, who said that Uncas had "no living prototype in our forests," and who denied authenticity to Cooper's rendering of Indian psychology and language. Cass's opinion, no doubt, was typical of those dealing directly with the Indians, those not affected by the romantic attitude long since current on the East coast. But on both the matter of psychology and language, Cooper had drawn, it now seems, on reliable contemporary authorities, and he was certainly not alone in his favorable view.

The most eminent defender of the Indian had been, in fact, Thomas Jefferson. His national feeling wounded by the declaration of the eminent French naturalist Buffon that ani-

---

[6] This late novel shows the arrival of civilization, long past the time of Natty's death—with towns and villages spotting the northern prairie, great wheatfields with mechanical reapers at work, old frontiersmen now solid businessmen and landholders, and Peter, once a great taker of scalps from the heads of palefaces, now a Christian convert uttering the gospel of peace.

mals in America (and men, even white men, as some were quick to add) were inferior to those of Europe, Jefferson, in his *Notes on the State of Virginia*, sprang to the defense of the Indian on all counts, from sexual vigor and the size of "the organs of generation" on to moral virtue and thence to intellect and artistic instinct. Jefferson, indeed, continued to dream of the day when paleface and redskin "would meet and blend together, to intermix, and become one people." Contrary to certain detractors of Cooper's Indians, Jefferson maintained that, in general, the race was superbly eloquent and declared that the famous speech by Chief Logan was as fine as any by Demosthenes or Cicero.[7]

[7] This speech appears in our section on Indian oratory. The reader should be aware that Logan's speech is of doubtful authenticity and that questions have been raised concerning Jefferson's connections with it. It should be noted, too, that Jefferson was much less certain of the possible attainments of the black man than of those of the red. Certainly, he never suggested amalgamation of the black and the white races—even though it is highly probable that he fathered children of mixed blood by a slave woman who had been the maid, and who may have been the half-sister, of his dead wife. (See Winthrop D. Jordan, *White over Black*, pp. 464–69; see also our text.)

William Byrd, whom we have already discussed, like

Jefferson would not, of course, suggest that all Indians were as heroic and eloquent as Chief Logan; he saw Logan as an indication of what the Indian might rise to. And this was the line of defense adopted by Cooper, who regarded Chingachgook and Uncas as representing, not the average, but the possibility of the Indian "gifts" raised to ideal proportions and set in the pathetic context of inevitable doom. The mythic Indian, like the mythic frontiersman, stood as a reproach to the civilization that would refuse to recognize and assimilate their "gifts" of reverence for nature and grateful humility before it.

Jefferson, strongly espoused the amalgamation of the white and red races. In *A History of the Dividing Line*, he wrote: "They [the settlers] had now made peace with the Indians, but there was one thing wanting to make that peace lasting. The Natives could by no means persuade themselves that the English were heartily their Friend, so long as they disdained to marry with them. And in earnest, had the English consulted their own Security and the good of the Colony—Had they intended either to Civilize or Convert these Gentiles, they would have brought their Stomachs to embrace this prudent Alliance. . . . Besides, the poor Indians would have had less reason to Complain that the English took away their Land, if they had received it by way of Portion with their Daughters."

BIOGRAPHICAL CHART

FURTHER READINGS

The Works of James Fenimore Cooper (1895–1900; 33 vols.)

James Franklin Beard, ed., *The Letters and Journals of James Fenimore Cooper* (1960–   )

Marius Bewley, *The Eccentric Design* (1959)

Henry W. Boynton, *James Fenimore Cooper* (1931)

Charles A. Brady, "James Fenimore Cooper: Myth-Maker and Christian Romancer," in *American Classics Reconsidered*, Harold C. Gardiner, ed. (1958)

Van Wyck Brooks, *The World of Washington Irving* (1944)

Mary E. Cunningham, ed., *James Fenimore Cooper:*

A Reappraisal (1954)

James Grossman, *James Fenimore Cooper* (1949)

D. H. Lawrence, *Studies in Classic American Literature* (1923)

Arthur Mizener, "The Deerslayer," in *Twelve Great American Novels* (1967)

Roy Harvey Pearce, "The Leatherstocking Tales Re-examined," *South Atlantic Quarterly* (October, 1947)

Donald Ringe, *James Fenimore Cooper* (1961)

Henry Nash Smith, *Virgin Land* (1957)

Robert E. Spiller, *Fenimore Cooper: Critic of His Times* (1931)

———, *James Fenimore Cooper* (1965)

NATTY BUMPPO AND HIS WORLD

We have discussed the Leatherstocking novels in the order of their composition, but they should be regarded in the order of the action they present. The series, read as a whole, covers the period from 1740 to shortly after 1800 and is a kind of prose epic of the westward conquest of the continent, with an overarching unity which compensates for the slack organization and flatness of some of the individual novels. This unity derives from the deeply ironic theme of loss against gain in the conquest, and will against fate, and comes to focus in the character of Natty as he, in the process of being shaped, all but unwittingly, to the heroic pattern of his destiny, learns the nature of his role.

1. *The Deerslayer* (1841): *Killing the First Indian.* [The subtitles are the editors'.] This novel is the last of the Leatherstocking series in date of writing, but is the first in chronology of action. This fact conceals the deep, gradually developing logic of Cooper's composition. With *The Pioneers* (1823) and *The Prairie* (1827), Cooper had been dealing with the pathetic and ironic contrast between the values of the victorious civilization and those embodied in the old and defeated frontiersman. Even if in *The Last of the Mohicans* (1826) we find Natty, with Chingachgook, in a vigorous prime, the title itself points to endings, and the novel is merely a glimpse of youth

caught between the two novels of age. Furthermore, though we have the love story of Uncas, and that of his death, there is little sense of a personal story for the hero himself, Natty. We see him doing daring deeds and exhibiting characteristic virtues, but we have no impression of how he has become the man he is.

With *The Pathfinder* and *The Deerslayer*, however, Cooper goes back to give a more personal story, and a sense of Natty's development in time. *The Deerslayer* is quite specifically a story of initiation—that theme obviously inherent in human experience but particularly emphasized in American literature with such characters as the hero of Melville's novel *Redburn* and that of his *Pierre, or, The Ambiguities*, Huck Finn in Mark Twain's novel, Nick Adams in Hemingway's stories, and Isaac McCaslin in Faulkner's *The Bear*. As for Deerslayer, he has come, with Chingachgook and Hurry Harry, to seek the Indian maiden Hist, beloved of Chingachgook, who is held prisoner by a Huron raiding party. The scene is Glimmerglass (the lake later to be the location of the settlement in *The Pioneers*), which is a spot remarkable for beauty and calm, with these qualities in symbolic contrast to the brutal facts that Deerslayer is about to confront.

The initiation of Deerslayer is threefold, involving death, money, and love. In fact, in the first episode, the theme of death and money are interwoven. Harry and another white man, a tough adventurer named Hutter, who had once been a pirate and who now holds the lake as his domain, try to involve Natty in their plan for the slaughter of the women and children in the Indian camp for the bounty money on scalps. These men represent for Cooper the rapacity, materialism, and hypocrisy of American civilization; they are men for whom the "money value," the bounty that the government will pay for scalps, is, in itself, all the moral justification they need. Natty refuses to participate but is as involved as a passive accomplice, for he is expected to bring his canoe ashore to pick them up. This passive involvement leads to a more active role, for when Harry and Hutter are captured, Deerslayer is left alone to protect the daughters of Hutter; to do so he must gain possession of the several canoes that the Hurons might use for an attack on the Hutter stronghold, a blockhouse of logs built on a shoal well offshore.

The subsequent scene (from Chap. 7), which is given below, is, according to Yvor Winters, "probably as great an achievement of its length as one will find in American fiction outside of Melville." Winters continues:

The prose is plain and factual, yet by rendering with a kind of bare precision the drifting of the canoes, the action of the water, and the caution with which Natty views the edge of the forest, Cooper communicates with a power that has rarely been equaled the tremendous and impersonal quiet of the virgin American wilderness.

We may note, too, the stages by which Deerslayer brings himself to kill the Huron, and the terms in which he finally accepts the act; and note that Deerslayer understands the Indian as fulfilling his "gifts," his nature and fate, as, in the end, Deerslayer understands himself as playing his own necessary role. In this matter of fated roles, when Deerslayer remarks, "say what you will for or ag'in 'em, a red-skin is by no means as sartain [certain] with powder and ball as a white man," we may take the larger implication to be that the Indian is doomed by his incapacity to understand the technology of civilization; and that the technology by which the white man conquers the Indian and the wilderness will be, in the end, ironically enough, the white man's own doom.

From The Deerslayer (1841)

As a matter of course, Deerslayer's attention was first given to the canoe ahead. It was already quite near the point, and a very few strokes of the paddle sufficed to tell him that it must touch before he could possibly overtake it. Just at this moment, too, the wind inopportunely freshened, rendering the drift of the light craft much more rapid and certain. Feeling the impossibility of preventing a contact with the land, the young man wisely determined not to heat himself with unnecessary exertions; but first looking to the priming of his piece, he proceeded slowly and warily toward the point, taking care to make a little circuit, that he might be exposed only on one side as he approached.

The canoe adrift, being directed by no such intelligence, pursued its proper way, and grounded on a small sunken rock at the distance of three or four yards from the shore. Just at that moment Deerslayer had got abreast of the point, and turned the bows of his own boat to the land, first casting loose his tow, that his movements might be unencumbered. The canoe hung an instant on the rock; then it rose a hair's-breadth on an almost imperceptible swell of the water, swung round, floated clear, and reached the strand. All this the young man noted, but it neither quickened his pulses nor hastened his hand. If any one had been lying in wait for the arrival of the waif, he must be seen, and the utmost caution in approaching the shore became indispensable; if no one was in ambush, hurry was unnecessary. The point being nearly diagonally opposite to the Indian encampment, he hoped the last, though the former was not only possible, but probable; for the savages were prompt in adopting all the expedients of their particular modes of warfare, and quite likely had many scouts searching the shores for crafts to carry them off to the castle. As a glance at the lake from any height or projection, would expose the smallest object on its surface, there was little hope that either of the canoes could pass unseen; and Indian sagacity needed no instruction to tell which way a boat or a log would drift when the direction of the wind was known. As Deerslayer drew nearer and nearer to the land, the stroke of his paddle grew slower, his eye became more watchful, and his ears and nostrils almost dilated with the effort to detect any lurking danger. 'Twas a trying moment for a novice, nor was there the encouragement which even the timid sometimes feel when conscious of being observed and commended. He was entirely alone, thrown on his own resources, and was cheered by no friendly eye, emboldened by no encouraging voice. Notwithstanding all these circumstances, the most experienced veteran in forest warfare could not have behaved better. Equally free from recklessness and hesitation, his advance was marked by a sort of philosophical prudence that appeared to render him superior to all motives but those which were best calculated to effect his purpose. Such was the commencement of a career in forest exploits that afterward rendered this man, in his way, and under the limits of his habits and opportunities, as renowned as many a hero whose name has adorned the pages of works more celebrated than legends simple as ours can ever become.

When about a hundred yards from the shore, Deerslayer rose in the canoe, gave three or four vigorous strokes with the paddle, sufficient of themselves to impel the bark to land, and then, quickly laying aside the instrument of labor, he seized that of war. He was in the very act of raising the rifle, when a sharp report was followed by the buzz of a bullet that passed so near his body as to cause him involuntarily to start. The next instant Deerslayer staggered, and fell his whole length in the bottom of the canoe. A yell—it came from a single voice—followed, and an Indian leaped from the bushes upon the open area of the point, bounding toward the canoe. This was the moment the young man desired. He rose on the instant and leveled his own rifle at his uncovered foe; but his finger hesitated about pulling the trigger on one whom he held at such a disadvantage. This little delay probably saved the life of the Indian, who bounded back into the cover as swiftly as he had broken out of it. In the meantime Deerslayer had been swiftly approaching the land, and his own canoe reached the point just as his enemy disappeared. As its movements had not been directed, it touched the shore a few yards from the other boat; and, though the rifle of his foe had to be loaded, there was not time to secure the prize and to carry it beyond danger before he would be exposed to another shot. Under the circumstances, therefore, he did not pause an instant, but dashed into the woods and sought a cover.

On the immediate point there was a small open area, partly in native grass, and partly beach, but a dense fringe of bushes lined its upper side. This narrow belt of dwarf vegetation passed, one issued immediately into the high and gloomy vaults of the forest. The land was tolerably level for a few hundred feet, and then it rose precipitously in a mountain-side. The trees were tall, large, and so free from underbrush that they resembled vast columns, irregularly scattered, upholding a dome of leaves. Although they stood tolerably close together for their ages and size, the eye could penetrate to considerable distances; and bodies of men, even, might have engaged beneath their cover with concert and intelligence.

Deerslayer knew that his adversary must be employed in reloading, unless he had fled. The former proved to be the case, for the young man had no sooner placed himself behind a tree, than he caught a glimpse of the arm of the Indian, his body being concealed by an oak, in the very act of forcing the leathered bullet home. Nothing would have been easier than to spring forward and decide the affair by a close assault on his unprepared foe; but every feeling of Deerslayer revolted at such a step, although his own life had just been attempted from a cover. He was yet unpracticed in the ruthless expedients of savage warfare, of which he knew nothing except by tradition and theory, and it struck him as an unfair advantage to assail an unarmed foe. His color had heightened, his eye frowned, his lips were compressed, and all his energies were collected and ready; but, instead of advancing to fire, he dropped his rifle to the usual position of a sportsman in readiness to catch his aim, and muttered to himself, unconscious that he was speaking:

"No, no—that may be red-skin warfare, but it's not a Christian's gift. Let the miscreant charge, and then we'll take it out like men; for the canoe he *must* not and *shall* not have. No, no; let him have time to load, and God will take care of the right!"

All this time the Indian had been so intent on his own movements, that he was even ignorant that his enemy was in the woods. His only apprehension was that the canoe would be recovered and carried away before he might be in readiness to prevent it. He had sought the cover from habit, but was within a few feet of the fringe of bushes, and could be at the margin of the forest in readiness to fire in a moment. The distance between him and his enemy was about fifty yards, and the trees were so arranged by Nature that the line of sight was not interrupted except by the particular trees behind which each party stood.

His rifle was no sooner loaded than the savage glanced around him, and advanced incautiously as regarded the real, but stealthily as respected the fancied, position of his enemy, until he was fairly exposed. Then Deerslayer stepped from behind his own cover, and hailed him.

"This-a-way, red-skin, this-a-way if you're looking for me," he called out. "I'm young in war, but not so young as to stand on an open beach to be shot down like an owl by daylight. It rests on yourself whether it's peace or war atween us; for my gifts are white gifts, and I'm not one of them that thinks it valiant to slay human mortals, singly, in the woods."

The savage was a good deal startled by this sudden discovery of the danger he ran. He had a little knowledge of English, however, and caught the drift of the other's meaning. He was also too well schooled to betray alarm, but, dropping the butt of his rifle to the earth with an air of confidence, he made a gesture of lofty courtesy. All this was done with the ease and self-possession of one accustomed to consider no man his superior. In the midst of this consummate acting, however, the volcano that raged within caused his eyes to glare and his nostrils to dilate like those of some wild beast that is suddenly prevented from taking the fatal leap.

"Two canoe," he said, in the deep, guttural tones of his race, holding up the number of fingers he mentioned by way of preventing mistakes: "one for you—one for me."

"No, no, Mingo, that will never do. You own neither, and neither shall you have, as long as I can prevent it. I know it's war atween your people and mine, but that's no reason why human mortals should slay each other, like savage creatur's that meet in the woods; go your way then, and leave me to go mine. The world is large enough for us both, and when we meet fairly in battle, why, the Lord will order the fate of each of us."

"Good!" exclaimed the Indian; "my brother missionary—great talk; all about Manitou."

"Not so—not so, warrior. I'm not good enough for the Moravians, and am too good for most of the other vagabonds that preach about in the woods. No, no, I'm only a hunter as yet, though afore the peace is made, 'tis like enough there'll be occasion to strike a blow at some of your people. Still, I wish it to be done in fair fight, and not in a quarrel about the ownership of a miserable canoe."

"Good! My brother very young—but he very wise. Little warrior—great talker. Chief, sometimes, in council."

"I don't know this, nor do I say it, Injin," returned Deerslayer, coloring a little at the ill-concealed sarcasm of the other's manner; "I look forward to a life in the woods, and I only hope it may be a peaceable one. All young men must go on the war-path, when there's occasion, but war isn't needfully massacre. I've seen enough of the last, this very night, to know that Providence frowns on it, and now I invite you to go your own way, while I go mine, and hope that we may part fri'nds."

"Good! My brother has two scalp—gray hair under t'other. Old wisdom—young tongue."

Here the savage advanced with confidence, his hand extended, his face smiling, and his whole bearing denoting amity and respect. Deerslayer met his offered friendship in a proper spirit, and they shook hands cordially, each endeavoring to assure the other of his sincerity and desire to be at peace.

"All have his own," said the Indian; "my canoe, mine; your canoe, your'n. Go look; if your'n, you keep; if mine, I keep."

"That's just, red-skin; though you must be wrong in thinking the canoe your property. Hows'ever, seein' is believin', and we'll go down to the shore, where you may look with your own eyes; for it's likely you'll object to trustin' altogether to mine."

The Indian uttered his favorite exclamation of "Good!" and then they walked, side by side, toward the shore. There was no apparent distrust in the manner of either, the Indian moving in advance as if he wished to show his companion that he did not fear turning his back to him. As they reached the open ground, the former pointed toward Deerslayer's boat and said, emphatically:

"No mine—pale-face canoe. *This* red-man's. No want other man's canoe—want his own."

"You're wrong, red-skin, you're altogether wrong. This canoe was left in old Hutter's keeping, and is his'n according to all law, red or white, till its owner comes to claim it. Here's the seats and stitching of the bark to speak for themselves. No man ever know'd an Injun to turn off such work."

"Good! My brother little ole—big wisdom. Injin no make him. White man's work."

"I'm glad you think so, for holding out to the contrary might have made ill blood atween us, every one having a right to take possession of his own. I'll just shove the canoe out of reach of dispute at once, as the quickest way of settling difficulties."

While Deerslayer was speaking he put a foot against the end of the light boat, and, giving a vigorous shove, he sent it out into the lake a hundred feet or more. where, taking the true current, it would necessarily float past the point, and be in no further danger of coming ashore. The savage started at this ready and decided expedient, and his companion saw that he cast a hurried and fierce glance at his own canoe, or that which contained the paddles. The change of manner, however, was but momentary, and then the Iroquois resumed his air of friendliness and a smile of satisfaction.

"Good!" he repeated, with stronger emphasis than ever. "Young head, old mind. Know how to settle quarrel. Farewell, brother. He go to house in water—muskrat house—Injin go to camp; tell chiefs no find canoe."

Deerslayer was not sorry to hear this proposal, for he felt anxious to join the females, and he took the offered hand of the Indian very willingly. The parting words were friendly, and while the red-man walked calmly toward the wood, with the rifle in the hollow of his arm, without once looking back in uneasiness or distrust, the white man moved toward the remaining canoe, carrying his piece in the same pacific manner, it is true, but keeping his eyes fastened on the movements of the other. This distrust, however, seemed to be altogether uncalled for, and, as if ashamed to have entertained it, the young man averted his look, and stepped carelessly up to his boat. Here he began to push the canoe from the shore, and to make his other preparations for departing. He might have been thus employed a minute, when, happening to turn his face toward the land, his quick and certain eye told him, at a glance, the imminent jeopardy in which his life was placed. The black, ferocious eyes of the savage were glancing on him, like those of the crouching tiger, through a small opening in the bushes, and the muzzle of his rifle seemed already to be opening in a line with his own body.

Then, indeed, the long practice of Deerslayer as a hunter did him good service. Accustomed to fire with the deer on the bound, and often when the precise position of the animal's body had in a manner to be guessed at, he used the same expedients here. To cock and poise his rifle were the acts of a single moment and a single motion; then, aiming almost without sighting, he fired into the bushes where he knew a body ought to be in order to sustain the appalling countenance which alone was visible. There was not time to raise the piece any higher or to take a more deliberate aim. So rapid were his movements, that both parties discharged their pieces at the same instant, the concussions mingling in one report. The mountains, indeed, gave back but a single echo. Deerslayer dropped his piece, and stood, with head erect, steady as one of the pines in the calm of a June morning, watching the result, while the savage gave the yell that has become historical for its appalling influence, leaped through the bushes, and came bounding across the open ground, flourishing a tomahawk. Still Deerslayer moved not, but stood with his unloaded rifle fallen against his shoulders, while, with a hunter's habits, his hands were mechanically feeling for the powder-horn and charger. When about forty feet from his enemy, the savage hurled his keen weapon; but it was with an eye so vacant, and a hand so unsteady and feeble, that the young man caught it by the handle as it was flying past him. At that instant the Indian staggered and fell his whole length on the ground.

"I know'd it—I know'd it!" exclaimed Deerslayer, who was already preparing to force a fresh bullet into his rifle; "I know'd it must come to this as soon as I had got the range from the creatur's eyes. A man sights suddenly and fires quick when his own life's in danger; yes, I know'd it would come to this. I was about the hundredth part of a second too quick for him, or it might have been bad for me. The riptyle's bullet has just grazed my side— but, say what you will for or ag'in 'em, a red-skin is by no means as sartain with powder and ball as a white man. Their gifts don't seem to lie that a-way. Even Chingachgook, great as he is in other matters, isn't downright deadly with the rifle."

By this time the piece was reloaded, and Deerslayer, after tossing the tomahawk into the canoe, advanced to his victim, and stood over him, leaning on his rifle, in melancholy attention. It was the first instance in which he had seen a man fall in battle—it was the first fellow-creature against whom he had ever seriously raised his own hand. The sensations were novel; and regret, with the freshness of our better feelings, mingled with his triumph. The Indian was not dead, though shot directly through the body. He lay on his back motionless, but his eyes, now full of consciousness, watched each action of his victor—as the fallen bird regards the fowler—jealous of every movement. The man probably expected the fatal blow which was to precede the loss of his scalp; or perhaps he anticipated that this latter act of cruelty would precede his death. Deerslayer read his thoughts; and he found a melancholy satisfaction in relieving the apprehensions of the helpless savage.

"No, no, red-skin," he said; "you've nothing more to fear from me. I am of a Christian stock, and scalping is not of my gifts. I'll just make sartain of your rifle, and then come back and do you what sarvice I can. Though here I can't stay much longer, as the crack of three rifles will be apt to bring some of your devils down upon me."

The close of this was said in a sort of a soliloquy, as the young man went in quest of the fallen rifle. The piece was found where its owner had dropped it, and was immediately put into the canoe. Laying his own rifle at its side Deerslayer then returned and stood over the Indian again.

"All inmity atween you and me's at an ind, red-skin," he said; "and you may set your heart at rest on the score of the scalp, or any further injury. My gifts are white, as I've told you; and I hope my conduct will be white also!"

Could looks have conveyed all they meant, it is probable Deerslayer's innocent vanity on the subject of color would have been rebuked a little; but he comprehended the gratitude that was expressed in the eyes of the dying savage, without in the least detecting the bitter sarcasm that struggled with the better feeling.

"Water!" ejaculated the thirsty and unfortunate creature; "give poor Injin water."

"Ay, water you shall have, if you drink the lake dry. I'll just carry you down to it, that you may take your fill. This is the way, they tell me, with all wounded people—water is their greatest comfort and delight."

So saying, Deerslayer raised the Indian in his arms, and carried him to the lake. Here he first helped him to take an attitude in which he could appease his burning thirst; after which he seated himself on a stone, and took the head of his wounded adversary in his own lap, and endeavored to soothe his anguish in the best manner he could.

"It would be sinful in me to tell you your time hadn't come, warrior," he commenced, "and therefore I'll not say it. You've passed the middle age already, and, considerin' the sort of lives ye lead, your days have been pretty well filled. The principal thing now is, to look forward to what comes next. Neither red-skin, nor pale-face, on the whole, calculates much on sleepin' forever; but both expect to live in another world. Each has his gifts, and will be judged by 'em, and, I suppose, you've thought these matters over enough, not to stand in need of sarmons when the trial comes. You'll find your happy hunting-grounds, if you've been a just Injin; if an onjust, you'll meet your desarts in another way. I've my own idees about these things; but you're too old and exper'enced to need any explanations from one as young as I."

"Good!" ejaculated the Indian, whose voice retained its depth even as life ebbed away; "young head—ole wisdom!"

"It's sometimes a consolation, when the ind comes, to know them we've harmed, or *tried* to harm, forgive us. I suppose natur' seeks this relief, by way of getting a pardon on 'arth; as we never can know whether he pardons, who is all in all, till judgment itself comes. It's soothing to know that *any* pardon at such times; and that, I conclude, is the secret. Now, as for myself, I overlook altogether your designs ag'in my life: first, because no harm came of 'em; next, because it's your gifts, and natur' and trainin', and I ought not to have trusted you at all; and, finally and chiefly, because I can bear no ill-will to a dying man, whether heathen or Christian. So put your heart at ease, so far as I'm consarned; you know best what other matters ought to trouble you, or what ought to give you satisfaction in so trying a moment."

It is probable that the Indian had some of the fearful glimpses of the unknown state of being which God in mercy seems at times to afford to all the human race; but they were necessarily in conformity with his habits and prejudices. Like most of his people, and like too many of our own, he thought more of dying in a way to gain applause among those he left than to secure a better state of existence hereafter. While Deerslayer was speaking, his mind was a little bewildered, though he felt that the intention was good; and when he had done, a regret passed over his spirit that none of his own tribe were present to witness his stoicism, under extreme bodily suffering, and the firmness with which he met his end. With the high innate courtesy that so often distinguishes the Indian warrior before he becomes corrupted by too much intercourse with the worst class of the white man, he endeavored to express his thankfulness for the other's good intentions, and to let him understand that they were appreciated.

"Good!" he repeated, for this was an English word much used by the savages—"good—young head; young *heart*, too. *Old* heart tough; no shed tear. Hear Indian when he die, and no want to lie —what he call him?"

"Deerslayer is the name I bear now, though the Delawares have said that, when I get back from this war-path, I shall have a more manly title, provided I can 'arn one."

"That good name for boy—poor name for warrior. He get better quick. No fear *there*"—the savage had strength sufficient, under the strong excitement he felt, to raise a hand and tap the young man on his breast—"eye sartain—finger lightning—aim, death—great warrior soon. No Deerslayer —Hawkeye—Hawkeye—Hawkeye. Shake hand."

Deerslayer—or Hawkeye, as the youth was then first named, for in after years he bore the appellation throughout all that region—Deerslayer took the hand of the savage, whose last breath was drawn in that attitude, gazing in admiration at the countenance of a stranger who had shown so much readiness, skill, and firmness, in a scene that was equally trying and novel. When the reader remembers it is the highest gratification an Indian can receive to see his enemy betray weakness, he will be better able to appreciate the conduct which had extorted so great a concession at such a moment.

"His spirit has fled!" said Deerslayer, in a suppressed, melancholy voice. "Ah's me! Well, to this we must all come, sooner or later; and he is happiest, let his skin be what color it may, who is best fitted to meet it. Here lies the body of no doubt a brave warrior, and the soul is already flying toward its heaven or hell, whether that be a happy hunting-ground, or a place scant of game; regions of glory, according to Moravian doctrine, or flames of fire! So it happens, too, as regards other matters. Here have old Hutter and Hurry Harry got themselves into difficulty, if they haven't got themselves into torment and death, and all for a bounty that luck offers to me in what many would think a lawful and suitable manner. But not a farthing of such money shall cross my hand. White I was born, and white will I die; clinging to the color to the last, even though the king's majesty, his governors, and all his councils, both at home and in the colonies,

forget from what they come, and where they hope to go, and all for a little advantage in warfare. No, no—warrior, hand of mine shall never molest your scalp, and so your soul may rest in peace on the p'int of making a decent appearance, when the body comes to join it, in your own land of spirits."

Deerslayer arose as soon as he had spoken. Then he placed the body of the dead man in a sitting posture, with its back against the little rock, taking the necessary care to prevent it from falling or in any way settling into an attitude that might be thought unseemly by the sensitive though wild notions of a savage. When this duty was performed, the young man stood gazing at the grim countenance of his fallen foe in a sort of melancholy abstraction. As was his practice, however, a habit gained by living so much alone in the forest, he then began again to give utterance to his thoughts and feelings aloud.

"I didn't wish your life, red-skin," he said, "but you left me no choice atween killing or being killed. Each party acted according to his gifts, I suppose, and blame can light on neither. You were treacherous, according to your natur' in war, and I was a little oversightful, as I'm apt to be in trusting others. Well, this is my first battle with a human mortal, though it's not likely to be the last. I have fou't most of the creatur's of the forest, such as bears, wolves, painters, and catamounts, but this is the beginning with the red-skins. If I was Injin born, now, I might tell of this, or carry in the scalp, and boast of the expl'ite afore the whole tribe; or, if my inimy had only been even a bear, 'twould have been nat'ral and proper to let everybody know what had happened; but I don't well see how I'm to let even Chingachgook into this secret, so long as it can be done only by boasting with a white tongue. And why should I wish to boast of it a'ter all? It's slaying a human, although he was a savage; and how do I know that he was a just Injin; and that he has not been taken away suddenly to anything but happy hunting-grounds? When it's onsartin whether good or evil has been done, the wisest thing is not to be boastful—still, I *should* like Chingachgook to know that I haven't discredited the Delawares or my training!"

Thus Deerslayer, the hunter, becomes the Warrior, and as Cooper puts it in the last chapter, "under the *sobriquet* of Hawkeye . . . made his fame spread far and near." Meanwhile, at the end of the novel, Judith, one of the daughters of old Hutter, offers her love to Natty, who refuses her for the life of the wilderness. Glimmerglass is left again to the Eden calm which Hawkeye, Chingachgook, and the young Uncas will again see, fifteen years later, as they go on their adventures recounted in *The Last of the Mohicans:*

> Here all was unchanged: the river still rushed through its bower of trees; the little rock was wasting away by the slow action of the waves in the course of centuries; the mountains stood in their native dress, dark, rich, and mysterious; while the sheet glistened in its solitude, a beautiful gem of the forest.

We know, however, that this natural peace is not to endure, for Glimmerglass is Lake Otsego on which, in *The Pioneers*, the settlement will appear and from which refuge, full of early memories, old Natty will be driven, in the turn of time, by the very civilization for which, as the young Deerslayer, he had opened the way. Looking back upon this conquest of the wilderness, and upon all human history, Cooper takes the perspective of orthodox Christianity, a view very different from any self-congratulation on "progress": "We live in a world of transgressions and selfishness, and no pictures that represent us otherwise can be true; though happily for human nature, gleamings of that pure spirit in whose likeness man has been fashioned are to be seen, relieving its deformities and mitigating, if not excusing, its crimes."

2. *The Last of the Mohicans* (1826): *The Pursuit.* This novel, set some fifteen years after *The Deerslayer*, deals with the campaign against the French and Indians of 1757, around Lake George. Here Natty, in his role as Hawkeye, shows his skill as a warrior. This novel is nearer

to a pure adventure story than any of the series, but one element sets it off from that category. If in *The Deerslayer* we have in Glimmerglass an image of nature as beautiful and calm in contrast to the brutality of civilized man, here we see nature in a more inimical aspect. Here is the backwash of European wars, which in this blind wilderness seem to have no meaning beyond the aimless ferocity of the "natural man." There are, of course, the "good" Indians like Chingachgook and Uncas, but the general impression here is of the savagery of man in a savage nature, a savagery which civilization, in the person of General Montcalm trying to control his red allies by the code of civilized warfare, is powerless to mitigate.

In this novel the role of Natty is that of the savior who can save only because he has submitted himself to the study of that nature that is more often merciless than merciful. There is, of course, the pervasive irony that the savior cannot, in the end, save himself from the even more merciless world of the palefaces. The novel is a teasing and ambiguous one, chiefly because we cannot be sure how much awareness is involved in the theme of the doubleness of nature and human nature, a theme which seems to foreshadow such modern works as *Heart of Darkness*, by Joseph Conrad (who, as we have said, admired Cooper).

The section given below (from Chap. 18) comes just after the powerful scene of the Indian massacre of the English who have surrendered at Fort William Henry; the Indians have captured Cora and Alice, the daughters of Munro, the commander of the Fort, and now Hawkeye, with Chingachgook, Uncas, Munro, and the lover of one of the girls, is in pursuit. The traces left by Cora may be derived from the story of those left by Daniel Boone's daughter, when she was captured by Shawnees.

From The Last of the Mohicans (1826)

The third day from the capture of the fort was drawing to a close, but the business of the narrative must still detain the reader on the shores of the "holy lake." When last seen, the environs of the works were filled with violence and uproar. They were now possessed by stillness and death.

The blood-stained conquerors had departed; and their camp, which had so lately rung with the merry rejoicings of a victorious army, lay a silent and deserted city of huts. The fortress was a smouldering ruin; charred rafters, fragments of exploded artillery, and rent mason-work, covering its earthen mounds in confused disorder.

A frightful change had also occurred in the season. The sun had hid its warmth behind an impenetrable mass of vapor, and hundreds of human forms, which had blackened beneath the fierce heats of August, were stiffening in their deformity, before the blasts of a premature November. The curling and spotless mists, which had been seen sailing above the hills towards the north, were now returning in an interminable dusky sheet, that was urged along by the fury of a tempest. The crowded mirror of the Horican was gone; and, in its place, the green and angry waters lashed the shores, as if indignantly casting back its impurities to the polluted strand. Still the clear fountain retained a portion of its charmed influence, but it reflected only the sombre gloom that fell from the impending heavens. That humid and congenial atmosphere which commonly adorned the view, veiling its harshness, and softening its asperities, had disappeared, and the northern air poured across the waste of water so harsh and unmingled, that nothing was left to be conjectured by the eye, or fashioned by the fancy.

The fiercer element had cropped the verdure of the plain, which looked as though it were scathed by the consuming lightning. But, here and there, a dark green tuft rose in the midst of the desolation; the earliest fruits of a soil that had been fattened with human blood. The whole landscape, which, seen by a favoring light, and in a genial temperature, had been found so lovely, appeared now like some pictured allegory of life, in which objects were arrayed in their harshest but truest colors, and without the relief of any shadowing.

The solitary and arid blades of grass arose from the passing gusts fearfully perceptible; the bold and rocky mountains were too distinct in their barrenness, and the eye even sought relief, in vain, by attempting to pierce the illimitable void of heaven, which was shut to its gaze by the dusky sheet of ragged and driving vapor.

The wind blew unequally; sometimes sweeping heavily along the ground, seeming to whisper its moanings in the cold ears of the dead, then rising in a shrill and mournful whistling, it entered the forest with a rush that filled the air with the leaves and branches it scattered in its path. Amid the unnatural shower, a few hungry ravens struggled with the gale; but no sooner was the green ocean of woods, which stretched beneath them, passed, than they gladly stopped, at random, to their hideous banquet.

In short, it was the scene of wildness and desolation; and it appeared as if all who had profanely entered it had been stricken, at a blow, by the relentless arm of death. But the prohibition had ceased; and for the first time since the perpetrators of those foul deeds which had assisted to disfigure the scene were gone, living human beings had now presumed to approach the place.

About an hour before the setting of the sun, on the day already mentioned, the forms of five men might have been seen issuing from the narrow vista of trees, where the path to the Hudson entered the forest, and advancing in the direction of the ruined works. At first their progress was slow and guarded, as though they entered with reluctance amid the horrors of the spot, or dreaded the renewal of its frightful incidents. A light figure preceded the rest of the party, with the caution and activity of a native; ascending every hillock to reconnoitre, and indicating, by gestures, to his companions, the route he deemed it most prudent to pursue. Nor were those in the rear wanting in every caution and foresight known to forest warfare. One among them, he also was an Indian, moved a little on one flank, and watched the margin of the woods, with eyes long accustomed to read the smallest sign of danger. The remaining three were white, though clad in vestments adapted, both in quality and color, to their present hazardous pursuit,—that of hanging, on the skirts of a retiring army in the wilderness.

The effects produced by the appalling sights that constantly arose in their path to the lake shore, were as different as the characters of the respective individuals who composed the party. The youth in front threw serious but furtive glances at the mangled victims, as he stepped lightly across the plain, afraid to exhibit his feelings, and yet too inexperienced to quell entirely their sudden and powerful influence. His red associate, however, was superior to such a weakness. He passed the groups of dead with a steadiness of purpose, and an eye so calm, that nothing but long and inveterate practice could enable him to maintain. The sensations produced in the minds of even the white men were different, though uniformly sorrowful. One, whose gray locks and furrowed lineaments, blending with a martial air and tread, betrayed, in spite of the disguise of a woodsman's dress, a man long experienced in scenes of war, was not ashamed to groan aloud, whenever a spectacle of more than usual horror came under his view. The young man at his elbow shuddered, but seemed to suppress his feelings in tenderness to his companion. Of them all, the straggler who brought up the rear appeared alone to betray his real thoughts, without fear of observation or dread of consequences. He gazed at the most appalling sight with eyes and muscles that knew not how to waver, but with execrations so bitter and deep as to denote how much he denounced the crime of his enemies.

The reader will perceive at once, in these respective characters, the Mohicans, and their white friend, the scout; together with Munro and Heyward. It was, in truth, the father in quest of his children, attended by the youth who felt so deep a stake in their happiness, and those brave and trusty foresters, who had already proved their skill and fidelity through the trying scenes related.

When Uncas, who moved in front, had reached the centre of the plain, he raised a cry that drew his companions in a body to the spot. The young warrior had halted over a group of females who lay in a cluster, a confused mass of dead. Notwithstanding the revolting horror of the exhibition, Munro and Heyward flew towards the festering heap, endeavoring, with a love that no unseemliness could extinguish, to discover whether any vestiges of those they sought were to be seen among the tattered and many-colored garments. The father and lover found instant relief in the search; though each was condemned again to experience the misery of an uncertainty that was hardly less insupportable than the most revolting truth. They were standing, silent and thoughtful, around the melancholy pile, when the scout approached. Eying the sad spectacle with an angry countenance, the sturdy woodsman, for the first time since his entering the plain, spoke intelligibly and aloud:—

"I have been on many a shocking field, and have followed a trail of blood for many miles," he said, "but never have I found the hand of the devil so plain as it is here to be seen! Revenge is an Indian feeling, and all who knew me know that there is no cross in my veins; but this much will I say—here, in the face of heaven, and with the power of the Lord so manifest in this howling wilderness—that should these Frenchers ever trust themselves again within the range of a ragged bullet, there is one rifle shall play its part, so long as flint will fire or powder burn! I leave the tomahawk and knife to such as have a natural gift to use them. What say you, Chingachgook," he added in Delaware; "shall the Hurons boast of this to their women when the deep snows come?"

A gleam of resentment flashed across the dark lineaments of the Mohican chief: he loosened his knife in his sheath; and then turning calmly from the sight, his countenance settled into a repose as deep as if he never knew the instigation of passion.

"Montcalm! Montcalm!" continued the deeply resentful and less self-restrained scout; "they say a time must come, when all the deeds done in the flesh will be seen at a single look; and that by eyes cleared from mortal infirmities. Woe betide the wretch who is born to behold this plain, with the judgment hanging about his soul! Ha—as I am a man of white blood, yonder lies a redskin, without the hair of his head where nature rooted it! Look to him, Delaware; it may be one of your missing people; and he should have burial like a stout warrior. I see it in your eye, Sagamore: a Huron pays for this, afore the fall winds have blown away the scent of the blood!"

Chingachgook approached the mutilated form, and turning it over, he found the distinguishing marks of one of those six allied tribes, or nations, as they were called, who, while they fought in the English ranks, were so deadly hostile to his own people. Spurning the loathsome object with his foot, he turned from it with the same indifference he would have quitted a brute carcass. The scout comprehended the action, and very deliberately pursued his own way, continuing, however, his denunciations against the French commander in the same resentful strain.

"Nothing but vast wisdom and onlimited power should dare to sweep off men in multitudes," he added; "for it is only the one that can know the necessity of the judgment; and what is there, short of the other, that can replace the creatures of the Lord? I hold it a sin to kill the second buck afore the first is eaten, unless a march in the front, or an ambushment, be contemplated. It is a different matter with a few warriors in open and rugged fight, for 't is their gift to die with the rifle or the tomahawk in hand; according as their natures may happen to be, white or red. Uncas, come this way, lad, and let the ravens settle upon the Mingo. I know, from often seeing it, that they have a craving for the flesh of an Oneida; and it is as well to let the bird follow the gift of its natural appetite."

"Hugh!" exclaimed the young Mohican, rising on the extremities of his feet, and gazing intently in his front, frightening the raven to some other prey, by the sound and the action.

"What is it, boy?" whispered the scout, lowering his tall form into a crouching attitude, like a panther about to take his leap; "God send it be a tardy Frencher, skulking for plunder. I do believe 'Killdeer' would take an oncommon range to-day!"

Uncas, without making any reply, bounded away from the spot, and in the next instant he was seen tearing from a bush, and waving in triumph, a fragment of the green riding-veil of Cora. The movement, the exhibition, and the cry, which again burst from the lips of the young Mohican, instantly drew the whole party about him.

"My child!" said Munro, speaking quick and wildly; "give me my child!"

"Uncas will try," was the short and touching answer.

The simple but meaning assurance was lost on the father, who seized the piece of gauze, and crushed it in his hand, while his eyes roamed fearfully among the bushes, as if he equally dreaded and hoped for the secrets they might reveal.

"Here are no dead," said Heyward; "the storm seems not to have passed this way."

"That's manifest; and clearer than the heavens above our heads," returned the undisturbed scout; "but either she, or they that have robbed her, have passed the bush; for I remember the rag she wore to hide a face that all did love to look upon. Uncas, you are right; the dark-hair has been here, and she has fled like a frightened fawn, to the wood; none who could fly would remain to be murdered. Let us search for the marks she left; for to Indian eyes, I sometimes think even a humming-bird leaves his trail in the air."

The young Mohican darted away at the suggestion, and the scout had hardly done speaking, before the former raised a cry of success from the margin of the forest. On reaching the spot, the anxious party perceived another portion of the veil fluttering on the lower branch of a beech.

"Softly, softly," said the scout, extending his long rifle in front of the eager Heyward; "we now know our work, but the beauty of the trail must not be deformed. A step too soon may give us hours of trouble. We have them though; that much is beyond denial."

"Bless ye, bless ye, worthy man!" exclaimed Munro; "whither, then, have they fled, and where are my babes?"

"The path they have taken depends on many chances. If they have gone alone, they are quite as likely to move in a circle as straight, and they may be within a dozen miles of us; but if the Hurons, or any of the French Indians, have laid hands on them, 't is probable they are now near the borders of the Canadas. But what matters that?" continued the deliberate scout, observing the powerful anxiety and disappointment the listeners exhibited; "here are the Mohicans and I on one end of the trail, and, rely on it, we find the other, though they should be a hundred leagues asunder! Gently, gently, Uncas, you are as impatient as a man in the settlements; you forget that light feet leave but faint marks!"

"Hugh!" exclaimed Chingachgook, who had been occupied in examining an opening that had been evidently made through the low underbrush, which skirted the forest; and who now stood erect, as he pointed downwards, in the attitude and with the air of a man who beheld a disgusting serpent.

"Here is the palpable impression of the footstep of a man," cried Heyward, bending over the indicated spot; "he has trod in the margin of this pool, and the mark cannot be mistaken. They are captives."

"Better so than left to starve in the wilderness," returned the scout; "and they will leave a wider trail. I would wager fifty beaver skins against as many flints, that the Mohicans and I enter their wigwams within the month! Stoop to it, Uncas, and try what you can make of the moccasin; for moccasin it plainly is, and no shoe."

The young Mohican bent over the track, and removing the scattered leaves from around the place, he examined it with much of that sort of scrutiny, that a money-dealer, in these days of pecuniary doubts, would bestow on a suspected due-bill. At length he arose from his knees, satisfied with the result of the examination.

"Well, boy," demanded the attentive scout, "what does it say? can you make anything of the tell-tale?"

"Le Renard Subtil!"

"Ha! that rampaging devil again! there never will be an end of his loping, till 'Killdeer' has said a friendly word to him."

Heyward reluctantly admitted the truth of this intelligence, and now expressed rather his hopes than his doubts by saying,—

"One moccasin is so much like another, it is probable there is some mistake."

"One moccasin like another! you may as well say

that one foot is like another; though we all know that some are long, and others short; some broad, and others narrow; some with high, and some with low insteps; some in-toed, and some out. One moccasin is no more like another than one book is like another; though they who can read in one are seldom able to tell the marks of the other. Which is all ordered for the best, giving to every man his natural advantages. Let me get down to it, Uncas; neither book nor moccasin is the worse for having two opinions, instead of one." The scout stooped to the task, and instantly added, "You are right, boy; here is the patch we saw so often in the other chase. And the fellow will drink when he can get an opportunity: your drinking Indian always learns to walk with a wider toe than the natural savage, it being the gift of a drunkard to straddle, whether of white or red skin. 'Tis just the length and breadth too! look at it, Sagamore: you measured the prints more than once, when we hunted the varmints from Glenn's to the healthsprings."

Chingachgook complied; and after finishing his short examination, he arose, and with a quiet demeanor, he merely pronounced the word—

"Magua!"

"Ay, 't is a settled thing; here then have passed the dark-hair and Magua."

"And not Alice?" demanded Heyward.

"Of her we have not yet seen the signs," returned the scout, looking closely around at the trees, the bushes, and the ground. "What have we there? Uncas, bring hither the thing you see dangling from yonder thorn-bush."

When the Indian had complied, the scout received the prize, and holding it on high, he laughed in his silent but heartfelt manner.

"'Tis the tooting we'pon of the singer! now we shall have a trail a priest might travel," he said. "Uncas, look for the marks of a shoe that is long enough to uphold six feet two of tottering human flesh. I begin to have some hopes of the fellow, since he has given up squalling to follow some better trade."

"At least, he has been faithful to his trust," said Heyward; "and Cora and Alice are not without a friend."

"Yes," said Hawkeye, dropping his rifle, and leaning on it with an air of visible contempt, "he will do their singing. Can he slay a buck for their dinner; journey by the moss on the beeches, or cut the throat of a Huron? If not, the first catbird he meets is the cleverest of the two. Well, boy, any signs of such a foundation?"

"Here is something like the footstep of one who has worn a shoe; can it be that of our friend?"

"Touch the leaves lightly, or you'll disconsart the formation. That! that is the print of a foot, but 't is the dark-hair's; and small it is, too, for one of such a noble height and grand appearance. The singer would cover it with his heel."

"Where! let me look on the footsteps of my child," said Munro, shoving the bushes aside, and bending fondly over the nearly obliterated impression. Though the tread, which had left the mark, had been light and rapid, it was still plainly visible. The aged soldier examined it with eyes that grew dim as he gazed; nor did he rise from his stooping posture until Heyward saw that he had watered the trace of his daughter's passage with a scalding tear. Willing to divert a distress which threatened each moment to break through the restraint of appearances, by giving the veteran something to do, the young man said to the scout,—

"As we now possess these infallible signs, let us commence our march. A moment, at such a time, will appear an age to the captives."

"It is not the swiftest leaping deer that gives the longest chase," returned Hawkeye, without moving his eyes from the different marks that had come under his view; "we know that the rampaging Huron has passed,—and the dark-hair,—and the singer,—but where is she of the yellow locks and blue eyes? Though little, and far from being as bold as her sister, she is fair to the view, and pleasant in discourse. Has she no friend, that none care for her?"

"God forbid she should ever want hundreds! Are we not now in her pursuit? for one, I will never cease the search till she be found."

"In that case we may have to journey by different paths; for here she has not passed, light and little as her footstep would be."

Heyward drew back, all his ardor to proceed seeming to vanish on the instant. Without attending to this sudden change in the other's humor, the scout, after musing a moment, continued,—

"There is no woman in this wilderness could leave such a print as that, but the dark-hair or her sister. We know that the first has been here, but where are the signs of the other? Let us push deeper on the trail, and if nothing offers, we must go back to the plain and strike another scent. Move on, Uncas, and keep your eyes on the dried leaves. I will watch the bushes, while your father shall run with a low nose to the ground. Move on, friends; the sun is getting behind the hills."

"Is there nothing that I can do?" demanded the anxious Heyward.

"You!" repeated the scout, who, with his red friends, was already advancing in the order he had prescribed; "yes, you can keep in our rear, and be careful not to cross the trail."

Before they had proceeded many rods, the Indians stopped, and appeared to gaze at some signs on the earth, with more than their usual keenness. Both father and son spoke quick and loud, now looking at the object of their mutual admiration, and now regarding each other with the most unequivocal pleasure.

"They have found the little foot!" exclaimed the scout, moving forward, without attending further to his own portion of the duty. "What have we here? An ambushment has been planted in the spot? No, by the truest rifle on the frontiers, here have been them one-sided horses again! Now the whole secret is out, and all is plain as the north star at midnight. Yes, here they have mounted. There the beasts have been bound to a sapling, in waiting; and yonder runs the broad path away to the north, in full sweep for the Canadas."

"But still there are no signs of Alice—of the younger Miss Munro,"—said Duncan.

"Unless the shining bauble Uncas has just lifted from the ground should prove one. Pass it this way, lad, that we may look at it."

Heyward instantly knew it for a trinket that Alice was fond of wearing, and which he recollected, with the tenacious memory of a lover, to have seen, on the fatal morning of the massacre, dangling from the fair neck of his mistress. He seized the highly prized jewel; and as he proclaimed the fact, it vanished from the eyes of the wondering scout, who in vain looked for it on the ground, long after it was warmly pressed against the beating heart of Duncan.

"Pshaw!" said the disappointed Hawkeye, ceasing to rake the leaves with the breech of his rifle; " 't is a certain sign of age, when the sight begins to weaken. Such a glittering gewgaw, and not to be seen! Well, well, I can squint along a clouded barrel yet, and that is enough to settle all disputes between me and the Mingos. I should like to find the thing too, if it were only to carry it to the right owner, and that would be bringing the two ends of what I call a long trail together,—for by this time the broad St. Lawrence, or, perhaps, the Great Lakes themselves, are atwixt us."

"So much the more reason why we should not delay our march," returned Heyward; "let us proceed."

"Young blood and hot blood, they say, are much the same thing. We are not about to start on a squirrel hunt, or to drive a deer into the Horican, but to outlie for days and nights, and to stretch across a wilderness where the feet of men seldom go, and where no bookish knowledge would carry you through harmless. An Indian never starts on such an expedition without smoking over his council-fire; and though a man of white blood, I honor their customs in this particular, seeing that they are deliberate and wise. We will, therefore, go back, and light our fire to-night in the ruins of the old fort, and in the morning we shall be fresh, and ready to undertake our work like men, and not like babbling women or eager boys."

Heyward saw, by the manner of the scout, that altercation would be useless. Munro had again sunk into that sort of apathy which had beset him since his late overwhelming misfortunes, and from which he was apparently to be roused only by some new and powerful excitement. Making a merit of necessity, the young man took the veteran by the arm, and followed in the footsteps of the Indians and the scout, who had already begun to retrace the path which conducted them to the plain.

---

3. *The Pathfinder* (1840): *Natty and Love.* This is the third of the novels concerned with Natty's youth. In *The Deerslayer*, we have seen Natty refuse the love offered by Judith Hutter, but here the theme of Natty's relation to love is more fully developed. In *The Deerslayer* Judith is clearly not appropriate for Natty, neither morally nor otherwise, and therefore, in that book, there is some uncertainty about the nature of his refusal. But now Cooper goes to great lengths to provide, in Mabel Dunham, the appropriate woman, in temperament, education, experience, and social class, and one to whom Natty is attracted and to whom he is bound by his promise to the girl's dying father. In other words, if Natty refuses Mabel, the appropriate mate, he is definitively refusing the world of civilization, society, and family in favor of the celibate freedom of the wilderness.

On the frontier there were men who, for one reason or another, simply withdrew from the responsibilities of society, but with Natty, the hero of an epic, a little more than this realistic concern is involved. Like Peter Pan who refuses to grow up, Natty is simply maintaining his identity; by remaining outside society, he can remain the symbol of certain values which perennially stand in critical contrast to society —a character, as Cooper called Natty in the preface of 1850, "that possessed little of civilization but its highest principles." Over against Natty we set Jasper, who, when he does marry Mabel, enters the world of civilization and becomes a successful merchant. Can we imagine Natty in such a career? The meaning would evaporate from all his past experience.

The scene here (from Chap. 24) is on Lake Ontario, two years after the action of *The Last of the Mohicans*.

From The Pathfinder (1840)

The occurrences of the last few days had been too exciting and had made too many demands on the fortitude of our heroine to leave her in the helplessness of grief. She mourned for her father, and she occasionally shuddered as she recalled the sudden death of Jennie and all the horrible scenes she had witnessed; but, on the whole, she had aroused herself, and was no longer in the deep depression that usually accompanies grief. Perhaps the overwhelming, almost stupefying sorrow that crushed poor June, and left her for nearly twenty-four hours in a state of stupor, assisted Mabel in conquering her own feelings, for she had felt called on to administer consolation to the young Indian woman. This she had done, in the quiet, soothing, insinuating way in which her sex usually exerts its influence on such occasions.

The morning of the third day was set for that on which the *Scud* was to sail. Jasper had made all his preparations; the different effects were embarked, and Mabel had taken leave of June—a painful and affectionate parting. In a word, all was ready, and every soul had left the island but the Indian woman, Pathfinder, Jasper and our heroine. The former had gone into a thicket to weep, and the three last were approaching the spot where three canoes lay, one of which was the property of June, and the other two were in waiting to carry the others off to the *Scud*. Pathfinder led the way, but when he drew near the shore, instead of taking the direction of the boats, he motioned to his companions to follow, and proceeded to a fallen tree that lay on the margin of the glade, and out of view of those in the cutter. Seating himself on the trunk, he signed to Mabel to take her place on one side of him and to Jasper to occupy the other.

"Sit down here, Mabel; sit down there, Eaudouce," he commenced, as soon as he had taken his own seat; "I've something that lies heavy on my mind, and now is the time to take it off, if it's ever to be done. Sit down, Mabel, and let me lighten my heart, if not my conscience, while I've the strength to do it."

The pause that succeeded lasted two or three minutes, and both the young people wondered what was to come next—the idea that Pathfinder could have any weight on his conscience seeming equally improbable to each.

"Mabel," our hero at length resumed, "we must talk plainly to each other afore we join your uncle in the cutter, where the Saltwater has slept every night since the last rally; for he says it's the only place in which a man can be sure of keeping the hair on his head, he does. Ah's me! what have I to do with these follies and sayings now? I try to be pleasant and to feel light-hearted, but the power of man can't make water run up stream. Mabel, you know that the sergeant, afore he left us, had settled it atween us two, that we were to become man and wife, and that we were to live together, and to love one another as long as the Lord was pleased to keep us both on 'arth; yes, and afterwards, too?"

Mabel's cheeks had regained a little of their ancient bloom in the fresh air of the morning: but at this unlooked-for-address they blanched again, nearly to the pallid hue which grief had imprinted there. Still she looked kindly, though seriously, at Pathfinder, and even endeavored to force a smile.

"Very true, my excellent friend"—she answered—"this was my poor father's wish, and I feel certain that a whole life devoted to your welfare and comforts could scarcely repay you for all you have done for us."

"I fear me, Mabel, that man and wife needs be bound together by a stronger tie than such feelings, I do. You have done nothing for me, or nothing of any account, and yet my very heart yearns toward you, it does; and therefore it seems likely that these feelings come from something besides saving scalps and guiding through woods."

Mabel's cheek had begun to glow again; and though she struggled hard to smile, her voice trembled a little as she answered:

"Had we not better postpone this conversation, Pathfinder?" she said; "we are not alone; and nothing is so unpleasant to a listener, they say, as family matters in which he feels no interest."

"It's because we are not alone, Mabel, or rather because Jasper is with us, that I wish to talk of this matter. The sergeant believed I might make a suitable companion for you, and, though I had misgivings about it—yes, I had many misgivings—he finally persuaded me into the idee, and things came round between us, as you know. But when you promised your father to marry me, Mabel, and gave me your hand so modestly but so prettily, there was one circumstance, as your uncle calls it, that you didn't know; and I've thought it right to tell you what it is before matters are finally settled. I've often taken a poor deer for my dinner, when good venison was not to be found; but it's as nat'ral not to take up with the worst when the best may be had."

"You speak in a way, Pathfinder, that is difficult to be understood. If this conversation is really necessary, I trust you will be more plain."

"Well, then, Mabel, I've been thinking it was quite likely, when you gave in to the sergeant's wishes, that you did not know the natur' of Jasper Western's feelings toward you?"

"Pathfinder!"—and Mabel's cheek now paled to the livid hue of death; then it flushed to the tint of crimson; and her whole frame shuddered. Pathfinder, however, was too intent on his own object to notice this agitation; and Eau-douce had hidden his face in his hands in time to shut out its view.

"I've been talking with the lad; and, on comparing his dreams with my dreams, his feelings with my feelings, and his wishes with my wishes, I fear we think too much alike concerning you for both of us to be very happy."

"Pathfinder—you forget—you should remember that we are betrothed!" said Mabel, hastily, and in a voice so low that it required acute attention in the listeners to catch the syllables. Indeed, the last word was not quite intelligible to the guide, and he confessed his ignorance by the usual:

"Anan?"

"You forget that we are to be married; and such allusions are improper as well as painful."

"Everything is proper that is right, Mabel; and everything is right that leads to justice and fair dealing; though it *is painful* enough, as you say—as I find on trial, I do. Now, Mabel, had you known that Eau-douce thinks of you in this way maybe you never would have consented to be married to one as old and as uncomely as I am."

"Why this cruel trial, Pathfinder, to what can all this lead? Jasper Western thinks no such thing; he says nothing—he feels nothing."

"Mabel!" burst from out of the young man's lips, in a way to betray the uncontrollable nature of his emotions, though he uttered not another syllable.

Mabel buried her face in both her hands; and the two sat like a pair of guilty beings, suddenly detected in the commission of some crime that involved the happiness of a common patron. At that instant, perhaps, Jasper himself was inclined to deny his passion, through an extreme unwillingness to grieve his friend; while Mabel, on whom this positive announcement of a fact that she had rather unconsciously hoped than believed came so unexpectedly, felt her mind momentarily bewildered, and she scarce knew whether to weep or to rejoice. Still, she was the first to speak; since Eau-douce could utter naught that would be disingenuous, or that would pain his friend.

"Pathfinder," she said, "you talk wildly. Why mention this at all?"

"Well, Mabel, if I talk wildly, I *am* half wild, you know; by natur', I fear, as well as by habit." As he said this, he endeavored to laugh in his usual noiseless way, but the effect produced a strange and discordant sound; and it appeared nearly to choke him. "Yes, I *must* be wild; I'll not attempt to deny it."

"Dearest Pathfinder!—my best, almost my only friend! you *cannot, do not* think I intended to say that!" interrupted Mabel, almost breathless in her haste to relieve his mortification—"if courage, truth, nobleness of soul and conduct, unyielding principles, and a hundred other excellent qualities, can render any man respectable, esteemed or beloved, your claims are inferior to those of no other human being."

"What tender and bewitching voices they have, Jasper!" resumed the guide, now laughing freely and naturally. "Yes, Natur' seems to have made them on purpose to sing in our ears when the music of the woods is silent! But we must come to a right understanding, we must. I ask you again, Mabel, if you had known that Jasper Western loves you as well as I do, or better perhaps—though that is scarce possible; that in his dreams he sees your face in the water of the lake; that he talks to you and of you in his sleep; fancies all that is beautiful like Mabel Dunham, and all that is good and virtuous; believes he never knowed happiness until he knowed you; could kiss the ground on which you have trod, and forgets all the joys of his calling to think of you, and of the delight of gazing at your beauty, and in listening to your voice, would you then have consented to marry me?"

Mabel could not have answered this question if she would; but, though her face was buried in her hands, the tint of the rushing blood was visible between the openings, and the suffusion seemed to impart itself to her very fingers. Still, Nature asserted her power, for there was a single instant when the astonished, almost terrified girl stole a glance at Jasper, as if distrusting Pathfinder's history of his feelings, read the truth of all he said in that furtive look, and instantly concealed her face again, as if she would hide it from observation forever.

"Take time to think, Mabel," the guide continued, "for it is a solemn thing to accept one man for a husband, while the thoughts and wishes lead to another. Jasper and I have talked this matter over freely and like old friends, and though I always knowed that we viewed most things pretty much alike, I couldn't have thought that we regarded any particular object with the very same eyes, as it might be, until we opened our minds to each other about you. Now, Jasper owns that the very first time he beheld you he thought you the sweetest and winningest creatur' he had ever met; that your voice sounded like murmuring water in his ears; that he fancied his sails were your garments, fluttering in the wind; that your laugh haunted him in his sleep; and that, ag'in and ag'in has he started up affrighted, because he has fancied some one wanted to force you out of the *Scud*, where he imagined you had taken up your abode. Nay, the lad has even acknowledged that he often weeps at the thought that you are likely to spend your days with another and not with him."

"Jasper!"

"It's solemn truth, Mabel, and it's right you should know it. Now stand up, and choose atween us. I do believe Eau-douce loves you as well as I do myself; he has tried to persuade me that he loves you better, but that I will not allow, for I do not think it possible; but I will own the boy loves you heart and soul, and he has a good right to be heard. The sergeant left me your protector, and not your tyrant. I told him that I would be a father

to you, as well as a husband, and it seems to me no feeling father would deny his child this small privilege. Stand up, Mabel, therefore, and speak your thoughts as freely as if I were the sergeant himself seeking your good, and nothing else."

Mabel dropped her hands, arose, and stood face to face with her two suitors, though the flush that was on her cheek was feverish, the evidence of excitement rather than of shame.

"What would you have, Pathfinder?" she asked. "Have I not already promised my poor father to do all you desire?"

"Then I desire this. Here I stand, a man of the forest, and of little l'arning, though I fear with an ambition beyond my desarts, and I'll do my endivors to do justice to both sides. In the first place, it is allowed that so far as feelings in your behalf are consarned we love you just the same; Jasper thinks his feelings *must* be the strongest, but this I cannot say, in honesty, for it doesn't seem to me that it *can* be true; else I would frankly and freely confess it, I would. So in this particular, Mabel, we are here before you on equal tarms. As for myself, being the oldest, I'll first say what little can be produced in my favor, as well as ag'in it. As a hunter, I do think there is no man near the lines than can outdo me. If venison or bear's meat, or even birds and fish, should ever be scarce in our cabin, it would be more likely to be owing to Natur' and Providence, than to any fault of mine. In short, it does seem to me that the woman who depended on me would never be likely to want for food. But I am fearful ignorant! It's true, I speak several tongues, such as they be, while I'm very far from being expart at my own. Then, my years are greater than your own, Mabel, and the circumstance that I was so long the sergeant's comrade can be no great merit in your eyes; I wish, too, I was more comely, I do; but we are all as Natur' made us, and the last thing that a man ought to lament, except on very special occasions, is his looks. When all is remembered, age, looks, l'arning, and habits, Mabel, conscience tells me I ought to confess that I'm altogether unfit for you, if not downright unworthy; and I would give up the hope, this minute, I would, if I didn't feel something pulling at my heart-strings which seems hard to undo."

"Pathfinder!—noble, generous Pathfinder!"—cried our heroine, seizing his hand, and kissing it with a species of holy reverence, "you do yourself injustice—you forget my poor father and your promise—you do not know *me!*"

"Now, here's Jasper," continued the guide, without allowing the girl's caresses to win him from his purpose; "with *him* the case is different. In the way of providing, as in that of loving, there's not much to choose atween us, for the lad is frugal, industrious, and careful. Then he is quite a scholar—knows the tongue of the Frenchers—reads many books, and some, I know, that you like to read yourself—can understand you at all times, which, perhaps, is more than I can say for myself."

"What of all this?"—interrupted Mabel, impatiently. "Why speak of it now—why speak of it at all?"

"Then the lad has a manner of letting his thoughts be known that I fear I can never equal. If there's anything on 'arth that would make my tongue bold and persuading, Mabel, I do think it's yourself; and yet, in our late conversations, Jasper has outdone me, even on this point, in a way to make me ashamed of myself. He has told me how simple you were, and how true-hearted, and kind-hearted; and how you looked down upon vanities, for though you might be the wife of more than one officer, as he thinks, that you cling to feeling, and would rather be true to yourself, and natur', than a colonel's lady. He fairly made my blood warm, he did, when he spoke of your having beauty without seeming ever to have looked upon it, and then the manner in which you moved about like a young fa'an, so nat'ral and so graceful like, without knowing it; and the truth and justice of your ideas, and the warmth and generosity of your heart——"

"Jasper!" interrupted Mabel, giving way to feelings that had gathered an ungovernable force by being so long pent, and falling into the young man's willing arms, weeping like a child, and almost as helpless. "Jasper!—Jasper!—why have you kept this from me?"

The answer of Eau-douce was not very intelligible, nor was the murmured dialogue that followed remarkable for coherency. But the language of affection is easily understood. The hour that succeeded passed like a very few minutes of ordinary life, so far as a computation of time was concerned; and when Mabel recollected herself, and bethought her of the existence of others, her uncle was pacing the cutter's deck in great impatience, and wondering why Jasper should be losing so much of a favorable wind. Her first thought was of him who was so likely to feel the recent betrayal of her real emotions.

"Oh! Jasper!" she exclaimed, like one suddenly self-convicted—"The Pathfinder."

Eau-douce fairly trembled, not with unmanly apprehension, but with the painful conviction of the pang he had given his friend; and he looked in all directions in the expectation of seeing his person. But Pathfinder had withdrawn, with a tact and delicacy that might have done credit to the sensibility and breeding of a courtier. For several minutes the two lovers sat silently awaiting his return, uncertain what propriety required of them, under circumstances so marked and so peculiar. At length they beheld their friend advancing slowly toward them, with a thoughtful and even pensive air.

"I now understand what you meant, Jasper, by speaking without a tongue, and hearing without an ear," he said, when close enough to the tree to be heard. "Yes, I understand it, now, I do, and a very pleasant sort of discourse it is, when one can hold it with Mabel Dunham. Ah's me! I told the sergeant I wasn't fit for her; that I was too old, too ignorant, and too wild, like—but he *would* have it otherwise."

Jasper and Mabel sat, resembling Milton's picture of our first parents, when the consciousness of sin first laid its leaden weight on their souls. Neither spoke, neither even moved; though both at that moment fancied they could part with their new-found happiness, in order to restore their friend to his peace of mind. Jasper was pale as death; but in Mabel, maiden modesty had caused the blood to mantle on her cheeks until their bloom was heightened to a richness that was scarce equaled in her hours of light-hearted buoyancy and joy. As the feeling, which, in her sex, always accompanies the security of love returned, threw its softness and tenderness over her countenance, she was singularly beautiful. Pathfinder gazed at her with an intenseness he did not endeavor to conceal, and then he fairly laughed in his own way, and with a sort of wild exultation, as men that are untutored are wont to express their delight. This momentary indulgence, however, was expiated by the pang that followed the sudden consciousness that this glorious young creature was lost to him forever. It required a full minute for this simple-minded being to recover from the shock of this conviction; and then he recovered his dignity of manner, speaking with gravity—almost with solemnity.

"I have always known, Mabel Dunham, that

men have their gifts," he said; "but I'd forgotten that it did not belong to mine to please the young, and beautiful, and l'arned. I hope the mistake has been no very heavy sin; and if it was, I've been heavily punished for it, I have. Nay, Mabel, I know what you'd say, but it's unnecessary; I feel it all, and that is as good as if I *heard* it all. I've had a bitter hour, Mabel—I've had a very bitter hour, lad——"

"Hour!" echoed Mabel, as the other first used the word, the tell-tale blood which had began to ebb toward her heart rushing again tumultuously to her very temples. "Surely not an hour, Pathfinder?"

"Hour!" exclaimed Jasper at the same instant—"no—no—my worthy friend, it is not ten minutes since you left us!"

"Well, it may be so; though to me it has seemed to be a day. I began to think, however, that the happy count time by minutes, and the miserable count it by months. But we will talk no more of this; it is all over now, and many words about it will make you no happier, while they will only tell me what I've lost; and quite likely how much I desarved to lose her. No—no—Mabel, 'tis useless to interrupt me; I admit it all, and your gainsaying it, though it be so well meant, cannot change my mind. Well, Jasper, she is yours; and though it's hard to think it, I do believe you'll make her happier than I could, for your gifts are better suited to do so, though I would have strived hard to do as much, if I knew myself, I would. I ought to have known better than to believe the sergeant; and I ought to have put faith in what Mabel told me at the head of the lake, for reason and judgment might have shown me its truth: but it is so pleasant to think what we wish, and mankind so easily overpersuade us when we overpersuade ourselves. But what's the use in talking of it, as I said afore? It's true, Mabel seemed to be consenting, though it all came from a wish to please her father, and from being skeary about the savages——"

"Pathfinder!"

"I understand you, Mabel, and have no hard feelings, I hav'n't. I sometimes think I should like to live in your neighborhood that I might look at your happiness; but on the whole it is better I should quit the Fifty-fifth altogether and go back to the Sixtieth, which is my natyve rejiment, as it might be. It would have been better, perhaps, had I never left, though my sarvices were much wanted in this quarter, and I'd been with some of the Fifty-fifth years agone—Sergeant Dunham, for instance, when he was in another corps. Still, Jasper, I do not regret that I have known you——"

"And me, Pathfinder!" impetuously interrupted Mabel—"do you regret having known *me?*—could I think so I should never be at peace with myself!"

"You, Mabel!" returned the guide, taking the hand of our heroine, and looking up into her countenance with guileless simplicity but earnest affection—"how could I be sorry that a ray of the sun came across the gloom of a cheerless day? that light has broken in upon darkness, though it remained so short a time? I do not flatter myself with being able to march quite as light-hearted as I once used to could, or to sleep as sound for some time to come; but I shall always remember how near I was to being undesarvedly happy, I shall. So far from blaming you, Mabel, I only blame myself for being so vain as to think it possible I could please such a creatur'; for sartainly you told me how it was when we talked it over on the mountain, and I ought to have believed you then; for I do suppose it's nat'ral that young women should know their own minds better than their fathers. Ah's me! It's settled now, and nothing remains but for me to take leave of you that you may depart; I feel that Master Cap must be impatient, and there is danger of his coming on shore to look for us all."

"To take leave!" exclaimed Mabel.

"Leave!" echoed Jasper, "you do not mean to quit us, my friend?"

"'Tis best, Mabel—'tis altogether best, Eau-douce; and it's wisest. I could live and die in your company if I only followed feeling; but if I follow reason, I shall quit you here. You will go back to Oswego, and become man and wife as soon as you arrive; for all that is determined with Master Cap, who hankers after the sea again, and who knows what is to happen: while I shall return to the wilderness and my Maker. Come, Mabel," continued Pathfinder, rising and drawing nearer to our heroine with grave decorum, "kiss me. Jasper will not grudge me one kiss: then we'll part."

"Oh! Pathfinder," exclaimed Mabel, falling into the arms of the guide and kissing his cheeks again and again, with a freedom and warmth she had been far from manifesting while held to the bosom of Jasper—"God bless you, dearest Pathfinder! You will come to us hereafter. We shall see you again. When old you will come to our dwelling and let me be a daughter to you?"

"Yes—that's it," returned the guide, almost gasping for breath; "I'll try to think of it in that way. You're more befitting to be my daughter than to be my wife, you are. Farewell, Jasper. Now we will go to the canoe; it's time you were on board."

The manner in which Pathfinder led the way to the shore was solemn and calm. As soon as he reached the canoe he again took Mabel by the hands, held her at the length of his own arms, and gazed wistfully into her face until the unbidden tears rolled out of the fountains of feeling, and trickled down his rugged cheeks in streams.

"Bless me, Pathfinder," said Mabel, kneeling reverently at his feet. "Oh! at least bless me before we part."

That untutored but noble-minded being did as she desired, and, aiding her to enter the canoe, seemed to tear himself away as one snaps a strong and obstinate cord. Before he retired, however, he took Jasper by the arm and led him a little aside, when he spoke as follows:

"You're kind of heart, and gentle by natur', Jasper; but we are both rough and wild, in comparison with that dear creatur'. Be careful of her, and never show the roughness of man's natur' to her soft disposition. You'll get to understand her in time; and the Lord who governs the lake and the forest alike—who looks upon virtue with a smile, and upon vice with a frown—keep you happy and worthy to be so!"

Pathfinder made a sign for his friends to depart; and he stood leaning on his rifle until the canoe had reached the side of the *Scud*. Mabel wept as if her heart would break; nor did her eyes once turn from the open spot in the glade, where the form of Pathfinder was to be seen, until the cutter had passed a point that completely shut out the island. When last in view, the sinewy frame of this extraordinary man was as motionless as if it were a statue set up in that solitary place to commemorate the scenes of which it has so lately been the witness.

---

4. *The Pioneers* (1823): *The Passenger Pigeons.* Here Natty, in 1793–94, in the period of Cooper's childhood, is an old man. In this, the next to the last tale in the Leatherstocking cycle, the thematic contrast between civilization and the wilderness is most sharply developed. For instance, the famous scene (from Chap. 22) of the wanton slaughter of the passenger pigeons by civilized men, which is given here, is in contrast, in the novel, to the punishment meted out to Natty by the civilized court for the crime of taking a deer for food.

From The Pioneers (1823)

If the heavens were alive with pigeons, the whole village seemed equally in motion with men, women, and children. Every species of fire-arms, from the French ducking-gun, with a barrel near six feet in length, to the common horseman's pistol, was to be seen in the hands of the men and boys; while bows and arrows, some made of the simple stick of walnut sapling, and others in a rude imitation of the ancient cross-bows, were carried by many of the latter.

The houses and the signs of life apparent in the village drove the alarmed birds, from the direct line of their flight, toward the mountains, along the sides and near the bases of which they were glancing in dense masses, equally wonderful by the rapidity of their motion, and their incredible numbers.

. . .

Among the sportsmen was the tall, gaunt form of Leatherstocking, walking over the field, with his rifle hanging on his arm, his dogs at his heels; the latter now scenting the dead or wounded birds that were beginning to tumble from the flocks, and then crouching under the legs of their master, as if they participated in his feelings at this wasteful and unsportsmanlike execution.

The reports of the fire-arms became rapid, whole volleys rising from the plain, as flocks of more than ordinary numbers darted over the opening, shadowing the field like a cloud; and then the light smoke of a single piece would issue from among the leafless bushes on the mountain, as death was hurled on the retreat of the affrighted birds, who were rising from a volley in a vain effort to escape. Arrows and missiles of every kind were in the midst of the flocks; and so numerous were the birds, and so low did they take their flight, that even long poles in the hands of those on the sides of the mountains were used to strike them to the earth.

During all this time Mr. Jones, who disdained the humble and ordinary means of destruction used by his companions, was busily occupied, aided by Benjamin, in making arrangements for an assault of more than ordinarily fatal character. Among the relics of the old military excursions, that occasionally are discovered throughout the different districts of the western part of New York, there had been found in Templeton, at its settlement, a small swivel, which would carry a ball of a pound weight. It was thought to have been deserted by a war party of the whites in one of their inroads into the Indian settlements, when, perhaps, convenience or their necessity induced them to leave such an incumbrance behind them in the woods. This miniature cannon had been released from the rust, and being mounted on little wheels, was now in a state for actual service. For several years it was the sole organ for extraordinary rejoicings used in those mountains. On the mornings of the Fourth of July it would be heard ringing among the hills; and even Captain Hollister, who was the highest authority in that part of the country on all such occasions, affirmed that, considering its dimensions, it was no despicable gun for a salute. It was somewhat the worse for the service it had performed, it is true, there being but a trifling difference in size between the touch-hole and the muzzle. Still, the grand conceptions of Richard had suggested the importance of such an instrument in hurling death at his nimble enemies. The swivel was dragged by a horse into a part of the open space that the sheriff thought most eligible for planting a battery of the kind, and Mr. Pump proceeded to load it. Several handfuls of duck-shot were placed on top of the powder, and the major-domo announced that his piece was ready for service.

. . .

Leatherstocking was a silent but uneasy spectator of all these proceedings, but was able to keep his sentiments to himself until he saw the introduction of the swivel into the sports.

"This comes of settling a country!" he said. "Here have I known the pigeon to fly for forty long years, and, till you made your clearings, there was nobody to skear or to hurt them. I loved to see them come into the woods, for they were company to a body, hurting nothing—being, as it was, as harmless as a garter-snake. But now it gives me sore thoughts when I hear the frighty things whizzing through the air, for I know it's only a motion to bring out all the brats of the village. Well, the Lord won't see the waste of his creatures for nothing, and right will be done to the pigeons, as well as others, by and by. There's Mr. Oliver, as bad as the rest of them, firing into the flocks as if he was shooting down nothing but Mingo warriors."

Among the sportsmen was Billy Kirby, who, armed with an old musket, was loading, and, without even looking into the air, was firing and shouting as his victims fell even on his own person. He heard the speech of Natty, and took upon himself to reply:

"What! old Leatherstocking," he cried, "grumbling at the loss of a few pigeons! If you had to sow your wheat twice, and three times, as I have done, you wouldn't be so massfully feeling toward the divils. Hurrah, boys! scatter the feathers! This is better than shooting at a turkey's head and neck, old fellow."

"It's better for you, maybe, Billy Kirby," replied the indignant old hunter, "and all them that don't know how to put a ball down a rifle barrel, or how to bring it up again with a true aim; but it's wicked to be shooting into flocks in this wasty manner, and none to do it who know how to knock over a single bird. If a body has a craving for pigeon's flesh, why, it's made the same as all other creatures, for man's eating; but not to kill twenty and eat one. When I want such a thing I go into the woods till I find one to my liking, and then I shoot him off the branches, without touching the feather of another, though there might be a hundred on the same tree. You couldn't do such a thing, Billy Kirby—you couldn't do it if you tried."

"What's that, old corn-stalk! you sapless stub!" cried the wood-chopper. "You have grown wordy, since the affair of the turkey; but if you are for a single shot, here goes at that bird which comes on by himself."

The fire from the distant part of the field had driven a single pigeon below the flock to which it belonged, and, frightened with the constant reports of the muskets, it was approaching the spot where the disputants stood, darting first from one side and then to the other, cutting the air with the swiftness of lightning, and making a noise with its wings not unlike the rushing of a bullet. Unfortunately for the wood-chopper, notwithstanding his vaunt, he did not see this bird until it was too late to fire as it approached, and he pulled the trigger at the unlucky moment when it was darting immediately over his head. The bird continued its course with the usual velocity.

Natty lowered his rifle from his arm when the challenge was made, and waiting a moment, until the terrified victim had got in a line with his eye, and had dropped near the bank of the lake, he raised it again with uncommon rapidity and fired. It might have been chance, or it might have been skill, that produced the result; it was probably a union of both; but the pigeon whirled over in the air, and fell into the lake with a broken wing. At the sound of his rifle, both his dogs started from his feet, and in a few minutes the "slut" brought out the bird, still alive.

The wonderful exploit of Leatherstocking was noised through the field with great rapidity, and the sportsmen gathered in to learn the truth of the report.

"What!" said young Edwards, "have you really killed a pigeon on the wing. Natty, with a single ball?"

"Haven't I killed loons before now, lad, that dive at the flash?" returned the hunter. "It's much better to kill only such as you want, without wasting your powder and lead, than to be firing into God's creatures in this wicked manner. But I came out for a bird, and you know the reason why I like small game, Mr. Oliver, and now I have got one I will go home, for I don't relish to see these wasty ways that you are all practysing, as if the least thing wasn't made for use, and not to destroy."

"Thou sayest well, Leatherstocking," cried Marmaduke, "and I begin to think it time to put an end to this work of destruction."

"Put an ind, Judge, to your clearings. A'n't the woods His work as well as the pigeons? Use, but don't waste. Wasn't the woods made for the beasts and birds to harbor in? and when man wanted their flesh, their skins, or their feathers, there's the place to seek them. But I'll go to the hut with my own game, for I wouldn't touch one of the harmless things that cover the ground here, looking up with their eyes on me as if they only wanted tongues to say their thoughts."

With this sentiment in his mouth, Leatherstocking threw his rifle over his arm, and, followed by his dogs, stepped across the clearing with great caution, taking care not to tread on one of the wounded birds in his path. He soon entered the bushes on the margin of the lake and was hid from view.

Whatever impression the morality of Natty made on the Judge, it was utterly lost on Richard. He availed himself of the gathering of the sportsmen to lay a plan for one "fell swoop" of destruction.

The musket men were drawn up in battle array, in a line extending on each side of his artillery, with orders to await the signal of firing from himself.

"Stand by, my lads," said Benjamin, who acted as an aid-de-camp on this occasion, "stand by, my hearties, and when Squire Dickens heaves out the signal to begin firing, d'ye see, you may open upon them in a broadside. Take care and fire low, boys, and you'll be sure to hull the flock."

"Fire low!" shouted Kirby: "hear the old fool! If we fire low, we may hit the stumps, but not ruffle a pigeon."

"How should you know, you lubber?" cried Benjamin, with a very unbecoming heat for an officer on the eve of battle—"how should you know, you grampus? Haven't I sailed aboard of the *Boadishy* for five years? and wasn't it a standing order to fire low, and to hull your enemy? Keep silence at your guns, boys, and mind the order that is passed."

The loud laughs of the musket men were silenced by the more authoritative voice of Richard, who called for attention and obedience to his signals.

Some millions of pigeons were supposed to have already passed that morning over the valley of Templeton; but nothing like the flock that was now approaching had been seen before. It extended from mountain to mountain in one solid blue mass, and the eye looked in vain, over the southern hills, to find its termination. The front of this living column was distinctly marked by a line but very slightly indented, so regular and even was the flight. Even Marmaduke forgot the morality of Leatherstocking as it approached, and, in common with the rest, brought his musket to a poise.

"Fire!" cried the sheriff, clapping a coal to the priming of the cannon. As half of Benjamin's charge escaped through the touch-hole, the whole volley of the musketry preceded the report of the swivel. On receiving this united discharge of small arms the front of the flock darted upward, while, at the same instant, myriads of those in the rear rushed with amazing rapidity into their places, so that, when the column of white smoke gushed from the mouth of the little cannon, an accumulated mass of objects was gliding over its point of direction. The roar of the gun echoed along the mountains, and died away to the north, like distant thunder, while the whole flock of alarmed birds seemed, for a moment, thrown into one disorderly and agitated mass. The air was filled with their irregular flight, layer rising above layer, far above the tops of the highest pines, none daring to advance beyond the dangerous pass; when, suddenly, some of the leaders of the feathered tribe shot across the valley, taking their flight directly over the village, and hundreds of thousands in their rear followed the example, deserting the eastern side of the plain to their persecutors and the slain.

"Victory!" shouted Richard, "victory! we have driven the enemy from the field."

"Not so, Dickon," said Marmaduke; "the field is covered with them; and, like the Leatherstocking, I see nothing but eyes, in every direction, as the innocent sufferers turn their heads in terror. Full one-half of those that have fallen are yet alive; and I think it is time to end the sport, if sport it be."

"Sport!" cried the sheriff; "it is princely sport!"

---

5. *The Prairie* (1827): *Two Deaths*. The first death is that of the squatter Ishmael Bush; and as the episode in *The Pioneers* of the slaughter of the pigeons is set against Natty's attitude toward nature, so here we find the character of Ishmael Bush serving the same function. Ishmael, like Hurry Harry and Hutter of *The Deerslayer*, is the type of brutal exploiter with no reverence for man or nature, setting up his own will against natural decency and the laws and sanctions of civilization. Rather, insofar as Ishmael draws on civilization, he uses only what will suit his will. For instance, he appeals to the worn fragments of a Bible in condemning his brother-in-law to death, finding there only a justification for his personal vengeance. Ishmael is, in one perspective, an example of the New England Puritanism that Cooper detested—using only a "fragment" of the Christian doctrine and tradition—the dire and vengeful part, with little emphasis on love, charity, and humility. And here we may indicate another parallel between Cooper and Faulkner, who regards his southern Puritans and Calvinists much as Cooper regards Ishmael. But Cooper, in spite of the unlovely role he assigns Ishmael, does recognize his integrity, toughness, and grandeur of scale, and therefore manages, in him, one of his most vital and impressive creations. Here is the episode (from Chap. 32) of the condemning and execution of the brother-in-law, who has murdered one of Ishmael's sons.

From The Prairie (1827)

When the squatter saw that all, even to the reviving Abiram, were busy in administering to their appetites, he gave his downcast partner a glance of his eye, and withdrew towards a distant roll of the land, which bounded the view towards the east. The meeting of the pair in this naked spot was like an interview held above the grave of their murdered son. Ishmael signed to his wife to take a seat beside him on a fragment of rock, and then followed a space during which neither seemed disposed to speak.

"We have journeyed together long, through good and bad," Ishmael at length commenced: "much have we had to try us, and some bitter cups have we been made to swallow, my woman; but nothing like this has ever before lain in my path."

"It is a heavy cross for a poor, misguided, and sinful woman to bear!" returned Esther, bowing her head to her knees, and partly concealing her face in her dress. "A heavy and a burdensome weight is this to be laid upon the shoulders of a sister and a mother!"

"Ay; therein lies the hardship of the case. I had brought my mind to the punishment of that houseless trapper, with no great strivings, for the man had done me few favors, and God forgive me if I suspected him wrongfully of much evil! This is, however, bringing shame in at one door of my cabin in order to drive it out at the other. But shall a son of mine be murdered, and he who did it go at large?—the boy would never rest!"

"Oh! Ishmael, we pushed the matter far! Had little been said, who would have been the wiser? Our consciences might then have been quiet."

"Eest'er," said the husband, turning on her a reproachful but still a dull regard, "the hour has been, my woman, when you thought another hand had done this wickedness."

"I did, I did! the Lord gave me the feeling as a punishment for my sins! but his mercy was not slow in lifting the veil; I looked into the book, Ishmael, and there I found the words of comfort."

"Have you that book at hand, woman? it may happen to advise in such a dreary business."

Esther fumbled in her pocket, and was not long in producing the fragment of a Bible which had been thumbed and smoke-dried till the print was nearly illegible. It was the only article in the nature of a book that was to be found among the chattels of the squatter, and it had been preserved by his wife as a melancholy relic of more prosperous, and possibly of more innocent days. She had long been in the habit of resorting to it under the pressure of such circumstances as were palpably beyond human redress, though her spirit and resolution rarely needed support under those that admitted of reparation through any of the ordinary means of reprisal. In this manner Esther had made a sort of convenient ally of the word of God; rarely troubling it for counsel, however, except when her own incompetency to avert an evil was too apparent to be disputed. We shall leave casuists to determine how far she resembled any other believers in this particular, and proceed directly with the matter before us.

"There are many awful passages in these pages, Ishmael," she said, when the volume was opened, and the leaves were slowly turning under her finger, "and some there ar' that teach the rules of punishment."

Her husband made a gesture for her to find one of those brief rules of conduct which have been received among all Christian nations as the direct mandates of the Creator, and which have been found so just, that even they who deny their high authority, admit their wisdom. Ishmael listened with grave attention as his companion read all those verses which her memory suggested, and which were thought applicable to the situation in which they found themselves. He made her show him the words, which he regarded with a sort of strange reverence. A resolution once taken was usually irrevocable in one who was moved with so much difficulty. He put his hand upon the book and closed the pages himself, as much as to apprise his wife that he was satisfied. Esther, who so well knew his character, trembled at the action, and casting a glance at his steady eye, she said—

"And yet, Ishmael, my blood and the blood of my children is in his veins! cannot mercy be shown?"

"Woman," he answered, sternly, "when we believed that miserable old trapper had done this deed, nothing was said of mercy!"

Esther made no reply, but folding her arms upon her breast she sat silent and thoughtful for many minutes. Then she once more turned her anxious gaze upon the countenance of her husband, where she found all passion and care apparently buried in the coldest apathy. Satisfied now that the fate of her brother was sealed, and possibly conscious how well he merited the punishment that was meditated, she no longer thought of mediation. No more words passed between them. Their eyes met for an instant, and then both arose and walked in profound silence towards the encampment.

The squatter found his children expecting his return in the usual listless manner with which they awaited all coming events. The cattle were already herded, and the horses in their gears in readiness to proceed, so soon as he should indicate that such was his pleasure. The children were already in their proper vehicle, and, in short, nothing delayed the departure but the absence of the parents of the wild brood.

"Abner," said the father, with the deliberation with which all his proceedings were characterized, "take the brother of your mother from the wagon, and let him stand on the 'arth."

Abiram issued from his place of concealment, trembling, it is true, but far from destitute of hopes as to his final success in appeasing the just resentment of his kinsman. After throwing a glance around him with the vain wish of finding a single countenance in which he might detect a solitary gleam of sympathy, he endeavored to smother those apprehensions that were by this time reviving in their original violence, by forcing a sort of friendly communication between himself and the squatter—

"The beasts are getting jaded, brother," he said; "and as we have made so good a march already, is it not time to 'camp? To my eye you may go far before a better place than this is found to pass the night in."

" 'Tis well you like it. Your tarry here ar' likely to be long. My sons, draw nigh and listen. Abiram White," he added, lifting his cap, and speaking with a solemnity and steadiness that rendered even his dull mien imposing, "you have slain my first-born, and according to the laws of God and man must you die!"

The kidnapper started at this terrible and sudden sentence, with the terror that one would exhibit who unexpectedly found himself in the grasp of a monster from whose power there was no retreat. Although filled with the most serious forebodings of what might be his lot, his courage had not been equal to look his danger in the face, and with the deceitful consolation with which timid tempers are apt to conceal their desperate condition from themselves, he had rather courted a treacherous relief in his cunning, than prepared himself for the worst.

"Die!" he repeated, in a voice that scarcely issued from his chest; "a man is surely safe among his kinsmen?"

"So thought my boy," returned the squatter, motioning for the team that contained his wife and the girls to proceed, as he very coolly examined the priming of his piece. "By the rifle did you destroy my son; it is fit and just that you meet your end by the same weapon."

Abiram stared about him with a gaze that bespoke an unsettled reason. He even laughed, as if he would not only persuade himself but others that what he heard was some pleasantry intended to try his nerves. But nowhere did his frightful merriment meet with an answering echo. All around was solemn and still. The visages of his nephews were excited, but cold towards him, and that of his former confederate frightfully determined. This very steadiness of mien was a thousand times more alarming and hopeless than any violence could have proved. The latter might possibly have touched his spirit and awakened resistance, but the former threw him entirely on the feeble resources of himself.

"Brother," he said, in a hurried, unnatural whisper, "did I hear you?"

"My words are plain, Abiram White: thou hast done murder, and for the same must thou die!"

"Esther! sister, sister, will you leave me! Oh! sister! do you hear my call?"

"I hear one speak from the grave!" returned the husky tones of Esther, as the wagon passed the spot where the criminal stood. "It is the voice of my first-born calling aloud for justice! God have mercy, God have mercy on your soul!"

The team slowly pursued its route, and the deserted Abiram now found himself deprived of the smallest vestige of hope. Still he could not summon fortitude to meet his death, and had not his limbs refused to aid him he would yet have attempted to fly. Then, by a sudden revolution from hope to utter despair, he fell upon his knees, and commenced a prayer in which cries for mercy to God and to his kinsman were wildly and blasphemously mingled. The sons of Ishmael turned away in horror at the disgusting spectacle, and even the stern nature of the squatter began to bend before so abject misery.

"May that which you ask of Him be granted," he said, "but a father can never forget a murdered child."

He was answered by the most humble appeals for time. A week, a day, an hour, were each implored with an earnestness commensurate to the value they receive when a whole life is compressed into their short duration. The squatter was troubled, and at length he yielded in part to the petitions of the criminal. His final purpose was not altered, though he changed the means. "Abner," he said, "mount the rock and look on every side that we may be sure none are nigh."

While his nephew was obeying this order, gleams of reviving hope were seen shooting across the quivering features of the kidnapper. The report was favorable, nothing having life, the retiring teams excepted, was to be seen. A messenger was, however, coming from the latter in great apparent haste. Ishmael awaited its arrival. He received from the hands of one of his wondering and frighted girls a fragment of that book which Esther had preserved with so much care. The squatter beckoned the child away, and placed the leaves in the hands of the criminal.

"Eest'er has sent you this," he said, "that in your last moments you may remember God."

"Bless her, bless her! a good and kind sister has she been to me! But time must be given that I may read: time, my brother, time!"

"Time shall not be wanting. You shall be your own executioner, and this miserable office shall pass away from my hands."

Ishmael proceeded to put his new resolution in force. The immediate apprehensions of the kidnapper were quieted by an assurance that he might yet live for days, though his punishment was inevitable. A reprieve to one abject and wretched as Abiram, temporarily produced the same effects as a pardon. He was even foremost in assisting in the appalling arrangements, and of all the actors in that solemn tragedy, his voice alone was facetious and jocular.

A thin shelf of the rock projected beneath one of the ragged arms of the willow. It was many feet from the ground, and admirably adapted to the purpose which, in fact, its appearance had suggested. On this little platform the criminal was placed, his arms bound at the elbows behind his back, beyond the possibility of liberation, with a proper cord leading from his neck to the limb of the tree. The latter was so placed, that when suspended the body could find no foot-hold. The fragment of the Bible was placed in his hands, and he was left to seek his consolation as he might from its pages.

"And now, Abiram White," said the squatter, when his sons had descended from completing this arrangement, "I give you a last and solemn asking. Death is before you in two shapes. With this rifle can your misery be cut short, or by that cord, sooner or later, must you meet your end."

"Let me yet live! Oh, Ishmael, you know not how sweet life is when the last moment draws so nigh!"

" 'Tis done," said the squatter, motioning for his assistants to follow the herds and teams. "And now, miserable man, that it may prove a consolation to your end, I forgive you my wrongs and leave you to your God."

Ishmael turned and pursued his way across the plain at his ordinary sluggish and ponderous gait. Though his head was bent a little towards the earth, his inactive mind did not prompt him to cast a look behind. Once, indeed, he thought he heard his name called in tones that were a little smothered, but they failed to make him pause.

At the spot where he and Esther had conferred he reached the boundary of the visible horizon from the rock. Here he stopped, and ventured a glance in the direction of the place he had just quitted. The sun was near dipping into the plains beyond, and its last rays lighted the naked branches of the willow. He saw the ragged outline of the whole drawn against the glowing heavens, and he even traced the still upright form of the being he had left to his misery. Turning the roll of the swell, he proceeded with the feelings of one who had been suddenly and violently separated from a recent confederate for ever.

Within a mile the squatter overtook his teams. His sons had found a place suited to the encampment for the night, and merely awaited his approach to confirm their choice. Few words were necessary to express his acquiescence. Everything passed in a silence more general and remarkable than ever. The chidings of Esther were not heard among her young, or if heard, they were more in the tones of softened admonition than in her usual upbraiding key.

No questions nor explanations passed between the husband and his wife. It was only as the latter was about to withdraw among her children for the night, that the former saw her taking a furtive look at the pan of his rifle. Ishmael bade his sons seek their rest, announcing his intention to look to the safety of the camp in person. When all was still, he walked out upon the prairie with a sort of sensation that he found his breathing among the tents too straitened. The night was well adapted to heighten the feelings which had been created by the events of the day.

The wind had risen with the moon, and it was occasionally sweeping over the plain in a manner that made it not difficult for the sentinel to imagine strange and unearthly sounds were mingling in the blasts. Yielding to the extraordinary impulses of which he was the subject, he cast a glance around to see that all were slumbering in security, and then he strayed towards the swell of land already mentioned. Here the squatter found himself at a point that commanded a view to the east and to the west. Light fleecy clouds were driving before the moon, which was cold and watery, though there were moments when its placid rays were shed from clear blue fields, seeming to soften objects to its own mild loveliness.

For the first time, in a life of so much wild adventure, Ishmael felt a keen sense of solitude. The naked prairies began to assume the forms of illimitable and dreary wastes, and the rushing of the wind sounded like the whisperings of the dead. It was not long before he thought a shriek was borne past him on a blast. It did not sound like a call from earth, but it swept frightfully through the upper air, mingled with the hoarse accompaniment of the wind. The teeth of the squatter were compressed, and his huge hand grasped the rifle, as if it would crush the metal. Then came a lull, a fresher blast, and a cry of horror that seemed to have been uttered at the very portals of his ears. A sort of echo burst involuntarily from his own lips, as men shout under unnatural excitement, and throwing his rifle across his shoulder, he proceeded towards the rock with the strides of a giant.

It was not often that the blood of Ishmael moved at the rate with which the fluid circulates in the veins of ordinary men; but now he felt it ready to gush from every pore in his body. The animal was aroused, in his most latent energies. Even as he advanced he heard those shrieks, which sometimes seemed ringing among the clouds, and sometimes passed so nigh, as to appear to brush the earth. At length there came a cry in which there could be no delusion, or to which the imagination could lend no horror. It appeared to fill each cranny of the air, as the visible horizon is often charged to fulness by one dazzling flash of the electric fluid. The name of God was distinctly audible, but it was awfully and blasphemously blended with sounds that may not be repeated.

The squatter stopped, and for a moment he covered his ears with his hands. When he withdrew the latter, a low and husky voice at his elbow asked in smothered tones—

"Ishmael, my man, heard ye nothing?"

"Hist!" returned the husband, laying a powerful arm on Esther, without manifesting the smallest surprise at the unlooked-for presence of his wife. "Hist, woman! if you have the fear of Heaven, be still!"

A profound silence succeeded. Though the wind rose and fell as before, its rushing was no longer mingled with those fearful cries. The sounds were imposing and solemn, but it was the solemnity and majesty of nature.

"Let us go on," said Esther; "all is hushed."

"Woman, what has brought you here?" demanded her husband, whose blood had returned into its former channels, and whose thoughts had already lost a portion of their excitement.

"Ishmael, he murdered our first-born: but it is not meet that the son of my mother should lie upon the ground, like the carrion of a dog."

"Follow!" returned the squatter, again grasping his rifle, and striding towards the rock. The distance was still considerable; and their approach, as they drew nigh the place of execution, was moderated by awe. Many minutes had passed before they reached a spot where they might distinguish the outlines of the dusky objects.

"Where have you put the body?" whispered Esther. "See, here are pick and spade, that a brother of mine may sleep in the bosom of the earth!"

The moon broke from behind a mass of clouds, and the eye of the woman was enabled to follow the finger of Ishmael. It pointed to a human form swinging in the wind, beneath the ragged and shining arm of the willow. Esther bent her head and veiled her eyes from the sight. But Ishmael drew nigher, and long contemplated his work in awe, though not in compunction. The leaves of the sacred book were scattered on the ground, and even a fragment of the shelf had been displaced by the kidnapper in his agony. But all was now in the stillness of death. The grim and convulsed countenance of the victim was at times brought full into the light of the moon, and again as the wind lulled, the fatal rope drew a dark line across its bright disk. The squatter raised his rifle with extreme care, and fired. The cord was cut, and the body came lumbering to the earth, a heavy and insensible mass.

Until now Esther had not moved nor spoken. But her hand was not slow to assist in the labor of the hour. The grave was soon dug. It was instantly made to receive its miserable tenant. As the lifeless form descended, Esther, who sustained the head, looked up into the face of her husband with an expression of anguish, and said—

"Ishmael, my man, it is very terrible! I cannot kiss the corpse of my father's child!"

The squatter laid his broad hand on the bosom of the dead, and said—

"Abiram White, we all have need of mercy; from my soul do I forgive you! May God in Heaven have pity on your sins!"

The woman bowed her face, and imprinted her lips long and fervently on the pallid forehead of her brother. After this came the falling clods and all the solemn sounds of filling a grave. Esther lingered on her knees, and Ishmael stood uncovered while the woman muttered a prayer. All was then finished.

The Death of Natty. In time of composition, this is only the third novel of the Leather-stocking cycle, but in point of action is the last. Now the aged Natty, just after acquisition of the Louisiana Territory (1803), having been driven from his old Glimmerglass by the settlement of Judge Temple, appears on the western plains. The character of Natty is nowhere so completely rendered as here, with full recognition of the realistic and humorous aspects (he is, after all, ignorant, garrulous, and somewhat vain), as well as the heroic and symbolic. And the episode of his death, in the presence of another kind of hero, the young soldier-explorer Middleton (who is a shadow image of Meriwether Lewis), is one of the most moving scenes in American fiction. The extract given here opens as Middleton rides into the camp of the Indians with whom Natty has spent his last days.

When they entered the town, its inhabitants were seen collected in an open space, where they were arranged with the customary deference to age and rank. The whole formed a large circle, in the centre of which were perhaps a dozen of the principal chiefs. Hard-Heart waved his hand as he approached, and, as the mass of bodies opened he rode through, followed by his companions. Here they dismounted; and as the beasts were led apart, the strangers found themselves environed by a thousand grave, composed, but solicitous faces.

Middleton gazed about him in growing concern, for no cry, no song, no shout welcomed him among a people, from whom he had so lately parted with regret. His uneasiness, not to say apprehensions, was shared by all his followers. Determination and stern resolution began to assume the place of anxiety in every eye, as each man silently felt for his arms, and assured himself that his several weapons were in a state for service. But there was no answering symptom of hostility on the part of their hosts. Hard-Heart beckoned for Middleton and Paul to follow, leading the way towards the cluster of forms that occupied the centre of the circle. Here the visitors found a solution of all the movements which had given them so much reason for apprehension.

The trapper was placed on a rude seat, which had been made, with studied care, to support his frame in an upright and easy attitude. The first glance of the eye told his former friends, that the old man was at length called upon to pay the last tribute of nature. His eye was glazed, and apparently as devoid of sight as of expression. His features were a little more sunken and strongly marked than formerly; but there, all change, so far as exterior was concerned, might be said to have ceased. His approaching end was not to be ascribed to any positive disease, but had been a gradual and mild decay of the physical powers. Life, it is true, still lingered in his system; but it was as if at times entirely ready to depart, and then it would appear to re-animate the sinking form, reluctant to give up the possession of a tenement that had never been corrupted by vice or undermined by disease. It would have been no violent fancy to have imagined that the spirit fluttered about the placid lips of the old woodsman, reluctant to depart from a shell that had so long given it an honest and honorable shelter.

His body was placed so as to let the light of the setting sun fall full upon the solemn features. His head was bare, the long thin locks of grey fluttering lightly in the evening breeze. His rifle lay upon his knee, and the other accoutrements of the chase were placed at his side, within reach of his hand. Between his feet lay the figure of a hound, with its head crouching to the earth, as if it slumbered; and so perfectly easy and natural was its position,

that a second glance was necessary to tell Middleton he saw only the skin of Hector, stuffed, by Indian tenderness and ingenuity, in a manner to represent the living animal. His own dog was playing at a distance with the child of Tachechana and Mahtoree. The mother herself stood at hand, holding in her arms a second offspring, that might boast of a parentage no less honorable than that which belonged to the son of Hard-Heart. Le Balafré was seated nigh the dying trapper, with every mark about his person that the hour of his own departure was not far distant. The rest of those immediately in the centre were aged men, who had apparently drawn near in order to observe the manner in which a just and fearless warrior would depart on the greatest of his journeys.

The old man was reaping the rewards of a life remarkable for temperance and activity, in a tranquil and placid death. His vigor in a manner endured to the very last. Decay, when it did occur, was rapid, but free from pain. He had hunted with the tribe in the spring, and even throughout most of the summer; when his limbs suddenly refused to perform their customary offices. A sympathizing weakness took possession of all his faculties; and the Pawnees believed that they were going to lose, in this unexpected manner, a sage and counsellor whom they had begun both to love and respect. But, as we have already said, the immortal occupant seemed unwilling to desert its tenement. The lamp of life flickered, without becoming extinguished. On the morning of the day on which Middleton arrived, there was a general reviving of the powers of the whole man. His tongue was again heard in wholesome maxims, and his eye from time to time recognised the persons of his friends. It merely proved to be a brief and final intercourse with the world, on the part of one who had already been considered, as to mental communion, to have taken his leave of it for ever.

When he had placed his guests in front of the dying man, Hard-Heart, after a pause, that proceeded as much from sorrow as decorum, leaned a little forward, and demanded—

"Does my father hear the words of his son?"

"Speak," returned the trapper, in tones that issued from his chest, but which were rendered awfully distinct by the stillness that reigned in the place. "I am about to depart from the village of the Loups, and shortly shall be beyond the reach of your voice."

"Let the wise chief have no cares for his journey," continued Hard-Heart, with an earnest solicitude that led him to forget, for the moment, that others were waiting to address his adopted parent; "a hundred Loups shall clear his path from briers."

"Pawnee, I die, as I have lived, a Christian man!" resumed the trapper, with a force of voice that had the same startling effect on his hearers as is produced by the trumpet, when its blast rises suddenly and freely on the air, after its obstructed sounds have been heard struggling in the distance: "as I came into life so will I leave it. Horses and arms are not needed to stand in the presence of the Great Spirit of my people. He knows my color, and according to my gifts will he judge my deeds."

"My father will tell my young men how many Mingoes he has struck, and what acts of valor and justice he has done, that they may know how to imitate him."

"A boastful tongue is not heard in the heaven of a white man!" solemnly returned the old man. "What I have done He has seen. His eyes are always open. That which has been well done will he remember; wherein I have been wrong will he not forget to chastise, though he will do the same in mercy. No, my son; a Pale-face may not sing his own praises, and hope to have them acceptable before his God!"

A little disappointed, the young partisan stepped modestly back, making way for the recent comers to approach. Middleton took one of the meagre hands of the trapper, and struggling to command his voice, he succeeded in announcing his presence.

The old man listened like one whose thoughts were dwelling on a very different subject; but when the other had succeeded in making him understand that he was present, an expression of joyful recognition passed over his faded features.

"I hope you have not so soon forgotten those whom you so materially served!" Middleton concluded. "It would pain me to think my hold on your memory was so light."

"Little that I have ever seen is forgotten," returned the trapper: "I am at the close of many weary days, but there is not one among them all that I could wish to overlook. I remember you, with the whole of your company; ay, and your gran'ther, that went before you. I am glad that you have come back upon these plains, for I had need of one who speaks the English, since little faith can be put in the traders of these regions. Will you do a favor to an old and dying man?"

"Name it," said Middleton; "it shall be done."

"It is a far journey to send such trifles," resumed the old man, who spoke at short intervals, as strength and breath permitted; "a far and weary journey is the same; but kindnesses and friendships are things not to be forgotten. There is a settlement among the Otsego hills—"

"I know the place," interrupted Middleton, observing that he spoke with increasing difficulty; "proceed to tell me what you would have done."

"Take this rifle, and pouch, and horn, and send them to the person whose name is graven on the plates of the stock,—a trader cut the letters with his knife,—for it is long that I have intended to send him such a token of my love!"

"It shall be so. Is there more that you could wish?"

"Little else have I to bestow. My traps I give to my Indian son; for honestly and kindly has he kept his faith. Let him stand before me."

Middleton explained to the chief what the trapper had said, and relinquished his own place to the other.

"Pawnee," continued the old man, always changing his language to suit the person he addressed, and not unfrequently according to the ideas he expressed, "it is a custom of my people for the father to leave his blessing with the son before he shuts his eyes for ever. This blessing I give to you; take it; for the prayers of a Christian man will never make the path of a just warrior to the blessed prairies either longer or more tangled. May the God of a white man look on your deeds with friendly eyes, and may you never commit an act that shall cause him to darken his face. I know not whether we shall ever meet again. There are many traditions concerning the place of Good Spirits. It is not for one like me, old and experienced though I am, to set up my opinions against a nation's. You believe in the blessed prairies, and I have faith in the sayings of my fathers. If both are true our parting will be final; but if it should prove that the same meaning is hid under different words, we shall yet stand together, Pawnee, before the face of your Wahcondah, who will then be no other than my God. There is much to be said in favor of both religions, for each seems suited to its own people, and no doubt it was so intended. I fear I have not altogether followed the gifts of my color, inasmuch as I find it a little painful to give up for ever the use of the rifle, and the comforts of the chase. But then the fault has been my own, seeing that it could not have been His. Ay, Hector," he continued, leaning forward a little, and feeling for the ears of the hound, "our parting has come at last, dog, and it will be a long hunt. You have been an honest, and a bold, and a faithful hound. Pawnee, you cannot slay the pup on my grave, for where a Christian dog falls there he lies for ever; but you can be kind to him after I am gone, for the love you bear his master."

"The words of my father are in my ears," returned the young partisan, making a grave and respectful gesture of assent.

"Do you hear what the chief has promised, dog!" demanded the trapper, making an effort to attract the notice of the insensible effigy of his hound. Receiving no answering look, nor hearing any friendly whine, the old man felt for the mouth, and endeavored to force his hand between the cold lips. The truth then flashed upon him, although he was far from perceiving the whole extent of the deception. Falling back in his seat, he hung his head, like one who felt a severe and unexpected shock. Profiting by this momentary forgetfulness, two young Indians removed the skin with the same delicacy of feeling that had induced them to attempt the pious fraud.

"The dog is dead!" muttered the trapper, after a pause of many minutes; "a hound has his time as well as a man; and well has he filled his days! Captain," he added, making an effort to wave his hand for Middleton, "I am glad you have come; for though kind, and well meaning according to the gifts of their color, these Indians are not the men to lay the head of a white man in his grave. I have been thinking, too, of this dog at my feet; it will not do to set forth the opinion that a Christian can expect to meet his hound again; still there can be little harm in placing what is left of so faithful a servant nigh the bones of his master."

"It shall be as you desire."

"I'm glad you think with me in this matter. In order, then, to save labor, lay the pup at my feet; or for that matter, put him side by side. A hunter need never be ashamed to be found in company with his dog!"

"I charge myself with your wish."

The old man made a long, and apparently a musing pause. At times he raised his eyes wistfully, as if he would again address Middleton, but some innate feeling appeared always to suppress his words. The other, who observed his hesitation, inquired in a way most likely to encourage him to proceed whether there was aught else that he could wish to have done.

"I am without kith or kin in the wide world!" the trapper answered: "when I am gone there will be an end of my race. We have never been chiefs; but honest, and useful in our way. I hope it cannot be denied we have always proved ourselves. My father lies buried near the sea, and the bones of his son will whiten on the prairies—"

"Name the spot, and your remains shall be placed by the side of your father," interrupted Middleton.

"Not so, not so, Captain. Let me sleep where I have lived—beyond the din of the settlements! Still I see no need why the grave of an honest man should be hid, like a Red-skin in his ambushment. I paid a man in the settlements to make and put a graven stone at the head of my father's resting-place. It was of the value of twelve beaver-skins, and cunningly and curiously was it carved! Then it told to all comers that the body of such a Christian lay beneath; and it spoke of his manner of life, of his years, and of his honesty. When we had done with the Frenchers in the old war I made a journey to the spot, in order to see that all was rightly performed, and glad I am to say, the workman had not forgotten his faith."

"And such a stone you would have at your grave!"

"I! no, no, I have no son but Hard-Heart, and it is little that an Indian knows of white fashions and usages. Besides, I am his debtor already, seeing it is so little I have done since I have lived in his tribe. The rifle might bring the value of such a thing—but then I know it will give the boy pleasure to hang the piece in his hall, for many is the deer and the bird that he has seen it destroy. No, no, the gun must be sent to him whose name is graven on the lock!"

"But there is one who would gladly prove his affection in the way you wish; he who owes you not only his own deliverance from so many dangers, but who inherits a heavy debt of gratitude from his ancestors. The stone shall be put at the head of your grave."

The old man extended his emaciated hand, and gave the other a squeeze of thanks.

"I thought you might be willing to do it, but I was backward in asking the favor," he said, "seeing that you are not of my kin. Put no boastful words on the same, but just the name, the age, and the time of the death, with something from the holy book; no more, no more. My name will then not be altogether lost on 'arth; I need no more."

Middleton intimated his assent, and then followed a pause that was only broken by distant and broken sentences from the dying man. He appeared now to have closed his accounts with the world, and to await merely for the final summons to quit it. Middleton and Hard-Heart placed themselves on the opposite sides of his seat, and watched with melancholy solicitude, the variations of his countenance. For two hours there was no very sensible alteration. The expression of his faded and time-worn features was that of a calm and dignified repose. From time to time he spoke, uttering some brief sentence in the way of advice, or asking some simple questions concerning those in whose fortunes he took a friendly interest. During the whole of that solemn and anxious period each individual of the tribe kept his place, in the most self-restrained patience. When the old man spoke, all bent their heads to listen; and when his words were uttered, they seemed to ponder on their wisdom and usefulness.

As the flame drew nigher to the socket his voice was hushed, and there were moments when his attendants doubted whether he still belonged to the living. Middleton, who watched each wavering expression of his weather-beaten visage, with the interest of a keen observer of human nature, softened by the tenderness of personal regard, fancied he could read the workings of the old man's soul in the strong lineaments of his countenance. Perhaps what the enlightened soldier took for the delusion of mistaken opinion did actually occur—for who has returned from that unknown world to explain by what forms, and in what manner, he was introduced into its awful precincts? Without pretending to explain what must ever be a mystery to the quick, we shall simply relate facts as they occurred.

The trapper had remained nearly motionless for an hour. His eyes alone had occasionally opened and shut. When opened, his gaze seemed fastened on the clouds which hung around the western horizon, reflecting the bright colors, and giving form and loveliness to the glorious tints of an American sunset. The hour—the calm beauty of the season—the occasion, all conspired to fill the spectators with solemn awe. Suddenly, while musing on the remarkable position in which he was placed,

Middleton felt the hand which he held grasp his own with incredible power, and the old man, supported on either side by his friends, rose upright to his feet. For a moment he looked about him, as if to invite all in presence to listen (the lingering remnant of human frailty), and then, with a fine military elevation of the head, and with a voice that might be heard in every part of that numerous assembly, he pronounced the word—

"Here!"

A movement so entirely unexpected, and the air of grandeur and humility which were so remarkably united in the mien of the trapper, together with the clear and uncommon force of his utterance, produced a short period of confusion in the faculties of all present. When Middleton and Hard-Heart, each of whom had involuntarily extended a hand to support the form of the old man, turned to him again, they found that the subject of their interest was removed for ever beyond the necessity of their care. They mournfully placed the body in its seat, and Le Balafré arose to announce the termination of the scene to the tribe. The voice of the old Indian seemed a sort of echo from that invisible world to which the meek spirit of the trapper had just departed.

"A valiant, a just, and a wise warrior, has gone on the path which will lead him to the blessed grounds of his people!" he said. "When the voice of the Wahcondah called him, he was ready to answer. Go, my children; remember the just chief of the Pale-faces, and clear your own tracks from briars!"

The grave was made beneath the shade of some noble oaks. It has been carefully watched to the present hour by the Pawnees of the Loup, and is often shown to the traveller and the trader as a spot where a just Whiteman sleeps. In due time the stone was placed at its head, with the simple inscription, which the trapper had himself requested. The only liberty, taken by Middleton, was to add—*"May no wanton hand ever disturb his remains!"*

COOPER AS A SOCIAL CRITIC

As we have pointed out, Cooper's fiction, even the Leatherstocking series, is heavily charged with criticism of American society. But *The American Democrat*, an analysis of American government and society, published in 1838, in the period after his return from Europe when Cooper was writing such novels as *Homeward Bound* and *Home As Found*, and was engaged in a long series of libel suits against the Whig newspapers, is the most succinct and systematic statement of his views.

It is clear that Cooper does not share the mystique of democracy which we shall often encounter in American literature—for example, in Whitman. Rather, he sees democracy as a practical arrangement for government, subject to special limitations and special hazards, a view which will later be encountered in the work of such writers as James Russell Lowell, Herman Melville, Henry James, Justice Holmes, T. S. Eliot, and Edmund Wilson. Cooper's basic position is set forth in his introduction to *The American Democrat*:

> The writer believes himself to be as good a democrat as there is in America. But his democracy is not of the impractical school. He prefers a democracy to any other system, on account of its comparative advantages, and not on account of its perfection.

The point to remember is that Cooper was criticizing democracy in order to defend democracy against its own defects.

From The American Democrat (1838)

ON THE DISADVANTAGES OF DEMOCRACY

Democracies are liable to popular impulses, which, necessarily arising from imperfect information, often work injustice from good motives. Tumults of the people are less apt to occur in democracies than under any other form of government, for, possessing the legal means of redressing themselves, there is less necessity to resort to force, but, public opinion constituting, virtually, the power of the state, measures are more apt to be influenced by sudden mutations of sentiment, than under systems where the rulers have better opportunities and more leisure for examination. There is more feeling and less design in the movements of masses than in those of small bodies, except as design emanates from demagogues and political managers.

The efforts of the masses that are struggling to obtain their rights, in monarchies and aristocracies, however, are not to be imputed to democracy; in such cases, the people use their natural weapon, force, merely because they are denied any participation in the legal authority.

When democracies are small, these impulses frequently do great injury to the public service, but in large states they are seldom of sufficient extent to produce results before there is time to feel the influence of reason. It is, therefore, one of the errors of politicians to imagine democracies more practicable in small than in large communities, an error that has probably arisen from the fact that, the ignorance of masses having hitherto put men at the mercy of the combinations of the affluent and intelligent, democracies have been permitted to exist only in countries insignificant by their wealth and numbers.

Large democracies, on the other hand, while less exposed to the principal evil of this form of government, than smaller, are unable to scrutinize and understand character with the severity and intelligence that are of so much importance in all representative governments, and consequently the people are peculiarly exposed to become the dupes of demagogues and political schemers, most of the crimes of democracies arising from the faults and designs of men of this character, rather than from the propensities of the people, who, having little temptation to do wrong, are seldom guilty of crimes except through ignorance.

Democracies are necessarily controlled by publick opinion, and failing of the means of obtaining power more honestly, the fraudulent and ambitious find a motive to mislead, and even to corrupt the common sentiment, to attain their ends. This is the greatest and most pervading danger of all large democracies, since it is sapping the foundations of society, by undermining its virtue. We see the effects of this baneful influence, in the openness and audacity with which men avow improper motives and improper acts, trusting to find support in a popular feeling, for while vicious influences are perhaps more admitted in other countries, than in America, in none are they so openly avowed.

It may also be urged against democracies, that, nothing being more corrupting than the management of human affairs, which are constantly demanding sacrifices of permanent principles to interests that are as constantly fluctuating, their people are exposed to assaults on their morals from this quarter, that the masses of other nations escape. It is probable, however, that this evil, while it ought properly to be enumerated as one of the disadvantages of the system, is more than counterbalanced by the main results, even on the score of morals.

The constant appeals to public opinion in a democracy, though excellent as a corrective of public vices, induce private hypocrisy, causing men to conceal their own convictions when opposed to those of the mass, the latter being seldom wholly right, or wholly wrong. A want of national manliness is a vice to be guarded against, for the man who would dare to resist a monarch, shrinks from opposing an entire community. That the latter is quite often wrong, however, is abundantly proved by the fact, that its own judgments fluctuate, as it reasons and thinks differently this year, or this month even, from what it reasoned and thought the last.

The tendency of democracies is, in all things, to mediocrity, since the tastes, knowledge and principles of the majority form the tribunal of appeal. This circumstance, while it certainly serves to elevate the average qualities of a nation, renders the introduction of a high standard difficult. Thus do we find in literature, the arts, architecture and in all acquired knowledge, a tendency in America to gravitate towards the common center in this, as in other things; lending a value and estimation to mediocrity that are not elsewhere given. It is fair to expect, however, that a foundation so broad, may in time sustain a superstructure of commensurate proportions, and that the influence of masses will in this, as in the other interests, have a generally beneficial effect. Still it should not be forgotten that, with the exception of those works, of which, as they appeal to human sympathies or the practices of men, an intelligent public is the best judge, the mass of no community is qualified to decide the most correctly on any thing, which, in its nature, is above its reach.

It is a besetting vice of democracies to substitute publick opinion for law. This is the usual form in which masses of men exhibit their tyranny. When the majority of the entire community commits this fault it is a sore grievance, but when local bodies, influenced by local interests, pretend to style themselves the publick, they are assuming powers that properly belong to the whole body of the people, and to them only under constitutional limitations. No tyranny of one, nor any tyranny of the few, is worse than this. All attempts in the publick, therefore, to do that which the publick has no right to do, should be frowned upon as the precise form in which tyranny is the most apt to be displayed in a democracy.

Democracies, depending so much on popular opinion are more liable to be influenced to their injury, through the management of foreign and hostile nations, than other governments. It is generally known that, in Europe, secret means are resorted to, to influence sentiment in this way, and we have witnessed in this country open appeals to the people, against the acts of their servants, in matters of foreign relations, made by foreign, not to say, hostile agents. Perhaps no stronger case can be cited of this weakness on the part of democracies, than is shown in this fact, for here we find men sufficiently audacious to build the hope of so far abusing opinion, as to persuade a people to act directly against their own dignity and interests.

The misleading of publick opinion in one way or another, is the parent of the principal disadvantages of a democracy, for in most instances it is first corrupting a community in order that it may be otherwise injured. Were it not for the counteracting influence of reason, which, in the end, seldom, perhaps never fails to assert its power, this defect would of itself, be sufficient to induce all discreet men to decide against ths form of government. The greater the danger, the greater the necessity that all well-intentioned and right-minded citizens should be on their guard against its influence.

It would be hazardous, however, to impute all the peculiar faults of American character, to the institutions, the country existing under so many unusual influences. If the latter were overlooked, one might be induced to think frankness and sincerity of character were less encouraged by popular institutions than was formerly supposed, close observers affirming that these qualities are less frequent here, than in most other countries. When the general ease of society is remembered, there is unquestionably more deception of opinion practised than one would naturally expect, but this failing is properly to be imputed to causes that have no necessary connection with democratical institutions, though men defer to publick opinion, right or wrong, quite as submissively as they defer to princes. Although truths are not smothered altogether in democracies, they are often temporarily abandoned under this malign influence, unless there is a powerful motive to sustain them at the moment. While we see in our own democracy this manifest disposition to defer to the wrong, in matters that are not properly subject to the common sentiment, in deference to the popular will of the hour, there is a singular boldness in the use of personalities, as if men avenged themselves for the restraints of the one case by a licentiousness that is without hazard.

The base feelings of detraction and envy have more room for exhibition, and perhaps a stronger incentive in a democracy, than in other forms of government, in which the people get accustomed to personal deference by the artificial distinctions of the institutions. This is the reason that men become impatient of all superiority in a democracy, and manifest a wish to prefer those who affect a deference to the publick, rather than those who are worthy.

ON THE PUBLICK

There is a disposition, under popular governments, to mistake the nature and authority of the publick. Publick opinion, as a matter of course, can only refer to that portion of the community that has cognizance of the particular circumstances it affects, but in all matters of law, of rights, and of principles, as they are connected with the general relations of society, the publick means the entire constituency, and that, too, only as it is authorized to act, by the fundamental laws, or the constitution. Thus the citizen who asserts his legal rights in opposition to the wishes of a neighborhood, is not opposing the publick, but maintaining its intentions, while the particular neighborhood is arrogating to itself a power that is confided to the whole body of the state.

Tyranny can only come from the publick, in a democracy, since individuals are powerless, possessing no more rights than it pleases the community to leave in their hands. The pretence that an individual oppresses the publick, is, to the last degree, absurd, since he can do no more than exercise his rights, as they are established by law; which law is enacted, administered and interpreted by the agents of the publick.

As every man forms a portion of the publick, if honest and influenced by right principles, the citizen will be cautious how he takes sides against particular members of the community, for he is both deciding in his own case, a circumstance under which few make impartial judges, and combining with the strong to oppress the weak.

In this country, in which political authority is the possession of the body that wields opinion, influences that elsewhere counteract each other, there is a strong and dangerous disposition to defer to the publick, in opposition to truth and justice. This is a penalty that is paid for liberty, and it depends on the very natural principle of flattering power. In a monarchy, adulation is paid to the prince; in a democracy to the people, or the publick. Neither hears the truth, as often as is wholesome, and both suffer for the want of the corrective. The man who resists the tyranny of a monarch, is often sustained by the voices of those around him; but he who opposes the innovations of the publick in a democracy, not only finds himself struggling with power, but with his own neighbors. It follows that the oppression of the publick is of the worst description, and all real lovers of liberty should take especial heed not to be accessaries to wrongs so hard to be borne. As between the publick and individuals, therefore, the true bias of a democrat, so far as there is any doubt of the real merits of the controversy, is to take sides with the latter. This is opposed to the popular notion, which is to fancy the man who maintains his rights against the popular will, an aristocrat, but it is none the less true; the popular will, in cases that affect popular pleasure, being quite as likely to be wrong, as an individual will, in cases that affect an individual interest.

It ought to be impressed, on every man's mind, in letters of brass, *"That, in a democracy, the publick has no power that is not expressly conceded by the institutions, and that this power, moreover, is only to be used under the forms prescribed by the constitution. All beyond this, is oppression, when it takes the character of acts, and not unfrequently when it is confined to opinion."* Society has less need of the corrective of publick opinion, under such a system, than under a narrow government, for possessing all the power, the body of the community, by framing the positive ordinances, is not compelled to check abuses by resisting, or overawing the laws. Great care should be had, therefore, to ascertain facts, before the citizen of a free country suffers himself to inflict the punishment of publick opinion, since it is aiding oppression in its worst form, when in error, and this too, without a sufficient object.

Another form of oppression practised by the publick, is arrogating to itself a right to inquire into, and to decide on the private acts of individuals, beyond the cognizance of the laws.

Men who have designs on the favor of the publick invite invasions on their privacy, a course that has rendered the community less scrupulous and delicate than it ought to be. All assumptions of a power to decide on conduct, that is unaccompanied by an authority to investigate facts, is adding the danger of committing rank injustice, to usurpation. The practice may make hypocrites, but it can never mend morals.

The publick, every where, is proverbially soulless. All feel when its rights, assumed or real, are invaded, but none feel its responsibilities. In republicks, the publick is, also, accused of ingratitude to its servants. This is true, few citizens of a democracy retaining the popular favor, without making a sacrifice of those principles, which conflict with popular caprices. The people, being sovereign, require the same flattery, the same humoring of their wishes, and the same sacrifices of truths, as a prince.

It is not more true, however, that the people in a democracy, are ungrateful, than that monarchs are ungrateful. The failing is common to all power, which, as a rule, is invariably as forgetful of services as it is exacting. The difference in the rewards of the servants of a prince, and the rewards of the servants of a democracy, is to be found in the greater vigilance of the first, who commonly sees the necessity of paying well. No dignities or honors conferred on a subject, moreover, can raise him to a level with his master, while a people reluctantly yield distinctions that elevate one of their own number above themselves.

In America, it is indispensable that every well wisher of true liberty should understand that acts of tyranny can only proceed from the publick. The publick, then, is to be watched, in this country, as, in other countries kings and aristocrats are to be watched.

The end of liberty is the happiness of man, and its means, that of leaving the greatest possible personal freedom of action, that comports with the general good. To supplant the exactions of the laws, therefore, by those of an unauthorized publick, is to establish restraints without the formalities and precision of legal requirements. It is putting the prejudices, provincialisms, ignorance and passions of a neighborhood in the place of statutes; or, it is establishing a power equally without general principles, and without responsibility.

Although the political liberty of this country is greater than that of nearly every other civilized nation, its personal liberty is said to be less. In other words, men are thought to be more under the control of extra-legal authority, and to defer more to those around them, in pursuing even their lawful and innocent occupations, than in almost every other country. That there is much truth in this opinion, all observant travellers agree, and it is a reproach to the moral civilization of the country that it should be so. It is not difficult to trace the causes of such a state of things, but the evil is none the less because it is satisfactorily explained. One principal reason, beyond a question, is the mistake that men are apt to make concerning the rights and powers of the publick in a popular government.

The pretence that the publick has a right to extend its jurisdiction beyond the reach of the laws, and without regard to the principles and restraints of the fundamental compact that binds society together, is, indeed, to verify the common accusation of the enemies of democracy, who affirm that, by substituting this form of government for that of a despotism, people are only replacing one tyrant by many. This saying is singularly false as respects the political action of our institutions, but society must advance farther, the country must collect more towns, a denser population, and possess a higher degree of general civilization, before it can be as confidently pronounced that it is untrue as respects the purely social.

The disgraceful desire to govern by means of mobs, which has lately become so prevalent, has arisen from misconceiving the rights of the publick. Men know that the publick, or the community, rules, and becoming impatient of any evil that presses on them, or which they fancy presses on them, they overstep all the forms of law, overlook deliberation and consultation, and set up their own local interests, and not unfrequently their passions, in the place of positive enactments and the institutions. It is scarcely predicting more than the truth will warrant, to say, that if this substitution of the caprices, motives and animosities of a portion of the publick, for the solemn ordinances of the entire legal publick, should continue, even those well affected to a popular government, will be obliged to combine with those who wish its downfall, in order to protect their persons and property, against the designs of the malevolent; for no civilized society can long exist, with an active power in its bosom that is stronger than the law.

3

A National Literature
and Romantic Individualism
1826–1861

In 1776 the hand of Thomas Jefferson wrote: "We hold these truths to be self-evident: that all men are created equal. . . ." In 1820, in the first great crisis over slavery, the same hand wrote: "This momentous question, like a fire bell in the night, awakened and filled me with terror. I considered it at once the knell of the Union."

These two utterances bracket the first period of the life of the young Republic, and in the next period, that between Jefferson's death, on July 4, 1826, and the firing on Fort Sumter, on April 12, 1861, the paradox of chattel slavery in a nation founded on the conception of the natural rights of man continued to be the central fact of national life. But the problem of how to give meaning to the dream of freedom and justice was not tidily confined to the fate of the black slave. It also appeared in many other forms during the period. It appeared in connection with the rise of Jacksonian democracy, which dramatized the problem of the possible tyranny of the majority and that of maintaining standards in a society based on a theory of egalitarianism. It appeared, too, with the rise of the industrial order, which raised, in an especially acute form, the problem of economic justice as related to freedom, and that of the human personality vis-à-vis the machine. And undergirding and overarching all such issues was the great philosophical and psychological reorientation demanded by the rise of science.

This was the age of the literary giants: Emerson, Hawthorne, Poe, Whitman, and Melville, who, along with lesser artists, consolidated and developed the new national literature of which Cooper had been the founding father. (Of course Cooper lived on into this age and did much of his best work in it.) These men, even Hawthorne and Poe, who at first glance seem more detached, were intensely of their time. Their work is both a record of, and a reaction to, all of its shocks and strains, and if through their work we best sense the *inwardness* of the age, it is, by the same token, necessary to gain some understanding of the age in order to sense the inwardness of the struggles that eventuated in their work.

One measure of the tremendous shifts in the structure of American life in the first half of the nineteenth century, and its most important political development, was the rise of Jacksonian democracy. In Revolutionary times, and even after, the word "democracy" was, to many ears, roughly synonymous with "anarchy." Democracy, declared Fisher Ames, a New England Federalist speaking in the accents of the old-time Puritan pulpit, "is an illuminated Hell that in the midst of remorse, horror and torture, rings with festivity; for experience shows, that one joy remains to the most malignant description of the damned, the power to make others wretched." Even Jefferson, who was regarded (by conservative citizens) as Antichrist and the fountainhead of anarchy, never applied the word "democrat" to himself—and he certainly did not use the word in the Declaration of Independence.[1] Even though, in one facet of his complex and sometimes paradoxical thinking about politics, he suggested that a revolution might be needed every twenty years, Jefferson agreed wholeheartedly with Washington that the "tumultuous populace of large cities are ever to be dreaded." Among the founding fathers there was certainly no consensus on the notion that the majority will is right, and they would have been appalled by the notion of universal suffrage. The voter in the new Republic was a man of property—or at least a taxpayer.

But powerful forces were afoot. The American Revolution proved to be an incitement to democracy. So, too, did the revolution in France. Both stirred up the nonpropertied American and provided him with an argument for full enfranchisement which was louder than words. American religion, too, after the Great Awakening (see pp. 83–84) of the middle of the eighteenth century, and the revivalism that became part of the back country and frontier culture, made for a democratization of life: if a man got "converted,"

---

[1] Jefferson did, however, allow his party to be called "Democratic-Republican"—with the second term perhaps disinfecting the first.

he was filled with the "spirit" and knew as much about politics, or anything else, as his rich and educated neighbor and therefore, in common justice, should have the vote.

Even so, the movement toward universal manhood suffrage was slow, state by state, and as late as 1820, Daniel Webster, along with the ex-President John Adams, was fighting a losing battle against it in a Massachusetts constitutional convention. The movement toward a political system in which the nomination of candidates would have some reference to the popular will was even slower.

The democratization of American politics was, in fact, a gradual and complex pragmatic growth, not a projection of theory, and one of the stimuli to that growth was fear. When James Fenimore Cooper, in *Notions of the Americans* (1828), observed that his countrymen were "getting clearly more democratic," he explained the event by saying that men in power were aware "that while the votes of a few thousand scattered individuals (the unpropertied) can make no great or lasting impression on the prosperity or policy of the country, their disaffection at being excluded might give a great deal of trouble." Democratization was, as the clear-headed, hardheaded, old ex-Federalist-turned-democrat indicates, as much a matter of prudence as of idealism.

The crisis came when, in 1824, Jackson first ran for the presidency. He won a plurality of the votes in a four-way contest, but lost to John Quincy Adams, the election having been thrown into the House of Representatives. The new states across the mountains felt cheated, for they had found their ideal in Jackson—a man of common origins but master of an elegant estate and of a high manner when occasion demanded, a man of hardihood, a duelist, a connoisseur of horseflesh, a breeder of fighting cocks, a soldier with a natural air of command, unimpeachable courage, and iron endurance, the hero of the Battle of New Orleans, a politician of pungent vocabulary, ruthless logic, and ferocious partisanship, and a husband of fanatical devotion to his Rachel.

In 1828, Jackson routed Adams and his supporters among the rich and well-born, the bankers, great merchants, and spokesmen of polite opinion in pulpit, editorial chair, college classroom, and drawing room. He took every electoral vote except those of New England. Jackson had forged a coalition between the trans-Appalachian woodsmen and farmers and the "tumultuous populace" of the eastern cities (though Jackson also drew some support from men of wealth in the East, especially in New York, and some from well-born New Englanders like Hawthorne and the Brahmin George Bancroft, the historian). In 1800, when Jefferson had won out over the elder Adams, the people had had a triumph, but now it was a different and more outlandish breed of people who thronged into the White House, on Inauguration Day, to celebrate.

This process of democratization, with all its crudities, injustices, and brutalities, was irreversible and was intimately associated with the development of the industrial system. By 1800 John Fitch's steamboat had given a successful demonstration, a spinning mill had been set up, Eli Whitney had patented his cotton gin, and David Wilkerson had invented a machine for making machines. Sixty years later the annual value of manufactures was at two billion dollars—the sum having doubled in the previous decade—and one third of the population, according to the census of 1860, were "supported, directly or indirectly, by manufacturing." By this time, too, the steam packet was driving the clipper ship from the seas, and railroads linked the western cities of Chicago, St. Louis, and Cincinnati with the eastern seaports. Telegraph lines crisscrossed the country, and newspapers, with advanced techniques for gathering news and for manufacturing and distributing their product, dramatically emphasized the growing democratic fluidity.

On the one hand, the industrial and technological developments worked to bind the country together, but on the other, they exacerbated and shifted into a new dimension the conflict between the North and South. When the period began, the spirit of Union, in spite of Jefferson's forebodings, was strong. Even John C. Calhoun, who was to become the architect of the philosophical and political program of the slaveholding South, began public life as a good Unionist and a firm believer in the "internal improvements" that would bind the country into a true nation. But the industrial developments that made such improvements more necessary and more readily available also increased, ironically enough, sectional tensions. The success of northern industry made slavery appear anomalous, and to the free labor of the North slavery became, in general, though with some peculiar shifts and crosscurrents, more and more repugnant—though, as we shall see, not necessarily on idealistic grounds. At the same time, the obvious success of the industrial order in the North drove the South more and more into desperation. Before the Civil War efforts toward industrialization in the agrarian South came to nothing. And the hard fact was that, by 1861, the worth of city property, including industrial plants, was considerably greater than that of all agricultural holdings in the entire nation—and most of that industrial urban property, along with a good deal of the nation's agricultural worth, was located above the Mason-Dixon line. The slaveholder's growing awareness that he was falling behind economically made him resort more and more to purely political solutions which left the root of his problems untouched.

One of the many ironical aspects of the North-South conflict was that the proslavery apologists, because they did stand outside the industrial system, could clearly see the brutalities and miseries that it entailed, the fact that the factory worker was becoming merely part of the machine, to be thrown on the junk heap when his usefulness was, even temporarily, gone. The analyses of capitalism and industrialism by southerners, such as George Fitzhugh, in *Cannibals All!* (1857), resemble those of Karl Marx. We are not to conclude, however, that in the period before the Civil War the only critical reaction to the industrial system came from the South. There was response, too, from many segments of northern society. Melville won special praise from Friedrich Engels, the friend and collaborator of Karl Marx, for his depiction of the slums of Liverpool, in *Redburn* (1849). Hawthorne wrote of the "crowds of pale-cheeked, slender girls who disturb the ear with the multiplicity of their short dry coughs . . . seamstresses who have plied the daily and nightly needle in the service of master tailors and close-fisted contractors until now it is almost time for each to hem the borders of her own shroud"; and went on to an almost Whitmanesque catalogue of "the prison, the insane asylum, the squalid chamber of the almshouse, the manufactory where the demon machinery annihilates the human soul." (But, playing no favorites, he added to his list of horrors "the cotton field where God's image becomes a beast of burden.")

Those at the bottom of the industrial heap naturally protested against the system. The new industrial city was being born, fed by domestic migration and by European immigration that, from a mere trickle in 1800, had grown to an annual half million by the time of the Civil War. The city, along with the new industrial town, was now packed with a toolless proletariat living on a daily wage and subject to the mysterious fluctuations of prosperity and money-panic characteristic of the industrial order. Westward migration was still something of a safety valve, but thinking men were beginning to fear the future, and meanwhile the "tumultuous populace" that Washington had dreaded were learning the meaning of politics and the rudiments of labor organizations.

Labor unions existed at the beginning of the century, and by the time of Jackson's presidency there was an attempt at national organization. An active labor press was developing and with it a lively intellectual debate that absorbed and adapted early European ideas of socialism; and after 1848, when the Communist Manifesto appeared, the doctrines of Marx began to circulate, and Marx himself did some writing for Horace Greeley's New York *Tribune*. It was, as a matter of fact, another foreigner, Fanny Wright, whom Walt Whitman remembered from his boyhood as announcing that the "war of classes" was upon the world: "It is the ridden people who are struggling to throw from their backs the 'booted and spurred' riders." Long after he had ceased to be a journalist for the Democrats and had become the poet of democracy, Whitman declared that Fanny Wright had "possessed herself" of him "body and soul." She was, however, only one of many educators of labor, native and foreign, and well before 1861 labor was on the way to becoming a potent factor in American life. But the question of slavery was more and more absorbing the energy of idealists and reformers, and the Civil War evidently fell right across what might have been a natural development of the labor movement.

Even so, by 1840 many men were aware of the incoherence and injustice of the new industrialism in America and had before their eyes the image of what was happening in England. Schemes for redeeming society, or establishing new societies, were epidemic. "Not a reading man but has a draft of a new community in his waistcoat pocket," Emerson wrote Carlyle in 1840. One scheme, land reform, would have set up an order of simple communities on public lands as a refuge for the dispossessed. But a more apocalyptic notion appeared in 1840 with Albert Brisbane, who published *The Social Destiny of Men*, adapted from the work of the French philosopher François Marie Charles Fourier, which was to prove highly influential.

Brisbane, brilliant, persuasive, neurotic, and epileptic, always looked, according to Whitman, "as if he were attempting to think out some problem a little too hard for him"; and the problem he was trying to think out was the same one that faces us today—that of how to restore to man, in the face of a technological society, his unity of being and a right relation to nature and to other men. Even in the relatively simple society of that time, Brisbane could say that "monotony, uniformity, intellectual inaction, and torpor reign: distrust, isolation, separation, conflict and antagonisms are almost universal. . . . Society is spiritually a desert." Brisbane set out to remedy the situation by establishing small communal organizations in which capital, labor, and talent would cooperate (according to an elaborate psychological analysis by Fourier, in which, by the way, the smallest return was assigned to labor) in producing necessary goods, with no nonproducers, such as middlemen, lawyers, and bankers, admitted. Society, then, would become an overall organization of these frictionless and happily balanced small units. More than forty "phalansteries" were founded by the "associationists"—and all came to grief.

There had been, of course, other communities in the same period that aimed to create an ideal society outside the industrial order—for example, New Harmony, Indiana, founded by the indefatigable Welsh philanthropist and reformer Robert Owen. New Harmony survived the ravages of human nature for only three years, but Brook Farm, founded in 1840, lasted longer, until 1847, and eventually shifted from its transcendentalist origins (see p. 444) into the more widely advertised Fourierist orbit. Hawthorne, though no more transcendentalist than Fourierist, went to Brook Farm, hoping for a retired and inexpensive life to which he might bring a bride, but he grew quickly weary of both the conversation and the shoveling of literal manure. He did, however, get a novel, *The Blithedale Romance*, out of his experience.

The idealism of the communal movement, generally considered, had sources beyond the social and economic. There was a specifically religious motive in, for instance, the Mormons' epic conquest of the West. But there were also the Perfectionists and the Millerites, both of which sects represent impulses that were, in less specific forms, at work in the age. The Perfectionists were a sect widely dispersed—as well they might have been, with their attractive doctrine of sanctified "free love." A certain John Humphrey Noyes, a cousin of Rutherford B. Hayes, the nineteenth President of the United States, well illustrates their principles.

As a divinity student at Yale, Noyes sought the way to perfection—"some specific for sin," as he put it in his diary—"whereby the curse would be exterminated once for all." He apparently found this spiritual "security," and imitated those members of the early Christian sect called antinomians; those who, convinced as they were of their own salvation, gave themselves over to drink and fornication with a clear conscience. As Noyes put it after a certain visit to the Gomorrah of New York, "I did nothing of which I had occasion to be ashamed, but I lost reputation with those who saw only the external attributes." Noyes came to public notice as the founder of the Oneida Community, in Madison County, New York, the most famous of all the Perfectionist colonies, where "complex marriage" ("free love" to the vulgar) was the rule, based on an idea that "if a man cannot love a woman and be happy in seeing her loved by others, he is a selfish man." "Special love," a marked preference for one person, was sternly forbidden; and when a virgin was ready to be instructed, the instructor was a gentleman of ripe experience and spiritual attainment (often Noyes himself) who would be more able than an immature cultist to imbue her with "the consciousness of having innocently exercised a pure and natural function of the spiritual plane."

Like other less gross antinomians of the period, some of them persons of literary fame, Noyes maintained that by what he called his "inspirational thought" he was in direct touch with the will of Christ; and, indeed, Noyes was simply a more dramatic and primitive manifestation of the belief in the direct personal revelation which was, as we shall see, characteristic of much of the thought of the age.

The Millerites, followers of a William Miller, shared one of the beliefs of the Perfectionists, that the Second Coming was at hand and the beginning of the millennium. But unlike Noyes, who merely prepared his disciples for the perfect world to come, Miller made the tactical mistake of claiming to know the precise date. By the morning of March 22, 1844, it was clear that his calculations were in error, and all the faithful who had assembled for the great event had to go back to the chores of ordinary living. This disappointment of the Millerites did not, however, end the hopefulness common to the various reformers of the period. They all drew on the same religious tradition and the dream of a millennium. America was, as Emerson declared in an address to the Mercantile Library Association of Boston, in 1844, "the country of the Future . . . of beginnings, of projects, of designs, of expectations," in the hands of a "sublime and friendly Destiny." He summed all up: "New thoughts, new things." And indeed it would be hard to overestimate the tonic effect that the sense of the beckoning future, like that of the beckoning distances of the vast continent, had on the American psyche.

The period was, then, a time of frenetic passion for reform. Established faiths—both political and religious—were breaking up, and men, the ignorant and the learned, were reaching out in all directions for meaning in life and for solutions for the problems of society. There was a babel of tongues and a confusion of prophecies. But all reforms, frivolous and profound, somehow flowed into one another, for they had all been generated in the same psychological matrix. In 1840, for instance, we find a great Convention of Friends of Universal Reform, which was attended by Dr. Channing, Bronson Alcott, Garrison, Theodore Parker, the poet Jones Very, and various other notables of New England, who for nine days bore witness, and whose proceedings Emerson reported, with equal-handed sympathy and irony, in the transcendentalist magazine the *Dial*.

It was perhaps because of the enormous tensions developing in this period that the expectation was for reform that would be total, universal, immediate, and apocalyptic. The ignorance of historical process and of human nature that permitted such expectations was considerable, as was the lack of a sense of proportion that would permit such faiths and panaceas as Amelia Bloomer's bloomers (worn by females in some of the Fourierist colonies), mesmerism, phrenology, hydropathy, the abjuring of tobacco or alcohol, or the eating of Dr. Graham's bread (a special table for "grahamites" was provided at Brook Farm) to be elevated to the same level of discourse as the abolition of slavery, the rights of women, and the problem of war.

But if, as William Lloyd Garrison said, there is a "unity of evil," then it could be argued that any social evil was connected at root with all others, and all had to be eradicated together. Meanwhile the evangelical fervor of the Great Awakening, along with Jonathan Edwards' doctrine of the "spiritual light," was now transferred into the secular arena and thus provided for the "enlightened" some of the secular satisfactions of personal vanity and the love of power. James Russell Lowell, whose first wife, Maria White, had led him from his natural bent of irony into the throbbing life of reformism, looked back in his late years and wrote, in his essay on Thoreau, that every form of "intellectual dyspepsia brought forth its gospel," and the reformers "stood ready at a moment's notice to reform anything but themselves." And even before the Civil War, Theodore Weld, one of the most committed and effective of abolitionists, withdrew from active propagandizing because, as he said to an admirer, he found that "he himself needed reforming" and that he "had been laboring to destroy evil in the same spirit as his antagonists."

In the great heyday of reform, however, men like Lowell, with his irony, Weld, with his self-scrutiny, and Emerson, with his Olympian detachment from human fumbling, were few. The intoxication of personal revelation and the certainty of being right made a heady brew. Promise was in the American air, and the millennial dream drew on old pieties, on the faith of the founding fathers, and on the same psychic energies, expansive optimism, and arrogant sense of being chosen by God (however "God" might be interpreted) that made the idea of manifest destiny seem perfectly natural, that set the American flag on the ramparts of Chapultepec in 1847 and seized an empire from Mexico,[2] and that led the Conestoga wagons across the plains. Energy is energy.

We should note, too, that the millennial dream was related not only to the expansive mind of the age, but to the impulse to "tinker," to invent, to short-cut nature and tradition. When Whittier said that Longfellow's "Psalm of Life" was greater than "all the dreams of Shelley, Keats, and Wordsworth," he gave as his reason that it was redolent "of the moral steam-enginery of an age of action." Whittier's phrase was beautifully apt—reformism was "moral steam-enginery." And behind this indigenous American impulse of "moral steam-enginery" were two other impulses. First, the scientific idea of general evolution that was being developed long before Darwin and second, the more specifically social idea implied by the founding fathers but succinctly put by the French philosopher the Comte de Saint-Simon, whose proud boast was that he had been a soldier under Washington and who predicted the inevitable "perfection of the social order."

---

[2] The Mexican War represents one of the points of crisis in the long swing toward the Civil War, subsequent ones including the Fugitive Slave Law of 1850, "Bleeding Kansas," and John Brown's raid on Harper's Ferry. The Mexican adventure struck antislavery people of all stripes as a high-handed attempt to expand the area open to slavery (which was indeed one of the things it was), and it provoked among abolitionists an impulse toward secession as a means of detaching themselves from the evil. It also provoked more general protest (see Lowell's *Biglow Papers* in our text), and even such a nonideological type as U. S. Grant was opposed to it, though of course he did serve. In the aftermath of the great imperialist expansion of the Mexican War, the vast wealth from the territory seized from Mexico, particularly California and Nevada, substantially helped finance the Union war effort.

If, looking back on that period, we find much of the reformism absurd, we must remind ourselves that history is never tidy, that in spite of all the frothy idiocies, hare-brained schemes, tin-horn fanaticism, and lust for power involved in the reformism of the age, real issues of the greatest practical and moral significance were sometimes at stake—women's rights, justice to labor, the rights of the minority against a majority, the relation of man to nature in the age of the machine, and, most dramatically, chattel slavery.

If, before 1860, chattel slavery was the most dramatic issue facing America, abolitionism represented the most dramatic force directed to the issue. It was a complex force, and it is worth trying to analyze it. The difficulty here is that abolitionism had many variants, both theoretical and practical; and to make matters worse, abolitionism, like any vital force, was constantly changing its forms, with many bitter factional struggles for power and control of policy. But we may best understand its essential nature by focusing attention on the radical group which is associated with the name of William Lloyd Garrison, even if it must be remembered, of course, that Garrison's own views did not remain the same from beginning to end.

To understand Garrison's form of abolitionism, or even abolitionism in general, the simplest way to start is to say what it was not.

First, abolitionism was not a general northern doctrine. The abolitionists were always, even during the Civil War, a minority. In the earlier days, in fact, the mobbing of abolitionists was not uncommon in the North, and the mobs, according to Leonard L. Richards' *"Gentlemen of Property and Standing": Anti-Abolition Mobs in Jacksonian America*, were carefully managed by "a well-organized nucleus of respectable, middle-class citizens" and were "usually led or engineered by the scions of old and socially dominant Northeastern families."

Though Garrison himself was manhandled by the "broadcloth mob" of Boston—that is, well-dressed businessmen—and Elijah Lovejoy was murdered by a mob, in 1837, in Illinois, mob action was generally supplemented by more polite devices. Charles Follen, professor of German at Harvard, lost his post for being an abolitionist, and Governor Edward Everett of Massachusetts, who later was to make the two-hour oration at Gettysburg that preceded Lincoln's two-minute address, asked the legislature for laws to stamp out abolitionism. Such antiabolitionism did not stop with the firing on Fort Sumter. When, in the middle of the Civil War, the Hutchinson Singers entertained the troops of the Army of the Potomac by singing the words Whittier had written to the tune of Luther's "Ein' Feste Burg Ist unser Gott," a hymn demanding the end of slavery, the performers were driven out of camp, and one of the federal officers who helped them on their way was, in fact, reported to have said that he didn't like abolitionists any better than he liked rebels—one perfectly logical position for a good Unionist.

Second, abolitionism and racism were not mutually exclusive. If by racism we understand the idea that the black (or any nonwhite race) is inherently inferior, then racism was as prevalent in the North as in the South, and the opposition to slavery, whether as emancipation or abolitionism, had no necessary connection with respect for, or acceptance of, the black.[3] As C. Vann Woodward has pointed out in "The Northern Crusade Against Slavery," it is clear that "race prejudice of various kinds was endemic among the white abolitionists," and this view is amply supported by recent researches; for example, the "free soil" movement both in the territories and among the stay-at-homes, according to E. H. Berwanger in *The Frontier Against Slavery*, was to a very considerable degree fed by feeling against blacks, and the fear of "free Negroes" motivated many a "Free Soiler." Even in "Bleeding Kansas," that bastion of liberty, the sad fact was sadly a fact. And in 1857, the free state of California was shipping black convicts back to New Orleans to be sold into slavery. Even Theodore Parker, a founding father of abolitionism, had said that "the Anglo-Saxon with common sense does not like the Africanization of America; he wishes the superior race to multiply rather than the inferior"; and Lincoln, though he became the Great Emancipator, could never accept the idea of racial equality.

Third, abolitionism was not the same thing as emancipationism, but was rather a special form of it. For instance, Jefferson, Emerson (for much of his career), Melville, Lincoln, and Robert E. Lee were emancipationists, but they were not abolitionists. The most obvious difference between emancipationism and abolitionism lay in the intensity of feeling involved, and this difference was associated with the question of contexts in which the problem of slavery might be regarded. For an emancipationist, the problem of slavery, no matter how important it was conceived to be, was to be treated in a general context—social, political, moral, and/or theological. For instance, Jefferson, in looking to the gradual emancipation of the slaves, placed the problem in a context of social continuity and political stability. And Lincoln, in taking the defense of the Union, not the freeing of the slaves, as the key issue in the Civil War, again considered the social and political contexts. But for an abolitionist the problem of slavery was paramount, central, burning, and immediate. The context did not matter.

Let us glance at this distinction in relation to theology. Behind abolitionism, as behind the antislavery impulse in general, often lay Christian theology. Both the emancipationist and the abolitionist might well regard slave-

---

[3] Ironically enough, at the fundamental level of mere physical acceptance, there was a great deal less racism in the South than in the North, as the mixture of blood will amply demonstrate, and as many works of southern literature—for instance, the novels of William Faulkner—will document. Whittier, like most abolitionists, was opposed to miscegenation.

holding as a sin, but for the latter, insofar as he thought theologically, it was the prime and unforgivable sin.[4] Benjamin Lay, a Quaker of the eighteenth century whom Whittier called the "irrepressible prophet," put it this way: "As God gave His only begotten Son, that whosoever believed in Him might have everlasting life; so the Devil gives his only begotten child, the Merchandize of Slaves and Souls of Men, that whosoever believes and trades in it might have everlasting Damnation." Slavery, according to Lay, was the "greatest sin in the world"—the "very worst part of the old Whores Merchandize, most filthy Whore of Whores, Babilon's Bastards." This particular theological interpretation, by making slavery the "greatest sin,"[5] implied that all other issues had to be strictly subordinated, not only for the benefit of the slave but to save the soul of the abolitionist: if he connived with sin he would be damned. The fear of personal damnation by connivance would rule out any attempt to work at practical solutions such as gradual emancipation or emancipation with compensation (none were, in fact, ever really tried, and the elaboration and complication of the debate about various schemes may have driven some antislavery people toward the basic simplicity of the abolitionist solution). In other words, a practical solution (to the benefit of the slave) might be rejected because inconsistent with the salvation of the soul of the abolitionist (or with an abstract moral point, that iniquity should not be rewarded, as by compensation for emancipation).

Associated with this theological approach was the notion of the "higher law,"[6]—of which government and other institutions, insofar as they in any way compromised with slavery, were in contravention.

The most immediate corollary of the doctrine of higher law would be that the slaveholder, as both a sinner and a criminal, stood outside the protection of ordinary secular law. This line of reasoning might justify the fomenting of insurrection and the approval of massacre; and it did lead to such legends as that southerners used black skulls for drinking bowls, in which Harriet Beecher Stowe and even Whittier believed, and to which the poet refers in "Amy Wentworth." More generally, the line of reasoning led to the

[4] See, for instance, in our text Hawthorne's "Ethan Brand" for a different primary sin.

[5] Many of slavery's advocates, too, found a theological basis for their position in the cursing of the descendants of Ham to be "hewers of wood and drawers of water" (Genesis 10:25).

[6] The "higher law" is, of course, a parallel to, or a version of, the transcendentalist's "intuition" and is not to be demonstrated but known only by direct revelation to the individual. It is to be sharply distinguished from the notion of "natural rights," of which, too, slavery was in violation; but both notions might lead to the same line of action in defying the state. The natural law would hold that the state cannot act to abridge natural rights, but the higher law, with its conviction of personal revelation, would give a cutting edge and intensity beyond the rationalistic theory.

vilification, not only of all southerners, but also of all men who failed to accept the abolitionist position, as murderers, thieves, adulterers, and whore-masters. To Wendell Phillips an emancipationist like Lincoln was simply the "slave-hound of Illinois," and even fellow abolitionists might come in for rough handling by those who had a nearer relation with the divine will: "Among the true, inner-seal Garrisonians," as John Jay Chapman puts it in his sympathetic study of Garrison, "the wrong kind of anti-slavery was always considered as anti-Christ." Garrison, that master of vilification, came to visit as much of his spleen on Frederick Douglass, the ex-slave and fellow abolitionist, as he ever visited on a slavemaster.

The second corollary of the doctrine of higher law would be to reinforce the rejection of political action. The idea that the revealed law was superior to anything in constitutions or on statute books would naturally lead to Garrison's gesture of publicly burning the Constitution as a "league with death and a covenant with hell," and to the sweeping notion that it was morally wrong even to try to work through institutions. The "pure" Garrisonian might hold to such a view through thick and thin on grounds of principle, but a number of abolitionists were more flexible, and it must be recognized that the attitude toward political involvement was often fluctuating, and at different times, according to shifts in circumstance, the same individual might hold different views. For instance, with the rise of the Republican party, in the later 1850's, a certain number of abolitionists, and others, who had previously abjured, or could not believe in the efficacy of, political action came to accept it. There now seemed some practical promise in it.

As for Garrison's position, it is argued by some recent historians that he was less concerned with theory than with results; that on the basis of his diagnosis of the situation, he knew that only the totally radical position would be effective (in contrast to the reformism of most abolitionists, that of Whittier, for example; see pp. 542–45) and that he was consciously engaged in a practical "revolutionary act."

In any case, Garrison got his total solution. War came, but it was a war fought on non-Garrisonian grounds, the North, with a Constitution that, like the Constitution of the Confederacy, defined a slave as property, and with a President who was an avowed racist and who had made a solemn and official promise not to interfere with slavery. Lincoln was a lawyer and decidedly not a "higher law" lawyer. But ironies accumulate, for in the end Garrison followed the Lincoln line. The moral of this story is, however, far from clear.

On the one hand, the moral may seem to be that in the world of fact and action, contexts, even when ignored, have a way of making themselves felt in the end. But whatever may be on the other hand, the moral is certainly not that the assertion—even the dogmatic assertion—of the individual conscience has no value or effect. Indeed, it is a chastening experience to realize that rational consensus eventuating in reform of even such an obvious, heinous, and anachronistic evil as chattel slavery is rare, and that the historical process often involves tragic collisions in which acts of conscience dramatize fundamental issues—sometimes, ironically, collisions of conscience against conscience.

If abolitionism—or at least one brand of it—set up, squarely and by principle, an absolute individualism and the "higher law" against the assumption of the majority will in a democratic society, it did so merely as one example of the philosophical tendency of the age. And this brings us to the question of transcendentalism.

Transcendentalism was a movement—philosophical, literary, and social—that emerged among New England intellectuals, mainly in the environs of Boston, in the 1830's. Underlying the philosophical, literary, and social manifestation, the root impulse of transcendentalism was, however, theological. By this time Puritan Calvinism had relaxed into Unitarianism, a belief not unlike the Deism of Franklin and Jefferson in its need to accommodate eighteenth-century thought to a theological framework; unitarianism was, in fact, the institutionalizing of a rationalistic humanism, with general cultural pretensions, perfumed by religious sentiment. That is, Unitarianism represented the triumph of the liberalism of the age against the old orthodoxy, a triumph which in New England had been prepared for by a "liberal Christianity" carrying the day against the spirit of Edwards and which, in the apt phrase of one scholar, marked a movement from "piety" in religious matters to a mere "moralism." But soon that "liberal Christianity," in its Unitarian guise, began to seem to some of the young little more than a new orthodoxy of smug social conformity that denied the spiritual and emotional depths of experience—"corpse-cold Unitarianism," as Emerson was to call it. The appetite for mystery and intensity left unsatisfied by Unitarianism was satisfied, to some degree at least, by the philosophical and literary works of the Romantic movement of Germany and England, some of which almost achieved the status of scripture to the transcendentalists; but, as Perry Miller, an authoritative student of the movement, says, the basic impulse behind transcendentalism was "a religious radicalism in revolt against a rational conservatism."

Here the word "radicalism" must not be taken, as is commonly done in our time, to mean merely an impulse toward sweeping and violent change, presumably of a left-wing variety. It is to be understood, more literally, as meaning a will to return to the "root"—here the "root" of Christianity, to "preach the Holy Ghost," as Margaret Fuller, a famous transcendentalist, put it, instead of "preaching Man"; to emphasize faith instead of understanding, revelation instead of reason, mysticism instead of rationalism. But, oddly enough in one perspective, this revolt, with what might well seem its obscurantist and illiberal aspects, was the work, as we have suggested, of the young. What the young were trying to do was to return to, or rediscover, what they regarded as a deeper "truth" of life than the "truth" of their "liberal" fathers. In this sense, the transcendentalists, whom Emerson called "the party of the Future" against "the party of the Past," were both revolutionary and reactionary, radical and conservative, and to understand them is to see this apparent paradox in historical terms.

To see transcendentalism in such terms demands that we regard it as more than the concern of a handful of men and women of special culture and talent—most notably Emerson and Thoreau[7]—removed from the hurly-burly of life. We must regard it, instead, as a response to the fundamental—if sometimes concealed—issues of the age which that handful of men and women had the gift of perceiving and analyzing. That is, transcendentalism represented a complex response to the democratization of American life, to the rise of science and the new technology, and to the new industrialism—to the whole question, in short, of the redefinition of the relation of man to nature and to other men that was being demanded by the course of history.

We must see, too, how the definition of those fundamental issues by the transcendentalists, and even how some of their particular attitudes toward the issues, could affect men who may seem to have opposed transcendentalism—men such as Hawthorne, Whitman, and Melville. Furthermore, and perhaps most importantly, we must try to see how the issues defined by the transcendentalists are related to our own time.

Even if transcendentalism did represent the revolt of the young, "the party of the Future," various older strains of thought flowed into it. Plato was for most transcendentalists the archetypal philosopher, and Emerson went so far as to say that "Plato is philosophy and philosophy is Plato." Too, the very name "transcendentalism" indicates the Platonic idealism according to which reality subsists beyond the appearances of the world. Like Plato, the transcendentalists held that the world is an expression of spirit, or

---

[7] Sometimes Emerson and Thoreau are regarded as peripheral to transcendentalism, but it is more by talent and character than by doctrine that they are to be distinguished from such members of the movement as Margaret Fuller, George Ripley, Orestes A. Bronson, Bronson Alcott, and William Henry Channing. Certainly, some students of the age, such as Perry Miller, regard Emerson and Thoreau as centrally important. In this connection, however, it must be remembered that there was no hard and fast body of doctrine, no orthodoxy, of transcendentalism.

mind, which, by definition, is sheer intelligibility and therefore good. But to Plato's influence must be added that of Immanuel Kant, who emphasized the "native spontaneity of the human mind" against the passive conception of the eighteenth-century psychology; and the influence of Coleridge, in a sense a disciple of Kant, and of other German and English Romantics who insisted on the importance of the sense of wonder, the antirationalism, and the primacy of the individual consciousness characteristic of the transcendentalists. In addition to all these nonindigenous influences, the transcendentalists carried on certain elements of New England Calvinism, especially its ethical seriousness and, more specifically, inherited one aspect of Jonathan Edwards' thought (see pp. 91–97), the doctrine of a "spiritual and divine light immediately imparted to the soul," by which the individual can know absolute truth.

So much for definable influences; but perhaps the best way to approach transcendentalism is to understand that when, on September 18, 1836, George Ripley, a scholar of Boston, later to be a founder of Brook Farm, convened in his study a congenial group of seekers, including Emerson, "to see how far it would be possible for earnest minds to meet," the meeting was not so much of minds as of temperaments, of yearnings, of aspirations, and of rejections, and that what emerged was not so much a philosophy as an atmosphere and a state of sensibility.

The rejections made by the earnest little group at their first meeting are significant. Emerson, looking back late in life on the movement, called it a reaction "against the too formal science, religion and social life of the earlier period." He had already confided to his journal that "Pure intellect is the pure devil when you have got off all the masks of Mephistopheles," and the rebels were concerned with a faculty that would give truth beyond that possible to the "pure devil" of intellect.

The too formal science against which the transcendentalists were rebelling was what the most learned American of his time, Theodore Parker, calls "sensationalism"—by which he meant the philosophy of empiricism of John Locke and David Hume, which had dominated the eighteenth century; Locke, and Hume after him, held that the mind begins as a blank page—a *tabula rasa*—and that all knowledge develops from sensation. As Parker, in attacking the doctrine, described it: "There is nothing in the intellect which was not first in the senses"—by intellect meaning the whole "consciousness of man." An idea, then, would be but a "transformed sensation."

The transcendentalists believed, on the contrary, that starting from sensation a man could know only the "facts of consciousness" and not ever anything of the existence of the material world. Worse, starting from sensation, man could never arrive at any truths about values. For the transcendentalists the only knowledge of any final worth would be absolutely "certain" knowledge—especially certain knowledge on moral questions; and this appetite for certainty in a world of flux and crumbling beliefs may be said to underlie the whole of their intellectual effort. And the key to such certain knowledge was man's faculty to intuit truth directly. It did not, they would maintain, have to come through the senses.

Our chief concern here is with the transcendentalists vis-à-vis the society of their time, but perhaps the best way to understand this is to begin with their conception of objective nature. By and large, they were, as we have said, Platonists, and Emerson, though he did, as he put it, "acquiesce entirely in the permanence of natural laws," held that "the question of the absolute existence of nature still remains open" and that "culture"[8] leads "man to attribute necessary existence to spirit" and "to esteem nature as an accident and an effect." Sometimes he was even inclined to believe that "all outward circumstance is but a dream and a shade"; and the tale goes that one day, discovered in the act of carrying in wood for his domestic arrangements, he remarked, "I suppose we must do this as if it were real."

Nature might be, then, merely a "divine dream from which we may presently awake to the glories and certainties of day." In this "divine dream" of nature (with the dreamer never quite specified), every "natural fact is a symbol of some spiritual fact," and the "whole of nature is a metaphor of the human mind"; and the end of man is, therefore, not to study nature as such, but to seek to engage the "spiritual fact" that nature symbolizes or to interpret the metaphorical burden. Man should not, that is, undertake to find truths about nature but to move through nature to the certainties thus afforded by his own intuition, his own "revelation."[9] For example, when Emerson became engrossed with the study of geology, he discerned that the excess of sandstone over coal and that of coal (a fossil of vegetables) over the fossils of animals represented a spiritual truth.

Even Thoreau, celebrated for his scrupulous attention to natural fact, was not, he confessed in a passage which in itself is a beautiful and brilliant little poem, finally concerned with things of Time (such as nature), but of Eternity:

> Time is but the stream I go a-fishing in. I drink at it; but when I drink I see the sandy bottom and detect how shallow it is. Its thin current slides away,

[8] Emerson clearly rejects from "culture" all that bears on scientific thought.

[9] The transcendentalist, according to the philosopher George Santayana, in his essay "The Genteel Tradition in American Philosophy" (see our accompanying volume), might love and respect nature, as Emerson did, but he loves it because what he takes to be nature "is his own work, a mirror in which he looks at himself and says (like a poet relishing his own verses), 'What a genius I am! Who would have thought there was such stuff in me?'"

but eternity remains. I would drink deep; fish in the sky, whose bottom is pebbly with stars.

Transcendentalism, in this dimension, represented a reaction not only against the Enlightenment of the eighteenth century, with Locke and Hume, but against the continuing development of science in the nineteenth century. It is interesting to compare this attitude toward science with that of the German Romantics of a couple of generations earlier. When the revolutionary scientific work *The System of Nature*, by Paul Henri d'Holbach (1770), reached Germany, Goethe wrote: "How hollow and empty did we feel in this melancholy, atheistical half night, in which the earth vanished with all its images, the heaven with all its stars." What the transcendentalist, like Goethe, wanted was his own version of nature with its "images"—neither the nature of common sense nor that of science, but a "romantic" nature, nature poeticized to please his spirit and taste. Upon receiving a letter from the Association for the Advancement of Science asking him what branch of service he was especially interested in, Thoreau wrote in his journal, under the date of March 5, 1853, that he couldn't properly answer, for the Association did not "believe in a science which deals with the higher laws." He was, he affirmed, "a mystic, a transcendentalist, and a natural philosopher" to boot. He was ultimately concerned with scientific fact only insofar as it was a doorway to the universal, and even at the time of the letter to the Association for the Advancement of Science he had not departed from his early application (in 1842, at Emerson's solicitation) of transcendental methodology to scientific fact in his "Natural History of Massachusetts," in which he concluded that "It is with science as with ethics, we cannot know truth by contrivance and method; the Baconian is as false as any other. . . ." We learn, he asserted, only "by direct intercourse and sympathy."

If for Thoreau nature held this secondary rank, it was only to be expected that by transcendentalists in general the observation of the facts of nature, especially the disciplined observation by the scientists and the disciplined process of generalizing abstractly from the facts, was likely to be taken as, on the one hand, a blasphemy against God (or the Over-Soul, to use Emerson's term) or, on the other, a demeaning of man. "Empirical science," says Emerson in *Nature*, his first book, "is apt to cloud the sight, and by the very knowledge of functions and processes to bereave the student of the manly contemplation of the whole." Both Emerson and Parker held a contempt for observation and for inductive reasoning based on it, Emerson proclaiming that the "astronomer, the geometer, rely on their irrefragable [because deductive] analyses, and disdain the results of observation." In other words, deductive reasoning, coming from the mind, asserts the creative primacy of the mind—like intuition. And associated with deduction against the vulgarity of observation and the fallibility of induction is set the personal vision of "wholeness"; for a "dream," Emerson says, "may let us deeper into the secret of nature than a hundred concerted experiments."

We must ask, even at the risk of a distraction, exactly what Emerson may mean in this particular assertion of the primacy of mind. Does he merely mean that, as with the case of the literal dream of the chemist Kekulé, who thus discovered the benzene ring, many scientific discoveries have come with visionary speed? Such discoveries, with their fascinating hints of how the creative mind works, are indeed a matter of record, but it is also a matter of record that no dream, vision, or intuition of any scientific importance has come to anyone who did not have training in science (just as no poems have come in dreams except to poets; see the introduction to Julia Ward Howe); and so we are back to observation and induction after all. The "dream" can come only, as the great scientist Pasteur puts it, to the "prepared spirit." Furthermore, if the "dream" does come to the "prepared spirit," it cannot be validated by the fact of its being a dream, but only by the vulgar tests of observation, experiment, and induction.

The transcendentalist's theory of nature and the attitude toward science had crucial consequences and parallels when he came to face society and its problems. First, the mere fact that nature was regarded as "an accident and an effect" of the reality of spirit, as "but a dream and a shade," would tend to drain events in the objective world, including human events, of their urgencies. Emerson, as a philosopher, sought a perch above the issues of the untidy—and unreal—world. "The relation of men of thought to society is," he declared, "always the same; they refuse that necessity of mediocre men, to take sides." There is, clearly, sound sense here; in a world of violent passion and irrational partisanship, the wise man does seek to give a detached judgment. But more than that is involved here, as will become clear as we look at a second consequence of the attitude toward nature.

If nature, insofar as it can be said to exist, is a manifestation of spirit, then, as Emerson says, "All things are moral," for, in "their boundless changes" they have an "unceasing reference to spiritual nature," and all "animal" functions "echo the Ten Commandments." In such a world evil could not, of course, exist. If Emerson might, in fits of weakness or realism, admit that "Famine, typhus, frost, war, suicide, and effete races must be reckoned calculable parts of the system of the world," he had at least a verbal formula for exorcism in his dictum, in the divinity school address, that good is "positive," while evil is "merely privitive." So he could say, in "Spiritual Laws," that "only the finite" has "wrought and suffered," while the "infinite lies stretched in smiling repose." His "whole philosophy," he summed up, "teaches acquiescence and optimism." He was, apparently, undisturbed when the Scots writer Thomas Carlyle, whom he greatly admired, warned him that he seemed to be "in danger of dividing" himself "from the facts of this present universe, in which alone, ugly as it is, can I find any anchorage, and soaring away after these Ideas, Beliefs, Revelations, and such like." And Carlyle added: "It is the whole Past and the whole Future, this same cotton-spinning, dollar-hunting, canting and shrieking, very wretched generation of ours. Come back into it, I tell you."

Emerson could not often be summoned back to the "finite" with its dollar-hunting and shrieking, for even if man was, after all, a part of nature, his important business was not with man or nature at the finite level, but with the "Over-Soul." It should be noted, however, that Emerson did, finally, accept the obligation of action; in spite of his earlier distaste for abolitionists, the question of slavery finally drew him into the world that "wrought and suffered." As Arthur Schlesinger, Jr., says in *The Age of Jackson*, when he came to an issue that he cared enough about, Emerson scuttled theory. Meanwhile, too, he had offered analyses and judgments on the life around him.

But on what terms might the transcendentalist *as transcendentalist* face the problems of the world of action? In matters of morals and politics, he could no more be satisfied with the empirical approach than in matters of science; this smacked of the "too formal" doctrine of Locke and Hume, which could give no "certain knowledge." In his famous essay "Transcendentalism," Parker deals at length with the whole question. The empirical approach depends on the "lamp of experience" for light and holds that there is no "final truth," only the appeal to history, tradition, and experience. And so Parker posits in the human psychology a specific "moral faculty" that tells a man what is right and just, so that he can, as Parker affirms, be "certain of it."

Furthermore, the empirical approach not only fails to give certainty, but involves the utilitarian notion that the moral thing is what "works well in the long run." In other words, you can no more look to the future for guidance than to the past.

In any case, since man can have the revelation of absolute truth, he should dismiss the whole matter of consequences. He should not look "to the consequences of virtue" as a test for it, for virtue is an "absolute good to be loved not for what it brings, but is." The only question a man must, therefore, ask himself is what "says conscience—what God?" This, with the obvious implication that the voice of conscience and the voice of God always issue identical instructions.

If we state the matter less theologically, the transcendentalist found in the mind itself intuitions that need no proofs, intimations that were guaranteed to be right by the very fact of their appearance in the mind. The moment when an intuition appeared might indeed be very thrilling, and the thrill itself might be taken as a proof of the "truth" received. One day James Russell Lowell, in the middle of a conversation, saw a whole system of thought rise up "like a vague Destiny looming from chaos." At the moment, he was so overwhelmed that the "very air seemed to waver to and fro with the presence of something I knew not what." Lowell promised himself that he would study his "revelation" through until he understood its "grandeur," but somehow, with his streak of worldliness and toughmindedness, he never got around to it.

A number of men—less imperfect transcendentalists than Lowell—did stand more staunchly by their "revelations." Such an intuition—whether the voice of moral faculty, conscience, or God—was, in Parker's words, to be placed "before all institutions, all laws, all traditions." The transcendentalist, with his Platonic bias and his conviction of possessing "absolute truths" about morals, politics, religion, and any other matter, might find himself withdrawn, apart in his "smiling repose," superior to the "finite" world which "wrought and suffered" and in which affairs were meanwhile being conducted by men not privy to "absolute truths." So Thoreau could say of the world around him that he would have none of its "dirty institutions." Margaret Fuller, the most famous female transcendentalist, who confessed to having an intellect the equal of any she had ever encountered and who was the queen of Brook Farm and the model of Zenobia in *The Blithedale Romance*, was, according to the Englishwoman Harriet Martineau, a perfect example of such superior withdrawal from actualities; "While Margaret Fuller and her adult pupils sat 'gorgeously dressed,' talking about Mars and Venus, Plato and Goethe, and fancying themselves the elect of the earth in intellect and refinement, the liberties of the republic were running out."

Sometimes, in fact, there was in the transcendentalists a streak of the excessive refinement and fastidious shrinking that prompts the hero of the play *Axel* (by Villiers de L'Isle-Adam, 1890) to say to his beloved, "As for living, our servants can do that for us."

As long as the transcendentalist stood outside society, the basic problems entailed by his notion of the intuition of absolute truth did not, in any practical sense, arise. But once he had left off letting his servants do his living for him and was in contact with other men—some of whom, perhaps, had their own convictions of absolute rightness—and had to face conflict with their views, how could he really know that his own intuition was unimpeachable? How, in the rough and tumble of things, could he distinguish the authenticity of one intuition from that of another? Parker faced this question in regard to the "transcendental moralist." The moralist, he admitted, might "take a transient impulse, personal and fugitive, for a universal law; follow a passion for a principle, and come to naught; surrender his manhood, his free will to his unreflecting instinct. . . ." Therefore, he concluded, men should be not "transcendental-mad," but "transcendental-wise."

But we are forced to go beyond such a merely verbal solution and ask on what ground does one distinguish the "transcendental-wise" from the "transcendental-mad"—in morality, science, or anything else. Are we forced to resort to the dreary, complex, unexciting, and uncertain tests disdained by the transcendentalist, who relies on his intuitions and absolutes? Are we forced to make judgments by experience, by observation, by science, by history, by society, by tradition, by utility, and by that most contemptible test of all, plain, commonsensical workableness?

If such dreary criteria are rejected, must we try to settle a matter merely by the intensity of conviction and the dogmatic vigor of assertion? Or should we try emulating Mr. Noyes, the patriarch of Perfectionism at his Oneida Community, who, when some of the faithful became spiritualists as well as perfectionists and began to receive absolute truths from the "other world," truths that sometimes conflicted with his own pronouncements on policy and discipline, simply pointed out that his own "inspirational thought" was in direct communication with the will of Christ.

The "thought" of the really convinced antinomian must, of course, always claim to identify itself with the will of Christ, God, the Over-Soul, Historical Necessity, or the Universe. Emerson, in fact, talked blissfully of the moment when man "shall cease to feel his boundaries but shall be so interfused by nature and shall so interfuse nature that the sun shall rise by his will as much as his own hand or foot do now." The will of the individual, in other words, thus becomes the law of the universe.

Let us turn to the relation of transcendentalism to some of the burning questions in the actual world.

Transcendentalism, a reaction, as we have seen, against the materialism of the "too formal" science of the old order, was also a reaction against the materialism of the new. The reaction was, however, complex and even paradoxical. As always, Emerson best exemplifies the situation of his time. On the one hand, he loathed the new economic and industrial order. Things were in the saddle, ambition was for the dollar, and all the values that the Emersonian individual should strive to embody seemed to be held in contempt. But on the other hand, Emerson, insofar as he followed his idealistic philosophy and what William James was to call his "soft determinism," could lie apart in his "smiling repose," and simply assume that, even though the finite "wrought and suffered," things of that realm were really working out very well, and very morally to boot.

To take a more practical angle on the situation, though Emerson objected to the "Lords of the loom," the new textile magnates, it did not follow that he objected to wealth *qua* wealth. For him, as for a long line of Americans, wealth could be regarded as a mark of virtue. Since an "eternal beneficent necessity is always bringing things right," since there is a "league between virtue and nature," and since success "consists in close appliance of the laws of the world, and since these laws are intellectual and moral," the rewards of success are the marks of virtue. In his essay "Nominalist and Realist," Emerson is very explicit: "Money . . . is in its effects and laws as beautiful as roses. Property keeps the accounts of the world and is always moral. Property will be found where the labor, the wisdom and the virtue have been in nations, in classes, and . . . in the individual also." So we have in this dimension of Emerson's thought, in memorable phrasing, a version of the economic Darwinism that was to be so dear to the heart of the age of the Robber Barons, and which has its roots in the Puritan conviction that material success may indicate election. As Perry Miller puts it, "Vice-Presidents of banks have been known to hang framed mottos from Emerson on the walls of their offices."

If Emerson was being illogical when he attacked the "Lords of the loom," he was being quite logical when, like most transcendentalists, he declined to champion labor against those Lords or against anybody else. The struggle for a ten-hour day, for instance, was not a transcendentalist's concern, nor was the matter of a living wage. "Do not tell me," said Emerson, "of my obligation to put all men in good situations. Are they my poor? I tell thee, foolish philanthropist, that I grudge the dollar, the dime, the cent I give to such men."

In the practical world, the rise of democracy, either the trans-Appalachian Jacksonian stripe or that of the eastern slums and factory towns, was what provoked the transcendentalist to his most significant reaction. With his unimpeachable intuition, the transcendentalist was concerned—as was, for instance, Cooper on other grounds (see pp. 320–23)—to protect his standards of justice, morality, intellect, and taste, as well as himself and his way of life, against the degradation of majority rule. Theodore Parker, a manly and forthright character, boasted of having protested "against the tyranny of the few over the many in Europe, and of the many over the few in America"; and here the transcendentalist would, ironically enough, find himself in bed with John C. Calhoun, with his doctrine of the concurrent majority (see the introduction to Calhoun), and with John Randolph of Roanoke, who declared, "I love liberty and hate equality." All the transcendentalists loathed the timidity, the craven spirit of conformity, which mass democracy runs the danger of breeding, and loathed the notion of quantitative, rather than qualitative, judgments.

It must be insisted, however, that Parker, along with the transcendentalists in general and James Fenimore Cooper, their contemporary critic of democracy, thought of himself as a democrat. The kind of democracy that he hoped for emerges dramatically in a passage from Emerson:

> Leave this hypocritical prating about the masses. Masses are rude, lame, unmade, pernicious in their demands and influence, and need not to be flattered, but to be schooled; I wish not to concede anything to them, but to tame, drill, divide, and break them up, and draw individuals out of them. The worst of charity is that the lives you are asked to preserve are not worth preserving. Masses! The calamity is the masses. I do not wish any mass at all, but honest men only, lovely, sweet, accomplished women only, and no shovel-handed, narrow-brained, gin-drinking million stockingers or lazzaroni at all. If government knew how, I should like to see it check, not multiply population. When it reaches its true law of action, man that is born will be hailed as essential. Away with this hurrah of masses, and let us have the considered vote of single men spoken on their honor and their conscience.

What Emerson is here concerned with is the shocking contrast between a democracy of the masses—with its mystique of the masses—and a democracy of real "individuals." On this point, taken in isolation, he is no different from Jefferson, and his "narrow-brained, gin-drinking million stockingers or lazzaroni" are simply a more eloquently defined version of the big-city mob that Jefferson, and Washington, had feared. Jefferson had naively hoped that his independent American farmer would be the "individual" in the new democracy[10] to give his "considered vote"; but by the time of Emerson that hope had grown quaint and threadbare. The American farmer hadn't quite lived up to expectations, and the cities were already bulging with their "shovel-handed," "gin-drinking" millions, and the tone of the passage conveys the sense of a desperation quite at variance from Emerson's "whole philosophy" that was supposed to teach "acquiescence and optimism."

What Emerson wanted was not a kingdom ruled by Plato's philosopher-king, but a democracy populated by philosopher-voters, with good manners and "lovely, sweet, accomplished" wives. But he found himself in America, in the middle of the nineteenth century, with the Whigs on one hand and the Democrats on the other, with the Lords of the loom on the one hand and the unshaven rabble on the other, and he scarcely knew which way to turn.

---

[10] Jefferson had held that the ideal political solution was not to give the vote apart from land, the hope being that ownership, making the voter economically independent, would make his vote responsible.

What could be done? Emerson says he would like to see population checked, but doesn't know how. So "school" them, he says, and this means to "tame, drill, divide, and break them up" in order to "draw individuals out of them." And, as an aside, we may say that this business of schooling America in general may be taken, in a way, as Emerson's mission. So we find his cajoling, his moments of rhetorical elevation, his tactics of shock and paradox, his metaphysics all conspiring to create a new awareness of the individual's possibility. But perhaps the most potent element in this process of schooling was the example set by Emerson—as by other transcendentalists—of a man heroically striving to lead the life of the mind.

But to return to the general question of the transcendentalist confronting the world. He might, for instance, see man as "divine," but such divine creatures were in the habit of making very un-divine political arrangements and indulging Satanic impulses. What, then, could a man do? Insist that he himself was *more* divine than his fellows—more equal, to paraphrase the old joke —and could distinguish "transcendental-wise" from "transcendental-mad"? Assuming this to be his view, and that he held, with Thoreau, the notion that "one with God is always a majority," what could he do, practically speaking, to make his "intuition" stick?

If, indeed, the gross-minded numerical majority didn't accept transcendental vote-counting, should the transcendentalist then repudiate the basic practical and institutionalized principle of "one man, one vote," and abjure the faith that in the clash of the free market of ideas truth will win out? Should he deny that to make the market of ideas free, one citizen must respect the next citizen's idea, even at the price of tolerating error, and must, further, be willing to admit the possibility of his own error? Should he deny the assumption that even conscience and conviction must be assumed to be not absolute but "educable," to be subject to discussion and criticism and the test of experience—even one's own conscience? If not, then the possibility must be faced that absolute conviction of rightness of "intuition" may well lead to the only absolute test experience knows—the test of absolute force.

To "draw individuals" out of the masses—that was what Emerson took to be his mission; and transcendentalism was, at its core, a philosophy of naked individualism, aimed at the creation of the new American, the self-reliant man (see pp. 711–17), complete and independent. In America there had been from the start, set over against the will to found a society, from the theocracy of early New England on to the new Republic of 1776, a vision of the freestanding, contextless individual to whom society was sometimes little more than a congregation of shadows. The emphasis might shift from one pole to the other, but both poles were always there. In the heyday of Puritanism, there was, for instance, the will to found the godly society in this world, but there was also the will to explore in sweat, prayer, and meditation the lonely world of the individual soul in its relation to God. But shifts did occur, and as the historian Edmund S. Morgan says, if the early American thought about God, the American of the late eighteenth century was thinking almost exclusively about statecraft—about the nature of society and how to make one. But as soon as the society got made, the pendulum began to swing back, and by the 1840's, Americans—in Concord and environs, at least—were thinking of neither God nor the state, but of the Self. And, in moments, even of the Self-as-God—detached, as we have seen, from nature, history, and society. The transcendentalist was, as the not very friendly critic George Santayana puts it, a "philosophical egotist"—concerned, as a more recent writer, Quentin Anderson says, with the "Imperial Self."

It is easy to point out the limitations of such a philosophy, but it must be remembered that central to it was the seminal idea of the creative power of mind. It must be granted, of course, that the transcendentalists did not originate this idea, that, as we have earlier suggested, they derived it from the German and English Romantics; but they did reformulate it and significantly adapted it to the American scene so that, among other consequences, we find it projected into the only native American school of philosophy, the pragmatism of William James (see our introduction). Furthermore, it cannot be gainsaid that transcendentalism, even in its extravagances in regard to the autonomy of the self, had something to do with creating the atmosphere in which might emerge the hero of the only literary work of tragic scale in nineteenth-century America. The hero is Ahab, cruising the universe in his pursuit of the white whale. The work is *Moby-Dick*, by Melville. That work's appearance ushered in the last decade before the Civil War. We may even say that the war was the murderous flourish and thrash of the great beast's tail.

To grasp the full significance and stature of the transcendentalists we must think of them in their moment of history, early in the development of the United States, when the modern world was assuming shape. The transcendentalists were, on the one hand, the young, the idealistic, those who were eager to break with the past and make a new world. They were, on the other hand, deeply embedded in their culture and their class, the old preindustrial elite of New England, the class of educated leadership, of teachers, scholars, clergymen and theologians, and doctors, with roots in the old system of farming and seaborne trade (not in manufacturing and banking), Congregationalism, Federalism, and the old distinctive stock that had respect for self-discipline, a full day's work, clean fields, sound learning, self-dependence, and hard money. (The grandfather of Theodore Parker was, for instance, the farmer who commanded the Minutemen at the Battle of Lexington.)

The cast of mind of these men was both an enormous asset and an enormous liability in dealing with their world. Even if they were in rebellion against what Emerson called the "formal" religion of the rationalistic Unitarianism in which they had been raised, their cast of mind was essentially religious and theological, supernatural and antinaturalistic, and their general education had been humanistic. This gave them a firm footing from which to criticize the defects of the new order; but at the same time they were completely ignorant of science, perhaps not of random facts and findings but of what is at stake in scientific thinking. Deduction and the Inner Light, a passion for absolutes, a contempt for consequences—these are not for the laboratory or for the scientific approach to a problem outside the laboratory in a modern society. The transcendentalists were also ignorant of history; they knew, of course, the historical "story," but they were not concerned with the nature of the forces operating in human affairs; their approach to history was not diagnostic but moralistic. They had lost their old-time theology, but they oddly clung to what is sometimes called the "devil theory of history." History was, to them, something like an old morality play, with Vices and Virtues aligned in debate for the human soul.

But every man must live in the limitations of his age, and the grandeur of his achievement depends on how he confronts the issues of his time in terms of its limitations. The achievement of the transcendentalists has a grandeur. They did confront, and helped define, the great issues of their time, and if they did not resolve those issues, we of the late twentieth century, who have not yet resolved them, are in no position to look down our noses at their effort. In fact, without their intellectual diagnosis we would lack much, and without their moral example, would lack much more.

Indeed, it is possible that certain issues are not to be resolved, but are to be lived into and, by the dialectic of life, merely transferred to new levels. For instance, democracy may exist only in the inevitable tension between the faith that makes institutions possible and the individual's faith in his own intuition. There is, clearly, no easy, abstract formula to resolve this tension. Again, there is the tension between egalitarianism (and the doctrine of the majority) and the need for standards—and sometimes for simple justice. Last, and perhaps most to their credit, the transcendentalists struggled with the problem of defining a ground for the affirmation of self in the face of the great machine of the world.

American history is the record of how men, including the transcendentalists, have tried to resolve—or to live with—such tensions. American literature finds in this fact, often in a concealed and indirect but nonetheless compelling form, one of its basic and most fruitful, and often one of its most tragic, themes.

EDGAR ALLAN POE (1809–1849)

There are good reasons for choosing Poe as the first of the writers to be discussed in this section of the book. A prime reason is that Poe exhibits in particularly sharp definition several features of his age. He was keenly conscious of the discontinuity between the Old and the New World. His commitment to the past was of a sort that made him the more sensitive to disturbing hints of the future. Though he wanted to find his place in a traditional society, his failure to do so may well have exacerbated his sense of lonely individualism. One supposes that he was pulled in opposite directions and that this tension was important in the production of his highly individual art—an art that revealed its full nature earlier and in more clearly defined forms than in the analogous productions of his contemporaries.

An inner conflict can be of enormous importance. The great twentieth-century Irish poet William Butler Yeats has remarked that out of our quarrel with others nothing better than rhetoric can come; great poetry issues only out of a quarrel with ourselves. In this connection, it will be useful to compare Poe with another southerner and near contemporary, William Gilmore Simms. Simms had no quarrel with himself. As we observed, he was largely content to chronicle the social and cultural development of his native section, to celebrate the quality of its life, and, later in his career, to defend that culture from outside attack. Simms's novels lack the subtle psychological insight and the tension that is the product of inner conflict, qualities that Cooper, at least in his best novels, expresses and qualities that we shall claim for the best work of Poe.[1]

Poe and Simms shared a good many ideas and acknowledged the same basic allegiances. Both men were sufficiently of their time and section to defend slavery. Both admired an aristocratic society, distrusted the leveling tendencies of democracy, and deplored the coarsening influence of mercantile life. In his tales and miscellaneous prose, Poe expresses his contempt for the utilitarian philosophy, for reformers, and for uplift movements generally. He does not believe in progress. He deplores America's increasing industrialization. In his more sardonic comments on democracy, he says that it amounts to the tyranny of a mob.[2] Clearly, Poe was no Jacksonian democrat.

As we shall see, he was not alone in his distrust of democracy and his distaste for the commercial spirit. The transcendentalists of New England, a group for whom Poe certainly had no liking, also were unhappy at the rise of the new industrial and mercantile power. Perry Miller, in his *Consciousness in Concord*,[3] remarks on the transcendentalists' "protest against the materiality of commercial New England." Up and down the land there were forces that tended to deprive the literary man of his former prestige and status. Miller remarks that something in the nature of "American society in the 1840's and 1850's" obliged "the literary voices of the era" to become, "in Melville's words, 'isolates.' Poe, of course, was a madman —in the opinion of his contemporaries; Whitman offended in ways too numerous to relate; Hawthorne," etc.[4]

Yet Poe's criticism of contemporary American culture cut deeper than that of his contemporaries, and his isolation was more nearly absolute than theirs. Emerson, in spite of his disdain for the rugged and pushing individualism of the lords of the cotton mills, ranked himself on the side of individualism, and Whitman could

---

[1] The quarrel of most of New England's men of letters was, of course, also a quarrel with "others," and their writing, along with that of Simms, equally lacks "insides." See, for example, the introductions to Longfellow and Lowell. But a great artist such as Nathaniel Hawthorne could arise, and Poe—in aspiration at least, if not in achievement—has some claim to be ranked with him.

[2] Killis Campbell, in his study *The Mind of Poe* (1933), has provided a convenient summary of Poe's opinions and prejudices; see especially pp. 137–38.

[3] 1958, p. 92; see also the introduction to 1826–61.

[4] *Op. cit.*, p. 117.

look with optimistic eye down democratic vistas. Poe could not. He probed the underlying assumptions of the new civilization developing on this side of the Atlantic. He questioned what was to be called by a later generation the American dream, and he foresaw some of the nightmares of twentieth-century man.

Writers abroad came to sense and appreciate these qualities far more quickly than did Poe's countrymen. The French poet Charles Baudelaire hailed Poe as a writer who had made profound discoveries about the human heart and had explored the potentialities of art to express them. Stephane Mallarmé, in a famous sonnet, "Le Tombeau d'Edgar Poe," saluted him as the archetypal poet, the man whose mission it was to redeem and refine the common language —to "give a purer meaning to the words of the tribe." Paul Valéry, in his admiration for Poe's discussion of poetics and critical theory, referred to him as "that great literary engineer."[5]

Yet Poe's American contemporaries failed to see these attributes, James Russell Lowell, though allowing him genius, estimated that element to be only a fraction of his makeup: Poe was in fact "two-fifths sheer fudge" (see *A Fable for Critics*). Emerson called him "the jingle man." A generation later, Henry James was to assert that "an enthusiasm for Poe is the mark of a decidedly primitive state of reflection."

Obviously there are problems here. The special virtues for which Baudelaire honored Poe were not obvious to Poe's countrymen, neither to the Virginia planter nor to the New England intellectual, and his contemporary popular appeal was based largely on rather different qualities. Moreover, in view of his general commitment to the values and ideas of his region, Poe ought to have been no more attractive to French men of letters like Baudelaire than was William Gilmore Simms. What possible inner tension could arise in this man who seemed, at least on the surface, to accept uncritically the values of an essentially conservative society, including its racism?[5]

Creativity is, of course, ultimately a mystery:

it is a confident man who believes he can explain the occurrence at a particular time of a Shakespeare or a Dante or even a Poe. Yet the circumstances of Poe's life may possibly throw some light on why his work differs so profoundly from that of Simms and of many other writers, northern as well as southern. Thus, it may have been Poe's very aspirations to become part of Virginia society that gave his life and his writing the particular turn which they took. For he merely hung on the fringes of that society. Since the Virginia of Poe's day was not particularly interested in literature, he could not hope to gain any satisfying accolade for distinction as a literary artist.[6]

The basic note of Poe's life was insecurity, an insecurity that began literally in the cradle. His grandfather, David Poe, an immigrant from Ireland, became a successful businessman and during the Revolutionary War, as a major in the quartermaster department, supplied provisions for the army. He was popularly known as "General Poe" and his services to the revolutionary cause included a loan of forty thousand dollars to the state, a sum that he never recovered. After the war his fortunes ebbed and any hope of establishing an illustrious family name dimmed still further when his son David ran away to become an actor.

The young David Poe joined a stage company in Boston and played opposite the beautiful Elizabeth Arnold, who had been before the footlights since early childhood and whose mother had been an actress in England. They were married in 1806 and continued their theatrical careers, though not always to critical acclaim. In 1807 their first child, William Henry Poe, was born, Mrs. Poe having continued to appear on the stage until late in her pregnancy. There seems to have been no question of her retiring from her career, and the infant Henry was

---

[5] See, for example, Sidney Kaplan's introduction to his edition of *The Narrative of Arthur Gordon Pym* (1960).

[6] Had Poe been more fully a part of the society that he claimed as his own, he might not have been thrown back into an imaginary world which he furnished forth with Gothic and other exotic properties. More cynical critics might even argue that had Poe been *fully* integrated into the planter society, he might not have been attracted to literature at all, finding his fulfillment in some career more highly valued by the Virginia planter society. He might even have become a Congressman or a major general.

brought to his Poe grandparents in Baltimore. Elizabeth Poe, pregnant again and criticized for appearing on the stage in that condition, continued to act until two weeks before Edgar was born (January 19, 1809). She returned to the stage three weeks after his birth.

Elizabeth was offered a job in New York and the Poes moved there, hoping to improve their fortunes, but secured only irregular work. David Poe's acting was severely criticized and, in his morbid sensitivity to criticism, he began to drink heavily. The problem was circular and hopeless. Before the child Edgar was a year old, his father had disappeared, leaving as his only legacy to his wife a third child, Rosalie, born in 1810.

Elizabeth Poe, now entirely responsible for the daily care as well as the support of her two younger children, continued with stage jobs in Charleston, in Norfolk, and in Richmond. There her health declined rapidly. She was befriended by two well-to-do Richmond ladies who brought her delicacies and became fond of the children. When she died in December, 1811, one of them took Rosalie into her home; the other, a Mrs. John Allan, took Edgar into hers. Thus the three Poe children were abandoned by their father, orphaned of their mother, and separated from each other in infancy. Although they knew of each other's existence and became acquainted during their later youth, their essential estrangement was to be lifelong.

Edgar was never legally adopted by the Allans —adoption was a rarity at this time—but he was given Allan as a middle name and was brought up as their son and presumed heir. Mrs. Allan, a kind and motherly woman but without brains or education, was dominated by her husband, a hardheaded Scots merchant. Allan was not only well-to-do; he had great prospects of wealth from the estate of his uncle, whose heir he was. The Allans lived well enough to be on visiting terms with the planter society of Richmond, but times became hard and Allan's business met with difficulties. As a consequence, he moved the family to England where he hoped to establish a branch of the business which would restore his fortunes. In this he was only partially successful. Allan did not become rich,

but there was enough to send Edgar to good schools and the boy profited from them. He showed there the facility for languages and the love of literature which were to shape his life, and it was at this time that he began to write verse.

After five years in England, the family returned to Richmond, worse off than when they had left. They lived humbly now, and Edgar, although entered in a decent school, was made to feel the scorn of some of his classmates for being a "players' brat" and the ward of a failed merchant.

When in 1825, on the death of his uncle, Allan inherited the expected fortune, he began to live on a rather grand scale and Edgar was entered in the University of Virginia. But Allan's attitude toward society and toward money was ambivalent. As for society, he was a kinless man in a kinship society, a Scots Presbyterian who kept mistresses and had several illegitimate children. As for money, what amount was proper for the support of a young gentleman at the University of Virginia? Allan thought very little. As a consequence Poe was embarrassed and in debt from the day of his arrival. He borrowed money, gambled to get funds to repay his debts, and got still deeper into debt.

Poe was not more dissolute than most of the students, and he was a scholar of real distinction; nevertheless he was in Allan's eyes a failure and a disgrace. At the end of the year he was withdrawn from the university and from then on between Poe and Allan there was an unending controversy about money. Was Poe's role that of foster son to John Allan and the presumed heir of his fortune? Or was he the worthless son of a worthless father, ungrateful to the Allans who had rescued him but who could throw him out at any time? Abandoned by his real father, scorned and ignored all his early life by the Poe family in Baltimore, Poe must have often questioned his identity. But problems of identity aside, now that he had been abandoned by his foster father, what was he to do?

He resolved to go to Boston. Though he left home penniless, he managed somehow to get there and, after real suffering, enlisted in the army under an assumed name. He served for two years, leaving to take an appointment at the military academy at West Point. By this time he had patched things up with John Allan, but after Mrs. Allan's death and her husband's subsequent remarriage, Poe despaired of ever becoming Allan's heir and decided to leave West Point. Since resignation was not allowed, he managed to get himself expelled (by failure to attend classes) and set out to support himself by writing, a particularly difficult thing to do in America in the first half of the nineteenth century.

He had, of course, been writing poems since he was a schoolboy, and a volume of poems, *Tamerlane and Other Poems*, was published in Boston in 1827, at the time of his army enlistment. In 1829 he published *Al Aaraaf, Tamerlane and Minor Poems*; and in 1831, *Poems*; but it was plain that verse could not provide him with a living and he was soon hard at work as an editor, first with the *Southern Literary Messenger*,[7] later with such magazines as *Graham's* and the *Broadway Journal*. But hack work—and a great deal of the writing that Poe did for the magazines has to be counted as such—was not well paid. His marriage in 1835 to his first cousin, Virginia Clemm, deepened his financial difficulties.

In 1829 Poe had looked up his relatives in Baltimore and there for the first time met his grandmother, her widowed daughter, Mrs. Maria Clemm, and Maria's two small children, Henry and Virginia. After the death of the grandmother, in whose house Mrs. Clemm had been living, Poe was concerned to provide a home for Mrs. Clemm and Virginia. This was accomplished by his marriage to Virginia, then not fourteen years old, and the three made up a *ménage à trois*, living happily together—save for Poe's almost chronic financial difficulties—until Virginia's death from tuberculosis in 1847.

The extreme youth of Poe's bride raised eyebrows at the time. To many present-day commentators it suggests that what Poe really yearned for was the mother and the family life of which he had been deprived. (Poe called Mrs.

Clemm "my own darling mother" and in his last letter to her he addressed her as "my dear dear Muddy.")[8]

With Poe's marriage he settled into what was to become the routine of his rather short life: trying to make a living with his pen, moving from one editorship to another, finding himself chronically in financial straits. The highlights of his melancholy record are detailed in our biographical chart.

During the nineteenth century, Poe was not well served by his biographers, and the notion that most of his difficulties were of his own making still persists. His first biographer, the Reverend Rufus Griswold, portrayed him as a thoroughly wicked man, a kind of American Satanist, whose example Griswold held up as a warning to others. At the other extreme, the French poet Baudelaire saw in Poe the sensitive young aristocrat, unable to cope with American materialism and so victimized by it. Later scholarship, however, has disproved Griswold's slanders and corrected Baudelaire's too romantic conjectures. Poe was not a moral monster nor was he an ineffectual genius, the victim of the crassness of the New World. He was a more than competent editor and by the standards of the day a quite successful journalist. But he was not an easy man to get on with; he let himself get involved in needless literary quarrels; his body had very little tolerance for alcohol; and he worked in a profession that was chancy and at the best not very well paid. He was often in financial difficulties, and the story that while his young wife was dying there was not money enough to provide a fire in their cottage may well be true.

When Poe was growing up, English Romanticism was at full tide and American writers too were producing Romantic poetry and fiction.

---

[7] John Pendleton Kennedy (see introduction to Kennedy) helped him secure this post.

[8] The circumstances of Poe's marriage and its aura of sexless coziness raise a question as to whether the marriage of Poe and Virginia was in fact ever consummated. Joseph Wood Krutch, in *Edgar Allan Poe: A Study in Genius* (1926), argues that Poe was impotent. On the other hand, William Bittner believes that Poe's union with Virginia was a true marriage; see his *Poe: A Biography* (1962).

In his exploitation of "Gothic" materials, Poe had an American forerunner, Charles Brockden Brown, whose work Poe knew and admired. (See the introduction to Brown.) As for British writers, Poe was familiar with Scott's novels and with the poetry of the great English Romantics. His *Tamerlane*, for example, is filled with echoes of Lord Byron's oriental tales in verse.

But, as we have said, it is likely that the circumstances of Poe's life may well account for the depth and intensity of his Romanticism and the special form it took: explorations of a world of dream and of nightmare rather than explorations of the American daylight scene. Moreover, to a man sensitized as Poe had been by his special experiences, what to other observers was only a daylight scene revealed itself as nightmare. Poe's fellow American Romantics were nourished by the contemplation of nature or of the world of the frontier, whether in its grand and desolate solitudes or as the home of the red men possessed of primitive violence and the poetry of action. But Poe's interests were not those of a Bryant or a Thoreau; he wrote only one tale of the American wilderness.[9] His imagination was stimulated by Europe and the ancient East—or by lands at the ends of the earth—as in *The Narrative of Arthur Gordon Pym.*

Poe remarks that beauty always has some element of strangeness in it and cites as his authority Francis Bacon. No one has ever been able to discover such a passage in Bacon's works, but there is no doubt that this formulation does express Poe's own profound conviction. For him, the needful vehicle for presenting his kind

of "strangeness" is the remote and the exotic. Yet Poe is no mere imitator of the English Gothic novelists. He takes their Gothicism up another notch. In Poe's stories the past is darker, more ominous, and lies on his heroes and heroines with a heavier weight than it does on those of Horace Walpole or Mrs. Radcliffe. The haunted castles of the Gothic novel were more remote from Poe than they were from Byron and Coleridge, and the very fact that the Atlantic rolled between him and those ruins allowed them to be more purely the creations of his own sensibility. As he remarked to a friend: "My terror is not from Germany but of the soul." Thus, though affected by the circumstances of his own life, his interest in a world of nightmare was related to a cultural situation that was just beginning to emerge in his own homeland and would not reveal its full character until the middle of the next century.

Yet this last statement which attributes a prophetic character to Poe may seem to contradict his conscious intentions as he confronted the hard realities of his life. Forced to make a living through his writing, he had to be on the alert for what might prove popular, and in his earliest stories he brazenly imitated all the current literary modes and fashions. For example, "King Pest" is a burlesque on an incident in *Vivian Grey* by the English novelist and statesman Benjamin Disraeli (1804–1881). "Loss of Breath" is a takeoff on the style of an American contemporary, John Hill Hewitt (1801–1890). In "A Tale of Jerusalem" he hits off the style of *Zillah, a Tale of Jerusalem,* a popular novel published in 1829 by Horace Smith (1779–1849). These stories and others were to make up a collection supposed to have been told by the members of the "Folio Club." At each meeting one member was to entertain the others by telling a story. The members bore such comic names as Chronologos Chronology, Solomon Seadrift, Mr. Rouge-et-noir, and so on.

As James Southall Wilson puts it, Poe carried out his apprenticeship as a writer of fiction by doing burlesques of popular stories and novels, and his "imitations [though] received ever since as original tales, were meant as de-

---

[9] One must not, however, jump to the conclusion that Poe was a man without muscles who had no experience of active, physical life. He was a good boxer and was proud of his abilities as a swimmer. He served for two years in the American army, not as an officer but as an enlisted man who worked his way up to the rank of sergeant major. Yet his army experience contributed very little more to his work than the physical setting for "The Gold Bug," Sullivan's Island, near Charleston, where he had been stationed for a time. Instinctively, Poe sought his material not in the American present but in the past, and ultimately in the depths of heightened and even aberrant psychic experience.

liberate burlesques and satires."[10] Thus, Poe learned to write "by imitating in burlesque the foibles of fashionable literature, from the epigrammatic cleverness of Bulwer and the extravagancies of the *Blackwood* article to what he considered the prose-poetic nonsense of the [New England] Transcendentalists or the frozen horrors of the German tale of terror."[11]

As evidence that many of his tales were written tongue-in-cheek, Wilson cites a letter from Poe to his friend John Pendleton Kennedy. Kennedy had denied an allegation that Poe's stories were intentionally satiric and then applied to the author for confirmation of his opinion. Poe replied: "Most of them were *intended* for half-banter, half-satire—although I might not fully acknowledge this to be their aim even to myself."

Banter and satire—especially if the satire is at the expense of fashions, social modes, and attitudes—imply intellectual judgment, not mere emotional response. Poe's qualifications ("half-banter, half-satire," not even fully acknowledged to himself) are in themselves highly significant. Perhaps they are meant merely to temper his disagreement with his friend's judgment; but they may very well point to a sophisticated and self-conscious artist who realized that he was at once inside and outside of his "bizarreries"— who, though caught up in these fantastic imaginings, was nevertheless judging them in some detachment.

One of Poe's most curious stories is entitled "Berenice." In this study in madness, the protagonist, like a good many of Poe's heroes, is afflicted with a "morbid irritability of those properties of the mind in metaphysical science termed the *attentive* . . . [manifesting itself in a] nervous *intensity of interest* with which, in my case, the powers of meditation . . . busied and buried themselves, in the contemplation of even the most ordinary objects of the universe."

The affected hero is in love with his cousin, a very beautiful woman with remarkably white gleaming teeth on which his "intensity of interest" becomes fixated. In his mania he begins to

believe that "their possession could alone . . . restore me to peace, in giving me back to reason."

Berenice falls ill with some vague but fatal malady and before the two can be married she is dead. After her burial, the hero, sitting in his room, comes to himself as if "newly awakened from a confused and exciting dream." A servant taps on the door and, wild with terror, enters to tell him that the grave of Berenice has been opened. He goes on to whisper of "a disfigured body, enshrouded, yet still breathing, still palpitating, still *alive!*"

The servant points to his master's garments which are muddy and bloodstained. There is a spade in the room and on the table a box.

> With a shriek I bounded to the table, and grasped the box that lay upon it. But I could not force it open; and in my tremor it slipped from my hands, and fell heavily, and burst into pieces; and from it, with a rattling sound, there rolled out some instruments of dental surgery, intermingled with thirty-two small, white and ivory-looking substances that were scattered to and fro about the floor.

When those "thirty-two small, white and ivory-looking substances"—all accounted for, apparently without cavities, gleaming testimony to Berenice's perfect dental hygiene—clatter on the floor, one is relieved to remember that this tale too was originally intended for the Folio Club. Nevertheless, there may remain a problem of just how one is to take it. As a bit of what we now call "black humor"? With a shriek of maniacal laughter to match the shriek of the mad teller of the tale? There is more than one kind of burlesque: some succeeds and some does not. To an editor[12] who remonstrated with Poe about "Berenice," Poe replied that his subject matter in truth was "far too horrible" but went on to indicate the kind of effect at which he had been aiming: ". . . the ludicrous heightened into the grotesque: the fearful colored into the horrible: the witty exaggerated into bur-

[10] *American Mercury*, 24 (1931), 215.
[11] *Op cit.*, p. 218.

[12] Thomas W. White. See Poe's letter to him, dated April 30, 1835.

lesque: the singular wrought out into the strange and mystical."

Suggestive as Poe's explanation is, it scarcely provides a solution. Is "Berenice" an example of the witty exaggerated into the burlesque? Or of the singular wrought out into the strange and mystical? It can scarcely be both. Or can it? Perhaps Poe was himself puzzled as to how he should describe what he was doing. But his letter to White would indicate that at least he knew what he was *not* doing. He was not trying to fabricate simply another horror story. He was trying to get beyond that effect, whatever that "beyond" might lead to. In any case, "Berenice" is clearly a preliminary study for such stories as "Ligeia" and "The Fall of the House of Usher," stories in which Poe has moved beyond a mere takeoff on an outmoded stereotype.[13]

One can learn a great deal about Poe's characteristic stage properties and the typical uses he makes of them from an examination of the setting of "Ligeia," his favorite among his tales (the text of which appears in this section). The heroine, Ligeia, is described as living in a "dim and decayed city by the Rhine." Poe's special angle of perspective reveals itself at once, for a nineteenth-century German living in the Rhine valley probably found its cities quite real, quite solid, and undecayed. Consciously or unconsciously, Poe enhances the remoteness of the city by not naming it. He even denies Ligeia a surname; he makes use of a studied vagueness.

After Ligeia's death, her widowed husband moves to England and sets up his household in a ruined abbey. Apparently he values the abbey's "gloomy and dreary grandeur," for he does not even clear from it the grasses and mosses that grow upon its stones. But inside the abbey, he makes great alterations, filling it with rich furniture, tapestries, and hangings. In doing so, he provides the kind of setting required for many of Poe's tales. In "Berenice," "Morella," "The Fall of the House of Usher," and "The Oval Portrait" one finds these same elaborate furnishings—most of which, by the way, are not at all "Gothic." Usually, a lamp burning scented oil hangs like a censer from the ceiling. Ottomans are disposed about the room. There are elaborate tapestries and heavy draperies, which, in their rustling, give "a hideous and uneasy intonation to the whole."[14] Poe may have genuinely admired such overstuffed and grandiloquent elegance. (He was evidently interested in interior decorating and wrote an essay entitled "The Philosophy of Furniture.") But in any case, grandly gloomy interiors provide the appropriate habitat for his heroes, so often morbidly melancholy or actually mad, and the proper setting for the return from the tomb of his Ligeias and Morellas and Madelines.

Sigfried Giedion, the Swiss architect and historian of culture, has some interesting comments to make on nineteenth-century taste in furniture and furnishings.[15] Though Giedion nowhere mentions Poe, the period rooms that he describes might very well be some of those found in Poe's tales. Giedion observes that the nineteenth century saw the increasing influence of the upholsterer, who more and more tended to "control the situation." "Picturesque disorder fascinated people, for it was the reflection of the chaotic state of feeling. The upholsterer, by embellishment of furniture and artistic hangings, sets up a fairy land to enchant the drabness of the industrial day."

---

[13] One more item in Poe's letter to White should be noted here. In defense of his writing "Berenice," Poe says, "To be appreciated you must be *read*, and these things [writings in "bad taste" like "Berenice"] are invariably sought after with avidity. They *are*, if you will take notice, the articles which find their way into other periodicals. . . ." He is speaking here as the practical man who has to make a living. He feels obliged to play up to the popular taste; but he means to pursue in the process his own purposes—and those purposes may include a little private fun at the expense of the public. This aspect of Poe ought to be kept in mind as a makeweight to our usual notion of the melancholy writer with the noble brow and an austerely ideal conception of art. This is the Poe who enjoyed contriving hoaxes. It was a deeply characteristic trait and one not lost on Baudelaire, who observes that "Poe was always great not only in his noble conceptions but also as a prankster."

[14] Such settings are not entirely peculiar to Poe. See the furnishings of Aylmer's apartment in Hawthorne's "The Birthmark" (pp. 478–79).

[15] *Mechanization Takes Command* (1948). See especially "The Nineteenth Century: Mechanization and Ruling Taste," pp. 329–89.

Giedion connects the ponderous armchairs and sofas and ottomans with what he calls an "orientalizing romanticism." He observes that "the Oriental influence must be counted on as one of the many strivings for escape that darkened the emotional life of the last century and gave it a tragic note. Man was not content to live in his own skin. This could lead to nothing but the grotesque." (Poe entitled his 1840 volume *Tales of the Grotesque and Arabesque.*)

It may be significant that some of Giedion's most interesting examples of nineteenth-century styles in furnishing come from France, the country that from the beginning saw in Poe the great pioneer artist. In particular, Giedion mentions Alfred de Musset's comment made in 1836: "We have left no imprint of our age either on our dwellings, on our gardens, or on anything else. We have culled something from every culture but our own. . . . We live off fragments." Did Poe think that the men of his own day were living off fragments? It would be hard to say. The issue here, however, is not how Poe might have phrased his account of the state of the culture, but rather the appropriateness of such settings to the particular examples of breakdown, frustration, and horror that he chose to depict.

At least one of Poe's characters in his tales of the grotesque is clearly aware of what the furnishings of his house mean and how they are related to his own state of mind. The hero of "The Assignation" tells his guests that

> to dream has been the business of my life. I have therefore framed for myself, as you see, a bower of dreams. . . . You behold around you, it is true, a medley of architectural embellishments. The chastity of Ionia is offended by antediluvian devices, and the sphinxes of Egypt are outstretched upon carpets of gold. Yet the effect is incongruous to the timid alone. Proprieties of place, and especially of time, are the bugbears which terrify mankind from contemplation of the magnificent. Once I was myself a decorist [that is, a person who venerates decorum]: but that sublimation of folly has palled upon my soul. All this is now the fitter for my purpose. Like these ara-

besque censers, my spirit is writhing in fire, and the delirium of this scene is fashioning me for the wild visions of that land of real dreams whither I am now rapidly departing.

His is the speech of a dying man, for he has poisoned himself in order to keep an assignation in the kingdom of death with his beautiful mistress.

The dying man's taste in furniture thoroughly accords with Giedion's account of the style of the period, in which there had occurred a "devaluation of symbols": all the miscellaneous lumber of the past is dumped together for merely decorative or spectacular effects.

Poe also beautifully dramatizes for us what Giedion calls "the demonic side of the nineteenth century." His tales are "oppressive with assassination and non-escape," or, as Giedion puts it in another passage, with "violence and death." (In virtue of his being able to dramatize the demonic side of the nineteenth century[16] as it expressed itself not only in America but in Europe, Poe shows himself to be neither the American provincial nor the American nationalist, but a writer moving within the mainstream of international literature.)

Many of Poe's characters are obsessed with a fear of death. Some of them strive to come back from the tomb; others are terrified of being buried alive or in fact are buried alive like Berenice or like Madeline in "The Fall of the House of Usher."[17] The two obsessions are, of course, actually the same: the horror of retain-

---

[16] The narrator of Poe's "Some Words with a Mummy" says, toward the end of the story: "The truth is, I am heartily sick of this life and of the nineteenth century in general. I am convinced that everything is going wrong." We have no right to assume that the teller of the tale necessarily expresses Poe's personal views; yet Poe may very well have felt, many times, sick of his own life and it may be that he also felt sick of the century into which he had been born.

[17] It has been noted how often this situation occurs in Poe's work: Ligeia and Morella also return or attempt to return from the tomb; the victim of "A Cask of Amontillado" is walled up alive; so also is the hero of *Arthur Gordon Pym*. So is the accusing black cat in the story that bears that title. One of Poe's stories is called "Premature Burial." If one adds to these stories those that describe related situations, the list could be greatly extended.

ing consciousness in a world that is dead—of living on in thought while still tied to one's own rotting body. Small wonder that in so many of Poe's tales the hero is already mad or is fighting off incipient madness.

As several writers of our own time have remarked, Poe combined primitivism and decadence; that is to say, he applied the freshness and energy that are associated with provincial rawness to the problems of an overrefined and hypercivilized consciousness. Poe's typical hero is consciously living (but with an abnormal energy) on the "fragments" of the past. We may cite the hero of "The Assignation" as a pertinent example. Because he is no longer committed to any particular tradition, he gathers around himself miscellaneous *objets d'art*, not because any of them has symbolic meaning for him, but because of their immediate decorative value or because their very random meaninglessness piques and amuses him.

Allen Tate, in his essay "Our Cousin, Mr. Poe,"[18] expresses in not very different terms Poe's preoccupation with the disintegration of culture. Poe, he says, more than any other writer "in England or the United States or, so far as I know, in France," gives us a vision of "dehumanized man." Tate goes on to specify what he means by the term *dehumanized*: Poe's characters are " 'dead to the world'; they are machines of sensation and will. . . ." This is Tate's way of coming at Giedion's point that men of the nineteenth century were not willing "to live in their own skins." For Poe's characters, the body is a mere machine:[19] it is effectively cut off from the consciousness which lives within, but aspires to live beyond, the body. The sensibility tries to cut itself loose from the flesh:[20] it refuses to be reconciled to the flesh and its mortal fate.

As a consequence, Poe's characters insist on living with an intensity that has no relation to the limitations imposed by biological and physical laws. In their fantastically gloomy though gorgeous settings, they seem never to eat or drink; they have no sensuous appetites of any kind. They do not work. Occasionally they read or play on musical instruments. They meditate a great deal. They speak to each other intensely and with passion. They seethe with all sorts of emotions, but their "living" is all in their heads—all a matter of intellect and imagination. Even so, they walk in fear of death, for though their consciousness manages rather successfully to float above the life of the body and of the senses, it cannot entirely cut its connection with the body; and this means that with the end of the body, consciousness itself will cease to be. It also means that Poe's characters sometimes fear that consciousness will *not* cease to be and that one will suffer the recurrent nightmare of being alive.

Consider Poe's typical heroines. They are usually afflicted with mysterious diseases. They visibly waste away before their lovers' eyes. A closer inspection reveals that they are not dying of spiritual anemia but rather of an intensity that drains the body of its energy. Their lovers or husbands can see that they are perishing and the heroines themselves are thoroughly aware of it, but the process cannot be halted. Yet Poe's heroines are not content to die; they are not willing to let go of their lovers, even though their relationships seem scarcely those of physical love: the lovers simply share an intense contemplation of each other. These women, "of monstrous will and intellect," as Tate describes them, in the end turn into vampires. They return from the tomb, literally as the Lady Madeline does, or by taking over the body of her husband's second wife, as Ligeia does, or by

---

18 *The Forlorn Demon* (1953), pp. 74–95.
19 Poe thus recognizes the split between the inner and outer worlds but he does not seem interested in the unification attempted by Romantics like Wordsworth. His way of dealing with the problem looks both backward and forward—back to an eighteenth-century sensibility and forward to the future as foreshadowed by Baudelaire.
20 In his essay 'The House of Poe," Richard Wilbur

gives this conflict a rather different inflection: "the poetic soul" seeks to detach itself "from earthly things, and regain [its] lost imaginative power—[its] power to commune with that supernal beauty" that it had known in childhood. See Robert Regan's *Poe: A Collection of Critical Essays* (1967), pp. 98–120.

appropriating the body of her own child, as Morella does.

Poe's characters do fear the final annihilation, the dread nothingness which always threatens them even while they are alive, since they have no real contact with the world of nature or with the world of religion, being purely intense sensibilities, sheer intelligences, operating in a vacuum. As Tate implies, these revenants who, like Ligeia, return from the tomb, are now the "undead" precisely because they were never truly alive. In fact, Tate says, "Poe is not interested in anything that is alive. Everything in Poe is dead: the houses, the rooms, the furniture. . . ." To say this is to overstate matters, and yet there is a very real sense in which the world depicted by Poe is a dead world. Typical examples are these somber mansions furnished—to use Giedion's phrase—like "operatic settings."[21] No one could conceivably drop crumbs on the oriental carpets or upset a teacup or open a window. The fact that Poe's characters occupy such stage sets hints that they are themselves dead, zombies of preternatural intuition and ravenous imagination, who are shut up in bodies which they do not really control and placed in environments with which they have no meaningful relationship.

One thinks of Roderick Usher spinning his morbid fancies as he sits within his melancholy house with its bleak walls and vacant eyelike windows and—not to forget the furnishings—in a room whose "general furniture [is] profuse, comfortless, antique, and tattered," a room lit-

[21] W. H. Auden has an interesting comment on this point. He writes: "Poe is sometimes attacked for the operatic quality of the prose and *decor* in his tales, but they are essential to preserving the illusion. His heroes cannot exist except operatically. Take, for instance, the following sentence from William Wilson:

> Let it suffice, that among spendthrifts I out-heroded Herod, and that, giving name to a multitude of novel follies, I added no brief appendix to the long catalogue of vices then usual in the most dissolute university in Europe.

In isolation, as a prose sentence, it is terrible, vague, verbose, the sense at the mercy of a conventional rhetorical rhythm. But dramatically, how right, how well it reveals the William Wilson who narrates the story in his real colors, as the fantastic self who hates and refuses contact with reality."

tered with "books and musical instruments" that fail, as the author says in so many words, "to give any vitality to the scene."

Death is a predominant theme also of Poe's poetry. One would expect it to be so in "The Conqueror Worm," the poem inserted in "Ligeia," that story about the horror of death. But death dominates his poetry generally. The setting of "The Raven," his most celebrated poem, is reminiscent of that of many of his tales: the disconsolate lover sits in an elaborate chamber, trying to find surcease from sorrow in his books and conducting a curious dialogue with his midnight visitant, perched on the "bust of Pallas above [his] chamber door." Death is also the theme of the curious poem "Ulalume," one of Poe's favorites, of "The Sleeper," and of "The City in the Sea."

Poe's typical hero, cut off from the world of nature, surrounded by "dead" furniture, living only in terms of an intense imagination, is unable to find in any human relationship an outlet for his feelings or in any human activity an occasion for his actions. Such a setting reflects a situation increasingly familiar to men of our century. More and more of us live in a world of abstractions—automated, computerized, cut off from nature. One might argue that Poe is the first writer to intimate "the world of the absurd," that antiuniverse which has come in for so much attention during the last quarter century.

Roderick Usher finds the interior world of his own consciousness far more exciting than the world outside him; indeed, his obsession with his own mental processes is precisely what cuts him off from the world of nature. Because Poe himself is much interested in the mysterious and baffling aspects of human consciousness, incipient madness and madness itself fascinate him, for he wants to understand that darker self that lurks behind the facade of rationality enjoined by society upon its members.

A typical "fireside poet" like Longfellow gave over the search into the darkness of the self and was willing to content himself with a more genial and comfortable scene. But Poe obviously was concerned with that search. The Gothic stage sets of his darker stories were not being used for their own sake but as a means to explore a terror which he quite truthfully insisted was "of the soul."

Yet if the world of Poe's imagination is haunted by death and if the tales in particular seem morbid and obsessed, why did they appeal to the audience of Poe's day? And can they have anything to say to us? The answer would have to be that in spite of their fantastic character they do, at some level, reveal what was going on in the psyche of nineteenth-century man and, even more pertinently, do predict what now goes on in the psyche of twentieth-century man. Something like a disintegration of personality was occurring in Poe's lifetime, and the strange horrors that Poe described produced correspondent echoes in the sensibilities of his contemporaries in America. Their spiritual baggage had been brought over from Europe; in transit it had suffered some damage and deterioration; and, in any case, it did not quite fit the developing conditions of the New World, a world which was at once more practical and more violent than the Old and which markedly lacked the ameliorating power of habitual custom and traditional social patterns.

This is not to argue that Poe's contemporaries were completely aware of the nature of their response to his work. They may have in fact been conscious of little more than the pleasure that men often take in the strange, the sensational, and the perversely Romantic.[22] But the ghost stories that Poe told to his contemporaries were ghost stories with a difference even though, by setting them in a remote and decadent Europe, Poe masked their application to the situation in America. Abroad, however, Baudelaire immediately found Poe's ghost stories relevant to *his* situation and in a very special way:

these stories pointed to a disintegration of which he was quite aware. So also the American reader of the twentieth century finds them relevant to the world in which he lives. Hart Crane, for example, who cherished the American dream and could be fervently optimistic about the future of American civilization, was also aware of the American nightmare, and in a section of *The Bridge* in which the New York subway is seen as a kind of hell—man dehumanized, spiritually gutted, hurtling through an insanely inhuman world—Poe is seen as a straphanger on the subway, his head nodding with the motion of the car. The poet, quoting from Poe's poem "The City in the Sea," asks himself:

. . . why do I often meet your visage here,
Your eyes like agate lanterns—on and on
Below the toothpaste and the dandruff ads?
—And did their riding eyes right through your
    side,
And did their eyes like unwashed platters ride?
And Death, aloft,—gigantically down
Probing through you—toward me, O evermore!
And when they dragged your retching flesh,
Your trembling hands that night through Balti-
    more—
That last night on the ballot rounds, did you
Shaking, did you deny the ticket, Poe?[23]

Poe's awareness of the disintegration of personality may be related to certain apparent con-

---

[22] Poe was quite right in noting that his audience had a craving for the sensational and the shocking. Yet this is not to deny that Poe's contemporary audience may have got some of his deeper implications as well. The sensational plots of the stories may have served—to use T. S. Eliot's words—"to keep the [reader's] mind diverted, while [the tale did] its work upon him." (See Eliot's *The Use of Poetry and the Use of Criticism*, 1933, p. 144.)

[23] The precise circumstances of Poe's death are not known. Poe left Richmond for Baltimore, presumably on September 27, 1849, and should have arrived in that city on September 28. Thomas H. Lane, a friend of Poe's, indicates that Poe then came on to Philadelphia to stop off with friends. But if he did so, he must have —prompted by reasons about which we can only conjecture—soon returned to Baltimore, for he was found there on October 3, semiconscious, and brought to the Washington College Hospital, where he died early on the morning of October 7. October 3 was an election day, and Arthur Hobson Quinn writes that "the fact that Poe was found in or near a polling place has given rise to vivid pictures, all problematical, of his having been drugged, taken from one polling place to another to be voted as a 'repeater,' and abandoned when his usefulness was over" (*Edgar Allan Poe: A Critical Biography*, 1941, p. 639). (See also John Pendleton Kennedy's account, pp. 268–69.) The dying man never recovered sufficiently to be able to tell what had happened to him.

traditions within his own personality—his fascination with the reasoning power as such, in spite of, yet perhaps finally because of, his obsession with the irrational side of the mind.[24]

Poe's interest in the powers of reason was intense and reveals itself in a number of ways. He fancied himself as a cryptographer, and the problem of breaking codes comes in for full attention in his story "The Gold Bug." In stories like "The Murders in the Rue Morgue" and "The Purloined Letter," reason is applied to the solution of a baffling crime. M. Dupin, given the case of the concealed letter, does not fiddle about with probing needles and magnifying glasses and other instruments with which to make an exhaustive search of the apartment which he reasons is bound to contain the letter in question. Dupin is not at all surprised to hear that such methods have already been tried and have failed. He sits in his own room to work out the solution in his head.

Some few of Poe's tales of nightmare terror come to happy endings precisely because the hero can think his way through a problem. Though the hero of "The Pit and the Pendulum" cannot, by his unaided efforts, save himself from the death intended for him, he uses his head to keep himself alive until help from the outside arrives; and the hero of "A Descent into the Maelstrom," without any outside help, does rescue himself from the very jaws of disaster. In fact, one kind of Poe-esque hero can be described as a man forced to fall back on the resources of his own mind, whether bound hand and foot as in "The Pit and the Pendulum" or clinging to a small boat as it whirls around the walls of the abyss as in "A Descent into the Maelstrom" or, less spectacularly, sitting quietly in his office like M. Dupin. In a way, the faith that one can—at least on some occasions—find through reasoning a way out of apparently hopeless situations is one of the most "American" things about Poe.

How good was Poe himself as a reasoner? Not very good, in the opinion of several recent scholars. C. C. Walcott dismisses Poe's logic as a mere "element of [his] style." Edward C. Wagenknecht tells us that "Poe was less concerned with accuracy than with the appearance of accuracy," though conceding that "this is just what the man of letters should be." Most of the experts who have read Poe's "Conversations of Eiros and Charmion" or his "Eureka" regard Poe's knowledge of science as rather superficial. Even in cryptography, a science to which Poe made certain public pretensions, his lore was not very deep. W. K. Wimsatt observes that "to study Poe at work on ciphers is to find not a wide knowledge and intricate method of procedure, but rather a kind of untrained wit, intuition which more quickly than accurately grasps the outlines of cryptic principles and immediately with confident imagination proclaims the whole. It is probable that whatever ciphers he did solve, he solved very rapidly." Wimsatt has also studied Poe on the subject of the mechanical chess player and comments that the picture of Poe that emerges is not that of "a detective drawing from observed facts a conclusion which squares with other facts," but that of "an imaginative writer, with the power of making bright and acceptable the drab-mechanic guesses of writers with an eye to reality."

In view of what has just been said, how deep was Poe's commitment to reason? On one level it was surely genuine enough. M. Dupin with his cool intellect is obviously one of Poe's personal heroes. But as for the general reasonableness of *Homo sapiens*, Poe had his reservations. Politically, he was a conservative—as indeed were other Americans of his generation, such as Irving, Cooper, and Hawthorne. Baudelaire was to praise Poe for having recovered human dignity from the shallowness of the optimistic reformers. (By contrast, Franklin,[25] who had been the idol of Frenchmen two generations earlier,

---

[24] Auden has noted this split. "The horror tales and the tales of ratiocination belong together, for the heroes of both exist as unitary states—Roderick Usher *reasons* as little as Auguste Dupin *feels*" (italics ours).

[25] Martha Banta, in "Benjamin, Edgar, Humbert, and Jay," *Yale Review* (Summer, 1971), pp. 532–49, has some interesting comments on the ways in which Franklin and Poe represent the polarities of the American character—and even of the American Dream.

was for Baudelaire "the inventor of a counting-house morality, the hero of a century devoted to materialism.")

At all events, Poe's regard for reason never deluded him into underestimating the dark depths of the soul. He was fascinated with the deviousness of the human being (as in "The Imp of the Perverse") and with its inner conflicts (as in "William Wilson"). He was intensely interested in the whole phenomenon of unconsciousness and the deeper realm of hidden motivations—what we should today call the unconscious.[26] These were the interests of the Romantic poets generally, but, as we have already observed, Poe forces the central issue further than most of his fellows in Romanticism, either American or British. He endeavors to explore even more deeply than they the depths of the psyche.

A poet like Wordsworth, by writing about peasants and children and idiots, attempts to get down to layers of the mind deeper than consciousness. So does Byron, who hints darkly at incest and nameless crimes. But it is Poe who takes this sense of horror one stage further: he attempts a rational examination of these irrational impulses and compulsive drives. He wants to bring reason to bear on areas which in his time were regarded as lying beyond its boundaries or else were ignored altogether. A French psychoanalyst, Marie Bonaparte, makes the bold conjecture that Poe actually predicted the development of psychoanalysis. She quotes a passage from Poe's "The Black Cat," in which the hero of that story conjectures: "Hereafter, perhaps, some intellect may be found which will reduce my phantasm to the common-place, some intellect more calm, more logical, and far less excitable than my own, which will perceive, in the circumstances I detail with awe, nothing more than an ordinary succession of very natural causes and effects." She remarks that "it is almost as though Poe had sensed the remote advent of psychoanalysis which, alone, has given us the means to reduce to a series of cause and

effect, emanating in fact, as he himself says, from 'homely and domestic happenings,' the dreadful phantasms that haunted his life and art."[27]

The most celebrated instance of Poe's application of the cool intellect to what has been commonly regarded as the stubbornly irrational and even suprarational, is his essay "The Philosophy of Composition" (included in our text), in which he describes the construction of his poem "The Raven." Everything from the prevailing mood and the specific subject matter down to the refrain, according to Poe, were deliberately calculated.

Even Baudelaire believed that Poe's account of the composition of this poem was written partly tongue-in-cheek, remarking that "after all a little charlatanism is always permitted to genius, and is even proper to it." Perhaps Poe did write tongue-in-cheek. It is hard to believe that any poet ever actually composed a poem in this fashion, and the very minuteness of the circumstantial detail makes the whole essay look suspiciously like a leg-pull. But René Wellek thinks that certain basic ideas were meant seriously; that is, "the elements of groping, experimenting, hard work, craftsmanship" did need emphasis "after the great romantic trust in the winds of inspiration."[28] The hard work, the experimenting, and the craftsmanship were precisely what Paul Valéry regarded as Poe's great contributions to the world of letters, for Poe combined logic with imagination and mysticism with calculation, and indeed, like the literary

---

[26] Hawthorne shows the same interest; see pp. 440–42.

[27] She has published a formidable psychoanalysis of Poe (*Edgar Poe: Étude Psychoanalytique*, Paris, 1933). An English translation appeared in 1949. For an amusing commentary on this study, see Mario Praz's "Poe and Psychoanalysis," *Sewanee Review*, 67 (Summer, 1960), 375–89.

[28] Wellek denies that Poe in his criticism was a "Romantic" at all. He concedes that Poe read such Romantics as Coleridge and A. W. Schlegel "and profited from their ideas, but centrally he rejected the dialectical and symbolist romantic creed and remained an eighteenth-century rationalist with occult leanings." (Wellek makes it plain, however, that Poe's influence on the French symbolist poets was real and important.) *A History of Modern Criticism* (1965), Vol. 3, pp. 159–63.

genius that he was, showed others how to utilize "all the resources of art."

Yet though Poe in "The Philosophy of Composition" preens himself as the unbelievably self-conscious and meticulous artist, was he in his own poetry and fiction meticulous enough? This has been the question at issue for generations. Inasmuch as there is a contradiction between Poe's high conception of art and his sometimes slovenly performance, it is of a piece with a whole congeries of fragmentations and contradictions that characterized Poe's life. More specific examination of this problem may well be deferred until we come to take a close look at particular poems. At this point, we shall give only a summarizing statement about Poe's general literary "situation" and his place in the development of American literature.

The crucial point is not the fragmentation within Poe's world and possibly within Poe himself, but his awareness of it and his attempt to deal with it. For both his awareness and his attempt to cope with the situation there is plenty of evidence, though Poe either did not choose—or perhaps was unable—to describe his sense of the situation as Baudelaire did or as a twentieth-century scholar and critic might now describe it. Such a description could be put thus: Poe imitated the authors whose work sold well, but he showed his true evaluation of them by burlesquing them and went on to find ways in which to employ their materials in order to express his own estimate of the cultural situation.

Though he was a provincial who coveted—and was denied—a secure place in an old-fashioned society, he resisted the temptation to exploit the local color of Virginia or, as a "national" author, that of the American scene. Poe's "American" quality is not a matter of the surface but an inward thing. It expresses itself in his employment of a certain perspective: he views the European tradition consciously *from the outside*. The break between the present and the past is taken for granted, and his recognition of it becomes the intellectual milieu in which his restless and deracinated characters live.

Poe sensed the change in the spiritual climate, and his fiction and verse—even the work that uses traditional settings—is really oriented toward the future. One can put the essential matter a little more succinctly still by saying that Poe grasped clearly the difference between traditional man and the new man (liberated? emancipated? alienated?) who was beginning to appear in America. That new man was also, needless to say, beginning to appear all over the world, as Baudelaire and Alfred de Musset were aware. (Perhaps this new man showed himself first in America or perhaps it was simply easier for one to make him out against an American background.)

Yet the view of Poe that we propose here does not require one to assume that Poe was fully conscious of all the implications of his stories and poems, or that he foresaw the appearance in the next century of books like Henry Miller's account of contemporary American civilization in *The Air-Conditioned Nightmare*. For a writer who cannot conceptualize the future may nevertheless be preternaturally sensitive, in the world of his own day, to currents that point toward that future world. Poe's imaginative works considered as a portent and a prophecy of things to come may perhaps be best described as a remarkably sensitive response to his environment.

BIOGRAPHICAL CHART

1809 Born, January 19, in Boston, the child of David and Elizabeth Poe, itinerant actors

1810 Elizabeth Poe, whose husband has by this time disappeared, brings her two younger children to Richmond, Virginia

1811 Poe's mother dies, and he is taken into the home of John Allan of Richmond

1815 Taken to England by the Allans

1815–20 Attends school at Stoke Newington

1820 Returns to Richmond; begins writing verse

1826 Attends University of Virginia; withdrawn after one term, heavily in debt
1827 Quarrels with Allan; goes to Boston, where *Tamerlane and Other Poems* is published; enlists in the army under an assumed name
1829 *Al Aaraaf, Tamerlane and Minor Poems*
1830 Enters West Point; disowned by Allan
1831 Arranges to be discharged from West Point; takes up residence in Baltimore with his aunt, Mrs. Maria Clemm, and her daughter Virginia; *Poems*
1832 "Metzengerstein"
1833 Wins a newspaper prize for "A MS. Found in a Bottle" and attracts some critical attention
1835 Joins the staff of the *Southern Literary Messenger*; alcoholism becomes severe; marries his thirteen-year-old cousin, Virginia Clemm
1836 Leaves the *Messenger*; moves to New York
1838 *The Narrative of Arthur Gordon Pym*; moves to Philadelphia
1839 Coedits *Burton's Gentleman's Magazine* (until

1840); *Tales of the Grotesque and Arabesque*
1841 Edits *Graham's Lady's and Gentleman's Magazine* (until 1842)
1843 "Murders in the Rue Morgue" and "The Man That Was Used Up"
1845 Joins the *Broadway Journal* and soon becomes editor and proprietor; *The Raven and Other Poems*
1846 *Broadway Journal* fails and the Poes move to Fordham; publishes sketches on the "Literati of New York" in *Godey's Lady's Book*
1847 Wins libel suit against the New York *Mirror*; wife dies, January 30
1848 Moves to Providence, Rhode Island, to court Helen Whitman; *Eureka*
1849 Returns to Richmond to begin work on his magazine, the *Stylus*; courts his childhood sweetheart (now a widow); disappears for five days in Baltimore; dies there shortly thereafter, October 7

FURTHER READINGS

James A. Harrison, ed., *The Complete Works of Edgar Allan Poe* (1902; 17 vols.)
J. W. Ostrom, ed., *The Letters of Edgar Allan Poe*, (1948)

Hervey Allen, *Israfel: the Life and Times of Edgar Allan Poe* (1926)
Margaret Alterton, *Origins of Poe's Critical Theory* (1965)
William T. Bandy, *The Influence and Reputation of Edgar Allan Poe in Europe* (1962)
Killis Campbell, *The Mind of Poe* (1933)
Daniel Hoffman, *Poe, Poe, Poe, Poe, Poe, Poe, Poe* (1972)
Joseph Wood Krutch, *Edgar Allan Poe: A Study in Genius* (1926)
Harry Levin, *The Power of Blackness: Hawthorne, Poe, Melville* (1958)
Arthur Hobson Quinn, *Edgar Allan Poe: A Critical Biography* (1941)

Patrick Francis Quinn, *The French Face of Edgar Poe* (1957)
Robert Regan, ed., *Poe: A Collection of Critical Essays* (1967)
David H. Rein, *Edgar Allan Poe: The Inner Pattern* (1960)
Floyd Stovall, *Edgar Poe the Poet: Essays New and Old on the Man and His Work* (1969)
Allen Tate, "The Angelic Imagination: Poe and the Power of Words," in *The Forlorn Demon* (1953)
Edward C. Wagenknecht, *Edgar Allan Poe: The Man Behind the Legend* (1963)
Richard Wilbur, "The House of Poe," *Anniversary Lectures*, Library of Congress (1959)
———, introductory essay in *Poe: Complete Poems* (1959)
William Carlos Williams, "Edgar Allan Poe," in *In the American Grain* (1925)
Yvor Winters, "Edgar Allan Poe: A Crisis in the History of American Obscurantism," in *In Defense of Reason* (1947)

Sonnet—To Science (1829)

It is interesting to compare this sonnet with other typical Romantic reactions to science. John Keats in his "Lamia" wrote:

> Do not all charms fly
> At the mere touch of cold philosophy?
> There was an awful rainbow once in heaven:

We know her woof, her texture; she is given
In the dull catalogue of common things.
Philosophy will clip an Angel's wings,
Conquer all mysteries by rule and line. . . .

Compare also Wordsworth's characterization (in "A Poet's Epitaph," 1799) of the natural philosopher as

a fingering slave,
One that would peep and botanize
Upon his mother's grave. . . .

But the student should also take into account Poe's later comment in which he associates imagination with mathematics, writing that "the highest order of the imaginative intellect is always preeminently mathematical."

Why preyest thou thus upon the poet's heart,
   Vulture, whose wings are dull realities?
How should he love thee? or how deem thee wise,
   Who wouldst not leave him in his wandering
To seek for treasure in the jewelled skies,
   Albeit he soared with an undaunted wing?
Hast thou not dragged Diana from her car?
   And driven the Hamadryad from the wood   10
To seek a shelter in some happier star?
   Hast thou not torn the Naiad from her flood,
The Elfin from the green grass, and from me
   The summer dream beneath the tamarind tree? *[handwritten: as from world.]*

[handwritten: There is beauty in eternity.]

Science! true daughter of Old Time thou art!
   Who alterest all things with thy peering eyes.

[handwritten: Poe turned inward to his own imagination. He was a dreamer and a poet, not a lover of money or material goods. In most of his poems material things decay and die. He is in a hurry to get to eternity. There is a great deal of horror but he is trying to distroy the material world. Very Gothic.]

To Helen (1831) *[handwritten: Macabre]*

Poe tells us that this poem was inspired by Mrs. Jane Stith Stanard, the mother of one of his schoolmates. The imagery is classical, with references to Helen of Troy, to Psyche (the maiden loved by Cupid), and perhaps, in the second stanza, to Ulysses brought back to his island home by the friendly Phaeacians. The manner of the poem is also "classical"; this is Poe's most restrained and balanced poem.

[handwritten: Lots of sculptural imagery. The rhythmic creation of beauty — poetry.]

Helen, thy beauty is to me *[handwritten: memory takes him]*
   Like those Nicéan barks of yore, *[handwritten: back to the age of Greece and Rome where art was appreciated.]*
That gently, o'er a perfumed sea,
   The weary, way-worn wanderer bore *[handwritten: female]*
To his own native shore. *[handwritten: beauty of Helen]*

On desperate seas long wont to roam,
   Thy hyacinth hair, thy classic face,
Thy Naiad airs have brought me home *[handwritten: nutty nymphs]*
   To the glory that was Greece, *[handwritten: beauty and art]*
And the grandeur that was Rome.   10

Lo! in yon brilliant window-niche *[handwritten: large might of army / military commotions]*
   How statue-like I see thee stand, *[handwritten: for beauty is frozen in stone forever.]*
The agate lamp within thy hand! *[handwritten: Soul / Mind]*
   Ah, Psyche, from the regions which *[handwritten: Illuminates spirit]*
Are Holy-Land! *[handwritten: of the spirit (classical countries) Greece and Rome beauty loving society]*

[handwritten right margin: Harry on one level, beauty on spiritual level fused together. Lots of demons, devils but also angels. Beauty can even arise from horror. Paradox.]

[handwritten: In his vision, he wants to go back. Helen is a symbol to bring him back.]

Israfel (1831)

Israfel was the Mohammedan angel with the sweetest voice. Poe had come upon a reference to him in Thomas Moore's *Lalla Rookh* but took his quotation from the *Koran* (to which Moore had referred in a note).

In Heaven a spirit doth dwell
   "Whose heart-strings are a lute;"
None sing so wildly well
   As the angel Israfel,
And the giddy stars (so legends tell)
Ceasing their hymns, attend the spell
   Of his voice, all mute.

Tottering above

In her highest noon,
   The enamoured moon   10
Blushes with love,
   While, to listen, the red levin
(With the rapid Pleiads, even,
   Which were seven,)
Pauses in Heaven.

And they say (the starry choir
   And the other listening things)
That Israfeli's fire
Is owing to that lyre
   By which he sits and sings—   20
The trembling living wire
Of those unusual strings.

But the skies that angel trod,
   Where deep thoughts are a duty—

Where Love's a grown-up God—
  Where the Houri glances are
Imbued with all the beauty
  Which we worship in a star.

Therefore, thou are not wrong,
  Israfeli, who despisest   30
An unimpassioned song;
To thee the laurels belong,
  Best bard, because the wisest!
Merrily live, and long!

The ecstasies above
  With thy burning measures suit—
Thy grief, thy joy, thy hate, thy love,

With the fervour of thy lute—
  Well may the stars be mute!

Yes, Heaven is thine; but this   40
  Is a world of sweets and sours;
  Our flowers are merely—flowers,
And the shadow of thy perfect bliss
  Is the sunshine of ours.

If I could dwell
Where Israfel
  Hath dwelt, and he were I,
He might not sing so wildly well
  A mortal melody,
While a bolder note than this might swell   50
  From my lyre within the sky.

The City in the Sea (1831)

The location of "The City in the Sea" is left sufficiently vague to allow full play to the reader's imagination. It obviously suggests buried empire and vanished glory. It may further suggest to the reader something like the fabled lost Atlantis or perhaps one of the wicked Cities of the Plain, destroyed by the Almighty with fire and brimstone (Genesis 19:24) and now, according to some legends, sunk beneath the waters of the Dead Sea. (A canceled passage in Poe's *Al Aaraaf*, 1829, refers to the Biblical city of Gomorrah as lying beneath the waters of the Dead Sea and thus may give a hint as to what specific "City in the Sea" Poe had in mind. In that case, however, it is curious that Poe locates it not, as we should expect from the viewpoint of America, in the East but "Far down within the dim West.") But the poet has not located it on a map or placed it in history. Though he has created an evocative atmosphere, he has also provided some very specific images and fresh and original phrasings. Death has perched itself on a proud tower in this city and thus can look "gigantically down." Death has gripped the city so thoroughly that it is bathed in an atmosphere heavier than that of air, an element that is windless and waveless. There are no seas anywhere "less hideously serene." All of this is brilliantly done, and though the theme is somber, one feels in the poem something of the vitality and exhilaration of high art.

Lo! Death has reared himself a throne
In a strange city lying alone
Far down within the dim West,
Where the good and the bad and the worst and the best
Have gone to their eternal rest.
There shrines and palaces and towers
(Time-eaten towers that tremble not!)
Resemble nothing that is ours.
Around, by lifting winds forgot,
Resignedly beneath the sky   10
The melancholy waters lie.

No rays from the holy heaven come down
On the long night-time of that town;
But light from out the lurid sea
Streams up the turrets silently—
Gleams up the pinnacles far and free—
Up domes—up spires—up kingly halls—
Up fanes—up Babylon-like walls—
Up shadowy long-forgotten bowers
Of sculptured ivy and stone flowers—
Up many and many a marvellous shrine   20
Whose wreathéd friezes intertwine
The viol, the violet, and the vine.

Resignedly beneath the sky
The melancholy waters lie.

So blend the turrets and shadows there
That all seem pendulous in air, *as if they are*
While from a proud tower in the town *hanging in*
Death looks gigantically down. *mid-ocean.*

There open fanes and gaping graves   30
Yawn level with the luminous waves;
But not the <u>riches</u> there that lie *frozen beauty*
In each idol's <u>diamond</u> eye— *not focusing on*
Not the gaily-jewelled dead *dollar value,*
Tempt the waters from their bed; *but beauty.*
For no ripples curl, alas!
Along that wilderness of glass—
No swellings tell that winds may be *Violates*
Upon some far-off happier sea— *not normal sea.* *its meter.*
pure Gothic horror

No heavings hint that winds have been *fuses* 40
On seas less <u>hideously serene</u>. *beauty and horror*
paradoxical
But lo, a stir is in the air!
The wave—there is a movement there!
As if the towers had thrust aside,
In slightly sinking, the dull tide—
As if their tops had feebly given
A void within the filmy Heaven.
The waves have now a redder glow—
The hours are breathing faint <u>and low</u>— *Time was even*
And when, amid no earthly moans, *coming on end.*
<u>Down, down</u> that town shall settle hence,   50
<u>Hell</u>, rising from a thousand thrones,
Shall do it reverence. *Hell and death—yet he*
makes it beautiful

The Sleeper (1831)

This poem constitutes a further instance in Poe's work of what he regarded as "the most poetical topic in the world . . . the death . . . of a beautiful woman. . . ." (See p. 429.) Though on one of Poe's familiar themes and though one of his favorite poems as a piece of workmanship, "The Sleeper" raises a number of questions. The person who speaks the poem obviously begins by taking the lady's sleep to be merely that, but by line 35 he is beginning to realize that hers is in fact the deep sleep of death. He exclaims at the strangeness of her pallor, at the strangeness of her dress (presumably he notices that it is really a shroud), and above all at the strangeness of the length of her tresses.

This last reference alludes to the fact that the hair continues to grow after death. Yet if this is what is meant, surely the claims of realism and common sense assert themselves. For if Irene is still reposing in her bed chamber, not yet buried, one wonders whether her hair would have had time to grow perceptibly. Again, what is one to make of the wish (expressed in lines 43–45) that the lady may lie forever "with unopened eye" so that she may not be terrified "While the pale sheeted ghosts go by"? In Shakespeare's play *Romeo and Juliet*, Juliet's fear that she may awaken too early in the tomb and be driven out of her mind by what she sees makes sense; but if Irene is truly dead, not like Juliet simply recovering from a sleeping potion, she will be a ghost herself and among her own kind.

Such lapses are the more curious in view of the fact that in his essay "The Philosophy of Composition" Poe stresses the need for the poet to keep steadily in view the effect to be wrought on the reader and his need to choose "such combinations of event, or tone, as shall best aid [him] in the construction of [the desired] effect." In reading a poem like "The Sleeper" one has the feeling that considerations of this sort are just precisely those with which Poe has insufficiently concerned himself. Indeed, most of his failures are what we should call today failures of "tone."

One should, however, point out that the last lines of this poem are quite effective though they are hardly consonant with those that have gone before. The reference to Irene as a little girl unimpressed by, and innocently irreverent toward, "her grand family funerals" ("grand" could be justified here as the adjective that the little girl herself would have used—tossing a stone at the tall vault and shuddering with delicious excitement at the noise that the stone made, imagining that she heard the sound of the dead groaning inside) provides a realistic detail and thus gives the poem a grounding in reality. But if this be true, the success of these last lines most unfortunately exposes the hollow grandiloquence of almost everything that precedes it. Imagine anyone seriously praying "Soft may the worms about her creep" (line 47)—as if it were possible for worms to be so noisy in their movements as to wake the dead!

At midnight, in the month of June,
I stand beneath the mystic moon.
An opiate vapour, dewy, dim,
Exhales from out her golden rim,
And, softly dripping, drop by drop,
Upon the quiet mountain top,
Steals drowsily and musically
Into the universal valley.
The rosemary nods upon the grave;
The lily lolls upon the wave;   10
Wrapping the fog about its breast,
The ruin moulders into rest;
Looking like Lethë, see! the lake
A conscious slumber seems to take,
And would not, for the world, awake.
All Beauty sleeps!—and lo! where lies
Irenë, with her Destinies!

Oh, lady bright! can it be right—
This window open to the night?
The wanton airs, from the tree-top   20
Laughingly through the lattice drop—
The bodiless airs, a wizard rout,
Flit through thy chamber in and out,
And wave the curtain canopy
So fitfully—so fearfully—
Above the closed and fringéd lid
'Neath which thy slumb'ring soul lies hid,

That, o'er the floor and down the wall,
Like ghosts the shadows rise and fall!
Oh, lady dear, hast thou no fear?   30
Why and what art thou dreaming here?
Sure thou art come o'er far-off seas,
A wonder to these garden trees!
Strange is thy pallor! strange thy dress!
Strange, above all, thy length of tress,
And this all solemn silentness!

The lady sleeps! Oh, may her sleep,
Which is enduring, so be deep!
Heaven have her in its sacred keep!
This chamber changed for one more holy,   40
This bed for one more melancholy,
I pray to God that she may lie
Forever with unopened eye,
While the pale sheeted ghosts go by!

My love, she sleeps! Oh, may her sleep,
As it is lasting, so be deep!
Soft may the worms about her creep!
Far in the forest, dim and old,
For her may some tall vault unfold—
Some vault that oft hath flung its black   50
And wingéd panels fluttering back,
Triumphant, o'er the crested palls,
Of her grand family funerals—
Some sepulchre, remote, alone,
Against whose portal she hath thrown,
In childhood, many an idle stone—
Some tomb from out whose sounding door
She ne'er shall force an echo more,
Thrilling to think, poor child of sin!
It was the dead who groaned within.   60

The Raven (1845)

"The Raven" was first published in the New York *Evening Mirror* for January 29, 1845. The poem quickly became sensationally popular. For Poe's account of how he composed it, see pages 427–32. In this account, however, Poe does not mention the obvious literary influences in the development of the poem. Some of them are Elizabeth Barrett Browning's "Lady Geraldine's Courtship," Dickens's novel *Barnaby Rudge*, in which Barnaby owns a talking raven named Grip, and perhaps most of all several poems by Thomas Holly Chivers (1809–1858), the Georgia-born physician who was Poe's friend

and who later charged that Poe had produced "The Raven" by plagiarizing his own work.

Plagiarism is perhaps too strong a word but stanzas from two of Chivers' poems will suggest the basis for his claims. The first example is from a poem on the death of Chivers' young daughter and is entitled "To Allegra Florence in Heaven."

As an egg, when broken, never
Can be mended, but must ever
Be the same crushed egg forever—
So shall this dark heart of mine!

Which, though broken, is still breaking,
And shall never more cease aching
For the sleep which has no waking—
For the sleep which now is thine!

(That Chivers prints his lines as tetrameters whereas Poe prints his as octameters is immaterial insofar as the *general* likeness of the meter and rhyme scheme is concerned.)

The second example is from a poem by Chivers entitled "Isadore":

Then the Voice again said: "Never
   Shall thy soul see Isadore!
God from thee thy love did sever—
He has damned thy soul forever!
   Wherefore then her loss deplore?
Thou shalt live in Hell forever!
   Heaven now holds thine Isadore!

These poems, to be sure, merely embody hints on which Poe was to improve, and the reader, appalled by the wild extravagance of much of Chivers' poetry, may well feel that it would be almost impossible for a competent writer not to improve upon them. But Chivers is not always as bad as this—though he is sometimes even more absurd.

It is amusing, and instructive with reference to the taste of the period, to know that Poe was not alone in striving for musicality in complicated meters and that there was at least one other poet in America who was willing to carry Poe-esque experiments with language even farther than Poe himself ever dared.

[marginal: Gothic   internal rhyme]

Once upon a midnight dreary, while I pondered, weak and weary,
Over many a quaint and curious volume of forgotten lore—
While I nodded, nearly napping, suddenly there came a tapping,
As of some one gently rapping, rapping at my chamber door.
"'Tis some visiter," I muttered, "tapping at my chamber door—
   Only this and nothing more."

Ah, distinctly I remember it was in the bleak December;

And each separate dying ember wrought its ghost upon the floor. *[marginal: reinforcing gothic horror.]*
Eagerly I wished the morrow;—vainly I had sought to borrow
From my books surcease of sorrow—sorrow for the lost Lenore— *[marginal: Trys to convince himself she is]* 10
For the rare and radiant maiden whom the angels name Lenore— *[marginal: in Heaven.]*
   Nameless *here* for evermore.

And the silken, sad, uncertain rustling of each purple curtain
Thrilled me—filled me with fantastic terrors never felt before;
So that now, to still the beating of my heart, I stood repeating
"'Tis some visiter entreating entrance at my chamber door—
Some late visiter entreating entrance at my chamber door;—
[marginal: Very normal but he is terrified]   This it is and nothing more."

Presently my soul grew stronger; hesitating then no longer,
"Sir," said I, "or Madam, truly your forgiveness I implore; 20
But the fact is I was napping, and so gently you came rapping,
And so faintly you came tapping, tapping at my chamber door,
That I scarce was sure I heard you"—here I opened wide the door;——
[marginal: No one there]   Darkness there and nothing more.

Deep into that darkness peering, long I stood there wondering, fearing,
Doubting, dreaming dreams no mortal ever dared to dream before;
But the silence was unbroken, and the stillness gave no token,
And the only word there spoken was the whispered word, "Lenore?"
This I whispered, and an echo murmured back the word "Lenore!"
   Merely this and nothing more. 30

Back into the chamber turning, all my soul within me burning,
Soon again I heard a tapping somewhat louder than before.
"Surely," said I, "surely that is something at my window lattice;
Let me see, then, what thereat is, and this mystery explore—

Let my heart be still a moment and this mystery
   explore;—
        'Tis the wind and nothing more!"

Open here I flung the shutter, when, with many a
   flirt and flutter,
In there stepped a stately Raven of the saintly days
   of yore;
Not the least obeisance made he; not a minute
   stopped or stayed he;
But, with mien of lord or lady, perched above my
   chamber door—   *shows no respect for speaker*
Perched upon a bust of Pallas just above my 40
   chamber door— *sculpture*   *goddess of wisdom*
        Perched, and sat, and nothing more.

Then this ebony bird beguiling my sad fancy into
   smiling,   *propriety* *prim and proper*
By the grave and stern decorum of the countenance
   it wore,
"Though thy crest be shorn and shaven, thou," I
   said, "art sure no craven, *coward — just because it fit*
Ghastly grim and ancient Raven wandering from
   the Nightly shore—
Tell me what thy lordly name is on the Night's
   Plutonian shore!" *neo — Raven symbolizes Hell.*
god of underworld   Quoth the Raven "Nevermore."
     Resounding NO!

Much I marvelled this ungainly fowl to hear discourse so plainly,
Though its answer little meaning—little relevancy
   bore; 50
For we cannot help agreeing that no living human
   being
Ever yet was blessed with seeing bird above his
   chamber door—
Bird or beast upon the sculptured bust above his
   chamber door,
      With such name as "Nevermore."

But the Raven, sitting lonely on the placid bust,
   spoke only
That one word, as if his soul in that one word he
   did outpour.
Nothing farther then he uttered—not a feather
   then he fluttered—
Till I scarcely more than muttered "Other friends
   have flown before—
On the morrow *he* will leave me, as my Hopes
   have flown before."
     Then the bird said "Nevermore." 60

Startled at the stillness broken by reply so aptly
   spoken,

"Doubtless," said I, "what it utters is its only stock
   and store
Caught from some unhappy master whom unmerciful Disaster
Followed fast and followed faster till his songs one
   burden bore— *funeral march (death)*
Till the dirges of his Hope that melancholy burden
   bore *negative view of things*
symbolized by "nevermore".   Of 'Never—nevermore.'"

But the Raven still beguiling all my fancy into
   smiling,
Straight I wheeled a cushioned seat in front of
   bird, and bust and door;
Then, upon the velvet sinking, I betook myself to
   linking
Fancy unto fancy, thinking what this ominous bird
   of yore— 70
What this grim, ungainly, ghastly, gaunt, and
   ominous bird of yore
     Meant in croaking "Nevermore."

This I sat engaged in guessing, but no syllable
   expressing
To the fowl whose fiery eyes now burned into my
   bosom's core; *like a devil or demon*
This and more I sat divining, with my head at
   ease reclining
On the cushion's velvet lining that the lamp-light
   gloated o'er,
But whose velvet-violet lining with the lamp-light
   gloating o'er,
    She shall press, ah, nevermore!
He can't forget Lenore
Then, methought, the air grew denser, perfumed
   from an unseen censer *incense burner*
Swung by Seraphim whose foot-falls tinkled on the
   tufted floor. *angels* 80
"Wretch," I cried, "thy God hath lent thee—by
   these angels he hath sent thee
Respite—respite and nepenthe from thy memories
   of Lenore; *medicine causes forgetfulness*
Quaff, oh quaff this kind nepenthe and forget this
   lost Lenore!" *that's not it at all.*
Bird says no,   Quoth the Raven "Nevermore."

"Prophet!" said I, "thing of evil!—prophet still, if
   bird or devil!—
Whether Tempter sent, or whether tempest tossed
   thee here ashore,
Desolate yet all undaunted, on this *deserted* desert land
   enchanted— *speaking of his own mind.*
On this home by Horror haunted—tell me truly, I
   implore— *his mind is haunted by horror.*

Terror is about to turn momentarily for a moment.

still a faced mind

He tortures by himself asking questions to which a negative answer will break his heart and hope.

Is there—*is* there balm in Gilead?—tell me—tell me,
    I implore!"

> Quoth the Raven "Nevermore." 90

"Prophet!" said I, "thing of evil!—prophet still, if
    bird or devil!
By that Heaven that bends above us—by that God
    we both adore—
Tell this soul with sorrow laden if, within the
    distant Aidenn,
It shall clasp a sainted maiden whom the angels
    name Lenore—
Clasp a rare and radiant maiden whom the angels
    name Lenore."

> Quoth the Raven "Nevermore."

"Be that word our sign of parting, bird or fiend!"
    I shrieked, upstarting—
"Get thee back into the tempest and the Night's
    Plutonian shore!

Ulalume (1847)

This poem was first published in the *American Review*. It was composed while Poe was living at Mamaroneck, New York. Weir was a painter who liked to paint the "misty mid region" around Mamaroneck. Auber is the name of the musician who composed "Le Lac des Fées." "Ulalume" is about lost love, though the "plot" is not easy to make out. Clearly it is a mood piece, relying heavily on the use of atmosphere and shadowy associations. An important element in building up this mood is the use of elaborate musical effects.

Poe is sometimes criticized for a mechanical use of metrical effects and for employing a kind of ready-made music. This is the principal indictment of Poe made by the late Aldous Huxley.

A quotation and a parody will illustrate the difference between ready-made music and music made to measure. I remember (I trust correctly) a simile of Milton's:

> Like that fair field
> Of Enna, where Proserpine gathering flowers,
> Herself a fairer flower, by gloomy Dis
> Was gathered, which cost Ceres all that pain
> To seek her through the world.

Leave no black plume as a token of that lie thy
    soul hath spoken!
Leave my loneliness unbroken!—quit the bust above
    my door! 100
Take thy beak from out my heart, and take thy
    form from off my door!"

> Quoth the Raven "Nevermore."

And the Raven, never flitting, still is sitting, *still* is
    sitting
On the pallid bust of Pallas just above my chamber
    door;
And his eyes have all the seeming of a demon's
    that is dreaming,
And the lamp-light o'er him streaming throws his
    shadow on the floor;
And my soul from out that shadow that lies floating
    on the floor
                    Shall be lifted—nevermore!

Rearranged according to their musical phrasing, these lines would have to be written thus:

> Like that fair field of Enna,
>   where Proserpine gathering flowers,
> Herself a fairer flower,
>   by gloomy Dis was gathered,
> Which cost Ceres all that pain
> To seek her through the world.

The contrast between the lyrical swiftness of the first four phrases, with that row of limping spondees which tells of Ceres's pain, is thrillingly appropriate. Bespoke, the music fits the sense like a glove.

How would Poe have written on the same theme? I have ventured to invent his opening stanza.

> It was noon in the fair field of Enna,
>   When Proserpina gathering flowers—
>   Herself the most fragrant of flowers,
> Was gathered away to Gehenna
>   By the Prince of Plutonian powers;
> Was borne down the windings of Brenner
>   To the gloom of his amorous bowers—
> Down the tortuous highway of Brenner
>   To the God's agapemonous bowers.

The parody is not too outrageous to be critically beside the point; and anyhow the music is genuine Poe. That permanent wave is unquestionably an *ondulation de chez Edgar*. The much too musical metre is (to change the metaphor once more) like a rich chasuble, so stiff with gold and gems that it stands unsupported, a carapace of jewelled sound, into which the sense, like some snotty little seminarist, irrelevantly creeps and is lost. This music of Poe's—how much less really musical it is than that which, out of his nearly neutral decasyllables, Milton fashioned on purpose to fit the slender beauty of Proserpine, the strength and swiftness of the ravisher and her mother's heavy, despairing sorrow!

The skies they were ashen and sober;
　　The leaves they were crispéd and sere—
　　The leaves they were withering and sere;
It was night, in the lonesome October
　　Of my most immemorial year:
It was hard by the dim lake of Auber,
　　In the misty mid region of Weir:—
It was down by the dank tarn of Auber,
　　In the ghoul-haunted woodland of Weir.

Here once, through an alley Titanic,　　　10
　　Of cypress, I roamed with my Soul—
　　Of cypress, with Psyche, my Soul.
These were days when my heart was volcanic
　　As the scoriac rivers that roll—
　　As the lavas that restlessly roll
Their sulphurous currents down Yaanek
　　In the ultimate climes of the Pole—
That groan as they roll down Mount Yaanek
　　In the realms of the Boreal Pole.

Our talk had been serious and sober,　　　20
　　But our thoughts they were palsied and sere—
　　Our memories were treacherous and sere;
For we knew not the month was October,
　　And we marked not the night of the year—
　　(Ah, night of all nights in the year!)
We noted not the dim lake of Auber,
　　(Though once we had journeyed down here)
Remembered not the dank tarn of Auber,
　　Nor the ghoul-haunted woodland of Weir.

And now, as the night was senescent　　　30
　　And star-dials pointed to morn—
　　As the star-dials hinted of morn—
At the end of our path a liquescent
　　And nebulous lustre was born,

Out of which a miraculous crescent
　　Arose with a duplicate horn—
Astarte's bediamonded crescent
　　Distinct with its duplicate horn.

And I said—"She is warmer than Dian;
　　She rolls through an ether of sighs—　　40
　　She revels in a region of sighs:
She has seen that the tears are not dry on
　　These cheeks, where the worm never dies
And has come past the stars of the Lion,
　　To point us the path to the skies—
　　To the Lethean peace of the skies—
Come up, in despite of the Lion,
　　To shine on us with her bright eyes—
Come up, through the lair of the Lion,
　　With love in her luminous eyes."　　50

But Psyche, uplifting her finger,
　　Said—"Sadly this star I mistrust—
　　Her pallor I strangely mistrust:—
Ah, hasten!—ah, let us not linger!
　　Ah, fly!—let us fly!—for we must."
In terror she spoke; letting sink her
　　Wings till they trailed in the dust—
In agony sobbed; letting sink her
　　Plumes till they trailed in the dust—
　　Till they sorrowfully trailed in the dust.　　60

I replied—"This is nothing but dreaming.
　　Let us on, by this tremulous light!
　　Let us bathe in this crystalline light!
Its Sibyllic splendor is beaming
　　With Hope and in Beauty to-night—
　　See!—it flickers up the sky through the night!
Ah, we safely may trust to its gleaming,
　　And be sure it will lead us aright—
We surely may trust to a gleaming
　　That cannot but guide us aright,　　70
Since it flickers up to Heaven through the night."

Thus I pacified Psyche and kissed her,
　　And tempted her out of her gloom—
　　And conquered her scruples and gloom;
And we passed to the end of the vista—
　　But were stopped by the door of a tomb—
　　By the door of a legended tomb;
And I said—"What is written, sweet sister,
　　On the door of this legended tomb?"
She replied—"Ulalume—Ulalume—　　80
　　'Tis the vault of thy lost Ulalume!"

Then my heart it grew ashen and sober
　　As the leaves that were crispéd and sere—
　　As the leaves that were withering and sere—

And I cried—"It was surely October
　　On *this* very night of last year
　　That I journeyed—I journeyed down here!—
　　That I brought a dread burden down here—
　　On this night, of all nights in the year,
　　Ah, what demon hath tempted me here?　　90
Well I know, now, this dim lake of Auber—
　　This misty mid region of Weir:—
Well I know, now, this dank tarn of Auber—
　　This ghoul-haunted woodland of Weir."

Said we then,—the two, then—"Ah, can it

Have been that the woodlandish ghouls—
　　The pitiful, the merciful ghouls,
To bar up our way and to ban it
　　From the secret that lies in these wolds—
　　From the thing that lies hidden in these
　　　　wolds—　　　　　　　　　　　　100
Have drawn up the spectre of a planet
　　From the limbo of lunary souls—
This sinfully scintillant planet
　　From the Hell of the planetary souls?"

Eldorado (1849)

This poem was first published in the magazine
the *Flag of Our Union*. The year 1849 was the
year of the gold rush in California. The excitement of the gold fever is probably reflected in
the title that Poe chose for this lyric, but here
the topical issue has been universalized and
given a timeless quality.

　　Gaily bedight,
　　A gallant knight,
In sunshine and in shadow,
　　Had journeyed long,
　　Singing a song,
In search of Eldorado.

　　But he grew old—
　　This knight so bold—

And o'er his heart a shadow
　　Fell as he found　　　　　　　　　　10
　　No spot of ground
That looked like Eldorado.

　　And, as his strength
　　Failed him at length,
He met a pilgrim shadow—
　　"Shadow," said he,
　　"Where can it be—
This land of Eldorado?"

　　"Over the Mountains
　　Of the Moon,　　　　　　　　　　　20
Down the Valley of the Shadow,
　　Ride, boldly ride,"
　　The shade replied,—
"If you seek for Eldorado."

The Bells (1849)

"The Bells" was published posthumously in the
Union Magazine for November, 1849. Mrs.
Mary Louise Shew, who was a kind friend of
the Poes and who helped nurse Virginia through
her last illness, suggested the poem to Poe after
they had listened to the chimes of Grace
Church in New York.

　　In this poem Poe strains every nerve to produce musical effects, to exploit onomatopoeia,
and to establish sharply contrasting moods. In
the nineteenth century "The Bells" was a great
showpiece for performance by both amateur and
professional elocutionists. But the student may

want to ask himself: Are the musical effects too
clamorous, too unsubtle, too "noisy"? Is there
a true wedding of sound and sense in this poem?
Or is not the sense drowned out by the sound?

　　　　　　　　　I
　　Hear the sledges with the bells—
　　　　Silver bells!
What a world of merriment their melody foretells!
　　How they tinkle, tinkle, tinkle,
　　　　In the icy air of night!
　　While the stars that oversprinkle
　　All the Heavens, seem to twinkle

With a crystalline delight;
Keeping time, time, time,
In a sort of Runic rhyme,   10
To the tintinnabulation that so musically wells
From the bells, bells, bells, bells,
Bells, bells, bells—
From the jingling and the tinkling of the
bells.

II

Hear the mellow wedding bells
Golden bells!
What a world of happiness their harmony foretells!
Through the balmy air of night
How they ring out their delight!—
From the molten-golden notes,   20
And all in tune,
What a liquid ditty floats
To the turtle-dove that listens, while she gloats
On the moon!
Oh, from out the sounding cells,
What a gush of euphony voluminously wells!
How it swells!
How it dwells
On the Future—how it tells
Of the rapture that impels   30
To the swinging and the ringing
Of the bells, bells, bells—
Of the bells, bells, bells, bells,
Bells, bells, bells—
To the rhyming and the chiming of the bells!

III

Hear the loud alarum bells—
Brazen bells!
What tale of terror, now, their turbulency tells!
In the startled ear of Night
How they scream out their affright!   40
Too much horrified to speak,
They can only shriek, shriek,
Out of tune,
In a clamorous appealing to the mercy of the fire—
In a mad expostulation with the deaf and frantic
fire,
Leaping higher, higher, higher,
With a desperate desire
And a resolute endeavor
Now—now to sit, or never,
By the side of the pale-faced moon.   50
Oh, the bells, bells, bells!
What a tale their terror tells
Of Despair!
How they clang and clash and roar!

What a horror they outpour
In the bosom of the palpitating air!
Yet the ear, it fully knows,
By the twanging
And the clanging,
How the danger ebbs and flows;   60
Yes, the ear distinctly tells,
In the jangling
And the wrangling,
How the danger sinks and swells,
By the sinking or the swelling in the anger of the
bells—
Of the bells—
Of the bells, bells, bells, bells,
Bells, bells, bells—
In the clamor and the clangor of the bells!

IV

Hear the tolling of the bells—   70
Iron bells!
What a world of solemn thought their monody
compels!
In the silence of the night
How we shiver with affright
At the melancholy meaning of the tone!
For every sound that floats
From the rust within their throats
Is a groan.
And the people—ah, the people
They that dwell up in the steeple   80
All alone,
And who, tolling, tolling, tolling,
In that muffled monotone,
Feel a glory in so rolling
On the human heart a stone—
They are neither man nor woman—
They are neither brute nor human,
They are Ghouls:—
And their king it is who tolls:—
And he rolls, rolls, rolls, rolls   90
A Pæan from the bells!
And his merry bosom swells
With the Pæan of the bells!
And he dances and he yells;
Keeping time, time, time,
In a sort of Runic rhyme,
To the Pæan of the bells:—
Of the bells:—
Keeping time, time, time,
In a sort of Runic rhyme,   100
To the throbbing of the bells—
Of the bells, bells, bells—

To the sobbing of the bells:—
Keeping time, time, time,
   As he knells, knells, knells,
In a happy Runic rhyme,
   To the rolling of the bells—

   Of the bells, bells, bells:—
     To the tolling of the bells—
  Of the bells, bells, bells, bells,   110
      Bells, bells, bells—
To the moaning and the groaning of the bells.

William Wilson (1839)

"William Wilson" was first published in *Burton's Gentleman's Magazine*. If "Ligeia" was Poe's own favorite story, "William Wilson" is probably the one most highly regarded by modern critics. Incidentally, William Wilson is made to attend a school kept by the Reverend Dr. Bransby. This was the school that Poe himself attended at Stoke Newington, in England, in 1815.

An account of the source of the story may be worth relating. Percy Bysshe Shelley, who had derived the story from the Spanish dramatist Calderon, related it to his friend Lord Byron, who, in turn, passed it on to Thomas Medwin. Medwin told the story to Washington Irving, who wrote an article on the subject entitled "An Unwritten Drama of Lord Byron." Poe picked up the idea from Irving.

The general psychological situation—one's awareness of another self which is his double, or antiself, or, as the Germans put it, his *Doppelgänger*—has, of course, continued to fascinate subsequent writers. One thinks, for example, of Oscar Wilde's *The Picture of Dorian Gray* and of Joseph Conrad's "The Secret Sharer" as well as of Dostoevski's *The Double* and his later novels.

> *What say of it? what say [of]* CONSCIENCE
>   *grim,*
> *That spectre in my path?*
>   CHAMBERLAYNE'S "PHARRONIDA"

Let me call myself, for the present, William Wilson. The fair page now lying before me need not be sullied with my real appellation. This has been already too much an object for the scorn—for the horror—for the destestation of my race. To the uttermost regions of the globe have not the indignant winds bruited its unparalleled infamy? Oh, outcast of all outcasts most abandoned!—to the earth art thou not forever dead? to its honors, to its flowers, to its golden aspirations?—and a cloud, dense, dismal, and limitless, does it not hang eternally between thy hopes and heaven?

I would not, if I could, here or to-day, embody a record of my later years of unspeakable misery, and unpardonable crime. This epoch—these later years—took unto themselves a sudden elevation in turpitude, whose origin alone it is my present purpose to assign. Men usually grow base by degrees. From me, in an instant, all virtue dropped bodily as a mantle. From comparatively trivial wickedness I passed, with the stride of a giant, into more than the enormities of an Elah-Gabalus. What chance —what one event brought this evil thing to pass, bear with me while I relate. Death approaches; and the shadow which foreruns him has thrown a softening influence over my spirit. I long, in passing through the dim valley, for the sympathy—I had nearly said for the pity—of my fellow men. I would fain have them believe that I have been, in some measure, the slave of circumstances beyond human control. I would wish them to seek out for me, in the details I am about to give, some little oasis of *fatality* amid a wilderness of error. I would have them allow—what they cannot refrain from allowing—that, although temptation may have erewhile existed as great, man was never *thus*, at least, tempted before—certainly, never *thus* fell. And is it therefore that he has never thus suffered? Have I not indeed been living in a dream? And am I not now dying a victim to the horror and the mystery of the wildest of all sublunary visions?

I am the descendant of a race whose imaginative and easily excitable temperament has at all times rendered them remarkable; and, in my earliest infancy, I gave evidence of having fully inherited the family character. As I advanced in years it was more strongly developed; becoming, for many reasons, a cause of serious disquietude to my friends, and of positive injury to myself. I grew self-willed, addicted to the wildest caprices, and a prey to the most ungovernable passions. Weak-minded, and beset with constitutional infirmities akin to my own, my parents could do but little to check the evil propensities which distinguished me. Some feeble and ill-directed efforts resulted in complete failure on their part, and, of course, in total triumph on mine. Thenceforward my voice was a household law; and at an age when few children have abandoned their leading-strings, I was left to the guidance of my own will, and became, in all but name, the master of my own actions.

My earliest recollections of a school-life, are connected with a large, rambling, Elizabethan house, in a misty-looking village of England, where were a vast number of gigantic and gnarled trees, and where all the houses were excessively ancient. In truth, it was a dream-like and spirit-soothing place, that venerable old town. At this moment, in fancy, I feel the refreshing chilliness of its deeply-shadowed avenues, inhale the fragrance of its thousand shrubberies, and thrill anew with undefinable delight, at the deep hollow note of the church-bell, breaking, each hour, with sullen and sudden roar, upon the stillness of the dusky atmosphere in which the fretted Gothic steeple lay imbedded and asleep.

It gives me, perhaps, as much of pleasure as I can now in any manner experience, to dwell upon minute recollections of the school and its concerns. Steeped in misery as I am—misery, alas! only too real—I shall be pardoned for seeking relief, however slight and temporary, in the weakness of a few rambling details. These, moreover, utterly trivial, and even ridiculous in themselves, assume, to my fancy, adventitious importance, as connected with a period and a locality when and where I recognize the first ambiguous monitions of the destiny which afterwards so fully overshadowed me. Let me then remember.

The house, I have said, was old and irregular. The grounds were extensive, and a high and solid brick wall, topped with a bed of mortar and broken glass, encompassed the whole. This prison-like rampart formed the limit of our domain; beyond it we saw but thrice a week—once every Saturday afternoon, when, attended by two ushers, we were permitted to take brief walks in a body through some of the neighbouring fields—and twice during Sunday, when we were paraded in the same formal manner to the morning and evening service in the one church of the village. Of this church the principal of our school was pastor. With how deep a spirit of wonder and perplexity was I wont to regard him from our remote pew in the gallery, as, with step solemn and slow, he ascended the pulpit! This reverend man, with countenance so demurely benign, with robes so glossy and so clerically flowing, with wig so minutely powdered, so rigid and so vast,—could this be he who, of late, with sour visage, and in snuffy habiliments, administered, ferule in hand, the Draconian laws of the academy? Oh, gigantic paradox, too utterly monstrous for solution!

At an angle of the ponderous wall frowned a more ponderous gate. It was riveted and studded with iron bolts, and surmounted with jagged iron spikes. What impressions of deep awe did it inspire! It was never opened save for the three periodical egressions and ingressions already mentioned; then, in every creak of its mighty hinges, we found a plenitude of mystery—a world of matter for solemn remark, or for more solemn meditation.

The extensive enclosure was irregular in form, having many capacious recesses. Of these, three or four of the largest constituted the play-ground. It was level, and covered with fine hard gravel. I well remember it had no trees, nor benches, nor any thing similar within it. Of course it was in the rear of the house. In front lay a small parterre, planted with box and other shrubs; but through this sacred division we passed only upon rare occasions indeed —such as a first advent to school or final departure thence, or perhaps, when a parent or friend having called for us, we joyfully took our way home for the Christmas or Midsummer holy-days.

But the house!—how quaint an old building was this!—to me how veritably a palace of enchantment! There was really no end to its windings—to its incomprehensible subdivisions. It was difficult, at any given time, to say with certainty upon which of its two stories one happened to be. From each room to every other there were sure to be found three or four steps either in ascent or descent. Then the lateral branches were innumerable—inconceivable—and so returning in upon themselves, that our most exact ideas in regard to the whole mansion were not very far different from those with which we pondered upon infinity. During the five years of my residence here, I was never able to ascertain with precision, in what remote locality lay the little sleeping apartment assigned to myself and some eighteen or twenty other scholars.

The school-room was the largest in the house—I could not help thinking, in the world. It was very long, narrow, and dismally low, with pointed

Gothic windows and a ceiling of oak. In a remote and terror-inspiring angle was a square enclosure of eight or ten feet, comprising the *sanctum,* "during hours," of our principal, the Reverend Dr. Bransby. It was a solid structure, with massy door, sooner than open which in the absence of the "Dominie," we would all have willingly perished by the *peine forte et dure.* In other angles were two other similar boxes, far less reverenced, indeed, but still greatly matters of awe. One of these was the pulpit of the "classical" usher, one of the "English and mathematical." Interspersed about the room, crossing and recrossing in endless irregularity, were innumerable benches and desks, black, ancient, and time-worn, piled desperately with much-bethumbed books, and so beseamed with initial letters, names at full length, grotesque figures, and other multiplied efforts of the knife, as to have entirely lost what little of original form might have been their portion in days long departed. A huge bucket with water stood at one extremity of the room, and a clock of stupendous dimensions at the other.

Encompassed by the massy walls of this venerable academy, I passed, yet not in tedium or disgust, the years of the third lustrum of my life. The teeming brain of childhood requires no external world of incident to occupy or amuse it; and the apparently dismal monotony of a school was replete with more intense excitement than my riper youth has derived from luxury, or my full manhood from crime. Yet I must believe that my first mental development had in it much of the uncommon—even much of the *outré.* Upon mankind at large the events of very early existence rarely leave in mature age any definite impression. All is gray shadow—a weak and irregular remembrance—an indistinct regathering of feeble pleasures and phantasmagoric pains. With me this is not so. In childhood I must have felt with the energy of a man what I now find stamped upon memory in lines as vivid, as deep, and as durable as the *exergues* of the Carthaginian medals.

Yet in fact—in the fact of the world's view—how little was there to remember! The morning's awakening, the nightly summons to bed; the connings, the recitations; the periodical half-holidays, and perambulations; the play-ground, with its broils, its pastimes, its intrigues;—these, by a mental sorcery long forgotten, were made to involve a wilderness of sensation, a world of rich incident, an universe of varied emotion, of excitement the most passionate and spirit-stirring, "*Oh, le bon temps, que ce siècle de fer!*" [Oh, what a fine era, this age of iron!]

In truth, the ardor, the enthusiasm, and the imperiousness of my disposition, soon rendered me a marked character among my schoolmates, and by slow, but natural gradations, gave me an ascendency over all not greatly older than myself;—over all with a single exception. This exception was found in the person of a scholar, who, although no relation, bore the same Christian and surname as myself;—a circumstance, in fact, little remarkable; for, notwithstanding a noble descent, mine was one of those everyday appellations which seem, by prescriptive right, to have been, time out of mind, the common property of the mob. In this narrative I have therefore designated myself as William Wilson,—a fictitious title not very dissimilar to the real. My namesake alone, of those who in school phraseology constituted "our set," presumed to compete with me in the studies of the class—in the sports and broils of the play-ground —to refuse implicit belief in my assertions, and submission to my will—indeed, to interfere with my arbitrary dictation in any respect whatsoever. If there is on earth a supreme and unqualified despotism, it is the despotism of a master mind in boyhood over the less energetic spirits of its companions.

Wilson's rebellion was to me a source of the greatest embarrassment;—the more so as, in spite of the bravado with which in public I made a point of treating him and his pretensions, I secretly felt that I feared him, and could not help thinking the equality which he maintained so easily with myself, a proof of his true superiority; since not to be overcome, cost me a perpetual struggle. Yet this superiority—even this equality—was in truth acknowledged by no one but myself; our associates, by some unaccountable blindness, seemed not even to suspect it. Indeed, his competition, his resistance, and especially his impertinent and dogged interference with my purposes, were not more pointed than private. He appeared to be destitute alike of the ambition which urged, and of the passionate energy of mind which enabled me to excel. In his rivalry he might have been supposed actuated solely by a whimsical desire to thwart, astonish, or mortify myself; although there were times when I could not help observing, with a feeling made up of wonder, abasement, and pique, that he mingled with his injuries, his insults, or his contradictions, a certain most inappropriate, and assuredly most unwelcome *affectionateness* of manner. I could only conceive this singular behavior to arise from a consummate self-conceit assuming the vulgar airs of patronage and protection.

Perhaps it was this latter trait in Wilson's conduct, conjoined with our identity of name, and the mere accident of our having entered the school upon the same day, which set afloat the notion that we were brothers, among the senior classes in the academy. These do not usually inquire with much strictness into the affairs of their juniors. I have before said, or should have said, that Wilson was not, in a most remote degree, connected with my family. But assuredly if we *had* been brothers we must have been twins; for, after leaving Dr. Bransby's, I casually learned that my namesake was born on the nineteenth of January, 1813—and this is a somewhat remarkable coincidence; for the day is precisely that of my own nativity.

It may seem strange that in spite of the continual anxiety occasioned me by the rivalry of Wilson, and his intolerable spirit of contradiction, I could not bring myself to hate him altogether. We had, to be sure, nearly every day a quarrel in which, yielding me publicly the palm of victory, he, in some manner, contrived to make me feel that it was he who had deserved it; yet a sense of pride on my part, and a veritable dignity on his own, kept us always upon what are called "speaking terms," while there were many points of strong congeniality in our tempers, operating to awake in me a sentiment which our position alone, perhaps, prevented from ripening into friendship. It is difficult, indeed, to define, or even to describe, my real feelings toward him. They formed a motley and heterogeneous admixture;—some petulant animosity, which was not yet hatred, some esteem, more respect, much fear, with a world of uneasy curiosity. To the moralist it will be unnecessary to say, in addition, that Wilson and myself were the most inseparable of companions.

It was no doubt the anomalous state of affairs existing between us, which turned all my attacks upon him, (and there were many, either open or covert) into the channel of banter or practical joke (giving pain while assuming the aspect of mere fun) rather than into a more serious and determined hostility. But my endeavours on this head were by no means uniformly successful, even when my plans were the most wittily concocted; for my namesake had much about him, in character, of that unassuming and quiet austerity which, while enjoying the poignancy of its own jokes, has no heel of Achilles in itself, and absolutely refuses to be laughed at. I could find, indeed, but one vulnerable point, and that, lying in a personal peculiarity, arising, perhaps, from constitutional disease, would have been spared by any antagonist less at his wit's end than myself;—my rival had a weakness in the faucial or guttural organs, which precluded him from raising his voice at any time *above a very low whisper*. Of this defect I did not fail to take what poor advantage lay in my power.

Wilson's retaliations in kind were many; and there was one form of his practical wit that disturbed me beyond measure. How his sagacity first discovered at all that so petty a thing would vex me, is a question I never could solve; but having discovered, he habitually practised the annoyance. I had always felt aversion to my uncourtly patronymic, and its very common, if not plebeian prænomen. The words were venom in my ears; and when, upon the day of my arrival, a second William Wilson came also to the academy, I felt angry with him for bearing the name, and doubly disgusted with the name because a stranger bore it, who would be the cause of its twofold repetition, who would be constantly in my presence, and whose concerns, in the ordinary routine of the school business, must inevitably, on account of the detestable coincidence, be often confounded with my own.

The feeling of vexation thus engendered grew stronger with every circumstance tending to show resemblance, moral or physical, between my rival and myself. I had not then discovered the remarkable fact that we were of the same age; but I saw that we were of the same height, and I perceived that we were even singularly alike in general contour of person and outline of feature. I was galled, too, by the rumor touching a relationship, which had grown current in the upper forms. In a word, nothing could more seriously disturb me, (although I scrupulously concealed such disturbance,) than any allusions to a similarity of mind, person, or condition existing between us. But, in truth, I had no reason to believe that (with the exception of the matter of relationship, and in the case of Wilson himself,) this similarity had ever been made a subject of comment, or even observed at all by our schoolfellows. That *he* observed it in all its bearings, and as fixedly as I, was apparent; but that he could discover in such circumstances so fruitful a field of annoyance, can only be attributed, as I said before, to his more than ordinary penetration.

His cue, which was to perfect an imitation of myself, lay both in words and in actions; and most admirably did he play his part. My dress it was an easy matter to copy; my gait and general manner were, without difficulty, appropriated; in spite of his constitutional defect, even my voice did not escape him. My louder tones were, of course, unattempted, but then the key, it was identical; *and his singular whisper, it grew the very echo of my own.*

How greatly this most exquisite portraiture harassed me, (for it could not justly be termed a caricature,) I will not now venture to describe. I had but one consolation—in the fact that the imitation, apparently, was noticed by myself alone, and that I had to endure only the knowing and strangely sarcastic smiles of my namesake himself. Satisfied with having produced in my bosom the intended effect, he seemed to chuckle in secret over the sting he had inflicted, and was characteristically disregardful of the public applause which the success of his witty endeavours might have so easily elicited. That the school, indeed, did not feel his design, perceive its accomplishment, and participate in his sneer, was, for many anxious months, a riddle I could not resolve. Perhaps the *gradation* of his copy rendered it not so readily perceptible; or, more possibly, I owed my security to the masterly air of the copyist, who, disdaining the letter, (which in a painting is all the obtuse can see,) gave but the full spirit of his original for my individual contemplation and chagrin.

I have already more than once spoken of the disgusting air of patronage which he assumed toward me, and of his frequent officious interference with my will. This interference often took the ungracious character of advice; advice not openly given, but hinted or insinuated. I received it with a repugnance which gained strength as I grew in years. Yet, at this distant day, let me do him the simple justice to acknowledge that I can recall no occasion when the suggestions of my rival were on the side of those errors or follies so usual to his immature age and seeming inexperience; that his moral sense, at least, if not his general talents and worldly wisdom, was far keener than my own; and that I might, to-day, have been a better and thus a happier man, had I less frequently rejected the counsels embodied in those meaning whispers which I then but too cordially hated and too bitterly despised.

As it was, I at length grew restive in the extreme under his distasteful supervision, and daily resented more and more openly what I considered his intolerable arrogance. I have said that, in the first years

of our connection as schoolmates, my feelings in regard to him might have been easily ripened into friendship: but, in the latter months of my residence at the academy, although the intrusion of his ordinary manner had, beyond doubt, in some measure, abated, my sentiments, in nearly similar proportion, partook very much of positive hatred. Upon one occasion he saw this, I think, and afterward avoided, or made a show of avoiding me.

It was about the same period, if I remember aright, that, in an altercation of violence with him, in which he was more than usually thrown off his guard, and spoke and acted with an openness of demeanor rather foreign to his nature, I discovered, or fancied I discovered, in his accent, in his air, and general appearance, a something which first startled, and then deeply interested me, by bringing to mind dim visions of my earliest infancy—wild, confused and thronging memories of a time when memory herself was yet unborn. I cannot better describe the sensation which oppressed me than by saying that I could with difficulty shake off the belief of my having been acquainted with the being who stood before me, at some epoch very long ago—some point of the past even infinitely remote. The delusion, however, faded rapidly as it came; and I mention it at all but to define the day of the last conversation I there held with my singular namesake.

The huge old house, with its countless subdivisions, had several large chambers communicating with each other, where slept the greater number of the students. There were, however, (as must necessarily happen in a building so awkwardly planned,) many little nooks or recesses, the odds and ends of the structure; and these the economic ingenuity of Dr. Bransby had also fitted up as dormitories; although, being the merest closets, they were capable of accommodating but a single individual. One of these small apartments was occupied by Wilson.

One night, about the close of my fifth year at the school, and immediately after the altercation just mentioned, finding every one wrapped in sleep, I arose from bed, and, lamp in hand, stole through a wilderness of narrow passages from my own bedroom to that of my rival. I had long been plotting one of those ill-natured pieces of practical wit at his expense in which I had hitherto been so uniformly unsuccessful. It was my intention, now, to put my scheme in operation, and I resolved to make him feel the whole extent of the malice with which I was imbued. Having reached his closet, I noiselessly entered, leaving the lamp, with a shade over it, on the outside. I advanced a step and listened to the sound of his tranquil breathing. Assured of his being asleep, I returned, took the light, and with it again approached the bed. Close curtains were around it, which, in the prosecution of my plan, I slowly and quietly withdrew, when the bright rays fell vividly upon the sleeper, and my eyes, at the same moment, upon his countenance. I looked;—and a numbness, an iciness of feeling instantly pervaded my frame. My breast heaved, my knees tottered, my whole spirit became possessed with an objectless yet intolerable horror. Gasping for breath, I lowered the lamp in still nearer proximity to the face. Were these—*these* the lineaments of William Wilson? I saw, indeed, that they were his, but I shook as if with a fit of the ague in fancying they were not. What *was* there about them to confound me in this manner? I gazed;—while my brain reeled with a multitude of incoherent thoughts. Not thus he appeared—assuredly not *thus*—in the vivacity of his waking hours. The same name! the same contour of person! the same day of arrival at the academy! And then his dogged and meaningless imitation of my gait, my voice, my habits, and my manner! Was it, in truth, within the bounds of human possibility, that *what I now saw* was the result, merely, of the habitual practice of this sarcastic imitation? Awe-stricken, and with a creeping shudder, I extinguished the lamp, passed silently from the chamber, and left, at once, the halls of that old academy, never to enter them again.

After a lapse of some months, spent at home in mere idleness, I found myself a student at Eton. The brief interval had been sufficient to enfeeble my remembrance of the events at Dr. Bransby's, or at least to effect a material change in the nature of the feelings with which I remembered them. The truth—the tragedy—of the drama was no more. I could now find room to doubt the evidence of my senses; and seldom called up the subject at all but with wonder at the extent of human credulity, and a smile at the vivid force of the imagination which I hereditarily possessed. Neither was this species of skepticism likely to be diminished by the character of the life I led at Eton. The vortex of thoughtless folly into which I there so immediately and so recklessly plunged, washed away all but the froth of my past hours, engulfed at once every solid or serious impression, and left to memory only the veriest levities of a formed existence.

I do not wish, however, to trace the course of my miserable profligacy here—a profligacy which set at defiance the laws, while it eluded the vigilance of the institution. Three years of folly, passed without profit, had but given me rooted habits of vice, and added, in a somewhat unusual degree, to my bodily stature, when, after a week of soulless dissipation, I invited a small party of the most dissolute students to a secret carousal in my chambers. We met at a late hour of the night; for our debaucheries were to be faithfully protracted until morning. The wine flowed freely, and there were not wanting other and perhaps more dangerous seductions; so that the grey dawn had already faintly appeared in the east while our delirious extravagance was at its height. Madly flushed with cards and intoxication, I was in the act of insisting upon a toast of more than wonted profanity, when my attention was suddenly diverted by the violent, although partial, unclosing of the door of the apartment, and by the eager voice of a servant from without. He said that some person, apparently in great haste, demanded to speak with me in the hall.

Wildly excited with wine, the unexpected interruption rather delighted than surprised me. I staggered forward at once, and a few steps brought me to the vestibule of the building. In this low and small room there hung no lamp; and now no light at all was admitted, save that of the exceedingly feeble dawn which made its way through the semicircular window. As I put my foot over the threshold, I became aware of the figure of a youth about my own height, and habited in a white kerseymere morning frock, cut in the novel fashion of the one I myself wore at the moment. This the faint light enabled me to perceive; but the features of his face I could not distinguish. Upon my entering he strode hurriedly up to me, and, seizing me by the arm with a gesture of petulant impatience, whispered the words "William Wilson!" in my ear.

I grew perfectly sober in an instant.

There was that in the manner of the stranger, and in the tremulous shake of his uplifted finger, as he held it between my eyes and the light, which filled me with unqualified amazement; but it was not this which had so violently moved me. It was the pregnancy of solemn admonition in the singular, low, hissing utterance; and, above all, it was the character, the tone, *the key*, of those few, simple, and familiar, yet *whispered* syllables, which came with a thousand thronging memories of by-gone days, and struck upon my soul with the shock of a galvanic battery. Ere I could recover the use of my senses he was gone.

Although this event failed not of a vivid effect upon my disordered imagination, yet was it evanescent as vivid. For some weeks, indeed, I busied myself in earnest inquiry, or was wrapped in a cloud of morbid speculation. I did not pretend to disguise from my perception the identity of the singular individual who thus perseveringly interfered with my affairs, and harassed me with his insinuated counsel. But who and what was this Wilson?—and whence came he?—and what were his purposes? Upon neither of these points could I be satisfied; merely ascertaining, in regard to him, that a sudden accident in his family had caused his removal from Dr. Bransby's academy on the afternoon of the day in which I myself had eloped. But in a brief period I ceased to think upon the subject; my attention being all absorbed in a contemplated departure for Oxford. Thither I soon went; the uncalculating vanity of my parents furnishing me with an outfit and annual establishment, which would enable me to indulge at will in the luxury already so dear to my heart,—to vie in profuseness of expenditure with the haughtiest heirs of the wealthiest earldoms in Great Britain.

Excited by such appliances to vice, my constitutional temperament broke forth with redoubled ardor, and I spurned even the common restraints of decency in the mad infatuation of my revels. But it were absurd to pause in the detail of my extravagance. Let it suffice, that among spendthrifts I out-Heroded Herod, and that, giving name to a multitude of novel follies, I added no brief appendix to the long catalogue of vices then usual in the most dissolute university of Europe.

It could hardly be credited, however, that I had, even here, so utterly fallen from the gentlemanly estate, as to seek acquaintance with the vilest arts of the gambler by profession, and, having become an adept in his despicable science, to practice it habitually as a means of increasing my already enormous income at the expense of the weak-minded among my fellow-collegians. Such, nevertheless, was the fact. And the very enormity of this offence against all manly and honourable sentiment proved, beyond doubt, the main if not the sole reason of the impunity with which it was committed. Who, indeed, among my most abandoned associates, would not rather have disputed the clearest evidence of his senses, than have suspected of such courses, the gay, the frank, the generous William Wilson—the noblest and most liberal commoner at Oxford—him whose follies (said his parasites) were but the follies of youth and unbridled fancy—whose errors but inimitable whim—whose darkest vice but a careless and dashing extravagance?

I had been now two years successfully busied in this way, when there came to the university a young *parvenu* nobleman, Glendinning—rich, said report, as Herodes Atticus—his riches, too, as easily acquired. I soon found him of weak intellect, and, of course, marked him as a fitting subject for my skill. I frequently engaged him in play, and contrived, with the gambler's usual art, to let him win considerable sums, the more effectually to entangle him in my snares. At length, my schemes being ripe, I met him (with the full intention that this meeting should be final and decisive) at the chambers of a fellow-commoner, (Mr. Preston,) equally intimate with both, but who, to do him justice, entertained not even a remote suspicion of my design. To give to this a better colouring, I had contrived to have assembled a party of some eight or ten, and was solicitously careful that the introduction of cards should appear accidental, and originate in the proposal of my contemplated dupe himself. To be brief upon a vile topic, none of the low finesse was omitted, so customary upon similar occasions, that it is a just matter for wonder how any are still found so besotted as to fall its victim.

We had protracted our sitting far into the night, and I had at length effected the manœuvre of getting Glendinning as my sole antagonist. The game, too, was my favorite *écarté*. The rest of the company, interested in the extent of our play, had abandoned their own cards, and were standing around us as spectators. The *parvenu*, who had been induced by my artifices in the early part of the evening, to drink deeply, now shuffled, dealt, or played, with a wild nervousness of manner for which his intoxication, I thought, might partially, but could not altogether account. In a very short period he had become my debtor to a large amount, when, having taken a long draught of port, he did precisely what I had been coolly anticipating—he proposed to double our already extravagant stakes. With a well-feigned show of reluctance, and not until after my repeated refusal had seduced him into some angry words which gave a color of *pique* to my compliance, did I finally comply. The result, of course, did but prove how entirely the prey was in my toils; in less than an hour he had quadrupled his debt. For some time his countenance had been losing the florid tinge lent it by the wine; but now, to my astonishment, I perceived that it had grown to a pallor truly fearful. I say, to my astonishment. Glendinning had been represented to my eager inquiries as immeasurably wealthy; and the sums which he had as yet lost, although in themselves vast, could not, I supposed, very seriously annoy, much less so violently affect him. That he was overcome by the wine just swallowed, was the idea which most readily presented itself; and, rather with a view to the preservation of my own character in the eyes of my associates, than from any less interested motive, I was about to insist, peremptorily, upon a discontinuance of the play, when some expressions at my elbow from among the company, and an ejaculation evincing utter despair on the part of Glendinning, gave me to understand that I had effected his total ruin under circumstances which, rendering him an object for the pity of all, should have protected him from the ill offices even of a fiend.

What now might have been my conduct it is difficult to say. The pitiable condition of my dupe had thrown an air of embarrassed gloom over all; and, for some moments, a profound silence was maintained, during which I could not help feeling my cheeks tingle with the many burning glances of scorn or reproach cast upon me by the less abandoned of the party. I will even own that an intolerable weight of anxiety was for a brief instant lifted from my bosom by the sudden and extraordinary interruption which ensued. The wide, heavy folding doors of the apartment were all at once thrown open, to their full extent, with a vigorous and rushing impetuosity that extinguished, as if by magic, every candle in the room. Their light, in dying, enabled us just to perceive that a stranger had entered, about my own height, and closely muffled in a cloak. The darkness, however, was now total; and we could only *feel* that he was standing in our midst. Before any one of us could recover from the extreme astonishment into which this rudeness had thrown all, we heard the voice of the intruder.

"Gentlemen," he said, in a low, distinct, and never-to-be-forgotten *whisper* which thrilled to the very marrow of my bones, "Gentlemen, I make no apology for this behavior, because in thus behaving, I am fulfilling a duty. You are, beyond doubt, uninformed of the true character of the person who has to-night won at *écarté* a large sum of money from Lord Glendinning. I will therefore put you upon an expeditious and decisive plan of obtaining this very necessary information. Please to examine, at your leisure, the inner linings of the cuff of his left sleeve, and the several little packages which may be found in the somewhat capacious pockets of his embroidered morning wrapper."

While he spoke, so profound was the stillness that one might have heard a pin drop upon the floor. In ceasing, he departed at once, and as abruptly as he had entered. Can I—shall I describe my sensations?—must I say that I felt all the horrors of the damned? Most assuredly I had little time given for reflection. Many hands roughly seized me upon the spot, and lights were immediately reprocured. A search ensued. In the lining of my sleeve were found all the court cards essential in *écarté*, and, in the pockets of my wrapper, a number of packs, fac-similes of those used at our sittings, with the single exception that mine were of the species called, technically, *arrondées;* the honours being slightly convex at the ends, the lower cards slightly convex at the sides. In this disposition, the dupe who cuts, as customary, at the length of the pack, will invariably find that he cuts his antagonist an honor; while the gambler, cutting at the breadth, will, as certainly, cut nothing for his victim which may count in the records of the game.

Any burst of indignation upon this discovery would have affected me less than the silent contempt, or the sarcastic composure, with which it was received.

"Mr. Wilson," said our host, stooping to remove from beneath his feet an exceedingly luxurious cloak of rare furs, "Mr. Wilson, this is your property." (The weather was cold; and, upon quitting my own room, I had thrown a cloak over my dressing wrapper, putting it off upon reaching the scene of play.) "I presume it is supererogatory to seek here (eyeing the folds of the garment with a bitter smile) for any farther evidence of your skill. Indeed, we have had enough. You will see the necessity, I hope, of quitting Oxford—at all events, of quitting instantly my chambers."

Abased, humbled to the dust as I then was, it is probable that I should have resented this galling language by immediate personal violence, had not my whole attention been at the moment arrested by a fact of the most startling character. The cloak which I had worn was of a rare description of fur; how rare, how extravagantly costly, I shall not venture to say. Its fashion, too, was of my own fantastic invention; for I was fastidious to an absurd degree of coxcombry, in matters of this frivolous nature. When, therefore, Mr. Preston reached me that which he had picked up upon the floor, and near the folding doors of the apartment, it was with an astonishment nearly bordering upon terror, that I perceived my own already hanging on my arm, (where I had no doubt unwittingly placed it,) and that the one presented me was but its exact counterpart in every, in even the minutest possible particular. The singular being who had so disastrously exposed me, had been muffled, I remembered, in a cloak; and none had been worn at all by any of the members of our party with the exception of myself. Retaining some presence of mind, I took the one offered me by Preston; placed it, unnoticed, over my own; left the apartment with a resolute scowl of defiance; and, next morning ere dawn of day, commenced a hurried journey from Oxford to the continent, in a perfect agony of horror and of shame.

I fled in vain. My evil destiny pursued me as if in exultation, and proved, indeed, that the exercise of its mysterious dominion had as yet only begun. Scarcely had I set foot in Paris, ere I had fresh evidence of the detestable interest taken by this Wilson in my concerns. Years flew, while I experienced no relief. Villain!—at Rome, with how untimely, yet with how spectral an officiousness, stepped he in between me and my ambition! at Vienna, too—at Berlin—and at Moscow! Where, in truth, had I *not* bitter cause to curse him within my heart? From his inscrutable tyranny did I at length flee, panic-stricken, as from a pestilence; and to the very ends of the earth *I fled in vain.*

And again, and again, in secret communion with my own spirit, would I demand the questions "Who is he—whence came he?—and what are his objects?" But no answer was there found. And then I scrutinized, with a minute scrutiny, the forms, and the methods, and the leading traits of his impertinent supervision. But even here there was very little upon which to base a conjecture. It was noticeable, indeed, that, in no one of the multiplied instances in which he had of late crossed my path, had he so crossed it except to frustrate those schemes, or to disturb those actions, which, if fully carried out, might have resulted in bitter mischief. Poor justification this, in truth, for an authority so imperiously assumed! Poor indemnity for natural rights of self-agency so pertinaciously, so insultingly denied!

I had also been forced to notice that my tormentor, for a very long period of time, (while scrupulously and with miraculous dexterity maintaining his whim of an identity of apparel with myself,) had so contrived it, in the execution of his varied interference with my will, that I saw not, at any moment, the features of his face. Be Wilson what he might, *this*, at least, was but the veriest of affectation, or of folly. Could he, for an instant, have supposed that, in my admonisher at Eton—in the destroyer of my honor at Oxford—in him who thwarted my ambition at Rome, my revenge at Paris, my passionate love at Naples, or what he falsely termed my avarice in Egypt,—that in this, my archenemy and evil genius, I could fail to recognize the William Wilson of my schoolboy days, —the namesake, the companion, the rival,—the hated and dreaded rival at Dr. Bransby's? Impossible!—But let me hasten to the last eventful scene of the drama.

Thus far I had succumbed supinely to this imperious domination. The sentiment of deep awe with which I habitually regarded the elevated character, the majestic wisdom, the apparent omnipresence and omnipotence of Wilson, added to a feeling of even terror, with which certain other traits in his nature and assumptions inspired me, had operated, hitherto, to impress me with an idea of my own utter weakness and helplessness, and to suggest an implicit, although bitterly reluctant submission to his arbitrary will. But, of late days, I had given myself up entirely to wine; and its maddening influence upon my hereditary temper rendered me more and more impatient of control. I began to murmur,—to hesitate,—to resist. And was it only fancy which induced me to believe that, with the increase of my own firmness, that of my tormentor underwent a proportional diminution? Be this as it may, I now began to feel the inspiration of a burning hope, and at length nurtured in my secret thoughts a stern and desperate resolution that I would submit no longer to be enslaved.

It was at Rome, during the Carnival of 18—, that I attended a masquerade in the palazzo of the Neapolitan Duke Di Broglio. I had indulged more freely than usual in the excesses of the wine-table; and now the suffocating atmosphere of the crowded rooms irritated me beyond endurance. The difficulty, too, of forcing my way through the mazes of the company contributed not a little to the ruffling of my temper; for I was anxiously seeking (let me not say with what unworthy motive) the young, the gay, the beautiful wife of the aged and doting Di Broglio. With a too unscrupulous confidence she had previously communicated to me the secret of the costume in which she would be habited and now, having caught a glimpse of her person, I was hurrying to make my way into her presence. —At this moment I felt a light hand placed upon my shoulder, and that ever-remembered, low, damnable *whisper* within my ear.

In an absolute frenzy of wrath, I turned at once upon him who had thus interrupted me, and seized him violently by the collar. He was attired, as I had expected, in a costume altogether similar to my own; wearing a Spanish cloak of blue velvet, begirt about the waist with a crimson belt sustaining a rapier. A mask of black silk entirely covered his face.

"Scoundrel!" I said, in a voice husky with rage, while every syllable I uttered seemed as new fuel to my fury, "scoundrel! imposter! accursed villain! you shall not—you *shall not* dog me unto death! Follow me, or I stab you where you stand!"—and I broke my way from the ballroom into a small antechamber adjoining, dragging him unresistingly with me as I went.

Upon entering, I thrust him furiously from me. He staggered against the wall, while I closed the door with an oath, and commanded him to draw. He hesitated but for an instant; then, with a slight sigh, drew in silence, and put himself upon his defence.

The contest was brief indeed. I was frantic with every species of wild excitement, and felt within my single arm the energy and power of a multitude. In a few seconds I forced him by sheer strength against the wainscoting, and thus, getting him at mercy, plunged my sword, with brute ferocity, repeatedly through and through his bosom.

At that instant some person tried the latch of the door. I hastened to prevent an intrusion, and then immediately returned to my dying antagonist. But what human language can adequately portray *that* astonishment, *that* horror which possessed me at the spectacle then presented to view? The brief moment in which I averted my eyes had been sufficient to produce, apparently, a material change in the arrangements at the upper or farther end of the room. A large mirror,—so at first it seemed to me in my confusion—now stood where none had been perceptible before; and as I stepped up to it in extremity of terror, mine own image, but with features all pale and dabbled in blood, advanced to meet me with a feeble and tottering gait.

Thus it appeared, I say, but was not. It was my antagonist—it was Wilson, who then stood before me in the agonies of his dissolution. His mask and cloak lay, where he had thrown them, upon the floor. Not a thread in all his raiment—not a line in all the marked and singular lineaments of his face which was not, even in the most absolute identity, *mine own!*

It was Wilson; but he spoke no longer in a whisper, and I could have fancied that I myself was speaking while he said:

"*You have conquered, and I yield. Yet, henceforward art thou also dead—dead to the World, to Heaven, and to Hope! In me didst thou exist—and, in my death, see by this image, which is thine own, how utterly thou hast murdered thyself.*"

A Descent into the Maelstrom (1841)

"A Descent into the Maelstrom" was published in *Graham's Magazine*. The Maelstrom (also known as the Moskoestrom) is a famous whirlpool just off the Norwegian coast, but it is neither so deep nor so dangerous as Poe's highly imaginative account would suggest. As a modern authority puts it: "Though dangerous in certain states of wind and tide, the tales of ships being swallowed in this whirlpool are fables."

> *The ways of God in Nature, as in Providence, are not as our ways; nor are the models that we frame any way commensurate to the vastness, profundity, and unsearchableness of His works,* which have a depth in them greater than the well of Democritus.
>
> JOSEPH GLANVILL

We had now reached the summit of the loftiest crag. For some minutes the old man seemed too much exhausted to speak.

"Not long ago," said he at length, "and I could have guided you on this route as well as the youngest of my sons; but, about three years past, there happened to me an event such as never happened before to mortal man—or at least such as no man ever survived to tell of—and the six hours of deadly terror which I then endured have broken me up body and soul. You suppose me a *very* old man—but I am not. It took less than a single day to change these hairs from a jetty black to white, to weaken my limbs, and to unstring my nerves, so that I tremble at the least exertion, and am frightened at a shadow. Do you know I can scarcely look over this little cliff without getting giddy?"

The "little cliff," upon whose edge he had so carelessly thrown himself down to rest that the weightier portion of his body hung over it, while he was only kept from falling by the tenure of his elbow on its extreme and slippery edge—this "little cliff" arose, a sheer unobstructed precipice of black shining rock, some fifteen or sixteen hundred feet from the world of crags beneath us. Nothing would have tempted me to within half a dozen yards of its brink. In truth so deeply was I excited by the perilous position of my companion, that I fell at full length upon the ground, clung to the shrubs around me, and dared not even glance upward at the sky—while I struggled in vain to divest myself of the idea that the very foundations of the mountain were in danger from the fury of the winds. It was long before I could reason myself into sufficient courage to sit up and look out into the distance.

"You must get over these fancies," said the guide, "for I have brought you here that you might have the best possible view of the scene of that event I mentioned—and to tell you the whole story with the spot just under your eye."

"We are now," he continued, in that particularizing manner which distinguished him—"we are now close upon the Norwegian coast—in the sixty-eighth degree of latitude—in the great province of Nordland—and in the dreary district of Lofoden. The mountain upon whose top we sit is Helseggen, the Cloudy. Now raise yourself up a little higher—hold on to the grass if you feel giddy—so—and look out, beyond the belt of vapor beneath us, into the sea."

I looked dizzily, and beheld a wide expanse of ocean, whose waters wore so inky a hue as to bring at once to my mind the Nubian geographer's account of the *Mare Tenebrarum*. A panorama more deplorably desolate no human imagination can conceive. To the right and left, as far as the eye could reach, there lay outstretched, like ramparts of the world, lines of horridly black and beetling cliff, whose character of gloom was but the more forcibly illustrated by the surf which reared high up against it its white and ghastly crest, howling and shrieking for ever. Just opposite the promontory upon whose apex we were placed, and at a distance of some five or six miles out at sea, there was visible a small, bleak-looking island; or, more properly, its position was discernible through the wilderness of surge in which it was enveloped. About two miles nearer the land, arose another of smaller size, hideously craggy and barren, and encompassed at various intervals by a cluster of dark rocks.

The appearance of the ocean, in the space be-

tween the more distant island and the shore, had something very unusual about it. Although, at the time, so strong a gale was blowing landward that a brig in the remote offing lay to under a double-reefed trysail, and constantly plunged her whole hull out of sight, still there was here nothing like a regular swell, but only a short, quick, angry cross dashing of water in every direction—as well in the teeth of the wind as otherwise. Of foam there was little except in the immediate vicinity of the rocks.

"The island in the distance," resumed the old man, "is called by the Norwegians Vurrgh. The one midway is Moskoe. That a mile to the northward is Ambaaren. Yonder are Iflesen, Hoeyholm, Kieldholm, Suarven, and Buckholm. Farther off—between Moskoe and Vurrgh—are Otterholm, Flimen, Sandflesen, and Skarholm. These are the true names of the places—but why it has been thought necessary to name them at all, is more than either you or I can understand. Do you hear any thing? Do you see any change in the water?"

We had now been about ten minutes upon the top of Helseggen, to which we had ascended from the interior of Lofoden, so that we had caught no glimpse of the sea until it had burst upon us from the summit. As the old man spoke, I became aware of a loud and gradually increasing sound, like the moaning of a vast herd of buffaloes upon an American prairie; and at the same moment I perceived that what seamen term the *chopping* character of the ocean beneath us, was rapidly changing into a current which set to the eastward. Even while I gazed, this current acquired a monstrous velocity. Each moment added to its speed—to its headlong impetuosity. In five minutes the whole sea, as far as Vurrgh, was lashed into ungovernable fury; but it was between Moskoe and the coast that the main uproar held its sway. Here the vast bed of the waters, seamed and scarred into a thousand conflicting channels, burst suddenly into phrensied convulsion—heaving, boiling, hissing—gyrating in gigantic and innumerable vortices, and all whirling and plunging on to the eastward with a rapidity which water never elsewhere assumes except in precipitous descents.

In a few minutes more, there came over the scene another radical alteration. The general surface grew somewhat more smooth, and the whirlpools, one by one, disappeared, while prodigious streaks of foam became apparent where none had been seen before. These streaks, at length, spreading out to a great distance, and entering into combination, took unto themselves the gyratory motion of the subsided vortices, and seemed to form the germ of another more vast. Suddenly—very suddenly—this assumed a distinct and definite existence, in a circle of more than half a mile in diameter. The edge of the whirl was represented by a broad belt of gleaming spray; but no particle of this slipped into the mouth of the terrific funnel, whose interior, as far as the eye could fathom it, was a smooth, shining, and jet-black wall of water, inclined to the horizon at an angle of some forty-five degrees, speeding dizzily round and round with a swaying and sweltering motion, and sending forth to the winds an appalling voice, half shriek, half roar, such as not even the mighty cataract of Niagara ever lifts up in its agony to Heaven.

The mountain trembled to its very base, and the rock rocked. I threw myself upon my face, and clung to the scant herbage in an excess of nervous agitation.

"This," said I at length, to the old man—"this *can* be nothing else than the great whirlpool of the Maelstrom."

"So it is sometimes termed," said he. "We Norwegians call it the Moskoestrom, from the island of Moskoe in the midway."

The ordinary accounts of this vortex had by no means prepared me for what I saw. That of Jonas Ramus, which is perhaps the most circumstantial of any, cannot impart the faintest conception either of the magnificence, or of the horror of the scene— or of the wild bewildering sense of *the novel* which confounds the beholder. I am not sure from what point of view the writer in question surveyed it, nor at what time; but it could neither have been from the summit of Helseggen, nor during a storm. There are some passages of his description, nevertheless, which may be quoted for their details, although their effect is exceedingly feeble in conveying an impression of the spectacle.

"Between Lofoden and Moskoe," he says, "the depth of the water is between thirty-six and forty fathoms; but on the other side, toward Ver (Vurrgh) this depth decreases so as not to afford a convenient passage for a vessel, without the risk of splitting on the rocks, which happens even in the calmest weather. When it is flood, the stream runs up the country between Lofoden and Moskoe with a boisterous rapidity; but the roar of its impetuous ebb to the sea is scarce equalled by the loudest and most dreadful cataracts; the noise being heard several leagues off, and the vortices or pits are of such an extent and depth, that if a ship comes within its attraction, it is inevitably absorbed and carried down to the bottom, and there beat to pieces against the rocks; and when the water relaxes, the fragments thereof are thrown up again. But these intervals of tranquillity are only at the turn of the ebb and flood, and in calm weather, and last but a quarter of an hour, its violence gradually returning. When the stream is most boisterous, and its fury heightened by a storm, it is dangerous to come within a Norway mile of it. Boats, yachts, and ships have been carried away by not guarding against it before they were within its reach. It likewise happens frequently, that whales come too near the stream, and are overpowered by its violence; and then it is impossible to describe their howlings and bellowings in their fruitless struggles to disengage themselves. A bear once, attempting to swim from Lofoden to Moskoe, was caught by the stream and borne down, while he roared terribly, so as to be heard on shore. Large stocks of firs and pine trees, after being absorbed by the current, rise again broken and torn to such a degree as if bristles grew upon them. This plainly shows the bottom to consist of craggy rocks, among which they are whirled to and fro. This stream is regulated by the flux and reflux of the sea—it being constantly high and low water every six hours. In the year 1645, early in the morning of Sexagesima Sunday, it raged with such noise and impetuosity that the very stones of the houses on the coast fell to the ground."

In regard to the depth of the water, I could not see how this could have been ascertained at all in the immediate vicinity of the vortex. The "forty fathoms" must have reference only to portions of the channel close upon the shore either of Moskoe or Lofoden. The depth in the centre of the Moskoestrom must be immeasurably greater; and no better proof of this fact is necessary than can be obtained from even the side-long glance into the abyss of the whirl which may be had from the highest crag of Helseggen. Looking down from this pinnacle upon the howling Phlegethon below, I could not help smiling at the simplicity with which the honest Jonas Ramus records, as a matter difficult of belief, the anecdotes of the whales and the bears; for it appeared to me, in fact, a self-evident thing, that the largest ships of the line in existence, coming within the influence of that deadly attraction, could resist it as little as a feather the hurricane, and must disappear bodily and at once.

The attempts to account for the phenomenon—

some of which, I remember, seemed to me sufficiently plausible in perusal—now wore a very different and unsatisfactory aspect. The idea generally received is that this, as well as three smaller vortices among the Feroe islands, "have no other cause than the collision of waves rising and falling, at flux and reflux, against a ridge of rocks and shelves, which confines the water so that it precipitates itself like a cataract; and thus the higher the flood rises, the deeper must the fall be, and the natural result of all is a whirlpool or vortex, the prodigious suction of which is sufficiently known by lesser experiments."—These are the words of the Encyclopædia Britannica. Kircher and others imagine that in the centre of the channel of the Maelstrom is an abyss penetrating the globe, and issuing in some very remote part—the Gulf of Bothnia being somewhat decidedly named in one instance. This opinion, idle in itself, was the one to which, as I gazed, my imagination most readily assented; and, mentioning it to the guide, I was rather surprised to hear him say that, although it was the view almost universally entertained of the subject by the Norwegians, it nevertheless was not his own. As to the former notion he confessed his inability to comprehend it; and here I agreed with him—for, however conclusive on paper, it becomes altogether unintelligible, and even absurd, amid the thunder of the abyss.

"You have had a good look at the whirl now," said the old man, "and if you will creep round this crag, so as to get in its lee, and deaden the roar of the water, I will tell you a story that will convince you I ought to know something of the Moskoestrom."

I placed myself as desired, and he proceeded.

"Myself and my two brothers once owned a schooner-rigged smack of about seventy tons burthen, with which we were in the habit of fishing among the islands beyond Moskoe, nearly to Vurrgh. In all violent eddies at sea there is good fishing, at proper opportunities, if one has only the courage to attempt it; but among the whole of the Lofoden coastmen, we three were the only ones who made a regular business of going out to the islands, as I tell you. The usual grounds are a great way lower down to the southward. There fish can be got at all hours, without much risk, and therefore these places are preferred. The choice spots over here among the rocks, however, not only yield the finest variety, but in far greater abundance; so that we often got in a single day, what the more

timid of the craft could not scrape together in a week. In fact, we made it a matter of desperate speculation—the risk of life standing instead of labor, and courage answering for capital.

"We kept the smack in a cove about five miles higher up the coast than this; and it was our practice, in fine weather, to take advantage of the fifteen minutes' slack to push across the main channel of the Moskoestrom, far above the pool, and then drop down upon anchorage somewhere near Otterholm, or Sandflesen, where the eddies are not so violent as elsewhere. Here we used to remain until nearly time for slack-water again, when we weighed and made for home. We never set out upon this expedition without a steady side wind for going and coming—one that we felt sure would not fail us before our return—and we seldom made a mis-calculation upon this point. Twice, during six years, we were forced to stay all night at anchor on account of a dead calm, which is a rare thing indeed just about here; and once we had to remain on the grounds nearly a week, starving to death, owing to a gale which blew up shortly after our arrival, and made the channel too boisterous to be thought of. Upon this occasion we should have been driven out to sea in spite of everything, (for the whirlpools threw us round and round so violently, that, at length, we fouled our anchor and dragged it) if it had not been that we drifted into one of the innumerable cross currents—here to-day and gone to-morrow—which drove us under the lee of Flimen, where, by good luck, we brought up.

"I could not tell you the twentieth part of the difficulties we encountered 'on the ground'—it is a bad spot to be in, even in good weather—but we made shift always to run the gauntlet of the Moskoestrom itself without accident; although at times my heart has been in my mouth when we happened to be a minute or so behind or before the slack. The wind sometimes was not as strong as we thought it at starting, and then we made rather less way than we could wish, while the current rendered the smack unmanageable. My eldest brother had a son eighteen years old, and I had two stout boys of my own. These would have been of great assistance at such times, in using the sweeps, as well as afterward in fishing—but, somehow, although we ran the risk ourselves, we had not the heart to let the young ones get into the danger—for, after all said and done, it *was* a horrible danger, and that is the truth.

"It is now within a few days of three years since

what I am going to tell you occurred. It was on the tenth of July, 18–, a day which the people of this part of the world will never forget—for it was one in which blew the most terrible hurricane that ever came out of the heavens. And yet all the morning, and indeed until late in the afternoon, there was a gentle and steady breeze from the south-west, while the sun shone brightly, so that the oldest seaman among us could not have foreseen what was to follow.

"The three of us—my two brothers and myself—had crossed over to the islands about two o'clock P.M., and soon nearly loaded the smack with fine fish, which, we all remarked, were more plenty that day than we had ever known them. It was just seven, *by my watch*, when we weighed and started for home, so as to make the worst of the Strom at slack water, which we knew would be at eight.

"We set out with a fresh wind on our starboard quarter, and for some time spanked along at a great rate, never dreaming of danger, for indeed we saw not the slightest reason to apprehend it. All at once we were taken aback by a breeze from over Helseggen. This was most unusual—something that had never happened to us before—and I began to feel a little uneasy, without exactly knowing why. We put the boat on the wind, but could make no headway at all for the eddies, and I was upon the point of proposing to return to the anchorage, when, looking astern, we saw the whole horizon covered with a singular copper-colored cloud that rose with the most amazing velocity.

"In the meantime the breeze that had headed us off fell away, and we were dead becalmed, drifting about in every direction. This state of things, however, did not last long enough to give us time to think about it. In less than a minute the storm was upon us—in less than two the sky was entirely overcast—and what with this and the driving spray, it became suddenly so dark that we could not see each other in the smack.

"Such a hurricane as then blew it is folly to attempt describing. The oldest seaman in Norway never experienced any thing like it. We had let our sails go by the run before it cleverly took us; but, at the first puff, both our masts went by the board as if they had been sawed off—the mainmast taking with it my youngest brother, who had lashed himself to it for safety.

"Our boat was the lightest feather of a thing that ever sat upon water. It had a complete flush deck, with only a small hatch near the bow, and this

hatch it had always been our custom to batten down when about to cross the Strom, by way of precaution against the chopping seas. But for this circumstance we should have foundered at once—for we lay entirely buried for some moments. How my elder brother escaped destruction I cannot say, for I never had an opportunity of ascertaining. For my part, as soon as I had let the foresail run, I threw myself flat on deck, with my feet against the narrow gunwale of the bow, and with my hands grasping a ring-bolt near the foot of the foremast. It was mere instinct that prompted me to do this—which was undoubtedly the very best thing I could have done—for I was too much flurried to think.

"For some moments we were completely deluged, as I say, and all this time I held my breath, and clung to the bolt. When I could stand it no longer I raised myself upon my knees, still keeping hold with my hands, and thus got my head clear. Presently our little boat gave herself a shake, just as a dog does in coming out of the water, and thus rid herself, in some measure, of the seas. I was now trying to get the better of the stupor that had come over me, and to collect my senses so as to see what was to be done, when I felt somebody grasp my arm. It was my elder brother, and my heart leaped for joy, for I had made sure that he was overboard—but the next moment all this joy was turned into horror—for he put his mouth close to my ear, and screamed out the word 'Moskoe-strom!'

"No one ever will know what my feelings were at that moment. I shook from head to foot as if I had had the most violent fit of the ague. I knew what he meant by that one word well enough—I knew what he wished to make me understand. With the wind that now drove us on, we were bound for the whirl of the Strom, and nothing could save us!

"You perceive that in crossing the Strom *channel*, we always went a long way up above the whirl, even in the calmest weather, and then had to wait and watch carefully for the slack—but now we were driving right upon the pool itself, and in such a hurricane as this! 'To be sure,' I thought, 'we shall get there just about the slack—there is some little hope in that'—but in the next moment I cursed myself for being so great a fool as to dream of hope at all. I knew very well that we were doomed, had we been ten times a ninety-gun ship.

"By this time the first fury of the tempest had spent itself, or perhaps we did not feel it so much, as we scudded before it, but at all events the seas, which at first had been kept down by the wind, and lay flat and frothing, now got up into absolute mountains. A singular change, too, had come over the heavens. Around in every direction it was still as black as pitch, but nearly overhead there burst out, all at once, a circular rift of clear sky—as clear as I ever saw—and of a deep bright blue—and through it there blazed forth the full moon with a lustre that I never before knew her to wear. She lit up every thing about us with the greatest distinctness—but, oh God, what a scene it was to light up!

"I now made one or two attempts to speak to my brother—but in some manner which I could not understand, the din had so increased that I could not make him hear a single word, although I screamed at the top of my voice in his ear. Presently he shook his head, looking as pale as death, and held up one of his fingers, as if to say '*listen!*'

"At first I could not make out what he meant—but soon a hideous thought flashed upon me. I dragged my watch from its fob. It was not going. I glanced at its face by the moonlight, and then burst into tears as I flung it far away into the ocean. *It had run down at seven o'clock! We were behind the time of the slack, and the whirl of the Strom was in full fury!*

"When a boat is well built, properly trimmed, and not deep laden, the waves in a strong gale, when she is going large, seem always to slip from beneath her—which appears very strange to a landsman—and this is what is called *riding*, in sea phrase.

"Well, so far we had ridden the swells very cleverly; but presently a gigantic sea happened to take us right under the counter, and bore us with it as it rose—up—up—as if into the sky. I would not have believed that any wave could rise so high. And then down we came with a sweep, a slide, and a plunge, that made me feel sick and dizzy, as if I was falling from some lofty mountain-top in a dream. But while we were up I had thrown a quick glance around—and that one glance was all sufficient. I saw our exact position in an instant. The Moskoestrom whirlpool was about a quarter of a mile dead ahead—but no more like the every-day Moskoestrom, than the whirl as you now see it, is like a mill-race. If I had not known where we were, and what we had to expect, I should not have recognised the place at all. As it was, I involuntarily closed my eyes in horror. The lids clenched themselves together as if in a spasm.

"It could not have been more than two minutes afterwards until we suddenly felt the waves subside, and were enveloped in foam. The boat made a sharp half turn to larboard, and then shot off in its new direction like a thunderbolt. At the same moment the roaring noise of the water was completely drowned in a kind of shrill shriek—such a sound as you might imagine given out by the water-pipes of many thousand steam-vessels, letting off their steam all together. We were now in the belt of surf that always surrounds the whirl; and I thought, of course, that another moment would plunge us into the abyss—down which we could only see indistinctly on account of the amazing velocity with which we were borne along. The boat did not seem to sink into the water at all, but to skim like an air-bubble upon the surface of the surge. Her starboard side was next the whirl, and on the larboard arose the world of ocean we had left. It stood like a huge writhing wall between us and the horizon.

"It may appear strange, but now, when we were in the very jaws of the gulf, I felt more composed than when we were only approaching it. Having made up my mind to hope no more, I got rid of a great deal of that terror which unmanned me at first. I suppose it was despair that strung my nerves.

"It may look like boasting—but what I tell you is truth—I began to reflect how magnificent a thing it was to die in such a manner, and how foolish it was in me to think of so paltry a consideration as my own individual life, in view of so wonderful a manifestation of God's power. I do believe that I blushed with shame when this idea crossed my mind. After a little while I became possessed with the keenest curiosity about the whirl itself. I positively felt a *wish* to explore its depths, even at the sacrifice I was going to make; and my principal grief was that I should never be able to tell my old companions on shore about the mysteries I should see. These, no doubt, were singular fancies to occupy a man's mind in such extremity—and I have often thought since, that the revolutions of the boat around the pool might have rendered me a little light-headed.

"There was another circumstance which tended to restore my self-possession; and this was the cessation of the wind, which could not reach us in our present situation—for, as you saw yourself, the belt of surf is considerably lower than the general bed of the ocean, and this latter now towered above us, a high, black, mountainous ridge. If you have never been at sea in a heavy gale, you can form no idea of the confusion of mind occasioned by the wind and spray together. They blind, deafen and strangle you, and take away all power of action or reflection. But we were now, in a great measure, rid of these annoyances—just as death-condemned felons in prison are allowed petty indulgences, forbidden them while their doom is yet uncertain.

"How often we made the circuit of the belt it is impossible to say. We careered round and round for perhaps an hour, flying rather than floating, getting gradually more and more into the middle of the surge, and then nearer and nearer to its horrible inner edge. All this time I had never let go of the ring-bolt. My brother was at the stern, holding on to a large empty water-cask which had been securely lashed under the coop of the counter, and was the only thing on deck that had not been swept overboard when the gale first took us. As we approached the brink of the pit he let go his hold upon this, and made for the ring, from which, in the agony of his terror, he endeavored to force my hands, as it was not large enough to afford us both a secure grasp. I never felt deeper grief than when I saw him attempt this act—although I knew he was a madman when he did it—a raving maniac through sheer fright. I did not care, however, to contest the point with him. I thought it could make no difference whether either of us held on at all; so I let him have the bolt, and went astern to the cask. This there was no great difficulty in doing; for the smack flew round steadily enough, and upon an even keel—only swaying to and fro, with the immense sweeps and swelters of the whirl. Scarcely had I secured myself in my new position, when we gave a wild lurch to starboard, and rushed headlong into the abyss. I muttered a hurried prayer to God, and thought all was over.

"As I felt the sickening sweep of the descent, I had instinctively tightened my hold upon the barrel, and closed my eyes. For some seconds I dared not open them—while I expected instant destruction, and wondered that I was not already in my death-struggles with the water. But moment after moment elapsed. I still lived. The sense of falling had ceased; and the motion of the vessel seemed much as it had been before while in the belt of foam, with the exception that she now lay more along. I took courage and looked once again upon the scene.

"Never shall I forget the sensations of awe, horror, and admiration with which I gazed about me.

The boat appeared to be hanging, as if by magic, midway down, upon the interior surface of a funnel vast in circumference, prodigious in depth, and whose perfectly smooth sides might have been mistaken for ebony, but for the bewildering rapidity with which they spun around, and for the gleaming and ghastly radiance they shot forth, as the rays of the full moon, from that circular rift amid the clouds which I have already described, streamed in a flood of golden glory along the black walls, and far away down into the inmost recesses of the abyss.

"At first I was too much confused to observe anything accurately. The general burst of terrific grandeur was all that I beheld. When I recovered myself a little, however, my gaze fell instinctively downward. In this direction I was able to obtain an unobstructed view, from the manner in which the smack hung on the inclined surface of the pool. She was quite upon an even keel—that is to say, her deck lay in a plane parallel with that of the water—but this latter sloped at an angle of more than forty-five degrees, so that we seemed to be lying upon our beam-ends. I could not help observing, nevertheless, that I had scarcely more difficulty in maintaining my hold and footing in this situation, than if we had been upon a dead level; and this, I suppose, was owing to the speed at which we revolved.

"The rays of the moon seemed to search the very bottom of the profound gulf; but still I could make out nothing distinctly, on account of a thick mist in which everything there was enveloped, and over which there hung a magnificent rainbow, like that narrow and tottering bridge which Mussulmen say is the only pathway between Time and Eternity. This mist, or spray, was no doubt occasioned by the clashing of the great walls of the funnel, as they all met together at the bottom—but the yell that went up to the Heavens from out of that mist, I dare not attempt to describe.

"Our first slide into the abyss itself, from the belt of foam above, had carried us to a great distance down the slope; but our farther descent was by no means proportionate. Round and round we swept—not with any uniform movement—but in dizzying swings and jerks, that sent us sometimes only a few hundred feet—sometimes nearly the complete circuit of the whirl. Our progress downward, at each revolution, was slow, but very perceptible.

"Looking about me upon the wide waste of liquid ebony on which we were thus borne, I perceived that our boat was not the only object in the embrace of the whirl. Both above and below us were visible fragments of vessels, large masses of building timber and trunks of trees, with many smaller articles, such as pieces of house furniture, broken boxes, barrels and staves. I have already described the unnatural curiosity which had taken the place of my original terrors. It appeared to grow upon me as I drew nearer and nearer to my dreadful doom. I now began to watch, with a strange interest, the numerous things that floated in our company. I *must* have been delirious—for I even sought *amusement* in speculating upon the relative velocities of their several descents toward the foam below. 'This fir tree,' I found myself at one time saying, 'will certainly be the next thing that takes the awful plunge and disappears,'—and then I was disappointed to find that the wreck of a Dutch merchant ship overtook it and went down before. At length, after making several guesses of this nature, and being deceived in all—this fact—the fact of my invariable miscalculation, set me upon a train of reflection that made my limbs again tremble, and my heart beat heavily once more.

"It was not a new terror that thus affected me, but the dawn of a more exciting *hope*. This hope arose partly from memory, and partly from present observation. I called to mind the great variety of buoyant matter that strewed the coast of Lofoden, having been absorbed and then thrown forth by the Moskoestrom. By far the greater number of the articles were shattered in the most extraordinary way—so chafed and roughened as to have the appearance of being stuck full of splinters—but then I distinctly recollected that there were *some* of them which were not disfigured at all. Now I could not account for this difference except by supposing that the roughened fragments were the only ones which had been *completely absorbed*—that the others had entered the whirl at so late a period of the tide, or, from some reason, had descended so slowly after entering, that they did not reach the bottom before the turn of the flood came, or of the ebb, as the case might be. I conceived it possible, in either instance, that they might thus be whirled up again to the level of the ocean, without undergoing the fate of those which had been drawn in more early or absorbed more rapidly. I made, also, three important observations. The first was, that as a general rule, the larger the bodies were, the more rapid their descent;—the second, that, between two masses of equal extent,

the one spherical, and the other *of any other shape*, the superiority in speed of descent was with the sphere;—the third, that, between two masses of equal size, the one cylindrical, and the other of any other shape, the cylinder was absorbed the more slowly.

"Since my escape, I have had several conversations on this subject with an old school-master of the district; and it was from him that I learned the use of the words 'cylinder' and 'sphere.' He explained to me—although I have forgotten the explanation—how what I observed was, in fact, the natural consequence of the forms of the floating fragments—and showed me how it happened that a cylinder, swimming in a vortex, offered more resistance to its suction, and was drawn in with greater difficulty than an equally bulky body, of any form whatever.

"There was one startling circumstance which went a great way in enforcing these observations, and rendering me anxious to turn them to account, and this was that, at every revolution, we passed something like a barrel, or else the broken yard or the mast of a vessel, while many of these things, which had been on our level when I first opened my eyes upon the wonders of the whirlpool, were now high up above us, and seemed to have moved but little from their original station.

"I no longer hesitated what to do. I resolved to lash myself securely to the water cask upon which I now held, to cut it loose from the counter, and to throw myself with it into the water. I attracted my brother's attention by signs, pointed to the floating barrels that came near us, and did everything in my power to make him understand what I was about to do. I thought at length that he comprehended my design—but, whether this was the case or not, he shook his head despairingly, and refused to move from his station by the ring-bolt. It was impossible to force him; the emergency admitted no delay; and so, with a bitter struggle, I resigned him to his fate, fastened myself to the cask by means of the lashings which secured it to the counter, and precipitated myself with it into the sea, without another moment's hesitation.

"The result was precisely what I had hoped it might be. As it is myself who now tell you this tale —as you see that I *did* escape—and as you are already in possession of the mode in which this escape was effected, and must therefore anticipate all that I have farther to say—I will bring my story quickly to conclusion. It might have been an hour, or thereabout, after my quitting the smack, when, having descended to a vast distance beneath me, it made three or four wild gyrations in rapid succession, and, bearing my loved brother with it, plunged headlong, at once and forever, into the chaos of foam below. The barrel to which I was attached sunk very little farther than half the distance between the bottom of the gulf and the spot at which I leaped overboard, before a great change took place in the character of the whirlpool. The slope of the sides of the vast funnel became momently less and less steep. The gyrations of the whirl grew, gradually, less and less violent. By degrees, the froth and the rainbow disappeared, and the bottom of the gulf seemed slowly to uprise. The sky was clear, the winds had gone down, and the full moon was setting radiantly in the west, when I found myself on the surface of the ocean, in full view of the shores of Lofoden, and above the spot where the pool of the Moskoestrom

had been. It was the hour of the slack—but the sea still heaved in mountainous waves from the effects of the hurricane. I was borne violently into the channel of the Strom, and in a few minutes, was hurried down the coast into the 'grounds' of the fishermen. A boat picked me up—exhausted from fatigue, and (now that the danger was removed) speechless from the memory of its horror. Those who drew me on board were my old mates and daily companions—but they knew me no more than they would have known a traveller from the spirit-land. My hair, which had been raven-black the day before, was as white as you see it now. They say too that the whole expression of my countenance had changed. I told them my story —they did not believe it. I now tell it to *you*—and I can scarcely expect you to put more faith in it than did the merry fishermen of Lofoden.''

The Purloined Letter (1845)

It has been observed that Poe has as good a claim as any to the invention of the detective story. "The Purloined Letter" was first published in the *Gift*. This is the third and last of Poe's stories about his detective, Monsieur Dupin.

T. O. Mabbott supplies a useful note for the modern reader in reminding him that at the time of this story separate envelopes for letters were rarely used. A message was written on one or more sheets of paper and these were so folded together that the outside sheet, one side of which was left blank, could be inscribed with the address and then folded so as to furnish a cover for the enclosed contents. The whole was sealed up with a blob of sealing wax. Dupin would not have found it difficult to change the shape of a letter of this sort.

> *Nil sapientiæ odiosius acumine nimio.*
> [Nothing is more troublesome than
>   too much keenness of discernment.]
>   SENECA

At Paris, just after dark one gusty evening in the autumn of 18—, I was enjoying the twofold luxury of meditation and a meerschaum, in company with

my friend C. Auguste Dupin, in his little back library, or book-closet, *au troisième, No. 33 Rue Dunôt, Faubourg St. Germain.* For one hour at least we had maintained a profound silence; while each, to any casual observer, might have seemed intently and exclusively occupied with the curling eddies of smoke that oppressed the atmosphere of the chamber. For myself, however, I was mentally discussing certain topics which had formed matter for conversation between us at an earlier period of the evening; I mean the affair of the Rue Morgue, and the mystery attending the murder of Marie Rogêt. I looked upon it, therefore, as something of a coincidence, when the door of our apartment was thrown open and admitted our old acquaintance, Monsieur G——, the Prefect of the Parisian police.

We gave him a hearty welcome; for there was nearly half as much of the entertaining as of the contemptible about the man, and we had not seen him for several years. We had been sitting in the dark, and Dupin now arose for the purpose of lighting a lamp, but sat down again, without doing so, upon G.'s saying that he had called to consult us, or rather to ask the opinion of my friend, about some official business which had occasioned a great deal of trouble.

"If it is any point requiring reflection," observed Dupin, as he forbore to enkindle the wick, "we shall examine it to better purpose in the dark."

"That is another of your odd notions," said the Prefect, who had a fashion of calling every thing "odd" that was beyond his comprehension, and thus lived amid an absolute legion of "oddities."

"Very true," said Dupin, as he supplied his visiter with a pipe, and rolled towards him a comfortable chair.

"And what is the difficulty now?" I asked. "Nothing more in the assassination way, I hope?"

"Oh no; nothing of that nature. The fact is, the business is *very* simple indeed, and I make no doubt that we can manage it sufficiently well ourselves; but then I thought Dupin would like to hear the details of it, because it is so excessively *odd*."

"Simple and odd," said Dupin.

"Why, yes; and not exactly that either. The fact is, we have all been a good deal puzzled because the affair *is* so simple, and yet baffles us altogether."

"Perhaps it is the very simplicity of the thing which puts you at fault," said my friend.

"What nonsense you *do* talk!" replied the Prefect, laughing heartily.

"Perhaps the mystery is a little *too* plain," said Dupin.

"Oh, good heavens! who ever heard of such an idea?"

"A little *too* self-evident."

"Ha! ha! ha!—ha! ha! ha!—ho! ho! ho"—roared our visiter, profoundly amused, "oh, Dupin, you will be the death of me yet!"

"And what, after all, *is* the matter on hand?" I asked.

"Why, I will tell you," replied the Prefect, as he gave a long, steady, and contemplative puff, and settled himself in his chair. "I will tell you in a few words; but, before I begin, let me caution you that this is an affair demanding the greatest secrecy, and that I should most probably lose the position I now hold, were it known that I confided it to any one."

"Proceed," said I.

"Or not," said Dupin.

"Well, then; I have received personal information, from a very high quarter, that a certain document of the last importance, has been purloined from the royal apartments. The individual who purloined it is known; this beyond a doubt; he was seen to take it. It is known, also, that it still remains in his possession."

"How is this known?" asked Dupin.

"It is clearly inferred," replied the Prefect, "from the nature of the document, and from the non-appearance of certain results which would at once arise from its passing *out* of the robber's possession;—that is to say, from his employing it as he must design in the end to employ it."

"Be a little more explicit," I said.

"Well, I may venture so far as to say that the paper gives its holder a certain power in a certain quarter where such power is immensely valuable." The Prefect was fond of the cant of diplomacy.

"Still I do not quite understand," said Dupin.

"No? Well; the disclosure of the document to a third person, who shall be nameless, would bring in question the honor of a personage of most exalted station; and this fact gives the holder of the document an ascendancy over the illustrious personage whose honor and peace are so jeopardized."

"But this ascendancy," I interposed, "would depend upon the robber's knowledge of the loser's knowledge of the robber. Who would dare—"

"The thief," said G., "is the Minister D——, who dares all things, those unbecoming as well as those becoming a man. The method of the theft was not less ingenious than bold. The document in question—a letter, to be frank—had been received by the personage robbed while alone in the royal *boudoir*. During its perusal she was suddenly interrupted by the entrance of the other exalted personage from whom especially it was her wish to conceal it. After a hurried and vain endeavor to thrust it in a drawer, she was forced to place it, open as it was, upon a table. The address, however, was uppermost, and, the contents thus unexposed, the letter escaped notice. At this juncture enters the Minister D——. His lynx eye immediately perceives the paper, recognizes the handwriting of the address, observes the confusion of the personage addressed, and fathoms her secret. After some business transactions, hurried through in his ordinary manner, he produces a letter somewhat similar to the one in question, opens it, pretends to read it, and then places it in close juxtaposition to the other. Again he converses, for some fifteen minutes, upon the public affairs. At length, in taking leave, he takes also from the table the letter to which he had no claim. Its rightful owner saw, but, of course, dared not call attention to the act, in the presence of the third personage who stood at her elbow. The minister decamped; leaving his own letter—one of no importance—upon the table."

"Here, then," said Dupin to me, "you have precisely what you demand to make the ascendancy complete—the robber's knowledge of the loser's knowledge of the robber."

"Yes," replied the Prefect; "and the power thus attained has, for some months past, been wielded, for political purposes, to a very dangerous extent. The personage robbed is more thoroughly convinced, every day, of the necessity of reclaiming her letter. But this, of course, cannot be done openly. In fine, driven to despair, she has committed the matter to me."

"Than whom," said Dupin, amid a perfect whirlwind of smoke, "no more sagacious agent could, I suppose, be desired, or even imagined."

"You flatter me," replied the Prefect; "but it is possible that some such opinion may have been entertained."

"It is clear," said I, "as you observe, that the letter is still in the possession of the minister; since it is this possession, and not any employment of the letter, which bestows the power. With the employment the power departs."

"True," said G.; "and upon this conviction I proceeded. My first care was to make thorough search of the minister's hotel; and here my chief embarrassment lay in the necessity of searching without his knowledge. Beyond all things, I have been warned of the danger which would result from giving him reason to suspect our design."

"But," said I, "you are quite *au fait* in these investigations. The Parisian police have done this thing often before."

"O yes; and for this reason I did not despair. The habits of the minister gave me, too, a great advantage. He is frequently absent from home all night. His servants are by no means numerous. They sleep at a distance from their master's apartment, and being chiefly Neapolitans, are readily made drunk. I have keys, as you know, with which I can open any chamber or cabinet in Paris. For three months a night has not passed, during the greater part of which I have not been engaged, personally, in ransacking the D—— Hôtel. My honor is interested, and, to mention a great secret, the reward is enormous. So I did not abandon the search until I had become fully satisfied that the thief is a more astute man than myself. I fancy that I have investigated every nook and corner of the premises in which it is possible that the paper can be concealed."

"But is it not possible," I suggested, "that although the letter may be in possession of the minister, as it unquestionably is, he may have concealed it elsewhere than upon his own premises?"

"This is barely possible," said Dupin. "The present peculiar condition of affairs at court, and especially of those intrigues in which D—— is known to be involved, would render the instant availability of the document—its susceptibility of being produced at a moment's notice—a point of nearly equal importance with its possession."

"Its susceptibility of being produced?" said I.

"That is to say, of being *destroyed*," said Dupin.

"True," I observed; "the paper is clearly then upon the premises. As for its being upon the person of the minister, we may consider that as out of the question."

"Entirely," said the Prefect. "He had been twice waylaid, as if by foot-pads, and his person rigorously searched under my own inspection."

"You might have spared yourself this trouble," said Dupin. "D——, I presume, is not altogether a fool, and, if not, must have anticipated these waylayings, as a matter of course."

"Not *altogether* a fool," said G., "but then he is a poet, which I take to be only one remove from a fool."

"True," said Dupin, after a long and thoughtful whiff from his meerschaum, "although I have been guilty of certain doggerel myself."

"Suppose you detail," said I, "the particulars of your search."

"Why the fact is, we took our time, and we searched *every where*. I have had long experience in these affairs. I took the entire building, room by room; devoting the nights of a whole week to each. We examined, first, the furniture of each apartment. We opened every possible drawer; and I presume you know that, to a properly trained police agent, such a thing as a *secret* drawer is impossible. Any man is a dolt who permits a 'secret' drawer to escape him in a search of this kind. The thing is *so* plain. There is a certain amount of bulk—of space—to be accounted for in every cabinet. Then we have accurate rules. The fiftieth part of a line could not escape us. After the cabinets we took the chairs. The cushions we probed with the fine long needles you have seen me employ. From the tables we removed the tops."

"Why so?"

"Sometimes the top of a table, or other similarly arranged piece of furniture, is removed by the person wishing to conceal an article; then the leg is excavated, the article deposited within the cavity, and the top replaced. The bottoms and tops of bedposts are employed in the same way."

"But could not the cavity be detected by sounding?" I asked.

"By no means, if, when the article is deposited,

a sufficient wadding of cotton be placed around it. Besides, in our case, we were obliged to proceed without noise."

"But you could not have removed—you could not have taken to pieces *all* articles of furniture in which it would have been possible to make a deposit in the manner you mention. A letter may be compressed into a thin spiral roll, not differing much in shape or bulk from a large knitting-needle, and in this form it might be inserted into the rung of a chair, for example. You did not take to pieces all the chairs?"

"Certainly not; but we did better—we examined the rungs of every chair in the hotel, and indeed the jointings of every description of furniture, by the aid of a most powerful microscope. Had there been any traces of recent disturbance we should not have failed to detect it instantly. A single grain of gimlet-dust, for example, would have been as obvious as an apple. Any disorder in the glueing— any unusual gaping in the joints—would have sufficed to insure detection."

"I presume you looked to the mirrors, between the boards and the plates, and you probed the beds and the bed-clothes, as well as the curtains and carpets."

"That of course; and when we had absolutely completed every particle of the furniture in this way, then we examined the house itself. We divided its entire surface into compartments, which we numbered, so that none might be missed; then we scrutinized each individual square inch throughout the premises, including the two houses immediately adjoining, with the microscope as before."

"The two houses adjoining!" I exclaimed; "you must have had a great deal of trouble."

"We had; but the reward offered is prodigious."

"You include the *grounds* about the houses?"

"All the grounds are paved with brick. They gave us comparatively little trouble. We examined the moss between the bricks, and found it undisturbed."

"You looked among D——'s papers, of course, and into the books of the library?"

"Certainly; we opened every package and parcel; we not only opened every book, but we turned over every leaf in each volume, not contenting ourselves with a mere shake, according to the fashion of some of our police officers. We also measured the thickness of every book-*cover*, with the most accurate admeasurement, and applied to each the most jealous scrutiny of the microscope. Had any

of the bindings been recently meddled with, it would have been utterly impossible that the fact should have escaped observation. Some five or six volumes, just from the hands of the binder, we carefully probed, longitudinally, with the needles."

"You explored the floors beneath the carpets?"

"Beyond doubt. We removed every carpet, and examined the boards with the microscope."

"And the paper on the walls?"

"Yes."

"You looked into the cellars?"

"We did."

"Then," I said, "you have been making a miscalculation, and the letter is *not* upon the premises as you suppose."

"I fear you are right there," said the Prefect. "And now, Dupin, what would you advise me to do?"

"To make a thorough re-search of the premises."

"That is absolutely needless," replied G——. "I am not more sure that I breathe than I am that the letter is not at the Hôtel."

"I have no better advice to give you," said Dupin. "You have, of course, an accurate description of the letter?"

"Oh, yes!"—And here the Prefect, producing a memorandum-book, proceeded to read aloud a minute account of the internal, and especially of the external, appearance of the missing document. Soon after finishing the perusal of this description, he took his departure, more entirely depressed in spirits than I had ever known the good gentleman before.

In about a month afterward he paid us another visit, and found us occupied very nearly as before. He took a pipe and a chair and entered into some ordinary conversation. At length I said;—

"Well, but G——, what of the purloined letter? I presume you have at last made up your mind that there is no such thing as overreaching the Minister?"

"Confound him, say I—yes; I made the reexamination, however, as Dupin suggested—but it was all labor lost, as I knew it would be."

"How much was the reward offered, did you say?" asked Dupin.

"Why, a very great deal—a *very* liberal reward— I don't like to say how much, precisely; but one thing I *will* say, that I wouldn't mind giving my individual check for fifty thousand francs to any one who could obtain me that letter. The fact is, it is becoming of more and more importance every day; and the reward has been lately doubled. If it were trebled, however, I could do no more than I have done."

"Why, yes," said Dupin, drawlingly, between the whiffs of his meerschaum, "I really—think, G——, you have not exerted yourself—to the utmost in this matter. You might—do a little more, I think, eh?"

"How?—in what way?"

"Why—puff, puff,—you might—puff, puff—employ counsel in the matter, eh?—puff, puff, puff. Do you remember the story they tell of Abernethy?"

"No; hang Abernethy!"

"To be sure! hang him and welcome. But, once upon a time, a certain rich miser conceived the design of spunging upon this Abernethy for a medical opinion. Getting up, for this purpose, an ordinary conversation in a private company, he insinuated his case to the physician, as that of an imaginary individual.

"'We will suppose,' said the miser, 'that his symptoms are such and such; now, doctor, what would *you* have directed him to take?'

"'Take!' said Abernethy, 'why, take *advice*, to be sure.'"

"But," said the Prefect, a little discomposed, "I am *perfectly* willing to take advice, and to pay for it. I would *really* give fifty thousand francs to any one who would aid me in the matter."

"In that case," replied Dupin, opening a drawer, and producing a check-book, "you may as well fill me up a check for the amount you mentioned. When you have signed it, I will hand you the letter."

I was astounded. The Prefect appeared absolutely thunder-stricken. For some minutes he remained speechless and motionless, looking incredulously at my friend with open mouth, and eyes that seemed starting from their sockets; then, apparently recovering himself in some measure, he seized a pen, and after several pauses and vacant stares, finally filled up and signed a check for fifty thousand francs, and handed it across the table to Dupin. The latter examined it carefully and deposited it in his pocket-book; then, unlocking an *escritoire*, took thence a letter and gave it to the Prefect. This functionary grasped it in a perfect agony of joy, opened it with a trembling hand, cast a rapid glance at its contents, and then, scrambling and struggling to the door, rushed at length unceremoniously from the room and from the house, without having uttered a syllable since Dupin had requested him to fill up the check.

When he had gone, my friend entered into some explanations.

"The Parisian police," he said, "are exceedingly able in their way. They are persevering, ingenious, cunning, and thoroughly versed in the knowledge which their duties seem chiefly to demand. Thus, when G—— detailed to us his mode of searching the premises at the Hôtel D——, I felt entire confidence in his having made a satisfactory investigation—so far as his labors extended."

"So far as his labors extended?" said I.

"Yes," said Dupin. "The measures adopted were not only the best of their kind, but carried out to absolute perfection. Had the letter been deposited within the range of their search, these fellows would, beyond a question, have found it."

I merely laughed—but he seemed quite serious in all that he said.

"The measures, then," he continued, "were good in their kind, and well executed; their defect lay in their being inapplicable to the case, and to the man. A certain set of highly ingenious resources are, with the Prefect, a sort of Proscrustean bed, to which he forcibly adapts his designs. But he perpetually errs by being too deep or too shallow, for the matter in hand; and many a schoolboy is a better reasoner than he. I knew one about eight years of age, whose success at guessing in the game of 'even and odd' attracted universal admiration. This game is simple, and is played with marbles. One player holds in his hand a number of these toys, and demands of another whether that number is even or odd. If the guess is right, the guesser wins one; if wrong, he loses one. The boy to whom I allude won all the marbles of the school. Of course he had some principle of guessing; and this lay in mere observation and admeasurement of the astuteness of his opponents. For example, an arrant simpleton is his opponent, and, holding up his closed hand, asks: 'Are they even or odd?' Our schoolboy replies, 'Odd,' and loses; but upon the second trial he wins, for he then says to himself, 'The simpleton had them even upon the first trial, and his amount of cunning is just sufficient to make him have them odd upon the second; I will therefore guess odd;'—he guesses odd, and wins. Now, with a simpleton a degree above the first, he would have reasoned thus: 'This fellow finds that in the first instance I guessed odd, and, in the second, he will propose to himself upon the first impulse, a simple variation from even to odd, as did the first simpleton; but then a second thought will suggest that this is too simple a variation, and finally he will decide upon putting it even as before. I will therefore guess even;'—he guesses even, and wins. Now this mode of reasoning in the schoolboy, whom his fellows termed 'lucky,'—what, in its last analysis, is it?"

"It is merely," I said, "an identification of the reasoner's intellect with that of his opponent."

"It is," said Dupin; "and, upon inquiring of the boy by what means he effected the *thorough* identification in which his success consisted, I received answer as follows: 'When I wish to find out how wise, or how stupid, or how good, or how wicked is any one, or what are his thoughts at the moment, I fashion the expression on my face, as accurately as possible, in accordance with the expression of his, and then wait to see what thoughts or sentiments arise in my mind or heart, as if to match or correspond with the expression.' This response of the schoolboy lies at the bottom of all the spurious profundity which has been attributed to Rochefoucault, to La Bougive, to Machiavelli, and to Campanella."

"And the identification," I said, "of the reasoner's intellect with that of his opponent, depends, if I understand you aright, upon the accuracy with which the opponent's intellect is admeasured."

"For its practical value it depends upon this," replied Dupin; "and the Prefect and his cohort fail so frequently, first, by default of this identification, and secondly, by ill-admeasurement, or rather through non-admeasurement, of the intellect with which they are engaged. They consider only their *own* ideas of ingenuity; and, in searching for anything hidden, advert only to the modes in which *they* would have hidden it. They are right in this much—that their own ingenuity is a faithful representative of that of *the mass*; but when the cunning of the individual felon is diverse in character from their own, the felon foils them, of course. This always happens when it is above their own, and very usually when it is below. They have no variation of principle in their investigations; at best, when urged by some unusual emergency—by some extraordinary reward—they extend or exaggerate their old modes of *practice*, without touching their principles. What, for example, in this case of D——, has been done to vary the principle of action? What is all this boring, and probing, and sounding, and scrutinizing with the microscope, and dividing the surface of the building into registered square inches—what is it all but an exaggeration *of the application* of one principle or set of principles of search, which are based upon the one set of notions regarding human ingenuity, to which the Prefect, in the long routine of his duty, has been accustomed? Do you not see he has taken it for granted that *all* men proceed to conceal a letter,—not exactly in a gimlet-hole bored in a chair-leg—but, at least, in *some* out-of-the-way hole or corner suggested by the same tenor of thought which would urge a man to secrete a letter in a gimlet-hole bored in a chair-leg? And do you not see also, that such *recherchés* nooks for concealment are adapted only for ordinary occasions, and would be adopted only by ordinary intellects; for, in all cases of concealment, a disposal of the article concealed—a disposal of it in this *recherché* manner—is, in the very first instance, presumable and presumed; and thus its discovery depends, not at all upon the acumen, but altogether upon the mere care, patience, and determination of the seekers; and where the case is of importance—or, what amounts to the same thing in the policial eyes, when the reward is of magnitude,—the qualities in question have *never* been known to fail. You will now understand what I meant in suggesting that, had the purloined letter been hidden anywhere within the limits of the Prefect's examination—in other words, had the principle of its concealment been comprehended within the principles of the Prefect—its discovery would have been a matter altogether beyond question. This functionary, however, has been thoroughly mystified; and the remote source of his defeat lies in the supposition that the Minister is a fool, because he has acquired renown as a poet. All fools are poets; this the Prefect *feels*; and he is merely guilty of a *non distributio medii* [a failure of logic] in thence inferring that all poets are fools."

"But is this really the poet?" I asked. "There are two brothers, I know; and both have attained reputation in letters. The Minister I believe has written learnedly on the Differential Calculus. He is a mathematician, and no poet."

"You are mistaken; I know him well; he is both. As poet *and* mathematician, he would reason well; as mere mathematician, he could not have reasoned at all, and thus would have been at the mercy of the Prefect."

"You surprise me," I said, "by these opinions, which have been contradicted by the voice of the world. You do not mean to set at naught the well-digested idea of centuries. The mathematical reason has long been regarded as *the* reason *par excellence*."

" '*Il y a à parier*,' " replied Dupin, quoting from

Chamfort, " '*que toute idée publique, toute convention reçue, est une sottise, car elle a convenue au plus grand nombre.*' [One could wager that every public idea, every accepted convention is a piece of foolishness for the very fact of its having been conceived by the masses.] The mathematicians, I grant you, have done their best to promulgate the popular error to which you allude, and which is none the less an error for its promulgation as truth. With an art worthy a better cause, for example, they have insinuated the term 'analysis' into application to algebra. The French are the originators of this particular deception; but if a term is of any importance—if words derive any value from applicability—then 'analysis' conveys 'algebra' about as much as, in Latin, '*ambitus*' implies 'ambition,' '*religio*' 'religion,' or '*homines honesti*,' a set of *honorable* men."

"You have a quarrel on hand, I see," said I, "with some of the algebraists of Paris; but proceed."

"I dispute the availability, and thus the value, of that reason which is cultivated in any especial form other than the abstractly logical. I dispute, in particular, the reason educed by mathematical study. The mathematics are the science of form and quantity; mathematical reasoning is merely logic applied to observation upon form and quantity. The great error lies in supposing that even the truths of what is called *pure* algebra, are abstract or general truths. And this error is so egregious that I am confounded at the universality with which it has been received. Mathematical axioms are *not* axioms of general truth. What is true of *relation*—of form and quantity—is often grossly false in regard to morals, for example. In this latter science it is very usually *un*true that the aggregated parts are equal to the whole. In chemistry also the axiom fails. In the consideration of motive it fails; for two motives, each of a given value, have not, necessarily, a value when united, equal to the sum of their values apart. There are numerous other mathematical truths which are only truths within the limits of *relation*. But the mathematician argues from his *finite truths*, through habit, as if they were of an absolutely general applicability—as the world indeed imagines them to be. Bryant, in his very learned 'Mythology,' mentions an analogous source of error, when he says that 'although the Pagan fables are not believed, yet we forget ourselves continually, and make inferences from them as existing realities.' With the algebraists, however, who are Pagans themselves, the 'Pagan fables' *are* believed, and the inferences are made, not so much

through lapse of memory as through an unaccountable addling of the brains. In short, I never yet encountered the mere mathematician who would be trusted out of equal roots, or one who did not clandestinely hold it as a point of his faith that $x^2 + px$ was absolutely and unconditionally equal to q. Say to one of these gentlemen, by way of experiment, if you please, that you believe occasions may occur where $x^2 + px$ is *not* altogether equal to q, and, having made him understand what you mean, get out of his reach as speedily as convenient, for, beyond doubt, he will endeavor to knock you down.

"I mean to say," continued Dupin, while I merely laughed at his last observations, "that if the Minister had been no more than a mathematician, the Prefect would have been under no necessity of giving me this check. I knew him, however, as both mathematician and poet, and my measures were adapted to his capacity, with reference to the circumstances by which he was surrounded. I knew him as a courtier, too, and as a bold *intriguant*. Such a man, I considered, could not fail to be aware of the ordinary policial modes of action. He could not have failed to anticipate—and events have proved that he did not fail to anticipate—the waylayings to which he was subjected. He must have foreseen, I reflected, the secret investigations of his premises. His frequent absences from home at night, which were hailed by the Prefect as certain aids to his success, I regarded only as *ruses*, to afford opportunity for thorough search to the police, and thus the sooner to impress them with the conviction to which G——, in fact, did finally arrive—the conviction that the letter was not upon the premises. I felt, also, that the whole train of thought, which I was at some pains in detailing to you just now, concerning the invariable principle of policial action in searches for articles concealed—I felt that this whole train of thought would necessarily pass through the mind of the Minister. It would imperatively lead him to despise all the ordinary *nooks* of concealment. *He* could not, I reflected, be so weak as not to see that the most intricate and remote recess of his hotel would be as open as his commonest closets to the eyes, to the probes, to the gimlets, and to the microscopes of the Prefect. I saw, in fine, that he would be driven, as a matter of course, to simplicity, if not deliberately induced as a matter of choice. You will remember, perhaps, how desperately the Prefect laughed when I suggested, upon our first interview, that it was just possible this mystery troubled him so much on account of its being so *very* self-evident."

"Yes," said I, "I remember his merriment well. I really thought he would have fallen into convulsions."

"The material world," continued Dupin, "abounds with very strict analogies to the immaterial; and thus some color or truth has been given to the rhetorical dogma, that metaphor, or simile, may be made to strengthen an argument as well as to embellish a description. The principle of the *vis inertiæ*, for example, seems to be identical in physics and metaphysics. It is not more true in the former, that a large body is with more difficulty set in motion than a smaller one, and that its subsequent *momentum* is commensurate with this difficulty, than it is, in the latter, that intellects of the vaster capacity, while more forcible, more constant, and more eventful in their movements than those of inferior grade, are yet the less readily moved, and more embarrassed and full of hesitation in the first few steps of their progress. Again: have you ever noticed which of the street signs, over the shop doors, are the most attractive of attention?"

"I have never given the matter a thought," I said.

"There is a game of puzzles," he resumed, "which is played upon a map. One party playing requires another to find a given word—the name of town, river, state or empire—any word, in short, upon the motley and perplexed surface of the chart. A novice in the game generally seeks to embarrass his opponents by giving them the most minutely lettered names; but the adept selects such words as stretch, in large characters, from one end of the chart to the other. These, like the over-largely lettered signs and placards of the street, escape observation by dint of being excessively obvious; and here the physical oversight is precisely analogous with the moral inapprehension by which the intellect suffers to pass unnoticed those considerations which are too obtrusively and too palpably self-evident. But this is a point, it appears, somewhat above or beneath the understanding of the Prefect. He never once thought it probable, or possible, that the Minister had deposited the letter immediately beneath the nose of the whole world, by way of best preventing any portion of that world from perceiving it.

"But the more I reflected upon the daring, dashing, and discriminating ingenuity of D——; upon the fact that the document must always have been *at hand*, if he intended to use it to good purpose;

and upon the decisive evidence, obtained by the Prefect, that it was not hidden within the limits of that dignitary's ordinary search—the more satisfied I became that, to conceal this letter, the Minister had resorted to the comprehensive and sagacious expedient of not attempting to conceal it at all.

"Full of these ideas, I prepared myself with a pair of green spectacles, and called one fine morning, quite by accident, at the Ministerial hotel. I found D—— at home, yawning, lounging, and dawdling, as usual, and pretending to be in the last extremity of *ennui*. He is, perhaps, the most really energetic human being now alive—but that is only when nobody sees him.

"To be even with him, I complained of my weak eyes, and lamented the necessity of the spectacles, under cover of which I cautiously and thoroughly surveyed the whole apartment, while seemingly intent only upon the conversation of my host.

"I paid especial attention to a large writing-table near which he sat, and upon which lay confusedly, some miscellaneous letters and other papers, with one or two musical instruments and a few books. Here, however, after a long and very deliberate scrutiny, I saw nothing to excite particular suspicion.

"At length my eyes, in going the circuit of the room, fell upon a trumpery filigree card-rack of pasteboard, that hung dangling by a dirty blue ribbon, from a little brass knob just beneath the middle of the mantel-piece. In this rack, which had three or four compartments, were five or six visiting cards and a solitary letter. This last was much soiled and crumpled. It was torn nearly in two, across the middle—as if a design, in the first instance, to tear it entirely up as worthless, had been altered, or stayed, in the second. It had a large black seal, bearing the D—— cipher *very* conspicuously, and was addressed, in a diminutive female hand, to D——, the minister, himself. It was thrust carelessly, and even, as it seemed, contemptuously, into one of the upper divisions of the rack.

"No sooner had I glanced at this letter than I concluded it to be that of which I was in search. To be sure, it was, to all appearance, radically different from the one of which the Prefect had read us so minute a description. Here the seal was large and black, with the D—— cipher; there it was small and red, with the ducal arms of the S—— family. Here, the address, to the Minister, was diminutive and feminine; there the superscription, to a certain royal personage, was markedly bold and decided; the size alone formed a point of correspondence. But, then, the *radicalness* of these differences, which was excessive; the dirt; the soiled and torn condition of the paper, so inconsistent with the *true* methodical habits of D——, and so suggestive of a design to delude the beholder into an idea of the worthlessness of the document; these things, together with the hyperobtrusive situation of this document, full in the view of every visiter, and thus exactly in accordance with the conclusions to which I had previously arrived; these things, I say, were strongly corroborative of suspicion, in one who came with the intention to suspect.

"I protracted my visit as long as possible, and, while I maintained a most animated discussion with the Minister, upon a topic which I knew well had never failed to interest and excite him, I kept my attention really riveted upon the letter. In this examination, I committed to memory its external appearance and arrangement in the rack; and also fell, at length, upon a discovery which set at rest whatever trivial doubt I might have entertained. In scrutinizing the edges of the paper, I observed them to be more *chafed* than seemed necessary. They presented the *broken* appearance which is manifested when a stiff paper, having been once folded and pressed with a folder, is refolded in a reversed direction, in the same creases or edges which had formed the original fold. This discovery was sufficient. It was clear to me that the letter had been turned, as a glove, inside out, re-directed, and re-sealed. I bade the Minister good morning, and took my departure at once, leaving a gold snuff-box upon the table.

"The next morning I called for the snuff-box, when we resumed, quite eagerly, the conversation of the preceding day. While thus engaged, however, a loud report, as if of a pistol, was heard immediately beneath the windows of the hotel, and was succeeded by a series of fearful screams, and the shoutings of a mob. D—— rushed to a casement, threw it open, and looked out. In the meantime I stepped to the card-rack, took the letter, put it in my pocket, and replaced it by a *fac-simile*, (so far as regards externals) which I had carefully prepared at my lodgings; imitating the D—— cipher, very readily, by means of a seal formed of bread.

"The disturbance in the street had been occasioned by the frantic behavior of a man with a musket. He had fired it among a crowd of women and children. It proved, however, to have been without ball, and the fellow was suffered to go his way as a lunatic or a drunkard. When he had gone, D—— came from the window, whither I had followed him immediately upon securing the object in view. Soon afterward I bade him farewell. The pretended lunatic was a man in my own pay."

"But what purpose had you," I asked, "in replacing the letter by a *fac-simile*? Would it not have been better, at the first visit, to have seized it openly, and departed?"

"D——," replied Dupin, "is a desperate man, and a man of nerve. His hotel, too, is not without attendants devoted to his interests. Had I made the wild attempt you suggest, I might never have left the Ministerial presence alive. The good people of Paris might have heard of me no more. But I had an object apart from these considerations. You know my political prepossessions. In this matter, I act as a partisan of the lady concerned. For eighteen months the Minister has had her in his power. She has now him in hers; since, being unaware that the letter is not in his possession, he will proceed with his exactions as if it was. Thus will he inevitably commit himself, at once, to his political destruction. His downfall, too, will not be more precipitate than awkward. It is all very well to talk about the *facilis descensus Averni*; but in all kinds of climbing, as Catalani said of singing, it is far more easy to get up than to come down. In the present instance I have no sympathy—at least no pity—for him who descends. He is that *monstrum horrendum*, an unprincipled man of genius. I confess, however, that I should like very well to know the precise character of his thoughts, when, being defied by her whom the Prefect terms 'a certain personage,' he is reduced to opening the letter which I left for him in the card-rack."

"How? did you put any thing particular in it?"

"Why—it did not seem altogether right to leave the interior blank—that would have been insulting. D——, at Vienna once, did me an evil turn, which I told him, quite good-humoredly, that I should remember. So, as I knew he would feel some curiosity in regard to the identity of the person who had outwitted him, I thought it a pity not to give him a clue. He is well acquainted with my MS., and I just copied into the middle of the blank sheet the words—

——Un dessein si funeste,
S'il n'est digne d'Atrée, est digne de Thyeste.

[Such a dreadful plan. If not worthy of Atreus, it is worthy of Thyestes.]

They are to be found in Crébillon's 'Atrée.' "

[handwritten top margin: union / separation / reunion / Death of a beautiful young woman. Eternal beauty restored / reunion of chief character with eternal beauty / death conquers the material world.]

The Fall of the House of Usher (1839)

[handwritten: Physical collapses symbolize triumph of spiritual world over material world.]

This story was first published in *Burton's Gentleman's Magazine*. As everyone has seen, Roderick Usher and the gloomy mansion that he inhabits are counterparts, each the expression of the other. The house with its "vacant eye-like windows" is actually described as if it were a human being. (In Usher's song, "The Haunted Palace," these analogies are pressed even further. The palace is a man's head with "Banners yellow" standing for his hair, "two luminous windows" for the eyes, "the fair palace door" glowing with "pearl and ruby" for the mouth, and even a whiff of perfumed hair oil: "Along the ramparts plumed and pallid/ A winged odour went away.") Roderick Usher has also another double, his sister Madeline. Brother and sister are knit together by various sorts of affinities and psychic ties. The illness of one sets up its repercussions in the psyche of the other; the death of one necessarily entails the death of the other. Thus sister, brother, and the House of Usher itself collapse together.

The richly symbolic material in this tale has stimulated the critics and literary scholars to unusual efforts. They have produced diverse interpretations, some of them very strained allegories indeed, none of them interpretations that we feel can be recommended wholeheartedly to the reader.

[handwritten: House of Usher stands for the Usher family and the House / Madeleine # Ligeia / Usher // narrator / When it falls, both fall. / gets gloomy mood]

> *Son cœur est un luth suspendu;*
> *Sitôt qu'on le touche il résonne.*
> [His heart is a hanging lute;
>   As soon as it is touched, it resounds.]
>   DE BÉRANGER

During the whole of a dull, dark, and soundless day in the autumn of the year, when the clouds hung oppressively low in the heavens, I had been passing alone, on horseback, through a singularly dreary tract of country, and at length found myself, as the shades of the evening drew on, within view of the melancholy House of Usher. I know not how it was—but, with the first glimpse of the building, a sense of insufferable gloom pervaded my spirit. I say insufferable; for the feeling was unrelieved by any of that half-pleasurable, because

poetic, sentiment, with which the mind usually receives even the sternest natural images of the desolate or terrible. I looked upon the scene before me—upon the mere house, and the simple landscape features of the domain—upon the bleak walls— upon the vacant eye-like windows—upon a few rank sedges—and upon a few white trunks of decayed trees—with an utter depression of soul which I can compare to no earthly sensation more properly than to the after-dream of the reveller upon opium—the bitter lapse into every-day life—the hideous dropping off of the veil. There was an iciness, a sinking, a sickening of the heart—an unredeemed dreariness of thought which no goading of the imagination could torture into aught of the sublime. What was it—I paused to think—what was it that so unnerved me in the contemplation of the House of Usher? It was a mystery all insoluble; nor could I grapple with the shadowy fancies that crowded upon me as I pondered. I was forced to fall back upon the unsatisfactory conclusion, that while, beyond doubt, there *are* combinations of very simple natural objects which have the power of thus affecting us, still the analysis of this power lies among considerations beyond our depth. It was possible, I reflected, that a mere different arrangement of the particulars of the scene, of the details of the picture, would be sufficient to modify, or perhaps to annihilate its capacity for sorrowful impression; and, acting upon this idea, I reined my horse to the precipitous brink of a black and lurid tarn that lay in unruffled lustre by the dwelling, and gazed down—but with a shudder even more thrilling than before—upon the remodelled and inverted images of the gray sedge, and the ghastly tree-stems, and the vacant and eye-like windows.

[handwritten margin: material world. / Mad. is Usher's spiritual counterpart / eyes are windows of the soul / House and Usher are identified / both collapse at same time]

Nevertheless, in this mansion of gloom I now proposed to myself a sojourn of some weeks. Its proprietor, Roderick Usher, had been one of my boon companions in boyhood; but many years had elapsed since our last meeting. A letter, however, had lately reached me in a distant part of the country—a letter from him—which, in its wildly importunate nature, had admitted of no other than a personal reply. The MS. gave evidence of nervous agitation. The writer spoke of acute bodily illness— of a mental disorder which oppressed him—and of an earnest desire to see me, as his best, and indeed his only personal friend, with a view of attempting, by the cheerfulness of my society, some alleviation

[handwritten bottom: typical of his style and technique. / that stories should have single emotional effect—horror / allegory of eternal beauty]

of his malady. It was the manner in which all this, and much more, was said—it was the apparent *heart* that went with his request—which allowed me no room for hesitation; and I accordingly obeyed forthwith what I still considered a very singular summons.

Although, as boys, we had been even intimate associates, yet I really knew little of my friend. His reserve had been always excessive and habitual. I was aware, however, that his very ancient family had been noted, time out of mind, for a peculiar sensibility of temperament, displaying itself, through long ages, in many works of exalted art, and manifested, of late, in repeated deeds of munificent yet unobtrusive charity, as well as in a passionate devotion to the intricacies, perhaps even more than to the orthodox and easily recognizable beauties, of musical science. I had learned, too, the very remarkable fact, that the stem of the Usher race, all time-honoured as it was, had put forth, at no period, any enduring branch; in other words, that the entire family lay in the direct line of descent, and had always, with very trifling and very temporary variation, so lain. It was this deficiency, I considered, while running over in thought the perfect keeping of the character of the premises with the accredited character of the people, and while speculating upon the possible influence which the one, in the long lapse of centuries, might have exercised upon the other—it was this deficiency, perhaps of collateral issue, and the consequent undeviating transmission, from sire to son, of the patrimony with the name, which had, at length, so identified the two as to merge the original title of the estate in the quaint and equivocal appellation of the "House of Usher"—an appellation which seemed to include, in the minds of the peasantry who used it, both the family and the family mansion.

I have said that the sole effect of my somewhat childish experiment—that of looking down within the tarn—had been to deepen the first singular impression. There can be no doubt that the consciousness of the rapid increase of my superstition—for why should I not so term it?—served mainly to accelerate the increase itself. Such, I have long known, is the paradoxical law of all sentiments having terror as a basis. And it might have been for this reason only, that, when I again uplifted my eyes to the house itself, from its image in the pool, there grew in my mind a strange fancy—a fancy so ridiculous, indeed, that I but mention it to show the vivid force of the sensations which oppressed me. I had so worked upon my imagination as really to believe that about the whole mansion and domain there hung an atmosphere peculiar to themselves and their immediate vicinity—an atmosphere which had no affinity with the air of heaven, but which had reeked up from the decayed trees, and the gray wall, and the silent tarn—a pestilent and mystic vapour, dull, sluggish, faintly discernible, and leaden-hued.

Shaking off from my spirit what *must* have been a dream, I scanned more narrowly the real aspect of the building. Its principal feature seemed to be that of an excessive antiquity. The discoloration of ages had been great. Minute fungi overspread the whole exterior, hanging in a fine tangled web-work from the eaves. Yet all this was apart from an extraordinary dilapidation. No portion of the masonry had fallen; and there appeared to be a wild inconsistency between its still perfect adaptation of parts, and the crumbling condition of the individual stones. In this there was much that reminded me of the spacious totality of old wood-work which has rotted for long years in some neglected vault, with no disturbance from the breath of the external air. Beyond this indication of extensive decay, however, the fabric gave little token of instability. Perhaps the eye of a scrutinizing observer might have discovered a barely perceptible fissure, which, extending from the roof of the building in front, made its way down the wall in a zigzag direction, until it became lost in the sullen waters of the tarn.

Noticing these things, I rode over a short causeway to the house. A servant in waiting took my horse, and I entered the Gothic archway of the hall. A valet, of stealthy step, thence conducted me, in silence, through many dark and intricate passages in my progress to the *studio* of his master. Much that I encountered on the way contributed, I know not how, to heighten the vague sentiments of which I have already spoken. While the objects around me—while the carvings of the ceilings, the sombre tapestries of the walls, the ebon blackness of the floors, and the phantasmagoric armorial trophies which rattled as I strode, were but matters to which, or to such as which, I had been accustomed from my infancy—while I hesitated not to acknowledge how familiar was all this—I still wondered to find how unfamiliar were the fancies which ordinary images were stirring up. On one of the staircases, I met the physician of the family. His countenance, I thought, wore a mingled expression of low cunning and perplexity. He accosted me with trepidation and passed on. The valet now threw open a door and ushered me into the presence of his master.

The room in which I found myself was very large and lofty. The windows were long, narrow, and pointed, and at so vast a distance from the black oaken floor as to be altogether inaccessible from within. Feeble gleams of encrimsoned light made their way through the trellissed panes, and served to render sufficiently distinct the more prominent objects around; the eye, however, struggled in vain to reach the remoter angles of the chamber, or the recesses of the vaulted and fretted ceiling. Dark draperies hung upon the walls. The general furniture was profuse, comfortless, antique, and tattered. Many books and musical instruments lay scattered about, but failed to give any vitality to the scene. I felt that I breathed an atmosphere of sorrow. An air of stern, deep, and irredeemable gloom hung over and pervaded all.

Upon my entrance, Usher arose from a sofa on which he had been lying at full length, and greeted me with a vivacious warmth which had much in it, I at first thought of an overdone cordiality—of the constrained effort of the *ennuyé* man of the world. A glance, however, at his countenance convinced me of his perfect sincerity. We sat down; and for some moments, while he spoke not, I gazed upon him with a feeling half of pity, half of awe. Surely, man had never before so terribly altered, in so brief a period, as had Roderick Usher! It was with difficulty that I could bring myself to admit the identity of the wan being before me with the companion of my early boyhood. Yet the character of his face had been at all times remarkable. A cadaverousness of complexion; an eye large, liquid, and luminous beyond comparison; lips somewhat thin and very pallid, but of a surprisingly beautiful curve; a nose of a delicate Hebrew model, but with a breadth of nostril unusual in similar formations; a finely moulded chin, speaking, in its want of prominence, of a want of moral energy; hair of a more than web-like softness and tenuity; these features, with an inordinate expansion above the regions of the temple, made up altogether a countenance not easily to be forgotten. And now in the mere exaggeration of the prevailing character of these features, and of the expression they were wont to convey, lay so much of change that I doubted to whom I spoke. The now ghastly pallor of the skin, and the now miraculous lustre of the eye, above all things startled and even awed me. The silken hair, too, had been suffered to grow all

unheeded, and as, in its wild gossamer texture, it floated rather than fell about the face, I could not, even with effort, connect its Arabesque expression with any idea of simple humanity.

In the manner of my friend I was at once struck with an incoherence—an inconsistency; and I soon found this to arise from a series of feeble and futile struggles to overcome an habitual trepidancy—an excessive nervous agitation. For something of this nature I had indeed been prepared, no less by his letter, than by reminiscences of certain boyish traits, and by conclusions deduced from his peculiar physical conformation and temperament. His action was alternately vivacious and sullen. His voice varied rapidly from a tremulous indecision (when the animal spirits seemed utterly in abeyance) to that species of energetic concision—that abrupt, weighty, unhurried, and hollow-sounding enunciation—that leaden, self-balanced, and perfectly modulated guttural utterance, which may be observed in the lost drunkard, or the irreclaimable eater of opium, during the periods of his most intense excitement.

It was thus that he spoke of the object of my visit, of his earnest desire to see me, and of the solace he expected me to afford him. He entered, at some length, into what he conceived to be the nature of his malady. It was, he said, a constitutional and a family evil, and one for which he despaired to find a remedy—a mere nervous affection, he immediately added, which would undoubtedly soon pass off. It displayed itself in a host of unnatural sensations. Some of these, as he detailed them, interested and bewildered me; although, perhaps, the terms and the general manner of their narration had their weight. He suffered much from a morbid acuteness of the senses; the most insipid food was alone endurable; he could wear only garments of certain texture; the odours of all flowers were oppressive; his eyes were tortured by even a faint light; and there were but peculiar sounds, and these from stringed instruments, which did not inspire him with horror.

To an anomalous species of terror I found him a bounden slave. "I shall perish," said he, "I *must* perish in this deplorable folly. Thus, thus, and not otherwise, shall I be lost. I dread the events of the future, not in themselves, but in their results. I shudder at the thought of any, even the most trivial, incident, which may operate upon this intolerable agitation of soul. I have, indeed, no abhorrence of danger, except in its absolute effect—in terror. In this unnerved—in this pitiable condition

—I feel that the period will sooner or later arrive when I must abandon life and reason together, in some struggle with the grim phantasm, FEAR."

I learned, moreover, at intervals, and through broken and equivocal hints, another singular feature of his mental condition. He was enchained by certain superstitious impressions in regard to the dwelling which he tenanted, and whence, for many years, he had never ventured forth—in regard to an influence whose suppositious force was conveyed in terms too shadowy here to be re-stated—an influence which some peculiarities in the mere form and substance of his family mansion had, by dint of long sufferance, he said, obtained over his spirit—an effect which the *physique* of the gray wall and turrets, and of the dim tarn into which they all looked down, had, at length, brought about upon the *morale* of his existence.

He admitted, however, although with hesitation, that much of the peculiar gloom which thus afflicted him could be traced to a more natural and far more palpable origin—to the severe and long-continued illness—indeed to the evidently approaching dissolution—of a tenderly beloved sister, his sole companion for long years, his last and only relative on earth. "Her decease," he said, with a bitterness which I can never forget, "would leave him (him the hopeless and the frail) the last of the ancient race of the Ushers." While he spoke, the lady Madeline (for so was she called) passed slowly through a remote portion of the apartment, and, without having noticed my presence, disappeared. I regarded her with an utter astonishment not unmingled with dread—and yet I found it impossible to account for such feelings. A sensation of stupor oppressed me, as my eyes followed her retreating steps. When a door, at length, closed upon her, my glance sought instinctively and eagerly the countenance of the brother—but he had buried his face in his hands, and I could only perceive that a far more than ordinary wanness had overspread the emaciated fingers through which trickled many passionate tears.

The disease of the lady Madeline had long baffled the skill of her physicians. A settled apathy, a gradual wasting away of the person, and frequent although transient affections of a partially cataleptical character were the unusual diagnosis. Hitherto she had steadily borne up against the pressure of her malady, and had not betaken herself finally to bed; but on the closing in of the evening of my arrival at the house, she succumbed (as her brother told me at night with inexpressible agitation) to

the prostrating power of the destroyer; and I learned that the glimpse I had obtained of her person would thus probably be the last I should obtain—that the lady, at least while living, would be seen by me no more.

For several days ensuing, her name was unmentioned by either Usher or myself: and during this period I was busied in earnest endeavours to alleviate the melancholy of my friend. We painted and read together, or I listened, as if in a dream, to the wild improvisations of his speaking guitar. And thus, as a closer and still closer intimacy admitted me more unreservedly into the recesses of his spirit, the more bitterly did I perceive the futility of all attempt at cheering a mind from which darkness, as if an inherent positive quality, poured forth upon all objects of the moral and physical universe in one unceasing radiation of gloom.

I shall ever bear about me a memory of the many solemn hours I thus spent alone with the master of the House of Usher. Yet I should fail in any attempt to convey an idea of the exact character of the studies, or of the occupations, in which he involved me, or led me the way. An excited and highly distempered ideality threw a sulphureous lustre over all. His long improvised dirges will ring forever in my ears. Among other things, I hold painfully in mind a certain singular perversion and amplification of the wild air of the last waltz of Von Weber. From the paintings over which his elaborate fancy brooded, and which grew, touch by touch, into vagueness at which I shuddered the more thrillingly, because I shuddered knowing not why;—from these paintings (vivid as their images now are before me) I would in vain endeavour to educe more than a small portion which should lie within the compass of merely written words. By the utter simplicity, by the nakedness of his designs, he arrested and overawed attention. If ever mortal painted an idea, that mortal was Roderick Usher. For me at least—in the circumstances then surrounding me—there arose out of the pure abstractions which the hypochondriac contrived to throw upon his canvas, an intensity of intolerable awe, no shadow of which I felt ever yet in the contemplation of the certainly glowing yet too concrete reveries of Fuseli.

One of the phantasmagoric conceptions of my friend, partaking not so rigidly of the spirit of abstraction, may be shadowed forth, although feebly, in words. A small picture presented the interior of an immensely long and rectangular vault or tunnel, with low walls, smooth, white, and without inter-

[handwritten top margin: He is soul-sick]

ruption or device. Certain accessory points of the design served well to convey the idea that this excavation lay at an exceeding depth below the surface of the earth. No outlet was observed in any portion of its vast extent, and no torch or other artificial source of light was discernible; yet a flood of intense rays rolled throughout, and bathed the whole in a ghastly and inappropriate splendour. *[handwritten: Hellish light]*

I have just spoken of that morbid condition of the auditory nerve which rendered all music intolerable to the sufferer, with the exception of certain effects of stringed instruments. It was, perhaps, the narrow limits to which he thus confined himself upon the guitar, which gave birth, in great measure, to the fantastic character of his performances. But the fervid *facility* of his *impromptus* could not be so accounted for. They must have been, and were, in the notes, as well as in the words of his wild fantasias (for he not unfrequently accompanied himself with rhymed verbal improvisations), the result of that intense mental collectedness and concentration to which I have previously alluded as observable only in particular moments of the highest artificial excitement. The words of one of these rhapsodies I have easily remembered. I was, perhaps, the more forcibly impressed with it, as he gave it, because, in the under or mystic current of its meaning, I fancied that I perceived, and for the first time, a full consciousness on the part of Usher, of the tottering of his lofty reason upon her throne. The verses, which were entitled "The Haunted Palace," ran very nearly, if not accurately, thus:

[handwritten left margin: palace & Head] *[handwritten: Corruption]* *[handwritten: mirrors what happens to Usher. allegorical poem within the allegory]*

I

In the greenest of our valleys,
   By good angels tenanted,
Once a fair and stately palace—
   Radiant palace—reared its head.
In the monarch Thought's dominion—
   It stood there!
Never seraph spread a pinion
   Over fabric half so fair.

[handwritten: good days]

II

Banners yellow, glorious, golden,
   On its roof did float and flow;
(This—all this—was in the olden
   Time long ago)
And every gentle air that dallied,
   In that sweet day,
Along the ramparts plumed and pallid,
   A winged odour went away.

[handwritten: what was once good is attacked by evil and goes down. material World]

[handwritten: everything is good and harmonious]

III

Wanderers in that happy valley
   Through two luminous windows saw *[handwritten: eyes in head]*
Spirits moving musically
   To a lute's well-tunèd law,
Round about a throne, where sitting
   (Porphyrogene!) *[handwritten: born to purple — born to be royal]*
In state his glory well befitting,
   The ruler of the realm was seen.

IV

And all with pearl and ruby glowing *[handwritten: teeth ... lips ... mouth]*
   Was the fair palace door,
Through which came flowing, flowing, flowing
   And sparkling evermore,
A troop of Echoes whose sweet duty
   Was but to sing,
In voices of surpassing beauty,
   The wit and wisdom of their king. *[handwritten: Out of his mouth comes beautiful words.]*

V *[handwritten: Shows the turn and corruption.]*

But evil things, in robes of sorrow,
   Assailed the monarch's high estate;
(Ah, let us mourn, for never morrow
   Shall dawn upon him, desolate!)
And, round about his home, the glory
   That blushed and bloomed
Is but a dim-remembered story
   Of the old time entombed.

[handwritten: Happy days are gone forever]

[handwritten: compare with 3]

VI

And travellers now within that valley,
   Through the red-litten windows see *[handwritten: blood-shot eyes suggesting evil and insanity.]*
Vast forms that move fantastically
   To a discordant melody; *[handwritten: was harmonious]*
While, like a rapid ghastly river,
   Through the pale door,
A hideous throng rush out forever,
   And laugh—but smile no more. *[handwritten: insane, wild, crazy laughter.]*

[handwritten: no harmonious smile]

I well remember that suggestions arising from this ballad, led us into a train of thought, wherein there became manifest an opinion of Usher's which I mention not so much on account of its novelty, (for other men have thought thus,) as on account of the pertinacity with which he maintained it. This opinion, in its general form, was that of the sentience of all vegetable things. But, in his disordered fancy, the idea had assumed a more daring character, and trespassed, under certain conditions, upon the kingdom of inorganization. I lack words to express the full extent, or the earnest *abandon* of his persuasion. The belief, however, was connected (as I have previously hinted) with the gray stones of the home of his forefathers. The conditions of the sentience had been here, he imagined, fulfilled in the method of collocation of these stones—in the order of their arrangement, as well as in that of the many *fungi* which overspread them, and of the decayed trees which stood around—above all, in the long undisturbed endurance of this arrangement, and in its reduplication in the still waters of the tarn. Its evidence—the evidence of the sentience—was to be seen, he said (and I here started as he spoke), in the gradual yet certain condensation of an atmosphere of their own about the waters and the walls. The result was discoverable, he added, in that silent yet importunate and terrible influence which for centuries had moulded the destinies of his family, and which made *him* what I now saw him—what he was. Such opinions need no comment, and I will make none.

Our books—the books which, for years, had formed no small portion of the mental existence of the invalid—were, as might be supposed, in strict keeping with his character of phantasm. We pored together over such works as the Ververt et Chartreuse of Gresset; the Belphegor of Machiavelli; the Heaven and Hell of Swedenborg; the Subterranean Voyage of Nicholas Klimm of Holberg; the Chiromancy of Robert Flud, of Jean D'Indaginé, and of De la Chambre; the Journey into the Blue Distance of Tieck; and the City of the Sun of Campanella. One favourite volume was a small octavo edition of the *Directorium Inquisitorum*, by the Dominican Eymeric de Gironne; and there were passages in Pomponius Mela, about the old African Satyrs and Ægipans, over which Usher would sit dreaming for hours. His chief delight, however, was found in the perusal of an exceedingly rare and curious book in quarto Gothic —the manual of a forgotten church—the *Vigiliæ Mortuorum secundum Chorum Ecclesiæ Maguntinæ*.

I could not help thinking of the wild ritual of this work, and of its probable influence upon the hypochondriac, when, one evening, having informed me abruptly that the lady Madeline was no more, he stated his intention of preserving her corpse for a fortnight, (previously to its final interment,) in one of the numerous vaults within the main walls of the building. The worldly reason, however, assigned for this singular proceeding, was one which I did not feel at liberty to dispute. The brother had been led to his resolution (so he told

me) by consideration of the unusual character of the malady of the deceased, of certain obtrusive and eager inquiries on the part of her medical men, and of the remote and exposed situation of the burial-ground of the family. I will not deny that when I called to mind the sinister countenance of the person whom I met upon the staircase, on the day of my arrival at the house, I had no desire to oppose what I regarded as at best but a harmless, and by no means an unnatural, precaution.

At the request of Usher, I personally aided him in the arrangements for the temporary entombment. The body having been encoffined, we two alone bore it to its rest. The vault in which we placed it (and which had been so long unopened that our torches, half smothered in its oppressive atmosphere, gave us little opportunity for investigation) was small, damp, and entirely without means of admission for light; lying, at great depth, immediately beneath that portion of the building in which was my own sleeping apartment. It had been used, apparently, in remote feudal times, for the worst purposes of a donjon-keep, and, in later days, as a place of deposit for powder, or some other highly combustible substance, as a portion of its floor, and the whole interior of a long archway through which we reached it, were carefully sheathed with copper. The door, of massive iron, had been, also, similarly protected. Its immense weight caused an unusually sharp grating sound, as it moved upon its hinges.

Having deposited our mournful burden upon tressels within this region of horror, we partially turned aside the yet unscrewed lid of the coffin, and looked upon the face of the tenant. A striking similitude between the brother and sister now first arrested my attention; and Usher, divining, perhaps, my thoughts, murmured out some few words from which I learned that the deceased and himself had been twins, and that sympathies of a scarcely intelligible nature had always existed between them. Our glances, however, rested not long upon the dead—for we could not regard her unawed. The disease which had thus entombed the lady in the maturity of youth, had left, as usual in all maladies of a strictly cataleptical character, the mockery of a faint blush upon the bosom and the face, and that suspiciously lingering smile upon the lip which is so terrible in death. We replaced and screwed down the lid, and, having secured the door of iron, made our way, with toil, into the scarcely less gloomy apartments of the upper portion of the house.

And now, some days of bitter grief having elapsed, an observable change came over the features of the mental disorder of my friend. His ordinary manner had vanished. His ordinary occupations were neglected or forgotten. He roamed from chamber to chamber with hurried, unequal, and objectless step. The pallor of his countenance had assumed, if possible, a more ghastly hue—but the luminousness of his eye had utterly gone out. The once occasional huskiness of his tone was heard no more; and a tremulous quaver, as if of extreme terror, habitually characterized his utterance. There were times, indeed, when I thought his unceasingly agitated mind was labouring with some oppressive secret, to divulge which he struggled for the necessary courage. At times, again, I was obliged to resolve all into the mere inexplicable vagaries of madness, for I beheld him gazing upon vacancy for long hours, in an attitude of the profoundest attention, as if listening to some imaginary sound. It was no wonder that his condition terrified—that it infected me. I felt creeping upon me, by slow yet certain degrees, the wild influences of his own fantastic yet impressive superstitions.

It was, especially, upon retiring to bed late in the night of the seventh or eighth day after the placing of the lady Madeline within the donjon, that I experienced the full power of such feelings. Sleep came not near my couch—while the hours waned and waned away. I struggled to reason off the nervousness which had dominion over me. I endeavoured to believe that much, if not all of what I felt, was due to the bewildering influence of the gloomy furniture of the room—of the dark and tattered draperies, which, tortured into motion by the breath of a rising tempest, swayed fitfully to and fro upon the walls, and rustled uneasily about the decorations of the bed. But my efforts were fruitless. An irrepressible tremour gradually pervaded my frame; and, at length, there sat upon my very heart an incubus of utterly causeless alarm. Shaking this off with a gasp and a struggle, I uplifted myself upon the pillows, and, peering earnestly within the intense darkness of the chamber, hearkened—I know not why, except that an instinctive spirit prompted me—to certain low and indefinite sounds which came, through the pauses of the storm, at long intervals, I knew not whence. Overpowered by an intense sentiment of horror, unaccountable yet unendurable, I threw on my clothes with haste, (for I felt that I should sleep no more during the night,) and endeavoured to arouse myself from the pitiable condition into which I had fallen, by pacing rapidly to and fro through the apartment.

I had taken but few turns in this manner, when a light step on an adjoining staircase arrested my attention. I presently recognised it as that of Usher. In an instant afterward he rapped, with a gentle touch, at my door, and entered, bearing a lamp. His countenance was, as usual, cadaverously wan—but, moreover, there was a species of mad hilarity in his eyes—an evidently restrained *hysteria* in his whole demeanour. His air appalled me—but anything was preferable to the solitude which I had so long endured, and I even welcomed his presence as a relief.

"And you have not seen it?" he said abruptly, after having stared about him for some moments in silence—"you have not then seen it?—but, stay! you shall." Thus speaking, and having carefully shaded his lamp, he hurried to one of the casements, and threw it freely open to the storm.

The impetuous fury of the entering gust nearly lifted us from our feet. It was, indeed, a tempestuous yet sternly beautiful night, and one wildly singular in its terror and its beauty. A whirlwind had apparently collected its force in our vicinity; for there were frequent and violent alterations in the direction of the wind; and the exceeding density of the clouds (which hung so low as to press upon the turrets of the house) did not prevent our perceiving the life-like velocity with which they flew careering from all points against each other, without passing away into the distance. I say that even their exceeding density did not prevent our perceiving this—yet we had no glimpse of the moon or stars—nor was there any flashing forth of the lightning. But the under surfaces of the huge masses of agitated vapour, as well as all terrestrial objects immediately around us, were glowing in the unnatural light of a faintly luminous and distinctly visible gaseous exhalation which hung about and enshrouded the mansion.

"You must not—you shall not behold this!" said I, shudderingly, to Usher, as I led him, with a gentle violence, from the window to a seat. "These appearances, which bewilder you, are merely electrical phenomena not uncommon—or it may be that they have their ghastly origin in the rank miasma of the tarn. Let us close this casement;—the air is chilling and dangerous to your frame. Here is one of your favourite romances. I will read, and you shall listen;—and so we will pass away this terrible night together."

The antique volume which I had taken up was

the "Mad Trist" of Sir Launcelot Canning; but I had called it a favourite of Usher's more in sad jest than in earnest; for, in truth, there is little in its uncouth and unimaginative prolixity which could have had interest for the lofty and spiritual ideality of my friend. It was, however, the only book immediately at hand; and I indulged a vague hope that the excitement which now agitated the hypochondriac, might find relief (for the history of mental disorder is full of similar anomalies) even in the extremeness of the folly which I could read. Could I have judged, indeed, by the wild overstrained air of vivacity with which he hearkened, or apparently hearkened, to the words of the tale, I might well have congratulated myself upon the success of my design.

I had arrived at that well-known portion of the story where Ethelred, the hero of the Trist, having sought in vain for peaceable admission into the dwelling of the hermit, proceeds to make good an entrance by force. Here, it will be remembered, the words of the narrative run thus:

"And Ethelred, who was by nature of a doughty heart, and who was now mighty withal, on account of the powerfulness of the wine which he had drunken, waited no longer to hold parley with the hermit, who, in sooth, was of an obstinate and maliceful turn, but, feeling the rain upon his shoulders, and fearing the rising of the tempest, uplifted his mace outright, and, with blows, made quickly room in the plankings of the door for his gauntleted hand; and now pulling therewith sturdily, he so cracked, and ripped, and tore all asunder, that the noise of the dry and hollow-sounding wood alarmed and reverberated throughout the forest."

At the termination of this sentence I started and, for a moment, paused; for it appeared to me (although I at once concluded that my excited fancy had deceived me)—it appeared to me that, from some very remote portion of the mansion, there came, indistinctly, to my ears, what might have been, in its exact similarity of character, the echo (but a stifled and dull one certainly) of the very cracking and ripping sound which Sir Launcelot had so particularly described. It was, beyond doubt, the coincidence alone which had arrested my attention; for, amid the rattling of the sashes of the casements, and the ordinary commingled noises of the still increasing storm, the sound, in itself, had nothing, surely, which should have interested or disturbed me. I continued the story:

"But the good champion Ethelred, now entering within the door, was sore enraged and amazed to perceive no signal of the maliceful hermit; but, in the stead thereof, a dragon of a scaly and prodigious demeanour, and of a fiery tongue, which sate in guard before a palace of gold, with a floor of silver; and upon the wall there hung a shield of shining brass with this legend enwritten—

Who entereth herein, a conqueror hath bin;
Who slayeth the dragon, the shield he shall win.

And Ethelred uplifted his mace, and struck upon the head of the dragon, which fell before him, and gave up his pesty breath, with a shriek so horrid and harsh, and withal so piercing, that Ethelred had fain to close his ears with his hands against the dreadful noise of it, the like whereof was never before heard."

Here again I paused abruptly, and now with a feeling of wild amazement—for there could be no doubt whatever that, in this instance, I did actually hear (although from what direction it proceeded I found it impossible to say) a low and apparently distant, but harsh, protracted, and most unusual screaming or grating sound—the exact counterpart of what my fancy had already conjured up for the dragon's unnatural shriek as described by the romancer.

Oppressed, as I certainly was, upon the occurrence of the second and most extraordinary coincidence, by a thousand conflicting sensations, in which wonder and extreme terror were predominant, I still retained sufficient presence of mind to avoid exciting, by any observation, the sensitive nervousness of my companion. I was by no means certain that he had noticed the sounds in question; although, assuredly, a strange alteration had, during the last few minutes, taken place in his demeanour. From a position fronting my own, he had gradually brought round his chair, so as to sit with his face to the door of the chamber; and thus I could but partially perceive his features, although I saw that his lips trembled as if he were murmuring inaudibly. His head had dropped upon his breast—yet I knew that he was not asleep, from the wide and rigid opening of the eye as I caught a glance of it in profile. The motion of his body, too, was at variance with this idea—for he rocked from side to side with a gentle yet constant and uniform sway. Having rapidly taken notice of all this, I resumed the narrative of Sir Launcelot, which thus proceeded:

"And now, the champion, having escaped from the terrible fury of the dragon, bethinking himself of the brazen shield, and of the breaking up of the enchantment which was upon it, removed the carcass from out of the way before him, and approached valorously over the silver pavement of the castle to where the shield was upon the wall; which in sooth tarried not for his full coming, but fell down at his feet upon the silver floor, with a mighty great and terrible ringing sound."

No sooner had these syllables passed my lips, than—as if a shield of brass had indeed, at the moment, fallen heavily upon a floor of silver—I became aware of a distinct, hollow, metallic, and clangorous, yet apparently muffled reverberation. Completely unnerved, I leaped to my feet; but the measured rocking movement of Usher was undisturbed. I rushed to the chair in which he sat. His eyes were bent fixedly before him, and throughout his whole countenance there reigned a stony rigidity. But, as I placed my hand upon his shoulder, there came a strong shudder over his whole person; a sickly smile quivered about his lips; and I saw that he spoke in a low, hurried, and gibbering murmur, as if unconscious of my presence. Bending closely over him, I at length drank in the hideous import of his words.

"Not hear it?—yes, I hear it, and *have* heard it. Long—long—long—many minutes, many hours, many days, have I heard it—yet I dared not—oh, pity me, miserable wretch that I am!—I dared not— I *dared* not speak! *We have put her living in the tomb!* Said I not that my senses were acute? I *now* tell you that I heard her first feeble movements in the hollow coffin. I heard them—many, many days ago—yet I dared not—I *dared not speak!* And now —to-night—Ethelred—ha! ha!—the breaking of the hermit's door, and the death-cry of the dragon, and the clangour of the shield!—say, rather, the rending of her coffin, and the grating of the iron hinges of her prison, and her struggles within the coppered archway of the vault! Oh whither shall I fly? Will she not be here anon? Is she not hurrying to upbraid me for my haste? Have I not heard her

footsteps on the stair? Do I not distinguish that heavy and horrible beating of her heart? MADMAN!"—here he sprang furiously to his feet, and shrieked out his syllables, as if in the effort he were giving up his soul—"MADMAN! I TELL YOU THAT SHE NOW STANDS WITHOUT THE DOOR!"

As if in the superhuman energy of his utterance there had been found the potency of a spell—the huge antique panels to which the speaker pointed threw slowly back, upon the instant, their ponderous and ebony jaws. It was the work of the rushing gust—but then without those doors there *did* stand the lofty and enshrouded figure of the lady Madeline of Usher. There was blood upon her white robes, and the evidence of some bitter struggle upon every portion of her emaciated frame. For a moment she remained trembling and reeling to and fro upon the threshold, then, with a low moaning cry, fell heavily inward upon the person of her brother, and in her violent and now final death-agonies, bore him to the floor a corpse, and a victim to the terrors he had anticipated.

From that chamber, and from that mansion, I fled aghast. The storm was still abroad in all its wrath as I found myself crossing the old causeway. Suddenly there shot along the path a wild light, and I turned to see whence a gleam so unusual could have issued; for the vast house and its shadows were alone behind me. The radiance was that of the full, setting, and blood-red moon, which now shone vividly through that once barely discernible fissure, of which I have before spoken as extending from the roof of the building, in a zigzag direction, to the base. While I gazed, this fissure rapidly widened—there came a fierce breath of the whirlwind—the entire orb of the satellite burst at once upon my sight—my brain reeled as I saw the mighty walls rushing asunder—there was a long tumultuous shouting sound like the voice of a thousand waters—and the deep and dank tarn at my feet closed sullenly and silently over the fragments of the "HOUSE OF USHER."

Ligeia (1838)

This story was first published in the Baltimore *American Museum.* Poe's friend, Philip Pendleton Cooke, was unhappy with its ending. He felt that Poe had demanded too much of the reader in asking him to believe that Ligeia

could actually have taken the material body of Rowena. Poe seems to have agreed with his friend, for in a letter of September 21, 1839, he wrote: "Touching Ligeia, you are right—all right—throughout. . . . I should have intimated that the *will* did not perfect its intention—there should have been a relapse—a final one—and Ligeia should be at length entombed as Rowena—the bodily alteration having gradually faded away." It may, however, be significant that though Poe on two separate occasions revised the story, he did not change the ending.

Professor Roy Basler would deny to Ligeia any of the powers of a witch, arguing that the apparent change in Rowena occurs only in the imagination of the narrator, a man who is obsessed with the idea that he can bring Ligeia back from the tomb. Indeed, Basler thinks that the story suggests that the narrator actually murdered Rowena.

Such an interpretation is tempting: it would get around the awkwardness of having to accept a literal transmogrification. Moreover, Poe, as we know, was always fascinated by the power of subjective states of mind. Nevertheless, there are difficulties with Basler's suggested interpretation as the thoughtful reader will discover.

And the will therein lieth, which dieth not. Who knoweth the mysteries of the will, with its vigor? For God is but a great will pervading all things by nature of its intentness. Man doth not yield himself to the angels, nor unto death utterly, save only through the weakness of his feeble will.

JOSEPH GLANVILL

I cannot, for my soul, remember how, when, or even precisely where, I first became acquainted with the lady Ligeia. Long years have since elapsed, and my memory is feeble through much suffering. Or, perhaps, I cannot *now* bring these points to mind, because, in truth, the character of my beloved, her rare learning, her singular yet placid cast of beauty, and the thrilling and enthralling eloquence of her low musical language, made their way into my heart by paces so steadily and stealthily progressive that they have been unnoticed and unknown. Yet I believe that I met her first and most frequently in some large, old, decaying city near the Rhine. Of her family—I have surely heard her speak. That it is of a remotely ancient date cannot be doubted. Ligeia! Ligeia! Buried in studies of a nature more than all else adapted to deaden impressions of the outward world, it is by

that sweet word alone—by Ligeia—that I bring before mine eyes in fancy the image of her who is no more. And now, while I write, a recollection flashes upon me that I have *never known* the paternal name of her who was my friend and my betrothed, and who became the partner of my studies, and finally the wife of my bosom. Was it a playful charge on the part of my Ligeia? or was it a test of my strength of affection, that I should institute no inquiries upon this point? or was it rather a caprice of my own—a wildly romantic offering on the shrine of the most passionate devotion? I but indistinctly recall the fact itself—what wonder that I have utterly forgotten the circumstances which originated or attended it? And, indeed, if ever that spirit which is entitled *Romance* —if ever she, the wan and the misty-winged *Ashtophet* of idolatrous Egypt, presided, as they tell, over marriages ill-omened, then most surely she presided over mine.

There is one dear topic, however, on which my memory fails me not. It is the *person* of Ligeia. In stature she was tall, somewhat slender, and, in her latter days, even emaciated. I would in vain attempt to portray the majesty, the quiet ease of her demeanor, or the incomprehensible lightness and elasticity of her footfall. She came and departed as a shadow. I was never made aware of her entrance into my closed study save by the dear music of her low sweet voice, as she placed her marble hand upon my shoulder. In beauty of face no maiden ever equalled her. It was the radiance of an opium-dream—an airy and spirit-lifting vision more wildly divine than the phantasies which hovered about the slumbering souls of the daughters of Delos. Yet her features were not of that regular mould which we have been falsely taught to worship in the classical labors of the heathen. "There is no exquisite beauty," says Bacon, Lord Verulam, speaking truly of all the forms and *genera* of beauty, "without some *strangeness* in the proportion." Yet, although I saw that the features of Ligeia were not of a classic regularity—although I perceived that her loveliness was indeed "exquisite," and felt that there was much of "strangeness" pervading it, yet I have tried in vain to detect the irregularity and to trace home my own perception of "the strange." I examined the contour of the lofty and pale forehead—it was faultless—how cold indeed that word when applied to a majesty so divine!—the skin rivalling the purest ivory, the commanding extent and repose, the gentle prominence of the regions above the temples; and then the raven-black, the glossy, the luxuriant and naturally-curling tresses, setting forth the full force of the Homeric epithet, "hyacinthine!" I looked at the delicate outlines of the nose—and nowhere but in the graceful medallions of the Hebrews had I beheld a similar perfection. There were the same luxurious smoothness of surface, the same scarcely perceptible tendency to the aquiline, the same harmoniously curved nostrils speaking the free spirit. I regarded the sweet mouth. Here was indeed the triumph of all things heavenly—the magnificent turn of the short upper lip—the soft, voluptuous slumber of the under—the dimples which sported, and the color which spoke—the teeth glancing back, with a brilliancy almost startling, every ray of the holy light which fell upon them in her serene and placid yet most exultingly radiant of all smiles. I scrutinized the formation of the chin—and, here too, I found the gentleness of breadth, the softness and the majesty, the fullness and the spirituality, of the Greek—the contour which the god Apollo revealed but in a dream, to Cleomenes, the son of the Athenian. And then I peered into the large eyes of Ligeia.

For eyes we have no models in the remotely antique. It might have been, too, that in these eyes of my beloved lay the secret to which Lord Verulam alludes. They were, I must believe, far larger than the ordinary eyes of our own race. They were even fuller than the fullest of the gazelle eyes of the tribe of the valley of Nourjahad. Yet it was only at intervals—in moments of intense excitement—that this peculiarity became more than slightly noticeable in Ligeia. And at such moments was her beauty—in my heated fancy thus it appeared perhaps—the beauty of beings either above or apart from the earth—the beauty of the fabulous Houri of the Turk. The hue of the orbs was the most brilliant of black, and, far over them, hung jetty lashes of great length. The brows, slightly irregular in outline, had the same tint. The "strangeness," however, which I found in the eyes, was of a nature distinct from the formation, or the color, or the brilliancy of the features, and must, after all, be referred to the *expression*. Ah, word of no meaning! behind whose vast latitude of mere sound we intrench our ignorance of so much of the spiritual. The expression of the eyes of Ligeia! How for long hours have I pondered upon it! How have I, through the whole of a midsummer night, struggled to fathom it! What was it—that something more profound than the well of Democritus—which lay far within the pupils of my beloved? What *was* it? I was possessed with a passion

to discover. Those eyes! those large, those shining, those divine orbs! they became to me twin stars of Leda, and I to them devoutest of astrologers.

There is no point, among the many incomprehensible anomalies of the science of mind, more thrillingly exciting than the fact—never, I believe, noticed in the schools—that in our endeavors to recall to memory something long forgotten, we often find ourselves *upon the very verge* of remembrance, without being able, in the end, to remember. And thus how frequently, in my intense scrutiny of Ligeia's eyes, have I felt approaching the full knowledge of their expression—felt it approaching—yet not quite be mine—and so at length entirely depart! And (strange, oh strangest mystery of all!) I found, in the commonest objects of the universe, a circle of analogies to that expression. I mean to say that, subsequently to the period when Ligeia's beauty passed into my spirit, there dwelling as in a shrine, I derived, from many existences in the material world, a sentiment such as I felt always aroused, within me, by her large and luminous orbs. Yet not the more could I define that sentiment, or analyze, or even steadily view it. I recognized it, let me repeat, sometimes in the survey of a rapidly growing vine—in the contemplation of a moth, a butterfly, a chrysalis, a stream of running water. I have felt it in the ocean; in the falling of a meteor. I have felt it in the glances of unusually aged people. And there are one or two stars in heaven—(one especially, a star of the sixth magnitude, double and changeable, to be found near the large star in Lyra) in a telescopic scrutiny of which I have been made aware of the feeling. I have been filled with it by certain sounds from stringed instruments, and not unfrequently by passages from books. Among innumerable other instances, I well remember something in a volume of Joseph Glanvill, which (perhaps from its quaintness—who shall say?) never failed to inspire me with the sentiment;—"And the will therein lieth, which dieth not. Who knoweth the mysteries of the will, with its vigor? For God is but a great will pervading all things by nature of its intentness. Man doth not yield him to the angels, nor unto death utterly, save only through the weakness of his feeble will."

Length of years and subsequent reflection, have enabled me to trace, indeed, some remote connection between this passage in the English moralist and a portion of the character of Ligeia. An *intensity* in thought, action, or speech, was possibly, in her, a result, or at least an index, of that gigantic volition which, during our long intercourse, failed to give other and more immediate evidence of its existence. Of all the women whom I have ever known, she, the outwardly calm, the ever-placid Ligeia, was the most violently a prey to the tumultuous vultures of stern passion. And of such passion I could form no estimate, save by the miraculous expansion of those eyes which at once so delighted and appalled me—by the almost magical melody, modulation, distinctness, and placidity of her very low voice—and by the fierce energy (rendered doubly effective by contrast with her manner of utterance) of the wild words which she habitually uttered.

I have spoken of the learning of Ligeia; it was immense—such as I have never known, in woman. In the classical tongues was she deeply proficient, and as far as my own acquaintance extended in regard to the modern dialects of Europe, I have never known her at fault. Indeed upon any theme of the most admired, because simply the most abstruse of the boasted erudition of the academy, have I *ever* found Ligeia at fault? How singularly —how thrillingly, this one point in the nature of my wife has forced itself, at this late period only, upon my attention! I said her knowledge was such as I have never known in woman—but where breathes the man who has traversed, and successfully, *all* the wide areas of moral, physical, and mathematical science? I saw not then what I now clearly perceive, that the acquisitions of Ligeia were gigantic, were astounding; yet I was sufficiently aware of her infinite supremacy to resign myself, with a child-like confidence, to her guidance through the chaotic world of metaphysical investigation at which I was most busily occupied during the earlier years of our marriage. With how vast a triumph—with how vivid a delight—with how much of all that is ethereal in hope—did I *feel*, as she bent over me in studies but little sought—but less known—that delicious vista by slow degrees expanding before me, down whose long, gorgeous, and all untrodden path, I might at length pass onward to the goal of a wisdom too divinely precious not to be forbidden!

How poignant, then, must have been the grief with which, after some years, I beheld my well-grounded expectations take wings to themselves and fly away! Without Ligeia I was but as a child groping benighted. Her presence, her readings alone, rendered vividly luminous the many mysteries of the transcendentalism in which we were immersed. Wanting the radiant lustre of her eyes, letters, lambent and golden, grew duller than Saturnian lead. And now those eyes shone less and less frequently upon the pages over which I pored. Ligeia grew ill. The wild eyes blazed with a too— too glorious effulgence; the pale fingers became of the transparent waxen hue of the grave; and the blue veins upon the lofty forehead swelled and sank impetuously with the tides of the most gentle emotion. I saw that she must die—and I struggled desperately in spirit with the grim Azrael. And the struggles of the passionate wife were, to my astonishment, even more energetic than my own. There had been much in her stern nature to impress me with the belief that, to her, death would have come without its terrors; but not so. Words are impotent to convey any just idea of the fierceness of resistance with which she wrestled with the Shadow. I groaned in anguish at the pitiable spectacle. I would have soothed—I would have reasoned; but, in the intensity of her wild desire for life,—for life—*but* for life—solace and reason were alike the uttermost folly. Yet not until the last instance, amid the most convulsive writhings of her fierce spirit, was shaken the external placidity of her demeanor. Her voice grew more gentle—grew more low—yet I would not wish to dwell upon the wild meaning of the quietly uttered words. My brain reeled as I hearkened entranced, to a melody more than mortal—to assumptions and aspirations which mortality had never before known.

That she loved me I should not have doubted; and I might have been easily aware that, in a bosom such as hers, love would have reigned no ordinary passion. But in death only was I fully impressed with the strength of her affection. For long hours, detaining my hand, would she pour out before me the overflowing of a heart whose more than passionate devotion amounted to idolatry. How had I deserved to be so blessed by such confessions?—how had I deserved to be so cursed with the removal of my beloved in the hour of her making them? But upon this subject I cannot bear to dilate. Let me say only, that in Ligeia's more than womanly abandonment to a love, alas! all unmerited, all unworthily bestowed, I at length recognized the principle of her longing with so wildly earnest a desire for the life which was now fleeing so rapidly away. It is this wild longing—it is this eager vehemence of desire for life—*but* for life— that I have no power to portray—no utterance capable of expressing.

At high noon of the night in which she departed, beckoning me, peremptorily, to her side, she bade me repeat certain verses composed by herself not many days before. I obeyed her.—They were these:

Lo! 'tis a gala night
    Within the lonesome latter years!
An angel throng, bewinged, bedight
    In veils, and drowned in tears,
Sit in a theatre, to see
    A play of hopes and fears,
While the orchestra breathes fitfully
    The music of the spheres.

Mimes, in the form of God on high,
    Mutter and mumble low,
And hither and thither fly—
    Mere puppets they, who come and go
At bidding of vast formless things
    That shift the scenery to and fro,
Flapping from out their Condor wings
    Invisible Wo!

That motley drama!—oh, be sure
    It shall not be forgot!
With its Phantom chased forever more,
    By a crowd that seize it not,
Through a circle that ever returneth in
    To the self-same spot,
And much of Madness and more of Sin
    And Horror the soul of the plot.

But see, amid the mimic rout,
    A crawling shape intrude!
A blood-red thing that writhes from out
    The scenic solitude!
It writhes!—it writhes!—with mortal pangs
    The mimes become its food,
And the seraphs sob at vermin fangs
    In human gore imbued.

Out—out are the lights—out all!
    And over each quivering form,
The curtain, a funeral pall,
    Comes down with the rush of a storm,
And the angels, all pallid and wan,
    Uprising, unveiling, affirm
That the play is the tragedy, "Man,"
    And its hero the Conqueror Worm.

"O God!" half shrieked Ligeia, leaping to her feet and extending her arms aloft with a spasmodic movement, as I made an end of these lines—"O God! O Divine Father!—shall these things be undeviatingly so?—shall this Conqueror be not once conquered? Are we not part and parcel in Thee? Who—who knoweth the mysteries of the will with its vigor? Man doth not yield him to the angels, *nor unto death utterly*, save only through the weakness of his feeble will."

And now, as if exhausted with emotion, she suffered her white arms to fall, and returned solemnly to her bed of death. And as she breathed her last sighs, there came mingled with them a low murmur from her lips. I bent to them my ear, and distinguished, again, the concluding words of the passage in Glanvill—"*Man doth not yield him to the angels, nor unto death utterly, save only through the weakness of his feeble will.*"

She died;—and I, crushed into the very dust with sorrow, could no longer endure the lonely desolation of my dwelling in the dim and decaying city by the Rhine. I had no lack of what the world calls wealth. Ligeia had brought me far more, very far more than ordinarily falls to the lot of mortals. After a few months, therefore, of weary and aimless wandering, I purchased, and put in some repair, an abbey, which I shall not name, in one of the wildest and least frequented portions of fair England. The gloomy and dreary grandeur of the building, the almost savage aspect of the domain, the many melancholy and time-honored memories connected with both, had much in unison with the feelings of utter abandonment which had driven me into that remote and unsocial region of the country. Yet although the external abbey, with its verdant decay hanging about it, suffered but little alteration, I gave way, with a child-like perversity, and perchance with a faint hope of alleviating my sorrows, to a display of more than regal magnificence within.—For such follies, even in childhood, I had imbibed a taste, and now they came back to me as if in the dotage of grief. Alas, I feel how much even of incipient madness might have been discovered in the gorgeous and fantastic draperies, in the solemn carvings of Egypt, in the wild cornices and furniture, in the Bedlam patterns of the carpets of tufted gold! I had become a bounden slave in the trammels of opium, and my labors and orders had taken a coloring from my dreams. But these absurdities I must not pause to detail. Let me speak only of that one chamber, ever accursed, whither, in a moment of mental alienation, I led from the altar as my bride—as the successor of the unforgotten Ligeia—the fair-haired and blue-eyed Lady Rowena Trevanion, of Tremaine.

There is no individual portion of the architecture and decoration of that bridal chamber which is not now visibly before me. Where were the souls of the haughty family of the bride, when, through thirst of gold, they permitted to pass the threshold of an apartment so bedecked, a maiden and a daughter so beloved? I have said that I minutely remember the details of the chamber—yet I am sadly forgetful on topics of deep moment—and here there was no system, no keeping, in the fantastic display, to take hold upon the memory. The room lay in a high turret of the castellated abbey, was pentagonal in shape, and of capacious size. Occupying the whole southern face of the pentagon was the sole window—an immense sheet of unbroken glass from Venice—a single pane, and tinted of a leaden hue, so that the rays of either the sun or moon, passing through it, fell with a ghastly lustre on the objects within. Over the upper portion of this huge window, extended the trellis-work of an aged vine which clambered up the massy walls of the turret. The ceiling, of gloomy-looking oak, was excessively lofty, vaulted, and elaborately fretted with the wildest and most grotesque specimens of a semi-Gothic, semi-Druidical device. From out the most central recess of this melancholy vaulting, depended, by a single chain of gold with long links, a huge censer of the same metal, Saracenic in pattern, and with many perforations so contrived that there writhed in and out of them, as if endued with a serpent vitality, a continual succession of parti-colored fires.

Some few ottomans and golden candelabra, of Eastern figure, were in various stations about—and there was the couch, too—the bridal couch—of an Indian model, and low, and sculptured of solid ebony, with a pall-like canopy above. In each of the angles of the chamber stood on end a gigantic sarcophagus of black granite, from the tombs of the kings over against Luxor, with their aged lids full of immemorial sculpture. But in the draping of the apartment lay, alas! the chief phantasy of all. The lofty walls, gigantic in height—even unproportionally so—were hung from summit to foot, in vast folds, with a heavy and massive-looking tapestry—tapestry of a material which was found alike as a carpet on the floor, as a covering for the ottomans and the ebony bed, as a canopy for the bed and as the gorgeous volutes of the curtains which partially shaded the window. The material was the richest cloth of gold. It was spotted all over, at irregular intervals, with arabesque figures, about a foot in diameter, and wrought upon the cloth in patterns of the most jetty black. But these figures partook of the true character of the arabesque only when regarded from a single point of view. By a

contrivance now common, and indeed traceable to a very remote period of antiquity, they were made changeable in aspect. To one entering the room, they bore the appearance of simple monstrosities; but upon a farther advance, this appearance gradually departed; and step by step, as the visitor moved his station in the chamber, he saw himself surrounded by an endless succession of the ghastly forms which belong to the superstition of the Norman, or arise in the guilty slumbers of the monk. The phantasmagoric effect was vastly heightened by the artificial introduction of a strong continual current of wind behind the draperies—giving a hideous and uneasy animation to the whole.

In halls such as these—in a bridal chamber such as this—I passed, with the Lady of Tremaine, the unhallowed hours of the first month of our marriage—passed them with but little disquietude. That my wife dreaded the fierce moodiness of my temper —that she shunned me and loved me but little— I could not help perceiving; but it gave me rather pleasure than otherwise. I loathed her with a hatred belonging more to demon than to man. My memory flew back, (oh, with what intensity of regret!) to Ligeia, the beloved, the august, the beautiful, the entombed. I revelled in recollections of her purity, of her wisdom, of her lofty, her ethereal nature, of her passionate, her idolatrous love. Now, then, did my spirit fully and freely burn with more than all the fires of her own. In the excitement of my opium dreams (for I was habitually fettered in the shackles of the drug) I would call aloud upon her name, during the silence of the night, or among the sheltered recesses of the glens by day, as if, through the wild eagerness, the solemn passion, the consuming ardor of my longing for the departed, I could restore her to the pathways she had abandoned—ah, could it be forever?—upon the earth.

About the commencement of the second month of the marriage, the Lady Rowena was attacked with sudden illness, from which her recovery was slow. The fever which consumed her rendered her nights uneasy; and in her perturbed state of half-slumber, she spoke of sounds, and of motions, in and above the chamber of the turret, which I concluded had no origin save in the distemper of her fancy, or perhaps in the phantasmagoric influences of the chamber itself. She became at length convalescent—finally well. Yet but a brief period elapsed, ere a second more violent disorder again threw her upon a bed of suffering; and from this attack her frame, at all times feeble, never altogether recovered. Her illnesses were, after this epoch, of alarming character, and of more alarming recurrence, defying alike the knowledge and the great exertions of her physicians. With the increase of the chronic disease which had thus, apparently, taken too sure hold upon her constitution to be eradicated by human means, I could not fail to observe a similar increase in the nervous irritation of her temperament, and in her excitability by trivial causes of fear. She spoke again, and now more frequently and pertinaciously, of the sounds—of the slight sounds—and of the unusual motions among the tapestries, to which she had formerly alluded.

One night, near the closing in of September, she pressed this distressing subject with more than usual emphasis upon my attention. She had just awakened from an unquiet slumber, and I had been watching, with feelings half of anxiety, half of vague terror, the workings of her emaciated countenance. I sat by the side of her ebony bed, upon one of the ottomans of India. She partly arose, and spoke, in an earnest low whisper, of sounds which she *then* heard, but which I could not hear—of motions which she *then* saw, but which I could not perceive. The wind was rushing hurriedly behind the tapestries, and I wished to show her (what, let me confess it, I could not *all* believe) that those almost inarticulate breathings, and those very gentle variations of the figures upon the wall, were but the natural effects of that customary rushing of the wind. But a deadly pallor, overspreading her face, had proved to me that my exertions to reassure her would be fruitless. She appeared to be fainting, and no attendants were within call. I remembered where was deposited a decanter of light wine which had been ordered by her physicians, and hastened across the chamber to procure it. But, as I stepped beneath the light of the censer, two circumstances of a startling nature attracted my attention. I had felt that some palpable although invisible object had passed lightly by my person; and I saw that there lay upon the golden carpet, in the very middle of the rich lustre thrown from the censer, a shadow—a faint, indefinite shadow of angelic aspect—such as might be fancied for the shadow of a shade. But I was wild with the excitement of an immoderate dose of opium, and heeded these things but little, nor spoke of them to Rowena. Having found the wine, I recrossed the chamber, and poured out a gobletful, which I held to the lips of the fainting lady. She had now partially recovered, however, and took the vessel herself, while I sank upon an ottoman

near me, with my eyes fastened upon her person. It was then that I became distinctly aware of a gentle foot-fall upon the carpet, and near the couch; and in a second thereafter, as Rowena was in the act of raising the wine to her lips, I saw, or may have dreamed that I saw, fall within the goblet, as if from some invisible spring in the atmosphere of the room, three or four large drops of a brilliant and ruby colored fluid. If this I saw—not so Rowena. She swallowed the wine unhesitatingly, and I forbore to speak to her of a circumstance which must, after all, I considered, have been but the suggestion of a vivid imagination, rendered morbidly active by the terror of the lady, by the opium, and by the hour.

Yet I cannot conceal it from my own perception that, immediately subsequent to the fall of the ruby-drops, a rapid change for the worse took place in the disorder of my wife; so that, on the third subsequent night, the hands of her menials prepared her for the tomb, and on the fourth, I sat alone, with her shrouded body, in that fantastic chamber which had received her as my bride.— Wild visions, opium-engendered, flitted, shadow-like, before me. I gazed with unquiet eye upon the sarcophagi in the angles of the room, upon the varying figures of the drapery, and upon the writhing of the parti-colored fires in the censer overhead. My eyes then fell, as I called to mind the circumstances of a former night, to the spot beneath the glare of the censer where I had seen the faint traces of the shadow. It was there, however, no longer; and breathing with greater freedom, I turned my glances to the pallid and rigid figure upon the bed. Then rushed upon me a thousand memories of Ligeia—and then came back upon my heart, with the turbulent violence of a flood, the whole of that unutterable woe with which I had regarded *her* thus enshrouded. The night waned; and still, with a bosom full of bitter thoughts of the one only and supremely beloved, I remained gazing upon the body of Rowena.

It might have been midnight, or perhaps earlier, or later, for I had taken no note of time, when a sob, low, gentle, but very distinct, startled me from my revery.—I *felt* that it came from the bed of ebony—the bed of death. I listened in an agony of superstitious terror—but there was no repetition of the sound. I strained my vision to detect any motion in the corpse—but there was not the slightest perceptible. Yet I could not have been deceived. I *had* heard the noise, however faint, and my soul was awakened within me. I resolutely and perseveringly kept my attention riveted upon the body. Many minutes elapsed before any circumstance occurred tending to throw light upon the mystery. At length it became evident that a slight, a very feeble, and barely noticeable tinge of color had flushed up within the cheeks, and along the sunken small veins of the eyelids. Through a species of unutterable horror and awe, for which the language of mortality has no sufficiently energetic expression, I felt my heart cease to beat, my limbs grow rigid where I sat. Yet a sense of duty finally operated to restore my self-possession. I could no longer doubt that we had been precipitate in our preparations—that Rowena still lived. It was necessary that some immediate exertion be made; yet the turret was altogether apart from the portion of the abbey tenanted by the servants—there were none within call—I had no means of summoning them to my aid without leaving the room for many minutes—and this I could not venture to do. I therefore struggled alone in my endeavors to call back the spirit still hovering. In a short period it was certain, however, that a relapse had taken place; the color disappeared from both eyelid and cheek, leaving a wanness even more than that of marble; the lips became doubly shrivelled and pinched up in the ghastly expression of death; a repulsive clamminess and coldness overspread rapidly the surface of the body; and all the usual rigorous stiffness immediately supervened. I fell back with a shudder upon the couch from which I had been so startlingly aroused, and again gave myself up to passionate waking visions of Ligeia.

An hour thus elapsed when (could it be possible?) I was a second time aware of some vague sound issuing from the region of the bed. I listened—in extremity of horror. The sound came again—it was a sigh. Rushing to the corpse, I saw—distinctly saw—a tremor upon the lips. In a minute afterward they relaxed, disclosing a bright line of pearly teeth. Amazement now struggled in my bosom with the profound awe which had hitherto reigned there alone. I felt that my vision grew dim, that my reason wandered; and it was only by a violent effort that I at length succeeded in nerving myself to the task which duty thus once more had pointed out. There was now a partial glow upon the forehead and upon the cheek and throat; a perceptible warmth pervaded the whole frame; there was even a slight pulsation at the heart. The lady *lived*; and with redoubled ardor I betook myself to the task of restoration. I chafed and bathed the temples and the hands, and used every exer-

tion which experience, and no little medical reading, could suggest. But in vain. Suddenly, the color fled, the pulsation ceased, the lips resumed the expression of the dead, and, in an instant afterward, the whole body took upon itself the icy chilliness, the livid hue, the intense rigidity, the sunken outline, and all the loathsome peculiarities of that which has been, for many days, a tenant of the tomb.

And again I sunk into visions of Ligeia—and again, (what marvel that I shudder while I write?) *again* there reached my ears a low sob from the region of the ebony bed. But why shall I minutely detail the unspeakable horrors of that night? Why shall I pause to relate how, time after time, until near the period of the gray dawn, this hideous drama of revivification was repeated; how each terrific relapse was only into a sterner and apparently more irredeemable death; how each agony wore the aspect of a struggle with some invisible foe; and how each struggle was succeeded by I know not what of wild change in the personal appearance of the corpse? Let me hurry to a conclusion.

The greater part of the fearful night had worn away, and she who had been dead once again stirred—and now more vigorously than hitherto, although arousing from a dissolution more appalling in its utter hopelessness than any. I had long ceased to struggle or to move, and remained sitting rigidly upon the ottoman, a helpless prey to a whirl of violent emotions, of which extreme awe was perhaps the least terrible, the least consuming. The corpse, I repeat, stirred, and now more vigorously than before. The hues of life flushed up with unwonted energy into the countenance—the limbs relaxed—and, save that the eyelids were yet pressed heavily together, and that the bandages and draperies of the grave still imparted their charnel character to the figure, I might have dreamed that Rowena had indeed shaken off, utterly, the fetters of Death. But if this idea was not, even then, altogether adopted, I could at least doubt no longer, when, arising from the bed, tottering, with feeble steps, with closed eyes, and with the manner of one bewildered in a dream, the thing that was enshrouded advanced boldly and palpably into the middle of the apartment.

I trembled not—I stirred not—for a crowd of unutterable fancies connected with the air, the stature, the demeanor of the figure, rushing hurriedly through my brain, had paralyzed—had chilled me into stone. I stirred not—but gazed upon the apparition. There was a mad disorder in my thoughts—a tumult unappeasable. Could it, indeed, be the *living* Rowena who confronted me? Could it, indeed, be Rowena *at all*—the fair-haired, the blue-eyed Lady Rowena Trevanion of Tremaine? Why, *why* should I doubt it? The bandage lay heavily about the mouth—but then might it not be the mouth of the breathing Lady of Tremaine? And the cheeks—there were the roses as in her noon of life—yes, these might indeed be the fair cheeks of the living Lady of Tremaine. And the chin, with its dimples, as in health, might it not be hers?—but *had she then grown taller since her malady?* What inex-

pressible madness seized me with that thought? One bound, and I had reached her feet! Shrinking from my touch, she let fall from her head, unloosened, the ghastly cerements which had confined it, and there streamed forth into the rushing atmosphere of the chamber huge masses of long and dishevelled hair; *it was blacker than the raven wings of midnight!* And now slowly opened *the eyes* of the figure which stood before me. "Here then, at least," I shrieked aloud, "can I never—can I never be mistaken—these are the full, and the black, and the wild eyes—of my lost love—of the Lady—of the LADY LIGEIA."

He is reunited with his only beloved.

Eternal beauty of the spirit conquers all. The beauty of the triumph of the spirit.

ghost story / horror level

allegorical level—say something about eternal beauty and the power of man's mind

The Masque of the Red Death (1842)

"The Masque of the Red Death" was first published in *Graham's Magazine*; it was reprinted (with some revisions) in the *Broadway Journal* in 1845. Our tradition is filled with stories of men's varied reactions to the onset of plague—a desperate attempt to escape it, or mournful resignation, or feverish gaiety induced by desire to live to the full every moment left before death strikes. Yet Poe would seem in this story to have primarily in mind Boccaccio's *Decameron*, in which a group of people take refuge in isolated villas away from the plague-infested city. They tell stories in order to pass the time until the plague has spent itself.

This tale is one of Poe's most characteristic. It constitutes a compendium of assorted Poe themes, symbolic motifs, and methods of presentation. "The Masque of the Red Death," more than most tales, invites and even seems to demand some kind of symbolic interpretation. Consider, for example, the seven sumptuous rooms, each furnished elaborately in terms of one key color; the gigantic clock of ebony with its spirit-chilling monotonous clang; the human beings who have got themselves up in elaborate disguises and who, when they are stopped in their motions by the clang of the clock, seem to be dreams "stiff-frozen." There have been many attempts, in spite of Poe's known antipathy to allegorizing (see p. 423), to find in this tale an elaborate allegory.

The reader may properly ask himself where the symbolic accent of the story falls. Is the problem one of discovering esoteric meanings? Or is there some fairly obvious symbolism, which in this story is pointed up and given a richer and more intricate meaning? For example, the clock clearly is the voice of time and the voice of time reminds most men of the inevitable advent of death, whether that death be near or remote, accomplished by the plague or by some other agency.

The reader might also ask himself whether this tale, which is so obviously a fantasy of some mythical princedom in Europe, is "American" at all. Yet may not the emphasis on doom, and the thoroughness and finality of the doom which befalls the prince and his subjects, have some relation to one of the obsessive themes of American literature?

The "Red Death" had long devastated the country. No pestilence had ever been so fatal, or so hideous. Blood was its Avatar and its seal—the redness and the horror of blood. There were sharp pains, and sudden dizziness, and then profuse bleeding at the pores, with dissolution. The scarlet stains upon the body and especially upon the face of the victim, were the pest ban which shut him out from the aid and from the sympathy of his fellowmen. And the whole seizure, progress and termination of the disease, were the incidents of half an hour.

But the Prince Prospero was happy and daunt-less and sagacious. When his dominions were half depopulated, he summoned to his presence a thou-sand hale and light-hearted friends from among the knights and dames of his court, and with these retired to the deep seclusion of one of his castel-lated abbeys. This was an extensive and magnificent structure, the creation of the prince's own eccentric yet august taste. A strong and lofty wall girdled it in. This wall had gates of iron. The courtiers, having entered, brought furnaces and massy ham-mers and welded the bolts. They resolved to leave means neither of ingress or egress to the sudden impulses of despair or of frenzy from within. The abbey was amply provisioned. With such precau-tions the courtiers might bid defiance to contagion. The external world could take care of itself. In the meantime it was folly to grieve, or to think. The prince had provided all the appliances of pleasure. There were buffoons, there were improvisatori, there were ballet-dancers, there were musicians, there was Beauty, there was wine. All these and security were within. Without was the "Red Death."

It was toward the close of the fifth or sixth month of his seclusion, and while the pestilence raged most furiously abroad, that the Prince Pros-pero entertained his thousand friends at a masked ball of the most unusual magnificence.

It was a voluptuous scene, that masquerade. But first let me tell of the rooms in which it was held. There were seven—an imperial suite. In many pal-aces, however, such suites form a long and straight vista, while the folding doors slide back nearly to the walls on either hand, so that the view of the whole extent is scarcely impeded. Here the case was very different; as might have been expected from the duke's love of the *bizarre*. The apart-ments were so irregularly disposed that the vision embraced but little more than one at a time. There was a sharp turn at every twenty or thirty yards, and at each turn a novel effect. To the right and left, in the middle of each wall, a tall and narrow Gothic window looked out upon a closed corridor which pursued the windings of the suite. These windows were of stained glass whose color varied in accordance with the prevailing hue of the deco-rations of the chamber into which it opened. That at the eastern extremity was hung, for example, in blue—and vividly blue were its windows. The sec-ond chamber was purple in its ornaments and tapestries, and here the panes were purple. The third was green throughout, and so were the case-ments. The fourth was furnished and lighted with

orange—the fifth with white—the sixth with violet. The seventh apartment was closely shrouded in black velvet tapestries that hung all over the ceil-ing and down the walls, falling in heavy folds upon a carpet of the same material and hue. But in this chamber only, the color of the windows failed to correspond with the decorations. The panes here were scarlet—a deep blood color. Now in no one of the seven apartments was there any lamp or can-delabrum, amid the profusion of golden ornaments that lay scattered to and fro or depended from the roof. There was no light of any kind emanating from lamp or candle within the suite of chambers. But in the corridors that followed the suite, there stood, opposite to each window, a heavy tripod, bearing a brazier of fire that projected its rays through the tinted glass and so glaringly illumined the room. And thus were produced a multitude of gaudy and fantastic appearances. But in the west-ern or black chamber the effect of the fire-light that streamed upon the dark hangings through the blood-tinted panes, was ghastly in the extreme, and produced so wild a look upon the countenances of those who entered, that there were few of the com-pany bold enough to set foot within its precincts at all.

It was in this apartment, also, that there stood against the western wall, a gigantic clock of ebony. Its pendulum swung to and fro with a dull, heavy, monotonous clang; and when the minute-hand made the circuit of the face, and the hour was to be stricken, there came from the brazen lungs of the clock a sound which was clear and loud and deep and exceedingly musical, but of so peculiar a note and emphasis that, at each lapse of an hour, the musicians of the orchestra were constrained to pause, momentarily, in their performance, to hearken to the sound; and thus the waltzers per-force ceased their evolutions; and there was a brief disconcert of the whole gay company; and, while the chimes of the clock yet rang, it was observed that the giddiest grew pale, and the more aged and sedate passed their hands over their brows as if in confused reverie or meditation. But when the echoes had fully ceased, a light laughter at once pervaded the assembly; the musicians looked at each other and smiled as if at their own nervous-ness and folly, and made whispering vows, each to the other, that the next chiming of the clock should produce in them no similar emotion; and then, after the lapse of sixty minutes, (which em-brace three thousand and six hundred seconds of the Time that flies,) there came yet another chiming of the clock, and then were the same disconcert and tremulousness and meditation as before.

But, in spite of these things, it was a gay and magnificent revel. The tastes of the duke were peculiar. He had a fine eye for colors and effects. He disregarded the *decora* of mere fashion. His plans were bold and fiery, and his conceptions glowed with barbaric lustre. There are some who would have thought him mad. His followers felt that he was not. It was necessary to hear and see and touch him to be *sure* that he was not.

He had directed, in great part, the moveable embellishments of the seven chambers, upon occasion of this great *fête*; and it was his own guiding taste which had given character to the masqueraders. Be sure they were grotesque. There were much glare and glitter and piquancy and phantasm— much of what has been since seen in "Hernani." There were arabesque figures with unsuited limbs and appointments. There were delirious fancies such as the madman fashions. There was much of the beautiful, much of the wanton, much of the *bizarre*, something of the terrible, and not a little of that which might have excited disgust. To and fro in the seven chambers there stalked, in fact, a multitude of dreams. And these—the dreams— writhed in and about, taking hue from the rooms, and causing the wild music of the orchestra to seem as the echo of their steps. And, anon, there strikes the ebony clock which stands in the hall of the velvet. And then, for a moment, all is still, and all is silent save the voice of the clock. The dreams are stiff-frozen as they stand. But the echoes of the chime die away—they have endured but an instant —and a light, half-subdued laughter floats after them as they depart. And now again the music swells, and the dreams live, and writhe to and fro more merrily than ever, taking hue from the many-tinted windows through which stream the rays from the tripods. But to the chamber which lies most westwardly of the seven, there are now none of the maskers who venture; for the night is waning away; and there flows a ruddier light through the blood-colored panes; and the blackness of the sable drapery appalls; and to him whose foot falls upon the sable carpet, there comes from the near clock of ebony a muffled peal more solemnly emphatic than any which reaches *their* ears who indulge in the more remote gaieties of the other apartments.

But these other apartments were densely crowded, and in them beat feverishly the heart of life. And the revel went whirlingly on, until at length there commenced the sounding of midnight upon the clock. And then the music ceased, as I have told; and the evolutions of the waltzers were quieted; and there was an uneasy cessation of all things as before. But now there were twelve strokes to be sounded by the bell of the clock; and thus it happened, perhaps, that more of thought crept, with more of time, into the meditations of the thoughtful among those who revelled. And thus, too, it happened, perhaps, that before the last echoes of the last chimes had utterly sunk into silence, there were many individuals in the crowd who had found leisure to become aware of the presence of a masked figure which had arrested the attention of no single individual before. And the rumor of this new presence having spread itself whisperingly around, there arose at length from the whole company a buzz, or murmur, expressive of disapprobation and surprise—then, finally, of terror, of horror, and of disgust.

In an assembly of phantasms such as I have painted, it may well be supposed that no ordinary appearance could have excited such sensation. In truth the masquerade license of the night was nearly unlimited; but the figure in question had out-Heroded Herod, and gone beyond the bounds of even the prince's indefinite decorum. There are chords in the hearts of the most reckless which cannot be touched without emotion. Even with the utterly lost, to whom life and death are equally jests, there are matters of which no jest can be made. The whole company, indeed, seemed now deeply to feel that in the costume and bearing of the stranger neither wit nor propriety existed. The figure was tall and gaunt, and shrouded from head to foot in the habiliments of the grave. The mask which concealed the visage was made so nearly to resemble the countenance of a stiffened corpse that the closest scrutiny must have had difficulty in detecting the cheat. And yet all this might have been endured, if not approved, by the mad revellers around. But the mummer had gone so far as to assume the type of the Red Death. His vesture was dabbled in *blood*—and his broad brow, with all the features of the face, was besprinkled with the scarlet horror.

When the eyes of Prince Prospero fell upon this spectral image (which with a slow and solemn movement, as if more fully to sustain its *rôle*, stalked to and fro among the waltzers) he was seen to be convulsed, in the first moment with a strong shudder either of terror or distaste; but, in the next, his brow reddened with rage.

"Who dares?" he demanded hoarsely of the courtiers who stood near him—"who dares insult us with this blasphemous mockery? Seize him and unmask him—that we may know whom we have to hang at sunrise, from the battlements!"

It was in the eastern or blue chamber in which stood the Prince Prospero as he uttered these words. They rang throughout the seven rooms loudly and clearly—for the prince was a bold and robust man, and the music had become hushed at the waving of his hand.

It was in the blue room where stood the prince, with a group of pale courtiers by his side. At first, as he spoke, there was a slight rushing movement of this group in the direction of the intruder, who at the moment was also near at hand, and now, with deliberate and stately step, made closer approach to the speaker. But from a certain nameless awe with which the mad assumptions of the mummer had inspired the whole party, there were found none who put forth hand to seize him; so that, unimpeded, he passed within a yard of the prince's person; and, while the vast assembly, as if with one impulse, shrank from the centres of the rooms to the walls, he made his way uninterruptedly, but with the same solemn and measured step which had distinguished him from the first, through the blue chamber to the purple—through the purple to the green—through the green to the orange—through this again to the white—and even thence to the violet, ere a decided movement had been made to arrest him. It was then, however, that the Prince Prospero, maddening with rage and the shame of his own momentary cowardice, rushed hurriedly through the six chambers, while none followed him on account of a deadly terror that had seized upon all. He bore aloft a drawn dagger, and had approached, in rapid impetuosity, to within three or four feet of the retreating figure, when the latter, having attained the extremity of the velvet apartment, turned suddenly and confronted his pursuer. There was a sharp cry—and the dagger dropped gleaming upon the sable carpet, upon which, instantly afterwards, fell prostrate in death the Prince Prospero. Then, summoning the wild courage of despair, a throng of the revellers at once threw themselves into the black apartment, and, seizing the mummer, whose tall figure stood erect and motionless within the shadow of the ebony clock, gasped in unutterable horror at finding the grave-cerements and corpse-like mask which they handled with so violent a rudeness, untenanted by any tangible form.

And now was acknowledged the presence of the Red Death. He had come like a thief in the night. And one by one dropped the revellers in the blood-bedewed halls of their revel, and died each in the despairing posture of his fall. And the life of the ebony clock went out with that of the last of the gay. And the flames of the tripods expired. And Darkness and Decay and the Red Death held illimitable dominion over all.

From Review of Nathaniel Hawthorne's Twice-Told Tales (1842)

Poe's review of Hawthorne's *Twice-Told Tales* was first printed in *Graham's Magazine* and was reprinted five years later in *Godey's Lady's Book.* (We have omitted from the version printed below a rather labored distinction concerning true originality as distinguished from peculiarity.)

It will be noticed that Poe's review, even with the cuts we have made, is discursive and even rambling. Poe talks about Hawthorne, to be sure, but he also writes at some length about what his notion of the "tale proper" is and expatiates on his theory that a long poem is an impossibility.

In the preface to my sketches of New York Literati, while speaking of the broad distinction between the seeming public and real private opinion respecting our authors, I thus alluded to Nathaniel Hawthorne:

"For example, Mr. Hawthorne, the author of 'Twice-Told Tales,' is scarcely recognized by the press or by the public, and when noticed at all, is noticed merely to be damned by faint praise. Now, my opinion of him is, that although his walk is limited and he is fairly to be charged with mannerism, treating all subjects in a similar tone, of dreamy *innuendo*, yet in this walk he evinces extraordinary genius, having no rival either in America or elsewhere; and this opinion I have never heard gainsaid by any one literary person in the country. That this opinion, however, is a spoken and not a written one, is referable to the facts, first, that Mr. Hawthorne is a poor man, and, secondly, that he *is not* an ubiquitous quack."

The reputation of the author of "Twice-Told Tales" has been confined, indeed, until very lately, to literary society; and I have not been wrong, perhaps, in citing him as *the* example, *par excellence*, in this country, of the privately-admired and publicly-unappreciated man of genius. Within the last year or two, it is true, an occasional critic has been urged, by honest indignation, into very warm approval. Mr. Webber, for instance, (than whom no one has a keener relish for that kind of writing which Mr. Hawthorne has best illustrated,) gave us, in a late number of "The American Review," a cordial and certainly a full tribute to his talents; and since the issue of the "Mosses from an Old Manse," criticisms of similar tone have been by no means infrequent in our more authoritative journals. I call to mind few reviews of Hawthorne published *before* the "Mosses." One I remember in "Arcturus" (edited by Mathews and Duyckinck) for May, 1841; another in the "American Monthly" (edited by Hoffman and Herbert) for March, 1838; a third in the ninety-sixth number of the "North American Review." These criticisms, however, seemed to have little effect on the popular taste—at least, if we are to form any idea of the popular taste by reference to its expression in the newspapers, or by the sale of the author's book. It was never the fashion (until lately) to speak of him in any summary of our best authors. The daily critics would say, on such occasions, "Is there not Irving and Cooper, and Bryant and Paulding, and —Smith?" or, "Have we not Halleck and Dana, and Longfellow and—Thompson?" or, "Can we not point triumphantly to our own Sprague, Willis, Channing, Bancroft, Prescott and—Jenkins?" but these unanswerable queries were never wound up by the name of Hawthorne.

Beyond doubt, this inappreciation of him on the part of the public arose chiefly from the two causes to which I have referred—from the facts that he is neither a man of wealth nor a quack;—but these are insufficient to account for the whole effect. No small portion of it is attributable to the very marked idiosyncrasy of Mr. Hawthorne himself. In one sense, and in great measure, to be peculiar is to be original, and than the true originality there is no higher literary virtue. This true or commendable originality, however, implies not the uniform, but the continuous peculiarity—a peculiarity springing from ever-active vigor of fancy—better still if from ever-present force of imagination, giving its own hue, its own character to everything it touches, and, especially, *self impelled to touch everything*.

It is often said, inconsiderately, that very original writers always fail in popularity—that such and such persons are too original to be comprehended by the mass. "Too peculiar," should be the phrase, "too idiosyncratic." It is, in fact, the excitable, undisciplined and childlike popular mind which most keenly feels the original. The criticism of the conservatives, of the hackneys, of the cultivated old clergymen of the "North American Review," is precisely the criticism which condemns and alone condemns it. "It becometh not a divine," saith Lord Coke, "to be of a fiery and salamandrine spirit." Their conscience allowing them to move nothing themselves, these dignitaries have a holy horror of being moved. "Give us *quietude*," they say. Opening their mouths with proper caution, they sigh forth the word "*Repose*." And this is, indeed, the one thing they should be permitted to enjoy, if only upon the Christian principle of give and take.

. . .

The "peculiarity" or sameness, or monotone of Hawthorne, would, in its mere character of "peculiarity," and without reference to what *is* the peculiarity, suffice to deprive him of all chance of popular appreciation. But at his failure to be appreciated, we can, *of course*, no longer wonder, when we find him monotonous at decidedly the worst of all possible points—at that point which, having the least concern with Nature, is the farthest removed from the popular intellect, from the popular sentiment and from the popular taste. I allude to the strain of allegory which completely overwhelms the greater number of his subjects, and which in some measure interferes with the direct conduct of absolutely all.

In defence of allegory, (however, or for whatever object, employed,) there is scarcely one respectable word to be said. Its best appeals are made to the fancy—that is to say, to our sense of adaptation, not of matters proper, but of matters improper for the purpose, of the real with the unreal; having never more of intelligible connection than has something with nothing, never half so much of effective affinity as has the substance for the shadow. The deepest emotion aroused within us by the happiest allegory, *as* allegory, is a very, very imperfectly satisfied sense of the writer's ingenuity in overcoming a difficulty we should have preferred his not having attempted to overcome. The fallacy of the idea that allegory, in any of its moods, can be made to enforce a truth—that metaphor, for example, may illustrate as well as embellish an argument—could be promptly demonstrated: the converse of the supposed fact might be shown, indeed, with very little trouble—but these are topics foreign to my present purpose. One thing is clear, that if allegory ever establishes a fact, it is by dint of overturning a fiction. Where the suggested meaning runs through the obvious one in a *very* profound under-current so as never to interfere with the upper one without our own volition, so as never to show itself unless *called* to the surface, there only, for the proper uses of fictitious narrative, is it available at all. Under the best circumstances, it must always interfere with that unity of effect which to the artist, is worth all the allegory in the world. Its vital injury, however, is rendered to the most vitally important point in fiction—that of earnestness or verisimilitude. That "The Pilgrim's Progress" is a ludicrously over-rated book, owing its seeming popularity to one or two of those accidents in critical literature which by the critical are sufficiently well understood, is a matter upon which no two thinking people disagree; but the pleasure derivable from it, in any sense, will be found in the direct ratio of the reader's capacity to smother its true purpose, in the direct ratio of his ability to keep the allegory out of sight, or of his *in*ability to comprehend it. Of allegory properly handled, judiciously subdued, seen only as a shadow or by suggestive glimpses, and making its nearest approach to truth in a not obtrusive and therefore not unpleasant *appositeness*, the "Undine" of De La Motte Fouqué is the best, and undoubtedly a very remarkable specimen.

The obvious causes, however, which have prevented Mr. Hawthorne's *popularity*, do not suffice to condemn him in the eyes of the few who belong properly to books, and to whom books, perhaps, do not quite so properly belong. These few estimate an author, not as do the public, altogether by what he does, but in great measure—indeed, even in the greatest measure—by what he evinces a capability of doing. In this view, Hawthorne stands among literary people in America much in the same light as did Coleridge in England. The few, also, through a certain warping of the taste, which long pondering upon books as books merely

never fails to induce, are not in condition to view the errors of a scholar as errors altogether. At any time these gentlemen are prone to think the public not right rather than an educated author wrong. But the simple truth is that the writer who aims at impressing the people, is *always* wrong when he fails in forcing that people to receive the impression. How far Mr. Hawthorne has addressed the people at all, is, of course, not a question for me to decide. His books afford strong internal evidence of having been written to himself and his particular friends alone.

There has long existed in literature a fatal and unfounded prejudice, which it will be the office of this age to overthrow—the idea that the mere bulk of a work must enter largely into our estimate of its merit. I do not suppose even the weakest of the quarterly reviewers weak enough to maintain that in a book's size or mass, abstractly considered, there is anything which especially calls for our admiration. A mountain, simply through the sensation of physical magnitude which it conveys, does, indeed, affect us with a sense of the sublime, but we cannot admit any such influence in the contemplation even of "The Columbiad." The Quarterlies themselves will not admit it. And yet, what else are we to understand by their continual prating about "sustained effort"? Granted that this sustained effort has accomplished an epic—let us then admire the effort, (if this be a thing admirable,) but certainly not the epic on the effort's account. Common sense, in the time to come, may possibly insist upon measuring a work of art rather by the object it fulfils, by the impression it makes, than by the time it took to fulfil the object, or by the extent of "sustained effort" which became necessary to produce the impression. The fact is, that perseverance is one thing and genius quite another; nor can all the transcendentalists in Heathendom confound them.

Full of its bulky ideas, the last number of the "North American Review," in what it imagines a criticism on Simms, "honestly avows that it has little opinion of the mere tale;" and the honesty of the avowal is in no slight degree guaranteed by the fact that this Review has never yet been known to put forth an opinion which was *not* a very little one indeed.

The tale proper affords the fairest field which can be afforded by the wide domains of mere prose, for the exercise of the highest genius. Were I bidden to say how this genius could be most advantageously employed for the best display of its powers, I should answer, without hesitation, "in the composition of a rhymed poem not to exceed in length what might be perused in an hour." Within this limit alone can the noblest order of poetry exist. I have discussed this topic elsewhere, and need here repeat only that the phrase "a long poem" embodies a paradox. A poem must intensely excite. Excitement is its province, its essentiality. Its value is in the ratio of its (elevating) excitement. But all excitement is, from a psychal necessity, transient. It cannot be sustained through a poem of great length. In the course of an hour's reading, at most, it flags, fails; and then the poem is, in effect, no longer such. Men admire, but are wearied with the "Paradise Lost;" for platitude follows platitude, *inevitably*, at regular interspaces, (the depressions between the waves of excitement,) until the poem, (which, properly considered, is but a succession of brief poems,) having been brought to an end, we discover that the sums of our pleasure and of displeasure have been very nearly equal. The absolute, ultimate or aggregate effect of any epic under the sun is, for these reasons, a nullity. "The Iliad," in its form of epic, has but an imaginary existence; granting it real, however, I can only say of it that it is based on a primitive sense of Art. Of the modern epic nothing can be so well said as that it is a blindfold imitation of a "come-by-chance." By and by these propositions will be understood as self-evident, and in the meantime will not be essentially damaged as truths by being generally condemned as falsities.

A poem *too* brief, on the other hand, may produce a sharp or vivid, but never a profound or enduring impression. Without a certain continuity, without a certain duration or repetition of the cause, the soul is seldom moved to the effect. There must be the dropping of the water on the rock. There must be the pressing steadily down of the stamp upon the wax. De Béranger has wrought brilliant things, pungent and spirit-stirring, but most of them are too immassive to have *momentum*, and, as so many feathers of fancy, have been blown aloft only to be whistled down the wind. Brevity, indeed, may degenerate into epigrammatism, but this danger does not prevent extreme length from being the one unpardonable sin.

Were I called upon, however, to designate that class of composition which, next to such a poem as I have suggested, should best fulfil the demands and serve the purposes of ambitious genius, should offer it the most advantageous field of exertion, and afford it the fairest opportunity of display, I should speak at once of the brief prose tale. History, philosophy, and other matters of that kind, we leave out of the question, of course. *Of course*, I say, and in spite of the gray-beards. These grave topics, to the end of time, will be best illustrated by what a discriminating world, turning up its nose at the drab pamphlets, has agreed to understand as *talent*. The ordinary novel is objectionable, from its length, for reasons analogous to those which render length objectionable in the poem. As the novel cannot be read at one sitting, it cannot avail itself of the immense benefit of *totality*. Worldly interests, intervening during the pauses of perusal, modify, counteract and annul the impressions intended. But simple cessation in reading would, of itself, be sufficient to destroy the true unity. In the brief tale, however, the author is enabled to carry out his full design without interruption. During the hour of perusal, the soul of the reader is at the writer's control.

A skilful artist has constructed a tale. He has not fashioned his thoughts to accommodate his incidents, but having deliberately conceived a certain *single effect* to be wrought, he then invents such incidents, he then combines such events, and discusses them in such tone as may best serve him in establishing this preconceived effect. If his very first sentence tend not to the out-bringing of this effect, then in his very first step has he committed a blunder. In the whole composition there should be no word written of which the tendency, direct or indirect, is not to the one pre-established design. And by such means, with such care and skill, a picture is at length painted which leaves in the mind of him who contemplates it with a kindred art, a sense of the fullest satisfaction. The idea of the tale, its thesis, has been presented unblemished, because undisturbed—an end absolutely demanded, yet, in the novel, altogether unattainable.

Of skilfully-constructed tales—I speak now without reference to other points, some of them more important than construction—there are very few American specimens. I am acquainted with no better one, upon the whole, than the "Murder Will Out" of Mr. Simms, and this has some glaring defects. The "Tales of a Traveler," by Irving, are graceful and impressive narratives—"The Young Italian" is especially good—but there is not one of the series which can be commended as a whole. In many of them the interest is subdivided and frittered away, and their conclusions are insufficiently *climactic*. In the higher requisites of composition, John Neal's magazine stories excel—I mean in vigor of thought, picturesque combination of incident, and so forth—but they ramble too much, and invariably break down just before coming to an end, as if the writer had received a sudden and irresistible summons to dinner, and thought it incumbent upon him to make a finish of his story before going. One of the happiest and best-sustained tales I have seen is "Jack Long; or, The Shot in the Eye," by Charles W. Webber, the assistant editor of Mr. Colton's "American Review." But in general skill of construction, the tales of Willis, I think, surpass those of any American writer—with the exception of Mr. Hawthorne.

I must defer to the better opportunity of a volume now in hand, a full discussion of his individual pieces, and hasten to conclude this paper with a summary of his merits and demerits.

He is peculiar and *not* original—unless in those detailed fancies and detached thoughts which his want of general originality will deprive of the appreciation due to them, in preventing them forever reaching the *public eye*. He is infinitely too fond of allegory, and can never hope for popularity so long as he persists in it. This he will not do, for allegory is at war with the whole tone of his nature, which disports itself never so well as when escaping from the mysticism of his Goodman Browns and White Old Maids into the hearty, genial, but still Indian-summer sunshine of his Wakefields and Little Annie's Rambles. Indeed, *his* spirit of "metaphor run-mad" is clearly imbibed from the phalanx and phalanstery atmosphere in which he has been so long struggling for breath. He has not half the material for the exclusiveness of authorship that he possesses for its universality. He has the purest style, the finest taste, the most available scholarship, the most delicate humor, the most touching pathos, the most radiant imagination, the most consummate ingenuity; and with these varied good qualities he has done *well* as a mystic. But is there any one of these qualities which should prevent his doing doubly as well in a career of honest, upright, sensible, prehensible and comprehensible things? Let him mend his pen, get a bottle of visible ink, come out from the Old Manse, cut Mr. Alcott, hang (if possible) the editor of "The Dial," and throw out of the window to the pigs all his odd numbers of "The North American Review."

The Philosophy of Composition (1850)

Though it is difficult to take completely seriously Poe's account of how he composed "The Raven," it would be a mistake to assume that "The Philosophy of Composition" does not include much that was central to Poe's conception of poetry or that it does not tell us a great deal about Poe's aesthetic.

In the first place, one notices how *practical* the emphasis is. The assumption is not that one is writing primarily to express himself or to make something that conforms to an ideal of beauty (though on p. 428 Poe gives at least lip service to this view) but that one is writing to produce a particular effect on the reader. This is one of the points stressed by René Wellek in his *History of Modern Criticism*. He writes: "Poe's ideal of planning for effect is, basically, a rhetorical concept that places aesthetic value on the emotional excitement caused by the poem. . . . Poe means by excitement literal nervous tension." Because he meant this, he can argue that "a long poem does not exist," for he refuses to accept as satisfactory a less intense or a more generalized kind of interest such as may exist during the course of a long novel.

One of the conclusions that Wellek draws from Poe's "rhetorical" concept of poetry is that Poe is much more a man of the eighteenth century than most of us have been willing to suppose. For example, according to Wellek, Poe had no grasp of organic unity. His is essentially "the eighteenth-century idea of unity as an impression or effect on the reader and not as something organically grown in the mind of the poet under the laws of nature." Furthermore, Poe's conception of the imagination is that of a power that is not creative but combinatory—a fact which helps account for his statement that "the truly imaginative [insights] are never otherwise than analytic" or that the "*highest* order of the imaginative intellect is always preeminently mathematical; and the converse."

If Wellek is right, and his judgment in such matters carries great weight, Poe's position here accords with what we have found true of other aspects of his general position: he is an essentially conservative American provincial and, in spite of the stimulus that he gave to later developments, still a man of the eighteenth century.

How, then, account for his role as pioneer and, specifically, how account for the esteem in which the French literary theorists have held him? Because, to quote Wellek once more, his "strange combination of mysticism and mathematics, sentimental aspiration and deliberate plotting for effect provided two important motifs for the theories of symbolism—music, with its suggestiveness and indefiniteness, and conscious craftsmanship, calculating virtuosity." These "oddly assorted strands" were woven "closely together in the theories of the French symbolists," who could add to them (from sources beyond Poe) "the concepts of symbol and creative imagination."

Charles Dickens, in a note now lying before me, alluding to an examination I once made of the mechanism of "Barnaby Rudge," says—"By the way, are you aware that Godwin wrote his 'Caleb Williams' backwards? He first involved his hero in a web of difficulties, forming the second volume, and then, for the first, cast about him for some mode of accounting for what had been done."

I cannot think this the *precise* mode of procedure on the part of Godwin—and indeed what he himself acknowledges, is not altogether in accordance with Mr. Dickens' idea—but the author of "Caleb Williams" was too good an artist not to perceive the advantage derivable from at least a somewhat similar process. Nothing is more clear than that every plot, worth the name, must be elaborated to its *dénouement* before anything be attempted with the pen. It is only with the *dénouement* constantly in view that we can give a plot its indispensable air of consequence, or causation, by making the incidents, and especially the tone at all points, tend to the development of the intention.

There is a radical error, I think, in the usual mode of constructing a story. Either history affords a thesis—or one is suggested by an incident of the day—or, at best, the author sets himself to work in the combination of striking events to form merely the basis of his narrative—designing, generally, to fill in with description, dialogue, or autorial comment, whatever crevices of fact, or action, may, from page to page, render themselves apparent.

I prefer commencing with the consideration of an *effect*. Keeping originality *always* in view—for he is false to himself who ventures to dispense with so obvious and so easily attainable a source of interest—I say to myself, in the first place, "Of the innumerable effects, or impressions, of which the heart, the intellect, or (more generally) the soul is susceptible, what one shall I, on the present occasion, select?" Having chosen a novel, first, and secondly a vivid effect, I consider whether it can be best wrought by incident or tone—whether by ordinary incidents and peculiar tone, or the converse, or by peculiarity both of incident and tone—afterward looking about me (or rather within) for such combinations of event, or tone, as shall best aid me in the construction of the effect.

I have often thought how interesting a magazine paper might be written by any author who would—that is to say who could—detail, step by step, the processes by which any one of his compositions attained its ultimate point of completion. Why such a paper has never been given to the world, I am much at a loss to say—but, perhaps, the autorial vanity has had more to do with the omission than any one other cause. Most writers—poets in especial—prefer having it understood that they compose by a species of fine frenzy—an ecstatic intuition—and would positively shudder at letting the public take a peep behind the scenes, at the elaborate and vacillating crudities of thought—at the true purposes seized only at the last moment—at the innumerable glimpses of idea that arrived not at the maturity of full view—at the fully matured fancies discarded in despair as unmanageable—at the cautious selections and rejections—at the painful erasures and interpolations—in a word, at the wheels and pinions—the tackle for scene-shifting—the step-ladders and demon-traps—the cock's feathers, the red paint and the black patches, which, in ninety-nine cases out of the hundred, constitute the properties of the literary *histrio*.

I am aware, on the other hand, that the case is by no means common, in which an author is at all in condition to retrace the steps by which his conclusions have been attained. In general, suggestions, having arisen pell-mell, are pursued and forgotten in a similar manner.

For my own part, I have neither sympathy with

the repugnance alluded to, nor, at any time the least difficulty in recalling to mind the progressive steps of any of my compositions; and, since the interest of an analysis, or reconstruction, such as I have considered a *desideratum*, is quite independent of any real or fancied interest in the thing analyzed, it will not be regarded as a breach of decorum on my part to show the *modus operandi* by which some one of my own works was put together. I select "The Raven," as most generally known. It is my design to render it manifest that no one point in its composition is referrable either to accident or intuition—that the work proceeded, step by step, to its completion with the precision and rigid consequence of a mathematical problem.

Let us dismiss, as irrelevant to the poem, *per se*, the circumstance—or say the necessity—which, in the first place, gave rise to the intention of composing *a* poem that should suit at once the popular and the critical taste.

We commence, then, with this intention.

The initial consideration was that of extent. If any literary work is too long to be read at one sitting, we must be content to dispense with the immensely important effect derivable from unity of impression—for, if two sittings be required, the affairs of the world interfere, and every thing like totality is at once destroyed. But since, *ceteris paribus*, no poet can afford to dispense with *any thing* that may advance his design, it but remains to be seen whether there is, in extent, any advantage to counterbalance the loss of unity which attends it. Here I say no, at once. What we term a long poem is, in fact, merely a succession of brief ones—that is to say, of brief poetical effects. It is needless to demonstrate that a poem is such, only inasmuch as it intensely excites, by elevating, the soul; and all intense excitements are, through a psychal necessity, brief. For this reason, at least one half of the "Paradise Lost" is essentially prose—a succession of poetical excitements interspersed, *inevitably*, with corresponding depressions—the whole being deprived, through the extremeness of its length, of the vastly important artistic element, totality, or unity, of effect.

It appears evident, then, that there is a distinct limit, as regards length, to all works of literary art —the limit of a single sitting—and that, although in certain classes of prose composition, such as "Robinson Crusoe," (demanding no unity,) this limit may be advantageously overpassed, it can never properly be overpassed in a poem. Within this limit, the extent of a poem may be made to bear

mathematical relation to its merit—in other words, to the excitement or elevation—again in other words, to the degree of the true poetical effect which it is capable of inducing; for it is clear that the brevity must be in direct ratio of the intensity of the intended effect:—this, with one proviso— that a certain degree of duration is absolutely requisite for the production of any effect at all.

Holding in view these considerations, as well as that degree of excitement which I deemed not above the popular, while not below the critical, taste, I reached at once what I conceived the proper *length* for my intended poem—a length of about one hundred lines. It is, in fact, a hundred and eight.

My next thought concerned the choice of an impression, or effect, to be conveyed: and here I may as well observe that, throughout the construction, I kept steadily in view the design of rendering the work *universally* appreciable. I should be carried too far out of my immediate topic were I to demonstrate a point upon which I have repeatedly insisted, and which, with the poetical, stands not in the slightest need of demonstration—the point, I mean, that Beauty is the sole legitimate province of the poem. A few words, however, in elucidation of my real meaning, which some of my friends have evinced a disposition to misrepresent. That pleasure which is at once the most intense, the most elevating, and the most pure, is, I believe, found in the contemplation of the beautiful. When, indeed, men speak of Beauty, they mean, precisely, not a quality, as is supposed, but an effect—they refer, in short, just to that intense and pure elevation of *soul—not* of intellect, or of heart—upon which I have commented, and which is experienced in consequence of contemplating "the beautiful." Now I designate Beauty as the province of the poem, merely because it is an obvious rule of Art that effects should be made to spring from direct causes—that objects should be attained through means best adapted for their attainment—no one as yet having been weak enough to deny that the peculiar elevation alluded to is *most readily* attained in the poem. Now the object, Truth, or the satisfaction of the intellect, and the object Passion, or the excitement of the heart, are, although attainable, to a certain extent, in poetry, far more readily attainable in prose. Truth, in fact, demands a precision, and Passion a *homeliness* (the truly passionate will comprehend me) which are absolutely antagonistic to that Beauty which, I maintain, is the excitement, or pleasurable elevation, of the soul. It by no means follows from any thing here said, that passion, or even truth, may not be introduced, and even profitably introduced, into a poem—for they may serve in elucidation, or aid the general effect, as do discords in music, by contrast—but the true artist will always contrive, first, to tone them into proper subservience to the predominant aim, and, secondly, to enveil them, as far as possible, in that Beauty which is the atmosphere and the essence of the poem.

Regarding, then, Beauty as my province, my next question referred to the *tone* of its highest manifestation—and all experience has shown that this tone is one of *sadness*. Beauty of whatever kind, in its supreme development, invariably excites the sensitive soul to tears. Melancholy is thus the most legitimate of all the poetical tones.

The length, the province, and the tone, being thus determined, I betook myself to ordinary induction, with the view of obtaining some artistic piquancy which might serve me as a key-note in the construction of the poem—some pivot upon which the whole structure might turn. In carefully thinking over all the usual artistic effects—or more properly *points*, in the theatrical sense—I did not fail to perceive immediately that no one had been so universally employed as that of the *refrain*. The universality of its employment sufficed to assure me of its intrinsic value, and spared me the necessity of submitting it to analysis. I considered it, however, with regard to its susceptibility of improvement, and soon saw it to be in a primitive condition. As commonly used, the *refrain*, or burden, not only is limited to lyric verse, but depends for its impression upon the force of monotone—both in sound and thought. The pleasure is deduced solely from the sense of identity—of repetition. I resolved to diversify, and so heighten, the effect, by adhering, in general, to the monotone of sound, while I continually varied that of thought: that is to say, I determined to produce continuously novel effects, by the variation *of the application* of the *refrain*—the *refrain* itself remaining, for the most part, unvaried.

These points being settled, I next bethought me of the *nature* of my *refrain*. Since its application was to be repeatedly varied, it was clear that the *refrain* itself must be brief, for there would have been an insurmountable difficulty in frequent variations of application in any sentence of length. In proportion to the brevity of the sentence, would, of course, be the facility of the variation. This led me at once to a single word as the best *refrain*.

The question now arose as to the *character* of the word. Having made up my mind to a *refrain*, the division of the poem into stanzas was, of course, a corollary: the *refrain* forming the close of each stanza. That such a close, to have force, must be sonorous and susceptible of protracted emphasis, admitted no doubt: and these considerations inevitably led me to the long *o* as the most sonorous vowel, in connection with *r* as the most producible consonant.

The sound of the *refrain* being thus determined, it became necessary to select a word embodying this sound, and at the same time in the fullest possible keeping with that melancholy which I had predetermined as the tone of the poem. In such a search it would have been absolutely impossible to overlook the word "Nevermore." In fact, it was the very first which presented itself.

The next *desideratum* was a pretext for the continuous use of the one word "nevermore." In observing the difficulty which I at once found in inventing a sufficiently plausible reason for its continuous repetition, I did not fail to perceive that this difficulty arose solely from the pre-assumption that the word was to be so continuously or monotonously spoken by a *human* being—I did not fail to perceive, in short, that the difficulty lay in the reconciliation of this monotony with the exercise of reason on the part of the creature repeating the word. Here, then, immediately arose the idea of a *non*-reasoning creature capable of speech; and, very naturally, a parrot, in the first instance, suggested itself, but was superseded forthwith by a Raven, as equally capable of speech, and infinitely more in keeping with the intended *tone*.

I had now gone so far as the conception of a Raven—the bird of ill omen—monotonously repeating the one word, "Nevermore," at the conclusion of each stanza, in a poem of melancholy tone, and in length about one hundred lines. Now, never losing sight of the object *supremeness*, or perfection, at all points, I asked myself—"Of all melancholy topics, what, according to the *universal* understanding of mankind, is the *most* melancholy?" Death was the obvious reply. "And when," I said, "is this most melancholy topic most poetical?" From what I have already explained at some length, the answer, here also, is obvious—"When it most closely allies itself to *Beauty*: the death, then, of a beautiful woman is, unquestionably, the most poetical topic in the world—and equally is it beyond doubt that the lips best suited for such topic are those of a bereaved lover."

I had now to combine the two ideas, of a lover lamenting his deceased mistress and a Raven continuously repeating the word "Nevermore."—I had to combine these, bearing in mind my design of varying, at every turn, the *application* of the word repeated; but the only intelligible mode of such combination is that of imagining the Raven employing the word in answer to the queries of the lover. And here it was that I saw at once the opportunity afforded for the effect on which I had been depending—that is to say, the effect of the *variation of application*. I saw that I could make the first query propounded by the lover—the first query to which the Raven should reply "Nevermore"—that I could make this first query a commonplace one —the second less so—the third still less, and so on —until at length the lover, startled from his original *nonchalance* by the melancholy character of the word itself—by its frequent repetition—and by a consideration of the ominous reputation of the fowl that uttered it—is at length excited to superstition, and wildly propounds queries of a far different character—queries whose solution he has passionately at heart—propounds them half in superstition and half in that species of despair which delights in self-torture—propounds them not altogether because he believes in the prophetic or demoniac character of the bird (which, reason assures him, is merely repeating a lesson learned by rote) but because he experiences a phrenzied pleasure in so modeling his questions as to receive from the *expected* "Nevermore" the most delicious because the most intolerable of sorrow. Perceiving the opportunity thus afforded me—or, more strictly, thus forced upon me in the progress of the construction —I first established in mind the climax, or concluding query—that query to which "Nevermore" should be in the last place an answer—that in reply to which this word "Nevermore" should involve the utmost conceivable amount of sorrow and despair.

Here then the poem may be said to have its beginning—at the end, where all works of art should begin—for it was here, at this point of my preconsideration, that I first put pen to paper in the composition of the stanza:

> "Prophet," said I, "thing of evil! prophet
>   still if bird or devil!
> By that heaven that bends above us—by
>   that God we both adore,
> Tell this soul with sorrow laden, if within
>   the distant Aidenn,
> It shall clasp a sainted maiden whom the
>   angels name Lenore—

> Clasp a rare and radiant maiden whom
>   the angels name Lenore."
> Quoth the Raven "Nevermore."

I composed this stanza, at this point, first that, by establishing the climax, I might the better vary and graduate, as regards seriousness and importance, the preceding queries of the lover—and, secondly, that I might definitely settle the rhythm, the metre, and the length and general arrangement of the stanza—as well as graduate the stanzas which were to precede, so that none of them might surpass this in rhythmical effect. Had I been able, in the subsequent composition, to construct more vigorous stanzas, I should, without scruple, have purposely enfeebled them, so as not to interfere with the climacteric effect.

And here I may as well say a few words of the versification. My first object (as usual) was originality. The extent to which this has been neglected, in versification, is one of the most unaccountable things in the world. Admitting that there is little possibility of variety in mere *rhythm*, it is still clear that the possible varieties of metre and stanza are absolutely infinite—and yet, *for centuries, no man, in verse, has ever done, or ever seemed to think of doing, an original thing.* The fact is, that originality (unless in minds of very unusual force) is by no means a matter, as some suppose, of impulse or intuition. In general, to be found, it must be elaborately sought, and although a positive merit of the highest class, demands in its attainment less of invention than negation.

Of course, I pretend to no originality in either the rhythm or metre of the "Raven." The former is trochaic—the latter is octameter acatalectic, alternating with heptameter catalectic repeated in the *refrain* of the fifth verse, and terminating with tetrameter catalectic. Less pedantically—the feet employed throughout (trochees) consist of a long syllable followed by a short: the first line of the stanza consists of eight of these feet—the second of seven and a half (in effect two-thirds)—the third of eight—the fourth of seven and a half—the fifth the same—the sixth three and a half. Now, each of these lines, taken individually, has been employed before, and what originality the "Raven" has, is in their *combination into stanza*; nothing even remotely approaching this combination has ever been attempted. The effect of this originality of combination is aided by other unusual, and some altogether novel effects, arising from an extension of the application of the principles of rhyme and alliteration.

The next point to be considered was the mode of bringing together the lover and the Raven—and the first branch of this consideration was the *locale*. For this the most natural suggestion might seem to be a forest, or the fields—but it has always appeared to me that a close *circumscription of space* is absolutely necessary to the effect of insulated incident:—it has the force of a frame to a picture. It has an indisputable moral power in keeping concentrated the attention, and, of course, must not be confounded with mere unity of place.

I determined, then, to place the lover in his chamber—in a chamber rendered sacred to him by memories of her who had frequented it. The room is represented as richly furnished—this in mere pursuance of the ideas I have already explained on the subject of Beauty, as the sole true poetical thesis.

The *locale* being thus determined, I had now to introduce the bird—and the thought of introducing him through the window, was inevitable. The idea of making the lover suppose, in the first instance, that the flapping of the wings of the bird against the shutter, is a "tapping" at the door, originated in a wish to increase, by prolonging, the reader's curiosity, and in a desire to admit the incidental effect arising from the lover's throwing open the door, finding all dark, and thence adopting the half-fancy that it was the spirit of his mistress that knocked.

I made the night tempestuous, first, to account for the Raven's seeking admission, and secondly, for the effect of contrast with the (physical) serenity within the chamber.

I made the bird alight on the bust of Pallas, also for the effect of contrast between the marble and the plumage—it being understood that the bust was absolutely *suggested* by the bird—the bust of *Pallas* being chosen, first, as most in keeping with the scholarship of the lover, and, secondly, for the sonorousness of the word, Pallas, itself.

About the middle of the poem, also, I have availed myself of the force of contrast, with a view of deepening the ultimate impression. For example, an air of the fantastic—approaching as nearly to the ludicrous as was admissible—is given to the Raven's entrance. He comes in "with many a flirt and flutter."

> Not the *least obeisance made he*—not a
>   moment stopped or stayed he,
> *But with mien of lord or lady*, perched
>   above my chamber door.

In the two stanzas which follow, the design is more obviously carried out:—

> Then this ebony bird beguiling my sad
>   fancy into smiling
> By the *grave and stern decorum of the*
>   *countenance it wore,*
> "Though thy *crest be shorn and shaven*
>   thou," I said, "art sure no craven,
> Ghastly grim and ancient Raven wandering
>   from the nightly shore—
> Tell me what thy lordly name is on the
>   Night's Plutonian shore?"
>   Quoth the Raven "Nevermore."

> Much I marvelled *this ungainly fowl* to
>   hear discourse so plainly
> Though its answer little meaning—
>   little relevancy bore;
> For we cannot help agreeing that no
>   living human being
> *Ever yet was blessed with seeing bird*
>   *above his chamber door—*
> *Bird or beast upon the sculptured bust*
>   *above his chamber door,*
>   With such name as "Nevermore."

The effect of the *dénouement* being thus provided for, I immediately drop the fantastic for a tone of the most profound seriousness:—this tone commencing in the stanza directly following the one last quoted, with the line,

> But the Raven, sitting lonely on that
>   placid bust, spoke only, etc.

From this epoch the lover no longer jests—no longer sees any thing even of the fantastic in the Raven's demeanor. He speaks of him as a "grim, ungainly, ghastly, gaunt, and ominous bird of yore," and feels the "fiery eyes" burning into his "bosom's core." This revolution of thought, or fancy, on the lover's part, is intended to induce a similar one on the part of the reader—to bring the mind into a proper frame for the *dénouement*—which is now brought about as rapidly and as *directly* as possible.

With the *dénouement* proper—with the Raven's reply, "Nevermore," to the lover's final demand if he shall meet his mistress in another world—the poem, in its obvious phase, that of a simple narrative, may be said to have its completion. So far, every thing is within the limits of the accountable —of the real. A raven, having learned by rote the single word "Nevermore," and having escaped from the custody of its owner, is driven at midnight, through the violence of a storm, to seek admission at a window from which a light still gleams—the chamber-window of a student, occupied half in poring over a volume, half in dreaming of a beloved mistress deceased. The casement being thrown open at the fluttering of the bird's wings, the bird itself perches on the most convenient seat out of the immediate reach of the student, who, amused by the incident and the oddity of the visitor's demeanor, demands of it, in jest and without looking for a reply, its name. The raven addressed, answers with its customary word, "Nevermore"—a word which finds immediate echo in the melancholy heart of the student, who, giving utterance aloud to certain thoughts suggested by the occasion, is again startled by the fowl's repetition of "Nevermore." The student now guesses the state of the case, but is impelled, as I have before explained, by the human thirst for self-torture, and in part by superstition, to propound such queries to the bird as will bring him, the lover, the most of the luxury of sorrow, through the anticipated answer "Nevermore." With the indulgence, to the extreme, of this self-torture, the narration, in what I have termed its first or obvious phase, has a natural termination, and so far there has been no overstepping of the limits of the real.

But in subjects so handled, however skilfully, or with however vivid an array of incident, there is always a certain hardness or nakedness, which repels the artistical eye. Two things are invariably required—first, some amount of complexity, or more properly, adaptation; and, secondly, some amount of suggestiveness—some under-current, however indefinite, of meaning. It is this latter, in especial, which imparts to a work of art so much of that *richness* (to borrow from colloquy a forcible term) which we are too fond of confounding with *the ideal*. It is the *excess* of the suggested meaning—it

is the rendering this the upper instead of the under current of the theme—which turns into prose (and that of the very flattest kind) the so called poetry of the so called transcendentalists.

Holding these opinions, I added the two concluding stanzas of the poem—their suggestiveness being thus made to pervade all the narrative which has preceded them. The under-current of meaning is rendered first apparent in the lines—

> "Take thy beak from out *my heart*, and
> take thy form from off my door!"
> Quoth the Raven "Nevermore!"

It will be observed that the words, "from out my heart," involve the first metaphorical expression in the poem. They, with the answer, "Nevermore," dispose the mind to seek a moral in all that has been previously narrated. The reader begins now to regard the Raven as emblematical—but it is not until the very last line of the very last stanza, that the intention of making him emblematical of *Mournful and Never-Ending Remembrance* is permitted distinctly to be seen:

> And the Raven, never flitting, still is
> sitting, still is sitting,
> On the pallid bust of Pallas, just above
> my chamber door;
> And his eyes have all the seeming of a
> demon's that is dreaming,
> And the lamplight o'er him streaming
> throws his shadow on the floor;
> And my soul *from out that shadow* that
> lies floating on the floor
> Shall be lifted—nevermore.

NATHANIEL HAWTHORNE (1804-1864)

Was there ever such a weary delay in obtaining the slightest recognition from the public, as in my case? I sat down by the wayside of life, like a man under enchantment, and a shrubbery sprung up around me, and the bushes grew to be saplings, and the saplings became trees, until no exit appeared possible, through the entangling depth of my obscurity.
(DEDICATION OF "THE SNOW IMAGE," TO HORATIO BRIDGE, 1851)

The relation of Hawthorne to himself, to his own work, to the public world which he addressed, and, in the end, to the fame which he found in the world, was, in each case, a teasing, uneasy, and paradoxical one; and this fact provided him with his recurrent theme, his fundamental insight, and his obsession. He lived in the right ratio—right for the fueling of his genius—between an attachment to his region and a detached assessment of it; between attraction to the past and its repudiation; between attraction to the world and contempt for its gifts; between a powerful attraction to women and a sexual flinch; between a faith in life and a corrosive skepticism; between a capacity for affection and an innate coldness; between aesthetic passion and moral concern; between a fascinated attentiveness to the realistic texture, forms, and characteristics of nature and human nature, and a compulsive flight from that welter of life toward abstract ideas; and between, most crucially of all, a deep knowledge of himself and an ignorance of himself instinctively cultivated in a fear of the darker potentialities of self.

The drama of such subjective tensions is played out objectively in the work. Hawthorne is the first American writer of fiction in whose work we can sense the inner relation of life to fiction—the relation which makes us deeply feel that fiction is more than an elegant amusement, a form of journalism or watered-down history, or a genteel parlor trick. Neither the tales of Washington Irving nor the novels of Cooper carry, in Hawthorne's way, a sense of the involvement of the creating personality. This is not to say that simply autobiographical fiction is the best. Shakespeare is not autobiographical —nor Dickens, nor Faulkner. On the contrary, they create a great variety of characters living in a variety of situations and facing a variety of issues. But the characters, situations, and issues are created with a passionate urgency of imagination which bespeaks the involvement, intellectual and emotional, of the creator and which, therefore, involves us. Hawthorne was the first American writer with this gift—or, as he himself might well have put it, this curse.

For this reason, we may say that Hawthorne discovered American literature in its inwardness, and that, in one sense, this role was as important as the work itself. Thus we may think of Hawthorne as a "culture hero"—the man discovering and enacting a role that changes the possibilities of a society, a role involving the deep sensibility by which experience may be newly grasped and values framed.

Though Hawthorne's inner drama was what fed his genius, the major events of his life, objectively considered, are unremarkable. He was born in Salem, Massachusetts, on July 4, 1804, of a family that had been prominent in the early days of the colony. The early Hathornes[1] were, it seems, of that type of "black, masterful men," as D. H. Lawrence calls them in *Studies in Classic American Literature*, who, in a "black revulsion" from the Old World, came over a "black sea." The founder of the family, William Hathorne, who arrived in 1630, "the bearded, sable-cloaked, and steeple-crowned progenitor" whom Hawthorne describes in the preamble to *The Scarlet Letter*, won fame as a soldier and judge, and as Mayor Hathorne appears in Hawthorne's sketch "Main Street," ordering a certain Quaker, Anne Coleman, to be bound to the tail of a cart and given ten stripes in Salem, ten in Boston, and ten in Dedham, and then driven off into the forest. The son John was also a judge, and in 1692 added to the family fame by his zealous part in the witch trials; and the bravery of David Hathorne, a captain in the continental navy and the grandfather of Nathaniel, was celebrated in a ballad. By 1804, however, the renown and prosperity of the family were in sad eclipse, and when four years later Hawthorne's father, a young sea captain, died at Surinam, his widow and three children were left dependent upon her relatives.

Certainly this contrast between the great past and the meager present had something to do with the boy's cast of mind. We hear of the self-aggrandizing fantasies which he told his sisters as tales to amuse them. And such tales were the first manifestations of the nostalgic appeal of a lost glory and a lost certainty of mission, the sense of a curse intertwined with the glory of the past, the proud alienation from the people who now occupied the big houses with less legitimate claim than a "Hathorne," the angry, compensatory ambition which, in itself, might be mystically accursed and which, therefore, should be denied in a ferocious, programmatic modesty.

---

[1] The *w* was added by Nathaniel to make the orthography conform to the pronunciation.

Hawthorne's isolation drew something not only from the fact of the family's collapse but from the way the other members of the family responded to it. The mother, a very young woman, withdrew into a grim and lifelong ritual of widowhood, isolating herself even in the isolation of the family. We do not know the precise relationship between Hawthorne and his mother—"whose grief," he reports, "outlasted even its vitality, and grew to be merely a torpid habit, and was saddest then"—but we do know that it was charged in a way which Hawthorne himself did not even suspect until his sudden and overmastering emotion at her death released him, as Mark Van Doren has suggested, for the supreme effort of composing *The Scarlet Letter*, the most moving and deeply human of his works.

At Bowdoin College, in the backwoods of Maine, not at fashionable Harvard, Hawthorne was "an idle student," as he was to say of himself, "negligent of college rules and the Procrustean details of academic life, rather choosing to nurse my own fancies than to dig into Greek roots. . . ." He learned to chew tobacco, was disciplined for card-playing and wine-bibbing and tavern-going (at the Falstaff and the Pumpkin), and in a letter home pictured himself as a lordly senior: "I have put on my gold watch-chain and purchased a cane; so that, with the aid of my new white gloves, I flatter myself that I make a most splendid appearance in the eyes of the pestilent little freshmen." He was, in fact, a young man of extraordinary charm and good looks, virile and poetic at the same time.

At Bowdoin, he belonged to the Athenaean literary society, which was "progressive" and "infected" with Jacksonian democracy. In the Athenaean, too, he found his devoted friends, loyal Democrats too—Jonathan Cilley, Franklin Pierce, and Horatio Bridge. Longfellow was then in Bowdoin with precocious fame as scholar and poet, but Hawthorne's preference for Cilley and Pierce, who were to become politicians, and for Bridge, who was to be a naval officer, conforms to a pattern in his character and life; he yearned, as he himself was to put it, to be "a man in society," to learn "the deep, warm secret" by

which other people seemed to live but which somehow eluded him. That secret was one possessed by active men, the kind of men he was to prefer to associate with, or, more commonly, to observe.

Hawthorne seems to have had little taste for literary and intellectual company, people who, he presumably felt, were wrapped up in words and abstractions. Worse, most of them did not even suspect the existence of another and darker secret, which Hawthorne could have imparted to them, the sense of the tragic tensions of life. Looking back on Bowdoin, Hawthorne was to say of the "finely dressed" Longfellow, recognized poet and "tremendous student," that he was "no more conscious of any earthly or spiritual trouble than a sunflower is." What he was to think of Emerson and his associates we shall come to.

Hawthorne graduated in the middle of his class. It is sometimes said that this position in the class has a sort of symbolic significance, that it may be taken as a rebellious and ironical declaration of averageness and normality, an expression of that somewhat morbid modesty, self-distrust, or self-effacement which was to become more and more characteristic of him, but which even now prompted him, the extraordinarily handsome young man, to refuse to have his silhouette made for the gallery of the class. It was the trait that prompted him too, shortly before graduation, to scotch a good report the family had had of him, by writing his sister Louisa: "I have thought much upon the subject, and have finally come to the conclusion that I shall never make a distinguished figure in the world, and all I hope or wish is to plod along with the multitude." As though mere averageness could impart the "deep, warm secret, the life within the life." If this letter to Louisa is straightforward and serious, there is in other letters of the period, as some biographers have pointed out, an element of irony, banter, and perverseness that would seem to screen the depth in which he fought out this issue—and other issues—with himself. And Cilley wrote of him: "I love Hawthorne; I admire him; but I do not know him. He lives in a mysterious world of thought and imagination which he never permits me to enter."

We have some evidence that in that "mysterious world" Hawthorne was facing the threat of his own ambition. Among other glimpses, we have that afforded by the title character of Hawthorne's first novel *Fanshawe,* a college story written shortly after he left Bowdoin, published anonymously, at the author's expense, in 1828, and then withdrawn; Fanshawe, the author writes,

> had hitherto deemed himself unconnected with the world, unconcerned in its feelings, and uninfluenced by it in any of his pursuits. In this respect he probably deceived himself. If his inmost heart could have been laid open, there would have been discovered that dream of undying fame, which, dream as it is, is more powerful than a thousand realities.

With such a "dream" Hawthorne, immediately after college, locked himself up in a southwest room on the third floor of a house on Herbert Street, in Salem. This was the famous "dismal chamber" under the eaves, where he isolated himself to discover his materials, his style, and his destiny.

At this time there was still the constant crying out for a literature worthy of the aspirations of the nation. Emerson's famous declaration of independence for American culture, his address "The American Scholar," was not to come until 1837, the year Hawthorne published his first book. We must remember this to understand the task which Hawthorne set himself when he entered that "dismal chamber." He saw himself set over against the "scribbling sons of John Bull," as he had called them—that is, he saw that he confronted the specific challenge of becoming an *American* writer.

In *Mosses from an Old Manse,* Hawthorne's second collection of tales (1846), appears a sketch called "A Select Party," in which a Man of Fancy entertains a party at "one of his castles in the air." Among the guests appears a young man "in poor attire," who turns out to be "the Master Genius for whom our country is looking anxiously into the mist of Time, as destined to fulfill the great mission of creating an American literature, hewing it, as it were, out of the unwrought granite of our intellectual quarries." The Genius, it develops,

> dwells as yet unhonored among men, unrecognized by those who have known him from his cradle; the noble countenance which should be distinguished by a halo diffused around it passes daily amid the throng of people toiling and troubling themselves about the trifles of a moment, and none pay reverence to the worker of immortality.

How much self-irony is here as an antidote for secret hope there is no way of saying, but here is as good a statement as any of the role which Hawthorne was proposing for himself, to hew an American literature out of the unwrought granite of the intellectual quarries.

And here is as good a statement as any of the life Hawthorne led in the thirteen years in Salem, passing "unhonored" and "unrecognized." He read widely, by one account every book in the library of the Salem Athenaeum—where he wouldn't go himself but sent his sister Elizabeth to fetch his reading matter. Isolated even from his mother and two sisters, even at meals sometimes, he worked day after day, going out late, often after dark, for an hour, whatever the weather, coming back to sup on a pint bowl of chocolate crumbled full of bread. In the summer he always took a trip, in New England, looking at the country and at all those strange folk who had the "deep, warm secret," putting down in his notebooks the fruit of his scrupulous observation just as though he would be able to write of such characters. And over the years, in a mood "half savage, half despairing," as Bridge puts in, he kept on writing. He was creating a new kind of fiction.

Aside from what his personal history and temperament had to do with that new fiction, we can tell something about it from his reading. For one thing, though he read ferociously, he read more or less at random. "I have indeed turned over a good many books," he later said to Longfellow, "but in so desultory a way that it cannot be called study, nor has it left me the fruits of study." He was, in other words, often reading to find the food of imagination, reading passively, as many writers do to lay the mind open to the glancing suggestions, reading with a kind of purposeful purposelessness.

In this spirit he soaked himself in the history of New England, in Felt's *Annals of Salem* and Cotton Mather's *Magnalia Christi Americana*, in which, as he put it, "true events and real personages move before the reader with the dreamy aspect which they wore in Cotton Mather's singular mind"—and were to wear in his own singular mind. He was steeped, too, in the work of the great English novelists of the eighteenth century—Fielding, Richardson, and Smollett—and had some acquaintance with the Romantic literature of Germany as well as with the English Romantics, such as De Quincey. He was reading the novels of Balzac as they appeared—though what effect the father of realism had on him is hard to guess. The fashionable Scott he knew well, and it is easy to see how Scott's fictional handling of the history of his own country would have had special concern for Hawthorne. One school of fiction which very early had special significance for Hawthorne's own work was the Gothic romance, as well as the work of the American imitator Charles Brockden Brown.

Hawthorne's reading of fiction did not have the desultory quality characteristic of much of his other reading. According to his sister Elizabeth, he set himself systematically to analyze fiction. Certainly, he knew that there are deep and subtle relations between fiction on the one hand and personality, society, and ethical values on the other; but in one perspective he also knew that fiction is also a matter of technical control. Passion, human meaning, inspiration, and the unconscious lie at one pole of any art; formal concern and technique lie at the other.

The kind of reading to which Hawthorne subjected himself in his apprenticeship bears on his style, too. In Bowdoin, he learned to write a Latin prose of remarkable purity and

read widely in French the classic dramatists, Racine, Molière, and Corneille, and Voltaire and Rousseau. His Latin and his French supported him in the forming of his style on the model of the Augustan writers of the eighteenth century. And here we may remark on the tension between the matter of Hawthorne's work and his style. The matter is essentially romantic, the mysterious depth of the soul, the scruples of guilt, shadowy and ambiguous psychological and moral issues, but the style he developed was a cool, detached, sometimes pretentious artprose. So in the contrast of matter and style is one more of the vibrant tensions in the work of Hawthorne which has made him congenial to the twentieth-century sensibility.

After five years of grinding discipline, Hawthorne was ready to give up his aspirations, but in 1830 a sketch, "The Hollow of Three Hills," was published in the Salem *Gazette*, and a little later "The Gentle Boy" was accepted by Samuel Griswold Goodrich, the publisher of the *Token*, one of the popular annuals of the period, those handsomely got-up little collections of romantic, sentimental, moralistic, and humorous tales, essays, and engravings. This was a start. But even if for the next several years Hawthorne's work regularly appeared there (over such pen names as Ashley A. Boyce, Oberon, M. Aubépine, and "The Author of 'The Gentle Boy' "), money remained a serious problem for the now not so young author, and worse, with his increasing sense of being estranged from normal experience, he began to feel himself a failure as a man.

But in 1837 the turn came. His Bowdoin friend Horatio Bridge secretly underwrote, to the amount of $250, the publication of a collection of his pieces, *Twice-Told Tales*. Longfellow wrote a fatuously uncomprehending but laudatory review of it in the influential *North American Review*, and the fame began.

What had Hawthorne actually achieved during the dozen years of his apprenticeship? Let us look at several pieces of the period, beginning with a fumbling example of his art, "Alice

Doane's Appeal." Though Hawthorne never thought well enough of this to put it in a collection, it is, in its very crudity, instructive, for it shows how Hawthorne, even in the early years, was reaching toward his subject and his insight. Here are the elements of incest, patricide, witchcraft, the haunted mind and the secret guilt, murder, the rising of the dead; all the elements from the Gothic romances are present, but they are already domesticated, put into seventeenth-century New England. They are domesticated in another way, too; in the frame of action, the "author" reads the tale to two female friends on Gallows Hill, a circumstance which in a deep but not explicit way associates the undefined guilt and curse of the story not only with the literal history of the region but implicitly with the author and his auditors. And so the past is not treated as quaint and romantic in its pastness: it is vitally interfused with the present.

Further, as more than one critic has pointed out, there is the fact that the brother Leonard Doane, who kills the sister's evil suitor, is aware that the suitor is his other, and therefore incestuous, self: "My soul had been conscious of the germ of all the fierce and deep passions, and of all the many varieties of wickedness, which accident had brought to their full maturity in him." But the dead lover also becomes, in a vision, the face of the dead father of Leonard Doane, with all the complexity of motivation thus implied. Hawthorne is already aiming at a "thickness" of effect and meaning in his work, with reference at many levels—at the ethical, the personal and psychological, the social, the historical. He wants the story to exist, as it were, as a tissue of interrelated meanings—the "meanings" somehow to be a reflex of their interrelations, in the interfusion of the "actual circumstance of life" and what in "The Hollow of Three Hills," another early piece, he called "dreams and madmen's reveries." But he would have said that truth can lie in such dreams and reveries and would have known that the dreamer and the madman was himself.

As much as Poe, Hawthorne early developed that kind of hallucinatory fiction characteristic of modernity. But he was also pioneering his own fiction, laying hand to themes and methods which allowed him to achieve the mastery of such stories as "The Gentle Boy" (1828), "Roger Malvin's Burial" (1830), "My Kinsman, Major Molineux" (1832), and "Young Goodman Brown" (1835).[2] These pieces, too, belong to Hawthorne's young manhood and in them it is easy to see what prompted him to write, in 1851, in the letter dedicating *The Snow Image* to Bridge:

In youth, men are apt to write more easily than they really know or feel; and the remainder of life may be not idly spent in realizing and convincing themselves of the wisdom which they uttered long ago. The truth that was only in the fancy then may have since become a substance in the mind and heart.

Here Hawthorne is saying that unconsciously —literally, out of the unconscious—a writer may find the meaning and the method which later, consciously, he may explore and develop; that is, in writing, a man may be discovering, among other things, himself. To have intuited this truth was one of Hawthorne's most brilliant achievements. But the truth, once intuited, was one that he could rarely bring himself to contemplate for long, and that gives us another of the deep paradoxes in his life and work. The work that reveals may also be used to conceal.

"The Gentle Boy" is one of the first tales in which Hawthorne's power appears. In a way, it prefigures *The Scarlet Letter*. It has the same deep grounding in the past, it presents the same outrage to humanity which Hawthorne considered implicit in Puritan society, and we can easily find here the qualities which make Austin Warren say that Hawthorne's "pictures are ancestral and prophetic," and we can find, too, the same ambivalence toward the past which

[2] Of these four stories only "The Gentle Boy" appears in *Twice-Told Tales*. "Roger Malvin's Burial" and "Young Goodman Brown" are in *Mosses from an Old Manse* (1846). The fourth is in *The Snow Image and Other Tales* (1852).

Hawthorne expressed in "Main Street": "Let us thank God for having given us such ancestors; and let each successive generation thank Him, not less fervently for being one step further from them in the march of ages." But at first glance the story seems to be a piece of straight realism, an episode from actual history, treated at the level of actuality without the tangential reference to "dreams" and "reveries." This literal singleness of vision is, in a way, deceptive, for there is another kind of depth which connects it with the more symbolic stories.

We may approach this notion by asking how questions of good and bad are deployed in the story. Casually regarded, the story would seem to present the inhuman Puritan rigor, of the sort we find in "The Maypole of Merry Mount" and *The Scarlet Letter*, set over against a gentle and humane Quakerism. (See the section on John Woolman.) We remember, however, that even in the historical introduction Hawthorne indicates a balancing of the "bad" between Puritans and Quakers. Let us look at the first sentence: "In the course of the year 1656, several of the people called Quakers, led, as they professed, by the inward movement of the spirit, made their appearance in New England." We cannot miss the irony in the phrase "as they professed" and so must consider what is the real content of "the inward movement of the spirit." Hawthorne then proceeds to say of the Quakers that their "enthusiasm, heightened almost to madness by the treatment which they received, produced actions contrary to the rules of decency, as well as of rational religion"—and there, though there may also be irony directed against the Puritans in the phrase "rational religion," the criticism of the Quakers is manifest. Furthermore, when Hawthorne mentions the execution of the father of the "Boy" and his fellow Quaker, he says that the Puritan government had "indulged" the victims, and his irony is double-edged, one edge being set against the motivations—we might say the combination of masochism and arrogance—in the victims themselves. We may recall, too, how Hawthorne

says of the Quakers that the "revengeful feelings were not less deep because they were inactive" or refers to Catharine's "unbridled fanaticism" and her "fierce and vindictive nature." As Hawthorne says elsewhere, the human being is better rendered by the wishes of the heart than by actions.

There is another criticism of the Quakers important in the story. Their fanaticism violates the "duties of the present life," that "deep, warm secret, the life within the life"; and this violation would be an example of the "unpardonable sin" which Hawthorne defines in his journal as "a want of love and reverence for the Human Soul," and which appears often in his work, most positively in "Ethan Brand."[3] In other words, though the Puritan rigor commits the same violation in a more obvious, objective, and brutal fashion, the Quaker, for all his professions, is no better. He, too, commits what we may call the sin of abstraction, of setting a scheme, a principle, against the human warmth.

This is not to say that life can be lived without abstractions, principles, schemes, theologies; if we cannot generalize, we cannot develop or inspect values. But it is to say that in the polarity which Hawthorne here explores, that between abstractions, however high and noble in their intent, and the "deep, warm secret," lies the potentiality of the most heart-rending tragedy. And so we have the ironic pattern of this story: the two abstractions, Puritanism and Quakerism, though seeming to be contrasted, one on the side of rigor and arrogance, the other on the side of love and humility, in reality conspire to destroy the Gentle Boy with his fund of "unappropriated love"—love that such a world does not know how to appropriate.

Certainly the boy carrying this "unappropriated love" is set in contrast to the unloving world, but we must wonder, in the context of

---

[3] In *The Scarlet Letter*, it appears in a more tangential way in Chillingworth (whose name is a "coldness") who has committed a sin worse than Dimmesdale's and Hester's, in that, as Dimmesdale says, he "has violated, in cold blood, the sanctity of a human heart."

the ironies of the story, how absolute is even this contrast. One answer would seem to lie in the sentence concerning Ilbrahim: "The disordered imaginations of both his father and mother had perhaps propagated a certain unhealthiness in the mind of the boy"—that is, his own taste for suffering, and the sense of suffering as a kind of inverted vengeance. This instinct would lead him, by a strand of hidden logic, to his friendship with another outcast, the cripple, and thus to the beating and his death. This irony can be paired with the more absolute irony in the fact that Catharine returns to her son and the "warm secret" only in the moment when she is ready to curse God for having "crushed my very heart in His Hand."

To sum up, the whole story, even according to this limited account, suggests appalling depths, both psychologically and philosophically, and it is hard to realize that for generations it was regarded as one of the author's more edifying and consoling productions. Hawthorne himself remarked of it that here he had been "led deeper into the universal heart than art has been able to follow." We can wonder if he ever knew exactly how deep.

The story ends with a return to the historical perspective. The persecution of the Quakers is abated. Even Catharine has become, in the settlement, an object of acceptance and pity. If left at this level, we might say that the story offers some notion of historical progress. But for the moment, let us consider the qualifying phrases attached to the acceptance and pity which Catharine receives:

> When the course of years had made the features of the unobtrusive mourner familiar in the settlement, she became a subject of not deep, but general interest; a being on whom the otherwise superfluous sympathies of all might be bestowed. Everyone spoke to her with that degree of pity which it is pleasant to experience.

They were even ready to bury her "with decent sadness and tears that were not painful." We shall find this same irony at the end of *The Scarlet Letter* in the qualified victory which Hester achieves.

To generalize, we may say that in the acceptance which Catharine receives we do not find a change of heart, merely a change in behavior, which people may now adopt as an emotional indulgence, like the tears that are "not painful"; the change in behavior is caused merely by the fact that the issues which had originally provoked the violence have now changed, and the violence remains, ready to be discharged elsewhere. We cannot, however, take this ironic view of history as one which Hawthorne dogmatically held; it too must be subjected to skeptical scrutiny, irony subjected to the test of irony, as we shall see in "My Kinsman, Major Molineux."

In this connection, as an aside, we may hazard that in Hawthorne's emotional involvement with the violence of the New England past is some feeling that in that violence there was a significance, a confronting of reality, which was lacking in the doctrines of transcendentalists, Brook Farmers, and Unitarians, and in Emerson. Such optimisms, along with that of most of the reformers whom he encountered, seemed too easy.[4] His suspicion of them is deeply rooted in the fictions, most obviously and schematically, perhaps, in "The Celestial Railroad" and "Earth's Holocaust," which are little more than straight allegories.

To return to the impulse which drew Hawthorne to the past, we may say that if there were violence and cruelty in that older society there was also, in that very fact, a sense of reality and grim meaningfulness, something that paradoxically appealed to the Hawthorne who could not find the "warm secret" and who, by the same token, could write, in an early journal, of the contemporary world: "The fight with the world, this struggle of a man among men—the agony of the universal effort to wrench the means of a living from a host of greedy competitors—all this seems to be like a dream to me."

---

[4] See our discussion of *The Scarlet Letter* for a further comparison of the thought of Hawthorne and the transcendentalists.

But the past was not a dream. It had, literally, happened. And blood, for fundamental convictions, had been shed there—and by men who had, as demonstrated by that fact, a sense of "reality."

In "The Gentle Boy," there is a narrative of literal events, with an analysis of the quite literal characters. The author reasons inductively from this to certain general notions about human nature. In "My Kinsman, Major Molineux," though the narrative has a literal dimension (Robin, a real lad, comes to the real city of Boston, and so on), certain elements, as we shall see, are inexplicable at a merely literal level; and this suggests that the literal elements are projections of a character's desires and dreams. We are dealing here with the interpenetration of the subjective and objective worlds, and the story is a "fable" rather than a "history." This difference, and the method by which psychological and moral "truths" are embodied rather than presented discursively, carries us closer to the center of Hawthorne's special genius.

"My Kinsman, Major Molineux" is obviously concerned with an initiation, Robin's struggle toward maturity. He comes to the city expecting to be protected by his father's cousin, but after certain mysterious and disturbing adventures finds himself thrown on his own resources, given the option of remaining in the city to rise in the world, if he can, by his own exertions and merits. The story ends with the option open. Into this simple scheme flow and intermingle the various kinds of meaning.

One kind of interpretation which, according to a number of critics, is involved is what we may somewhat loosely term the Freudian.[5] Critics who take this approach to the story say, characteristically, that the overt content does not account for its great force, that we must look for the elements that play upon the unconscious of the reader (however consciously the

author may or may not have worked such elements into the story). By this reading, the story presents a young man in typical rebellion—and as is typical, a largely unconscious rebellion—against the repressive figure of the father, with more or less emphasis on an implicit Oedipal conflict; and this theme, it seems reasonable to assume, is one of Hawthorne's central concerns and is, for example, embodied in the recurrent themes of patricide and incest that first appear, as we have seen, in "Alice Doane's Appeal."

To summarize this reading, we begin by pointing out that more than the literal father is involved; various persons take a paternal role. First, there is the kinsman in town, who represents not only help and protection, but authority. The vigorous lad, though wanting help, also characteristically wants freedom and unconsciously postpones as long as possible the finding of the kinsman. For example, he "forgets," in a typically Freudian fashion, to ask the ferryman the way to Molineux's house. When he does accost a stranger, he is rebuffed with what appears to be irrational violence, and the scene provokes, from the barber's helpers who see it, the first outburst of that inimical laughter that will accompany Robin's progress.

Here, if the story is to make sense, we must ask the meaning of the man's rebuff of Robin. The man is "in years," habitually strikes his staff down with a peremptory perpendicular thrust, and regularly utters "two successive hems" of a "sepulchral" intonation; furthermore, when for no good reason he threatens Robin with the stocks, he says, "I have authority, I have—hem-hem—authority." So the old man is another image of the father. In the tavern (where Robin is drawn as much by the smell of food as by desire for directions and where he promises himself he will sit some day, that is, when he is "grown up"), he again encounters a threatening figure in the man with the bulging forehead, and when he mentions to the tavernmaster his kinsman's name, the previously obsequious fellow threatens him as though he were a lad running away from indenture; Robin is, in fact, in his half-avowed desires, a runaway bondservant—that is, a "son"

[5] Hawthorne was, of course, dead more than a generation before Freud's work was available. Freud himself freely granted, insisted on rather, the fact that the fundamental insights of his psychology had long been achieved.

—and in one sense, Robin "dreams" the threat.

For a time now Robin makes no further effort to get directions, this with some shadow of justification after the rebuffs; but when we reach the mean streets, we begin to sense more completely that the rebuffs provide him with an alibi for acting on his secret desires. Here he certainly could not expect to find the house of Molineux, and when he encounters the pretty trollop with the red petticoat, the inviting eye, and the absurdly improbable story about this being the house of the rich Major, and the Major asleep upstairs, it begins to emerge that what Robin is really seeking is sexual freedom. But, dismissing the merely literal level, is it so absurdly improbable that the trollop should say that this is the Major's house? For the Major is a "father," and is not this the "dream" version, the "projection," of the son's fascinated and envious feelings about the father's sexual world? And by this token the inviting prostitute, the father's mistress, is the projection of the son's secret Oedipal desires—desires which he knows are guilty, for at some sound the woman suddenly releases his hand and disappears. Then suddenly there appears the watch, threatening him with the stocks, and his sense of guilt is thus embodied in another father figure, armed with his significant iron-shod stave.

After the nightmare scene of the street deserted by all except the wandering bands of men with outlandish attire and strange gibberish, Robin again encounters the man with the bulging forehead from the tavern, who had seemed to have some strange knowledge of him. His face now painted half-black and half-red "as if two individual devils, a fiend of fire and a fiend of darkness, had united themselves," the man greets him with another threat, but then, in a mysterious complicity, tells him to wait there and he will see his kinsman pass.

Now follows the scene of Robin's peering into the church window, where moonlight strikes the Bible, and Robin, in his guiltiness, is aware of the graves in the churchyard and his own loneliness—his sense of loss, in other words, of the old protection. Then, longing for that protection, he tries to imagine how his father and the family would have spent "that evening of ambiguity," in religious devotions and family affections; and in his distress at now being forever excluded from that circle—that is, at having to grow up—he cries out: "Am I here, or there?" Is he, in other words, grown up or not?

Waking from a confused dream, Robin sees another man and addresses him in a "lamentable cry" (no longer the brash and demanding adolescent, but the lost child), and the stranger speaks to him in a kind voice as "my good lad," in the role of a father to whom, now, Robin can tell his story. Then Robin hears the sound of the mob, which he at first takes to be "some prodigious merrymaking"—which in a sense it is, for there appears the Major, in the midst of the howling mob, on a cart, in "tarred-and-feathered dignity," his ruin the mark of the lad's secretly desired victory over the "father." But Robin is at first ambivalently struck by "pity and terror," before he bursts into the loudest laughter of all the throng, the throng which appears "as a dream broken forth from some feverish brain." The laughter is the mark of his release from the long inner struggle. Meanwhile, among all the figures of the evening who now reappear, there is the trollop in the red petticoat twitching his arm, to confirm, as it were, his victory.

But it is not yet quite a victory. After the street is empty of the throng, Robin, shaken and exhausted, wants to leave the city and asks the kindly gentleman the way to the ferry and, shall we say, the safety of home. Then the gentleman, the kindly father who no longer uses authority, gives him the option of remaining in the world and trying to rise without help—that is, to become an adult.

This summary has omitted certain relevant details. For instance, we may take the inimical laughter that follows Robin everywhere as not only an echo of his own guilt, but also as an echo of his fear and shame at the absurd temerity of his attempt to become a man. Again, the angry man who finally appears painted like a devil is to be the destroyer of the father, a devil to be feared as a mark of guilt but also the evil one who will do the lad's secretly wished work for him. And another corroborative detail appears in the oak cudgel, a phallic symbol, the natural woodsman's weapon with the threat of which the lad, in his callow arrogance, thinks to conquer all the complex difficulties of the city—that is, the adult world.

Assuming that some such account as this is acceptable as one line of the story, we may well ask what it stacks up to, what it, in itself, means. Is it merely descriptive, diagnostic, or does Hawthorne take some evaluative attitude toward this process inherent in life? The answer lies, it would seem, in an extension of the ambivalence of feeling in Robin himself. The process of repudiating the father—of growing up—is necessary; but in the very moment of victory, there is "pity and terror"—human pity, we are tempted to say, for the inevitable victim and terror for the self who, as human, is bound to undergo, in time, the same fate. In the life process, which in one perspective can be viewed as a "senseless uproar" and "frenzied merriment,"[6] there is, if we regard the victim as an individual, the trampling "on an old man's heart." To put it another way, remembering that "pity and terror"[7] is the formulation sacred to tragedy, Hawthorne is seeing the natural life process as, in one perspective, tragic: pain is inevitably involved, and in the victim there is tragic dignity, like that of a "dead potentate, mighty no more but majestic in his agony"— even if the "majesty" is simply the illusion that is carried over from the nursery.

[6] We notice that the first old man whom Robin accosts, and whom we have here taken in the role of the authoritative father, now participates in the mirth at the Major's expense. Is there a contradiction between the role of father and this lack of sympathy with the dethronement of another "father," Molineux? Presumably not, for the victim is always isolated in his personal story, with all the rest of the world, including those who have suffered and will suffer, caught up in the wild and heartless celebration of the process. In any case, a role—say the role of the old man—is not fixed, is not an identity. As the wise and kindly father whom Robin last encounters says to him: "May not a man have several faces, Robin, as well as two complexions?"

[7] Melville, we shall see, used the same formulation in his *Supplement to Battle-Pieces*, his poems of the Civil War.

This Freudian "meaning" is, as we have said, only one of the several which flow into the story, and it clearly does not account for all the elements in it. The Freudian approach deals with a natural process, presumably, but the process occurs in a social, moral, and philosophical context and, in fact, has come to exist only in such contexts. So we may look at the story in, for example, the light of its "moral" theme. Robin is initiated into adulthood, but the full initiation involves the confrontation with evil, not merely the Freudian guilts but evil as a force operative in the world and in the heart.

The boy came into the city armed with his club and his "shrewdness," but this is a world where neither force nor ordinary common sense avails. He is, as one critic, Daniel Hoffman, has put it (in *Form and Fable in American Fiction*), a kind of parody of the smart Yankee— Brother Jonathan, the peddlers of folk anecdote, Jack Downing, Sam Slick (see pp. 1087–94)— and, we may add, of the hero posited by Emerson's essay "Self-Reliance." To quote Hoffman, Robin is "the Great American Boob, the naif whose odyssey leads him, all uncomprehending, into the dark center of experience." In his callow arrogance, and in his stupid trust in cudgel and shrewdness, Robin has not even been able to recognize the image of the Devil in the man with the painted face, and in the end, in his "mental inebriety," by his joining, by his shout: "the loudest there," with the nightmare procession, he surrenders himself, for the moment in any case, to that horrid ringleader who had fixed his glance full upon him as he rode past. When he is left shaken and confused, ready to go home, the option the wise stranger leaves with him is the fundamental *moral* option: to go home, that is, to flee into a dream of innocence, which would really be ignorance and cowardice, or to stay in the city and, in experience and moral awareness, to try to deal with the hard terms of actuality.

In the historical setting we find another line of meaning that flows into the story. The setting presents, in embryo, the story of a revolution—

the American Revolution[8]—and an image of revolution in general. The kinsman is not only a "father," but also a royal governor, or at least a representative of such power. So in the historical theme, we find a parallel to the Freudian and moral themes. The first feature of Hawthorne's treatment to strike us is the strange inversion of the officially patriotic view which occurs elsewhere in his work. Here the leader of the patriots is, in one aspect, the Devil, the patriots themselves are a dehumanized mob, a nightmare crew, and Molineux, politically the representative of oppression, appears "majestic still in his agony." In the interpretation of the historical process of revolution, we have a parallel with Hawthorne's attitude toward the "revolution" of achieving maturity: both involve a tragic paradox, there are human costs in the process, and both processes, like that of moral initiation, involve the problem of evil.

We must not take it, however, that the story necessarily implies that revolution, any more than the growing up of a lad, is wrong or bad. As a matter of fact, a strong case has been made, again by Daniel Hoffman, that the riotous and violent "merrymaking" is to be taken symbolically as a kind of Saturnalia, and the painted ringleader as a Lord of Misrule; and this would imply that after the debauch, necessary to the rebirth of society, order will be restored and the roots of continuity rediscovered. If this idea is acceptable, it provides merely another ambiguity of the "night of ambiguities." It would in no wise cancel the import of the story that the part of wisdom is to recognize the paradoxical aspects of reality and to confront the tragic tension at its core. And we may take the story, too, as a rebuke to the easy chauvinism, the democratic mystique, the doctrine of manifest destiny, the belief in automatic progress, and the moral complacency parading as philosophy which characterized much American life of Hawthorne's time and, it must be added, of our time too.

Let us look at one last element in the story.

Several critics have emphasized the importance of the inimical laughter which pursues Robin until the moment when he finally joins in that "tremendous ridicule."[9] We have seen how, in one dimension, the laughter can be taken as an echo, self-directed, of Robin's fear, guilt, and shame; how, in another, it embodies the depersonalized cruelty of the natural and historical process; and how, in another, it expresses the purgation of the Saturnalia.

But as it aimlessly echoes through the complex arches and vaultings of the story, its most pervasive and profound effect, the effect to be emphasized here, is to establish a counterpoint of tonality for the meaning of the story. Anthony Trollope, writing in praise of *The Scarlet Letter*, makes a remark that, at first glance, seems peculiar; he says that in the novel is "a touch of burlesque—not as to the suffering of the sufferers, but as to the great question whether it signifies much in what way we suffer. . . . Hawthorne seems to ridicule the very woes which he expends himself in depicting." And in *The House of the Seven Gables*, Hawthorne refers to the "tragic power of laughter." Of "My Kinsman, Major Molineux," we may even say, not too fancifully, that in the "tremendous ridicule" we hear the story laughing at itself, laughing so boisterously at the tragic awareness of life that the Man in the Moon, at his distance, or with his irony, finds all frolicsome. But this would be only one last ambiguity. For the tragic awareness would, in our human perspective, remain.

In considering the various themes that are involved in "My Kinsman, Major Molineux," we must, in the end, insist on the interpenetration of all the themes. After all, the story is quite solidly set in history and in the consciousness of Robin, and all the meanings are merely functions of his literal story. In other words, we are not dealing with the standard type of allegory but with a pervasive and massive symbolism, the basic symbol being the story

---

[8] The first development of this interpretation was by Q. D. Leavis, "Hawthorne as Poet," *Sewanee Review* (Spring, 1951).

[9] See also "Young Goodman Brown" and the inimical laughter heard in the forest by the young man as he hurries to his evil appointment.

itself which, in its literalism, absorbs and fuses the various kinds of import. It is well to remember that in "The Antique Ring," when the storyteller is asked what thought he would embody in the ring, we have the answer: "You know that I can never separate the idea from the symbol in which it manifests itself."[10]

The publication of *Twice-Told Tales* brought Hawthorne not only some fame but a fiancée to boot, a young lady of a good family of cultural pretensions. Sophia Peabody herself had sensibility, a little literary and artistic talent, and considerable piety, and was a near invalid— a fact which may well have some psychological significance for both the man and his work.[11] In any case, Hawthorne now faced the prospect of responsibilities.

"The world," as he put it, "called me forth" —called him forth to social life in the cultivated Peabody circle and to a job as measurer of coal and salt at the Boston custom house. By 1841, however, Hawthorne had had enough of that custom house and, with the notion of providing a home for a wife, bought shares in Brook Farm, that idealistic colony devoted to healthy labor, communal living, and intellectual pursuits. (See pp. 330–31.) He shoveled a great deal of manure, milked and foddered cows, including a "transcendental heifer" belonging to Margaret Fuller, listened to interminable conversations by reformers of various stripes, said little, and kept a journal.

The high-minded conversation of Brook Farm had a deadening effect on Hawthorne's creative impulse. He withdrew from the project, married anyway, in 1843, and moved to Concord, into

the Old Manse, where he occupied the study in which Emerson had written his first book, *Nature*. The house and the quiet of the locality pleased Hawthorne, but here, too, he found something of the same qualities which had made Brook Farm intolerable: "Never was a poor little country village infested with such a variety of queer, strangely dressed, oddly behaved mortals, most of whom took upon themselves to be important agents of the world's destiny, yet were simply bores of the first water." Thoreau was a good companion for walks and talks and had "great qualities of intellect and character"; but even he could be "the most unmalleable fellow alive—the most tedious, tiresome, and intolerable—the narrowest and most notional." As for Emerson, "that everlasting rejector of all that is, and seeker for he knows not what," Hawthorne remarked that earlier he could have demanded "of this prophet the master word that would solve me the riddle of the universe, but now, being happy, I felt as if there were no questions to be put, and therefore admired Emerson as a poet of deep beauty and austere tenderness, but sought nothing from him as a philosopher."

Hawthorne and Emerson could not, in fact, manage conversation together; Emerson put in his journal that Hawthorne's fiction was "not good for anything,"[12] and Henry James, with remarkable precision of imagery, was to explain

---

10 This notion is like the doctrine of symbolism of Coleridge, and other Romantics, who take the true symbol (as distinguished from the items of allegory) as "participating" in the "reality" which it represents. In this early story Hawthorne managed to create a fiction in which the symbol and the reality interfuse. In this connection, see too Paul Tillich's analysis of the symbolism of the Cross, in *Christ and Culture*.

11 The strong, vital women in Hawthorne's work, like Zenobia in *The Blithedale Romance*, Miriam in *The Marble Faun*, and Hester in *The Scarlet Letter*, are dark, passionate temptresses, perilous to have to do with— especially for a man of uneasy disposition.

12 Precisely the opposite of Emerson's view was taken by Melville in a review of *Mosses from an Old Manse*, in 1850, and more emphatically in a review of *The House of the Seven Gables*, which, though Poe had taken Hawthorne very seriously and praised him, presented the first fundamental insight into Hawthorne's special quality:

He [Hawthorne] says NO! in thunder; but the Devil himself cannot make him say *yes*. For all men who say *yes*, lie; and all men who say *no*—why, they are in the happy condition of judicious, unencumbered travellers in Europe; they cross the frontiers into Eternity with nothing but a carpetbag,—that is to say, the Ego.

From the "tornadoed Atlantic" of his own being, Melville sensed the "power of blackness" in Hawthorne, the "sense of Innate Depravity and Original Sin, from whose visitations . . . no deeply thinking mind is always and wholly free." The men were for a brief time closely associated, and one of Melville's more beautiful poems is on the death of Hawthorne. See pp. 819 and 927.

this lack of comprehension by saying that "Emerson, as a spiritual sun-worshipper, could have attached but a moderate value to Hawthorne's catlike faculty of seeing in the dark." James added, by way of further explanation, that for Emerson the idea of sin was the "soul's mumps and measles"—a disease of childhood. It should be clear what Hawthorne would make of this.

By the fall of 1845 Hawthorne left Concord. Through the friendly offices of Bridge and Pierce he was shortly to receive the appointment as surveyor of customs at Salem. In this period, in spite of the demands of his post, he managed to write several new tales, including "The Snow Image," another tale dealing, like "The Artist of the Beautiful," with the relation of the artist to the world, "The Great Stone Face," which tangentially touches on the same theme, and "Ethan Brand." Ethan is another example of the obsessed hero who, as we have seen, appears again and again in Hawthorne's fiction—Goodman Brown, Aylmer, Warland, Rappaccini, and Chillingworth in *The Scarlet Letter*. Such obsessions alienate a person from the human community, but more than alienation may be involved. Ethan Brand, in his obsessions, has committed a crime against humanity. In his search for the Unpardonable Sin, he has committed it by treating human beings "with cold remorseless purpose," as "the subject of a psychological experiment." He had disturbed the "counterpoise between his mind and his heart" and, by making his Idea all, had "lost his hold of the magnetic chain of humanity" and had, thus, become a "fiend."

Ethan Brand is, of course, no artist, but the way in which Hawthorne gives the diagnosis of his sin describes what Hawthorne took to be the moral danger that he feared in the practice of his art. "He was no longer a brother, and opening the chambers or the dungeons of our common nature by the key of holy sympathy, which gave him a right to share in all of its secrets; he was now a cold observer . . . converting man and woman to be his puppets." This period, in which Hawthorne seems to

have been most eaten by doubts about the nature of art, was to lead shortly to his greatest artistic achievement. Often, in fact, the doubts became the subject matter of his work, with the surrogate self, often an artist, in the role of the protagonist.

In 1849 Hawthorne lost his post at the custom house. Sophia, in secret, had saved a little money, and on this he began *The Scarlet Letter*. When, only a few weeks after he lost the post, his mother died, there followed the emotional upheaval which, he said, he himself could not understand. Some years later, looking back on this period of the composition of *The Scarlet Letter*, Hawthorne said that he was "in a very nervous state then, having gone through diversity of direction, while writing it. I think I have never overcome my adamant in any other instance."[13]

When Hawthorne read this new book to his wife, it "sent her to bed with a grievous headache"—as well it might, for there must have been a considerable shock to find revealed here a man whom, in the years of marriage, she had never realized existed and whom she had been unable to sense behind the cool facade of the tales. The book was, as he dolorously put it, fearing that it would never be generally acceptable, "positively a hell-fired story, into which I found it almost impossible to throw a cheering light."

Why did Sophia Hawthorne take to her bed with a "grievous headache"? Why did Emerson,

[13] This is a significant reference to the allegorical tale in *The Snow Image*, "The Man of Adamant." Richard Digby, a Puritan romantic obsessed with spiritual pride and suffering appropriately from a disease by which calcium was deposited in his heart, withdraws into a sepulchral cave and refuses to be enticed forth by human love or any interpretation of religion different from his own; a century later his calcified form, "a repulsive personage," is found seated in the cave. To interpret Hawthorne's remark, then, we should say that before the death of his mother he had suffered from some stony inhibition of his emotional life, from which the shock of her death released him for his fullest expression. But it is not to be suggested that the death of the mother accounts for the conception of *The Scarlet Letter* or for the beginning of work on it. The death simply made certain forces available to the labor.

when asked what he thought of the novel, murmur "Ghastly, ghastly"? Why did Julian Hawthorne declare, upon rereading the work, long after Hawthorne's death, that he found it impossible to reconcile the father he had known with the author of the fiction? And why did the author himself refer to it, in a different tonality we may be sure, as "hell-fired"? The answer to these questions would bring us close to the significance of the novel, but the only way to approach an answer is through the novel itself.

The Scarlet Letter is another example of Hawthorne's inclination to treat violent materials in the long perspective of the past. In this work Hawthorne not only takes his materials from the past, in which the violence may be regarded at arm's length, but omits what might have been the most violently emotional phase of the story —the account of the growth of passion, the temptation, and the fall. Indeed, he does not even begin with the story itself, but with the introductory discussion of the custom house, which serves as a screen between the reader and the possible intensity of action, as a distancing device. Then, when he does enter the story proper, he opens with the first stage of the long train of consequences, the moment when Hester steps forth from the jail to face public shame. Even this is introduced by a kind of prologue, which puts the event in the perspective of meaning as contrasted with a direct shock to the emotions: the scene of the throng of men in "sad-colored garments" contrasted with the wild rose bush blooming at the very door of the jail, "in token that the deep heart of Nature could pity and be kind." So we have here in this contrast the first indication of the thematic tension, which represents an intellectualizing of emotion.

The same contrast is to be developed, more deeply and ironically, in the fact that the women waiting at the jail, who, as women, should "naturally" exhibit some sympathy and understanding for Hester's plight, are more savage than the men in their condemnation: that is, there is a contrast between their natural role and their social role. To continue, when

Hester does appear, the scarlet A on her bosom presents a variation on the same thematic line; for embroidered in gold thread with a "gorgeous luxuriance of fancy," it is—"naturally," shall we say?—an object of beauty, while socially considered it is a badge of infamy.

This set of contrasts, we shall see as the story develops, will lead us to another and deeper paradox, in that the act which is a "sin" is also presented as the source of deepened understanding and development. This, however, is to run ahead of ourselves, and for the moment what we see is that when the woman steps forth, who we have learned from the crowd is a creature to be reviled (and at the moment that is all we do know about her), she appears, surprisingly enough, in a beauty and pride which make "a halo of the misfortune and ignominy." The point here is simply to observe how freighted with meaning are the details of the narrative and how coherently these suggestions will be developed.

If we look at the first three chapters, we find a marvelously compact and exciting introductory scene; for *The Scarlet Letter* is, in point of fact, the first American novel to be truly "composed," in the sense that we shall find Henry James using the term; that is, the first novel to consider form as, in itself, an expression of emotion and meaning. In connection with the structure of the novel, we must note that in this first scene Hester stands on the scaffold. This fact is of the deepest significance, for the scaffold is crucial to the whole conception. With this opening scene, the great scene of Dimmesdale's midnight vigil on it (in Chap. 12, at the middle of the novel), and the denouement and Dimmesdale's death on it at the end, the scaffold becomes the seminal image of the novel, the locus of both agony and vision.

Now, at the beginning, Hester, standing on the scaffold, experiences, in a flash of memory, the "entire track along which she had been treading since her happy infancy"—aware, however vaguely, of a pattern in her fate. Across the crowd she suddenly sees the old man who is her husband, and who, as though an incarnation of her past, seems to be summoned by her thoughts of it. His identity is not yet divulged to us, but from the sinister tone of his questioning of a bystander, we get what exposition we need, getting it as an action thrusting forward (as the old man, referring to Hester's unknown partner in guilt, threatens, "He will be known"), not as mere exposition. Then, as the apex of this "triangular" scene, we first see Dimmesdale, placed high with the great and powerful of the state who judge and administer judgment: poor Dimmesdale, whose sermon to Hester now, with all its doubleness of motivation and of meaning, is a dynamic development of, and a guide to, his private drama.

Chapter 4, with the scene between Hester and Chillingworth, may be taken as the last phase of the first movement of the novel. Here Chillingworth defines for himself, and for us, his role, and forces Hester into her decision to keep silent about his identity, a decision which gives the key to the future action. The novel is now in train: we have a masterful piece of exposition, the characters established in their archetypal stances, with a maximum of economy in presenting the past and a maximum of suspense in the thrust toward the future.

After the essentially dramatic exposition of the first four chapters, there is a second movement, this of generalized narrative rather than scene, analytical rather than dramatic. Here we have a description of the kind of life Hester works out for herself in the "charmed circle" of her moral isolation and, as a corollary, a further presentation of her character. Why has she remained in Boston to be a "type of shame"? Because here she has encountered reality; "her sin, her ignominy, were the roots which she had struck in the soil." But there was another motive, although she "hid the secret from herself." Dimmesdale is here, with whom "she deemed herself connected in a union . . . that would bring them together before the bar of final judgment, and make that their marriage altar, for a joint futurity of endless retribution." So in the very idea of "endless retribution" with her lover there enters an element of sexual gratification, torment as ecstasy, a thing totally removed from the idea of true penitence; it

was an idea that "the tempter of souls" thrust upon her, and then "laughed at the passionate and desperate joy with which she seized, and then strove to cast it from her."

Meanwhile, Hester lives by doing sewing and performing acts of charity, even for those who revile her in the moment of accepting it. She was a "martyr," but she "forbore to pray for her enemies lest, in spite of her forgiving aspiration, the words of blessing should stubbornly twist themselves into a curse." She felt, too, that the letter had "endowed her with a new sense," that it "gave her a sympathetic knowledge of the hidden sin in other hearts." In regard to this she was torn between the temptation to believe that all "purity" was a "lie,"[14] and the impulse to "believe that no fellow mortal was guilty like herself." (But she will, at the end, develop another option in which she will rest: that of using the knowledge coming from "sin" as a means to assist and comfort others.)

The only society possible to her is little Pearl. She dresses the child gorgeously, the richness of color being an expression of that part of her own nature otherwise suppressed. The child, often presented as little more than an allegory, is a kind of elf, outside the ordinary world, a child of "nature" who says to Hester, "I have no Heavenly Father." There comes a time when the authorities are about to remove Pearl from Hester's care, and only the arguments advanced by Dimmesdale prevent this, a fact which confirms Chillingworth in his suspicions of the minister's guilt.

In the second movement of the novel, too, the course of the relation of Dimmesdale and Chillingworth is traced. Dimmesdale is living in anguish. Tormented by his guilt and by his weakness in not bringing himself to confess it, he can still self-deceivingly argue that there are men who, though guilty, retain "a zeal for God's glory and man's welfare," and therefore "shrink from displaying themselves black and filthy in the view of men," because by this course "no evil of the past can be redeemed by

[14] This theme appears again in Chapter 22 in the behavior of Dimmesdale after his meeting with Hester in the forest. See also "Young Goodman Brown."

better service." He keeps a scourge in his closet and pitilessly brings blood to his own shoulders, all the while laughing bitterly. But all his acts of penance are fruitless; there is, he says, "penance" but not "penitence," only a "mockery of penitence." In other words, as in Hester's thought of union in the torture of "endless retribution," there is, in Dimmesdale's pangs of penance, a kind of sexual gratification.

Even as he suffers, Dimmesdale has achieved "a brilliant popularity in his sacred office," having "won it indeed by his sorrows," for, in a kind of parallel to Hester's notion that she could intuit the guilt in the hearts of others, Dimmesdale's "burden" is what makes "his sympathies so intimate with the sinful brotherhood of mankind" that his pain issues in "gushes of sad, persuasive eloquence."

As a result of his torment, Dimmesdale's health fails, and the learned stranger Chillingworth moves into the same house with him, ostensibly to save him for the greater glory of God and of New England. He is there, of course, out of his desire for vengeance, which now amounts to a mania, a mania intertwined with Chillingworth's intellectual passion for anatomizing the soul and body of the sufferer. Dimmesdale, out of the morbidity of his sensibility, is aware of an inimical agency but cannot identify it.

With Chapter 12, the second movement of the novel ends, the long section of generalized narration and analysis being concluded by the night scene in which Dimmesdale, forecasting the climactic scene at the end of the novel, mounts the scaffold. Now, "in this vain show of expiation," Dimmesdale is "overcome with a great horror of mind, as if the universe were gazing at a scarlet token on his naked breast," where in fact there had long been "the gnawing and poisonous tooth of bodily pain." In his agony Dimmesdale shrieks, and then, being sure that his voice has summoned the whole town to see his shame, he exclaims, with an echo of the Biblical account of the crucifixion, "It is done!" The town does not rouse itself to witness Dimmesdale's agony (as it will in the end), but there is the ghostlike appearance of the old

governor at his window and at another the head of his sister, the witch, and then, in the street, unaware of him, the Reverend Mr. Wilson, who has been praying by the side of the dying old Governor Winthrop.

It is the passing of Mr. Wilson that stirs up the wild self-torturing humor in Dimmesdale which again appears (Chap. 22) after the forest scene with Hester; and this "grisly sense of the humorous" summons up his vision of what the morning will reveal:

The neighbourhood would begin to rouse itself. The earliest riser, coming forth in the dim twilight, would perceive a vaguely defined figure aloft on the place of shame; and, half crazed betwixt alarm and curiosity, would go, knocking from door to door, summoning all the people to behold the ghost—as he needs must think it—of some defunct transgressor. A dusky tumult would flap its wings from one house to another. Then—the morning light still waxing stronger—old patriarchs would rise up in great haste, each in his flannel gown, and matronly dames, without pausing to put off their night-gear. The whole tribe of decorous personages, who had never heretofore been seen with a single hair of their heads awry, would start into public view, with the disorder of a nightmare in their aspects. Old Governor Bellingham would come grimly forth, with his King James's ruff fastened askew; and Mistress Hibbins, with some twigs of the forest clinging to her skirts, and looking sourer than ever, as having hardly got a wink of sleep after her night ride; and good Father Wilson, too, after spending half the night at a death-bed, and liking ill to be disturbed, thus early, out of his dreams about the glorified saints. Hither, likewise, would come the elders and deacons of Mr. Dimmesdale's church, and the young virgins who so idolized their minister, and had made a shrine for him in their white bosoms; which, now, by the by, in their hurry and confusion, they would scantly have given themselves time to cover with their kerchiefs. All people, in a word, would come stumbling over their thresholds, and turning up their amazed and horror-stricken visages around the scaffold.

At this Dimmesdale, "to his own infinite alarm," burst out into wild laughter, and this laughter, as by the logic of dream, evokes the "light, airy, childish" laughter of Pearl, the "good" witch (unlike the sister of Governor Bellingham), the child who is of nature, who has "no Heavenly Father." And there is Hester, who, with Pearl, ascends the scaffold to stand by his side. Then the red meteor flames in the sky, and in that red glare appears Chillingworth, who has come, he says, to lead Dimmesdale home.

The scaffold scene not only brings to focus, there at the middle of the novel, all the forces that, in their complexity and ambiguity, are at work, but also provides a new thrust of plot. For the scene impels Hester to seek out her husband to persuade him to have mercy on his victim. Chillingworth refuses, but he offers an insight into himself and his private story. He is, he says, now a "fiend," and he demands: "Who made me so?" To which Hester, shuddering at a new sense of guilt, replies: "It was myself." But even the "fiend" can see the pity of their situation: "Peradventure, hadst thou met earlier with a better love than mine, this evil had not been. I pity thee for the good that has been wasted in thy nature."

But when Hester says that she pities him for the same reason and makes a last plea that, to save his own soul, he release Dimmesdale, he can only reply that "it has all been a dark necessity." And in one of the most important thematic statements of the novel, he continues: "Ye that have wronged me are not sinful, save in a kind of typical illusion; neither am I fiend-like who have snatched a fiend's office from his hand. It is our fate. Let the black flower blossom as it may!"

The refusal of Chillingworth to relinquish Dimmesdale justifies Hester, she feels, in breaking her promise not to divulge his identity, and so prepares for the end of the third movement of the novel in the forest scene (Chap. 17), in which the strong and vital Hester attempts to save Dimmesdale by persuading him to flee from America and seek a new life and which comes to a climax when she snatches the A from her bosom and casts it away.

This scene, in the beautiful interpenetration of elements in the structure of the work, not only provides a forward thrust for action (it prepares for the end), but interprets the past. We had never seen, or been told anything about, the relation of the lovers before the opening of the novel, but now, in this "natural" forest scene, we understand how Hester, in her "natural" strength and vitality, is the "seducer" of Dimmesdale, and we understand that it must have been this way, however unconsciously, in the beginning of their story before the novel opens. We understand more precisely than before another element of both structure and meaning: the tension, in life and in man, between "nature" and "idea," the doom of man's essential division of flesh and spirit.

Other elements are to emerge in the fourth movement. In the forest scene itself we notice the reaction of little Pearl, who will not cross the brook to her mother and Dimmesdale until the A is restored to its place—to declare Hester's identity (and, for that matter, Dimmesdale's too). The forest scene throws a special light on the split between flesh and spirit. It would seem that man, in seeking the freedom of nature (discarding the A and preparing to flee), loses his identity, that is, his moral history. But, at the same time, in the ambiguity of experience, we see that the most immediate consequence of this decision to discard the mark of guilt and to flee to make a new life (by discarding penance without having achieved penitence) is the great burst of "natural" energy for the nearly moribund Dimmesdale.

Associated with this energy as he rushes homeward is a kind of diabolic humor, like that observed on the midnight scaffold, which now amounts to a parody of Dimmesdale's gift of intuitive sympathy for the sinful hearts of others and which now expresses itself in a desire to entrap others in their own corruption—to whisper a wicked joke in the ear of a young girl or an atheistical argument into that of a poor widow who has nothing left but her Christian faith. Dimmesdale experiences, in other words, a sudden release of his suppressed sexual energy which had been spent in penance and which now comes out in an anarchic denial of all "purity"; but he is still so much the man of faith that he can think of his new energy only in terms of the joy of Christian conversion— "risen up all made anew, and with new powers to glorify Him that hath been merciful." (And this little passage may be put in balance with the last words of Dimmesdale in the climactic scene of the novel.) This is a parody of conversion, and as such the carrier of a double irony. First, Dimmesdale does not realize the nature of the "joy," not even when it eventuates in the anarchic obscenities. Second, Dimmesdale does not realize that he, being the "religionist" he is, cannot escape into the guiltlessness of pure nature. He is doomed to penitence— doomed, as it were, to be saved. This is his "dark necessity."

Another consequence flows from the forest scene. As the new "joy" of Dimmesdale bursts forth into the obscene comedy on the way homeward, so, once in his chamber, it bursts forth in the composition of the election day sermon that he will give before his flight into "guiltlessness." As he sits in his chamber, and sees his old Bible there, he thinks of himself as he had once been; and he "eyes that former self with scornful, pitying, but half-envious curiosity." Even as he repudiates that old pious self, his pen is racing ahead as though beyond his control. What if this eloquence, which soon all auditors will consider divinely inspired, springs from the same energy that had been bursting out in the anarchic obscenities? Hawthorne would certainly not regard this as a simple irony undercutting the validity and spirituality of the sermon. There is an irony, to be sure, but an irony involving the very doubleness of human nature.

The fifth, and last, movement of the novel begins with a public gathering, which architecturally balances the scene outside the jail at the beginning of the story. Hester and Pearl are now in the crowd waiting for the great procession to the church where Dimmesdale will give his sermon. Here Hester encounters the captain of the Bristol ship that is to take her, Pearl, and her lover away (the captain, let us note, is "outside" society and its values, a creature of the wild ocean like a creature of the unredeemed forest, where the Devil lurks and witches foregather); but from him, the agent of freedom, she gets the news, not of freedom and guiltlessness, but of pursuing guilt in the person of Chillingworth, who has found out the secret of their intended flight and taken passage on the same ship.

A second shock awaits Hester when she sees Dimmesdale in the procession, suddenly seeming far beyond her among the great, his mind "far and deep in its own region" and his eyes not sparing even a glance for her. Her spirit sinks with "the idea that all must have been delusion." And upon her thoughts, to compound this distress, there breaks Mistress Hibbins, the witch, speaking of the Black Man in the forest and how Dimmesdale had signed a bond there with him.

At the time of the sermon, with symbolic appropriateness, Hester is outside the church, standing by the scaffold of the pillory, with the sense in her "that her whole orb of life . . . was connected with this spot, as the one point that gave it unity"—as it gives the novel unity. As she stands there, she cannot hear the actual words of the sermon, only the flow of the minister's peculiarly musical and expressive voice, with an "essential character of plaintiveness." The fact that she cannot hear the words has symbolic significance, of course, for, in a sense, she and her lover do not speak the same language. They belong to different dimensions of life that scarcely intersect—only in their "love." His obsessed spirituality, which is his "necessary" story, is not for her. So what she hears is not a message from his dimension, but the "whisper, or the shriek, as it might be conceived, of suffering humanity." And it is the same secret voice of "suffering humanity," not the message, that provokes the "rapture" of the congregation—though ironically enough, they think they are moved by the message which foretells "a high and glorious destiny" for the settlers in New England, that "newly gathered people of the Lord."

When, after the sermon, Dimmesdale summons Hester and Pearl to the scaffold with him for the climactic scene of the confession, several features should be remarked. First, the role of Chillingworth, we now see, is not to uncover the sinner, but to prevent the confession, for in the confession his victim "escapes" him. Second, in Dimmesdale's penitent confession there is, in the very ecstasy of self-abasement, a kind of egotism; he is, he proclaims, the "one sinner of the world." Third, as a corollary of this egotism, when Hester, from the depth of her feeling, cries out for assurance that they will meet in the immortal life, Dimmesdale replies that the "law" has been broken and it may be vain to hope for a "pure reunion." He does add that God is merciful, but with this reference to mercy his egotism totally reasserts itself, and the mercy now referred to is to be directed at Dimmesdale alone. If God had not mercifully given Dimmesdale the "burning torture" on his breast, the company of the "dark, terrible old man," and death in "triumphant ignominy," then he "had been lost forever."

Poor Hester is utterly forgotten. In fact, we should add that if the confession is an "escape" from Chillingworth, it is also, in a deeper fashion, an "escape" from Hester—from nature, from flesh, from passion, from sexuality, from, in the end, woman, who is the unclean one, the temptress. So even in the heroic moment, there is a deep ambiguity.

It is easy to see how if a reader ignores all the characters except Dimmesdale, if he does not attend very closely to what Dimmesdale does and says, and if he accepts Dimmesdale's values as Hawthorne's, he can take *The Scarlet Letter* as *merely* a story of conscience and redemption. But clearly Sophia with her "grievous headache," Emerson with his "Ghastly, ghastly," and Hawthorne with his "hell-fired" saw more. Each in his own way saw the tragic tensions, the pitiful instances of waste, the irremediable

askewness of life which the story, taken as a whole, delineates.

Taken as a whole: that is the point. Even in Dimmesdale's story there are ambiguities. How much, for instance, is there of spiritual aspiration, and how much of fear of nature, fear of his own nature, sexual incertitude, and narcissism? But whatever Dimmesdale may actually be taken to be, he is only part of the pattern of the novel. Chillingworth, for instance, is a thematic and psychological counterpoint to him; and even, in the novel, a structural counterpoint, for the relation of each to Hester gives one principle of the action, and one principle of balance to the action. Psychologically and thematically, their roles are even more significant. Both are men "outside" of nature, Chillingworth with his passion for study (to be directed, of course, to the good of mankind) and Dimmesdale with his aspiration to spirituality (so as to be a model for the redemption of mankind). When Chillingworth comes to the vital Hester he is already old, twisted, withered, and all but impotent, and if Dimmesdale discovers passion with her, there is inevitably the self-loathing we find expressed in the fact that part of his penance is to stare at his own face in a mirror. If Chillingworth, out of envy of what he takes to be the successful lover, and in his outraged vanity, devotes himself to the torture of Dimmesdale, then we find as a parallel Dimmesdale's obsessively gratifying process of self-torture. In the end, the two men are more important to each other than Hester is to either; theirs is the truest "marriage."

Hester's story is one of penance, it is clear. She accepts her role as the outcast, the revulsion of society, and the insults from even those unfortunates whom she succors, but she does this out of pride rather than humility. She has, in fact, stayed here for reasons having nothing to do with penance, to be near Dimmesdale and, perhaps more importantly, to fulfill some obscure sense of what Hawthorne calls the "unity" of her life and what we might call her identity. Further, her isolation has freed her mind to speculate about the nature of society and to decide that society is not fixed by God in immutable law but is subject to change. This is not penance; and certainly not penitence.

Hawthorne says, indeed, that Hester had in her the making of a harsh prophetess who might attempt to create the future. It is this strain of coldness and harshness developed in her adversity, in her "battle" with the world, which he deplores, even as he admires her courage. This point is reinforced in the last scaffold scene. When Pearl, as though aroused by the "great scene of grief," comes out of the "spell" to kiss at last her father's lips, Hawthorne says that her tears "were the pledge that she would grow up in human joy and sorrow, nor forever do battle with the world, but be a woman in it."

The scaffold scene, then, would say that Hester has been forced to do battle with the world and that part of her tragedy lies in the consequent hardening of her womanliness; only in the meeting with Dimmesdale in the forest, where love is again "aroused," does her natural womanliness return: "Such was the sympathy of Nature—that wild, heathen nature of the forest, never subjugated by human law, nor illumined by higher truth."[15]

Hester, strong, vital, beautiful, is indeed the wonderful "natural" creature, but even so another source of her tragedy lies in the fact that she cannot be merely "natural." Here we must consider that the men she has accepted are not men we would reasonably expect as her sexual partners. We can argue that accident and social conditions may well have played a part here, and this is true; but *dramatically* regarded, what we have is the natural woman yearning, as it were, toward a condition beyond her "naturalness." Dramatically, psychologically, and thematically regarded, it is not an accident that Hester takes up with the old and twisted Chillingworth, and when she deserts him, it is for the pale, beautiful Dimmesdale and his pathologically sensitive conscience and narcissistic spirituality, instead of for some strapping officer of militia who would wear his religion more lightly, could gratify her appetites more single-mindedly, and could sleep better o' nights. From the very start there has been an askewness in her fate, an askewness that Chillingworth recognizes when he says, "hadst thou met with a better love than mine, this evil had not been." But what he does not recognize is the possibility that there may also be a reason why "naturalness" yearns beyond "nature."

The last chapter is balanced, as a kind of epilogue, against the first, which, as we have said, serves as a prologue. The climactic scaffold scene must, then, be regarded in the context of this conclusion. The meaning of Dimmesdale's confession is, in this epilogue, subjected to debate, and the mere fact qualifies the interpretation of the whole story. There is, too, considerable complexity in the way the story of Chillingworth is worked out. Deprived of the terrible meaning of his own life, he withers away, but in the very withering he provides means for Pearl to achieve her life. As heiress to his fortune, she goes to Europe, marries a nobleman, and as we are given to understand, fulfills the prediction that she would not "do battle with the world, but be a woman in it." This may be taken as a happy normality coming out of the distorted lives—but if so, then with what illogicality, and after what waste! Pearl's happiness can scarcely be taken to discount the grief of all the others.

As for Hester, can the final meaning of her life be taken to discount the grief? She returns from Europe to resume her life in the withdrawn cottage and resumes, by her own choice, the scarlet letter—for only thus could she feel that her own life had found meaning. Now as she distributes comfort and counsel to women suffering from "wounded, wasted, wronged, misplaced, or erring and sinful passion," she assures them that a "brighter period" would come when the relation of man and woman would be "on a surer ground of mutual happiness." This, we must observe, is at the farthest remove from penitence, for the message that Hester, by implication, gives the suffering women is not that they are "sinners" in need of redemption, but that they are victims of a social order that violates nature.

---

[15] This scene has strong parallels with the scene in *Billy Budd* where the chaplain meditates on the "innocence" of the "barbarian" boy.

How seriously are we, the readers, to take this prediction that would give to the novel, at least in a qualified way, a "happy ending"? Not very seriously, for by a last strange irony Hester, whose identity and vision have been made possible only by her "sin," can say that the prophetess of the new dispensation must be a woman "lofty, pure, and beautiful," and wise too, but, unlike Hester herself, not wise through a "dusky grief." This would be a world freed of all guilt, a world of natural joy. It is her dream, but scarcely the world Hawthorne envisaged.

In this connection, it may be recalled that, just as *The Scarlet Letter* was often misread as a cautionary tale of sin and conscience, it could also be misread as a tract in which Hester is primarily a martyr for the liberation of women —and of men, too—from a sexually repressive society. Such was the transcendentalist interpretation in a review of the novel by a certain George Bailey Loring, a young physician, writing in Theodore Parker's *Massachusetts Quarterly Review*—transcendentalist insofar as the doctrines of "intuition" and "self-reliance" were taken by a significant segment of the public to imply sexual release from the sanctions of both church and state.

This element of the conflict between the individual and society is clearly present in *The Scarlet Letter*, and it is reasonable to suppose that the influence of the transcendentalists may have sharpened it in Hawthorne's mind, but Hawthorne's specific concern with the rigor of Puritan society, as with the complex tensions of sexual encounters, long antedated the initial meeting of earnest seekers in George Ripley's study. In fact, the meaning of the drama of *The Scarlet Letter* is far more tangled and profound that young Dr. Loring ever imagined and bears no simple relation to transcendental reformism.

In the opening paragraphs of "Rappaccini's Daughter," we find a more instructive statement of Hawthorne's own notion of his position vis-à-vis the transcendentalists. Here, in the whimsical remarks about Monsieur de l'Aubépine— the mask of Hawthorne—it is said that he holds a position "between the Transcendentalists . . .

and the great body of pen-and-ink men who address the intellect and sympathies of the multitude." Monsieur de l'Aubépine is said to be "too popular to satisfy the spiritual or metaphysical requirements" of the transcendentalists, and "too shadowy" for the multitude— for, shall we say, *l'homme moyen et sensuel.* In other words, the concern of Hawthorne lies in the tensions between the demands of spirit and those of nature; and it is precisely on this issue that *The Scarlet Letter*—as well as of much other work of Hawthorne, for instance, "Rappaccini's Daughter"—revolves. The transcendentalists had, in their several and various ways, insisted upon this issue, and Hawthorne was with them in grasping its immediate urgency for the age. But his own view was far different from that of the transcendentalists, for it was profoundly ironical in seeing the tensions between the two realms as the very essence of life—its tragedy, and glory, and even comedy.

Even nature, which, in the novel, is thematically set against the sanctions of society, cannot be taken simply. The forest is a haunt of evil as well as of good, and the wishes of the heart may be wicked as well as benign. In the tale "Earth's Holocaust," for example, when all the marks of evil and vanity have been consigned to the flames, the world is not purged; there remains the human heart. In that world of ambiguities, there is, inevitably, a terrible illogic. Good and bad may be intertwined; good may be wasted; accident, not justice, rules. Man is doomed to live in a world where nature is denied and human nature distorted, and—most shatteringly of all—in a world where love and hate may be "the same thing at bottom," and even vice or virtue may represent nothing more than what Chillingworth calls "a typical illusion." But men must live by the logic of their illusions, as best they can—Dimmesdale by his, Hester by hers, and Chillingworth by his. That is their last and darkest "necessity." What compensation is possible in such a world comes from the human capacity for achieving scale and grandeur even in illusion, one might say by insisting on the coherence of the illusion, and from the capacity for giving pity.

This is the hell-firedness of *The Scarlet Letter*.

The book, which appeared in 1850, was, in spite of the hell-firedness, a success. Hawthorne was famous and, within limits, made money. A year later, *The House of the Seven Gables*, another success, was before the public as well as another collection of tales, *The Snow Image*. In 1852 *The Blithedale Romance*, derived from his experience at Brook Farm, appeared, and the next year *Tanglewood Tales for Boys and Girls*.

To this same period (in 1852) belongs the biography of Franklin Pierce which Hawthorne wrote as his contribution to his friend's successful campaign for the presidency. Here on a specific political issue we observe Hawthorne's general distrust of "reformers." He praised Pierce as a man—and a northerner—"who dared to love that great and sacred reality—his whole united, country—better than the mustiness of philanthropic theory." On the matter of slavery, he took the legal view that the Constitution guaranteed it to the southern states, at their option—a view which Lincoln also was to take.[16] But what is more important to observe is his remark that slavery might be

> one of those evils which divine Providence does not leave to be removed by human contrivances, but which in its own good time, by some means impossible to be anticipated, but of the simplest and easiest operation, when all its uses have been fulfilled, it causes to vanish like a dream.

And he continued: "There is no instance in all history, of the human will and intellect having perfected any great moral reform by methods which it adopted to that end."

In one perspective, this passage, so consistent with Hawthorne's ironical view of history in general, and of revolution in particular, makes sound sense: however compelling the dream of establishing the City of God among men, the effort can be made only by the hands of man and the resulting community is always populated merely by men, with their same old unregenerated hearts. But in another perspective the passage shows that, for all his immersion in history, Hawthorne—unlike another ironist, Melville—had not speculated on the need for, and nature of, action in history. For one thing, Hawthorne would imply that the workings of "divine Providence" are not to be thought of as occurring through the agency of human hands. In any case, for Hawthorne, history often seemed more like a tale told than an openended demand for the gamble of action. Furthermore, this passage specifically indicates a profound failure on Hawthorne's part to diagnose the deep and self-compounding tensions in the America of his time. He was, in another context, to complain that the "actual" always eluded him. Here, certainly, it did.

As a result of his contribution to the victory of the Democrats in 1852, Hawthorne was appointed as consul to Liverpool, an arrangement which he hoped would make him financially independent. He found the duties onerous and the life there unsatisfactory—as, in a deepseated restlessness, he sooner or later found life in every place he ever lived. He traveled widely in England but made few contacts in literary and artistic circles, and these not with the great. He was struck by the beauty of the countryside and the Dickensian horror of the slums. The sense of the past, which had been at the very root of his literary inspiration in America, for a time fascinated him here, but even this became, by way of reaction, sometimes a burden and a provocation to nausea. In the British Museum he wished that the Elgin marbles were burned to lime,[17] for in the record of the past he found the same moral risk of losing touch with the magnetic chain of humanity that he found in his role as artist. His increasing unease with museums and galleries, though less streaked with brash chauvinism and a resentful sense of American inferiority, ends by reminding us of

---

[16] And to which Calhoun had given a philosophical ground in the doctrine of "concurrent majorities."

[17] One is led to speculate that the burning to lime here has more than an accidental link, a thematic one, with "Ethan Brand."

Mark Twain's attitude toward Europe and the European past. But he conscientiously kept his journals, from which later, in 1863, *Our Old Home*, a book on England, was to emerge. He even toyed with the project of a romance having to do, in a way that suggests the work of Henry James, with the conflict between American and English values; but he found it impossible to write fiction there, and for him that activity was always, however disturbing the fact might be to his conscience, and consciousness, the center of reality.

By January, 1858, Hawthorne, with his family, was in Rome, where, after the first excitements, he was depressed by "its weary pavements, its little life, pressed down by a weight of death." He dutifully continued to do the museums and galleries, trying to establish contact with their contents and sometimes failing as dismally as when, in American prudery, he argued against the nude on the grounds that one doesn't ordinarily encounter naked people or when, in a burst of patriotism and party loyalty as a good Democrat, he cried out: "I wish it had been possible for Raphael to paint General Jackson."

In Rome and Florence, he associated with the colony of American artists, trying to instruct himself and absorbing materials for *The Marble Faun*. He actually began to work on this, his last significant novel, which, like the projected English novel, deals with a conflict between American values and those of the Old World. Specifically it sets American innocence, and the Puritan tradition, in the double context of Catholicism and that pagan spirit which had antedated and managed to survive Catholicism. The germ of the story is, of course, an obsessive theme: the initiation, through evil, into moral awareness.

In 1860, Hawthorne, after seven years of exile, came home. He was coming back with some money saved, with the journals, and with the conviction that the great effort of the seven years, *The Marble Faun*, had, by his standards, failed. During the long exile, his fundamental division of feeling—in which, one is tempted to hazard, his irony found its blind, undiffer-

entiated roots—had constantly expressed itself in relation to the country from which he had been so long separated. At one moment he might find English life intolerable or indulge in bursts of patriotic fervor, but at another he could write (to Ticknor, a partner in the firm of Ticknor and Fields, his publishers): "The United States are fit for many excellent purposes, but they certainly are not fit to live in." And now, on shipboard, he said: "I should like to sail on and on forever, and never touch the shore again. . . ."

The shore he was soon to touch was that of an America of exacerbated idealisms, fanaticisms, and political passions—full of all the aspects of life which he most detested. The shore was that, too, of an America where the political party to which he had given his lifelong loyalty and the ex-President who was his old friend were discredited, and where Abraham Lincoln, who was shortly to be the candidate of the new party that had arisen since his departure in 1853, represented a western America with which Hawthorne had no familiarity. The long exile had certainly cut him off from the life of his country, but it is possible to argue that the exile and the coming of war simply gave an objective frame for, and an aggravation to, a deepening personal distress.

In any case, as the war came on, he felt himself more and more out of tune with the world. He might indeed write to Bridge that the war had "a beneficial effect upon my spirits" and say that "it was delightful to share in the heroic sentiment of the time, and to feel that I had a country—a consciousness which seemed to make me young again." But this was a mood—even in the letter it is put in the past tense—and his most considered statement appears in an article, "Chiefly About War Matters," written as a result of a trip to Washington, in March, 1862, as a member of a delegation from Massachusetts to call upon Lincoln. The article, which, with certain deletions insisted upon by Fields, the editor, appeared in the *Atlantic Monthly* in July, 1862, is notable, in particular, for his view about Emerson and John Brown—a view, by the way, which Lincoln shared—and his ironical prediction about the kind of America to come after the Union victory. But, in a more general sense, it is notable for its tone of detachment, even alienation, from the violent world he was living in.

The general tone of "Chiefly About War Matters" was, in fact, finding a dramatization in the novel Hawthorne was then trying to write. That work, *Septimius Felton*, has as hero a man who, at the very moment of the world-shaking battle of Concord at the beginning of the American Revolution, simply withdraws:

> Septimius went into his house, and sat in his study for some hours, in that unpleasant state of feeling which a man of brooding thought is apt to experience when the world around him is in a state of intense action, which he finds it impossible to sympathize with. There seemed to be a stream rushing past him, by which, even if he plunged into the midst of it, he could not be wet. He felt himself strangely ajar with the human race, and would have given much either to be in full accord with it, or to be separated from it forever.

How could Hawthorne finish such a story? He did not. This was not a story laid in the past to be interpreted at leisure. It was the story that he was living and found intolerable.

Hawthorne was withdrawing from more than the Civil War. Now, back at Concord, all efforts to resume life failed. He did make some feeble efforts to enter the world, but the elder Henry James, father of the novelist, could write of him that, on a social occasion, he had the "look all the time, to one who doesn't know him, of a rogue who suddenly finds himself in the company of detectives."

As for work, nothing went well. He did manage to convert his English journals into a book, *Our Old Home*, but he could not push through a piece of fiction. After *Septimius Felton* had proved too much for him, he tried another novel, and when that bogged down, yet another, *The Dolliver Romance*, but by February, 1864, ready to give up, he wrote Fields: "I cannot finish it unless a great change comes over me.

. . . I am not low-spirited, nor fanciful, nor freakish, but look what seem to be realities in the face, and am ready to take whatever may come."

His health, previously robust, was mysteriously declining. Now, not quite sixty, he seemed an old man. He had refused to see a doctor, and this stubbornness, combined with his acute sense of alienation, has led to the speculation that in his decline there was a significant psychosomatic factor. Certainly, his own astute awareness of the relation of body and psyche invites such speculation. He had, for instance, written: "Wherever there is a heart and intellect, the diseases of the physical frame are tinged with the peculiarities of these. In Arthur Dimmesdale, thought and imagination were so active and sensibility so intense, that the bodily infirmity would be likely to have its groundwork there."

On the night of May 18, 1864, on a trip under the guardianship of Pierce in a search for some alleviation or distraction, he died, soundlessly, in his sleep. Pierce found the body, with, as he recounted, the "position and face perfectly natural." There is something symbolically appropriate, something consistent with the temper of his own work, in the fact that he died alone, in a hotel room, in the middle of the national tragedy of the war, and that the body was found by the inept, discredited, and, in the minds of some, almost treasonable ex-President.

And there is an appropriate irony, again something in the temper of his own work, in the fact that among the pallbearers at the funeral in Concord was Emerson. The irony in the fact of Emerson's presence is compounded by the anomalous remark in his letter of sympathy to the widow that he had been "sternly disappointed" in Hawthorne's work.

There is reason to believe that Hawthorne, though for reasons different from Emerson's, was "sternly disappointed" in his own work. It is not merely that his work and fame had not salved an abiding life-dissatisfaction—the feeling that would make him write to Longfellow, in his last phase at Concord, "You can tell far better than I whether there is ever anything worth having in literary reputation, and whether the best achievements seem to have any substance after they grow cold." Hawthorne's basic feelings, however related to that life-dissatisfaction, took the form of an uncertainty of the relation of art to reality. The ingrained irony and skepticism, with which, as we have seen, he dramatized this relation, applied even more rigorously to himself. In one part of himself he wanted to be a solid citizen, "to plod along," as he had put it in that deeply sincere and deeply disingenuous college letter to Louisa, "with the multitude." But often, in despair of entering the common human circle, with its "warm secret," he could see art as a substitute and say that "the most desirable mode of existence might be that of a spiritualized Paul Pry hovering invisible round men and women, witnessing their deeds, searching their hearts, borrowing brightness from their felicity and shade from their sorrow, and retaining no emotion peculiar to himself." And out of this same despair of participating in reality, Hawthorne could write, in 1851, of *Twice-Told Tales*: "They have the pale tint of flowers that blossomed in too retired a shade—the coolness of a meditative habit, which diffuses itself through the feeling and observation of every sketch. Instead of passion there is sentiment."

The same impulse toward the safety of the average which he wrote of to Louisa made him hope, as he reported, that *The Scarlet Letter* would have a happy ending; and the use of the word *hope* is the language of a man working against the inner logic of his materials—and of himself. The kind of fiction that—at the social level of his being anyway—he wanted to write was not what he was deeply compelled to write. For instance, he could say to Fields about the novelist Trollope:

It is odd enough that my own individual taste is for quite another class of novels than those which I myself am able to write. . . . They [the works of Trollope] precisely suit my taste; solid and substantial, whether on the strength of beef and through the inspiration of ale, and just as real as if some giant had hewn a great lump out of the earth and put it under a glass case, with all its inhabitants going about their daily business. . . .

In the preface to *Our Old Home*, even that late in his life, Hawthorne was still bewailing the fact that he had not been able to engage the sort of world Trollope could deal with: "The Present, the Immediate of the Actual, has proved too potent for me." And even in the moment of his great triumph, at the time of *The Scarlet Letter*, as though from a perversely resolute need of his nature, he complained that he had missed "reality"; in speaking of the daily life in the custom house, he says:

The wise effort would have been, to diffuse thought and imagination through the opaque substance of today, and thus to make it a bright transparency. . . . A better book than I shall ever write was there; leaf after leaf presenting itself to me, just as it was written out by the reality of the flitting hour, and vanishing as fast as written, only because my brain wanted the insight and my hand the cunning to transcribe it.

To transcribe it: the very phrase tells the story. He could not transcribe; he was cursed with creation. And he could create only by his own inner laws.

Yet, ironically, Hawthorne did possess this power of transcription, but he was able to use it only when he was keeping a journal or writing a letter—not creating fiction; he did have this same gift for rendering the literal surface of that common reality which he so yearned to join and which he so much admired Trollope and others for being able to render. He himself could describe to the life a cranky character in back-country New England or present as convincingly as ever Trollope could a dinner of the Lord Mayor of Liverpool. The point is that once Hawthorne left the level of documentation and began to write fiction, he had to confront his own genius, and that genius demanded, and the complexity of his own innermost nature compelled, that he engage his materials at a level far deeper than that of documentation. In fiction he could use only such materials as could stand transportation into his own peculiar province and could be imaged there in conformity with the laws of that province, his own inner laws.

One of those laws dictated that all material to be useful to him be regarded from a certain perspective of distances, and this meant, as a corollary, that he had to abjure certain materials too grossly rooted in the "opaque world of today." A complex of factors in his family history and in his psychological makeup forced him to turn from the present and seek certainties and compensations in the past, and those factors, in the end, defined the laws of his imagination.

He tried over and over again to break those laws, but he always broke them at his own risk, as, for instance, in *The Blithedale Romance.* Hawthorne's use of the past implied, however, certain paradoxes. On the one hand, he felt a need for accuracy. He wanted the right detail, the mooring in firm fact—or at least the illusion of a mooring in fact, as in the "Custom House," which so anomalously and in such a contradictory spirit appears as the preface to *The Scarlet Letter*; at the same time, he was, by turning to the past, repudiating the demand for factuality which is the present. Again, though he turned to tales of violence and passion, the violence and passion had to be in the past, for, as he put it, poetry "is a plant that thrives best in spots where blood has been spilt long ago." We may say that Hawthorne, though yearning toward violence and passion, could deal only with the image of violence, the reflection of passion. Involvement, even the sense of involvement, was not, in spite of all his yearnings, for him, and what he could give was, in the end, the spiritual shape, the moral profile, the "meaning." It is characteristic that *The Scarlet Letter* begins, not in the period of love encounters between Hester and Dimmesdale, but with the moment when consequences must be dealt with.

Hawthorne's attempt to describe the kind of book he was doomed to write tells us something

of this province of his imagination. The "romance," as he distinguished it from the novel, is what he undertook to write. A famous passage from the preface to *The Marble Faun* gives one key to the distinction. He says that he had chosen Italy

> as affording a sort of poetic or faery precinct, where actualities would not be too terribly insisted upon as they are, and must needs be, in America. No author, without a trial, can conceive of the difficulty of writing a romance about a country where there is no shadow, no antiquity, no mystery, no picturesque and gloomy wrong, nor anything but a commonplace prosperity, in broad and simple daylight, as is happily the case with my native land.[18]

Distance in space, distance in time, shadowy uncertainty—these are the requisites. In the "faery precinct" Hawthorne can avoid being distracted by the demands of an urgent present and can devote himself to tracing the inner reality, which, in that shadowy light, will be both clearer in outline—that is, more typical— and more massively ambiguous in meaning than would be true in a narrative committed to reporting the "opaque substance of today." This difference comes very clear if we think of the contrast between an ordinary historical novel and one of Hawthorne's fictions grounded in history. The novelist—at least the novelist as Hawthorne conceived him in contrast to the writer of romances—would be concerned, in large part at least, with recreating the actualities of the past, aiming at the involvement of the

---

[18] Later Henry James was to voice something of the same complaint about American life. And there is the ironical expression of it in Robert Frost's poem "New Hampshire":

I don't know what to say about the people.
For art's sake one could almost wish them worse
Rather than better. How are we to write
The Russian novel in America
As long as life goes so unterribly?
There is the pinch from which our only outcry
In literature today is heard to come.
We get what little misery we can
Out of not having cause for misery.
It makes the guild of novel writers sick
To be expected to be Dostoevskis
On nothing worse than too much luck and comfort.

reader in the urgencies of the recreated world. But the writer of romance would use the actualities of the past as a means of validating and generalizing—at a distance for clarity of outline —the moral and psychological drama. *The historical novelist aims, then, at converting the past into a kind of virtual present; the writer of romance aims at converting the past into a myth for the present.*

The "faery precinct," the "neutral ground" between the mind and the world, between the idea and nature, between the past and the present—that was his province. There his imagination might arrive at its truth beyond the truth of fact. And here we have, in this shadowy territory, something very like the half-light or moonlight by which, according to Coleridge and some of the other Romantics, imaginative truth can be envisioned.

We have seen how, in one sense, fiction is for Hawthorne, as it was for Poe, another alienated man, a projection of his problem of relating himself to "reality." The work of art is, for the alienated man, his crucial connection with that world beyond him, and it is no wonder that Hawthorne's fiction should carry some of the complexity and tensions of his dilemma vis-à-vis that world. In its best exemplars, his fiction was multiphase, "thick," with various levels of meaning, referring to his own inner, personal story, his own obsessive concerns, as well as to moral, philosophical, and psychological generalizations, and to the world beyond presented in the objective story as told. It was this need for "thickness" that dictated what he called his "blasted allegories"—or what we may call his symbolic fictions. For only by such a symbolic method can be condensed a complex of meanings, as in "My Kinsman, Major Molineux," "Young Goodman Brown," or *The Scarlet Letter*, where the implications are not only massive but often contradictory and paradoxical, as in life itself.

The fact that Hawthorne was aware of the intuitive and obscure process by which his work was characteristically composed, and of the contradictory and paradoxical nature of the result, is indicated in the introductory passage of "Wake-field." Referring to the germ episode from which the story developed, he says that he had brooded upon it for a long time without being able to specify its meaning. He writes: "When ever any subject so forcibly affects the mind, time is well spent in thinking of it. . . ." He trusts, he continues, "that there will be a pervading spirit and a moral, even should we fail to find them, done up neatly, and condensed into the final sentence." He implies, therefore, that he writes not *from* a predetermined meaning ("moral" in his terminology), but *toward* a meaning, creation thus being a process of discovery, ultimately of self-discovery.

We know, however, that Hawthorne was never sure how far to trust either his practice or his theorizing. For instance, in 1854, in a letter to Field, he says: "I am not quite sure that I entirely comprehend my own meaning in some of these blasted allegories." There may well have been, as some critics have suggested, a split in Hawthorne between his rationalistic eighteenth-century education and cast of mind (which might find allegory congenial, in that allegory involves rather mechanically point-to-point equations of meaning) and his tendency toward symbolism, with its density and condensation of meaning.[19] Symbolism, as Charles Feidelson, Jr., puts it, defied the "analysis of his mind" and "at once fascinated and horrified him." Yet why, we may well ask, should symbolism, the only method by which his genius succeeded in fully delivering itself, have "horrified" him?

It did so for the very fact that, as both method and created object, it involved that fullest delivery which his genius could make. With this, then, we come to the obsessive concern of Hawthorne's works: the struggle to achieve self-knowledge. His fictions are constantly concerned with "secrets"—the secret curse, the secret motive, the secret guilt, the secret penance, the secret potion, formula, or elixir, the secret behind the various masks of vice or virtue—which the world wears, and even the "warm secret" of common human happiness. Hawthorne did not, without reason, refer

[19] There is something of the same split in Poe. See pp. 362–65.

to himself as a Paul Pry, but if his fictions represent his prying into the secrets of others, they also represent, even more fully, his prying into his own secret life. His stories are always stories of someone caught in delusions, obsessions, and compulsions and struggling, consciously or unconsciously, toward freedom and peace; and we may reasonably take it that the root story of a writer's work reflects, however indirectly, the root story of a writer's life. The work is, necessarily, part of the life.

But the "horror" of symbolism which Feidelson notes in Hawthorne leads straight to the many stories about artists (or artist figures), such as "The Artist of the Beautiful," "The Snow Image," "Ethan Brand," "The Birthmark," and "Rappaccini's Daughter." On one hand, Hawthorne could be contemptuous of art, as in "The Artist of the Beautiful," because the artist, out of weakness and frustration, deals in illusion and not reality. On the other hand, he could fear art as somehow destructive—the "somehow" varying from instance to instance, but getting one of the clearest statements in relation to Ethan Brand, an artist figure: "He was no longer a brother, and opening the chambers of the dungeons of our common nature by the key of holy sympathy, which gave him a right to share in all its secrets; he was now a cold observer . . . converting man and woman to be his puppets." But contempt and fear both represent repudiations of art: art "reveals," and one of the most terrible things it reveals, we may add, is not that the artist converts man and woman into puppets, but that the artist may become a "puppet" caught in a process that he has initiated but cannot control.

When there is a struggle for self-knowledge, it may well be that it is undertaken in the face of a guilty fear of success in that very struggle: the knowledge may be too terrible to bear. If that dangerous knowledge is discovered through, and embodied in, symbolism, then the fear of that knowledge may readily be transformed into a fear of the symbolism involving it—especially if the writer, as Hawthorne says of himself, is not always able, or willing, to fully decipher the burden of the symbol.

The knowledge represented in Hawthorne's work involved, over and over again, images of a peculiar violence and a peculiar aura—incest, patricide, murder, betrayal, mysterious guilts, thwarted or perverted sexualities. Fresh from the effort of creating *The Scarlet Letter*, Hawthorne called it a "hell-fired story," but all of his work, except the most trivial pieces, are, in the same sense, "hell-fired." They are all images of the mystic dream that all men, in one way or another, pass through if they are to reach manhood; this is the fascination the fictions have carried, even if the cool style and the air, equally deceptive, of the author as a detached moralist have helped generations of readers to deceive themselves about the nature of the fascination they felt.

The first glory of Hawthorne's art is that through it he managed to distinguish and render images of that infinitely complicated process by which self-knowledge may be approached. The second glory is that out of the personal struggle he managed to create images which, without losing the urgency of the individual (author or character), embodied the relevance of the typical, and which, in such typicality, serve as mirrors of haunting revelation to us all.

Caught in the painful intensity of his own fate as artist and as man, Hawthorne sometimes felt that the effort "to typicalize" would bleach out reality from his work and leave but the "pale tint of flowers that blossom in too retired a shade," but it was, in another sense, only by the effort to achieve typicality that he could, in some degree, be relieved of that intensity. If he could not sink himself in the "multitude" whom he assumed to have the "warm secret" of the untroubled, unreflecting, natural joy of life (or the ignorance of life, as he would sometimes have put it), he might find relief in projecting his own plight as typical and thus enter another communion: he might enter the communion of the generalized human fate, of what he called "our common nature," and in that find, perhaps, the warmth of pity given and the strength of fortitude achieved.

A third glory of Hawthorne's art is that, in creating the first American fiction of "inwardness," of what Henry James, in reference to him, called the "deeper psychology," Hawthorne also caught and dramatized a fundamental change in American life, for he often set his characters, as in *The Scarlet Letter*, in conflict with society. It may be said that Leatherstocking, too, is in conflict with society, and in a sense he is. But the difference is that with Leatherstocking there is a minimum of "inwardness," while in Hawthorne the inward and the outward dramas are intricately intertwined and constitute, in fact, a coherent dialectic. And this dialectic of inward and outward dramas is what distinguishes Hawthorne's achievement from the work of Poe; for with Poe there is only the drama of "inwardness."

But there is another glory of Hawthorne's art: it is art.

BIOGRAPHICAL CHART

1804 Born, July 4, in Salem, Massachusetts; descended on both sides from prominent New England ancestors

1808 Father, a sea captain, dies at Surinam, leaving the family dependent on relatives

1821–25 Attends Bowdoin College, with Longfellow and Franklin Pierce his classmates; upon graduation returns to Salem and spends the next twelve years in seclusion

1828 *Fanshawe: A Tale*, published anonymously at his own expense

1837 *Twice-Told Tales*

1839 Becomes engaged to Sophia Peabody

1839–40 Works as a measurer in the Boston custom house

1841 Joins Brook Farm community, West Roxbury, Massachusetts; invests over a thousand dollars in the venture but withdraws by the end of the year

1842–45 Marries; lives at the Old Manse, Concord

1846 *Mosses from an Old Manse*

1846–49 Works as a surveyor in the Salem custom house

1850 *The Scarlet Letter*; friendship with Herman Melville (see our essay on Melville)

1851 *The House of the Seven Gables* and *The Snow Image*

1852 *The Blithedale Romance*; campaign biography of Franklin Pierce

1853–57 Serves as United States consul at Liverpool

1857–59 Rome and Florence

1860 *The Marble Faun*; returns to the United States

1863 *Our Old Home*

1864 Dies, May 19, in Plymouth, New Hampshire, leaving four unfinished novels: *The Ancestral Footstep, Dr. Grimshawe's Secret, Septimus Felton,* and *The Dolliver Romance*

FURTHER READINGS

A definitive edition of the works of Hawthorne, edited by the late William Charvat *et al.*, is in the process of being issued. Meanwhile the standard edition is The Old Manse Edition (1904; 22 vols.).

Randall Stewart, ed., *American Notebooks* (1932; 1960)

Newton Arvin, *Hawthorne* (1929)
Marius Bewley, *The Complex Fate* (1952)
———, *The Eccentric Design* (1959)
Agnes Donohue, ed., *Casebook on the Hawthorne Question* (1962)
Charles Feidelson, Jr., *Symbolism and American Literature* (1953)
Leslie Fiedler, *Love and Death in the American Novel* (1960)
Daniel G. Hoffman, *Form and Fable in American Fiction* (1961)
Henry James, *Hawthorne* (1879)

A. N. Kaul, *The American Vision* (1963)
Harry Levin, *The Power of Blackness: Hawthorne, Poe, Melville* (1958)
R. W. B. Lewis, *The American Adam: Innocence, Tragedy, and Tradition in the Nineteenth Century* (1955)
F. O. Matthiessen, *American Renaissance* (1941)
Randall Stewart, *Nathaniel Hawthorne: A Biography* (1948)
Arlin Turner, *Nathaniel Hawthorne: An Introduction and Interpretation* (1961)
Mark Van Doren, *Nathaniel Hawthorne: A Critical Biography* (1949)
Edward C. Wagenknecht, *Nathaniel Hawthorne: Man and Writer* (1961)
Hyatt Waggoner, *Hawthorne: A Critical Study* (1955)
Austin Warren, *Rage for Order* (1948)
Yvor Winters, *Maule's Curse* (1947)

The Gentle Boy (1828)

In the course of the year 1656, several of the people called Quakers, led, as they professed, by the inward movement of the spirit, made their appearance in New England. Their reputation, as holders of mystic and pernicious principles, having spread before them, the Puritans early endeavored to banish, and to prevent the further intrusion of the rising sect. But the measures by which it was intended to purge the land of heresy, though more than sufficiently vigorous, were entirely unsuccessful. The Quakers, esteeming persecution as a divine call to the post of danger, laid claim to a holy courage, unknown to the Puritans themselves, who had shunned the cross, by providing for the peaceable exercise of their religion in a distant wilderness. Though it was the singular fact, that every nation of the earth rejected the wandering enthusiasts who practised peace towards all men, the place of greatest uneasiness and peril, and therefore, in their eyes the most eligible, was the province of Massachusetts Bay.

The fines, imprisonments, and stripes, liberally distributed by our pious forefathers; the popular antipathy, so strong that it endured nearly a hundred years after actual persecution had ceased, were attractions as powerful for the Quakers, as peace, honor, and reward, would have been for the worldly minded. Every European vessel brought new cargoes of the sect, eager to testify against the oppression which they hoped to share; and when shipmasters were restrained by heavy fines from affording them passage, they made long and circuitous journeys through the Indian country, and appeared in the province as if conveyed by a supernatural power. Their enthusiasm, heightened almost to madness by the treatment which they received, produced actions contrary to the rules of decency, as well as of rational religion, and presented a singular contrast to the calm and staid deportment of their sectarian successors of the present day. The command of the spirit, inaudible except to the soul, and not to be controverted on grounds of human wisdom, was made a plea for most indecorous exhibitions, which, abstractedly considered, well deserved the moderate chastisement of the rod. These extravagances, and the persecution which was at once their cause and consequence, continued to increase, till, in the year 1659, the government of Massachusetts Bay indulged two members of the Quaker sect with the crown of martyrdom.

An indelible stain of blood is upon the hands of all who consented to this act, but a large share of the awful responsibility must rest upon the person then at the head of the government. He was a man of narrow mind and imperfect education, and his uncompromising bigotry was made hot and mischievous by violent and hasty passions; he exerted his influence indecorously and unjustifiably to compass the death of the enthusiasts; and his whole conduct, in respect to them, was marked by brutal cruelty. The Quakers, whose revengeful feelings were not less deep because they were inactive, remembered this man and his associates in after times. The historian of the sect affirms that, by the wrath of Heaven, a blight fell upon the land in the vicinity of the "bloody town" of Boston, so that no wheat would grow there; and he takes his stand, as it were, among the graves of the ancient persecutors, and triumphantly recounts the judgments that overtook them, in old age or at the parting hour. He tells us that they died suddenly and violently and in madness; but nothing can exceed the bitter mockery with which he records the loathsome disease, and "death by rottenness," of the fierce and cruel governor.

On the evening of the autumn day that had witnessed the martyrdom of two men of the Quaker persuasion, a Puritan settler was returning from the metropolis to the neighboring country town in which he resided. The air was cool, the sky clear, and the lingering twilight was made brighter by the rays of a young moon, which had now nearly reached the verge of the horizon. The traveller, a man of middle age, wrapped in a gray frieze cloak, quickened his pace when he had reached the outskirts of the town, for a gloomy extent of nearly four miles lay between him and his home. The low, straw-thatched houses were scattered at considerable intervals along the road, and the country having been settled but about thirty years, the tracts of original forest still bore no small proportion to the cultivated ground. The autumn wind wandered among the branches, whirling away the leaves from all except the pine-trees, and moaning as if it lamented the desolation of which it was the instrument. The road had penetrated the mass of woods that lay nearest to the town, and was just emerging into an open space, when the traveller's ears were saluted by a sound more mournful than even that of the wind. It was like the wailing of some one in distress, and it seemed to proceed from beneath a tall and lonely fir-tree, in the centre of a cleared but uninclosed and uncultivated field. The Puritan could not but remember that this was the very spot which had been made accursed a few hours before by the execution of the Quakers, whose bodies had been thrown together into one hasty grave, beneath the tree on which they suffered. He struggled, however, against the superstitious fears which belonged to the age, and compelled himself to pause and listen.

"The voice is most likely mortal, nor have I cause to tremble if it be otherwise," thought he, straining his eyes through the dim moonlight. "Methinks it is like the wailing of a child; some infant, it may be, which has strayed from its mother, and chanced upon this place of death. For the ease of mine own conscience I must search this matter out."

He therefore left the path, and walked somewhat fearfully across the field. Though now so desolate, its soil was pressed down and trampled by the thousand footsteps of those who had witnessed the spectacle of that day, all of whom had now retired, leaving the dead to their loneliness. The traveller at length reached the fir-tree, which from the middle upward was covered with living branches, although a scaffold had been erected beneath, and other preparations made for the work of death. Under this unhappy tree, which in after times was believed to drop poison with its dew, sat the one solitary mourner for innocent blood. It was a slender and light clad little boy, who leaned his face upon a hillock of fresh-turned and half-frozen earth, and wailed bitterly, yet in a suppressed tone, as if his grief might receive the punishment of crime. The Puritan, whose approach had been unperceived, laid his hand upon the child's shoulder, and addressed him compassionately.

"You have chosen a dreary lodging, my poor boy, and no wonder you weep," said he. "But dry your eyes, and tell me where your mother dwells. I promise you, if the journey be not too far, I will leave you in her arms to-night."

The boy had hushed his wailing at once, and turned his face upward to the stranger. It was a pale, bright-eyed countenance, certainly not more than six years old, but sorrow, fear, and want had destroyed much of its infantile expression. The Puritan seeing the boy's frightened gaze, and feeling that he trembled under his hand, endeavored to reassure him.

"Nay, if I intended to do you harm, little lad, the readiest way were to leave you here. What! you do not fear to sit beneath the gallows on a new-made grave, and yet you tremble at a friend's touch. Take heart, child, and tell me what is your name and where is your home?"

"Friend," replied the little boy, in a sweet though faltering voice, "they call me Ilbrahim, and my home is here."

The pale, spiritual face, the eyes that seemed to mingle with the moonlight, the sweet, airy voice, and the outlandish name, almost made the Puritan believe that the boy was in truth a being which had sprung up out of the grave on which he sat. But perceiving that the apparition stood the test of a short mental prayer, and remembering that the arm which he had touched was lifelike, he adopted a more rational supposition. "The poor child is stricken in his intellect," thought he, "but verily his words are fearful in a place like this." He then spoke soothingly, intending to humor the boy's fantasy.

"Your home will scarce be comfortable, Ilbrahim, this cold autumn night, and I fear you are ill-provided with food. I am hastening to a warm supper and bed, and if you will go with me you shall share them!"

"I thank thee, friend, but though I be hungry, and shivering with cold, thou wilt not give me food nor lodging," replied the boy, in the quiet tone which despair had taught him, even so young. "My father was of the people whom all men hate. They have laid him under this heap of earth, and here is my home."

The Puritan, who had laid hold of little Ilbrahim's hand, relinquished it as if he were touching a loathsome reptile. But he possessed a compassionate heart, which not even religious prejudice could harden into stone.

"God forbid that I should leave this child to perish, though he comes of the accursed sect," said he to himself. "Do we not all spring from an evil root? Are we not all in darkness till the light doth shine upon us? He shall not perish, neither in body, nor, if prayer and instruction may avail for him, in soul." He then spoke aloud and kindly to Ilbrahim, who had again hid his face in the cold earth of the grave. "Was every door in the land shut against you, my child, that you have wandered to this unhallowed spot?"

"They drove me forth from the prison when they took my father thence," said the boy, "and I stood afar off watching the crowd of people, and when they were gone I came hither, and found only his grave. I knew that my father was sleeping here, and I said this shall be my home."

"No, child, no; not while I have a roof over my head, or a morsel to share with you!" exclaimed the Puritan, whose sympathies were now fully excited. "Rise up and come with me, and fear not any harm."

The boy wept afresh, and clung to the heap of earth as if the cold heart beneath it were warmer to him than any in a living breast. The traveller, however, continued to entreat him tenderly, and seeming to acquire some degree of confidence, he at length arose. But his slender limbs tottered with weakness, his little head grew dizzy, and he leaned against the tree of death for support.

"My poor boy, are you so feeble?" said the Puritan. "When did you taste food last?"

"I ate of bread and water with my father in the prison," replied Ilbrahim, "but they brought him none neither yesterday nor to-day, saying that he had eaten enough to bear him to his journey's end. Trouble not thyself for my hunger, kind friend, for I have lacked food many times ere now."

The traveller took the child in his arms and wrapped his cloak about him, while his heart stirred with shame and anger against the gratuitous cruelty of the instruments in this persecution. In the awakened warmth of his feelings he resolved that, at whatever risk, he would not forsake the poor little defenceless being whom Heaven had confided to his care. With this determination he left the accursed field, and resumed the homeward path from which the wailing of the boy had called him. The light and motionless burden scarcely impeded his progress, and he soon beheld the fire rays from the windows of the cottage which he, a native of a distant clime, had built in the western wilderness. It was surrounded by a considerable extent of cultivated ground, and the dwelling was situated in the nook of a wood-covered hill, whither it seemed to have crept for protection.

"Look up, child," said the Puritan to Ilbrahim, whose faint head had sunk upon his shoulders, "there is our home."

At the word "home," a thrill passed through the child's frame, but he continued silent. A few moments brought them to a cottage door, at which the owner knocked; for at that early period, when savages were wandering everywhere among the settlers, bolt and bar were indispensable to the security of a dwelling. The summons was answered by a bond-servant, a coarse-clad and dull-featured piece of humanity, who, after ascertaining that his master was the applicant, undid the door, and held a flaring pine-knot torch to light him in. Farther back in the passage-way, the red blaze discovered a matronly woman, but no little crowd of children came bounding forth to greet their father's return. As the Puritan entered, he thrust aside his cloak, and displayed Ilbrahim's face to the female.

"Dorothy, here is a little outcast, whom Providence hath put into our hands," observed he. "Be kind to him, even as if he were of those dear ones who have departed from us."

"What pale and bright-eyed little boy is this, Tobias?" she inquired. "Is he one whom the wilderness folk have ravished from some Christian mother?"

"No, Dorothy, this poor child is no captive from the wilderness," he replied. "The heathen savage would have given him to eat of his scanty morsel, and to drink of his birchen cup; but Christian men, alas! had cast him out to die."

Then he told her how he had found him beneath the gallows, upon his father's grave; and how his heart had prompted him, like the speaking of an inward voice, to take the little outcast home, and be kind unto him. He acknowledged his resolution to feed and clothe him, as if he were his own child, and to afford him the instruction which should counteract the pernicious errors hitherto instilled into his infant mind. Dorothy was gifted with even a quicker tenderness than her husband, and she approved of all his doings and intentions.

"Have you a mother, dear child?" she inquired.

The tears burst forth from his full heart, as he attempted to reply; but Dorothy at length understood that he had a mother, who, like the rest of her sect, was a persecuted wanderer. She had been taken from the prison a short time before, carried into the uninhabited wilderness, and left to perish there by hunger or wild beasts. This was no uncommon method of disposing of the Quakers, and they were accustomed to boast that the inhabitants of the desert were more hospitable to them than civilized man.

"Fear not, little boy, you shall not need a mother, and a kind one," said Dorothy, when she had gathered this information. "Dry your tears, Ilbrahim, and be my child, as I will be your mother."

The good woman prepared the little bed, from which her own children had successively been borne to another resting-place. Before Ilbrahim would consent to occupy it, he knelt down, and as Dorothy listened to his simple and affecting prayer, she marvelled how the parents that had taught it to him could have been judged worthy of death. When the boy had fallen asleep, she bent over his pale and spiritual countenance, pressed a kiss upon his white brow, drew the bedclothes up about his neck, and went away with a pensive gladness in her heart.

Tobias Pearson was not among the earliest emigrants from the old country. He had remained in England during the first years of the civil war, in which he had borne some share as a cornet of dragoons, under Cromwell. But when the ambitious designs of his leader began to develop themselves, he quitted the army of the Parliament, and sought a refuge from the strife, which was no longer holy, among the people of his persuasion in the colony of Massachusetts. A more worldly consideration had perhaps an influence in drawing him thither; for New England offered advantages to men of unprosperous fortunes, as well as to dissatisfied religionists, and Pearson had hitherto found it difficult to provide for a wife and increasing family. To this supposed impurity of motive the more bigoted Puritans were inclined to impute the removal by death of all the children, for whose earthly good the father had been over-thoughtful. They had left their native country blooming like roses, and like roses they had perished in a foreign soil. Those expounders of the ways of Providence, who had thus judged their brother, and attributed his domestic sorrows to his sin, were not more charitable when they saw him and Dorothy endeavoring to fill up the void in their hearts by the adoption of an infant of the accursed sect. Nor did they fail to communicate their disapprobation to Tobias; but the latter, in reply, merely pointed at the little, quiet, lovely boy, whose appearance and deportment were indeed as powerful arguments as could possibly have been adduced in his own favor. Even his beauty, however, and his winning manners, sometimes produced an effect ultimately unfavorable; for the bigots, when the outer surfaces of their iron hearts had been softened and again grew hard, affirmed that no merely natural cause could have so worked upon them.

Their antipathy to the poor infant was also increased by the ill success of divers theological discussions, in which it was attempted to convince him of the errors of his sect. Ilbrahim, it is true, was not a skilful controversialist; but the feeling of his religion was strong as instinct in him, and he could neither be enticed nor driven from the faith which his father had died for. The odium of this stubbornness was shared in a great measure

by the child's protectors, insomuch that Tobias and Dorothy very shortly began to experience a most bitter species of persecution, in the cold regards of many a friend whom they had valued. The common people manifested their opinions more openly. Pearson was a man of some consideration, being a representative to the General Court, and an approved lieutenant in the trainbands, yet within a week after his adoption of Ilbrahim he had been both hissed and hooted. Once, also, when walking through a solitary piece of woods, he heard a loud voice from some invisible speaker; and it cried, "What shall be done to the backslider? Lo! the scourge is knotted for him, even the whip of nine cords, and every cord three knots!" These insults irritated Pearson's temper for the moment; they entered also into his heart, and became imperceptible but powerful workers towards an end which his most secret thought had not yet whispered.

On the second Sabbath after Ilbrahim became a member of their family, Pearson and his wife deemed it proper that he should appear with them at public worship. They had anticipated some opposition to this measure from the boy, but he prepared himself in silence, and at the appointed hour was clad in the new mourning suit which Dorothy had wrought for him. As the parish was then, and during many subsequent years, unprovided with a bell, the signal for the commencement of religious exercises was the beat of a drum. At the first sound of that martial call to the place of holy and quiet thoughts, Tobias and Dorothy set forth, each holding a hand of little Ilbrahim, like two parents linked together by the infant of their love. On their path through the leafless woods they were overtaken by many persons of their acquaintance, all of whom avoided them, and passed by on the other side; but a severer trial awaited their constancy when they had descended the hill, and drew near the pine-built and undecorated house of prayer. Around the door, from which the drummer still sent forth his thundering summons, was drawn up a formidable phalanx, including several of the oldest members of the congregation, many of the middle aged, and nearly all the younger males. Pearson found it difficult to sustain their united and disapproving gaze, but Dorothy, whose mind was differently circumstanced, merely drew the boy closer to her, and faltered not in her approach. As they entered the door, they overheard the muttered sentiments of the assemblage, and when the reviling voices of the little children smote Ilbrahim's ear, he wept.

The interior aspect of the meeting-house was rude. The low ceiling, the unplastered walls, the naked wood work, and the undraperied pulpit, offered nothing to excite the devotion, which, without such external aids, often remains latent in the heart. The floor of the building was occupied by rows of long, cushionless benches, supplying the place of pews, and the broad aisle formed a sexual division, impassable except by children beneath a certain age.

Pearson and Dorothy separated at the door of the meeting-house, and Ilbrahim, being within the years of infancy, was retained under the care of the latter. The wrinkled beldams involved themselves in their rusty cloaks as he passed by; even the mild-featured maidens seemed to dread contamination; and many a stern old man arose, and turned his repulsive and unheavenly countenance upon the gentle boy, as if the sanctuary were polluted by his presence. He was a sweet infant of the skies that had strayed away from his home, and all the inhabitants of this miserable world closed up their impure hearts against him, drew back their earth-soiled garments from his touch, and said, "We are holier than thou."

Ilbrahim, seated by the side of his adopted mother, and retaining fast hold of her hand, assumed a grave and decorous demeanor, such as might befit a person of matured taste and understanding, who should find himself in a temple dedicated to some worship which he did not recognize, but felt himself bound to respect. The exercises had not yet commenced, however, when the boy's attention was arrested by an event, apparently of trifling interest. A woman, having her face muffled in a hood, and a cloak drawn completely about her form, advanced slowly up the broad aisle and took a place upon the foremost bench. Ilbrahim's faint color varied, his nerves fluttered, he was unable to turn his eyes from the muffled female.

When the preliminary prayer and hymn were over, the minister arose, and having turned the hour-glass which stood by the great Bible, commenced his discourse. He was now well stricken in years, a man of pale, thin countenance, and his gray hairs were closely covered by a black velvet skullcap. In his younger days he had practically learned the meaning of persecution from Archbishop Laud, and he was not now disposed to forget the lesson against which he had murmured then. Introducing the often discussed subject of the Quakers, he gave a history of that sect, and a description of their tenets, in which error predominated, and prejudice distorted the aspect of what was true. He adverted to the recent measures in the province, and cautioned his hearers of weaker parts against calling in question the just severity which God-fearing magistrates had at length been compelled to exercise. He spoke of the danger of pity, in some cases a commendable and Christian virtue, but inapplicable to this pernicious sect. He observed that such was their devilish obstinacy in error, that even the little children, the sucking babes, were hardened and desperate heretics. He affirmed that no man, without Heaven's especial warrant, should attempt their conversion, lest while he lent his hand to draw them from the slough, he should be precipitated into its lowest depths.

The sands of the second hour were principally in the lower half of the glass when the sermon concluded. An approving murmur followed, and the clergyman, having given out a hymn, took his seat with much self-congratulation, and endeavored to read the effect of his eloquence in the visages of the people. But while voices from all parts of the house were tuning themselves to sing, a scene occurred, which, though not very unusual at that period in the province, happened to be without precedent in this parish.

The muffled female, who had hitherto sat motionless in the front rank of the audience, now arose, and with slow, stately, and unwavering step, ascended the pulpit stairs. The quiverings of incipient harmony were hushed, and the divine sat in speechless and almost terrified astonishment, while she undid the door, and stood up in the sacred desk from which his maledictions had just been thundered. She then divested herself of the cloak and hood, and appeared in a most singular array. A shapeless robe of sackcloth was girded about her waist with a knotted cord; her raven hair fell down upon her shoulders, and its blackness was defiled by pale streaks of ashes, which she had strown upon her head. Her eyebrows, dark and strongly defined, added to the deathly whiteness of a countenance, which, emaciated with want, and wild with enthusiasm and strange sorrows, retained no trace of earlier beauty. This figure stood gazing earnestly on the audience, and there was no sound, nor any movement, except a faint shuddering which every man observed in his neighbor, but was scarcely conscious of in himself. At length, when her fit of inspiration came, she spoke, for the first few moments, in a low voice, and not invariably distinct utterance. Her discourse gave evidence of an imagination hopelessly entangled with her reason; it was a vague and incomprehensible rhapsody, which, however, seemed to spread its own atmosphere round the hearer's soul, and to move his feelings by some influence unconnected with the words. As she proceeded, beautiful but shadowy images would sometimes be seen, like bright things moving in a turbid river; or a strong and singularly-shaped idea leaped forth, and seized at once on the understanding or the heart. But the course of her unearthly eloquence soon led her to the persecutions of her sect, and from thence the step was short to her own peculiar sorrows. She was naturally a woman of mighty passions, and hatred and revenge now wrapped themselves in the garb of piety; the character of her speech was changed, her images became distinct though wild, and her denunciations had an almost hellish bitterness.

"The Governor and his mighty men," she said, "have gathered together, taking counsel among themselves and saying, 'What shall we do unto this people—even unto the people that have come into this land to put our iniquity to the blush?' And lo! the devil entereth into the council chamber, like a lame man of low stature and gravely apparelled, with a dark and twisted countenance, and a bright, downcast eye. And he standeth up among the rulers; yea, he goeth to and fro, whispering to each; and every man lends his ear, for his word is 'Slay, slay!' But I say unto ye, Woe to them that slay! Woe to them that shed the blood of saints! Woe to them that have slain the husband, and cast forth the child, the tender infant, to wander homeless and hungry and cold, till he die; and have saved the mother alive, in the cruelty of their tender mercies! Woe to them in their lifetime! cursed are they in the delight and pleasure of their hearts! Woe to them in their death hour, whether it come swiftly with blood and violence, or after long and lingering pain! Woe, in the dark house, in the rottenness of the grave, when the children's children shall revile the ashes of the fathers! Woe, woe, woe, at the judgment, when all the persecuted and all the slain in this bloody land, and the father, the mother, and the child, shall await them in a day that they cannot escape! Seed of the faith, seed of the faith, ye whose hearts are moving with a power that ye know not, arise, wash your hands of this innocent blood! Lift your voices, chosen ones; cry aloud, and call down a woe and a judgment with me!"

Having thus given vent to the flood of malignity which she mistook for inspiration, the speaker was silent. Her voice was succeeded by the hysteric shrieks of several women, but the feelings of the audience generally had not been drawn onward in the current with her own. They remained stupefied, stranded as it were, in the midst of a torrent, which deafened them by its roaring, but might not move them by its violence. The clergyman, who could not hitherto have ejected the usurper of his pulpit otherwise than by bodily force, now addressed her in the tone of just indignation and legitimate authority.

"Get you down, woman, from the holy place which you profane," he said. "Is it to the Lord's house that you come to pour forth the foulness of your heart and the inspiration of the devil? Get you down, and remember that the sentence of death is on you; yea, and shall be executed, were it but for this day's work!"

"I go, friend, I go, for the voice hath had its utterance," replied she, in a depressed and even mild tone. "I have done my mission unto thee and to thy people. Reward me with stripes, imprisonment, or death, as ye shall be permitted."

The weakness of exhausted passion caused her steps to totter as she descended the pulpit stairs. The people, in the meanwhile, were stirring to and fro on the floor of the house, whispering among themselves, and glancing towards the intruder. Many of them now recognized her as the woman who had assaulted the Governor with frightful language as he passed by the window of her prison; they knew, also, that she was adjudged to suffer death, and had been preserved only by an involuntary banishment into the wilderness. The new outrage, by which she had provoked her fate, seemed to render further lenity impossible; and a gentleman in military dress, with a stout man of inferior rank, drew towards the door of the meeting-house, and awaited her approach.

Scarcely did her feet press the floor, however, when an unexpected scene occurred. In that moment of her peril, when every eye frowned with death, a little timid boy pressed forth, and threw his arms round his mother.

"I am here, mother; it is I, and I will go with thee to prison," he exclaimed.

She gazed at him with a doubtful and almost frightened expression, for she knew that the boy had been cast out to perish, and she had not hoped to see his face again. She feared, perhaps, that it was but one of the happy visions with which her excited fancy had often deceived her, in the solitude of the desert or in prison. But when she felt his hand warm within her own, and heard his little eloquence of childish love, she began to know that she was yet a mother.

"Blessed art thou, my son," she sobbed. "My heart was withered; yea, dead with thee and with thy father; and now it leaps as in the first moment when I pressed thee to my bosom."

She knelt down and embraced him again and again, while the joy that could find no words expressed itself in broken accents, like the bubbles gushing up to vanish at the surface of a deep fountain. The sorrows of past years, and the darker peril that was nigh, cast not a shadow on the brightness of that fleeting moment. Soon, however, the spectators saw a change upon her face, as the consciousness of her sad estate returned, and grief supplied the fount of tears which joy had opened. By the words she uttered, it would seem that the indulgence of natural love had given her mind a momentary sense of its errors, and made her know how far she had strayed from duty in following the dictates of a wild fanaticism.

"In a doleful hour art thou returned to me, poor boy," she said, "for thy mother's path has gone darkening onward, till now the end is death. Son, son, I have borne thee in my arms when my limbs were tottering, and I have fed thee with the food that I was fainting for; yet I have ill performed a mother's part by thee in life, and now I leave thee no inheritance but woe and shame. Thou wilt go seeking through the world, and find all hearts closed against thee and their sweet affections turned to bitterness for my sake. My child, my child, how many a pang awaits thy gentle spirit, and I the cause of all!"

She hid her face on Ilbrahim's head, and her long, raven hair, discolored with the ashes of her mourning, fell down about him like a veil. A low and interrupted moan was the voice of her heart's anguish, and it did not fail to move the sympathies of many who mistook their involuntary virtue for a sin. Sobs were audible in the female section of the house, and every man who was a father drew his hand across his eyes. Tobias Pearson was agitated and uneasy, but a certain feeling like the consciousness of guilt oppressed him, so that he could not go forth and offer himself as the protector of the child. Dorothy, however, had watched her husband's eye. Her mind was free from the influence that had begun to work on his, and she drew near the Quaker woman, and addressed her in the hearing of all the congregation.

"Stranger, trust this boy to me, and I will be his mother," she said, taking Ilbrahim's hand. "Providence has signally marked out my husband to protect him, and he has fed at our table and lodged under our roof now many days, till our hearts have grown very strongly unto him. Leave the tender child with us, and be at ease concerning his welfare."

The Quaker rose from the ground, but drew the boy closer to her, while she gazed earnestly in Dorothy's face. Her mild but saddened features, and neat matronly attire, harmonized together, and were like a verse of fireside poetry. Her very aspect proved that she was blameless, so far as mortal could be so, in respect to God and man; while the enthusiast, in her robe of sackcloth and girdle of knotted cord, had as evidently violated the duties of the present life and the future, by fixing her attention wholly on the latter. The two females, as they held each a hand of Ilbrahim, formed a practical allegory; it was rational piety and unbridled fanaticism contending for the empire of a young heart.

"Thou art not of our people," said the Quaker, mournfully.

"No, we are not of your people," replied Dorothy, with mildness, "but we are Christians, looking upward to the same heaven with you. Doubt not that your boy shall meet you there, if there be a blessing on our tender and prayerful guidance of him. Thither, I trust, my own children have gone before me, for I also have been a mother; I am no longer so," she added, in a faltering tone, "and your son will have all my care."

"But will ye lead him in the path which his parents have trodden?" demanded the Quaker. "Can ye teach him the enlightened faith which his father has died for, and for which I, even I, am soon to become an unworthy martyr? The boy has been baptized in blood; will ye keep the mark fresh and ruddy upon his forehead?"

"I will not deceive you," answered Dorothy. "If your child become our child, we must breed him up in the instruction which Heaven has imparted to us; we must pray for him the prayers of our own faith; we must do towards him according to the dictates of our own consciences, and not of yours. Were we to act otherwise, we should abuse your trust, even in complying with your wishes."

The mother looked down upon her boy with a troubled countenance, and then turned her eyes upward to heaven. She seemed to pray internally, and the contention of her soul was evident.

"Friend," she said at length to Dorothy, "I

doubt not that my son shall receive all earthly tenderness at thy hands. Nay, I will believe that even thy imperfect lights may guide him to a better world, for surely thou art on the path thither. But thou hast spoken of a husband. Doth he stand here among this multitude of people? Let him come forth, for I must know to whom I commit this most precious trust."

She turned her face upon the male auditors, and after a momentary delay, Tobias Pearson came forth from among them. The Quaker saw the dress which marked his military rank, and shook her head; but then she noted the hesitating air, the eyes that struggled with her own, and were vanquished; the color that went and came, and could find no resting-place. As she gazed, an unmirthful smile spread over her features, like sunshine that grows melancholy in some desolate spot. Her lips moved inaudibly, but at length she spake.

"I hear it, I hear it. The voice speaketh within me and saith, 'Leave thy child, Catharine, for his place is here, and go hence, for I have other work for thee. Break the bonds of natural affection, martyr thy love, and know that in all these things eternal wisdom hath its ends.' I go, friends; I go. Take ye my boy, my precious jewel. I go hence, trusting that all shall be well, and that even for his infant hands there is a labor in the vineyard."

She knelt down and whispered to Ilbrahim, who at first struggled and clung to his mother, with sobs and tears, but remained passive when she had kissed his cheek and arisen from the ground. Having held her hands over his head in mental prayer, she was ready to depart.

"Farewell, friends in mine extremity," she said to Pearson and his wife; "the good deed ye have done me is a treasure laid up in heaven, to be returned a thousand-fold hereafter. And farewell ye, mine enemies, to whom it is not permitted to harm so much as a hair of my head, nor to stay my footsteps even for a moment. The day is coming when ye shall call upon me to witness for ye to this one sin uncommitted, and I will rise up and answer."

She turned her steps toward the door, and the men, who had stationed themselves to guard it, withdrew, and suffered her to pass. A general sentiment of pity overcame the virulence of religious hatred. Sanctified by her love and her affliction, she went forth, and all the people gazed after her till she had journeyed up the hill, and was lost behind its brow. She went, the apostle of her own unquiet heart, to renew the wanderings of past years. For her voice had been already heard in many lands of Christendom; and she had pined in the cells of a Catholic Inquisition before she felt the lash and lay in the dungeons of the Puritans. Her mission had extended also to the followers of the Prophet, and from them she had received the courtesy and kindness which all the contending sects of our purer religion united to deny her. Her husband and herself had resided many months in Turkey, where even the Sultan's countenance was gracious to them; in that pagan land, too, was Ilbrahim's birthplace, and his oriental name was a mark of gratitude for the good deeds of an unbeliever.

When Pearson and his wife had thus acquired all the rights over Ilbrahim that could be delegated, their affection for him became like the memory of their native land, or their mild sorrow for the dead, a piece of the immovable furniture of their hearts. The boy, also, after a week or two of mental disquiet, began to gratify his protectors by many inadvertent proofs that he considered them as parents, and their house as home. Before the winter snows were melted, the persecuted infant, the little wanderer from a remote and heathen country, seemed native in the New England cottage, and inseparable from the warmth and security of its hearth. Under the influence of kind treatment, and in the consciousness that he was loved, Ilbrahim's demeanor lost a premature manliness, which had resulted from his earlier situation; he became more childlike, and his natural character displayed itself with freedom. It was in many respects a beautiful one, yet the disordered imaginations of both his father and mother had perhaps propagated a certain unhealthiness in the mind of the boy. In his general state, Ilbrahim would derive enjoyment from the most trifling events, and from every object about him; he seemed to discover rich treasures of happiness, by a faculty analogous to that of the witch hazel, which points to hidden gold where all is barren to the eye. His airy gayety, coming to him from a thousand sources, communicated itself to the family, and Ilbrahim was like a domesticated sunbeam, brightening moody countenances, and chasing away the gloom from the dark corners of the cottage.

On the other hand, as the susceptibility of pleasure is also that of pain, the exuberant cheerfulness of the boy's prevailing temper sometimes yielded to moments of deep depression. His sorrows could not always be followed up to their original source, but most frequently they appeared to flow, though Ilbrahim was young to be sad for such a cause, from wounded love. The flightiness of his mirth rendered him often guilty of offences against the decorum of a Puritan household, and on these occasions he did not invariably escape rebuke. But the slightest word of real bitterness, which he was infallible in distinguishing from pretended anger, seemed to sink into his heart and poison all his enjoyments, till he became sensible that he was entirely forgiven. Of the malice, which generally accompanies a superfluity of sensitiveness, Ilbrahim was altogether destitute: when trodden upon, he would not turn; when wounded, he could but die. His mind was wanting in the stamina for self-support; it was a plant that would twine beautifully round something stronger than itself, but if repulsed, or torn away, it had no choice but to wither on the ground. Dorothy's acuteness taught her that severity would crush the spirit of the child, and she nurtured him with the gentle care of one who handles a butterfly. Her husband manifested an equal affection, although it grew daily less productive of familiar caresses.

The feelings of the neighboring people, in regard to the Quaker infant and his protectors, had not undergone a favorable change, in spite of the momentary triumph which the desolate mother had obtained over their sympathies. The scorn and bitterness, of which he was the object, were very grievous to Ilbrahim, especially when any circumstance made him sensible that the children, his equals in age, partook of the enmity of their parents. His tender and social nature had already overflowed in attachments to everything about him, and still there was a residue of unappropriated love, which he yearned to bestow upon the little ones who were taught to hate him. As the warm days of spring came on, Ilbrahim was accustomed to remain for hours, silent and inactive, within hearing of the children's voices at their play; yet, with his usual delicacy of feeling, he avoided their notice, and would flee and hide himself from the smallest individual among them. Chance, however, at length seemed to open a medium of communication between his heart and theirs; it was by means of a boy about two years older than Ilbrahim, who was injured by a fall from a tree in the vicinity of Pearson's habitation. As the sufferer's own home was at some distance, Dorothy willingly received him under her roof, and became his tender and careful nurse.

Ilbrahim was the unconscious possessor of much skill in physiognomy, and it would have deterred him, in other circumstances, from attempting to make a friend of this boy. The countenance of the latter immediately impressed a beholder disagreeably, but it required some examination to discover that the cause was a very slight distortion of the mouth, and the irregular, broken line, and near approach of the eyebrows. Analogous, perhaps, to these trifling deformities, was an almost imperceptible twist of every joint, and the uneven prominence of the breast; forming a body, regular in its general outline, but faulty in almost all its details. The disposition of the boy was sullen and reserved, and the village schoolmaster stigmatized him as obtuse in intellect; although, at a later period of life, he evinced ambition and very peculiar talents. But whatever might be his personal or moral irregularities, Ilbrahim's heart seized upon, and clung to him, from the moment that he was brought wounded into the cottage; the child of persecution seemed to compare his own fate with that of the sufferer, and to feel that even different modes of misfortune had created a sort of relationship between them. Food, rest, and the fresh air, for which he languished, were neglected; he nestled continually by the bedside of the little stranger, and, with a fond jealousy, endeavored to be the medium of all the cares that were bestowed upon him. As the boy became convalescent, Ilbrahim contrived games suitable to his situation, or amused him by a faculty which he had perhaps breathed in with the air of his barbaric birthplace. It was that of reciting imaginary adventures, on the spur of the moment, and apparently in inexhaustible succession. His tales were of course monstrous, disjointed, and without aim; but they were curious on account of a vein of human tenderness which ran through them all, and was like a sweet, familiar face, encountered in the midst of wild and unearthly scenery. The auditor paid much attention to these romances, and sometimes interrupted them by brief remarks upon the incidents, displaying shrewdness above his years, mingled with a moral obliquity which grated very harshly against Ilbrahim's instinctive rectitude. Nothing, however, could arrest the progress of the latter's affection, and there were many proofs that it met with a response from the dark and stubborn nature on which it was lavished. The boy's parents at length removed him, to complete his cure under their own roof.

Ilbrahim did not visit his new friend after his departure; but he made anxious and continual inquiries respecting him, and informed himself of the day when he was to reappear among his playmates. On a pleasant summer afternoon, the children of the neighborhood had assembled in the little forest-crowned amphitheatre behind the meeting-house, and the recovering invalid was there, leaning on a staff. The glee of a score of untainted bosoms was heard in light and airy voices, which danced among the trees like sunshine become audible; the grown men of this weary world, as they journeyed by the spot, marvelled why life, beginning in such brightness, should proceed in gloom; and their hearts, or their imaginations, answered them and said, that the bliss of childhood gushes from its innocence. But it happened that an unexpected addition was made to the heavenly little band. It was Ilbrahim, who came towards the children with a look of sweet confidence on his fair and spiritual face, as if, having manifested his love to one of them, he had no longer to fear a repulse from their society. A hush came over their mirth the moment they beheld him, and they stood whispering to each other while he drew nigh; but, all at once, the devil of their fathers entered into the unbreeched fanatics, and sending up a fierce, shrill cry, they rushed upon the poor Quaker child. In an instant, he was the centre of a brood of baby-fiends, who lifted sticks against him, pelted him with stones, and displayed an instinct of destruction far more loathsome than the bloodthirstiness of manhood.

The invalid, in the meanwhile, stood apart from the tumult, crying out with a loud voice, "Fear not, Ilbrahim, come hither and take my hand;" and his unhappy friend endeavored to obey him. After watching the victim's struggling approach with a calm smile and unabashed eye, the foul-hearted little villain lifted his staff and struck Ilbrahim on the mouth, so forcibly that the blood issued in a stream. The poor child's arms had been raised to guard his head from the storm of blows; but now he dropped them at once. His persecutors beat him down, trampled upon him, dragged him by his long, fair locks, and Ilbrahim was on the point of becoming as veritable a martyr as ever entered bleeding into heaven. The uproar, however, attracted the notice of a few neighbors, who put themselves to the trouble of rescuing the little heretic, and of conveying him to Pearson's door.

Ilbrahim's bodily harm was severe, but long and careful nursing accomplished his recovery; the injury done to his sensitive spirit was more serious, though not so visible. Its signs were principally of a negative character, and to be discovered only by those who had previously known him. His gait was thenceforth slow, even, and unvaried by the sudden bursts of sprightlier motion, which had once corresponded to his overflowing gladness; his countenance was heavier, and its former play of expression, the dance of sunshine reflected from moving water, was destroyed by the cloud over his existence; his notice was attracted in a far less degree by passing events, and he appeared to find greater difficulty in comprehending what was new to him than at a happier period. A stranger, founding his judgment upon these circumstances, would have said that the dulness of the child's intellect widely contradicted the promise of his features; but the secret was in the direction of Ilbrahim's thoughts, which were brooding within him when they should naturally have been wandering abroad. An attempt of Dorothy to revive his former sportiveness was the single occasion on which his quiet demeanor yielded to a violent display of grief; he burst into passionate weeping, and ran and hid himself, for his heart had become so miserably sore that even the hand of kindness tortured it like fire. Sometimes, at night and probably in his dreams, he was heard to cry "Mother! Mother!" as if her place, which a stranger had supplied while Ilbrahim was happy, admitted of no substitute in his extreme affliction. Perhaps, among the many life-weary wretches then upon the earth, there was not one who combined innocence and misery like this poor, broken-hearted infant, so soon the victim of his own heavenly nature.

While this melancholy change had taken place in Ilbrahim, one of an earlier origin and of different character had come to its perfection in his adopted father. The incident with which this tale commences found Pearson in a state of religious dulness, yet mentally disquieted, and longing for a more fervid faith than he possessed. The first effect of his kindness to Ilbrahim was to produce a softened feeling, and incipient love for the child's whole sect; but joined to this, and resulting perhaps from self-suspicion, was a proud and ostentatious contempt of all their tenets and practical extravagances. In the course of much thought, however, for the subject struggled irresistibly into his mind, the foolishness of the doctrine began to be less evident, and the points which had particularly offended his reason assumed another aspect, or vanished entirely away. The work within him appeared to go on even while he slept, and that which had been a doubt, when he laid down to rest, would often hold the place of a truth, confirmed by some forgotten demonstration, when he recalled his thoughts in the morning. But while he was thus becoming assimilated to the enthusiasts, his contempt, in nowise decreasing towards them, grew very fierce against himself; he imagined, also, that every face of his acquaintance wore a sneer, and that every word addressed to him was a gibe. Such was his state of mind at the period of Ilbrahim's misfortune; and the emotions consequent upon that event completed the change, of which the child had been the original instrument.

In the mean time, neither the fierceness of the persecutors, nor the infatuation of their victims, had decreased. The dungeons were never empty; the streets of almost every village echoed daily with the lash; the life of a woman, whose mild and Christian spirit no cruelty could embitter, had been sacrificed; and more innocent blood was yet to pollute the hands that were so often raised in prayer. Early after the Restoration, the English Quakers represented to Charles II that a "vein of blood was open in his dominions;" but though the displeasure of the voluptuous king was roused, his interference was not prompt. And now the tale must stride forward over many months, leaving Pearson to encounter ignominy and misfortune; his wife to a firm endurance of a thousand sorrows; poor Ilbrahim to pine and droop like a cankered rosebud; his mother to wander on a mistaken errand, neglectful of the holiest trust which can be committed to a woman.

A winter evening, a night of storm, had darkened over Pearson's habitation, and there were no cheerful faces to drive the gloom from his broad hearth. The fire, it is true, sent forth a glowing heat and a ruddy light, and large logs, dripping with half-melted snow, lay ready to be cast upon the embers. But the apartment was saddened in its aspect by the absence of much of the homely wealth which had once adorned it; for the exaction of repeated fines, and his own neglect of temporal affairs, had greatly impoverished the owner. And with the furniture of peace, the implements of war had likewise disappeared; the sword was broken, the helm and cuirass were cast away forever; the soldier had done with battles, and might not lift so much as his naked hand to guard his head. But the Holy Book remained, and the table on which it rested was drawn before the fire, while two of the persecuted sect sought comfort from its pages.

He who listened, while the other read, was the master of the house, now emaciated in form, and altered as to the expression and healthiness of his countenance; for his mind had dwelt too long among visionary thoughts, and his body had been worn by imprisonment and stripes. The hale and weather-beaten old man who sat beside him had sustained less injury from a far longer course of the same mode of life. In person he was tall and dignified, and, which alone would have made him hateful to the Puritans, his gray locks fell from beneath the broad-brimmed hat, and rested on his shoulders. As the old man read the sacred page the snow drifted against the windows, or eddied in at the crevices of the door, while a blast kept laughing in the chimney, and the blaze leaped fiercely up to seek it. And sometimes, when the wind struck the hill at a certain angle, and swept down by the cottage across the wintry plain, its voice was the most doleful that can be conceived; it came as if the Past were speaking, as if the Dead had contributed each a whisper, as if the Desolation of Ages were breathed in that one lamenting sound.

The Quaker at length closed the book, retaining however his hand between the pages which he had been reading, while he looked steadfastly at Pearson. The attitude and features of the latter might have indicated the endurance of bodily pain; he leaned his forehead on his hands, his teeth were firmly closed, and his frame was tremulous at intervals with a nervous agitation.

"Friend Tobias," inquired the old man, compassionately, "hast thou found no comfort in these many blessed passages of Scripture?"

"Thy voice has fallen on my ear like a sound afar off and indistinct," replied Pearson without lifting his eyes. "Yea, and when I have hearkened carefully the words seemed cold and lifeless, and intended for another and a lesser grief than mine. Remove the book," he added, in a tone of sullen bitterness. "I have no part in its consolations, and they do but fret my sorrow the more."

"Nay, feeble brother, be not as one who hath never known the light," said the elder Quaker earnestly, but with mildness. "Art thou he that wouldst be content to give all, and endure all, for conscience' sake; desiring even peculiar trials, that thy faith might be purified and thy heart weaned from worldly desires? And wilt thou sink beneath an affliction which happens alike to them that have their portion here below, and to them that lay up treasure in heaven? Faint not, for thy burden is yet light."

"It is heavy! It is heavier than I can bear!" exclaimed Pearson, with the impatience of a variable spirit. "From my youth upward I have been a man marked out for wrath; and year by year, yea, day after day, I have endured sorrows such as others know not in their lifetime. And now I speak not of the love that has been turned to hatred, the honor to ignominy, the ease and plentifulness of all things to danger, want, and nakedness. All this I could have borne, and counted myself blessed. But when my heart was desolate with many losses I fixed it upon the child of a stranger, and he became dearer to me than all my buried ones; and now he too must die as if my love were poison. Verily, I am an accursed man, and I will lay me down in the dust and lift up my head no more."

"Thou sinnest, brother, but it is not for me to rebuke thee; for I also have had my hours of darkness, wherein I have murmured against the cross," said the old Quaker. He continued, perhaps in the hope of distracting his companion's thoughts from his own sorrows. "Even of late was the light obscured within me, when the men of blood had banished me on pain of death, and the constables led me onward from village to village towards the wilderness. A strong and cruel hand was wielding the knotted cords; they sunk deep into the flesh, and thou mightst have tracked every reel and totter of my footsteps by the blood that followed. As we went on"—

"Have I not borne all this; and have I murmured?" interrupted Pearson impatiently.

"Nay, friend, but hear me," continued the other "As we journeyed on, night darkened on our path, so that no man could see the rage of the persecutors or the constancy of my endurance, though Heaven forbid that I should glory therein. The lights began to glimmer in the cottage windows, and I could discern the inmates as they gathered in comfort and security, every man with his wife and children by their own evening hearth. At length we came to a tract of fertile land; in the dim light, the forest was not visible around it; and behold! there was a straw-thatched dwelling, which bore the very aspect of my home, far over the wild ocean, far in our own England. Then came bitter thoughts upon me; yea, remembrances that were like death to my soul. The happiness of my early days was painted to me; the disquiet of my manhood, the altered faith of my declining years. I remembered how I had been moved to go forth a wanderer when my daughter, the youngest, the dearest of my flock, lay on her dying bed, and."—

"Couldst thou obey the command at such a moment?" exclaimed Pearson, shuddering.

"Yea, yea," replied the old man hurriedly. "I was kneeling by her bedside when the voice spoke loud within me; but immediately I rose, and took my staff, and gat me gone. Oh! that it were permitted me to forget her woful look when I thus withdrew my arm, and left her journeying through the dark valley alone! for her soul was faint, and she had leaned upon my prayers. Now in that night of horror I was assailed by the thought that I had been an erring Christian and a cruel parent; yea, even my daughter, with her pale, dying features, seemed to stand by me and whisper, 'Father, you are deceived; go home and shelter your gray head.' O Thou, to whom I have looked in my farthest wanderings," continued the Quaker, raising his agitated eyes to heaven, "inflict not upon the bloodiest of our persecutors the unmitigated agony of my soul, when I believed that all I had done and suffered for Thee was at the instigation of a mocking fiend! But I yielded not; I knelt down and wrestled with the tempter, while the scourge bit more fiercely into the flesh. My prayer was heard, and I went on in peace and joy towards the wilderness."

The old man, though his fanaticism had generally all the calmness of reason, was deeply moved while reciting this tale; and his unwonted emotion seemed to rebuke and keep down that of his companion. They sat in silence, with their faces to the fire, imagining, perhaps, in its red embers new scenes of persecution yet to be encountered. The snow still drifted hard against the windows, and sometimes, as the blaze of the logs had gradually sunk, came down the spacious chimney and hissed upon the hearth. A cautious footstep might now and then be heard in a neighboring apartment, and the sound invariably drew the eyes of both Quakers to the door which led thither. When a fierce and riotous gust of wind had led his thoughts, by a natural association, to homeless travellers on such a night, Pearson resumed the conversation.

"I have well-nigh sunk under my own share of this trial," observed he, sighing heavily; "yet I would that it might be doubled to me, if so the child's mother could be spared. Her wounds have been deep and many, but this will be the sorest of all."

"Fear not for Catharine," replied the old Quaker, "for I know that valiant woman, and have seen how she can bear the cross. A mother's heart, indeed, is strong in her, and may seem to contend mightily with her faith; but soon she will stand up and give thanks that her son has been thus early an accepted sacrifice. The boy hath done his work, and she will feel that he is taken hence in kindness both to him and her. Blessed, blessed are they that with so little suffering can enter into peace!"

The fitful rush of the wind was now disturbed by a portentous sound; it was a quick and heavy knocking at the outer door. Pearson's wan countenance grew paler, for many a visit of persecution had taught him what to dread; the old man, on the other hand, stood up erect, and his glance was firm as that of the tried soldier who awaits his enemy.

"The men of blood have come to seek me," he observed with calmness. "They have heard how I was moved to return from banishment; and now am I to be led to prison, and thence to death. It is an end I have long looked for. I will open unto them, lest they say, 'Lo, he feareth!' "

"Nay, I will present myself before them," said Pearson, with recovered fortitude. "It may be that they seek me alone, and know not that thou abidest with me."

"Let us go boldly, both one and the other," rejoined his companion. "It is not fitting that thou or I should shrink."

They therefore proceeded through the entry to the door, which they opened, bidding the applicant "Come in, in God's name!" A furious blast of wind drove the storm into their faces, and extinguished the lamp; they had barely time to discern a figure, so white from head to foot with the drifted snow that it seemed like Winter's self, come in human shape, to seek refuge from its own desolation.

"Enter, friend, and do thy errand, be it what it may," said Pearson. "It must needs be pressing, since thou comest on such a bitter night."

"Peace be with this household," said the stranger, when they stood on the floor of the inner apartment.

Pearson started, the elder Quaker stirred the slumbering embers of the fire till they sent up a clear and lofty blaze; it was a female voice that had spoken; it was a female form that shone out, cold and wintry, in that comfortable light.

"Catharine, blessed woman!" exclaimed the old man, "art thou come to this darkened land again? art thou come to bear a valiant testimony as in former years? The scourge hath not prevailed against thee, and from the dungeon hast thou come forth triumphant; but strengthen, strengthen now thy heart, Catharine, for Heaven will prove thee

yet this once, ere thou go to thy reward."

"Rejoice, friends!" she replied. "Thou who hast long been of our people, and thou whom a little child hath led to us, rejoice! Lo! I come, the messenger of glad tidings, for the day of persecution is overpast. The heart of the king, even Charles, hath been moved in gentleness towards us, and he hath sent forth his letters to stay the hands of the men of blood. A ship's company of our friends hath arrived at yonder town, and I also sailed joyfully among them."

As Catharine spoke, her eyes were roaming about the room, in search of him for whose sake security was dear to her. Pearson made a silent appeal to the old man, nor did the latter shrink from the painful task assigned him.

"Sister," he began, in a softened yet perfectly calm tone, "thou tellest us of His love, manifested in temporal good; and now must we speak to thee of that selfsame love, displayed in chastenings. Hitherto, Catharine, thou hast been as one journeying in a darksome and difficult path, and leading an infant by the hand; fain wouldst thou have looked heavenward continually, but still the cares of that little child have drawn thine eyes and thy affections to the earth. Sister! go on rejoicing, for his tottering footsteps shall impede thine own no more."

But the unhappy mother was not thus to be consoled; she shook like a leaf, she turned white as the very snow that hung drifted into her hair. The firm old man extended his hand and held her up, keeping his eye upon hers, as if to repress any outbreak of passion.

"I am a woman, I am but a woman; will He try me above my strength?" said Catharine very quickly, and almost in a whisper. "I have been wounded sore: I have suffered much; many things in the body; many in the mind; crucified in myself, and in them that were dearest to me. Surely," added she, with a long shudder, "He hath spared me in this one thing." She broke forth with sudden and irrepressible violence. "Tell me, man of cold heart, what has God done to me? Hath He cast me down, never to rise again? Hath He crushed my very heart in his hand? And thou, to whom I committed my child, how hast thou fulfilled thy trust? Give me back the boy, well, sound, alive, alive; or earth and Heaven shall avenge me!"

The agonized shriek of Catharine was answered by the faint, the very faint, voice of a child.

On this day it had become evident to Pearson, to his aged guest, and to Dorothy, that Ilbrahim's brief and troubled-pilgrimage drew near its close. The two former would willingly have remained by him, to make use of the prayers and pious discourses which they deemed appropriate to the time, and which, if they be impotent as to the departing traveller's reception in the world whither it goes, may at least sustain him in bidding adieu to earth. But though Ilbrahim uttered no complaint, he was disturbed by the faces that looked upon him; so that Dorothy's entreaties, and their own conviction that the child's feet might tread heaven's pavement and not soil it, had induced the two Quakers to remove. Ilbrahim then closed his eyes and grew calm, and, except for now and then a kind and low word to his nurse, might have been thought to slumber. As nightfall came on, however, and the storm began to rise, something seemed to trouble the repose of the boy's mind, and to render his sense of hearing active and acute. If a passing wind lingered to shake the casement, he strove to turn his head towards it; if the door jarred to and fro upon its hinges, he looked long and anxiously thitherward; if the heavy voice of the old man, as he read the Scriptures, rose but a little higher, the child almost held his dying breath to listen; if a snow-drift swept by the cottage, with a sound like the trailing of a garment, Ilbrahim seemed to watch that some visitant should enter.

But, after a little time, he relinquished whatever secret hope had agitated him, and with one low, complaining whisper, turned his cheek upon the pillow. He then addressed Dorothy with his usual sweetness, and besought her to draw near him; she did so, and Ilbrahim took her hand in both of his, grasping it with a gentle pressure, as if to assure himself that he retained it. At intervals, and without disturbing the repose of his countenance, a very faint trembling passed over him from head to foot, as if a mild but somewhat cool wind had breathed upon him, and made him shiver. As the boy thus led her by the hand, in his quiet progress over the borders of eternity, Dorothy almost imagined that she could discern the near, though dim, delightfulness of the home he was about to reach; she would not have enticed the little wanderer back, though she bemoaned herself that she must leave him and return. But just when Ilbrahim's feet were pressing on the soil of Paradise he heard a voice behind him, and it recalled him a few, few paces of the weary path which he had travelled. As Dorothy looked upon his features, she perceived that their placid expression was again disturbed; her own thoughts had been so wrapped in him,

that all sounds of the storm, and of human speech, were lost to her; but when Catharine's shriek pierced through the room, the boy strove to raise himself.

"Friend, she is come! Open unto her!" cried he.

In a moment his mother was kneeling by the bedside; she drew Ilbrahim to her bosom, and he nestled there, with no violence of joy, but contentedly, as if he were hushing himself to sleep. He looked into her face, and reading its agony, said, with feeble earnestness, "Mourn not, dearest mother. I am happy now." And with these words the gentle boy was dead.

The king's mandate to stay the New England persecutors was effectual in preventing further martyrdoms; but the colonial authorities, trusting in the remoteness of their situation, and perhaps in the supposed instability of the royal government, shortly renewed their severities in all other respects. Catharine's fanaticism had become wilder by the sundering of all human ties; and wherever a scourge was lifted there was she to receive the blow; and whenever a dungeon was unbarred thither she came, to cast herself upon the floor. But in process of time a more Christian spirit—a spirit of forbearance, though not of cordiality or approbation—began to pervade the land in regard to the persecuted sect. And then, when the rigid old Pilgrims eyed her rather in pity than in wrath; when the matrons fed her with the fragments of their children's food, and offered her a lodging on a hard and lowly bed; when no little crowd of schoolboys left their sports to cast stones after the roving enthusiast; then did Catharine return to Pearson's dwelling and made that her home.

As if Ilbrahim's sweetness yet lingered round his ashes; as if his gentle spirit came down from heaven to teach his parent a true religion, her fierce and vindictive nature was softened by the same griefs which had once irritated it. When the course of years had made the features of the unobtrusive mourner familiar in the settlement, she became a subject of not deep, but general, interest; a being on whom the otherwise superfluous sympathies of all might be bestowed. Every one spoke of her with that degree of pity which it is pleasant to experience; every one was ready to do her the little kindnesses which are not costly, yet manifest good will; and when at last she died, a long train of her once bitter persecutors followed her, with decent sadness and tears that were not painful, to her place by Ilbrahim's green and sunken grave.

The Birthmark (1843)

In the latter part of the last century there lived a man of science, an eminent proficient in every branch of natural philosophy, who not long before our story opens had made experience of a spiritual affinity more attractive than any chemical one. He had left his laboratory to the care of an assistant, cleared his fine countenance from the furnace smoke, washed the stain of acids from his fingers, and persuaded a beautiful woman to become his wife. In those days when the comparatively recent discovery of electricity and other kindred mysteries of Nature seemed to open paths into the region of miracle, it was not unusual for the love of science to rival the love of woman in its depth and absorbing energy. The higher intellect, the imagination, the spirit, and even the heart might all find their congenial aliment in pursuits which, as some of their ardent votaries believed, would ascend from one step of powerful intelligence to another, until the philosopher should lay his hand on the secret of creative force and perhaps make new worlds for himself. We know not whether Aylmer possessed this degree of faith in man's ultimate control over Nature. He had devoted himself, however, too unreservedly to scientific studies ever to be weaned from them by any second passion. His love for his young wife might prove the stronger of the two; but it could only be by intertwining itself with his love of science, and uniting the strength of the latter to his own.

Such a union accordingly took place, and was attended with truly remarkable consequences and a deeply impressive moral. One day, very soon after their marriage, Aylmer sat gazing at his wife with a trouble in his countenance that grew stronger until he spoke.

"Georgiana," said he, "has it never occurred to you that the mark upon your cheek might be removed?"

"No, indeed," said she, smiling; but perceiving the seriousness of his manner, she blushed deeply. "To tell you the truth it has been so often called a charm that I was simple enough to imagine it might be so."

"Ah, upon another face perhaps it might," replied her husband; "but never on yours. No, dearest Georgiana, you came so nearly perfect from the hand of Nature that this slightest possible defect, which we hesitate whether to term a defect or a beauty, shocks me, as being the visible mark of earthly imperfection."

"Shocks you, my husband!" cried Georgiana, deeply hurt; at first reddening with momentary anger, but then bursting into tears. "Then why did you take me from my mother's side? You cannot love what shocks you!"

To explain this conversation it must be mentioned that in the centre of Georgiana's left cheek there was a singular mark, deeply interwoven, as it were, with the texture and substance of her face. In the usual state of her complexion—a healthy though delicate bloom—the mark wore a tint of deeper crimson, which imperfectly defined its shape amid the surrounding rosiness. When she blushed it gradually became more indistinct, and finally vanished amid the triumphant rush of blood that bathed the whole cheek with its brilliant glow. But if any shifting motion caused her to turn pale there was the mark again, a crimson stain upon the snow, in what Aylmer sometimes deemed an almost fearful distinctness. Its shape bore not a little similarity to the human hand, though of the smallest pygmy size. Georgiana's lovers were wont to say that some fairy at her birth hour had laid her tiny hand upon the infant's cheek, and left this impress there in token of the magic endowments that were to give her such sway over all hearts. Many a desperate swain would have risked life for the privilege of pressing his lips to the mysterious hand. It must not be concealed, however, that the impression wrought by this fairy sign manual varied exceedingly, according to the difference of temperament in the beholders. Some fastidious persons—but they were exclusively of her own sex—affirmed that the bloody hand, as they chose to call it, quite destroyed the effect of Georgiana's beauty, and rendered her countenance even hideous. But it would be as reasonable to say that one of those small blue stains which sometimes occur in the purest statuary marble would convert the Eve of Powers to a monster. Masculine observers, if the birthmark did not heighten their admiration, contented themselves with wishing it away, that the world might possess one living specimen of ideal loveliness without the semblance of a flaw. After his marriage,—for he thought little or nothing of the matter before,—Aylmer discovered that this was the case with himself.

Had she been less beautiful,—if Envy's self could have found aught else to sneer at,—he might have felt his affection heightened by the prettiness of this mimic hand, now vaguely portrayed, now lost, now stealing forth again and glimmering to and fro with every pulse of emotion that throbbed within her heart; but seeing her otherwise so perfect, he found this one defect grow more and more intolerable with every moment of their united lives. It was the fatal flaw of humanity which Nature, in one shape or another, stamps ineffaceably on all her productions, either to imply that they are temporary and finite, or that their perfection must be wrought by toil and pain. The crimson hand expressed the ineludible gripe in which mortality clutches the highest and purest of earthly mould, degrading them into kindred with the lowest, and even with the very brutes, like whom their visible frames return to dust. In this manner, selecting it as the symbol of his wife's liability to sin, sorrow, decay, and death, Aylmer's sombre imagination was not long in rendering the birthmark a frightful object, causing him more trouble and horror than ever Georgiana's beauty, whether of soul or sense, had given him delight.

At all the seasons which should have been their happiest, he invariably and without intending it, nay, in spite of a purpose to the contrary, reverted to this one disastrous topic. Trifling as it at first appeared, it so connected itself with innumerable trains of thought and modes of feeling that it became the central point of all. With the morning twilight Aylmer opened his eyes upon his wife's face and recognized the symbol of imperfection; and when they sat together at the evening hearth his eyes wandered stealthily to her cheek, and beheld, flickering with the blaze of the wood fire, the spectral hand that wrote mortality where he would fain have worshipped. Georgiana soon learned to shudder at his gaze. It needed but a glance with the peculiar expression that his face often wore to change the roses of her cheek into a deathlike paleness, amid which the crimson hand was brought strongly out, like a bass-relief of ruby on the whitest marble.

Late one night when the lights were growing dim, so as hardly to betray the stain on the poor wife's cheek, she herself, for the first time, voluntarily took up the subject.

"Do you remember, my dear Aylmer," said she, with a feeble attempt at a smile, "have you any recollection of a dream last night about this odious hand?"

"None! none whatever!" replied Aylmer, starting; but then he added, in a dry, cold tone, affected for the sake of concealing the real depth of his emotion, "I might well dream of it; for before I fell asleep it had taken a pretty firm hold of my fancy."

"And you did dream of it?" continued Georgiana, hastily; for she dreaded lest a gush of tears should interrupt what she had to say. "A terrible dream! I wonder that you can forget it. Is it possible to forget this one expression?—'It is in her heart now; we must have it out!' Reflect, my husband; for by all means I would have you recall that dream."

The mind is in a sad state when Sleep, the all-involving, cannot confine her spectres within the dim region of her sway, but suffers them to break forth, affrighting this actual life with secrets that perchance belong to a deeper one. Aylmer now remembered his dream. He had fancied himself with his servant Aminadab, attempting an operation for the removal of the birthmark; but the deeper went the knife, the deeper sank the hand, until at length its tiny grasp appeared to have caught hold of Georgiana's heart; whence, however, her husband was inexorably resolved to cut or wrench it away.

When the dream had shaped itself perfectly in his memory, Aylmer sat in his wife's presence with a guilty feeling. Truth often finds its way to the mind close muffled in robes of sleep, and then speaks with uncompromising directness of matters in regard to which we practise an unconscious self-deception during our waking moments. Until now he had not been aware of the tyrannizing influence acquired by one idea over his mind, and of the lengths which he might find in his heart to go for the sake of giving himself peace.

"Aylmer," resumed Georgiana, solemnly, "I know not what may be the cost to both of us to rid me of this fatal birthmark. Perhaps its removal may cause cureless deformity; or it may be the stain goes as deep as life itself. Again: do we know that there is a possibility, on any terms, of unclasping the firm gripe of this little hand which was laid upon me before I came into the world?"

"Dearest Georgiana, I have spent much thought upon the subject," hastily interrupted Aylmer. "I am convinced of the perfect practicability of its removal."

"If there be the remotest possibility of it," continued Georgiana, "let the attempt be made at whatever risk. Danger is nothing to me; for life, while this hateful mark makes me the object of your horror and disgust,—life is a burden which I would fling down with joy. Either remove this dreadful hand, or take my wretched life! You have deep science. All the world bears witness of it. You have achieved great wonders. Cannot you remove this little, little mark, which I cover with the tips of two small fingers? Is this beyond your power, for the sake of your own peace, and to save your poor wife from madness?"

"Noblest, dearest, tenderest wife," cried Aylmer, rapturously, "doubt not my power. I have already given this matter the deepest thought—thought which might almost have enlightened me to create a being less perfect that yourself. Georgiana, you have led me deeper than ever into the heart of science. I feel myself fully competent to render this dear cheek as faultless as its fellow; and then, most beloved, what will be my triumph when I shall have corrected what Nature left imperfect in her fairest work! Even Pygmalion, when his sculptured woman assumed life, felt not greater ecstasy than mine will be."

"It is resolved, then," said Georgiana, faintly smiling. "And, Aylmer, spare me not, though you should find the birthmark take refuge in my heart at last."

Her husband tenderly kissed her cheek—her right cheek—not that which bore the impress of the crimson hand.

The next day Aylmer apprised his wife of a plan that he had formed whereby he might have opportunity for the intense thought and constant watchfulness which the proposed operation would require; while Georgiana, likewise, would enjoy the perfect repose essential to its success. They were to seclude themselves in the extensive apartments occupied by Aylmer as a laboratory, and where, during his toilsome youth, he had made discoveries in the elemental powers of Nature that had roused the admiration of all the learned societies in Europe. Seated calmly in this laboratory, the pale philosopher had investigated the secrets of the highest cloud region and of the profoundest mines; he had satisfied himself of the causes that kindled and kept alive the fires of the volcano; and had explained the mystery of fountains, and how it is that they gush forth, some so bright and pure, and others with such rich medicinal virtues, from the dark bosom of the earth. Here, too, at an earlier period, he had studied the wonders of the human frame, and attempted to fathom the very process by which Nature assimilates all her precious influences from earth and air, and from the spiritual world, to create and foster man, her masterpiece. The latter pursuit, however, Aylmer had long laid aside in unwilling recognition of the truth—against which all seekers sooner or later stumble—that our

great creative Mother, while she amuses us with apparently working in the broadest sunshine, is yet severely careful to keep her own secrets, and, in spite of her pretended openness, shows us nothing but results. She permits us, indeed, to mar, but seldom to mend, and, like a jealous patentee, on no account to make. Now, however, Aylmer resumed these half-forgotten investigations; not, of course, with such hopes or wishes as first suggested them; but because they involved much physiological truth and lay in the path of his proposed scheme for the treatment of Georgiana.

As he led her over the threshold of the laboratory, Georgiana was cold and tremulous. Aylmer looked cheerfully into her face, with intent to reassure her, but was so startled with the intense glow of the birthmark upon the whiteness of her cheek that he could not restrain a strong convulsive shudder. His wife fainted.

"Aminadab! Aminadab!" shouted Aylmer, stamping violently on the floor.

Forthwith there issued from an inner apartment a man of low stature, but bulky frame, with shaggy hair hanging about his visage, which was grimed with the vapors of the furnace. This personage had been Aylmer's underworker during his whole scientific career, and was admirably fitted for that office by his great mechanical readiness, and the skill with which, while incapable of comprehending a single principle, he executed all the details of his master's experiments. With his vast strength, his shaggy hair, his smoky aspect, and the indescribable earthiness that incrusted him, he seemed to represent man's physical nature; while Aylmer's slender figure, and pale, intellectual face, were no less apt a type of the spiritual element.

"Throw open the door of the boudoir, Aminadab," said Aylmer, "and burn a pastil."

"Yes, master," answered Aminadab, looking intently at the lifeless form of Georgiana; and then he muttered to himself, "If she were my wife, I'd never part with that birthmark."

When Georgiana recovered consciousness she found herself breathing an atmosphere of penetrating fragrance, the gentle potency of which had recalled her from her deathlike faintness. The scene around her looked like enchantment. Aylmer had converted those smoky, dingy, sombre rooms, where he had spent his brightest years in recondite pursuits, into a series of beautiful apartments not unfit to be the secluded abode of a lovely woman. The walls were hung with gorgeous curtains, which imparted the combination of grandeur and grace that no other species of adornment can achieve;

and as they fell from the ceiling to the floor, their rich and ponderous folds, concealing all angles and straight lines, appeared to shut in the scene from infinite space. For aught Georgiana knew, it might be a pavilion among the clouds. And Aylmer, excluding the sunshine, which would have interfered with his chemical processes, had supplied its place with perfumed lamps, emitting flames of various hue, but all uniting in a soft, impurpled radiance. He now knelt by his wife's side, watching her earnestly, but without alarm; for he was confident in his science, and felt that he could draw a magic circle round her within which no evil might intrude.

"Where am I? Ah, I remember," said Georgiana, faintly; and she placed her hand over her cheek to hide the terrible mark from her husband's eyes.

"Fear not, dearest!" exclaimed he. "Do not shrink from me! Believe me, Georgiana, I even rejoice in this single imperfection, since it will be such a rapture to remove it."

"Oh, spare me!" sadly replied his wife. "Pray do not look at it again. I never can forget that convulsive shudder."

In order to soothe Georgiana, and, as it were, to release her mind from the burden of actual things, Aylmer now put in practice some of the light and playful secrets which science had taught him among its profounder lore. Airy figures, absolutely bodiless ideas, and forms of unsubstantial beauty came and danced before her, imprinting their momentary footsteps on beams of light. Though she had some indistinct idea of the method of these optical phenomena, still the illusion was almost perfect enough to warrant the belief that her husband possessed sway over the spiritual world. Then again, when she felt a wish to look forth from her seclusion, immediately, as if her thoughts were answered, the procession of external existence flitted across a screen. The scenery and the figures of actual life were perfectly represented, but with that bewitching, yet indescribable difference which always makes a picture, an image, or a shadow so much more attractive than the original. When wearied of this, Aylmer bade her cast her eyes upon a vessel containing a quantity of earth. She did so, with little interest at first; but was soon startled to perceive the germ of a plant shooting upward from the soil. Then came the slender stalk; the leaves gradually unfolded themselves; and amid them was a perfect and lovely flower.

"It is magical!" cried Georgiana. "I dare not touch it."

"Nay, pluck it," answered Aylmer,—"pluck it, and inhale its brief perfume while you may. The flower will wither in a few moments and leave nothing save its brown seed vessels; but thence may be perpetuated a race as ephemeral as itself."

But Georgiana had no sooner touched the flower than the whole plant suffered a blight, its leaves turning coal-black as if by the agency of fire.

"There was too powerful a stimulus," said Aylmer, thoughtfully.

To make up for this abortive experiment, he proposed to take her portrait by a scientific process of his own invention. It was to be effected by rays of light striking upon a polished plate of metal. Georgiana assented; but, on looking at the result, was affrighted to find the features of the portrait blurred and indefinable; while the minute figure of a hand appeared where the cheek should have been. Aylmer snatched the metallic plate and threw it into a jar of corrosive acid.

Soon, however, he forgot these mortifying failures. In the intervals of study and chemical experiment he came to her flushed and exhausted, but seemed invigorated by her presence, and spoke in glowing language of the resources of his art. He gave a history of the long dynasty of the alchemists, who spent so many ages in quest of the universal solvent by which the golden principle might be elicited from all things vile and base. Aylmer appeared to believe that, by the plainest scientific logic, it was altogether within the limits of possibility to discover this long-sought medium; "but," he added, "a philosopher who should go deep enough to acquire the power would attain too lofty a wisdom to stoop to the exercise of it." Not less singular were his opinions in regard to the elixir vitæ. He more than intimated that it was at his option to concoct a liquid that should prolong life for years, perhaps interminably; but that it would produce a discord in Nature which all the world, and chiefly the quaffer of the immortal nostrum, would find cause to curse.

"Aylmer, are you in earnest?" asked Georgiana, looking at him with amazement and fear. "It is terrible to possess such power, or even to dream of possessing it."

"Oh, do not tremble, my love," said her husband. "I would not wrong either you or myself by working such inharmonious effects upon our lives; but I would have you consider how trifling, in comparison, is the skill requisite to remove this little hand."

At the mention of the birthmark, Georgiana, as

usual, shrank as if a redhot iron had touched her cheek.

Again Aylmer applied himself to his labors. She could hear his voice in the distant furnace room giving directions to Aminadab, whose harsh, uncouth, misshapen tones were audible in response, more like the grunt or growl of a brute than human speech. After hours of absence, Aylmer reappeared and proposed that she should now examine his cabinet of chemical products and natural treasures of the earth. Among the former he showed her a small vial, in which, he remarked, was contained a gentle yet most powerful fragrance, capable of impregnating all the breezes that blow across a kingdom. They were of inestimable value, the contents of that little vial; and, as he said so, he threw some of the perfume into the air and filled the room with piercing and invigorating delight.

"And what is this?" asked Georgiana, pointing to a small crystal globe containing a gold-colored liquid. "It is so beautiful to the eye that I could imagine it the elixir of life."

"In one sense it is," replied Aylmer; "or, rather, the elixir of immortality. It is the most precious poison that ever was concocted in this world. By its aid I could apportion the lifetime of any mortal at whom you might point your finger. The strength of the dose would determine whether he were to linger out years, or drop dead in the midst of a breath. No king on his guarded throne could keep his life if I, in my private station, should deem that the welfare of millions justified me in depriving him of it."

"Why do you keep such a terrific drug?" inquired Georgiana in horror.

"Do not mistrust me, dearest," said her husband, smiling; "its virtuous potency is yet greater than its harmful one. But see! here is a powerful cosmetic. With a few drops of this in a vase of water, freckles may be washed away as easily as the hands are cleansed. A stronger infusion would take the blood out of the cheek, and leave the rosiest beauty a pale ghost."

"Is it with this lotion that you intend to bathe my cheek?" asked Georgiana, anxiously.

"Oh, no," hastily replied her husband; "this is merely superficial. Your case demands a remedy that shall go deeper."

In his interviews with Georgiana, Aylmer generally made minute inquiries as to her sensations and whether the confinement of the rooms and the temperature of the atmosphere agreed with her. These questions had such a particular drift that

Georgiana began to conjecture that she was already subjected to certain physical influences, either breathed in with the fragrant air or taken with her food. She fancied likewise, but it might be altogether fancy, that there was a stirring up of her system—a strange, indefinite sensation creeping through her veins, and tingling, half painfully, half pleasurably, at her heart. Still, whenever she dared to look into the mirror, there she beheld herself pale as a white rose and with the crimson birthmark stamped upon her cheek. Not even Aylmer now hated it so much as she.

To dispel the tedium of the hours which her husband found it necessary to devote to the processes of combination and analysis, Georgiana turned over the volumes of his scientific library. In many dark old tomes she met with chapters full of romance and poetry. They were the works of the philosophers of the middle ages, such as Albertus Magnus, Cornelius Agrippa, Paracelsus, and the famous friar who created the prophetic Brazen Head. All these antique naturalists stood in advance of their centuries, yet were imbued with some of their credulity, and therefore were believed, and perhaps imagined themselves to have acquired from the investigation of Nature a power above Nature, and from physics a sway over the spiritual world. Hardly less curious and imaginative were the early volumes of the Transactions of the Royal Society, in which the members, knowing little of the limits of natural possibility, were continually recording wonders or proposing methods whereby wonders might be wrought.

But to Georgiana the most engrossing volume was a large folio from her husband's own hand, in which he had recorded every experiment of his scientific career, its original aim, the methods adopted for its development, and its final success or failure, with the circumstances to which either event was attributable. The book, in truth, was both the history and emblem of his ardent, ambitious, imaginative, yet practical and laborious life. He handled physical details as if there were nothing beyond them; yet spiritualized them all, and redeemed himself from materialism by his strong and eager aspiration towards the infinite. In his grasp the veriest clod of earth assumed a soul. Georgiana, as she read, reverenced Aylmer and loved him more profoundly than ever, but with a less entire dependence on his judgment than heretofore. Much as he had accomplished, she could not but observe that his most splendid successes were almost invariably failures, if compared with the ideal at which he aimed. His brightest diamonds were the merest pebbles, and felt to be so by himself, in comparison with the inestimable gems which lay hidden beyond his reach. The volume, rich with achievements that had won renown for its author, was yet as melancholy a record as ever mortal hand had penned. It was the sad confession and continual exemplification of the shortcomings of the composite man, the spirit burdened with clay and working in matter, and of the despair that assails the higher nature at finding itself so miserably thwarted by the earthly part. Perhaps every man of genius in whatever sphere might recognize the image of his own experience in Aylmer's journal.

So deeply did these reflections affect Georgiana that she laid her face upon the open volume and burst into tears. In this situation she was found by her husband.

"It is dangerous to read in a sorcerer's books," said he with a smile, though his countenance was uneasy and displeased. "Georgiana, there are pages in that volume which I can scarcely glance over and keep my senses. Take heed lest it prove as detrimental to you."

"It has made me worship you more than ever," said she.

"Ah, wait for this one success," rejoined he, "then worship me if you will. I shall deem myself hardly unworthy of it. But come, I have sought you for the luxury of your voice. Sing to me, dearest."

So she poured out the liquid music of her voice to quench the thirst of his spirit. He then took his leave with a boyish exuberance of gayety, assuring her that her seclusion would endure but a little longer, and that the result was already certain. Scarcely had he departed when Georgiana felt irresistibly impelled to follow him. She had forgotten to inform Aylmer of a symptom which for two or three hours past had begun to excite her attention. It was a sensation in the fatal birthmark, not painful, but which induced a restlessness throughout her system. Hastening after her husband, she intruded for the first time into the laboratory.

The first thing that struck her eye was the furnace, that hot and feverish worker, with the intense glow of its fire, which by the quantities of soot clustered above it seemed to have been burning for ages. There was a distilling apparatus in full operation. Around the room were retorts, tubes, cylinders, crucibles, and other apparatus of chemical research. An electrical machine stood ready for immediate use. The atmosphere felt oppressively close, and was tainted with gaseous odors which had been tormented forth by the processes of science. The severe and homely simplicity of the apartment, with its naked walls and brick pavement, looked strange, accustomed as Georgiana had become to the fantastic elegance of her boudoir. But what chiefly, indeed almost solely, drew her attention, was the aspect of Aylmer himself.

He was pale as death, anxious and absorbed, and hung over the furnace as if it depended upon his utmost watchfulness whether the liquid which it was distilling should be the draught of immortal happiness or misery. How different from the sanguine and joyous mien that he had assumed for Georgiana's encouragement!

"Carefully now, Aminadab; carefully, thou human machine; carefully, thou man of clay!" muttered Aylmer, more to himself than his assistant. "Now, if there be a thought too much or too little, it is all over."

"Ho! ho!" mumbled Aminadab. "Look, master! look!"

Aylmer raised his eyes hastily, and at first reddened, then grew paler than ever, on beholding Georgiana. He rushed towards her and seized her arm with a gripe that left the print of his fingers upon it.

"Why do you come hither? Have you no trust in your husband?" cried he, impetuously. "Would you throw the blight of that fatal birthmark over my labors? It is not well done. Go, prying woman, go!"

"Nay, Aylmer," said Georgiana with the firmness of which she possessed no stinted endowment, "it is not you that have a right to complain. You mistrust your wife; you have concealed the anxiety with which you watch the development of this experiment. Think not so unworthily of me, my husband. Tell me all the risk we run, and fear not that I shall shrink; for my share in it is far less than your own."

"No, no, Georgiana!" said Aylmer, impatiently; "it must not be."

"I submit," replied she calmly. "And, Aylmer, I shall quaff whatever draught you bring me; but it will be on the same principle that would induce me to take a dose of poison if offered by your hand."

"My noble wife," said Aylmer, deeply moved, "I knew not the height and depth of your nature until now. Nothing shall be concealed. Know, then, that this crimson hand, superficial as it seems, has clutched its grasp into your being with a strength of which I had no previous conception. I have already administered agents powerful enough to do aught except to change your entire physical system. Only one thing remains to be tried. If that fail us we are ruined."

"Why did you hesitate to tell me this?" asked she.

"Because, Georgiana," said Aylmer, in a low voice, "there is danger."

"Danger? There is but one danger—that this horrible stigma shall be left upon my cheek!" cried Georgiana. "Remove it, remove it, whatever be the cost, or we shall both go mad!"

"Heaven knows your words are too true," said Aylmer, sadly. "And now, dearest, return to your boudoir. In a little while all will be tested."

He conducted her back and took leave of her with a solemn tenderness which spoke far more than his words how much was now at stake. After his departure Georgiana became rapt in musings. She considered the character of Aylmer, and did it completer justice than at any previous moment. Her heart exulted, while it trembled, at his honorable love—so pure and lofty that it would accept nothing less than perfection nor miserably make itself contented with an earthlier nature than he had dreamed of. She felt how much more precious was such a sentiment than that meaner kind which would have borne with the imperfection for her sake, and have been guilty of treason to holy love by degrading its perfect idea to the level of the actual; and with her whole spirit she prayed that, for a single moment, she might satisfy his highest and deepest conception. Longer than one moment she well knew it could not be; for his spirit was ever on the march, ever ascending, and each instant required something that was beyond the scope of the instant before.

The sound of her husband's footsteps aroused her. He bore a crystal goblet containing a liquor colorless as water, but bright enough to be the draught of immortality. Aylmer was pale; but it seemed rather the consequence of a highly-wrought state of mind and tension of spirit than of fear or doubt.

"The concoction of the draught has been perfect," said he, in answer to Georgiana's look. "Unless all my science have deceived me, it cannot fail."

"Save on your account, my dearest Aylmer," observed his wife, "I might wish to put off this birthmark of mortality by relinquishing mortality itself in preference to any other mode. Life is but a sad possession to those who have attained precisely the degree of moral advancement at which I

stand. Were I weaker and blinder it might be happiness. Were I stronger, it might be endured hopefully. But, being what I find myself, methinks I am of all mortals the most fit to die."

"You are fit for heaven without tasting death!" replied her husband. "But why do we speak of dying? The draught cannot fail. Behold its effect upon this plant."

On the window seat there stood a geranium diseased with yellow blotches, which had overspread all its leaves. Aylmer poured a small quantity of the liquid upon the soil in which it grew. In a little time, when the roots of the plant had taken up the moisture, the unsightly blotches began to be extinguished in a living verdure.

"There needed no proof," said Georgiana, quietly. "Give me the goblet. I joyfully stake all upon your word."

"Drink, then, thou lofty creature!" exclaimed Aylmer, with fervid admiration. "There is no taint of imperfection on thy spirit. Thy sensible frame, too, shall soon be all perfect."

She quaffed the liquid and returned the goblet to his hand.

"It is grateful," said she with a placid smile. "Methinks it is like water from a heavenly fountain; for it contains I know not what of unobtrusive fragrance and deliciousness. It allays a feverish thirst that had parched me for many days. Now, dearest, let me sleep. My earthly senses are closing over my spirit like the leaves around the heart of a rose at sunset."

She spoke the last words with a gentle reluctance, as if it required almost more energy than she could command to pronounce the faint and lingering syllables. Scarcely had they loitered through her lips ere she was lost in slumber. Aylmer sat by her side, watching her aspect with the emotions proper to a man the whole value of whose existence was involved in the process now to be tested. Mingled with this mood, however, was the philosophic investigation characteristic of the man of science. Not the minutest symptom escaped him. A heightened flush of the cheek, a slight irregularity of breath, a quiver of the eyelid, a hardly perceptible tremor through the frame,—such were the details which, as the moments passed, he wrote down in his folio volume. Intense thought had set its stamp upon every previous page of that volume, but the thoughts of years were all concentrated upon the last.

While thus employed, he failed not to gaze often at the fatal hand, and not without a shudder.

Yet once, by a strange and unaccountable impulse, he pressed it with his lips. His spirit recoiled, however, in the very act; and Georgiana, out of the midst of her deep sleep, moved uneasily and murmured as if in remonstrance. Again Aylmer resumed his watch. Nor was it without avail. The crimson hand, which at first had been strongly visible upon the marble paleness of Georgiana's cheek, now grew more faintly outlined. She remained not less pale than ever; but the birthmark, with every breath that came and went, lost somewhat of its former distinctness. Its presence had been awful; its departure was more awful still. Watch the stain of the rainbow fading out of the sky, and you will know how that mysterious symbol passed away.

"By Heaven! it is well-nigh gone!" said Aylmer to himself, in almost irrepressible ecstasy. "I can scarcely trace it now. Success! success! And now it is like the faintest rose color. The lightest flush of blood across her cheek would overcome it. But she is so pale!"

He drew aside the window curtain and suffered the light of natural day to fall into the room and rest upon her cheek. At the same time he heard a gross, hoarse chuckle, which he had long known as his servant Aminadab's expression of delight.

"Ah, clod! ah, earthly mass!" cried Aylmer, laughing in a sort of frenzy, "you have served me well! Matter and spirit—earth and heaven—have both done their part in this! Laugh, thing of the senses! You have earned the right to laugh."

These exclamations broke Georgiana's sleep. She slowly unclosed her eyes and gazed into the mirror which her husband had arranged for that purpose. A faint smile flitted over her lips when she recognized how barely perceptible was now that crimson

hand which had once blazed forth with such disastrous brilliancy as to scare away all their happiness. But then her eyes sought Aylmer's face with a trouble and anxiety that he could by no means account for.

"My poor Aylmer!" murmured she.

"Poor? Nay, richest, happiest, most favored!" exclaimed he. "My peerless bride, it is successful! You are perfect!"

"My poor Aylmer," she repeated, with a more than human tenderness, "you have aimed loftily; you have done nobly. Do not repent that with so high and pure a feeling, you have rejected the best the earth could offer. Aylmer, dearest Aylmer, I am dying!"

Alas! it was too true! The fatal hand had grappled with the mystery of life, and was the bond by which an angelic spirit kept itself in union with a mortal frame. As the last crimson tint of the birthmark—that sole token of human imperfection—faded from her cheek, the parting breath of the now perfect woman passed into the atmosphere, and her soul, lingering a moment near her husband, took its heavenward flight. Then a hoarse, chuckling laugh was heard again! Thus ever does the gross fatality of earth exult in its invariable triumph over the immortal essence which, in this dim sphere of half development, demands the completeness of a higher state. Yet, had Aylmer reached a profounder wisdom, he need not thus have flung away the happiness which would have woven his mortal life of the selfsame texture with the celestial. The momentary circumstance was too strong for him; he failed to look beyond the shadowy scope of time, and, living once for all in eternity, to find the perfect future in the present.

Young Goodman Brown (1835)

Young Goodman Brown came forth at sunset into the street at Salem village; but put his head back, after crossing the threshold, to exchange a parting kiss with his young wife. And Faith, as the wife was aptly named, thrust her own pretty head into the street, letting the wind play with the pink ribbons of her cap while she called to Goodman Brown.

"Dearest heart," whispered she, softly and rather sadly, when her lips were close to his ear, "prithee put off your journey until sunrise and sleep in your own bed to-night. A lone woman is troubled with

such dreams and such thoughts that she's afeard of herself sometimes. Pray tarry with me this night, dear husband, of all nights in the year."

"My love and my Faith," replied young Goodman Brown, "of all nights in the year, this one night must I tarry away from thee. My journey, as thou callest it, forth and back again, must needs be done 'twixt now and sunrise. What, my sweet, pretty wife, dost thou doubt me already, and we but three months married?"

"Then God bless you!" said Faith, with the pink

[handwritten annotations: "This horrible insight that everyone is evil changes his life and he sees the dark side of nature. The devil looks like an extension of Brown. The devil is in everyone. Innate Depravity. Story is an allegory about the discovery of innate depravity—story told trough symbols. allegory. Devil is the father symbols. Everyone is at the Devil's meeting. Brown recognizes the bond of evil between the people." "Sounds like Halloween night."]

ribbons; "and may you find all well when you come back."

"Amen!" cried Goodman Brown. "Say thy prayers, dear Faith, and go to bed at dusk, and no harm will come to thee."

So they parted; and the young man pursued his way until, being about to turn the corner by the meeting-house, he looked back and saw the head of Faith still peeping after him with a melancholy air, in spite of her pink ribbons.

"Poor little Faith!" thought he, for his heart smote him. "What a wretch am I to leave her on such an errand! She talks of dreams, too. Methought as she spoke there was trouble in her face, as if a dream had warned her what work is to be done tonight. But no, no; 't would kill her to think it. Well, she's a blessed angel on earth; and after this one night I'll cling to her skirts and follow her to heaven."

With this excellent resolve for the future, Goodman Brown felt himself justified in making more haste on his present evil purpose. He had taken a dreary road, darkened by all the gloomiest trees of the forest, which barely stood aside to let the narrow path creep through, and closed immediately behind. It was all as lonely as could be; and there is this peculiarity in such a solitude, that the traveller knows not who may be concealed by the innumerable trunks and the thick boughs overhead; so that with lonely footsteps he may yet be passing through an unseen multitude.

"There may be a devilish Indian behind every tree," said Goodman Brown to himself; and he glanced fearfully behind him as he added, "What if the devil himself should be at my very elbow!"

His head being turned back, he passed a crook of the road, and, looking forward again, beheld the figure of a man, in grave and decent attire, seated at the foot of an old tree. He arose at Goodman Brown's approach and walked onward side by side with him.

"You are late, Goodman Brown," said he. "The clock of the Old South was striking as I came through Boston, and that is full fifteen minutes agone."

"Faith kept me back a while," replied the young man, with a tremor in his voice, caused by the sudden appearance of his companion, though not wholly unexpected.

It was now deep dusk in the forest, and deepest in that part of it where these two were journeying. As nearly as could be discerned, the second traveller was about fifty years old, apparently in the

same rank of life as Goodman Brown, and bearing a considerable resemblance to him, though perhaps more in expression than features. Still they might have been taken for father and son. And yet, though the elder person was as simply clad as the younger, and as simple in manner too, he had an indescribable air of one who knew the world, and who would not have felt abashed at the governor's dinner table or in King William's court, were it possible that his affairs should call him thither. But the only thing about him that could be fixed upon as remarkable was his staff, which bore the likeness of a great black snake, so curiously wrought that it might almost be seen to twist and wriggle itself like a living serpent. This, of course, must have been an ocular deception, assisted by the uncertain light.

"Come, Goodman Brown," cried his fellow-traveller, "this is a dull pace for the beginning of a journey. Take my staff, if you are so soon weary."

"Friend," said the other, exchanging his slow pace for a full stop, "having kept covenant by meeting thee here, it is my purpose now to return whence I came. I have scruples touching the matter thou wot'st of."

"Sayest thou so?" replied he of the serpent, smiling apart. "Let us walk on, nevertheless, reasoning as we go; and if I convince thee not thou shalt turn back. We are but a little way in the forest yet."

"Too far! too far!" exclaimed the goodman, unconsciously resuming his walk. "My father never went into the woods on such an errand, nor his father before him. We have been a race of honest men and good Christians since the days of the martyrs; and shall I be the first of the name of Brown that ever took this path and kept"—

"Such company, thou wouldst say," observed the elder person, interpreting his pause. "Well said, Goodman Brown! I have been as well acquainted with your family as with ever a one among the Puritans; and that's no trifle to say. I helped your grandfather, the constable, when he lashed the Quaker woman so smartly through the streets of Salem; and it was I that brought your father a pitch-pine knot, kindled at my own hearth, to set fire to an Indian village, in King Philip's war. They were my good friends, both; and many a pleasant walk have we had along this path, and returned merrily after midnight. I would fain be friends with you for their sake."

"If it be as thou sayest," replied Goodman Brown, "I marvel they never spoke of these matters;

or, verily, I marvel not, seeing that the least rumor of the sort would have driven them from New England. We are a people of prayer, and good works to boot, and abide no such wickedness."

"Wickedness or not," said the traveller with the twisted staff, "I have a very general acquaintance here in New England. The deacons of many a church have drunk the communion wine with me; the selectmen of divers towns make me their chairman; and a majority of the Great and General Court are firm supporters of my interest. The governor and I, too—But these are state secrets."

"Can this be so?" cried Goodman Brown, with a stare of amazement at his undisturbed companion. "Howbeit, I have nothing to do with the governor and council; they have their own ways, and are no rule for a simple husbandman like me. But, were I to go on with thee, how should I meet the eye of that good old man, our minister, at Salem village? Oh, his voice would make me tremble both Sabbath day and lecture day."

Thus far the elder traveller had listened with due gravity; but now burst into a fit of irrepressible mirth, shaking himself so violently that his snake-like staff actually seemed to wriggle in sympathy.

"Ha! ha! ha!" shouted he again and again; then composing himself, "Well, go on, Goodman Brown, go on; but, prithee, don't kill me with laughing."

"Well, then, to end the matter at once," said Goodman Brown, considerably nettled, "there is my wife, Faith. It would break her dear little heart; and I'd rather break my own."

"Nay, if that be the case," answered the other, "e'en go thy ways, Goodman Brown. I would not for twenty old women like the one hobbling before us that Faith should come to any harm."

As he spoke he pointed his staff at a female figure on the path, in whom Goodman Brown recognized a very pious and exemplary dame, who had taught him his catechism in youth, and was still his moral and spiritual adviser, jointly with the minister and Deacon Gookin.

"A marvel, truly, that Goody Cloyse should be so far in the wilderness at nightfall," said he. "But with your leave, friend, I shall take a cut through the woods until we have left this Christian woman behind. Being a stranger to you, she might ask whom I was consorting with and whither I was going."

"Be it so," said his fellow-traveller. "Betake you to the woods, and let me keep the path."

Accordingly the young man turned aside, but took care to watch his companion, who advanced softly along the road until he had come within a staff's length of the old dame. She, meanwhile, was making the best of her way, with singular speed for so aged a woman, and mumbling some indistinct words—a prayer, doubtless—as she went. The traveller put forth his staff and touched her withered neck with what seemed the serpent's tail.

"The devil!" screamed the pious old lady.

"Then Goody Cloyse knows her old friend?" observed the traveller, confronting her and leaning on his writhing stick.

"Ah, forsooth, and is it your worship indeed?" cried the good dame. "Yea, truly is it, and in the very image of my old gossip, Goodman Brown, the grandfather of the silly fellow that now is. But—would your worship believe it?—my broomstick hath strangely disappeared, stolen, as I suspect, by that unhanged witch, Goody Cory, and that, too, when I was all anointed with the juice of smallage, and cinquefoil, and wolf's bane"—

"Mingled with fine wheat and the fat of a new-born babe," said the shape of old Goodman Brown.

"Ah, your worship knows the recipe," cried the old lady, cackling aloud. "So, as I was saying, being all ready for the meeting, and no horse to ride on, I made up my mind to foot it; for they tell me there is a nice young man to be taken into communion to-night. But now your good worship will lend me your arm, and we shall be there in a twinkling."

"That can hardly be," answered her friend. "I may not spare you my arm, Goody Cloyse; but here is my staff, if you will."

So saying, he threw it down at her feet, where, perhaps, it assumed life, being one of the rods which its owner had formerly lent to the Egyptian magi. Of this fact, however, Goodman Brown could not take cognizance. He had cast up his eyes in astonishment, and, looking down again, beheld neither Goody Cloyse nor the serpentine staff, but his fellow-traveller alone, who waited for him as calmly as if nothing had happened.

"That old woman taught me my catechism," said the young man; and there was a world of meaning in this simple comment.

They continued to walk onward, while the elder traveller exhorted his companion to make good speed and persevere in the path, discoursing so aptly that his arguments seemed rather to spring up in the bosom of his auditor than to be suggested by himself. As they went, he plucked a branch of maple to serve for a walking stick, and began to strip it of the twigs and little boughs, which were wet with evening dew. The moment his fingers touched them they became strangely withered and dried up as with a week's sunshine. Thus the pair proceeded, at a good free pace, until suddenly, in a gloomy hollow of the road, Goodman Brown sat himself down on the stump of a tree and refused to go any farther.

"Friend," said he, stubbornly, "my mind is made up. Not another step will I budge on this errand. What if a wretched old woman do choose to go to the devil when I thought she was going to heaven: is that any reason why I should quit my dear Faith and go after her?" *pun on name*

"You will think better of this by and by," said his acquaintance, composedly. "Sit here and rest yourself a while; and when you feel like moving again, there is my staff to help you along."

Without more words, he threw his companion the maple stick, and was as speedily out of sight as if he had vanished into the deepening gloom. The young man sat a few moments by the roadside, applauding himself greatly, and thinking with how clear a conscience he should meet the minister in his morning walk, nor shrink from the eye of good old Deacon Gookin. And what calm sleep would be his that very night, which was to have been spent so wickedly, but so purely and sweetly now, in the arms of Faith! Amidst these pleasant and praiseworthy meditations, Goodman Brown heard the tramp of horses along the road, and deemed it advisable to conceal himself within the verge of the forest, conscious of the guilty purpose that had brought him thither, though now so happily turned from it.

On came the hoof tramps and the voices of the riders, two grave old voices, conversing soberly as they drew near. These mingled sounds appeared to pass along the road, within a few yards of the young man's hiding-place; but, owing doubtless to the depth of the gloom at that particular spot, neither the travellers nor their steeds were visible. Though their figures brushed the small boughs by the wayside, it could not be seen that they intercepted, even for a moment, the faint gleam from the strip of bright sky athwart which they must have passed. Goodman Brown alternately crouched and stood on tiptoe, pulling aside the branches and thrusting forth his head as far as he durst without discerning so much as a shadow. It vexed him the more, because he could have sworn, were such a thing possible, that he recognized the voices of the minister and Deacon Gookin, jogging along quietly, as they were wont to do, when bound to

some ordination or ecclesiastical council. While yet within hearing, one of the riders stopped to pluck a switch.

"Of the two, reverend sir," said the voice like the deacon's, "I had rather miss an ordination dinner than to-night's meeting. They tell me that some of our community are to be here from Falmouth and beyond, and others from Connecticut and Rhode Island, besides several of the Indian powwows, who, after their fashion, know almost as much deviltry as the best of us. Moreover, there is a goodly young woman to be taken into communion." *Obviously Faith*

"Mighty well, Deacon Gookin!" replied the solemn old tones of the minister. "Spur up, or we shall be late. Nothing can be done, you know, until I get on the ground."

The hoofs clattered again; and the voices, talking so strangely in the empty air, passed on through the forest, where no church had ever been gathered or solitary Christian prayed. Whither, then, could these holy men be journeying so deep into the heathen wilderness? Young Goodman Brown caught hold of a tree for support, being ready to sink down on the ground, faint and overburdened with the heavy sickness of his heart. He looked up to the sky, doubting whether there really was a heaven above him. Yet there was the blue arch, and the stars brightening in it.

"With heaven above and Faith below, I will yet stand firm against the devil!" cried Goodman Brown.

While he still gazed upward into the deep arch of the firmament and had lifted his hands to pray, a cloud, though no wind was stirring, hurried across the zenith and hid the brightening stars. The blue sky was still visible, except directly overhead, where this black mass of cloud was sweeping swiftly northward. Aloft in the air, as if from the depths of the cloud, came a confused and doubtful sound of voices. Once the listener fancied that he could distinguish the accents of towns-people of his own, men and women, both pious and ungodly, many of whom he had met at the communion table, and had seen others rioting at the tavern. The next moment, so indistinct were the sounds, he doubted whether he had heard aught but the murmur of the old forest, whispering without a wind. Then came a stronger swell of those familiar tones, heard daily in the sunshine at Salem village, but never until now from a cloud of night. There was one voice, of a young woman, uttering lamentations, yet with an uncertain sorrow, and entreating for some favor, which, perhaps, it would grieve her to obtain; and all the unseen multitude, both saints and sinners, seemed to encourage her onward.

"Faith!" shouted Goodman Brown, in a voice of agony and desperation; and the echoes of the forest mocked him, crying, "Faith! Faith!" as if bewildered wretches were seeking her all through the wilderness.

The cry of grief, rage, and terror was yet piercing the night, when the unhappy husband held his breath for a response. There was a scream, drowned immediately in a louder murmur of voices, fading into far-off laughter, as the dark cloud swept away, leaving the clear and silent sky above Goodman Brown. But something fluttered lightly down through the air and caught on the branch of a tree. The young man seized it, and beheld a pink ribbon.

"My Faith is gone!" cried he, after one stupefied moment. "There is no good on earth; and sin is but a name. Come, devil; for to thee is this world given."

And, maddened with despair, so that he laughed loud and long, did Goodman Brown grasp his staff and set forth again, at such a rate that he seemed to fly along the forest path rather than to walk or run. The road grew wilder and drearier and more faintly traced, and vanished at length, leaving him in the heart of the dark wilderness, still rushing onward with the instinct that guides mortal man to evil. The whole forest was peopled with frightful sounds—the creaking of the trees, the howling of wild beasts, and the yell of Indians; while sometimes the wind tolled like a distant church bell, and sometimes gave a broad roar around the traveller, as if all Nature were laughing him to scorn. But he was himself the chief horror of the scene, and shrank not from its other horrors.

"Ha! ha! ha!" roared Goodman Brown when the wind laughed at him. "Let us hear which will laugh loudest. Think not to frighten me with your deviltry. Come witch, come wizard, come Indian powwow, come devil himself, and here comes Goodman Brown. You may as well fear him as he fears you."

In truth, all through the haunted forest there could be nothing more frightful than the figure of Goodman Brown. On he flew among the black pines, brandishing his staff with frenzied gestures, now giving vent to an inspiration of horrid blasphemy, and now shouting forth such laughter as set all the echoes of the forest laughing like demons around him. The fiend in his own shape is less hideous than when he rages in the breast of man. Thus sped the demoniac on his course, until, quivering among the trees, he saw a red light before him, as when the felled trunks and branches of a clearing have been set on fire, and throw up their lurid blaze against the sky, at the hour of midnight. He paused, in a lull of the tempest that had driven him onward, and heard the swell of what seemed a hymn, rolling solemnly from a distance with the weight of many voices. He knew the tune; it was a familiar one in the choir of the village meeting-house. The verse died heavily away, and was lengthened by a chorus, not of human voices, but of all the sounds of the benighted wilderness pealing in awful harmony together. Goodman Brown cried out, and his cry was lost to his own ear by its unison with the cry of the desert.

In the interval of silence he stole forward until the light glared full upon his eyes. At one extremity of an open space, hemmed in by the dark wall of the forest, arose a rock, bearing some rude, natural resemblance either to an altar or a pulpit, and surrounded by four blazing pines, their tops aflame, their stems untouched, like candles at an evening meeting. The mass of foliage that had overgrown the summit of the rock was all on fire, blazing high into the night and fitfully illuminating the whole field. Each pendent twig and leafy festoon was in a blaze. As the red light arose and fell, a numerous congregation alternately shone forth, then disappeared in shadow, and again grew, as it were, out of the darkness, peopling the heart of the solitary woods at once.

"A grave and dark-clad company," quoth Goodman Brown.

In truth they were such. Among them, quivering to and fro between gloom and splendor, appeared faces that would be seen next day at the council board of the province, and others which, Sabbath after Sabbath, looked devoutly heavenward, and benignantly over the crowded pews, from the holiest pulpits in the land. Some affirm that the lady of the governor was there. At least there were high dames well known to her, and wives of honored husbands, and widows, a great multitude, and ancient maidens, all of excellent repute, and fair young girls, who trembled lest their mothers should espy them. Either the sudden gleams of light flashing over the obscure field bedazzled Goodman Brown, or he recognized a score of the church members of Salem village famous for their especial sanctity. Good old Deacon Gookin had arrived, and waited at the skirts of that venerable saint, his revered pastor. But, irreverently consorting with these grave, reputable, and pious people, these elders of the church, these chaste dames and dewy virgins, there were men of dissolute lives and women of spotted fame, wretches given over to all mean and filthy vice, and suspected even of horrid crimes. It was strange to see that the good shrank not from the wicked, nor were the sinners abashed by the saints. Scattered also among their pale-faced enemies were the Indian priests, or powwows, who had often scared their native forest with more hideous incantations than any known to English witchcraft.

"But where is <u>Faith</u>?" thought Goodman Brown: and, as <u>hope</u> came into his heart, he trembled.

Another verse of the hymn arose, a slow and mournful strain, such as the pious love, but joined to words which expressed all that our nature can conceive of sin, and darkly hinted at far more. Unfathomable to mere mortals is the lore of fiends. Verse after verse was sung; and still the chorus of the desert swelled between like the deepest tone of a mighty organ; and with the final peal of that dreadful anthem there came a sound, as if the roaring wind, the rushing streams, the howling beasts, and every other voice of the unconcerted wilderness were mingling and according with the voice of guilty man in homage to the prince of all. The four blazing pines threw up a loftier flame, and obscurely discovered shapes and visages of horror on the smoke wreaths above the impious assembly. At the same moment the fire on the rock shot redly forth and formed a glowing arch above its base, where now appeared a figure. With reverence be it spoken, the figure bore no slight similitude, both in garb and manner, to some grave divine of the New England churches.

"Bring forth the converts!" cried a voice that echoed through the field and rolled into the forest.

At the word, Goodman Brown stepped forth from the shadow of the trees and approached the congregation, with whom he felt a loathful brotherhood by the sympathy of all that was wicked in his heart. He could have well-nigh sworn that the shape of his own dead father beckoned him to advance, looking downward from a smoke wreath, while a woman, with dim features of despair, threw out her hand to warn him back. Was it his mother? But he had no power to retreat one step, nor to resist, even in thought, when the minister and good old Deacon Gookin seized his arms and led him to the blazing rock. Thither came also the slender form of a veiled female, led between Goody Cloyse, that pious teacher of the catechism, and Martha Carrier, who had received the devil's promise to be queen of hell. A rampant hag was she. And there stood the proselytes beneath the canopy of fire.

"Welcome, my children," said the dark figure, "to the communion of your race. Ye have found thus young your nature and your destiny. My children, look behind you!"

They turned; and flashing forth, as it were, in a sheet of flame, the fiend worshippers were seen; the smile of welcome gleamed darkly on every visage.

"There," resumed the sable form, "are all whom ye have reverenced from youth. Ye deemed them holier than yourselves, and shrank from your own sin, contrasting it with their lives of righteousness and prayerful aspirations heavenward. Yet here are they all in my worshipping assembly. This night it shall be granted you to know their secret deeds: how hoary-bearded elders of the church have whispered wanton words to the young maids of their households; how many a woman, eager for widows' weeds, has given her husband a drink at bedtime and let him sleep his last sleep in her bosom; how beardless youths have made haste to inherit their fathers' wealth; and how fair damsels—blush not, sweet ones—have dug little graves in the garden, and bidden me, the sole guest, to an infant's funeral. By the sympathy of your human hearts for sin ye shall scent out all the places—whether in church, bed-chamber, street, field, or forest—where crime has been committed, and shall exult to behold the whole earth one stain of guilt, one mighty blood spot. Far more than this. It shall be yours to penetrate, in every bosom, the deep mystery of sin, the fountain of all wicked arts, and which inexhaustibly supplies more evil impulses than human power—than my power at its utmost—can make manifest in deeds. And now, my children, look upon each other."

They did so; and, by the blaze of the hell-kindled torches, the wretched man beheld his Faith, and the wife her husband, trembling before that unhallowed altar.

"Lo, there ye stand, my children," said the figure, in a deep and solemn tone, almost sad with its despairing awfulness, as if his once angelic nature could yet mourn for our miserable race. "Depending upon one another's hearts, ye had still hoped that virtue were not all a dream. Now are ye undeceived. Evil is the nature of mankind. Evil must be your only happiness. Welcome again, my children, to the communion of your race."

"Welcome," repeated the fiend worshippers, in one cry of despair and triumph.

And there they stood, the only pair, as it seemed, who were yet hesitating on the verge of wickedness in this dark world. A basin was hollowed, naturally, in the rock. Did it contain water, reddened by the lurid light? or was it blood? or, perchance, a liquid flame? Herein did the shape of evil dip his hand and prepare to lay the mark of baptism upon their foreheads, that they might be partakers of the mystery of sin, more conscious of the secret guilt of others, both in deed and thought, than they could now be of their own. The husband cast one look at his pale wife, and Faith at him. What polluted wretches would the next glance show them to each other, shuddering alike at what they disclosed and what they saw!

"Faith! Faith!" cried the husband, "look up to heaven, and resist the wicked one."

Whether Faith obeyed he knew not. Hardly had he spoken when he found himself amid calm night and solitude, listening to a roar of the wind which died heavily away through the forest. He staggered against the rock, and felt it chill and damp; while a hanging twig, that had been all on fire, besprinkled his cheek with the coldest dew.

The next morning young Goodman Brown came slowly into the street of Salem village, staring around him like a bewildered man. The good old minister was taking a walk along the graveyard to get an appetite for breakfast and meditate his sermon, and bestowed a blessing, as he passed, on Goodman Brown. He shrank from the venerable saint as if to avoid an anathema. Old Deacon Gookin was at domestic worship, and the holy words of his prayer were heard through the open window. "What God doth the wizard pray to?" quoth Goodman Brown. Goody Cloyse, that excel-

lent old Christian, stood in the early sunshine at her own lattice, catechizing a little girl who had brought her a pint of morning's milk. Goodman Brown snatched away the child as from the grasp of the fiend himself. Turning the corner by the meeting-house, he spied the head of Faith, with the pink ribbons, gazing anxiously forth, and bursting into such joy at sight of him that she skipped along the street and almost kissed her husband before the whole village. But Goodman Brown looked sternly and sadly into her face, and passed on without a greeting.

Had Goodman Brown fallen asleep in the forest and only dreamed a wild dream of a witch-meeting?

Be it so if you will; but, alas! it was a dream of evil omen for young Goodman Brown. A stern, a sad, a darkly meditative, a distrustful, if not a desperate man did he become from the night of that fearful dream. On the Sabbath day, when the congregation were singing a holy psalm, he could not listen because an anthem of sin rushed loudly upon his ear and drowned all the blessed strain. When the minister spoke from the pulpit with power and fervid eloquence, and, with his hand on the open Bible, of the sacred truths of our religion, and of saint-like lives and triumphant deaths, and of future bliss or misery unutterable, then did Goodman Brown turn pale, dreading lest the roof should thunder down upon the gray blasphemer and his hearers. Often, awaking suddenly at midnight, he shrank from the bosom of Faith; and at morning or eventide, when the family knelt down at prayer, he scowled and muttered to himself, and gazed sternly at his wife, and turned away. And when he had lived long, and was borne to his grave a hoary corpse, followed by Faith, an aged woman, and children and grandchildren, a goodly procession, besides neighbors not a few, they carved no hopeful verse upon his tombstone, for his dying hour was gloom.

Roger Malvin's Burial (1830)

One of the few incidents of Indian warfare naturally susceptible of the moonlight of romance was that expedition undertaken for the defence of the frontiers in the year 1725, which resulted in the well-remembered "Lovell's Fight." Imagination, by casting certain circumstances judicially into the shade, may see much to admire in the heroism of a little band who gave battle to twice their num-

ber in the heart of the enemy's country. The open bravery displayed by both parties was in accordance with civilized ideas of valor; and chivalry itself might not blush to record the deeds of one or two individuals. The battle, though so fatal to those who fought, was not unfortunate in its consequences to the country; for it broke the strength of a tribe and conduced to the peace which subsisted during several ensuing years. History and tradition are unusually minute in their memorials of this affair; and the captain of a scouting party of frontier men has acquired as actual a military renown as many a victorious leader of thousands. Some of the incidents contained in the following pages will be recognized, notwithstanding the substitution of fictitious names, by such as have heard, from old men's lips, the fate of the few combatants who were in a condition to retreat after "Lovell's Fight."

The early sunbeams hovered cheerfully upon the tree-tops, beneath which two weary and wounded men had stretched their limbs the night before. Their bed of withered oak leaves was strewn upon the small level space, at the foot of a rock, situated near the summit of one of the gentle swells by which the face of the country is there diversified. The mass of granite, rearing its smooth, flat surface fifteen or twenty feet above their heads, was not unlike a gigantic gravestone, upon which the veins seemed to form an inscription in forgotten characters. On a tract of several acres around this rock, oaks and other hard-wood trees had supplied the place of the pines, which were the usual growth of the land; and a young and vigorous sapling stood close beside the travellers.

The severe wound of the elder man had probably deprived him of sleep; for, so soon as the first ray of sunshine rested on the top of the highest tree, he reared himself painfully from his recumbent posture and sat erect. The deep lines of his countenance and the scattered gray of his hair marked him as past the middle age; but his muscular frame would, but for the effects of his wound, have been as capable of sustaining fatigue as in the early vigor of life. Languor and exhaustion now sat upon his haggard features; and the despairing glance which he sent forward through the depths of the forest proved his own conviction that his pilgrimage was at an end. He next turned his eyes to the companion who reclined by his side. The youth—for he had scarcely attained the years of manhood—lay, with his head upon his arm, in the embrace of an unquiet sleep, which a thrill of pain from his wounds seemed each moment on the point of breaking. His right hand grasped a musket; and, to judge from the violent action of his features, his slumbers were bringing back a vision of the conflict of which he was one of the few survivors. A shout—deep and loud in his dreaming fancy—found its way in an imperfect murmur

to his lips; and, starting even at the slight sound of his own voice, he suddenly awoke. The first act of reviving recollection was to make anxious inquiries respecting the condition of his wounded fellow-traveller. The latter shook his head.

"Reuben, my boy," said he, "this rock beneath which we sit will serve for an old hunter's gravestone. There is many and many a long mile of howling wilderness before us yet; nor would it avail me anything if the smoke of my own chimney were but on the other side of that swell of land. The Indian bullet was deadlier than I thought."

"You are weary with our three days' travel," replied the youth, "and a little longer rest will recruit you. Sit you here while I search the woods for the herbs and roots that must be our sustenance; and, having eaten, you shall lean on me, and we will turn our faces homeward. I doubt not that, with my help, you can attain to some one of the frontier garrisons."

"There is not two days' life in me, Reuben," said the other, calmly, "and I will no longer burden you with my useless body, when you can scarcely support your own. Your wounds are deep and your strength is failing fast; yet, if you hasten onward alone, you may be preserved. For me there is no hope, and I will await death here."

"If it must be so, I will remain and watch by you," said Reuben, resolutely.

"No, my son, no," rejoined his companion. "Let the wish of a dying man have weight with you; give me one grasp of your hand, and get you hence. Think you that my last moments will be eased by the thought that I leave you to die a more lingering death? I have loved you like a father, Reuben; and at a time like this I should have something of a father's authority. I charge you to be gone that I may die in peace."

"And because you have been a father to me, should I therefore leave you to perish and to lie unburied in the wilderness?" exclaimed the youth. "No; if your end be in truth approaching, I will watch by you and receive your parting words. I will dig a grave here by the rock, in which, if my weakness overcome me, we will rest together; or, if Heaven gives me strength, I will seek my way home."

"In the cities and wherever men dwell," replied the other, "they bury their dead in the earth; they hide them from the sight of the living; but here, where no step may pass perhaps for a hundred years, wherefore should I not rest beneath the open sky, covered only by the oak leaves when the autumn winds shall strew them? And for a monument, here is this gray rock, on which my dying hand shall carve the name of Roger Malvin; and the traveller in days to come will know that here sleeps a hunter and a warrior. Tarry not, then, for a folly like this, but hasten away, if not for your own sake, for hers who will else be desolate."

Malvin spoke the last few words in a faltering voice, and their effect upon his companion was strongly visible. They reminded him that there were other and less questionable duties than that of sharing the fate of a man whom his death could not benefit. Nor can it be affirmed that no selfish feeling strove to enter Reuben's heart, though the consciousness made him more earnestly resist his companion's entreaties.

"How terrible to wait the slow approach of death in this solitude!" exclaimed he. "A brave man does not shrink in the battle; and, when friends stand round the bed, even women may die composedly; but here"—

"I shall not shrink even here, Reuben Bourne," interrupted Malvin. "I am a man of no weak heart, and, if I were, there is a surer support than that of earthly friends. You are young, and life is dear to you. Your last moments will need comfort far more than mine; and when you have laid me in the earth, and are alone, and night is settling on the forest, you will feel all the bitterness of the death that may now be escaped. But I will urge no selfish motive to your generous nature. Leave me for my sake, that, having said a prayer for your safety, I may have space to settle my account undisturbed by worldly sorrows."

"And your daughter,—how shall I dare to meet her eye?" exclaimed Reuben. "She will ask the fate of her father, whose life I vowed to defend with my own. Must I tell her that he travelled three days' march with me from the field of battle and that then I left him to perish in the wilderness? Were it not better to lie down and die by your side than to return safe and say this to Dorcas?"

"Tell my daughter," said Roger Malvin, "that, though yourself sore wounded, and weak, and weary, you led my tottering footsteps many a mile, and left me only at my earnest entreaty, because I would not have your blood upon my soul. Tell her that through pain and danger you were faithful, and that, if your lifeblood could have saved me, it would have flowed to its last drop; and tell her that you will be something dearer than a father, and that my blessing is with you both, and

that my dying eyes can see a long and pleasant path in which you will journey together."

As Malvin spoke he almost raised himself from the ground, and the energy of his concluding words seemed to fill the wild and lonely forest with a vision of happiness; but, when he sank exhausted upon his bed of oak leaves, the light which had kindled in Reuben's eye was quenched. He felt as if it were both sin and folly to think of happiness at such a moment. His companion watched his changing countenance, and sought with generous art to wile him to his own good.

"Perhaps I deceive myself in regard to the time I have to live," he resumed. "It may be that, with speedy assistance, I might recover of my wound. The foremost fugitives must, ere this, have carried tidings of our fatal battle to the frontiers, and parties will be out to succor those in like condition with ourselves. Should you meet one of these and guide them hither, who can tell but that I may sit by my own fireside again?"

A mournful smile strayed across the features of the dying man as he insinuated that unfounded hope,—which, however, was not without its effect on Reuben. No merely selfish motive, nor even the desolate condition of Dorcas, could have induced him to desert his companion at such a moment— but his wishes seized on the thought that Malvin's life might be preserved, and his sanguine nature heightened almost to certainty the remote possibility of procuring human aid.

"Surely there is reason, weighty reason, to hope that friends are not far distant," he said, half aloud. "There fled one coward, unwounded, in the beginning of the fight, and most probably he made good speed. Every true man on the frontier would shoulder his musket at the news; and, though no party may range so far into the woods as this, I shall perhaps encounter them in one day's march. Counsel me faithfully," he added, turning to Malvin, in distrust of his own motives. "Were your situation mine, would you desert me while life remained?"

"It is now twenty years," replied Roger Malvin, —sighing, however, as he secretly acknowledged the wide dissimilarity between the two cases,—"it is now twenty years since I escaped with one dear friend from Indian captivity near Montreal. We journeyed many days through the woods, till at length overcome with hunger and weariness, my friend lay down and besought me to leave him; for he knew that, if I remained, we both must perish; and, with but little hope of obtaining succor, I heaped a pillow of dry leaves beneath his head and hastened on."

"And did you return in time to save him?" asked Reuben, hanging on Malvin's words as if they were to be prophetic of his own success.

"I did," answered the other. "I came upon the camp of a hunting party before sunset of the same day. I guided them to the spot where my comrade was expecting death; and he is now a hale and hearty man upon his own farm, far within the frontiers, while I lie wounded here in the depths of the wilderness."

This example, powerful in affecting Reuben's decision, was aided, unconsciously to himself, by the hidden strength of many another motive. Roger Malvin perceived that the victory was nearly won.

"Now, go, my son, and Heaven prosper you!" he said. "Turn not back with your friends when you meet them, lest your wounds and weariness overcome you; but send hitherward two or three, that may be spared, to search for me; and believe me, Reuben, my heart will be lighter with every step you take towards home." Yet there was, perhaps, a change both in his countenance and voice as he spoke thus; for, after all, it was a ghastly fate to be left expiring in the wilderness.

Reuben Bourne, but half convinced that he was acting rightly, at length raised himself from the ground and prepared himself for his departure. And first, though contrary to Malvin's wishes, he collected a stock of roots and herbs, which had been their only food during the last two days. This useless supply he placed within reach of the dying man, for whom, also, he swept together a bed of dry oak leaves. Then climbing to the summit of the rock, which on one side was rough and broken, he bent the oak sapling downward, and bound his handkerchief to the topmost branch. This precaution was not unnecessary to direct any who might come in search of Malvin; for every part of the rock, except its broad, smooth front, was concealed at a little distance by the dense undergrowth of the forest. The handkerchief had been the bandage of a wound upon Reuben's arm; and, as he bound it to the tree, he vowed by the blood that stained it that he would return, either to save his companion's life or to lay his body in the grave. He then descended, and stood, with downcast eyes, to receive Roger Malvin's parting words.

The experience of the latter suggested much and minute advice respecting the youth's journey through the trackless forest. Upon this subject he spoke with calm earnestness, as if he were sending Reuben to the battle or the chase while he himself remained secure at home, and not as if the human countenance that was about to leave him were the last he would ever behold. But his firmness was shaken before he concluded.

"Carry my blessing to Dorcas, and say that my last prayer shall be for her and you. Bid her to have no hard thoughts because you left me here," —Reuben's heart smote him,—"for that your life would not have weighed with you if its sacrifice could have done me good. She will marry you after she has mourned a little while for her father; and Heaven grant you long and happy days, and may your children's children stand round your death bed! And, Reuben," added he, as the weakness of mortality made its way at last, "return, when your wounds are healed and your weariness refreshed,—return to this wild rock, and lay my bones in the grave, and say a prayer over them."

An almost superstitious regard, arising perhaps from the customs of the Indians, whose war was with the dead as well as the living, was paid by the frontier inhabitants to the rites of sepulture; and there are many instances of the sacrifice of life in the attempt to bury those who had fallen by the "sword of the wilderness." Reuben, therefore, felt the full importance of the promise which he most solemnly made to return and perform Roger Malvin's obsequies. It was remarkable that the latter, speaking his whole heart in his parting words, no longer endeavored to persuade the youth that even the speediest succor might avail to the preservation of his life. Reuben was internally convinced that he should see Malvin's living face no more. His generous nature would fain have delayed him, at whatever risk, till the dying scene were past; but the desire of existence and the hope of happiness had strengthened in his heart, and he was unable to resist them.

"It is enough," said Roger Malvin, having listened to Reuben's promise. "Go, and God speed you!"

The youth pressed his hand in silence, turned, and was departing. His slow and faltering steps, however, had borne him but a little way before Malvin's voice recalled him.

"Reuben, Reuben," said he, faintly; and Reuben returned and knelt down by the dying man.

"Raise me, and let me lean against the rock," was his last request. "My face will be turned towards home, and I shall see you a moment longer as you pass among the trees."

Reuben, having made the desired alteration in his companion's posture, again began his solitary pilgrimage. He walked more hastily at first than was consistent with his strength; for a sort of guilty feeling, which sometimes torments men in their most justifiable acts, caused him to seek concealment from Malvin's eyes; but after he had trodden far upon the rustling forest leaves he crept back, impelled by a wild and painful curiosity, and, sheltered by the earthy roots of an uptorn tree, gazed earnestly at the desolate man. The morning sun was unclouded, and the trees and shrubs imbibed the sweet air of the month of May; yet there seemed a gloom on Nature's face, as if she sympathized with mortal pain and sorrow. Roger Malvin's hands were uplifted in a fervent prayer, some of the words of which stole through the stillness of the woods and entered Reuben's heart, torturing it with an unutterable pang. They were the broken accents of a petition for his own happiness and that of Dorcas; and, as the youth listened, conscience, or something in its similitude, pleaded strongly with him to return and lie down again by the rock. He felt how hard was the doom of the kind and generous being whom he had deserted in his extremity. Death would come like the slow approach of a corpse, stealing gradually towards him through the forest, and showing its ghastly and motionless features from behind a nearer and yet a nearer tree. But such must have been Reuben's own fate had he tarried another sunset; and who shall impute blame to him if he shrink from so useless a sacrifice? As he gave a parting look, a breeze waved the little banner upon the sapling oak and reminded Reuben of his vow.

Many circumstances combined to retard the wounded traveller in his way to the frontiers. On the second day the clouds, gathering densely over the sky, precluded the possibility of regulating his course by the position of the sun; and he knew not but that every effort of his almost exhausted strength was removing him farther from the home he sought. His scanty sustenance was supplied by the berries and other spontaneous products of the forest. Herds of deer, it is true, sometimes bounded past him, and partridges frequently whirred up before his footsteps; but his ammunition had been expended in the fight, and he had no means of slaying them. His wounds, irritated by the constant exertion in which lay the only hope of life, wore away his strength and at intervals confused his reason. But, even in the wanderings of intellect,

Reuben's young heart clung strongly to existence; and it was only through absolute incapacity of motion that he at last sank down beneath a tree, compelled there to await death.

In this situation he was discovered by a party who, upon the first intelligence of the fight, had been despatched to the relief of the survivors. They conveyed him to the nearest settlement, which chanced to be that of his own residence.

Dorcas, in the simplicity of the olden time, watched by the bedside of her wounded lover, and administered all those comforts that are in the sole gift of woman's heart and hand. During several days Reuben's recollection strayed drowsily among the perils and hardships through which he had passed, and he was incapable of returning definite answers to the inquiries with which many were eager to harass him. No authentic particulars of the battle had yet been circulated; nor could mothers, wives, and children tell whether their loved ones were detained by captivity or by the stronger chain of death. Dorcas nourished her apprehensions in silence till one afternoon when Reuben awoke from an unquiet sleep, and seemed to recognize her more perfectly than at any previous time. She saw that his intellect had become composed, and she could no longer restrain her filial anxiety.

"My father, Reuben?" she began; but the change in her lover's countenance made her pause.

The youth shrank as if with a bitter pain, and the blood gushed vividly into his wan and hollow cheeks. His first impulse was to cover his face; but apparently with a desperate effort, he half raised himself and spoke vehemently, defending himself against an imaginary accusation.

"Your father was sore wounded in the battle, Dorcas; and he bade me not burden myself with him, but only to lead him to the lakeside, that he might quench his thirst and die. But I would not desert the old man in his extremity, and, though bleeding myself, I supported him; I gave him half my strength, and led him away with me. For three days we journeyed on together, and your father was sustained beyond my hopes, but, awaking at sunrise on the fourth day, I found him faint and exhausted; he was unable to proceed; his life had ebbed away fast; and"—

"He died!" exclaimed Dorcas, faintly.

Reuben felt it impossible to acknowledge that his selfish love of life had hurried him away before her father's fate was decided. He spoke not; he only bowed his head; and, between shame and exhaustion, sank back and hid his face in the pillow.

Dorcas wept when her fears were thus confirmed; but the shock, as it had been long anticipated, was on that account the less violent.

"You dug a grave for my poor father in the wilderness, Reuben?" was the question by which her filial piety manifested itself.

"My hands were weak; but I did what I could," replied the youth in a smothered tone. "There stands a noble tombstone above his head; and I would to Heaven I slept as soundly as he!"

Dorcas, perceiving the wildness of his latter words, inquired no further at the time; but her heart found ease in the thought that Roger Malvin had not lacked such funeral rites as it was possible to bestow. The tale of Reuben's courage and fidelity lost nothing when she communicated it to her friends; and the poor youth, tottering from his sick chamber to breathe the sunny air, experienced from every tongue the miserable and humiliating torture of unmerited praise. All acknowledged that he might worthily demand the hand of the fair maiden to whose father he had been "faithful unto death;" and, as my tale is not of love, it shall suffice to say that in the space of a few months Reuben became the husband of Dorcas Malvin. During the marriage ceremony the bride was covered with blushes, but the bridegroom's face was pale.

There was now in the breast of Reuben Bourne an incommunicable thought—something which he was to conceal most heedfully from her whom he most loved and trusted. He regretted, deeply and bitterly, the moral cowardice that had restrained his words when he was about to disclose the truth to Dorcas; but pride, the fear of losing her affection, the dread of universal scorn, forbade him to rectify this falsehood. He felt that for leaving Roger Malvin he deserved no censure. His presence, the gratuitous sacrifice of his own life, would have added only another and a needless agony to the last moments of the dying man; but concealment had imparted to a justifiable act much of the secret effect of guilt; and Reuben, while reason told him that he had done right, experienced in no small degree the mental horrors which punish the perpetrator of undiscovered crime. By a certain association of ideas, he at times almost imagined himself a murderer. For years, also, a thought would occasionally recur, which, though he perceived all its folly and extravagance, he had not power to banish from his mind. It was a haunting and torturing fancy that his father-in-law was yet sitting at the foot of the rock, on the withered forest leaves, alive, and awaiting his pledged assistance. These mental deceptions, however, came and went, nor did he ever mistake them for realities; but in the calmest and clearest moods of his mind he was conscious that he had a deep vow unredeemed, and that an unburied corpse was calling to him out of the wilderness. Yet such was the consequence of his prevarication that he could not obey the call. It was now too late to require the assistance of Roger Malvin's friends in performing his long-deferred sepulture; and superstitious fears, of which none were more susceptible than the people of the outward settlements, forbade Reuben to go alone. Neither did he know where in the pathless and illimitable forest to seek that smooth and lettered rock at the base of which the body lay: his remembrance of every portion of his travel thence was indistinct, and the latter part had left no impression upon his mind. There was, however, a continual impulse, a voice audible only to himself, commanding him to go forth and redeem his vow; and he had a strange impression that, were he to make the trial, he would be led straight to Malvin's bones. But year after year that summons, unheard but felt, was disobeyed. His one secret thought became like a chain binding down his spirit and like a serpent gnawing into his heart; and he was transformed into a sad and downcast yet irritable man.

In the course of a few years after their marriage changes began to be visible in the external prosperity of Reuben and Dorcas. The only riches of the former had been his stout heart and strong arm; but the latter, her father's sole heiress, had made her husband master of a farm, under older cultivation, larger, and better stocked than most of the frontier establishments. Reuben Bourne, however, was a neglectful husband-man; and, while the lands of the other settlers became annually more fruitful, his deteriorated in the same proportion. The discouragements to agriculture were greatly lessened by the cessation of Indian war, during which men held the plough in one hand and the musket in the other, and were fortunate if the products of their dangerous labor were not destroyed, either in the field or in the barn, by the savage enemy. But Reuben did not profit by the altered condition of the country; nor can it be denied that his intervals of industrious attention to his affairs were but scantily rewarded with success. The irritability by which he had recently become distinguished was another cause of his declining prosperity, as it occasioned frequent quarrels in his

unavoidable intercourse with the neighboring settlers. The results of these were innumerable lawsuits; for the people of New England, in the
earliest stages and wildest circumstances of the
country, adopted, whenever attainable, the legal
mode of deciding their differences. To be brief,
the world did not go well with Reuben Bourne;
and, though not till many years after his marriage,
he was finally a ruined man, with but one remaining expedient against the evil fate that had pursued him. He was to throw sunlight into some
deep recess of the forest, and seek subsistence from
the virgin bosom of the wilderness.

The only child of Reuben and Dorcas was a son,
now arrived at the age of fifteen years, beautiful
in youth, and giving promise of a glorious manhood. He was peculiarly qualified for, and already
began to excel in, the wild accomplishments of
frontier life. His foot was fleet, his aim true, his
apprehension quick, his heart glad and high; and
all who anticipated the return of Indian war spoke
of Cyrus Bourne as a future leader in the land.
The boy was loved by his father with a deep and
silent strength, as if whatever was good and happy
in his own nature had been transferred to his child,
carrying his affections with it. Even Dorcas, though
loving and beloved, was far less dear to him; for
Reuben's secret thoughts and insulated emotions
had gradually made him a selfish man, and he
could no longer love deeply except where he saw
or imagined some reflection or likeness of his own
mind. In Cyrus he recognized what he had himself been in other days; and at intervals he seemed
to partake of the boy's spirit, and to be revived
with a fresh and happy life. Reuben was accompanied by his son in the expedition, for the purpose of selecting a tract of land and felling and
burning the timber, which necessarily preceded
the removal of the household gods. Two months
of autumn were thus occupied, after which Reuben
Bourne and his young hunter returned to spend
their last winter in the settlements.

It was early in the month of May that the little
family snapped asunder whatever tendrils of affections had clung to inanimate objects, and bade
farewell to the few who, in the blight of fortune,
called themselves their friends. The sadness of the
parting moment had, to each of the pilgrims, its
peculiar alleviations. Reuben, a moody man, and
misanthropic because unhappy, strode onward with
his usual stern brow and downcast eye, feeling few
regrets and disdaining to acknowledge any. Dorcas,
while she wept abundantly over the broken ties
by which her simple and affectionate nature had
bound itself to everything, felt that the inhabitants
of her inmost heart moved on with her, and that
all else would be supplied wherever she might go.
And the boy dashed one tear-drop from his eye,
and thought of the adventurous pleasures of the
untrodden forest.

Oh, who, in the enthusiasm of a daydream, has
not wished that he were a wanderer in a world of
summer wilderness, with one fair and gentle being
hanging lightly on his arm? In youth his free and
exulting step would know no barrier but the rolling
ocean or the snow-topped mountains; calmer manhood would choose a home where Nature had
strewn a double wealth in the vale of some transparent stream; and when hoary age, after long,
long years of that pure life, stole on and found
him there, it would find him the father of a race,
the patriarch of a people, the founder of a mighty
nation yet to be. When death, like the sweet sleep
which we welcome after a day of happiness, came
over him, his far descendants would mourn over
the venerated dust. Enveloped by tradition in mysterious attributes, the men of future generations
would call him godlike; and remote posterity
would see him standing, dimly glorious, far up the
valley of a hundred centuries.

The tangled and gloomy forest through which
the personages of my tale were wandering differed
widely from the dreamer's land of fantasy; yet
there was something in their way of life that Nature asserted as her own, and the gnawing cares
which went with them from the world were all
that now obstructed their happiness. One stout
and shaggy steed, the bearer of all their wealth,
did not shrink from the added weight of Dorcas;
although her hardy breeding sustained her, during
the latter part of each day's journey, by her husband's side. Reuben and his son, their muskets on
their shoulders and their axes slung behind them,
kept an unwearied pace, each watching with a
hunter's eye for the game that supplied their food.
When hunger bade, they halted and prepared their
meal on the bank of some unpolluted forest brook,
which, as they knelt down with thirsty lips to
drink, murmured a sweet unwillingness, like a
maiden at love's first kiss. They slept beneath a
hut of branches, and awoke at peep of light refreshed for the toils of another day. Dorcas and
the boy went on joyously, and even Reuben's spirit
shone at intervals with an outward gladness; but
inwardly there was a cold, cold sorrow, which he

compared to the snowdrifts lying deep in the glens and hollows of the rivulets while the leaves were brightly green above.

Cyrus Bourne was sufficiently skilled in the travel of the woods to observe that his father did not adhere to the course they had pursued in their expedition of the preceding autumn. They were now keeping farther to the north, striking out more directly from the settlements, and into a region of which savage beasts and savage men were as yet the sole possessors. The boy sometimes hinted his opinions upon the subject, and Reuben listened attentively, and once or twice altered the direction of their march in accordance with his son's counsel; but, having so done, he seemed ill at ease. His quick and wandering glances were sent forward, apparently in search of enemies lurking behind the tree trunks; and, seeing nothing there, he would cast his eyes backwards as if in fear of some pursuer. Cyrus, perceiving that his father gradually resumed the old direction, forbore to interfere; nor, though something began to weigh upon his heart, did his adventurous nature permit him to regret the increased length and the mystery of their way.

On the afternoon of the fifth day they halted, and made their simple encampment nearly an hour before sunset. The face of the country, for the last few miles, had been diversified by swells of land resembling huge waves of a petrified sea; and in one of the corresponding hollows, a wild and romantic spot, had the family reared their hut and kindled their fire. There is something chilling, and yet heart-warming, in the thought of these three, united by strong bands of love and insulated from all that breathe beside. The dark and gloomy pines looked down upon them, and, as the wind swept through their tops, a pitying sound was heard in the forest; or did those old trees groan in fear that men were come to lay the axe to their roots at last? Reuben and his son, while Dorcas made ready their meal, proposed to wander out in search of game, of which that day's march had afforded no supply. The boy, promising not to quit the vicinity of the encampment, bounded off with a step as light and elastic as that of the deer he hoped to slay; while his father, feeling a transient happiness as he gazed after him, was about to pursue an opposite direction. Dorcas, in the meanwhile, had seated herself near their fire of fallen branches, upon the mossgrown and mouldering trunk of a tree uprooted years before. Her employment, diversified by an occasional glance at the pot, now beginning to simmer over the blaze, was the perusal of the current year's Massachusetts Almanac, which, with the exception of an old black-letter Bible, comprised all the literary wealth of the family. None pay a greater regard to arbitrary divisions of time than those who are excluded from society; and Dorcas mentioned, as if the information were of importance, that it was now the twelfth of May. Her husband started.

"The twelfth of May! I should remember it well," muttered he, while many thoughts occasioned a momentary confusion in his mind. "Where am I? Whither am I wandering? Where did I leave him?"

Dorcas, too well accustomed to her husband's wayward moods to note any peculiarity of demeanor, now laid aside the almanac and addressed him in that mournful tone which the tender hearted appropriate to griefs long cold and dead.

"It was near this time of the month, eighteen years ago, that my poor father left this world for a better. He had a kind arm to hold his head and a kind voice to cheer him. Reuben, in his last moments; and the thought of the faithful care you took of him has comforted me many a time since. Oh, death would have been awful to a solitary man in a wild place like this!"

"Pray Heaven, Dorcas," said Reuben, in a broken voice,—"pray Heaven that neither of us three dies solitary and lies unburied in this howling wilderness!" And he hastened away, leaving her to watch the fire beneath the gloomy pines.

Reuben Bourne's rapid pace gradually slackened as the pang, unintentionally inflicted by the words of Dorcas, became less acute. Many strange reflections, however, thronged upon him; and, straying onward rather like a sleep walker than a hunter, it was attributable to no care of his own that his devious course kept him in the vicinity of the encampment. His steps were imperceptibly led almost in a circle; nor did he observe that he was on the verge of a tract of land heavily timbered, but not with pine-trees. The place of the latter was here supplied by oaks and other of the harder woods; and around their roots clustered a dense and bushy under-growth, leaving, however, barren spaces between the trees, thick strewn with withered leaves. Whenever the rustling of the branches or the creaking of the trunks made a sound, as if the forest were waking from slumber, Reuben instinctively raised the musket that rested on his arm, and cast a quick, sharp glance on every side; but, convinced by a partial observation that no animal was near, he would again give himself up to his thoughts. He was musing on the strange influence that had led him away from his premeditated course, and so far into the depths of the wilderness. Unable to penetrate to the secret place of his soul where his motives lay hidden, he believed that a supernatural voice had called him onward, and that a supernatural power had obstructed his retreat. He trusted that it was Heaven's intent to afford him an opportunity of expiating his sin; he hoped that he might find the bones so long unburied; and that, having laid the earth over them, peace would throw its sunlight into the sepulchre of his heart. From these thoughts he was aroused by a rustling in the forest at some distance from the spot to which he had wandered. Perceiving the motion of some object behind a thick veil of undergrowth, he fired, with the instinct of a hunter and the aim of a practised marksman. A low moan, which told his success, and by which even animals can express their dying agony, was unheeded by Reuben Bourne. What were the recollections now breaking upon him?

The thicket into which Reuben had fired was near the summit of a swell of land, and was clustered around the base of a rock, which, in the shape and smoothness of one of its surfaces, was not unlike a gigantic gravestone. As if reflected in a mirror, its likeness was in Reuben's memory. He even recognized the veins which seemed to form an inscription in forgotten characters: everything remained the same, except that a thick covert of bushes shrouded the lower part of the rock, and would have hidden Roger Malvin had he still been sitting there. Yet in the next moment Reuben's eye was caught by another change that time had effected since he last stood where he was now standing again behind the earthy roots of the uptorn tree. The sapling to which he had bound the bloodstained symbol of his vow had increased and strengthened into an oak, far indeed from its maturity, but with no mean spread of shadowy branches. There was one singularity observable in this tree which made Reuben tremble. The middle and lower branches were in luxuriant life, and an excess of vegetation had fringed the trunk almost to the ground; but a blight had apparently stricken the upper part of the oak, and the very topmost bough was withered, sapless, and utterly dead. Reuben remembered how the little banner had fluttered on that topmost bough, when it was green and lovely, eighteen years before. Whose guilt had blasted it?

Dorcas, after the departure of the two hunters, continued her preparations for their evening repast. Her sylvan table was the moss-covered trunk of a large fallen tree, on the broadest part of which she had spread a snow-white cloth and arranged what were left of the bright pewter vessels that had been her pride in the settlements. It had a strange aspect, that one little spot of homely comfort in the desolate heart of Nature. The sunshine yet lingered upon the higher branches of the trees that grew on rising ground; but the shadows of evening had deepened into the hollow where the encampment was made, and the firelight began to redden as it gleamed up the tall trunks of the pines or hovered on the dense and obscure mass of foliage that circled round the spot. The heart of Dorcas was not sad; for she felt that it was better to journey in the wilderness with two whom she loved than to be a lonely woman in a crowd that cared not for her. As she busied herself in arranging seats of mouldering wood, covered with leaves, for Reuben and her son, her voice danced through the gloomy forest in the measure of a song that she had learned in youth. The rude melody, the production of a bard who won no name, was descriptive of a winter evening in a frontier cottage, when, secured from savage inroad by the high-piled snow-drifts, the family rejoiced by their own fireside. The whole song possessed the nameless charm peculiar to unborrowed thought, but four continually-recurring lines shone out from the rest like the blaze of the hearth whose joys they celebrated. Into them, working magic with a few simple words, the poet had instilled the very essence of domestic love and household happiness, and they were poetry and picture joined in one. As Dorcas sang, the walls of her forsaken home seemed to encircle her; she no longer saw the gloomy pines, nor heard the wind which still, as she began each verse, sent a heavy breath through the branches, and died away in a hollow moan from the burden of the song. She was aroused by the report of a gun in the vicinity of the encampment; and either the sudden sound, or her loneliness by the glowing fire, caused her to tremble violently. The next moment she laughed in the pride of a mother's heart.

"My beautiful young hunter! My boy has slain a deer!" she exclaimed, recollecting that in the direction whence the shot proceeded Cyrus had gone to the chase.

She waited a reasonable time to hear her son's light step bounding over the rustling leaves to tell of his success. But he did not immediately appear; and she sent her cheerful voice among the trees in search of him.

"Cyrus! Cyrus!"

His coming was still delayed; and she determined, as the report had apparently been very near, to seek for him in person. Her assistance, also, might be necessary in bringing home the venison which she flattered herself he had obtained. She therefore set forward, directing her steps by the long-past sound, and singing as she went, in order that the boy might be aware of her approach and run to meet her. From behind the trunk of every tree, and from every hiding-place in the thick foliage of the undergrowth, she hoped to discover the countenance of her son, laughing with the sportive mischief that is born of affection. The sun was now beneath the horizon, and the light that came down among the leaves was sufficiently dim to create many illusions in her expecting fancy. Several times she seemed indistinctly to see his face gazing out from among the leaves; and once she imagined that he stood beckoning to her at the base of a craggy rock. Keeping her eyes on this object, however, it proved to be no more than the trunk of an oak fringed to the very ground with little branches, one of which, thrust out farther than the rest, was shaken by the breeze. Making her way round the foot of the rock, she suddenly found herself close to her husband, who had approached in another direction. Leaning upon the butt of his gun, the muzzle of which rested upon the withered leaves, he was apparently absorbed in the contemplation of some object at his feet.

"How is this Reuben? Have you slain the deer and fallen asleep over him?" exclaimed Dorcas, laughing cheerfully, on her first slight observation of his posture and appearance.

He stirred not, neither did he turn his eyes towards her; and a cold, shuddering fear, indefinite in its source and object, began to creep into her blood. She now perceived that her husband's face was ghastly pale, and his features were rigid, as if incapable of assuming any other expression than the strong despair which had hardened upon them. He gave not the slightest evidence that he was aware of her approach.

"For the love of Heaven, Reuben, speak to me!" cried Dorcas; and the strange sound of her own voice affrighted her even more than the dead silence.

Her husband started, stared into her face, drew her to the front of the rock, and pointed with his finger.

Oh, there lay the boy, asleep, but dreamless, upon the fallen forest leaves! His cheek rested upon his arm—his curled locks were thrown back from his brow—his limbs were slightly relaxed. Had a sudden weariness overcome the youthful hunter? Would his mother's voice arouse him? She knew that it was death.

"This broad rock is the gravestone of your near kindred, Dorcas," said her husband. "Your tears will fall at once over your father and your son."

She heard him not. With one wild shriek, that seemed to force its way from the sufferer's inmost soul, she sank insensible by the side of her dead boy. At that moment the withered topmost bough of the oak loosened itself in the stilly air, and fell in soft, light fragments upon the rock, upon the leaves, upon Reuben, upon his wife and child, and upon Roger Malvin's bones. Then Reuben's heart was stricken, and the tears gushed out like water from a rock. The vow that the wounded youth had made the blighted man had come to redeem. His sin was expiated,—the curse was gone from him; and in the hour when he had shed blood dearer to him than his own, a prayer, the first for years, went up to Heaven from the lips of Reuben Bourne.

Ethan Brand: A Chapter from an Abortive Romance (1850)

Bartram the lime-burner, a rough, heavy-looking man, begrimed with charcoal, sat watching his kiln at nightfall, while his little son played at building houses with the scattered fragments of marble, when, on the hill-side below them, they heard a roar of laughter, not mirthful, but slow, and even solemn, like a wind shaking the boughs of the forest.

"Father, what is that?" asked the little boy, leaving his play, and pressing betwixt his father's knees.

"Oh, some drunken man, I suppose," answered

the lime-burner; "some merry fellow from the bar-room in the village, who dared not laugh loud enough within doors lest he should blow the roof of the house off. So here he is, shaking his jolly sides at the foot of Graylock."

"But, father," said the child, more sensitive than the obtuse, middle-aged clown, "he does not laugh like a man that is glad. So the noise frightens me!"

"Don't be a fool, child!" cried his father, gruffly. "You will never make a man, I do believe; there is too much of your mother in you. I have known the rustling of a leaf startle you. Hark! Here comes the merry fellow now. You shall see that there is no harm in him."

Bartram and his little son, while they were talking thus, sat watching the same lime-kiln that had been the scene of Ethan Brand's solitary and meditative life, before he began his search for the Unpardonable Sin. Many years, as we have seen, had now elapsed, since that portentous night when the *Idea* was first developed. The kiln, however, on the mountain-side, stood unimpaired, and was in nothing changed since he had thrown his dark thoughts into the intense glow of its furnace, and melted them, as it were, into the one thought that took possession of his life. It was a rude, round, tower-like structure about twenty feet high, heavily built of rough stones, and with a hillock of earth heaped about the larger part of its circumference; so that the blocks and fragments of marble might be drawn by cart-loads, and thrown in at the top. There was an opening at the bottom of the tower, like an oven-mouth, but large enough to admit a man in a stooping posture, and provided with a massive iron door. With the smoke and jets of flame issuing from the chinks and crevices of this door, which seemed to give admittance into the hill-side, it resembled nothing so much as the private entrance to the infernal regions, which the shepherds of the Delectable Mountains were accustomed to show to pilgrims.

There are many such lime-kilns in that tract of country, for the purpose of burning the white marble which composes a large part of the substance of the hills. Some of them, built years ago, and long deserted, with weeds growing in the vacant round of the interior, which is open to the sky, and grass and wild-flowers rooting themselves into the chinks of the stones, look already like relics of antiquity, and may yet be overspread with the lichens of centuries to come. Others, where the lime-burner still feeds his daily and night-long fire, afford points of interest to the wanderer among the hills, who seats himself on a log of wood or a fragment of marble, to hold a chat with the solitary man. It is a lonesome, and, when the character is inclined to thought, may be an intensely thoughtful occupation; as it proved in the case of Ethan Brand, who had mused to such strange purpose, in days gone by, while the fire in this very kiln was burning.

The man who now watched the fire was of a different order, and troubled himself with no thoughts save the very few that were requisite to his business. At frequent intervals, he flung back the clashing weight of the iron door, and, turning his face from the insufferable glare, thrust in huge logs of oak, or stirred the immense brands with a long pole. Within the furnace were seen the curling and riotous flames, and the burning marble, almost molten with the intensity of heat; while without, the reflection of the fire quivered on the dark intricacy of the surrounding forest, and showed in the foreground a bright and ruddy little picture of the hut, the spring beside its door, the athletic and coal-begrimed figure of the lime-burner, and the half-frightened child, shrinking into the protection of his father's shadow. And when, again, the iron door was closed, then reappeared the tender light of the half-full moon, which vainly strove to trace out the indistinct shapes of the neighboring mountains; and, in the upper sky, there was a flitting congregation of clouds, still faintly tinged with the rosy sunset, though thus far down into the valley the sunshine had vanished long and long ago.

The little boy now crept still closer to his father, as footsteps were heard ascending the hill-side, and a human form thrust aside the bushes that clustered beneath the trees.

"Halloo! who is it?" cried the lime-burner, vexed at his son's timidity, yet half infected by it. "Come forward, and show yourself, like a man, or I'll fling this chunk of marble at your head!"

"You offer me a rough welcome," said a gloomy voice, as the unknown man drew nigh. "Yet I neither claim nor desire a kinder one, even at my own fireside."

To obtain a distincter view, Bartram threw open the iron door of the kiln, whence immediately issued a gush of fierce light, that smote full upon the stranger's face and figure. To a careless eye there appeared nothing very remarkable in his aspect, which was that of a man in a coarse, brown, country-made suit of clothes, tall and thin, with the staff and heavy shoes of a wayfarer. As he advanced, he fixed his eyes—which were very bright—intently upon the brightness of the furnace, as if he beheld, or expected to behold, some object worthy of note within it.

"Good evening, stranger," said the lime-burner; "whence come you, so late in the day?"

"I come from my search," answered the wayfarer; "for, at last, it is finished."

"Drunk!—or crazy!" muttered Bartram to himself. "I shall have trouble with the fellow. The sooner I drive him away, the better."

The little boy, all in a tremble, whispered to his father, and begged him to shut the door of the kiln, so that there might not be so much light; for that there was something in the man's face which he was afraid to look at, yet could not look away from. And, indeed, even the lime-burner's dull and torpid sense began to be impressed by an indescribable something in that thin, rugged, thoughtful visage, with the grizzled hair hanging wildly about it, and those deeply sunken eyes, which gleamed like fires within the entrance of a mysterious cavern. But, as he closed the door, the stranger turned towards him, and spoke in a quiet, familiar way, that made Bartram feel as if he were a sane and sensible man, after all.

"Your task draws to an end, I see," said he. "This marble has already been burning three days. A few hours more will convert the stone to lime."

"Why, who are you?" exclaimed the lime-burner. "You seem as well acquainted with my business as I am myself."

"And well I may be," said the stranger; "for I followed the same craft many a long year, and here, too, on this very spot. But you are a newcomer in these parts. Did you never hear of Ethan Brand?"

"The man that went in search of the Unpardonable Sin?" asked Bartram, with a laugh.

"The same," answered the stranger. "He has found what he sought, and therefore he comes back again."

"What! then you are Ethan Brand himself?" cried the lime-burner, in amazement. "I am a newcomer here, as you say, and they call it eighteen years since you left the foot of Graylock. But, I can tell you, the good folks still talk about Ethan Brand, in the village yonder, and what a strange errand took him away from his lime-kiln. Well, and so you have found the Unpardonable Sin?"

"Even so!" said the stranger, calmly.

"If the question is a fair one," proceeded Bartram, "where might it be?"

Ethan Brand laid his finger on his own heart.

"Here!" replied he.

And then, without mirth in his countenance, but as if moved by an involuntary recognition of the infinite absurdity of seeking throughout the world for what was the closest of all things to himself, and looking into every heart, save his own, for what was hidden in no other breast, he broke into a laugh of scorn. It was the same slow, heavy laugh, that had almost appalled the lime-burner when it heralded the wayfarer's approach.

The solitary mountain-side was made dismal by it. Laughter, when out of place, mistimed, or bursting forth from a disordered state of feeling, may be the most terrible modulation of the human voice. The laughter of one asleep, even if it be a little child,—the madman's laugh,—the wild, screaming laugh of a born idiot,—are sounds that we sometimes tremble to hear, and would always willingly forget. Poets have imagined no utterance of fiends or hobgoblins so fearfully appropriate as a laugh. And even the obtuse lime-burner felt his nerves shaken, as this strange man looked inward at his own heart, and burst into laughter that rolled away into the night, and was indistinctly reverberated among the hills.

"Joe," said he to his little son, "scamper down to the tavern in the village, and tell the jolly fellows there that Ethan Brand has come back, and that he has found the Unpardonable Sin!"

The boy darted away on his errand, to which Ethan Brand made no objection, nor seemed hardly to notice it. He sat on a log of wood, looking steadfastly at the iron door of the kiln. When the child was out of sight, and his swift and light footsteps ceased to be heard treading first on the fallen leaves and then on the rocky mountain-path, the lime-burner began to regret his departure. He felt that the little fellow's presence had been a barrier between his guest and himself, and that he must now deal, heart to heart, with a man who, on his own confession, had committed the one only crime for which Heaven could afford no mercy. That crime, in its indistinct blackness, seemed to overshadow him. The lime-burner's own sins rose up within him, and made his memory riotous with a throng of evil shapes that asserted their kindred with the Master Sin, whatever it might be, which it was within the scope of man's corrupted nature to conceive and cherish. They were all of one family; they went to and fro between his breast and Ethan Brand's, and carried dark greetings from one to the other.

Then Bartram remembered the stories which had grown traditional in reference to this strange man, who had come upon him like a shadow of the night, and was making himself at home in his old place, after so long absence, that the dead people, dead and buried for years, would have had more right to be at home, in any familiar spot, than he. Ethan Brand, it was said, had conversed with Satan himself in the lurid blaze of this very kiln. The legend had been matter of mirth heretofore, but looked grisly now. According to this tale, before Ethan Brand departed on his search, he had been accustomed to evoke a fiend from the hot furnace of the lime-kiln, night after night, in order to confer with him about the Unpardonable Sin; the man and the fiend each laboring to frame the image of some mode of guilt which could neither be atoned for nor forgiven. And, with the first gleam of light upon the mountain-top, the fiend crept in at the iron door, there to abide the intensest element of fire until again summoned forth to share in the dreadful task of extending man's possible guilt beyond the scope of Heaven's else infinite mercy.

While the lime-burner was struggling with the horror of these thoughts, Ethan Brand rose from the log, and flung open the door of the kiln. The action was in such accordance with the idea in Bartram's mind, that he almost expected to see the Evil One issue forth, red-hot, from the raging furnace.

"Hold! hold!" cried he, with a tremulous attempt to laugh; for he was ashamed of his fears, although they overmastered him. "Don't, for mercy's sake, bring out your Devil now!"

"Man!" sternly replied Ethan Brand, "what need have I of the Devil? I have left him behind me, on my track. It is with such half-way sinners as you that he busies himself. Fear not, because I open the door. I do but act by old custom, and am going to trim your fire, like a lime-burner, as I was once."

He stirred the vast coals, thrust in more wood, and bent forward to gaze into the hollow prison-house of the fire, regardless of the fierce glow that reddened upon his face. The lime-burner sat watching him, and half suspected this strange guest of a purpose, if not to evoke a fiend, at least to plunge bodily into the flames, and thus vanish from the sight of man. Ethan Brand, however, drew quietly back, and closed the door of the kiln.

"I have looked," said he, "into many a human heart that was seven times hotter with sinful passions than yonder furnace is with fire. But I found not there what I sought. No, not the Unpardonable Sin!"

"What is the Unpardonable Sin?" asked the lime-burner; and then he shrank farther from his companion, trembling lest his question should be answered.

"It is a sin that grew within my own breast," replied Ethan Brand, standing erect, with a pride that distinguishes all enthusiasts of his stamp. "A sin that grew nowhere else! The sin of an intellect that triumphed over the sense of brotherhood with man and reverence for God, and sacrificed everything to its own mighty claims! The only sin that deserves a recompense of immortal agony! Freely, were it to do again, would I incur the guilt. Unshrinkingly I accept the retribution!"

"The man's head is turned," muttered the lime-burner to himself. "He may be a sinner like the rest of us,—nothing more likely,—but, I'll be sworn, he is a madman too."

Nevertheless, he felt uncomfortable at his situation, alone with Ethan Brand on the wild mountain-side, and was right glad to hear the rough murmur of tongues, and the footsteps of what seemed a pretty numerous party, stumbling over the stones and rustling through the underbrush. Soon appeared the whole lazy regiment that was wont to infest the village tavern, comprehending three or four individuals who had drunk flip beside the bar-room fire through all the winters, and smoked their pipes beneath the stoop through all the summers, since Ethan Brand's departure. Laughing boisterously, and mingling all their voices together in unceremonious talk, they now burst into the moonshine and narrow streaks of firelight that illuminated the open space before the lime-kiln. Bartram set the door ajar again, flooding the spot with light, that the whole company might get a fair view of Ethan Brand, and he of them.

There, among other old acquaintances, was a once ubiquitous man, now almost extinct, but whom we were formerly sure to encounter at the hotel of every thriving village throughout the country. It was the stage-agent. The present specimen of the genus was a wilted and smoke-dried man, wrinkled and red-nosed, in a smartly cut, brown, bobtailed coat, with brass buttons, who, for a length of time unknown, had kept his desk and corner in the bar-room, and was still puffing what seemed to be the same cigar that he had lighted twenty years before. He had great fame as a dry joker, though, perhaps, less on account of any intrinsic humor than from a certain flavor of brandy-toddy and tobacco-smoke, which impregnated all his ideas and expressions, as well as his person. Another well-remembered, though strangely altered, face was that of Lawyer Giles, as people still called him in courtesy; an elderly ragamuffin, in his soiled shirt-sleeves and tow-cloth trousers. This poor fellow had been an attorney, in what he called his better days, a sharp practitioner, and in great vogue among the village litigants; but flip, and sling, and toddy, and cocktails, imbibed at all hours, morning, noon, and night, had caused him to slide from intellectual to various kinds and degrees of bodily labor, till at last, to adopt his own phrase, he slid into a soap-vat. In other words, Giles was now a soap-boiler, in a small way. He had come to be but the fragment of a human being, a part of one foot having been chopped off by an axe, and an entire hand torn away by the devilish grip of a steam-engine. Yet, though the corporeal hand was gone, a spiritual member remained; for, stretching forth the stump, Giles steadfastly averred that he felt an invisible thumb and fingers with as vivid a sensation as before the real ones were amputated. A maimed and miserable wretch he was; but one, nevertheless, whom the world could not trample on, and had no right to scorn, either in this or any previous stage of his misfortunes, since he had still kept up the courage and spirit of a man, asked nothing in charity, and with his one hand—and that the left one—fought a stern battle against want and hostile circumstances.

Among the throng, too, came another personage, who, with certain points of similarity to Lawyer Giles, had many more of difference. It was the village doctor; a man of some fifty years, whom, at an earlier period of his life, we introduced as paying a professional visit to Ethan Brand during the latter's supposed insanity. He was now a purple-visaged, rude, and brutal, yet half-gentlemanly figure, with something wild, ruined, and desperate in his talk, and in all the details of his gesture and manners. Brandy possessed this man like an evil spirit, and made him as surly and savage as a wild beast, and as miserable as a lost soul; but there was supposed to be in him such wonderful skill, such native gifts of healing, beyond any which medical science could impart, that society caught hold of him, and would not let him sink out of its reach. So, swaying to and fro upon his horse, and grumbling thick accents at the bedside, he visited all the sick-chambers for miles about among the moun-

tain towns, and sometimes raised a dying man, as it were, by miracle, or quite as often, no doubt, sent his patient to a grave that was dug many a year too soon. The doctor had an everlasting pipe in his mouth, and, as somebody said, in allusion to his habit of swearing, it was always alight with hell-fire.

These three worthies pressed forward, and greeted Ethan Brand each after his own fashion, earnestly inviting him to partake of the contents of a certain black bottle, in which, as they averred, he would find something far better worth seeking for than the Unpardonable Sin. No mind, which has wrought itself by intense and solitary meditation into a high state of enthusiasm, can endure the kind of contact with low and vulgar modes of thought and feeling to which Ethan Brand was now subjected. It made him doubt—and, strange to say, it was a painful doubt—whether he had indeed found the Unpardonable Sin, and found it within himself. The whole question on which he had exhausted life, and more than life, looked like a delusion.

"Leave me," he said bitterly, "ye brute beasts, that have made yourselves so, shrivelling up your souls with fiery liquors! I have done with you. Years and years ago, I groped into your hearts and found nothing there for my purpose. Get ye gone!"

"Why, you uncivil scoundrel," cried the fierce doctor, "is that the way you respond to the kindness of your best friends? Then let me tell you the truth. You have no more found the Unpardonable Sin than yonder boy Joe has. You are but a crazy fellow,—I told you so twenty years ago,—neither better nor worse than a crazy fellow, and the fit companion of old Humphrey, here!"

He pointed to an old man, shabbily dressed, with long white hair, thin visage, and unsteady eyes. For some years past this aged person had been wandering about among the hills, inquiring of all travellers whom he met for his daughter. The girl, it seemed, had gone off with a company of circus-performers, and occasionally tidings of her came to the village, and fine stories were told of her glittering appearance as she rode on horseback in the ring, or performed marvellous feats on the tight-rope.

The white-haired father now approached Ethan Brand, and gazed unsteadily into his face.

"They tell me you have been all over the earth," said he, wringing his hands with earnestness. "You must have seen my daughter, for she makes a grand figure in the world, and everybody goes to see her. Did she send any word to her old father, or say when she was coming back?"

Ethan Brand's eye quailed beneath the old man's. That daughter, from whom he so earnestly desired a word of greeting, was the Esther of our tale, the very girl whom, with such cold and remorseless purpose, Ethan Brand had made the subject of a psychological experiment, and wasted, absorbed, and perhaps annihilated her soul, in the process.

"Yes," murmured he, turning away from the hoary wanderer, "it is no delusion. There is an Unpardonable Sin!"

While these things were passing, a merry scene was going forward in the area of cheerful light, beside the spring and before the door of the hut. A number of the youth of the village, young men and girls, had hurried up the hill-side, impelled by curiosity to see Ethan Brand, the hero of so many a legend familiar to their childhood. Finding nothing, however, very remarkable in his aspect,—nothing but a sunburnt wayfarer, in plain garb and dusty shoes, who sat looking into the fire as if he fancied pictures among the coals,—these young people speedily grew tired of observing him. As it happened, there was other amusement at hand. An old German Jew travelling with a diorama on his back, was passing down the mountain-road towards the village just as the party turned aside from it, and, in hopes of eking out the profits of the day, the showman had kept them company to the lime-kiln.

"Come, old Dutchman," cried one of the young men, "let us see your pictures, if you can swear they are worth looking at!"

"Oh yes, Captain," answered the Jew,—whether as a matter of courtesy or craft, he styled everybody Captain,—"I shall show you, indeed, some very superb pictures!"

So, placing his box in a proper position, he invited the young men and girls to look through the glass orifices of the machine, and proceeded to exhibit a series of the most outrageous scratchings and daubings, as specimens of the fine arts, that ever an itinerant showman had the face to impose upon his circle of spectators. The pictures were worn out, moreover, tattered, full of cracks and wrinkles, dingy with tobacco-smoke, and otherwise in a most pitiable condition. Some purported to be cities, public edifices, and ruined castles in Europe; others represented Napoleon's battles and Nelson's sea-fights; and in the midst of these would be seen a gigantic, brown, hairy hand,—which might have been mistaken for the Hand of Destiny, though, in truth, it was only the showman's,—pointing its forefinger to various scenes of the conflict, while its owner gave historical illustrations. When, with much merriment at its abominable deficiency of merit, the exhibition was concluded, the German bade little Joe put his head into the box. Viewed through the magnifying-glasses, the boy's round, rosy visage assumed the strangest imaginable aspect of an immense Titanic child, the mouth grinning broadly, and the eyes and every other feature overflowing with fun at the joke. Suddenly, however, that merry face turned pale, and its expression changed to horror, for this easily impressed and excitable child had become sensible that the eye of Ethan Brand was fixed upon him through the glass.

"You make the little man to be afraid, Captain," said the German Jew, turning up the dark and strong outline of his visage from his stooping posture. "But look again, and, by chance, I shall cause you to see somewhat that is very fine, upon my word!"

Ethan Brand gazed into the box for an instant, and then starting back, looked fixedly at the German. What had he seen? Nothing, apparently; for a curious youth, who had peeped in almost at the same moment, beheld only a vacant space of canvas.

"I remember you now," muttered Ethan Brand to the showman.

"Ah, Captain," whispered the Jew of Nuremburg, with a dark smile, "I find it to be a heavy matter in my show-box,—this Unpardonable Sin! By my faith, Captain, it has wearied my shoulders, this long day, to carry it over the mountain."

"Peace," answered Ethan Brand, sternly, "or get thee into the furnace yonder!"

The Jew's exhibition had scarcely concluded, when a great, elderly dog—who seemed to be his own master, as no person in the company laid claim to him—saw fit to render himself the object of public notice. Hitherto, he had shown himself a very quiet, well-disposed old dog, going round from one to another, and, by way of being sociable, offering his rough head to be patted by any kindly hand that would take so much trouble. But now, all of a sudden, this grave and venerable quadruped, of his own mere motion, and without the slightest suggestion from anybody else, began to run round after his tail, which, to heighten the absurdity of the proceeding, was a great deal shorter than it should have been. Never was seen such headlong eagerness in pursuit of an object that could not possibly be attained; never was heard such a tremendous outbreak of growling, snarling, barking, and snapping,—as if one end of the ridiculous brute's body were at deadly and most unforgivable enmity with the other. Faster and faster, round about went the cur; and faster and still faster fled the unapproachable brevity of his tail; and louder and fiercer grew his yells of rage and animosity; until, utterly exhausted, and as far from the goal as ever, the foolish old dog ceased his performance as suddenly as he had begun it. The next moment he was as mild, quiet, sensible, and respectable in his deportment, as when he first scraped acquaintance with the company.

As may be supposed, the exhibition was greeted with universal laughter, clapping of hands, and shouts of encore, to which the canine performer responded by wagging all that there was to wag of his tail, but appeared totally unable to repeat his very successful effort to amuse the spectators.

Meanwhile, Ethan Brand had resumed his seat upon the log, and moved, it might be, by a perception of some remote analogy between his own case and that of this self-pursuing cur, he broke into the awful laugh, which, more than any other token, expressed the condition of his inward being. From that moment, the merriment of the party was at an end; they stood aghast, dreading lest the inauspicious sound should be reverberated around the horizon, and that mountain would thunder it to mountain, and so the horror be prolonged upon their ears. Then, whispering one to another that it was late,—that the moon was almost down,—that the August night was growing chill,—they hurried homewards, leaving the lime-burner and little Joe to deal as they might with their unwelcome guest. Save for these three human beings, the open space on the hill-side was a solitude, set in a vast gloom of forest. Beyond that darksome verge, the firelight glimmered on the stately trunks and almost black foliage of pines, intermixed with the lighter verdure of sapling oaks, maples, and poplars, while here and there lay the gigantic corpses of dead trees, decaying on the leaf-strewn soil. And it seemed to little Joe—a timorous and imaginative child—that the silent forest was holding its breath until some fearful thing should happen.

Ethan Brand thrust more wood into the fire, and closed the door of the kiln; then looking over his shoulder at the lime-burner and his son, he bade, rather than advised, them to retire to rest.

"For myself, I cannot sleep," said he. "I have matters that it concerns me to meditate upon. I will watch the fire, as I used to do in the old time."

"And call the Devil out of the furnace to keep you company, I suppose," muttered Bartram, who had been making intimate acquaintance with the black bottle above mentioned. "But watch, if you like, and call as many devils as you like! For my part, I shall be all the better for a snooze. Come, Joe!"

As the boy followed his father into the hut, he looked back at the wayfarer, and the tears came into his eyes, for his tender spirit had an intuition of the bleak and terrible loneliness in which this man had enveloped himself.

When they had gone, Ethan Brand sat listening to the crackling of the kindled wood, and looking at the little spirts of fire that issued through the chinks of the door. These trifles, however, once so familiar, had but the slightest hold of his attention, while deep within his mind he was reviewing the gradual but marvellous change that had been wrought upon him by the search to which he had devoted himself. He remembered how the night dew had fallen upon him,—how the dark forest had whispered to him,—how the stars had gleamed upon him,—a simple and loving man, watching his fire in the years gone by, and ever musing as it burned. He remembered with what tenderness, with what love and sympathy for mankind, and what pity for human guilt and woe, he had first begun to contemplate those ideas which afterwards became the inspiration of his life; with what reverence he had then looked into the heart of man, viewing it as a temple originally divine, and, however desecrated, still to be held sacred by a brother; with what awful fear he had deprecated the success of his pursuit, and prayed that the Unpardonable Sin might never be revealed to him. Then ensued that vast intellectual development, which, in its progress, disturbed the counterpoise between his mind and heart. The Idea that possessed his life had operated as a means of education; it had gone on cultivating his powers to the highest point of which they were susceptible; it had raised him from the level of an unlettered laborer to stand on a star-lit eminence, whither the philosophers of the earth, laden with the lore of universities, might vainly strive to clamber after him. So much for the intellect! But where was the heart? That, indeed, had withered,—had contracted,—had hardened,—had perished! It had ceased to partake of the universal throb. He had lost his hold of the magnetic chain of humanity. He was no longer a brother-man, opening the chambers or the dungeons of our common nature by the key of holy sympathy, which gave him a right to share in all its secrets; he was now a cold observer, looking on mankind as the subject of his experiment, and, at length, converting man and woman to be his puppets, and pulling the wires that moved them to such degrees of crime as were demanded for his study.

Thus Ethan Brand became a fiend. He began to be so from the moment that his moral nature had ceased to keep the pace of improvement with his intellect. And now, as his highest effort and inevitable development,—as the bright and gorgeous flower, and rich, delicious fruit of his life's labor,—he had produced the Unpardonable Sin!

"What more have I to seek? what more to achieve?" said Ethan Brand to himself. "My task is done, and well done!"

Starting from the log with a certain alacrity in his gait and ascending the hillock of earth that was raised against the stone circumference of the lime-kiln, he thus reached the top of the structure. It was a space of perhaps ten feet across, from edge to edge, presenting a view of the upper surface of the immense mass of broken marble with which the kiln was heaped. All these innumerable blocks and fragments of marble were red-hot and vividly on fire, sending up great spouts of blue flame, which quivered aloft and danced madly, as within a magic circle, and sank and rose again, with continual and multitudinous activity. As the lonely man bent forward over this terrible body of fire, the blasting heat smote up against his person with a breath that, it might be supposed, would have scorched and shrivelled him up in a moment.

Ethan Brand stood erect, and raised his arms on high. The blue flames played upon his face, and imparted the wild and ghastly light which alone could have suited its expression; it was that of a fiend on the verge of plunging into his gulf of intensest torment.

"O Mother Earth," cried he, "who art no more my Mother, and into whose bosom this frame shall never be resolved! O mankind, whose brotherhood I have cast off, and trampled thy great heart beneath my feet! O stars of heaven, that shone on me of old, as if to light me onward and upward!—farewell all, and forever. Come, deadly element of Fire,—henceforth my familiar friend! Embrace me, as I do thee!"

That night the sound of a fearful peal of laughter rolled heavily through the sleep of the lime-burner and his little son; dim shapes of horror and anguish haunted their dreams, and seemed still present in the rude hovel, when they opened their eyes to the daylight.

"Up, boy, up!" cried the lime-burner, staring about him. "Thank Heaven, the night is gone, at last; and rather than pass another, I would watch my lime-kiln, wide awake, for a twelve-month. This Ethan Brand, with his humbug of an Unpardonable Sin, has done me no such mighty favor, in taking my place!"

He issued from the hut, followed by little Joe, who kept fast hold of his father's hand. The early sunshine was already pouring its gold upon the mountain-tops, and though the valleys were still in shadow, they smiled cheerfully in the promise of the bright day that was hastening onward. The village, completely shut in by hills, which swelled away gently about it, looked as if it had rested peacefully in the hollow of the great hand of Providence. Every dwelling was distinctly visible; the little spires of the two churches pointed upwards, and caught a fore-glimmering of brightness from the sun-gilt skies upon their gilded weathercocks. The tavern was astir, and the figure of the old, smoke-dried stage-agent, cigar in mouth, was seen beneath the stoop. Old Graylock was glorified with a golden cloud upon his head. Scattered likewise over the breasts of the surrounding mountains, there were heaps of hoary mist, in fantastic shapes, some of them far down into the valley, others high up towards the summits, and still others, of the same family of mist or cloud, hovering in the gold radiance of the upper atmosphere. Stepping from one to another of the clouds that rested on the hills, and thence to the loftier brotherhood that sailed in air, it seemed almost as if a mortal man might thus ascend into the heavenly regions. Earth was so mingled with sky that it was a day-dream to look at it.

To supply that charm of the familiar and homely, which Nature so readily adopts into a scene like this, the stage-coach was rattling down the mountain-road, and the driver sounded his horn, while Echo caught up the notes, and intertwined them into a rich and varied and elaborate harmony, of which the original performer could lay claim to little share. The great hills played a concert among themselves, each contributing a strain of airy sweetness.

Little Joe's face brightened at once.

"Dear father," cried he, skipping cheerily to and fro, "that strange man is gone, and the sky and the mountains all seem glad of it!"

"Yes," growled the lime-burner, with an oath, "but he has let the fire go down, and no thanks to him if five hundred bushels of lime are not spoiled. If I catch the fellow hereabouts again, I shall feel like tossing him into the furnace!"

With his long pole in his hand, he ascended to the top of the kiln. After a moment's pause, he called to his son.

"Come up here, Joe!" said he.

So little Joe ran up the hillock, and stood by his father's side. The marble was all burnt into perfect, snow-white lime. But on its surface, in the midst of the circle,—snow-white too, and thoroughly converted into lime,—lay a human skeleton, in the attitude of a person who, after long toil, lies down to long repose. Within the ribs—strange to say—was the shape of a human heart.

"Was the fellow's heart made of marble?" cried Bartram, in some perplexity at this phenomenon. "At any rate, it is burnt into what looks like special good lime; and, taking all the bones together, my kiln is half a bushel the richer for him."

So saying, the rude lime-burner lifted his pole, and letting it fall upon the skeleton, the relics of Ethan Brand were crumbled into fragments.

My Kinsman, Major Molineux (1832)

After the kings of Great Britain had assumed the right of appointing the colonial governors, the measures of the latter seldom met with the ready and general approbation which had been paid to those of their predecessors, under the original charters. The people looked with most jealous scrutiny to the exercise of power which did not emanate from themselves, and they usually rewarded their rulers with slender gratitude for the compliances by which, in softening their instructions from beyond the sea, they had incurred the reprehension of those who gave them. The annals of Massachusetts Bay will inform us, that of six governors in the space of about forty years from the surrender of the old charter, under James II, two were imprisoned by a popular insurrection; a third, as Hutchinson inclines to believe, was driven from the province by the whizzing of a musket-ball; a fourth, in the opinion of the same historian, was hastened to his grave by continual bickerings with the House of Representatives; and the remaining two, as well as their successors, till the Revolution, were favored with few and brief intervals of peaceful sway. The inferior members of the court party, in times of high political excitement, led scarcely a more desirable life. These remarks may serve as a preface to the following adventures, which chanced upon a summer night, not far from a hundred years ago. The reader, in order to avoid a long and dry detail of colonial affairs, is requested to dispense with an account of the train of circumstances that had caused much temporary inflammation of the popular mind.

It was near nine o'clock of a moonlight evening, when a boat crossed the ferry with a single passenger, who had obtained his conveyance at that unusual hour by the promise of an extra fare. While he stood on the landing-place, searching in either pocket for the means of fulfilling his agreement, the ferryman lifted a lantern, by the aid of which, and the newly risen moon, he took a very accurate survey of the stranger's figure. He was a youth of barely eighteen years, evidently country-bred, and now, as it should seem, upon his first visit to town. He was clad in a coarse gray coat, well worn, but in excellent repair; his under garments were durably constructed of leather, and fitted tight to a pair of serviceable and well-shaped limbs; his stockings of blue yarn were the incontrovertible work of a mother or a sister; and on his head was a three-cornered hat, which in its better days had perhaps sheltered the graver brow of the lad's father. Under his left arm was a heavy cudgel formed of an oak sapling, and retaining a part of the hardened root; and his equipment was completed by a wallet, not so abundantly stocked as to incommode the vigorous shoulders on which it hung. Brown, curly hair, well-shaped features, and bright, cheerful eyes were nature's gifts, and worth all that art could have done for his adornment.

The youth, one of whose names was Robin, finally drew from his pocket the half of a little province bill of five shillings, which, in the depreciation in that sort of currency, did but satisfy the ferryman's demand, with the surplus of a sexangular piece of parchment, valued at three pence. He then walked forward into the town, with as light a step as if his day's journey had not already exceeded thirty miles, and with as eager an eye as if he were entering London city, instead of the little metropolis of a New England colony. Before Robin had proceeded far, however, it occurred to him that he knew not whither to direct his steps; so he paused, and looked up and down the narrow street, scrutinizing the small and mean wooden buildings that were scattered on either side.

"This low hovel cannot be my kinsman's dwelling," thought he, "nor yonder old house, where the moonlight enters at the broken casement; and truly I see none hereabouts that might be worthy of him. It would have been wise to inquire my way of the ferryman, and doubtless he would have gone with me, and earned a shilling from the Major for his pains. But the next man I meet will do as well."

He resumed his walk, and was glad to perceive that the street now became wider, and the houses more respectable in their appearance. He soon discerned a figure moving on moderately in advance, and hastened his steps to overtake it. As Robin drew nigh, he saw that the passenger was a man in years, with a full periwig of gray hair, a wide-skirted coat of dark cloth, and silk stockings rolled above his knees. He carried a long and polished cane, which he struck down perpendicularly before him at every step; and at regular intervals he uttered two successive hems, of a peculiarly solemn and sepulchral intonation. Having made these observations, Robin laid hold of the skirt of the old man's coat, just when the light from the open door and windows of a barber's shop fell upon both their figures.

"Good evening to you, honored sir," said he, making a low bow, and still retaining his hold of the skirt. "I pray you tell me whereabouts is the dwelling of my kinsman, Major Molineux."

The youth's question was uttered very loudly; and one of the barbers, whose razor was descending on a well-soaped chin, and another who was dressing a Ramillies wig, left their occupations, and came to the door. The citizen, in the mean time, turned a long-favored countenance upon Robin, and answered him in a tone of excessive anger and annoyance. His two sepulchral hems, however, broke into the very centre of his rebuke, with most singular effect, like a thought of the cold grave obtruding among wrathful passions.

"Let go my garment, fellow! I tell you, I know not the man you speak of. What! I have authority, I have—hem, hem—authority; and if this be the respect you show for your betters, your feet shall be brought acquainted with the stocks by daylight, tomorrow morning!"

Robin released the old man's skirt, and hastened away, pursued by an ill-mannered roar of laughter from the barber's shop. He was at first considerably surprised by the result of his question, but, being a shrewd youth, soon thought himself able to account for the mystery.

"This is some country representative," was his conclusion, "who has never seen the inside of my kinsman's door, and lacks the breeding to answer a stranger civilly. The man is old, or verily—I might be tempted to turn back and smite him on the nose. Ah, Robin, Robin! even the barber's boys laugh at you for choosing such a guide! You will be wiser in time, friend Robin."

He now became entangled in a succession of crooked and narrow streets, which crossed each other, and meandered at no great distance from the water-side. The smell of tar was obvious to his nostrils, the masts of vessels pierced the moonlight above the tops of the buildings, and the numerous signs, which Robin paused to read, informed him that he was near the centre of business. But the streets were empty, the shops were closed, and lights were visible only in the second stories of a few dwelling-houses. At length, on the corner of a narrow lane, through which he was passing, he beheld the broad countenance of a British hero swinging before the door of an inn, whence proceeded the voices of many guests. The casement of one of the lower windows was thrown back, and a very thin curtain permitted Robin to distinguish a party at supper, round a well-furnished table. The fragrance of the good cheer steamed forth into the outer air, and the youth could not fail to recollect that the last remnant of his travelling stock of provision had yielded to his morning appetite, and that noon had found and left him dinnerless.

"Oh, that a parchment three-penny might give me a right to sit down at yonder table!" said Robin, with a sigh. "But the Major will make me welcome to the best of his victuals; so I will even step boldly in, and inquire my way to his dwelling."

He entered the tavern, and was guided by the murmur of voices and the fumes of tobacco to the public-room. It was a long and low apartment, with oaken walls, grown dark in the continual smoke, and a floor which was thickly sanded, but of no immaculate purity. A number of persons— the larger part of whom appeared to be mariners, or in some way connected with the sea—occupied the wooden benches, or leather-bottomed chairs, conversing on various matters, and occasionally lending their attention to some topic of general interest. Three or four little groups were draining as many bowls of punch, which the West India trade had long since made a familiar drink in the colony. Others, who had the appearance of men who lived by regular and laborious handicraft, pre- ferred the insulated bliss of an unshared potation, and became more taciturn under its influence. Nearly all, in short, evinced a predilection for the Good Creature in some of its various shapes, for this is a vice to which, as Fast Day sermons of a hundred years ago will testify, we have a long hereditary claim. The only guests to whom Robin's sympathies inclined him were two or three sheep- ish countrymen, who were using the inn somewhat after the fashion of a Turkish caravansary; they had gotten themselves into the darkest corner of the room, and heedless of the Nicotian atmosphere, were supping on the bread of their own ovens, and the bacon cured in their own chimney-smoke. But though Robin felt a sort of brotherhood with these strangers, his eyes were attracted from them to a person who stood near the door, holding whispered conversation with a group of ill-dressed associates. His features were separately striking almost to grotesqueness, and the whole face left a deep im- pression on the memory. The forehead bulged out into a double prominence, with a vale between; the nose came boldly forth in an irregular curve, and its bridge was of more than a finger's breadth; the eyebrows were deep and shaggy, and the eyes glowed beneath them like fire in a cave.

While Robin deliberated of whom to inquire re- specting his kinsman's dwelling, he was accosted by the innkeeper, a little man in a stained white apron, who had come to pay his professional wel- come to the stranger. Being in the second genera- tion from a French Protestant, he seemed to have inherited the courtesy of his parent nation; but no variety of circumstances was ever known to change his voice from the one shrill note in which he now addressed Robin.

"From the country, I presume, sir?" said he, with a profound bow. "Beg leave to congratulate you on your arrival, and trust you intend a long stay with us. Fine town here, sir, beautiful build-

ings, and much that may interest a stranger. May I hope for the honor of your commands in respect to supper?"

"The man sees a family likeness! the rogue has guessed that I am related to the Major!" thought Robin, who had hitherto experienced little super- fluous civility.

All eyes were now turned on the country lad, standing at the door, in his worn three-cornered hat, gray coat, leather breeches, and blue yarn stockings, leaning on an oaken cudgel, and bearing a wallet on his back.

Robin replied to the courteous innkeeper, with such an assumption of confidence as befitted the Major's relative. "My honest friend," he said, "I shall make it a point to patronize your house on some occasion, when"—here he could not help low- ering his voice—"when I may have more than a parchment three-pence in my pocket. My present business," continued he, speaking with lofty con- fidence, "is merely to inquire my way to the dwell- ing of my kinsman, Major Molineux."

There was a sudden and general movement in the room, which Robin interpreted as expressing the eagerness of each individual to become his guide. But the innkeeper turned his eyes to a written paper on the wall, which he read, or seemed to read, with occasional recurrences to the young man's figure.

"What have we here?" said he, breaking his speech into little dry fragments. " 'Left the house of the subscriber, bounden servant, Hezekiah Mudge, —had on, when he went away, gray coat, leather breeches, master's third-best hat. One pound cur- rency reward to whosoever shall lodge him in any jail of the province.' Better trudge, boy; better trudge!"

Robin had begun to draw his hand towards the lighter end of the oak cudgel, but a strange hostility in every countenance induced him to re- linquish his purpose of breaking the courteous innkeeper's head. As he turned to leave the room, he encountered a sneering glance from the bold- featured personage whom he had before noticed; and no sooner was he beyond the door, than he heard a general laugh, in which the innkeeper's voice might be distinguished, like the dropping of small stones into a kettle.

"Now, is it not strange," thought Robin, with his usual shrewdness,—"is it not strange that the confession on an empty pocket should outweigh the name of my kinsman, Major Molineux? Oh, if I had one of those grinning rascals in the woods, where I and my oak sapling grew up together, I would teach him that my arm is heavy though my purse is light!"

On turning the corner of the narrow lane, Robin found himself in a spacious street, with an unbroken line of lofty houses on each side, and a steepled building at the upper end, whence the ringing of a bell announced the hour of nine. The light of the moon, and the lamps from the numerous shop-windows, discovered people promenading on the pavement, and amongst them Robin hoped to recognize his hitherto inscrutable relative. The result of his former inquiries made him unwilling to hazard another, in a scene of such publicity, and he determined to walk slowly and silently up the street, thrusting his face close to that of every elderly gentleman, in search of the Major's lineaments. In his progress, Robin encountered many gay and gallant figures. Embroidered garments of showy colors, enormous periwigs, gold-laced hats, and silver-hilted swords glided past him and dazzled his optics. Travelled youths, imitators of the European fine gentlemen of the period, trod jauntily along, half dancing to the fashionable tunes which they hummed, and making poor Robin ashamed of his quiet and natural gait. At length, after many pauses to examine the gorgeous display of goods in the shop-windows, and after suffering some rebukes for the impertinence of his scrutiny into people's faces, the Major's kinsman found himself near the steepled building, still unsuccessful in his search. As yet, however, he had seen only one side of the thronged street; so Robin crossed, and continued the same sort of inquisition down the opposite pavement, with stronger hopes than the philosopher seeking an honest man, but with no better fortune. He had arrived about midway towards the lower end, from which his course began, when he overheard the approach of some one who struck down a cane on the flag-stones at every step, uttering, at regular intervals, two sepulchral hems.

"Mercy on us!" quoth Robin, recognizing the sound.

Turning a corner, which chanced to be close at his right hand, he hastened to pursue his researches in some other part of the town. His patience now was wearing low, and he seemed to feel more fatigue from his rambles since he crossed the ferry, than from his journey of several days on the other side. Hunger also pleaded loudly within him, and Robin began to balance the propriety of demanding, violently, and with lifted cudgel, the necessary guidance from the first solitary passenger whom he should meet. While a resolution to this effect was gaining strength, he entered a street of mean appearance, on either side of which a row of ill-built houses was straggling towards the harbor. The moonlight fell upon no passenger along the whole extent, but in the third domicile which Robin passed there was a half-opened door, and his keen glance detected a woman's garments within.

"My luck may be better here," said he to himself.

Accordingly, he approached the door, and beheld it shut closer as he did so; yet an open space remained, sufficing for the fair occupant to observe the stranger, without a corresponding display on her part. All that Robin could discern was a strip of scarlet petticoat, and the occasional sparkle of an eye, as if the moonbeams were trembling on some bright thing.

"Pretty mistress," for I may call her so with a good conscience, thought the shrewd youth, since I know nothing to the contrary,—"my sweet pretty mistress, will you be kind enough to tell me whereabouts I must seek the dwelling of my kinsman, Major Molineux?"

Robin's voice was plaintive and winning, and the female, seeing nothing to be shunned in the handsome country youth, thrust open the door, and came forth into the moonlight. She was a dainty little figure, with a white neck, round arms, and a slender waist, at the extremity of which her scarlet petticoat jutted out over a hoop, as if she were standing in a balloon. Moreover, her face was oval and pretty, her hair dark beneath the little cap, and her bright eyes possessed a sly freedom, which triumphed over those of Robin.

"Major Molineux dwells here," said this fair woman.

Now, her voice was the sweetest Robin had heard that night, the airy counterpart of a stream of melted silver; yet he could not help doubting whether that sweet voice spoke Gospel truth. He looked up and down the mean street, and then surveyed the house before which they stood. It was a small, dark edifice of two stories, the second of which projected over the lower floor, and the front apartment had the aspect of a shop for petty commodities.

"Now, truly, I am in luck," replied Robin, cunningly, "and so indeed is my kinsman, the Major, in having so pretty a housekeeper. But I prithee trouble him to step to the door; I will deliver him a message from his friends in the country, and then go back to my lodgings at the inn."

"Nay, the Major has been abed this hour or more," said the lady of the scarlet petticoat; "and it would be to little purpose to disturb him to-night, seeing his evening draught was of the strongest. But he is a kind-hearted man, and it would be as much as my life's worth to let a kinsman of his turn away from the door. You are the good old gentleman's very picture, and I could swear that was his rainy-weather hat. Also he has garments very much resembling those leather small-clothes. But come in, I pray, for I bid you hearty welcome in his name."

So saying, the fair and hospitable dame took our hero by the hand; and the touch was light, and the force was gentleness, and though Robin read in her eyes what he did not hear in her words, yet the slender-waisted woman in the scarlet petticoat proved stronger than the athletic country youth. She had drawn his half-willing footsteps nearly to the threshold, when the opening of a door in the neighborhood startled the Major's housekeeper, and, leaving the Major's kinsman, she vanished speedily into her own domicile. A heavy yawn preceded the appearance of a man, who, like the Moonshine of Pyramus and Thisbe, carried a lantern, needlessly aiding his sister luminary in the heavens. As he walked sleepily up the street, he turned his broad, dull face on Robin, and displayed a long staff, spiked at the end.

"Home, vagabond, home!" said the watchman, in accents that seemed to fall asleep as soon as they were uttered. "Home, or we'll set you in the stocks by peep of day!"

"This is the second hint of the kind," thought Robin. "I wish they would end my difficulties, by setting me there to-night."

Nevertheless, the youth felt an instinctive antipathy towards the guardian of midnight order, which at first prevented him from asking his usual question. But just when the man was about to vanish behind the corner, Robin resolved not to lose the opportunity, and shouted lustily after him,—

"I say, friend! will you guide me to the house of my kinsman, Major Molineux?"

The watchman made no reply, but turned the corner and was gone; yet Robin seemed to hear the sound of drowsy laughter stealing along the solitary street. At that moment, also, a pleasant titter saluted him from the open window above his head; he looked up, and caught the sparkle of a saucy eye; a round arm beckoned to him, and next he heard light footsteps descending the staircase within. But Robin, being of the household of a New England clergyman, was a good youth, as well as a shrewd one; so he resisted temptation, and fled away.

He now roamed desperately, and at random, through the town, almost ready to believe that a spell was on him, like that by which a wizard of his country had once kept three pursuers wandering, a whole winter night, within twenty paces of the cottage which they sought. The streets lay before him, strange and desolate, and the lights were extinguished in almost every house. Twice, however, little parties of men, among whom Robin distinguished individuals in outlandish attire, came hurrying along; but, though on both occasions they paused to address him, such intercourse did not at all enlighten his perplexity. They did but utter a few words in some language of which Robin knew nothing, and perceiving his inability to answer, bestowed a curse upon him in plain English and hastened away. Finally, the lad determined to knock at the door of every mansion that might appear worthy to be occupied by his kinsman, trusting that perseverance would overcome the fatality that had hitherto thwarted him. Firm in this resolve, he was passing beneath the walls of a church, which formed the corner of two streets, when, as he turned into the shade of its steeple, he encountered a bulky stranger, muffled in a cloak. The man was proceeding with the speed of earnest business, but Robin planted himself full before him, holding the oak cudgel with both hands across his body as a bar to further passage.

"Halt, honest man, and answer me a question," said he, very resolutely. "Tell me, this instant, whereabouts is the dwelling of my kinsman, Major Molineux!"

"Keep your tongue between your teeth, fool, and let me pass!" said a deep, gruff voice, which Robin partly remembered. "Let me pass, I say, or I'll strike you to the earth!"

"No, no, neighbor!" cried Robin, flourishing his cudgel, and then thrusting its larger end close to the man's muffled face. "No, no, I'm not the fool you take me for, nor do you pass till I have an answer to my question. Whereabouts is the dwelling of my kinsman, Major Molineux?"

The stranger, instead of attempting to force his passage, stepped back into the moonlight, unmuffled his face, and stared full into that of Robin.

"Watch here an hour, and Major Molineux will pass by," said he.

Robin gazed with dismay and astonishment on the unprecedented physiognomy of the speaker.

The forehead with its double prominence, the broad hooked nose, the shaggy eyebrows, and fiery eyes were those which he had noticed at the inn, but the man's complexion had undergone a singular, or, more properly, a twofold change. One side of the face blazed an intense red, while the other was black as midnight, the division line being in the broad bridge of the nose; and a mouth which seemed to extend from ear to ear was black or red, in contrast to the color of the cheek. The effect was as if two individual devils, a fiend of fire and a fiend of darkness, had united themselves to form this infernal visage. The stranger grinned in Robin's face, muffled his party-colored features, and was out of sight in a moment.

"Strange things we travellers see!" ejaculated Robin.

He seated himself, however, upon the steps of the church-door, resolving to wait the appointed time for his kinsman. A few moments were consumed in philosophical speculations upon the species of man who had just left him; but having settled this point shrewdly, rationally, and satisfactorily, he was compelled to look elsewhere for his amusement. And first he threw his eyes along the street. It was of more respectable appearance than most of those into which he had wandered; and the moon, creating, like the imaginative power, a beautiful strangeness in familiar objects, gave something of romance to a scene that might not have possessed it in the light of day. The irregular and often quaint architecture of the houses, some of whose roofs were broken into numerous little peaks, while others ascended, steep and narrow, into a single point, and others again were square; the pure snow-white of some of their complexions, the aged darkness of others, and the thousand sparklings, reflected from bright substances in the walls of many; these matters engaged Robin's attention for a while, and then began to grow wearisome. Next he endeavored to define the forms of distant objects, starting away, with almost ghostly indistinctness, just as his eye appeared to grasp them; and finally he took a minute survey of an edifice which stood on the opposite side of the street, directly in front of the church-door, where he was stationed. It was a large, square mansion, distinguished from its neighbors by a balcony, which rested on tall pillars, and by an elaborate Gothic window, communicating therewith.

"Perhaps this is the very house I have been seeking," thought Robin.

Then he strove to speed away the time, by listening to a murmur which swept continually along the street, yet was scarcely audible, except to an unaccustomed ear like his; it was a low, dull, dreamy sound, compounded of many noises, each of which was at too great a distance to be separately heard. Robin marvelled at this snore of a sleeping town, and marvelled more whenever its continuity was broken by now and then a distant shout, apparently loud where it originated. But altogether it was a sleep-inspiring sound, and, to shake off its drowsy influence, Robin arose, and climbed a window-frame, that he might view the interior of the church. There the moonbeams came trembling in, and fell down upon the deserted pews, and extended along the quiet aisles. A fainter yet more awful radiance was hovering around the pulpit, and one solitary ray had dared to rest upon the open page of the great Bible. Had nature, in that deep hour, become a worshipper in the house which man had builded? Or was that heavenly light the visible sanctity of the place,—visible because no earthly and impure feet were within the walls? The scene made Robin's heart shiver with a sensation of loneliness stronger than he had ever felt in the remotest depths of his native woods; so he turned away and sat down again before the door. There were graves around the church, and now an uneasy thought obtruded into Robin's breast. What if the object of his search, which had been so often and so strangely thwarted, were all the time mouldering in his shroud? What if his kinsman should glide through yonder gate, and nod and smile to him in dimly passing by?

"Oh that any breathing thing were here with me!" said Robin.

Recalling his thoughts from this uncomfortable track, he sent them over forest, hill, and stream, and attempted to imagine how that evening of ambiguity and weariness had been spent by his father's household. He pictured them assembled at the door, beneath the tree, the great old tree, which had been spared for its huge twisted trunk and venerable shade, when a thousand leafy brethren fell. There, at the going down of the summer sun, it was his father's custom to perform domestic worship, that the neighbors might come and join with him like brothers of the family, and that the wayfaring man might pause to drink at that fountain, and keep his heart pure by freshening the memory of home. Robin distinguished the seat of every individual of the little audience; he saw the good man in the midst, holding the Scriptures in the golden light that fell from the western clouds; he beheld him close the book and all rise up to pray. He heard the old thanksgivings for daily mercies, the old supplications for their continuance, to which he had so often listened in weariness, but which were now among his dear remembrances. He perceived the slight inequality of his father's voice when he came to speak of the absent one; he noted how his mother turned her face to the broad and knotted trunk; how his elder brother scorned, because the beard was rough upon his upper lip, to permit his features to be moved; how the younger sister drew down a low hanging branch before her eyes; and how the little one of all, whose sports had hitherto broken the decorum of the scene, understood the prayer for her playmate, and burst into clamorous grief. Then he saw them go in at the door; and when Robin would have entered also, the latch tinkled into its place, and he was excluded from his home.

"Am I here, or there?" cried Robin, starting; for all at once, when his thoughts had become visible and audible in a dream, the long, wide, solitary street shone out before him.

He aroused himself, and endeavored to fix his attention steadily upon the large edifice which he had surveyed before. But still his mind kept vibrating between fancy and reality; by turns, the pillars of the balcony lengthened into the tall, bare stems of pines, dwindled down to human figures, settled again into their true shape and size, and then commenced a new succession of changes. For a single moment, when he deemed himself awake, he could have sworn that a visage—one which he seemed to remember, yet could not absolutely name as his kinsman's—was looking towards him from the Gothic window. A deeper sleep wrestled with and nearly overcame him, but fled at the sound of footsteps along the opposite pavement. Robin rubbed his eyes, discerned a man passing at the foot of the balcony, and addressed him in a loud, peevish, and lamentable cry.

"Hallo, friend! must I wait here all night for my kinsman, Major Molineux?"

The sleeping echoes awoke, and answered the voice; and the passenger, barely able to discern a figure sitting in the oblique shade of the steeple, traversed the street to obtain a nearer view. He was himself a gentleman in his prime, of open, intelligent, cheerful, and altogether prepossessing countenance. Perceiving a country youth, apparently homeless and without friends, he accosted him in a tone of real kindness, which had become strange to Robin's ears.

"Well, my good lad, who are you sitting here?" inquired he. "Can I be of service to you in any way?"

"I am afraid not, sir," replied Robin, despondingly; "yet I shall take it kindly, if you'll answer me a single question. I've been searching, half the night, for one Major Molineux; now, sir, is there really such a person in these parts, or am I dreaming?"

"Major Molineux! The name is not altogether strange to me," said the gentleman, smiling. "Have you any objection to telling me the nature of your business with him?"

Then Robin briefly related that his father was a clergyman, settled on a small salary, at a long distance back in the country, and that he and Major Molineux were brothers' children. The Major, having inherited riches, and acquired civil and military rank, had visited his cousin, in great pomp, a year or two before; had manifested much interest in Robin and an elder brother, and, being childless himself, had thrown out hints respecting the future establishment of one of them in life. The elder brother was destined to succeed to the farm which his father cultivated in the interval of sacred duties; it was therefore determined that Robin should profit by his kinsman's generous intentions, especially as he seemed to be rather the favorite, and was thought to possess other necessary endowments.

"For I have the name of being a shrewd youth," observed Robin, in this part of his story.

"I doubt not you deserve it," replied his new friend, good-naturedly; "but pray proceed."

"Well, sir, being nearly eighteen years old, and well grown, as you see," continued Robin, drawing himself up to his full height, "I thought it high time to begin the world. So my mother and sister put me in handsome trim, and my father gave me half the remnant of his last year's salary, and five days ago I started for this place, to pay the Major a visit. But, would you believe it, sir! I crossed the ferry a little after dark, and have yet found nobody that would show me the way to his dwelling; only, an hour or two since, I was told to wait here, and Major Molineux would pass by."

"Can you describe the man who told you this?" inquired the gentleman.

"Oh, he was a very ill-favored fellow, sir," replied Robin, "with two great bumps on his forehead, a hook nose, fiery eyes; and, what struck me as the strangest, his face was of two different colors. Do you happen to know such a man, sir?"

"Not intimately," answered the stranger, "but I chanced to meet him a little time previous to your stopping me. I believe you may trust his word, and that the Major will very shortly pass through this street. In the mean time, as I have a singular curiosity to witness your meeting, I will sit down here upon the steps and bear you company."

He seated himself accordingly, and soon engaged his companion in animated discourse. It was but of brief continuance, however, for a noise of shouting, which had long been remotely audible, drew so much nearer that Robin inquired its cause.

"What may be the meaning of this uproar?" asked he. "Truly, if your town be always as noisy, I shall find little sleep while I am an inhabitant."

"Why, indeed, friend Robin, there do appear to be three or four riotous fellows abroad to-night," replied the gentleman. "You must not expect all the stillness of your native woods here in our streets. But the watch will shortly be at the heels of these lads and"—

"Ay, and set them in the stocks by peep of day," interrupted Robin, recollecting his own encounter with the drowsy lantern-bearer. "But, dear sir, if I may trust my ears, an army of watchmen would never make head against such a multitude of rioters. There were at least a thousand voices went up to make that one shout."

"May not a man have several voices, Robin, as well as two complexions?" said his friend.

"Perhaps a man may; but Heaven forbid that a woman should!" responded the shrewd youth, thinking of the seductive tones of the Major's housekeeper.

The sounds of a trumpet in some neighboring street now became so evident and continual, that Robin's curiosity was strongly excited. In addition to the shouts, he heard frequent bursts from many instruments of discord, and a wild and confused laughter filled up the intervals. Robin rose from the steps, and looked wistfully towards a point whither people seemed to be hastening.

"Surely some prodigious merry-making is going on," exclaimed he. "I have laughed very little since I left home, sir, and should be sorry to lose an opportunity. Shall we step round the corner by that darkish house, and take our share of the fun?"

"Sit down again, sit down, good Robin," replied the gentleman, laying his hand on the skirt of the gray coat. "You forget that we must wait here for your kinsman; and there is reason to believe that he will pass by, in the course of a very few moments."

The near approach of the uproar had now disturbed the neighborhood; windows flew open on all sides; and many heads, in the attire of the pillow, and confused by sleep suddenly broken, were protruded to the gaze of whoever had leisure to observe them. Eager voices hailed each other from house to house, all demanding the explanation, which not a soul could give. Half-dressed men hurried towards the unknown commotion, stumbling as they went over the stone steps that thrust themselves into the narrow foot-walk. The shouts, the laughter, and the tuneless bray, the antipodes of music, came onwards with increasing din, till scattered individuals, and then denser bodies, began to appear round a corner at the distance of a hundred yards.

"Will you recognize your kinsman, if he passes in this crowd?" inquired the gentleman.

"Indeed, I can't warrant it, sir; but I'll take my stand here, and keep a bright lookout," answered Robin, descending to the outer edge of the pavement.

A mighty stream of people now emptied into the street, and came rolling slowly towards the church. A single horseman wheeled the corner in the midst of them, and close behind him came a band of fearful wind-instruments, sending forth a fresher discord now that no intervening buildings kept it from the ear. Then a redder light disturbed the moonbeams, and a dense multitude of torches shone along the street, concealing, by their glare, whatever object they illuminated. The single horseman, clad in a military dress, and bearing a drawn sword, rode onward as the leader, and, by his fierce and variegated countenance, appeared like war personified; the red of one cheek was an emblem of fire and sword; the blackness of the other betokened the mourning that attends them. In his train were wild figures in the Indian dress, and many fantastic shapes without a model, giving the whole march a visionary air, as if a dream had broken forth from some feverish brain, and were sweeping visibly through the midnight streets. A mass of people, inactive, except as applauding spectators, hemmed the procession in; and several women ran along the sidewalk, piercing the confusion of heavier sounds with their shrill voices of mirth or terror.

"The double-faced fellow has his eye upon me," muttered Robin, with an indefinite but an uncomfortable idea that he was himself to bear a part in the pageantry.

The leader turned himself in the saddle, and

fixed his glance full upon the country youth, as the steed went slowly by. When Robin had freed his eyes from those fiery ones, the musicians were passing before him, and the torches were close at hand; but the unsteady brightness of the latter formed a veil which he could not penetrate. The rattling of wheels over the stones sometimes found its way to his ear, and confused traces of a human form appeared at intervals, and then melted into the vivid light. A moment more, and the leader thundered a command to halt: the trumpets vomited a horrid breath, and then held their peace; the shouts and laughter of the people died away, and there remained only a universal hum, allied to silence. Right before Robin's eyes was an uncovered cart. There the torches blazed the brightest, there the moon shone out like day, and there, in tar-and-feathery dignity, sat his kinsman, Major Molineux!

He was an elderly man, of large and majestic person, and strong, square features, betokening a steady soul; but steady as it was, his enemies had found means to shake it. His face was pale as death, and far more ghastly; the broad forehead was contracted in his agony, so that his eyebrows formed one grizzled line; his eyes were red and wild, and the foam hung white upon his quivering lip. His whole frame was agitated by a quick and continual tremor, which his pride strove to quell, even in those circumstances of overwhelming humiliation. But perhaps the bitterest pang of all was when his eyes met those of Robin; for he evidently knew him on the instant, as the youth stood witnessing the foul disgrace of a head grown gray in honor. They stared at each other in silence, and Robin's knees shook, and his hair bristled, with a mixture of pity and terror. Soon, however, a bewildering excitement began to seize upon his mind; the preceding adventures of the night, the unexpected appearance of the crowd, the torches, the confused din and the hush that followed, the spectre of his kinsman reviled by that great multitude,—all this, and, more than all, a perception of tremendous ridicule in the whole scene, affected him with a sort of mental inebrity. At that moment a voice of sluggish merriment saluted Robin's ears; he turned instinctively, and just behind the corner of the church stood the lantern-bearer, rubbing his eyes, and drowsily enjoying the lad's amazement. Then he heard a peal of laughter like the ringing of silvery bells; a woman twitched his arm, a saucy eye met his, and he saw the lady of the scarlet petticoat. A sharp, dry cachinnation

appealed to his memory, and, standing on tiptoe in the crowd, with his white apron over his head, he beheld the courteous little innkeeper. And lastly, there sailed over the heads of the multitude a great, broad laugh, broken in the midst by two sepulchral hems; thus, "Haw, haw, haw,—hem, hem,—haw, haw, haw, haw!"

The sound proceeded from the balcony of the opposite edifice, and thither Robin turned his eyes. In front of the Gothic window stood the old citizen, wrapped in a wide gown, his gray periwig exchanged for a nightcap, which was thrust back from his forehead, and his silk stockings hanging about his legs. He supported himself on his polished cane in a fit of convulsive merriment, which manifested itself on his solemn old features like a funny inscription on a tombstone. Then Robin seemed to hear the voices of the barbers, of the guests of the inn, and of all who had made sport of him that night. The contagion was spreading among the multitude, when all at once, it seized upon Robin, and he sent forth a shout of laughter that echoed through the street,—every man shook his sides, every man emptied his lungs, but Robin's shout was the loudest there. The cloud-spirits peeped from their silvery islands, as the congregated mirth went roaring up the sky! The Man in the Moon heard the far bellow. "Oho," quoth he, "the old earth is frolicsome to-night!"

When there was a momentary calm in that tempestuous sea of sound, the leader gave the sign, the procession resumed its march. On they went, like fiends that throng in mockery around some dead potentate, mighty no more, but majestic still in his agony. On they went, in counterfeited pomp, in senseless uproar, in frenzied merriment, trampling all on an old man's heart. On swept the tumults, and left a silent street behind.

"Well, Robin, are you dreaming?" inquired the gentleman, laying his hand on the youth's shoulder.

Robin started, and withdrew his arm from the stone post to which he had instinctively clung, as the living stream rolled by him. His cheek was somewhat pale, and his eye not quite as lively as in the earlier part of the evening.

"Will you be kind enough to show me the way to the ferry?" said he, after a moment's pause.

"You have, then, adopted a new subject of inquiry?" observed his companion, with a smile.

"Why, yes, sir," replied Robin, rather dryly. "Thanks to you, and to my other friends, I have at last met my kinsman, and he will scarce desire to see my face again. I begin to grow weary of a town life, sir. Will you show me the way to the ferry?"

"No, my good friend Robin,—not to-night, at least," said the gentleman. "Some few days hence, if you wish it, I will speed you on your journey. Or, if you prefer to remain with us, perhaps, as you are a shrewd youth, you may rise in the world without the help of your kinsman, Major Molineux."

Rappaccini's Daughter (1844)

[From the writings of Aubépine.]

We do not remember to have seen any translated specimens of the productions of M. de l'Aubépine —a fact the less to be wondered at, as his very name is unknown to many of his own countrymen as well as to the student of foreign literature. As a writer, he seems to occupy an unfortunate position between the Transcendentalists (who, under one name or another, have their share in all the current literature of the world) and the great body of pen-and-ink men who address the intellect and sympathies of the multitude. If not too refined, at all events too remote, too shadowy, and unsubstantial in his modes of development to suit the taste of the latter class, and yet too popular to satisfy the spiritual or metaphysical requisitions of the former, he must necessarily find himself without an audience, except here and there an individual or possibly an isolated clique. His writings, to do them justice, are not altogether destitute of fancy and originality; they might have won him greater reputation but for an inveterate love of allegory, which is apt to invest his plots and characters with the aspect of scenery and people in the clouds and to steal away the human warmth out of his conceptions. His fictions are sometimes historical, sometimes of the present day, and sometimes, so far as can be discovered, have little or no reference either to time or space. In any case, he generally contents himself with a very slight embroidery of outward manners,—the faintest possible counterfeit of real life,—and endeavors to create an interest by some less obvious peculiarity of the subject. Occasionally a breath of Nature, a raindrop of pathos and tenderness, or a gleam of humor will find its way into the midst of his fantastic imagery, and make us feel as if, after all, we were yet within the limits of our native earth. We will only add to this very cursory notice that M. de l'Aubépine's productions, if the reader chance to take them in precisely the proper point of view, may amuse a leisure hour as well as those of a brighter man; if otherwise, they can hardly fail to look excessively like nonsense.

Our author is voluminous; he continues to write and publish with as much praiseworthy and indefatigable prolixity as if his efforts were crowned with the brilliant success that so justly attends those of Eugene Sue. His first appearance was by a collection of stories in a long series of volumes entitled *Contes deux fois racontées*. The titles of some of his more recent works (we quote from memory) are as follows: *Le Voyage Céleste à Chemin de Fer*, 3 tom., 1838. *Le nouveau Père Adam et la nouvelle Mère Eve*, 2 tom., 1839. *Roderic; ou le Serpent à l'estomac*, 2 tom., 1840. *Le Culte du Feu*, a folio volume of ponderous research into the religion and ritual of the old Persian Ghebers, published in 1841. *La Soirée du Chateau en Espagne*, 1 tom. 8vo., 1842; and *L'Artiste du Beau; ou le Papillon Mécanique*, 5 tom. 4to., 1843. Our somewhat wearisome perusal of this startling catalogue of volumes has left behind it a certain personal affection and sympathy, though by no means admiration, for M. de l'Aubépine; and we would fain do the little in our power towards introducing him favorably to the American public. The ensuing tale is a translation of his *Beatrice; ou la Belle Empoisonneuse*, recently published in *La Revue Anti-Aristocratique*. This journal, edited by the Comte de Bearhaven, has for some years past led the defence of liberal principles and popular rights with a faithfulness and ability worthy of all praise.

A young man, named Giovanni Guasconti, came, very long ago, from the more southern region of Italy, to pursue his studies at the University of Padua. Giovanni, who had but a scanty supply of gold ducats in his pocket, took lodgings in a high and gloomy chamber of an old edifice which looked not unworthy to have been the palace of a Paduan noble, and which, in fact, exhibited over its entrance the armorial bearings of a family long since extinct. The young stranger, who was not unstudied in the great poem of his country, recollected that one of the ancestors of this family, and perhaps an occupant of this very mansion, had been pictured by Dante as a partaker of the immortal agonies of his Inferno. These reminiscences and associations, together with the tendency to heartbreak natural to a young man for the first time out of his native sphere, caused Giovanni to sigh heavily as he looked around the desolate and ill-furnished apartment.

"Holy Virgin, signor!" cried old Dame Lisabetta, who, won by the youth's remarkable beauty of person, was kindly endeavoring to give the chamber a habitable air, "what a sigh was that to come out of a young man's heart! Do you find this old mansion gloomy? For the love of Heaven, then, put your head out of the window, and you will see as bright sunshine as you have left in Naples."

Guasconti mechanically did as the old woman advised, but could not quite agree with her that the Paduan sunshine was as cheerful as that of southern Italy. Such as it was, however, it fell upon a garden beneath the window and expended its fostering influences on a variety of plants, which seemed to have been cultivated with exceeding care.

"Does this garden belong to the house?" asked Giovanni.

"Heaven forbid, signor, unless it were fruitful of better pot herbs than any that grow there now," answered old Lisabetta. "No; that garden is cultivated by the own hands of Signor Giacomo Rappaccini, the famous doctor, who, I warrant him, has been heard of as far as Naples. It is said that he distils these plants into medicines that are as potent as a charm. Oftentimes you may see the signor doctor at work, and perchance the signora, his daughter, too, gathering the strange flowers that grow in the garden."

The old woman had now done what she could for the aspect of the chamber; and, commending the young man to the protection of the saints, took her departure.

Giovanni still found no better occupation than to look down into the garden beneath his window. From its appearance, he judged it to be one of those botanic gardens which were of earlier date in Padua than elsewhere in Italy or in the world. Or, not improbably, it might once have been the pleasure-place of an opulent family; for there was the ruin of a marble fountain in the centre, sculptured with rare art, but so wofully shattered that it was impossible to trace the original design from the chaos of remaining fragments. The water, however, continued to gush and sparkle into the sunbeams as cheerfully as ever. A little gurgling sound ascended to the young man's window and made him feel as if the fountain were an immortal spirit, that sung its song unceasingly and without heeding the vicissitudes around it, while one century imbodied it in marble and another scattered the perishable garniture on the soil. All about the pool into which the water subsided grew various plants, that seemed to require a plentiful supply of moisture for the nourishment of gigantic leaves, and, in some instances, flowers gorgeously magnificent. There was one shrub in particular, set in a marble vase in the midst of the pool, that bore a profusion of purple blossoms, each of which had the lustre and richness of a gem; and the whole together made a show so resplendent that it seemed enough to illuminate the garden, even had there been no sunshine. Every portion of the soil was peopled with plants and herbs, which, if less beautiful, still bore tokens of assiduous care, as if all had their individual virtues, known to the scientific mind that fostered them. Some were placed in urns, rich with old carving, and others in common garden pots; some crept serpent-like along the ground or climbed on high, using whatever means of ascent was offered them. One plant had wreathed itself round a statue of Vertumnus, which was thus quite veiled and shrouded in a drapery of hanging foliage, so happily arranged that it might have served a sculptor for a study.

While Giovanni stood at the window he heard a rustling behind a screen of leaves, and became aware that a person was at work in the garden. His figure soon emerged into view, and showed itself to be that of no common laborer, but a tall, emaciated, sallow, and sickly-looking man, dressed in a scholar's garb of black. He was beyond the middle term of life, with gray hair, a thin, gray beard, and a face singularly marked with intellect and cultivation, but which could never, even in his more youthful days, have expressed much warmth of heart.

Nothing could exceed the intentness with which this scientific gardener examined every shrub which grew in his path: it seemed as if he was looking into their inmost nature, making observations in regard to their creative essence, and discovering why one leaf grew in this shape and another in that, and wherefore such and such flowers differed among themselves in hue and perfume. Nevertheless, in spite of this deep intelligence on his part, there was no approach to intimacy between himself and these vegetable existences. On the contrary, he avoided their actual touch or the direct inhaling of their odors with a caution that impressed Giovanni most disagreeably; for the man's demeanor was that of one walking among malignant influences, such as savage beasts, or deadly snakes, or evil spirits, which, should he allow them one moment of license, would wreak upon him some terrible fatality. It was strangely frightful to the young man's imagination to see this air of insecurity in a person cultivating a garden, that most simple and innocent of human toils, and which had been alike the joy and labor of the unfallen parents of the race. Was this garden, then, the Eden of the present world? And this man, with such a perception of harm in what his own hands caused to grow,—was he the Adam?

The distrustful gardener, while plucking away the dead leaves or pruning the too luxuriant growth of the shrubs, defended his hands with a pair of thick gloves. Nor were these his only armor. When, in his walk through the garden, he came to the magnificent plant that hung its purple gems beside the marble fountain, he placed a kind of mask over his mouth and nostrils, as if all this beauty did but conceal a deadlier malice; but, finding his task still too dangerous, he drew back, removed the mask, and called loudly, but in the infirm voice of a person affected with inward disease,—

"Beatrice! Beatrice!"

"Here am I, my father. What would you?" cried a rich and youthful voice from the window of the opposite house—a voice as rich as a tropical sunset, and which made Giovanni, though he knew not why, think of deep hues of purple or crimson and of perfumes heavily delectable. "Are you in the garden?"

"Yes, Beatrice," answered the gardener; "and I need your help."

Soon there emerged from under a sculptured portal the figure of a young girl, arrayed with as much richness of taste as the most splendid of the flowers, beautiful as the day, and with a bloom so deep and vivid that one shade more would have been too much. She looked redundant with life, health, and energy; all of which attributes were bound down and compressed, as it were, and girdled tensely, in their luxuriance, by her virgin zone. Yet Giovanni's fancy must have grown morbid while he looked down into the garden; for the impression which the fair stranger made upon him

was as if there were another flower, the human sister of those vegetable ones, as beautiful as they, more beautiful than the richest of them, but still to be touched only with a glove, nor to be approached without a mask. As Beatrice came down the garden path, it was observable that she handled and inhaled the odor of several of the plants which her father had most sedulously avoided.

"Here, Beatrice," said the latter, "see how many needful offices require to be done to our chief treasure. Yet, shattered as I am, my life might pay the penalty of approaching it so closely as circumstances demand. Henceforth, I fear, this plant must be consigned to your sole charge."

"And gladly will I undertake it," cried again the rich tones of the young lady, as she bent towards the magnificent plant and opened her arms as if to embrace it. "Yes, my sister, my splendor, it shall be Beatrice's task to nurse and serve thee; and thou shalt reward her with thy kisses and perfumed breath, which to her is as the breath of life."

Then, with all the tenderness in her manner that was so strikingly expressed in her words, she busied herself with such attentions as the plant seemed to require; and Giovanni, at his lofty window, rubbed his eyes, and almost doubted whether it were a girl tending her favorite flower, or one sister performing the duties of affection to another. The scene soon terminated. Whether Dr. Rappaccini had finished his labors in the garden, or that his watchful eye had caught the stranger's face, he now took his daughter's arm and retired. Night was already closing in; oppressive exhalations seemed to proceed from the plants and steal upward past the open window; and Giovanni, closing the lattice, went to his couch and dreamed of a rich flower and beautiful girl. Flower and maiden were different, and yet the same, and fraught with some strange peril in either shape.

But there is an influence in the light of morning that tends to rectify whatever errors of fancy, or even of judgment, we may have incurred during the sun's decline, or among the shadows of the night, or in the less wholesome glow of moonshine. Giovanni's first movement, on starting from sleep, was to throw open the window and gaze down into the garden which his dreams had made so fertile of mysteries. He was surprised, and a little ashamed, to find how real and matter-of-fact an affair it proved to be, in the first rays of the sun which gilded the dewdrops that hung upon leaf and blossom, and, while giving a brighter beauty to each rare flower, brought every thing within the limits of ordinary experience. The young man rejoiced that, in the heart of the barren city, he had the privilege of overlooking this spot of lovely and luxuriant vegetation. It would serve, he said to himself, as a symbolic language to keep him in communication with Nature. Neither the sickly and thoughtworn Dr. Giacomo Rappaccini, it is true, nor his brilliant daughter, were now visible; so that Giovanni could not determine how much of the singularity which he attributed to both was due to their own qualities and how much to his wonder-working fancy; but he was inclined to take a most rational view of the whole matter.

In the course of the day he paid his respects to Signor Pietro Baglioni, professor of medicine in the university, a physician of eminent repute, to whom Giovanni had brought a letter of introduction. The professor was an elderly personage, apparently of genial nature and habits that might almost be called jovial. He kept the young man to dinner, and made himself very agreeable by the freedom and liveliness of his conversation, especially when warmed by a flask or two of Tuscan wine. Giovanni, conceiving that men of science, inhabitants of the same city, must needs be on familiar terms with one another, took an opportunity to mention the name of Dr. Rappaccini. But the professor did not respond with so much cordiality as he had anticipated.

"Ill would it become a teacher of the divine art of medicine," said Professor Pietro Baglioni, in answer to a question of Giovanni, "to withhold due and well-considered praise of a physician so eminently skilled as Rappaccini; but, on the other hand, I should answer it but scantily to my conscience were I to permit a worthy youth like yourself, Signor Giovanni, the son of an ancient friend, to imbibe erroneous ideas respecting a man who might hereafter chance to hold your life and death in his hands. The truth is, our worshipful Dr. Rappaccini has as much science as any member of the faculty—with perhaps one single exception —in Padua, or all Italy; but there are certain grave objections to his professional character."

"And what are they?" asked the young man.

"Has my friend Giovanni any disease of body or heart, that he is so inquisitive about physicians?" said the professor, with a smile. "But as for Rappaccini, it is said of him—and I, who know the man well, can answer for its truth—that he cares infinitely more for science than for mankind. His patients are interesting to him only as subjects for some new experiment. He would sacrifice human life, his own among the rest, or whatever else was dearest to him, for the sake of adding so much as a grain of mustard seed to the great heap of his accumulated knowledge."

"Methinks he is an awful man indeed," remarked Guasconti, mentally recalling the cold and purely intellectual aspect of Rappaccini. "And yet, worshipful professor, is it not a noble spirit? Are there many men capable of so spiritual a love of science?"

"God forbid," answered the professor, somewhat testily; "at least, unless they take sounder views of the healing art than those adopted by Rappaccini. It is his theory that all medicinal virtues are comprised within those substances which we term vegetable poisons. These he cultivates with his own hands, and is said even to have produced new varieties of poison more horribly deleterious than Nature, without the assistance of this learned person, would ever have plagued the world withal. That the signor doctor does less mischief than might be expected with such dangerous substances, is undeniable. Now and then, it must be owned, he has effected, or seemed to effect, a marvellous cure; but, to tell you my private mind, Signor Giovanni, he should receive little credit for such instances of success,—they being probably the work of chance,—but should be held strictly accountable for his failures, which may justly be considered his own work."

The youth might have taken Baglioni's opinions with many grains of allowance had he known that there was a professional warfare of long continuance between him and Dr. Rappaccini, in which the latter was generally thought to have gained the advantage. If the reader be inclined to judge for himself, we refer him to certain black-letter tracts on both sides, preserved in the medical department of the University of Padua.

"I know not, most learned professor," returned Giovanni, after musing on what had been said of Rappaccini's exclusive zeal for science,—"I know not how dearly this physician may love his art; but surely there is one object more dear to him. He has a daughter."

"Aha!" cried the professor, with a laugh. "So now our friend Giovanni's secret is out. You have heard of this daughter, whom all the young men in Padua are wild about, though not half a dozen have ever had the good hap to see her face. I know little of the Signora Beatrice save that Rappaccini is said to have instructed her deeply in his science, and that, young and beautiful as fame reports her, she is already qualified to fill a professor's chair. Perchance her father destines her for mine! Other absurd rumors there be, not worth talking about or listening to. So now, Signor Giovanni, drink off your glass of lachryma."

Guasconti returned to his lodgings somewhat heated with the wine he had quaffed, and which caused his brain to swim with strange fantasies in reference to Dr. Rappaccini and the beautiful Beatrice. On his way, happening to pass by a florist's, he bought a fresh bouquet of flowers.

Ascending to his chamber, he seated himself near the window, but within the shadow thrown by the depth of the wall, so that he could look down into the garden with little risk of being discovered. All beneath his eye was a solitude. The strange plants were basking in the sunshine, and now and then nodding gently to one another, as if in acknowledgment of sympathy and kindred. In the midst, by the shattered fountain, grew the magnificent shrub, with its purple gems clustering all over it; they glowed in the air, and gleamed back again out of the depths of the pool, which thus seemed to overflow with colored radiance from the rich reflection that was steeped in it. At first, as we have said, the garden was a solitude. Soon, however,—as Giovanni had half hoped, half feared, would be the case,—a figure appeared beneath the antique sculptured portal, and came down between the rows of plants, inhaling their various perfumes as if she were one of those beings of old classic fable that lived upon sweet odors. On again beholding Beatrice, the young man was even startled to perceive how much her beauty exceeded his recollection of it; so brilliant, so vivid, was its character, that she glowed amid the sunlight, and, as Giovanni whispered to himself, positively illuminated the more shadowy intervals of the garden path. Her face being now more revealed than on the former occasion, he was struck by its expression of simplicity and sweetness—qualities that had not entered into his idea of her character, and which made him ask anew what manner of mortal she might be. Nor did he fail again to observe, or imagine, an analogy between the beautiful girl and the gorgeous shrub that hung its gemlike flowers over the fountain—a resemblance which Beatrice seemed to have indulged a fantastic humor in heightening, both by the arrangement of her dress and the selection of its hues.

Approaching the shrub, she threw open her arms, as with a passionate ardor, and drew its branches into an intimate embrace—so intimate that her features were hidden in its leafy bosom and her glistening ringlets all intermingled with the flowers.

"Give me thy breath, my sister," exclaimed Beatrice; "for I am faint with common air. And give me this flower of thine, which I separate with gentlest fingers from the stem and place it close beside my heart."

With these words the beautiful daughter of Rappaccini plucked one of the richest blossoms of the shrub, and was about to fasten it in her bosom. But now, unless Giovanni's draughts of wine had bewildered his senses, a singular incident occurred. A small orange-colored reptile, of the lizard or chameleon species, chanced to be creeping along the path, just at the feet of Beatrice. It appeared to Giovanni,—but, at the distance from which he gazed, he could scarcely have seen anything so minute,—it appeared to him, however, that a drop or two of moisture from the broken stem of the flower descended upon the lizard's head. For an instant the reptile contorted itself violently, and then lay motionless in the sunshine. Beatrice observed this remarkable phenomenon, and crossed herself, sadly, but without surprise; nor did she therefore hesitate to arrange the fatal flower in her bosom. There it blushed, and almost glimmered with the dazzling effect of a precious stone, adding to her dress and aspect the one appropriate charm which nothing else in the world could have supplied. But Giovanni, out of the shadow of his window, bent forward and shrank back, and murmured and trembled.

"Am I awake? Have I my senses?" said he to himself. "What is this being? Beautiful shall I call her, or inexpressibly terrible?"

Beatrice now strayed carelessly through the garden, approaching closer beneath Giovanni's window, so that he was compelled to thrust his head quite out of its concealment in order to gratify the intense and painful curiosity which she excited. At this moment there came a beautiful insect over the garden wall: it had, perhaps, wandered through the city, and found no flowers or verdure among those antique haunts of men until the heavy perfumes of Dr. Rappaccini's shrubs had lured it from afar. Without alighting on the flowers this winged brightness seemed to be attracted by Beatrice, and lingered in the air and fluttered about her head. Now, here it could not be but that Giovanni Guasconti's eyes deceived him. Be that as it might, he fancied that, while Beatrice was gazing at the insect with childish delight, it grew faint and fell at her feet; its bright wings shivered; it was dead—from no cause that he could discern, unless it were the atmosphere of her breath. Again Beatrice crossed herself and sighed heavily as she bent over the dead insect.

An impulsive movement of Giovanni drew her eyes to the window. There she beheld the beautiful head of the young man—rather a Grecian than an Italian head, with fair, regular features, and a glistening of gold among his ringlets—gazing down upon her like a being that hovered in mid air. Scarcely knowing what he did, Giovanni threw down the bouquet which he had hitherto held in his hand.

"Signora," said he, "there are pure and healthful flowers. Wear them for the sake of Giovanni Guasconti."

"Thanks, signor," replied Beatrice, with her rich voice, that came forth as it were like a gush of music, and with a mirthful expression half childish and half womanlike. "I accept your gift, and would fain recompense it with this precious purple flower; but, if I toss it into the air, it will not reach you. So Signor Guasconti must even content himself with my thanks."

She lifted the bouquet from the ground, and then, as if inwardly ashamed at having stepped aside from her maidenly reserve to respond to a stranger's greeting, passed swiftly homeward through the garden. But, few as the moments were, it seemed to Giovanni, when she was on the point of vanishing beneath the sculptured portal, that his beautiful bouquet was already beginning to wither in her grasp. It was an idle thought; there could be no possibility of distinguishing a faded flower from a fresh one at so great a distance.

For many days after this incident the young man avoided the window that looked into Dr. Rappaccini's garden, as if something ugly and monstrous would have blasted his eyesight had he been betrayed into a glance. He felt conscious of having put himself, to a certain extent, within the influence of an unintelligible power by the communication which he had opend with Beatrice. The wisest course would have been, if his heart were in any real danger, to quit his lodgings and Padua itself at once; the next wiser, to have accustomed himself, as far as possible, to the familiar and daylight view of Beatrice—thus bringing her rigidly and systematically within the limits of ordinary experi-

ence. Least of all, while avoiding her sight, ought Giovanni to have remained so near this extraordinary being that the proximity and possibility even of intercourse should give a kind of substance and reality to the wild vagaries which his imagination ran riot continually in producing. Guasconti had not a deep heart—or, at all events, its depths were not sounded now; but he had a quick fancy, and an ardent southern temperament, which rose every instant to a higher fever pitch. Whether or no Beatrice possessed those terrible attributes, that fatal breath, the affinity with those so beautiful and deadly flowers which were indicated by what Giovanni had witnessed, she had at least instilled a fierce and subtle poison into his system. It was not love, although her rich beauty was a madness to him; nor horror, even while he fancied her spirit to be imbued with the same baneful essence that seemed to pervade her physical frame; but a wild offspring of both love and horror that had each parent in it, and burned like one and shivered like the other. Giovanni knew not what to dread; still less did he know what to hope; yet hope and dread kept a continual warfare in his breast, alternately vanquishing one another and starting up afresh to renew the contest. Blessed are all simple emotions, be they dark or bright! It is the lurid intermixture of the two that produces the illuminating blaze of the infernal regions.

Sometimes he endeavored to assuage the fever of his spirit by a rapid walk through the streets of Padua or beyond its gates: his footsteps kept time with the throbbings of his brain, so that the walk was apt to accelerate itself to a race. One day he found himself arrested; his arm was seized by a portly personage, who had turned back on recognizing the young man and expended much breath in overtaking him.

"Signor Giovanni! Stay, my young friend!" cried he. "Have you forgotten me? That might well be the case if I were as much altered as yourself."

It was Baglioni, whom Giovanni had avoided ever since their first meeting, from a doubt that the professor's sagacity would look too deeply into his secrets. Endeavoring to recover himself, he stared forth wildly from his inner world into the outer one and spoke like a man in a dream.

"Yes; I am Giovanni Guasconti. You are Professor Pietro Baglioni. Now let me pass!"

"Not yet, not yet, Signor Giovanni Guasconti," said the professor, smiling, but at the same time scrutinizing the youth with an earnest glance.

"What! did I grow up side by side with your father? and shall his son pass me like a stranger in these old streets of Padua? Stand still, Signor Giovanni; for we must have a word or two before we part."

"Speedily, then, most worshipful professor, speedily," said Giovanni, with feverish impatience. "Does not your worship see that I am in haste?"

Now, while he was speaking there came a man in black along the street, stooping and moving feebly like a person in inferior health. His face was all overspread with a most sickly and sallow hue, but yet so pervaded with an expression of piercing and active intellect that an observer might easily have overlooked the merely physical attributes and have seen only this wonderful energy. As he passed, this person exchanged a cold and distant salutation with Baglioni, but fixed his eyes upon Giovanni with an intentness that seemed to bring out whatever was within him worthy of notice. Nevertheless, there was a peculiar quietness in the look, as if taking merely a speculative, not a human, interest in the young man.

"It is Dr. Rappaccini!" whispered the professor when the stranger had passed. "Has he ever seen your face before?"

"Not that I know," answered Giovanni, starting at the name.

"He *has* seen you! he must have seen you!" said Baglioni, hastily. "For some purpose or other, this man of science is making a study of you. I know that look of his! It is the same that coldly illuminates his face as he bends over a bird, a mouse, or a butterfly; which, in pursuance of some experiment, he has killed by the perfume of a flower; a look as deep as Nature itself, but without Nature's warmth of love. Signor Giovanni, I will stake my life upon it, you are the subject of one of Rappaccini's experiments!"

"Will you make a fool of me?" cried Giovanni, passionately. "*That*, signor professor, were an untoward experiment."

"Patience! patience!" replied the imperturbable professor. "I tell thee, my poor Giovanni, that Rappaccini has a scientific interest in thee. Thou hast fallen into fearful hands! And the Signora Beatrice,—what part does she act in this mystery?"

But Guasconti, finding Baglioni's pertinacity intolerable, here broke away, and was gone before the professor could again seize his arm. He looked after the young man intently and shook his head.

"This must not be," said Baglioni to himself. "The youth is the son of my old friend, and shall not come to any harm from which the arcana of medical science can preserve him. Besides, it is too insufferable an impertinence in Rappaccini thus to snatch the lad out of my own hands, as I may say, and make use of him for his infernal experiments. This daughter of his! It shall be looked to. Perchance, most learned Rappaccini, I may foil you where you little dream of it!"

Meanwhile Giovanni had pursued a circuitous route, and at length found himself at the door of his lodgings. As he crossed the threshold he was met by old Lisabetta, who smirked and smiled, and was evidently desirous to attract his attention; vainly, however, as the ebullition of his feelings had momentarily subsided into a cold and dull vacuity. He turned his eyes full upon the withered face that was puckering itself into a smile, but seemed to behold it not. The old dame, therefore, laid her grasp upon his cloak.

"Signor! signor!" whispered she, still with a smile over the whole breadth of her visage, so that it looked not unlike a grotesque carving in wood, darkened by centuries. "Listen, signor! There is a private entrance into the garden!"

"What do you say?" exclaimed Giovanni, turning quickly about, as if an inanimate thing should start into feverish life. "A private entrance into Dr. Rappaccini's garden?"

"Hush! hush! not so loud!" whispered Lisabetta, putting her hand over his mouth. "Yes; into the worshipful doctor's garden, where you may see all his fine shrubbery. Many a young man in Padua would give gold to be admitted among those flowers."

Giovanni put a piece of gold into her hand.

"Show me the way," said he.

A surmise, probably excited by his conversation with Baglioni, crossed his mind, that this interposition of old Lisabetta might perchance be connected with the intrigue, whatever were its nature, in which the professor seemed to suppose that Dr. Rappaccini was involving him. But such a suspicion, though it disturbed Giovanni, was inadequate to restrain him. The instant that he was aware of the possibility of approaching Beatrice, it seemed an absolute necessity of his existence to do so. It mattered not whether she were angel or demon; he was irrevocably within her sphere, and must obey the law that whirled him onward, in ever-lessening circles, towards a result which he did not attempt to foreshadow; and yet, strange to say, there came across him a sudden doubt whether this intense interest on his part were not delusory;

whether it were really of so deep and positive a nature as to justify him in now thrusting himself into an incalculable position; whether it were not merely the fantasy of a young man's brain, only slightly or not at all connected with his heart.

He paused, hesitated, turned half about, but again went on. His withered guide led him along several obscure passages, and finally undid a door, through which, as it was opened, there came the sight and sound of rustling leaves, with the broken sunshine glimmering among them. Giovanni stepped forth, and, forcing himself through the entanglement of a shrub that wreathed its tendrils over the hidden entrance, stood beneath his own window in the open area of Dr. Rappaccini's garden.

How often is it the case that, when impossibilities have come to pass and dreams have condensed their misty substance into tangible realities, we find ourselves calm, and even coldly self-possessed, amid circumstances which it would have been a delirium of joy or agony to anticipate! Fate delights to thwart us thus. Passion will choose his own time to rush upon the scene, and lingers sluggishly behind when an appropriate adjustment of events would seem to summon his appearance. So was it now with Giovanni. Day after day his pulses had throbbed with feverish blood at the improbable idea of an interview with Beatrice, and of standing with her, face to face, in this very garden, basking in the Oriental sunshine of her beauty, and snatching from her full gaze the mystery which he deemed the riddle of his own existence. But now there was a singular and untimely equanimity within his breast. He threw a glance around the garden to discover if Beatrice or her father were present, and, perceiving that he was alone, began a critical observation of the plants.

The aspect of one and all of them dissatisfied him; their gorgeousness seemed fierce, passionate, and even unnatural. There was hardly an individual shrub which a wanderer, straying by himself through a forest, would not have been startled to find growing wild, as if an unearthly face had glared at him out of the thicket. Several also would have shocked a delicate instinct by an appearance of artificialness indicating that there had been such commixture, and, as it were, adultery of various vegetable species, that the production was no longer of God's making, but the monstrous offspring of man's depraved fancy, glowing with only an evil mockery of beauty. They were probably the result of experiment, which in one or two cases had succeeded in mingling plants individually lovely into a compound possessing the questionable and ominous character that distinguished the whole growth of the garden. In fine, Giovanni recognized but two or three plants in the collection, and those of a kind that he well knew to be poisonous. While busy with these contemplations he heard the rustling of a silken garment, and, turning, beheld Beatrice emerging from beneath the sculptured portal.

Giovanni had not considered with himself what should be his deportment; whether he should apologize for his intrusion into the garden, or assume that he was there with the privity at least, if not by the desire, of Dr. Rappaccini or his daughter; but Beatrice's manner placed him at his ease, though leaving him still in doubt by what agency he had gained admittance. She came lightly along the path and met him near the broken fountain. There was surprise in her face, but brightened by a simple and kind expression of pleasure.

"You are a connoisseur in flowers, signor," said Beatrice, with a smile, alluding to the bouquet which he had flung her from the window. "It is no marvel, therefore, if the sight of my father's rare collection has tempted you to take a nearer view. If he were here, he could tell you many strange and interesting facts as to the nature and habits of these shrubs; for he has spent a lifetime in such studies, and this garden is his world."

"And yourself, lady," observed Giovanni, "if fame says true,—you likewise are deeply skilled in the virtues indicated by these rich blossoms and these spicy perfumes. Would you deign to be my instructress, I should prove an apter scholar than if taught by Signor Rappaccini himself."

"Are there such idle rumors?" asked Beatrice, with the music of a pleasant laugh. "Do people say that I am skilled in my father's science of plants? What a jest is there! No; though I have grown up among these flowers, I know no more of them than their hues and perfume; and sometimes methinks I would fain rid myself of even that small knowledge. There are many flowers here, and those not the least brilliant, that shock and offend me when they meet my eye. But pray, signor, do not believe these stories about my science. Believe nothing of me save what you see with your own eyes."

"And must I believe all that I have seen with my own eyes?" asked Giovanni, pointedly, while the recollection of former scenes made him shrink. "No, signora; you demand too little of me. Bid me believe nothing save what comes from your own lips."

It would appear that Beatrice understood him. There came a deep flush to her cheek; but she looked full into Giovanni's eyes, and responded to his gaze of uneasy suspicion with a queenlike haughtiness.

"I do so bid you, signor," she replied. "Forget whatever you may have fancied in regard to me. If true to the outward senses, still it may be false in its essence; but the words of Beatrice Rappaccini's lips are true from the depths of the heart outward. Those you may believe."

A fervor glowed in her whole aspect and beamed upon Giovanni's consciousness like the light of truth itself; but while she spoke there was a fragrance in the atmosphere around her, rich and delightful, though evanescent, yet which the young man, from an indefinable reluctance, scarcely dared to draw into his lungs. It might be the odor of the flowers. Could it be Beatrice's breath which thus embalmed her words with a strange richness, as if by steeping them in her heart? A faintness passed like a shadow over Giovanni and flitted away; he seemed to gaze through the beautiful girl's eyes into her transparent soul, and felt no more doubt or fear.

The tinge of passion that had colored Beatrice's manner vanished; she became gay, and appeared to derive a pure delight from her communion with the youth not unlike what the maiden of a lonely island might have felt conversing with a voyager from the civilized world. Evidently her experience of life had been confined within the limits of that garden. She talked now about matters as simple as the daylight or summer clouds, and now asked questions in reference to the city, or Giovanni's distant home, his friends, his mother, and his sisters—questions indicating such seclusion, and such lack of familiarity with modes and forms, that Giovanni responded as if to an infant. Her spirit gushed out before him like a fresh rill that was just catching its first glimpse of the sunlight and wondering at the reflections of earth and sky which were flung into its bosom. There came thoughts, too, from a deep source, and fantasies of a gemlike brilliancy, as if diamonds and rubies sparkled upward among the bubbles of the fountain. Ever and anon there gleamed across the young man's mind a sense of wonder that he should be walking side by side with the being who had so wrought upon his imagination, whom he had idealized in such hues of terror, in whom he had positively witnessed such manifestations of dreadful attributes—that he should be conversing with Beatrice like a brother, and should find her

so human and so maidenlike. But such reflections were only momentary; the effect of her character was too real not to make itself familiar at once.

In this free intercourse they had strayed through the garden, and now, after many turns among its avenues, were come to the shattered fountain, beside which grew the magnificent shrub, with its treasury of glowing blossoms. A fragrance was diffused from it which Giovanni recognized as identical with that which he had attributed to Beatrice's breath, but incomparably more powerful. As her eyes fell upon it, Giovanni beheld her press her hand to her bosom as if her heart were throbbing suddenly and painfully.

"For the first time in my life," murmured she, addressing the shrub, "I had forgotten thee."

"I remember, signora," said Giovanni, "that you once promised to reward me with one of these living gems for the bouquet which I had the happy boldness to fling to your feet. Permit me now to pluck it as a memorial of this interview."

He made a step towards the shrub with extended hand; but Beatrice darted forward, uttering a shriek that went through his heart like a dagger. She caught his hand and drew it back with the whole force of her slender figure. Giovanni felt her touch thrilling through his fibres.

"Touch it not!" exclaimed she, in a voice of agony. "Not for thy life! It is fatal!"

Then, hiding her face, she fled from him and vanished beneath the sculptured portal. As Giovanni followed her with his eyes, he beheld the emaciated figure and pale intelligence of Dr. Rappaccini, who had been watching the scene, he knew not how long, within the shadow of the entrance.

No sooner was Guasconti alone in his chamber than the image of Beatrice came back to his passionate musings, invested with all the witchery that had been gathering around it ever since his first glimpse of her, and now likewise imbued with a tender warmth of girlish womanhood. She was human; her nature was endowed with all gentle and feminine qualities; she was worthiest to be worshipped; she was capable, surely, on her part, of the height and heroism of love. Those tokens which he had hitherto considered as proofs of a frightful peculiarity in her physical and moral system were now either forgotten or by the subtle sophistry of passion transmitted into a golden crown of enchantment, rendering Beatrice the more admirable by so much as she was the more unique. Whatever had looked ugly was now beautiful; or, if incapable of such a change, it stole away and hid itself among those shapeless half ideas which throng the dim region beyond the daylight of our perfect consciousness. Thus did he spend the night, nor fell asleep until the dawn had began to awake the slumbering flowers in Dr. Rappaccini's garden, whither Giovanni's dreams doubtless led him. Up rose the sun in his due season, and, flinging his beams upon the young man's eyelids, awoke him to a sense of pain. When thoroughly aroused, he became sensible of a burning and tingling agony in his hand—in his right hand—the very hand which Beatrice had grasped in her own when he was on the point of plucking one of the gemlike flowers. On the back of that hand there was now a purple print like that of four small fingers, and the likeness of a slender thumb upon his wrist.

O, how stubbornly does love,—or even that cunning semblance of love which flourishes in the imagination, but strikes no depth of root into the heart,—how stubbornly does it hold its faith until the moment comes when it is doomed to vanish into thin mist! Giovanni wrapped a handkerchief about his hand and wondered what evil thing had stung him, and soon forgot his pain in a revery of Beatrice.

After the first interview, a second was in the inevitable course of what we call fate. A third; a fourth; and a meeting with Beatrice in the garden was no longer an incident in Giovanni's daily life, but the whole space in which he might be said to live; for the anticipation and memory of that ecstatic hour made up the remainder. Nor was it otherwise with the daughter of Rappaccini. She watched for the youth's appearance and flew to his side with confidence as unreserved as if they had been playmates from early infancy—as if they were such playmates still. If, by any unwonted chance, he failed to come at the appointed moment, she stood beneath the window and sent up the rich sweetness of her tones to float around him in his chamber and echo and reverberate throughout his heart: "Giovanni! Giovanni! Why tarriest thou? Come down!" And down he hastened into that Eden of poisonous flowers.

But, with all this intimate familiarity, there was still a reserve in Beatrice's demeanor, so rigidly and invariably sustained that the idea of infringing it scarcely occurred to his imagination. By all appreciable signs, they loved; they had looked love with eyes that conveyed the holy secret from the depths of one soul into the depths of the other, as if it were too sacred to be whispered by the way; they had even spoken love in those gushes of passion when their spirits darted forth in articulated breath like tongues of long hidden flame; and yet there had been no seal of lips, no clasp of hands, nor any slightest caress such as love claims and hallows. He had never touched one of the gleaming ringlets of her hair; her garment—so marked was the physical barrier between them—had never been waved against him by a breeze. On the few occasions when Giovanni had seemed tempted to overstep the limit, Beatrice grew so sad, so stern, and withal wore such a look of desolate separation, shuddering at itself, that not a spoken word was requisite to repel him. At such times he was startled at the horrible suspicions that rose, monster-like, out of the caverns of his heart and stared him in the face; his love grew thin and faint as the morning mist; his doubts alone had substance. But, when Beatrice's face brightened again after the momentary shadow, she was transformed at once from the mysterious, questionable being whom he had watched with so much awe and horror; she was now the beautiful and unsophisticated girl whom he felt that his spirit knew with a certainty beyond all other knowledge.

A considerable time had now passed since Giovanni's last meeting with Baglioni. One morning, however, he was disagreeably surprised by a visit from the professor, whom he had scarcely thought of for whole weeks, and would willingly have forgotten still longer. Given up as he had long been to a pervading excitement, he could tolerate no companions except upon condition of their perfect sympathy with his present state of feeling. Such sympathy was not to be expected from Professor Baglioni.

The visitor chatted carelessly for a few moments about the gossip of the city and the university, and then took up another topic.

"I have been reading an old classic author lately," said he, "and met with a story that strangely interested me. Possibly you may remember it. It is of an Indian prince, who sent a beautiful woman as a present to Alexander the Great. She was as lovely as the dawn and gorgeous as the sunset; but what especially distinguished her was a certain rich perfume in her breath—richer than a garden of Persian roses. Alexander, as was natural to a youthful conqueror, fell in love at first sight with this magnificent stranger; but a certain sage physician, happening to be present, discovered a terrible secret in regard to her."

"And what was that?" asked Giovanni, turning his eyes downward to avoid those of the professor.

"That this lovely woman," continued Baglioni,

with emphasis, "had been nourished with poisons from her birth upward, until her whole nature was so imbued with them that she herself had become the deadliest poison in existence. Poison was her element of life. With that rich perfume of her breath she blasted the very air. Her love would have been poison—her embrace death. Is not this a marvellous tale?"

"A childish fable," answered Giovanni, nervously starting from his chair. "I marvel how your worship finds time to read such nonsense among your graver studies."

"By the by," said the professor, looking uneasily about him, "what singular fragrance is this in your apartment? Is it the perfume of your gloves? It is faint, but delicious; and yet, after all, by no means agreeable. Were I to breathe it long, methinks it would make me ill. It is like the breath of a flower; but I see no flowers in the chamber."

"Nor are there any," replied Giovanni, who had turned pale as the professor spoke; "nor, I think, is there any fragrance except in your worship's imagination. Odors, being a sort of element combined of the sensual and the spiritual, are apt to deceive us in this manner. The recollection of a perfume, the bare idea of it, may easily be mistaken for a present reality."

"Ay; but my sober imagination does not often play such tricks," said Baglioni; "and, were I to fancy any kind of odor, it would be that of some vile apothecary drug, wherewith my fingers are likely enough to be imbued. Our worshipful friend Rappaccini, as I have heard, tinctures his medicaments with odors richer than those of Araby. Doubtless, likewise, the fair and learned Signora Beatrice would minister to her patients with draughts as sweet as a maiden's breath; but woe to him that sips them!"

Giovanni's face evinced many contending emotions. The tone in which the professor alluded to the pure and lovely daughter of Rappaccini was a torture to his soul; and yet the intimation of a view of her character, opposite to his own, gave instantaneous distinctness to a thousand dim suspicions, which now grinned at him like so many demons. But he strove hard to quell them and to respond to Baglioni with a true lover's perfect faith.

"Signor professor," said he, "you were my father's friend; perchance, too, it is your purpose to act a friendly part towards his son. I would fain feel nothing towards you save respect and deference; but I pray you to observe, signor, that there is one subject on which we must not speak. You know not the Signora Beatrice. You cannot, there-

fore, estimate the wrong—the blasphemy, I may even say—that is offered to her character by a light or injurious word."

"Giovanni! my poor Giovanni!" answered the professor, with a calm expression of pity, "I know this wretched girl far better than yourself. You shall hear the truth in respect to the poisoner Rappaccini and his poisonous daughter; yes, poisonous as she is beautiful. Listen; for, even should you do violence to my gray hairs, it shall not silence me. That old fable of the Indian woman has become a truth by the deep and deadly science of Rappaccini and in the person of the lovely Beatrice."

Giovanni groaned and hid his face.

"Her father," continued Baglioni, "was not restrained by natural affection from offering up his child in this horrible manner as the victim of his insane zeal for science; for, let us do him justice, he is as true a man of science as ever distilled his own heart in an alembic. What, then, will be your fate? Beyond a doubt you are selected as the material of some new experiment. Perhaps the result is to be death; perhaps a fate more awful still. Rappaccini, with what he calls the interest of science before his eyes, will hesitate at nothing."

"It is a dream," muttered Giovanni to himself; "surely it is a dream."

"But," resumed the professor, "be of good cheer, son of my friend. It is not yet too late for the rescue. Possibly we may even succeed in bringing back this miserable child within the limits of ordinary nature, from which her father's madness has estranged her. Behold this little silver vase! It was wrought by the hands of the renowned Benvenuto Cellini, and is well worthy to be a love gift to the fairest dame in Italy. But its contents are invaluable. One little sip of this antidote would have rendered the most virulent poisons of the Borgias innocuous. Doubt not that it will be as efficacious against those of Rappaccini. Bestow the vase, and the precious liquid within it, on your Beatrice, and hopefully await the result."

Baglioni laid a small, exquisitely wrought silver vial on the table and withdrew, leaving what he had said to produce its effect upon the young man's mind.

"We will thwart Rappaccini yet," thought he, chuckling to himself, as he descended the stairs; "but, let us confess the truth of him, he is a wonderful man—a wonderful man indeed; a vile empiric, however, in his practice, and therefore not to be tolerated by those who respect the good old rules of the medical profession."

Throughout Giovanni's whole acquaintance with Beatrice, he had occasionally, as we have said, been haunted by dark surmises as to her character; yet so thoroughly had she made herself felt by him as a simple, natural, most affectionate, and guileless creature, that the image now held up by Professor Baglioni looked as strange and incredible as if it were not in accordance with his own original conception. True, there were ugly recollections connected with his first glimpses of the beautiful girl; he could not quite forget the bouquet that withered in her grasp, and the insect that perished amid the sunny air, by no ostensible agency save the fragrance of her breath. These incidents, however, dissolving in the pure light of her character, had no longer the efficacy of facts, but were acknowledged as mistaken fantasies, by whatever testimony of the senses they might appear to be substantiated. There is something truer and more real than what we can see with the eyes and touch with the finger. On such better evidence had Giovanni founded his confidence in Beatrice, though rather by the necessary force of her high attributes than by any deep and generous faith on his part. But now his spirit was incapable of sustaining itself at the height to which the early enthusiasm of passion had exalted it; he fell down, grovelling among earthly doubts, and defiled therewith the pure whiteness of Beatrice's image. Not that he gave her up! he did but distrust. He resolved to institute some decisive test that should satisfy him, once for all, whether there were those dreadful peculiarities in her physical nature which could not be supposed to exist without some corresponding monstrosity of soul. His eyes, gazing down afar, might have deceived him as to the lizard, the insect, and the flowers; but if he could witness, at the distance of a few paces, the sudden blight of one fresh and beautiful flower in Beatrice's hand, there would be room for no further question. With this idea he hastened to the florist's and purchased a bouquet that was still gemmed with the morning dewdrops.

It was now the customary hour of his daily interview with Beatrice. Before descending into the garden, Giovanni failed not to look at his figure in the mirror—a vanity to be expected in a beautiful young man, yet, as displaying itself at that troubled and feverish moment, the token of a certain shallowness of feeling and insincerity of character. He did gaze, however, and said to himself that his features had never before possessed so rich a grace, nor his eyes such vivacity, nor his cheeks so warm a hue of superabundant life.

"At least," thought he, "her poison has not yet insinuated itself into my system. I am no flower to perish in her grasp."

With that thought he turned his eyes on the bouquet, which he had never once laid aside from his hand. A thrill of indefinable horror shot through his frame on perceiving that those dewy flowers were already beginning to droop; they wore the aspect of things that had been fresh and lovely yesterday. Giovanni grew white as marble, and stood motionless before the mirror, staring at his own reflection there as at the likeness of something frightful. He remembered Baglioni's remark about the fragrance that seemed to pervade the chamber. It must have been the poison in his breath! Then he shuddered—shuddered at himself. Recovering from his stupor, he began to watch with curious eye a spider that was busily at work hanging its web from the antique cornice of the apartment, crossing and recrossing the artful system of interwoven lines—as vigorous and active a spider as ever dangled from an old ceiling. Giovanni bent towards the insect, and emitted a deep, long breath. The spider suddenly ceased its toil; the web vibrated with a tremor originating in the body of the small artisan. Again Giovanni sent forth a breath, deeper, longer, and imbued with a venomous feeling out of his heart: he knew not whether he were wicked, or only desperate. The spider made a convulsive gripe with his limbs and hung dead across the window.

"Accursed! accursed!" muttered Giovanni, addressing himself. "Hast thou grown so poisonous that this deadly insect perishes by thy breath?"

At that moment a rich, sweet voice came floating up from the garden.

"Giovanni! Giovanni! It is past the hour! Why tarriest thou? Come down!"

"Yes," muttered Giovanni again. "She is the only being whom my breath may not slay! Would that it might!"

He rushed down, and in an instant was standing before the bright and loving eyes of Beatrice. A moment ago his wrath and despair had been so fierce that he could have desired nothing so much as to wither her by a glance; but with her actual presence there came influences which had too real an existence to be at once shaken off; recollections of the delicate and benign power of her feminine nature, which had so often enveloped him in a religious calm; recollections of many a holy and passionate outgush of her heart, when the pure fountain had been unsealed from its depths and made visible in its transparency to his mental eye;

recollections which, had Giovanni known how to estimate them, would have assured him that all this ugly mystery was but an earthly illusion, and that, whatever mist of evil might seem to have gathered over her, the real Beatrice was a heavenly angel. Incapable as he was of such high faith, still her presence had not utterly lost its magic. Giovanni's rage was quelled into an aspect of sullen insensibility. Beatrice, with a quick spiritual sense, immediately felt that there was a gulf of blackness between them which neither he nor she could pass. They walked on together, sad and silent, and came thus to the marble fountain and to its pool of water on the ground, in the midst of which grew the shrub that bore gemlike blossoms. Giovanni was affrighted at the eager enjoyment—the appetite, as it were—with which he found himself inhaling the fragrance of the flowers.

"Beatrice," asked he, abruptly, "whence came this shrub?"

"My father created it," answered she, with simplicity.

"Created it! created it!" repeated Giovanni. "What mean you, Beatrice?"

"He is a man fearfully acquainted with the secrets of Nature," replied Beatrice; "and, at the hour when I first drew breath, this plant sprang from the soil, the offspring of his science, of his intellect, while I was but his earthly child. Approach it not!" continued she, observing with terror that Giovanni was drawing nearer to the shrub. "It has qualities that you little dream of. But I, dearest Giovanni,—I grew up and blossomed with the plant and was nourished with its breath. It was my sister, and I loved it with a human affection; for, alas!—hast thou not suspected it?—there was an awful doom."

Here Giovanni frowned so darkly upon her that Beatrice paused and trembled. But her faith in his tenderness reassured her, and made her blush that she had doubted for an instant.

"There was an awful doom," she continued, "the effect of my father's fatal love of science, which estranged me from all society of my kind. Until Heaven sent thee, dearest Giovanni, O, how lonely was thy poor Beatrice!"

"Was it a hard doom?" asked Giovanni, fixing his eyes upon her.

"Only of late have I known how hard it was," answered she, tenderly. "O, yes; but my heart was torpid, and therefore quiet."

Giovanni's rage broke forth from his sullen gloom like a lightning flash out of a dark cloud.

"Accursed one!" cried he, with venomous scorn and anger. "And, finding thy solitude wearisome, thou hast severed me likewise from all the warmth of life and enticed me into thy region of unspeakable horror!"

"Giovanni!" exclaimed Beatrice, turning her large bright eyes upon his face. The force of his words had not found its way into her mind; she was merely thunderstruck.

"Yes, poisonous thing!" repeated Giovanni, beside himself with passion. "Thou hast done it! Thou hast blasted me! Thou hast filled my veins with poison! Thou hast made me as hateful, as ugly, as loathsome and deadly a creature as thyself—a world's wonder of hideous monstrosity! Now, if our breath be happily as fatal to ourselves as to all others, let us join our lips in one kiss of unutterable hatred, and so die!"

"What has befallen me?" murmured Beatrice, with a low moan out of her heart. "Holy Virgin, pity me, a poor heart-broken child!"

"Thou,—dost thou pray?" cried Giovanni, still with the same fiendish scorn. "Thy very prayers, as they come from thy lips, taint the atmosphere with death. Yes, yes; let us pray! Let us to church and dip our fingers in the holy water at the portal! They that come after us will perish as by a pestilence! Let us sign crosses in the air! It will be scattering curses abroad in the likeness of holy symbols!"

"Giovanni," said Beatrice, calmly, for her grief was beyond passion, "why dost thou join thyself with me thus in those terrible words? I, it is true, am the horrible thing thou namest me. But thou,—what hast thou to do, save with one other shudder at my hideous misery to go forth out of the garden and mingle with thy race, and forget that there ever crawled on earth such a monster as poor Beatrice?"

"Dost thou pretend ignorance?" asked Giovanni, scowling upon her. "Behold! this power have I gained from the pure daughter of Rappaccini."

There was a swarm of summer insects flitting through the air in search of the food promised by the flower odors of the fatal garden. They circled round Giovanni's head, and were evidently attracted towards him by the same influence which had drawn them for an instant within the sphere of the shrubs. He sent forth a breath among them, and smiled bitterly at Beatrice as at least a score of the insects fell dead upon the ground.

"I see it! I see it!" shrieked Beatrice. "It is my father's fatal science! No, no, Giovanni; it was not I! Never! never! I dreamed only to love thee and be with thee a little time, and so to let thee pass away, leaving but thine image in mine heart; for, Giovanni, believe it, though my body be nourished with poison, my spirit is God's creature, and craves love as its daily food. But my father,—he has united us in this fearful sympathy. Yes; spurn me, tread upon me, kill me! O, what is death after such words as thine? But it was not I. Not for a world of bliss would I have done it."

Giovanni's passion had exhausted itself in its outburst from his lips. There now came across him a sense, mournful, and not without tenderness, of the intimate and peculiar relationship between Beatrice and himself. They stood, as it were, in an utter solitude, which would be made none the less solitary by the densest throng of human life. Ought not, then, the desert of humanity around them to press this insulated pair closer together? If they should be cruel to one another, who was there to be kind to them? Besides, thought Giovanni, might there not still be a hope of his returning within the limits of ordinary nature, and leading Beatrice, the redeemed Beatrice, by the hand? O, weak, and selfish, and unworthy spirit, that could dream of an earthly union and earthly happiness as possible, after such deep love had been so bitterly wronged as was Beatrice's love by Giovanni's blighting words! No, no; there could be no such hope. She must pass heavily, with that broken heart, across the borders of Time—she must bathe her hurts in some fount of paradise, and forget her grief in the light of immortality, and *there* be well.

But Giovanni did not know it.

"Dear Beatrice," said he, approaching her, while she shrank away as always at his approach, but now with a different impulse, "dearest Beatrice, our fate is not yet so desperate. Behold! there is a medicine, potent, as a wise physician has assured me, and almost divine in its efficacy. It is composed of ingredients the most opposite to those by which thy awful father has brought this calamity upon thee and me. It is distilled of blessed herbs. Shall we not quaff it together, and thus be purified from evil?"

"Give it me!" said Beatrice, extending her hand to receive the little silver vial which Giovanni took from his bosom. She added, with a peculiar emphasis, "I will drink; but do thou await the result."

She put Baglioni's antidote to her lips; and, at the same moment, the figure of Rappaccini emerged from the portal and came slowly towards the marble fountain. As he drew near, the pale man of science seemed to gaze with a triumphant expression at the beautiful youth and maiden, as might

an artist who should spend his life in achieving a picture or a group of statuary and finally be satisfied with his success. He paused; his bent form grew erect with conscious power; he spread out his hands over them in the attitude of a father imploring a blessing upon his children; but those were the same hands that had thrown poison into the stream of their lives. Giovanni trembled. Beatrice shuddered nervously, and pressed her hand upon her heart.

"My daughter," said Rappaccini, "thou art no longer lonely in the world. Pluck one of those precious gems from thy sister shrub and bid thy bridegroom wear it in his bosom. It will not harm him now. My science and the sympathy between thee and him have so wrought within his system that he now stands apart from common men, as thou dost, daughter of my pride and triumph, from ordinary women. Pass on, then, through the world, most dear to one another and dreadful to all besides!"

"My father," said Beatrice, feebly,—and still as she spoke she kept her hand upon her heart,—"wherefore didst thou inflict this miserable doom upon thy child?"

"Miserable!" exclaimed Rappaccini. "What mean you, foolish girl? Dost thou deem it misery to be endowed with marvellous gifts against which no power nor strength could avail an enemy—misery, to be able to quell the mightiest with a breath—misery, to be as terrible as thou art beautiful? Wouldst thou, then, have preferred the condition of a weak woman, exposed to all evil and capable of none?"

"I would fain have been loved, not feared," murmured Beatrice, sinking down upon the ground. "But now it matters not. I am going, father, where the evil which thou hast striven to mingle with my being will pass away like a dream—like the fragrance of these poisonous flowers, which will no longer taint my breath among the flowers of Eden. Farewell, Giovanni! Thy words of hatred are like lead within my heart; but they, too, will fall away as I ascend. O, was there not, from the first, more poison in thy nature than in mine?"

To Beatrice,—so radically had her earthly part been wrought upon by Rappaccini's skill,—as poison had been life, so the powerful antidote was death; and thus the poor victim of man's ingenuity and of thwarted nature, and of the fatality that attends all such efforts of perverted wisdom, perished there, at the feet of her father and Giovanni. Just at that moment Professor Pietro Baglioni looked forth from the window, and called loudly, in a tone of triumph mixed with horror, to the thunderstricken man of science,—

"Rappaccini! Rappaccini! and is *this* the upshot of your experiment?"

From Chiefly About War Matters (1862)

"Chiefly About War Matters" is a very strange document, deeply indicative of the failing of Hawthorne's sense of life—for instance, in the sometimes forced and painfully frivolous ironies. The editor of the *Atlantic* no doubt acted wisely in suppressing certain passages; Hawthorne accepted the suppression, but, by way of a kind of revenge, wrote certain footnotes to account for the deletions. The description of Lincoln given here was one of the passages suppressed in the original publication.

There is no remoteness of life and thought, no hermetically sealed seclusion, except, possibly, that of the grave, into which the disturbing influences of this war do not penetrate. Of course, the general heart-quake of the country long ago knocked at my cottage-door, and compelled me, reluctantly, to suspend the contemplation of certain fantasies, to which, according to my harmless custom, I was endeavoring to give a sufficiently life-like aspect to admit of their figuring in a romance. As I make no pretensions to state-craft or soldiership, and could promote the common weal neither by valor nor counsel, it seemed, at first, a pity that I should be debarred from such unsubstantial business as I had contrived for myself, since nothing more genuine was to be substituted for it. But I magnanimously considered that there is a kind of treason in insulating one's self from the universal fear and sorrow, and thinking one's idle thoughts in the dread time of civil war; and could a man be so cold and hard-hearted, he would better deserve to be sent to Fort Warren than many who have found their way thither on the score of violent, but misdirected sympathies. I remembered the touching rebuke administered by King Charles to that rural squire the echo of whose hunting-horn came to the poor monarch's ear on the morning before a battle, where the sovereignty and constitution of England were to be set at a stake. So I gave myself

up to reading newspapers and listening to the click of the telegraph, like other people; until, after a great many months of such pastime, it grew so abominably irksome that I determined to look a little more closely at matters with my own eyes.

. . .

Even supposing the war should end to-morrow, and the army melt into the mass of the population within the year, what an incalculable preponderance will there be of military titles and pretensions for at least half a century to come? Every country-neighborhood will have its general or two, its three or four colonels, half a dozen majors, and captains without end,—besides non-commissioned officers and privates, more than the recruiting offices ever knew of,—all with their campaign-stories, which will become the staple of fire-side-talk forevermore. Military merit, or rather, since that is not so readily estimated, military notoriety, will be the measure of all claims to civil distinction. One bullet-headed general will succeed another in the Presidential chair; and veterans will hold the offices at home and abroad, and sit in Congress and the state legislatures, and fill all the avenues of public life. And yet I do not speak of this deprecatingly, since, very likely, it may substitute something more real and genuine, instead of the many shams on which men have heretofore founded their claims to public regard; but it behooves civilians to consider their wretched prospects in the future, and assume the military button before it is too late.[1]

. . .

Of course, there was one other personage, in the class of statesmen, whom I should have been truly mortified to leave Washington without seeing; since (temporarily, at least, and by force of

[1] For the fear that the Civil War, even with the victory of the North, will endanger democracy, see Herman Melville's poem "The Conflict of Convictions," lines 73–90, in our text.

circumstances) he was the man of men. But a private grief had built up a barrier about him, impeding the customary free intercourse of Americans with their chief magistrate; so that I might have come away without a glimpse of his very remarkable physiognomy, save for a semi-official opportunity of which I was glad to take advantage. The fact is, we were invited to annex ourselves, as supernumeraries, to a deputation that was about to wait upon the President, from a Massachusetts whip-factory, with a present of a splendid whip.

Our immediate party consisted only of four or five (including Major Ben Perley Poore, with his notebook and pencil), but we were joined by several other persons, who seemed to have been lounging about the precincts of the White House, under the spacious porch, or within the hall, and who swarmed in with us to take the chances of a presentation. Nine o'clock had been appointed as the time for receiving the deputation, and we were punctual to the moment; but not so the President, who sent us word that he was eating his breakfast, and would come as soon as he could. His appetite, we were glad to think, must have been a pretty fair one; for we waited about half an hour in one of the antechambers, and then were ushered into a reception-room, in one corner of which sat the Secretaries of War and of the Treasury, expecting, like ourselves, the termination of the Presidential breakfast. During this interval there were several new additions to our group, one or two of whom were in a working-garb, so that we formed a very miscellaneous collection of people, mostly unknown to each other, and without any common sponsor, but all with an equal right to look our head-servant in the face.

By and by there was a little stir on the staircase and in the passage-way, and in lounged a tall, loose-jointed figure, of an exaggerated Yankee port and demeanor, whom (as being about the homeliest man I ever saw, yet by no means repulsive or disagreeable) it was impossible not to recognize as Uncle Abe.

Unquestionably, Western man though he be, and Kentuckian by birth, President Lincoln is the essential representative of all Yankees, and the veritable specimen, physically, of what the world seems determined to regard as our characteristic qualities. It is the strangest and yet the fittest thing in the jumble of human vicissitudes, that he, out of so many millions, unlooked for, unselected by any intelligible process that could be based upon his genuine qualities, unknown to those who chose him, and unsuspected of what endowments may adapt him for his tremendous responsibility, should have found the way open for him to fling his lank personality into the chair of state,—where, I presume, it was his first impulse to throw his legs on the council-table, and tell the Cabinet Ministers a story. There is no describing his lengthy awkwardness nor the uncouthness of his movement; and yet it seemed as if I had been in the habit of seeing him daily, and had shaken hands with him a thousand times in some village street; so true was he to the aspect of the pattern American, though with a certain extravagance which, possibly, I exaggerated still further by the delighted eagerness with which I took it in. If put to guess his calling and livelihood, I should have taken him for a country schoolmaster as soon as anything else. He was dressed in a rusty black frock-coat and pantaloons, unbrushed, and worn so faithfully that the suit had adapted itself to the curves and angularities of his figure, and had grown to be an outer skin of the man. He had shabby slippers on his feet. His hair was black, still unmixed with gray, stiff, somewhat bushy, and had apparently been acquainted with neither brush nor comb that morning, after the disarrangement of the pillow; and as to a night-cap, Uncle Abe probably knows nothing of such effeminacies. His complexion is dark and sallow, betokening, I fear, an insalubrious atmosphere around the White House; he has thick black eyebrows and an impending brow; his nose is large, and the lines about his mouth are very strongly defined.

The whole physiognomy is as coarse a one as you would meet anywhere in the length and breadth of the States; but, withal, it is redeemed, illuminated, softened, and brightened by a kindly though serious look out of his eyes, and an expression of homely sagacity, that seems weighted with rich results of village experience. A great deal of native sense; no bookish cultivation, no refinement; honest at heart, and thoroughly so, and yet, in some sort, sly,—at least, endowed with a sort of tact and wisdom that are akin to craft, and would impel him, I think, to take an antagonist in flank, rather than to make a bull-run at him right in front. But, on the whole, I like this sallow, queer, sagacious visage, with the homely human sympathies that warmed it; and, for my small share in the matter, would as lief have Uncle Abe for a ruler as any man whom it would have been practicable to put in his place.

.   .   .

. . . It is a strange thing in human life, that the greatest errors both of men and women often spring from their sweetest and most generous qualities; and so, undoubtedly, thousands of warm-hearted, sympathetic, and impulsive persons have joined the Rebels, not from any real zeal for the cause, but because, between two conflicting loyalties, they chose that which necessarily lay nearest the heart. There never existed any other government against which treason was so easy, and could defend itself by such plausible arguments, as against that of the United States. The anomaly of two allegiances (of which that of the State comes nearest home to a man's feelings, and includes the altar and the hearth, while the General Government claims his devotion only to an airy mode of law, and has no symbol but a flag) is exceedingly mischievous in this point of view; for it has converted crowds of honest people into traitors, who seem to themselves not merely innocent, but patriotic, and who die for a bad cause with as quiet a conscience as if it were the best. In the vast extent of our country,—too vast by far to be taken into one small human heart,—we inevitably limit to our own State, or, at farthest, to our own section, that sentiment of physical love for the soil which renders an Englishman, for example, so intensely sensitive to the dignity and well-being of his little island, that one hostile foot, treading anywhere upon it, would make a bruise on each individual breast. If a man loves his own State, therefore, and is content to be ruined with her, let us shoot him, if we can, but allow him an honorable burial in the soil he fights for.

. . .

One very pregnant token of a social system thoroughly disturbed was presented by a party of contrabands, escaping out of the mysterious depths of Secessia; and its strangeness consisted in the leisurely delay with which they trudged forward, as dreading no pursuer, and encountering nobody to turn them back. They were unlike the specimens of their race whom we are accustomed to see at the North, and, in my judgment, were far more agreeable. So rudely were they attired,—as if their garb had grown upon them spontaneously,—so picturesquely natural in manners, and wearing such a crust of primeval simplicity (which is quite polished away from the northern black man), that they seemed a kind of creature by themselves, not altogether human, but perhaps quite as good, and

akin to the fauns and rustic deities of olden times. I wonder whether I shall excite anybody's wrath by saying this. It is no great matter. At all events, I felt most kindly towards these poor fugitives, but knew not precisely what to wish in their behalf, nor in the least how to help them. For the sake of the manhood which is latent in them, I would not have turned them back; but I should have felt almost as reluctant, on their own account, to hasten them forward to the stranger's land; and I think my prevalent idea was, that, whoever may be benefited by the results of this war, it will not be the present generation of negroes, the childhood of whose race is now gone forever, and who must henceforth fight a hard battle with the world, on very unequal terms. On behalf of my own race, I am glad and can only hope that an inscrutable Providence means good to both parties.

There is an historical circumstance, known to few, that connects the children of the Puritans with these Africans of Virginia in a very singular way. They are our brethren, as being lineal descendants from the Mayflower, the fated womb of which, in her first voyage, sent forth a brood of Pilgrims on Plymouth Rock, and, in a subsequent one, spawned slaves upon the Southern soil,[2]—a monstrous birth, but with which we have an instinctive sense of kindred, and so are stirred by an irresistible impulse to attempt their rescue, even at the cost of blood and ruin. The character of our sacred ship, I fear, may suffer a little by this revelation; but we must let her white progeny offset her dark one,—and two such portents never sprang from an identical source before.

. . .

. . . He was on General McClellan's staff, and a gallant cavalier, high-booted, with a revolver in his belt, and mounted on a noble horse, which trotted hard and high without disturbing the rider in his accustomed seat. His face had a healthy hue of exposure and an expression of careless hardihood; and, as I looked at him, it seemed to me that the war had brought good fortune to the youth of this epoch, if to none beside; since they now make it their daily business to ride a horse and handle a sword, instead of lounging listlessly through the duties, occupations, pleasures—all tedious alike—to which the artificial state of society

---

[2] The editors have been unable to substantiate the historical accuracy of Hawthorne's assertion that the *Mayflower* was later used as a slave ship.

limits a peaceful generation. The atmosphere of the camp and the smoke of the battlefield are morally invigorating; the hardy virtues flourish in them, the nonsense dies like a wilted weed. The enervating effects of centuries of civilization vanish at once, and leave these young men to enjoy a life of hardship, and the exhilarating sense of danger,— to kill men blamelessly, or to be killed gloriously, —and to be happy in following out their native instincts of destruction, precisely in the spirit of Homer's heroes, only with some considerable change of mode. One touch of Nature makes not only the whole world, but all time, akin. Set men face to face, with weapons in their hands, and they are as ready to slaughter one another now, after playing at peace and good-will for so many years, as in the rudest ages, that never heard of peace-societies, and thought no wine so delicious as what they quaffed from an enemy's skull. . . .

. . .

. . . The Provost-Marshal [of Harper's Ferry] kindly sent a corporal to guide us to the little building which John Brown seized upon as his fortress, and which, after it was stormed by the United States marines, became his temporary prison. It is an old engine-house, rusty and shabby, like every other work of man's hands in this God-forsaken town, and stands fronting upon the river, only a short distance from the bank, nearly at the point where the pontoon-bridge touches the Virginia shore. In its front wall, on each side of the door, are two or three ragged loop-holes, which John Brown perforated for his defence, knocking out merely a brick or two, so as to give himself and his garrison a sight over their rifles. Through these orifices the sturdy old man dealt a good deal of deadly mischief among his assailants, until they broke down the door by thrusting against it with a ladder, and tumbled headlong in upon him. I shall not pretend to be an admirer of old John Brown, any farther than sympathy with Whittier's excellent ballad about him may go; nor did I expect ever to shrink so unutterably from any apothegm of a sage, whose happy lips have uttered a hundred golden sentences, as from that saying (perhaps falsely attributed to so honored a source), that the death of this blood-stained fanatic has "made the Gallows as venerable as the Cross!" Nobody was ever more justly hanged. He won his martyrdom fairly, and took it firmly. He himself, I am persuaded (such was his natural integrity),

would have acknowledged that Virginia had a right to take the life which he had staked and lost; although it would have been better for her, in the hour that is fast coming, if she could generously have forgotten the criminality of his attempt in its enormous folly. On the other hand, any common-sensible man, looking at the matter unsentimentally, must have felt a certain intellectual satisfaction in seeing him hanged, if it were only in requital of his preposterous miscalculation of possibilities.

. . .

On her quarter-deck,[3] an elderly flag-officer was pacing to and fro, with a self-conscious dignity to which a touch of the gout or rheumatism perhaps contributed a little additional stiffness. He seemed to be a gallant gentleman, but of the old, slow, and pompous school of naval worthies, who have grown up amid rules, forms, and etiquette which were adopted full-blown from the British navy into ours, and are somewhat too cumbrous for the quick spirit of to-day. This order of nautical heroes will probably go down, along with the ships in which they fought valorously and strutted most intolerably. How can an admiral condescend to go to sea in an iron pot? What space and elbow-room can be found for quarter-deck dignity in the cramped lookout of the Monitor, or even in the twenty-feet diameter of her cheese-box? All the pomp and splendor of naval warfare are gone by. Henceforth there must come up a race of engine-men and smoke-blackened cannoneers, who will hammer away at their enemies under the direction of a single pair of eyes; and even heroism—so deadly a gripe is Science laying on our noble possibilities—will become a quality of very minor importance, when its possessor cannot break through the iron crust of his own armament and give the world a glimpse of it.

At no great distance from the Minnesota lay the strangest-looking craft I ever saw. It was a platform of iron, so nearly on a level with the water that the swash of the waves broke over it, under the impulse of a very moderate breeze; and on this platform was raised a circular structure, likewise of iron, and rather broad and capacious, but of no great height. It could not be called a vessel at all;

[3] Of the *Minnesota*, at Hampton Roads. The *Minnesota* had been in the squadron attacked by the Confederate ironclad *Virginia* (converted from the federal *Merrimack*) when, on March 8, 1862, it had sunk the *Cumberland* and the *Congress* [Editors' footnote.]

it was a machine,—and I have seen one of somewhat similar appearance employed in cleaning out the docks; or, for lack of a better similitude, it looked like a gigantic rat-trap. It was ugly, questionable, suspicious, evidently mischievous,—nay, I will allow myself to call it devilish; for this was the new war-fiend, destined, along with others of the same breed, to annihilate whole navies and batter down all supremacies. The wooden walls of Old England cease to exist, and a whole history of naval renown reaches its period, now that the monitor comes smoking into view; while the billows dash over what seems her deck, and storms bury even her turret in green water, as she burrows and snorts along, oftener under the surface than above. The singularity of the object has betrayed me into a more ambitious vein of description than I often indulge; and, after all, I might as well have contented myself with simply saying that she looked very queer.

Going on board, we were surprised at the extent and convenience of her interior accommodations. There is a spacious ward-room, nine or ten feet in height, besides a private cabin for the commander, and sleeping accommodations on an ample scale; the whole well lighted and ventilated, though beneath the surface of the water. Forward, or aft (for it is impossible to tell stem from stern), the crew are relatively quite as well provided for as the officers. It was like finding a palace, with all its conveniences, under the sea. The inaccessibility, the apparent impregnability, of this submerged iron fortress are most satisfactory; the officers and crew get down through a little hole in the deck, hermetically seal themselves, and go below; and until they see fit to reappear, there would seem to be no power given to man whereby they can be brought to light. A storm of cannon-shot damages them no more than a handful of dried peas. We saw the shotmarks made by the great artillery of the Merrimack on the outer casing of the iron tower; they were about the breadth and depth of shallow saucers, almost imperceptible dents, with no corresponding bulge on the interior surface.

. . .

From these various excursions, and a good many others (including one to Manassas), we gained a pretty lively idea of what was going on; but, after all, if compelled to pass a rainy day in the hall and parlors of Willard's Hotel, it proved about as profitably spent as if we had floundered through

miles of Virginia mud, in quest of interesting matter. This hotel, in fact, may be much more justly called the centre of Washington and the Union than either the Capitol, the White House, or the State Department. Everybody may be seen there. It is the meeting-place of the true representatives of the country,—not such as are chosen blindly and amiss by electors who take a folded ballot from the hand of a local politician, and thrust it into the ballot-box unread, but men who gravitate or are attracted hither by real business, or a native impulse to breathe the intensest atmosphere of the nation's life, or a genuine anxiety to see how this life-and-death struggle is going to deal with us. Nor these only, but all manner of loafers. Never, in any other spot, was there such a miscellany of people. You exchange nods with governors of sovereign States; you elbow illustrious men, and tread on the toes of generals; you hear statesmen and orators speaking in their familiar tones. You are mixed up with office-seekers, wire-pullers, inventors, artists, poets, prosers (including editors, army-correspondents, *attachés* of foreign journals, and long-winded talkers), clerks, diplomatists, mail-contractors, railway-directors, until your own identity is lost among them. Occasionally you talk with a man whom you have never before heard of, and are struck by the brightness of a thought, and fancy that there is more wisdom hidden among the obscure than is anywhere revealed among the famous. You adopt the universal habit of the place, and call for a mint-julep, a whiskey-skin, a gin-cocktail, a brandy-smash, or a glass of pure Old Rye; for the conviviality of Washington sets in at an early hour, and, so far as I had an opportunity of observing, never terminates at any hour, and all these drinks are continually in request by almost all these people. A constant atmosphere of cigar-smoke, too, envelops the motley crowd, and forms a sympathetic medium, in which men meet more closely and talk more frankly than in any other kind of air. If legislators would smoke in session, they might speak truer words, and fewer of them, and bring about more valuable results.

. . .

Looking round at these poor prisoners, therefore, it struck me as an immense absurdity that they should fancy us their enemies; since, whether we intend it so or no, they have a far greater stake on our success than we can possibly have. For ourselves, the balance of advantages between defeat and triumph may admit of question. For them, all truly valuable things are dependent on our complete success; for thence would come the regeneration of a people,—the removal of a foul scurf that has overgrown their life, and keeps them in a state of disease and decrepitude, one of the chief symptoms of which is, that, the more they suffer and are debased, the more they imagine themselves strong and beautiful. No human effort, on a grand scale, has ever yet resulted according to the purpose of its projectors. The advantages are always incidental. Man's accidents are God's purposes. We miss the good we sought, and do the good we little cared for.

From The American Notebooks of Nathaniel Hawthorne (1842-45)

A life, generally of a grave hue, may be said to be *embroidered* with occasional sports and fantasies.

A Father Confessor—his reflections on character, and the contrast of the inward man with the outward, as he looks round on his congregation—all whose secret sins are known to him.[1]

A person with an ice-cold hand—his right hand; which people ever afterwards remember, when once they have grasped it.

A stove possessed by a Devil.

A [. . .] death, which may be supposed to be the affliction of his own heart.

A physician for the cure of moral diseases.

Fancy pictures of familiar places, which one has never been in—as the green-room of a theatre &c.

The famous characters of history—to imagine their spirits now extant on earth, in the guise of various public or private personages.

The case quoted in Combe's Physiology, from Pinel, of a young man of great talents and profound knowledge of chemistry, who had in view some new discovery of importance. In order to put his mind into the highest possible activity, he shut himself up, for several successive days, and used various methods of excitement; he had a singing girl with him; he drank spirits; smelled penetrating odors, sprinkled cologne-water round the room &c

&c. Eight days thus passed, when he was seized with a fit of frenzy, which terminated in mania.

Flesh and Blood—a firm of butchers.

Miss Polly Syllable—a schoolmistress.

Mankind are earthen jugs with spirit in them.

Tender Love, Tough Love, which is better.

A spendthrift—in one sense he has his money's worth, by the purchase of large lots of repentance and other dolorous commodities.

Men's accidents are God's purposes. S.A.H.[2]

To sit at the gate of Heaven, and watch persons, as they apply for admittance, some gaining it, others being thrust away.

To point out the moral slavery of one who deems himself a freeman.

A stray leaf from the book of Fate, picked up in the street.

The streak of sunshine journeying through the prisoner's cell; it may be considered as something sent from heaven to keep the soul alive and glad within him. And there is something equivalent to this sunbeam in the darkest circumstances; as flowers, which figuratively grew in Paradise, in the dusky room of a poor maiden in a great city; the child, with its sunny smile, is a cherub. God does not let us live any where or any how on earth, without placing something of Heaven close at hand, by rightly using and considering which, the earthly darkness or trouble will vanish, and all be Heaven.

A moral philosopher to buy a slave, or other-

---

[1] Hawthorne's interest in the confessional is best evidenced in *The Marble Faun*, chap. xxxix, where Hilda tells her secret to a Father Confessor. According to Lowell, it had been part of Hawthorne's plan in *The Scarlet Letter* to make Dimmesdale confess to a Catholic priest. See Lowell's letter to Miss Norton, June 12, 1860, in *Letters of James Russell Lowell*, ed. Charles Eliot Norton (New York, 1894), I, 302. And Lowell was sorry that Hawthorne did not carry out the plan; he thought it would have been "psychologically admirable." It is clear that Hawthorne's interest in the subject steadily increased, and, gaining sufficient strength to overcome an inherited reluctance, found ultimate expression in *The Marble Faun*. [Footnotes throughout are Randall Stewart's.]

[2] This apothegm was inscribed on the glass of one of the windows of Hawthorne's study in the Old Manse with the signature, "Sophia A. Hawthorne 1843." In "Chiefly About War Matters" (1862), Hawthorne used this aphorism, adding an ironic footnote: "The author seems to imagine that he has compressed a great deal of meaning into these little, hard, dry pellets of aphoristic wisdom. We disagree with him. The counsels of wise and good men are often coincident with the purposes of Providence; and the present war promises to illustrate our remark."

wise get possession of a human being, and to use him for the sake of experiment, by trying the operation of a certain vice on him.[3]

When the reformation of the world is complete, a fire shall be made of the gallows; and the Hangman shall come and sit down by it, in solitude and despair. To him shall come the Last Thief, the Last Prostitute, the Last Drunkard, and other representatives of past crime and vice; and they shall hold a dismal merry-making, quaffing the contents of the Drunkard's last Brandy Bottle.[4]

The human Heart to be allegorized as a cavern; at the entrance there is sunshine, and flowers growing about it. You step within, but a short distance, and begin to find yourself surrounded with a terrible gloom, and monsters of divers kinds; it seems like Hell itself. You are bewildered, and wander long without hope. At last a light strikes upon you. You press towards it yon, and find yourself in a region that seems, in some sort, to reproduce the flowers and sunny beauty of the entrance, but all perfect. These are the depths of the heart, or of human nature, bright and peaceful; the gloom and terror may lie deep; but deeper still is the eternal beauty.[5]

A man, in his progress through life, picks up various matters, time, care, habit, riches &c. until at last he staggers along under a heavy burthen.

To have a life-long desire for a certain object, which shall appear to be the one thing essential to happiness. At last that object is attained, but proves to be merely incidental to a more important affair; and that affair is the greatest evil fortune that can occur. For instance, all through the winter I had wished to sit in the dusk of Evening, by the flickering firelight, with my wife, instead of beside a dismal stove. At last, this has come to pass; but it was owing to her illness, and our having no chamber with a stove, fit to receive her.

Generosity is the flower of Justice. S.A.H.

Madame Calderon de la B (in *Life in Mexico*) speaks of persons who have been inoculated with the venom of rattlesnakes, by pricking them in various places with the tooth. These persons are thus secured forever after against the bite of any venomous reptile. They have the power of calling snakes, and feel great pleasure in playing with and handling them. Their own bite becomes poisonous to people not inoculated in the same manner. Thus a part of the serpent's nature appears to be transfused into them.[6]

An Auction (perhaps in Vanity Fair) of offices, honors, and all sorts of things considered desirable by mankind; together with things eternally valuable, which shall be considered by most people as worthless lumber.[7]

An examination of wits and poets at a police-court; and they to be sentenced by the Judge to various penalties, as fines, the house of correction, whipping &c, according to the worst offenses of which they were guilty.

A volume bound in cowhide. It should treat of breeding cattle, or some other coarse subject.

A young girl inherits a family grave-yard—that being all that remains of rich hereditary possessions.[8]

An interview between General Charles Lee, of the Revolution, and his sister, the Foundress and Mother of the sect of Shakers.[9]

---

[3] Compare the case of Ethan Brand, who "wasted, absorbed, and perhaps annihilated" the soul of a young girl in the process of a "psychological experiment."

[4] In "Earth's Holocaust" (1844), the hangman, the last thief, the last murderer, and the last toper gather around the fire into which the gallows and many other objects have been cast by the reformers, and attempt to relieve their despondency by drinking out of the brandy bottle which the toper has rescued from the general destruction.

[5] The figure comparing the human heart to a cavern occurs several times in stories and sketches which were published within a comparatively short period after this entry: in "The Christmas Banquet" (1844), ". . . the gloomy mysteries of the human heart, through which I have wandered like one astray in a dark cavern . . ."; in "Rappaccini's Daughter" (1844), ". . . he was startled at the horrible suspicions that rose, monster-like, out of the caverns of his heart . . ."; in "The Old Manse" (1846), "We have been standing on the greensward, but just within the cavern's mouth. . . ."

[6] See Mme C[alderon] de la B[arca], *Life in Mexico* . . . (Boston, 1843), II, 414. This passage suggests an analogy to "Rappaccini's Daughter" (1844), in which Beatrice, imbued with the poison of flowers, becomes poisonous to others.

[7] This suggestion was developed in "The Celestial Railroad," which was published in the *Democratic Review*, XII (May, 1843), 515–523. The passage which is an expansion of this note is found in *Mosses from an Old Manse*. Hawthorne derived the idea of the note from Bunyan's description of Vanity Fair. See *The Pilgrim's Progress* (Everyman's Library), p. 104.

[8] The dwindling of hereditary possessions is a favorite idea with Hawthorne.

[9] Hawthorne was in error in supposing that Charles Lee (1731–82), who was a General in the American Revolutionary army, and Ann Lee (1736–84), who founded the sect of the Shakers, were brother and sister.

For a child's sketch, perhaps, the life of a city Dove; or perhaps of a flock of doves, flying about the streets, and sometimes alighting on church steeples; on the eaves of lofty houses &c.

The greater picturesqueness and reality of backyards, and everything appertaining to the rear of a house; as compared with the front, which is fitted up for the public eye. There is much to be learnt, always, by getting a glimpse at rears. When the direction of a road has been altered, so as to pass the rear of farm-houses, instead of the front, a very noticeable aspect is presented.

A sketch—the devouring of the old country residences by the overgrown monster of a city. For instance, Mr. Beekman's ancestral residence was originally several miles from the city of New-York; but the pavements kept creeping nearer and nearer; till now the house is removed, and a street runs directly through what was once its hall.

The print in blood of a naked foot to be traced through the street of a town.

An essay on various kinds of death, together with the just-before and just-after.

The majesty of death to be exemplified in a beggar, who, after being seen, humble and cringing, in the streets of a city, for many years, at length, by some means or other, gets admittance into a rich man's mansion, and there dies—assuming state, and striking awe into the breasts of those who had looked down upon him.[10]

To write a dream, which shall resemble the real course of a dream, with all its inconsistency, its strange transformations, which are all taken as a matter of course, its eccentricities and aimlessness— with nevertheless a leading idea running through the whole. Up to this old age of the world, no such thing ever has been written.[11]

To allegorize life with a masquerade, and represent mankind generally as masquers. Here and there, a natural face may appear.

Sketch of a personage with the malignity of a witch, and doing the mischief attributed to one— but by natural means; breaking off love-affairs, teaching children vices, ruining men of wealth, &c.

With an emblematical divining-rod to seek for emblematic gold—that is for Truth—for what of Heaven is left on earth.

A task for a subjugated fiend—to gather up all the fallen autumnal leaves of a forest, assort them, and affix each one to a twig where it originally grew.

A vision of Grub-street, forming an allegory of the literary world.

The emerging from their lurking-places of evil-characters, on some occasion suited to their action—they having been quite unknown to the world hitherto. For instance, the French Revolution brought out such wretches.

The advantages of a longer life than is allotted to mortals—the many things that might then be accomplished;—to which one life-time is inadequate, and for which the time spent is therefore lost; a successor being unable to take up the task when we drop it.

George First had promised the Duchess of Kendall, his mistress, that, if possible, he would pay her a visit, after death. Accordingly, a large raven flew into the window of her villa at Isleworth. She believed it to be his soul, and treated it ever after with all respect and tenderness, till either she or the bird died.—Walpole's Reminiscences.

The history of an Alms-House in a country village, from the eve of its foundation downward—a record of the remarkable occupants of it; and extracts from interesting portions of its annals. The rich of one generation might, in the next, seek for a home there, either in their own persons or those of their representatives. Perhaps the son and heir of the founder might have no better refuge. There should be occasional sunshine let into the story; for instance, the good fortune of some nameless infant, educated there, and discovered finally to be the child of wealthy parents.

Ladislaus, King of Naples, beseiging [*sic*] the city of Florence, agreed to show mercy, provided the inhabitants would deliver to him a certain virgin of famous beauty, the daughter of a physician of the city. When she was sent to the king— every one contributing something to adorn her in the richest manner—her father gave her a perfumed handkerchief, at that time a universal decoration, richly wrought. This handkerchief was poisoned with his utmost art; and in their first embrace, the poison being received into their pores, opened by heat,—it killed them both—"converting their warm sweat into a cold sweat, they presently died in one another's arms."—Cotton's Montaigne.

---

[10] The fundamental situation of a beggar in a rich man's house may have been suggested by *The Taming of the Shrew.*

[11] "The Celestial Railroad," which is told as a dream and ends with the awakening of the narrator, may have been Hawthorne's attempt to carry out the plan suggested here. Hawthorne had never read, perhaps, Chaucer's *Book of the Duchess.*

Pearl—the English of Margaret—a pretty name for a girl in a story.[12]

The conversation of the steeples of a city, when the bells are ringing on Sunday—Calvinist, Episcopalian, Unitarian &c.

Of a bitter satirist—of Swift, for instance—it might be said, that the person or thing, on which his satire fell, shrivelled up, as if the Devil had spit on it.

Allston's picture of Belshazzar's Feast—with reference to the advantages, or otherwise, of having life assured to us, till we could finish important tasks on which we were engaged.

Visits to Castles in the Air—Chateaus en Espagne &c—with remarks on that sort of architecture.

To consider a piece of gold as a sort of talisman —or as containing within itself all the forms of enjoyment that it can purchase—so that they might appear, by some fantastical chemical process, as visions.

To personify If—But—And—Though—&c.

The fount of Tears—a traveller to discover it, and other similar localities.

Benvenuto Cellini saw a salamander in the household fire. It was shown him by his father, in his childhood.

A man seeks for something excellent, and seeks it in the wrong way, and in a wrong spirit, and finds something horrible—as for instance, he seeks for treasure, and finds a dead body—for the gold that somebody has hidden, and brings to light his accumulated sins.

An auction of second hands—then moralizing how the fashion of this world passeth away.

Noted people in a town:—as the town-crier—the old fruit-man—the constable—the oyster-seller—the fish-man—the scissors-grinder—&c &c &c.

The Magic Ray of Sunshine, for a child's story: —the sunshine circling round through a prisoner's cell, from his high and narrow window. He keeps his soul alive and cheerful by means of it, it typifying [sic] cheerfulness; and when he is released, he takes up the ray of Sunshine and carries it away with him; and it enables him to discover treasures all over the world, in places where nobody else would think of looking for any.

A young man finds a portion of the skeleton of a Mammoth; he begins by degrees to become interested in completing it; searches round the world for the means of doing so; spends youth and manhood in the pursuit; and in old age has nothing to show for his life, but this skeleton.

For the Virtuoso's Collection—the pen with which Faust signed away his salvation, with a drop of blood dried on it.

For a child's sketch—a meeting with all the personages mentioned in Mother Goose's Melodies, and other juvenile stories.

Great expectation to be entertained in the allegorical Grub-street of the appearance of the great American writer. Or a search warrant to be sent thither to catch a poet. On the former supposition, he shall be discovered under some most unlikely form; or shall be supposed to have lived and died unrecognized.

An old man to promise a youth a treasure of gold;—and to keep his promise by teaching him practically a Golden Rule.

A valuable jewel to be buried in the grave of a beloved person, or thrown over with a corpse at sea, or deposited under the foundation-stone of an edifice—and to be afterward met with by the former owner, in the possession of some one.

In moods of heavy despondency, one feels as if it would be delightful to sink down in some quiet spot, and lie there forever, letting the soil gradually accumulate and form a little hillock over us, and the grass and perhaps flowers gather over it. At such times, death is too much of an event to be wished for;—we have not spirits to encounter it; but choose to pass out of existence in this sluggish way.

A noted gambler had acquired such self-command, that, in the most desperate circumstances of his game, no change of feature ever betrayed him;—only there was a slight scar upon his forehead, which, at such moments, assumed a deep blood-red hue. Thus, in playing at Brag, for instance, his antagonist could judge from this index, when he had a bad hand. At last, discovering what it was that betrayed him, he covered the scar with a green silk shade.

A dream, the other night, that the world had become dissatisfied with the inaccurate manner in which facts are reported, and had employed me, with a salary of a thousand dollars, to relate things of public importance exactly as they happen.

A person who has all the qualities of a friend, except that he invariably fails you at the pinch.

---

[12] The name was given about seven years later to the child of Hester Prynne in *The Scarlet Letter*.

JOHN GREENLEAF WHITTIER (1807-1892)

John Greenleaf Whittier, of the founding stock of New England, was born in Haverhill, Massachusetts, on December 17, 1807, in a substantial farmhouse for which the first Whittier, his great-grandfather, had hewed the oak beams. John Greenleaf, frail and suffering from an injury resulting from overexertion, loved the land but loathed the work on it and early had a passion for study. His verses began early, too, and one of them sets forth the ambition that was to dominate his youth:

> And must I always swing the flail,
> And help to fill the milking pail?
> I wish to go away to school,
> I do not wish to be a fool.

Because of these verses, Whittier's boyhood circumstances, and his admiration for Burns, certain critics have been tempted to think of Whittier, as more than one European critic has thought of Robert Frost, as a "peasant poet." The Whittiers were farmers, certainly; and if they were not exactly poor, they were not rich. But when Jefferson thought of his independent farmer, he was not thinking of a peasant; he was thinking of a type central to a whole society. And when the poet Whittier looked backward on the family past he saw the "founding fathers" of a whole new world—a whole society—and if anything characterized his early manhood, it was an almost pathological ambition to take his "rightful" place in that whole society.

The house of the Quaker farmer at Haverhill had books, and the son reached out for others, for Milton, who was to become a personal rather than a poetic model, and such un-Quakerish works as the stage plays of Shakespeare.[1] By the age of fourteen, Whittier had heard a Scot, "a pawky auld carle," singing songs of Robert Burns at the kitchen hearth of the Whittiers, and in the same year, the schoolmaster, Joshua Coffin, sat in the same spot and read from a volume of Burns, which he then lent to the young listener. "This was about the first poetry I had ever read," Whittier was to say, "with the exception of that of the Bible (of which I had been a close student) and it had a lasting influence upon me." It was thus by Burns that Whittier's eyes were opened to the land around him as the proper subject matter of poetry.

It was not only to nature that Burns opened the boy's eyes. He was already steeped in the legends and folklore of his region, but Burns showed that this, too, was the stuff of poetry. So Whittier, as early as Hawthorne, and earlier than Longfellow, was to turn to the past of New England for subject matter, and by 1831, in a poem called "New England," was expressing his ambition to be the poet of his region. His first volume, a mixture of eleven poems and seven prose pieces, published in 1831 in Hartford, was called *Legends of New England*.[2]

To return to Whittier's literary beginnings, Milton and Burns were not the only models he proposed to himself. There was the flood of contemporary trash, American and English, from writers like Felicia Hemans, Lydia Sigourney, N. P. Willis, the elder Dana, Lydia Maria Child, Bernard Barton, and John Pierpont. The marks of their incorrigible gabble remained on Whittier's sensibility more indelibly than those

---

[1] There was no Shakespeare in the little library at the Whittier farmhouse. But even if that library was limited, it was not that of a stupid or illiterate family. It included, naturally, the Bible, the works of William Penn and other Quakers, and of John Bunyan—but also various accounts of exotic travel, works of history, and Lindley Murray's *English Reader . . . Selected from the Best Writers*. At an early age Whittier could tell the whole story of the Bible from Genesis to Revelation and had vast amounts of it by heart.

[2] In 1849 Whittier published, too, a prose work *Leaves from Margaret Smith's Journal*, a charming reconstruction of early American life.

made by the work of even the idolized Burns; and it is highly probable that Whittier, in spite of the fact that he was to deplore "the imbecility of our poetry," could not nicely distinguish the poetic level of Burns from that of, say, Lydia Sigourney, the "sweet singer of Hartford," who was his friend. He could write, too, of Longfellow's "A Psalm of Life": "These nine simple verses are worth more than all the dreams of Shelley, Keats, and Wordsworth. They are alive and vigorous with the spirit of the day in which we live—the moral steam enginery of an age of action." Whenever "moral steam enginery" came in the door, whatever taste Whittier did happen to have went precipitously out the window. "Strictly speaking," as Hawthorne put it, "Whittier did not care much for literature."[3] And, if a letter written late in life is to be believed, he cared less for poetry than prose: "I regard good prose writing as really better than rhyme."

But, in addition to all the other poets good and bad that Whittier read, there was, inevitably, Byron, and it was under the aegis of Byron that Whittier, with a poem called "The Exile's Departure," written when he was eighteen, first found his way into print. His elder sister Mary had secretly sent the poem, with only the signature "W," to the *Free Press*, the newspaper at Newburyport.

The editor was William Lloyd Garrison, then only twenty-one, destined to become the most famous of the abolitionists (see pp. 1031–34), who now, having discovered the identity of "W," drove fourteen miles to the Whittier farm, burst in upon the family, and lectured John Whittier on his duty to give the son "every facility for the development of his remarkable genius." To this oratory of a beardless youth, old John Whittier replied: "Sir, poetry will not give him bread."

Nevertheless, the father did allow his son to

enroll in the Haverhill Academy, just then established. Two sessions saw the end of his formal education, but by this time his poetry had appeared in distant places like Boston, Hartford, and Philadelphia. Whittier was, in fact, something of a local celebrity, had friends and admirers, and was inflamed with ambition and the ignorant confidence that the world was his for the reaching out. He felt "a consciousness of slumbering powers."

Whittier had already had some experience in the office of the local newspaper, and it was to be through journalism that he became a writer. Anxious to take a hand in the "moral steam enginery" of the age, he aspired to the editorship of the *National Philanthropist* of Boston, the first prohibition paper in the country, which Garrison had been editing. Alcohol had not proved a worthy challenge to Garrison's mettle, and now he was resigning from the *Philanthropist* to establish, in Bennington, Vermont, the *Journal of the Times*, which was to take as its twin targets slavery and war. Though Garrison sponsored Whittier as his successor in the crusade for prohibition, this did not work out; but Whittier did get a second-best job as editor of the *American Manufacturer* of Boston.

The *Manufacturer* was a weekly dedicated to the support of Henry Clay and the Whig party, especially to the policy of a high protective tariff. But Whittier, who, while still hoping for the editorship of the *Philanthropist*, had written to a friend that he would "rather have the memory" of a reformer "than the undying fame of Byron," promptly grafted the cause of prohibition onto that of a high tariff, and the first poem he wrote for his editorial column was an un-Byronic ditty entitled "Take Back the Bowl!"

In the *Manufacturer*, however, Whittier knew his duty to fight for high tariffs and the "American System" of the Whigs. As one of Whittier's biographers, John A. Pollard, has pointed out, Whittier, in spite of the fact that he had been raised in the tradition of Jeffersonian democracy, failed to grasp the contradiction between Whig capitalism and his own inherited principles and assumed that what was good for New England loom-masters was good for New England in gen-

---

[3] As good a proof of this as any is the fact that Whittier found Hawthorne merely a pleasant teller of tales. It is not too hard to believe that Whittier would have instinctively flinched from the inwardness and shadows of Hawthorne's work. In fact, he may have lived only by such a refusal to regard inwardness and shadows.

eral and, in fact, for the human race at large. Whittier's Quaker pacifism made him regard Jackson, a soldier and duelist, as the "blood-thirsty old man at the head of our government" and blinded him to some of the economic and social implications of Jacksonian democracy as contrasted with "Whiggery."

Meanwhile, Whittier had made something of a reputation as a partisan editor, and though poems poured out in unabated flow, his personal ambitions were more and more political. The conclusion is not far short of inevitable that he was using his facility in verse as a device for success rather than using poetry as a way of coming to grips with experience. He wrote poems by the bushel and got himself extravagantly praised for them—and why not? He had become a master of the garrulous vapidity which was in general fashion.

But poetry was not enough. Whittier wanted some great, overwhelming, apocalyptic success, a success that he probably could not, or dared not, define for himself, a success that would be the very justification for life. "I would have fame visit me *now*, or not at all," he wrote Lydia Sigourney. Again, in a most extraordinary essay, "The Nervous Man," in 1833, he speaks through his character:

> Time has dealt hardly with my boyhood's muse. Poetry has been to me a beautiful delusion. It was something woven of my young fancies, and reality has destroyed it. I can, indeed, make rhymes now, as mechanically as a mason piles one brick above another; but the glow of feeling, the hope, the ardor, the excitement have passed away forever. I have long thought, or rather the world hath *made* me think, that poetry is too trifling, too insignificant a pursuit for the matured intellect of sober manhood.

With some rational sense of his own limitations (he knew that what he knew was how to pile the bricks) was paradoxically coupled a self-pity and an air of grievance against the world that had not adequately rewarded the poet, by the age of twenty-five, with that overwhelming and life-justifying success. So he wrote

Lydia Sigourney that politics was "the only field now open." He turned to politics for the prize, not merely by clinging to Clay's coattails, to which he pinned wildly adulatory effusions such as "Star of the West," but by trying to run for office himself.

For the moment, nothing came of Whittier's political projects, and nothing came of the love affairs that belong to the same period of his attempt to enter the great world. Whittier, in spite of a certain frailty, was tall, handsome, and attractive to women; and he himself was greatly attracted to women and was rather inclined to insist on the fact. But he remained a bachelor. In the series of love affairs, in the period before 1833, a pattern seems to emerge. The girls were non-Quaker, good-looking, popular, and above Whittier's station, both financially and socially; that is, the choice of sweethearts seems to have been consistent with his worldly and un-Quakerish ambitions. Some biographers take at face value Whittier's statement, made late in life, that he refused matrimony because of "the care of an aged mother, and the duty owed to a sister [Elizabeth] in delicate health," but his explanation does not quite square with the facts; he did not reject matrimony—the girls, with one possible exception, seem to have rejected him. As an index to wounded self-esteem, frustrated ambition, and a considerable talent for boyish self-dramatization, we have this passage, which, though it dates back to 1828, cannot be without significance in relation to more than poetry:

> . . . *I will quit poetry and everything else of a literary nature,* for I am sick at heart of the business. . . . Insult has maddened me. The friendless boy has been mocked at; and, years ago, he vowed to triumph over the scorners of his boyish endeavors. With the unescapable sense of wrong burning like a volcano in the recesses of his spirit, he has striven to accomplish this vow, until his heart has grown weary of the struggle. . . .

There is no way to be sure what went on in Whittier's heart, or in his romances. In 1857, in a poem called "My Namesake," looking back on his youth, he said of himself:

> His eye was beauty's powerless slave,
>   And his the ear which discord pains;
> Few guessed beneath his aspect grave
>   What passions strove in chains.

Though Whittier was aware of the existence of the "chains," we cannot know exactly what they were. It may even be that Whittier, consciously choosing girls that fitted his "passions" and his vaulting ambition, was unconsciously choosing girls who would be certain to turn him, and his Quakerism, down. Whittier did, it is true, have a protracted, complex relationship with one Quaker lady, Elizabeth Lloyd, to which we shall recur. But this was after he had given up his worldly ambitions and had made, as we shall see, his commitment to abolitionism as a way of life.

The change in the way of life may have made some difference in the kind of girl Whittier, in this second phase, found congenial: poetesses, dabblers in art, abolitionists, hero-worshipers, and protégés. But the old pattern of behavior did not change. In the same period when Whittier had written "The Nervous Man," he composed another remarkable piece of what seems to be undeclared self-analysis; it is called "The Male Coquette," and it is hard not to believe that it predicted the role he was doomed to play until the end.

In any case, there was some deep inner conflict in Whittier, with fits of self-pity and depression, breakdowns and withdrawals from the world, violent chronic headaches and insomnia. A breakdown in 1831 sent Whittier from Hartford and his editorship back to Haverhill. But here, again, Garrison appeared. Already he had done a hitch in a Baltimore jail (unable to pay a judgment for libelously accusing a shipmaster of carrying a cargo of slaves), had founded, in January, 1831, the *Liberator*, the most famous of abolitionist papers, and had written the pamphlet *Thoughts on African Colonization*. Now, in the spring of 1833, Garrison wrote Whittier a direct appeal: "The cause is worthy of Gabriel, yea, the God of hosts places himself at its head.

Whittier, enlist!—Your talents, zeal, influence—all are needed."

Whittier was ready now, as he put it, to knock "Pegasus on the head, as a tanner does his bark-mill donkey, when he is past service." Years later, after the Civil War, in the poem "The Tent on the Beach," Whittier wrote, with something less than full historical accuracy, of his shift in direction:

> And one there was, a dreamer born,
>   Who, with a mission to fulfil,
> Had left the Muses' haunts to turn
>   The crank of an opinion-mill,
> Making his rustic reed of song
> A weapon in the war with wrong.

A more candid account appears in a letter to E. L. Godkin, the editor of the *Nation*: "I cannot be sufficiently grateful to the Divine Providence that so early called my attention to the great interests of humanity, saving me from the poor ambitions and miserable jealousies of a selfish pursuit of literary reputation." And, he added, from "the pain of disappointment and the temptation to envy." Whittier had, apparently already suffered enough from those things, as well as from other wounds to ego and ambition, and the relief from suffering was what he must have been referring to when, late in life, he said that the question was not what he had done for abolitionism but what abolitionism had done for him.

In spite of the fact that many Quakers had been slaveholders and some, especially the sea-going Quakers of the southwest of England, had been in the slave trade (there was an English slave ship of the eighteenth century called *The Willing Quaker*), the tradition that Whittier directly inherited was that of Benjamin Lay and John Woolman (see pp. 140–53), whose anti-slavery writings were fundamental documents in the history of abolitionism. It was a tradition of brotherhood understood in quite simple and literal terms, and so his entrance into the abolition movement was a natural act, as was his repudiation of ambition and the reduction of poetry, so dangerously tied to the physical world and human passions, to the safe role of a mere "weapon in the war with wrong." But if abolitionism was for Whittier both a catharsis of and a refuge from his ambitions and his passions, the internal tensions in the movement, both philosophical and practical, set up a new problem. Whittier spent a large part of his active life trying to master, resolve, or mediate these tensions. He was a man of peace and a man of reason, and this world of abolitionism was no more cut to his measure than the old world he had repudiated. But he survived, and out of the struggle seemed to gain sweetness of spirit.

Whittier began his career as an abolitionist in 1833, by writing, and publishing out of his own thinly furnished pocket, a well-argued pamphlet, *Justice and Expediency*, in which he expressed the conviction that the "withering concentration of public opinion upon the slave system is alone needed for its total annihilation." At the end of that year, he attended the convention in Philadelphia that founded the American Anti-Slavery Society and had an important hand in drawing up the platform, which disavowed all violence and any attempt to foment servile insurrection. All his life it was a point of pride for him that he had been one of the original signers of this "Declaration."

From this time on, Whittier was constantly engaged in the cause of abolitionism, as a writer of both prose and verse, as a member, briefly, of the lower house of the Massachusetts legislature, as an editor of a series of antislavery papers, and as an organizer and speaker. He came to know contumely, mob violence—and, in the end, the formidable wrath and contempt of Garrison.

Whittier, in opposition to the Garrisonian abolitionists, had become more and more firm in his belief in political action, that is, in the belief that man is, among other things, a member of society. For instance, in a letter to his publisher, J. T. Fields, he rejected the radical individualism of Thoreau's *Walden*, which he called "capital reading, but very wicked and heathenish," and added that the "moral of it seems to be that if a man is willing to sink himself into a woodchuck he can live as cheaply as that quadruped; but after all, for me, I prefer walking on two legs."[4] Whittier saw man among men, in his social as well as in other dimensions, and as the proper object of appeal to reason rather than the target for insult; and nothing could more infuriate the radical Garrison, who was publicly to accuse Whittier of being a traitor to principle. The final crisis came when the "political" wing of the original American Anti-Slavery Society split off to form the American and Foreign Anti-Slavery Society, and to this Whittier, in spite of his depression over the estrangement from his old friend, devoted his energies for some years as an editor, propagandist, and political manipulator.

As the tensions mounted during the 1850's, Whittier held as best he could to his principles of institutional reform and political action—and to his Quaker pacifism. He never compromised on the question of slavery, but he steadily insisted on viewing the question in human and institutional contexts. When news of John Brown's raid on Harper's Ferry broke, Whittier wrote an article in which he expressed his "emphatic condemnation" of "this and all similar attempts to promote the goal of freedom by the evil of servile strife and civil war." At the same time, however, he analyzed the danger which the South created for itself by trying to justify the internal contradiction between freedom and slavery in its system, and the tension in his feelings is indicated when he declared, at a meeting called at the time of John Brown's hanging, that he could not help but "wish success to all slave insurrections," for an insurrection was—and here he took a wild leap into a realm of transcendental logic—"one way to get up to the sublime principle of non-resistance." In other words, on this test matter of the raid on Harper's Ferry, Whittier—in his original editorial, at least—agreed with Lincoln and not with Emerson, Thoreau, or Garrison.

There is, in fact, a general similarity between

---

[4] Something of the distaste for radical individualism that made Whittier reject Thoreau may have contributed to a revulsion from Whitman so intense that he flung *Leaves of Grass* into the fire. But he may, in addition, have been offended by the realism of Whitman and by the aura of sexuality.

Whittier's views and those of Lincoln. As early as 1833, in his *Justice and Expediency*, Whittier pointed out the internal contradiction created by the presence of slavery in the United States and declared that "Liberty and slavery cannot dwell in harmony together." He saw the psychological and economic issues raised by this coexistence of free and slave labor. He also held the view that Christianity and civilization had placed slavery "on a moral quarantine." In summary, he agreed with Lincoln that if the extension of slavery was stopped, it would die out in the slave states without forceful intervention. Though Whittier had some sympathy with those antislavery people who would resort to a northern secession from the Union rather than connive in the annexation of Texas, he fundamentally saw the Union as necessary to the termination of slavery.

When the Civil War was over, Whittier saw, as many could not, that the war had not automatically solved the problem of freedom. Though rejoicing in the fact of emancipation, he could write, in a letter to Lydia Maria Child, that the "emancipation that came by military necessity and enforced by bayonets, was not the emancipation for which we worked and prayed."

When Whittier, at the age of twenty-six, came to knock "Pegasus on the head," the creature he laid low was, indeed, not much better than the tanner's superannuated donkey. Whittier had the knack, as he put it in "The Nervous Man," for making rhymes "as mechanically as a mason piles one brick above another," but nothing that he wrote had the inwardness, the organic quality, of poetry. Even when he was able to strike out poetic phrases, images, or effects, he was not able to organize a poem; his poems usually began anywhere and ended when the author got tired. If occasionally we see a poem begin with a real sense of poetry, the poetry gets quickly lost in some abstract idea.

For a poet of natural sensibility, subtlety, and depth to dedicate his work to propaganda would probably result in a coarsening of style and a blunting of effects, for the essence of propaganda is to refuse qualifications and complexity.

But Whittier had, by 1833, shown little sensibility, subtlety, or depth, and his style was coarse to a degree. He had nothing to lose and stood to gain certain things. To be effective, propaganda, if it is to be more than random vituperation, has to make a point, and the point has to be held in view from the start; the piece has to show some sense of organization and control, the very thing Whittier's poems had lacked.

But his prose had not lacked this quality, or, in fact, a sense of the biting phrase; now his verse could absorb the virtues of his prose. It could learn, in addition to a sense of point, something of the poetic pungency of phrase and image, and the precision that sometimes marked the prose. He had referred to his poems as "fancies," and that is what they were, no more. Now he began to relate poetry, though blunderingly enough, to reality, but it was ten years— 1843—before he was able to produce propaganda as good as "Massachusetts to Virginia." It was effective propaganda; it had content and was organized to make a point, and here Whittier had at least avoided his besetting sin of wandering and padding.

But Whittier had to wait seven years before, at the age of forty-two, he could write his first really fine poem, the famous "Ichabod"—a poem in which, as we shall see, he could fuse a deep personal impulse with his politics. On March 7, 1850, Daniel Webster, Senator from Massachusetts, spoke on behalf of the more stringent Fugitive Slave Bill that had just been introduced by Whittier's ex-idol Henry Clay; and the poem laments the loss of the more recent and significant idol.

The effectiveness of "Ichabod," certainly one of the most telling poems of personal attack in English, is largely due to the subtlety of dramatization. At the center of the dramatization lies a division of feeling on the part of the poet; the poem is not a simple piece of vituperation, but represents a tension between old trust and new disappointment, old admiration and new rejection, the past and the present. The Biblical allusion in the title sets this up: "And she named the child Ichabod, saying, the glory is departed from Israel" (I Samuel 4:21). The glory has departed, but grief rather than rage, respect for the man who was once the vessel of glory rather than contempt, pity for his frailty rather than condemnation—these are the emotions recommended as appropriate. We may note that not only are they appropriate as a generosity of attitude; they are also the emotions that are basically condescending, that put the holder of the emotions above the object of them, and that make the most destructive assault on the ego of the object. If Webster had been motivated by ambition, then pity would be the one attitude his pride could not forgive.

The Biblical allusion at the end offers a brilliant and concrete summary of the complexity of feeling in the poem. As Notley Sinclair Maddox has pointed out (*Explicator*, April 1960), the last stanza is based on Genesis 9:20-25. Noah, in his old age, plants a vineyard, drinks the wine, and is found drunk and naked in his tent by his youngest son Ham, who merely reports the fact to his brothers Shem and Japheth. Out of filial piety, they go to cover Noah's shame, but "their faces were backward, and they saw not their father's nakedness." Ham, for having looked upon Noah's nakedness, is cursed as a "servant of servants" to his "brethren."

The allusion works as a complex and precise metaphor: the great Webster of the past, who, in the time of the debate with Robert Young Hayne (1830), had opposed the slave power and thus established his reputation, has now become obsessed with ambition (drunk with wine) and has exposed the nakedness of human pride and frailty. The conduct of Shem and Japheth sums up, of course, the attitude recommended by the poet. As an ironical adjunct, we may remember that the Biblical episode was used from many a pulpit as a theological defense of slavery, Ham, accursed as a "servant of servants," being, presumably, the forefather of the black race—though, according to modern scholarship, Ham stands for the progenitor of the Canaanites, not the black race.

We may look back at the first stanza to see another complex and effective metaphor, suggested rather than presented. The light is withdrawn, and the light is identified, by the appositive construction, with the "glory" of Webster's gray hair—the glory being the achievement of age and the respect due to honorable age, but also the image of a literal light, an aureole about the head coming like a glow from the literal gray hair. This image fuses with that of the "fallen angel" of line 27 and the dimness of the "dim, dishonored brow" in lines 19-20. In other words, by suggestion, one of the things that holds the poem together (as contrasted with the logical sequence of the statement) is the image of the angel Lucifer, the light-bearer, fallen by excess of pride. Then in lines 29-30, the light image, introduced in the first stanza with the aureole about the gray hair, appears as an inward light shed outward, the "soul" that had once shone from Webster's eyes (he had remarkably large and lustrous dark eyes). But the soul is now dead, the light "withdrawn," and we have by suggestion a death's head with the eyes hollow and blank. How subtly the abstract ideas of "faith" and "honor" are drawn into this image, and how subtly the image itself is related to the continuing play of variations of the idea of light and dark.

From the point of view of technique this poem is, next to "Telling the Bees," Whittier's most perfectly controlled and subtle composition. This is true not only of the dramatic ordering and interplay of imagery, but also of the handling of rhythm as related to meter and stanza, and to the verbal texture. For Whittier, in those rare moments when he could shut out the inane gabble of the sweet singers, could hear the true voice of feeling. But how rarely he heard—or trusted—the voice of feeling. He was, we may hazard, afraid of feeling. Unless, of course, feeling had been properly disinfected.

In the "war with wrong," Whittier wrote a number of poems that were, in their moment, effectively composed, but only three, aside from "Ichabod," that survive to us as poetry. To one, "Song of Slaves in the Desert," we shall return, but the others too, especially the "Letter from a Missionary of the Methodist Episcopal Church South, in Kansas, to a Distinguished Politician," mark significant moments in Whittier's poetic development.

The "Letter" may enlighten us about the relation of Whittier's poetic education to his activity as a journalist and propagandist. The poem, as the title indicates, grew out of the struggle between the proslavery and the free-state forces for the control of "Bleeding Kansas." Though the poem appeared in 1854, four years after "Ichabod," it shows us more clearly than the earlier piece how the realism, wit, and irony of Whittier's prose could be absorbed into a composition that is both tendentious and poetic. The tendentious element is converted into poetry by the force of its dramatization—as in the case of "Ichabod"—but here specifically by an ironic ventriloquism, the device of having the "Letter" come from the pen of the godly missionary. (See lines 1–22, p. 560.) By the ventriloquism the poem achieves a control of style, a fluctuating tension between the requirements of verse and those of "speech," as basis for the variations of tone that set up the sudden poetic, and ironic, effect at the end. (See lines 59–90, p. 561.)

Here quite obviously the ventriloquism is what gives the poem a "voice," and the fact instructs us how Whittier, less obviously, develops through dramatization a voice in "Ichabod." The voice of a poem is effective—is resonant—insofar as it bespeaks a life behind that voice, implies a dramatic issue by which that life is defined. We have spoken of the complexity of feeling behind the voice of "Ichabod," and in the present instance we find such a complexity in the character of the missionary himself. At first glance, we have the simple irony of the evil man cloaking himself in the language of the good. But another irony, and deeper, is implicit in the poem: the missionary may not be evil, after all; he may even be, in a sense, "good"—that is, be speaking in perfect sincerity, a man good but misguided; and thus we have the fundamental irony of the relation of evil and good in human character, action, and history. Whittier was a polemicist, and a very astute one, as the "Letter" in its primary irony exemplifies. But he was also a devout Quaker, and by fits and starts a poet, and his creed, like

his art, would necessarily give a grounding for the secondary, and deeper, irony, an irony that implies humility and forgiveness.

What we have been saying is that by repudiating poetry Whittier became a poet. His image of knocking Pegasus on the head tells a deeper truth than he knew; by getting rid of the "poetical" notion of poetry, he was able, eventually, to ground his poetry on experience. In the years of his crusade and of the Civil War, he was learning this, even though the process was slow, and after a triumph such as the small masterpiece "Telling the Bees" he could fall back into the dreary repetitiveness which characterizes much of the eight volumes of verse he published between 1843 and 1860.

What were the subjects, what were the occasions, that might release this creative energy?

We may begin our attempt to answer the question by stating what we have hinted at earlier: that there was, almost certainly, a deep streak of grievance and undischarged anger in Whittier, for which the abolitionist poems and editorials could allow a hallowed—and disinfected—expression; simple indignation at fate could become "righteous indignation," and the biting sarcasm could be redeemed by the very savagery of the bite. But at what was the grievance directed?

For an answer we may turn to the obsessive subjects of Whittier's poems. The first and most obvious subject is the nostalgia for the childhood past. Whittier was, as he shrewdly saw himself in a poem called "Questions of Life," an "over-wearied child," seeking in "cool and shade his peace to find," in flight

> From vain philosophies, that try
> The sevenfold gates of mystery,
> And, baffled ever, babble still,
> Word-prodigal of fate and will.

As a young man hot with passion and ambition, and later as a journalist, agitator, and propagandist, he had struggled with the world, but there had always been the yearning for total peace which could be imaged in the

Quaker meetinghouse or, more deeply, in childhood, as he summarized it in "To My Sister":

> And, knowing how my life hath been
> A weary work of tongue and pen,
> A long, harsh strife with strong-willed men,
>   Thou wilt not chide my turning
> To con, at times, an idle rhyme,
> To pluck a flower from childhood's clime,
> Or listen, at Life's noonday chime,
>   For the sweet bells of Morning!

The thing from which he fled but did not mention was, of course, inner struggle, more protracted and more bitter than the outer with "strong-willed men" (as he put in the poem "To My Sister") to which he had to steel himself, the collapses, and the grinding headaches.

Almost everyone has an Eden time to look back on, even if it never existed and he has to create it for his own delusion; but for Whittier the need to dwell on this lost Eden was more marked than is ordinary. If the simple indignation against a fate that had deprived him of the security of childhood could be transmuted into righteous indignation, both forms of indignation could be redeemed in a dream of Eden innocence. This was one of the subjects that could summon up Whittier's deepest feeling and release his fullest poetic power.

But there is another obsessive theme in Whittier's work—that of the lost girl, a child or a beloved, who may or may not, in the course of the poem, be recovered. The girl may be simply lost in time, as in "My Playmate," but in many poems, as in "Maud Muller," she may be lost by reason of a social or religious difference. This subject, especially with the social or religious bar, is repeated over and over and clearly echoes Whittier's personal life, but taken by itself it never really touched the springs of true poetry in him; it belonged too literally, no doubt, and too poignantly to the world of frustration. In real life Whittier had worked out the sexual problem and had survived by finding the right kind of action for himself, a "sanctified" action, and this action could, as we have seen, contribute to some of his best poetry; but more characteristically, his poetic powers were released by the refuge in assuagement, the flight into Eden, and this was at once his great limitation and the source of his success. But his fullest successes came when the theme of the lost girl was absorbed into the theme of childhood nostalgia, directly, as in "Telling the Bees," or indirectly, as in *Snow-Bound*, so as to mitigate the pang of the sexual overtones. We shall return to this question, with those poems.

In the light of the two obsessive themes, let us review some of the more important poems leading up to *Snow-Bound*. The germ of Whittier's great summarizing poem may be found in "To My Old Schoolmaster," which was written just after the poetic breakthrough with "Ichabod." It can be taken as the germ not merely because it turns back to the early years of the poet's life, but because Joshua Coffin, the schoolmaster, was associated with certain events that we may regard as Whittier's rites of passage. It was Coffin who, when Whittier was a boy of fourteen, sat by the family fire and read aloud from Burns. It was Coffin who was with Whittier at the founding of the American Anti-Slavery Society in Philadelphia, in 1833. It was Coffin who early encouraged Whittier's historical and antiquarian interests (a fact that explains certain passages in the poem) and shared in his religious sense of the world; and in this last connection, it is logical to assume that when, late in life, Coffin, a sweet-natured and devout man, fell prey to the conviction that he was not among the "elect" and would be damned, the fact would stir the aging Whittier's deepest feelings about the meaning of his own experience. Be that as it may, when Coffin died, in June, 1864, just before the death of Whittier's sister Elizabeth, which provoked *Snow-Bound*, Whittier felt, as he said in a letter, that he had lost "another of the old landmarks of the past." This bereavement would be absorbed into the more catastrophic one about to occur, just as the figure of Coffin would be absorbed into that of the schoolmaster in the poem that is ordinarily taken to refer, as we shall see, to a certain George Haskell.

Though "To My Old Schoolmaster" is a germ

of *Snow-Bound*, an even earlier poem, "Song of Slaves in the Desert" of 1847, indicates more clearly the relation of the poems inspired by Whittier's "war on wrong" to the poems of personal inspiration. The "Song," the best poem done by Whittier up to that time, dramatizes the homesickness of the slaves, the theme of nostalgia, and since the slaves are, specifically, female, affords, too, the first example of the theme of the lost girl.

To illustrate how deeply, and often unconsciously, the theme of nostalgia pervades Whittier's poetry, let us return to "Ichabod" to see what new dimensions the piece may exhibit. To begin with, the title declares that the theme is a lament for departed glory. Literally the glory is that of Webster, who has betrayed his trust, but also involved is the "glory" of those who trusted, who had trailed their own clouds of glory, not of strength and dedication, but of innocence, simplicity, and faith. The followers are, shall we say, children betrayed by their natural protector, for as the Biblical reference indicates, they are the sons of the drunken Noah. In the massiveness of the image, however, the father betrays the sons not only by wine but by death, for it is a death's head with empty eye-sockets that is the most striking fact of the poem. Here the evitable moral betrayal is equated, imagistically, with the inevitable and morally irrelevant fact of death. But by the same token, as a conversion of the proposition, the fact of death in the morally irrelevant course of nature is, too, a moral betrayal. The child, in other words, cannot forgive the course of nature—the fate—that leaves him defenseless.

In connection with this purely latent content of the imagery, we may remark that Whittier, in looking back on the composition of the poem, claimed that he had recognized in Webster's act the "forecast of evil consequences" and knew the "horror of such a vision." For him this was the moment of confronting the grim actuality of life. It was, as it were, a political rite of passage. Here the protector has become the betrayer—has "died." So, in this recognition of the terrible isolation of maturity, "Ichabod," too, takes its place in the massive cluster of poems

treating the nostalgia of childhood that prevision *Snow-Bound*.[5]

Let us glance at a later poem, "The Pipes at Lucknow: An Incident of the Sepoy Mutiny," that seems, at first glance, even more unrelated to the theme of childhood than does "Ichabod." But as "Ichabod" is associated with "To My Old Schoolmaster," a more explicit poem of childhood, so "Lucknow" is associated with "Telling the Bees." If we translate "Lucknow," we have something like this: the Scots have left home (that is, have grown up) and are now beleaguered.

> Day by day the Indian tiger
> Louder yelled, and nearer crept;
> Round and round the jungle-serpent
> Near and nearer circles swept.

The "Indian tiger" and the "jungle-serpent" are melodramatic versions of the "strong-willed men" and other manifestations of the adult world that Whittier had steeled himself to cope with, and from which he had turned, as the Scots turn now, on hearing the pipes, to seek assuagement in the vision of home. As another factor in this equation, we may recall that Whittier had early identified his father's rocky acres with the Scotland of Burns, and so the mystic "pipes o' Havelock" are the pipes of Haverhill.

---

[5] "Ichabod" has thematic parallels with Hawthorne's great story "My Kinsman, Major Molineux." Both concern the degrading of a "father," Noah—as—Webster in his drunkenness and the Major at the hands of the mob. Both concern the son's involvement in the degrading: Whittier repudiates Webster even as Robin joins the mob in repudiating Molineux. Both works concern a betrayal by the father: Webster of his political trust, and Molineux, less precisely, in being an agent of the king and not of the colonists (that is, children). Both concern what Hawthorne calls a majesty in ruins and in this connection involve deep ambivalences of the son toward the father. And in both, the son is thrown back upon his own resources, Whittier as is implied in his comment on the poem, and Robin quite specifically when he is offered the chance of going home or staying in Boston to "rise" by his own "efforts."

There is, probably, one great difference between the two works. It is hard not to believe that Hawthorne was conscious of what is at stake in his work, and it is hard to believe that Whittier was not unconscious of certain implications in "Ichabod."

With one difference: the pipes of Havelock announce not merely a vision of assuagement but also a vengeful carnage to be wrought on all those evil forces and persons that had robbed the child of "home," on the "strong-willed men" and the "Indian tiger" and the "jungle-serpent." Furthermore, since in the inner darkness, where their dramas are enacted, desire, fear, and hatred know no logic or justice beyond their own incorrigible natures, we may see distorted in the dark face of the "Indian tiger" and the "jungle-serpent" the dark faces of those poor slaves in Dixie—for it was all their fault. They were the enemy. If it had not been for them Whittier would never have been drawn forth from the daydreams and neurotic indulgences of his youth into the broad daylight of mature and objective action.

Whittier, it should be remembered, recognized in himself an appetite for violence. "I have still strong suspicions," he would write in one of his essays, "The Training," "that somewhat of the old Norman blood, something of the grim Berserker spirit, has been bequeathed to me." So, paradoxically, but in the deepest logic of his nature, this strain of violence is provoked against these forces that would threaten the "peace" of childhood, and it is by the gentle "air of Auld Lang Syne" rising above the "cruel roll of war-drums" that the vengeful slaughter is justified and the gentle Quaker poet breaks blamelessly out in warlike glee in such lines as

And the tartan clove the turban,
   As the Goomtee cleaves the plain.

"Lucknow" seems more in the spirit of Kipling than of the saint of Amesbury, the abolitionist, and the libertarian poet who, in this very period, was writing poems deeply concerned with the freedom of Italians ("From Perugia," 1858, and "Italy," 1860) though not with that of Sepoys. But it is, as we have said, paradoxically even nearer that gentle little masterpiece of nostalgia, "Telling the Bees." Both would seem to be conditioned by the same traumatic event, the death of Whittier's mother, which occurred in December, 1857.

The setting of the poem is a scrupulous re-creation of the farmstead where Whittier spent his youth, as Samuel T. Pickard, in his *Life and Letters of Whittier*, reports in 1894:

There were beehives on the garden terrace near the wellsweep, occupied, perhaps, by the descendants of Thomas Whittier's bees. The approach to the house from over the northern shoulder of Job's Hill by a path that was in constant use in his boyhood, and is still in existence, is accurately described in the poem. The "gap in the old wall" is still to be seen, and "the stepping-stones in the shallow brook" are still in use. His sister's garden was down by the brookside in front of the house, and her daffodils are perpetuated, and may now be found in their season each year in that place. The red-barred gate, the poplars, the cattle-yard with "the white horns tossing over the wall,"—these were all part of Whittier's boy life on the old farm. Even the touch of "the sundown's blaze on her window-pane" is realistic. The only place from which the blaze of the setting sun could be seen reflected in the windows of the old mansion was from the path so perfectly described, and no doubt the poet had often noticed the phenomenon in his youth while approaching the house in this direction.

The poem was composed almost thirty years after Whittier had gone out into the world, and some twenty-two years after he had sold the home place and moved the family to Amesbury. Not only the same nostalgia that informs *Snow-Bound* is part of the motivation of this poem, but also the same literalism. But more than mere literalism seems to be involved in the strange fact that Whittier keeps his sister Mary —or at least her name—in the poem and keeps her there to kill her off; and there is, of course, the strange fact that he cast a shadowy self— the "I" of the poem—in the role of the lover of Mary, again playing here with the theme of lost love, of the lost girl, but bringing the story within the family circle, curiously coalescing the youthful yearning for sexual love and the childhood yearning for love and security within the family circle. And all this at a time when Mary was very much alive.

Just as the shock of his mother's death turned Whittier's imagination back to the boyhood home and presumably released the energy for "Telling the Bees," so the death of his sister Elizabeth lies behind *Snow-Bound*. The relation of Whittier to this sister, who shared his literary and other tastes, who herself wrote verses, who was a spirited and humorous person, and who, as a spinster, was a companion to his bachelorhood, was of a more intimate kind even than that of Whittier to his mother. When she died, on September 3, 1864, Whittier said, "the great motive of my life seems lost." Five years before Elizabeth's death there had been another crisis in Whittier's life, the end of his second and final romance with Elizabeth Lloyd, whom we have already mentioned. The relation with her was not merely another of his frustrated romances. He had known her for some twenty-five years, from the time when he was thirty. She was good-looking, wrote verses, painted pictures, believed ardently in abolition, and was a Quaker to boot. She even fell in love with him, if we can judge from letters written toward the end of her first connection with him: "Spirit, silent, dumb and cold! What hath possessed thee?" Or: "Do come, Greenleaf! I am almost forgetting how thee looks and seems." But at that earlier time Greenleaf had been beating one of his strategic retreats; so she cut her losses, got to work and made a literary reputation of sorts, married a non-Quaker and got "read out of meeting."

After her husband's death, however, Elizabeth Lloyd, now Howell, reappeared in Whittier's life. They became constant companions. Both suffered from severe headaches but found that if they caressed each other's hair and massaged each other's brows, the headaches would go away. Or at least Whittier's headache would, and he proposed to her. She refused him, but not definitively, and the dalliance went on. Even a quarrel about Quakerism did not end it. But it did end, and in later years the lady

nursed a grievance and spoke bitterly of the old sweetheart.

Whittier had scarcely escaped from Elizabeth Lloyd's healing hands when his sister Elizabeth died. If he still clung to the explanation that his long bachelorhood had been due to "the care of an aged mother, and the duty owed a sister in delicate health," its last vestige of plausibility was now removed. He was now truly alone, with no landmarks left from the Edenic past. There was only memory, and so here nostalgia merges with the subject of not one, but two, "lost girls"—the two Elizabeths— to furnish the poet with the materials for his masterpiece.[6]

Before the end of the month in which Elizabeth died, Whittier sent to the *Atlantic* a poem which he said had "beguiled some weary hours." It was "The Vanishers," based on a legend he had read in Schoolcraft's famous *History, Condition, and Prospects of the American Indians*, about the beautiful spirits who fleetingly appear to beckon the living on to what Whittier calls "The Sunset of the Blest." To the Vanishers, Whittier likens the beloved dead:

> Gentle eyes we closed below,
> Tender voices heard once more,
> Smile and call us, as they go
> On and onward, still before.

The poem is, in its basic impulse, the first draft of *Snow-Bound*. It offers the last of the specific elements to be absorbed into that summarizing work.

In a very special way *Snow-Bound* does summarize Whittier's life and work. We have already noted the theme of childhood nostalgia that leads to *Snow-Bound*, but as early as 1830, in "The Frost Spirit," we find the key situation of the family gathered about a fire while the "evil power" of the winter storm (and of the world) goes shrieking by. Whittier, too, had long been fumbling toward his great question of how to find in the contemplation of the past

---

[6] The strange identification here—or merging—of the sister with the lost beloved repeats the pattern of "Telling the Bees."

a meaning for the future, as in "The Garrison of Cape Ann":

The great eventful Present hides the Past; but
  through the din
Of its loud life hints and echoes from the life
  behind steal in;
And the lore of home and fireside, and the
  legendary rhyme,
Make the task of duty lighter which the true man
  owes his time.

As for the relation to the poet's personal life, *Snow-Bound* came at the moment when, for Whittier, the options of life seemed to be closing. It came after the old inhibition had forbidden his seeking solace from Elizabeth Lloyd's healing hands—and this as he neared the age of sixty when the repudiation of the solace must have seemed catastrophically final; and after the death of the sister had deprived him of his "life-motive." It came, too, toward the end of the Civil War, when he could foresee the victory of the cause to which he had given his energies for more than thirty years and which had, in a sense, served as his justification for life and as a substitute for other aspects of life. Now the joy of victory would, necessarily, carry with it a sense of emptiness. Furthermore, Whittier recognized, as we have seen, that the victory itself would come in terms sadly different from those of which he had dreamed.

If *Snow-Bound* is a summarizing poem for Whittier, it came, also, at a summarizing moment for the country. It came when the country—at least, the North—was poised on the threshold of a new life, the world of technology, big industry, big business, finance capitalism, and urban values; and at that moment, caught up in the promises of the future, the new breed of Americans could afford to look back on their innocent beginnings. The new breed could afford to pay for the indulgence of nostalgia; in fact, in the new affluence, they paid quite well for it. The book appeared on February 17, 1866,[7] and the success was immediate. The poor man was, overnight, modestly rich.

---

[7] Melville's book of poems on the Civil War, *Battle-*

The scene of the poem, the "Flemish picture" as Whittier calls it, the modest genre piece, is rendered with precise and loving care, and this had its simple nostalgic appeal for the generation who had come to town and made it, and a somewhat different appeal, compensatory and comforting, no doubt, for the generation that had stayed in the country and had not made it. But the poem is not simple, and it is likely that the appeals would have been far less strong and permanent if Whittier had not set the "idyl" in certain "perspectives" of deeper interpretation. In other words, it can be said of this poem, as of most poetry, that the effect does not depend so much on the thing looked at as on the way of the looking. True, if there is nothing to look at, there can be no looking, but the way of the looking determines the kind of feeling that fuses with the object looked at.

Before we speak of the particular "perspectives" in which the poem is set, we may say that there is a preliminary and general one. This general perspective, specified in Whittier's dedicatory note to his "Winter Idyl," denies that the poem is a mere "poem." The poem, that is, is offered as autobiography, with all the validation of fact. In other words, the impulse that had appeared in "The Vanishers" as fanciful is here given a grounding in the real world, and in presenting that world the poem explores a complex idea, how different from the vague emotion of "The Vanishers," concerning the human relation to Time.

The reality of that literal world is most obviously certified by the lovingly and precisely observed details: the faces sharpened by cold, the "clashing horn on horn" of the restless cattle in the barn, the "grizzled squirrel" dropping his shell, the "board nails snapping in the frost" at night. This general base of the style is low, depending on precision of rendering

---

Pieces, appeared almost simultaneously, and was a crashing failure. As *Snow-Bound* seemed to dwell merely on the simplicity of the past, *Battle-Pieces* analyzed some of the painful complexities of the war and the present, and recognized some of the painful paradoxes in the glowing promises of the future: not what the public wanted to hear. See pp. 911–17.

rather than on the shock and brilliance of language or image; but from this base certain positive poetic effects emerge as accents and point of focus. For instance:

A chill no coat, however stout,
Of homespun stuff could quite shut out,
A hard, dull bitterness of cold,
That checked, mid-vein, the circling race
Of life-blood in the sharpened face,
The coming of the snow-storm told.
The wind blew east; we heard the roar
Of Ocean on his wintry shore,
And felt the strong pulse throbbing there
Beat with low rhythm our inland air.

Associated with this background realism of the style of the poem we find a firm realism in the drawing of character. Three of the portraits are sharp and memorable, accented against the other members of the group and at the same time bearing thematic relations to them: the spinster aunt, the schoolmaster, and Harriet Livermore.

The aunt, who had a tragic love affair but who, as the poem states, has found reconciliation with life, bears a thematic relation to both Elizabeth Whittier and Whittier himself. The schoolmaster, whose name Whittier could not remember until near the end of his life, was a George Haskell, who later became a doctor, practiced in Illinois and New Jersey, and died in 1876 without even knowing, presumably, of his role in the poem; but as we have pointed out, there are echoes here, too, of Joshua Coffin. As for Harriet Livermore, Whittier's note identifies her. The fact that the "warm, dark languish of her eyes" might change to rage is amply documented by the fact that at one time, before the scene of *Snow-Bound*, she had been converted to Quakerism, but during an argument with another Quaker on a point of doctrine asserted her theological view by seizing a length of stove wood and laying out her antagonist. This, of course, ended her connection with the sect. In her restless search for a satisfying religion, she represents one strain of thought in nineteenth-century America, and as a "woman tropical, intense," and at the same time concerned with ideas and beliefs, she is of the type of Margaret Fuller, the model for Zenobia in *The Blithedale Romance* of Hawthorne.

To return to the structure of the poem, there are three particular "perspectives"—ways in which the material is to be viewed—that can be localized in the body of the work. These perspectives operate as inserts that indicate the stages of the dialectic of this poem. The first appears in lines 175 to 211, the second in lines 400 to 437, and the third in lines 715 to the end.

The first section of the poem (up to the first perspective) presents a generalized setting, the coming of the storm, the first night, the first day, and the second night. Here the outside world is given full value in contrast to the interior, especially in the following passage, which is set between two close-ups of the hearthside, that Eden spot surrounded by the dark world:

The moon above the eastern wood
Shone at its full; the hill-range stood
Transfigured in the silver flood,
Its blown snows flashing cold and keen,
Dead white, save where some sharp ravine
Took shadow, or the sombre green
Of hemlocks turned to pitchy black
Against the whiteness at their back.
For such a world and such a night
Most fitting that unwarming light,
Which only seemed where'er it fell
To make the coldness visible.

The setting, as we have said, is generalized; the individual characters have not yet emerged, the father having appeared in only one line of description and as a voice ordering the boys (John and his only brother Matthew) to dig a path, with the group at the fireside only an undifferentiated "we" (line 156). This section ends with the sharp focus on the mug of cider simmering between the feet of the andirons and the apples sputtering—the literal fire, the literal comfort against the threat of literal darkness and cold outside.

Now, with line 175, the first perspective is introduced:

What matter how the night behaved?
What matter how the north-wind raved?
Blow high, blow low, not all its snow
Could quench our hearth-fire's ruddy glow.

But immediately, even as he affirms the inviolability of the fireside world, the poet cries out:

O Time and Change!—with hair as gray
As was my sire's that winter day,
How strange it seems, with so much gone
Of life and love, to still live on!

From this remembered scene by the fireside only two of the participants survive, the poet and his brother (Matthew), who are now as gray as the father at that snowfall of long ago; for all are caught in Time, in this less beneficent snowfall that whitens every head, as the implied image seems to say. Given this process of the repetition of the life pattern of Time and Change, what, the poet asks, can survive? The answer is that "Love can never lose its own."

After the first perspective has thus developed a new meaning from the scene of simple nostalgia by the fire, the poem becomes a gallery of individual portraits, the father, the mother, the uncle, the aunt, the elder sister (Mary), and the younger (Elizabeth), the schoolmaster, and Harriet Livermore. That is, each individual brings into the poem a specific dramatization of the problem of Time. In the simplest dimension, they offer continuity and repetition: they, the old, were once young, and now sitting by the fire, with the young, tell of youth remembered against the background of age. More specifically, each of the old has had to try to come to terms with Time, and, to quote from "To My Old Schoolmaster," "we/what our fathers are shall be." Each portrait involves an aspect of the work of Time.

When the family portraits have been completed, the second perspective is introduced; this is concerned primarily with the recent bereavement, with the absent Elizabeth, and with the poet's personal future as he walks toward the night and sees (as an echo from "The Vanishers") Elizabeth's beckoning hand. Thus out of the theme of Time and Change emerges the theme of the Future, which is to be developed in the portraits of the schoolmaster and Harriet Livermore.

The first will make his peace in Time, by identifying himself with progressive social good (which, as a matter of fact, George Haskell had done by 1866). Harriet Livermore, though seeking, by her theological questing, a peace out of Time, has found no peace in Time, presumably because she cannot seek in the right spirit; with the "love within her mute" she cannot identify herself with the real needs of the world about her (as Aunt Mercy can and George Haskell will); she is caught in the "tangled skein of will and fate," and can only hope for a peace in Divine forgiveness, out of Time. After the portrait of Harriet Livermore, we find the contrast in the mother's attitude at the good-night scene: unlike Harriet, she finds peace in the here-and-now, "food and shelter, warmth and health" and love, with no "vain prayers" but a willingness to act practically in the world. This is followed with the peace of night and the "reconciled" dream of summer in the middle of the winter, an image of both past and future in the turn of Time.

With dawn, the present—not the past, not the future—appears, with its obligations, joys, and promises. Here there is a lag in the structure of the poem. When the snowbound ones awake to the sound of "merry voices high and clear," the poem should, logically, move toward its fulfillment. But instead, after the active intrusion of the world and the present, we have the section beginning "So days went on" (line 674), and then the dead "filler" for some twenty lines. Whittier's literalism, his fidelity to irrelevant fact rather than to relevant meaning and appropriate structure of the whole, here almost destroys both the emotional and the thematic thrust, and it is due only to the power of the last movement that the poem is not irretrievably damaged.[8]

---

[8] There are, in fact, other lags and fillers in the poem. For instance, there are repetitions in the two barn scenes (lines 21–30 and 81–92); it "happened" this way, so back we go to the barn for the retake. There are patches,

The third "perspective" (lines 715–59), which ends the poem, is introduced by these eloquent lines:

> Clasp, Angel of the backward look
> And folded wings of ashen gray
> And voice of echoes far away,
> The brazen covers of thy book;

Then follow certain new considerations. What is the relation between the dream of the past and the obligations and actions of the future? The answer is, of course, in the sense of continuity of human experience, found when one stretches the "hands of memory" to the "wood-fire's blaze" of the past; it is thus that one may discover the meaningfulness of obligation and action in Time, even as he discovers, in the specific memories of the past, an image for the values out of Time. The "idyl" is more than a "Flemish picture"; it is an image, and a dialectic, of one of life's most fundamental questions that is summed up in the haunting simplicity of the end:

> Sit with me by the homestead hearth,
> And stretch the hands of memory forth
>   To warm them at the wood-fire's blaze!
> And thanks untraced to lips unknown
> Shall greet me like the odors blown
> From unseen meadows newly mown,
> Or lilies floating in some pond,
> Wood-fringed, the wayside gaze beyond;
> The traveller owns the grateful sense
> Of sweetness near, he knows not whence,
> And, pausing, takes with forehead bare
> The benediction of the air.

As a corollary to the third "perspective" generally considered, Whittier has, however, ventured a specific application. He refers not merely to the action in the future, in general, in relation to the past, but also, quite clearly, to the Civil War and the new order with its "larger hopes and graver fears"—the new order of "throngful city ways" as contrasted with the old agrarian

way of life and thought. He invites the "worldling"—the man who, irreligiously, would see no meaning in the shared experience of human history, which to Whittier would have been a form of revelation—to seek in the past not only a sense of personal renewal and continuity, but also a sense of the continuity of the new order with the American past. This idea is clearly related to Whittier's conviction, already mentioned, that the course of development for America should be the fulfilling of the "implied intent" of the Constitution in particular, of the American revelation in general, and of God's will. And we may add that Whittier, by this, also gives another "perspective" in which his poem is to be read.

If we leave *Snow-Bound*, the poem, and go back again to its springs in Whittier's personal story, we may find that it recapitulates in a new form an old issue. The story of his youth is one of entrapments—and of his failure to break out into the world of mature action. In love, politics, and poetry, he was constantly being involved in a deep, inner struggle, with the self-pity, the outrage, the headaches, the breakdowns. He was, to no avail, trying to break out of the "past" of childhood into the "future" of manhood—to achieve, in other words, a self.

The ambition that drove him to try to break out of the entrapments became, in itself, paradoxically, another entrapment—another dead hand of the past laid on him. He cried out, "now, now!"—not even knowing what he cried out for, from what need, or for what reality. But nothing worked out, not love, or politics, or even poetry, that common substitute for success of a more immediate order. In poetry, in fact, he could only pile up words as a mason piles up bricks; he could only repeat, compulsively, the dreary clichés; his meter-making machine ground on, and nothing that came out was, he knew, real: his poems were only "fancies," as he called them, only an echo of the past, not his own present. And if he set out with the declared intention of being the poet of New England, his sense of its history was mere antiquarianism, mere quaintness: no sense of an

---

too, where the mason piling bricks takes over from the poet, with monotonous versification; for instance, in lines 263–75.

abiding human reality. Again he was trapped in the past. All his passions strove, as he put it, "in chains." He found release from what he called "the pain of disappointment and the temptation to envy" only in repudiating the self, and all the self stood for, in order to save the self. He had found a cause which, since it had absorbed, shall we hazard, all the inner forces of the "past" that had thwarted his desires, could free him into some "future" of action.

So much for the story of the young Whittier. But what of the old?

He had, in the end, fallen into another entrapment of the past. All action—and the possibility of continuing life—had been withdrawn: the solacing hands of Elizabeth Lloyd, the "great motive of . . . life" that the other Elizabeth represented, old friends such as Joshua Coffin, even the "cause" to which he had given his life and which had given his life meaning. Only memory—the past—was left. To live—to have a future—he had to refight the old battle of his youth on a new and more difficult terrain. He had to find a new way to make the past nourish the future.

It could not be the old way. The old way had been, in a sense, merely a surrender. By it, Whittier had indeed found a future, a life of action. But the victory had been incomplete, and the costs great; for we must remember that the grinding headaches continued and that the solacing hands of Elizabeth Lloyd had been, in the end, impossible for him.

The new way was more radical. That is, Whittier undertook to see the problem of the past and future as generalized rather than personal, as an issue confronting America, not only himself: furthermore, to see it *sub specie aeternitatis*, as an aspect of man's fate. And he came to see that man's fate is that he must learn to accept and use his past completely, knowingly, rather than to permit himself to be used, ignorantly, by it.

Having struggled for years with the deep difficulties of his own life, Whittier at last found a way to fruitfully regard them, and *Snow-Bound* is the monument of this personal victory. No,

it may be the dynamic image of the very process by which the victory itself was achieved. But there is another way in which we may regard it. It sets Whittier into relation to an obsessive and continuing theme in our literature, a theme that most powerfully appears in Cooper, Hawthorne, Melville, and Faulkner: What does the past mean to an American?

Whittier, though without the scale and power of Cooper, Hawthorne, Melville, and Faulkner, and though he was singularly lacking in their sense of historical and philosophic irony, yet shared their deep intuition of what it meant to be an American. Further, he shared their intuitive capacity to see personal fate as an image for a general cultural and philosophic situation. *Snow-Bound* sets his star in their constellation. If it is less commanding than any of theirs, it yet shines with a clear and authentic light.

Whittier lived some twenty-five years after *Snow-Bound* and wrote voluminously. But, as always, the flashes of poetry were intermittent: "Abraham Davenport," "The Prelude," "The Hive at Gettysburg," "The Pressed Gentian," "At Last," and "To Oliver Wendell Holmes." To these might be added the elegy on Conductor Bradley ("A railway conductor who lost his life in an accident on a Connecticut railway, May 9, 1873"), which may claim immortality of a sort scarcely intended by the poet—as a work of grotesque humor and unconscious parody and self-parody. The world would be poorer without this accidental triumph of what we may call inspired bathos. The opening stanzas run:

Conductor Bradley, (always may his name
Be said with reverence!) as the swift doom came,
Smitten to death, a crushed and mangled frame,

Sank, with the brake he grasped just where he
    stood
To do the utmost that a brave man could,
And die, if needful, as a true man should.

Men stooped above him; women dropped their
    tears

On that poor wreck beyond all hopes or fears,
Lost in the strength and glory of his years.

What heard they? Lo! the ghastly lips of pain,
Dead to all thought save duty's, moved again;
"Put out the signals for the other train!"[9]

Whittier had lived into a world totally strange to him. The world of industrialism and finance capitalism, of strikes and strikebreaking, meant no more to him than it would have to Emerson. But his fame was worldwide: the abolitionist, the hero, the humorist (for he was that, too, in his way), and to top it all, a sort of minor saint in outmoded Quaker dress. The house at Amesbury had long since become a point of pilgrimage, and many of the pilgrims were female, and often marriageable, or fancied themselves so. In Whittier's continuing bachelorhood, with a series of female friends and admirers, there ran a strain of flirtatiousness that more than one lady seems to have taken too seriously. The old fierce ambition had now shrunk to a small vanity that gratified itself in an excessive number of sittings for photographs and some devious tricks of self-advertisement, such as writing an interview with himself and disguising the identity of the interviewer, or doing the laudatory entry under his name in an encyclopedia of biography. So, too, the old passion that had striven "in chains" now flickered on in these little erotic charades. His ego needed these things even at the time when he had long since won the real battle against himself and fate, and even now when he could, without blame, turn his feelings and imagination to the safe past of the child by the fireside. Or perhaps now, as age drew on, he needed these old charades more than ever.

Whittier died September 7, 1892, after a brief illness and a paralytic stroke. He was buried in the section of the cemetery at Amesbury reserved for Friends. The grave was lined with fern and goldenrod, and the coffin was lowered to rest on a bed of roses. Nearby were the graves of the members of the family who had sat at the fireside in *Snow-Bound*.

---

[9] A comparison with folk songs about heroism in railroading—for instance, with "Casey Jones" or "The Wreck of the Old Ninety-Seven"—will indicate what makes Whittier's poem comic. In the folk songs the language belongs to the world of the event celebrated; with Whittier, the language is that of a world so remote that it seems pretentious and false and gives the impression not of the heroic, but of the mock-heroic. See our accompanying volume.

BIOGRAPHICAL CHART

1807 Born, December 17, in Haverhill, Massachusetts, second child of John and Abigail Hussey Whittier
1826 "The Exile's Departure," Whittier's first poem, sent to the *Newburyport Free Press*, by Mary, and published there by William Lloyd Garrison
1827 Enrolls at Haverhill Academy
1828 Becomes editor of the *American Manufacturer*, in Boston, a pro-Clay paper
1830 Edits *Haverhill Gazette*; in June becomes editor of the *New England Weekly Review*, at Hartford, Connecticut; father dies
1831 *Legends of New England*, Whittier's first book
1832 Returns to Haverhill; ill health
1833 Conversion to militant abolitionism by Garrison; antislavery pamphlet *Justice and Expediency*; delegate to National Anti-Slavery Convention at Philadelphia; prominent in proceedings as a secretary and member of a committee drafting the Declaration of Sentiments

1835 Elected to Massachusetts legislature
1836 Edits *Haverhill Gazette*; sells family farm and moves to Amesbury
1843 *Lays of My Home and Other Poems*
1846 *Voices of Freedom*
1847 Contributing editor to *National Era*, in Washington
1850 *Old Portraits and Modern Sketches*
1857 *Poetical Works*; mother dies
1860 *Home Ballads, Poems and Lyrics*
1863 *In War Time and Other Poems*
1866 *Snow-Bound*
1867 *The Tent on the Beach and Other Poems*
1869 *Among the Hills and Other Poems*
1871 *The Journal of John Woolman*
1887 Eightieth birthday celebrated as a national event
1892 Dies, September 7

FURTHER READINGS

Edwin H. Cady and Harry Hayden Clark, eds., *Whittier on Writers and Writing: The Uncollected Critical Writings of John Greenleaf Whittier* (1950)

Horace E. Scudder, ed., *The Writings of John Greenleaf Whittier* (1888–89; reissued 1904; 7 vols.)

Whitman Bennett, *Whittier: Bard of Freedom* (1941)

Thomas Franklin Currier, ed., *Elizabeth Lloyd and the Whittiers: A Budget of Letters* (1939)

Norman Foerster, *Nature in American Literature* (1923)

Howard Mumford Jones, "Whittier Reconsidered," *Essex Institute Historical Collections* (October, 1957)

Lewis Leary, *John Greenleaf Whittier* (1961)

Perry Miller, "John Greenleaf Whittier: The Conscience in Poetry," *Harvard Review* (1964)

Albert Mordell, *Quaker Militant: John Greenleaf Whittier* (1933)

Paul Elmer More, *Shelburne Essays:* Third Series (1907)

John B. Pickard, *John Greenleaf Whittier: An Introduction and Interpretation* (1961)

Samuel T. Pickard, *Life and Letters of John Greenleaf Whittier* (1894; 2 vols.)

John A. Pollard, *John Greenleaf Whittier: Friend of Man* (1949)

Edward C. Wagenknecht, *John Greenleaf Whittier: A Portrait in Paradox* (1967)

Hyatt Waggoner, "What I Had I Gave: Another Look at Whittier," *Essex Institute Historical Collections* (January, 1959)

Massachusetts to Virginia (1843)

This poem grew out of the case of George Latimer, a slave who had escaped to Boston and was taken by the authorities there to be returned to his master in Virginia. An attempt to gain the right of trial by jury for Latimer failed. The case was nationally important, and a petition with some sixty-five thousand signatures was sent from Massachusetts to Congress asking for such amendment as might be necessary to relieve free states from the legal obligation to return runaways. Whittier's poem was first presented to the public at a mass meeting, on January 2, 1843, at Ipswich, Massachusetts.

The blast from Freedom's Northern hills, upon
    its Southern way,
Bears greeting to Virginia from Massachusetts
    Bay:—
No word of haughty challenging, nor battle
    bugle's peal,
Nor steady tread of marching files, nor clang
    of horsemen's steel.

No trains of deep-mouthed cannon along our
    highways go,—
Around our silent arsenals untrodden lies
    the snow;
And to the land-breeze of our ports, upon
    their errands far,
A thousand sails of commerce swell, but
    none are spread for war.

We hear thy threats, Virginia! thy stormy
    words and high,
Swell harshly on the Southern winds which   10
    melt along our sky;
Yet, not one brown, hard hand foregoes its
    honest labor here,
No hewer of our mountain oaks suspends his
    axe in fear.

Wild are the waves which lash the reefs along
    St. George's bank,—
Cold on the shore of Labrador the fog lies
    white and dank;
Through storm, and wave, and blinding mist,
    stout are the hearts which man
The fishing-smacks of Marblehead, the
    sea-boats of Cape Ann.

The cold north light and wintry sun glare
    on their icy forms,
Bent grimly o'er their straining lines or
    wrestling with the storms;
Free as the winds they drive before, rough
    as the waves they roam,
They laugh to scorn the slaver's threat against   20
    their rocky home.

What means the Old Dominion? Hath she
    forgot the day
When o'er her conquered valleys swept the
    Briton's steel array?
How side by side, with sons of hers, the
    Massachusetts men

Encountered Tarleton's charge of fire, and
    stout Cornwallis, then?

Forgets she how the Bay State, in answer
    to the call
Of her old House of Burgesses, spoke out
    from Faneuil Hall?
When, echoing back her Henry's cry, came
    pulsing on each breath
Of Northern winds, the thrilling sounds of
    "LIBERTY OR DEATH!"

What asks the Old Dominion? If now her
    sons have proved
False to their fathers' memory,—false to   30
    the faith they loved,
If she can scoff at Freedom, and its great
    charter spurn,
Must we of Massachusetts from truth and
    duty turn?

We hunt your bondmen, flying from Slavery's
    hateful hell,—
Our voices, at your bidding, take up the
    bloodhound's yell,—
We gather, at your summons, above our
    fathers' graves,
From Freedom's holy altar-horns to tear your
    wretched slaves!

Thank God! not yet so vilely can
    Massachusetts bow;
The spirit of her early time is with her
    even now;
Dream not because her Pilgrim blood moves
    slow and calm and cool,
She thus can stoop her chainless neck,   40
    a sister's slave and tool!

All that a *sister* State should do, all that a
    free State may,
Heart, hand, and purse we proffer, as in
    our early day;
But that one dark loathsome burden ye must
    stagger with alone,
And reap the bitter harvest which ye yourselves
    have sown!

Hold, while ye may, your struggling slaves,
    and burden God's free air
With women's shriek beneath the lash, and
    manhood's wild despair;
Cling closer to the "cleaving curse" that writes
    upon your plains

The blasting of Almighty wrath against a land
    of chains.

Still shame your gallant ancestry, the
    cavaliers of old,
By watching round the shambles where   50
    human flesh is sold,—
Gloat o'er the new-born child, and count
    his market value, when
The maddened mother's cry of woe shall
    pierce the slaver's den!

Lower than plummet soundeth, sink the
    Virginia name;
Plant, if ye will, your fathers' graves with
    rankest weeds of shame;
Be, if ye will, the scandal of God's fair
    universe,—
We wash our hands forever of your sin and
    shame and curse.

A voice from lips whereon the coal from
    Freedom's shrine hath been,
Thrilled, as but yesterday, the hearts of
    Berkshire's mountain men:
The echoes of that solemn voice are sadly
    lingering still
In all our sunny valleys, on every windswept   60
    hill.

And when the prowling man-thief came
    hunting for his prey
Beneath the very shadow of Bunker's
    shaft of gray,
How, through the free lips of the son,
    the father's warning spoke;
How, from its bonds of trade and sect,
    the Pilgrim city broke!

A hundred thousand right arms were lifted
    up on high,—
A hundred thousand voices sent back their
    loud reply;
Through the thronged towns of Essex the
    startling summons rang,
And up from bench and loom and wheel
    her young mechanics sprang!

The voice of free, broad Middlesex,—of
    thousands as of one,—
The shaft of Bunker calling to that of   70
    Lexington,—
From Norfolk's ancient villages, from
    Plymouth's rocky bound

To where Nantucket feels the arms of
    ocean close her round;—

From rich and rural Worcester, where
    through the calm repose
Of cultured vales and fringing woods the
    gentle Nashua flows,
To where Wachuset's wintry blasts the
    mountain larches stir,
Swelled up to Heaven the thrilling cry of
    "God save Latimer!"

And sandy Barnstable rose up, wet with
    the salt sea spray,—
And Bristol sent her answering shout down
    Narragansett Bay!
Along the broad Connecticut old Hampden
    felt the thrill,
And the cheer of Hampshire's woodmen   80
    swept down from Holyoke Hill.

The voice of Massachusetts! Of her free sons
    and daughters,—
Deep calling unto deep aloud,—the sound
    of many waters!
Against the burden of that voice what tyrant
    power shall stand?
No fetters in the Bay State! No slave
    upon her land!

Look to it well, Virginians! In calmness
    we have borne,
In answer to our faith and trust, your insult
    and your scorn;
You've spurned our kindest counsels,—you've
    hunted for our lives,—
And shaken round our hearths and homes
    your manacles and gyves!

We wage no war,—we lift no arm,—we fling
    no torch within
The fire-damps of the quaking mine beneath   90
    your soil of sin;
We leave ye with your bondmen, to
    wrestle, while ye can,
With the strong upward tendencies and
    godlike soul of man!

But for us and for our children, the vow
    which we have given
For freedom and humanity is registered
    in heaven;
No slave-hunt in our borders,—no pirate
    on our strand!
No fetters in the Bay State,—no slave
    upon our land!

Song of Slaves in the Desert (1847, 1856)

Whittier gives the following note on the poem:

Sebah, Oasis of Fezzan, 10th March, 1846.—
This evening the female slaves were unusually
excited in singing, and I had the curiosity to
ask my negro servant Said, what they were
singing about. As many of them were natives
of his own country, he had no difficulty in
translating the Manara or Bornou language.
I had often asked the Moors to translate their
songs for me, but got no satisfactory account
from them. Said at first said, "Oh, they sing
of *Rubee*" (God). "What do you mean?" I
replied, impatiently. "Oh, don't you know?"
he continued, "they asked God to give them
their *Atka*" (certificate of freedom). I inquired, "Is that all?" Said: "No; they say,
'Where are we going? The world is large. O

God! *Where are we going? O God!*'" I inquired, "What else?" Said: "They remember
their country, Bornou, and say, '*Bornou was*
a pleasant country, full of good things; but
this is a bad country, and we are miserable!'"
"Do they say anything else?" Said: "No; they
repeat these words over and over again, and
add, 'O God! give us our *Atka, and let us*
return again to our dear home!'" — *Richard-*
son's Journal in Africa.

This is one of Whittier's more successful
poems and is certainly, with "Ichabod" and
"Letter," one of the three pieces of propaganda
that comes across as poetry. Here Whittier succeeds in finding a language for the slave women
that is simple without being banal or senti-

mental and is content to give a direct dramatic expression of their feeling, without editorializing.

Where are we going? where are we going,
    Where are we going, Rubee?
Lord of peoples, lord of lands,
Look across these shining sands,
Through the furnace of the noon,
Through the white light of the moon.
Strong the Ghiblee wind is blowing,
Strange and large the world is growing!
Speak and tell us where we are going,
    Where are we going, Rubee?   10

Bornou land was rich and good,
Wells of water, fields of food,
Dourra fields, and bloom of bean,
And the palm-tree cool and green:
Bornou land we see no longer,
Here we thirst and here we hunger,
Here the Moor-man smites in anger:
    Where are we going, Rubee?

When we went from Bornou land,
We were like the leaves and sand,   20
We were many, we are few;
Life has one, and death has two:
Whitened bones our path are showing,
Thou All-seeing, thou All-knowing!
Hear us, tell us, where are we going,
    Where are we going, Rubee?

Moons of marches from our eyes
Bornou land behind us lies;
Stranger round us day by day
Bends the desert circle gray;   30
Wild the waves of sand are flowing,
Hot the winds above them blowing,—
Lord of all things! where are we going?
    Where are we going, Rubee?

We are weak, but Thou art strong;
Short our lives, but Thine is long;
We are blind, but Thou hast eyes;
We are fools, but Thou art wise!
Thou, our morrow's pathway knowing
Through the strange world round us growing,   40
Hear us, tell us where are we going,
    Where are we going, Rubee?

Ichabod (1850)

So fallen! so lost! the light withdrawn
    Which once he wore!
The glory from his gray hairs gone
    Forevermore!

Revile him not, the Tempter hath
    A snare for all;
And pitying tears, not scorn and wrath,
    Befit his fall!

Oh, dumb be passion's stormy rage,
    When he who might   10
Have lighted up and led his age,
    Falls back in night.

Scorn! would the angels laugh, to mark
    A bright soul driven,
Fiend-goaded, down the endless dark,
    From hope and heaven!

Let not the land once proud of him
    Insult him now,

Nor brand with deeper shame his dim,
    Dishonored brow.   20

But let its humbled sons, instead,
    From sea to lake,
A long lament, as for the dead,
    In sadness make.

Of all we loved and honored, naught
    Save power remains:
A fallen angel's pride of thought,
    Still strong in chains.

All else is gone; from those great eyes
    The soul has fled: 30
When faith is lost, when honor dies,
    The man is dead!

Then, pay the reverence of old days
    To his dead fame;
Walk backward, with averted gaze,
    And hide the shame!

First-Day Thoughts (1853)

In calm and cool and silence, once again
  I find my old accustomed place among
  My brethren, where, perchance, no human
    tongue
  Shall utter words; where never hymn is sung,
  Nor deep-toned organ blown, nor censer
    swung,
Nor dim light falling through the pictured
    pane!
There, syllabled by silence, let me hear
The still small voice which reached the
    prophet's ear;
Read in my heart a still diviner law
Than Israel's leader on his tables saw!   10

There let me strive with each besetting sin,
  Recall my wandering fancies, and restrain
  The sore disquiet of a restless brain,
  And, as the path of duty is made plain,
May grace be given that I may walk therein,
  Not like the hireling, for his selfish gain,
With backward glances and reluctant tread,
Making a merit of his coward dread,
  But, cheerful, in the light around me
    thrown,
  Walking as one to pleasant service led;   20
  Doing God's will as if it were my own,
Yet trusting not in mine, but in His strength
    alone!

Letter from a Missionary of the Methodist Episcopal Church South, in Kansas, to a Distinguished Politician (1854)

This poem has for its background the struggle, in the 1850's, between Free-Soilers and southern immigrants for the control of the Kansas Territory. The struggle was a rehearsal for the Civil War and was often marked by a peculiar brutality on both sides, the two most famous episodes being the burning of the settlement of Lawrence by southern raiders and the massacre performed by John Brown and his sons at Pottawatomie.

Douglas Mission, August, 1854

Last week—the Lord be praised for all His
    mercies
To His unworthy servant!—I arrived
Safe at the Mission, via Westport where
I tarried over night, to aid in forming
A Vigilance Committee, to send back,
In shirts of tar, and feather-doublets quilted
With forty stripes save one, all Yankee comers
Uncircumcised and Gentile, aliens from
The Commonwealth of Israel, who despise
The prize of the high calling of the saints,   10
Who plant amidst this heathen wilderness

Pure gospel institutions, sanctified
By patriarchal use. The meeting opened
With prayer, as was most fitting. Half an
    hour,
Or thereaway, I groaned, and strove, and
    wrestled,
As Jacob did at Penuel, till the power
Fell on the people, and they cried "Amen!"
"Glory to God!" and stamped and clapped
    their hands;
And the rough river boatmen wiped their
    eyes;
"Go it, old hoss!" they cried, and cursed   20
    the niggers—
Fulfilling thus the word of prophecy,
"Cursëd be Canaan." After prayer, the meeting
Chose a committee—good and pious men—
A Presbyterian Elder, Baptist deacon,
A local preacher, three or four class-leaders,
Anxious inquirers, and renewed backsliders,
A score in all—to watch the river ferry,
(As they of old did watch the fords of Jordan,)
And cut off all whose Yankee tongues refuse
The Shibboleth of the Nebraska bill.   30
And then, in answer to repeated calls,
I gave a brief account of what I saw
In Washington; and truly many hearts

Rejoiced to know the President, and you
And all the Cabinet regularly hear
The gospel message of a Sunday morning,
Drinking with thirsty souls of the sincere
Milk of the Word. Glory! Amen, and Selah!

Here, at the Mission, all things have gone
    well:
The brother who, throughout my absence, acted   40
As overseer, assures me that the crops
Never were better. I have lost one negro,
A first-rate hand, but obstinate and sullen.
He ran away some time last spring, and hid
In the river timber. There my Indian converts
Found him, and treed and shot him. For
    the rest,
The heathens round about begin to feel
The influence of our pious ministrations
And works of love; and some of them already
Have purchased negroes, and are settling   50
    down
As sober Christians! Bless the Lord for this!
I know it will rejoice you. You, I hear,
Are on the eve of visiting Chicago,
To fight with the wild beasts of Ephesus,
Long John, and Dutch Free-Soilers.
    May your arm
Be clothed with strength, and on your tongue
    be found
The sweet oil of persuasion. So desires
Your brother and co-laborer. Amen!

    P. S. All's lost. Even while I write these lines,

The Yankee abolitionists are coming   60
Upon us like a flood—grim, stalwart men,
Each face set like a flint of Plymouth Rock
Against our institutions—staking out
Their farm lots on the wooded Wakarusa,
Or squatting by the mellow-bottomed Kansas;
The pioneers of mightier multitudes,
The small rain-patter, ere the thunder shower
Drowns the dry prairies. Hope from man is not.
Oh, for a quiet berth at Washington,
Snug naval chaplaincy, or clerkship, where   70
These rumors of free labor and free soil
Might never meet me more. Better to be
Door-keeper in the White House, than to dwell
Amidst these Yankee tents, that, whitening,
    show
On the green prairie like a fleet becalmed.
Methinks I hear a voice come up the river
From those far bayous where the alligators
Mount guard around the camping filibusters:
"Shake off the dust of Kansas. Turn to Cuba—
(That golden orange just about to fall,   80
O'er-ripe, into the Democratic lap;)
Keep pace with Providence, or, as we say,
Manifest destiny. Go forth and follow
The message of *our* gospel, thither borne
Upon the point of Quitman's bowie knife,
And the persuasive lips of Colt's revolvers.
There may'st thou, underneath thy vine and
    fig-tree,
Watch thy increase of sugar cane and negroes,
Calm as a patriarch in his eastern tent!"
Amen: So mote it be. So prays your friend.   90

Maud Muller (1854)

Maud Muller, on a summer's day,
Raked the meadow sweet with hay.

Beneath her torn hat glowed the wealth
Of simple beauty and rustic health.

Singing, she wrought, and her merry glee
The mock-bird echoed from his tree.

But when she glanced to the far-off town,
White from its hill-slope looking down,

The sweet song died, and a vague unrest
And a nameless longing filled her breast,—   10

A wish, that she hardly dared to own,
For something better than she had known.

The Judge rode slowly down the lane,
Smoothing his horse's chestnut mane.

He drew his bridle in the shade
Of the apple-tree, to greet the maid,

And asked a draught from the spring that
    flowed
Through the meadow across the road.

She stooped where the cool spring bubbled up,
And filled for him her small tin cup,   20

And blushed as she gave it, looking down
On her feet so bare, and her tattered gown.

"Thanks!" said the Judge; "a sweeter draught
From a fairer hand was never quaffed."

He spoke of the grass and flowers and trees,
Of the singing birds and the humming bees;

Then talked of the haying, and wondered
    whether
The cloud in the west would bring foul
    weather.

And Maud forgot her brier-torn gown,
And her graceful ankles bare and brown;   30

And listened, while a pleased surprise
Looked from her long-lashed hazel eyes.

At last, like one who for delay
Seeks a vain excuse, he rode away.

Maud Muller looked and sighed: "Ah me!
That I the Judge's bride might be!

"He would dress me up in silks so fine,
And praise and toast me at his wine.

"My father should wear a broadcloth coat;
My brother should sail a painted boat.   40

"I'd dress my mother so grand and gay,
And the baby should have a new toy each day.

"And I'd feed the hungry and clothe the poor,
And all should bless me who left our door."

The Judge looked back as he climbed the hill,
And saw Maud Muller standing still.

"A form more fair, a face more sweet,
Ne'er hath it been my lot to meet.

"And her modest answer and graceful air
Show her wise and good as she is fair.   50

"Would she were mine, and I to-day,
Like her, a harvester of hay;

"No doubtful balance of rights and wrongs,
Nor weary lawyers with endless tongues,

"But low of cattle and song of birds,
And health and quiet and loving words."

But he thought of his sisters, proud and cold,
And his mother, vain of her rank and gold.

So, closing his heart, the Judge rode on,
And Maud was left in the field alone.   60

But the lawyers smiled that afternoon,
When he hummed in court an old love-tune;

And the young girl mused beside the well
Till the rain on the unraked clover fell.

He wedded a wife of richest dower,
Who lived for fashion, as he for power.

Yet oft, in his marble hearth's bright glow,
He watched a picture come and go;

And sweet Maud Muller's hazel eyes
Looked out in their innocent surprise.   70

Oft, when the wine in his glass was red,
He longed for the wayside well instead;

And closed his eyes on his garnished rooms
To dream of meadows and clover-blooms.

And the proud man sighed, with a secret pain,
"Ah, that I were free again!

"Free as when I rode that day,
Where the barefoot maiden raked her hay."

She wedded a man unlearned and poor,
And many children played round her door.   80

But care and sorrow, and childbirth pain,
Left their traces on heart and brain.

And oft, when the summer sun shone hot
On the new-mown hay in the meadow lot,

And she heard the little spring brook fall
Over the roadside, through the wall,

In the shade of the apple-tree again
She saw a rider draw his rein;

And, gazing down with timid grace,
She felt his pleased eyes read her face.   90

Sometimes her narrow kitchen walls
Stretched away into stately halls;

The weary wheel to a spinnet turned,
The tallow candle an astral burned,

And for him who sat by the chimney lug,
Dozing and grumbling o'er pipe and mug,

A manly form at her side she saw,
And joy was duty and love was law.

Then she took up her burden of life again
Saying only, "It might have been."   100

Alas for maiden, alas for Judge,
For rich repiner and household drudge!

God pity them both! and pity us all,
Who vainly the dreams of youth recall.

For of all sad words of tongue or pen,
The saddest are these: "It might have been!"

Ah, well! for us all some sweet hope lies
Deeply buried from human eyes;

And, in the hereafter, angels may
Roll the stone from its grave away!   110

Skipper Ireson's Ride (1857)

In 1857 the *Atlantic Monthly* was founded as a magazine that, though nonpartisan, would be directed toward liberal reform, including the abolition of slavery, as was attested by the fact that Whittier, as well as Harriet Beecher Stowe, was associated with the project, and James Russell Lowell was the editor. Whittier contributed a now forgotten poem to the first issue, but just after that appeared, he sent in what he called a "bit of Yankee ballad."

Back at the Haverhill Academy, a fellow student from Marblehead had given Whittier what he was later to call a "fragment of rhyme," the song which Captain Ireson had, presumably, been forced to sing as the bereaved women of Marblehead escorted his cart:

Oi, Flood Oierson, for tellin' a loi
Was torred and feathered above my pi.

Oi, Flood Oierson, for leavin' a wrack
Was torred and feathered all over my back.

Oi, Flood Oierson, for my hord hort
Was torred and feathered and cor'd in a cort.

Oi, Flood Oierson, in all my glory
Was torred and feathered and cor'd in a dory.

Whittier began his ballad in 1828 but happily for the result waited some thirty years to finish it. Even so, one of the most telling strokes comes from Lowell, who wrote Whittier that he was setting the poem up with dialect in the refrain. Whittier accepted the idea, but only for those lines which were directly quoted from the women; and he made the further change of striking out the word *was* at the first of the next to the last line, an effective revision.

As for the facts of Skipper Ireson's case, it developed that he, according to a history of Marblehead, published in 1879 by Samuel Roades, was cruelly maligned in Whittier's poem. Whittier wrote to the author saying that his ballad was "pure fancy" and added, "I certainly would not knowingly do injustice to any one, living or dead."

Of all the rides since the birth of time,
Told in story or sung in rhyme,—
On Apuleius's Golden Ass,
Or one-eyed Calender's horse of brass,
Witch astride of a human back,
Islam's prophet on Al-Borák,—
The strangest ride that ever was sped
Was Ireson's, out from Marblehead!
   Old Floyd Ireson, for his hard heart,
   Tarred and feathered and carried in a cart   10
   By the women of Marblehead!

Body of turkey, head of owl,
Wings a-droop like a rained-on fowl,
Feathered and ruffled in every part,
Skipper Ireson stood in the cart.
Scores of women, old and young,
Strong of muscle, and glib of tongue,
Pushed and pulled up the rocky lane,
Shouting and singing the shrill refrain:
   "Here's Flud Oirson, fur his horrd horrt,   20
   Torr'd an' futherr'd an' corr'd in a corrt
   By the women o' Morble'ead!"

Wrinkled scolds with hands on hips,
Girls in bloom of cheek and lips,
Wild-eyed, free-limbed, such as chase
Bacchus round some antique vase,
Brief of skirt, with ankles bare,
Loose of kerchief and loose of hair,
With conch-shells blowing and fish-horns'
   twang,
Over and over the Maenads sang: 30
   "Here's Flud Oirson, fur his horrd horrt,
   Torr'd an' futherr'd an' corr'd in a corrt
   By the women o' Morble'ead!"

Small pity for him!—He sailed away
From a leaking ship in Chaleur Bay,—
Sailed away from a sinking wreck,
With his own town's-people on her deck!
"Lay by! lay by!" they called to him.
Back he answered, "Sink or swim!
Brag of your catch of fish again!"   40
And off he sailed through the fog and rain!
   Old Floyd Ireson, for his hard heart,
   Tarred and feathered and carried in a cart
   By the women of Marblehead!

Fathoms deep in dark Chaleur
That wreck shall lie forevermore.

Mother and sister, wife and maid,
Looked from the rocks of Marblehead
Over the moaning and rainy sea,—
Looked for the coming that might not be!   50
What did the winds and the sea-birds say
Of the cruel captain who sailed away—?
  Old Floyd Ireson, for his hard heart,
  Tarred and feathered and carried in a cart
    By the women of Marblehead!

Through the street, on either side,
Up flew windows, doors swung wide;
Sharp-tongued spinsters, old wives gray,
Treble lent the fish-horn's bray.
Sea-worn grandsires, cripple-bound,   60
Hulks of old sailors run aground,
Shook head, and fist, and hat, and cane,
And cracked with curses the hoarse refrain:
  "Here's Flud Oirson, fur his horrd horrt,
  Torr'd an' futherr'd an' corr'd in a corrt
    By the women o' Morble'ead!"

Sweetly along the Salem road
Bloom of orchard and lilac showed.
Little the wicked skipper knew
Of the fields so green and the sky so blue.   70
Riding there in his sorry trim,
Like an Indian idol glum and grim,
Scarcely he seemed the sound to hear

Of voices shouting, far and near:
  "Here's Flud Oirson, fur his horrd horrt,
  Torr'd an' futherr'd an' corr'd in a corrt
    By the women o' Morble'ead!"

"Hear me, neighbors!" at last he cried,—
"What to me is this noisy ride?
What is the shame that clothes the skin   80
To the nameless horror that lives within?
Waking or sleeping, I see a wreck,
And hear a cry from a reeling deck!
Hate me and curse me,—I only dread
The hand of God and the face of the dead!"
  Said old Floyd Ireson, for his hard heart,
  Tarred and feathered and carried in a cart
    By the women of Marblehead!

Then the wife of the skipper lost at sea
Said, "God has touched him!—why should   90
    we?"
Said an old wife mourning her only son,
"Cut the rogue's tether and let him run!"
So with soft relentings and rude excuse,
Half scorn, half pity, they cut him loose,
And gave him a cloak to hide him in,
And left him alone with his shame and sin.
  Poor Floyd Ireson, for his hard heart,
  Tarred and feathered and carried in a cart
    By the women of Marblehead!

The Pipes at Lucknow: An Incident of the Sepoy Mutiny (1858)

Pipes of the misty moorlands,
  Voice of the glens and hills;
The droning of the torrents,
  The treble of the rills;
Not the braes of bloom and heather,
  Nor the mountains dark with rain,
Nor maiden bower, nor border tower,
  Have heard your sweetest strain!

Dear to the Lowland reaper,
  And plaided mountaineer,—   10
To the cottage and the castle
  The Scottish pipes are dear;—
Sweet sounds the ancient pibroch
  O'er mountain, loch, and glade;
But the sweetest of all music
  The pipes at Lucknow played.

Day by day the Indian tiger
  Louder yelled, and nearer crept;
Round and round the jungle-serpent

Near and nearer circles swept.   20
"Pray for rescue, wives and mothers,—
  Pray to-day!" the soldier said;
"To-morrow, death's between us
  And the wrong and shame we dread."

Oh, they listened, looked, and waited,
  Till their hope became despair;
And the sobs of low bewailing
  Filled the pauses of their prayer.
Then up spake a Scottish maiden,
  With her ear unto the ground: 30
"Dinna ye hear it?—dinna ye hear it?
  The pipes o' Havelock sound!"

Hushed the wounded man his groaning;
  Hushed the wife her little ones;
Alone they heard the drum-roll
  And the roar of Sepoy guns.
But to sounds of home and childhood
  The Highland ear was true;—

As her mother's cradle-crooning
  The mountain pipes she knew.   40

Like the march of soundless music
  Through the vision of the seer,
More of feeling than of hearing,
  Of the heart than of the ear,
She knew the droning pibroch,
  She knew the Campbell's call:
"Hark! hear ye no MacGregor's,
  The grandest o' them all!"

Oh, they listened, dumb and breathless,
  And they caught the sound at last;   50
Faint and far beyond the Goomtee
  Rose and fell the piper's blast!
Then a burst of wild thanksgiving
  Mingled woman's voice and man's;
"God be praised!—the march of Havelock!
  The piping of the clans!"

Louder, nearer, fierce as vengeance,
  Sharp and shrill as swords at strife,
Came the wild MacGregor's clan-call,

Stinging all the air to life.   60
But when the far-off dust-cloud
  To plaided legions grew,
Full tenderly and blithesomely
  The pipes of rescue blew!

Round the silver domes of Lucknow,
  Moslem mosque and Pagan shrine,
Breathed the air to Britons dearest,
  The air of Auld Lang Syne.
O'er the cruel roll of war-drums
  Rose that sweet and homelike strain;   70
And the tartan clove the turban,
  As the Goomtee cleaves the plain

Dear to the corn-land reaper
  And plaided mountaineer,—
To the cottage and the castle
  The piper's song is dear.
Sweet sounds the Gaelic pibroch
  O'er mountain, glen, and glade;
But the sweetest of all music
  The Pipes at Lucknow played!   80

Telling the Bees (1858)

The poem is based on the superstitious custom which the colonists had brought from England and which, in Whittier's lifetime, still persisted in parts of back-country New England: that of telling the family's bees when a death occurred in the house and of draping the hives with a trailer of black in order to keep the swarms from leaving.

Here is the place; right over the hill
  Runs the path I took;
You can see the gap in the old wall still,
  And the stepping-stones in the shallow
    brook.

There is the house, with the gate red-barred,
  And the poplars tall;
And the barn's brown length, and the
    cattle-yard,
  And the white horns tossing above the wall.

There are the beehives ranged in the sun;
  And down by the brink   10
Of the brook are her poor flowers, weed-o'errun,
  Pansy and daffodil, rose and pink.

A year has gone, as the tortoise goes,
  Heavy and slow;
And the same rose blows, and the same
    sun glows,
  And the same brook sings of a year ago.

There's the same sweet clover-smell in the
    breeze;
  And the June sun warm
Tangles his wings of fire in the trees,
  Setting, as then, over Fernside farm.   20

1 mind me how with a lover's care
  From my Sunday coat
I brushed off the burrs, and smoothed my hair,
  And cooled at the brookside my brow
    and throat.

Since we parted, a month had passed,—
  To love, a year;
Down through the beeches I looked at last
  On the little red gate and the well-sweep
    near.

I can see it all now,—the slantwise rain
  Of light through the leaves,   30

The sundown's blaze on her window-pane,
  The bloom of her roses under the eaves.

Just the same as a month before,—
  The house and the trees,
The barn's brown gable, the vine by the
      door,—
  Nothing changed but the hives of bees.

Before them, under the garden wall,
  Forward and back,
Went drearily singing the chore-girl small,
  Draping each hive with a shred of black.   40

Trembling, I listened: the summer sun
  Had the chill of snow;

For I knew she was telling the bees of one
  Gone on the journey we all must go!

Then I said to myself, "My Mary weeps
  For the dead to-day:
Haply her blind old grandsire sleeps
  The fret and the pain of his age away."

But her dog whined low; on the doorway sill,
  With his cane to his chin,   50
The old man sat; and the chore-girl still
  Sung to the bees stealing out and in.

And the song she was singing ever since
  In my ear sounds on:—
"Stay at home, pretty bees, fly not hence!
  Mistress Mary is dead and gone!"

My Playmate (1860)

The pines were dark on Ramoth hill,
  Their song was soft and low;
The blossoms in the sweet May wind
  Were falling like the snow.

The blossoms drifted at our feet,
  The orchard birds sang clear;
The sweetest and the saddest day
  It seemed of all the year.

For, more to me than birds or flowers,
  My playmate left her home,   10
And took with her the laughing spring,
  The music and the bloom.

She kissed the lips of kith and kin,
  She laid her hand in mine:
What more could ask the bashful boy
  Who fed her father's kine?

She left us in the bloom of May:
  The constant years told o'er
Their seasons with as sweet May morns,
  But she came back no more.   20

I walk, with noiseless feet, the round
  Of uneventful years;
Still o'er and o'er I sow the spring
  And reap the autumn ears.

She lives where all the golden year
  Her summer roses blow;
The dusky children of the sun
  Before her come and go.

There haply with her jewelled hands
  She smooths her silken gown,—   30
No more the homespun lap wherein
  I shook the walnuts down.

The wild grapes wait us by the brook,
  The brown nuts on the hill,
And still the May-day flowers make sweet
  The woods of Follymill.

The lilies blossom in the pond,
  The bird builds in the tree,
The dark pines sing on Ramoth hill
  The slow song of the sea.   40

I wonder if she thinks of them,
  And how the old time seems,—
If ever the pines of Ramoth wood
  Are sounding in her dreams.

I see her face, I hear her voice;
  Does she remember mine?
And what to her is now the boy
  Who fed her father's kine?

What cares she that the orioles build
  For other eyes than ours,—   50
That other hands with nuts are filled,
  And other laps with flowers?

O playmate in the golden time!
  Our mossy seat is green,
Its fringing violets blossom yet,
  The old trees o'er it lean.

The winds so sweet with birch and fern
 A sweeter memory blow;
And there in spring the veeries sing
 The song of long ago.   60

And still the pines of Ramoth wood
 Are moaning like the sea,—
The moaning of the sea of change
 Between myself and thee!

Barbara Frietchie (1863)

Up from the meadows rich with corn,
Clear in the cool September morn,

The clustered spires of Frederick stand
Green-walled by the hills of Maryland.

Round about them orchards sweep,
Apple and peach tree fruited deep,

Fair as the garden of the Lord
To the eyes of the famished rebel horde,

On that pleasant morn of the early fall
When Lee marched over the mountain wall;   10

Over the mountains winding down,
Horse and foot, into Frederick town.

Forty flags with their silver stars,
Forty flags with their crimson bars,

Flapped in the morning wind: the sun
Of noon looked down, and saw not one.

Up rose old Barbara Frietchie then,
Bowed with her fourscore years and ten;

Bravest of all in Frederick town,
She took up the flag the men hauled down.   20

In her attic window the staff she set,
To show that one heart was loyal yet.

Up the street came the rebel tread,
Stonewall Jackson riding ahead.

Under his slouched hat left and right
He glanced; the old flag met his sight.

"Halt!"—the dust-brown ranks stood fast.
"Fire!"—out blazed the rifle-blast.

It shivered the window, pane and sash;
It rent the banner with seam and gash.   30

Quick, as it fell, from the broken staff
Dame Barbara snatched the silken scarf.

She leaned far out on the window-sill,
And shook it forth with a royal will.

"Shoot, if you must, this old gray head,
But spare your country's flag," she said.

A shade of sadness, a blush of shame,
Over the face of the leader came;

The nobler nature within him stirred
To life at that woman's deed and word;   40

"Who touches a hair of yon gray head
Dies like a dog! March on!" he said.

All day long through Frederick street
Sounded the tread of marching feet:

All day long that free flag tost
Over the heads of the rebel host.

Ever its torn folds rose and fell
On the loyal winds that loved it well;

And through the hill-gaps sunset light
Shone over it with a warm good-night.   50

Barbara Frietchie's work is o'er,
And the Rebel rides on his raids no more.

Honor to her! and let a tear
Fall, for her sake, on Stonewall's bier.

Over Barbara Frietchie's grave,
Flag of Freedom and Union, wave!

Peace and order and beauty draw
Round thy symbol of light and law;

And ever the stars above look down
On thy stars below in Frederick town!   60

Laus Deo (1865)

On January 31, 1865, the Senate passed the resolution proposing the Thirteenth Amendment, abolishing slavery. On February 2, at Amesbury, while Whittier was sitting in the silence of the regular Fifth Day meeting of the Friends, he heard the bells and cannon proclaiming the event, and the poem "wrote itself, or rather sang itself," as he later described the process. This rapidity of composition was unusual for him. In spite of the slackness and roughness of much of his work, he wrote slowly and with effort.

The ratification of the Thirteenth Amendment was not officially proclaimed until December 18 of the same year.

It is done!
Clang of bell and roar of gun
Send the tidings up and down.
How the belfries rock and reel!
How the great guns, peal on peal,
Fling the joy from town to town!

Ring, O bells!
Every stroke exulting tells
Of the burial hour of crime.
Loud and long, that all may hear,   10
Ring for every listening ear
Of Eternity and Time!

Let us kneel:
God's own voice is in that peal,
And this spot is holy ground.
Lord, forgive us! What are we,
That our eyes this glory see,
That our ears have heard the sound!

For the Lord
On the whirlwind is abroad;   20
In the earthquake He has spoken;
He has smitten with His thunder
The iron walls asunder,
And the gates of brass are broken!

Loud and long
Lift the old exulting song;
Sing with Miriam by the sea,
He has cast the mighty down;

Horse and rider sink and drown;
"He hath triumphed gloriously!"   30

Did we dare,
In our agony of prayer,
Ask for more than He has done?
When was ever his right hand
Over any time or land
Stretched as now beneath the sun?

How they pale,
Ancient myth and song and tale,
In this wonder of our days,
When the cruel rod of war   40
Blossoms white with righteous law,
And the wrath of man is praise!

Blotted out!
All within and all about
Shall a fresher life begin;
Freer breathe the universe
As it rolls its heavy curse
On the dead and buried sin!

It is done!
In the circuit of the sun   50
Shall the sound thereof go forth.
It shall bid the sad rejoice,
It shall give the dumb a voice,
It shall belt with joy the earth!

Ring and swing,
Bells of joy! On morning's wing
Send the song of praise abroad!
With a sound of broken chains
Tell the nations that He reigns,
Who alone is Lord and God!   60

Snow-Bound: A Winter Idyl (1866)

To the Memory of the Household It Describes
This Poem Is Dedicated by the Author

The inmates of the family at the Whittier
homestead who are referred to in the poem
were my father, mother, my brother and
two sisters, and my uncle and aunt, both unmarried. In addition, there was the district
schoolmaster, who boarded with us. The "not
unfeared, half-welcome guest" was Harriet
Livermore, daughter of Judge Livermore, of
New Hampshire, a young woman of fine natu-

ral ability, enthusiastic, eccentric, with slight
control over her violent temper, which sometimes made her religious profession doubtful.
She was equally ready to exhort in school-
house prayer-meetings and dance in a Washington ball-room, while her father was a
member of congress. She early embraced the
doctrine of the Second Advent, and felt it
her duty to proclaim the Lord's speedy coming. With this message she crossed the Atlantic and spent the greater part of a long
life in traveling over Europe and Asia. She

lived some time with Lady Hester Stanhope, a woman as fantastic and mentally strained as herself, on the slope of Mt. Lebanon, but finally quarrelled with her in regard to two white horses with red marks on their backs which suggested the idea of saddles, on which her titled hostess expected to ride into Jerusalem with the Lord. A friend of mine found her, when quite an old woman, wandering in Syria with a tribe of Arabs, who with the Oriental notion that madness is inspiration, accepted her as their prophetess and leader. At the time referred to in *Snow-Bound* she was boarding at the Rocks Village, about two miles from us.

In my boyhood, in our lonely farm-house, we had scanty resources of information; few books and only a small weekly newspaper. Our only annual was the Almanac. Under such circumstances story-telling was a necessary resource in the long winter evenings. My father when a young man had traversed the wilderness to Canada, and could tell us of his adventures with Indians and wild beasts, and of his sojourn in the French villages. My uncle was ready with his record of hunting and fishing and, it must be confessed, with stories which he at least half-believed, of witchcraft and apparitions. My mother, who was born in the Indian-haunted region of Somersworth, New Hampshire, between Dover and Portsmouth, told us of the inroads of the savages, and the narrow escape of her ancestors. She described strange people who lived on the Piscataqua and Cocheco, among whom was Bantam the sorcerer. I have in my possession the wizard's "conjuring book," which he solemnly opened when consulted. It is a copy of Cornelius Agrippa's *Magic*, printed in 1651, dedicated to Dr. Robert Child, who, like Michael Scott, had learned

> "the art of glammorie
> In Padua beyond the sea,"

and who is famous in the annals of Massachusetts, where he was at one time a resident, as the first man who dared petition the General Court for liberty of conscience. The full title of the book is *Three Books of Occult Philosophy, by Henry Cornelius Agrippa, Knight, Doctor of both Laws, Counsellor to Caesar's Sacred Majesty and Judge of the Prerogative Court.*

"As the Spirits of Darkness be stronger in the dark, so Good Spirits, which be Angels of Light, are augmented not only by the Divine light of the Sun, but also by our common VVood Fire: and as the Celestial Fire drives away dark spirits, so also this our Fire of VVood doth the same." Cor. Agrippa, *Occult Philosophy*, Book I, ch. v.

"Announced by all the trumpets of the sky,
Arrives the snow, and, driving o'er the fields,
Seems nowhere to alight: the whited air
Hides hills and woods, the river, and the heaven,
And veils the farm-house at the garden's end.
The sled and traveller stopped, the courier's feet
Delayed, all friends shut out, the housemates sit
Around the radiant fireplace, enclosed
In a tumultuous privacy of storm."
Emerson, "The Snow-Storm"

The sun that brief December day
Rose cheerless over hills of gray,
And, darkly circled, gave at noon
A sadder light than waning moon.
Slow tracing down the thickening sky
Its mute and ominous prophecy,
A portent seeming less than threat,
It sank from sight before it set.
A chill no coat, however stout,
Of homespun stuff could quite shut out,   10
A hard, dull bitterness of cold,
That checked, mid-vein, the circling race
Of life-blood in the sharpened face,
The coming of the snow-storm told.
The wind blew east; we heard the roar
Of Ocean on his wintry shore,
And felt the strong pulse throbbing there
Beat with low rhythm our inland air.

Meanwhile we did our nightly chores,—
Brought in the wood from out of doors,—   20
Littered the stalls, and from the mows
Raked down the herd's-grass for the cows:
Heard the horse whinnying for his corn;
And, sharply clashing horn on horn,

Impatient down the stanchion rows
The cattle shake their walnut bows;
While, peering from his early perch
Upon the scaffold's pole of birch,
The cock his crested helmet bent
And down his querulous challenge sent.   30

Unwarmed by any sunset light
The gray day darkened into night,
A night made hoary with the swarm
And whirl-dance of the blinding storm,
As zigzag, wavering to and fro,
Crossed and recrossed the winged snow:
And ere the early bedtime came
The white drift piled the window-frame,
And through the glass the clothes-line posts
Looked in like tall and sheeted ghosts.   40

So all night long the storm roared on:
The morning broke without a sun;
In tiny spherule traced with lines
Of Nature's geometric signs,
In starry flake, and pellicle,
All day the hoary meteor fell;
And, when the second morning shone,
We looked upon a world unknown,
On nothing we could call our own.
Around the glistening wonder bent   50
The blue walls of the firmament,
No cloud above, no earth below,—
A universe of sky and snow!
The old familiar sights of ours
Took marvellous shapes; strange domes
          and towers
Rose up where sty or corn-crib stood,
Or garden-wall, or belt of wood;
A smooth white mound the brush-pile showed,
A fenceless drift what once was road;
The bridle-post an old man sat   60
With loose-flung coat and high cocked hat;
The well-curb had a Chinese roof;
And even the long sweep, high aloof,
In its slant splendor, seemed to tell
Of Pisa's leaning miracle.

A prompt, decisive man, no breath
Our father wasted: "Boys, a path!"
Well pleased, (for when did farmer boy
Count such a summons less than joy?)
Our buskins on our feet we drew;   70
With mittened hands, and caps drawn low,
To guard our necks and ears from snow,
We cut the solid whiteness through.
And, where the drift was deepest, made

A tunnel walled and overlaid
With dazzling crystal: we had read
Of rare Aladdin's wondrous cave,
And to our own his name we gave,
With many a wish the luck were ours
To test his lamp's supernal powers.   80
We reached the barn with merry din,
And roused the prisoned brutes within.
The old horse thrust his long head out,
And grave with wonder gazed about;
The cock his lusty greeting said,
And forth his speckled harem led;
The oxen lashed their tails, and hooked,
And mild reproach of hunger looked;
The hornèd patriarch of the sheep,
Like Egypt's Amun roused from sleep,   90
Shook his sage head with gesture mute,
And emphasized with stamp of foot.

All day the gusty north-wind bore
The loosening drift its breath before;
Low circling round its southern zone,
The sun through dazzling snow-mist shone.
No church-bell lent its Christian tone
To the savage air, no social smoke
Curled over woods of snow-hung oak.
A solitude made more intense   100
By dreary-voicèd elements,
The shrieking of the mindless wind,
The moaning tree-boughs swaying blind,
And on the glass the unmeaning beat
Of ghostly finger-tips of sleet.
Beyond the circle of our hearth
No welcome sound of toil or mirth
Unbound the spell, and testified
Of human life and thought outside.
We minded that the sharpest ear   110
The buried brooklet could not hear,
The music of whose liquid lip
Had been to us companionship,
And, in our lonely life, had grown
To have an almost human tone.

As night drew on, and, from the crest
Of wooded knolls that ridged the west,
The sun, a snow-blown traveller, sank
From sight beneath the smothering bank,
We piled, with care, our nightly stack   120
Of wood against the chimney-back,—
The oaken log, green, huge, and thick,
And on its top the stout back-stick;
The knotty forestick laid apart,
And filled between with curious art

The ragged brush; then, hovering near,
We watched the first red blaze appear,
Heard the sharp crackle, caught the gleam
On whitewashed wall and sagging beam,
Until the old, rude-furnished room   130
Burst, flower-like, into rosy bloom;
While radiant with a mimic flame
Outside the sparkling drift became,
And through the bare-boughed lilac-tree
Our own warm hearth seemed blazing free.
The crane and pendant trammels showed,
The Turks' heads on the andirons glowed;
While childish fancy, prompt to tell
The meaning of the miracle,
Whispered the old rhyme: *"Under the tree,*   140
When fire outdoors burns merrily,
There the witches are making tea."

The moon above the eastern wood
Shone at its full; the hill-range stood
Transfigured in the silver flood,
Its blown snows flashing cold and keen,
Dead white, save where some sharp ravine
Took shadow, or the sombre green
Of hemlocks turned to pitchy black
Against the whiteness at their back.   150
For such a world and such a night
Most fitting that unwarming light,
Which only seemed where'er it fell
To make the coldness visible.

Shut in from all the world without,
We sat the clean-winged hearth about,
Content to let the north wind roar
In baffled rage at pane and door,
While the red logs before us beat
The frost-line back with tropic heat;   160
And ever, when a louder blast
Shook beam and rafter as it passed,
The merrier up its roaring draught
The great throat of the chimney laughed;
The house-dog on his paws outspread
Laid to the fire his drowsy head,
The cat's dark silhouette on the wall
A couchant tiger's seemed to fall;
And, for the winter fireside meet,
Between the andirons' straddling feet,   170
The mug of cider simmered slow,
The apples sputtered in a row,
And, close at hand, the basket stood
With nuts from brown October's wood.

What matter how the night behaved?
What matter how the north-wind raved?

Blow high, blow low, not all its snow
Could quench our hearth-fire's ruddy glow.
O Time and Change!—with hair as gray
As was my sire's that winter day,   180
How strange it seems, with so much gone
Of life and love, to still live on!
Ah, brother! only I and thou
Are left of all that circle now,—
The dear home faces whereupon
That fitful firelight paled and shone.
Henceforward, listen as we will,
The voices of that hearth are still;
Look where we may, the wide earth o'er,
Those lighted faces smile no more.   190
We tread the paths their feet have worn,
    We sit beneath their orchard trees,
    We hear, like them, the hum of bees
And rustle of the bladed corn;
We turn the pages that they read,
    Their written words we linger o'er,
But in the sun they cast no shade,
No voice is heard, no sign is made,
    No step is on the conscious floor!
Yet Love will dream, and Faith will trust,   200
(Since He who knows our need is just,)
That somehow, somewhere, meet we must.
Alas for him who never sees
The stars shine through his cypress-trees!
Who, hopeless, lays his dead away,
Nor looks to see the breaking day
Across the mournful marbles play!
Who hath not learned, in hours of faith,
    The truth to flesh and sense unknown,
That Life is ever lord of Death,   210
    And Love can never lose its own!

We sped the time with stories old,
Wrought puzzles out, and riddles told,
Or stammered from our school-book lore
"The Chief of Gambia's golden shore."
How often since, when all the land
Was clay in Slavery's shaping hand,
As if a far-blown trumpet stirred
The languorous sin-sick air, I heard:
"Does not the voice of reason cry,   220
    Claim the first right which Nature gave,
From the red scourge of bondage fly,
    Nor deign to live a burdened slave!"
Our father rode again his ride
On Memphremagog's wooded side;
Sat down again to moose and samp
In trapper's hut and Indian camp;
Lived o'er the old idyllic ease

Beneath St. François' hemlock-trees;
Again for him the moonlight shone   230
On Norman cap and bodiced zone;
Again he heard the violin play
Which led the village dance away.
And mingled in its merry whirl
The grandam and the laughing girl.
Or, nearer home, our steps he led
Where Salisbury's level marshes spread
    Mile-wide as flies the laden bee;
Where merry mowers, hale and strong,
Swept, scythe on scythe, their swaths along   240
    The low green prairies of the sea.
We shared the fishing off Boar's Head,
    And round the rocky Isles of Shoals
    The hake-broil on the drift-wood coals;
The chowder on the sand-beach made,
Dipped by the hungry, steaming hot,
With spoons of clam-shell from the pot.
We heard the tales of witchcraft old,
And dream and sign and marvel told
To sleepy listeners as they lay   250
Stretched idly on the salted hay,
Adrift along the winding shores,
When favoring breezes deigned to blow
The square sail of the gundelow
And idle lay the useless oars.

Our mother, while she turned her wheel
Or run the new-knit stocking-heel,
Told how the Indian hordes came down
At midnight on Cocheco town,
And how her own great-uncle bore   260
His cruel scalp-mark to fourscore.
Recalling, in her fitting phrase,
    So rich and picturesque and free,
    (The common unrhymed poetry
Of simple life and country ways,)
The story of her early days,—
She made us welcome to her home;
Old hearths grew wide to give us room;
We stole with her a frightened look
At the gray wizard's conjuring-book,   270
The fame whereof went far and wide
Through all the simple country side;
We heard the hawks at twilight play,
The boat-horn on Piscataqua,
The loon's weird laughter far away;
We fished her little trout-brook, knew
What flowers in wood and meadow grew,
What sunny hillsides autumn-brown
She climbed to shake the ripe nuts down,
Saw where in sheltered cove and bay   280

The ducks' black squadron anchored lay,
And heard the wild geese calling loud
Beneath the gray November cloud.
Then, haply, with a look more grave,
And soberer tone, some tale she gave
From painful Sewel[l]'s ancient tome,
Beloved in every Quaker home,
Of faith fire-winged by martyrdom,
Or Chalkley's Journal, old and quaint,—
Gentlest of skippers, rare sea-saint!—   290
Who, when the dreary calms prevailed,
And water-butt and bread-cask failed,
And cruel, hungry eyes pursued
His portly presence mad for food,
With dark hints muttered under breath
Of casting lots for life or death,
Offered, if Heaven withheld supplies,
To be himself the sacrifice.
Then, suddenly, as if to save
The good man from his living grave,   300
A ripple on the water grew,
A school of porpoise flashed in view.
"Take, eat," he said, "and be content;
These fishes in my stead are sent
By Him who gave the tangled ram
To spare the child of Abraham."

Our uncle, innocent of books,
Was rich in lore of fields and brooks,
The ancient teachers never dumb
Of Nature's unhoused lyceum.   310
In moons and tides and weather wise,
He read the clouds as prophecies,
And foul or fair could well divine,
By many an occult hint and sign,
Holding the cunning-warded keys
To all the woodcraft mysteries;
Himself to Nature's heart so near
That all her voices in his ear
Of beast or bird had meanings clear,
Like Apollonius of old,   320
Who knew the tales the sparrows told,
Or Hermes who interpreted
What the sage cranes of Nilus said;
A simple, guileless, childlike man,
Content to live where life began;
Strong only on his native grounds,
The little world of sights and sounds
Whose girdle was the parish bounds,
Whereof his fondly partial pride
The common features magnified,   330
As Surrey hills to mountains grew
In White of Selborne's loving view,—

He told how teal and loon he shot,
And how the eagle's eggs he got,
The feats on pond and river done,
The prodigies of rod and gun;
Till, warming with the tales he told,
Forgotten was the outside cold,
The bitter wind unheeded blew,
From ripening corn the pigeons flew,   340
The partridge drummed i' the wood, the mink
Went fishing down the river-brink.
In fields with bean or clover gay,
The woodchuck, like a hermit gray,
  Peered from the doorway of his cell;
The muskrat plied the mason's trade,
And tier by tier his mud-walls laid;
And from the shagbark overhead
  The grizzled squirrel dropped his shell.

Next, the dear aunt, whose smile of cheer   350
And voice in dreams I see and hear,—
The sweetest woman ever Fate
Perverse denied a household mate,
Who, lonely, homeless, not the less
Found peace in love's unselfishness,
And welcome wheresoe'er she went,
A calm and gracious element,
Whose presence seemed the sweet income
And womanly atmosphere of home,—
Called up here girlhood memories,   360
The huskings and the apple-bees,
The sleigh-rides and the summer sails,
Weaving through all the poor details
And homespun warp of circumstance
A golden woof-thread of romance.
For well she kept her genial mood
And simple faith of maidenhood;
Before her still a cloud-land lay,
The mirage loomed across her way;
The morning dew, that dries so soon   370
With others, glistened at her noon;
Through years of toil and soil and care,
From glossy tress to thin gray hair,
All unprofaned she held apart
The virgin fancies of the heart.
Be shame to him of woman born
Who hath for such but thought of scorn.

There, too, our elder sister plied
Her evening task the stand beside;
A full, rich nature, free to trust,   380
Truthful and almost sternly just,
Impulsive, earnest, prompt to act,

And make her generous thought a fact,
Keeping with many a light disguise
The secret of self-sacrifice.
O heart sore-tried! thou hast the best
That Heaven itself could give thee,—rest,
Rest from all bitter thoughts and things!
  How many a poor one's blessing went
  With thee beneath the low green tent   390
Whose curtain never outward swings!

As one who held herself a part
Of all she saw, and let her heart
  Against the household bosom lean,
Upon the motley-braided mat
Our youngest and our dearest sat,
Lifting her large, sweet, asking eyes,
  Now bathed in the unfading green
And holy peace of Paradise.
Oh, looking from some heavenly hill,   400
  Or from the shade of saintly palms,
  Or silver reach of river calms,
Do those large eyes behold me still?
With me one little year ago:—
The chill weight of the winter snow
  For months upon her grave has lain;
And now, when summer south-winds blow
  And brier and harebell bloom again,
I tread the pleasant paths we trod,
I see the violet-sprinkled sod   410
Whereon she leaned, too frail and weak
The hillside flowers she loved to seek,
Yet following me where'er I went
With dark eyes full of love's content.
The birds are glad; the brier-rose fills
The air with sweetness; all the hills
Stretch green to June's unclouded sky;
But still I wait with ear and eye
For something gone which should be nigh,
A loss in all familiar things,   420
In flower that blooms, and bird that sings.
And yet, dear heart! remembering thee,
  Am I not richer than of old?
Safe in thy immortality,
  What change can reach the wealth I hold?
  What chance can mar the pearl and gold
Thy love hath left in trust with me?
And while in life's late afternoon,
  Where cool and long the shadows grow,
I walk to meet the night that soon   430
  Shall shape and shadow overflow,
I cannot feel that thou art far,
Since near at need the angels are;
And when the sunset gates unbar,

Shall I not see thee waiting stand,
And, white against the evening star,
    The welcome of thy beckoning hand?

Brisk wielder of the birch and rule,
The master of the district school
Held at the fire his favored place,   440
Its warm glow lit a laughing face
Fresh-hued and fair, where scarce appeared
The uncertain prophecy of beard.
He teased the mitten-blinded cat,
Played cross-pins on my uncle's hat,
Sang songs, and told us what befalls
In classic Dartmouth's college halls.
Born the wild Northern hills among,
From whence his yeoman father wrung
By patient toil subsistence scant,   450
Not competence and yet not want,
He early gained the power to pay
His cheerful, self-reliant way;
Could doff at ease his scholar's gown
To peddle wares from town to town;
Or through the long vacation's reach
In lonely lowland districts teach,
Where all the droll experience found
At stranger hearths in boarding round,
The moonlit skater's keen delight,   460
The sleigh-drive through the frosty night,
The rustic party, with its rough
Accompaniment of blind-man's-buff,
And whirling-plate, and forfeits paid,
His winter task a pastime made.
Happy the snow-locked homes wherein
He tuned his merry violin,
Or played the athlete in the barn,
Or held the good dame's winding-yarn,
Or mirth-provoking versions told   470
Of classic legends rare and old,
Wherein the scenes of Greece and Rome
Had all the commonplace of home,
And little seemed at best the odds
'Twixt Yankee pedlers and old gods;
Where Pindus-born Arachthus took
The guise of any grist-mill brook,
And dread Olympus at his will
Became a huckleberry hill.

A careless boy that night he seemed;   480
    But at his desk he had the look
And air of one who wisely schemed,
    And hostage from the future took
    In trainèd thought and lore of book
Large-brained, clear-eyed,—of such as he

Shall Freedom's young apostles be,
Who, following in War's bloody trail,
Shall every lingering wrong assail;
All chains from limb and spirit strike,
Uplift the black and white alike;   490
Scatter before their swift advance
The darkness and the ignorance,
The pride, the lust, the squalid sloth,
Which nurtured Treason's monstrous growth,
Made murder pastime, and the hell
Of prison-torture possible;
The cruel lie of caste refute,
Old forms remould, and substitute
For Slavery's lash the freeman's will,
For blind routine, wise-handed skill;   500
A school-house plant on every hill,
Stretching in radiate nerve-lines thence
The quick wires of intelligence;
Till North and South together brought
Shall own the same electric thought,
In peace a common flag salute,
And, side by side in labor's free
And unresentful rivalry,
Harvest the fields wherein they fought.

Another guest that winter night   510
Flashed back from lustrous eyes the light.
Unmarked by time, and yet not young,
The honeyed music of her tongue
And words of meekness scarcely told
A nature passionate and bold,
Strong, self-concentred, spurning guide,
Its milder features dwarfed beside
Her unbent will's majestic pride.
She sat among us, at the best,
A not unfeared, half-welcome guest,   520
Rebuking with her cultured phrase
Our homeliness of words and ways.
A certain pard-like, treacherous grace
    Swayed the lithe limbs and dropped the
        lash,
    Lent the white teeth their dazzling flash;
    And under low brows, black with night,
    Rayed out at times a dangerous light;
The sharp heat-lightnings of her face
Presaging ill to him whom Fate
Condemned to share her love or hate.   530
A woman tropical, intense
In thought and act, in soul and sense,
She blended in a like degree
The vixen and the devotee,
Revealing with each freak or feint
    The temper of Petruchio's Kate,

The raptures of Siena's saint.
Her tapering hand and rounded wrist
Had facile power to form a fist;
The warm, dark languish of her eyes   540
Was never safe from wrath's surprise.
Brows saintly calm and lips devout
Knew every change of scowl and pout;
And the sweet voice had notes more high
And shrill for social battle-cry.

Since then what old cathedral town
Has missed her pilgrim staff and gown,
What convent-gate has held its lock
Against the challenge of her knock!
Through Smyrna's plague-hushed thorough-
     fares,   550
Up sea-set Malta's rocky stairs,
Gray olive slopes of hills that hem
     Thy tombs and shrines, Jerusalem,
Or startling on her desert throne
The crazy Queen of Lebanon
With claims fantastic as her own,
Her tireless feet have held their way;
And still, unrestful, bowed, and gray,
She watches under Eastern skies,
     With hope each day renewed and fresh,   560
     The Lord's quick coming in the flesh,
Whereof she dreams and prophesies!

Where'er her troubled path may be,
     The Lord's sweet pity with her go!
The outward wayward life we see,
     The hidden springs we may not know.
Nor is it given us to discern
     What threads the fatal sisters spun,
     Through what ancestral years has run
The sorrow with the woman born,   570
What forged her cruel chain of moods,
What set her feet in solitudes,
     And held the love within her mute,
What mingled madness in the blood,
     A life-long discord and annoy,
     Waters of tears with oil of joy,
And hid within the folded bud
     Perversities of flower and fruit.
It is not ours to separate
     The tangled skein of will and fate,   580
To show what metes and bounds should
     stand
Upon the soul's debatable land,
And between choice and Providence
Divide the circle of events;
But He who knows our frame is just,

Merciful and compassionate,
And full of sweet assurances
And hope for all the language is,
That He remembereth we are dust!

At last the great logs, crumbling low,   590
Sent out a dull and duller glow,
The bull's-eye watch that hung in view,
Ticking its weary circuit through,
Pointed with mutely warning sign
Its black hand to the hour of nine.
That sign the pleasant circle broke:
My uncle ceased his pipe to smoke,
Knocked from its bowl the refuse gray,
And laid it tenderly away;
Then roused himself to safely cover   600
The dull red brands with ashes over.
And while, with care, our mother laid
The work aside, her steps she stayed
One moment, seeking to express
Her grateful sense of happiness
For food and shelter, warmth and health,
And love's contentment more than wealth,
With simple wishes (not the weak,
Vain prayers which no fulfilment seek,
But such as warm the generous heart,   610
O'er-prompt to do with Heaven its part)
That none might lack, that bitter night,
For bread and clothing, warmth and light.

Within our beds awhile we heard
The wind that round the gables roared,
With now and then a ruder shock,
Which made our very bedsteads rock.
We heard the loosened clapboards tost,
The board-nails snapping in the frost;
And on us, through the unplastered wall,   620
Felt the light sifted snow-flakes fall.
But sleep stole on, as sleep will do
When hearts are light and life is new;
Faint and more faint the murmurs grew,
Till in the summer-land of dreams
They softened to the sound of streams,
Low stir of leaves, and dip of oars,
And lapsing waves on quiet shores.

Next morn we wakened with the shout
Of merry voices high and clear;   630
And saw the teamsters drawing near
To break the drifted highways out.
Down the long hillside treading slow
We saw the half-buried oxen go,
Shaking the snow from heads uptost,
Their straining nostrils white with frost.

Before our door the straggling train
Drew up, an added team to gain.
The elders threshed their hands a-cold,
 Passed, with the cider-mug, their jokes 640
 From lip to lip; the younger folks
Down the loose snow-banks, wrestling, rolled,
Then toiled again the cavalcade
 O'er windy hill, through clogged ravine,
 And woodland paths that wound between
Low drooping pine-boughs winter-weighed.
From every barn a team afoot,
At every house a new recruit,
Where, drawn by Nature's subtlest law,
Haply the watchful young men saw 650
Sweet doorway pictures of the curls
And curious eyes of merry girls,
Lifting their hands in mock defence
Against the snow-ball's compliments,
And reading in each missive tost
The charm with Eden never lost.

We heard once more the sleigh-bells' sound;
 And, following where the teamsters led,
The wise old Doctor went his round,
Just pausing at our door to say, 660
In the brief autocratic way
Of one who, prompt at Duty's call,
Was free to urge her claim on all,
 That some poor neighbor sick abed
At night our mother's aid would need.
For, one in generous thought and deed,
 What mattered in the sufferer's sight
 The Quaker matron's inward light,
The Doctor's mail of Calvin's creed?
All hearts confess the saints elect 670
 Who, twain in faith, in love agree,
And melt not in an acid sect
 The Christian pearl of charity!

So days went on: a week had passed
Since the great world was heard from last.
The Almanac we studied o'er,
Read and reread our little store
Of books and pamphlets, scarce a score;
One harmless novel, mostly hid
From younger eyes, a book forbid, 680
And poetry, (or good or bad,
A single book was all we had,)
Where Ellwood's meek, drab-skirted Muse,
 A stranger to the heathen Nine,
 Sang, with a somewhat nasal whine,
The wars of David and the Jews.
At last the floundering carrier bore

The village paper to our door.
Lo! broadening outward as we read,
To warmer zones the horizon spread; 690
In panoramic length unrolled
We saw the marvels that it told.
Before us passed the painted Creeks,
 And daft McGregor on his raids
 In Costa Rica's everglades.
And up Taygetos winding slow
Rode Ypsilanti's Mainote Greeks,
A Turk's head at each saddle-bow!
Welcome to us its week-old news,
Its corner for the rustic Muse, 700
 Its monthly gauge of snow and rain,
Its record, mingling in a breath
The wedding bell and dirge of death;
Jest, anecdote, and love-lorn tale,
The latest culprit sent to jail;
Its hue and cry of stolen and lost,
Its vendue sales and goods at cost,
 And traffic calling loud for gain.
We felt the stir of hall and street,
The pulse of life that round us beat; 710
The chill embargo of the snow
Was melted in the genial glow;
Wide swung again our ice-locked door,
And all the world was ours once more!

Clasp, Angel of the backward look
 And folded wings of ashen gray
 And voice of echoes far away,
The brazen covers of thy book;
The weird palimpsest old and vast,
Wherein thou hid'st the spectral past; 720
Where, closely mingling, pale and glow
The characters of joy and woe;
The monographs of outlived years,
Or smile-illumed or dim with tears,
 Green hills of life that slope to death,
And haunts of home, whose vistaed trees
Shade off to mournful cypresses
 With the white amaranths underneath.
Even while I look, I can but heed
 The restless sands' incessant fall, 730
Importunate hours that hours succeed,
Each clamorous with its own sharp need,
 And duty keeping pace with all.
Shut down and clasp the heavy lids;
I hear again the voice that bids
The dreamer leave his dream midway
For larger hopes and graver fears;
Life greatens in these later years,
The century's aloe flowers to-day!

Yet, haply, in some lull of life,   740
Some Truce of God, which breaks its strife,
The worldling's eyes shall gather dew,
    Dreaming in throngful city ways
Of winter joys his boyhood knew;
And dear and early friends—the few
Who yet remain—shall pause to view
    These Flemish pictures of old days;
Sit with me by the homestead hearth,
And stretch the hands of memory forth

To warm them at the wood-fire's blaze!   750
And thanks untraced to lips unknown
Shall greet me like the odors blown
From unseen meadows newly mown,
Or lilies floating in some pond,
Wood-fringed, the wayside gaze beyond;
The traveller owns the grateful sense
Of sweetness near, he knows not whence,
And, pausing, takes with forehead bare
The benediction of the air.

Abraham Davenport (1866)

Whittier, with his usual literalism, remarks in a note on the poem that this event of Davenport's "sturdy protest" on the "Dark Day" of May 19, 1780, is "a matter of history." Whittier's imagination, in fact, always worked best on a short tether.

As for this poem, it illustrates at its highest pitch Whittier's talent for sketching a character. It also shows a talent for narrative and dramatic effects which rarely comes into play in his ballads, where it would seem to be most in order. There is a splendid comment on the poem in an essay called "Whittier Reconsidered," by Howard Mumford Jones:

> The secret of the excellence of "Abraham Davenport" lies in its fusion *of low relief with salient observations*. The metrical tone is faint, like Crabbe's, but the pattern is always *there*, is always gently persistent so that it can carry even the formal description of the threatening sky without melodrama. Against its gentle beat various important observations seem projected by an impulse that is partly respect, partly humor. We laugh at what we love, and, obviously, Whittier loves Abraham Davenport and can therefore afford to laugh at him a little. Note the amusing repetition of verbs placed first in the line, towards the end of the second section— "roosted," "lowed," "flitted," and then the variation that follows—"men prayed and women wept." The deliberate simplicity of

> "Bring in the candles." And they brought them in.

> cannot be bettered in its place, nor can the contrast between the husky voice and shaking hands of the Speaker and the mock solemnity of

> > An act to amend an act to regulate
> > The shad and alewise fisheries.

> The writer is so at ease with his material, he can take time out for a little play with figures of speech and figures of arithmetic; and even the last line, which in another poem—say, "Conductor Bradley"—might be tedious, is caught up in the wonderful atmosphere of irony and heroism, admiration and anti-climax Whittier achieves. Indeed, the irony of the penultimate

> > A witness to the ages as they pass

> might be that of Frost or Robinson.

The critic is right. This poem, like certain passages in *Snow-Bound*, is one of discovery. On a few occasions, Whittier made, or seemed on the verge of making, a breakthrough of the staggering sort made by Whitman, Emily Dickinson, and Melville. One is almost tempted to say that Whittier knew too little about poetry and that what he knew, he knew in the wrong way, just as Longfellow knew too much and knew it in the wrong way. Neither, in other words, trusted himself; neither had "innocence," in the way that Whitman, Dickinson, or Melville did—or Milton, for that matter, for "learning" has little to do with this question. The kind of innocence we mean here is an openness to experience—a thing that sometimes learning may help to achieve and ignorance may prevent.

In the old days (a custom laid aside
With breeches and cocked hats) the people sent
Their wisest men to make the public laws.
And so, from a brown homestead, where the Sound
Drinks the small tribute of the Mianas,
Waved over by the woods of Rippowams,
And hallowed by pure lives and tranquil deaths,
Stamford sent up to the councils of the State
Wisdom and grace in Abraham Davenport.

'Twas on a May-day of the far old year   10
Seventeen hundred eighty, that there fell
Over the bloom and sweet life of the Spring,
Over the fresh earth and the heaven of noon,
A horror of great darkness, like the night
In day of which the Norland sagas tell,—
The Twilight of the Gods. The low-hung sky
Was black with ominous clouds, save where its rim
Was fringed with a dull glow, like that which climbs
The crater's sides from the red hell below.
Birds ceased to sing, and all the barn-yard fowls   20
Roosted; the cattle at the pasture bars
Lowed, and looked homeward; bats on leathern wings
Flitted abroad; the sounds of labor died;
Men prayed, and women wept; all ears grew sharp
To hear the doom-blast of the trumpet shatter
The black sky, that the dreadful face of Christ
Might look from the rent clouds, not as he looked
A loving guest at Bethany, but stern
As Justice and inexorable Law.

Meanwhile in the old State House, dim as ghosts   30
Sat the lawgivers of Connecticut,
Trembling beneath their legislative robes.
"It is the Lord's Great Day! Let us adjourn,"
Some said; and then, as if with one accord,
All eyes were turned to Abraham Davenport.
He rose, slow cleaving with his steady voice
The intolerable hush. "This well may be
The Day of Judgment which the world awaits;
But be it so or not, I only know
My present duty, and my Lord's command   40
To occupy till He come. So at the post
Where He hath set me in his providence,
I choose, for one, to meet Him face to face,—
No faithless servant frightened from my task,
But ready when the Lord of the harvest calls;
And therefore, with all reverence, I would say,
Let God do his work, we will see to ours.
Bring in the candles." And they brought them in.

Then by the flaring lights the Speaker read,
Albeit with husky voice and shaking hands,   50
An act to amend an act to regulate
The shad and alewive fisheries. Whereupon
Wisely and well spake Abraham Davenport,
Straight to the questions, with no figures of speech
Save the ten Arab signs, yet not without
The shrewd dry humor natural to the man:
His awe-struck colleagues listening all the while,
Between the pauses of his argument,
To hear the thunder of the wrath of God
Break from the hollow trumpet of the cloud.   60

And there he stands in memory to this day,
Erect, self-poised, a rugged face, half seen
Against the background of unnatural dark,
A witness to the ages as they pass,
That simple duty hath no place for fear.

The Hive at Gettysburg (1869)

In the old Hebrew myth the lion's frame,
    So terrible alive,
Bleached by the desert's sun and wind, became
    The wandering wild bees' hive;
And he who, lone and naked-handed, tore

Those jaws of death apart,
In after time drew forth their honeyed store
    To strengthen his strong heart.
Dead seemed the legend: but it only slept
    To wake beneath our sky;   10

Just on the spot whence ravening Treason
  crept
  Back to its lair to die,
Bleeding and torn from Freedom's mountain
  bounds,
  A stained and shattered drum
Is now the hive where, on their flowery
  rounds,
  The wild bees go and come.

Unchallenged by a ghostly sentinel,
  They wander wide and far,
Along green hillsides, sown with shot and
  shell,
  Through vales once choked with war.   20

The low reveille of their battle-drum
  Disturbs no morning prayer:
  With deeper peace in summer noons their
    hum
  Fills all the drowsy air.

And Samson's riddle is our own to-day,
  Of sweetness from the strong,
Of union, peace, and freedom plucked away
  From the rent jaws of wrong.
From Treason's death we draw a purer life,
  As, from the beast he slew,   30
A sweetness sweeter for his bitter strife
  The old-time athlete drew!

Among the Hills: Prelude (1868)

This "Prelude" introduces one of Whittier's several ballads about love across a social and economic bar. The ballad itself, beyond this biographical echo, is not interesting, but the "Prelude" is notable in several ways. For one thing, the nostalgic emotion of *Snow-Bound* reappears here, though more fitfully, and modified, especially in the section of lines 45 to 98, by realistic and witty effects. For another thing, the fluidity and variety in the handling of the blank verse (a form Whittier rarely used) is in contrast to the patter of much of his work; and this fact suggests that he had allowed himself to be trapped into a mechanical repetitiousness which throttled technical and, one might say, spiritual possibilities. In general, this blank verse is superior to his rhymed verse, but he apparently needed the rhyme and the tight stanza. Perhaps he needed the "bricks" ready shaped to his hand; they were "safer."

Along the roadside, like the flowers of gold
That tawny Incas for their gardens wrought,
Heavy with sunshine droops the goldenrod,
And the red pennons of the cardinal-flowers
Hang motionless upon their upright staves.
The sky is hot and hazy, and the wind,
Wing-weary with its long flight from the
  south,
Unfelt; yet, closely scanned, yon maple leaf
With faintest motion, as one stirs in dreams,

Confesses it. The locust by the wall   10
Stabs the noon-silence with his sharp alarm.
A single hay-cart down the dusty road
Creaks slowly, with its driver fast asleep
On the load's top. Against the neighboring
  hill,
Huddled along the stone wall's shady side,
The sheep show white, as if a snowdrift still
Defied the dog-star. Through the open door
A drowsy smell of flowers—gray heliotrope,
And white sweet clover, and shy mignonette—
Comes faintly in, and silent chorus lends   20
To the pervading symphony of peace.

No time is this for hands long overworn
To task their strength: and (unto Him be
  praise
Who giveth quietness!) the stress and strain
Of years that did the work of centuries
Have ceased, and we can draw our breath once
  more
Freely and full. So, as yon harvesters
Make glad their nooning underneath the elms
With tale and riddle and old snatch of song,
I lay aside grave themes, and idly turn   30
The leaves of memory's sketch-book, dreaming
  o'er
Old summer pictures of the quiet hills,
And human life, as quiet, at their feet.

And yet not idly all. A farmer's son,
Proud of field-lore and harvest craft, and
  feeling
All their fine possibilities, how rich
And restful even poverty and toil

Become when beauty, harmony, and love
Sit at their humble hearth as angels sat
At evening in the patriarch's tent, when man   40
Makes labor noble, and his farmer's frock
The symbol of a Christian chivalry
Tender and just and generous to her
Who clothes with grace all duty; still, I know
Too well the picture has another side,—
How wearily the grind of toil goes on
Where love is wanting, how the eye and ear
And heart are starved amidst the plenitude
Of nature, and how hard and colorless
Is life without an atmosphere. I look   50
Across the lapse of half a century,
And call to mind old homesteads, where no
    flower
Told that the spring had come, but evil weeds,
Nightshade and rough-leaved burdock in the
    place
Of the sweet doorway greeting of the rose
And honeysuckle, where the house walls
    seemed
Blistering in sun, without a tree or vine
To cast the tremulous shadow of its leaves
Across the curtainless windows, from whose
    panes
Fluttered the signal rags of shiftlessness.   60
Within, the cluttered kitchen floor, unwashed
(Broom-clean I think they called it); the best
    room
Stifling with cellar-damp, shut from the air
Save the inevitable sampler hung
In hot midsummer bookless, pictureless
Over the fireplace, or a mourning piece,
A green-haired woman, peony-cheeked, be-
    neath
Impossible willows; the wide-throated hearth
Bristling with faded pine-boughs half con-
    cealing
The piled-up rubbish at the chimney's back;   70
And, in sad keeping with all things about
    them
Shrill, querulous women, sour and sullen men,
Untidy, loveless, old before their time,
With scarce a human interest save their own
Monotonous round of small economies,
Or the poor scandal of the neighborhood;
Blind to the beauty everywhere revealed,
Treading the May-flowers with regardless feet;
For them the song-sparrow and the bobolink
Sang not, nor winds made music in the leaves;   80
For them in vain October's holocaust
Burned, gold and crimson, over all the hills,

The sacramental mystery of the woods.
Church-goers, fearful of the unseen Powers,
But grumbling over pulpit-tax and pew-rent,
Saving, as shrewd economists, their souls
And winter pork with the least possible outlay
Of salt and sanctity; in daily life
Showing as little actual comprehension
Of Christian charity and love and duty,   90
As if the Sermon on the Mount had been
Outdated like a last year's almanac:
Rich in broad woodlands and in half-tilled
    fields,
And yet so pinched and bare and comfortless,
The veriest straggler limping on his rounds,
The sun and air his sole inheritance,
Laughed at a poverty that paid its taxes,
And hugged his rags in self-complacency!

Not such should be the homesteads of a land
Where whoso wisely wills and acts may dwell   100
As king and lawgiver, in broad-acred state,
With beauty, art, taste, culture, books, to
    make
His hour of leisure richer than a life
Of fourscore to the barons of old time,
Our yeoman should be equal to his home
Set in the fair, green valleys, purple walled,
A man to match his mountains, not to creep
Dwarfed and abased below them. I would
    fain
In this light way (of which I needs must own
With the knife-grinder of whom Canning   110
    sings,
"Story, God bless you! I have none to tell
    you!")
Invite the eye to see and heart to feel
The beauty and the joy within their reach,—
Home, and home loves, and the beatitudes
Of nature free to all. Haply in years
That wait to take the places of our own,
Heard where some breezy balcony looks down
On happy homes, or where the lake in the
    moon
Sleeps dreaming of the mountains, fair as
    Ruth,
In the old Hebrew pastoral, at the feet   120
Of Boaz, even this simple lay of mine
May seem the burden of a prophecy,
Finding its late fulfilment in a change
Slow as the oak's growth, lifting manhood up
Through broader culture, finer manners, love,
And reverence, to the level of the hills.
O Golden Age, whose light is of the dawn,

And not of sunset, forward, not behind,
Flood the new heavens and earth, and with
  thee bring
All the old virtues, whatsoever things   130
Are pure and honest and of good repute,
But add thereto whatever bard has sung
Or seer has told of when in trance and dream
They saw the Happy Isles of prophecy!
Let Justice hold her scale, and Truth divide
Between the right and wrong; but give the
  heart
The freedom of its fair inheritance;
Let the poor prisoner, cramped and starved
  so long,
At Nature's table feast his ear and eye
With joy and wonder; let all harmonies   140

Of sound, form, color, motion, wait upon
The princely guest, whether in soft attire
Of leisure clad, or the coarse frock of toil,
And, lending life to the dead form of faith,
Give human nature reverence for the sake
Of One who bore it, making it divine
With the ineffable tenderness of God;
Let common need, the brotherhood of prayer,
The heirship of an unknown destiny,
The unsolved mystery round about us, make   150
A man more precious than the gold of Ophir.
Sacred, inviolate, unto whom all things
Should minister, as outward types and signs
Of the eternal beauty which fulfils
The one great purpose of creation, Love,
The sole necessity of Earth and Heaven!

In School-Days (1870)

Still sits the school-house by the road,
  A ragged beggar sunning;
Around it still the sumachs grow,
  And blackberry-vines are running.

Within, the master's desk is seen,
  Deep scarred by raps official;
The warping floor, the battered seats,
  The jack-knife's carved initial;

The charcoal frescos on its wall;
  Its door's worn sill, betraying   10
The feet that, creeping slow to school,
  Went storming out to playing!

Long years ago a winter sun
  Shone over it at setting;
Lit up its western window-panes,
  And low eaves' icy fretting.

It touched the tangled golden curls,
  And brown eyes full of grieving,
Of one who still her steps delayed
  When all the school were leaving.   20

For near her stood the little boy
  Her childish favor singled:

His cap pulled low upon a face
  Where pride and shame were mingled

Pushing with restless feet the snow
  To right and left, he lingered;—
As restlessly her tiny hands
  The blue-checked apron fingered.

He saw her lift her eyes; he felt
  The soft hand's light caressing,   30
And heard the tremble of her voice,
  As if a fault confessing.

"I'm sorry that I spelt the word:
  I hate to go above you,
Because,"—the brown eyes lower fell,—
  "Because, you see, I love you!"

Still memory to a gray-haired man
  That sweet child-face is showing.
Dear girl! the grasses on her grave
  Have forty years been growing!   40

He lives to learn, in life's hard school,
  How few who pass above him
Lament their trumph and his loss,
  Like her,—because they love him.

The Pressed Gentian (1876)

This poem affords one of the rare instances in which we can see, if not an influence from, at least an affinity with the seventeenth-century poets whom Whittier read. The poem is based on the sort of "conceit" the earlier poets had used, and Whittier develops it in much the same way, but without the degree of complication and precision characteristic of the best "metaphysical" poetry of the seventeenth century, or the dramatic intensity.

The time of gifts has come again,
And, on my northern window-pane,
Outlined against the day's brief light,
A Christmas token hangs in sight.
The wayside travellers, as they pass,
Mark the gray disk of clouded glass;
And the dull blankness seems, perchance,
Folly to their wise ignorance.

They cannot from their outlook see
The perfect grace it hath for me;   10
For there the flower, whose fringes through
The frosty breath of autumn blew,
Turns from without its face of bloom

To the warm tropic of my room,
As fair as when beside its brook
The hue of bending skies it took.

So from the trodden ways of earth,
Seem some sweet souls who veil their worth,
And offer to the careless glance
The clouding gray of circumstance.   20
They blossom best where hearth-fires burn,
To loving eyes alone they turn
The flowers of inward grace, that hide
Their beauty from the world outside.

But deeper meanings come to me,
My half-immortal flower, from thee!
Man judges from a partial view,
None ever yet his brother knew;
The Eternal Eye that sees the whole
May better read the darkened soul,   30
And find, to outward sense denied,
The flower upon its inmost side!

At Last (1882)

When on my day of life the night is falling,
    And, in the winds from unsunned spaces
        blown,
I hear far voices out of darkness calling
    My feet to paths unknown,

Thou who hast made my home of life so
        pleasant,
    Leave not its tenant when its walls decay;
O Love Divine, O Helper ever present,
    Be Thou my strength and stay!

Be near me when all else is from me drifting;
    Earth, sky, home's pictures, days of shade
        and shine,   10
And kindly faces to my own uplifting
    The love which answers mine.

I have but Thee, my Father! let Thy spirit
    Be with me then to comfort and uphold;
No gate of pearl, no branch of palm I merit,

Nor street of shining gold.

Suffice it if—my good and ill unreckoned,
    And both forgiven through Thy abounding
        grace—
I find myself by hands familiar beckoned
    Unto my fitting place.   20

Some humble door among Thy many mansions,
    Some sheltering shade where sin and striving
        cease,
And flows forever through heaven's green expansions
    The river of Thy peace.

There, from the music round about me stealing,
    I fain would learn the new and holy song,
And find at last, beneath Thy trees of healing,
    The life for which I long.

To Oliver Wendell Holmes (1892)

Even before the death of Lowell, in August, 1891, Whittier and Holmes were often bracketed together, and Whittier wrote Holmes:

"Ever since I heard the sad news of Lowell's death, I have been thinking of thee, and longing to see thee, for we are now standing alone."

They were the last of the group of famous writers to appear in New England before the Civil War, and as they were more and more alone, the warmth of their friendship increased. On the occasion of Whittier's eighty-fourth birthday, December 17, 1891, Holmes wrote him a complimentary letter in which he said:

At our age we must live chiefly in the past; happy is he who has a past like yours to look back upon. It is one of the felicitous incidents —I will not say accidents—of my life that the lapse of time has brought us very near together, so that I frequently find myself honored by my name being mentioned in near connection with your own.

Whittier's poem to Holmes was written in the summer of 1892, when he was very feeble and verging toward his last illness. His last letter to Holmes concerned the poem: "I wrote the verse in a great hurry, as I knew the time of publication in the Atlantic for September was near. . . . It was written on the hottest day of the season, and that must excuse its defects." The letter is dated August 26. Whittier died on September 7. Holmes wrote a tribute to him, which begins:

Thou, too, has left us. While with heads bowed low,
    And sorrowing hearts, we mourned our summer's dead,
The flying season bent its Parthian bow,
    And yet again our mingled tears were shed.

Holmes survived Whittier by two years.

Among the thousands who with hail and cheer
    Will welcome thy new year,
How few of all have passed, as thou and I,
    So many milestones by!

We have grown old together; we have seen,
    Our youth and age between,
Two generations leave us, and to-day
    We with the third hold way,

Loving and loved. If thought must backward run
    To those who, one by one,   10

In the great silence and the dark beyond
    Vanished with farewells fond,

Unseen, not lost; our grateful memories still
    Their vacant places fill,
And with the full-voiced greeting of new friends
    A tenderer whisper blends.

Linked close in a pathetic brotherhood
    Of mingled ill and good,
Of joy and grief, of grandeur and of shame,
    For pity more than blame,—   20

The gift is thine the weary world to make
    More cheerful for thy sake,
Soothing the ears its Miserere pains,
    With the old Hellenic strains,

Lighting the sullen face of discontent
    With smiles for blessing sent.
Enough of selfish wailing has been had,
    Thank God! for notes more glad.

Life is indeed no holiday; therein
    Are want, and woe, and sin   30
Death and its nameless fears, and over all
    Our pitying tears must fall.

Sorrow is real; but the counterfeit
    Which folly brings to it,
We need thy wit and wisdom to resist,
    O rarest Optimist!

Thy hand, old friend! the service of our days,
    In differing moods and ways,
May prove to those who follow in our train
    Not valueless nor vain.   40

Far off, and faint as echoes of a dream,
    The songs of boyhood seem,
Yet on our autumn boughs, unflown with spring,
    The evening thrushes sing.

The hour draws near, howe'er delayed and late,
    When at the Eternal Gate
We leave the words and works we call our own,
    And lift void hands alone

For love to fill. Our nakedness of soul
    Brings to that Gate no toll;   50
Giftless we come to Him, who all things gives,
    And live because He lives.

HENRY WADSWORTH LONGFELLOW
(1807–1882)

One might say that if Longfellow had not been born, the times would have created him. When, in 1807, Longfellow was born, the rigors of Puritanism had long since been relaxed, and the more recent ardors of the Revolution were being absorbed into the new period of commercial and industrial development and national consolidation. This was also the period when America, of which New England felt itself to be the prime manifestation, was trying to create an American literature, and at the same time, paradoxically enough, was reaching out to establish contact with the older culture of Europe. Longfellow was the nearly perfect embodiment of the various impulses of the time, but with their tensions and raw edges mollified; he was, in fact, so well endowed with a genius for easy synthesis that his role of reconciliator in the midst of the strains of transition seemed painless and natural. And the role absorbed the man.

Not only the time but the place of Longfellow's birth was a determinant of this role. Portland—with Maine still a territory of Massachusetts—touched, on the one hand, the thriving, pushing world of the counting house and seaborne trade, with strange tongues spoken in the streets and, on the other hand, the farms and forests of the frontier. Years later, when Longfellow had achieved a greater "eminence in literature" than even his boyhood dreams had promised him, he wrote his finest poem, "My Lost Youth," about the Portland of his boyhood, "the beautiful town . . . seated by the sea." On March 30, 1855, he was to make the entry in his journal: "Wrote the poem; and am rather pleased with it, and with the bringing in of the two lines of the old Lapland song. 'A boy's will is the wind's will,/And the thoughts of youth are long, long thoughts.'"

Nostalgic yearnings and the tug of European scholarship—it is symbolically apt that the distinguished professor of languages, stung to the beautiful poem by nocturnal memories of the little city of his boyhood, should preen himself on having adapted his haunting refrain not, as a matter of fact, from the original language but from a German translation by Herder. Portland and the German version of the Lapland song: the whole story of his role is there. In this rare instance the role was dominated by the man, for the personal urgency and the memory of Portland absorbed and informed the little trophy of scholarship on which the author prided himself in the journal. It would not often be the case.

The history of the family into which the poet was born was also appropriate for his role. The scholar and poet who was to bring American letters into easy relation with Europe, and who was to be honored by Queen Victoria's conversation and a bust in Westminster Abbey, had his roots deep in the American past. His paternal grandfather had been a distinguished lawyer and jurist, and a member of the Massachusetts legislature. His father, a graduate of Harvard and a trustee of the new Bowdoin College, was also a lawyer and member of Congress with a handsome brick house in Portland and a piano. The maternal line of Wadsworth was even more noteworthy, including John Alden and Priscilla Mullens (for whom the poet secured a modest niche in the American pantheon by writing *The Courtship of Miles Standish*), and two military heroes, Peleg Wadsworth, a general in the Revolution, and Henry Wadsworth, who, as a lieutenant on the *Intrepid*, was lost in the harbor of Tripoli when, in 1804, the vessel was blown up to prevent its capture. The Wadsworths not only gave the poet the glamor of military tradition; on the great holdings of the old general the boy got some acquaintance with the lonely life of forest and frontiersman's cabin which reached back to the time before the towns like Portland, with brick houses and pianos, had come to be.

Longfellow's life was an almost unbroken series of professional successes. His career at Bowdoin (the entrance examinations for which he passed at fourteen) was exemplary. Already he had local fame as a poet, and in his commencement oration, "Our Native Writers," he promised himself that in a society where there had been no profession of letters he would, to the "utter abandonment of everything else," give himself with "a noble self-devotion to the cause of literature." His father, pointing out the hard fact that America had not yet achieved the margin of money and leisure to support a literature, urged the law. Longfellow compromised for one more year of literary study, this to be at Harvard, before settling down.

But luck—so different from the luck that immured Hawthorne in his dismal chamber under the eaves—played into his hands. Bowdoin was to establish a chair of modern languages, and the post was offered to the new graduate, with the stipulation that he should go to Europe to prepare himself. In 1829, having learned Spanish, French, Italian, and German, he came back to Bowdoin. He wrote textbooks (no suitable ones then existing in English), scholarly articles, and, as an imitation of Washington Irving's *Sketch Book*, a prose account of his travels called *Outre-Mer*. At Bowdoin there was little temptation to do anything but work; after the wider horizons of Madrid, Paris, and Rome, he was bored to distraction by the local conversation, which was conducted solely in English.

Luck, however, was with him again. The eminent scholar George Ticknor—the founding father of the study of modern languages in America—was resigning his post at Harvard, and Longfellow was appointed to succeed him. Again, he went to Europe before taking up his duties. On this trip occurred the first of the personal tragedies that punctuated the career of professional success. Longfellow's wife suffered a miscarriage and died shortly afterward. But before his return to America—lucky again—he met and fell in love with the young lady, Fanny Appleton, whose hand, after several years, he was to win.

Back at Cambridge he became a lodger in the handsome Craigie House, the home of the widow of Andrew Craigie, of Washington's staff. Longfellow's career at Harvard, in spite of comment provoked by his tendency to foreign foppishness, and a growing impatience with the routine of the profession, was a great public success, and his literary career, in spite of bouts of bad health and eye strain, which he shrewdly took as psychosomatic in origin, led him rapidly to fame. In 1839 he published *Hyperion,* a prose romance after the reigning German fashion and, like his earlier *Outre-Mer,* an echo of both his foreign travels and the picturesque legends that had fired his imagination and were to become the subject matter of so much of his later poetry. The work also contained hints of his continuing pursuit of Fanny Appleton, not well enough disguised to prevent a little stir at his indelicacy, an indelicacy that may, in fact, have contributed to the considerable popularity of the work.

In the same year, Longfellow achieved a more significant success. His first volume of verse, *Voices of the Night,* appeared, containing "Hymn to the Night" and "A Psalm of Life,"[1] and the fame thus secured was compounded in 1841 by *Ballads and Other Poems,* in which appeared "The Wreck of the Hesperus," "The Skeleton in Armor," "The Village Blacksmith," and "Excelsior."

If further confirmation of his luck was needed, it came in 1843, with his marriage to Fanny Appleton. She was not only good-looking, charming, appropriately intellectual, and devoted; she was also—or would be—rich, and in handsome earnest of the fact her father bought Craigie House and presented it to the happy pair. For they were happy—in the six children, in the professional triumphs, in a host of friends, in world fame, in the elegance of their house and the variety of its wine closet. One day in 1861, George William Curtis, driving with Dr. Oliver Wendell Holmes, remarked that he trembled to look at Craigie House, which they were then passing, for the Longfellows "had

---

[1] Also in the volume, adumbrating one of Longfellow's most significant achievements, were translations of parts of four cantos of Dante's *Purgatorio*.

their happiness so perfect that no change, of all changes that must come to them, could fail to be for the worse." Some days later, the light dress Mrs. Longfellow was wearing caught fire and she was burned to death. Longfellow was severely injured trying to save her.

From prostrating grief, Longfellow took refuge in translating the *Divina Commedia* of Dante, which he had begun twenty years earlier. Around the work on Dante gathered, on Wednesday evenings, a group of learned friends —James Russell Lowell, Charles Eliot Norton, William Dean Howells, and James Thomas Fields—who served as critics. Also conspiring to numb the pain of bereavement were other projects, other friends, and, of course, the inevitable distractions of fame: the visits of eminent foreigners such as Dickens, Trollope, Dom Pedro II, Emperor of Brazil, and Mikhail Bakunin, the Russian anarchist just escaped from Siberia; foreign travel; and a flood of honors, including an LL.D. from Cambridge, a D.C.L. from Oxford, and the summons to an audience with Queen Victoria.

In college, Longfellow had written to his father: "I most eagerly aspire after future eminence in literature, my whole soul burns most ardently after it, and every earthly thought centers in it." In spite of the fact that success came easily to him, and in spite of his talent for insulating himself from unpleasant criticism, he did occasionally suffer, along the way, from "despair" at the "utter impossibility . . . to lay hold upon anything permanent." At the end, however, he seems to have felt himself securely at the top. On his seventy-fourth birthday he makes this entry in his journal:

I am surrounded by roses and lilies. Flowers everywhere,—

And that which should accompany old age, As honor, love, obedience, troops of friends.

He was a success and may happily have forgotten another entry made earlier in his *Table Talk*: "Every man is some sort of a failure to himself."

Longfellow died on March 24, 1882. We have

the tale from William Dean Howells, who was present at the snowy burial in Mount Auburn Cemetery, that Emerson, now in his dotage, turned to his daughter and said: "The gentleman we have just been burying was a sweet and beautiful soul; but I forget his name."[2]

Until the First World War, Longfellow was, in the popular mind, the "poet" of America. Even as late as the centenary of Longfellow's birth, eminent critics could predict an enduring fame for this gentle Jove, domesticated out of his thunderbolts, seated on the New England Olympus. Nor had his fame been confined to America. By the turn of the century *Hiawatha* had been translated into twelve languages, including Latin; and the bust was, of course, in Westminster Abbey.

But the First World War was a charnel pit for literary reputations as well as for the bones of the millions butchered on the Somme and at Verdun. Longfellow's easy and uncritical cosmopolitanism, his notion of history as a series of picturesque tales, and his belief in the mystic efficacy of meter and of a gentle Unitarian faith with no wrenching intensities, could seem nothing less than comic to a generation of philosophers, historians, poets, and thoughtful citizens who had begun to suspect that the war might be the debacle of Western civilization and a ghastly unmasking of a tragic truth that had lain behind the Victorian gospel of progress. One expression of the new apprehension was *Hugh Selwyn Mauberley*, in which Ezra Pound called civilization "an old bitch gone in the teeth"; and *The Waste Land* of T. S. Eliot became the dominant image of the period.

What place, in general, could the so-called fireside poets—Whittier, Lowell, and, supremely, Longfellow—have in a time when a new version of the American "fireside" was being presented in Sherwood Anderson's *Winesburg, Ohio*, Sinclair Lewis's *Main Street*, and Theodore Dreiser's *An American Tragedy*, and when the Freudian doctrines of infant sexuality and the Oedipus complex were topics of conversation in

[2] Back in the days when he had been able to remember the name, Emerson had called Longfellow "a trivial, to make my meaning plainer, say, a vulgar poet."

middle-class parlors, speakeasies, and college cafeterias? As Hawthorne and Melville took on a new dimension in the 1920's and continued to offer more and more to the contemporary sensibility, Longfellow lost not only his accepted stature but relevance. In studying him, then, we confront the question: What originally accounted for his reputation?

We have already remarked that Longfellow's role might be said to have been created by his time and place. If Irving represents one stage toward the creation of a national literature, Cooper a second, and Hawthorne a third, then Longfellow, in his treatment of American materials, represents a very strange fourth. For one thing, by the time he turned to his officially American materials, in *Evangeline* (1847), those materials had long since become the subject of a sentimental tradition. This was especially true of the Indian, that most American of all materials, which gave Longfellow his most famous poem, *Hiawatha* (1855). Freneau, antedating Cooper, had celebrated the pathos of the redskin in "The Indian Burying Ground," a note to be struck later by Lydia Sigourney in "Our Aborigines." The Indian, now merely a menace on some far-removed frontier held by expendable illiterates, had become a fit subject for tears. But he could also be tenderly regarded in another dimension. Henry Schoolcraft, whose fame rests on his anthropological researches among the Indians, was also a poet of sorts, and in "The Birchen Canoe," he struck on a subject to be celebrated for more than a century on the advertising calendars of groceries, insurance companies, and mortuary parlors, for here, to the charm of canoe and blue waters, he joined the theme of romantic love:

The builder knew well, in his wild, merry mood,
  A smile from his sweet-love to win,
And he sang as he sewed the green bark to the
    wood,
  Leen ata nee saugein.[3]

But there was another kind of sentimentalizing of the Indian. He had become not merely

---

[3] Which he translates in a footnote as "You only I love."

the figure of pathos and of unspoiled natural love, but also a figure of noble, tragic, and heroic stance, as a flood of dull poems imitated from Walter Scott's poems of Border and Highland warfare indicate. His manly virtues were assumed to have entered, by some mystical osmosis, into the blood of the victorious paleface—as the force of the slain enemy, according to the belief of some primitive people, can be absorbed if one eats him. The general attitude toward the great chief Tecumseh, who, before his defeat at Tippecanoe, had posed the last Indian threat east of the Mississippi, is evidence that this kind of romanticizing was not a merely literary matter; for instance, the infant who was to be General Sherman, of Civil War fame, was named for him.

If the Indian had, in several ways, been sentimentalized, Longfellow finished the job by dehumanizing him completely. That is, he turned him into a sort of culture spirit floating vaguely and edifyingly in the background of the by then not-so-young Republic. And that was what he did, too, with Evangeline, and with John Alden, Priscilla Mullens, and the hero of *The Courtship of Miles Standish* (1858). He had none of the philosophical bent and epic sweep of Cooper, and none of the moral and psychological rigor of Hawthorne, any more than he had their talent for making the past significant to the present. In that period just before the Civil War when, in tragic conflict and tension, the American past was catching up with the present, he waved the wand of his magically hypnotic hexameters and transmuted the past into a charming distraction from the grim realities of the living moment.

Critics sometimes say that Longfellow's poetry achieved a new realism in this period, but even if, in *The Courtship*, he does backhandedly admit to the bloodthirstiness of the Puritan in Indian fighting, his realism characteristically had to do with such small details as would give the pleasure of recognition to a quiet domestic eye. In the period that saw the power and reality of *The Scarlet Letter*, *Moby-Dick*, and *Leaves of Grass*, Longfellow's gift was to bring the American story into the glow of the family hearth, gentling and sweetening the material, creating a blend of sentiment, pathos, and discreet humor, converting history into pastoral.

What were the spiritual demands of that fireside audience whose measure, even with his first book of poems, Longfellow had so shrewdly taken? To begin with, almost everything conspired to focus literature on the family. In frontier times, the family had been, and in the later agrarian development continued to be, the basic economic unit. The fact that Puritanism (and now Victorian evangelistic Christianity), in both the northern and southern versions, was utterly prudish put emphasis on the family, in whose precincts sex could be redeemed and, as it were, licensed, by calling it something else.

On the frontier, especially in the South, there had been, of course, a great deal of promiscuity, and later the fact of slavery modified sexual morality in the South; but wherever the middle class—the carriers of commerce and industry—became dominant, the sanctity of the home was the mark of respectability and social solidity. As the old theological rigors relaxed, the idea of sexual morality, in the narrowest sense, became the index of all virtue—in popular opinion at least the one requisite for prosperity in this world and salvation in the next. In addition, democratic nationalism glorified—as it does today with a nauseating commercialism—the American "home"; it was the seed bed of the virtues that make democracy function, and in itself a solid moral demonstration of the superiority of democracy over the aristocratic feudalism of Europe.[4]

If the audience for the poet was at this fireside, the poet could not forget that the most sacred member of the family circle was the mother, and next to her the nubile daughter, who should not be made to blush. For a long time American literature was, quite literally, feminized. If the glorification of sexual passion for its own sake, in however idealized a form, had no proper place by the fireside, then certainly any celebration of vice and crime, even by the ethereal Shelley,[5] who could declare incest the most poetical of subjects, or by the more mundane Byron, whose own conduct was not above reproach, was not admissible. Even *The Scarlet Letter* did not escape criticism on grounds of impurity. Melville's *Moby-Dick* found few readers in a feminized society, and his *Pierre, or, The Ambiguities* outraged that society—chiefly by rumor, since few read it. Poe was suspect, and it is no accident that his chief influence on literature in the nineteenth century was in France, by way of the poet Charles Baudelaire.

Sexual passion, certainly, had no place by the fireside—but neither did depth of passion of any kind. And quite logically, too: all kinds of violent feeling are, at some level, akin. So even if sexual passion in itself was not presented, the mere tumult of the soul was somewhat reprehensible, for if it did no other harm, it might distract one from practical affairs.

If passion was frowned upon, tender sensibility and tearful emotionalism were not. The eighteenth century had been a time when it was fashionable to exploit what Plato calls the unmanly appetite for tears, from the "sentimental drama" of Richard Steele and the novels

---

[4] In the period before the Civil War, this same sense of superiority was, in the North, directed toward the South, it being held that the institution of slavery, as one aspect of southern feudalism, corrupted the home—in fact, according to most abolitionists, converting every plantation, in the words of William Lloyd Garrison, into a "brothel." So even the antislavery impulse was grafted on to the mystique of the sanctity of the fireside. Concubinage was not uncommon in the South, but, paradoxically, one of its effects was, by putting the white woman on a pedestal, distinguishing her, that is, from mere sexual appetite, to emphasize the "sanctity" of the fireside.

[5] Shelley and Keats were relatively unknown in America before the 1840's. Byron was constantly under attack by critics and clergymen, who, as a matter of fact, may have contributed to his considerable readership and the titillating vogue of the Byronic stance. In 1831, Longfellow, who certainly had no strain of the Byronic in his makeup, remarked that every town had "its little Byron, its self-tormenting scoffer at morality, its gloomy misanthropist in song." In regard to the general picture we have been describing, the treatment of sex and the attitude toward womanhood were features of the Anglo-Saxon world of the time—and to a degree of bourgeois Europe. It was merely intensified here.

of Richardson, for example, forward to the poetry of Ossian and nonliterary manifestations such as the religious movement of John Wesley and the rise of Methodism. By the time of Longfellow's youth, the new tearfulness of the Romantic movement was in full tide, and *The Sorrows of Werther*, by Goethe, had become a handbook for weeping. Too, as we have seen, Charles Brockden Brown, in his novel *Wieland*, had presented a heroine who, for tears and fainting fits, could match anything the English or German Romantics had to offer.

As for the poets, they might well have taken their slogan from "The Silkworm," that example of debased Wordsworthianism by Sarah J. Hale, the last line of which reads: "We need but hearts to feel." The range of feeling celebrated was not great—a sweet melancholy, a grief luxurious rather than bitter—but there was some variety in the objects and occasions which might provoke the fashionable reaction. Fitz-Greene Halleck, in a song from *Fanny*, wrote:

Today the forest leaves are green;
    They'll wither on the morrow,
And the maiden's laugh be changed, ere long,
    To the widow's wail of sorrow.

Richard Henry Dana, in 124 lines of blank verse, mourns for "The Dying Raven," concluding:

He who the lily clothes in simple glory,
He who doth hear the raven's cry for food,
Hath on our hearts, with hand invisible,
In signs mysterious, written what alone
Our *hearts* may read—Death bring thee rest,
    poor bird.

Samuel Woodworth, in a poem that has gained him a wide but anonymous fame, celebrated "The Old Oaken Bucket" as a focus for childhood. Childhood, in fact, was a favorite stimulus for feeling. Lydia Sigourney, who had a long reign in annuals and magazines, ends her lament "The Death of an Infant" with a note of consolation:

But there beamed a smile
So fixed and holy from that cherub brow—

Death gazed, and left it there;—He dared not steal
The signet-ring of Heaven.

L. M. Davidson enunciates, in "The Smile of Innocence," a doctrine that would have horrified the founding fathers of American Puritanism, who took infant damnation as a cornerstone of faith; as Davidson says, the infant

    . . . smiles what it can never speak,
A heart devoid of sin.

Family solidarity is a compelling subject, as is well illustrated in "The Family Meeting," by Charles Sprague:

    We are all here!
        Father, mother,
    Sister, brother,
All who hold each other dear;
Each chair is filled—we're all *at home*:
Tonight let no cold stranger come . . .

The character who speaks in Mrs. Sigourney's "Power of Maternal Piety" declares that

    In foreign lands I travelled wide,
        My pulse was beating high,
    Vice spread her meshes at my side,
        And pleasure lured my eye.

But he heard, as "from the lowly sea," his mother's voice admonishing him:

    "My son—my only one—beware!
        Nor sin against thy God."

Mrs. Hale, who often seems to be doubling for Mrs. Sigourney, warns a son in "The Light of Home":

My boy, thou wilt dream the world is fair,
    And thy spirit will sigh to roam;
And thou must go: but never when there,
    Forget the light of home.

Against the expansion of the new country and the centrifugal pull of the West, the sea, and the wicked city, there was "home"—the glowing fireside with the windows shut against the old fear of the forest and the new challenge of destiny.[6] But the dear notion of "home" shut another kind of window too. In the days of Puritan rigor, even by the glowing fireside, the individual might turn his eyes from the coals, as from warmth of human companionship, and search out the darkness of the self and sweat for the salvation of his own soul. Now by the soft dictate of the tyrannical fireside, that window was shut too. That window was the one most tightly shut. For somehow it was guessed that that window opened on the most seductive, dark, lonely, and terrifying landscape of all.

America was moving toward the time when it would be through with the soul. Except insofar as the soul could be officialized, ritualized, and put to work.

In the "Prelude" to *Voices of the Night*, Longfellow, paraphrasing Sir Philip Sidney,[7] wrote:

> Look, then, into thine heart and write,
>   Yes, into life's deep stream!
> All forms of sorrow and delight,
> All solemn Voices of the Night—
>   Be these henceforth thy theme.

Longfellow thus made a promise, and no promise was ever more rashly made. The one thing Longfellow could not do was look into his heart. He saw no deeper than what might be termed the "social heart," which reflected faithfully the officially accepted values of the world around, and the only "voices of the night" he might hear, or at least long listen to, were those that soothed. The poetry that came forth was a poetry that soothed: it soothed because it told the reader that whatever voices of the night he might happen to hear were sweetly

applauding echoes, mellowed by distance and diminution, of the brazen mandates of the broad day. The fund of unfocused, not understood, unanalyzed, and anarchic emotion which surged in the breast was thus interpreted, socialized, and harnessed.[8]

It is easy to see how the work of Longfellow was a sort of extension of the poems we have been irreverently inspecting. Poems like "The Village Blacksmith" and "The Children's Hour" avowedly belong to such a world, and the kind of sentiment offered even in poems made of sterner stuff, such as "The Skeleton in Armor" or "The Wreck of the Hesperus," does not violate the taboos of the fireside. We can see, too, how in "Seaweed" Longfellow begins by composing a beautifully wrought objective poem, with feeling deeply implicit in it, and then halfway through, as though terrified by his own achievement, grafts on a moral acceptable to the audience, and to himself. In that act, he converts the very poem which had signaled a moment of freedom into a new declaration of the old bondage, turning it into an apology, as it were, for "fireside poetry," and the very subject, at least the official subject, now becomes the taming of violent feeling down to "household words." There were, no doubt, storms in the being of Longfellow, but the poems that were the record of them were, like the seaweed, brought to rest in some quiet little cove.

Within this range of feeling Longfellow could, in fact, achieve his characteristic triumphs. The elegiac, the relaxed, the sad complacency of the heart that looks out from a safe corner on action long past, long distant, or irrelevant—within this range of feeling Longfellow could be, authentically, a poet. This was the poet who wrote "My Lost Youth," "The Jewish Cemetery at Newport," "In the Churchyard at Cambridge," "Seaweed," some of the sonnets, some fragments of *Christus*, "The Tide Rises, the Tide Falls," and "Jugurtha."

---

[6] In one sense Whittier is one of the fireside poets, but in *Snow-Bound*, its setting the archetypal "fireside" poem, he converts the characteristic withdrawal from action into a philosophy of action—the past as providing the thrust for the future.

[7] The first sonnet in Sidney's *Astrophel and Stella* ends:

> Thus, great with child to speak, and helpless in my throes,
> Biting my truant pen, beating myself for spite;
> "Fool," said my Muse to me, "look in thy heart, and write!"

[8] It is strange to see in Poe, who was among the first American writers to open the inward windows on those terrors that were "not of Germany but of the soul," a split, a tension, between the terrors and the yearning for the safety of the—for him—desexualized fireside. Or was it? See p. 355.

Longfellow ritualized, and refined, the presentation of accepted attitudes and feelings. When such accepted feelings and attitudes happened to coincide for a fleeting moment with something of the secret surge of personal life we have the poetry. All poetry depends, we might hazard, on such a coincidence—more especially on the coincidence that creates conflict. But Longfellow could function only when the coincidence was one of identification, not conflict, and usually the coincidence was not of enough emotional significance to create anything—merely intellectual, merely a situation about which Longfellow could say what he thought he *ought* to feel.

Furthermore, Longfellow, unlike all but a few poets of the least consequence, obdurately and compulsively denied the very existence of that secret surge of life. He had the need to create, but he could not bring himself to face the basic condition of creation, to undertake what the truly creative poet, of any scale, undertakes—to try to understand the secret surge, and the world. He could not, it would seem, undertake the deepest risk: that of identity.

If what we have said of Longfellow's work is true, then we must deal with an important question: What did the readers of 1839 find in *Voices of the Night* to make them feel that this poetry was new, vital, and exciting, a step beyond the Sigourneys and Davidsons? For that was what many readers did feel. For one thing, as we have seen in the "Prelude," Longfellow offered to those who, consciously or unconsciously, chafed at the taboos implicit in the official themes and feelings the promise of a deeper experience, of contact with the thrilling and perhaps forbidden reality hinted at in the very title of the volume and in "Hymn to the Night" and "The Light of Stars."

If the volume did not fulfill the hinted promise of contact with a deeper and darker reality, it did give a substitute satisfaction that, in a sense, might distract the reader from his disappointment. In place of the relaxed sensibility and the celebration of easy sentiment and the abstract and pietistic moralizing of the period

in which he had grown up, Longfellow did affirm in "A Psalm of Life" the masculine creed of action, without reference to "enjoyment" or "sorrow," as a means of creating values; and this affirmation, a primitive manifestation of the philosophy of pragmatism of two generations later, brought to focus a diffuse and floating possibility in American life. Furthermore, since the philosophy of energy entails the risks of defeat, "A Psalm of Life" is counterpointed by the masculine stoicism of "The Light of Stars."

In other words, both poems indicated a new role for poetry—with, for the moment, a centrifugal motion away from the fireside. It gave it a new kind of social reference and did, in fact, indicate a new dimension of emotional life. The creed of action and the creed of stoicism might distract from the promise of a search for a deeper reality, but here was, by way of compensation, another thrill of novelty. The poet was—or rather, said he was—returning poetry from the feminized atmosphere of the fireside to the outer world of manly conflict and endurance—the world in which forests were cut down, canals dug, cotton gins invented, and redskins killed. He was praised for giving poetry a new "intellectual quality."[9]

As a matter of fact, Longfellow did not, in the end, return poetry to the world of manly conquest and endurance. It remained for Whit-

---

[9] In Longfellow's novel *Kavanagh* (1849), the brash young man Hathaway, declares: "We want a national literature commensurate with our mountains and rivers. . . . We want a national epic that shall correspond to the size of the country. . . . We want a national drama in which scope shall be given to our gigantic ideas and to the unparalleled activity of our people. . . . In a word, we want a national literature altogether shaggy and unshorn, that shall shake the earth, like a herd of buffaloes thundering over the prairies." Here Longfellow is satirizing the extravagance of literary nationalism, and Hathaway's interlocutory remarks that "a man will not necessarily be a great poet because he lives near a great mountain." But when the main character Kavanagh comes back from studying the old masters in Europe, he is more than half inclined to agree with Hathaway.

In other words, Longfellow was aware of certain complications in regard to an indigenous and "manly" literature, and no doubt, after his own immersion in Europe and its masterpieces, he came back to America in a mood similar to Kavanagh's, ready to write "A Psalm of Life"

man and Melville to do that—and to do it at the same time that they explored an inward landscape, as did Emily Dickinson. As for Longfellow, this was simply the second exciting promise—like the promise to look into his heart—that he reneged on. Passion became pathos and thought became platitude.

Beyond the excitement of the early promises of new contact and new attitudes, there was, however, another factor that gave Longfellow a public. He could, at times, write verse. If we look back at the examples from Fitz-Greene Halleck, Richard Henry Dana, Lydia Sigourney *et al.*, and set against their mechanical patter the first stanza of "Hymn to the Night," with its rhythmic thrust and variety, its vibrance of verbal texture, we may better understand how Poe could exclaim that "no poem ever opened with a beauty more august." However exaggerated the praise may be, Poe might, with equal justification, have been referring to the last stanza of "Hymn to the Night," to the first two stanzas of "The Light of Stars," or to the last stanza of "Midnight Mass." The other work in *Voices of the Night* strikes the modern ear as mediocre or worse, but in spite of vapid phrasing, confusion in metaphor, and the obvious sentiments and ideas, these poems, in the context of the time, offered a possibility of poetry. And that is, at any time, much.

Facility—that was Longfellow's fatal gift, and one he cultivated with suicidal devotion. He could so readily write an almost-poem, a shadow-poem that looked so much better than somebody else's shadow-poem of the same style, that he rarely tried to do more. Paul Elmer More once said that the weakness of Longfellow's

genius was "an absence of resistance." At one level, the lack of resistance manifested itself merely in the competent gabble of much of his verse. As long as the metrical movement continued, Longfellow never lingered, apparently, to seek a more precise phrase or more pregnant metaphor. His mind was primarily a prose mind, abstract and generalizing, wedded to the world as data and not as reality, and he had only the most meager conception of how outward reality might relate to the world within. Therefore he could write automatically, as it were, the kind of prefabricated, paste-strip pseudo-poetry perfectly exemplified in this stanza from "Prelude":

> Athwart the *swinging branches* cast,
>   *Soft rays of sunshine* pour;
> Then comes the *fearful wintry blast*,
> Our hopes, *like withered leaves*, fall fast;
> *Pallid* lips say, "It is past!
>   We can *return no more!*"

It is all a tissue of cliché, as our italicizing indicates.

Longfellow's latter-day Unitarianism was remote from the shock and shiver of experience. Occasionally, as for instance in *Evangeline*, he might report the objective world with some felicity; but he could rarely, if ever, give a sense of immanence. Least of all could he turn inward and try to break through the crust of the conventional self that concealed the real and unacknowledged self struggling, with a throttled voice, to find utterance, the buried self whose struggles were made manifest only in a pervasive and unaimed melancholy which could usually be disposed of by feeding it into the hopper of his meter-machine and turning the crank as rapidly as possible.

But, sometimes, in spite of all he could do to prevent it, Longfellow's gaze might be hypnotically fixed on the snowflake, on the seaweed, or on the swell and fall of the tide, and suddenly he would see the mystic worth of the world. He might even forget to crank the meter-machine. In those rare moments a poem might happen.

---

and utter a call to action appropriate to booming America and what Whittier called, in connection with Longfellow's poem, an "age of moral steam-enginery." But with Longfellow the "old masters" won out after all, and the best he could do to Americanize literature was to fix on a subject like Hiawatha or Miles Standish. The "old masters" won out, after all, not the mountains and the buffalo. But the theory of the "shaggy and unshorn" literature as appropriate for America has never died. See the idea of the "national novel" and Carl Sandburg and Thomas Wolfe in our accompanying volume.

BIOGRAPHICAL CHART

1807 Born, February 27, in Portland, Maine
1825 Graduates from Bowdoin College in same class as Hawthorne; already a published poet, he reads law in the Portland office of his father, a distinguished lawyer and member of Congress
1826–29 Travels to Europe to study in France, Spain, Italy, and Germany
1829 Professor of modern languages at Bowdoin
1831 Marries Mary Storer Potter of Portland, September 14
1835 *Outre-Mer*; travels in England, Scandinavia, Germany, and Holland; wife dies in Rotterdam
1836 Returns to America; begins career at Harvard, which continues for eighteen years
1839 *Hyperion* and *Voices of the Night*
1841 *Ballads and Other Poems*
1842 Europe; visits Dickens; writes *Poems on Slavery* on return voyage
1843 Marries Frances Elizabeth Appleton, July 13; *The Spanish Student*

1845 *Poems* and *The Belfry of Bruges and Other Poems*
1847 *Evangeline*
1849 *Kavanagh: A Tale*, and *The Seaside and the Fireside*
1855 *The Song of Hiawatha*
1858 *The Courtship of Miles Standish and Other Poems*
1861 Wife dies of burns suffered in a home accident
1863 *Tales of a Wayside Inn*
1865–67 Three-volume translation of *The Divine Comedy* of Dante
1868–69 Tours Europe, as international celebrity; receives honorary degrees from Oxford and Cambridge
1872 *Christus: A Mystery* and *Three Books of Songs*
1878 *Kéramos and Other Poems*
1880 *Ultima Thule*
1882 *In the Harbor*; dies, March 24

FURTHER READINGS

The Complete Works of Henry Wadsworth Longfellow (1904) (no editor cited)

Newton Arvin, *Longfellow: His Life and Work* (1963)
Van Wyck Brooks, *The Flowering of New England, 1815–1865* (1936)
Edward Hirsh, *Henry Wadsworth Longfellow* (1964)
William Dean Howells, *Literary Friends and Acquaintances* (1900)
Samuel Longfellow, *Life of Henry Wadsworth Longfellow* (1891; 3 vols.)
James Russell Lowell, *The Function of the Poet and Other Essays* (1920)

Paul Elmer More, "The Centenary of Longfellow," in *Shelburne Essays: Fifth Series* (1908)
Howard Nemerov, "On Longfellow," in *Poetry and Fiction* (1963)
Charles Eliot Norton, *Henry Wadsworth Longfellow: A Sketch of His Life* (1907)
Lawrance Thompson, *Young Longfellow, 1807–1843* (1938)
Edward C. Wagenknecht, *Longfellow: A Full-Length Portrait* (1955)
———, *Henry Wadsworth Longfellow: Portrait of an American Humanist* (1966)
Cecil B. Williams, *Henry Wadsworth Longfellow* (1964)

Hymn to the Night (1839)

Ἀσπασίη, τρίλλιστος

[Well pleasing, most welcome]

I heard the trailing garments of the Night
  Sweep through her marble halls!
I saw her sable skirts all fringed with light
  From the celestial walls!

I felt her presence, by its spell of might,
  Stoop o'er me from above;

The calm, majestic presence of the Night,
  As of the one I love.
I heard the sounds of sorrow and delight,
  The manifold, soft chimes,   10
That fill the haunted chambers of the Night,
  Like some old poet's rhymes.

From the cool cisterns of the midnight air
  My spirit drank repose;

The fountain of perpetual peace flows there,—
  From those deep cisterns flows.

O holy Night! from thee I learn to bear
  What man has borne before!
Thou layest thy finger on the lips of Care,
  And they complain no more.   20

Peace! Peace! Orestes-like I breathe this
    prayer!
  Descend with broad-winged flight,
The welcome, the thrice-prayed for, the
    most fair,
  The best-beloved Night!

A Psalm of Life:
What the Heart of the Young Man Said to the Psalmist (1839)

In 1837 Frances Appleton had rejected Longfellow's suit. This seems to have precipitated some sort of crisis in Longfellow's life. The vague poetical and nocturnal yearnings which he had cultivated under the influence of German Romanticism, especially of Novalis, and of Dante, as he misunderstood and romanticized him, were in conflict with the notion of manly, objective, and practical action presented by Goethe (and, one might say, stipulated for success in American life). Failure in his courtship accentuated the inner struggle which Longfellow had been suffering in the attempt to find his way in life, and out of this came "A Psalm of Life"—a poem, as Lawrance Thompson points out in *Young Longfellow*, of intense personal motivation. *Hyperion*, too, sprang from the same impulse. Of that book, Longfellow wrote his friend Greene:

> I had the glorious satisfaction of writing it; and thereby gained a great victory, *not* over the "dark Ladie" but over myself. I now once more rejoice in my freedom; and am no longer the thrall of anyone. I have great faith in one's writing himself clear from a passion—giving vent to a pent-up fire.

In that moment at least, Longfellow seemed to understand something of the relation of poetry and life. But what he had learned, he could later remember, if at all, only with the greatest difficulty. Or perhaps he found it too uncomfortable, or dangerous, to remember it.

Tell me not, in mournful numbers,
  Life is but an empty dream!—

For the soul is dead that slumbers,
  And things are not what they seem.

Life is real! Life is earnest!
  And the grave is not its goal;
Dust thou art, to dust returnest,
  Was not spoken of the soul.

Not enjoyment, and not sorrow,
  Is our destined end or way;   10
But to act, that each to-morrow
  Find us farther than to-day.

Art is long, and Time is fleeting,
  And our hearts, though stout and brave,
Still, like muffled drums, are beating
  Funeral marches to the grave.

In the world's broad field of battle,
  In the bivouac of Life,
Be not like dumb, driven cattle!
  Be a hero in the strife!   20

Trust no Future, howe'er pleasant!
  Let the dead Past bury its dead!
Act,—act in the living Present!
  Heart within, and God o'erhead!

Lives of great men all remind us
  We can make our lives sublime,
And, departing, leave behind us
  Footprints on the sands of time;

Footprints, that perhaps another,
  Sailing o'er life's solemn main,   30
A forlorn and shipwrecked brother,
  Seeing, shall take heart again.

Let us, then, be up and doing,
  With a heart for any fate;
Still achieving, still pursuing,
  Learn to labor and to wait.

The Light of Stars (1839)

The night is come, but not too soon;
  And sinking silently,
All silently, the little moon
  Drops down behind the sky.

There is no light in earth or heaven
  But the cold light of stars;
And the first watch of night is given
  To the red planet Mars.

Is it the tender star of love?
  The star of love and dreams?   10
Oh no! from that blue tent above
  A hero's armor gleams.

And earnest thoughts within me rise,
  When I behold afar,
Suspended in the evening skies,
  The shield of that red star.

O star of strength! I see thee stand
  And smile upon my pain;

Thou beckonest with thy mailèd hand,
  And I am strong again.   20

Within my breast there is no light
  But the cold light of stars;
I give the first watch of the night
  To the red planet Mars.

The star of the unconquered will,
  He rises in my breast,
Serene, and resolute, and still,
  And calm, and self-possessed.

And thou, too, whosoe'er thou art,
  That readest this brief psalm,   30
As one by one thy hopes depart,
  Be resolute and calm.

Oh, fear not in a world like this,
  And thou shalt know erelong,
Know how sublime a thing it is
  To suffer and be strong.

Seaweed (1845)

When descends on the Atlantic
  The gigantic
Storm-wind of the equinox,
Landward in his wrath he scourges
  The toiling surges,
Laden with seaweed from the rocks:

From Bermuda's reefs; from edges
  Of sunken ledges,
In some far-off, bright Azore;
From Bahama, and the dashing,   10
  Silver-flashing
Surges of San Salvador;

From the tumbling surf, that buries
  The Orkneyan skerries,
Answering the hoarse Hebrides;
And from wrecks of ships, and drifting
  Spars, uplifting
On the desolate, rainy seas;—

Ever drifting, drifting, drifting
  On the shifting   20
Currents of the restless main;
Till in sheltered coves, and reaches
  Of sandy beaches,
All have found repose again.

So when storms of wild emotion
  Strike the ocean
Of the poet's soul, erelong
From each cave and rocky fastness,
  In its vastness,
Floats some fragment of a song: 30

From the far-off isles enchanted,
  Heaven has planted
With the golden fruit of Truth;
From the flashing surf, whose vision
  Gleams Elysian
In the tropic clime of Youth;

From the strong Will, and the Endeavor
  That forever
Wrestle with the tides of Fate;
From the wreck of Hopes far-scattered,   40
  Tempest-shattered,
Floating waste and desolate;—

Ever drifting, drifting, drifting
  On the shifting
Currents of the restless heart;
Till at length in books recorded,
  They, like hoarded
Household words, no more depart.

Rain in Summer (1845)

How beautiful is the rain!
After the dust and heat,
In the broad and fiery street,
In the narrow lane,
How beautiful is the rain!

How it clatters along the roofs,
Like the tramp of hoofs!
How it gushes and struggles out
From the throat of the overflowing spout!

Across the window-pane   10
It pours and pours;
And swift and wide,
With a muddy tide,
Like a river down the gutter roars
The rain, the welcome rain!

The sick man from his chamber looks
At the twisted brooks;
He can feel the cool
Breath of each little pool;
His fevered brain   20
Grows calm again,
And he breathes a blessing on the rain.

From the neighboring school
Come the boys,
With more than their wonted noise
And commotion;
And down the wet streets
Sail their mimic fleets,
Till the treacherous pool
Ingulfs them in its whirling   30
And turbulent ocean.

In the country, on every side,
Where far and wide,
Like a leopard's tawny and spotted hide,
Stretches the plain,
To the dry grass and the drier grain
How welcome is the rain!

In the furrowed land
The toilsome and patient oxen stand;
Lifting the yoke-encumbered head,   40
With their dilated nostrils spread,
They silently inhale
The clover-scented gale,
And the vapors that arise
From the well-watered and smoking soil.
For this rest in the furrow after toil
Their large and lustrous eyes

Seem to thank the Lord,
More than man's spoken word.

Near at hand,   50
From under the sheltering trees,
The farmer sees
His pastures, and his fields of grain,
As they bend their tops
To the numberless beating drops
Of the incessant rain.
He counts it as no sin
That he sees therein
Only his own thrift and gain.

These, and far more than these,   60
The Poet sees!
He can behold
Aquarius old
Walking the fenceless fields of air;
And from each ample fold
Of the clouds about him rolled
Scattering everywhere
The showery rain,
As the farmer scatters his grain.

He can behold   70
Things manifold
That have not yet been wholly told,—
Have not been wholly sung nor said.
For his thought, that never stops,
Follows the water-drops
Down to the graves of the dead,
Down through chasms and gulfs profound,
To the dreary fountain-head
Of lakes and rivers under ground;
And sees them, when the rain is done,   80
On the bridge of colors seven
Climbing up once more to heaven,
Opposite the setting sun.

Thus the Seer,
With vision clear,
Sees forms appear and disappear,
In the perpetual round of strange,
Mysterious change
From birth to death, from death to birth,
From earth to heaven, from heaven to earth;   90
Till glimpses more sublime
Of things, unseen before,
Unto his wondering eyes reveal
The Universe, as an immeasurable wheel
Turning forevermore
In the rapid and rushing river of Time.

The Bridge (1845)

I stood on the bridge at midnight,
  As the clocks were striking the hour,
And the moon rose o'er the city,
  Behind the dark church-tower.

I saw her bright reflection
  In the waters under me,
Like a golden goblet falling
  And sinking into the sea.

And far in the hazy distance
  Of that lovely night in June,   10
The blaze of the flaming furnace
  Gleamed redder than the moon.

Among the long, black rafters
  The wavering shadows lay,
And the current that came from the ocean
  Seemed to lift and bear them away;

As, sweeping and eddying through them,
  Rose the belated tide,
And, streaming into the moonlight,
  The seaweed floated wide.   20

And like those waters rushing
  Among the wooden piers,
A flood of thoughts came o'er me
  That filled my eyes with tears.

How often, oh how often,
  In the days that had gone by,
I had stood on that bridge at midnight
  And gazed on that wave and sky!

How often, oh how often,
  I had wished that the ebbing tide   30

Would bear me away on its bosom
  O'er the ocean wild and wide!

For my heart was hot and restless,
  And my life was full of care,
And the burden laid upon me
  Seemed greater than I could bear.

But now it has fallen from me,
  It is buried in the sea;
And only the sorrow of others
  Throws its shadow over me.   40

Yet whenever I cross the river
  On its bridge with wooden piers,
Like the odor of brine from the ocean
  Comes the thought of other years.

And I think how many thousands
  Of care-encumbered men,
Each bearing his burden of sorrow,
  Have crossed the bridge since then.

I see the long procession
  Still passing to and fro,   50
The young heart hot and restless,
  And the old subdued and slow!

And forever and forever,
  As long as the river flows,
As long as the heart has passions,
  As long as life has woes;

The moon and its broken reflection
  And its shadows shall appear,
As the symbol of love in heaven,
  And its wavering image here.   60

The Children's Hour (1850)

Between the dark and the daylight,
  When the night is beginning to lower,
Comes a pause in the day's occupations,
  That is known as the Children's Hour.

I hear in the chamber above me
  The patter of little feet,
The sound of a door that is opened,
  And voices soft and sweet.

From my study I see in the lamplight,
  Descending the broad hall stair,   10

Grave Alice, and laughing Allegra,
  And Edith with golden hair.

A whisper, and then a silence:
  Yet I know by their merry eyes
They are plotting and planning together
  To take me by surprise.

A sudden rush from the stairway,
  A sudden raid from the hall!
By three doors left unguarded
  They enter my castle wall!   20

They climb up into my turret
  O'er the arms and back of my chair;
If I try to escape, they surround me;
  They seem to be everywhere.

They almost devour me with kisses,
  Their arms about me entwine,
Till I think of the Bishop of Bingen
  In his Mouse-Tower on the Rhine!
Do you think, O blue-eyed banditti,
  Because you have scaled the wall,   30

Such an old mustache as I am
  Is not a match for you all!

I have you fast in my fortress,
  And will not let you depart,
But put you down into the dungeon
  In the round-tower of my heart.

And there will I keep you forever,
  Yes, forever and a day,
Till the walls shall crumble to ruin,
  And moulder in dust away!   40

The Jewish Cemetery at Newport (1854)

How strange it seems! These Hebrews in
    their graves,
  Close by the street of this fair seaport town,
Silent beside the never-silent waves,
  At rest in all this moving up and down!

The trees are white with dust, that o'er their
    sleep
  Wave their broad curtains in the
      south-wind's breath,
While underneath these leafy tents they keep
  The long, mysterious Exodus of Death.

And these sepulchral stones, so old and brown,
  That pave with level flags their burial-place,   10
Seem like the tablets of the Law, thrown down
  And broken by Moses at the mountain's
      base.

The very names recorded here are strange,
  Of foreign accent, and of different climes;
Alvares and Rivera interchange
  With Abraham and Jacob of old times.

"Blessed be God, for he created Death!"
  The mourners said, "and Death is rest
      and peace;"
Then added, in the certainty of faith,
  "And giveth Life that nevermore shall
      cease."   20

Closed are the portals of their Synagogue,[1]
  No Psalms of David now the silence break,
No Rabbi reads the ancient Decalogue
  In the grand dialect the Prophets spake.

---

[1] The "portals" of the Newport Synagogue are now
open.

Gone are the living, but the dead remain,
  And not neglected; for a hand unseen,
Scattering its bounty, like a summer rain,
  Still keeps their graves and their
      remembrance green.

How came they here? What burst of
      Christian hate,
  What persecution, merciless and blind,   30
Drove o'er the sea—that desert desolate—
  These Ishmaels and Hagars of mankind?

They lived in narrow streets and lanes obscure,
  Ghetto and Judenstrass, in mirk and mire;
Taught in the school of patience to endure
  The life of anguish and the death of fire.

All their lives long, with the unleavened bread
  And bitter herbs of exile and its fears,
The wasting famine of the heart they fed,
  And slaked its thirst with marah of
      their tears.   40

Anathema maranatha! was the cry
  That rang from town to town, from
      street to street;
At every gate the accursed Mordecai
  Was mocked and jeered, and spurned by
      Christian feet.

Pride and humiliation hand in hand
  Walked with them through the world
      where'er they went;
Trampled and beaten were they as the sand,
  And yet unshaken as the continent.

For in the background figures vague and vast
  Of patriarchs and of prophets rose sublime,   50

And all the great traditions of the Past
   They saw reflected in the coming time.

And thus forever with reverted look
   The mystic volume of the world they read,
Spelling it backward, like a Hebrew book,

Till life became a Legend of the Dead.

But ah! what once has been shall be no more!
   The groaning earth in travail and in pain
Brings forth its races, but does not restore,
   And the dead nations never rise again.   60

In the Churchyard at Cambridge (1853)

In the village churchyard she lies,
Dust is in her beautiful eyes,
   No more she breathes, nor feels, nor stirs;
At her feet and at her head
Lies a slave to attend the dead,
   But their dust is white as hers.

Was she, a lady of high degree,
So much in love with the vanity
   And foolish pomp of this world of ours?
Or was it Christian charity,   10
And lowliness and humility,
   The richest and rarest of all dowers?

Who shall tell us? No one speaks;
No color shoots into those cheeks,
   Either of anger or of pride,
At the rude question we have asked:
Nor will the mystery be unmasked
   By those who are sleeping at her side.

Hereafter?—And do you think to look
On the terrible pages of that Book   20
   To find her failings, faults, and errors?
Ah, you will then have other cares,
In your own shortcomings and despairs,
   In your own secret sins and terrors!

My Lost Youth (1855)

Often I think of the beautiful town
   That is seated by the sea;
Often in thought go up and down
The pleasant streets of that dear old town,
   And my youth comes back to me.
     And a verse of a Lapland song
     Is haunting my memory still:
     "A boy's will is the wind's will,
And the thoughts of youth are long,
     long thoughts."

I can see the shadowy lines of its trees,   10
   And catch, in sudden gleams,
The sheen of the far-surrounding seas,
And islands that were the Hesperides
   Of all my boyish dreams.
     And the burden of that old song,
     It murmurs and whispers still:
     "A boy's will is the wind's will,
And the thoughts of youth are long,
     long thoughts."

I remember the black wharves and the slips,
   And the sea-tides tossing free;   20
And Spanish sailors with bearded lips,
And the beauty and mystery of the ships,

   And the magic of the sea.
     And the voice of that wayward song
     Is singing and saying still:
     "A boy's will is the wind's will,
And the thoughts of youth are long,
     long thoughts."

I remember the bulwarks by the shore,
   And the fort upon the hill;
The sunrise gun, with its hollow roar,   30
The drum-beat repeated o'er and o'er,
   And the bugle wild and shrill.
     And the music of that old song
     Throbs in my memory still:
     "A boy's will is the wind's will,
And the thoughts of youth are long,
     long thoughts."

I remember the sea-fight far away,
   How it thundered o'er the tide!
And the dead captains, as they lay
In their graves, o'erlooking the tranquil bay,   40
   Where they in battle died.
     And the sound of that mournful song
     Goes through me with a thrill:
     "A boy's will is the wind's will,

And the thoughts of youth are long,
    long thoughts."

I can see the breezy dome of groves,
    The shadows of Deering's Woods;
And the friendships old and the early loves
Come back with a Sabbath sound, as of doves
    In quiet neighborhoods.   50
      And the verse of that sweet old song,
      It flutters and murmurs still:
      "A boy's will is the wind's will,
And the thoughts of youth are long,
    long thoughts."

I remember the gleams and glooms that dart
    Across the school-boy's brain;
The song and the silence in the heart,
That in part are prophecies, and in part
    Are longings wild and vain.
      And the voice of that fitful song   60
      Sings on, and is never still:
      "A boy's will is the wind's will,
And the thoughts of youth are long,
    long thoughts."

There are things of which I may not speak;
    There are dreams that cannot die;
There are thoughts that make the strong
    heart weak,
And bring a pallor into the cheek,

And a mist before the eye.
    And the words of that fatal song
    Come over me like a chill: 70
    "A boy's will is the wind's will,
And the thoughts of youth are long,
    long thoughts."

Strange to me now are the forms I meet
    When I visit the dear old town;
But the native air is pure and sweet,
And the trees that o'ershadow each
      well-known street,
    As they balance up and down,
      Are singing the beautiful song,
      Are sighing and whispering still:
      "A boy's will is the wind's will,   80
And the thoughts of youth are long,
    long thoughts."

And Deering's Woods are fresh and fair,
    And with joy that is almost pain
My heart goes back to wander there,
And among the dreams of the days that were,
    I find my lost youth again.
      And the strange and beautiful song,
      The groves are repeating it still:
      "A boy's will is the wind's will,
And the thoughts of youth are long,
    long thoughts."   90

Snow-Flakes (1863)

Out of the bosom of the Air,
    Out of the cloud-folds of her garments
      shaken,
Over the woodlands brown and bare,
    Over the harvest-fields forsaken,
      Silent, and soft, and slow
      Descends the snow.

Even as our cloudy fancies take
    Suddenly shape in some divine expression,
Even as the troubled heart doth make

In the white countenance confession,   10
    The troubled sky reveals
    The grief it feels.

This is the poem of the air,
    Slowly in silent syllables recorded;
This is the secret of despair,
    Long in its cloudy bosom hoarded,
      Now whispered and revealed
      To wood and field.

Killed at the Ford (1867)

He is dead, the beautiful youth,
The heart of honor, the tongue of truth,
He, the life and light of us all,
Whose voice was blithe as a bugle-call,
Whom all eyes followed with one consent,

The cheer of whose laugh, and whose
    pleasant word,
Hushed all murmurs of discontent.

Only last night, as we rode along,

Down the dark of the mountain gap,
To visit the picket-guard at the ford,   10
Little dreaming of any mishap,
He was humming the words of some old song:
"Two red roses he had on his cap
And another he bore at the point of his sword."

Sudden and swift a whistling ball
Came out of a wood, and the voice was still;
Something I heard in the darkness fall,
And for a moment my blood grew chill;
I spake in a whisper, as he who speaks
In a room where some one is lying dead;   20
But he made no answer to what I said.

We lifted him up to his saddle again,

And through the mire and the mist and the rain
Carried him back to the silent camp,
And laid him as if asleep on his bed;
And I saw by the light of the surgeon's lamp
Two white roses upon his cheeks,
And one, just over his heart, blood-red!

And I saw in a vision how far and fleet
That fatal bullet went speeding forth,   30
Till it reached a town in the distant North,
Till it reached a house in a sunny street,
Till it reached a heart that ceased to beat
Without a murmur, without a cry;
And a bell was tolled, in that far-off town,
For one who had passed from cross to crown,
And the neighbors wondered that she should die.

Jugurtha (1880)

How cold are thy baths, Apollo!
    Cried the African monarch, the splendid,
As down to his death in the hollow
    Dark dungeons of Rome he descended,
    Uncrowned, unthroned, unattended;
How cold are thy baths, Apollo!

How cold are thy baths, Apollo!
    Cried the Poet, unknown, unbefriended,
As the vision, that lured him to follow,
    With the mist and the darkness blended,   10
    And the dream of his life was ended;
How cold are thy baths, Apollo!

Divina Commedia (1867)

1

Oft have I seen at some cathedral door
    A laborer, pausing in the dust and heat,
    Lay down his burden, and with reverent feet
    Enter, and cross himself, and on the floor
Kneel to repeat his paternoster o'er;
    Far off the noises of the world retreat;
    The loud vociferations of the street
    Become an undistinguishable roar.
So, as I enter here from day to day,
    And leave my burden at this minster gate,   10
    Kneeling in prayer, and not ashamed to pray,
The tumult of the time disconsolate
    To inarticulate murmurs dies away,
    While the eternal ages watch and wait.

2

How strange the sculptures that adorn these
        towers!
    This crowd of statues, in whose folded
        sleeves
    Birds build their nests; while canopied
        with leaves

Parvis and portal bloom like trellised bowers,
And the vast minster seems a cross of flowers!
    But fiends and dragons on the
        gargoyled eaves   20
    Watch the dead Christ between the living
        thieves,
    And, underneath, the traitor Judas lowers!
Ah! from what agonies of heart and brain,
    What exultations trampling on despair,
    What tenderness, what tears, what hate
        of wrong,
What passionate outcry of a soul in pain,
    Uprose this poem of the earth and air,
    This mediæval miracle of song!

3

I enter, and I see thee in the gloom
    Of the long aisles, O poet saturnine!   30
    And strive to make my steps keep pace
        with thine.
    The air is filled with some unknown
        perfume;
The congregation of the dead make room

For thee to pass; the votive tapers shine;
   Like rooks that haunt Ravenna's groves
      of pine
   The hovering echoes fly from tomb to tomb.
From the confessionals I hear arise
   Rehearsals of forgotten tragedies,
   And lamentations from the crypts below;
And then a voice celestial that begins   40
   With the pathetic words, "Although
      your sins
   As scarlet be," and ends with "as the snow."

4

With snow-white veil and garments as of flame,
   She stands before thee, who so long ago
   Filled thy young heart with passion and
      the woe
   From which thy song and all its
      splendors came;
And while with stern rebuke she speaks
      thy name,
   The ice about thy heart melts as the snow
   On mountain heights, and in swift overflow
   Comes gushing from thy lips in sobs of shame. 50
Thou makest full confession; and a gleam,
   As of the dawn on some dark forest cast,
   Seems on thy lifted forehead to increase;
Lethe and Eunoe—the remembered dream
   And the forgotten sorrow—bring at last
   That perfect pardon which is perfect peace.

5

I lift mine eyes, and all the windows blaze

With forms of Saints and holy men who died,
   Here martyred and hereafter glorified;
   And the great Rose upon its leaves displays   60
Christ's Triumph, and the angelic roundelays,
   With splendor upon splendor multiplied;
   And Beatrice again at Dante's side
No more rebukes, but smiles her words
      of praise.
And then the organ sounds, and unseen choirs
   Sing the old Latin hymns of peace and love
   And benedictions of the Holy Ghost;
And the melodious bells among the spires
   O'er all the house-tops and through
      heaven above
   Proclaim the elevation of the Host!   70

6

O star of morning and of liberty!
   O bringer of the light, whose splendor shines
   Above the darkness of the Apennines,
   Forerunner of the day that is to be!
The voices of the city and the sea,
   The voices of the mountains and the pines,
   Repeat thy son, till the familiar lines
   Are footpaths for the thought of Italy!
Thy fame is blown abroad from all the heights,
   Through all the nations, and a sound is heard, 80
   As of a mighty wind, and men devout,
Strangers of Rome, and the new proselytes,
   In their own language hear thy
      wondrous word,
   And many are amazed and many doubt.

The Cross of Snow (1879)

In the long, sleepless watches of the night,
   A gentle face—the face of one long dead—
   Looks at me from the wall, where round
     its head
   The night-lamp casts a halo of pale light.
Here in this room she died; and soul
     more white
   Never through martyrdom of fire was led
   To its repose; nor can in books be read

The legend of a life more benedight.
There is a mountain in the distant West
   That, sun-defying, in its deep ravines   10
   Displays a cross of snow upon its side.
Such is the cross I wear upon my breast
   These eighteen years, through all the
     changing scenes
   And seasons, changeless since the day
     she died.

Chaucer (1875)

An old man in a lodge within a park;
   The chamber walls depicted all around
   With portraitures of huntsman, hawk,
     and hound,

And the hurt deer. He listeneth to the lark,
Whose song comes with the sunshine through
     the dark
   Of painted glass in leaden lattice bound;

He listeneth and he laugheth at the sound,
 Then writeth in a book like any clerk.
He is the poet of the dawn, who wrote
 The Canterbury Tales, and his old age   10

Made beautiful with song; and as I read
I hear the crowing cock, I hear the note
 Of lark and linnet, and from every page
 Rise odors of ploughed field or flowery mead.

Shakespeare (1875)

A vision as of crowded city streets,
 With human life in endless overflow;
 Thunder of thoroughfares; trumpets
  that blow
To battle; clamor, in obscure retreats,
Of sailors landed from their anchored fleets;
 Tolling of bells in turrets, and below
 Voices of children, and bright flowers
  that throw

O'er garden-walls their intermingled sweets!
This vision comes to me when I unfold
 The volume of the Poet paramount,   10
 Whom all the Muses loved, not one alone;—
Into his hands they put the lyre of gold,
 And, crowned with sacred laurel at
  their fount,
 Placed him as Musagetes on their throne.

Milton (1875)

I pace the sounding sea-beach and behold
 How the voluminous billows roll and run,
 Upheaving and subsiding, while the sun
 Shines through their sheeted emerald
  far unrolled,
And the ninth wave, slow gathering fold by fold
 All its loose-flowing garments into one,
 Plunges upon the shore, and floods the dun

Pale reach of sands, and changes them
  to gold.
So in majestic cadence rise and fall
 The mighty undulations of thy song,   10
 O sightless bard, England's Mæonides!
And ever and anon, high over all
 Uplifted, a ninth wave superb and strong,
 Floods all the soul with its melodious seas.

The Tide Rises, The Tide Falls (1880)

The tide rises, the tide falls,
The twilight darkens, the curlew calls;
Along the sea-sands damp and brown
The traveller hastens toward the town,
 And the tide rises, the tide falls.

Darkness settles on roofs and walls,
But the sea, the sea in the darkness calls;
The little waves, with their soft, white hands,

Efface the footprints in the sands,
 And the tide rises, the tide falls.   10

The morning breaks; the steeds in their stalls
Stamp and neigh, as the hostler calls;
The day returns, but nevermore
Returns the traveller to the shore,
 And the tide rises, the tide falls.

JAMES RUSSELL LOWELL (1819–1891)

James Russell Lowell was born in 1819 and died in 1891. At his birth, Cambridge was scarcely more than a village, and if it was some- what special because of Harvard College and a high percentage of the aristocratic families later to be known as Brahmins, it still had vices, virtues, and loyalties more regional than national, the tone of life of a village, the moral rigor of the Puritan tradition (now somewhat modified by Unitarianism and seaborne trade), and a democratic atmosphere made comfortable, or even possible, by homogeneity of blood—Anglo–Saxon, of course.

By the time of Lowell's death, that world was little more than a romantic memory to be propagated in schoolrooms of the Middle West. The Civil War had been fought; the Negro slave had been emancipated and, by a gentleman's agreement of the white South and the white North, had been condemned to a second-class citizenship and a third-class economic status; the new industrial America had been born; the flood of immigration from Europe had hardened the tradition of old America into a social snobbery; and the old idealism about the future of American democracy had often given place to a cynical individualism, sometimes justifying itself by the new theories of Darwin. Many of the finest intelligences, such men as Whitman, Mark Twain, Henry Adams, Brooks Adams, and Henry James, were deeply distressed about American life, and pessimistic about its future.

The life of Lowell, in other words, reached from the New England village to the world of mass production, expanding technology, finance capitalism, and social revolution. Lowell was significantly involved in many aspects of the life of his century, and better, perhaps, than any other writer of his time may serve as an index to the shifting relation of literature to the world from which it sprang. He serves all the better as such an index in that he is a literary figure rather than a maker of literature, a man of taste rather than talent, of sensibility rather than passion, of yearning rather than creative compulsion, an appreciative monger of ideas rather than their maker.

Though of far less weight than Matthew Arnold in England, he greatly resembles him: he was the poet whose talent dried up and who, with backward pangs and a stoical sense of duty, accepted the compensatory function of a teacher, public servant, and civilizer.

The Lowell family was old in New England and distinguished. The father of James Russell, Dr. Charles Lowell, was a Unitarian clergyman, a man of considerable learning and great sweetness of spirit who, in spite of this sweetness, was tough enough to put the "higher law"—the voice of personal conscience—above the demands, even the laws, of society. In the period of James Russell's youth, when respectable opinion in New England generally accepted slavery, his father had the courage to put on public record, even in the prayers offered in his church, his abhorrence of that institution. The effect of the father's personality was fundamental in the son's life; and its influence was confirmed by that of Maria White, whom Lowell married in 1844. She was a very charming and intelligent young woman, with literary tastes, an inclination toward transcendentalism, and a passionate commitment to abolitionism.

By this time Lowell was practicing law with little, and literature with considerable, success. When twenty-two, he had published his first book of poems, *A Year's Life*, and by 1843, when he was twenty-four, his second, *Poems*, which prompted Poe to say that Lowell had "given evidence of at least as high poetical genius as anyone in America—if not a loftier genius than any." His work was appearing in the best magazines, and he had founded his own, the *Pioneer*, in the first issue of which appeared Poe's "The Tell-Tale Heart," and later two other famous pieces by him, "Notes on English Verse" and "Lenore." Lowell had even made headway as a critic, with *Conversations on the Old Poets*.

By this time, too, the young man had announced himself as a reformer; and poetry, he grandly proclaimed in "L'Envoi," would be the instrument of reform:

Never had poets such high call before,
Never can poets hope for higher one,
And, if they be but faithful to their trust,
Earth will remember them with love and joy,
And O, far better, God will not forget.
For he who settles Freedom's principles
Writes the death-warrant of all tyranny.

Poetry, however, was not the only instrument for reform that came to the hand of this particular young poet; there was his prose in the abolitionist press, the *National Anti-Slavery Standard* and the *Liberty Bell*. Nor was abolition his only reforming concern. In a sonnet called "Sub Pondere Crescit," he wrote, "The hope of Truth grows stronger day by day," and the Truth involved not only the freeing of the slaves, but woman's suffrage, the improvement of factory conditions (he had written earlier of "factory children thin"), temperance (he had overcome Maria's ladylike scruples against actually carrying a banner at a temperance rally), the abolishing of capital punishment, and the promotion of Dr. Graham's health bread. He was the child of the reforming age that, years later, he was ironically to describe in his essay on Thoreau.

In spite of this wide range of interest and the pressing need to do journalism to keep the pot boiling (the antislavery articles did considerable service to Mammon as well as to God), in spite of the death of his first child, the early years of Lowell's married life saw a massive production of verse. A second volume of *Poems* appeared late in 1847. Within a year, three other books appeared, *A Fable for Critics, The Biglow Papers,* and *The Vision of Sir Launfal.* Lowell's fame as a poet seemed assured.

At this point, when Lowell was only a little past thirty, he entered the world. The death of another child drove him and Maria to Europe for distraction and a broadening of vision. He was appointed to succeed Longfellow as Professor of Modern Languages at Harvard and, after a year studying German abroad, assumed those duties. He even became a member of the executive committee of the Massachusetts Anti-Slavery Society. In 1857 he was made the first editor of the *Atlantic Monthly,* a new magazine of "literature, art and politics," which, under his direction, achieved immediate influence.

With a vengeance, Lowell was in the world, and something of a public figure, but he was now alone in his success, for Maria had died. The bustle of life afforded distraction from his prolonged grief, and poetry, which might have prompted periods of withdrawal, was now rare. He had lost the knack for it—and a knack was really all that he had ever had.

The world he moved in was one of high distinction. At the Saturday Club, in a gathering famous for witty conversation, good wine, and high intellectual achievement, he hobnobbed with Emerson, Hawthorne, Whittier, Longfellow, Oliver Wendell Holmes, the geologist Louis Agassiz, the mathematician Benjamin Peirce, and the historians John Lothrop Motley and W. H. Prescott. Abroad, his name was in full flower. In 1873, he received an honorary doctorate from Oxford, followed shortly by one from Cambridge. Four years later he became minister to Spain and subsequently to England, a post he was to hold for five years. There, in spite of the lingering illness and death of his second wife, he served his country well, and his reputation for charm and wit made him in great demand as an after-dinner speaker. Even after this period, the recollection of his personal success there, and the friendships he had made drew him back again and again. America seemed dull and crude:

I frankly confess that I like England immensely, I find men of leisure at every turn, men who are profound scholars, who think for themselves, with whom interchange of ideas is an inspiration. Where there is one such man in America there are a dozen here. Do you wonder I like it? The contrast is not fault on the part of our country: it is the consequence of youth and the struggle for material existence.

Even the great fame and constant adulation he found in America could not quite redeem it. In 1891, with that fame yet uncrumbling, he died.

The fame has badly crumbled now, and in the general decline it is strange to remember that poetry was the keystone of its arch. It is, in fact, difficult to salvage much from the massive production of verse. *The Vision of Sir Launfal,* which was once on every parlor table in the land, now appears only in the mustier corners of attics. If the banging rhythms of "The Present Crisis" once stirred pulses, in later days few readers have found in its brew of evangelical religion, apocalyptic social thought, and vest-pocket history either poetical elevation or political wisdom:

> Once to every man or nation comes the moment to decide
> In the strife of Truth with Falsehood for the good or evil side;
> Some great cause, God's new Messiah, offering each the bloom or blight,
> Puts the goats upon the left hand, and the sheep upon the right,
> And the choice goes on forever 'twixt that darkness and that light.

The "Ode Recited at the Harvard Commemoration" on July 21, 1865, on which tardy burst of poetic and patriotic fervor Lowell staked his all, is scarcely superior to his "Ode Written for the Celebration of the Introduction of the Cochituate Water into the City of Boston." With one exception, the poems of grief over which generations wept now merely embarrass the reader who happens to remember that real death and real anguish lay behind such lines as these from "The Changeling":

> I had a little daughter,
>   And she was given to me
> To lead me gently backward
>   To the Heavenly Father's knee.

In a poem called "An Incident in a Railway Car," Lowell says that "All thought begins in feeling," and such a notion, even if an overstatement of a psychological fact, does suggest a significant truth about poetry—that a poem involves a complex and vital fusion of feeling and thought, a fusion that comes into being only in terms of the special medium in which it exists. But Lowell had a very feeble instinct for the language of poetry and so could rarely get beyond the stage of an unfocused generalized emotion in which a poem might begin. What focus the emotion might achieve would be in a stale situation or stale image, and to this Lowell would attach, by some obvious, mechanical means, a stale idea. Having no sense

of the medium as a function of imagination, he wound up with no vital fusion of feeling and thought—only a generalized presentation of emotion to which would be attached a "truth," inevitably noble or comforting, and inevitably trivial because not realized in the poem itself.

But Lowell did have, it must be said to his credit, a remarkable degree of self-awareness. In *A Fable for Critics*, he could say of himself:

> There is Lowell, who's striving Parnassus to climb
> With a whole bale of *isms* tied together with rhyme,
> He might get on alone, spite of brambles and boulders,
> But he can't with that bundle he has on his shoulders,
> The top of the hill he will never come nigh reaching
> Till he learns the distinction 'twixt singing and preaching;
> His lyre has some chords that would ring pretty well,
> But he'd rather by half, make a drum of the shell,
> And rattle away till he's old as Methusalem,
> At the head of a march to the last new Jerusalem.

In addition to the rare moments when Lowell stumbled, as it were, into poetry, as in "She Came and Went," his achievement depends on a kind of peripheral, or secondary, poetry—*A Fable for Critics* and *The Biglow Papers*. Such works are what we may call a "poetry of commentary," not a "poetry of realization," and as such depend for effect on the astuteness of observation and wittiness of turn.[1] By reason of this very limitation, the *Fable* and the *Papers* offered scope for the qualities which Lowell could best exercise. Such poetry demands astuteness of observation, and Lowell was an extremely intelligent man with an instructed passion for both literature and politics, the sub-

---

[1] Such categories must be taken as provisional: for instance, *The Dunciad*, of Alexander Pope, and some of the satires of John Dryden and Byron's *Don Juan* might be said to be a poetry of commentary, but they reach beyond that.

jects, respectively, of the *Fable* and the *Papers*. Such subjects demand wit, and that was the gift—a high-spirited and gay, rather than sarcastic and destructive, wit—with which Lowell was most generously endowed.

On the technical side, neither the *Fable* nor the *Papers* made any demand for subtle expressiveness. In the whacking meters of the *Fable*, Lowell's defect of ear became a virtue, and in the *Papers*, the interest in the contortions of dialect took precedence over ordinary poetic considerations. Nor can the fact that both poems are wordy, marred by digressions and often by forced and jejune wit, seriously hurt them. For one thing, the poems depend not on the whole but on parts for their effect, for instance, on the individual portraits in the *Fable*, and on single turns and thrusts in the *Papers*. It is a pervading tone, atmosphere, and attitude that provides what sense of unity there is, not an organization of materials or the development of a theme.

Indeed, the charm of the *Fable* lies in the spirit of rollicking improvisation, and the most outrageous pun or wrenched rhyme justifies itself in this ebullience. As for the *Papers*, the fact that solecisms and other expressions of mother wit are put into the mouths of the rural characters to whom, in spite of sturdy virtues and common sense, the writer (or reader) condescends somewhat, serves to make certain defects dramatically acceptable: we do not, as it were, blame Lowell; we blame the uninstructed speakers for their *gaucherie* and even take a relish in our superiority to it. In fact, this sometimes uneasy fusion of faith in the good sense and integrity of the uninstructed speaker with condescension toward him and his cultural limitations reminds one of the contrast that William Dean Howells once pointed out between his own sense of democracy, which was of the heart, and that of Lowell, which, he said, was of the head.

Both the *Fable* and the *Papers* are works of a charming, clever, high-spirited young gentleman whose élan at charades and witty horseplay had once delighted the circle of cultivated young people in which he and Maria White moved. If those poems are taken in the proper spirit, the modern reader can still find them interesting and agreeable. But the reader of the 1840's found more.

With regard to the *Fable*, we should say that by then there had developed in America, especially in New England and New York City, a consciousness of the "new literature" which really extended beyond persons of merely literary inclination. Interest in the new literature ramified into national pride, the democratic faith, moral aspirations, and reforming zeal. Literature was important news, but it was gossip, too, and the *Fable*, with its not-too-serious summaries and handy critical tags, appealed at the levels of both serious news and gossip. It condescended a little to literature, for the tone of the piece implied that writers were a little bit like the worthy but clownish Hosea Biglow *et al.*, who were already being condescended to in the early installments of the *Papers*. The nonliterary reader was put at his ease: writers were to be admired, certainly in a community of culture like Boston, but they were not at the real center of power. Even if a writer was a Harvard professor, like Longfellow, and might have good connections and move in good society, his salary was only $600 a year. As for other writers who were merely writers, like Whittier or Hawthorne or Thoreau, some of them made even less money, and worse, they sometimes pretended not even to care about money or position at all and might be generally eccentric. Lowell, in his role of newsmonger, critic, and charming, well-placed, witty young man of the world, detaches himself from his other self, the poor, blundering Lowell the poet, and this fact dramatizes the amiable condescension which informs the whole work.

The *Papers*, even more precisely than the *Fable*, came at the right moment, the first one appearing in June, 1846, in the *Courier*, of Boston, in the middle of the Mexican War. The war, which in New England was widely regarded as a vicious device of southern politicians and the Democratic party to acquire territory for the expansion of slavery, provided the context in which Lowell scored his great success. When he wrote the first *Paper*, a satirical attack on recruiting in New England, in the dialect of the untutored village poet Hosea Biglow, he had no intention of doing more than the one dramatized editorial. But the reception was so warm, the topic so congenial to his deepest convictions, and the form so liberating to his spirit of charade and improvisation, and, perhaps, to some nostalgic yearning for old simplicities, that after the lapse of more than a year he resumed and, in quick succession, did the rest of what is now the First Series.

The book appeared in 1848, with an elaborate framework provided by the mythical Reverend Homer Wilbur, the minister of the village of Jaalam, a creation of comic pedantry, piety, and a good heart, who acts as sponsor for the work of his "talented young parishioner." The framework, in principle, was a good idea; it localized the poems, gave a context for them, and fixed more nicely the distance between Boston and the world of Hosea Biglow. It also enriched, in the person of Homer Wilbur, the humor of the work—and would have enriched it more except for an intolerable prolixity, which is too often obviously not Wilbur's but the author's.

In fact, it is not clear how much self-humor Lowell put into the character of Wilbur. It has been surmised that Wilbur, in his pedantry, is modeled on one Barzillai Frost, who tutored Lowell when, as a student at Harvard, he was sent down to disciplinary rustication in the wilds of Concord; but Lowell had a tendency to self-satire, manifested, as we have seen, in the portrait of "Lowell" in the *Fable*, and it would have been quite in character for him to make comedy of his own incipient pedantry.

But such humor at the expense of himself as pedant would lead to another aspect of Wilbur-as-Lowell. Parson Wilbur would stand as whipping boy for Lowell as the sponsor of Hosea, for the comedy of Wilbur lies in the irrelevancy of his pedantry to Hosea's uninstructed shrewdness. In other words, in the figure of Wilbur, Lowell projects the comedy of his own relation to the world of Hosea; the fact, indeed, that

he knows himself to be ultimately outside of Hosea's world but not entirely superior to it.

This topic suggests Lowell's relation to the rise of realism, to the use of local color and folk elements, particularly humor and dialect, to the interest in the low-class hero. The *Papers* are an early contribution to a developing tradition of realism which combined a number of different impulses and interests, but Lowell was to make other, though indirect, contributions to this tradition. For one thing, in the 1850's, as editor of the *Atlantic*, he sponsored the new realism and local color and was the discoverer of William Dean Howells, the first important novelist of that school. For another, the growing prestige of Lowell gave special weight to his theorizing on one aspect of the new realism. In the fascinating introduction to the Second Series of the *Biglow Papers*, which appeared during the Civil War, Lowell approached the subject at the level of language. The educated and half-educated classes in America, he says, spoke and wrote a language starched by the grammarians or corrupted into bombast by politicians and journalists, while the common language remained "racy with life and vigor and originality." This debasing of the language was occurring, even though the "first postulate of an original literature is that a people should use their language instinctively and unconsciously, as if it were a lively part of their growth and personality, not as the mere torpid boon of education or inheritance." Then, with wit, relish, and learning, Lowell surveys a number of metaphoric turns, angular words, and grainy pronunciations in Yankee speech, praising the first for freshness and perceptiveness and the second and third for a sense of the historical continuity of language. In a passage in his most charming vein, he says:

> The dialect was native, was spoken all about me when a boy, at a time when an Irish day-laborer was as rare as an American one now. Since then I have made a study of it so far as opportunity allowed. But when I write in it, it is as in another tongue, and I am carried back far beyond any studies of it to long-ago noonings in my father's hay-fields, and to the

talk of Sam and Job over their jug of *black-strap* under the shadow of the ash-tree which still dapples the grass whence they have been gone so long.

Lowell looked back with nostalgia on the language of Sam and Job, but in spite of his appreciation he had not made the language his own. For a language is more than words, and the *Papers* remain somehow a little like the exhibition cabinet of a butterfly collector; the specimens are all there, exact and beautiful, but dead. This comes painfully clear as soon as we leave the parts of the *Papers* concerned with satire and turn to those in which Lowell, following the urgings of his friend the English poet Arthur Hugh Clough to write "some Yankee Pastorals," has aimed at "more sentiment and a higher tone without foregoing the advantages offered by the dialect."

Take the following passage from the *Papers* entitled "Sunthin' in the Pastoral Line":

I, country-born an' bred, know where to find
Some blooms that make the season suit the
    mind,
An' seem to metch the doubtin' blue-bird's
    notes,—
Half-vent'rin' liverworts in furry coats,
Bloodroots, whose rolled-up leaves ef you oncurl,
Each of 'em's cradle to a baby-pearl,—
But these are jes' Spring's pickets; sure ez sin,
The rebble frosts'll try to drive 'em in;
For half our May's so awfully like May n't,
'twould rile a Shaker or an evrige saint.

Now let us "un-dialect" the passage:

I, country-born and bred, know where to find
Some blooms that make the season suit the
    mind,
And seem to match the doubting bluebird's
    notes,—
Half-venturing liverworts in furry coats,
Bloodroots, whose rolled-up leaves if you uncurl,
Each of them's cradle to a baby pearl,—
But these are just Spring's pickets; sure as sin,
The rebel frosts will try to drive them in;
For half our May's so awfully like May ain't,
It would rile a Shaker or an average saint.

What we have now is simply some fairly attractive verse about the uncertain New England spring, with nothing, except perhaps the last line, to suggest anything of the racy "life, vigor, and originality" for which Lowell had praised the common speech.[2] To go further, we find that in this poem of "more sentiment and a higher tone," Lowell has a tendency to pull away into something conventionally poetic, as when he says that the "maple crimsons to a coral reef" (a line that betrays considerable ignorance of coral reefs), or says the blooming lime trees "drows'ly simmer with the bees' sweet trade" (a line which has merit, but a merit, in the phrase "bees' sweet trade," entirely false to Hosea). Or, again in the same poem, Lowell plasters dialect on a passage that seems to come directly out of his reading in the English metaphysical poets of the seventeenth century:

Our lives in sleep are some like streams that
    glide
'Twixt flesh an' sperrit boundin' on each side,
Where both shores' shadders kind o' mix an'
    mingle
In sunthin' thet ain't jes' like either single:
An' when you cast off moorin's from Today,
An' down towards To-Morrer drift away,
The imiges thet tengle on the stream
Make a new upside-down'ard world o' dream.

In other words, once outside the political and satirical passages, which deal with objective matters of public concern, Lowell's "native language" does not serve him. For matters of opinion he may penetrate the world of Sam and Job at their "noonings," but not for matters of feeling and sensibility. As for the poem that Lowell took to be his best attempt at a Yankee Pastoral, "The Courtin'," it is saved only by its casual unpretentiousness.

As we have already noticed, the same thing held true of Whittier. He, more intimately than

[2] In contrast with the mechanical and burdensome effect of Lowell's attempt to give the impression of common speech, see Robert Frost's narrative poems, such as "The Death of the Hired Man," "The Mountain," "Home Burial," and "Snow."

Lowell, knew the "native language," with its vitality and originality, but when he came to write poetry, he lost it; for years we find the "native language" only in his letters or, patchily, in his journalism. Both Whittier, the Quaker farmboy, and Lowell, the Harvard-bred aristocrat, were equally victims of the notion that literature, especially poetry, is outside the churn and plunge of life and speaks a different and idealized language—a more "genteel" language. In fact, by the same notion, literature was thought to deal with only certain subjects, equally "genteel." We shall encounter this notion later in the philosopher Santayana's discussion of what is called the "genteel tradition." (The essay is reprinted in our accompanying volume.)

Perhaps the best way to locate Lowell as a critic is to contrast him with Poe on the one hand and with Emerson on the other. Poe, as we have seen, was specifically concerned with literature as an art; he wanted to understand the methods of literature and the meaning of those methods in making literature what it is and not something else. He undertook to develop a method of technical analysis and to relate it to a philosophical theory of literature—a full aesthetic. He failed in this grandiose scheme but emphasized for America an awareness of what had always been one of the poles of criticism.

To turn to Emerson, though his essays may be pieces of literature, they can scarcely be called literary criticism, even when they refer to literature. They are concerned with general ideas about the nature of man and the values by which he should live, about his relation to nature and to society. They embody what was a genuinely new and compelling vision of the possibilities of man, especially of man on the American continent. One aspect of this vision was the relation of literature to life, as a thing made from life and a thing making life. In other words, we have here another pole of literary criticism, not developed and applied, but stated.

Both Poe and Emerson stand—and stood, in a revolutionary way—for a significant view of

literature. But it is hard to know exactly what Lowell does stand for. In one sense, it may be said that, in criticism, he stands for too many things, a group of more or less unrelated awarenesses rather than formulated ideas. For instance, though Lowell has none of the talent of Poe for analyzing literary values, he does realize the disastrous consequences of a confusion of values in American taste. Where Poe tries to correct taste by establishing aesthetic and psychological principles, Lowell merely calls attention to the work of masters—Shakespeare, Cervantes, Dante, Spenser, Chaucer, Dryden, Fielding, Wordsworth—without trying to define the qualities that make them masters, usually taking refuge in generalizations about genius. And when he does focus on some precise point, like the metrics of Milton, Wyatt, or Surrey, he is apt to be equally blunt of ear and understanding. Some of the masters he treats had been, themselves, critics of great significance, but Lowell, apparently, could learn little from that department of their mastership.

On the broader concerns characteristic of Emerson's criticism, Lowell usually contents himself with an easy moralizing. His essays often give an elaborate biographical background of the writer who is the subject, but in general he merely comments on some vaguely assumed connection between the writer's personal virtues and those of his work. When Lowell finds that one of his literary heroes—one as strange for him as Henry Fielding—was a man of loose habits, he simply struggles to make the best of it. Even for his own period, Lowell seems peculiarly unaware of the complexity of the relation between the life of the writer and his work. When he goes further, as in the essay on Chaucer, or that on Pope, and presents a relatively extended and informed piece of literary, or general, history, he makes no real effort to penetrate into the relation between a society and the literature that comes out of it.

In the actual presentation of his material and ideas, Lowell is often very slack and confusing. The fact that Lowell, unlike Poe and Emerson, has no dominating concern, only a number of concerns more or less unrelated and competing, is often reflected in the organization of an essay. Lowell seems to have a teacher's laudable impulse to tell all about the subject that he himself finds so fascinating, but this sense for the "aboutness" of a subject is rarely converted into a direct confrontation with it. Furthermore, the impulse to tell all about a subject is compounded by an incorrigible loquacity. Sometimes he is merely carried on a flood of language, and sometimes a language of a peculiarly vapid sort —far from the color and terseness of Sam and Job in their "noonings."

All this would seem to suggest that Lowell is a critic of no importance. He is, as a matter of fact, of considerable importance, if we regard him from a certain angle. As the successor of Ticknor and Longfellow at Harvard, his function was to break the narrow and provincial classicism that had made Emerson demand why a man should be required to spend twelve of the best years of his life studying languages that led to nothing, to provide some sense of the richness of the modern achievement, and to put the live culture of raw America into some rela-tion with the live culture of the mature world beyond. In his essays, Lowell undertook to do what his predecessors had not done, to extend his obligation as teacher beyond the bounds of his classroom, to point out to American society that world beyond itself. If we see the essays in this light, they assume a new significance in our history, and even some of the qualities which seem unfortunate holdovers from the classrooms are justified; the essays are addressed to a classroom, after all—to the great one beyond the bounds of Harvard.

Lowell's interest in literature may have been unfocused, but it was passionate. If he could not treat literature with rigor, he could at least treat it with an infectious appreciation. If he was not in any philosophical sense a critic, but only a man of taste, he did manage to convey something of his own enthusiasm. If he had no central, seminal idea, at least his range of awareness tended to open the minds of his readers to new experiences and new issues, however unclearly defined or feebly resolved. He was a civilizer.

BIOGRAPHICAL CHART

1819 Born, February 22, in Cambridge, Massachusetts
1834–38 Attends Harvard; "rusticated" for misbehavior to Concord; meets Emerson and Thoreau
1838–40 Attends Harvard Law School
1841 *A Year's Life and Other Poems*
1843 Establishes the *Pioneer*, with Robert Carter; magazine fails
1844 Marries Maria White, ardent abolitionist; *Poems*
1845 *Conversations on Some of the Old Poets*
1847 *Poems*
1848 *A Fable for Critics; The Vision of Sir Launfal; The Biglow Papers* (First Series)
1851–52 Travels in Europe
1853 Maria White Lowell dies
1855 Becomes professor at Harvard, succeeding Long-fellow

1856 Travels in Germany and Italy
1857 Edits new *Atlantic Monthly* (until 1861); marries Frances Dunlap
1864 Coedits the *North American Review* (until 1872)
1865 "Ode Recited at the Harvard Commemoration"
1867 *The Biglow Papers* (Second Series)
1870 *Among My Books*
1872 Resigns professorship; travels in Europe
1877–80 Serves as minister to Spain
1880–85 Serves as minister to England
1885 Wife dies in London after long mental illness; returns to Cambridge
1887 *Democracy and Other Addresses*
1891 Dies, August 12, in Cambridge

FURTHER READINGS

Charles Eliot Norton, ed., *The Writings of James Russell Lowell* (1890; 11 vols.)
H. H. Clark and Norman Foerster, eds., *Representative Selections* (1947)

Van Wyck Brooks, *The Flowering of New England, 1815–1865* (1936)
Martin Duberman, *James Russell Lowell* (1966)
Norman Foerster, "The Creed of Lowell as a Literary

Critic," *Studies in Philology* (July, 1927)
Ferris Greenslet, *James Russell Lowell, His Life and Work* (1905)
T. W. Higginson, *Old Cambridge* (1899)
Leon Howard, *Victorian Knight-Errant: A Study of the Early Literary Career of James Russell Lowell* (1952)
William Dean Howells, *Literary Friends and Acquaintances* (1900)

Henry James, "James Russell Lowell," in *The American Essays of Henry James*, Leon Edel, ed. (1950)
R. C. Nye, "Lowell and American Speech," *Philological Quarterly* (July, 1939)
Austin Warren, "Lowell on Thoreau," *Studies in Philology* (July, 1930)
René Wellek, *A History of Modern Criticism* (1965), Vol. 4

From A Fable for Critics (1848)

"There comes Emerson first, whose rich
    words, every one,
Are like gold nails in temples to hang
    trophies on,
Whose prose is grand verse, while his verse,
    the Lord knows,
Is some of it pr— No, 't is not even prose;
I'm speaking of metres; some poems have
    welled
From those rare depths of soul that have
    ne'er been excelled;
They're not epics, but that doesn't matter
    a pin,
In creating, the only hard thing's to begin;
A grass-blade's no easier to make than an oak;
If you've once found the way, you've achieved
    the grand stroke;   10
In the worst of his poems are mines of
    rich matter,
But thrown in a heap with a crash and
    a clatter;
Now it is not one thing nor another alone
Makes a poem, but rather the general tone,
The something pervading, uniting the whole,
The before unconceived, unconceivable soul,
So that just in removing this trifle or that, you
Take away, as it were, a chief limb of the statue;
Roots, wood, bark, and leaves singly perfect
    may be,
But, clapt hodge-podge together, they don't
    make a tree.   20

"But, to come back to Emerson (whom,
    by the way,
I believe we left waiting),—his is, we may say,
A Greek head on right Yankee shoulders,
    whose range
Has Olympus for one pole, for t' other the
    Exchange;
He seems, to my thinking (although I'm afraid

The comparison must, long ere this, have
    been made),
A Plotinus-Montaigne, where the Egyptian's
    gold mist
And the Gascon's shrewd wit cheek-by-jowl
    coexist;
All admire, and yet scarcely six converts he's got
To I don't (nor they either) exactly know what;   30
For though he builds glorious temples, 't is odd
He leaves never a doorway to get in a god.
'T is refreshing to old-fashioned people like me
To meet such a primitive Pagan as he,
In whose mind all creation is duly respected
As parts of himself—just a little projected;
And who's willing to worship the stars and
    the sun,
A convert to—nothing but Emerson.
So perfect a balance there is in his head,
That he talks of things sometimes as if they
    were dead;   40
Life, nature, love, God, and affairs of that sort,
He looks at as merely ideas; in short,
As if they were fossils stuck round in a cabinet,
Of such vast extent that our earth's a mere
    dab in it;
Composed just as he is inclined to conjecture
    her,
Namely, one part pure earth, ninety-nine parts
    pure lecturer;
You are filled with delight at his clear
    demonstration,
Each figure, word, gesture, just fits the occasion,
With the quiet precision of science he'll
    sort 'em,
But you can't help suspecting the whole a
    post mortem.   50

"There are persons, mole-blind to the soul's
    make and style,

Who insist on a likeness 'twixt him and
    Carlyle;
To compare him with Plato would be
    vastly fairer,
Carlyle's the more burly, but E. is the rarer;
He sees fewer objects, but clearlier, truelier,
If C.'s as original, E.'s more peculiar;
That he's more of a man you might say
    of the one,
Of the other he's more of an Emerson;
C.'s the Titan, as shaggy of mind as of limb,—
E. the clear-eyed Olympian, rapid and slim;   60
The one's two thirds Norseman, the other
    half Greek,
Where the one's most abounding, the other's
    to seek;
C.'s generals require to be seen in the mass,—
E.'s specialties gain if enlarged by the glass;
C. gives nature and God his own fits of
    the blues,
And rims common-sense things with mystical
    hues,—
E. sits in a mystery calm and intense,
And looks coolly around him with sharp
    common-sense;
C. shows you how every-day matters unite
With the dim transdiurnal recesses of night,—   70
While E., in a plain, preternatural way,
Makes mysteries matters of mere every day;
C. draws all his characters quite *à la* Fuseli,—
Not sketching their bundles of muscles and
    thews illy,
He paints with a brush so untamed and profuse,
They seem nothing but bundles of muscles
    and thews;
E. is rather like Flaxman, lines strait and severe,
And a colorless outline, but full, round,
    and clear;—
To the men he thinks worthy he frankly
    accords
The design of a white marble statue in words.   80
C. labors to get at the centre, and then
Take a reckoning from there of his actions
    and men;
E. calmly assumes the said centre as granted,
And, given himself, has whatever is wanted.

"He has imitators in scores, who omit
No part of the man but his wisdom and wit,—
Who go carefully o'er the sky-blue of his brain,
And when he has skimmed it once, skim
    it again;

If at all they resemble him, you may be sure
    it is
Because their shoals mirror his mists and
    obscurities,   90
As a mud-puddle seems deep as heaven for
    a minute,
While a cloud that floats o'er is reflected
    within it.

           · · ·

"There comes ——,[1] for instance; to see
    him's rare sport,
Tread in Emerson's tracks with legs painfully
    short;
How he jumps, how he strains, and gets red
    in the face,
To keep step with the mystagogue's natural
    pace!
He follows as close as a stick to a rocket,
His fingers exploring the prophet's each
    pocket.
Fie, for shame, brother bard; with good
    fruit of your own,
Can't you let Neighbor Emerson's orchards
    alone?   100
Besides, 't is no use, you'll not find e'en
    a core,—
—— has picked up all the windfalls before.
They might strip every tree, and E. never
    would catch 'em,
His Hesperides have no rude dragon to
    watch 'em;
When they send him a dishful, and ask him
    to try 'em,
He never suspects how the sly rogues
    came by 'em;
He wonders why 't is there are none such his
    trees on,
And thinks 'em the best he has tasted this
    season.

           · · ·

"There is Hawthorne, with genius so
    shrinking and rare
That you hardly at first see the strength
    that is there;   110
A frame so robust, with a nature so sweet,
So earnest, so graceful, so lithe and so fleet,
Is worth a descent from Olympus to meet;
'Tis as if a rough oak that for ages had stood,

---

[1] Here Lowell refers to Thoreau.

With his gnarled bony branches like ribs of
    the wood,
Should bloom, after cycles of struggle
    and scathe,
With a single anemone trembly and rathe;
His strength is so tender, his wildness so meek,
That a suitable parallel sets one to seek,—
He's a John Bunyan Fouqué, a Puritan Tieck;   120
When Nature was shaping him, clay was
    not granted
For making so full-sized a man as she wanted,
So, to fill out her model, a little she spared
From some finer-grained stuff for a woman
    prepared,
And she could not have hit a more excellent
    plan
For making him fully and perfectly man.
The success of her scheme gave her so much
    delight,
That she tried it again, shortly after, in
    Dwight;
Only, while she was kneading and shaping
    the clay,
She sang to her work in her sweet childish way,   130
And found, when she'd put the last touch
    to his soul,
That the music had somehow got mixed
    with the whole.

. . .

"Here's Cooper, who's written six volumes
    to show
He's as good as a lord: well, let's grant that
    he's so;
If a person prefer that description of praise,
Why, a coronet's certainly cheaper than bays;
But he need take no pains to convince us
    he's not
(As his enemies say) the American Scott.
Choose any twelve men, and let C. read aloud
That one of his novels of which he's most
    proud,   140
And I'd lay any bet that, without ever
    quitting
Their box, they'd be all, to a man, for
    acquitting.
He has drawn you one character, though,
    that is new,
One wildflower he's plucked that is wet with
    the dew
Of this fresh Western world, and, the thing
    not to mince,

He has done naught but copy it ill ever since;
His Indians, with proper respect be it said,
Are just Natty Bumppo, daubed over with red,
And his very Long Toms are the same
    useful Nat,
Rigged up in duck pants and a sou'wester hat   150
(Though once in a Coffin, a good chance
    was found
To have slipped the old fellow away
    underground).
All his other men-figures are clothes upon
    sticks,
The *dernière chemise* of a man in a fix
(As a captain besieged, when his garrison's
    small,
Sets up caps upon poles to be seen o'er
    the wall);
And the women he draws from one model
    don't vary,
All sappy as maples and flat as a prairie.
When a character's wanted, he goes to
    the task
As a cooper would do in composing a cask   160
He picks out the staves, of their qualities
    heedful,
Just hoops them together as tight as is
    needful,
And, if the best fortune should crown
    the attempt, he
Has made at the most something wooden
    and empty.

"Don't suppose I would underrate Cooper's
    abilities;
If I thought you'd do that, I should feel
    very ill at ease;
The men who have given to *one* character life
And objective existence are not very rife;
You may number them all, both prose-writers
    and singers,
Without overrunning the bounds of your
    fingers,   170
And Natty won't go to oblivion quicker
Than Adams the parson or Primrose the vicar.

"There is one thing in Cooper I like, too,
    and that is
That on manners he lectures his countrymen
    gratis;
Not precisely so either, because, for a rarity,
He is paid for his tickets in unpopularity.
Now he may overcharge his American pictures,

But you'll grant there's a good deal of truth
    in his strictures;
And I honor the man who is willing to sink
Half his present repute for the freedom
    to think,   180
And, when he has thought, be his cause
    strong or weak,
Will risk t' other half for the freedom
    to speak,
Caring naught for what vengeance the mob
    has in store,
Let that mob be the upper ten thousand
    or lower.

. . .

"There comes Poe, with his raven, like
    Barnaby Rudge,
Three fifths of him genius and two fifths
    sheer fudge,
Who talks like a book of iambs and
    pentameters,
In a way to make people of common sense
    damn metres,
Who has written some things quite the best of
    their kind,
But the heart somehow seems all squeezed
    out by the mind, . . .   190

. . .

"But what's that? a mass-meeting? No,
    there come in lots,
The American Bulwers, Disraelis, and Scotts,
And in short the American everything elses,
Each charging the others with envies and
    jealousies;—

By the way, 'tis a fact that displays what
    profusions
Of all kinds of greatness bless free institutions,
That while the Old World has produced
    barely eight
Of such poets as all men agree to call great,
And of other great characters hardly a score
(One might safely say less than that rather
    than more),   200
With you every year a whole crop is begotten,
They're as much of a staple as corn is,
    or cotton;
Why, there's scarcely a huddle of log-huts
    and shanties
That has not brought forth its own Miltons
    and Dantes;
I myself know ten Byrons, one Coleridge,
    three Shelleys,
Two Raphaels, six Titians, (I think) one
    Apelles,
Leonardos and Rubenses plenty as lichens,
One (but that one is plenty) American
    Dickens,
A whole flock of Lambs, any number
    of Tennysons,—
In short, if a man has the luck to have
    any sons,   210
He may feel pretty certain that one out of
    twain
Will be some very great person over again.
There is one inconvenience in all this,
    which lies
In the fact that by contrast we estimate size,
And, where there are none except Titans,
    great stature
Is only the normal proceeding of nature."

From The Biglow Papers (1846)

NO. I. A LETTER

FROM MR. EZEKIEL BIGLOW OF JAALAM TO THE
HON. JOSEPH T. BUCKINGHAM, EDITOR OF THE
BOSTON COURIER, INCLOSING A POEM OF HIS SON,
MR. HOSEA BIGLOW.

                    JAYLEM, june 1846
MISTER EDDYTER:—Our Hosea wuz down to Boston
last week, and he see a cruetin Sarjunt a struttin
round as popler as a hen with 1 chicking, with 2
fellers a drummin and fifin arter him like all nater.

the sarjunt he thout Hosea hed n't gut his i teeth
cut cos he looked a kindo's though he 'd jest com
down, so he cal'lated to hook him in, but Hosy
wood n't take none o' his sarse for all he hed much
as 20 Rooster's tales stuck onto his hat and eena-
most enuf brass a bobbin up and down on his
shoulders and figureed onto his coat and trousis,
let alone wut nater hed sot in his featers, to make
a 6 pounder out on.

    wal, Hosea he com home considerabal riled, and

arter I' d gone to bed I heern Him a thrashin round like a short-tailed Bull in fli-time. The old Woman ses she to me ses she, Zekle, ses she, our Hosee's gut the chollery or suthin anuther ses she, don't you Bee skeered, ses I, he's oney amakin pottery ses i, he's ollers on hand at that ere busynes like Da & martin, and shure enuf, cum mornin, Hosy he cum down stares full chizzle, hare on eend and cote tales flyin, and sot rite of to go reed his varses to Parson Wilbur bein he haint aney grate shows o' book larnin himself, bimeby he cum back and sed the parson wuz dreffle tickled with 'em as i hoop you will Be, and said they wuz True grit.

Hosea ses taint hardly fair to call 'em hisn now, cos the parson kind o' slicked off sum o' the last varses, but he told Hosee he did n't want to put his ore in to tetch to the Rest on 'em, bein they wuz verry well As thay wuz, and then Hosy ses he sed suthin a nuther about Simplex Mundishes or sum sech feller, but I guess Hosea kind o' did n't hear him, for I never hearn o' nobody o' that name in this villadge, and I 've lived here man and boy 76 year cum next tater diggin, and thair aint no wheres a kitting spryer 'n I be.

If you print 'em I wish you 'd jest let folks know who hosy's father is, cos my ant Keziah used to say it's nater to be curus ses she, she aint livin though and he's a likely kind o' lad.

 EZEKIEL BIGLOW

Thrash away, you'll *hev* to rattle
    On them kittle-drums o' yourn,—
'Taint a knowin' kind o' cattle
    Thet is ketched with mouldy corn;
Put in stiff, you fifer feller,
    Let folks see how spry you be,—
Guess you'll toot till you are yeller
    'Fore you git ahold o' me!

Thet air flag's a leetle rotten,
    Hope it aint your Sunday's best;—   10
Fact! it takes a sight o' cotton
    To stuff out a soger's chest:
Sence we farmers hev to pay fer 't,
    Ef you must wear humps like these,
S'posin' you should try salt hay fer 't,
    It would du ez slick ez grease.

'T would n't suit them Southun fellers,
    They 're a dreffle graspin' set,
We must ollers blow the bellers
    Wen they want their irons het;   20
May be it's all right ez preachin',
    But *my* narves it kind o' grates,

Wen I see the overreachin'
    O' them nigger-drivin' States.

Them thet rule us, them slave-traders,
    Haint they cut a thunderin' swarth
(Helped by Yankee renegaders),
    Thru the vartu o' the North!
We begin to think it 's nater
    To take sarse an' not be riled;—   30
Who 'd expect to see a tater
    All on eend at bein' biled?

Ez fer war, I call it murder,—
    There you hev it plain an' flat;
I don't want to go no furder
    Than my Testyment fer that;
God hez sed so plump an' fairly,
    It 's ez long ez it is broad,
An' you 've gut to git up airly
    Ef you want to take in God.   40

'Taint your eppyletts an' feathers
    Make the thing a grain more right;
'Taint afollerin' your bell-wethers
    Will excuse ye in His sight;
Ef you take a sword an' dror it,
    An' go stick a feller thru,
Guv'ment aint to answer for it,
    God 'll send the bill to you.

Wut 's the use o' meetin'-goin'
    Every Sabbath, wet or dry,   50
Ef it's right to go amowin'
    But it 's curus Christian dooty
I dunno but wut it's pooty
    Trainin' round in bobtail coats,—
But it 's curus Christian dooty
    This 'ere cuttin' folks's throats.

They may talk o' Freedom's airy
    Tell they're pupple in the face,—
It 's a grand gret cemetary
    Fer the barthrights of our race;   60
They jest want this Californy
    So 's to lug new slave-states in
To abuse ye, an' to scorn ye,
    An' to plunder ye like sin.

Aint it cute to see a Yankee
    Take sech everlastin' pains,
All to git the Devil's thankee
    Helpin' on 'em weld their chains?
Wy, it 's jest ez clear ez figgers,
    Clear ez one an' one make two,   70
Chaps thet make black slaves o' niggers
    Want to make wite slaves o' you.

Tell ye jest the eend I 've come to
  Arter cipherin' plaguy smart,
An' it makes a handy sum, tu,
  Any gump could larn by heart;
Laborin' man an' laborin' woman
  Hev one glory an' one shame.
Ev'y thin' thet 's done inhuman
  Injers all on 'em the same.   80

'Taint by turnin' out to hack folks
  You 're agoin' to git your right,
Nor by lookin' down on black folks
  Coz you 're put upon by wite;
Slavery aint o' nary color,
  'Taint the hide thet makes it wus,
All it keers fer in a feller
  'S jest to make him fill its pus.

Want to tackle *me* in, du ye?
  I expect you 'll hev to wait;   90
Wen cold lead puts daylight thru ye
  You 'll begin to kal'late;
S'pose the crows wun't fall to pickin'
  All the carkiss from your bones,
Coz you helped to give a lickin'
  To them poor half-Spanish drones?

Jest go home an' ask our Nancy
  Wether I'd be sech a goose
Ez to jine ye,—guess you 'd fancy
  The eternal bung wuz loose!   100
She wants me fer home consumption,
  Let alone the hay's to mow,—
Ef you 're arter folks o' gumption,
  You 've a darned long row to hoe.

Take them editors thet 's crowin'
  Like a cockerel three months old,—
Don't ketch any on 'em goin',
  Though they *be* so blasted bold;
Aint they a prime lot o' fellers?
  'Fore they think on 't guess they'll sprout   110
(Like a peach thet 's got the yellers),
  With the meanness bustin' out.

Wal, go 'long to help 'em stealin'
  Bigger pens to cram with slaves,
Help the men thet 's ollers dealin'
  Insults on your fathers' graves;
Help the strong to grind the feeble,
  Help the many agin the few,
Help the men thet call your people
  Witewashed slaves an' peddlin' crew!   120

Massachusetts, God forgive her,

She 's akneelin' with the rest,
She, thet ough' to ha' clung ferever
  In her grand old eagle-nest;
She thet ough' to stand so fearless
  W'ile the wracks are round her hurled,
Holdin' up a beacon peerless
  To the oppressed of all the world!

Ha'n't they sold your colored seamen?
  Ha'n't they made your env'ys w'iz?   130
Wut'll make ye act like freemen?
  Wut'll git your dander riz?
Come, I 'll tell ye wut I'm thinkin'
  Is our dooty in this fix,
They 'd ha' done 't ez quick ez winkin'
  In the days o' seventy-six.

Clang the bells in every steeple,
  Call all true men to disown
The tradoocers of our people,
  The enslavers o' their own;   140
Let our dear old Bay State proudly
  Put the trumpet to her mouth,
Let her ring this messidge loudly
  In the ears of all the South:—

"I'll return ye good fer evil
  Much ez we frail mortils can,
But I wun 't go help the Devil
  Makin' man the cus o' man;
Call me coward, call me traiter,
  Jest ez suits your mean idees,—
Here I stand a tyrant-hater,
  An' the friend o' God an' Peace!"

Ef I 'd *my* way I hed ruther
  We should go to work an' part,
They take one way, we take t' other,
  Guess it would n't break my heart;   150
Man hed ough' to put asunder
  Them thet God has noways jined;
An' I should n't gretly wonder
  Ef there 's thousands o' my mind.

[The first recruiting sergeant on record I conceive to have been that individual who is mentioned in the Book of Job as *going to and fro in the earth, and walking up and down in it.* Bishop Latimer will have him to have been a bishop, but to me that other calling would appear more congenial. The sect of Cainites is not yet extinct, who esteemed the first-born of Adam to be the most worthy, not only because of that privilege of primogeniture, but inasmuch as he was able to overcome and slay his younger brother. That was a wise saying of the famous Marquis Pescara to the Papal Legate, that *it was impossible for men to serve Mars and Christ at the same time.* Yet in time past the profession of arms was judged to be κατ' ἐξοχήν [the occupation most befitting] that of a gentleman, nor does this opinion want for strenuous upholders even in our day. Must we suppose, then, that the profession of Christianity was only intended for losels, or, at best, to afford an opening for plebeian ambition? Or shall we hold with that nicely metaphysical Pomeranian, Captain Vratz, who was Count Königsmark's chief instrument in the murder of Mr. Thynne, that the Scheme of Salvation has been arranged with an especial eye to the necessities of the upper classes, and that "God would consider *a gentleman* and deal with him suitably to the condition and profession he had placed him in"? It may be said of us all, *Exemplo plus quam ratione vivimus* [We live more by example than by calculation].—H.W.]

After the Burial (1850)

Yes, faith is a goodly anchor;
When skies are sweet as a psalm,
At the bows it lolls so stalwart,
In its bluff, broad-shouldered calm.

And when over breakers to leeward
The tattered surges are hurled,
It may keep our head to the tempest,
With its grip on the base of the world.

But, after the shipwreck, tell me
What help in its iron thews,   10
Still true to the broken hawser,
Deep down among sea-weed and ooze?

In the breaking gulfs of sorrow,
When the helpless feet stretch out
And find in the deeps of darkness
No footing so solid as doubt,

Then better one spar of Memory,
One broken plank of the Past,
That our human heart may cling to,
Though hopeless of shore at last!   20

To the spirit its splendid conjectures,
To the flesh its sweet despair,
Its tears o'er the thin-worn locket
With its anguish of deathless hair!

Immortal? I feel it and know it,
Who doubts it of such as she?

But that is the pang's very secret,—
Immortal away from me.

There's a narrow ridge in the graveyard
Would scarce stay a child in his race,   30
But to me and my thought it is wider
Than the star-sown vague of Space.

Your logic, my friend, is perfect,
Your moral most drearily true;
But, since the earth clashed on *her* coffin,
I keep hearing that, and not you.

Console if you will, I can bear it;
'T is a well-meant alms of breath;
But not all the preaching since Adam
Has made Death other than Death.   40

It is pagan; but wait till you feel it,—
That jar of our earth, that dull shock
When the ploughshare of deeper passion
Tears down to our primitive rock.

Communion in spirit! Forgive me,
But I, who am earthy and weak,
Would give all my incomes from dreamland
For a touch of her hand on my cheek.

That little shoe in the corner,
So worn and wrinkled and brown,   50
With its emptiness confutes you,
And argues your wisdom down.

She Came and Went (1849)

As a twig trembles, which a bird
  Lights on to sing, then leaves unbent,
So is my memory thrilled and stirred;—
  I only know she came and went.

As clasps some lake, by gusts unriven,
  The blue dome's measureless content,

So my soul held that moment's heaven;—
  I only know she came and went.

As, at one bound, our swift spring heaps
  The orchards full of bloom and scent,   10
So clove her May my wintry sleeps;—
  I only know she came and went.

An angel stood and met my gaze,
   Through the low doorway of my tent;
The tent is struck, the vision stays;—
   I only know she came and went.

Oh, when the room grows slowly dim,
   And life's last oil is nearly spent,
One gush of light these eyes will brim,
   Only to think she came and went.   20

Thoreau (1865)

What contemporary, if he was in the fighting period of his life, (since Nature sets limits about her conscription for spiritual fields, as the state does in physical warfare,) will ever forget what was somewhat vaguely called the "Transcendental Movement" of thirty years ago? Apparently set astir by Carlyle's essays on the "Signs of the Times," and on "History," the final and more immediate impulse seemed to be given by "Sartor Resartus." At least the republication in Boston of that wonderful Abraham à Sancta Clara sermon on Lear's text of the miserable forked radish gave the signal for a sudden mental and moral mutiny. *Ecce nunc tempus acceptabile!* [Now is the proper time!] was shouted on all hands with every variety of emphasis, and by voices of every conceivable pitch, representing the three sexes of men, women, and Lady Mary Wortley Montagues. The nameless eagle of the tree Ygdrasil was about to sit at last, and wild-eyed enthusiasts rushed from all sides, each eager to thrust under the mystic bird that chalk egg from which the new and fairer Creation was to be hatched in due time. *Redeunt Saturnia regna* [the Saturnian age returns],—so far was certain, though in what shape, or by what methods, was still a matter of debate. Every possible form of intellectual and physical dyspepsia brought forth its gospel. Bran had its prophets, and the presartorial simplicity of Adam its martyrs, tailored impromptu from the tar-pot by incensed neighbors, and sent forth to illustrate the "feathered Mercury," as defined by Webster and Worcester. Plainness of speech was carried to a pitch that would have taken away the breath of George Fox; and even swearing had its evangelists, who answered a simple inquiry after their health with an elaborate ingenuity of imprecation that might have been honorably mentioned by Marlborough in general orders. Everybody had a mission (with a capital M) to attend to everybody-else's business. No brain but had its private maggot, which must have found pitiably short commons sometimes. Not a few impecunious zealots abjured the use of money

(unless earned by other people), professing to live on the internal revenues of the spirit. Some had an assurance of instant millennium so soon as hooks and eyes should be substituted for buttons. Communities were established where everything was to be common but common-sense. Men renounced their old gods, and hesitated only whether to bestow their furloughed allegiance on Thor or Budh. Conventions were held for every hitherto inconceivable purpose. The belated gift of tongues, as among the Fifth Monarchy men, spread like a contagion, rendering its victims incomprehensible to all Christian men; whether equally so to the most distant possible heathen or not was unexperimented, though many would have subscribed liberally that a fair trial might be made. It was the pentecost of Shinar. The day of utterances reproduced the day of rebuses and anagrams, and there was nothing so simple that uncial letters and the style of Diphilus the Labyrinth could not turn it into a riddle. Many foreign revolutionists out of work added to the general misunderstanding their contribution of broken English in every most ingenious form of fracture. All stood ready at a moment's notice to reform everything but themselves. The general motto was:—

   "And we'll *talk* with them, too,
And take upon 's the mystery of things
As if we were God's spies."

Nature is always kind enough to give even her clouds a humorous lining. I have barely hinted at the comic side of the affair, for the material was endless. This was the whistle and trailing fuse of the shell, but there was a very solid and serious kernel, full of the most deadly explosiveness. Thoughtful men divined it, but the generality suspected nothing. The word "transcendental" then was the maid of all work for those who could not think, as "Pre-Raphaelite" has been more recently for people of the same limited housekeeping. The truth is, that there was a much nearer metaphysical relation and a much more distant æsthetic and literary relation between Carlyle and the Apostles of the Newness, as they were called in New England, than has commonly been supposed. Both represented the reaction and revolt against *Philisterei*, a renewal of the old battle begun in modern times by Erasmus and Reuchlin, and continued by Lessing, Goethe, and, in a far narrower sense, by Heine in Germany, and of which Fielding, Sterne, and Wordsworth in different ways have been the leaders in England. It was simply a struggle for fresh air, in which, if the windows could not be opened, there was danger that panes would be broken, though painted with images of saints and martyrs. Light, colored by these reverend effigies, was none the more respirable for being picturesque. There is only one thing better than tradition, and that is the original and eternal life out of which all tradition takes its rise. It was this life which the reformers demanded, with more or less clearness of consciousness and expression, life in politics, life in literature, life in religion. Of what use to import a gospel from Judæa, if we leave behind the soul that made it possible, the God who keeps it forever real and present? Surely Abana and Pharpar *are* better than Jordan, if a living faith be mixed with those waters and none with these.

Scotch Presbyterianism as a motive of spiritual progress was dead; New England Puritanism was in like manner dead; in other words, Protestantism had made its fortune and no longer protested; but till Carlyle spoke out in the Old World and Emerson in the New, no one had dared to proclaim, *Le roi est mort: vive le roi!* The meaning of which proclamation was essentially this: the vital spirit has long since departed out of this form once so kingly, and the great seal has been in commission long enough; but meanwhile the soul of man, from which all power emanates and to which it reverts, still survives in undiminished royalty; God still survives, little as you gentlemen of the Commission seem to be aware of it,—nay, will possibly outlive the whole of you, incredible as it may appear. The truth is, that both Scotch Presbyterianism and New England Puritanism made their new avatar in Carlyle and Emerson, the heralds of their formal decease, and the tendency of the one toward Authority and of the other toward Independency might have been prophesied by whoever had studied history. The necessity was not so much in the men as in the principles they represented and the traditions which overruled them. The Puritanism of the past found its unwill-

ing poet in Hawthorne, the rarest creative imagination of the century, the rarest in some ideal respects since Shakespeare; but the Puritanism that cannot die, the Puritanism that made New England what it is, and is destined to make America what it should be, found its voice in Emerson. Though holding himself aloof from all active partnership in movements of reform, he has been the sleeping partner who has supplied a great part of their capital.

The artistic range of Emerson is narrow, as every well-read critic must feel at once; and so is that of Æschylus, so is that of Dante, so is that of Montaigne, so is that of Schiller, so is that of nearly every one except Shakespeare; but there is a gauge of height no less than of breadth, of individuality as well as of comprehensiveness, and, above all, there is the standard of genetic power, the test of the masculine as distinguished from the receptive minds. There are staminate plants in literature, that make no fine show of fruit, but without whose pollen, quintessence of fructifying gold, the garden had been barren. Emerson's mind is emphatically one of these, and there is no man to whom our æsthetic culture owes so much. The Puritan revolt had made us ecclesiastically and the Revolution politically independent, but we were still socially and intellectually moored to English thought, till Emerson cut the cable and gave us a chance at the dangers and the glories of blue water. No man young enough to have felt it can forget or cease to be grateful for the mental and moral *nudge* which he received from the writings of his high-minded and brave-spirited countryman. That we agree with him, or that he always agrees with himself, is aside from the question; but that he arouses in us something that we are the better for having awakened, whether that something be of opposition or assent, that he speaks always to what is highest and least selfish in us, few Americans of the generation younger than his own would be disposed to deny. His oration before the Phi Beta Kappa Society at Cambridge, some thirty years ago, was an event without any former parallel in our literary annals, a scene to be always treasured in the memory for its picturesqueness and its inspiration. What crowded and breathless aisles, what windows clustering with eager heads, what enthusiasm of approval, what grim silence of foregone dissent! It was our Yankee version of a lecture by Abelard, our Harvard parallel to the last public appearances of Schelling.

I said that the Transcendental Movement was the protestant spirit of Puritanism seeking a new outlet and an escape from forms and creeds which compressed rather than expressed it. In its motives, its preaching, and its results, it differed radically from the doctrine of Carlyle. The Scotchman, with all his genius, and his humor gigantesque as that of Rabelais, has grown shriller and shriller with years, degenerating sometimes into a common scold, and emptying very unsavory vials of wrath on the head of the sturdy British Socrates of worldly common-sense. The teaching of Emerson tended much more exclusively to self-culture and the independent development of the individual man. It seemed to many almost Pythagorean in its voluntary seclusion from commonwealth affairs. Both Carlyle and Emerson were disciples of Goethe, but Emerson in a far truer sense; and while the one, from his bias toward the eccentric, has degenerated more and more into mannerism, the other has clarified steadily toward perfection of style,—exquisite fineness of material, unobtrusive lowness of tone and simplicity of fashion, the most high-bred garb of expression. Whatever may be said of his thought, nothing can be finer than the delicious limpidness of his phrase. If it was ever questionable whether democracy could develop a gentleman, the problem has been affirmatively solved at last. Carlyle, in his cynicism and his admiration of force in and for itself, has become at last positively inhuman; Emerson, reverencing strength, seeking the highest outcome of the individual, has found that society and politics are also main elements in the attainment of the desired end, and has drawn steadily manward and world-ward. The two men represent respectively those grand personifications in the drama of Æschylus, Βία and Κράτος [might; strength].

Among the pistillate plants kindled to fruitage by the Emersonian pollen, Thoreau is thus far the most remarkable; and it is something eminently fitting that his posthumous works should be offered us by Emerson, for they are strawberries from his own garden. A singular mixture of varieties, indeed, there is;—alpine, some of them, with the flavor of rare mountain air; others wood, tasting of sunny roadside banks or shy openings in the forest; and not a few seedlings swollen hugely by culture, but lacking the fine natural aroma of the more modest kinds. Strange books these are of his, and interesting in many ways,—instructive chiefly as showing how considerable a crop may be raised on a comparatively narrow close of mind, and how much a man may make of his life if he will assiduously follow it, though perhaps never truly finding it at last.

I have just been renewing my recollection of Mr. Thoreau's writings, and have read through his six volumes in the order of their production. I shall try to give an adequate report of their impression upon me both as critic and as mere reader. He seems to me to have been a man with so high a conceit of himself that he accepted without questioning, and insisted on our accepting, his defects and weaknesses of character as virtues and powers peculiar to himself. Was he indolent, he finds none of the activities which attract or employ the rest of mankind worthy of him. Was he wanting in the qualities that make success, it is success that is contemptible, and not himself that lacks persistency and purpose. Was he poor, money was an unmixed evil. Did his life seem a selfish one, he condemns doing good as one of the weakest of superstitions. To be of use was with him the most killing bait of the wily tempter Uselessness. He had no faculty of generalization from outside of himself, or at least no experience which would supply the material of such, and he makes his own whim the law, his own range the horizon of the universe. He condemns a world, the hollowness of whose satisfactions he had never had the means of testing, and we recognize Apemantus behind the mask of Timon. He had little active imagination; of the receptive he had much. His appreciation is of the highest quality; his critical power, from want of continuity of mind, very limited and inadequate. He somewhere cites a simile from Ossian, as an example of the superiority of the old poetry to the new, though, even were the historic evidence less convincing, the sentimental melancholy of those poems should be conclusive of their modernness. He had none of the artistic mastery which controls a great work to the serene balance of completeness, but exquisite mechanical skill in the shaping of sentences and paragraphs, or (more rarely) short bits of verse for the expression of a detached thought, sentiment, or image. His works give one the feeling of a sky full of stars,—something impressive and exhilarating certainly, something high overhead and freckled thickly with spots of isolated brightness; but whether these have any mutual relation with each other, or have any concern with our mundane matters, is for the most part matter of conjecture,—astrology as yet, and not astronomy.

It is curious, considering what Thoreau after-

wards became, that he was not by nature an observer. He only saw the things he looked for, and
was less poet than naturalist. Till he built his
Walden shanty, he did not know that the hickory
grew in Concord. Till he went to Maine, he had
never seen phosphorescent wood, a phenomenon
early familiar to most country boys. At forty he
speaks of the seeding of the pine as a new discovery, though one should have thought that its gold-
dust of blowing pollen might have earlier drawn
his eye. Neither his attention nor his genius was
of the spontaneous kind. He discovered nothing.
He thought everything a discovery of his own, from
moonlight to the planting of acorns and nuts by
squirrels. This is a defect in his character, but one
of his chief charms as a writer. Everything grows
fresh under his hand. He delved in his mind and
nature; he planted them with all manner of native
and foreign seeds, and reaped assiduously. He was
not merely solitary, he would be isolated, and succeeded at last in almost persuading himself that he
was autochthonous. He valued everything in proportion as he fancied it to be exclusively his own.
He complains in "Walden" that there is no one in
Concord with whom he could talk of Oriental
literature, though the man was living within two
miles of his hut who had introduced him to it.
This intellectual selfishness becomes sometimes almost painful in reading him. He lacked that
generosity of "communication" which Johnson admired in Burke. De Quincey tells us that Wordsworth was impatient when any one else spoke of
mountains, as if he had a peculiar property in
them. And we can readily understand why it should
be so: no one is satisfied with another's appreciation of his mistress. But Thoreau seems to have
prized a lofty way of thinking (often we should be
inclined to call it a remote one) not so much because it was good in itself as because he wished few
to share it with him. It seems now and then as if
he did not seek to lure others up "above our lower
region of turmoil," but to leave his own name cut
on the mountain peak as the first climber. This
itch of originality infects his thought and style. To
be misty is not to be mystic. He turns common-
places end for end, and fancies it makes something
new of them. As we walk down Park Street, our
eye is caught by Dr. Winship's dumb-bells, one of
which bears an inscription testifying that it is the
heaviest ever put up at arm's length by any athlete;
and in reading Mr. Thoreau's books we cannot help
feeling as if he sometimes invited our attention to
a particular sophism or paradox as the biggest yet

maintained by any single writer. He seeks, at all
risks, for perversity of thought, and revives the age
of *concetti* while he fancies himself going back
to a pre-classical nature. "A day," he says, "passed
in the society of those Greek sages, such as described in the Banquet of Xenophon, would not be
comparable with the dry wit of decayed cranberry-
vines and the fresh Attic salt of the moss-beds."
It is not so much the True that he loves as the
Out-of-the-Way. As the Brazen Age shows itself
in other men by exaggeration of phrase, so in him
by extravagance of statement. He wishes always to
trump your suit and to *ruff* when you least expect it. Do you love Nature because she is beautiful? He will find a better argument in her ugliness.
Are you tired of the artificial man? He instantly
dresses you up an ideal in a Penobscot Indian,
and attributes to this creature of his otherwise-
mindedness as peculiarities things that are common to all woodsmen, white or red, and this simply
because he has not studied the pale-faced variety.

This notion of an absolute originality, as if one
could have a patent-right in it, is an absurdity. A
man cannot escape in thought, any more than he
can in language, from the past and the present.
As no one ever invents a word, and yet language
somehow grows by general contribution and necessity, so it is with thought. Mr. Thoreau seems to
me to insist in public on going back to flint and
steel, when there is a match-box in his pocket
which he knows very well how to use at a pinch.
Originality consists in power of digesting and assimilating thought, so that they become part of
our life and substance. Montaigne, for example,
is one of the most original of authors, though he
helped himself to ideas in every direction. But
they turn to blood and coloring in his style, and
give a freshness of complexion that is forever
charming. In Thoreau much seems yet to be foreign and unassimilated, showing itself in symptoms
of indigestion. A preacher-up of Nature, we now
and then detect under the surly and stoic garb
something of the sophist and the sentimentalizer.
I am far from implying that this was conscious on
his part. But it is much easier for a man to impose
on himself when he measures only with himself.
A greater familiarity with ordinary men would have
done Thoreau good, by showing him how many
fine qualities are common to the race. The radical
vice of his theory of life was that he confounded
physical with spiritual remoteness from men. A
man is far enough withdrawn from his fellows if
he keep himself clear of their weaknesses. He is

not so truly withdrawn as exiled, if he refuse to share in their strength. "Solitude," says Cowley, "can be well fitted and set right but upon a very few persons. They must have enough knowledge of the world to see the vanity of it, and enough virtue to despise all vanity." It is a morbid self-consciousness that pronounces the world of men empty and worthless before trying it, the instinctive evasion of one who is sensible of some innate weakness, and retorts the accusation of it before any has made it but himself. To a healthy mind, the world is a constant challenge of opportunity. Mr. Thoreau had not a healthy mind, or he would not have been so fond of prescribing. His whole life was a search for the doctor. The old mystics had a wiser sense of what the world was worth. They ordained a severe apprenticeship to law, and even ceremonial, in order to the gaining of freedom and mastery over these. Seven years of service for Rachel were to be rewarded at last with Leah. Seven other years of faithfulness with her were to win them at last the true bride of their souls. Active Life was with them the only path to the Contemplative.

Thoreau had no humor, and this implies that he was a sorry logician. Himself an artist in rhetoric, he confounds thought with style when he undertakes to speak of the latter. He was forever talking of getting away from the world, but he must be always near enough to it, nay, to the Concord corner of it, to feel the impression he makes there. He verifies the shrewd remark of Sainte-Beuve, "On touche encore à son temps et très-fort, même quand on le repousse." [One remains a creature of his time even in rejecting it.] This egotism of his is a Stylites pillar after all, a seclusion which keeps him in the public eye. The dignity of man is an excellent thing, but therefore to hold one's self too sacred and precious is the reverse of excellent. There is something delightfully absurd in six volumes addressed to a world of such "vulgar fellows" as Thoreau affirmed his fellowmen to be. I once had a glimpse of a genuine solitary who spent his winters one hundred and fifty miles beyond all human communication, and there dwelt with his rifle as his only confidant. Compared with this, the shanty on Walden Pond has something the air, it must be confessed, of the Hermitage of La Chevrette. I do not believe that the way to a true cosmopolitanism carries one into the woods or the society of musquashes. Perhaps the narrowest provincialism is that of Self; that of Kleinwinkel is nothing to it. The natural man, like the singing birds, comes out of the forest as inevitably as the natural bear and the wildcat stick there. To seek to be natural implies a consciousness that forbids all naturalness forever. It is as easy—and no easier—to be natural in a *salon* as in a swamp, if one do not aim at it, for what we call unnaturalness always has its spring in a man's thinking too much about himself. "It is impossible," said Turgot, "for a vulgar man to be simple."

I look upon a great deal of the modern sentimentalism about Nature as a mark of disease. It is one more symptom of the general liver-complaint. To a man of wholesome constitution the wilderness is well enough for a mood or a vacation, but not for a habit of life. Those who have most loudly advertised their passion for seclusion and their intimacy with nature, from Petrarch down, have been mostly sentimentalists, unreal men, misanthropes on the spindle side, solacing an uneasy suspicion of themselves by professing contempt for their kind. They make demands on the world in advance proportioned to their inward measure of their own merit, and are angry that the world pays only by the visible measure of performance. It is true of Rousseau, the modern founder of the sect, true of Saint Pierre, his intellectual child, and of Châteaubriand, his grandchild, the inventor, we might almost say, of the primitive forest, and who first was touched by the solemn falling of a tree from natural decay in the windless silence of the woods. It is a very shallow view that affirms trees and rocks to be healthy, and cannot see that men in communities are just as true to the laws of their organization and destiny; that can tolerate the puffin and the fox, but not the fool and the knave; that would shun politics because of its demagogues, and snuff up the stench of the obscene fungus. The divine life of Nature is more wonderful, more various, more sublime in man than in any other of her works, and the wisdom that is gained by commerce with men, as Montaigne and Shakespeare gained it, or with one's own soul among men, as Dante, is the most delightful, as it is the most precious, of all. In outward nature it is still man that interests us, and we care far less for the things seen than the way in which they are seen by poetic eyes like Wordsworth's or Thoreau's, and the reflections they cast there. To hear the to-do that is often made over the simple fact that a man sees the image of himself in the outward world, one is reminded of a savage when he for the first time catches a glimpse of himself in a looking-glass. "Venerable child of Nature," we are tempted to say, "to whose science in the invention of the tobacco-pipe, to whose art in the tattooing of thine undegenerate hide not yet enslaved by tailors, we are slowly striving to climb back, the miracle thou beholdest is sold in my unhappy country for a shilling!" If matters go on as they have done, and everybody must needs blab of all the favors that have been done him by roadside and riverbrink and woodland walk, as if to kiss and tell were no longer treachery, it will be a positive refreshment to meet a man who is as superbly indifferent to Nature as she is to him. By and by we shall have John Smith, of No. –12 –12th Street, advertising that he is not the J. S. who saw a cow-lily on Thursday last, as he never saw one in his life, would not see one if he could, and is prepared to prove an alibi on the day in question.

Solitary communion with Nature does not seem to have been sanitary or sweetening in its influence on Thoreau's character. On the contrary, his letters show him more cynical as he grew older. While he studied with respectful attention the minks and woodchucks, his neighbors, he looked with utter contempt on the august drama of destiny of which his country was the scene, and on which the curtain had already risen. He was converting us back to a state of nature "so eloquently," as Voltaire said of Rousseau, "that he almost persuaded us to go on all fours," while the wiser fates were making it possible for us to walk erect for the first time. Had he conversed more with his fellows, his sympathies would have widened with the assurance that his peculiar genius had more appreciation, and his writings a larger circle of readers, or at least a warmer one, than he dreamed of. We have the highest testimony [1] to the natural sweetness, sincerity, and nobleness of his temper, and in his books an equally irrefragable one to the rare quality of his mind. He was not a strong thinker, but a sensitive feeler. Yet his mind strikes us as cold and wintry in its purity. A light snow has fallen everywhere in which he seems to come on the track of the shier sensations that would elsewhere leave no trace. We think greater compression would have done more for his fame. A feeling of sameness comes over us as we read so much. Trifles are recorded with an over-minute punctuality and conscientiousness of detail. He registers the state of his personal thermometer thirteen times a day. We cannot help thinking sometimes of the man who

"Watches, starves, freezes, and sweats
To learn but catechisms and alphabets
Of unconcerning things, matters of fact,"

and sometimes of the saying of the Persian poet, that "when the owl would boast, he boasts of catching mice at the edge of a hole." We could readily part with some of his affectations. It was well enough for Pythagoras to say, once for all, "When I was Euphorbus at the siege of Troy"; not so well for Thoreau to travesty it into "When I was a shepherd on the plains of Assyria." A naïve thing said over again is anything but naïve. But with every exception, there is no writing comparable with Thoreau's in kind, that is comparable with it in degree where it is best; where it disengages itself, that is, from the tangled roots and dead leaves of a second-hand Orientalism, and runs limpid and smooth and broadening as it runs, a mirror for whatever is grand and lovely in both worlds.

George Sand says neatly, that "Art is not a study of positive reality," (*actuality* were the fitter word,) "but a seeking after ideal truth." It would be doing very inadequate justice to Thoreau if we left it to be inferred that this ideal element did not exist in him, and that too in larger proportion, if less obtrusive, than his nature-worship. He took nature as the mountain-path to an ideal world. If the path wind a good deal, if he record too faithfully every trip over a root, if he botanize somewhat wearisomely, he gives us now and then superb outlooks from some jutting crag, and brings us out at last into an illimitable ether, where the breathing is not difficult for those who have any true touch of the climbing spirit. His shanty-life was a mere impossibility, so far as his own conception of it goes, as an entire independency of mankind. The tub of Diogenes had a sounder bottom. Thoreau's experiment actually presupposed all that complicated civilization which it theoretically abjured. He squatted on another man's land; he borrows an axe; his boards, his nails, his bricks, his mortar, his books, his lamp, his fish-hooks, his plough, his hoe, all turn state's evidence against him as an accomplice in the sin of that artificial civilization which rendered it possible that such a person as Henry D. Thoreau should exist at all. *Magnis tamen excidit ausis* [Nevertheless, it was at great undertakings that he failed]. His aim was a noble and a useful one, in the direction of "plain living and high thinking." It was a practical sermon on Emerson's text that "things are in the saddle

---

[1] Mr. Emerson, in the Biographical Sketch prefixed to the *Excursions* [Lowell].

and ride mankind," an attempt to solve Carlyle's problem (condensed from Johnson) of "lessening your denominator." His whole life was a rebuke of the waste and aimlessness of our American luxury, which is an abject enslavement to tawdry upholstery. He had "fine translunary things" in him. His better style as a writer is in keeping with the simplicity and purity of his life. We have said that his range was narrow, but to be a master is to be a master. He had caught his English at its living source, among the poets and prose-writers of its best days; his literature was extensive and recondite; his quotations are always nuggets of the purest ore: there are sentences of his as perfect as anything in the language, and thoughts as clearly crystallized; his metaphors and images are always fresh from the soil; he had watched Nature like a detective who is to go upon the stand; as we read him, it seems as if all-out-of-doors had kept a diary and become its own Montaigne; we look at the landscape as in a Claude Lorraine glass; compared with his, all other books of similar aim, even White's "Selborne," seem dry as a country clergyman's meteorological journal in an old almanac. He belongs with Donne and Browne and Novalis; if not with the originally creative men, with the scarcely smaller class who are peculiar, and whose leaves shed their invisible thought-seed like ferns.

OLIVER WENDELL HOLMES (1809–1894)

Like Longfellow and Lowell, Oliver Wendell Holmes can probably tell us more about the pervasive cultural climate of nineteenth-century Boston—and perhaps that of New England—than can more powerful and searching intellects or more adventurous imaginations. For the minor writer reflects the general coloration of the period, and his individual qualities are not sufficiently striking to distract us from what is typical. Holmes not only was a minor writer; he was not even a professional man of letters in the sense that Longfellow and Lowell were. He wrote for pleasure and essentially in the spirit of the accomplished amateur. His training was scientific, and his profession was medicine. Thus, his literary work was executed with his left hand—though it proved to be so adept as to justify the claim that the man to whom it belonged was ambidextrous.

By family background and nurture Holmes was well prepared to reflect the characteristic ethos of the civilization of Boston. Though his father was Connecticut-born and was educated at Yale College, he had moved to Cambridge when he was called to become minister of its First Congregational Church. There he married a Cambridge girl, the daughter of Judge Oliver Wendell. In 1809 their first son, Oliver, was born in a house just north of Harvard Yard, and in due time Oliver graduated from Harvard College.

Again like Longfellow and Lowell, by spending some years in Europe Holmes had acquired a perspective that allowed him to see his provincial culture with a measure of detachment. For some two and a half years he studied medicine in Paris before he returned to practice in Boston, later to become one of the more distinguished professors in the Harvard Medical School. He was the author of several scientific papers, one of which would today be called a "breakthrough": it established the fact that puerperal fever was spread by contact. Thus as a scientist and physician Holmes was in touch with his culture at points beyond the reach of a Longfellow or a Lowell. Throughout his life Holmes studied the culture of Boston thoughtfully, if yet with loving amusement. (See below, for example, his account of the "Brahmin Caste.")

The Boston of Holmes's day was worth the study. It was a genuine cultural capital and one whose great literary flowering coincided with the period of Holmes's own maturity. His best prose reflects the bright and witty conversation of his circle of Boston friends. *The Autocrat of the Breakfast Table*, one supposes, mirrors rather faithfully—though of course in a more concentrated form—the kind of talk to be heard at the Saturday Club. (See p. 605 above.) Most of Holmes's poetry is frankly topical and occasional, and many of the occasions that he celebrated have to do with the life of Boston and its environs.

Boston, to be sure, was not the only literary center among the American cities. Philadelphia had been a publishing center since Franklin set up his press there in 1728, and, as one would expect of the home city of the American Philosophical Society, it was particularly important for scientific studies. It boasted men like Dr. Benjamin Rush, a pioneer in medical science, Benjamin Barton, the great botanist, and Joseph Priestley, the British-born chemist who arrived in 1794 and lived out his life there.

The great days of New York as the literary capital of the nation were not to arrive until the middle of the nineteenth century, but much earlier that city might claim writers like Cooper and Irving and lesser figures like James Kirke Paulding and Nathaniel Parker Willis, as well as Halleck and Drake (see pp. 201–4). Moreover, as a thriving port and business city, New York was already beginning to attract writers from other regions, such as Bryant from New England and Poe from Virginia. Further south there were literary centers like Baltimore (with William Wirt, Edward Coote Pinkney, and John Pendleton Kennedy) and Charleston.

Charleston is of particular interest here, for its resemblance to Boston in some characteristics makes it almost the perfect foil to set off certain features of Boston life. Each city absolutely dominated its cultural area. Holmes's Autocrat comments on the statement that "Boston State-House is the hub of the solar-system." Though he takes note of the way in which local pride everywhere manifests itself, he is willing to concede that Boston does have "some right to look down on the mob of cities." The Autocrat is here surely stating Holmes's own view of the matter. Many a Bostonian did regard his city as the hub of the universe.

Charleston too had its pride, seeing itself as a city-state on the Greek model, expressing, and giving focus to, the whole social, political, and artistic life of the South Carolina low country. Both Boston and Charleston had their great families, but Charleston probably came even closer to being what a sociologist would call an old-fashioned "kinship society." But the resemblance between the two cities pretty well exhausts itself in the fact that each was thoroughly expressive of its cultural region.

The cultures themselves were sharply different in almost every regard—economic, social, and political—though we shall be concerned here with only the artistic and literary life.

Charleston had its arts, but they were not primarily literary. Its most authentic cultural expression is to be found in its architecture, its gardens, its social life, and such informal arts as letter writing and conversation. See, for example, the excerpts in our text from the diary of Mary Boykin Chesnut. Mrs. Chesnut lived on one of the great plantations outside Charleston, was related to many important people, knew everybody in Charleston and the country about, and was an amateur writer of great natural talent. Her diary is not only richly informative about the culture of Charleston: it remains today highly readable—more successful as "literature" than most of the high-flown attempts at that special commodity.

Charleston had in Simms its principal novelist and a half generation later would have its poets, Henry Timrod (1826–1867) and Paul Hamilton Hayne (1830–1886), but its culture was not "literary" in the sense in which Boston's was. Simms was aware of his countrymen's lack of appreciation of literary distinction and Hayne was eager—though, to be sure, *after* the debacle of the Civil War—to move to the Northeast.

What is at stake here is not the failure of Simms to produce great fiction or of Hayne to write significant poetry. The Boston writers discussed in this section—Longfellow, Lowell, and Holmes—were not first-rate literary artists either, but they had an audience that read for more than mere entertainment. Literature, for their readers—even *belles lettres*—did mesh with significant interests. It was not viewed as primarily an ornament which could be dismissed in the stress of really important affairs or put aside when more energetic and exciting pastimes were at hand.

Thomas Bailey Aldrich (1836–1907), a minor literary figure of the mid-century, provides an excellent definition of Boston's special literary character. In a letter written in 1866 he describes to a friend the difference between New York and Boston:

> There is a finer intellectual atmosphere here [in Boston] than in our city. It is true, a poor literary man could not earn his salt, or more than that, out of pure literary labor in Boston; but then he couldn't do it in New York, unless he turned *journalist*. The people of Boston are full-blooded *readers*, appreciative, trained. The humble man of letters has a position here which he doesn't have in New York. To be known as an able writer is to have the choicest society opened to you. Just as an officer in the Navy (providing he is a gentleman) is the social equal of everybody—so a knight of the quill here is supposed necessarily to be a gentleman. In New York—he's a Bohemian! outside of his personal friends he has no standing.

Perhaps nothing was more characteristic of the cultural flavor of Boston than the Saturday Club, a group that met each month for lunch and conversation. At a typical gathering one might sit down with men of letters like Lowell, Longfellow, and Emerson; with scientists like Louis Agassiz and Benjamin Peirce; with musicians like Thomas Dwight; with historians like John Lothrop Motley; and with lawyers like Rockwood Hoar and Richard Henry Dana, the latter being also the author of the American classic *Two Years Before the Mast*. Henry James, the father of William, the psychologist, and Henry, Jr., the novelist, tells of meeting Nathaniel Hawthorne there on at least one occasion.

E. P. Whipple describes one of the livelier meetings of the Club: on this occasion Motley made a statement with which Holmes immediately disagreed, only to have Lowell break in to state his difference with both men. Whipple writes:

> Still, in the incessant din of voices, every point made by one was replied to by another or ridiculed by a third, and was instantly followed by new statements, counter-statements, arguments and counter-arguments, hits and retorts, all germane to the matter, and all directed toward a definite end. The curiosity of the contest was that none of the combatants repeated anything which had once been thrown out as irrelevant, and that . . . the course of the discussion was as clear to the mind as though there had been a minute's pause between statement and reply. . . . The other members of the Club looked on in mute wonder while witnessing these feats of intellectual and vocal gymnastics. (*Early Years of the Saturday Club*, 1918, pp. 91–92)

A pleasant story, which may well be true, nicely illustrates the feeling of intimacy and the sense of community that obtained. It seems that Dr. Holmes was examining William James in anatomy when James was standing for his degree in medicine. Holmes asked James one or two questions, each of which James answered correctly, and then exclaimed: "Good, good; that's enough. Now tell me, how is your dear old father?"

Yet Holmes—and probably most of his confreres in the Saturday Club—intellectually alert as they were, nevertheless failed to comprehend the important economic and social changes which were taking place in the nation. They were not alone, of course, in this failure of perception and comprehension; few Americans seem to have sensed what was occurring during the latter part of the nineteenth century. In fact, not many understood the implications of the Civil War itself, interpreting it merely on the constitutional level of preserving the union or on the moral level of freeing the slaves. The fact that the conflict had as one of its results a tremendous speeding up—and redefining—of the process of industrialization and finance-capitalism was scarcely comprehended.[1]

In general Holmes tended to be a conservative and a rather conventional conservative at that. He manifested a liberal spirit only in scientific work and in his conception of the nature of ultimate truth. During the period in which New England was powerfully agitated by the abolitionists, Holmes would have no part in their program. Evidently he found the abolitionists noisy and obstreperous and believed them not likely to accomplish very much by their conduct. Moreover, he felt that the situation was not as bad as they painted it, and in any case he hoped that time and historical developments would rid the nation of the curse of slavery without resort having to be made to the violent actions toward which the abolitionists were obviously driving. There is no reason to attribute Holmes's stand on abolitionism either to indifference or to moral cowardice. His attitude toward the evils of society and the various political modes for dealing with them was of a piece with the rest of his training and temperament. When the Civil War did break out, Holmes was wholehearted in his commitment to the Union and to the necessity of prosecuting the war with all vigor. He sent his son (who in 1902 was to become Chief Justice of the Supreme Court of the United States) into the conflict with his blessing and took great pride in his son's career as a Union soldier.

Holmes was a remarkably agile occasional poet. He was the official poet of Harvard's class

---

[1] If David Donald is correct in saying that the abolitionists were on the whole descended from professional men and were somewhat resentful at being elbowed out of political and moral leadership by the rising class of bankers and manufacturers (see his *Lincoln Reconsidered*, 1959), then their attack on slavery takes on a certain irony. For a principal economic consequence of the Civil War was the establishment of the power of the corporations and the delivery of the new Republican party over to Big Business. If one protests that this was not at all what the idealists desired, the reply is that this is precisely the point to be made: few Americans, including the abolitionists and the professional class generally, saw very clearly the complex consequences of the causes they supported.

of 1829 and continued through his lifetime to write of Harvard men and Harvard occasions. But he could supply poems for any other occasions, and his collected works are filled with such odd titles as "At the Banquet to the Grand Duke Alexis" and "Hymn Written for the Great Central Fair in Philadelphia, 1864." Unfortunately, the final reputation of a topical and occasional poet usually varies inversely with his contemporary popularity. A few of Holmes's poems do endure—those that deal with universal topics and those that treat their local and special subjects with so much finesse that we make the application to ourselves.

Holmes's prose has held up a good deal better than his poetry. This is particularly true of quasi-fictional essays of the sort to be found in *The Autocrat of the Breakfast Table*. This witty and entertaining work owes something to the papers that Joseph Addison contributed to the *Spectator* and something to the personal essays of Charles Lamb. The subtitle of *The Autocrat*, "Every Man His Own Boswell," points to still another model, the talk of Samuel Johnson as recorded in Boswell's famous life of the great man. Holmes's title suggests that the Autocrat, lacking a Boswell, proposes to be his own recorder.

Like Addison, Holmes provides a fictional character to utter what he has to say. The Autocrat's audience (for the indefatigable talker requires attentive listeners) consists of his fellow boarders at the breakfast table—the schoolmistress, the landlady's nineteen-year-old daughter, the "old gentleman," the divinity student. (The Addison of the *Spectator* papers, one remembers, arranged something similar: there was a club gathered about the "Spectator.") Holmes's Autocrat addresses his remarks now to one, now to another of the breakfasters; on occasion he may have timid questions put to him; he is sometimes interrupted by one of the bolder of his companions.

The talk is, on the whole, quite good and runs over every kind of subject from art to science, from the trivial to the profound. Holmes enjoyed good talk and by every account was a most entertaining conversationalist. Because human nature changes so little, such talk is perennially attractive, and much of Holmes's writing of this sort—for he produced other series such as *The Professor at the Breakfast Table* (1860), *The Poet at the Breakfast Table* (1872), and *Over the Teacups* (1891)—is still thoroughly readable.

In his *Autocrat* papers Holmes gives us the flavor of spontaneous talk, basically a monologue with occasional interruptions. Yet what we are reading is in fact very different from the random and sprawling stuff that might be picked up by a tape recorder. The style may seem artless but is in fact a conscious work of art.

The first five paragraphs (see pp. 639–40) provide a good illustration. The sentences tend to be short. They often say something that is mildly startling. It is an aphoristic style which at times sounds like a pleasant (though serious) parody of Emerson's essays. But the succession of terse and simple sentences on occasion rises to the effective rhetorical complication of a sentence like the following: "Unpretending mediocrity is good, and genius is glorious; but a weak flavor of genius in an essentially common person is detestable."

The Autocrat is urbane; he frequently speaks with tongue in cheek. He is often ironical, as in the sly observation that "men of genius may even associate together and continue to think highly of each other." But he can also (as in the second paragraph) adopt the bluff knock-'em-down style of Dr. Samuel Johnson. When, for example, the divinity student "abuses" his liberty "by presuming to say that Leibnitz had the same observation," the Autocrat floors him with a direct contradiction: "No, sir, I replied, he has not. But he said a mighty good thing about mathematics, that sounds something like it, and you found it, *not in the original*, but quoted by Dr. Thomas Reid."

The Autocrat is the master of ingenious analogies and is adept at using the concrete language of metaphor. Sometimes the metaphor is condensed, as in the fifth paragraph, where he refers to "the broken-winded novel, or spavined verse" of certain mediocrities, implying that their fiction and verses were like broken-down

nags incapable of winning any horse race. Sometimes the metaphor is brilliantly elaborated, as when Holmes puts the case persuasively against the essentially common place person who has only "a weak flavor of genius." That weak flavor, he says, "spoils the grand neutrality of a common place character, as the rinsings of an unwashed wine-glass spoil a draught of fair water." The talk of the Autocrat may not be profound or deeply moving, but the prose is alive and the mind and personality sparkle through his long semi-monologue.

One of the most interesting aspects of Holmes and certainly one of his boldest experiments was his writing of three psychological novels. The first of these, *Elsie Venner*, tells the story of a girl who would probably today be called a manic-depressive. Holmes's purpose in writing this novel was to dispose of any theological explanation for the girl's strange and, as it might appear to some people, even diabolical conduct. He accounts for her behavior in purely naturalistic terms: before Elsie's birth, her mother had been bitten by a rattlesnake and the narrator supposes that the shock to the mother (and perhaps the venom of the serpent) had affected the child in the womb. The twentieth-century reader will find this explanation fantastic, but he will not find fantastic Holmes's attempt to explore the problem of abnormal behavior, to try to understand it, and to find its origin either in the effect of chemical substances on the body or in the psychic conditioning that the infant has received.

It must be said that neither *Elsie Venner* nor Holmes's other psychological novels (*The Guardian Angel* and *A Mortal Antipathy*) are successful as fiction. Holmes is so clumsily bent on making his point didactically that he is not able to mediate his insights through a plausible dramatic form. Yet, though lacking literary merit, these novels do embody Holmes's own practical experience as a physician, and they do constitute, in intent at least, a real anticipation of modern attitudes toward the treatment of the mentally ill.

Holmes once remarked that we ought to treat "bad men as if they were insane. They are *in-sane*, out of health, morally." This view of the matter represents a shocking departure from earlier Puritan doctrines about the nature of man. The Holmes family in itself provides an apt illustration of what was happening to New England Puritanism through the course of the nineteenth century. Of Holmes's grandfather, a surgeon, we know nothing to make us think that he held other than orthodox religious views. Holmes's father was a clergyman and his views were far from radical, though they were too liberal for his Calvinist congregation and got him into trouble. This experience was not lost on the son, Oliver Wendell, who became, as his novels show, seriously concerned to loosen what remained of the bonds of Calvinism and to beget a more liberal attitude toward human delinquency. But the elder Holmes never quite freed himself from certain Puritan inhibitions. To the end of his life he did not permit himself to read novels on Sunday until after sundown—that is, until what he reckoned was the end of the Sabbath day. It is not until we come to *his* son, the man destined to be a justice of the Supreme Court, that we get something like a final emancipation in which the stern New England creed has disappeared completely in favor of a skeptical humanism.

The attitude expressed in Holmes's novels was part of an increasingly humanistic attitude which Holmes shared with a good many other New Englanders of his generation. He remarks that " 'Nature' and 'Grace' have been contrasted with each other" as the "hostile Divinities in the Pantheon of post-classical polytheism." But fortunately for mankind, Darwinism had now removed "the traditional curse from that helpless infant lying in his mother's arms. . . . We have everything to hope from the future. . . . We are entering on a new era . . . the Revival of Humanity. . . . Sin, like disease, is a vital process. . . . It must be studied as a section of anthropology."

Holmes, then, is an optimist: nature, including human nature, is good; history holds out hope for mankind. These conceptions constituted for Holmes a liberation. He saw the race as now standing in the dawn of a new day. A general optimism about man and his purposes—an optimism which even the horrors of the Civil War had not been able seriously to shake—was to become complacent and to mellow into what George Santayana would later call the "genteel tradition." Calvinism he defined as the "expression of the agonized conscience." Santayana would contend, further, that when the sense of sin evaporates, the virtues generated by Calvinism—earnest endeavor, searchings of the spirit, rigorous self-discipline—hold on merely as unconscious habits, or are consciously justified simply because they are said to make a man healthy, wealthy, and wise, or—for poorer motives still—simply because they have in times past been the attributes of all decent, genteel people.

BIOGRAPHICAL CHART

1809	Born, August 29, in Cambridge, Massachusetts
1824	Enters Phillips Academy, Andover, Massachusetts
1825	Enters Harvard College
1830	Publishes "Old Ironsides" in the *Boston Daily Advertiser*; begins the private study of medicine in Boston
1833	Continues study of medicine in Paris, where he remains for two years, traveling intermittently in France, Holland, Italy, Switzerland, and England
1836	Receives M.D. from Harvard; begins to practice medicine; *Poems*
1838	Appointed professor of anatomy at Dartmouth College
1840	Marries Amelia Lee Jackson; returns to Boston
1843	"The Contagiousness of Puerperal Fever," his most significant contribution to medicine
1847	Appointed Parkman Professor of Anatomy and Physiology at the Harvard Medical School
1857	Publishes the main series of "The Autocrat of the Breakfast Table" in the *Atlantic Monthly*; later publishes them in book form (1858)
1860	*The Professor at the Breakfast Table*
1861	*Elsie Venner*
1867	*The Guardian Angel*
1886	Visits Europe; receives honorary degrees from various universities
1891	*Over the Teacups*
1894	Dies, October 7, in Boston

FURTHER READINGS

The Writings of Oliver Wendell Holmes (1896; 15 vols.; including John T. Morse, *Life and Letters of Holmes*) (no editor cited)

S. I. Hayakawa and H. M. Jones, eds., *Oliver Wendell Holmes: Representative Selections* (1939)

Hildegarde Hawthorne, *The Happy Autocrat: A Life of Oliver Wendell Holmes* (1938)

Eleanor M. Tilton, *The Amiable Autocrat: A Biography of Oliver Wendell Holmes* (1947)

John Greenleaf Whittier, "Mirth and Medicine," in *Literary Recreations and Miscellanies* (1854)

From Elsie Venner (1861)

THE BRAHMIN CASTE OF NEW ENGLAND

"The Brahmin Caste of New England" constitutes Chapter 1 of Holmes's novel *Elsie Venner*; but this chapter, which Holmes devised to introduce one of his characters, can be read as an essay. Holmes, by the way, was the first to use the term "Brahmin" in this fashion. Through the transcendentalists New England had become much interested in India and Indian philosophy, and since India was famous for its caste system, Holmes borrowed the name of the highest cast of India to designate the "aristocracy" of Boston.

There is nothing in New England corresponding at all to the feudal aristocracies of the Old World. Whether it be owing to the stock from which we were derived, or to the practical working of our institutions, or to the abrogation of the technical "law and honor," which draws a sharp line between the personally responsible class of "gentlemen" and the unnamed multitude of those who are not expected to risk their lives for an abstraction,— whatever be the cause, we have no such aristocracy here as that which grew up out of the military systems of the Middle Ages.

What we mean by "aristocracy" is merely the richer part of the community, that live in the tallest houses, drive real carriages, (not "kerridges,") kid-glove their hands, and French-bonnet their ladies' heads, give parties where the persons who call them by the above title are not invited, and have a provokingly easy way of dressing, walking, talking, and nodding to people, as if they felt entirely at home, and would not be embarrassed in the least, if they met the Governor, or even the President of the United States, face to face. Some of these great folks are really well-bred, some of them are only purse-proud and assuming,—but they form a class, and are named as above in the common speech.

It is in the nature of large fortunes to diminish rapidly, when subdivided and distributed. A million is the unit of wealth, now and here in America. It splits into four handsome properties; each of these into four good inheritances; these, again, into scanty competences for four ancient maidens, —with whom it is best the family should die out, unless it can begin again as its great-grandfather did. Now a million is a kind of golden cheese, which represents in a compendious form the summer's growth of a fat meadow of craft or commerce; and as this kind of meadow rarely bears more than one crop, it is pretty certain that sons and grandsons will not get another golden cheese out of it, whether they milk the same cows or turn in new ones. In other words, the millionocracy, considered in a large way, is not at all an affair of persons and families, but a perpetual fact of money with a variable human element, which a philosopher might leave out of consideration without falling into serious error. Of course, this trivial and fugitive fact of personal wealth does not create a permanent class, unless some special means are taken to arrest the process of disintegration in the third generation. This is so rarely done, at least successfully, that one need not live a very long life to see most of the rich families he knew in childhood more or less reduced, and the millions shifted into the hands of the country-boys who were sweeping stores and carrying parcels when the now decayed gentry were driving their chariots, eating their venison over silver chafing-dishes, drinking Madeira chilled in embossed coolers, wearing their hair in powder, and casing their legs in long boots with silken tassels.

There is, however, in New England, an aristocracy, if you choose to call it so, which has a far greater character of permanence. It has grown to be a *caste*,—not in any odious sense,—but, by the repetition of the same influences, generation after generation, it has acquired a distinct organization and physiognomy, which not to recognize is mere stupidity, and not to be willing to describe would show a distrust of the good-nature and intelligence of our readers, who like to have us see all we can and tell all we see.

If you will look carefully at any class of students in one of our colleges, you will have no difficulty in selecting specimens of two different aspects of youthful manhood. Of course I shall choose extreme cases to illustrate the contrast between them. In the first, the figure is perhaps robust, but often otherwise,—inelegant, partly from careless attitudes, partly from ill-dressing,—the face is uncouth in feature, or at least common,—the mouth coarse and unformed,—the eye unsympathetic, even if bright,—the movements of the face are clumsy, like those of the limbs,—the voice is unmusical,—and the enunciation as if the words were coarse castings, instead of fine carvings. The youth of the other aspect is commonly slender,—his face is smooth, and apt to be pallid,—his features are regular and of a certain delicacy,—his eye is bright and quick,—his lips play over the thought he utters as a pianist's fingers dance over their music,—and his whole air, though it may be timid, and even awkward, has nothing clownish. If you are a teacher, you know what to expect from each of these young men. With equal willingness, the first will be slow at learning; the second will take to his books as a pointer or a setter to his field-work.

The first youth is the common country-boy, whose race has been bred to bodily labor. Nature has adapted the family organization to the kind of life it has lived. The hands and feet by constant use have got more than their share of development,—the organs of thought and expression less than their share. The finer instincts are latent and must be developed. A youth of this kind is raw material in its first stage of elaboration. You must not expect too much of any such. Many of them have force of will and character, and become distinguished in practical life; but very few of them ever become great scholars. A scholar is, in a large proportion of cases, the son of scholars or scholarly persons.

That is exactly what the other young man is. He comes of the *Brahmin caste of New England*. This is the harmless, inoffensive, untitled aristocracy referred to, and which many readers will at once acknowledge. There are races of scholars among us, in which aptitude for learning, and all these marks of it I have spoken of, are congenital and hereditary. Their names are always on some college catalogue or other. They break out every generation or two in some learned labor which calls them up after they seem to have died out. At last some newer name takes their place, it may be,—but you inquire a little and you find it is the blood of the Edwardses or the Chauncys or the Ellerys or some of the old historic scholars, disguised under the altered name of a female descendant.

There probably is not an experienced instructor anywhere in our Northern States who will not recognize at once the truth of this general distinction. But the reader who has never been a teacher will very probably object, that some of our most illustrious public men have come direct from the homespun-clad class of the people,—and he may, perhaps, even find a noted scholar or two whose parents were masters of the English alphabet, but of no other.

It is not fair to pit a few chosen families against the great multitude of those who are continually working their way up into the intellectual classes. The results which are habitually reached by hereditary training are occasionally brought about without it. There are natural filters as well as artificial ones; and though the great rivers are commonly more or less turbid, if you will look long enough, you may find a spring that sparkles as no water does which drips through your apparatus of sands and sponges. So there are families which refine themselves into intellectual aptitude without having had much opportunity for intellectual acquirements. A series of felicitous crosses develops an improved strain of blood, and reaches its maximum perfection at last in the large uncombed youth who goes to college and startles the hereditary class-leaders by striding past them all. That is Nature's republicanism; thank God for it, but do not let it make you illogical. The race of the hereditary scholar has exchanged a certain portion of its animal vigor for its new instincts, and it is hard to lead men without a good deal of animal vigor. The scholar who comes by Nature's special grace from an unworn stock of broad-chested sires and deep-bosomed mothers must always overmatch an equal intelligence with a compromised and lowered vitality. A man's breathing and digestive apparatus (one is tempted to add *muscular*) are just as important to him on the floor of the Senate as his thinking organs. You broke down in your great speech, did you? Yes, your grandfather had an attack of dyspepsia in '82, after working too hard on

his famous Election Sermon. All this does not touch the main fact: our scholars come chiefly from a privileged order, just as our best fruits come from well-known grafts,—though now and then a seedling apple, like the Northern Spy, or a seedling pear, like the Seckel, springs from a nameless ancestry and grows to be the pride of all the gardens in the land.

Old Ironsides (1830)

Holmes's great facility in writing verse is well illustrated by this poem. "Old Ironsides," his most famous occasional poem, was literally dashed off. We are told that when Holmes read in a newspaper in 1830 that the frigate *Constitution* had been condemned to destruction by the navy department, on "a scrap of paper, with a lead pencil, he rapidly shaped the impetuous stanzas of 'Old Ironsides'" (John T. Morse, *Life and Letters of Holmes*, 1896). Later on, after the poem's great success, Holmes revised it to advantage, and it is the revised version which is printed here. The poem achieved its purpose and the order to dismantle the old warship was revoked.

Ay, tear her tattered ensign down!
  Long has it waved on high,
And many an eye has danced to see
  That banner in the sky;

Beneath it rung the battle shout,
  And burst the cannon's roar;—
The meteor of the ocean air
  Shall sweep the clouds no more!

Her deck, once red with heroes' blood,　　　　10
  Where knelt the vanquished foe,
When winds were hurrying o'er the flood,
  And waves were white below,
No more shall feel the victor's tread,
  Or know the conquered knee;—
The harpies of the shore shall pluck
  The eagle of the sea!

Oh, better that her shattered hulk
  Should sink beneath the wave;
Her thunder shook the mighty deep,
  And there should be her grave;　　　　20
Nail to the mast her holy flag,
  Set every threadbare sail,
And give her to the god of storms,
  The lightning and the gale!

The Last Leaf (1831)

Holmes's own note tells us that it "was suggested by the sight of a figure well known to Bostonians, that of Major Thomas Melville, 'the last of the cocked hats,' as he was sometimes called. . . . He was often pointed out as one of the 'Indians' of the famous 'Boston Tea-Party' of 1774." Major Melville (1751–1832) was Herman Melville's grandfather.

I saw him once before,
As he passed by the door,
  And again

The pavement stones resound,
As he totters o'er the ground
  With his cane.

They say that in his prime,
Ere the pruning-knife of Time
  Cut him down,
Not a better man was found　　　　10
By the Crier on his round
  Through the town.

But now he walks the streets,
And he looks at all he meets
  Sad and wan,
And he shakes his feeble head,

That it seems as if he said,
     "They are gone."

The mossy marbles rest
On the lips that he has prest   20
     In their bloom,
And the names he loved to hear
Have been carved for many a year
     On the tomb.

My grandmamma has said—
Poor old lady, she is dead
     Long ago—
That he had a Roman nose,
And his cheek was like a rose
     In the snow;   30

But now his nose is thin,
And it rests upon his chin

Like a staff,
And a crook is in his back,
And a melancholy crack
     In his laugh.

I know it is a sin
For me to sit and grin
     At him here;
But the old three-cornered hat,   40
And the breeches, and all that,
     Are so queer!

And if I should live to be
The last leaf upon the tree
     In the spring,
Let them smile, as I do now,
At the old forsaken bough
     Where I cling.

The Chambered Nautilus (1858)

"The Chambered Nautilus" first appeared as one of the poems recited by the Autocrat of the Breakfast Table in the fourth section of that work. In a note Holmes suggests that we "need not trouble ourselves about the distinction between this [the Pearly Nautilus] and the Paper Nautilus, the *Argonauta* of the ancients. The name applied to both shows that each has long been compared to a ship. . . ."

In drawing an analogy between the development of the nautilus and the development of man's soul, it is possible that Holmes had in mind a passage in which Emerson likens man's growth to that of a shellfish "which crawls out of its beautiful but stony case, because it no longer admits of growth, and slowly forms itself a new house."

Many readers have found "The Chambered Nautilus" to be Holmes's most successful poem in the high style. The first three stanzas provide brilliant realizations of the voyages of the ship of pearl. Some readers, however, may feel that Holmes flattens the poem toward didacticism in the last two stanzas. It would be interesting to try to characterize the tone of the fourth stanza.

This is the ship of pearl, which, poets feign,
     Sails the unshadowed main,—
     The venturous bark that flings

On the sweet summer wind its purpled wings
In gulfs enchanted, where the Siren sings,
     And coral reefs lie bare,
Where the cold sea-maids rise to sun their
     streaming hair.

Its webs of living gauze no more unfurl;
     Wrecked is the ship of pearl!
     And every chambered cell,   10
Where its dim dreaming life was wont to
     dwell,
As the frail tenant shaped his growing shell,
     Before thee lies revealed,—
Its irised ceiling rent, its sunless crypt unsealed!

Year after year beheld the silent toil
     That spread his lustrous coil;
     Still, as the spiral grew,
He left the past year's dwelling for the new,
Stole with soft step its shining archway
     through,
     Built up its idle door,   20
Stretched in his last-found home, and knew
     the old no more.

Thanks for the heavenly message brought by
     thee,
     Child of the wandering sea,
     Cast from her lap, forlorn!
From thy dead lips a clearer note is born
Than ever Triton blew from wreathèd horn!
     While on mine ear it rings,

Through the deep caves of thought I hear a
    voice that sings:—

Build thee more stately mansions, O my soul,
    As the swift seasons roll!   30
    Leave thy low-vaulted past!

Let each new temple, nobler than the last,
Shut thee from heaven with a dome more vast,
    Till thou at length art free,
Leaving thine outgrown shell by life's unrest-
    ing sea!

The Deacon's Masterpiece, or, the Wonderful "One-Hoss-Shay": A Logical Story (1858)

This poem was recited by the Autocrat. Holmes
set a good deal of store by the subtitle, "A
Logical Story." The poem is a good-natured
spoof on the spinning out of "logical" systems.
In spite of the tradition that Holmes here meant
to twit the ice-cold logic of Calvinism, there
seems no evidence either in his letters or in the
context of *The Autocrat* to warrant that supposition.

Holmes, in his note on the poem, writes that
it "is conceivable that a being of an order
superior to humanity should so understand the
conditions of matter that he could construct a
machine which would go to pieces, if not into
its constituent atoms, at a given moment of the
future. The mind may take a certain pleasure in
this picture of the impossible."

Yet since the deacon's intention is to build a
shay in which no one part is weaker than the
rest, it is curious that his concern as described
in the poem seems to be not so much to match
the endurance of the various parts so that no
one of them will outlast the rest but rather to
get the strongest and most enduring of every
kind of material that is to go into the shay.
Perhaps this is a hypercritical objection. But the
reader might do well to ask himself whether the
last ten lines are sufficiently prepared for.

Have you heard of the wonderful one-hoss-
    shay,
That was built in such a logical way
It ran a hundred years to a day,
And then, of a sudden, it—ah, but stay,
I'll tell you what happened without delay,
Scaring the parson into fits,
Frightening people out of their wits,—
Have you ever heard of that, I say?

Seventeen hundred and fifty-five,
Georgius Secundus was then alive,—   10
Snuffy old drone from the German hive;
That was the year when Lisbon-town
Saw the earth open and gulp her down,
And Braddock's army was done so brown,
Left without a scalp to its crown.
It was on the terrible earthquake-day
That the Deacon finished the one-hoss-shay.

Now in building of chaises, I tell you what,
There is always *somewhere* a weakest spot,—
In hub, tire, felloe, in spring or thill,   20
In panel, or crossbar, or floor, or sill,
In screw, bolt, thoroughbrace,—lurking still,
Find it somewhere you must and will,—
Above or below, or within or without,—
And that's the reason, beyond a doubt,
A chaise *breaks down*, but does n't *wear out*.

But the Deacon swore (as Deacons do,
With an "I dew vum," or an "I tell *yeou*,")
He would build one shay to beat the taown
'n' the keounty 'n' all the kentry raoun';   30
It should be so built that it *couldn'* break
    daown,
—"Fur," said the Deacon, "'t 's mighty plain
Thut the weakes' place mus' stan' the strain;
'n' the way t' fix it, uz I maintain,
    Is only jest
T' make that place uz strong uz the rest."

So the Deacon inquired of the village folk
Where he could find the strongest oak,
That could n't be split nor bent nor broke,—
That was for spokes and floor and sills;   40
He sent for lancewood to make the thills;
The crossbars were ash, from the straightest
    trees,
The panels of white-wood, that cuts like
    cheese,
But lasts like iron for things like these;
The hubs of logs from the "Settler's ellum,"—

Last of its timber,—they could n't sell 'em,
Never an axe had seen their chips,
And the wedges flew from between their lips,
Their blunt ends frizzled like celery-tips;
Step and prop-iron, bolt and screw,   50
Spring, tire, axle, and linchpin too,
Steel of the finest, bright and blue;
Thoroughbrace bison-skin, thick and wide;
Boot, top, dasher, from tough old hide
Found in the pit when the tanner died.
That was the way he "put her through."—
"There!" said the Deacon, "naow she 'll dew."

Do! I tell you, I rather guess
She was a wonder, and nothing less!
Colts grew horses, beards turned gray,   60
Deacon and deaconess dropped away,
Children and grand-children—where were
    they?
But there stood the stout old one-hoss-shay
As fresh as on Lisbon-earthquake-day!

Eighteen hundred;—it came and found
The Deacon's Masterpiece strong and sound.
Eighteen hundred increased by ten;—
"Hahnsum kerridge" they called it then.
Eighteen hundred and twenty came;—
Running as usual; much the same.   70
Thirty and forty at last arrive,
And then come fifty, and FIFTY-FIVE.

Little of all we value here
Wakes on the morn of its hundredth year
Without both feeling and looking queer.
In fact, there 's nothing that keeps its youth,
So far as I know, but a tree and truth.
(This is a moral that runs at large;
Take it.—You 're welcome.—No extra charge.)

FIRST OF NOVEMBER,—the Earthquake-day.—   80
There are traces of age in the one-hoss-shay,
A general flavor of mild decay,

But nothing local, as one may say.
There could n't be,—for the Deacon's art
Had made it so like in every part
That there was n't a chance for one to start.
For the wheels were just as strong as the thills,
And the floor was just as strong as the sills,
And the panels just as strong as the floor,
And the whippletree neither less nor more,   90
And the back-crossbar as strong as the fore,
And spring and axle and hub *encore*.
And yet, *as a whole*, it is past a doubt
In another hour it will be *worn out!*

First of November, 'Fifty-five!
This morning the parson takes a drive.
Now, small boys, get out of the way!
Here comes the wonderful one-hoss-shay,
Drawn by a rat-tailed, ewe-necked bay.
"Huddup!" said the parson.—Off went they.   100

The parson was working his Sunday's text,—
Had got to *fifthly*, and stopped perplexed
At what the—Moses—was coming next.
All at once the horse stood still,
Close by the meet'n'-house on the hill.
—First a shiver, and then a thrill,
Then something decidedly like a spill,—
And the parson was sitting upon a rock,
At half-past nine by the meet'n'-house clock,—
Just the hour of the Earthquake shock!   110
—What do you think the parson found,
When he got up and stared around?
The poor old chaise in a heap or mound,
As if it had been to the mill and ground.
You see, of course, if you 're not a dunce,
How it went to pieces all at once,—
All at once, and nothing first,—
Just as bubbles do when they burst.

End of the wonderful one-hoss-shay.
Logic is logic. That 's all I say.   120

Dorothy Q (1871)

Holmes himself provides the appropriate background information in his prose introduction to the poem. The reader will note that the "rapier thrust" referred to in Holmes's introduction was that inflicted on the painting by a British soldier during the Revolutionary War, an event mentioned in the poem itself.

I cannot tell the story of Dorothy Q. more simply in prose than I have told it in verse, but I can add something to it.

Dorothy was the daughter of Judge Edmund Quincy, and the niece of Josiah Quincy, junior, the young patriot and orator who died just before the American Revolution, of which he was one of the most eloquent and effective promoters. The son of the latter, Josiah Quincy, the first mayor of Boston bearing that name, lived to a great age, one of the most useful and honored citizens of his time.

The canvas of the painting was so much decayed that it had to be replaced by a new one, in doing which the rapier thrust was of course filled up.

Grandmother's mother: her age, I guess,
Thirteen summers, or something less;
Girlish bust, but womanly air;
Smooth, square forehead with uprolled hair;
Lips that lover has never kissed;
Taper fingers and slender wrist;
Hanging sleeves of stiff brocade;
So they painted the little maid.

On her hand a parrot green
Sits unmoving and broods serene.   10
Hold up the canvas full in view,—
Look! there's a rent the light shines through,
Dark with a century's fringe of dust,—
That was a Red-Coat's rapier-thrust!
Such is the tale the lady old,
Dorothy's daughter's daughter, told.

Who the painter was none may tell,—
One whose best was not over well;
Hard and dry, it must be confessed,
Flat as a rose that has long been pressed;   20
Yet in her cheek the hues are bright,
Dainty colors of red and white,
And in her slender shape are seen
Hint and promise of stately mien.

Look not on her with eyes of scorn,—
Dorothy Q. was a lady born!
Ay! since the galloping Normans came,
England's annals have known her name;
And still to the three-hilled rebel town
Dear is that ancient name's renown,   30
For many a civic wreath they won,
The youthful sire and the gray-haired son.

O Damsel Dorothy! Dorothy Q.!

Strange is the gift that I owe to you;
Such a gift as never a king
Save to daughter or son might bring,—
All my tenure of heart and hand,
All my title to house and land;
Mother and sister and child and wife
And joy and sorrow and death and life!   40

What if a hundred years ago
Those close-shut lips had answered No,
When forth the tremulous question came
That cost the maiden her Norman name,
And under the folds that look so still
The bodice swelled with the bosom's thrill?
Should I be I, or would it be
One tenth another, to nine tenths me?

Soft is the breath of a maiden's Yes:
Not the light gossamer stirs with less;   50
But never a cable that holds so fast
Through all the battles of wave and blast,
And never an echo of speech or song
That lives in the babbling air so long!
There were tones in the voice that whispered
            then
You may hear to-day in a hundred men.

O lady and lover, how faint and far
Your images hover,—and here we are,
Solid and stirring in flesh and bone,—
Edward's and Dorothy's—all their own,—   60
A goodly record for Time to show
Of a syllable spoken so long ago!—
Shall I bless you, Dorothy, or forgive
For the tender whisper that bade me live?

It shall be a blessing, my little maid!
I will heal the stab of the Red-Coat's blade,
And freshen the gold of the tarnished frame,
And gild with a rhyme your household name;
So you shall smile on us brave and bright
As first you greeted the morning's light,   70
And live untroubled by woes and fears
Through a second youth of a hundred years.

One Country (1865)

"One Country" is a fair sample of Holmes's patriotic verse. As the editors of the American Writers Series volume on Holmes put it, "A small dictionary of poetic bromides could be made up from [Holmes's Civil War] verses:

'*Stain Not the Scroll that Emblazoned Their Fame!*'; '*Fair Heritage Spotless Descended*'; '*Freedom Stands Gasping*'; '*God Calls You— Answer Now*'; '*Let the Fountain of Mercy Flow Alike for Helpless Friend and Foe*'; '*Hark! 'Tis*

the Voice'; 'What if the Storm-Clouds Blow?';
'And Is the Old Flag Flying Still?'; 'Blow,
Trumpets, Your Summons, Till Sluggards
Awake!'"

One country! Treason's writhing asp
Struck madly at her girdle's clasp,
And Hatred wrenched with might and main
To rend its welded links in twain,
While Mammon hugged his golden calf
Content to take one broken half,
While thankless churls stood idly by
And heard unmoved a nation's cry!

One country! "Nay,"—the tyrant crew
Shrieked from their dens,—"it shall be two!   10
Ill bodes to us this monstrous birth,
That scowls on all the thrones of earth,
Too broad yon starry cluster shines,

Too proudly tower the New-World pines,
Tear down the 'banner of the free,'
And cleave their land from sea to sea!"

One country still, though foe and "friend"
Our seamless empire strove to rend;
Safe! safe! though all the fiends of hell
Join the red murderers' battle-yell!   20
What though the lifted sabres gleam,
The cannons frown by shore and stream,—
The sabres clash, the cannons thrill,
In wild accord, One country still!

One country! in her stress and strain
We heard the breaking of a chain!
Look where the conquering Nation swings
Her iron flail,—its shivered rings!
Forged by the rebels' crimson hand,
That bolt of wrath shall scourge the land   30
Till Peace proclaims on sea and shore
One Country now and evermore!

The Boys (1859)

Holmes was elected poet of his Harvard class
(1829). In the years that followed he was
diligent in supplying poems for the annual re-
unions of the class. "The Boys" is the poem
that he read at the thirtieth reunion. The student may not be much interested in the specific
identities of Holmes's classmates; yet Holmes's
note identifying them provides a dramatic indication of the power of Harvard influence and
of the general cohesiveness of the society of
which it was the intellectual center. Holmes's
note reads:

> The members of the Harvard College class of
> 1829 referred to in this poem are: "Doctor,"
> Francis Thomas; "Judge," G. T. Bigelow,
> Chief Justice of the Supreme Court of Massa-
> chusetts; "Speaker," Hon. Francis B. Crown-
> inshield, Speaker of the Massachusetts House
> of Representatives; "Mr. Mayor," G. W.
> Richardson, of Worcester, Mass.; "Member
> of Congress," Hon. George T. Davis; "Rev-
> erend," James Freeman Clarke; "boy with the
> grave mathematical look," Benjamin Peirce;
> "boy with a three-decker brain," Judge Benja-
> min R. Curtis, of the Supreme Court of the
> United States; "nice youngster of excellent

pith," S. F. Smith, author of "My Country,
'tis of Thee."

Has there any old fellow got mixed with the
    boys?
If there has, take him out, without making a
    noise.
Hang the Almanac's cheat and the Catalogue's
    spite!
Old Time is a liar! We're twenty to-night!

We're twenty! We're twenty! Who says we
    are more?
He's tipsy,—young jackanapes!—show him the
    door!
"Gray temples at twenty?"—Yes! *white* if we
    please;
Where the snow-flakes fall thickest there's
    nothing can freeze!

Was it snowing I spoke of? Excuse the mis-
    take!
Look close,—you will see not a sign of a flake!   10
We want some new garlands for those we
    have shed,—
And these are white roses in place of the red.

We've a trick, we young fellows, you may
    have been told

Of talking (in public) as if we were old:—
That boy we call "Doctor," and this we call
  "Judge";
It's a neat little fiction,—of course it's all fudge.

That fellow's the "Speaker,"—the one on the
  right;
"Mr. Mayor," my young one, how are you to-
  night?
That's our "Member of Congress," we say
  when we chaff;
There's the "Reverend" What's his name?—
  don't make me laugh.   20

That boy with the grave mathematical look
Made believe he had written a wonderful book,
And the Royal Society thought it was *true!*
So they chose him right in; a good joke it was,
  too!

There's a boy, we pretend, with a three-decker
  brain,
That could harness a team with a logical
  chain;
When he spoke for our manhood in syllabled
  fire,
We called him "The Justice," but now he's
  "The Squire."

And there's a nice youngster of excellent pith,—
Fate tried to conceal him by naming him
  Smith;   30

But he shouted a song for the brave and the
  free,—
Just read on his medal, "My country," "of
  thee!"

You hear that boy laughing?—You think he's
  all fun;
But the angels laugh, too, at the good he has
  done;
The children laugh loud as they troop to his
  call,
And the poor man that knows him laughs
  loudest of all!

Yes, we're boys,—always playing with tongue
  or with pen,—
And I sometimes have asked,—Shall we ever
  be men?
Shall we always be youthful, and laughing,
  and gay,
Till the last dear companion drops smiling
  away?   40

Then here's to our boyhood, its gold and its
  gray!
The stars of its winter, the dews of its May!
And when we have done with our life-lasting
  toys,
Dear Father, take care of thy children, the
  Boys!

From The Autocrat of the Breakfast Table (1858)

The Autocrat of the Breakfast Table was published serially in the *Atlantic Monthly*, the first installment appearing in November, 1857. *The Autocrat* appeared in book form in 1858.

The "interruption" to which the first sentence alludes had lasted some twenty-five years. Holmes had published in the *New England Magazine* (1831 and 1832) two articles entitled "The Autocrat of the Breakfast Table." When Holmes resumed *The Autocrat* a quarter-century later, he did not alter the general plan, but a glance at the two early numbers will show how much his Autocrat grew in wisdom and urbanity during the long interruption.

I

I was just going to say, when I was interrupted, that one of the many ways of classifying minds is under the heads of arithmetical and algebraical intellects. All economical and practical wisdom is an extension or variation of the following arithmetical formula: $2 + 2 = 4$. Every philosophical proposition has the more general character of the expression $a + b = c$. We are mere operatives, empirics, and egotists, until we learn to think in letters instead of figures.

They all stared. There is a divinity student lately come among us to whom I commonly address remarks like the above, allowing him to take a certain share in the conversation, so far as assent or pertinent questions are involved. He abused his liberty on this occasion by presuming to say that Leibnitz had the same observation.—No, sir, I replied, he has not. But he said a mighty good thing about mathematics, that sounds something like it, and you found it, *not in the original*, but quoted by Dr. Thomas Reid. I will tell the company what he did say, one of these days.

—If I belong to a Society of Mutual Admiration? —I blush to say that I do not at this present moment. I once did, however. It was the first association to which I ever heard the term applied; a body of scientific young men in a great foreign city[1] who admired their teacher, and to some extent each other. Many of them deserved it; they have become famous since. It amuses me to hear the talk of one of those beings described by Thackeray [*Book of Snobs*]—

"Letters four do form his name"—

about a social development which belongs to the very noblest stage of civilization. All generous companies of artists, authors, philanthropists, men of science, are, or ought to be, Societies of Mutual Admiration. A man of genius, or any kind of superiority, is not debarred from admiring the

---

[1] The "body of scientific young men in a great foreign city" was the Société d'Observation Medicale, of Paris, of which M. Louis was president, and MM. Barth, Grisotte, and our own Dr. Bowditch were members. They agreed in admiring their justly-honored president, and thought highly of some of their associates, who have since made good their promise of distinction.

About the time when these papers were published, the Saturday Club was founded, or, rather, found itself in existence, without any organization, almost without parentage. It was natural enough that such men as Emerson, Longfellow, Agassiz, Peirce, with Hawthorne, Motley, Sumner, when within reach, and others who would be good company for them, should meet and dine together once in a while, as they did, in point of fact, every month, and as some who are still living, with other and newer members, still meet and dine. If some of them had not admired each other they would have been exceptions in the world of letters and science. The club deserves being remembered for having no constitution or by-laws, for making no speeches, reading no papers, observing no ceremonies, coming and going at will without remark, and acting out, though it did not proclaim the motto, "Shall I not take mine ease in mine inn?" There was and is nothing of the Bohemian element about this club, but it has had many good times and not a little good talking [Holmes].

same quality in another, nor the other from returning his admiration. They may even associate together and continue to think highly of each other. And so of a dozen such men, if any one place is fortunate enough to hold so many. The being referred to above assumes several false premises. First, that men of talent necessarily hate each other. Secondly, that intimate knowledge or habitual association destroys our admiration of persons whom we esteemed highly at a distance. Thirdly, that a circle of clever fellows, who meet together to dine and have a good time, have signed a constitutional compact to glorify themselves and to put down him and the fraction of the human race not belonging to their number. Fourthly, that it is an outrage that he is not asked to join them.

Here the company laughed a good deal, and the old gentleman who sits opposite said: "That's it! that's it!"

I continued, for I was in the talking vein. As to clever people's hating each other, I think *a little* extra talent does sometimes make people jealous. They become irritated by perpetual attempts and failures, and it hurts their tempers and dispositions. Unpretending mediocrity is good, and genius is glorious; but a weak flavor of genius in an essentially common person is detestable. It spoils the grand neutrality of a commonplace character, as the rinsings of an unwashed wine-glass spoil a draught of fair water. No wonder the poor fellow we spoke of, who always belongs to this class of slightly flavored mediocrities, is puzzled and vexed by the strange sight of a dozen men of capacity working and playing together in harmony. He and his fellows are always fighting. With them familiarity naturally breeds contempt. If they ever praise each other's bad drawings, or broken-winded novels, or spavined verses, nobody ever supposed it was from admiration; it was simply a contract between themselves and a publisher or dealer.

If the Mutuals have really nothing among them worth admiring, that alters the question. But if they are men with noble powers and qualities, let me tell you, that, next to youthful love and family affections, there is no human sentiment better than that which unites the Societies of Mutual Admiration. And what would literature or art be without such associations? Who can tell what we owe to the Mutual Admiration Society of which Shakespeare, and Ben Jonson, and Beaumont and Fletcher were members? Or to that of which Addison and Steele formed the centre, and which gave us the Spectator? Or to that where Johnson, and Goldsmith, and Burke, and Reynolds, and Beauclerk, and Boswell, most admiring among all admirers, met together? Was there any great harm in the fact that the Irvings and Paulding wrote in company? or any unpardonable cabal in the literary union of Verplanck and Bryant and Sands, and as many more as they chose to associate with them?

The poor creature does not know what he is talking about when he abuses this noblest of institutions. Let him inspect its mysteries through the knot-hole he has secured, but not use that orifice as a medium for his popgun. Such a society is the crown of a literary metropolis; if a town has not material for it, and spirit and good feeling enough to organize it, it is a mere caravansary, fit for a man of genius to lodge in, but not to live in. Foolish people hate and dread and envy such an association of men of varied powers and influence, because it is lofty, serene, impregnable, and, by the necessity of the case, exclusive. Wise ones are prouder of the title M.S.M.A. than of all their other honors put together.

—All generous minds have a horror of what are commonly called "facts." They are the brute beasts of the intellectual domain. Who does not know fellows that always have an ill-conditioned fact or two which they lead after them into decent company like so many bull-dogs, ready to let them slip at every ingenious suggestion, or convenient generalization, or pleasant fancy? I allow no "facts" at this table. What! Because bread is good and wholesome, and necessary and nourishing, shall you thrust a crumb into my windpipe while I am talking? Do not these muscles of mine represent a hundred loaves of bread? and is not my thought the abstract of ten thousand of these crumbs of truth with which you would choke off my speech?

(The above remark must be conditioned and qualified for the vulgar mind. The reader will, of course, understand the precise amount of seasoning which must be added to it before he adopts it as one of the axioms of his life. The speaker disclaims all responsibility for its abuse in incompetent hands.)

This business of conversation is a very serious matter. There are men whom it weakens one to talk with an hour more than a day's fasting would do. Mark this which I am going to say, for it is as good as a working professional man's advice, and costs you nothing: It is better to lose a pint of blood from your veins than to have a nerve tapped. Nobody measures your nervous force as it runs away, nor bandages your brain and marrow after the operation.

There are men of *esprit* who are excessively exhausting to some people. They are the talkers who have what may be called *jerky* minds. Their thoughts do not run in the natural order of sequence. They say bright things on all possible subjects, but their zigzags rack you to death. After a jolting half-hour with one of these jerky companions, talking with a dull friend affords great relief. It is like taking the cat in your lap after holding a squirrel.

What a comfort a dull but kindly person is, to be sure, at times! A ground-glass shade over a gas-lamp does not bring more solace to our dazzled eyes than such a one to our minds. . . .

—The men of genius that I fancy most, have erectile heads like the cobra-di-capello. You remember what they tell of William Pinkney, the great pleader; how in his eloquent paroxysms the veins of his neck would swell and his face flush and his eyes glitter, until he seemed on the verge of apoplexy. The hydraulic arrangements for supplying the brain with blood are only second in importance to its own organization. The bulbous-headed fellows who steam well when they are at work are the men that draw big audiences and give us marrowy books and pictures. It is a good sign to have one's feet grow cold when he is writing. A great writer and speaker once told me that he often wrote with his feet in hot water; but for this, *all* his blood would have run into his head, as the mercury sometimes withdraws into the ball of a thermometer.

—You don't suppose that my remarks made at this table are like so many postage-stamps, do you, —each to be only once uttered? If you do, you are mistaken. He must be a poor creature who does not often repeat himself. Imagine the author of the excellent piece of advice, "Know thyself," never alluding to that sentiment again during the course of a protracted existence! Why, the truths a man carries about with him are his tools; and do you think a carpenter is bound to use the same plane but once to smooth a knotty board with, or to hang up his hammer after it has driven its first nail? I shall never repeat a conversation, but an idea often. I shall use the same types when I like, but not commonly the same stereotypes. A thought is often original, though you have uttered it a hundred times. It has come to you over a new route, by a new and express train of associations.

Sometimes, but rarely, one may be caught making the same speech twice over, and yet be held blameless. Thus, a certain lecturer, after performing in an inland city, where dwells a *Littératrice* of note, was invited to meet her and others over the social teacup. She pleasantly referred to his many wanderings in his new occupation. "Yes," he replied, "I am like the Huma, the bird that never lights, being always in the cars, as he is always on the wing."—Years elapsed. The lecturer visited the same place once more for the same purpose. Another social cup after the lecture, and a second meeting with the distinguished lady. "You are constantly going from place to place," she said.—"Yes," he answered, "I am like the Huma,"—and finished the sentence as before.

What horrors, when it flashed over him that he had made this fine speech, word for word, twice over! Yet it was not true, as the lady might perhaps have fairly inferred, that he had embellished his conversation with the Huma daily during that whole interval of years. On the contrary, he had never once thought of the odious fowl until the recurrence of precisely the same circumstances brought up precisely the same idea. He ought to have been proud of the accuracy of his mental adjustments. Given certain factors, and a sound brain should always evolve the same fixed product with the certainty of Babbage's calculating machine.

—What a satire, by the way, is that machine on the mere mathematician! A Frankenstein-monster, a thing without brains and without heart, too stupid to make a blunder; which turns out results like a corn-sheller, and never grows any wiser or better, though it grind a thousand bushels of them!

I have an immense respect for a man of talents *plus* "the mathematics." But the calculating power alone should seem to be the least human of qualities, and to have the smallest amount of reason in it; since a machine can be made to do the work of three or four calculators, and better than any one of them. Sometimes I have been troubled that I had not a deeper intuitive apprehension of the relations of numbers. But the triumph of the ciphering hand-organ has consoled me. I always fancy I can hear the wheels clicking in a calculator's brain. The power of dealing with numbers is a kind of "detached lever" arrangement, which may be put into a mighty poor watch. I suppose it is about as common as the power of moving the ears voluntarily, which is a moderately rare endowment.

—Little localized powers, and little narrow streaks of specialized knowledge, are things men are very apt to be conceited about. Nature is very wise; but for this encouraging principle how many small talents and little accomplishments would be neglected! Talk about conceit as much as you like, it is to human character what salt is to the ocean; it keeps it sweet, and renders it endurable. Say rather it is like the natural unguent of the sea-fowl's plumage, which enables him to shed the rain that falls on him and the wave in which he dips. When one has had *all* his conceit taken out of him, when he has lost *all* his illusions, his feathers will soon soak through, and he will fly no more.

"So you admire conceited people, do you?" said the young lady who has come to the city to be finished off for—the duties of life.

I am afraid you do not study logic at your school, my dear. It does not follow that I wish to be pickled in brine because I like a salt-water plunge at Nahant. I say that conceit is just as natural a thing to human minds as a centre is to a circle. But little-minded people's thoughts move in such small circles that five minutes' conversation gives you an arc long enough to determine their whole curve. An arc in the movement of a large intellect does not sensibly differ from a straight line. Even if it have the third vowel as its centre, it does not soon betray it. The highest thought, that is, is the most seemingly impersonal; it does not obviously imply any individual centre.

Audacious self-esteem, with good ground for it, is always imposing. What resplendent beauty that must have been which could have authorized Phryne to "peel" in the way she did! What fine speeches are those two: *"Non omnis moriar"* [I shall not wholly die], and "I have taken all knowledge to be my province"! Even in common people, conceit has the virtue of making them cheerful; the man who thinks his wife, his baby, his house, his horse, his dog, and himself severally unequalled, is almost sure to be a good-humored person, though liable to be tedious at times.

—What are the great faults of conversation? Want of ideas, want of words, want of manners, are the principal ones, I suppose you think. I don't doubt it, but I will tell you what I have found spoil more good talks than anything else;—long arguments on special points between people who differ on the fundamental principles upon which these points depend. No men can have satisfactory relations with each other until they have agreed on certain *ultimata* of belief not to be disturbed in ordinary conversation, and unless they have sense enough to trace the secondary questions depending upon these ultimate beliefs to their source. In short, just as a written constitution is essential to the best social order; so a code of finalities is a necessary condition of profitable talk between two persons. Talking is like playing on the harp; there is as much in laying the hand on the strings to stop their vibrations as in twanging them to bring out their music.

—Do you mean to say the pun-question is not clearly settled in your minds? Let me lay down the law upon the subject. Life and language are alike sacred. Homicide and *verbicide*—that is, violent treatment of a word with fatal results to its legitimate meaning, which is its life—are alike forbidden. Manslaughter, which is the meaning of the one, is the same as man's laughter, which is the end of the other. A pun is *primâ facie* an insult to the person you are talking with. It implies utter indifference to or sublime contempt for his remarks, no matter how serious. I speak of total depravity, and one says all that is written on the subject is deep raving. I have committed my self-respect by talking with such a person. I should like to commit him, but cannot, because he is a nuisance. Or I speak of geological convulsions, and he asks me what was the cosine of Noah's ark; also, whether the Deluge was not a deal huger than any modern inundation.

A pun does not commonly justify a blow in return. But if a blow were given for such a cause, and death ensued, the jury would be judges both of the facts and of the pun, and might, if the latter were of an aggravated character, return a verdict of justifiable homicide. Thus, in a case lately decided before Miller, J., Doe presented Roe a subscription paper, and urged the claims of suffering humanity. Roe replied by asking, When charity was like a top? It was in evidence that Doe preserved a dignified silence. Roe then said, "When it begins to hum." Doe then—and not till then—struck Roe, and his head happening to hit a bound volume of the Monthly Rag-Bag and Stolen Miscellany, intense mortification ensued, with a fatal result. The chief laid down his notions of the law to his brother justices, who unanimously replied, "Jest so." The chief rejoined, that no man should jest so without being punished for it, and charged for the prisoner, who was acquitted, and the pun ordered to be burned by the sheriff. The bound volume was forfeited as a deodand, but not claimed.

People that make puns are like wanton boys that put coppers on the railroad tracks. They amuse themselves and other children, but their little trick may upset a freight train of conversation for the sake of a battered witticism.

I will thank you, B. F., to bring down two books, of which I will mark the places on this slip of paper. (While he is gone, I may say that this boy, our landlady's youngest, is called Benjamin Franklin, after the celebrated philosopher of that name. A highly merited compliment.)

I wished to refer to two eminent authorities. Now be so good as to listen. The great moralist says: "To trifle with the vocabulary which is the vehicle of social intercourse is to tamper with the currency of human intelligence. He who would violate the sanctities of his mother tongue would invade the recesses of the paternal till without remorse, and repeat the banquet of Saturn without an indigestion."

And, once more, listen to the historian. "The Puritans hated puns. The Bishops were notoriously addicted to them. The Lords Temporal carried them to the verge of license. Majesty itself must have its Royal quibble. 'Ye be burly, my Lord of Burleigh,' said Queen Elizabeth, 'but ye shall make less stir in our realm than my Lord of Leicester.' The gravest wisdom and the highest breeding lent their sanction to the practice. Lord Bacon playfully declared himself a descendant of 'Og, the King of Bashan.' Sir Philip Sidney, with his last breath, reproached the soldier who brought him water, for wasting a casque full upon a dying man. A courtier, who saw Othello performed at the Globe Theatre, remarked, that the blackamoor was a brute, and not a man. 'Thou hast reason,' replied a great Lord, 'according to Plato his saying; for this be a two-legged animal *with* feathers.' The fatal habit became universal. The language was corrupted. The infection spread to the national conscience. Political double-dealings naturally grew out of verbal double meanings. The teeth of the new dragon were sown by Cadmus who introduced the alphabet of equivocation. What was levity in the time of the Tudors grew to regicide and revolution in the age of the Stuarts."

Who was that boarder that just whispered something about the Macaulay-flowers of literature?—There was a dead silence.—I said calmly, I shall

henceforth consider any interruption by a pun as a
hint to change my boarding-house. Do not plead
my example. If *I* have used any such, it has been
only as a Spartan father would show up a drunken
helot. We have done with them. . . .

What do *you* think of my verses, my friends?—Is
that piece an impromptu? said my landlady's
daughter. (Aet. 19. Tender-eyed blonde. Long
ringlets. Cameo pin. Gold pencil-case on a chain.
Locket. Bracelet. Album. Autograph book. Ac-
cordeon. Reads Byron, Tupper, and Sylvanus
Cobb, Junior, while her mother makes the pud-
dings. Says "Yes?" when you tell her anything.)—
Oui et non, ma petite,—Yes and no, my child. . . .

I did not address the following remark to her,
and I trust, from her limited range of reading, she
will never see it; I said it softly to my next neighbor.

When a young female wears a flat circular side-
curl, gummed on each temple,—when she walks
with a male, not arm in arm, but his arm against
the back of hers,—and when she says "Yes?" with
the note of interrogation, you are generally safe
in asking her what wages she gets, and who the
"feller" was you saw her with.

"What were you whispering?" said the daughter
of the house, moistening her lips, as she spoke, in
a very engaging manner.

"I was only laying down a principle of social
diagnosis."

"Yes?" . . .

—We are the Romans of the modern world,—
the great assimilating people. Conflicts and conquests are of course necessary accidents with us, as
with our prototypes. And so we come to their style
of weapon. Our army sword is the short, stiff,
pointed *gladius* of the Romans; and the American
bowie-knife is the same tool, modified to meet the
daily wants of civil society. I announce at this table
an axiom not to be found in Montesquieu or the
journals of Congress:—

The race that shortens its weapons lengthens its
boundaries.

Corollary. It was the Polish *lance* that left Poland at last with nothing of her own to bound.

> "Dropped from her nerveless grasp
>   the *shattered spear!*"

What business had Sarmatia to be fighting for
liberty with a fifteen-foot pole between her and the
breasts of her enemies? If she had but clutched
the old Roman and young American weapon, and
come to close quarters, there might have been a
chance for her; but it would have spoiled the best
passage in "The Pleasures of Hope."

—Self-made men?—Well, yes. Of course every
body likes and respects self-made men. It is a great
deal better to be made in that way than not to be
made at all. Are any of you younger people old
enough to remember that Irishman's house on the
marsh at Cambridgeport, which house he built
from drain to chimney-top with his own hands? It
took him a good many years to build it, and one
could see that it was a little out of plumb, and a
little wavy in outline, and a little queer and uncertain in general aspect. A regular hand could
certainly have built a better house; but it was a
very good house for a "self-made" carpenter's
house, and people praised it, and said how remarkably well the Irishman had succeeded. They
never thought of praising the fine blocks of houses
a little farther on.

Your self-made man, whittled into shape with
his own jack-knife, deserves more credit, if that is
all, than the regular engine-turned article, shaped
by the most approved pattern, and French-polished
by society and travel. But as to saying that one is
every way the equal of the other, that is another
matter. The right of strict social discrimination of
all things and persons, according to their merits,
native or acquired, is one of the most precious
republican privileges. I take the liberty to exercise
it when I say that, *other things being equal*, in
most relations of life I prefer a man of family.

What do I mean by a man of family?—O, I'll
give you a general idea of what I mean. Let us give
him a first-rate fit out; it costs us nothing.

Four or five generations of gentlemen and gen-
tlewomen; among them a member of his Majesty's
Council for the Province, a Governor or so, one or
two Doctors of Divinity, a member of Congress,
not later than the time of long boots with tassels.

Family portraits. The member of the Council,
by Smibert. The great merchant-uncle, by Copley,
full length, sitting in his arm-chair, in a velvet cap
and flowered robe, with a globe by him, to show
the range of his commercial transactions, and letters with large red seals lying round, one directed
conspicuously to The Honorable, etc., etc. Great-
grandmother, by the same artist; brown satin, lace
very fine, hands superlative; grand old lady, stiffish,
but imposing. Her mother, artist unknown; flat,
angular, hanging sleeves; parrot on fist. A pair of

Stuarts, viz., 1. A superb, full-blown, mediæval gentleman, with a fiery dash of Tory blood in his veins, tempered down with that of a fine old rebel grandmother, and warmed up with the best of old India Madeira; his face is one flame of ruddy sunshine; his ruffled shirt rushes out of his bosom with an impetuous generosity, as if it would drag his heart after it; and his smile is good for twenty thousand dollars to the Hospital, besides ample bequests to all relatives and dependants. 2. Lady of the same; remarkable cap; high waist, as in time of Empire; bust *à la Josephine;* wisps of curls, like celery-tips, at sides of forehead; complexion clear and warm, like rose-cordial. As for the miniatures by Malbone, we don't count them in the gallery.

Books, too, with the names of old college-students in them,—family names;—you will find them at the head of their respective classes in the days when students took rank on the catalogue from their parents' condition. Elzevirs, with the Latinized appellations of youthful progenitors, and *Hic liber est meus* [This is my book] on the title-page. A set of Hogarth's original plates. Pope, original edition, 15 volumes, London, 1717. Barrow on the lower shelves, in folio. Tillotson on the upper, in a little dark platoon of octo-decimos.

Some family silver; a string of wedding and funeral rings; the arms of the family curiously blazoned; the same in worsted, by a maiden aunt. . . .

No, my friends, I go (always, other things being equal) for the man who inherits family traditions and the cumulative humanities of at least four or five generations. Above all things, as a child, he should have tumbled about in a library. All men are afraid of books, who have not handled them from infancy. Do you suppose our dear *didascalos* over there ever read *Poli Synopsis,* or consulted *Castelli Lexicon,* while he was growing up to their stature? Not he; but virtue passed through the hem of their parchment and leather garments whenever he touched them, as the precious drugs sweated through the bat's handle in the Arabian story. I tell you he is at home wherever he smells the invigorating fragrance of Russia leather. No self-made man feels so. One may, it is true, have all the antecedents I have spoken of, and yet be a boor or a shabby fellow. One may have none of them, and yet be fit for councils and courts. Then let them change places. Our social arrangement has this great beauty, that its strata shift up and down as they change specific gravity, without being clogged by layers of prescription. But I still insist on my

democratic liberty of choice, and I go for the man with the gallery of family portraits against the one with the twenty-five-cent daguerreotype, unless I find out that the last is the better of the two. . . .

II

I really believe some people save their bright thoughts as being too precious for conversation. What do you think an admiring friend said the other day to one that was talking good things,— good enough to print? "Why," said he, "you are wasting merchantable literature, a cash article, at the rate, as nearly as I can tell, of fifty dollars an hour." The talker took him to the window and asked him to look out and tell what he saw.

"Nothing but a very dusty street," he said, "and a man driving a sprinkling-machine through it."

"Why don't you tell the man he is wasting that water? What would be the state of the highways of life, if we did not drive our *thought-sprinklers* through them with the valves open, sometimes?

"Besides, there is another thing about this talking, which you forget. It shapes our thoughts for us;—the waves of conversation roll them as the surf rolls the pebbles on the shore. Let me modify the image a little. I rough out my thoughts in talk as an artist models in clay. Spoken language is so plastic,—you can pat and coax, and spread and shave, and rub out, and fill up, and stick on so easily, when you work that soft material, that there is nothing like it for modelling. Out of it come the shapes which you turn into marble or bronze in your immortal books, if you happen to write such. Or, to use another illustration, writing or printing is like shooting with a rifle; you may hit your reader's mind, or miss it;—but talking is like playing at a mark with the pipe of an engine; if it is within reach, and you have time enough, you can't help hitting it."

The company agreed that this last illustration was of superior excellence, or, in the phrase used by them, "Fust-rate." I acknowledged the compliment, but gently rebuked the expression. "Fustrate," "prime," "a prime article," "a superior piece of goods," "a handsome garment," "a gent in a flowered vest,"—all such expressions are final. They blast the lineage of him or her who utters them, for generations up and down. . . .

—It is an odd idea, that almost all our people

have had a professional education. To become a doctor a man must study some three years and hear a thousand lectures, more or less. Just how much study it takes to make a lawyer I cannot say, but probably not more than this. Now, most decent people hear one hundred lectures or sermons (discourses) on theology every year,—and this, twenty, thirty, fifty years together. They read a great many religious books besides. The clergy, however, rarely hear any sermons except what they preach themselves. A dull preacher might be conceived, therefore, to lapse into a state of *quasi* heathenism, simply for want of religious instruction. And, on the other hand, an attentive and intelligent hearer, listening to a succession of wise teachers, might become actually better educated in theology than any one of them. We are all theological students, and more of us qualified as doctors of divinity than have received degrees at any of the universities.

It is not strange, therefore, that very good people should often find it difficult, if not impossible, to keep their attention fixed upon a sermon treating feebly a subject which they have thought vigorously about for years, and heard able men discuss scores of times. I have often noticed, however, that a hopelessly dull discourse acts *inductively*, as electricians would say, in developing strong mental currents. I am ashamed to think with what accompaniments and variations and flourishes I have sometimes followed the droning of a heavy speaker, —not willingly,—for my habit is reverential,—but as a necessary result of a slight continuous impression on the senses and the mind, which kept both in action without furnishing the food they required to work upon. If you ever saw a crow with a king-bird after him, you will get an image of a dull speaker and a lively listener. The bird in sable plumage flaps heavily along his straightforward course, while the other sails round him, over him, under him, leaves him, comes back again, tweaks out a black feather, shoots away once more, never losing sight of him, and finally reaches the crow's perch at the same time the crow does, having cut a perfect labyrinth of loops and knots and spirals while the slow fowl was painfully working from one end of his straight line to the other.

(I think these remarks were received rather coolly. A temporary boarder from the country, consisting of a somewhat more than middle-aged female, with a parchment forehead and a dry little "frisette" shingling it, a sallow neck with a necklace of gold beads, a black dress too rusty for recent grief, and contours in basso-rilievo, left the table

prematurely, and was reported to have been very virulent about what I said. So I went to my good old minister, and repeated the remarks, as nearly as I could remember them, to him. He laughed good-naturedly, and said there was considerable truth in them. He thought he could tell when people's minds were wandering, by their looks. In the earlier years of his ministry he had sometimes noticed this, when he was preaching;—very little of late years. Sometimes, when his colleague was preaching, he observed this kind of inattention; but after all, it was not so very unnatural. I will say, by the way, that it is a rule I have long followed, to tell my worst thoughts to my minister, and my best thoughts to the young people I talk with.)

—I want to make a literary confession now, which I believe nobody has made before me. . . . . Now I never wrote a "good" line in my life, but the moment after it was written it seemed a hundred years old. Very commonly I had a sudden conviction that I had seen it somewhere. Possibly I may have sometimes unconsciously stolen it, but I do not remember that I ever once detected any historical truth in these sudden convictions of the antiquity of my new thought or phrase. I have learned utterly to distrust them, and never allow them to bully me out of a thought or line.

This is the philosophy of it. (Here the number of the company was diminished by a small secession.) Any new formula which suddenly emerges in our consciousness has its roots in long trains of thought; it is virtually old when it first makes its appearance among the recognized growths of our intellect. Any crystalline group of musical words has had a long and still period to form in. Here is one theory.

But there is a larger law which perhaps comprehends these facts. It is this. The rapidity with which ideas grow old in our memories is in a direct ratio to the squares of their importance. Their apparent age runs up miraculously, like the value of diamonds, as they increase in magnitude. A great calamity, for instance, is as old as the trilobites an hour after it has happened. It stains backward through all the leaves we have turned over in the book of life, before its blot of tears or of blood is dry on the page we are turning. For this we seem to have lived; it was foreshadowed in dreams that we leaped out of in the cold sweat of terror; in the "dissolving views" of dark day-visions; all omens pointed to it; all paths led to it. After the tossing half-forgetfulness of the first sleep that follows such an event, it comes upon us afresh, as a surprise, at waking; in a few moments it is old again,—old as eternity.

[I wish I had not said all this then and there. I might have known better. The pale schoolmistress, in her mourning dress, was looking at me, as I noticed, with a wild sort of expression. All at once the blood dropped out of her cheeks as the mercury drops from a broken barometer-tube, and she melted away from her seat like an image of snow; a slung-shot could not have brought her down better. God forgive me!

After this little episode, I continued, to some few who remained balancing teaspoons on the edges of cups, twirling knives, or tilting upon the hind legs of their chairs until their heads reached the wall, where they left gratuitous advertisements of various popular cosmetics.]

When a person is suddenly thrust into any strange, new position of trial, he finds the place fits him as if he had been measured for it. He has committed a great crime, for instance, and is sent to the State Prison. The traditions, prescriptions, limitations, privileges, all the sharp conditions of his new life, stamp themselves upon his consciousness as the signet on soft wax;—a single pressure is enough. Let me strengthen the image a little. Did you ever happen to see that most soft-spoken and velvet-handed steam-engine at the Mint? The smooth piston slides backward and forward as a lady might slip her delicate finger in and out of a ring. The engine lays one of *its* fingers calmly, but firmly, upon a bit of metal; it is a coin now, and will remember that touch, and tell a new race about it, when the date upon it is crusted over with twenty centuries. So it is that a great silent-moving misery puts a new stamp on us in an hour or a moment, —as sharp an impression as if it had taken half a lifetime to engrave it. . . .

Here is a little poem I sent a short time since to a committee for a certain celebration. I understood that it was to be a festive and convivial occasion, and ordered myself accordingly. It seems the president of the day was what is called a "teetotaller." I received a note from him in the following words, containing the copy subjoined, with the emendations annexed to it.

"Dear Sir,—your poem gives good satisfaction to the committee. The sentiments expressed with reference to liquor are not, however, those generally entertained by this community. I have therefore consulted the clergyman of this place, who has made some slight changes, which he thinks will remove all objections, and keep the valuable portions of the poem. Please to inform me of your charge for said poem. Our means are limited, etc., etc., etc.

"Yours with respect."

Here it is,—with the slight alterations.

Come! fill a fresh bumper,—for why should we go
    logwood
While the ~~nectar~~ still reddens our cups as they flow!
   decoction
Pour out the ~~rich juices~~ still bright with the sun,
     eye-stuff
Till o'er the brimmed crystal the ~~rubies~~ shall run.

  half-ripened apples
The ~~purple-globed~~ clusters their life-dews have bled;
     taste   *sugar of lead*
How sweet is the ~~breath~~ of the ~~fragrance they shed!~~
    rank poisons   *wines!!!*
For summer's ~~last roses~~ lie hid in the ~~wines~~
   stable-boys smoking long-nines.
That were garnered by ~~maidens who laughed through the vines~~

  scowl   *howl*   *scoff*   *sneer*
Then a ~~smile~~, and a ~~glass~~, and a ~~toast~~, and a ~~cheer~~,
  strychnine and whiskey, and ratsbane and beer
For all ~~the good wine, and we've some of it here~~
In cellar, in pantry, in attic, in hall,
Down, down, with the tyrant that masters us all!
~~Long live the gay servant that laughs for us all!~~

The company said I had been shabbily treated, and advised me to charge the committee double, —which I did. But as I never got my pay, I don't know that it made much difference. I am a very particular person about having all I write printed as I write it. I require to see a proof, a revise, a re-revise, and a double re-revise, or fourth-proof rectified impression of all my productions, especially verse. A misprint kills a sensitive author. An intentional change of his text murders him. No wonder so many poets die young!

I have nothing more to report at this time, except two pieces of advice I gave to the young women at table. One relates to a vulgarism of language, which I grieve to say is sometimes heard even from female lips. The other is of more serious purport, and applies to such as contemplate a change of condition,—matrimony, in fact.

—The woman who "calc'lates" is lost.
—Put not your trust in money, but put your money in trust.

HARRIET BEECHER STOWE (1811–1896)

Harriet Beecher Stowe sums up a good deal of the New England character in its admirable as well as some of its more exasperating manifestations. She had a bright mind and a very facile pen, yet lacked any profound literary gift. Her piety, which was genuine, did not prevent her from being much concerned with the world, particularly the world of literary and social distinction. She was deeply idealistic but also very practical. She took care of an intellectual husband not noted for his practicality, who was also something of a hypochondriac, and she managed a household full of growing children. She gave herself passionately to good causes but knew the financial worth of her writings, and she kept a sharp eye on fees and royalties—in short, she managed to combine in one small person the virtues traditionally divided between the sisters Martha and Mary, the Scriptural representatives of the practical and contemplative life.

Mrs. Stowe's literary career, like that of Oliver Wendell Holmes, can tell us a good deal about the culture of her region during the nineteenth century. She and Holmes were almost exact contemporaries. They were friends. But though Mrs. Stowe was a popular and influential novelist and though her *Uncle Tom's Cabin* remains one of the great fictional best sellers of all time, she cannot be regarded, any more than Holmes, as a writer of major stature.

Harriet Beecher Stowe was born in the pleasant village of Litchfield, Connecticut, in 1811, the daughter of Lyman Beecher, a prominent Congregational clergyman. She was to become the wife of Calvin Stowe, another clergyman, celebrated for his learning. Her brother was Henry Ward Beecher, probably the greatest pulpit orator of the day. Mrs. Stowe, therefore, came out of the very heart of New England Puritanism and grew up, not in relatively liberal Boston, but in New England's Puritan hinterland. Yet, like Holmes, Mrs. Stowe was to move away from Puritanism, though not in the direction of Unitarianism. She ended her life as an Episcopalian.

In 1832, when Harriet was just twenty-one, her father removed to Cincinnati to become head of the Lane Theological Seminary, and there in 1836 she married Calvin Stowe. Cincinnati was just across the Ohio River from Kentucky, a slave state, and there one saw from time to time escaped slaves and heard frequent stories about them. Moreover, Harriet visited friends in Kentucky. What she saw and heard during this period bore fruit some twenty years later when she produced *Uncle Tom's Cabin*.

She began to write early, in 1834 won a prize for her first short story, and contributed extensively to the magazines, especially to those of an evangelical character. Her husband recognized her talent and encouraged her to pursue her writing career.[1] In 1849 Calvin Stowe was appointed to the faculty of Bowdoin College in Brunswick, Maine. There Mrs. Stowe, during a Sunday communion service, had a sudden vision of an old and ragged slave being cruelly beaten, a vision so vivid that she immediately wrote down what she had seen. This narrative became the germ of *Uncle Tom's Cabin*. The

[1] Practical considerations were also involved: in this period of their lives, the Stowes' income was so meager that Mrs. Stowe's earnings were important in making ends meet.

novel was serialized in the *National Era* (1851–52) and in 1852 was issued as a book.[2]

The success of *Uncle Tom's Cabin* was immediate. In view of the book's powerful impact, it is amusing to note that the abolitionists at first considered it too easy on slavery and, more surprising still, that at the very beginning southerners saw little reason to resent it. The sale of the book, abroad as at home, was tremendous. Mrs. Stowe had sent copies to Englishmen like Charles Dickens, Lord Macaulay, Charles Kingsley, and even to the Prince Consort, but she could scarcely have dreamed that it would have such a spectacular success. It was issued in England by forty different publishers and the English sales, most of them pirated editions, amounted to a million and a half copies. On the continent, too, it was widely read, translated into twenty languages, and received the plaudits of such figures as George Sand in France, Turgenev in Russia, Heinrich Heine in Germany, and Fredrika Bremer in Sweden. The novel was speedily dramatized in both England and the United States and "Tom" shows lasted on in America until the end of the century.

Mrs. Stowe made a triumphal tour of England, where she was received by the intellectuals, the political leaders, and the nobility. The plaudits of the great obviously pleased her very much; on the other hand, it is only fair to observe that she and her husband managed on the whole to keep matters in proper perspective. For example, at a packed meeting at Exeter Hall in London in 1853 several of the speakers made Mrs. Stowe's appearance the occasion for self-congratulatory observations (England had emancipated its slaves in the West Indies) and

of sharp anti-American attacks (the United States still countenanced slavery). Then Calvin Stowe got to his feet and pointed out that since England consumed 80 percent of American slave-grown cotton, she was thus jointly responsible for slavery in America and asked the crowd: "Are you willing to sacrifice one penny of your profits for the sake of doing away with this cursed business?" He had heard a great deal of talk about the conscience of cotton-growers, but "has the cotton-consumer no conscience?"

The political effects of *Uncle Tom's Cabin* were momentous: it provided for the imagination concrete and passionately conceived scenes in which the vague general dislike for slavery could realize itself. The novel mobilized northern sentiment against a new and more stringent fugitive slave act that had been passed only the year before, and it secured the suffrages of many a northern citizen who had previously paid little attention to the diatribes of the abolitionists. It may well be true that President Lincoln, on meeting Mrs. Stowe, said: "So this is the little lady who made this big war!"

Uncle Tom's Cabin soon called forth answers from southern writers, in books like the anonymous *The North and the South or Slavery and Its Contrasts: A Tale of Real Life* (1852), L. G. Smith's *Uncle Tom's Cabin as It Is, or Life at the South* (1852?), *Tit for Tat, by a Lady of New Orleans* (1856), and Joseph Addison Turner's *The Old Plantation: A Poem* (1862).[3] Yet William Gilmore Simms wrote in the *Southern Quarterly Review* (for January, 1854) that Mrs. Stowe's novel "considered wholly aside from the slavery question, is a story of great and striking, though coarse, attraction"; and another southern observer, writing in a book entitled *Uncle Tom at Home* (1853), went so far as to say that Mrs. Stowe in her treatment of the South had been "far too good to us."

Mrs. Stowe was surprised at the increasingly hostile response from the South, for it seemed to her that she had gone out of her way to be

[2] Four years later, in 1856, Mrs. Stowe published another novel with a Negro as a hero, *Dred*, the story of a slave insurrection loosely based on the slave revolt led by Nat Turner in 1831. Though one might suspect that the shrewd business sense of Mrs. Stowe had led her to choose a title capitalizing on the Dred Scott decision, that case was not adjudicated until a few months after the book's publication. Dred, Mrs. Stowe herself pointed out, was the name of one of Nat Turner's followers. *Dred* was not nearly as popular as *Uncle Tom's Cabin*, though in our day the treatment of the same event in William Styron's *The Confessions of Nat Turner* (1967) has been a best seller.

[3] Olmsted tells us how he saw *Uncle Tom's Cabin* sold to passengers on a Red River steamboat in Louisiana. See p. 1073.

fair. She had given a not unpleasant picture of Uncle Tom's life as a slave in Kentucky. Even when he has been sold down the river, his new owner, Augustine St. Clare, turns out to be a kindly and essentially decent man who deplores slavery but is baffled about how to get rid of the institution. The great villain of the novel, the insufferable Simon Legree, Mrs. Stowe deliberately portrayed as a Yankee, who has come South to make his fortune. Moreover, Mrs. Stowe was evidently fascinated with southern society and apparently honestly liked the South. As the author of *Uncle Remus*, Joel Chandler Harris, pointed out: "All the worthy and beautiful characters in her book—Uncle Tom, Little Eva, the beloved Master, and the rest—are the products of the system the text of the book is all the time condemning."

The particular horror that *Uncle Tom's Cabin* was intended to expose was the breakup and separation of families which the southern slave laws permitted and which certainly occurred. The emotional power of the book comes from the portrayal of such situations: a father is torn from his family and a mother is tormented by hearing the screams of the child that has been separated from her. As Mrs. Stowe was to put it in her *Key to Uncle Tom's Cabin* (1853): "Human nature is no worse at the South than at the North; but law at the South distinctly provides for and protects the worst abuses to which that nature is liable."

Uncle Tom's Cabin cannot be really understood unless one sees it as issuing from the evangelical Christianity of Mrs. Stowe's day. Her religious position represents a modification of the earlier Calvinism of New England. As it is put in a recent article, "The spiritual discipline of Calvinism had become too intellectually rigorous and morally severe for a sentimental people. Mrs. Stowe's book exemplified the convergence of the popular cults of home, love, and instant salvation which transformed Protestantism into a culture-religion."[4] Slavery's blackest sins were its violations of love and the sanctity of the home. It cruelly separated husband and wife, mother and child. Perhaps men could be brought by strong emotional appeals to a conviction of their complicity in the sin of slavery, and Mrs. Stowe evidently hoped that through a portrayal of its evils some of her readers would be "converted"—perhaps instantaneously—to the cause of right and truth.

Uncle Tom himself was converted at a revival meeting. His conversion experience endures, even unto death. He is a true Christian martyr, and Mrs. Stowe sees him as exhibiting the faith of the primitive martyrs of the Church. (If "Uncle Tom-ism" has come to mean, in present-day usage, cringing subservience, then it must be made plain that the author did not see her hero as an "Uncle Tom." She saw him rather as the completely dedicated Christian who has taken Christ's teachings literally and who has the courage to abide by them.)

Mrs. Stowe's particular version of Christianity had a powerful influence on her notion of what ought to be done and could be done in a practical way about slavery. Abolitionism was something that came to her rather late, and hers was of a far less doctrinaire kind than that of firebrands like William Lloyd Garrison. What she urged was that the United States as a Christian nation should put its Christianity into practice. Specifically she wanted the churches of the northern states to defy the Fugitive Slave Law of 1850, to educate the escaped slaves, and then to assist them to get to Liberia so that they could set up a true Christian republic there. (See below her "Concluding Remarks," which constitute the last chapter of *Uncle Tom's Cabin*.)

As one can see, Mrs. Stowe is not arguing for integration. She believed the ideal political state for the Negro should be created by Negroes in Africa, not in the United States. *Uncle Tom's Cabin* was in its intention not radical but moderate and, with reference to the southern and border states, conciliatory. In the last sentence of her book, Mrs. Stowe says that both the North and the South have been guilty before God, that the Christian churches have heavy accounts to answer to, and that the time

---

[4] Cushing Strout, "*Uncle Tom's Cabin* and the Portent of Millennium," *Yale Review*, 57 (Spring, 1968), 581. In this general connection, see also the discussion of Longfellow and the fireside poets, pp. 586–92.

is short if "this Union [is] to be saved. . . ." This last phrase is ominous, for though Mrs. Stowe could not clearly foresee the events of 1861, like a great many other sensitive observers, she feared catastrophe might well be near at hand.

Not for nothing was Mrs. Stowe the child of a culture that believed in its holy mission to establish churches that were to be like "golden candlesticks" shining in the darkness of the American wilderness, but her culture was also aware of the awful possibility that the Lord might suddenly remove those candlesticks "out of their places" because of sloth or other wickedness and so expressed that anxiety in a poem like *The Day of Doom* (reprinted in this text).

Though the last sentence of *Uncle Tom's Cabin* sounds an ominous note, the novel begins optimistically. In the preface to the first edition Mrs. Stowe tells her reader that "another and better day is dawning; every influence of literature, of poetry and of art, in our times, is becoming more and more in unison with a great master chord of Christianity, 'good will to man.'" Actually, the two notes—of woeful apprehension and of joyful expectation—both relate to the prophecy of the Second Coming of Christ which is to usher in the millennium. For if Christ is to come in judgment, separating the nations "one from another as a shepherd separates the sheep from the goats," and if He will order those set on His left hand to depart from Him "into the eternal fire prepared for the devil and his angels," He will also on that great day invite those that He places on His right hand to enter into the kingdom prepared for them "from the foundation of the world." He will thus institute the rule of perfect peace and goodness.

The earlier Calvinism had stressed the Day of Judgment and the punishment to be inflicted on the wicked. A more mellowed Calvinism tended to stress the golden age to come. It is the latter stress that is more congenial to Mrs. Stowe. In her *Poganuc People* she says that "the star of hope in the eyes of the New En-gland clergy" was the promise of the "triumph of goodness and a perfected world."

It is probably not too much to say that America from the beginning has lived in terms of a millennial expectation. As Mrs. Stowe says of one of her characters, the little New Englander Dolly (in *Poganuc People*), "No Jewish maiden ever grew up with a more earnest faith that she belonged to a consecrated race, of people especially called and chosen of God for some great work on earth."[5] On the New England shore in particular, a serious attempt had been made to create a state modeled on the prescriptions of God Himself as recorded in His Holy Scripture.

Cushing Strout, in the article already cited, stresses the millennial hopes and fears as the spiritual background of *Uncle Tom's Cabin*. He writes (p. 379) that Mrs. Stowe's

passionate faith in the Second Coming wavered between the optimistic hopes of the post-millennialists and the apocalyptic fears of the pre-millennialists, but the eschatological expectation is always present. . . .

In her pages Negro Christians live in hope, whites live in fear. St. Clare's mother told him of a millennium that was coming, "when Christ should reign, and all men should be free and happy." He [St. Clare, the southern plantation owner] concludes that "all this sighing and groaning, and stirring among the dry bones foretells what she used to tell me was coming." He reads the signs in a "mustering among the masses, the world over," a singular observation for a plantation master. St. Clare wonders: "But who may abide the day of His appearing?" [Mrs. Stowe, his]

[5] The New England Puritans had a strong sense of affinity with the Jews. Calvin Stowe wore a skull cap and Mrs. Stowe referred to him as "My rabbi." Protestantism had from the beginning placed a heavy emphasis on the Old Testament scriptures, and the Puritans of New England drew an analogy between the mission of Israel and their own keenly felt sense of mission in the New World. Edmund Wilson has an interesting discussion of these matters in *A Piece of My Mind* (1956). See "The Jews," especially pp. 90–107. See also the subject of Judaism in our discussions of Bret Harte and Gertrude Stein in the accompanying volume.

creator completes the portentous quotation in her postscript: "for that day shall burn as an oven: and he shall appear as swift witness against those that oppress the hireling in his wages, the widow and the fatherless, and that *turn aside the stranger in his right: and he shall break in pieces the oppressor.*" Christians might pray for the coming Kingdom but they should remember in fear and trembling that in this last convulsion "prophecy associates, in dread fellowship, the *day of vengeance* with the year of his redeemed."

Millennialism, of course, was firmly rooted in the Puritan culture of New England. (For a mid-nineteenth-century expression of such attitudes and expectations, see the account of Julia Ward Howe's "Battle Hymn of the Republic" in this text.) Millennialism was gradually to become detached from Christianity and more and more secularized. In its secularized form, it remains a potent force in our American culture. We fight wars to end war, or to make the world safe for democracy, or to establish the four freedoms, which include freedom from fear itself! Apocalyptic imagery suffused the rhetoric of the civil rights movement. It is, for example, brilliantly used in James Baldwin's *The Fire Next Time*. Americans feel instinctively that it is possible somehow to legislate morality, to eliminate evils of every kind, and to devise—here upon this earth and in our time—the perfect society. We shall scarcely understand ourselves and our basic motivations and hopes unless we recognize how deeply rooted in American culture is the millennial appeal. This is not to say that attempts, even against odds, to better the human lot are to be abandoned. Quite the contrary. But it is to say that self-righteousness and delusion and omnipotence make a heady brew and that, in the end, a heroism that acts in some awareness of human limitations may be more heroic than that fostered by self-deception.

How good is *Uncle Tom's Cabin* as a novel? Not very good, if we judge it by the highest fictional standards. It is essentially the work of a dedicated "amateur"—of a person passionately involved in the issues with which her novel deals. The writing is often careless. Some of the big scenes like the death of Little Eva are mawkishly sentimental; the author frequently intrudes with didactic comments; she rarely hesitates to pluck at the reader's sleeve to tell him how he ought to react to this or that happening.

The novel is not only often sentimental but also melodramatic. (Perhaps it was faults like this that Simms had in mind in applying the adjective "coarse.") Mrs. Stowe on occasion told friends that not she but God wrote *Uncle Tom's Cabin*. She may very well have had this conviction, but the faults and limitations of Mrs. Stowe as God's amanuensis clearly show in the novel—perhaps the more so because with her eye on the burning vision, she paid the less attention to the precise terms in which she set it down.

Even so, Mrs. Stowe had certain virtues as a novelist. Her work has narrative drive and often displays a talent for fresh and vivid presentation of a scene. As Edmund Wilson puts it:

> She can make us see a person and hear him talk, and she can render a scene or a landscape by a process that can only be likened to a flinging out of handfuls of words which succeed in conveying with a precision that is rather surprising in view of the looseness of her language, of her having no sense whatever of the construction of a sentence of a paragraph, and hardly even a sense of syntax. . . . It is as if she were communicating directly— that is, without the artist's deliberate skill— the perceptions of a sensitive woman. She had a natural mimetic gift, which is exhibited not merely in her dialogue but sometimes also in descriptions . . . through a poetic appropriateness of the language (*Patriotic Gore*, 1962, pp. 34–35).

Thus, though not a skillful literary artist, Mrs. Stowe was in a very real sense a born writer. She had published a great deal before the runaway success of *Uncle Tom's Cabin,* and she continued to write for the rest of her life. Titles like *Sunny Memories of Foreign Lands* (1854), *Religious Poems* (1867), and *Our Famous Women* (1884) will suggest the miscellaneous character of her work.

Mrs. Stowe's last crusade was undertaken in behalf of Lady Byron. On her first visit to England in 1853, she had met Lady Byron, the poet's widow. The acquaintance later ripened into friendship. In 1869, nine years after Lady Byron's death, Mrs. Stowe published an article entitled "The True Story of Lady Byron's Life." (In 1870 the article was expanded into a book entitled *Lady Byron Vindicated.*) In this article Mrs. Stowe told the public that Lady Byron had confided to her that the real cause of her separation from Lord Byron was the incest committed by Lord Byron with his sister, Augusta Leigh. Many people on both sides of the Atlantic, but particularly in England, were outraged and accused Mrs. Stowe of scandalmongering. She was revealing—by her own admission—information that had been given to her in confidence, concerning matters that Lady Byron herself had chosen not to make public. Mrs. Stowe was charged with seeking to exploit a great and honored name in order to produce another best seller.

There is no good reason to question Mrs. Stowe's basic motives. She felt that Lady Byron had been misunderstood and mistreated and, jealous for her friend's reputation, meant to vindicate her. But at the time, Mrs. Stowe's literary reputation suffered severely because of her Byron revelations.

We began this introduction by suggesting parallels between Mrs. Stowe and Oliver Wendell Holmes as representatives of New England's literary and social culture. Mrs. Stowe's desire to do good, her passion to set things right, are sufficiently typical of the culture of which she was a product. Indeed, here it is she rather than Holmes (with his skittishness about abolitionism and other causes) who tends to be the more truly representative. But there is another aspect of Mrs. Stowe's importance in representing New England culture and this aspect is worth careful consideration, for it is here that some of her own best literary work is to be found. It is her portrayal of New England life, particularly that of the towns and villages in the eighteenth century and in the early part of the nineteenth century. If Holmes was oriented toward Boston and is at his best in writing about it, Mrs. Stowe writes with loving perception about the New England folkways and the New England society with which she had been personally familiar as a child or which she came to form through the stories of her husband and of her friends.

One of the best of these works is the novel *The Minister's Wooing,* published in 1859. It has a seaport setting, derived from the actual city of Newport, Rhode Island. Another such novel is *Oldtown Folks* (1869). Mrs. Stowe calls it a "résumé of the whole spirit and body of New England." The model for Oldtown was South Natick, Massachusetts, birthplace of her husband, Calvin Stowe. In *Poganuc People* (1878), Mrs. Stowe is remembering principally her home town of Litchfield as she had known it as a little girl and as a young woman.

In such studies Mrs. Stowe follows in a tradition that goes back to Seba Smith, the Maine author who wrote under the name of "Major Jack Downing." (See pp. 1091–94.) Smith's satiric sketches began to appear in the 1830's and became very popular. In the exploitation of this kind of Yankee humor, Smith had his successors in T. C. Haliburton ("Sam Slick"), C. F. Browne ("Artemus Ward"), and James Russell Lowell ("Hosea Biglow"). In Mrs. Stowe's use of such folk and village material there is less satire and less broad humor. Her work points toward the local-color stories and sketches of later writers like Sarah Orne Jewett. (Miss Jewett was in fact roused to authorship by reading *Poganuc People.*) It is perhaps in this area that Harriet Beecher Stowe comes closest to achieving serious literary art.

BIOGRAPHICAL CHART

1811   Born, June 14, in Litchfield, Connecticut, daughter of Lyman Beecher, Congregationalist minister

1832   Beechers move to Cincinnati, Ohio

1834   Publishes "Prize Tale, a New England Sketch" in *Western Monthly Magazine*

1836   Marries Calvin Ellis Stowe, professor of Biblical literature

1836–50   Lives in Cincinnati; visits Kentucky plantations; becomes interested in abolition

1850   Moves to Brunswick, Maine, when Calvin Stowe receives a professorship at Bowdoin; visits her brother Edward, whose fierce antislavery sermons turn her totally to the abolitionist movement

1851   *Uncle Tom's Cabin* serialized in the *National Era*

1852   *Uncle Tom's Cabin* published in book form

1853   Responds to the critics with *A Key to Uncle Tom's Cabin;* travels to England amidst great popular acclaim

1856   *Dred, a Tale of the Great Dismal Swamp*

1859   *The Minister's Wooing*

1863   Moves to Hartford, Connecticut

1869   *Oldtown Folks;* publishes "The True Story of Lady Byron's Life" in the *Atlantic Monthly,* accusing Byron of incest; article enlarged into book form the next year

1878   *Poganuc People*

1886   Calvin Stowe dies; Mrs. Stowe lapses into mental torpidity and senility

1896   Dies, July 1, in Hartford

FURTHER READINGS

The Writings of Harriet Beecher Stowe (1896; 16 vols.) (no editor cited)

John A. Woods, ed., *Uncle Tom's Cabin* (1965; available in paperback)

James Baldwin, "Everybody's Protest Novel," *Partisan Review* 16 (1949)

Alice C. Crozier, *The Novels of Harriet Beecher Stowe* (1969)

Charles H. Foster, *The Rungless Ladder: Harriet Beecher Stowe and New England Puritanism* (1954)

Charles Edward Stowe, *Harriet Beecher Stowe: The Story of Her Life,* (1911)

Edward C. Wagenknecht, *Harriet Beecher Stowe: The Known and the Unknown,* (1965)

Forrest Wilson, *Crusader in Crinoline: The Life of Harriet Beecher Stowe* (1941)

From Uncle Tom's Cabin (1852)

As we have already remarked, certain experiences of the Stowes while living in Cincinnati provided Mrs. Stowe with materials for her novel. For example, the Stowes harbored for a time a Negro girl who, though she told them she was free, turned out to be sought by her master. Mrs. Stowe's husband and brother arranged for her escape. This girl was the original for Eliza Harris, the slave girl who in the novel makes her hair-raising escape over the icy Ohio River to freedom.

A younger brother of Mrs. Stowe worked for a time as a clerk in New Orleans and returned from time to time to Cincinnati with stories about life on the plantations of Louisiana. He was Mrs. Stowe's principal source for the Louisiana scenes in the novel.

Chapter 28 (printed below) has its setting in the New Orleans home of Augustine St. Clare, who has great wealth and owns many slaves. When Uncle Tom had been parted from his wife and children in Kentucky and sold down the river, St. Clare had purchased him at the insistence of his little daughter, Eva, who had seen something of Uncle Tom on the Mississippi steamboat which was also bringing the St. Clares home.

Miss Ophelia, St. Clare's cousin, is a visitor from Vermont. Her presence in the novel allows Mrs. Stowe to point some contrasts between two people who, though blood relatives, had been nurtured in different cultures: Miss Ophelia, the straitlaced, somewhat doctrinaire New England-bred woman and her cousin St.

Clare, a man brought up in a slave-owning society and so influenced by its customs and attitudes.

St. Clare as a realist sees no easy way out of his situation as a slaveholder, but he is far from blind and insensitive to the moral implications of his position, and he is not untouched by human sympathies. He has, as Mrs. Stowe evidently felt a great many decent people in the South had, a bad conscience about the whole slave system.

By having St. Clare's death come suddenly and melodramatically, Mrs. Stowe provides herself with an illustration of another terrible defect in the slave system. St. Clare's personal good intentions are brought to nothing, for his wife, a spoiled, cruel, and—as we should call her today—neurotic woman, does not carry out St. Clare's wish to give Uncle Tom his freedom but instead proceeds to sell him to the despicable Simon Legree, who will finally have him beaten to death.

Chapter 45 is printed in this text immediately after Chapter 28. Mrs. Stowe entitled it "Concluding Remarks" and this is precisely what it is, for it has no real part in the fictional fabric of the novel. We do the story no violence, therefore, in excerpting it from the narrative context. The whole novel indeed is filled with such asides and preachments. Mrs. Stowe's "Remarks" constitutes an important statement about possible solutions for the problem of slavery in the United States.

CHAPTER 28: REUNION

Week after week glided away in the St. Clare mansion, and the waves of life settled back to their usual flow, where that little bark had gone down.[1] For how imperiously, how coolly, in disregard of all one's feeling, does the hard, cold, uninteresting course of daily realities move on! Still must we eat, and drink, and sleep, and wake again,—still bargain, buy, sell, ask and answer questions,—pursue, in short, a thousand shadows, though all interest in them be over; the cold mechanical habit of living remaining, after all vital interest in it has fled.

All the interests and hopes of St. Clare's life had unconsciously wound themselves around this child. It was for Eva that he had managed his property; it was for Eva that he had planned the disposal of his time; and, to do this and that for Eva,—to buy, improve, alter, and arrange, or dispose something for her,—had been so long his habit, that now she was gone, there seemed nothing to be thought of, and nothing to be done.

True, there was another life,—a life which, once believed in, stands as a solemn, significant figure before the otherwise unmeaning ciphers of time, changing them to orders of mysterious, untold value. St. Clare knew this well; and often, in many a weary hour, he heard that slender, childish voice calling him to the skies, and saw that little hand pointing to him the way of life; but a heavy lethargy of sorrow lay on him,—he could not arise. He had one of those natures which could better and more clearly conceive of religious things from its own perceptions and instincts, than many a matter-of-fact and practical Christian. The gift to appreciate and the sense to feel the finer shades and relations of moral things, often seems an attribute of those whose whole life shows a careless disregard of them. Hence Moore, Byron, Goethe, often speak words more wisely descriptive of the true religious sentiment, than another man, whose whole life is governed by it. In such minds, disregard of religion is a more fearful treason,—a more deadly sin.

St. Clare had never pretended to govern himself by any religious obligation; and a certain fineness of nature gave him such an instinctive view of the extent of the requirements of Christianity, that he shrank, by anticipation, from what he felt would be the exactions of his own conscience, if he once did resolve to assume them. For, so inconsistent is human nature, especially in the ideal, that not to undertake a thing at all seems better than to undertake and come short.

Still St. Clare was, in many respects, another man. He read his little Eva's Bible seriously and honestly; he thought more soberly and practically of his relations to his servants,—enough to make him extremely dissatisfied with both his past and present course; and one thing he did, soon after his return to New Orleans, and that was to commence the legal steps necessary to Tom's emancipation, which was to be perfected as soon as he could get through the necessary formalities. Meantime, he attached himself to Tom more and more,

---

[1] The death of St. Clare's little daughter, Eva [editors' note].

every day. In all the wide world, there was nothing that seemed to remind him so much of Eva; and he would insist on keeping him constantly about him, and, fastidious and unapproachable as he was with regard to his deeper feelings, he almost thought aloud to Tom. Nor would any one have wondered at it, who had seen the expression of affection and devotion with which Tom continually followed his young master.

'Well, Tom,' said St. Clare, the day after he had commenced the legal formalities for his enfranchisement, 'I'm going to make a free man of you; —so, have your trunk packed, and get ready to set out for Kentucky.'

The sudden light of joy that shone in Tom's face as he raised his hands to heaven, his emphatic 'Bless the Lord!' rather discomposed St. Clare; he did not like it that Tom should be so ready to leave him.

'You haven't had such very bad times here, that you need be in such a rapture, Tom,' he said, drily.

'No, no, Mas'r! 'tan't that,—it's bein' a *free man!* That's what I'm joyin' for.'

'Why, Tom, don't you think, for your own part, you've been better off than to be free?'

'*No, indeed,* Mas'r St. Clare,' said Tom, with a flash of energy. 'No, indeed!'

'Why, Tom, you couldn't possibly have earned, by your work, such clothes and such living as I have given you.'

'Knows all that, Mas'r St. Clare; Mas'r's been too good; but, Mas'r, I'd rather have poor clothes, poor house, poor everything, and have 'em *mine,* than have the best, and have 'em any man's else,—I had *so,* Mas'r; I think it's natur, Mas'r.'

'I suppose so, Tom, and you'll be going off and leaving me, in a month or so,' he added, rather discontentedly. 'Though why you shouldn't, no mortal knows,' he said, in a gayer tone; and, getting up, he began to walk the floor.

'Not while Mas'r is in trouble,' said Tom. 'I'll stay with Mas'r as long as he wants me,—so as I can be any use.'

'Not while I'm in trouble, Tom?' said St. Clare, looking sadly out of the window. . . . 'And when will *my* trouble be over?'

'When Mas'r St. Clare's a Christian,' said Tom.

'And you really mean to stay by till that day comes?' said St. Clare, half smiling, as he turned from the window, and laid his hand on Tom's shoulder. 'Ah, Tom, you soft, silly boy! I won't keep you till that day. Go home to your wife and children, and give my love to all.'

'I 's faith to believe that day will come,' said Tom, earnestly, and with tears in his eyes; 'the Lord has a work for Mas'r.'

'A work, hey?' said St. Clare; 'well, now, Tom, give me your views on what sort of a work it is;—let's hear.'

'Why, even a poor fellow like me has a work from the Lord; and Mas'r St. Clare, that has larnin, and riches, and friends,—how much he might do for the Lord!'

'Tom, you seem to think the Lord needs a great deal done for him,' said St. Clare, smiling.

'We does for the Lord when we does for his critturs,' said Tom.

'Good theology, Tom; better than Dr. B. preaches, I dare swear,' said St. Clare.

The conversation was here interrupted by the announcement of some visiters.

Marie St. Clare felt the loss of Eva as deeply as she could feel anything; and, as she was a woman that had a great faculty of making everybody unhappy when she was, her immediate attendants had still stronger reason to regret the loss of their young mistress, whose winning ways and gentle intercessions had so often been a shield to them from the tyrannical and selfish exactions of her mother. Poor old Mammy, in particular, whose heart, severed from all natural domestic ties, had consoled itself with this one beautiful being, was almost heart-broken. She cried day and night, and was, from excess of sorrow, less skilful and alert in her ministrations on her mistress than usual, which drew down a constant storm of invectives on her defenceless head.

Miss Ophelia felt the loss; but, in her good and honest heart, it bore fruit unto everlasting life. She was more softened, more gentle; and, though equally assiduous in every duty, it was with a chastened and quiet air, as one who communed with her own heart not in vain. She was more diligent in teaching Topsy,—taught her mainly from the Bible,—did not any longer shrink from her touch, or manifest an ill-repressed disgust, because she felt none. She viewed her now through the softened medium that Eva's hand had first held before her eyes, and saw in her only an immortal creature, whom God had sent to be led by her to glory and virtue. Topsy did not become at once a saint; but the life and death of Eva did work a marked change in her. The callous indifference was gone; there was now sensibility, hope, desire, and the striving for good,—a strife irregular, interrupted, suspended oft, but yet renewed again.

One day, when Topsy had been sent for by Miss Ophelia, she came, hastily thrusting something into her bosom.

'What are you doing there, you limb? You've been stealing something, I'll be bound,' said the imperious little Rosa, who had been sent to call her, seizing her, at the same time, roughly by the arm.

'You go 'long, Miss Rosa!' said Topsy, pulling from her; ' 'tan't none o' your business!'

'None o' your sa'ce!' said Rosa. 'I saw you hiding something,—I know yer tricks,' and Rosa seized her arm, and tried to force her hand into her bosom, while Topsy, enraged, kicked and fought valiantly for what she considered her rights. The clamor and confusion of the battle drew Miss Ophelia and St. Clare both to the spot.

'She's been stealing!' said Rosa.

'I han't, neither!' vociferated Topsy, sobbing with passion.

'Give me that, whatever it is!' said Miss Ophelia, firmly.

Topsy hesitated; but, on a second order, pulled out of her bosom a little parcel done up in the foot of one or her own old stockings.

Miss Ophelia turned it out. There was a small book, which had been given to Topsy by Eva, containing a single verse of Scripture, arranged for every day in the year, and in a paper the curl of hair that she had given her on that memorable day when she had taken her last farewell.

St. Clare was a good deal affected at the sight of it; the little book had been rolled in a long strip of black crape, torn from the funeral weeds.

'What did you wrap *this* round the book for?' said St. Clare, holding up the crape.

''Cause,—cause,—cause 't was Miss Eva. O, don't take 'em away, please!' she said; and, sitting flat down on the floor, and putting her apron over her head, she began to sob vehemently.

It was a curious mixture of the pathetic and the ludicrous,—the little old stocking,—black crape,—text-book,—fair, soft curl,—and Topsy's utter distress.

St. Clare smiled; but there were tears in his eyes, as he said,

'Come, come,—don't cry; you shall have them!' and, putting them together, he threw them into her lap, and drew Miss Ophelia with him into the parlor.

'I really think you can make something of that concern,' he said, pointing with his thumb backward over his shoulder. 'Any mind that is capable of a *real sorrow* is capable of good. You must try and do something with her.'

'The child has improved greatly,' said Miss Ophelia. 'I have great hopes of her; but, Augustine,' she said, laying her hand on his arm, 'one thing I want to ask; whose is this child to be?—yours or mine?'

'Why, I gave her to *you*,' said Augustine.

'But not legally;—I want her to be mine legally,' said Miss Ophelia.

'Whew! cousin,' said Augustine. 'What will the Abolition Society think? They'll have a day of fasting appointed for this backsliding, if you become a slave-holder!'

'O, nonsense! I want her mine, that I may have a right to take her to the free States, and give her her liberty, that all I am trying to do be not undone.'

'O, cousin, what an awful "doing evil that good may come"! I can't encourage it.'

'I don't want you to joke, but to reason,' said Miss Ophelia. 'There is no use in my trying to make this child a Christian child, unless I save her from all the chances and reverses of slavery; and, if you really are willing I should have her, I want you to give me a deed of gift, or some legal paper.'

'Well, well,' said St. Clare, 'I will;' and he sat down, and unfolded a newspaper to read.

'But I want it done now,' said Miss Ophelia.

'What's your hurry?'

'Because now is the only time there ever is to do a thing in,' said Miss Ophelia. 'Come, now, here's paper, pen, and ink; just write a paper.'

St. Clare, like most men of his class of mind, cordially hated the present tense of action, generally; and, therefore, he was considerably annoyed by Miss Ophelia's downrightness.

'Why, what's the matter?' said he. 'Can't you take my word? One would think you had taken lessons of the Jews, coming at a fellow so!'

'I want to make sure of it,' said Miss Ophelia. 'You may die, or fail, and then Topsy be hustled off to auction, spite of all I can do.'

'Really, you are quite provident. Well, seeing I'm in the hands of a Yankee, there is nothing for it but to concede;' and St. Clare rapidly wrote off a deed of gift, which, as he was well versed in the forms of law, he could easily do, and signed his name to it in sprawling capitals, concluding by a tremendous flourish.

'There, isn't that black and white, now, Miss Vermont?' he said, as he handed it to her.

'Good boy,' said Miss Ophelia, smiling. 'But must it not be witnessed?'

'O, bother!—yes. Here,' he said, opening the door into Marie's apartment, 'Marie, Cousin wants your autograph; just put your name down here.'

'What's this?' said Marie, as she ran over, the paper. 'Ridiculous! I thought Cousin was too pious for such horrid things,' she added, as she carelessly wrote her name; 'but, if she has a fancy for that article, I am sure she's welcome.'

'There, now, she's yours, body and soul,' said St. Clare, handing the paper.

'No more mine now than she was before,' said Miss Ophelia. 'Nobody but God has a right to give her to me; but I can protect her now.'

'Well, she's yours by a fiction of law, then,' said St. Clare, as he turned back into the parlor, and sat down to his paper.

Miss Ophelia, who seldom sat much in Marie's company, followed him into the parlor, having first carefully laid away the paper.

'Augustine,' she said, suddenly, as she sat knitting, 'have you ever made any provision for your servants, in case of your death?'

'No,' said St. Clare, as he read on.

'Then all your indulgence to them may prove a great cruelty, by and by.'

St. Clare had often thought the same thing himself; but he answered, negligently,

'Well, I mean to make a provision, by and by.'

'When?' said Miss Ophelia.

'O, one of these days.'

'What if you should die first?'

'Cousin, what's the matter?' said St. Clare, laying down his paper and looking at her. 'Do you think I show symptoms of yellow fever or cholera, that you are making post mortem arrangements with such zeal?'

' "In the midst of life we are in death," ' said Miss Ophelia.

St. Clare rose up, and laying the paper down, carelessly, walked to the door that stood open on the verandah, to put an end to a conversation that was not agreeable to him. Mechanically, he repeated the last word again,—'*Death!*'—and, as he leaned against the railings, and watched the sparkling water as it rose and fell in the fountain; and, as in a dim and dizzy haze, saw flowers and trees and vases of the courts, he repeated again the mystic word so common in every mouth, yet of such fearful power,—'*Death!*' 'Strange that there should be such a word,' he said, 'and such a thing, and we ever forget it; that one should be living, warm and beautiful, full of hopes, desires and wants, one day, and the next be gone, utterly gone, and forever!'

It was a warm, golden evening; and, as he walked to the other end of the verandah, he saw Tom busily intent on his Bible, pointing, as he did so, with his finger to each successive word, and whispering them to himself with an earnest air.

'Want me to read to you, Tom?' said St. Clare, seating himself carelessly by him.

'If Mas'r pleases,' said Tom, gratefully, 'Mas'r makes it so much plainer.'

St. Clare took the book and glanced at the place, and began reading one of the passages which Tom had designated by the heavy marks around it. It ran as follows:

'When the Son of man shall come in his glory, and all his holy angels with him, then shall he sit upon the throne of his glory: and before him shall be gathered all nations; and he shall separate them one from another, as a shepherd divideth his sheep from the goats.' St. Clare read on in an animated voice, till he came to the last of the verses.

'Then shall the king say unto them on his left hand, Depart from me, ye cursed, into everlasting fire: for I was an hungered, and ye gave me no meat: I was thirsty, and ye gave me no drink: I was a stranger, and ye took me not in: naked, and ye clothed me not: I was sick, and in prison, and ye visited me not. Then shall they answer unto Him, Lord when saw we thee an hungered, or athirst, or a stranger, or naked, or sick, or in prison, and did not minister unto thee? Then shall he say unto them, Inasmuch as ye did it not to one of the least of these my brethren, ye did it not to me.'

St. Clare seemed struck with this last passage, for he read it twice,—the second time slowly, and as if he were revolving the words in his mind.

'Tom,' he said, 'these folks that get such hard measure seem to have been doing just what I have,—living good, easy, respectable lives; and not troubling themselves to inquire how many of their brethren were hungry or athirst, or sick, or in prison.'

Tom did not answer.

St. Clare rose up and walked thoughtfully up and down the verandah, seeming to forget everything in his own thoughts; so absorbed was he, that Tom had to remind him twice that the tea-bell had rung, before he could get his attention.

St. Clare was absent and thoughtful, all tea-time. After tea, he and Marie and Miss Ophelia took possession of the parlor, almost in silence.

Marie disposed herself on a lounge, under a silken mosquito curtain, and was soon sound asleep. Miss Ophelia silently busied herself with her knitting. St. Clare sat down to the piano, and began playing a soft and melancholy movement with the Æolian accompaniment. He seemed in a deep reverie, and to be soliloquizing to himself by music. After a little, he opened one of the drawers, took out an old music-book whose leaves were yellow with age, and began turning it over.

'There,' he said to Miss Ophelia, 'this was one of my mother's books,—and here is her handwriting, —come and look at it. She copied and arranged this from Mozart's Requiem.' Miss Ophelia came accordingly.

'It was something she used to sing often,' said St. Clare. 'I think I can hear her now.'

He struck a few majestic chords, and began singing that grand old Latin piece, the 'Dies Iræ.'

Tom, who was listening in the outer verandah, was drawn by the sound to the very door, where he stood earnestly. He did not understand the words, of course; but the music and manner of singing appeared to affect him strongly, especially when St. Clare sang the more pathetic parts. Tom would have sympathized more heartily, if he had known the meaning of the beautiful words:

> Recordare Jesu pie
> Quod sum causa tuæ viæ
> Ne me perdas, illa die
> Querens me sedisti lassus
> Redemisti crucem passus
> Tantus labor non sit cassus.[2]

St. Clare threw a deep and pathetic expression into the words; for the shadowy veil of years seemed drawn away, and he seemed to hear his mother's voice leading his. Voice and instrument seemed both living, and threw out with vivid sympathy those strains which the ethereal Mozart first conceived as his own dying requiem.

When St. Clare had done singing, he sat leaning his head upon his hand a few moments, and then began walking up and down the floor.

---

[2] These lines have been thus rather inadequately translated:

> Think, O Jesus, for what reason
> Thou endured'st earth's spite and treason,
> Nor me lose, in that dread season;
> Seeking me, thy worn feet hasted,
> On the cross thy soul death tasted,
> Let not all these toils be wasted [Stowe].

'What a sublime conception is that of a last judgment!' said he,—'a righting of all the wrongs of ages!—a solving of all moral problems, by an unanswerable wisdom! It is, indeed, a wonderful image.'

'It is a fearful one to us,' said Miss Ophelia.

'It ought to be to me, I suppose,' said St. Clare, stopping, thoughtfully. 'I was reading to Tom, this afternoon, that chapter in Matthew that gives an account of it, and I have been quite struck with it. One should have expected some terrible enormities charged to those who are excluded from Heaven, as the reason; but no,—they are condemned for *not* doing positive good, as if that included every possible harm.'

'Perhaps,' said Miss Ophelia, 'it is impossible for a person who does no good not to do harm.'

'And what,' said St. Clare, speaking abstractedly, but with deep feeling, 'what shall be said of one whose own heart, whose education, and the wants of society, have called in vain to some noble purpose; who has floated on, a dreamy, neutral spectator of the struggles, agonies, and wrongs of man, when he should have been a worker?'

'I should say,' said Miss Ophelia, 'that he ought to repent, and begin now.'

'Always practical and to the point!' said St. Clare, his face breaking out into a smile. 'You never leave me any time for general reflections, Cousin; you always bring me short up against the actual present; you have a kind of eternal *now*, always in your mind.'

'*Now* is all the time I have anything to do with,' said Miss Ophelia.

'Dear little Eva,—poor child!' said St. Clare, 'she had set her little simple soul on a good work for me.'

It was the first time since Eva's death that he had ever said as many words as these of her, and he spoke now evidently repressing very strong feeling.

'My view of Christianity is such,' he added, 'that I think no man can consistently profess it without throwing the whole weight of his being against this monstrous system of injustice that lies at the foundation of all our society; and, if need be, sacrificing himself in the battle. That is, I mean that I could not be a Christian otherwise, though I have certainly had intercourse with a great many enlightened and Christian people who did no such thing; and I confess that the apathy of religious people on this subject, their want of perception of wrongs that filled me with horror, have engendered in me more scepticism than any other thing.'

'If you knew all this,' said Miss Ophelia, 'why didn't you do it?'

'O, because I have had only that kind of benevolence which consists in lying on a sofa, and cursing the church and clergy for not being martyrs and confessors. One can see, you know, very easily, how others ought to be martyrs.'

'Well, are you going to do differently now?' said Miss Ophelia.

'God only knows the future,' said St. Clare. 'I am braver than I was, because I have lost all; and he who has nothing to lose can afford all risks.'

'And what are you going to do?'

'My duty, I hope, to the poor and lowly, as fast as I find it out,' said St. Clare, 'beginning with my own servants, for whom I have yet done nothing; and, perhaps, at some future day, it may appear that I can do something for a whole class; something to save my country from the disgrace of that false position in which she now stands before all civilized nations.'

'Do you suppose it possible that a nation ever will voluntarily emancipate?' said Miss Ophelia.

'I don't know,' said St. Clare. 'This is a day of great deeds. Heroism and disinterestedness are rising up, here and there, in the earth. The Hungarian nobles set free millions of serfs, at an immense pecuniary loss; and, perhaps, among us may be found generous spirits, who do not estimate honor and justice by dollars and cents.'

'I hardly think so,' said Miss Ophelia.

'But, suppose we should rise up to-morrow and emancipate, who would educate these millions, and teach them how to use their freedom? They never would rise to do much among us. The fact is, we are too lazy and unpractical, ourselves, ever to give them much of an idea of that industry and energy which is necessary to form them into men. They will have to go north, where labor is the fashion,—the universal custom; and tell me, now, is there enough Christian philanthropy, among your northern states, to bear with the process of their education and elevation? You send thousands of dollars to foreign missions; but could you endure to have the heathen sent into your towns and villages, and give your time, and thoughts, and money, to raise them to the Christian standard? That's what I want to know. If we emancipate, are you willing to educate? How many families, in your town, would take a negro man and woman, teach them, bear with them, and seek to make them Christians? How many merchants would take Adolph, if I wanted to make him a clerk; or mechanics, if I wanted him taught a trade? If I wanted to put Jane and Rosa to a school, how many schools are there in the northern states that would take them in? how many families that would board them? and yet they are as white as many a woman, north or south. You see, Cousin, I want justice done us. We are in a bad position. We are the more *obvious* oppressors of the negro; but the unchristian prejudice of the north is an oppressor almost equally severe.'

'Well, Cousin, I know it is so,' said Miss Ophelia,—'I know it was so with me, till I saw that it was my duty to overcome it; but, I trust I have overcome it; and I know there are many good people at the north, who in this matter need only to be *taught* what their duty is, to do it. It would certainly be a greater self-denial to receive heathen among us, than to send missionaries to them; but I think we would do it.'

'*You* would, I know,' said St. Clare. 'I'd like to see anything you wouldn't do, if you thought it your duty!'

'Well, I'm not uncommonly good,' said Miss Ophelia. 'Others would, if they saw things as I do. I intend to take Topsy home, when I go. I suppose our folks will wonder, at first; but I think they will be brought to see as I do. Besides, I know there are many people at the north who do exactly what you said.'

'Yes, but they are a minority; and, if we should begin to emancipate to any extent, we should soon hear from you.'

Miss Ophelia did not reply. There was a pause of some moments; and St. Clare's countenance was overcast by a sad, dreamy expression.

'I don't know what makes me think of my mother so much, to-night,' he said. 'I have a strange kind of feeling, as if she were near me. I keep thinking of things she used to say. Strange, what brings these past things so vividly back to us, sometimes!'

St. Clare walked up and down the room for some minutes more, and then said,

'I believe I'll go down street, a few moments, and hear the news, to-night.'

He took his hat, and passed out.

Tom followed him to the passage, out of the court, and asked if he should attend him.

'No, my boy,' said St. Clare. 'I shall be back in an hour.'

Tom sat down in the verandah. It was a beautiful moonlight evening, and he sat watching the rising and falling spray of the fountain, and listening to its murmur. Tom thought of his home, and than he should soon be a free man, and able to return to it at will. He thought how he should work to buy his wife and boys. He felt the muscles of his brawny arms with a sort of joy, as he thought they would soon belong to himself, and how much they could do to work out the freedom of his family. Then he thought of his noble young master, and, ever second to that, came the habitual prayer that he had always offered for him; and then his thoughts passed on to the beautiful Eva, whom he now thought of among the angels; and he thought till he almost fancied that that bright face and golden hair were looking upon him, out of the spray of the fountain. And, so musing, he fell asleep, and dreamed he saw her coming bounding towards him, just as she used to come, with a wreath of jessamine in her hair, her cheeks bright, and her eyes radiant with delight; but, as he looked, she seemed to rise from the ground; her cheeks wore a paler hue,—her eyes had a deep, divine radiance, a golden halo seemed around her head,—and she vanished from his sight; and Tom was awakened by a loud knocking, and a sound of many voices at the gate.

He hastened to undo it; and, with smothered voices and heavy tread, came several men, bringing a body, wrapped in a cloak, and lying on a shutter. The light of the lamp fell full on the face; and Tom gave a wild cry of amazement and despair, that rung through all the galleries, as the men advanced, with their burden, to the open parlor door, where Miss Ophelia still sat knitting.

St. Clare had turned into a cafe, to look over an evening paper. As he was reading, an affray arose between two gentlemen in the room, who were both partially intoxicated. St. Clare and one or two others made an effort to separate them, and St. Clare received a fatal stab in the side with a bowie-knife, which he was attempting to wrest from one of them.

The house was full of cries and lamentations, shrieks and screams; servants frantically tearing their hair, throwing themselves on the ground, or running distractedly about, lamenting. Tom and Miss Ophelia alone seemed to have any presence of mind; for Marie was in strong hysteric convulsions. At Miss Ophelia's direction, one of the lounges in the parlor was hastily prepared, and the bleeding form laid upon it. St. Clare had fainted, through pain and loss of blood; but, as Miss Ophelia applied restoratives, he revived, opened his eyes, looked fixedly on them, looked earnestly around the room, his eyes travelling wistfully over every object, and finally they rested on his mother's picture.

The physician now arrived, and made his examination. It was evident, from the expression of his face, that there was no hope; but he applied himself to dressing the wound, and he and Miss Ophelia and Tom proceeded composedly with this work, amid the lamentations and sobs and cries of the affrighted servants, who had clustered about the doors and windows of the verandah.

'Now,' said the physician, 'we must turn all these creatures out; all depends on his being kept quiet.'

St. Clare opened his eyes, and looked fixedly on the distressed beings, whom Miss Ophelia and the doctor were trying to urge from the apartment. 'Poor creatures!' he said, and an expression of bitter self-reproach passed over his face. Adolph absolutely refused to go. Terror had deprived him of all presence of mind; he threw himself along on the floor, and nothing could persuade him to rise. The rest yielded to Miss Ophelia's urgent representations, that their master's safety depended on their stillness and obedience.

St. Clare could say but little; he lay with his eyes shut, but it was evident that he wrestled with bitter thoughts. After a while, he laid his hand on Tom's, who was kneeling beside him, and said, 'Tom! poor fellow!'

'What, Mas'r?' said Tom, earnestly.

'I am dying!' said St. Clare, pressing his hand; 'pray!'

'If you would like a clergyman—' said the physician.

St. Clare hastily shook his head, and said again to Tom, more earnestly, 'Pray!'

And Tom did pray, with all his mind and strength, for the soul that was passing,—the soul that seemed looking so steadily and mournfully from those large, melancholy blue eyes. It was literally prayer offered with strong crying and tears.

When Tom ceased to speak, St. Clare reached out and took his hand, looking earnestly at him, but saying nothing. He closed his eyes, but still retained his hold; for, in the gates of eternity, the black hand and the white hold each other with an equal clasp. He murmured softly to himself, at broken intervals,

Recordare Jesu pie—

. . .

Ne me perdas—ille die
Querens me—sedisti lassus.

It was evident that the words he had been singing that evening were passing through his mind,—words of entreaty addressed to Infinite Pity. His lips moved at intervals, as parts of the hymn fell brokenly from them.

'His mind is wandering,' said the doctor.

'No! it is coming home, at last!' said St. Clare, energetically; 'at last! at last!'

The effort of speaking exhausted him. The sinking paleness of death fell on him; but with it there fell, as if shed from the wings of some pitying spirit, a beautiful expression of peace, like that of a wearied child who sleeps.

So he lay for a few moments. They saw that the mighty hand was on him. Just before the spirit parted, he opened his eyes, with a sudden light, as of joy and recognition, and said '*Mother!*' and then he was gone!

CHAPTER 45: CONCLUDING REMARKS

The writer has often been inquired of, by correspondents from different parts of the country, whether this narrative is a true one; and to these inquiries she will give one general answer.

The separate incidents that compose the narrative are, to a very great extent, authentic, occurring, many of them, either under her own observation, or that of her personal friends. She or her friends have observed characters the counterpart of almost all that are here introduced; and many of the sayings are word for word as heard herself, or reported to her.

The personal appearance of Eliza, the character ascribed to her, are sketches drawn from life. The incorruptible fidelity, piety and honesty, of Uncle Tom, had more than one development, to her personal knowledge. Some of the most deeply tragic and romantic, some of the most terrible incidents, have also their parallel in reality. The incident of the mother's crossing the Ohio river on the ice is a well-known fact. The story of 'old Prue,' in the second volume [which begins with Chap. 19], was an incident that fell under the personal observation of a brother of the writer, then collecting-clerk to

a large mercantile house, in New Orleans. From the same source was derived the character of the planter Legree. Of him her brother thus wrote, speaking of visiting his plantation, on a collecting tour: 'He actually made me feel of his fist, which was like a blacksmith's hammer, or a nodule of iron, telling me that it was "calloused with knocking down niggers." When I left the plantation, I drew a long breath, and felt as if I had escaped from an ogre's den.'

That the tragical fate of Tom, also, has too many times had its parallel, there are living witnesses, all over our land, to testify. Let it be remembered that in all southern states it is a principle of jurisprudence that no person of colored lineage can testify in a suit against a white, and it will be easy to see that such a case may occur, wherever there is a man whose passions outweigh his interests, and a slave who has manhood or principle enough to resist his will. There is, actually, nothing to protect the slave's life, but the *character* of the master. Facts too shocking to be contemplated occasionally force their way to the public ear, and the comment that one often hears made on them is more shocking than the thing itself. It is said, 'Very likely such cases may now and then occur, but they are no sample of general practice.' If the laws of New England were so arranged that a master could *now and then* torture an apprentice to death, would it be received with equal composure? Would it be said, 'These cases are rare, and no samples of general practice'? This injustice is an *inherent* one in the slave system,—it cannot exist without it.

The public and shameless sale of beautiful mulatto and quadroon girls has acquired a notoriety, from the incidents following the capture of the Pearl. We extract the following from the speech of Hon. Horace Mann, one of the legal counsel for the defendants in that case. He says: 'In that company of seventy-six persons, who attempted, in 1848, to escape from the District of Columbia in the schooner Pearl, and whose officers I assisted in defending, there were several young and healthy girls, who had those peculiar attractions of form and feature which connoisseurs prize so highly. Elizabeth Russel was one of them. She immediately fell into the slave-trader's fangs, and was doomed for the New Orleans market. The hearts of those that saw her were touched with pity for her fate. They offered eighteen hundred dollars to redeem her; and some there were who offered to give, that would not have much left after the gift; but the fiend of a slave-trader was inexorable. She was despatched to New Orleans; but, when about half way there, God had mercy on her, and smote her with death. There were two girls named Edmundson in the same company. When about to be sent to the same market, an older sister went to the shambles, to plead with the wretch who owned them, for the love of God, to spare his victims. He bantered her, telling what fine dresses and fine furniture they would have. "Yes," she said, "that may do very well in this life, but what will become of them in the next?" They too were sent to New Orleans; but were afterwards redeemed, at an enormous ransom, and brought back.' Is it not plain, from this, that the histories of Emmeline and Cassy may have many counterparts?

Justice, too, obliges the author to state that the fairness of mind and generosity attributed to St. Clare are not without a parallel, as the following anecdote will show. A few years since, a young southern gentleman was in Cincinnati, with a favorite servant, who had been his personal attendant from a boy. The young man took advantage of this opportunity to secure his own freedom, and fled to the protection of a Quaker, who was quite noted in affairs of this kind. The owner was exceedingly indignant. He had always treated the slave with such indulgence, and his confidence in his affection was such, that he believed he must have been practised upon to induce him to revolt from him. He visited the Quaker, in high anger; but, being possessed of uncommon candor and fairness, was soon quieted by his arguments and representations. It was a side of the subject which he never had heard,—never had thought on; and he immediately told the Quaker that, if his slave would, to his own face, say that it was his desire to be free, he would liberate him. An interview was forthwith procured, and Nathan was asked by his young master whether he had ever had any reason to complain of his treatment, in any respect.

'No, Mas'r,' said Nathan; 'you've always been good to me.'

'Well, then, why do you want to leave me?'

'Mas'r may die, and then who get me?—I'd rather be a free man.'

After some deliberation, the young master replied, 'Nathan, in your place, I think I should feel very much so, myself. You are free.'

He immediately made him out free papers; deposited a sum of money in the hands of the Quaker, to be judiciously used in assisting him to start in life, and left a very sensible and kind letter of advice to the young man. That letter was for some time in the writer's hands.

The author hopes she has done justice to that nobility, generosity, and humanity, which in many cases characterize individuals at the South. Such instances save us from utter despair of our kind. But, she asks any person, who knows the world, are such characters *common*, anywhere?

For many years of her life, the author avoided all reading upon or allusion to the subject of slavery, considering it as too painful to be inquired into, and one which advancing light and civilization would certainly live down. But, since the legislative act of 1850, when she heard, with perfect surprise and consternation, Christian and humane people actually recommending the remanding escaped fugitives into slavery, as a duty binding on good citizens,—when she heard, on all hands, from kind, compassionate and estimable people, in the free states of the North, deliberations and discussions as to what Christian duty could be on this head,—she could only think, These men and Christians cannot know what slavery is; if they did, such a question could never be open for discussion. And from this arose a desire to exhibit it in a *living dramatic reality*. She has endeavored to show it fairly, in its best and its worst phases. In its *best* aspect, she has, perhaps, been successful; but, oh! who shall say what yet remains untold in that valley and shadow of death, that lies the other side?

To you, generous, noble-minded men and women, of the South,—you, whose virtue, and magnanimity and purity of character, are the greater for the severer trial it has encountered,— to you is her appeal. Have you not, in your own secret souls, in your own private conversings, felt that there are woes and evils, in this accursed system, far beyond what are here shadowed, or can be shadowed? Can it be otherwise? Is *man* ever a creature to be trusted with wholly irresponsible power? And does not the slave system, by denying the slave all legal right of testimony, make every individual owner an irresponsible despot? Can anybody fail to make the inference what the practical result will be? If there is, as we admit, a public sentiment among you, men of honor, justice and humanity, is there not also another kind of public sentiment among the ruffian, the brutal and debased? And cannot the ruffian, the brutal, the debased, by slave law, own just as many slaves as the best and purest? Are the honorable, the just, the high-minded and compassionate, the majority anywhere in this world?

The slave-trade is now, by American law, considered as piracy. But a slave-trade, as systematic as ever was carried on on the coast of Africa, is an inevitable attendant and result of American slavery. And its heart-break and its horrors, *can* they be told?

The writer has given only a faint shadow, a dim picture, of the anguish and despair that are, at this very moment, riving thousands of hearts, shattering thousands of families, and driving a helpless and sensitive race to frenzy and despair. There are those living who know the mothers whom this accursed traffic has driven to the murder of their children; and themselves seeking in death a shelter from woes more dreaded than death. Nothing of tragedy can be written, can be spoken, can be conceived, that equals the frightful reality of scenes daily and hourly acting on our shores, beneath the shadow of American law, and the shadow of the cross of Christ.

And now, men and women of America, is this a thing to be trifled with, apologized for, and passed over in silence? Farmers of Massachusetts, of New Hampshire, of Vermont, of Connecticut, who read this book by the blaze of your winter-evening fire,—strong-hearted, generous sailors and ship-owners of Maine,—is this a thing for you to countenance and encourage? Brave and generous men of New York, farmers of rich and joyous Ohio, and ye of the wide prairie states,—answer, is this a thing for you to protect and countenance? And you, mothers of America,—you, who have learned, by the cradles of your own children, to love and feel for all mankind,—by the sacred love you bear your child; by your joy in his beautiful, spotless infancy; by the motherly pity and tenderness with which you guide his growing years; by the anxieties of his education; by the prayers you breathe for his soul's eternal good;—I beseech you, pity the mother who has all your affections, and not one legal right to protect, guide, or educate, the child of her bosom! By the sick hour of your child; by those dying eyes, which you can never forget; by those last cries, that wrung your heart when you could neither help nor save; by the desolation of that empty cradle, that silent nursery, —I beseech you, pity those mothers that are constantly made childless by the American slave-trade! And say, mothers of America, is this a thing to be

defended, sympathized with, passed over in silence?

Do you say that the people of the free states have nothing to do with it, and can do nothing? Would to God this were true! But it is not true. The people of the free states have defended, encouraged, and participated; and are more guilty for it, before God, than the South, in that they have *not* the apology of education or custom.

If the mothers of the free states had all felt as they should, in times past, the sons of the free states would not have been the holders, and, proverbially, the hardest masters of slaves; the sons of the free states would not have connived at the extension of slavery, in our national body; the sons of the free states would not, as they do, trade the souls and bodies of men as an equivalent to money, in their mercantile dealings. There are multitudes of slaves temporarily owned, and sold again, by merchants in northern cities; and shall the whole guilt or obloquy of slavery fall only on the South?

Northern men, northern mothers, northern Christians, have something more to do than denounce their brethren at the South; they have to look to the evil among themselves.

But, what can any individual do? Of that, every individual can judge. There is one thing that every individual can do,—they can see to it that *they feel right*. An atmosphere of sympathetic influence encircles every human being; and the man or woman who *feels* strongly, healthily and justly, on the great interests of humanity, is a constant benefactor to the human race. See, then, to your sympathies in this matter! Are they in harmony with the sympathies of Christ? or are they swayed and perverted by the sophistries of worldly policy?

Christian men and women of the North! still further,—you have another power; you can *pray!* Do you believe in prayer? or has it become an indistinct apostolic tradition? You pray for the heathen abroad; pray also for the heathen at home. And pray for those distressed Christians whose whole chance of religious improvement is an accident of trade and sale; from whom any adherence to the morals of Christianity is, in many cases, an impossibility, unless they have given them, from above, the courage and grace of martyrdom.

But, still more. On the shores of our free states are emerging the poor, shattered, broken remnants of families,—men and women, escaped, by miraculous providences, from the surges of slavery,—feeble in knowledge, and, in many cases, infirm in moral constitution, from a system which confounds and confuses every principle of Christianity and morality. They come to seek a refuge among you; they come to seek education, knowledge, Christianity.

What do you owe to these poor unfortunates, oh Christians? Does not every American Christian owe to the African race some effort at reparation for the wrongs that the American nation has brought upon them? Shall the doors of churches and school-houses be shut upon them? Shall states arise and shake them out? Shall the church of Christ hear in silence the taunt that is thrown at them, and shrink away from the helpless hand that they stretch out; and, by her silence, encourage the cruelty that would chase them from our borders? If it must be so, it will be a mournful spectacle. If it must be so, the country will have reason to tremble, when it remembers that the fate of nations is in the hands of One who is very pitiful, and of tender compassion.

Do you say, 'We don't want them here; let them go to Africa'?

That the providence of God has provided a refuge in Africa, is, indeed, a great and noticeable fact; but that is no reason why the church of Christ should throw off that responsibility to this outcast race which her profession demands of her.

To fill up Liberia with an ignorant, inexperienced, half-barbarized race, just escaped from the chains of slavery, would be only to prolong, for ages, the period of struggle and conflict which attends the inception of new enterprises. Let the church of the north receive these poor sufferers in the spirit of Christ; receive them to the educating advantages of Christian republican society and schools, until they have attained to somewhat of a moral and intellectual maturity, and then assist them in their passage to those shores, where they may put in practice the lessons they have learned in America.

There is a body of men at the north, comparatively small, who have been doing this; and, as the result, this country has already seen examples of men, formerly slaves, who have rapidly acquired property, reputation, and education. Talent has been developed, which, considering the circumstances, is certainly remarkable; and, for moral traits of honesty, kindness, tenderness of feeling,— for heroic efforts and self-denials, endured for the ransom of brethren and friends yet in slavery,— they have been remarkable to a degree that, considering the influence under which they were born, is surprising.

The writer has lived, for many years, on the frontier-line of slave states, and has had great op-

portunities of observation among those who formerly were slaves. They have been in her family as servants; and, in default of any other school to receive them, she has, in many cases, had them instructed in a family school, with her own children. She has also the testimony of missionaries, among the fugitives in Canada, in coincidence with her own experience; and her deductions, with regard to the capabilities of the race, are encouraging in the highest degree.

The first desire of the emancipated slave, generally, is for *education*. There is nothing that they are not willing to give or do to have their children instructed; and, so far as the writer has observed herself, or taken the testimony of teachers among them, they are remarkably intelligent and quick to learn. The results of schools, founded for them by benevolent individuals in Cincinnati, fully establish this.

The author gives the following statement of facts, on the authority of Professor C. E. Stowe, then of Lane Seminary, Ohio, with regard to emancipated slaves, now resident in Cincinnati; given to show the capability of the race, even without any very particular assistance or encouragement.

The initial letters alone are given. They are all residents of Cincinnati.

'B——. Furniture maker; twenty years in the city; worth ten thousand dollars, all his own earnings; a Baptist.

'C——. Full black; stolen from Africa; sold in New Orleans; been free fifteen years; paid for himself six hundred dollars; a farmer; owns several farms in Indiana; Presbyterian; probably worth fifteen or twenty thousand dollars, all earned by himself.

'K——. Full black; dealer in real estate; worth thirty thousand dollars; about forty years old; free six years; paid eighteen hundred dollars for his family; member of the Baptist church; received a legacy from his master, which he has taken good care of, and increased.

'G——. Full black; coal dealer; about thirty years old; worth eighteen thousand dollars; paid for himself twice, being once defrauded to the amount of sixteen hundred dollars; made all his money by his own efforts—much of it while a slave, hiring his time of his master, and doing business for himself; a fine, gentlemanly fellow.

'W——. Three-fourths black; barber and waiter; from Kentucky; nineteen years free; paid for self and family over three thousand dollars; deacon in the Baptist church.

'G. D——. Three-fourths black; white-washer; from Kentucky; nine years free; paid fifteen hundred dollars for self and family; recently died, aged sixty; worth six thousand dollars.'

Professor Stowe says, 'With all these, except G——, I have been, for some years, personally acquainted, and make my statements from my own knowledge.'

The writer well remembers an aged colored woman, who was employed as a washerwoman in her father's family. The daughter of this woman married a slave. She was a remarkably active and capable young woman, and, by her industry and thrift, and the most persevering self-denial, raised nine hundred dollars for her husband's freedom, which she paid, as she raised it, into the hands of his master. She yet wanted a hundred dollars of the price, when he died. She never recovered any of the money.

These are but few facts, among multitudes which might be adduced, to show the self-denial, energy, patience, and honesty, which the slave has exhibited in a state of freedom.

And let it be remembered that these individuals have thus bravely succeeded in conquering for themselves comparative wealth and social position, in the face of every disadvantage and discouragement. The colored man, by the law of Ohio, cannot be a voter, and, till within a few years, was even denied the right of testimony in legal suits with the white. Nor are these instances confined to the State of Ohio. In all states of the Union we see men, but yesterday burst from the shackles of slavery, who, by a self-educating force, which cannot be too much admired, have risen to highly respectable stations in society. Pennington, among clergymen, Douglas and Ward, among editors, are well known instances.

If this persecuted race, with every discouragement and disadvantage, have done thus much, how much more they might do, if the Christian church would act towards them in the spirit of her Lord!

This is an age of the world when nations are trembling and convulsed. A mighty influence is abroad, surging and heaving the world, as with an earthquake. And is America safe? Every nation that carries in its bosom great and unredressed injustice has in it the elements of this last convulsion.

For what is this mighty influence thus rousing in all nations and languages those groanings that cannot be uttered, for man's freedom and equality?

O, Church of Christ, read the signs of the times! Is not this power the spirit of Him whose kingdom is yet to come, and whose will to be done on earth as it is in heaven?

But who may abide the day of his appearing? 'for that day shall burn as an oven: and he shall appear as a swift witness against those that oppress the hireling in his wages, the widow and the fatherless, and that *turn aside the stranger in his right:* and he shall break in pieces the oppressor.'

Are not these dread words for a nation bearing in her bosom so mighty an injustice? Christians! every time that you pray that the kingdom of Christ may come, can you forget that prophecy associates, in dread fellowship, the *day of vengeance* with the year of his redeemed?

A day of grace is yet held out to us. Both North and South have been guilty before God; and the *Christian church* has a heavy account to answer. Not by combining together, to protect injustice and cruelty, and making a common capital of sin, is this Union to be saved,—but by repentance, justice and mercy; for, not surer is the eternal law by which the millstone sinks in the ocean, than that stronger law, by which injustice and cruelty shall bring on nations the wrath of Almighty God!

From Poganuc People (1878)

This novel is the account of Dolly Cushing's childhood, girlhood, and eventual marriage. Dolly's story owes a great deal to Mrs. Stowe's own early life.

The chapter that follows (Chap. 18), entitled

"Dolly's 'Fourth,' " is a good example of Mrs. Stowe's descriptions of village life and farm life in the New England of her girlhood. In the Litchfield that she is remembering here, the power of Calvinism was waning, the Calvinists themselves were mellowing somewhat, and the Episcopal church was beginning to strengthen. The time is the early 1820's.

CHAPTER 18: DOLLY'S "FOURTH"

Bang! went the cannon on the green, just as the first red streak appeared over Poganuc hills, and open flew Dolly's great blue eyes. Every boy in town was out of bed as if he had been fired out of a pop-gun, and into his clothes and out on the green with a celerity scarcely short of the miraculous. Dolly's little toilet took more time; but she, too, was soon out upon the scene with her curls in a wild, unbrushed tangle, her little breast swelling and beating with a great enthusiasm for General Washington and liberty and her country, all of which were somehow to be illustrated and honored that day in Poganuc.

As the first rays of the rising sun struck the stars and stripes floating over the Court-house, and the sound of distant drum and fife announced the coming in of the Poganuc Rangers, Dolly was so excited that she burst into tears.

"What in the world are you crying for, Dolly?" said Bill rather impatiently. "I don't see any thing to cry about."

"I can't help it, Will," said Dolly, wiping her eyes, "it's so glorious!"

"If that isn't just like a girl!" said Bill. Contempt could go no farther, and Dolly retreated abashed. She was a girl—there was no help for that; but for this one day she envied the boys— the happy boys who might some day grow up and fight for their country, and do something glorious like General Washington. Meanwhile, from mouth to mouth, every one was giving in advance an idea of what the splendors of the day were to be.

"I tell ye," said Abe Bowles, "this 'ere's goin' to be a reel slam-bang, this 'ere is. Colonel Davenport is a goin' to review the troops, and wear the very same uniform he wore at Long Island."

"Yes," said Liph Kingsley, "and old Cæsar's goin' to wear his uniform and wait on the colonel. Tell ye what, the old snowball is on his high heels this morning—got a suit of the colonel's old uniform. Won't he strut and show his ivories!"

"Hulloa, boys, there's going to be a sham fight; Hiel told me so," said Bob Cushing. "Some are going to be British and some Americans, and the Americans are going to whip the British and make 'em run."

"Tell ye what," said Jake Freeman, "there'll be a bangin' and poppin'! won't there, boys!"

"Oh," said Dolly, who irrepressibly was following her brothers into the throng, "they won't *really* shoot anybody, will they?"

"Oh no, they'll only fire powder, of course," said Bill majestically, "don't you know that?"

Dolly was rebuked and relieved at once.

"I say, boys," said Nabby, appearing suddenly among the throng, "your ma says you must come right home to breakfast this minit; and you, Dolly Cushing, what are you out here for, round among the fellers like a tom-boy? Come right home."

"Why, Nabby, I wanted to see!" pleaded Dolly.

"Oh yes, you're allers up to everything and into everything, and your hair not brushed nor nothin'. You'll see it all in good time—come right away. Don't be a-lookin' at them trainers, now," she added, giving herself, however, a good observing glance to where across the green a knot of the Poganuc Rangers were collecting, and where Hiel, in full glory of his uniform, with his gold epaulets and cocked hat, was as busy and impressive as became the situation.

"Oh, Nabby, do look; there's Hiel," cried Dolly.

"Yes, yes; I see plain enough there's Hiel," said Nabby; "he thinks he's mighty grand, I suppose. He'll be conceiteder'n ever, I expect."

Just at that moment Hiel, recognizing Nabby, took off his gold-laced hat and bowed with a graceful flourish.

Nabby returned a patronizing little nod, and either the morning dawn, or the recent heat of the kitchen fire, or *something*, flushed her cheeks. It was to be remarked in evidence of the presence of mind that distinguishes the female sex that, though she had been sent out on a hurried errand to call the children, yet she had on her best bonnet, and every curl of her hair had evidently been carefully and properly attended to that morning.

"Of course, I wasn't going to look like a fright," she soliloquized. "Not that I care for any of 'em; but looks is looks any time o' day."

At the minister's breakfast-table the approaching solemnities were discussed. The procession was to form at the Court-house at nine o'clock. Democrats and Federalists had united to distribute impartially as possible the honors of the day. As Col. Davenport, the only real live revolutionary officer the county boasted, was an essential element of the show, and as he was a staunch Federalist, it was necessary to be conciliatory. Then there was the Federal ex-Governor to sit on the platform with the newly elected Democratic Governor. The services were in the Meeting-house, as the largest building in town; and Dr. Cushing was appointed to make the opening prayer. As a compliment to the Episcopal Church the Federal members of the committee allotted a closing prayer to the Reverend Simeon Coan.

That young man, however, faithful to the logic of his creed, politely declined joining in public services where his assisting might be held to recognize the ordination of an unauthorized sectarian preacher, and so the Rev. Dr. Goodman, of Skantic, was appointed in his place.

Squire Lewis was observed slightly to elevate his eye-brows and shrug his shoulders as he communicated to the committee the grounds of his rector's refusal. He was in fact annoyed, and a little embarrassed, by the dry, amused expression of Sheriff Dennie's countenance.

"Oh, speak it all out; never fear, Lewis," he said. "I like to see a man face the music. Your minister is a logical fellow, and keeps straight up to what he teaches. You old Episcopalians were getting loose in your ideas; you needed cording up."

"There's such a thing as cording too tight and breaking a string sometimes," muttered the Squire, who was not well pleased at the scruple that kept his church unrepresented in the exercises.

The domestic arrangements for the parson's family were announced at the breakfast table. The boys were endowed with the magnificent sum of six cents each and turned loose for the day, with the parting admonition to keep clear of powder—a most hopeless and unnecessary charge, since powder was the very heart and essence of all the glory of the day.

At an early hour the bell of the Meeting-house rang out over all the neighboring hills and valleys; the summons was replied to by streams of wagons on the roads leading to Poganuc for a square of ten miles round. Not merely Poganuc—North, South, East, West, and Center—was in motion, but several adjacent towns and villages sent forth their trainers—bands of militia, who rose about midnight and marched till morning to be on time.

By nine o'clock nominally (but far nearer to ten really) the procession started from the Court-house with drum and fife and banners. Dolly had been committed for the day to the charge of Nabby, who should see that she took no harm, and engineer for her the best chances of seeing all that went on; while Mrs. Cushing, relieved of this care, took her seat quietly among the matron-age of Poganuc and waited for the entrance of the procession. But Dolly saw them start from the Court-house, with beat of drum and peal of fife; and Dolly saw the banners, and saw Colonel Davenport with his white hair and splendid physique, now more splendid in the blue and gold of his military dress; and they all marched with majestic tread towards the meeting-house. Then Nabby hurried with her charge and got for her a seat by herself in the front singers' seat in the gallery, where she could see them all file in and take their seats on the platform. Nabby had been one of the flowers of this singers' seat before her father's change of base had transferred her to the Episcopal Church, and her presence to-day was welcomed by many old friends—for Nabby had a good, strong clear voice of her own, and was no small addition to the choral force.

The services opened by the national Puritan psalm:

"Let children hear the mighty deeds
Which God performed of old,
Which in our younger years we saw
And which our fathers told.

"Our lips shall teach them to our sons,
And they again to theirs,
That generations yet unborn
May teach them to their heirs.

"That they may learn, in God alone
Their hope securely stands;
That they may ne'er his laws forget,
But practice his commands."

The wild warble of "St. Martin's," the appointed tune whose wings bore these words, swelled and billowed and reverberated through the house, carrying with it that indefinable thrill which always fills a house when deep emotions are touched—deepest among people habitually reserved and reticent of outward demonstration. It was this solemn undertone, this mysterious, throbbing sub-bass of repressed emotion, which gave the power and effect to the Puritan music. After the singing came Dr. Cushing's prayer—which was a recounting of God's mercies to New England from the beginning, and of his deliverances from her enemies, and of petitions for the glorious future of the United States of America—that they might be chosen vessels, commissioned to bear the light of liberty and religion through all the earth and to bring in the great millennial day, when wars should cease and the whole world, released from the thraldom of evil, should rejoice in the light of the Lord.

The millennium was ever the star of hope in the eyes of the New England clergy: their faces were set eastward, towards the dawn of that day, and the cheerfulness of those anticipations illuminated the hard tenets of their theology with a rosy glow. They were children of the morning. The Doctor, however, did not fail to make use of his privilege to give some very decided political hits, and some petitions arose which caused sensation between the different parties. The New England clergyman on these occasions had his political antagonists at decided advantage. If he could not speak at them he could pray at them, and of course there was no reply to an impeachment in the court of heaven. So when the Doctor's prayer was over, glances were interchanged, showing the satisfaction or dissatisfaction, as might be, of the listeners.

And now rose Colonel Davenport to read the Declaration of Independence. Standing square and erect, his head thrown back, he read in a resonant and emphatic voice that great enunciation upon which American national existence was founded.

Dolly had never heard it before, and even now had but a vague idea of what was meant by some parts of it; but she gathered enough from the recital of the abuses and injuries which had driven her nation to this course to feel herself swelling with indignation, and ready with all her little mind and strength to applaud that concluding Declaration of Independence which the Colonel rendered with resounding majesty. She was as ready as any of them to pledge her "life, fortune and sacred honor" for such a cause. The heroic element was strong in Dolly; it had come down by "ordinary generation" from a line of Puritan ancestry, and just now it swelled her little frame and brightened her cheeks and made her long to do something, she scarce knew what; to fight for her country or to make some declaration on her own account.

But now came the oration of the day, pronounced by a lively young Virginia law student in the office of Judge Gridley. It was as ornate and flowery, as full of patriotism and promise, as has been the always approved style of such productions. The bird of our nation received the usual appropriate flourishes, flew upward and sun-ward, waved his pinions, gazed with undaunted eye on the brightness, and did all other things appointed for the American Eagle to do on the Fourth of July. It was a nicely-written classical composition, and eminently satisfactory to the audience; and Dolly, without any very direct conception of its exact meaning, was delighted with it, and so were all the Poganuc People.

Then came the singing of an elaborate anthem, on which the choir had been practicing for a month beforehand and in which the various parts ran, and skipped, and hopped, and chased each other round and round, and performed all sorts of unheard-of trills and quavers and musical evolutions, with a heartiness of self-satisfaction that was charming to witness.

Then, when all was over, the procession marched out—the magnates on the stage to a dinner, and the Poganuc military to refresh themselves at Glazier's, preparatory to the grand review in the afternoon.

Dolly spent her six cents for ginger-bread, and walked unwearyingly the rounds of sight-seeing with Nabby, her soul inly uplifted with the grandeur of the occasion.

In the afternoon came the military display; and Colonel Davenport on his white horse reviewed the troops; and just behind him, also mounted, was old Cato, with his gold-laced hat and plume, his buff breeches and long-tailed blue coat. On the whole, this solemn black attendant formed a striking and picturesque addition to the scene. And so there were marching and counter-marching and military evolutions of all kinds, and Hiel, with his Poganuc Rangers, figured conspicuously in the eyes of all.

It was a dangerous sight for Nabby. She really could not help feeling a secret awe for Hiel, as if he had been wafted away from her into some higher sphere; he looked so very determined and martial that she began to admit that he might carry any fortress that he set himself seriously to attack. After the regular review came the sham fight, which was in fact but an organized military frolic. Some of the West Poganuc youth had dressed themselves as Indians, and other companies, drawn by lot, were to personate the British, and there was skirmishing and fighting and running, to the wild and crazy delight of the boys. A fort, which had been previously constructed of bushes and trees, was furiously attacked by British and Indians, and set on fire; and then the Americans bursting out scattered both the fire and the forces, and performed prodigies of valor.

In short, it was a Day of days to Dolly and the children, and when sober twilight drew on they came home intoxicated with patriotism and sight-seeing.

On her way home Dolly was spied out by her old friend Judge Gridley, who always delighted to have a gossip with her.

"Ha, my little Dolly, are you out to-day?"

"To be sure, sir," said Dolly; "indeed I'm out. Oh, hasn't it been glorious! I've never been so happy in my life. I never heard the Declaration of Independence before."

"Well, and what do you think of it?" asked the Judge.

"I never heard anything like it," said Dolly. "I didn't know before how they did abuse us, and wasn't it grand that we wouldn't bear it! I never heard anything so splendid as that last part."

"You would have made a good soldier."

"If I were a man I would. Only think of it, Colonel Davenport fought in the war! I'm so glad we can see one man that did. If we had lived then, I know my papa and all my brothers would have fought; we would have had 'liberty or death.'"

Dolly pronounced these words, which she had heard in the oration, with a quivering eagerness. The old Judge gave her cheek a friendly pinch.

"You'll do," he said; "but now you must let Nabby here get you home and quiet you down, or you won't sleep all night. Good by, Pussy."

And so went off Dolly's Fourth of July.

But Hiel made an evening call at the parsonage in his full regimentals; and stayed to a late hour unreproved. There were occasions when even the nine o'clock bell did not send a young fellow home. This appeared to be one of them.

RALPH WALDO EMERSON (1803–1882)

Ralph Waldo Emerson is, somehow, the *indispensable* figure in American literary history. He is by no means the strongest or most broadly ranging of our writers, nor is he our most consummate artist. It has indeed been rightly said about Emerson that he never quite found the proper literary form for the play of his mind and imagination; and perhaps no form exists for the lightning flashes of intuition and insight, of suggestive wit and moral challenge that mark Emerson at his best. But the themes he sounded most frequently will always be found close to the center of any fair account of the continuity and development of American literature.

Emerson provides, for example, the first revealing link between the Romantic spirit of his own day and certain long-buried and occasionally eruptive aspects of Puritanism. The American Romantic movement was, among other things, another of those periodic upsurges of feeling, of a yearning for emotional fulfillment, that have regularly countered the periodic cultural control of the rationalistic and scientific mind. Those impulses, we recall, led to the Great Awakening in 1735 and to the spread of evangelical Christianity in the later eighteenth century. Emerson's early essays, lectures, and addresses sparked a sort of Awakening among the literati and intellectuals of New England, though an Awakening far less frenzied and much more decorous than the one that the sermons of Jonathan Edwards gave rise to. It was, moreover, a primarily literary phenomenon (with important religious ingredients) and found expression in tales and poems and essays. But just as Edwards stirred again those spiritual fears and hungers which the Puritans had taken note of but the Enlightenment tended to ignore or suppress, so Emerson gave voice to the spiritual and imaginative frustration of his own generation.

Emerson's effect upon his contemporaries was of course prodigious, even if we credit him only with saying persuasively and charmingly and repeatedly what many others were already thinking and struggling to formulate. Whitman admitted that, as a poet, he had been "simmering" for a long time before the essays of Emerson brought him "to a boil." To both Whitman and Emily Dickinson, Emerson bequeathed—or made accessible—the notion of poetry as the power capable of transforming our habits of perception and hence of lighting up the world we live in, in new ways. Upon Hawthorne and Melville, Emerson had an indispensable *negative* influence: that is, by meditating Emerson's confidence in human nature, his serene assurance of man's ability to shape a high and happy destiny, they clarified their own tragic vision, their sense of irresolvable ambiguity and contradiction in human experience. As to Emerson's friend and neighbor, Thoreau, his entire career might almost be described as Emersonianism getting down to brass tacks—Thoreau tried to practice, as a way of life on the shores of Walden Pond and elsewhere, what Emerson had been preaching. In our century, traces of Emerson can be found in the work of writers as radically diverse as William James, John Dos Passos, and Robert Frost—though, again, "Emerson" is sometimes only a convenient label for a visionary Romantic strain, or a commitment to democratic idealism, that Emerson first and best enunciated.

If Emerson's centrality has not always been recognized, it is in part because of a certain shiftiness and evasiveness in his expression—he abhorred systems, distrusted flat and unequivocal statements, and famously denounced a foolish consistency as merely the hobgoblin of the small-minded. It is also because of serious limitations in his vision—he seems to leave out so much of experience and reality that was of such major significance for Edwards, for Hawthorne and Melville, for Henry James and Faulkner, and for ourselves. "There were certain chords in Emerson," Henry James remarked, "that did not vibrate at all." James confessed an ironic astonishment at learning (from a biography of Emerson) that Emerson "could see nothing in Shelley, Aristophanes, Don Quixote, Miss Austen, Dickens," that he never read a novel and that he found nothing of interest in Dante (neither of those latter claims is strictly true, though Emerson can be quoted in defense of them). The confession of so broad an insensibility, James said, "is a large allowance to have to make for a man of letters." But the fact was, James believed, that Emerson "had no great sense of wrong . . . no sense of the dark, the foul, the

base"; he had only "a kind of hearsay, uninformed acquaintance with the disorders" of the spirit.

That is an eloquent summary of the persisting image. Nor is it entirely misleading. For while, in his essays and lectures, Emerson displayed a highly developed awareness of contrariety—more than any man of his time—we rarely feel any vital *tension* between the conflicting elements at any given moment. Emerson listened cheerfully, he tells us, to "the clangor and jangle of contrary tendencies," and no one pointed more often to the "doubleness" that runs through the world and through human nature and experience. It was a doubleness reflected in the two realms inhabited by the human spirit—which, borrowing the terms from Kant, Emerson often called the Reason and the Understanding; in the alternating need for solitude and for society; in a conviction of One-ness in the universe (as of Beauty, Truth, Goodness, and Moral Law) and the constant apprehension of multiplicity and diversity. "All the universe over," he wrote in his journal in 1842, "there is just one thing, that old double"; and he ruminated somewhat sadly, in "The Transcendentalist," on "this double consciousness," on "the two lives, of the understanding and the soul, which we lead," and which never seem to "meet and measure each other." It was the very function and responsibility of what Emerson called "the scholar" to mediate between the contrary tendencies. Yet each must be allowed to press its claim. What appeared to Hawthorne and Melville, in different ways, as real contradictions, as the "yeas" and the "nays" of a culture, seem in Emerson to be simply competing "yeas."

But that is the voice that speaks in the essays and lectures, and especially the earlier ones: Emerson's public or platform voice, as it were. Emerson's more private writings, his journals and his poems, sometimes suggest another mood. He did possess a sense of pain, of suffering, partly as a result of incidents in his own life; and he had a sense of psychological depredations—that is, of the negations and absences and blanks in certain individual natures.

But in the course of time there was something deeper still: a growing awareness of human limitation so potent that Stephen Whicher, in the best account yet written of Emerson's intellectual development (*Freedom and Fate*, 1953), could, in view of it, attribute to the later Emerson a tragic consciousness. For having once believed that the human spirit was radically free, that the domain of Freedom was indeed his natural home, Emerson went on to discover that man belonged equally to the domain of Necessity and that the spiritual achievement he had formerly dreamed of (the fragmented self reunited and capable of ever larger visions of universal truth) was not accessible to him or to any man.

The force of that discovery made its way slowly into the essays and never received full expression there, except possibly in the essay called "Fate" (1852). What we get in such later essays is not the shock of new dark insight, but the painfully achieved acceptance of it, and after the pain has been largely expunged. This, too, has helped to obscure Emerson's centrality and to falsify and simplify his real and oscillating view of things. But even Melville (for whom the only Emerson was always the early Emerson), after commenting to himself about Emerson's apparently willful ignorance of evil, added characteristically: "Still, these essays are noble." And James, after explaining the defects of Emerson's "genius" by reference to the intellectual and literary sparseness of the Boston he had grown up in, added: "The genius itself it seems to me impossible to contest—I mean the genius for seeing character as a real and supreme thing. . . . No one has had so steady and constant, and above all so natural, a vision of what we require and what we are capable of in the way of aspiration and independence."

The first of the modest climacterics in Emerson's life occurred in 1832, when he resigned as minister of the Second Church in Boston. He was twenty-nine at the time, and the act was a decided break with the tradition of his family, which had supplied the Boston area with a long line of ministers, including Emerson's

father (William) and his grandfather. His mother (Ruth Ripley) was a gentle and pious woman, possessed—in the words of her sister-in-law—of a "whole assemblage of mild and amiable virtues," yet lacking in "those energies —those keen vibrations of soul . . . which give to life all the zest of enjoyment!" That same sister-in-law, Mary Moody Emerson, had immense energy, both mental and physical, and she made a greater impact on the young Emerson than anyone else in his family. "She had the misfortune," Emerson said of his aunt in a fond memoir, "of spinning with a greater velocity than any of the other tops." From Mary Moody, Emerson could learn a devotion to human freedom, but on the religious issue she was a staunch Calvinist and fought her nephew's gradual defection every step of the way.

At Harvard, from which Emerson graduated in 1821, he had had a most undistinguished career, ending up thirtieth in a class of fifty-nine. It was in college that he dropped his first name, thereafter to be called Waldo by his family and his few intimates. But at college he began his readings in Plato and the Platonists and in Montaigne—writings which nourished the two dimensions of Emerson, the idealistic and the down-to-earth, the searcher for the universal Moral Law and the observer of contemporary life and manners. (Lowell, in *A Fable for Critics*, acutely referred to Emerson as a "Plotinus-Montaigne.") After college, he had drifted almost automatically into theological study, began preaching in 1826, and in March, 1829, was ordained junior pastor at the Second Church in Boston with the expectation of soon becoming the senior, on the retirement of Henry Ware. But all the while, something in him had been working away from every kind of religious orthodoxy.

Emerson had never had any stomach for Calvinism, with its doctrine of "hereditary depravity" and its belief in divine retribution. But as early as 1823, Emerson's vaguely "liberal" religious thinking became focused by the sermons of William Ellery Channing—that small, shy, sickly, and much beloved minister of the

Federal Street Church in Boston, and the leading voice of New England Unitarianism. Channing, in his own person, showed how a man might discard most of the orthodox tenets while remaining within the church; and for Emerson and those who felt as he did, Channing was "the star of the American Church" and "one of those men who vindicate the power of the American race to produce greatness." From Channing, Emerson learned the supremacy of direct intuition—especially of God as revealed in nature—over discursive reasoning. "The beauty and glory of God's works," Channing maintained, "are revealed to the mind by a light beaming from itself." And that God *was* to be looked for in nature and not in formal theology and ritualistic practices, Channing was supremely confident. So convinced, Channing suggested—in a way that Emerson would carry to an optimistic extreme—that for a spirit in tune with God, evil tends to disappear.

> We discern more and more of God in every thing, from the frail flower to the everlasting stars. Even in evil, that dark cloud which hangs over the creation, we discern rays of light and hope, and gradually come to see, in suffering, the temptation, proofs and instruments of the sublimest purposes of wisdom and love.

But Channing hung on to a belief in historical Christianity, in the unique figure of Jesus, and in the miracles as recorded in the Bible. For the younger generation, Emerson outstanding among them, those beliefs too would have to be abandoned.

It may be that an event in Emerson's private life did even more than these intellectual influences to bring about the final break. In the fall of 1829, Emerson had married Ellen Tucker, an intelligent, talented, womanly, but unhappily ailing, girl of seventeen. It was the one passion of his life: "I am enamored of thy loveliness," he wrote her, "love-sick with thy sweet beauty." In less than two years, Ellen died of tuberculosis of the lungs. For months afterwards, Emerson walked down every morning to visit her grave, and on one evening in 1832 he tore open her

coffin. Soon after that, he preached a sermon in which he declared that the sacrament of communion (or the Lord's Supper) had no authority in the Bible or anywhere else, that the language of Jesus was purely figurative and had been misunderstood by St. Paul, and that the entire rite was out of date. He followed with his written resignation and sailed for Europe. His maternal grandfather expressed the opinion that Emerson had literally gone insane.

Emerson recovered only gradually from the loss of Ellen, and in a certain sense he may never have recovered from it altogether—or at least from what that event revealed to him about fatality. The first journal passages which eventually went into "Self-Reliance" were written in 1832; others made part of lectures in the middle and late thirties; and when the essay itself finally appeared in 1841, the knowing might have discerned beneath its dithyrambic urgings a hard-won victory over personal grief. The signs of emotional struggle are even more striking in "Fate," a decade later. William James is a valuable witness here. When James suffered two calamities within weeks of each other in the winter of 1870—a nervous collapse followed or possibly caused by the death of a beloved cousin—he fought his way back to sanity and stability in good part with the aid of Emerson. In language borrowed directly from Emerson, James admonished himself to "Ascend to some sort of partnership with fate, and since tragedy is at the heart of us, go to meet it, work it in to our ends"—a paraphrase of Emerson's staunch assertion in "Fate" that " 'Tis the best use of Fate to teach a fatal courage. . . . For if fate is so prevailing, man is a part of it, and can confront fate with fate." It was spiritual consolation of that sort that James acknowledged in his "Address at the Emerson Centenary in Concord" in 1903, when he celebrated Emerson as the heartener and the sustainer of his youth and envisioned him as stepping forth resolutely " 'Gainst death and all oblivious enmity."[1]

---

[1] In the larger Jamesian perspective, of course, Emerson would be regarded as "tender-minded," to use one of the two terms—the other being "tough-minded"—by

On his return from Europe in the fall of 1833, Emerson took up preaching again. But he was now more interested in public lecturing, at which he became extraordinarily adept and which brought him a much needed income (though the eventual settlement of Ellen's estate left him modestly well-off). Out of the lectures, and the journal notes which went into them and then elaborated upon them, he slowly composed his first book, *Nature*, which appeared in 1836 and was the decisive turning point in his intellectual life. Forwarding it to Carlyle—whom he had met and talked with at length on his European journey—Emerson called the book "an entering wedge . . . for something more worthy and significant." Carlyle replied warmly that "I call it rather the Foundation and Ground-plan on which you may build whatsoever of great and true has been given you to build," and added that it was a "true Apocalypse." *Nature* is all of that and more: the ground plan for a large segment of Emerson's world view, and his own little book of revelations. It is also, and despite its rhetorical flaws—the awkward combination of divinity school scholasticism (firstly, secondly, and so on) with a now rather stale bardic fervor—one of the most important documents in the history of American letters.

---

which James, in *Pragmatism*, roughly distinguished the two basic philosophical temperaments. The tender-minded thinker, according to James, was (in his own words) intellectualistic, idealistic, optimistic, religious, "free-willist," and so on. For all James's modifications, the list of attributes adds up to a thoroughly unsatisfactory picture of Emerson, or indeed of any other idealist philosopher from Plato onward. Valuing above all else practicality and common sense, James not only had no stomach for idealism, he had little comprehension of it, or of the dialectical role it can play in the amelioration of the "real" world. Much as he revered Emerson along certain lines, James also contributed to the long-standing misconception of his father's old friend. Henry James, Sr.—though on one occasion he addressed Emerson with affectionate exasperation as "You man without a handle"—had a breadth of view which was able to embrace both Emerson and Jonathan Edwards; and William's brother Henry, Jr., as we have seen, was able to see through Emerson's limitations to his image of the genuinely moral personality.

Emerson is often alleged to have had an inadequate sense of man as a fallen being, and in a Puritan perspective—as we have seen, in the partially Puritan perspective of Henry James—the charge is true. Yet much of *Nature* is given over to a scathing account of what Emerson saw as man's fallen condition. Man has become "the dwarf of himself"; he is "a god in ruins." Man is divided from himself, and he is divided from everything that is not himself—from what Emerson calls "nature." But the reason for this unhappy state of things is not an inherited corruption of the heart (the very mention of the doctrine of original depravity used to set Emerson stammering). It was what, in a letter to Margaret Fuller, Emerson called "opthalmia"—a deficiency in human vision. Man *looks* in the wrong direction and at the wrong things and in the wrong way.

Man looks backward: "our age is retrospective," *Nature* begins; and by the very title of the last section, "Prospects," Emerson urges the human glance to reverse direction and look forward. Men live, Emerson continues, and they organize their response on the basis of outworn opinions and institutionalized beliefs; but such a life is passive and secondhand, almost a mode of death. Emerson summons his readers to seek "an original relation to the universe," to attempt an active, direct, and personal perception of nature—of the physical nature which surrounds one on a country walk, and of the ideal nature which, in Emerson's view, lies behind and beyond that actuality. To do so is to draw upon psychic energies long untapped; for one of the great troubles with contemporary man, as Emerson would put it two years later in his talk to the Harvard Divinity School, is that he had "become near-sighted" and could "only attend to what addresses his senses." Man had, in other words, been seduced by the theory of John Locke; but Emerson, following Channing, rejected Locke's "sensational" psychology and insisted upon man's power to arrive at a direct apprehension of transcendent reality. Such an apprehension, finally—the ultimate cure for "opthalmia"—was possible only for a spirit in harmony with itself. Hence these key sentences near the end of *Nature:*

> The problem of restoring to the world original and eternal beauty is solved by the redemption of the soul. The ruin or the blank that we see when we look at nature, is in our own eye. The axis of vision is not coincident with the axis of things, and so they appear not transparent but opaque. The reason why the world lacks unity, and lies broken and in heaps, is because man is disunited with himself.

The reunited soul is what, elsewhere, Emerson identified as "the active soul," declaring it to be "the one thing in the world, of value." The activities of that soul, as spelled out in the course of *Nature,* are multiple; but we may notice two functions in particular—functions of what, more generally, we may call "the visionary act." The act is "integrative": observing the many, the truly observant eye composes them into a one—Emerson's immediate and homely example being the landscape which, though "indubitably made up of some twenty or thirty farms," strikes the active perceiver (he "whose eyes can integrate all the parts") as unified. The active soul, furthermore, transfigures what it gazes upon. In *Nature,* Emerson elaborates upon this conviction until, in the exalted conclusion, he surveys the transfiguration of the entire world as accomplished at last by the restored human vision: "So fast will all disagreeable appearances, swine, spiders, snakes, pests, mad-houses, prisons, enemies, vanish; they are temporary and shall be no more seen."

Even Emerson rarely reached such a peak of confidence in the human possibility. Yet in "Circles" (1841), he may have outstripped himself. "Circles" is, in fact, an essay which insists, sometimes with blazing eloquence, upon the soul's need and its capacity to reach ever further into the unknown, to push ever beyond any moment or stage of understanding it may have arrived at.

> The life of man is a self-evolving circle, which, from a ring imperceptibly small, rushes on all sides outwards to new and larger circles, and that without end. The extent to which this generation of circles, wheel without wheel, will go, depends on the force or truth of the individual soul. For it is the inert effort of each thought, having formed itself into a circular wave of circumstance, as for instance an empire, rules of an art, a local usage, a religious rite,—to heap itself on that ridge and to solidify and hem in the life. But if the soul is quick and strong it bursts over that boundary on all sides and expands another orbit on the great deep, which also runs up into a high wave, with attempt again to stop and to bind. But the heart refuses to be imprisoned.

Those stirring words and that commitment to the endless, on-pressing pursuit of spiritual insight would be echoed in Romantic poets from Whitman ("O farther, farther sail!") to Hart Crane ("Thy purpose—still one shore beyond desire!/The sea's green crying towers a-sway, Beyond . . ."). More immediately, such passages served to galvanize proponents of something called "transcendentalism."

Emerson once said: "I cannot define, and care not to define," and the New England movement he helped inaugurate and give a certain shape to displays an almost willful lack of definition. In the general introduction to the period 1826–1861, we have offered some preliminary observations on transcendentalism; here we may have a look at some of its representatives, its native origins, its characteristics and tendencies.

Transcendentalism involved the varied and even disparate writings of a remarkably small group of men and women (hardly more than a dozen of them are really worth remembering), mostly living in or near Boston, from roughly 1820 to 1850. They met and discussed an assortment of ideas at one another's homes; they wrote essays and poems; they founded a quarterly journal, the *Dial,* which, as Emerson recalled in "Historic Notes of Life and Letters in New England," "enjoyed its obscurity for four years"; they founded the utopian community at Brook Farm, which lasted little more; they pronounced on philosophy and religion, on politics and literature, on history and economics; they translated from the German. In "Historic Notes," Emerson lists some of the first comers: Margaret Fuller, first editor of the *Dial*, enthusiastic Goethian, an intense, vulnerable, perhaps tragic woman; Theodore Parker, the fiery spirited theologian—"our Savonarola," Emerson called him, "the stout Reformer to urge and defend every cause of humanity with and for the humblest of mankind"; George Ripley, of Brook Farm; James Freeman Clarke, one of the few who transplanted to the West, where (in Cincinnati) he edited the transcendentalizing *Western Messenger*; Frederic Henry Hedge, mediator between German idealistic philosophy and literature and the New England mind; Orestes A. Brownson, magisterial, aggressive, tireless editor (of the *Boston Quarterly Review*), writer, scholar, layer-down of the law on a myriad of subjects, and man of many Christian creeds—eventually, to the dismay of his fellow transcendentalists, a Roman Catholic; Bronson Alcott, educator and Platonist (and the father of Louisa May Alcott, the author of *Little Women*), "a pure idealist," in Emerson's words, "not at all a man of letters, nor of any practical talent, nor a writer of books."

They had little in common as to purpose or program. One of their minor members defined transcendentalism, with a vague wave of the hand, as "a little beyond"; and indeed one senses a push of mind and imagination *beyond* previous American limits. They pushed in particular beyond the rather cautious liberalism, in religion and social thought, of the previous generation. They were mostly younger Unitarians in increasing rebellion against the vestigial orthodoxy of the older Unitarians—one of the most striking examples in American cultural history of the generation gap. "There are always two parties," Emerson wrote, "the party of the Past and the party of the Future"; there is always a generation gap, but "at times the resistance is reanimated, the schism runs under the world and appears in Literature, Philosophy, Church, State and social customs." Emerson

dated this widening gap from about 1820 for twenty years thereafter.

Apart from a shared rebelliousness, there was no clearly defined goal either of an intellectual or social nature, though the Boston establishment feared and suspected one.

> There was no concert [Emerson insisted], and only here and there two or three men or women who read and wrote, each alone, with unusual vivacity. Perhaps they only agreed in having fallen upon Coleridge and Wordsworth and Goethe, then on Carlyle, with pleasure and sympathy.

The transcendentalists thus introduced English and European Romanticism into New England —or anyhow, helped along a process already under way. They tended to value intuition and inspiration over rational discourse; and if they were much concerned with moral character, they were no less concerned with the unfettered flights of the imagination. They were, most of them, idealists in the stricter and philosophical meaning of the word and believed the material world to be less real and of course infinitely less important than the ideal world, which was the domain of the moral law and of perfect beauty. They were all of them idealists in the looser sense, with heady expectations of the emancipation of the spirit (from the past, from received ideas, from creeds and schools) and of the forthcoming creation of a new community among men.

But they were Romantics in New England. Transcendentalism was above all (in James's paraphrase of Emerson's biographer), a "remarkable outburst of Romanticism on Puritan ground." The same perception was nicely voiced by that member of the little group quoted by Emerson who said that the conversation of the transcendentalists "seemed to him like going to heaven on a swing." And Emerson overcame his own distaste for definition in the excellent formula that transcendentalism was "a Saturnalia of faith." All these phrases indicate the same thing: that transcendentalism was fundamentally a religious movement, and one that had its roots in the old New England Puritan consciousness. It was a religious movement imbued with Romantic attitudes and emphases, and it expressed itself as often in poems about natural phenomena as in essays about God-in-nature. But it was a movement which sought and sometimes found literary terms to release much of the ecstasy and a little of the terror that had inhered in Puritanism; it was a Saturnalian revulsion from the cold pieties of contemporary Protestantism, those of the Unitarians not least cold among them. What it recoiled from was perhaps best expressed in the despairing little cry of Margaret Fuller, after observing a Unitarian congregation on a Sunday morning: "That crowd of upturned faces, with their look of unintelligent complacency!" As against that, the transcendentalists yearned for the kind of experience recorded by Emerson in the early pages of *Nature*—when, crossing Boston Common at twilight on an overcast day, he was suddenly seized with exhilaration and felt "glad to the brink of fear."

It will do no harm to use the word "transcendentalism" quite loosely, to include all New England idealists of whatever special interest. But it can be noted that strictly speaking Thoreau was not a transcendentalist (though on occasion he called himself one), if only because he cannot be imagined belonging to any movement whatever and was far more at home in the woods than conversing over tea in other people's houses. ("I take to the woods," he once wrote, "as the homesick go home.") Emerson's relation to the group is more interestingly ambiguous.

In his essay "The Transcendentalist," Emerson applied the label only to those among the idealists who responded to the conformity, injustice, placidity, and materialism of American society by simply dropping out and withdrawing into silence. These were, Emerson suggested, the self-displaced.

their solitary and fastidious manners not only withdraw them from the conversation, but from the labors of the world; they are not good citizens, not good members of society; unwillingly they bear their part of the public and private burdens; they do not willingly share in the public charities, in the public religious rites, in the abolition of the slave-trade, or in the temperance society.

It was a shrewd analysis and not without a sort of sympathetic irony. Concerned as always to reconcile the world of lofty thought with the world of daily activity, Emerson concluded that "the good and wise must learn to act, and carry salvation to the combatants and demagogues in the dusty arena below." How far Emerson followed his own advice we shall see in a moment; here it should be said that his analysis would have been even shrewder if he had fully understood that those most angrily pursuing "the abolition of the slave-trade" might also be displaced idealists. It was by no means impossible that a man—Theodore Parker, for example—who in one perspective could be called a "transcendentalist" could be found, in another context, taking the most radical abolitionist line.

In 1837, the year after the appearance of *Nature*, Emerson delivered the annual Phi Beta Kappa address at Harvard and reflected on the nature and role of "the American scholar." The speech was hailed immediately as the declaration of *literary* independence from the Old World, the long-awaited cultural consequence of political independence. Much was made of its resounding call to the native imagination: "We have listened too long to the courtly muses of Europe. The spirit of the American freeman is already suspected to be timid, imitative, tame. . . . We will walk on our own feet; we will work with our own hands; we will speak our own minds." But though one can still catch some of the excitement that enlivened the rhetoric, that phase of the address is of largely historical interest today. What can or should still stir us is Emerson's image of the "scholar"—as "Man-thinking," not simply a brain at work but a whole personality vigorously exercising its active soul. Doing so, the "scholar" becomes the great mediator between the world of thought and the world of everyday affairs. The scholar, Emerson says, "is one who raises himself from private considerations and breathes and lives on public and illustrious thoughts. He is the world's eye. He is the world's heart." That remarkable description—of the scholar as the dedicated vessel of perception and compassion for his fellow men—may better be appreciated if we think of the frequent tendency today to belittle the life of the mind as dangerous or irrelevant, of the talk about "long-haired intellectuals" and the vulgar concept of "brains incorporated," the subjection of mental talent to the immediate needs of science-for-business. One notices, too, Emerson's stress on the *democratic* nature of the American scholar (the European muses were "courtly" or monarchical), of his concern with "the common . . . the familiar, the low," his respect for "the single person."

In July of the year following, Emerson talked to the graduating class of the Harvard Divinity School and stirred up the angriest hornets' nest of his career. His attack on traditional and historical Christianity as against the "moral sentiment" innate in every man aroused the orthodox to a kind of fury and seemed to threaten the foundations of the entire church, as indeed it did. In the opening moments of the address, Emerson subtly led his listeners to the intuition of divinity by allowing his vision to rise gracefully from the beauty of the immediate physical setting to the realm of the "divine laws." The extended passage is as good an example as may be found in Emerson's writings of what might be meant by "going to heaven on a swing"—a heightening of one's view from the here-and-now to a glimpse of heaven through the force of dialectical play, the to-and-fro swing of the mind as it oscillates upward. Then, in a brilliant twist, Emerson accused the traditionalists of suggesting what we now call "the death of God." "Men have come to speak of the revelation as somewhat long ago given and done, as if God were dead." He pointed to the almost complete loss of religious ecstasy and terror in the stale air of dull orthodox preaching and proclaimed the capacity and as it were the religious right of every individual to experience a direct and immediate revelation of God—by himself, for himself, here on the spot.

The Protestants pounced on Emerson at once, and none more savagely than the Unitarians. The latter felt and expressed that peculiar outrage that liberals have always felt when the younger generation, pushing beyond them in liberality of thought (in whatever field), seems to regard *them* as the enemy rather than the conservatives whom the earlier liberals had taken such pride in breaking away from. Andrews Norton of Harvard, an influential and conservative Biblical scholar, labeled the address "the latest form of infidelity," and Emerson was elsewhere denounced as an atheist, a pantheist, a corrupter of the young. Nathan Hale, Jr., wanted to kick all the ministers he could find for inviting Emerson to talk in the first place; another gentleman enjoined all New Englanders "to abhor and abominate R. W. Emerson as a sort of mad dog." Emerson would not be asked back to Harvard for forty years. But despite some private anguish, his public face remained unperturbed.

The ideal Emersonian figure was three-dimensional. He was not only a scholar (or seer), and a preacher (or inspirer). He was also a "sayer"; and to complete our survey we should take account of Emerson's definition—in the essay of that name—of "the poet." Emerson's poet is first of all a "democratic" personality; a representative man. "He stands among partial men," Emerson says in one of his most artful summaries, "for the complete man, and apprises us not of his wealth but of the common wealth." He makes accessible to men a wealth of insight into things and into the human soul which is the common legacy of all, though few have normally availed themselves of it. And this he does by tapping his own hidden spiritual and imaginative resources—"by unlocking, at all risks, his human doors." The poetry that flows therefrom has the force of revelation and of emancipation. "Poets are thus liberating gods," Emerson insists. "Men have really got a new sense, and found within their world another world, or nest of worlds; for the metamorphosis once seen, we divine that it does not stop."

The poet is the great changer of things, or rather of the human perception of things. His poetry is an act of metamorphosis, of transfiguration; it is indeed the poet who can best bring about that revolution of consciousness called for in *Nature*. Emerson was aware of the temptation, no less strong in his age than in ours, to seek "the higher consciousness" through artificial means. The immense desire to unlock one's human doors is the reason, Emerson observes, "why bards love wine, mead, narcotics, coffee, tea, opium, the fumes of sandalwood and tobacco. . . . But never can any advantage be taken of nature by a trick. . . . That is not inspiration, which we owe to narcotics, but some counterfeit excitement and fury."

But Emerson, writing in the early 1840's, admitted that he "looked in vain for the poet whom I describe." The actual poet was exactly like the actual man as he appeared in *Nature*: the mere dwarf of his real or potential self. "We have yet had no genius in America, with tyrannous eye, which knew the value of our incomparable materials, and saw, in the barbarism and materialism of the times, another carnival of the same gods. . . ." A little over a decade after "The Poet" was published, Whitman would be inspired by the Emersonian message, would draw on its language for the preface to the first edition of *Leaves of Grass*, and would offer a body of poetry which Emerson immediately recognized as the American revelation he had awaited.

"The Poet" was contained in *Essays: Second Series*, in 1844, a volume which solidified once and for all his reputation, here and abroad, as possessing the most inspiriting voice that had yet been heard on this continent. In fact, however, as we realize in retrospect, the period of Emerson's untrammeled confidence in the human capacity to reunite the self and hence to know, to create, to enlarge morally was already over, and somewhat darker days lay ahead. We shall come back to this. But by 1844, Emerson had also come as close to perfecting his literary style as he ever would.

Emerson's style is easy to enjoy, and even to be exhilarated by; but it is uncommonly hard to analyze. He was fundamentally a writer of sentences. This is literally true, in that his es-

says were revisions of his lectures which in turn were made up of sentences—sometimes stray sentences—culled from his journals. It is because the journals were, essentially, modes of self-communication that the personal note sounded so strongly, and to audiences so appealingly, in his public performances. But Emerson was also a writer of *sententiae*; his work characteristically releases a barrage of maxims of every variety, crisp "sayings" about the human condition and human aspiration, condensed bits of wisdom in the manner of the essays of Francis Bacon. It was to just this kind of writing that he was drawn from his young manhood on: before his twenty-first birthday, he was stating his preference for "those books which collect and embody the wisdom of their times, and so mark the stages of human improvement. Such are the Proverbs of Solomon, the Essays of Montaigne, and eminently the Essays of Bacon."

The origins of Emerson's curiously limpid scatter-shot style may be found not only in the books of the sort Emerson listed, but also in the tradition of pulpit-rhetoric in New England, and in the fairly well-defined conventions of oratory. Emerson, addressing a packed lecture hall or presenting his books to the public, saw himself engaged in an enterprise once assumed by the preacher (and to which, in the talk to the Harvard Divinity School, he recalled the preacher), and now the province of the orator. "He believed," F. O. Matthiessen remarked in a searching analysis of Emerson's style (*American Renaissance*, 1941), "that the orator could speak both more directly and more deeply to men, breaking down their reserves, tugging them through the barriers of themselves, bringing to articulation their own confused thoughts, flooding them with a sudden surprise that the moment of their life was so rich."

The task of orator, so conceived, required him simultaneously to stir the senses of his listeners and to move their minds and imaginations; and it is here that we perceive Emerson's genuine originality. For if Jonathan Edwards, to name the most powerful rhetorician among Emerson's predecessors, likewise sought to engage (or assault) both dimensions of the psyche, Emerson at his best was capable both of headier abstractions and of a more pungent concreteness than Edwards. If he could say with grand simplicity that "All the universe over, there is just one thing, this old double," he could also pile up little verbal heaps of concrete phenomena, linked by a recurring prose rhythm: "What would we really know the meaning of? The meal in the firkin; the milk in the pan; the ballad in the street; the news of the boat; the glance of the eye; the form and gait of the body." And if he could intone his belief that "If the soul is quick and strong it bursts over that boundary and expands another orbit on the great deep," he could also complain about his friend Bronson Alcott that Alcott was so bent on expanding another orbit on the vast sea of knowledge that he missed "the poetry that is in man's life, the poorest pastoral clownish life; the light that shines on a man's hat, in a child's spoon."

Emerson's predilection for the spacious generality was, in short, held in check by a commitment to the actual. Or better (as George Santayana recognized), his verbal ventures into the empyrean were regularly followed by a return to the immediacies of experience. By the same token, if he indulged in the soaring speculations of the Neoplatonists he so admired, he was also a long-standing addict of Montaigne, and once told Alcott that the kind of book he would most like to read or even write would, like Montaigne's, be "full of fun, poetry, business, divinity, philosophy, anecdotes, smut," and would be composed "of bone and marrow, or cornbarn and flour barrel, of wife, of friend, and valet, of things nearest and next." Behind that ambition lay a theory of language.

If Emerson was fundamentally a writer of sentences, he was perhaps even more fundamentally a writer of words; and words, as he declared in *Nature*, "are signs of natural facts." Natural facts, he went on, are symbols of spiritual facts, and nature in general is a symbol of spirit in general—more often than he would have liked, Emerson's mind leaped beyond natural facts to enter the world of spirit, leaving

the facts far behind. But he always loved words that engaged particularities and that had vitality and punch to them. "I confess to some pleasure," he told himself in 1840, "from the stinging rhetoric of a rattling oath in the mouth of truckmen and teamsters. How laconic and brisk it is by the side of a page from the *North American Review*. Cut these words and they would bleed; they are vascular and alive; they walk and run." That passage, incidentally, was put to typical use by Emerson: the sentences and several which followed were incorporated a few years later into a lecture on Montaigne—the reference to oaths being deleted—and appeared in print in *Representative Men* in 1850.[2]

[2] Compare the remarks of Lowell, in the second series of the *Biglow Papers*, on the language of the American common people as being "racy with life and vigor and originality," as against that of the academics, the politicians, and the literary journals (see pp. 608–9). Lowell's analysis of American speech was written during the Civil War and very likely derived in part from Emerson's essay on Montaigne. It is also likely that Lowell's recollections of "the talk of Sam and Job over their jug of blackstrap," while undoubtedly autobiographical, also owed something to Emerson's quite magnificent poem "Monadnoc."

In "Monadnoc," Emerson speaks of the "mountain men" with whom he had visited: "Coarse and boisterous, yet mild,/Strong as giant, slow as child"; and he suggests that these vigorous uncouth creatures are the ones who can teach Americans a living speech.

> Yet, will you learn our ancient speech,
> These the masters who can teach.
> Fourscore or a hundred words
> All their vocal muse affords;
> But they turn them in a fashion
> Past clerks' or statesmen's art or passion.
>
>   . . .
> Rude poets of the tavern hearth,
> Squandering your unquoted mirth,
> Which keeps the ground and never soars,
> While Jake retorts and Reuben roars;
> Scoff of yeoman strong and stark,
> Goes like bullet to its mark;
> While the solid curse and jeer
> Never balk the waiting ear.

In "Eloquence" (*Letters and Social Aims*, 1876), Emerson returned to the theme: "The speech of the man in the street is invariably strong, nor can you mend it by making it what you call parliamentary."

This concern with a vital and expressive native language was shared by Whitman, among others, and was one of the most striking phases of the coming into being of an American literature.

Individual words, for Emerson, combined easily enough into individual sentences: a larger problem was to bring together sentences into paragraphs, and larger yet to conjoin paragraphs into whole compositions. Any estimate of Emerson's success in this regard would involve an entire theory of aesthetics and would pit the classical against the romantic temper. Emerson, according to Matthiessen, was seeking for himself a "form without boundaries," an ambition which in the classical perspective is simply self-defeating. For Emerson's mind genially refused to be guided by the rules of logic, to *develop* an idea point by logical point, to enunciate a well-worked-out doctrine. It did not deal with ideas at all, properly speaking, but preferred to play around an intuition, to dart imaginatively at a fresh perception, to express itself (in the words of Harold Bloom) in "the rhapsode's impatient rushes." Yet if there is nothing resembling system-building in the essays, or even logical expansion in the paragraphs, one senses in them an extraordinary thrust and agility of mind, now sliding sideways, now vaulting forward, hastening back and forth between the high and the commonplace—and accumulating into a message, a moral or spiritual imperative, which the speaker at least for the moment convinces us is of the greatest urgency.

Consider the most famous passage in "Self-Reliance":

Trust thyself: every heart vibrates to that iron string. Accept the place the divine providence has found for you, the society of your contemporaries, the connection of events. Great men have always done so, and confided themselves childlike to the genius of their age, betraying their perception that the absolutely trustworthy was seated at their heart, working through their hands, predominating in all their being. And we are now men, and must accept in the highest mind the same transcendent destiny; and not minors and invalids in a protected corner, not cowards fleeing before a revolution, but guides, redeemers and benefactors, obeying the Almighty effort and advancing on Chaos and the Dark.

Two imperatives, seemingly contradictory: trust your own self, and trust the historical and personal environment providence has placed you in; a glance at "great men" who have yielded to "the genius of their age"—is this the same or not the same as providence, and are either or both identical with the "absolutely trustworthy" and with the Almighty, with its capital A? Statements as of actual fact—"every heart vibrates," "we are now men . . . and not minors or invalids"—which are obviously ideal aspirations; the mounting suggestion that what is to be trusted—the inner self, providence, the age's genius, the Almighty—are only aspects of a single power running through nature and man. This kind of discourse reveals what the exceedingly Romantic and Emersonian poet Hart Crane (in "Legend") called *bright* logic," the "logic" of metaphor, instinct, guess, free association. No one manipulated that nonlogical logic more cunningly than Emerson.

The size and even the shape of an essay by Emerson depended, one feels, on the amount of time originally allotted him in the auditorium and on the fertility of the impulse that went into it. When his time was up, or when the impulse was exhausted, the essay drew to its conclusion. But however his essays may be judged as finished works of literary art, there can be little doubting that Emerson was almost matchless in English as a prose-poet of sentences that quicken the mind and challenge the imagination. Here is a random assortment of them, each designed to unsettle or bestir, and when juxtaposed reflecting Emerson's serene indifference to philosophical consistency:

The ruin or blank that we see when we look at nature is on our own eye. . . . The true doctrine of omnipresence is that God reappears with all his parts in every moss and cobweb. . . . We are as much strangers in nature as we are aliens from God. . . . In every work of genius we recognize our own rejected thoughts; they come back to us with a certain alienated majesty. . . . Sleep lingers all our lifetime about our eyes, as night hovers all day in the boughs of the fir-tree. . . . It is very unhappy, but too late to be helped, the discovery we have made that we exist. That discovery is called the Fall of Man. . . . Character is higher than intellect. Thinking is the function, Living is the functionary. . . . In love, in art, in avarice, in politics, in labor, in games, we study to utter our painful secret. The man is only half himself, the other half is his expression.

Emerson once said that he was "not a good subject for autobiography," and his external life was indeed lacking dramatic circumstance or change. In the wake of his two books of essays, he was in constant demand as a lecturer. He became our first distinguished lecture-tourist, speaking on public platforms in St. Louis, Buffalo, and Pittsburgh, then in Canada and the Middle West, eventually in California and along the West Coast. He thus faithfully performed his role as an American scholar, spreading his stimulating word to large segments of American society (though on one occasion, after delivering a particularly rousing message, he confessed to having heard a voice—his own inner voice—murmuring in his ear: "Why so hot, little man?"). But Emerson's real life was an inward one, the life of Man-thinking. Perhaps the saddest moment in the personal life was the death, in 1842, of Emerson's five-year-old son Waldo. It was this event, in part, that caused Emerson to modify the confident idealism of his early years.

The essay "Experience" (1844) is to a considerable degree a poignant recanting of that idealism, a listing no longer of the visionary resources of man but rather of the possibly insuperable obstacles to vision. One of the worst of these is temperament—the given in each man's psychological nature, his natural tendencies and leanings. Temperament is a sort of prison; it "shuts us in a prison of glass which we cannot see"; and far from believing now that each man has the capacity for ultimate perception, Emerson, at his gloomiest, seems to think that each man is slave to the fateful necessities of his own nature and can see no more than his temperament permits. But what cuts the individual off even more from true insight is subjectivity, the individual's unhappy consciousness of himself *as* a wholly separate and individual being. "It is very unhappy, but too late to be helped," Emerson remarks, "the discovery we have made that we exist. That discovery is called the Fall of Man." For as soon as we arrive at such a realization, we begin to suspect our perceptions—of other men, of the world around us, of nature, of society, of the moral law—exactly because they are ours, only ours. We begin to doubt that the axis of *our* vision, in the phrases of *Nature*, ever can become coincident with the axis of things. "Experience" ends with a certain resurgence of optimism, a restated confidence in "sanity and revelations"; but there is notably less assurance than before.

"Experience" is one major piece of evidence that Emerson should be dissociated from any conviction about the absolute sovereignty of the individual mind—or individual spirit, or conscience—for in this essay he had explored in detail a number of reasons for distrusting that mind. There is no doubt that he distrusted institutions too, when they came into conflict with conscience, and he was suspicious of the institutionally oriented person; he had seen too many examples of institutions outliving their relevance. (See also, below, his essay "Society and Solitude.") We have remarked in the general introduction to this section that the pull of private conscience and a faith in private intuition provide one part of an indispensable tension in American cultural history, with an allegiance to institutions and an awareness of the complexities of social history providing the other. In this regard, there is no doubt that Emerson gave a certain primacy to intuition and conscience. If he had a fairly minimal interest in history, he was also very clear in his mind that it is all too possible to become *too* aware of historical complexities—paralyzingly aware—and too reverential of the ways in which society traditionally organizes itself. But he was never a champion of the arrogantly, absolutistically assertive self. Granted that with diligence the commentator can show Emerson saying almost anything about any important issue; and granted that Emerson's remarks have been sometimes irresponsibly taken, in later generations, as the warrant for otherwise unjustifiable actions; nonetheless, Emerson's overriding purpose, in encouraging each individual to discover and realize his own nature, did not envisage the subjugation of other natures by the imposing self. Robert Frost understood this very well when he said that it was Emerson who had "disabused me of my notion . . . that the truth would make me free. My truth will bind you slave to me." Emerson, Frost concluded roundly, "didn't want converts and followers."

A chart of Emerson's intellectual evolution would (to recapitulate) reveal a kind of swinging motion between Freedom and Necessity, or between Power and Fate—the pairs of moral and psychological terms that he used to identify what elsewhere, in working out a theory of knowledge, he called Reason and Understanding. During the great period 1832–1841—the period of *Nature*, the most famous of the addresses, and *Essays: First Series*—Emerson fairly chanted a soaring confidence in the soul's freedom and its power to thrust ever further into the mystery of being and to straighten itself into an ever more vigorous moral posture. The tug of necessity, as a phenomenon in everyday affairs, was acknowledged in these years, but almost as though it were a self-imposed necessity, an *unnecessary* necessity which the daring soul could always overcome. This is the Emerson his own generation recognized, and the one we mostly encounter in histories of American literature. But the figure thus established must be modified by the tone of the writings from about 1842 onward. For in the wake of his son's death, and due also perhaps to the unshakable burden of sorrow over Ellen, with whatever personal reasons we may not yet know about, Emerson began to perceive Necessity or Fate (he employed the words almost interchangeably) as an irreducible and unconquerable reality in experience.[3]

Throughout the later decades of his life—with the inexplicable exception of the year 1846, when Emerson's spirit was, briefly, again flooded with assurance about his and every man's imaginative and intellectual power—Emerson appraised the human condition as caught between an irrepressible desire for a vision of truth and a somber recognition of limitation, or Fate. A remarkable journal entry in 1842, soon after the death of Waldo, first declared this view of things and set the tone for "Experience," "Fate," "Montaigne: or, The Skeptic," and a host of writings in the darker, or more skeptical, or more acquiescent vein. It is Emerson at his grandest and most courageous:

In short, there ought to be no such thing as Fate. As long as we use this word, it is a sign of our impotence and that we are not yet ourselves. There is now a sublime revelation in each of us which makes us so strangely aware and certain of our riches that although I have never since I was born for so much as one moment expressed the truth, and although I have never heard the expression of it from any other, I know that the whole is here,—the wealth of the Universe is for me, everything is explicable and practicable for me. And yet whilst I adore this ineffable life which is at my heart, it will not condescend to gossip with me, it will not announce to me any particulars of science, it will not enter into the details of my biography, and say to me why I have a son and daughters born to me, or why my son dies in his sixth year of joy. Herein, then, I have this latent omniscience coexistent with omni-ignorance. Moreover, whilst this Deity glows at the heart, and by his unlimited presentiments gives me all Power, I know that tomorrow will be as this day, I am a dwarf, and I remain a dwarf. That is to say, I believe in

---

[3] In a passage quoted earlier from "Fate," Emerson declared: "If fate is so prevailing, man is a part of it, and can confront fate with fate." Here again Emerson reflected his persistent link with the Puritan tradition, however different his language and general style might be from those of the seventeenth-century writers. The Puritans accommodated themselves to the doctrine of predestination (their version of the theories of "necessity" and "fate") by proclaiming that even if their every action had been predetermined by God, they were by the same token participants in this grand divine process—in Emerson's words, they were "part of it."

Fate. As long as I am weak, I shall talk of Fate; whenever the God fills me with his fulness, I shall see the disappearance of Fate.

I am *defeated* all the time; yet to *Victory* I am born.

This was the germ of the essay "Fate," and it was the anguished yet heroic manifesto that lay behind the writings and the public utterances of the years following. For neither grief, bewilderment, nor skepticism prevented Emerson from a steady spate of writing and lecturing. There is less bite and much less joyful rebelliousness to Emerson's writing in the 1850's. But if he accepted, or was reconciled to, more of the historic world he lived in, he also explored it more widely—for example, in the essay "France, or Urbanity" (1854) and in the little book he wrote after a prolonged visit to England, *English Traits*. (During that visit, Emerson took sharp issue with Carlyle because of the latter's enthusiasm for Cromwell; Carlyle "rose like a great Norse giant from his chair" and heaped scorn on Emerson's democratic faith; but the two remained reasonably amicable correspondents thereafter.) Only the intensifying question of slavery brought back the old impassioned and prophetic Emerson—a prophet now entered fully into "the dusty arena below."

Emerson's abhorrence of the institution of slavery was long-standing, as was his profound compassion for Negroes everywhere—even if they were free, even if they were rich ("Of what use are riches to them?" he wrote in his journal, in 1838. "They never go without being insulted.") His second wife, Lydian, was even more of an abolitionist than he and probably helped draw him into the cause. By the mid-forties, he was lecturing on the emancipation of the slaves in the West Indies and fraternizing with the most vehement of the abolitionists, William Lloyd Garrison. The Compromise of 1850 and the Fugitive Slave Law the same year were final straws. The latter Emerson described as a "filthy enactment" which he would resolutely not obey; and lecturing on it in Concord, he urged buying the freedom of American Negro slaves—if it cost two billion dollars; every free man would have to give up his luxuries,

and the church to melt down its plate. Thus would America "dig away this accursed mountain of sorrow once and forever out of the world." While John Brown was awaiting sentence (and execution) in late 1859, Emerson saluted him as "The Saint, whose fate yet hangs in suspense, but whose martyrdom, if it shall be perfected, will make the gallows as glorious as the cross."

But if Emerson were one of the heroes—in some sense *the* hero—of New England reformers, he himself always distrusted organized reform movements. He slackened betimes in his anti-slavery energy, and told himself in his journal that "I have other slaves to free than those negroes, to wit, imprisoned spirits, imprisoned thoughts"—only to berate himself for his backsliding. In the late 1850's Emerson apparently read a little of Karl Marx, but his self-reliant and idealistic spirit was hardly framed to accept, or even to comprehend, the doctrines of collectivism and dialectical materialism. On the matter of women's rights—the other major social issue, along with slavery, in the prewar years—Emerson responded typically: "I should vote for every franchise for women,—vote that they should hold property, and vote, yes & be eligible to all offices as men . . . (but) I should not wish women to wish political functions, nor, if granted assume them." On utopian communities, especially the Fourierist experiments, he was wittily skeptical, asserting again the primacy of the individual over every attempt to organize him—either his body, or his life, or his mind. Emerson's lecture "New England Reformers" contains the best compilation of his contradictory attitudes in these matters; and where in "The Transcendentalist" he chided the idealists for withdrawing from life, in "New England Reformers" he stresses rather the need "to be lifted to some higher platform, that man may see beyond his present fear the transalpine good." Much as he sympathized with the impulses behind the conflicting reformist movements of his day, Emerson found reformers "partial"—each bent on improving only a single aspect of the human condition, rather than the condition itself—and found little value in their tendency to work collectively and through "associations."

His private circle of friends during the 1840's and the 1850's included several others in that galaxy of writers who brought about what F. O. Matthiessen has called the American literary renaissance. Thoreau was his friend and neighbor, sometimes his house guest; Mrs. Emerson used to take him pies when he was living at Walden Pond. Soon after Thoreau's death in 1862, Emerson wrote a memorial essay about him, praising his robust common sense, his love of physical nature ("he knew the country like a fox or a bird"), and his love of truth. "He was a speaker and actor of truth, born such, and was ever running into dramatic situations from this cause," Emerson recalled, and he told again the story of Thoreau's refusal to pay his tax in 1847 and his vigorous speech in support of John Brown. Emerson only regretted that Thoreau was not more active yet. "He seemed born for great enterprise and command," Emerson said, but "he had no ambition. Wanting this, instead of engineering for all America, he was the captain of a huckleberry party."

Thoreau was fourteen years younger than Emerson (though Emerson would outlive him by two decades), and as such was inevitably a follower along intellectual lines—though anything but a disciple, Thoreau having even less an instinct for discipleship than Emerson. Emerson himself sized their relationship in terms close to those we have used above: "Emersonianism getting down to brass tacks." The few persons whose companionship he most valued, Emerson wrote in 1852, were those "who give flesh to what were mere thoughts. . . . Thoreau," he went on, "gives me in flesh and blood and pertinacious Saxon belief my own ethics. He is far more real, and daily practically obeying them than I, and fortifies my memory at all times with an affirmative experience which refuses to be set aside."

Hawthorne was a Concord neighbor for several years, his home being at the opposite end of the village from the Emersons'. Emerson was intrigued by him, but mystified as well, and he worried in his journals over the growing popularity of Hawthorne's dark romances—it must, he concluded, be the quality of the man that appealed, since it could hardly be Hawthorne's obsession with sin. Emerson said as much to Sophia Hawthorne, in a somewhat odd letter of condolence after her husband's death in the spring of 1864. "He was always a mine of hope to me," Emerson wrote, "and I promised myself a rich future in achieving at some day, when we should both be less engaged to tyrannical studies and habitudes, an unreserved intercourse with him. . . . As he always appeared to me superior to his own performances, I counted this yet untold force an insurance of a long life."

Hawthorne, for his part, also admitted that he had not been in Emerson's company as often as he might have liked, but that the occasional encounters were memorable. "It was good . . . to meet him in the wood-paths, or sometimes in our avenue, with that pure intellectual gleam diffused about his presence, like the garment of a shining one. . . ." (Henry James, quoting that passage in his biography of Hawthorne, wondered ironically whether Hawthorne's sense of his neighbor's "shining" element was matched by a perception on Emerson's side of the novelist's dark luminosity and concluded that "Emerson, as a sort of spiritual sun-worshipper, could have attached but a moderate value to Hawthorne's cat-like faculty of seeing in the dark.") Only once, and then very tellingly, did Hawthorne pronounce a strenuous disagreement with Emerson. This was after the execution of John Brown and Emerson's public apotheosizing of the radical leader. Never, Hawthorne declared, "did I expect to shrink so unutterably from any apothegm of a sage whose happy lips have uttered a hundred golden sentences, as from that saying . . . that the death of this blood-stained fanatic has 'made the Gallows as venerable as the Cross!' Nobody was ever more justly hanged. He won his martyrdom fairly, and took it fairly."

There were, meanwhile, visits exchanged with Bronson Alcott. Emerson enjoyed the far reaches of Alcott's speculative mind, but felt, as we have seen, that he had too little touch with the concrete, the here and now, and that a kind of vaporous impracticality had been the undoing of Alcott's communal experiment at Fruitlands. And in Boston, finally, there was the Saturday Club, which Emerson helped found in 1856 and where he could converse at comfortable leisure with persons as congenial as Dr. Oliver Wendell Holmes and, on a rare occasion, with Henry James, Sr.

Reflecting on the opposing pulls of such social intercourse and a natural impulse toward solitude, Emerson summed up the dilemma in an essay of the late fifties called, precisely, "Society and Solitude." He was concerned especially with the man of powerful creative imagination, whether in art or in science, with the social ineptitude of genius ("Dante was very bad company, and was never invited to dinner"), and the need for self-protection. Emerson was being, we may be sure, more than a little autobiographical, when he argued that "One protects himself by solitude, and one by courtesy, and one by an acid, worldly manner—each concealing how he can the thinness of his skin and his incapacity for strict association." And yet once again, as he had in different tones in "The American Scholar" and "The Transcendentalist," Emerson reaffirmed the necessity of the human being as such, and even more for Manthinking, to take part in the company of men and to stay close to the things of this world. "This banishment to the rocks and echoes no metaphysics can make just or tolerable"; and as for the poet, "If you would learn to write, it is in the street you must learn." Emerson ended by acknowledging one of the large contradictions between which man must exert himself. "Nature delights to put us between extreme antagonisms, and our safety is in the skill with which we keep the diagonal line. Solitude is impracticable, and society fatal." It is, Emerson admitted, a dilemma as old as Archimedes in classical Greece; but it is also, somehow, a peculiarly difficult problem in America, where the man of talent inhabits a country in which privacy is feared, but nourishing intimacy seems next to impossible.

During the Civil War, Emerson was driven by a kind of sublime fury against slavery and a religious devotion to the northern cause; he was enormously active both on the Concord scene and as far away as Washington, where he met Lincoln—about whom he would speak glowingly a few days after the President's assassination. In 1870, he was invited to lecture at Harvard, the first time since the episode of the "Divinity School Address"; he presented a series called "The Natural History of the Intellect." One of the most pungent of his later writings was the retrospective "Notes of Life and Letters in New England," in which the aging speaker surveyed the time of his greatest intellectual exuberance. But Emerson's faculties began to fail in the 1870's, a failure due in part to a very damaging fire in his house in 1872. He died in April, 1882. The hordes that came to the funeral by special trains and carriages heard a series of eulogies which, with subsequent memorial essays, enshrined the Emerson of *Nature* and "Self-Reliance"—as that figure so undeniably deserved to be—but discreetly ignored the less rousing but arguably no less significant figure that Emerson had become.

That same benign and encouraging figure is the one we mostly encounter in standard histories of American philosophy. Here he tends to appear fleetingly, now as the apostle of self-reliance, now as the expert observer of the character of his age (both of which he of course was), but not a writer whose propositions need to be taken very seriously. Among the professional philosophers in this country who have dealt with Emerson (certain continental thinkers, Nietzsche especially, have revered him), George Santayana has been the most gracefully severe. Santayana devoted a number of his handsomest pages (in *Interpretations of Poetry and Religion*, 1900—note the title) to denying to Emerson the name of "philosopher." "At bottom, he had no doctrine at all. . . . He was far from being, like a Plato or an Aristotle, past master in the art and the science of life." Santayana found Emerson all of a piece with the German idealists, for whom Santayana had the strongest intellectual dislike; though he granted Emerson a plasticity and a spontaneity of mind that was all his own. Santayana was one of the first to understand, though he did not approve, that what most preoccupied Emerson was the imagination—"Imagination, indeed, is his single theme"; and he was quick to praise the "constant renewal of sincerity which kept Emerson's imagination near to experience." But it was not, Santayana concluded, any originality of thought by which Emerson might endure, rather an originality and a beauty of expression.

For John Dewey it was, if not precisely the originality, at least the ever fresh immediacy of Emerson's thought that made him "the one citizen of the New World fit to have his name uttered in the same breath with that of Plato." Emerson was of paramount importance to Dewey, as in certain respects he had been to William James: both made out in Emerson's writings the basic ingredients of what James called pragmatism, and Dewey instrumentalism. For both, it was a matter of referring everything, every doctrine ancient and modern, "to the immediate life," in Dewey's words; of submitting every idea "to the test of trial by the service rendered the present and immediate experience." Uniquely, Dewey felt, Emerson could make one believe that

> the Idea is no longer either an academic toy nor even a gleam of poetry, but a literal report of the experience of the hour as that is enriched and reinforced for the individual through the tale of history, the appliance of science, the gossip of conversation and the exchange of commerce (*Characters and Events*, Vol. 1, 1929).

This talent for speaking directly to the individual—to any individual of whatever station—was what made Emerson, according to Dewey, the supreme philosopher of democracy, the poetic champion of the common man.

The same perceptions and the same sense of shared commitment led William James to call Emerson the heartener and sustainer of his youth, though James, as has been said, discerned more clearly than Dewey the personal suffering Emerson had to overcome before he could achieve the intellectual self-reliance he bequeathed to all men. Yet Emerson himself believed that the future of thought, and by extension perhaps the future reputation of his own thought, belonged rather to the poets than the philosophers. "I think that philosophy is still rude and elementary," he wrote; "it will one day be taught by poets. The poet is in the right attitude; he is believing; the philosopher, after some struggle, having only reasons for believing." It has been, anyhow, among the poets that the current of Emersonianism has run most visibly: Whitman and Emily Dickinson, later Edwin Arlington Robinson, later still Wallace Stevens and Hart Crane, and younger writers just coming into view.[4]

But perhaps Robert Frost can have the last word as to whether Emerson should be taken primarily as a philosopher or a poet. On receiving the Emerson-Thoreau medal before the American Academy of Arts and Sciences, in 1959, Frost remarked (talking in the same scatter-shot manner that characterized Emerson's platform performance) that "Naturally on this proud occasion I should like to make myself as much of an Emersonian as I can. Let me see," he went on, "if I can't go a long way." He owed more to Emerson than to anyone, Frost said, "for troubled thoughts about freedom," and it had been Emerson ("never mind how and where") who had "disabused me of my notion I may have been brought up to that the truth would make me free. My truth will bind you slave to me. He didn't want converts and followers." But then Frost went pretty nearly all the way:

> I suppose I have always thought I'd like to name in verse some day my four greatest Americans: George Washington, the general and statesman; Thomas Jefferson, the political thinker; Abraham Lincoln, the martyr and savior; and fourth, Ralph Waldo Emerson, the poet. I take these names because they are going around the world. They are not just local. Emerson's has gone as a poetic

---

4 For traces of Emerson in the work of these poets, see the introductory comments on each.

philosopher or as a philosophic poet, my favorite kind of both.

In a lecture delivered during a tour of this country in 1886 (and published in *Discourses in America*, 1896), Matthew Arnold—while establishing some of the critical clichés about Emerson that have persisted almost to this day —remarked that the most important writing in English during the nineteenth century had been the poems of Wordsworth and the essays of Emerson.

Insofar as one shares the claim for Emerson, it becomes peculiarly hard to make a selection among his work in the essay form. One wants to represent something of his intellectual development—hence *Nature*, "The American Scholar," and "Self-Reliance"; and one wants also to show something of the springy dialectic of his mind— here *Nature* pairs with "Experience," as otherwise "Circles," if chosen, might have had its surging confidence matched by the tough honesty about human limitation expressed in "Fate." The Emerson whom audiences thronged to for his analyses of current movements in society and culture appears here in "The Transcen-

dentalist"—but that essay, to get its full force, should be juxtaposed with "New England Reformers." Emerson's genius for inspecting the genius of other individuals is displayed in "Thoreau," but that genius showed no less boldly in his essays on Montaigne, on Napoleon, on Shakespeare.

Others among Emerson's essays announce in their titles themes of peculiar relevance to this decade—education, wealth, friendship, society and solitude. Yet, faced with the difficulty of having to make choices, one is comforted by the realization that the essential Emerson is likely to be present in any essay he ever wrote, indeed on almost every page—no invocation of freedom without a darting glance at necessity, no acknowledgment of fate without a sidelong allusion to spiritual power, no discussion of social reformers or of exiles from society which does not say that the ones are too close and the others have become too remote from the social challenges of the day; no meditation on men in the abstract that does not pounce, for illustration, on some sharply outlined individual, and no individual who is not taken as representative of some major human potentiality.

BIOGRAPHICAL CHART

1803 Born, May 25, in Boston, Massachusetts
1821 Graduated from Harvard College
1826 Begins preaching in Boston
1829 Ordained junior pastor at Second Church, Boston; marries Ellen Tucker (who dies two years later)
1832 Resigns from Second Church
1832–33 Travels in Europe; meets Carlyle, Wordsworth, and others
1834 Settles in Concord; lectures in Boston and Concord on *Biography*; marries Lydia Jackson (called Lydian thereafter)
1836 *Nature*; son Waldo is born
1837 "The American Scholar"
1838 Address to the Harvard Divinity School
1841 *Essays: First Series*
1841–42 Lectures on *The Times*, including "The Transcendentalist"
1842 Waldo dies
1844 *Essays: Second Series*
1847 *Poems*
1847–48 Travels in France and England; has controversy with Carlyle

1850 *Representative Men*
1851 Address denouncing the Fugitive Slave Law of 1850, to the citizens of Concord
1856 *English Traits*; helps found the Saturday Club in Boston
1859 Lectures in Boston on "Courage," saluting John Brown as a saint and a martyr; Brown executed a month later, on December 2, and Emerson, with Thoreau and Alcott, holds a quiet meeting of commemoration in Concord
1860 *The Conduct of Life*
1862 "Thoreau"
1867 *May-Day and Other Pieces*
1870 Invited to lecture at Harvard for the first time since 1838; delivers a series called "The Natural History of the Intellect"
1872 House burns down
1872–73 Travels in Europe and the Near East to recover physical and mental health
1880 Lectures at Concord on "Historic Notes of Life and Letters in New England"
1882 Dies, April 27, in Concord

FURTHER READINGS

Brooks Atkinson, ed., *The Complete Essays and Other Writings of Ralph Waldo Emerson* (1950)

Edward Waldo Emerson, ed., *The Complete Works of Ralph Waldo Emerson* (1903)

Alfred R. Ferguson et al., eds., *The Collected Works of Ralph Waldo Emerson* (12 vols.; CEAA edition); this work, one volume of which has already been published, will become the standard edition

William H. Gilman et al., eds., *The Journals and Miscellaneous Notebooks of Ralph Waldo Emerson* (16 vols.; CEAA edition); this work, ten volumes of which have already been published, will become the standard edition

Alfred Kazin and Daniel Aaron, eds., *Ralph Waldo Emerson: A Modern Anthology* (1959)

Ralph L. Rusk, ed., *The Letters of Ralph Waldo Emerson* (1939)

Joseph Slater, ed., *The Correspondence of Emerson and Carlyle* (1964)

Newton Arvin, "The House of Pain: Emerson's Tragic Sense," in *The American Pantheon* (1966)

Jonathan Bishop, *Emerson on the Soul* (1964)

Van Wyck Brooks, *Emerson and Others* (1927)

———, *The Flowering of New England, 1815–1865* (1936)

———, *The Life of Emerson* (1932)

Kenneth W. Cameron, *Emerson Among His Contemporaries* (1967)

Michael Cowan, *City of the West: Emerson, America and Urban Metaphor* (1967)

Vivian C. Hopkins, *Spires of Form: A Study of Emerson's Aesthetic Theory* (1951)

Milton R. Konwitz and Stephen E. Whicher, *Emerson: A Collection of Critical Essays* (1962)

Perry Miller, *The American Transcendentalists* (1957)

———, "From Edwards to Emerson," in *Errand into the Wilderness* (1964)

———, *The Transcendentalists: An Anthology* (1950; 1967)

Sherman Paul, *Emerson's Angle of Vision: Man and Nature in American Experience* (1952)

Joel Porte, *Emerson and Thoreau: Transcendentalists in Conflict* (1966)

Ralph L. Rusk, *The Life of Ralph Waldo Emerson* (1949)

F. B. Sanborn, ed., *The Genius and Character of Emerson* (1885)

Stephen E. Whicher, *Freedom and Fate: An Inner Life of Ralph Waldo Emerson* (1953)

From Nature (1836)

For general comment on this crucial essay, see the introduction. We might take special notice here of the Emersonian theme of miraculous perception—"The invariable mark of wisdom," Emerson says near the end of *Nature*, "is to see the miraculous in the common." It would be interesting to compare that idea with Jonathan Edwards' insistence that the commonest aspects of physical nature can be seen as images or shadows of divine things, including (among such divine things) the miracles of Jesus Christ. In nineteenth-century American Romanticism, miraculous perception was a frequently sounded theme. We encounter it readily enough in *Walden*, in the poems of Emily Dickinson, somewhat obscurely in *Moby-Dick*, and most openly in *Leaves of Grass* ("And a mouse is a miracle to stagger sextillions of infidels"). But with all these writers, the theme is involved with certain convictions about democracy—see, for example, the first of the chapters called "Knights and Squires" in *Moby-Dick*.

> *"Nature is but an image or imitation of wisdom, the last thing of the soul; nature being a thing which doth only do, but not know."*—PLOTINUS
>
> (Motto of 1836)

> *A subtle chain of countless rings*
> *The next unto the farthest brings;*
> *The eye reads omens where it goes,*
> *And speaks all languages the rose;*
> *And, striving to be man, the worm*
> *Mounts through all the spires of form.*
> (Motto of 1849)

Introduction

Our age is retrospective. It builds the sepulchres of the fathers. It writes biographies, histories, and criticism. The foregoing generations beheld God and nature face to face; we, through their eyes. Why should not we also enjoy an original relation to the universe? Why should not we have a poetry and philosophy of insight and not of tradition, and a religion by revelation to us, and not the history of theirs? Embosomed for a season in nature, whose floods of life stream around and through us, and invite us, by the powers they supply, to action proportioned to nature, why should we grope among the dry bones of the past, or put the living generation into masquerade out of its faded wardrobe? The sun shines today also. There is more wool and flax in the fields. There are new lands, new men, new thoughts. Let us demand our own works and laws and worship.

Undoubtedly we have no questions to ask which are unanswerable. We must trust the perfection of the creation so far as to believe that whatever curiosity the order of things has awakened in our minds, the order of things can satisfy. Every man's condition is a solution in hieroglyphic to those inquiries he would put. He acts it as life, before he apprehends it as truth. In like manner, nature is already, in its forms and tendencies, describing its own design. Let us interrogate the great apparition that shines so peacefully around us. Let us inquire, to what end is nature?

All science has one aim, namely, to find a theory of nature. We have theories of races and of functions, but scarcely yet a remote approach to an idea of creation. We are now so far from the road to truth, that religious teachers dispute and hate each other, and speculative men are esteemed unsound and frivolous. But to a sound judgment, the most abstract truth is the most practical. Whenever a true theory appears, it will be its own evidence. Its test is, that it will explain all phenomena. Now many are thought not only unexplained but inexplicable; as language, sleep, madness, dreams, beasts, sex.

Philosophically considered, the universe is composed of Nature and the Soul. Strictly speaking, therefore, all that is separate from us, all which Philosophy distinguishes as the NOT ME, that is, both nature and art, all other men and my own body, must be ranked under this name, NATURE. In enumerating the values of nature and casting up their sum, I shall use the word in both senses; —in its common and in its philosophical import. In inquiries so general as our present one, the inaccuracy is not material; no confusion of thought will occur. *Nature*, in the common sense, refers to essences unchanged by man; space, the air, the river, the leaf. *Art* is applied to the mixture of his will with the same things, as in a house, a canal, a statue, a picture. But his operations taken together are so insignificant, a little chipping, baking, patching, and washing, that in an impression so grand as that of the world on the human mind, they do not vary the result.

1. Nature

To go into solitude, a man needs to retire as much from his chamber as from society. I am not solitary whilst I read and write, though nobody is with me. But if a man would be alone, let him look at the stars. The rays that come from those heavenly worlds will separate between him and what he touches. One might think the atmosphere was made transparent with this design, to give man, in the heavenly bodies, the perpetual presence of the sublime. Seen in the streets of cities, how great they are! If the stars should appear one night in a thousand years, how would men believe and adore; and preserve for many generations the remembrance of the city of God which had been shown! But every night come out these envoys of beauty, and light the universe with their admonishing smile.

The stars awaken a certain reverence, because though always present, they are inaccessible; but all natural objects make a kindred impression, when the mind is open to their influence. Nature never wears a mean appearance. Neither does the wisest man extort her secret, and lose his curiosity by finding out all her perfection. Nature never became a toy to a wise spirit. The flowers, the animals, the mountains, reflected the wisdom of his best hour, as much as they had delighted the simplicity of his childhood.

When we speak of nature in this manner, we have a distinct but most poetical sense in the mind. We mean the integrity of impression made by manifold natural objects. It is this which distinguishes the stick of timber of the wood-cutter from the tree of the poet. The charming landscape which I saw this morning is indubitably made up of some twenty or thirty farms. Miller owns this field, Locke that, and Manning the woodland beyond. But none of them owns the landscape. There is a property in the horizon which no man has but he whose eye can integrate all the parts, that is, the poet. This is the best part of these men's farms, yet to this their warranty-deeds give no title.

To speak truly, few adult persons can see nature. Most persons do not see the sun. At least they have a very superficial seeing. The sun illuminates only the eye of the man, but shines into the eye and the heart of the child. The lover of nature is he whose inward and outward senses are still truly adjusted to each other; who has retained the spirit of infancy even into the era of manhood. His intercourse with heaven and earth becomes part of his daily food. In the presence of nature a wild delight runs through the man, in spite of real sorrows. Nature says,—he is my creature, and maugre all his impertinent griefs, he shall be glad with me. Not the sun or the summer alone, but every hour and season yields its tribute of delight; for every hour and change corresponds to and authorizes a different state of the mind, from breathless noon to grimmest midnight. Nature is a setting that fits equally well a comic or a mourning piece. In good health, the air is a cordial of incredible virtue. Crossing a bare common, in snow puddles, at twilight, under a clouded sky, without having in my thoughts any occurrence of special good fortune, I have enjoyed a perfect exhilaration. I am glad to the brink of fear. In the woods, too, a man casts off his years, as the snake his slough, and at what period soever of life is always a child. In the woods is perpetual youth. Within these plantations of God, a decorum and sanctity reign, a perennial festival is dressed, and the guest sees not how he should tire of them in a thousand years. In the woods, we return to reason and faith. There I feel that nothing can befall me in life,—no disgrace, no calamity (leaving me my eyes), which nature cannot repair. Standing on the bare ground, —my head bathed by the blithe air and uplifted into infinite space,—all mean egotism vanishes. I become a transparent eyeball; I am nothing; I see all; the currents of the Universal Being circulate through me; I am part or parcel of God. The name of the nearest friend sounds then foreign and accidental: to be brothers, to be acquaintances, master or servant, is then a trifle and a disturbance. I am the lover of uncontained and immortal beauty. In the wilderness, I find something more dear and connate than in streets or villages. In the tranquil landscape, and especially in the distant line of the horizon, man beholds somewhat as beautiful as his own nature.

The greatest delight which the fields and woods minister is the suggestion of an occult relation between man and the vegetable. I am not alone and unacknowledged. They nod to me, and I to them. The waving of the boughs in the storm is new to me and old. It takes me by surprise, and yet is not unknown. Its effect is like that of a higher thought or a better emotion coming over me, when I deemed I was thinking justly or doing right.

Yet it is certain that the power to produce this delight does not reside in nature, but in man, or in a harmony of both. It is necessary to use these pleasures with great temperance. For nature is not always tricked in holiday attire, but the same scene which yesterday breathed perfume and glittered as for the frolic of the nymphs is overspread with melancholy today. Nature always wears the colors of the spirit. To a man laboring under calamity, the heat of his own fire hath sadness in it. Then there is a kind of contempt of the landscape felt by him who has just lost by death a dear friend. The sky is less grand as it shuts down over less worth in the population.

2. Commodity

Whoever considers the final cause of the world will discern a multitude of uses that enter as parts into that result. They all admit of being thrown into one of the following classes: Commodity; Beauty; Language; and Discipline.

Under the general name of commodity, I rank all those advantages which our senses owe to nature. This, of course, is a benefit which is temporary and mediate, not ultimate, like its service to the soul. Yet although low, it is perfect in its kind, and is the only use of nature which all men apprehend. The misery of man appears like childish petulance, when we explore the steady and prodigal provision that has been made for his support and delight on this green ball which floats him through the heavens. What angels invented these splendid ornaments, these rich conveniences, this ocean of air above, this ocean of water beneath, this firmament of earth between? this zodiac of lights, this tent of dropping clouds, this striped coat of climates, this four-fold year? Beasts, fire, water, stones, and corn serve him. The field is at once his floor, his work-yard, his play-ground, his garden, and his bed.

> "More servants wait on man
> Than he'll take notice of."

Nature, in its ministry to man, is not only the material, but is also the process and the result. All the parts incessantly work into each other's hands for the profit of man. The wind sows the seed; the sun evaporates the sea; the wind blows the vapor to the field; the ice, on the other side of the planet, condenses rain on this; the rain feeds the plant; the plant feeds the animal; and thus the endless circulations of the divine charity nourish man.

The useful arts are reproductions or new combinations by the wit of man, of the same natural benefactors. He no longer waits for favoring gales, but by means of steam, he realizes the fable of Aeolus's bag, and carries the two and thirty winds in the boiler of his boat. To diminish friction, he paves the road with iron bars, and, mounting a coach with a ship-load of men, animals, and merchandise behind him, he darts through the country, from town to town, like an eagle or a swallow through the air. By the aggregate of these aids, how is the face of the world changed, from the era of Noah to that of Napoleon! The private poor man hath cities, ships, canals, bridges, built for him. He goes to the post-office, and the human race run on his errands; to the book-shop, and the human race read and write of all that happens, for him; to the court-house, and nations repair his wrongs. He sets his house upon the road, and the human race go forth every morning, and shovel out the snow, and cut a path for him.

But there is no need of specifying particulars in this class of uses. The catalogue is endless, and the examples so obvious, that I shall leave them to the reader's reflection, with the general remark, that this mercenary benefit is one which has respect to a farther good. A man is fed, not that he may be fed, but that he may work.

3. Beauty

A nobler want of man is served by nature, namely, the love of Beauty.

The ancient Greeks called the world Κόσμος [order], beauty. Such is the constitution of all things, or such the plastic power of the human eye, that the primary forms, as the sky, the mountain, the tree, the animal, give us a delight *in and for themselves;* a pleasure arising from outline, color, motion, and grouping. This seems partly owing to the eye itself. The eye is the best of artists. By the mutual action of its structure and of the laws of light, perspective is produced, which integrates every mass of objects, of what character soever, into a well colored and shaded globe, so that where the particular objects are mean and unaffecting, the landscape which they compose is round and symmetrical. And as the eye is the best composer, so light is the first of painters. There is no object so foul that intense light will not make beautiful. And the stimulus it affords to the sense, and a sort of infinitude which it hath, like space and time, make all matter gay. Even the corpse has its own beauty. But besides this general grace diffused over nature, almost all the individual forms are agreeable to the eye, as is proved by our endless imitations of some of them, as the acorn, the grape, the pine-cone, the wheat-ear, the egg, the wings and forms of most birds, the lion's claw, the serpent, the butterfly, sea-shells, flames, clouds, buds, leaves, and the forms of many trees, as the palm.

For better consideration, we may distribute the aspects of Beauty in a threefold manner.

1. First, the simple perception of natural forms is a delight. The influence of the forms and actions in nature is so needful to man, that, in its lowest functions, it seems to lie on the confines of commodity and beauty. To the body and mind which have been cramped by noxious work or company, nature is medicinal and restores their tone. The tradesman, the attorney comes out of the din and craft of the street and sees the sky and the woods, and is a man again. In their eternal calm, he finds himself. The health of the eye seems to demand a horizon. We are never tired, so long as we can see far enough.

But in other hours, Nature satisfies by its loveliness, and without any mixture of corporeal benefit. I see the spectacle of morning from the hilltop over against my house, from daybreak to sunrise, with emotions which an angel might share. The long slender bars of cloud float like fishes in the sea of crimson light. From the earth, as a shore, I look out into that silent sea. I seem to partake its rapid transformations; the active enchantment reaches my dust, and I dilate and conspire with the morning wind. How does Nature deify us with a few and cheap elements! Give me health and a day, and I will make the pomp of emperors ridiculous. The dawn is my Assyria; the sunset and moonrise my Paphos, and unimaginable realms of faerie; broad noon shall be my England of the senses and the understanding; the night shall be my Germany of mystic philosophy and dreams.

Not less excellent, except for our less susceptibility in the afternoon, was the charm, last evening, of a January sunset. The western clouds divided and subdivided themselves into pink flakes modulated with tints of unspeakable softness, and the air had so much life and sweetness that it was a pain to come within doors. What was it that nature would say? Was there no meaning in the live repose of the valley behind the mill, and which Homer or Shakespeare could not re-form for me in words? The leafless trees become spires of flame in the sunset, with the blue cast for their background, and the stars of the dead calices of flowers, and every withered stem and stubble rimed with frost, contribute something to the mute music.

The inhabitants of cities suppose that the country landscape is pleasant only half the year. I please myself with the graces of the winter scenery, and believe that we are as much touched by it as by the genial influences of summer. To the attentive eye, each moment of the year has its own beauty, and in the same field, it beholds, every hour, a picture which was never seen before, and which shall never be seen again. The heavens change every moment, and reflect their glory or gloom on the plains beneath. The state of the crop in the surrounding farms alters the expression of the earth from week to week. The succession of native plants in the pastures and roadsides, which makes the silent clock by which time tells the summer hours, will make even the divisions of the day sensible to a keen observer. The tribes of birds and insects, like the plants punctual to their time, follow each other, and the year has room for all. By watercourses, the variety is greater. In July, the blue pontederia or pickerel-weed blooms in large beds in the shallow parts of our pleasant river, and swarms with yellow butterflies in continual motion. Art cannot rival this pomp of purple and gold. Indeed the river is a perpetual gala, and boasts each month a new ornament.

But this beauty of Nature which is seen and felt as beauty, is the least part. The shows of day, the dewy morning, the rainbow, mountains, orchards in blossom, stars, moonlight, shadows in still water, and the like, if too eagerly hunted, become shows merely, and mock us with their unreality. Go out of the house to see the moon, and 'tis mere tinsel; it will not please as when its light shines upon your necessary journey. The beauty that shimmers in the yellow afternoons of October, who ever could clutch it? Go forth to find it, and it is gone; 'tis only a mirage as you look from the windows of diligence.

2. The presence of a higher, namely, of the spiritual element is essential to its perfection. The high and divine beauty which can be loved without effeminacy, is that which is found in combination with the human will. Beauty is the mark God sets upon virtue. Every natural action is graceful. Every heroic act is also decent, and causes the place and the bystanders to shine. We are taught by great actions that the universe is the property of every individual in it. Every rational creature has all nature for his dowry and estate. It is his, if he will. He may divest himself of it; he may creep into a corner, and abdicate his kingdom, as most men do, but he is entitled to the world by his constitution. In proportion to the energy of his thought and will, he takes up the world into himself. "All those things for which men plough, build, or sail, obey virtue," said Sallust. "The winds and waves," said Gibbon, "are always on the side of the ablest navigators." So are the sun and moon and all the stars of heaven. When a noble act is done,—perchance in a scene of great natural beauty; when Leonidas and his three hundred martyrs consume one day in dying, and the sun and moon come each and look at them once in the steep defile of Thermopylae; when Arnold Winkelried, in the high Alps, under the shadow of the avalanche, gathers in his side a sheaf of Austrian spears to break the line for his comrades; are not these heroes entitled to add the beauty of the scene to the beauty of the deed? When the bark of Columbus nears the shore of America;—before it the beach lined with savages, fleeing out of all their huts of cane; the sea behind; and the purple mountains of the Indian Archipelago around, can we separate the man from the living picture? Does not the New World clothe his form with her palm-groves and savannahs as fit drapery? Ever does natural beauty steal in like air, and envelope great actions. When Sir Harry Vane was dragged up the Tower-hill, sitting on a sled, to suffer death as the champion of the English laws, one of the multitude cried out to him, "You never sate on so glorious a seat!" Charles II, to intimidate the citizens of London, caused the patriot Lord Russell to be drawn in an open coach through the principal streets of the city on his way to the scaffold. "But," his biographer says, "the multitude imagined they saw liberty and virtue sitting by his side." In private places, among sordid objects, an act of truth or heroism seems at once to draw to itself the sky as its temple, the sun as its candle. Nature stretches out her arms to embrace man, only let his thoughts be of equal greatness. Willingly does she follow his steps with the rose and the violet, and bend her lines of grandeur and grace to the decoration of her darling child. Only let his thoughts be of equal scope, and

the frame will suit the picture. A virtuous man is in unison with her works, and makes the central figure of the visible sphere. Homer, Pindar, Socrates, Phocion, associate themselves fitly in our memory with the geography and climate of Greece. The visible heavens and earth sympathize with Jesus. And in common life whosoever has seen a person of powerful character and happy genius, will have remarked how easily he took all things along with him,—the persons, the opinions, and the day, and nature become ancillary to a man.

3. There is still another aspect under which the beauty of the world may be viewed, namely, as it becomes an object of the intellect. Beside the relation of things to virtue, they have a relation to thought. The intellect searches out the absolute order of things as they stand in the mind of God, and without the colors of affection. The intellectual and the active powers seem to succeed each other, and the exclusive activity of the one generates the exclusive activity of the other. There is something unfriendly in each to the other, but they are like the alternate periods of feeding and working in animals; each prepares and will be followed by the other. Therefore does beauty, which, in relation to actions, as we have seen, comes unsought, and comes because it is unsought, remain for the apprehension and pursuit of the intellect; and then again, in its turn, of the active power. Nothing divine dies. All good is eternally reproductive. The beauty of nature re-forms itself in the mind, and not for barren contemplation, but for new creation.

All men are in some degree impressed by the face of the world; some men even to delight. This love of beauty is Taste. Others have the same love in such excess, that, not content with admiring, they seek to embody it in new forms. The creation of beauty is Art.

The production of a work of art throws a light upon the mystery of humanity. A work of art is an abstract or epitome of the world. It is the result or expression of nature, in miniature. For although the works of nature are innumerable and all different, the result or the expression of them all is similar and single. Nature is a sea of forms radically alike and even unique. A leaf, a sunbeam, a landscape, the ocean, make an analogous impression on the mind. What is common to them all,—that perfectness and harmony, is beauty. The standard of beauty is the entire circuit of natural forms,—the totality of nature; which the Italians expressed by defining beauty "il più nell' uno" [the many in

one]. Nothing is quite beautiful alone; nothing but is beautiful in the whole. A single object is only so far beautiful as it suggests this universal grace. The poet, the painter, the sculptor, the musician, the architect, seek each to concentrate this radiance of the world on one point, and each in his several work to satisfy the love of beauty which stimulates him to produce. Thus is Art a nature passed through the alembic of man. Thus in art does Nature work through the will of a man filled with the beauty of her first works.

The world thus exists to the soul to satisfy the desire of beauty. This element I call an ultimate end. No reason can be asked or given why the soul seeks beauty. Beauty, in its largest and profoundest sense, is one expression for the universe. God is the all-fair. Truth, and goodness, and beauty, are but different faces of the same All. But beauty in nature is not ultimate. It is the herald of inward and eternal beauty, and is not alone a solid and satisfactory good. It must stand as a part, and not as yet the last or highest expression of the final cause of Nature.

4. Language

Language is a third use which Nature subserves to man. Nature is the vehicle of thought, and in a simple, double, and threefold degree.

1. Words are signs of natural facts.

2. Particular natural facts are symbols of particular spiritual facts.

3. Nature is the symbol of spirit.

1. Words are signs of natural facts. The use of natural history is to give us aid in supernatural history; the use of the outer creation, to give us language for the beings and changes of the inward creation. Every word which is used to express a moral or intellectual fact, if traced to its root, is found to be borrowed from some material appearance. *Right* means *straight; wrong* means *twisted. Spirit* primarily means *wind; transgression,* the *crossing of a line; supercilious,* the *raising of the eyebrow.* We say the *heart* to express emotion, the *head* to denote thought; and *thought* and *emotion* are words borrowed from sensible things, and now appropriated to spiritual nature. Most of the process by which this transformation is made, is hidden from us in the remote time when language was framed; but the same tendency may be daily observed in children. Children and savages use only nouns or names of things, which they con-

vert into verbs, and apply to analogous mental acts.

2. But this origin of all words that convey a spiritual import,—so conspicuous a fact in the history of language,—is our least debt to nature. It is not words only that are emblematic; it is things which are emblematic. Every natural fact is a symbol of some spiritual fact. Every appearance in nature corresponds to some state of the mind, and that state of the mind can only be described by presenting that natural appearance as its picture. An enraged man is a lion, a cunning man is a fox, a firm man is a rock, a learned man is a torch. A lamb is innocence; a snake is subtle spite; flowers express to us the delicate affections. Light and darkness are our familiar expression for knowledge and ignorance; and heat for love. Visible distance behind and before us, is respectively our image of memory and hope.

Who looks upon a river in a meditative hour and is not reminded of the flux of all things? Throw a stone into the stream, and the circles that propagate themselves are the beautiful type of all influence. Man is conscious of a universal soul within or behind his individual life, wherein, as in a firmament, the natures of Justice, Truth, Love, Freedom, arise and shine. This universal soul he calls Reason: it is not mine, or thine, or his, but we are its; we are its property and men. And the blue sky in which the private earth is buried, the sky with its eternal calm, and full of everlasting orbs, is the type of Reason. That which intellectually considered we call Reason, considered in relation to nature, we call Spirit. Spirit is the Creator. Spirit hath life in itself. And man in all ages and countries embodies it in his language as the FATHER.

It is easily seen that there is nothing lucky or capricious in these analogies, but that they are constant, and pervade nature. These are not the dreams of a few poets, here and there, but man is an analogist, and studies relations in all objects. He is placed in the center of beings, and a ray of relation passes from every other being to him. And neither can man be understood without these objects, nor these objects without man. All the facts in natural history taken by themselves, have no value, but are barren, like a single sex. But marry it to human history, and it is full of life. Whole floras, all Linnaeus' and Buffon's volumes, are dry catalogues of facts; but the most trivial of these facts, the habit of a plant, the organs, or work, or noise of an insect, applied to the illustration of a fact in intellectual philosophy, or in any way associated to human nature, affects us in the most lively and agreeable manner. The seed of a plant,—to what affecting analogies in the nature of man is that little fruit made use of, in all discourse, up to the voice of Paul, who calls the human corpse a seed, —"It is sown a natural body; it is raised a spiritual body." The motion of the earth round its axis and round the sun, makes the day and the year. These are certain amounts of brute light and heat. But is there no intent of an analogy between man's life and the seasons? And do the seasons gain no grandeur or pathos from that analogy? The instincts of the ant are very unimportant considered as the ant's; but the moment a ray of relation is seen to extend from it to man, and the little drudge is seen to be a monitor, a little body with a mighty heart, then all its habits, even that said to be recently observed, that it never sleeps, become sublime.

Because of this radical correspondence between visible things and human thoughts, savages, who have only what is necessary, converse in figures. As we go back in history, language becomes more picturesque, until its infancy, when it is all poetry; or all spiritual facts are represented by natural symbols. The same symbols are found to make the original elements of all languages. It has moveover been observed, that the idioms of all languages approach each other in passages of the greatest eloquence and power. And as this is the first language, so is it the last. This immediate dependence of language upon nature, this conversion of an outward phenomenon into a type of somewhat in human life, never loses its power to affect us. It is this which gives that piquancy to the conversation of a strong-natured farmer or back-woodsman, which all men relish.

A man's power to connect his thought with its proper symbol, and so to utter it, depends on the simplicity of his character, that is, upon his love of truth and his desire to communicate it without loss. The corruption of man is followed by the corruption of language. When simplicity of character and the sovereignty of ideas is broken up by the prevalence of secondary desires,—the desire of riches, of pleasure, of power, and of praise,—and duplicity and falsehood take place of simplicity and truth, the power over nature as an interpreter of the will is in a degree lost; new imagery ceases to be created, and old words are perverted to stand for things which are not; a paper currency is employed, when there is no bullion in the vaults. In due time the fraud is manifest, and words lose all power to stimulate the understanding or the affections. Hundreds of writers may be found in every long-civilized nation who for a short time believe and make others believe that they see and utter truths, who do not of themselves clothe one thought in its natural garment, but who feed unconsciously on the language created by the primary writers of the country, those, namely, who hold primarily on nature.

But wise men pierce this rotten diction and fasten words again to visible things; so that picturesque language is at once a commanding certificate that he who employs it is a man in alliance with truth and God. The moment our discourse rises above the ground line of familiar facts and is inflamed with passion or exalted by thought, it clothes itself in images. A man conversing in earnest, if he watch his intellectual processes, will find that a material image more or less luminous arises in his mind, contemporaneous with every thought, which furnishes the vestment of the thought. Hence, good writing and brilliant discourse are perpetual allegories. This imagery is spontaneous. It is the blending of experience with the present action of the mind. It is proper creation. It is the working of the Original Cause through the instruments he has already made.

These facts may suggest the advantage which the country-life possesses, for a powerful mind, over the artificial and curtailed life of cities. We know more from nature than we can at will communicate. Its light flows into the mind evermore, and we forget its presence. The poet, the orator, bred in the woods, whose senses have been nourished by their fair and appeasing changes, year after year, without design and without heed,—shall not lose their lesson altogether, in the roar of cities or the broil of politics. Long hereafter, amidst agitation and terror in national councils,—in the hour of revolution,—these solemn images shall reappear in their morning lustre, as fit symbols and words of the thoughts which the passing events shall awaken. At the call of a noble sentiment, again the woods wave, the pines murmur, the river rolls and shines, and the cattle low upon the mountains, as he saw and heard them in his infancy. And with these forms, the spells of persuasion, the keys of power are put into his hands.

3. We are thus assisted by natural objects in the expression of particular meanings. But how great a language to convey such pepper-corn informations! Did it need such noble races of creatures, this profusion of forms, this host of orbs in heaven, to furnish man with the dictionary and grammar of his municipal speech? Whilst we use this grand cipher to expedite the affairs of our pot and kettle, we feel that we have not yet put it to its use, neither are able. We are like travelers using the cinders of a volcano to roast their eggs. Whilst we see that it always stands ready to clothe what we would say, we cannot avoid the question whether the characters are not significant of themselves. Have mountains, and waves, and skies, no significance but what we consciously give them when we employ them as emblems of our thoughts? The world is emblematic. Parts of speech are metaphors, because the whole of nature is a metaphor of the human mind. The laws of moral nature answer to those of matter as face to face in a glass. "The visible world and the relation of its parts, is the dial plate of the invisible." The axioms of physics translate the laws of ethics. Thus, "the whole is greater than its part"; "reaction is equal to action"; "the smallest weight may be made to lift the greatest, the difference of weight being compensated by time"; and many the like propositions, which have an ethical as well as physical sense. These propositions have a much more extensive and universal sense when applied to human life, than when confined to technical use.

In like manner, the memorable words of history and the proverbs of nations consist usually of a natural fact, selected as a picture or parable of a moral truth. Thus; A rolling stone gathers no moss; A bird in the hand is worth two in the bush; A cripple in the right way will beat a racer in the wrong; Make hay while the sun shines; 'Tis hard to carry a full cup even; Vinegar is the son of wine; The last ounce broke the camel's back; Long-lived trees make roots first;—and the like. In their primary sense these are trivial facts, but we repeat them for the value of their analogical import. What is true of proverbs, is true of all fables, parables, and allegories.

This relation between the mind and matter is not fancied by some poet, but stands in the will of God, and so is free to be known by all men. It appears to men, or it does not appear. When in fortunate hours we ponder this miracle, the wise man doubts if at all other times he is not blind and deaf;

> "Can such things be,
> And overcome us like a summer's cloud,
> Without our special wonder?"

for the universe becomes transparent, and the light of higher laws than its own shines through it. It is the standing problem which has exercised the wonder and the study of every fine genius since the world began; from the era of the Egyptians and the Brahmins to that of Pythagoras, of Plato, of Bacon, of Leibnitz, of Swedenborg. There sits the Sphinx at the road-side, and from age to age, as each prophet comes by, he tries his fortune at reading her riddle. There seems to be a necessity in spirit to manifest itself in material forms; and day and night, river and storm, beast and bird, acid and alkali, preëxist in necessary Ideas in the mind of God, and are what they are by virtue of preceding affections in the world of spirit. A Fact is the end or last issue of spirit. The visible creation is the terminus or the circumference of the invisible world. "Material objects," said a French philosopher, "are necessarily kinds of *scoriae* [dross] of the substantial thoughts of the Creator, which must always preserve an exact relation to their first origin; in other words, visible nature must have a spiritual and moral side."

This doctrine is abstruse, and though the images of "garment," "scoriae," "mirror," etc., may stimulate the fancy, we must summon the aid of subtler and more vital expositors to make it plain. "Every scripture is to be interpreted by the same spirit which gave it forth,"—is the fundamental law of criticism. A life in harmony with Nature, the love of truth and of virtue, will purge the eyes to understand her text. By degrees we may come to know the primitive sense of the permanent objects of nature, so that the world shall be to us an open book, and every form significant of its hidden life and final cause.

A new interest surprises us, whilst, under the view now suggested, we contemplate the fearful extent and multitude of objects; since "every object rightly seen, unlocks a new faculty of the soul." That which was unconscious truth, becomes, when interpreted and defined in an object, a part of the domain of knowledge,—a new weapon in the magazine of power.

. . .

6. Idealism

Thus is the unspeakable but intelligible and practicable meaning of the world conveyed to man, the immortal pupil, in every object of sense. To this one end of Discipline, all parts of nature conspire.

A noble doubt perpetually suggests itself,— whether this end be not the Final Cause of the Universe; and whether nature outwardly exists. It is a sufficient account of that Appearance we call the World, that God will teach a human mind, and so makes it the receiver of a certain number of congruent sensations, which we call sun and moon, man and woman, house and trade. In my utter impotence to test the authenticity of the report of my senses, to know whether the impressions they make on me correspond with outlying objects, what difference does it make, whether Orion is up there in heaven, or some god paints the image in the firmament of the soul? The relations of parts and the end of the whole remaining the same, what is the difference, whether land and sea interact, and worlds revolve and intermingle without number or end,—deep yawning under deep, and galaxy balancing galaxy, throughout absolute space,—or whether, without relations of time and space, the same appearances are inscribed in the constant faith of man? Whether nature enjoy a substantial existence without, or is only in the apocalypse of the mind, it is alike useful and alike venerable to me. Be it what it may, it is ideal to me so long as I cannot try the accuracy of my senses.

The frivolous make themselves merry with the Ideal theory, as if its consequences were burlesque; as if it affected the stability of nature. It surely does not. God never jests with us, and will not compromise the end of nature by permitting any inconsequence in its procession. Any distrust of the permanence of laws would paralyze the faculties of man. Their permanence is sacredly respected, and his faith therein is perfect. The wheels and springs of man are all set to the hypothesis of the permanence of nature. We are not built like a ship to be tossed, but like a house to stand. It is a natural consequence of this structure, that so long as the active powers predominate over the reflective, we resist with indignation any hint that nature is more short-lived or mutable than spirit. The broker, the wheelwright, the carpenter, the tollman, are much displeased at the intimation.

But whilst we acquiesce entirely in the permanence of natural laws, the question of the absolute existence of nature still remains open. It is the uniform effect of culture on the human mind, not to shake our faith in the stability of particular phenomena, as of heat, water, azote; but to lead us to regard nature as a phenomenon, not a substance; to attribute necessary existence to spirit; to esteem nature as an accident and an effect.

To the senses and the unrenewed understanding,

belongs a sort of instinctive belief in the absolute existence of nature. In their view man and nature are indissolubly joined. Things are ultimates, and they never look beyond their sphere. The presence of Reason mars this faith. The first effort of thought tends to relax this despotism of the senses which binds us to nature as if we were a part of it, and shows us nature aloof, and, as it were, afloat. Until this higher agency intervened, the animal eye sees, with wonderful accuracy, sharp outlines and colored surfaces. When the eye of Reason opens, to outline and surface are at once added grace and expression. These proceed from imagination and affection, and abate somewhat of the angular distinctness of objects. If the Reason be stimulated to more earnest vision, outlines and surfaces become transparent, and are no longer seen; causes and spirits are seen through them. The best moments of life are these delicious awakenings of the higher powers, and the reverential withdrawing of nature before its God.

Let us proceed to indicate the effects of culture.

1. Our first institution [instruction] in the Ideal philosophy is a hint from Nature herself.

Nature is made to conspire with spirit to emancipate us. Certain mechanical changes, a small alteration in our local position, apprizes us of a dualism. We are strangely affected by seeing the shore from a moving ship, from a balloon, or through the tints of an unusual sky. The least change in our point of view gives the whole world a pictorial air. A man who seldom rides, needs only to get into a coach and traverse his own town, to turn the street into a puppet-show. The men, the women,—talking, running, bartering, fighting,—the earnest mechanic, the lounger, the beggar, the boys, the dogs are unrealized at once, or, at least, wholly detached from all relation to the observer, and seen as apparent, not substantial beings. What new thoughts are suggested by seeing a face of country quite familiar, in the rapid movement of the railroad car! Nay, the most wonted objects, (make a very slight change in the point of vision), please us most.

. . . But I own there is something ungrateful in expanding too curiously the particulars of the general proposition, that all culture tends to imbue us with idealism. I have no hostility to nature, but a child's love to it. I expand and live in the warm day like corn and melons. Let us speak her fair. I do not wish to fling stones at my beautiful mother, nor soil my gentle nest. I only wish to indicate the true position of nature in regard to man, wherein to establish man all right education tends; as the ground which to attain is the object of human life, that is, of man's connection with nature. Culture inverts the vulgar views of nature, and brings the mind to call that apparent which it uses to call real, and that real which it uses to call visionary. Children, it is true, believe in the external world. The belief that it appears only, is an afterthought, but with culture this faith will as surely arise on the mind as did the first.

The advantage of the ideal theory over the popular faith is this, that it presents the world in precisely that view which is most desirable to the mind. It is, in fact, the view which Reason, both speculative and practical, that is, philosophy and virtue take. For seen in the light of thought, the world always is phenomenal; and virtue subordinates it to the mind. Idealism sees the world in God. It beholds the whole circle of persons and things, of actions and events, of country and religion, not as painfully accumulated, atom after atom, act after act, in an aged creeping Past, but as one vast picture which God paints on the instant eternity for the contemplation of the soul. Therefore the soul holds itself off from a too trivial and microscopic study of the universal tablet. It respects the end too much to immerse itself in the means. It sees something more important in Christianity than the scandals of ecclesiastical history or the niceties of criticism; and, very incurious concerning persons or miracles, and not at all disturbed by chasms of historical evidence, it accepts from God the phenomenon, as it finds it, as the pure and awful form of religion in the world. It is not hot and passionate at the appearance of what it calls its own good or bad fortune, at the union or opposition of other persons. No man is its enemy. It accepts whatsoever befalls, as part of its lesson. It is a watcher more than a doer, and it is a doer, only that it may the better watch.

7. Spirit

It is essential to a true theory of nature and of man, that it should contain somewhat progressive. Uses that are exhausted or that may be, and facts that end in the statement, cannot be all that is true of this brave lodging wherein man is harbored, and wherein all his faculties find appropriate and endless exercise. And all the uses of nature admit of being summed in one, which yields the activity of man an infinite scope. Through all its kingdoms, to the suburbs and outskirts of things, it is faithful to the cause whence it had its origin. It always speaks of Spirit. It suggests the absolute. It is a perpetual effect. It is a great shadow pointing always to the sun behind us.

The aspect of Nature is devout. Like the figure of Jesus, she stands with bended head, and hands folded upon the breast. The happiest man is he who learns from nature the lesson of worship.

Of that ineffable essence which we call Spirit, he that thinks most, will say least. We can foresee God in the coarse, and, as it were, distant phenomena of matter; but when we try to define and describe himself, both language and thought desert us, and we are as helpless as fools and savages. That essence refuses to be recorded in propositions, but when man has worshipped him intellectually, the noblest ministry of nature is to stand as the apparition of God. It is the organ through which the universal spirit speaks to the individual, and strives to lead back the individual to it.

When we consider Spirit, we see that the views already presented do not include the whole circumference of man. We must add some related thoughts.

Three problems are put by nature to the mind: What is matter? Whence is it? and Whereto? The first of these questions only, the ideal theory answers. Idealism saith: matter is a phenomenon, not a substance. Idealism acquaints us with the total disparity between the evidence of our own being and the evidence of the world's being. The one is perfect; the other, incapable of any assurance; the mind is a part of the nature of things; the world is a divine dream, from which we may presently awake to the glories and certainties of day. Idealism is a hypothesis to account for nature by other principles than those of carpentry and chemistry. Yet, if it only deny the existence of matter, it does not satisfy the demands of the spirit. It leaves God out of me. It leaves me in the splendid labyrinth of my perceptions, to wander without end. Then the heart resists it, because it balks the affections in denying substantive being to men and women. Nature is so pervaded with human life that there is something of humanity in all and in every particular. But this theory makes nature foreign to me, and does not account for that consanguinity which we acknowledge to it.

Let it stand then, in the present state of our knowledge, merely as a useful introductory hypothesis, serving to apprize us of the eternal distinction between the soul and the world.

But when, following the invisible steps of thought, we come to inquire, Whence is matter? and Whereto? many truths arise to us out of the recesses of consciousness. We learn that the highest is present to the soul of man; that the dread universal essence, which is not wisdom, or love, or beauty, or power, but all in one, and each entirely, is that for which all things exist, and that by which they are; that spirit creates; that behind nature, throughout nature, spirit is present; one and not compound it does not act upon us from without, that is, in space and time, but spiritually, or through ourselves: therefore, that spirit, that is, the Supreme Being, does not build up nature around us, but puts it forth through us, as the life of the tree puts forth new branches and leaves through the pores of the old. As a plant upon the earth, so a man rests upon the bosom of God; he is nourished by unfailing fountains, and draws at his need inexhaustible power. Who can set bounds to the possibilities of man? Once inhale the upper air, being admitted to behold the absolute natures of justice and truth, and we learn that man has access to the entire mind of the Creator, is himself the creator in the finite. This view, which admonishes me where the sources of wisdom and power lie, and points to virtue as to

"The golden key
Which opes the palace of eternity,"

carries upon its face the highest certificate of truth, because it animates me to create my own world through the purification of my soul.

The world proceeds from the same spirit as the body of man. It is a remoter and inferior incarnation of God, a projection of God in the unconscious. But it differs from the body in one important respect. It is not, like that, now subjected to the human will. Its serene order is inviolable by us. It is, therefore, to us, the present expositor of the divine mind. It is a fixed point whereby we may measure our departure. As we degenerate, the contrast between us and our house is more evident. We are as much strangers in nature as we are aliens from God. We do not understand the notes of birds. The fox and the deer run away from us; the bear and tiger rend us. We do not know the uses of more than a few plants, as corn and the apple, the potato and the vine. Is not the landscape, every glimpse of which hath a grandeur, a face of him? Yet this may show us what discord is between man and nature, for you cannot freely admire a noble landscape if laborers are digging in the field hard by. The poet finds something ridiculous in his delight until he is out of the sight of men.

8. Prospects

In inquiries respecting the laws of the world and the frame of things, the highest reason is always the truest. That which seems faintly possible, it is so refined, is often faint and dim because it is deepest seated in the mind among the eternal verities. Empirical science is apt to cloud the sight, and by the very knowledge of functions and processes to bereave the student of the manly contemplation of the whole. The savant becomes unpoetic. But the best read naturalist who lends an entire and devout attention to truth, will see that there remains much to learn of his relation to the world, and that it is not to be learned by any addition or subtraction or other comparison of known quantities, but is arrived at by untaught sallies of the spirit, by a continual self-recovery, and by entire humility. He will perceive that there are far more excellent qualities in the student than preciseness and infallibility; that a guess is often more fruitful than an indisputable affirmation, and that a dream may let us deeper into the secret of nature than a hundred concerted experiments.

For the problems to be solved are precisely those which the physiologist and the naturalist omit to state. It is not so pertinent to man to know all the individuals of the animal kingdom, as it is to know whence and whereto is this tyrannizing unity in his constitution, which evermore separates and classifies things, endeavoring to reduce the most diverse to one form. When I behold a rich landscape, it is less to my purpose to recite correctly the order and superposition of the strata, than to know why all thought of multitude is lost in a tranquil sense of unity. I cannot greatly honor minuteness in details, so long as there is no hint to explain the relation between things and thoughts; no ray upon the *metaphysics* of conchology, of botany, of the arts, to show the relation of the forms of flowers, shells, animals, architecture, to the mind, and build science upon ideas. In a cabinet of natural history, we become sensible of a certain occult recognition and sympathy in regard to the most unwieldly and eccentric forms of beast, fish, and insect. The American who has been confined, in his own country, to the sight of buildings designed after foreign models, is surprised on entering York Minster or St. Peter's at Rome, by the feeling that these structures are imitations also,—faint copies of an invisible archetype. Nor has science sufficient humanity, so long as the naturalist overlooks that wonderful congruity which subsists between man and the world; of which he is lord, not because he is the most subtile inhabitant, but because he is its head and heart, and finds something of himself in every great and small thing, in every mountain stratum, in every new law of color, fact of astronomy, or atmospheric influence which observation or analysis lays open. A perception of this mystery inspires the muse of George Herbert, the beautiful psalmist of the seventeenth century. The following lines are part of his little poem on Man.

"Man is all symmetry,
Full of proportions, one limb to another,
  And all to all the world besides.
  Each part may call the farthest, brother;
For head with foot hath private amity,
  And both with moons and tides.

"Nothing hath got so far
But man hath caught and kept it as his prey;
  His eyes dismount the highest star:
  He is in little all the sphere.
Herbs gladly cure our flesh, because that they
  Find their acquaintance there.

"For us, the winds do blow,
The earth doth rest, heaven move, and fountains flow;
  Nothing we see, but means our good,
  As our delight, or as our treasure;
The whole is either our cupboard of food,
  Or cabinet of pleasure.

"The stars have us to bed:
Night draws the curtain; which the sun withdraws.
  Music and light attend our head.
  All things unto our flesh are kind,
In their descent and being; to our mind,
  In their ascent and cause.

"More servants wait on man
Than he'll take notice of. In every path,
  He treads down that which doth befriend him
  When sickness makes him pale and wan.
Oh mighty love! Man is one world, and hath
  Another to attend him."

The perception of this class of truths makes the attraction which draws men to science, but the end is lost sight of in attention to the means. In view of this half-sight of science, we accept the sentence of Plato, that "poetry comes nearer to vital truth than history." Every surmise and vaticination of the mind is entitled to a certain respect, and we learn to prefer imperfect theories, and sentences which contain glimpses of truth, to digested systems which have no one valuable suggestion. A wise writer will feel that the ends of study and composition are best answered by announcing undiscovered regions of thought, and so communicating, through hope, new activity to the torpid spirit.

I shall therefore conclude this essay with some traditions of man and nature, which a certain poet sang to me; and which, as they have always been in the world, and perhaps reappear to every bard, may be both history and prophecy.

"The foundations of man are not in matter, but in spirit. But the element of spirit is eternity. To it, therefore, the longest series of events, the oldest chronologies are young and recent. In the cycle of the universal man, from whom the known individuals proceed, centuries are points, and all history is but the epoch of one degradation.

"We distrust and deny inwardly our sympathy with nature. We own and disown our relation to it, by turns. We are like Nebuchadnezzar, dethroned, bereft of reason, and eating grass like an ox. But who can set limits to the remedial force of spirit?

"A man is a god in ruins. When men are innocent, life shall be longer, and shall pass into the immortal as gently as we awake from dreams. Now, the world would be insane and rabid, if these disorganizations should last for hundreds of years. It is kept in check by death and infancy. Infancy is the perpetual Messiah, which comes into the arms of fallen men, and pleads with them to return to paradise.

"Man is the dwarf of himself. Once he was permeated and dissolved by spirit. He filled nature with his overflowing currents. Out from him sprang the sun and moon; from man the sun, from woman the moon. The laws of his mind, the periods of his actions externized themselves into day and night, into the year and the seasons. But, having made for himself this huge shell, his waters retired; he no longer fills the veins and veinlets; he is shrunk to a drop. He sees that the structure still fits him, but fits him colossally. Say, rather, once it fitted him, now it corresponds to him from far and on high. He adores timidly his own work. Now is man the follower of the sun, and woman the follower of the moon. Yet sometimes he starts in his slumber, and wonders at himself and his

house, and muses strangely at the resemblance betwixt him and it. He perceives that if his law is still paramount, if still he have elemental power, if his word is sterling yet in nature, it is not conscious power, it is not inferior but superior to his will. It is instinct." Thus my Orphic poet sang.

At present, man applies to nature but half his force. He works on the world with his understanding alone. He lives in it and masters it by a penny-wisdom; and he that works most in it is but a half-man, and whilst his arms are strong and his digestion good, his mind is imbruted, and he is a selfish savage. His relation to nature, his power over it, is through the understanding, as by manure; the economic use of fire, wind, water, and the mariner's needle; steam, coal, chemical agriculture; the repairs of the human body by the dentist and the surgeon. This is such a resumption of power as if a banished king should buy his territories inch by inch, instead of vaulting at once into his throne. Meantime, in the thick darkness, there are not wanting gleams of a better light,—occasional examples of the action of man upon nature with his entire force,—with reason as well as understanding. Such examples are, the traditions of miracles in the earliest antiquity of all nations; the history of Jesus Christ; the achievements of a principle, as in religious and political revolutions, and in the abolition of the slave-trade; the miracles of enthusiasm, as those reported of Swedenborg, Hohenlohe, and the Shakers; many obscure and yet contested facts, now arranged under the name of Animal Magnetism; prayer; eloquence; self-healing; and the wisdom of children. These are examples of Reason's momentary grasp of the scepter; the exertions of a power which exists not in time or space, but an instantaneous in-streaming causing power. The difference between the actual and the ideal force of man is happily figured by the schoolmen, in saying, that the knowledge of man is an evening knowledge, *vespertina cognitio*, but that of God is a morning knowledge, *matutina cognitio*.

The problem of restoring to the world original and eternal beauty is solved by the redemption of the soul. The ruin or the blank that we see when we look at nature, is in our own eye. The axis of vision is not coincident with the axis of things, and so they appear not transparent but opaque. The reason why the world lacks unity, and lies broken and in heaps, is because man is disunited with himself. He cannot be a naturalist until he satisfies all the demands of the spirit. Love is as much its demand as perception. Indeed, neither can be perfect without the other. In the uttermost meaning of the words, thought is devout, and devotion is thought. Deep calls unto deep. But in actual life, the marriage is not celebrated. There are innocent men who worship God after the tradition of their fathers, but their sense of duty has not yet extended to the use of all their faculties. And there are patient naturalists, but they freeze their subject under the wintry light of the understanding. Is not prayer also a study of truth,—a sally of the soul into the unfound infinite? No man ever prayed heartily without learning something. But when a faithful thinker, resolute to detach every object from personal relations and see it in the light of thought, shall, at the same time, kindle science with the fire of the holiest affections, then will God go forth anew into the creation.

It will not need, when the mind is prepared for study, to search for objects. The invariable mark of wisdom is to see the miraculous in the common. What is a day? What is a year? What is summer? What is woman? What is a child? What is sleep? To our blindness, these things seem unaffecting. We make fables to hide the baldness of the fact and conform it, as we say, to the higher law of the mind. But when the fact is seen under the light of an idea, the gaudy fable fades and shrivels. We behold the real higher law. To the wise, therefore, a fact is true poetry, and the most beautiful of fables. These wonders are brought to our own door. You also are a man. Man and woman and their social life, poverty, labor, sleep, fear, fortune, are known to you. Learn that none of these things is superficial, but that each phenomenon has its roots in the faculties and affections of the mind. Whilst the abstract question occupies your intellect, nature brings it in the concrete to be solved by your hands. It were a wise inquiry for the closet, to compare, point by point, especially at remarkable crises in life, our daily history with the rise and progress of ideas in the mind.

So shall we come to look at the world with new eyes. It shall answer the endless inquiry of the intellect,—What is truth? and of the affections,—What is good? by yielding itself passive to the educated Will. Then shall come to pass what my poet said: "Nature is not fixed but fluid. Spirit alters, molds, makes it. The immobility or bruteness of nature is the absence of spirit; to pure spirit it is fluid, it is volatile, it is obedient. Every spirit builds itself a house, and beyond its house a world, and beyond its world a heaven. Know then that the world exists for you. For you is the phenomenon perfect. What we are, that only can we see. All that Adam had, all that Caesar could, you have and can do. Adam called his house, heaven and earth; Caesar called his house, Rome; you perhaps call yours, a cobbler's trade; a hundred acres of ploughed land; or a scholar's garret. Yet line for line and point for point your dominion is as great as theirs, though without fine names. Build therefore your own world. As fast as you conform your life to the pure idea in your mind, that will unfold its great proportions. A correspondent revolution in things will attend the influx of the spirit. So fast will disagreeable appearances, swine, spiders, snakes, pests, mad-houses, prisons, enemies, vanish; they are temporary and shall be no more seen. The sordor and filths of nature, the sun shall dry up and the wind exhale. As when the summer comes from the south the snow-banks melt and the face of the earth becomes green before it, so shall the advancing spirit create its ornaments along its path, and carry with it the beauty it visits and the song which enchants it; it shall draw beautiful faces, warm hearts, wise discourse, and heroic acts, around its way, until evil is no more seen. The kingdom of man over nature, which cometh not with observation,—a dominion such as now is beyond his dream of God,—he shall enter without more wonder than the blind man feels who is gradually restored to perfect sight."

The American Scholar (1837)

In the annual Phi Beta Kappa address at Harvard, delivered on August 31, 1837, Emerson raised, among those other matters mentioned in the introduction, the question of "action"—"Action is with the scholar subordinate, but it is essential." If Emerson did not exactly mean the

man of letters taking active part in the political struggles of his day, he did have in mind a necessary watchfulness over those struggles, an explicit taking of sides, and bearing of witness. Emerson might not have marched on the Pentagon in protest against our military policy, but he can well be imagined making that protest in a lecture hall two blocks away. In addition, of course, action was invaluable for Emerson's scholar because by brushing against the actualities of historical life the scholar could vitalize and quicken the vocabulary with which he wrote.

Mr. President and Gentlemen:

I greet you on the recommencement of our literary year. Our anniversary is one of hope, and, perhaps, not enough of labor. We do not meet for games of strength or skill, for the recitation of histories, tragedies, and odes, like the ancient Greeks; for parliaments of love and poesy, like the Troubadours; nor for the advancement of science, like our contemporaries in the British and European capitals. Thus far, our holiday has been simply a friendly sign of the survival of the love of letters amongst a people too busy to give to letters any more. As such it is precious as the sign of an indestructible instinct. Perhaps the time is already come when it ought to be, and will be, something else; when the sluggard intellect of this continent will look from under its iron lids and fill the postponed expectation of the world with something better than the exertions of mechanical skill. Our day of dependence, our long apprenticeship to the learning of other lands, draws to a close. The millions that around us are rushing into life, cannot always be fed on the sere remains of foreign harvests. Events, actions arise, that must be sung, that will sing themselves. Who can doubt that poetry will revive and lead in a new age, as the star in the constellation Harp, which now flames in our zenith, astronomers announce, shall one day be the polestar for a thousand years?

In this hope I accept the topic which not only usage but the nature of our association seem to prescribe to this day—the AMERICAN SCHOLAR. Year by year we come up hither to read one more chapter of his biography. Let us inquire what light new days and events have thrown on his character and his hopes.

It is one of those fables which out of an unknown antiquity convey an unlooked-for wisdom, that the gods, in the beginning, divided Man into men, that he might be more helpful to himself; just as the hand was divided into fingers, the better to answer its end.

The old fable covers a doctrine ever new and sublime; that there is One Man—present to all particular men only partially, or through one faculty; and that you must take the whole society to find the whole man. Man is not a farmer, or a professor, or an engineer, but he is all. Man is priest, and scholar, and statesman, and producer, and soldier. In the *divided* or social state these functions are parcelled out to individuals, each of whom aims to do his stint of the joint work, whilst each other performs his. The fable implies that the individual, to possess himself, must sometimes return from his own labor to embrace all the other laborers. But, unfortunately, this original unit, this fountain of power, has been so distributed to multitudes, has been so minutely subdivided and peddled out, that it is spilled into drops, and cannot be gathered. The state of society is one in which the members have suffered amputation from the trunk, and strut about so many walking monsters—a good finger, a neck, a stomach, an elbow, but never a man.

Man is thus metamorphosed into a thing, into many things. The planter, who is Man sent out into the field to gather food, is seldom cheered by any idea of the true dignity of his ministry. He sees his bushel and his cart, and nothing beyond, and sinks into the farmer, instead of Man on the farm. The tradesman scarcely ever gives an ideal worth to his work, but is ridden by the routine of his craft, and the soul is subject to dollars. The priest becomes a form; the attorney a statute-book; the mechanic a machine; the sailor a rope of the ship.

In this distribution of functions the scholar is the delegated intellect. In the right state he is *Man Thinking*. In the degenerate state, when the victim of society, he tends to become a mere thinker, or still worse, the parrot of other men's thinking.

In this view of him, as Man Thinking, the theory of his office is contained. Him Nature solicits with all her placid, all her monitory pictures; him the past instructs; him the future invites. Is not indeed every man a student, and do not all things exist for the student's behoof? And, finally, is not the true scholar the only true master? But the old oracle said, "All things have two handles: beware of the wrong one." In life, too often, the scholar errs with mankind and forfeits his privilege. Let us see him in his school, and consider him in reference to the main influences he receives.

I. The first in time and the first in importance of the influences upon the mind is that of nature. Every day, the sun; and, after sunset, Night and her stars. Ever the winds blow; ever the grass grows. Every day, men and women, conversing—beholding and beholden. The scholar is he of all men whom this spectacle most engages. He must settle its value in his mind. What is nature to him? There is never a beginning, there is never an end, to the inexplicable continuity of this web of God, but always circular power returning into itself. Therein it resembles his own spirit, whose beginning, whose ending, he never can find—so entire, so boundless. Far too as her splendors shine, system on system shooting like rays, upward, downward, without centre, without circumference—in the mass and in the particle, Nature hastens to render account of herself to the mind. Classification begins. To the young mind every thing is individual, stands by itself. By and by, it finds how to join two things and see in them one nature; then three, then three thousand; and so, tyrannized over by its own unifying instinct, it goes on tying things together, diminishing anomalies, discovering roots running under ground whereby contrary and remote things cohere and flower out from one stem. It presently learns that since the dawn of history there has been a constant accumulation and classifying of facts. But what is classification but the perceiving that these objects are not chaotic, and are not foreign, but have a law which is also a law of the human mind? The astronomer discovers that geometry, a pure abstraction of the human mind, is the measure of planetary motion. The chemist finds proportions and intelligible method throughout matter; and science is nothing but the finding of analogy, identity, in the most remote parts. The ambitious soul sits down before each refractory fact; one after another reduces all strange constitutions, all new powers, to their class and their law, and goes on forever to animate the last fibre of organization, the outskirts of nature, by insight.

Thus to him, to this schoolboy under the bending dome of day, is suggested that he and it proceed from one root; one is leaf and one is flower; relation, sympathy, stirring in every vein. And what is that root? Is not that the soul of his soul? A thought too bold; a dream too wild. Yet when this spiritual light shall have revealed the law of more earthly natures—when he has learned to worship the soul, and to see that the natural philosophy that now is, is only the first gropings of its gigantic hand, he shall look forward to an ever expanding knowledge as to a becoming creator. He shall see that nature is the opposite of the soul, answering to it part for part. One is seal and one is print.

Its beauty is the beauty of his own mind. Its laws are the laws of his own mind. Nature then becomes to him the measure of his attainments. So much of nature as he is ignorant of, so much of his own mind does he not yet possess. And, in fine, the ancient precept, "Know thyself," and the modern precept, "Study nature," become at last one maxim.

II. The next great influence into the spirit of the scholar is the mind of the Past—in whatever form, whether of literature, of art, of institutions, that mind is inscribed. Books are the best type of influence of the past, and perhaps we shall get at the truth—learn the amount of this influence more conveniently—by considering their value alone.

The theory of books is noble. The scholar of the first age received into him the world around; brooded thereon; gave it the new arrangement of his own mind, and uttered it again. It came into him life; it went out from him truth. It came to him short-lived actions; it went out from him immortal thoughts. It came to him business; it went from him poetry. It was dead fact; now, it is quick thought. It can stand, and it can go. It now endures, it now flies, it now inspires. Precisely in proportion to the depth of mind from which it issued, so high does it soar, so long does it sing.

Or, I might say, it depends on how far the process had gone, of transmuting life into truth. In proportion to the completeness of the distillation, so will the purity and imperishableness of the product be. But none is quite perfect. As no air-pump can by any means make a perfect vacuum, so neither can any artist entirely exclude the conventional, the local, the perishable from his book, or write a book of pure thought, that shall be as efficient, in all respects, to a remote posterity, as to contemporaries, or rather to the second age. Each age, it is found, must write its own books; or rather, each generation for the next succeeding. The books of an older period will not fit this.

Yet hence arises a grave mischief. The sacredness which attaches to the act of creation, the act of thought, is transferred to the record. The poet chanting was felt to be a divine man: henceforth the chant is divine also. The writer was a just and wise spirit: henceforward it is settled the book is perfect; as love of the hero corrupts into worship of his statue. Instantly the book becomes noxious: the guide is a tyrant. The sluggish and perverted mind of the multitude, slow to open to the incursions of Reason, having once so opened, having once received this book, stands upon it, and makes an outcry if it is disparaged. Colleges are built on it. Books are written on it by thinkers, not by Man Thinking; by men of talent, that is, who start wrong, who set out from accepted dogmas, not from their own sight of principles. Meek young men grow up in libraries, believing it their duty to accept the views which Cicero, which Locke, which Bacon, have given; forgetful that Cicero, Locke, and Bacon were only young men in libraries when they wrote these books.

Hence, instead of Man Thinking, we have the bookworm. Hence the book-learned class, who value books, as such; not as related to nature and the human constitution, but as making a sort of Third Estate with the world and the soul. Hence the restorers of readings, the emendators, the bibliomaniacs of all degrees.

Books are the best of things, well used; abused, among the worst. What is the right use? What is the one end which all means go to effect? They are for nothing but to inspire. I had better never see a book than to be warped by its attraction clean out of my own orbit, and made a satellite instead of a system. The one thing in the world, of value, is the active soul. This every man is entitled to; this every man contains within him, although in almost all men obstructed and as yet unborn. The soul active sees absolute truth and utters truth, or creates. In this action it is genius; not the privilege of here and there a favorite, but the sound estate of every man. In its essence it is progressive. The book, the college, the school of art, the institution of any kind, stop with some past utterance of genius. This is good, say they—let us hold by this. They pin me down. They look backward and not forward. But genius looks forward: the eyes of man are set in his forehead, not in his hindhead: man hopes: genius creates. Whatever talents may be, if the man create not, the pure efflux of the Deity is not his; cinders and smoke there may be, but not yet flame. There are creative manners, there are creative actions, and creative words; manners, actions, words, that is, indicative of no custom or authority, but springing spontaneous from the mind's own sense of good and fair.

On the other part, instead of being its own seer, let it receive from another mind its truth, though it were in torrents of light, without periods of solitude, inquest, and self-recovery, and a fatal disservice is done. Genius is always sufficiently the enemy of genius by over-influence. The literature of every nation bears me witness. The English dramatic poets have Shakspearized now for two hundred years.

Undoubtedly there is a right way of reading, so it be sternly subordinated. Man Thinking must not be subdued by his instruments. Books are for the scholar's idle times. When he can read God directly, the hour is too precious to be wasted in other men's transcripts of their readings. But when the intervals of darkness come, as come they must—when the sun is hid and the stars withdraw their shining—we repair to the lamps which were kindled by their ray, to guide our steps to the East again, where the dawn is. We hear, that we may speak. The Arabian proverb says, "A fig tree, looking on a fig tree, becometh fruitful."

It is remarkable, the character of the pleasure we derive from the best books. They impress us with the conviction that one nature wrote and the same reads. We read the verses of one of the great English poets, of Chaucer, of Marvell, of Dryden, with the most modern joy—with a pleasure, I mean, which is in great part caused by the abstraction of all *time* from their verses. There is some awe mixed with the joy of our surprise, when this poet, who lived in some past world, two or three hundred years ago, says that which lies close to my own soul, that which I also had well-nigh thought and said. But for the evidence thence afforded to the philosophical doctrine of the identity of all minds, we should suppose some preëstablished harmony, some foresight of souls that were to be, and some preparation of stores for their future wants, like the fact observed in insects, who lay up food before death for the young grub they shall never see.

I would not be hurried by any love of system, by any exaggeration of instincts, to underrate the Book. We all know, that as the human body can be nourished on any food, though it were boiled grass and the broth of shoes, so the human mind can be fed by any knowledge. And great and heroic men have existed who had almost no other information than by the printed page. I only would say that it needs a strong head to bear that diet. One must be an inventor to read well. As the proverb says, "He that would bring home the wealth of the Indies, must carry out the wealth of the Indies." There is then creative reading as well as creative writing. When the mind is braced by labor and invention, the page of whatever book we read becomes luminous with manifold allusion. Every sentence is doubly significant, and the sense of our author is as broad as the world. We then see, what is always true, that as the seer's hour of vision is short and rare among heavy days and months, so is its record, perchance, the least part of his volume. The discerning will read, in his Plato or Shakspeare, only that least part—only the authentic utterances of the oracles; all the rest he rejects, were it never so many times Plato's and Shakspeare's.

Of course there is a portion of reading quite indispensable to a wise man. History and exact science he must learn by laborious reading. Colleges, in like manner, have their indispensable office—to teach elements. But they can only highly serve us when they aim not to drill, but to create; when they gather from far every ray of various genius to their hospitable halls, and by the concentrated fires, set the hearts of their youth on flame. Thought and knowledge are natures in which apparatus and pretension avail nothing. Gowns and pecuniary foundations, though of towns of gold, can never countervail the least sentence or syllable of wit. Forget this, and our American colleges will recede in their public importance, whilst they grow richer every year.

III. There goes in the world a notion that the scholar should be a recluse, a valetudinarian—as unfit for any handiwork or public labor as a penknife for an axe. The so-called "practical men" sneer at speculative men, as if, because they speculate or *see*, they could do nothing. I have heard it said that the clergy—who are always, more universally than any other class, the scholars of their day—are addressed as women; that the rough, spontaneous conversation of men they do not hear, but only a mincing and diluted speech. They are often virtually disfranchised; and indeed there are advocates for their celibacy. As far as this is true of the studious classes, it is not just and wise. Action is with the scholar subordinate, but it is essential. Without it he is not yet man. Without it thought can never ripen into truth. Whilst the world hangs before the eye as a cloud of beauty, we cannot even see its beauty. Inaction is cowardice, but there can be no scholar without the heroic mind. The preamble of thought, the transition through which it passes from the unconscious to the conscious, is action. Only so much do I know, as I have lived. Instantly we know whose words are loaded with life, and whose not.

The world—this shadow of the soul, or *other me* —lies wide around. Its attractions are the keys which unlock my thoughts and make me acquainted with myself. I run eagerly into this resounding tumult. I grasp the hands of those next me, and take my place in the ring to suffer and to work, taught by an instinct that so shall the dumb abyss be vocal with speech. I pierce its order; I dissipate its fear; I dispose of it within the circuit of my expanding life. So much only of life as I know by experience, so much of the wilderness have I vanquished and planted, or so far have I extended my being, my dominion. I do not see how any man can afford, for the sake of his nerves and his nap, to spare any action in which he can partake. It is pearls and rubies to his discourse. Drudgery, calamity, exasperation, want, are instructors in eloquence and wisdom. The true scholar grudges every opportunity of action past by, as a loss of power. It is the raw material out of which the intellect moulds her splendid products. A strange process too, this by which experience is converted into thought, as a mulberry leaf is converted into satin. The manufacture goes forward at all hours.

The actions and events of our childhood and youth are now matters of calmest observation. They lie like fair pictures in the air. Not so with our recent actions—with the business which we now have in hand. On this we are quite unable to speculate. Our affections as yet circulate through it. We no more feel or know it than we feel the feet, or the hand, or the brain of our body. The new deed is yet a part of life—remains for a time immersed in our unconscious life. In some contemplative hour it detaches itself from the life like a ripe fruit, to become a thought of the mind. Instantly it is raised, transfigured; the corruptible has put on incorruption. Henceforth it is an object of beauty, however base its origin and neighborhood. Observe too the impossibility of antedating this act. In its grub state, it cannot fly, it cannot shine, it is a dull grub. But suddenly, without observation, the selfsame thing unfurls beautiful wings, and is an angel of wisdom. So is there no fact, no event, in our private history, which shall not, sooner or later, lose its adhesive, inert form, and astonish us by soaring from our body into the empyrean. Cradle and infancy, school and playground, the fear of boys, and dogs, and ferrules, the love of little maids and berries, and many another fact that once filled the whole sky, are gone already; friend and relative, profession and party, town and country, nation and world, must also soar and sing.

Of course, he who has put forth his total strength in fit actions has the richest return of wisdom. I will not shut myself out of this globe of action, and transplant an oak into a flowerpot, there to hunger and pine; nor trust the revenue of some single faculty, and exhaust one vein of thought, much like those Savoyards, who, getting their livelihood by carving shepherds, shepherdesses, and smoking Dutchmen, for all Europe, went out one day to the mountain to find stock, and discovered that they had whittled up the last of their pine trees. Authors we have, in numbers, who have written out their vein, and who, moved by a commendable prudence, sail for Greece or Palestine, follow the trapper into the prairie, or ramble round Algiers, to replenish their merchantable stock.

If it were only for a vocabulary, the scholar would be covetous of action. Life is our dictionary. Years are well spent in country labors; in town; in the insight into trades and manufactures; in frank intercourse with many men and women; in science; in art; to the one end of mastering in all their facts a language by which to illustrate and embody our perceptions. I learn immediately from any speaker how much he has already lived, through the poverty or the splendor of his speech. Life lies behind us as the quarry from whence we get tiles and copestones for the masonry of to-day. This is the way to learn grammar. Colleges and books only copy the language which the field and the workyard made.

But the final value of action, like that of books, and better than books, is that it is a resource. That great principle of Undulation in nature, that shows itself in the inspiring and expiring of the breath; in desire and satiety; in the ebb and flow of the sea; in day and night; in heat and cold; and as yet more deeply ingrained in every atom and every fluid, is known to us under the name of Polarity—these "fits of easy transmission and reflection," as Newton called them, are the law of nature because they are the law of spirit.

The mind now thinks, now acts, and each fit reproduces the other. When the artist has exhausted his materials, when the fancy no longer paints, when thoughts are no longer apprehended and books are a weariness—he has always the resources *to live*. Character is higher than intellect. Thinking is the function. Living is the functionary. The stream retreats to its source. A great soul will be strong to live, as well as strong to think. Does he lack organ or medium to impart his truths? He can still fall back on this elemental force of living them. This is a total act. Thinking is a partial act. Let the grandeur of justice shine in his affairs. Let the beauty of affection cheer his lowly roof. Those

"far from fame," who dwell and act with him, will feel the force of his constitution in the doings and passages of the day better than it can be measured by any public and designed display. Time shall teach him that the scholar loses no hour which the man lives. Herein he unfolds the sacred germ of his instinct, screened from influence. What is lost in seemliness is gained in strength. Not out of those on whom systems of education have exhausted their culture, comes the helpful giant to destroy the old or to build the new, but out of unhandselled savage nature; out of terrible Druids and Berserkers come at last Alfred and Shakspeare.

I hear therefore with joy whatever is beginning to be said of the dignity and necessity of labor to every citizen. There is virtue yet in the hoe and the spade, for learned as well as for unlearned hands. And labor is everywhere welcome; always we are invited to work; only be this limitation observed, that a man shall not for the sake of wider activity sacrifice any opinion to the popular judgments and modes of action.

I have now spoken of the education of the scholar by nature, by books, and by action. It remains to say somewhat of his duties.

They are such as become Man Thinking. They may all be comprised in self-trust. The office of the scholar is to cheer, to raise, and to guide men by showing them facts amidst appearances. He plies the slow, unhonored, and unpaid task of observation. Flamsteed and Herschel, in their glazed observatories, may catalogue the stars with the praise of all men, and the results being splendid and useful, honor is sure. But he, in his private observatory, cataloguing obscure and nebulous stars of the human mind, which as yet no man has thought of as such—watching days and months sometimes for a few facts; correcting still his old records; must relinquish display and immediate fame. In the long period of his preparation he must betray often an ignorance and shiftlessness in popular arts, incurring the disdain of the able who shoulder him aside. Long he must stammer in his speech; often forego the living for the dead. Worse yet, he must escape—how often!—poverty and solitude. For the ease and pleasure of treading the old road, accepting the fashions, the education, the religion of society, he takes the cross of making his own, and, of course, the self-accusation, the faint heart, the frequent uncertainty and loss of time, which are the nettles and tangling vines in the way of the self-relying and self-directed; and the state of virtual hostility in which he seems to stand to society, and especially to educated society. For all this loss and scorn, what offset? He is to find consolation in exercising the highest functions of human nature. He is one who raises himself from private considerations and breathes and lives on public and illustrious thoughts. He is the world's eye. He is the world's heart. He is to resist the vulgar prosperity that retrogrades ever to barbarism, by preserving and communicating heroic sentiments, noble biographies, melodious verse, and the conclusions of history. Whatsoever oracles the human heart, in all emergencies, in all solemn hours, has uttered as its commentary on the world of actions—these he shall receive and impart. And whatsoever new verdict Reason from her inviolable seat pronounces on the passing men and events of to-day—this he shall hear and promulgate.

These being his functions, it becomes him to feel all confidence in himself, and to defer never to the popular cry. He and he only knows the world. The world of any moment is the merest appearance. Some great decorum, some fetish of a government, some ephemeral trade, or war, or man, is cried up by half mankind and cried down by the other half, as if all depended on this particular up or down. The odds are that the whole question is not worth the poorest thought which the scholar has lost in listening to the controversy. Let him not quit his belief that a popgun is a popgun, though the ancient and honorable of the earth affirm it to be the crack of doom. In silence, in steadiness, in severe abstraction, let him hold by himself; add observation to observation, patient of neglect, patient of reproach, and bide his own time, —happy enough if he can satisfy himself alone that this day he has seen something truly. Success treads on every right step. For the instinct is sure, that prompts him to tell his brother what he thinks. He then learns that in going down into the secrets of his own mind he has descended into the secrets of all minds. He learns that he who has mastered any law in his private thoughts, is master to that extent of all men whose language he speaks, and of all into whose language his own can be translated. The poet, in utter solitude remembering his spontaneous thoughts and recording them, is found to have recorded that which men in crowded cities find true for them also. The orator distrusts at first the fitness of his frank confessions, his want of knowledge of the persons he addresses, until he finds that he is the complement of his hearers;

—that they drink his words because he fulfils for them their own nature; the deeper he dives into his privatest, secretest presentiment, to his wonder he finds this is the most acceptable, most public, and universally true. The people delight in it; the better part of every man feels, This is my music; this is myself.

In self-trust all the virtues are comprehended. Free should the scholar be,—free and brave. Free even to the definition of freedom, "without any hindrance that does not arise out of his own constitution." Brave; for fear is a thing which a scholar by his very function puts behind him. Fear always springs from ignorance. It is a shame to him if his tranquillity, amid dangerous times, arise from the presumption that like children and women his is a protected class; or if he seek a temporary peace by the diversion of his thoughts from politics or vexed questions, hiding his head like an ostrich in the flowering bushes, peeping into miscroscopes, and turning rhymes, as a boy whistles to keep his courage up. So is the danger a danger still; so is the fear worse. Manlike let him turn and face it. Let him look into its eye and search its nature, inspect its origin,—see the whelping of this lion,—which lies no great way back; he will then find in himself a perfect comprehension of its nature and extent; he will have made his hands meet on the other side, and can henceforth defy it and pass on superior. The world is his who can see through its pretension. What deafness, what stone-blind custom, what overgrown error you behold is there only by sufferance,—by your sufferance. See it to be a lie, and you have already dealt it its mortal blow.

Yes, we are the cowed,—we the trustless. It is a mischievous notion that we are come late into nature; that the world was finished a long time ago. As the world was plastic and fluid in the hands of God, so it is ever to so much of his attributes as we bring to it. To ignorance and sin, it is flint. They adapt themselves to it as they may; but in proportion as a man has any thing in him divine, the firmament flows before him and takes his signet and form. Not he is great who can alter matter, but he who can alter my state of mind. They are the kings of the world who give the color of their present thought to all nature and all art, and persuade men by the cheerful serenity of their carrying the matter, that this thing which they do is the apple which the ages have desired to pluck, now at last ripe, and inviting nations to the harvest. The great man makes the great thing. Wherever Macdonald sits, there is the head of the table. Linnaeus makes botany the most alluring of studies, and wins it from the farmer and the herb-woman; Davy, chemistry; Cuvier, fossils. The day is always his who works in it with serenity and great aims. The unstable estimates of men crowd to him whose mind is filled with a truth, as the heaped waves of the Atlantic follow the moon.

For this self-trust, the reason is deeper than can be fathomed,—darker than can be enlightened. I might not carry with me the feeling of my audience in stating my own belief. But I have already shown the ground of my hope, in adverting to the doctrine that man is one. I believe man has been wronged; he has wronged himself. He has almost lost the light than can lead him back to his prerogatives. Men are become of no account. Men in history, men in the world of today, are bugs, are spawn, and are called "the mass" and "the herd." In a century, in a millennium, one or two men; that is to say, one or two approximations to the right state of every man. All the rest behold in the hero or the poet their own green and crude being, —ripened; yes, and are content to be less, so *that* may attain to its full stature. What a testimony, full of grandeur, full of pity, is borne to the demands of his own nature, by the poor clansman, the poor partisan, who rejoices in the glory of his chief. The poor and the low find some amends to their immense moral capacity, for their acquiescence in a political and social inferiority. They are content to be brushed like flies from the path of a great person, so that justice shall be done by him to that common nature which it is the dearest desire of all to see enlarged and glorified. They sun themselves in the great man's light, and feel it to be their own element. They cast the dignity of man from their downtrod selves upon the shoulders of a hero, and will perish to add one drop of blood to make that great heart beat, those giant sinews combat and conquer. He lives for us, and we live in him.

Men, such as they are, very naturally seek money or power; and power because it is as good as money, —the "spoils," so called, "of office." And why not? for they aspire to the highest, and this, in their sleep-walking, they dream is highest. Wake them and they shall quit the false good and leap to the true, and leave governments to clerks and desks. This revolution is to be wrought by the gradual domestication of the idea of Culture. The main enterprise of the world for splendor, for extent, is the upbuilding of a man. Here are the materials strewn along the ground. The private life of one man shall be a more illustrious monarchy, more formidable to its enemy, more sweet and serene in its influence to its friend, than any kingdom in history. For a man, rightly viewed, comprehendeth the particular natures of all men. Each philosopher, each bard, each actor has only done for me, as by a delegate, what one day I can do for myself. The books which once we valued more than the apple of the eye, we have quite exhausted. What is that but saying that we have come up with the point of view which the universal mind took through the eyes of one scribe; we have been that man, and have passed on. First, one, then another, we drain all cisterns, and waxing greater by all these supplies, we crave a better and more abundant food. The man has never lived that can feed us ever. The human mind cannot be enshrined in a person who shall set a barrier on any one side to this unbounded, unboundable empire. It is one central fire, which, flaming now out of the lips of Etna, lightens the capes of Sicily, and now out of the throat of Vesuvius, illuminates the towers and vineyards of Naples. It is one light which beams out of a thousand stars. It is one soul which animates all men.

But I have dwelt perhaps tediously upon this abstraction of the Scholar. I ought not to delay longer to add what I have to say of nearer reference to the time and to this country.

Historically, there is thought to be a difference in the ideas which predominate over successive epochs, and there are data for marking the genius of the Classic, of the Romantic, and now of the Reflective or Philosophical age. With the views I have intimated of the oneness or the identity of the mind through all individuals, I do not much dwell on these differences. In fact, I believe each individual passes through all three. The boy is a Greek; the youth, romantic; the adult, reflective. I deny not, however, that a revolution in the leading idea may be distinctly enough traced.

Our age is bewailed as the age of Introversion. Must that needs be evil? We, it seems, are critical; we are embarrassed with second thoughts; we cannot enjoy any thing for hankering to know whereof the pleasure consists; we are lined with eyes; we see with our feet; the time is infected with Hamlet's unhappiness,—

"Sicklied o'er with the pale cast of thought."

It is so bad then? Sight is the last thing to be

pitied. Would we be blind? Do we fear lest we should outsee nature and God, and drink truth dry? I look upon the discontent of the literary class as a mere announcement of the fact that they find themselves not in the state of mind of their fathers, and regret the coming state as untried; as a boy dreads the water before he has learned that he can swim. If there is any period one would desire to be born in, is it not the age of Revolution; when the old and the new stand side by side and admit of being compared; when the energies of all men are searched by fear and by hope; when the historic glories of the old can be compensated by the rich possibilities of the new era? This time, like all times, is a very good one, if we but know what to do with it.

I read with some joy of the auspicious signs of the coming days, as they glimmer already through poetry and art, through philosophy and science, through church and state.

One of these signs is the fact that the same movement which effected the elevation of what was called the lowest class in the state, assumed in literature a very marked and as benign an aspect. Instead of the sublime and beautiful, the near, the low, the common, was explored and poetized. That which had been negligently trodden under foot by those who were harnessing and provisioning themselves for long journeys into far countries, is suddenly found to be richer than all foreign parts. The literature of the poor, the feelings of the child, the philosophy of the street, the meaning of household life, are the topics of the time. It is a great stride. It is a sign—is it not?—of new vigor when the extremities are made active, when currents of warm life run into the hands and the feet. I ask not for the great, the remote, the romantic; what is doing in Italy or Arabia; what is Greek art, or Provençal minstrelsy; I embrace the common, I explore and sit at the feet of the familiar, the low. Give me insight into today, and you may have the antique and future worlds. What would we really know the meaning of? The meal in the firkin; the milk in the pan; the ballad in the street; the news of the boat; the glance of the eye; the form and the gait of the body;—show me the ultimate reason of these matters; show me the sublime presence of the highest spiritual cause lurking, as always it does lurk, in these suburbs and extremities of nature; let me see every trifle bristling with the polarity that ranges it instantly on an eternal law; and the shop, the plough, and the ledger referred to the like

cause by which light undulates and poets sing;—and the world lies no longer a dull miscellany and lumber-room, but has form and order; there is no trifle, there is no puzzle, but one design unites and animates the farthest pinnacle and the lowest trench.

This idea has inspired the genius of Goldsmith, Burns, Cowper, and, in a newer time, of Goethe, Wordsworth and Carlyle. This idea they have differently followed and with various success. In contrast with their writing, the style of Pope, of Johnson, of Gibbon, looks cold and pedantic. This writing is blood-warm. Man is surprised to find that things near are not less beautiful and wondrous than things remote. The near explains the far. The drop is a small ocean. A man is related to all nature. This perception of the worth of the vulgar is fruitful in discoveries. Goethe, in this very thing the most modern of the moderns, has shown us, as none ever did, the genius of the ancients.

There is one man of genius who has done much for this philosophy of life, whose literary value has never yet been rightly estimated;—I mean Emanuel Swedenborg. The most imaginative of men, yet writing with the precision of a mathematician, he endeavored to engraft a purely philosophical Ethics on the popular Christianity of his time. Such an attempt of course must have difficulty which no genius could surmount. But he saw and showed the connection between nature and the affections of the soul. He pierced the emblematic or spiritual character of the visible, audible, tangible world. Especially did his shade-loving muse hover over and interpret the lower parts of nature; he showed the mysterious bond that allies moral evil to the foul material forms, and has given in epical parables a theory of insanity, of beasts, of unclean and fearful things.

Another sign of our times, also marked by an analogous political movement, is the new importance given to the single person. Every thing that tends to insulate the individual,—to surround him with barriers of natural respect, so that each man shall feel the world is his, and man shall treat with man as a sovereign state with a sovereign state,—tends to true union as well as greatness. "I learned," said the melancholy Pestalozzi, "that no man in God's wide earth is either willing or able to help any other man." Help must come from the bosom alone. The scholar is that man who must take up into himself all the ability of the time, all the contributions of the past, all the hopes

of the future. He must be an university of knowledges. If there be one lesson more than another
which should pierce his ear, it is, The world is
nothing, the man is all; in yourself is the law of all
nature, and you know not yet how a globule of sap
ascends; in yourself slumbers the whole of Reason;
it is for you to know all; it is for you to dare all.
Mr. President and Gentlemen, this confidence in
the unsearched might of man belongs, by all motives, by all prophecy, by all preparation, to the
American Scholar. We have listened too long to
the courtly muses of Europe. The spirit of the
American freeman is already suspected to be timid,
imitative, tame. Public and private avarice make
the air we breathe thick and fat. The scholar is
decent, indolent, complaisant. See already the
tragic consequence. The mind of this country,
taught to aim at low objects, eats upon itself. There
is no work for any but the decorous and the complaisant. Young men of the fairest promise, who
begin life upon our shores, inflated by the mountain winds, shined upon by all the stars of God,
find the earth below not in unison with these, but
are hindered from action by the disgust which the
principles on which business is managed inspire,
and turn drudges, or die of disgust, some of them
suicides. What is the remedy? They did not yet
see, and thousands of young men as hopeful now
crowding to the barriers for the career do not yet
see, that if the single man plant himself indomitably on his instincts, and there abide, the huge
world will come round to him. Patience,—patience;
with the shades of all the good and great for company; and for solace the perspective of your own
infinite life; and for work the study and the communication of principles, the making those instincts prevalent, the conversion of the world. It
is not the chief disgrace in the world, not to be an
unit;—not to be reckoned one character;—not to
yield that peculiar fruit which each man was
created to bear, but to be reckoned in the gross,
in the hundred, or the thousand, of the party, the
section, to which we belong; and our opinion
predicted geographically, as the north, or the
south? Not so, brothers and friends—please God,
ours shall not be so. We will walk on our own feet;
we will work with our own hands; we will speak
our own minds. The study of letters shall be no
longer a name for pity, for doubt, and for sensual
indulgence. The dread of man and the love of man
shall be a wall of defence and a wreath of joy
around all. A nation of men will for the first time
exist, because each believes himself inspired by
the Divine Soul which also inspires all men.

From Self-Reliance (1841)

"Self-Reliance" is the best known of Emerson's
essays, but it has by no means always been the
most admired. It proved inspirational to Emerson's contemporaries, but it fell into growing
disrepute when its essential doctrine was
adopted by business tycoons and the lords of
American financial life as a thoroughly respectable justification for their sometimes ruthless
methods of procedure. Later, in the 1920's
and 1930's, "Self Reliance" became associated
with rugged individualism and was regarded
with the utmost hostility by those who believed
in the necessity of collective and communal action—first, to resist a kind of "takeover" of
American life by big business; later to combat
the economic depression and the attendant cultural crises. It was, indeed, at this time that
Emerson's general reputation was at its lowest.

More recently, however, in the fifties and
sixties, when the most dangerous threat within
American society has become the obliteration of
individuality by bigness in government, business,
the military-industrial complex, and elsewhere,
Emerson's appeal to self-reliance rings again
with much of its initial nobility. It will never be
a total theory of life for most people, though a
few here and there seem bent on trying to live
by it; but it will always be an irreducibly important portion of such a theory.

The editors have risked deleting the latter
pages of this essay (and a few pages earlier),
where Emerson reflects, in a topical manner, on
the implications for social change of his principle of self-trust. The pages are eminently worth
reading, for they show Emerson expanding
characteristically on the temper of the times;
but they are, perhaps, of chiefly historical interest.

"Ne te quæsiveris extra."
[Seek not beyond yourself.]

*Man is his own star; and the soul that can
Render an honest and a perfect man,
Commands all light, all influence, all fate;
Nothing to him falls early or too late.
Our acts our angels are, or good or ill,
Our fatal shadows that walk by us still.*

Epilogue to Beaumont and Fletcher's
Honest Man's Fortune.

*Cast the bantling on the rocks,
Suckle him with the she-wolf's teat,
Wintered with the hawk and fox,
Power and speed be hands and feet.*

I read the other day some verses written by an eminent painter which were original and not conventional. The soul always hears an admonition in such lines, let the subject be what it may. The sentiment they instil is of more value than any thought they may contain. To believe your own thought, to believe that what is true for you in your private heart is true for all men—that is genius. Speak your latent conviction, and it shall be the universal sense; for the inmost in due time becomes the outmost, and our first thought is rendered back to us by the trumpets of the Last Judgment. Familiar as the voice of the mind is to each, the highest merit we ascribe to Moses, Plato and Milton is that they set at naught books and traditions, and spoke not what men, but what *they* thought. A man should learn to detect and watch that gleam of light which flashes across his mind from within, more than the lustre of the firmament of bards and sages. Yet he dismisses without notice his thought, because it is his. In every work of genius we recognize our own rejected thoughts; they come back to us with a certain alienated majesty. Great works of art have no more affecting lesson for us than this. They teach us to abide by our spontaneous impression with good-humored inflexibility then most when the whole cry of voices is on the other side. Else to-morrow a stranger will say with masterly good sense precisely what we have thought and felt all the time, and we shall be forced to take with shame our own opinion from another.

There is a time in every man's education when he arrives at the conviction that envy is ignorance; that imitation is suicide; that he must take himself for better for worse as his portion; that though the wide universe is full of good, no kernel of nourishing corn can come to him but through his toil bestowed on that plot of ground which is given to him to till. The power which resides in him is new in nature, and none but he knows what that is which he can do, nor does he know until he has tried. Not for nothing one face, one character, one fact, makes much impression on him, and another none. This sculpture in the memory is not without preëstablished harmony. The eye was placed where one ray should fall, that it might testify of that particular ray. We but half express ourselves, and are ashamed of that divine idea which each of us represents. It may be safely trusted as proportionate and of good issues, so it be faithfully imparted, but God will not have his work made manifest by cowards. A man is relieved and gay when he has put his heart into his work and done his best; but what he has said or done otherwise shall give him no peace. It is a deliverance which does not deliver. In the attempt his genius deserts him; no muse befriends; no invention, no hope.

Trust thyself: every heart vibrates to that iron string. Accept the place the divine providence has found for you, the society of your contemporaries, the connection of events. Great men have always done so, and confided themselves childlike to the genius of their age, betraying their perception that the absolutely trustworthy was seated at their heart, working through their hands, predominating in all their being. And we are now men, and must accept in the highest mind the same transcendent destiny; and not minors and invalids in a protected corner, not cowards fleeing before a revolution, but guides, redeemers and benefactors, obeying the Almighty effort and advancing on Chaos and the Dark.

What pretty oracles nature yields us on this text in the face and behavior of children, babes, and even brutes! That divided and rebel mind, that distrust of a sentiment because our arithmetic has computed the strength and means opposed to our purpose, these have not. Their mind being whole, their eye is as yet unconquered; and when we look in their faces we are disconcerted. Infancy conforms to nobody; all conform to it; so that one babe commonly makes four or five out of the adults who prattle and play to it. So God has armed youth and puberty and manhood no less with its own piquancy and charm, and made it enviable and gracious and its claims not to be put by, if it will stand by itself. Do not think the youth has no force, because he cannot speak to you and me. Hark! in the next room his voice is sufficiently clear and emphatic. It seems he knows how to speak to his contemporaries. Bashful or bold

There is no evil, only a lack of good.

only within my own heart and mind can I find the truth.

Optimistic view of man.

then, he will know how to make us seniors very unnecessary.

The nonchalance of boys who are sure of a dinner, and would disdain as much as a lord to do or say aught to conciliate one, is the healthy attitude of human nature. A boy is in the parlor what the pit is in the playhouse; independent, irresponsible, looking out from his corner on such people and facts as pass by, he tries and sentences them on their merits, in the swift, summary way of boys, as good, bad, interesting, silly, eloquent, troublesome. He cumbers himself never about consequences, about interests; he gives an independent, genuine verdict. You must court him; he does not court you. But the man is as it were clapped into jail by his consciousness. As soon as he has once acted or spoken with *éclat* he is a committed person, watched by the sympathy or the hatred of hundreds, whose affections must now enter into his account. There is no Lethe for this. Ah, that he could pass again into his neutrality! Who can thus avoid all pledges and, having observed, observe again from the same unaffected, unbiased, unbribable, unaffrighted innocence—must always be formidable. He would utter opinions on all passing affairs, which being seen to be not private but necessary, would sink like darts into the ear of men and put them in fear.

These are the voices which we hear in solitude, but they grow faint and inaudible as we enter into the world. Society everywhere is in conspiracy against the manhood of every one of its members. Society is a joint-stock company, in which the members agree, for the better securing of his bread to each shareholder, to surrender the liberty and culture of the eater. The virtue in most request is conformity. Self-reliance is its aversion. It loves not realities and creators, but names and customs.

Whoso would be a man, must be a nonconformist. He who would gather immortal palms must not be hindered by the name of goodness, but must explore if it be goodness. Nothing is at last sacred but the integrity of your own mind. Absolve you to yourself, and you shall have the suffrage of the world. I remember an answer which when quite young I was prompted to make to a valued adviser who was wont to importune me with the dear old doctrines of the church. On my saying, "What have I to do with the sacredness of traditions, if I live wholly from within?" my friend suggested— "But these impulses may be from below, not from above." I replied, "They do not seem to me to be such; but if I am the Devil's child, I will live then

The more security the less freedom.

from the Devil." No law can be sacred to me but that of my nature. Good and bad are but names very readily transferable to that or this; the only right is what is after my constitution; the only wrong what is against it. A man is to carry himself in the presence of all opposition as if every thing were titular and ephemeral but he. I am ashamed to think how easily we capitulate to badges and names, to large societies and dead institutions. Every decent and well-spoken individual affects and sways me more than is right. I ought to go upright and vital, and speak the rude truth in all ways. If malice and vanity wear the coat of philanthropy, shall that pass? If an angry bigot assumes this bountiful cause of Abolition, and comes to me with his last news from Barbadoes, why should I not say to him, 'Go love thy infant; love thy woodchopper; be good-natured and modest; have that grace; and never varnish your hard, uncharitable ambition with this incredible tenderness for black folk a thousand miles off. Thy love afar is spite at home.' Rough and graceless would be such greeting, but truth is handsomer than the affectation of love. Your goodness must have some edge to it— else it is none. The doctrine of hatred must be preached, as the counteraction of the doctrine of love, when that pules and whines. I shun father and mother and wife and brother when my genius calls me. I would write on the lintels of the doorpost, *Whim*. I hope it is somewhat better than whim at last, but we cannot spend the day in explanation. Expect me not to show cause why I seek or exclude company. Then again, do not tell me, as a good man did to-day, of my obligation to put all poor men in good situations. Are they *my* poor? I tell thee, thou foolish philanthropist, that I grudge the dollar, the dime, the cent I give to such men as do not belong to me and to whom I do not belong. There is a class of persons to whom by all spiritual affinity I am bought and sold; for them I will go to prison if need be; but your miscellaneous popular charities; the education at college of fools; the building of meeting-houses to the vain end to which many now stand; alms to sots, and the thousand-fold Relief Societies; though I confess with shame I sometimes succumb and give the dollar, it is a wicked dollar, which by and by I shall have the manhood to withhold.

Virtues are, in the popular estimate, rather the exception than the rule. There is the man *and* his virtues. Men do what is called a good action, as some piece of courage or charity, much as they would pay a fine in expiation of daily non-appear-

They are relative

It takes great inner strength to be a nonconformist.

ance on parade. Their works are done as an apology or extenuation of their living in the world—as invalids and the insane pay a high board. Their virtues are penances. I do not wish to expiate, but to live. My life is for itself and not for a spectacle. I much prefer that it should be of a lower strain, so it be genuine and equal, than that it should be glittering and unsteady. I wish it to be sound and sweet, and not to need diet and bleeding. I ask primary evidence that you are a man, and refuse this appeal from the man to his actions. I know that for myself it makes no difference whether I do or forbear those actions which are reckoned excellent. I cannot consent to pay for a privilege where I have intrinsic right. Few and mean as my gifts may be, I actually am, and do not need for my own assurance or the assurance of my fellows any secondary testimony.

What I must do is all that concerns me, not what the people think. This rule, equally arduous in actual and in intellectual life, may serve for the whole distinction between greatness and meanness. It is the harder because you will always find those who think they know what is your duty better than you know it. It is easy in the world to live after the world's opinion; it is easy in solitude to live after our own; but the great man is he who in the midst of the crowd keeps with perfect sweetness the independence of solitude.

The objection to conforming to usages that have become dead to you is that it scatters your force. It loses your time and blurs the impression of your character. If you maintain a dead church, contribute to a dead Bible-society, vote with a great party either for the government or against it, spread your table like base housekeepers—under all these screens I have difficulty to detect the precise man you are: and of course so much force is withdrawn from your proper life. But do your work, and I shall know you. Do your work, and you shall reinforce yourself. A man must consider what a blindman's-buff is this game of conformity. If I know your sect I anticipate your argument. I hear a preacher announce for his text and topic the expediency of one of the institutions of his church. Do I not know beforehand that not possibly can he say a new and spontaneous word? Do I not know that with all this ostentation of examining the grounds of the institution he will do no such thing? Do I not know that he is pledged to himself not to look but at one side, the permitted side, not as a man, but as a parish minister? He is a retained attorney, and these airs of the bench are the emptiest affectation. Well, most men have bound their eyes with one or another handkerchief, and attached themselves to some one of these communities of opinion. This conformity makes them not false in a few particulars, authors of a few lies, but false in all particulars. Their every truth is not quite true. Their two is not the real two, their four not the real four; so that every word they say chagrins us and we know not where to begin to set them right. Meantime nature is not slow to equip us in the prison-uniform of the party to which we adhere. We come to wear one cut of face and figure, and acquire by degrees the gentlest asinine expression. There is a mortifying experience in particular, which does not fail to wreak itself also in the general history; I mean "the foolish face of praise," the forced smile which we put on in company where we do not feel at ease, in answer to conversation which does not interest us. The muscles, not spontaneously moved but moved by a low usurping wilfulness, grow tight about the outline of the face, with the most disagreeable sensation.

For nonconformity the world whips you with its displeasure. And therefore a man must know how to estimate a sour face. The by-standers look askance on him in the public street or in the friend's parlor. If this aversion had its origin in contempt and resistance like his own he might well go home with a sad countenance; but the sour faces of the multitude, like their sweet faces, have no deep cause, but are put on and off as the wind blows and a newspaper directs. Yet is the discontent of the multitude more formidable than that of the senate and the college. It is easy enough for a firm man who knows the world to brook the rage of the cultivated classes. Their rage is decorous and prudent, for they are timid, as being very vulnerable themselves. But when to their feminine rage the indignation of the people is added, when the ignorant and the poor are aroused, when the unintelligent brute force that lies at the bottom of society is made to growl and mow, it needs the habit of magnanimity and religion to treat it godlike as a trifle of no concernment.

The other terror that scares us from self-trust is our consistency; a reverence for our past act or word because the eyes of others have no other data for computing our orbit than our past acts, and we are loth to disappoint them.

But why should you keep your head over your shoulder? Why drag about this corpse of your memory, lest you contradict somewhat you have

[handwritten top margin: Essay is memorable expression of philosophical ideas]

stated in this or that public place? Suppose you should contradict yourself; what then? It seems to be a rule of wisdom never to rely on your memory alone, scarcely even in acts of pure memory, but to bring the past for judgment into the thousand-eyed present, and live ever in a new day. In your metaphysics you have denied personality to the Deity, yet when the devout motions of the soul come, yield to them heart and life, though they should clothe God with shape and color. Leave your theory, as Joseph his coat in the hand of the harlot, and flee.

A foolish consistency is the hobgoblin of little minds, adored by little statesmen and philosophers and divines. With consistency a great soul has simply nothing to do. He may as well concern himself with his shadow on the wall. Speak what you think now in hard words and to-morrow speak what to-morrow thinks in hard words again, though it contradict every thing you said to-day.—'Ah, so you shall be sure to be misunderstood.'—Is it so bad then to be misunderstood? Pythagoras was misunderstood, and Socrates, and Jesus, and Luther, and Copernicus, and Galileo, and Newton, and every pure and wise spirit that ever took flesh. To be great is to be misunderstood.

. . .

. . . Here is the fountain of action and of thought. Here are the lungs of that inspiration which giveth man wisdom and which cannot be denied without impiety and atheism. We lie in the lap of immense intelligence, which makes us receivers of its truth and organs of its activity. When we discern justice, when we discern truth, we do nothing of ourselves, but allow a passage to its beams. If we ask whence this comes, if we seek to pry into the soul that causes, all philosophy is at fault. Its presence or its absence is all we can affirm. Every man discriminates between the voluntary acts of his mind and his involuntary perceptions, and knows that to his involuntary perceptions a perfect faith is due. He may err in the expression of them, but he knows that these things are so, like day and night, not to be disputed. My wilful actions and acquisitions are but roving; the idlest reverie, the faintest native emotion, command my curiosity and respect. Thoughtless people contradict as readily the statement of perceptions as of opinions, or rather much more readily; for they do not distinguish between perception and notion. They fancy that I choose to see this or that thing. But perception is not whimsical, but fatal. If I see

a trait, my children will see it after me, and in course of time all mankind—although it may chance that no one has seen it before me. For my perception of it is as much a fact as the sun.

The relations of the soul to the divine spirit are so pure that it is profane to seek to interpose helps. It must be that when God speaketh he should communicate, not one thing, but all things; should fill the world with his voice; should scatter forth light, nature, time, souls, from the centre of the present thought; and new date and new create the whole. Whenever a mind is simple and receives a divine wisdom, old things pass away—means, teachers, texts, temples fall; it lives now, and absorbs past and future into the present hour. All things are made sacred by relation to it—one as much as another. All things are dissolved to their centre by their cause, and in the universal miracle petty and particular miracles disappear. If therefore a man claims to know and speak of God and carries you backward to the phraseology of some old mouldered nation in another country, in another world, believe him not. Is the acorn better than the oak which is its fulness and completion? Is the parent better than the child into whom he has cast his ripened being? Whence then this worship of the past? The centuries are conspirators against the sanity and authority of the soul. Time and space are but physiological colors which the eye makes, but the soul is light: where it is, is day; where it was, is night; and history is an impertinence and an injury if it be any thing more than a cheerful apologue or parable of my being and becoming. Man is timid and apologetic; he is no longer upright; he dares not say 'I think,' 'I am,' but quotes some saint or sage. He is ashamed before the blade of grass or the blowing rose. These roses under my window make no reference to former roses or to better ones; they are for what they are; they exist with God to-day. There is no time to them. There is simply the rose; it is perfect in every moment of its existence. Before a leaf-bud has burst, its whole life acts; in the full-blown flower there is no more; in the leafless root there is no less. Its nature is satisfied and it satisfies nature in all moments alike. But man postpones or remembers; he does not live in the present, but with reverted eye laments the past, or, heedless of the riches that surround him, stands on tiptoe to foresee the future. He cannot be happy and strong until he too lives with nature in the present above time. This should be plain enough. Yet see what

[handwritten marginal notes, bottom and side margins:]
Why worship the past? It is no better than the present. All is one.
To live above time. no past present or future. All time is one.
This should be plain enough — works for moral people.
The physical world just because you can't see it doesn't mean it isn't there.
The eye fools you into believing.
all time is one. Now is forever.
He did not follow English models. The past has nothing good to tell us.
what we see with our eyes are but colors that the eye makes and illusion. The soul is the original prism. It is part of being and oneness.

strong intellects dare not yet hear God himself unless he speak the phraseology of I know not what David, or Jeremiah, or Paul. We shall not always set so great a price on a few texts, on a few lives. We are like children who repeat by rote the sentences of grandames and tutors, and, as they grow older, of the men of talents and character they chance to see—painfully recollecting the exact words they spoke; afterwards, when they come into the point of view which those had who uttered these sayings, they understand them and are willing to let the words go; for at any time they can use words as good when occasion comes. If we live truly, we shall see truly. It is as easy for the strong man to be strong, as it is for the weak to be weak. When we have new perception, we shall gladly disburden the memory of its hoarded treasures as old rubbish. When a man lives with God, his voice shall be as sweet as the murmur of the brook and the rustle of the corn.

And now at last the highest truth on this subject remains unsaid; probably cannot be said; for all that we say is the far-off remembering of the intuition. That thought by what I can now nearest approach to say it, is this. When good is near you, when you have life in yourself, it is not by any known or accustomed way; you shall not discern the footprints of any other; you shall not see the face of man; you shall not hear any name; the way, the thought, the good, shall be wholly strange and new. It shall exclude example and experience. You take the way from man, not to man. All persons that ever existed are its forgotten ministers. Fear and hope are alike beneath it. There is somewhat low even in hope. In the hour of vision there is nothing that can be called gratitude, nor properly joy. The soul raised over passion beholds identity and eternal causation, perceives the self-existence of Truth and Right, and calms itself with knowing that all things go well. Vast spaces of nature, the Atlantic Ocean, the South Sea; long intervals of time, years, centuries, are of no account. This which I think and feel underlay every former state of life and circumstances, as it does underlie my present, and what is called life and what is called death.

Life only avails, not the having lived. Power ceases in the instant of repose; it resides in the moment of transition from a past to a new state, in the shooting of the gulf, in the darting to an aim. This one fact the world hates; that the soul *becomes*; for that forever degrades the past, turns all riches to poverty, all reputation to a shame, con-

founds the saint with the rogue, shoves Jesus and Judas equally aside. Why then do we prate of self-reliance? Inasmuch as the soul is present there will be power not confident but agent. To talk of reliance is a poor external way of speaking. Speak rather of that which relies because it works and is. Who has more obedience than I masters me, though he should not raise his finger. Round him I must revolve by the gravitation of spirits. We fancy it rhetoric when we speak of eminent virtue. We do not yet see that virtue is Height, and that a man or a company of men, plastic and permeable to principles, by the law of nature must overpower and ride all cities, nations, kings, rich men, poets, who are not.

This is the ultimate fact which we so quickly reach on this, as on every topic, the resolution of all into the ever-blessed ONE. Self-existence is the attribute of the Supreme Cause, and it constitutes the measure of good by the degree in which it enters into all lower forms. All things real are so by so much virtue as they contain. Commerce, husbandry, hunting, whaling, war, eloquence, personal weight, are somewhat, and engage my respect as examples of its presence and impure action. I see the same law working in nature for conservation and growth. Power is, in nature, the essential measure of right. Nature suffers nothing to remain in her kingdoms which cannot help itself. The genesis and maturation of a planet, its poise and orbit, the bended tree recovering itself from the strong wind, the vital resources of every animal and vegetable, are demonstrations of the self-sufficing and therefore self-relying soul.

Thus all concentrates: let us not rove; let us sit at home with the cause. Let us stun and astonish the intruding rabble of men and books and institutions by a simple declaration of the divine fact. Bid the invaders take the shoes from off their feet, for God is here within. Let our simplicity judge them, and our docility to our own law demonstrate the poverty of nature and fortune beside our native riches.

But now we are a mob. Man does not stand in awe of man, nor is his genius admonished to stay at home, to put itself in communication with the internal ocean, but it goes abroad to beg a cup of water of the urns of other men. We must go alone; I like the silent church before the service begins, better than any preaching. How far off, how cool, how chaste the persons look, begirt each one with a precinct or sanctuary! So let us always sit. Why should we assume the faults of our friend, or wife, or father, or child, because they sit around our hearth, or are said to have the same blood? All men have my blood and I all men's. Not for that will I adopt their petulance or folly, even to the extent of being ashamed of it. But your isolation must not be mechanical, but spiritual, that is, must be elevation. At times the whole world seems to be in conspiracy to importune you with emphatic trifles. Friend, client, child, sickness, fear, want, charity, all knock at once at thy closet door and say—'Come out unto us.' But keep thy state; come not into their confusion. The power men possess to annoy me I give them by a weak curiosity. No man can come near me but through my act. "What we love that we have, but by desire we bereave ourselves of the love."

If we cannot at once rise to the sanctities of obedience and faith, let us at least resist our temptations; let us enter into the state of war and wake Thor and Woden, courage and constancy, in our Saxon breasts. This is to be done in our smooth times by speaking the truth. Check this lying hospitality and lying affection. Live no longer to the expectation of these deceived and deceiving people with whom we converse. Say to them, 'O father, O mother, O wife, O brother, O friend, I have lived with you after appearances hitherto. Henceforward I am the truth's. Be it known unto you that henceforward I obey no law less than the eternal law. I will have no covenants but proximities. I shall endeavor to nourish my parents, to support my family, to be the chaste husband of one wife—but these relations I must fill after a new and unprecedented way. I appeal from your customs. I must be myself. I cannot break myself any longer for you, or you. If you can love me for what I am, we shall be the happier. If you cannot, I will still seek to deserve that you should. I will not hide my tastes or aversions. I will so trust that what is deep is holy, that I will do strongly before the sun and moon whatever inly rejoices me and the heart ap-

points. If you are noble, I will love you; if you are not, I will not hurt you and myself by hypocritical attentions. If you are true, but not in the same truth with me, cleave to your companions; I will seek my own. I do this not selfishly but humbly and truly. It is alike your interest, and mine, and all men's, however long we have dwelt in lies, to live in truth. Does this sound harsh to-day? You will soon love what is dictated by your nature as well as mine, and if we follow the truth it will bring us out safe at last.'—But so may you give these friends pain. Yes, but I cannot sell my liberty and my power, to save their sensibility. Besides, all persons have their moments of reason, when they look out into the region of absolute truth; then will they justify me and do the same thing.

The populace think that your rejection of popular standards is a rejection of all standard, and mere antinomianism; and the bold sensualist will use the name of philosophy to gild his crimes. But the law of consciousness abides. There are two confessionals, in one or the other of which we must be shriven. You may fulfil your round of duties by clearing yourself in the *direct*, or in the *reflex* way. Consider whether you have satisfied your relations to father, mother, cousin, neighbor, town, cat and dog—whether any of these can upbraid you. But I may also neglect this reflex standard and absolve me to myself. I have my own stern claims and perfect circle. It denies the name of duty to many offices that are called duties. But if I can discharge its debts it enables me to dispense with the popular code. If any one imagines that this law is lax, let him keep its commandment one day.

And truly it demands something godlike in him who has cast off the common motives of humanity and has ventured to trust himself for a taskmaster. High be his heart, faithful his will, clear his sight, that he may in good earnest be doctrine, society, law, to himself, that a simple purpose may be to him as strong as iron necessity is to others!

The Transcendentalist (1842)

This is the fourth in a series of eight lectures on "The Times" delivered by Emerson at the Masonic Temple in Boston during the winter of 1841–42. As we remarked in the introduction, it should be placed alongside "New England Reformers," in *Essays: Second Series*. Emerson

to some extent dissociated himself in this essay from the transcendental movement; for while sharing in the transcendentalists' idealistic faith, he selects for emphasis the impulse to withdraw from society, to "drop out" and leave the social and political challenges of the day to others. In

"New England Reformers," he amiably chides the reformers for refusing to take the long and the high view and to be too engrossed in meeting those immediate challenges.

Emerson's approach, however, leads him to one of his most moving statements about what he called "the double consciousness," whereby man alternates between "the understanding" and an absorption in everyday affairs, within the domain of the necessitated; and "the soul" or "the reason" and meditation on the higher laws of truth and beauty and goodness, within the domain of freedom. Emerson's language may not be our own, but we have all surely experienced that same sense of alternation between areas where our thought is unimpeded and areas where our thought is coerced.

The first thing we have to say respecting what are called *new views* here in New England, at the present time, is, that they are not new, but the very oldest of thoughts cast into the mould of these new times. The light is always identical in its composition, but it falls on a great variety of objects, and by so falling is first revealed to us, not in its own form, for it is formless, but in theirs; in like manner, thought only appears in the objects it classifies. What is popularly called Transcendentalism among us, is Idealism; Idealism as it appears in 1842. As thinkers, mankind have ever divided into two sects, Materialists and Idealists; the first class founding on experience, the second on consciousness; the first class beginning to think from the data of the senses, the second class perceive that the senses are not final, and say, The senses give us representations of things, but what are the things themselves, they cannot tell. The materialist insists on facts, on history, on the force of circumstances and the animal wants of man; the idealist on the power of Thought and of Will, on inspiration, on miracle, on individual culture. These two modes of thinking are both natural, but the idealist contends that his way of thinking is in higher nature. He concedes all that the other affirms, admits the impressions of sense, admits their coherency, their use and beauty, and then asks the materialist for his grounds of assurance that things are as his senses represent them. But I, he says, affirm facts not affected by the illusions of sense, facts which are of the same nature as the

faculty which reports them, and not liable to doubt; facts which in their first appearance to us assume a native superiority to material facts, degrading these into a language by which the first are to be spoken; facts which it only needs a retirement from the senses to discern. Every materialist will be an idealist; but an idealist can never go backward to be a materialist.

The idealist, in speaking of events, sees them as spirits. He does not deny the sensuous fact: by no means; but he will not see that alone. He does not deny the presence of this table, this chair, and the walls of this room, but he looks at these things as the reverse side of the tapestry, as the *other end*, each being a sequel or completion of a spiritual fact which nearly concerns him. This manner of looking at things transfers every object in nature from an independent and anomalous position without there, into the consciousness. Even the materialist Condillac, perhaps the most logical expounder of materialism, was constrained to say, "Though we should soar into the heavens, though we should sink into the abyss, we never go out of ourselves; it is always our own thoughts that we perceive." What more could an idealist say?

The materialist, secure in the certainty of sensation, mocks at fine-spun theories, at star-gazers and dreams, and believes that his life is solid, that he at least takes nothing for granted, but knows where he stands, and what he does. Yet how easy it is to show him that he also is a phantom walking and working amid phantoms, and that he need only ask a question or two beyond his daily questions to find his solid universe growing dim and impalpable before his sense. The sturdy capitalist, no matter how deep and square on blocks of Quincy granite he lays the foundations of his banking-house or Exchange, must set it, at last, not on a cube corresponding to the angles of his structure, but on a mass of unknown materials and solidity, red-hot, or white-hot perhaps at the core, which rounds off to an almost perfect sphericity, and lies floating in soft air, and goes spinning away, dragging bank and banker with it at a rate of thousands of miles the hour, he knows not whither—a bit of bullet, now glimmering, now darkling through a small cubic space on the edge of an unimaginable pit of emptiness. And this wild balloon, in which his whole venture is embarked, is a just symbol of his whole state and faculty. One thing at least, he says, is certain, and does not give me the headache, that figures do not lie; the multiplication table has been hitherto found unimpeachable truth; and, moreover, if I put a gold eagle in my safe, I find it again to-morrow; but for these thoughts, I know not whence they are. They change and pass away. But ask him why he believes that an uniform experience will continue uniform, or on what grounds he founds his faith in his figures, and he will perceive that his mental fabric is built up on just as strange and quaking foundations as his proud edifice of stone.

In the order of thought, the materialist takes his departure from the external world, and esteems a man as one product of that. The idealist takes his departure from his consciousness, and reckons the world an appearance. The materialist respects sensible masses, Society, Government, social art and luxury, every establishment, every mass, whether majority of numbers, or extent of space, or amount of objects, every social action. The idealist has another measure, which is metaphysical, namely the *rank* which things themselves take in his consciousness; not at all the size or appearance. Mind is the only reality, of which men and all other natures are better or worse reflectors. Nature, literature, history, are only subjective phenomena. Although in his action overpowered by the laws of action, and so, warmly co-operating with men, even preferring them to himself, yet when he speaks scientifically, or after the order of thought, he is constrained to degrade persons into representatives of truths. He does not respect labor, or the products of labor, namely property, otherwise than as a manifold symbol, illustrating with wonderful fidelity of details the laws of being; he does not respect government, except as far as it reiterates the law of his mind; nor the church, nor charities, nor arts, for themselves; but hears, as at a vast distance, what they say, as if his consciousness would speak to him through a pantomimic scene. His thought—that is the Universe. His experience inclines him to behold the procession of facts you call the world, as flowing perpetually outward from an invisible, unsounded centre in himself, centre alike of him and of them, and necessitating him to regard all things as having a subjective or relative existence, relative to that aforesaid Unknown Centre of him.

From this transfer of the world into the consciousness, this beholding of all things in the mind, follow easily his whole ethics. It is simpler to be self-dependent. The height, the deity of man is to be self-sustained, to need no gift, no foreign force. Society is good when it does not violate me, but best when it is likest to solitude. Everything real is self-existent. Everything divine shares the self-existence of Deity. All that you call the world is the shadow of that substance which you are, the perpetual creation of the powers of thought, of those that are dependent and of those that are independent of your will. Do not cumber yourself with fruitless pains to mend and remedy remote effects; let the soul be erect, and all things will go well. You think me the child of my circumstances: I make my circumstances. Let any thought or motive of mine be different from that they are, the difference will transform my condition and economy. I—this thought which is called I—is the mould into which the world is poured like melted wax. The mould is invisible, but the world betrays the shape of the mould. You call it the power of circumstance, but it is the power of me. Am I in harmony with myself? my position will seem to you just and commanding. Am I vicious and insane? my fortunes will seem to you obscure and descending. As I am, so shall I associate, and so shall I act; Cæsar's history will paint out Cæsar. Jesus acted so, because he thought so. I do not wish to overlook or to gainsay any reality; I say I make my circumstance; but if you ask me, Whence am I? I feel like other men my relation to that Fact which cannot be spoken, or defined, nor even thought, but which exists, and will exist.

The Transcendentalist adopts the whole connection of spiritual doctrine. He believes in miracle, in the perpetual openness of the human mind to new influx of light and power; he believes in inspiration, and in ecstasy. He wishes that the spiritual principle should be suffered to demonstrate itself to the end, in all possible applications to the state of man, without the admission of anything unspiritual; that is, anything positive, dogmatic, personal. Thus the spiritual measure of inspiration is the depth of the thought, and never, who said it? And so he resists all attempts to palm other rules and measures on the spirit than its own.

In action he easily incurs the charge of antinomianism by his avowal that he, who has the Law-giver, may with safety not only neglect, but even contravene every written commandment. In the play of Othello, the expiring Desdemona absolves her husband of the murder, to her attendant Emilia. Afterwards, when Emilia charges him with the crime, Othello exclaims,

"You heard her say herself it was not I."

Emilia replies,

"The more angel she, and thou the blacker devil."

Of this fine incident, Jacobi, the Transcendental moralist, makes use, with other parallel instances, in his reply to Fichte. Jacobi, refusing all measure of right and wrong except the determinations of the private spirit, remarks that there is no crime but has sometimes been a virtue. "I," he says, "am that atheist, that godless person who, in opposition to an imaginary doctrine of calculation, would lie as the dying Desdemona lied; would lie and deceive, as Pylades when he personated Orestes; would assassinate like Timoleon; would perjure myself like Epaminondas and John de Witt; I would resolve on suicide like Cato; I would commit sacrilege with David; yea, and pluck ears of corn on the Sabbath, for no other reason than that I was fainting for lack of food. For I have assurance in myself that in pardoning these faults according to the letter, man exerts the sovereign right which the majesty of his being confers on him; he sets the seal of his divine nature to the grace he accords."

In like manner, if there is anything grand and daring in human thought or virtue, any reliance on the vast, the unknown; any presentiment, any extravagance of faith, the spiritualist adopts it as most in nature. The oriental mind has always tended to this largeness. Buddhism is an expression of it. The Buddhist who thanks no man, who says, "Do not flatter your benefactors," but who, in his conviction that every good deed can by no possibility escape its reward, will not deceive the benefactor by pretending that he has done more than he should, is a Transcendentalist.

You will see by this sketch that there is no such thing as a Transcendental *party*; that there is no pure Transcendentalist; that we know of none but prophets and heralds of such a philosophy; that all who by strong bias of nature have leaned to the spiritual side in doctrine, have stopped short of their goal. We have had many harbingers and forerunners; but of a purely spiritual life, history has afforded no example. I mean we have yet no man who has leaned entirely on his character, and eaten angels' food; who, trusting to his sentiments, found life made of miracles; who, working for universal aims, found himself fed, he knew not how; clothed, sheltered, and weaponed, he knew not how, and yet it was done by his own hands. Only in the instinct of the lower animals we find the suggestion of the methods of it, and something higher than our understanding. The squirrel hoards nuts and the bee gathers honey, without knowing what they do, and they are thus provided for without selfishness or disgrace.

Shall we say then that Transcendentalism is the Saturnalia or excess of Faith; the presentiment of a faith proper to man in his integrity, excessive only when his imperfect obedience hinders the satisfaction of his wish? Nature is transcendental, exists primarily, necessarily, ever works and advances, yet takes no thought for the morrow. Man owns the dignity of the life which throbs around him, in chemistry, and tree, and animal, and in the involuntary functions of his own body; yet he is balked when he tries to fling himself into this enchanted circle, where all is done without degradation. Yet genius and virtue predict in man the same absence of private ends and of condescension to circumstances, united with every trait and talent of beauty and power.

This way of thinking, falling on Roman times, made Stoic philosophers; falling on despotic times, made patriot Catos and Brutuses; falling on superstitious times, made prophets and apostles; on popish times, made protestants and ascetic monks, preachers of Faith against the preachers of Works; on prelatical times, made Puritans and Quakers; and falling on Unitarian and commercial times, makes the peculiar shades of Idealism which we know.

It is well known to most of my audience that the Idealism of the present day acquired the name of Transcendental from the use of that term by Immanuel Kant, of Königsberg, who replied to the skeptical philosophy of Locke, which insisted that there was nothing in the intellect which was not previously in the experience of the senses, by showing that there was a very important class of ideas or imperative forms, which did not come by experience, but through which experience was acquired; that these were intuitions of the mind itself; and he denominated them *Transcendental* forms. The extraordinary profoundness and precision of that man's thinking have given vogue to his nomenclature, in Europe and America, to that extent that whatever belongs to the class of intuitive thought is popularly called at the present day *Transcendental*.

Although, as we have said, there is no pure Transcendentalist, yet the tendency to respect the intuitions and to give them, at least in our creed, all authority over our experience, has deeply colored the conversation and poetry of the present day; and the history of genius and of religion in these times, though impure, and as yet not incarnated in any powerful individual, will be the history of this tendency.

It is a sign of our times, conspicuous to the coarsest observer, that many intelligent and religious persons withdraw themselves from the common labors and competitions of the market and the caucus, and betake themselves to a certain solitary and critical way of living, from which no solid fruit has yet appeared to justify their separation. They hold themselves aloof: they feel the disproportion between their faculties and the work offered them, and they prefer to ramble in the country and perish of ennui, to the degradation of such charities and such ambitions as the city can propose to them. They are striking work, and crying out for somewhat worthy to do! What they do is done only because they are overpowered by the humanities that speak on all sides; and they consent to such labor as is open to them, though to their lofty dream the writing of Iliads or Hamlets, or the building of cities or empires seems drudgery.

Now every one must do after his kind, be he asp or angel, and these must. The question which a wise man and a student of modern history will ask, is, what that kind is? And truly, as in ecclesiastical history we take so much pains to know what the Gnostics, what the Essenes, what the Manichees, and what the Reformers believed, it would not misbecome us to inquire nearer home, what these companions and contemporaries of ours think and do, at least so far as these thoughts and actions appear to be not accidental and personal, but common to many, and the inevitable flower of the Tree of Time. Our American literature and spiritual history are, we confess, in the optative mood; but whoso knows these seething brains, these admirable radicals, these unsocial worshippers, these talkers who talk the sun and moon away, will believe that this heresy cannot pass away without leaving its mark.

They are lonely; the spirit of their writing and conversation is lonely; they repel influences; they shun general society; they incline to shut themselves in their chamber in the house, to live in the country rather than in the town, and to find their tasks and amusements in solitude. Society, to be sure, does not like this very well; it saith, Whoso goes to walk alone, accuses the whole world; he declares all to be unfit to be his companions; it is very uncivil, nay, insulting; Society will retaliate. Meantime, this retirement does not proceed from any whim on the part of these separators; but if any one will take pains to talk with them, he will find that this part is chosen both from temperament and from principle; with some unwillingness too, and as a choice of the less of two evils; for these persons are not by nature melancholy, sour, and unsocial—they are not stockish or brute—but joyous, susceptible, affectionate; they have even more than others a great wish to be loved. Like the young Mozart, they are rather ready to cry ten times a day, "But are you sure you love me?" Nay, if they tell you their whole thought, they will own that love seems to them the last and highest gift of nature; that there are persons whom in their hearts they daily thank for existing—persons whose faces are perhaps unknown to them, but whose fame and spirit have penetrated their solitude—and for whose sake they wish to exist. To behold the beauty of another character, which inspires a new interest in our own; to behold the beauty lodged in a human being, with such vivacity of apprehension that I am instantly forced home to inquire if I am not deformity itself; to behold in another the expression of a love so high that it assures itself—assures itself also to me against every possible casualty except my unworthiness; these are degrees on the scale of human happiness to which they have ascended; and it is a fidelity to this sentiment which has made common association distasteful to them. They wish a just and even fellowship, or none. They cannot gossip with you, and they do not wish, as they are sincere and religious, to gratify any mere curiosity which you may entertain. Like fairies, they do not wish to be spoken of. Love me, they say, but do not ask who is my cousin and my uncle. If you do not need to hear my thought, because you can read it in my face and behavior, then I will tell it you from sunrise to sunset. If you cannot divine it, you would not understand what I say. I will not molest myself for you. I do not wish to be profaned.

And yet, it seems as if this loneliness, and not this love, would prevail in their circumstances, because of the extravagant demand they make on human nature. That, indeed, constitutes a new feature in their portrait, that they are the most exacting and extortionate critics. Their quarrel with every man they meet is not with his kind, but with his degree. There is not enough of him—that is the only fault. They prolong their privilege of childhood in this wise; of doing nothing, but making immense demands on all the gladiators in the lists of action and fame. They make us feel the strange disappointment which overcasts every human youth. So many promising youths, and never a finished man! The profound nature will have a savage rudeness; the delicate one will be shallow, or the victim of sensibility; the richly accomplished will have some capital absurdity; and so every piece has a crack. 'T is strange, but this masterpiece is the result of such an extreme delicacy that the most unobserved flaw in the boy will neutralize the most aspiring genius, and spoil the work. Talk with a seaman of the hazards to life in his profession and he will ask you, 'Where are the old sailors? Do you not see that all are young men?' And we, on this sea of human thought, in like manner inquire, Where are the old idealists? where are they who represented to the last generation that extravagant hope which a few happy aspirants suggest to ours? In looking at the class of counsel, and power, and wealth, and at the matronage of the land, amidst all the prudence and all the triviality, one asks, Where are they who represented genius, virtue, the invisible and heavenly world, to these? Are they dead—taken in early ripeness to the gods —as ancient wisdom foretold their fate? Or did the high idea die out of them, and leave their unperfumed body as its tomb and tablet, announcing to all that the celestial inhabitant, who once gave them beauty, had departed? Will it be better with the new generation? We easily predict a fair future to each new candidate who enters the lists, but we are frivolous and volatile, and by low aims and ill example do what we can to defeat this hope. Then these youths bring us a rough but effectual aid. By their unconcealed dissatisfaction they expose our poverty and the insignificance of man to man. A man is a poor limitary benefactor. He ought to be a shower of benefits—a great influence, which should never let his brother go, but should refresh old merits continually with new ones; so that though absent he should never be out of my mind, his name never far from my lips; but if the earth should open at my side, or my last hour were come, his name should be the prayer I should utter to the Universe. But in our experience, man is cheap and friendship wants its deep sense. We affect to dwell with our friends in their absence, but we do not; when deed, word, or letter comes not, they let us go. These exacting children advertise us of our wants. There is no compliment, no smooth speech with them; they pay you only this one compliment, of insatiable expectation; they aspire, they severely exact, and if they only stand fast in this watchtower, and persist in demanding unto the end, and without end, then are they terrible friends, whereof poet and priest cannot choose but stand in awe;

and what if they eat clouds, and drink wind, they have not been without service to the race of man.

With this passion for what is great and extraordinary, it cannot be wondered at that they are repelled by vulgarity and frivolity in people. They say to themselves, It is better to be alone than in bad company. And it is really a wish to be met— the wish to find society for their hope and religion —which prompts them to shun what is called society. They feel that they are never so fit for friendship as when they have quitted mankind and taken themselves to friend. A picture, a book, a favorite spot in the hills or the woods which they can people with the fair and worthy creation of the fancy, can give them often forms so vivid that these for the time shall seem real, and society the illusion.

But their solitary and fastidious manners not only withdraw them from the conversation, but from the labors of the world; they are not good citizens, not good members of society; unwillingly they bear their part of the public and private burdens; they do not willingly share in the public charities, in the public religious rites, in the enterprises of education, of missions foreign and domestic, in the abolition of the slave-trade, or in the temperance society. They do not even like to vote. The philanthropists inquire whether Transcendentalism does not mean sloth: they had as lief hear that their friend is dead, as that he is a Transcendentalist; for then is he paralyzed, and can never do anything for humanity. What right, cries the good world, has the man of genius to retreat from work, and indulge himself? The popular literary creed seems to be, 'I am a sublime genius; I ought not therefore to labor.' But genius is the power to labor better and more availably. Deserve thy genius: exalt it. The good, the illuminated, sit apart from the rest, censuring their dulness and vices, as if they thought that by sitting very grand in their chairs, the very brokers, attorneys, and congressmen would see the error of their ways, and flock to them. But the good and wise must learn to act, and carry salvation to the combatants and demagogues in the dusty arena below.

On the part of these children it is replied that life and their faculty seem to them gifts too rich to be squandered on such trifles as you propose to them. What you call your fundamental institutions, your great and holy causes, seem to them great abuses, and, when nearly seen, paltry matters. Each 'cause' as it is called—say Abolition, Temperance, say Calvinism, or Unitarianism—becomes speedily a little shop, where the article, let it have been at first never so subtle and ethereal, is now made up into portable and convenient cakes, and retailed in small quantities to suit purchasers. You make very free use of these words 'great' and 'holy,' but few things appear to them such. Few persons have any magnificence of nature to inspire enthusiasm, and the philanthropies and charities have a certain air of quackery. As to the general course of living, and the daily employments of men, they cannot see much virtue in these, since they are parts of this vicious circle; and as no great ends are answered by the men, there is nothing noble in the arts by which they are maintained. Nay, they have made the experiment and found that from the liberal professions to the coarsest manual labor, and from the courtesies of the academy and the college to the conventions of the cotillion-room and the morning call, there is a spirit of cowardly compromise and seeming which intimates a frightful skepticism, a life without love, and an activity without an aim.

Unless the action is necessary, unless it is adequate, I do not wish to perform it. I do not wish to do one thing but once. I do not love routine. Once possessed of the principle, it is equally easy to make four or forty thousand applications of it. A great man will be content to have indicated in any the slightest manner his perception of the reigning Idea of his time, and will leave to those who like it the multiplication of examples. When he has hit the white, the rest may shatter the target. Every thing admonishes us how needlessly long life is. Every moment of a hero so raises and cheers us that a twelvemonth is an age. All that the brave Xanthus brings home from his wars is the recollection that at the storming of Samos, "in the heat of the battle, Pericles smiled on me, and passed on to another detachment." It is the quality of the moment, not the number of days, of events, or of actors, but imports.

New, we confess, and by no means happy, is our condition: if you want the aid of our labor, we ourselves stand in greater want of the labor. We are miserable with inaction. We perish of rest and rust: but we do not like your work.

'Then,' says the world, 'show me your own.'

'We have none.'

'What will you do, then?' cries the world.

'We will wait.'

'How long?'

'Until the Universe beckons and calls us to work.'

'But whilst you wait, you grow old and useless.'

'Be it so: I can sit in a corner and *perish* (as you call it), but I will not move until I have the highest command. If no call should come for years, for centuries, then I know that the want of the Universe is the attestation of faith by my abstinence. Your virtuous projects, so called, do not cheer me. I know that which shall come will cheer me. If I cannot work, at least I need not lie. All that is clearly due today is not to lie. In other places other men have encountered sharp trials, and have behaved themselves well. The martyrs were sawn asunder, or hung alive on meat-hooks. Cannot we screw our courage to patience and truth, and without complaint, or even with good-humor, await our turn of action in the Infinite Counsels?'

But to come a little closer to the secret of these persons, we must say that to them it seems a very easy matter to answer the objections of the man of the world, but not so easy to dispose of the doubts and objections that occur to themselves. They are exercised in their own spirit with queries which acquaint them with all adversity, and with the trials of the bravest heroes. When I asked them concerning their private experience, they answered somewhat in this wise: It is not to be denied that there must be some wide difference between my faith and other faith; and mine is a certain brief experience, which surprised me in the highway or in the market, in some place, at some time—whether in the body or out of the body. God knoweth—and made me aware that I had played the fool with fools all this time, but that law existed for me and for all; that to me belonged trust, a child's trust and obedience, and the worship of ideas, and I should never be fool more. Well, in the space of an hour probably, I was let down from this height; I was at my old tricks, the selfish member of a selfish society. My life is superficial, takes no root in the deep world; I ask, When shall I die and be relieved of the responsibility of seeing a Universe I do not use? I wish to exchange this flash-of-lightning faith for continuous daylight, this fever-glow for a benign climate.

These two states of thought diverge every moment, and stand in wild contrast. To him who looks at his life from these moments of illumination, it will seem that he skulks and plays a mean, shiftless and subaltern part in the world. That is to be done which he has not skill to do, or to be said which others can say better, and he lies by, or occupies his hands with some plaything, until his hour comes again. Much of our reading, much of our labor, seems mere waiting; it was not that we were born for. Any other could do it as well or better. So little skill enters into these works, so little do they mix with the divine life, that it really signifies little what we do, whether we turn a grindstone, or ride, or run, or make fortunes, or govern the state. The worst feature of this double consciousness is, that the two lives, of the understanding and of the soul, which we lead, really show very little relation to each other; never meet and measure each other: one prevails now, all buzz and din; and the other prevails then, all infinitude and paradise; and, with the progress of life, the two discover no greater disposition to reconcile themselves. Yet, what is my faith? What am I? What but a thought of serenity and independence, an abode in the deep blue sky? Presently the clouds shut down again; yet we retain the belief that this pretty web we weave will at last be overshot and reticulated with veins of the blue, and that the moments will characterize the days. Patience, then, is for us, is it not? Patience, and still patience. When we pass, as presently we shall, into some new infinitude, out of this Iceland of negations, it will please us to reflect that though we had few virtues or consolations, we bore with our indigence, nor once strove to repair it with hypocrisy or false heat of any kind.

But this class are not sufficiently characterized if we omit to add that they are lovers and worshippers of Beauty. In the eternal trinity of Truth, Goodness, and Beauty, each in its perfection including the three, they prefer to make Beauty the sign and head. Something of the same taste is observable in all the moral movements of the time, in the religious and benevolent enterprises. They have a liberal, even an æsthetic spirit. A reference to Beauty in action sounds, to be sure, a little hollow and ridiculous in the ears of the old church. In politics, it has often sufficed, when they treated of justice, if they kept the bounds of selfish calculation. If they granted restitution, it was prudence which granted it. But the justice which is now claimed for the black, and the pauper, and the drunkard, is for Beauty—is for a necessity to the soul of the agent, not of the beneficiary. I say this is the tendency, not yet the realization. Our virtue totters and trips, does not yet walk firmly. Its representatives are austere; they preach and denounce; their rectitude is not yet a grace. They are still liable to that slight taint of burlesque which in our strange world attaches to the zealot. A saint

should be as dear as the apple of the eye. Yet we are tempted to smile, and we flee from the working to the speculative reformer, to escape that same slight ridicule. Alas for these days of derision and criticism! We call the Beautiful the highest, because it appears to us the golden mean, escaping the dowdiness of the good and the heartlessness of the true. They are lovers of nature also, and find an indemnity in the inviolable order of the world for the violated order and grace of man.

There is, no doubt, a great deal of well-founded objection to be spoken or felt against the sayings and doings of this class, some of whose traits we have selected; no doubt they will lay themselves open to criticism and to lampoons, and as ridiculous stories will be to be told of them as of any. There will be cant and pretension; there will be subtilty and moonshine. These persons are of unequal strength, and do not all prosper. They complain that everything around them must be denied; and if feeble, it takes all their strength to deny, before they can begin to lead their own life. Grave seniors insist on their respect to this institution and that usage; to an obsolete history; to some vocation, or college, or etiquette, or beneficiary, or charity, or morning or evening call, which they resist as what does not concern them. But it costs such sleepless nights, alienations and misgivings— they have so many moods about it; these old guardians never change *their* minds; they have but one mood on the subject, namely, that Antony is very perverse—that it is quite as much as Antony can do to assert his rights, abstain from what he thinks foolish, and keep his temper. He cannot help the reaction of this injustice in his own mind. He is braced-up and stilted; all freedom and flowing genius, all sallies of wit and frolic nature are quite out of the question; it is well if he can keep from lying, injustice, and suicide. This is no time for gaiety and grace. His strength and spirits are wasted in rejection. But the strong spirits overpower those around them without effort. Their thought and emotion comes in like a flood, quite withdraws them from all notice of these carping critics; they surrender themselves with glad heart to the heavenly guide, and only by implication reject the clamorous nonsense of the hour. Grave seniors talk to the deaf—church and old book mumble and ritualize to an unheeding, preoccupied and advancing mind, and thus they by happiness of greater momentum lose no time, but take the right road at first.

But all these of whom I speak are not proficients;

they are novices; they only show the road in which man should travel, when the soul has greater health and prowess. Yet let them feel the dignity of their charge, and deserve a larger power. Their heart is the ark in which the fire is concealed which shall burn in the broader and universal flame. Let them obey the Genius then most when his impulse is wildest; then most when he seems to lead to uninhabitable deserts of thought and life; for the path which the hero travels alone is the highway of health and benefit to mankind. What is the privilege and nobility of our nature but its persistency, through its power to attach itself to what is permanent?

Society also has its duties in reference to this class, and must behold them with what charity it can. Possibly some benefit may yet accrue from them to the state. In our Mechanics' Fair, there must be not only bridges, ploughs, carpenters' planes, and baking troughs, but also some few finer instruments—rain-gauges, thermometers, and telescopes; and in society, besides farmers, sailors, and weavers, there must be a few persons of purer fire kept specially as gauges and meters of character; persons of a fine, detecting instinct, who note the smallest accumulations of wit and feeling in the bystander. Perhaps too there might be room for the exciters and monitors; collectors of the heavenly spark, with power to convey the electricity to others. Or, as the storm-tossed vessel at sea speaks the frigate or 'line packet' to learn its longitude, so it may not be without its advantage that we should now and then encounter rare and gifted men, to compare the points of our spiritual compass, and verify our bearings from superior chronometers.

Amidst the downward tendency and proneness of things, when every voice is raised for a new road or another statute or a subscription of stock; for an improvement in dress, or in dentistry; for a new house or a larger business; for a political party, or the division of an estate; will you not tolerate one or two solitary voices in the land, speaking for thoughts and principles not marketable or perishable? Soon these improvements and mechanical inventions will be superseded; these modes of living lost out of memory; these cities rotted, ruined by war, by new inventions, by new seats of trade, or the geologic changes: all gone, like the shells which sprinkle the sea-beach with a white colony to-day, forever renewed to be forever destroyed. But the thoughts which these few hermits strove to proclaim by silence as well as by speech, not only by what they did, but by what they forbore to do, shall abide in beauty and strength, to reorganize themselves in nature, to invest themselves anew in other, perhaps higher endowed and happier mixed clay than ours, in fuller union with the surrounding system.

Experience (1844)

The relative but poignant skepticism of this essay should be matched, as we have said in the introduction, with the exuberant faith of *Nature*, some eight years earlier. Stephen Whicher has called "Experience" "probably [Emerson's] strongest essay," and in our own confused and skeptical time we are likely to agree.

We draw attention to one of Emerson's most profound and most beguiling statements, a few pages before the end of "Experience": "It is very unhappy, but too late to be helped, the discovery we have made that we exist. That discovery is called the Fall of Man." On the most elementary level, this insight can be illustrated in the observable change of a very young child from natural spontaneity to a certain coy and posturing self-consciousness. The child has discovered, however dimly, that it is a separate self. Emerson's friend Henry James, Sr., the father of William and Henry James, constructed an entire theory of the psychological history of man after (presumably) watching the passage from innocence to self-hood in his children. For the older James, the fall of man was precisely this acquisition of self-awareness, which manifested itself, in the maturing individual, in egotism and self-righteousness. (We do not, of course, mean to imply that these perceptions were reached for the first time in history by Emerson and James. They are presumably as old as human society, when the first father watched the first child acting up. In *intellectual* history, they probably appear first in St. Augustine's *Confessions*. But for various reasons—some of them suggested in the general introduction to the period 1826–1861—the emergence of the self in the individual life, the growth of self-consciousness, was of special and sometimes disturbing import for certain observers in the American nineteenth century.) Human salvation, James argued in various books, involved the shedding of selfhood (a strenuous experience which James called "vastation") and the entrance into what James defined somewhat mystically as "the divine-natural humanity."

Society, to borrow the title of James's most important treatise, was "the redeemed form of man." It is noteworthy that Emerson, in his speculations, never fully envisaged, or anyhow never fully embraced, such a theory of social salvation. He remained committed to the primacy of the individual soul, however imprisoned—as he says in "Experience"—the soul may be in its own subjectivity and peculiarity of temperament. Forays into society and social intercourse were necessary and valuable, but temporary; society, in a later phrase, was mainly a useful place to visit.

But as an exploration of subjectivity, temperament, illusion, and other barriers to true perception, and for the haunting quality of its rhetoric, "Experience" deserves to be pondered at length. Nothing Emerson wrote speaks more directly to our condition.

> *The lords of life, the lords of life,—*
> *I saw them pass*
> *In their own guise,*
> *Like and unlike,*
> *Portly and grim,—*
> *Use and Surprise,*
> *Surface and Dream,*
> *Succession swift and spectral Wrong,*
> *Temperament without a tongue,*
> *And the inventor of the game*
> *Omnipresent without name;—*
> *Some to see, some to be guessed,*
> *They marched from east to west:*
> *Little man, least of all,*
> *Among the legs of his guardians tall,*
> *Walked about with puzzled look.*
> *Him by the hand dear Nature took;*
> *Dearest Nature, strong and kind,*
> *Whispered, "Darling, never mind!*
> *Tomorrow they will wear another face,*
> *The founder thou; these are thy race!"*

Where do we find ourselves? In a series of which we do not know the extremes, and believe that it has none. We wake and find ourselves on a stair; there are stairs below us, which we seem to have ascended; there are stairs above us, many a one, which go upward and out of sight. But the Genius which according to the old belief stands at the door by which we enter, and gives us the lethe to drink, that we may tell no tales, mixed the cup too strongly, and we cannot shake off the lethargy now at noonday. Sleep lingers all our lifetime about our eyes, as night hovers all day in the boughs of the fir-tree. All things swim and glitter. Our life is not so much threatened as our perception. Ghost-like we glide through nature, and should not know our place again. Did our birth fall in some fit of indigence and frugality in nature, that she was so sparing of her fire and so liberal of her earth that it appears to us that we lack the affirmative principle, and though we have health and reason, yet we have no superfluity of spirit for new creation? We have enough to live and bring the year about, but not an ounce to impart or to invest. Ah that our Genius were a little more of a genius! We are like millers on the lower levels of a stream, when the factories above them have exhausted the water. We too fancy that the upper people must have raised their dams.

If any of us knew what we were doing, or where we are going, then when we think we best know! We do not know today whether we are busy or idle. In times when we thought ourselves indolent, we have afterwards discovered that much was accomplished and much was begun in us. All our days are so unprofitable while they pass, that 'tis wonderful where or when we ever got anything of this which we call wisdom, poetry, virtue. We never got it on any dated calendar day. Some heavenly days must have been intercalated somewhere, like those that Hermes won with dice of the Moon, that Osiris might be born. It is said all martyrdoms looked mean when they were suffered. Every ship is a romantic object, except that we sail in. Embark, and the romance quits our vessel and hangs on every other sail in the horizon. Our life looks trivial, and we shun to record it. Men seem to have learned of the horizon the art of perpetual retreating and reference. "Yonder uplands are rich pasturage, and my neighbor has fertile meadow, but my field," says the querulous farmer, "only holds the world together." I quote another man's saying; unluckily that other withdraws himself in the same way, and quotes me. 'Tis the trick of nature thus to degrade today; a good deal of buzz, and somewhere a result slipped magically in. Every roof is agreeable to the eye until it is lifted; then we find tragedy and moaning women and hard-eyed husbands and deluges of lethe, and the men ask, "What's the news?" as if the old were so bad. How many individuals can we count in society? how many actions? how many opinions? So much of our time is preparation, so much is routine, and so much retrospect, that the pith of each man's genius contracts itself to a very few hours. The history of literature—take the net result of Tiraboschi, Warton, or Schlegel—is a sum of very few ideas and of very few original tales; all the rest being variation of these. So in this great society wide lying around us, a critical analysis would find very few spontaneous actions. It is almost all custom and gross sense. There are even few opinions, and these seem organic in the speakers, and do not disturb the universal necessity.

What opium is instilled into all disaster! It shows formidable as we approach it, but there is at last no rough rasping friction, but the most slippery sliding surfaces; we fall soft on a thought; *Ate Dea* is gentle,—

> "Over men's heads walking aloft,
> With tender feet treading so soft."

People grieve and bemoan themselves, but it is not half so bad with them as they say. There are moods in which we court suffering, in the hope that here at least we shall find reality, sharp peaks and edges of truth. But it turns out to be scene-painting and counterfeit. The only thing grief has taught me is to know how shallow it is. That, like all the rest, plays about the surface, and never introduces me into the reality, for contact with which we would even pay the costly price of sons and lovers. Was it Boscovich who found out that bodies never come in contact? Well, souls never touch their objects. An innavigable sea washes with silent waves between us and the things we aim at and converse with. Grief too will make us idealists. In the death of my son, now more than two years ago, I seem to have lost a beautiful estate,—no more. I cannot get it nearer to me. If tomorrow I should be informed of the bankruptcy of my principal debtors, the loss of my property would be a great inconvenience to me, perhaps, for many years; but it would leave me as it found me,—neither better nor worse. So is it with this calamity; it does not touch me; something which I fancied was a part of me, which could not be torn away without tearing me nor enlarged without enriching me, falls off from me and leaves no scar. It was caducous. I grieve that grief can teach me nothing, nor carry me one step into real nature. The Indian who was laid under a curse that the wind should not blow on him, nor water flow to him, nor fire burn him, is a type of us all. The dearest events are summer-rain, and we the Para coats that shed every drop. Nothing is left us now but death. We look to that with a grim satisfaction, saying, There at least is reality that will not dodge us.

I take this evanescence and lubricity of all objects, which lets them slip through our fingers then when we clutch hardest, to be the most unhandsome part of our condition. Nature does not like to be observed, and likes that we should be her fools and playmates. We may have the sphere for our cricket-ball, but not a berry for our philosophy. Direct strokes she never gave us power to make; all our blows glance, all our hits are accidents. Our relations to each other are oblique and casual.

Dream delivers us to dream, and there is no end to illusion. Life is a train of moods like a string of beads, and as we pass through them they prove to be many-colored lenses which paint the world their own hue, and each shows only what lies in its focus. From the mountain you see the mountain. We animate what we can, and we see only what we animate. Nature and books belong to the eyes that see them. It depends on the mood of the man whether he shall see the sunset or the fine poem. There are always sunsets, and there is always genius; but only a few hours so serene that we can relish nature or criticism. The more or less depends on structure or temperament. Temperament is the iron wire on which the beads are strung. Of what use is fortune or talent to a cold and defective nature? Who cares what sensibility or discrimination a man has at some time shown, if he falls asleep in his chair? or if he laugh and giggle? or if he apologize? or is infected with egotism? or thinks of his dollar? or cannot go by food? or has gotten a child in his boyhood? Of what use is genius, if the organ is too convex or too concave and cannot find a focal distance within the actual horizon of human life? Of what use, if the brain is too cold or too hot, and the man does not care enough for results to stimulate him to experiment, and hold him up in it? or if the web is too finely woven, too irritable by pleasure and pain, so that life stagnates from too much reception without due outlet? Of what use to make heroic vows of amendment, if the same old law-breaker is to keep them? What cheer can the religious sentiment yield, when that is suspected to be secretly dependent on the seasons of the year and the state of the blood? I knew a witty physician who found the creed in the biliary duct, and used to affirm that if there was disease in the liver, the man became a Calvinist, and if that organ was sound, he became a Unitarian. Very mortifying is the reluctant experience that some unfriendly excess or imbecility neutralizes the promise of genius. We see young men who owe us a new world, so readily and lavishly they promise, but they never acquit the debt; they die young and dodge the account; or if they live they lose themselves in the crowd.

Temperament also enters fully into the system of illusions and shuts us in a prison of glass which we cannot see. There is an optical illusion about every person we meet. In truth they are all creatures of given temperament, which will appear in a given character, whose boundaries they will never pass; but we look at them, they seem alive, and we presume there is impulse in them. In the moment it seems impulse; in the year, in the lifetime, it turns out to be a certain uniform tune which the revolving barrel of the music-box must play. Men resist the conclusion in the morning, but adopt it as the evening wears on, that temper prevails over everything of time, place and condition, and is inconsumable in the flames of religion. Some modifications the moral sentiment avails to impose, but the individual texture holds its dominion, if not to bias the moral judgments, yet to fix the measure of activity and of enjoyment.

I thus express the law as it is read from the platform of ordinary life, but must not leave it without noticing the capital exception. For temperament is a power which no man willingly hears any one praise but himself. On the platform of physics we cannot resist the contracting influences of so-called science. Temperament puts all divinity to rout. I know the mental proclivity of physicians. I hear the chuckle of the phrenologists. Theoretic kidnappers and slave-drivers, they esteem each man the victim of another, who winds him round his finger by knowing the law of his being; and, by such cheap signboards as the color of his beard or the slope of his occiput, reads the inventory of his fortunes and character. The grossest ignorance does not disgust like this impudent knowingness. The physicians say they are not materialists; but they are:— Spirit is matter reduced to an extreme thinness: O so thin!—But the definition of *spiritual* should

be, *that which is its own evidence.* What notions do they attach to love! what to religion! One would not willingly pronounce these words in their hearing, and give them the occasion to profane them. I saw a gracious gentleman who adapts his conversation to the form of the head of the man he talks with! I had fancied that the value of life lay in its inscrutable possibilities; in the fact that I never know, in addressing myself to a new individual, what may befall me. I hold the keys of my castle in my hand, ready to throw them at the feet of my lord, whenever and in what disguise soever he shall appear, I know he is in the neighborhood, hidden among vagabonds. Shall I preclude my future by taking a high seat and kindly adapting my conversation to the shape of heads? When I come to that, the doctors shall buy me for a cent. —"But, sir, medical history; the report to the Institute; the proven facts."—I distrust the facts and the inferences. Temperament is the veto or limitation-power in the constitution, very justly applied to restrain an opposite excess in the constitution, but absurdly offered as a bar to original equity. When virtue is in presence, all subordinate powers sleep. On its own level, or in view of nature, temperament is final. I see not, if one be once caught in this trap of so-called sciences, any escape for the man from the links of the chain of physical necessity. Given such an embryo, such a history must follow. On this platform one lives in a sty of sensualism, and would soon come to suicide. But it is impossible that the creative power should exclude itself. Into every intelligence there is a door which is never closed, through which the creator passes. The intellect, seeker of absolute truth, or the heart, lover of absolute good, intervenes for our succor, and at one whisper of these high powers we awake from ineffectual struggles with this nightmare. We hurl it into its own hell, and cannot again contract ourselves to so base a state.

The secret of the illusoriness is in the necessity of a succession of moods or objects. Gladly we would anchor, but the anchorage is quicksand. This onward trick of nature is too strong for us: *Pero si muove* [And yet, it does move]. When at night I look at the moon and stars, I seem stationary, and they to hurry. Our love of the real draws us to permanence, but health of body consists in circulation, and sanity of mind in variety or facility of association. We need change of objects. Dedication to one thought is quickly odious. We house with the insane, and must humor them; then conversation dies out. Once I took such delight in Montaigne that I thought I should not need any other book; before that, in Shakespeare; then in Plutarch; then in Plotinus; at one time in Bacon; afterwards in Goethe; even in Bettine; but now I turn the pages of either of them languidly, whilst I still cherish their genius. So with pictures; each will bear an emphasis of attention once, which it cannot retain, though we fain would continue to be pleased in that manner. How strongly I have felt of pictures that when you have seen one well, you must take your leave of it; you shall never see it again. I have had good lessons from pictures which I have since seen without emotion or remark. A deduction must be made from the opinion which even the wise express on a new book or occurrence. Their opinion gives me tidings of their mood, and some vague guess at the new fact, but is nowise to be trusted as the lasting relation between that intellect and that thing. The child asks, "Mamma, why don't I like the story as well as when you told it me yesterday?" Alas! child, it is even so with the oldest cherubim of knowledge. But will it answer thy question to say, Because thou wert born to a whole and this story is a particular? The reason of the pain this discovery causes us (and we make it late in respect to works of art and intellect) is the plaint of tragedy which murmurs from it in regard to persons, to friendship and love.

That immobility and absence of elasticity which we find in the arts, we find with more pain in the artist. There is no power of expansion in men. Our friends early appear to us as representatives of certain ideas which they never pass or exceed. They stand on the brink of the ocean of thought and power, but they never take the single step that would bring them there. A man is like a bit of Labrador spar, which has no lustre as you turn it in your hand until you come to a particular angle; then it shows deep and beautiful colors. There is no adaptation or universal applicability in men, but each has his special talent, and the mastery of successful men consists in adroitly keeping themselves where and when that turn shall be oftenest to be practised. We do what we must, and call it by the best names we can, and would fain have the praise of having intended the result which ensues. I cannot recall any form of man who is not superfluous sometimes. But is not this pitiful? Life is not worth the taking, to do tricks in.

Of course it needs the whole society to give the symmetry we seek. "The party-colored wheel must revolve very fast to appear white." Something is

earned too by conversing with so much folly and defect. In fine, whoever loses, we are always of the gaining party. Divinity is behind our failures and follies also. The plays of children are nonsense, but very educative nonsense. So it is with the largest and solemnest things, with commerce, government, church, marriage, and so with the history of every man's bread, and the ways by which he is to come by it. Like a bird which alights nowhere, but hops perpetually from bough to bough, is the Power which abides in no man and in no woman, but for a moment speaks from this one, and for another moment from that one.

But what help from these fineries or pedantries? What help from thought? Life is not dialectics. We, I think, in these times, have had lessons enough of the futility of criticism. Our young people have thought and written much on labor and reform, and for all that they have written, neither the world nor themselves have got on a step. Intellectual tasting of life will not supersede muscular activity. If a man should consider the nicety of the passage of a piece of bread down his throat, he would starve. At Education Farm the noblest theory of life sat on the noblest figures of young men and maidens, quite powerless and melancholy. It would not rake or pitch a ton of hay; it would not rub down a horse; and the men and maidens it left pale and hungry. A political orator wittily compared our party promises to western roads, which opened stately enough, with planted trees on either side to tempt the traveler, but soon became narrow and narrower and ended in a squirrel-track and ran up a tree. So does culture with us; it ends in headache. Unspeakably sad and barren does life look to those who a few months ago were dazzled with the splendor of the promise of the times. "There is now no longer any right course of action nor any self-devotion left among the Iranis." Objections and criticism we have had our fill of. There are objections to every course of life and action, and the practical wisdom infers an indifferency, from the omnipresence of objection. The whole frame of things preaches indifferency. Do not craze yourself with thinking, but go about your business anywhere. Life is not intellectual or critical, but sturdy. Its chief good is for well-mixed people who can enjoy what they find, without question. Nature hates peeping, and our mothers speak her very sense when they say, "Children, eat your victuals, and say no more of it." To fill the hour, —that is happiness; to fill the hour and leave no crevice for a repentance or an approval. We live amid surfaces, and the true art of life is to skate well on them. Under the oldest moldiest conventions a man of native force prospers just as well as in the newest world, and that by skill of handling and treatment. He can take hold anywhere. Life itself is a mixture of power and form, and will not bear the least excess of either. To finish the moment, to find the journey's end in every step of the road, to live the greatest number of good hours, is wisdom. It is not the part of men, but of fanatics, or of mathematicians if you will, to say that, the shortness of life considered, it is not worth caring whether for so short a duration we were sprawling in want or sitting high. Since our office is with moments, let us husband them. Five minutes of today are worth as much to me as five minutes in the next millennium. Let us be poised, and wise, and our own, today. Let us treat the men and women well; treat them as if they were real; perhaps they are. Men live in their fancy, like drunkards whose hands are too soft and tremulous for successful labor. It is a tempest of fancies, and the only ballast I know is a respect to the present hour. Without any shadow of doubt, amidst this vertigo of shows and politics, I settle myself ever the firmer in the creed that we should not postpone and refer and wish, but do broad justice where we are, by whomsoever we deal with, accepting our actual companions and circumstances, however humble or odious, as the mystic officials to whom the universe has delegated its whole pleasure for us. If these are mean and malignant, their contentment, which is the last victory of justice, is a more satisfying echo to the heart than the voice of poets and the casual sympathy of admirable persons. I think that however a thoughtful man may suffer from the defects and absurdities of his company, he cannot without affectation deny to any set of men and women a sensibility to extraordinary merit. The coarse and frivolous have an instinct of superiority, if they have not a sympathy, and honor it in their blind capricious way with sincere homage.

The fine young people despise life, but in me, and in such as with me are free from dyspepsia, and to whom a day is a sound and solid good, it is a great excess of politeness to look scornful and to cry for company. I am grown by sympathy a little eager and sentimental, but leave me alone and I should relish every hour and what it brought me, the potluck of the day, as heartily as the oldest gossip in the bar-room. I am thankful for small mercies. I compared notes with one of my friends who expects everything of the universe and is disappointed when anything is less than the best, and I found that I begin at the other extreme, expecting nothing, and am always full of thanks for moderate goods. I accept the clangor and jangle of contrary tendencies. I find my account in sots and bores also. They give a reality to the circumjacent picture which such a vanishing meteorous appearance can ill spare. In the morning I awake and find the old world, wife, babes and mother, Concord and Boston, the dear old spiritual world and even the dear old devil not far off. If we will take the good we find, asking no questions, we shall have heaping measures. The great gifts are not got by analysis. Everything good is on the highway. The middle region of our being is the temperate zone. We may climb into the thin and cold realm of pure geometry and lifeless science, or sink into that of sensation. Between these extremes is the equator of life, of thought, of spirit, of poetry,— a narrow belt. Moreover, in popular experience everything good is on the highway. A collector peeps into all the picture-shops of Europe for a landscape of Poussin, a crayon-sketch of Salvator; but the Transfiguration, the Last Judgment, the Communion of Saint Jerome, and what are as transcendent as these, are on the walls of the Vatican, the Uffizi, or the Louvre, where every footman may see them; to say nothing of Nature's pictures in every street, of sunsets and sunrises every day, and the sculpture of the human body never absent. A collector recently bought at public auction, in London, for one hundred and fifty-seven guineas, an autograph of Shakespeare; but for nothing a school-boy can read Hamlet and can detect secrets of highest concernment yet unpublished therein. I think I will never read any but the commonest books,—the Bible, Homer, Dante, Shakespeare and Milton. Then we are impatient of so public a life and planet, and run hither and thither for nooks and secrets. The imagination delights in the woodcraft of Indians, trappers and bee-hunters. We fancy that we are strangers, and not so intimately domesticated in the planet as the wild man and the wild beast and bird. But the exclusion reaches them also; reaches the climbing, flying, gliding, feathered and four-footed man. Fox and woodchuck, hawk and snipe and bittern, when nearly seen, have no more root in the deep world than man, and are just such superficial tenants of the globe. Then the new molecular philosophy shows astronomical interspaces betwixt atom and atom, shows that the world is all outside; it has no inside.

The mid-world is best. Nature, as we know her, is no saint. The lights of the church, the ascetics, Gentoos and corn-eaters, she does not distinguish by any favor. She comes eating and drinking and sinning. Her darlings, the great, the strong, the beautiful, are not children of our law; do not come out of the Sunday School, nor weigh their food, nor punctually keep the commandments. If we will be strong with her strength we must not harbor such disconsolate consciences, borrowed too from the consciences of other nations. We must set up the strong present tense against all the rumors of wrath, past or to come. So many things are unsettled which it is of the first importance to settle; —and, pending their settlement, we will do as we do. Whilst the debate goes forward on the equity of commerce, and will not be closed for a century or two, New and Old England may keep shop. Law of copyright and international copyright is to be discussed, and in the interim we will sell our books for the most we can. Expediency of literature, reason of literature, lawfulness of writing down a thought, is questioned; much is to say on both sides, and, while the fight waxes hot, thou, dearest scholar, stick to thy foolish task, add a line every hour, and between whiles add a line. Right to hold land, right of property, is disputed, and the conventions convene, and before the vote is taken, dig away in your garden, and spend your earnings as a waif or godsend to all serene and beautiful purposes. Life itself is a bubble and a skepticism, and a sleep within a sleep. Grant it, and as much more as they will,—but thou, God's darling! heed thy private dream; thou wilt not be missed in the scorning and skepticism; there are enough of them; stay there in thy closet and toil until the rest are agreed what to do about it. Thy sickness, they say, and thy puny habit require that thou do this or avoid that, but know that thy life is a flitting state, a tent for a night, and do thou, sick or well, finish that stint. Thou art sick, but shalt not be worse, and the universe, which holds thee dear, shall be the better.

Human life is made up of the two elements, power and form, and the proportion must be invariably kept if we would have it sweet and sound. Each of these elements in excess makes a mischief as hurtful as its defect. Everything runs to excess; every good quality is noxious if unmixed, and, to carry the danger to the edge of ruin, nature causes each man's peculiarity to superabound. Here, among the farms, we adduce the scholars as examples of this treachery. They are nature's victims of expression. You who see the artist, the orator, the poet, too near, and find their life no more excellent than that of mechanics or farmers, and themselves victims of partiality, very hollow and haggard, and pronounce them failures, not heroes, but quacks,—conclude very reasonably that these arts are not for man, but are disease. Yet nature will not bear you out. Irresistible nature made men such, and makes legions more of such, every day. You love the boy reading in a book, gazing at a drawing or a cast; yet what are these millions who read and behold, but incipient writers and sculptors? Add a little more of that quality which now reads and sees, and they will seize the pen and chisel. And if one remembers how innocently he began to be an artist, he perceives that nature joined with his enemy. A man is a golden impossibility. The line he must walk is a hair's breadth. The wise through excess of wisdom is made a fool.

How easily, if fate would suffer it, we might keep forever these beautiful limits, and adjust ourselves, once for all, to the perfect calculation of the kingdom of known cause and effect. In the street and in the newspapers, life appears so plain a business that manly resolution and adherence to the multiplication-table through all weathers will insure success. But ah! presently comes a day, or is it only a half-hour, with its angel-whispering,—which discomfits the conclusions of nations and of years! Tomorrow again every thing looks real and angular, the habitual standards are reinstated, common-sense is as rare as genius,—is the basis of genius, and experience is hands and feet to every enterprise;—and yet, he who should do his business on this understanding would be quickly bankrupt. Power keeps quite another road than the turnpikes of choice and will; namely the subterranean and invisible tunnels and channels of life. It is ridiculous that we are diplomatists, and doctors, and considerate people; there are no dupes like these. Life is a series of surprises, and would not be worth taking or keeping if it were not. God delights to isolate us every day, and hide from us the past and the future. We would look about us, but with grand politeness he draws down before us an impenetrable screen of purest sky, and another behind us of purest sky. "You will not remember," he seems to say, "and you will not expect." All good conversation, manners and action come from a spontaneity which forgets usages and makes the moment great. Nature hates calculators; her methods are saltatory and impulsive. Man lives by pulses; our organic movements are such; and the chemical and ethereal agents are undulatory and alternate; and the mind goes antagonizing on, and never prospers but by fits. We thrive by casualties. Our chief experiences have been casual. The most attractive class of people are those who are powerful obliquely and not by the direct stroke; men of genius, but not yet accredited; one gets the cheer of their light without paying too great a tax. Theirs is the beauty of the bird or the morning light, and not of art. In the thought of genius there is always a surprise; and the moral sentiment is well called "the newness," for it is never other; as new to the oldest intelligence as to the young child;—"the kingdom that cometh without observation." In like manner, for practical success, there must not be too much design. A man will not be observed in doing that which he can do best. There is a certain magic about his properest action which stupefies your powers of observation, so that though it is done before you, you wist not of it. The art of life has a pudency, and will not be exposed. Every man is an impossibility until he is born; every thing impossible until we see a success. The ardors of piety agree at last with the coldest skepticism,— that nothing is of us or our works,—that all is of God. Nature will not spare us the smallest leaf of laurel. All writing comes by the grace of God, and all doing and having. I would gladly be moral and keep due metes and bounds, which I dearly love, and allow the most to the will of man; but I have set my heart on honesty in this chapter, and I can see nothing at last, in success or failure, than more or less of vital force supplied from the Eternal. The results of life are uncalculated and uncalculable. The years teach much which the days never know. The persons who compose our company converse, and come and go, and design and execute many things, and somewhat comes of it all, but an unlooked-for result. The individual is always mistaken. He designed many things, and drew in other persons as coadjutors, quarreled with some or all, blundered much, and something is done; all are a little advanced, but the individual is always mistaken. It turns out somewhat new and very unlike what he promised himself.

The ancients, struck with this irreducibleness of the elements of human life to calculation, exalted Chance into a divinity; but that is to stay too long at the spark, which glitters truly at one point, but the universe is warm with the latency of the same fire. The miracle of life which will not be expounded but will remain a miracle, introduces a new element. In the growth of the embryo, Sir Everard Home I think noticed that the evolution was not from one central point, but coactive from three or more points. Life has no memory. That which proceeds in succession might be remembered, but that which is coexistent, or ejaculated from a deeper cause, as yet far from being conscious, knows not its own tendency. So is it with us, now skeptical or without unity, because immersed in forms and effects all seeming to be of equal yet hostile value, and now religious, whilst in the reception of spiritual law. Bear with these distractions, with this coetaneous growth of the parts; they will one day be *members*, and obey one will. On that one will, on that secret cause, they nail our attention and hope. Life is hereby melted into an expectation or a religion. Underneath the inharmonious and trivial particulars, is a musical perfection: the Ideal journeying always with us, the heaven without rent or seam. Do but observe the mode of our illumination. When I converse with a profound mind, or if at any time being alone I have good thoughts, I do not at once arrive at satisfactions, as when, being thirsty, I drink water; or go to the fire, being cold; no! but I am at first apprised of my vicinity to a new and excellent region of life. By persisting to read or to think, this region gives further sign of itself, as it were in flashes of light, in sudden discoveries of its profound beauty and repose, as if the clouds that covered it parted at intervals and showed the approaching traveler the inland mountains, with the tranquil eternal meadows spread at their base, whereon flocks graze and shepherds pipe and dance. But every insight from this realm of thought is felt as initial, and promises a sequel. I do not make it; I arrive there, and behold what was there already. I make! O no! I clap my hands in infantine joy and amazement before the first opening to me of this august magnificence, old with the love and homage of innumerable ages, young with the life of life, the sunbright Mecca of the desert. And what a future it opens! I feel a new heart beating with the love of the new beauty. I am ready to die out of nature and be born again into this new yet unapproachable America I have found in the West:—

"Since neither now nor yesterday began
These thoughts, which have been ever, nor yet can
A man be found who their first entrance knew."

If I have described life as a flux of moods, I must now add that there is that in us which changes not and which ranks all sensations and states of mind. The consciousness in each man is a sliding scale, which identifies him now with the First Cause, and now with the flesh of his body; life above life, in infinite degrees. The sentiment from which it sprung determines the dignity of any deed, and the question ever is, not what you have done or forborne, but at whose command you have done or forborne it.

Fortune, Minerva, Muse, Holy Ghost,—these are quaint names, too narrow to cover this unbounded substance. The baffled intellect must still kneel before this cause, which refuses to be named,—ineffable cause, which every fine genius has essayed to represent by some emphatic symbol, as, Thales by water, Anaximenes by air, Anaxagoras by (Noûs) thought, Zoroaster by fire, Jesus and the moderns by love; and the metaphor of each has become a national religion. The Chinese Mencius has not been the least successful in his generalization. "I fully understand language," he said, "and nourish well my vast-flowing vigor."—"I beg to ask what you call vast-flowing vigor?" said his companion. "The explanation," replied Mencius, "is difficult. This vigor is supremely great, and in the highest degree unbending. Nourish it correctly and do it no injury, and it will fill up the vacancy between heaven and earth. This vigor accords with and assists justice and reason, and leaves no hunger."—In our more correct writing we give to this generalization the name of Being, and thereby confess that we have arrived as far as we can go. Suffice it for the joy of the universe that we have not arrived at a wall, but at interminable oceans. Our life seems not present so much as prospective; not for the affairs on which it is wasted, but as a hint of this vast-flowing vigor. Most of life seems to be mere advertisement of faculty; information is given us not to sell ourselves cheap; that we are very great. So, in particulars, our greatness is always in a tendency or direction, not in an action. It is for us to believe in the rule, not in the exception. The noble are thus known from the ignoble. So in accepting the leading of the sentiments, it is not what we believe concerning the immortality of the soul or the like, but *the universal impulse to believe*, that is the material circumstance and is the principal fact in the history of the globe. Shall we describe this cause as that which works directly? The spirit is not helpless or needful of mediate organs. It has plentiful powers and direct effects. I am explained without explaining, I am felt without acting, and where I am not. Therefore all just persons are satisfied with their own praise. They refuse to explain themselves, and are content that new actions should do them that office. They believe that we communicate without speech and above speech, and that no right action of ours is quite unaffecting to our friends, at whatever distance; for the influence of action is not to be measured by miles. Why should I fret myself because a circumstance has occurred which hinders my presence where I was expected? If I am not at the meeting, my presence where I am should be as useful to the commonwealth of friendship and wisdom, as would be my presence in that place. I exert the same quality of power in all places. Thus journeys the mighty Ideal before us; it never was known to fall into the rear. No man ever came to an experience which was satiating, but his good is tidings of a better. Onward and onward! In liberated moments we know that a new picture of life and duty is already possible; the elements already exist in many minds around you of a doctrine of life which shall transcend any written record we have. The new statement will comprise the skepticisms as well as the faiths of society, and out of unbeliefs a creed shall be formed. For skepticisms are not gratuitous or lawless, but are limitations of the affirmative statement, and the new philosophy must take them in and make affirmations outside of them, just as much as it must include the oldest beliefs.

It is very unhappy, but too late to be helped, the discovery we have made that we exist. That discovery is called the Fall of Man. Ever afterwards we suspect our instruments. We have learned that we do not see directly, but mediately, and that we have no means of correcting these colored and distorting lenses which we are, or of computing the amount of their errors. Perhaps these subject-lenses have a creative power; perhaps there are no objects. Once we lived in what we saw; now, the rapaciousness of this new power, which threatens to absorb all things, engages us. Nature, art, persons, letters, religions, objects, successively tumble in, and God is but one of its ideas. Nature and literature are subjective phenomena; every evil and every good thing is a shadow which we cast. The street is full of humiliations to the proud. As the fop contrived to dress his bailiffs in his livery and make them wait on his guests at table, so the chagrins which the bad heart gives off as bubbles, at once take form as ladies and gentlemen in the street, shopmen or bar-keepers in hotels, and threaten or insult whatever is threatenable and insultable in us. 'Tis the same with our idolatries. People forget that it is the eye which makes the horizon, and the rounding mind's eye which makes this or that man a type or representative of humanity, with the name of hero or saint. Jesus, the "providential man," is a good man on whom many people are agreed that these optical laws shall take effect. By love on one part and by forbearance to press objection on the other part, it is for a time settled that we will look at him in the center of the horizon, and ascribe to him the properties that will attach to any man so seen. But the longest love or aversion has a speedy term. The great and crescive self, rooted in absolute nature, supplants all relative existence and ruins the kingdom of mortal friendship and love. Marriage (in what is called the spiritual world) is impossible, because of the inequality between every subject and every object. The subject is the receiver of Godhead, and at every comparison must feel his being enhanced by that cryptic might. Though not in energy, yet by presence, this magazine of substance cannot be otherwise than felt; nor can any force of intellect attribute to the object the proper deity which sleeps or wakes forever in every subject. Never can love make consciousness and ascription equal in force. There will be the same gulf between every me and thee as between the original and the picture. The universe is the bride of the soul. All private sympathy is partial. Two human beings are like globes, which can touch only in a point, and whilst they remain in contact all other points of each of the spheres are inert; their turn must also come, and the longer a particular union lasts the more energy of appetency the parts not in union acquire.

Life will be imaged, but cannot be divided nor doubled. Any invasion of its unity would be chaos. The soul is not twin-born but the only begotten, and though revealing itself as child in time, child in appearance, is of a fatal and universal power, admitting no co-life. Every day, every act betrays the ill-concealed deity. We believe in ourselves as we do not believe in others. We permit all things to ourselves, and that which we call sin in others is experiment for us. It is an instance of our faith in ourselves that men never speak of crime as lightly as they think; or every man thinks a latitude safe for himself which is no wise to be indulged to another. The act looks very differently on the inside and on the outside; in its quality and in its consequences. Murder in the murderer is no such

ruinous thought as poets and romancers will have it; it does not unsettle him or fright him from his ordinary notice of trifles; it is an act quite easy to be contemplated; but in its sequel it turns out to be a horrible jangle and confounding of all relations. Especially the crimes that spring from love seem right and fair from the actor's point of view, but when acted are found destructive of society. No man at last believes that he can be lost, or that the crime in him is as black as in the felon. Because the intellect qualifies in our own case the moral judgments. For there is no crime to the intellect. That is antinomian or hypernomian, and judges law as well as fact. "It is worse than a crime, it is a blunder," said Napoleon, speaking the language of the intellect. To it, the world is a problem in mathematics or the science of quantity, and it leaves out praise and blame and all weak emotions. All stealing is comparative. If you come to absolutes, pray who does not steal? Saints are sad, because they behold sin (even when they speculate) from the point of view of the conscience, and not of the intellect; a confusion of thought. Sin, seen from the thought, is a diminution, or *less*; seen from the conscience or will, it is pravity or *bad*. The intellect names it shade, absence of light, and no essence. The conscience must feel it as essence, essential evil. This it is not; it has an objective existence, but no subjective.

Thus inevitably does the universe wear our color, and every object fall successively into the subject itself. The subject exists, the subject enlarges; all things sooner or later fall into place. As I am, so I see; use what language we will, we can never say anything but what we are; Hermes, Cadmus, Columbus, Newton, Bonaparte, are the mind's ministers. Instead of feeling a poverty when we encounter a great man, let us treat the new-comer like a traveling geologist who passes through our estate and shows us good slate, or limestone, or anthracite, in our brush pasture. The partial action of each strong mind in one direction is a telescope for the objects on which it is pointed. But every other part of knowledge is to be pushed to the same extravagance, ere the soul attains her due sphericity. Do you see that kitten chasing so prettily her own tail? If you could look with her eyes you might see her surrounded with hundreds of figures performing complex dramas, with tragic and comic issues, long conversations, many characters, many ups and downs of fate,—and meantime it is only puss and her tail. How long before our masquerade will end its noise of tambourines, laughter and shouting, and we shall find it was a solitary performance? A subject and an object,—it takes so much to make the galvanic circuit complete, but magnitude adds nothing. What imports it whether it is Kepler and the sphere, Columbus and America, a reader and his book, or puss with her tail?

It is true that all the muses and love and religion hate these developments, and will find a way to punish the chemist who publishes in the parlor the secrets of the laboratory. And we cannot say too little of our constitutional necessity of seeing things under private aspects, or saturated with our humors. And yet is the God the native of these bleak rocks. That need makes in morals the capital virtue of self-trust. We must hold hard to this poverty, however scandalous, and by more vigorous self-recoveries, after the sallies of action, possess our axis more firmly. The life of truth is cold and so far mournful; but it is not the slave of tears, contritions and perturbations. It does not attempt another's work, nor adopt another's facts. It is a main lesson of wisdom to know your own from another's. I have learned that I cannot dispose of other people's facts; but I possess such a key to my own as persuades me, against all their denials, that they also have a key to theirs. A sympathetic person is placed in the dilemma of a swimmer among drowning men, who all catch at him, and if he give so much as a leg or a finger they will drown him. They wish to be saved from the mischiefs of their vices, but not from their vices. Charity would be wasted on this poor waiting on the symptoms. A wise and hardy physician will say, *Come out of that*, as the first condition of advice.

In this our talking America we are ruined by our good nature and listening on all sides. This compliance takes away the power of being greatly useful. A man should not be able to look other than directly and forthright. A preoccupied attention is the only answer to the importunate frivolity of other people; an attention, and to an aim which makes their wants frivolous. This is a divine answer, and leaves no appeal and no hard thoughts. In Flaxman's drawing of the Eumenides of Aeschylus, Orestes supplicates Apollo, whilst the Furies sleep on the threshold. The face of the god expresses a shade of regret and compassion, but is calm with the conviction of the irreconcilableness of the two spheres. He is born into other politics, into the eternal and beautiful. The man at his feet asks for his interest in turmoils of the earth, into which his nature cannot enter. And the Eumenides there

lying express pictorially this disparity. The god is surcharged with his divine destiny.

Illusion, Temperament, Succession, Surface, Surprise, Reality, Subjectiveness,—these are threads on the loom of time, these are the lords of life. I dare not assume to give their order, but I name them as I find them in my way. I know better than to claim any completeness for my picture. I am a fragment, and this is a fragment of me. I can very confidently announce one or another law, which throws itself into relief and form, but I am too young yet by some ages to compile a code. I gossip for my hour concerning the eternal politics. I have seen many fair pictures not in vain. A wonderful time I have lived in. I am not the novice I was fourteen, nor yet seven years ago. Let who will ask, Where is the fruit? I find a private fruit sufficient. This a fruit,—that I should not ask for a rash effect from meditations, counsels and the hiving of truths. I should feel it pitiful to demand a result on this town and country, an overt effect on the instant month and year. The effect is deep and secular as the cause. It works on periods in which mortal lifetime is lost. All I know is reception; I am and I have: but I do not get, and when I have fancied I had gotten anything, I found I did not. I worship with wonder the great Fortune. My reception has been so large, that I am not annoyed by receiving this or that superabundantly. I say to the Genius, if he will pardon the proverb, *In for a mill, in for a million*. When I receive a new gift, I do not macerate my body to make the account square, for if I should die I could not make the account square. The benefit overran the merit the first day, and has overrun the merit ever since. The merit itself, so-called, I reckon part of the receiving.

Also that hankering after an overt or practical effect seems to me an apostasy. In good earnest I am willing to spare this most unnecessary deal of doing. Life wears to me a visionary face. Hardest roughest action is visionary also. It is but a choice between soft and turbulent dreams. People disparage knowing and the intellectual life, and urge doing. I am very content with knowing, if only I could know. That is an august entertainment, and would suffice me a great while. To know a little would be worth the expense of this world. I hear always the law of Adrastia, "that every soul which had acquired any truth, should be safe from harm until another period."

I know that the world I converse with in the city

and in the farms, is not the world I *think*. I observe that difference, and shall observe it. One day I shall know the value and law of this discrepance. But I have not found that much was gained by manipular attempts to realize the world of thought. Many eager persons successively make an experiment in this way, and make themselves ridiculous. They acquire democratic manners, they foam at the mouth, they hate and deny. Worse, I observe that in the history of mankind there is never a solitary example of success,—taking their own tests of success. I say this polemically, or in reply to the inquiry, Why not realize your world? But far be from me the despair which prejudges the law by a paltry empiricism;—since there never was a right endeavor but it succeeded. Patience and pa-

tience, we shall win at the last. We must be very suspicious of the deceptions of the element of time. It takes a good deal of time to eat or to sleep, or to earn a hundred dollars and a very little time to entertain a hope and an insight which becomes the light of our life. We dress our garden, eat our dinners, discuss the household with our wives, and these things make no impression, are forgotten next week; but, in the solitude to which every man is always returning, he has a sanity and revelations which in his passage into new worlds he will carry with him. Never mind the ridicule, never mind the defeat; up again, old heart!—it seems to say,—there is victory yet for all justice; and the true romance which the world exists to realize will be the transformation of genius into practical power.

From Thoreau (1862)

Thoreau died in May, 1862, in Concord, at the age of forty-four, and Emerson made the funeral address (with certain additions, it was published a few months later in the *Atlantic Monthly*). As Emerson says here, Thoreau had been a remarkably healthy man for most of his life and had kept himself perfectly fit by his spartan mode of life. But consumption ran in his family, and Thoreau was stricken by it in the winter of 1862 after sitting out in the snow for long hours counting the growth rings on some stumps.

Emerson had known Thoreau (whom he probably called "Thurugh," in the New England way) for a quarter of a century, and the two had been as intimate as either permitted any other human being to be—which was not very intimate. Emerson's address does not omit mention of the abrasive side of Thoreau's nature, his congenital impulses to contradict whatever statement an interlocutor might make, his prickly independence. But all that is absorbed within the warm and high esteem Emerson had for this extraordinary individual, whose genius Emerson had been the first to detect—and which he had every opportunity to observe at close hand, in his own house and on his own estate. (Other aspects of the relation between

the two men are discussed in the introductions to the writings of each.)

Henry David Thoreau was the last male descendant of a French ancestor who came to this country from the Isle of Guernsey. His character exhibited occasional traits drawn from this blood, in singular combination with a very strong Saxon genius.

He was born in Concord, Massachusetts, on the 12th of July, 1817. He was graduated at Harvard College in 1837, but without any literary distinction. An iconoclast in literature, he seldom thanked colleges for their service to him, holding them in small esteem, whilst yet his debt to them was important. After leaving the University, he joined his brother in teaching a private school, which he soon renounced. His father was a manufacturer of lead-pencils, and Henry applied himself for a time to this craft, believing he could make a better pencil than was then in use. After completing his experiments, he exhibited his work to chemists and artists in Boston, and having obtained their certificates to its excellence and to its equality with the best London manufacture, he returned home contented. His friends congratulated him that he had now opened his way to fortune. But he replied that he should never make another pencil. "Why should I? I would not do again what I have done once." He resumed his endless walks and miscellaneous studies, making every day some new acquaintance with Nature, though as yet never speaking of zoölogy or botany, since, though very studious of natural facts, he was incurious of technical and textual science.

At this time, a strong, healthy youth, fresh from college, whilst all his companions were choosing their profession, or eager to begin some lucrative employment, it was inevitable that his thoughts should be exercised on the same question, and it required rare decision to refuse all the accustomed paths and keep his solitary freedom at the cost of disappointing the natural expectations of his family and friends: all the more difficult that he had a perfect probity, was exact in securing his own independence, and in holding every man to the like duty. But Thoreau never faltered. He was a born protestant. He declined to give up his large ambition of knowledge and action for any narrow craft or profession, aiming at a much more comprehensive calling, the art of living well. If he slighted and defied the opinions of others, it was only that he was more intent to reconcile his practice with his own belief. Never idle or self-indulgent, he preferred, when he wanted money, earning it by some piece of manual labor agreeable to him, as building a boat or a fence, planting, grafting, surveying or other short work, to any long engagements. With his hardy habits and few wants, his skill in wood-craft, and his powerful arithmetic, he was very competent to live in any part of the world. It would cost him less time to supply his wants than another. He was therefore secure of his leisure.

A natural skill for mensuration, growing out of his mathematical knowledge and his habit of ascertaining the measures and distances of objects which interested him, the size of trees, the depth and extent of ponds and rivers, the height of mountains and the air-line distance of his favorite summits,—this, and his intimate knowledge of the territory about Concord, made him drift into the profession of land-surveyor. It had the advantage for him that it led him continually into new and secluded grounds, and helped his studies of Nature. His accuracy and skill in this work were readily appreciated, and he found all the employment he wanted.

He could easily solve the problems of the surveyor, but he was daily beset with graver questions, which he manfully confronted. He interrogated every custom, and wished to settle all his practice on an ideal foundation. He was a protestant à outrance, and few lives contain so many renunciations. He was bred to no profession; he never married; he lived alone; he never went to church; he never voted; he refused to pay a tax to the State; he ate no flesh, he drank no wine, he never knew the use of tobacco; and, though a naturalist, he used neither trap nor gun. He chose, wisely no doubt for himself, to be the bachelor of thought and Nature. He had no talent for wealth, and knew how to be poor without the least hint of squalor or inelegance. Perhaps he fell into his way of living without forecasting it much, but approved it with later wisdom. "I am often reminded," he wrote in his journal, "that if I had bestowed on me the wealth of Crœsus, my aims must be still the same, and my means essentially the same." He had no temptations to fight against, —no appetites, no passions, no taste for elegant trifles. A fine house, dress, the manners and talk of highly cultivated people were all thrown away on him. He much preferred a good Indian, and considered these refinements as impediments to conversation, wishing to meet his companion on the simplest terms. He declined invitations to dinner-parties, because there each was in every one's way, and he could not meet the individuals to any purpose. "They make their pride," he said, "in making their dinner cost much; I make my pride in making my dinner cost little." When asked at table what dish he preferred, he answered, "The nearest." He did not like the taste of wine, and never had a vice in his life. He said,—"I have a faint recollection of pleasure derived from smoking dried lily-stems, before I was a man. I had commonly a supply of these. I have never smoked anything more noxious."

He chose to be rich by making his wants few, and supplying them himself. In his travels, he used the railroad only to get over so much country as was unimportant to the present purpose, walking hundreds of miles, avoiding taverns, buying a lodging in farmers' and fishermen's houses, as cheaper, and more agreeable to him, and because there he could better find the men and the information he wanted.

There was somewhat military in his nature, not to be subdued, always manly and able, but rarely tender, as if he did not feel himself except in opposition. He wanted a fallacy to expose, a blunder to pillory, I may say required a little sense of victory, a roll of the drum, to call his powers into full exercise. It cost him nothing to say No; indeed he found it much easier than to say Yes.

It seemed as if his first instinct on hearing a proposition was to controvert it, so impatient was he of the limitations of our daily thought. This habit, of course, is a little chilling to the social affections; and though the companion would in the end acquit him of any malice or untruth, yet it mars conversation. Hence, no equal companion stood in affectionate relations with one so pure and guileless. "I love Henry," said one of his friends, "but I cannot like him; and as for taking his arm, I should as soon think of taking the arm of an elm-tree."

Yet, hermit and stoic as he was, he was really fond of sympathy, and threw himself heartily and childlike into the company of young people whom he loved, and whom he delighted to entertain, as he only could, with the varied and endless anecdotes of his experiences by field and river: and he was always ready to lead a huckleberry-party or a search for chestnuts or grapes. Talking, one day, of a public discourse, Henry remarked that whatever succeeded with the audience was bad. I said, "Who would not like to write something which all can read, like Robinson Crusoe? and who does not see with regret that his page is not solid with a right materialistic treatment, which delights everybody?" Henry objected, of course, and vaunted the better lectures which reached only a few persons. But, at supper, a young girl, understanding that he was to lecture at the Lyceum, sharply asked him, "Whether his lecture would be a nice, interesting story, such as she wished to hear, or whether it was one of those old philosophical things that she did not care about." Henry turned to her, and bethought himself, and, I saw, was trying to believe that he had matter that might fit her and her brother, who were to sit up and go to the lecture, if it was a good one for them.

He was a speaker and actor of the truth, born such, and was ever running into dramatic situations from this cause. In any circumstance it interested all bystanders to know what part Henry would take, and what he would say; and he did not disappoint expectation, but used an original judgment on each emergency. In 1845 he built himself a small framed house on the shores of Walden Pond, and lived there two years alone, a life of labor and study. This action was quite native and fit for him. No one who knew him would tax him with affectation. He was more unlike his neighbors in his thought than in his action. As soon as he had exhausted the advantages of that solitude, he abandoned it. In 1847, not approving some uses to which the public expenditure was applied, he refused to pay his town tax, and was put in jail. A friend paid the tax for him, and he was released. The like annoyance was threatened the next year. But as his friends paid the tax, notwithstanding his protest, I believe he ceased to resist. No opposition or ridicule had any weight with him. He coldly and fully stated his opinion without affecting to believe that it was the opinion of the company. It was of no consequence if every one present held the opposite opinion. On one occasion he went to the University Library to procure some books. The librarian refused to lend them. Mr. Thoreau repaired to the President, who stated to him the rules and usages, which permitted the loan of books to resident graduates, to clergymen who were alumni, and to some others resident within a circle of ten miles' radius from the College. Mr. Thoreau explained to the President that the railroad had destroyed the old scale of distances,—that the library was useless, yes, and President and College useless, on the terms of his rules,—that the one benefit he owed to the College was its library,—that, at this moment, not only his want of books was imperative, but he wanted a large number of books, and assured him that he, Thoreau, and not the librarian, was the proper custodian of these. In short, the President found the petitioner so formidable, and the rules getting to look so ridiculous, that he ended by giving him a privilege which in his hands proved unlimited thereafter.

No truer American existed than Thoreau. His preference of his country and condition was genuine, and his aversation from English and European manners and tastes almost reached contempt. He listened impatiently to news or *bonmots* gleaned from London circles; and though he tried to be civil, these anecdotes fatigued him. The men were all imitating each other, and on a small mould. Why can they not live as far apart as possible, and each be a man by himself? What he sought was the most energetic nature; and he wished to go to Oregon, not to London. "In every part of Great Britain," he wrote in his diary, "are discovered traces of the Romans, their funereal urns, their camps, their roads, their dwellings. But New England, at least, is not based on any Roman ruins. We have not to lay the foundations of our houses on the ashes of a former civilization."

But idealist as he was, standing for abolition of slavery, abolition of tariffs, almost for abolition of government, it is needless to say he found himself not only unrepresented in actual politics, but almost equally opposed to every class of reformers. Yet he paid the tribute of his uniform respect to the Anti-Slavery party. One man, whose personal acquaintance he had formed, he honored with exceptional regard. Before the first friendly word had been spoken for Captain John Brown, he sent notices to most houses in Concord that he would speak in a public hall on the condition and character of John Brown, on Sunday evening, and invited all people to come. The Republican Committee, the Abolitionist Committee, sent him word that it was premature and not advisable. He replied,—"I did not send to you for advice, but to announce that I am to speak." The hall was filled at an early hour by people of all parties, and his earnest eulogy of the hero was heard by all respectfully, by many with a sympathy that surprised themselves.

It was said of Plotinus that he was ashamed of his body, and 't is very likely he had good reason for it,—that his body was a bad servant, and he had not skill in dealing with the material world, as happens often to men of abstract intellect. But Mr. Thoreau was equipped with a most adapted and serviceable body. He was of short stature, firmly built, of light complexion, with strong, serious blue eyes, and a grave aspect,—his face covered in the late years with a becoming beard. His senses were acute, his frame well-knit and hardy, his hands strong and skilful in the use of tools. And there was a wonderful fitness of body and mind. He could pace sixteen rods more accurately than another man could measure them with rod and chain. He could find his path in the woods at night, he said, better by his feet than his eyes. He could estimate the measure of a tree very well by his eye; he could estimate the weight of a calf or a pig, like a dealer. From a box containing a bushel or more of loose pencils, he could take up with his hands fast enough just a dozen pencils at every grasp. He was a good swimmer, runner, skater, boatman, and would probably outwalk most countrymen in a day's journey. And the relation of body to mind was still finer than we have indicated. He said he wanted every stride his legs made. The length of his walk uniformly made the length of his writing. If shut up in the house he did not write at all.

He had a strong common sense, like that which Rose Flammock, the weaver's daughter in Scott's romance, commends in her father, as resembling a yardstick, which, whilst it measures dowlas and diaper, can equally well measure tapestry and cloth of gold. He had always a new resource. When I

was planting forest trees, and had procured half a peck of acorns, he said that only a small portion of them would be sound, and proceeded to examine them and select the sound ones. But finding this took time, he said, "I think if you put them all into water the good ones will sink"; which experiment we tried with success. He could plan a garden or a house or a barn; would have been competent to lead a "Pacific Exploring Expedition"; could give judicious counsel in the gravest private or public affairs.

He lived for the day, not cumbered and mortified by his memory. If he brought you yesterday a new proposition, he would bring you to-day another not less revolutionary. A very industrious man, and setting, like all highly organized men, a high value on his time, he seemed the only man of leisure in town, always ready for any excursion that promised well, or for conversation prolonged into late hours. His trenchant sense was never stopped by his rules of daily prudence, but was always up to the new occasion. He liked and used the simplest food, yet, when some one urged a vegetable diet, Thoreau thought all diets a very small matter, saying that "the man who shoots the buffalo lives better than the man who boards at the Graham House." He said,—"You can sleep near the railroad, and never be disturbed: Nature knows very well what sounds are worth attending to, and has made up her mind not to hear the railroad-whistle. But things respect the devout mind, and a mental ecstasy was never interrupted." He noted what repeatedly befell him, that, after receiving from a distance a rare plant, he would presently find the same in his own haunts. And those pieces of luck which happen only to good players happened to him. One day, walking with a stranger, who inquired where Indian arrowheads could be found, he replied, "Everywhere," and, stooping forward, picked one on the instant from the ground. At Mount Washington, in Tuckerman's Ravine, Thoreau had a bad fall, and sprained his foot. As he was in the act of getting up from his fall, he saw for the first time the leaves of the *Arnica mollis*.

His robust common sense, armed with stout hands, keen perceptions and strong will, cannot yet account for the superiority which shone in his simple and hidden life. I must add the cardinal fact, that there was an excellent wisdom in him, proper to a rare class of men, which showed him the material world as a means and symbol. This discovery, which sometimes yields to poets a certain casual and interrupted light, serving for the ornament of their writing, was in him an unsleeping insight; and whatever faults or obstructions of temperament might cloud it, he was not disobedient to the heavenly vision. In his youth, he said, one day, "The other world is all my art; my pencils will draw no other; my jack-knife will cut nothing else; I do not use it as a means." This was the muse and genius that ruled his opinions, conversation, studies, work and course of life. This made him a searching judge of men. At first glance he measured his companion, and, though insensible to some fine traits of culture, could very well report his weight and calibre. And this made the impression of genius which his conversation sometimes gave.

He understood the matter in hand at a glance, and saw the limitations and poverty of those he talked with, so that nothing seemed concealed from such terrible eyes. I have repeatedly known young men of sensibility converted in a moment to the belief that this was the man they were in search of, the man of men, who could tell them all they should do. His own dealing with them was never affectionate, but superior, didactic, scorning their petty ways,—very slowly conceding, or not conceding at all, the promise of his society at their houses, or even at his own. "Would he not walk with them?" "He did not know. There was nothing so important to him as his walk; he had no walks to throw away on company." Visits were offered him from respectful parties, but he declined them. Admiring friends offered to carry him at their own cost to the Yellowstone River,—to the West Indies,—to South America. . . .

. . .

His poetry might be bad or good; he no doubt wanted a lyric facility and technical skill, but he had the source of poetry in his spiritual perception. He was a good reader and critic, and his judgment on poetry was to the ground of it. He could not be deceived as to the presence or absence of the poetic element in any composition, and his thirst for this made him negligent and perhaps scornful of superficial graces. He would pass by many delicate rhythms, but he would have detected every live stanza or line in a volume and knew very well where to find an equal poetic charm in prose. He was so enamoured of the spiritual beauty that he held all actual written poems in very light esteem in the comparison. He admired Æschylus and Pindar; but when some one was commending them, he said that Æschylus and the Greeks, in describing Apollo and Orpheus, had given no song, or no good one. "They ought not to have moved trees, but to have chanted to the gods such a hymn as would have sung all their old ideas out of their heads, and new ones in." His own verses are often rude and defective. The gold does not yet run pure, is drossy and crude. The thyme and marjoram are not yet honey. But if he want lyric fineness and technical merits, if he have not the poetic temperament, he never lacks the causal thought, showing that his genius was better than his talent. He knew the worth of the Imagination for the uplifting and consolation of human life, and liked to throw every thought into a symbol. The fact you tell is of no value, but only the impression. For this reason his presence was poetic, always piqued the curiosity to know more deeply the secrets of his mind. He had many reserves, an unwillingness to exhibit to profane eyes what was still sacred in his own, and knew well how to throw a poetic veil over his experience. All readers of Walden will remember his mythical record of his disappointments:—

"I long ago lost a hound, a bay horse and a turtle-dove, and am still on their trail. Many are the travellers I have spoken concerning them, describing their tracks, and what calls they answered to. I have met one or two who have heard the hound; and the tramp of the horse, and even seen the dove disappear behind a cloud; and they seemed as anxious to recover them as if they had lost them themselves."

His riddles were worth the reading, and I confide that if at any time I do not understand the expression, it is yet just. Such was the wealth of his truth that it was not worth his while to use words in vain. His poem entitled "Sympathy" reveals the tenderness under that triple steel of stoicism, and the intellectual subtility it could animate. His classic poem on "Smoke" suggests Simonides, but is better than any poem of Simonides. His biography is in his verses. His habitual thought makes all his poetry a hymn to the Cause of causes, the Spirit which vivifies and controls his own:—

"I hearing get, who had but ears,
And sight, who had but eyes before;
I moments live, who lived but years,
And truth discern, who knew but learning's lore."

And still more in these religious lines:—

"Now chiefly is my natal hour,
And only now my prime of life;
I will not doubt the love untold,
Which not my worth nor want have bought,
Which wooed me young, and wooes me old,
And to this evening hath me brought."

Whilst he used in his writings a certain petulance of remark in reference to churches or churchmen, he was a person of a rare, tender and absolute religion, a person incapable of any profanation, by act or by thought. Of course, the same isolation which belonged to his original thinking and living detached him from the social religious forms. This is neither to be censured nor regretted. Aristotle long ago explained it, when he said, "One who surpasses his fellow citizens in virtue is no longer a part of the city. Their law is not for him, since he is a law to himself."

Thoreau was sincerity itself, and might fortify the convictions of prophets in the ethical laws by his holy living. It was an affirmative experience which refused to be set aside. A truth-speaker he, capable of the most deep and strict conversation; a physician to the wounds of any soul; a friend, knowing not only the secret of friendship, but almost worshipped by those few persons who resorted to him as their confessor and prophet, and knew the deep value of his mind and great heart. He thought that without religion or devotion of some kind nothing great was ever accomplished: and he thought that the bigoted sectarian had better bear this in mind.

His virtues, of course, sometimes ran into extremes. It was easy to trace to the inexorable demand on all for exact truth that austerity which made this willing hermit more solitary even than he wished. Himself of a perfect probity, he required not less of others. He had a disgust at crime, and no worldly success would cover it. He detected paltering as readily in dignified and prosperous persons as in beggars, and with equal scorn. Such dangerous frankness was in his dealing that his admirers called him "that terrible Thoreau," as if he spoke when silent, and was still present when he had departed. I think the severity of his ideal interfered to deprive him of a healthy sufficiency of human society.

The habit of a realist to find things the reverse of their appearance inclined him to put every statement in a paradox. A certain habit of antagonism defaced his earlier writings,—a trick of rhetoric not quite outgrown in his later, of substituting for the obvious word and thought its diametrical opposite. He praised wild mountains and winter forests for their domestic air, in snow and ice he would find sultriness, and commended the wilderness for resembling Rome and Paris. "It was so dry, that you might call it wet."

The tendency to magnify the moment, to read all the laws of Nature in the one object or one combination under your eye, is of course comic to those who do not share the philosopher's perception of identity. To him there was no such thing as size. The pond was a small ocean; the Atlantic, a large Walden Pond. He referred every minute fact to cosmical laws. Though he meant to be just, he seemed haunted by a certain chronic assumption that the science of the day pretended completeness, and he had just found out that the *savans* had neglected to discriminate a particular botanical variety, had failed to describe the seeds or count the sepals. "That is to say," we replied, "the blockheads were not born in Concord; but who said they were? It was their unspeakable misfortune to be born in London, or Paris, or Rome; but, poor fellows, they did what they could, considering that they never saw Bateman's Pond, or Nine-Acre Corner, or Becky Stow's Swamp; besides, what were you sent into the world for, but to add this observation?"

Had his genius been only contemplative, he had been fitted to his life, but with his energy and practical ability he seemed born for great enterprise and for command; and I so much regret the loss of his rare powers of action, that I cannot help counting it a fault in him that he had no ambition. Wanting this, instead of engineering for all America, he was the captain of a huckleberry-party. Pounding beans is good to the end of pounding empires one of these days; but if, at the end of years, it is still only beans!

But these foibles, real or apparent, were fast vanishing in the incessant growth of a spirit so robust and wise, and which effaced its defeats with new triumphs. His study of Nature was a perpetual ornament to him, and inspired his friends with curiosity to see the world through his eyes, and to hear his adventures. They possessed every kind of interest.

He had many elegancies of his own, whilst he scoffed at conventional elegance. Thus, he could not bear to hear the sound of his own steps, the grit of gravel; and therefore never willingly walked in the road, but in the grass, on mountains and in woods. His senses were acute, and he remarked that by night every dwelling-house gives out bad air, like a slaughter-house. He liked the pure fragrance of melilot. He honored certain plants with special regard, and, over all, the pond-lily,—then, the gentian, and the *Mikania scandens*, and "life-everlasting," and a bass-tree which he visited every year when it bloomed, in the middle of July. He thought the scent a more oracular inquisition than the sight,—more oracular and trustworthy. The scent, of course, reveals what is concealed from the other senses. By it he detected earthiness. He delighted in echoes, and said they were almost the only kind of kindred voices that he heard.

From Historic Notes of Life and Letters in New England (1880)

This lecture, delivered in Concord in 1880, was, Emerson said, his "100th lecture before the Lyceum." A very large audience "rose en masse to meet him," according to the lyceum secretary's report; and although Emerson was now seventy-seven years old, he read "with a clearness and vigor remarkable, considering his advanced age."

It seems probable that the lecture consisted of comments and reminiscences written at earlier moments and was pieced together for the occasion by Emerson with the help of his daughter and secretary, Ellen Tucker Emerson. Only the first part of it is given here; the balance has to do, in a somewhat rambling way, with the Brook Farm experiment.

The ancient manners were giving way. There grew a certain tenderness on the people, not before remarked. Children had been repressed and kept in the background; now they were considered, cosseted and pampered. I recall the remark of a witty physician who remembered the hardships of his own youth; he said, "It was a misfortune to have been born when children were nothing, and to live till men were nothing."

There are always two parties, the party of the Past and the party of the Future; the Establishment and the Movement. At times the resistance is reanimated, the schism runs under the world and appears in Literature, Philosophy, Church, State and social customs. It is not easy to date these eras of activity with any precision, but in this region one made itself remarked, say in 1820 and the twenty years following.

It seemed a war between intellect and affection; a crack in Nature, which split every church in Christendom into Papal and Protestant; Calvinism into Old and New schools; Quakerism into Old and New; brought new divisions in politics; as the new conscience touching temperance and slavery. The key to the period appeared to be that the mind had become aware of itself. Men grew reflective and intellectual. There was a new consciousness. The former generations acted under the belief that a shining social prosperity was the beatitude of man, and sacrificed uniformly the citizen to the State. The modern mind believed that the nation existed for the individual, for the guardianship and education of every man. This idea, roughly written in revolutions and national movements, in the mind of the philosopher had far more precision; the individual is the world.

This perception is a sword such as was never drawn before. It divides and detaches bone and marrow, soul and body, yea, almost the man from himself. It is the age of severance, of dissociation, of freedom, of analysis, of detachment. Every man for himself. The public speaker disclaims speaking for any other; he answers only for himself. The social sentiments are weak; the sentiment of patriotism is weak; veneration is low; the natural affections feebler than they were. People grow philosophical about native land and parents and relations. There is an universal resistance to ties and ligaments once supposed essential to civil society. The new race is stiff, heady and rebellious; they are fanatics in freedom; they hate tolls, taxes, turnpikes, banks, hierarchies, governors, yea, almost laws. They have a neck of unspeakable tenderness; it winces at a hair. They rebel against theological as against political dogmas; against mediation, or saints, or any nobility in the unseen.

The age tends to solitude. The association of the time is accidental and momentary and hypocritical, the detachment intrinsic and progressive.

The association is for power, merely,—for means; the end being the enlargement and independency of the individual. Anciently, society was in the course of things. There was a Sacred Band, a Theban Phalanx. There can be none now. College classes, military corps, or trades-unions may fancy themselves indissoluble for a moment, over their wine; but it is a painted hoop, and has no girth. The age of arithmetic and of criticism has set in. The structures of old faith in every department of society a few centuries have sufficed to destroy. Astrology, magic, palmistry, are long gone. The very last ghost is laid. Demonology is on its last legs. Prerogative, government, goes to pieces day by day. Europe is strewn with wrecks; a constitution once a week. In social manners and morals the revolution is just as evident. In the law courts, crimes of fraud have taken the place of crimes of force. The stockholder has stepped into the place of the warlike baron. The nobles shall not any longer, as feudal lords, have power of life and death over the churls, but now, in another shape, as capitalists, shall in all love and peace eat them up as before. Nay, government itself becomes the resort of those whom government was invented to restrain. "Are there any brigands on the road?" inquired the traveler in France. "Oh, no, set your heart at rest on that point," said the landlord; "what should these fellows keep the highway for, when they can rob just as effectually, and much more at their ease, in the bureaus of office?"

In literature the effect appeared in the decided tendency of criticism. The most remarkable literary work of the age has for its hero and subject precisely this introversion: I mean the poem of Faust. In philosophy, Immanuel Kant has made the best catalogue of the human faculties and the best analysis of the mind. Hegel also, especially. In science the French *savant*, exact, pitiless, with barometer, crucible, chemic test and calculus in hand, travels into all nooks and islands, to weigh, to analyze and report. And chemistry, which is the analysis of matter, has taught us that we eat gas, drink gas, tread on gas, and are gas. The same decomposition has changed the whole face of physics; the like in all arts, modes. Authority falls, in Church, College, Courts of Law, Faculties, Medicine. Experiment is credible; antiquity is grown ridiculous.

It marked itself by a certain predominance of the intellect in the balance of powers. The warm swart Earth-spirit which made the strength of past ages, mightier than it knew, with instincts instead of science, like a mother yielding food from her own breast instead of preparing it through chemic and culinary skill,—warm negro ages of sentiment and vegetation,—all gone; another hour had struck and other forms arose. Instead of the social existence which all shared, was now separation. Every one for himself; driven to find all his resources, hopes, rewards, society and deity within himself.

The young men were born with knives in their brain, a tendency to introversion, self-dissection, anatomizing of motives. The popular religion of our fathers had received many severe shocks from the new times; from the Arminians, which was the current name of the backsliders from Calvinism, sixty years ago; then from the English philosophic theologians, Hartley and Priestley and Belsham, the followers of Locke; and then I should say much later from the slow but extraordinary influence of Swedenborg; a man of prodigious mind, though as I think tainted with a certain suspicion of insanity, and therefore generally disowned, but exerting a singular power over an important intellectual class; then the powerful influence of the genius and character of Dr. Channing.

Germany had created criticism in vain for us until 1820, when Edward Everett returned from his five years in Europe, and brought to Cambridge his rich results, which no one was so fitted by natural grace and the splendor of his rhetoric to introduce and recommend. He made us for the first time acquainted with Wolff's theory of the Homeric writings, with the criticism of Heyne. The novelty of the learning lost nothing in the skill and genius of his relation, and the rudest undergraduate found a new morning opened to him in the lecture-room of Harvard Hall.

There was an influence on the young people from the genius of Everett which was almost comparable to that of Pericles in Athens. He had an inspiration which did not go beyond his head, but which made him the master of elegance. If any of my readers were at that period in Boston or Cambridge, they will easily remember his radiant beauty of person, of a classic style, his heavy large eye, marble lids, which gave the impression of mass which the slightness of his form needed; sculptured lips; a voice of such rich tones, such precise and perfect utterance, that, although slightly nasal, it was the most mellow and beautiful and correct of all the instruments of the time. The word that he spoke, in the manner in which he spoke it, became current and classical in New England. He had a great talent for collecting facts, and for bringing those he had to bear with ingenious felicity on the topic of the moment. Let him rise to speak on what occasion soever, a fact had always just transpired which composed, with some other fact well known to the audience, the most pregnant and happy coincidence. It was remarked that for a man who threw out so many facts he was seldom convicted of a blunder. He had a good deal of special learning, and all his learning was available for purposes of the hour. It was all new learning, that wonderfully took and stimulated the young men. It was so coldly and weightily communicated from so commanding a platform, as if in the consciousness and consideration of all history and all learning,—adorned with so many simple and austere beauties of expression, and enriched with so many excellent digressions and significant quotations that, though nothing could be conceived beforehand less attractive or indeed less fit for green boys from Connecticut, New Hampshire and Massachusetts, with their unripe Latin and Greek reading, than exegetical discourses in the style of Voss and Wolff and Ruhnken, on the Orphic and Ante-Homeric remains,—yet this learning instantly took the highest place to our imagination in our unoccupied American Parnassus. All his auditors felt the extreme beauty and dignity of the manner, and even the coarsest were contented to go punctually to listen, for the manner, when they had found out that the subject-matter was not for them. In the lecture-room, he abstained from all ornament, and pleased himself with the play of detailing erudition in a style of perfect simplicity. In the pulpit (for he was then a clergyman) he made amends to himself and his auditor for the self-denial of the professor's chair, and, with an infantine simplicity still, of manner, he gave the reins to his florid, quaint and affluent fancy.

Then was exhibited all the richness of a rhetoric which we have never seen rivalled in this country. Wonderful how memorable were words made which were only pleasing pictures, and covered no new or valid thoughts. He abounded in sentences, in wit, in satire, in splendid allusion, in quotation impossible to forget, in daring imagery, in parable and even in a sort of defying experiment of his own wit and skill in giving an oracular weight to Hebrew or Rabbinical words;—feats which no man could better accomplish, such was his self-command and the security of his manner.

All his speech was music, and with such variety and invention that the ear was never tired. Especially beautiful were his poetic quotations. He delighted in quoting Milton, and with such sweet modulation that he seemed to give as much beauty as he borrowed; and whatever he quoted will be remembered by any who heard him, with inseparable association with his voice and genius. He had nothing in common with vulgarity and infirmity, but speaking, walking, sitting, was as much aloof and uncommon as a star. The smallest anecdote of his behavior or conversation was eagerly caught and repeated, and every young scholar could recite brilliant sentences from his sermons, with mimicry, good or bad, of his voice. This influence went much farther, for he who was heard with such throbbing hearts and sparkling eyes in the lighted and crowded churches, did not let go his hearers when the church was dismissed, but the bright image of that eloquent form followed the boy home to his bed-chamber; and not a sentence was written in academic exercises, not a declamation attempted in the college chapel, but showed the omnipresence of his genius to youthful heads. This made every youth his defender, and boys filled their mouths with arguments to prove that the orator had a heart. This was a triumph of Rhetoric. It was not the intellectual or the moral principles which he had to teach. It was not thoughts. When Massachusetts was full of his fame it was not contended that he had thrown any truths into circulation. But his power lay in the magic of form; it was in the graces of manner; in a new perception of Grecian beauty, to which he opened our eyes. There was that finish about this person which is about women, and which distinguishes every piece of genius from the works of talent,—that these last are more or less matured in every degree of completeness according to the time bestowed on them, but works of genius in their first and slightest form are still wholes. In every public discourse there was nothing left for the indulgence of his hearer, no marks of late hours and anxious, unfinished study, but the goddess of grace had breathed on the work a last fragrancy and glitter.

By a series of lectures largely and fashionably attended for two winters in Boston he made a beginning of popular literary and miscellaneous lecturing, which in that region at least had important results. It is acquiring greater importance every day, and becoming a national institution. I am quite certain that this purely literary influence was of the first importance to the American mind.

In the pulpit Dr. Frothingham, an excellent classical and German scholar, had already made us acquainted, if prudently, with the genius of Eichhorn's theologic criticism. And Professor Norton a little later gave form and method to the like studies in the then infant Divinity School. But I think the paramount source of the religious revolution was Modern Science; beginning with Copernicus, who destroyed the pagan fictions of the Church, by showing mankind that the earth on which we live was not the centre of the Universe, around which the sun and stars revolved every day, and thus fitted to be the platform on which the Drama of the Divine Judgment was played before the assembled Angels of Heaven,— "the scaffold of the divine vengeance" Saurin called it,—but a little scrap of a planet, rushing round the sun in our system, which in turn was too minute to be seen at the distance of many stars which we behold. Astronomy taught us our insignificance in Nature; showed that our sacred as our profane history had been written in gross ignorance of the laws, which were far grander than we knew; and compelled a certain extension and uplifting of our views of the Deity and his Providence. This correction of our superstitions was confirmed by the new science of Geology, and the whole train of discoveries in every department. But we presently saw also that the religious nature in man was not affected by these errors in his understanding. The religious sentiment made nothing of bulk or size, or far or near; triumphed over time as well as space; and every lesson of humility, or justice, or charity, which the old ignorant saints had taught him, was still forever true.

Whether from these influences, or whether by a reaction of the general mind against the too formal science, religion and social life of the earlier period,—there was, in the first quarter of our nineteenth century, a certain sharpness of criticism, an eagerness for reform, which showed itself in every quarter. It appeared in the popularity of Lavater's Physiognomy, now almost forgotten. Gall and Spurzheim's Phrenology laid a rough hand on the mysteries of animal and spiritual nature, dragging down every sacred secret to a street show. The attempt was coarse and odious to scientific men, but had a certain truth in it; it felt connection where the professors denied it, and was a leading to a truth which had not yet been announced. On the heels of this intruder

came Mesmerism, which broke into the inmost shrines, attempted the explanation of miracle and prophecy, as well as of creation. What could be more revolting to the contemplative philosopher! But a certain success attended it, against all expectation. It was human, it was genial, it affirmed unity and connection between remote points, and as such was excellent criticism on the narrow and dead classification of what passed for science; and the joy with which it was greeted was an instinct of the people which no true philosopher would fail to profit by. But while society remained in doubt between the indignation of the old school and the audacity of the new, a higher note sounded. Unexpected aid from high quarters came to iconoclasts. The German poet Goethe revolted against the science of the day, against French and English science, declared war against the great name of Newton, proposed his own new and simple optics; in Botany, his simple theory of metamorphosis;—the eye of a leaf is all; every part of the plant from root to fruit is only a modified leaf, the branch of a tree is nothing but a leaf whose serratures have become twigs. He extended this into anatomy and animal life, and his views were accepted. The revolt became a revolution. Schelling and Oken introduced their ideal natural philosophy, Hegel his metaphysics, and extended it to Civil History.

The result in literature and the general mind was a return to law; in science, in politics, in social life; as distinguished from the profligate manners and politics of earlier times. The age was moral. Every immorality is a departure from nature, and is punished by natural loss and deformity. The popularity of Combe's Constitution of Man; the humanity which was the aim of all the multitudinous works of Dickens; the tendency even of Punch's caricature, was all on the side of the people. There was a breath of new air, much vague expectation, a consciousness of power not yet finding its determinate aim.

I attribute much importance to two papers of Dr. Channing, one on Milton and one on Napoleon, which were the first specimens in this country of that large criticism which in England had given power and fame to the Edinburgh Review. They were widely read, and of course immediately fruitful in provoking emulation which lifted the style of Journalism. Dr. Channing, whilst he lived, was the star of the American Church, and we then thought, if we do not still think, that he left no successor in the pulpit. He could never be reported, for his eye and voice could not be printed, and his discourses lose their best in losing them. He was made for the public; his cold temperament made him the most unprofitable private companion; but all America would have been impoverished in wanting him. We could not then spare a single word he uttered in public, not so much as the reading a lesson in Scripture, or a hymn, and it is curious that his printed writings are almost a history of the times; as there was no great public interest, political, literary or even economical (for he wrote on the Tariff), on which he did not leave some printed record of his brave and thoughtful opinion. A poor little invalid all his life, he is yet one of those men who vindicate the power of the American race to produce greatness.

Dr. Channing took counsel in 18[34] with George Ripley, to the point whether it were possible to bring cultivated, thoughtful people together, and make society that deserved the name. He had earlier talked with Dr. John Collins Warren on the like purpose, who admitted the wisdom of the design and undertook to aid him in making the experiment. Dr. Channing repaired to Dr. Warren's house on the appointed evening, with large thoughts which he wished to open. He found a well-chosen assembly of gentlemen variously distinguished; there was mutual greeting and introduction, and they were chatting agreeably on indifferent matters and drawing gently towards their great expectation, when a side-door opened, the whole company streamed in to an oyster supper, crowned by excellent wines; and so ended the first attempt to establish aesthetic society in Boston.

Some time afterwards Dr. Channing opened his mind to Mr. and Mrs. Ripley, and with some care they invited a limited party of ladies and gentlemen. I had the honor to be present. Though I recall the fact, I do not retain any instant consequence of this attempt, or any connection between it and the new zeal of the friends who at that time began to be drawn together by sympathy of studies and of aspiration. Margaret Fuller, George Ripley, Dr. Convers Francis, Theodore Parker, Dr. Hedge, Mr. Brownson, James Freeman Clarke, William H. Channing and many others, gradually drew together and from time to time spent an afternoon at each other's houses in a serious conversation. With them was always one well-known form, a pure idealist, not at all a man of letters, nor of any practical talent, nor a writer of books; a man quite too cold and contemplative for the alliances of friendship, with rare simplicity and grandeur of perception, who read Plato as an equal, and inspired his companions only in proportion as they were intellectual,—whilst the men of talent complained of the want of point and precision in this abstract and religious thinker.

These fine conversations, of course, were incomprehensible to some in the company, and they had their revenge in their little joke. One declared that "It seemed to him like going to heaven in a swing"; another reported that, at a knotty point in the discourse, a sympathizing Englishman with a squeaking voice interrupted with the question, "Mr. Alcott, a lady near me desires to inquire whether omnipotence abnegates attribute?"

I think there prevailed at that time a general belief in Boston that there was some concert of *doctrinaires* to establish certain opinions and inaugurate some movement in literature, philosophy and religion, of which design the supposed conspirators were quite innocent; for there was no concert, and only here and there two or three men or women who read and wrote, each alone, with unusual vivacity. Perhaps they only agreed in having fallen upon Coleridge and Wordsworth and Goethe, then on Carlyle, with pleasure and sympathy. Otherwise, their education and reading were not marked, but had the American superficialness, and their studies were solitary. I suppose all of them were surprised at this rumor of a school or sect, and certainly at the name of Transcendentalism, given nobody knows by whom, or when it was first applied. As these persons became in the common chances of society acquainted with each other, there resulted certainly strong friendships, which of course were exclusive in proportion to their heat: and perhaps those persons who were mutually the best friends were the most private and had no ambition of publishing their letters, diaries or conversation.

From that time meetings were held for conversation, with very little form, from house to house, of people engaged in studies, fond of books, and watchful of all the intellectual light from whatever quarter it flowed. Nothing could be less formal, yet the intelligence and character and varied ability of the company gave it some notoriety and perhaps waked curiosity as to its aims and results.

Nothing more serious came of it than the modest quarterly journal called The Dial, which, under the editorship of Margaret Fuller, and later of some other, enjoyed its obscurity for four years.

All its papers were unpaid contributions, and it was rather a work of friendship among the narrow circle of students than the organ of any party. Perhaps its writers were its chief readers: yet it contained some noble papers by Margaret Fuller, and some numbers had an instant exhausting sale, because of papers by Theodore Parker.

Theodore Parker was our Savonarola, an excellent scholar, in frank and affectionate communication with the best minds of his day, yet the tribune of the people, and the stout Reformer to urge and defend every cause of humanity with and for the humblest of mankind. He was no artist. Highly refined persons might easily miss in him the element of beauty. What he said was mere fact, almost offended you, so bald and detached; little cared he. He stood altogether for practical truth; and so to the last. He used every day and hour of his short life, and his character appeared in the last moments with the same firm control as in the midday of strength. I habitually apply to him the words of a French philosopher who speaks of "the man of Nature who abominates the steam-engine and the factory. His vast lungs breathe independence with the air of the mountains and the woods."

Emerson used the word "poet" loosely, to mean any person whose imagination could find a significant unity in experience, a meaningful order among objects perceived—the poem "Each and All," included here, is in effect a statement about the poetic act. (In a later day, Wallace Stevens would identify the poet in a somewhat similar way.) But there is no doubt that Emerson aspired above all to be a poet in the conventional sense of the word, and one sign of this is his persistent deprecation of his poem-making abilities. Literary history has for the most part taken him at his word; but as the Neoromantic revival makes its headway in our time, in universities and among critics and practicing poets, Emerson's poetry appears to be earning for itself an appreciative admiration which is probably long overdue. Harold Bloom touches on this at several moments in *The Ringers in the Tower* (1971) and elsewhere; and even as we write, the first full-length study of Emerson's verse ever attempted is in the making (by Hyatt Wagoner). It seems likely that as a poet Emerson will eventually rank above Thoreau and not very far below Melville —with whom, here as always, Emerson provides a stimulating contrast. The work of none of those three poets, in any case, should ever again be obliterated by the enormous accomplishments of Whitman and Emily Dickinson.

Aspects of Emerson's theory of poetry—like all his "theories," this one must be pieced together out of random and often superficially inconsistent references—can be found in *Nature*, in "The Poet," in asides and innuendoes in other essays, and scattered through the journal. Many of these have been alluded to in the introduction, and some are reconsidered in the headnotes following.

An important element in that theory is suggested by the statement in *Nature* that words are signs of natural facts, that the latter are symbols of spiritual facts, and that nature is a symbol of spirit. Emerson is at his best, both in poetry and in prose, not only when the words are "vascular and alive," in his own phrase, but also when the facts hang on to their factuality and do not evaporate into a pure symbolism of spirit. Emerson knew as much and knew that he could not always—perhaps only infrequently —maintain that delicate tension. When he did so, he was America's first symbolist poet in the modern manner.

Emerson also said, famously, that it is not meter but a meter-making argument that makes a genuine poem. This is in part the saying of a man whose ear for meter was notably imperfect (see the remarks on "Merlin," below). But it is also a healthy statement about the importance of poetic conventions and about what has become known as the doctrine of "organic form" —the doctrine that shape in a poem should grow naturally out of content.

Two volumes of verse were published in Emerson's lifetime: *Poems* (1847) and *May-Day and Other Pieces* (1867). To those, the poet's son Edward Emerson added a number of uncollected pieces for an edition of 1883. No complete edition of Emerson's poetry has yet appeared, though one exists in manuscript (see note on "The River").

The River (1827)

This poem was included in the section called "Poems of Youth and Early Manhood" in the volume of Emerson's poetry edited by his son Edward W. Emerson. The latter tells us that "The River" was inspired by a summer afternoon in the orchard running down behind the manse to the Concord River. Emerson was just beginning to meditate "signing off" from the Unitarian church (which he finally did in 1831); and the poem reflects his impulse to turn back from the institutionalized world to the spiritually restorative immersion in nature.

"The River" belongs, no doubt knowingly, to the tradition of English landscape poetry, and in particular of "river poetry" (for example, Coleridge's "Sonnet: To the River Otter")—a tradition which explored the vicissitudes in the relation between the individual psyche and the nature that surrounded it. It also belongs to the larger tradition wherein the poet returns, in fact or in memory, to the scenes of his childhood, to recover that sense of awe, of refreshed revelation, that the adult and rational life had mostly expunged. Wordsworth's "Ode: Intimations of Immortality" is the supreme instance of this experience, and it was probably the chief poetic resource for the New England idealists.

Rather unlike the English Romantics, however, Emerson—while feeling himself welcomed by his father's fields and the old remembered surroundings, and while sensing the currents of sympathy that flow between them and him—knows that he cannot again be entirely a part of that natural scene and does not regret the fact.

> These are the same, but I am not the same,
> But wiser than I was, and wise enough
> Not to regret the changes, tho' they cost
> Me many a sigh.

Emerson's attitude here is not unlike that of Hart Crane, in "Passage":

> Where the cedar leaf divides the sky
> I heard the sea.
> In sapphire arenas of the hills
> I was promised an improved infancy.

Carl F. Straud, the editor of the definitive text of Emerson's poetry (unpublished Yale dissertation, 1965), has established that the opening word of "The River" is "awed" rather than, as it has hitherto appeared, "and."

Awed I behold once more
My old familiar haunts; here the blue river,
The same blue wonder that my infant eye
Admired, sage doubting whence the traveller
     came,—
Whence brought his sunny bubbles ere he
     washed
The fragrant flag-roots in my father's fields,
And where thereafter in the world he went.
Look, here he is, unaltered, save that now
He hath broke his banks and flooded all the
     vales
With his redundant waves.   10
Here is the rock where, yet a simple child,
I caught with bended pin my earliest fish,
Much triumphing,—and these the fields
Over whose flowers I chased the butterfly,
A blooming hunter of a fairy fine.
And hark! where overhead the ancient crows
Hold their sour conversation in the sky:—
These are the same, but I am not the same,
But wiser than I was, and wise enough
Not to regret the changes, tho' they cost   20
Me many a sigh. Oh, call not Nature dumb;
These trees and stones are audible to me,
These idle flowers, that tremble in the wind,
I understand their faery syllables,
And all their sad significance. The wind,
That rustles down the well-known forest road—
It hath a sound more eloquent than speech.
The stream, the trees, the grass, the sighing
     wind,
All of them utter sounds of 'monishment
And grave parental love.   30
They are not of our race, they seem to say,
And yet have knowledge of our moral race,
And somewhat of majestic sympathy,
Something of pity for the puny clay,
That holds and boasts the immeasurable mind.
I feel as I were welcome to these trees
After long months of weary wandering,
Acknowledged by their hospitable boughs;
They know me as their son, for side by side,
They were coeval with my ancestors,   40

Adorned with them my country's primitive times,

And soon may give my dust their funeral shade.

Each and All (1839)

"Each and All" draws upon an 1834 journal entry which tells of Emerson bringing home some colored shells, only to discover that, divorced from their original surroundings, they had lost their charm. "Thence I learned," he added, "that Composition was more important than beauty of individual forms to Effect. On the shore they lay wet and social, by the sea and under the sky." The word "social" is adroitly introduced there and suggests that Emerson was himself aware of a certain highly significant analogy, one which later critics have sometimes noticed—for example, F. O. Matthiessen in his remark that "The problem of Emerson's prose was the same as that of his philosophy, how to reconcile the individual with society, how to join his sentences into a paragraph."

Both the social and the aesthetic challenge are implicit in "Each and All," but the emphasis is on what Emerson calls "composition"—the creative uniting of objects into a "perfect whole."

It was, incidentally, in connection with line 19 that Edward Emerson quoted his father as confessing that "I think sometimes that my lack of musical ear is made good to me through my eyes; what others hear I see." Emerson rarely says "I hear," and when he does he usually means "I see." By contrast, to take a modern example, Hart Crane invokes hearing quite as often as he does seeing; the two senses, for Crane, were equivalent sources for detecting ideal harmony.

Little thinks, in the field, yon red-cloaked clown
Of thee from the hill-top looking down;
The heifer that lows in the upland farm,
Far-heard, lows not thine ear to charm;
The sexton, tolling his bell at noon,
Deems not that great Napoleon
Stops his horse, and lists with delight,
Whilst his files sweep round yon Alpine height;
Nor knowest thou what argument
Thy life to thy neighbor's creed has lent.   10
All are needed by each one;
Nothing is fair or good alone.
I thought the sparrow's note from heaven,
Singing at dawn on the alder bough;
I brought him home, in his nest, at even;
He sings the song, but it cheers not now,
For I did not bring home the river and sky;—
He sang to my ear,—they sang to my eye.
The delicate shells lay on the shore;
The bubbles of the latest wave   20
Fresh pearls to their enamel gave,
And the bellowing of the savage sea
Greeted their safe escape to me.
I wiped away the weeds and foam,
I fetched my sea-born treasures home;
But the poor, unsightly, noisome things
Had left their beauty on the shore
With the sun and the sand and the wild uproar.
The lover watched his graceful maid,
As 'mid the virgin train she strayed,   30
Nor knew her beauty's best attire
Was woven still by the snow-white choir.
At last she came to his hermitage,
Like the bird from the woodlands to the cage;—
The gay enchantment was undone,
A gentle wife, but fairy none.
Then I said, 'I covet truth;
Beauty is unripe childhood's cheat;
I leave it behind with the games of youth:'—
As I spoke, beneath my feet   40
The ground-pine curled its pretty wreath,
Running over the club-moss burrs;
I inhaled the violet's breath;
Around me stood the oaks and firs;
Pine-cones and acorns lay on the ground;
Over me soared the eternal sky,
Full of light and of deity;
Again I saw, again I heard,
The rolling river, the morning bird;—
Beauty through my senses stole;   50
I yielded myself to the perfect whole.

Uriel (1847)

On one level, "Uriel" is Emerson's response to the uproar that followed his address to the Harvard Divinity School in July, 1838. "The young deities" are the divinity students; "The stern old war-gods" are the outraged orthodox ministers, led by Andrews Norton—who did indeed believe that the Emersonian doctrine would introduce intellectual chaos into their tidy, rational world of discourses.

Plotinian and Pythagorean elements also have their play in this strange and powerful poem. In general, "Uriel" suggests the shattering impact of a truly revolutionary metaphysic: the huge dismay among those committed to the old system; the sadness of the person who uttered the idea; the reverberations that will not cease: "And a blush tinged the upper sky,/And the gods shook, they knew not why."

Robert Frost, who always enjoyed upsetting the establishment, has called "Uriel" "the greatest Western poem yet."

It fell in the ancient periods
　Which the brooding soul surveys,
Or ever the wild Time coined itself
　Into calendar months and days.

This was the lapse of Uriel,
Which in Paradise befell.
Once, among the Pleiads walking,
Seyd overheard the young gods talking;
And the treason, too long pent,
To his ears was evident.　　　　　　10
The young deities discussed
Laws of form, and metre just,
Orb, quintessence, and sunbeams,
What subsisteth, and what seems.
One, with low tones that decide,
And doubt and reverend use defied,
With a look that solved the sphere,
And stirred the devils everywhere,
Gave his sentiment divine
Against the being of a line.　　　　　　20
'Line in nature is not found;
Unit and universe are round;
In vain produced, all rays return;
Evil will bless, and ice will burn.'
As Uriel spoke with piercing eye,
A shudder ran around the sky;
The stern old war-gods shook their heads,
The seraphs frowned from myrtle-beds;
Seemed to the holy festival
The rash word boded ill to all;　　　　　　30
The balance-beam of Fate was bent;
The bounds of good and ill were rent;
Strong Hades could not keep his own,
But all slid to confusion.
A sad self-knowledge, withering, fell
On the beauty of Uriel;
In heaven once eminent, the god
Withdrew, that hour, into his cloud;
Whether doomed to long gyration
In the sea of generation,　　　　　　40
Or by knowledge grown too bright
To hit the nerve of feebler sight.
Straightway, a forgetting wind
Stole over the celestial kind,
And their lips the secret kept,
If in ashes the fire-seed slept.
But now and then, truth-speaking things
Shamed the angels' veiling wings;
And, shrilling from the solar course,
Or from fruit of chemic force,　　　　　　50
Procession of a soul in matter,
Or the speeding change of water,
Or out of the good of evil born,
Came Uriel's voice of cherub scorn,
And a blush tinged the upper sky,
And the gods shook, they knew not why.

Forerunners (1847)

The forerunners are, literally, the winds, blowing forth each morning, strewing the flowers as they pass, dancing on the far hills. But they are also the winds seen within the Romantic convention of "the correspondent breeze": the unseen forces of inspiration and insight. Here they are imaginings and intimations, the sense of possible spiritual adventure and miracle. Characteristically of Emerson they are jubilant and utter sounds of "harp-like laughter"; they are the source of a "peace that hallows rudest ways." And they are particularly audible in sleep.

Long I followed happy guides,
I could never reach their sides;
Their step is forth, and, ere the day
Breaks up their leaguer, and away.
Keen my sense, my heart was young,
Right good-will my sinews strung,
But no speed of mine avails
To hurt upon their shining trails.
On and away, their hasting feet
Make the morning proud and sweet;   10
Flowers they strew,—I catch the scent;
Or tone of silver instrument
Leaves on the wind melodious trace;
Yet I could never see their face.
On eastern hills I see their smokes,
Mixed with mist by distant lochs,
I met many travellers

Who the road had surely kept;
They saw not my fine revellers,—
These had crossed them while they slept.   20
Some had heard their fair report,
In the country or the court.
Fleetest couriers alive
Never yet could once arrive,
As they went or they returned,
At the house where these sojourned.
Sometimes their strong speed they slacken,
Though they are not overtaken;
In sleep their jubilant troop is near,—
I tuneful voices overhear;   30
It may be in wood or waste,—
At unawares 't is come and past.
Their near camp my spirit knows
By signs gracious as rainbows.
I thenceforward and long after
Listen for their harp-like laughter,
And carry in my heart, for days,
Peace that hallows rudest ways.

The Humble-Bee (1847)

The central lines of this superb poem occur in the second stanza:

> Wait, I prithee, till I come
> Within earshot of thy hum,—
> All without is martyrdom.

Emily Dickinson might have written the lines, though to somewhat different effect. For anyone (this poem says) who has experienced the healing immersion in nature, the rest of life seems a desolation; and when beset by the woes and wants that "torture us," one longs to fade back into that soothing relationship. "The humble-bee and the pine-warbler," Emerson remarked in 1837, during a period of national financial crisis, "seems to me the proper objects of attention in these disastrous times." But the poem is far more than a celebration of a temporary escape from worry. The domain of the free-flying bee and the world of grief and deprivation are symbols of those areas of experience Emerson habitually contrasted: Freedom and Necessity.

Burly, dozing humble-bee,
Where thou art is clime for me.
Let them sail for Porto Rique,
Far-off heats through seas to seek;
I will follow thee alone,
Thou animated torrid-zone!
Zigzag steerer, desert cheerer,
Let me chase thy waving lines;
Keep me nearer, me thy hearer,
Singing over shrubs and vines.   10

Insect lover of the sun,
Joy of thy dominion!
Sailor of the atmosphere;
Swimmer through the waves of air;
Voyager of light and noon;
Epicurean of June;
Wait, I prithee, till I come
Within earshot of thy hum,—
All without is martyrdom.

When the south wind, in May days,   20
With a net of shining haze
Silvers the horizon wall,
And with softness touching all,
Tints the human countenance

With a color of romance,
And infusing subtle heats,
Turns the sod to violets,
Thou, in sunny solitudes,
Rover of the underwoods,
The green silence dost displace   30
With thy mellow, breezy bass.

Hot midsummer's petted crone,
Sweet to me thy drowsy tone
Tells of countless sunny hours,
Long days, and solid banks of flowers;
Of gulfs of sweetness without bound
In Indian wildernesses found;
Of Syrian peace, immortal leisure,
Firmest cheer, and bird-like pleasure.

Aught unsavory or unclean   40
Hath my insect never seen;
But violets and bilberry bells,
Maple-sap and daffodels,

Grass with green flag half-mast high,
Succory to match the sky,
Columbine with horn of honey,
Scented fern, and agrimony,
Clover, catchfly, adder's-tongue
And brier-roses, dwelt among;
All beside was unknown waste,   50
All was picture as he passed.

Wiser far than human seer,
Yellow-breeched philosopher!
Seeing only what is fair,
Sipping only what is sweet,
Thou dost mock at fate and care,
Leave the chaff, and take the wheat.
When the fierce northwestern blast
Cools sea and land so far and fast,
Thou already slumberest deep;   60
Woe and want thou canst outsleep;
Want and woe, which torture us,
Thy sleep makes ridiculous.

The Snow-Storm (1835)

In 1832, Emerson declared: "I will make a lecture on God's architecture, one of his beautiful works, a Day. I will draw a sketch of a winter's day." Luckily, in this, perhaps Emerson's finest short poem, he celebrated not God's but nature's architecture, contrasting its swift, organic, nonmathematical method to the work-a-day logic of the buildings of man: "the frolic architecture of the snow."

Anyone who has seen a snowstorm in the New England countryside will recognize the powerful accuracy of the first stanza. But what gives the poem its great and special quality is the movement from that realistic description to the near-*sur*realism of the second part.

John Greenleaf Whittier, though he was often impatient with Emerson as a thinker, appropriately quoted the first stanza of this poem in his introduction to his own masterpiece *Snow-Bound.*

Announced by all the trumpets of the sky,
Arrives the snow, and, driving o'er the fields,
Seems nowhere to alight: the whited air
Hides hills and woods, the river, and the
    heaven,

And veils the farm-house at the garden's end.
The sled and traveller stopped, the courier's
    feet
Delayed, all friends shut out, the housemates
    sit
Around the radiant fireplace, enclosed
In a tumultuous privacy of storm.

Come see the north wind's masonry.   10
Out of an unseen quarry evermore
Furnished with tile, the fierce artificer
Curves his white bastions with projected roof
Round every windward stake, or tree, or door.
Speeding, the myriad-handed, his wild work
So fanciful, so savage, nought cares he
For number or proportion. Mockingly,
On coop or kennel he hangs Parian wreaths;
A swan-like form invests the hidden thorn;
Fills up the farmer's lane from wall to wall,   20
Maugre the farmer's sighs; and at the gate
A tapering turret overtops the work.
And when his hours are numbered, and the
    world
Is all his own, retiring, as he were not,
Leaves, when the sun appears, astonished Art
To mimic in slow structures, stone by stone,
Built in an age, the mad wind's night-work,
The frolic architecture of the snow.

Merlin (1847)

William Carlos Williams once said that every English-language poet after Whitman must show cause why the iambic is the meter most suited to his verse. But if the immense influence of Whitman's often free-moving poetry is indeed responsible for the great loosening up of American prosody—and hence the great opening up of innumerable new poetic possibilities—it was, as almost always, Emerson who led the way. Emerson both announced and exemplified the first breakthrough in prosody, and "Merlin I" is his major manifesto. True poetry (or music), he here proclaims, should beat with the pulse of life and of nature; not by inherited, conventional rhythms, but striking like the flood. True poetry should carry the spirit heavenward by the sharp surprises of its innovations —as Emerson seeks to do in the final stanza of "Merlin I," when he departs almost casually, almost contemptuously, from what had been essentially a three-beat line to a meandering line of seven beats.

Emerson was equivocal as to whether "Merlin II" was to be regarded as a separate poem or the second section of the same poem, and the editors have followed the example of Harold Bloom in presenting "Merlin II" as a continuation. In any case, "Merlin II," about the rhyming of things, may be taken as the rhyme to "Merlin I." Poems, like thoughts, come also hand in hand.

The "double stars" (or binary stars) in the first stanza of "Merlin II" has a continuing history in Romantic literature, and can be found, for example, as the image of the perfect relation between male and female in D. H. Lawrence's *Women in Love.*

I

Thy trivial harp will never please
Or fill my craving ear;
Its chords should ring as blows the breeze,
Free, peremptory, clear.
No jingling serenader's art,
Nor tinkle of piano strings,
Can make the wild blood start

In its mystic springs.
The kingly bard
Must smite the chords rudely and hard,   10
As with hammer or with mace;
That they may render back
Artful thunder, which conveys
Secrets of the solar track,
Sparks of the supersolar blaze.
Merlin's blows are strokes of fate,
Chiming with the forest tone,
When boughs buffet boughs in the wood;
Chiming with the gasp and moan
Of the ice-imprisoned flood;   20
With the pulse of manly hearts;
With the voice of orators;
With the din of city arts;
With the cannonade of wars;
With the marches of the brave;
And prayers of might from martyrs' cave.

Great is the art,
Great be the manners, of the bard.
He shall not his brain encumber
With the coil of rhythm and number;   30
But, leaving rule and pale forethought,
He shall aye climb
For his rhyme.
'Pass in, pass in,' the angels say,
'In to the upper doors,
Nor count compartments of the floors,
But mount to paradise
By the stairway of surprise.'

Blameless master of the games,
King of sport that never shames,   40
He shall daily joy dispense
Hid in song's sweet influence.
Forms more cheerly live and go,
What time the subtle mind
Sings aloud the tune whereto
Their pulses beat,
And march their feet,
And their members are combined.

By Sybarites beguiled,
He shall no task decline;   50
Merlin's mighty line
Extremes of nature reconciled,—
Bereaved a tyrant of his will,
And made the lion mild.
Songs can the tempest still,
Scattered on the stormy air,

Mould the year to fair increase,
And bring in poetic peace.

He shall not seek to weave,
In weak, unhappy times,   60
Efficacious rhymes;
Wait his returning strength.
Bird that from the nadir's floor
To the zenith's top can soar,—
The soaring orbit of the muse exceeds that
    journey's length.
Nor profane affect to hit
Or compass that, by meddling wit,
Which only the propitious mind
Publishes when 't is inclined.
There are open hours   70
When the God's will sallies free,
And the dull idiot might see
The flowing fortunes of a thousand years;—
Sudden, at unawares,
Self-moved, fly-to the doors,
Nor sword of angels could reveal
What they conceal.

II

The rhyme of the poet
Modulates the king's affairs;
Balance-loving Nature   80
Made all things in pairs.
To every foot its antipode;
Each color with its counter glowed;
To every tone beat answering tones,
Higher or graver;
Flavor gladly blends with flavor;
Leaf answers leaf upon the bough;
And match the paired cotyledons.
Hands to hands, and feet to feet,
In one body grooms and brides;   90
Eldest rite, two married sides
In every mortal meet.

Light's far furnace shines,
Smelting balls and bars,
Forging double stars,
Glittering twins and trines.
The animals are sick with love,
Lovesick with rhyme;
Each with all propitious Time
Into chorus wove.   100

Like the dancers' ordered band,
Thoughts come also hand in hand;
In equal couples mated,
Or else alternated;
Adding by their mutual gage,
One to other, health and age.
Solitary fancies go
Short-lived wandering to and fro,
Most like to bachelors,
Or an ungiven maid,   110
Not ancestors,
With no posterity to make the lie afraid,
Or keep truth undecayed.
Perfect-paired as eagle's wings,
Justice is the rhyme of things;
Trade and counting use
The self-same tuneful muse;
And Nemesis,
Who with even matches odd,
Who athwart space redresses   120
The partial wrong,
Fills the just period,
And finishes the song.

Subtle rhymes, with ruin rife,
Murmur in the house of life,
Sung by the Sisters as they spin;
In perfect time and measure they
Build and unbuild our echoing clay.
As the two twilights of the day
Fold us music-drunken in.   130

Bacchus (1847)

To his own copy of this poem. Emerson attached a line from Plato: "The man who is his own master knocks in vain at the door of Poetry"; and in a lecture on poetry, he spoke of "a wise surrender to the currents of Nature, a noble passion which will not let us halt, but hurries us into the stream of things."

The poet, according to Emerson, has need of what today is called an "expanded consciousness"; but here, as in "The Poet," Emerson austerely rejects drugs, alcohol, and other artificial stimuli to such expansion. The wine he calls for is altogether of the spirit that flows through reality.

This wine is above all, and at first sight surprisingly, a "remembering wine." It puts things back as they should be: it requites, repairs, refreshes, recuts; it "cure[s] the old despair." What the wine restores is at once the vision of life when young, and the vision of life at the dawn of time, when men had not fallen, and were still gods.

It has been suggested by several critics that Emily Dickinson's sparkling poem "I taste a liquor never brewed" is in part a parody of "Bacchus," saying more frolicsomely and startlingly what Emerson is saying a bit portentously. But each poem has its own independent excellence, and each is thoroughly typical of the author.

"The lote" in the final stanza is the leaf of the lotus, which Odysseus's crew munched upon to their near disaster. Its effect in Homer is lethargy, a loss of will; Emerson connects it with the old deadly sin of sloth, or immobilizing despair.

Bring me wine, but wine which never grew
In the belly of the grape,
Or grew on vine whose tap-roots, reaching through
Under the Andes to the Cape,
Suffer no savor of the earth to scape.

Let its grapes the morn salute
From a nocturnal root,
Which feels the acrid juice
Of Styx and Erebus;
And turns the woe of Night,   10
By its own craft, to a more rich delight.

We buy ashes for bread;
We buy diluted wine;
Give me of the true,—
Whose ample leaves and tendrils curled
Among the silver hills of heaven
Draw everlasting dew;
Wine of wine,
Blood of the world,
Form of forms, and mould of statures,   20
That I intoxicated,
And by the draught assimilated,
May float at pleasure through all natures;

The bird-language rightly spell,
And that which roses say so well.

Wine that is shed
Like the torrents of the sun
Up the horizon walls,
Or like the Atlantic streams, which run
When the South Sea calls.   30

Water and bread,
Food which needs no transmuting,
Rainbow-flowering, wisdom-fruiting,
Wine which is already man,
Food which teach and reason can.

Wine which Music is,—
Music and wine are one,—
That I, drinking this,
Shall hear far Chaos talk with me;
Kings unborn shall walk with me;   40
And the poor grass shall plot and plan
What it will do when it is man.
Quickened so, will I unlock
Every crypt of every rock.

I thank the joyful juice
For all I know;—
Winds of remembering
Of the ancient being blow,
And seeming-solid walls of use
Open and flow.   50

Pour, Bacchus! the remembering wine;
Retrieve the loss of me and mine!
Vine for vine be antidote,
And the grape requite the lote!
Haste to cure the old despair,—
Reason in Nature's lotus drenched,
The memory of ages quenched;
Give them again to shine;
Let wine repair what this undid;
And where the infection slid,   60
A dazzling memory revive;
Refresh the faded tints,
Recut the aged prints,
And write my old adventures with the pen
Which on the first day drew,
Upon the tablets blue,
The dancing Pleiads and eternal men.

Concord Hymn (1837)

The first stanza of this poem, with its drumbeat eloquence, contains Emerson's best-known lines.

"I am not a shriner," Frost remarked, accepting the Emerson-Thoreau medal in 1939, "but two things I never happen on unmoved: one, this poem on stone"—that is, on the monument in Concord—"and the other the tall shaft seen from Lafayette Park across the White House in Washington."

SUNG AT THE COMPLETION OF THE BATTLE
MONUMENT, JULY 4, 1837

By the rude bridge that arched the flood,
   Their flag to April's breeze unfurled,
Here once the embattled farmers stood
   And fired the shot heard round the world.

The foe long since in silence slept;
   Alike the conqueror silent sleeps;
And Time the ruined bridge has swept

Brahma (1857)

Of several sources for this mysterious but compelling work, a quotation from the *Bhagavad
Gita* is perhaps most relevant: "He who believes that this spirit can kill, and he who
thinks it can be killed, both of these are wrong
in judgment. It neither kills nor is killed. It is
not born nor dies at any time. It has no origin,
nor will it ever have an origin. Unborn, changeless, eternal, both as to future and past time,
it is not slain when the body is killed."

"The strong gods" and "the sacred Seven"
are also elements drawn from the *Bhagavad
Gita*.

According to a story current in Emerson's lifetime, a little girl was asked by her teacher to
memorize and recite one of Mr. Emerson's
poems. She chose "Brahma," and when the
surprised teacher asked why, the child replied:

Days (1857)

Resonance here combines with a nearly perfect
restraint to make this one of Emerson's finest
poems. Everything is in the tone, and in the
overtone.

The days are "hypocritic" presumably in the
root sense of being actors or dissemblers. But
a question might be raised as to whether the
day's scorn, in the final line, is entirely justified.
Were the morning wishes—evidently for things
grander than "a few heroes and apples"—necessarily the proper ones? While Emerson can suggest on occasion (for example, in "Merlin I")

Down the dark stream which seaward
   creeps.

On this green bank, by this soft stream,
   We set to-day a votive stone;   10
That memory may their deed redeem,
   When, like our sires, our sons are gone.

Spirit, that made those heroes dare
   To die, and leave their children free,
Bid Time and Nature gently spare
   The shaft we raise to them and thee.

"Because it's the easiest to understand. It simply means that God is everywhere."

If the red slayer think he slays,
   Or if the slain think he is slain,
They know not well the subtle ways
   I keep, and pass, and turn again.

Far or forgot to me is near;
   Shadow and sunlight are the same;
The vanished gods to me appear;
   And one to me are shame and fame.

They reckon ill who leave me out;
   When me they fly, I am the wings;   10
I am the doubter and the doubt,
   And I the hymn the Brahmin sings.

The strong gods pine for my abode,
   And pine in vain the sacred Seven;
But thou, meek lover of the good!
   Find me, and turn thy back on heaven.

that only the greatest themes are suitable for
poetry, he can also insist, elsewhere, that poetry
should deal with the low and the familiar. More
widely, while at times Emerson seems to urge
men to live heroically, he can also at other
times admonish them to make the most of
what is at hand about them.

Daughters of Time, the hypocritic Days,
Muffled and dumb like barefoot dervishes,
And marching single in an endless file,
Bring diadems and fagots in their hands.

[handwritten at top:] When he forgets his morning aspirations, he turns his back on intuition. Mind tells you apples and herbs are better than stars and skies. He becomes pragmatic and practical and less idealistic - *ideal* principles are more important ~~then~~ than money.

To each they offer gifts after his will, *[handwritten: in accordance with]*
Bread, kingdoms, stars, and sky that holds
   them all.
I, in my pleached garden, watched the pomp, *[handwritten: intrinsic]*

[handwritten below left:] got lazy and takes what he can get. Grabs too hastily. Didn't hold out for good stuff.

Terminus (1867)

This poem will surprise anyone who still believes that Emerson was always and altogether committed to the belief that there were no boundaries to the mind's capacity to grow. For many years, as we have tried to show in the introduction, Emerson had been admitting to an increasing awareness of limitations in experience, of modes of psychic imprisonment. Here the mood is acquiescent—more, it is softly celebrational, in a salute to the god of boundaries that would even satisfy W. H. Auden, the contemporary poet who has been most respectful of that deity.

It is time to be old,
To take in sail:—
The god of bounds,
Who sets to seas a shore,
Came to me in his fatal rounds,
And said: 'No more!
No farther shoot
Thy broad ambitious branches, and thy root.
Fancy departs: no more invent;
Contract thy firmament   10
To compass of a tent.
There's not enough for this and that,
Make thy option which of two;

Forgot my morning wishes, hastily *[handwritten: childhood]*
Took a few herbs and apples, and the Day
Turned and departed silent. I, too late,   10
Under her solemn fillet saw the scorn.

[handwritten right:] He could have had anything but he took the lower things.

[handwritten:] The day has great scorn for the man that traded great things for material goods. We make the compromises of life as we get older. We settle for less.

Economize the failing river,
Not the less revere the Giver,
Leave the many and hold the few.
Timely wise accept the terms,
Soften the fall with wary foot;
A little while
Still plan and smile,   20
And,—fault of novel germs,—
Mature the unfallen fruit.
Curse, if thou wilt, thy sires,
Bad husbands of their fires,
Who, when they gave thee breath,
Failed to bequeath
The needful sinew stark as once,
The Baresark marrow to thy bones,
But left a legacy of ebbing veins,
Inconstant heat and nerveless reins,—   30
Amid the Muses, left thee deaf and dumb,
Amid the gladiators, halt and numb.'

   As the bird trims her to the gale,
I trim myself to the storm of time,
I man the rudder, reef the sail,
Obey the voice at eve obeyed at prime:
'Lowly faithful, banish fear,
Right onward drive unharmed;
The port, well worth the cruise, is near,
And every wave is charmed.'   40

HENRY DAVID THOREAU (1817–1862)

Henry David Thoreau, as a man and as a writer, has proved to be thoroughly central to the American experience. More than most nineteenth-century writers, and certainly more than any of the other New England transcendentalists, he continues to appeal to Americans of the present day. His building and furnishing of his cabin, so circumstantially described in *Walden*, or, *Life in the Woods*, aligns him with the strong do-it-yourself strain in contemporary America. He appeals also to the streak of romantic primitivism still deeply embedded in American culture, a primitivism which shows itself, to take one example, in the current vogue for "folk songs." A good many devotees of the folk song probably come from the affluent American suburbs, and not all of them would seriously consider abandoning the elaborate machinery and multifarious gadgets that sustain modern civilization. Yet the attraction toward some sort of naked and primitive nature is genuine, and men and women who might in fact be very unhappy in Thoreau's cabin do respond quite sincerely to the idea of the cabin and of a life that is uncluttered and free.

It is scarcely surprising, of course, that those who feel a nostalgia for an older America should find their hero in Thoreau or that he should be admired by the old-fashioned Jeffersonian democrat who takes seriously Jefferson's fear of the meaningless complexity of cities and of their power to corrupt. But Thoreau is also the hero of the young radical who is oriented quite positively toward an urban-industrial culture. The young radical assigns prophetic authority to the Thoreau who went to jail rather than pay his poll tax to a government which countenanced slavery, who spoke in defense of John Brown and wrote a justification of civil disobedience. Abroad, Thoreau's admirers are of a comparable variety. It was under the inspiration of *Walden* that the young Irish poet William Butler Yeats wrote his first successful poem, "The Lake Isle of Innisfree," and it was from Thoreau's essay on civil disobedience that the political idealist Mahatma Gandhi derived the key idea he used to win the independence of India.

Keeping in mind the divergent appeals associated with Thoreau, we should not find it strange that he so often seems inconsistent with himself. He was certainly no system builder. Yet in spite of inconsistencies and occasional contradictions, Thoreau shows in his writings one central concern which runs through his various observations, comments, and aperçus: the relation of means to ends. Thoreau believed that most men, in their frantic pursuit of the means for living, had lost sight of the true ends of life. If all one's time and energy were devoted to the machinery for living, what would be left for life itself? How much "machinery" was actually required for a good life? Surely the amount would depend on what one considered a good life to be—and indeed what he considered life

itself to be. Many men actually had no authentic life. To Thoreau it was plain that most men were expending most of their time and waking thoughts in acquiring food, clothing, and shelter far in excess of what, by any reasonable standard, they required.

Two sentences in *Walden* bear directly on this point. Thoreau defines "the cost of a thing" as "the amount of what I will call life which is required to be exchanged for it, immediately or in the long run." A little later, he observes that this "spending of the best part of one's life earning money in order to enjoy questionable liberty during the least valuable part of it, reminds me of the Englishman who went to India to make a fortune first, in order that he might return to England and live the life of a poet. He should have gone up garret at once."

Where did Thoreau come by such ideas? One does not deny for a moment their "American" quality; yet his ideas on work and leisure were not held by a majority of Americans—who had been busy killing Indians, felling the forests, sailing clipper ships, farming, shopkeeping, and running for political office. Thoreau's Concord neighbors, for example, were puzzled by his going off to live in the woods, and most of them misunderstood the meaning of his experiment in simplifying his life. They were inclined to reproach him for being idle and lazy. The doctrine of work is of long standing, firmly rooted in the New England tradition and certainly was still powerful in the Concord of Thoreau's day.

The source of some of Thoreau's key concepts may be found in his education as a classics scholar.[1] Thoreau knew that the ancient Greeks had pondered the problems of the good life, and one supposes that he had been deeply impressed with their solution. In one of his poems, he seems to touch on precisely this matter:

> When life contracts into a vulgar span,
> And human nature tries to be a man,

[1] After attending the Concord Academy, he went on to Harvard, where he was an honor student and where he gained a sound grounding not only in Greek and Latin, which he came to read with ease, but also in modern languages such as German, Italian, French, and Spanish.

I thank the gods for Greece,
That permanent realm of peace.

Just how had the Athenians solved the problem of work and leisure? An authority of our own day, Professor H. D. F. Kitto (in *The Greeks*, 1951), puts the answer in amusingly concrete terms. He suggests that his reader try to calculate how much of his "working time is concerned in helping him pay for things which the Greeks simply did without"—things like "settees, collars and ties, bed clothes, laid-on water, tobacco, tea and the Civil Service," and he asks his reader to

reflect on the time-using occupations that we follow and [the ancient Greek] did not—reading books and newspapers, traveling daily to work, pottering about the house, mowing the lawn. . . . We get up at seven, and what with shaving, having breakfast, and putting on the complicated panoply which we wear, we are not ready for anything until 8:30. The Greek got up as soon as it was light, shook out the blanket in which he had slept, draped it elegantly around himself as a suit, had a beard and no breakfast, and was ready to face the world in five minutes. The afternoon, in fact, was not the middle of his day, but very near the end of it.

Kitto's account oversimplifies the situation, but not greatly so. In any case, Thoreau was intensely interested in how much he could simplify his own. One might regard the Walden experiment as a North American adaptation of what the Athenian citizen had already achieved in the fifth century B.C.

The problem of ends and means is, of course, intimately related to other matters such as the proper use of time, the distinction between idleness and leisure, contemplation and wholeness of mind, true and false perceptions of reality, and other aspects of an attainment of the good life. In his writings, Thoreau ranges over this whole intellectual terrain. Thus, in *Walden* he writes:

Most men . . . are so occupied with the factitious cares and superfluously coarse labours of life that its finer fruits cannot be plucked by them. Their fingers, from excessive toil, are too clumsy and tremble too much for that. Actually, the labouring man has not leisure for a true integrity day by day; he cannot afford to sustain the manliest relations to men; his labour would be depreciated in the market. He has no time to be anything but a machine.

Thoreau puts the matter here pithily and with a felicitous metaphor. Fingers rendered clumsy from "excessive labour" and wearied by it are unable to pluck the "finer fruits of life." Genuine integrity requires leisure. The true manliness of men expresses itself in works of the spirit—not in the action of the body used as if it were merely a machine.

Thoreau's experience at Walden tested and confirmed these sentiments, and in reading *Walden* and the *Journals* we shall have abundant opportunity to observe how he phrased these insights into the nature of reality. Yet it may be expedient to forgo for the moment Thoreau's characteristic way of putting matters in favor of a condensed statement of what was his essential position. A contemporary book, by Josef Pieper, significantly entitled *Leisure: The Basis of Culture* (1952), presents ideas which might be Thoreau's own, though the author never mentions Thoreau and perhaps has never read him. There are two further advantages in making use of this twentieth-century defense of leisure: (1) it will indicate how fresh and indeed contemporary Thoreau's basic ideas still are, and (2) since the author invokes the names of not only the great thinkers of ancient Greece but also those of the Middle Ages, citation of his book will indicate that Thoreau's ideas are also fully in the tradition of our Western civilization.

Pieper makes the bold assertion that leisure is nothing less than "the preserve of freedom . . . and of that undiminished humanity which views the world as a whole" and does not confine itself to more limited and specialized views, such as those that regard a noble forest as only so many board feet of lumber, or two lovers clasping hands as two anthropoid mammals, quietly sweating, palm to palm, as one of Aldous Huxley's poems has it.

Leisure differs radically from mere idleness. In fact, an idle or lazy man is unable to experience leisure. Why? Because, as Pieper points out, "leisure is only possible . . . to a man [who is] at one with himself, [and] who is also at one with the world."[2] The man who has not come to terms with himself is restless. He feels the need to "kill time," for time hangs heavy on his hands. Such a man cannot contemplate the world about him, accepting with joy the reality of the creation and celebrating it. Nature, far from being a realm of endless fascination, bores him to death. Because he is not really at home in his world, he cannot find a meaningful activity to which to give himself. (Thoreau in his life at Walden Pond did not find time hanging heavy on his hands. In addition to exploring nature and exploring himself, he did a great deal of creative work. It was during his stay at Walden that he completed the manuscript of his first book, *A Week on the Concord and Merrimack Rivers.*)

Leisure has a special relation to silence, solitude, and contemplation—all of them essential ingredients in Thoreau's fruitful experience in the Walden woods. For example, Pieper observes that "silence . . . is the prerequisite of the apprehension of reality." It is easy to see why this must be true, for "leisure is a receptive attitude of mind, a contemplative attitude, and it is not only the occasion but also the capacity for steeping oneself in the whole of creation."

Walden provides plenty of illustrations of just such observations. The visitors to Walden, Thoreau soon discovered, fell into two classes—those with receptive minds and those others who brought with them only their restless, distracted selves.

Girls and boys and young women [Thoreau tells us] generally seemed glad to be in the woods. They looked in the pond and at the flowers, and improved their time. Men of business, even farmers, thought only of soli-

tude and employment, and of the great distance at which I dwelt from something or other; and though they said that they loved a ramble in the woods occasionally, it was obvious that they did not. Restless, committed men, whose time was all taken up in getting a living or keeping it; ministers who spoke of God as if they enjoyed a monopoly of the subject, who could not bear all kinds of opinions; doctors, lawyers, uneasy housekeepers who pried into my cupboard and bed when I was out,—how came Mrs. —— to know that my sheets were not as clean as hers?— young men who had ceased to be young, and had concluded that it was safest to follow the beaten track of the professions,—all these generally said that it was not possible to do so much good in my position.

Thoreau believed that most of the people around him had so far lost the capacity for silence, receptivity, and wonder, and had become so much involved in the processes of getting on in the world, that they were leading "lives of quiet desperation." (Pieper, by the way, says that "despair and the incapacity for leisure" are twins.)

Thus, in spite of the freshness and vigor of Thoreau's mode of statement, his view of leisure was deeply traditional, and it was shared by notable American writers of his own time and later. Cooper's theory of the gentleman (see p. 284) embodies the idea of a creative leisure out of which the norms for true living emerge. Thoreau's contemporary, Whitman, frankly avowed that he meant to "loaf and invite my soul." A generation later, Mark Twain was to portray in Huck Finn and his companion Jim, floating down the Mississippi River, the achievement of genuine (as opposed to pretended) aesthetic experience and a true spiritual response to human life. Later still and closer to our own time, the case for leisure has been put in dramatic terms by writers as diverse as Henry James, Sherwood Anderson, Ernest Hemingway, and William Faulkner.

We have remarked earlier that Thoreau might

[2] Emerson makes the same point.

have derived his characteristic ideas about leisure and the good life from his training in Greek philosophy and literature, but of course his own temperament and genius played an important part in his fixing on these ideas and developing them as he did. After all, some of Thoreau's classmates at Harvard had studied the same books that he had studied but were not induced thereby to venture on a Walden experiment or enabled to write the books that Thoreau wrote. It goes without saying that Thoreau's own cast of mind and sensibility were of the utmost importance. One remembers Emerson's admiring remark that Thoreau "knew the country like a fox or a bird."

Another factor important in shaping Thoreau's spiritual quest and his literary style was the social and intellectual environment of early nineteenth-century America. The New World in which Thoreau found himself seemed to offer mankind a second chance. The first settlers of New England had believed this: here on a new continent they could set up the kind of state ordained by the Holy Scriptures and thus provide scope for the realization of a truly pure worship of God. Their descendants a century and a half later were still inspired by the promise of America but their hope had begun to take a rather different form. For Thoreau and intellectuals like him, the truly crippling fetters were not the ecclesiastical forms of the Old World—popes and bishops, fixed forms of worship and state-enforced tithes, fortunate as it was that their forefathers had been able to break them. The task set for the present was to break out of fetters of a different sort—those that had to do with church doctrine itself. Some of the most pernicious doctrine had to do with New England's Calvinist inheritance—for example, the belief that man was stained with an indelible original sin. Men like Emerson had come to believe on the contrary that man was a creature essentially good and that one had every right to be optimistic about him and his future. Such was the special intellectual climate in which a vigorous young thinker like Thoreau could grow up, and, as a very special part of the intellectual scene, there was Emerson himself.

Quite early he became Thoreau's philosopher, guide, and friend.

Thoreau first met Emerson in 1837. In 1841 he went to live in Emerson's home, and it was on land owned by Emerson on the shores of Walden Pond that Thoreau erected his cabin and carried out the famous experiment recorded in *Walden.* (One may describe it as an attempt to see whether one could practice the solitude that Emerson had said was impracticable.)

One should note in particular the impact made upon Thoreau by Emerson's essay *Nature.* In the light of Emerson's doctrine, man did not stand at the mercy of nature nor did he need to consider her alien and aloof. Nature was in fact a reflection—a bodying forth—of man's own spirit. Moreover, no longer did one have to regard philosophy and poetry as at odds with each other. The true philosopher and the true poet, Emerson had argued, were one and the same. Many aspects of Emerson's essay fitted Thoreau's own interests and attitudes toward nature. In any case, the sentiments expressed by Emerson stimulated the younger man to explore nature for himself and gave him sanction and justification for doing so.

After Thoreau had become a part of the Emerson household, friends and acquaintances took it for granted that he was Emerson's disciple and that Thoreau's thought, though pitched in a rather different key, simply echoed Emerson's. This was Emerson's own view. An entry in his journal for 1841 reads: "told Henry Thoreau that . . . he does not disclose new matter. I am very familiar with all his thoughts, —they are my own quite originally expressed."

At the suggestion of Emerson, Thoreau in 1837 began to keep a journal of his own and continued to make entries in it to the end of his life. His journal is filled with philosophical observations, factual records of some of his trips, and his thoughts about himself and about other people. It also contains much of Thoreau's verse. It is an intimate and a rather complete record of his life. Among other things, it represents the raw materials or semi-worked materials out of which he developed the various books and essays that he was to publish.

Entries in Thoreau's journal, especially the early ones, show him accepting the role of Emerson's pupil and disciple.[3] For example, in 1839 Thoreau wrote: "We are one virtue, one truth, one beauty. All nature is our satellite, whose light is dull and reflected. She is subaltern to us,—an episode to our poem; for we are primary, and radiate light and heat to the system." That is to say, nature simply reflects man's spirit as the moon reflects light borrowed from the sun.

Later, however, Thoreau was less confident that nature was a mere "subaltern" to man. For one thing, by temperament Thoreau savored nature and enjoyed it for its own sake far more than Emerson ever did. One can't imagine Emerson chasing a fox, as Thoreau once did through the winter snow, simply to see what the fox would do, or seriously thinking of eating a woodchuck, not merely out of curiosity as to what it would taste like, but as a means of immersing himself more deeply in the wild creation. At any rate, Thoreau was later willing to set down in his journal statements that pretty well inverted Emerson's conception of nature as subordinate to man. In 1852 Thoreau wrote:

I would fain let man go by and behold a universe in which man is but as a grain of sand. . . . I do not value any view of the universe into which man and the institutions of man enter very largely and absorb much of the attention. Man is but the place where I stand, and the prospect hence is infinite. [Nature] is not a chamber of mirrors which reflect me. When I reflect [Is Thoreau punning?], I find that there is other than me.

A recent study of Emerson and Thoreau puts the difference between the two men thus: "Emerson was a pious Platonist who went to nature for confirmation and illustration of his a priori ethical system, not for mystic ecstasy inseparable from its ineffable meaning." What Emerson really wanted from the natural world was not "a moment of sublime illumination" but "a quick whiff of the moral law" (Joel Porte, *Emerson and Thoreau: Transcendentalists in Conflict*, 1966, p. 62).

This statement makes for a neat contrast between Thoreau and his mentor; but do Thoreau's writings on nature quite bear out so sharp an antithesis? Did Thoreau actually go to nature primarily for "mystic ecstasy" or for "sublime illumination"? An honest answer will have to be: not always and certainly not consistently. Thoreau's attitudes toward nature shifted with his shifting experiences and with his shifting moods. Perhaps our best course here will be simply to note the infrared and ultraviolet extremes of what is in fact a rich spectrum of attitudes. At one extreme, we find a Thoreau who in method and spirit is close to the scientific naturalist, alert, observant, and absorbed in contemplating the natural fact that has caught his attention. Thus, in the following journal entry Thoreau describes a Joe-Pye-weed:

A eupatorium from Hubbard's Bridge causeway answers to E[upatorium] purpureum, except in these doubtful points, that the former has four leaves in a whorl, is unequally serrate, the stem is nearly filled with a thin pith, the corymb is not merely terminal, florets eight and nine. Differs from verticillatum in the stem being not solid, and I perceive no difference between calyx and corolla in color, if I know what the two are. It may be one of the intermediate varieties referred to.

At the other extreme, we find a Thoreau who employs nature as a means for exploring his inner self as he observes that self responding to the manifold of influences that play upon his senses and upon his spirit. For example, in the *Week* he writes:

These simple sounds related us to the stars. Ay, there was a logic in them so convincing that the combined sense of mankind could never make me doubt their conclusions. I

---

[3] In an essay on Thoreau noted for its acerbity (see pp. 619–25), Lowell could see in him little more than an inept and rather ungrateful imitator of Emerson. Thoreau's literary fruits are "strawberries from [Emerson's] own garden." See also the figure that Thoreau cuts in Lowell's *A Fable for Critics*, p. 613.

stop my habitual thinking, as if the plow had suddenly run deeper in its furrow through the crust of the world. How can I go on, who have just stepped over such a bottomless sky-light in the bog of my life? Suddenly old Time winked at me,—Ah, you know me, you rogue,—and news had come that IT was well. That ancient universe is in such capital health, I think undoubtedly it will never die. Heal yourselves, doctors, by God I live.

> Then idle Time ran gadding by
> And left me with Eternity alone;
> I hear beyond the range of sound,
> I see beyond the verge of sight. . . .

In like spirit Thoreau can write (in *Walden*) that "Time is but the stream I go a-fishing in. . . . Its thin current slips away, but eternity remains." Such passages seem quite as "Platonic" as anything in Emerson.

In certain moods, however, Thoreau feels passionately the attraction of nature. He believes that he can lose himself in it and yearns to do so. In his boyhood, he tells us, his life was an ecstasy. It might be William Wordsworth himself speaking when Thoreau laments: "in youth, before I lost any of my senses, I can remember that I was all alive, and inhabited my body with inexpressible satisfaction; both its weariness and its refreshment were sweet to me." Yet Thoreau could also write, in a very different mood and on another occasion: "We soon get through with Nature. She excites an expectation which she cannot satisfy."

Yet even in his dissatisfaction with nature, Thoreau's attitude differs from Emerson's: Thoreau's is less purely moral in its interest,[4] less disposed to see nature as merely ancillary to man's life of thought and action. Sometimes, in the joy that he takes in the scene about him, he comes close to a kind of poetic naturalism.

---

[4] Thoreau did not suffer "moralists" gladly. In his journal he complains: "Why always insist that men incline to the moral side of their being? Our life is not all moral." Or he will observe: "The best thought is not only without sombreness, but even without morality. The universe lies outspread in floods of white light to it. The moral aspect of nature is a jaundiced reflection from man."

In 1842 Hawthorne set down in one of his notebooks: "Mr. Thoreau is a keen and delicate observer of nature,—a genuine observer,—which, I suspect, is about as rare a character as even an original poet," and in 1845, in a letter to a friend, he wrote: "The only way . . . in which [Thoreau] could ever approach the popular mind, would be by writing a book of simple observation of nature. . . ." Yet Hawthorne believed that there was only "one chance in a thousand that he might write [any] . . . excellent and readable book." It was with delighted surprise, therefore, that Hawthorne read *Walden* when it appeared in 1854, for it more than fulfilled his notion of the kind of book that he thought Thoreau should attempt.

In his sympathies, Hawthorne seems to have felt closer to Thoreau than to Emerson. Yet he is frank to remark in his journal, as we have noted earlier, that Thoreau was the "most unmalleable fellow alive—the most tedious, tiresome, and intolerable." Another entry indicates that he was well aware that Thoreau could be a difficult friend. After a pleasant conversation with Emerson, he records that "Mr. Emerson appears to have suffered some inconveniencing from his experience of Mr. Thoreau as an inmate [of his home]. It may be that such a sturdy and uncompromising person is fitter to meet occasionally in the open air, than to have as a permanent guest at table and fireside."

In asking certain questions of nature, Thoreau addressed himself to the primary topic of all the great Romantics of the nineteenth century, not only American Romantics like Emerson, but those across the Atlantic, like Wordsworth and Goethe. We might remind ourselves of what was said earlier about the fundamental concern of all Romantics: their concern with "nature" was continuous with their concern for human nature. This is what Thoreau meant in saying that his primary purpose in going to Walden Pond was not economic—it "was not to live cheaply nor to live dearly there, but to transact some private business with the fewest obstacles." And that private business had finally to do with his coming to an understanding of himself. The evidence for this statement lies in all of his writing, but it is perhaps easiest to discern in his journal.

Thoreau's first book, *A Week on the Concord and Merrimack Rivers,* was made up in large part of a reworking of the sort of material to be found in his journal. The manuscript of the *Week* was completed by the time Thoreau left Walden in September, 1847. The trip on the Concord and the Merrimack had been taken by Thoreau in company with his brother John[5] some years earlier, in August, 1839. The *Week* was not published, however, until 1849 (at Thoreau's own expense). Relatively few copies were sold, and though some of his friends praised the book, it gained him no literary fame. Its failure played a part in delaying Thoreau's publication of *Walden* which, though completed in its first draft by 1849, did not appear until 1854. In the meantime, Thoreau supported himself by hiring out as a painter, carpenter, day laborer, or working in the family pencil factory.

Walden is a condensed and somewhat formalized account of an experience—some of it recorded in the journal—which had ended some seven years before. Was the Walden experiment successful? For Thoreau the answer was obviously yes. Yet if this simplifying of life and this jettisoning of unnecessary machinery worked for Thoreau, would it have worked for other men? Here, the honest and realistic answer has to be that for a great many men it would not have worked at all. Thoreau did not claim that his plan would have worked for everyone; he makes it very plain that the experiment was personal and private, though he did believe that his experience at Walden might suggest to other men how to find a meaningful life suitable for *them*.

Thoreau was unmarried. He and his brother John had both fallen in love with a girl named Ellen Sewall, and in 1840 each of the brothers had proposed to her and had been rejected. Had Henry been accepted, would he have built his cabin by Walden Pond? Two cannot really live as cheaply as one, and moreover the frugal

and austere life from which Thoreau drew so much spiritual sustenance would have been drastically transformed if the cabin had contained a wife and perhaps children.

Even the average bachelor, unencumbered by a family, might well have failed to get from the Walden experience what Thoreau got. He brought to his semi-hermitage a mind filled with ideas and stocked with abundant learning, materials upon which he could draw for his meditations and his self-communings. More important still, he brought with him a spiritual discipline that allowed him to thrive on plain living and high thinking. Such inner resources, and the mental and moral discipline that allow one to make fruitful use of them, do not spring naturally from a simple life in the woods. It is no denigration of the eighteenth- and nineteenth-century pioneers on the American frontier to observe that their manner of life, though it produced much of value, produced no Thoreaus.

A man of less introspective cast and of more vigorous appetites, including a more powerful sexual appetite, might have found his life in the woods boring and irksome—one that said nothing to him at all; or if it did speak to him, one that said something quite different from what it said to Thoreau. Those who have read Joseph Conrad's *Heart of Darkness* will remember the sort of thing that the African wilderness "whispered to Kurtz," things "about himself that he did not know, things of which he had no conception till he took counsel with [that] great solitude." What we think we are deriving from nature is usually simply what we have projected upon her. Nature reveals to us what is in our own hearts.

In this general connection, two other matters concerning Thoreau's cultural heritage have to be kept in mind. Thoreau's attitude toward nature is obviously quasi-religious. The Walden adventure was undertaken because he was concerned to discover life's ultimate values. If he felt that a church-bound community which pretended to live by the letter of orthodox theology had missed the real point of religion, he shared the community's basic orientation: a yearning for "salvation" through attaining to the truth

---

[5] The brothers were devoted to each other, and the death of John in 1842 affected Henry deeply.

about man's final destiny. Though Thoreau's truth was not that of his church-going neighbors, he believed along with them that men must seek truth because it was promised that the truth would make men free.

Moreover, though the bonds of orthodoxy had loosened for Thoreau as they had for Emerson and for most of the other transcendentalists, the Christian terms and symbols still carried, for him and for his readers, great emotional power. That power could actually be intensified if one put those sacred terms and symbols into startlingly new contexts. The reader could thus be shocked into new apprehension of what, in some deep though perhaps unorthodox sense, he had believed all his life.

In the matter of literary style, this cultural situation held great advantages for Thoreau. He did not have to develop a new vocabulary. He was in the enviable position of a writer who inherits terms that have adequate precision and great emotional weight and thus is freed for his proper and special task of weaving them into a disturbingly fresh statement. By putting the old terms into new verbal patterns, he could realize their pent-up power.

Thoreau profited from his cultural situation more as a prose writer perhaps than as a poet. At the beginning of his career as a writer, however, he had apparently thought of himself as primarily a poet. His earliest publications were poems, and he wove a good deal of his verse into his prose works, notably, for example, into his *Week on the Concord and Merrimack Rivers*. Thoreau is clearly a genuine poet, a poet of God's making, sounding the authentic note, embodying sharp insights in fresh and powerful metaphors, and often hitting off the unforgettable phrase. But he was also an awkward poet, and some of his verse reads, one is tempted to say, like inspired doggerel.

Other poets, including some very fine ones, have shown a similar awkwardness. One thinks of Herman Melville and, on the other side of the Atlantic, of Thomas Hardy, of whose style T. S. Eliot has written that "at times . . . it touches sublimity without ever having passed through the stage of being good." One might

add to these names that of Emily Dickinson, remembering that a good deal of her verse is unfinished, or seems unfinished, and reads as if it had been dashed off—the work of genius, to be sure, but scribbled down and sometimes broken off rather than brought to a conclusion.

Why should this be? Was it because the American poets of the nineteenth century were unable any longer to accommodate their style, with naturalness and ease, to the English tradition of poetry? Did the very virtues of those who thought and felt deeply push them into clumsy blunderings? Such a generalization would not be easy to establish. The question as to whether some of the most gifted American poets of the period constitute a kind of awkward squad in the ranks of the poets writing in English has already been touched on in discussing the poetry of Bryant, Whittier, and Lowell. But Thoreau's own poetic left-handedness is sufficiently obvious and rather easily illustrated, not merely from some of his weaker poems such as "My Boots,"[6] but from some of his very best. Even poems as fine as "Let Such Pure Hate Still Underprop" or "The Fall of the Leaf" are not fully integrated: the poet has not finally resolved the dissonances into an all-embracing harmony.

In his prose, however, Thoreau succeeds in forging an authentic style of great power. It is not, to be sure, a style which manifests an obvious ordonnance. Like Emerson, Thoreau seems to write sentence by sentence with no special concern to marshal his sentences into paragraphs, or his paragraphs into a carefully organized argument. But what brilliant sen-

---

[6] Anon with gaping fearlessness they quaff
    The dewy nectar with a natural thirst,
    Or wet their leathern lungs where cranberries
      lurk,
    With sweeter wine than Chian, Lesbian, or
      Falernian far.
    Theirs was the inward lustre that bespeaks
    An open sole—unknowing to exclude
    The cheerful day—a worthier glory far
    Than that which gilds the outmost rind with
      darkness visible—
    Virtues that fast abide through lapse of years,
    Rather rubbed in than off.

tences they are! The narrative or the description or the meditation in question does not languish: the prose is charged with vitality. The reader, under the spell of this rich and powerful personality, finds the talk pungent and persuasive and does not worry about whether it has a clear articulation or whether it moves forward to a foreordained goal.

In his prose, moreover, Thoreau brilliantly solves the problem of tonal unity. He is on the same page raconteur, anecdotist, gadfly, and sage. He can tease his orthodox friends by parodying the very language of orthodoxy. Thus, in *Walden* he writes: "Our manners have been corrupted by communication with the saints. Our hymn-books resound with a melodious cursing of God and enduring him forever. One would say that even the prophets and redeemers had rather consoled the fears than confirmed the hopes of man. But there is nowhere recorded a simple and irrepressible satisfaction with the gift of life, any memorable praise of God."

The success of any parody, of course, depends upon the reader's being quite familiar—as Thoreau's readers were—with what is being mimicked. Thoreau's "communication with the saints" recalls the phrase "the communion of saints" in the Apostle's Creed; "cursing God and enduring him forever" mockingly echoes the language of a passage in the Shorter Catechism: "Man's chief end is to glorify God and to enjoy Him forever." The effectiveness of Thoreau's irony, the brilliance with which he subverts traditional Christianity,[7] the series of minor shocks calculated to jar the casual reader into attention—all of these depend upon the fact that the reader shares with Thoreau a common vocabulary that can be twisted, parodied, and mildly, or radically, subverted.

To take another example: in the chapter of *Walden* entitled "Spring," Thoreau makes the point that nature is immortal. He sums up a brilliant description of a spring day by saying:

[7] In *Walden* Thoreau writes: "The greater part of what my neighbors call good I believe in my soul to be bad, and if I repent anything, it is very likely to be my good behavior. What demon possessed me that I behaved so well?"

Ah, I have penetrated to those meadows on the morning of many a first spring day, jumping from hummock to hummock, from willow root to willow root, when the wild river valley and the woods were bathed in so pure and bright a light as would have waked the dead, if they had been slumbering in their graves, as some suppose. There needs no stronger proof of immortality. All things must live in such a light. O Death, where was thy sting? O Grave, where was thy victory, then?

In his first epistle to the Corinthians, St. Paul exclaims: "O Death, where is thy sting? O grave where is thy victory?" and, going on to observe that "The sting of death is sin," he praises God "who giveth thus the victory through our Lord Jesus Christ." Thoreau makes a brilliant adaptation of this passage to his own purposes. His borrowing from St. Paul was, of course, calculated to raise the hackles of his neighbors, for Thoreau's warrant of immortality here is not Christ's atoning for man's sin but the imperishability of matter throughout all its various permutations. Individual flowers, birds, and beasts die in the natural process of things, but nature itself is undying.

One ought not to suggest that Thoreau's style consists merely or even mainly of devices for administering minor shocks to the godly. His target is the conventionally minded man of whatever creed or program. In any case, administering shocks is only the negative aspect of his prose: its positive qualities are freshness, vigor, and an exhilarating concreteness. Thoreau's prose is that of a well-read man, who knows his Latin and Greek authors and is steeped in the Bible, who is thoroughly at home in the English classics, and who has obviously read widely in the various literatures of the world. But he also knows—and shares with his chosen audience— an intimate knowledge of field and farm, flora and fauna, and the experience of living in an early nineteenth-century New England village. When he generalizes he is never at a loss for a pertinent, concrete illustration, a pithy figure of speech, drawn from common experience, robustly particular. On the other hand, when he writes simply and straightforwardly, he is able—by making an allusion or through some turn of phrase or by summoning up a quotation—to associate his point with traditional wisdom enunciated by the poet or the prophet or the philosopher of old.

Thoreau's dissatisfaction with the Puritan hymnal because it did not record "a simple irrepressible satisfaction with the gift of life" and his ability to find in nature itself on a fine spring morning the real proof of immortality are characteristic of his thought. He is incorrigibly optimistic about man and his possibilities. *Walden* concludes with a notable affirmation of this sort: "The light which puts out our eyes is darkness to us. Only that day dawns to which we are awake. There is more day to dawn. The sun is but a morning star."

A sense of man's limitations and of the impossibility of his ever perfecting himself by his own efforts—all that is implied by the orthodox doctrine of original sin, the peculiar heritage of New England Puritanism—has been dropped as an idea now emptied of meaning. No one of the New England intellectuals of his day dismissed it more thoroughly than did Thoreau. In his optimism, he has indeed to be accounted as one of the patron saints of present-day Americans who believe that no problem is finally insoluble and that American know-how and good intentions and courageous resolve will suffice to remove any impediment to man's aspirations.

For all that he has such firmly held opinions, Thoreau is remarkably undoctrinaire. He is not concerned to lead a movement or to run for office or even to preach a sermon to his fellows, though he is willing for his fellows to profit from the example of his own conduct. In *Walden* he specifically disclaims any desire to proselytize others to his own way of life. On the very first page he explains to his readers that he would

not talk so much about myself if there were any body else whom I knew so well. Unfortunately, I am confined to this theme by the narrowness of my experience. Moreover, I, on my side, require of every writer, first or last, a simple and sincere account of his own life, and not merely what he has heard of other men's lives. . . . Perhaps these pages [of *Walden*] are more particularly addressed to poor students. As for the rest of my readers, they will accept such portions as apply to them.

In short, Thoreau tells us that no one need put on the coat that he has tailored unless it fits, and indeed those who are likely to find it too snug are not even encouraged to try it on, for he adds: "I trust that none will stretch the seams in putting on the coat, for it may do good service to him whom it fits."

More specifically still, he writes:

I would not have any one adopt *my* mode of living on any account; for, besides that before he has fairly learned it I may have found out another for myself, I desire that there may be as many different persons in the world as possible; but I would have each one be very careful to find out and pursue *his own* way, and not his father's or his mother's or his neighbor's instead.

Yet one may ask whether what we have said about Thoreau's lack of concern for politics is not contradicted by his own political actions during his last years. He refused to comply with the Fugitive Slave Law when it was enacted in 1850 and from time to time harbored fugitive slaves. He met John Brown when Brown visited Concord in 1857, and after Brown's raid on Harper's Ferry and his capture and condemnation to the gallows, Thoreau defended Brown's conduct publicly in speeches made in Concord and in Boston.

One may answer that these actions are certainly quite explicit and fully "political" in their effect in spite of the fact that Thoreau refused to lobby for a political bill or to run for office himself. It was this *attitude* that Emerson had in mind when he lamented Thoreau's failure to employ his talents in enterprises of breadth and scope. He was content, Emerson said, to be "the captain of a huckleberry-party."

Yet Emerson's judgment may overestimate

Thoreau's fitness for public life as well as underestimate the long-range effect of Thoreau's own way of making his protest. Whatever the truth here, Thoreau's way of reacting is thoroughly consonant with his whole attitude toward life. He will follow conscience and his own notion of the truth even if this calls for partial withdrawal from the community, as did his life at *Walden*, or from the state, as when he preferred jail to paying his poll tax. He is belligerently nonconformist. When we come to consider "Civil Disobedience" more particularly, we shall see that Thoreau was prepared to abandon democratic discussion and to retire into his own estimate of what the truth was.

How well did Thoreau's optimism survive his later years when he was confronted with what must have seemed to him the criminal indifference to public morality of most of his fellow citizens? There are some hints that he may have been constrained to qualify his optimism somewhat, but he never really gave it up. His political dissent was part and parcel of his special kind of nonconformity and that itself was founded upon a deep-seated belief in man.

It has been argued that Thoreau, having in effect abandoned orthodox Christianity and not being satisfied with an Emersonian moralism, made for himself a kind of aesthetic religion. Joel Porte claims that what Thoreau yearned for was a purely sensuous life. In *A Week on the Concord and Merrimack Rivers* Thoreau wrote: "I see, smell, taste, hear, feel, that everlasting Something to which we are allied, at once our maker, our abode, our destiny, our very Selves; the one historic truth, the most remarkable fact which can become the distinct and uninvited subject of our thought, the actual glory of the universe. . . ." Thus, Porte claims that Thoreau's real affinities are with a poet like John Keats, who said that he yearned for a "life of sensations, not of thought," and further proposes (p. 172) that we should regard Thoreau as a forerunner of Walter Pater. (Porte has in mind such passages [in Pater's *Studies in the History of the Renaissance*] as "The service of philosophy, of speculative culture, towards the human spirit is to rouse, to startle it to

a life of constant and eager observation. . . . Not the fruit of experience, but experience itself, is the end.")

The reasoning that lies behind Porte's statement can bear a little elaboration. The argument might be said to run like this: the man who worships nature and revels in the world of the senses will find the chief threat to such happiness in the gradual dulling of his senses and the prospect of the eventual dissolution of his body. If he believes that his most intense happiness is to be found, not in a world of pure idea and not in any afterlife, but in an acute sensing of the world of nature, then the dulling of the ears, the dimming of the eyes, and the aging of the body generally do threaten such happiness, and the idea of death will become almost intolerable to him. Thus, Porte can go on to say that Thoreau's theory of art was "a theory built on the illusory hope of perennial youth and in frantic defiance of the exigencies of age."

Porte is able to find in Thoreau's writings, particularly in his journal, plenty of passages that support such an interpretation. Among them are entries that suggest that Thoreau, more than most men, found the idea of death intolerable. Perry Miller, too, comments on Thoreau's apparent unwillingness to dwell on the subject of death and the body's decomposition. He finds in Thoreau a dread of death and wonders whether Thoreau's attitude does not come "from some deep twisted compulsion. Is the rejection of death that runs through [Thoreau's journal] truly a circumvention or the elaborate disguise of a wish?" (*Consciousness in Concord*, 1958, p. 66).

Porte goes so far as to say that it was Thoreau's fear of death that accounts for his "excessive dislike of houses" since to Thoreau's imagination "a house is always a tomb." If one could accept such an interpretation—it strikes us as somewhat fanciful—it might make Poe's almost morbid concern with being buried alive seem not so much a personal aberration as an aspect of the general spiritual climate of the early nineteenth century. One recalls also Emerson's attempt to open his first wife's grave.

For Thoreau, as for most of the other Romantics, British and American, the problem of uniting the self with the world outside the self is complicated by the problem of consciousness. The happy animal, with its keen senses and its apparently complete rapport with nature, can indeed revel in the world of the senses, for it lacks man's complex consciousness and his sense of the death that will some day bring to an end the world of sensation. Thus, it is man's consciousness that cuts him off from full immersion in those delights of nature, and yet it is that same consciousness that gives a special savor and massive intensity to them.

This paradox is implicit in all romantic experience. Thoreau sometimes feels that he would like to be a woodchuck or a fox, living in a kind of timeless present as a creature almost submerged in nature. Yet he is sufficiently the philosopher not really to want to exchange places with the woodchuck—even if that were possible. Since the paradox is implicit in the whole of romantic experience, small wonder that the entries in Thoreau's journal, made at various times and in various moods, provide a whole spectrum of attitudes toward nature.

In any case, what we know of Thoreau's deathbed casts some doubt on the idea that his concern for death was excessive or morbid. It is said that when Thoreau's Aunt Maria asked him whether he had made his peace with God, his answer was "Why, Aunt, I didn't know we'd ever quarreled." This does not sound like the answer of a man terrified of death; nor does that other story in which Thoreau, on his deathbed, replies to a friend who asked him whether his thoughts had turned to the hereafter: "One world at a time." The reply also suggests a man whose past preoccupation with "this-worldliness" does not cause him to panic about the next world when he is about to leave this one. Thoreau's writings, like the Scriptures, can be quoted to "prove" almost anything. We are probably on safe ground if we allow for a certain amount of contradiction, apparent or real, and do not insist on trying to pin him down to any systematic world view.

Perry Miller sees in Thoreau a fastidious temperament, husbanding its strength, preserving its own privacy, holding itself aloof from embarrassing involvements. Throughout his journal one finds him, so Miller says, "circumventing death, evading woman,[8] discounting friendship," and, by convincing himself in advance that certain things were not possible for him to attain, making it impossible for him ever to be "seduced by the moments he loved so passionately." In *Walden* Thoreau wrote: "Rather than love, than money, than fame, give me truth," and, we may add, Thoreau's was a lonely truth. Yet Miller does not attempt to force such an interpretation on his reader. In fact, he tells us that in approaching the concluding pages of *Walden,* as so often in Thoreau's writings, "every reader is on his own."

It may indeed be impossible to sum up this remarkable man. It is probably not really accurate to describe him as a democratic voice or as a Romantic visionary. He is too much the anarchic individualist to fit the first category; too earthy, to fit the second. He was, truth to tell, an eccentric—independent to the point of crankiness, though rarely the surly or cross-grained or self-obsessed crank.

His style beautifully reflects the man. It is a remarkable style, learned *and* homely, eloquent *and* salty, exalted but never unctuously rhetorical. As a writer he possessed great natural gifts; yet how shrewd he was to get himself born at precisely the right time and in precisely the right place. The orthodoxy of an earlier New England would have found for him a role that would probably have curbed his wit and solemnified him. A generation later on, the more general watering down of the old New England values might well have left him stranded in the genteel tradition.

---

[8] Miller writes (*Consciousness in Concord,* p. 86): "It may at least be posed as a question whether Henry Thoreau in his Concord hamlet of 1840 had the slightest inclination to offer himself as husband to Ellen Sewall. If he did, then it was in the certainty of being refused, and so an inexpensive way to gain an increment in consciousness."

BIOGRAPHICAL CHART

1817 Born, July 12, in Concord, Massachusetts

1833 After preparation at the Concord Academy, enters Harvard

1837 Graduates from Harvard; begins teaching school in Concord, but resigns after dispute over corporal discipline; begins journal

1838 With his brother John, establishes a private academy; delivers a Concord Lyceum address on "Society"

1839 Travels with his brother down the Concord River and then up the Merrimack River

1841 Brother's illness forces the closing of their school; lives with Ralph Waldo Emerson and his family, serving as handyman and editorial assistant at the *Dial*

1843 Tutor in the household of William Emerson; moves with them to Staten Island, N.Y.

1844 Returns to Concord and in 1845 begins residence in a small hut on Emerson's property near Walden Pond; arrested for failure to pay his poll tax

1846 First journey to the Maine woods; begins writing *Walden*

1847 Leaves Walden; returns to the Emersons; first draft of *A Week on the Concord and Merrimack Rivers*

1849 "Resistance to Civil Government" (later "Civil Disobedience") published in *Aesthetic Papers*; the *Week* privately published; returns to his father's house, his last permanent residence; tours Cape Cod

1850 Visits Canada

1851 Helps a fugitive slave to escape to Canada

1854 *Walden*

1857 Final trip to Maine; meets John Brown at Emerson's home

1859 Defends John Brown publicly in Concord and Boston

1861 Travels to Minnesota for his health, observes the Middle West

1862 Dies, May 6, in Concord

FURTHER READINGS

Carl Bode, ed., *The Collected Poems of Henry Thoreau* (1943)

Walter Harding and Carl Bode, eds., *The Correspondence of Henry David Thoreau* (1958)

J. Lyndon Shanley, *The Making of Walden and the Text of the First Version* (1957)

———— et al., eds., *The Writings of Henry D. Thoreau* (25 vols.; CEAA edition); this work, three volumes of which have already been published, will become the standard edition

Philip Van Doren Stern, ed., *The Annotated Walden* (1971)

Bradford Torrey and F. B. Sanborn, eds., *The Writings of Henry David Thoreau* (1906; 20 vols.); a new edition of the last fourteen volumes (F. H. Allen, ed.), containing the journal, appeared in 1949 and was reissued in two volumes in 1962

Brooks Atkinson, *Henry Thoreau, the Cosmic Yankee* (1927)

Henry Seidel Canby, *Thoreau* (1939)

William Ellery Channing, *Thoreau: The Poet Naturalist* (1873)

Wendell Glick, ed., *The Recognition of Henry David Thoreau* (1969)

Walter R. Harding, *A Thoreau Handbook* (1959)

Lauriat Lane, ed., *Approaches to Walden* (1961)

Perry Miller, *Consciousness in Concord* (1958)

Sherman Paul, *The Shores of America: Thoreau's Inward Exploration* (1958)

————, *Thoreau: A Collection of Critical Essays* (1962)

Joel Porte, *Emerson and Thoreau: Transcendentalists in Conflict* (1966)

Leo Stoller, *After Walden: Thoreau's Changing Views on Economic Man* (1957)

From the Journals

At Emerson's suggestion, Thoreau began to keep a journal in 1837; the first entry is dated October 22. Thoreau continued his journal throughout his lifetime, the last entries being recorded only a few months before his death in 1862. Since Thoreau did not envisage publishing his journal, it is an intimate recording of his opinions of events and people, and a record of the growth of his own mind. Moreover, because he kept it only as a convenience to himself, it is a melange of notations about what he did and whom he saw, of his own opinions of people and events, of passages quoted from books that interested him, of private meditations and portions of his verse as well as prose. The full journal amounts to about two million words.

Selections from the journal began to be published in the 1880's, but it was not until 1906 that Houghton Mifflin issued the *Journals* in an edition of fourteen volumes (reissued in 1949). An early volume (July 30, 1840, to January 22, 1841) was not available to the Houghton Mifflin editors and has only recently been published by Perry Miller under the title *Consciousness in Concord* (1958). A second volume, containing entries for part of 1846, has not yet been published.

Thoreau used his journal as source material for works like the *Week* and *Walden*. The student may find it interesting to compare the entries for July 5–7, 1845 below, with the corresponding passages from *Walden* (in this text, pp. 777–78). For the student who would like to read more of the *Journals* than can be included here but who does not wish to tackle a fourteen-volume work, there are a number of volumes of selections, for example, *The Heart of Thoreau's Journals*, edited by Odell Shepard (1927).

July 5, 1845. Saturday. Walden.—Yesterday I came here to live. My house makes me think of some mountain houses I have seen, which seemed to have a fresher auroral atmosphere about them, as I fancy of the halls of Olympus. I lodged at the house of a saw-miller last summer, on the Caatskill Mountains, high up as Pine Orchard, in the blueberry and raspberry region, where the quiet and cleanliness and coolness seemed to be all one,— which had their ambrosial character. He was the miller of the Kaaterskill Falls. They were a clean and wholesome family, inside and out, like their house. The latter was not plastered, only lathed, and the inner doors were not hung. The house seemed high-placed, airy, and perfumed, fit to entertain a travelling god. It was so high, indeed, that all the music, the broken strains, the waifs and accompaniments of tunes, that swept over the ridge of the Caatskills, passed through its aisles. Could not man be man in such an abode? And would he ever find out this grovelling life? It was

the very light and atmosphere in which the works of Grecian art were composed, and in which they rest. They have appropriated to themselves a loftier hall than mortals ever occupy, at least on a level with the mountain-brows of the world. There was wanting a little of the glare of the lower vales, and in its place a pure twilight as became the precincts of heaven. Yet so equable and calm was the season there that you could not tell whether it was morning or noon or evening. Always there was the sound of the morning cricket.

July 6, 1845. I wish to meet the facts of life— the vital facts, which are the phenomena or actuality the gods meant to show us—face to face, and so I came down here. Life! who knows what it is, what it does? If I am not quite right here, I am less wrong than before; and now let us see what they will have. The preacher, instead of vexing the ears of drowsy farmers on their day of rest, at the end of the week.—for Sunday always seemed to me like a fit conclusion of an ill-spent week and not the fresh and brave beginning of a new one,—with this one other draggletail and postponed affair of a sermon, from thirdly to fifteenthly, should teach them with a thundering voice pause and simplicity. "Stop! Avast! Why so fast?" In all studies we go not forward but rather backward with redoubled pauses. We always study antiques with silence and reflection. Even time has a depth, and below its surface the waves do not lapse and roar. I wonder men can be so frivolous almost as to attend to the gross form of negro slavery, there are so many keen and subtle masters who subject us both. Self-emancipation in the West Indies of a man's thinking and imagining provinces, which should be more than his island territory,—one emancipated heart and intellect! It would knock off the fetters from a million slaves.

July 7, 1845. I am glad to remember to-night, as I sit by my door, that I too am at least a remote descendant of that heroic race of men of whom there is tradition. I too sit here on the shore of my Ithaca, a fellow-wanderer and survivor of Ulysses. How symbolical, significant of I know not what, the pitch pine stands here before my door! Unlike any glyph I have seen sculptured or painted yet, one of Nature's later designs, yet perfect as her Grecian art. There it is, a done tree. Who can mend it? And now where is the generation of heroes whose lives are to pass amid these our northern pines, whose exploits shall appeal to posterity pictured amid these strong and shaggy forms? Shall there be only arrows and bows to go with these pines on some pipe-stone quarry at length? There is something more respectable than railroads in these simple relics of the Indian race. What hieroglyphs shall we add to the pipe-stone quarry?

If we can forget, we have done somewhat; if we can remember, we have done somewhat. Let us remember this.

The Great Spirit makes indifferent all times and places. The place where he is seen is always the same, and indescribably pleasant to all our senses. We had allowed only neighboring and transient circumstances to make our occasions. They were, in fact, the causes of our distractions. But nearest to all things is that power which fashions their being. Next to us the grandest laws are being enacted and administered. Next to us is not the workman whom we have hired, but ever the workman whose work we are. He is at work, not in my backyard, but inconceivably nearer than that. We are the subjects of an experiment how singular! Can we not dispense with the society of our gossips a little while under these circumstances?

My auxiliaries are the dews and rains,—to water this dry soil,—and genial fatness in the soil itself, which for the most part is lean and effete. My enemies are worms, cool days, and most of all woodchucks. They have nibbled for me an eighth of an acre clean. I plant in faith, and they reap. This is the tax I pay for ousting johnswort and the rest. But soon the surviving beans will be too tough for woodchucks, and then they will go forward to meet new foes.

October, 1850. Cultivate poverty like sage, like a garden herb. Do not trouble yourself to get new things, whether clothes or friends. That is dissipation. Turn the old; return to them. Things do not change; we change. If I were confined to a corner in a garret all my days, like a spider, the world would be just as large to me while I had my thoughts.

Undated, 1851. English literature from the days of the minstrels to the Lake Poets, Chaucer and Spenser and Shakspeare and Milton included, breathes no quite fresh and in this sense, wild strain. It is an essentially tame and civilized literature, reflecting Greece and Rome. Her wilderness is a greenwood, her wild man a Robin Hood. There is plenty of genial love of nature in her poets, but not so much of nature herself. Her chronicles inform us when her wild animals, but not when the wild man in her, became extinct. There was need of America.

August 22, 1851. It is the fault of some excellent writers—De Quincey's first impressions on seeing London suggest it to me—that they express themselves with too great fullness and detail. They give the most faithful, natural, and lifelike account of their sensations, mental and physical, but they lack moderation and sententiousness. They do not affect us by an ineffectual earnestness and a reserve of meaning, like a stutterer; they say all they mean. Their sentences are not concentrated and nutty. Sentences which suggest far more than they say, which have an atmosphere about them, which do not merely report an old, but make a new, impression; sentences which suggest as many things and are as durable as a Roman aqueduct; to frame these, that is the art of writing. Sentences which are expensive, towards which so many volumes, so much life, went; which lie like boulders on the page, up and down or across; which contain the seed of other sentences, not mere repetition, but creation; which a man might sell his grounds and castles to build. If De Quincey had suggested each of his pages in a sentence and passed on, it would have been far more excellent writing. His style is nowhere kinked and knotted up into something hard and significant, which you could swallow like a diamond, without digesting.

September 4, 1851. To have a hut here, and a footpath to the brook! For roads, I think that a poet cannot tolerate more than a footpath through the fields; that is wide enough, and for purposes of winged poesy suffices. It is not for the muse to speak of cart-paths. I would fain travel by a footpath round the world. I do not ask the railroads of commerce, not even the cart-paths of the farmer. Pray, what other path would you have than a footpath? What else should wear a path? This is the track of man alone. What more suggestive to the pensive walker? One walks in a wheeltrack with less emotion; he is at a greater distance from man; but this footpath was, perchance, worn by the bare feet of human beings, and he cannot but think with interest of them.

October 1, 5 P.M., 1851. Just put a fugitive slave, who has taken the name of Henry Williams, into the cars for Canada. He escaped from Stafford County, Virginia, to Boston last October; has been in Shadrach's place at the Cornhill Coffee-House; had been corresponding through an agent with his master, who is his father, about buying himself, his master asking $600, but he having been able to raise only $500. Heard that there were writs out for two Williamses, fugitives, and was informed by his fellow-servants and employer that Augerhole

Burns and others of the police had called for him when he was out. Accordingly fled to Concord last night on foot, bringing a letter to our family from Mr. Lovejoy of Cambridge and another which Garrison had formerly given him on another occasion. He lodged with us, and waited in the house till funds were collected with which to forward him. Intended to dispatch him at noon through to Burlington, but when I went to buy his ticket, saw one at the depot who looked and behaved so much like a Boston policeman that I did not venture that time. An intelligent and very well-behaved man, a mulatto.

November 13, 1851. Just spent a couple of hours (eight to ten) with Miss Mary Emerson at Holbrook's. The wittiest and most vivacious woman that I know, certainly that woman among my acquaintance whom it is most profitable to meet, the least frivolous, who will most surely provoke to good conversation and the expression of what is in you. She is singular, among women at least, in being really and perseveringly interested to know what thinkers think. She relates herself surely to the intellectual where she goes. It is perhaps her greatest praise and peculiarity that she, more surely than any other woman, gives her companion occasion to utter his best thought. In spite of her own biases, she can entertain a large thought with hospitality, and is not prevented by an intellectuality in it, as women commonly are. In short, she is a genius, as woman seldom is, reminding you less often of her sex than any woman whom I know. In that sense she is capable of a masculine appreciation of poetry and philosophy. I never talked with any other woman who I thought accompanied me so far in describing a poetic experience. Miss Fuller is the only woman I think of in this connection, and of her rather from her fame than from any knowledge of her. Miss Emerson expressed to-night a singular want of respect for her own sex, saying that they were frivolous almost without exception, that woman was the weaker vessel, etc.; that into whatever family she might go, she depended more upon the 'clown' for society than upon the lady of the house. Men are more likely to have opinions of their own.

December 12, 1851. Ah, dear nature, the mere remembrance, after a short forgetfulness, of the pine woods! I come to it as a hungry man to a crust of bread.

January 24, 1852. If thou art a writer, write as if thy time were short, for it is indeed short at the longest. Improve each occasion when thy soul is reached. Drain the cup of inspiration to its last dregs. Fear no intemperance in that, for the years will come when otherwise thou wilt regret opportunities unimproved. The spring will not last forever. These fertile and expanding seasons of thy life, when the rain reaches thy root, when thy vigor shoots, when thy flower is budding, shall be fewer and farther between. Again I say, Remember thy Creator in the days of thy youth. Use and commit to life what you cannot commit to memory. I hear the tones of my sister's piano below. It reminds me of strains which once I heard more frequently, when, possessed with the inaudible rhythm, I sought my chamber in the cold and communed with my own thoughts. I feel as if I then received the gifts of the gods with too much indifference. Why did I not cultivate those fields they introduced me to? Does nothing withstand the inevitable march of time? Why did I not use my eyes when I stood on Pisgah? Now I hear those strains but seldom. My rhythmical mood does not endure. I cannot draw from it and return to it in my thought as to a well all the evening or the morning. I cannot dip my pen in it. I cannot work the vein, it is so fine and volatile. Ah, sweet, ineffable reminiscences!

January 30, Friday, 1852. I doubt if Emerson could trundle a wheelbarrow through the streets, because it would be out of character. One needs to have a comprehensive character. . . .

I am afraid to travel much or to famous places, lest it might completely dissipate the mind. Then I am sure that what we observe at home, if we observe anything, is of more importance than what we observe abroad. The far-fetched is of the least value. What we observe in travelling are to some extent the accidents of the body, but [what] we observe when sitting at home are, in the same proportion, phenomena of the mind itself. A wakeful night will yield as much thought as a long journey. If I try thoughts by their quality, not their quantity, I may find that a restless night will yield more than the longest journey.

February 11, 1852. I have lived some thirty-odd years on this planet, and I have yet to hear the first syllable of valuable or even earnest advice from my seniors. They have told me nothing, and probably can tell me nothing to the purpose. There is life, an experiment untried by me, and it does not avail me that you have tried it. If I have any valuable experience, I am sure to reflect that this my mentors said nothing about. What were mysteries to the child remain mysteries to the old man.

May 23, 1853. At Loring's Wood heard and saw a tanager. That contrast of a red bird with the green pines and the blue sky! Even when I have heard his note and look for him and find the bloody fellow, sitting on a dead twig of a pine, I am always startled. (They seem to love the darkest and thickest pines.) That incredible red, with the green and blue, as if these were the trinity we wanted. Yet with his hoarse note he pays for his color. I am transported; these are not the woods I ordinarily walk in. He sunk Concord in his thought. How he enhances the wildness and wealth of the woods! This and the emperor moth make the tropical phenomena of our zone. There is warmth in the pewee's strain, but this bird's colors and his note tell of Brazil.

From Walden, or, Life in the Woods (1854)

When Thoreau decided to live in the woods at Walden Pond he did not propose to become a hermit. The little cabin that he built was in easy walking distance of Concord and only twenty miles from Boston itself. He was in touch with neighbors and had many visitors, but the solitude that his location provided and the opportunity it gave him to cultivate his own garden answered almost perfectly to the terms of his experiment in living. Thoreau's decision to retire to Walden was not made on sudden impulse. For a long time he had thought about the possibility of living in the woods and when Emerson purchased fourteen acres on the shores of the pond in 1845, he found an opportunity to act upon his long-cherished plan. It was in March, 1845, Thoreau tells us, that he borrowed an axe and began to fell trees for his cabin. By July 4, he was able to move into it and set up housekeeping. He lived at Walden for exactly two years, two months, and two days.

In writing his book about the Walden experience, however, Thoreau wisely compressed the two years into one. The book begins with summer and moves through the round of the seasons—autumn, winter, and spring. Thoreau, thus, does not record his various experiences in literal sequence, but composes like an artist, omitting some items, amplifying others, reordering his material where necessary, and, in general, shaping his work in the interest of producing a particular effect.

It has been remarked earlier that Thoreau seems to write sentence by sentence rather than paragraph by paragraph and that there is no obvious plan of logical progression. In a sense this is true enough, and the brilliant sentence is indeed the hallmark of Thoreau's style. But it has been argued quite persuasively that a more subtle plan of organization does underlie the surface detail of *Walden* and that part is so related to part that the work has a truly organic unity. (See, for example, J. Lyndon Shanley, *The Making of Walden*, 1957.) Not only is the rhythm of *Walden* that of the seasons of the year, but individual chapters reflect the sequence of day and night. For example, the chapter entitled "Sounds" begins with the various sounds of the afternoon and goes on to record those of the evening and night, ending with the cockcrow at dawn.

The following list of the titles of chapters will suggest something of the arrangement as well as the subject matter of the book. The chapters marked with an asterisk are printed in whole or in part in this text.

*Economy
Where I Lived, and What I Lived For
Reading
Sounds
*Solitude
Visitors
The Bean-Field
*The Village
*The Ponds
Baker Farm
Higher Laws
Brute Neighbors
House-Warming
Former Inhabitants; and Winter Visitors
Winter Animals
The Pond in Winter
Spring
*Conclusion

ECONOMY

When I wrote the following pages, or rather the bulk of them, I lived alone, in the woods, a mile from any neighbor, in a house which I had built myself, on the shore of Walden Pond, in Concord, Massachusetts, and earned my living by the labor of my hands only. I lived there two years and two months. At present I am a sojourner in civilized life again.

I should not obtrude my affairs so much on the notice of my readers if very particular inquiries had not been made by my townsmen concerning my mode of life, which some would call impertinent, though they do not appear to me at all impertinent, but, considering the circumstances, very natural and pertinent. Some have asked what I got to eat; if I did not feel lonesome; if I was not afraid; and the like. Others have been curious to learn what portion of my income I devoted to charitable purposes; and some, who have large families, how many poor children I maintained. I will therefore ask those of my readers who feel no particular interest in me to pardon me if I undertake to answer some of these questions in this book. In most books, the I, or first person, is omitted; in this it will be retained; that, in respect to egotism, is the main difference. We commonly do not remember that it is, after all, always the first person that is speaking. I should not talk so much about myself if there were any body else whom I knew so well. Unfortunately, I am confined to this theme by the narrowness of my experience. Moreover, I, on my side, require of every writer, first or last, a simple and sincere account of his own life, and not merely what he has heard of other men's lives; some such account as he would send to his kindred from a distant land; for if he has lived sincerely, it must have been in a distant land to me. Perhaps these pages are more particularly addressed to poor students. As for the rest of my readers, they will accept such portions as apply to them. I trust that none will stretch the seams in putting on the coat, for it may do good service to him whom it fits.

. . .

The mass of men lead lives of quiet desperation. What is called resignation is confirmed desperation. From the desperate city you go into the desperate country, and have to console yourself with the bravery of minks and muskrats. A stereotyped but unconscious despair is concealed even under what are called the games and amusements of mankind. There is no play in them, for this comes after work. But it is a characteristic of wisdom not to do desperate things.

When we consider what, to use the words of the catechism, is the chief end of man, and what are the true necessaries and means of life, it appears as if men had deliberately chosen the common mode of living because they preferred it to any other. Yet they honestly think there is no choice left. But alert and healthy natures remember that the sun rose clear. It is never too late to give up our prejudices. No way of thinking or doing, however ancient, can be trusted without proof. What every body echoes or in silence passes by as true to-day may turn out to be falsehood to-morrow, mere smoke of opinion, which some had trusted for a cloud that would sprinkle fertilizing rain on their fields. What old people say you cannot do you try and find that you can. Old deeds for old people, and new deeds for new. Old people did not know enough once, perchance, to fetch fresh fuel to keep the fire a-going; new people put a little dry wood under a pot, and are whirled round the globe with the speed of birds, in a way to kill old people, as the phrase is. Age is no better, hardly so well, qualified for an instructor as youth, for it has not profited so much as it has lost. One may almost doubt if the wisest man has learned any thing of absolute value by living. Practically, the old have no very important advice to give the young, their own experience has been so partial, and their lives have been such miserable failures, for private reasons, as they must believe; and it may be that they have some faith left which belies that experience, and they are only less young than they were. I have lived some thirty years on this planet, and I have yet to hear the first syllable of valuable or even earnest advice from my seniors. They have told me nothing, and probably cannot tell me any thing, to the purpose. Here is life, an experiment to a great extent untried by me; but it does not avail me that they have tried it. If I have any experience which I think valuable, I am sure to reflect that this my Mentors said nothing about.

One farmer says to me, "You cannot live on vegetable food solely, for it furnishes nothing to make bones with;" and so he religiously devotes a part of his day to supplying his system with the raw material of bones; walking all the while he talks behind his oxen, which, with vegetable-made bones, jerk him and his lumbering plough along in spite of every obstacle. Some things are really necessaries of life in some circles, the most helpless and diseased, which in others are luxuries merely, and in others still are entirely unknown.

The whole ground of human life seems to some to have been gone over by their predecessors, both the heights and the valleys, and all things to have been cared for. According to Evelyn, "the wise Solomon prescribed ordinances for the very distances of trees; and the Roman prætors have decided how often you may go into your neighbor's land to gather the acorns which fall on it without trespass, and what share belongs to that neighbor." Hippocrates has even left directions how we should cut our nails; that is, even with the ends of the fingers, neither shorter nor longer. Undoubtedly the very tedium and ennui which presume to have exhausted the variety and the joys of life are as old as Adam. But man's capacities have never been measured; nor are we to judge of what he can do by any precedents, so little has been tried. Whatever have been thy failures hitherto, "be not afflicted, my child, for who shall assign to thee what thou hast left undone?"

. . .

Finding that my fellow-citizens were not likely to offer me any room in the court house, or any curacy or living any where else, but I must shift for myself, I turned my face more exclusively than ever to the woods, where I was better known. I determined to go into business at once, and not wait to acquire the usual capital, using such slender means as I had already got. My purpose in going to Walden Pond was not to live cheaply nor to live dearly there, but to transact some private business with the fewest obstacles; to be hindered from accomplishing which for want of a little common sense, a little enterprise and business talent, appeared not so sad as foolish.

. . .

Near the end of March, 1845, I borrowed an axe and went down to the woods by Walden Pond, nearest to where I intended to build my house, and began to cut down some tall arrowy white pines, still in their youth, for timber. It is difficult to begin without borrowing, but perhaps it is the most generous course thus to permit your fellow-men to have an interest in your enterprise. The owner of the axe, as he released his hold on it, said that it was the apple of his eye; but I returned it sharper than I received it. It was a pleasant hillside where I worked, covered with pine woods, through which I looked out on the pond, and a small open field in the woods where pines and hickories were springing up. The ice in the pond was not yet dissolved, though there were some open spaces, and it was all dark colored and saturated with water. There were some slight flurries of snow during the days that I worked there; but for the most part when I came out on to the railroad, on my way home, its yellow sand heap stretched away gleaming in the hazy atmosphere, and the rails shone in the spring sun, and I heard the lark and pewee and other birds already come to commence another year with us. They were pleasant spring days, in which the winter of man's discontent was thawing as well as the earth, and the life that had lain torpid began to stretch itself. One day, when my axe had come off and I had cut a green hickory for a wedge, driving it with a stone, and had placed the whole to soak in a pond hole in order to swell the wood, I saw a striped snake run into the water, and he lay on the bottom, apparently without inconvenience, as long as I staid there, or more than a quarter of an hour; perhaps because he had not yet fairly come out of the torpid state. It appeared to me that for a like reason men remain in their present low and primitive condition; but if they should feel the influence of the spring of springs arousing them, they would of necessity rise to a higher and more ethereal life. I had previously seen the snakes in frosty mornings in my path with portions of their bodies still numb and inflexible, waiting for the sun to thaw them. On the 1st of April it rained and melted the ice, and in the early part of the day, which was very foggy, I heard a stray goose groping about over the pond and cackling as if lost, or like the spirit of the fog.

So I went on for some days cutting and hewing timber, and also studs and rafters, all with my narrow axe, not having many communicable or scholar-like thoughts, singing to myself,—

Men say they know many things;
But lo! they have taken wings,—
The arts and sciences,
And a thousand appliances;
The wind that blows
Is all that any body knows.

I hewed the main timbers six inches square, most of the studs on two sides only, and the rafters and floor timbers on one side, leaving the rest of the bark on, so that they were just as straight and much stronger than sawed ones. Each stick was carefully mortised or tenoned by its stump, for I had borrowed other tools by this time. My days in the woods were not very long ones; yet I usually carried my dinner of bread and butter, and read the newspaper in which it was wrapped, at noon, sitting amid the green pine boughs which I had cut off, and to my bread was imparted some of their fragrance, for my hands were covered with a thick coat of pitch. Before I had done I was more the friend than the foe of the pine tree, though I had cut down some of them, having become better acquainted with it. Sometimes a rambler in the wood was attracted by the sound of my axe, and we chatted pleasantly over the chips which I had made.

By the middle of April, for I made no haste in my work, but rather made the most of it, my house was framed and ready for the raising. I had already bought the shanty of James Collins, an Irishman who worked on the Fitchburg Railroad, for boards. James Collins' shanty was considered an uncommonly fine one. When I called to see it he was not at home. I walked about the outside, at first unobserved from within, the window was so deep and high. It was of small dimensions, with a peaked cottage roof, and not much else to be seen, the dirt being raised five feet all around as if it were a compost heap. The roof was the soundest part, though a good deal warped and made brittle by the sun. Doorsill there was none, but a perennial passage for the hens under the door board. Mrs. C. came to the door and asked me to view it from the inside. The hens were driven in by my approach. It was dark, and had a dirt floor for the most part, dank, clammy, and aguish, only here a board and there a board which would not bear removal. She lighted a lamp to show me the inside of the roof and the walls, and also that the board floor extended under the bed, warning me not to step into the cellar, a sort of dust hole two feet deep. In her own words, they were "good boards overhead, good boards all around, and a good window,"—of two whole squares originally, only the cat had passed out that way lately. There was a stove, a bed, and a place to sit, an infant in the house where it was born, a silk parasol, gilt-framed looking-glass, and a patent new coffee mill nailed to an oak sapling, all told. The bargain was soon concluded, for James had in the mean while returned. I to pay four dollars and twenty-five cents to-night, he to vacate at five to-morrow morning, selling to nobody else mean while: I to take possession at six. It were well, he said, to be there early, and anticipate certain indistinct but wholly unjust claims on the score of ground rent and fuel. This he assured me was the only encumbrance. At six I passed him and his family on the road. One large bundle held their all,—bed, coffee-mill, looking-glass, hens,—all but the cat, she took to the woods and became a wild cat, and, as I learned afterward, trod in a trap set for woodchucks, and so became a dead cat at last.

I took down this dwelling the same morning, drawing the nails, and removed it to the pond side by small cartloads, spreading the boards on the grass there to bleach and warp back again in the sun. One early thrush gave me a note or two as I drove along the woodland path. I was informed treacherously by a young Patrick that neighbor Seeley, an Irishman, in the intervals of the carting, transferred the still tolerable, straight, and drivable nails, staples, and spikes to his pocket, and then stood when I came back to pass the time of day, and look freshly up, unconcerned, with spring thoughts, at the devastation; there being a dearth of work, as he said. He was there to represent spectatordom, and help make this seemingly insignificant event one with the removal of the gods of Troy.

I dug my cellar in the side of a hill sloping to the south, where a woodchuck had formerly dug his burrow, down through sumach and blackberry roots, and the lowest stain of vegetation, six feet square by seven deep, to a fine sand where potatoes would not freeze in any winter. The sides were left shelving, and not stoned; but the sun having never shone on them, the sand still keeps its place. It was but two hours' work. I took particular pleasure in this breaking of ground, for in almost all latitudes men dig into the earth for an equable temperature. Under the most splendid house in the city is still to be found the cellar where they store their roots as of old, and long after the superstructure has disappeared posterity remark its dent in the earth. The house is still but a sort of porch at the entrance of a burrow.

At length, in the beginning of May, with the help of some of my acquaintances, rather to improve so good an occasion for neighborliness than from any necessity, I set up the frame of my house. No man was ever more honored in the character of his raisers than I. They are destined, I trust, to assist at the raising of loftier structures one day. I began to occupy my house on the 4th of July, as soon as it was boarded and roofed, for the boards were carefully feather-edged and lapped, so that it was perfectly impervious to rain; but before boarding I laid the foundation of a chimney at one end, bringing two cartloads of stones up the hill from the pond in my arms. I built the chimney after my hoeing in the fall, before a fire became necessary for warmth, doing my cooking in the mean while out of doors on the ground, early in the morning: which mode I still think is in some respects more convenient and agreeable than the usual one. When it stormed before my bread was baked, I fixed a few boards over the fire, and sat under them to watch my loaf, and passed some pleasant hours in that way. In those days, when my hands were much employed, I read but little, but the least scraps of paper which lay on the ground, my holder, or tablecloth, afforded me as much entertainment, in fact answered the same purpose as the Iliad.

. . .

Before winter I built a chimney, and shingled the sides of my house, which were already impervious to rain, with imperfect and sappy shingles made of the first slice of the log, whose edges I was obliged to straighten with a plane.

I have thus a tight shingled and plastered house, ten feet wide by fifteen long, and eight-feet posts, with a garret and a closet, a large window on each side, two trap doors, one door at the end, and a brick fireplace opposite. The exact cost of my house, paying the usual price for such materials as I used, but not counting the work, all of which was done by myself, was as follows; and I give the details because very few are able to tell exactly what their houses cost, and fewer still, if any, the separate cost of the various materials which compose them:—

Boards	$8 03½,	Mostly shanty boards.
Refuse shingles for roof and sides	4 00	
Laths	1 25	
Two second-hand windows with glass	2 43	
One thousand old brick	4 00	
Two casks of lime	2 40	That was high.
Hair	0 31	More than I needed.
Mantle-tree iron	0 15	
Nails	3 90	
Hinges and screws	0 14	
Latch	0 10	
Chalk	0 01	
Transportation	1 40	I carried a good part on my back.
In all	$28 12½	

These are all the materials excepting the timber, stones and sand, which I claimed by squatter's right. I have also a small wood-shed adjoining, made chiefly of the stuff which was left after building the house.

I intend to build me a house which will surpass any on the main street in Concord in grandeur and luxury, as soon as it pleases me as much and will cost me no more than my present one.

I thus found that the student who wishes for a shelter can obtain one for a lifetime at an expense not greater than the rent which he now pays annually. If I seem to boast more than is becoming, my excuse is that I brag for humanity rather than for myself; and my shortcomings and inconsistencies do not affect the truth of my statement. Notwithstanding much cant and hypocrisy,—chaff which I find it difficult to separate from my wheat, but for which I am as sorry as any man,—I will breathe freely and stretch myself in this respect, it is such a relief to both the moral and physical system; and I am resolved that I will not through humility become the devil's attorney. I will endeavor to speak a good word for the truth. At Cambridge [Harvard] College the mere rent of a student's room, which is only a little larger than my own, is thirty dollars each year, though the corporation had the advantage of building thirty-two side by side and under one roof, and the occupant suffers the inconvenience of many and noisy neighbors, and perhaps a residence in the fourth story. I cannot but think that if we had more true wisdom in these respects, not only less education would be needed, because, forsooth, more would already have been acquired, but the pecuniary expense of getting an education would in a great measure vanish. Those conveniences which the student requires at Cambridge or elsewhere cost him or somebody else ten times as great a sacrifice of life as they would with proper management on both sides. Those things for which the most money is demanded are never the things which the student most wants. Tuition, for instance, is an important item in the term bill, while for the far more valuable education which he gets by associating with the most cultivated of his contemporaries no charge is made. The mode of founding a college is, commonly, to get up a subscription of dollars and cents, and then following blindly the principles of a division of labor to its extreme, a principle which should never be followed but with circumspection,—to call in a contractor who makes this a subject of speculation, and he employs Irishmen or other operatives actually to lay the foundations, while the students that are to be are said to be fitting themselves for it; and for these oversights successive generations have to pay. I think that it would be *better than this,* for the students, or those who desire to be benefited by it, even to lay the foundation themselves. The student who secures his coveted leisure and retirement by systematically shirking any labor necessary to man obtains but an ignoble and unprofitable leisure, defrauding himself of the experience which alone can make leisure fruitful. "But," says one, "you do not mean that the students should go to work with their hands instead of their heads?" I do not mean that exactly, but I mean something which he might think a good deal like that; I mean that they should not *play* life, or *study* it merely, while the community supports them at this expensive game, but earnestly *live* it from beginning to end. How could youths better learn to live than by at once trying the experiment of living? Methinks this would exercise their minds as much as mathematics. If I wished a boy to know something about the arts and sciences, for instance, I would not pursue the common course, which is merely to send him into the neighbourhood of some professor, where anything is professed and practised but the art of life;—to survey the world through a telescope or a microscope, and never with his natural eye; to study chemistry, and not learn how his bread is made, or mechanics, and not learn how it is earned; to discover new satellites to Neptune, and not detect the motes in his eyes, or to what vagabond he is a satellite himself; or to be devoured by the monsters that swarm all around him, while contemplating the monsters in a drop of vinegar. Which would have advanced the most at the end of a month—the boy who had made his own jack-knife from the ore which he had dug and smelted, reading as much as would be necessary for this,—or the boy who had attended the lectures on metallurgy at the Institute in the mean while,

and had received a Rogers' penknife from his father? Which would be most likely to cut his fingers?—To my astonishment I was informed on leaving college that I had studied navigation!—why, if I had taken one turn down the harbour I should have known more about it. Even the *poor* student studies and is taught only *political* economy, while that economy of living which is synonymous with philosophy is not even sincerely professed in our colleges. The consequence is, that while he is reading Adam Smith, Ricardo, and Say, he runs his father in debt irretrievably.

As with our colleges, so with a hundred "modern improvements:" there is an illusion about them; there is not always a positive advance. The devil goes on exacting compound interest to the last for his early share and numerous succeeding investments in them. Our inventions are wont to be pretty toys, which distract our attention from serious things. They are but improved means to an unimproved end, an end which it was already but too easy to arrive at—as railroads lead to Boston or New York. We are in great haste to construct a magnetic telegraph from Maine to Texas; but Maine and Texas, it may be, have nothing important to communicate. Either is in such a predicament as the man who was earnest to be introduced to a distinguished deaf woman, but when he was presented, and one end of her ear trumpet was put into his hand, had nothing to say. As if the main object were to talk fast and not to talk sensibly. We are eager to tunnel under the Atlantic and bring the old world some weeks nearer to the new; but perchance the first news that will leak through into the broad, flapping American ear will be that the Princess Adelaide has the whooping cough. After all, the man whose horse trots a mile in a minute does not carry the most important messages: he is not an evangelist, nor does he come round eating locusts and wild honey. I doubt if Flying Childers ever carried a peck of corn to mill.

One says to me, "I wonder that you do not lay up money; you love to travel; you might take the cars and go to Fitchburg to-day and see the country." But I am wiser than that. I have learned that the swiftest traveller is he that goes a-foot. I say to my friend, Suppose we try who will get there first. The distance is thirty miles; the fare ninety cents. That is almost a day's wages. I remember when wages were sixty cents a-day for labourers on this very road. Well, I start now on foot, and get there before night; I have travelled at that rate by the week together. You will in the mean while have earned your fare, and arrive there some time to-morrow, or possibly this evening, if you are lucky enough to get a job in season. Instead of going to Fitchburg, you will be working here the greater part of the day. And so, if the railroad reached round the world, I think that I should keep ahead of you; and as for seeing the country and getting experience of that kind, I should have to cut your acquaintance altogether.

Such is the universal law, which no man can ever outwit, and with regard to the railroad even we may say it is as broad as it is long. To make a railroad round the world available to all mankind is equivalent to grading the whole surface of the planet. Men have an indistinct notion that if they keep up this activity of joint stocks and spades long enough all will at length ride somewhere, in next to no time, and for nothing; but though a crowd rushes to the depôt, and the conductor shouts "All aboard!" when the smoke is blown away and the vapour condensed, it will be perceived that a few are riding, but the rest are run over,—and it will be called, and will be, "A melancholy accident." No doubt they can ride at last who shall have earned their fare, that is, if they survive, so long, but they will probably have lost their elasticity and desire to travel by that time. This spending of the best part of one's life earning money in order to enjoy a questionable liberty during the least valuable part of it, reminds me of the Englishman who went to India to make a fortune first, in order that he might return to England and live the life of a poet. He should have gone up garret at once. "What!" exclaim a million Irishmen, starting up from all the shanties in the land, "is not this railroad which we have built a good thing?" Yes, I answer, *comparatively* good—that is, you might have done worse; but I wish, as you are brothers of mine, that you could have spent your time better than digging in this dirt.

Before I finished my house, wishing to earn ten or twelve dollars by some honest and agreeable method, in order to meet my unusual expenses, I planted about two acres and a-half of light and sandy soil near it chiefly with beans, but also a small part with potatoes, corn, peas, and turnips. The whole lot contains eleven acres, mostly growing up to pines and hickories, and was sold the preceding season for eight dollars and eight cents an acre. One farmer said that it was "good for nothing but to raise cheeping squirrels on." I put no manure on this land, not being the owner, but merely a squatter, and not expecting to cultivate so much again, and I did not quite hoe it all once. I got out several cords of stumps in ploughing, which supplied me with fuel for a long time, and left small circles of virgin mould, easily distinguishable through the summer by the greater luxuriance of the beans there. The dead and for the most part unmerchantable wood behind my house, and the driftwood from the pond, have supplied the remainder of my fuel. I was obliged to hire a team and a man for the ploughing, though I held the plough myself. My farm outgoes for the first season were, for implements, seed, work, &c., $14 72½. The seed corn was given me. This never costs anything to speak of, unless you plant more than enough. I got twelve bushels of beans, and eighteen bushels of potatoes, beside some peas and sweet corn. The yellow corn and turnips were too late to come to anything. My whole income from the farm was

		$23 44.
Deducting the outgoes,	. .	14 72½
There are left,	. . . .	8 71½,

beside produce consumed and on hand at the time this estimate was made of the value of $4 50,—the amount on hand much more than balancing a little grass which I did not raise. All things considered, that is, considering the importance of a man's soul and of to-day, notwithstanding the short time occupied by my experiment, nay, partly even because of its transient character, I believe that that was doing better than any farmer in Concord did that year.

SOLITUDE

. . .

I have a great deal of company in my house; especially in the morning, when nobody calls. Let me suggest a few comparisons, that some one may convey an idea of my situation. I am no more lonely than the loon in the pond that laughs so loud, or than Walden Pond itself. What company has that lonely lake, I pray? And yet it has not the blue devils, but the blue angels in it, in the azure tint of its waters. The sun is alone, except in thick weather, when there sometimes appear to be two, but one is a mock sun. God is alone,—but the devil, he is far from being alone; he sees a great deal of company; he is legion. I am no more lonely than a single mullein or dandelion in a pasture, or a bean leaf, or sorrel, or a horse-fly, or a humble-bee. I am no more lonely than the Mill Brook, or a weathercock, or the north star, or the south wind, or an April shower, or a January thaw, or the first spider in a new house.

I have occasional visits in the long winter evenings, when the snow falls fast and the wind howls in the wood, from an old settler and original proprietor, who is reported to have dug Walden Pond, and stoned it, and fringed it with pine woods; who tells me stories of old time and of new eternity; and between us we manage to pass a cheerful evening with social mirth and pleasant views of things, even without apples or cider,—a most wise and humorous friend, whom I love much, who keeps himself more secret than ever did Goffe or Whalley; and though he is thought to be dead, none can show where he is buried. An elderly dame, too, dwells in my neighborhood, invisible to most persons, in whose odorous herb garden I love to stroll sometimes, gathering simples and listening to her fables; for she has a genius of unequalled fertility, and her memory runs back farther than mythology, and she can tell me the original of every fable, and on what fact every one is founded, for the incidents occurred when she was young. A ruddy and lusty old dame, who delights in all weathers and seasons, and is likely to outlive all her children yet.

The indescribable innocence and beneficence of Nature,—of sun and wind and rain, of summer and winter,—such health, such cheer, they afford forever! and such sympathy have they ever with our race, that all Nature would be affected, and the sun's brightness fade, and the winds would sigh humanely, and the clouds rain tears, and the woods shed their leaves and put on mourning in midsummer, if any man should ever for a just cause grieve. Shall I not have intelligence with the earth? Am I not partly leaves and vegetable mould myself?

What is the pill which will keep us well, serene, contented? Not my or thy great-grandfather's, but our great-grandmother Nature's universal, vegetable, botanic medicines, by which she has kept herself young always, outlived so many old Parrs in her day, and fed her health with their decaying fatness. For my panacea, instead of one of those quack vials of a mixture dipped from Acheron and the Dead Sea, which come out of those long shallow black-schooner looking wagons which we some-times see made to carry bottles, let me have a draught of undiluted morning air. Morning air! If men will not drink of this at the fountainhead of the day, why, then, we must even bottle up some and sell it in the shops, for the benefit of those who have lost their subscription ticket to morning time in this world. But remember, it will not keep quite till noon-day even in the coolest cellar, but drive out the stopples long ere that and follow westward the steps of Aurora. I am no worshipper of Hygeia, who was the daughter of that old herb-doctor Æsculapius, and who is represented on monuments holding a serpent in one hand, and in the other a cup out of which the serpent sometimes drinks; but rather of Hebe, cupbearer to Jupiter, who was the daughter of Juno and wild lettuce, and who had the power of restoring gods and men to the vigor of youth. She was probably the only thoroughly sound-conditioned, healthy, and robust young lady that ever walked the globe, and wherever she came it was spring.

THE VILLAGE

After hoeing, or perhaps reading and writing, in the forenoon, I usually bathed again in the pond, swimming across one of its coves for a stint, and washed the dust of labor from my person, or smoothed out the last wrinkle which study had made, and for the afternoon was absolutely free. Every day or two I strolled to the village to hear some of the gossip which is incessantly going on there, circulating either from mouth to mouth, or from newspaper to newspaper, and which, taken in homœopathic doses, was really as refreshing in its way as the rustle of leaves and the peeping of frogs. As I walked in the woods to see the birds and squirrels, so I walked in the village to see the men and boys; instead of the wind among the pines I heard the carts rattle. In one direction from my house there was a colony of muskrats in the river meadows; under the grove of elms and buttonwoods in the other horizon was a village of busy men, as curious to me as if they had been prairie dogs, each sitting at the mouth of its burrow, or running over to a neighbor's to gossip. I went there frequently to observe their habits. The village appeared to me a great news room; and on one side, to support it, as once at Redding & Company's on State Street [Boston], they kept nuts and raisins, or salt and meal and other groceries. Some have such a vast appetite for the former commodity, that is, the news, and such sound digestive organs, that they can sit forever in public avenues without stirring, and let it simmer and whisper through them like the Etesian winds, or as if inhaling either, it only producing numbness and insensibility to pain,—otherwise it would often be painful to hear,—without affecting the consciousness. I hardly ever failed, when I rambled through the village, to see a row of such worthies, either sitting on a ladder sunning themselves, with their bodies inclined forward and their eyes glancing along the line this way and that, from time to time, with a voluptuous expression, or else leaning against a barn with their hands in their pockets, like caryatides, as if to prop it up. They, being commonly out of doors, heard whatever was in the wind. These are the coarsest mills, in which all gossip is first rudely digested or cracked up before it is emptied into finer and more delicate hoppers within doors. I observed that the vitals of the village were the grocery, the bar-room, the post-office, and the bank; and, as a necessary part of the machinery, they kept a bell, a big gun, and a fire-engine, at convenient places; and the houses were so arranged as to make the most of mankind, in lanes and fronting one another, so that every traveller had to run the gantlet, and every man, woman, and child might get a lick at him. Of course, those who were stationed nearest to the head of the line, where they could most see and be seen, and have the first blow at him, paid the highest prices for their places; and the few straggling inhabitants in the outskirts, where long gaps in the line began to occur, and the traveller could get over walls or turn aside into cow paths, and so escape, paid a very slight ground or window tax. Signs were hung out on all sides to allure him; some to catch him by the appetite, as the tavern and victualling cellar; some by the fancy, as the dry goods store and the jeweller's; and others by the hair or the feet or the skirts, as the barber, the shoemaker, or the tailor. Besides, there was a still more terrible standing invitation to call at every one of these houses, and company expected about these times. For the most part I escaped wonderfully from these dangers, either by proceeding at once boldly and without deliberation to the goal, as is recommended to those who run the gantlet, or by keeping my thoughts on high things, like Orpheus, who, "loudly singing the praises of the gods to his lyre, drowned the voices of the Sirens, and kept out of danger." Sometimes I bolted suddenly, and nobody could tell my whereabouts, for I did not stand much

about gracefulness, and never hesitated at a gap in a fence. I was even accustomed to make an irruption into some houses, where I was well entertained, and after learning the kernels and very last sieveful of news, what had subsided, the prospects of war and peace, and whether the world was likely to hold together much longer, I was let out through the rear avenues, and so escaped to the woods again.

It was very pleasant, when I staid late in town, to launch myself into the night, especially if it was dark and tempestuous, and set sail from some bright village parlor or lecture room, with a bag of rye or Indian meal upon my shoulder, for my snug harbor in the woods, having made all tight without and withdrawn under hatches with a merry crew of thoughts, leaving only my outer man at the helm, or even tying up the helm when it was plain sailing. I had many a genial thought by the cabin fire "as I sailed." I was never cast away nor distressed in any weather, though I encountered some severe storms. It is darker in the woods, even in common nights, than most suppose. I frequently had to look up at the opening between the trees above the path in order to learn my route, and, where there was no cart-path, to feel with my feet the faint track which I had worn, or steer by the known relation of particular trees which I felt with my hands, passing between two pines for instance, not more than eighteen inches apart, in the midst of the woods, invariably in the darkest night. Sometimes, after coming home thus late in a dark and muggy night, when my feet felt the path which my eyes could not see, dreaming and absent-minded all the way, until I was aroused by having to raise my hand to lift the latch, I have not been able to recall a single step of my walk, and I have thought that perhaps my body would find its way home if its master should forsake it, as the hand finds its way to the mouth without assistance. Several times, when a visitor chanced to stay into evening, and it proved a dark night, I was obliged to conduct him to the cart-path in the rear of the house, and then point out to him the direction he was to pursue, and in keeping which he was to be guided rather by his feet than his eyes. One very dark night I directed thus on their way two young men who had been fishing in the pond. They lived about a mile off through the woods, and were quite used to the route. A day or two after one of them told me that they wandered about the greater part of the night, close by their own premises, and did not get home till toward morning, by which time, as there had been several heavy showers in the mean while, and the leaves were very wet, they were drenched to their skins. I have heard of many going astray even in the village streets, when the darkness was so thick that you could cut it with a knife, as the saying is. Some who live in the outskirts, having come to town a-shopping in their wagons, have been obliged to put up for the night; and gentlemen and ladies making a call have gone half a mile out of their way, feeling the sidewalk only with their feet, and not knowing when they turned. It is a surprising and memorable, as well as valuable experience, to be lost in the woods any time. Often in a snow storm, even by day, one will come out upon a well-known road and yet find it impossible to tell which way leads to the village. Though he knows that he has travelled it a thousand times, he cannot recognize a feature in it, but it is as strange to him as if it were a road in Siberia. By night, of course, the perplexity is infinitely greater. In our most trivial walks, we are constantly, though unconsciously, steering like pilots by certain well-known beacons and headlands, and if we go beyond our usual course we still carry in our minds the bearing of some neighboring cape; and not till we are completely lost, or turned round,—for a man needs only to be turned round once with his eyes shut in this world to be lost,—do we appreciate the vastness and strangeness of Nature. Every man has to learn the points of compass again as often as he awakes, whether from sleep or any abstraction. Not till we are lost, in other words, not till we have lost the world, do we begin to find ourselves, and realize where we are and the infinite extent of our relations.

One afternoon, near the end of the first summer, when I went to the village to get a shoe from the cobbler's, I was seized and put into jail, because, as I have elsewhere related, I did not pay a tax to, or recognize the authority of, the state which buys and sells men, women, and children, like cattle at the door of its senate-house. I had gone down to the woods for other purposes. But, wherever a man goes, men will pursue and paw him with their dirty institutions, and, if they can, constrain him to belong to their desperate odd-fellow society. It is true, I might have resisted forcibly with more or less effect, might have run "amok" against society; but I preferred that society should run "amok" against me, it being the desperate party. However, I was released the next day, obtained my mended shoe, and returned to the woods in season to get my dinner of huckleberries on Fair-Haven Hill. I was never molested by any person but those who represented the state. I had no lock nor bolt but for the desk which held my papers, not even a nail to put over my latch or windows. I never fastened my door night or day, though I was to be absent several days; not even when the next fall I spent a fortnight in the woods of Maine. And yet my house was more respected than if it had been surrounded by a file of soldiers. The tired rambler could rest and warm himself by my fire, the literary amuse himself with the few books on my table, or the curious, by opening my closet door, see what was left of my dinner, and what prospect I had of a supper. Yet, though many people of every class came this way to the pond, I suffered no serious inconvenience from these sources, and I never missed any thing but one small book, a volume of Homer, which perhaps was improperly gilded, and this I trust a soldier of our camp has found by this time. I am convinced, that if all men were to live as simply as I then did, thieving and robbery would be unknown. These take place only in communities where some have got more than is sufficient while others have not enough. The Pope's Homers would soon get properly distributed.—

> *"Nec bella fuerunt,*
> *Faginus astabat dum scyphus ante dapes."*

> *"Nor wars did men molest,*
> *When only beechen bowls were in request."*

"You who govern public affairs, what need have you to employ punishments? Love virtue, and the people will be virtuous. The virtues of a superior man are like the wind; the virtues of a common man are like the grass; the grass, when the wind passes over it, bends."

THE PONDS

. . .

In warm evenings I frequently sat in the boat playing the flute, and saw the perch, which I seemed to have charmed, hovering around me, and the moon travelling over the ribbed bottom, which was strewed with the wrecks of the forest. Formerly I had come to this pond adventurously, from time to time, in dark summer nights, with a companion, and making a fire close to the water's edge, which we thought attracted the fishes, we caught pouts with a bunch of worms strung on a thread; and when we had done, far in the night, threw the burning brands high into the air like skyrockets, which, coming down into the pond, were quenched with a loud hissing, and we were suddenly groping in total darkness. Through this, whistling a tune, we took our way to the haunts of men again. But now I had made my home by the shore.

Sometimes, after staying in a village parlor till the family had all retired, I have returned to the woods, and, partly with a view to the next day's dinner, spent the hours of midnight fishing from a boat by moonlight, serenaded by owls and foxes, and hearing, from time to time, the creaking note of some unknown bird close at hand. These experiences were very memorable and valuable to me,—anchored in forty feet of water, and twenty or thirty rods from the shore, surrounded sometimes by thousands of small perch and shiners, dimpling the surface with their tails in the moonlight, and communicating by a long flaxen line with mysterious nocturnal fishes which had their dwelling forty feet below, or sometimes dragging sixty feet of line about the pond as I drifted in the gentle night breeze, now and then feeling a slight vibration along it, indicative of some life prowling about its extremity, of dull uncertain blundering purpose there, and slow to make up its mind. At length you slowly raise, pulling hand over hand, some horned pout squeaking and squirming to the upper air. It was very queer, especially in dark nights, when your thoughts had wandered to vast and cosmogonal themes in other spheres, to feel this faint jerk, which came to interrupt your dreams and link you to Nature again. It seemed as if I might next cast my line upward into the air, as well as downward into this element which was scarcely more dense. Thus I caught two fishes as it were with one hook.

The scenery of Walden is on a humble scale, and, though very beautiful, does not approach to grandeur, nor can it much concern one who has not long frequented it or lived by its shore; yet this pond is so remarkable for its depth and purity as to merit a particular description. It is a clear and deep green well, half a mile long and a mile and three quarters in circumference, and contains about sixty-one and a half acres; a perennial spring in the midst of pine and oak woods, without any visible inlet or outlet except by the clouds and evaporation. The surrounding hills rise abruptly from the water to the height of forty to eighty feet, though on the south-east and east they attain to about one hundred and one hundred and fifty feet respectively, within a quarter and a third of a mile. They are exclusively woodland. All our Concord waters have two colors at least, one when viewed at a distance, and another, more proper, close at hand. The first depends more on the light, and follows the sky. In clear weather, in summer, they appear blue at a little distance, especially if agitated, and at a great distance all appear alike. In stormy weather they are sometimes of a dark slate color. The sea, however, is said to be blue one day and green another without any perceptible change in the atmosphere. I have seen our river, when, the landscape being covered with snow, both water and ice were almost as green as grass. Some consider blue "to be the color of pure water, whether liquid or solid." But, looking directly down into our waters from a boat, they are seen to be of very different colors. Walden is blue at one time and green at another, even from the same point of view. Lying between the earth and the heavens, it partakes of the color of both. . . . Yet a single glass of its water held up to the light is as colorless as an equal quantity of air. It is well known that a large plate of glass will have a green tint, owing, as the makers say, to its "body," but a small piece of the same will be colorless. How large a body of Walden water would be required to reflect a green tint I have never proved. The water of our river is black or a very dark brown to one looking directly down on it, and, like that of most ponds, imparts to the body of one bathing in it a yellowish tinge; but this water is of such crystalline purity that the body of the bather appears of an alabaster whiteness, still more unnatural, which, as the limbs are magnified and distorted withal, produces a monstrous effect, making fit studies for a Michael Angelo.

The water is so transparent that the bottom can easily be discerned at the depth of twenty-five or thirty feet. Paddling over it, you may see many feet beneath the surface the schools of perch and shiners, perhaps only an inch long, yet the former easily distinguished by their transverse bars, and you think that they must be ascetic fish that find a subsistence there. Once, in the winter, many years ago, when I had been cutting holes through the ice in order to catch pickerel, as I stepped ashore I tossed my axe back on to the ice, but, as if some evil genius had directed it, it slid four or five rods directly into one of the holes, where the water was twenty-five feet deep. Out of curiosity, I lay down on the ice and looked through the hole, until I saw the axe a little on one side, standing on its head, with its helve erect and gently swaying to and fro with the pulse of the pond; and there it might have stood erect and swaying till in the course of time the handle rotted off, if I had not disturbed it. Making another hole directly over it with an ice chisel which I had, and cutting down the longest birch which I could find in the neighborhood with my knife, I made a slip-noose, which I attached to its end, and, letting it down carefully, passed it over the knob of the handle, and drew it by a line along the birch, and so pulled the axe out again.

The shore is composed of a belt of smooth rounded white stones like paving stones, excepting one or two short sand beaches, and is so steep that in many places a single leap will carry you into water over your head; and were it not for its remarkable transparency, that would be the last to be seen of its bottom till it rose on the opposite side. Some think it is bottomless. It is nowhere muddy, and a casual observer would say that there were no weeds at all in it; and of noticeable plants, except in the little meadows recently overflowed, which do not properly belong to it, a closer scrutiny does not detect a flag nor a bulrush, nor even a lily, yellow or white, but only a few small heart-leaves and potamogetons, and perhaps a water-target or two; all which however a bather might not perceive; and these plants are clean and bright like the element they grow in. The stones extend a rod or two into the water, and then the bottom is pure sand, except in the deepest parts, where there is usually a little sediment, probably from the decay of the leaves which have been wafted on to it so many successive falls, and a bright green weed is brought up on anchors even in mid-winter.

We have one other pond just like this, White Pond in Nine Acre Corner, about two and a half miles westerly; but, though I am acquainted with most of the ponds within a dozen miles of this centre, I do not know a third of this pure and well-like character. Successive nations perchance have drank at, admired, and fathomed it, and passed away, and still its water is green and pellucid as ever. Not an intermitting spring! Perhaps on that spring morning when Adam and Eve were driven out of Eden Walden Pond was already in existence, and even then breaking up in a gentle spring rain accompanied with mist and a southerly wind, and covered with myriads of ducks and geese, which had not heard of the fall, when still such pure lakes sufficed them. Even then it had commenced to rise and fall, and had clarified its waters and colored them of the hue they now wear, and obtained a patent of heaven to be the only Walden Pond in the world and distiller of celestial dews. Who knows in how many unremembered nations' literatures this has been the Castalian Fountain? or what nymphs presided over it in the Golden Age? It is a gem of the first water which Concord wears in her coronet.

. . .

The pond rises and falls, but whether regularly or not, and within what period, nobody knows, though, as usual, many pretend to know. It is commonly higher in the winter and lower in the summer, though not corresponding to the general wet and dryness. I can remember when it was a foot or two lower, and also when it was at least five feet higher, than when I lived by it. There is a narrow sand-bar running into it, with very deep water on one side, on which I helped boil a kettle of chowder, some six rods from the main shore, about the year 1824, which it has not been possible to do for twenty-five years; and on the other hand, my friends used to listen with incredulity when I told them, that a few years later I was accustomed to fish from a boat in a secluded cove in the woods, fifteen rods from the only shore they knew, which place was long since converted into a meadow. But the pond has risen steadily for two years, and now, in the summer of '52, is just five feet higher than when I lived there, or as high as it was thirty years ago, and fishing goes on again in the meadow. This makes a difference of level, at the outside, of six or seven feet; and yet the water shed by the surrounding hills is insignificant in amount, and this overflow must be referred to causes which affect the deep springs. This same summer the pond has begun to fall again. It is remarkable that this fluctuation, whether periodical or not, appears thus to require many years for its accomplishment. I have observed one rise and a part of two falls, and I expect that a dozen or fifteen years hence the water will again be as low as I have ever known it. Flints' Pond, a mile eastward, allowing for the disturbance occasioned by its inlets and outlets, and the smaller intermediate ponds also, sympathize with Walden, and recently attained their greatest height at the same time with the latter. The same is true, as far as my observation goes, of White Pond.

This rise and fall of Walden at long intervals serves this use at least; the water standing at this great height for a year or more, though it makes it difficult to walk round it, kills the shrubs and trees which have sprung up about its edge since the last rise, pitch-pines, birches, alders, aspens, and others, and, falling again, leaves an unobstructed shore; for unlike many ponds and all waters which are subject to a daily tide, its shore is cleanest when the water is lowest. On the side of the pond next my house, a row of pitch-pines fifteen feet high has been killed and tipped over as if by a lever, and thus a stop put to their encroachments; and their size indicates how many years have elapsed since the last rise to this height. By this fluctuation the pond asserts its title to a shore, and thus the *shore* is *shorn*, and the trees cannot hold it by right of possession. These are the lips of the lake on which no beard grows. It licks its chaps from time to time. When the water is at its height, the alders, willows, and maples send forth a mass of fibrous red roots several feet long from all sides of their stems in the water, and to the height of three or four feet from the ground, in the effort to maintain themselves; and I have known the high-blueberry bushes about the shore, which commonly produce no fruit, bear an abundant crop under these circumstances.

Some have been puzzled to tell how the shore became so regularly paved. My townsmen have all heard the tradition, the oldest people tell me that they heard it in their youth, that anciently the Indians were holding a pow-wow upon a hill here, which rose as high into the heavens as the pond now sinks deep into the earth, and they used much profanity, as the story goes, though this vice is one of which the Indians were never guilty, and while they were thus engaged the hill shook and suddenly sank, and only one old squaw, named Walden, escaped and from her the pond was named. It has been conjectured that when the hill shook these stones rolled down its side and became the present shore. It is very certain, at any rate, that once there was no pond here, and now there is one; and this Indian fable does not in any respect conflict with the account of that ancient settler whom I have mentioned, who remembers so well when he first came here with his divining rod, saw a thin vapor rising from the sward, and the hazel pointed steadily downward, and he concluded to dig a well here. As for the stones, many still think that they are hardly to be accounted for by the action of the waves on these hills; but I observe that the surrounding hills are remarkably full of the same kind of stones, so that they have been obliged to pile them up in walls on both sides of the railroad cut nearest the pond; and, moreover, there are most stones where the shore is most abrupt; so that, unfortunately, it is no longer a mystery to me. I detect the paver. If the name was not derived from that of some English locality,— Saffron Walden, for instance,—one might suppose that it was called, originally, *Walled-in* Pond.

. . .

In such a day, in September or October, Walden is a perfect forest mirror, set round with stones as precious to my eye as if fewer or rarer. Nothing so fair, so pure, and at the same time so large, as a lake, perchance, lies on the surface of the earth. Sky water. It needs no fence. Nations come and go without defiling it. It is a mirror which no stone can crack, whose quicksilver will never wear off, whose gilding Nature continually repairs; no storms, no dust, can dim its surface ever fresh;—a mirror in which all impurity presented to it sinks, swept and dusted by the sun's hazy brush,—this the light dust-cloth,—which retains no breath that is breathed on it, but sends its own to float as clouds high above its surface, and be reflected in its bosom still.

A field of water betrays the spirit that is in the air. It is continually receiving new life and motion from above. It is intermediate in its nature between land and sky. On land only the grass and trees wave, but the water itself is rippled by the wind. I see where the breeze dashes across it by the streaks or flakes of light. It is remarkable that we can look down on its surface. We shall, perhaps, look down thus on the surface of air at length, and mark where a still subtler spirit sweeps over it.

The skaters and water-bugs finally disappear in the latter part of October, when the severe frosts have come; and then in November, usually, in a calm day, there is absolutely nothing to ripple the surface. One November afternoon, in the calm at the end of a rain storm of several days' duration, when the sky was still completely overcast and the air was full of mist, I observed that the pond was remarkably smooth, so that it was difficult to distinguish its surface; though it no longer reflected the bright tints of October, but the sombre November colors of the surrounding hills. Though I passed over it as gently as possible, the slight undulations produced by my boat extended almost as far as I could see, and gave a ribbed appearance to the reflections. But, as I was looking over the surface, I saw here and there at a distance a faint glimmer, as if some skater insects which had escaped the frosts might be collected there, or, perchance, the surface, being so smooth, betrayed where a spring welled up from the bottom. Paddling gently to one of these places, I was surprised to find myself surrounded by myriads of small perch, about five inches long, of a rich bronze color in the green water, sporting there and constantly rising to the surface and dimpling it, sometimes leaving bubbles on it. In such transparent and seemingly bottomless water, reflecting the clouds, I seemed to be floating through the air as in a balloon, and their swimming impressed me as a kind of flight or hovering, as if they were a compact flock of birds passing just beneath my level on the right or left, their fins, like sails, set all around them. There were many such schools in the pond, apparently improving the short season before winter would draw an icy shutter over their broad skylight, sometimes giving to the surface an appearance as if a slight breeze struck it, or a few rain-drops fell there. When I approached carelessly and alarmed them, they made a sudden plash and rippling with their tails, as if one had struck the water with a brushy bough, and instantly took refuge in the depths. At length the wind rose, the mist increased, and the waves began to run, and the perch leaped much higher than before, half out of water, a hundred black points, three inches long, at once above the surface. Even as late as the fifth of December, one year, I saw some dimples on the surface, and thinking it was going to rain hard immediately, the air being full of mist, I made haste to take my place at the oars and row homeward; already the rain seemed rapidly increasing, though I felt none on my cheek, and I anticipated a thorough soaking. But suddenly the dimples ceased, for they were produced by the perch, which the noise of my oars had scared into the depths, and I saw their schools dimly disappearing; so I spent a dry afternoon after all.

. . .

Now the trunks of trees on the bottom, and the old log canoe, and the dark surrounding woods, are gone, and the villagers, who scarcely know where it lies, instead of going to the pond to bathe or drink, are thinking to bring its water, which should be as sacred as the Ganges at least, to the village in a pipe, to wash their dishes with!—to earn their Walden by the turning of a cock or drawing of a plug! That devilish Iron Horse, whose ear-rending neigh is heard throughout the town, has muddied the Boiling Spring with his foot, and he it is that has browsed off all the woods on Walden shore; that Trojan horse, with a thousand men in his belly, introduced by mercenary Greeks! Where is the country's champion, the Moore of Moore Hall, to meet him at the Deep Cut and thrust an avenging lance between the ribs of the bloated pest?

Nevertheless, of all the characters I have known, perhaps Walden wears best, and best preserves its purity. Many men have been likened to it, but few deserve that honor. Though the woodchoppers have laid bare first this shore and then that, and the Irish have built their sties by it, and the railroad has infringed on its border, and the icemen have skimmed it once, it is itself unchanged, the same water which my youthful eyes fell on; all the change is in me. It has not acquired one permanent wrinkle after all its ripples. It is perennially young, and I may stand and see a swallow dip apparently to pick an insect from its surface as of yore. It struck me again to-night, as if I had not seen it almost daily for more than twenty years,— Why, here is Walden, the same woodland lake that I discovered so many years ago; where a forest was cut down last winter another is springing up by its shore as lustily as ever; the same thought is welling up to its surface that was then; it is the same liquid joy and happiness to itself and its Maker, ay, and it *may* be to me. It is the work of a brave man surely, in whom there was no guile! He rounded this water with his hand, deepened and clarified it in his thought, and in his will bequeathed it to Concord. I see by its face that it is visited by the same reflection; and I can almost say, Walden, is it you?

It is no dream of mine,
To ornament a line;
I cannot come nearer to God and Heaven
Than I live to Walden even.
I am its stony shore,
And the breeze that passes o'er;
In the hollow of my hand
Are its water and its sand,
And its deepest resort
Lies high in my thought.

The cars never pause to look at it; yet I fancy that the engineers and firemen and brakemen, and those passengers who have a season ticket and see it often, are better men for the sight. The engineer does not forget at night, or his nature does not, that he has beheld this vision of serenity and purity once at least during the day. Though seen but once, it helps to wash out State-street and the engine's soot. One proposes that it be called "God's Drop."

I have said that Walden has no visible inlet nor outlet, but it is on the one hand distantly and indirectly related to Flints' Pond, which is more elevated, by a chain of small ponds coming from that quarter, and on the other directly and manifestly to Concord River, which is lower, by a similar chain of ponds through which in some other geological period it may have flowed, and by a little digging, which God forbid, it can be made to flow thither again. If by living thus reserved and austere, like a hermit in the woods, so long, it has acquired such wonderful purity, who would not regret that the comparatively impure waters of Flints' Pond should be mingled with it, or itself should ever go to waste its sweetness in the ocean wave?

.   .   .

CONCLUSION

.   .   .

I left the woods for as good a reason as I went there. Perhaps it seemed to me that I had several more lives to live, and could not spare any more time for that one. It is remarkable how easily and insensibly we fall into a particular route, and make a beaten track for ourselves. I had not lived there a week before my feet wore a path from my door to the pond-side; and though it is five or six years since I trod it, it is still quite distinct. It is true, I fear that others may have fallen into it, and so helped to keep it open. The surface of the earth is soft and impressible by the feet of men; and so with the paths which the mind travels. How worn and dusty, then, must be the highways of the world, how deep the ruts of tradition and conformity! I did not wish to take a cabin passage, but rather to go before the mast and on the deck of the world, for there I could best see the moonlight amid the mountains. I do not wish to go below now.

I learned this, at least, by my experiment; that if one advances confidently in the direction of his dreams, and endeavors to live the life which he has imagined, he will meet with a success unexpected in common hours. He will put some things behind, will pass an invisible boundary; new, universal, and more liberal laws will begin to establish themselves around and within him; or the old laws be expanded, and interpreted in his favor in a more liberal sense, and he will live with the license of a higher order of beings. In proportion as he simplifies his life, the laws of the universe will appear less complex, and solitude will not be solitude, nor poverty poverty, nor weakness weakness. If you have built castles in the air, your work need not be lost; that is where they should be. Now put the foundations under them.

It is a ridiculous demand which England and America make, that you shall speak so that they can understand you. Neither men nor toad-stools grow so. As if that were important, and there were not enough to understand you without them. As if Nature could support but one order of understandings, could not sustain birds as well as quadrupeds, flying as well as creeping things, and *hush* and *who*, which Bright can understand, were the best English. As if there were safety in stupidity alone. I fear chiefly lest my expression may not be *extravagant* enough, may not wander far enough beyond the narrow limits of my daily experience, so as to be adequate to the truth of which I have been convinced. *Extra vagance!* it depends on how you are yarded. The migrating buffalo, which seeks new pastures in another latitude, is not extravagant like the cow which kicks over the pail, leaps the cow-yard fence, and runs after her calf, in milking time. I desire to speak somewhere *without* bounds; like a man in a waking moment, to men in their waking moments; for I am convinced that I cannot exaggerate enough even to lay the foundation of a true expression. Who that has heard a strain of music feared then lest he should speak extravagantly any more forever? In view of the future or possible, we should live quite laxly and undefined in front, our outlines dim and misty on that side; as our shadows reveal an insensible perspiration toward the sun. The volatile truth of our words should continually betray the inadequacy of the residual statement. Their truth is instantly *translated*; its literal monument alone remains. The words which express our faith and piety are not definite; yet they are significant and fragrant like frankincense to superior natures.

Why level downward to our dullest perception always, and praise that as common sense? The commonest sense is the sense of men asleep, which they express by snoring. Sometimes we are inclined to class those who are once-and-a-half witted with the half-witted, because we appreciate only a third part of their wit. Some would find fault with the morning-red, if they ever got up early enough. "They pretend," as I hear, "that the verses of Kabir have four different senses; illusion, spirit, intellect, and the exoteric doctrine of the Vedas;" but in this part of the world it is considered a ground for complaint if a man's writings admit of more than one interpretation. While England endeavors to cure the potato-rot, will not any endeavor to cure the brain-rot, which prevails so much more widely and fatally?

I do not suppose that I have attained to obscurity, but I should be proud if no more fatal fault were found with my pages on this score than was found with the Walden ice. Southern customers objected to its blue color, which is the evidence of its purity, as if it were muddy, and preferred the Cambridge ice, which is white, but tastes of weeds. The purity men love is like the mists which envelop the earth, and not like the azure ether beyond.

Some are dinning in our ears that we Americans, and moderns generally, are intellectual dwarfs compared with the ancients, or even the Elizabethan men. But what is that to the purpose? A living dog is better than a dead lion. Shall a man go and hang himself because he belongs to the race of pygmies, and not be the biggest pygmy that he can? Let every one mind his own business, and endeavor to be what he was made.

Why should we be in such desperate haste to succeed, and in such desperate enterprises? If a man does not keep pace with his companions, perhaps it is because he hears a different drummer. Let him step to the music which he hears, however measured or far away. It is not important that he should mature as soon as an apple-tree or an oak. Shall he turn his spring into summer? If the condition of things which we were made for is not yet, what were any reality which we can substitute? We will not be shipwrecked on a vain reality. Shall we with pains erect a heaven of blue glass over ourselves, though when it is done we shall be sure to gaze still at the true ethereal heaven far above, as if the former were not?

There was an artist in the city of Kouroo who was disposed to strive after perfection. One day it came into his mind to make a staff. Having considered that in an imperfect work time is an ingredient, but into a perfect work time does not enter, he said to himself, It shall be perfect in all respects, though I should do nothing else in my life. He proceeded instantly to the forest for wood, being resolved that it should not be made of unsuitable material; and as he searched for and rejected stick after stick, his friends gradually deserted him, for they grew old in their works and died, but he grew not older by a moment. His singleness of purpose and resolution, and his elevated piety, endowed him, without his knowledge, with perennial youth. As he made no compromise with Time, Time kept out of his way, and only sighed at a distance because he could not overcome him. Before he had found a stock in all respects suitable the city of Kouroo was a hoary ruin, and he sat on one of its mounds to peel the stick. Before he had given it the proper shape the dynasty of the Candahars was at an end, and with the point of the stick he wrote the name of the last of that race in the sand, and then resumed his work. By the time he had smoothed and polished the staff Kalpa was no longer the pole-star; and ere he had put on the ferule and the head adorned with precious stones, Brahma had awoke and slumbered many times. But why do I stay to mention these things? When the finishing stroke was put to his work, it suddenly expanded before the eyes of the astonished artist into the fairest of all the creations of Brahma. He had made a new system in making a staff, a world with full and fair proportions; in which, though the old cities and dynasties had passed away, fairer and more glorious ones had taken their places. And now he saw by the heap of shavings still fresh at his feet, that, for him and his work, the former lapse of time had been an illusion, and that no more time had elapsed than is required for a single scintillation from the brain of Brahma to fall on and inflame the tinder of a mortal brain. The material was pure, and his art was pure; how could the result be other than wonderful?

No face which we can give to a matter will stead us so well at last as the truth. This alone wears well. For the most part, we are not where we are, but in a false position. Through an infirmity of our natures, we suppose a case, and put ourselves into it, and hence are in two cases at the same time, and it is doubly difficult to get out. In sane moments we regard only the facts, the case that is. Say what you have to say, not what you ought. Any truth is better than make-believe. Tom Hyde, the tinker, standing on the gallows, was asked if he had any thing to say. "Tell the tailors," said he, "to remember to make a knot in their thread before they take the first stitch." His companion's prayer is forgotten.

However mean your life is, meet it and live it; do not shun it and call it hard names. It is not so bad as you are. It looks poorest when you are richest. The fault-finder will find faults even in paradise. Love your life, poor as it is. You may perhaps have some pleasant, thrilling, glorious hours, even in a poor-house. The setting sun is reflected from the windows of the alms-house as brightly as from the rich man's abode; the snow melts before its door as early in the spring. I do not see but a quiet mind may live as contentedly there, and have as cheering thoughts, as in a palace. The town's poor seem to me often to live the most independent lives of any. May be they are simply great enough to receive without misgiving. Most think that they are above being supported by the town; but it oftener happens that they are not above supporting themselves by dishonest means, which should be more disreputable. Cultivate poverty like a garden herb, like sage. Do not trouble yourself much to get new things, whether clothes or friends. Turn the old; return to them. Things do not change; we change. Sell your clothes and keep your thoughts. God will see that you do not want society. If I were confined to a corner of a garret all my days, like a spider, the world would be just as large to me while I had my thoughts about me. The philosopher said: "From an army of three divisions one can take away its general, and put it in disorder; from the man the most abject and vulgar one cannot take away his thought." Do not seek so anxiously to be developed, to subject yourself to many influences to be played on; it is all dissipation. Humility like darkness reveals the heavenly lights. The shadows of poverty and meanness gather around us, "and lo! creation widens to our view." We are often reminded that if there were bestowed on us the wealth of Crœsus, our aims must still be the same, and our means essentially the same. Moreover, if you are restricted in your range by poverty, if you cannot buy books and newspapers, for instance, you are but confined to the most significant and vital experiences; you are compelled to deal with the material which yields the most sugar and the most starch. It is life near the bone where it is sweetest. You are defended from being a trifler.

No man loses ever on a lower level by magnanimity on a higher. Superfluous wealth can buy superfluities only. Money is not required to buy one necessary of the soul.

I live in the angle of a leaden wall, into whose composition was poured a little alloy of bell metal. Often, in the repose of my mid-day, there reaches my ears a confused *tintinnabulum* from without. It is the noise of my contemporaries. My neighbors tell me of their adventures with famous gentlemen and ladies, what notabilities they met at the dinner-table; but I am no more interested in such things than in the contents of the Daily Times. The interest and the conversation are about costume and manners chiefly; but a goose is a goose still, dress it as you will. They tell me of California and Texas, of England and the Indies, of the Hon. Mr. — of Georgia or of Massachusetts, all transient and fleeting phenomena, till I am ready to leap from their court-yard like the Mameluke bey. I delight to come to my bearings,—not walk in procession with pomp and parade, in a conspicuous place, but to walk even with the Builder of the universe, if I may,—not to live in this restless, nervous, bustling, trivial Nineteenth Century, but stand or sit thoughtfully while it goes by. What are men celebrating? They are all on a committee of arrangements, and hourly expect a speech from somebody. God is only the president of the day, and Webster is his orator. I love to weigh, to settle, to gravitate toward that which most strongly and rightfully attracts me;—not hang by the beam of the scale and try to weigh less,—not suppose a case, but take the case that is; to travel the only path I can, and that on which no power can resist me. It affords me no satisfaction to commence to spring an arch before I have got a solid foundation. Let us not play at kittlybenders. There is a solid bottom every where. We read that the traveller asked the boy if the swamp before him had a hard bottom. The boy replied that it had. But presently the traveller's horse sank in up to the girths, and he observed to the boy, "I thought you said that this bog had a hard bottom." "So it has," answered the latter, "but you have not got half way to it yet." So it is with the bogs and quicksands of society; but he is an old boy that knows it. Only what is thought said or done at a certain rare coincidence is good. I would not be one of those who will foolishly drive a nail into mere lath and plastering; such a deed would keep me awake nights. Give me a hammer, and let me feel for the furring. Do not depend on the putty. Drive a nail home and clinch it so faithfully that you can wake up in the night and think of your work with satisfaction,—a work at which you would not be ashamed to invoke the Muse. So will help you God, and so only. Every nail driven should be as another rivet in the machine of the universe, you carrying on the work.

Rather than love, than money, than fame, give me truth. I sat at a table where were rich food and wine in abundance, and obsequious attendance, but sincerity and truth were not; and I went away hungry from the inhospitable board. The hospitality was as cold as the ices. I thought that there was no need of ice to freeze them. They talked to me of the age of the wine and the fame of the vintage; but I thought of an older, a newer, and purer wine, of a more glorious vintage, which they had not got, and could not buy. The style, the house and grounds and "entertainment" pass for nothing with me. I called on the king, but he made me wait in his hall, and conducted like a man incapacitated for hospitality. There was a man in my neighborhood who lived in a hollow tree. His manners were truly regal. I should have done better had I called on him.

How long shall we sit in our porticoes practising idle and musty virtues, which any work would make impertinent? As if one were to begin the day with long-suffering, and hire a man to hoe his potatoes; and in the afternoon go forth to practice Christian meekness and charity with goodness aforethought! Consider the China pride and stagnant self-complacency of mankind. This generation reclines a little to congratulate itself on being the last of an illustrious line; and in Boston and London and Paris and Rome, thinking of its long descent, it speaks of its progress in art and science and literature with satisfaction. There are the Records of the Philosophical Societies, and the public Eulogies of *Great Men!* It is the good Adam contemplating his own virtue. "Yes, we have done great deeds, and sung divine songs, which shall never die,"—that is, as long as *we* can remember them. The learned societies and great men of Assyria,—where are they? What youthful philosophers and experimentalists we are! There is not one of my readers who has yet lived a whole human life. These may be but the spring months in the life of the race. If we have had the seven-years' itch, we have not seen the seventeen-year locust yet in Concord. We are acquainted with a mere pellicle of the globe on which we live. Most have not delved six feet beneath the surface, nor

leaped as many above it. We know not where we are. Beside, we are sound asleep nearly half our time. Yet we esteem ourselves wise, and have an established order on the surface. Truly, we are deep thinkers, we are ambitious spirits! As I stand over the insect crawling amid the pine needles on the forest floor, and endeavoring to conceal itself from my sight, and ask myself why it will cherish those humble thoughts, and hide its head from me who might, perhaps, be its benefactor, and impart to its race some cheering information, I am reminded of the greater Benefactor and Intelligence that stands over me the human insect.

There is an incessant influx of novelty into the world, and yet we tolerate incredible dulness. I need only suggest what kind of sermons are still listened to in the most enlightened countries. There are such words as joy and sorrow, but they are only the burden of a psalm, sung with a nasal twang, while we believe in the ordinary and mean. We think that we can change our clothes only. It is said that the British Empire is very large and respectable, and that the United States are a first-rate power. We do not believe that a tide rises and falls behind every man which can float the British Empire like a chip, if he should ever harbor it in his mind. Who knows what sort of seventeen-year locust will next come out of the ground? The government of the world I live in was not framed, like that of Britain, in after-dinner conversations over the wine.

The life in us is like the water in the river. It may rise this year higher than man has ever known it, and flood the parched uplands; even this may be the eventful year, which will drown out all our muskrats. It was not always dry land where we dwell. I see far inland the banks which the stream anciently washed, before science began to record its freshets. Every one has heard the story which has gone the rounds of New England, of a strong and beautiful bug which came out of the dry leaf of an old table of apple-tree wood, which had stood in a farmer's kitchen for sixty years, first in Connecticut, and afterward in Massachusetts,— from an egg deposited in the living tree many years earlier still, as appeared by counting the annual layers beyond it; which was heard gnawing out for several weeks, hatched perchance by the heat of an urn. Who does not feel his faith in a resurrection and immortality strengthened by hearing of this? Who knows what beautiful and winged life, whose egg has been buried for ages under many concentric layers of woodenness in the dead dry life of society, deposited at first in the alburnum of the green and living tree, which has been gradually converted into the semblance of its well-seasoned tomb,—heard perchance gnawing out now for years by the astonished family of man, as they sat round the festive board,—may unexpectedly come forth from amidst society's most trivial and hand-selled furniture, to enjoy its perfect summer life at last!

I do not say that John or Jonathan will realize all this; but such is the character of that morrow which mere lapse of time can never make to dawn. The light which puts out our eyes is darkness to us. Only that day dawns to which we are awake. There is more day to dawn. The sun is but a morning star.

[handwritten: Thoreau showed his activism. He becomes darker after going to jail. He was trying to dramatize his high ideas and he gets through in jail for it. He is less optimistic about human nature than the "safe" teacher.]

Civil Disobedience (1849)

In July, 1846, Thoreau refused, in protest against the government's condoning slavery, to pay his poll tax. Though the Concord constable, a long-time friend of Thoreau's, offered to pay the tax for him, Thoreau continued to refuse payment and the constable was compelled to arrest him. Thoreau spent the night in jail, but he was released the next morning when someone, probably his aunt, paid the tax for him, though he was not happy at the interference in his behalf that had cut short his protest. The incident inspired Thoreau to write the essay usually known as "Civil Disobedience." Thoreau first delivered it as a lecture in 1848. It was later printed in Elizabeth Peabody's magazine, *Aesthetic Papers*, in 1849.

[handwritten left margin: He was protesting slavery and the Mexico war by not paying his poll taxes]

Beginning by affirming the Jeffersonian position that "That government is best which governs least," Thoreau at once extends the principle to its ideal limit: "that government is best which governs not at all." Thoreau's notion here can easily be subsumed under his concern with means and ends. A government is merely a means to serve an end: the welfare and freedom of the people. If the means gets in the way of that end, then it is machinery that does far more harm than good. In fact, Thoreau argued that the relative success of the American experiment up to his time was due to the "character inherited by the American people" and that what they had accomplished would actually have been greater "if the government had not sometimes got in its way."

Yet Thoreau quickly comes down from this idealistic "no-government" position to speak "practically and as a citizen." As such, he asks not at once for "no government," but he does ask at once for "a better government." Thoreau is aware that though all men "recognize the right of revolution," many would argue that in the present situation the "tyranny" of government or "its inefficiency" is not unendurable. For this argument Thoreau has an answer: the fact that one sixth of the population are slaves proves that the present situation is unendurable. The situation underlines the necessity for a radical change. As Thoreau puts it, "I simply wish to refuse allegiance to the State, to withdraw and stand aloof from it effectually. . . . In fact, I quietly declare war with the State, after my fashion, though I will still make what use and get what advantage of her I can, as is usual in such cases."

How carefully thought out is Thoreau's case for civil disobedience? How thorough is his analysis of the circumstances under which refusal to obey the law is justified? In an "Occasional Paper" published by the Center for the Study of Democratic Institutions, Harry Kalven, Jr., of the University of Chicago Law School, notes that Thoreau fails to discuss a number of very important points. For instance, Thoreau says nothing about one's need to accept punishment meted out by the state, the position taken by Socrates in the fifth century B.C. and by Mahatma Gandhi in the twentieth century. Thoreau also fails to discuss "the counter-value of order." Kalven thinks that this omission is deliberate, for in his opinion Thoreau "sees no real utility to the State. The State is not a natural condition of human life; it does not have a decent, civilized purpose. To [Thoreau] jail becomes, metaphorically, a ground outside the State: to go to jail is a way of withdrawing

[handwritten bottom, numbered:]
[left margin: rules to be followed]
1. You have to be sincerely opposed to a law, not just because you it hurts you. It has to be a bad law
2. Break the law deliberately
3. Accept the punishment and arouse the conscious of the people.
4. The pressure will be brought to bear on the lawmakers; law changes

*most people don't emphathize if they are satisfied
people would rather not bother*

so they just turn their backs

from the State." And Kalven says, by way of summary, that in this essay "Thoreau is primarily interested in seceding from Massachusetts."

So much for the omissions. On the positive side, Kalven points out that Thoreau makes three "novel emphases." The first of these is Thoreau's assumption that his case is perfectly clear on its merits. It does not need to be argued. The second is Thoreau's suggestion that perhaps there "should be a constitutional limitation on the majority vote if any given vote is against the conscience of the individual." That is, Thoreau maintains that any action "to which a man adheres as a matter of conscience should be constitutionally immune from the power of the majority." The third emphasis is expressed in Thoreau's contempt for those who merely hold an opinion and do nothing further about it or even who merely cast their votes and then do nothing further about it. Thoreau has scant patience for those who "will wait, well disposed, for others to remedy the evil, that they may no longer have it to regret." Nor does Thoreau have much more patience for those who "give only a cheap vote, and a feeble countenance, and a Godspeed, to the right, as it goes by them."

Kalven comes to the conclusion that, even though "analytically" the essay leaves almost everything to be desired, it turns out to be "great, in fact breathtakingly brilliant, writing." Indeed, Kalven goes on to say that perhaps the essay "is so effective just because it is so poor analytically," for it does not undertake to be "a cold, analytic balancing of the considerations that would warrant disobeying the law." On the contrary, it is "a burst of simple, spontaneous insight, rather loosely handled, done with a good deal of irony, and uncomplicated by any counter considerations at all. It is exhilarating, like civil disobedience itself."

A more severe judgment comes from Austin Warren, himself a good New Englander. He writes that he finds the end of Thoreau's imprisonment anticlimactic.

It is hard for me to see the bravery and logic of this famous incident. If this was "passive resistance" to some particular action or in-

action of the state of which Thoreau disapproved, surely he should have stayed in jail and urged others to join him there in his protest. Why allow someone else—Emerson or his sister—to pay the tax? Out of deference to their individual right to pay? This seems individualism not only absurd but immoral. Dorothy Day and her "Catholic Workers" have served out their jail sentences when, on principle, they refused to obey New York's rules for air-raid or whatever.

In 1849 Thoreau published his now famous essay called "Civil Disobedience," confusing and difficult even to summarize, let alone defend or refute. Gandhi, the Reverend Martin Luther King, and Dorothy Day, all "passive resisters" of our century, appear to have made something more consistent out of Thoreau's essay than did Thoreau (*The New England Conscience*, 1966, p. 111).

Erwin T. Griswold, a former dean of the Harvard Law School, has made a somewhat detailed comment on the "secession" from society which he finds implicit in Thoreau's "Civil Disobedience."

Henry David Thoreau is generally regarded as the most notable American exponent of civil disobedience, and all of us share admiration for his determination. But we must not ignore the vital aspect of Thoreau's nonconformity—his passionate attempt to dissociate himself from society.

Thoreau's poignant attitude was charming enough in mid-nineteenth century America. But, it was, essentially, an effort to withdraw from the realities of life, and it was, I suggest, myopic even then. . . . Unlike a member of a purely artificial group, like a . . . country club, a citizen cannot resign from the "social compact" because he protests policies of the regime. Now . . . we must be even more cognizant that there is nothing noble or salutary about foredoomed attempts to abdicate membership in society. Complex problems demand rational attention that can come only from personal focus on solutions. . . .

In determining whether and when to exercise the moral right to disobey the dictates of the law, it must also be recognized that society not only does not, but cannot, recognize this determination as entitled to legal privilege. It is part of the Gandhian tradition of civil disobedience that the sincerity of the individual's conscience presupposes that the law will punish this assertion of personal principle. . . . Thus, it is of the essence of law that it is equally applied to all . . . irrespective of personal motive. For this reason, if one contemplates civil disobedience out of moral conviction, he should not be surprised and must not be bitter if a criminal conviction ensues. And he must accept the fact that organized society cannot endure on any other basis. His hope is that he may aid in getting the law changed. But, if he does not succeed in that, he cannot complain if the law is applied to him . . . (*Tulanian*, May, 1966).

The reader might ask himself how close Kalven and Griswold are in agreement. Are they making what is essentially the same point? With regard to political theory in general, is Thoreau a democrat or an anarchist? Is there any evidence to suggest that Thoreau had thought very deeply about the difference between the two philosophies?

The reader might also look back at Emerson's criticism of the transcendentalists: their solution for the ills of society was to "drop out." Is Thoreau's own solution a form of "drop-out"?

I heartily accept the motto, "That government is best which governs least"; and I should like to see it acted up to more rapidly and systematically. Carried out, it finally amounts to this, which also I believe—"That government is best which governs not at all"; and when men are prepared for it, that will be the kind of government which they will have. Government is at best but an expedient; but most governments are usually, and all governments are sometimes, inexpedient. The objections which have been brought against a standing army, and they are many and weighty, and deserve to prevail, may also at last be brought against a standing government. The standing army is only an arm of the standing government. The government itself, which is only the mode which the people have chosen to execute their will, is equally liable to be abused and perverted before the people can act through it. Witness the present Mexican war, the work of comparatively a few individuals using the standing government as their tool; for, in the outset, the people would not have consented to this measure.

This American government—what is it but a tradition, though a recent one, endeavoring to transmit itself unimpaired to posterity, but each instant losing some of its integrity? It has not the vitality and force of a single living man; for a single man can bend it to his will. It is a sort of wooden gun to the people themselves. But it is not the less necessary for this; for the people must have some complicated machinery or other, and hear its din, to satisfy that idea of government which they have. Governments show thus how successfully men can be imposed on, even impose on themselves, for their own advantage. It is excellent, we must all allow. Yet this government never of itself furthered any enterprise, but by the alacrity with which it got out of its way. *It* does not keep the country free. *It* does not settle the West. *It* does not educate. The character inherent in the American people has done all that has been accomplished; and it would have done somewhat more, if the government had not sometimes got in its way. For government is an expedient by which men would fain succeed in letting one another alone; and, as has been said, when it is most expedient, the governed are most let alone by it. Trade and commerce, if they were not made of india-rubber, would never manage to bounce over the obstacles which legislators are continually putting in their way; and, if one were to judge these men wholly by the effects of their actions and not partly by their intentions, they would deserve to be classed and punished with those mischievous persons who put obstructions on the railroads.

But, to speak practically and as a citizen, unlike those who call themselves no-government men, I ask for, not at once no government, but *at once* a better government. Let every man make known what kind of government would command his respect, and that will be one step toward obtaining it.

After all, the practical reason why, when the power is once in the hands of the people, a majority are permitted, and for a long period continue, to rule is not because they are most likely

[handwritten: majority rules because they are the strongest; not always because they are right.]

[handwritten: He makes a distinction between the "law" and "right". Not all laws are morally right.]

to be in the right, nor because this seems fairest to the minority, but because they are physically the strongest. But a government in which the majority rule in all cases cannot be based on justice, even as far as men understand it. Can there not be a government in which majorities do not virtually decide right and wrong, but conscience?—in which majorities decide only those questions to which the rule of expediency is applicable? Must the citizen ever for a moment, or in the least degree, resign his conscience to the legislator? Why has every man a conscience, then? I think that we should be men first, and subjects afterward. It is not desirable to cultivate a respect for the law, so much as for the right. The only obligation which I have a right to assume is to do at any time what I think right. It is truly enough said that a corporation has no conscience; but a corporation of conscientious men is a corporation *with* a conscience. Law never made men a whit more just; and, by means of their respect for it, even the well-disposed are daily made the agents of injustice. A common and natural result of an undue respect for law is, that you may see a file of soldiers, colonel, captain, corporal, privates, powder-monkeys, and all, marching in admirable order over hill and dale to the wars, against their wills, ay, against their common sense and consciences, which makes it very steep marching indeed, and produces a palpitation of the heart. They have no doubt that it is a damnable business in which they are concerned; they are all peaceably inclined. Now, what are they? Men at all? or small movable forts and magazines, at the service of some unscrupulous man in power? Visit the Navy Yard, and behold a marine, such a man as an American government can make, or such as it can make a man with its black arts—a mere shadow and reminiscence of humanity, a man laid out alive and standing, and already, as one may say, buried under arms with funeral accompaniments, though it may be,

[handwritten: go off to war because of got orders]

Not a drum was heard, not a funeral note,
As his corse to the rampart we hurried;
Not a soldier discharged his farewell shot
O'er the grave where our hero we buried.

The mass of men serve the state thus, not as men mainly, but as machines, with their bodies. They are the standing army, and the militia, jailers, constables, *posse comitatus*, etc. In most cases there is no free exercise whatever of the judgment or of the moral sense; but they put themselves

[handwritten: Don't exercise judgment or moral sense.]

on a level with wood and earth and stones; and wooden men can perhaps be manufactured that will serve the purpose as well. Such command no more respect than men of straw or a lump of dirt. They have the same sort of worth only as horses and dogs. Yet such as these even are commonly esteemed good citizens. Others—as most legislators, politicians, lawyers, ministers, and office-holders—serve the state chiefly with their heads; and, as they rarely make any moral distinctions, they are as likely to serve the devil, without *intending* it, as God. A very few—as heroes, patriots, martyrs, reformers in the great sense, and *men*—serve the state with their consciences also, and so necessarily resist it for the most part; and they are commonly treated as enemies by it. A wise man will only be useful as a man, and will not submit to be "clay," and "stop a hole to keep the wind away," but leave that office to his dust at least:

*[handwritten: *]*

I am too high-born to be propertied,
To be a secondary at control,
Or useful serving-man and instrument
To any sovereign state throughout the world.

He who gives himself entirely to his fellow men appears to them useless and selfish; but he who gives himself partially to them is pronounced a benefactor and philanthropist.

How does it become a man to behave toward this American government today? I answer, that he cannot without disgrace be associated with it. I cannot for an instant recognize that political organization as *my* government which is the *slave's* government also.

All men recognize the right of revolution; that is, the right to refuse allegiance to, and to resist, the government, when its tyranny or its inefficiency are great and unendurable. But almost all say that such is not the case now. But such was the case, they think, in the Revolution of '75. If one were to tell me that this was a bad government because it taxed certain foreign commodities brought to its ports, it is most probable that I should not make an ado about it, for I can do without them. All machines have their friction; and possibly this does enough good to counterbalance the evil. At any rate, it is a great evil to make a stir about it. But when the friction comes to have its machine, and oppression and robbery are organized, I say, let us not have such a machine any longer. In other words, when a sixth of the population of a nation which has undertaken to be the refuge of

[handwritten margin note: There are so many people who don't support war or slavery but they still pay taxes.]

liberty are slaves, and a whole country is unjustly overrun and conquered by a foreign army, and subjected to military law, I think that it is not too soon for honest men to rebel and revolutionize. What makes this duty the more urgent is the fact that the country so overrun is not our own, but ours is the invading army.

Paley, a common authority with many on moral questions, in his chapter on the "Duty of Submission to Civil Government," resolves all civil obligation into expediency; and he proceeds to say that "so long as the interest of the whole society requires it, that is, so long as the established government cannot be resisted or changed without public inconveniency, it is the will of God . . . that the established government be obeyed—and no longer. This principle being admitted, the justice of every particular case of resistance is reduced to a computation of the quantity of the danger and grievance on the one side, and of the probability and expense of redressing it on the other." Of this, he says, every man shall judge for himself. But Paley appears never to have contemplated those cases to which the rule of expediency does not apply, in which a people, as well as an individual, must do justice, cost what it may. If I have unjustly wrested a plank from a drowning man, I must restore it to him though I drown myself. This, according to Paley, would be inconvenient. But he that would save his life, in such a case, shall lose it. This people must cease to hold slaves, and to make war on Mexico, though it cost them their existence as a people.

In their practice, nations agree with Paley; but does anyone think that Massachusetts does exactly what is right at the present crisis?

> *A drab of state, a cloth-o'-silver slut,*
> *To have her train borne up, and her soul*
> *trail in the dirt.*

Practically speaking, the opponents to a reform in Massachusetts are not a hundred thousand politicians at the South, but a hundred thousand merchants and farmers here, who are more interested in commerce and agriculture than they are in humanity, and are not prepared to do justice to the slave and to Mexico, *cost what it may*. I quarrel not with far-off foes, but with those who, near at home, co-operate with, and do the bidding of, those far away, and without whom the latter would be harmless. We are accustomed to say, that the

mass of men are unprepared; but improvement is slow, because the few are not materially wiser or better than the many. It is not so important that many should be as good as you, as that there be some absolute goodness somewhere; for that will leaven the whole lump. There are thousands who are *in opinion* opposed to slavery and to the war, who yet in effect do nothing to put an end to them; who, esteeming themselves children of Washington and Franklin, sit down with their hands in their pockets, and say that they know not what to do, and do nothing; who even postpone the question of freedom to the question of free trade, and quietly read the prices-current along with the latest advices from Mexico, after dinner, and, it may be, fall asleep over them both. What is the price-current of an honest man and patriot today? They hesitate, and they regret, and sometimes they petition; but they do nothing in earnest and with effect. They will wait, well disposed, for others to remedy the evil, that they may no longer have it to regret. At most, they give only a cheap vote, and a feeble countenance and Godspeed, to the right, as it goes by them. There are nine hundred and ninety-nine patrons of virtue to one virtuous man. But it is easier to deal with the real possessor of a thing than with the temporary guardian of it.

[handwritten margin note: maybe doesn't believe organized wisdom]

All voting is a sort of gaming, like checkers or backgammon, with a slight moral tinge to it, a playing with right and wrong, with moral questions; and betting naturally accompanies it. The character of the voters is not staked. I cast my vote, perchance, as I think right; but I am not vitally concerned that that right should prevail. I am willing to leave it to the majority. Its obligation, therefore, never exceeds that of expediency. Even voting *for the right* is *doing* nothing for it. It is only expressing to men feebly your desire that it should prevail. A wise man will not leave the right to the mercy of chance, nor wish it to prevail through the power of the majority. There is but little virtue in the action of masses of men. When the majority shall at length vote for the abolition of slavery, it will be because they are indifferent to slavery, or because there is but little slavery left to be abolished by their vote. *They* will then be the only slaves. Only *his* vote can hasten the abolition of slavery who asserts his own freedom by his vote.

I hear of a convention to be held at Baltimore, or elsewhere, for the selection of a candidate for the Presidency, made up chiefly of editors, and men who are politicians by profession; but I think, what is it to any independent, intelligent, and respectable man what decision they may come to? Shall we not have the advantage of his wisdom and honesty, nevertheless? Can we not count upon some independent votes? Are there not many individuals in the country who do not attend conventions? But no: I find that the respectable man, so called, has immediately drifted from his position, and despairs of his country, when his country has more reason to despair of him. He forthwith adopts one of the candidates thus selected as the only *available* one, thus proving that he is himself *available* for any purposes of the demagogue. His vote is of no more worth than that of any unprincipled foreigner or hireling native, who may have been bought. O for a man who is a *man*, and, as my neighbor says, has a bone in his back which you cannot pass your hand through! Our statistics are at fault: the population has been returned too large. How many *men* are there to a square thousand miles in this country? Hardly one. Does not America offer any inducement for men to settle here? The American has dwindled into an Odd Fellow—one who may be known by the development of his organ of gregariousness, and a manifest lack of intellect and cheerful self-reliance; whose first and chief concern, on coming into the world, is to see that the almshouses are in good repair; and, before yet he has lawfully donned the virile garb, to collect a fund for the support of the widows and orphans that may be; who, in short, ventures to live only by the aid of the Mutual Insurance company, which has promised to bury him decently.

It is not a man's duty, as a matter of course, to devote himself to the eradication of any, even the most enormous, wrong; he may still properly have other concerns to engage him; but it is his duty, at least, to wash his hands of it, and, if he gives it no thought longer, not to give it practically his support. If I devote myself to other pursuits and contemplations, I must first see, at least, that I do not pursue them sitting upon another man's shoulders. I must get off him first, that he may pursue his contemplations too. See what gross inconsistency is tolerated. I have heard some of my townsmen say, "I should like to have them order me out to help put down an insurrection of the slaves, or to march to Mexico—see if I would go"; and yet these very men have each directly by their allegiance, and so indirectly, at least, by their money, furnished a substitute. The soldier is applauded who refuses to serve in an unjust war by

those who do not refuse to sustain the unjust government which makes the war; is applauded by those whose own act and authority he disregards and sets at naught; as if the state were penitent to that degree that it hired one to scourge it while it sinned, but not to that degree that it left off sinning for a moment. Thus, under the name of Order and Civil Government, we are all made at last to pay homage to and support our own meanness. After the first blush of sin comes its indifference; and from immoral it becomes, as it were, *un*moral, and quite unnecessary to that life which he have made.

The broadest and most prevalent error requires the most disinterested virtue to sustain it. The slight reproach to which the virtue of patriotism is commonly liable, the noble are most likely to incur. Those who, while they disapprove of the character and measures of a government, yield to it their allegiance and support are undoubtedly its most conscientious supporters, and so frequently the most serious obstacles to reform. Some are petitioning the State to dissolve the Union, to disregard the requisitions of the President. Why do they not dissolve it themselves—the union between themselves and the State—and refuse to pay their quota into its treasury? Do not they stand in the same relation to the State that the State does to the Union? And have not the same reasons prevented the State from resisting the Union which have prevented them from resisting the State?

How can a man be satisfied to entertain an opinion merely, and enjoy *it*? Is there any enjoyment in it, if his opinion is that he is aggrieved? If you are cheated out of a single dollar by your neighbor, you do not rest satisfied with knowing that you are cheated, or with saying that you are cheated, or even with petitioning him to pay you your due; but you take effectual steps at once to obtain the full amount, and see that you are never cheated again. Action from principle, the perception and the performance of right, changes things and relations; it is essentially revolutionary, and does not consist wholly with anything which was. It not only divides States and churches, it divides families; ay, it divides the *individual*, separating the diabolical in him from the divine.

Unjust laws exist: shall we be content to obey them, or shall we endeavor to amend them, and obey them until we have succeeded, or shall we transgress them at once? Men generally, under such a government as this, think that they ought to wait until they have persuaded the majority to alter them. They think that, if they should resist, the remedy would be worse than the evil. But it is the fault of the government itself that the remedy *is* worse than the evil. *It* makes it worse. Why is it not more apt to anticipate and provide for reform? Why does it not cherish its wise minority? Why does it cry and resist before it is hurt? Why does it not encourage its citizens to be on the alert to point out its faults, and *do better* than it would have them? Why does it always crucify Christ, and excommunicate Copernicus and Luther, and pronounce Washington and Franklin rebels?

One would think, that a deliberate and practical denial of its authority was the only offence never contemplated by government; else, why has it not assigned its definite, its suitable and proportionate, penalty? If a man who has no property refuses but once to earn nine shillings for the State, he is put in prison for a period unlimited by any law that I know, and determined only by the discretion of those who placed him there; but if he should steal ninety times nine shillings from the State, he is soon permitted to go at large again.

If the injustice is part of the necessary friction of the machine of government, let it go, let it go: perchance it will wear smooth—certainly the machine will wear out. If the injustice has a spring, or a pulley, or a rope, or a crank, exclusively for itself, then perhaps you may consider whether the remedy will not be worse than the evil; but if it is of such a nature that it requires you to be the agent of injustice to another, then, I say, break the law. Let your life be a counter-friction to stop the machine. What I have to do is to see, at any rate, that I do not lend myself to the wrong which I condemn.

As for adopting the ways which the State has provided for remedying the evil, I know not of such ways. They take too much time, and a man's life will be gone. I have other affairs to attend to. I came into this world, not chiefly to make this a good place to live in, but to live in it, be it good or bad. A man has not everything to do, but something, and because he cannot do *everything*, it is not necessary that he should do *something* wrong. It is not my business to be petitioning the Governor or the Legislature any more than it is theirs to petition me; and if they should not hear my petition, what should I do them? But in this case the State has provided no way: its very Constitution is the evil. This may seem to be harsh and stubborn and unconciliatory; but it is to treat with the utmost kindness and consideration the only

spirit that can appreciate or deserves it. So is all change for the better, like birth and death, which convulse the body.

I do not hesitate to say, that those who call themselves Abolitionists should at once effectually withdraw their support, both in person and property, from the government of Massachusetts, and not wait till they constitute a majority of one, before they suffer the right to prevail through them. I think that it is enough if they have God on their side, without waiting for that other one. Moreover, any man more right than his neighbors constitutes a majority of one already.

I meet this American government, or its representative, the State government, directly, and face to face, once a year—no more—in the person of its tax-gatherer; this is the only mode in which a man situated as I am necessarily meets it; and it then says distinctly, Recognize me; and the simplest, the most effectual, and, in the present posture of affairs, the indispensablest mode of treating with it on this head, of expressing your little satisfaction with and love for it, is to deny it then. My civil neighbor, the tax-gatherer, is the very man I have to deal with—for it is, after all, with men and not with parchment that I quarrel—and he has voluntarily chosen to be an agent of the government. How shall he ever know well what he is and does as an officer of the government, or as a man, until he is obliged to consider whether he shall treat me, his neighbor, for whom he has respect, as a neighbor and well-disposed man, or as a maniac and disturber of the peace, and see if he can get over this obstruction to his neighborliness without a ruder and more impetuous thought or speech corresponding with his action. I know this well, that if one thousand, if one hundred, if ten men whom I could name—if ten *honest* men only—ay, if *one* HONEST man, in this State of Massachusetts, *ceasing to hold slaves*, were actually to withdraw from this copartnership, and be locked up in the county jail therefor, it would be the abolition of slavery in America. For it matters not how small the beginning may seem to be: what is once well done is done forever. But we love better to talk about it: that we say is our mission. Reform keeps many scores of newspapers in its service, but not one man. If my esteemed neighbor, the State's ambassador, who will devote his days to the settlement of the question of human rights in the Council Chamber, instead of being threatened with the prisons of Carolina, were to sit down the prisoner of Massachusetts, that State which is so anxious to foist the sin of slavery upon her sister—though at present she can discover only an act of inhospitality to be the ground of a quarrel with her—the Legislature would not wholly waive the subject the following winter.

Under a government which imprisons any unjustly, the true place for a just man is also a prison. The proper place today, the only place which Massachusetts has provided for her freer and less desponding spirits, is in her prisons, to be put out and locked out of the State by her own act, as they have already put themselves out by their principles. It is there that the fugitive slave, and the Mexican prisoner on parole, and the Indian come to plead the wrongs of his race should find them; on that separate, but more free and honorable, ground, where the State places those who are not *with* her, but *against* her—the only house in a slave State in which a free man can abide with honor. If any think that their influence would be lost there, and their voices no longer afflict the ear of the State, that they would not be as an enemy within its walls, they do not know by how much truth is stronger than error, nor how much more eloquently and effectively he can combat injustice who has experienced a little in his own person. Cast your whole vote, not a strip of paper merely, but your whole influence. A minority is powerless while it conforms to the majority; it is not even a minority then; but it is irresistible when it clogs by its whole weight. If the alternative is to keep all just men in prison, or give up war and slavery, the State will not hesitate which to choose. If a thousand men were not to pay their tax-bills this year, that would not be a violent and bloody measure, as it would be to pay them, and enable the State to commit violence and shed innocent blood. This is, in fact, the definition of a peaceable revolution, if any such is possible. If the tax-gatherer, or any other public officer, asks me, as one has done, "But what shall I do?" my answer is, "If you really wish to do anything, resign your office." When the subject has refused allegiance, and the officer has resigned his office, then the revolution is accomplished. But even suppose blood should flow. Is there not a sort of blood shed when the conscience is wounded? Through this wound a man's real manhood and immortality flow out, and he bleeds to an everlasting death. I see this blood flowing now.

I have contemplated the imprisonment of the offender, rather than the seizure of his goods—though both will serve the same purpose—because

they who assert the purest right, and consequently are most dangerous to a corrupt State, commonly have not spent much time in accumulating property. To such the State renders comparatively small service, and a slight tax is wont to appear exorbitant, particularly if they are obliged to earn it by special labor with their hands. If there were one who lived wholly without the use of money, the State itself would hesitate to demand it of him. But the rich man—not to make any invidious comparison—is always sold to the institution which makes him rich. Absolutely speaking, the more money, the less virtue; for money comes between a man and his objects, and obtains them for him; and it was certainly no great virtue to obtain it. It puts to rest many questions which he would otherwise be taxed to answer; while the only new question which it puts is the hard but superfluous one, how to spend it. Thus his moral ground is taken from under his feet. The opportunities of living are diminished in proportion as what are called the "means" are increased. The best thing a man can do for his culture when he is rich is to endeavor to carry out those schemes which he entertained when he was poor. Christ answered the Herodians according to their condition. "Show me the tribute-money," said he—and one took a penny out of his pocket—if you use money which has the image of Caesar on it, and which he has made current and valuable, that is, *if you are men of the State*, and gladly enjoy the advantages of Caesar's government, then pay him back some of his own when he demands it. "Render therefore to Caesar that which is Caesar's, and to God those things which are God's"—leaving them no wiser than before as to which was which; for they did not wish to know.

When I converse with the freest of my neighbors, I perceive that, whatever they may say about the magnitude and seriousness of the question, and their regard for the public tranquillity, the long and the short of the matter is, that they cannot spare the protection of the existing government, and they dread the consequences to their property and families of disobedience to it. For my own part, I should not like to think that I ever rely on the protection of the State. But, if I deny the authority of the State when it presents its tax bill, it will soon take and waste all my property, and so harass me and my children without end. This is hard. This makes it impossible for a man to live honestly, and at the same time comfortably, in outward respects. It will not be worth the while

money is power and power corrupts

to accumulate property; that would be sure to go again. You must hire or squat somewhere, and raise but a small crop, and eat that soon. You must live within yourself, and depend upon yourself always tucked up and ready for a start, and not have many affairs. A man may grow rich in Turkey even, if he will be in all respects a good subject of the Turkish government. Confucius said: "If a state is governed by the principles of reason, poverty and misery are subjects of shame; if a state is not governed by the principles of reason, riches and honors are the subjects of shame." No: until I want the protection of Massachusetts to be extended to me in some distant Southern port, where my liberty is endangered, or until I am bent solely on building up an estate at home by peaceful enterprise, I can afford to refuse allegiance to Massachusetts, and her right to my property and life. It costs me less in every sense to incur the penalty of disobedience to the State than it would to obey. I should feel as if I were worth less in that case.

Some years ago, the State met me in behalf of the Church, and commanded me to pay a certain sum toward the support of a clergyman whose preaching my father attended, but never I myself. "Pay," it said, "or be locked up in the jail." I declined to pay. But, unfortunately, another man saw fit to pay it. I did not see why the schoolmaster should be taxed to support the priest, and not the priest the schoolmaster; for I was not the State's schoolmaster, but I supported myself by voluntary subscription. I did not see why the lyceum should not present its tax bill, and have the State to back its demand, as well as the Church. However, at the request of the selectmen, I condescended to make some such statement as this in writing: "Know all men by these presents, that I, Henry Thoreau, do not wish to be regarded as a member of any incorporated society which I have not joined." This I gave to the town clerk; and he has it. The State, having thus learned that I did not wish to be regarded as a member of that church, has never made a like demand on me since; though it said that it must adhere to its original presumption that time. If I had known how to name them, I should then have signed off in detail from all the societies which I never signed on to; but I did not know where to find a complete list.

I have paid no poll-tax for six years. I was put into a jail once on this account, for one night; and, as I stood considering the walls of solid stone, two or three feet thick, the door of wood and iron, a foot thick, and the iron grating which strained the light, I could not help being struck with the foolishness of that institution which treated me as if I were mere flesh and blood and bones, to be locked up. I wondered that it should have concluded at length that this was the best use it could put me to, and had never thought to avail itself of my services in some way. I saw that, if there was a wall of stone between me and my townsmen, there was a still more difficult one to climb or break through before they could get to be as free as I was. I did not for a moment feel confined, and the walls seemed a great waste of stone and mortar. I felt as if I alone of all my townsmen had paid my tax. They plainly did not know how to treat me, but behaved like persons who are underbred. In every threat and in every compliment there was a blunder; for they thought that my chief desire was to stand the other side of that stone wall. I could not but smile to see how industriously they locked the door on my meditations, which followed them out again without let or hindrance, and *they* were really all that was dangerous. As they could not reach me, they had resolved to punish my body; just as boys, if they cannot come at some person against whom they have a spite, will abuse his dog. I saw that the State was half-witted, that it was timid as a lone woman with her silver spoons, and that it did not know its friends from its foes, and I lost all my remaining respect for it, and pitied it.

Thus the State never intentionally confronts a man's sense, intellectual or moral, but only his body, his senses. It is not armed with superior wit or honesty, but with superior physical strength. I was not born to be forced. I will breathe after my own fashion. Let us see who is the strongest. What force has a multitude? They only can force me who obey a higher law than I. They force me to become like themselves. I do not hear of *men* being *forced* to live this way or that by masses of men. What sort of life were that to live? When I meet a government which says to me, "Your money or your life," why should I be in haste to give it my money? It may be in a great strait, and not know what to do: I cannot help that. It must help itself; do as I do. It is not worth the while to snivel about it. I am not responsible for the successful working of the machinery of society. I am not the son of the engineer. I perceive that, when an acorn and a chestnut fall side by side, the one does not remain inert to make way for the other, but both obey their own laws, and spring and grow and flourish as best they can, till one, perchance, overshadows and destroys the other. If a plant cannot live according to its nature, it dies; and so a man.

The night in prison was novel and interesting enough. The prisoners in their shirtsleeves were enjoying a chat and the evening air in the doorway, when I entered. But the jailer said, "Come, boys, it is time to lock up"; and so they dispersed, and I heard the sound of their steps returning into the hollow apartments. My room-mate was introduced to me by the jailer as "a first-rate fellow and a clever man." When the door was locked, he showed me where to hang my hat, and how he managed matters there. The rooms were whitewashed once a month; and this one, at least, was the whitest, most simply furnished, and probably the neatest apartment in the town. He naturally wanted to know where I came from, and what brought me there; and, when I had told him, I asked him in my turn how he came there, presuming him to be an honest man, of course; and, as the world goes, I believe he was. "Why," said he, "they accuse me of burning a barn; but I never did it." As near as I could discover, he had probably gone to bed in a barn when drunk, and smoked his pipe there; and so a barn was burnt. He had the reputation of being a clever man, had been there some three months waiting for his trial to come on, and would have to wait as much longer; but he was quite domesticated and contented, since he got his board for nothing, and thought that he was well treated.

He occupied one window, and I the other; and I saw that if one stayed there long, his principal business would be to look out the window. I had soon read all the tracts that were left there, and examined where former prisoners had broken out, and where a grate had been sawed off, and heard the history of the various occupants of that room; for I found that even here there was a history and a gossip which never circulated beyond the walls of the jail. Probably this is the only house in the town where verses are composed, which are afterward printed in a circular form, but not published. I was shown quite a long list of verses which were composed by some young men who had been detected in an attempt to escape, who avenged themselves by singing them.

I pumped my fellow-prisoner as dry as I could, for fear I should never see him again; but at length he showed me which was my bed, and left me to blow out the lamp.

It was like traveling into a far country, such as I had never expected to behold, to lie there for one night. It seemed to me that I never had heard the town clock strike before, nor the evening sounds of the village; for we slept with the windows open, which were inside the grating. It was to see my native village in the light of the Middle Ages, and our Concord was turned into a Rhine stream, and visions of knights and castles passed before me. They were the voices of old burghers that I heard in the streets. I was an involuntary spectator and auditor of whatever was done and said in the kitchen of the adjacent village inn—a wholly new and rare experience to me. It was a closer view of my native town. I was fairly inside of it. I never had seen its institutions before. This is one of its peculiar institutions; for it is a shire town. I began to comprehend what its inhabitants were about.

In the morning, our breakfasts were put through the hole in the door, in small oblong-square tin pans, made to fit, and holding a pint of chocolate, with brown bread, and an iron spoon. When they called for the vessels again, I was green enough to return what bread I had left; but my comrade seized it, and said that I should lay that up for lunch or dinner. Soon after he was let out to work at haying in a neighboring field, whither he went every day, and would not be back till noon; so he bade me good-day, saying that he doubted if he should see me again.

When I came out of prison—for some one interfered, and paid that tax—I did not perceive that great changes had taken place on the common, such as he observed who went in a youth and emerged a tottering and gray-headed man; and yet a change had to my eyes come over the scene—the town, and State, and country—greater than any that mere time could effect. I saw yet more distinctly the State in which I lived. I saw to what extent the people among whom I lived could be trusted as good neighbors and friends; that their friendship was for summer weather only; that they did not greatly propose to do right; that they were a distinct race from me by their prejudices and superstitions, as the Chinamen and Malays are; that in their sacrifices to humanity they ran no risks, not even to their property; that after all they were not so noble but they treated the thief as he had treated them, and hoped, by a certain outward observance and a few prayers, and by walking in a particular straight though useless path from time to time, to save their souls. This may be to judge my neighbors harshly; for I believe that many of them are not aware that they have such an institution as the jail in their village.

It was formerly the custom in our village, when a poor debtor came out of jail, for his acquaintances to salute him, looking through their fingers, which were crossed to represent the grating of a jail window, "How do ye do?" My neighbors did not thus salute me, but first looked at me, and then at one another, as if I had returned from a long journey. I was put into jail as I was going to the shoemaker's to get a shoe which was mended. When I was let out the next morning, I proceeded to finish my errand, and, having put on my mended shoe, joined a huckleberry party, who were impatient to put themselves under my conduct; and in half an hour—for the horse was soon tackled—was in the midst of a huckleberry field, on one of our highest hills, two miles off, and then the State was nowhere to be seen.

This is the whole history of "My Prisons."

I have never declined paying the highway tax, because I am as desirous of being a good neighbor as I am of being a bad subject; and as for supporting schools, I am doing my part to educate my fellow-countrymen now. It is for no particular item in the tax bill that I refuse to pay it. I simply wish to refuse allegiance to the State, to withdraw and stand aloof from it effectually. I do not care to trace the course of my dollar, if I could, till it buys a man or a musket to shoot one with—the dollar is innocent—but I am concerned to trace the effects of my allegiance. In fact, I quietly declare war with the State, after my fashion, though I will still make what use and get what advantage of her I can, as is usual in such cases.

If others pay the tax which is demanded of me, from a sympathy with the State, they do but what they have already done in their own case, or rather they abet injustice to a greater extent than the State requires. If they pay the tax from a mistaken interest in the individual taxed, to save his property, or prevent his going to jail, it is because they have not considered wisely how far they let their private feelings interfere with the public good.

This, then, is my position at present. But one cannot be too much on his guard in such a case, lest his action be biased by obstinacy or an undue regard for the opinions of men. Let him see that he does only what belongs to himself and to the hour.

I think sometimes, Why, this people mean well, they are only ignorant; they would do better if they knew how: why give your neighbors this pain to treat you as they are not inclined to? But I think again, This is no reason why I should do as they do, or permit others to suffer much greater pain of a different kind. Again, I sometimes say to myself, When many millions of men, without heat, without ill will, without personal feeling of any kind, demand of you a few shillings only, without the possibility, such is their constitution, of retracting or altering their present demand, and without the possibility, on your side, of appeal to any other millions, why expose yourself to this overwhelming brute force? You do not resist cold and hunger, the winds and the waves, thus obstinately; you quietly submit to a thousand similar necessities. You do not put your head into the fire. But just in proportion as I regard this as not wholly a brute force, but partly a human force, and consider that I have relations to those millions as to so many millions of men, and not of mere brute or inanimate things, I see that appeal is possible, first and instantaneously, from them to the Maker of them, and, secondly, from them to themselves. But if I put my head deliberately into the fire, there is no appeal to fire or to the Maker of fire, and I have only myself to blame. If I could convince myself that I have any right to be satisfied with men as they are, and to treat them accordingly, and not according, in some respects, to my requisitions and expectations of what they and I ought to be, then, like a good Mussulman and fatalist, I should endeavor to be satisfied with things as they are, and say it is the will of God. And, above all, there is this difference between resisting this and a purely brute or natural force, that I can resist this with some effect; but I cannot expect, like Orpheus, to change the nature of the rocks and trees and beasts.

I do not wish to quarrel with any man or nation. I do not wish to split hairs, to make fine distinctions, or set myself up as better than my neighbors. I seek rather, I may say, even an excuse for conforming to the laws of the land. I am but too ready to conform to them. Indeed, I have reason to suspect myself on this head; and each year, as the tax-gatherer comes round, I find myself disposed to review the acts and position of the general and State governments, and the spirit of the people, to discover a pretext for conformity.

We must affect our country as our parents,
And if at any time we alienate
Our love or industry from doing it honor,

We must respect effects and teach the soul
Matter of conscience and religion,
And not desire of rule or benefit.

I believe that the State will soon be able to take all my work of this sort out of my hands, and then I shall be no better a patriot than my fellow-countrymen. Seen from a lower point of view, the Constitution, with all its faults, is very good; the law and the courts are very respectable; even this State and this American government are, in many respects, very admirable, and rare things, to be thankful for, such as a great many have described them; but seen from a point of view a little higher, they are what I have described them; seen from a higher still, and the highest, who shall say what they are, or that they are worth looking at or thinking of at all?

However, the government does not concern me much, and I shall bestow the fewest possible thoughts on it. It is not many moments that I live under a government, even in this world. If a man is thought-free, fancy-free, imagination-free, that which *is not* never for a long time appearing *to be* to him, unwise rulers or reformers cannot fatally interrupt him.

I know that most men think differently from myself; but those whose lives are by profession devoted to the study of these or kindred subjects content me as little as any. Statesmen and legislators, standing so completely within the institution, never distinctly and nakedly behold it. They speak of moving society, but have no resting-place without it. They may be men of a certain experience and discrimination, and have no doubt invented ingenious and even useful systems, for which we sincerely thank them; but all their wit and usefulness lie within certain not very wide limits. They are wont to forget that the world is not governed by policy and expediency. Webster never goes behind government, and so cannot speak with authority about it. His words are wisdom to those legislators who contemplate no essential reform in the existing government; but for thinkers, and those who legislate for all time, he never once glances at the subject. I know of those whose serene and wise speculations on this theme would soon reveal the limits of his mind's range and hospitality. Yet, compared with the cheap professions of most reformers, and the still cheaper wisdom and eloquence of politicians in general, his are almost the only sensible and valuable words, and we thank Heaven for him. Comparatively, he is always strong, original, and, above all, practical. Still, his quality is not wisdom, but prudence. The lawyer's truth is not Truth, but consistency or a consistent expediency. Truth is always in harmony with herself, and is not concerned chiefly to reveal the justice that may consist with wrong-doing. He well deserves to be called, as he has been called, the Defender of the Constitution. There are really no blows to be given by him but defensive ones. He is not a leader, but a follower. His leaders are the men of '87. "I have never made an effort," he says, "and never propose to make an effort; I have never countenanced an effort, and never mean to countenance an effort, to disturb the arrangement as originally made, by which the various States came into the Union." Still thinking of the sanction which the Constitution gives to slavery, he says, "Because it was a part of the original compact—let it stand." Notwithstanding his special acuteness and ability, he is unable to take a fact out of its merely political relations, and behold it as it lies absolutely to be disposed of by the intellect—what, for instance, it behooves a man to do here in America today with regard to slavery—but ventures, or is driven, to make some such desperate answer as the following, while professing to speak absolutely, and as a private man—from which what new and singular code of social duties might be inferred? "The manner," says he, "in which the governments of those States where slavery exists are to regulate it is for their own consideration, under their responsibility to their constituents, to the general laws of propriety, humanity, and justice, and to God. Associations formed elsewhere, springing from a feeling of humanity, or any other cause, have nothing whatever to do with it. They have never received any encouragement from me, and they never will."

They who know of no purer sources of truth, who have traced up its stream no higher, stand, and wisely stand, by the Bible and the Constitution, and drink at it there with reverence and humility; but they who behold where it comes trickling into this lake or that pool, gird up their loins once more, and continue their pilgrimage toward its fountainhead.

No man with a genius for legislation has appeared in America. They are rare in the history of the world. There are orators, politicians, and eloquent men, by the thousand; but the speaker has not yet opened his mouth to speak who is capable of settling the much-vexed questions of the day. We love eloquence for its own sake, and not for any truth which it may utter, or any heroism it may inspire. Our legislators have not yet learned the comparative value of free trade and of freedom, of union, and of rectitude, to a nation. They have no genius or talent for comparatively humble questions of taxation and finance, commerce and manufactures and agriculture. If we were left solely to the wordy wit of legislators in Congress for our guidance, uncorrected by the seasonable experience and the effectual complaints of the people, America would not long retain her rank among the nations. For eighteen hundred years, though perchance I have no right to say it, the New Testament has been written; yet where is the legislator who has wisdom and practical talent enough to avail himself of the light which it sheds on the science of legislation?

The authority of government, even such as I am willing to submit to—for I will cheerfully obey those who know and can do better than I, and in many things even those who neither know nor can do so well—is still an impure one: to be strictly just, it must have the sanction and consent of the governed. It can have no pure right over my person and property but what I concede to it. The

progress from an absolute to a limited monarchy, from a limited monarchy to a democracy, is a progress toward a true respect for the individual. Even the Chinese philosopher was wise enough to regard the individual as the basis of the empire. Is a democracy, such as we know it, the last improvement possible in government? Is it not possible to take a step further towards recognizing and organizing the rights of man? There will never be a really free and enlightened State until the State comes to recognize the individual as a higher and independent power, from which all its own power and authority are derived, and treats him accordingly. I please myself with imagining a State at last which can afford to be just to all men, and to treat the individual with respect as a neighbor; which even would not think it inconsistent with its own repose if a few were to live aloof from it, not meddling with it, nor embraced by it, who fulfilled all the duties of neighbors and fellow men. A State which bore this kind of fruit, and suffered it to drop off as fast as it ripened, would prepare the way for a still more perfect and glorious State, which also I have imagined, but not yet anywhere seen.

The Inward Morning (1842)

This poem (divided into and treated as two separate lyrics in Thoreau's journal for November 30, 1841, and December 12, 1841) was published in the October, 1842, number of the *Dial*. In this poem the great theme of the English Romantic poets, the relation of man's spirit to nature, a relationship in which one both gives to and receives from the other, is resolved in favor of what may be called a "projectionist" view of the matter: that is, a light coming out of man's own mind throws upon nature, as upon a screen, the hues that nature only seems to wear. In the first stanza, Thoreau states this view of the matter by means of a rather startlingly matter-of-fact metaphor. The various kinds of clothing that outward nature wears are stored ("packed") in the poet's own mind. Just as the light of the sun chases away the night, stirs up the morning breeze, and awakens the birds, so a light coming out of man's spirit animates nature and gives it its

special qualities. "The Inward Morning" is thus one of Thoreau's most Emersonian poems.

The concrete detail has been sharply observed, and the adjectives and adverbs used are striking. They set the tone of the poem. The pine tree is characterized as "patient." The light is said to have told something to the forest trees "nimbly." What it has told them is probably the same sort of "cheerful morning news" that the poet has heard within his "inmost soul."

Packed in my mind lie all the clothes
   Which outward nature wears,
And in its fashion's hourly change
   It all things else repairs.

In vain I look for change abroad,
   And can no difference find,
Till some new ray of peace uncalled
   Illumes my inmost mind.

What is it gilds the trees and clouds,

And paints the heavens so gay,   10
But yonder fast-abiding light
  With its unchanging ray?

Lo, when the sun streams through the wood,
  Upon a winter's morn,
Where'er his silent beams intrude
  The murky night is gone.

How could the patient pine have known
  The morning breeze would come,
Or humble flowers anticipate
  The insect's noonday hum,—   20

Till the new light with morning cheer
  From far streamed through the aisles,
And nimbly told the forest trees

For many stretching miles?

I've heard within my inmost soul
  Such cheerful morning news,
In the horizon of my mind
  Have seen such orient hues,

As in the twilight of the dawn,
  When the first birds awake,   30
Are heard within some silent wood,
  Where they the small twigs break,

Or in the eastern skies are seen,
  Before the sun appears,
The harbingers of summer heats
  Which from afar he bears.

My Books I'd Fain Cast Off, I Cannot Read (1842)

This poem was first published in the *Dial*. The third line is clumsy. In the fourth, "targe" for *target* is a "literary" and rather forced usage, at that. One cannot imagine a New Englander of Thoreau's day using the word in conversation. In the fourth stanza, the playfulness which treats as Homeric the contest between the red ants and the black ants and discerns in one of them a champion like Ajax in the *Iliad* is too ponderous. Ants, it is true, do have remarkable strength for their size and can move something heavier than themselves, but fighting ants don't heave objects at their adversaries as Ajax did when he lifted a great stone from the battle-field, "swung it round his head and cast it with all his might" at Hector.

   And yet, for all the incidental awkwardness, the poem has some charming touches: for example, the speaker's remark that now he has "*business* with this drop of dew" or his vivid description of the rainy wind "Shaking down crystals on the leaves below."

My books I'd fain cast off, I cannot read,
'Twixt every page my thoughts go stray at large
Down in the meadow, where is richer feed,
And will not mind to hit their proper targe.

Plutarch was good, and so was Homer too,
Our Shakespeare's life were rich to live again,
What Plutarch read, that was not good nor true,
Now Shakespeare's books, unless his books
  were men.

Here while I lie beneath this walnut bough,
What care I for the Greeks or for Troy town,   10
If juster battles are enacted now
Between the ants upon this hummock's crown?

Bid Homer wait till I the issue learn,
If red or black the gods will favor most,
Or yonder Ajax will the phalanx turn,
Struggling to heave some rock against the host.

Tell Shakespeare to attend some leisure hour,
For now I've business with this drop of dew,
And see you not, the clouds prepare a shower,—
I'll meet him shortly when the sky is blue.   20

This bed of herd's-grass and wild oats was spread
Last year with nicer skill than monarchs use,
A clover tuft is pillow for my head,
And violets quite overtop my shoes.

And now the cordial clouds have shut all in,
And gently swells the wind to say all's well,
The scattered drops are falling fast and thin,
Some in the pool, some in the flower-bell.

I am well drenched upon my bed of oats;
But see that globe come rolling down its stem,   30
Now like a lonely planet there it floats,
And now it sinks into my garment's hem.

Drip drip the trees for all the country round,
And richness rare distils from every bough,

The wind alone it is makes every sound,
Shaking down crystals on the leaves below.

For shame the sun will never show himself,

Who could not with his beams e'er melt me so,
My dripping locks,—they would become an elf,
Who in a beaded coat does gayly go.   40

I Mark the Summer's Swift Decline (1842)

Thoreau entered this poem in his journal. The
editor of the *Collected Poems* conjectures that
the date of composition was probably 1842.
These verses constitute a kind of set piece: for
example, the closing line, "And sing the requiem
of the dying year," echoes a dozen English
poems of the late eighteenth and the early
nineteenth centuries. But how resonant and
powerfully stimulating to the imagination is line
4: "The aged year turns on its couch of leaves."

Such imaginative perceptions as this one are the
special mark of Thoreau's finest poetry.

I mark the summer's swift decline
The springing sward its grave clothes weaves
Whose rustling woods the gales confine
The aged year turns on its couch of leaves.

Oh could I catch the sounds remote
Could I but tell to human ear—
The strains which on the breezes float
And sing the requiem of the dying year.

Fog (1843)

Dull water spirit—and Protean god
Descended cloud fast anchored to the earth
That drawest too much air for shallow coasts
Thou ocean branch that flowest to the sun
Incense of earth, perfumed with flowers—

Spirit of lakes and rivers, seas and rills
Come to revisit now thy native scenes
Night thoughts of earth—dream drapery
Dew cloth and fairy napkin
Thou wind-blown meadow of the air.   10

Pray to What Earth Does This Sweet Cold Belong (1843)

F. B. Sanborn tells us that this poem was included in the manuscript of "A Winter Walk,"
but was omitted by Emerson when he published that essay in the October, 1843, number
of the *Dial*. In this poem the sensitive observer
of Walden Pond reveals himself in such passages as "The moon goes up by leaps," "The
snow dust still emits a silvery light," and "By
the brooksides . . ./The crystals shoot and
form." But the poet is not content to rest in the
presentation of such details. He is concerned to
define the difference between nature and himself, the human observer. In this poem, Thoreau
might almost be thinking of the famous passage
in Plotinus: "Should anyone interrogate [na-
ture], how she works, if graciously she vouchsafe
to listen and speak, she will reply, it behooves

thee not to disquiet me with interrogatories, but
to understand in silence even as I am silent, and
work without words." Unlike the human being
who is oppressed by the sense of duties to be
performed and who is sometimes nipped by an
uneasy conscience, nature carries out its ministrations quietly and unerringly. Observed in
such a context, even the cold of winter will seem
sweet, and winter will appear to take possession
of the earth, not violently and rudely, but "by
gentlest summer means."

Pray to what earth does this sweet cold belong,
Which asks no duties and no conscience?
The moon goes up by leaps her cheerful path
In some far summer stratum of the sky,

While stars with their cold shine bedot her way.
The fields gleam mildly back upon the sky,
And far and near upon the leafless shrubs
The snow dust still emits a silvery light.
Under the hedge, where drift banks are their
   screen,
The titmice now pursue their downy dreams,   10

As often in the sweltering summer nights
The bee doth drop asleep in the flower cup,
When evening overtakes him with his load.
By the brooksides, in the still genial night,
The more adventurous wanderer may hear
The crystals shoot and form, and winter slow
Increase his rule by gentlest summer means.

The Fall of the Leaf (1863)

This poem was published a year after Thoreau's death, in 1863 in the *Boston Commonwealth*—stanzas 1–4 on October 9 as "The Fall of the Leaf," and stanzas 5–16 on November 6 as "The Soul's Season." One of the interesting features of the poem is that it contains more than do most of Thoreau's writings touches of conventional Christian piety. The opening lines thank God for the seasons of the year and even for the dreaded season of winter because God is "plainest seen upon the shortest days." In stanza 11, the falling autumn leaf is said to obey "its Maker's call."

There are trite and well-worn figures: for example, the singing of the insects is called "Nature's lullaby." But the poem also contains a number of bold comparisons, some of them somewhat forced, like that in stanza 6, in which the shadows thrown by the trees are likened to sentries "gently protecting them," or that in the last stanza, in which the trees shorn of their leaves are likened to knights on a battlefield bravely awaiting the "charge of Winter's cavalry," or as austerely garbed Roman citizens, now "Discumbered of their Persian luxury."

Yet though the poem is disconcertingly uneven, it has, one repeats, some wonderful things in it. Notice, for example, "Since Summer's garishness is gone," the nicely observed natural detail in stanza 7, and the elaborate—and successful—"metaphysical" conceit in stanza 15:

The threadbare trees, so poor and thin—
They are no wealthier than I;

The reader will probably have noticed other memorable phrases and lines. He may, however, find that he needs to read some passages more than once, for example, stanza 3 or 14, in order to get the meaning. The poet's assertion (in stanza 14) that "The crisped and yellow leaves around/Are hue and texture of my mood" is readily intelligible and brilliantly said, but what does the poet mean by calling the "rough burrs . . . on the ground" his "heirlooms"?

Thank God who seasons thus the year,
   And sometimes kindly slants his rays;
For in his winter he's most near
   And plainest seen upon the shortest days.

Who gently tempers now his heats,
   And then his harsher cold, lest we
Should surfeit on the summer's sweets,
   Or pine upon the winter's crudity.

A sober mind will walk alone,
   Apart from nature, if need be,   10
And only its own seasons own;
   For nature leaving its humanity.

Sometimes a late autumnal thought
   Has crossed my mind in green July,
And to its early freshness brought
   Late ripened fruits, and an autumnal sky.

The evening of the year draws on,
   The fields a later aspect wear;
Since Summer's garishness is gone,
   Some grains of night tincture the noontide air.   20

Behold! the shadows of the trees
   Now circle wider 'bout their stem,
Like sentries that by slow degrees
   Perform their rounds, gently protecting them.

And as the year doth decline,
   The sun allows a scantier light;
Behind each needle of the pine
   There lurks a small auxiliar to the night.

I hear the cricket's slumbrous lay
   Around, beneath me, and on high;   30
It rocks the night, it soothes the day,
   And everywhere is Nature's lullaby.

But most he chirps beneath the sod,
   When he has made his winter bed;
His creak grown fainter but more broad,
   A film of autumn o'er the summer spread.

Small birds, in fleets migrating by,
   Now beat across some meadow's bay,
And as they tack and veer on high,
   With faint and hurried click beguile the way.   40

Far in the woods, these golden days,
   Some leaf obeys its Maker's call;
And through their hollow aisles it plays
   With delicate touch the prelude of the Fall.

Gently withdrawing from its stem,
   It lightly lays itself along
Where the same hand hath pillowed them,

Resigned to sleep upon the old year's throng.

The loneliest birch is brown and sere,
   The furthest pool is strewn with leaves,   50
Which float upon their watery bier,
   Where is no eye that sees, no heart that
     grieves.

The jay screams through the chestnut wood;
   The crisped and yellow leaves around
Are hue and texture of my mood—
   And these rough burrs my heirlooms on the
     ground.

The threadbare trees, so poor and thin—
   They are no wealthier than I;
But with as brave a core within
   They rear their boughs to the October sky.   60

Poor knights they are which bravely wait
   The charge of Winter's cavalry,
Keeping a simple Roman state,
   Discumbered of their Persian luxury.

Let Such Pure Hate Still Underprop (1841)

This poem was first published in the *Dial*. It may seem curious that a poem which will celebrate love should begin by asking that "pure hate" may still underprop that "love." Yet if such boldness makes for obscurity, particularly in the early part of the poem, the general drift of the poem is obvious enough. The two friends are to be completely sincere with each other. Each is to say what he really thinks in the confidence that anything less than complete candor will be unworthy of the relationship which binds them together.

Though the first five stanzas, with their bold imagery and rather violent statements, do not hang together in every respect—or at least do not *obviously* hang together—the other stanzas do. Love is seen as winning the day, unconquerable, able to penetrate any defense and to bridge any yawning chasm.

The dominant figure used by Thoreau is that of a moated castle. In his isolation, every man, and especially the man who asks a great deal of friendship and cannot easily permit another to enter into his inner self, is like such a castle. But love, the sort of love that Thoreau is talk-

ing about, is formidable. If no "trivial bridge of words" will avail to span the moat that cuts each person apart from his fellows, love at least can be counted upon to win entrance. The figure of the sun, a force that cannot be kept out, bathing the gloomy stronghold in light, investing the fortress with its rays, "says," by implication and suggestion, all that Thoreau needs to say here. The reader might explore this image and ask himself why the line "And shine along the wall" is so powerfully suggestive. He might also try to determine the other sources of the poem's strength.

              "Friends, Romans, Countrymen,
                       and Lovers."

Let such pure hate still underprop
Our love, that we may be
Each other's conscience,
And have our sympathy
Mainly from thence.

We'll one another treat like gods,
And all the faith we have
In virtue and in truth, bestow

On either, and suspicion leave
To gods below. 10

Two solitary stars,—
Unmeasured systems far
Between us roll,
But by our conscious light we are
Determined to one pole.

What need confound the sphere,—
Love can afford to wait,
For it no hour's too late
That witnesseth one duty's end,
Or to another doth beginning lend. 20

It will subserve no use,
More than the tints of flowers,
Only the independent guest
Frequents its bowers,
Inherits its bequest.

No speech though kind has it,
But kinder silence doles
Unto its mates,
By night consoles,
By day congratulates. 30

What saith the tongue to tongue?
What heareth ear of ear?
By the decrees of fate
From year to year,
Does it communicate.

Pathless the gulf of feeling yawns,—

No trivial bridge of words,
Or arch of boldest span,
Can leap the moat that girds
The sincere man. 40

No show of bolts and bars
Can keep the foeman out,
Or 'scape his secret mine
Who entered with the doubt
That drew the line.

No warder at the gate
Can let the friendly in,
But, like the sun, o'er all
He will the castle win,
And shine along the wall. 50

There's nothing in the world I know
That can escape from love,
For every depth it goes below,
And every height above.
It waits as waits the sky,
Until the clouds go by,
Yet shines serenely on
With an eternal day,
Alike when they are gone,
And when they stay. 60

Implacable is Love,—
Foes may be bought or teased
From their hostile intent,
But he goes unappeased
Who is on kindness bent.

HERMAN MELVILLE (1819–1891)

We cannot say about Herman Melville, in any literal sense, what we have said about Hawthorne—that he enacted a literary role which changed the possibilities of society, and that this role was involved in part with his relation to the public world he addressed and to the fame which he found in that world. Of these two supreme American writers of romance (and sometime friends), Melville had undoubtedly the greater genius; there is more drive, urgency, and scope in his writing; and while Hawthorne's work is thick with the most fertile paradoxes and ironies, in Melville's we sense rather the unending and extraordinarily creative struggle between fierce and irresolvable contradictions—the contradictory realities of good and evil, freedom and fate, knowledge and the unknowable, belief and nonbelief, the life of safety and common sense and the life of dangerous, perhaps catastrophic pursuit of ultimate truth.

But Hawthorne really did address a public world, a world which, as time passed, listened to him ever more intently; and we need only the example of Henry James to see the profound effectiveness of Hawthorne's work in showing his countrymen and his fellow artists how (as we have said) experience may be newly grasped and values framed. But after a brief period of great popularity, Melville lost almost all contact with the public world. From *Moby-Dick* (1851) onward, he lived and wrote in a kind of absolute silence, the very type of isolated writer, yet heroic, energetic, and uncomplaining to the end. He died quite unnoticed in 1891, the manuscript of his final masterpiece *Billy Budd* stored away somewhere in a trunk, and it was not until almost half a century later that the range and depth of his accomplishment began to be recognized, along with the nearly violent originality of his imagination and the matchless vigor of his mind. We know now that he was—that he *is*—one of America's literary giants; even more than Hawthorne, perhaps, he is now and all so belatedly established as a man and a writer whose sensibility really does change and enlarge our sense of life's possibilities.

Melville's first book, *Typee* (1846), was an immense and immediate success, and Melville told a correspondent that he felt like the person (he was thinking of Byron) who "woke one morning and found himself famous." *Omoo* (1847), the sequel to *Typee*, was as well received; but readers stumbled a little over the untraditional allegory in *Mardi* (1849), and they were puzzled by some parts of *Redburn* (1849). *Moby-Dick* simply baffled and annoyed them: here was a splendid yarn about whaling that had gotten hopelessly lost in obscure metaphysical rangings. *Pierre, or, The Ambiguities* (1852) was dismissed as hysterical lunacy, further degraded by its incestuous and suicidal elements. As to Melville's career, the rest, as we have said, is silence. *Israel Potter* (1855), *The Confidence Man* (1857), most of the tales of the 1850's, *Battle-Pieces* (1866), *Clarel* (1876), and Melville's other and later poems: all of these, as he once said about *Clarel* to one of his rare admirers, were "eminently adapted for unpopularity."

For all his dry irony, "adapted" was the right word. There was nothing accidental in Melville's loss of popularity. He knew from the beginning that if he could go on writing books like *Typee* —though he also knew that much in that book had gone unappreciated—he could hang on to his public following. But the integrity of his imagination forbade him to write more *Typees*. That was the safe way, the easy way, the self-protective way; but it was not Melville's way. "What I feel most moved to write," he told Hawthorne in the summer of 1851, while in the midst of *Moby-Dick*, "that is banned—and it will not pay. Yet, altogether, write the *other* way I cannot." He felt compelled to reach out constantly in his writing for new dimensions of experience, new exertions of mind, new horizons of insight—to take the adventurous but radically dangerous way, and to risk, as he was perfectly aware that he would, literary defeat and public alienation. These two fundamentally opposed views of the literary career (the safe and the daring) are reflected, along with other alternative modes of life, in the great contrast between the harbor and the open sea described by Ishmael in Chapter 23 of *Moby-Dick* ("The Lee Shore"). "The port," Ishmael says, "would fain give succor; the port is pitiful; in the port is safety, comfort, hearthstone, supper, warm blankets, friends, all that's kind to our mortalities." But under certain circumstances, a ship must flee the harbor, as a man and a writer must flee the easy channels of expression. For

all deep, earnest thinking is but the intrepid effort of the soul to keep the open independence of her sea; while the wildest winds of heaven and earth conspire to cast her on the treacherous slavish shore. But as in landlessness alone resides the highest truth, shoreless, indefinite as God—so, better is it to perish in that howling infinite than be ingloriously dashed upon the lee, even if that were safety!

As a literary figure in his own lifetime, Melville may be said to have perished, and to have done so almost deliberately, as matter of firmest principle—and so, "gloriously." But there is a major irony—and one that says a great deal about American literary culture—in Melville's lack of recognition, or rather in the total loss of the public recognition once granted him. For Melville deeply believed that the *immediate* recognition of literary achievement was not only important for the individual writer, it gave indispensable encouragement to "the whole brotherhood" of writers and could lead, in America, to the more general recognition that American literature was an existing fact. Writing about Hawthorne in the August, 1850, issue of the *Literary World*, Melville besought his countrymen not to delay acknowledging the author of *Mosses from an Old Manse*. "Give not over to future generations the glad duty of acknowledging him for what he is," especially since "by confessing him, you thereby confess others; you brace the whole brotherhood. For genius, all over the world, stands hand in hand, and one shock of recognition runs the whole circle round."

Melville's failure to be so acknowledged in his lifetime cannot be laid entirely to an inhospitality to the tragic imagination on the part of his contemporary readers. Such a theory is disputed at once by the impact of *The Scarlet Letter*. But Hawthorne's tragic vision was more nearly accessible to readers; it engaged the local and familiar, even the quotidian, where Melville's was exotic and metaphysical—and the latter, the strenuous imaginative concern with "deep, earnest thinking," was no doubt the more damaging. By contrast with Hawthorne's, moreover, Melville's imagination was at times coercive. Hawthorne invited the reader, for example, to decide whether Dimmesdale did or did not have the letter A engraved on his chest, and if so whether it was self-imposed or a freak of nature.[1] Melville, for all his distrust of allegory and for all his determination to imbed his tales in the demonstrably factual, rather asks us to accept the extraordinary—whether of motivation or event—as given. But the same qualities—the exotic, the metaphysical, the coercive—which made Melville seem either bewildering or for-

bidding in his own time were the ones that exerted the strongest appeal in a later day.

No one thought harder than Melville about the relation between a writer and his historical culture. It was the "American-ness" of Hawthorne that, in the essay cited, Melville particularly extolled and identified by beguilingly American metaphors: "If you travel inland into his deep and noble nature, you will hear the far roar of his Niagara," and so on. Among the attributes of the genuinely American writer, Melville places stress on two. The first is originality: the writer who wishes to be truly American should avoid imitation at all costs, particularly imitation of the eighteenth-century English authors (Irving is cited as a smooth and carefully pleasing imitator of Goldsmith). The second is the expression of fundamental humanity. "Let him write like a man, for then he will be sure to write like an American." And doing so, he will join those writers "who breathe that unshackled democratic spirit of Christianity in all things"—who bespeak in every phase of their writing a deep belief in the essential freedom of mind and equality of spirit of all human beings.

Such a belief permeates Melville's work. He was concerned artistically (Richard Chase has made the point) not with men in social contexts, more than half shaped and determined by institutions and traditions, ranked according to birth, wealth, influence. He was not, that is, concerned with writing the novel of manners. He was concerned rather with certain basic and enduring qualities of human nature and experience and thought—with what, in a letter to Hawthorne, he called "the tragedies of human thought in its own unbiased, native and profounder workings." To concentrate on those workings—wherein men are, potentially at least, free and equal—is, to Melville's mind, to express an unshackled and democratic and Christian spirit.

Melville was, in short, concerned with truth; and in this respect he is not only one of the most American, he is perhaps the most *Western* of our great writers. Melville's teacher at the Albany school he briefly attended remembered

[1] See Lionel Trilling's essay "Our Hawthorne," in *Hawthorne Centenary Essays* (1964).

him as a lad "strict in his truthfulness." But it was more than a passion for factual accuracy and scrupulous honesty, though these were always important. It was a driving search for, as it were, the very truth about things, the truth that lay somewhere amid those clashing contradictions we have listed earlier. In an essay called "The Spirit of Western Literature," the German critic Hans-Egon Holthusen has argued effectively that what characterizes Western as against Eastern literature is exactly its dramatization of the thrust toward ultimate truth; and he adduces, as representative heroes of Western literature, the figures of Oedipus, Hamlet, Don Juan, and Faust. To that company one should surely add the figure of Captain Ahab. And on its outskirts we can similarly locate other memorable and typical Melvillian inventions: Taji in the allegorical romance *Mardi*; Ishmael; Pierre Glendinning; Captain Vere in *Billy Budd*; the speaking voice in the poem "The Conflict of Convictions"; the stricken star-gazing woman in "After the Pleasure Party"; and others still. All these characters are caught up in the drama of the quest for truth. And each of them, in his or her way, is led to suspect what Ishmael had discovered: that "in the landlessness alone resides the highest truth, shoreless, indefinite as God."

Herman Melville was born in New York City in 1819, the second son of Allan Melville and Maria Gansevoort Melville. Both parents were well-born, in early nineteenth-century American terms: Maria came from one of the solid, healthy, Dutch, Hudson River mercantile clans; Allan from a somewhat more unstable and romantic but no less affluent Boston family. There were revolutionary heroes on both sides: General Peter Gansevoort, the doughty defender of Fort Stanwix against the British and Indians (the old general is reverently remembered in the portrait of General Glendinning in *Pierre*); and Herman's remarkable grandfather, Major Melville, who took part in the Boston Tea Party, was later appointed surveyor of ports in Boston by Washington, and survived to totter about the city, a familiar figure much given to watch-

ing houses burn down—and indeed to die of this at last, from overexposure while attending a fire in his early eighties. (Major Melville is slenderly immortalized in Oliver Wendell Holmes's poem, "The Last Leaf.") If inheritance means anything, we can account for a good deal in the mature Melville's sometimes enormously excitable and yet staunchly durable temperament by this diverse background.

The first decade of Herman's life was passed in reasonable comfort and, as far as externals went, contentment, within a sizable and rather closely knit family. Catastrophe struck for the first time in the summer of 1830, when Allan Melville went bankrupt after an unwise investment. The family had to repair abruptly to Albany, where they were taken in and given succor by relatives. There followed a period of racking economic, and hence social, uncertainty. There were moments when things seemed a bit better, and Herman and his brothers could be sent to the well-regarded Albany Academy; but these were regularly succeeded by moments when things were obviously worse—until Allan Melville, in January, 1832, collapsed under the intolerable strain, took to his bed, finally went quite insane, and, after two weeks, died.

It is impossible to measure the immediate effect of this experience upon Melville the boy, about to enter adolescence, or the long-range effect upon Melville the man and the writer of genius. With Melville, we have to reckon with someone for whom love—not love in the abstract, but immediate and personal love: parental love, married love, masculine love, filial love— was a driving necessity of existence. And we have to reckon with someone for whom such love was, more often than not, either subtly denied or forcibly removed. Certainly, one of the major themes of Melville's fiction is the child's search for his father—most prominently in *Moby-Dick* ("Where is the foundling's father hidden?" muses Ishmael), but also in *Redburn*, and more obscurely in *Billy Budd*. In those stories, Melville may be seen as making an intense imaginative effort to re-ally himself symbolically with the father he had adored. At the same time, Melville the boy seems to have felt—

not surprisingly—that he had been incomprehensibly betrayed and abandoned by his father; and from this feeling there later issued the counter-theme of defiance. This is the dramatic message of Ahab in *Moby-Dick*, when, addressing the gleaming fires that had tipped the three lightning-rod-ends on each of the three masts, he declares: "Thou art my fiery father," and "I now know that thy right worship is defiance. To neither love nor reverence wilt thou be kind."

Beyond that basic contradiction of attitude, the early experience of sudden bankruptcy and then his father's collapse into madness and death gave Melville his first sense not only of the utter precariousness of the human situation but also of the tormenting mystery of things. It led him not only to seek out his father, symbolically, in his fiction, but to search for the truth about human life that lay behind the necessity of the search itself. It led him to wonder about human freedom: whether the individual life were not, after all, a self-determining affair but rather something controlled by invisible, perhaps unknowable and maybe malignant forces—"the Arch-Principals," as he would half-jestingly call them.

Melville brought to that search and that speculation more than a mixture of filial love and resentment and a sheer energy of mind. He also brought a certain Calvinistic view of human nature and destiny, something he inherited from his mother. Melville's relation to Maria Gansevoort is not the least of the contradictions that beset him. Always an austere, reserved, and humorless woman, Maria became only more so after her husband's death and through subsequent years of humiliating poverty; and at just the time when Herman's love-obsessed nature most reached out for her, she remained maternally aloof. There is no doubt that Herman loved *her*, perhaps too much or in a manner not the healthiest. For example, the birth certificate of Melville's son Stanwix lists the mother as Maria, that is, Melville's own mother, though it is not certain whether the slip was Freudian, and Melville's (in dictation), or that of the pen of the county clerk. What is clear is that, as well as love, Melville must have felt surges of resentment toward his mother. But Melville never doubted the value of his mother's Calvinist indoctrination.

Perhaps "indoctrination" is too strong a word. But Herman, with his brothers and sisters, on the insistence of their mother, regularly attended the Dutch Reformed Church in New York and Albany (Allan Melville, during his lifetime, made no effort to impose his pallid Unitarian beliefs upon the children). They listened week after week to the sermons and the reading of the catechism; and the doctrines they heard enunciated were in the strictest mode of orthodox Calvinism. We can disentangle a few of the key ideas Melville received from his exposure—always remembering that we are talking not about Calvinist doctrines in their pure form, but in the shape they assumed in Melville's active imagination.

There was, first, the theme of Original Sin and human depravity. Speaking of what he called Hawthorne's "power of blackness," Melville wrote that it

> derives its force from its appeal to that Calvinistic sense of Innate Depravity and Original Sin, from whose visitations in some shape or other, no deeply thinking mind is always and wholly free. For, in certain moods, no man can weigh this world without throwing in something, somehow like Original Sin, to strike the uneven balance.

One notices both the strength of the thought and the hesitancy of its application: "something, somehow like Original Sin." In *Billy Budd*, near the end of his life, Melville would appeal rather to the Platonic idea of "Natural Depravity," which "though savoring of Calvinism, by no means involves Calvin's dogma as to total mankind." Melville's experience would teach him, so he felt, that while all men might be flawed, only some few men were genuinely evil. But there is a hint too, in the longer passage just quoted as well as in several of his poems, that beyond mere human sinfulness there may be a portion of metaphysical evil in the world at large, in the nature of things.

He was led, as well, to reflect upon the Calvinist conviction that human life was entirely predetermined and unfolded within the grand design of an omnipotent God. Over this, Melville would characteristically brood, oscillating between acceptance and rejection of the harsh assumption, at once dramatizing it and challenging it in his fiction. The nature and, more important, the knowability of God provided another and more tormenting mystery, and if Calvinism focused attention on that mystery it did not help Melville solve it. There would be moments when Melville considered the most fearsome alternative of all—namely, that all these questions were finally meaningless, that there simply was no rational order in the universe, nothing to believe in, nothing to either worship or hate, only a vast universal blank. (See the discussion of *Clarel*, Melville's theological epic, p. 917.)

But if Melville brought to his writing and his imaginative quest a certain set of theological concerns—as both a maternal bequest, so to speak, and a main component of the inherited American religious culture of his time—he also brought something altogether different, and no less crucial. He brought his own personal experiences during his late adolescence and young manhood. In the years just after his father's death, Herman paid long visits to his beloved uncle Tom Melville, on his farm near Pittsfield in the Berkshires. The nephew would later recall his uncle with great affection in a short story called "The Happy Failure," a story that captured a good part of Melville's mood in the mid-fifties. Melville also tried his hand at schoolteaching in the Berkshires; but he returned often enough to his immediate family, which had now moved (in an act of "downward mobility") to the village of Lansingburg, near Troy—enough to be thoroughly unsettled by the dreary atmosphere of the impoverished and sunless household. And so, in 1839, he did what so many young Americans in his generation dreamed of, and some succeeded in doing—he ran away to sea.

On the first of his voyages, Melville served as cabin boy aboard the merchant vessel *St. Lawrence*, which left New York, bound for Liverpool, in June, 1839. During the next five years—until the fall of 1844—he journied in a variety of ships, in a variety of menial functions; but it was his experiences on board a series of whalers, and his later meditation on them and imaginative renderings *of* them, that meant by far the most to him. He sailed on the whaler *Acushnet*, from Buzzards Bay (at the edge of Cape Cod) bound for the South Pacific, in January, 1841; and it was from the *Acushnet*, eighteen months later, that Melville jumped ship to spend a few weeks among the "cannibals" in the Typee valley in the Marquesas. He escaped from the valley to join the whaler *Lucy Ann* in July or August, 1842, and went with her as far as Tahiti. In January, 1843, he worked his way to Hawaii on the whaler *Charles and Henry*. The last of Melville's youthful voyages was as an enlisted sailor on the American man-of-war, *United States*, a ship once commanded by Stephen Decatur; polishing brass, keeping watch, and taking part in gun drill on the *United States*, Melville made his way from Hawaii once again through the South Pacific, touching at several South American ports before making the long trip back to the harbor of Boston in early October, 1844.

Speaking through the voice of Ishmael, Melville remarks early in *Moby-Dick* (Chap. 24) that "a whale-ship was my Yale College and my Harvard." The words should be taken more precisely than sometimes they are. It is true that until his family met with disaster Melville had hoped to go to one of the leading American colleges. But he is not saying here that he went a-whaling *instead of* attending college. He is saying that his experiences on a number of whalers constituted *his* higher education. Just as Emerson and Thoreau went to Harvard, there to read Plato and Montaigne and to study such textbooks on rhetoric and theology as would serve their eventual intellectual purposes; and as Hawthorne attended Bowdoin and read Spenser and Bunyan and other writers whom he could draw upon for his own brand of fictional allegory; so Melville found preeminently in the life at sea and the whale chase (but also in his other sea-going and ship-jumping adventures) the elements out of which he would forge his great creations.

Among the main ingredients in Melville's education were, of course, the sea itself, especially the vast reaches of the Pacific ocean; the hunt, especially the hunting of the whale; the extreme vicissitudes of physical nature; masculine friendship and (on the *United States* at least) persistent homosexuality; cruelty amounting to sadism (particularly on the part of the captain of the *Acushnet*, whose answer to the mildest complaint was "the butt-end of a handspike"); iniquity; the lure of the exotic; and, in the Typee valley, the mixed attractions of the pastoral and idyllic. But two things should be said at once about those ingredients. First, and to underscore the obvious, they were not gleanings from books; they were actual, immediate, and personal experiences. Melville was an indefatigable reader; his own work is stuffed with echoes and borrowings from world literature (especially classical, Elizabethan, and seventeenth-century English literature); and later stories like *Israel Potter*, "Benito Cereno," and *Billy Budd* were based on the writings of others. Nonetheless, Melville stands at the head of that list of American writers—it includes Stephen Crane and Hemingway—who came initially to the literary life out of the adventurous life, and in Melville's case an adventurous life which followed upon a deeply disturbing family life. Second, however, those ingredients expanded so rapidly into powerful images, within Melville's highly active imagination, that it is hardly possible, as it were, to catch any one of them pure. The sea, to take a single example, was not only the Pacific or Atlantic ocean; it was, in Ishmael's words, "the image of the ungraspable phantom of life"—and had evidently seemed so to Melville since the time when, as a boy, he used to stroll along the New York waterfront with his father. And in the most violent storms at sea, Melville could get his first intuitions of that "landlessness"—and more, of that "howling infinite"—wherein a man might wrestle with ultimate truth.

We can carry our speculations further. Considering now the whole of Melville's "education" up to the fall of 1844, we can say that it included two of the most primary components in American culture. Sailing westward and southwestward, Melville absorbed the American fascination with space and movement; with the West; with the frontier; with the romantic and the escape from civilization. These were indispensable aids to the imagination; but his *mind*, as we have said, was imbued with another large aspect of the culture, the somber hypotheses of orthodox Calvinism. It was an extraordinary combination, one perfectly adapted for a writer of Melville's peculiar genius; but one also eminently adapted, as he would discover, to make literary creations that were to prove increasingly unpalatable to his contemporaries.

In 1844, Melville was back with his family in Lansingburg, New York. There is little record of his doings for the next two years, and for a simple reason. Melville was now embarked upon a life that was increasingly inward. His adventures now became adventures of the mind; he was caught up henceforth in "the tragedies of thought." He had, in short, begun to write. Melville's only publication to this point had been a couple of interesting juvenilia (one of them dealing with a "fair charmer" who had let him down), which he submitted to a Lansingburg newspaper not long before he boarded the *St. Lawrence*. Now, however, he began to produce at a speed which, considering the extraordinary quality of the work, must be unmatched in American literary history—seven novels (or "romances") in six years, between *Typee* in 1846 and *Pierre* in 1852; with *Israel Potter*, *The Confidence Man*, and *The Piazza Tales* in the short five years following *Pierre*. If there is something breathtaking in that achievement, there is also something disconcerting—to crowd a lifetime of writing into so short a span! Melville himself, as we shall see, thought he had written himself out with *Moby-Dick*, and again a few years after that. It was an explosion of energy that would have exhausted Shakespeare; and one wonders whether a different pace—a different creative patience—might have resulted in a more protracted career of writing. But Melville, as he said, wrote in the only way he could. And in any event, despite the legend that has grown up about him, Melville's writing career by no means ended in the late fifties; it did not end until his death.

In 1847, Melville moved to the city, settling in a house on lower Fourth Avenue. He was married by this time to Elizabeth Shaw of Boston, the daughter of Lemuel Shaw, Chief Justice of Massachusetts, and an exceedingly distinguished and influential jurist. Judge Shaw had been a good friend of Allan Melville's, and a warm and constant benefactor of the Melville family after the disaster; Melville dedicated *Typee* to him. Newton Arvin may well be right in his suggestion that, in choosing Lizzie Shaw to be his wife, Melville was in part choosing Lemuel Shaw to be his father-in-law—a substitute father, that is, for the vanished Allan. Lizzie was a homebody; amiable, unintellectual; absorbed by housekeeping chores and the modest social round. She was proud of her husband's work, as years went by, but she could hardly have understood much of it—especially those passages which wittily or scornfully condemned the married life. But she was a completely devoted and loyal wife, and never more so than during the periods of crisis and frustration of Melville's later decades. And if there were tensions and bewilderments in the early married years— Melville's relation to women was always vexed and obscurely modified by his strong attraction to men—there seems to have been much serenity and a genuine happiness in the later ones.

It would be wrong to consider the five novels which preceded *Moby-Dick* as simply creative stages en route to that titanic masterpiece. Each of them can be read and enjoyed separately; each has its own special points of intellectual and aesthetic interest, each its own unique source of compulsion, and each no doubt its own larger or smaller blemishes. But Melville, as we have said, was always thrusting onward, thrusting deeper into the mysteries of self, nature, reality—or at any rate always attempting to. Even *Moby-Dick*, though it is of course incomparably Melville's greatest work and very likely the greatest work of fiction yet produced in this country—even *Moby-Dick* can, in one

perspective, be seen as one enormous stage in Melville's unending search for certainty. So there is a justification in taking the fictional predecessors of *Moby-Dick* as important moments in a larger process. (The present essay, it should be remarked, deals almost exclusively with Melville's *fiction*. A discussion of his poetry follows thereafter.)

Typee and *Mardi*, so inspected, make a suggestive pair. *Typee* is essentially an autobiographical narrative crowded with well-remembered and handsomely assembled factual detail —and with larger "meanings" and implications hovering and gliding, only intermittently and partially visible, beneath the exotic surface. *Mardi*, on the other hand, after a brief stretch of straightforward, almost journalistic, narrative, shifts abruptly into a world of total fantasy and an allegorical tour of some imaginary islands where—in an atmosphere quite devoid of actuality—the allegorical figures engage in philosophical debates and ruminations. These were the uneasy alternatives between which Melville's creative powers swung in his first efforts—either ideas tended to lie hidden beneath the color and weight of the actual and the personally experienced; or the actual had to be abandoned in order to get on with the pursuit of ideas.

Both definitions to be sure are reductive and misleading. *Typee*, for all its density of fact, reveals large areas of significance without undue prodding; and the allegorical landscape in *Mardi* is vivified by details taken from Melville's observation of Polynesian life. The narrative of *Typee* remains closely bound to Melville's adventures in 1842 when he jumped ship with a seventeen-year-old lad named Toby Greene and plunged into the interior of the Nuku-Hiva island, there to spend several weeks—at once a guest and a prisoner—with a tribe of Polynesians. Melville had suffered a leg wound, and Toby Greene went back to the harbor settlement for medicine, only to be shanghaied onto another whaler. But he turned up later in the United States and testified to the "entire accuracy" of Melville's account insofar as he could judge; anthropologists since, including Sir James Frazer (author of *The Golden Bough*), have similarly praised the verisimilitude of Melville's descriptions. But at the same time, we recognize in *Typee*, as its truthful narrative proceeds, a major example of a persistent American literary genre —the genre of the pastoral, the story of the retreat from "civilization," especially one which, in the 1840's, was beginning to be invaded by technology and burgeoning cities and with all the apparatus and rhetoric of material progress. Thoreau's *Walden* is an eminently superior and much more knowing contribution to this genre, and so is *Huckleberry Finn*. But Melville's discovery of the idyllic life and his vigorous critique of American society from his island viewpoint contain one or two unusual features.

For one thing, the plunge into the interior of Nuku-Hiva is—as imaginatively recollected by Melville and as presented by him in *Typee*—an inward journey, a plunge into the deeper interiors of the self, and more impressively so than Melville fully realized. Meditating his actual experience, Melville saw in it, without quite *seeing* that he saw, a symbol of the descent into the unconscious, down to that mysterious realm where primordial thoughts bestir themselves and where myths arise. *Typee* never marshals those thoughts, nor does it project any one of those myths; but the impulse is there and would be fulfilled in due time. For another thing, however, Melville's pastoral imagination is much more complex and dialectical than, say, that of Thoreau; it included typically something of its own opposite. While enjoying the physical beauties of the island and its inhabitants, the pleasures of the sensual life and the erotic companionship of the maiden Fayaway, Melville did not lose his rigor of mind, nor forget those hypotheses by which, he had learned, life might in part be measured. So if, in a desperate venture, he made his escape from Typee, it was not only because he felt some real fear that he might be killed, or because he was conscious of a savagery and barbarism that mingled oddly with the Polynesian charm and smiling good nature. It was above all because of an incurable deficiency in the Polynesian temperament, a lack even of an awareness of some of the realities that most concerned him. "There seemed,"

he wrote, "to be no cares, griefs, troubles, or vexation in all Typee." But care and grief were part of the truth of experience. *Typee* is an American pastoral which includes a severe critique of the pastoral.

Mardi, flawed as it is by a disjunction between fact and allegory, is Melville's first boldly explicit attempt to lay siege to truth—or anyhow to certain *truths*, of a moral and political and aesthetic and sexual nature. It is, as Hawthorne said about it to Evert Duyckinck (a minor author and editor of the *Literary World*), a rich book, "with depths in it here and there that compel a man to swim for his life"; though not every reader may be inclined to take the initial dive. Such narrative line as remains after the opening section involves the pursuit by Taji (as the cerebral Yankee sailor comes to be renamed) after the fair Yillah, the representative, presumably, of innocence and perhaps the rational, a pursuit often interrupted by the expectably dark Hautia, who stands for the powerful temptations of disorder and the irrational. At the end, when, with Yillah still in the far distance, Taji sets off alone upon the open seas, it is disorder and irresolvable ambiguity that appear to define the world explored. Such must have been the troubled conviction of Melville in the summer of 1849. But the importance of *Mardi* may lie finally in the array of incompatible literary modes with which Melville experiments in the course of the book, in his intense if momentarily unsuccessful search for the literary form in which experience, imagination, and idea could be fused. Journalistic narrative, romantic allegory, symbolism both potent and petty, philosophical satire in a manner akin to *Gulliver's Travels*, debates and meditations along the way that possibly echo *Rasselas*, legends and rituals transplanted from the Marquesas to the nonworld of *Mardi*—these fail to coalesce; the book is a sort of junkyard of modes and styles; but the extraordinary amalgam of *Moby-Dick* is only just out of reach.

In *Redburn*, the amalgam begins to take shape. The story in *Redburn* goes back to Melville's first ocean voyage, as a cabin boy on the merchant ship *St. Lawrence*; but Melville obviously felt much freer to invent and interpolate than hitherto. If *Redburn* is superior to all the other novels prior to *Moby-Dick*, it is partly because, though it is firmly rooted in personal experience, Melville is less tied down by the autobiographical than in *Typee* (or its easy-going sequel, *Omoo*); and while a number of the abstract problems of *Mardi* are again puzzled over, they tend in *Redburn* to appear in dramatic form, by means of character and incident. Death, for example, is not brooded over but is embodied—in the wildly drunken sailor who throws himself overboard on the voyage out, in the Portuguese sailor who is discovered dead in his bunk on the voyage back, in the murder of a prostitute in a Liverpool bar; and in the reencountered fact—as of something not yet fully faced up to—of the death of Redburn's father.

If death punctuates the narrative in *Redburn*, sickness permeates it. The physical epidemic that breaks out on the trip back, and kills many of the passengers in the overcrowded steerage, has its correlative in the moral disease that is first noted in the deceitful pawnshop-keeper in New York, swells into the horrors of moral corruption observed by young Redburn along the docks and in "the booble alleys" of Liverpool, and is brilliantly focused in the malignant, dying mate Jackson. Jackson, who is no more than "the foul lees and dregs of a man," is Melville's first truly striking and memorable characterization. Weak and wasted, he is nonetheless the crew's bully; he is a genuinely wicked man, but his wickedness, as Redburn dimly perceives, "seemed to spring from his woe"; and in his dire complexity, he personifies something more than merely moral and human badness—something at once stricken and diabolical, something of metaphysical evil and of anguish.

What is notable about *Redburn* is that all these themes of sickness and death and evil and grief and madness are at once artfully related to each other and subordinated to the main theme of the book. If *Typee* is an American pastoral which is also an American antipastoral, and if *Mardi* plays over some of the most important ideas and considerations current in the America of the 1840's, *Redburn* is a major contribution to another primary American genre—the literature of initiation, of the young person's introduction to the buffeting realities of life and of society, to the mysteries of the human tribe. The theme of initiation was prevalent enough in European writing, especially in the nineteenth century—one need only think of *The Red and the Black*, or *Great Expectations*, or *The Sorrows of Werther*; and it is, of course, a literary theme that derives at great distance from the actual initiation rites of primitive tribes. But the American imagination, with its sense of the constant possibility of fresh beginnings, seems to have been peculiarly obsessed by it. Cooper in *The Deerslayer* and Hawthorne in stories like "Young Goodman Brown," "My Kinsman, Major Molyneux," and "The Gentle Boy" somewhat anticipate Melville; and after Melville, the theme would be returned to again and again by Henry James, Mark Twain, Dreiser, Fitzgerald, Faulkner, and in our time by Ralph Ellison, Saul Bellow, and John Barth, among many others.

In this large, native context, *Redburn* stands out because of the bleak nature of the reality that forces itself upon the boy's awareness. It is a reality almost entirely composed of sickness and death and malignancy—and loss. The loss is that of Redburn's father, whom the boy only half-consciously searches for, as he wanders through Liverpool, guidebook in hand. He feels that he is "performing a filial pilgrimage," retracing the steps he and his father had followed in the same city years before; and so strong is this impression that he almost expects to overtake his father around the next corner. All this is pure invention on Melville's part (as are most of the other incidents we have mentioned); Melville and his father were never in Liverpool together. But it is part of Melville's imaginative and symbolic struggle to repossess himself of his lost parent, only to realize with a finality that the father "had gone whither no son's search could find him in this world." Redburn himself remains relatively untouched by the discovery, but Melville, reliving it, did not; in *Moby-Dick* the remembered loss would be a source of fury and defiance.

In the summer of 1850, Melville, with his wife and young son, moved to Pittsfield to stay, first in the house that had belonged to Melville's Uncle Tom, and then in a farmhouse Melville bought and named Arrowhead. Scarcely more than a month later, on an expedition to Monument Mountain, Melville was introduced to Nathaniel Hawthorne, and there began one of the most remarkable, if also one of the briefest, friendships in American literary history. It was no doubt more intense, even passionate, on Melville's side. He felt that he had at last met someone whose mind and imagination paralleled his own, and that in Hawthorne's presence he could lay himself bare of all his bursting ideas, his profoundly tragic intuitions, his colossal creative aspirations. He could, he felt, indulge with Hawthorne in "ontological heroics"; and he wrote his new friend that "when the big hearts strike together, the concussion is a little stunning." Hawthorne was too reserved and self-contained to reply altogether in kind; but he—and, it must be added, his wife Sophia—gave Melville the keenest sympathy and understanding he would ever receive.

Writing about Hawthorne in the *Literary World* and writing a series of letters *to* Hawthorne, Melville not only gave vent to some exceedingly acute remarks about literature and American culture generally. He also managed to take these occasions to concentrate his own creative energies and clarify his own ideas. Reading and rereading Hawthorne, moreover (and discussing these matters with him, one supposes), Melville made fresh discoveries about his craft: the manipulation of symbol, the presentation of the dramatic scene or even the dramatic gesture, the way meditation and narrative can intermingle, the moral and aesthetic courage that the writing of tragedy requires. Melville had begun *Moby-Dick* before he met Hawthorne; he finished it in July, 1851, and dedicated it with all propriety to his neighbor.

There is good evidence that Melville shifted and enormously enlarged his conception of *Moby-Dick* in the course of writing it, to the point that what might have been a superior *Redburn* became a world masterpiece *sui gen-* eris. It is impossible to explain how or why this happened, though Melville's reading provides some tangential clues. Before and during the time of composition, Melville had been reading Greek tragedy, especially the *Oresteia* of Aeschylus, and he had been immersed in the tragedies of Shakespeare—in the essay on Hawthorne, he refers specifically and tellingly to King Lear, Hamlet, Iago, and Timon of Athens. He had also been reading epic poetry, Homer obviously, but also the *Lusiads*, that splendid modern epic of the sea by the Portuguese poet, Camoëns. And in the philosophical dictionary of Pierre Bayle, Melville had been learning about a number of philosophical creeds and religious sects, among them such ancient "heretical" groups as the Manicheans and the Gnostics.

All this suggests something about the ingredients of *Moby-Dick*, as a way of identifying the work, if not of grasping it. *Moby-Dick* is epic in scope and in the sheer abundance of its materials, and it contains several of the grand, traditional epic conventions—the long and arduous journey and the great battle, for example. But much of the novel is dramatically shaped; much of it, indeed, is staged: the scenes on the quarter-deck, the sharp personal confrontations, the soliloquies; while phrases and images from Shakespeare flow through the astonishingly supple rhetoric. It is—or better, the epic contains—a *tragic* drama, a tragedy of pride and pursuit and revenge which, though it is fleshed out in the most palpable and violent manner, is nonetheless a tragedy of thought in the mind's profoundest workings.

It should be remarked at this point that, though *Moby-Dick* is in many ways the most remarkable American book about life at sea, it was by no means the first. Cooper had written his two sea romances, *The Pilot* (1823, a story of derring-do set in the revolutionary period, with a title figure based in part upon John Paul Jones) and *The Red Rover* (1827, a tale of piracy, conflicting loyalties, and sensationally revealed blood relationships, in the years before the Revolution). There had been quasi-scientific studies of whales and whaling, and personal reminiscences like *Etchings of a Whaling Cruise* (1846), by a young Kentuckian, John Ross Brown, who, like Melville, had shipped out of New Bedford; Melville reviewed the book.[2] Other writings were of more immediate importance for Melville. It was from *A Mariner's Sketches* (1830) by a New Englander named Nathaniel Ames that Melville drew the most memorable incident in *White-Jacket*, when the young hero loses his balance and plunges into the depths of the sea. The account by Owen Chase of the catastrophe that befell the Nantucket whaler *Essex* in 1820, when it was ripped into and sunk by a sperm whale, "had," Melville said, "a surprising effect upon me."[3] And it was in an article by J. N. Reynolds about "an old bull whale, of prodigious size and strength," known by awe-struck whale hunters as Mocha Dick and also, because of his color (he was "white as wool"), as the White Whale of the Pacific—it was here that Melville gathered the image which would enlarge into Moby-Dick. But above all, there had been what Melville called "my friend Dana's unmatchable *Two Years Before the Mast*." (See pp. 1080–87 for a discussion of Dana's work and an excerpt from *Two Years Before the Mast*.)

Moby-Dick is a sea-haunted novel, and exactly because, as Ishmael says in the opening chapter, the sea—for those who are drawn to it—is "the image of the ungraspable phantom of life." Melville's great work is about the pursuit of that phantom, an attempt to seek out the mystery which seems to lie—malevolently or benevolently, as the case may prove—at the heart of human experience. On one level, in other words, the search is an intellectual one, an act of the mind in its quest for what Melville, in Chapter 23, calls "the highest truth," a

truth only discoverable in a metaphorical "landlessness." But that very metaphor springs from Melville's creative strategy. Drawing both on his personal experience and his immensely powerful vivifying and dramatizing imagination, Melville cast the mental adventure in the form of a sea voyage—the long voyage of the *Pequod* from Nantucket down the coast of South America, around the Cape of Good Hope, and up through the China Seas to the North Pacific. As charted by the *Pequod*'s commander, the monomaniacal Captain Ahab, the voyage is a "fiery hunt" for one particular whale, the great beast Moby-Dick; for to Ahab, the white whale is the very embodiment of the ultimate mystery. He is the ungraspable phantom seemingly made accessible to human attack.

Moby-Dick is much too large and various, too crowded with contrasting incidents and competing ideas, too rich in metaphor and symbol to be taken account of in a relatively brief commentary. For that reason, however, it may be more helpful to pause over a few moments characteristic of the diversity of this bursting narrative, rather than to attempt an abstract and thus inevitably a reductive overall interpretation. By so doing, we can give some sense of the way Melville establishes his themes and expands upon them, how he identifies and matches the two outsize antagonists (Ahab and Moby-Dick), how he thickens the context and deploys his rhetoric and finally carries the story into the final grand encounter. Our concern, in short, is as much with the manner of treatment as with the things treated. It is with Melville as an artist.

The 135 chapters of *Moby-Dick* do not divide tidily, in the classical mode, into a beginning, a middle, and an end. The book, nonetheless, can be said to have smaller and larger "stages" —stages distinguished more by the prevailing tone and atmosphere in each than by any carefully wrought turn in the action. Three of the larger phases may be made out, and the first of these runs through Chapter 42, "The Whiteness of the Whale." Here the emphasis is all upon mystery and the inescapable challenge of the unknown. The young man who asks us to

---

[2] Melville's review of Brown's book is included in *Herman Melville: Representative Selections*, edited by Willard Thorp (1938).

[3] *Narrative of the Most Extraordinary and Distressing Shipwreck of the Whale-Ship Essex*. The author, Owen Chase, had been first mate on the *Essex* and one of five survivors of the disaster. Melville was given the book by Chase's young son whom he met aboard the *Acushnet*.

call him Ishmael (after the truculent character in Genesis whose hand, it is prophesied, "will be against every man, and every man's hand against him") takes to the sea in a mood at once aggressive and suicidal, because the sea lures him on with its mute promise of containing an explanation of life and hence of his own malaise. The nature both of Ishmael's condition and of his quest is suggested by the atmosphere of gloom and darkness that hangs over the New Bedford scene which is his first stopping point, and by the air of ambiguity which pervades all the phenomena observed. The season is winter; the night is dismal; the streets are dreary, and the buildings "blocks of darkness." Entering what looks like a public house, Ishmael finds he has stumbled into a Negro church, where a hundred black faces turn to stare at him, and a black minister is preaching about "the blackness of darkness."

As a seeker after truth, Ishmael moves in a world dense with puzzles and portents, with objects which—as one peers at them through the dimness—refuse to convey a clear message or to reveal their true identity. Surveying a sign which says "The Spouter-Inn:—Peter Coffin," Ishmael reflects uneasily that for a man about to set forth on a whaling voyage, the conjunction of "spouter" and "coffin" may be ominous. Inside, his attention is drawn to a dark, indistinct painting. Perhaps this "boggy, soggy" picture shows an actual whale impaling himself on the mastheads of a ship; but just possibly it describes instead the battle of the four primal elements, or it is an allegorical rendering of the breaking up of the icebound stream of time. Actual disaster at sea is thus obscurely associated with metaphysical speculations. The literal and the intellectual journies are made to run ever more closely parallel.

Ishmael, we eventually realize, serves primarily to introduce the theme of the quest, and before very long he gives way to a far more troubled and determined figure—Ahab, who towers over all other seekers after truth in the novel even as Moby-Dick looms over all the other whales encountered. Before Ahab appears, in fact, Ishmael has made his peace with life and found

the explanation he had been straining after. The explanation, in his case, is human friendship: in the form of a pagan harpooner named Queequeg. Seated with Queequeg in the little room they share in the Spouter Inn, he begins to feel "a melting" in him.

> No more my splintered heart and maddened hand were turned against the wolfish world. This soothing savage had redeemed it. There he sat, his very indifference speaking a nature in which there lurked no civilized hypocrisies and bland deceits. Wild he was; a very sight of sights to see; yet I began to feel myself mysteriously drawn to him.

Thereafter, Ishmael can be seen as representing essential or common humanity and to have opted for the life symbolized in Chapter 23 by the harbor—the domain of "safety, comfort, hearthstone, supper, warm blankets, friends, all that's kind to our mortalities." The latter word means the natural limitations and infirmities which all but the most extraordinary men are wise to acknowledge and to agree to live with. Within them, it can be added, Ishmael, now at peace, is able to exercise a good deal of high good humor, of a kind which oddly colors the narrative style of the early chapters for all their content of gloom, and which Ahab admits he is wholly bereft of.[4]

But Ahab is exactly one of those extraordinary men who indomitably (or insanely) refuse to accept the limitations humanity is otherwise confined by. He is also, by general agreement, the most powerful creation in American literature. Apart perhaps from Faulkner's Thomas Sutpen in *Absalom, Absalom!* one looks in vain for another fictional hero, tragic or not, who remotely approaches him in stature.

We get our first glimpse of him in Chapter 28, and the force of that dramatic appearance derives in good part from the muscular intensity

---

[4] The jaunty style of the early chapters, as it plays off against the solemnity of a flow of Biblical, Shakespearean, and Miltonic allusions and borrowings, reflects of course the Ishmael who has survived the final calamity, who has lived and returned to land to tell his story.

of the language with which he is immediately invested. Of a sudden, on a morning several days out from Nantucket, and after remaining invisible during that period, "Captain Ahab stood upon his quarter-deck."

There seemed no sign of common bodily illness about him, nor of the recovery from any. He looked like a man cut away from the stake, when the fire has overrunningly wasted all the limbs without consuming them, or taking away one particle from their compacted aged robustness. His whole high, broad form, seemed made of solid bronze, and shaped in an unalterable mould, like Cellini's cast of Perseus. Threading its way out from among his gray hairs, and continuing right down one side of his tawny scorched face and neck till it disappeared in his clothing, you saw a slender rod-like mark, lividly whitish. It resembled that perpendicular seam sometimes made in the straight, lofty trunk of a great tree, when the upper lightning tearingly darts down it, and without wrenching a single twig, peels and grooves out the bark from top to bottom, ere running off into the soil, leaving the tree still greenly alive, but branded. . . .

I was struck with the singular posture he maintained. Upon each side of the Pequod's quarter-deck, and pretty close to the mizzen shrouds, there was an auger hole, bored about half an inch or so, into the plank. His bone leg steadied in that hole; one arm elevated, and holding by a shroud; Captain Ahab stood erect, looking straight out beyond the ship's ever-pitching prow. There was an infinity of firmest fortitude, a determinate, unsurrenderable wilfulness, in the fixed and fearless, forward dedication of that glance. Not a word he spoke; nor did his officers say ought to him; though by all their minutest gestures and expression, they plainly showed the uneasy, if not painful, consciousness of being under a troubled master-eye. And not only that, but moody stricken Ahab stood before them with a crucifixion in his face; in all the nameless regal overbearing dignity of some mighty woe.

But the force of that language itself, as of the human figure it introduces, derives from the context that has been building and thickening. Take, for example, one of the qualities attributed to Ahab: "an infinity of firmest fortitude." Ahab enters a fictional world in which the theme of courage has been sounded time and again. There was Queequeg's calm bravery, on the trip from New Bedford to Nantucket, in diving to rescue an oafish stranger who had fallen overboard. Each of the assorted "knights and squires" (to borrow the title of Chapter 26)—the three mates and the three harpooners on the *Pequod*—is characterized and ranked according to the kind and degree of his courage. It is in the wake of these clustering allusions that Ahab, when he at last comes into view, can be seen as possessing a courage beyond anything the other figures can display. And "the fixed and fearless, forward dedication of his *glance*" suggests—in a novel in which the act of perceiving or trying to perceive has taken on such high metaphysical meaning—that Ahab is capable of facing up not only to physical danger but to spiritual terrors as well. It is this, Melville remarks, which sets him apart even from Starbuck, who is the bravest member of the crew when it comes to the normal perils of life at sea.

Or take Ahab's as yet unexplained grief: he is "moody" and "stricken"; there is "a crucifixion in his face"; he seems smitten by "some mighty woe." The theme of suffering has also been prevalent from the opening chapter, and Ishmael's recollection of nearly suicidal despondency which had driven him to sea. It had been reinforced by the sight of the silent quenchless grief of the women in the New Bedford chapel whom Ishmael had seen mourning for the husbands and brothers lost at sea; and by the account of the "despair" and "black distress" experienced by Jonah, in the hymn intoned by Father Mapple in the same chapel. Ahab's grief, measured against such feelings, goes as far beyond them (context and language makes us understand) as his courage goes beyond Starbuck's.

Ahab's "regal" quality—his "regal overbearing dignity"—has been verbally prepared for by the labeling of the mates and harpooners "knights and squires," that is, the entourage of a monarch, and Queequeg has been revealed as a member of royalty on his native island. But Melville's language *adds* to these moral, spiritual, and social calculations certain elements in Ahab which combine in a huge contradiction. His "determinate, unsurrenderable wilfulness" associates him with Satan in one of Melville's favorite works of literature, Milton's *Paradise Lost* (with his self-professed "unconquerable will"); and the "crucifixion in his face" associates him with Jesus. Ahab—regal, fearless, grief-stricken—is at once Satanic and Christ-like, such language insinuates; he has the potential either to destroy or to redeem the world he presides over.

While incident, character, and language have thus been creating a vital frame within which Ahab can stand forth in the fullness of his utterly exceptional nature, they have simultaneously been creating a frame for Moby-Dick—who, comparably, is immeasurably superior to all other sea beasts in his size, his cunning, his ferocity, and his seeming ubiquity. This process began with the prologue-listing of the various names for the whale in a series of languages and literary quotations about Leviathan, and has gone forward with a spirited and jocular defense of the nobility of the whaling industry, and a celebration of the whale as, allegedly, the supreme phenomenon in literature and history.

The first great wave of the novel, in fact, exhausts itself in the paired chapters which concentrate on the title figure—"Moby-Dick" and "The Whiteness of the Whale." The former is a model study of symbol-making—of how one particular whale had come to symbolize what it did in the consciousness of mariners generally and of Ahab in particular; of how *this* whale had grown to such proportions in the minds of those who had had dealings with it. Critics who have assigned "meanings" to Moby-Dick have sometimes paid insufficient attention to what Melville is doing here, and have declared the whale to mean, flatly, this thing or that— as though a certain significance inhered in the creature quite apart from the consciousness of its human observers. Such fixity of meaning was possible in an age—for example, the age of

Dante and the *Divine Comedy*—when writers and readers shared the same beliefs and could interpret experience by the same set of symbols. By the mid-nineteenth century, as Melville well knew, this situation no longer obtained: symbolic meaning varied with the intellectual and imaginative temper of the onlooker, and this fluidity of significance was, precisely, a key factor in the search for truth which the novel is steadily enacting. In the later chapter called "The Doubloon," Ishmael muses that "some certain significance lurks in all things"—for this is also a premise of the book—but then he goes on to demonstrate that every man will derive the meanings his character and experience prepare him for.

To Ahab, in his violence of spirit, the white whale has come to represent "All that maddens and torments; all that stirs up the lees of things; all truth with malice in it; all that cracks the sinews and cakes the brain; all the subtle demonisms of life and thought; all evil. . . ." Ahab is a New Englander of profoundest symbol-making imagination—a fictional descendant of Jonathan Edwards: "O Nature, and O soul of man!" he reflects in Chapter 70: "how far beyond all utterance are your linked analogies!" A naturally somber individual, Ahab has been led by an earlier savage encounter with Moby-Dick (the episode in which he lost his leg) to focus upon the whale "all the general rage and hate felt by his whole race from Adam down."

For the *Pequod*'s captain as for certain others, it is the whale's intelligence that is peculiarly unnerving: "that unexampled, intelligent malignity," the "infernal aforethought of ferocity." Yet to the unimaginative Starbuck, the whale is no more than a "dumb beast." What he is for Ishmael—who, unlike Ahab, is a New Yorker by origin—is shown in the chapter on the whale's whiteness.

That chapter begins with a rhetorical triumph: a long list of the kindly, beautiful, and beneficent associations of the color white—concluding with the abrupt and total psychological turn of the main clause: "There yet lurks an elusive something in the innermost idea of this hue, which strikes more of panic to the soul than that redness which affrights the blood." But Melville in these lines is accomplishing much more than a splendid rhetorical stunt. He is effecting an astonishing psychological and even cultural reversal. In 1851, as earlier and later, it was of course blackness rather than whiteness that struck panic to so many souls—that is, the souls of so many white men. But here, adducing the terror aroused by the color white, Ishmael can even insist that his reaction is not unique and that men everywhere, and animals too, have often responded to whiteness as though it stood for the "demonism of the world."[5] Among American writers, only Poe, in the spectral white apparition at the close of *The Narrative of Arthur Gordon Pym*, anticipated Melville in this venturesome perception, and not many since have followed up on it. But Melville's mind habitually moved between extreme polarities and was impelled by a sense of their proximity and interaction—of the way one might arise out of the other, as storm out of calm and light out of darkness. The concept of blackness would, for Melville, carry within it the concept of whiteness; and the appeal of whiteness would be almost a source of its terror.

In the same way, Melville's dialectical thrust advances at the end of this chapter to the point where the blackness of darkness has been replaced—as a sort of ultimate horror—by the blankness of whiteness. To Ishmael, whiteness means heartlessness, and worse, an emptiness in the universe. It suggests something in one perspective more terrible than evil: sheer nothingness, a total void of meaning; a "palsied universe" which "lies before us like a leper."

The second and longest of the three main stages of *Moby-Dick* runs from Chapter 43 to about Chapter 106 (it can be stressed again that, except for the literal beginning and con-

clusion of the novel, the boundaries of its several stages are indistinct). Here Melville surveys almost every aspect of life aboard a whaling vessel. Whales are sighted, pursued, and captured; and while one of them is being dismembered, Melville takes the occasion to inspect its physical characteristics, finding in each of them the grounds for intellectual meditation (the whale's eyes, for instance, are so far apart that they pick up two images, rather than a single one, as men do—they thus may have, Ishmael speculates, a double or dialectical vision). Other ships are encountered, and in some cases messages are exchanged. There are soliloquies, dialogues, choral passages; there are minor adventures and misadventures. We become familiar with every corner of the *Pequod* and with the odd vocabulary of mariners and their sailing lore. In this section, the world—the sea world—of *Moby-Dick* comes fully into being.

There are untold narrative and rhetorical splendors in this part of the novel, but the whole of it, one feels, is in fact clearing the way for the final stage. It is as though all the other aspects of whales and whale-hunting, of seamanship and voyaging, had to be experienced and described before the story could concentrate again on its main action—the pursuit of Moby-Dick. Beginning with the carving of a new ivory leg for Ahab by the ship's carpenter, and then the forging of the great harpoon by the blacksmith (Chapters 107 through 113), the momentum picks up; and from then on, everything contributes to the reality and the meaning of the final battle—the three-day "chase" of the white whale. Baptizing the harpoon in the blood of the three pagan harpooners, Ahab shouts: "Ego non baptizo te in nomine patris sed in nomine diaboli!" ("not in the name of the father but in the name of the devil")—thus investing the climactic encounter with the quality of an assault upon the ultimate demonic element in life.

It is indeed in the last stage of *Moby-Dick* that the array of meanings the story has been throwing off at every turn come together and form a coherent pattern. As an example of this, we can take the richly suggestive and extremely

---

[5] As a literary source, Melville may have had in mind the Elizabethan and Jacobean image of "the white devil" (as in John Webster's play of that name)—the wicked person who hides his malignity behind a fair and gracious mask. Something of this dissembling quality is observed in Moby-Dick.

histrionic address to the fire in Chapter 119 ("The Candles").

Passing through the Japanese seas, the *Pequod* has run into a typhoon; and flashes of lightning, striking the yardarms and the lightning-rod-ends atop the three masts, have kindled a series of gleaming fires: vivid balls of electrical energy known as "corposants" ("holy bodies"). Ahab, standing erect and glaring upward, one foot resting on the crouching figure of a mysterious person called Fedallah,[6] begins to speak in a kind of fierce exultation: "O! thou clear spirit of fire. . . ." In his sonorous speech, Melville can be heard simultaneously manipulating several different motifs.

Critics who have disagreed in their interpretations of the whale as symbol have also found a disconcerting assortment of *overall* meanings in the novel as a whole. They have quite correctly made out various "levels of meaning"; but what is sometimes forgotten is that such levels should relate to one another; they should be higher and lower embodiments of the same theme or principle. Otherwise, they are not *levels* at all, but a hodgepodge of unconnected or conflicting significations. What is at issue is the integrity of the writer's imagination, his capacity to order and unify the multiple issues he is engaged with. Put to the test, Melville's imaginative integrity—in this passage at least—was nearly absolute. And what links the several dimensions of meaning one can make out in Ahab's address is the principle of authority: both the expression of authority and, much more, the defiance of it. It is in the latter guise that the pursuit of the white whale appears at this moment.

We begin with the indispensable actuality, the literal level which alone can give rise to higher meanings. There is an actual ship and an actual storm; actual bursts of electrical energy;

and an actual old whaling captain. Ahab's posture, his foot on the kneeling Parsee, is the mute announcement of *his* authority, his total command aboard the *Pequod*. But as he makes his dark allusions to father and mother ("Thou art but my fiery father; my sweet mother, I know not"), and to love and reverence and hate ("To neither love nor reverence wilt thou be kind; and e'en for hate thou canst but kill"), one begins to sense that in Ahab's declamations to the impersonal fire there is a strong personal component—on Ahab's part, but even more on Melville's. One this second level, one ventures, Melville—perhaps only half-consciously—is projecting his feelings about his own parents. He is remembering how, years before, he had longed to love and revere them, and how he had felt betrayed by his father (in the latter's madness and death) and had never truly come to know his mother. Newton Arvin, in his exemplary analysis of *Moby-Dick*, calls this the "oneiric" level, drawing on the Greek word for "dream," and he suggests that Melville, speaking through Ahab, goes beyond defiance of an actual father to a rejection of the parental principle itself.

Above the literal and psychological levels, we discern another mode of defiance—an affirmation of proud and unyielding individual sovereignty. "In the midst of the personified impersonal," Ahab calls out, "a personality stands here . . . and though thou launchest navies of full-freighted worlds, there's that in here that still remains indifferent." This might be called the American theme: the assertion of the democratic American belief in the sovereignty of the single person, the irreducible self; and of unending resistance to any form of nonhuman repression or coercion, whether it be by a faceless society or a dehumanized political power.

The language reflects a self-confidence verging on fatal pride, what was known in Greek tragedy as "hubris."[7] But as it does so, it also draws the scene onto another and highest level. Here it

---

[6] Fedallah is a "Parsee," that is, a Persian follower of Zoroaster, and an adherent of the Gnostic faith—the belief that the world is controlled by two eternal, and eternally warring, principles of good and evil, or light and darkness. Ahab speaks of him as "my bad angel," and he seems to be the human embodiment of Ahab's darker side.

[7] Ahab, at this stage, clearly represents the furthest extreme of that "imperial self," the affirmat⁚ ⁙f which had characterized Melville's generation, or ⁙ me parts of it.

enacts the ultimate relation between man and the universe. This is the level often called "mythic," where action and speech represent some final account of all-encompassing reality and man's participation in it. Ahab acknowledges that reality as something wholly inimical and destructive: "I own thy speechless, placeless power. . . . Thou canst blind. . . . Thou canst consume." But against that awful power, he flings taunts and jeers and even implies that there may be yet a power *behind* the power of total malignity: "There is some unsuffusing thing beyond thee, thou clear spirit, to whom all thy eternity is but time, all thy creativeness mechanical."

For all the well-nigh overwhelming intensity of Ahab's language, with its Shakespearean thrust and inventiveness, it is not to be supposed that Ahab's is at last the controlling voice in *Moby-Dick*. There is *no* controlling voice in the novel—unless it be that of Ishmael. As the action moves to its climax, Ahab assumes an ever greater stature and evinces ever greater courage and determination: but it is a stature beyond the limits of mortal men, it has smashed the boundaries of logic and reason, and it is catastrophic in effect. When the chase is over, Ahab has gone to his death helplessly tied to the back of the white whale; the *Pequod* has been splintered and sunk, and every member of its crew is drowned—except Ishmael. He is picked up after two days by a passing ship, in an act of fellow feeling and kindness of the sort Ahab had so violently rejected.

Ishmael, one imagines, returns to land at once chastened and restored, and now willing, after his supreme adventure, to live within the limits of human possibility. But he will never deny the nobility of Ahab's character or his mission, however both may be streaked with madness. He knows that, as the ship's owner says early in the book, if Ahab is "ungodly," he is also "godlike." Even while safe on shore, he realizes—and here surely Melville himself is speaking—that Ahab was committed, in his fatally crazy way, to the highest principle upon which man can act, can make the choices which determine his life: "As in landlessness alone resides the highest truth, shoreless, indefinite as God—so, better it is to perish in that howling infinite, than be ingloriously dashed upon the lee, even if that were safety!"

"I have written a wicked book," Melville told Hawthorne after completing *Moby-Dick*, "and I feel as spotless as the lamb." The implication was that having brought to perfect ending (as a part of him must have known) the magnificent account of Ahab's pursuit of the white whale, Melville had purged himself of such demonism as he may have felt lurking in his own nature. But he had another reaction as well: of a sort of exhausted fulfillment, as of creative energies finally played out. "Until I was twenty-five, I had no development at all," he wrote his friend. "From my twenty-fifth year I date my life"—that is, from 1844, his return from voyaging, and the start of his creative career. "Three weeks have scarcely passed, at any time between then and now, that I have not unfolded within myself. But I feel that I am now come to the inmost leaf of the bulb, and that shortly the flower must fall to the mould." The flower did not fall, though it diminished somewhat. It is true that in the forty years remaining to him, Melville produced nothing of the stature of *Moby-Dick*; but that is a little like saying that Dante, had he lived longer, would probably never have written anything to equal the *Divine Comedy*. In fact, Melville began to work far too quickly on the novel *Pierre*, which appeared within a year after *Moby-Dick*—and was rejected with derision or alarm, where it was not greeted with silence. In his bitterness and bewilderment, Melville seems to have asked Hawthorne for more solace than perhaps any man could have given him. The friendship, at any rate, started to cool, though the two men met and talked and exchanged literary ideas as before; and though Melville made a point of visiting the Hawthornes in Liverpool in 1856, after Hawthorne had been appointed consul there and when Melville was on his way to the Holy Land. Melville was to feel, as he says in the little poem "Monody," that he and Hawthorne had been, somehow, "estranged in life/And neither in the wrong." In *Clarel*, he would reflect further on the vicissitudes of their relationship.

The 1850's were a peculiarly harried time for Melville, no doubt the worst period of his life. In addition to his rapidly vanishing prestige, there were severe practical problems. He was forever in debt, and with a growing family to take care of—two sons and two daughters by 1855—he might well say, as he did to Hawthorne, that "dollars damn me." At one time, he tried unsuccessfully with the help of Hawthorne, Dana, and others to get a consulship. At another, he tried his hand at lecturing; but he was an indifferent speaker and could not conceal his contempt for the whole enterprise. He was frequently in ill health, and at one period both his mother and his wife, and probably Melville himself, suspected that he was on the verge of insanity. His mother attributed her son's seeming mental instability to "constant indoor confinement—constant working of the brain and excitement of the imagination" (a woman friend recalled telling him in 1851 that the recluse life he was leading made his friends think him slightly insane—he replied that long ago he came to the same conclusion himself). Dr. Holmes was called in to examine him, with no positive results.[8] Then, in 1856, barely staving off a breakdown, Melville scraped together enough money to embark on a long and to some degree curative trip to England, Italy, and Palestine.

Yet during these bedeviled and desperately disappointing years, Melville never ceased writing: partly for the few dollars a new work might (with luck) bring in; partly because his bruised imagination could not long lie dormant; partly in order to explain himself *to* himself, in a sort of secret self-communion, and to explore further the treacherous world that had injured him. *Israel Potter*, a still insufficiently known novel that has its own rich Melvillian rewards, appeared in 1855; and the following year Melville completed *The Confidence Man*, a work of

dizzying virtuosity and the most far-reaching apocalyptic satire about which opinions continue to differ but which may well, eventually, stand closest to *Moby-Dick* in the Melville canon. And between 1853 and 1856, Melville produced eighteen shorter fictional pieces (as well as a certain amount of nonfictional prose), half a dozen of which were collected in *The Piazza Tales* of 1856. Thereafter, until *Billy Budd* near the end of his life, Melville's creative energy would be devoted entirely to poetry.

Melville returned from his trip to Palestine—on which he would draw heavily in the long philosophical poem *Clarel* twenty years later—in relatively good health and good humor. His fortunes, however, had undergone no change for the better. We will consider later the effect upon him of the outbreak of the Civil War in 1861. Here we need only remark that in 1863, Melville, with his family, moved back to New York City, to a house on East Twenty-sixth Street; and in 1866, he at last received a government appointment of sorts, as district inspector of customs in New York. Each morning, he walked across to one of the North River piers, to examine (at four dollars a day) freight and passengers' luggage from incoming vessels—a *métier* absolutely unconnected with his inner life or with the poems he labored over at his desk in the evenings.

But the "Arch-Principals," having escorted Melville through a disaster-ridden and adventurous youth to a heady initial success and on to successive failures as a novelist and a poet, were not done with him yet. In 1867, less than a year after Melville was taken on as Inspector Number 75, his son Malcolm was found one morning behind a locked door in the Melville home, a presumptive suicide, a bullet in his head and a pistol in his hand. Malcolm had been a wayward, mutinous young man, and the tension between father and son had at times been extreme. Melville's obscurely guilty parental feeling could hardly have been palliated by the conclusion of the coroner's jury that Malcolm's self-shooting was not *clearly* "by premeditation or consciously done." Then, almost twenty years later, Melville, now sixty-seven, was brought

---

[8] All this is recounted, in an old-gaffer tone that just conceals the sense of desperation, in "I and My Chimney."

the news that his second son Stanwix had died at the age of thirty-five in San Francisco—the last destination of that unhappy, physically and psychologically, unstable wanderer, that (to Melville) bitterly disappointing lost son.

The same year, by some sort of ironic recompense, Lizzie Melville came into a modest inheritance. Melville was able to retire, and he began work almost at once upon what turned out to be *Billy Budd*. It is anything but surprising that this, Melville's last piece of writing and his first work of fiction in three decades, should be invested not only with a sense of the past, slowly and thoughtfully reflected on with an eye to its legendary quality as well as to the violence so often done to the truth about it; but also with a complex and deeply personal consciousness of the relations between fathers and sons.

Melville was not a master of the shorter fictional forms in the sense that Hawthorne and Henry James and Hemingway were masters. The shorter pieces of Melville—most of them written in the 1850's—resemble rather those of Dostoevski. They have the air of being sheer and almost random chunks of experience. But they are unforgettably solid chunks; and under inspection they reveal Melville's major themes at work in fresh formulations and new complexities. We can here refer to only a few of them, and only most briefly.

"Bartleby the Scrivener" is the most craftsmanlike among them, and it may also be the most autobiographical. The story of the fading scrivener—who, against every demand and request of his bemused employer, prefers "not to"—is, in part, one suspects, Melville's way of responding to literary failure, in the wake of the harsh reception accorded to *Moby-Dick* and *Pierre*. In Bartleby's obdurate "I would prefer not to," we hear the much stronger voice of Melville insisting again that "write the *other* way, I cannot," and by implication "I *will* not." But there may well be more buried elements of autobiography in "Bartleby." In a brilliant tour de force called "I and Bartleby," Henry A. Murray has listed a number of similarities be-

tween Bartleby and the Melville of 1853: both were scriveners, or writers; both worked through the day and strained their eyes; both were silent and stubborn-minded; both were at times of a suicidal inclination; and both struck onlookers as verging on insanity. Murray concludes by suggesting that at the heart of the story is Melville's deeply restive feeling about his marriage to Lizzie Shaw—that the literal and the metaphorical wall that hems in Bartleby (the wall for Melville, as Murray points out, being a regular symbol of some unsurpassable barrier) stands for the marriage and the family responsibilities by which Melville felt cramped and confined.

It is a main virtue of Murray's discussion that it is not limited to biography and psychoanalysis. Those latter are carefully balanced by considerations of literary history and formal criticism. For any but the best-informed reader, indeed, the strength and appeal of "Bartleby" lie in the story as such. The story is a fable of sorts—that is, an extended but self-enclosed anecdote that obviously surges with meaning, but a meaning about which none can be unquestionably sure. We may take it perhaps as a very low-keyed reenactment of some of the themes Melville was most concerned with, and which received their grandest treatment in *Moby-Dick*. Bartleby, spiritually shattered by some unknown previous experience, is as it were a forlorn and desolate Ahab; and if he cannot say, like Ahab smiting his breast, "There's that in here that still remains indifferent," he can at least say in an almost inaudible voice, and to whatever request or hint of pressure, "I would prefer not to."

The lawyer in turn is asked to respond with a patience, an understanding, and a Christian charity simply beyond the possibilities of any ordinary human being. Like most of Melville's fiction, "Bartleby" provides us with certain irresolvable contradictions, as forming the essence of the universal human predicament. Someone once said (see below) that in one perspective *Billy Budd* is about "the injustice of justice" and "Bartleby" might be seen as dramatizing the unfeasibility of the Christian ethic as radically interpreted. It is the lawyer's duty, no doubt, to protect and shelter his neighbor Bartleby; but kindly as he is, he lacks the patience of an actual saint and allows Bartleby to be carried off and imprisoned, there to decline silently into death. One suspects, however, that the lawyer—though he dimly recognizes that the moral burden demanded of him was greater than anyone could be expected to shoulder—advances into old age incurably troubled in spirit.

"The Encantadas" is a small masterpiece in the Melvillian genre of the inverted pastoral: the bleak and blasted landscape, explored with such typically scientific precision in its sketches, is the symbol, Melville suggests, of some dreadful calamity that has afflicted the human condition—"in no world but a fallen one," he tells us, "could such lands exist." And from the very heart of this waste land there arises the heroic figure of Hunilla, the Chola widow, solitary, abandoned, living on without hope, yet with a supreme capacity—like the tortoises observed upon the islands—for endurance. For one recurring theme in the stories of the fifties is that to live is to suffer, but to suffer is to endure.

"The Tartarus of Maids" is more purely allegorical—the process of making paper (Melville is recalling his actual visits to a paper mill in nearby Dalton, Massachusetts) as the production of a human child. The story is not entirely successful, and in some ways it is repellent, partly because of Melville's evident revulsion from certain aspects of the sexual act and of the human body. But it has great fascination, especially when the symbolism moves beyond the sexual and the biological to suggest Melville's Romantic hostility to technology and machinery as most dangerous enemies of the human spirit —a hostility to what Blake called "the dark Satanic mills," here seen as "machinery . . . menially served by human beings." And beyond that the paper-making machines appear as the engines of fate: "What made the thing I saw so specially terrible to me," remarks the narrator, "was the metallic necessity, the unbudging fatality which governed it."

In "Benito Cereno," the drama of opposition (or dramatized polarities) that we discover in almost everything Melville ever wrote is peculiarly powerful, and for many readers peculiarly baffling. The central polarity is between appearance and reality—concretely, between the apparent situation on board the half-derelict Spanish ship, the *San Dominick*, the apparent relation between black man and white man, between slave and master, obedience and command; and the reality of all that. But there is also a profound contradiction between the two portions of narrative: the first, as seen through the myopic, innocent, and, for Melville, typically American eyes of Captain Delano, who boards the ship, explores it, talks with its Captain and his Negro "servant" Babo, and departs without ever gaining more than a fleeting impression of the truth; and the second, the dryly legalistic recorded testimony at the trial of Babo and his black fellow mutineers.

Melville's point in juxtaposing these two so different narrative modes and voices seems to be this: that neither version of the events contains the truth. No reader doubts that Delano's version is false, that he got everything wrong way round; but we should recognize that the legal version is equally remote from the full reality of the adventure. We are presumably intended to accept Don Benito's statement of the external facts, the process of revolt and of massacre, the names and numbers of those that killed and were killed. But for Melville, facts were not truth, and wrongly handled could be an obstacle to truth. The Spaniard was quite unequipped to understand the raging desire of the Negroes for freedom, the murderous animosity that slavery begot in them; even as Captain Delano was too kindhearted to grasp the force of a lust for liberty intensified into evil. Neither narrative expresses anything like the truth of the affair; and yet this is a curious instance of two falsehoods making a truth between them: a truth contained in the continuing tension between contradictory versions.

It is only with regard to the insistently dialectical nature of Melville's mind and imagination, so handsomely displayed in "Benito Cereno," that we can ourselves understand his attitude to the black race. Melville, personally, was as little racist as any white American in his generation, though he took little active part in the abolitionist movement (or any other political or reformist movement). *Moby-Dick* is alone sufficient testimony on this score: with the figures of Pip, the black cabin boy, and of Queequeg, after rescuing an insolent white man, puffing on his pipe, and seeming to say "It's a mutual, joint-stock world in all meridians. We cannibals must help these Christians"; not to mention the extraordinary discourse on the terror not of blackness, but of whiteness. But if Melville's personal experience of all races and conditions of men around the world had obliterated the slightest hint of any racism he might have inherited, and turned him into a wholehearted egalitarian, he was nonetheless perfectly aware of the appalling fact of Negro slavery, and of its consequences. Apart from "Benito Cereno," there is also, as an example, "The Bell-Tower," a little Gothic melodrama about a machine which mysteriously turns on its inventor and destroys him—Melville, by the motto he supplied at the head of the story, pointed explicitly to the analogy intended: "Like Negroes, these powers own man sullenly; mindful of their higher master; while serving, plot revenge."

But for Melville, black men—like white men, like any men—were, as human beings, not notably less prone than other human beings to the vices, and even the evils, of humanity. The injustice of slavery had not made black men immune to the nature of man. A writer eager for popularity with liberal readers might have tried to make them seem so; but Melville had long since abandoned any dream of popularity—and in any case, not even a black slave could be exempted from Melville's sense of the polarities between which truth all so precariously resides.[9]

The final entry in the manuscript of *Billy Budd* is a date: April 15, 1891 (a few months before Melville's death). But Melville had not in fact completed work on the story (see our headnote), and the version we are offering, probably definitive, is the result of a brilliant act of creative scholarship by Harrison Hayford and Merton M. Sealts, Jr. Some of the changes from earlier versions are suggestive. The standard text hitherto, for example, began with a short chapter on the revolutionary atmosphere in Europe at the time of action, 1797, following the French Revolution, the mutinies at Spithead and the Nore, and the first exploits of Napoleon—later described as a "portentous upstart from the revolutionary chaos who seemed in act of fulfilling judgment prefigured in the Apocalypse." The new version begins with allusions to the figure known generally as "the handsome sailor," and goes on at once to introduce an example thereof, Billy Budd himself. Melville had chosen, it seems, to filter the tense and mutiny-ridden atmosphere throughout his narrative. But that atmosphere is as palpable as can be, and it is what both determines the fate of young Billy and gives it its enlarged significance. Similarly, by subtly associating his peaceable common sailor with the spectacular Horatio Nelson, "the greatest sailor since the world began," Melville accomplishes again that democratic enlargement of stature that we noticed in *Moby Dick*, where he ascribed "tragic graces" to "meanest mariners" and invested a shaggy old whaling captain with the dignity of a Shakespearean king. Passionate drama, Melville here remarks, does not need a "palatial stage," but can be observed "down among the groundlings," where "the circumstances that provoke it, however trivial or mean, are no measure of its power."

The power of *Billy Budd* can be measured in part by the vital complexity of the three central characters and of their interrelation. Billy, Claggart, and Captain Vere may, at first sight, appear extremely oversimplified inventions, bare

[9] For a different reading of "Benito Cereno" and a different appraisal of Melville's view of the race question in the 1850's, see Sidney Kaplan's careful and reluctant indictment in "Herman Melville and the American Na-

tional Sin" (*Journal of Negro History*, Nos. 41–42, 1957).

instances of certain basic human possibilities: pure innocence, pure evil, pure rationality. But Melville's sense of human ambiguity was never more evident, and each of the three is a study in contradiction. Billy is indeed an innocent: "an upright barbarian," who might have posed in the nude "for a statue of a young Adam before the Fall"—that is, before man's acquisition of knowledge and of the distinction between good and evil. But for all his comeliness and goodness, and his unconscious moral authority, Billy has a serious defect: a tendency to sudden and overpowering fury, a burst of rage which robs him of speech and leaves him stuttering hopelessly. At such times, Billy becomes violent, almost homicidal: on the *Rights-of-Man* he gave a fearful drubbing to a bullying sailor who had dug him in the ribs; on the *Bellipotent*, when approached to take part in a pretended mutiny, he almost throws the "mysterious emissary" overboard. As for Claggart, he is identified by Melville as a representative of that rare phenomenon, "Natural Depravity: a depravity according to nature." He has in him "the mania of an evil nature," and his nature is consumed by envy, rage, and despair at Billy's simple and inexperienced goodness. "Yet in an aesthetic way he saw the charm" of Billy's radiant innocence, "the courageous free-and-easy temper of it, and fain would have shared it, but he despaired of it." There are even times when Claggart's expression, as he gazes after the handsome sailor, is "meditative and melancholy," and his eyes are "strangely suffused with incipient feverish tears." "Then would Claggart look like the man of sorrows. Yes, and sometimes the melancholy expression would have in it a touch of soft yearning, as if Claggart would have loved Billy but for fate and ban." One recalls Ahab's yearning for intimacy with Starbuck; and, indeed, there is in Claggart something of Ahab's special complexity (as there is of the grief-stricken evil-souled Jackson in *Redburn*). All my means are sane, Ahab tells himself; only my purpose is mad; and about the naturally depraved, Melville declares in *Billy Budd*, that though they may pursue "an aim which in wantonness of atrocity would seem to partake

of the insane," yet "the method and the outward proceeding are always perfectly rational." Claggart's determination to destroy Billy is, moreover, regarded by the master-at-arms as a mission of revenge—upon a goodness he alone on the *Bellipotent* is capable of apprehending, and he alone perhaps is entirely powerless to share.[10]

Captain Edward Fairfax ("Starry") Vere is without question a rational, humorless, bookish man; a perfect product of the Enlightenment; an aristocratic leader, born and bred to command; judicious, impersonal, imperturbable. But at the moment of crisis—after Billy has struck Claggart dead with a single blow on the forehead—this austerely self-controlled man, overcome as it seems by the unredeemable enormity of the event, almost literally goes out of his mind. His excited ejaculations to the hastily summoned surgeon suggest to the latter's professional eye that Vere has been "suddenly affected in his mind"; and Vere's immediate convoking of a drumhead court only strengthens the suspicion.

Never were three fictional characters more imaginatively conceived as fated to participate in one another's doom. Yet, by a kind of final paradox, no one of the three fully understands the nature of the doom that has overtaken him. That understanding is reserved for the alert reader. In no other work (except possibly *The Confidence Man*) does Melville place such a charge upon the reader—for it is, really, in the reader's mind alone that the action truly unfolds, as a coherent pattern of incidents acted out by a set of clearly defined individuals. It is with the intention of engaging the reader as an active participant in his story that Melville constantly and slyly introduces new and hitherto unknown characteristics of Billy, Claggart, and Captain Vere—each new feature upsetting the view we had taken of the characters. The process continues until, in our confusion, we become conscious that something far more intricate is

---

[10] It is tempting to pursue the analogy further, and to suggest that to Claggart the pink-cheeked sailor represents a maddening mystery not unlike that which the white whale represented to Ahab.

occurring than we had supposed, or that any one of the persons involved is capable of grasping.

Certain facts can always be brought to bear upon *Billy Budd* and its meaning. There was the Melville family story about the American training brig *Somers*, the mutiny which allegedly broke out aboard her in December, 1842, and the hearing (it was really not a trial) presided over by Melville's cousin Guert Gansevoort, which hastily condemned three men, including midshipman Philip Spencer, to be hanged at daybreak. (Melville had alluded to the *Somers* in *White-Jacket*, and Gansevoort appears in *John Marr and Other Sailors*.) Interest in the case had been revived, while Melville was writing *Billy Budd*, by two articles in 1888 and 1889, and there are several striking parallels between the historical episode and the fiction. Spencer, the ne'er-do-well son of the then Secretary of War, was afflicted by a severe squint (analogous to Billy's stutter), which gave him, Gansevoort said later, "the most infernal expression I ever beheld on a human face," an expression which satisfied Gansevoort of the eighteen-year-old boy's guilt. Mackenzie, captain of the brig, was, like Vere, suspected of mental imbalance at the time of the hearing; and his entire conduct of the affair lacked legality or precedent.

But *Billy Budd* is hardly to be interpreted by appeals to history (the two articles just cited appeared after the story had pretty much assumed its final shape) or to customary naval procedures. The story's grip upon Melville's imagination and ours comes from deeper sources. On the personal level, one ventures, the story reflects the force of Melville's freshly aroused feelings about his unfortunate sons, and his paternal relation to them. Much is made, in the opening pages of *Billy Budd*, of Billy's aristocratic features, and the strong indication that his was "a lineage in direct contradiction to his lot"; "nobility of descent was as evident in him as in a blood horse." Some critics have even suggested that Captain Vere, who had taken a fatherly attitude to the handsome sailor all along, is in fact the boy's father, and that in the scene in which Vere tells Billy

about the trial verdict—a scene Melville apparently could not bring himself to write—he reveals as much to him.[11] If so, we can make out in the unfolding drama Melville's recognition of his own deeply ambiguous relation with his two unfortunate sons—his recognition, moreover, that he *as a father* and Malcolm and Stanwix *as sons* were equally doomed; and that, in that very recognition, there was the basis for a final and permanent reconciliation. Melville's filial defiance, so resonantly declared by Ahab in *Moby-Dick*, was thus converted at the end into a paternal embrace, the more poignant for its deep consciousness of unavertible disaster.

On a more public level, so to speak, *Billy Budd* has to do with what the poet Delmore Schwartz once described as "the injustice of justice." Caught in a grinding dilemma between the requirements of military duty and the stirrings of moral scruple and human compassion (not to mention the powerful buried feelings of an Abraham for an Isaac), and between the dictates of the naval code and the urgings of private conscience, Vere guides the troubled court toward the sentence of death. Under the circumstances, the sentence was coldly just: Billy had in literal fact performed a murderous act of mutiny, and to acquit him would have been to encourage further uprisings in the fleet (in the shadow of the *Nore* mutiny) at just the time when an invasion from France was threatening. The sentence was also profoundly, unspeakably unjust: Claggart's accusation was an evil lie, and Billy struck out only in mute expression of his outrage, with no intention whatever of serious harm.

There are other levels and perspectives. About *Billy Budd*, one might say what Mark Van Doren said about *The Tempest*: "Bring any set of symbols close to this play, and they light up, as in an electric field." We need only mention the religious and mythological strain the story constantly suggests. More than one critic has

---

[11] The biological fact of Billy's paternity is of course much less important than the thematic fact. That Vere is *like*—and feels like—a father to Billy is all we need to reckon with.

ventured the guess that in *Billy Budd* Melville was drawing upon the Celtic mythology he had been reading about in Matthew Arnold's study *Celtic Literature*, and within which the "Celtic Apollo," as Arnold's source called him, was known as *Beli* and *Budd*—a sun god sacrificed as an insurance of victory during time of war.[12] Melville, here as always, discerns and discloses in "trivial or mean" circumstances the outline of most far-reaching drama.

There is another presence, finally, which gives *Billy Budd* its ultimate significance, and this is the presence of Herman Melville himself—Melville, speaking in his own voice through the pages, brooding over the events and personal-ities, and the mysterious contradictions they represent; brooding aloud over history and fiction and legend; reflecting about "this matter of writing" and "the symmetry of form attainable in pure fiction"; ruminating without intellectual rancor on the vitiation of moral and religious ideas ("the doctrine of man's fall . . . is a doctrine now popularly ignored," and "dark sayings" about "the mysteries of iniquity" only alienate the modern reader). It is Melville who provides us with "the inside narrative" of Billy Budd, Claggart, and Captain Vere, and who then quotes in an almost expressionless manner the atrociously erroneous "outside" newspaper report of the episode, with its allusions to "the extreme depravity of the criminal" and the "respectable and discreet" character of the victim. It is Melville, too, who watches, in conclusion, as the events drift into legend and become imbedded in song and story.[13] To the day of his death, Melville remained fascinated above all by the greatest of human problems—the problem of finding and of devising language to convey the truth about things.

[12] See H. Bruce Franklin, *The Wake of the Gods*; Richard Chase, editor, *Melville*; and Harold Beaver, editor, *Herman Melville: Billy Budd, Sailor and Other Stories* (1967, p. 457). Arnold's source was Sir Edward Davies, *The Mythology and Rites of the British Druids*. The figure and role of the old Danish sailor, referred to by Melville as "an old Merlin," add to the Druidic atmosphere.

One dimension of *Billy Budd* which we are not inclined to emphasize is the sexual. Claggart's attraction to Billy is without doubt homosexual in part; and Melville's language occasionally lends itself to sexual interpretation. But all this is surely far less compelling than the moral and metaphysical aspect.

[13] The poem "Billy in the Darbies" (in irons) is an integral part of *Billy Budd*. Comment upon it will be found in the section following.

BIOGRAPHICAL CHART

1819   Born, August 1, in New York City, son of Allan Melville, a prosperous importer of good family, and Maria Gansevoort

1830   Moves to Albany after failure of father's business

1832   Father dies, mad; period in Albany Classical School, and as schoolteacher

1838   Moves to Lansingburg, N.Y.; studies surveying

1839   First writing published in *Democratic Press and Lansingburg Advertiser*, "Fragments from a Writing Desk"; first voyage, in crew of *St. Lawrence*, New York to Liverpool

1841   Ships as seaman on whaler *Acushnet*, New Bedford for South Seas

1842   Deserts July 9, in Marquesas Islands, with Richard Greene; period in the Typee Valley, with cannibals; escape on another whaler

1843   Enlists in American navy, at Honolulu (mustered out following year)

1846   *Typee*

1847   *Omoo*; marries Elizabeth Shaw, daughter of Chief Justice Lemuel Shaw, of Boston, August 4; home in New York City

1849   *Mardi* and *Redburn*

1850   *White-Jacket*; buys Arrowhead, farm near Pittsfield, Massachusetts; intimacy with Hawthorne

1851   *Moby-Dick*, relative failure

1852   *Pierre, or, The Ambiguities*, failure

1855   *Israel Potter*

1856   *The Piazza Tales*; trip to Holy Land, with visit to Hawthorne at Liverpool

1857   *The Confidence Man*; returns from abroad; first of three seasons as lecturer

1860   Voyages for health to San Francisco on clipper *Meteor*, commanded by his brother Thomas

1863   Moves to New York City

1866   *Battle-Pieces and Aspects of the War*, another failure; becomes customs inspector

1867 Malcolm dies, possibly a suicide
1876 *Clarel*
1885 Resigns post at customs house; probably begins *Billy Budd*
1886 Stanwix dies in San Francisco
1888 *John Marr and Other Sailors* published privately,

in edition of twenty-five copies
1891 *Timoleon* printed privately, in edition of twenty-five copies; *Billy Budd* left but not in a final version; dies, September 28
1924 *Billy Budd* published

FURTHER READINGS

The Works of Herman Melville (1922–24; 16 vols.) (no editor cited)

Harold Beaver, ed., *Herman Melville: Billy Budd, Sailor and Other Stories* (1967)

Charles Feidelson, ed., *Moby-Dick or the Whale* (1964)

Harrison Hayford et al., eds., *The Writings of Herman Melville* (15 vols.; CEAA edition); this work, six volumes of which have already been published, will become the standard edition

Harrison Hayford and Hershel Parker, eds., *Moby-Dick: An Authoritative Text* (1967)

Harrison Hayford and Merton M. Sealts, Jr., eds., *Billy Budd, Sailor* (1963)

R. W. B. Lewis, ed., *The Confidence Man* (1964)

Jay Leyda, ed., *The Complete Stories of Herman Melville* (1949)

Henry A. Murray, ed., *Pierre, or, The Ambiguities* (1949)

Robert Penn Warren, ed., *Selected Poems of Herman Melville* (1970)

Newton Arvin, *Herman Melville* (1950)

W. H. Auden, "Herman Melville," in *Another Time* (1940)

Warner Berthoff, *The Example of Melville* (1962)

Paul Brodtkorb, Jr., *Ishmael's White World: A Phenomenological Reading of Moby-Dick* (1965)

Richard Chase, *The American Novel and Its Tradition* (1957)

——, ed., *Melville: A Collection of Critical Essays* (1962)

Merrill R. Davis, *Melville's Mardi: A Chartless Voyage* (1952)

Charles Feidelson, *Symbolism in American Literature* (1953)

H. Bruce Franklin, *The Wake of the Gods* (1963)

Robert L. Gale, *Plots and Characters in the Fiction and Narrative Poetry of Herman Melville* (1969)

William H. Gilman, *Melville's Early Life and Redburn* (1951)

Leon Howard, *Herman Melville* (1951)

Jay Leyda, *The Melville Log* (1951)

Perry Miller, *The Raven and the Whale* (1956)

Lewis Mumford, *Herman Melville* (1929)

Charles Olson, *Call Me Ishmael* (1947)

William E. Sedgwick *Herman Melville: The Tragedy of Mind* (1955)

Lawrance Thompson, *Melville's Quarrel with God* (1952)

Howard P. Vincent, *The Trying-Out of Moby Dick* (1949)

Raymond Weaver, *Herman Melville: Mariner and Mystic* (1921)

Yvor Winters, *In Defense of Reason* (1947)

Hawthorne and His Mosses (1850)

Melville's review of Hawthorne's *Mosses from an Old Manse* appeared in the *Literary World*. It was a key moment both in Melville's imaginative development and in his relationship with Hawthorne. Some comments on the essay will be found in the early pages of the introduction to Melville.

A papered chamber in a fine old farmhouse, a mile from any other dwelling, and dipped to the eaves in foliage—surrounded by mountains, old woods, and Indian pools,—this surely, is the place to write of Hawthorne. Some charm is in this northern air, for love and duty seem both impelling to the task. A man of a deep and noble nature has seized me in this seclusion. His wild, witch-voice rings through me; or, in softer cadences, I seem to hear it in the songs of the hillside birds that sing in the larch trees at my window.

Would that all excellent books were foundlings, without father or mother, that so it might be we could glorify them, without including their ostensible authors! Nor would any true man take exception to this; least of all, he who writes, "When the artist rises high enough to achieve the beautiful, the symbol by which he makes it perceptible to mortal senses becomes of little value in his eyes, while his spirit possesses itself in the enjoyment of the reality."

But more than this. I know not what would be the right name to put on the title-page of an excellent book; but this I feel, that the names of all fine authors are fictitious ones, far more so than that of Junius; simply standing, as they do, for the mystical ever-eluding spirit of all beauty, which ubiquitously possesses men of genius. Purely imaginative as this fancy may appear, it nevertheless seems to receive some warranty from the fact, that on a personal interview no great author has ever come up to the idea of his reader. But that dust of which our bodies are composed, how can it fitly express the nobler intelligences among us? With reverence be it spoken, that not even in the case of one deemed more than man, not even in our Saviour, did his visible frame betoken anything of the augustness of the nature within. Else, how could those Jewish eyewitnesses fail to see heaven in his glance!

It is curious how a man may travel along a country road, and yet miss the grandest or sweetest of prospects by reason of an intervening hedge, so like all other hedges, as in no way to hint of the wide landscape beyond. So has it been with me concerning the enchanting landscape in the soul of this Hawthorne, this most excellent Man of Mosses. His Old Manse has been written now four years, but I never read it till a day or two since. I had seen it in the book-stores—heard of it often—even had it recommended to me by a tasteful friend, as a rare, quiet book, perhaps too deserving of popularity to be popular. But there are so many books called "excellent," and so much unpopular merit, that amid the thick stir of other things, the hint of my tasteful friend was disregarded and for four years the Mosses on the Old Manse never refreshed me with their perennial green. It may be, however, that all this while the book, likewise, was only improving in flavor and body. At any rate, it so chanced that this long procrastination eventuated in a happy result. At breakfast the other day, a mountain girl, a cousin of mine, who for the last two weeks has every morning helped me to strawberries and raspberries, which, like the roses and pearls in the fairy tale, seemed to fall into the saucer from those strawberry beds, her cheeks—this delightful creature, this charming Cherry says to me—"I see you spend your mornings in the haymow; and yesterday I found there Dwight's *Travels in New England*. Now I have something far better than that, some-

thing more congenial to our summer on these hills. Take these raspberries, and then I will give you some moss." "Moss!" said I. "Yes, and you must take it to the barn with you, and good-by to Dwight."

With that she left me, and soon returned with a volume, verdantly bound, and garnished with a curious frontispiece in green; nothing less than a fragment of real moss, cunningly pressed to a fly-leaf. "Why, this," said I, spilling my raspberries, "this is the *Mosses from an Old Manse*." "Yes," said cousin Cherry, "yes, it is that flowery Hawthorne." "Hawthorne and Mosses," said I, "no more is it morning: it is July in the country: and I am off for the barn."

Stretched on that new mown clover, the hillside breeze blowing over me through the wide barn door, and soothed by the hum of the bees in the meadows around, how magically stole over me this Mossy Man! and how amply, how bountifully, did he redeem that delicious promise to his guests in the Old Manse, of whom it is written: "Others could give them pleasure, or amusement, or instruction—these could be picked up anywhere; but it was for me to give them rest—rest, in a life of trouble! What better could be done for those weary and world-worn spirits? . . . what better could be done for anybody who came within our magic circle than to throw the spell of a tranquil spirit over him?" So all that day, half-buried in the new clover, I watched this Hawthorne's "Assyrian dawn, and Paphian sunset and moonrise from the summit of our eastern hill."

The soft ravishments of the man spun me round about in a web of dreams, and when the book was closed, when the spell was over, this wizard "dismissed me with but misty reminiscences, as if I had been dreaming of him."

What a wild moonlight of contemplative humor bathes that Old Manse!—the rich and rare distilment of a spicy and slowly-oozing heart. No rollicking rudeness, no gross fun fed on fat dinners, and bred in the lees of wine,—but a humor so spiritually gentle, so high, so deep, and yet so richly relishable, that it were hardly inappropriate in an angel. It is the very religion of mirth; for nothing so human but it may be advanced to that. The orchard of the Old Manse seems the visible type of the fine mind that has described it—those twisted and contorted old trees, "they stretch out their crooked branches, and take such hold of the imagination that we remember them as humorists and odd-fellows." And then, as surrounded by these grotesque forms, and hushed in the noonday repose of this Hawthorne's spell, how aptly might the still fall of his ruddy thoughts into your soul be symbolized by: "In the stillest afternoon, if I listened, the thump of a great apple was audible, falling without a breath of wind, from the mere necessity of perfect ripeness." For no less ripe than ruddy are the apples of the thoughts and fancies in this sweet Man of Mosses.

Buds and Bird Voices. What a delicious thing is that; "Will the world ever be so decayed, that spring may not renew its greenness?" And the *Fire Worship.* Was ever the hearth so glorified into an altar before? The mere title of that piece is better than any common work in fifty folio volumes. How exquisite is this: "Nor did it lessen the charm of his soft, familiar courtesy and helpfulness that the mighty spirit, were opportunity offered him, would run riot through the peaceful house, wrap its inmates in his terrible embrace, and leave nothing of them save their whitened bones. This possibility of mad destruction only made his domestic kindness the more beautiful and touching. It was so sweet of him, being endowed with such power, to dwell day after day, and one long lonesome night after another, on the dusky hearth, only now and then betraying his wild nature by thrusting his red tongue out of the chimney-top! True, he had done much mischief in the world, and was pretty certain to do more; but his warm heart atoned for all. He was kindly to the race of man; and they pardoned his characteristic imperfections."

But he has still other apples, not quite so ruddy, though full as ripe:—apples, that have been left to wither on the tree, after the pleasant autumn gathering is past. The sketch of *The Old Apple Dealer* is conceived in the subtlest spirit of sadness; he whose "subdued and nerveless boyhood prefigured his abortive prime, which likewise contained within itself the prophecy and image of his lean and torpid age." Such touches as are in this piece cannot proceed from any common heart. They argue such a depth of tenderness, such a boundless sympathy with all forms of being, such an omnipresent love, that we must needs say that this Hawthorne is here almost alone in his generation,—at least, in the artistic manifestation of these things. Still more. Such touches as these—and many, very many similar ones, all through his chapters—furnish clues whereby we enter a little way into the intricate, profound heart where they originated. And we see that suffering, some time or other and in some

shape or other,—this only can enable any man to depict it in others. All over him, Hawthorne's melancholy rests like an Indian-summer, which, though bathing a whole country in one softness, still reveals the distinctive hue of every towering hill and each far-winding vale.

But it is the least part of genius that attracts admiration. Where Hawthorne is known, he seems to be deemed a pleasant writer, with a pleasant style,—a sequestered, harmless man, from whom any deep and weighty thing would hardly be anticipated—a man who means no meanings. But there is no man, in whom humor and love, like mountain peaks, soar to such a rapt height as to receive the irradiations of the upper skies;—there is no man in whom humor and love are developed in that high form called genius; no such man can exist without also possessing, as the indispensable complement of these, a great, deep intellect, which drops down into the universe like a plummet. Or, love and humor are only the eyes through which such an intellect views this world. The great beauty in such a mind is but the product of its strength. What, to all readers, can be more charming than the piece entitled *Monsieur du Miroir*; and to a reader at all capable of fully fathoming it, what, at the same time, can possess more mystical depth of meaning?—yes, there he sits and looks at me,—this "shape of mystery," this "identical MONSIEUR DU MIROIR!" "Methinks I should tremble now were his wizard power of gliding through all impediments in search of me to place him suddenly before my eyes."

How profound, nay, appalling, is the moral evolved by the *Earth's Holocaust*; where—beginning with the hollow follies and affectations of the world,—all vanities and empty theories and forms are, one after another, and by an admirably graduated, growing comprehensiveness, thrown into the allegorical fire, till, at length, nothing is left but the all-engendering heart of man; which remaining still unconsumed, the great conflagration is naught.

Of a piece with this, is the *Intelligence Office*, a wondrous symbolizing of the secret workings in men's souls. There are other sketches still more charged with ponderous import.

The Christmas Banquet, and *The Bosom Serpent,* would be fine subjects for a curious and elaborate analysis, touching the conjectural parts of the mind that produced them. For spite of all the Indian-summer sunlight on the hither side of Hawthorne's soul, the other side—like the dark half of the physical sphere—is shrouded in a blackness, ten times black. But this darkness but gives more effect to the ever-moving dawn, that forever advances through it, and circumnavigates his world. Whether Hawthorne has simply availed himself of this mystical blackness as a means to the wondrous effects he makes it to produce in his lights and shades; or whether there really lurks in him, perhaps unknown to himself, a touch of Puritanic gloom,—this, I cannot altogether tell. Certain it is, however, that this great power of blackness in him derives its force from its appeals to that Calvinistic sense of Innate Depravity and Original Sin, from whose visitations, in some shape or other, no deeply thinking mind is always and wholly free. For, in certain moods, no man can weigh this world without throwing in something, somehow like Original Sin, to strike the uneven balance. At all events, perhaps no writer has ever wielded this terrific thought with greater terror than this same harmless Hawthorne. Still more: this black conceit pervades him through and through. You may be witched by his sunlight,—transported by the bright gildings in the skies he builds over you; but there is the blackness of darkness beyond; and even his bright gildings but fringe and play upon the edges of thunder-clouds. In one word, the world is mistaken in this Nathaniel Hawthorne. He himself must often have smiled at its absurd misconception of him. He is immeasurably deeper than the plummet of the mere critic. For it is not the brain that can test such a man; it is only the heart. You cannot come to know greatness by inspecting it; there is no glimpse to be caught of it, except by intuition; you need not ring it, you but touch it, and you find it is gold.

Now, it is that blackness in Hawthorne, of which I have spoken that so fixes and fascinates me. It may be, nevertheless, that it is too largely developed in him. Perhaps he does not give us a ray of light for every shade of his dark. But however this may be, this blackness it is that furnishes the infinite obscure of his background,—that background, against which Shakspeare plays his grandest conceits, the things that have made for Shakspeare his loftiest but most circumscribed renown, as the profoundest of thinkers. For by philosophers Shakspeare is not adored, as the great man of tragedy and comedy:—"Off with his head; so much for Buckingham!" This sort of rant interlined by another hand, brings down the house,—those mistaken souls, who dream of Shakspeare as a mere man of Richard the Third humps and Macbeth daggers. But it is those deep far-away things in him; those occasional flashings-forth of the initiative Truth in him; those short, quick probings at the very axis of reality;—these are the things that make Shakspeare, Shakspeare. Through the mouths of the dark characters of Hamlet, Timon, Lear, and Iago, he craftily says, or sometimes insinuates the things which we feel to be so terrifically true, that it were all but madness for any good man, in his own proper character, to utter, or even hint of them. Tormented into desperation, Lear, the frantic king, tears off the mask, and speaks the same madness of vital truth. But, as I before said, it is the least part of genius that attracts admiration. And so, much of the blind, unbridled admiration that has been heaped upon Shakspeare, has been lavished upon the least part of him. And few of his endless commentators and critics seem to have remembered, or even perceived, that the immediate products of a great mind are not so great as that undeveloped and sometimes undevelopable yet dimly-discernible greatness, to which those immediate products are but the infallible indices. In Shakspeare's tomb lies infinitely more than Shakspeare ever wrote. And if I magnify Shakspeare, it is not so much for what he did do as for what he did not do, or refrained from doing. For in this world of lies, Truth is forced to fly like a scared white doe in the woodlands; and only by cunning glimpses will she reveal herself, as in Shakspeare and other masters of the great Art of Telling the Truth,—even though it be covertly and by snatches.

But if this view of the all-popular Shakspeare be seldom taken by his readers, and if very few who extol him have ever read him deeply, or perhaps, only have seen him on the tricky stage (which alone made, and is still making him his mere mob renown)—if few men have time, or patience, or palate, for the spiritual truth as it is in that great genius—it is then no matter of surprise, that in a contemporaneous age, Nathaniel Hawthorne is a man as yet almost utterly mistaken among men. Here and there, in some quiet armchair in the noisy town, or some deep nook among the noiseless mountains, he may be appreciated for something of what he is. But unlike Shakspeare, who was forced to the contrary course by circumstances, Hawthorne (either from simple disinclination, or else from inaptitude) refrains from all the popularizing noise and show of broad farce and blood-besmeared tragedy; content with the still, rich utterance of a great intellect in repose, and which sends few thoughts into circulation, except they be arterialized at his large warm lungs, and expanded in his honest heart.

Nor need you fix upon that blackness in him, if it suit you not. Nor, indeed, will all readers discern it; for it is, mostly, insinuated to those who may best understand it, and account for it; it is not obtruded upon every one alike.

Some may start to read of Shakspeare and Hawthorne on the same page. They may say, that if an illustration were needed, a lesser light might have sufficed to elucidate this Hawthorne, this small man of yesterday. But I am not willingly one of those who, as touching Shakspeare at least, exemplify the maxim of Rochefoucauld, that "we exalt the reputation of some, in order to depress that of others";—who, to teach all noble-souled aspirants that there is no hope for them, pronounce Shakspeare absolutely unapproachable. But Shakspeare has been approached. There are minds that have gone as far as Shakspeare into the universe. And hardly a mortal man, who, at some time or other, has not felt as great thoughts in him as any you will find in Hamlet. We must not inferentially malign mankind for the sake of any one man, whoever he may be. This is too cheap a purchase of contentment for conscious mediocrity to make. Besides, this absolute and unconditional adoration of Shakspeare has grown to be a part of our Anglo-Saxon superstitions. The Thirty-Nine Articles are now Forty. Intolerance has come to exist in this matter. You must believe in Shakspeare's unapproachability, or quit the country. But what sort of a belief is this for an American, a man who is bound to carry republican progressiveness into Literature as well as into Life? Believe me, my friends, that men, not very much inferior to Shakspeare are this day being born on the banks of the Ohio. And the day will come when you shall say, Who reads a book by an Englishman that is a modern? The great mistake seems to be, that even with those Americans who look forward to the coming of a great literary genius among us, they somehow fancy he will come in the costume of Queen Elizabeth's day; be a writer of dramas founded upon old English history or the tales of Boccaccio. Whereas, great geniuses are parts of the times, they themselves are the times, and possess a corresponding coloring. It is of a piece with the Jews, who, while their Shiloh was meekly walking in their streets, were still praying for his magnificent coming; looking for him in a chariot, who was already among them on an ass. Nor must we forget that, in his own lifetime, Shakspeare was not

Shakspeare, but only Master William Shakspeare of the shrewd, thriving, business firm of Condell, Shakspeare and Co., proprietors of the Globe Theatre in London; and by a courtly author, of the name of Chettle, was looked at as an "upstart crow," beautified "with other birds' feathers." For, mark it well, imitation is often the first charge brought against originality. Why this is so, there is not space to set forth here. You must have plenty of sea-room to tell the Truth in; especially when it seems to have an aspect of newness, as America did in 1492, though it was then just as old, and perhaps older than Asia, only those sagacious philosophers, the common sailors, had never seen it before, swearing it was all water and moonshine there.

Now I do not say that Nathaniel of Salem is a greater man than William of Avon, or as great. But the difference between the two men is by no means immeasurable. Not a very great deal more, and Nathaniel were verily William.

This, too, I mean, that if Shakspeare has not been equalled, give the world time, and he is sure to be surpassed in one hemisphere or the other. Nor will it at all do to say that the world is getting grey and grizzled now, and has lost that fresh charm which she wore of old, and by virtue of which the great poets of past times made themselves what we esteem them to be. Not so. The world is as young to-day as when it was created; and this Vermont morning dew is as wet to my feet, as Eden's dew to Adam's. Nor has nature been all over ransacked by our progenitors, so that no new charms and mysteries remain for this latter generation to find. Far from it. The trillionth part has not yet been said; and all that has been said, but multiplies the avenues to what remains to be said. It is not so much paucity as superabundance of material that seems to incapacitate modern authors.

Let America, then, prize and cherish her writers; yea, let her glorify them. They are not so many in number as to exhaust her goodwill. And while she has good kith and kin of her own, to take to her bosom, let her not lavish her embraces upon the household of an alien. For believe it or not, England after all, is in many things an alien to us. China has more bonds of real love for us than she. But even were there no strong literary individualities among us, as there are some dozens at least, nevertheless, let America first praise mediocrity even, in her children, before she praises (for everywhere, merit demands acknowledgment from every one) the best excellence in the children of any other land. Let her own authors, I say, have the priority of appreciation. I was much pleased with a hot-headed Carolina cousin of mine, who once said,—"If there were no other American to stand by, in literature, why, then, I would stand by Pop Emmons and his *Fredoniad*, and till a better epic came along, swear it was not very far behind the *Iliad*." Take away the words, and in spirit he was sound.

Not that American genius needs patronage in order to expand. For that explosive sort of stuff will expand though screwed up in a vice, and burst it, though it were triple steel. It is for the nation's sake, and not for her authors' sake, that I would have America be heedful of the increasing greatness among her writers. For how great the shame, if other nations should be before her, in crowning her heroes of the pen! But this is almost the case now. American authors have received more just and discriminating praise (however loftily and ridiculously given, in certain cases) even from some Englishmen, than from their own countrymen. There are hardly five critics in America; and several of them are asleep. As for patronage, it is the American author who now patronizes his country, and not his country him. And if at times some among them appeal to the people for more recognition, it is not always with selfish motives, but patriotic ones.

It is true, that but few of them as yet have evinced that decided originality which merits great praise. But that graceful writer, who perhaps of all Americans has received the most plaudits from his own country for his productions,—that very popular and amiable writer, however good and self-reliant in many things, perhaps owes his chief reputation to the self-acknowledged imitation of a foreign model, and to the studied avoidance of all topics but smooth ones. But it is better to fail in originality, than to succeed in imitation. He who has never failed somewhere, that man cannot be great. Failure is the true test of greatness. And if it be said, that continual success is a proof that a man wisely knows his powers,—it is only to be added, that, in that case, he knows them to be small. Let us believe it, then, once for all, that there is no hope for us in these smooth, pleasing writers that know their powers. Without malice, but to speak the plain fact, they but furnish an appendix to Goldsmith, and other English authors. And we want no American Goldsmiths, nay, we want no American Miltons. It were the vilest thing you

could say of a true American author, that he were an American Tompkins. Call him an American and have done, for you cannot say a nobler thing of him. But it is not meant that all American writers should studiously cleave to nationality in their writings; only this, no American writer should write like an Englishman or a Frenchman; let him write like a man, for then he will be sure to write like an American. Let us away with this leaven of literary flunkeyism towards England. If either must play the flunkey in this thing, let England do it, not us. While we are rapidly preparing for that political supremacy among the nations which prophetically awaits us at the close of the present century, in a literary point of view, we are deplorably unprepared for it; and we seem studious to remain so. Hitherto, reasons might have existed why this should be; but no good reason exists now. And all that is requisite to amendment in this matter, is simply this; that while fully acknowledging all excellence everywhere, we should refrain from unduly lauding foreign writers, and, at the same time, duly recognize the meritorious writers that are our own;—those writers who breathe that unshackled, democratic spirit of Christianity in all things, which now takes the practical lead in this world, though at the same time led by ourselves—us Americans. Let us boldly condemn all imitation, though it comes to us graceful and fragrant as the morning; and foster all originality though at first it be crabbed and ugly as our own pine knots. And if any of our authors fail, or seem to fail, then, in the words of my Carolina cousin, let us clap him on the shoulder and back him against all Europe for his second round. The truth is, that in one point of view this matter of a national literature has come to pass with us, that in some sense we must turn bullies, else the day is lost, or superiority so far beyond us, that we can hardly say it will ever be ours.

And now, my countrymen, as an excellent author of your own flesh and blood,—an unimitating, and, perhaps, in his way, an inimitable man—whom better can I commend to you, in the first place, than Nathaniel Hawthorne. He is one of the new, and far better generation of your writers. The smell of young beeches and hemlocks is upon him; your own broad prairies are in his soul; and if you travel away inland into his deep and noble nature, you will hear the far roar of his Niagara. Give not over to future generations the glad duty of acknowledging him for what he is. Take that joy to yourself, in your own generation;

and so shall he feel those grateful impulses on him, that may possibly prompt him to the full flower of some still greater achievement in your eyes. And by confessing him you thereby confess others; you brace the whole brotherhood. For genius, all over the world, stands hand in hand, and one shock of recognition runs the whole circle round.

In treating of Hawthorne, or rather of Hawthorne in his writings (for I never saw the man; and in the chances of a quiet plantation life, remote from his haunts, perhaps never shall); in treating of his works, I say, I have thus far omitted all mention of his *Twice Told Tales*, and *Scarlet Letter*. Both are excellent, but full of such manifold, strange, and diffusive beauties, that time would all but fail me to point the half of them out. But there are things in those two books, which, had they been written in England a century ago, Nathaniel Hawthorne had utterly displaced many of the bright names we now revere on authority. But I am content to leave Hawthorne to himself, and to the infallible finding of posterity; and however great may be the praise I have bestowed upon him, I feel that in so doing I have served and honored myself, than him. For, at bottom, great excellence is praise enough to itself; but the feeling of a sincere and appreciative love and admiration towards it, this is relieved by utterance, and warm, honest praise ever leaves a pleasant flavor in the mouth; and it is an honorable thing to confess to what is honorable in others.

But I cannot leave my subject yet. No man can read a fine author, and relish him to his very bones while he reads, without subsequently fancying to himself some ideal image of the man and his mind. And if you rightly look for it, you will almost always find that the author himself has somewhere furnished you with his own picture. For poets (whether in prose or verse), being painters by nature, are like their brethren of the pencil, the true portrait-painters, who, in the multitude of likenesses to be sketched, do not invariably omit their own; and in all high instances, they paint them without any vanity, though at times with a lurking something that would take several pages to properly define.

I submit it, then, to those best acquainted with the man personally, whether the following is not Nathaniel Hawthorne;—and to himself, whether something involved in it does not express the temper of his mind,—that lasting temper of all true, candid men—a seeker, not a finder yet:

A man now entered, in neglected attire, with the aspect of a thinker, but somewhat too roughhewn and brawny for a scholar. His face was full of sturdy vigor, with some finer and keener attribute beneath; though harsh at first, it was tempered with the glow of a large, warm heart, which had force enough to heat his powerful intellect through and through. He advanced to the Intelligencer, and looked at him with a glance of such stern sincerity, that perhaps few secrets were beyond its scope.

"I seek for Truth," said he.

Twenty-four hours have elapsed since writing the foregoing. I have just returned from the haymow, charged more and more with love and admiration of Hawthorne. For I have just been gleaning through the Mosses, picking up many things here and there that had previously escaped me. And I found that but to glean after this man, is better than to be in at the harvest of others. To be frank (though, perhaps, rather foolish) notwithstanding what I wrote yesterday of these Mosses, I had not then culled them all; but had, nevertheless, been sufficiently sensible of the subtle essence in them, as to write as I did. To what infinite height of loving wonder and admiration I may yet be borne, when by repeatedly banqueting on these Mosses I shall have thoroughly incorporated their whole stuff into my being—that, I cannot tell. But already I feel that this Hawthorne has dropped germinous seeds into my soul. He expands and deepens down, the more I contemplate him; and further and further, shoots his strong New England roots into the hot soil in my Southern soul.

By careful reference to the table of contents, I now find that I have gone through all the sketches; but that when I yesterday wrote, I had not at all read two particular pieces, to which I now desire to call special attention—*A Select Party* and *Young Goodman Brown*. Here, be it said to all those whom this poor fugitive scrawl of mine may tempt to the perusal of the Mosses, that they must on no account suffer themselves to be trifled with, disappointed, or deceived by the triviality of many of the titles to these sketches. For in more than one instance, the title utterly belies the piece. It is as if rustic demijohns containing the very best and costliest of Falernian and Tokay, were labelled "Cider," "Perry," and "Elderberry wine." The truth seems to be, that like many other geniuses, this Man of Mosses takes great delight in hoodwinking the world,—at least, with respect to himself. Personally, I doubt not that he rather prefers to be generally esteemed but a so-so sort of author; being willing to reserve the thorough and acute appreciation of what he is, to that party most qualified to judge—that is, to himself. Besides, at the bottom of their natures, men like Hawthorne, in many things, deem the plaudits of the public such strong presumptive evidence of mediocrity in the object of them, that it would in some degree render them doubtful of their own powers, did they hear much and vociferous braying concerning them in the public pastures. True, I have been braying myself (if you please to be witty enough to have it so), but then I claim to be the first that has so brayed in this particular matter; and, therefore, while pleading guilty to the charge, still claim all the merit due to originality.

But with whatever motive, playful or profound, Nathaniel Hawthorne has chosen to entitle his pieces in the manner he has, it is certain that some of them are directly calculated to deceive—egregiously deceive, the superficial skimmer of pages. To be downright and candid once more, let me cheerfully say, that two of these titles did dolefully dupe no less an eager-eyed reader than myself; and that, too, after I had been impressed with a sense of the great depth and breadth of this American man. "Who in the name of thunder" (as the country people say in this neighborhood), "who in the name of thunder, would anticipate any marvel in a piece entitled *Young Goodman Brown?*" You would of course suppose that it was a simple little tale, intended as a supplement to *Goody Two Shoes.* Whereas, it is deep as Dante; nor can you finish it, without addressing the author in his own words—"It shall be yours to penetrate, in every bosom, the deep mystery of sin". . . . And with Young Goodman, too, in allegorical pursuit of his Puritan wife, you cry out in your anguish:

"Faith!" shouted Goodman Brown, in a voice of agony and desperation; and the echoes of the forest mocked him, crying, "Faith! Faith!" as if bewildered wretches were seeking her all through the wilderness.

Now this same piece entitled *Young Goodman Brown*, is one of the two that I had not all read yesterday; and I allude to it now, because it is, in itself, such a strong positive illustration of the blackness in Hawthorne, which I had assumed from the mere occasional shadows of it; as revealed in several of the other sketches. But had I previously perused *Young Goodman Brown*, I should have been at no pains to draw the conclusion, which I came to at a time when I was ignorant that the book contained one such direct and unqualified manifestation of it.

The other piece of the two referred to, is entitled *A Select Party*, which, in my first simplicity upon originally taking hold of the book, I fancied must treat of some pumpkin-pie party in old Salem; or some chowder party on Cape Cod. Whereas, by all the gods of Peedee, it is the sweetest and sublimest thing that has been written since Spenser wrote. Nay, there is nothing in Spenser that surpasses it, perhaps nothing that equals it. And the test is this. Read any canto in *The Faerie Queene* and then read *A Select Party*, and decide which pleases you most,—that is, if you are qualified to judge. Do not be frightened at this; for when Spenser was alive, he was thought of very much as Hawthorne is now,—was generally accounted just such a "gentle" harmless man. It may be, that to common eyes, the sublimity of Hawthorne seems lost in his sweetness,—as perhaps in that same *Select Party* of his; for whom he has builded so august a dome of sunset clouds, and served them on richer plate than Belshazzar when he banqueted his lords in Babylon.

But my chief business now, is to point out a particular page in this piece, having reference to an honored guest, who under the name of the Master Genius, but in the guise "of a young man of poor attire, with no insignia of rank or acknowledged eminence," is introduced to the Man of Fancy, who is the giver of the feast. Now, the page having reference to this Master Genius, so happily expresses much of what I yesterday wrote, touching the coming of the literary Shiloh of America, that I cannot but be charmed by the coincidence; especially, when it shows such a parity of ideas, at least in this one point, between a man like Hawthorne and a man like me.

And here, let me throw out another conceit of mine touching this American Shiloh, or Master Genius, as Hawthorne calls him. May it not be, that this commanding mind has not been, is not, and never will be, individually developed in any one man? And would it, indeed, appear so unreasonable to suppose, that this great fulness and overflowing may be, or may be destined to be, shared by a plurality of men of genius? Surely, to take the very greatest example on record, Shakspeare cannot be regarded as in himself the concretion of all the genius of his time; nor as so immeasurably beyond Marlowe, Webster, Ford, Beaumont, Jonson, that these great men can be said to share none of his power? For one, I conceive that there were dramatists in Elizabeth's day, between whom and Shakspeare the distance was by no means great. Let any one, hitherto little acquainted with those neglected old authors, for the first time read them thoroughly, or even read Charles Lamb's *Specimens* of them, and he will be amazed at the wondrous ability of those Anaks of men, and shocked at this renewed example of the fact, that Fortune has more to do with fame than merit,—though, without merit, lasting fame there can be none.

Nevertheless, it would argue too ill of my country were this maxim to hold good concerning Nathaniel Hawthorne, a man, who already, in some few minds has shed "such a light as never illuminates the earth save when a great heart burns as the household fire of a grand intellect."

The words are his,—in the *Select Party*; and they are a magnificent setting to a coincident sentiment of my own, but ramblingly expressed yesterday, in reference to himself. Gainsay it who will, as I now write, I am Posterity speaking by proxy—and after times will make it more than good, when I declare, that the American, who up to the present day has evinced, in literature, the largest brain with the largest heart, that man is Nathaniel Hawthorne. Moreover, that whatever Nathaniel Hawthorne may hereafter write, *Mosses from an*

Old Manse will be ultimately accounted his masterpiece. For there is a sure, though secret sign in some works which proves the culmination of the powers (only the developable ones, however) that produced them. But I am by no means desirous of the glory of a prophet. I pray Heaven that Hawthorne may yet prove me an impostor in this prediction. Especially, as I somehow cling to the strange fancy, that, in all men, hiddenly reside certain wondrous, occult properties—as in some plants and minerals—which by some happy but very rare accident (as bronze was discovered by the melting of the iron and brass at the burning of Corinth) may chance to be called forth here on earth; not entirely waiting for their better discovery in the more congenial, blessed atmosphere of heaven.

Once more—for it is hard to be finite upon an infinite subject, and all subjects are infinite. By some people this entire scrawl of mine may be esteemed altogether unnecessary, inasmuch "as years ago" (they may say) "we found out the rich and rare stuff in this Hawthorne, who you now parade forth, as if only you *yourself* were the discoverer of this Portuguese diamond in your literature." But even granting all this—and adding to it, the assumption that the books of Hawthorne have sold by the five thousand,—what does that signify? They should be sold by the hundred thousand; and read by the million; and admired by every one who is capable of admiration.

Bartleby the Scrivener (1853)

I am a rather elderly man. The nature of my avocations, for the last thirty years, has brought me into more than ordinary contact with what would seem an interesting and somewhat singular set of men, of whom, as yet, nothing, that I know of, has ever been written—I mean, the law-copyists, or scriveners. I have known very many of them, professionally and privately, and, if I pleased, could relate divers histories, at which good-natured gentlemen might smile, and sentimental souls might weep. But I waive the biographies of all other scriveners, for a few passages in the life of Bartleby, who was a scrivener, the strangest I ever saw, or heard of. While, of other law-copyists, I might write the complete life, of Bartleby nothing of that sort can be done. I believe that no materials exist, for a full and satisfactory biography of this man.

It is an irreparable loss to literature. Bartleby was one of those beings of whom nothing is ascertainable, except from the original sources, and, in his case, those are very small. What my own astonished eyes saw of Bartleby, *that* is all I know of him, except, indeed, one vague report, which will appear in the sequel.

Ere introducing the scrivener, as he first appeared to me, it is fit I make some mention of myself, my *employés*, my business, my chambers, and general surroundings; because some such description is indispensable to an adequate understanding of the chief character about to be presented. Imprimis: I am a man who, from his youth upwards, has been filled with a profound conviction that the easiest way of life is the best. Hence, though I belong to a profession proverbially energetic and nervous, even to turbulence, at times, yet nothing of that sort have I ever suffered to invade my peace. I am one of those unambitious lawyers who never address a jury, or in any way draw down public applause; but, in the cool tranquillity of a snug retreat, do a snug business among rich men's bonds, and mortgages, and title-deeds. All who know me, consider me an eminently *safe* man. The late John Jacob Astor, a personage little given to poetic enthusiasm, had no hesitation in pronouncing my first grand point to be prudence; my next, method. I do not speak it in vanity, but simply record the fact, that I was not unemployed in my profession by the late John Jacob Astor; a name which, I admit, I love to repeat; for it hath a rounded and orbicular sound to it, and rings like unto bullion. I will freely add, that I was not insensible to the late John Jacob Astor's good opinion.

Some time prior to the period at which this little history begins, my avocations had been largely increased. The good old office, now extinct in the State of New York, of a Master in Chancery, had been conferred upon me. It was not a very arduous office, but very pleasantly remunerative. I seldom lose my temper; much more seldom indulge in dangerous indignation at wrongs and outrages; but I must be permitted to be rash here and declare, that I consider the sudden and violent abrogation of the office of Master in Chancery, by the new Constitution, as a —— premature act; inasmuch as I had counted upon a life-lease of the profits, whereas I only received those of a few short years. But this is by the way.

My chambers were up stairs, at No. — Wall Street. At one end, they looked upon the white wall of the interior of a spacious sky-light shaft, penetrating the building from top to bottom.

This view might have been considered rather tame than otherwise, deficient in what landscape painters call "life." But, if so, the view from the other end of my chambers offered, at least, a contrast, if nothing more. In that direction, my windows commanded an unobstructed view of a lofty brick wall, black by age and everlasting shade; which wall required no spy-glass to bring out its lurking beauties, but, for the benefit of all near-sighted spectators, was pushed up to within ten feet of my window-panes. Owing to the great height of the surrounding buildings, and my chambers being on the second floor, the interval between this wall and mine not a little resembled a huge square cistern.

At the period just preceding the advent of Bartleby, I had two persons as copyists in my employment, and a promising lad as an office-boy. First, Turkey; second, Nippers; third, Ginger Nut. These may seem names, the like of which are not usually found in the Dictionary. In truth, they were nicknames, mutually conferred upon each other by my three clerks, and were deemed expressive of their respective persons or characters. Turkey was a short, pursy Englishman, of about my own age— that is, somewhere not far from sixty. In the morning, one might say, his face was of a fine florid hue, but after twelve o'clock, meridian—his dinner hour—it blazed like a grate full of Christmas coals; and continued blazing—but, as it were, with a gradual wane—till six o'clock, P.M., or thereabouts; after which, I saw no more of the proprietor of the face, which, gaining its meridian with the sun, seemed to set with it, to rise, culminate, and decline the following day, with the like regularity and undiminished glory. There are many singular coincidences I have known in the course of my life, not the least among which was the fact, that, exactly when Turkey displayed his fullest beams from his red and radiant countenance, just then, too, at that critical moment, began the daily period when I considered his business capacities as seriously disturbed for the remainder of the twenty-four hours. Not that he was absolutely idle, or averse to business then; far from it. The difficulty was, he was apt to be altogether too energetic. There was a strange, inflamed, flurried, flighty recklessness of activity about him. He would be incautious in dipping his pen into his inkstand. All his blots upon my documents were dropped there after twelve o'clock, meridian. Indeed, not only would he be reckless, and sadly given to making blots in the afternoon, but, some days, he went further, and was rather noisy. At such times, too, his face flamed with augmented blazonry, as if cannel coal had been heaped on anthracite. He made an unpleasant racket with his chair; spilled his sand-box; in mending his pens, impatiently split them all to pieces, and threw them on the floor in a sudden passion; stood up, and leaned over his table, boxing his papers about in a most indecorous manner, very sad to behold in an elderly man like him. Nevertheless, as he was in many ways a most valuable person to me, and all the time before twelve o'clock, meridian, was the quickest, steadiest creature, too, accomplishing a great deal of work in a style not easily to be matched—for these reasons, I was willing to overlook his eccentricities, though, indeed, occasionally, I remonstrated with him. I did this very gently, however, because, though the civilest, nay, the blandest and most reverential of men in the morning, yet, in the afternoon, he was disposed, upon provocation, to be slightly rash with his tongue—in fact, insolent. Now, valuing his morning services as I did, and resolved not to lose them —yet, at the same time, made uncomfortable by his inflamed ways after twelve o'clock—and being a man of peace, unwilling by my admonitions to call forth unseemly retorts from him, I took upon me, one Saturday noon (he was always worse on Saturdays) to hint to him, very kindly, that, perhaps, now that he was growing old, it might be well to abridge his labors; in short, he need not come to my chambers after twelve o'clock, but, dinner over, had best go home to his lodgings, and rest himself till tea-time. But no; he insisted upon his afternoon devotions. His countenance became intolerably fervid, as he oratorically assured me—gesticulating with a long ruler at the other end of the room—that if his services in the morning were useful, how indispensable, then, in the afternoon?

"With submission, sir," said Turkey, on this occasion, "I consider myself your right-hand man. In the morning I but marshal and deploy my columns; but in the afternoon I put myself at their head, and gallantly charge the foe, thus"— and he made a violent thrust with the ruler.

"But the blots, Turkey," intimated I.

"True; but, with submission, sir, behold these hairs! I am getting old. Surely, sir, a blot or two of a warm afternoon is not to be severely urged against gray hairs. Old age—even if it blot the page —is honorable. With submission, sir, we *both* are getting old."

This appeal to my fellow-feeling was hardly to be resisted. At all events, I saw that go he would not. So, I made up my mind to let him stay, resolving, nevertheless, to see to it that, during the afternoon, he had to do with my less important papers.

Nippers, the second on my list, was a whiskered, sallow, and, upon the whole, rather piratical-looking young man, of about five-and-twenty. I always deemed him the victim of two evil powers—ambition and indigestion. The ambition was evinced by a certain impatience of the duties of a mere copyist, an unwarrantable usurpation of strictly professional affairs, such as the original drawing up of legal documents. The indigestion seemed betokened in an occasional nervous testiness and grinning irritability, causing the teeth to audibly grind together over mistakes committed in copying; unnecessary maledictions, hissed, rather than spoken, in the heat of business; and especially by a continual discontent with the height of the table where he worked. Though of a very ingenious mechanical turn, Nippers could never get this table to suit him. He put chips under it, blocks of various sorts, bits of pasteboard, and at last went so far as to attempt an exquisite adjustment, by final pieces of folded blotting-paper. But no invention would answer. If, for the sake of easing his back, he brought the table-lid at a sharp angle well up towards his chin, and wrote there like a man using the steep roof of a Dutch house for his desk, then he declared that it stopped the circulation in his arms. If now he lowered the table to his waistbands, and stooped over it in writing, then there was a sore aching in his back. In short, the truth of the matter was, Nippers knew not what he wanted. Or, if he wanted anything, it was to be rid of a scrivener's table altogether. Among the manifestations of his diseased ambition was a fondness he had for receiving visits from certain ambiguous-looking fellows in seedy coats, whom he called his clients. Indeed, I was aware that not only was he, at times, considerable of a ward-politician, but he occasionally did a little business at the Justices' courts, and was not unknown on the steps of the Tombs. I have good reason to believe, however, that one individual who called upon him at my chambers, and who, with a grand air, he insisted was his client, was no other than a dun, and the alleged title-deed, a bill. But, with all his failings, and the annoyances he caused me, Nippers, like his compatriot Turkey, was a very useful man to me; wrote a neat, swift hand; and, when he chose, was not deficient in a gentlemanly sort of deportment. Added to this, he always dressed in a gentlemanly sort of way; and so, incidentally, reflected credit upon my chambers. Whereas, with respect to Turkey, I had much ado to keep him from being a reproach to me. His clothes were apt to look oily, and smell of eating-houses. He wore his pantaloons very loose and baggy in summer. His coats were execrable; his hat not to be handled. But while the hat was a thing of indifference to me, inasmuch as his natural civility and deference, as a dependent Englishman, always led him to doff it the moment he entered the room, yet his coat was another matter. Concerning his coats, I reasoned with him; but with no effect. The truth was, I suppose, that a man with so small an income could not afford to sport such a lustrous face and a lustrous coat at one and the same time. As Nippers one observed, Turkey's money went chiefly for red ink. One winter day, I presented Turkey with a highly respectable-looking coat of my own—a padded gray coat, of a most comfortable warmth, and which buttoned straight up from the knee to the neck. I thought Turkey would appreciate the favor, and abate his rashness and obstreperousness of afternoons. But no; I verily believe that buttoning himself up in so downy and blanket-like a coat had a pernicious effect upon him—upon the same principle that too much oats are bad for horses. In fact, precisely as a rash, restive horse is said to feel his oats, so Turkey felt his coat. It made him insolent. He was a man whom prosperity harmed.

Though, concerning the self-indulgent habits of Turkey, I had my own private surmises, yet, touching Nippers, I was well persuaded that, whatever might be his faults in other respects, he was, at least, a temperate young man. But, indeed, nature herself seemed to have been his vintner, and, at his birth, charged him so thoroughly with an irritable, brandy-like disposition, that all subsequent potations were needless. When I consider how, amid the stillness of my chambers, Nippers would sometimes impatiently rise from his seat, and stooping over his table, spread his arms wide apart, seize the whole desk, and move it, and jerk it, with a grim, grinding motion on the floor, as if the table were a perverse voluntary agent, intent on thwarting and vexing him, I plainly perceive that, for Nippers, brandy-and-water were altogether superfluous.

It was fortunate for me that, owing to its peculiar cause—indigestion—the irritability and consequent nervousness of Nippers were mainly observable in the morning, while in the afternoon he was comparatively mild. So that, Turkey's paroxysms only coming on about twelve o'clock, I never had to do with their eccentricities at one time. Their fits relieved each other, like guards. When Nippers's was on, Turkey's was off; and *vice versa*. This was a good natural arrangement, under the circumstances.

Ginger Nut, the third on my list, was a lad, some twelve years old. His father was a carman, ambitious of seeing his son on the bench instead of a cart, before he died. So he sent him to my office, as student at law, errand-boy, cleaner and sweeper, at the rate of one dollar a week. He had a little desk to himself, but he did not use it much. Upon inspection, the drawer exhibited a great array of the shells of various sorts of nuts. Indeed, to this quick-witted youth, the whole noble science of the law was contained in a nut-shell. Not the least among the employments of Ginger Nut, as well as one which he discharged with the most alacrity, was his duty as cake and apple purveyor for Turkey and Nippers. Copying law-papers being proverbially a dry, husky sort of business, my two scriveners were fain to moisten their mouths very often with Spitzenbergs, to be had at the numerous stalls nigh the Custom House and Post Office. Also, they sent Ginger Nut very frequently for that peculiar cake—small, flat, round, and very spicy—after which he had been named by them. Of a cold morning, when business was but dull, Turkey would gobble up scores of these cakes, as if they were mere wafers—indeed, they sell them at the rate of six or eight for a penny—the scrape of his pen blending with the crunching of the crisp particles in his mouth. Of all the fiery afternoon blunders and flurried rashnesses of Turkey, was his once moistening a ginger-cake between his lips, and clapping it on to a mortgage, for a seal. I came within an ace of dismissing him then. But he mollified me by making an oriental bow, and saying—

"With submission, sir, it was generous of me to find you in stationery on my own account."

Now my original business—that of a conveyancer and title hunter, and drawer-up of recondite documents of all sorts—was considerably increased by receiving the Master's office. There was now great work for scriveners. Not only must I push the clerks already with me, but I must have additional help.

In answer to my advertisement, a motionless young man one morning stood upon my office threshold, the door being open, for it was summer. I can see that figure now—pallidly neat, pitiably respectable, incurably forlorn! It was Bartleby.

After a few words touching his qualifications, I engaged him, glad to have among my corps of copyists a man of so singularly sedate an aspect, which I thought might operate beneficially upon the flighty temper of Turkey, and the fiery one of Nippers.

I should have stated before that ground-glass folding-doors divided my premises into two parts, one of which was occupied by my scriveners, the other by myself. According to my humor, I threw open these doors, or closed them. I resolved to assign Bartleby a corner by the folding-doors, but on my side of them, so as to have this quiet man within easy call, in case any trifling thing was to be done. I placed his desk close up to a small side-window in that part of the room, a window which originally had afforded a lateral view of certain grimy backyards and bricks, but which, owing to subsequent erections, commanded at present no view at all, though it gave some light. Within three feet of the panes was a wall, and the light came down from far above, between two lofty buildings, as from a very small opening in a dome. Still further to a satisfactory arrangement, I procured a high green folding screen, which might entirely isolate Bartleby from my sight, though not remove him from my voice. And thus, in a manner, privacy and society were conjoined.

At first, Bartleby did an extraordinary quantity of writing. As if long famishing for something to copy, he seemed to gorge himself on my documents. There was no pause for digestion. He ran a day and night line, copying by sun-light and by candle-light. I should have been quite delighted with his application, had he been cheerfully industrious. But he wrote on silently, palely, mechanically.

It is, of course, an indispensable part of a scrivener's business to verify the accuracy of his copy, word by word. Where there are two or more scriveners in an office, they assist each other in this examination, one reading from the copy, the other holding the original. It is a very dull, wearisome, and lethargic affair. I can readily imagine that, to some sanguine temperaments, it would be altogether intolerable. For example, I cannot credit that the mettlesome poet, Byron, would have contentedly sat down with Bartleby to examine a law document of, say five hundred pages, closely written in a crimpy hand.

Now and then, in the haste of business, it had been my habit to assist in comparing some brief document myself, calling Turkey or Nippers for this purpose. One object I had, in placing Bartleby so handy to me behind the screen, was, to avail myself of his services on such trivial occasions. It was on the third day, I think, of his being with me, and before any necessity had arisen for having his own writing examined, that, being much hurried to complete a small affair I had in hand, I abruptly called to Bartleby. In my haste and natural expectancy of instant compliance, I sat with my head bent over the original on my desk, and my right hand sideways, and somewhat ner-

vously extended with the copy, so that, immediately upon emerging from his retreat, Bartleby might snatch it and proceed to business without the least delay.

In this very attitude did I sit when I called to him, rapidly stating what it was I wanted him to do—namely, to examine a small paper with me. Imagine my surprise, nay, my consternation, when, without moving from his privacy, Bartleby, in a singularly mild, firm voice, replied, "I would prefer not to."

I sat awhile in perfect silence, rallying my stunned faculties. Immediately it occurred to me that my ears had deceived me, or Bartleby had entirely misunderstood my meaning. I repeated my request in the clearest tone I could assume; but in quite as clear a one came the previous reply, "I would prefer not to."

"Prefer not to," echoed I, rising in high excitement, and crossing the room with a stride. "What do you mean? Are you moon-struck? I want you to help me compare this sheet here—take it," and I thrust it towards him.

"I would prefer not to," said he.

I looked at him steadfastly. His face was leanly composed; his gray eye dimly calm. Not a wrinkle of agitation rippled him. Had there been the least uneasiness, anger, impatience or impertinence in his manner, in other words, had there been anything ordinarily human about him, doubtless I should have violently dismissed him from the premises. But as it was, I should have as soon thought of turning my pale plaster-of-paris bust of Cicero out of doors. I stood gazing at him awhile, as he went on with his own writing, and then reseated myself at my desk. This is very strange, thought I. What had one best do? But my business hurried me. I concluded to forget the matter for the present, reserving it for my future leisure. So, calling Nippers from the other room, the paper was speedily examined.

A few days after this, Bartleby concluded four lengthy documents, being quadruplicates of a week's testimony taken before me in my High Court of Chancery. It became necessary to examine them. It was an important suit, and great accuracy was imperative. Having all things arranged, I called Turkey, Nippers and Ginger Nut, from the next room, meaning to place the four copies in the hands of my four clerks, while I should read from the original. Accordingly, Turkey, Nippers, and Ginger Nut had taken their seats in a row, each with his document in his hand, when I called to Bartleby to join this interesting group.

"Bartleby! quick, I am waiting."

I heard a slow scrape of his chair legs on the uncarpeted floor, and soon he appeared standing at the entrance of his hermitage.

"What is wanted?" said he, mildly.

"The copies, the copies," said I, hurriedly. "We are going to examine them. There"—and I held towards him the fourth quadruplicate.

"I would prefer not to," he said, and gently disappeared behind the screen.

For a few moments I was turned into a pillar of salt, standing at the head of my seated column of clerks. Recovering myself, I advanced towards the screen, and demanded the reason for such extraordinary conduct.

"*Why* do you refuse?"

"I would prefer not to."

With any other man I should have flown outright into a dreadful passion, scorned all further words, and thrust him ignominiously from my presence. But there was something about Bartleby that not only strangely disarmed me, but, in a wonderful manner, touched and disconcerted me. I began to reason with him.

"These are your own copies we are about to examine. It is labor saving to you, because one examination will answer for your four papers. It is common usage. Every copyist is bound to help examine his copy. Is it not so? Will you not speak? Answer!"

"I prefer not to," he replied in a flute-like tone. It seemed to me that, while I had been addressing him, he carefully revolved every statement that I made; fully comprehended the meaning; could not gainsay the irresistible conclusion; but, at the same time, some paramount consideration prevailed with him to reply as he did.

"You are decided, then, not to comply with my request—a request made according to common usage and common sense?"

He briefly gave me to understand, that on that point my judgment was sound. Yes: his decision was irreversible.

It is not seldom the case that, when a man is browbeaten in some unprecedented and violently unreasonable way, he begins to stagger in his own plainest faith. He begins, as it were, vaguely to surmise that, wonderful as it may be, all the justice and all the reason is on the other side. Accord-

ingly, if any disinterested persons are present, he turns to them for some reinforcement for his own faltering mind.

"Turkey," said I, "what do you think of this? Am I not right?"

"With submission, sir," said Turkey, in his blandest tone, "I think that you are."

"Nippers," said I, "what do *you* think of it?"

"I think I should kick him out of the office."

(The reader of nice perceptions will here perceive that, it being morning, Turkey's answer is couched in polite and tranquil terms, but Nippers replies in ill-tempered ones. Or, to repeat a previous sentence, Nippers's ugly mood was on duty, and Turkey's off.)

"Ginger Nut," said I, willing to enlist the smallest suffrage in my behalf, "what do *you* think of it?"

"I think, sir, he's a little *luny*," replied Ginger Nut, with a grin.

"You hear what they say," said I, turning towards the screen, "come forth and do your duty."

But he vouchsafed no reply. I pondered a moment in sore perplexity. But once more business hurried me. I determined again to postpone the consideration of this dilemma to my future leisure. With a little trouble we made out to examine the papers without Bartleby, though at every page or two Turkey deferentially dropped his opinion, that this proceeding was quite out of the common; while Nippers, twitching in his chair with a dyspeptic nervousness, ground out, between his set teeth, occasional hissing maledictions against the stubborn oaf behind the screen. And for his (Nippers's) part, this was the first and the last time he would do another man's business without pay.

Meanwhile Bartleby sat in his hermitage, oblivious to everything but his own peculiar business there.

Some days passed, the scrivener being employed upon another lengthy work. His late remarkable conduct led me to regard his ways narrowly. I observed that he never went to dinner; indeed, that he never went anywhere. As yet I had never, of my personal knowledge, known him to be outside of my office. He was a perpetual sentry in the corner. At about eleven o'clock though, in the morning, I noticed that Ginger Nut would advance toward the opening in Bartleby's screen, as if silently beckoned thither by a gesture invisible to me where I sat. The boy would then leave the office, jingling a few pence, and reappear with a handful of ginger-nuts, which he delivered in the hermitage, receiving two of the cakes for his trouble.

He lives, then, on ginger-nuts, thought I; never eats a dinner, properly speaking; he must be a vegetarian, then; but no; he never eats even vegetables, he eats nothing but ginger-nuts. My mind then ran on in reveries concerning the probable effects upon the human constitution of living entirely on ginger-nuts. Ginger-nuts are so called, because they contain ginger as one of their peculiar constituents, and the final flavoring one. Now, what was ginger? A hot, spicy thing. Was Bartleby hot and spicy? Not at all. Ginger, then, had no effect upon Bartleby. Probably he preferred it should have none.

Nothing so aggravates an earnest person as a passive resistance. If the individual so resisted be of a not inhumane temper, and the resisting one perfectly harmless in his passivity, then, in the better moods of the former, he will endeavor charitably to construe to his imagination what proves impossible to be solved by his judgment. Even so, for the most part, I regarded Bartleby and his ways. Poor fellow! thought I, he means no mischief; it is plain he intends no insolence; his aspect sufficiently evinces that his eccentricities are involuntary. He is useful to me. I can get along with him. If I turn him away, the chances are he will fall in with some less indulgent employer, and then he will be rudely treated, and perhaps driven forth miserably to starve. Yes. Here I can cheaply purchase a delicious self-approval. To befriend Bartleby; to humor him in his strange wilfulness, will cost me little or nothing, while I lay up in my soul what will eventually prove a sweet morsel for my conscience. But this mood was not invariable with me. The passiveness of Bartleby sometimes irritated me. I felt strangely goaded on to encounter him in new opposition—to elicit some angry spark from him answerable to my own. But, indeed, I might as well have essayed to strike fire with my knuckles against a bit of Windsor soap. But one afternoon the evil impulse in me mastered me, and the following little scene ensued:

"Bartleby," said I, "when those papers are all copied, I will compare them with you."

"I would prefer not to."

"How? Surely you do not mean to persist in that mulish vagary?"

No answer.

I threw open the folding-doors near by, and, turning upon Turkey and Nippers, exclaimed:

"Bartleby a second time says, he won't examine his papers. What do you think of it, Turkey?"

It was afternoon, be it remembered. Turkey sat glowing like a brass boiler, his bald head steaming; his hands reeling among his blotted papers.

"Think of it?" roared Turkey. "I think I'll just step behind his screen, and black his eyes for him!"

So saying, Turkey rose to his feet and threw his arms into a pugilistic position. He was hurrying away to make good his promise, when I detained him, alarmed at the effect of incautiously rousing Turkey's combativeness after dinner.

"Sit down, Turkey," said I, "and hear what Nippers has to say. What do you think of it, Nippers? Would I not be justified in immediately dismissing Bartleby?"

"Excuse me, that is for you to decide, sir. I think his conduct quite unusual, and, indeed, unjust, as regards Turkey and myself. But it may only be a passing whim."

"Ah," exclaimed I, "you have strangely changed your mind, then—you speak very gently of him now."

"All beer," cried Turkey; "gentleness is effects of beer—Nippers and I dined together to-day. You see how gentle I am, sir. Shall I go and black his eyes?"

"You refer to Bartleby, I suppose. No, not today, Turkey," I replied; "pray, put up your fists."

I closed the doors, and again advanced towards Bartleby. I felt additional incentives tempting me to my fate. I burned to be rebelled against again. I remembered that Bartleby never left the office.

"Bartleby," said I, "Ginger Nut is away; just step around to the Post Office, won't you?" (it was but a three minutes' walk) "and see if there is anything for me."

"I would prefer not to."

"You *will* not?"

"I *prefer* not."

I staggered to my desk, and sat there in a deep study. My blind inveteracy returned. Was there any other thing in which I could procure myself to be ignominiously repulsed by this lean, penniless wight?—my hired clerk? What added thing is there, perfectly reasonable, that he will be sure to refuse to do?

"Bartleby!"

No answer.

"Bartleby," in a louder tone.

No answer.

"Bartleby," I roared.

Like a very ghost, agreeably to the laws of magical invocation, at the third summons, he appeared at the entrance of his hermitage.

"Go to the next room, and tell Nippers to come to me."

"I prefer not to," he respectfully and slowly said, and mildly disappeared.

"Very good, Bartleby," said I, in a quiet sort of serenely-severe self-possessed tone, intimating the unalterable purpose of some terrible retribution very close at hand. At the moment I half intended something of the kind. But upon the whole, as it was drawing towards my dinner-hour, I thought it best to put on my hat and walk home for the day, suffering much from perplexity and distress of mind.

Shall I acknowledge it? The conclusion of this whole business was, that it soon became a fixed fact of my chambers, that a pale young scrivener, by the name of Bartleby, had a desk there; that he copied for me at the usual rate of four cents a folio (one hundred words); but he was permanently exempt from examining the work done by him, that duty being transferred to Turkey and Nippers, out of compliment, doubtless, to their superior acuteness; moreover, said Bartleby was never, on any account, to be dispatched on the most trivial errand of any sort; and that even if entreated to take upon him such a matter, it was generally understood that he would "prefer not to" —in other words, that he would refuse point-blank.

As days passed on, I became considerably reconciled to Bartleby. His steadiness, his freedom from all dissipation, his incessant industry (except when he chose to throw himself into a standing revery behind his screen), his great stillness, his unalterableness of demeanor under all circumstances, made him a valuable acquisition. One prime thing was this—*he was always there*—first in the morning, continually through the day, and the last at night. I had a singular confidence in his honesty. I felt my most precious papers perfectly safe in his hands. Sometimes, to be sure, I could not, for the very soul of me, avoid falling into sudden spasmodic passions with him. For it was exceeding difficult to bear in mind all the time those strange peculiarities, privileges, and unheard-of exemptions, forming the tacit stipulations on Bartleby's part under which he remained in my office. Now and then, in the eagerness of dispatching pressing business, I would inadvertently summon Bartleby, in a short, rapid tone, to put his finger, say, on the incipient tie of a bit of red tape with which I was about compressing some papers. Of course, from behind the screen the usual answer, "I prefer not to," was sure to come; and then, how could a human creature, with the common infirmities of our nature, refrain from bitterly exclaiming upon such perverseness—such unreasonableness? However, every added repulse of this sort which I received only tended to lessen the probability of my repeating the inadvertence.

Here it must be said, that, according to the custom of most legal gentlemen occupying chambers in densely-populated law buildings, there were several keys to my door. One was kept by a woman residing in the attic, which person weekly scrubbed and daily swept and dusted my apartments. Another was kept by Turkey for convenience sake. The third I sometimes carried in my own pocket. The fourth I knew not who had.

Now, one Sunday morning I happened to go to Trinity Church, to hear a celebrated preacher, and finding myself rather early on the ground I thought I would walk round to my chambers for a while. Luckily I had my key with me; but upon applying it to the lock, I found it resisted by something inserted from the inside. Quite surprised, I called out; when to my consternation a key was turned from within; and thrusting his lean visage at me, and holding the door ajar, the apparition of Bartleby appeared, in his shirt-sleeves, and otherwise in a strangely tattered deshabille, saying quietly that he was sorry, but he was deeply engaged just then, and—preferred not admitting me at present. In a brief word or two, he moreover added, that perhaps I had better walk round the block two or three times, and by that time he would probably have concluded his affairs.

Now, the utterly unsurmised appearance of Bartleby, tenanting my law-chambers of a Sunday morning, with his cadaverously gentlemanly *nonchalance*, yet withal firm and self-possessed, had such a strange effect upon me, that incontinently I slunk away from my own door, and did as desired. But not without sundry twinges of impotent rebellion against the mild effrontery of this unaccountable scrivener. Indeed, it was his wonderful mildness chiefly, which not only disarmed me, but unmanned me, as it were. For I consider that one, for the time, is a sort of unmanned when he tranquilly permits his hired clerk to dictate to him, and order him away from his own premises. Furthermore, I was full of uneasiness as to what Bartleby could possibly be doing in my office in his shirt-sleeves, and in an otherwise dismantled condition of a Sunday morning. Was anything amiss going on? Nay, that was out of the question. It was not to be thought of for a moment that Bartleby was an immoral person. But what could he be doing there?—copying? Nay again, whatever might be his eccentricities, Bartleby was an eminently decorous person. He would be the last man to sit down to his desk in any state approaching to nudity. Besides, it was Sunday; and there was something about Bartleby that forbade the supposition that he would by any secular occupation violate the proprieties of the day.

Nevertheless, my mind was not pacified; and full of a restless curiosity, at last I returned to the door. Without hindrance I inserted my key, opened it, and entered. Bartleby was not to be seen. I looked round anxiously, peeped behind his screen; but it was very plain that he was gone. Upon more closely examining the place, I surmised that for an indefinite period Bartleby must have ate, dressed, and slept in my office, and that too without plate, mirror, or bed. The cushioned seat of a rickety old sofa in one corner bore the faint impress of a lean, reclining form. Rolled away under his desk, I found a blanket; under the empty grate, a blacking box and brush; on a chair, a tin basin, with soap and a ragged towel; in a newspaper a few crumbs of ginger-nuts and a morsel of cheese. Yes, thought I, it is evident enough that Bartleby has been making his home here, keeping bachelor's hall all by himself. Immediately then the thought came sweeping across me, what miserable friendlessness and loneliness are here revealed! His poverty is great; but his solitude, how horrible! Think of it. Of a Sunday, Wall Street is deserted as Petra; and every night of every day it is an emptiness. This building, too, which of week-days hums with industry and life, at nightfall echoes with sheer vacancy, and all through Sunday is forlorn. And here Bartleby makes his home; sole spectator of a solitude which he has seen all populous—a sort of innocent and transformed Marius brooding among the ruins of Carthage!

For the first time in my life a feeling of overpowering stinging melancholy seized me. Before, I had never experienced aught but a not unpleasing sadness. The bond of a common humanity now drew me irresistibly to gloom. A fraternal melancholy! For both I and Bartleby were sons of Adam.

I remembered the bright silks and sparkling faces I had seen that day, in gala trim, swan-like sailing down the Missisipi of Broadway; and I contrasted them with the pallid copyist, and thought to myself, Ah, happiness courts the light, so we deem the world is gay; but misery hides aloof, so we deem that misery there is none. These sad fancyings—chimeras, doubtless, of a sick and silly brain—led on to other and more special thoughts, concerning the eccentricities of Bartleby. Presentiments of strange discoveries hovered round me. The scrivener's pale form appeared to me laid out, among uncaring strangers, in its shivering winding-sheet.

Suddenly I was attracted by Bartleby's closed desk, the key in open sight left in the lock.

I mean no mischief, seek the gratification of no heartless curiosity, thought I; besides, the desk is mine, and its contents, too, so I will make bold to look within. Everything was methodically arranged, the papers smoothly placed. The pigeon-holes were deep, and removing the files of documents, I groped into their recesses. Presently I felt something there, and dragged it out. It was an old bandanna handkerchief, heavy and knotted. I opened it, and saw it was a saving's bank.

I now recalled all the quiet mysteries which I had noted in the man. I remembered that he never spoke but to answer; that, though at intervals he had considerable time to himself, yet I had never seen him reading—no, not even a newspaper; that for long periods he would stand looking out, at his pale window behind the screen, upon the dead brick wall; I was quite sure he never visited any refectory or eating-house; while his pale face clearly indicated that he never drank beer like Turkey, or tea and coffee even, like other men; that he never went anywhere in particular that I could learn; never went out for a walk, unless, indeed, that was the case at present; that he had declined telling who he was, or whence he came, or whether he had any relatives in the world; that though so thin and pale, he never complained of ill-health. And more than all, I remembered a certain unconscious air of pallid—how shall I call it?—of pallid haughtiness, say, or rather an austere reserve about him, which had positively awed me into my tame compliance with his eccentricities, when I had feared to ask him to do the slightest incidental thing for me, even though I might know, from his long-continued motionlessness, that behind his screen he must be standing in one of those dead-wall reveries of his.

Revolving all these things, and coupling them with the recently discovered fact, that he made my office his constant abiding place and home, and not forgetful of his morbid moodiness; revolving all these things, a prudential feeling began to steal over me. My first emotions had been those of pure melancholy and sincerest pity; but just in proportion as the forlornness of Bartleby grew and grew to my imagination, did that same melancholy merge into fear, that pity into repulsion. So true it is, and so terrible, too, that up to a certain point the thought or sight of misery enlists our best affections; but, in certain special cases, beyond that point it does not. They err who would assert that invariably this is owing to the inherent selfishness of the human heart. It rather proceeds from a certain hopelessness of remedying excessive and organic ill. To a sensitive being, pity is not seldom pain. And when at last it is perceived that such pity cannot lead to effectual succor, common sense bids the soul be rid of it. What I saw that morning persuaded me that the scrivener was the victim of innate and incurable disorder. I might give alms to his body; but his body did not pain him; it was his soul that suffered, and his soul I could not reach.

I did not accomplish the purpose of going to Trinity Church that morning. Somehow, the things I had seen disqualified me for the time from church-going. I walked homeward, thinking what I would do with Bartleby. Finally, I resolved upon this—I would put certain calm questions to him the next morning, touching his history, etc., and if he declined to answer them openly and unreservedly (and I supposed he would prefer not), then to give him a twenty dollar bill over and above whatever I might owe him, and tell him his services were no longer required; but that if in any other way I could assist him, I would be happy to do so, especially if he desired to return to his native place, wherever that might be, I would willingly help to defray the expenses. Moreover, if, after reaching home, he found himself at any time in want of aid, a letter from him would be sure of a reply.

The next morning came.

"Bartleby," said I, gently calling to him behind his screen.

No reply.

"Bartleby," said I, in a still gentler tone, "come here; I am not going to ask you to do anything you would prefer not to do—I simply wish to speak to you."

Upon this he noiselessly slid into view.

"Will you tell me, Bartleby, where you were born?"

"I would prefer not to."

"Will you tell me *anything* about yourself?"

"I would prefer not to."

"But what reasonable objection can you have to speak to me? I feel friendly towards you."

He did not look at me while I spoke, but kept his glance fixed upon my bust of Cicero, which, as I then sat, was directly behind me, some six inches above my head.

"What is your answer, Bartleby?" said I, after waiting a considerable time for a reply, during which his countenance remained immovable, only there was the faintest conceivable tremor of the white attenuated mouth.

"At present I prefer to give no answer," he said, and retired into his hermitage.

It was rather weak in me I confess, but his manner, on this occasion, nettled me. Not only did there seem to lurk in it a certain calm disdain, but his perverseness seemed ungrateful, considering the undeniable good usage and indulgence he had received from me.

Again I sat ruminating what I should do. Mortified as I was at his behavior, and resolved as I had been to dismiss him when I entered my office, nevertheless I strangely felt something superstitious knocking at my heart, and forbidding me to carry out my purpose, and denouncing me for a villain if I dared to breathe one bitter word against this forlornest of mankind. At last, familiarly drawing my chair behind his screen, I sat down and said: "Bartleby, never mind, then, about revealing your history; but let me entreat you, as a friend, to comply as far as may be with the usages of this office. Say now, you will help to examine papers to-morrow or next day: in short, say now, that in a day or two you will begin to be a little reasonable:—say so, Bartleby."

"At present I would prefer not to be a little reasonable," was his mildly cadaverous reply.

Just then the folding-doors opened, and Nippers approached. He seemed suffering from an unusually bad night's rest, induced by severer indigestion than common. He overheard those final words of Bartleby.

"*Prefer not*, eh?" gritted Nippers—"I'd *prefer* him, if I were you, sir," addressing me—"I'd *prefer* him; I'd give him preferences, the stubborn mule! What is it, sir, pray, that he *prefers* not to do now?"

Bartleby moved not a limb.

"Mr. Nippers," said I, "I'd prefer that you would withdraw for the present."

Somehow, of late, I had got into the way of involuntarily using this word "prefer" upon all sorts of not exactly suitable occasions. And I trembled to think that my contact with the scrivener had already and seriously affected me in a mental way. And what further and deeper aberration might it not yet produce? This apprehension had not been without efficacy in determining me to summary measures.

As Nippers, looking very sour and sulky, was departing, Turkey blandly and deferentially approached.

"With submission, sir," said he, "yesterday I was thinking about Bartleby here, and I think that if he would but prefer to take a quart of good ale every day, it would do much towards mending him, and enabling him to assist in examining his papers."

"So you have got the word, too," said I, slightly excited.

"With submission, what word, sir?" asked Turkey, respectfully crowding himself into the contracted space behind the screen, and by so doing, making me jostle the scrivener. "What word, sir?"

"I would prefer to be left alone here," said Bartleby, as if offended at being mobbed in his privacy.

"*That's* the word, Turkey," said I—"*that's* it."

"Oh, *prefer*? oh yes—queer word. I never use it myself. But, sir, as I was saying, if he would but prefer—"

"Turkey," interrupted I, "you will please withdraw."

"Oh certainly, sir, if you prefer that I should."

As he opened the folding-door to retire, Nippers at his desk caught a glimpse of me, and asked whether I would prefer to have a certain paper copied on blue paper or white. He did not in the least roguishly accent the word "prefer." It was plain that it involuntarily rolled from his tongue. I thought to myself, surely I must get rid of a demented man, who already has in some degree turned the tongues, if not the heads of myself and clerks. But I thought it prudent not to break the dismission at once.

The next day I noticed that Bartleby did nothing but stand at his window in his dead-wall revery. Upon asking him why he did not write, he said that he had decided upon doing no more writing.

"Why, how now? what next?" exclaimed I, "do no more writing?"

"No more."

"And what is the reason?"

"Do you not see the reason for yourself?" he indifferently replied.

I looked steadfastly at him, and perceived that his eyes looked dull and glazed. Instantly it occurred to me, that his unexampled diligence in copying by his dim window for the first few weeks of his stay with me might have temporarily impaired his vision.

I was touched. I said something in condolence with him. I hinted that of course he did wisely in abstaining from writing for a while; and urged him to embrace that opportunity of taking wholesome exercise in the open air. This, however, he did not do. A few days after this, my other clerks being absent, and being in a great hurry to dispatch certain letters by the mail, I thought that, having nothing else earthly to do, Bartleby would surely be less inflexible than usual, and carry these letters to the post-office. But he blankly declined. So, much to my inconvenience, I went myself.

Still added days went by. Whether Bartleby's eyes improved or not, I could not say. To all appearance, I thought they did. But when I asked him if they did, he vouchsafed no answer. At all events, he would do no copying. At last, in reply to my urgings, he informed me that he had permanently given up copying.

"What!" exclaimed I; "suppose your eyes should get entirely well—better than ever before—would you not copy then?"

"I have given up copying," he answered, and slid aside.

He remained as ever, a fixture in my chamber. Nay—if that were possible—he became still more of a fixture than before. What was to be done? He would do nothing in the office; why should he stay there? In plain fact, he had now become a millstone to me, not only useless as a necklace, but afflictive to bear. Yet I was sorry for him. I speak less than truth when I say that, on his own account, he occasioned me uneasiness. If he would but have named a single relative or friend, I would instantly have written, and urged their taking the poor fellow away to some convenient retreat. But he seemed alone, absolutely alone in the universe. A bit of wreck in the mid-Atlantic. At length, necessities connected with my business tyrannized over all other considerations. Decently as I could,

I told Bartleby that in six days' time he must unconditionally leave the office. I warned him to take measures, in the interval, for procuring some other abode. I offered to assist him in this endeavor, if he himself would but take the first step towards a removal. "And when you finally quit me, Bartleby," added I, "I shall see that you go not away entirely unprovided. Six days from this hour, remember."

At the expiration of that period, I peeped behind the screen, and lo! Bartleby was there.

I buttoned up my coat, balanced myself; advanced slowly towards him, touched his shoulder, and said, "The time has come; you must quit this place; I am sorry for you; here is money; but you must go."

"I would prefer not," he replied, with his back still towards me.

"You *must*."

He remained silent.

Now I had an unbounded confidence in this man's common honesty. He had frequently restored to me sixpences and shillings carelessly dropped upon the floor, for I am apt to be very reckless in such shirt-button affairs. The proceeding, then, which followed will not be deemed extraordinary.

"Bartleby," said I, "I owe you twelve dollars on account; here are thirty-two; the odd twenty are yours—Will you take it?" and I handed the bills towards him.

But he made no motion.

"I will leave them here, then," putting them under a weight on the table. Then taking my hat and cane and going to the door, I tranquilly turned and added—"After you have removed your things from these offices, Bartleby, you will of course lock the door—since every one is now gone for the day but you—and if you please, slip your key underneath the mat, so that I may have it in the morning. I shall not see you again; so good-bye to you. If, hereafter, in your new place of abode, I can be of any service to you, do not fail to advise me by letter. Good-bye, Bartleby, and fare you well."

But he answered not a word; like the last column of some ruined temple, he remained standing mute and solitary in the middle of the otherwise deserted room.

As I walked home in a pensive mood, my vanity got the better of my pity. I could not but highly plume myself on my masterly management in getting rid of Bartleby. Masterly I call it, and such it must appear to any dispassionate thinker. The beauty of my procedure seemed to consist in its perfect quietness. There was no vulgar bullying, no bravado of any sort, no choleric hectoring, and striding to and fro across the apartment, jerking out vehement commands for Bartleby to bundle himself off with his beggarly traps. Nothing of the kind. Without loudly bidding Bartleby depart—as an inferior genius might have done—I *assumed* the ground that depart he must; and upon that assumption built all I had to say. The more I thought over my procedure, the more I was charmed with it. Nevertheless, next morning, upon awakening, I had my doubts—I had somehow slept off the fumes of vanity. One of the coolest and wisest hours a man has, is just after he awakes in the morning. My procedure seemed as sagacious as ever—but only in theory. How it would prove in practice—there was the rub. It was truly a beautiful thought to have assumed Bartleby's departure; but, after all, that assumption was simply my own, and none of Bartleby's. The great point was, not whether I had assumed that he would quit me, but whether he would prefer so to do. He was more a man of preferences than assumptions.

After breakfast, I walked down town, arguing the probabilities *pro* and *con*. One moment I thought it would prove a miserable failure, and Bartleby would be found all alive at my office as usual; the next moment it seemed certain that I should find his chair empty. And so I kept veering about. At the corner of Broadway and Canal Street, I saw quite an excited group of people standing in earnest conversation.

"I'll take odds he doesn't," said a voice as I passed.

"Doesn't go?—done!" said I, "put up your money."

I was instinctively putting my hand in my pocket to produce my own, when I remembered that this was an election day. The words I had overheard bore no reference to Bartleby, but to the success or non-success of some candidate for the mayoralty. In my intent frame of mind, I had, as it were, imagined that all Broadway shared in my excitement, and were debating the same question with me. I passed on, very thankful that the uproar of the street screened my momentary absentmindedness.

As I had intended, I was earlier than usual at my office door. I stood listening for a moment. All was still. He must be gone. I tried the knob.

[handwritten top margin: Lawyer's conscious is at stake, but finally his greed wins out.]

The door was locked. Yes, my procedure had worked to a charm; he indeed must be vanished. Yet a certain melancholy mixed with this: I was almost sorry for my brilliant success. I was fumbling under the door mat for the key, which Bartleby was to have left there for me, when accidently my knee knocked against a panel, producing a summoning sound, and in response a voice came to me from within—"Not yet; I am occupied."

It was Bartleby.

I was thunderstruck. For an instant I stood like the man who, pipe in mouth, was killed one cloudless afternoon long ago in Virginia, by summer lightning; at his own warm open window he was killed, and remained leaning out there upon the dreamy afternoon, till some one touched him, when he fell.

"Not gone!" I murmured at last. But again obeying that wondrous ascendancy which the inscrutable scrivener had over me, and from which ascendancy, for all my chafing, I could not completely escape, I slowly went down stairs and out into the street, and while walking round the block, considered what I should next do in this unheard-of perplexity. Turn the man out by an actual thrusting I could not; to drive him away by calling him names would not do; calling in the police was an unpleasant idea; and yet, permit him to enjoy his cadaverous triumph over me—this, too, I could not think of. What was to be done? or, if nothing could be done, was there anything further that I could *assume* in the matter? Yes, as before I had prospectively assumed that Bartleby would depart, so now I might retrospectively assume that departed he was. In the legitimate carrying out of this assumption, I might enter my office in a great hurry, and pretending not to see Bartleby at all, walk straight against him as if he were air. Such a proceeding would in a singular degree have the appearance of a home-thrust. It was hardly possible that Bartleby could withstand such an application of the doctrine of assumptions. But upon second thoughts the success of the plan seemed rather dubious. I resolved to argue the matter over with him again.

"Bartleby," said I, entering the office, with a quietly severe expression. "I am seriously displeased. I am pained, Bartleby. I had thought better of you. I had imagined you of such a gentlemanly organization, that in any delicate dilemma a slight hint would suffice—in short, an assumption. But it appears I am deceived. Why," I added, unaffectedly starting, "you have not even touched that money yet," pointing to it, just where I had left it the evening previous.

He answered nothing.

"Will you, or will you not, quit me?" I now demanded in a sudden passion, advancing close to him. *[handwritten: passive resistance to rules of society]*

"I would prefer *not* to quit you," he replied, gently emphasizing the *not*.

"What earthly right have you to stay here? Do you pay any rent? Do you pay my taxes? Or is this property yours?" *[handwritten: Thinking of money and property]*

He answered nothing. *[handwritten: rights rather than people]*

"Are you ready to go on and write now? Are *[handwritten: right]* your eyes recovered? Could you copy a small paper for me this morning? or help examine a few lines? or step round to the post-office? In a word, will you do anything at all, to give a coloring to your refusal to depart the premises?"

He silently retired into his hermitage.

I was now in such a state of nervous resentment that I thought it but prudent to check myself at present from further demonstrations. Bartleby and I were alone. I remembered the tragedy of the unfortunate Adams and the still more unfortunate Colt in the solitary office of the latter; and how poor Colt, being dreadfully incensed by Adams, and imprudently permitting himself to get wildly excited, was at unawares hurried into his fatal act—an act which certainly no man could possibly deplore more than the actor himself. Often it had occurred to me in my ponderings upon the subject that had that altercation taken place in the public street, or at a private residence, it would not have terminated as it did. It was the circumstance of being alone in a solitary office, up stairs, of a building entirely unhallowed by humanizing domestic associations—an uncarpeted office, doubtless, of a dusty, haggard sort of appearance—this it must have been, which greatly helped to enhance the irritable desperation of the hapless Colt.

But when this old Adam of resentment rose in me and tempted me concerning Bartleby, I grappled him and threw him. How? Why, simply by recalling the divine injunction: "A new commandment give I unto you, that ye love one another." Yes, this it was that saved me. Aside from higher considerations, charity often operates as a vastly wise and prudent principle—a great safeguard to its possessor. Men have committed murder for jealousy's sake, and anger's sake, and hatred's sake, and selfishness' sake, and spiritual pride's sake; but no man, that ever I heard of, ever committed a diabolical murder for sweet charity's sake. Mere self-interest, then, if no better motive can be enlisted, should, especially with high-tempered men, prompt all beings to charity and philanthropy. At any rate, upon the occasion in question, I strove to drown my exasperated feelings towards the scrivener by benevolently construing his conduct. Poor fellow, poor fellow! thought I, he don't mean anything; and besides, he has seen hard times, and ought to be indulged.

I endeavored, also, immediately to occupy myself, and at the same time to comfort my despondency. I tried to fancy, that in the course of the morning, at such time as might prove agreeable to him, Bartleby, of his own free accord, would emerge from his hermitage and take up some decided line of march in the direction of the door. But no. Half-past twelve o'clock came; Turkey began to glow in the face, overturn his inkstand, and become generally obstreperous; Nippers abated down into quietude and courtesy; Ginger Nut munched his noon apple; and Bartleby remained standing at his window in one of his profoundest dead-wall reveries. Will it be credited? Ought I to acknowledge it? That afternoon I left the office without saying one further word to him.

Some days now passed, during which, at leisure intervals I looked a little into "Edwards on the Will," and "Priestley on Necessity." Under the circumstances, those books induced a salutary feeling. Gradually I slid into the persuasion that these troubles of mine, touching the scrivener, had been all predestined from eternity, and Bartleby was billeted upon me for some mysterious purpose of an all-wise Providence, which it was not for a mere mortal like me to fathom. Yes, Bartleby, stay there behind your screen, thought I; I shall persecute you no more; you are harmless and noiseless as any of these old chairs; in short, I never feel so private as when I know you are here. At last I see it, I feel it; I penetrate to the predestinated purpose of my life. I am content. Others may have loftier parts to enact; but my mission in this world, Bartleby, is to furnish you with office-room for such period as you may see fit to remain.

I believe that this wise and blessed frame of mind would have continued with me, had it not been for the unsolicited and uncharitable remarks obtruded upon me by my professional friends who visited the rooms. But thus it often is, that the constant friction of illiberal minds wears out at last the best resolves of the more generous. Though to be sure, when I reflected upon it, it was not strange that people entering my office should be struck by the peculiar aspect of the unaccountable Bartleby, and so be tempted to throw out some sinister observations concerning him. Sometimes an attorney, having business with me, and calling at my office, and finding no one but the scrivener there, would undertake to obtain some sort of precise information from him touching my whereabouts; but without heeding his idle talk, Bartleby would remain standing immovable in the middle of the room. So after contemplating him in that position for a time, the attorney would depart, no wiser than he came.

Also, when a reference was going on, and the room full of lawyers and witnesses, and business driving fast, some deeply-occupied legal gentleman present, seeing Bartleby wholly unemployed, would request him to run round to his (the legal gentleman's) office and fetch some papers for him. Thereupon, Bartleby would tranquilly decline, and yet remain idle as before. Then the lawyer would give a great stare, and turn to me. And what could I say? At last I was made aware that all through the circle of my professional acquaintance, a whisper of wonder was running round, having reference to the strange creature I kept at my office. This worried me very much. And as the idea came upon me of his possibly turning out a long-lived man, and keep occupying my chambers, and denying my authority; and perplexing my visitors; and scandalizing my professional reputation; and casting a general gloom over the premises; keeping soul and body together to the last upon his savings (for doubtless he spent but half a dime a day), and in the end perhaps outlive me, and claim possession of my office by right of his perpetual occupancy: as all these dark anticipations crowded upon me more and more, and my friends continually intruded their relentless remarks upon the apparition in my room; a great change was wrought in me. I resolved to gather all my faculties together, and forever rid me of this intolerable incubus.

Ere revolving any complicated project, however, adapted to this end, I first simply suggested to Bartleby the propriety of his permanent departure. In a calm and serious tone, I commended the idea to his careful and mature consideration. But, having taken three days to meditate upon it, he apprised me, that his original determination remained the same; in short, that he still preferred to abide with me.

What shall I do? I now said to myself, buttoning up my coat to the last button. What shall I do? what ought I to do? what does conscience say

I *should* do with this man, or, rather, ~~ghost~~. Rid myself of him, I must; go, he shall. But how? You will not thrust him, the poor, pale, passive mortal —you will not thrust such a helpless creature out of your door? you will not dishonor yourself by such cruelty? No, I will not, I cannot do that. Rather would I let him live and die here, and then mason up his remains in the wall. What, then, will you do? For all your coaxing, he will not budge. Bribes he leaves under your own paper-weight on your table; in short, it is quite plain that he prefers to cling to you.

Then something severe, something unusual must be done. What! surely you will not have him collared by a constable, and commit his innocent pallor to the common jail? And upon what ground could you procure such a thing to be done?—a vagrant, is he? What! he a vagrant, a wanderer, who refuses to budge? It is because he will *not* be a vagrant, then, that you seek to count him *as* a vagrant. That is too absurd. No visible means of support: there I have him. Wrong again: for indubitably he *does* support himself, and that is the only unanswerable proof that any man can show of his possessing the means so to do. No more, then. Since he will not quit me, I must quit him. I will change my offices; I will move elsewhere, and give him fair notice, that if I find him on my new premises I will then proceed against him as a common trespasser.

Acting accordingly, next day I thus addressed him: "I find these chambers too far from the City Hall; the air is unwholesome. In a word, I propose to remove my offices next week, and shall no longer require your services. I tell you this now, in order that you may seek another place."

He made no reply, and nothing more was said.

On the appointed day I engaged carts and men, proceeded to my chambers, and, having but little furniture, everything was removed in a few hours. Throughout, the scrivener remained standing behind the screen, which I directed to be removed the last thing. It was withdrawn; and, being folded up like a huge folio, left him the motionless occupant of a naked room. I stood in the entry watching him a moment, while something from within me upbraided me.

I re-entered, with my hand in my pocket—and—and my heart in my mouth.

"Good-bye, Bartleby; I am going—good-bye, and God some way bless you; and take that," slipping something in his hand. But it dropped upon the floor, and then—strange to say—I tore myself from him whom I had so longed to be rid of.

Established in my new quarters, for a day or two I kept the door locked, and started at every footfall in the passages. When I returned to my rooms, after any little absence, I would pause at the threshold for an instant, and attentively listen, ere applying my key. But these fears were needless. Bartleby never came nigh me.

I thought all was going well, when a perturbed-looking stranger visited me, inquiring whether I was the person who had recently occupied rooms at No. — Wall Street.

Full of forebodings, I replied that I was.

"Then, sir," said the stranger, who proved a lawyer, "you are responsible for the man you left there. He refuses to do any copying; he refuses to do anything; he says he prefers not to; and he refuses to quit the premises."

"I am very sorry, sir," said I, with assumed tranquillity, but an inward tremor. "but, really, the man you allude to is nothing to me—he is no relation or apprentice of mine, that you should hold me responsible for him."

"In mercy's name, who is he?"

"I certainly cannot inform you. I know nothing about him. Formerly I employed him as a copyist; but he has done nothing for me now for some time past."

"I shall settle him, then—good morning, sir."

Several days passed, and I heard nothing more; and, though I often felt a charitable prompting to call at the place and see poor Bartleby, yet a certain squeamishness, of I know not what, withheld me.

All is over with him, by this time, thought I, at last, when, through another week, no further intelligence reached me. But, coming to my room the day after, I found several persons waiting at my door in a high state of nervous excitement.

"That's the man—here he comes," cried the foremost one, whom I recognized as the lawyer who had previously called upon me alone.

"You must take him away, sir, at once," cried a portly person among them, advancing upon me, and whom I knew to be the landlord of No. — Wall Street. "These gentlemen, my tenants, cannot stand it any longer; Mr. B——," pointing to the lawyer, "has turned him out of his room, and he now persists in haunting the building generally, sitting upon the banisters of the stairs by day, and sleeping in the entry by night. Everybody is concerned; clients are leaving the offices; some fears are entertained of a mob; something you must do, and that without delay."

Aghast at this torrent, I fell back before it, and would fain have locked myself in my new quarters. In vain I persisted that Bartleby was nothing to me —no more than to any one else. In vain—I was the last person known to have anything to do with him, and they held me to the terrible account. Fearful, then, of being exposed in the papers (as one person present obscurely threatened), I considered the matter, and, at length, said, that if the lawyer would give me a confidential interview with the scrivener, in his (the lawyer's) own room, I would, that afternoon, strive my best to rid them of the nuisance they complained of.

Going up stairs to my old haunt, there was Bartleby silently sitting upon the banister at the landing.

"What are you doing here, Bartleby?" said I.

"Sitting upon the banister," he mildly replied.

I motioned him into the lawyer's room, who then left us.

"Bartleby," said I, "are you aware that you are the cause of great tribulation to me, by persisting in occupying the entry after being dismissed from the office?"

No answer.

"Now one of two things must take place. Either you must do something, or something must be done to you. Now what sort of business would you like to engage in? Would you like to re-engage in copying for some one?"

"No; I would prefer not to make any change."

"Would you like a clerkship in a dry-goods store?"

"There is too much confinement about that. No, I would not like a clerkship; but I am not particular."

"Too much confinement," I cried, "why, you keep yourself confined all the time!"

"I would prefer not to take a clerkship," he rejoined, as if to settle that little item at once.

"How would a bar-tender's business suit you? There is no trying of the eye-sight in that."

"I would not like it at all; though, as I said before, I am not particular."

His unwonted wordiness inspired me. I returned to the charge.

"Well, then, would you like to travel through the country collecting bills for the merchants? That would improve your health."

"No, I would prefer to be doing something else."

"How, then, would going as a companion to Europe, to entertain some young gentleman with your conversation—how would that suit you?"

"Not at all. It does not strike me that there is anything definite about that. I like to be stationary. But I am not particular."

"Stationary you shall be, then," I cried, now losing all patience, and, for the first time in all my exasperating connection with him, fairly flying into a passion. "If you do not go away from these premises before night, I shall feel bound—indeed, I *am* bound—to—to—to quit the premises myself!" I rather absurdly concluded, knowing not with what possible threat to try to frighten his immobility into compliance. Despairing of all further efforts, I was precipitately leaving him, when a final thought occurred to me—one which had not been wholly unindulged before.

"Bartleby," said I, in the kindest tone I could assume under such exciting circumstances, "will you go home with me now—not to my office, but my dwelling—and remain there till we can conclude upon some convenient arrangement for you at our leisure? Come, let us start now, right away."

"No: at present I would prefer not to make any change at all."

I answered nothing; but, effectually dodging every one by the suddenness and rapidity of my flight, rushed from the building, ran up Wall Street towards Broadway, and, jumping into the first omnibus, was soon removed from pursuit. As soon as tranquillity returned, I distinctly perceived that I had now done all that I possibly could, both in respect to the demands of the landlord and his tenants, and with regard to my own desire and sense of duty, to benefit Bartleby, and shield him from rude persecution. I now strove to be entirely care-free and quiescent; and my conscience justified me in the attempt; though, indeed, it was not so successful as I could have wished. So fearful was I of being again hunted out by the incensed landlord and his exasperated tenants, that, surrendering my business to Nippers, for a few days, I drove about the upper part of the town and through the suburbs, in my rockaway; crossed over to Jersey City and Hoboken, and paid fugitive visits to Manhattanville and Astoria. In fact, I almost lived in my rockaway for the time.

When again I entered my office, lo, a note from the landlord lay upon the desk. I opened it with

[handwritten margin note: sounds Christian but He has no intention of bringing him home for good.]

trembling hands. It informed me that the writer had sent to the police, and had Bartleby removed to the Tombs as a vagrant. Moreover, since I knew more about him than any one else, he wished me to appear at that place, and make a suitable statement of the facts. These tidings had a conflicting effect upon me. At first I was indignant; but, at last, almost approved. The landlord's energetic, summary disposition, had led him to adopt a procedure which I do not think I would have decided upon myself; and yet, as a last resort, under such peculiar circumstances, it seemed the only plan.

As I afterwards learned, the poor scrivener, when told that he must be conducted to the Tombs, offered not the slightest obstacle, but, in his pale, unmoving way, silently acquiesced.

Some of the compassionate and curious bystanders joined the party; and headed by one of the constables arm-in-arm with Bartleby, the silent procession filed its way through all the noise, and heat, and joy of the roaring thoroughfares at noon.

The same day I received the note, I went to the Tombs, or, to speak more properly, the Halls of Justice. Seeking the right officer, I stated the purpose of my call, and was informed that the individual I described was, indeed, within. I then assured the functionary that Bartleby was a perfectly honest man, and greatly to be compassionated, however unaccountably eccentric. I narrated all I knew, and closed by suggesting the idea of letting him remain in as indulgent confinement as possible, till something less harsh might be done—though, indeed, I hardly knew what. At all events, if nothing else could be decided upon, the almshouse must receive him. I then begged to have an interview.

Being under no disgraceful charge, and quite serene and harmless in all his ways, they had permitted him freely to wander about the prison, and, especially, in the inclosed grass-platted yards thereof. And so I found him there, standing all alone in the quietest of the yards, his face towards a high wall, while all around, from the narrow slits of the jail windows, I thought I saw peering out upon him the eyes of murderers and thieves.

"Bartleby!"

"I know you," he said, without looking round— "and I want nothing to say to you."

"It was not I that brought you here, Bartleby," said I, keenly pained at his implied suspicion. "And to you, this should not be so vile a place. Nothing reproachful attaches to you by being here. And see, it is not so sad a place as one might

think. Look, there is the sky, and here is the grass."

"I know where I am," he replied, but would say nothing more, and so I left him.

As I entered the corridor again, a broad meat-like man, in an apron, accosted me, and, jerking his thumb over his shoulder, said—"Is that your friend?"

"Yes."

"Does he want to starve? If he does, let him live on the prison fare, that's all."

"Who are you?" asked I, not knowing what to make of such an unofficially speaking person in such a place.

"I am the grub-man. Such gentlemen as have friends here, hire me to provide them with something good to eat."

"Is this so?" said I, turning to the turnkey.

He said it was.

"Well, then," said I, slipping some silver into the grub-man's hands (for so they called him), "I want you to give particular attention to my friend there; let him have the best dinner you can get. And you must be as polite to him as possible."

"Introduce me, will you?" said the grub-man, looking at me with an expression which seemed to say he was all impatience for an opportunity to give a specimen of his breeding.

Thinking it would prove of benefit to the scrivener, I acquiesced; and, asking the grub-man his name, went up with him to Bartleby.

"Bartleby, this is a friend; you will find him very useful to you."

"Your sarvant, sir, your sarvant," said the grub-man, making a low salutation behind his apron. "Hope you find it pleasant here, sir; nice grounds—cool apartments—hope you'll stay with us some time—try to make it agreeable. What will you have for dinner to-day?"

"I prefer not to dine to-day," said Bartleby, turning away. "It would disagree with me; I am unused to dinners." So saying, he slowly moved to the other side of the inclosure, and took up a position fronting the dead-wall.

"How's this?" said the grub-man, addressing me with a stare of astonishment. "He's odd, ain't he?"

"I think he is a little deranged," said I, sadly.

"Deranged? deranged is it? Well, now, upon my word, I thought that friend of yourn was a gentleman forger; they are always pale and genteel-like, them forgers. I can't help pity 'em—can't help it, sir. Did you know Monroe Edwards?" he added, touchingly, and paused. Then, laying his hand

[handwritten top margin: If the best of us can't stand up for life, there is no hope for any of us.]

piteously on my shoulder, sighed, "he died of consumption at Sing-Sing. So you weren't acquainted with Monroe?"

"No, I was never socially acquainted with any forgers. But I cannot stop longer. Look to my friend yonder. You will not lose by it. I will see you again."

Some few days after this, I again obtained admission to the Tombs, and went through the corridors in quest of Bartleby; but without finding him.

"I saw him coming from his cell not long ago," said a turnkey, "may be he's gone to loiter in the yards."

So I went in that direction.

"Are you looking for the silent man?" said another turnkey, passing me. "Yonder he lies—sleeping in the yard there. 'Tis not twenty minutes since I saw him lie down."

The yard was entirely quiet. It was not accessible to the common prisoners. The surrounding walls, of amazing thickness, kept off all sounds behind them. The Egyptian character of the masonry weighed upon me with its gloom. But a soft imprisoned turf grew under foot. The heart of the eternal pyramids, it seemed, wherein, by some strange magic, through the clefts, grass-seed, dropped by birds, had sprung.

Strangely huddled at the base of the wall, his knees drawn up, and lying on his side, his head touching the cold stones, I saw the wasted Bartleby. But nothing stirred. I paused; then went close up to him; stooped over, and saw that his dim eyes were open; otherwise he seemed profoundly sleeping. Something prompted me to touch him. I felt his hand, when a tingling shiver ran up my arm and down my spine to my feet.

The round face of the grub-man peered upon me now. "His dinner is ready. Won't he dine to-day, either? Or does he live without dining?"

"Lives without dining," said I, and closed the eyes.

"Eh!—He's asleep, ain't he?"

"With kings and counselors," murmured I.

[handwritten: Suggesting democracy in afterlife. Everyone is equal in death. Oneness.]

There would seem little need for proceeding further in this history. Imagination will readily supply the meagre recital of poor Bartleby's interment. But, ere parting with the reader, let me say, that if this little narrative has sufficiently interested him, to awaken curiosity as to who Bartleby was, and what manner of life he led prior to the present narrator's making his acquaintance, I can only reply, that in such curiosity I fully share, but am wholly unable to gratify it. Yet here I hardly know whether I should divulge one little item of rumor, which came to my ear a few months after the scrivener's decease. Upon what basis it rested, I could never ascertain; and hence, how true it is I cannot now tell. But, inasmuch as this vague report has not been without a certain suggestive interest to me, however sad, it may prove the same with some others; and so I will briefly mention it. The report was this: that Bartleby had been a subordinate clerk in the Dead Letter Office at Washington, from which he had been suddenly removed by a change in the administration. When I think over this rumor, hardly can I express the emotions which seize me. Dead letters! does it not sound like dead men? Conceive a man by nature and misfortune prone to a pallid hopelessness, can any business seem more fitted to heighten it than that of continually handling these dead letters, and assorting them for the flames? For by the cart-load they are annually burned. Sometimes from out the folded paper the pale clerk takes a ring—the finger it was meant for, perhaps, moulders in the grave; a bank-note sent in swiftest charity—he whom it would relieve, nor eats nor hungers any more; pardon for those who died despairing; hope for those who died unhoping; good tidings for those who died stifled by unrelieved calamities. On errands of life, these letters speed to death.

[handwritten right margin: The letters were things that could have saved somebody. They are Bartleby.]

Ah, Bartleby! Ah, humanity!

[handwritten: Ah is sad – the tragedy and pity of it all. He couldn't fit in and was a threat to establishment. Loss of Christ is loss of humanity. If we can't save Christ we can't save ourselves. Always putting #1 first.]

From The Confidence Man (1857)

The Confidence Man has only quite recently begun to come into its own—possibly because it communicates more readily to our own age than to any American age preceding. It virtually created the genre which seems so peculiarly suited to the temper of our times: that is, the genre of apocalyptic satire (a larger and more meaningful genre than what is sometimes called "black comedy"). Mark Twain's *The Mysterious Stranger* belongs to this genre; and, coming closer to the present, Nathanael West's *The Day of the Locust*, John Barth's *The Sot-Weed Factor*, and Thomas Pynchon's *The Crying of Lot Forty-Nine*.

To these and other works, Melville, in *The Confidence Man*, bequeathed the vision of an apocalypse no less terrible for being enormously comic, the self-extinction of a world characterized by deceit and thronging with imposters and masqueraders. Central to this vision is the image of charity, the greatest of Christian virtues, fatally curdled into hatred and distrust. And prowling through such a world—feeding on it, but more importantly forcing it to declare itself for what it is—is the figure of the confidence man: the man of many roles and guises, and the first "metamorphic hero" (or hero of multiple identities) in American literary history.

The first of our two selections introduces that hero in his guises, successively, of a deaf-mute and a cripple named Black Guinea. The latter's list of the persons on board the ironically named riverboat, the *Fidèle*, is a partial list of the identities the confidence man will assume before the day is over: a nice gentleman with a weed, a gentleman with a gray coat and white tie, a "yarb-doctor" (herb-doctor), and so on. It might be added that Melville's presentation of his archetypal hustler as a crippled black beggar adds a kind of final ferocious irony to his treatment over the years of the issue of race in American society.

Yet matching that irony—as though to do total justice to the savagery inherent in so much of the white American temperament—is the bland discussion, in the second of our selections, of "the metaphysics of Indian-hating." This episode speaks for itself, though it might be explained that "the cosmopolitan"—to whom the remarks are addressed—is the last and the most imposing of the identities taken on by the title figure.

Even in perusing these brief selections, the reader should beware: for the most accomplished confidence man in the book is Melville himself, its author; and his first potential victim is the unwary reader. The narrative is at every turn a cunning assault upon our intellectual lazi-ness, our habits of thoughts, our predispositions. In any given sentence, a clause may be undercut by the clause that follows it, and the latter further undercut by its successor—as in the twisty description of the man who talks about Indian-hating to the cosmopolitan: "Though his teeth were singularly good, those same ungracious ones might have hinted that they were too good to be true; or rather, were not so good as they might be; since the best false teeth are those made with at least two or three blemishes, the more to look like life." A fairly elaborate essay could be devoted to the rhetorical divagations and the broad insinuations (for example, about truth and falsehood in human life) of that single sentence.

The action of *The Confidence Man* takes place on April 1, between dawn and midnight on the Feast of All Fools; and by an odd coincidence it was published on April 1 in 1857. Melville had finished the book the year before, and he was by this date in Venice, en route to the Holy Land, on the trip he took (see the introduction above) to restore his health. It was his last work of fiction before *Billy Budd* thirty years later. All the writing he did in the years between was in lyric, narrative, and meditational poetry.

CHAPTER 1

A Mute Goes Aboard a Boat on the Mississippi

At sunrise on a first of April, there appeared, suddenly as Manco Capac at the lake Titicaca, a man in cream-colors, at the water-side in the city of St. Louis.

His cheek was fair, his chin downy, his hair flaxen, his hat a white fur one, with a long fleecy nap. He had neither trunk, valise, carpet-bag, nor parcel. No porter followed him. He was unaccompanied by friends. From the shrugged shoulders, titters, whispers, wonderings of the crowd, it was plain that he was, in the extremest sense of the word, a stranger.

In the same moment with his advent, he stepped aboard the favorite steamer Fidèle, on the point of starting for New Orleans. Stared at, but unsaluted, with the air of one neither courting nor shunning regard, but evenly pursuing the path of duty, lead it through solitudes or cities, he held on his way along the lower deck until he chanced to come to a placard nigh the captain's office, offering a reward for the capture of a mysterious imposter, supposed to have recently arrived from the East; quite an original genius in his vocation, as would appear, though wherein his originality consisted was not clearly given; but what purported to be a careful description of his person followed.

As if it had been a theatre-bill, crowds were gathered about the announcement, and among them certain chevaliers, whose eyes, it was plain, were on the capitals, or, at least, earnestly seeking sight of them from behind intervening coats; but as for their fingers, they were enveloped in some myth; though, during a chance interval, one of these chevaliers somewhat showed his hand in purchasing from another chevalier, ex-officio a peddler of money-belts, one of his popular safe-guards, while another peddler, who was still another versatile chevalier, hawked, in the thick of the throng, the lives of Measan, the bandit of Ohio, Murrel, the pirate of the Mississippi, and the brothers Harpe, the Thugs of the Green River country, in Kentucky—creatures, with others of the sort, one and all exterminated at the time, and for the most part, like the hunted generations of wolves in the same regions, leaving comparatively few successors; which would seem cause for unalloyed gratulation, and is such to all except those who think that in new countries, where the wolves are killed off, the foxes increase.

Pausing at this spot, the stranger so far succeeded in threading his way, as at last to plant himself just beside the placard, when, producing a small slate and tracing some words upon it, he held it up before him on a level with the placard, so that they who read the one might read the other. The words were these:—

"Charity thinketh no evil."

As, in gaining his place, some little perseverance, not to say persistence, of a mildly inoffensive sort, had been unavoidable, it was not with the best relish that the crowd regarded his apparent intrusion; and upon a more attentive survey, perceiving no badge of authority about him, but rather something quite the contrary—he being of an aspect so singularly innocent; an aspect, too, which they took to be somehow inappropriate to the time and place, and inclining to the notion that his writing was of much the same sort: in short, taking him for some strange kind of simpleton, harmless enough, would he keep to himself, but not wholly unobnoxious as an intruder—they made no scruple to jostle him aside; while one, less kind than the rest, or more of a wag, by an unobserved stroke, dexterously flattened down his fleecy hat upon his head. Without readjusting it, the stranger quietly turned, and writing anew upon the slate, again held it up:—

"Charity suffereth long, and is kind."

Illy pleased with his pertinacity, as they thought it, the crowd a second time thrust him aside, and not without epithets and some buffets, all of which were unresented. But, as if at last despairing of so difficult an adventure, wherein one, apparently a non-resistant, sought to impose his presence upon fighting characters, the stranger now moved slowly away, yet not before altering his writing to this:—

"Charity endureth all things."

Shield-like bearing his slate before him, amid stares and jeers he moved slowly up and down, at his turning points again changing his inscription to—

"Charity believeth all things."

and then—

"Charity never faileth."

The word charity, as originally traced, remained throughout uneffaced, not unlike the left-hand numeral of a printed date, otherwise left for convenience in blank.

To some observers, the singularity, if not lunacy, of the stranger was heightened by his muteness, and, perhaps also, by the contrast to his proceedings afforded in the actions—quite in the wonted and sensible order of things—of the barber of the boat, whose quarters, under a smoking-saloon, and over against a bar-room, was next door but two to the captain's office. As if the long, wide, covered deck, hereabouts built up on both sides with shop-like windowed spaces, were some Constantinople arcade or bazaar, where more than one trade is plied, this river barber, aproned and slippered, but rather crusty-looking for the moment, it may be from being newly out of bed, was throwing open his premises for the day, and suitably arranging the exterior. With business-like dispatch, having rattled down his shutters, and at a palm-tree angle set out in the iron fixture his little ornamental pole, and this without overmuch tenderness for the elbows and toes of the crowd, he concluded his operations by bidding people stand still more aside, when, jumping on a stool, he hung over his door, on the customary nail, a gaudy sort of illuminated pasteboard sign, skillfully executed by himself, gilt with the likeness of a razor elbowed in readiness to shave, and also, for the public benefit, with two words not unfrequently seen ashore gracing other shops besides barbers':—

"No TRUST."

An inscription which, though in a sense not less intrusive than the contrasted ones of the stranger, did not, as it seemed, provoke any corresponding derision or surprise, much less indignation; and still less, to all appearances, did it gain for the inscriber the repute of being a simpleton.

Meanwhile, he with the slate continued moving slowly up and down, not without causing some stares to change into jeers, and some jeers into pushes, and some pushes into punches; when suddenly, in one of his turns, he was hailed from behind by two porters carrying a large trunk; but as the summons, though loud, was without effect, they accidentally or otherwise swung their burden against him, nearly overthrowing him; when, by a quick start, a peculiar inarticulate moan, and a pathetic telegraphing of his fingers, he involuntarily betrayed that he was not alone dumb, but also deaf.

Presently, as if not wholly unaffected by his reception thus far, he went forward, seating himself in a retired spot on the forecastle, nigh the foot of a ladder there leading to a deck above, up and down which ladder some of the boatmen, in discharge of their duties, were occasionally going.

From his betaking himself to this humble quarter, it was evident that, as a deck-passenger, the stranger, simple though he seemed, was not entirely ignorant of his place, though his taking a deck-passage might have been partly for convenience; as, from his having no luggage, it was probable that his destination was one of the small wayside landings within a few hours' sail. But, though he might not have a long way to go, yet he seemed already to have come from a very long distance.

Though neither soiled nor slovenly, his cream-colored suit had a tossed look, almost linty, as if, traveling night and day from some far country beyond the prairies, he had long been without the solace of a bed. His aspect was at once gentle and

jaded, and, from the moment of seating himself, increasing in tired abstraction and dreaminess. Gradually overtaken by slumber, his flaxen head drooped, his whole lamb-like figure relaxed, and, half reclining against the ladder's foot, lay motionless, as some sugar-snow in March, which, softly stealing down over night, with its white placidity startles the brown farmer peering out from his threshold at day-break.

CHAPTER 2

Showing That Many Men Have Many Minds

"Odd fish!"

"Poor fellow!"

"Who can he be?"

"Casper Hauser."

"Bless my soul!"

"Uncommon countenance."

"Green prophet from Utah."

"Humbug!"

"Singular innocence."

"Means something."

"Spirit-rapper."

"Moon-calf."

"Piteous."

"Trying to enlist interest."

"Beware of him."

"Fast asleep here, and, doubtless, pick-pockets on board."

"Kind of daylight Endymion."

"Escaped convict, worn out with dodging."

"Jacob dreaming at Luz."

Such the epitaphic comments, conflictingly spoken or thought, of a miscellaneous company, who, assembled on the overlooking, cross-wise balcony at the forward end of the upper deck near by, had not witnessed preceding occurrences.

Meantime, like some enchanted man in his grave, happily oblivious of all gossip, whether chiseled or chatted, the deaf and dumb stranger still tranquilly slept, while now the boat started on her voyage.

The great ship-canal of Ving-King-Ching, in the Flowery Kingdom, seems the Mississippi in parts, where, amply flowing between low, vine-tangled banks, flat as tow-paths, it bears the huge toppling steamers, bedizened and lacquered within like imperial junks.

Pierced along its great white bulk with two tiers of small embrasure-like windows, well above the waterline, the Fidèle, though, might at distance have been taken by strangers for some whitewashed fort on a floating isle.

Merchants on 'change seem the passengers that buzz on her decks, while, from quarters unseen, comes a murmur as of bees in the comb. Fine promenades, domed saloons, long galleries, sunny balconies, confidential passages, bridal chambers, staterooms plenty as pigeon-holes, and out-of-the-way retreats like secret drawers in an escritoire, present like facilities for publicity or privacy. Auctioneer or coiner, with equal ease, might somewhere here drive his trade.

Though her voyage of twelve hundred miles extends from apple to orange, from clime to clime, yet, like any small ferryboat, to right and left, at every landing, the huge Fidèle still receives additional passengers in exchange for those that disembark; so that, though always full of strangers, she continually, in some degree, adds to, or replaces them with strangers still more strange; like Rio Janeiro fountain, fed from the Cocovarde mountains, which is ever overflowing with strange waters, but never with the same strange particles in every part.

Though hitherto, as has been seen, the man in cream-colors had by no means passed unobserved, yet by stealing into retirement, and there going asleep and continuing so, he seemed to have courted oblivion, a boon not often withheld from so humble an applicant as he. Those staring crowds on the shore were now left far behind, seen dimly clustering like swallows on eaves; while the passengers' attention was soon drawn away to the rapidly shooting high bluffs and shot-towers on the Missouri shore, or the bluff-looking Missourians and towering Kentuckians among the throngs on the decks.

By-and-by—two or three random stoppages having been made, and the last transient memory of the slumberer vanished, and he himself, not unlikely, waked up and landed ere now—the crowd, as is usual, began in all parts to break up from a concourse into various clusters or squads, which in some cases disintegrated again into quartettes, trios, and couples, or even solitaires; involuntarily submitting to that natural law which ordains dissolution equally to the mass, as in time to the member.

As among Chaucer's Canterbury pilgrims, or those oriental ones crossing the Red Sea towards Mecca in the festival month, there was no lack of variety. Natives of all sorts, and foreigners; men of business and men of pleasure; parlor men and back-woodsmen; farm-hunters and fame-hunters; heiress-hunters, gold-hunters, buffalo-hunters, bee-hunters, happiness-hunters, truth-hunters, and still keener hunters after all these hunters. Fine ladies in slippers, and moccasined squaws; Northern speculators and Eastern philosophers; English, Irish, German, Scotch, Danes; Santa Fé traders in striped blankets, and Broadway bucks in cravats of cloth of gold; fine-looking Kentucky boatmen, and Japanese-looking Mississippi cotton-planters; Quakers in full drab, and United States soldiers in full regimentals; slaves, black, mulatto, quadroon; modish young Spanish Creoles, and old-fashioned French Jews; Mormons and Papists; Dives and Lazarus; jesters and mourners, teetotalers and convivialists, deacons and blacklegs; hard-shell Baptists and clay-eaters; grinning negroes, and Sioux chiefs solemn as high-priests. In short, a piebald parliament, an Anacharsis Cloots congress of all kinds of that multiform pilgrim species, man.

As pine, beech, birch, ash, hackmatack, hemlock, spruce, bass-wood, maple, interweave their foliage in the natural wood, so these varieties of mortals blended their varieties of visage and garb. A Tartar-like picturesqueness; a sort of pagan abandonment and assurance. Here reigned the dashing and all-fusing spirit of the West, whose type is the Mississippi itself, which, uniting the streams of the most distant and opposite zones, pours them along, helter-skelter, in one cosmopolitan and confident tide.

CHAPTER 3

In Which a Variety of Characters Appear

In the forward part of the boat, not the least attractive object, for a time, was a grotesque negro cripple, in tow-cloth attire and an old coal-sifter of a tambourine in his hand, who, owing to something wrong about his legs, was, in effect, cut down to the stature of a Newfoundland dog; his knotted black fleece and good-natured, honest black face rubbing against the upper part of people's thighs as he made shift to shuffle about, making music, such as it was, and raising a smile even from the gravest. It was curious to see him, out of his very deformity, indigence, and houselessness, so cheerily endured, raising mirth in some of that crowd, whose own purses, hearths, hearts, all their possessions, sound limbs included, could not make gay.

"What is your name, old boy?" said a purple-faced drover, putting his large purple hand on the cripple's bushy wool, as if it were the curled forehead of a black steer.

"Der Black Guinea dey calls me, sar."

"And who is your master, Guinea?"

"Oh sar, I am der dog widout massa."

"A free dog, eh? Well, on your account, I'm sorry for that, Guinea. Dogs without masters fare hard."

"So dey do, sar; so dey do. But you see, sar, dese here legs? What ge'mman want to own dese here legs?"

"But where do you live?"

"All 'long shore, sar; dough now I'se going to see brodder at der landing; but chiefly I libs in der city."

"St. Louis, ah? Where do you sleep there of nights?"

"On der floor of der good baker's oven, sar."

"In an oven? whose, pray? What baker, I should like to know, bakes such black bread in his oven, alongside of his nice white rolls, too. Who is that too charitable baker, pray?"

"Dar he be," with a broad grin lifting his tambourine high over his head.

"The sun is the baker, eh?"

"Yes sar, in der city dat good baker warms der stones for dis ole darkie when he sleeps out on der pabements o' nights."

"But that must be in the summer only, old boy. How about winter, when the cold Cossacks come clattering and jingling? How about winter, old boy?"

"Den dis poor old darkie shakes werry bad, I tell you, sar. Oh sar, oh! don't speak ob der winter," he added, with a reminiscent shiver, shuffling off into the thickest of the crowd, like a half-frozen black sheep nudging itself a cozy berth in the heart of the white flock.

Thus far not very many pennies had been given him, and, used at last to his strange looks, the less polite passengers of those in that part of the boat began to get their fill of him as a curious object; when suddenly the negro more than revived their first interest by an expedient which, whether by chance or design, was a singular temptation at once to *diversion* and charity, though, even more than his crippled limbs, it put him on a canine footing. In short, as in appearance he seemed a dog, so now, in a merry way, like a dog he began to be treated. Still shuffling among the crowd, now and then he would pause, throwing back his head and opening his mouth like an elephant for tossed apples at a menagerie; when, making a space before him, people would have a bout at a strange sort of pitch-penny game, the cripple's mouth being at once target and purse, and he hailing each expertly-caught copper with a cracked bravura from his tambourine. To be the subject of alms-giving is trying, and to feel in duty bound to appear cheerfully grateful under the trial, must be still more so; but whatever his secret emotions, he swallowed them, while still retaining each copper this side the œsophagus. And nearly always he grinned, and only once or twice did he wince, which was when certain coins, tossed by more playful almoners, came inconveniently nigh to his teeth, an accident whose unwelcomeness was not unedged by the circumstance that the pennies thus thrown proved buttons.

While this game of charity was yet at its height, a limping, gimlet-eyed, sour-faced person—it may be some discharged custom-house officer, who, suddenly stripped of convenient means of support, had concluded to be avenged on government and humanity by making himself miserable for life, either by hating or suspecting everything and everybody—this shallow unfortunate, after sundry sorry observations of the negro, began to croak out something about his deformity being a sham, got up for financial purposes, which immediately threw a damp upon the frolic benignities of the pitch-penny players.

But that these suspicions came from one who himself on a wooden leg went halt, this did not appear to strike anybody present. That cripples, above all men should be companionable, or, at least, refrain from picking a fellow-limper to pieces, in short, should have a little sympathy in common misfortune, seemed not to occur to the company.

Meantime, the negro's countenance, before marked with even more than patient good-nature, drooped into a heavy-hearted expression, full of the most painful distress. So far abased beneath its proper physical level, that Newfoundland-dog face turned in passively hopeless appeal, as if instinct told it that the right or the wrong might not have overmuch to do with whatever wayward mood superior intelligences might yield to.

But instinct, though knowing, is yet a teacher set below reason, which itself says, in the grave words of Lysander in the comedy, after Puck has made a sage of him with his spell:—

"The will of man is by his reason swayed."

So that, suddenly change as people may, in their dispositions, it is not always waywardness, but improved judgment, which, as in Lysander's case, or the present, operates with them.

Yes, they began to scrutinize the negro curiously enough; when, emboldened by this evidence of the efficacy of his words, the wooden-legged man hobbled up to the negro, and, with the air of a beadle, would, to prove his alleged imposture on the spot, have stripped him and then driven him away, but was prevented by the crowd's clamor, now taking part with the poor fellow, against one who had just before turned nearly all minds the other way. So he with the wooden leg was forced to retire; when the rest, finding themselves left sole judges in the case, could not resist the opportunity of acting the part: not because it is a human weakness to take pleasure in sitting in judgment upon one in a box, as surely this unfortunate negro now was, but that it strangely sharpens human perceptions, when, instead of standing by and having their fellow-feelings touched by the sight of an alleged culprit severely handled by some one justiciary, a crowd suddenly come to be all justiciaries in the same case themselves; as in Arkansas once, a man proved guilty, by law, of murder, but whose condemnation was deemed unjust by the people, so that they rescued him to try him themselves; whereupon, they, as it turned out, found him even guiltier than the court had done, and forthwith proceeded to execution; so that the gallows presented the truly warning spectacle of a man hanged by his friends.

But not to such extremities, or anything like them, did the present crowd come; they, for the time, being content with putting the negro fairly and discreetly to the question; among other things, asking him, had he any documentary proof, any plain paper about him, attesting that his case was not a spurious one.

"No, no, dis poor ole darkie haint none o' dem waloable papers," he wailed.

"But is there not some one who can speak a good word for you?" here said a person newly arrived from another part of the boat, a young Episcopal clergyman, in a long, straight-bodied black coat; small in stature, but manly; with a clear face and blue eye; innocence, tenderness, and good sense triumvirate in his air.

"Oh yes, oh yes, ge'mmen," he eagerly answered, as if his memory, before suddenly frozen up by cold charity, as suddenly thawed back into fluidity at the first kindly word. "Oh yes, oh yes, dar is

aboard here a werry nice, good ge'mman wid a weed, and a ge'mman in a gray coat and white tie, what knows all about me; and a ge'mman wid a big book, too; and a yarb-doctor; and a ge'mman in a yaller west; and a ge'mman wid a brass plate; and a ge'mman in a wiolet robe; and a ge'mman as is a sodjer; and ever so many good, kind, honest ge'mmen more abord what knows me and will speak for me, God bress 'em; yes, and what knows me as well as dis poor old darkie knows hisself, God bress him! Oh, find 'em, find 'em," he earnestly added, "and let 'em come quick, and show you all, ge'mmen, dat dis poor ole darkie is werry well wordy of all you kind ge'mmen's kind confidence."

"But how are we to find all these people in this great crowd?" was the question of a bystander, umbrella in hand; a middle-aged person, a country merchant apparently, whose natural good-feeling had been made at least cautious by the unnatural ill-feeling of the discharged custom-house officer.

"Where are we to find them?" half-rebukefully echoed the young Episcopal clergyman. "I will go find one to begin with," he quickly added, and, with kind haste suiting the action to the word, away he went.

"Wild goose chase!" croaked he with the wooden leg, now again drawing nigh. "Don't believe there's a soul of them aboard. Did ever beggar have such heaps of fine friends? He can walk fast enough when he tries, a good deal faster than I; but he can lie yet faster. He's some white operator, betwisted and painted up for a decoy. He and his friends are all humbugs."

"Have you no charity, friend?" here in self-subdued tones, singularly contrasted with his unsubdued person, said a Methodist minister, advancing; a tall, muscular, martial-looking man, a Tennesseean by birth, who in the Mexican war had been volunteer chaplain to a volunteer rifle-regiment.

"Charity is one thing, and truth is another," rejoined he with the wooden leg: "he's a rascal, I say."

"But why not, friend, put as charitable a construction as one can upon the poor fellow?" said the soldier-like Methodist, with increased difficulty maintaining a pacific demeanor towards one whose own asperity seemed so little to entitle him to it: "he looks honest, don't he?"

"Looks are one thing, and facts are another," snapped out the other perversely; "and as to your constructions, what construction can you put upon a rascal, but that a rascal he is?"

"Be not such a Canada thistle," urged the Methodist, with something less of patience than before. "Charity, man, charity."

"To where it belongs with your charity! to heaven with it!" again snapped out the other, diabolically; "here on earth, true charity dotes, and false charity plots. Who betrays a fool with a kiss, the charitable fool has the charity to believe is in love with him, and the charitable knave on the stand gives charitable testimony for his comrade in the box."

"Surely, friend," returned the noble Methodist, with much ado restraining his still waxing indignation—"surely, to say the least, you forget yourself. Apply it home," he continued, with exterior calmness tremulous with inkept emotion. "Suppose, now, I should exercise no charity in judging your own character by the words which have fallen from you; what sort of vile, pitiless man do you think I would take you for?"

"No doubt"—with a grin—"some such pitiless man as has lost his piety in much the same way that the jockey loses his honesty."

"And how is that, friend?" still conscientiously holding back the old Adam in him, as if it were a mastiff he had by the neck.

"Never you mind how it is"—with a sneer; "but all horses aint virtuous, no more than all men kind; and come close to, and much dealt with, some things are catching. When you find me a virtuous jockey, I will find you a benevolent wise man."

"Some insinuation there."

"More fool you that are puzzled by it."

"Reprobate!" cried the other, his indignation now at last almost boiling over; "godless reprobate! if charity did not restrain me, I could call you by names you deserve."

"Could you, indeed?" with an insolent sneer.

"Yea, and teach you charity on the spot," cried the goaded Methodist, suddenly catching this exasperating opponent by his shabby coat-collar, and shaking him till his timber-toe clattered on the deck like a nine-pin. "You took me for a noncombatant, did you?—thought, seedy coward that you are, that you could abuse a Christian with impunity. You find your mistake"—with another hearty shake.

"Well said and better done, church militant!" cried a voice.

"The white cravat against the world!" cried another.

"Bravo, bravo!" chorused many voices, with like enthusiasm taking sides with the resolute champion.

"You fools!" cried he with the wooden leg, writhing himself loose and inflamedly turning upon the throng; "you flock of fools, under this captain of fools, in this ship of fools!"

.   .   .

CHAPTER 25

The Cosmopolitan Makes an Acquaintance

In the act of retiring, the cosmopolitan was met by a passenger, who, with the bluff *abord* of the West, thus addressed him, though a stranger.

"Queer 'coon, your friend. Had a little skrimmage with him myself. Rather entertaining old 'coon, if he wasn't so deuced analytical. Reminded me somehow of what I've heard about Colonel John Moredock, of Illinois, only your friend ain't quite so good a fellow at bottom, I should think."

It was in the semicircular porch of a cabin, opening a recess from the deck, lit by a zoned lamp swung overhead, and sending its light vertically down, like the sun at noon. Beneath the lamp stood the speaker, affording to any one disposed to it no unfavorable chance for scrutiny; but the glance now resting on him betrayed no such rudeness.

A man neither tall nor stout, neither short nor gaunt; but with a body fitted, as by measure, to the service of his mind. For the rest, one less favored perhaps in his features than his clothes; and of these the beauty may have been less in the fit than the cut; to say nothing of the fineness of the nap, seeming out of the keeping with something the reverse of fine in the skin; and the unsuitableness of a violet vest, sending up sunset hues to a countenance betokening a kind of bilious habit.

But, upon the whole, it could not be fairly said that his appearance was unprepossessing; indeed, to the congenial, it would have been doubtless not uncongenial; while to others, it could not fail to be at least curiously interesting, from the warm air of florid cordiality, contrasting itself with one knows not what kind of aguish sallowness of saving discretion lurking behind it. Ungracious critics might have thought that the manner flushed the man, something in the same fictitious way that the vest flushed the cheek. And though his teeth were singularly good, those same ungracious ones might have hinted that they were too good to be true; or rather, were not so good as they might be; since the best false teeth are those made with at least two or three blemishes, the more to look like life. But fortunately for better constructions, no such critics had the stranger now in eye; only the cosmopolitan, who, after, in the first place, acknowledging his advances with a mute salute—in which acknowledgment, if there seemed less of spirit than in his way of accosting the Missourian, it was probably because of the saddening sequel of that late interview—thus now replied: "Colonel John Moredock," repeating the words abstractedly; "that surname recalls reminiscences. Pray," with enlivened air, "was he anyway connected with the Moredocks of Moredock Hall, Northamptonshire, England?"

"I know no more of the Moredocks of Moredock Hall than of the Burdocks of Burdock Hut," returned the other, with the air somehow of one whose fortunes had been of his own making; "all I know is, that the late Colonel John Moredock was a famous one in his time; eye like Lochiel's; finger like a trigger; nerve like a catamount's; and with but two little oddities—seldom stirred without his rifle, and hated Indians like snakes."

"Your Moredock, then, would seem a Moredock of Misanthrope Hall—the Woods. No very sleek creature, the colonel, I fancy."

"Sleek or not, he was no uncombed one, but silky bearded and curly headed, and to all but Indians juicy as a peach. But Indians—how the late Colonel John Moredock, Indian-hater of Illinois, did hate Indians, to be sure!"

"Never heard of such a thing. Hate Indians? Why should he or anybody else hate Indians? I admire Indians. Indians I have always heard to be one of the finest of the primitive races, possessed of many heroic virtues. Some noble women, too. When I think of Pocahontas, I am ready to love Indians. Then there's Massasoit, and Philip of Mount Hope, and Tecumseh, and Red-Jacket, and Logan—all heroes; and there's the Five Nations, and Araucanians—federations and communities of heroes. God bless me; hate Indians? Surely the late Colonel John Moredock must have wandered in his mind."

"Wandered in the woods considerably, but

never wandered elsewhere, that I ever heard."

"Are you in earnest? Was there ever one who so made it his particular mission to hate Indians that, to designate him, a special word has been coined—Indian-hater?"

"Even so."

"Dear me, you take it very calmly.—But really, I would like to know something about this Indian-hating. I can hardly believe such a thing to be. Could you favor me with a little history of the extraordinary man you mentioned?"

"With all my heart," and immediately stepping from the porch, gestured the cosmopolitan to a settee near by, on deck. "There, sir, sit you there, and I will sit here beside you—you desire to hear of Colonel John Moredock. Well, a day in my boyhood is marked with a white stone—the day I saw the colonel's rifle, powder-horn attached, hanging in a cabin on the West bank of the Wabash river. I was going westward a long journey through the wilderness with my father. It was nigh noon, and we had stopped at the cabin to unsaddle and bait. The man at the cabin pointed out the rifle, and told whose it was, adding that the colonel was that moment sleeping on wolf-skins in the corn-loft above, so we must not talk very loud, for the colonel had been out all night hunting (Indians, mind), and it would be cruel to disturb his sleep. Curious to see one so famous, we waited two hours over, in hopes he would come forth; but he did not. So, it being necessary to get to the next cabin before nightfall, we had at last to ride off without the wished-for satisfaction. Though, to tell the truth, I, for one, did not go away entirely ungratified, for, while my father was watering the horses, I slipped back into the cabin, and stepping a round or two up the ladder, pushed my head through the trap, and peered about. Not much light in the loft; but off, in the further corner, I saw what I took to be the wolf-skins, and on them a bundle of something, like a drift of leaves; and at one end, what seemed a moss-ball; and over it, deer-antlers branched; and close by, a small squirrel sprang out from a maple-bowl of nuts, brushed the moss-ball with his tail, through a hole, and vanished, squeaking. That bit of woodland scene was all I saw. No Colonel Moredock there, unless that moss-ball was his curly head, seen in the back view. I would have gone clear up, but the man below had warned me, that though, from his camping habits, the colonel could sleep through thunder, he was for the same cause amazing quick to waken at the sound of footsteps, however soft, and especially if human."

"Excuse me," said the other, softly laying his hand on the narrator's wrist, "but I fear the colonel was of a distrustful nature—little or no confidence. He *was* a little suspicious-minded, wasn't he?"

"Not a bit. Knew too much. Suspected nobody, but was not ignorant of Indians. Well: though, as you may gather, I never fully saw the man, yet, have I, one way and another, heard about as much of him as any other; in particular, have I heard his history again and again from my father's friend, James Hall, the judge, you know. In every company being called upon to give this history, which none could better do, the judge at last fell into a style so methodic, you would have thought he spoke less to mere auditors than to an invisible amanuensis; seemed talking for the press; very impressive way with him indeed. And I, having an equally impressible memory, think that, upon a pinch, I can render you the judge upon the colonel almost word for word."

"Do so, by all means," said the cosmopolitan, well pleased.

"Shall I give you the judge's philosophy, and all?"

"As to that," rejoined the other gravely, pausing over the pipe-bowl he was filling, "the desirableness, to a man of a certain mind, of having another man's philosophy given, depends considerably upon what school of philosophy that other man belongs to. Of what school or system was the judge, pray?"

"Why, though he knew how to read and write, the judge never had much schooling. But, I should say he belonged, if anything, to the free-school system. Yes, a true patriot, the judge went in strong for free-schools."

"In philosophy? The man of a certain mind, then, while respecting the judge's patriotism, and not blind to the judge's capacity for narrative, such as he may prove to have, might, perhaps, with prudence, waive an opinion of the judge's probable philosophy. But I am no rigorist; proceed, I beg; his philosophy or not, as you please."

"Well, I would mostly skip that part, only, to begin, some reconnoitering of the ground in a philosophical way the judge always deemed indispensable with strangers. For you must know that Indian-hating was no monopoly of Colonel Moredock's; but a passion, in one form or other, and to a degree, greater or less, largely shared among the class to which he belonged. And Indian-hating still exists; and, no doubt, will continue to exist, so long as Indians do. Indian-hating, then, shall be my first theme, and Colonel Moredock, the Indian-hater, my next and last."

With which the stranger, settling himself in his seat, commenced—the hearer paying marked regard, slowly smoking, his glance, meanwhile, steadfastly abstracted towards the deck, but his right ear so disposed towards the speaker that each word came through as little atmospheric intervention as possible. To intensify the sense of hearing, he seemed to sink the sense of sight. No complaisance of mere speech could have been so flattering, or expressed such striking politeness as this mute eloquence of thoroughly digesting attention.

CHAPTER 26

Containing the Metaphysics of Indian-Hating, According to the Views of One Evidently Not So Prepossessed as Rousseau in Favor of Savages

"The judge always began in these words: 'The backwoodsman's hatred of the Indian has been a topic for some remark. In the earlier times of the frontier the passion was thought to be readily accounted for. But Indian rapine having mostly ceased through regions where it once prevailed, the philanthropist is surprised that Indian-hating has not in like degree ceased with it. He wonders why the backwoodsman still regards the red man in much the same spirit that a jury does a murderer, or a trapper a wild cat—a creature, in whose behalf mercy were not wisdom; truce is vain; he must be executed.

" 'A curious point,' the judge would continue, 'which perhaps not everybody, even upon explanation, may fully understand; while, in order for any one to approach to an understanding, it is necessary for him to learn, or if he already know, to bear in mind, what manner of man the backwoodsman is; as for what manner of man the Indian is, many know, either from history or experience.

" 'The backwoodsman is a lonely man. He is a thoughtful man. He is a man strong and unsophisticated. Impulsive, he is what some might call unprincipled. At any rate, he is self-willed; being one who less hearkens to what others may say about things, than looks for himself, to see what are things themselves. If in straits, there are few to help; he must depend upon himself; he must continually look to himself. Hence self-reliance, to the degree of standing by his own judgment, though it stand alone. Not that he deems himself infallible; too many mistakes in following trials prove the contrary; but he thinks that nature destines such sagacity as she has given him, as she destines it to the 'possum. To these fellow-beings of the wilds their untutored sagacity is their best dependence. If with either it prove faulty, if the 'possum's betray it to the trap, or the backwoodsman's mislead him into ambuscade, there are consequences to be undergone, but no self-blame. As with the 'possum, instincts prevail with the backwoodsman over precepts. Like the 'possum, the backwoodsman presents the spectacle of a creature dwelling exclusively among the works of God, yet these, truth must confess, breed little in him of a godly mind. Small bowing and scraping is his, further than when with bent knee he points his rifle, or picks its flint. With few companions, solitude by necessity his lengthened lot, he stands the trial—no slight one, since, next to dying, solitude, rightly borne, is perhaps of fortitude the most rigorous test. But not merely is the backwoodsman content to be alone, but in no few cases is anxious to be so. The sight of smoke ten miles off is provocation to one more remove from man, one step deeper into nature. Is it that he feels that whatever man may be, man is not the universe? that glory, beauty, kindness, are not all engrossed by him? that as the presence of man frights birds away, so, many bird-like thoughts? Be that how it will, the backwoodsman is not without some fineness to his nature. Hairy Orson as he looks, it may be with him as with the Shetland seal—beneath the bristles lurks the fur.

" 'Though held in a sort of barbarian, the backwoodsman would seem to America what Alexander was to Asia—captain in the vanguard of conquering civilization. Whatever the nation's growing opulence or power, does it not lackey his heels? Pathfinder, provider of security to those who come after him, for himself he asks nothing but hardship. Worthy to be compared with Moses in the Exodus, or the Emperor Julian in Gaul, who on foot, and bare-browed, at the head of covered or mounted legions, marched so through the elements, day after day. The tide of emigration, let it roll as it will, never overwhelms the backwoodsman into itself; he rides upon advance, as the Polynesian upon the comb of the surf.

" 'Thus, though he keep moving on through life,

he maintains with respect to nature much the same unaltered relation throughout; with her creatures, too, including panthers and Indians. Hence, it is not unlikely that, accurate as the theory of the Peace Congress may be with respect to those two varieties of beings, among others, yet the backwoodsman might be qualified to throw out some practical suggestions.

" 'As the child born to a backwoodsman must in turn lead his father's life—a life which, as related to humanity, is related mainly to Indians—it is thought best not to mince matters, out of delicacy; but to tell the boy pretty plainly what an Indian is, and what he must expect from him. For however charitable it may be to view Indians as members of the Society of Friends, yet to affirm them such to one ignorant of Indians, whose lonely path lies a long way through their lands, this, in the event, might prove not only injudicious but cruel. At least something of this kind would seem the maxim upon which backwoods' education is based. Accordingly, if in youth the backwoodsman incline to knowledge, as is generally the case, he hears little from his schoolmasters, the old chroniclers of the forest, but histories of Indian lying, Indian theft, Indian double-dealing, Indian fraud and perfidy, Indian want of conscience, Indian blood-thirstiness, Indian diabolism—histories which, though of wild woods, are almost as full of things unangelic as the Newgate Calendar or the Annals of Europe. In these Indian narratives and traditions the lad is thoroughly grounded. "As the twig is bent the tree's inclined." The instinct of antipathy against an Indian grows in the backwoodsman with the sense of good and bad, right and wrong. In one breath he learns that a brother is to be loved, and an Indian to be hated.

" 'Such are the facts,' the judge would say, 'upon which, if one seek to moralize, he must do so with an eye to them. It is terrible that one creature should so regard another, should make it conscience to abhor an entire race. It is terrible; but is it surprising? Surprising, that one should hate a race which he believes to be red from a cause akin to that which makes some tribes of garden insects green? A race whose name is upon the frontier a *memento mori*; painted to him in every evil light; now a horse-thief like those in Moyamensing; now an assassin like a New York rowdy; now a treaty-breaker like an Austrian; now a Palmer with poisoned arrows; now a judicial murderer and Jeffries, after a fierce farce of trial condemning his victim to bloody death; or a Jew with hospitable speeches cozening some fainting stranger into ambuscade, there to burke him, and account it a deed grateful to Manitou, his god.

" 'Still, all this is less advanced as truths of the Indians than as examples of the backwoodsman's impression of them—in which the charitable may think he does them some injustice. Certain it is, the Indians themselves think so; quite unanimously, too. The Indians, indeed, protest against the backwoodsman's view of them; and some think that one cause of their returning his antipathy so sincerely as they do, is their moral indignation at being so libeled by him, as they really believe and say. But whether, on this or any point, the Indians should be permitted to testify for themselves, to the exclusion of other testimony, is a question that may be left to the Supreme Court. At any rate, it has been observed that when an Indian becomes a genuine proselyte to Christianity (such cases, however, not being very many; though, indeed, entire tribes are sometimes nominally brought to the true light,) he will not in that case conceal his enlightened conviction, that his race's portion by nature is total depravity; and, in that way, as much as admits that the backwoodsman's worst idea of it is not very far from true; while, on the other hand, those red men who are the greatest sticklers for the theory of Indian virtue, and Indian loving-kindness, are sometimes the arrantest horse-thieves and tomahawkers among them. So, at least, avers the backwoodsman. And though, knowing the Indian nature, as he thinks he does, he fancies he is not ignorant that an Indian may in some points deceive himself almost as effectually as in bush-tactics he can another, yet his theory and his practice as above contrasted seem to involve an inconsistency so extreme, that the backwoodsman only accounts for it on the supposition that when a tomahawking red man advances the notion of the benignity of the red race, it is but part and parcel with that subtle strategy which he finds so useful in war, in hunting, and the general conduct of life.'

"In further explanation of that deep abhorrence with which the backwoodsman regards the savage, the judge used to think it might perhaps a little help, to consider what kind of stimulus to it is furnished in those forest histories and traditions before spoken of. In which behalf, he would tell the story of the little colony of Wrights and Weavers, originally seven cousins from Virginia, who, after successive removals with their families, at last established themselves near the southern frontier of the Bloody Ground, Kentucky: 'They were strong, brave men; but, unlike many of the pioneers in those days, theirs was no love of conflict for conflict's sake. Step by step they had been lured to their lonely resting-place by the ever-beckoning seductions of a fertile and virgin land, with a singular exemption, during the march, from Indian molestation. But clearings made and houses built, the bright shield was soon to turn its other side. After repeated persecutions and eventual hostilities, forced on them by a dwindled tribe in their neighborhood—persecutions resulting in loss of crops and cattle; hostilities in which they lost two of their number, illy to be spared, besides others getting painful wounds—the five remaining cousins made, with some serious concessions, a kind of treaty with Mocmohoc, the chief—being to this induced by the harryings of the enemy, leaving them no peace. But they were further prompted, indeed, first incited, by the suddenly changed ways of Mocmohoc, who, though hitherto deemed a savage almost perfidious as Cæsar Borgia, yet now put on a seeming the reverse of this, engaging to bury the hatchet, smoke the pipe, and be friends forever; not friends in the mere sense of renouncing enmity, but in the sense of kindliness, active and familiar.

" 'But what the chief now seemed, did not wholly blind them to what the chief had been; so that, though in no small degree influenced by his change of bearing, they still distrusted him enough to covenant with him, among other articles on their side, that though friendly visits should be exchanged between the wigwams and the cabins, yet the five cousins should never, on any account, be expected to enter the chief's lodge together. The intention was, though they reserved it, that if ever, under the guise of amity, the chief should mean them mischief, and effect it, it should be but partially; so that some of the five might survive, not only for their families' sake, but also for retribution's. Nevertheless, Mocmohoc did, upon a time, with such fine art and pleasing carriage win their confidence, that he brought them all together to a feast of bear's meat, and there, by stratagem, ended them. Years after, over their calcined bones and those of all their families, the chief, reproached for his treachery by a proud hunter whom he had made captive, jeered out, "Treachery? pale face! 'Twas they who broke their covenant first, in coming all together; they that broke it first, in trusting Mocmohoc." '

"At this point the judge would pause, and lifting

his hand, and rolling his eyes, exclaim in a solemn enough voice, 'Circling wiles and bloody lusts. The acuteness and genius of the chief but made him the more atrocious.'

"After another pause, he would begin an imaginary kind of dialogue between a backwoodsman and a questioner:

" 'But are all Indians like Mocmohoc?—Not all have proved such; but in the least harmful may lie his germ. There is an Indian nature. "Indian blood is in me," is the half-breed's threat.—But are not some Indians kind?—Yes, but kind Indians are mostly lazy, and reputed simple—at all events are seldom chiefs; chiefs among the red men being taken from the active, and those accounted wise. Hence, with small promotion, kind Indians have but proportionate influence. And kind Indians may be forced to do unkind biddings. So "beware the Indian, kind or unkind," said Daniel Boone, who lost his sons by them.—But, have all you backwoodsmen been some way victimized by Indians? —No.—Well, and in certain cases may not at least some few of you be favored by them?—Yes, but scarce one among us so self-important, or so selfish-minded, as to hold his personal exemption from Indian outrage such a set-off against the contrary experience of so many others, as that he must needs, in a general way, think well of Indians; or, if he do, an arrow in his flank might suggest a pertinent doubt.

" 'In short,' according to the judge, 'if we at all credit the backwoodsman, his feeling against Indians, to be taken aright, must be considered as being not so much on his own account as on others', or jointly on both accounts. True it is, scarce a family he knows but some member of it, or connection, has been by Indians maimed or scalped. What avails, then, that some one Indian, or some two or three, treat a backwoodsman friendly-like? He fears me, he thinks. Take my rifle from me, give him motive, and what will come? Or if not so, how know I what involuntary preparations may be going on in him for things as unbeknown in present time to him as me—a sort of chemical preparation in the soul for malice, as chemical preparation in the body for malady.'

"Not that the backwoodsman ever used those words, you see, but the judge found him expression for his meaning. And this point he would conclude with saying, that, 'what is called a "friendly Indian" is a very rare sort of creature; and well it was so, for no ruthlessness exceeds that of a "friendly Indian" turned enemy. A coward friend, he makes a valiant foe.

" 'But, thus far the passion in question has been viewed in a general way as that of a community. When in his due share of this the backwoodsman adds his private passion, we have then the stock out of which is formed, if formed at all, the Indian-hater *par excellence*.'

"The Indian-hater *par excellence* the judge defined to be one 'who, having with his mother's milk drank in small love for red men, in youth or early manhood, ere the sensibilities become osseous, receives at their hand some signal outrage, or, which in effect is much the same, some of his kin have, or some friend. Now, nature all around him by her solitudes wooing or bidding him muse upon this matter, he accordingly does so, till the thought develops such attraction, that much as straggling vapors troop from all sides to a storm-cloud, so straggling thoughts of other outrages troop to the nucleus thought, assimilate with it, and swell it. At last, taking counsel with the elements, he comes to his resolution. An intenser Hannibal, he makes a vow, the hate of which is a vortex from whose suction scarce the remotest chip of the guilty race may reasonably feel secure. Next, he declares himself and settles his temporal affairs. With the solemnity of a Spaniard turned monk, he takes leave of his kin; or rather, these leave-takings have something of the still more impressive finality of death-bed adieus. Last, he commits himself to the forest primeval; there, so long as life shall be his, to act upon a calm, cloistered scheme of strategical, implacable, and lonesome vengeance. Ever on the noiseless trail; cool, collected, patient; less seen than felt; snuffing, smelling—a Leather-stocking Nemesis. In the settlements he will not be seen again; in eyes of old companions tears may start at some chance thing that speaks of him; but they never look for him, nor call; they know he will not come. Suns and seasons fleet; the tiger-lily blows and falls; babes are born and leap in their mothers' arms; but, the Indian-hater is good as gone to his long home, and "Terror" is his epitaph.'

"Here the judge, not unaffected, would pause again, but presently resume: 'How evident that in strict speech there can be no biography of an Indian-hater *par excellence*, any more than one of a sword-fish, or other deep-sea denizen; or, which is still less imaginable, one of a dead man. The career of the Indian-hater *par excellence* has the impenetrability of the fate of a lost steamer. Doubtless, events, terrible ones, have happened, must have happened; but the powers that be in nature have taken order that they shall never become news.

" 'But, luckily for the curious, there is a species of diluted Indian-hater, one whose heart proves not so steely as his brain. Soft enticements of domestic life too often draw him from the ascetic trail; a monk who apostatizes to the world at times. Like a mariner, too, though much abroad, he may have a wife and family in some green harbor which he does not forget. It is with him as with the Papist converts in Senegal; fasting and mortification prove hard to bear.'

"The judge, with his usual judgment, always thought that the intense solitude to which the Indian-hater consigns himself, has, by its overawing influence, no little to do with relaxing his vow. He would relate instances where, after some months' lonely scoutings, the Indian-hater is suddenly seized with a sort of calenture; hurries openly towards the first smoke, though he knows it is an Indian's, announces himself as a lost hunter, gives the savage his rifle, throws himself upon his charity, embraces him with much affection, imploring the privilege of living a while in his sweet companionship. What is too often the sequel of so distempered a procedure may be best known by those who best know the Indian. Upon the whole, the judge, by two and thirty good and sufficient reasons, would maintain that there was no known vocation whose consistent following calls for such self-containings as that of the Indian-hater *par excellence*. In the highest view, he considered such a soul one peeping out but once an age.

"For the diluted Indian-hater, although the vacations he permits himself impair the keeping of the character, yet, it should not be overlooked that this is the man who, by his very infirmity, enables us to form surmises, however inadequate, of what Indian-hating in its perfection is."

Billy Budd, Sailor

The manuscript of *Billy Budd*, the story Melville left unfinished at the time of his death in 1891, lay undiscovered among his belongings until 1924. It was then turned up by Raymond Weaver, at work on a doctoral dissertation about Melville, when Elizabeth Melville Metcalf gave him permission to look through her great-grandfather's papers. In 1948, F. Baron Freeman prepared a much revised edition of *Billy Budd*; and *corrigenda* were added to that version in 1953 by Elizabeth Freeman. Finally, in 1962, Harrison Hayford and Merton M. Sealts, Jr., brought out *Billy Budd, Sailor: An Inside Narrative*. This is probably as definitive an edition as we shall ever have.

Hayford and Sealts juxtapose what they call "the Genetic Text . . . , an exact transcription of what appeared in the *Billy Budd* manuscript at the time of Melville's death," and a "Reading Text," the actual wording "that in our judgment most closely approximates Melville's final intention had a new fair copy been made without his engaging in further expansion or revision." We have called this edition an act of creative scholarship, since in at least a marginal way the editors have taken part in the writing of this remarkable story, the last work by America's greatest writer of fiction. The case was not as difficult, perhaps, as that of Emily Dickinson's poems, since she often gave no indication of her choice among alternate scribbled lines or stanzas; Melville's intentions can, with the most painstaking scrutiny, usually be made out. But it is a most notable editorial achievement, and we are grateful indeed to be allowed to make use of it.

In the earliest phase of composition, Melville envisaged Billy not as an innocent youth, but as the "Captain of a gun's crew in a seventy-four" (a man-of-war mounting seventy-four guns), who was "condemned at sea to be hung as the ringleader of an incipient mutiny." He was, in fact, only the subject of a headnote to accompany the poem "Billy in the Darbies," itself presumably quite different from the poem as we now have it. The major changes in the story took place, apparently, in 1886 and 1887, when Billy became the radiant young foretopman, Claggart was introduced as his adversary, and Vere, though still rather shadowy, appeared in the background.

Some of the other changes can be mentioned. We have alluded, in our general introduction, to the deletion of what, in the previous standard version of *Billy Budd*, had been a prefatory reflection on the French Revolution, Napoleon, the mutinies in the British fleet, and the widespread air of unrest throughout Europe. Previous versions, too, retained Melville's first name for Vere's ship, the *Indomitable*; Hayford and Sealts make clear that Melville planned to change that name (and did so part way through the manuscript) to *Bellipotent*—perhaps to make more constant one's awareness of that imminent threat of war that so affects the action (the new name is suggestive of power and pride in a time of war). Like two of the other original chapters, what is now Chapter 13 was headed by what looked like a title: "Pale ire, envy and despair"—words used by Milton to describe Satan in *Paradise Lost*, Book 4 ("Thus while he spake, each passion dimm'd his face,/Thrice changed with pale ire, envy and despair"), and intended obviously to associate Claggart's play of contrasting emotions with those of Milton's fallen angel. Melville must have decided that he did not need to lean upon Milton, but could achieve his effect by his own descriptive language.

More important than any of this, perhaps, is the location of the "outside narrative," the report in the naval chronicle about "the extreme depravity of the criminal," William Budd, and the "respectable and discreet" character and "strong patriotic impulse" of Budd's victim, John Claggart. At one stage in the writing, the narrative *concluded* with this news story. Had Melville left it so, *Billy Budd* would have ended on a note of scathing and unmitigated irony, and with the implication that Billy's death was an event without meaning and without dignity, a subject at most for bitter laughter. Some critics of Melville, indeed, offer just such an "ironic" reading of the novel. But Melville chose instead to conclude by watching the story of Billy Budd become a legendary memory, to take on some-

thing like the proportions of a religious experience (to Billy's deckmates, a chip from the spar from which he had been hung "was as a piece of the Cross") and be enshrined in a ballad. (For some further discussion of the poem "Billy in the Darbies," see our section on Melville's poetry.)

1

In the time before steamships, or then more frequently than now, a stroller along the docks of any considerable seaport would occasionally have his attention arrested by a group of bronzed mariners, man-of-war's men or merchant sailors in holiday attire, ashore on liberty. In certain instances they would flank, or like a bodyguard quite surround, some superior figure of their own class, moving along with them like Aldebaran among the lesser lights of his constellation. That signal object was the "Handsome Sailor" of the less prosaic time alike of the military and merchant navies. With no perceptible trace of the vainglorious about him, rather with the offhand unaffectedness of natural regality, he seemed to accept the spontaneous homage of his shipmates.

A somewhat remarkable instance recurs to me. In Liverpool, now half a century ago, I saw under the shadow of the great dingy street-wall of Prince's Dock (an obstruction long since removed) a common sailor so intensely black that he must needs have been a native African of the unadulterate blood of Ham—a symmetric figure much above the average height. The two ends of a gay silk handkerchief thrown loose about the neck danced upon the displayed ebony of his chest, in his ears were big hoops of gold, and a Highland bonnet with a tartan band set off his shapely head. It was a hot noon in July; and his face, lustrous with perspiration, beamed with barbaric good humor. In jovial sallies right and left, his white teeth flashing into view, he rollicked along, the center of a company of his shipmates. These were made up of such an assortment of tribes and complexions as would have well fitted them to be marched up by Anacharsis Cloots before the bar of the first French Assembly as Representatives of the Human Race. At each spontaneous tribute rendered by the wayfarers to this black pagod of a fellow—the tribute of a pause and stare, and less frequently an exclamation—the motley retinue showed that they took that sort of pride in the evoker of it which the Assyrian priests doubtless showed for their grand sculptured Bull when the faithful prostrated themselves.

To return. If in some cases a bit of a nautical Murat in setting forth his person ashore, the Handsome Sailor of the period in question evinced nothing of the dandified Billy-be-Dam, an amusing character all but extinct now, but occasionally to be encountered, and in a form yet more amusing than the original, at the tiller of the boats on the tempestuous Erie Canal or, more likely, vaporing in the groggeries along the towpath. Invariably a proficient in his perilous calling, he was also more or less of a mighty boxer or wrestler. It was strength and beauty. Tales of his prowess were recited. Ashore he was the champion; afloat the spokesman; on every suitable occasion always foremost. Close-reefing topsails in a gale, there he was, astride the weather yardarm-end, foot in the Flemish horse as stirrup, both hands tugging at the earing as at a bridle, in very much the attitude of young Alexander curbing the fiery Bucephalus. A superb figure, tossed up as by the horns of Taurus against the thunderous sky, cheerily hallooing to the strenuous file along the spar.

The moral nature was seldom out of keeping with the physical make. Indeed, except as toned by the former, the comeliness and power, always attractive in masculine conjunction, hardly could have drawn the sort of honest homage the Handsome Sailor in some examples received from his less gifted associates.

Such a cynosure, at least in aspect, and something such too in nature, though with important variations made apparent as the story proceeds, was welkin-eyed Billy Budd—or Baby Budd, as more familiarly, under circumstances hereafter to be given, he at last came to be called—aged twenty-one, a foretopman of the British fleet toward the close of the last decade of the eighteenth century. It was not very long prior to the time of the narration that follows that he had entered the King's service, having been impressed on the Narrow Seas from a homeward-bound English merchantman into a seventy-four outward bound, H.M.S. *Bellipotent*; which ship, as was not unusual in those hurried days, having been obliged to put to sea short of her proper complement of men. Plump upon Billy at first sight in the gangway the boarding officer, Lieutenant Ratcliffe, pounced, even before the merchantman's crew was formerly mus-

tered on the quarter-deck for his deliberate inspection. And him only he elected. For whether it was because the other men when ranged before him showed to ill advantage after Billy, or whether he had some scruples in view of the merchantman's being rather short-handed, however it might be, the officer contented himself with his first spontaneous choice. To the surprise of the ship's company, though much to the lieutenant's satisfaction, Billy made no demur. But, indeed, any demur would have been as idle as the protest of a goldfinch popped into a cage.

Noting this uncomplaining acquiescence, all but cheerful, one might say, the shipmaster turned a surprised glance of silent reproach at the sailor. The shipmaster was one of those worthy mortals found in every vocation, even the humbler ones—the sort of person whom everybody agrees in calling "a respectable man." And—nor so strange to report as it may appear to be—though a ploughman of the troubled waters, lifelong contending with the intractable elements, there was nothing this honest soul at heart loved better than simple peace and quiet. For the rest, he was fifty or thereabouts, a little inclined to corpulence, a prepossessing face, unwhiskered, and of an agreeable color—a rather full face, humanely intelligent in expression. On a fair day with a fair wind and all going well, a certain musical chime in his voice seemed to be the veritable unobstructed outcome of the innermost man. He had much prudence, much conscientiousness, and there were occasions when these virtues were the cause of overmuch disquietude in him. On a passage, so long as his craft was in any proximity to land, no sleep for Captain Graveling. He took to heart those serious responsibilities not so heavily borne by some shipmasters.

Now while Billy Budd was down in the forecastle getting his kit together, the *Bellipotent*'s lieutenant, burly and bluff, nowise disconcerted by Captain Graveling's omitting to proffer the customary hospitalities on an occasion so unwelcome to him, an omission simply caused by preoccupation of thought, unceremoniously invited himself into the cabin, and also to a flask from the spirit locker, a receptacle which his experienced eye instantly discovered. In fact he was one of those sea dogs in whom all the hardship and peril of naval life in the great prolonged wars of his time never impaired the natural instinct for sensuous enjoyment. His duty he always faithfully did; but duty is sometimes a dry obligation, and he was for irrigating its aridity, whensoever possible, with a fertilizing decoction of strong waters. For the cabin's proprietor there was nothing left but to play the part of the enforced host with whatever grace and alacrity were practicable. As necessary adjuncts to the flask, he silently placed tumbler and water jug before the irrepressible guest. But excusing himself from partaking just then, he dismally watched the unembarrassed officer deliberately diluting his grog a little, then tossing it off in three swallows, pushing the empty tumbler away, yet not so far as to be beyond easy reach, at the same time settling himself in his seat and smacking his lips with high satisfaction, looking straight at the host.

These proceedings over, the master broke the silence; and there lurked a rueful reproach in the tone of his voice: "Lieutenant, you are going to take my best man from me, the jewel of 'em."

"Yes, I know," rejoined the other, immediately drawing back the tumbler preliminary to a replenishing. "Yes, I know. Sorry."

"Beg pardon, but you don't understand, Lieutenant. See here, now. Before I shipped that young fellow, my forecastle was a rat-pit of quarrels. It was black times, I tell you, aboard the *Rights* here. I was worried to that degree my pipe had no comfort for me. But Billy came; and it was like a Catholic priest striking peace in an Irish shindy. Not that he preached to them or said or did anything in particular; but a virtue went out of him, sugaring the sour ones. They took to him like hornets to treacle; all but the buffer of the gang, the big shaggy chap with the fire-red whiskers. He indeed, out of envy, perhaps, of the newcomer, and thinking such a 'sweet and pleasant fellow,' as he mockingly designated him to the others, could hardly have the spirit of a gamecock, must needs bestir himself in trying to get up an ugly row with him. Billy forebore with him and reasoned with him in a pleasant way—he is something like myself, Lieutenant, to whom aught like a quarrel is hateful—but nothing served. So, in the second dogwatch one day, the Red Whiskers in presence of the others, under pretense of showing Billy just whence a sirloin steak was cut—for the fellow had once been a butcher—insultingly gave him a dig under the ribs. Quick as lightning Billy let fly his arm. I dare say he never meant to do quite as much as he did, but anyhow he gave the burly fool a terrible drubbing. It took about half a minute, I should think. And, lord bless you, the lubber was astonished at the celerity. And will you believe it, Lieutenant, the Red Whiskers now really loves Billy—loves him, or is the biggest hypocrite that ever I heard of. But they all love him. Some of 'em do his washing, darn his old trousers for him; the carpenter is at odd times making a pretty little chest of drawers for him. Anybody will do anything for Billy Budd; and it's the happy family here. But now, Lieutenant, if that young fellow goes—I know how it will be aboard the *Rights*. Not again very soon shall I, coming up from dinner, lean over the capstan smoking a quiet pipe—no, not very soon again, I think. Ay, Lieutenant, you are going to take away the jewel of 'em; you are going to take away my peacemaker!" And with that the good soul had really some ado in checking a rising sob.

"Well," said the lieutenant, who had listened with amused interest to all this and now was waxing merry with his tipple; "well, blessed are the peacemakers, especially the fighting peacemakers. And such are the seventy-four beauties some of which you see poking their noses out of the portholes of yonder warship lying to for me," pointing through the cabin window at the *Bellipotent.* "But courage! Don't look so downhearted, man. Why, I pledge you in advance the royal approbation. Rest assured that His Majesty will be delighted to know that in a time when his hardtack is not sought for by sailors with such avidity as should be, a time also when some shipmasters privily resent the borrowing from them a tar or two for the service; His Majesty, I say, will be delighted to learn that *one* shipmaster at least cheerfully surrenders to the King the flower of his flock, a sailor who with equal loyalty makes no dissent.— But where's my beauty? Ah," looking through the cabin's open door, "here he comes; and, by Jove, lugging along his chest—Apollo with his portmanteau!—My man," stepping out to him, "you can't take that big box aboard a warship. The boxes there are mostly shot boxes. Put your duds in a bag, lad. Boot and saddle for the cavalryman, bag and hammock for the man-of-war's man."

The transfer from chest to bag was made. And, after seeing his man into the cutter and then following him down, the lieutenant pushed off from the *Rights-of-Man.* That was the merchant ship's name, though by her master and crew abbreviated in sailor fashion into the *Rights.* The hardheaded Dundee owner was a staunch admirer of Thomas Paine, whose book in rejoinder to Burke's arraignment of the French Revolution had then been published for some time and had gone everywhere. In christening his vessel after the title of Paine's volume the man of Dundee was something like his contemporary shipowner, Stephen Girard of Philadelphia, whose sympathies, alike with his native land and its liberal philosophers, he evinced by naming his ships after Voltaire, Diderot, and so forth.

But now, when the boat swept under the merchantman's stern, and officer and oarsmen were noting—some bitterly and others with a grin—the name emblazoned there; just then it was that the new recruit jumped up from the bow where the coxswain had directed him to sit, and waving hat to his silent shipmates sorrowfully looking over at him from the taffrail, bade the lads a genial good-bye. Then, making a salutation as to the ship herself, "And good-bye to you too, old *Rights-of-Man*."

"Down, sir!" roared the lieutenant, instantly assuming all the rigor of his rank, though with difficulty repressing a smile.

To be sure, Billy's action was a terrible breach of naval decorum. But in that decorum he had never been instructed; in consideration of which the lieutenant would hardly have been so energetic in reproof but for the concluding farewell to the ship. This he rather took as meant to convey a covert sally on the new recruit's part, a sly slur at impressment in general, and that of himself in especial. And yet, more likely, if satire it was in effect, it was hardly so by intention, for Billy, though happily endowed with the gaiety of high health, youth, and a free heart, was yet by no means of a satirical turn. The will to it and the sinister dexterity were alike wanting. To deal in double meanings and insinuations of any sort was quite foreign to his nature.

As to his enforced enlistment, that he seemed to take pretty much as he was wont to take any vicissitude of weather. Like the animals, though no philosopher, he was, without knowing it, practically a fatalist. And it may be that he rather liked this adventurous turn in his affairs, which promised an opening into novel scenes and martial excitements.

Aboard the *Bellipotent* our merchant sailor was forthwith rated as an able seaman and assigned to the starboard watch of the foretop. He was soon at home in the service, not at all disliked for his unpretentious good looks and a sort of genial happy-go-lucky air. No merrier man in his mess: in marked contrast to certain other individuals included like himself among the impressed portion of the ship's company; for these when not actively

employed were sometimes, and more particularly in the last dogwatch when the drawing near of twilight induced revery, apt to fall into a saddish mood which in some partook of sullenness. But they were not so young as our foretopman, and no few of them must have known a hearth of some sort, others may have had wives and children left, too probably, in uncertain circumstances, and hardly any but must have had acknowledged kith and kin, while for Billy, as will shortly be seen, his entire family was practically invested in himself.

2

Though our new-made foretopman was well received in the top and on the gun decks, hardly here was he that cynosure he had previously been among those minor ship's companies of the merchant marine, with which companies only had he hitherto consorted.

He was young; and despite his all but fully developed frame, in aspect looked even younger than he really was, owing to a lingering adolescent expression in the as yet smooth face all but feminine in purity of natural complexion but where, thanks to his seagoing, the lily was quite suppressed and the rose had some ado visibly to flush through the tan.

To one essentially such a novice in the complexities of factitious life, the abrupt transition from his former and simpler sphere to the ampler and more knowing world of a great warship; this might well have abashed him had there been any conceit or vanity in his composition. Among her miscellaneous multitude, the *Bellipotent* mustered several individuals who however inferior in grade were of no common natural stamp, sailors more signally susceptive of that air which continuous martial discipline and repeated presence in battle can in some degree impart even to the average man. As the Handsome Sailor, Billy Budd's position aboard the seventy-four was something analogous to that of a rustic beauty transplanted from the provinces and brought into competition with the highborn dames of the court. But this change of circumstances he scarce noted. As little did he observe that something about him provoked an ambiguous smile in one or two harder faces among the bluejackets. Nor less unaware was he of the peculiar favorable effect his person and demeanor had upon the more intelligent gentlemen of the quarter-deck. Nor could this well have been otherwise. Cast in a mold peculiar to the finest physical examples of those Englishmen in whom the Saxon strain would seem not at all to partake of any Norman or other admixture, he showed in face that humane look of reposeful good nature which the Greek sculptor in some instances gave to his heroic strong man, Hercules. But this again was subtly modified by another and pervasive quality. The ear, small and shapely, the arch of the foot, the curve in mouth and nostril, even the indurated hand dyed to the orange-tawny of the toucan's bill, a hand telling alike of the halyards and tar bucket; but, above all, something in the mobile expression, and every chance attitude and movement, something suggestive of a mother eminently favored by Love and the Graces; all this strangely indicated a lineage in direct contradiction to his lot. The mysteriousness here became less mysterious through a matter of fact elicited when Billy at the capstan was being formally mustered into the service. Asked by the officer, a small, brisk little gentleman as it chanced, among other questions, his place of birth, he replied, "Please, sir, I don't know."

"Don't know where you were born? Who was your father?"

"God knows, sir."

Struck by the straightforward simplicity of these replies, the officer next asked, "Do you know anything about your beginning?"

"No, sir. But I have heard that I was found in a pretty silk-lined basket hanging one morning from the knocker of a good man's door in Bristol."

"*Found*, say you? Well," throwing back his head and looking up and down the new recruit; "well, it turns out to have been a pretty good find. Hope they'll find some more like you, my man; the fleet sadly needs them."

Yes, Billy Budd was a foundling, a presumable by-blow, and, evidently, no ignoble one. Noble descent was as evident in him as in a blood horse.

For the rest, with little or no sharpness of faculty or any trace of the wisdom of the serpent, nor yet quite a dove, he possessed that kind and degree of intelligence going along with the unconventional rectitude of a sound human creature, one to whom not yet has been proffered the questionable apple of knowledge. He was illiterate; he could not read, but he could sing, and like the illiterate nightingale was sometimes the composer of his own song.

Of self-consciousness he seemed to have little or none, or about as much as we may reasonably impute to a dog of Saint Bernard's breed.

Habitually living with the elements and knowing little more of the land than as a beach, or, rather, that portion of the terraqueous globe providentially set apart for dance-houses, doxies, and tapsters, in short what sailors call a "fiddler's green," his simple nature remained unsophisticated by those moral obliquities which are not in every case incompatible with that manufacturable thing known as respectability. But are sailors, frequenters of fiddlers' greens, without vices? No; but less often than with landsmen do their vices, so called, partake of crookedness of heart, seeming less to proceed from viciousness than exuberance of vitality after long constraint: frank manifestations in accordance with natural law. By his original constitution aided by the co-operating influences of his lot, Billy in many respects was little more than a sort of upright barbarian, much such perhaps as Adam presumably might have been ere the urbane Serpent wriggled himself into his company.

And here be it submitted that apparently going to corroborate the doctrine of man's Fall, a doctrine now popularly ignored, it is observable that where certain virtues pristine and unadulterate peculiarly characterize anybody in the external uniform of civilization, they will upon scrutiny seem not to be derived from custom or convention, but rather to be out of keeping with these, as if indeed exceptionally transmitted from a period prior to Cain's city and citified man. The character marked by such qualities has to an unvitiated taste an untampered-with flavor like that of berries, while the man thoroughly civilized, even in a fair specimen of the breed, has to the same moral palate a questionable smack as of a compounded wine. To any stray inheritor of these primitive qualities found, like Caspar Hauser, wandering dazed in any Christian capital of our time, the good-natured poet's famous invocation, near two thousand years ago, of the good rustic out of his latitude in the Rome of the Caesars, still appropriately holds:

Honest and poor, faithful in word and thought,
What hath thee, Fabian, to the city brought?

Though our Handsome Sailor had as much of masculine beauty as one can expect anywhere to see; nevertheless, like the beautiful woman in one of Hawthorne's minor tales, there was just one thing amiss in him. No visible blemish indeed, as with the lady; no, but an occasional liability to a vocal defect. Though in the hour of elemental uproar or peril he was everything that a sailor should be, yet under sudden provocation of strong heart-feeling his voice, otherwise singularly musical, as if expressive of the harmony within, was apt to develop an organic hesitancy, in fact more or less of a stutter or even worse. In this particular Billy was a striking instance that the arch interferer, the envious marplot of Eden, still has more or less to do with every human consignment to this planet of Earth. In every case, one way or another he is sure to slip in his little card, as much as to remind us—I too have a hand here.

The avowal of such an imperfection in the Handsome Sailor should be evidence not alone that he is not presented as a conventional hero, but also that the story in which he is the main figure is no romance.

3

At the time of Billy Budd's arbitrary enlistment into the *Bellipotent* that ship was on her way to join the Mediterranean fleet. No long time elapsed before the junction was effected. As one of that fleet the seventy-four participated in its movements, though at times on account of her superior sailing qualities, in the absence of frigates, dispatched on separate duty as a scout and at times on less temporary service. But with all this the story has little concernment, restricted as it is to the inner life of one particular ship and the career of an individual sailor.

It was the summer of 1797. In the April of that year had occurred the commotion at Spithead followed in May by a second and yet more serious outbreak in the fleet at the Nore. The latter is known, and without exaggeration in the epithet, as "the Great Mutiny." It was indeed a demonstration more menacing to England than the contemporary manifestoes and conquering and proselyting armies of the French Directory. To the British Empire the Nore Mutiny was what a strike in the fire brigade would be to London threatened by general arson. In a crisis when the kingdom might well have anticipated the famous signal that some years later published along the naval line of battle what it was that upon occasion England expected of Englishmen; *that* was the time when at the mastheads of the three-deckers and seventy-fours moored in her own roadstead—a fleet the right arm of a Power then all but the sole free conservative one of the Old World—the bluejackets, to be

numbered by thousands, ran up with huzzas the British colors with the union and cross wiped out; by that cancellation transmuting the flag of founded law and freedom defined, into the enemy's red meteor of unbridled and unbounded revolt. Reasonable discontent growing out of practical grievances in the fleet had been ignited into irrational combustion as by live cinders blown across the Channel from France in flames.

The event converted into irony for a time those spirited strains of Dibdin—as a song-writer no mean auxiliary to the English government at that European conjuncture—strains celebrating, among other things, the patriotic devotion of the British tar: "And as for my life, 'tis the King's!"

Such an episode in the Island's grand naval story her naval historians naturally abridge, one of them (William James) candidly acknowledging that fain would he pass it over did not "impartiality forbid fastidiousness." And yet his mention is less a narration than a reference, having to do hardly at all with details. Nor are these readily to be found in the libraries. Like some other events in every age befalling states everywhere, including America, the Great Mutiny was of such character that national pride along with views of policy would fain shade it off into the historical background. Such events cannot be ignored, but there is a considerate way of historically treating them. If a well-constituted individual refrains from blazoning aught amiss or calamitous in his family, a nation in the like circumstance may without reproach be equally discreet.

Though after parleyings between government and the ring-leaders, and concessions by the former as to some glaring abuses, the first uprising—that at Spithead—with difficulty was put down, or matters for the time pacified; yet at the Nore the unforeseen renewal of insurrection on a yet larger scale, and emphasized in the conferences that ensued by demands deemed by the authorities not only inadmissible but aggressively insolent, indicated—if the Red Flag did not sufficiently do so —what was the spirit animating the men. Final suppression, however, there was; but only made possible perhaps by the unswerving loyalty of the marine corps and a voluntary resumption of loyalty among influential sections of the crews.

To some extent the Nore Mutiny may be regarded as analogous to the distempering eruption of contagious fever in a frame constitutionally sound, and which anon throws it off.

At all events, of these thousands of mutineers

were some of the tars who not so very long after-wards—whether wholly prompted thereto by pa-triotism, or pugnacious instinct, or by both—helped to win a coronet for Nelson at the Nile, and the naval crown of crowns for him at Trafalgar. To the mutineers, those battles and especially Tra-falgar were a plenary absolution and a grand one. For all that goes to make up scenic naval display and heroic magnificence in arms, those battles, especially Trafalgar, stand unmatched in human annals.

4

In this matter of writing, resolve as one may to keep to the main road, some bypaths have an en-ticement not readily to be withstood. I am going to err into such a bypath. If the reader will keep me company I shall be glad. At the least, we can promise ourselves that pleasure which is wickedly said to be in sinning, for a literary sin the di-vergence will be.

Very likely it is no new remark that the inven-tions of our time have at last brought about a change in sea warfare in degree corresponding to the revolution in all warfare effected by the original introduction from China into Europe of gun-powder. The first European firearm, a clumsy con-trivance, was, as is well known, scouted by no few of the knights as a base implement, good enough peradventure for weavers too craven to stand up crossing steel with steel in frank fight. But as ashore knightly valor, though shorn of its blazonry, did not cease with the knights, neither on the seas —though nowadays in encounters there a certain kind of displayed gallantry be fallen out of date as hardly applicable under changed circumstances —did the nobler qualities of such naval magnates as Don John of Austria, Doria, Van Tromp, Jean Bart, the long line of British admirals, and the American Decaturs of 1812 become obsolete with their wooden walls.

Nevertheless, to anybody who can hold the Present at its worth without being inappreciative of the Past, it may be forgiven, if to such an one the solitary old hulk at Portsmouth, Nelson's *Victory*, seems to float there, not alone as the de-caying monument of a fame incorruptible, but also as a poetic reproach, softened by its pic-turesqueness, to the *Monitors* and yet mightier hulls of the European ironclads. And this not altogether

because such craft are unsightly, unavoidably lack-ing the symmetry and grand lines of the old battle-ships, but equally for other reasons.

There are some, perhaps, who while not alto-gether inaccessible to that poetic reproach just alluded to, may yet on behalf of the new order be disposed to parry it; and this to the extent of icono-clasm, if need be. For example, prompted by the sight of the star inserted in the *Victory's* quarter-deck designating the spot where the Great Sailor fell, these martial utilitarians may suggest consider-ations implying that Nelson's ornate publication of his person in battle was not only unnecessary, but not military, nay, savored of foolhardiness and vanity. They may add, too, that at Trafalgar it was in effect nothing less than a challenge to death; and death came; and that but for his bravado the victorious admiral might possibly have survived the battle, and so, instead of having his sagacious dy-ing injunctions overruled by his immediate suc-cessor in command, he himself when the contest was decided might have brought his shattered fleet to anchor, a proceeding which might have averted the deplorable loss of life by shipwreck in the ele-mental tempest that followed the martial one.

Well, should we set aside the more than dis-putable point whether for various reasons it was possible to anchor the fleet, then plausibly enough the Benthamites of war may urge the above. But the *might-have-been* is but boggy ground to build on. And, certainly, in foresight as to the larger issue of an encounter, and anxious preparations for it—buoying the deadly way and mapping it out, as at Copenhagen—few commanders have been so painstakingly circumspect as this same reckless de-clarer of his person in fight.

Personal prudence, even when dictated by quite other than selfish considerations, surely is no spe-cial virtue in a military man; while an excessive love of glory, impassioning a less burning impulse, the honest sense of duty, is the first. If the name *Wellington* is not so much of a trumpet to the blood as the simpler name *Nelson*, the reason for this may perhaps be inferred from the above. Alfred in his funeral ode on the victor of Waterloo ventures not to call him the greatest soldier of all time, though in the same ode he invokes Nelson as "the greatest sailor since our world began."

At Trafalgar Nelson on the brink of opening the fight sat down and wrote his last brief will and testament. If under the presentiment of the most magnificent of all victories to be crowned by his own glorious death, a sort of priestly motive led him to dress his person in the jewelled vouchers of his own shining deeds; if thus to have adorned himself for the altar and the sacrifice were indeed vainglory, then affectation and fustian is each more heroic line in the great epics and dramas, since in such lines the poet but embodies in verse those exaltations of sentiment that a nature like Nelson, the opportunity being given, vitalizes into acts.

5

Yes, the outbreak at the Nore was put down. But not every grievance was redressed. If the contractors, for example, were no longer permitted to ply some practices peculiar to their tribe everywhere, such as providing shoddy cloth, rations not sound, or false in the measure; not the less impressment, for one thing, went on. By custom sanctioned for centuries, and judicially maintained by a Lord Chancellor as late as Mansfield, that mode of manning the fleet, a mode now fallen into a sort of abeyance but never formally renounced, it was not practicable to give up in those years. Its abrogation would have crippled the indispensable fleet, one wholly under canvas, no steam power, its innumerable sails and thousands of cannon, everything in short, worked by muscle alone; a fleet the more insatiate in demand for men, because then multiplying its ships of all grades against contingencies present and to come of the convulsed Continent.

Discontent foreran the Two Mutinies, and more or less it lurkingly survived them. Hence it was not unreasonable to apprehend some return of trouble sporadic or general. One instance of such apprehensions: In the same year with this story, Nelson, then Rear Admiral Sir Horatio, being with the fleet off the Spanish coast, was directed by the admiral in command to shift his pennant from the *Captain* to the *Theseus*; and for this reason: that the latter ship having newly arrived on the station from home, where it had taken part in the Great Mutiny, danger was apprehended from the temper of the men; and it was thought that an officer like Nelson was the one, not indeed to terrorize the crew into base subjection, but to win them, by force of his mere presence and heroic personality, back to an allegiance if not as enthusiastic as his own yet as true.

So it was that for a time, on more than one quarter-deck, anxiety did exist. At sea, precautionary vigilance was strained against relapse. At short notice an engagement might come on. When

it did, the lieutenants assigned to batteries felt it incumbent on them, in some instances, to stand with drawn swords behind the men working the guns.

6

But on board the seventy-four in which Billy now swung his hammock, very little in the manner of the men and nothing obvious in the demeanor of the officers would have suggested to an ordinary observer that the Great Mutiny was a recent event. In their general bearing and conduct the commissioned officers of a warship naturally take their tone from the commander, that is if he have that ascendancy of character that ought to be his.

Captain the Honorable Edward Fairfax Vere, to give his full title, was a bachelor of forty or thereabouts, a sailor of distinction even in a time prolific of renowned seamen. Though allied to the higher nobility, his advancement had not been altogether owing to influences connected with that circumstance. He had seen much service, been in various engagements, always acquitting himself as an officer mindful of the welfare of his men, but never tolerating an infraction of discipline; thoroughly versed in the science of his profession, and intrepid to the verge of temerity, though never injudiciously so. For his gallantry in the West Indian waters as flag lieutenant under Rodney in that admiral's crowning victory over De Grasse, he was made a post captain.

Ashore, in the garb of a civilian, scarce anyone would have taken him for a sailor, more especially that he never garnished unprofessional talk with nautical terms, and grave in his bearing, evinced little appreciation of mere humor. It was not out of keeping with these traits that on a passage when nothing demanded his paramount action, he was the most undemonstrative of men. Any landsman observing this gentleman not conspicuous by his stature and wearing no pronounced insignia, emerging from his cabin to the open deck, and noting the silent deference of the officers retiring to leeward, might have taken him for the King's guest, a civilian aboard the King's ship, some highly honorable discreet envoy on his way to an important post. But in fact this unobtrusiveness of demeanor may have proceeded from a certain unaffected modesty of manhood sometimes accompanying a resolute nature, a modesty evinced at all times not calling for pronounced action, which shown in any rank of life suggests a virtue aristocratic in kind. As with some others engaged in various departments of the world's more heroic activities, Captain Vere though practical enough upon occasion would at times betray a certain dreaminess of mood. Standing alone on the weather side of the quarter-deck, one hand holding by the rigging, he would absently gaze off at the blank sea. At the presentation to him then of some minor matter interrupting the current of his thoughts, he would show more or less irascibility; but instantly he would control it.

In the navy he was popularly known by the appellation "Starry Vere." How such a designation happened to fall upon one who whatever his sterling qualities was without any brilliant ones, was in this wise: A favorite kinsman, Lord Denton, a freehearted fellow, had been the first to meet and congratulate him upon his return to England from his West Indian cruise; and but the day previous turning over a copy of Andrew Marvell's poems had lighted, not for the first time, however, upon the lines entitled "Appleton House," the name of one of the seats of their common ancestor, a hero in the German wars of the seventeenth century, in which poem occur the lines:

> This 'tis to have been from the first
> In a domestic heaven nursed,
> Under the discipline severe
> Of Fairfax and the starry Vere.

And so, upon embracing his cousin fresh from Rodney's great victory wherein he had played so gallant a part, brimming over with just family pride in the sailor of their house, he exuberantly exclaimed, "Give ye joy, Ed; give ye joy, my starry Vere!" This got currency, and the novel prefix serving in familiar parlance readily to distinguish the *Bellipotent*'s captain from another Vere his senior, a distant relative, an officer of like rank in the navy, it remained permanently attached to the surname.

7

In view of the part that the commander of the *Bellipotent* plays in scenes shortly to follow, it may be well to fill out that sketch of him outlined in the previous chapter.

Aside from his qualities as a sea officer Captain Vere was an exceptional character. Unlike no few of England's renowned sailors, long and arduous service with signal devotion to it had not resulted in absorbing and *salting* the entire man. He had a marked leaning toward everything intellectual. He loved books, never going to sea without a newly replenished library, compact but of the best. The isolated leisure, in some cases so wearisome, falling at intervals to commanders even during a war cruise, never was tedious to Captain Vere. With nothing of that literary taste which less heeds the thing conveyed than the vehicle, his bias was toward those books to which every serious mind of superior order occupying any active post of authority in the world naturally inclines: books treating of actual men and events no matter of what era—history, biography, and unconventional writers like Montaigne, who, free from cant and convention, honestly and in the spirit of common sense philosophize upon realities. In this line of reading he found confirmation of his own more reserved thoughts—confirmation which he had vainly sought in social converse, so that as touching most fundamental topics, there had got to be established in him some positive convictions which he forefelt would abide in him essentially unmodified so long as his intelligent part remained unimpaired. In view of the troubled period in which his lot was cast, this was well for him. His settled convictions were as a dike against those invading waters of novel opinion social, political, and otherwise, which carried away as in a torrent no few minds in those days, minds by nature not inferior to his own. While other members of that aristocracy to which by birth he belonged were incensed at the innovators mainly because their theories were inimical to the privileged classes, Captain Vere disinterestedly opposed them not alone because they seemed to him insusceptible of embodiment in lasting institutions, but at war with the peace of the world and the true welfare of mankind.

With minds less stored than his and less earnest, some officers of his rank, with whom at times he would necessarily consort, found him lacking in the companionable quality, a dry and bookish gentleman, as they deemed. Upon any chance withdrawal from their company one would be apt to say to another something like this: "Vere is a noble fellow, Starry Vere. 'Spite the gazettes, Sir Horatio" (meaning him who became Lord Nelson) "is at bottom scarce a better seaman or fighter. But between you and me now, don't you think there is a queer streak of the pedantic running through him? Yes, like the King's yarn in a coil of navy rope?"

Some apparent ground there was for this sort of confidential criticism; since not only did the captain's discourse never fall into the jocosely familiar, but in illustrating of any point touching the stirring personages and events of the time he would be as apt to cite some historic character or incident of antiquity as he would be to cite from the moderns. He seemed unmindful of the circumstance that to his bluff company such remote allusions, however pertinent they might really be, were altogether alien to men whose reading was mainly confined to the journals. But considerateness in such matters is not easy to natures constituted like Captain Vere's. Their honesty prescribes to them directness, sometimes far-reaching like that of a migratory fowl that in its flight never heeds when it crosses a frontier.

8

The lieutenants and other commissioned gentlemen forming Captain Vere's staff it is not necessary here to particularize, nor needs it to make any mention of any of the warrant officers. But among the petty officers was one who, having much to do with the story, may as well be forthwith introduced. His portrait I essay, but shall never hit it. This was John Claggart, the master-at-arms. But that sea title may to landsmen seem somewhat equivocal. Originally, doubtless, that petty officer's function was the instruction of the men in the use of arms, sword or cutlass. But very long ago, owing to the advance in gunnery making hand-to-hand encounters less frequent and giving to niter and sulphur the pre-eminence over steel, that function ceased; the master-at-arms of a great warship becoming a sort of chief of police charged among other matters with the duty of preserving order on the populous lower gun decks.

Claggart was a man about five-and-thirty, somewhat spare and tall, yet of no ill figure upon the whole. His hand was too small and shapely to have been accustomed to hard toil. The face was a notable one, the features all except the chin cleanly cut as those on a Greek medallion; yet the chin, beardless as Tecumseh's, had something of strange protuberant broadness in its make that recalled the prints of the Reverend Dr. Titus Oates, the historic deponent with the clerical drawl in the time of Charles II and the fraud of the alleged Popish Plot. It served Claggart in his office that his eye could cast a tutoring glance. His brow was of the sort phrenologically associated with more than average intellect; silken jet curls partly clustering over it, making a foil to the pallor below, a pallor tinged with a faint shade of amber akin to the hue of time-tinted marbles of old. This complexion, singularly contrasting with the red or deeply bronzed visages of the sailors, and in part the result of his official seclusion from the sunlight, though it was not exactly displeasing, nevertheless seemed to hint of something defective or abnormal in the constitution and blood. But his general aspect and manner were so suggestive of an education and career incongruous with his naval function that when not actively engaged in it he looked like a man of high quality, social and moral, who for reasons of his own was keeping incog. Nothing was known of his former life. It might be that he was an Englishman; and yet there lurked a bit of accent in his speech suggesting that possibly he was not such by birth, but through naturalization in early childhood. Among certain grizzled sea gossips of the gun decks and forecastle went a rumor perdue that the master-at-arms was a *chevalier* who had volunteered into the King's navy by way of compounding for some mysterious swindle whereof he had been arraigned at the King's Bench. The fact that nobody could substantiate this report was, of course, nothing against its secret currency. Such a rumor once started on the gun decks in reference to almost anyone below the rank of a commissioned officer would, during the period assigned to this narrative, have seemed not altogether wanting in credibility to the tarry old wiseacres of a man-of-war crew. And indeed a man of Claggart's accomplishments, without prior nautical experience entering the navy at mature life, as he did, and necessarily allotted at the start to the lowest grade in it; a man too who never made allusion to his previous life ashore; these were circumstances which in the dearth of exact knowledge as to his true antecedents opened to the invidious a vague field for unfavorable surmise.

But the sailors' dogwatch gossip concerning him derived a vague plausibility from the fact that now for some period the British navy could so little afford to be squeamish in the matter of keeping up the muster rolls, that not only were press gangs notoriously abroad both afloat and ashore, but there was little or no secret about another matter, namely, that the London police were at liberty to capture any able-bodied suspect, any questionable fellow at large, and summarily ship him to the dockyard or fleet. Furthermore, even among voluntary enlistments there were instances where the motive thereto partook neither of patriotic impulse nor yet of a random desire to experience a bit of sea life and martial adventure. Insolvent debtors of minor grade, together with the promiscuous lame ducks of morality, found in the navy a convenient and secure refuge, secure because, once enlisted aboard a King's ship, they were as much in sanctuary as the transgressor of the Middle Ages harboring himself under the shadow of the altar. Such sanctioned irregularities, which for obvious reasons the government would hardly think to parade at the time and which consequently, and as affecting the least influential class of mankind, have all but dropped into oblivion, lend color to something for the truth whereof I do not vouch, and hence have some scruple in stating; something I remember having seen in print though the book I cannot recall; but the same thing was personally communicated to me now more than forty years ago by an old pensioner in a cocked hat with whom I had a most interesting talk on the terrace at Greenwich, a Baltimore Negro, a Trafalgar man. It was to this effect: In the case of a warship short of hands whose speedy sailing was imperative, the deficient quota, in lack of any other way of making it good, would be eked out by drafts culled direct from the jails. For reasons previously suggested it would not perhaps be easy at the present day directly to prove or disprove the allegation. But allowed as a verity, how significant would it be of England's straits at the time confronted by those wars which like a flight of harpies rose shrieking from the din and dust of the fallen Bastille. That era appears measurably clear to us who look back at it, and but read of it. But to the grandfathers of us graybeards, the more thoughtful of them, the genius of it presented an aspect like that of Camoëns' Spirit of the Cape, an eclipsing menace mysterious and prodigious. Not America was exempt from apprehension. At the height of Napoleon's unexampled conquests, there were Americans who had fought at Bunker Hill who looked forward to the possibility that the Atlantic might prove no barrier against the ultimate schemes of this French portentous upstart from the revolutionary chaos who seemed in act of fulfilling judgment prefigured in the Apocalypse.

But the less credence was to be given to the gun-deck talk touching Claggart, seeing that no man holding his office in a man-of-war can ever hope to be popular with the crew. Besides, in derogatory comments upon anyone against whom they have a grudge, or for any reason or no reason mislike, sailors are much like landsmen: they are apt to exaggerate or romance it.

About as much was really known to the *Bellipotent*'s tars of the master-at-arms' career before entering the service as an astronomer knows about a comet's travels prior to its first observable appearance in the sky. The verdict of the sea quidnuncs has been cited only by way of showing what sort of moral impression the man made upon rude uncultivated natures whose conceptions of human wickedness were necessarily of the narrowest, limited to ideas of vulgar rascality—a thief among the swinging hammocks during a night watch, or the man-brokers and land-sharks of the seaports.

It was no gossip, however, but fact that though, as before hinted, Claggart upon his entrance into the navy was, as a novice, assigned to the least honorable section of a man-of-war's crew, embracing the drudgery, he did not long remain there. The superior capacity he immediately evinced, his constitutional sobriety, an ingratiating deference to superiors, together with a peculiar ferreting genius manifested on a singular occasion; all this, capped by a certain austere patriotism, abruptly advanced him to the position of master-at-arms.

Of this maritime chief of police the ship's corporals, so called, were the immediate subordinates, and compliant ones; and this, as is to be noted in some business departments ashore, almost to a degree inconsistent with entire moral volition. His place put various converging wires of underground influence under the chief's control, capable when astutely worked through his understrappers of operating to the mysterious discomfort, if nothing worse, of any of the sea commonalty.

9

Life in the foretop well agreed with Billy Budd. There, when not actually engaged on the yards yet higher aloft, the topmen, who as such had been picked out for youth and activity, constituted an aerial club lounging at ease against the smaller stun'sails rolled up into cushions, spinning yarns like the lazy gods, and frequently amused with what was going on in the busy world of the decks below. No wonder then that a young fellow of Billy's disposition was well content in such society. Giving no cause of offense to anybody, he was always alert at a call. So in the merchant service it had been with him. But now such a punctiliousness in duty was shown that his topmates would some-times good-naturedly laugh at him for it. This heightened alacrity had its cause, namely, the im-pression made upon him by the first formal gang-way-punishment he had ever witnessed, which be-fell the day following his impressment. It had been incurred by a little fellow, young, a novice after-guardsman absent from his assigned post when the ship was being put about; a dereliction result-ing in a rather serious hitch to that maneuver, one demanding instantaneous promptitude in letting go and making fast. When Billy saw the culprit's naked back under the scourge, gridironed with red welts and worse, when he marked the dire expres-sion in the liberated man's face as with his woolen shirt flung over him by the executioner he rushed forward from the spot to bury himself in the crowd, Billy was horrified. He resolved that never through remissness would he make himself liable to such a visitation or do or omit aught that might merit even verbal reproof. What then was his sur-prise and concern when ultimately he found him-self getting into petty trouble occasionally about such matters as the stowage of his bag or some-thing amiss in his hammock, matters under the police oversight of the ship's corporals of the lower decks, and which brought down on him a vague threat from one of them.

So heedful in all things as he was, how could this be? He could not understand it, and it more than vexed him. When he spoke to his young top-mates about it they were either lightly incredulous or found something comical in his unconcealed anxiety. "Is it your bag, Billy?" said one. "Well, sew yourself up in it, bully boy, and then you'll be sure to know if anybody meddles with it."

Now there was a veteran aboard who because his years began to disqualify him for more active work had been recently assigned duty as main-mastman in his watch, looking to the gear belayed at the rail roundabout that great spar near the deck. At off-times the foretopman had picked up some acquaintance with him, and now in his trouble it occurred to him that he might be the sort of person to go to for wise counsel. He was an old Dansker long anglicized in the service, of few words, many wrinkles, and some honorable scars. His wizened face, time-tinted and weather-stained to the complexion of an antique parchment, was here and there peppered blue by the chance explo-sion of a gun cartridge in action.

He was an *Agamemnon* man, some two years prior to the time of this story having served under Nelson when still captain in that ship immortal

in naval memory, which dismantled and in part broken up to her bare ribs is seen a grand skeleton in Haden's etching. As one of a boarding party from the *Agamemnon* he had received a cut slant-wise along one temple and cheek leaving a long pale scar like a streak of dawn's light falling athwart the dark visage. It was on account of that scar and the affair in which it was known that he had received it, as well as from his blue-peppered complexion, that the Dansker went among the *Bellipotent's* crew by the name of "Board-Her-in-the-Smoke."

Now the first time that his small weasel eyes happened to light on Billy Budd, a certain grim internal merriment set all his ancient wrinkles into antic play. Was it that his eccentric unsentimental old sapience, primitive in its kind, saw or thought it saw something which in contrast with the war-ship's environment looked oddly incongruous in the Handsome Sailor? But after slyly studying him at intervals, the old Merlin's equivocal merriment was modified; for now when the twain would meet, it would start in his face a quizzing sort of look, but it would be but momentary and sometimes replaced by an expression of speculative query as to what might eventually befall a nature like that, dropped into a world not without some mantraps and against whose subtleties simple courage lack-ing experience and address, and without any touch of defensive ugliness, is of little avail; and where such innocence as man is capable of does yet in a moral emergency not always sharpen the faculties or enlighten the will.

However it was, the Dansker in his ascetic way rather took to Billy. Nor was this only because of a certain philosophic interest in such a character. There was another cause. While the old man's eccentricities, sometimes bordering on the ursine, repelled the juniors, Billy, undeterred thereby, revering him as a salt hero, would make advances, never passing the old *Agamemnon* man without a salutation marked by that respect which is seldom lost on the aged, however crabbed at times or whatever their station in life.

There was a vein of dry humor, or what not, in the mastman; and, whether in freak of patri-archal irony touching Billy's youth and athletic frame, or for some other and more recondite rea-son, from the first in addressing him he always substituted *Baby* for Billy, the Dansker in fact being the originator of the name by which the foretopman eventually became known aboard ship.

Well then, in his mysterious little difficulty going in quest of the wrinkled one, Billy found him off duty in a dogwatch ruminating by himself, seated on a shot box of the upper gun deck, now and then surveying with a somewhat cynical regard certain of the more swaggering promenaders there. Billy recounted his trouble, again wondering how it all happened. The salt seer attentively listened, accompanying the foretopman's recital with queer twitchings of his wrinkles and problematical little sparkles of his small ferret eyes. Making an end of his story, the foretopman asked, "And now, Dansker, do tell me what you think of it."

The old man, shoving up the front of his tarpaulin and deliberately rubbing the long slant scar at the point where it entered the thin hair, laconically said, "Baby Budd, *Jemmy Legs*" (meaning the master-at-arms) "is down on you."

"*Jemmy Legs!*" ejaculated Billy, his welkin eyes expanding. "What for? Why, he calls me 'the sweet and pleasant young fellow,' they tell me."

"Does he so?" grinned the grizzled one; then said, "Ay, Baby lad, a sweet voice has Jemmy Legs."

"No, not always. But to me he has. I seldom pass him but there comes a pleasant word."

"And that's because he's down upon you, Baby Budd."

Such reiteration, along with the manner of it, incomprehensible to a novice, disturbed Billy almost as much as the mystery for which he had sought explanation. Something less unpleasingly oracular he tried to extract; but the old sea Chiron, thinking perhaps that for the nonce he had sufficiently instructed his young Achilles, pursed his lips, gathered all his wrinkles together, and would commit himself to nothing further.

Years, and those experiences which befall certain shrewder men subordinated lifelong to the will of superiors, all this had developed in the Dansker the pithy guarded cynicism that was his leading characteristic.

10

The next day an incident served to confirm Billy Budd in his incredulity as to the Dansker's strange summing up of the case submitted. The ship at noon, going large before the wind, was rolling on her course, and he below at dinner and engaged in some sportful talk with the members of his mess, chanced in a sudden lurch to spill the entire contents of his soup pan upon the new-scrubbed deck. Claggart, the master-at-arms, official rattan

in hand, happened to be passing along the battery in a bay of which the mess was lodged, and the greasy liquid streamed just across his path. Stepping over it, he was proceeding on his way without comment, since the matter was nothing to take notice of under the circumstances, when he happened to observe who it was that had done the spilling. His countenance changed. Pausing, he was about the ejaculate something hasty at the sailor, but checked himself, and pointing down to the streaming soup, playfully tapped him from behind with his rattan, saying in a low musical voice peculiar to him at times, "Handsomely done, my lad! And handsome is as handsome did it, too!" And with that passed on. Not noted by Billy as not coming within his view was the involuntary smile, or rather grimace, that accompanied Claggart's equivocal words. Aridly it drew down the thin corners of his shapely mouth. But everybody taking his remark as meant for humorous, and at which therefore as coming from a superior they were bound to laugh "with counterfeited glee," acted accordingly; and Billy, tickled, it may be, by the allusion to his being the Handsome Sailor, merrily joined in; then addressing his messmates exclaimed, "There now, who says that Jemmy Legs is down on me!"

"And who said he was, Beauty?" demanded one Donald with some surprise. Whereat the foretopman looked a little foolish, recalling that it was only one person, Board-Her-in-the-Smoke, who had suggested what to him was the smoky idea that this master-at-arms was in any peculiar way hostile to him. Meantime that functionary, resuming his path, must have momentarily worn some expression less guarded than that of the bitter smile, usurping the face from the heart—some distorting expression perhaps, for a drummer-boy heedlessly frolicking along from the opposite direction and chancing to come into light collision with his person was strangely disconcerted by his aspect. Nor was the impression lessened when the official, impetuously giving him a sharp cut with the rattan, vehemently exclaimed, "Look where you go!"

11

What was the matter with the master-at-arms? And, be the matter what it might, how could it have direct relation to Billy Budd, with whom prior to the affair of the spilled soup he had never come into any special contact official or otherwise? What indeed could the trouble have to do with one so little inclined to give offense as the merchant-ship's "peacemaker," even him who in Claggart's own phrase was "the sweet and pleasant young fellow"? Yes, why should Jemmy Legs, to borrow the Dansker's expression, be "down" on the Handsome Sailor? But, at heart and not for nothing, as the late chance encounter may indicate to the discerning, down on him, secretly down on him, he assuredly was.

Now to invent something touching the more private career of Claggart, something involving Billy Budd, of which something the latter should be wholly ignorant, some romantic incident implying that Claggart's knowledge of the young bluejacket began at some period anterior to catching sight of him on board the seventy-four—all this, not so difficult to do, might avail in a way more or less interesting to account for whatever of enigma may appear to lurk in the case. But in fact there was nothing of the sort. And yet the cause necessarily to be assumed as the sole one assignable is in its very realism as much charged with that prime element of Radcliffian romance, the mysterious, as any that the ingenuity of the author of *The Mysteries of Udolpho* could devise. For what can more partake of the mysterious than an antipathy spontaneous and profound such as is evoked in certain exceptional mortals by the mere aspect of some other mortal, however harmless he may be, if not called forth by this very harmlessness itself?

Now there can exist no irritating juxtaposition of dissimilar personalities comparable to that which is possible aboard a great warship fully manned and at sea. There, every day among all ranks, almost every man comes into more or less of contact with almost every other man. Wholly there to avoid even the sight of an aggravating object one must needs give it Jonah's toss or jump overboard himself. Imagine how all this might eventually operate on some peculiar human creature the direct reverse of a saint!

But for the adequate comprehending of Claggart by a normal nature these hints are insufficient. To pass from a normal nature to him one must cross "the deadly space between." And this is best done by indirection.

Long ago an honest scholar, my senior, said to me in reference to one who like himself is now no more, a man so unimpeachably respectable that against him nothing was ever openly said though among the few something was whispered, "Yes, X—— is a nut not to be cracked by the tap of a lady's fan. You are aware that I am the adherent of no organized religion, much less of any philosophy built into a system. Well, for all that, I think that to try and get into X——, enter his labyrinth and get out again, without a clue derived from some source other that what is known as 'knowledge of the world'—that were hardly possible, at least for me."

"Why," said I, "X——, however singular a study to some, is yet human, and knowledge of the world assuredly implies the knowledge of human nature, and in most of its varieties."

"Yes, but a superficial knowledge of it, serving ordinary purposes. But for anything deeper, I am not certain whether to know the world and to know human nature be not two distinct branches of knowledge, which while they may coexist in the same heart, yet either may exist with little or nothing of the other. Nay, in an average man of the world, his constant rubbing with it blunts that finer spiritual insight indispensable to the understanding of the essential in certain exceptional characters, whether evil ones or good. In a matter of some importance I have seen a girl wind an old lawyer about her little finger. Nor was it the dotage of senile love. Nothing of the sort. But he knew law better than he knew the girl's heart. Coke and Blackstone hardly shed so much light into obscure spiritual places as the Hebrew prophets. And who were they? Mostly recluses."

At the time, my inexperience was such that I did not quite see the drift of all this. It may be that I see it now. And, indeed, if that lexicon which is based on Holy Writ were any longer popular, one might with less difficulty define and denominate certain phenomenal men. As it is, one must turn to some authority not liable to the charge of being tinctured with the biblical element.

In a list of definitions included in the authentic translation of Plato, a list attributed to him, occurs this: "Natural Depravity: a depravity according to nature," a definition which, though savoring of Calvinism, by no means involves Calvin's dogma as to total mankind. Evidently its intent makes it applicable but to individuals. Not many are the examples of this depravity which the gallows and jail supply. At any rate, for notable instances, since these have no vulgar alloy of the brute in them, but invariably are dominated by intellectuality, one must go elsewhere. Civilization, especially if of the austerer sort, is auspicious to it. It folds itself in the mantle of respectability. It has its certain negative virtues serving as silent auxiliaries. It never allows wine to get within its guard. It is not going too far to say that it is without vices or small sins. There is a phenomenal pride in it that excludes them. It is never mercenary or avaricious. In short, the depravity here meant partakes nothing of the sordid or sensual. It is serious, but free from acerbity. Though no flatterer of mankind it never speaks ill of it.

But the thing which in eminent instances signalizes so exceptional a nature is this: Though the man's even temper and discreet bearing would seem to intimate a mind peculiarly subject to the law of reason, not the less in heart he would seem to riot in complete exemption from that law, having apparently little to do with reason further than to employ it as an ambidexter implement for effecting the irrational. That is to say: Toward the accomplishment of an aim which in wantonness of atrocity would seem to partake of the insane, he will direct a cool judgment sagacious and sound. These men are madmen, and of the most dangerous sort, for their lunacy is not continuous, but occasional, evoked by some special object; it is protectively secretive, which is as much as to say it is self-contained, so that when, moreover, most active it is to the average mind not distinguishable from sanity, and for the reason above suggested: that whatever its aims may be—and the aim is never declared—the method and the outward proceeding are always perfectly rational.

Now something such an one was Claggart, in whom was the mania of an evil nature, not engendered by vicious training or corrupting books or licentious living, but born with him and innate, in short "a depravity according to nature."

Dark sayings are these, some will say. But why? Is it because they somewhat savor of Holy Writ in its phrase "mystery of iniquity"? If they do, such savor was far enough from being intended, for little will it commend these pages to many a reader of today.

The point of the present story turning on the hidden nature of the master-at-arms has necessitated this chapter. With an added hint or two in connection with the incident at the mess, the resumed narrative must be left to vindicate, as it may, its own credibility.

12

That Claggart's figure was not amiss, and his face, save the chin, well molded, has already been said. Of these favorable points he seemed not insensible, for he was not only neat but careful in his dress. But the form of Billy Budd was heroic: and if his face was without the intellectual look of the pallid Claggart's, not the less was it lit, like his, from within, though from a different source. The bonfire in his heart made luminous the rose-tan in his cheek.

In view of the marked contrast between the persons of the twain, it is more than probable that when the master-at-arms in the scene last given applied to the sailor the proverb "Handsome is as handsome does," he there let escape an ironic inkling, not caught by the young sailors who heard it, as to what it was that had first moved him against Billy, namely, his significant personal beauty.

Now envy and antipathy, passions irreconcilable in reason, nevertheless in fact may spring conjoined like Chang and Eng in one birth. Is Envy then such a monster? Well, though many an arraigned mortal has in hopes of mitigated penalty pleaded guilty to horrible actions, did ever anybody seriously confess to envy? Something there is in it universally felt to be more shameful than even felonious crime. And not only does everybody disown it, but the better sort are inclined to incredulity when it is in earnest imputed to an intelligent man. But since its lodgment is in the heart not the brain, no degree of intellect supplies a guarantee against it. But Claggart's was no vulgar form of the passion. Nor, as directed toward Billy Budd, did it partake of that streak of apprehensive jealousy that marred Saul's visage perturbedly brooding on the comely young David. Claggart's envy struck deeper. If askance he eyed the good looks, cheery health, and frank enjoyment of young life in Billy Budd, it was because these went along with a nature that, as Claggart magnetically felt, had in its simplicity never willed malice or experienced the reactionary bite of that serpent. To him, the spirit lodged within Billy, and looking out from his welkin eyes as from windows, that ineffability it was which made the dimple in his dyed cheek, suppled his joints, and dancing in his yellow curls made him pre-eminently the Handsome Sailor. One person excepted, the master-at-arms was perhaps the only man in the ship intellectually capable of adequately appreciating the moral phenomenon presented in Billy Budd. And the insight but intensified his passion, which assuming various secret forms within him, at times assumed that of cynic disdain, disdain of innocence—to be nothing more than innocent! Yet in an aesthetic way he saw the charm of it, the courageous free-and-easy temper of it, and fain would have shared it, but he despaired of it.

With no power to annul the elemental evil in him, though readily enough he could hide it; apprehending the good, but powerless to be it; a nature like Claggart's, surcharged with energy as such natures almost invariably are, what recourse is left to it but to recoil upon itself and, like the scorpion for which the Creator alone is responsible, act out to the end the part allotted it.

13

Passion, and passion in its profoundest, is not a thing demanding a palatial stage whereon to play its part. Down among the groundlings, among the beggars and rakers of the garbage, profound passion is enacted. And the circumstances that provoke it, however trivial or mean, are no measure of its power. In the present instance the stage is a scrubbed gun deck, and one of the external provocations of man-of-war's man's spilled soup.

Now when the master-at-arms noticed whence came that greasy fluid streaming before his feet, he must have taken it—to some extent wilfully, perhaps—not for the mere accident it assuredly was, but for the sly escape of a spontaneous feeling on Billy's part more or less answering to the antipathy on his own. In effect a foolish demonstration, he must have thought, and very harmless, like the futile kick of a heifer, which yet were the heifer a shod stallion would not be so harmless. Even so was it that into the gall of Claggart's envy he infused the vitriol of his contempt. But the incident confirmed to him certain telltale reports purveyed to his ear by "Squeak," one of his more cunning corporals, a grizzled little man, so nicknamed by the sailors on account of his squeaky voice and sharp visage ferreting about the dark corners of the lower decks after interlopers, satirically suggesting to them the idea of a rat in a cellar.

From his chief's employing him as an implicit tool in laying little traps for the worriment of the foretopman—for it was from the master-at-arms that the petty persecutions heretofore adverted to had proceeded—the corporal, having naturally enough concluded that his master could have no love for the sailor, made it his business, faithful understrapper that he was, to foment the ill blood by perverting to his chief certain innocent frolics of the good-natured foretopman, besides inventing for his mouth sundry contumelious epithets he claimed to have overheard him let fall. The master-at-arms never suspected the veracity of these reports, more especially as to the epithets, for he well knew how secretly unpopular may become a master-at-arms, at least a master-at-arms of those days, zealous in his function, and how the bluejackets shoot at him in private their raillery and wit; the nickname by which he goes among them (Jemmy Legs) implying under the form of merriment their cherished disrespect and dislike. But in view of the greediness of hate for pabulum it hardly needed a purveyor to feed Claggart's passion.

An uncommon prudence is habitual with the subtler depravity, for it has everything to hide. And in case of an injury but suspected, its secretiveness voluntarily cuts it off from enlightenment or disillusion; and, not unreluctantly, action is taken upon surmise as upon certainty. And the retaliation is apt to be in monstrous disproportion to the supposed offense; for when in anybody was revenge in its exactions aught else but an inordinate usurer? But how with Claggart's conscience? For though consciences are unlike as foreheads, every intelligence, not excluding the scriptural devils who "believe and tremble," has one. But Claggart's conscience being but the lawyer to his will, made ogres of trifles, probably arguing that the motive imputed to Billy in spilling the soup just when he did, together with the epithets alleged, these, if nothing more, made a strong case against him; nay, justified animosity into a sort of retributive righteousness. The Pharisee is the Guy Fawkes prowling in the hid chambers underlying some natures like Claggart's. And they can really form no conception of an unreciprocated malice. Probably the master-at-arms' clandestine persecution of Billy was started to try the temper of the man; but it had not developed any quality in him that enmity could make official use of or even pervert into plausible self-justification; so that the occurrence at the mess, petty if it were, was a welcome one to that peculiar conscience assigned to be the private mentor of Claggart; and, for the rest, not improbably it put him upon new experiments.

14

Not many days after the last incident narrated, something befell Billy Budd that more graveled him than aught that had previously occurred.

It was a warm night for the latitude; and the foretopman, whose watch at the time was properly below, was dozing on the uppermost deck whither he had ascended from his hot hammock, one of hundreds suspended so closely wedged together over a lower gun deck that there was little or no swing to them. He lay as in the shadow of a hillside, stretched under the lee of the booms, a piled ridge of spare spars amidships between foremast and mainmast among which the ship's largest boat, the launch, was stowed. Alongside of three other slumberers from below, he lay near that end of the booms which approaches the foremast; his station aloft on duty as a foretopman being just over the deck-station of the forecastlemen, entitling him according to usage to make himself more or less at home in that neighborhood.

Presently he was stirred into semiconsciousness by somebody, who must have previously sounded the sleep of the others, touching his shoulder, and then, as the foretopman raised his head, breathing into his ear in a quick whisper, "Slip into the lee forechains, Billy; there is something in the wind. Don't speak. Quick, I will meet you there," and disappearing.

Now Billy, like sundry other essentially good-natured ones, had some of the weaknesses inseparable from essential good nature; and among these was a reluctance, almost an incapacity of plumply saying *no* to an abrupt proposition not obviously absurd on the face of it, nor obviously unfriendly, nor iniquitous. And being of warm blood, he had not the phlegm tacitly to negative any proposition by unresponsive inaction. Like his sense of fear, his apprehension as to aught outside of the honest and natural was seldom very quick. Besides, upon the present occasion, the drowse from his sleep still hung upon him.

However it was, he mechanically rose and, sleepily wondering what could be in the wind, betook himself to the designated place, a narrow platform, one of six, outside of the high bulwarks and screened by the great deadeyes and multiple columned lanyards of the shrouds and backstays; and, in a great warship of that time, of dimensions commensurate to the hull's magnitude; a tarry balcony in short, overhanging the sea, and so secluded that one mariner of the *Bellipotent*, a Nonconformist old tar of a serious turn, made it even in daytime his private oratory.

In this retired nook the stranger soon joined Billy Budd. There was no moon as yet; a haze obscured the starlight. He could not distinctly see the stranger's face. Yet from something in the outline and carriage, Billy took him, and correctly, for one of the afterguard.

"Hist! Billy," said the man, in the same quick cautionary whisper as before. "You were impressed, weren't you? Well, so was I"; and he paused, as to mark the effect. But Billy, not knowing exactly what to make of this, said nothing. Then the other: "We are not the only impressed ones, Billy. There's a gang of us.—Couldn't you—help—at a pinch?"

"What do you mean?" demanded Billy, here thoroughly shaking off his drowse.

"Hist, hist!" the hurried whisper now growing husky. "See here," and the man held up two small objects faintly twinkling in the night-light; "see, they are yours, Billy, if you'll only——"

But Billy broke in, and in his resentful eagerness to deliver himself his vocal infirmity somewhat intruded. "D–d–damme, I don't know what you are d–d–driving at, or what you mean, but you had better g–g–go where you belong!" For the moment the fellow, as confounded, did not stir; and Billy, springing to his feet, said, "If you d–don't start, I'll t–t–toss you back over the r–rail!" There was no mistaking this, and the mysterious emissary decamped, disappearing in the direction of the mainmast in the shadow of the booms.

"Hallo, what's the matter?" here came growling from a forecastleman awakened from his deck-doze by Billy's raised voice. And as the foretopman reappeared and was recognized by him: "Ah, Beauty, is it you? Well, something must have been the matter, for you st–st–stuttered."

"Oh," rejoined Billy, now mastering the impediment, "I found an afterguardsman in our part of the ship here, and I bid him be off where he belongs."

"And is that all you did about it, Foretopman?" gruffly demanded another, an irascible old fellow of brick-colored visage and hair who was known to his associate forecastlemen as "Red Pepper." "Such sneaks I should like to marry to the gunner's daughter!"—by that expression meaning that he would like to subject them to disciplinary castigation over a gun.

However, Billy's rendering of the matter satisfactorily accounted to these inquirers for the brief commotion, since of all the sections of a ship's company the forecastlemen, veterans for the most part and bigoted in their sea prejudices, are the most jealous in resenting territorial encroachments, especially on the part of any of the afterguard, of whom they have but a sorry opinion—chiefly landsmen, never going aloft except to reef or furl the mainsail, and in no wise competent to handle a marlinspike or turn in a deadeye, say.

15

This incident sorely puzzled Billy Budd. It was an entirely new experience, the first time in his life that he had ever been personally approached in underhand intriguing fashion. Prior to this encounter he had known nothing of the afterguardsman, the two men being stationed wide apart, one forward and aloft during his watch, the other on deck and aft.

What could it mean? And could they really be guineas, those two glittering objects the interloper had held up to his (Billy's) eyes? Where could the fellow get guineas? Why, even spare buttons are not so plentiful at sea. The more he turned the matter over, the more he was nonplussed, and made uneasy and discomfited. In his disgustful recoil from an overture which, though he but ill comprehended, he instinctively knew must involve evil of some sort, Billy Budd was like a young horse fresh from the pasture suddenly inhaling a vile whiff from some chemical factory, and by repeated snortings trying to get it out of his nostrils and lungs. This frame of mind barred all desire of holding further parley with the fellow, even were it but for the purpose of gaining some enlightenment as to his design in approaching him. And yet he was not without natural curiosity to see how such a visitor in the dark would look in broad day.

He espied him the following afternoon in his first dogwatch below, one of the smokers on that forward part of the upper gun deck allotted to the pipe. He recognized him by his general cut and build more than by his round freckled face and glassy eyes of pale blue, veiled with lashes all but white. And yet Billy was a bit uncertain whether indeed it were he—yonder chap about his own age chatting and laughing in freehearted way, leaning against a gun; a genial young fellow enough to look at, and something of a rattlebrain, to all appearance. Rather chubby too for a sailor, even an afterguardsman. In short, the last man in the world, one would think, to be overburdened with thoughts, especially those perilous thoughts that must needs belong to a conspirator in any serious project, or even to the underling of such a conspirator.

Although Billy was not aware of it, the fellow, with a side-long watchful glance, had perceived Billy first, and then noting that Billy was looking at him, thereupon nodded a familiar sort of friendly recognition as to an old acquaintance, without interrupting the talk he was engaged in with the group of smokers. A day or two afterwards, chancing in the evening promenade on a gun deck to pass Billy, he offered a flying word of good-fellowship, as it were, which by its unexpectedness, and equivocalness under the circumstances, so embarrassed Billy that he knew not how to respond to it, and let it go unnoticed.

Billy was now left more at a loss than before. The ineffectual speculations into which he was led were so disturbingly alien to him that he did his best to smother them. It never entered his mind that here was a matter which, from its extreme questionableness, it was his duty as a loyal bluejacket to report in the proper quarter. And, probably, had such a step been suggested to him, he would have been deterred from taking it by the thought, one of novice magnanimity, that it would savor overmuch of the dirty work of a telltale. He kept the thing to himself. Yet upon one occasion he could not forbear a little disburdening himself to the old Dansker, tempted thereto perhaps by the influence of a balmy night when the ship lay becalmed; the twain, silent for the most part, sitting together on deck, their heads propped against the bulwarks. But it was only a partial and anonymous account that Billy gave, the unfounded scruples above referred to preventing full disclosure to anybody. Upon hearing Billy's version, the sage Dansker seemed to divine more than he was told; and after a little meditation, during which his wrinkles were pursed as into a point, quite effacing for the time that quizzing expression his face sometimes wore: "Didn't I say so, Baby Budd?"

"Say what?" demanded Billy.

"Why, *Jemmy Legs* is *down* on you."

"And what," rejoined Billy in amazement, "has *Jemmy Legs* to do with that cracked afterguardsman?"

"Ho, it was an afterguardsman, then. A cat's-paw, a cat's-paw!" And with that exclamation, whether it had reference to a light puff of air just then coming over the calm sea, or a subtler relation to the afterguardsman, there is no telling, the old Merlin gave a twisting wrench with his black teeth at his plug of tobacco, vouchsafing no reply to Billy's impetuous question, though now repeated, for it was his wont to relapse into grim silence when interrogated in skeptical sort as to any of his sententious oracles, not always very clear ones, rather partaking of that obscurity which invests most Delphic deliverances from any quarter.

Long experience had very likely brought this old man to that bitter prudence which never interferes in aught and never gives advice.

16

Yes, despite the Dansker's pithy insistence as to the master-at-arms being at the bottom of these strange experiences of Billy on board the *Bellipotent*, the young sailor was ready to ascribe them to almost anybody but the man who, to use Billy's own expression, "always had a pleasant word for him." This is to be wondered at. Yet not so much to be wondered at. In certain matters, some sailors even in mature life remain unsophisticated enough. But a young seafarer of the disposition of our athletic foretopman is much of a child-man. And yet a child's utter innocence is but its blank ignorance, and the innocence more or less wanes as intelligence waxes. But in Billy Budd intelligence, such as it was, had advanced while yet his simple-mindedness remained for the most part unaffected. Experience is a teacher indeed; yet did Billy's years make his experience small. Besides, he had none of that intuitive knowledge of the bad which in natures not good or incompletely so foreruns experience, and therefore may pertain, as in some instances it too clearly does pertain, even to youth.

And what could Billy know of man except of man as a mere sailor? And the old-fashioned sailor, the veritable man before the mast, the sailor from boyhood up, he, though indeed of the same species as a landsman, is in some respects singularly distinct from him. The sailor is frankness, the landsman is finesse. Life is not a game with the sailor, demanding the long head—no intricate game of chess where few moves are made in straight-forwardness and ends are attained by indirection, an oblique, tedious, barren game hardly worth that poor candle burnt out in playing it.

Yes, as a class, sailors are in character a juvenile race. Even their deviations are marked by juvenility, this more especially holding true with the sailors of Billy's time. Then too, certain things which apply to all sailors do more pointedly oper-ate here and there upon the junior one. Every sailor, too, is accustomed to obey orders without debating them; his life afloat is externally ruled for him; he is not brought into that promiscuous commerce with mankind where unobstructed free agency on equal terms—equal superficially, at least—soon teaches one that unless upon occasion he exercise a distrust keen in proportion to the fairness of the appearance, some foul turn may be served him. A ruled undemonstrative distrustfulness is so habitual, not with businessmen so much as with men who know their kind in less shallow relations than business, namely, certain men of the world, that they come at last to employ it all but unconsciously; and some of them would very likely feel real surprise at being charged with it as one of their general characteristics.

17

But after the little matter at the mess Billy Budd no more found himself in strange trouble at times about his hammock or his clothes bag or what not. As to that smile that occasionally sunned him, and the pleasant passing word, these were, if not more frequent, yet if anything more pronounced than before.

But for all that, there were certain other demonstrations now. When Claggart's unobserved glance happened to light on belted Billy rolling along the upper gun deck in the leisure of the second dog-watch, exchanging passing broadsides of fun with other young promenaders in the crowd, that glance would follow the cheerful sea Hyperion with a settled meditative and melancholy expression, his eyes strangely suffused with incipient feverish tears. Then would Claggart look like the man of sorrows. Yes, and sometimes the melancholy expression would have in it a touch of soft yearning, as if Claggart could even have loved Billy but for fate and ban. But this was an evanescence, and quickly repented of, as it were, by an immitigable look, pinching and shriveling the visage into the momentary semblance of a wrinkled walnut. But sometimes catching sight in advance of the foretopman coming in his direction, he would, upon their nearing, step aside a little to let him pass, dwelling upon Billy for the moment with the glittering dental satire of a Guise. But upon any abrupt unforeseen encounter a red light would flash forth from his eye like a spark from an anvil in a dusk smithy. That quick, fierce light was a strange one, darted from orbs which in repose were of a color nearest approaching a deeper violet, the softest of shades.

Though some of these caprices of the pit could not but be observed by their object, yet were they beyond the construing of such a nature. And the thews of Billy were hardly compatible with that sort of sensitive spiritual organization which in some cases instinctively conveys to ignorant innocence an admonition of the proximity of the malign. He thought the master-at-arms acted in a manner rather queer at times. That was all. But the occasional frank air and pleasant word went for what they purported to be, the young sailor never having heard as yet of the "too fair-spoken man."

Had the foretopman been conscious of having done or said anything to provoke the ill will of the official, it would have been different with him, and his sight might have been purged if not sharpened. As it was, innocence was his blinder.

So was it with him in yet another matter. Two minor officers, the armorer and captain of the hold, with whom he had never exchanged a word, his position in the ship not bringing him into contact with them, these men now for the first began to cast upon Billy, when they chanced to encounter him, that peculiar glance which evidences that the man from whom it comes has been some way tampered with, and to the prejudice of him upon whom the glance lights. Never did it occur to Billy as a thing to be noted or a thing suspicious, though he well knew the fact, that the armorer and captain of the hold, with the ship's yeoman, apothecary, and others of that grade, were by naval usage messmates of the master-at-arms, men with ears convenient to his confidential tongue.

But the general popularity that came from our Handsome Sailor's manly forwardness upon occasion and irresistible good nature, indicating no mental superiority tending to excite an invidious feeling, this good will on the part of most of his shipmates made him the less to concern himself about such mute aspects toward him as those whereto allusion has just been made, aspects he could not so fathom as to infer their whole import.

As to the afterguardsman, though Billy for reasons already given necessarily saw little of him, yet when the two did happen to meet, invariably came the fellow's offhand cheerful recognition, sometimes accompanied by a passing pleasant word or two. Whatever that equivocal young person's original design may really have been, or the design of

which he might have been the deputy, certain it was from his manner upon these occasions that he had wholly dropped it.

It was as if his precocity of crookedness (and every vulgar villain is precocious) had for once deceived him, and the man he had sought to entrap as a simpleton had through his very simplicity ignominiously baffled him.

But shrewd ones may opine that it was hardly possible for Billy to refrain from going up to the afterguardsman and bluntly demanding to know his purpose in the initial interview so abruptly closed in the forechains. Shrewd ones may also think it but natural in Billy to set about sounding some of the other impressed men of the ship in order to discover what basis, if any, there was for the emissary's obscure suggestions as to plotting disaffection aboard. Yes, shrewd ones may so think. But something more, or rather something else than mere shrewdness is perhaps needful for the due understanding of such a character as Billy Budd's.

As to Claggart, the monomania in the man—if that indeed it were—as involuntarily disclosed by starts in the manifestations detailed, yet in general covered over by his self-contained and rational demeanor; this, like a subterranean fire, was eating its way deeper and deeper in him. Something decisive must come of it.

18

After the mysterious interview in the forechains, the one so abruptly ended there by Billy, nothing especially germane to the story occurred until the events now about to be narrated.

Elsewhere it has been said that in the lack of frigates (of course better sailers than line-of-battle ships) in the English squadron up the Straits at that period, the *Bellipotent* 74 was occasionally employed not only as an available substitute for a scout, but at times on detached service of more important kind. This was not alone because of her sailing qualities, not common in a ship of her rate, but quite as much, probably, that the character of her commander, it was thought, specially adapted him for any duty where under unforeseen difficulties a prompt initiative might have to be taken in some matter demanding knowledge and ability in addition to those qualities implied in good seamanship. It was on an expedition of the latter sort, a somewhat distant one, and when the *Bellipotent* was almost at her furthest remove from the fleet, that in the latter part of an afternoon watch she unexpectedly came in sight of a ship of the enemy. It proved to be a frigate. The latter, perceiving through the glass that the weight of men and metal would be heavily against her, invoking her light heels crowded sail to get away. After a chase urged almost against hope and lasting until about the middle of the first dogwatch, she signally succeeded in effecting her escape.

Not long after the pursuit had been given up, and ere the excitement incident thereto had altogether waned away, the master-at-arms, ascending from his cavernous sphere, made his appearance cap in hand by the mainmast respectfully waiting the notice of Captain Vere, then solitary walking the weather side of the quarter-deck, doubtless somewhat chafed at the failure of the pursuit. The spot where Claggart stood was the place allotted to men of lesser grades seeking some more particular interview either with the officer of the deck or the captain himself. But from the latter it was not often that a sailor or petty officer of those days would seek a hearing; only some exceptional cause would, according to established custom, have warranted that.

Presently, just as the commander, absorbed in his reflections, was on the point of turning aft in his promenade, he became sensible of Claggart's presence, and saw the doffed cap held in deferential expectancy. Here be it said that Captain Vere's personal knowledge of this petty officer had only begun at the time of the ship's last sailing from home, Claggart then for the first, in transfer from a ship detained for repairs, supplying on board the *Bellipotent* the place of a previous master-at-arms disabled and ashore.

No sooner did the commander observe who it was that now deferentially stood awaiting his notice than a peculiar expression came over him. It was not unlike that which uncontrollably will flit across the countenance of one at unawares encountering a person who, though known to him indeed, has hardly been long enough known for thorough knowledge, but something in whose aspect nevertheless now for the first provokes a vaguely repellent distaste. But coming to a stand and resuming much of his wonted official manner, save that a sort of impatience lurked in the intonation of the opening word, he said "Well? What is it, Master-at-arms?"

With the air of a subordinate grieved at the necessity of being a messenger of ill tidings, and while conscientiously determined to be frank yet equally resolved upon shunning overstatement, Claggart at this invitation, or rather summons to disburden, spoke up. What he said, conveyed in the language of no uneducated man, was to the effect following, if not altogether in these words, namely, that during the chase and preparations for the possible encounter he had seen enough to convince him that at least one sailor aboard was a dangerous character in a ship mustering some who not only had taken a guilty part in the late serious troubles, but others also who, like the man in question, had entered His Majesty's service under another form than enlistment.

At this point Captain Vere with some impatience interrupted him: "Be direct, man; say *impressed men.*"

Claggart made a gesture of subservience, and proceeded. Quite lately he (Claggart) had begun to suspect that on the gun decks some sort of movement prompted by the sailor in question was covertly going on, but he had not thought himself warranted in reporting the suspicion so long as it remained indistinct. But from what he had that afternoon observed in the man referred to, the suspicion of something clandestine going on had advanced to a point less removed from certainty. He deeply felt, he added, the serious responsibility assumed in making a report involving such possible consequences to the individual mainly concerned, besides tending to augment those natural anxieties which every naval commander must feel in view of extraordinary outbreaks so recent as those which, he sorrowfully said it, it needed not to name.

Now at the first broaching of the matter Captain Vere, taken by surprise, could not wholly dissemble his disquietude. But as Claggart went on, the former's aspect changed into restiveness under something in the testifier's manner in giving his testimony. However, he refrained from interrupting him. And Claggart, continuing, concluded with this: "God forbid, your honor, that the *Bellipotent's* should be the experience of the ——"

"Never mind that!" here peremptorily broke in the superior, his face altering with anger, instinctively divining the ship that the other was about to name, one in which the Nore Mutiny had assumed a singularly tragical character that for a time jeopardized the life of its commander. Under the circumstances he was indignant at the purposed allusion. When the commissioned officers themselves were on all occasions very heedful how they referred to the recent events in the fleet, for a petty officer unnecessarily to allude to them in the presence of his captain, this struck him as a most immodest presumption. Besides, to his quick sense of self-respect it even looked under the circumstances something like an attempt to alarm him. Nor at first was he without some surprise that one who so far as he had hitherto come under his notice had shown considerable tact in his function should in this particular evince such lack of it.

But these thoughts and kindred dubious ones flitting across his mind were suddenly replaced by an intuitional surmise which, though as yet obscure in form, served practically to affect his reception of the ill tidings. Certain it is that, long versed in everything pertaining to the complicated gun-deck life, which like every other form of life has its secret mines and dubious side, the side popularly disclaimed, Captain Vere did not permit himself to be unduly disturbed by the general tenor of his subordinate's report.

Furthermore, if in view of recent events prompt action should be taken at the first palpable sign of recurring insubordination, for all that, not judicious would it be, he thought, to keep the idea of lingering disaffection alive by undue forwardness in crediting an informer, even if his own subordinate and charged among other things with police surveillance of the crew. This feeling would not perhaps have so prevailed with him were it not that upon a prior occasion the patriotic zeal officially evinced by Claggart had somewhat irritated him as appearing rather supersensible and strained. Furthermore, something even in the official's self-possessed and somewhat ostentatious manner in making his specifications strangely reminded him of a bandsman, a perjurous witness in a capital case before a court-martial ashore of which when a lieutenant he (Captain Vere) had been a member.

Now the peremptory check given to Claggart in the matter of the arrested allusion was quickly followed up by this: "You say that there is at least one dangerous man aboard. Name him."

"William Budd, a foretopman, your honor."

"William Budd!" repeated Captain Vere with unfeigned astonishment. "And mean you the man that Lieutenant Ratcliffe took from the merchantman not very long ago, the young fellow who seems to be so popular with the men—Billy, the Handsome Sailor, as they call him?"

"The same, your honor; but for all his youth and good looks, a deep one. Not for nothing does he insinuate himself into the good will of his ship-mates, since at the least they will at a pinch say—all hands will—a good word for him, and at all hazards. Did Lieutenant Ratcliffe happen to tell your honor of that adroit fling of Budd's, jumping up in the cutter's bow under the merchantman's stern when he was being taken off? It is even masked by that sort of good-humored air that at heart he resents his impressment. You have but noted his fair cheek. A mantrap may be under the ruddy-tipped daisies."

Now the Handsome Sailor as a signal figure among the crew had naturally enough attracted the captain's attention from the first. Though in general not very demonstrative to his officers, he had congratulated Lieutenant Ratcliffe upon his good fortune in lighting on such a fine specimen of the *genus homo*, who in the nude might have posed for a statue of young Adam before the Fall. As to Billy's adieu to the ship *Rights-of-Man*, which the boarding lieutenant had indeed reported to him, but, in a deferential way, more as a good story than aught else, Captain Vere, though mistakenly understanding it as a satiric sally, had but thought so much the better of the impressed man for it; as a military sailor, admiring the spirit that could take an arbitrary enlistment so merrily and sensibly. The foretopman's conduct, too, so far as it had fallen under the captain's notice, had confirmed the first happy augury, while the new recruit's qualities as a "sailor-man" seemed to be such that he had thought of recommending him to the executive officer for promotion to a place that would more frequently bring him under his own observation, namely, the captaincy of the mizzentop, replacing there in the starboard watch a man not so young whom partly for that reason he deemed less fitted for the post. Be it parenthesized here that since the mizzentopmen have not to handle such breadths of heavy canvas as the lower sails on the mainmast and foremast, a young man if of the right stuff not only seems best adapted to duty there, but in fact is generally selected for the captaincy of that top, and the company under him are light hands and often but striplings. In sum, Captain Vere had from the beginning deemed Billy Budd to be what in the naval parlance of the time was called a "King's bargain": that is to say, for His Britannic Majesty's navy a capital investment at small outlay or none at all.

After a brief pause, during which the reminiscences above mentioned passed vividly through his mind and he weighed the import of Claggart's last suggestion conveyed in the phrase "mantrap under the daisies," and the more he weighed it the less reliance he felt in the informer's good faith, suddenly he turned upon him and in a low voice demanded: "Do you come to me, Master-at-arms, with so foggy a tale? As to Budd, cite me an act or spoken word of his confirmatory of what you in general charge against him. Stay," drawing nearer to him; "heed what you speak. Just now, and in a case like this, there is a yardarm-end for the false witness."

"Ah, your honor!" sighed Claggart, mildly shaking his shapely head as in sad deprecation of such unmerited severity of tone. Then, bridling—erecting himself as in virtuous self-assertion—he circumstantially alleged certain words and acts which collectively, if credited, led to presumptions mortally inculpating Budd. And for some of these averments, he added, substantiating proof was not far.

With gray eyes impatient and distrustful essaying to fathom to the bottom Claggart's calm violet ones, Captain Vere again heard him out; then for the moment stood ruminating. The mood he evinced, Claggart—himself for the time liberated from the other's scrutiny—steadily regarded with a look difficult to render: a look curious of the operation of his tactics, a look such as might have been that of the spokesman of the envious children of Jacob deceptively imposing upon the troubled patriarch the blood-dyed coat of young Joseph.

Though something exceptional in the moral quality of Captain Vere made him, in earnest encounter with a fellow man, a veritable touchstone of that man's essential nature, yet now as to Claggart and what was really going on in him his feeling partook less of intuitional conviction than of strong suspicion clogged by strange dubieties. The perplexity he evinced proceeded less from aught touching the man informed against—as Claggart doubtless opined—than from considerations how best to act in regard to the informer. At first, indeed, he was naturally for summoning that substantiation of his allegations which Claggart said was at hand. But such a proceeding would result in the matter at once getting abroad, which in the present stage of it, he thought, might undesirably affect the ship's company. If Claggart was a false witness—that closed the affair. And therefore, before trying the accusation, he would first practically test the accuser; and he thought this could be done in a quiet, undemonstrative way.

The measure he determined upon involved a shifting of the scene, a transfer to a place less exposed to observation than the broad quarter-deck. For although the few gun-room officers there at the time had, in due observance of naval etiquette, withdrawn to leeward the moment Captain Vere had begun his promenade on the deck's weather side; and though during the colloquy with Claggart they of course ventured not to diminish the distance; and though throughout the interview Captain Vere's voice was far from high, and Claggart's silvery and low; and the wind in the cordage and the wash of the sea helped the more to put them beyond earshot; nevertheless, the interview's continuance already had attracted observation from some topmen aloft and other sailors in the waist or further forward.

Having determined upon his measures, Captain Vere forthwith took action. Abruptly turning to Claggart, he asked, "Master-at-arms, is it now Budd's watch aloft?"

"No, your honor."

Whereupon, "Mr. Wilkes!" summoning the nearest midshipman. "Tell Albert to come to me." Albert was the captain's hammock-boy, a sort of sea valet in whose discretion and fidelity his master had much confidence. The lad appeared.

"You know Budd, the foretopman?"

"I do, sir."

"Go find him. It is his watch off. Manage to tell him out of earshot that he is wanted aft. Contrive it that he speaks to nobody. Keep him in talk yourself. And not till you get well aft here, not till then let him know that the place where he is wanted is my cabin. You understand. Go.—Master-at-arms, show yourself on the decks below, and when you think it time for Albert to be coming with his man, stand by quietly to follow the sailor in."

19

Now when the foretopman found himself in the cabin, closeted there, as it were, with the captain and Claggart, he was surprised enough. But it was a surprise unaccompanied by apprehension or distrust. To an immature nature essentially honest and humane, forewarning intimations of subtler danger from one's kind come tardily if at all. The only thing that took shape in the young sailor's mind was this: Yes, the captain, I have always thought, looks kindly upon me. Wonder if he's going to make me his coxswain. I should like that.

And may be now he is going to ask the master-at-arms about me.

"Shut the door there, sentry," said the commander; "stand without, and let nobody come in. —Now, Master-at-arms, tell this man to his face what you told of him to me," and stood prepared to scrutinize the mutually confronting visages.

With the measured step and calm collected air of an asylum physician approaching in the public hall some patient beginning to show indications of a coming paroxysm, Claggart deliberately advanced within short range of Billy and, mesmerically looking him in the eye, briefly recapitulated the accusation.

Not at first did Billy take it in. When he did, the rose-tan of his cheek looked struck as by white leprosy. He stood like one impaled and gagged. Meanwhile the accuser's eyes, removing not as yet from the blue dilated ones, underwent a phenomenal change, their wonted rich violet color blurring into a muddy purple. Those lights of human intelligence, losing human expression, were gelidly protruding like the alien eyes of certain uncatalogued creatures of the deep. The first mesmeristic glance was one of serpent fascination; the last was as the paralyzing lurch of the torpedo fish.

"Speak, man!" said Captain Vere to the transfixed one, struck by his aspect even more than by Claggart's. "Speak! Defend yourself!" Which appeal caused but a strange dumb gesturing and gurgling in Billy; amazement at such an accusation so suddenly sprung on inexperienced nonage; this, and, it may be, horror of the accuser's eyes, serving to bring out his lurking defect and in this instance for the time intensifying it into a convulsed tongue-tie; while the intent head and entire form straining forward in an agony of ineffectual eagerness to obey the injunction to speak and defend himself, gave an expression to the face like that of a condemned vestal priestess in the moment of being buried alive, and in the first struggle against suffocation.

Though at the time Captain Vere was quite ignorant of Billy's liability to vocal impediment, he now immediately divined it, since vividly Billy's aspect recalled to him that of a bright young schoolmate of his whom he had once seen struck by much the same startling impotence in the act of eagerly rising in the class to be foremost in response to a testing question put to it by the master. Going close up to the young sailor, and laying a soothing hand on his shoulder, he said, "There is no hurry, my boy. Take your time, take your time." Contrary to the effect intended, these words so fatherly in tone, doubtless touching Billy's heart to the quick, prompted yet more violent efforts at utterance—efforts soon ending for the time in confirming the paralysis, and bringing to his face an expression which was as a crucifixion to behold. The next instant, quick as the flame from a discharged cannon at night, his right arm shot out, and Claggart dropped to the deck. Whether intentionally or but owing to the young athlete's superior height, the blow had taken effect full upon the forehead, so shapely and intellectual-looking a feature in the master-at-arms; so that the body fell over lengthwise, like a heavy plank tilted from erectness. A gasp or two, and he lay motionless.

"Fated boy," breathed Captain Vere in tone so low as to be almost a whisper, "what have you done! But here, help me."

The twain raised the felled one from the loins up into a sitting position. The spare form flexibly acquiesced, but inertly. It was like handling a dead snake. They lowered it back. Regaining erectness, Captain Vere with one hand covering his face stood to all appearance as impassive as the object at his feet. Was he absorbed in taking in all the bearings of the event and what was best not only now at once to be done, but also in the sequel? Slowly he uncovered his face; and the effect was as if the moon emerging from eclipse should reappear with quite another aspect than that which had gone into hiding. The father in him, manifested towards Billy thus far in the scene, was replaced by the military disciplinarian. In his official tone he bade the foretopman retire to a stateroom aft (pointing it out), and there remain till thence summoned. This order Billy in silence mechanically obeyed. Then going to the cabin door where it opened on the quarter-deck, Captain Vere said to the sentry without, "Tell somebody to send Albert here." When the lad appeared, his master so contrived it that he should not catch sight of the prone one. "Albert," he said to him, "tell the surgeon I wish to see him. You need not come back till called."

When the surgeon entered—a self-poised character of that grave sense and experience that hardly anything could take him aback—Captain Vere advanced to meet him, thus unconsciously intercepting his view of Claggart, and, interrupting the other's wonted ceremonious salutation, said, "Nay. Tell me how it is with yonder man," directing his attention to the prostrate one.

The surgeon looked, and for all his self-command somewhat started at the abrupt revelation. On Claggart's always pallid complexion, thick black blood was now oozing from nostril and ear. To the gazer's professional eye it was unmistakably no living man that he saw.

"Is it so, then?" said Captain Vere, intently watching him. "I thought it. But verify it." Whereupon the customary tests confirmed the surgeon's first glance, who now, looking up in unfeigned concern, cast a look of intense inquisitiveness upon his superior. But Captain Vere, with one hand to his brow, was standing motionless. Suddenly, catching the surgeon's arm convulsively, he exclaimed, pointing down to the body, "It is the divine judgment on Ananias! Look!"

Disturbed by the excited manner he had never before observed in the *Bellipotent*'s captain, and as yet wholly ignorant of the affair, the prudent surgeon nevertheless held his peace, only again looking an earnest interrogatory as to what it was that had resulted in such a tragedy.

But Captain Vere was now again motionless, standing absorbed in thought. Again starting, he vehemently exclaimed, "Struck dead by an angel of God! Yet the angel must hang!"

At these passionate interjections, mere incoherences to the listener as yet unapprised of the antecedents, the surgeon was profoundly discomposed. But now, as recollecting himself, Captain Vere in less passionate tone briefly related the circumstances leading up to the event. "But come; we must dispatch," he added. "Help me to remove him" (meaning the body) "to yonder compartment," designating one opposite that where the foretopman remained immured. Anew disturbed by a request that, as implying a desire for secrecy, seemed unaccountably strange to him, there was nothing for the subordinate to do but comply.

"Go now," said Captain Vere with something of his wonted manner. "Go now. I presently shall call a drumhead court. Tell the lieutenants what has happened, and tell Mr. Mordant" (meaning the captain of marines), "and charge them to keep the matter to themselves."

20

Full of disquietude and misgiving, the surgeon left the cabin. Was Captain Vere suddenly affected in his mind, or was it but a transient excitement, brought about by so strange and extraordinary a tragedy? As to the drumhead court, it struck the surgeon as impolitic, if nothing more. The thing to do, he thought, was to place Billy Budd in confinement, and in a way dictated by usage, and postpone further action in so extraordinary a case to such time as they should rejoin the squadron, and then refer it to the admiral. He recalled the unwonted agitation of Captain Vere and his excited exclamations, so at variance with his normal manner. Was he unhinged?

But assuming that he is, it is not so susceptible of proof. What then can the surgeon do? No more trying situation is conceivable than that of an officer subordinate under a captain whom he suspects to be not mad, indeed, but yet not quite unaffected in his intellects. To argue his order to him would be insolence. To resist him would be mutiny.

In obedience to Captain Vere, he communicated what had happened to the lieutenants and captain of marines, saying nothing as to the captain's state. They fully shared his own surprise and concern. Like him too, they seemed to think that such a matter should be referred to the admiral.

21

Who in the rainbow can draw the line where the violet tint ends and the orange tint begins? Distinctly we see the difference of the colors, but where exactly does the one first blendingly enter into the other? So with sanity and insanity. In pronounced cases there is no question about them. But in some supposed cases, in various degrees supposedly less pronounced, to draw the exact line of demarcation few will undertake, though for a fee becoming considerate some professional experts will. There is nothing namable but that some men will, or undertake to, do it for pay.

Whether Captain Vere, as the surgeon professionally and privately surmised, was really the sudden victim of any degree of aberration, every one must determine for himself by such light as this narrative may afford.

That the unhappy event which has been narrated could not have happened at a worse juncture was but too true. For it was close on the heel of the suppressed insurrections, an aftertime very critical to naval authority, demanding from every English sea commander two qualities not readily interfusable—prudence and rigor. Moreover, there was something crucial in the case.

In the jugglery of circumstances preceding and attending the event on board the *Bellipotent*, and in the light of that martial code whereby it was formally to be judged, innocence and guilt personified in Claggart and Budd in effect changed places. In a legal view the apparent victim of the tragedy was he who had sought to victimize a man blameless; and the indisputable deed of the latter, navally regarded, constituted the most henious of military crimes. Yet more. The essential right and wrong involved in the matter, the clearer that might be, so much the worse for the responsibility of a loyal sea commander, inasmuch as he was not authorized to determine the matter on that primitive basis.

Small wonder then that the *Bellipotent*'s captain, though in general a man of rapid decision, felt that circumspectness not less than promptitude was necessary. Until he could decide upon his course, and in each detail; and not only so, but until the concluding measure was upon the point of being enacted, he deemed it advisable, in view of all the circumstances, to guard as much as possible against publicity. Here he may or may not have erred. Certain it is, however, that subsequently in the confidential talk of more than one or two gun rooms and cabins he was not a little criticized by some officers, a fact imputed by his friends and vehemently by his cousin Jack Denton to professional jealousy of Starry Vere. Some imaginative ground for invidious comment there was. The maintenance of secrecy in the matter, the confining all knowledge of it for a time to the place where the homicide occurred, the quarter-deck cabin; in these particulars lurked some resemblance to the policy adopted in those tragedies of the palace which have occurred more than once in the capital founded by Peter the Barbarian.

The case indeed was such that fain would the *Bellipotent*'s captain have deferred taking any action whatever respecting it further than to keep the foretopman a close prisoner till the ship rejoined the squadron and then submitting the matter to the judgment of his admiral.

But a true military officer is in one particular like a true monk. Not with more of self-abnegation will the latter keep his vows of monastic obedience than the former his vows of allegiance to martial duty.

Feeling that unless quick action was taken on it, the deed of the foretopman, so soon as it should be known on the gun decks, would tend to awaken any slumbering embers of the Nore among the crew, a sense of the urgency of the case overruled in Captain Vere every other consideration. But though a conscientious disciplinarian, he was no lover of authority for mere authority's sake. Very far was he from embracing opportunities for monopolizing to himself the perils of moral responsibility, none at least that could properly be referred to an official superior or shared with him by his official equals or even subordinates. So thinking, he was glad it would not be at variance with usage to turn the matter over to a summary court of his own officers, reserving to himself, as the one on whom the ultimate accountability would rest, the right of maintaining a supervision of it, or formally or informally interposing at need. Accordingly a drumhead court was summarily convened, he electing the individuals composing it: the first lieutenant, the captain of marines, and the sailing master.

In associating an officer of marines with the sea lieutenant and the sailing master in a case having to do with a sailor, the commander perhaps deviated from general custom. He was prompted thereto by the circumstance that he took that soldier to be a judicious person, thoughtful, and not altogether incapable of grappling with a difficult case unprecedented in his prior experience. Yet even as to him he was not without some latent misgiving, for withal he was an extremely good-natured man, an enjoyer of his dinner, a sound sleeper, and inclined to obesity—a man who though he would always maintain his manhood in battle might not prove altogether reliable in a moral dilemma involving aught of the tragic. As to the first lieutenant and the sailing master, Captain Vere could not but be aware that though honest natures, of approved gallantry upon occasion, their intelligence was mostly confined to the matter of active seamanship and the fighting demands of their profession.

The court was held in the same cabin where the unfortunate affair had taken place. This cabin, the commander's, embraced the entire area under the poop deck. Aft, and on either side, was a small stateroom, the one now temporarily a jail and the other a dead-house, and a yet smaller compartment, leaving a space between expanding forward into a goodly oblong of length coinciding with the ship's beam. A skylight of moderate dimension was overhead, and at each end of the oblong space were two sashed porthole windows easily convertible back into embrasures for short carronades.

All being quickly in readiness, Billy Budd was arraigned, Captain Vere necessarily appearing as the sole witness in the case, and as such temporarily sinking his rank, though singularly maintaining it in a matter apparently trivial, namely, that he testified from the ship's weather side, with that object having caused the court to sit on the lee side. Concisely he narrated all that had led up to the catastrophe, omitting nothing in Claggart's accusation and deposing as to the manner in which the prisoner had received it. At this testimony the three officers glanced with no little surprise at Billy Budd, the last man they would have suspected either of the mutinous design alleged by Claggart or the undeniable deed he himself had done. The first lieutenant, taking judicial primacy and turning toward the prisoner, said: "Captain Vere has spoken. Is it or is it not as Captain Vere says?"

In response came syllables not so much impeded in the utterance as might have been anticipated. They were these: "Captain Vere tells the truth. It is just as Captain Vere says, but it is not as the master-at-arms said. I have eaten the King's bread and I am true to the King."

"I believe you, my man," said the witness, his voice indicating a suppressed emotion not otherwise betrayed.

"God will bless you for that, your honor!" not without stammering said Billy, and all but broke down. But immediately he was recalled to self-control by another question, to which with the same emotional difficulty of utterance he said, "No, there was no malice between us. I never bore malice against the master-at-arms. I am sorry that he is dead. I did not mean to kill him. Could I have used my tongue I would not have struck him. But he foully lied to my face and in presence of my captain, and I had to say something, and I could only say it with a blow, God help me!"

In the impulsive aboveboard manner of the frank one the court saw confirmed all that was implied in words that just previously had perplexed them, coming as they did from the testifier to the tragedy and promptly following Billy's impassioned disclaimer of mutinous intent—Captain Vere's words, "I believe you, my man."

Next it was asked of him whether he knew of or suspected aught savoring of incipient trouble (meaning mutiny, though the explicit term was avoided) going on in any section of the ship's company.

The reply lingered. This was naturally imputed by the court to the same vocal embarrassment which had retarded or obstructed previous answers. But in main it was otherwise here, the question immediately recalling to Billy's mind the interview with the afterguardsman in the forechains. But an innate repugnance to playing a part at all approaching that of an informer against one's own shipmates—the same erring sense of uninstructed honor which had stood in the way of his reporting the matter at the time, though as a loyal man-of-war's man it was incumbent on him, and failure so to do, if charged against him and proven, would have subjected him to the heaviest of penalties; this, with the blind feeling now his that nothing really was being hatched, prevailed with him. When the answer came it was a negative.

"One question more," said the officer of marines, now first speaking and with a troubled earnestness. "You tell us that what the master-at-arms said against you was a lie. Now why should he have so lied, so maliciously lied, since you declare there was no malice between you?"

At that question, unintentionally touching on a spiritual sphere wholly obscure to Billy's thoughts, he was nonplussed, evincing a confusion indeed that some observers, such as can readily be imagined, would have construed into involuntary evidence of hidden guilt. Nevertheless, he strove some way to answer, but all at once relinquished the vain endeavor, at the same time turning an appealing glance towards Captain Vere as deeming him his best helper and friend. Captain Vere, who had been seated for a time, rose to his feet, addressing the interrogator. "The question you put to him comes naturally enough. But how can he rightly answer it?—or anybody else, unless indeed it be he who lies within there," designating the compartment where lay the corpse. "But the prone one there will not rise to our summons. In effect, though, as it seems to me, the point you make is hardly material. Quite aside from any conceivable motive actuating the master-at-arms, and irrespective of the provocation to the blow, a martial court must needs in the present case confine its attention to the blow's consequence, which consequence justly is to be deemed not otherwise than as the striker's deed."

This utterance, the full significance of which it was not at all likely that Billy took in, nevertheless caused him to turn a wistful interrogative look toward the speaker, a look in its dumb expressiveness not unlike that which a dog of generous breed might turn upon his master, seeking in his face some elucidation of a previous gesture ambiguous to the canine intelligence. Nor was the same utterance without marked effect upon the three officers, more especially the soldier. Couched in it seemed to them a meaning unanticipated, involving a prejudgment on the speaker's part. It served to augment a mental disturbance previously evident enough.

The soldier once more spoke, in a tone of suggestive dubiety addressing at once his associates and Captain Vere: "Nobody is present—none of the ship's company, I mean—who might shed lateral light, if any is to be had, upon what remains mysterious in this matter."

"That is thoughtfully put," said Captain Vere; "I see your drift. Ay, there is a mystery; but, to use a scriptural phrase, it is a 'mystery of iniquity,' a matter for psychologic theologians to discuss. But what has a military court to do with it? Not to add that for us any possible investigation of it is cut off by the lasting tongue-tie of—him—in yonder," again designating the mortuary stateroom. "The prisoner's deed—with that alone we have to do."

To this, and particularly the closing reiteration, the marine soldier, knowing not how aptly to reply, sadly abstained from saying aught. The first lieutenant, who at the outset had not unnaturally assumed primacy in the court, now overrulingly instructed by a glance from Captain Vere, a glance more effective than words, resumed that primacy. Turning to the prisoner, "Budd," he said, and scarce in equable tones, "Budd, if you have aught further to say for yourself, say it now."

Upon this the young sailor turned another quick glance toward Captain Vere; then, as taking a hint from that aspect, a hint confirming his own instinct that silence was now best, replied to the lieutenant, "I have said all, sir."

The marine—the same who had been the sentinel without the cabin door at the time that the foretopman, followed by the master-at-arms, entered it—he, standing by the sailor throughout these judicial proceedings, was now directed to take him back to the after compartment originally assigned to the prisoner and his custodian. As the twain disappeared from view, the three officers, as partially liberated from some inward constraint associated with Billy's mere presence, simultaneously stirred in their seats. They exchanged looks of troubled indecision, yet feeling that decide they must and without long delay. For Captain Vere, he for the time stood—unconsciously with his back toward them, apparently in one of his absent fits—gazing out from a sashed porthole to windward upon the monotonous blank of the twilight sea.

But the court's silence continuing, broken only at moments by brief consultations, in low earnest tones, this served to arouse him and energize him. Turning, he to-and-fro paced the cabin athwart; in the returning ascent to windward climbing the slant deck in the ship's lee roll, without knowing it symbolizing thus in his action a mind resolute to surmount difficulties even if against primitive instincts strong as the wind and the sea. Presently he came to a stand before the three. After scanning their faces he stood less as mustering his thoughts for expression than as one inly deliberating how best to put them to well-meaning men not intellectually mature, men with whom it was necessary to demonstrate certain principles that were axioms to himself. Similar impatience as to talking is perhaps one reason that deters some minds from addressing any popular assemblies.

When speak he did, something, both in the substance of what he said and his manner of saying it, showed the influence of unshared studies modifying and tempering the practical training of an active career. This, along with his phraseology, now and then was suggestive of the grounds whereon rested that imputation of a certain pedantry socially alleged against him by certain naval men of wholly practical cast, captains who nevertheless would frankly concede that His Majesty's navy mustered no more efficient officer of their grade than Starry Vere.

What he said was to this effect: "Hitherto I have been but the witness, little more; and I should hardly think now to take another tone, that of your coadjutor for the time, did I not perceive in you—at the crisis too—a troubled hesitancy, proceeding, I doubt not, from the clash of military duty with moral scruple—scruple vitalized by compassion. For the compassion, how can I otherwise than share it? But, mindful of paramount obligations, I strive against scruples that may tend to enervate decision. Not, gentlemen, that I hide from myself that the case is in exceptional one. Speculatively regarded, it well might be referred to a jury of casuists. But for us here, acting not as casuists or moralists, it is a case practical, and under martial law practically to be dealt with.

"But your scruples: do they move as in a dusk? Challenge them. Make them advance and declare themselves. Come now; do they import something like this: If, mindless of palliating circumstances, we are bound to regard the death of the master-at-arms as the prisoner's deed, then does that deed constitute a capital crime whereof the penalty is a mortal one. But in natural justice is nothing but the prisoner's overt act to be considered? How can we adjudge to summary and shameful death a fellow creature innocent before God, and whom we feel to be so?—Does that state it aright? You sign sad assent. Well, I too feel that, the full force of that. It is Nature. But do these buttons that we wear attest that our allegiance is to Nature? No, to the King. Though the ocean, which is inviolate Nature primeval, though this be the element where we move and have our being as sailors, yet as the King's officers lies our duty in a sphere correspondingly natural? So little is that true, that in receiving our commissions we in the most important regards ceased to be natural free agents. When war is declared are we the commissioned fighters previously consulted? We fight at command. If our judgments approve the war, that is but coincidence. So in other particulars. So now. For suppose condemnation to follow these present proceedings. Would it be so much we ourselves that would condemn as it would be martial law operating through us? For that law and the rigor of it, we are not responsible. Our vowed responsibility is in this: That however pitilessly that law may operate in any instances, we nevertheless adhere to it and administer it.

"But the exceptional in the matter moves the hearts within you. Even so too is mine moved. But let not warm hearts betray heads that should be cool. Ashore in a criminal case, will an upright judge allow himself off the bench to be waylaid by some tender kinswoman of the accused seeking to touch him with her tearful plea? Well, the heart here, sometimes the feminine in man, is as that piteous woman, and hard though it be, she must be ruled out."

He paused, earnestly studying them for a moment; then resumed.

"But something in your aspect seems to urge that it is not solely the heart that moves in you, but also the conscience, the private conscience. But tell me whether or not, occupying the position we do, private conscience should not yield to that imperial one formulated in the code under which alone we officially proceed?"

Here the three men moved in their seats, less convinced than agitated by the course of an argument troubling but the more the spontaneous conflict within.

Perceiving which, the speaker paused for a moment; then abruptly changing his tone, went on.

"To steady us a bit, let us recur to the facts.—In wartime at sea a man-of-war's man strikes his superior in grade, and the blow kills. Apart from its effect the blow itself is, according to the Articles of War, a capital crime. Furthermore ———"

"Ay, sir," emotionally broke in the officer of marines, "in one sense it was. But surely Budd purposed neither mutiny nor homicide."

"Surely not, my good man. And before a court less arbitrary and more merciful than a martial one, that plea would largely extenuate. At the Last Assizes it shall acquit. But how here? We proceed under the law of the Mutiny Act. In feature no child can resemble his father more than that Act resembles in spirit the thing from which it derives—War. In His Majesty's service—in this ship, indeed—there are Englishmen forced to fight for the King against their will. Against their conscience, for aught we know. Though as their fellow creatures some of us may appreciate their position, yet as navy officers what reck we of it? Still less recks the enemy. Our impressed men he would fain cut down in the same swath with our volunteers. As regards the enemy's naval conscripts, some of whom may even share our own abhorrence of the regicidal French Directory, it is the same on our side. War looks but to the frontage, the appearance. And the Mutiny Act, War's child, takes after the father. Budd's intent or non-intent is nothing to the purpose.

"But while, put to it by those anxieties in you which I cannot but respect, I only repeat myself—while thus strangely we prolong proceedings that should be summary—the enemy may be sighted and an engagement result. We must do; and one of two things must we do—condemn or let go."

"Can we not convict and yet mitigate the penalty?" asked the sailing master, here speaking, and falteringly, for the first.

"Gentlemen, were that clearly lawful for us under the circumstances, consider the consequences of such clemency. The people" (meaning the ship's company) "have native sense; most of them are familiar with our naval usage and tradition; and how would they take it? Even could you explain to them—which our official position forbids—they, long molded by arbitrary discipline, have not that kind of intelligent responsiveness that might qualify them to comprehend and discriminate. No, to the people the foretopman's deed, however it be worded in the announcement, will be plain homicide committed in a flagrant act of mutiny. What penalty for that should follow, they know. But it does not follow. *Why?* they will ruminate. You know what sailors are. Will they not revert to the recent outbreak at the Nore? Ay. They know the well-founded alarm—the panic it struck throughout England. Your clement sentence they would account pusillanimous. They would think that we flinch, that we are afraid of them—afraid of practicing a lawful rigor singularly demanded at this juncture, lest it should provoke new troubles. What shame to us such a conjecture on their part, and how deadly to discipline. You see then, whither, prompted by duty and the law, I steadfastly drive. But I beseech you, my friends, do not take me amiss. I feel as you do for this unfortunate boy. But did he know our hearts, I take him to be of that generous nature that he would feel even for us on whom in this military necessity so heavy a compulsion is laid."

With that, crossing the deck he resumed his place by the sashed porthole, tacitly leaving the three to come to a decision. On the cabin's opposite side the troubled court sat silent. Loyal lieges, plain and practical, though at bottom they dissented from some points Captain Vere had put to them, they were without the faculty, hardly had the inclination, to gainsay one whom they felt to be an earnest man, one too not less their superior in mind than in naval rank. But it is not improbable that even such of his words as were not without influence over them, less came home to them than his closing appeal to their instinct as sea officers: in the forethought he threw out as to the practical consequences to discipline, considering the unconfirmed tone of the fleet at the time, should a man-of-war's man's violent killing at sea of a superior in grade be allowed to pass for aught else than a capital crime demanding prompt infliction of the penalty.

Not unlikely they were brought to something more or less akin to that harassed frame of mind which in the year 1842 actuated the commander of the U.S. brig-of-war *Somers* to resolve, under the so-called Articles of War, Articles modeled upon the English Mutiny Act, to resolve upon the execution at sea of a midshipman and two sailors as mutineers designing the seizure of the brig. Which resolution was carried out though in a time of peace and without not many days' sail of home. An act vindicated by a naval court of inquiry subsequently convened ashore. History, and here cited without comment. True, the circumstances on board the *Somers* were different from those on board the *Bellipotent*. But the urgency felt, well-warranted or otherwise, was much the same.

Says a writer whom few know, "Forty years after a battle it is easy for a noncombatant to reason about how it ought to have been fought. It is another thing personally and under fire to have to direct the fighting while involved in the obscuring smoke of it. Much so with respect to other emergencies involving considerations both practical and moral, and when it is imperative promptly to act. The greater the fog the more it imperils the steamer, and speed is put on though at the hazard of running somebody down. Little ween the snug card players in the cabin of the responsibilities of the sleepless man on the bridge."

In brief, Billy Budd was formally convicted and sentenced to be hung at the yardarm in the early morning watch, it being now night. Otherwise, as is customary in such cases, the sentence would forthwith have been carried out. In wartime on the field or in the fleet, a mortal punishment decreed by a drumhead court—on the field sometimes decreed by but a nod from the general—follows without delay on the heel of conviction, without appeal.

22

It was Captain Vere himself who of his own motion communicated the finding of the court to the prisoner, for that purpose going to the compartment where he was in custody and bidding the marine there to withdraw for the time.

Beyond the communication of the sentence, what took place at this interview was never known. But in view of the character of the twain briefly closeted in that stateroom, each radically sharing in the rarer qualities of our nature—so rare indeed as to be all but incredible to average minds however much cultivated—some conjectures may be ventured.

It would have been in consonance with the spirit of Captain Vere should he on this occasion have concealed nothing from the condemned one —should he indeed have frankly disclosed to him the part he himself had played in bringing about the decision, at the same time revealing his actuating motives. On Billy's side it is not improbable that such a confession would have been received in much the same spirit that prompted it. Not without a sort of joy, indeed, he might have appreciated the brave opinion of him implied in his captain's making such a confidant of him. Nor, as to the sentence itself, could he have been insensible that it was imparted to him as to one not afraid to die. Even more may have been. Captain Vere in end may have developed the passion sometimes latent under an exterior stoical or indifferent. He was old enough to have been Billy's father. The austere devotee of military duty, letting himself melt back into what remains primeval in our formalized humanity, may in end have caught Billy to his heart, even as Abraham may have caught young Isaac on the brink of resolutely offering him up in obedience to the exacting behest. But there is no telling the sacrament, seldom if in any case revealed to the gadding world, wherever under circumstances at all akin to those here attempted to be set forth two of great Nature's nobler order embrace. There is privacy at the time, inviolable to the survivor; and holy oblivion, the sequel to each diviner magnanimity, providentially covers all at last.

The first to encounter Captain Vere in act of leaving the compartment was the senior lieutenant. The face he beheld, for the moment one expressive of the agony of the strong, was to that officer, though a man of fifty, a startling revelation. That the condemned one suffered less than he who mainly had effected the condemnation was apparently indicated by the former's exclamation in the scene soon perforce to be touched upon.

23

Of a series of incidents within a brief term rapidly following each other, the adequate narration may take up a term less brief, especially if explanation or comment here and there seem requisite to the better understanding of such incidents. Between the entrance into the cabin of him who never left it alive, and him who when he did leave it left it as one condemned to die; between this and the closeted interview just given, less than an hour and a half had elapsed. It was an interval long enough, however, to awaken speculations among no few of the ship's company as to what it was that could be detaining in the cabin the master-at-arms and the sailor; for a rumor that both of them had been seen to enter it and neither of them had been seen to emerge, this rumor had got abroad upon the gun decks and in the tops,

the people of a great warship being in one respect like villagers, taking microscopic note of every outward movement or non-movement going on. When therefore, in weather not at all tempestuous, all hands were called in the second dogwatch, a summons under such circumstances not usual in those hours, the crew were not wholly unprepared for some announcement extraordinary, one having connection too with the continued absence of the two men from their wonted haunts.

There was a moderate sea at the time; and the moon, newly risen and near to being at its full, silvered the white spar deck wherever not blotted by the clear-cut shadows horizontally thrown of fixtures and moving men. On either side the quarter-deck the marine guard under arms was drawn up; and Captain Vere, standing in his place surrounded by all the wardroom officers, addressed his men. In so doing, his manner showed neither more nor less than that properly pertaining to his supreme position aboard his own ship. In clear terms and concise he told them what had taken place in the cabin: that the master-at-arms was dead, that he who had killed him had been already tried by a summary court and condemned to death, and that the execution would take place in the early morning watch. The word *mutiny* was not named in what he said. He refrained too from making the occasion an opportunity for any preachment as to the maintenance of discipline, thinking perhaps that under existing circumstances in the navy the consequence of violating discipline should be made to speak for itself.

Their captain's announcement was listened to by the throng of standing sailors in a dumbness like that of a seated congregation of believers in hell listening to the clergyman's announcement of his Calvinistic text.

At the close, however, a confused murmur went up. It began to wax. All but instantly, then, at a sign, it was pierced and suppressed by shrill whistles of the boatswain and his mates. The word was given to about ship.

To be prepared for burial Claggart's body was delivered to certain petty officers of his mess. And here, not to clog the sequel with lateral matters, it may be added that at a suitable hour, the master-at-arms was committed to the sea with every funeral honor properly belonging to his naval grade.

In this proceeding as in every public one growing out of the tragedy strict adherence to usage was observed. Nor in any point could it have been at all deviated from, either with respect to Claggart or Billy Budd, without begetting undesirable speculations in the ship's company, sailors, and more particularly men-of-war's men, being of all men the greatest sticklers for usage. For similar cause, all communication between Captain Vere and the condemned one ended with the closeted interview already given, the latter being now surrendered to the ordinary routine preliminary to the end. His transfer under guard from the captain's quarters was effected without unusual precautions —at least no visible ones. If possible, not to let the men so much as surmise that their officers anticipate aught amiss from them is the tacit rule in a military ship. And the more that some sort of trouble should really be apprehended, the more do the officers keep that apprehension to themselves, though not the less unostentatious vigilance may be augmented. In the present instance, the sentry placed over the prisoner had strict orders to let no one have communication with him but the chaplain. And certain unobtrusive measures were taken absolutely to insure this point.

24

In a seventy-four of the old order the deck known as the upper gun deck was the one covered over by the spar deck, which last, though not without its armament, was for the most part exposed to the weather. In general it was at all hours free from hammocks; those of the crew swinging on the lower gun deck and berth deck, the latter being not only a dormitory but also the place for the stowing of the sailors' bags, and on both sides lined with the large chests or movable pantries of the many messes of the men.

On the starboard side of the *Bellipotent's* upper gun deck, behold Billy Budd under sentry lying prone in irons in one of the bays formed by the regular spacing of the guns comprising the batteries on either side. All these pieces were of the heavier caliber of that period. Mounted on lumbering wooden carriages, they were hampered with cumbersome harness of breeching and strong side-tackles for running them out. Guns and carriages, together with the long rammers and shorter linstocks lodged in loops overhead—all these, as customary, were painted black; and the heavy hempen breechings, tarred to the same tint, wore the like livery of the undertakers. In contrast with the fu-

nereal hew of these surroundings, the prone sailor's exterior apparel, white jumper and white duck trousers, each more or less soiled, dimly glimmered in the obscure light of the bay like a patch of discolored snow in early April lingering at some upland cave's black mouth. In effect he is already in his shroud, or the garments that shall serve him in lieu of one. Over him but scarce illuminating him, two battle lanterns swing from two massive beams of the deck above. Fed with the oil supplied by the war contractors (whose gains, honest or otherwise, are in every land an anticipated portion of the harvest of death), with flickering splashes of dirty yellow light they pollute the pale moonshine all but ineffectually struggling in obstructed flecks through the open ports from which the tampioned cannon protrude. Other lanterns at intervals serve but to bring out somewhat the obscurer bays which, like small confessionals or side-chapels in a cathedral, branch from the long dim-vistaed broad aisle between the two batteries of that covered tier.

Such was the deck where now lay the Handsome Sailor. Through the rose-tan of his complexion no pallor could have shown. It would have taken days of sequestration from the winds and the sun to have brought about the effacement of that. But the skeleton in the cheekbone at the point of its angle was just beginning delicately to be defined under the warm-tinted skin. In fervid hearts self-contained, some brief experiences devour our human tissue as secret fire in a ship's hold consumes cotton in the bale.

But now lying between the two guns, as nipped in the vice of fate, Billy's agony, mainly proceeding from a generous young heart's virgin experience of the diabolical incarnate and effective in some men —the tension of that agony was over now. It survived not the something healing in the closeted interview with Captain Vere. Without movement, he lay as in a trance, that adolescent expression previously noted as his taking on something akin to the look of a slumbering child in the cradle when the warm hearth-glow of the still chamber at night plays on the dimples that at whiles mysteriously form in the cheek, silently coming and going there. For now and then in the gyved one's trance a serene happy light born of some wandering reminiscence or dream would diffuse itself over his face, and then wane away only anew to return.

The chaplain, coming to see him and finding him thus, and perceiving no sign that he was conscious of his presence, attentively regarded him for a space, then slipping aside, withdrew for the time, peradventure feeling that even he, the minister of Christ though receiving his stipend from Mars, had no consolation to proffer which could result in a peace transcending that which he beheld. But in the small hours he came again. And the prisoner, now awake to his surroundings, noticed his approach, and civilly, all but cheerfully, welcomed him. But it was to little purpose that in the interview following, the good man sought to bring Billy Budd to some godly understanding that he must die, and at dawn. True, Billy himself freely referred to his death as a thing close at hand; but it was something in the way that children will refer to death in general, who yet among their other sports will play a funeral with hearse and mourners.

Not that like children Billy was incapable of conceiving what death really is. No, but he was wholly without irrational fear of it, a fear more prevalent in highly civilized communities than those so-called barbarous ones which in all respects stand nearer to unadulterate Nature. And, as elsewhere said, a barbarian Billy radically was—as much so, for all the costume, as his countrymen the British captives, living trophies, made to march in the Roman triumph of Germanicus. Quite as much so as those later barbarians, young men probably, and picked specimens among the earlier British converts to Christianity, at least nominally such, taken to Rome (as today converts from lesser isles of the sea may be taken to London), of whom the Pope of that time, admiring the strangeness of their personal beauty so unlike the Italian stamp, their clear ruddy complexion and curled flaxen locks, exclaimed, "Angles" (meaning *English*, the modern derivative), "Angles, do you call them? And is it because they look so like angels?" Had it been later in time, one would think that the Pope had in mind Fra Angelico's seraphs, some of whom, plucking apples in gardens of the Hesperides, have the faint rosebud complexion of the more beautiful English girls.

If in vain the good chaplain sought to impress the young barbarian with ideas of death akin to those conveyed in the skull, dial, and crossbones on old tombstones, equally futile to all appearance were his efforts to bring home to him the thought of salvation and a Savior. Billy listened, but less out of awe or reverence, perhaps, than from a certain natural politeness, doubtless at bottom regarding all that in much the same way that most mariners of his class take any discourse abstract

or out of the common tone of the workaday world. And this sailor way of taking clerical discourse is not wholly unlike the way in which the primer of Christianity, full of transcendent miracles, was received long ago on tropic isles by any superior *savage*, so called—a Tahitian, say, of Captain Cook's time or shortly after that time. Out of natural courtesy he received, but did not appropriate. It was like a gift placed in the palm of an outreached hand upon which the fingers do not close.

But the *Bellipotent*'s chaplain was a discreet man possessing the good sense of a good heart. So he insisted not in his vocation here. At the instance of Captain Vere, a lieutenant had apprised him of pretty much everything as to Billy; and since he felt that innocence was even a better thing than religion wherewith to go to Judgment, he reluctantly withdrew; but in his emotion not without first performing an act strange enough in an Englishman, and under the circumstances yet more so in any regular priest. Stooping over, he kissed on the fair cheek his fellow man, a felon in martial law, one whom though on the confines of death he felt he could never convert to a dogma; nor for all that did he fear for his future.

Marvel not that having been made acquainted with the young sailor's essential innocence the worthy man lifted not a finger to avert the doom of such a martyr to martial discipline. So to do would not only have been as idle as invoking the desert, but would also have been an audacious transgression of the bounds of his function, one as exactly prescribed to him by military law as that of the boatswain or any other naval officer. Bluntly put, a chaplain is the minister of the Prince of Peace serving in the host of the God of War—Mars. As such, he is as incongruous as a musket would be on the altar at Christmas. Why, then, is he there? Because he indirectly subserves the purpose attested by the cannon; because too he lends the sanction of the religion of the meek to that which practically is the abrogation of everything but brute Force.

25

The night so luminous on the spar deck, but otherwise on the cavernous ones below, levels so like the tiered galleries in a coal mine—the luminous night passed away. But like the prophet in the chariot disappearing in heaven and dropping his mantle to Elisha, the withdrawing night transferred its pale robe to the breaking day. A meek, shy light appeared in the East, where stretched a diaphanous fleece of white furrowed vapor. That light slowly waxed. Suddenly *eight bells* was struck aft, responded to by one louder metallic stroke from forward. It was four o'clock in the morning. Instantly the silver whistles were heard summoning all hands to witness punishment. Up through the great hatchways rimmed with racks of heavy shot the watch below came pouring, overspreading with the watch already on deck the space between the mainmast and foremast including that occupied by the capacious launch and the black booms tiered on either side of it, boat and booms making a summit of observation for the powderboys and younger tars. A different group comprising one watch of topmen leaned over the rail of that sea balcony, no small one in a seventy-four, looking down on the crowd below. Man or boy, none spake but in whisper, and few spake at all. Captain Vere—as before, the central figure among the assembled commissioned officers—stood nigh the break of the poop deck facing forward. Just below him on the quarter-deck the marines in full equipment were drawn up much as at the scene of the promulgated sentence.

At sea in the old time, the execution by halter of a military sailor was generally from the foreyard. In the present instance, for special reasons the mainyard was assigned. Under an arm of that yard the prisoner was presently brought up, the chaplain attending him. It was noted at the time, and remarked upon afterwards, that in this final scene the good man evinced little or nothing of the perfunctory. Brief speech indeed he had with the condemned one, but the genuine Gospel was less on his tongue than in his aspect and manner towards him. The final preparations personal to the latter being speedily brought to an end by two boatswain's mates, the consummation impended. Billy stood facing aft. At the penultimate moment, his words, his only ones, words wholly unobstructed in the utterance, were these: "God bless Captain Vere!" Syllables so unanticipated coming from one with the ignominious hemp about his neck—a conventional felon's benediction directed aft towards the quarters of honor; syllables too delivered in the clear melody of a singing bird on the point of launching from the twig—had a phenomenal effect, not unenhanced by the rare personal beauty of the young sailor, spiritualized now through late experiences so poignantly profound.

Without volition, as it were, as if indeed the ship's populace were but the vehicles of some vocal current electric, with one voice from alow and aloft came a resonant sympathetic echo: "God bless Captain Vere!" And yet at that instant Billy alone must have been in their hearts, even as in their eyes.

At the pronounced words and the spontaneous echo that voluminously rebounded them, Captain Vere, either through stoic self-control or a sort of momentary paralysis induced by emotional shock, stood erectly rigid as a musket in the ship-armorer's rack.

The hull, deliberately recovering from the periodic roll to leeward, was just regaining an even keel when the last signal, a preconcerted dumb one, was given. At the same moment it chanced that a vapory fleece hanging low in the East was shot through with a soft glory as of the fleece of the Lamb of God seen in mystical vision, and simultaneously therewith, watched by the wedged mass of upturned faces, Billy ascended; and, ascending, took the full rose of the dawn.

In the pinioned figure arrived at the yard-end, to the wonder of all no motion was apparent, none save that created by the slow roll of the hull in moderate weather, so majestic in a great ship ponderously cannoned.

26

When some days afterwards, in reference to the singularity just mentioned, the purser, a rather ruddy, rotund person more accurate as an accountant than profound as a philosopher, said at mess to the surgeon, "What testimony to the force lodged in will power," the latter, saturnine, spare, and tall, one in whom a discreet causticity went along with a manner less genial than polite, replied, "Your pardon, Mr. Purser. In a hanging scientifically conducted—and under special orders I myself directed how Budd's was to be effected—any movement following the completed suspension and originating in the body suspended, such movement indicates mechanical spasm in the muscular system. Hence the absence of that is no more attributable to will power, as you call it, than to horsepower—begging your pardon."

"But this muscular spasm you speak of, is not that in a degree more or less invariable in these cases?"

"Assuredly so, Mr. Purser."

"How then, my good sir, do you account for its absence in this instance?"

"Mr. Purser, it is clear that your sense of the singularity in this matter equals not mine. You account for it by what you call will power—a term not yet included in the lexicon of science. For me, I do not, with my present knowledge, pretend to account for it at all. Even should we assume the hypothesis that at the first touch of the halyards the action of Budd's heart, intensified by extraordinary emotion at its climax, abruptly stopped, much like a watch when in carelessly winding it up you strain at the finish, thus snapping the chain—even under that hypothesis how account for the phenomenon that followed?"

"You admit, then, that the absence of spasmodic movement was phenomenal."

"It was phenomenal, Mr. Purser, in the sense that it was an appearance the cause of which is not immediately to be assigned."

"But tell me, my dear sir," pertinaciously continued the other, "was the man's death effected by the halter, or was it a species of euthanasia?"

"*Euthanasia*, Mr. Purser, is something like your *will power*: I doubt its authenticity as a scientific term—begging your pardon again. It is at once imaginative and metaphysical—in short, Greek.— But," abruptly changing his tone, "there is a case in the sick bay that I do not care to leave to my assistants. Beg your pardon, but excuse me." And rising from the mess he formally withdrew.

27

The silence at the moment of execution and for a moment or two continuing thereafter, a silence but emphasized by the regular wash of the sea against the hull or the flutter of a sail caused by the helmsman's eyes being tempted astray, this emphasized silence was gradually disturbed by a sound not easily to be verbally rendered. Whoever has heard the freshet-wave of a torrent suddenly swelled by pouring showers in tropical mountains, showers not shared by the plain; whoever has heard the first muffled murmur of its sloping advance through precipitous woods may form some conception of the sound now heard. The seeming remoteness of its source was because of its murmurous indistinctness, since it came from close by, even from the men massed on the ship's open deck. Being inarticulate, it was dubious in significance further than it seemed to indicate some capricious revulsion of thought or feeling such as mobs ashore are liable to, in the present instance possibly implying a sullen revocation on the men's part of their involuntary echoing of Billy's benediction. But ere the murmur had time to wax into clamor it was met by a strategic command, the more telling that it came with abrupt unexpectedness: "Pipe down the starboard watch, Boatswain, and see that they go."

Shrill as the shriek of the sea hawk, the silver whistles of the boatswain and his mates pierced that ominous low sound, dissipating it; and yielding to the mechanism of discipline the throng was thinned by one-half. For the remainder, most of them were set to temporary employments connected with trimming the yards and so forth, business readily to be got up to serve occasion by any officer of the deck.

Now each proceeding that follows a mortal sentence pronounced at sea by a drumhead court is characterized by promptitude not perceptibly merging into hurry, though bordering that. The hammock, the one which had been Billy's bed when alive, having already been ballasted with shot and otherwise prepared to serve for his canvas coffin, the last offices of the sea undertakers, the sailmaker's mates, were now speedily completed. When everything was in readiness a second call for all hands, made necessary by the strategic movement before mentioned, was sounded, now to witness burial.

The details of this closing formality it needs not to give. But when the tilted plank let slide its freight into the sea, a second strange human murmur was heard, blended now with another inarticulate sound proceeding from certain larger seafowl who, their attention having been attracted by the peculiar commotion in the water resulting from the heavy sloped dive of the shotted hammock into the sea, flew screaming to the spot. So near the hull did they come, that the stridor or bony creak of their gaunt double-jointed pinions was audible. As the ship under light airs passed on, leaving the burial spot astern, they still kept circling it low down with the moving shadow of their outstretched wings and the croaked requiem of their cries.

Upon sailors as superstitious as those of the age preceding ours, men-of-war's men too who had just beheld the prodigy of repose in the form suspended in air, and now foundering in the deeps; to such mariners the action of the seafowl, though dictated by mere animal greed for prey, was big with no prosaic significance. An uncertain movement began among them, in which some encroachment was made. It was tolerated but for a moment. For suddenly the drum beat to quarters, which familiar sound happening at least twice every day, had upon the present occasion a signal peremptoriness in it. True martial discipline long continued superinduces in average man a sort of impulse whose operation at the official word of command much resembles in its promptitude the effect of an instinct.

The drumbeat dissolved the multitude, distributing most of them along the batteries of the two covered gun decks. There, as wonted, the guns' crews stood by their respective cannon erect and silent. In due course the first officer, sword under arm and standing in his place on the quarter-deck, formally received the successive reports of the sworded lieutenants commanding the sections of batteries below; the last of which reports being made, the summed report he delivered with the customary salute to the commander. All this occupied time, which in the present case was the object in beating to quarters at an hour prior to the customary one. That such variance from usage was authorized by an officer like Captain Vere, a martinet as some deemed him, was evidence of the necessity for unusual action implied in what he deemed to be temporarily the mood of his men. "With mankind," he would say, "forms, measured forms, are everything; and that is the import couched in the story of Orpheus with his lyre spellbinding the wild denizens of the wood." And this he once applied to the disruption of forms going on across the Channel and the consequences thereof.

At this unwonted muster at quarters, all proceeded as at the regular hour. The band on the quarter-deck played a sacred air, after which the chaplain went through the customary morning service. That done, the drum beat the retreat; and toned by music and religious rites subserving the discipline and purposes of war, the men in their wonted orderly manner dispersed to the places allotted them when not at the guns.

And now it was full day. The fleece of low-hanging vapor had vanished, licked up by the sun that late had so glorified it. And the circumambient air in the clearness of its serenity was like smooth white marble in the polished block not yet removed from the marble-dealer's yard.

28

The symmetry of form attainable in pure fiction cannot so readily be achieved in a narration essentially having less to do with fable than with fact. Truth uncompromisingly told will always have its ragged edges; hence the conclusion of such a narration is apt to be less finished than an architectural finial.

How it fared with the Handsome Sailor during the year of the Great Mutiny has been faithfully given. But though properly the story ends with his life, something in way of sequel will not be amiss. Three brief chapters will suffice.

In the general rechristening under the Directory of the craft originally forming the navy of the French monarchy, the *St. Louis* line-of-battle ship was named the *Athée* (the *Atheist*). Such a name, like some other substituted ones in the Revolutionary fleet, while proclaiming the infidel audacity of the ruling power, was yet, though not so intended to be, the aptest name, if one consider it, ever given to a warship; far more so indeed than the *Devastation*, the *Erebus* (the *Hell*), and similar names bestowed upon fighting ships.

On the return passage to the English fleet from the detached cruise during which occurred the events already recorded, the *Bellipotent* fell in with the *Athée*. An engagement ensued, during which Captain Vere, in the act of putting his ship alongside the enemy with a view of throwing his boarders across her bulwarks, was hit by a musket ball from a porthole of the enemy's main cabin. More than disabled, he dropped to the deck and was carried below to the same cockpit where some of his men already lay. The senior lieutenant took command. Under him the enemy was finally captured, and though much crippled was by rare good fortune successfully taken into Gibraltar, an English port not very distant from the scene of the fight. There, Captain Vere with the rest of the wounded was put ashore. He lingered for some days, but the end came. Unhappily he was cut off too early for the Nile and Trafalgar. The spirit that 'spite its philosophic austerity may yet have indulged in the most secret of all passions, ambition, never attained to the fulness of fame.

Not long before death, while lying under the influence of that magical drug which, soothing the physical frame, mysteriously operates on the subtler element in man, he was heard to murmur words inexplicable to his attendant: "Billy Budd, Billy Budd." That these were not the accents of remorse would seem clear from what the attendant said to the *Bellipotent*'s senior officer of marines, who, as the most reluctant to condemn of the members of the drumhead court, too well knew, though here he kept the knowledge to himself, who Billy Budd was.

29

Some few weeks after the execution, among other matters under the head of "News from the Mediterranean," there appeared in a naval chronicle of the time, an authorized weekly publication, an account of the affair. It was doubtless for the most part written in good faith, though the medium, partly rumor, through which the facts must have reached the writer served to deflect and in part falsify them. The account was as follows:

"On the tenth of the last month a deplorable occurrence took place on board H.M.S. *Bellipotent*. John Claggart, the ship's master-at-arms, discovering that some sort of plot was incipient among an inferior section of the ship's company, and that the ringleader was one William Budd; he, Claggart, in the act of arraigning the man before the captain, was vindictively stabbed to the heart by the suddenly drawn sheath knife of Budd.

"The deed and the implement employed sufficiently suggest that though mustered into the service under an English name the assassin was no Englishman, but one of those aliens adopting English cognomens whom the present extraordinary necessities of the service have caused to be admitted into it in considerable numbers.

"The enormity of the crime and the extreme depravity of the criminal appear the greater in view of the character of the victim, a middle-aged man respectable and discreet, belonging to that minor official grade, the petty officers, upon whom, as none know better than the commissioned gentlemen, the efficiency of His Majesty's navy so largely depends. His function was a responsible one, at once onerous and thankless; and his fidelity in it the greater because of his strong patriotic impulse. In this instance as in so many other instances in these days, the character of this unfortunate man signally refutes, if refutation were needed, that peevish saying attributed to the late Dr. Johnson, that patriotism is the last refuge of a scoundrel.

"The criminal paid the penalty of his crime. The promptitude of the punishment has proved salutary. Nothing amiss is now apprehended aboard H.M.S. *Bellipotent*."

The above, appearing in a publication now long ago superannuated and forgotten, is all that hitherto has stood in human record to attest what manner of men respectively were John Claggart and Billy Budd.

30

Everything is for a term venerated in navies. Any tangible object associated with some striking incident of the service is converted into a monument. The spar from which the foretopman was suspended was for some few years kept trace of by the bluejackets. Their knowledges followed it from ship to dockyard and again from dockyard to ship, still pursuing it even when at last reduced to a mere dockyard boom. To them a chip of it was as a piece of the Cross. Ignorant though they were of the secret facts of the tragedy, and not thinking but that the penalty was somehow unavoidably inflicted from the naval point of view, for all that, they instinctively felt that Billy was a sort of man as incapable of mutiny as of wilful murder. They recalled the fresh young image of the Handsome Sailor, that face never deformed by a sneer or subtler vile freak of the heart within. This impression of him was doubtless deepened by the fact that he was gone, and in a measure mysteriously gone. On the gun decks of the *Bellipotent* the general estimate of his nature and its unconscious simplicity eventually found rude utterance from another foretopman, one of his own watch, gifted, as some sailors are, with an artless *poetic* temperament. The tarry hand made some lines which, after circulating among the shipboard crews for a while, finally got rudely printed at Portsmouth as a ballad. The title given to it was the sailor's.

Billy in the Darbies

Good of the chaplain to enter Lone Bay
And down on his marrowbones here and pray
For the likes just o' me, Billy Budd.—But, look:
Through the port comes the moonshine astray!

It tips the guard's cutlass and silvers this nook;
But 'twill die in the dawning of Billy's last day.
A jewel-block they'll make of me tomorrow,
Pendant pearl from the yardarm-end
Like the eardrop I gave to Bristol Molly—
O, 'tis me, not the sentence they'll suspend.
Ay, ay, all is up; and I must up too,
Early in the morning, aloft from alow.
On an empty stomach now never it would do.
They'll give me a nibble—bit o' biscuit ere I go.
Sure, a messmate will reach me the last parting
    cup;
But, turning heads away from the hoist and the
    belay,
Heaven knows who will have the running of
    me up!
No pipe to those halyards.—But aren't it all sham?
A blur's in my eyes; it is dreaming that I am.
A hatchet to my hawser? All adrift to go?
The drum roll to grog, and Billy never know?
But Donald he has promised to stand by the plank;
So I'll shake a friendly hand ere I sink.
But—no! It is dead then I'll be, come to think.
I remember Taff the Welshman when he sank.
And his cheek it was like the budding pink.
But me they'll lash in hammock, drop me deep.
Fathoms down, fathoms down, how I'll dream fast
    asleep.
I feel it stealing now. Sentry, are you there?
Just ease these darbies at the wrist,
And roll me over fair!
I am sleepy, and the oozy weeds about me twist.[1]

If we are to understand Melville's poetry, we must see it against the backdrop of his defeat as a writer of fiction, from which he suffered not only the pangs of rejection, but the associated distress of ill health and no doubt, since his father, after failure, had died mad, the fear of madness.

While running before the spanking breeze of his great creative period, Melville, in *White-Jacket*, had written: "Sailor or landsman, there is some sort of Cape Horn for all. Boys! beware of it; prepare for it in time. Graybeards! thank God it is passed." And among the late poems there is "Old Counsel of the Young Master of a Wrecked California Clipper" (1885):

[1] For a discussion of "Billy in the Darbies" turn to p. 929.

Come out of the Golden Gate,
Go round the Horn with streamers,
Carry royals early and late;
But, brother, be not over-elate—
All hands save ship! has startled dreamers.

Melville's poetry belongs to the second half of his life after he had rounded his Horn. The theme was to be with him until his death.[1]

Meanwhile, as a distraction from overwork, Melville went on a journey, in 1856, to the Holy Land. He had touched bottom and was now seeking some belief by which life could be considered, and his own life rebuilt; and his poetry, in one dimension, may be read as a record of that search. In youth, Melville had fled from the Western world into a land of savage and innocent beauty, an Eden lost in the misty time before civilization. Now he was going back to touch base on the spot which had been the seed bed of the spiritual life of the Western world. As the Pacific Eden had given him a vision of "natural" joy out of time, in contrast to modern civilization, so the Holy Land gave him a vision of man's effort to reach, out of time, the joy of supernatural certainties, in contrast with the flickering aim of modernity. The two adventures gave him the poles of his thought and art. What meaning or reconciliation might man find in "nature"? What in "spirit"? Many of Melville's poems, including his epic *Clarel*, draw direct inspiration from his journey of 1856, and almost all are concerned with these questions.

For ten years after the journey Melville worked ferociously to school himself in the art he was undertaking so late. He had, as his novels show, great poetic powers, but he had little sense of the technique of verse, and it was not until 1866 that his first collection of poems was

[1] In his poem "Herman Melville," W. H. Auden refers to this theme:
    Goodness existed: that was the new knowledge
    His terror had to blow itself quite out
    To let him see it; but it was the gale had blown him
    Past the Cape Horn of sensible success
    Which cries: "This rock is Eden. Shipwreck here."
The "rock is Eden" in that only through the knowledge of reality gained by disaster can man enter the true paradise.

published. This volume, *Battle-Pieces and Aspects of the War*, which came out of the Civil War, is a remarkable document in American poetry and American history, but it is also to be remarked in the personal history of the author.

The war seems to have tapped in Melville old, nigh-forgotten energies, to have enabled him to sublimate in the national tragedy his personal distress. In 1861 he was 42 and not in good health, and active service was not possible for him; but he followed the war with intense concern and may even have decided to make himself into the poet of the war, with the hope of reestablishing his practical as well as literary fortunes.

Battle-Pieces reads like a log of the conflict, in chronological order from the execution of John Brown to the Reconstruction, but very few of the poems were composed before the end of the war, and then not in a chronological order. In his preface Melville says that the poems are "as manifold as are the moods of involuntary meditation—moods variable and at times widely in variance." And he adds: "I seem in most of these verses, to have but placed a harp in a window and noted the contrasting airs which vagrant winds have played upon the strings." But the winds that touch the harp all blow from Melville's soul, and the contrasting airs that come from the strings constitute a dialectic. The book is not a log of the war, but a log of Melville's attempts to make sense of the war—and of life.

The Civil War gave Melville the kind of athletic, overmastering subject which he always needed for his best work, and if he also needed to have a germ drawn from actuality, the germ here was bloodily certified by actuality. But such a subject drawn from actuality would serve his needs only if the centrifugal whirl toward violent action was perfectly balanced by the centripetal pull toward an inwardness of apparently unresolvable mystery, or tormenting ambiguity. Of such issues, the war offered God's—and the devil's—plenty.

This complexity in the subject itself had a deep psychological consistency with the kind of style toward which Melville had already been groping in his poems written (though not published) before the war, a style drawn from English metaphysical poetry of the seventeenth century. But now he ceased to be merely imitative. He was aiming at a style rich and yet shot through with prosaisms, sometimes casual and open and sometimes dense and intellectually freighted, fluid and yet various because following the contours of his subject, or, rather, the contours of his complex feelings about the subject.

For instance, in "The March into Virginia," each section has its own characteristic rhythm, weight of line, and tone. In the first section, where the subject is generalized, we find the passage built up line by line, almost every line a sort of apothegm. The second section, presenting the gay march, the characteristic rhythm, based on tetrameter, which had been heavily clogged before, becomes brisk and light:

> The banners play, the bugles call,
> The air is blue and prodigal.

Or:

> So they gayly go to fight,
> Chatting left and laughing right.

But set immediately against this is the movement of the last section:

> But some who this blithe mood present,
>   As on in lightsome files they fare,
> Shall die experienced ere three days are spent—
>   Perish, enlightened by the vollied glare;
> Or shame survive, and, like to adamant,
>   The throe of Second Manassas share.

Here with the first line we have the heavy succession of monosyllables, with retarded, scarcely resolved accentuation, and then the slow uncoiling of the complex rhythm of the entire passage. But let us notice that the second line, referring again to the uninstructed gaiety of the march, repeats, in a kind of ironic contrast, the characteristic movement of the second section: "As on in lightsome files they fare." With the next line, the meter shifts from tetrameter to pentameter, and then the last three lines go increasingly heavy and retarded, an effect based primarily on a dramatic handling of forced pauses, vowel weightings, and unresolved accentuation.[2]

"The March into Virginia" is deeply coherent, dramatically and intellectually. It is ordered by a series of contrasts among detail as well as among sections, with great subtlety of implication. The "picnic party" is a march to death. The ignorance and innocence of youth are all that makes war possible (and there is an echo of the Melvillian irony: Is it all that makes life possible?); but only in "experience," in "knowledge," can the true "adamant" of life be forged. Yet the cost of such experience may be death. To take another set of paradoxes, the transitory "rapture" of youthful action is always about to enter "story," to become legend or history, dying, as it were, into significance or glory.

Furthermore, the phrasing has the same density of references. How brilliant are the lines:

> In Bacchic glee they file toward Fate,
> Moloch's uninitiate.

Significantly, no line could be simpler than "No berrying party, pleasure-wooed"—but "berrying party," with its atmosphere of rural gaiety and sunburned youthfulness, is really a secret, and grim, pun: *burying* party, the echo of the military phrase. Or to turn to another detail, the pleasure that woos the picnickers—the "rapture"—is a complex one: vanity, dreams of glory, a sense of adventure, a sense of duty, the need to test the self, a "glad surmise of battle's unknown mysteries," which involve death and the "pleasure" of death, with all the overtones of that notion.

Or let us look at the word "enlightened" in the line "Perish, enlightened by the vollied glare." To perish in the moment of enlightenment, of knowledge—in a blaze of knowledge, which, for all its deadliness, is somehow a blaze of fulfillment, of glory, a glare of glory, with both the benign and inimical implications of the word "glare." And part of that enlightenment is self-knowledge. Once the nature of the

terms of life and of the self are clear, one can bear the "throe." So here the poem goes back to Melville's old obsessive theme. First Manassas is like the Horn which must be rounded if man is to be fully a man.

Few of Melville's poems are as deeply coherent as "The March into Virginia," but some of the principles of its style do appear rather generally: for instance, the use of realistic detail, which in other poems is carried even further. But not merely the fact of such detail deserves comment; more important is the way in which such prosaic materials are played against conventional poetic elements. The contrast occurs, of course, at the level of vocabulary, for Melville, as Newton Arvin has pointed out in his biography, was given to combining poeticisms like *fair, deem,* and *wight* with technical terms like *caloric, escheat,* and *integral,* and with various coined words.

But vocabulary merely affords the starting point for stylistic contrasts. Take the first stanza of "Malvern Hill":

> Ye elms that wave on Malvern Hill
>   In prime of morn and May,
> Recall ye how McClellan's men
>   Here stood at bay?
> While deep within yon forest dim
>   Our rigid comrades lay—
> Some with the cartridge in their mouth,
> Others with fixed arms lifted South—
>   Invoking so
> The cypress glades? Ah wilds of woe!

Here, in the midst of the rather conventional poetic materials at the beginning of the poem, we find the realistic detail of the cartridge clenched in the teeth of a dead man, held there as he prepared for loading; and this detail suddenly vivifies the whole passage.

But there are contrasts among poems, too, as in the pairing of two of the pieces suggested by the fight between the *Monitor* and the *Virginia.* (See pp. 920–21.) The first of the poems, celebrating the *Temeraire* of Lord Nelson's famous fleet, has a conventional style, well illustrated by the ending:

---

[2] The last line is, strictly speaking, tetrameter, but pauses and weightings are such that it "feels" like pentameter—has the "time" of pentameter.

But fame has nailed your battle-flags—
　Your ghost it sails before:
O, the navies old and oaken,
　O, the Temeraire no more!

This poem is immediately followed by "A Utilitarian View of the Monitor's Fight," which begins, "Plain be the phrase." The plainness of the language and style of the poem is determined, as it were, by the subject matter—appropriate to the "blacksmith's fray," in which

　. . . all went on by crank,
　　Pivot, and screw,
　And calculations of caloric.

But the poem ends with an internal stylistic contrast, a brilliant metaphor which snatches it from the jaws of prose:

Wars shall yet be, and to the end;
　But war-paint shows the streaks of weather;
War yet shall be, but warriors
Are now but operatives; War's made
　Less grand than Peace,
And a singe runs through the lace and feather.

Melville saw another kind of singe running through the lace and feather of life. Not only is there the inevitable test of the passage around the "Horn"; in the course of all life, there is a doubleness in things. If nature seems beneficent and beautiful, that is only one aspect, for, as it is put in "Misgivings," there is "Nature's darker side."

Such doubleness lies in history too. If man must exert will to try to control events, he may find that even when he seems to act effectively, the process in which his will operates may be only a mask for a secret process of which he has suspected nothing. So we find it said in "Misgivings":

And storms are formed behind the storm we
　feel:
The hemlock shakes in the rafter, the oak in the
　driving keel.

And in "The Conflict of Convictions," the wind of history "spins against the way it drives." For example, by the victory of "Right" in the Civil War, certain undreamed-of forces may be released so that,

Power unanointed may come—
Dominion (unsought by the free)
　And the Iron Dome,
Stronger for stress and strain,
Fling her huge shadow athwart the main;
But the Founders' dream shall flee.

There are other polarities and ambiguities in life. A decision presumably made on idealistic grounds may simply be the reflex of a historical situation. In "The Slain Collegians," the young men of both North and South are "swept by the winds of their place and time." Even if an ethical distinction is to be made at the level of the "cause" for which war is being waged, at another level, such a distinction is irrelevant:

Warred one for Right and one for Wrong?
So be it; but they both were young—
　Each grape to his cluster clung,
　All their elegies are sung.

Each youth was doomed to cling to his cluster, and in this fact is implicit the polarity of "ideology" ("Law," "Right," or even "Destiny") against human values, human suffering, human aspiration, qualities of personality and spirit.

The human bond may be as important as the bond of ideology. As "On the Photograph of a Corps Commander" puts it:

Nothing can lift the heart of man
Like manhood in a fellow-man.

And the fellow-man may be a fellow, not by ideology, but only in his manhood. A recognition of the human community is an essential virtue, and the human community is, in one perspective, a community of guilt, as we find in "The Swamp Angel," the poem of the bombardment of Charleston, South Carolina:

Who weeps for the woeful City
　Let him weep for our guilty kind;
Who joys at her wild despairing—
　Christ, the Forgiver, convert his mind.

The most painful polarity of all is that be-

tween all values and the blank fact of annihilation.[3] As in "Sheridan at Cedar Creek,"

> There is glory for the brave
> Who lead, and nobly save,
> But no knowledge in the grave
> Where the nameless followers sleep.

But the same fact of annihilation—the subject
on which Melville had brooded so much—which
appears in this poem as mere blankness may
elsewhere be regarded as a peace, with the
problem of values in the flux of history resolved,
however perilously and equivocally, in the context of natural process. For instance, in "Malvern Hill" the elms remember the horror and
heroism of the battle,

> *But sap and twig will fill:*
> *Wag the world how it will,*
> *Leaves must be green in Spring.*

But if death is blankness—or even blankness
regarded as elegiac peace—how can values be
found in action desperately foredoomed to
blankness? The answer is by a stoicism at once
self-assertive and self-denying. It is self-assertive
in the will to endure, and by endurance to define its own value, outside of time, as in the
poem on the prisoners who died at Andersonville, in Georgia, "On a Natural Monument":

> Their fame is this: they did endure—
> Endure, when fortitude was vain
> To kindle any approving strain
> Which they might hear. To these who rest,
> This healing sleep alone was sure.

But stoicism may be self-denying in the will to
sink the personal pain in a compassionate and
ennobling awareness of the general human lot,
as in another poem on a forgotten monument,
"An Uninscribed Monument":

[3] The horror of annihilation is important in *Moby-
Dick*, as in the discussion of "The Whiteness of the
Whale," and in Ishmael's fear of the "nothing-making
palsied color." Melville had brooded much upon the
theme, and by 1856, when he visited Hawthorne at
Liverpool (where Hawthorne was now consul), he
could say, according to his friend's journal, that he was
prepared to accept annihilation.

> Thou who beholdest, if thy thought,
> Not narrowed down to personal cheer,
> Take in the import of the quiet here—
>   The after-quiet—the calm full fraught;
> Thou too wilt silent stand—
> Silent as I, and lonesome as the land.

We cannot be too schematic about polarities
such as we have been discussing. One pair
shades into another. One pole does not cancel
out its opposite. All belong to the complex texture of life as lived, to the density and equivocalness of experience. But to live in any full sense
demands the effort to comprehend this complexity of texture, this density and equivocalness of
experience, and yet not forfeit the ability to act.
The man who can act, but who, at the same
time, "sees through it," who has a sense of the
tragedy of the human plight—that is the hero
for Melville. For instance, "The College Colonel":

> But all through the Seven Days' Fight,
>   And deep in the Wilderness grim,
> And in the field-hospital tent,
>   And Petersburg crater, and dim
> Lean brooding in Libby, there came—
> Ah heaven!—what *truth* to him.

Beyond his personal experience and personal
heroism and the official celebration, what the
young colonel sees is the tragic complexity of
man's fate: the painful limit of man's ideological constructions and rational vision; for one
aspect of man's fate is the inevitability of evil,
the cost of action, the blind doom which underlies all the superstructures which he erects and
must trust in—the secret force which shakes the
"oak in the driving keel."

In many poems this idea of the ever-presence
of evil—evil, shall we say, as the cost of good?—
appears; for instance, in "Commemorative of a
Naval Victory," a poem which one is tempted
to call great:

But seldom the laurel wreath is seen
  Unmixed with pensive pansies dark;
There's a light and a shadow on every man
  Who at last attains his lifted mark—

Nursing through night the ethereal spark.
Elate he never can be;
He feels that spirits which glad had hailed his
    worth,
    Sleep in oblivion.—The shark
Glides white through the phosphorous sea.

Many themes are absorbed here into the ghastly whiteness and imperial ease of the gliding shark.

Whitman and Melville are the poets of the Civil War, but the difference between them is instructive. Before discussing that difference, three things should be said. First, the comparison is of them as poets of the war—though, of course, the poetry of the war cannot be entirely isolated from the body of work of either man. Second, Whitman is the bigger poet. Third, the distinction is one of emphases rather than of absolute differences.

Whiman's poetry of the war is primarily "synthetic." That is, he gives strong representational images—cavalry crossing a ford or a bivouac at night or a dressing station—which draw into focus and unify whatever attitudes and emotions are already available in the reader. If there are tensions and contradictions lurking among these attitudes, such tensions and contradictions are absorbed, purged in the vivid, overmastering immediacy of the image. As for his generalizations and comments, we shall shortly be sampling them. Melville's poetry, on the other hand, is analytic. It does give strong representational images, too; and we have noted Melville's realistic sense, which he shares with Whitman. But Melville often strives to analyze the implications of his images and the attitudes evoked by them; and this dialectic of imagery, and of statement, actually exploits the resistance a reader might have to the poem.

By way of comparison, we may turn to some of Whitman's poetry not of the war, say, in "Song of Myself" (reprinted in this text), and point out that the magnificent and often dramatically moving catalogues of persons and events involve enormous variety and testify to a will to find values in all life and to possess all life, and absorb it. Whitman has the true poetic eye, and poetic sympathy, to present his items without divesting them of their intrinsic and characteristic values, but he never sharpens issues among them that might make possession and absorption difficult. What he does is to celebrate, ultimately, not the items but the will to possess, to absorb. On the other hand, for Melville, the poetry lies in a conflict of values, an inner conflict, and that is what he feels driven, ultimately, to deal with.

To take a simple instance, this from the war poetry, when Whitman writes a poem about the death letter from the front, the powerful "Come Up from the Fields, Father," the family is safely northern, on a farm in Ohio, and the northern reader whom Whitman wrote for could find his patriotism, his selfish interests, and all his human and humane feelings mobilized together and focused in the image—"ritualized." This is not to say that Whitman merely manipulates what are called stock responses in the reader, but it is to say that he is characteristically more concerned with intensity and purity of feeling than with complexity or painful richness.

To return to the poem, if Melville had written it, the farm might very well have been in Georgia, and the dead son one of those "Slain Collegians" about whom he did write a poem: then the northern reader, whose own son had been habitually shot at by the now dead Georgia lad, might have had some divisions of attitude to deal with. Like all decent poetry, that of Melville aims at the moment of poise, of synthesis, but for him the poise and the synthesis are hard-won, and often incomplete and provisional, and the awareness of that fact is, in a sense, the point, the "truth," of the poetry. To summarize, Whitman, in his poems of the war, is ritualistic, Melville is dramatic, ultimately tragic.

The differences we have been talking about in relation to the poetry have some parallel in the difference between their respective brands of Unionism. For Whitman, the Union was a mystique. One aspect of this mystique was, of course, Whitman's democratic faith. Another was his passion for power, not power for himself, but his passion for participation in the power of a unity. In one sense, Whitman welcomed such power merely because it was power, even if he could think of it, too, as susceptible of being "spiritualized" in one way or another, one day or another.

In "Long, Too Long, America," Whitman exhorts America to show the world "what your children en-masse really are." In "Over the Carnage Rose Prophetic a Voice," he says that "affection shall resolve the problems of freedom yet," but the reward offered for this achievement is to be power:

Those who love each other shall become invincible,
They shall yet make Columbia victorious.

If, in "From Paumanok Starting I Fly Like a Bird," Whitman promises to sing the songs of the individual states, he finds it necessary

To sing first (to the tap of the war-drum if need be),
The idea of all, of the Western world one and inseparable.[4]

The "idea of all" becomes, easily, "an idea only," and in "Song of the Banner at Daybreak," Whitman hails the flag waving high in the air as "an idea only"—the pure idea in which all is absorbed, the abstraction in which all distinctions are wiped out:

Valueless, object of eyes, over all and demanding all—
(absolute owner of all)—O banner and pennant!
I too leave the rest—great as it is, it is nothing—houses,
machines are nothing, I see them not,
I see but you, O warlike pennant! O banner so broad, with stripes,
I sing you only,
Flapping up there in the wind.

The making of distinctions—that is the very

center of Melville's poetry, and of Melville's Unionism. He was a Unionist, but he did not see the Union in mystical terms, or as an absolute, however much a part of his nature may have yearned for that easy solution. There were human values beyond mere unity by the achievement of which the Union must justify itself. Hence, in one perspective at least, the Union could be regarded by Melville as a political arrangement serving certain ends—which it might serve well or ill.[5] As a political arrangement, it might very well, in the ironical course of destiny, change its nature, and the very "power," which Whitman hymned as the blessing to be derived from Union, might well be the bane; in victory, in power, as we have seen, the "Founders' dream" might flee—a chilling thought that does not disturb Whitman in his poetry of the war, though he does discover some sobering second thoughts in *Democratic Vistas*.

More radically, in "The House-Top," the poem on the draft riots of 1863 in New York City, and their bloody suppression, Melville calls into question the very premise of the democratic faith which was a corollary of Whitman's Unionism. To suppress the general anarchy, "Wise Draco" comes and with grape-shot corroborates "Calvin's creed" as well as the "cynic tyrannies of honest kings."

. . . and the Town, redeemed,
Gives thanks devout; nor, being thankful, heeds
The grimy slur on the Republic's faith implied,
Which holds that Man is naturally good,
And—more—is Nature's Roman, never to be scourged.

When *Battle-Pieces* appeared, Melville was in desperate need of money as well as appreciation. But it failed, and as a last resort he became, at the age of 47, at the wage of four dollars a day, an inspector in the customs house of the Port of New York. This practical and literary disaster was compounded, as we have already seen, by the suicide of his elder son, Malcolm, with whom he had had difficult relations.

[4] Which, by the same logic, and by "the tap of the war-drum if need be," might be taken to include Canada and Mexico—as well as the Louisiana Purchase and California.

[5] It may be remarked that in this "unitarian" view of the Union Melville's thought resembles that of Cooper. See pp. 320–23.

In this situation, Melville occupied himself for some ten years, insofar as his duties would permit, with his long poem *Clarel,* a poem devoted to the problem of finding meaning in the life of the modern world. On his journey to the Holy Land, he had encountered a land of poverty and death, Jerusalem "like a cold grey eye in a cold old man," and the landscape a desolation; but this ruined land had once been the land of milk and honey, the source of the spiritual life of the Western world. His poem is about a number of people who, like himself, have come here to try to rediscover the "living waters," each representing some aspect of the modern world; among them a disillusioned revolutionist; an ex-Confederate soldier, of Catholic background and of some Indian blood; a Jewish geologist who believes in nothing but science; an Anglican clergyman who believes in automatic progress; an adventurer rather like Melville himself; a figure resembling Hawthorne; and Clarel, the hero, a young divinity student seeking to renew his faith who falls in love with a Jewish girl. The whole poem is, one may say, a kind of charade of modern attitudes and beliefs. What Clarel, the student, comes to accept—and what, presumably, represents Melville's attitude at the time—is best summarized in the "Epilogue," an attitude which, in a new perspective and with a new tonality, stems from the combination of skepticism, stoicism, and compassion found in *Battle-Pieces.*

Clarel, even more positively than *Battle-Pieces,* failed to find a public or to redeem Melville's reputation, and in many ways it fails as a poem. It is inordinately long, much of the writing is slack and hurried, the handling of the action is weak. But, for all its shortcomings, it remains a powerful document of Melville's mind and of the meaning of modernity; and in this last sense it may be taken as a forerunner —though an unread forerunner—of many works, especially of Eliot's *The Waste Land.*

For some years after the publication of *Clarel,* Melville continued at the customs house, but in 1885 an inheritance of his wife's permitted him to retire, and in 1888 to issue a private edition of his poems, of only twenty-five copies. This volume, *John Marr and Other Sailors,* in addition to some of the pieces written before 1861, also contained later work, including some of his finest poems, poems showing a new dimension of experience and of technical development. The remaining years of his life were spent on new poems and in the slow development of *Billy Budd,* his last fiction, which was left unpublished until 1924. In 1891, the year of his death, he issued another collection of poems, *Timoleon,* again in twenty-five copies.

It was not until the 1920's that Melville's fiction began to receive serious consideration and appraisal, and it was not for another decade that the poetry was regarded as more than an unworthy appendage to the achievement in prose. Even now there is no consensus as to its value. If the eminent poet Randall Jarrell can say that Melville, Whitman, and Dickinson are the "best poets of the nineteenth century," adding that Melville's poetry has been grotesquely underestimated, the eminent critic Edmund Wilson can refer to *Battle-Pieces* as merely "versified journalism"—"a chronicle of the patriotic feelings of an anxious middle-aged non-combatant." The present writers are inclined to agree with Jarrell rather than Wilson, but in any case, in spite of awkwardnesses and lapses in technique, the poetry of Melville has become, at the least, a compelling document of our literary, and general, history. It cannot be ignored.

The Portent (1859)

"The Portent" is a kind of prologue to *Battle-Pieces,* as John Brown's raid was to the Civil War. The word "weird" has the sense of possessing the power of directing fate as well as that of suggesting the unearthly and supernatural; and the old man at the rope end with his beard streaming like the trail of a meteor appears as an omen. In this complex relation to the course

of events, Brown is "weird" in the same sense
as the Weird Sisters in *Macbeth*.

Hanging from the beam,
  Slowly swaying (such the law),
Gaunt the shadow on your green,
  Shenandoah!
The cut is on the crown

(Lo, John Brown),
And the stabs shall heal no more.

Hidden in the cap
  Is the anguish none can draw;
So your future veils its face,   10
  Shenandoah!
But the streaming beard is shown
(Weird John Brown),
The meteor of the war.

Misgivings (1860)

The image of the autumn storm develops the
idea of "The Portent." We may even take the
word "brown" in the second line as a kind of
pun, linking this poem to that about John
Brown.

The word "shouts" is more than a casual
descriptive metaphor. In its obvious sense, it
identifies the literal storms with human violence
feared in the future, but, in a deeper sense, as
is developed further in the last two lines of the
poem, it relates the impending human violence
to the blind forces of nature, suggesting the
idea that historical process may be beyond rational and ethical considerations, may be a kind
of "fate"—a weather of the world.

When ocean-clouds over inland hills
  Sweep storming in late autumn brown,
And horror the sodden valley fills,
  And the spire falls crashing in the town,
I muse upon my country's ills—
  The tempest bursting from the waste of Time
On the world's fairest hope linked with man's
  foulest crime.

Nature's dark side is heeded now—
  (Ah! optimist-cheer disheartened flown)—
A child may read the moody brow   10
  Of yon black mountain lone.
With shouts and torrents down the gorges
  go,
And storms are formed behind the storm
  we feel:
The hemlock shakes in the rafter, the oak in
  the driving keel.

The Conflict of Convictions (1861)

Melville's note gives the general background of
the poem:

> The gloomy lull of the early part of the winter
> of 1860–1 seeming big with final disaster to
> our institutions, affected some minds that be-
> lieved them to constitute one of the great
> hopes of mankind, much as the eclipse that
> came over the promise of the first French
> Revolution affected kindred natures, throwing
> them for the time into doubts and misgivings
> universal.

It is to this, of course, that the "latter fall" (line
6) refers, with, also, a reference to Milton's
Paradise Lost.

The lines involving the "Iron Dome" need
some explanation. The original dome of the
Capitol had been made of wood but was replaced during the Civil War by a dome constructed of two iron shells, one of cast iron and
one of wrought iron. The poem (though written
long after placing of the new dome) is dramatically set before the beginning of the armed conflict, which means that the reference to the
dome is anachronistic; but presumably Melville
needed it as a symbol for the new power state
that he predicted would arise after the victory, a
state in which the ideals of the old Republic
would be lost.

On starry heights
  A bugle wails the long recall;
Derision stirs the deep abyss,
  Heaven's ominous silence over all.
Return, return, O eager Hope,
  And face man's latter fall.
Events, they make the dreamers quail;
Satan's old age is strong and hale,
A disciplined captain, gray in skill,
And Raphael a white enthusiast still;   10
Dashed aims, at which Christ's martyrs pale,
  Shall Mammon's slaves fulfill?

    (*Dismantle the fort,*
Cut down the fleet—
Battle no more shall be!
While the fields for fight in æons to come
Congeal beneath the sea.)

The terrors of truth and dart of death
  To faith alike are vain;
Though comets, gone a thousand years,   20
    Return again,
Patient she stands—she can no more—
And waits, nor heeds she waxes hoar.

    (*At a stony gate,*
A statue of stone,
Weed overgrown—
Long 'twill wait!)

But God his former mind retains,
  Confirms his old decree;
The generations are inured to pains,   30
  And strong Necessity
Surges, and heaps Time's strand with wrecks.
  The People spread like a weedy grass,
  The thing they will they bring to pass,
And prosper to the apoplex.
The rout it herds around the heart,
  The ghost is yielded in the gloom;
Kings wag their heads—Now save thyself
  Who wouldst rebuild the world in bloom.

    (*Tide-mark*   40
And top of the ages' strife,
Verge where they called the world to come,
The last advance of life—
Ha ha, the rust on the Iron Dome!)

Nay, but revere the hid event;
  In the cloud a sword is girded on,
I mark a twinkling in the tent

Of Michael the warrior one.
Senior wisdom suits not now,
The light is on the youthful brow.   50

    (*Ay, in caves the miner see:*
His forehead bears a blinking light;
Darkness so he feebly braves—
A meagre wight!)

But He who rules is old—is old;
Ah! faith is warm, but heaven with age is cold.

    (*Ho, ho, ho ho,*
The cloistered doubt
Of olden times
Is blurted out!)   60

The Ancient of Days forever is young,
  Forever the scheme of Nature thrives;
I know a wind in purpose strong—
  It spins *against* the way it drives.
What if the gulfs their slimed foundations
    bare?
So deep must the stones be hurled
Whereon the throes of ages rear
The final empire and the happier world.

    (*The poor old Past,*
The Future's slave,   70
She drudged through pain and crime
To bring about the blissful Prime,
Then—perished. There's a grave!)

  Power unanointed may come—
Dominion (unsought by the free)
  And the Iron Dome,
Stronger for stress and strain,
Fling her huge shadow athwart the main;
But the Founders' dream shall flee.
Age after age shall be   80
As age after age has been,
(From man's changeless heart their way
    they win);
And death be busy with all who strive—
Death, with silent negative.

    Yea and Nay—
    Each hath his say;
    But God He keeps the middle way.
    None was by
    When He spread the sky;
    Wisdom is vain, and prophesy.   90

The March into Virginia (1861)

In July, 1861, General Irving McDowell moved out of Washington to engage the Confederates. The federal army, operating against an inferior force, had total confidence, and the march resembled a picnic more than a military action, with politicians and their ladies in carriages, supplied with hampers of food and champagne, out to witness the victory. At Bull Run, after much confusion among the green troops of both sides, Thomas J. Jackson's command held "like a stonewall," and the federal army fled back to Washington in total rout. This, the first important battle of the war, is officially known as the First Battle of Manassas. The Second Battle of Manassas (1862), referred to in the last line of the poem, was also a defeat for the federal army.

Did all the lets and bars appear
  To every just or larger end,
Whence should come the trust and cheer?
  Youth must its ignorant impulse lend—
Age finds place in the rear.
  All wars are boyish, and are fought by boys,
The champions and enthusiasts of the state:
  Turbid ardors and vain joys
    Not barrenly abate—

Stimulants to the power mature,   10
  Preparatives of fate.

Who here forecasteth the event?
What heart but spurns at precedent
  And warnings of the wise,
Contemned foreclosures of surprise?

The banners play, the bugles call,
The air is blue and prodigal.
  No berrying party, pleasure-wooed,
No picnic party in the May,
Ever went less loth than they   20
  Into that leafy neighborhood.
In Bacchic glee they file toward Fate,
Moloch's uninitiate;
Expectancy, and glad surmise
Of battle's unknown mysteries.
All they feel is this: 'tis glory,
A rapture sharp, though transitory,
Yet lasting in belaureled story.
So they gayly go to fight,
Chatting left and laughing right.   30

But some who this blithe mood present,
  As on in lightsome files they fare,
Shall die experienced ere three days are spent—
  Perish, enlightened by the vollied glare;
Or shame survive, and, like to adamant,
  The throe of Second Manassas share.

Ball's Bluff: A Reverie (1861)

One noonday, at my window in the town,
  I saw a sight—saddest that eyes can see—
Young soldiers marching lustily
    Unto the wars,
With fifes, and flags in mottoed pageantry;
  While all the porches, walks, and doors
Were rich with ladies cheering royally.

They moved like Juny morning on the wave,
  Their hearts were fresh as clover in its prime
  (It was the breezy summer time),   10
    Life throbbed so strong,

How should they dream that Death in a rosy
    clime
  Would come to thin their shining throng?
Youth feels immortal, like the gods sublime.

Weeks passed; and at my window, leaving bed,
  By night I mused, of easeful sleep bereft,
  On those brave boys (Ah War! thy theft);
    Some marching feet
Found pause at last by cliffs Potomac cleft;
  Wakeful I mused, while in the street   20
Far footfalls died away till none were left.

A Utilitarian View of the Monitor's Fight (1862)

On March 8, 1862, the Confederate ironclad *Virginia*, rebuilt from the federal frigate *Merri-* *mack*, entered Hampton Roads, where the federal blockade fleet lay. Sinking the *Cumberland*

and burning the *Congress*, the *Virginia* demonstrated her superiority to wooden ships. The next day she returned to finish off the fleet, but was challenged by the *Monitor*, the first federal ironclad, just arrived from New York, designed by the Swedish inventor John Ericsson. For three hours the two craft slugged it out, for a tactical draw, in the first battle between ironclads.

Plain be the phrase, yet apt the verse,
  More ponderous than nimble;
For since grimed War here laid aside
His Orient pomp, 'twould ill befit
    Overmuch to ply
  The rhyme's barbaric cymbal.

Hail to victory without the gaud
  Of glory; zeal that needs no fans
Of banners; plain mechanic power
Plied cogently in War now placed—   10

Where War belongs—
  Among the trades and artisans.

Yet this was battle, and intense—
  Beyond the strife of fleets heroic;
Deadlier, closer, calm 'mid storm;
No passion; all went on by crank,
    Pivot, and screw,
  And calculations of caloric.

Needless to dwell; the story's known.
  The ringing of those plates on plates   20
Still ringeth round the world—
The clangor of that blacksmiths' fray.
    The anvil-din
  Resounds this message from the Fates:

War shall yet be, and to the end;
  But war-paint shows the streaks of weather;
War yet shall be, but warriors
Are now but operatives; War's made
    Less grand than Peace,
  And a singe runs through lace and feather.   30

Shiloh: A Requiem (1862)

On April 6, 1862, the Confederates surprised the federal army at Shiloh Church, near Savannah, Tennessee, and nearly drove it into the Tennessee River. The second day, following the arrival of federal reinforcements, there was a bloody and indecisive action, after which the Confederates withdrew. Grant had managed, by the slimmest margin, to hold the field, and his recently gained reputation weathered the savage attacks on his generalship.

As Hennig Cohen, an editor of Melville, points out: "The structure of the poem is circular, a counterpart of the wheeling swallows at the beginning and end of what is grammatically a single sentence"—a structure which can be taken as appropriate for the sense of absorption of the human struggle into the cycle of nature.

The idea we find so wonderfully put in line 16 echoes, of course, the "vollied glare" of "The March into Virginia." Here, however, the enlightenment from the bullet is simpler and somewhat different from that of the earlier poem: at morning, men were deluded in thinking themselves foes, in accepting certain political and ideological views, but now, with the undeceiving bullet, they are reconciled in the natural lot of man.

Skimming lightly, wheeling still,
  The swallows fly low
Over the field in clouded days,
  The forest-field of Shiloh—
Over the field where April rain
Solaced the parched ones stretched in pain
Through the pause of night
That followed the Sunday fight
  Around the church of Shiloh—
The church so lone, the log-built one,   10
That echoed to many a parting groan
    And natural prayer
Of dying foemen mingled there—
Foemen at morn, but friends at eve—
  Fame or country least their care:
(What like a bullet can undeceive!)
  But now they lie low,
While over them the swallows skim,
  And all is hushed at Shiloh.

The House-Top: A Night Piece (1863)

On July 13, 1863, following the Conscription Act, rioting, amounting almost to revolutionary action, broke out in New York City. Though there was considerable pro-southern sympathy in the city, the basic motive was class resentment against the provision allowing the purchase of immunity from the draft on the payment of $300. (Among those who bought immunity was Grover Cleveland.) The most obvious targets for the resentment were Negroes, of whom a number were tortured and lynched in the streets. Order was not restored until troops fresh from the battle of Gettysburg were brought and cannon were turned on the mob. The event, indicating as it did deep tensions within the Union, was to be largely ignored by historians and swept under the rug; but those tensions are the subject matter of Melville's poem.

No sleep.　The sultriness pervades the air
And binds the brain—a dense oppression, such
As tawny tigers feel in matted shades,
Vexing their blood and making apt for ravage.

Beneath the stars the roofy desert spreads
Vacant as Libya.　All is hushed near by.
Yet fitfully from far breaks a mixed surf
Of muffled sound, the Atheist roar of riot.
Yonder, where parching Sirius set in drought,
Balefully glares red Arson—there—and there.　　10
The Town is taken by its rats—ship-rats
And rats of the wharves.　All civil charms
And priestly spells which late held hearts in
　　awe—
Fear-bound, subjected to a better sway
Than sway of self; these like a dream dissolve,
And man rebounds whole æons back in nature.
Hail to the low dull rumble, dull and dead,
And ponderous drag that shakes the wall.
Wise Draco comes, deep in the midnight roll
Of black artillery; he comes, though late;　　20
In code corroborating Calvin's creed
And cynic tyrannies of honest kings;
He comes, nor parlies; and the Town, redeemed,
Gives thanks devout; nor, being thankful, heeds
The grimy slur on the Republic's faith implied,
Which holds that Man is naturally good,
And—more—is Nature's Roman, never to be
　　scourged.

The College Colonel (1866)

The hero is William Francis Bartlett, who, as a student at Harvard, had enlisted. In August, 1863, Melville saw him parade his command in Pittsfield, Massachusetts, though in the poem he refers to experiences that Bartlett was to have subsequent to this date. The "truth" at the end of the poem has a relation to the "vollied glare" of "The March into Virginia." Melville's characteristic hero is the man who, seeing the complexity and ambiguity of human nature and experience, can still define an ideal and act on it.

He rides at their head;
　A crutch by his saddle just slants in view,
One slung arm is in splints, you see,
　Yet he guides his strong steed—how coldly
　　too.

He brings his regiment home—
　Not as they filed two years before,
But a remnant half-tattered, and battered,
　　and worn,
Like castaway sailors, who—stunned
　　By the surf's loud roar,
　Their mates dragged back and seen no more—　10
Again and again breast the surge,
　And at last crawl, spent, to shore.

A still rigidity and pale—
　An Indian aloofness lones his brow;
He has lived a thousand years
Compressed in battle's pains and prayers,
　Marches and watches slow.

There are welcoming shouts, and flags;
　Old men off hat to the Boy,
Wreaths from gay balconies fall at his feet,　　20
　But to *him*—there comes alloy.

It is not that a leg is lost,
  It is not that an arm is maimed,
It is not that the fever has racked—
  Self he has long disclaimed.

But all through the Seven Days' Fight,

And deep in the Wilderness grim,
And in the field-hospital tent,
  And Petersburg crater, and dim
Lean brooding in Libby, there came—   30
  Ah heaven!—what *truth* to him.

A Requiem for Soldiers Lost in Ocean Transports (1866)

When, after storms that woodlands rue,
  To valleys comes atoning dawn,
The robins blithe their orchard-sports renew;
  And meadow-larks, no more withdrawn,
Caroling fly in the languid blue;
The while, from many a hid recess,
Alert to partake the blessedness,
The pouring mites their airy dance pursue.
  So, after ocean's ghastly gales,
When laughing light of hoyden morning
    breaks,   10
    Every finny hider wakes—
From vaults profound swims up with
    glittering scales;
Through the delightsome sea he sails,

With shoals of shining tiny things
Frolic on every wave that flings
  Against the prow its showery spray;
All creatures joying in the morn,
Save them forever from joyance torn,
  Whose bark was lost where now the
      dolphins play;
Save them that by the fabled shore,   20
  Down the pale stream are washed away,
Far to the reef of bones are borne;
  And never revisits them the light,
Nor sight of long-sought land and pilot more;
  Nor heed they now the lone bird's flight
Round the lone spar where mid-sea surges pour.

An Uninscribed Monument on One of the Battlefields of the Wilderness (1866)

Silence and Solitude may hint
  (Whose home is in yon piny wood)
What I, though tableted, could never tell—
The din which here befell,
  And striving of the multitude.
The iron cones and spheres of death
  Set round me in their rust,
    These, too, if just;

Shall speak with more than animated breath.
  Thou who beholdest, if thy thought,   10
Not narrowed down to personal cheer,
Take in the import of the quiet here—
  The after-quiet—the calm full fraught;
Thou too wilt silent stand—
Silent as I, and lonesome as the land.

On a Natural Monument in a Field of Georgia (1866)

Andersonville, in Georgia, was a Confederate
camp for military prisoners. Some fifteen thousand men died there of disease and starvation.
This poem, like "An Uninscribed Monument,"
deals with the nameless dead.

No trophy this—a Stone unhewn,
  And stands where here the field immures
The nameless brave whose palms are won.

Outcast they sleep; yet fame is nigh—
  Pure fame of deeds, not doers;
Nor deeds of men who bleeding die
  In cheer of hymns that round them float:
In happy dreams such close the eye.
But withering famine slowly wore,
  And slowly fell disease did gloat.   10
Even Nature's self did aid deny;
They choked in horror the pensive sigh.
  Yea, off from home sad Memory bore

(Though anguished Yearning heaved that way),
Lest wreck of reason might befall.
 As men in gales shun the lee shore,
Though there the homestead be, and call,
And thitherward winds and waters sway—
As such lorn mariners, so fared they.

But naught shall now their peace molest. 20
 Their fame is this: they did endure—
Endure, when fortitude was vain
To kindle any approving strain
Which they might hear. To these who rest,
 This healing sleep alone was sure.

Commemorative of a Naval Victory (1866)

Sailors there are of gentlest breed,
 Yet strong, like every goodly thing;
The discipline of arms refines,
 And the wave gives tempering.
 The damasked blade its beam can fling;
It lends the last grave grace:
The hawk, the hound, and sworded nobleman
 In Titian's picture for a king,
Are of hunter or warrior race.

In social halls a favored guest 10
 In years that follow victory won,
How sweet to feel your festal fame
 In woman's glance instinctive thrown:
 Repose is yours—your deed is known,

It musks the amber wine;
It lives, and sheds a light from storied days
 Rich as October sunsets brown,
Which make the barren place to shine.

But seldom the laurel wreath is seen
 Unmixed with pensive pansies dark; 20
There's a light and a shadow on every man
 Who at last attains his lifted mark—
 Nursing through night the ethereal spark.
Elate he never can be;
He feels that spirits which glad had hailed
  his worth,
 Sleep in oblivion.—The shark
Glides white through the phosphorus sea.

Epilogue (from Clarel) (1876)

If Luther's day expand to Darwin's year,
Shall that exclude the hope—foreclose the fear?

 Unmoved by all the claims our times
  avow,
The ancient Sphinx still keeps the porch
 of shade;
And comes Despair, whom not her calm
 may cow,
And coldly on that adamantine brow
Scrawls undeterred his bitter pasquinade.
But Faith (who from the scrawl indignant
 turns)
With blood warm oozing from her wounded
 trust,
Inscribes even on her shards of broken urns 10
The sign o' the cross—*the spirit above the dust!*

 Yea, ape and angel, strife and old debate—
The harps of heaven and dreary gongs of hell;
Science the feud can only aggravate—
No umpire she betwixt the chimes and knell:
The running battle of the star and clod
Shall run forever—if there be no God.

 Degrees we know, unknown in days before;
The light is greater, hence the shadow more;
And tantalized and apprehensive Man 20
Appealing—Wherefore ripen us to pain?
Seems there the spokesman of dumb Nature's
 train.
 But through such strange illusions have
  they passed
Who in life's pilgrimage have baffled striven—
Even death may prove unreal at the last,
And stoics be astounded into heaven.

 Then keep thy heart, though yet but
  ill-resigned—
Clarel, thy heart, the issues there but mind;
That like the crocus budding through the
 snow—
That like a swimmer rising from the deep— 30
That like a burning secret which doth go
Even from the bosom that would hoard
 and keep;
Emerge thou mayst from the last whelming
 sea,
And prove that death but routs life into victory.

John Marr (1888)

The poem is preceded by a long headnote in prose recounting how the sailor John Marr, too old for the sea, came to the prairie country of the Middle West, there lost his wife and child by a fever, and now lives in isolation from his neighbors, who cannot understand or sympathize with him and his memories of the sea, which to them is but "a rumor traditional and vague." In his loneliness, John Marr invokes his dead shipmates—"striving as it were, to get into verbal communication with them, or, under yet stronger illusion, reproaching them for their silence." The poem is his "reproach" to them.

Since as in night's deck-watch ye show,
Why, lads, so silent here to me,
Your watchmate of times long ago?

Once, for all the darkling sea,
You your voices raised how clearly,
Striking in when tempest sung;
Hoisting up the storm-sail cheerly,
Life is storm—let storm! you rung.
Taking things as fated merely,
Child-like though the world ye spanned;   10
Nor holding unto life too dearly,
Ye who held your lives in hand—
Skimmers, who on oceans four
Petrels were, and larks ashore.

O, not from memory lightly flung,
Forgot, like strains no more availing,
The heart to music haughtier strung;
Nay, frequent near me, never staleing,
Whose good feeling kept ye young.
Like tides that enter creek or stream,   20
Ye come, ye visit me, or seem
Swimming out from seas of faces,
Alien myriads memory traces,
To enfold me in a dream!

I yearn as ye. But rafts that strain,
Parted, shall they lock again?
Twined we were, entwined, then riven,
Ever to new embracements driven,
Shifting gulf-weed of the main!
And how if one here shift no more,   30
Lodged by the flinging surge ashore?

Nor less, as now, in eve's decline,
Your shadowy fellowship is mine.
Ye float around me, form and feature:—
Tattooings, ear-rings, love-locks curled;
Barbarians of man's simpler nature,
Unworldly servers of the world.
Yea, present all, and dear to me,
Though shades, or scouring China's sea.

Whither, whither, merchant-sailors,   40
Whitherward now in roaring gales?
Competing still, ye huntsman-whalers,
In leviathan's wake what boat prevails?
And man-of-war's men, whereaway?
If now no dinned drum beat to quarters
On the wilds of midnight waters—
Foemen looming through the spray;
Do yet your gangway lanterns, streaming,
Vainly strive to pierce below,
When, tilted from the slant plank gleaming,   50
A brother you see to darkness go?

But, gunmates lashed in shotted canvas,
If where long watch-below ye keep,
Never the shrill *"All hands up hammocks!"*
Breaks the spell that charms your sleep,
And summoning trumps might vainly call,
And booming guns implore—
A beat, a heart-beat musters all,
One heart-beat at heart-core.
It musters. But to clasp, retain;   60
To see you at the halyards main—
To hear your chorus once again!

Tom Deadlight (1888)

Melville's note on the poem reads:

During a tempest encountered homeward-bound from the Mediterranean, a grizzled petty-officer, one of the two captains of the forecastle, dying at night in his hammock, swung in the *sick-bay* under the tiered gun-decks of the British *Dreadnaught*, 98, wandering in his mind, though with glimpses of sanity, and starting up at whiles, sings by snatches his good-bye and last injunctions to two messmates, his watchers, one of whom fans the fevered tar with the flap of his old sou'-wester. Some names and phrases, with here and there a line, or part of one; these, in his aberration, wrested into incoherency from their original connection and import, he involuntarily derives, as he does the measure, from a famous old sea-ditty, whose cadences, long rife, and now humming in the collapsing brain, attune the last flutterings of distempered thought.

Farewell and adieu to you noble hearties,—
  Farewell and adieu to you ladies of Spain,
For I 've received orders for to sail for the
    Deadman,
  But hope with the grand fleet to see you
    again.

I have hove my ship to, with main-top-sail
  aback, boys;
  I have hove my ship to, for to strike
    soundings clear—
The black scud a'flying; but, by God's blessing,
  dam' me,
  Right up the Channel for the Deadman
    I'll steer.

I have worried through the waters that are
  called the Doldrums,
  And growled at Sargasso that clogs while   10
    ye grope—
Blast my eyes, but the light-ship is hid by the
  mist, lads:—

Flying Dutchman—odds bobbs—off the
  Cape of Good Hope!

But what's this I feel that is fanning my
  cheek, Matt?
  The white goney's wing?—how she rolls!—
    't is the Cape!—
Give my kit to the mess, Jock, for kin
  none is mine, none;
  And tell *Holy Joe* to avast with the crape.

Dead reckoning, says *Joe*, it won't do to go by;
  But they doused all the glims, Matt, in sky
    t' other night.
Dead reckoning is good for to sail for the
  Deadman;
  And Tom Deadlight he thinks it may   20
    reckon near right.

The signal!—it streams for the grand fleet to
  anchor.
  The captains—the trumpets—the hullabaloo!
Stand by for blue-blazes, and mind your shank-
  painters,
  For the Lord High Admiral, he 's squinting
    at you!

But give me my *tot*, Matt, before I roll over;
  Jock, let's have your flipper, it 's good for
    to feel;
And don't sew me up without *baccy* in
  mouth, boys,
  And don't blubber like lubbers when I turn
    up my keel.

The Man-of-War Hawk (1888)

Yon black man-of-war hawk that wheels in
  the light
O'er the black ship's white sky-s'l, sunned
  cloud to the sight,
Have we low-flyers wings to ascend to his
  height?

No arrow can reach him; nor thought can
  attain
To the placid supreme in the sweep of his
  reign.

The Tuft of Kelp (1888)

All dripping in tangles green,
  Cast up by a lonely sea,

If purer for that, O Weed,
  Bitterer, too, are ye?

The Maldive Shark (1888)

About the Shark, phlegmatical one,
Pale sot of the Maldive sea,
The sleek little pilot-fish, azure and slim,
How alert in attendance be.
From his saw-pit of mouth, from his charnel of
    maw
They have nothing of harm to dread;
But liquidly glide on his ghastly flank
Or before his Gorgonian head;
Or lurk in the port of serrated teeth

In white triple tiers of glittering gates,   10
And there find a haven when peril 's abroad,
An asylum in jaws of the Fates!
They are friends; and friendly they guide him
    to prey,
Yet never partake of the treat—
Eyes and brains to the dotard lethargic and
    dull,
Pale ravener of horrible meat.

The Ravaged Villa (1891)

In shards the sylvan vases lie,
    Their links of dance undone,
And brambles wither by thy brim,
    Choked fountain of the sun!

The spider in the laurel spins,
    The weed exiles the flower:
And, flung to kiln, Apollo's bust
    Makes lime for Mammon's tower.

Monody (1864)

"Monody" was written on the death of Hawthorne, which occurred May 19, 1864; it was inscribed in Melville's copy of Hawthorne's last book, *Our Old Home*, and not published until the *Timoleon* volume of 1891.

The friendship between Hawthorne and Melville began in the summer of 1850, at Stockbridge, Massachusetts, and, as we have already observed, Melville had found in Hawthorne's work a tremendous stimulation and a validation of his own powers and his will to probe the ambiguous depth of human nature. He dedicated *Moby-Dick* to Hawthorne and could write in a letter to him that "the Godhead is broken up like bread at the Supper, and that we are the pieces."

To have known him, to have loved him
    After loneness long;
And then to be estranged in life,
    And neither in the wrong;
And now for death to set his seal—
    Ease me, a little ease, my song!

By wintry hills his hermit-mound
    The sheeted snow-drifts drape,
And houseless there the snow-bird flits
    Beneath the fir-trees' crape: 10
Glazed now with ice the cloistral vine
    That hid the shyest grape.

Pontoosuce

Pontoosuc (without the final *e*) is the name of a lake near Pittsfield, Massachusetts, in the neighborhood where for some fifteen years Melville had a farm. The poem was left among Melville's papers at his death, in the form of unfinished worksheets, a fact that accounts for some of the roughnesses and confusions in it. In spite of the unfinished condition, the poem is one of the stronger of his pieces. The date is uncertain.

Crowning a bluff where gleams the lake below,
Some pillared pines in well-spaced order stand
And like an open temple show,
And here in best of seasons bland,
Autumnal noon-tide, I look out
From dusk arcades on sunshine all about.

Beyond the Lake, in upland cheer
Fields, pastoral fields, and barns appear,
They skirt the hills where lonely roads
Revealed in links thro' tiers of woods   10
Wind up to indistinct abodes
And faery-peopled neighborhoods;
While further fainter mountains keep
Hazed in romance impenetrably deep.

Look, corn in stacks, on many a farm,
And orchards ripe in languorous charm,
As dreamy Nature, feeling sure
Of all her genial labor done,
And the last mellow fruitage won,
Would idle out her term mature;   20
Reposing like a thing reclined
In kinship with man's meditative mind.

For me, within the brown arcade—
Rich life, methought; sweet here in shade
And pleasant abroad in air!—But, nay,
A counter thought intrusive played,
A thought as old as thought itself,
And who shall lay it on the shelf!—
I felt the beauty bless the day
In opulence of autumn's dower;   30
But evanescence will not stay!
A year ago was such an hour,
As this, which but foreruns the blast
Shall sweep these live leaves to the dead leaves past.

All dies!—
          I stood in revery long.
Then, to forget death's ancient wrong,
I turned me in the brown arcade,
And there by chance in lateral glade
I saw low tawny mounds in lines   40
Relics of trunks of stately pines
Ranked erst in colonnades where, lo!
Erect succeeding pillars show!

All dies! and not alone
The aspiring trees and men and grass;
The poet's forms of beauty pass,
And noblest deeds they are undone,
Even truth itself decays, and lo,

From truth's sad ashes fraud and falsehood
    grow.

All dies!   50
The workman dies, and after him, the work;
Like to these pines whose graves I trace,
Statue and statuary fall upon their face:
In very amaranths the worm doth lurk,
Even stars, Chaldæans say, have left their
    place.
Andes and Apalachee tell
Of havoc ere our Adam fell,
And present Nature as a moss doth show
On the ruins of the Nature of the æons of
    long ago.

But look—and hark!   60
          Adown the glade,
Where light and shadow sport at will,
Who cometh vocal, and arrayed
As in the first pale tints of morn—
So pure, rose-clear, and fresh and chill!
Some ground-pine sprigs her brow adorn,
The earthy rootlets tangled clinging.
Over tufts of moss which dead things made,
Under vital twigs which danced or swayed,
Along she floats, and lightly singing: 70

"Dies, all dies!
The grass it dies, but in vernal rain
Up it springs and it lives again;
Over and over, again and again
It lives, it dies and it lives again.
Who sighs that all dies?
Summer and winter, and pleasure and pain
And everything everywhere in God's reign,
They end, and anon they begin again:
Wane and wax, wax and wane: 80
Over and over and over amain
End, ever end, and begin again—
End, ever end, and forever and ever begin
    again!"

She ceased, and nearer slid, and hung
In dewy guise; then softlier sung:
"Since light and shade are equal set
And all revolves, nor more ye know;
Ah, why should tears the pale cheek fret
For aught that waneth here below.
Let go, let go!"   90
With that, her warm lips thrilled me through,
She kissed me, while her chaplet cold
Its rootlets brushed against my brow

With all their humid clinging mould.
She vanished, leaving fragrant breath

And warmth and chill of wedded life and death.

Billy in the Darbies

"Billy in the Darbies" is, as we have seen, intimately entwined with the novel and depends on that narrative for its full effect. But at the same time it is a coherent and powerful poem, and in that sense is self-contained, probably Melville's most perfect poem. For the text of the poem see pages 909–10.

On the one hand it is presented as a broadside ballad, composed, we are told, by a semi-literate sailor, and on the other it is a high poetic elegy, like "Lycidas," and much of the power of the poem comes from the interplay of these disparate elements. But, dramatically considered, the musings of the doomed boy constitute the poem, and it is the psychology of Billy that gives the poem its basic structure.

The poem begins with the contrast between the prayer of the chaplain and the moonlight stealing in, a contrast which suggests the problem of reconciliation in theological terms against reconciliation in natural terms. And this second implication would lead us to the two images of the body of Billy: one is of the body swung "aloft from alow," and has, as we shall see, certain associations with a Christ image, and the other is of the body sleeping in the oozy weeds. The contrast between a theological reconciliation and one in nature returns us, of course, to the issue at the end of *Clarel.*

The image of the "jewel block" gives the next point of focus in the poem. Literally, a jewel block is the pulley at the end of the main and fore topsail yards, but Billy, in a blend of self-pity and self-commanding humor, stumbles upon the pun, and for us he becomes the "jewel," glimmering and pure—"pendant," both as pearl and executed man, "precious" as the jewel and as the "hanged man," which is Christ.

But the pearl is also the eardrop given to Bristol Molly, and this thought returns Billy, and us, to the warm actuality of life, giving us Billy as the young sailor and his girl, who was,

no doubt, no more virtuous than she needed to be—Billy as Billy and no Christ figure after all. And this flash of realism reminds us of the grim facts of the case, with the pun on the word "suspend." From this word Billy turns again to the idea of life and warmth, toward his messmates, with the sense of the human community of affection and shared labor, but also with an overtone of the Catholic sacrament of the viaticum, in which bread and wine are given to the dying person. This, of course, is related to the prose account of the hanging, with Billy's body taking "the full rose of the dawn," and with the sailors of the fleet later treating a chip from the death spar like "a piece of the Cross." But we should remember that this Christ image is to be taken in the context of the realistic event, and this suggests that we turn to the notion in "Via Crucis," one of the cantos of *Clarel,* that all men (and beasts too) are "cross-bearers."

In relation to the Christ image we must also remember that the actual body, which had suffered, is last seen on the sea floor, in shackles. What are we to make of this? If we look closely at the passage, we see that Billy is treated like a drowsy child, falling to sleep—that is, falling into the peace of nature. He will sink, he tells us, "fathoms down," not only into the sea but into sleep. The phrase "just ease," used to the sentry does not imply pain, merely a request to make things just a little bit more comfortable —with some hint of Billy in the role of a child and the sentry as a nurse. We must observe, too, that the statement that Billy is sleepy is not put in opposition to the weeds into which he sinks; elements are connected by "and," not separated by "but," and the weeds are "with" the sleep, not against it.

This effect is made more significant by another factor, the prevailing vowel run of the whole passage, from line 27 to the end. In line 27 the *e* of *me* is repeated in the second *me,* and again in *deep*. This is picked up in line 28 with *dream* and *asleep*; in line 29 with *feel* and *stealing*; in line 30 with *ease* and *these*; in line 31 with *me*; and in line 32 with *sleepy*, *weeds*, and again *me*. This is not to suggest that a certain sound automatically carries a specific content, as in a code (*weeds* is neither sleepy nor wakeful), but it is to say that here the sound has been specifically charged with a series of related meanings, beginning with *me*, which is Billy: *me-deep-dream-asleep-feel-stealing-ease-these-sleepy*. By the time we come to *weeds* the literal meaning of the word has been impregnated with what we may call the audio-symbolic meaning; and thus the inimical meaning of the weeds as fetters binding the dead man is interpenetrated and substantially canceled by the beneficent meaning, a meaning last echoed in *me* just before the word *twist*. Even the inimical word *twist* is merely a reminder, as it were, of the pain overpassed, the cost of peace. The whole effect reminds us of the same notion in certain poems in *Battle-Pieces*.

WALT WHITMAN (1819–1892)

Whitman's relation to his age is another special instance of the paradoxes surrounding the poet in an expanding democratic society. Politically, and even more psychologically, he was every inch a democrat and what used to be known as a freethinker. His father was acquainted with Tom Paine and admired him; Whitman himself listened appreciatively to the discourses on the freeing of the slaves, women's rights, and other critical social issues by the Scottish-born Frances Wright (see pp. 329–30); in 1848, he defended the free soil principle so vehemently in the Brooklyn *Eagle* that the editor fired him, and three decades later he was giving his support to the first serious workers' strikes. Yet to call him "the poet of democracy" is to invoke a formula that needs careful modification.

There is no doubt that, by inheritance and temperament, Whitman was genuinely committed to the democratic principles of freedom, equality, and human brotherhood, and he took pride in being himself a man of the people and the son of a small-time farmer. He had an almost mystical devotion to the American Union (as his Civil War poems make manifest) and had every belief in its future greatness—which he sometimes, though by no means always, confused with sheer bigness. He dedicated the 1871 edition of his life-long book *Leaves of Grass* to the "Vast, composite, electric, *Democratic Nationality*," whatever that might be. Even T. S. Eliot, who found most of Whitman's poetry slovenly and baneful in its influence, acknowledged Whitman's genius for "making America as it was . . . into something grand and significant." Nonetheless, at his poetic best, during the fifties and sixties, Whitman performed that transmutation *indirectly*—by talking, or seeming to talk, primarily about himself, his own aspirations, excitements, and experiences; with the firm intuition that in doing so he was speaking for every man. "I celebrate myself, and sing myself," he said at the start of his most famous long poem; and went on at once to insist:

And what I assume you shall assume,
For every atom belonging to me as good belongs
　　to you.

During his great period, Whitman was perhaps the poet of the democracy of the psychic life. His poetry obliquely reflected the moral and psychological consequences of the democratic principles, for the inward spirit of the individual and for its relation to the inward reality of others.

The themes of freedom, equality, and fraternity, for example, are sounded less compellingly (because more explicitly) in the satiric outburst of 1854 provoked by the arrest in Boston of a runaway slave than by those passages in which the humble, the twisted, and the oppressed are invited to join the human race as honored equals:

> This is the meal equally set, this the meat for
>   natural hunger,
> It is for the wicked just the same as the
>   righteous, I make appointments with all,
> I will not have a single person slighted or left
>   away,
>
>   . . .
>
> Through me many long dumb voices,
> Voices of the interminable generations of
>   prisoners and slaves,
> Voices of the diseas'd and despairing and of
>   thieves and dwarfs,
>
>   . . .
>
> Through me forbidden voices,
> Voices of sexes and lusts, voices veil'd and I
>   remove the veil,
> Voices indecent by me clarified and trans-
>   figur'd.

As those last lines indicate, Whitman was thoroughly aware of the immense power of the sexual impulse. Hawthorne of course, and Melville even more, had a consciousness of human sexuality, but neither spoke with the freedom and candor Whitman allowed himself:

> The torment, the irritable tide that will not
>   be at rest,
> The like of the same I feel, the like of the
>   same in others,
> The young man that flushes and flushes, and
>   the young woman that flushes and flushes,

Melville once said that "the Declaration of Independence makes a difference"—meaning that the American writer was at liberty to speak forthrightly on any subject he chose. Whitman —as Emerson and Thoreau realized—was the first fully to exemplify that difference.

But it may well be that Whitman is most arresting as a democratic *poet* when he presents us not only with poetic formulations of freedom and equality ("This is the meal equally set"), but also with poetic equivalents of those themes. Freedom is announced in the very rhythms and structures of his free-flowing lines—that is, in the free verse he espoused, and about which we shall have more to say: verse emancipated from what Whitman regarded as the tyranny of traditional metrics, verse allowed to uncoil and to contract according to the play of feeling and observation. And absolute equality is postulated by the simple device of juxtaposing—as syntactical equals, as equal poetic units—the lowliest and the mightiest in American society:

> The prostitute draggles her shawl, her bonnet
>   bobs on her tipsy and pimpled neck,
> The crowd laugh at her blackguard oaths, the
>   men jeer and wink to each other,
> (Miserable! I do not laugh at your oath nor
>   jeer you;),
> The President holding a cabinet council is
>   surrounded by the great secretaries,

By such devices and urgent professions of belief, Whitman hoped to have a transforming effect upon his country. He had as lofty a view as Shelley of the poet's capacity, and responsibility, to legislate the opinions and feelings of mankind, and in *Democratic Vistas* (1871) he declared roundly that poets could do more than all the statesmen and generals combined to give significant shape to their culture. But Whitman lived to see the grand potentials of pre–Civil War America dissipated in the chaotic vulgarity of the Gilded Age. (See pp. 944–45.) And he himself, as a poet, never had the liberating and unifying effect he so devoutly desired.

To be sure, many of those who fought against the sometimes brutal materialism of the country and engaged in the struggle for social justice— especially the idealistic radicals in the first decades of this century—cited Whitman as their hero and prophet. "Fifty years after the first publication of *Leaves of Grass*," one of them recalled, "the words of Whitman . . . were the neutral air we breathed, whether we had read them or not." Max Eastman, editor of the forceful communist periodical the *Masses*, said that "We have drunk of the universe in Walt

Whitman's poetry," and as late as 1932 John Dos Passos could claim that "Walt Whitman's a hell of a lot more revolutionary than any Russian poet I've ever heard of."

But as a poet, for most readers and over too long a period of time, Whitman was chiefly known as the author of "O Captain, My Captain!" the worst and least characteristic poem he ever wrote. The final paradox, however, is this: all along, Whitman's poetry, designed to gain a vast audience, was speaking to the intimate reality of separate and individual readers —as it were, the solitary singer (to borrow his own phrase) to the solitary listener. There have always been readers who come upon Whitman with the shock of a personal and private discovery. Among these latter have been some of the finest poets of this century: Edwin Arlington Robinson, who addressed a sonnet to Whitman; Hart Crane, in whose long poem *The Bridge* Whitman is the resident genius; and Wallace Stevens, who put to his own use Whitman's conviction (which Whitman in turn took partly from Emerson) that poetry is man's major resource for "redeeming" and ordering the world.

It is, in any case, in those poems in which Whitman's psychic life, welling out into poetry, communicates with the psychic life of other individuals that we find the great American poet of the nineteenth century, and perhaps, as many readers feel, the greatest poet so far produced in this country.

Walt Whitman, who was born on Long Island in 1819, pursued as wayward a path to literature as did Herman Melville, and to his equal artistic good fortune. Parental inheritance counted rather less for Whitman than for Melville. Whitman's mother was a kindly, mild-tempered woman of Dutch and Quaker descent, and the aging poet, reflecting on his ancestry, once observed that "like the Quakers, the Dutch are very practical and materialistic . . . but are terribly transcendental and cloudy too." The mixture of the practical and the transcendental, not to mention the cloudy, is of course often very striking in Whitman's poetry; but it was if

anything only a vague and general maternal legacy. Whitman was devoted to his mother; he remembered his father (in "There Was a Child Went Forth") as manly but also as mean-spirited and unjust; he was at once liberal and narrow-minded, an unsuccessful and possibly an inept farmer. The incipient poet could learn more from witnessing the afflictions of his brothers and sisters, who suffered a horrendous series of calamities. One of his brothers contracted syphilis and died in an insane asylum; another, also diseased, became a drunkard and married a prostitute. A younger brother was born an idiot, and a sister suffered from incurable melancholy. They became for Whitman closely experienced instances of the victimization by life and figured in the compassionate catalogue of "Song of Myself": "The lunatic is carried at last to the asylum a confirm'd case. . . . The prostitute draggles her shawl. . . . Voices of the diseas'd and despairing. . . ."

The family moved into Brooklyn in 1823; but over the years Whitman was constantly drawn back to Long Island and to its shoreline. The shore was one of Whitman's characteristic habitats—the mysterious frontier, as it seemed to him, of the solid and the liquid, of the known and the unknown. He would tramp along the shore chanting verses from Greek and Latin epic poetry; and he remarked in his old age that the only reason he was not overwhelmed by Homer and Virgil was that he read and recited them not in a library, but "in the full presence of Nature . . . with the sea rolling in." The sea and the land and poetry: it was a quintessential combination for Whitman and provided the pattern of some of his most memorable poems—among them, "Out of the Cradle Endlessly Rocking" and "As I Ebb'd with the Ocean of Life." Whitman, in his prime, became a master of what Paul Fussell has called "The American Shore Ode": a genre practiced by Emerson, Lanier, Eliot, Stevens, and others as well; and one which, in Fussell's words, related "the wholeness and flux of the sea to the discreteness and fixity of land objects," seeming to suggest the reconciliation of several kinds of dualism. The major dualisms that Whitman sought to reconcile, especially in these poems, have been indicated by Wallace Stevens in "Like Decorations in a Nigger Cemetery":

. . . Walt Whitman walking along the ruddy shore.
. . . singing and chanting the things that are part of him,
The worlds that were and will be, death and day.

For Whitman it was, therefore, not the sea itself that aroused him, as it did Melville; much less did he have any relish for "the howling infinite," the mortally dangerous "landlessness" in which Melville symbolically pursued ultimate truth. It was rather the borderline *between* land and sea, observing which the imagination might reconcile the past and the future, time and the timeless, life and death.

But there were other habitats and activities. After he quit school in 1831, Whitman engaged in a series of jobs—printer's assistant, printer, schoolteacher, handyman. Even these minor experiences would be of some value for his poetry: Whitman would be fascinated, for example, by the poetic effect of certain printing devices, by the visual separation or squeezing together of the items in his long catalogues. More important, however, was the profession of journalism, which he entered after moving to Manhattan in 1841, and which he followed there and in Brooklyn for nearly fifteen years—on a series of New York newspapers and as editor of the Brooklyn *Eagle* (1846–48) and of the Brooklyn *Freeman* (1849–50). One of the main qualities of Whitman's early verse, especially "Song of Myself," is that it is *reportorial*, as though Whitman were telling us what he had seen and "covered" as he made his journalistic rounds, notebook and pencil in hand:

The suicide sprawls on the bloody floor of the bedroom,
I witness the corpse with its dabbled hair, I note where the pistol has fallen.

. . .

The hurrahs for popular favorites, the fury of rous'd mobs,

The flap of the curtain'd litter, a sick man inside borne to the hospital,
The meeting of enemies, the sudden oath, the blows and fall,
The excited crowd, the policeman with his star quickly working his passage to the centre of the crowd,

Whitman's newspaper training, along with his remarkable precision of observed detail ("the corpse with its *dabbled*"—that is, bespattered—"hair"), explains something about the often crowded surfaces of Whitman's poetry, and about his relation to his materials. On a certain level, Whitman was a "realist"; he was a devotee of concrete actualities; though he characteristically moved on to disclose in those actualities a portion of the awe-inspiring, even the miraculous. With Whittier, Whitman was one of the first of those American writers who—like Mark Twain and Stephen Crane, Dreiser and Hemingway—came to the creative life after a serious stint of journalism and who, however they might enlarge upon it, always retained a fidelity to an initially realistic vision of things.

We should add still other Whitmanian *personae* during his formative years. The stroller along the shore, for example, was also the elegantly attired wanderer through the city streets; and the compassionate brother was also a political activist, one always ready to stand up and be counted. As we have said, he argued the case for excluding Negro slavery from the territories so heatedly, in 1848, that he was dismissed from the *Eagle*.[1] Whitman thereupon made his first extensive trip across America, traveling as far south and west as New Orleans, where he paused for a three-month job with the *Crescent*. He absorbed the rivers and lakes and hills as he passed them, and the dockhands and laborers and riverboat attendants, with the same loving, absorptive intentness he had given to the turmoil of Manhattan. Out of all this, Whitman

---

[1] It was also rumored that he had kicked a visiting politician downstairs. The Brooklyn *Eagle* denied editorially that there had been any political motivation in Whitman's dismissal, and as to the alleged incident the editor remarked contemptuously: "He is too indolent to kick a musketo [sic]."

developed imperceptibly from a New Yorker
and Brooklynite into that larger entity, an
American—his imagination increasingly hospitable to whole gobbets of sheer Americana, of
personalities and professions, geography and
history.

Whitman returned north to become editor-
in-chief of the Brooklyn *Freeman;* but a year
later (1850), after expressing fierce indignation
over the Fugitive Slave Law (which Emerson,
it will be recalled, denounced as an atrocious
act), he quit the newspaper and withdrew from
the public scene. He lived quietly with his family, sleeping late (according to his brother
George), doing a bit of writing "if he took the
notion," and earning an occasional dollar by
carpentry. The latter occupation gave him the
last of his pre-poetic roles: the role of the simple,
independent American workingman, as indicated by the picture facing the title page of the
first edition of *Leaves of Grass*. But, in fact, from
1850 onward the greatest of Whitman's roles,
and the one that drew upon all the others, was
a-borning. This was the role of the American
poet.

Whitman had long since determined to be
some kind of a writer, and in the early forties
he had published several short stories, signed
"Walter Whitman." They were crudely moralistic and unimpressive—surprisingly so, when
one considers that Whitman might quite likely
have made a first-class novelist. We have mentioned his feeling for vivid detail and his newspaper experience (and it should be noted that,
apart from Whittier, the other names we linked
with his in this respect were in fact all writers
of fiction). In addition, he often displayed a
genuine talent for narrative. His account of John
Paul Jones and the massacre at Goliad, Texas,
in "Song of Myself" and his poignant pictures
of General Washington saying farewell to his
troops and of the visit to his home of the Indian
squaw in "The Sleepers" suggest a capacity for
compelling human imagery that could have
been a major fictional resource.

In any event, Whitman gradually turned to
poetry and took to jotting in his notebook subjects for poems and experiments in language
and metrics. In the later forties and early fifties,

he was reading and reviewing books by Emerson, Carlyle, Goethe; and he was studying the
standard English poets (Whitman's *taste* in
poetry was traditional enough) as well as Americans like Bryant and Poe. The essays of Emerson were probably the main stimulus for the
poet-to-be, particularly, to judge from Whitman's own theory and practice, *Nature*, "The
American Scholar," and "The Poet." It was
from these that Whitman took the conception
of the poet as more, or other, than a maker of
verses—as indeed the visionary emancipator of
the human spirit, as (in Emerson's phrase) "a
liberating god." In a lecture called "Art and
Artists" at the Brooklyn Art Institute in 1851,
Whitman went so far as to compare the artist
to Socrates and by implication to Christ.

In "Song of Myself," Whitman suggests—
and his biographers are inclined to believe it—
that sometime in the 1850's, perhaps in 1853,
he experienced a kind of mystical seizure that
at last released his full creative powers. Speaking from one part of himself to another—the
actual Whitman as it were speaking to his inner
genius—he describes the experiences and the
vision it produced in section 5:

I mind how once we lay such a transparent sum-
    mer morning,
How you settled your head athwart my hips and
    gently turn'd over upon me,
And parted the shirt from my bosom-bone, and
    plunged your tongue to my bare-stript heart,
And reach'd till you felt my beard, and reach'd
    till you held my feet.

Swiftly arose and spread around me the peace
    and knowledge that pass all the arguments
    of the earth,
And I know that the hand of God is the prom-
    ise of my own,
And I know that the spirit of God is the brother
    of my own,
And that all the men ever born are also my
    brothers, and the women my sisters and
    lovers,
And that a kelson of the creation is love,

Such experiences are of course impossible to
document or even to appraise very carefully,

especially when, as here, they take the curious form of what sounds like rapturous love-making leading to a vision of the universal binding power of love. But granting all the invaluable and successive states of Whitman's "higher education," one still looks for something like a miracle to explain the transformation of Walter Whitman, journeyman and occasional scribbler, into Walt Whitman, the poet. Within two years, anyhow, of that "transparent summer morning," Whitman published by his own hand at his own expense what is still the most remarkable first volume of poetry brought out in this country, a little collection of twelve poems, with a long and erratically punctuated preface, called *Leaves of Grass*.

Among those first poems, three—"There Was a Child Went Forth," "Song of Myself," and "The Sleepers" (to use the titles Whitman later gave them)—may be considered here in the order indicated; for they amount to an unfolding but increasingly *inward* autobiography. "There Was a Child Went Forth" is in fact valuable on the strictly biographical level, as it tells us of Whitman's first years, his parents and teachers and friends, the life of nature and farming which surrounded him then ("the early lilacs . . . the noisy brood of the farmyard . . . the apple-trees cover'd with blossoms"), the wharves and ferries and schooner and "hurrying tumbling waves" he used to watch so affectionately. But the poem is, of course, the memory of a young person's initiation into life, like other stories and poems we have come upon and will later be discussing; and what is important is the way all the elements observed are not *merely* observed (and remembered), but become integral parts of the boy's reality, his consciousness, his imagination. More: the process at work is not simply one of absorption; it is also one of sympathetic identification. While the elements "became part of him," at the same time "the first object he look'd upon, that object he became."

Certain passages in Wordsworth's *The Prelude* describe an almost exactly similar double process; and other English Romantic poets could be cited as expressing the same identification. But in the America of Whitman's day, if

Emerson and Thoreau could voice their harmony with nature, others like Poe and Hawthorne and Melville suggested an at least occasional estrangement from their environment, a sense of otherness and even of hostility in the reality that surrounded them. So there was nothing merely fashionable or conventional in Whitman's expressed sense of oneness with his natural world. This is not to imply, of course, that such a sense inevitably gives rise to a greater kind of poetry than its opposite. But the fact is that Whitman's assertion of an unimpeded intimacy between his young self and the world the child goes forth into was hard-won, poetically speaking; and it is the more persuasive since it is conveyed hardly less by technique than by statement. The twin process is enacted by lines that alternately lengthen and stretch into the outer world (as it were) and recoil back into the internality of the boy. In "There Was a Child Went Forth," it is the lengthening and forthgoing movement that predominates; we shall observe the virtual opposite in "As I Ebb'd with the Ocean of Life" in 1860.

"Song of Myself," which occupied sixty-three pages in the first edition, is autobiographical in a more subtle as well as more broadly reaching manner. Here Whitman seems to be telling us most indirectly how he as an individual man (identified in the third stanza as "now thirty-seven years old in perfect health") became a poet, and a poet who, as in Emerson's definition, eventually takes to himself the attributes and functions of the old outmoded divinities. The poem, we may say, is about the birth of a poet and belongs to the genre (sometimes called that of "the birth of Apollo") especially prevalent in English-language poetry from the late eighteenth century onward. So conceived, "Song of Myself" may also be seen as one major instance of what Roy Harvey Pearce has argued (in *The Continuity of American Poetry*) is the distinctively modern and Romantic version of the old epic mode. An epic of this modern sort, according to Pearce, does not—perhaps because it cannot—address itself to ancient times and a mythic story, as in Virgil's *Aeneid* or the medieval *Song of Roland*. Rather, it attempts to perform the traditional epic function by introducing us to a hero, or better a heroic presence or spirit, suitable to the present and the future condition of things: in effect, a heroic being who will be instrumental in shaping that condition—in other words, a great poet.

But to say that "Song of Myself" enacts the birth of such a poet-hero should not suggest that the poem gives us a "story," at least in the usual sense of that word. The entire poem, in fact, is cast in the present tense; and to speak more precisely, Whitman is not so much describing the coming into being of the poet as he is engaged in making more *visible* the nature and attributes of his hero, along with his habits of perception, his attitudes, his complex of relationships. Whitman is not rehearsing the actual life story we have touched upon earlier; he is exploring himself within his world and within a continuing present—by example, as it were: by acting poetically. The much-vexed question of the "form" of "Song of Myself" may be answered by remarking that the poem does not have a dramatic form in the classical manner, a clear unfolding action with a beginning, middle, and end; instead, it consists of a series of emotional pulsations, of attitudinal posturings, of mercurially shifting responses—many of them exceedingly and artfully elusive, and all of them adding up at last to the complete profile of the poetic figure.

Whitman's ideal poet, like Whitman himself, not only believes in the democratic principles; he enacts them. In the preface to the 1855 edition, Whitman assigns to the American poet the task of investing all phenomena with an absolute equality of value: "Of all mankind, the great poet is the equable man. . . . He is the equalizer of his age and land." Whitman thereupon presents as of equal worth and interest such disparate entities as "the multiplication table . . . old age . . . the carpenter's trade . . . the grand-opera." In "Song of Myself," he will sometimes state the principle flatly: "I am the poet of the Body, and I am the poet of the Soul. . . . I am the poet of the woman the same as the man"—well-justified claims that were not without their shock value in a literary culture that was at once overwhelmingly male

in its orientation and at the same time tended to deny (in its Puritanic idealism) the reality of the body. Elsewhere, as we have remarked, instead of asserting equality, Whitman simply "equalizes"—by bringing together within the same poetic breath a prostitute and a president, a Missouri peddler and the crew of a fishing boat. Even when, near the end of the poem, Whitman's poet begins to take on the characteristics of divinity—

Taking myself the exact dimensions of Jehovah,
Lithographing Kronos, Zeus his son, and Hercules his grandson,
Buying drafts of Osiris, Belus, Brahma, Buddha

—even then, he attributes the same divine quality to each of his readers and his fellow men.[2]

At every turn, moreover, Whitman declares the actual and the spiritual freedom of all persons of whatever social degree or race or condition in American society; and by declaring it, he helps make it a little more true. Such at least is the intention: for "Song of Myself" aspires to be an act of liberation, a poem which so works upon its readers as to emancipate them from whatever fetters of mind and inherited attitude (undue allegiance to the past, for example, or unthinking acceptance of things as they are) and whatever drowsiness of spirit they may be afflicted by. The liberating purpose is reflected as well in the technical freedom we have touched on earlier: freedom from rhyme, freedom of rhythm, flexibility of line length and stanzaic structure. Even in his apprentice poems Whitman had broken free of the standard English-verse meter of iambic pentameter; and every American poet after him, William Carlos Williams was to say, has had to show cause why the iambic is the metrical foot best suited to him. (The operative phrase there is, of course, "show cause." Most American poets of quality after Whitman have shown excellent cause for employing the iambic, by doing so to great

---

[2] Belus, whose name one notices in the list of gods, is the same Druidic "Apollo" whom Melville may have had in mind in coining the name of his scapegoat hero Billy Budd.

effect: among them, Robinson, Eliot, Frost, Stevens, and Hart Crane.)

Whitman's gift of "free verse" to American poetry has been anything but an unmixed blessing. Lesser poets, taking Whitman as their warrant, have sometimes offered a sort of nonpoetry with no rhythmic pattern at all: prose so arranged on the page as to have, misleadingly, the look of poetry. But Whitman understood, perhaps intuitively, that if free verse is to be not only free but also verse it must be felt working against what might be called a "shadow poem"—that is, a poetic construct with conventional meter. In "Song of Myself," he achieves this effect most obviously by allowing a conventional line of verse to be followed by or merged into a longer line in which the basic meter is partly broken up. Thus, in section 3:

The little one sleeps in its cradle,
I lift the gauze and look a long time, and silently brush away flies with my hand.

Those lines are succeeded by another pair which reverse the order of conventional and unconventional:

The youngster and the red-faced girl turn aside
    up the bushy hill,
I peeringly view them from the top.

After two more lines which unsettle our metrical expectancies a little further—

The suicide sprawls on the bloody floor of the
    bedroom,
I witness the corpse with its dabbled hair, I note
    where the pistol has fallen

—Whitman has arrived at the point where he can present, and we can accept, an entire passage of nonconventional verse:

The blab of the pave, tires of carts, sluff of boot-
    soles, talk of the promenades,
The heavy omnibus, the driver with his interro-
    gating thumb, the clank of the shod horses
    on the granite floor,
The snow-sleighs, clinking, shouted jokes, pelts
    of snow-balls,

and so on. Whitman's poetry at its best, as

here, shows that free verse is if anything a more delicate matter than verse composed in traditional meters, and harder to write.

"Whoever walks a furlong without sympathy," Whitman says resolutely, "walks to his own funeral drest in his shroud." The life without sympathy is a death-in-life: for Whitman, the democratic motif of fraternity appears as all-embracing compassion. He is one with the wounded slave, with thieves and dwarfs, with the wretched of the earth: "I am the man, I suffer'd, I was there." For the kelson—the metaphorical binding force—of the creation, Whitman believed, is love; and Whitman's poetry, when it engages suffering and grief, moves always to heal and assuage—to bind or fuse, both by sentiment and by technique, the discordant elements.

If the great poet is, in his poetic manner, a great democrat, it is because of his capacity for a special kind of perception, for looking at things in a unique way. "He is a seer," Whitman says in the 1855 preface, going back to one of the oldest definitions of the poet, and one brought back into favor by Romantic theory. "What the eyesight does to the rest he does to the rest. Who knows the curious mystery of eyesight?" This was the lesson of Emerson, who spoke in *Nature* of the poet's "attentive eye," and who said of the American scholar (and by implication of the poet) that he was "the world's eye" as well as "the world's heart." To act as the eyesight of mankind, according to both Emerson and Whitman, was to exercise the faculty of "miraculous" perception, of seeing the extraordinary in the here-and-now (as Jonathan Edwards discovered evidences of the supernatural in the natural world). Whitman, at his typical best, could lead out from closely observed realistic detail to the revelation of miracle:

I believe a leaf of grass is no less than the
    journey-work of the stars
And the pismire is equally perfect, and a grain
    of sand, and the egg of the wren,
And the tree-toad is a chef-d'oeuvre for the
    highest,

And the running blackberry would adorn the
    parlors of heaven,
And the narrowest hinge in my hand puts to
    scorn all machinery,
And the cow crunching with depress'd head sur-
    passes any statue,
And a mouse is miracle enough to stagger sextil-
    lions of infidels.

The passage is brilliant; and it is, again, the
sharp particularity—for example, "the cow
crunching with depress'd head"—that gives rise
to the sense of awe (an awe, on the reader's
part, not only at the world's miracles, but at
Whitman's talent for such particularity). Whitman was probably wise, however, not to extend
the catalogue, for when everything is regarded
as miraculous everything begins to look rather
commonplace. There is a danger, too, of sounding at last a bit ridiculous by insisting too long
and too loudly on the grandiosity of the trivial;
but this danger is beautifully averted by a final
line which satirizes its own tendency to absurd
exaggeration.[3]

    Two other aspects of Whitman's vision are
manifested in "Song of Myself." There is his
vigorous contempt for the sentimental piety of
the day:

I think I could turn and live with animals, they
    are so placid and self-contained,
I stand and look at them long and long.

They do not sweat and whine about their condi-
    tion,
They do not lie awake in the dark and weep for
    their sins,
They do not make me sick discussing their duty
    to God,

Too, although "Song of Myself" is certainly
Whitman's supreme poem of life and of day,

---

[3] The danger referred to—to clarify the point—was not
avoided by E. E. Cummings when he wrote: "A pretty
girl that naked is/Is worth a million statues." In most
situations, the contention is perfectly sound; but it
would hardly satisfy a person engaged in preparing an exhibition of statuary. Whitman, it should be acknowledged, by no means succeeded in avoiding this danger on
all occasions; his humor did not always hold him in
check.

there are also moments of death and darkness
in it. The emerging poet suffers spasms of doubt
and anxiety, even of panic, until (in section 38)
he feels himself stunned and then crucified.
But he experiences at once the movement of
rebirth, as "gashes heal" and "fastenings roll
from me," and he rises from the psychic grave
to "troop forth replenish'd with supreme power."
    "The Sleepers" concludes Whitman's early
autobiographical explorations. He moves here
beyond the explicit reminiscing of "There Was
a Child Went Forth" and the complex presentation of himself as the poet he had become in
"Song of Myself," to touch deeper and more
troubled levels. "The Sleepers" is indeed Whitman's masterpiece in the genre we have called
"the inward journey," a genre (it will be recalled) which goes back to the Puritan habit of
self-inquiry, and to the need, in the words of
the Puritan writer Thomas Hooker, for every
individual to search out "the frame of his own
heart" and examine unflinchingly "the windings
and turnings of his own ways." In describing
such self-inquiry, Hooker deftly invoked the
metaphor of the spiritual traveler; and Whitman's poem does the same: "I wander all night
in my visions,/Stepping with light feet, swiftly
and noiselessly stepping and stopping." But
where Hooker aimed at "a true sight of sin,"
Whitman begins—in a superbly chosen string
of adjectives—with a true sense of guilt and of
psychic disorder: "Wandering and confused,
lost to myself, ill-assorted, contradictory." There
is perhaps an element of sexual shame in this
fractured condition: the journey metaphor in
"The Sleepers" may well imply (as Richard
Chase has suggested) a descent into the unconscious where, in a dream of terror and bewilderment, the ego or conscious self confronts the
lawless energies of the id and feels its very
existence threatened.
    Nonetheless, the dominant impulse in this
poem, as everywhere else in the 1855 *Leaves of
Grass*, is toward psychic recovery and self-assurance, toward a wholeness of *self* that produces
a sense of harmony and reconciliation throughout the surrounding *world*. The poem concludes
with a vision of union and love between Asiatic

and African, European and American, learned and unlearned, lover and mistress, father and son, teacher and student, slave and master. More persuasively even than Emerson himself in *Nature*, Whitman demonstrates in "The Sleepers" the Emersonian belief that only for the reunited self, the redeemed soul, can "original and eternal beauty" be restored to the broken world at large.

The second edition of *Leaves of Grass* appeared less than a year after the first—in June, 1856; and the twenty new poems Whitman had added indicate that during the intervening months, Whitman had been almost beside himself with excitement. The excitement was due in part to the very fact of having published his first volume and to its generally very favorable reception. It was due in particular to a letter from Emerson, who wrote Whitman that *Leaves of Grass* was "the most extraordinary piece of wit and wisdom that America has yet contributed," with "incomparable things said incomparably well in it." The 1856 edition, in fact, displayed on its back cover one sentence from that letter (and Emerson was to grumble that, had he known of Whitman's intention to use it, he would have modified the sentence —in Emerson's phrase, have "enlarged the *but*"): "I greet you at the beginning of a great career."

But Whitman's excitement came from sources much deeper than the mere enjoyment of recognition in high literary places. It came from the profound conviction of poetic genius and of enormous creative powers within himself. Abandoning every other form of activity, Whitman now, as he told Bronson Alcott, who had come down from Concord to pay his respects, only "lived to make pomes," to exercise and to control as best he might the tremendous imaginative force he felt welling up inside him. He had become seized, moreover, with the intoxicating conviction—as expressed, for example, in "Spontaneous Me"—that his own poetic fertility and the fertility of nature were intimately associated, were almost one and the same thing. Such a conviction produced a sense of exhilaration

amounting to awe and verging on a sort of sacred terror—in a way not entirely dissimilar to the experience recorded by Emerson in *Nature*: "Crossing a bare common, in snow puddles, at twilight . . . , I have enjoyed a perfect exhilaration. I am glad to the brink of fear." Identifying his poetic self with the deepest creative currents of nature, Whitman, too, was sometimes glad to the brink of fear.

In retrospect, one realizes that "Crossing Brooklyn Ferry" represents the peak of this visionary intoxication and the most complete merging of the flow of the poet's consciousness with the flow of reality—of human, natural, and man-made reality. It is a poetic experience of the absolute and mystical "oneness" of all times and places, all people and things—a oneness seen as an eternal onward flow, and created by the integrating power of the poet's vision. In section 3, for example, we notice the eleven successive lines beginning with the word "watched" or such equivalents as "saw," "had my eyes dazzled by," and "look'd on." What we may miss is the fact that those reiterated verbs of seeing are performing an action—they are drawing together into a "simple, compact well-join'd scheme" the myriad objects so precisely observed ("the fine centrifugal spokes of light round the shape of my head in the sunlit water . . . the sailors at work in the rigging . . . the flags of all nations . . . the gray walls of the granite storehouses by the docks"). And as Whitman's vision performs its unifying and transfiguring function, so the objects perceived have their transfiguring effect upon *him*: they are "glories strung like beads on my smallest sights and hearings"; they are "dumb, beautiful ministers" to his spiritual and imaginative aspirations and "furnish" their "parts toward eternity . . . toward the soul." Even on this peak of intensity, Whitman is not unmindful of the dark side of experience, for this too he shares with all people in all times and places. On him too "the dark patches fall"; he also, like all mankind, had "blabb'd, blush'd, resented, lied, stole, grudged," and he is even willing to doubt the value of that very force—his creative energy —which had led him to this peak. But all such considerations are finally swept away in the flow of reality, exuberance, and perception.

In the year immediately following the 1856 edition, Whitman wrote about seventy new poems—the products of a still immense over-flow of the energy that had gone into the great poems of the first two editions. But then there came a silence, evidently a pause in creative activity, from the beginning of 1858 till December, 1859, when, in the December issue of the New York *Saturday Press*, Whitman published a poem called "A Child's Reminiscence," later "Out of the Cradle Endlessly Rocking." Two years, or even a little less, is hardly a long space of time for a normal poet to lie fallow; but in the light of Whitman's extraordinary fertility from about 1853 onward, it calls for an attempt at explanation.

For one thing, Whitman had again moved out into the public world, as editor-in-chief of the Brooklyn *Daily Times* (from May, 1857, to June, 1859); and he spent many hours strolling along lower Broadway, his favorite human haunt, or sitting in Pfaff's popular Swiss restaurant watching the (mostly literary) clientele. Whitman's mother once told Bronson Alcott that her son was "always going out and coming in," a most precise formula on the literal level, whether as an observation of Whitman's daily round, or as testimony to the larger rhythms of his career with its alternation of public involvement and private self-communion. It is also a formula that can be applied to his poetry, to the flow and ebb of consciousness within it, the thrust and recoil of his rhythms, the manifest impulse alternately to press outward to fuse with external reality and to retire inward to explore the recesses of his psyche. But during the period in question, the actual outgoing gesture—the return to journalism—had a somewhat different quality than before; sound as his editorial opinions may seem to us, there is something oddly disturbed in some of his writings. Nor did he, for nearly two years, "come in" to write "pomes"; and when he did again begin to write, the poetry resulting is charged with the desolating sense of loss and of death. That sense provides the keynote of the 1860 edition of *Leaves of Grass*.

Whitman's best-informed biographers are persuasive in arguing that one serious cause both of the period of silence and the death-oriented poetry that followed was a homosexual love affair—an affair that, however fulfilling at moments, also brought with it feelings of guilt and, when it ended (the lover apparently abandoning the poet), feelings of despair. Poems like "A Hand-Mirror" and "Hours Continuing Long, Sore and Heavy-Hearted" (the latter significantly deleted by Whitman in the later editions of *Leaves of Grass*) seem undeniable evidence of the sexual adventure and its aftermath. But Whitman's characteristic attitude to experience—his own or anyone else's—was one of tolerance and forgiveness, even celebration. "What blurt is this about virtue and about vice?" he asks, typically, in "Song of Myself." "Evil propels me and reform of evil propels me, I stand indifferent." Guilt was not, accordingly, an emotion he would long sustain. The emotion of loss—the loss of a loved one—may very well have been much harder to overcome. And we may surmise that the feeling was gravely compounded—as the first great wave of creativity spent itself—by a desperate fear that he had also lost his poetic powers. For a poet who had associated his own fertility with that of nature's, a poet who like Shelley and other Romantics really did believe that the poet was "the son of God" and the hero and savior of mankind, no apprehension could be more terrible.

And consequently no achievement could be more triumphant than the poetry—in 1859 and 1860—that Whitman made out of his sense of perhaps multiple bereavement. If the identifying title phrase of 1855 had been "There Was a Child *Went Forth*," the mood of the 1860 edition of *Leaves of Grass* was set by the title "As I *Ebb'd* with the Ocean of Life." And if the inspiriting conviction earlier had been that of the absolute supremacy of *life*, the representative assertion in 1860 was (in "Scented Herbage of My Breast") that "now it is conveyed to me that you [death] are . . . the real reality." "It appears to me that I am dying," Whitman said in "So Long," his presumed farewell to poetry: "My songs cease, I abandon them." On the contrary, his songs were just starting up again—but now they sprang from the consciousness of death. The theme of the new poems was the discovery that death—psychic death, emotional loss, creative exhaustion—could be the very source of human understanding and of poetry.

Such is exactly the theme of "Out of the Cradle Endlessly Rocking." This is one of Whitman's great "shore odes" and declares itself so to be at the end of its first long, hovering, accretive stanza:

A man, yet by these tears a little boy again,
Throwing myself on the sand, confronting the
    waves,
I, chanter of pains and joys, uniter of here and
    hereafter,
Taking all hints to use them, but swiftly leaping
    beyond them,
A reminiscence sing.

Much of the poem's strategy and purpose is implicit in those lines. To begin with, the narrative perspective in "Out of the Cradle" is as intricate as that in a story by Henry James, and for cogent reasons.[4] The poem is indeed a reminiscence: a forty-year-old man recalling an experience of his childhood, when he was on the verge of adolescence. But that experience is in turn vicarious: the boy watching with mounting compassion and understanding the unhappy love affair of two other beings, two mockingbirds from Alabama—the she-bird disappearing one day, the he-bird exchanging through the summer evenings his song of inconsolable anguish with the whispering sounds of the sea.

[4] The poem's meaningful complexity of structure may be a main reason why James was especially drawn to it. Edith Wharton in her memoir *A Backward Glance* (the title taken from Whitman's own memoir) recalls James reading and reciting Whitman's poetry before a small enraptured audience at her home in the Berkshires. The climax was James's crooning recitation of "Out of the Cradle." "A great genius, a very great genius," James murmured when he had finished; then, with a typical Jamesian twist and twinkle, he added: "One can only deplore his too great familiarity with the foreign languages."

This technique is not merely a matter of distancing the sad event, the bird's loss of his mate, as though Whitman were summoning his resources to push away his own recent personal loss (as of course he is also doing). It is rather that the poem's eventual revelation arises from the difference between the anguished bird and the watchful boy, and the difference between that same boy and the middle-aged poet. The bird is imprisoned within the pain of his loss, and cannot see beyond it. He is trapped in time; and for all its loveliness, his continuing lament ends in darkness and sorrow, in the sense of blind futility.

O darkness! O in vain!
O I am very sick and sorrowful.

O throat! O throbbing heart!
And I singing uselessly, uselessly all the night.

Listening to those cries, "the boy ecstatic" has his first poetic intimations. He becomes an "outsetting bard" (the essence of "Out of the Cradle" is caught by the punning distinction between "bird" and "bard"): "My own songs awakened from that hour." At the time, however, the boy was too young to take in the full import of his experience, or to perceive the relation between loss and death on the one hand and poetic inspiration on the other. It requires the mature man, looking back, to give voice to the ultimate revelation; and doing so, he also comes to terms at last with his own immediate bereavement.

That revelation, which can hardly be paraphrased, has to do with the reconciliation of opposites and the ensuing consciousness of totality. The man as poet is not, like the bird, a singer simply of the sorrowful here-and-now. He is liberated and liberating, for his is the poetic vision that unites "pains *and* joys," time *and* the release from time. He is the spokesman above all of the reconciliation of death and life, and of the perception that death is an integral element in the on-going process of life. This is not to belittle death, much less to deny its grand reality—as Whitman had been inclined to do in his first "morning" poems. It is rather to receive death reverently, even rapturously, as one of the supreme facts of experience. This is the message the sea whispers to the child, the longed-for "clew" to an understanding of the human situation which the sea grants the boy as it rustles at his feet and creeps (like death itself) slowly up to his head: "Death, death, death, death, death." It should be added that, along with the poem's beauty of structure and of verbal music, "Out of the Cradle" contains a profound and, so to say, profoundly un-American psychological suggestion—namely, that the first full, unevasive, and conscious acceptance of death is indeed the beginning of human wisdom, as, in certain gifted cases, it may also be the beginning of poetry.

In *Democratic Vistas* (1871), Whitman would argue shrewdly that because of its obsession with material success, America stood in particular need of poets who would "make great poems of death." In "As I Ebb'd with the Ocean of Life"—another of his shore odes—Whitman contributed another remarkable example of the genre. The reader is invited to make his own analysis of this important and difficult poem, which some critics regard as Whitman's finest single work. We will only stress again—as a way of charting the curve of Whitman's developing imagination—the fundamental contrast between it and "There Was a Child Went Forth." The earlier poem enacts a going forth; the later one, an ebbing. The earlier poem is set in the spring of the year, and amid lilacs and morning-glories; in "As I Ebb'd," the poet is found "musing late in the autumn day," surrounded not by spring blossomings but (in another string of stunningly precise observations) by:

Chaff, straw, splinters of wood, weeds, and the
    sea-gluten,
Scum, scales from shining rocks, leaves of salt-
    lettuce, left by the tide,

In the poetic motion of "There Was a Child Went Forth," one senses a constant growth and enlargement; in "As I Ebb'd," there is a sense of dwindling and diminution, of rhythms falling away into silence.

The occasion of the later poem seems not to be the loss or death of a loved one, as in "Out of the Cradle," but the feared loss or death of creative energy, of the capacity to write new poems. The condition of the self as described in "As I Ebb'd" is at an opposite extreme from that perfect interior union reflected in section 5 of "Song of Myself." The actual "me" is now almost wholly separated from "the Real Me," which we may take to be the deepest source of creative inspiration and human insight. Everything the poet has written now strikes him as a worthless object of mockery. The extraordinary accomplishment of the poem lies, as it were, in its denial of its own manifest content. Whitman has in effect written a great poem which takes off from a confessed inability to write poetry or even to believe in poetry any longer. We leave it open whether the mysterious language of the last stanza does in fact announce —rather than simply *display*—a total recovery of creative power.

"When Lilacs Last in the Dooryard Bloom'd" —which appeared in a volume called *Drum-Taps* in 1865, before being incorporated into the 1867 *Leaves of Grass*—is probably not Whitman's masterpiece among his poems of death, though it has often been so judged. But it may constitute Whitman's most impressive act of poetic reconciliation. It was occasioned, of course, by the assassination of Abraham Lincoln, and the long passage of the funeral train from Washington to Springfield, Illinois. The poem is a remarkable fusion of public event and private response, and before commenting on it we should recall the public turn Whitman's life had again taken.

The outbreak of the Civil War in April, 1861, drew Whitman once more into the public world. In December, 1862, he journeyed to Falmouth, Virginia, where his brother Jeff was recovering from wounds; and he spent some eight days in the battle area. The experience moved him to assume his own role in the war—the active and exceedingly typical role of a "wound-dresser" in the Washington hospitals: a healer-priest of sorts, like the one he had described as part of the profile of the poet in "Song of Myself." Performing this admirable, even heroic role, Whitman visited the injured, wrote their letters, changed their bandages, lifted their spirits, and literally held them in his arms as they died.

The poems Whitman wrote during the war alternate between images of actual wound-dressing and those which record moments and glimpses in the front lines—cavalry crossing a ford, a bivouac at night, a night-long vigil beside a slain comrade. But even these latter, as we suggested in comparing Whitman's war poetry, in an earlier section, with that of Melville, can be seen as poems of healing: in the sense that they seek to mitigate feelings of horror or grief and to purge such tensions as exist within readers' attitudes toward the phenomena of war. In "Bivouac on a Mountain Side," for example, the agents of war—the soldiers and horses—blur shadowlike into the natural landscape, the terraced mountain sides and the clinging cedars, while "far out of reach . . . the eternal stars" begin to appear. The arresting feature of "When Lilacs Last in the Dooryard Bloom'd" is just its slow, delicate, and (poetically speaking) utterly honest reconciliation of the emotional responses to the death of President Lincoln.

The challenge is set by the historic fact that Lincoln was assassinated in the spring of the year. In the other two death poems we have considered, there was no contradiction between season and experience: the song in "Out of the Cradle" arises from "the Ninth-month" (that is, September) "midnight"; and the disconsolate wanderer in "As I Ebb'd" is "musing late in the autumn day." But Lincoln was struck down at the very moment that physical nature was coming alive, when lilacs were blooming in the yard; and the poet knows that every year he will be confronted by the contradictory feelings aroused by the annual rebirth and the remembered death of his beloved leader.

Ever-returning spring, trinity sure to me you
    bring,
Lilac blooming perennial and drooping star in
    the west,
And thought of him I love.

It is the elements of that trinity that—within

the poem, and by poetic means—must be reconciled: the symbol of spring, the symbol of the dying President (a *western* star, for Lincoln of Illinois), the poet's personal love and grief. But as the poem progresses, it is rather the contradictions that are stressed. Section 5 begins: "Over the breast of the spring," but its single sentence ends with the image of the endlessly journeying coffin. To the coffin that moves westward in section 6 and over fourteen lines crowded with draped flags and somber faces and mournful voices, the poet in a final brief line offers a tiny sprig of lilac. Gazing up at the drooping, disappearing star in section 8, the poet's soul sinks almost to oblivion, his voice all but silenced.

The poem's spirit of reconciliation is a gray-brown thrush and the "carol of death" that he sings, as the poet listens in wonderment, amid "the fragrant cedars and the ghostly pines." The thrush is also, of course, the spirit of poetry—of Whitman's kind of death poetry. As against the sorrowful mockingbird hopelessly caught in his own grief in "Out of the Cradle," the thrush is capable, like the true poet, of absorbing the reality of death into the larger reality of "the fathomless universe." He is a poet who finds in the outlet of a melodious song about death the very warrant for death itself, and the means not only of accepting but even of rejoicing in it. "Death's outlet song" (section 16) becomes a "victorious song," because it can unite death and life, reconcile the irrevocable loss and the ever-returning spring, and transform the poet's feelings by bringing them into harmony with the elements reconciled. The union, at the poem's close, is total and permanent:

Lilac and star and bird twined with the chant
    of my soul,
There in the fragrant pines and the cedars dusk
    and dim.

Whitman remained in Washington for some years after the war, until 1873, working in a series of government jobs—from one of which, in the Indian bureau, he was summarily dismissed in 1865 when the bureau chief happened upon a copy of *Leaves of Grass* and was scandalized by its sexual, not to say genitalian, frankness. In 1873,

Whitman, still only fifty-four years old, suffered a stroke that left him partly paralyzed. On a painful journey north, he paused more or less by chance in Camden, New Jersey, and there he lived until his death in 1892.

Whitman's performance as a wound-dresser was, as we have said, humane and admirable to the point of the heroic; and his years of government service were (as *Democratic Vistas* would show) highly educational. But it cannot be said that the decade spent in the capital of the United States was beneficial for Whitman's poetic art. His best poetry—whether of "day" or of "death"—depended upon a sort of mobile balance, a constant intermovement or flow between himself and the phenomenal world: the self very closely observing and then often transfiguring the world, while the world's phenomena poured in upon him "as glories strung like beads" upon his sight and hearing. This balance was a matter of the greatest delicacy; and critical discussions of Whitman—too conscious, perhaps, of the bearded bluffness of his public persona as well as the expansiveness of his sayings—have sometimes overlooked his genius for the delicate. In any event, the Washington experience seems to have upset the balance; and in Whitman's later poetry, the world outpulls the imagining self, and hazy abstractions tend to obscure the actual. He began to write "Chants Democratic" and talk about "these states"; the 1871 edition of *Leaves of Grass* was dedicated to the "Vast, composite, electric *Democratic Nationality*," one of the most depressingly bombastic phrases Whitman ever coined. And already with the 1867 edition, he had begun the task of editing the early poems, toning them down, deleting passages that struck him as too candid or self-revealing, shifting the poems out of their original and significant sequence.

During his Camden years, Whitman became the object of a cult both in this country and in Europe. It is gratifying that Whitman in his own lifetime was appreciated and even worshiped (though only in small circles) as he so deserved to be; and the many glimpses we have of the aging bard, in various reminiscences, show us a person of high good humor, continuing

devotion to literature and its role in a democratic culture, and almost incredible stamina. Still, it is unfortunate that the cult established as its poet-hero the patriotic and "cosmic" Whitman, rather than Whitman the poet of flow and ebb, the reconciler of pain and joy. It was this cosmic Whitman against whom later poets like T. S. Eliot reacted, and not without some warrant: for the later or "cosmic" Whitman—the Whitman after, say, 1866—was a poet who to some degree had lost his hold on, or faith in, the realistic vision. Whitman could still, to be sure, write "pomes" that would guarantee the enduring reputation of a lesser artist, but more and more rarely. "Passage to India" can stand as representative of the faults and virtues of Whitman in the last decades of his life. We have not thought it necessary, in the interests of giving a full picture of Whitman, to include in our selections examples of his work at its poetical flabbiest; but it should be remembered that of all great modern poets in English, none wrote more bad poems—puffy or awkward or verbally pompous or pathetic, as the case may be—than he.

The best of Whitman in the latter years is probably in his prose, of which there was a good deal: *Democratic Vistas* (1871), *Specimen Days and Collect* (1882), and the autobiographical *A Backward Glance O'er Travel'd Roads* (1888). The first of these, though overblown and disorganized, is a major document—the first thoroughgoing survey of the American Republic in "the Gilded Age," that period of chaotic economic development, of financial greed and of many kinds of gross corruption following the Civil War (and in fact begun during and because of the war). Among others, Mark Twain, Henry James, and Henry Adams would also give an account of this disreputable but fascinating moment in our national history; but none would offer as scathing an indictment of postwar America as Whitman:

I say we had best look our times and lands searchingly in the face, like a physician diagnosing some deep disease. Never was there, perhaps, more hollowness at heart than at present, and here in the United States. Genuine belief seems to have left us. The underlying principles of the States are not honestly believ'd in, (for all this hectic glow, and these melodramatic screamings) nor is humanity itself believ'd in. What penetrating eye does not everywhere see through the mask? The spectacle is appalling. We live in an atmosphere of hypocrisy throughout. The men believe not in the women, nor the women in the men. A scornful superciliousness rules in literature.

With the passing years, Whitman became only more deeply troubled about America's future. "If the United States, like the countries of the Old World," he wrote eight years after *Democratic Vistas*, "are also to grow vast crops of poor, desperate, dissatisfied, nomadic, miserably-waged populations, such as we see looming upon us of late years . . . then our republican experiment, notwithstanding all its surface-success, is at heart an unhealthy failure." Those strong words occurred in an undelivered lecture called "The Tramp and Strike Questions," which Whitman wrote in support of the great railroad strike of 1879, and after American soldiers had for the first time fired upon American workingmen. With an acuteness and a persisting democratic conviction shared by few of his contemporaries—Howells would be virtually ostracized for supporting the participants in the Haymarket riots in 1886[5]—Whitman declared that "the great American revolution of 1776 was simply a great strike, successful for its immediate object." And he saw the mounting challenge no less in hard, concrete, economic terms than in a spiritual perspective:

Beneath the whole political world, what most presses and perplexes today, sending vastest results affecting the future, is not the abstract question of democracy, but of social and economic organization, the treatment of workingpeople by employers, and all that goes along with it—not only the wages-payment part, but

[5] For further comments on those episodes, see the general introduction to Part 4 and the introduction to Howells.

a certain spirit and principle, to vivify anew these relations.

But Whitman continued to believe in the unifying and vitalizing role of poetry and the poets—more generally, of literature—in the enormous work of giving or restoring health to the nation. In a climactic moment in *Democratic Vistas*, he put forward his most unmodified claim in this regard:

It must still be reiterated, as . . . the deep lesson of history and time, that all else in the contribution of a nation or age, through its politics, materials, heroic personalities, military *éclat*, etc., remains crude, and defers, in any close and thoroughgoing estimate, until vitalized by national, original archetypes in literature. They only put the nation in form, finally tell anything—prove, complete anything—perpetuate anything.

Whitman supplied no few of the most striking and original archetypes in our literature, although by 1871 he seems to have half-forgotten that they were components or manifestations of an archetypal *self*—that they were not "national," or not initially so. Whitman's vision of America—in "Song of Myself," in "The Sleepers," in "When Lilacs Last in the Dooryard Bloom'd"—was something he arrived at only after what Emerson would have called the redemption, or the reunification, of his own soul. Only then did the American world draw itself together—put itself "in form"—under his gaze. In those poems, and in all his supreme poems, Whitman spoke first to the private individual, the secret sharer of his poetry, his experience, his personality. For that other self must likewise awaken spiritually, come to himself, plunge at last into the ocean of life:

Sit a while dear son,

· · ·

Long enough have you dream'd contemptible dreams,
Now I wash the gum from your eyes,
You must habit yourself to the dazzle of light and of every moment of your life.

Long have you timidly waded holding a plank
  by the shore,
Now I will you to be a bold swimmer,

To jump off in the midst of the sea, rise
again, nod to me, shout, and laughingly
dash with your hair.

BIOGRAPHICAL CHART

1819 Born, May 31, in Huntington, Long Island
1823 Moves with his family to Brooklyn
ca. 1830 Formal schooling ends
1832 Becomes printer's devil in the offices of the Long Island *Patriot*
1836 Wanders about on Long Island, teaching briefly, doing occasional editorial work until 1841
1841–48 Works with various Brooklyn newspapers, notably the Brooklyn *Eagle*, contributing mostly stories
1842 *Franklin Evan*, a temperance novel
1846 Becomes editor of the *Eagle*
1848 Loses his position as editor for protests against the Democrats' failures to deal adequately with slavery issues; travels across the country to work in New Orleans for the *Crescent*; leaves after three months; for the next fifteen years publishes sporadically in various Brooklyn newspapers, doing occasional editorial work as well
1855 *Leaves of Grass*
1856 Second edition of *Leaves of Grass*
1857 Edits the Brooklyn *Times* (until 1859)
1860 Third edition of *Leaves of Grass*
1862 Publishes a series of articles dealing with the Broadway Hospital, in which he had served as male nurse; leaves Brooklyn for Washington, D.C., to find his brother wounded in action in the Civil War; begins personal efforts at caring for wounded soldiers
1865 *Walt Whitman's Drum-Taps*; given a minor government clerkship, then fired, probably because of his literary reputation; hired by the office of the attorney general
1867 Fourth edition of *Leaves of Grass*
1868 W. M. Rossetti publishes a British edition of *Leaves of Grass*
1871 Fifth edition of *Leaves of Grass*
1873 Suffers a paralytic stroke; takes up residence in Camden, New Jersey; mother dies
1875 *Memoranda During the War*
1876 Sixth edition of *Leaves of Grass*; *Two Rivulets*; publishes and circulates a self-written article describing his destitution that results in increased interest in his books
1879 Travels to Colorado
1881 Seventh edition of *Leaves of Grass*; visits Boston
1882 Eighth edition of *Leaves of Grass*; *Specimen Days and Collect*
1883 First official biography appears by Richard Maurice Bucke
1888 Ninth edition of *Leaves of Grass*; *November Boughs*; suffers another stroke
1891 Tenth edition of *Leaves of Grass*
1892 Dies, March 26, in Camden, New Jersey

FURTHER READINGS

Gay Wilson Allen, *Walt Whitman Handbook* (1946)
———— and E. Sculley Bradley, eds., *The Collected Writings of Walt Whitman* (18 vols.; CEAA edition); this work, ten volumes of which have already been published, will become the standard edition
R. M. Bucke, T. B. Harned, and H. L. Traubel, eds., *The Complete Writings of Walt Whitman* (1926)
Malcolm Cowley, ed., *Leaves of Grass* (1960)
Leslie Fiedler, ed., *Whitman* (1959)
Emory Holloway, ed., *Leaves of Grass* (1925)
————, *Uncollected Poetry and Prose of Walt Whitman* (1921)
Roy Harvey Pearce, *Leaves of Grass* (1961; facsimile edition of 1860 text)

Gay Wilson Allen, *The Solitary Singer: A Critical Biography of Walt Whitman* (1955)

————, *Walt Whitman* (1969)
————, *Walt Whitman as Man, Poet and Legend* (1961)
Newton Arvin, *Whitman* (1938)
Roger Asselineau, *The Evolution of Walt Whitman* (1960)
John Burroughs, *Whitman: A Study* (1896)
Richard V. Chase, *Walt Whitman* (1961)
————, *Walt Whitman Reconsidered* (1955)
Milton Hindus, ed., *Leaves of Grass One Hundred Years After* (1955)
R. W. B., Lewis, ed., *The Presence of Walt Whitman* (1965)
Edwin H. Miller, ed., *A Century of Whitman Criticism* (1969)

James Miller, Jr., *A Critical Guide to Leaves of Grass* (1957)

Perry Miller, *The Life of the Mind in America* (1965)

Francis Murphy, ed., *Walt Whitman: A Critical Anthology* (1969)

Roy Harvey Pearce, *Whitman: A Collection of Critical Essays* (1962)

Frederick Schyberg, *Walt Whitman* (1951)

Mark Van Doren, Gay Wilson Allen, and David Daiches, *Walt Whitman: Man, Poet, Philosopher* (1955)

Song of Myself (1855)

This was the first poem in the 1855 edition of *Leaves of Grass*. It appeared without title and without section numbers. In our introduction, we suggested guardedly that the subject of "Song of Myself" might be taken to be "the birth of the poet"—the process by which a particular man became a poet, and then the process by which the poet assumes a godlike quality and becomes *the* poet in the Emersonian and Whitmanian view of that figure. In this connection, the first process perhaps carries through section 17; the revelation of the human aspects of the poet are revealed in the sections following through 32; and the "apotheosis" occurs thereafter. But it is not very fruitful to attempt this kind of analysis of "Song of Myself," for the poem does not have the sort of structure that yields to the classical mode of criticism. One should seek, rather, to gain a sense of the varying *rhythm* of the poem—the ebb and flow of emotion within it, the shift of mood, the alternation between moments of intensity and moments of relaxation.

One may gather a sense of the archetypal nature of the poetic experience in "Song of Myself" by considering what is superficially a very different and very remote experience—that of the "shaman," or medicine man, in certain extremely primitive African and Asian tribes. Writing about this curious figure, in *Myths, Dreams and Mysteries* (1960), Mircea Eliade remarks:

> By means of special techniques, the shamans endeavor to rise above the present condition of man—that is of *man corrupted*—and to re-enter the state of primordial man described to us in the paradisiac myths. . . . The shaman is above all the specialist in ecstasy. It is owing to his capacity for ecstasies—that

is, because he is able, at will, to pass out of his body and undertake mystical journeys through all the cosmic regions—that the shaman is a healer, and a director of souls as well as a mystic and visionary. . . . Only the shaman is able to pursue the wandering soul of the sick person, capture it and bring it back into the body. . . . In a word, the shaman is the great specialist in *spiritual questions*, it is he who knows better than anyone else the numerous dramas, the risks and dangers of the soul.

The healer, the director of souls, the mystic and visionary: all these are aspects of Whitman's poet; he too is a specialist in ecstasy; and his departure from his body and mystical journey through the cosmic regions is recounted in detail in section 33 of "Song of Myself" ("I visit the orchards of spheres" and so on).

Professor Eliade describes a "shamanic session" in language that almost describes the process at work in "Song of Myself":

> First, an appeal to the auxiliary spirits, which, more often than not, are those of animals, and a dialogue with them in a *secret language*; secondly, drum-playing and a dance, preparatory to the mystic journey; and thirdly, a trance (real or simulated) during which the shaman's soul is believed to have left the body.

These items are easily located in Whitman's poem: for example, the congress with animals in section 14 (some, Whitman says there, may find the wild gander's *ya-honk* meaningless, "but I listening close,/Find its purpose"); the drum-playing in section 18 ("With music strong I come, with my cornets and my drums"); the mystic journey.

[handwritten top margin: Whitman – poet of democracy, early feminist. He's unconventional. The whole tone, not just context, is American. Lived in Brooklyn. everything and the value of nothing. the price of everything. A cynic is a man who knows the price of everything and the value of nothing. Cynical – distrustful of society; one has good motives.]

To observe these similarities should not, of course, be to force "Song of Myself" into some deforming traditional pattern. After meditating the analogy suggested, one should turn to the altogether different perspective of Randall Jarrell's brilliant and spirited essay "Some Lines from Whitman." Jarrell declares, with effective Whitmanian exaggeration, that "one finds half (Whitman's) best work" in "Song of Myself" and almost makes the reader believe it by a most illuminating analysis of a number of passages from the poem. The value, as well as the charm, of Jarrell's discussion lies in his sure sense of the limits of criticism. After quoting the passage that ends "I am the man, I suf-

fered, I was there," Jarrell says: "In the last lines of this quotation Whitman has reached—as great writers always reach—a point at which criticism seems not only unnecessary but absurd: these lines are so good that even admiration feels like insolence." At the same time, no one has been more acute or wittier about Whitman's worst passages than Jarrell.

It can be added, incidentally, that the line in the first section of "Song of Myself" which identifies the poet as being thirty-seven years old was inserted long after the 1855 edition of *Leaves of Grass* and is inaccurate. Whitman was, in fact, thirty-six in 1855.

[handwritten: Exultant tone; life is wonderful; life deserves celebration. He is a mystic – believes in oneness of being. free verse. context: slavery, feminism]

1

I celebrate myself, and sing myself, *[individualism]*
And what I assume you shall assume, *[we are all one]*
For every atom belonging to me as good belongs to you. *[there is good in everyone. We are all part of same creation]*

[relaxed] I loafe and invite my soul,
I lean and loafe at my ease observing a spear of summer grass.

My tongue, every atom of my blood, form'd from this soil, this air, *[American soil and air. long line of]*
Born here of parents born here from parents the same, and their parents the same,
I, now thirty-seven years old in perfect health begin, *[full of energy and Americans. vitality. Life is the best form of education]*
Hoping to cease not till death. *[very non-conformist. against formal education]*

Creeds and schools in abeyance, *[old ways of believing. temporary suspension or of an activity or ruling. to be enough]*
Retiring back a while sufficed at what they are, but never forgotten, *[you have to build on past. they were good enough for their time. No worshipping of past. Believes in brotherhood of man.]*
I harbor for good or bad, I permit to speak at every hazard, *[all part of oneness. He will not be censored. Speaks out boldly whatever the hazard.]*
Nature without check with original energy. *[vitality]*

[handwritten: No attempt to suppress. May be shocking; will be frank]

2

Houses and rooms are full of perfumes, the shelves are crowded with perfumes,
I breathe the fragrance myself and know it and like it,
The distillation would intoxicate me also, but I shall not let it.

The atmosphere is not a perfume, it has no taste of the distillation, it is odorless, *[Everything natural.]*
It is for my mouth forever, I am in love with it, *[clothes disguise humanity. "Whatever is according to]*
I will go to the bank by the wood and become undisguised and naked, *[my nature is right."]*
I am mad for it to be in contact with me.

The smoke of my own breath, *[Speaking of anatomy and nature together.]*
Echoes, ripples, buzz'd whispers, love-root, silk-thread, crotch and vine,
My respiration and inspiration, the beating of my heart, the passing of blood and air through my
    lungs, *[normal living]*
The sniff of green leaves and dry leaves, and of the shore and dark-color'd sea-rocks, and of hay in the
    barn, *[various aspects of landscape]*
The sound of the belch'd words of my voice loos'd to the eddies of the wind, *[a little whirlpool or whirling]*
A few light kisses, a few embraces, a reaching around of arms,

10

Joie-de-vivre - tone of the speaker

The play of shine and shade on the trees as the supple boughs wag,
The delight alone or in the rush of the streets, or along the fields and hill-sides,
The feeling of health, the full-moon trill, the song of me rising from bed and meeting the sun.

Have you reckon'd a thousand acres much? have you reckon'd the earth much?
Have you practis'd so long to learn to read?
Have you felt so proud to get at the meaning of poems?

Stop this day and night with me and you shall possess the origin of all poems, 20
You shall possess the good of the earth and sun, (there are millions of suns left,)
You shall no longer take things at second or third hand, nor look through the eyes of the dead, nor
   feed on the spectres in books,
You shall not look through my eyes either, nor take things from me,
You shall listen to all sides and filter them from your self.

I have heard what the talkers were talking, the talk of the beginning and the end,
But I do not talk of the beginning or the end.

There was never any more inception than there is now,
Nor any more youth or age than there is now,
And will never be any more perfection than there is now,
Nor any more heaven or hell than there is now.

Urge and urge and urge,
Always the procreant urge of the world.
Out of the dimness opposite equals advance, always substance and increase, always sex,
Always a knit of identity, always distinction, always a breed of life. 10
To elaborate is no avail, learn'd and unlearn'd feel that it is so.

Sure as the most certain sure, plumb in the uprights, well entretied, braced in the beams,
Stout as a horse, affectionate, haughty, electrical,
I and this mystery here we stand.
Clear and sweet is my soul, and clear and sweet is all that is not my soul.

Lack one lacks both, and the unseen is proved by the seen,
Till that becomes unseen and receives proof in its turn.
Showing the best and dividing it from the worst age vexes age,
Knowing the perfect fitness and equanimity of things, while they discuss I am silent, and go bathe
   and admire myself. 20

Welcome is every organ and attribute of me, and of any man hearty and clean,
Not an inch nor a particle of an inch is vile, and none shall be less familiar than the rest.

I am satisfied—I see, dance, laugh, sing;
As the hugging and loving bed-fellow sleeps at my side through the night, and withdraws at the peep
   of the day with stealthy tread,
Leaving me baskets cover'd with white towels swelling the house with their plenty,
Shall I postpone my acceptation and realization and scream at my eyes,
That they turn from gazing after and down the road,
And forthwith cipher and show me to a cent,
Exactly the value of one and exactly the value of two, and which is ahead?

4

Trippers and askers surround me,
People I meet, the effect upon me of my early life or the ward and city I live in, or the nation,
The latest dates, discoveries, inventions, societies, authors old and new,
The real or fancied indifference of some man or woman I love,
My dinner, dress, associates, looks, compliments, dues,
The real or fancied indifference of some man or woman I love,
The sickness of one of my folks or of myself, or ill-doing or loss or lack of money, or depressions or
    exaltations,
Battles, the horrors of fratricidal war, the fever of doubtful news, the fitful events;
These come to me days and nights and go from me again,
But they are not the Me myself.   10

Apart from the pulling and hauling stands what I am,
Stands amused, complacent, compassionating, idle, unitary,
Looks down, is erect, or bends an arm on an impalpable certain rest,
Looking with side-curved head curious what will come next,
Both in and out of the game and watching and wondering at it.
Backward I see in my own days where I sweated through fog with linguists and contenders,
I have no mockings or arguments, I witness and wait.

5

I believe in you my soul, the other I am must not abase itself to you,
And you must not be abased to the other.

Loafe with me on the grass, loose the stop from your throat,
Not words, not music or rhyme I want, not custom or lecture, not even the best,
Only the lull I like, the hum of your valvèd voice.

I mind how once we lay such a transparent summer morning,
How you settled your head athwart my hips and gently turn'd over upon me,
And parted the shirt from my bosom-bone, and plunged your tongue to my bare-stript heart,
And reach'd till you felt my beard, and reach'd till you held my feet.

Swiftly arose and spread around me the peace and knowledge that pass all the argument of the
    earth,   10
And I know that the hand of God is the promise of my own,
And I know that the spirit of God is the brother of my own,
And that all the men ever born are also my brothers, and the women my sisters and lovers,
And that a kelson of the creation is love,
And limitless are leaves stiff or drooping in the fields,
And brown ants in the little wells beneath them,
And mossy scabs of the worm fence, heap'd stones, elder, mullein and poke-weed.

6

A child said What is the grass? fetching it to me with full hands;
How could I answer the child? I do not know what it is any more than he.

I guess it must be the flag of my disposition, out of hopeful green stuff woven.

Or I guess it is the handkerchief of the Lord,
A scented gift and remembrancer designedly dropt,
Bearing the owner's name someway in the corners, that we may see and remark, and say Whose?

Or I guess the grass is itself a child, the produced babe of the vegetation.

Or I guess it is a uniform hieroglyphic, *symbol*

And it means, Sprouting alike in broad zones and narrow zones, *wide lawns and tiny lawns*

Growing among black folks as among white,   10

Kanuck, Tuckahoe, Congressman, Cuff, I give them the same, I receive them the same. *It is becoming*

Canadians, Indian, white, Irish — all are one   *part of the*

And now it seems to me the beautiful uncut hair of graves. *Symbolic of ongoing life*   *universe*

Tenderly will I use you curling grass,

It may be you transpire from the breasts of young men, *may have fought, become known*

It may be if I had known them I would have loved them,

It may be you are from old people, or from offspring taken soon out of their mother's laps.

And here you are the mothers' laps.

This grass is very dark to be from the white heads of old mothers,

Darker than the colorless beards of old men,

Dark to come from under the faint red roofs of mouths. *Grass represents hair*   20

O I perceive after all so many uttering tongues, *linguists*

And I perceive they do not come from the roofs of mouths for nothing.

I wish I could translate the hints about the dead young men and women, *what has become of the young*

And the hints about old men and mothers, and the offspring taken soon out of their laps. *and old?*

What do you think has become of the young and old men? *Life goes on after death as*

And what do you think has become of the women and children? *symbolized by grass growing on*

                                                                                                                        graves

They are alive and well somewhere,

The smallest sprout shows there is really no death, *Very optimistic. Life goes on.*

And if ever there was it led forward life, and does not wait at the end to arrest it, *Death is a gateway to*

And ceas'd the moment life appear'd. *more life.*   30

All goes onward and outward, nothing collapses, *Optimistic; country was growing.*

And to die is different from what any one supposed, and luckier. *happy*

most people think it is horrible to die.

To die is a happy thing.

7

Has any one supposed it lucky to be born?

I hasten to inform him or her it is just as lucky to die, and I know it.

part of oneness   *equating women as just as valuable as men*

I pass death with the dying and birth with the new-wash'd babe, and am not contain'd

between my hat and boots, *only the body is contained there, not his soul.*

they are full

And peruse manifold objects, no two alike and every one good, *optimism*

The earth good and the stars good, and their adjuncts all good. *optimism*

a secondary + inessential addition

I am not an earth nor an adjunct of an earth, *brotherhood element*

I am the mate and companion of people, all just as immortal and fathomless as myself,

(They do not know how immortal, but I know.)

Every kind for itself and its own, for me mine male and female, *reconciling opposites, pulling everything*

For me those that have been boys and that love women, *together.*   10

For me the man that is proud and feels how it stings to be slighted,

For me the sweet-heart and the old maid, for me mothers and the mothers of mothers, *women are as*

For me lips that have smiled, eyes that have shed tears, *important as*

For me children and the begetters of children. *men.*

sees dignity no matter what the age

Undrape! you are not guilty to me, nor stale nor discarded, *Clothing is a façade that conceals*

I see through the broadcloth and gingham whether or no, *humanity. He*

And am around, tenacious, acquisitive, tireless, and cannot be shaken away. *wants to see*

holding firmly   *easy to*   *all-seeing spirit of the universe. the real person*

persistent   *acquire*

He sees babies 8   *Babies are symbolic of rebirth.*

The little one sleeps in its cradle,
I lift the gauze and look a long time, and silently brush away flies with my hand.

The youngster and the red-faced girl turn aside up the bushy hill, *love*
I peeringly view them from the top.

The suicide sprawls on the bloody floor of the bedroom,   *death*
I witness the corpse with its dabbled hair, I note where the pistol has fallen.

The blab of the pave, tires of carts, sluff of boot-soles, talk of the promenaders,
The heavy omnibus, the driver with his interrogating thumb, the clank of the shod horses on the
    granite floor,
The snow-sleighs, clinking, shouted jokes, pelts of snow-balls,
The hurrahs for popular favorites, the fury of rous'd mobs,
The flap of the curtain'd litter, a sick man inside borne to the hospital,   10
The meeting of enemies, the sudden oath, the blows and fall,
The excited crowd, the policeman with his star quickly working his passage to the centre of the
    crowd,
The impassive stones that receive and return so many echoes,
What groans of over-fed or half-starv'd who fall sunstruck or in fits,
What exclamations of women taken suddenly who hurry home and give birth to babes, *proper behavior*
What living and buried speech is always vibrating here, what howls restrain'd by decorum,
Arrests of criminals, slights, adulterous offers made, acceptances, rejections with convex lips,
I mind them or the show or resonance of them—I come and I depart. *He is like a shadow, a spirit*
    of presence;
    everywhere at the
    same time.

9

The big doors of the country barn stand open and ready,
The dried grass of the harvest-time loads the slow-drawn wagon,
The clear light plays on the brown gray and green intertinged,
The armfuls are pack'd to the sagging mow.

I am there, I help, I came stretch'd atop of the load,
I felt its soft jolts, one leg reclined on the other,
I jump from the cross-beams and seize the clover and timothy,
And roll head over heels and tangle my hair full of wisps.

10 *Plays several roles.*

Alone far in the wilds and mountains I hunt,
Wandering amazed at my own lightness and glee, *joie de vivre*
In the late afternoon choosing a safe spot to pass the night,
Kindling a fire and broiling the fresh-kill'd game,
Falling asleep on the gather'd leaves with my dog and gun by my side.

The Yankee clipper is under her sky-sails, she cuts the sparkle and scud,
My eyes settle the land, I bend at her prow or shout joyously from the deck.

The boatmen and clam-diggers arose early and stopt for me,
I tuck'd my trowser-ends in my boots and went and had a good time;
You should have been with us that day round the chowder-kettle.

I saw the marriage of the trapper in the open air in the far west, the bride was a red girl,
Her father and his friends sat near cross-legged and dumbly smoking, they had moccasins to their feet
    and large thick blankets hanging from their shoulders,   10

[handwritten: paradoxism / quranic —]
[handwritten top: Great Dignity / Indians were considered inferior / Tone of approval and acceptance / Shows dignity of the persecuted]

On a bank lounged the trapper, he was drest mostly in skins, his luxuriant beard and curls protected his
    neck, he held his bride by the hand,
She had long eyelashes, her head was bare, her coarse straight locks descended upon her voluptuous *[handwritten: sensuous]*
    limbs and reach'd to her feet.

The runaway slave came to my house and stopt outside, *[handwritten: structured free verse – can't have chaos]*
I heard his motions crackling the twigs of the woodpile, *[handwritten: good free verse has structure]*
Through the swung half-door of the kitchen I saw him limpsy and weak,
And went where he sat on a log and led him in and assured him,
And brought water and fill'd a tub for his sweated body and bruis'd feet,
And gave him a room that enter'd from my own, and gave him some coarse clean clothes,   20
And remember perfectly well his revolving eyes and his awkwardness,
And remember putting plasters on the galls of his neck and ankles;
He staid with me a week before he was recuperated and pass'd north, *[handwritten: to Canada]*
I had him sit next me at table, my fire-lock lean'd in the corner. *[handwritten: gun]*
[handwritten: equality]
[handwritten: shows he trusts the slave and will protect him because fugitive slave law was in effect. / 3/5 comp. supported slavery / Slave trade]

11

Twenty-eight young men bathe by the shore,
Twenty-eight young men and all so friendly;
Twenty-eight years of womanly life and all so lonesome.
[handwritten: Whitman projects his vision into this woman.]

She owns the fine house by the rise of the bank,
She hides handsome and richly drest aft the blinds of the window.

Which of the young men does she like the best?
Ah the homeliest of them is beautiful to her.

Where are you off to, lady? for I see you, *[handwritten: Eye of the universe]*
You splash in the water there, yet stay stock still in your room. *[handwritten: fantasy]*

Dancing and laughing along the beach came the twenty-ninth bather, *[handwritten: was very shocking / typical Whitman]*
The rest did not see her, but she saw them and loved them.   10

The beards of the young men glisten'd with wet, it ran from their long hair,
Little streams pass'd all over their bodies.

An unseen hand also pass'd over their bodies,
It descended tremblingly from their temples and ribs.

The young men float on their backs, their white bellies bulge to the sun, they do not ask who seizes
    fast to them,
They do not know who puffs and declines with pendant and bending arch,
They do not think whom they souse with spray.

12

The butcher-boy puts off his killing-clothes, or sharpens his knife at the stall in the market,
I loiter enjoying his repartee and his shuffle and break-down.

Blacksmiths with grimed and hairy chests environ the anvil,
Each has main-sledge, they are all out, there is a great heat in the fire.

From the cinder-strew'd threshold I follow their movements,
The lithe sheer of their waists plays even with their massive arms,
Overhand the hammers swing, overhand so slow, overhand so sure,
They do not hasten, each man hits in his place.

13

The negro holds firmly the reins of his four horses, the block swags underneath on its tied-over chain,
The negro that drives the long dray of the stone-yard, steady and tall he stands pois'd on one leg on the string-piece,
His blue shirt exposes his ample neck and breast and loosens over his hip-band,
His glance is calm and commanding, he tosses the slouch of his hat away from his forehead,
The sun falls on his crispy hair and mustache, falls on the black of his polish'd and perfect limbs.

I behold the picturesque giant and love him, and I do not stop there,
I go with the team also.

In me the caresser of life wherever moving, backward as well as forward sluing,
To niches aside and junior bending, not a person or object missing,
Absorbing all to myself and for this song.   10

Oxen that rattle the yoke and chain or halt in the leafy shade, what is that you express in your eyes?
It seems to me more than all the print I have read in my life.

My tread scares the wood-drake and wood-duck on my distant and day-long ramble,
They rise together, they slowly circle around.

I believe in those wing'd purposes,
And acknowledge red, yellow, white, playing within me,
And consider green and violet and the tufted crown intentional,
And do not call the tortoise unworthy because she is not something else,
And the jay in the woods never studied the gamut, yet trills pretty well to me,
And the look of the bay mare shames silliness out of me.   20

14

The wild gander leads his flock through the cool night,
Ya-honk he says, and sounds it down to me like an invitation,
The pert may suppose it meaningless, but I listening close,
Find its purpose and place up there toward the wintry sky.

The sharp-hoof'd moose of the north, the cat on the house-sill, the chickadee, the prairie-dog,
The litter of the grunting sow as they tug at her teats,
The brood of the turkey-hen and she with her half-spread wings,
I see in them and myself the same old law.

The press of my foot to the earth springs a hundred affections,
They scorn the best I can do to relate them.   10

I am enamour'd of growing out-doors,
Of men that live among cattle or taste of the ocean or woods,
Of the builders and steerers of ships and the wielders of axes and mauls, and the drivers of horses,
I can eat and sleep with them week in and week out.

What is commonest, cheapest, nearest, easiest, is Me,
Me going in for my chances, spending for vast returns,
Adorning myself to bestow myself on the first that will take me,
Not asking the sky to come down to my good will,
Scattering it freely forever.

15

The pure contralto sings in the organ loft,
The carpenter dresses his plank, the tongue of his foreplane whistles its wild ascending lisp,

The married and unmarried children ride home to their Thanksgiving dinner,
The pilot seizes the king-pin, he heaves down with a strong arm,
The mate stands braced in the whale-boat, lance and harpoon are ready,
The duck-shooter walks by silent and cautious stretches,
The deacons are ordain'd with cross'd hands at the altar,
The spinning-girl retreats and advances to the hum of the big wheel,
The farmer stops by the bars as he walks on a First-day loafe and looks at the oats and rye,
The lunatic is carried at last to the asylum a confirm'd case,   10
(He will never sleep any more as he did in the cot in his mother's bedroom;)
The jour printer with gray head and gaunt jaws works at his case,
He turns his quid of tobacco while his eyes blurr with the manuscript;
The malform'd limbs are tied to the surgeon's table,
What is removed drops horribly in a pail;
The quadroon girl is sold at the auction-stand, the drunkard nods by the bar-room stove,
The machinist rolls up his sleeves, the policeman travels his beat, the gate-keeper marks who pass,
The young fellow drives the express-wagon, (I love him, though I do not know him;)
The half-breed straps on his light boots to compete in the race,
The western turkey-shooting draws old and young, some lean on their rifles, some sit on logs,   20
Out from the crowd steps the marksman, takes his position, levels his piece;
The groups of newly-come immigrants cover the wharf or levee,
As the wooly-pates hoe in the sugar-field, the overseer views them from his saddle,
The bugle calls in the ball-room, the gentlemen run for their partners, the dancers bow to each other,
The youth lies awake in the cedar-roof'd garret and harks to the musical rain,
The Wolverine sets traps on the creek that helps fill the Huron,
The squaw wrapt in her yellow-hemm'd cloth is offering moccasins and bead-bags for sale,
The connoisseur peers along the exhibition-gallery with half-shut eyes bent sideways,
As the deck-hands make fast the steamboat the plank is thrown for the shore-going passengers,
The young sister holds out the skein while the elder sister winds it off in a ball, and stops now and then
    for knots,   30
The one-year wife is recovering and happy having a week ago borne her first child,
The clean-hair'd Yankee girl works with her sewing-machine or in the factory or mill,
The paving-man leans on his two-handed rammer, the reporter's lead flies swiftly over the note-book, the
    sign-painter is lettering with blue and gold.
The canal boy trots on the tow-path, the book-keeper counts at his desk, the shoemaker waxes his thread,
The conductor beats time for the band and all the performers follow him,
The child is baptized, the convert is making his first professions,
The regatta is spread on the bay, the race is begun, (how the white sails sparkle!)
The drover watching his drove sings out to them that would stray,
The pedler sweats with his pack on his back, (the purchaser higgling about the odd cent;)
The bride unrumples her white dress, the minute-hand of the clock moves slowly,   40
The opium-eater reclines with rigid head and just-open'd lips,
The prostitute draggles her shawl, her bonnet bobs on her tipsy and pimpled neck,
The crowd laugh at her blackguard oaths, the men jeer and wink to each other,
(Miserable! I do not laugh at your oaths nor jeer you;)
The President holding a cabinet council is surrounded by the great Secretaries,
On the piazza walk three matrons stately and friendly with twined arms,
The crew of the fish-smack pack repeated layers of halibut in the hold,
The Missourian crosses the plains toting his wares and his cattle,
As the fare-collector goes through the train he gives notice by the jingling of loose change,
The floor-men are laying the floor, the tinners are tinning the roof, the masons are calling for mortar,   50
In single file each shouldering his hod pass onward the laborers;

Seasons pursuing each other the indescribable crowd is gather'd, it is the fourth of Seventh-month, (what salutes of cannon and small arms!)
Seasons pursuing each other the plougher ploughs, the mower mows, and the winter-grain falls in the ground;
Off on the lakes the pike-fisher watches and waits by the hole in the frozen surface,
The stumps stand thick round the clearing, the squatter strikes deep with his axe,
Flatboatmen make fast towards dusk near the cotton-wood or pecan-trees,
Coon-seekers go through the regions of the Red river or through those drain'd by the Tennessee, or through those of the Arkansas,
Torches shine in the dark that hangs on the Chattahooche or Altamahaw,
Patriarchs sit at supper with sons and grandsons and great-grandsons around them,
In walls of adobie, in canvas tents, rest hunters and trappers after their day's sport,   60
The city sleeps and the country sleeps,
The living sleep for their time, the dead sleep for their time,
The old husband sleeps by his wife and the young husband sleeps by his wife;
And these tend inward to me, and I tend outward to them,
And such as it is to be of these more or less I am,
And of these one and all I weave the song of myself.

16 *reconciling opposites*

I am of old and young, of the foolish as much as the wise,
Regardless of others, ever regardful of others,
Maternal as well as paternal, a child as well as a man,
Stuff'd with the stuff that is coarse and stuff'd with the stuff that is fine,
One of the Nation of many nations, the smallest the same and the largest the same,
A Southerner soon as a Northerner, a planter nonchalant and hospitable down by the Oconee I live,
A Yankee bound my own way ready for trade, my joints the limberest joints on earth and the sternest joints on earth,
A Kentuckian walking the vale of the Elkhorn in my deerskin leggings, a Louisianian or Georgian,
A boatman over lakes or bays or along coasts, a Hoosier, Badger, Buckeye;
At home on Kanadian snow-shoes or up in the bush, or with fishermen off Newfoundland,   10
At home in the fleet of ice-boats, sailing with the rest and tacking,
At home on the hills of Vermont or in the woods of Maine, or the Texan ranch,
Comrade of Californians, comrade of free North-Westerners, (loving their big proportions,)
Comrade of raftsmen and coalmen, comrade of all who shake hands and welcome to drink and meat,
A learner with the simplest, a teacher of the thoughtfullest,
A novice beginning yet experient of myriads of seasons,
Of every hue and caste am I, of every rank and religion,
A farmer, mechanic, artist, gentleman, sailor, quaker,
Prisoner, fancy-man, rowdy, lawyer, physician, priest.
I resist any thing better than my own diversity,   20
Breathe the air but leave plenty after me,
And am not stuck up, and am in my place.
(The moth and the fish-eggs are in their place,
The bright suns I see and the dark suns I cannot see are in their place,
The palpable is in its place and the impalpable in its place.)

17

These are really the thoughts of all men in all ages and lands, they are not original with me,
If they are not yours as much as mine they are nothing, or next to nothing.

If they are not the riddle and the untying of the riddle they are nothing,
If they are not just as close as they are distant they are nothing.

This is the grass that grows wherever the land is and the water is,
This the common air that bathes the globe.

18

With music strong I come, with my cornets and my drums,
I play not marches for accepted victors only, I play marches for conquer'd and slain persons.

Have you heard that it was good to gain the day?
I also say it is good to fall, battles are lost in the same spirit in which they are won.

I beat and pound for the dead,
I blow through my embouchures my loudest and gayest for them.

Vivas to those who have fail'd!
And to those whose war-vessels sank in the sea!
And to those themselves who sank in the sea!
And to all generals that lost engagements, and all overcome heroes!   10
And the numberless unknown heroes equal to the greatest heroes known!

19

This is the meal equally set, this the meat for natural hunger,
It is for the wicked just the same as the righteous, I make appointments with all,
I will not have a single person slighted or left away,
The kept-woman, sponger, thief, are hereby invited,
The heavy-lipp'd slave is invited, the venerealee is invited;
There shall be no difference between them and the rest.

This is the press of a bashful hand, this the float and odor of hair,
This the touch of my lips to yours, this the murmur of yearning,
This the far-off depth and height reflecting my own face,
This the thoughtful merge of myself, and the outlet again.   10

Do you guess I have some intricate purpose?
Well I have, for the Fourth-month showers have, and the mica on the side of a rock has.

Do you take it I would astonish?
Does the daylight astonish? does the early redstart twittering through the woods?
Do I astonish more than they?

This hour I tell things in confidence,
I might not tell everybody, but I will tell you.

20

Who goes there? hankering, gross, mystical, nude;
How is it I extract strength from the beef I eat?

What is a man anyhow? what am I? what are you?

All I mark as my own you shall offset it with your own,
Else it were time lost listening to me.

I do not snivel that snivel the world over,
The months are vacuums and the ground but wallow and filth.

Whimpering and truckling fold with powders for invalids, conformity goes to the fourth-remov'd,
I wear my hat as I please indoors or out.

Why should I pray? why should I venerate and be ceremonious?   10

Having pried through the strata, analyzed to a hair, counsel'd with doctors and calculated close,
I find no sweeter fat than sticks to my own bones.

In all people I see myself, none more and not one a barley-corn less,
And the good or bad I say of myself I say of them.

I know I am solid and sound,
To me the converging objects of the universe perpetually flow,
All are written to me, and I must get what the writing means.

I know I am deathless,
I know this orbit of mine cannot be swept by a carpenter's compass,
I know I shall not pass like a child's carlacue cut with a burnt stick at night.   20

I know I am august,
I do not trouble my spirit to vindicate itself or be understood,
I see that the elementary laws never apologize,
(I reckon I behave no prouder than the level I plant my house by, after all.)

I exist as I am, that is enough,
If no other in the world be aware I sit content,
And if each and all be aware I sit content.

One world is aware and by far the largest to me, and that is myself,
And whether I come to my own to-day or in ten thousand or ten million years,
I can cheerfully take it now, or with equal cheerfulness I can wait.   30

My foothold is tenon'd and mortis'd in granite,
I laugh at what you call dissolution,
And I know the amplitude of time.

21

I am the poet of the Body and I am the poet of the Soul, *Physical vs. Spiritual – shocking to celebrate the body*
The pleasures of heaven are with me and the pains of hell are with me, *no hell. Optimist as something good*
The first I graft and increase upon myself, the latter I translate into a new tongue. *doesn't* *rather than be something to be covered.*
transplanting of skin, bone
I am the poet of the woman the same as the man, *shocking. women believe in*
And I say it is as great to be a woman as to be a man, *were inferior it a*
And I say there is nothing greater than the mother of men.

I chant the chant of dilation or pride, *speech* *optimism – bigger and better, country is getting bigger*
We have had ducking and deprecating about enough, *put down*
I show that size is only development.

Have you outstript the rest? are you the President? *as high as you can get.*   10
It is a trifle, they will more than arrive there every one, and still pass on. *Death will prove that everyone is the same,*
Because of the oneness of being we are all the same.
I am he that walks with the tender and growing night, *and since death is life*
I call to the earth and sea half-held by the night. *we are all equal in life as well.*
love of the beauty of the earth from spirits view
Press close bare-bosom'd night—press close magnetic nourishing night!
Night of south winds—night of the large few stars!
Still nodding night—mad naked summer night.

It is time we stood up and stopped thinking we were second rate to England and Europe.

NIETZSCHE {
extremely romantic – wildness
Wild Romantic group – DIONYSIAN
Prefers quietness and serenity – APOLLONIAN
}

Smile O voluptuous cool-breath'd earth!
Earth of the slumbering and liquid trees! *Parallelism*
Earth of departed sunset—earth of the mountains misty-topt!
Earth of the vitreous pour of the full moon just tinged with blue! 20
Earth of shine and dark mottling the tide of the river! *perfectly clear*
Earth of the limpid gray of clouds brighter and clearer for my sake!
Far-swooping elbow'd earth—rich apple-blossom'd earth!
Smile, for your lover comes. *Lover of Earth (role-playing)*
Very extravagant — overly generous
Prodigal, you have given me love—therefore I to you give love! *Every force of nature has an opposite*
O unspeakable passionate love. *and equal force*
Very romantic *Give love for love.*

22

You sea! I resign myself to you also—I guess what you mean,
I behold from the beach your crooked inviting fingers,
I believe you refuse to go back without feeling of me,
We must have a turn together, I undress, hurry me out of sight of the land,
Cushion me soft, rock me in billowy drowse,
Dash me with amorous wet, I can repay you.

Sea of stretch'd ground-swells,
Sea breathing broad and convulsive breaths,
Sea of the brine of life and of unshovel'd yet always-ready graves,
Howler and scooper of storms, capricious and dainty sea, 10
I am integral with you, I too am of one phase and of all phases.

Partaker of influx and efflux, I, extoller of hate and conciliation,
Extoller of amies and those that sleep in each others' arms,

I am he attesting sympathy,
(Shall I make my list of things in the house and skip the house that supports them?)

I am not the poet of goodness only, I do not decline to be the poet of wickedness also.

What blurt is this about virtue and about vice?
Evil propels me and reform of evil propels me, I stand indifferent,
My gait is no fault-finder's or rejecter's gait,
I moisten the roots of all that has grown. 20

Did you fear some scrofula out of the unflagging pregnancy?
Did you guess the celestial laws are yet to be work'd over and rectified?

I find one side a balance and the antipodal side a balance,
Soft doctrine as steady help as stable doctrine,
Thoughts and deeds of the present our rouse and early start.

This minute that comes to me over the past decillions,
There is no better than it and now.

What behaved well in the past or behaves well to-day is not such a wonder,
The wonder is always and always how there can be a mean man or an infidel.

23

Endless unfolding of words of ages!
And mine a word of the modern, the word En-Masse.

A word of the faith that never balks,
Here or henceforward it is all the same to me, I accept Time absolutely.

It alone is without flaw, it alone rounds and completes all,
That mystic baffling wonder alone completes all.

I accept Reality and dare not question it,
Materialism first and last imbuing.

Hurrah for positive science! long live exact demonstration!
Fetch stonecrop mixt with cedar and branches of lilac,   10
This is the lexicographer, this the chemist, this made of grammar of the old cartouches,
These mariners put the ship through dangerous unknown seas,
This is the geologist, this works with the scalpel, and this is a mathematician.

Gentlemen, to you the first honors always!
Your facts are useful, and yet they are not my dwelling,
I but enter by them to an area of my dwelling.

Less the reminders of properties told my words,
And more the reminders they of life untold, and of freedom and extrication,
And make short account of neuters and geldings, and favor men and women fully equipt,
And beat the gong of revolt, and stop with fugitives and them that plot and conspire.   20

24

Walt Whitman, a kosmos, of Manhattan the son,
Turbulent, fleshy, sensual, eating, drinking and breeding,
No sentimentalist, no stander above men and women or apart from them,
No more modest than immodest.

Unscrew the locks from the doors!
Unscrew the doors themselves from their jambs!

Whoever degrades another degrades me,
And whatever is done or said returns at last to me.

Through me the afflatus surging and surging, through me the current and index.
I speak the pass-word primeval, I give the sign of democracy,   10
By God! I will accept nothing which all cannot have their counterpart of on the same terms.

Through me many long dumb voices,
Voices of the interminable generations of prisoners and slaves,
Voices of the diseas'd and despairing and of thieves and dwarfs,
Voices of cycles of preparation and accretion,
And of the threads that connect the stars, and of wombs and of the father-stuff,
And of the rights of them the others are down upon,
Of the deform'd, trivial, flat, foolish, despised,
Fog in the air, beetles rolling balls of dung.

Through me forbidden voices,
Voices of sexes and lusts, voices veil'd and I remove the veil,   20
Voices indecent by me clarified and transfigur'd.

I do not press my fingers across my mouth,
I keep as delicate around the bowels as around the head and heart,
Copulation is no more rank to me than death is.

I believe in the flesh and the appetites, *Goes with line I*

Seeing, hearing, feeling, are miracles, and each part and tag of me is a miracle. *physiological functions*

Divine am I inside and out, and I make holy whatever I touch or am touch'd from, *blending with*

The scent of these arm-pits aroma finer than prayer, *smell is natural* *universe*

This head more than churches, bibles, and all the creeds. *no attempt to hide* 30

He is against established religion

If I worship one thing more than another it shall be the spread of my own body, or any part of it,

Translucent mould of me it shall be you!

Shaded ledges and rests it shall be you!

Firm masculine colter it shall be you!

Whatever goes to the tilth of me it shall be you! *father*

You my rich blood! your milky stream pale strippings of my life!

Breast that presses against other breasts it shall be you!

My brain it shall be your occult convolutions! *curves*

Root of wash'd sweet-flag! timorous pond-snipe! nest of guarded duplicate eggs! it shall be you! *combining sex with nature*

Mix'd tussled hay of head, beard, brawn, it shall be you!

Trickling sap of maple, fibre of manly wheat, it shall be you! 40

Sun so generous it shall be you! *Sun is a male symbol*

Vapors lighting and shading my face it shall be you!

You sweaty brooks and dews it shall be you!

Winds whose soft-tickling genitals rub against me it shall be you! *running naked through the air*

Broad muscular fields, branches of live oak, loving lounger in my winding paths, it shall be you!

Hands I have taken, face I have kiss'd, mortal I have ever touch'd, it shall be you. *Gives bodily imagery to nature*

I dote on myself, there is that lot of me and all so luscious,

Each moment and whatever happens thrills me with joy,

I cannot tell how my ankles bend, nor whence the cause of my faintest wish, *miracle of life* 50

Nor the cause of the friendship I emit, nor the cause of the friendship I take again.

not just body, it is relationships

That I walk up my stoop, I pause to consider if it really be,

A morning-glory at my window satisfies me more than the metaphysics of books. *philosophy (god, soul, source of life) as well.*

To behold the day-break! *flower*

The little light fades the immense and diaphanous shadows, *translucent*

The air tastes good to my palate.

Hefts of the moving world at innocent gambols silently rising freshly exuding, *romps* *oozing* *Talking about*

Scooting obliquely high and low. *clouds*

Something I cannot see puts upward libidinous prongs, *at an angle (slant)* *having to do with sex* *raining*

Seas of bright juice suffuse heaven. 60

The earth by the sky staid with, the daily close of their junction, *sunrise*

The heav'd challenge from the east that moment over my head,

The mocking taunt, See then whether you shall be master! *man gets big head as his technology grows*

man should know his place
man is child of universe, not controller

25

Dazzling and tremendous how quick the sun-rise would kill me,

If I could not now and always send sun-rise out of me.

We also ascend dazzling and tremendous as the sun,

We found our own O my soul in the calm and cool of the daybreak.

My voice goes after what my eyes cannot reach,

With the twirl of my tongue I encompass worlds and volumes of worlds.

Speech is the twin of my vision, it is unequal to measure itself,
It provokes me forever, it says sarcastically,
Walt you contain enough, why don't you let it out then?

Come now I will not be tantalized, you conceive too much of articulation,   10
Do you not know O speech how the buds beneath you are folded?
Waiting in gloom, protected by frost,
The dirt receding before my prophetical screams,
I underlying causes to balance them at last,
My knowledge my live parts, it keeping tally with the meaning of all things,
Happiness, (which whoever hears me let him or her set out in search of this day.)

My final merit I refuse you, I refuse putting from me what I really am,
Encompass worlds, but never try to encompass me,
I crowd your sleekest and best by simply looking toward you.

Writing and talk do not prove me,   20
I carry the plenum of proof and every thing else in my face,
With the hush of my lips I wholly confound the skeptic.

26

Now I will do nothing but listen,
To accrue what I hear into this song, to let sounds contribute toward it.
I hear bravuras of birds, bustle of growing wheat, gossip of flames, clack of sticks cooking my meals,

I hear the sound I love, the sound of the human voice,
I hear all sounds running together, combined, fused or following,
Sounds of the city and sounds out of the city, sounds of the day and night,
Talkative young ones to those that like them, the loud laugh of work-people at their meals,
The angry base of disjointed friendship, the faint tones of the sick,
The judge with hands tight to the desk, his pallid lips pronouncing a death-sentence,
The heave'e'yo of stevedores unlading ships by the wharves, the refrain of the anchor-lifters,   10
The ring of alarm-bells, the cry of fire, the whirr of swift-streaking engines and hose-carts with premonitory tinkles and color'd lights,
The steam-whistle, the solid roll of the train of approaching cars,
The slow march play'd at the head of the association marching two and two,
(They go to guard some corpse, the flag-tops are draped with black muslin.)

I hear the violoncello, ('tis the young man's heart's complaint,)
I hear the key'd cornet, it glides quickly in through my ears,
It shakes mad-sweet pangs through my belly and breast.

I hear the chorus, it is a grand opera,
Ah this indeed is music—this suits me.

A tenor large and fresh as the creation fills me,   20
The orbic flex of his mouth is pouring and filling me full.

I hear the train'd soprano (what work with hers is this?)
The orchestra whirls me wider than Uranus flies,
It wrenches such ardors from me I did not know I possess'd them,
It sails me, I dab with bare feet, they are lick'd by the indolent waves,
I am cut by bitter and angry hail, I lose my breath,
Steep'd amid honey'd morphine, my windpipe throttled in fakes of death,
At length let up again to feel the puzzle of puzzles,
And that we call Being.

27

To be in any form, what is that?
(Round and round we go, all of us, and ever come back thither,)
If nothing lay more develop'd the quahaug in its callous shell were enough.

Mine is no callous shell,
I have instant conductors all over me whether I pass or stop,
They seize every object and lead it harmlessly through me.

I merely stir, press, feel with my fingers, and am happy,
To touch my person to some one else's is about as much as I can stand.

28

Is this then a touch? quivering me to a new identity,
Flames and ether making a rush for my veins,
Treacherous tip of me reaching and crowding to help them,
My flesh and blood playing out lightning to strike what is hardly different from myself,
On all sides prurient provokers stiffening my limbs,
Straining the udder of my heart for its withheld drip,
Behaving licentious toward me, taking no denial,
Depriving me of my best as for a purpose,
Unbuttoning my clothes, holding me by the bare waist,
Deluding my confusion with the calm of the sunlight and pasture-fields,   10
Immodestly sliding the fellow-senses away,
They bribed to swap off with touch and go and graze at the edges of me,
No consideration, no regard for my draining strength or my anger,
Fetching the rest of the herd around to enjoy them a while,
Then all uniting to stand on a headland and worry me.

The sentries desert every other part of me,
They have left me helpless to a red marauder,
They all come to the headland to witness and assist against me.

I am given up by traitors,
I talk wildly, I have lost my wits, I and nobody else am the greatest traitor,   20
I went myself first to the headland, my own hands carried me there.

You villain touch! what are you doing? my breath is tight in its throat,
Unclench your floodgates, you are too much for me.

29

Blind loving wrestling touch, sheath'd hooded sharp-tooth'd touch!
Did it make you ache so, leaving me?

Parting track'd by arriving, perpetual payment of perpetual loan,
Rich showering rain, and recompense richer afterward.

Sprouts take and accumulate, stand by the curb prolific and vital,
Landscapes projected masculine, full-sized and golden.

30

All truths wait in all things,
They neither hasten their own delivery nor resist it,
They do not need the obstetric forceps of the surgeon,
The insignificant is as big to me as any,
(What is less or more than a touch?)

Logic and sermons never convince,
The damp of the night drives deeper into my soul.

(Only what proves itself to every man and woman is so,
Only what nobody denies is so.)

A minute and a drop of me settle my brain,   10
I believe the soggy clods shall become lovers and lamps,
And a compend of compends is the meat of a man or woman,
And a summit and flower there is the feeling they have for each other,
And they are to branch boundlessly out of that lesson until it becomes omnific,
And until one and all shall delight us, and we them.

31

I believe a leaf of grass is no less than the journey-work of the stars,
And the pismire is equally perfect, and a grain of sand, and the egg of the wren,
And the tree-toad is a chef-d'œuvre for the highest,
And the running blackberry would adorn the parlors of heaven,
And the narrowest hinge in my hand puts to scorn all machinery,
And the cow crunching with depress'd head surpasses any statue,
And a mouse is miracle enough to stagger sextillions of infidels.

I find I incorporate gneiss, coal, long-threaded moss, fruits, grains, esculent roots,
And am stucco'd with quadrupeds and birds all over,
And have distanced what is behind me for good reasons,   10
But call any thing back again when I desire it.

In vain the speeding or shyness,
In vain the plutonic rocks send their old heat against my approach,
In vain the mastodon retreats beneath its own powder'd bones,
In vain objects stand leagues off and assume manifold shapes,
In vain the ocean settling in hollows and the great monsters lying low,
In vain the buzzard houses herself with the sky,
In vain the snake slides through the creepers and logs,
In vain the elk takes to the inner passes of the woods,
In vain the razor-bill'd auk sails far north to Labrador,   20
I follow quickly, I ascend to the nest in the fissure of the cliff.

32

Not very optimistic

I think I could turn and live with animals, they're so placid and self-contain'd,
I stand and look at them long and long. *He thinks animals are better than people*

They do not sweat and whine about their condition,
They do not lie awake in the dark and weep for their sins,
They do not make me sick discussing their duty to God, *fanatics, hypocrites   Doesn't make them any better as people.*
Not one is dissatisfied, not one is demented with the mania of owning things,   *façade of*
Not one kneels to another, nor to his kind that lived thousands of years ago,
Not one is respectable or unhappy over the whole earth.
Undress, unscrew doors - attack on respectability   respect.
So they show their relations to me and I accept them,
They bring me tokens of myself, they evince them plainly in their possession. *theory of evolution*   10
show

I wonder where they get those tokens,
Did I pass that way huge times ago and negligently drop them? *Before scientists knew about stages of evolution in womb.*

Myself moving forward then and now and forever,

Onward and upward.
Evolution is very optimistic

attack on materialism   why worship past?

Gathering and showing more always and with velocity,   *Gets more optimistic*
Infinite and omnigenous, and the like of these among them,
Not too exclusive toward the reachers of my remembrancers,
Picking out here one that I love, and now go with him on brotherly terms.

A gigantic beauty of a stallion, fresh and responsive to my caresses,
Head high in the forehead, wide between the ears,
Limbs glossy and supple, tail dusting the ground,   20
Eyes full of sparkling wickedness, ears finely cut, flexibly moving.

His nostrils dilate as my heels embrace him.
His well-built limbs tremble with pleasure as we race around and return,

I but use you a minute, then I resign you, stallion,
Why do I need your paces when I myself out-gallop them?   *I passed animals a long time ago.*
Even as I stand or sit passing faster than you.

Hypocrisy of religious right.

33

Space and Time! now I see it is true, what I guess'd at,
What I guess'd when I loaf'd on the grass,
What I guess'd while I lay alone in my bed,
And again as I walk'd the beach under the paling stars of the morning.

My ties and ballasts leave me, my elbows rest in sea-gaps,
I skirt sierras, my palms cover continents,
I am afoot with my vision.

By the city's quadrangular houses—in log huts, camping with lumbermen,
Along the ruts of the turnpike, along the dry gulch and rivulet bed,
Weeding my onion-patch or hoeing rows of carrots and parsnips, crossing savannas, trailing in
    forests,   10
Prospecting, gold-digging, girdling the trees of a new purchase,
Scorch'd ankle-deep by the hot sand, hauling my boat down the shallow river,
Where the panther walks to and fro on a limb overhead, where the buck turns furiously at the hunter,
Where the rattlesnake suns his flabby length on a rock, where the otter is feeding on fish,
Where the alligator in his tough pimples sleeps by the bayou,
Where the black bear is searching for roots or honey, where the beaver pats the mud with his paddle-
    shaped tail;
Over the growing sugar, over the yellow-flower'd cotton plant, over the rice in its low moist field,
Over the sharp-peak'd farm house, with its scallop'd scum and slender shoots from the gutters,
Over the western persimmon, over the long-leav'd corn, over the delicate blue-flower flax,
Over the white and brown buckwheat, a hummer and buzzer there with the rest,   20
Over the dusky green of the rye as it ripples and shades in the breeze;
Scaling mountains, pulling myself cautiously up, holding on by low scragged limbs,
Walking the path worn in the grass and beat through the leaves of the brush,
Where the quail is whistling betwixt the woods and the wheat-lot,
Where the bat flies in the Seventh-month eve, where the great gold-bug drops through the dark,
Where the brook puts out of the roots of the old tree and flows to the meadow,
Where cattle stand and shake away flies with the tremulous shuddering of their hides,
Where the cheese-cloth hangs in the kitchen, where andirons straddle the hearth-slab, where cobwebs
    fall in festoons from the rafters;
Where trip-hammers crash, where the press is whirling its cylinders,
Where the human heart beats with terrible throes under its ribs,   30
Where the pear-shaped balloon is floating aloft, (floating in it myself and looking composedly down,)

Where the life-car is drawn on the slip-noose, where the heat hatches pale-green eggs in the dented
  sand,
Where the she-whale swims with her calf and never forsakes it,
Where the steam-ship trails hind-ways its long pennant of smoke,
Where the fin of the shark cuts like a black chip out of the water,
Where the half-burn'd brig is riding on unknown currents,
Where shells grow to her slimy deck, where the dead are corrupting below;
Where the dense-starr'd flag is borne at the head of the regiments,
Approaching Manhattan up by the long-stretching island,
Under Niagara, the cataract falling like a veil over my countenance,   40
Upon a door-step, upon the horse-block of hard wood outside,
Upon the race-course, or enjoying picnics or jigs or a good game of base-ball,
At he-festivals, with blackguard jibes, ironical license, bull-dances, drinking, laughter,
At the cider-mill tasting the sweets of the brown mash, sucking the juice through a straw,
At apple-peelings wanting kisses for all the red fruit I find,
At musters, beach-parties, friendly bees, huskings, house-raisings;
Where the mocking-bird sounds his delicious gurgles, cackles, screams, weeps,
Where the hay-rick stands in the barn-yard, where the dry-stalks are scatter'd, where the brood-cow
  waits in the hovel,
Where the bull advances to do his masculine work, where the stud to the mare, where the cock is
  treading the hen,
Where the heifers browse, where geese nip their food with short jerks,   50
Where sun-down shadows lengthen over the limitless and lonesome prairie,
Where herds of buffalo make a crawling spread of the square miles far and near,
Where the humming-bird shimmers, where the neck of the long-lived swan is curving and winding,
Where the laughing-gull scoots by the shore, where she laughs her near-human laugh,
Where bee-hives range on a gray bench in the garden half hid by the high weeds,
Where band-neck'd partridges roost in a ring on the ground with their heads out,
Where burial coaches enter the arch'd gates of a cemetery,
Where winter wolves bark amid wastes of snow and icicled trees,
Where the yellow-crown'd heron comes to the edge of the marsh at night and feeds upon small crabs,
Where the splash of swimmers and divers cools the warm noon,   60
Where the katy-did works her chromatic reed on the walnut-tree over the well,
Through patches of citrons and cucumbers with silver-wired leaves,
Through the salt-lick or orange glade, or under conical firs,
Through the gymnasium, through the curtain'd saloon, through the office or public hall;
Pleas'd with the native and pleas'd with the foreign, pleas'd with the new and old,
Pleas'd with the homely woman as well as the handsome,
Pleas'd with the quakeress as she puts off her bonnet and talks melodiously,
Pleas'd with the tune of the choir of the whitewash'd church,
Pleas'd with the earnest words of the sweating Methodist preacher, impress'd seriously at the camp-
  meeting;
Looking in at the shop-windows of Broadway the whole forenoon, flatting the flesh of my nose on the
  thick plate glass,   70
Wandering the same afternoon with my face turn'd up to the clouds, or down a lane or along the beach,
My right and left arms round the sides of two friends, and I in the middle;
Coming home with the silent and dark-cheek'd bush-boy, (behind me he rides at the drape of the day,)
Far from the settlements studying the print of animals' feet, or the moccasin print,
By the cot in the hospital reaching lemonade to a feverish patient,
Nigh the coffin'd corpse when all is still, examining with a candle;
Voyaging to every port to dicker and adventure,
Hurrying with the modern crowd as eager and fickle as any,

Hot toward one I hate, ready in my madness to knife him,
Solitary at midnight in my back yard, my thoughts gone from me a long while,   80
Walking the old hills of Judæa with the beautiful gentle God by my side,
Speeding through space, speeding through heaven and the stars,
Speeding amid the seven satellites and the broad ring, and the diameter of eighty thousand miles,
Speeding with tail'd meteors, throwing fire-balls like the rest,
Carrying the crescent child that carries its own full mother in its belly,
Storming, enjoying, planning, loving, cautioning,
Backing and filling, appearing and disappearing,
I tread day and night such roads.

I visit the orchards of spheres and look at the product,
And look at quintillions ripen'd and look at quintillions green.   90

I fly those flights of a fluid and swallowing soul,
My course runs below the soundings of plummets.

I help myself to material and immaterial,
No guard can shut me off, no law prevent me.

I anchor my ship for a little while only,
My messengers continually cruise away or bring their returns to me.

I go hunting polar furs and the seal, leaping chasms with a pike-pointed staff, clinging to topples of
    brittle and blue.

I ascend to the foretruck,
I take my place late at night in the crow's-nest,
We sail the arctic sea, it is plenty light enough,   100
Through the clear atmosphere I stretch around on the wonderful beauty,
The enormous masses of ice pass me and I pass them, the scenery is plain in all directions,
The white-topt mountains show in the distance, I fling out my fancies toward them,
We are approaching some great battle-field in which we are soon to be engaged,
We pass the colossal outposts of the encampment, we pass with still feet and caution,
Or we are entering by the suburbs some vast and ruin'd city,
The blocks and fallen architecture more than all the living cities of the globe.

I am a free companion, I bivouac by invading watchfires,
I turn the bridegroom out of bed and stay with the bride myself,
I tighten her all night to my thighs and lips.   110

My voice is the wife's voice, the screech by the rail of the stairs,
They fetch my man's body up dripping and drown'd.

I understand the large hearts of heroes,
The courage of present times and all times,
How the skipper saw the crowded and rudderless wreck of the steam-ship, and Death chasing it up and
    down the storm,
How he knuckled tight and gave not back an inch, and was faithful of days and faithful of nights,
And chalk'd in large letters on a board, *Be of good cheer, we will not desert you;*
How he follow'd with them and tack'd with them three days and would not give it up,
How he saved the drifting company at last,
How the lank loose-gown'd women look'd when boated from the side of their prepared graves,   120
How the silent old-faced infants and the lifted sick, and the sharp-lipp'd unshaved men;
All this I swallow, it tastes good, I like it well, it becomes mine,
I am the man, I suffer'd, I was there.

The disdain and calmness of martyrs,
The mother of old, condemn'd for a witch, burnt with dry wood, her children gazing on,
The hounded slave that flags in the race, leans by the fence, blowing cover'd with sweat,
The twinges that sting like needles his legs and neck, the murderous buckshot and the bullets,
All these I feel or am.

I am the hounded slave, I wince at the bite of the dogs,
Hell and despair are upon me, crack and again crack the marksmen,   130
I clutch the rails of the fence, my gore dribs, thinn'd with the ooze of my skin,
I fall on the weeds and stones,
The riders spur their unwilling horses, haul close,
Taunt my dizzy ears and beat me violently over the head with whip-stocks.

Agonies are one of my changes of garments.
I do not ask the wounded person how he feels, I myself become the wounded person,
My hurts turn livid upon me as I lean on a cane and observe.

I am the mash'd fireman with breast-bone broken,
Tumbling walls buried me in their debris,
Heat and smoke I inspired, I heard the yelling shouts of my comrades,   140
I heard the distant click of their picks and shovels,
They have clear'd the beams away, they tenderly lift me forth.

I lie in the night air in my red shirt, the pervading hush is for my sake,
Painless after all I lie exhausted but not so unhappy,
White and beautiful are the faces around me, the heads are bared of their fire-caps,
The kneeling crowd fades with the light of the torches.

Distant and dead resuscitate,
They show me as the dial or move as the hands of me, I am the clock myself.

I am an old artillerist, I tell of my fort's bombardment,
I am there again.   150

Again the long roll of the drummers,
Again the attacking cannon, mortars,
Again to my listening ears the cannon responsive.

I take part, I see and hear the whole,
The cries, curses, roar, the plaudits for well-aim'd shots,
The ambulanza slowly passing trailing its red drip,
Workmen searching after damages, making indispensable repairs,
The fall of grenades through the rent roof, the fan-shaped explosion,
The whizz of limbs, heads, stone, wood, iron, high in the air.

Again gurgles the mouth of my dying general, he furiously waves with his hand,   160
He gasps through the clot *Mind not me—mind—the entrenchments.*

34

Now I tell what I knew in Texas in my early youth,
(I tell not the fall of Alamo,
Not one escaped to tell the fall of Alamo,
The hundred and fifty are dumb yet at Alamo,)
'Tis the tale of the murder in cold blood of four hundred and twelve young men.

Retreating they had form'd in a hollow square with their baggage for breastworks,
Nine hundred lives out of the surrounding enemy's, nine times their number, was the price they took in advance,
Their colonel was wounded and their ammunition gone,
They treated for an honorable capitulation, receiv'd writing and seal, gave up their arms and march'd back prisoners of war.

They were the glory of the race of rangers,   10
Matchless with horse, rifle, song, supper, courtship,
Large, turbulent, generous, handsome, proud, and affectionate,
Bearded, sunburnt, drest in the free costume of hunters,
Not a single one over thirty years of age.

The second First-day morning they were brought out in squads and massacred, it was beautiful early summer,
The work commenced about five o'clock and was over by eight.

None obey'd the command to kneel,
Some made a mad and helpless rush, some stood stark and straight,
A few fell at once, shot in the temple or heart, the living and dead lay together,
The maim'd and mangled dug in the dirt, the new-comers saw them there,   20
Some half-kill'd attempted to crawl away,
These were despatch'd with bayonets or batter'd with the blunts of muskets.
A youth not seventeen years old seiz'd his assassin till two more came to release him,
The three were all torn and cover'd with the boy's blood.

At eleven o'clock began the burning of the bodies;
This is the tale of the murder of the four hundred and twelve young men.

35

Would you hear of an old-time sea-fight?
Would you learn who won by the light of the moon and stars?
List to the yarn, as my grandmother's father the sailor told it to me.

Our foe was no skulk in his ship I tell you, (said he,)
His was the surly English pluck, and there is no tougher or truer, and never was, and never will be;
Along the lower'd eve he came horribly raking us.

We closed with him, the yards entangled, the cannon touch'd,
My captain lash'd fast with his own hands.

We had receiv'd some eighteen pound shots under the water,
On our lower-gun-deck two large pieces had burst at the first fire, killing all around and blowing up over-head.   10

Fighting at sun-down, fighting at dark,
Ten o'clock at night, the full moon well up, our leaks on the gain, and five feet of water reported,
The master-at-arms loosing the prisoners confined in the after-hold to give them a chance for them-selves.

The transmit to and from the magazine is now stopt by the sentinels,
They see so many strange faces they do not know whom to trust.

Our frigate takes fire,
The other asks if we demand quarter?
If our colors are struck and the fighting done?

Now I laugh content, for I hear the voice of my little captain,
We have not struck, he composedly cries, *we have just begun our part of the fighting.*   20

Only three guns are in use,
One is directed by the captain himself against the enemy's main-mast,
Two well serv'd with grape and canister silence his musketry and clear his decks.

The tops alone second the fire of this little battery, especially the main-top,
They hold out bravely during the whole of the action.

Not a moment's cease,
The leaks gain fast on the pumps, the fire eats toward the powder-magazine.

One of the pumps has been shot away, it is generally thought we are sinking.

Serene stands the little captain,
He is not hurried, his voice is neither high nor low,   30
His eyes give more light to us than our battle-lanterns.

Toward twelve there in the beams of the moon they surrender to us.

36

Stretch'd and still lies the midnight,
Two great hulls motionless on the breast of the darkness,
Our vessel riddled and slowly sinking, preparations to pass to the one we have conquer'd,
The captain on the quarter-deck coldly giving his orders through a countenance white as a sheet,
Near by the corpse of the child that serv'd in the cabin,
The dead face of an old salt with long white hair and carefully curl'd whiskers,
The flames spite of all that can be done flickering aloft and below,
The husky voices of the two or three officers yet fit for duty,
Formless stacks of bodies and bodies by themselves, dabs of flesh upon the masts and spars,
Cut of cordage, dangle of rigging, slight shock of the soothe of waves,   10
Black and impassive guns, litter of powder-parcels, strong scent,
A few large stars overhead, silent and mournful shining,
Delicate sniffs of sea-breeze, smells of sedgy grass and fields by the shore, death-messages given in charge to survivors,
The hiss of the surgeon's knife, the gnawing teeth of his saw,
Wheeze, cluck, swash of falling blood, short wild scream, and long, dull, tapering groan,
These so, these irretrievable.

37

You laggards there on guard! look to your arms!
In at the conquer'd doors they crowd! I am possess'd!
Embody all presences outlaw'd or suffering,
See myself in prison shaped like another man,
And feel the dull unintermitted pain.

For me the keepers of convicts shoulder their carbines and keep watch,
It is I let out in the morning and barr'd at night.

Not a mutineer walks handcuff'd to jail but I am handcuff'd to him and walk by his side,
(I am less the jolly one there, and more the silent one with sweat on my twitching lips.)

Not a youngster is taken for larceny but I go up too, and am tried and sentenced.   10

Not a cholera patient lies at the last gasp but I also lie at the last gasp,
My face is ash-color'd, my sinews gnarl, away from me people retreat.

Askers embody themselves in me and I am embodied in them,
I project my hat, sit shame-faced, and beg.

38

Enough! enough! enough!
Somehow I have been stunn'd. Stand back!
Give me a little time beyond my cuff'd head, slumbers, dreams, gaping,
I discover myself on the verge of a usual mistake.

That I could forget the mockers and insults!
That I could forget the trickling tears and the blows of the bludgeons and hammers!
That I could look with a separate look on my own crucifixion and bloody crowning.

I remember now,
I resume the overstaid fraction,
The grave of rock multiplies what has been confided to it, or to any graves,   10
Corpses rise, gashes heal, fastenings roll from me.

I troop forth replenish'd with supreme power, one of an average unending procession,
Inland and sea-coast we go, and pass all boundary lines,
Our swift ordinances on their way over the whole earth,
The blossoms we wear in our hats the growth of thousands of years.

Eleves, I salute you! come forward!
Continue your annotations, continue your questionings.

39

The friendly and flowing savage, who is he?
Is he waiting for civilization, or past it and mastering it?

Is he some Southwesterner rais'd out-doors? is he Kanadian?
Is he from the Mississippi country? Iowa, Oregon, California?
The mountains? prairie-life, bush-life? or sailor from the sea?

Wherever he goes men and women accept and desire him,
They desire he should like them, touch them, speak to them, stay with them.

Behavior lawless as snow-flakes, words simple as grass, uncomb'd head, laughter, and naiveté,
Slow-stepping feet, common features, common modes and emanations,
They descend in new forms from the tips of his fingers,   10
They are wafted with the odor of his body or breath, they fly out of the glance of his eyes.

40

Flaunt of the sunshine I need not your bask—lie over!
You light surfaces only, I force surfaces and depths also.

Earth! you seem to look for something at my hands,
Say, old top-knot, what do you want?

Man or woman, I might tell how I like you, but cannot,
And might tell what it is in me and what it is in you, but cannot,
And might tell that pining I have, that pulse of my nights and days.

Behold, I do not give lectures or a little charity,
When I give I give myself.

You there, impotent, loose in the knees,   10
Open your scarf'd chops till I blow grit within you,
Spread your palms and lift the flaps of your pockets,
I am not to be denied, I compel, I have stores plenty and to spare,
And any thing I have I bestow.

I do not ask who you are, that is not important to me,
You can do nothing and be nothing but what I will infold you.

To cotton-field drudge or cleaner of privies I lean,
On his right cheek I put the family kiss,
And in my soul I swear I never will deny him.

On women fit for conception I start bigger and nimbler babes,   20
(This day I am jetting the stuff of far more arrogant republics.)

To any one dying, thither I speed and twist the knob of the door,
Turn the bed-clothes toward the foot of the bed,
Let the physician and the priest go home.

I seize the descending man and raise him with resistless will,
O despairer, here is my neck,
By God, you shall not go down! hang your whole weight upon me.

I dilate you with tremendous breath, I buoy you up,
Every room of the house do I fill with an arm'd force,
Lovers of me, bafflers of graves.   30

Sleep—I and they keep guard all night,
Not doubt, not decease shall dare to lay finger upon you,
I have embraced you, and henceforth possess you to myself,
And when you rise in the morning you will find what I tell you is so.

41

I am he bringing help for the sick as they pant on their backs,
And for strong upright men I bring yet more needed help.

I heard what was said of the universe,
Heard it and heard it of several thousand years;
It is middling well as far as it goes—but is that all?

Magnifying and applying come I,
Outbidding at the start the old cautious hucksters,
Taking myself the exact dimensions of Jehovah,
Lithographing Kronos, Zeus his son, and Hercules his grandson,
Buying drafts of Osiris, Isis, Belus, Brahma, Buddha,   10
In my portfolio placing Manito loose, Allah on a leaf, the crucifix engraved,
With Odin and the hideous-faced Mexitli and every idol and image,
Taking them all for what they are worth and not a cent more,
Admitting they were alive and did the work of their days,
(They bore mites as for unfledg'd birds who have now to rise and fly and sing for themselves,)
Accepting the rough deific sketches to fill out better in myself, bestowing them freely on each man and
    woman I see,

Discovering as much or more in a framer framing a house,
Putting higher claims for him there with his roll'd-up sleeves driving the mallet and chisel,
Not objecting to special revelations, considering a curl of smoke or a hair on the back of my hand just
    as curious as any revelation,
Lads ahold of fire-engines and hook-and-ladder ropes no less to me than the gods of the antique wars,   20
Minding their voices peal through the crash of destruction,
Their brawny limbs passing safe over charr'd laths, their white foreheads whole and unhurt out of the
    flames;
By the mechanic's wife with her babe at her nipple interceding for every person born,
Three scythes at harvest whizzing in a row from three lusty angels with shirts bagg'd out at their waists,
The snag-tooth'd hostler with red hair redeeming sins past and to come,
Selling all he possesses, traveling on foot to fee lawyers for his brother and sit by him while he is tried
    for forgery;
What was strewn in the amplest strewing the square rod about me, and not filling the square rod then,
The bull and the bug never worshipp'd half enough,
Dung and dirt more admirable than was dream'd,
The supernatural of no account, myself waiting my time to be one of the supremes,   30
The day getting ready for me when I shall do as much good as the best, and be as prodigious;
By my life-lumps! becoming already a creator,
Putting myself here and now to the ambush'd womb of the shadows.

42

A call in the midst of the crowd,
My own voice, orotund sweeping and final.

Come my children,
Come my boys and girls, my women, household and intimates,
Now the performer launches his nerve, he has pass'd his prelude on the reeds within.

Easily written loose-finger'd chords—I feel the thrum of your climax and close.

My head slues round on my neck,
Music rolls, but not from the organ,
Folks are around me, but they are no household of mine.

Ever the hard unsunk ground,   10
Ever the eaters and drinkers, ever the upward and downward sun, ever the air and the ceaseless tides,
Ever myself and my neighbors, refreshing, wicked, real,
Ever the old inexplicable query, ever that thorn'd thumb, that breath of itches and thirsts,
Ever the vexer's *hoot! hoot!* till we find where the sly one hides and bring him forth,
Ever love, ever the sobbing liquid of life,
Ever the bandage under the chin, ever the trestles of death.

Here and there with dimes on the eyes walking,
To feed the greed of the belly the brains liberally spooning,
Tickets buying, taking, selling, but in to the feast never once going,
Many sweating, ploughing, thrashing, and then the chaff for payment receiving,   20
A few idly owning, and they the wheat continually claiming.

This is the city and I am one of the citizens,
Whatever interests the rest interests me, politics, wars, markets, newspapers, schools,
The mayor and councils, banks, tariffs, steamships, factories, stocks, stores, real estate and personal
    estate.

The little plentiful manikins skipping around in collars and tail'd coats,

I am aware who they are, (they are positively not worms or fleas,)
I acknowledge the duplicates of myself, the weakest and shallowest is deathless with me,
What I do and say the same waits for them,
Every thought that flounders in me the same flounders in them.

I know perfectly well my own egotism,   30
Know my omnivorous lines and must not write any less,
And would fetch you whoever you are flush with myself.

Not words of routine this song of mine,
But abruptly to question, to leap beyond yet nearer bring;
This printed and bound book—but the printer and the printing-office boy?
The well-taken photographs—but your wife or friend close and solid in your arms?
The black ship mail'd with iron, her mighty guns in her turrets—but the pluck of the captain and
    engineers?
In the houses the dishes and fare and furniture—but the host and hostess, and the look out of their
    eyes?
The sky up there—yet here or next door, or across the way?
The saints and sages in history—but you yourself?   40
Sermons, creeds, theology—but the fathomless human brain,
And what is reason? and what is love? and what is life?

43

I do not despise you priests, all time, the world over,
My faith is the greatest of faiths and the least of faiths,
Enclosing worship ancient and modern and all between ancient and modern,
Believing I shall come again upon the earth after five thousand years,
Waiting responses from oracles, honoring the gods, saluting the sun,
Making a fetich of the first rock or stump, powowing with sticks in the circle of obis,
Helping the llama or brahmin as he trims the lamps of the idols,
Dancing yet through the streets in a phallic procession, rapt and austere in the woods a gymnosophist,
Drinking mead from the skull-cup, to Shastas and Vedas admirant, minding the Koran,
Walking the teokallis, spotted with gore from the stone and knife, beating the serpent-skin drum,   10
Accepting the Gospels, accepting him that was crucified, knowing assuredly that he is divine,
To the mass kneeling or the puritan's prayer rising, or sitting patiently in a pew,
Ranting and frothing in my insane crisis, or waiting dead-like till my spirit arouses me,
Looking forth on pavement and land, or outside of pavement and land,
Belonging to the winders of the circuit of circuits.

One of that centripetal and centrifugal gang I turn and talk like a man leaving charges before a journey.

Down-hearted doubters dull and excluded,
Frivolous, sullen, moping, angry, affected, dishearten'd, atheistical,
I know every one of you, I know the sea of torment, doubt, despair and unbelief.

How the flukes splash!   20
How they contort rapid as lightning, with spasms and spouts of blood!

Be at peace bloody flukes of doubters and sullen mopers,
I take my place among you as much as among any,
The past is the push of you, me, all, precisely the same,
And what is yet untried and afterward is for you, me, all precisely the same.

I do not know what is untried and afterward,
But I know it will in its turn prove sufficient, and cannot fail.

Each who passes is consider'd, each who stops is consider'd, not a single one can it fail.

It cannot fail the young man who died and was buried,
Nor the young woman who died and was put by his side,
Nor the little child that peep'd in at the door, and then drew back and was never seen again,
Nor the old man who has lived without purpose, and feels it with bitterness worse than gall,
Nor him in the poor house tubercled by rum and the bad disorder,
Nor the numberless slaughter'd and wreck'd, nor the brutish koboo call'd the ordure of humanity,
Nor the sacs merely floating with open mouths for food to slip in,
Nor any thing in the earth, or down in the oldest graves of the earth,
Nor any thing in the myriads of spheres, nor the myriads of myriads that inhabit them,
Nor the present, nor the least wisp that is known.

44

It is time to explain myself—let us stand up.

What is known I strip away,
I launch all men and women forward with me into the Unknown.

The clock indicates the moment—but what does eternity indicate?

We have thus far exhausted trillions of winters and summers,
There are trillions ahead, and trillions ahead of them.

Births have brought us richness and variety,
And other births will bring us richness and variety.

I do not call one greater and one smaller,
That which fills its period and place is equal to any.

Were mankind murderous or jealous upon you, my brother, my sister?
I am sorry for you, they are not murderous or jealous upon me,
All has been gentle with me, I keep no account with lamentation,
(What have I to do with lamentation?)

I am an acme of things accomplish'd, and I an encloser of things to be.

My feet strike an apex of the apices of the stairs,
On every step bunches of ages, and larger bunches between the steps,
All below duly travel'd, and still I mount and mount.

Rise after rise bow the phantoms behind me,
Afar down I see the huge first Nothing, I know I was even there,
I waited unseen and always, and slept through the lethargic mist,
And took my time, and took no hurt from the fetid carbon.

Long I was hugg'd close—long and long.

Immense have been the preparations for me,
Faithful and friendly the arms that have help'd me.

Cycles ferried my cradle, rowing and rowing like cheerful boatmen,
For room to me stars kept aside in their own rings,
They sent influences to look after what was to hold me.

Before I was born out of my mother generations guided me,
My embryo has never been torpid, nothing could overlay it.

For it the nebula cohered to an orb,
The long slow strata piled to rest it on,
Vast vegetables gave it sustenance,
Monstrous sauroids transported it in their mouths and deposited it with care.

All forces have been steadily employ'd to complete and delight me,
Now on this spot I stand with my robust soul!

45

O span of youth! ever-push'd elasticity!
O manhood, balanced, florid and full.

My lovers suffocate me,
Crowding my lips, thick in the pores of my skin,
Jostling me through streets and public halls, coming naked to me at night,
Crying by day *Ahoy!* from the rocks of the river, swinging and chirping over my head,
Calling my name from flower-beds, vines, tangled underbrush,
Lighting on every moment of my life,
Bussing my body with soft balsamic busses,
Noiselessly passing handfuls out of their hearts and giving them to be mine.   10

Old age superbly rising! O welcome, ineffable grace of dying days!

Every condition promulges not only itself, it promulges what grows after and out of itself,
And the dark hush promulges as much as any.

I open my scuttle at night and see the far-sprinkled systems,
And all I see multiplied as high as I can cipher edge but the rim of the farther systems.

Wider and wider they spread, expanding, always expanding,
Outward and outward and forever outward.

My sun has his sun and round him obediently wheels,
He joins with his partners a group of superior circuit,
And greater sets follow, making specks of the greatest inside them.   20

There is no stoppage and never can be stoppage,
If I, you, and the worlds, and all beneath or upon their surfaces, were this moment reduced back to a
    pallid float, it would not avail in the long run,
We should surely bring up again where we now stand,
And surely go as much farther, and then farther and farther.

A few quadrillions of eras, a few octillions of cubic leagues, do not hazard the span or make it impatient,
They are but parts, any thing is but a part.

See ever so far, there is limitless space outside of that,
Count ever so much, there is limitless time around that.

My rendezvous is appointed, it is certain,
The Lord will be there and wait till I come on perfect terms,   30
The great Camerado, the lover true for whom I pine will be there.

46

I know I have the best of time and space, and was never measured and never will be measured.

I tramp a perpetual journey, (come listen all!)
My signs are a rain-proof coat, good shoes, and a staff cut from the woods,

No friend of mine takes his ease in my chair,
I have no chair, no church, no philosophy,
I lead no man to a dinner-table, library, exchange,
But each man and each woman of you I lead upon a knoll,
My left hand hooking you round the waist,
My right hand pointing to landscapes of continents and the public road.

Not I, nor any one else can travel that road for you,   10
You must travel it for yourself.

It is not far, it is within reach,
Perhaps you have been on it since you were born and did not know,
Perhaps it is everywhere on water and on land.

Shoulder your duds dear son, and I will mine, and let us hasten forth,
Wonderful cities and free nations we shall fetch as we go.

If you tire, give me both burdens, and rest the chuff of your hand on my hip,
And in due time you shall repay the same service to me,
For after we start we never lie by again.

This day before dawn I ascended a hill and look'd at the crowded heaven,   20
And I said to my spirit *When we become the enfolders of those orbs, and the pleasure and knowledge of*
    every thing in them, shall we be fill'd and satisfied then?
And my spirit said *No, we but level that lift to pass and continue beyond.*

You are also asking me questions and I hear you,
I answer that I cannot answer, you must find out for yourself.

Sit a while dear son,
Here are biscuits to eat and here is milk to drink,
But as soon as you sleep and renew yourself in sweet clothes, I kiss you with a good-by kiss and open the
    gate for your egress hence.

Long enough have you dream'd contemptible dreams,
Now I wash the gum from your eyes,
You must habit yourself to the dazzle of the light and of every moment of your life.   30

Long have you timidly waded holding a plank by the shore,
Now I will you to be a bold swimmer,
To jump off in the midst of the sea, rise again, nod to me, shout, and laughingly dash with your hair.

47

I am the teacher of athletes,
He that by me spreads a wider breast than my own proves the width of my own,
He most honors my style who learns under it to destroy the teacher.

The boy I love, the same becomes a man not through derived power, but in his own right,
Wicked rather than virtuous out of conformity or fear,
Fond of his sweetheart, relishing well his steak,
Unrequited love or a slight cutting him worse than sharp steel cuts,
First-rate to ride, to fight, to hit the bull's eye, to sail a skiff, to sing a song or play on the banjo,
Preferring scars and the beard and faces pitted with small-pox over all latherers,
And those well-tann'd to those that keep out of the sun.   10

I teach straying from me, yet who can stray from me?
I follow you whoever you are from the present hour,

My words itch at your ears till you understand them.

I do not say these things for a dollar or to fill up the time while I wait for a boat,
(It is you talking just as much as myself, I act as the tongue of you,
Tied in your mouth, in mine it begins to be loosen'd.)

I swear I will never again mention love or death inside a house,
And I swear I will never translate myself at all, only to him or her who privately stays with me in the
    open air.

If you would understand me go to the heights or water-shore,
The nearest gnat is an explanation, and a drop or motion of waves a key,   20
The maul, the oar, the hand-saw, second my words.

No shutter'd room or school can commune with me,
But roughs and little children better than they.

The young mechanic is closest to me, he knows me well,
The woodman that takes his axe and jug with him shall take me with him all day,
The farm-boy ploughing in the field feels good at the sound of my voice,
In vessels that sail my words sail, I go with fishermen and seamen and love them.

The soldier camp'd or upon the march is mine,
On the night ere the pending battle many seek me, and I do not fail them,
On that solemn night (it may be their last) those that know me seek me.   30

My face rubs to the hunter's face when he lies down alone in his blanket,
The driver thinking of me does not mind the jolt of his wagon,
The young mother and old mother comprehend me,
The girl and the wife rest the needle a moment and forget where they are,
They and all would resume what I have told them.

48

I have said that the soul is not more than the body,
And I have said that the body is not more than the soul,
And nothing, not God, is greater to one than one's self is,
And whoever walks a furlong without sympathy walks to his own funeral drest in his shroud,
And I or you pocketless of a dime may purchase the pick of the earth,
And to glance with an eye or show a bean in its pod confounds the learning of all times,
And there is no trade or employment but the young man following it may become a hero,
And there is no object so soft but it makes a hub for the wheel'd universe,
And I say to any man or woman, Let your soul stand cool and composed before a million universes.

And I say to mankind, Be not curious about God,   10
For I who am curious about each am not curious about God,
(No array of terms can say how much I am at peace about God and about death.)

I hear and behold God in every object, yet understand God not in the least,
Nor do I understand who there can be more wonderful than myself.

Why should I wish to see God better than this day?
I see something of God each hour of the twenty-four, and each moment then,
In the faces of men and women I see God, and in my own face in the glass,
I find letters from God dropt in the street, and every one is sign'd by God's name,
And I leave them where they are, for I know that wheresoe'er I go   20
Others will punctually come for ever and ever.

49

And as to you Death, and you bitter hug of mortality, it is idle to try to alarm me.

To his work without flinching the accoucheur comes,
I see the elder-hand pressing receiving supporting,
I recline by the sills of the exquisite flexible doors,
And mark the outlet, and mark the relief and escape.

And as to you Corpse I think you are good manure, but that does not offend me,
I smell the white roses sweet-scented and growing,
I reach to the leafy lips, I reach to the polish'd breasts of melons.

And as to you Life I reckon you are the leavings of many deaths,
(No doubt I have died myself ten thousand times before.)   10

I hear you whispering there O stars of heaven,
O suns—O grass of graves—O perpetual transfers and promotions,
If you do not say any thing how can I say any thing?

Of the turbid pool that lies in the autumn forest,
Of the moon that descends the steeps of the soughing twilight,
Toss, sparkles of day and dusk—toss on the black stems that decay in the muck,
Toss to the moaning gibberish of the dry limbs.

I ascend from the moon, I ascend from the night,
I perceive that the ghastly glimmer is noonday sunbeams reflected,
And debouch to the steady and central from the offspring great or small.   20

50

There is that in me—I do not know what it is—but I know it is in me.

Wrench'd and sweaty—calm and cool then my body becomes,
I sleep—I sleep long.

I do not know it—it is without name—it is a word unsaid,
It is not in any dictionary, utterance, symbol.

Something it swings on more than the earth I swing on,
To it the creation is the friend whose embracing awakes me.

Perhaps I might tell more. Outlines! I plead for my brothers and sisters.

Do you see O my brothers and sisters?
It is not chaos or death—it is form, union, plan—it is eternal life—it is Happiness.   10

51

The past and present wilt—I have fill'd them, emptied them,
And proceed to fill my next fold of the future.

Listener up there! what have you to confide to me?
Look in my face while I snuff the sidle of evening,
(Talk honestly, no one else hears you, and I stay only a minute longer.)

Do I contradict myself?
Very well then I contradict myself,
(I am large, I contain multitudes.)

I concentrate toward them that are nigh, I wait on the door-slab.

Who has done his day's work? who will soonest be through with his supper?   10
Who wishes to walk with me?

Will you speak before I am gone? will you prove already too late?

52

The spotted hawk swoops by and accuses me, he complains of my gab and my loitering.   *He's talking*
Natural like a hawk   *been too much.*
I too am not a bit tamed, I too am untranslatable,
I sound my barbaric yawp over the roofs of the world.   *Better is to be a barb. than a*   *too so-called*
                                                                                                                       "civilized"
The last scud of day holds back for me, *death*   *person.*
It flings my likeness after the rest and true as any on the shadow'd wilds,
It coaxes me to the vapor and the dusk.   *lose physical appearance*

                           old man
I depart as air, I shake my white locks at the runaway sun,
I effuse my flesh in eddies, and drift it in lacy jags.
give off (emit)
I bequeath myself to the dirt to grow from the grass I love, *He loves grass because it is*
If you want me again look for me under your boot-soles.   *symbolic of rebirth.*   10

You will hardly know who I am or what I mean,
But I shall be good health to you nevertheless,
And filter and fibre your blood.
                understand
Failing to fetch me at first keep encouraged,
Missing me one place search another,
I stop somewhere waiting for you.   *witness and wait (for death)*
                                                Death has come now and
                                                he waits for us.

There Was a Child Went Forth (1855)

This poem appeared, untitled, almost as a fragment of a longer untitled poem in the last pages of the 1855 edition of *Leaves of Grass*. It can stand alone easily enough as a distinctive and brilliant poem; but it may also help to think of it as one moment in a continuing poetic expression—a moment when the poet's imagination, playing somewhat haphazardly over a variety of things, suddenly reverts without warning to certain childhood memories.

There was a child went forth every day,
And the first object he look'd upon, that object he became,
And that object became part of him for the day or a certain part of the day,
Or for many years or stretching cycles of years.

The early lilacs became part of this child,
And grass and white and red morning-glories, and white and red clover, and the song of the phœbe bird,
And the Third-month lambs and the sow's pink-faint litter, and the mare's foal and the cow's calf,
And the noisy brood of the barnyard or by the mire of the pond-side,
And the fish suspending themselves so curiously below there, and the beautiful curious liquid,
And the water-plants with their graceful flat heads, all became part of him.   10

The field-sprouts of Fourth-month and Fifth-month became part of him,
Winter-grain sprouts and those of the light-yellow corn, and the esculent roots of the garden,
And the apple-trees cover'd with blossoms and the fruit afterward, and wood-berries, and the commonest
    weeds by the road,

And the old drunkard staggering home from the outhouse of the tavern whence he had lately risen,
And the schoolmistress that pass'd on her way to the school,
And the friendly boys that pass'd, and the quarrelsome boys,
And the tidy and fresh-cheek'd girls, and the barefoot negro boy and girl,
And all the changes of city and country wherever he went.

His own parents, he that had father'd him and she that had conceiv'd him in her womb and birth'd him,
They gave this child more of themselves than that,   20
They gave him afterward every day, they became part of him.

The mother at home quietly placing the dishes on the supper-table,
The mother with mild words, clean her cap and gown, a wholesome odor falling off her person and clothes as she walks by,
The father, strong, self-sufficient, manly, mean, anger'd, unjust,
The blow, the quick loud word, the tight bargain, the crafty lure,
The family usages, the language, the company, the furniture, the yearning and swelling heart,
Affection that will not be gainsay'd, the sense of what is real, the thought if after all it should prove unreal,
The doubts of day-time and the doubts of night-time, the curious whether and how,
Whether that which appears so is so, or is it all flashes and specks?
Men and women crowding fast in the streets, if they are not dashes and specks what are they?   30
The streets themselves and the façades of houses, and goods in the windows,
Vehicles, teams, the heavy-plank'd wharves, the huge crossing at the ferries,
The village on the highland seen from afar at sunset, the river between,
Shadows, aureola and mist, the light falling on roofs and gables of white or brown two miles off,
The schooner near by sleepily dropping down the tide, the little boat slack-tow'd astern,
The hurrying tumbling waves, quick-broken crests, slapping,
The strata of color'd clouds, the long bar of maroon-tint away solitary by itself, the spread of purity it lies motionless in,
The horizon's edge, the flying sea-crow, the fragrance of salt marsh and shore mud,
These became part of that child who went forth every day, and who now goes, and will always go forth every day.

The Sleepers (1855)

We present this poem exactly as it appeared in 1855. Notice the different effect of the typography and language of this version as against that of the later and standard version—for example, in the first stanza, which customarily looks and reads like this:

I wander all night in my vision,
Stepping with light feet, swiftly and noiselessly stepping and stopping,
Bending with open eyes over the shut eyes of sleepers,
Wandering and confused, lost to myself, ill-assorted, contradictory,

Pausing, gazing, bending, and stopping.

The section (in the 1855 version) beginning "O hotcheeked and blushing!" and continuing for eleven lines was deleted by Whitman in the 1867 edition and all subsequent editions. The section beginning "Now Lucifer was not dead" and the seven following lines were also deleted. It can be noted that our interpretation of "The Sleepers" assumes the inclusion of those sections and is indeed partly based upon them.

I wander all night in my vision,
Stepping with light feet . . . . swiftly and noiselessly stepping and stopping,

Bending with open eyes over the shut eyes of sleepers;
Wandering and confused . . . . lost to myself . . . . ill-assorted . . . . contradictory,
Pausing and gazing and bending and stopping.

How solemn they look there, stretched and still;
How quiet they breathe, the little children in their cradles.

The wretched features of ennuyees, the white features of corpses, the livid faces of drunkards, the sick-gray
    faces of onanists,
The gashed bodies on battlefields, the insane in their strong-doored rooms, the sacred idiots,
The newborn emerging from gates and the dying emerging from gates,   10
The night pervades them and enfolds them.

The married couple sleep calmly in their bed, he with his palm on the hip of the wife, and she with her
    palm on the hip of the husband,
The sisters sleep lovingly side by side in their bed,
The men sleep lovingly side by side in theirs,
And the mother sleeps with her little child carefully wrapped.

The blind sleep, and the deaf and dumb sleep,
The prisoner sleeps well in the prison . . . . the runaway son sleeps,
The murderer that is to be hung next day . . . . how does he sleep?
And the murdered person . . . . how does he sleep?

The female that loves unrequited sleeps,   20
And the male that loves unrequited sleeps;
The head of the moneymaker that plotted all day sleeps,
And the enraged and treacherous dispositions sleep.

I stand with drooping eyes by the worstsuffering and restless,
I pass my hands soothingly to and fro a few inches from them;
The restless sink in their beds . . . . they fitfully sleep.

The earth recedes from me into the night,
I saw that it was beautiful . . . . and I see that what is not the earth is beautiful.

I go from bedside to bedside . . . . I sleep close with the other sleepers, each in turn;
I dream in my dream all the dreams of the other dreamers,   30
And I become the other dreamers.

I am a dance . . . . Play up there! the fit is whirling me fast.

I am the everlaughing . . . . it is new moon and twilight,
I see the hiding of douceurs . . . . I see nimble ghosts whichever way I look,
Cache and cache again deep in the ground and sea, and where it is neither ground or sea.

Well do they do their jobs, those journeymen divine,
Only from me can they hide nothing and would not if they could;
I reckon I am their boss, and they make me a pet besides,
And surround me, and lead me and run ahead when I walk,
And lift their cunning covers and signify me with stretched arms, and resume the way;   40
Onward we move, a gay gang of blackguards with mirthshouting music and wildflapping pennants of joy.

I am the actor and the actress . . . . the voter . . the politician,
The emigrant and the exile . . . the criminal that stood in the box,
He who has been famous, and he who shall be famous after today,
The stammerer . . . . the wellformed person . . the wasted or feeble person.

I am she who adorned herself and folded her hair expectantly,
My truant lover has come and it is dark.

Double yourself and receive me darkness,
Receive me and my lover too . . . . he will not let me go without him.

I roll myself upon you as upon a bed . . . . I resign myself to the dusk.   50

He whom I call answers me and takes the place of my lover,
He rises with me silently from the bed.

Darkness you are gentler than my lover . . . . his flesh was sweaty and panting,
I feel the hot moisture yet that he left me.

My hands are spread forth . . I pass them in all directions,
I would sound up the shadowy shore to which you are journeying.

Be careful, darkness . . . . already, what was it touched me?
I thought my lover had gone . . . . else darkness and he are one,
I hear the heart-beat . . . . I follow . . I fade away.

O hotcheeked and blushing! O foolish hectic!   60
O for pity's sake, no one must see me now! . . . . my clothes were stolen while I was abed,
Now I am thrust forth, where shall I run?

Pier that I saw dimly last night when I looked from the windows,
Pier out from the main, let me catch myself with you and stay . . . . I will not chafe you;
I feel ashamed to go naked about the world,
And am curious to know where my feet stand . . . . and what is this flooding me, childhood or manhood
    . . . . and the hunger that crosses the bridge between.

The cloth laps a first sweet eating and drinking,
Laps life-swelling yolks . . . . laps ear of rose-corn, milky and just ripened:
The white teeth stay, and the boss-tooth advances in darkness,
And liquor is spilled on lips and bosoms by touching glasses, and the best liquor afterward.   70

I descend my western course . . . . my sinews are flaccid,
Perfume and youth course through me, and I am their wake.

It is my face yellow and wrinkled instead of the old woman's,
I sit low in a strawbottom chair and carefully darn my grandson's stockings.

It is I too . . . . the sleepless widow looking out on the winter midnight,
I see the sparkles of starshine on the icy and pallid earth.

A shroud I see—and I am the shroud . . . . I wrap a body and lie in the coffin;
It is dark here underground . . . . it is not evil or pain here . . . . it is blank here, for reasons.

It seems to me that everything in the light and air ought to be happy;
Whoever is not in his coffin and the dark grave, let him know he has enough.   80

I see a beautiful gigantic swimmer swimming naked through the eddies of the sea,
His brown hair lies close and even to his head . . . . he strikes out with courageous arms . . . . he urges
    himself with his legs.
I see his white body . . . . I see his undaunted eyes;
I hate the swift-running eddies that would dash him headforemost on the rocks.

What are you doing you ruffianly red-trickled waves?
Will you kill the courageous giant? Will you kill him in the prime of his middle age?

Steady and long he struggles;
He is baffled and banged and bruised . . . . he holds out while his strength holds out,
The slapping eddies are spotted with his blood . . . . they bear him away . . . . they roll him and swing him and turn him:
His beautiful body is borne in the circling eddies . . . . it is continually bruised on rocks,   90
Swiftly and out of sight is borne the brave corpse.

I turn but do not extricate myself;
Confused . . . . a pastreading . . . . another, but with darkness yet.

The beach is cut by the razory ice-wind . . . . the wreck-guns sounds,
The tempest lulls and the moon comes floundering through the drifts.

I look where the ship helplessly heads end on . . . . I hear the burst as she strikes . . I hear the howls of dismay . . . . they grow fainter and fainter.

I cannot aid with my wringing fingers;
I can but rush to the surf and let it drench me and freeze upon me.

I search with the crowd . . . . not one of the company is washed to us alive;
In the morning I help pick up the dead and lay them in rows in a barn.   100

Now of the old war-days . . the defeat at Brooklyn;
Washington stands inside the lines . . he stands on the entrenched hills amid a crowd of officers,
His face is cold and damp . . . . he cannot repress the weeping drops . . . . he lifts the glass perpetually to his eyes . . . . the color is blanched from his cheeks,
He sees the slaughter of the southern braves confided to him by their parents.

The same at last and at last when peace is declared,
He stands in the room of the old tavern . . . . the wellbeloved soldiers all pass through.

The officers speechless and slow draw near in their turns,
The chief encircles their necks with his arm and kisses them on the cheek,
He kisses lightly the wet cheeks one after another . . . . he shakes hands and bids goodbye to the army.

Now I tell what my mother told me today as we sat at dinner together,   110
Of when she was a nearly grown girl living home with her parents on the old homestead.

A red squaw came one breakfastime to the old homestead,
On her back she carried a bundle of rushes for rushbottoming chairs;
Her hair straight shiny coarse black and profuse halfenveloped her face,
Her step was free and elastic . . . . her voice sounded exquisitely as she spoke.

My mother looked in delight and amazement at the stranger,
She looked at the beauty of her tallborne face and full and pliant limbs,
The more she looked upon her she loved her,
Never before had she seen such wonderful beauty and purity;
She made her sit on a bench by the jamb of the fireplace . . . . she cooked food for her,   120
She had no work to give her but she gave her remembrance and fondness.

The red squaw staid all the forenoon, and toward the middle of the afternoon she went away;
O my mother was loth to have her go away,
All the week she thought of her . . . . she watched for her many a month,
She remembered her many a winter and many a summer,
But the red squaw never came nor was heard of there again.

Now Lucifer was not dead . . . . or if he was I am his sorrowful terrible heir;
I have been wronged . . . . I am oppressed . . . . I hate him that oppresses me,

I will either destroy him, or he shall release me.

Damn him! how he does defile me,   130
How he informs against my brother and sister and takes pay for their blood,
How he laughs when I look down the bend after the steamboat that carries away my woman.

Now the vast dusk bulk that is the whale's bulk . . . . it seems mine,
Warily, sportsman! though I lie so sleepy and sluggish, my tap is death.

A show of the summer softness . . . . a contact of something unseen . . . . an amour of the light and air;
I am jealous and overwhelmed with friendliness,
And will go gallivant with the light and the air myself,
And have an unseen something to be in contact with them also.

O love and summer! you are in the dreams and in me,
Autumn and winter are in the dreams . . . . the farmer goes with his thrift,   140
The droves and crops increase . . . . the barns are wellfilled.

Elements merge in the night . . . . ships make tacks in the dreams . . . . the sailor sails . . . . the
    exile returns home,
The fugitive returns unharmed . . . . the immigrant is back beyond months and years;
The poor Irishman lives in the simple house of his childhood, with the wellknown neighbors and faces,
They warmly welcome him . . . . he is barefoot again . . . . he forgets he is welloff;
The Dutchman voyages home, and the Scotchman and Welchman voyage home . . and the native of
    the Mediterranean voyages home;
To every port of England and France and Spain enter wellfilled ships;
The Swiss foots it toward his hills . . . . the Prussian goes his way, and the Hungarian his way, and the
    Pole goes his way,
The Swede returns, and the Dane and Norwegian return.

The homeward bound and the outward bound,   150
The beautiful lost swimmer, the ennuyee, the onanist, the female that loves unrequited, the moneymaker,
The actor and actress . . those through with their parts and those waiting to commence,
The affectionate boy, the husband and wife, the voter, the nominee that is chosen and the nominee that
    has failed,
The great already known, and the great anytime after to day,
The stammerer, the sick, the perfectformed, the homely,
The criminal that stood in the box, the judge that sat and sentenced him, the fluent lawyers, the jury, the
    audience,
The laugher and weeper, the dancer, the midnight widow, the red squaw,
The consumptive, the erysipalite, the idiot, he that is wronged,
The antipodes, and every one between this and them in the dark,
I swear they are averaged now . . . . one is no better than the other,   160
The night and sleep have likened them and restored them.

I swear they are all beautiful,
Every one that sleeps is beautiful . . . . every thing in the dim night is beautiful,
The wildest and bloodiest is over and all is peace.

Peace is always beautiful,
The myth of heaven indicates peace and night.

The myth of heaven indicates the soul;
The soul is always beautiful . . . . it appears more or it appears less . . . . it comes or lags behind,
It comes from its embowered garden and looks pleasantly on itself and encloses the world;
Perfect and clean the genitals previously jetting, and perfect and clean the womb cohering,   170

The head wellgrown and proportioned and plumb, and the bowels and joints proportioned and plumb.

The soul is always beautiful,
The universe is duly in order . . . . every thing is in its place,
What is arrived is in its place, and what waits is in its place;
The twisted skull waits . . . . the watery or rotten blood waits,
The child of the glutton or venerealee waits long, and the child of the drunkard waits long, and the drunk-
    ard himself waits long,
The sleepers that lived and died wait . . . . the far advanced are to go on in their turns, and the far
    behind are to go on in their turns,
The diverse shall be no less diverse, but they shall flow and unite . . . . they unite now.

The sleepers are very beautiful as they lie unclothed,
They flow hand in hand over the whole earth from east to west as they lie unclothed;   180
The Asiatic and African are hand in hand . . . . the European and American are hand in hand,
Learned and unlearned are hand in hand . . and male and female are hand in hand;
The bare arm of the girl crosses the bare breast of her lover . . . . they press close without lust . . . .
    his lips press her neck,
The father holds his grown or ungrown son in his arms with measureless love . . . . and the son holds
    the father in his arms with measureless love,
The white hair of the mother shines on the white wrist of the daughter,
The breath of the boy goes with the breath of the man . . . . friend is inarmed by friend,
The scholar kisses the teacher and the teacher kisses the scholar . . . . the wronged is made right,
The call of the slave is one with the master's call . . and the master salutes the slave,
The felon steps forth from the prison . . . . the insane becomes sane . . . . the suffering of sick per-
    sons is relieved,
The sweatings and fevers stop . . the throat that was unsound is sound . . the lungs of the consump-
    tive are resumed . . the poor distressed head is free,   190
The joints of the rheumatic move as smoothly as ever, and smoother than ever,
Stiflings and passages open . . . . the paralysed become supple,
The swelled and convulsed and congested awake to themselves in condition,
They pass the invigoration of the night and the chemistry of the night and awake.

I too pass from the night;
I stay awhile away O night, but I return to you again and love you;
Why should I be afraid to trust myself to you?
I am not afraid . . . . I have been well brought forward by you;
I love the rich running day, but I do not desert her in whom I lay so long:
I know not how I came of you, and I know not where I go with you . . . . but I know I came well and
    shall go well.   200

I will stop only a time with the night . . . . and rise betimes.

I will duly pass the day O my mother and duly return to you;
Not you will yield forth the dawn again more surely than you will yield forth me again,
Not the womb yields the babe in its time more surely than I shall be yielded from you in my time.

Spontaneous Me (1856)

Spontaneous me, Nature,
The loving day, the mounting sun, the friend I am happy with,
The arm of my friend hanging idly over my shoulder,
The hillside whiten'd with blossoms of the mountain ash,

The same late in autumn, the hues of red, yellow, drab, purple, and light and dark green,
The rich coverlet of the grass, animals and birds, the private untrimm'd bank, the primitive apples, the
  pebble-stones,
Beautiful dripping fragments, the negligent list of one after another as I happen to call them to me or
  think of them,
The real poems, (what we call poems being merely pictures,)
The poems of the privacy of the night, and of men like me,
This poem drooping shy and unseen that I always carry, and that all men carry,   10
(Know once for all, avow'd on purpose, wherever are men like me, are our lusty lurking masculine poems,)
Love-thoughts, love-juice, love-odor, love-yielding, love-climbers, and the climbing sap,
Arms and hands of love, lips of love, phallic thumb of love, breasts of love, bellies press'd and glued to-
  gether with love,
Earth of chaste love, life that is only life after love,
The body of my love, the body of the woman I love, the body of the man, the body of the earth,
Soft forenoon airs that blow from the south-west,
The hairy wild-bee that murmurs and hankers up and down, that gripes the full-grown lady-flower, curves
  upon her with amorous firm legs, takes his will of her, and holds himself tremulous and tight till he
  is satisfied;
The wet of woods through the early hours,
Two sleepers at night lying close together as they sleep, one with an arm slanting down across and below
  the waist of the other,
The smell of apples, aromas from crush'd sage-plant, mint, birch-bark,   20
The boy's longings, the glow and pressure as he confides to me what he was dreaming,
The dead leaf whirling its spiral whirl and falling still and content to the ground,
The no-form'd stings that sights, people, objects, sting me with,
The hubb'd sting of myself, stinging me as much as it ever can any one,
The sensitive, orbic, underlapp'd brothers, that only privileged feelers may be intimate where they are,
The curious roamer, the hand roaming all over the body, the bashful withdrawing of flesh where the fin-
  gers soothingly pause and edge themselves,
The limpid liquid within the young man,
The vex'd corrosion so pensive and so painful,
The torment, the irritable tide that will not be at rest,
The like of the same I feel, the like of the same in others,   30
The young man that flushes and flushes, and the young woman that flushes and flushes,
The young man that wakes deep at night, the hot hand seeking to repress what would master him,
The mystic amorous night, the strange half-welcome pangs, visions, sweats,
The pulse pounding through palms and trembling encircling fingers, the young man all color'd, red, ashamed,
  angry;
The souse upon me of my lover the sea, as I lie willing and naked,
The merriment of the twin babes that crawl over the grass in the sun, the mother never turning her vigi-
  lant eyes from them,
The walnut-trunk, the walnut-husks, and the ripening or ripen'd long-round walnuts,
The continence of vegetables, birds, animals,
The consequent meanness of me should I skulk or find myself indecent, while birds and animals never once
  skulk or find themselves indecent,
The great chastity of paternity, to match the great chastity of maternity,   40
The oath of procreation I have sworn, my Adamic and fresh daughters,
The greed that eats me day and night with hungry gnaw, till I saturate what shall produce boys to fill my
  place when I am through,
The wholesome relief, repose, content,
And this bunch pluck'd at random from myself,
It has done its work—I toss it carelessly to fall where it may.

Crossing Brooklyn Ferry (1856)

The very title of this poem—which is, to quote Randall Jarrell, one of Whitman's "immortal masterpieces"—is peculiar and suggestive. What the poet is *crossing* is, of course, not Brooklyn Ferry but the East River from Brooklyn to Manhattan. It would be more correct, grammatically, to speak of "Crossing on Brooklyn Ferry"; but Whitman had a habit of omitting prepositions: "I mind how we lay [on] such a transparent summer morning" and "Taking [to] myself the exact dimensions of Jehovah" in "Song of Myself"; "the sea whisper'd [to] me" in "Out of the Cradle Endlessly Rocking."

1

Flood-tide below me! I see you face to face!
Clouds of the west—sun there half an hour high—I see you also face to face.

Crowds of men and women attired in the usual costumes, how curious you are to me!
On the ferry-boats the hundreds and hundreds that cross, returning home, are more curious to me than you suppose,
And you that shall cross from shore to shore years hence are more to me, and more in my meditations, than you might suppose.

2

The impalpable sustenance of me from all things at all hours of the day,
The simple, compact, well-join'd scheme, myself disintegrated, every one disintegrated yet part of the scheme,
The similitudes of the past and those of the future,
The glories strung like beads on my smallest sights and hearings, on the walk in the street and the passage over the river,
The current rushing so swiftly and swimming with me far away,
The others that are to follow me, the ties between me and them,
The certainty of others, the life, love, sight, hearing of others.

Others will enter the gates of the ferry and cross from shore to shore,
Others will watch the run of the flood-tide,
Others will see the shipping of Manhattan north and west, and the heights of Brooklyn to the south and east,   10
Others will see the islands large and small;
Fifty years hence, others will see them as they cross, the sun half an hour high,
A hundred years hence, or ever so many hundred years hence, others will see them,
Will enjoy the sunset, the pouring-in of the flood-tide, the falling-back to the sea of the ebb-tide.

3

It avails not, time nor place—distance avails not,
I am with you, you men and women of a generation, or ever so many generations hence,
Just as you feel when you look on the river and sky, so I felt,
Just as any of you is one of a living crowd, I was one of a crowd,
Just as you are refresh'd by the gladness of the river and the bright flow, I was refresh'd,
Just as you stand and lean on the rail, yet hurry with the swift current, I stood yet was hurried,
Just as you look on the numberless masts of ships and the thick-stemm'd pipes of steamboats, I look'd.

I too many and many a time cross'd the river of old,
Watched the Twelfth-month sea-gulls, saw them high in the air floating with motionless wings, oscillating their bodies,

Saw how the glistening yellow lit up parts of their bodies and left the rest in strong shadow,   10
Saw the slow-wheeling circles and the gradual edging toward the south,
Saw the reflection of the summer sky in the water,
Had my eyes dazzled by the shimmering track of beams,
Look'd at the fine centrifugal spokes of light round the shape of my head in the sunlit water,
Look'd on the haze on the hills southward and south-westward,
Look'd on the vapor as it flew in fleeces tinged with violet,
Look'd toward the lower bay to notice the vessels arriving,
Saw their approach, saw aboard those that were near me,
Saw the white sails of schooners and sloops, saw the ships at anchor,
The sailors at work in the rigging or out astride the spars,   20
The round masts, the swinging motion of the hulls, the slender serpentine pennants,
The large and small steamers in motion, the pilots in their pilot-houses,
The white wake left by the passage, the quick tremulous whirl of the wheels,
The flags of all nations, the falling of them at sunset,
The scallop-edged waves in the twilight, the ladled cups, the frolicsome crests and glistening,
The stretch afar growing dimmer and dimmer, the gray walls of the granite storehouses by the docks,
On the river the shadowy group, the big steam-tug closely flank'd on each side by the barges, the hay-boat, the belated lighter,
On the neighboring shore the fires from the foundry chimneys burning high and glaringly into the night,
Casting their flicker of black contrasted with wild red and yellow light over the tops of houses, and down into the clefts of streets.

4

These and all else were to me the same as they are to you,
I loved well those cities, loved well the stately and rapid river,
The men and women I saw were all near to me,
Others the same—others who look back on me because I look'd forward to them,
(The time will come, though I stop here to-day and to-night.)

5

What is it then between us?
What is the count of the scores or hundreds of years between us?

Whatever it is, it avails not—distance avails not, and place avails not,
I too lived, Brooklyn of ample hills was mine,
I too walk'd the streets of Manhattan island, and bathed in the waters around it,
I too felt the curious abrupt questionings stir within me.
In the day among crowds of people sometimes they came upon me,
In my walks home late at night or as I lay in my bed they came upon me,
I too had been struck from the float forever held in solution,
I too had receiv'd identity by my body,   10
That I was I knew was of my body, and what I should be I knew I should be of my body.

6

It is not upon you alone the dark patches fall,
The dark threw its patches down upon me also,
The best I had done seem'd to me blank and suspicious,
My great thoughts as I supposed them, were they not in reality meagre?
Nor is it you alone who know what it is to be evil,
I am he who knew what it was to be evil,
I too knitted the old knot of contrariety,
Blabb'd, blush'd, resented, lied, stole, grudg'd,

Had guile, anger, lust, hot wishes I dared not speak,
Was wayward, vain, greedy, shallow, sly, cowardly, malignant,   10
The wolf, the snake, the hog, not wanting in me,
The cheating look, the frivolous word, the adulterous wish, not wanting,
Refusals, hates, postponements, meanness, laziness, none of these wanting,
Was one with the rest, the days and haps of the rest,
Was call'd by my nighest name by clear loud voices of young men as they saw me approaching or passing,
Felt their arms on my neck as I stood, or the negligent leaning of their flesh against me as I sat,
Saw many I loved in the street or ferry-boat or public assembly, yet never told them a word,
Lived the same life with the rest, the same old laughing, gnawing, sleeping,
Play'd the part that still looks back on the actor or actress,
The same old role, the role that is what we make it, as great as we like,   20
Or as small as we like, or both great and small.

7

Closer yet I approach you,
What thought you have of me now, I had as much of you—I laid in my stores in advance,
I consider'd long and seriously of you before you were born.

Who was to know what should come home to me?
Who knows but I am enjoying this?
Who knows, for all the distance, but I am as good as looking at you now, for all you cannot see me?

8

Ah, what can ever be more stately and admirable to me than mast-hemm'd Manhattan?
River and sunset and scallop-edg'd waves of flood-tide?
The sea-gulls oscillating their bodies, the hay-boat in the twilight, and the belated lighter?
What gods can exceed these that clasp me by the hand, and with voices I love call me promptly and
    loudly by my nighest name as I approach?
What is more subtle than this which ties me to the woman or man that looks in my face?
Which fuses me into you now, and pours my meaning into you?

We understand then do we not?
What I promis'd without mentioning it, have you not accepted?
What the study could not teach—what the preaching could not accomplish is accomplish'd, is it not?

9

Flow on, river! flow with the flood-tide, and ebb with the ebb-tide!
Frolic on, crested and scallop-edg'd waves!
Gorgeous clouds of the sunset! drench with your splendor me, or the men and women generations after
    me!
Cross from shore to shore, countless crowds of passengers!
Stand up, tall masts of Mannahatta! stand up, beautiful hills of Brooklyn!
Throb, baffled and curious brain! throw out questions and answers!
Suspend here and everywhere, eternal float of solution!
Gaze, loving and thirsting eyes, in the house or street or public assembly!
Sound out, voices of young men! loudly and musically call me by my nighest name!
Live, old life! play the part that looks back on the actor or actress!   10
Play the old role, the role that is great or small according as one makes it!
Consider, you who peruse me, whether I may not in unknown ways be looking upon you;
Be firm, rail over the river, to support those who lean idly, yet haste with the hasting current;
Fly on, sea-birds! fly sideways, or wheel in large circles high in the air;

Receive the summer sky, you water, and faithfully hold it till all downcast eyes have time to take it from you!

Diverge, fine spokes of light, from the shape of my head, or any one's head, in the sunlit water!

Come on, ships from the lower bay! pass up or down, white-sail'd schooners, sloops, lighters!

Flaunt away, flags of all nations! be duly lower'd at sunset!

Burn high your fires, foundry chimneys! cast black shadows at nightfall! cast red and yellow light over the tops of the houses!

Appearances, now or henceforth, indicate what you are,   20

You necessary film, continue to envelop the soul,

About my body for me, and your body for you, be hung our divinest aromas,

Thrive, cities—bring your freight, bring your shows, ample and sufficient rivers,

Expand, being than which none else is perhaps more spiritual,

Keep your places, objects than which none else is more lasting.

You have waited, you always wait, you dumb, beautiful ministers,

We receive you with free sense at last, and are insatiate henceforward,

Not you any more shall be able to foil us, or withhold yourselves from us,

We use you, and do not cast you aside—we plant you permanently within us,

We fathom you not—we love you—there is perfection in you also,   30

You furnish your parts toward eternity,

Great or small, you furnish your parts toward the soul.

Out of the Cradle Endlessly Rocking (1881)

This poem first appeared as "A Child's Reminiscence" in the New York *Saturday Press* on December 24, 1859; and a slightly different version was included in the 1860 edition of *Leaves of Grass*. The latter began as follows:

Out of the rocked cradle,
Out of the mocking-bird's throat, the musical shuttle,
Out of the boy's mother's womb, and from the nipples of her breasts,
Out of the Ninth Month midnight,
Over the sterile sands, and the fields beyond, where the child,
  leaving his bed, wandered alone, bareheaded, barefoot,

In the 1860 version, the line "O give me the clew! (it lurks in the night here somewhere)" was followed by

O if I am to have so much, let me have more!
O a word! O what is my destination!
O I fear it is henceforth chaos!
O how joys, dreads, convolutions, human shapes, and all shapes,

spring as from graves around me!
O phantoms! you cover all the land, and all the sea!
O I cannot see in the dimness whether you smile or frown upon me!
O vapor, a look, a word! O well-beloved!
O you dear women's and men's phantoms!

All but the first of those lines were deleted by Whitman in the 1881 edition, which contained the version we are printing. The deletion is exceptionally interesting, since it is fairly certain that Whitman was giving voice, in those lines, to his own feelings of grief and bewilderment at the loss or departure of his lover (at the same time, no less interestingly, seeking to cover up his personal emotion by alluding to a variety of "phantoms").

The 1881 version shows a number of other deletions and emendations. For a general comment and for a line-by-line comparison of the 1860 and 1881 versions, see *The Presence of Walt Whitman*.

Out of the cradle endlessly rocking,
Out of the mocking-bird's throat, the musical shuttle,
Out of the Ninth-month midnight,
Over the sterile sands and the fields beyond, where the child leaving his bed wander'd alone, bare-
    headed, barefoot,
Down from the shower'd halo,
Up from the mystic play of shadows twining and twisting as if they were alive,
Out from the patches of briers and blackberries,
From the memories of the bird that chanted to me,
From your memories sad brother, from the fitful risings and fallings I heard,
From under that yellow half-moon late-risen and swollen as if with tears,   10
From those beginning notes of yearning and love there in the mist,
From the thousand responses of my heart never to cease,
From the myriad thence-arous'd words,
From the word stronger and more delicious than any,
From such as now they start the scene revisiting,
As a flock, twittering, rising, or overhead passing,
Borne hither, ere all eludes me, hurriedly,
A man, yet by these tears a little boy again,
Throwing myself on the sand, confronting the waves,
I, chanter of pains and joys, uniter of here and hereafter,   20
Taking all hints to use them, but swiftly leaping beyond them,
A reminiscence sing.

Once Paumanok,
When the lilac-scent was in the air and Fifth-month grass was growing,
Up this seashore in some briers,
Two feather'd guests from Alabama, two together,
And their nest, and four light-green eggs spotted with brown,
And every day the he-bird to and fro near at hand,
And every day the she-bird crouch'd on her nest, silent, with bright eyes,
And every day I, a curious boy, never too close, never disturbing them,   30
Cautiously peering, absorbing, translating.

Shine! shine! shine!
Pour down your warmth, great sun!
While we bask, we two together.

Two together!
Winds blow south, or winds blow north,
Day come white, or night come black,
Home, or rivers and mountains from home,
Singing all time, minding no time,   40
While we two keep together.

Till of a sudden,
May-be kill'd, unknown to her mate,
One forenoon the she-bird crouch'd not on the nest,
Nor return'd that afternoon, nor the next,
Nor ever appear'd again.

And thenceforward all summer in the sound of the sea,
And at night under the full of the moon in calmer weather,
Over the hoarse surging of the sea,

Or flitting from brier to brier by day,
I saw, I heard at intervals the remaining one, the he-bird,   50
The solitary guest from Alabama.

Blow! blow! blow!
Blow up sea-winds along Paumanok's shore;
I wait and I wait till you blow my mate to me.

Yes, when the stars glisten'd,
All night long on the prong of a moss-scallop'd stake,
Down almost amid the slapping waves,
Sat the lone singer wonderful causing tears.

He call'd on his mate,
He pour'd forth the meanings which I of all men know.   60

Yes my brother I know,
The rest might not, but I have treasur'd every note,
For more than once dimly down to the beach gliding,
Silent, avoiding the moonbeams, blending myself with the shadows,
Recalling now the obscure shapes, the echoes, the sounds and sights after their sorts,
The white arms out in the breakers tirelessly tossing,
I, with bare feet, a child, the wind wafting my hair,
Listen'd long and long.

Listen'd to keep, to sing, now translating the notes,
Following you my brother.   70

Soothe! soothe! soothe!
Close on its wave soothes the wave behind,
And again another behind embracing and lapping, every one close,
But my love soothes not me, not me.

Low hangs the moon, it rose late,
It is lagging—O I think it is heavy with love, with love.

O madly the sea pushes upon the land,
With love, with love.

O night! do I not see my love fluttering out among the breakers?
What is that little black thing I see there in the white?   80

Loud! loud! loud!
Loud I call to you, my love!

High and clear I shoot my voice over the waves,
Surely you must know who is here, is here,
You must know who I am, my love.

Low-hanging moon!
What is that dusky spot in your brown yellow?
O it is the shape, the shape of my mate!
O moon do not keep her from me any longer.

Land! land! O land!   90
Whichever way I turn, O I think you could give me my mate back again if you only would,
For I am almost sure I see her dimly whichever way I look.

O rising stars!
Perhaps the one I want so much will rise, will rise with some of you.

O throat! O trembling throat!
Sound clearer through the atmosphere!
Pierce the woods, the earth,
Somewhere listening to catch you must be the one I want.

Shake out carols!
Solitary here, the night's carols!   100
Carols of lonesome love! death's carols!
Carols under that lagging, yellow, waning moon!
O under that moon where she droops almost down into the sea!
O reckless despairing carols.

But soft! sink low!
Soft! let me just murmur,
And do you wait a moment you husky-nois'd sea,
For somewhere I believe I heard my mate responding to me,
So faint, I must be still, be still to listen,
But not altogether still, for then she might not come immediately to me.   110

Hither my love!
Here I am! here!
With this just-sustain'd note I announce myself to you,
This gentle call is for you my love, for you.

Do not be decoy'd elsewhere,
That is the whistle of the wind, it is not my voice,
That is the fluttering, the fluttering of the spray,
Those are the shadows of leaves.

O darkness! O in vain!
O I am very sick and sorrowful.   120

O brown halo in the sky near the moon, drooping upon the sea!
O troubled reflection in the sea!
O throat! O throbbing heart!
And I singing uselessly, uselessly all the night.

O past! O happy life! O songs of joy!
In the air, in the woods, over fields,
Loved! loved! loved! loved! loved!
But my mate no more, no more with me!
We two together no more.

The aria sinking,   130
All else continuing, the stars shining,
The winds blowing, the notes of the bird continuous echoing,
With angry moans the fierce old mother incessantly moaning,
On the sands of Paumanok's shore gray and rustling,
The yellow half-moon enlarged, sagging down, drooping, the face of the sea almost
     touching,
The boy ecstatic, with his bare feet the waves, with his hair the atmosphere dallying,

The love in the heart long pent, now loose, now at last tumultuously bursting,
The aria's meaning, the ears, the soul, swiftly depositing,
The strange tears down the cheeks coursing,
The colloquy there, the trio, each uttering,   140
The undertone, the savage old mother incessantly crying,
To the boy's soul's questions sullenly timing, some drown'd secret hissing,
To the outsetting bard.

Demon or bird! (said the boy's soul,)
Is it indeed toward your mate you sing? or is it really to me?
For I, that was a child, my tongue's use sleeping, now I have heard you,
Now in a moment I know what I am for, I awake,
And already a thousand singers, a thousand songs, clearer, louder and more sorrowful than yours,
A thousand warbling echoes have started to life within me, never to die.

O you singer solitary, singing by yourself, projecting me,   150

O solitary me listening, never more shall I cease perpetuating you,
Never more shall I escape, never more the reverberations,
Never more the cries of unsatisfied love be absent from me,
Never again leave me to be the peaceful child I was before what there in the night,
By the sea under the yellow and sagging moon,
The messenger there arous'd, the fire, the sweet hell within,
The unknown want, the destiny of me.

O give me the clew! (it lurks in the night here somewhere,)
O if I am to have so much, let me have more!

A word then, (for I will conquer it,)   160
The word final, superior to all,
Subtle, sent up—what is it?—I listen;
Are you whispering it, and have been all the time, you sea waves?
Is that it from your liquid rims and wet sands?

Whereto answering, the sea,
Delaying not, hurrying not,
Whisper'd me through the night, and very plainly before daybreak,
Lisp'd to me the low and delicious word death,
And again death, death, death, death,
Hissing melodious, neither like the bird nor like my arous'd child's heart,   170
But edging near as privately for me rustling at my feet,
Creeping thence steadily up to my ears and laving me softly all over
Death, death, death, death, death.

Which I do not forget,
But fuse the song of my dusky demon and brother,
That he sang to me in the moonlight on Paumanok's gray beach,
With the thousand responsive songs at random,
My own songs awaked from that hour,
And with them the key, the word up from the waves,
The word of the sweetest song and all songs,   180
That strong and delicious word which, creeping to my feet,
(Or like some old crone rocking the cradle, swathed in sweet garments, bending aside,)
The sea whisper'd me.

As I Ebb'd with the Ocean of Life (1860)

1

As I ebb'd with the ocean of life,
As I wended the shores I know,
As I walk'd where the ripples continually wash you Paumanok,
Where they rustle up hoarse and sibilant,
Where the fierce old mother endlessly cries for her castaways,
I musing late in the autumn day, gazing off southward,
Held by this electric self out of the pride of which I utter poems,
Was seiz'd by the spirit that trails in the lines underfoot,
The rim, the sediment that stands for all the water and all the land of the globe.

Fascinated, my eyes reverting from the south, dropt, to follow those slender windrows,   10
Chaff, straw, splinters of wood, weeds, and the sea-gluten,
Scum, scales from shining rocks, leaves of salt-lettuce, left by the tide,
Miles walking, the sound of breaking waves the other side of me,
Paumanok there and then as I thought the old thought of likenesses,
These you presented to me you fish-shaped island,
As I wended the shores I know,
As I walk'd with that electric self seeking types.

2

As I wend to the shores I know not,
As I list to the dirge, the voices of men and women wreck'd,
As I inhale the impalpable breezes that set in upon me,
As the ocean so mysterious rolls toward me closer and closer,
I too but signify at the utmost a little wash'd-up drift,
A few sands and dead leaves to gather,
Gather, and merge myself as part of the sands and drift.

O baffled, balk'd, bent to the very earth,
Oppress'd with myself that I have dared to open my mouth,
Aware now that amid all that blab whose echoes recoil upon me I have not once had the least idea who
    or what I am,   10
But that before all my arrogant poems the real Me stands yet untouch'd, untold, altogether unreach'd,
Withdrawn far, mocking me with mock-congratulatory signs and bows,
With peals of distant ironical laughter at every word I have written,
Pointing in silence to these songs, and then to the sand beneath.

I perceive I have not really understood any thing, not a single object, and that no man ever can,
Nature here in sight of the sea taking advantage of me to dart upon me and sting me,
Because I have dared to open my mouth to sing at all.

3

You oceans both, I close with you,
We murmur alike reproachfully rolling sands and drift, knowing not why,
These little shreds indeed standing for you and me and all.

You friable shore with trails of debris,
You fish-shaped island, I take what is underfoot,
What is yours is mine my father.

I too Paumanok,

I too have bubbled up, floated the measureless float, and been wash'd on your shores,
I too am but a trail of drift and debris,
I too leave little wrecks upon you, you fish-shaped island.   10

I throw myself upon your breast my father,
I cling to you so that you cannot unloose me,
I hold you so firm till you answer me something.

Kiss me my father,
Touch me with your lips as I touch those I love,
Breathe to me while I hold you close the secret of the murmuring I envy.

4

Ebb, ocean of life, (the flow will return,)
Cease not your moaning you fierce old mother,
Endlessly cry for your castaways, but fear not, deny not me,
Rustle not up so hoarse and angry against my feet as I touch you or gather from you.

I mean tenderly by you and all,
I gather for myself and for this phantom looking down where we lead, and following me and mine.

Me and mine, loose windrows, little corpses,
Froth, snowy white, and bubbles,
(See, from my dead lips the ooze exuding at last,
See, the prismatic colors glistening and rolling,)   10
Tufts of straw, sands, fragments,
Buoy'd hither from many moods, one contradicting another,
From the storm, the long calm, the darkness, the swell,
Musing, pondering, a breath, a briny tear, a dab of liquid or soil,
Up just as much out of fathomless workings fermented and thrown,
A limp blossom or two, torn, just as much over waves floating, drifted at random,
Just as much for us that sobbing dirge of Nature,
Just as much whence we come that blare of the cloud-trumpets,
We, capricious, brought hither we know not whence, spread out before you,
You up there walking or sitting,   20
Whoever you are, we too lie in drifts at your feet.

Cavalry Crossing a Ford (1867)

A line in long array where they wind betwixt green islands,
They take a serpentine course, their arms flash in the sun—hark to the musical clank,
Behold the silvery river, in it the splashing horses loitering stop to drink,
Behold the brown-faced men, each group, each person a picture, the negligent rest on
  the saddles,
Some emerge on the opposite bank, others are just entering the ford—while,
Scarlet and blue and snowy white,
The guidon flags flutter gayly in the wind.

Bivouac on a Mountain Side (1867)

I see before me now a traveling army halting,
Below a fertile valley spread, with barns and the orchards of summer,

Behind, the terraced sides of a mountain, abrupt, in places rising high,
Broken, with rocks, with clinging cedars, with tall shapes dingily seen,
The numerous camp-fires scatter'd near and far, some away up on the mountain,
The shadowy forms of men and horses, looming, large-sized, flickering,
And over all the sky—the sky! far, far out of reach, studded, breaking out, the eternal stars.

Vigil Strange I Kept on the Field One Night (1867)

Vigil strange I kept on the field one night;
When you my son and my comrade dropt at my side that day,
One look I but gave which your dear eyes return'd with a look I shall never forget,
One touch of your hand to mine O boy, reach'd up as you lay on the ground,
Then onward I sped in the battle, the even-contested battle,
Till late in the night reliev'd to the place at last again I made my way,
Found you in death so cold dear comrade, found your body son of responding kisses, (never again on earth responding,)
Bared your face in the starlight, curious the scene, cool blew the moderate night-wind,
Long there and then in vigil I stood, dimly around me the battlefield spreading,
Vigil wondrous and vigil sweet there in the fragrant silent night,   10
But not a tear fell, not even a long-drawn sigh, long, long I gazed,
Then on the earth partially reclining sat by your side leaning my chin in my hands,
Passing sweet hours, immortal and mystic hours with you dearest comrade—not a tear, not a word,
Vigil of silence, love and death, vigil for you my son and my soldier,
As onward silently stars aloft, eastward new ones upward stole,
Vigil final for you brave boy, (I could not save you, swift was your death,
I faithfully loved you and cared for you living, I think we shall surely meet again,)
Till at latest lingering of the night, indeed just as the dawn appear'd,
My comrade I wrapt in his blanket, envelop'd well his form,
Folded the blanket well, tucking it carefully over head and carefully under feet,   20
And there and then and bathed by the rising sun, my son in his grave, in his rude-dug grave I deposited,
Ending my vigil strange with that, vigil of night and battle-field dim,
Vigil for boy of responding kisses, (never again on earth responding,)
Vigil for comrade swiftly slain, vigil I never forget, how as day brighten'd,
I rose from the chill ground and folded my soldier well in his blanket,
And buried him where he fell.

When Lilacs Last in the Dooryard Bloom'd (1867)

1

When lilacs last in the dooryard bloom'd,
And the great star early droop'd in the western sky in the night,
I mourn'd, and yet shall mourn with ever-returning spring.

Ever-returning spring, trinity sure to me you bring,
Lilac blooming perennial and drooping star in the west,
And thought of him I love.

2

O powerful western fallen star!
O shades of night—O moody, tearful night!

O great star disappear'd—O the black murk that hides the star!
O cruel hands that hold me powerless—O helpless soul of me!
O harsh surrounding cloud that will not free my soul.

3

In the dooryard fronting an old farm-house near the white-wash'd palings,
Stands the lilac-bush tall-growing with heart-shaped leaves of rich green,
With many a pointed blossom rising delicate, with the perfume strong I love,
With every leaf a miracle—and from this bush in the dooryard,
With delicate-color'd blossoms and heart-shaped leaves of rich green,
A sprig with its flower I break.

4

In the swamp in secluded recesses,
A shy and hidden bird is warbling a song.

Solitary the thrush,
The hermit withdrawn to himself, avoiding the settlements,
Sings by himself a song.

Song of the bleeding throat,
Death's outlet song of life, (for well dear brother I know,
If thou was not granted to sing thou would'st surely die.)

5

Over the breast of the spring, the land, amid cities,
Amid lanes and through old woods, where lately the violets peep'd from the ground, spotting the gray debris,
Amid the grass in the fields each side of the lanes, passing the endless grass,
Passing the yellow-spear'd wheat, every grain from its shroud in the dark-brown fields uprisen,
Passing the apple-tree blows of white and pink in the orchards,
Carrying a corpse to where it shall rest in the grave,
Night and day journeys a coffin.

6

Coffin that passes through lanes and streets,
Through day and night with the great cloud darkening the land,
With the pomp of the inloop'd flags with the cities draped in black,
With the show of the States themselves as of crape-veil'd women standing,
With processions long and winding and the flambeaus of the night,
With the countless torches lit, with the silent sea of faces and the unbared heads,
With the waiting depot, the arriving coffin, and the sombre faces,
With dirges through the night, with the thousand voices rising strong and solemn,
With all the mournful voices of the dirges pour'd around the coffin,
The dim-lit churches and the shuddering organs—where amid these you journey,   10
With the tolling tolling bells' perpetual clang,
Here, coffin that slowly passes,
I give you my sprig of lilac.

7

(Nor for you, for one alone,
Blossoms and branches green to coffins all I bring,
For fresh as the morning, thus would I chant a song for you O sane and sacred death.

All over bouquets of roses,
O death, I cover you over with roses and early lilies,
But mostly and now the lilac that blooms the first,
Copious I break, I break the sprigs from the bushes,
With loaded arms I come, pouring for you,
For you and the coffins all of you O death.)

8

O western orb sailing the heaven,
Now I know what you must have meant as a month since I walk'd,
As I walk'd in silence the transparent shadowy night,
As I saw you had something to tell as you bent to me night after night,
As you droop'd from the sky low down as if to my side, (while the other stars all look'd on,)
As we wander'd together the solemn night, (for something I know not what kept me from sleep,)
As the night advanced, and I saw on the rim of the west how full you were of woe,
As I stood on the rising ground in the breeze in the cool transparent night,
As I watch'd where you pass'd and was lost in the netherward black of the night,
As my soul in its trouble dissatisfied sank, as where you sad orb,   10
Concluded, dropt in the night, and was gone.

9

Sing on there in the swamp,
O singer bashful and tender, I hear your notes, I hear your call,
I hear, I come presently, I understand you,
But a moment I linger, for the lustrous star has detain'd me,
The star my departing comrade holds and detains me.

10

O how shall I warble myself for the dead one there I loved?
And how shall I deck my song for the large sweet soul that has gone?
And what shall my perfume be for the grave of him I love?

Sea-winds blown from east and west,
Blown from the Eastern sea and blown from the Western sea, till there on the prairies meeting,
These and with these and the breath of my chant,
I'll perfume the grave of him I love.

11

O what shall I hang on the chamber walls?
And what shall the pictures be that I hang on the walls,
To adorn the burial-house of him I love?

Pictures of growing spring and farms and homes,
With the Fourth-month eve at sundown, and the gray smoke lucid and bright,
With floods of the yellow gold of the gorgeous, indolent, sinking sun, burning, expanding the air,
With the fresh sweet herbage under foot, and the pale green leaves of the trees prolific,
In the distance the flowing glaze, the breast of the river, with a wind-dapple here and there,
With ranging hills on the banks, with many a line against the sky, and shadows,
And the city at hand with dwellings so dense, and stacks of chimneys,
And all the scenes of life and the workshops, and the workmen homeward returning.

12

Lo, body and soul—this land,
My own Manhattan with spires, and the sparkling and hurrying tides, and the ships,

The varied and ample land, the South and the North in the light, Ohio's shores and flashing Missouri,
And ever the far-spreading prairies cover'd with grass and corn.

Lo, the most excellent sun so calm and haughty,
The violet and purple morn with just-felt breezes,
The gentle soft-born measureless light,
The miracle spreading bathing all, the fulfill'd noon,
The coming eve delicious, the welcome night and the stars,
Over my cities shining all, enveloping man and land.   10

13

Sing on, sing on you gray-brown bird,
Sing from the swamps, the recesses, pour your chant from the bushes,
Limitless out of the dusk, out of the cedars and pines.

Sing on dearest brother, warble your reedy song,
Loud human song, with voice of uttermost woe.

O liquid and free and tender!
O wild and loose to my soul—O wondrous singer!
You only I hear—yet the star holds me, (but will soon depart,)
Yet the lilac with mastering odor holds me.

14

Now while I sat in the day and look'd forth,
In the close of the day with its light and the fields of spring, and the farmers preparing their crops,
In the large unconscious scenery of my land with its lakes and forests,
In the heavenly aerial beauty, (after the perturb'd winds and the storms,)
Under the arching heavens of the afternoon swift passing, and the voices of children and women,
The many-moving sea-tides, and I saw the ships how they sail'd,
And the summer approaching with richness, and the fields all busy with labor,
And the infinite separate houses, how they all went on, each with its meals and minutia of daily usages,
And the streets how their throbbings throbb'd, and the cities pent—lo, then and there,
Falling upon them all and among them all, enveloping me with the rest,   10
Appear'd the cloud, appear'd the long black trail,
And I knew death, its thought, and the sacred knowledge of death.

Then with the knowledge of death as walking one side of me,
And the thought of death close-walking the other side of me,
And I in the middle as with companions, and as holding the hands of companions,
I fled forth to the hiding receiving night that talks not,
Down to the shores of the water, the path by the swamp in the dimness,
To the solemn shadowy cedars and ghostly pines so still.

And the singer so shy to the rest receiv'd me,
The gray-brown bird I know receiv'd us comrades three,   20
And he sang the carol of death, and a verse for him I love.

From deep secluded recesses,
From the fragrant cedars and the ghostly pines so still,
Came the carol of the bird.

And the charm of the carol rapt me,
As I held as if by their hands my comrades in the night,
And the voice of my spirit tallied the song of the bird.

Come lovely and soothing death,
Undulate round the world, serenely arriving, arriving,
In the day, in the night, to all, to each,   30
Sooner or later delicate death.

Prais'd be the fathomless universe,
For life and joy, and for objects and knowledge curious,
And for love, sweet love—but praise! praise! praise!
For the sure-enwinding arms of cool-enfolding death.

Dark mother always gliding near with soft feet,
Have none chanted for thee a chant of fullest welcome?
Then I chant it for thee, I glorify thee above all,
I bring thee a song that when thou must indeed come, come unfalteringly.

Approach strong deliveress,   40
When it is so, when thou hast taken them I joyously sing the dead,
Lost in the loving floating ocean of thee,
Laved in the flood of thy bliss O death.

From me to thee glad serenades,
Dances for thee I propose saluting thee, adornments and feastings for thee,
And the sights of the open landscape and the high-spread sky are fitting,
And life and the fields, and the huge and thoughtful night.

The night in silence under many a star,
The ocean shore and the husky whispering wave whose voice I know,
And the soul turning to thee O vast and well-veil'd death,   50
And the body gratefully nestling close to thee.

Over the tree-tops I float thee a song,
Over the rising and sinking waves, over the myriad fields and the prairies wide,
Over the dense-pack'd cities all and the teeming wharves and ways,
I float this carol with joy, with joy to thee O death.

                                              15

To the tally of my soul,
Loud and strong kept up the gray-brown bird,
With pure deliberate notes spreading filling the night.

Loud in the pines and cedars dim,
Clear in the freshness moist and the swamp-perfume,
And I with my comrades there in the night.

While my sight that was bound in my eyes unclosed,
As to long panoramas of visions.

And I saw askant the armies,
I saw as in noiseless dreams hundreds of battle-flags,   10
Borne through the smoke of the battles and pierc'd with missiles I saw them,
And carried hither and yon through the smoke, and torn and bloody,
And at last but a few shreds left on the staffs, (and all in silence,)
And the staffs all splinter'd and broken.

I saw battle-corpses, myriads of them,
And the white skeletons of young men, I saw them,

I saw the debris and debris of all the slain soldiers of the war,
But I saw they were not as was thought,
They themselves were fully at rest, they suffer'd not,
The living remain'd and suffer'd, the mother suffered,   20
And the wife and the child and the musing comrade suffer'd,
And the armies that remain'd suffer'd.

16

Passing the visions, passing the night,
Passing, unloosing the hold of my comrades' hands,
Passing the song of the hermit bird and the tallying song of my soul,
Victorious song, death's outlet song, yet varying ever-altering song.
As low and wailing, yet clear the notes, rising and falling, flooding the night,
Sadly sinking and fainting, as warning and warning, and yet again bursting with joy,
Covering the earth and filling the spread of the heaven,
As that powerful psalm in the night I heard from recesses,
Passing, I leave thee lilac with heart-shaped leaves,
I leave thee there in the door-yard, blooming, returning with spring.   10

I cease from any song for thee,
From my gaze on thee in the west, fronting the west, communing with thee,
O comrade lustrous with silver face in the night.

Yet each to keep and all, retrievements out of the night,
The song, the wondrous chant of the gray-brown bird,
And the tallying chant, the echo arous'd in my soul,
With the lustrous and drooping star with the countenance full of woe,
With the holders holding my hand nearing the call of the bird,
Comrades mine and I in the midst, and their memory ever to keep, for the dead I loved so well,
For the sweetest, wisest soul of all my days and lands—and this for his dear sake,   20
Lilac and star and bird twined with the chant of my soul,
There in the fragrant pines and the cedars dusk and dim.

From the Preface to the 1855 Edition of Leaves of Grass

America does not repel the past or what it has produced under its forms or amid other politics or the idea of castes or the old religions . . . accepts the lesson with calmness . . . is not so impatient as has been supposed that the slough still sticks to opinions and manners and literature while the life which served its requirements has passed into the new life of the new forms . . . perceives that the corpse is slowly borne from the eating and sleeping rooms of the house . . . perceives that it waits a little while in the door . . . that it was fittest for its days . . . that its action has descended to the stalwart and wellshaped heir who approaches . . . and that he shall be fittest for his days.

The Americans of all nations at any time upon the earth have probably the fullest poetical nature. The United States themselves are essentially the greatest poem. In the history of the earth hitherto the largest and most stirring appear tame and orderly to their ampler largeness and stir. Here at last is something in the doings of man that corresponds with the broadcast doings of the day and night.[1] Here is not merely a nation but a teeming nation of nations. Here is action untied from strings necessarily blind to particulars and details magnificently moving in vast masses. Here is the hospitality which forever indicates heroes. . . .

[1] A phrase which bears striking resemblance to Nick Carraway's musing on the meaning of America to its first settlers in Fitzgerald's *The Great Gatsby*.

Here are the roughs and beards and space and ruggedness and nonchalance that the soul loves. Here the performance disdaining the trivial unapproached in the tremendous audacity of its crowds and groupings and the push of its perspective spreads with crampless and flowing breadth and showers its prolific and splendid extravagance. One sees it must indeed own the riches of the summer and winter, and need never be bankrupt while corn grows from the ground or the orchards drop apples or the bays contain fish or men beget children upon women.

Other states indicate themselves in their deputies . . . but the genius of the United States is not best or most in its executives or legislatures, nor in its ambassadors or authors or colleges or churches or parlors, nor even in its newspapers or inventors . . . but always most in the common people. Their manners speech dress friendships— the freshness and candor of their physiognomy— the picturesque looseness of their carriage . . . their deathless attachment to freedom—their aversion to anything indecorous or soft or mean—the practical acknowledgment of the citizens of one state by the citizens of all other states—the fierceness of their roused resentment—their curiosity and welcome of novelty—their self-esteem and wonderful sympathy—their susceptibility to a slight—the air they have of persons who never knew how it felt to stand in the presence of superiors—the fluency of their speech—their delight in music, the sure symptom of manly tenderness and native elegance of soul . . . their good temper and openhandedness—the terrible significance of their elections—the President's taking off his hat to them not they to him—these too are unrhymed poetry. It awaits the gigantic and generous treatment worthy of it.

The largeness of nature or the nation were monstrous without a corresponding largeness and generosity of the spirit of the citizen. Not nature nor swarming states nor streets and steamships nor prosperous business nor farms nor capital nor learning may suffice for the ideal of man . . . nor suffice the poet. No reminiscences may suffice either. A live nation can always cut a deep mark and can have the best authority the cheapest . . . namely from its own soul. This is the sum of the profitable uses of individuals or states and of present action and grandeur and of the subjects of poets.—As if it were necessary to trot back generation after generation to the eastern records! As if the beauty and sacredness of the demonstrable must fall behind that of the mythical! As if men do not make their mark out of any times! As if the opening of the western continent by discovery and what has transpired since in North and South America were less than the small theatre of the antique or the aimless sleepwalking of the middle ages! The pride of the United States leaves the wealth and finesse of the cities and all returns of commerce and agriculture and all the magnitude of geography or shows of exterior victory to enjoy the breed of fullsized men or one fullsized man unconquerable and simple.

The American poets are to enclose old and new for America is the race of races. Of them a bard is to be commensurate with a people. To him the other continents arrive as contributions . . . he gives them reception for their sake and his own sake. His spirit responds to his country's spirit . . . he incarnates its geography and natural life and rivers and lakes. Mississippi with annual freshets and changing chutes, Missouri and Columbia and Ohio and Saint Lawrence with the falls and beautiful masculine Hudson, do not embouchure where they spend themselves more than they embouchure into him. The blue breadth over the inland sea of Virginia and Maryland and the sea off Massachusetts and Maine and over Manhattan bay and over Champlain and Erie and over Ontario and Huron and Michigan and Superior, and over the Texas and Mexican and Floridian and Cuban seas and over the seas off California and Oregon, is not tallied by the blue breadth of the waters below more than the breadth of above and below is tallied by him. When the long Atlantic coast stretches longer and the Pacific coast stretches longer he easily stretches with them north or south. He spans between them also from east to west and reflects what is between them. On him rise solid growths that offset the growths of pine and cedar and hemlock and liveoak and locust and chestnut and cypress and hickory and limetree and cottonwood and tuliptree and cactus and wildvine and tamarind and persimmon . . . and tangles as tangled as any canebrake or swamp . . . and forests coated with transparent ice and icicles hanging from the boughs and crackling in the wind . . . and sides and peaks of mountains . . . and pasturage sweet and free as savannah or upland or prairie . . . with flights and songs and screams that answer those of the wildpigeon and highhold and orchard-oriole and coot and surf-duck and redshouldered-hawk and fish-hawk and white-ibis and indian-hen and cat-owl and water-pheasant and qua-bird and pied-sheldrake and blackbird and mockingbird and buzzard and condor and nightheron and eagle. To him the hereditary countenance descends both mother's and father's. To him enter the essences of the real things and past and present events—of the enormous diversity of temperature and agriculture and mines—the tribes of red aborigines—the weather-beaten vessels entering new ports or making landings on rocky coasts—the first settlements north or south—the rapid stature and muscle—the haughty defiance of '76, and the war and peace and formation of the constitution . . . the union always surrounded by blatherers and always calm and impregnable—the perpetual coming of immigrants—the wharf-hem'd cities and superior marine—the unsurveyed interior—the loghouses and clearings and wild animals and hunters and trappers . . . the free commerce—the fisheries and whaling and gold-digging—the endless gestation of new states—the convening of Congress every December, the members duly coming up from all climates and the uttermost parts . . . the noble character of the young mechanics and of all free American workmen and workwomen . . . the general ardor and friendliness and enterprise—the perfect equality of the female with the male . . . the large amativeness—the fluid movement of the population—the factories and mercantile life and laborsaving machinery—the Yankee swap—the New-York firemen and the target excursion—the southern plantation life—the character of the northeast and of the northwest and southwest—slavery and the tremulous spreading of hands to protect it, and the stern opposition to it which shall never cease till it ceases or the speaking of tongues and the moving of lips cease. For such the expression of the American poet is to be transcendant and new. It is to be indirect and not direct or descriptive or epic. Its quality goes through these to much more. Let the age and wars of other nations be chanted and their eras and characters be illustrated and that finish the verse. Not so the great psalm of the republic. Here the theme is creative and has vista. Here comes one among the well-beloved stonecutters and plans with decision and science and sees the solid and beautiful forms of the future where there are now no solid forms.

Of all nations the United States with veins full of poetical stuff most need poets and will doubtless have the greatest and use them the greatest. Their Presidents shall not be their common referee so much as their poets shall. Of all mankind the great poet is the equable man. Not in him but off from him things are grotesque or eccentric or fail of their sanity. Nothing out of its place is good and nothing in its place is bad. He bestows on every object or quality its fit proportions neither more nor less. He is the arbiter of the diverse and he is the key. He is the equalizer of his age and land . . . he supplies what wants supplying and checks what wants checking. If peace is the routine out of him speaks the spirit of peace, large, rich, thrifty, building vast and populous cities, encouraging agriculture and the arts and commerce—lighting the study of man, the soul, immortality—federal, state or municipal government, marriage, health, free trade, inter-travel by land and sea . . . nothing too close, nothing too far off . . . the stars not too far off. In war he is the most deadly force of the war. Who recruits him recruits horse and foot . . . he fetches parks of artillery the best that engineer ever knew. If the time becomes slothful and heavy he knows how to arouse it . . . he can make every word he speaks draw blood. Whatever stagnates in the flat of custom or obedience or legislation he never stagnates. Obedience does not master him, he masters it. High up out of reach he stands turning a concentrated light . . . he turns the pivot with his finger . . . he baffles the swiftest runners as he stands and easily overtakes and envelops them. The time straying toward infidelity and confections and persiflage he withholds by his steady faith . . . he spreads out his dishes . . . he offers the sweet firmfibred meat that grows men and women. His brain is the ultimate brain. He is no arguer . . . he is judgment. He judges not as the judge judges but as the sun falling around a helpless thing. As he sees the farthest he has the most faith. His thoughts are the hymns of the praise of things. In the talk on the soul and eternity and God off of his equal plane he is silent. He sees eternity less like a play with a prologue and denouement . . . he sees eternity in men and women . . . he does not see men and women as dreams or dots. Faith is the antiseptic of the soul . . . it pervades the common people and preserves them . . . they never give up believing and expecting and trusting There is that indescribable freshness and unconsciousness about an illiterate person that humbles and mocks the power of the noblest expressive genius. The poet sees for a certainty how one not a great artist may be just as sacred as the greatest artist. . . . The power to destroy or remould is freely used by him but never the power of attack. What is past is past. If he does not expose superior models and prove himself by every step he takes he is not what is wanted. The presence of the greatest poet conquers . . . not parleying or struggling or any prepared attempts. Now he has passed that way see after him! there is not left any vestige of despair or misanthropy or cunning or exclusiveness or the ignominy of a nativity or color or delusion of hell or the necessity of hell . . . and no man thenceforward shall be degraded for ignorance or weakness or sin.

The greatest poet hardly knows pettiness or triviality. If he breathes into any thing that was before thought small it dilates with the grandeur and life of the universe. He is a seer . . . he is individual . . . he is complete in himself . . . the others are as good as he, only he sees it and they do not. He is not one of the chorus . . . he does not stop for any regulations . . . he is the president of regulation. What the eyesight does to the rest he does to the rest. Who knows the curious mystery of the eyesight? The other senses corroborate themselves, but this is removed from any proof but its own and foreruns the identities of the spiritual world. A single glance of it mocks all the investigations of man and all the instruments and books of the earth and all reasoning. What is marvelous? what is unlikely? what is impossible or baseless or vague? after you have once just opened the space of a peachpit and given audience to far and near and to the sunset and had all things enter with electric swiftness softly and duly without confusion or jostling or jam.

The land and sea, the animals fishes and birds, the sky of heaven and the orbs, the forests mountains and rivers, are not small themes . . . but folks expect of the poet to indicate more than the beauty and dignity which always attach to dumb real objects . . . they expect him to indicate the path between reality and their souls. Men and women perceive the beauty well enough . . . probably as well as he. The passionate tenacity of hunters, woodmen, early risers, cultivators of gardens and orchards and fields, the love of healthy women for the manly form, seafaring persons, drivers of horses, the passion for light and the open air, all is an old varied sign of the unfailing perception of

beauty and of a residence of the poetic in outdoor people. They can never be assisted by poets to perceive . . . some may but they never can. The poetic quality is not marshalled in rhyme or uniformity or abstract addresses to things nor in melancholy complaints or good precepts, but is the life of these and much else and is in the soul. The profit of rhyme is that it drops seeds of a sweeter and more luxuriant rhyme, and of uniformity that it conveys itself into its own roots in the ground out of sight. The rhyme and uniformity of perfect poems show the free growth of metrical laws and bud from them as unerringly and loosely as lilacs or roses on a bush, and take shapes as compact as the shapes of chestnuts and oranges and melons and pears, and shed the perfume impalpable to form. The fluency and ornaments of the finest poems or music of orations or recitations are not independent but dependent. All beauty comes from beautiful blood and a beautiful brain. If the greatnesses are in conjunction in a man or woman it is enough . . . the fact will prevail through the universe . . . but the gaggery and gilt of a million years will not prevail. Who troubles himself about his ornaments or fluency is lost. This is what you shall do: Love the earth and sun and the animals, despise riches, give alms to every one that asks, stand up for the stupid and crazy, devote your income and labor to others, hate tyrants, argue not concerning God, have patience and indulgence toward the people, take off your hat to nothing known or unknown or to any man or number of men, go freely with powerful uneducated persons and with the young and with the mothers of families, read these leaves in the open air every season of every year of your life, reexamine all you have been told at school or church or in any book, dismiss whatever insults your own soul, and your very flesh shall be a great poem and have the richest fluency not only in its words but in the silent lines of its lips and face and between the lashes of your eyes and in every motion and joint of your body. . . . The poet shall not spend his time in unneeded work. He shall know that the ground is always plowed and manured . . . others may not know it but he shall. He shall go directly to the creation. His trust shall master the trust of everything he touches . . . and shall master all attachment.

The known universe has one complete lover and that is the greatest poet. He consumes an eternal passion and is indifferent which chance happens and which possible contingency of fortune or misfortune and persuades daily and hourly his delicious pay. What balks or breaks others is fuel for his burning progress to contact and amorous joy. Other proportions of the reception of pleasure dwindle to nothing to his proportions. All expected from heaven or from the highest he is rapport with in the sight of the daybreak or a scene of the winterwoods or the presence of children playing or with his arm round the neck of a man or woman. His love above all love has leisure and expanse . . . he leaves room ahead of himself. He is no irresolute or suspicious lover . . . he is sure . . . . he scorns intervals. His experience and the showers and thrills are not for nothing. Nothing can jar him . . . suffering and darkness cannot—death and fear cannot. To him complaint and jealousy and envy are corpses buried and rotten in the earth . . . he saw them buried. The sea is not surer of the shore or the shore of the sea than he is of the fruition of his love and of all perfection and beauty.

From Democratic Vistas (1871)

It may be claim'd, (and I admit the weight of the claim,) that common and general worldly prosperity, and a populace well-to-do, and with all life's material comforts, is the main thing, and is enough. It may be argued that our republic is, in performance, really enacting today the grandest arts, poems, etc., by beating up the wilderness into fertile farms, and in her railroads, ships, machinery, etc. And it may be ask'd, Are these not better, indeed, for America, than any utterances even of greatest rhapsode, artist, or literatus?

I too hail those achievements with pride and joy: then answer that the soul of man will not with such only—nay, not with such at all—be finally satisfied; but needs what, (standing on these and on all things, as the feet stand on the ground), is addressed to the loftiest, to itself alone.

Out of such considerations, such truths, arises for treatment in these Vistas the important question of character, of an American stock-personality, with literatures and arts for outlets and return-expressions, and, of course, to correspond, within outlines common to all. To these, the main affair, the thinkers of the United States, in general so acute, have either given feeblest attention, or have remain'd, and remain, in a state of somnolence.

For my part, I would alarm and caution even the political and business reader, and to the utmost extent, against the prevailing delusion that the establishment of free political institutions, and plentiful intellectual smartness, with general good order, physical plenty, industry, etc. (desirable and precious advantages as they all are), do, of themselves, determine and yield to our experiment of democracy the fruitage of success. With such advantages at present fully, or almost fully, possess'd —the Union just issued victorious, from the struggle with the only foes it need ever fear (namely, those within itself, the interior ones), and with unprecedented materialistic advancement—society, in these States, is canker'd, crude, superstitious and rotten. Political, or law-made society is, and private, or voluntary society, is also. In any vigor, the element of the moral conscience, the most important, the verteber to State or man, seems to me either entirely lacking, or seriously enfeebled or ungrown.

I say we had best look our times and lands searchingly in the face, like a physician diagnosing some deep disease. Never was there, perhaps, more hollowness at heart than at present, and here in the United States. Genuine belief seems to have left us. The underlying principles of the States are not honestly believ'd in (for all this hectic glow, and these melodramatic screamings), nor is humanity itself believ'd in. What penetrating eye does not everywhere see through the mask? The spectacle is appalling. We live in an atmosphere of hypocrisy throughout. The men believe not in the women, nor the women in the men. A scornful superciliousness rules in literature. The aim of all the *littérateurs* is to find something to make fun of. A lot of churches, sects, etc., the most dismal phantasms I know, usurp the name of religion. Conversation is a mass of badinage. From deceit in the spirit, the mother of all false deeds, the offspring is already incalculable. An acute and candid person, in the revenue department in Washington, who is led by the course of his employment to regularly visit the cities, north, south, and west, to investigate frauds, has talked much with me about his discoveries. The depravity of the business classes of our country is not less than has been supposed, but infinitely greater. The official services of America, national, state, and municipal, in all their branches and departments, except the judiciary, are saturated in corruption, bribery, falsehood, maladministration; and the judiciary is tainted. The great cities reek with respectable as much as non-respectable robbery and scoundrelism. In fashionable life, flippancy, tepid amours, weak infidelism, small aims, or no aims at all, only to kill time. In business (this all-devouring modern word, business), the one sole object is, by any means, pecuniary gain. The magician's serpent in the fable ate up all the other serpents; and moneymaking is our magician's serpent, remaining today sole master of the field. The best class we show, is but a mob of fashionably dress'd speculators and vulgarians. True, indeed, behind this fantastic farce, enacted on the visible stage of society, solid things and stupendous labors are to be discover'd, existing crudely and going on in the background, to advance and tell themselves in time. Yet the truths are none the less terrible. I say that our New World democracy, however great a success in uplifting the masses out of their sloughs, in materialistic development, products, and in a certain highly deceptive superficial popular intellectuality, is, so far, an almost complete failure in its social aspects, and in really grand religious, moral, literary, and æsthetic results. In vain do we march with unprecedented strides to empire so colossal, outvying the antique, beyond Alexander's, beyond the proudest sway of Rome. In vain have we annex'd Texas, California, Alaska, and reach north for Canada and south for Cuba. It is as if we were somehow being endow'd with a vast and more and more thoroughly appointed body, and then left with little or no soul.

Let me illustrate further, as I write, with current observation, localities, etc. The subject is important, and will bear repetition. After an absence, I am now again (September 1870) in New York City and Brooklyn, on a few weeks' vacation. The splendor, picturesqueness, and oceanic amplitude and rush of these great cities, the unsurpassed situation, rivers and bay, sparkling sea-tides, costly and lofty new buildings, façades of marble and iron, of original grandeur and elegance of design, with the masses of gay color, the preponderance of white and blue, the flags flying, the endless ships, the tumultuous streets, Broadway, the heavy, low,

musical roar, hardly ever intermitted, even at night; the jobbers' houses, the rich shops, the wharves, the great Central Park, and the Brooklyn Park of hills (as I wander among them this beautiful fall weather, musing, watching, absorbing)—the assemblages of the citizens in their groups, conversations, trades, evening amusements, or along the by-quarters—these, I say, and the like of these, completely satisfy my senses of power, fullness, motion, etc., and give me, through such senses and appetites, and through my æsthetic conscience, a continued exaltation and absolute fulfillment. Always and more and more, as I cross the East and North rivers, the ferries, or with the pilots in their pilot-houses, or pass an hour in Wall Street, or the Gold Exchange, I realize (if we must admit such partialisms) that not Nature alone is great in her fields of freedom and the open air, in her storms, the shows of night and day, the mountains, forests, sea—but in the artificial, the work of man too is equally great—in this profusion of teeming humanity—in these ingenuities, streets, goods, houses, ships—these hurrying, feverish, electric crowds of men, their complicated business genius (not least among the geniuses), and all this mighty, many-threaded wealth and industry concentrated here.

But sternly discarding, shutting our eyes to the glow and grandeur of the general superficial effect, coming down to what is of the only real importance, Personalities, and examining minutely, we question, we ask, Are there, indeed, *men* here worthy the name? Are there athletes? Are there perfect women, to match the generous material luxuriance? Is there a pervading atmosphere of beautiful manners? Are there crops of fine youths, and majestic old persons? Are there arts worthy freedom and a rich people? Is there a great moral and religious civilization—the only justification of a great material one? Confess that to severe eyes, using the moral microscope upon humanity, a sort of dry and flat Sahara appears, these cities, crowded with petty grotesques, malformations, phantoms, playing meaningless antics. Confess that everywhere, in shop, street, church, theatre, barroom, official chair, are pervading flippancy and vulgarity, low cunning infidelity—everywhere the youth puny, impudent, foppish, prematurely ripe—everywhere an abnormal libidinousness, unhealthy forms male, female, painted, padded, dyed, chignon'd, muddy complexions, bad blood, the capacity for good motherhood decreasing or de-ceas'd, shallow motions of beauty, with a range of manners, or rather lack of manners (considering the advantages enjoy'd), probably the meanest to be seen in the world.

Of all this, and these lamentable conditions, to breathe into them the breath recuperative of sane and heroic life, I say a new-founded literature, not merely to copy and reflect existing surfaces, or pander to what is called taste—not only to amuse, pass away time, celebrate the beautiful, the refined, the past, or exhibit technical, rhythmic, or grammatical dexterity—but a literature underlying life, religious, consistent with science, handling the elements and forces with competent power, teaching and training men—and, as perhaps the most precious of its results, achieving the entire redemption of woman out of these incredible holds and webs of silliness, millinery, and every kind of dyspeptic depletion—and thus insuring to the States a strong and sweet Female Race, a race of perfect Mothers—is what is needed.

And now, in the full conception of these facts and points, and all that they infer, pro and con—with yet unshaken faith in the elements of the American masses, the composites, of both sexes, and even consider'd as individuals—and ever recognizing in them the broadest bases of the best literary and æsthetic appreciation—I proceed with my speculations, Vistas.

. . .

Approaching thus the momentous spaces, and considering with reference to a new and greater personalism, the needs and possibilities of American imaginative literature, through the medium-light of what we have already broach'd, it will at once be appreciated that a vast gulf of difference separates the present accepted condition of these spaces, inclusive of what is floating in them, from any condition adjusted to, or fit for, the world, the America, there sought to be indicated, and the copious races of complete men and women along these Vistas crudely outlined. It is, in some sort, no less a difference than lies between that long-continued nebular state and vagueness of the astronomical worlds, compared with the subsequent state, the definitely-form'd worlds themselves, duly compacted, clustering in systems, hung up there, chandeliers of the universe, beholding and mutually lit by each other's lights, serving for ground of all substantial foothold, all vulgar uses—yet serv-

ing still more as an undying chain and echelon of spiritual proofs and shows. A boundless field to fill! A new creation, with needed orbic works launch'd forth, to revolve in free and lawful circuits—to move, self-poised, through the ether, and shine like heaven's own suns! With such, and nothing less, we suggest that New World literature, fit to rise upon, cohere, and signalize in time, these States.

What, however, do we more definitely mean by New World literature? Are we not doing well enough here already? Are not the United States this day busily using, working, more printer's type, more presses than any other country? uttering and absorbing more publications than any other? Do not our publishers fatten quicker and deeper? (helping themselves, under shelter of a delusive and sneaking law, or rather absence of law, to most of their forage, poetical, pictorial, historical, romantic, even comic, without money and without price—and fiercely resisting the timidest proposal to pay for it). Many will come under this delusion—but my purpose is to dispel it. I say that a nation may hold and circulate rivers and oceans of very readable print, journals, magazines, novels, library books, "poetry," &c.—such as the States today possess and circulate—of unquestionable aid and value—hundreds of new volumes annually composed and brought out here, respectable enough, indeed unsurpass'd in smartness and erudition—with further hundreds, or rather millions (as by free forage or theft aforementioned), also thrown into the market—and yet, all the while, the said nation, land, strictly speaking, may possess no literature at all.

Repeating our inquiry, what, then, do we mean by real literature? especially the democratic literature of the future? Hard questions to meet. The clues are inferential and turn us to the past. At best, we can only offer suggestions, comparisons, circuits.

It must still be reiterated, as, for the purpose of these memoranda, the deep lesson of history and time, that all else in the contributions of a nation or age, through its politics, materials, heroic personalities, military *éclat*, etc., remains crude, and defers, in any close and thorough-going estimate, until vitalized by national, original achetypes in literature. They only put the nation in form, finally tell anything—prove, complete anything—perpetuate anything. Without doubt, some of the richest and most powerful and populous communities of the antique world, and some of the grandest personalities and events, have, to after and present times, left themselves entirely unbequeath'd. Doubtless, greater than any that have come down to us, were among those lands, heroisms, persons, that have not come down to us at all, even by name, date, or location. Others have arrived safely, as from voyages over wide, century-stretching seas. The little ships, the miracles that have buoy'd them, and by incredible chances safely convey'd them (or the best of them, their meaning and essence) over long wastes, darkness, lethargy, ignorance, etc., have been a few inscriptions—a few immortal compositions, small in size, yet compassing what measureless values of reminiscence, contemporary portraitures, manners, idioms and beliefs, with deepest inference, hint, thought, to tie and touch forever the old, new body, and the old, new soul! These! and still these! bearing the freight so dear—dearer than pride—dearer than love. All the best experience of humanity, folded, saved, freighted to us here. Some of these tiny ships we call Old and New Testament, Homer, Aeschylus, Plato, Juvenal, etc. Precious minims! I think, if we were forced to choose, rather than have you, and the likes of you, and what belongs to, and has grown of you, blotted out and gone, we could better afford, appalling as that would be, to lose all actual ships, this day fasten'd by wharf, or floating on wave, and see them, with all their cargoes, scuttled and sent to the bottom.

Gathered by geniuses of city, race or age, and put by them in highest of art's forms, namely, the literary form, the peculiar combinations and the outshows of that city, age, or race, its particular modes of the universal attributes and passions, its faiths, heroes, lovers and gods, wars, traditions, struggles, crimes, emotions, joys (for the subtle spirit of these), having been pass'd on to us to illumine our own selfhood, and its experiences— what they supply, indispensable and highest, if taken away, nothing else in all the world's boundless storehouses could make up to us, or ever again return.

For us, along the great highways of time, those monuments stand—those forms of majesty and beauty. For us those beacons burn through all the nights. Unknown Egyptians, graving hieroglyphs; Hindus, with hymn and apothegm and endless epic; Hebrew prophet, with spirituality, as in flashes of lightning, conscience like red-hot iron, plaintive songs and screams of vengeance for tyrannies and enslavement; Christ, with bent head, brooding love

and peace, like a dove; Greek, creating eternal shapes of physical and æsthetic proportion; Roman, lord of satire, the sword, and the codex;—of the figures, some far off and veil'd, others nearer and visible; Dante, stalking with lean form, nothing but fiber, not a grain of superfluous flesh; Angelo, and the great painters, architects, musicians; rich Shakspere, luxuriant as the sun, artist and singer of feudalism in its sunset, with all the gorgeous colors, owner thereof, and using them at will; and so to such as German Kant and Hegel, where they, though near us, leaping over the ages, sit again, impassive, imperturbable, like the Egyptian gods. Of these, and the like of these, is it too much, indeed, to return to our favorite figure, and view them as orbs and systems of orbs, moving in free paths in the spaces of that other heaven, the kosmic intellect, the soul?

Ye powerful and resplendent ones! ye were, in your atmospheres, grown not for America, but rather for her foes, the feudal and the old—while our genius is democratic and modern. Yet could ye, indeed, but breathe your breath of life into our New World's nostrils—not to enslave us as now, but, for our needs, to breed a spirit like your own —perhaps (dare we to say it?) to dominate, even destroy, what you yourselves have left! On your plane, and no less, but even higher and wider, must we mete and measure for today and here. I demand races of orbic bards, with unconditioned, uncompromising sway. Come forth, sweet democratic despots of the west!

By points like these we, in reflection, token what we mean by any land's or people's genuine literature. And thus compared and tested, judging amid the influence of loftiest products only, what do our current copious fields of print, covering in manifold forms, the United States, better, for an analogy, present, than, as in certain regions of the sea, those spreading, undulating masses of squid, through which the whale swimming, with head half out, feeds?

Not but that doubtless our current so-called literature, (like an endless supply of small coin,) performs a certain service, and maybe too, the service needed for the time, (the preparation-service, as children learn to spell). Everybody reads, and truly nearly everybody writes, either books, or for the magazines or journals. The matter has magnitude, too, after a sort. But is it really advancing? or, has it advanced for a long while? There is something impressive about the huge editions of the dailies and weeklies, the mountain-stacks of white paper piled in the press-vaults, and the proud, crashing, ten-cylinder presses, which I can stand and watch any time by the half hour. Then (though the States in the field of imagination present not a single first-class work, not a single great literatus), the main objects, to amuse, to titillate, to pass away time, to circulate the news, and rumors of news, to rhyme, and read rhyme, are yet attain'd, and on a scale of infinity. Today, in books, in the rivalry of writers, especially novelists, success (so-called) is for him or her who strikes the mean flat average, the sensational appetite for stimulus, incident, persiflage, etc., and depicts, to the common caliber, sensual, exterior life. To such, or the luckiest of them, as we see, the audiences are limitless and profitable; but they cease presently. While this day, or any day, to workmen portraying interior or spiritual life, the audiences were limited, and often laggard—but they last forever.

Compared with the past, our modern science soars, and our journals serve—but ideal and even ordinary romantic literature, does not, I think, substantially advance. Behold the prolific brood of the contemporary novel, magazine tale, theatre play, etc. The same endless thread of tangled and superlative love-story, inherited, apparently from the Amadises and Palmerins of the 13th, 14th, and 15th centuries over there in Europe. The costumes and associations brought down to date, the seasoning hotter and more varied, the dragons and ogres left out—but the *thing*, I should say, has not advanced—is just as sensational, just as strain'd—remains about the same, nor more, nor less.

What is the reason our time, our lands, that we see no fresh local courage, sanity, of our own—the Mississippi, stalwart Western men, real mental and physical facts, Southerners, etc., in the body of our literature? especially the poetic part of it. But always, instead, a parcel of dandies and ennuyees, dapper little gentlemen from abroad, who flood us with their thin sentiment of parlors, parasols, piano songs, tinkling rhymes, the five-hundredth importation—or whimpering and crying about something, chasing one aborted conceit after another, and forever occupied in dyspeptic amours with dyspeptic women. While, current and novel, the grandest events and revolutions, and stormiest passions of history, are crossing today with unparalleled rapidity and magnificence over the stages of our own and all the continents, offering new materials, opening new vistas, with largest needs,

inviting the daring launching forth of conceptions in literature, inspired by them, soaring in highest regions, serving art in its highest (which is only the other name for serving God, and serving humanity), where is the man of letters, where is the book, with any nobler aim than to follow in the old track, repeat what has been said before—and, as its utmost triumph, sell well, and be erudite or elegant?

Mark the roads, the processes, through which these States have arrived, standing easy, henceforth ever-equal, ever-compact, in their range today. European adventures? the most antique? Asiatic or African? old history—miracles—romances? Rather, our own unquestion'd facts. They hasten, incredible, blazing bright as fire. From the deeds and days of Columbus down to the present, and including the present—and especially the late Secession War—when I con them, I feel, every leaf, like stopping to see if I have not made a mistake, and fall'n on the splendid figments of some dream. But it is no dream. We stand, live, move, in the huge flow of our age's materialism—in its spirituality. We have founded for us the most positive of lands. The founders have pass'd to other spheres—but what are these terrible duties they have left us?

Their policies the United States have, in my opinion, with all their faults, already substantially establish'd, for good, on their own native, sound, long-vista'd principles, never to be overturn'd, offering a sure basis for all the rest. With that, their future religious forms, sociology, literature, teachers, schools, costumes, etc., are of course to make a compact whole, uniform, on tallying principles. For how can we remain, divided, contradicting ourselves this way?[1] I say we can only attain harmony and stability by consulting ensemble and the ethic purports, and faithfully building upon them. For the New World, indeed, after two grand stages of preparation-strata, I perceive that now a third stage,

---

[1] Note, today, an instructive, curious spectacle and conflict. Science (twin, in its fields, of Democracy in its) —Science, testing absolutely all thoughts, all works, has already burst well upon the world—a sun, mounting, most illuminating, most glorious—surely never again to set. But against it, deeply entrench'd, holding possession, yet remains (not only through the churches and schools, but by imaginative literature, and unregenerative poetry), the fossil theology of the mythic-materialistic, superstitious, untaught and credulous, fable-loving, primitive ages of humanity [Whitman].

being ready for (and without which the other two were useless), with unmistakable signs appears. The First stage was the planning and putting on record the political foundation rights of immense masses of people—indeed all people—in the organization of republican National, State, and municipal governments, all constructed with reference to each, and each to all. This is the American programme, not for classes, but for universal man, and is embodied in the compacts of the Declaration of Independence, and, as it began and has now grown, with its amendments, the Federal Constitution—and in the State governments, with all their interiors, and with general suffrage; those having the sense not only of what is in themselves, but that their certain several things started, planted, hundreds of others in the same direction duly arise and follow. The Second stage relates to material prosperity, wealth, produce, laborsaving machines, iron, cotton, local, State, and continental railways, intercommunication and trade with all lands, steamships, mining, general employment, organization of great cities, cheap appliances for comfort, numberless technical schools, books, newspapers, a currency for money circulation, etc. The Third stage, rising out of the previous ones, to make them and all illustrious, I, now, for one, promulge, announcing a native expression-spirit, getting into form, adult, and through mentality, for these States, self-contain'd, different from others, more expansive, more rich and free, to be evidenced by original authors and poets to come, by American personalities, plenty of them, male and female, traversing the States, none excepted—and by native superber tableaux and growths of language, songs, operas, orations, lectures, architecture—and by a sublime and serious Religious Democracy sternly taking command, dissolving the old, sloughing off surfaces, and from its own interior and vital principles, reconstructing, democratizing society.

. . .

In the future of these States must arise poets immenser far, and make great poems of death. The poems of life are great, but there must be the poems of the purports of life, not only in itself, but beyond itself. I have eulogized Homer, the sacred bards of Jewry, Aeschylus, Juvenal, Shakspere, etc., and acknowledged their inestimable value. But (with perhaps the exception in some, not all respects, of the second-mention'd) I say there must, for future and democratic purposes, appear poets (dare I say so?) of higher class even, than any of those—poets not only possess'd of the religious fire and abandon of Isaiah, luxuriant in the epic talent of Homer, or for proud characters as in Shakspere, but consistent with the Hegelian formulas, and consistent with modern science. America needs, and the world needs, a class of bards who will, now and ever, so link and tally the rational physical being of man, with the ensembles of time and space, and with this vast and multiform show, Nature, surrounding him, ever tantalizing him, equally a part, and yet not a part of him, as to essentially harmonize, satisfy, and put at rest. Faith, very old, now scared away by science, must be restored, brought back by the same power that caused her departure—restored with new sway, deeper, wider, higher than ever. Surely, this universal ennui, this coward fear, this shuddering at death, these low, degrading views, are not always to rule the spirit pervading future society, as it has the past, and does the present. What the Roman Lucretius sought most nobly, yet all too blindly, negatively to do for his age and its successors, must be done positively by some great coming literatus, especially poet, who, while remaining fully poet, will absorb whatever science indicates, with spiritualism, and out of them, and out of his own genius, will compose the great poem of death. Then will man indeed confront Nature, and confront time and space, both with science, and *con amore*, and take his right place, prepared for life, master of fortune and misfortune. And then that which was long wanted will be supplied, and the ship that had it not before in all her voyages, will have an anchor.

There are still other standards, suggestions, for products of high literatuses. That which really balances and conserves the social and political world is not so much legislation, police, treaties, and dread of punishment, as the latent eternal intuitional sense, in humanity, of fairness, manliness, decorum, etc. Indeed, this perennial regulation, control, and oversight, by self-suppliance, is *sine qua non* to democracy; and a highest, widest aim of democratic literature may well be to bring forth, cultivate, brace, and strengthen this sense, in individuals and society. A strong mastership of the general inferior self by the superior self, is to be aided, secured, indirectly, but surely, by the literatus, in his works, shaping, for individual or aggregate democracy, a great passionate body, in and along with which goes a great masterful spirit.

And still, providing for contingencies, I fain confront the fact, the need of powerful native philosophs and orators and bards, these States, as rallying points to come, in times of danger, and to fend off ruin and defection. For history is long, long, long. Shift and turn the combinations of the statement as we may, the problem of the future of America is in certain respects as dark as it is vast. Pride, competition, segregation, vicious wilfulness, and license beyond example, brood already upon us. Unwieldly and immense, who shall hold in behemoth? who bridle leviathan? Flaunt it as we choose, athwart and over the roads of our progress loom huge uncertainty, and dreadful, threatening gloom. It is useless to deny it: Democracy grows rankly up the thickest, noxious, deadliest plants and fruits of all—brings worse and worse invaders —needs newer, larger, stronger, keener compensations and compellers.

Our lands, embracing so much (embracing indeed the whole, rejecting none), hold in their breast that flame also, capable of consuming themselves, consuming us all. Short as the span of our national life has been, already have death and downfall crowded close upon us—and will again crowd close, no doubt, even if warded off. Ages to come may never know, but I know, how narrowly during the late Secession War—and more than once, and more than twice or thrice—our Nationality (wherein bound up, as in a ship in a storm, depended, and yet depend, all our best life, all hope, all value), just grazed, just by a hair escaped destruction. Alas! to think of them! the agony and bloody sweat of certain of those hours! those cruel, sharp, suspended crises!

Even today, amid these whirls, incredible flippancy, and blind fury of parties, infidelity, entire lack of first-class captains and leaders, added to the plentiful meanness and vulgarity of the ostensible masses—that problem, the labor question, beginning to open like a yawning gulf, rapidly widening every year—what prospect have we? We sail a dangerous sea of seething currents, cross and undercurrents, vortices—all so dark, untried—and whither shall we turn? It seems as if the Almighty had spread before this nation charts of imperial destinies, dazzling as the sun, yet with many a deep intestine difficulty, and human aggregate of cankerous imperfection—saying, lo! the roads, the only plans of development, long and varied with all terrible balks and ebullitions. You said in your soul, I will be empire of empires, overshadowing all else,

past and present, putting the history of Old-World dynasties, conquests behind me, as of no account— making a new history, a history of democracy, making old history a dwarf—I alone inaugurating largeness, culminating time. If these, O lands of America, are indeed the prizes, the determination of your soul, be it so. But behold the cost, and already specimens of the cost. Thought you greatness was to ripen for you like a pear? If you would have greatness, know that you must conquer it through ages, centuries—must pay for it with a proportionate price. For you too, as for all lands, the struggle, the traitor, the wily person in office, scrofulous wealth, the surfeit of prosperity, the demonism of greed, the hell of passion, the decay of faith, the long postponement, the fossil-like lethargy, the ceaseless need of revolutions, prophets, thunderstorms, deaths, births, new projections and invigorations of ideas and men.

Yet I have dream'd, merged in that hidden-tangled problem of our fate, whose long unraveling stretches mysteriously through time—dream'd out, portray'd, hinted already—a little or a larger band—a band of brave and true, unprecedented yet —arm'd and equipt at every point—the members separated, it may be, by different dates and States, or south, or north, or east, or west—Pacific, Atlantic, Southern, Canadian—a year, a century here, and other centuries there—but always one, compact in soul, conscience-conserving, God-inculcating, inspired achievers, not only in literature, the greatest art, but achievers in all art—a new, undying order, dynasty, from age to age transmitted—a band, a class, at least as fit to cope with current years, our dangers, needs, as those who, for their times, so long, so well, in armor or in cowl, upheld and made illustrious, that far-back feudal, priestly world. To offset chivalry, indeed, those vanish'd countless knights, old altars, abbeys, priests, ages and strings of ages, a knightlier and more sacred cause today demands, and shall supply, in a New World, to larger, grander work, more than the counterpart and tally of them.

Arrived now, definitely, at an apex for these Vistas, I confess that the promulgation and belief in such a class or institution—a new and greater literatus order—its possibility, (nay certainty,) underlies these entire speculations—and that the rest, the other parts, as superstructures, are all founded upon it. It really seems to me the condition, not only of our future national and democratic development, but of our perpetuation. In the highly artificial and materialistic bases of modern civilization, with the corresponding arrangements and methods of living, the force-infusion of intellect alone, the depraving influences of riches just as much as poverty, the absence of all high ideals in character—with the long series of tendencies, shapings, which few are strong enough to resist, and which now seem, with steam-engine speed, to be everywhere turning out the generations of humanity like uniform iron castings—all of which, as compared with the feudal ages, we can yet do nothing better than accept, make the best of, and even welcome, upon the whole, for their oceanic practical grandeur, and their restless wholesale kneading of the masses—I say of all this tremendous and dominant play of solely materialistic bearings upon current life in the United States, with the results as already seen, accumulating, and reaching far into the future, that they must either be confronted and met by at least an equally subtle and tremendous force-infusion for purposes of spiritualization, for the pure conscience, for genuine æsthetics, and for absolute and primal manliness and womanliness—or else our modern civilization, with all its improvements, is in vain, and we are on the road to a destiny, a status, equivalent, in its real world, to that of the fabled damned.

Prospecting thus the coming unsped days, and that new order in them—marking the endless train of exercise, development, unwind, in nation as in man, which life is for—we see, fore-indicated, amid these prospects and hopes, new law-forces of spoken and written language—not merely the pedagogue-forms, correct, regular, familiar with precedents, made for matters of outside propriety, fine words, thoughts definitely told out—but a language fann'd by the breath of Nature, which leaps overhead, cares mostly for impetus and effects, and for what it plants and invigorates to grow—tallies life and character, and seldomer tells a things than suggests or necessitates it. In fact, a new theory of literary composition for imaginative works of the very first class, and especially for highest poems, is the sole course open to these States. Books are to be call'd for, and supplied, on the assumption that the process of reading is not a half-sleep, but, in highest sense, an exercise, a gymnast's struggle; that the reader is to do something for himself, must be on the alert, must himself or herself construct indeed the poem, argument, history, metaphysical essay—the text furnishing the hints, the clue, the start or framework. Not the book needs so much to be the complete thing, but the reader of the book does. That were to make a nation of supple and athletic minds, well-train'd, intuitive, used to depend on themselves, and not on a few coteries of writers.

Investigating here, we see, not that it is a little thing we have, in having the bequeath'd libraries, countless shelves of volumes, records, etc.; yet how serious the danger, depending entirely on them, of the bloodless vein, the nerveless arm, the false application, at second or third hand. We see that the real interest of this people of ours in the theology, history, poetry, politics, and personal models of the past (the British islands, for instance, and indeed all the past), is not necessarily to mold ourselves or our literature upon them, but to attain fuller, more definite comparisons, warnings, and the insight to ourselves, our own present, and our own far grander, different, future history, religion, social customs, etc. We see that almost everything that has been written, sung, or stated, of old, with reference to humanity under the feudal and oriental institutes, religions, and for other lands, needs to be rewritten, resung, restated, in terms consistent with the institution of these States, and to come in range and obedient uniformity with them.

We see, as in the universes of the material kosmos, after meteorological, vegetable, and animal cycles, man at last arises, born through them, to prove them, concentrate them, to turn upon them with wonder and love—to command them, adorn them, and carry them upward into superior realms—so, out of the series of the preceding social and political universes, now arise these States. We see that while many were supposing things established and completed, really the grandest things always remain; and discover that the work of the New World is not ended, but only fairly begun.

We see our land, America, her literature, æsthetics, etc., as, substantially, the getting in form, or effusement and statement, of deepest basic elements and loftiest final meanings, of history and man—and the portrayal (under the eternal laws and conditions of beauty) of our own physiognomy, the subjective tie and expression of the objective, as from our own combination, continuation, and points of view—and the deposit and record of the national mentality, character, appeals, heroism, wars, and even liberties—where these, and all, culminate in native literary and artistic formulation, to be perpetuated; and not having which native, first-class formulation, she will flounder about, and her other, however imposing, eminent greatness, prove merely a passing gleam; but truly having which, she will understand herself, live nobly, nobly contribute, emanate, and, swinging, poised safely on herself, illumin'd and illuming, become a full-form'd world, and divine Mother not only of material but spiritual worlds, in ceaseless succession through time—the main thing being the average, the bodily, the concrete, the democratic, the popular, on which all the superstructures of the future are to permanently rest.

Literature of the

Nonliterary World

When we think of literature our first thought is of poetry, drama, fiction, and criticism, written down and published. But *within* these categories there is another body of material, chiefly poetry and fiction, which was not written down and published but which circulated by word of mouth, and which, if later written down and published, represents an offshoot from an oral tradition. Here we find such things as the ballads of the southern mountains, the "Negro spirituals," the "tall tales" of the old frontier. Too, in our scrutiny of the Puritans, we have already seen that *outside* the categories of fiction, poetry, and drama, there is a vast body of writing, sometimes of great artistic excellence and general significance. Examples of such writing in the previous sections were Franklin's *Autobiography*, the travel accounts of Meriwether Lewis and William Byrd, and the essays and correspondence of Thomas Jefferson. Here, in addition to such kinds of writing, we include history, journalism, and oratory, as well as the black and white folk songs. In the second volume of this work there will again appear sections of what we may call the literature of the nonliterary world.

Since we are engaged primarily in the study of the formal literature of America, we may well ask why we should be concerned at all with such informal literature. The answer is simple. Literature—formal literature—does not exist in a vacuum. Every piece of literature has come into being out of a particular society, in a particular place and time, and is read by us in our particular society and place and time. It is true that literature, because of some basic uniformity of human nature and human experience, may speak to us across great distances of time and space and in spite of great historical and social differences, but even so, the more we know about the particular world from which a piece of literature comes, the clearer and deeper will be its voice and our response. Ultimately we cannot divorce literature from history—economic, political, technological, or social history.

There is, however, another and more intimate relation between formal and informal literature. As formal literature does not exist distinct from, say, the economic or political aspects of the practical world it springs from, so that practical world does not exist distinct from the various impulses of feeling, intellect, and imagination that fulfill themselves in formal literature. There is here, too, a continuity and uniformity between the world of formal literature and the world of practical action. The brutal life of the keelboats on the Mississippi in the early days of the nineteenth century gave a Homeric mythology, out of chattel slavery came the Negro spiritual, and when Lincoln wrote the Gettysburg Address, it came in powerful rhythms that were not concocted by a team of ghost writers surrounded by a bevy of secretaries, but out of a life experience.

In this section, and in those of this kind that will follow, we have tried to give selections that carry, in their different ways, something of the context of the world of urgent practicality and historical action. We have, furthermore, chosen items which, in their different ways, exhibit literary quality—which give some impression of the general world of feeling and sensibility from which the literature of the period springs. If we do not understand what we may call this continuity of sensibility, we cannot really understand our literature—Whitman or Mark Twain or Dreiser or Faulkner or the newly concocted "folk ballad" sung in a student demonstration.

Political Writing

The question of slavery was the point around which American political thought in the first half of the nineteenth century revolved, and it was only natural that the literature of the period should have felt the impact of the forces that were rending society. We have seen something of that impact on writers like Emerson, Hawthorne, Whittier, Thoreau, and Lowell, and the shock of the Civil War itself was even more profound and made an even more indelible impression on literature. It is hard to imagine what Whitman, Melville (as poet), and even Emily Dickinson would have been without the war, and the influence has been felt on literature into our own time. The writers we now prepare to discuss are not, however, literary men; they are men who produced a powerful literature of the nonliterary world of action.

JOHN C. CALHOUN (1782–1850)

John C. Calhoun, a South Carolinian, was one of the political giants of the period before the Civil War, one of the triumvirate of orators, including Henry Clay and Daniel Webster, which dominated the Senate. As a young man Calhoun devoted himself to programs which were national in scope and which would, it was assumed, bind the country into a closer union: internal improvements, a national bank, high tariffs to encourage manufacturing. But by 1829, under the pressure of rising sectional tensions and animosities, he could frame the Doctrine of Nullification. From then until his death, with his formidable powers of logic and debate, he was the chief spokesman for the South and its theorist of government.

FURTHER READINGS

John M. Anderson, ed., *Calhoun: Basic Documents* (1952)

Richard K. Crallé, ed., *A Disquisition On Government* (1943)

Robert L. Meriwether, ed., *Papers* (1959–69)

Frederic Bancroft, *Calhoun and the South Carolina Nullification Movement* (1928)

Gerald Mortimer Caspers, *John C. Calhoun, Opportunist: A Reappraisal* (1960)

Margaret L. Coit, *John C. Calhoun: American Portrait* (1950)

Richard Nelson Current, *John C. Calhoun* (1966)

Christopher Hollis, *The American Heresy* (1927)

Gaillard Hunt, *John C. Calhoun* (1908)

Gerald White Johnson, *America's Silver Age: The Statecraft of Clay-Webster-Calhoun* (1939)

Henry Cabot Lodge, *The Democracy of the Constitution, and Other Addresses and Essays* (1915)

August Oran Spain, *The Political Theory of John C. Calhoun* (1951)

John L. Thomas, ed., *John C. Calhoun: A Profile* (1968)

Charles Maurice Wiltse, *John C. Calhoun* (1944–51; 3 vols.)

From A Disquisition on Government (1851)

In *A Disquisition on Government*, Calhoun undertakes to expound the theory of the concurrent majority as opposed to the numerical majority. Along with Emerson, Theodore Parker, Thoreau, and many others, Calhoun feared the tyranny of numbers and sought to develop a theory that would protect minority rights by recognizing "interest groups" (for example, a state). A majority *within* an interest group would have the right to accept or reject a given law within its sphere of interest or governance. The right to do so, Calhoun argued, was implied in the Constitution and was necessary to preserve the unity of a nation embracing so many diverse groups.

To perfect society, it is necessary to develop the faculties, intellectual and moral, with which man is endowed. But the main spring to their development, and, through this, to progress, improvement and civilization, with all their blessings, is the desire of individuals to better their condition. For this purpose, liberty and security are indispensable. Liberty leaves each free to pursue the course he may deem best to promote his interest and happiness, as far as it may be compatible with the primary end for which government is ordained;—while security gives assurance to each, that he shall not be deprived of the fruits of his exertions to better his condition. These combined, give to this desire the strongest impulse of which it is susceptible. For, to extend liberty beyond the limits assigned, would be to weaken the government and to render it incompetent to fulfil its primary end—the protection of society against dangers, internal and external. The effect of this would be, insecurity; and, of insecurity—to weaken the impulse of individuals to better their condition, and thereby retard progress and improvement. On the other hand, to extend the powers of the government, so as to contract the sphere assigned to liberty, would have the same effect, by disabling individuals in their efforts to better their condition.

Herein is to be found the principle which assigns to power and liberty their proper spheres, and reconciles each to the other under all circumstances. For, if power be necessary to secure to liberty the fruits of its exertions, liberty, in turn, repays power with interest, by increasing population, wealth, and other advantages, which progress and improvement bestow on the community. By thus assigning to each its appropriate sphere, all conflicts between them cease; and each is made to co-operate with and assist the other, in fulfilling the great ends for which government is ordained.

But the principle, applied to different communities, will assign to them different limits. It will assign a larger sphere to power and a more contracted one to liberty, or the reverse, according to circumstances. To the former, there must ever be allotted, under all circumstances, a sphere sufficiently large to protect the community against danger from without and violence and anarchy within. The residuum belongs to liberty. More cannot be safely or rightly allotted to it.

But some communities require a far greater amount of power than others to protect them against anarchy and external dangers; and, of course, the sphere of liberty in such, must be proportionally contracted. The causes calculated to enlarge the one and contract the other, are numerous and various. Some are physical—such as open and exposed frontiers, surrounded by powerful and hostile neighbors. Others are moral—such as the different degrees of intelligence, patriotism, and virtue among the mass of the community, and their experience and proficiency in the art of self-government. Of these, the moral are, by far, the most influential. A community may possess all the necessary moral qualifications, in so high a degree, as to be capable of self-government under the most adverse circumstances; while, on the other hand, another may be so sunk in ignorance and vice, as to be incapable of forming a conception of liberty, or of living, even when most favored by circumstances, under any other than an absolute and despotic government.

The principle, in all communities, according to these numerous and various causes, assigns to power and liberty their proper spheres. To allow to liberty, in any case, a sphere of action more extended than this assigns, would lead to anarchy; and this, probably, in the end, to a contraction instead of an enlargement of its sphere. Liberty, then, when forced on a people unfit for it, would, instead of a blessing, be a curse; as it would, in its reaction, lead directly to anarchy—the greatest of all curses. No people, indeed, can long enjoy more liberty than that to which their situation and advanced intelligence and morals fairly entitle them. If more than this be allowed, they must soon fall into confusion and disorder—to be followed, if not by anarchy and despotism, by a change to a form of government more simple and absolute; and, therefore, better suited to their condition. And hence, although it may be true, that a people may not have as much liberty as they are fairly entitled to, and are capable of enjoying—yet the reverse is unquestionably true—that no people can long possess more than they are fairly entitled to.

Liberty, indeed, though among the greatest of blessings, is not so great as that of protection; inasmuch, as the end of the former is the progress and improvement of the race—while that of the latter is its preservation and perpetuation. And hence, when the two come into conflict, liberty must, and ever ought, to yield to protection; as the existence of the race is of greater moment than its improvement.

It follows, from what has been stated, that it is a great and dangerous error to suppose that all people are equally entitled to liberty. It is a reward to be earned, not a blessing to be gratuitously lavished on all alike—a reward reserved for the intelligent, the patriotic, the virtuous and deserving—and not a boon to be bestowed on a people too ignorant, degraded and vicious, to be capable either of appreciating or of enjoying it. Nor is it any disparagement to liberty, that such is, and ought to be the case. On the contrary, its greatest praise—its proudest distinction is, that an all-wise Providence has reserved it, as the noblest and highest reward for the development of our faculties, moral and intellectual. A reward more appropriate than liberty could not be conferred on the deserving—nor a punishment inflicted on the undeserving more just, than to be subject to lawless and despotic rule. This dispensation seems to be the result of some fixed law—and every effort to disturb or defeat it, by attempting to elevate a people in the scale of liberty, above the point to which they are entitled to rise, must ever prove abortive, and end in disappointment. The progress of a people rising from a lower to a higher point in the scale of liberty, is necessarily slow—and by attempting to precipitate, we either retard, or permanently defeat it.

There is another error, not less great and dangerous, usually associated with the one which has just been considered. I refer to the opinion, that liberty and equality are so intimately united, that liberty cannot be perfect without perfect equality.

That they are united to a certain extent—and that equality of citizens, in the eyes of the law, is essential to liberty in a popular government, is conceded. But to go further, and make equality of *condition* essential to liberty, would be to destroy both liberty and progress. The reason is, that inequality of condition, while it is a necessary consequence of liberty is, at the same time, indispensable to progress. In order to understand why this is so, it is necessary to bear in mind, that the main spring to progress is, the desire of individuals to better their condition; and that the strongest impulse which can be given to it is, to leave individuals free to exert themselves in the manner they may deem best for that purpose, as far at least as it can be done consistently with the ends for which government is ordained—and to secure to all the fruits of their exertions. Now, as individuals differ greatly from each other, in intelligence, sagacity, energy, perseverance, skill, habits of industry and economy, physical power, position and opportunity—the necessary effect of leaving all free to exert themselves to better their condition, must be a corresponding inequality between those who may possess these qualities and advantages in a high degree, and those who may be deficient in them. The only means by which this result can be prevented are, either to impose such restrictions on the exertions of those who may possess them in a high degree, as will place them on a level with those who do not; or to deprive them of the fruits of their exertions. But to impose such restrictions on them would be destructive of liberty—while, to deprive them of the fruits of their exertions, would be to destroy the desire of bettering their condition. It is, indeed, this inequality of condition between the front and rear ranks, in the march of progress, which gives so strong an impulse to the former to maintain their position, and to the latter to press forward into their files. This gives to progress its greatest impulse. To force the front rank back to the rear, or attempt to push forward the rear into line with the front, by the interposition of the government, would put an end to the

impulse, and effectually arrest the march of progress.

These great and dangerous errors have their origin in the prevalent opinion that all men are born free and equal—than which nothing can be more unfounded and false. It rests upon the assumption of a fact, which is contrary to universal observation, in whatever light it may be regarded. It is, indeed, difficult to explain how an opinion so destitute of all sound reason, ever could have been so extensively entertained, unless we regard it as being confounded with another, which has some semblance of truth—but which, when properly understood, is not less false and dangerous. I refer to the assertion, that all men are equal in the state of nature; meaning, by a state of nature, a state of individuality, supposed to have existed prior to the social and political state; and in which men lived apart and independent of each other. If such a state ever did exist, all men would have been, indeed, free and equal in it; that is, free to do as they pleased, and exempt from the authority or control of others—as, by supposition, it existed anterior to society and government. But such a state is purely hypothetical. It never did, nor can exist; as it is inconsistent with the preservation and perpetuation of the race. It is, therefore, a great misnomer to call it *the state of nature*. Instead of being the natural state of man, it is, of all conceivable states, the most opposed to his nature—most repugnant to his feelings, and most incompatible with his wants. His natural state is, the social and political—the one for which his Creator made him, and the only one in which he can preserve and perfect his race. As, then, there never was such a state as the, so-called, state of nature, and never can be, it follows, that men, instead of being born in it, are born in the social and political state; and of course, instead of being born free and equal, are born subject, not only to parental authority, but to the laws and institutions of the country where born, and under whose protection they draw their first breath. With these remarks, I return from this digression, to resume the thread of the discourse.

It follows, from all that has been said, that the more perfectly a government combines power and liberty—that is, the greater its power and the more enlarged and secure the liberty of individuals, the more perfectly it fulfils the ends for which government is ordained. To show, then, that the government of the concurrent majority is better calculated to fulfil them than that of the numerical, it is only necessary to explain why the former is better suited to combine a higher degree of power, and a wider scope of liberty than the latter. I shall begin with the former.

The concurrent majority, then, is better suited to enlarge and secure the bounds of liberty, because it is better suited to prevent government from passing beyond its proper limits, and to restrict it to its primary end—the protection of the community. But in doing this, it leaves, necessarily, all beyond it open and free to individual exertions; and thus enlarges and secures the sphere of liberty to the greatest extent which the condition of the community will admit, as has been explained. The tendency of government to pass beyond its proper limits is what exposes liberty to danger, and renders it insecure; and it is the strong counteraction of governments of the concurrent majority to this tendency which makes them so favorable to liberty. On the contrary, those of the numerical, instead of opposing and counteracting this tendency, add to it increased strength, in consequence of the violent party struggles incident to them, as has been fully explained. And hence their encroachments on liberty, and the danger to which it is exposed under such governments.

So great, indeed, is the difference between the two in this respect, that liberty is little more than a name under all governments of the absolute form, including that of the numerical majority; and can only have a secure and durable existence under those of the concurrent or constitutional form. The latter, by giving to each portion of the community which may be unequally affected by its action, a negative on the others, prevents all partial or local legislation, and restricts its action to such measures as are designed for the protection and the good of the whole. In doing this, it secures, at the same time, the rights and liberty of the people, regarded individually; as each portion consists of those who, whatever may be the diversity of interests among themselves, have the same interest in reference to the action of the government.

Such being the case, the interest of each individual may be safely confided to the majority, or voice of his portion, against that of all others, and, of course, the government itself. It is only through an organism which vests each with a negative, in some one form or another, that those who have like interests in preventing the government from passing beyond its proper sphere, and encroaching on the rights and liberty of individuals, can cooperate peaceably and effectually in resisting the encroachments of power, and thereby preserve their rights and liberty. Individual resistance is too feeble, and the difficulty of concert and co-operation too great unaided by such an organism, to oppose, successfully, the organized power of government, with all the means of the community at its disposal; especially in populous countries of great extent; where concert and co-operation are almost impossible. Even when the oppression of the government comes to be too great to be borne, and force is resorted to in order to overthrow it, the result is rarely ever followed by the establishment of liberty. The force sufficient to overthrow an oppressive government is usually sufficient to establish one equally, or more, oppressive in its place. And hence, in no governments, except those that rest on the principle of the concurrent or constitutional majority, can the people guard their liberty against power; and hence, also, when lost, the great difficulty and uncertainty of regaining it by force.

It may be further affirmed that, being more favorable to the enlargement and security of liberty, governments of the concurrent, must necessarily be more favorable to progress, development, improvement, and civilization—and, of course, to the increase of power which results from, and depends on these, than those of the numerical majority.

GEORGE FITZHUGH (1806–1881)

George Fitzhugh was descended from a distinguished Virginia family which, by his time, had come upon reduced circumstances. He, however, married advantageously and, though he had little formal education, became a successful lawyer and a social philosopher and polemicist who had considerable impact on his time. His first book was *Sociology for the South, or, The*

Failure of Free Society, which appeared in 1854; *Cannibals All! or, Slaves Without Masters* came in 1857.

Fitzhugh's views were based on the belief that it is wiser to trust the experience of the past and a knowledge of human nature than to follow the theories of philosophers eager to create an ideal society.[1] For instance, he saw the American Revolution as the work of historical forces culminating in a colonial revolt and believed that the society in revolt was grounded on institutions which, naturally developed and tested by time in the mother country, "would have lasted for many ages, had not thoughtless, half-informed, speculative men, like Jefferson, succeeded in basing them on such inflammable materials" as "the bombastic absurdity in the Declaration of Independence about the inalienable rights of man."

Fitzhugh, thus, was profoundly skeptical of the doctrines of the perfectibility of man, of progress, and of egalitarianism. The truth, as he saw it, is that "men are not born physically, morally, or intellectually equal," and this truth had to be recognized by government and by the social order. It is extremely important to recognize that for him this position led not to the condoning of unbridled individualism and unrestricted competition, but to the idea that the function of government and society is to protect the weak from the strong and guard them against the inequities of nature. In fact, he held that the form of government and of society least likely to protect the weak was the new order of industrialism and capitalism arising in the North, with its glorification of individualism and competition.

Fitzhugh's analysis of capitalism, sketchy as it is, or of the history of liberalism, has much in common with that of Karl Marx. Fitzhugh was, in fact, acquainted with the Communist Manifesto and could grant "much of truth, justice, and good sense to the 'Communists.'" And he was close to the theory of Marx when he stated "that *Labor makes values, and Wit exploitates and accumulates them.*

[1] Set this in contrast to the views of Theodore Parker and other transcendentalists. See pp. 675–76.

It is of interest to observe that some of the arguments of Fitzhugh continue to reappear in analyses made by contemporary historians. For instance, J. H. Plumb, professor of Modern English History at Cambridge University, England, and certainly no defender of slavery, writes that abolitionism arose primarily among members of an industrial society (in England) whose interest was to create "a pool of laboring men . . . selling their labor on a free market" as a means of keeping down the wage scale. (The same interest would presumably condition attitudes in America.) Plumb adds: "Manufacturers' attitudes were rarely as crudely materialistic as this, any more than were those of the slaveholders. Many were devoted to their workers, helped them in harsh times, and developed a patriarchal attitude, but this did not change the basic situation." Whatever paternalistic and humane attitudes did exist, this working class, Plumb asserts, "was treated often with a callousness which was no less evil than that of slavery."

As a critic of industrialism, Fitzhugh was far in advance of his own time. But as a defender of the South, he could go no further than to hope for an amelioration of a system which only as a historical pessimist could he accept. He could, in the end, defend it only as a lesser of evils in a world which was populated by "Cannibals all."

But Fitzhugh, unlike most defenders of slavery, or most of its enemies, was not a racist. Nor was he a secessionist. Least of all, as a lover of Don Quixote and Falstaff, was he a fanatic. In fact, he could say that "all of the greatest and darkest crimes of recorded history have been perpetrated by men 'terribly in earnest.' blindly attempting to fulfill, what they considered, some moral, political, or religious duty." He would not, however, exempt the South from this curse. And, not being himself a fanatic, he worked, after the war, for the Freedmen's Bureau—a fact that scarcely squares with William Dean Howells' use of him as a model for the character Mr. Woodburn in the novel *A Hazard of New Fortunes* (see accompanying volume), an attractive old bigot who writes articles urging the restoration of slavery.

FURTHER READINGS

Edmund Wilson, *Patriotic Gore* (1962)

Harvey Wish, *George Fitzhugh, Propagandist of the*

Old South (1943)

C. Vann Woodward, ed., *Cannibals All!* (1960)

From Cannibals All! or, Slaves Without Masters (1857)

CHAPTER 1

The Universal Trade

We are all, North and South, engaged in the White Slave Trade, and he who succeeds best, is esteemed most respectable. It is far more cruel than the Black Slave Trade, because it exacts more of its slaves, and neither protects nor governs them. We boast, that it exacts more, when we say, "that the *profits* made from employing free labor are greater than those from slave labor." The profits, made from free labor, are the amount of the products of such labor, which the employer, by means of the command which capital or skill gives him, takes away, exacts or "exploitates" from the free laborer. The profits of slave labor are that portion of the products of such labor which the power of the master enables him to appropriate. These profits are less, because the master allows the slave to retain a larger share of the results of his own labor, than do the employers of free labor. But we not only boast that the White Slave Trade is more exacting and fraudulent (in fact, though not in intention) than Black Slavery; but we also boast, that it is more cruel, in leaving the laborer to take care of himself and family out of the pittance which skill or capital have allowed him to retain. When the day's labor is ended, he is free, but is overburdened with the cares of family and household, which make his freedom an empty and delusive mockery. But his employer is really free, and may enjoy the profits made by others' labor, without a care, or a trouble, as to their well-being. The negro slave is free, too, when the labors of the day are over, and free in mind as well as body; for the master provides food, raiment, house, fuel, and everything else necessary to the physical well-being of himself and family. The master's labors commence just when the slave's end. No wonder men should prefer white slavery to capital, to negro slavery, since it is more profitable, and is free from all the cares and labors of black slave-holding.

Now, reader, if you wish to know yourself—to "descant on your own deformity"—read on. But if you would cherish self-conceit, self-esteem, or self-appreciation, throw down our book; for we will dispel illusions which have promoted your happiness, and shew you that what you have considered and practiced as virtue, is little better than moral Cannibalism. But you will find yourself in numerous and respectable company; for all good and respectable people are "Cannibals all," who do not labor, or who are successfully trying to live without labor, on the unrequited labor of other people:—Whilst low, bad, and disreputable people, are those who labor to support themselves, and to support said respectable people besides. Throwing the negro slaves out of the account, and society is divided in Christendom into four classes: The rich, or independent respectable people, who live well and labor not at all; the professional and skillful respectable people who do a little light work, for enormous wages; the poor hard-working people, who support every body, and starve themselves; and the poor thieves, swindlers and sturdy beggars, who live like gentlemen, without labor, on the labor of other people. The gentlemen exploitate, which being done on a large scale, and requiring a great many victims, is highly respectable—whilst the rogues and beggars take so little from others, that they fare little better than those who labor.

But, reader, we do not wish to fire into the flock. "Thou art the man!" You are a Cannibal! and if a successful one, pride yourself on the number of your victims, quite as much as any Feejee chieftain, who breakfasts, dines and sups on human flesh.—And your conscience smites you, if you have failed to succeed, quite as much as his, when he returns from an unsuccessful foray.

Probably, you are a lawyer, or a merchant, or a doctor, who have made by your business fifty thousand dollars, and retired to live on your capital. But, mark! not to spend your capital. That would be vulgar, disreputable, criminal. That would be, to live by your own labor; for your capital is your amassed labor. That would be, to do as common working men do; for they take the pittance which their employers leave them, to live on. They live by labor; for they exchange the results of their own labor for the products of other people's labor. It is, no doubt, an honest, vulgar way of living; but not at all a respectable way. The respectable way of living is, to make other people work for you, and to pay them nothing for so doing—and to have no concern about them after their work is done. Hence, white slave-holding is much more respectable than negro slavery—for the master works nearly as hard for the negro, as he for the master. But you, my virtuous, respectable reader, exact three thousand dollars per annum from white labor, (for your income is the product of white labor) and make not one cent of return in any form. You retain your capital, and never labor, and yet live in luxury on the labor of others. Capital commands labor, as the master does the slave. Neither pays for labor; but the master permits the slave to retain a larger allowance from the proceeds of his own labor, and hence "free labor is cheaper than slave labor." You, with the command over labor which your capital gives you, are a slave owner—a master, without the obligations of a master. They who work for you, who create your income, are slaves, without the rights of slaves. Slaves without a master! Whilst you were engaged in amassing your capital, in seeking to become independent, you were in the White Slave Trade. To become independent, is to be able to make other people support you, without being obliged to labor for *them.* Now, what man in society is not seeking to attain this situation? He who attains it, is a slave owner, in the worst sense. He who is in pursuit of it, is engaged in the slave trade. You, reader, belong to the one or other class. The men without property, in free society, are theoretically in a worse condition than slaves. Practically, their condition corresponds with this theory, as history and statistics every where demonstrate. The capitalists, in free society, live in ten times the luxury and show that Southern masters do, because the slaves to capital work harder and cost less, than negro slaves.

The negro slaves of the South are the happiest, and, in some sense, the freest people in the world. The children and the aged and infirm work not at all, and yet have all the comforts and necessaries of life provided for them. They enjoy liberty, because they are oppressed neither by care nor labor.

The women do little hard work, and are protected from the despotism of their husbands by their masters. The negro men and stout boys work, on the average, in good weather, not more than nine hours a day. The balance of their time is spent in perfect abandon. Besides, they have their Sabbaths and holidays. White men, with so much of license and liberty, would die of ennui; but negroes luxuriate in corporeal and mental repose. With their faces upturned to the sun, they can sleep at any hour; and quiet sleep is the greatest of human enjoyments. "Blessed be the man who invented sleep." 'Tis happiness in itself—and results from contentment with the present, and confident assurance of the future. We do not know whether free laborers ever sleep. They are fools to do so; for whilst they sleep, the wily and watchful capitalist is devising means to ensnare and exploitate them. The free laborer must work or starve. He is more of a slave than the negro, because he works longer and harder for less allowance than the slave, and has no holiday, because the cares of life with him begin when its labors end. He has no liberty, and not a single right. We know, 'tis often said, air and water, are common property, which all have equal right to participate and enjoy; but this is utterly false. The appropriation of the lands carries with it the appropriation of all on or about the lands, *usque ad cœlum, aut ad inferos* [even unto heaven, or unto hell]. A man cannot breathe the air, without a place to breathe it from, and all places are appropriated. All water is private property "to the middle of the stream," except the ocean, and that is not fit to drink.

Free laborers have not a thousandth part of the rights and liberties of negro slaves. Indeed, they have not a single right or a single liberty, unless it be the right or liberty to die. But the reader may think that he and other capitalists and employers are freer than negro slaves. Your capital would soon vanish, if you dared indulge in the liberty and abandon of negroes. You hold your wealth and position by the tenure of constant watchfulness, care and circumspection. You never labor; but you are never free.

Where a few own the soil, they have unlimited power over the balance of society, until domestic slavery comes in, to compel them to permit this balance of society to draw a sufficient and comfortable living from "terra mater." Free society, asserts the right of a few to the earth—slavery, maintains that it belongs, in different degrees, to all.

But, reader, well may you follow the slave trade.

It is the only trade worth following, and slaves the only property worth owning. All other is worthless, a mere *caput mortuum* [death's head], except in so far as it vests the owner with the power to command the labors of others—to enslave them. Give you a palace, ten thousand acres of land, sumptuous clothes, equipage and every other luxury; and with your artificial wants, you are poorer than Robinson Crusoe, or the lowest working man, if you have no slaves to capital, or domestic slaves. Your capital will not bring you an income of a cent, nor supply one of your wants, without labor. Labor is indispensable to give value to property, and if you owned every thing else, and did not own labor, you would be poor. But fifty thousand dollars means, and is, fifty thousand dollars worth of slaves. You can command, without touching on that capital, three thousand dollars' worth of labor per annum. You could do no more were you to buy slaves with it, and then you would be cumbered with the cares of governing and providing for them. You are a slaveholder now, to the amount of fifty thousand dollars, with all the advantages, and none of the cares and responsibilities of a master.

"Property in man" is what all are struggling to obtain. Why should they not be obliged to take care of man, their property, as they do of their horses and their hounds, their cattle and their sheep. Now, under the delusive name of liberty, you work him, "from morn to dewy eve"—from infancy to old age—then turn him out to starve. You treat your horses and hounds better. Capital is a cruel master. The free slave trade, the commonest, yet the cruelest of trades.

THE ANTISLAVERY MOVEMENT BEFORE GARRISON

The first stirrings of the antislavery movement in America began before the Revolution in the attempt of certain Quakers to purge the Society of Friends of its errors—some Quakers having been, as a matter of fact, not only holders of slaves, but among the most successful slave-traders doing business off the African coast. (A ship named *The Willing Quaker* was one of the most famous.) John Woolman, whose journals, as we have seen, Whittier was to edit, and Anthony Benezet worked tirelessly among Quakers, and their influence spread, in fact, far beyond the membership of the sect; it was they who early analyzed the special relation of racism and slavery that characterized the institution in this country.

In addition to the movement among the Quakers, the wave of revivalism known as the Great Awakening, which swept America in the middle of the eighteenth century, raised new questions about the nature of slavery. For the first time slaves were Christianized in massive numbers and participated with the whites in the bursts of wild enthusiasm nurtured by the revivals. In the racially mixed meetings, blacks even became exhorters and preachers, for in this orgiastic religion, literacy, for white or black, was as irrelevant as theological training to the workings of the "Spirit."

To this Protestant egalitarianism, the Revolution added the doctrine of the natural rights of man, which gave a new philosophical context for the antislavery impulse. The paradox between the struggle of the colonials against British tyranny and their own holding of slaves became a commonplace of argument. For instance, in relation to the Declaration of Independence and the American victory, the Quaker David Cooper could write: "We need not now turn over the libraries of Europe for authorities to prove that blacks are born equally free with whites: It is declared and recorded as the sense of America."[1]

The only way out of the paradox created by the doctrine of the rights of man was to deny that the black men were men—or to assert that if they were of the genus man, they were of an

---

[1] George Washington, a better general than a philosopher, was relatively untroubled by the paradox of white rights and black slavery. As late as 1774, he could write that "the crisis is arrived when we must assert our rights or submit to every imposition, that can be heaped upon us, till custom and use shall make us tame as abject slaves, as the blacks we rule over with such arbitrary sway."

inferior species. But this solution was countered by another idea in which the Revolution was deeply rooted—the "environmentalist" notion well expressed by Benjamin Rush, a famous physician and scientist of the time: "Human Nature is the same in all Ages and Countries; and all the difference we perceive in its Characters in respect to Virtue and Vice, Knowledge and Ignorance, may be accounted for from Climate, Country, Degree of Civilization, form of Government, or other accidental causes."

Environmentalism was a notion peculiarly appropriate to a people newly self-conscious and newly conscious of a vast and rich continent and of a system of government that offered the liberty to exploit and enjoy that continent. In such a geographical and social environment, man would reach a new level of development, and a vision of ultimate perfection might be cherished. But, conversely, those groups which had lagged behind—notably, according to the views of the time, the blacks of Africa and the slaves in America—had done so, not because of lack of natural endowment, but because of a defective environment.

It was only natural that those who opposed slavery on religious grounds or on the grounds of natural rights should find support in environmentalist theory, and for proof should seize on examples of intellectual achievement by blacks. For instance, the poems of Phillis Wheatley (see pp. 199–200), born in Africa and as a child bought by a Boston family, were widely admired as a proof that black genius merely needed a favorable environment for its flowering. There were numerous examples to be cited, such as the ministers John Chavis (who studied at Princeton) and Absalom Jones, or the "African Calculator," Thomas Fuller, who had been brought to America as a slave, at the age of 14. Benjamin Banneker, born free in Maryland, was, however, the most famous example of intellectual achievement among Negroes in the postrevolutionary period, instructing himself in languages (with a command of Greek and Latin, and a practical knowledge of French and German), mathematics, and astronomy and becoming a member of the commission for sur-

veying the newly authorized National District in which the capitol was to be built. But his most widely recognized achievement was his series of almanacs, issued from 1791 to 1796, which was approved by David Rittenhouse, the most eminent American astronomer, and prefaced by James McHenry, of Baltimore, known for his scientific education and admired as soldier and statesman. McHenry declared that he regarded "this Negro as a striking contradiction to Mr. [David] Hume's doctrine, that 'the Negroes are naturally inferior to the whites, and unsusceptible of attainments in arts and sciences.'"

To Hume's doctrine, McHenry might have added Jefferson's doubts concerning the capacity of Negroes in arts and sciences, for, though the author of *Notes on the State of Virginia* (see pp. 172–75) was opposed to slavery as violating the natural rights of man (and as degrading to white morals and character), and though he declared the Indian "to be in body and mind equal to the whiteman [sic],"[2] he was not convinced that environment explained the apparent inferiority of the blacks and waited for more scientific evidence on the question. Knowing Jefferson's views, Banneker sent a copy of the first almanac to him, with a letter suggesting that the work might be taken as evidence of intellectual capacity among Negroes, and in this connection remarked on the institution of slavery. To this Jefferson replied courteously, but with an implication that he did not take this piece of evidence as final; and in a letter to a French correspondent, after praising the accomplishments of Banneker, he added: "I shall be delighted to see these instances of moral eminence so multiplied as to prove that the want of talents observed in them [Negroes] is merely the effect of their degraded condition, and not proceeding from any difference in the structure of the parts on which intellect depends."

Even if Jefferson did not take the example of Banneker as conclusive, it was he who was responsible for the appointment of Banneker to

[2] In a letter to the Marquis de Chastellux, in 1785.

the commission to survey the National District.

In the first decade after the founding of the Republic, the liberalizing principles of the Revolution were dominant, and slavery, it was generally assumed, would die out. But around the turn of the century this assumption was called into question. Many factors were contributing to the hardening of the system, but two may be mentioned. The first was the series of horrors attending the revolution that made Santo Domingo a black state, an event that almost hamstrung the antislavery movement in the United States.[3] The second factor was economic; even though slavery was already established in the Deep South, the invention of the cotton gin, by making the production of cotton vastly more profitable, effectively countered any tendency to free the slaves. Manumission, which had been not uncommon, now became legally difficult. In Virginia, for instance, the freedman had to leave the state within a year or be recommitted to slavery; but the laws of the bordering states, Kentucky, Ohio, Delaware, and Maryland, for-

[3] This negative effect was not modified by the fact that the system of forced labor instituted under the succession of black regimes differed little, except in name, from the brutal system which it replaced, with the driver's whip replaced by the cocomacombo, a stick.

bade his entry there. So where, therefore, might he go? The free Negro was, indeed, as little desired in the North as in the South, and though slavery did not exist there, a rigorous social discrimination, with, generally speaking, deprivation of the franchise, did. In other words, both slavery and racism, with all the attendant paradoxes, were becoming more firmly established in the new Republic, which proclaimed equality and freedom.

Even during the Revolution, these paradoxes had been clearly recognized by many blacks—and how could it have been otherwise when blacks were regularly enlisted in the American army, and when those who were slaves might thus earn their freedom?[4] As early as 1777 Negro petitioners in Massachusetts had appealed to "that very principle from which America has acted" in the Revolution. But whatever hope blacks had had from the Revolution began to gutter in the atmosphere of the new century. It is in this context that we may read the *Appeal*, by David Walker, which is sometimes described as the Declaration of Independence of the Black American.

[4] But blacks might also earn their freedom by joining the British. Lord Dunmore raised black troops in Virginia.

FURTHER READINGS

Herbert Aptheker, *One Continual Cry* (1965)
David Brion Davis, *The Problem of Slavery in Western Culture* (1966)
Melvin Drimmer, ed., *Black History: A Reappraisal* (1968)
Dwight Lowell Dumond, *Anti-Slavery* (1961)
Stanley Elkins, *Slavery* (1964)

Eugene D. Genovese, *The Political Economy of Slavery* (1965)
Winthrop D. Jordan, *White over Black* (1968)
Kenneth Stampp, *The Peculiar Institution: Slavery in the Ante-Bellum South* (1956)
Allen Weinstein, ed., *American Negro Slavery: A Modern Reader* (1968)

DAVID WALKER (1785–1830)

David Walker was born in Wilmington, North Carolina. His father was a slave, but since the law declared that a child followed the condition of the mother, he was born free. When young, he wandered about the South, but finally settled in Boston, where he modestly prospered with a clothing store. In 1829 he first published his *Appeal*; in 1830, the last year of his life, two more editions appeared. It was reissued in 1848.

The *Appeal*, with its prediction of violent revolt, caused considerable excitement in the South, especially since the insurrection under the leadership of Nat Turner, the best organized and most nearly successful of the slave risings, came shortly after its publication. The Gover-

nor of Georgia tried to persuade the Mayor of Boston to suppress the pamphlet. When this was refused, certain private citizens in Georgia offered a reward of $1000 for Walker dead and $10,000 for him alive. It has been surmised that his sudden death shortly thereafter resulted from poison.[1]

[1] See Dwight Lowell Dumond, *Anti-Slavery* (1961), pp. 158, 329.

From the Appeal (1829)

ARTICLE I:

Our Wretchedness in Consequence of Slavery

My beloved brethren:—The Indians of North and of South America—the Greeks—the Irish, subjected under the king of Great Britain—the Jews, that ancient people of the Lord—the inhabitants of the islands of the sea—in fine, all the inhabitants of the earth, (except however, the sons of Africa) are called *men*, and of course are, and ought to be free. But we, (coloured people) and our children are *brutes!!* and of course are, and *ought to be* SLAVES to the American people and their children forever!! to dig their mines and work their farms; and thus go on enriching them, from one generation to another with our *blood* and our *tears!!!!*

I promised in a preceding page to demonstrate to the satisfaction of the most incredulous, that we, (coloured people of these United States of America) are the *most wretched, degraded* and *abject* set of beings that *ever lived* since the world began, and that the white American having reduced us to the wretched state of *slavery*, treat us in that condition *more cruel* (they being an enlighted and Christian people,) than any heathen nation did any people whom it had reduced to our condition. These affirmations are so well confirmed in the minds of all unprejudiced men, who have taken the trouble to read histories, that they need no elucidation from me. But to put them beyond all doubt, I refer you in the first place to the children of Jacob, or of Israel in Egypt, under Pharaoh and his people. Some of my brethren do not know who Pharaoh and the Egyptians were—I know it to be a fact, that some of them take the Egyptians to have been a gang of *devils*, not knowing any better, and that they (Egyptians) having got pos-

session of the Lord's people, treated them *nearly* as cruel as *Christian Americans* do us, at the present day. For the information of such, I would only mention that the Egyptians, were Africans or coloured people, such as we are—some of them yellow and others dark—a mixture of Ethiopians and the natives of Egypt—about the same as you see the coloured people of the United States at the present day.—I say, I call your attention then, to the children of Jacob, while I point out particularly to you his son Joseph, among the rest, in Egypt.

"And Pharaoh, said unto Joseph, thou shalt be "over my house, and according unto thy word "shall all my people be ruled: only in the throne "will I be greater than thou."

"And Pharaoh said unto Joseph, see, I have set "thee over all the land of Egypt."

"And Pharaoh said unto Joseph, I am Pharaoh, "and without thee shall no man lift up his hand "or foot in all the land of Egypt."

Now I appeal to heaven and to earth, and particularly to the American people themselves, who cease not to declare that our condition is not *hard*, and that we are comparatively satisfied to rest in wretchedness and misery, under them and their children. Not, indeed, to show me a coloured President, a Governor, a Legislator, a Senator, a Mayor, or an Attorney at the Bar.—But to show me a man of colour, who holds the low office of a Constable, or one who sits in a Juror Box, even on a case of one of his wretched brethren, throughout this great Republic!!—But let us pass Joseph the son of Israel a little farther in review, as he existed with that heathen nation.

"And Pharaoh called Joseph's name Zaphnath-

"paaneah; and he gave him to wife Asenath the "daughter of Potipherah priest of On. And Joseph "went out over all the land of Egypt."

Compare the above, with the American institutions. Do they not institute laws to prohibit us from marrying among the whites? I would wish, candidly, however, before the Lord, to be understood, that I would not give a *pinch of snuff* to be married to any white person I ever saw in all the days of my life. And I do say it, that the black man, or man of colour, who will leave his own colour (provided he can get one, who is good for any thing) and marry a white woman, to be a double slave to her, just because she is *white*, ought to be treated by her as he surely will be, viz: as a NIGER ! ! ! ! It is not, indeed, what I care about inter-marriages with the whites, which induced me to pass this subject in review; for the Lord knows, that there is a day coming when they will be glad enough to get into the company of the blacks, notwithstanding, we are, in this generation, levelled by them, almost on a level with the brute creation: and some of us they treat even worse than they do the brutes that perish. I only made this extract to show how much lower we are held, and how much more cruel we are treated by the Americans, than were the children of Jacob, by the Egyptians.—We will notice the sufferings of Israel some further, under *heathen Pharaoh*, compared with ours under the *enlightened Christians of America.*

"And Pharaoh spake unto Joseph, saying, thy "father and thy brethren are come unto thee:"

"The land of Egypt is before thee: in the best "of the land make thy father and brethren to "dwell; in the land of Goshen let them dwell: and "if thou knowest any men of activity among them, "then make them rulers over my cattle."

I ask those people who treat us so *well*, Oh! I ask them, where is the most barren spot of land which they have given unto us? Israel had the most fertile land in all Egypt. Need I mention the very notorious fact, that I have known a poor man of colour, who laboured night and day, to acquire a little money, and having acquired it, he vested it in a small piece of land, and got him a house erected thereon, and having paid for the whole, he moved his family into it, where he was suffered to remain but nine months, when he was cheated out of his property by a white man, and driven out of door! And is not this the case generally? Can a man of colour buy a piece of land and keep it peaceably? Will not some white man

try to get it from him, even if it is in a *mud hole?* I need not comment any farther on a subject, which all, both black and white, will readily admit. But I must, really, observe that in this very city, when a man of colour dies, if he owned any real estate it most generally falls into the hands of some white person. The wife and children of the deceased may weep and lament if they please, but the estate will be kept snug enough by its white possessor.

But to prove farther that the condition of the Israelites was better under the Egyptians than ours is under the whites. I call upon the professing Christians, I call upon the philanthropist, I call upon the very tyrant himself, to show me a page of history, either sacred or profane, on which a verse can be found, which maintains, that the Egyptians heaped the *insupportable insult* upon the children of Israel, by telling them that they were not of the *human family.* Can the whites deny this charge? Have they not, after having reduced us to the deplorable condition of slaves under their feet, held us up as descending originally from the tribes of *Monkeys* or *Orang-Outangs?* O! my God! I appeal to every man of feeling—is not this insupportable? Is it not heaping the most gross insult upon our miseries, because they have got us under their feet and we cannot help ourselves? Oh! pity us we pray thee, Lord Jesus, Master.—Has Mr. Jefferson declared to the world, that we are inferior to the whites, both in the endowments of our bodies and of minds? It is indeed surprising, that a man of such great learning, combined with such excellent natural parts, should speak so of a set of men in chains. I do not know what to compare it to, unless, like putting one wild deer in an iron cage, where it will be secured, and hold another by the side of the same, then let it go, and expect the one in the cage to run as fast as the one at liberty. So far, my brethren, were the Egyptians from heaping these insults upon their slaves, that Pharaoh's daughter took Moses, a son of Israel for her own, as will appear by the following.

"And Pharaoh's daughter said unto her, [Moses' "mother] take this child away, and nurse it for me, "and I will pay thee thy wages. And the woman "took the child [Moses] and nursed it.

"And the child grew, and she brought him unto "Pharaoh's daughter and he became her son. And "she called his name Moses: and she said because "I drew him out of the water."

In all probability, Moses would have become

Prince Regent to the throne, and no doubt, in process of time but he would have been seated on the throne of Egypt. But he had rather suffer shame, with the people of God, than to enjoy pleasures with that wicked people for a season. O! that the coloured people were long since of Moses' excellent disposition, instead of courting favour with, and telling news and lies to our *natural enemies*, against each other—aiding them to keep their hellish chains of slavery upon us. Would we not long before this time, have been respectable men, instead of such wretched victims of oppression as we are? Would they be able to drag our mothers, our fathers, our wives, our children and ourselves, around the world in chains and handcuffs as they do, to dig up gold and silver for them and theirs? This question, my brethren, I leave for you to digest; and may God Almighty force it home to your hearts. Remember that unless you are united, keeping your tongues within your teeth, you will be afraid to trust your secrets to each other, and thus perpetuate our miseries under the *Christians ! ! ! ! !*

. . .

. . . But is Mr. Jefferson's assertions true? viz. "that it is unfortunate for us that our Creator has been pleased to make us *black*." We will not take his say so, for the fact. The world will have an opportunity to see whether it is unfortunate for us, that our Creator *has made us* darker than the *whites*.

Fear not the number and education of our *enemies*, against whom we shall have to contend for our lawful right; guaranteed to us by our Maker; for why should we be afraid, when God is, and will continue, (if we continue humble) to be on our side?

The man who would not fight under our Lord and Master Jesus Christ, in the glorious and heavenly cause of freedom and of God—to be delivered from the most wretched, abject and servile slavery, that ever a people was afflicted with since the foundation of the world, to the present day —ought to be kept with all of his children or family, in slavery, or in chains, to be butchered by his *cruel enemies*.

I saw a paragraph, a few years since, in a South Carolina paper, which, speaking of the barbarity of the Turks, it said: "The Turks are the most "barbarous people in the world—they treat the "Greeks more like *brutes* than human beings."

And in the same paper was an advertisement, which said: "Eight well built Virginia and Mary-"land *Negro fellows* and four *wenches* will posi-"tively be *sold* this day, *to the highest bidder!*" And what astonished me still more was, to see in this same *humane* paper ! ! the cuts of three men, with clubs and budgets on their backs, and an advertisement offering a considerable sum of money for their apprehension and delivery. I declare, it is really so amusing to hear the Southerners and Westerners of this country talk about *barbarity*, that it is positively enough to make a man *smile*.

. . .

The world knows, that slavery as it existed among the Romans, (which was the primary cause of their destruction) was, comparatively speaking, no more than a *cypher*, when compared with ours under the Americans. Indeed I should not have noticed the Roman slaves, had not the very learned and penetrating Mr. Jefferson said, "when a master was murdered, all his slaves in the same house, or within hearing, were condemned to death."—Here let me ask Mr. Jefferson, (but he is gone to answer at the bar of God, for the deeds done in his body while living,) I therefore ask the whole American people, had I not rather die, or be put to death, than to be a slave to any tyrant, who takes not only my own, but my wife and children's lives by the inches? Yea, would I meet death with avidity far! far!! in preference to such *servile submission* to the murderous hands of tyrants. Mr. Jefferson's very severe remarks on us have been so extensively argued upon by men whose attainments in literature, I shall never be able to reach, that I would not have meddled with it, were it not to solicit each of my brethren, who has the spirit of a man, to buy a copy of Mr. Jefferson's "Notes on Virginia," and put it in the hand of his son. For let no one of us suppose that the refutations which have been written by our white friends are enough —they are *whites*—we are *blacks*. We, and the world wish to see the charges of Mr. Jefferson refuted by the blacks *themselves*, according to their chance; for we must remember that what the whites have written respecting this subject, is other men's labours, and did not emanate from the blacks. I know well, that there are some talents and learning among the coloured people of this country, which we have not a chance to develope, in consequence of oppression; but our oppression ought not to hinder us from acquiring all we can. For we will have a chance to develope them by and by. God will not suffer us, always to be oppressed. Our sufferings will come to an *end,* in spite of all the Americans this side of *eternity.* Then we will want all the learning and talents among ourselves, and perhaps more, to govern ourselves.—"Every dog must have its day," the American's is coming to an end.

. . .

The whites have always been an unjust, jealous, unmerciful, avaricious and blood-thirsty set of beings, always seeking after power and authority.— We view them all over the confederacy of Greece, where they were first known to be any thing, (in consequence of education) we see them there, cutting each other's throats—trying to subject each other to wretchedness and misery—to effect which, they used all kinds of deceitful, unfair, and unmerciful means. We view them next in Rome, where the spirit of tyranny and deceit raged still higher. We view them in Gaul, Spain, and in Britain.—In fine, we view them all over Europe, together with what were scattered about in Asia and Africa, as heathens, and we see them acting more like devils than accountable men. But some may ask, did not the blacks of Africa, and the mulattoes of Asia, go on in the same way as did the whites of Europe. I answer, no—they never were half so avaricious, deceitful and unmerciful as the whites, according to their knowledge.

But we will leave the whites or Europeans as heathens, and take a view of them as Christians, in which capacity we see them as cruel, if not more so than ever. In fact, take them as a body, they are ten times more. cruel, avaricious and unmerciful than ever they were; for while they were heathens, they were bad enough it is true, but it is positively a fact that they were not quite so audacious as to go and take vessel loads of men, women and children, and in cold blood, and through devilishness, throw them into the sea,

and murder them in all kind of ways. While they were heathens, they were too ignorant for such barbarity. But being Christians, enlightened and sensible, they are completely prepared for such hellish cruelties. Now suppose God were to give them more sense, what would they do? If it were possible, would they not *dethrone* Jehovah and seat themselves upon his throne? I therefore, in the name and fear of the Lord God of Heaven and of earth, divested of prejudice either on the side of my colour or that of the whites, advance my suspicion of them, whether they are *as good by nature* as we are or not. Their actions, since they were known as a people, have been the reverse, I do indeed suspect them, but this, as I before observed, is shut up with the Lord, we cannot exactly tell, it will be proved in succeeding generations.— The whites have had the essence of the gospel as it was preached by my master and his apostles— the Ethiopians have not, who are to have it in its meridian splendor—the Lord will give it to them to their satisfaction. I hope and pray my God, that they will make good use of it, that it may be well with them.[1]

[1] It is my solemn belief, that if ever the world becomes Christianized, (which must certainly take place before long) it will be through the means, under God of the *Blacks,* who are now held in wretchedness, and degradation, by the white *Christians* of the world, who before they learn to do justice to us before our Maker— and be reconciled to us, and reconcile us to them, and by that means have clear consciencies before God and man. —Send out Missionaries to convert the Heathens, many of whom after they cease to worship gods, which neither see nor hear, become ten times more the children of Hell, then ever they were, why is what the reason? Why the reason is obvious, they must learn to do justice at home, before they go into distant lands, to display their charity, Christianity, and benevolence; when they learn to do justice, God will accept their offering, (no man may think that I am against Missionaries for I am not, my object is to see justice done at home, before we go to convert the Heathens) [Walker].

WILLIAM LLOYD GARRISON (1805–1879)

William Lloyd Garrison was born at Newburyport, Massachusetts, was trained as a printer, but in early youth became imbued with the

passion for general reform which characterized the period and which, as we have seen, affected such writers as Whittier and Lowell. (See pp.

539, 604.) Only gradually, out of a welter of issues—woman's rights, temperance, peace, and general moral regeneration—did Garrison come to focus on the abolition of slavery as his special mission.

As was only natural, given the historical moment, he began as an advocate of gradual emancipation by legislative action of the individual slave states, and of the colonization of the freedmen in Africa. But by the time he founded the *Liberator*, in January, 1831, at Boston, he was urging immediate emancipation and was violently opposed to colonization as an insult to the Negro, a violation of his right to citizenship, and treason to his cause. In 1832, Garrison founded, in Boston, the first antislavery society based on the principles of immediate abolition; the next year he was a moving spirit in founding the American Anti-Slavery Society and was, with Whittier, whom he had drawn into active abolitionism, one of the authors of its constitution.

Garrison became the most famous of the abolition leaders. He was also the most radical and intransigent. He regarded slavery only as a sin and had no concern with any social or political contexts. Garrison was, in fact, woefully ignorant of history and law, the American Constitution, and earlier literature of the antislavery movement; moreover, he was contemptuous of ideas not his own or of facts that did not gibe with his opinions. He opposed any attempt to work politically, and on this point split the antislavery movement and, incidentally, alienated himself from his great convert Whittier. He demanded that the North sever connections with the South, a policy that would seem to place the fear of moral contamination of the self above the desire to do good for the slaves thus abandoned. Finally, on July 4, 1854, at Framingham, Massachusetts, he publicly burned the Constitution as a "covenant with death and an agreement with hell." It was only natural that the followers of Garrison should, when war came, regard Lincoln with abhorrence, or at best with profound distrust; it was Wendell Phillips, a follower of Garrison, who called Lincoln "the slave-hound from Illinois."

It is difficult to assess the actual power that Garrison exerted. He clearly had a genius for propaganda, but it was the learned Theodore Weld, not he, who wrote the greatest and most influential abolitionist documents. Furthermore, Garrison's violence of language, his readiness to attribute base motives to others, even to his closest associates, his disregard for fact, his self-righteousness, and more than a hint of blood-lust alienated many, as did his apparent lack of concern with the human needs of individual Negroes, even escaping slaves. But, in the complexity of his nature, there was, too, a great capacity for empathy with suffering—even if a highly selected variety of suffering.

As the slavery issue, in the 1850's and during the war, became more and more involved with historical, economic, and political issues, Garrison, it has been argued, seemed more and more irrelevant to the world of action. Dwight Lowell Dumond, the author of the most recent and comprehensive history of the antislavery movement, calls Garrison's basic antipolitical policy "ill considered and without justification, playing into the hands of the proslavery men." He sums up Garrison as "a man of distinctly narrow limitations among the giants of the antislavery movement," and of his contribution remarks: "It was neither a large nor overpowering one, and sometimes it was a negative one."

But some historians, notably Aileen S. Kraditor, in *Means and Ends in American Abolitionism*, hold that Garrison's radicalism—that is, his view that only the destruction of the system whose racism made slavery possible could solve the fundamental problem of the black man in America—was the realistic view and that, in the long run, his method of agitation for an absolute solution was effective.

No doubt Garrison's absolutism is what has made his fame, in our time, outstrip that of all other antislavery leaders, even among—perhaps especially among—those who know little of what he actually believed or did. He became, perhaps because of his very narrowness, the incarnate dramatization of an issue; and that was enough. And he had eloquence, even when it was, as his fellow-worker Theodore Weld described it, "the vibration of serpents' tongues." We print here the famous editorial in the first issue of the *Liberator*, which Garrison founded and which was for years his personal mouthpiece.

FURTHER READINGS

Works (1905) (no editor cited)
Truman Nelson, ed., *The Liberator* (1966)

John J. Chapman, *William Lloyd Garrison* (1913)
Martin Duberman, *The Anti-Slavery Vanguard: New Essays on the Abolitionists* (1965)
Dwight Lowell Dumond, *Anti-Slavery* (1961)
Francis Jackson Garrison and Wendell Phillips Garrison, *The Life of Lloyd Garrison* (1894)
Aileen S. Kraditor, *Means and Ends in American Abolitionism* (1967)

Russell Blaine Nye, *William Lloyd Garrison and the Humanitarian Reformers* (1955)
Benjamin P. Thomas, *Theodore Weld, Crusader for Freedom* (1950)
John L. Thomas, *The Liberator: William Lloyd Garrison* (1963)
Austin Warren, "William Lloyd Garrison," in *The New England Conscience* (1967)
C. Vann Woodward, "The Anti-Slavery Myth," *American Scholar* (Spring, 1962)

Editorial from the Liberator (1831)

In the month of August, I issued proposals for publishing 'THE LIBERATOR' in Washington city; but the enterprise, though hailed in different sections of the country, was palsied by public indifference. Since that time, the removal of the *Genius of Universal Emancipation* to the Seat of Government has rendered less imperious the establishment of a similar periodical in that quarter.

During my recent tour for the purpose of exciting the minds of the people by a series of discourses on the subject of slavery, every place that I visited gave fresh evidence of the fact, that a greater revolution in public sentiment was to be effected in the free states—*and particularly in New-England*—than at the south. I found contempt more bitter, opposition more active, detraction more relentless, prejudice more stubborn, and apathy more frozen, than among slave owners themselves. Of course, there were individual exceptions to the contrary. This state of things afflicted, but did not dishearten me. I determined, at every hazard, to lift up the standard of emancipation in the eyes of the nation, *within sight of Bunker Hill and in the birth place of liberty*. That standard is now unfurled; and long may it float, unhurt by the spoliations of time or the missiles of a desperate foe—yea, till every chain be broken, and every bondman set free! Let southern oppressors tremble—let their secret abettors tremble

—let their northern apologists tremble—let all the enemies of the persecuted blacks tremble.

I deem the publication of my original Prospectus[1] unnecessary, as it has obtained a wide circulation. The principles therein inculcated will be steadily pursued in this paper, excepting that I shall not array myself as the political partisan of any man. In defending the great cause of human rights, I wish to derive the assistance of all religions and of all parties.

Assenting to the 'self-evident truth' maintained in the American Declaration of Independence, 'that all men are created equal, and endowed by their Creator with certain inalienable rights—among which are life, liberty and the pursuit of happiness,' I shall strenuously contend for the immediate enfranchisement of our slave population. In Park-street Church, on the Fourth of July, 1829, in an address on slavery, I unreflectingly assented to the popular but pernicious doctrine of *gradual* abolition. I seize this opportunity to make a full and unequivocal recantation, and thus publicly to ask pardon of my God, of my country, and of my brethren the poor slaves, for having uttered

---

[1] I would here offer my grateful acknowledgments to those editors who so promptly and generously inserted my Proposals. They must give me an available opportunity to repay their liberality [Garrison].

a sentiment so full of timidity, injustice and absurdity. A similar recantation, from my pen, was published in the Genius of Universal Emancipation at Baltimore, in September, 1829. My conscience is now satisfied.

I am aware, that many object to the severity of my language; but is there not cause for severity? I *will be* as harsh as truth, and as uncompromising as justice. On this subject, I do not wish to think, or speak, or write, with moderation. No! no! Tell a man whose house is on fire, to give a moderate alarm; tell him to moderately rescue his wife from the hands of the ravisher; tell the mother to gradually extricate her babe from the fire into which it has fallen;—but urge me not to use moderation in a cause like the present. I am in earnest—I will not equivocate—I will not excuse—I will not retreat a single inch—AND I WILL BE HEARD. The apathy of the people is enough to make every statue leap from its pedestal, and to hasten the resurrection of the dead.

It is pretended, that I am retarding the cause of emancipation by the coarseness of my invective, and the precipitancy of my measures. *The charge is not true.* On this question my influence,—hum-ble as it is,—is felt at this moment to a considerable extent, and shall be felt in coming years—not perniciously, but beneficially—not as a curse, but as a blessing; and posterity will bear testimony that I was right. I desire to thank God, that he enables me to disregard 'the fear of man which bringeth a snare,' and to speak his truth in its simplicity and power.

And here I close with this fresh dedication:

'Oppression! I have seen thee, face to face,
And met thy cruel eye and cloudy brow;
But thy soul-withering glance I fear not now—
For dread to prouder feelings doth give place
Of deep abhorrence! Scorning the disgrace
Of slavish knees that at thy footstool bow,
I also kneel—but with far other bow
Do hail thee and thy herd of hirelings base:—
I swear, while life-blood warms my throbbing veins,
Still to oppose and thwart, with heart and hand,
Thy brutalizing sway—till Afric's chains
Are burst, and Freedom rules the rescued land,—
Trampling Oppression and his iron rod:
Such is the vow I take—SO HELP ME GOD!'

FREDERICK DOUGLASS (1817?–1895)

Frederick Douglass was the most famous of a number of Negroes active in the antislavery movement in the period between David Walker's *Appeal* and the Civil War. The others whose writings are worthy of mention are Henry Highland Garnet, the grandson of an African chief, born a slave in Maryland, who became the rival of Douglass and whose speech at a Negro antislavery convention in 1843, calling for a black insurrection, was printed and distributed by John Brown at his own expense; and Richard J. Hinton, who, in 1894, published a life of John Brown.

Douglass was born a slave, on a plantation on the eastern shore of Maryland, was early sent to Baltimore, and there, with the relative freedom of the city, learned to read and write; by the time he was twenty-one he escaped to Massachusetts. His intellectual power and gift of oratory were early recognized, and he was hired as an agent for the Anti-Slavery Society. He had an impressive presence, great natural dignity, and a magnificent voice, and under the tutelage of William Lloyd Garrison and the famous Wendell Phillips rapidly attracted national attention as an orator.

Meanwhile, Douglass was asserting his independence, even against his early sponsor Garrison. First, Douglass supported the idea of political action as against Garrison's more apocalyptic approach, and, second, he founded a newspaper, the *North Star*, which, as a specifically Negro organ, outraged Garrison's commitment to what would now be called "integration." The upshot was that Garrison pursued him with enduring rancor and vengeful attempts to destroy him. In this same period, and almost, it may be said, as an offshoot of his work as a propagandist, Douglass was writing his *Autobiography*. The first version, a rather simple narrative, appeared in 1845, and the second, much more detailed and showing Douglass at his accomplished best as a writer, in 1855.

As orator, journalist, and autobiographer Douglass was clearly a figure of distinction, but all three activities were, for the age he lived in, aspects of a role that was of more significance than any particular achievement: he was the living example of what the black man, once free, might become.

It was inevitable that, once the Civil War came, the influence of the abolitionists as such should wane, but, even so, Douglass remained of considerable importance. In the early phase of the conflict, he effectively attacked Lincoln for his failure to declare the slaves free and for general incompetence; later, as the war assumed a new dimension after the Emancipation Proclamation, Douglass aided in recruiting black troops (a policy frowned upon by most civilians as well as military men in the North, but finally accepted by Lincoln).

With the coming of peace, many white abolitionists became victims of technological unemployment and now, having made their theoretical point, did not feel themselves deeply concerned with the fate of the individual black man under the new political and economic dispensation. Yet this altered situation, especially as segregation developed, demanded new channels of communication between the races. Thus, at all levels, from the local community to the national scene, the so-called Negro leader—usually a preacher, ward boss, or college president—made his appearance. Willy-nilly, Douglass, as the most famous black in the country, found himself in the somewhat uneasy role of national spokesman for the black world. He sat in councils of the great, wielded considerable political influence, and crowned his public career with the post of minister to Haiti. He died in 1895, having passed the mantle of leadership to Booker T. Washington, who would later write Douglass's biography.

For all his importance in the history of the antislavery movement, Douglass is now perhaps more important for his role in the development of black literature. The second version of the *Autobiography* (he published a third in 1881 which, except for bringing the factual record up to date, is of little consequence) remains one of the most vivid and readable of the works in that genre. Furthermore, though it is not the first autobiography written by an American slave,[1] it was the first to make a general impact. It did so not only because of its intrinsic merit but because of its timing: feelings about slavery were now approaching a crisis. Since the abolitionists were quick to see the importance of such work as propaganda, the "slave narrative" —real or spurious[2]—became a feature of the literature of the time.

But the fundamental importance of Douglass's *Autobiography* survives beyond its time and its ostensible purpose. It is a compelling human document and, in a sense, introduced autobiography as a characteristic form for black writers, from Booker T. Washington, through W. E. B. Du Bois and James Weldon Johnson, to Richard Wright and James Baldwin. In the early period the slave had one powerfully overriding story to tell: his own. The slave inhabited a shadowy world, and his story had, inevitably, the drama of "notes from underground." In fact, the slave was a chattel, legally a thing and not a man, and the great impact of his story came when the "invisible man" was, shockingly, revealed as visible. When the Fourteenth

[1] Among the most popular of the early autobiographies was *The Narrative of Moses Roper's Adventures and Escape from American Slavery* (1837), which by 1856 had gone through ten editions and been translated into Celtic.

[2] Other autobiographies which might be mentioned are those of Josiah Henson and William Wells Brown. Henson's character was said to have served as a partial model for Harriet Beecher Stowe's Uncle Tom, and Brown went on to author *Clotel; or the President's Daughter, A Narrative of Slave Life in the United States* (1853), the first novel by an American black. Of the narratives whose spuriousness has definitely been established, two of the more popular were *The Memoirs of Archy Moore* and *The Autobiography of a Female Slave*, both written by whites.

Amendment finally came, it worked not to end the story the black man had to tell, but to complicate it with an additional irony. The amendment declared, officially, that the black man was now above ground and visible, and from that day to this the theme of black autobiography has been ironically double: to show that, contrary to official declaration and the moral complacency of the white world, the black man *is* underground and invisible, and to show too that, though in that condition, he can still be revealed as existing and visible—but in a way quite different from what would be officially expected.

All autobiography, presumably, aims at exploring the identity of the author, but with the black author—in America, at least—the situation is somewhat different. The black autobiographer —from slave times to the present—has had to establish the very fact that he had an authentic identity. It is, then, dramatically right that the hero of black autobiography might not even know who his father was and in a later period, after slavery, was often the abandoned son, or the son who lived on terms of desperate strain with the father. The story the black autobiographer has to tell is a form of the classic existential story of our age.

FURTHER READINGS

Frederick Douglass, *My Bondage and My Freedom* (1855)
——, *My Life and Times* (1881; 1941)
——, *Narrative of the Life of Frederick Douglass* (1845)

Philip S. Foner, *Frederick Douglass, a Biography* (1964)

——, *The Life and Writings of Frederick Douglass* (1950–55)
Charles H. Nichols, "Who Read the Slave Narratives," *Phylon* (Summer, 1959)
Benjamin Quarles, *Frederick Douglass* (1948)
M. W. Starling, *The Slave Narrative: Its Place in American Literary History*

From My Bondage and My Freedom (1855)

FROM CHAPTER 1

In Talbot county, Eastern Shore, Maryland, near Easton, the county town of that county, there is a small district of country, thinly populated, and remarkable for nothing that I know of more than for the worn-out, sandy, desert-like appearance of its soil, the general dilapidation of its farms and fences, the indigent and spiritless character of its inhabitants, and the prevalence of ague and fever.

The name of this singularly unpromising and truly famine stricken district is Tuckahoe, a name well known to all Marylanders, black and white. It was given to this section of country probably, at the first, merely in derision; or it may possibly have been applied to it, as I have heard, because some one of its earlier inhabitants had been guilty of the petty meanness of stealing a hoe—or taking a hoe—that did not belong to him. Eastern Shore men usually pronounce the word *took*, as *tuck*; *Took-a-hoe*, therefore, is, in Maryland parlance, *Tuckahoe*. But, whatever may have been its origin

—and about this I will not be positive—that name has stuck to the district in question; and it is seldom mentioned but with contempt and derision, on account of the barrenness of its soil, and the ignorance, indolence, and poverty of its people. Decay and ruin are everywhere visible, and the thin population of the place would have quitted it long ago, but for the Choptank river, which runs through it, from which they take abundance of shad and herring, and plenty of ague and fever.

It was in this dull, flat, and unthrifty district, or neighborhood, surrounded by a white population of the lowest order, indolent and drunken to a proverb, and among slaves, who seemed to ask, *"Oh! what's the use?"* every time they lifted a hoe, that I—without any fault of mine—was born, and spent the first years of my childhood.

The reader will pardon so much about the place of my birth, on the score that it is always a fact of some importance to know where a man is born, if, indeed, it be important to know anything about him. In regard to the *time* of my birth, I cannot be as definite as I have been respecting the *place.* Nor, indeed, can I impart much knowledge concerning my parents. Genealogical trees do not flourish among slaves. A person of some consequence here in the north, sometimes designated *father*, is literally abolished in slave law and slave practice. It is only once in a while that an exception is found to this statement. I never met with a slave who could tell me how old he was. Few slave-mothers know anything of the months of the year, nor of the days of the month. They keep no family records, with marriages, births, and deaths. They measure the ages of their children by spring time, winter time, harvest time, planting time, and the like; but these soon become undistinguishable and forgotten. Like other slaves, I cannot tell how old I am. This destitution was among my earliest troubles. I learned when I grew up, that my master—and this is the case with masters generally —allowed no questions to be put to him, by which a slave might learn his age. Such questions are deemed evidence of impatience, and even of impudent curiosity. From certain events, however, the dates of which I have since learned, I suppose myself to have been born about the year 1817.

The first experience of life with me that I now remember—and I remember it but hazily—began in the family of my grandmother and grandfather, Betsey and Isaac Baily. They were quite advanced in life, and had long lived on the spot where they then resided. They were considered old settlers in the neighborhood, and, from certain circumstances, I infer that my grandmother, especially, was held in high esteem, far higher than is the lot of most colored persons in the slave states. She was a good nurse, and a capital hand at making nets for catching shad and herring; and these nets were in great demand, not only in Tuckahoe, but at Denton and Hillsboro, neighboring villages. She was not only good at making the nets, but was also somewhat famous for her good fortune in taking the fishes referred to. I have known her to be in the water half the day. Grandmother was likewise more provident than most of her neighbors in the preservation of seedling sweet potatoes, and it happened to her—as it will happen to any careful and thrifty person residing in an ignorant and improvident community—to enjoy the reputation of having been born to "good luck." Her "good luck" was owing to the exceeding care which she took in preventing the succulent root from getting bruised

in the digging, and in placing it beyond the reach of frost, by actually burying it under the hearth of her cabin during the winter months. In the time of planting sweet potatoes, "Grandmother Betty," as she was familiarly called, was sent for in all directions, simply to place the seedling potatoes in the hills; for superstition had it, that if "Grandmamma Betty but touches them at planting, they will be sure to grow and flourish." This high reputation was full of advantage to her, and to the children around her. Though Tuckahoe had but few of the good things of life, yet of such as it did possess grandmother got a full share, in the way of presents. If good potato crops came after her planting, she was not forgotten by those for whom she planted; and as she was remembered by others, so she remembered the hungry little ones around her.

The dwelling of my grandmother and grandfather had few pretensions. It was a log hut, or cabin, built of clay, wood, and straw. At a distance it resembled—though it was much smaller, less commodious and less substantial—the cabins erected in the western states by the first settlers. To my child's eye, however, it was a noble structure, admirably adapted to promote the comforts and conveniences of its inmates. A few rough, Virginia fence-rails, flung loosely over the rafters above, answered the triple purpose of floors, ceilings, and bedsteads. To be sure, this upper apartment was reached only by a ladder—but what in the world for climbing could be better than a ladder? To me, this ladder was really a high invention, and possessed a sort of charm as I played with delight upon the rounds of it. In this little hut there was a large family of children: I dare not say how many. My grandmother—whether because too old for field service, or because she had so faithfully discharged the duties of her station in early life, I know not—enjoyed the high privilege of living in a cabin, separate from the quarter, with no other burden than her own support, and the necessary care of the little children, imposed. She evidently esteemed it a great fortune to live so. The children were not her own, but her grandchildren—the children of her daughters. She took delight in having them around her, and in attending to their few wants. The practice of separating children from their mothers, and hiring the latter out at distances too great to admit of their meeting, except at long intervals, is a marked feature of the cruelty and barbarity of the slave system. But it is in harmony with the grand aim of slavery, which, always and everywhere, is to reduce man to a level with the brute. It is a successful method of obliterating from the mind and heart of the slave, all just ideas of the sacredness of *the family*, as an institution.

. . .

Living here, with my dear old grandmother and grandfather, it was a long time before I knew myself to be *a slave*. I knew many other things before I knew that. Grandmother and grandfather were the greatest people in the world to me; and being with them so snugly in their own little cabin—I supposed it be their own—knowing no higher authority over me or the other children than the authority of grandmamma, for a time there was nothing to disturb me; but, as I grew larger and older, I learned by degrees the sad fact, that the "little hut," and the lot on which it stood, belonged not to my dear old grandparents, but to some person who lived a great distance off, and who was called, by grandmother, "Old Master." I further learned the sadder fact, that not only the house and lot, but that grandmother herself, (grandfather was free,) and all the little children around her, belonged to this mysterious personage, called by grandmother, with every mark of reverence, "Old Master." Thus early did clouds and shadows begin to fall upon my path. Once on the track—troubles never come singly—I was not long in finding out another fact, still more grievous to my childish heart. I was told that this "old master," whose name seemed ever to be mentioned with fear and shuddering, only allowed the children to live with grandmother for a limited time, and that in fact as soon as they were big enough, they were promptly taken away, to live with the said "old master." These were distressing revelations indeed; and though I was quite too young to comprehend the full import of the intelligence, and mostly spent my childhood days in gleesome sports with the other children, a shade of disquiet rested upon me.

. . .

Children have their sorrows as well as men and women; and it would be well to remember this in our dealings with them. Slave-children *are* children, and prove no exceptions to the general rule. The liability to be separated from my grandmother, seldom or never to see her again, haunted me. I dreaded the thought of going to live with that mysterious "old master," whose name I never heard mentioned with affection, but always with fear. I look back to this as among the heaviest of my childhood's sorrows. My grandmother! my grandmother! and the little hut, and the joyous circle under her care, but especially *she*, who made us sorry when she left us but for an hour, and glad on her return,—how could I leave her and the good old home?

But the sorrows of childhood, like the pleasures of after life, are transient. It is not even within the power of slavery to write *indelible* sorrow, at a single dash, over the heart of a child.

"The tear down childhood's cheek that flows,
Is like the dew-drop on the rose,—
When next the summer breeze comes by,
And waves the bush,—the flower is dry."

There is, after all, but little difference in the measure of contentment felt by the slave-child neglected and the slaveholder's child cared for and petted. The spirit of the All Just mercifully holds the balance for the young.

The slaveholder, having nothing to fear from impotent childhood, easily affords to refrain from cruel inflictions; and if cold and hunger do not pierce the tender frame, the first seven or eight years of the slave-boy's life are about as full of sweet content as those of the most favored and petted *white* children of the slaveholder. The slave-boy escapes many troubles which befall and vex his white brother. He seldom has to listen to lectures on propriety of behavior, or on anything else. He is never chided for handling his little knife and fork improperly or awkwardly, for he uses none. He is never reprimanded for soiling the table-cloth, for he takes his meals on the clay floor. He never has the misfortune, in his games or sports, of soiling or tearing his clothes, for he has almost none to soil or tear. He is never expected to act like a nice little gentleman, for he is only a rude little slave. Thus, freed from all restraint, the slave-boy can be, in his life and conduct, a genuine boy, doing whatever his boyish nature suggests; enacting, by turns, all the strange antics and freaks of horses, dogs, pigs, and barn-door fowls, without in any manner compromising his dignity, or incurring reproach of any sort. He literally runs wild; has no pretty little verses to learn in the nursery; no nice little speeches to make for aunts, uncles, or cousins, to show how smart he is; and, if he can only manage to keep out of the way of the heavy feet and fists of the older slave boys, he may trot on, in his joyous and roguish tricks, as happy as any little heathen under the palm trees of Africa. . . .

FROM CHAPTER 6

I have already referred to the business-like aspect of Col. Lloyd's plantation. This business-like appearance was much increased on the two days at the end of each month, when the slaves from the different farms came to get their monthly allowance of meal and meat. These were gala days for the slaves, and there was much rivalry among them as to *who* should be elected to go up to the great house farm for the allowance, and, indeed, to attend to any business at this, (for them,) the capital. The beauty and grandeur of the place, its numerous slave population, and the fact that Harry, Peter and Jake—the sailors of the sloop—almost always kept, privately, little trinkets which they bought at Baltimore, to sell, made it a privilege to come to the great house farm. Being selected, too, for this office, was deemed a high honor. It was taken as a proof of confidence and favor; but, probably, the chief motive of the competitors for the place, was, a desire to break the dull monotony of the field, and to get beyond the overseer's eye and lash. Once on the road with an ox team, and seated on the tongue of his cart, with no overseer to look after him, the slave was comparatively free; and, if thoughtful, he had time to think. Slaves are generally expected to sing as well as to work. A silent slave is not liked by masters or overseers. *"Make a noise," "make a noise,"* and *"bear a hand,"* are the words usually addressed to the slaves when there is silence amongst them. This may account for the almost constant singing heard in the southern states. There was, generally, more or less singing among the teamsters, as it was one means of letting the overseer know where they were, and that they were moving on with the work. But, on allowance day, those who visited the great house farm were peculiarly excited and noisy. While on their way, they would make the dense old woods, for miles around, reverberate with their wild notes. These were not always merry because they were wild. On the contrary, they were mostly of a plaintive cast, and told a tale of grief and sorrow. In the most boisterous outbursts of rapturous sentiment, there was ever a tinge of deep melancholy. I have never heard any songs like those anywhere since I left slavery, except when in Ireland. There I heard the same *wailing notes*, and was

much affected by them. It was during the famine of 1845–6. In all the songs of the slaves, there was ever some expression in praise of the great house farm; something which would flatter the pride of the owner, and, possibly, draw a favorable glance from him.

> "I am going away to the great house farm,
>   O yea! O yea! O yea!
> My old master is a good old master,
>   Oh yea! O yea! O yea!"

This they would sing, with other words of their own improvising—jargon to others, but full of meaning to themselves. I have sometimes thought, that the mere hearing of these songs would do more to impress truly spiritual-minded men and women with the soul-crushing and death-dealing character of slavery, than the reading of whole volumes of its mere physical cruelties. They speak to the heart and to the soul of the thoughtful. I cannot better express my sense of them now, than ten years ago, when, in sketching my life, I thus spoke of this feature of my plantation experience:

"I did not, when a slave, understand the deep meanings of those rude, and apparently incoherent songs. I was myself within the circle, so that I neither saw nor heard as those without might see and hear. They told a tale which was then altogether beyond my feeble comprehension; they were tones, loud, long and deep, breathing the prayer and complaint of souls boiling over wtih the bitterest anguish. Every tone was a testimony against slavery, and a prayer to God for deliverance from chains. The hearing of those wild notes always depressed my spirits, and filled my heart with ineffable sadness. The mere recurrence, even now, afflicts my spirit, and while I am writing these lines, my tears are falling. To those songs I trace my first glimmering conceptions of the dehumanizing character of slavery. I can never get rid of that conception. Those songs still follow me, to deepen my hatred of slavery, and quicken my sympathies for my brethren in bonds. If any one wishes to be impressed with a sense of the soul-killing power of slavery, let him go to Col. Lloyd's plantation, and, on allowance day, place himself in the deep, pine woods, and there let him, in silence, thoughtfully analyze the sounds that shall pass through the chambers of his soul, and if he is not thus impressed, it will only be because 'there is no flesh in his obdurate heart.'"

The remark is not unfrequently made, that slaves are the most contented and happy laborers in the world. They dance and sing, and make all manner of joyful noises—so they do; but it is a great mistake to suppose them happy because they sing. The songs of the slave represent the sorrows, rather than the joys, of his heart; and he is relieved by them, only as an aching heart is relieved by its tears. Such is the constitution of the human mind, that, when pressed to extremes, it often avails itself of the most opposite methods. Extremes meet in mind as in matter. When the slaves on board of the "Pearl" were overtaken, arrested, and carried to prison—their hopes for freedom blasted—as they marched in chains they sang, and found (as Emily Edmunson tells us) a melancholy relief in singing. The singing of a man cast away on a desolate island, might be as appropriately considered an evidence of his contentment and happiness, as the singing of a slave. Sorrow and desolation have their songs, as well as joy and peace. Slaves sing more to *make* themselves happy, than to express their happiness.

. . .

FROM CHAPTER 10

. . . My new mistress happily proved to be all she *seemed* to be, when, with her husband, she met me at the door, with a most beaming, benignant countenance. She was, naturally, of an excellent disposition, kind, gentle and cheerful. The supercilious contempt for the rights and feelings of the slave, and the petulance and bad humor which generally characterize slaveholding ladies, were all quite absent from kind "Miss" Sophia's manner and bearing toward me. She had, in truth, never been a slaveholder, but had—a thing quite unusual in the south—depended almost entirely upon her own industry for a living. To this fact the dear lady, no doubt, owed the excellent preservation of her natural goodness of heart, for slavery can change a saint into a sinner, and an angel into a demon. I hardly knew how to behave toward "Miss Sophia," as I used to call Mrs. Hugh Auld. I had been treated as a *pig* on the plantation; I was treated as a *child* now. I could not even approach her as I had formerly approached Mrs. Thomas Auld. How could I hang down my head, and speak with bated breath, when there was no pride to scorn me, no coldness to repel me, and no hatred to inspire me with fear? I therefore soon learned to regard her as something more akin to a mother, than a slaveholding mistress. The crouching servility of a slave, usually so acceptable a quality to the haughty slaveholder, was not understood nor desired by this gentle woman. So far from deeming it impudent in a slave to look her straight in the face, as some slaveholding ladies do, she seemed ever to say, "look up, child; don't be afraid; see, I am full of kindness and good will toward you." The hands belonging to Col. Lloyd's sloop, esteemed it a great privilege to be the bearers of parcels or messages to my new mistress; for whenever they came, they were sure of a most kind and pleasant reception. If little Thomas was her son, and her most dearly beloved child, she, for a time, at least, made me something like his half-brother in her affections. If dear Tommy was exalted to a place on his mother's knee, "Foddy" was honored by a place at his mother's side. Nor did he lack the caressing strokes of her gentle hand, to convince him that, though *motherless*, he was not *friendless*. Mrs. Auld was not only a kind-hearted woman, but she was remarkably pious; frequent in her attendance of public worship, much given to reading the bible, and to chanting hymns of praise, when alone. Mr. Hugh Auld was altogether a different character. He cared very little about religion, knew more of the world, and was more of the world, than his wife. He set out, doubtless, to be—as the world goes—a respectable man, and to get on by becoming a successful ship builder, in that city of ship building. This was his ambition, and it fully occupied him. I was, of course, of very little consequence to him, compared with what I was to good Mrs. Auld; and, when he smiled upon me, as he sometimes did, the smile was borrowed from his lovely wife, and, like all borrowed light, was transient, and vanished with the source whence it was derived. While I must characterize Master Hugh as being a very sour man, and of forbidding appearance, it is due to him to acknowledge, that he was never very cruel to me, according to the notion of cruelty in Maryland. The first year or two which I spent in his house, he left me almost exclusively to the management of his wife. She was my lawgiver. In hands so tender as hers, and in the absence of the cruelties of the plantation, I became, both physically and mentally, much more sensitive to good and ill treatment; and, perhaps, suffered more from a frown from my mistress, than I formerly did from a cuff at the hands of Aunt Katy. Instead of the cold, damp floor of my old master's kitchen, I found myself on carpets; for the corn bag in winter, I now had a good straw bed, well furnished with covers; for the coarse corn-meal in the morning, I now had good bread, and mush occasionally; for my poor tow-linen shirt, reaching to my knees, I had good, clean clothes. I was really well off. My employment was to run of errands, and to take care of Tommy; to prevent his getting in the way of carriages, and to keep him out of harm's way generally. Tommy, and I, and his mother, got on swimmingly together, for a time. I say *for a time,* because the fatal poison of irresponsible power, and the natural influence of slavery customs, were not long in making a suitable impression on the gentle and loving disposition of my excellent mistress. At first, Mrs. Auld evidently regarded me simply as a child, like any other child; she had not come to regard me as *property.* This latter thought was a thing of conventional growth. The first was natural and spontaneous. A noble nature, like hers, could not, instantly, be wholly perverted; and it took several years to change the natural sweetness of her temper into fretful bitterness. In her worst estate, however, there were, during the first seven years I lived with her, occasional returns of her former kindly disposition.

The frequent hearing of my mistress reading the bible—for she often read aloud when her husband was absent—soon awakened my curiosity in respect to this *mystery* of reading, and roused in me the desire to learn. Having no fear of my kind mistress before my eyes, (she had then given me no reason to fear,) I frankly asked her to teach me to read; and, without hesitation, the dear woman began the task, and very soon, by her assistance, I was master of the alphabet, and could spell words of three or four letters. My mistress seemed almost as proud of my progress, as if I had been her own child; and, supposing that her husband would be as well pleased, she made no secret of what she was doing for me. Indeed, she exultingly told him of the aptness of her pupil, of her intention to persevere in teaching me, and of the duty which she felt it to teach me, at least to read *the bible.* Here arose the first cloud over my Baltimore prospects, the precursor of drenching rains and chilling blasts.

Master Hugh was amazed at the simplicity of his spouse, and, probably for the first time, he unfolded to her the true philosophy of slavery, and the peculiar rules necessary to be observed by masters and mistresses, in the management of their human chattels. Mr. Auld promptly forbade the continuance of her instruction; telling her, in the first place, that the thing itself was unlawful; that it was also unsafe, and could only lead to mischief. To use his own words, further, he said, "if you give a nigger an inch, he will take an ell;" "he should know nothing but the will of his master, and learn to obey it." "Learning would spoil the best nigger in the world;" "if you teach that nigger—speaking of myself—how to read the bible, there will be no keeping him;" "it would forever unfit him for the duties of a slave;" and "as to himself, learning would do him no good, but probably, a great deal of harm—making him disconsolate and unhappy." "If you learn him now to read, he'll want to know how to write; and, this accomplished, he'll be running away with himself." Such was the tenor of Master Hugh's oracular exposition of the true philosophy of training a human chattel; and it must be confessed that he very clearly comprehended the nature and the requirements of the relation of master and slave. His discourse was the first decidedly antislavery lecture to which it had been my lot to listen. Mrs. Auld evidently felt the force of his remarks; and, like an obedient wife, began to shape her course in the direction indicated by her husband. The effect of his words, *on me,* was neither slight nor transitory. His iron sentences—cold and harsh—sunk deep into my heart, and stirred up not only my feelings into a sort of rebellion, but awakened within me a slumbering train of vital thought. It was a new and special revelation, dispelling a painful mystery, against which my youthful understanding had struggled, and struggled in vain, to wit: the *white* man's power to perpetuate the enslavement of the *black* man. "Very well," thought I; "knowledge unfits a child to be a slave." I instinctively assented to the proposition; and from that moment I understood the direct pathway from slavery to freedom. This was just what I needed; and I got it at a time, and from a source, whence I least expected it. I was saddened at the thought of losing the assistance of my kind mistress; but the information, so instantly derived, to some extent compensated me for the loss I had sustained in this direction. Wise as Mr. Auld was, he evidently underrated my comprehension, and had little idea of the use to which I was capable of putting the impressive lesson he was giving to his wife. *He* wanted me to be *a slave;* I had already voted against that on the home plantation of Col. Lloyd. That which he most loved I most hated; and the very determination which he expressed to keep me in ignorance, only rendered me the more resolute in seeking intelligence. In learning to read, therefore, I am not sure that I do not owe quite as much to the opposition of my master, as to the kindly assistance of my amiable mistress. I acknowledge the benefit rendered me by the one, and by the other; believing, that but for my mistress, I might have grown up in ignorance.

. . .

FROM CHAPTER 11

. . . In ceasing to instruct me, she must begin to justify herself *to* herself; and, once consenting to take sides in such a debate, she was riveted to her position. One needs very little knowledge of moral philosophy, to see *where* my mistress now landed. She finally became even more violent in her opposition to my learning to read, than was her husband himself. She was not satisfied with simply doing as *well* as her husband had commanded her, but seemed resolved to better his instruction. Nothing appeared to make my poor mistress—after her turning toward the downward path—more angry, than seeing me, seated in some nook or corner, quietly reading a book or a newspaper. I have had her rush at me, with the utmost fury, and snatch from my hand such newspaper or book, with something of the wrath and consternation which a traitor might be supposed to feel on being discovered in a plot by some dangerous spy.

Mrs. Auld was an apt woman, and the advice of her husband, and her own experience, soon demonstrated, to her entire satisfaction, that education and slavery are incompatible with each other. When this conviction was thoroughly established, I was most narrowly watched in all my movements. If I remained in a separate room from the family for any considerable length of time, I was sure to be suspected of having a book, and was at once called upon to give an account of myself. All this, however, was entirely *too late*. The first, and never to be retraced, step had been taken. In teaching me the alphabet, in the days of her simplicity and kindness, my mistress had given me the *"inch,"* and now, no ordinary precaution could prevent me from taking the *"ell."*

Seized with a determination to learn to read, at any cost, I hit upon many expedients to accomplish the desired end. The plea which I mainly adopted, and the one by which I was most successful, was that of using my young white playmates, with whom I met in the street, as teachers. I used to carry, almost constantly, a copy of Webster's spelling book in my pocket; and, when sent of errands, or when play time was allowed me, I would step, with my young friends, aside, and take a lesson in spelling. I generally paid my *tuition fee* to the boys, with bread, which I also carried in my pocket. For a single biscuit, any of my hungry little comrades would give me a lesson more valuable to me than bread. Not every one, however, demanded this consideration, for there were those who took pleasure in teaching me, whenever I had a chance to be taught by them. I am strongly tempted to give the names of two or three of those little boys, as a slight testimonial of the gratitude and affection I bear them, but prudence forbids; not that it would injure me, but it might, possibly, embarrass them; for it is almost an unpardonable offense to do any thing, directly or indirectly, to promote a slave's freedom, in a slave state. It is enough to say, of my warm-hearted little play fellows, that they lived on Philpot street, very near Durgin & Bailey's shipyard.

Although slavery was a delicate subject, and very cautiously talked about among grown up people in Maryland, I frequently talked about it—and that very freely—with the white boys. I would, sometimes, say to them, while seated on a curb stone or a cellar door, "I wish I could be free, as you will be when you get to be men." "You will be free, you know, as soon as you are twenty-one, and can go where you like, but I am a slave for life. Have I not as good a right to be free as you have?" Words like these, I observed, always troubled them; and I had no small satisfaction in wringing from the boys, occasionally, that fresh and bitter condemnation of slavery, that springs from nature, unseared and unperverted. Of all consciences, let me have those to deal with which have not been bewildered by the cares of life. I do not remember ever to have met with a *boy*, while I was in slavery, who defended the slave system; but I have often had boys to console me, with the hope that something would yet occur, by which I might be made free. Over and over again, they have told me, that "they believed *I* had as good a right to be free as *they* had;" and that "they did not believe God ever made any one to be a slave." The reader will easily see, that such little conversations with my play fellows, had no tendency to weaken my love of liberty, nor to render me contented with my condition as a slave.

JOHN BROWN (1800–1859)

John Brown was born in Connecticut, but was raised in the newly opened region of the Western Reserve, now Ohio. He was intelligent, rigorous, and ambitious, but his life was for many years a record of failures, sometimes tainted with a hint of financial dishonesty. The habit of failure prompted him to be on the move, always with a new project, and in 1855 he went to the Territory of Kansas, but this time not on just another business project. There something like guerrilla war prevailed between the free-state men and the proslavery men, and Brown's intention was to make himself a leader. of the first faction. As a result of his exploits in Kansas he did come to national reputation, even if he concealed from his idealistic admirers in the East his most noteworthy exploit, the Pottawatomie massacre. In that most brutal episode of that brutal time and place five men were taken from their beds and chopped down—not primarily as punishment for acts of their own but as examples.

In 1859, without disclosing the true nature of his design, John Brown raised money from the "Secret Six" (see p. 1159), prominent and wealthy antislavery men in the North, chiefly in Boston, and led a raid upon Harper's Ferry, Virginia (now West Virginia), with the intention of seizing the United States arsenal there, arming the local slaves, and leading a general insurrection. The first victim was, ironically enough, not a slaveholder but a free Negro of Harper's Ferry; no slaves rose, and Brown was taken by a detachment of marines under the command of Colonel Robert E. Lee and, with those of his men who had survived the fighting, was tried by the state of Virginia. In the early part of the trial, Brown, in spite of the fact that his party was heavily armed and had killed a man at the opening of the raid, and that he was well supplied with pikes to distribute to slaves, claimed that no violence had ever been intended; but at some point in the proceedings his attitude changed and he welcomed the role of martyr, not allowing his defense to use the plea of insanity.[1] He was convicted and hanged. In the latter part of the trial, and while awaiting execution, Brown conducted himself with great dignity and spoke with eloquence.

The raid, especially since it was financed by prominent northern citizens, drove many southerners of moderate opinion to feel that bloody conspiracies were being hatched against them, provoked in many quarters hysterical fears of insurrection, and in general strengthened the influence of the "fire-eaters." Although there were massive anti-Brown rallies in New York and elsewhere in the North, in that section, and even in Europe, Brown became the great martyr of

---

[1] Among close relatives who were, according to affidavits collected for Brown's defense, insane, completely or intermittently, were a grandmother, his mother, five uncles and aunts, one niece, six first cousins, and two sons. The two sons were, however, by his first wife, who was insane. Nineteen affidavits signed by relatives, friends, and an old business associate declared that Brown himself was mad; an uncle swore that Brown had, for twenty years, suffered from fits of insanity.

Though a number of historians, some of great eminence, have accepted the affidavits, the most recent biographer of Brown, Stephen B. Oates, is inclined to discount them, on two grounds: they were assembled for the purpose of saving Brown's life, and they can scarcely be said to represent clinical findings. Oates is especially concerned to attack the psychoanalytic interpretation by Allan Nevins (*The Emergence of Lincoln*, Vol. 2) of Brown as suffering from "ambitious paranoia."

In one sense, the affidavits, whatever may be made of them, are not finally important. Brown stated, over and over, that he regarded himself the appointed agent of God, to be judged by God alone, not by man, and according to Mrs. Doyle, in her eyewitness account of the killing of her husband and sons, Brown "said if a man stood between him and what he considered right, he would take his life as coolly as he would eat his breakfast." The question is, simply, whether we take Brown to be, in Theodore Parker's words, "transcendental-wise" or "transcendental-mad" (see pp. 345–46) —a question not to be settled merely by clinical analysis.

the abolitionist cause. Louisa May Alcott, resident of Concord and author of *Little Women*, named him "Saint John the Just." Wendell Phillips called Brown "the impersonation of God's law." A little later, from Italy, Garibaldi greeted Lincoln, no doubt to Lincoln's great surprise, as the heir of the aspirations of Christ and John Brown. We have already encountered the views of Emerson, Lowell, Longfellow, and Thoreau. Thoreau, in fact, proclaimed that

those who did not appreciate John Brown did not have "ethereal natures"; by this standard, Hawthorne, Whittier, and Lincoln did not have ethereal natures.

But whatever John Brown actually was, the raid on Harper's Ferry was a crucial event in the long drift toward the Civil War, and when war did come, John Brown became a symbol, and a song by which men marched to die. The symbol, and the song, absorbed the man.

FURTHER READINGS

James C. Malin, *John Brown and the Legend of Fifty-Six* (1942)
Allan Nevins, *The Emergence of Lincoln*, Vol. 2 (1950)
Stephen B. Oates, *To Purge This Land with Blood: A Biography of John Brown* (1970)

Oswald Garrison Villard, *John Brown* (1911)
Hill Peebles Wilson, *John Brown: Soldier of Fortune* (1913)
C. Vann Woodward "John Brown's Private War," in *The Burden of Southern History* (1960)

Letter to Mary Brown and Children

Charlestown, Jefferson Co, Va.
31st Oct. [1859]

My dear Wife, & Children every One

I suppose you have learned before this by the newspapers that Two weeks ago today we were fighting for our lives at Harpers ferry: that during the fight Watson was mortally wounded; Oliver killed, Wm Thompson killed, & Dauphin slightly wounded. That on the following day I was taken prisoner immediately after which I received several Sabre-cuts in my head; & Bayonet stabs in my body. As nearly as I can learn Watson died of his wound on Wednesday the 2d or on Thursday the 3d day after I was taken.

Dauphin was killed when I was taken; & Anderson I suppose also. I have since been tried, & found guilty of Treason, etc; and of murder in the first degree. I have not yet received my sentence. No others of the company with whom you were acquainted were, so far as *I can learn*, either killed or taken. Under all these terrible calamities; I feel quite cheerful in the assurance that God reigns; & will overrule all for his glory; & the best possible good. I feel *no* consciousness of *guilt* in the matter: nor even mortifycation on account of my imprisonment; & irons; & I feel perfectly sure that

very soon no member of my family will feel any possible disposition to "blush on my account." Already dear friends at a distance with kindest sympathy are cheering me with the assurance that *posterity* at least will do me justice. I shall commend you all together, with my beloved; but bereaved daughters in law, to their sympathies which I do not doubt will reach you.

I also commend you all to Him "whose mercy endureth forever:" to the God of my *fathers* "whose I am; & whom I serve." "He will never leave you nor forsake you," unless you forsake Him. Finally my dearly beloved be of good comfort. Be sure to remember *& to follow my advice* & my example too; so far as it has been consistent with the holy religion of Jesus Christ in which I remain a most firm, & humble believer. Never forget the poor nor think anything you bestow on them to be lost, to you even though they may be as *black* as Ebedmelch the Ethiopean eunuch who cared for Jeremiah in the pit of the dungeon; or as *black* as the one to whom Phillip preached Christ. Be sure to entertain strangers, for thereby some have—"Remember them that are in bonds as bound with them." I am in charge of a jailor *like* the one who took charge of "Paul & Silas;" & you may rest assured that both *kind hearts* & *kind faces* are more or less about me; whilst thousands are thirsting for my blood. "These *light* afflictions which are but *for a moment* shall work out for us a *far more exceeding & eternal* weight of Glory." I hope to be able to write to you again. My wounds are doing well. Copy this, & send it to your sorrow stricken brothers, Ruth; to comfort them. Write me a few words in regard to the welfare of all. God Almighty bless you all: & "make you joyful in the midst of all your tribulations." Write to

John Brown Charlestown Jefferson Co, Va, care of Capt John Avis.

Your Affectionate Husband, & Father,

P S Yesterday Nov 2d I was sentenced to be hanged on Decem 2d next. Do not grieve on my account. I am still quite cheerful. God bless you all.

Yours ever

Letter to E. Brown

Charlestown, Jefferson County, Va.
Nov. 1, 1859

My Dear Friend E. B. of R. I.: Your most cheering letter of the 27th of Oct. is received, and may the Lord reward you a thousand fold for the kind feeling you express toward me; but more especially for your fidelity to the "poor that cry, and those that have no help." For this I am a prisoner in bonds. It is solely my own fault, in a military point of view, that we met with our disaster—I mean that I mingled with our prisoners and so far sympathized with them and their families that I neglected my duty *in other* respects. But God's will, not mine, be done.

You know that Christ once armed Peter. So also in my case, I think he put a sword into my hand, and there continued it, so long as he saw best, and then kindly took it from me. I mean when I first went to Kansas. I wish you could know with what cheerfulness I am now wielding the "Sword of the Spirit" on the right hand and on the left. I bless God that it proves "mighty to the pulling down of strongholds." I always loved my Quaker friends, and I commend to their kind regard my poor, bereaved widowed wife, and my daughters and daughters-in-law, whose husbands fell at my side. One is a mother and the other likely to become so

soon. They, as well as my own sorrow-stricken daughter[s], are left very poor, and have much greater need of sympathy than I, who, through Infinite Grace and the kindness of strangers, am "joyful in all my tribulations."

Dear sister, write them at North Elba, Essex Co., N.Y., to comfort their sad hearts. Direct to Mary A. Brown, wife of John Brown. There is also another—a widow, wife of Thompson, who fell with my poor boys in the affair at Harper's Ferry, at the same place.

I do not feel conscious of guilt in taking up arms; and had it been in behalf of the rich and powerful, the intelligent, the great—as men count greatness—of those who form enactments to suit themselves and corrupt others, or some of their friends, that I interfered, suffered, sacrificed, and fell, it would have been doing very well. But enough of this.

These light afflictions which endure for a moment, shall work out for me *a far more exceeding and eternal weight of glory.* I would be very grateful for another letter from you. My wounds are healing.
Farewell. God will surely attend to his own cause in the best possible way and time, and he will not forget the work of his own hands.

Your friend,

Letter to Mary Brown

Charlestown Jefferson Co. Va.
10th Nov. 1859

My Dear devoted Wife
I have just learned from Mr. Hoyt of Boston that he saw you with dear kind friends in Phila-

delphia on your return trip you had so far made in the expectation of again seeing me in this world of "sin & sorrow." I need not tell you that I had a great desire to see you again: but that many strong objections exist in my mind against it. I have before alluded to them in what I have said in my other letters (which I hope you will soon get) & will not now repeat them; as it is exceedingly laborious for me to write at all. I am under renewed obligation to you my ever faithful & beloved wife, for heeding what may be my last but earnest request. I have before given you a very brief statement of the fall of our dear sons; & other friends. Full particulars relating to our disaster; I cannot now give: & may never give *probably*. I am greatly comforted by learning of the kindness already shown you; & allow me *humbly* to repeat the language of a far greater man & better sinner than I. "I have been young; & now am old: yet have I not seen the righteous forsaken nor his seed begging bread." I will here say that the sacrifizes *you*; & I, have been called to make in behalf of the *cause we love* the *cause of God; & of humanity*: do not seem to me as at all too great. I have been *whiped* as the saying *is*; but am sure I can recover all the lost capital occasioned by that disaster; by only hanging a few moments by the neck; & I feel quite determined to make the utmost possible out of a defeat. I am dayly & hourly striving to gather up what little I may from the wreck. I mean to write you as *much & as often* as I have Strength (or may be permitted to write.) "Be of good cheer:" in the world we must have tribulation: but the *cords* that have bound *you* as well as I; to earth: have been many of them severed already. Let us with sincere gratitude receive all that "our Father in Heaven" may send us; for "he doeth all things well." *You* must kiss our dear children and grandchildren for me. May the "God of my fathers" be the God, & father of all—"To him be everlasting praise." "Although the fig tree shall not blossom: neither shall fruit be in the vines: the labour of the olive shall fail, and the fields shall yield no meat: the flock shall be cut off from the fold, and there shall be no herd in the stalls: yet *I will rejoice* in the Lord, I will joy in the God of my salvation." I want dear Ruth; or *Anne*; to send copies (when they can) to their deeply afflicted brothers, of all I write. I cannot muster strength to write them all. If after Virginia has applied the finishing stroke to the picture already made of me (in order to "*establish Justice*") you can afford to meet the expence & trouble of coming on here to gather up the bones of our beloved sons, & of your husband; and the people here will suffer you to do so; I should be entirely willing. I have just received a most welcome letter from a dear old- friend of my youth; Rev. H. L. Vail of Litchfield, Connecticut. Will you get some kind friend to copy this letter to you & send him very plain as all the acknowledgement I have *now* strength to make him; & the other kind friends he mentions. I cannot write my friends as I would do; if I had strength. Will you answer to Jeremiah in the same way *for the present* a letter I have received from him? Write me wont you? God bless you all

Your affectionate Husband

The Last Paper Written by John Brown, Handed to One of the Guards on the Morning of His Execution

Charlestown, Va., Dec. 2, 1859

I, John Brown, am now quite *certain* that the crimes of this *guilty land* will never be purged away but with *blood*. I had, as I now think vainly, flattered myself that without very much bloodshed it might be done.

ABRAHAM LINCOLN (1809–1865)

Abraham Lincoln was born in the "knob" country of Kentucky, knew the poverty and hardship of the backwoods, and as a result of taking a flatboat down to New Orleans, knew the life of the Mississippi. Later he would know the life of a settlement in Illinois, storekeeping, splitting rails, managing a little mill, and then, after years of study at night, practicing law on a country circuit. If Shakespeare, the Bible, John Bunyan, and Defoe were in his head, the tales and the idiom of the frontier were there too (he was later to remark that all his best stories came from country people); and if the gangling bumpkin with the melancholy face did (contrary to legend) become the successful attorney who tried important railroad and business cases, he was still remembered as the wrestler who, in the open patch of ground near Orfutt's store, had thrown the formidable champion of Clarey's Grove and who won the bet that he could lift a barrel of whisky and drink from the bunghole. Allowing for regional and personal differences, he belongs to the same race as Longstreet, Crockett, and the thousands of young lawyers and politicians who had their roots deep in the back country. Lincoln did not, like Longstreet, put his tales in a book and get an honorary degree from Yale, but he did carry them into cabinet meetings where, though they were not universally appreciated, they served, as his friend Lamon reports, as "labor-saving contrivances" to cut through pomposity, pretentious argument, and formality to get to the core of an issue; and some critics profess to hear, behind the choice language of his greatest speeches, the rhythms of the tall tale. But this is not to be taken to mean, as Edmund Wilson has put it, that Lincoln was "a folksy and jocular countryman swapping yarns at the village store." Though he had fully immersed himself in that world, he had always known that he was not of it, and had no intention of remaining in it.

The question of slavery and the Union lay not only at the center of the political career of Lincoln, but, for a long period, close to the central concerns of literature. Furthermore, Lincoln himself, as both man and symbol, was inextricably involved with these concerns and in that role became a subject of literature. It is worthwhile, then, to point out, however briefly, the relation of the Great Emancipator to those questions.

As early as 1837, when Lincoln was only 28 and was a Whig representative in the general assembly in Illinois, he was one of the two members who opposed a resolution affirming the legality of slavery and who countered with the statement that "slavery is founded on both injustice and bad policy," adding, however, that "the promulgation of abolition doctrines tends rather to increase than to abate its evils." Thus Lincoln early held that slavery was morally wrong, but disassociated himself from the abolitionists who wished to treat the moral question outside of legal, political, and social contexts.

This distinction runs throughout Lincoln's subsequent career. He did *not* favor an unqualified repeal of the Fugitive Slave Laws; and though he opposed slavery in the territories, he did not, in theory, oppose the admission of states in which slavery had been legally established by their constitutions; and he held that Congress had "no power, under the Constitution, to interfere with the institution of slavery in the different states." He would have had no sympathy for Thoreau's civil disobedience, and while Emerson proclaimed that John Brown had "made the gallows glorious as the Cross," Lincoln merely said, according to the newspaper report of his speech, that he believed "the attack of Brown wrong for two reasons. It was a violation of law and it was futile as far as any effect it might have on the extinction of a great evil." When the Emancipation Proclamation came, on January 1, 1863, it came strictly as a war measure of limited applicability, and only after long hesitation and doubt as to the Proclamation's constitutionality. Lincoln believed in the Constitution and detested the anarchic attitude symbolized by Garrison's burning of that document, or for the appeal many abolitionists made to the "Higher Law."

A second distinction that Lincoln insisted on is that between his personal feelings and moral preferences on one hand and his role as a public official bound by an oath of office on the other. In 1864, in a letter to the editor of a newspaper in Kentucky, after reference to his personal distaste for slavery, he said: "And yet I have never understood that the Presidency conferred upon me an unrestricted right to act officially upon this judgment and feeling. It was in the oath

I took that I would, to the best of my ability, preserve, protect, and defend the Constitution of the United States. I understood, too, that in ordinary civil administration the oath even forbade me to practically indulge my primary abstract judgments on the moral question of slavery."

A third aspect of the attitude toward slavery appears in relation to the Union. As Lincoln put his oath to defend the Constitution above his "abstract judgment," so, as a corollary, he put his obligation to maintain the Union—the very Union which Garrisonian abolitionists would have dissolved even before it was dissolved by southern secessionists—above his desire to emancipate the slaves.

But the defense of the Union was, for Lincoln, more than a corollary of the oath. If the "government of the people, by the people, for the people" should "perish from the earth," there would be no freedom for anyone—including those who were, at the moment, slaves. By this line of argument, the survival of the Union as the fundamental embodiment of, and instrumentality for, freedom, would take precedence over all other considerations. By such logic, Lincoln's moral sense would seem to come to terms with his constitutional view and, it may be added, with his political sense—for a crusade against slavery was the last thing to be popular as a war aim. The popular aim was to maintain the Union, and that for reasons sometimes more complex and less grandiose than those expressed by Lincoln. When in 1862, pressed by Horace Greeley, the influential editor of the New York Tribune, he could reply, in a famous letter:

I would save the Union. I would save it the shortest way under the Constitution. The sooner the national authority can be restored, the nearer the Union will be "the Union as it was." If there be those who would not save the Union, unless they could at the same time save slavery, I do not agree with them. If there be those who would not save the Union unless they could at the same time destroy slavery, I do not agree with them. My paramount object in this struggle is to save the Union, and is not either to save or to destroy slavery. If I could save the Union without freeing any slave, I would do it, and if I could save it by freeing all the slaves I would do it; and if I could save it by freeing some and leaving others alone I would also do that.

Alexander Stephens, the Vice President of the Confederacy, was to say that the Union, for Lincoln, had risen to the sublimity of religious mysticism. Though hard-core abolitionists were more likely to regard Lincoln as a "slave-hound" —to quote Wendell Phillips, the great abolitionist orator—than a religious mystic, it was this view of the Union which Lincoln did manage to impose on the imagination of a number of his countrymen and which we find widely echoed in literature, notably in Whitman.

Lincoln's view of the Union implied that the war was being fought not merely to conquer and occupy territory, but to reestablish a community of common interests that had once existed. But Lincoln hinted more than once at another dimension of that community that had led to the struggle and that continued in the struggle. For instance, in a letter of 1864 to the editor in Kentucky, he says: "If God now wills the removal of a great wrong, and wills also that we of the North, as well as the South, shall pay fairly for our complicity in that wrong, impartial history will find therein new cause to attest and revere the justice and goodness of God." What we find here, and elsewhere, is the notion of a community in guilt—a complicity that belongs to the general human lot.

There is one more dimension. Carl Sandburg, the poet and biographer of Lincoln, suggests that in the Gettysburg Address, when Lincoln says that the "brave men, living and dead, who struggled here" had consecrated the spot, he may well be referring not merely to "brave Union men," but to both Union and Confederate soldiers bound together in that community of heroism. It is these lost notions of community that most deeply affected our literature.

To turn to the story of Lincoln as a literary man, it is well to remember that when he was young and feeling his way into the world, he wrote a few poems that are not without merit. But his literary genius, though nourished by a life-long reading of poetry, lay in prose. That genius depended for its fruition, however, on another kind of genius—a genuis for self-comprehension and self-discipline. Lincoln was a man of unsleeping ambition, but just as his will to power was modified by the realization that power achieves its fullest exercise in the context of moral awareness, so language as an instrument of power might be most effective if it involved those precisions and depths made possible by aesthetic awareness. If Lincoln had the will of a man of power he also had the sensibility of an artist.

That combination is well illustrated in a letter by his old law partner William Herndon:

> Mr. Lincoln's habits, methods of reading law, politics, poetry, etc., etc., were to come into the office, pick up books, newspapers, etc., and to sprawl himself out on the sofa, chairs, etc., and read aloud, much to my annoyance. I have asked him often why he did so and his invariable reply was: "I catch the idea by two senses, for when I read aloud I hear what is read and I see it; and hence two senses get it and I remember it better, if I do not understand it better."

The point is not that Lincoln read poetry in his law office, but that he read aloud, to "catch the idea by two senses"; in other words, if he read with the practical man's concern for the "idea," he also had the instinct to immerse himself in the medium in which the idea was embodied. As far as we can make out, Lincoln did have a need for literature; in the same way as he had a need for the comic art of the spoken tale, without which, he once said, he might have gone crazy, he had a need, even in the darkest and most crowded days of the war, for reading, studying, and memorizing Shakespeare. Study had been a life-long habit, and his early study of rhetoric had given him a coolly calculated intellectual base for his own compositions. In this connection Edmund Wilson analyzes a passage from a private letter written when Lincoln was thirty-three:

> "The second [cause of his correspondent's

melancholy] is, the absence of all business and conversation of friends, which might divert your mind, and give it occasional rest from that intensity of thought, which will sometimes wear the sweetest idea threadbare and turn it to the bitterness of death." Here, in the final phrases, the balance of vowels and consonants, the assonance and alliteration, the progression from the long "e"s of "sweetest idea," over which one would want to linger, to the short and closed vowels of "bitterness of death," which chill the lyrical rhythm and bite it off at the end.

Lincoln's writing is characteristically directed to practical occasions, and this practical motive did indeed limit the range of application of his artistic powers; but it did not prevent his creative imagination from seizing on and embodying in language the deepest dimensions of meaning, intellectual and emotional, in an occasion. In actuality, he did not, apparently, feel a vindictive distinction between the practical and the artistic realms. He had been bred up in the tradition of eighteenth-century rationalism, and that remained the bias of his mind. Shakespeare and the Bible were fundamental to him, but neither encourages romantic self-dramatization or romantic self-indulgence, and neither encourages a division between the sense of beauty and the sense of reality. If Lincoln as a young man, took Henry Clay as his model for eloquence, he admired his eloquence as eloquence with a purpose: "All his efforts were for practical effect. He never spoke merely to be heard."

For Lincoln's temperament a better schooling than he had could scarcely be devised: it provided the poles of eloquence and logic, of imagination and wit, of a sense of human aspiration and a respect for the hard actualities of life. He was, as we have said, soaked in Shakespeare and the Bible, but that elevation of language was countered by the cool precision of the language of *Pilgrim's Progress* and *Robinson Crusoe*, and later, when he studied law, by the surgical logicality of *Blackstone's Commentaries* and the Olympian irony of Gibbon's *Decline and Fall of the Roman Empire*. Behind this world of books lay, too, the world of the frontier, with on the one hand its own combination of the language of fact, and the metaphors of fact, drawn from the transactions of daily activity, and on the other hand a boisterous language of imagination and wit.

Such was the background of Lincoln's accomplishment, but it must be remembered that the accomplishment came of ambition and will that manifested themselves in devoted study—a habit that, in the back country, was often interpreted as laziness. Lincoln's kinsman Dennis Hankins called him "a very lazy man" and explained by adding that he was "always reading, scribbling, ciphering, and writing poetry." There is no evidence that Lincoln's mind was peculiarly quick, and in this connection it is significant to remember that Lincoln was not a fluent impromptu speaker. Quite the contrary, his impromptu speeches were dull and flat. As he said, he had to think with a pencil. He was a "writer," and he needed the writer's detachment and time to search his own feelings and marshal his thoughts into a composition. In other words, a limitation of mind may well have driven him to those stolen hours of solitude that made the Gettysburg Address immortal.

Lincoln did not have one style; he had several, but all were grounded in his sense of the occasion for which he was writing, a matter of business to a politician or rebuke or praise to a general, an expression of condolence to a bereaved mother, a report to Congress, or a ceremonial address such as that at Gettysburg or at the second inauguration. He never forgot the ideal he had found realized in Clay, that language is not to be spoken "merely to be heard," nor written as a matter of vanity and self-indulgence. It must be consistent with the deeper implications of the occasion and must be adapted to the particular audience. The hours spent in the stores, doggeries, inns, and taverns swapping tales with some higgledy-piggledy gathering of the back country had given him a rigorous education in assessing the response of an audience, for the spoken tale is a fine and demanding art, calling for subtle shades in narrative, characterization, and comic effect.

The base of Lincoln's style, too, remained a simple, bare, factual language, with imagery drawn from the world of that language. When, in the early days of the war, it was reported to him that General McClellan was willing to serve as his adviser in government, Lincoln reflected on the man who, when his horse happened to kick up and got a foot caught in the stirrup, said to the animal, "If you are going to get on, I will get off." McClellan's pretensions could scarcely survive that story. Lincoln could use such language and imagery to cut through the technical language of the military world and ironically reduce its pomposities in order to specify the central nature of a problem. For instance, there is the letter to General Hooker, who, after his defeat at Chancellorsville, was prepared to take risks to redeem his reputation:

> If he [Lee] should leave a rear force at Fredericksburg, tempting you to fall upon it, it would fight in entrenchments, and have you at a disadvantage, and so, man for man, worst you at that point, while his main force would in some way be getting an advantage of you northward. In one word, I would not take any risk of being entangled upon the river, like an ox jumped over a fence, and liable to be torn by dogs, front and rear, without a fair chance to gore one way or kick the other.

But from the base of such simple, bare, factual language, Lincoln could erect the elevated effects of the Gettysburg Address.

FURTHER READINGS

Roy Basler, ed., *The Collected Works of Abraham Lincoln* (1953)

Roy Basler, *The Lincoln Legend* (1935)
Albert J. Beveridge, *Abraham Lincoln* (1928)

Courtland Canby, ed., *Lincoln and the Civil War* (1960)
Herbert Joseph Edwards and John Erskine Hankins, *Lincoln the Writer* (1962)
Lloyd Lewis, *Myths After Lincoln* (1929)

Allan Nevins, *The Emergence of Lincoln* (1950)
David Potter, "The Lincoln Theme and American Historiography," in *The South and Sectional Conflict* (1968)
Carl Sandburg, *Abraham Lincoln* (1926; 1939)

Dixon Wecter, "The Democrat as Hero," in *The Hero in America* (1941)
Edmund Wilson, "Abraham Lincoln," in *Patriotic Gore* (1962)

Letter to Colonel Allen

During Lincoln's campaign for the legislature in 1836, a certain Colonel Allen gave dark hints concerning his fitness for office. Lincoln's reply is composed in simple language, but beneath that simple surface it is very precise, and there is a complex control of tone that makes the letter a masterpiece of sustained and destructive irony.

New Salem, June 21, 1836

I am told that during my absence last week, you passed through this place, and stated publicly, that you were in possession of a fact or facts, which, if known to the public, would entirely destroy the prospects of N. W. Edwards and myself at the ensuing election; but that through favour to us, you should forbear to divulge them.

No one has needed favours more than I, and generally, few have been less unwilling to accept them; but in this case, favour to me would be injustice to the public, and therefore I must beg your pardon for declining it. That I once had the confidence of the people of Sangamon is sufficiently evident, and if I have since done anything, either by design or misadventure, which if known, would subject me to a forfeiture of that confidence, he that knows that thing, and conceals it, is a traitor to his country's interest.

I find myself wholly unable to form any conjecture of what fact or facts, real or supposed, you spoke; but my opinion of your veracity will not permit me for a moment to doubt that you at least believed what you said.

I am flattered with the personal regard you manifested for me, but I do hope that, on more mature reflection, you will view the public interest as a paramount consideration, and, therefore, determine to let the worst come.

I here assure you that the candid statement of facts, on your part, however low it may sink me, shall never break the tie of personal friendship between us.

I wish an answer to this, and you are at liberty to publish both if you choose.

Very Respectfully,

Letter to General Hooker

Irony was not an obviously prevailing characteristic of the writings of Lincoln, but Lincoln was a humorist, and irony, no doubt, played its part in his famous tales. The Marquis de Chambrun, among others, noted a "trace of irony always to be found in his wit," and the ironical turn of mind may sporadically appear in letters not generally ironical. A letter to General Carl Schurz provides a nice instance. Schurz, who dearly loved speechmaking, applied to Lincoln to be relieved of active duty in the army in order to take part in the presidential campaign of 1864. To this request, Lincoln replied: "I perceive no objection to your making a political speech when you are where one is to be made, but quite surely speaking in the North and fighting in the South, at the same time, are not possible." Or later, concerning Schurz, Lincoln wrote to Andrew Johnson, then Governor of Tennessee, in the same tone: "I appreciate him certainly as highly as you do; but you can never know until you have the trial, how difficult it is to find a *place* for an officer of so high a rank, when there is no place seeking *him*."

The irony in the following letter to Hooker concerning dictatorship was not lost on Fighting Joe; it brought tears to his eyes; and no doubt the irony seemed more poignant after he had lost the battle of Chancellorsville, and was removed.

Executive Mansion
Washington, January 26, 1863

I have placed you at the head of the Army of the Potomac. Of course I have done this upon what appears to me to be sufficient reasons. And yet I think it best for you to know that there are some things in regard to which I am not quite satisfied with you. I believe you to be a brave and skillful soldier, which, of course, I like. I also believe you do not mix politics with your profession, in which you are right. You have confidence in yourself, which is a valuable, if not an indispensable quality. You are ambitious, which, within reasonable bounds, does good rather than harm. But I think that during Gen. Burnside's command of the army, you have taken counsel of your ambition, and thwarted him as much as you could, in which you did a great wrong to the country, and to a most meritorious and honorable brother officer. I have heard, in such a way as to believe it, of your recently saying that both the army and the government needed a dictator. Of course it was not *for* this, but in spite of it, that I have given you the command. Only those generals who gain successes can set up dictators. What I now ask of you is military success, and I will risk the dictatorship. The government will support you to the utmost of its ability, which is neither more nor less than it has done and will do for all commanders. I much fear that the spirit which you have aided to infuse into the army, of criticizing their commander, and withholding confidence from him, will now turn upon you. I shall assist you, as far as I can, to put it down. Neither you, nor Napoleon, if he were alive again, could get any good out of an army while such a spirit prevails in it.

And now beware of rashness. Beware of rashness, but with energy, and sleepless vigilance, go forward, and give us victories.

Yours very truly,

From Cooper Institute Address (1860)

The debate, in 1859, between Stephen A. Douglas, the "Little Giant," and Lincoln, in the campaign for the United States Senate, made Lincoln a national figure, even if Douglas won the election. The appearance of Lincoln at the Cooper Institute in New York, on February 27, 1860, was crucial for his presidential ambitions. He was known, but this was his first appearance in the East, where it was generally supposed that the untutored lawyer from Illinois would bring to this more sophisticated audience the spread-eagle bombast of the frontier. What he offered was an argument of rigorous structure in a plain style which could accommodate both subtle irony and controlled eloquence.

The excerpt offered here appears in the second half of the address. The text is that revised for publication, after its delivery.

And now, if they would listen—as I suppose they will not—I would address a few words to the Southern people.

I would say to them:—You consider yourselves a reasonable and a just people; and I consider that in the general qualities of reason and justice you are not inferior to any other people. Still, when you speak of us Republicans, you do so only to denounce us as reptiles, or, at the best, as no better than outlaws. You will grant a hearing to pirates or murderers, but nothing like it to "Black Republicans." In all your contentions with one another, each of you deems an unconditional condemnation of "Black Republicanism" as the first thing to be attended to. Indeed, such condemnation of us seems to be an indispensable prerequisite—license, so to speak—among you to be admitted or permitted to speak at all. Now, can you, or not, be prevailed upon to pause and to consider whether this is quite just to us, or even to yourselves? Bring forward your charges and specifications, and then be patient long enough to hear us deny or justify.

You say we are sectional. We deny it. That makes an issue; and the burden of proof is upon you. You produce your proof; and what is it? Why, that our party has no existence in your section—gets no votes in your section. The fact is substantially true; but does it prove the issue? If it does, then in case we should, without change of principle, begin to get votes in your section, we should thereby cease to be sectional. You cannot escape this conclusion; and yet, are you willing to abide by it? If you are, you will probably soon find that we have ceased to be sectional, for we shall get votes in your section this very year. You will then begin to discover, as the truth plainly is, that your proof does not touch the issue. The fact that we get no votes in your section, is a fact of your making, and not of ours. And if there be fault in that fact, that fault is primarily yours, and remains until you show that we repel you by some wrong principle or practice. If we do repel you by any wrong principle or practice, the fault is ours; but this brings you to where you ought to have started —to a discussion of the right or wrong of our principle. If our principle, put in practice, would wrong your section for the benefit of ours, or for any other object, then our principle, and we with it, are sectional, and are justly opposed and denounced as such. Meet us, then, on the question of whether our principle, put in practice, would wrong your section; and so meet it as if it were possible that something may be said on our side. Do you accept the challenge? No! Then you really believe that the principle which "our fathers who framed the Government under which we live" thought so clearly right as to adopt it, and indorse it again and again, upon their official oaths, is in fact so clearly wrong as to demand your condemnation without a moment's consideration.

Some of you delight to flaunt in our faces the warning against sectional parties given by Washington in his Farewell Address. Less than eight years before Washington gave that warning, he had, as President of the United States, approved and signed an act of Congress, enforcing the prohibition of slavery in the Northwestern Territory, which act embodied the policy of the Government upon that subject up to and at the very moment he penned that warning; and about one year after he penned it, he wrote LaFayette that he considered that prohibition a wise measure, expressing in the same connection his hope that we should at some time have a confederacy of free States.

Bearing this in mind, and seeing that sectionalism has since arisen upon this same subject, is that warning a weapon in your hands against us, or in our hands against you? Could Washington himself speak, would he cast the blame of that sectionalism upon us, who sustain his policy, or upon you who repudiate it? We respect that warning of Washington, and we commend it to you, together with his example pointing to the right application of it.

But you say you are conservative—eminently conservative—while we are revolutionary, destructive, or something of the sort. What is conservatism? Is it not adherence to the old and tried, against the new and untried? We stick to, contend for, the identical old policy on the point in controversy which was adopted by "our fathers who framed the Government under which we live;" while you with one accord reject, and scout, and spit upon that old policy, and insist upon substituting something new. True, you disagree among yourselves as to what that substitute shall be. You are divided on new propositions and plans, but you are unanimous in rejecting and denouncing the old policy of the fathers. Some of you are for reviving the foreign slave trade; some for a Congressional Slave-Code for the Territories; some for Congress forbidding the Territories to prohibit Slavery within their limits; some for maintaining Slavery in the Territories through the judiciary; some for the "gur-reat pur-rinciple" that "if one man would enslave another, no third man should object," fantastically called "Popular Sovereignty;" but never a man among you is in favor of federal prohibition of slavery in federal territories, according to the practice of "our fathers who framed the Government under which we live." Not one of all your various plans can show a precedent or an advocate in the century within which our Government originated. Consider, then, whether your claim of conservatism for yourselves, and your charge of destructiveness against us, are based on the most clear and stable foundations.

Again, you say we have made the slavery question more prominent than it formerly was. We deny it. We admit that it is more prominent, but we deny that we made it so. It was not we, but you, who discarded the old policy of the fathers. We resisted, and still resist, your innovation; and thence comes the greater prominence of the question. Would you have that question reduced to its former proportions? Go back to that old policy. What has been will be again, under the same conditions. If you would have the peace of the old times, readopt the precepts and policy of the old times.

You charge that we stir up insurrections among your slaves. We deny it; and what is your proof? Harper's Ferry! John Brown!! John Brown was no Republican; and you have failed to implicate a single Republican in his Harper's Ferry enterprise, If any member of our party is guilty in that matter, you know it or you do not know it. If you do know it, you are inexcusable for not designating the man and proving the fact. If you do not know it, you are inexcusable for asserting it, and especially for persisting in the assertion after you have tried and failed to make the proof. You need not be told that persisting in a charge which one does not know to be true, is simply malicious slander.

Some of you admit that no Republican designedly aided or encouraged the Harper's Ferry affair, but still insist that our doctrines and declarations necessarily lead to such results. We do not believe it. We know we hold to no doctrine, and make no declaration, which were not held to and made by "our fathers who framed the Government under which we live." You never dealt fairly by us in relation to this affair. When it occurred, some important State elections were near at hand, and you were in evident glee with the belief that, by charging the blame upon us, you could get an advantage of us in those elections. The elections came, and your expectations were not quite fulfilled. Every Republican man knew that, as to himself at least, your charge was a slander, and he was not much inclined by it to cast his vote in your favor. Republican doctrines and declarations are accompanied with a continual protest against any interference whatever with your slaves, or with you about your slaves. Surely, this does not encourage them to revolt. True, we do, in common with "our fathers, who framed the Government under which we live," declare our belief that slavery is wrong; but the slaves do not hear us declare even this. For anything we say or do, the slaves would scarcely know there is a Republican party. I believe they would not, in fact, generally know it but for your misrepresentations of us, in their hearing. In your political contests among yourselves, each faction charges the other with sympathy with Black Republicanism; and then, to give point to the charge, defines Black Republicanism to simply be insurrection, blood and thunder among the slaves.

·   ·   ·

In the language of Mr. Jefferson, uttered many years ago, "It is still in our power to direct the process of emancipation, and deportation, peaceably, and in such slow degrees, as that the evil will wear off insensibly; and their places be, *pari passu*, filled up by free white laborers. If, on the contrary, it is left to force itself on, human nature must shudder at the prospect held up."

Mr. Jefferson did not mean to say, nor do I, that the power of emancipation is in the Federal Government. He spoke of Virginia; and, as to the power of emancipation, I speak of the slave-holding States only. The Federal Government, however, as we insist, has the power of restraining the extension of the institution—the power to insure that a slave insurrection shall never occur on any American soil which is now free from slavery.

John Brown's effort was peculiar. It was not a slave insurrection. It was an attempt by white men to get up a revolt among slaves, in which the slaves refused to participate. In fact, it was so absurd that the slaves, with all their ignorance, saw plainly enough it could not succeed. That affair, in its philosophy, corresponds with the many attempts, related in history, at the assassination of kings and emperors. An enthusiast broods over the oppression of a people till he fancies himself commissioned by Heaven to liberate them. He ventures the attempt, which ends in little else than his own execution. Orsini's attempt on Louis Napoleon, and John Brown's attempt at Harper's Ferry were, in their philosophy, precisely the same. The eagerness to cast blame on old England in the one case, and on New England in the other, does not disprove the sameness of the two things.

And how much would it avail you, if you could, by the use of John Brown, Helper's Book, and the like, break up the Republican organization? Human action can be modified to some extent, but human nature cannot be changed. There is a judgment and a feeling against slavery in this nation, which cast at least a million and a half of votes. You cannot destroy that judgment and feeling—that sentiment—by breaking up the political organization which rallies around it. You can scarcely scatter and disperse an army which has been formed into order in the face of your heaviest fire; but if you could, how much would you gain by forcing the sentiment which created it out of the peaceful channel of the ballot-box, into some other channel? What would that other channel probably be? Would the number of John Browns be lessened or enlarged by the operation?

Gettysburg Address (1863)

The dedication of the cemetery at Gettysburg (November 19, 1863) was shot through with ironies. For the main event, the oration, the commissioners had no difficulty in deciding on Edward Everett, the first American to hold a Ph.D. (from Göttingen), who had been minister to Great Britain, Secretary of State, Senator from Massachusetts, and president of Harvard, and who was generally acclaimed as the foremost orator of the time. They had hoped to have an ode to follow his oration, but having failed to entice Longfellow, Whittier, Bryant, and even the now forgotten George Boker, they invited Lincoln to fill the dead space on the program and make a "few remarks," even though, as one commissioner later divulged, there was doubt "as to his ability to speak upon such a grave and solemn occasion." Indeed, Lincoln had no reputation for eloquence, and even at late as 1863 the educated public would have agreed with Harriet Beecher Stowe's estimate of him as "a plain working man of the people, with no more culture, instruction, or education than any such working man might obtain for himself." Furthermore, his political prestige, in spite of the victory at Gettysburg, was now at its nadir.

The address may well be the peak of eloquence and poetic power offered at any public occasion in America, but we do not even know for sure where and when it was written. A part was certainly composed at Washington, and, though the old tale that the whole was written on the back of an envelope on the train trip to Gettysburg is definitely not true, Lincoln may have done some work on it under those circumstances. That night, at Gettysburg, in the house of Judge David Wills, Lincoln presumably finished his first draft and read it to Secretary Seward; next morning he copied it. When, that afternoon, he delivered it, he made an important addition, the phrase "under God," in the last sentence.

It is not entirely clear, furthermore, what reception the piece got. Benjamin B. French, who was the author of the hymn for the occasion and who was on the platform, reports that "a hurricane of applause" met "every word." Joseph L. Gilbert, who covered the event for the Associated Press, reports that of the "tumultuous outbursts of enthusiasm" supposed to have greeted the address, he "heard none" and adds that there was "no outward manifestation of feeling." The truth may lie somewhere between these versions; in any case the audience, being stunned by Everett's two-hour performance, which was probably much nearer to their taste for grandeur, could have had a minimum of sensibility and energy left for Lincoln, who had finished his 270 words and sat down before they could well focus their attention.

As for Lincoln himself, he immediately remarked to a companion on the platform that the address would "not scour"—and there is a characteristic beauty in the contrast between the elevation of the address and this phrase drawn from farming on the prairie, it there being used to describe the situation when soil too wet and sticky would not fold from the plowshare. A considerable number of newspapers agreed that the address would not "scour." By way of comfort, however, Lincoln could remember that the great Dr. Everett had generously congratulated him.

A good deal has been written about the sources of the address, and many parallels, one from Periclean Athens, have been adduced for the memorable last sentence. It is likely that Lincoln drew it from a speech by the learned clergyman Theodore Parker, delivered at the New England Anti-Slavery Convention, in Boston, in 1850: "There is what I call the American idea. This idea demands, as the proximate organization thereof, a democracy,—that is, a government of all the people, by all the people, for all the people. . . ."

For the same passage in the address we are sometimes referred to the peroration of Daniel Webster's reply to Hayne, in the Senate on January 26, 1830.

Lincoln, of course, knew this famous speech,

and it may have been one of the things that early fed his conception of the Union, but there are no verbal parallels. In fact, Webster's speech belongs to the grandiloquent, soaring style to which Lincoln's style, even in its elevated moments, was antithetical. Can we imagine Webster, in an intense utterance, using the word "proposition" (which, by the way, made Matthew Arnold fling down the address unread), with its implications of the coldly mathematical, of impersonal precision? But these implications are what Lincoln did want, and from them stems the power of the absorbed metaphor that such a "proposition" is what is being tested by the utmost rigor of bloody proof in the Civil War—a metaphor worthy of John Donne or Shakespeare. The word "proposition" is, too, one of the prosy, realistic elements on which the more elevated thrusts are based. In this connection, we may compare the sweeping, swooping rhythms of Webster, in the quotation below, with the controlled and complex rhythms of the last paragraph of the address before the powerful release in the final sentence.

When my eyes shall be turned to behold for the last time the sun in heaven, may I not see him shining on the broken and dishonored fragments of a once glorious Union; on States dissevered, discordant, belligerent; on a land rent with civil feuds, or drenched, it may be, in fraternal blood. Let their last feeble and lingering glance behold the gorgeous ensign of the republic, now known and honored throughout the earth, stand full high advanced, its arms and trophies streaming in their original luster, not a stripe erased or polluted, not a single star obscured, bearing for its motto no such miserable interrogatory as "What is all this worth?" nor those other words of delusion and folly, "Liberty first and Union afterwards," but everywhere, spread over all in characters of living light blazing on all its ample folds, as they float over the sea and over the land, and in every wind under the whole heavens, that other sentiment, dear to every true American heart—Liberty *and* Union, now and forever, one and inseparable!

Lincoln wrote at least six copies of the address. The first draft is the one begun at Washington and finished at Gettysburg. The second is that prepared, at Gettysburg, for delivery. The last version, prepared some months after the occasion, was to be bound with the oration by Everett and auctioned off for a patriotic purpose. This definitive version is printed here below, followed by the first and second versions, the order of which is, however, in dispute among scholars.

———————

Four score and seven years ago our fathers brought forth on this continent, a new nation, conceived in Liberty, and dedicated to the proposition that all men are created equal.

Now we are engaged in a great civil war, testing whether that nation, or any nation so conceived and so dedicated, can long endure. We are met on a great battle-field of that war. We have come to dedicate a portion of that field, as a final resting place for those who here gave their lives that that nation might live. It is altogether fitting and proper that we should do this.

But, in a larger sense, we can not dedicate—we can not consecrate—we can not hallow—this ground. The brave men, living and dead, who struggled here, have consecrated it, far above our poor power to add or detract. The world will little note, nor long remember what we say here, but it can never forget what they did here. It is for us the living, rather, to be dedicated here to the unfinished work which they who fought here have thus far so nobly advanced. It is rather for us to be here dedicated to the great task remaining before us—that from these honored dead we take increased devotion to that cause for which they gave the last full measure of devotion—that we here highly resolve that these dead shall not have died in vain—that this nation, under God, shall have a new birth of freedom—and that government of the people, by the people, for the people, shall not perish from the earth.

FIRST(?) DRAFT

"Four score and seven years ago our fathers brought forth, upon this continent, a new nation, conceived in liberty, and dedicated to the proposition that 'all men are created equal'

"Now we are engaged in a great civil war, testing whether that nation, or any nation so conceived, and so dedicated, can long endure. We are met on a great battle field of that war. We have come to dedicate a portion of it, as a final resting place for those who died here, that the nation might live. This we may, in all propriety do. But, in a larger sense, we can not dedicate—we can not consecrate—we can not hallow, this ground—The brave men, living and dead, who struggled here, have hallowed it, far above our poor power to add or detract. The world will little note, nor long remember what we say here; while it can never forget what they *did* here.

"It is rather for us, the living, ~~to stand here,~~ to the great task remaining before us—that, from these honored dead we take increased devotion to that cause for which they here, gave the last full measure of devotion—that we here highly resolve these dead shall not have died in vain; that the nation, shall have a new birth of freedom, and that government of the people by the people for the people, shall not perish from the earth."

SECOND(?) DRAFT

"Four score and seven years ago our fathers brought forth, upon this continent, a new nation, conceived in Liberty, and dedicated to the proposition that all men are created equal.

"Now we are engaged in a great civil war, testing whether that nation, or any nation, so conceived, and so dedicated, can long endure. We are met here on a great battle-field of that war. We have come ~~are met~~ to dedicate a portion of it as ~~the~~ a final resting place ~~of~~ for those who here gave their lives that that nation might live. It is altogether fitting and proper that we should do this.

"But in a larger sense we can not dedicate—we can not consecrate—we can not hallow this ground. The brave men, living and dead, who struggled here, have consecrated it far above our poor power to add or detract. The world will little note, nor long remember, what we say here, but can never forget what they did here. It is for us, the living, rather to be dedicated here to the unfinished work which they have, thus far, so nobly carried on. It is rather for us to be here dedicated to the great task remaining before us—that from these honored dead we take increased devotion to that cause for which they here gave ~~gave~~ the last full measure of devotion—that we here highly resolve that these dead shall not have died in vain; that this nation shall have a new birth of freedom; and that this government of the people, by the people, for the people, shall not perish from the earth."

Letter to Mrs. Bixby

The war department files, to which Lincoln alludes in his letter to Mrs. Bixby, showed that five of her sons had died in battle. But they were in error. Two had died in combat; a third had been captured and exchanged; a fourth had been captured and elected to join the southern army and was officially listed as a deserter; the fifth, who had enlisted as eighteen years old, was discharged on his mother's oath that he was only sixteen and had fits of insanity. These facts, of course, do not impair the eloquence of the letter.

There has been some debate, too, about the authenticity of this, the most famous letter of Lincoln. It has been maintained that John Hay, who served as secretary to Lincoln and was later his biographer, composed the letter, the original of which has never been discovered. But Hay, late in life, stated that the letter was genuine, and that is the view taken by Roy P. Basler, the editor of the works of Lincoln.

Observe the complex implications of the word "beguile." And compare the rhythmic structure with that of the letter to Colonel Allen, and of that to General Hooker.

Executive Mansion,
Washington, Nov. 21, 1864

I have been shown in the files of the war Department a statement of the Adjutant General of

Massachusetts, that you are the mother of five sons who have died gloriously on the field of battle.

I feel how weak and fruitless must be any word of mine which should attempt to beguile you from the grief of a loss so overwhelming. But I cannot refrain from tendering to you the consolation that may be found in the thanks of the Republic they died to save.

I pray that our Heavenly Father may assuage the anguish of your bereavement, and leave you only the cherished memory of the loved and lost, and the solemn pride that must be yours, to have laid so costly a sacrifice upon the altar of Freedom.

Yours, very sincerely and respectfully,

Second Inaugural Address (1865)

By the time this address was delivered the war was clearly won, and Lincoln's thoughts were more and more turning to what kind of Union might now be possible in actuality after it had been asserted in the field at bayonet point. It was already clear that he was to be at loggerheads with the Radicals in Congress, but he was, by death, to be spared the consequences of peace and politics. The letter to Thurlow Weed is a strange sidelight on his feelings. The address itself invites comparison with Melville's *Supplement to Battle-Pieces*, a prose addendum to his volume of poetry.

At this second appearing to take the oath of the presidential office, there is less occasion for an extended address than there was at the first. Then a statement, somewhat in detail, of a course to be pursued, seemed fitting and proper. Now, at the expiration of four years, during which public declarations have been constantly called forth on every point and phase of the great contest which still absorbs the attention, and engrosses the energies of the nation, little that is new could be presented. The progress of our arms, upon which all else chiefly depends, is as well known to the public as to myself; and it is, I trust, reasonably satisfactory and encouraging to all. With high hope for the future, no prediction in regard to it is ventured.

On the occasion corresponding to this four years ago, all thoughts were anxiously directed to an impending civil war. All dreaded it—all sought to avert it. While the inaugeral [sic] address was being delivered from this place, devoted altogether to *saving* the Union without war, insurgent agents were in the city seeking to *destroy* it without war—seeking to dissole [sic] the Union, and divide effects, by negotiation. Both parties deprecated war; but one of them would *make* war rather than let the nation survive; and the other would *accept* war rather than let it perish. And the war came.

One eighth of the whole population were colored slaves, not distributed generally over the Union, but localized in the Southern part of it. These slaves constituted a peculiar and powerful interest. All knew that this interest was, somehow, the cause of the war. To strengthen, perpetuate, and extend this interest was the object for which the insurgents would rend the Union, even by war; while the government claimed no right to do more than to restrict the territorial enlargement of it. Neither party expected for the war, the magnitude, or the duration, which it has already attained. Neither anticipated that the *cause* of the conflict might cease with, or even before, the conflict itself should cease. Each looked for an easier triumph, and a result less fundamental and astounding. Both read the same Bible, and pray to the same God; and each invokes His aid against the other. It may seem strange that any men should dare to ask a just God's assistance in wringing their bread from the sweat of other men's faces; but let us judge not that we be not judged. The prayers of both could not be answered; that of neither has been answered fully. The Almighty has his own purposes. "Woe unto the world because of offences! for it must needs be that offences come; but woe to that man by whom the offence cometh!" If we shall suppose that American Slavery is one of those offences which, in the providence of God, must needs come, but which, having continued through His appointed time, He now wills to remove, and that He gives to both North and South, this terrible war, as the woe due to those by whom the offence came, shall we discern therein any departure from those divine attributes which the believers in a Living God always ascribe to Him? Fondly do we hope—fervently do we pray—

that this mighty scourge of war may speedily pass away. Yet, if God wills that it continue, until all the wealth piled by the bond-man's two hundred and fifty years of unrequited toil shall be sunk, and until every drop of blood drawn with the lash, shall be paid by another drawn with the sword, as was said three thousand years ago, so still it must be said "the judgments of the Lord, are true and righteous altogether"

With malice toward none; with charity for all; with firmness in the right, as God gives us to see the right, let us strive on to finish the work we are in; to bind up the nation's wounds; to care for him who shall have borne the battle, and for his widow, and his orphan—to do all which may achieve and cherish a just and lasting peace, among ourselves, and with all nations.

Letter to Thurlow Weed

Executive Mansion,
Washington, March 15, 1865

Every one likes a compliment. Thank you for yours on my little notification speech, and on the recent Inaugeral [sic] Address. I expect the latter to wear as well as—perhaps better than—anything I have produced; but I believe it is not immediately popular. Men are not flattered by being

shown that there has been a difference of purpose between the Almighty and them. To deny it, however, in this case, is to deny that there is a God governing the world. It is a truth which I thought needed to be told; and as whatever of humiliation there is in it, falls most directly on myself, I thought others might afford for me to tell it.

Yours truly

ROBERT E. LEE (1807–1870)

Robert E. Lee was descended from two of the most notable families of Virginia, and he was to marry into a third, his wife being the great-granddaughter of Martha Washington and the heiress of Arlington—which was seized by the federal government during the Civil War (the mementoes of Washington belonging to the family were hawked about the streets of the capital) and is now the National Cemetery. Lee's father, Light-Horse Harry Lee, was a famous and dashing commander in the Revolution and a close friend of George Washington, and the son seems always to have devotedly held the ideal of Washington in his mind. His own career was, from the first, exemplary, including second place in his class at West Point (where he was called the Marble Model) and distinguished service in the Mexican War.

When the Civil War began, Lee was offered command of the first army that was to be put

into the field by the federal government. He refused the appointment. Though, like many Virginians and other southerners, he disapproved of slavery (Lee had freed all of his own slaves long before the Civil War began, and during its course also freed those he had acquired by marriage), and though he was opposed to secession ("I must say that I am one of those dull creatures that cannot see the good of secession," he said on April 19, 1861, when he heard the news that Virginia had withdrawn from the Union), he felt he had no choice but to follow the fortunes of his state into the Confederacy.

The Confederacy did not award him a military rank equal to that which he had declined in the Union army, and the beginning of his career in the Civil War was attended by indifferent success; but in the end it was his genius for command and the charisma of his personality that sustained Confederate arms. Two days before Appomattox he said that he had never believed in the possibility of victory. "But," he added, "such considerations really made with me no difference."

After the war Lee stood for reconciliation. An indictment for treason was not pursued against him, and he participated in the general amnesty of 1868. Because of his great fame he had long since had opportunities offered from business-men of the North to commercialize his name, but his honor forbade him. Believing that education was the surest way to rebuild the shattered society of the South, he became president of Washington College, in Lexington, Virginia, the college now known as Washington and Lee. He devoted himself to rebuilding the college and using his great prestige for a peaceful re-ordering of the South. He died in 1870.

FURTHER READINGS

Robert E. Lee, Jr., *Recollections and Letters of General Robert E. Lee* (1924)

William E. Dodd, *Lincoln and Lee* (1928)
Clifford Dowdy, *Lee* (1965)

Douglas Southall Freeman, *Robert E. Lee* (1934; 4 vols.)
Dixon Wecter, "Lee: The Aristocrat as Hero," in *The Hero in America* (1941)
Edmund Wilson, "Robert E. Lee," in *Patriotic Gore* (1962)

Farewell Address to the Troops

Headquarters Army of Northern Virginia
10th April 1865

After four years of arduous service marked by unsurpassed courage and fortitude the Army of Northern Virginia has been compelled to yield to overwhelming numbers and resources.

I need not tell the survivors of so many hard fought battles, who have remained steadfast to the last, that I have consented to this result from no distrust of them. But feeling that valor and devotion could accomplish nothing that could compensate for the loss that would have accompanied the continuance of the contest, I determined to avoid the useless sacrifice of those whose past services have endeared them to their country.

By the terms of the agreement Officers and men can return to their homes and remain there until exchanged. You will take with you the satisfaction that proceeds from the consciousness of duty faithfully performed and I earnestly pray that a merciful God will extend to you his blessing and protection.

With an unceasing admiration of your constancy and devotion to your country and a grateful remembrance of your kind and generous consideration of myself, I bid you all an affectionate farewell.

Letter to Matthew Maury

Near Cartersville, Va.
September 8, 1865

I have just received your letter of the 8th ult. We have certainly not found our form of government all that was anticipated by its original founders, but that may be partly our effect in expecting too much and partly in the absence of virtue in the people. As long as virtue was dominant in the republic so long was the happiness of the people secure. I can not, however, despair of it yet. I look forward to better days and trust that time and experience, the great teachers of men, under the guidance of an ever-merciful God, may save us from destruction and restore to us the bright hopes and prospects of the past.

The thought of abandoning the country and all that must be left in it is abhorrent to my feelings, and I prefer to struggle for its restoration and share its fate rather than to give up all as lost. I have a great admiration for Mexico. The salubrity of its climate, the fertility of its soil and the magnificence of its scenery possess for me great charms; but I still look with delight upon the mountains of my native state. To remove our people with their domestics to a portion of Mexico which would be favorable to them would be a work of much difficulty. Did they possess the means and could the system of apprenticeship you suggest be established, the United States Government I think would interpose obstacles; and under the circumstances there would be difficulty in persuading the freedmen to emigrate.

Those citizens who can leave the country and others who may be compelled to do so will reap the fruits of your considerate labor; but I shall be very sorry if your presence be lost to Virginia. She has now need for all her sons and can ill afford to spare you. I am very much obliged to you for all you have done for us, and hope your labors in the future may be as efficacious as in the past and that your separation from us may not be permanent.

The Natural Setting: Travel Literature

From the earliest times—beginning with Captain John Smith and Jamestown—there has been a rich literature of travel in America. (See, for example, Byrd, etc., earlier in this volume.) The selections to follow are from three classics of the period of the first half of the nineteenth century, a period peculiarly fruitful in this form.

JOHN JAMES AUDUBON (1785–1851)

Legend was to have it that Jean Jacques Audubon, of mysterious origin, was the lost Dauphin of France, but he was, in fact, the illegitimate son of a French sea captain, temporarily a merchant and slave trader in Santo Domingo, and his Creole mistress, who died shortly after the child's birth in 1785. The boy was raised in France, by the legal wife of the captain, who had been patiently waiting while he was far away making his fortune. The fortune was made, then lost; and the boy, who cared not at all for any profitable study, only for fishing, hunting, collecting specimens, and drawing, was sent off to Pennsylvania, where the father still owned a farm, to learn English as some preparation for a commercial career.

The early years of the spoiled and headstrong John James tell a story of idleness, ineptitude, bad judgment, and ill fortune, the ill fortune redeemed only by the marriage to a woman with enough devotion and toughness of spirit to survive the fate of being his wife. Failure by failure, Audubon was driven toward his own fated role, and his greatness. His only passion was for the woods, the streams, the study of the creatures that lived there, and the paintings he could make of them, especially of birds. For years this was an aimless passion, but in Louisville, Kentucky, in March, 1810, a stranger came into the store that Audubon was operating, introduced himself as Alexander Wilson, the author of *American Ornithology*, and asked if Audubon, who he understood was interested in birds, would care to subscribe for the work, two volumes of which he had there to exhibit. Audubon did not subscribe, but he now had at least a vague notion of his own direction. He was less and less able to discipline himself to his business, and spent more and more time in fishing and hunting, in seeking the company of men who had known that life a little earlier, before the country began to fill up (he claimed to have actually hunted with Daniel Boone, when Boone was an old man on a visit back to Kentucky), and in drawing. He may have had no special talent as an artist, but the passion was there. It took the place of discipline, and in the end his dream of a collection of "true" paintings of the birds of North America fully possessed him. He became a lonely wanderer, with dog, gun, and sketch box, in the forest or on the rivers contemplating "the beauties of that nature, from which I have certainly derived my greatest pleasures." Meanwhile his wife Lucy and the children waited, poor and sometimes hungry, for the pittance that he might now and then be able to send as a return for doing a portrait or giving some lessons in painting.

Later, when the collection of paintings of birds had been finished, he became a wanderer of another sort, from city to city, even in England, armed with letters of introduction or merely with his obsession, seeking subscribers who would finance the enormously expensive production of the work, waiting day after day in the lobbies and halls of the rich and influential, sometimes enduring contempt and even insult.

In the end, the work was published; but even now his obsession was scarcely diminished, and he embarked on the project of doing a parallel work on the animals of North America. Though now aging, he made a trip West, into the Yellowstone country, hunted buffalo, and saw Indians, even a war party. Then he flung the last of his furious energies into preparing *The Viviparous Quadrupeds of North America*.

He was famous now, much sought after, and rich, and Lucy and the family, including grandchildren, were settled on a handsome estate just north of New York City. But the years of hardship now, suddenly, took their toll. He was losing his sight and could not paint. His mind began to wander, then failed. For several years he lived a shadowy, childlike life. In 1851, after a stroke, he died.

In one of his remarkable journals (1820), Audubon wrote:

Ever since a boy I have had an astonishing desire to see much of the world and particularly to acquire a true knowledge of the birds of North America, consequently, I hunted whenever I had an opportunity, and drew every new specimen as I could, or dared *steal time* from my business.

Deep in himself Audubon knew that the ordinary world of business was not for him, and in the same journal he recognized his deepest longing:

I saw here [at the confluence of the Ohio and the Mississippi] two Indians in a canoe, they spoke some French, had bear traps, uncommonly clean kept, a few venison hams, a gun, and looked so independent, free and unconcerned with the world that I gazed on them, admired their spirits, and wished for their condition.

Audubon came very near to fulfilling his "astonishing desire to see much of the world"—at least that world that was his dream. His dream was not unique. For two hundred years, men had been dreaming of the Eden beauty of the great forests, the majestically uncoiling rivers, and the endless plains of the inner America. For some that dream had been of a land to be possessed and exploited for the use of civilization, but for others it was of a land in which man could joyfully enter nature.

If Audubon, seeing the Indians in the canoe, could wish for "their condition," he knew that the wish was, ultimately, vain; the country was being occupied, the forest was being cut down, the rivers were already fouled, the buffalo herds butchered. There was a tension in his soul about the whole question, as in this passage from a description of the Ohio—"la belle rivière"—in his *Delineations of American Scenery and Character*:

When I think of these times [his early years in Kentucky], and call back to my mind the grandeur and beauty of those almost uninhabited shores; when I picture to myself the dense and lofty summits of the forest, that everywhere spread along the hills, and overhung the margins of the stream, unmolested by the axe of the settler; when I know how dearly purchased the safe navigation of that river has been by the blood of many worthy Virginians; when I see that no longer any Aborigines are to be found there, and that the vast herds of elk, deer and buffaloes which once pastured on these hills and in these valleys, making for themselves great roads to the several salt-springs, have ceased to exist; when I reflect that all this grand portion of our Union, instead of being in a state of nature, is now more or less covered with villages, farms and towns, where the din of hammers and machinery is constantly heard; that the woods are fast disappearing under the axe by day, and the fire by night; that hundreds of steam-boats are gliding to and fro, over the whole length of the majestic river, forcing commerce to take root and to prosper at every spot; when I see the surplus population of Europe coming to assist in the destruction of the forest, and transplanting civilization into its darkest recesses;—when I remember that these extraordinary changes have all taken place in the short period of twenty years, I pause, wonder, and, although I know all to be fact, can scarcely believe its reality.

Whether these changes are for the better or for the worse, I shall not pretend to say; but in whatever way my conclusions may incline, I feel with regret that there are on record no satisfactory accounts of the state of that portion of the country, from the time when our people first settled in it. This has not been because no one in America is able to accomplish such an undertaking. Our Irvings and our Coopers have proved themselves fully competent for the task. It has more probably been because the changes have succeeded each other with such rapidity, as almost to rival the movements of their pen. However, it is not too late yet; and I sincerely hope that either or both of them will ere long furnish the generations to come with those delightful descriptions which they are so well qualified to give, of the original state of a country that has been so rapidly forced to change her form and attire under the influence of increasing population. Yes, I hope to read, ere I close my earthly career, accounts from those delightful writers of the progress of civilization in our western country. They will speak of the Clarks, the Croghans, the Boones, and many other men of great and daring enterprise. They will analyze, as it were, into each component part, the country as it once existed, and will render the picture, as it ought to be, immortal.

Audubon knew that it was too late for his dream of man's sinking joyfully into nature, and he could even praise, though in somewhat ambiguous inflections, the course of history that had rendered even the dream anachronistic. Now he could only hope for a faithful record, and a fitting monument, to render "immortal" the world that had once provoked that dream. He could scarcely have guessed that his own life would be such a record, and such a monument.

FURTHER READINGS

Maria H. Audubon, *Audubon and His Travels* (1960)
Howard Corning, ed., *Journal of John James Audubon, Made During His Trip to New Orleans in 1820–21* (1929)
———, *Journal of John James Audubon, 1840–43* (1929)
J. F. McDermott, ed., *Audubon in the West* (1965)
Francis Hobart Herrick, ed., *Delineations of American Scenery and Character* (1926)
Donald Culross Peattie, ed., *Audubon's America* (1940)

Alexander B. Adams, *Audubon* (1966)
John Burroughs, *John James Audubon* (1908)
Alice E. Ford, *John James Audubon* (1964)
Francis Hobart Herrick, *Audubon the Naturalist* (1968)

From Ornithological Biography (1839)

The achievement of Audubon as a naturalist and artist outweighs his literary reputation. But even from the first publication of his *Ornithological Biography* (1839), his literary work did receive appreciation. In *Blackwood's Magazine*, the reviewer could say: "Audubon, who had written but little even in his native tongue, under a powerful motive took to writing English, and he was not long in learning to write it well, not only with fluency but with eloquence." The literary achievement, like the artistic, seems to have sprung not from an easy and precocious talent, but from the "powerful motive"—the passionate commitment. But, whatever its source, the achievement is there, the embodiment of a deep life-sense.

Audubon's most consistent writing is in the *Ornithological Biography*, but the journals are fascinating as a document of the life and personality and are occasionally lit by felicitous and interesting passages of description or narrative, by a startling perception of "true knowledge," or by a bright phrase.

THE PRAIRIE

On my return from the Upper Mississippi, I found myself obliged to cross one of the wide Prairies, which, in that portion of the United States vary the appearance of the country. The weather was fine, all around me was as fresh and blooming as if it had just issued from the bosom of nature. My knapsack, my gun, and my dog, were all I had for baggage and company. But, although well moccasined, I moved slowly along, attracted by the brilliancy of the flowers, and the gambols of the fawns around their dams, to all appearance as thoughtless of danger as I felt myself.

My march was of long duration; I saw the sun sinking beneath the horizon long before I could perceive any appearance of woodland, and nothing in the shape of man had I met with that day. The track which I followed was only an old Indian trace, and as darkness overshadowed the prairie, I felt some desire to reach at least a copse, in which I might lie down to rest. The Night-hawks were skimming over and around me, attracted by the buzzing wings of the beetles which form their food, and the distant howling of wolves gave me some hope that I should soon arrive at the skirts of some woodland.

I did so, and almost at the same instant a firelight attracting my eye, I moved towards it, full of confidence that it proceeded from the camp of some wandering Indians. I was mistaken:—I discovered by its glare that it was from the hearth of a small log cabin, and that a tall figure passed and repassed between it and me, as if busily engaged in household arrangements.

I reached the spot, and presenting myself at the door, asked the tall figure, which proved to be a woman, if I might take shelter under her roof for the night. Her voice was gruff, and her attire negligently thrown around her. She answered in the affirmative. I walked in, took a wooden stool, and quietly seated myself by the fire. The next object that attracted my notice was a finely formed young Indian, resting his head between his hands, with his elbows on his knees. A long bow rested against the log wall near him, while a quantity of arrows and two or three raccoon skins lay at his feet. He moved not; he apparently breathed not. Accustomed to the habits of the Indians, and knowing that they pay little attention to the approach of civilized strangers (a circumstance which in some countries is considered as evincing the apathy of their character), I addressed him in French, a language not unfrequently partially known to the people in that neigborhood. He raised his head, pointed to one of his eyes with his finger, and gave me a significant glance with the other. His face was covered with blood. The fact was, that an hour before this, as he was in the act of discharging an arrow at a raccoon in the top of a tree, the arrow had split upon the cord, and sprung back with such violence into his right eye as to destroy it for ever.

Feeling hungry, I inquired what sort of fare I might expect. Such a thing as a bed was not to be seen, but many large untanned bear and buffalo hides lay piled in a corner. I drew a fine time-piece from my breast, and told the woman that it was late, and that I was fatigued. She had espyed my watch, the richness of which seemed to operate upon her feelings with electric quickness. She told me that there was plenty of venison and jerked buffalo meat, and that on removing the ashes I should find a cake. But my watch had struck her fancy, and her curiosity had to be gratified by an immediate sight of it. I took off the gold chain that secured it from around my neck, and presented it to her. She was all ecstasy, spoke of its beauty, asked me its value, and put the chain round her brawny neck, saying how happy the possession of such a watch should make her. Thoughtless, and, as I fancied myself, in so retired a spot, secure, I paid little attention to her talk or her movements. I helped my dog to a good supper of venison, and was not long in satisfying the demands of my own appetite.

The Indian rose from his seat, as if in extreme suffering. He passed and repassed me several times, and once pinched me on the side so violently, that the pain nearly brought forth an exclamation of anger. I looked at him. His eye met mine; but his look was so forbidding, that it struck a chill into the more nervous part of my system. He again seated himself, drew his butcher-knife from its greasy scabbard, examined its edge, as I would do that of a razor suspected dull, replaced it, and again taking his tomahawk from his back, filled the pipe of it with tobacco, and sent me expressive glances whenever our hostess chanced to have her back towards us.

Never until that moment had my senses been awakened to the danger which I now suspected to be about me. I returned glance for glance to my companion, and rested well assured that, whatever enemies I might have, he was not of their number.

I asked the woman for my watch, wound it up, and under pretence of wishing to see how the weather might probably [be] on the morrow, took up my gun, and walked out of the cabin. I slipped a ball into each barrel, scraped the edges of my flints, renewed the primings, and returning to the hut, gave a favourable account of my observations. I took a few bearskins, made a pallet of them, and calling my faithful dog to my side, lay down, with my gun close to my body, and in a few minutes was, to all appearances, fast asleep.

A short time had elapsed, when some voices were heard, and from the corner of my eyes I saw two athletic youths making their entrance, bearing a dead stag on a pole. They disposed of their burden, and asking for whisky, helped themselves freely to it. Observing me and the wounded Indian, they asked who I was, and why the devil that rascal (meaning the Indian, who, they knew, understood not a word of English) was in the house.

The mother—for so she proved to be, bade them speak less loudly, made mention of my watch, and took them to a corner, where a conversation took place, the purport of which it required little shrewdness in me to guess. I tapped my dog gently. He moved his tail, and with indescribable pleasure I saw his fine eyes alternately fixed on me and raised towards the trio in the corner. I felt that he perceived danger in my situation. The Indian exchanged a last glance with me.

The lads had eaten and drunk themselves into such condition, that I already looked upon them as *hors de combat*; and the frequent visits of the whisky bottle to the ugly mouth of their dam I hoped would soon reduce her to a like state. Judge of my astonishment, reader, when I saw this incarnate fiend take a large carving-knife, and go to the grindstone to whet its edge. I saw her pour the water on the turning machine, and watched her working away with the dangerous instrument, until the sweat covered every part of my body, in despite of my determination to defend myself to the last. Her task finished, she walked to her reeling sons, and said. "There, that'll soon settle him! Boys, kill yon ———, and then for the watch."

I turned, cocked my gun-locks silently, touched my faithful companion, and lay ready to start up and shoot the first who might attempt my life. The moment was fast approaching, and that night might have been my last in this world, had not Providence made preparations for my rescue. All was ready. The infernal hag was advancing slowly, probably contemplating the best way of despatching me, whilst her sons should be engaged with the Indian. I was several times on the eve of rising and shooting her on the spot:—but she was not to be punished thus. The door was suddenly opened, and there entered two stout travellers, each with a long rifle on his shoulder. I bounced up on my feet, and making them most heartily welcome, told them how well it was for me that they should have arrived at that moment. The tale was told in a minute. The drunken sons were secured, and the woman, in spite of her defence and vociferations, shared the same fate. The Indian fairly danced with joy, and gave us to understand that, as he could not sleep for pain, he would watch over us. You may suppose we slept much less than we talked. The two strangers gave me an account of their once having been themselves in a somewhat similar situation. Day came, fair and rosy, and with it the punishment of our captives.

They were now quite sobered. Their feet were

unbound, but their arms were still securely tied. We marched them into the woods off the road, and having used them as Regulators were wont to use such delinquents, we set fire to the cabin, gave all the skins and implements to the young Indian warrior, and proceeded, well pleased, towards the settlements.

During upwards of twenty-five years, when my wanderings extended to all parts of our country, this was the only time at which my life was in danger from my fellow creatures. Indeed, so little risk do travellers run in the United States, that no one born there ever dreams of any to be encountered on the road; and I can only account for this occurrence by supposing that the inhabitants of the cabin were not Americans.

Will you believe, reader, that not many miles from the place where this adventure happened, and where fifteen years ago, no habitation belonging to civilized man was expected, and very few ever seen, large roads are now laid out, cultivation has converted the woods into fertile fields, taverns have been erected, and much of what we Americans call comfort is to be met with. So fast does improvement proceed in our abundant and free country.

. . . .

KENTUCKY SPORTS

We have individuals in Kentucky, that even there are considered wonderful adepts in the management of the rifle. To *drive a nail* is a common feat, not more thought of by the Kentuckians than to cut off a wild turkey's head, at a distance of a hundred yards. Others will *bark* off squirrels one after another, until satisfied with the number procured. Some, less intent on destroying game, may be seen under night *snuffing a candle* at the distance of fifty yards, off-hand, without extinguishing it. I have been told that some have proved so expert and cool, as to make choice of the eye of a foe at a wonderful distance, boasting beforehand of the sureness of their piece, which has afterwards been fully proved when the enemy's head has been examined!

Having resided some years in Kentucky, and having more than once been witness of rifle sport, I will present you with the results of my observation, leaving you to judge how far rifle-shooting is understood in that State.

Several individuals who conceive themselves expert in the management of the gun, are often seen to meet for the purpose of displaying their skill, and betting a trifling sum, put up a target, in the centre of which a common-sized nail is hammered for about two-thirds of its length. The marksmen make choice of what they consider a proper distance, which may be forty paces. Each man cleans the interior of his tube, which is called *wiping* it, places a ball in the palm of his hand, pouring as much powder from his horn upon it as will cover it. This quantity is supposed to be sufficient for any distance within a hundred yards. A shot which comes very close to the nail is considered as that of an indifferent marksman; the bending of the nail is, of course, somewhat better; but nothing less than hitting it right on the head is satisfactory. Well, kind reader, one out of three shots generally hits the nail, and should the shooters amount to half a dozen, two nails are frequently needed before each can have a shot. Those who drive the nail have a further trial amongst themselves, and the two best shots of these generally settle the affair, when all the sportsmen adjourn to some house, and spend an hour or two in friendly intercourse, appointing, before they part, a day for another trial. This is technically termed *Driving the Nail*.

Barking off squirrels is delightful sport, and in my opinion requires a greater degree of accuracy than any other. I first witnessed this manner of procuring squirrels whilst near the town of Frankfort. The performer was the celebrated Daniel Boon. We walked out together, and followed the rocky margins of the Kentucky River, until we reached a piece of flat land thickly covered with black walnuts, oaks and hickories. As the general mast was a good one that year, squirrels were seen gamboling on every tree around us. My companion, a stout, hale, and athletic man, dressed in a homespun hunting-shirt, bare-legged and moccasined, carried a long and heavy rifle, which, as he was loading it, he said had proved efficient in all his former undertakings, and which he hoped would not fail on this occasion, as he felt proud to show me his skill. The gun was wiped, the powder measured, the ball patched with six-hundred-thread linen, and the charge sent home with a hickory rod. We moved not a step from the place, for the squirrels were so numerous that it was unnecessary to go after them. Boon pointed to one of these animals which had observed us, and was crouched on a branch about fifty paces distant, and bade me mark well the spot where the ball should hit. He raised his piece gradually, until the *bead* (that being the name given by the Kentuckians to the *sight*) of the barrel was brought to a line with the spot which he intended to hit. The whip-like report resounded through the woods and along the hills in repeated echoes. Judge of my surprise, when I perceived that the ball had hit the piece of the bark immediately beneath the squirrel, and shivered it into splinters, the concussion produced by which had killed the animal, and sent it whirling through the air, as if it had been blown up by explosion of a powder magazine. Boon kept up his firing, and before many hours had elapsed, we had procured as many squirrels as we wished; for you must know, that to load a rifle requires only a moment, and that if it is wiped once after each shot, it will do duty for hours. Since that first interview with our veteran Boon, I have seen many other individuals perform the same feat.

The *snuffing of a candle* with a ball, I first had an opportunity of seeing near the banks of Green River, not far from a large pigeon-roost, to which I had previously made a visit. I heard many reports of guns during the early part of a dark night, and knowing them to be those of rifles, I went towards the spot to ascertain the cause. On reaching the place, I was welcomed by a dozen of tall stout men, who told me they were exercising, for the purpose of enabling them to shoot under night at the reflected light from the eyes of a deer or wolf, by torch-light, of which I shall give you an account somewhere else. A fire was blazing near, the smoke of which rose curling among the thick foliage of the trees. At a distance which rendered it scarcely dstinguishable, stood a burning candle,

as if intended for an offering to the goddess of night, but which in reality was only fifty yards from the spot on which we all stood. One man was within a few yards of it, to watch the effects of the shots, as well as to light the candle should it chance to go out, or to replace it should the shot cut it across. Each marksmen shot in his turn. Some never hit either the snuff or the candle, and were congratulated with a loud laugh; while others actually snuffed the candle without putting it out, and were recompensed for their dexterity by numerous hurrahs. One of them, who was particularly expert, was very fortunate, and snuffed the candle three times out of seven, whilst all the other shots either put out the candle, or cut it immediately under the light.

Of the feats performed by the Kentuckians with the rifle, I could say more than might be expedient on the present occasion. In every thinly peopled portion of the State, it is rare to meet one without a gun of that description, as well as a tomahawk. By way of recreation they often cut off a piece of the bark of a tree, make a target of it, using a little powder wetted with water or saliva for the bull's eye, and shoot into the mark all the balls they have about them, picking them out of the wood again.

After what I have said, you may easily imagine with what ease a Kentuckian procures game, or dispatches an enemy, more especially when I tell you that every one in the State is accustomed to handle the rifle from the time when he is first able to shoulder it until near the close of his career. That murderous weapon is the means of procuring them subsistence during all their wild and extensive rambles, and is the source of their principal sports and pleasures.

On the Dakota Prairies (1843)

July 6, Thursday [1843]. Whilst we were sitting at the back gate of the fort, we saw a parcel of Indians coming towards the place, yelling and singing what Mr. Culbertson told me was the song of the scalp dance; we saw through the telescope that they were fourteen in number, with their faces painted black, and that it was a detachment of a war party. When within a hundred yards they all stopped, as if awaiting an invitation; we did not hurry as to this, and they seated themselves

on the ground and looked at us, while Mr. Culbertson sent Mr. Denig to ask them to come in by the front gate of the fort, and put them in the Indian house, a sort of camp for the fellows. They all looked miserably poor, filthy beyond description, and their black faces and foully smelling Buffalo robes made them appear to me like so many devils. The leader, who was well known to be a famous rascal, and was painted red, was a tall, well-formed man. The party had only three poor guns, and a few had coarse, common lances; every man had a knife, and the leader was armed with a stick in which were inserted three blades of butcher's-knives; a blow from this weapon would doubtless kill a man. Some of the squaws of the fort, having found that they were Assiniboins, went to meet them; they took one of these, and painted her face black, as a sign of friendship. Most of these mighty warriors had a lump of fresh Buffalo meat slung on his back, which was all traded for by Mr. Larpenteur, who gave them in exchange some dried meat, not worth the notice of Harris's dog, and some tobacco.

July 7, Friday. This morning the dirty Indians, who could have washed had they so minded, were beating the tambour and singing their miserable scalp song, until Mr. Culbertson ordered the drum taken away, and gave them more tobacco and some vermilion to bedaub their faces. They were permitted to remain about the fort the remainder of the day, and the night coming they will again be sheltered; but they must depart to-morrow morning.

August 10, Thursday. Although I have said much about Buffalo running, and butchering in general, I have not given the particular manner in which the latter is performed by the hunters of this country—I mean the white hunters—and I will now try to do so. The moment that the Buffalo is dead, three or four hunters, their faces and hands often covered with gunpowder, and with pipes lighted, place the animal on its belly, and by drawing out each fore and hind leg, fix the body so that it cannot fall down again; an incision is made near the root of the tail, immediately above the root in fact, and the skin cut to the neck, and taken off in the roughest manner imaginable, downwards and on both sides at the same time.

The knives are going in all directions, and many wounds occur to the hands and fingers, but are rarely attended to at this time. The pipe of one man has perhaps given out, and with his bloody hands he takes the one of his nearest companion, who has his own hands equally bloody. Now one breaks in the skull of the bull, and with bloody fingers draws out the hot brains and swallows them with peculiar zest; another has now reached the liver, and is gobbling down enormous pieces of it; whilst, perhaps, a third, who has come to the paunch, is feeding luxuriously on some—to me—disgusting-looking offal. But the main business proceeds. The flesh is taken off from the sides of the boss, or hump bones, from where these bones

begin to the very neck, and the hump itself is thus destroyed. The hunters give the name of 'hump' to the mere bones when slightly covered by flesh; and it is cooked, and very good when fat, young, and well broiled. The pieces of flesh taken from the sides of these bones are called *filets*, and are the best portion of the animal when properly cooked. The fore-quarters, or shoulders, are taken off, as well as the hind ones, and the sides, covered by a thin portion of flesh called the *depouille*, are taken out. Then the ribs are broken off at the vertebrae, as well as the boss bones. The marrow-bones, which are those of the fore and hind legs only, are cut out last. The feet usually remain attached to these; the paunch is stripped of its covering of layers of fat, the head and the backbone are left to the Wolves, the pipes are all emptied, the hands, faces, and clothes all bloody, and now a glass of grog is often enjoyed, as the stripping off the skins and flesh of three or four animals is truly very hard work.

In some cases when no water was near, our supper was cooked without our being washed, and it was not until we had travelled several miles the next morning that we had any opportunity of cleaning ourselves; and yet, despite everything, we are all hungry, eat heartily, and sleep soundly. When the wind is high and the Buffaloes run towards it, the hunter's guns very often snap, and it is during their exertions to replenish their pans, that the powder flies and sticks to the moisture every moment accumulating on their faces; but nothing stops these daring and usually powerful men, who the moment the chase is ended, leap from their horses, let them graze, and begin their butcher-like work.

August 11, Friday. The activity of Buffaloes is almost beyond belief; they can climb the steep defiles of the Mauvaises Terres in hundreds of places where men cannot follow them, and it is a fine sight to see a large gang of them proceeding along these defiles four or five hundred feet above the level of the bottoms, and from which pathway if one of the number makes a mis-step or accidentally slips, he goes down rolling over and over, and breaks his neck ere the level ground is reached. The thing that troubles them most is crossing rivers on the ice; their hoofs slip from side to side, they become frightened, and stretch their four legs apart to support the body, and in such situations the Indians and white hunters easily approach, and stab them to the heart, or cut the ham-strings, when they become an easy prey.

When in large gangs those in the centre are supported by those on the outposts, and if the stream is not large, reach the shore and readily escape.

Indians of different tribes hunt the Buffalo in different ways; some hunt on horseback, and use arrows altogether; they are rarely expert in reloading the gun in the close race. Others hunt on foot, using guns, arrows, or both. Others follow with patient perseverance, and kill them also. But I will give you the manner pursued by the Mandans. Twenty to fifty men start, as the occasion suits, each provided with two horses, one of which is a pack-horse, the other fit for the chase. They have quivers with from twenty to fifty arrows, according to the wealth of the hunter. They ride the pack horse bareback, and travel on, till they see the game, when they leave the pack-horse, and leap on the hunter, and start at full speed and soon find themselves amid the Buffaloes, on the flanks of the herd, and on both sides. When within a few yards the arrow is sent, they shoot at a Buffalo somewhat ahead of them, and send the arrow in an oblique manner, so as to pass through the lights. If the blood rushes out of the nose and mouth the animal is fatally wounded, and they shoot no more; if not, a second, and perhaps a third arrow, is sent before this happens.

The buffaloes on starting carry the tail close in between the legs, but when wounded they switch it about, especially if they wish to fight, and then the hunter's horse shies off and lets the mad animal breathe awhile. If shot through the heart, they occasionally fall dead on the instant; sometimes, if not hit in the right place, a dozen arrows will not stop them. When wounded and mad they turn suddenly round upon the hunter, and rush upon him in such a quick and furious manner that if horse and rider are not both on the alert, the former is overtaken, hooked and overthrown, the hunter pitched off, trampled and gored to death. Although the Buffalo is such a large animal, and to all appearance a clumsy one, it can turn with the quickness of thought, and when once enraged, will rarely give up the chase until avenged for the wound it has received. If, however, the hunter is expert, and the horse fleet, they outrun the bull, and it returns to the herd. Usually the greater number of the gang is killed, but it very rarely happens that some of them do not escape.

This however is not the case when the animal is pounded, especially by the Gros Ventres, Black Feet, and Assiniboins. These pounds are called 'parks,' and the Buffaloes are made to enter them in the following manner: The park is sometimes round and sometimes square, this depending much on the ground where it is put up; at the end of the park is what is called a *precipice* of some fifteen feet or more as may be found. It is approached by a funnel-shaped passage, which like the park itself is strongly built of logs, brushwood, and pickets, and when all is ready a young man, very swift of foot, starts at daylight covered over with a Buffalo robe and wearing a Buffalo headdress. The moment he sees the herd to be taken, he bellows like a young calf, and makes his way slowly towards the contracted part of the funnel, imitating the cry of the calf, at frequent intervals. The Buffaloes advance after the decoy; about a dozen mounted hunters are yelling and galloping behind them, and along both flanks of the herd, forcing them by these means to enter the mouth of the funnel.

Women and children are placed behind the fences of the funnel to frighten the cattle, and as soon as the young man who acts as decoy feels assured that the game is in a fair way to follow to the bank or 'precipice,' he runs or leaps down the bank, over the barricade, and either rests, or joins in the fray. The poor Buffaloes, usually headed by a large bull, proceed, leap down the bank in haste and confusion, the Indians all yelling and pursuing till every bull, cow, and calf is impounded. Although this is done at all seasons, it is more general in October or November, when the hides are good and salable.

Now the warriors are all assembled by the pen, calumets are lighted, and the chief smokes to the Great Spirit, the four points of the compass, and lastly to the Buffaloes. The pipe is passed from mouth to mouth in succession, and as soon as this ceremony is ended, the destruction commences. Guns shoot, arrows fly in all directions, and the hunters being on the outside of the enclosure, destroy the whole gang, before they jump over to clean and skin the murdered herd. Even the children shoot small, short arrows to assist in the destruction.

It happens sometimes however, that the leader of the herd will be restless at the sight of the precipices, and if the fence is weak will break through it, and all his fellows follow him, and escape. The same thing sometimes takes place in the pen, for so full does this become occasionally that the animals touch each other, and as they cannot move, the very weight against the fence of the pen is quite enough to break it through; the smallest aperture is sufficient, for in a few minutes it becomes wide, and all the beasts are seen scampering over the prairies, leaving the poor Indians starving and discomfited.

Mr. Kipp told me that while travelling from Lake Travers to the Mandans, in the month of August, he rode in a heavily laden cart for six successive days through masses of Buffaloes, which divided for the cart, allowing it to pass without opposition. He has seen the immense prairie back of Fort Clark look black to the tops of the hills, though the ground was covered with snow, so crowded was it with these animals; and the masses probably extended much further. In fact it is *impossible to describe or even conceive* the vast multitudes of these animals that exist even now, and feed on these ocean-like prairies.

FREDERICK LAW OLMSTED (1822–1903)

Frederick Law Olmsted is best remembered as a landscape architect, especially as responsible for the plan of Central Park in New York, but his books on travel in the South, in the decade before the Civil War, provide an indispensable view of that world which he found so strange but which he made such efforts to understand and record honestly. His record comes through the eyes of an emancipationist—not an abolitionist.

FURTHER READINGS

Frederick Law Olmsted, A *Journey in the Backcountry* (1860)
———, A *Journey in the Seaboard Slave States* (1860)
———, A *Journey Through Texas* (1857)
———, *The Cotton Kingdom* (an abridgment of the three previous books; 1860)

Frederick Law Olmstead, Jr., *Frederick Law Olmsted, Landscape Architect* (1922)
Broadus Mitchell, *Frederick Law Olmsted, a Critic of the Old South* (1924)

From A Journey in the Seaboard Slave States (1860)

A TOBACCO PLANTATION

Half an hour after this I arrived at the negro-quarters—a little hamlet of ten or twelve small and dilapidated cabins. Just beyond them was a plain farm-gate, at which several negroes were standing; one of them, a well-made man, with an intelligent countenance and prompt manner, directed me how to find my way to his owner's house. It was still nearly a mile distant; and yet, until I arrived in its immediate vicinity, I saw no cultivated field, and but one clearing. In the edge of this clearing, a number of negroes, male and female, lay stretched out upon the ground near a small smoking charcoal pit. Their master afterwards informed me that they were burning charcoal for the plantation blacksmith, using the time allowed them for holidays—from Christmas to New Year's—to earn a little money for themselves in this way. He paid them by the bushel for it. When I said that I supposed he allowed them to take what wood they chose for this purpose, he replied that he had five hundred acres covered with wood, which he would be very glad to have any one burn, or clear off in any way. Cannot some Yankee contrive a method of concentrating some of the valuable properties of this old-field pine, so that they may be profitably brought into use in more cultivated regions? Charcoal is now brought to New York from Virginia; but when made from pine it is not very valuable, and will only bear transportation from the banks of the navigable rivers, whence it can be shipped, at one movement, to New York. Turpentine does not flow in sufficient quantity from this variety of the pine to be profitably collected and for lumber it is of very small value.

Mr. W.'s house was an old family mansion, which he had himself remodeled in the Grecian style and furnished with a large wooden portico. An oak forest had originally occupied the ground where it stood; but this having been cleared and the soil worn out in cultivation by the previous proprietors, pine woods now surrounded it in every direction, a square of a few acres only being kept clear immediately about it. A number of the old oaks still stood in the rear of the house, and, until Mr. W. commenced his improvements, there had been some in its front. These, however, he had cut away, as interfering with the symmetry of his grounds, and in place of them had planted ailanthus trees in parallel rows.

On three sides of the outer part of the cleared square there was a row of large and comfortable-looking negro-quarters, stables, tobacco-houses, and other offices, built of logs.

Mr. W. was one of the few large planters, of his vicinity, who still made the culture of tobacco their principal business. He said there was a general prejudice against tobacco, in all the tidewater region of the State, because it was through the culture of tobacco that the once fertile soils had been impoverished; but he did not believe that, at the present value of negroes, their labor could be applied to the culture of grain, with any profit, except under peculiarly favorable circumstances. Possibly, the use of guano might make wheat a paying crop, but he still doubted. He had not used it, himself. Tobacco required fresh land, and was rapidly exhausting, but it returned more money, for the labor used upon it, than anything else; enough more, in his opinion, to pay for the wearing out of the land. If he was well-paid for it, he did not know why he should not wear out his land.

His tobacco-fields were nearly all in a distant and lower part of his plantation; land which had been neglected before his time, in a great measure, because it had been sometimes flooded, and was, much of the year, too wet for cultivation. He was draining and clearing it, and it now brought good crops.

He had had an Irish gang draining for him, by contract. He thought a negro could do twice as much work, in a day, as an Irishman. He had not stood over them and seen them at work, but judged entirely from the amount they accomplished: he thought a good gang of negroes would have got on twice as fast. He was sure they must have "trifled" a great deal, or they would have accomplished more than they had. He complained much, also, of their sprees and quarrels. I asked why he should employ Irishmen, in preference to doing the work with his own hands. "It's dangerous work (unhealthy?), and a negro's life is too valuable to be risked at it. If a negro dies, it's a considerable loss, you know."

He afterwards said that his negroes never worked so hard as to tire themselves—always were lively, and ready to go off on a frolic at night. He did not think they ever did half a fair day's work. They could not be made to work hard: they never would lay out their strength freely, and it was impossible to make them do it.

This is just what I have thought when I have seen slaves at work—they seem to go through the motions of labor without putting strength into them. They keep their powers in reserve for their own use at night, perhaps.

Mr. W. also said that he cultivated only the coarser and lower-priced sorts of tobacco, because the finer sorts required more pains-taking and discretion than it was possible to make a large gang of negroes use. "You can make a nigger work," he said, *"but you cannot make him think."*

Although Mr. W. was very wealthy (or, at least, would be considered so anywhere at the North), and was a gentleman of education, his style of living was very farmer-like, and thoroughly Southern. On their plantations, generally, the Virginia gentlemen seem to drop their full-dress and constrained town-habits, and to live a free, rustic, shooting-jacket life. We dined in a room that extended out, rearwardly, from the house, and which, in a Northern establishment, would have been the kitchen. The cooking was done in a detached log-cabin, and the dishes brought some distance, through the open air, by the servants. The outer door was left constantly open, though there was a fire in an enormous old fire-place, large enough, if it could have been distributed sufficiently, to have lasted a New York seamstress the best part of the winter. By the door, there was indiscriminate admittance to negro-children and fox-hounds, and, on an average, there were four of these, grinning or licking their chops, on either side of my chair, all the time I was at the table. A stout woman acted as head waitress, employing two handsome little mulatto boys as her aids in communicating with the kitchen, from which relays of hot corn-bread, of an excellence quite new to me, were brought at frequent intervals.[1] There was no other bread, and but one vegetable served—sweet potato, roasted in ashes, and this, I thought, was the best sweet potato, also, that I ever had eaten; but there were four preparations of swine's flesh, besides fried fowls, fried eggs, cold roast turkey, and opossum, cooked, I know not how, but it somewhat resembled baked sucking-pig. The only beverages on the table were milk and whisky.

I was pressed to stay several days with Mr. W., and should have been glad to have accepted such hospitality, had not another engagement prevented. When I was about to leave, an old servant was directed to get a horse, and go with me, as guide, to the rail-road station at Col. Gillin's. He followed behind me, and I had great difficulty in inducing him to ride near enough to converse with me. I wished to ascertain from him how old the different stages of the old-field forest-growth, by the side of our road, might be; but, for a long time, he was, or pretended to be, unable to comprehend my questions. When he did so, the most accurate information he could give me was, that he reckoned such a field (in which the pines were now some sixty feet high) had been planted with tobacco the year his old master bought him. He thought he was about twenty years old then, and now he was forty. He had every appearance of being seventy.

He frequently told me there was no need for him to go any further, and that it was a dead, straight road to the station, without any forks. As he appeared very eager to return, I was at length foolish enough to allow myself to be prevailed upon to dispense with his guidance; gave him a quarter of a dollar for his time that I had employed, and went on alone.

[1] There is probably some choice in the sort of corn used. The best cornbread that I have eaten was made simply by wetting coarse meal with pure water, adding only a little salt, and baking in the form of a breakfast-roll. The addition of milk, butter, or eggs, damages it. I speak now from experience—having been, in my second journey in the South, often obliged to make my own bread. The only care required, except not to burn it, is to make sure, if possible—which it was not, generally, in Texas—that the corn is not mouldy [Olmsted].

RED RIVER EMIGRANT CRAFT

On Saturday morning I found that two boats, the Swamp Fox and the St. Charles, were advertised to leave in the evening, for Shreveport, on the Red River. I went to the levee, and, finding the St. Charles to be the best of the two, I asked her clerk if I could engage a state-room. There was just one state-room berth left unengaged; I was requested to place my name against its number on the passenger-book—and did so, understanding that it was thus secured for me.

Having taken leave of my friends, I had my baggage brought down, and went on board at half-past three—the boat being advertised to sail at four. Four o'clock passed, and freight was still being taken on—a fire had been made in the furnace, and the boat's big bell was rung. I noticed that the Swamp Fox was also firing up, and that her bell rang whenever ours did—though she was not advertised to sail till five. At length, when five o'clock came, the clerk told me he thought, perhaps, they would not be able to get off at all that night—there was so much freight still to come on board. Six o'clock arrived, and he felt certain that, if they did get off that night, it would not be till very late. At half-past six, he said the captain had not come on board yet, and he was quite sure they would not be able to get off that night. I prepared to return to the hotel, and asked if they would leave in the morning. He thought not. He was confident they would not. He was positive they could not leave now, before Monday, at twelve o'clock—I might rely upon it.

Monday morning, *The Picayune* stated, editorially, that the floating palace, the St. Charles, would leave for Shreveport, at five o'clock, and, if anybody wanted to make a quick and luxurious trip up Red River, with a jolly soul, Captain Lickup was in command. It also stated, in another paragraph, that, if any of its friends had business up Red River, Captain Pitchup was a whole-souled veteran in that trade, and was going up with that remarkably low-draft favorite, the Swamp Fox, to leave at four o'clock that evening. Both boats were also announced, in the advertising columns, to leave at four o'clock.

As the clerk had told me the St. Charles would leave at noon, however, I thought there might have been a misprint in the newspaper announcements, and so went on board again before twelve. The clerk informed me that the newspaper was right—they had finally concluded not to sail till four o'clock. Before four, I returned again, and the boat again fired up, and rang her bell. So did the Swamp Fox. Neither, however, was quite ready to leave at four o'clock. Not quite ready at five. Even at six—not yet quite ready. At seven, the fires having burned out in the furnace, and the stevedores having gone away, leaving a quantity of freight yet on the dock, without advising this time with the clerk, I had my baggage re-transferred to the hotel.

A similar performance was repeated on Tuesday.

On Wednesday, I found the berth I had engaged occupied by a very strong man, who was not very polite, when I informed him that I believed there was some mistake—that the berth he was using had been engaged to me. I went to the clerk, who said that he was sorry, but that, as I had not staid on board at night, and had not paid for the berth, he had not been sure that I should go, and he had, therefore, given it to the gentleman who now had it in possession, and whom, he thought, it would not be best to try to reason out of it. He was very busy, he observed, because the boat was going to start at four o'clock; if I would now pay him the price of passage, he would do the best he could for me. When he had time to examine, he could probably put me in some state-room, if not quite as good a one as that I had lost. I could, at any rate, put my baggage in his private state-room, until the boat got off, and then he would make some satisfactory arrangements for me. I inquired if it was quite certain that the boat would get off at four; for I had been asked to dine with a friend, at three o'clock. There was not the smallest doubt that she would leave at four. They were all ready, at that moment, and only waited till four, because the agent had advertised that they would—merely a technical point of honor.

But, by some error of calculation, I suppose, she didn't go at four. Nor at five. Nor at six.

At seven o'clock, the Swamp Fox and the St. Charles were both discharging dense smoke from their chimneys, blowing steam, and ringing bells. It was apparent that each was making every exertion to get off before the other. The captains of both boats stood at the break of the hurricane deck, as if they were waiting impatiently for mails to come on board.

The St. Charles was crowded with passengers, and her decks were piled high with freight. Bumboatmen, about the bows, were offering shells, and oranges, and bananas; and newsboys, and peddlers,

and tract distributers, were squeezing about with their wares among the passengers. I had confidence in their instinct; there had been no such numbers of them the previous evenings, and I made up my mind, although past seven o'clock, that the St. Charles would not let her fires go down again.

Among the peddlers there were two of "cheap literature," and among their yellow covers, each had two or three copies of the cheap edition (pamphlet) of Uncle Tom's Cabin. They did not cry it out as they did the other books they had, but held it forth among others, so its title could be seen. One of them told me he carried it because gentlemen often inquired for it, and he sold a good many: at least three copies were sold to passengers on the boat. Another young man, who looked like a beneficiary of the Education Society, endeavoring to pass a college vacation in a useful and profitable manner, was peddling a Bible Defense of Slavery, which he made eloquent appeals, in the manner of a pastoral visit, to us, each personally, to purchase. He said it was prepared by a clergyman of Kentucky, and every slave-holder ought to possess it. When he came to me, I told him that I owned no slaves, and therefore had no occasion for it. He answered that the world was before me, and I perhaps yet might own many of them. I replied so decidedly that I should not, that he appeared to be satisfied that my conscience would not need the book, and turned back again to a man sitting beside me, who had before refused to look at it. He now urged again that he should do so, and forced it into his hands, open at the title-page on which was a vignette, representing a circle of colored gentlemen and ladies, sitting around a fire-place, with a white person standing behind them, like a servant, reading from a book. "Here we see the African race as it is in America, under the blessed—"

"Now you go to hell! I've told you three times, as civilly as I could, I didn't want your book. If you bring it here again I'll throw it overboard. I own niggers; and I calculate to own more of 'em, if I can get 'em, but I don't want any damned preachin' about it."

That was the last I saw of the book-peddler.

It was twenty minutes after seven when the captain observed, scanning the levee in every direction, to see if there was another cart or carriage coming toward us, "No use waiting any longer, I reckon: throw off, Mr. Heady." (The Swamp

Fox did not leave, I afterwards heard, till Saturday.)

We backed out, winded round head up, and as we began to breast the current, a dozen of the negro boat-hands, standing on the freight, piled up on the low forecastle, began to sing, waving hats and handkerchiefs, and shirts lashed to poles, towards the people who stood on the sterns of the steam-boats at the levee. After losing a few lines, I copied literally into my note-book:

"Ye see dem boat way dah ahead.
    Chorus.—Oahoiohieu.
De San Charles is arter 'em, dey mus go behine.
    Cho.—Oahoiohieu.
So stir up dah, my livelies, stir her up; (pointing to the furnaces).
    Cho.—Oahoiohieu.
Dey's burnin' not'n but fat and rosum.
    Cho.—Oahoiohieu.
Oh, we is gwine up de Red River, oh!
    Cho.—Oahoiohieu.
Oh, we mus part from you dah asho'.
    Cho.—Oahoiohieu.
Give my lub to Dinah, oh!
    Cho.—Oahoiohieu.
For we is gwine up de Red River.
    Cho.—Oahoiohieu.
Yes, we is gwine up de Red River.
    Cho.—Oahoiohieu.
Oh we must part from you dah oh.
    Cho.—Oahoiohieu."

After the conclusion of this song, and after the negroes had left the bows, and were coming aft along the guards, we passed two or three colored nurses, walking with children on the river bank; as we did so the singers jumped on some cotton bales, bowed very low to them, took off their hats, and swung and waved them, and renewed their song:

God bless you all, dah! ladies!
    Oh, John come down in de holler,
Farwell, de Lord be wid you, honey,
    Oh, John, come down, &c.
Done cry yerself to def,
    Oh, John, &c.
I'm gwine down to New Orleans,
    Oh, John, &c.
I'll come back, dough, bime-by,
    Oh, John, &c,

So far-you-well, my honey,
    Oh, John, &c.
Far-you-well, all you dah, shore,
    Oh, John, &c.
And save your cotton for de Dalmo!
    Oh, John, &c.

As soon as the song was ended, I went into the cabin to remind the clerk to obtain a berth for me. I found two brilliant supper tables reaching the whole length of the long cabin, and a file of men standing on each side of both of them, ready to take seats as soon as the signal was given.

The clerk was in his room, with two other men, and appeared to be more occupied than ever. His manner was, I thought, now rather cool, not to say rude; and he very distinctly informed me that every berth was occupied, and he didn't know where I was to sleep. He judged I was able to take care of myself; and if I was not, he was quite sure that he had too much to do to give all his time to my surveillance. I then went to the captain, and told him that I thought myself entitled to a berth. I had paid for one, and should not have taken passage in the boat, if it had not been promised me. I was not disposed to fight for it, particularly as the gentleman occupying the berth engaged to me was a good deal bigger fellow than I, and also carried a bigger knife; but I thought the clerk was accountable to me for a berth, and I begged that he would inform him so. He replied that the clerk probably knew his business; he had nothing to do with it; and walked away from me. I then addressed myself to a second clerk, or sub-officer of some denomination, who more good-naturedly informed me that half the company were in the same condition as myself, and I needn't be alarmed, cots would be provided for us.

As I saw that the supper-table was likely to be crowded, I asked if there would be a second table. "Yes, they'll keep on eatin' till they all get through." I walked the deck till I saw those who had been first seated at the table coming out; then going in, I found the table still crowded, while many stood waiting to take seats as fast as any were vacated. I obtained one for myself at length, and had no sooner occupied it than two half-intoxicated and garrulous men took the adjoining stools.

It was near nine o'clock before the tables were cleared away, and immediately afterwards the waiters began to rig a framework for sleeping-cots in their place. These cots were simply canvas shelves, five feet and a half long, two wide, and less than two feet apart, perpendicularly. A waiter, whose good will I had purchased at the supper-table, gave me a hint to secure one of them for myself, as soon as they were erected, by putting my hat in it. I did so, and saw that others did the same. I chose a cot as near as possible to the midship doors of the cabin, perceiving that there was not likely to be the best possible air, after all the passengers were laid up for the night, in this compact manner.

Nearly as fast as the cots were ready they were occupied. To make sure that mine was not stolen from me, I also, without much undressing, laid myself away. A single blanket was the only bed-clothing provided. I had not lain long, before I was driven, by an exceedingly offensive smell, to search for a cleaner neighborhood; but I found all the cots fore and aft were either occupied or engaged. I immediately returned, and that I might have a dernier resort, left my shawl in that I had first obtained.

In the forward part of the cabin there was a bar, a stove, a table, and a placard of rules, forbidding smoking, gambling, and swearing in the cabin, and a close company of drinkers, smokers, card-players, and constant swearers. I went out, and stepped down to the boiler-deck. The boat had been provided with very poor wood, and the firemen were crowding it into the furnaces whenever they could find room for it, driving smaller sticks between the larger ones at the top, by a battering-ram method.

. . .

As I came to the bows again, and was about to ascend to the cabin, two men came down, one of whom I recognized to have been my cot neighbor. "Where's a bucket?" said he; "by thunder! this fellow was so strong I could not sleep by him, so I stumped him to come down and wash his feet." "I am much obliged to you," said I, and I was, very much; the man had been lying in the cot beneath mine, which I now returned to, and soon fell asleep.

I awoke about midnight. There was an unusual jar in the boat, and an evident excitement among people talking on deck. I rolled out of my cot, and stepped out on to the gallery. The steamboat "Kimball" was running head-and-head with us, and so close that one might have jumped easily from our paddle-box on to her guards. A few other passengers had turned out beside myself, and most of the waiters were leaning on the rail of the gallery. Occasionally a few words of banter passed between them and the waiters of the Kimball; below, the firemen were shouting as they crowded the furnaces, and some one could be heard cheering them: "Shove her up, boys! Shove her up! Give her hell!" "She's got to hold a conversation with us before she gets by, anyhow," said one of the negroes. "Ye har' that ar' whistlin'," said a white man; "tell ye thar ain't any too much water in her bilers when ye har that." I laughed silently, but was not without a slight expectant sensation, which Mr. Burke would have called sublime. At length the Kimball slowly drew ahead, crossed our bow, and the contest was given up. "De ole lady too heavy," said a waiter; "if I could pitch a few ton of dat freight off her bow, I'd bet de Kimball would be askin' her to show de way, mighty quick."

. . .

I was sitting one day on the forward gallery, watching a pair of ducks, that were alternately floating on the river, and flying further ahead as the steamer approached them. A man standing near me drew a long barreled and very finely-finished pistol from his coat pocket, and, resting it against a stanchion, took aim at them. They were, I judged, full the boat's own length—not less than two hundred feet—from us and were just raising their wings to fly, when he fired. One of them only rose; the other flapped round and round, and when within ten yards of the boat, dived. The bullet had broken its wing. So remarkable a shot excited, of course, not a little admiration and conversation. Half a dozen other men drew pistols, or revolvers, which they appeared to carry habitually, and several were fired at floating chips, or objects on the shore. I saw no more remarkable shooting, however; and that the duck should have been hit at such a distance, was generally considered a piece of luck. A man who had been "in the Rangers" said that all his company could put a ball into a tree, the size of a man's body, at sixty paces, at every shot, with Colt's army revolver, not taking steady aim, but firing at the jerk of the arm. He did not believe that any dueling pistol could be fired with more accuracy.

. . .

On the third day, just after the dinner-bell had rung, and most of the passengers had gone into the cabin, I was sitting alone on the gallery, reading a pamphlet, when a well-dressed, middle-aged man accosted me.

"Is that the book they call Uncle Tom's Cabin, you are reading, sir?"

"No, sir."

"I did not know but it was; I see that there are two or three gentlemen on board that have got it. I suppose I might have got it in New Orleans: I wish I had. Have you ever seen it, sir?"

"Yes, sir."

"I'm told it shows up Slavery in very high colors."

"Yes, sir, it shows the evils of Slavery very strongly."

He took a chair near me, and said that, if it represented extreme cases as if they were general, it was not fair.

Perceiving that he was disposed to discuss the matter, I said that I was a Northern man, and perhaps not very well able to judge; but that I thought that a certain degree of cruelty was necessary to make slave-labor profitable, and that not many were disposed to be more severe than they thought necessary. I believed there was very little wanton cruelty.

He answered, that northern men were much mistaken in supposing that slaves were generally ill-treated. He was a merchant, and owned a plantation, and he just wished I could see his negroes.

"Why, sir," said he, "my niggers' children all go regularly to a Sunday-school, just the same as my own, and learn verses, and catechism, and hymns. Every one of my grown-up niggers are pious, every one of them, and members of the church. I've got an old man that can pray—— well, sir, I only wish I had as good a gift at praying! I wish you could just hear him pray. There are cases in which niggers are badly used; but they are not common. There are brutes everywhere. You have men, at the North, who whip their wives —and they kill them, sometimes."

"Certainly, we have, sir; there are plenty of brutes at the North; but our law, you must remember, does not compel women to submit themselves to their power, nor refuse to receive their testimony against them. A wife, cruelly treated, can escape from her husband, and can compel him to give her subsistence, and to cease from doing her harm. A woman could defend herself against her husband's cruelty, and the law would sustain her."

"It would not be safe to receive negroes' testimony against white people; they would be always plotting against their masters, if you did."

"Wives are not always plotting against their husbands."

"Husband and wife is a very different thing from master and slave."

"Your remark, that a bad man might whip his wife, suggested an analogy, sir."

"If the law was to forbid whipping altogether, the authority of the master would be at an end."

"And if you allow bad men to own slaves, and allow them to whip them, and deny the slave the privilege of resisting cruelty, and refuse testimony, except from those most unlikely to witness cruelty from a master, on his own plantation, to his own slave, do you not show that you think it is necessary to permit cruelty, in order to sustain the authority of masters, in general, over their slaves? That is, you establish cruelty as a necessity of Slavery—do you not?"

"No more than it is of marriage, because men may whip their wives cruelly."

"Excuse me, sir; the law does all it can, to prevent cruelty between husband and wife; between master and slave it does not, because it cannot, without weakening the necessary authority of the master—that is, without destroying Slavery. It is, therefore, a fair argument against Slavery, to show how cruelly this necessity, of sustaining the authority of cruel and passionate men over their slaves, sometimes operates. Some people have thought that a similar argument lay against some of our Northern laws, with regard to marriage. No one objected to the case being argued, and scores of books, some of them novels, have been written about it; and, in consequence, these laws have been repealed, and marriage has become a simple civil contract, with every relic of involuntary servitude abolished, as far as the civil law is concerned."

He asked what it was *Uncle Tom* "tried to make out."

I narrated the Red River episode, and asked if such things could not possibly occur.

"Yes," replied he; "but very rarely. I don't know a man, in my parish, that could do such a thing. There are two men, though, in ——, bad enough to do it, I believe; but it isn't a likely story, at all. In the first place, no colored woman would be likely to offer any resistance, if a white man should want to seduce her."

After further conversation, he said, that a planter had been tried for injuring one of his negroes, at the Court in his parish, the preceding summer. He had had, among his girls, a *favorite*, and suspecting that she was unduly kind to one of his men, under an impulse of jealousy, he mutilated him. There was not sufficient testimony to convict him; "but," he said "everybody believes he was guilty, and ought to have been punished. Nobody thinks there was any good reason for his being jealous of the boy."

I said this story corroborated the truthfulness of Uncle Tom's Cabin; it showed that it was all possible.

"Yes," he answered, "perhaps it may; but, then, nobody would have any respect for a man that would treat his niggers cruelly."

I wondered, as I went into dinner, and glanced at the long rows of surly faces, how many men there were there, whose passions would be much restrained by the fear of losing the respect of their neighbors.

I think very few of them would be very much controlled by such an influence, but I should do them injustice if I neglected to add my conviction, that as a general rule the slaves of this rough, strait-forward pioneer class, enjoy privileges and are less liable to severe labor or excessive punishment than the majority of those belonging to wealthy proprietors, who work on large plantations under overseers. They are less well provided for and are more neglected in every way; but I am inclined to think that the greatest kindness that can be done to a slave, is to neglect him and so encourage, if not force him, to exercise some care over himself.

．　．　．

LA PLACÉE

There is one, among the multitudinous classifications of society in New Orleans, which is a very peculiar and characteristic result of the prejudices, vices, and customs of the various elements of color, class, and nation, which have been there brought together.

I refer to a class composed of the illegitimate offspring of white men and colored women (mulattoes or quadroons), who, from habits of early life, the advantages of education, and the use of wealth, are too much superior to the negroes, in general, to associate with them, and are not allowed by law, or the popular prejudice, to marry white people. The girls are frequently sent to Paris to be educated, and are very accomplished. They are generally pretty, and often handsome. I have rarely, if ever, met more beautiful women, than one or two of them, that I saw by chance, in the streets. They are much better formed, and have a much more graceful and elegant carriage than Americans in general, while they seem to have commonly inherited or acquired much of the taste and skill, in the selection and arrangement, and the way of wearing dresses and ornaments, that is the especial distinction of the women of Paris. Their beauty and attractiveness being their fortune, they cultivate and cherish with diligence every charm or accomplishment they are possessed of.

Of course, men are attracted by them, associate with them, are captivated, and become attached to them, and, not being able to marry them legally, and with the usual forms and securities for constancy, make such arrangements "as can be agreed upon." When a man makes a declaration of love to a girl of this class, she will admit or deny, as the case may be, her happiness in receiving it; but, supposing she is favorably disposed, she will usually refer the applicant to her mother. The mother inquires, like a Countess of Kew, into the circumstances of the suitor; ascertains whether he is able to maintain a family, and, if satisfied with him, in these and other respects, requires from him security that he will support her daughter in a style suitable to the habits she has been bred to, and that, if he should ever leave her, he will give her a certain sum for her future support, and a certain additional sum for each of the children she shall then have.

The wealth, thus secured, will, of course, vary—as in society with higher assumptions of morality—with the value of the lady in the market; that is, with her attractiveness, and the number and value of other suitors she may have, or may reasonably expect. Of course, I do not mean that love has nothing at all to do with it; but love is sedulously restrained, and held firmly in hand, until the road of competency is seen to be clear, with less humbug than our English custom requires about it. Everything being satisfactorily arranged, a tenement in a certain quarter of the town is usually hired, and the couple move into it and go to house-keeping—living as if they were married. The woman is not, of course, to be wholly deprived of the society of others—her former acquaintances are continued, and she sustains her relations as daughter, sister, and friend. Of course, too, her husband (she calls him so—why shouldn't she?) will be likely to continue, also, more or less in, and form a part of, this kind of society. There are parties and balls—*bals masqués*—and all the movements and customs of other fashionable society, which they can enjoy in it, if they wish.[2] The women of this sort are represented to be exceedingly affectionate in disposition, and constant beyond reproach.

During all the time a man sustains this relation, he will commonly be moving, also, in reputable society on the other side of the town; not improbably, eventually he marries, and has a family establishment elsewhere. Before doing this, he may separate from his *placée* (so she is termed). If so, he pays her according to agreement, and as much more, perhaps, as his affection for her, or his sense of the cruelty of the proceeding, may lead him to; and she has the world before her again, in the position of a widow. Many men continue, for a long time, to support both establishments—particularly, if their legal marriage is one *de convenance*. But many others form so strong attachments, that the relation is never discontinued, but becomes, indeed, that of marriage, except that it is not legalized or solemnized. These men leave their estate, at death, to their children, to whom they may have previously given every advantage of edu-

2   THE GLOBE BALL ROOM,
  Corner of St. Claude and St. Peter streets,
          abreast of the Old Basin,
WILL OPEN THIS EVENING, October 16, when
  a Society Ball will be given.
No ladies admitted without masks.
Gentlemen, fifty cents—Ladies, gratis.
Doors open at 9½ o'clock. Ball to commence at
10 o'clock.
No person admitted with weapons, by order of the
Council.
A superior orchestra has been engaged for the season.
The public may be assured of the most strict order, as
there will be at all times, an efficient police in attendance.
Attached to the establishment is a superior Bar, well
stocked with wines and liquors; also, a Restaurant,
where may be had all such delicacies as the market
affords.
All ladies are requested to procure free tickets in the
Mask Room, as no lady will be admitted into the ball
room without one.

                  A. WHITLOCK, Manager.

cation they could command. What becomes of the boys, I am not informed; the girls, sometimes, are removed to other countries, where their color does not prevent their living reputable lives; but, of course, mainly continue in the same society, and are fated to a life similar to that of their mothers.

I have described this custom as it was described to me; I need hardly say in only its best aspects. The crime and heart-breaking sorrow that must frequently result from it, must be evident to every reflective reader.

A gentleman, of New England education, gave me the following account of his acquaintance with the quadroon society. On first coming to New Orleans, he was drawn into the social circles usually frequented by New England people, and some time afterwards was introduced by a friend to a quadroon family, in which there were three pretty and accomplished young women. They were intelligent and well informed; their musical taste was especially well cultivated; they were interested in the literature of the day, and their conversation upon it was characterized by good sense and refined discrimination. He never saw any indication of a want of purity of character or delicacy of feeling in them. He was much attracted by them, and for some time visited them very frequently. Having then discontinued his intimacy, at length one of the girls asked him why he did not come to see them as often as he had formerly done. He frankly replied that he had found their society so fascinating, that he had thought it best to restrict himself in the enjoyment of it, lest it should become necessary to his happiness; and out of regard to his general plans of life, and the feelings of his friends, he could not permit himself to indulge the purpose to be united to one of them, according to the usual custom with their class. The young woman was evidently much pained, but not at all offended, and immediately acknowledged and commended the propriety and good sense of his resolution.

One reason which leads this way of living to be frequently adopted by unmarried men, who come to New Orleans to carry on business, is, that it is much cheaper than living at hotels and boarding-houses. As no young man ordinarily dare think of marrying, until he has made a fortune to support the extravagant style of house-keeping, and gratify the expensive tastes of young women, as fashion is now educating them, many are obliged to make up their minds never to marry. Such a one undertook to show me that it was cheaper for him to *placer* than to live in any other way that he could be expected to in New Orleans. He hired, at a low rent, two apartments in the older part of the town; his placée did not, except occasionally, require a servant; she did the marketing, and performed all the ordinary duties of house-keeping herself; she took care of his clothes, and in every way was economical and saving in her habits—it being her interest, if her affection for him were not sufficient, to make him as much comfort and as little expense as possible, that he might be the more strongly attached to her, and have the less occasion to leave her. He concluded by assuring me that whatever might be said against it, it certainly was better than the way in which most young men lived who depended on salaries in New York.

. . .

EPISODES

No Room

The house was well filled with guests, and my friend and myself were told that we must sleep together. In the room containing our bed, there were three other beds; and although the outside of the house was pierced with windows, nowhere more than four feet apart, not one of them opened out of our room. A door opened into the hall, another into the dining-room, and at the side of our bed was a window into the dining-room, through which, betimes in the morning, we could, with our heads on our pillows, see the girls setting the breakfast-tables. Both the doors were provided with glass windows, without curtains. Hither, about eleven o'clock, we *retired*. Soon afterwards, hearing something moving under the bed, I asked, "Who's there?" and was answered by a girl, who was burrowing for eggs; part of the stores of the establishment being kept in boxes, in this convenient locality. Later, I was awakened by a stranger attempting to enter my bed. I expostulated, and he replied that it was his bed, and nobody else had a right to his place in it. Who was I, he asked, angrily, and where was his partner. "Here I am," answered a voice from another bed; and without another word, he left us. I slept but little, and woke feverish, and with a headache, caused by the want of ventilation.

Fights

While at the dinner-table, a man asked, as one might at the North, if the steamer had arrived, if there had been "any fights to-day?" After dinner, while we were sitting on the gallery, loud cursing, and threatening voices were heard in the direction of the bar-room, which, as at Nachitoches, was detached, and at a little distance from the hotel. The company, except myself and the other New-Yorker, immediately ran towards it. After ten minutes, one returned, and said:

"I don't believe there'll be any fight; they are both cowards."

"Are they preparing for a fight?"

"O, yes; they are loading pistols in the coffee-room, and there's a man outside, in the street, who has a revolver and a knife, and who is challenging another to come out. He swears he'll wait there till he does come out; but in my opinion he'll think better of it, when he finds that the other feller's got pistols, too."

"What's the occasion of the quarrel?"

"Why, the man in the street says the other one insulted him this morning, and that he had his hand on his knife, at the very moment he did so, so he couldn't reply. And now he says he's ready to talk with him, and he wants to have him come out, and as many of his friends as are a mind to may come with him; he's got enough for all of 'em, he says. He's got two revolvers, I believe."

We did not hear how it ended; but, about an hour afterwards, I saw three men, with pistols in their hands, coming from the bar-room.

The next day, I saw, in the streets of the same town, two boys running from another, who was pursuing them with a large, open dirk-knife in his hand, and every appearance of ungovernable rage in his face.

The boat, for which I was waiting, not arriving, I asked the landlady—who appeared to be a German Jewess—if I could not have a better sleeping-room. She showed me one, which she said I might use for a single night; but, if I remained another, I must not refuse to give it up. It had been occupied by another gentleman, and she thought he might return the next day, and would want it again; and, if I remained in it, he would be very angry that they had not reserved it for him, although they were under no obligation to. "He is a dangerous man," she observed, "and my husband, he's a quick-tempered man, and, if they get to quarreling about it, there'll be knives about, sure. It always frightens me to see knives drawn."

A Texas Drover's Religion

A Texas drover, who staid over night at the hotel, being asked, as he was about to leave in the morn-ing, if he was not going to have his horse shod, replied:

"No sir! it'll be a damned long spell 'fore I pay for having a horse shod. I reckon if God Almighty had thought it right hosses should have iron on thar feet, he'd a put it thar himself. I don't pretend to be a pious man myself; but I a'nt a-goin' to run agin the will of God Almighty, though thar's some, that calls themselves ministers of Christ, that does it."

RICHARD HENRY DANA, JR. (1815–1882)

Richard Henry Dana, Jr., came from a long line of Boston and Cambridge Brahmins, some of whom had shown a modest aptitude for letters—like Dana's father, an occasional poet who helped found the *North American Review*. During his second year at Harvard in 1834, young Dana was afflicted with eye trouble; and when no physician seemed able to improve matters, he determined to attempt a cure on his own, "by an entire change of life," as he would put it, "and by a long absence from books, with plenty of hard work, plain food, and open air." He signed on to the brig *Pilgrim* and sailed from Boston in August, 1834. The ship made the long passage around Cape Horn and up the California coast; after some months of shore duty collecting cargo, Dana transferred to the bigger and more seaworthy merchant vessel, the *Alert*, worked his way back with her, and arrived in the Boston harbor in September, 1836. His account of his two years "before the mast" appeared in 1840.

Dana's *Two Years Before the Mast* is a book of travel in two senses. It is first an account of sea faring and of a strange and exotic world—California under the old Spanish regime. But it is, more importantly, the account of a journey, factual and psychological, into another world equally exotic—that of a deliberately declassed Brahmin to the world of the forecastle.

At the outset of the book, Dana is at pains to stress the *realistic* nature of his narrative. He cites Cooper's two romances and observes that almost all the stories of sea life written under their influence were by naval officers or passengers. With the single exception of Ames's *A Mariner's Sketches* (which Dana found "entertaining, but hasty and desultory"), there had not yet been, he goes on, an accurate picture of the daily life of a common sailor. "*A voice from the forecastle* has hardly yet been heard"; and it is his purpose, Dana declares, "to present the life of a common sailor as it really is—the light and the dark together."

Dana was almost entirely successful in carrying out this intention, and *Two Years Before the Mast* soon won the position it has steadily held as a minor classic of American literature. It can also be reckoned the first American work of literary realism—nonfictional realism to be sure, as against the realistic fiction which flourished a generation later, in the age of Howells. Dana's is a realism which reaches back, as well, to the sober reporting and the hard factuality of Daniel Defoe, to his *Journal of the Plague Year* and to his only slightly more "fictive" *Robinson Crusoe*, a volume Dana particularly cherished.[1] But the restrained precision of Dana's

---

[1] Dana felt, he acknowledges, a peculiar attachment to the South Pacific island Juan Fernandez, since—apart from the romantic outline of its mountains and the beauty of its greenery—he recognized it as the place

style is constantly enlivened by current slang, which he employs with italics: "to *show off*," "to get *thick* with," "to *jaw*" (that latter word, incidentally, being a favorite of Emerson's). And the wealth of carefully chosen detail by which Dana renders the variable physical settings and the routines of life aboard ship and on shore heighten those descriptions into a kind of spare poetry.

He effectively suggests the psychological effect of the open sea (its "boundlessness" and "unknown depth" give one "a feeling of loneliness, of dread") as in describing the violent storms—the snow, hail and drenching rains—which almost submerge the *Pilgrim* off Cape Horn. He watches the denizens of the ocean, dolphins in particular, and whales—scores of whales off San Pedro, one of which surfaced so near the brig that it struck the ship's cable and made the whole vessel shake alarmingly.[2] He explores the whole range of seamanship, but always in terms of action and immediate experience—on one occasion, when he performs the difficult feat of climbing aloft to send down a "royal-yard," he recalls that he "heard the 'well done' of the mate, when the yard reached the deck, with as much satisfaction as I ever felt at Cambridge on seeing a '*bene*' at the foot of a Latin exercise."

Dana is no less assured and exact in his portrayals of the coastal towns of California where the *Pilgrim* puts in—Santa Barbara, San Pedro, San Diego, San Francisco, and the others; in glimpses of the Californians, with their racial intermixtures, their hierarchic society, and their idyllic slothfulness. He makes a good story of the four months he spent ashore in California, working in the company's "hide-house," preparing hides to be shipped back to Boston (there to be converted into leather goods which would be returned to California for sale to its indolent inhabitants). But it is in its pictures of the other members of the crew on the *Pilgrim* that *Two Years Before the Mast* at once achieves its greatest fidelity to recognizable human life and realizes itself as art.

Speaking of the shipmates Dana introduces us to, Mark Van Doren has said: "Each one of them here is a portrait from the life, and one cannot doubt the painter's accuracy. The heart of the book is after all in them: in their singing, their grumbling, their washing and sewing, their fatigue, their heroism whenever heroism was in order." As for heroism, it was called for not only during hazardous weather, or when (as once happened) a whale almost upset the little "gig" on which Dana and others were returning to the *Pilgrim* at San Diego. It also took courage to stand up to Captain Thompson, the officer in charge of the *Pilgrim* and later the *Alert*: a man of violent temper and sometimes of savage cruelty, consumed by his sense of absolute power. Dana gives a nearly unbearable account of the flogging of a heavy-witted midwestern sailor named Sam, to whom Thompson had taken an irrational dislike, and then of John, a Swede, who had quietly questioned the captain's right to inflict such punishment.

Meanwhile, there is the childlike Sandwich-Islander, Hope, who becomes touchingly dependent on Dana; and the shabby cultivated English gentleman, George Marsh, the black sheep of his genteel family, but for Dana an amiable and stimulating companion. Thinking back on Marsh, Dana formulates thoughts that have been frequently quoted:

He is one of those cases which are more numerous than those suppose who have never lived anywhere but in their own homes, and never walked but in one line from their cradles to their graves. We must come down from our heights, and leave our straight paths for the by-ways and low places of life, if we would learn truths by strong contrasts; and in hovels, in forecastles, and among our own outcasts in foreign lands, see what has been wrought

---

where Crusoe's real life original, Alexander Selkirk, had undergone his many adventures.

[2] Dana reports at one point that whaling vessels and their crews were somewhat looked down on by regular merchant seamen as engaged in an inferior enterprise. It is in his consciousness of this that Melville, in *Moby-Dick*, goes to such length to elevate whale-hunting to one of the grand human undertakings. Ironically, the *Alert*, the ship Dana remembered so fondly, was converted into a whaler some years after Dana had sailed on her. During the Civil War, it was captured by the Confederate vessel *Alabama*.

among our fellow-creatures by accident, hardship or vice.

There, of course, speaks the Harvard man and the Boston Brahmin, preening himself a little at having undergone exotic experiences denied to his peers. But there also speaks the literary artist who has learned at first-hand that the truths of life, as Melville would say in *Billy Budd*, are to be found down among the "groundlings" as much as up amidst the prominent and the powerful. In fact, in addition to its intrinsic interest, *Two Years Before the Mast* points ahead to the titanic achievement of *Moby-Dick*.

To turn from the crew of the *Pequod* that Melville immortalized, and from his shipmates of other, more literal cruises, we find Dana has his own virtue—that of the sober, sympathetic observer.

The most remarkable member of the crew, for Dana, was a man named Tom Harris, and Dana's recollection of him is perhaps the best passage in the book.

From Two Years Before the Mast (1840)

This leads me to speak of my watchmate for nine months—and, taking him all in all, the most remarkable man I had ever seen—Tom Harris. An hour, every night while lying in port, Harris and I had the deck to ourselves, and walking fore and aft, night after night, for months, I learned his character and history, and more about foreign nations, the habits of different people, and especially the secrets of sailors' lives and hardships, and also of practical seamanship (in which he was abundantly capable of instructing me) than I could ever have learned elsewhere. His memory was perfect, seeming to form a regular chain, reaching from his earliest childhood up to the time I knew him, without a link wanting. His power of calculation, too, was extraordinary. I called myself pretty quick at figures, and had been through a course of mathematical studies; but, working by my head, I was unable to keep within sight of this man, who had never been beyond his arithmetic. He carried in his head, not only a log-book of the voyage, which was complete and accurate, and from which no one thought of appealing, but also an accurate registry of the cargo, knowing where each thing was stowed, and how many hides we took in at each port.

One night he made a rough calculation of the number of hides that could be stowed in the lower hold, between the fore and main masts, taking the depth of hold and breadth of beam (for he knew the dimensions of every part of a ship before he had been long on board), and the average area and thickness of a hide; and he came surprisingly near the number, as it afterwards turned out. The mate frequently came to him to know the capacity of different parts of the vessel, and he could tell the sailmaker very nearly the amount of canvas he would want for each sail in the ship; for he knew the hoist of every mast, and spread of each sail, on the head and foot, in feet and inches. When we were at sea, he kept a running account, in his head, of the ship's way—the number of knots and the courses; and, if the courses did not vary much during the twenty-four hours, by taking the whole progress and allowing so many eighths southing or northing, to so many easting or westing, he would make up his reckoning just before the captain took the sun at noon, and often came very near the mark. He had, in his chest, several volumes giving accounts of inventions in mechanics, which he read with great pleasure, and made himself master of. I doubt if he forgot anything that he read. The only thing in the way of poetry that he ever read was Falconer's "Shipwreck," which he was charmed with, and pages of which he could repeat. He said he could recall the name of every sailor that had ever been his shipmate, and also of every vessel, captain, and officer, and the principal dates of each voyage; and a sailor whom we afterwards fell in with, who had been in a ship with Harris nearly twelve years before, was much surprised at having Harris tell him things about himself which he had entirely forgotten. His facts, whether dates or events, no one thought of disputing; and his opinions few of the sailors dared to oppose, for, right or wrong, he always had the best of the argument with them. His reasoning powers were striking. I have had harder work maintaining an argument with him in a watch, even when I knew myself to be right, and he was only doubting, than I ever had before, not from his obstinacy, but from his acuteness. Give him only a little knowledge of his subject, and, among all the young men of my acquaintance at college, there is not one whom I had not rather meet in an argument than this man. I never answered a question from him, or advanced an opinion to him, without thinking more than once. With an iron memory, he seemed to have your whole past conversation at command, and if you said a thing now which ill agreed with something you had said months before, he was sure to have you on the hip. In fact, I felt, when with him, that I was with no common man. I had a positive respect for his powers of mind, and thought, often, that if half the pains had been spent upon his education which are thrown away yearly, in our colleges, he would have made his mark. Like many self-taught men of real merit, he overrated the value of a regular education; and this I often told him, though I had profited by his error; for he always treated me with respect, and often unnecessarily gave way to me, from an over-estimate of my knowledge. For the intellectual capacities of all the rest of the crew—captain and all—he had a sovereign contempt. He was a far better sailor, and probably a better navigator, than the captain, and had more brains than all the after part of the ship put together. The sailors said, "Tom's got a head as long as the bowsprit," and if any one fell into an argument with him, they would call out: "Ah, Jack! you had better drop that as you would a hot potato, for Tom will turn you inside out before you know it!"

I recollect his posing me once on the subject of the Corn Laws. I was called to stand my watch, and, coming on deck, found him there before me; and we began, as usual, to walk fore and aft, in the waist. He talked about the Corn Laws; asked me my opinion about them, which I gave him, and my reasons, my small stock of which I set forth to the best advantage, supposing his knowledge on the subject must be less than mine, if, indeed, he had any at all. When I had got through, he took the liberty of differing from me, and brought arguments and facts which were new to me, and to which I was unable to reply. I confessed that I knew almost nothing of the subject, and expressed my surprise at the extent of his information. He said that, a number of years before, while at a boarding-house in Liverpool, he had fallen in with a pamphlet on the subject, and, as it contained calculations, had read it very care-

fully, and had ever since wished to find some one who could add to his stock of knowledge on the question. Although it was many years since he had seen the book, and it was a subject with which he had had no previous acquaintance, yet he had the chain of reasoning, founded upon principles of political economy, fully in his memory; and his facts, so far as I could judge, were correct; at least, he stated them with precision. The principles of the steam-engine, too, he was familiar with, having been several months on board a steamboat, and made himself master of its secrets. He knew every lunar star in both hemispheres, and was a master of the quadrant and sextant. The men said he could take a meridian altitude of the sun from a tar bucket. Such was the man, who, at forty, was still a dog before the mast, at twelve dollars a month. The reason of this was to be found in his past life, as I had it, at different times, from himself.

He was an Englishman, a native of Ilfracomb, in Devonshire. His father was skipper of a small coaster from Bristol, and, dying, left him, when quite young, to the care of his mother, by whose exertions he received a common-school education, passing his winters at school and his summers in the coasting trade until his seventeenth year, when he left home to go upon foreign voyages. Of his mother he spoke with the greatest respect, and said that she was a woman of a strong mind, and had an excellent system of education, which had made respectable men of his three brothers, and failed in him only from his own indomitable obstinacy. One thing he mentioned, in which he said his mother differed from all other mothers that he had ever seen disciplining their children; that was, that when he was out of humour and refused to eat, instead of putting his plate away, saying that his hunger would bring him to it in time, she would stand over him and oblige him to eat it—every mouthful of it. It was no fault of hers that he was what I saw him; and so great was his sense of gratitude for her efforts, though unsuccessful, that he determined, when the voyage should end, to embark for home with all the wages he should get, to spend with and for his mother, if perchance he should find her alive.

After leaving home, he had spent nearly twenty years sailing upon all sorts of voyages, generally out of the ports of New York and Boston. Twenty years of vice! Every sin that a sailor knows, he had gone to the bottom of. Several times he had been hauled up in the hospitals, and as often the great strength of his constitution had brought him out again in health. Several times, too, from his acknowledged capacity, he had been promoted to the office of chief mate, and as often his conduct when in port, especially his drunkenness, which neither fear nor ambition could induce him to abandon, put him back into the forecastle. One night, when giving me an account of his life, and lamenting the years of manhood he had thrown away, "There," said he, "in the forecastle, at the foot of those steps, a chest of old clothes is the result of twenty-two years of hard labour and exposure—worked like a horse, and treated like a dog." As he had grown older, he began to feel the necessity of some provision for his later years, and came gradually to the conviction that rum had been his worst enemy. One night, in Havana, a young shipmate of his was brought aboard drunk, with a dangerous gash in his head, and his money and new clothes stripped from him. Harris had been in hundreds of such scenes as these, but in his then state of mind it fixed his determination, and he resolved never to taste a drop of strong drink of any kind. He signed no pledge, and made no vow, but relied on his own strength of purpose. The first thing with him was to reason, and then a resolution, and the thing was done. The date of his resolution he knew, of course, to the very hour —it was three years before I became acquainted with him; and during all that time nothing stronger than cider or coffee had passed his lips. The sailors never thought of enticing Tom to take a glass, any more than they would of talking to the ship's compass. He was now a temperate man for life, and capable of filling any berth in a ship, and many a high station there is on shore which is held by a meaner man.

He understood the management of a ship upon scientific principles, and could give the reasons for hauling every rope; and a long experience, added to careful observation at the time, gave him a knowledge of the expedients and resorts for times of hazard for which I became much indebted to him, as he took the greatest pleasure in opening his stores of information to me, in return for what I was enabled to do for him. Stories of tyranny and hardship which had driven men to piracy; of the incredible ignorance of masters and mates, and of horrid brutality to the sick, dead, and dying; as well as of the secret knavery and impositions practised upon seamen by connivance of the owners, landlords, and officers—all these he had,

and I could not but believe them; for he made the impression of an exact man, to whom exaggeration was falsehood; and his statements were always credited. I remember, among other things, his speaking of a captain whom I had known by report who never handed a thing to a sailor, but put it on deck and kicked it to him; and of another, who was highly connected in Boston, who absolutely murdered a lad from Boston, who went out with him before the mast to Sumatra, by keeping him hard at work while ill of the coast fever, and obliging him to sleep in the close steerage. (The same captain has since died of the same fever on the same coast.)

In fact, taking together all that I learned from him of seamanship, of the history of sailors' lives, of practical wisdom, and of human nature under new circumstances and strange forms of life—a great history from which many are shut out—I would not part with the hours I spent in the watch with that man for the gift of many hours to be passed in study and intercourse with even the best of society.

———

To get the full flavor, the sharp yet eloquent realism, of those pages, they may be juxtaposed with Melville's first description of the chief mate Starbuck, in *Moby-Dick* (Chap. 26). All the difference between realism, or Dana's brand of it, and romance fiction, or Melville's possibly unique mode of it, can be seen in the comparison. Harris is presented in the round, solidly imbedded in geographical and family background, with a sketch of his special qualities, a careful outline of his career, a distinct impression of the man as human, all too human. Starbuck, though he comes to us at first as a clearly defined individual, soon takes on a representative character—a typical mixture of bravery and superstition, and of bravery on a practical rather than a spiritual level; and with this consideration, Melville flexes his rhetorical muscles to invoke the "just Spirit of Equality" and the beneficent ghosts of John Bunyan, Cervantes, and (for good American measure) Andrew Jackson.

———

The chief mate of the Pequod was Starbuck, a native of Nantucket, and a Quaker by descent. He was a long, earnest man, and though born on an

icy coast, seemed well adapted to endure hot latitudes, his flesh being hard as twice-baked biscuit.
Transported to the Indies, his live blood would not
spoil like bottled ale. He must have been born
in some time of general drought and famine, or
upon one of those fast days for which his state is
famous. Only some thirty arid summers had he
seen; those summers had dried up all his physical
superfluousness. But this, his thinness, so to speak,
seemed no more the token of wasting anxieties and
cares, than it seemed the indication of any bodily
blight. It was merely the condensation of the man.
He was by no means ill-looking; quite the contrary.
His pure tight skin was an excellent fit; and closely
wrapped up in it, and embalmed with inner health
and strength, like a revivified Egyptian, this Starbuck seemed prepared to endure for long ages to
come, and to endure always, as now; for be it
Polar snow or torrid sun, like a patent chronom-
eter, his interior vitality was warranted to do well
in all climates. Looking into his eyes, you seemed
to see there the yet lingering images of those
thousand-fold perils he had calmly confronted
through life. A staid, steadfast man, whose life for
the most part was a telling pantomime of action,
and not a tame chapter of sounds. Yet, for all his
hardy sobriety and fortitude, there were certain
qualities in him which at times affected, and in
some cases seemed well nigh to overbalance all
the rest. Uncommonly conscientious for a seaman,
and endued with a deep natural reverence, the
wild watery loneliness of his life did therefore
strongly incline him to superstition; but to that
sort of superstition, which in some organizations
seems rather to spring, somehow, from intelligence
than from ignorance. Outward portents and inward presentiments were his. And if at times these
things bent the welded iron of his soul, much
more did his far-away domestic memories of his
young Cape wife and child, tend to bend him still
more from the original ruggedness of his nature,
and open him still further to those latent influences which, in some honest-hearted men, restrain
the gush of dare-devil daring, so often evinced by
others in the more perilous vicissitudes of the
fishery. "I will have no man in my boat," said
Starbuck, "who is not afraid of a whale." By this,
he seemed to mean, not only that the most reliable and useful courage was that which arises from
the fair estimation of the encountered peril, but
that an utterly fearless man is a far more dangerous comrade than a coward.

"Aye, aye," said Stubb, the second mate, "Starbuck, there, is as careful a man as you'll find anywhere in this fishery." But we shall ere long see
what that word "careful" precisely means when
used by a man like Stubb, or almost any other
whale hunter.

Starbuck was no crusader after perils; in him
courage was not a sentiment; but a thing simply
useful to him, and always at hand upon all mortally practical occasions. Besides, he thought, perhaps, that in this business of whaling, courage was
one of the great staple outfits of the ship, like her
beef and her bread, and not to be foolishly wasted.
Wherefore he had no fancy for lowering for whales
after sun-down; nor for persisting in fighting a fish
that too much persisted in fighting him. For,
thought Starbuck, I am here in this critical ocean
to kill whales for my living, and not to be killed
by them for theirs; and that hundreds of men had
been so killed Starbuck well knew. What doom
was his own father's? Where, in the bottomless
deeps, could he find the torn limbs of his brother?

With memories like these in him, and moreover, given to a certain superstitiousness, as has
been said; the courage of this Starbuck which
could, nevertheless, still flourish, must indeed have
been extreme. But it was not in reasonable nature
that a man so organized, and with such terrible
experiences and remembrances as he had; it was
not in nature that these things should fail in la-
tently engendering an element in him, which,
under suitable circumstances, would break out
from its confinement, and burn all his courage up.
And brave as he might be, it was that sort of
bravery chiefly, visible in some intrepid men,
which, while generally abiding firm in the conflict
with seas, or winds, or whales, or any of the ordinary irrational horrors of the world, yet cannot
withstand those more terrific, because more spiritual terrors, which sometimes menace you from
the concentrating brow of an enraged and mighty
man.

But were the coming narrative to reveal, in any
instance, the complete abasement of poor Starbuck's fortitude, scarce might I have the heart to
write it; for it is a thing most sorrowful, nay
shocking, to expose the fall of valor in the soul.
Men may seem detestable as joint stock-companies
and nations; knaves, fools, and murderers there
may be; men may have mean and meagre faces;
but man, in the ideal, is so noble and so sparkling,
such a grand and glowing creature, that over any

ignominious blemish in him all his fellows should run to throw their costliest robes. That immaculate manliness we feel within ourselves, so far within us, that it remains intact though all the outer character seem gone; bleeds with keenest anguish at the undraped spectacle of a valor-ruined man. Nor can piety itself, at such a shameful sight, completely stifle her upbraidings against the permitting stars. But this august dignity I treat of, is not the dignity of kings and robes, but that abounding dignity which has no robed investiture. Thou shalt see it shining in the arm that wields a pick or drives a spike; that democratic dignity which, on all hands, radiates without end from God; Himself! The great God absolute! The centre and circumference of all democracy! His omnipresence, our divine equality!

If, then, to meanest mariners, and renegades and castaways, I shall hereafter ascribe high qualities, though dark; weave round them tragic graces; if even the most mournful, perchance the most abased, among them all, shall at times lift himself to the exalted mounts; if I shall touch that workman's arm with some ethereal light; if I shall spread a rainbow over his disastrous set of sun; then against all mortal critics bear me out in it, thou just Spirit of Equality, which hast spread one royal mantle of humanity over all my kind! Bear me out in it, thou great democratic God! who didst not refuse to the swart convict, Bunyan, the pale, poetic pearl; Thou who didst clothe with doubly hammered leaves of finest gold, the stumped and paupered arm of old Cervantes; Thou who didst pick up Andrew Jackson from the pebbles; who didst hurl him upon a war-horse; who didst thunder him higher than a throne! Thou who, in all Thy mighty, earthly marchings, ever cullest Thy selectest champions from the kingly commons; bear me out in it, O God!

In the later portions of *Two Years Before the Mast*, the narrative takes on what might be called a deeper realism—a realism of psychic response and development. During the weary months ashore in California, Dana could imagine nothing more soul-satisfying than the first view of the Boston harbor, and the first feel of the Boston wharf under his feet. From his lowly position, shut off from the counsels of the authorities, Dana hears rumors and counter-rumors of plans and cancellations, delays which would keep him in California for a year or more, proposed changes in destination. Dana is nowhere more accurate than here, in giving a sense of the confusing and worrisome feel of things for an underling in any institution characterized by a strict hierarchical structure and severe discipline. When, finally, he is transferred to the *Alert*, which is bound for home, the transaction leaves Dana uneasy: he is aware that the change was only approved because he—or his father—has influential friends in Boston; for the first time since his earliest apprentice days two years before, he is made conscious of a separation between himself and his new friends. Excitement, nonetheless, rises in him as the *Alert* sails up the eastern coast and the lights of Cape Cod are sighted. But then, of a sudden, when the ship anchors in Boston, Dana is overcome by a feeling of apathy. He can barely bring himself to pack his gear and walk, numbly, down the gangplank.

Writing in the late 1830's, Dana explained his mood of almost paralyzing indifference by the general theory that "there is probably so much of excitement in prolonged expectation that the quiet realizing of it produces a momentary stagnation of feeling as well as of effort." That may well be; but in his innermost self the young Dana may have had an intuition that the remainder of his life would feel anticlimactic. He was returning to a pattern of existence long prepared for him—an elegant, comfortable, and inescapable trap composed of Harvard, Boston society, and other familiar ingredients. Such, anyhow, turned out to be the case. He completed Harvard and went on to law school there; he became a moderately liberal lawyer and "Free-soiler," worked against the Fugitive Slave Law, and held a few minor offices in government. But the continued popularity of *Two Years Before the Mast* only embittered its aging author. When the Senate refused his appointment as minister to England in 1876, Dana exclaimed: "My life has been a failure. . . . My great success—my book—was a boy's work, done before I came to the Bar."

The book was, certainly, the work of a young man not yet twenty-five, but it is a thoroughly adult accomplishment. *Two Years Before the*

Mast is in fact one of those rare books—American literature has a few others of the kind to show—which has the power to appeal at once to the adventure-loving adolescent and to the art-loving person of mature years. It appealed greatly to Herman Melville. But Dana's environment closed in upon him, and never again would he have the opportunity, or take the risk, of venturing out to "learn truths by strong contrasts."

Tale and Character

In discussing the early novel in America, especially the work of Charles Brockden Brown, we have remarked how little sense we feel of the American scene or American types—how little of what Whitman calls "that taste of identity and locality which is so dear in literature." When Hugh Henry Brackenridge, who had more of a bent for realistic observation than Brown showed, came to write *Modern Chivalry*, a work Henry Adams was to call a "more thoroughly American book than any written before 1833," he complained that he had to use an Irish character, Teague O'Regan, because the "American has, in fact, yet no character; neither the clown nor the gentleman." Or, as we have seen Robert Frost put it, in "The Gift Outright," "The land was ours before we were the land's"—that is, before the American knew himself as fully the creature of a special place and society.

The specialness of the American had been, in fact, recognized by outsiders long before he himself had a very clear notion of it. It had been, for instance, recognized—and recognized quite unflatteringly—by the British, who applied to the colonial the name of "Yankee," the name which the colonial then defiantly and humorously adopted.[1] But this was only the beginning of a recognition of identity. The character of the Yankee had to be filled out, and that meant a long process of self-scrutiny. The Yankees were, however, inhabitants of only one section of a large country, and so the question of American identity involved, too, the recognition of differences among kinds of Americans. Here, as in the case of the satirical recognition of the Yankee by the British, the observations of foreigners sharpened the self-awareness of the American. The Europeans seriously inspected the American claim to have a new world and a new society, and in a great spate of travel books they discussed the topic. Americans were often outraged by what visitors thought, but even outrage could sharpen the American's need to scrutinize himself and, in so doing, to distinguish among the rich variety of types being produced here.

[1] The origin of "Yankee" is obscure. It may have been given by the Dutch settlers of New Amsterdam to the inhabitants of Connecticut and other New Englanders on their border in the seventeenth century.

The process was, however, slow, and the beginnings are not to be found in formal literature. Even when Washington Irving, in *A History of New York* (1809), distinguished Yankees and Virginians, he was very short on realistic detail and used a method and style he had learned from English writers of the eighteenth century. Meanwhile, however, in unliterary literature such as almanacs, especially *The Old Farmer's Almanac* (which began in 1793 and still continues), in joke books, and in newspaper sketches the native world was being reported, with increasing shrewdness of eye and increasing appreciation of that world's humorous aspects. That is, the sense of realism and the sense of humor worked together. By the time of *The Sketch Book* (1819), Washington Irving had learned to see the world around him and write of it in a style more nearly American, and in *The Spy*, by Cooper (1821), we find, especially in the low characters, a sense of the American peculiarities. Formal literature was, at last, beginning to profit from the lessons of the informal literature, as well as from the models of realism, local color, and humor found in certain new models from England, Walter Scott, Maria Edgeworth, and Bulwer Lytton.

The influence of the informal literature did not end there—for, in fact, that influence is a never-ending process. The Yankee did not achieve full stature until a newspaper editor of Portland, Maine, one Seba Smith, invented Jack Downing, who began his career in 1830, and until, strangely enough, a foreigner, a judge of the Supreme Court of Nova Scotia, Thomas Chandler Haliburton, invented Sam Slick, a somewhat less engaging character than Jack. Out of Jack and Sam, lines run in many directions—straight from Jack, for example, to James Russell Lowell's *Biglow Papers* and collaterally to Robin in Hawthorne's story "My Kinsman, Major Molineux."

If we may regard informal literature as a sort of matrix for formal literature, we may also regard habits of speech, characteristic concerns of conversation, and oral styles of narration as the matrix of informal literature, and when we turn from New England to the region known as the Old Southwest nothing could be more obvious. There we can clearly see the rich relation of ways of life to oral tradition, to informal literature, and, thence, to formal literature.

The Old Southwest was an enormous and various country—the southern states of the Mississippi Valley and the Gulf states as far east as Georgia, and in that country there was an enormous variety of racial and cultural strands, of clearly marked ways of life, and of social tensions. There were cotton plantations and mountain cabins, sugar plantations and scrub farms, the high-bred Creoles of New Orleans and the Acadian Cajuns of the bayous, the half-horse, half-alligator keelboatmen and the swells, gamblers, pilots, and roustabouts of the steamboats, the Natchez Trace with circuit riders and maniacal cutthroats like the Harpe brothers and land pirates like Murrell, who dreamed an empire. There were transplanted aristocrats from Virginia, and pseudo-aristocrats, cotton snobs, duelists, land sharks, peddlers, Yankee schoolteachers, black slaves, and tribeless Indians. It was a world of violence and drama, of great fortune in flush times and general ruination in bad, of rigid social distinctions and a paradoxical social fluidity, of murderous intensities and quixotic generosity, of rampant individualism and social responsibility, of chivalric honor and unspeakable depravity.

This world of variety and contrast was, also, a world of motion, and the varieties and contrasts were constantly and kaleidoscopically falling into new patterns. The "Kentucky screamer" fresh off a keel boat might jostle the Creole dandy of New Orleans, and Davy Crockett, from the cane brakes of Tennessee, might crack his joke in the corridors of the Capitol. Jefferson Davis might rise from a log cabin at Fairview, Kentucky, to a planter's mansion in Mississippi and thence to the presidency of the Confederacy. On big court day, the young lawyer, in black broadcloth, might squat on his heels in the shade of the maple by the hitching rack in the square, and pass the bottle or play mumblety-peg with an unshaven character wearing a coonskin cap and toting a Decherd rifle. The Governor of Tennessee, after a quarrel with his bride, might flee to hide his grief among the Indians in the wilds of Arkansas. A bishop might be a distiller on the side, a little boy scarcely tall enough for his eyes to peer over the edge of a faro table might, as Joseph G. Baldwin relates in *Flush Times in Alabama*, pay a stranger ten dollars to hold him up level while he tried his luck at the game, and a card sharper might die in the odor of sanctity. Anything might happen in that world, and indeed did.

One of the things that happened was the development of a language of peculiar fluency, pith, poetry, and grotesquerie. Sober records give us some hint of how that language grew out of life, and support the evidence in the tales themselves. James Hall, a writer of fiction who flourished during the 1830's, says of the frontiersman:

> Though usually taciturn in the presence of strangers, he is communicative to his friend or guest, has often strong colloquial powers, with quaint, singular, figurative, and even eloquent forms of expression. His language, which is commonly brief, sententious, and abrupt, becomes, when excited by the interest of the subject or by passion, highly expletive, and redundant with exaggerated forms and figures of comparison. When he swears . . . he does swear in earnest, his philology becomes concentrated, and explodes with appalling energy. . . . (*The Harpe's Head,* 1833)

The literary significance of this world and this language was recognized as early as 1836 by the *Southern Quarterly Review*:

> For perfect originality we must turn to the Southwest, for there grows a hardy and generous nature, untaught, unsophisticated, warm, ardent, impetuous, which is yet destined to unfold great destinies in art and literature for the country it endows. It is an original and vigorous nature, rough but rich, illiterate but fresh—full of virgin glow and enthusiasm—yearning after great things and impetuous in their attainment.

The drama of life and language combined to bring the tales, comic or violent, into being, and the very brutality, hardship, blankness, and boredom of much of the life helped to perpetuate their existence. Out of the hardship and brutality sprang a crazy pride in endurance and strength which found expression in mythic characters who could outscream seven catamounts hung up by their tails like a bunch of wild grapes, or grin a grizzly bear out of countenance until he would follow tame as an old coon dog. And out of the same brutality and hardship came a humor that transcended the cramping condition of life even while recognizing it, that glorified or turned into comedy the violent and ugly, and that in a wild poetry might affirm man's spirit and thus convert realism into fantasy.

As for the blankness and boredom which characterized much of frontier life, it was such a void that the tale-telling filled.

FURTHER READINGS

S. P. Avery, *The Harp of a Thousand Strings* (1858)

Joseph G. Baldwin, *Flush Times in Alabama* (1853)

Walter Blair, *Native American Humor* (1937)

———, *Tall Tale America* (1944)

——— and Franklin J. Meine, *Mike Fink, King of the Mississippi Keelboatmen* (1933)

B. A. Botkin, *Treasury of American Folklore* (1944)

T. A. Burke, ed., *Polly Peablossom's Wedding; and Other Tales* (1851)

Thomas D. Clark, *Rampaging Frontier* (1939)

Bernard De Voto, *Mark Twain's America* (1932)

George Washington Harris, *Sut Lovingood*, Brom Weber, ed. (1954)

Arthur Palmer Hudson, ed., *Humor of the Old Deep South* (1936)

M. Thomas Inge, ed., *High Times and Hard Times* (1967)

Augustus Baldwin Longstreet, *Georgia Scenes* (1835; 1940)

Frank L. Owsley, *Plain Folk of the South*, Chaps. 3–4 (1949)

V. L. Parrington, *The Romantic Revolution in America, 1800–1860* (1927)

William T. Porter, ed., *The Big Bear of Arkansas and Other Sketches* (1945)

Milton Rickels, *George Washington Harris* (1965)

Constance Rourke, *American Humor* (1931)

———, *Davy Crockett* (1934)

Henry Nash Smith, *Virgin Land*, Chaps. 11–13 (1950)

Jennette Tandy, *Crackerbox Philosophers in American Humor and Satire* (1925)

John Donald Wade, *Augustus Baldwin Longstreet* (1924)

Henry Watterson, ed., *Oddities in Southern Life and Character* (1882)

Alice Wyman, *Two American Pioneers* (1927)

SEBA SMITH (1792–1868)

Seba Smith came at the moment when the idea of the Yankee character was ready to crystallize. The outlines of the Yankee were already set; he was rural, laconic, full of common sense and against all newfangledness, independent in spirit, holding shrewd beneath his air of innocence, given to wry humor that came with no smile. Seba Smith, in the *Daily Courier* of Portland, Maine, gave him a name, Jack Downing, and a role, that of the cracker-barrel philosopher, a role that has survived for the Yankee even as late as the poetry of Robert Frost. Though the fictional Jack Downing made his fame as a cracker-barrel philosopher, he had begun his career, quite appropriately for a Yankee, as a peddler with a load of hoop poles and axe handles brought from the country. Jack survived thirty years in the *Daily Courier*, and during that time was enshrined in three volumes, the first and most famous of which is *The Life and Writings of Major Jack Downing* (1834).

From The Life and Writings of Major Jack Downing (1834)

When we read about great men, we always want to know something about the place where they live; therefore I shall begin my history with a short account of Downingville, the place where I was born and brought up.

Downingville is a snug, tidy sort of a village, situated in a valley about two miles long, and a mile and a half wide, scooped out between two large rugged hills that lie to the east and west, having a thick forest of trees to the north, and a clear pond of water, with a sandy beach, to the south. It is about three miles from the main road as you go back into the country, and is *jest about in the middle of down east*. It contains by this time a pretty considerable number of inhabitants, though my grandfather Downing was the first person that settled there, jest after he got back from sogering in the revolutionary war. It has a school house, and a tavern, and a minister, and a doctor, and a blacksmith, and a shoe-maker, and folks that work at most all sorts of trades. They have n't got any meetin house up yet, but the school house is pretty large and does very well to hold meetins in, and they have meetins very regular every Sunday, the men filling up all the seats on one side of the school house and the women on the other.

They have n't got any lawyer in Downingville; there was one come once and sot out to settle there, and hired a room and put a sign up over the door with his name on it, and the word OFFICE in great large letters, so big you could read 'em clear across the road. A meeting of the inhabitants was called at the school house the next day, and after chawing the matter over awhile, it was unanimously agreed if the man wanted an office he should go somewhere else for it, for as for having an office-seeker in Downingville they never would. So they voted that he should leave the town in twenty-four hours, or they would take him down to the pond and duck him, and ride him out of town on a rail. A committee of twenty of the stoutest men in Downingville was appointed to carry the message to him, at which he prudently took the hint, and packed up and cleared out that afternoon. All the quarrels, and disputes and law-cases are always left out to uncle Joshua Downing, and he settles them all, by and large, at two shillings apiece, except where they have come to blows, and then he charges two and sixpence apiece.

The land in Downingville is most capital rich land, and bears excellent crops. I would 'nt pretend to say it 's equal to some land I 've hearn tell of away off in Ohio, where the corn grows so tall they have to go up on a ladder to pick the ears off; and where a boy fell into the hole that his father had dug a beet out of, and they had to let down a bed-cord to draw him up again; and where pigs are so plenty that they run about the farms ready roasted, and some of 'em with knives and forks in their backs for any body who wants to eat. I would n't pretend that Downingville is any such sort of a place as that; but this I do say, he that is diligent and will plant his potatoes and corn early, and hoe them well, may always get a good crop, and live above board.

. . .

. . . As I said afore, my grandfather was the first settler in Downingville. When he got through sogering in the revolutionary war, he took a notion he 'd go and pick him out a good lot of land away down east to settle on, where there was land enough to be had jest for whistling for it, and where his boys would have a chance to do something in the world. So he took grandmother and the two boys, for father and Uncle Joshua were all the boys he had then, and packed them into a horse waggon, and took an axe and a hoe and a shovel, and some victuals, and a bed tick to put some straw in, and a gun and some blankets and one thing another, and started off down east. He drove away into Maine till he got clear to the end of the road, and then he picked his way along through the woods and round the pond five miles further, till he got to the very spot where Downingville now is, and there he stopt and baited his horse, and while grandmother and the boys sot down and took a bit of a luncheon, grandfather went away up top of one of the hills to take a view of the country. And when he come down again, says he, I guess we may as well ontackle, for I dont believe we shall find a better place if we travel all summer. So he ontackled the old horse, and took the waggon and turned it over against a great oak tree, and put some bushes up round it and made a pretty comfortable sort of a house for 'em to sleep in a few nights, and then he took his axe and slashed away amongst the trees. But that old oak never was cut down; it 's the very same one that stands out a little ways in front of grandfather's house now. And poor old grandmother as long as she lived, for she 's been dead about five years, always made a practice once a year, when the day come round that they first camped under the old oak, to have the table carried out and set under the tree, and all hands, children and grand-children, had to go and eat supper there, and the good old lady always used to tell over the whole story how she slept eight nights under the waggon, and how they were the sweetest nights' rest she ever had.

Well, grandfather he smashed away among the trees, and he soon had a half a dozen acres of 'em sprawling, and while they were drying in the sun he went to work and built him a snug little log house, and made two stools to set on, one for him and one for grandmother, and a couple of blocks for the boys. He made a stone fireplace in one corner of the house, and left a hole in one corner of the roof for the smoke to go out, and he got it all fixed as nice as a new pin, and then they moved into it; and I've heard grandmother say more than a hundred times, that she raly believed she took more comfort in that log house, than ever a queen took in a palace.

When the leaves and the twigs of the trees that grandfather had cut down had got considerable dry in the sun, he went out one warm clear afternoon and set fire to 'em. The wind was blowing a considerable of a breeze from the southward, and the fire spread almost as fast as a horse could run. Grandmother used to say it was the grandest sight she ever see, to see them are six acres of trees all in a light flame at once, and the fire streaming up as high as the tallest pines, sometimes in a broad red sheet, and sometimes in narrow strips that went up rolling and bending like ten thousand fiery dragon's tongues. After the fire had gone through it grandfather went to work to clear it up. He picked up the limbs and bits that were left and threw 'em in heaps and sot fire to 'em again, and he laid sticks across the large logs that were too heavy to move, and *niggered* them off with fire, and then roolled them up in piles and sot fire to 'em again and burnt 'em all up smack smooth. Then he went to work and planted the ground all over to corn, and potatoes, and punkins, and beans, and squashes, and round near the house he planted water-millions, and mush-millions, and cowcumbers, and beats and carrots and tarnips; and grandmother carried out a whole apron full of seeds of all kinds of arbs that ever grew in old Massachusetts, and sowed 'em all round, and they come up as thick as hops.

After this the family of old Mr. Zebedee Downing always lived like heroes and never knew what it was to be in want. They had ten children, and a smart likely set of boys and gals they were too, and they all lived to grow up, and were all married and well to do in the world.

. . .

I believe I was born somewhere about the year seventeen hundred and ninety-five, more or less, and mother says I was the smartest baby that she ever see. I dont speak of this by way of bragging, ·but as I am writing a history to go before the world, I'm bound to be impartial. She says before I was a week old I showed that I was real grit, and could kick and scream two hours upon the stretch, and not seem to be the least bit tired that ever was. But I dont remember any thing about this. The first I remember, I found myself one cold November day, when I was about five years old, bareheaded and barefoot, sliding on the ice. It had been a snapping cold night, and in the morning the pond was all froze over as smooth as glass, and hard enough to bear a horse. All the boys in the neighborhood, and most all the gals, turned out and had a fine frolic that day, sliding and running on the pond. Most of the larger boys had shoes, but we little fellers that want big enough to wear shoes had to tuff it out as well as we could. I carried a great pine chip in my hand, and when my feet got so cold I could n't stand it no longer, I'd put the chip down and stand on that a little while and warm 'em, and then at it to sliding again like a two year old.

. . .

We used to have a school in Downingville about three months in the winter season and two months in the summer, and I went to the winter school three winters, from the time I was twelve till I was fifteen. And I was called about the best scholar of my age that there was in school. But to be impartial, I must confess the praise did n't always all belong to me, for I used sometimes to work headwork a little in order to get the name of being a smart scholar. One instance of it was in reading. I got along in reading so well, that the master said I read better than some of the boys that were considerable older than I, and that had been to school a dozen winters. But the way I managed it was this. There was cousin Obediah was the best reader there was in school, and as clever a boy as one in a thousand, only his father had n't got no orchard. So I used to carry a great apple to school in my pocket every day and give ·to him to get him to set behind me when I was reading, where he could peak into my book, and when I come to a hard word, have him whisper it to me, and then I read it out loud. Well, one day I was reading along so, pretty glib, and at last I come to a pesky great long crooked word, that I could n't make head nor tail to it. So I waited for Obediah. But it proved to be a match for Obediah.

He peaked, and squinted, and choked, and I was catching my breath and waiting for him to speak; and at last he found he could do nothing with it, and says he 'skip it.' The moment I heard the sound I bawled out, *skip it*. What's that? said the master, looking at me as queer as though he had catched a weazel asleep. I stopt and looked at the word again, and poked my tongue out, and waited for Obediah. Well, Obediah give me a hunch, and whispered again, 'skip it.' Then I bawled out again, *skip it*. At that the master and about one half the scholars yaw-hawed right out. I could n't stand that; and I dropt the book and streaked it out of school, and pulled foot for home as fast as I could go, and I never showed my head in school again from that day to this. But for all that, I made out to pick up a pretty good education. I got so I could read and spell like a fox, and could cypher as far as the rule of three. And when I got to be about twenty years old, I was strongly talked of one winter for schoolmaster. But as a good many of the same boys and gals would go to me, that were in the school when I read 'skip it,' I did n't dare to venture it for fear there would be a sort of a snickering among 'em whenever any of the scholars come to a hard word.

So I jogged along with father on the farm. But let me be doing what I would, whether it was hoeing potatoes, or pitching hay, or making stone wall, or junking and piling logs, I never could feel exactly easy; some thing seemed to keep ringing in my ears all the time, and saying I was made to do something else in the world besides this. And an old woman that come along and told fortunes, when she come to tell mine, said that wherever I should go and whatever I should undertake to do, I should always get to the top of the ladder. I believe I have mentioned it somewhere in one of my letters. Well, this made me keep a thinking so much the harder, and wondering what I should be in the world, and although I used to stick to my work as steady as any of the boys, yet I used to feel as uneasy as a fish out of water. But what made me think most about it was father. He always used to stand to it I was smarter than common boys, and used to tell mother she might depend upon it, if I lived and nothing did n't happen to me, I should some day or other raise the name of the Downings higher than it ever had been yet.

. . .

Well, I kept jogging along on the farm after the same old sort, year after year, so long, and there did n't nothing happen to me, that sometimes I almost begun to give it up, and think sure enough it was all nothing but a dream. Still I kept having spells that I felt terrible uneasy, and was tempted forty times to pack up and go and seek my fortune. I might tell a good deal more about my life, and my uncles and ants and cousins, and the rest of the neighbors: but I begin to feel a most tired of writing my life, and believe I shall have to serve it pretty much as I planted my watermillion seeds. And that was this. When I was about six or seven years old, our folks give me a pint of watermillion seeds and told me to go out into the field and plant 'em for myself, and I might have all I could raise. So off I goes tickled enough. And I went to work and punched little holes down in the ground and put in one seed to time along in a row, three or four inches apart, till I got about half the seeds planted. It was rather a warm afternoon and I begun to feel a little tired, so I took and dug a hole and poured the rest of the seeds all in together, and covered 'em up, and went into the house. Well, mother asked me if I 'd planted my seeds; yes mam, says I. What, all of 'em, says she? Yes mam, says I. But you 've been very spry, says she, how did you get them done so quick? Oh says I, easy enough; I planted 'em in a *hill and a row*. And when they begun to come up they found 'em in a hill and a row sure enough. So I believe I shall have to pour the rest of my life into a hill, and let it go.

To come then right to the pint—I dont mean the pint of watermillion seeds, but the pint in my life which seemed to be the turning pint—In the fall of the year 1829 I took it into my head I 'd go to Portland. I had heard a good deal about Portland, what a fine place it was, and how the folks got rich there proper fast; and that fall there was a couple of new papers come up to Downingville from there, called the Portland Courier and Family Reader; and they told a good many queer kind of things about Portland and one thing another; and all at once it popped into my head, and I up and told father, and says I, I 'm going to Portland whether or no; and I'll see what this world is made of yet. Father stared a little at first, and said he was afraid I should get lost; but when he see I was bent upon it, he give it up; and he stepped to his chist and opened the till, and took out a dollar and give it to me, and says he, Jack, this is all I can do for you; but go, and lead an honest life, and I believe I shall hear good of you yet. He turned and walked across the room, but I could see the tears start into his eyes, and mother sot down and had a hearty crying spell. This made me feel rather bad for a minute or two, and I almost had a mind to give it up; and then again father's dream came into my mind, and I mustered up courage, and declared I 'd go. So I tackled up the old horse and packed in a load of ax handles and a few notions, and mother fried me some dough-nuts and put 'em into a box along with some cheese and sassages, and ropped me up another shirt, for I told her I did n't know how long I should be gone; and after I got all rigged out, I went round and bid all the neighbors good bye, and jumped in and drove off for Portland.

DAVY CROCKETT (1786–1836)

Davy Crockett was a real man and really did some of the things Jack Downing did only fictionally. He really was the back-country man come to town, from the cane brakes of Tennessee to Washington; he really was a soldier, this in the Creek War, and again at the Alamo, where he fell to Mexican bullet and bayonet; he really did get elected to office, as a state legislator, and then as Congressman for two terms; and he really did know President Jackson.

There is another big difference between Davy and Jack. Where Jack really was the bumpkin funny because of his innocence, Davy quite deliberately played the game of bumpkin ignorance as a device of humor—humor which was not, in the end, at his own expense. He was, literally, a hunter and frontiersman, but he was self-taught and extremely intelligent. He had physical courage, and the courage of his principles, as he proved in standing up against his old commanding officer and his political sponsor, President Jackson, on the issue of the removal of the southern Indians to the West, and on the issue of the United States Bank. As a result of his struggle against Jackson, he lost his seat in Congress and went to Texas and his death.

Crockett's fame as a hunter and teller of tales had spread far beyond Tennessee and the bars of Washington. He was a national legend. In 1833 appeared a book called *Sketches and Eccentricities of Col. David Crockett, of West Tennessee,* followed in rapid succession by *A Narrative of the Life of David Crockett, of the State of Tennessee, An Account of Col. Crockett's Tour to the North and Down East,* and *Col. Crockett's Exploits and Adventures in Texas.* It is not certain what hand Crockett himself had in the several books. The *Narrative* is generally accepted as autobiography, retouched and developed but essentially his and in his language, and the *Sketches* may be taken as his in a somewhat more indirect fashion. In *Tour* he is often supposed to have had some hand, and it is even suggested by Constance Rourke, in her biography of Crockett, that the author of the *Exploits,* whoever he was, must have had access to letters written by Crockett from Texas, or perhaps even to a diary taken from his body at the Alamo and recovered by Americans at the battle of San Jacinto.

Whatever degree of responsibility Crockett had for the books, they spread his fame, as did two plays, *The Lion of the West* and *The Kentuckian,* by James Kirke Paulding (who had been a collaborator of Irving in the *Salmagundi* papers), in both of which the hero was a Colonel Nimrod Wildfire, a great hunter in a coonskin cap, who spoke the frontier lingo attributed to Crockett; and when Crockett appeared at the theater in Washington for a performance, he received a great ovation. As for ovations, the tour recorded in the *Account* evoked enormous popular response. The moment was right, the romance of the frontier and the forest had been discovered, as the popularity of Cooper was proving, and Crockett, who was the coonskin hero in the flesh, had the talent to play the role to the hilt.

It has been argued, for example, by V. L. Parrington in *Main Currents in American Thought,* a famous study of American literature, that Crockett's reputation was artificially created by the Whig party because Crockett, a Jackson man who had defected, gave them a counterweight to Jackson's appeal in the back country. Furthermore, it is argued that Crockett was merely a common backwoods type, "an assertive, opinionated, likeable fellow, ready to fight, drink, dance, shoot or brag, the biggest frog in a very small puddle," and that "the best joke he ever played he played on posterity that has swallowed the myth whole and persists in setting a romantic halo on his coonskin cap."

The real Crockett, whatever else he was, was not the "myth." A myth is never "real," for if it were real, it would not be a myth. A myth, however, has its own relation to reality. It interprets reality, makes it possible for man to grasp and accept reality. This myth was the heroic, mock-heroic, and grotesquely comic dream that somehow made the brutality, hardship, cramp, and ugliness of the frontier endurable, even desirable.

In his autobiographical writing, Crockett was in the process of creating a myth not only out of the substance of that life but out of the substance of himself, even as he was in the process of creating a language for the myth out of the language of life. And in that lies his significance, a significance amply attested by the fact that long after Davy himself was dead, far off at the Alamo, and his books were forgotten, the myth continued to grow, in the Crockett *Almanacs* and by word of mouth, self-generating, growing ever more preposterous until at last we have the Crockett who said that to cook bear steaks you ought to "salt 'em in a hail storm, pepper 'em with buckshot, and then broil 'em with a flash o' lightnin'," and whose gizzard was a wasp's nest and who breathed out rifle balls, who swallowed a lightning bolt to cure himself of being in love, and who drank the Gulf of Mexico dry to make Texas handier for annexation.

If, in fact, Davy Crockett was the biggest frog in a puddle, that puddle was the American imagination.

From A Narrative of the Life of David Crockett (1834)

While on the subject of election matters, I will just relate a little anecdote about myself, which will show the people to the east, how we manage these things on the frontiers. It was when I first run for Congress; I was then in favor of the Hero, for he had chalked out his course so sleek in his letter to the Tennessee legislature, that, like Sam Patch, says I, "there can be no mistake in him," and so I went ahead. No one dreamt about the monster and the deposites at that time, and so, as I afterward found, many, like myself, were taken in by these fair promises, which were worth about as much as a flash in the pan when you have a fair shot at a fat bear.

But I am losing sight of my story. Well, I started off to the Cross Roads, dressed in my hunting shirt, and my rifle on my shoulder. Many of our constituents had assembled there to get a taste of the quality of the candidates at orating. Job Snelling, a gander-shanked Yankee, who had been caught somewhere about Plymouth Bay, and been shipped to the west with a cargo of codfish and rum, erected a large shantee, and set up shop for the occasion. A large posse of the voters had assembled before I arrived, and my opponent had already made considerable headway with his speechifying and his treating, when they spied me about a rifle shot from the camp, sauntering along as if I was not a party in business. "There comes Crockett," cried one. "Let us hear the colonel," cried another, and so I mounted the stump that had been cut down for the occasion, and began to bushwhack in the most approved style.

I had not been up long before there was such an uproar in the crowd that I could not hear my own voice, and some of my constituents let me know, that they could not listen to me on such a dry subject as the welfare of the nation, until they had something to drink, and that I must treat them. Accordingly I jumped down from the rostrum, and led the way to the shantee, followed by my constituents, shouting, "Huzza for Crockett," and "Crocket for ever!"

When we entered the shantee, Job was busy dealing out his rum in a style that showed he was making a good day's work of it, and I called for a quart of the best, but the crooked critur returned no other answer than by pointing to a board over the bar, on which he had chalked in large letters, "*Pay to-day and trust to-morrow.*" Now that idea brought me up all standing; it was a sort of corner-ing in which there was no back out, for ready money in the west, in those times, was the shyest thing in all natur, and it was most particularly shy with me on that occasion.

The voters seeing my predicament, fell off to the other side, and I was left deserted and alone, as the Government will be, when he no longer has any offices to bestow. I saw, as plain as day, that the tide of popular opinion was against me, and that, unless I got some rum speedily, I should lose my election as sure as there are snakes in Virginny,—and it must be done soon, or even burnt brandy wouldn't save me. So I walked away from the shantee, but in another guess sort from the way I entered it, for on this occasion I had no train after me, and not a voice shouted, "Huzza for Crockett." Popularity sometimes depends on a very small matter indeed; in this particular it was worth a quart of New England rum, and no more.

Well, knowing that a crisis was at hand, I struck into the woods with my rifle on my shoulder, my best friend in time of need, and as good fortune would have it, I had not been out more than a quarter of an hour before I treed a fat coon, and in the pulling of a trigger, he lay dead at the root of the tree. I soon whipped his hairy jacket off his back, and again bent my steps towards the shantee, and walked up to the bar, but not alone, for this time I had half a dozen of my constituents at my heels. I threw down the coon skin upon the counter, and called for a quart, and Job, though busy in dealing out rum, forgot to point at his chalked rules and regulations, for he knew that a coon was as good a legal tender for a quart, in the west, as a New York shilling, any day in the year.

My constituents now flocked about me, and cried, "Huzza for Crockett," "Crockett for ever," and finding the tide had taken a turn, I told them several yarns, to get them in a good humor, and having soon dispatched the value of the coon, I went out and mounted the stump, without opposition, and a clear majority of the voters followed me to hear what I had to offer for the good of the nation. Before I was half through, one of my constituents moved that they would hear the balance of my speech, after they had washed down the first part with some more of Job Snelling's extract of cornstalk and molasses, and the question being put, it was carried unanimously. It wasn't considered necessary to tell the yeas and nays, so we adjourned to the shantee, and on the way I began to reckon that the fate of the nation pretty much depended upon my shooting another coon.

While standing at the bar, feeling sort of bashful while Job's rules and regulations stared me in the face, I cast down my eyes, and discovered one end of the coon skin sticking between the logs that supported the bar. Job had slung it there in the hurry of business. I gave it a sort of quick jerk, and it followed my hand as natural as if I had been the rightful owner. I slapped it on the counter, and Job, little dreaming that he was barking up the wrong tree, shoved along another bottle, which my constituents quickly disposed of with great good humor, for some of them saw the trick, and then we withdrew to the rostrum to discuss the affairs of the nation.

I don't know how it was, but the voters soon became dry again, and nothing would do, but we must adjourn to the shantee, and as luck would have it, the coon skin was still sticking between the logs, as if Job had flung it there on purpose to tempt me. I was not slow in raising it to the counter, the rum followed of course, and I wish I may be shot, if I didn't, before the day was over, get ten quarts for the same identical skin, and from a fellow, too, who in those parts was considered as sharp as a steel trap, and as bright as a pewter button.

This joke secured me my election, for it soon circulated like smoke among my constituents, and they allowed, with one accord, that the man who could get the whip hand of Job Snelling in fair trade, could outwit Old Nick himself, and was the real grit for them in Congress. Job was by no means popular; he boasted of always being wide awake, and that any one who could take him in, was free to do so, for he came from a stock, that sleeping or waking had always one eye open, and the other not more than half closed. The whole family were geniuses. His father was the inventor of wooden nutmegs, by which Job said he might have made a fortune, if he had only taken out a patent and kept the business in his own hands; his mother Patience manufactured the first white oak pumpkin seeds of the mammoth kind, and turned a pretty penny the first season; and his aunt Prudence was the first to discover that corn husks, steeped into tobacco water, would make as handsome Spanish wrappers as ever came from Havana, and that oak leaves would answer all the purpose of filling, for no one could discover the difference except the man who smoked them, and then it would be too late to make a stir about it. Job, himself, bragged of having made some useful discoveries; the most profitable of which was the art of converting mahogany sawdust into cayenne pepper, which he said was a profitable and safe business; for the people have been so long accustomed to having dust thrown in their eyes, that there wasn't much danger of being found out.

The way I got to the blind side of the Yankee merchant, was pretty generally known before election day, and the result was, that my opponent might as well have whistled jigs to a milestone, as attempt to beat up for votes in that district. I beat him out and out, quite back into the old year, and there was scarce enough left of him, after the canvass was over, to make a small grease spot. He disappeared without even leaving a mark behind; and such will be the fate of Adam Huntsman, if there is a fair fight and no gouging.

After the election was over, I sent Snelling the price of the rum, but took good care to keep the fact from the knowledge of my constituents. Job refused the money, and sent me word, that it did him good to be taken in occasionally, as it served to brighten his ideas; but I afterwards learnt when he found out the trick that had been played upon him, he put all the rum I had ordered, in his bill against my opponent, who, being elated with the speeches he had made on the affairs of the nation, could not descend to examine into the particulars of a bill of a vender of rum in the small way.

From Sketches and Eccentricities of Col. David Crockett, of West Tennessee (1833)

CROCKETT'S BRAG

I'm that same David Crockett, fresh from the backwoods, half-horse, half-alligator, a little touched with the snapping-turtle; can wade the Mississippi, leap the Ohio, ride upon a streak of lightning, and slip without a scratch down a honey locust; can whip my weight in wild cats,—and if any gentleman pleases, for a ten dollar bill, he may throw in a panther,—hug a bear too close for comfort, and eat any man opposed to Jackson.

A VOTE FOR CROCKETT

"I had taken old Betsy," said he, "and straggled off to the banks of the Mississippi river; and meeting with no game, I didn't like it. I felt mighty wolfish about the head and ears, and thought I would spile if I wasn't kivured up in salt, for I hadn't had a fight in ten days; and I cum acrost a fellow floatin' down stream settin' in the stern of his boat fast asleep. Said I, 'Hello, stranger! if you don't take keer your boat will run away with you'—and he looked up; and said he, 'I don't value you.' He looked up at me slantendicler, and I looked down upon him slantendicler; and he took out a chaw of turbaccur, and said he, 'I don't value you that.' Said I, 'Cum ashore, I can whip you—I've been trying to git a fight all the mornin' '; and the varmint flapped his wings and crowed like a chicken. I ris up, shook my mane, and neighed like a horse. He run his boat plump head foremost ashore. I stood still and sot my triggurs, that is, took off my shurt, and tied my galluses tight around my waist—and at it we went. He was a right smart coon, but hardly a bait for such a fellur as me. I put it to him mighty droll. In ten minutes he yelled enough, and swore I was a ripstavur. Said I, 'Ain't I the yaller flower of the forest! And I am all brimstone but the head and ears, and that's aquafortis.' Said he, 'Stranger, you are a beauty: and if I know'd your name, I'd vote for you next election.' Said I, 'I'm that same David Crockett. You know what I'm made of. I've got the closest shootin' rifle, the best 'coon dog, the biggest ticlur [knife; presumably a bowie knife], and the ruffest racking horse in the district. I can kill more lickur, fool more varmints, and cool out more men than any man you can find in all Kentucky.' Said he, 'Good morin', stranger—I'm satisfied.' Said I, 'Good mornin', sir; I feel much better since our meetin' '; but after I got away a piece, I said, 'Hello, friend, don't forget that vote.' "

GRINNING THE BARK OFF A TREE

That Colonel Crockett could avail himself, in electioneering, of the advantages which well applied satire ensures, the following anecdote will sufficiently prove:

In the canvass of the Congressional election of 18—, Mr. ***** was the Colonel's opponent—a gentleman of the most pleasing and conciliating manners—who seldom addressed a person or a company without wearing upon his countenance a peculiarly good humoured smile. The colonel, to counteract the influence of this winning attribute, thus alluded to it in a stump speech:

"Yes, gentlemen, he may get some votes by *grinning*, for he can *outgrin me*—and you know I ain't slow—and to prove to you that I am not, I will tell you an anecdote. I was concerned myself—and I was fooled a little of the wickedest. You all know I love hunting. Well, I discovered a long time ago that a 'coon couldn't stand my grin. I could bring one tumbling down from the highest tree. I never wasted powder and lead, when I wanted one of the creatures. Well, as I was walking out one night, a few hundred yards from my house, looking carelessly about me, I saw a 'coon planted upon one of the highest limbs of an old tree. The night was very *moony* and clear, and old Ratler was with me; but Ratler won't bark at a 'coon—he's a queer dog in that way. So, I thought I'd bring the lark down in the usual way, *by a grin.* I set myself—and, after grinning at the 'coon a reasonable time, found that he didn't come down. I wondered what was the reason—and I took another steady grin at him. Still he was *there.* It made me a little mad; so I felt round and got an old limb about five feet long, and, planting one end upon the ground, I placed my chin upon the other, and took *a rest.* I then grinned my best for about five minutes; but the cursed 'coon hung on. So, finding I could not bring him down by grinning, I determined to have him—for I thought he must be a droll chap. I went over to the house, got my axe, returned to the tree, saw the 'coon still there, and began to cut away. Down it come, and I ran forward; but d–n the 'coon was there to be seen. I found that what I had taken for one, was a large knot upon the branch of the tree and, upon looking at it closely, I saw that *I had grinned all the bark off, and left the knot perfectly smooth.*

"Now, fellow-citizens," continued the Colonel, "you must be convinced that, in the *grinning line*, I myself am not slow—yet, when I look upon my opponent's countenance, I must admit that he is my superior. You must all admit it. Therefore, be wide awake—look sharp—and do not let him grin you out of your votes."

From the Crockett Almanacs (1835–56)

The treatment of woman in the tall tales is full of complexities and ambivalences. In the hard world of the frontier, the girl might turn into a toothless hag before the age of twenty, and the woman who survived the rigors of life might have to thank a masculine hardihood or even brutishness. So, out of a deep rancor at being deprived of the feminine and beautiful, and as a vaunting of sexuality superior to that of the genteel world in which appetite had to be stimulated by beauty, perfume, and furbelows, and in which woman was worshiped on her pedestal rather than possessed, the creators of the tall tale glorified the ugly and often brutish man-woman, who was both monstrous and, sometimes, comic. At the same time, the tall tale, in regard to sex and woman, had elements of a realistic satire directed against the romantic pretensions of gentility. The situation here, in a tale from the *Crockett Almanac*, is a parallel to that in certain "blues" and black jazz songs, for instance.

A PRETTY PREDICAMENT

When I was a big boy, that had jist begun to go a galling, I got astray in the woods one arternoon; and being wandering about a good deel, and got pretty considerable soaked by a grist of rain, I sot down on to a stump, and begun to wring out my leggin's, and shake the drops off of my raccoon cap.

Whilst I was on the stump, I got kind of sleepy, and so laid my head back in the crotch of a young tree that growed behind me, and shot up my eyes. I had laid out of doors for many a night before, with a sky blanket over me—so I got to sleep pretty soon, and fell to snoring most beautiful. So somehow, or somehow else, I did not wake till near sundown; and I don't know when I should have waked, had it not been for somebody tugging at my hair. As soon as I felt this, though I wan't more than half awake, I begun

to feel to see if my thum' nail was on, as that was all the ammunition I had about me. I lay still, to see what the feller would be at. The first idee I had was that a cussed Ingun was fixing to take off my scalp; so I thought I'd wait till I begun to feel the pint of his knife scraping against the skin, and then I should have full proof agin him, and could jerk out his copper-coloured liver with the law all on my side. At last I felt such a hard twitch, that I roared right out, but when I found my head was squeezed so tight in the crotch that I could not get it out, I felt like a gone sucker. I felt raal ridiculous, I can assure you; so I began to talk to the varmint, and told him to help me get my head out, like a man, and I would give him five dollars before I killed him.

At last my hair begun to come out by the roots, and then I was mad to be took advantage of in that way. I swore at the varmint, till the tree shed all its leaves, and the sky turned yaller. So, in a few minutes, I heerd a voice, and then a gall cum running up, and axed what was the matter. She soon saw what was to pay, and told me that the eagles were tearing out my hair to build nests with. I told her I had endured more than a dead possum could stand already, and that if she would drive off the eagles, I would make her a present of an iron comb.

"That I will," says she; "for I am a she steamboat, and have doubled up a crocodile in my day."

So she pulled up a small sapling by the roots, and went to work as if she hadn't another minnit to live. She knocked down two of the varmints, and screamed the rest out of sight. Then I told her the predicament I was in; and she said she would loosen the hold that the crotch had on my head. So she took and reached out her arm into a rattlesnake's hole, and pulled out three or four of them. She tied 'em awl together, and made a strong rope out of 'em. She tied one eend of the snakes to the top of one branch, and pulled as if she was trying to haul the multiplication table apart. The tightness about my head began to be different altogether, and I hauled out my cocoanut, though I left a piece of one of my ears behind.

As soon as I was clear, I could not tell which

way to look for the sun, and I was afeared I should fall into the sky, for I did not know which way was up, and which way was down. Then I looked at the gal that had got me loose—she was a strapper: she was as tall as a sapling, and had an arm like a keel boat's tiller. So I looked at her like all wrath, and as she cum down from the tree, I says to her:

"I wish I may be utterly onswoggled if I don't know how to hate an Ingun or love a gal as well as any he this side of roaring river. I fell in love with three gals at once at a log rolling, and as for tea squalls my heart never shut pan for a minnit at a time; so if you will marry me, I will forgive the tree and the eagles for your sake."

Then she turned as white as an egg-shell, and I seed that her heart was busting, and I run up to her, like a squirrel to his hole, and gave her a buss that sounded louder than a musket. So her spunk was all gone, and she took my arm as tame as a pigeon, and we cut out for her father's house. She complained that I hung too heavy on her arm, for I was enermost used up after laying so long between the branches. So she took up a stone that would weigh about fifty pound, and put it in her pocket on the other side to balance agin my weight, and so she moved along as upright as a steamboat. She told me that her Sunday bonnet was a hornet's nest garnished with wolves' tails and eagles' feathers, and that she wore a bran new goun, made of a whole bear's-hide, the tail serving for a train. She said she could drink of the branch without a cup, could shoot a wild goose flying, and wade the Mississippi without wetting herself. She said she could not play on the piane, nor sing like a nightingale, but she could outscream a catamount and jump over her own shadow; she had good strong horse sense and new a woodchuck from a skunk. So I was pleased with her, and offered her all my plunder if she would let me split the difference and call her Mrs. Crockett.

She kinder said she must insult her father before she went so fur as to marry. So she took me into another room to introduce me to another beau that she had. He was setting on the edge of a grindstone at the back part of the room with his heels on the mantel-piece! He had the skullbone of a catamount for a snuff-box, and he was dressed like he had been used to seeing hard times. I got a side squint into one of his pockets, and saw it was full of eyes that had been gouged from people of my acquaintance. I knew my jig was up, for such a feller could outcourt me, and I thort the gal brot me in on proppus to have a fight. So I turned off, and threatened to call agin; and I cut through the bushes like a pint of whiskey among forty men.

SUNRISE IN HIS POCKET

One January morning it was so all screwen cold that the forest trees were stiff and they couldn't shake, and the very daybreak froze fast as it was trying to dawn. The tinder box in my cabin would no more ketch fire than a sunk raft at the bottom of the sea. Well, seein' daylight war so far behind time I thought creation war in a fair way for freezen fast: so, thinks I, I must strike a little fire from my fingers, light my pipe, an' travel out a few leagues, and see about it. Then I brought my knuckles together like two thunderclouds, but the sparks froze up afore I could begin to collect 'em, so out I walked, whistlin' "Fire in the mountains!" as I went along in three double quick time. Well, arter I had walked about twenty miles up the Peak O'Day and Daybreak Hill I soon discovered what war the matter. The airth had actually friz fast on her axes, and couldn't turn round; the sun had got jammed between two cakes o' ice under the wheels, an' thar he had been shinin' an' workin' to get loose till he friz fast in his cold sweat. C-r-e-a-t-i-o-n! thought I, this ar the toughest sort of suspension, an' it mustn't be endured. Somethin' must be done, or human creation is done for. It war then so anteluvian an' premature cold that my upper and lower teeth an' tongue war all collapsed together as tight as a friz oyster; but I took a fresh twenty-pound bear off my back that I'd picked up on my road, and beat the animal agin the ice till the hot ile began to walk out on him at all sides. I then took an' held him over the airth's axes an' squeezed him till I'd thawed 'em loose, poured about a ton on't over the sun's face, give the airth's cog-wheel one kick backward till I got the sun loose—whistled "Push along, keep movin'!" an' in about fifteen seconds the airth gave a grunt, an' began movin'. The sun walked up beautiful, salutin' me with sich a wind o' gratitude that it made me sneeze. I lit my pipe by the blaze o' his top-knot, shouldered my bear, an' walked home, introducin' people to the fresh daylight with a piece of sunrise in my pocket.

AUGUSTUS BALDWIN LONGSTREET
(1790–1870)

Augustus Baldwin Longstreet was born in Augusta, Georgia, of parents who had recently immigrated from New Jersey. As a matter of fact, there was in that period a considerable immigration to Georgia from the East, especially to that section of Georgia that was scarcely past the frontier stage. Longstreet, after a Georgia boyhood, attended Yale, and then studied law in Connecticut; but he returned to Georgia to make his career. The career was varied and distinguished—lawyer, judge, journalist, politician, inventor, minister, university president, writer. He was also a good horseman, a fine shot, and, like James Fenimore Cooper's father and Abraham Lincoln, a wrestler. In other words, he had the personal skills that would make him acceptable to those rough members of the community who might care little for his professional accomplishments.

Longstreet himself was certainly not one of the back-country men whom he writes about. It is one of the ironies of history that the writers who put into print the humor and tall tales of the Old Southwest were not men of the people; they were usually professional men and usually anti-Jackson in politics. Even though Crockett was definitely a man of the people, he wound up against Jackson, a wild man domesticated and petted by the Whigs. And there is often a tone of condescension, of indulgent amusement from a safe distance, in the work of these immortalizers of the barbaric yawp of the frontier. It is not until we reach Mark Twain

that the strength of imagination conquers the distance between the writer and his low-born subject—though George Washington Harris had, in a sense, prepared the way.

But if there was distance between the humorist of the Old Southwest and the common man, there was also a certain intimacy. The Whig humorists knew their world and, like Longstreet, had an incorrigible curiosity about the raw but richly complex life about them, and a broad tolerance even for its brutalities. They might be proud but they were not squeamish. These lawyers and doctors and newspaper men in the Southwest and up the Mississippi Valley kept a sharp eye on the county court houses, boarding houses, grog shops, and doggeries of the little towns and converted local absurdities and disasters into tales. Longstreet, unlike many another young lawyer, wrote his tales down and published them in newspapers, beginning in 1833; and his book *Georgia Scenes* (1835) made him famous, North and South. Poe, reviewing it, said that if this book were published in England it would make a fortune for its author, and added: "Seldom—perhaps never in our lives—have we laughed immoderately over any rural book." And Poe was not a critic to be ordinarily overwhelmed by rustic japes and bumpkin humor. Yale confirmed Longstreet's reputation by conferring on him the honorary degree of Doctor of Laws; but, nevertheless, he soon turned from literature to the next of his multifarious interests.

The Gander Pulling (1835)

In the year 1798 I resided in the city of Augusta and, upon visiting the market-house one morning in that year, my attention was called to the following notice, stuck upon one of the pillars of the building.

> "*advurtysement.*

"Thos woo wish To be inform heareof, is heareof notyfide that edwd. Prator will giv a gander pullin, jis this side of harisburg, on Satterday of thes pressents munth to All woo mout wish to partak tharof.

"e Prator, thos wishin to purtak

will cum yearly, as the pullin will begin soon.

"e. p."

If I am asked why "jis this side of harisburg" was selected for the promised feat instead of the city of Augusta, I answer from conjecture, but with some confidence, because the ground chosen was near the central point between four rival towns, the citizens of all which *"mout wish to partak tharof;"* namely, Augusta, Springfield, Harrisburg, and Campbellton. Not that each was the rival of all the others, but that the first and the last were competitors, and each of the others backed the pretensions of its nearest neighbour. Harrisburg sided with Campbellton, *not because she had any interest in seeing the business of the two states centre upon the bank of the river, nearly opposite to her*; but because, like the "Union Democratic Republican Party of Georgia," she thought, after the adoption of the Federal Constitution, that the several towns of the confederacy should no longer be "separated" by the distinction of local party; but that, laying down all former prejudices and jealousies as a sacrifice on the altar of their country, they should become united in a *single body*, for the maintenance of those principles which they deemed essential to the *public welfare*.

Springfield, on the other hand, espoused the State Rights' creed. She admitted that, under the Federal Compact, she ought to love the sister states very much; but that, under the *Social Compact*, she ought to love her own state a little more; and she thought the two compacts perfectly reconcilable to each other. Instead of the towns of the several states getting into *single bodies* to preserve the *public welfare*, her doctrine was, that they should be kept in *separate bodies* to preserve the *private welfare*. She admitted frankly, that, living, as she always had lived, right amid gullies, vapours, fogs, creeks, and lagoons, she was wholly incapable of comprehending that expansive kind of benevolence, which taught her to love people whom she knew nothing about, as much as her next-door neighbours and friends. Until, therefore, she should learn it from the practical operation of the Federal Compact, she would stick to the oldfashioned Scotch love, which she understood perfectly, and "go in" for Augusta, live or die, hit or miss, right or wrong. As in the days of Mr. Jefferson, the Springfield doctrines prevailed, Campbellton was literally *nullified*; insomuch that, ten years ago, there was not a house left to mark the spot where once flourished this active, busy little village. Those who are curious to know where Springfield stood at the time of which I am speaking, have only to take their position at the intersection of Broad and Marbury streets, in the city of Augusta, and they will be in the very heart of old Springfield. Sixty steps west, and as many east of this position, will measure the whole length of this Jeffersonian republican village, which never boasted of more than four dwelling-houses; and Broad-street measures its width, if we exclude kitchens and stables. And, while upon this subject, since it has been predicted by a man for whose opinions I entertain the profoundest respect[1] (especially since the prediction), that my writings will be read with increased interest a hundred years to come; and as I can see no good reason, if this be true, why they should not be read a thousand years hence with more interest, I will take the liberty of dropping a word here to the curious reader of the year 1933. He will certainly wish to know the site of Harrisburg (seeing it is doomed, at no distant period, to share the fate of Springfield) and of Campbellton.

Supposing, then, that if the great fire in Augusta, on the 3d of April, 1829, did not destroy that city, nothing will; I select this as a permanent object.

In 1798, Campbell-street was the western verge of Augusta, a limit to which it had advanced but a few years before, from Jackson-street. Thence to Springfield led a large road, now built up on either side, and forming a continuation of Broad-street. This road was cut across obliquely by a deep gully, the bed of which was an almost impassable bog, which entered the road about one hundred yards below Collock-street on the south, and left it about thirty yards below Collock-street on the north side of now Broad-street. It was called Campbell's Gully, from the name of the gentleman through whose possessions and near whose dwelling it wound its way to the river. Following the direction of Broad-street from Springfield westward, 1347 yards, will bring you to Harrisburg, which had nothing to boast of over Springfield but a warehouse for the storage of tobacco, then the staple of Georgia. Continue the same direction 700 yards, then face to your right hand, and follow your nose directly across Savannah river, and, upon ascending the opposite bank, you will be in the busiest part of Campbellton in 1798. Between Harrisburg and Springfield, and 1143 yards from the latter, there runs a stream which may be per-

[1] The Editor of the "Hickory Nut" [Longstreet].

petual. At the time just mentioned, it flowed between banks twelve or fourteen feet high, and was then called, as it still is, 'Hawk's Gully.'"[2]

Now Mr. Prator, like the most successful politician of the present day, was on all sides in a doubtful contest; and, accordingly, he laid off his gander-pulling ground on the nearest suitable unappropriated spot to the centre point between Springfield and Harrisburg. This was between Harrisburg and Hawk's Gully, to the south of the road, and embraced part of the road, but within 100 yards of Harrisburg.

When "*Satterday of thes pressents munth*" rolled round, I determined to go to the gander-pulling. When I reached the spot, a considerable number of persons, of different ages, sexes, sizes, and complexions, had collected from the rival towns and the country around. But few females were there, however; and those few were from the lowest walks of life.

A circular path of about forty yards diameter had already been laid out; over which, from two posts about ten feet apart, stretched a rope, the middle of which was directly over the path. The rope hung loosely, so as to allow it, with the weight of a gander attached to it, to vibrate in an arc of four or five feet span, and so as to bring the breast of the gander within barely easy reach of a man of middle stature on a horse of common size.

A hat was now handed to such as wished to enter the list; and they threw into it twenty-five cents each; this sum was the victor's prize.

The devoted gander was now produced; and Mr. Prator, having first tied his feet together with a strong cord, proceeded to the *neck-greasing*. Abhorrent as it may be to all who respect the tenderer relations of life, *Mrs.* Prator had actually prepared a gourd of *goose*-grease for this very purpose. For myself, when I saw Ned dip his hands into the grease, and commence stroking down the feathers from breast to head, my thoughts took a melancholy turn. They dwelt in sadness upon the many conjugal felicities which had probably been shared between the *greasess* and the *greasee*. I could see him as he stood by her side, through many a chilly day and cheerless night, when she was warming into life the offspring of their mutual loves, and

repelled, with chivalrous spirit, every invasion of the consecrated spot which she had selected for her incubation. I could see him moving with patriarchal dignity by the side of his loved one, at the head of a smiling, prattling group, the rich reward of their mutual care, to the luxuries of the meadow or to the recreations of the pool. And now, alas! an extract from the smoking sacrifice of his bosom friend was desecrated to the unholy purpose of making his neck "a fit object" for Cruelty to reach "her quick, unerring fingers at." Ye friends of the sacred tie! judge what were my feelings when, in the midst of these reflections, the voice of James Prator thundered on mine ear, "Darn his old dodging soul; brother Ned! grease his neck till a fly can't light on it!"

Ned, having fulfilled his brother Jim's request as well as he could, attached the victim of his cruelty to the rope, directly over the path. On each side of the gander was stationed a man, whose office it was to lash forward any horse which might linger there for a moment; for, by the rules of the ring, all pulling was to be done at a brisk canter.

The word was now given for the competitors to mount and take their places on the ring. Eight appeared: Tall Zubley Zin, mounted upon Sally Spitfire; Arch Odum, mounted on Bull and Ingons (onions); Nathan Perdew, on Hellcat; James Dickson, on Nigger; David Williams, on Gridiron; Fat John Fulger, on Slouch; Gorham Bostwick, on Gimlet; and Turner Hammond, on 'Possum.

"Come, *gentlemen*," said Commandant Prator, "fall in. All of you get behind one another, sort o' in a row."

All came into the track very kindly but Sally Spitfire and Gridiron. The former, as soon as she saw a general movement of horses, took it for granted there was mischief brewing, and, because she could not tell where it lay, she concluded it lay everywhere, and therefore took fright at everything.

Gridiron was a grave horse; but a suspicious eye which he cast to the right and left, wherever he moved, showed that "he was wide awake," and that "nobody better not go fooling with him," as his owner sometimes used to say. He took a sober but rather intense view of things; insomuch that, in his contemplations, he passed over the track three times before he could be prevailed upon to stop in it. He stopped at last, however; and when he was made to understand that this was all that was required of him for the present, he surrendered his suspicions at once, with a counte-

---

[2] It took its name from an old man by the name of Hawk, who lived in a log hut on a small knoll on the eastern side of the gully and about 100 yards south of the Harrisburg road [Longstreet].

nance which seemed plainly to say, "Oh, if this is all you want, I've no objection to it."

It was long before Miss Spitfire could be prevailed upon to do the like.

"Get another horse, Zube," said one; "Sal will never do for a gander pullin."

"I won't," said Zube. "If she won't do, I'll make her do. I want a nag that goes off with a spring; so that, when I get a hold, she'll cut the neck in two like a steel-trap."

At length Sally was rather flung than coaxed into the track, directly ahead of Gridiron.

"Now, gentlemen," said the master of the ceremonies, "no man's to make a grab till all's been once round; and when the first man *are* got round, then the whole twist and tucking of you grab away as you come under ("Look here, Jim Fulger! you better not stand too close to that gander, I tell you"), one after another. Now blaze away!" (the command for an onset of every kind with people of this order).

Off they went, Miss Sally delighted; for she now thought the whole parade would end in nothing more nor less than her favourite amusement, a race. But Gridiron's visage pronounced this the most nonsensical business that ever a horse of sense was engaged in since the world began.

For the first three rounds Zubly was wholly occupied in restraining Sally to her place; but he lost nothing by this, for the gander had escaped unhurt. On completing his third round, Zube reached forth his long arm, grabbed the gander by the neck with a firmness which seemed likely to defy *goose-grease*, and, at the same instant, he involuntarily gave Sally a sudden check. She raised her head, which before had been kept nearly touching her leader's hocks, and for the first time saw the gander in the act of descending upon her; at the same moment she received two pealing lashes from the whippers. The way she now broke for Springfield "is nothing to nobody." As Zube dashed down the road, the whole Circus raised a whoop after him. This started, about twenty dogs, hounds, curs, and pointers, in full chase of him (for no one moved without his dog in those days). The dogs alarmed some belled cattle, which were grazing on Zube's path, just as he reached them; these joined him, with tails up and a tremendous rattling. Just beyond these went three tobacco-rollers, at distances of fifty and a hundred yards apart; each of whom gave Zube a terrific whoop, scream, or yell as he passed.

He went in and out of Hawk's Gully like a trap-ball, and was in Springfield "in less than no time." Here he was encouraged onward by a new recruit of dogs; but they gave up the chase as hopeless before they cleared the village. Just beyond Springfield, what should Sally encounter but a flock of geese! the tribe to which she owed all her misfortunes. She stopped suddenly, and Zube went over her head with the last acquired velocity. He was up in a moment, and the activity with which he pursued Sally satisfied every spectator that he was unhurt.

Gridiron, who had witnessed Miss Sally's treatment with astonishment and indignation, resolved not to pass between the posts until the whole matter should be explained to his satisfaction. He therefore stopped short, and, by very intelligible looks, demanded of the whippers whether, if he passed between them, he was to be treated as Miss Spitfire had been? The whippers gave him no satisfaction, and his rider signified, by reiterated thumps of the heel, that he should go through whether he would or not. Of these, however, Gridiron seemed to know nothing. In the midst of the conference, Gridiron's eye lit upon the oscillating gander, and every moment's survey of it begat in him a growing interest, as his slowly rising head, suppressed breath, and projected ears plainly evinced. After a short examination, he heaved a sigh, and looked behind him to see if the way was clear. It was plain that his mind was now made up; but, to satisfy the world that he would do nothing rashly, he took another view, and then wheeled and went for Harrisburg as if he had set in for a year's running. Nobody whooped at Gridiron, for all saw that his running was purely the result of philosophic deduction. The reader will not suppose all this consumed half the time which has been consumed in telling it, though it might have been so without interrupting the amusement; for Miss Spitfire's flight had completely suspended it for a time.

The remaining competitors now went on with the sport. A few rounds showed plainly that Odum or Bostwick would be the victor; but which, no one could tell. Whenever either of them came round, the gander's neck was sure of a severe wrench. Many a half pint of Jamaica was staked upon them, besides other things. The poor gander withstood many a strong pull before his wailings ceased. At length, however, they were hushed by Odum. Then came Bostwick, and broke the neck. The next grasp of Odum, it was thought, would bear away the head; but it did not. Then Bostwick was sure of it; but he missed it. Now Odum must surely have it. All is interest and animation; the horses sweep round with redoubled speed; every eye is upon Odum; his backers smiling, Bostwick's trembling. To the rope he comes; lifts his hand; when, lo! Fat John Fulger had borne it away the second before. All were astonished, all disappointed, and some were vexed a little; for it was now clear that, "if it hadn't o' been for his great, fat, greasy paw," to use their own language, "Odum would have gained the victory." Others cursed "that long-legged Zube Zin, who was so high he didn't know when his feet were cold, for bringing such a nag as Sal Spitfire to a gander pullen; for if he'd o' been in his place, it would o' flung Bostwick right where that *gourd o'* hogs lard (Fulger) was."

Fulger's conduct was little calculated to reconcile them to their disappointment.

"Come here, Neddy Prater," said he, with a triumphant smile; "let your Uncle Johnny put his potato stealer (hand) into that hat, and tickle the chins of them *are* shiners a little! Oh you little shinings sons o' bitches! walk into your Mas' Johnny's pocket, and jingle so as Arch Odum and Gory Bostwick may hear you! You hear 'em, Gory?

Boys, don't pull with *men* any more. I've just got my hand in; I wish I had a pond full o' ganders here now, jist to show how I could make their heads fly. Bet all I've won, you may hang three upon that rope, and I'll set Slouch at full speed, and take off the heads of all three the first grab; two with my hands and one with my teeth."

Thus he went on, but really there was no boasting in all this; it was all fun; for John knew, and all were convinced that he knew, that his success was entirely the result of accident. John was really "a good-natured fellow," and his *cavorting* had an effect directly opposite to that which the reader would suppose it had; it reconciled all to their disappointment save one. I except little Billy Mixen, of Spirit Creek; who had staked the net proceeds of six quarts of huckleberries upon Odum, which he had been long keeping for a safe bet. *He* could not be reconciled until he fretted himself into a pretty little *piney*-woods fight, in which he got whipped; and then he went home perfectly satisfied. Fulger spent all his winnings with Prator in treats to the company; made most of them drunk, and thereby produced four Georgia *rotations*; after which all parted good friends.

MIKE FINK (1770?–1823?)

There was a real Mike Fink, who was born at Fort Pitt, later Pittsburgh. His local fame was as a scout, Indian fighter, and marksman, but he was to become not a legend of the frontier, but of the keelboats. The keelboat was a long narrow craft that ran the Ohio and Mississippi in the days before steam, taking cargoes down to New Orleans. It was steered by a great sweep and, as occasion demanded, propelled by poling; the power was brawn, sweat, and the pride of the keelboatman in being able to endure the murderous rigors of that life. The keelboatmen, with shoulders humped with muscle like a bull buffalo, with Homeric appetites for bragging, fighting, and women, and with no inhibitions, were a race apart.

That race, of course, did not long survive the coming of the steamboat. The first steamboat to intrude upon their realm was the *New Orleans*, which passed down the Ohio and Mississippi in the winter of 1811–12; and soon after that the famous song of the boatmen, which seemed to foretell their own passing out of life into legend, was heard no more:

> Hard upon the beech oar!—
> She moves too slow!
> All the way to Shawneetown—
> Long time ago.

Mike Fink, unlike Davy Crockett, had no hand in creating his own legend. The episodes come from many anonymous sources, but in part from "The Last of the Boatmen," by Morgan Neville, who lifted tales "from the campfire and steamboat saloon" and who claimed to have known the historical Mike, even though, in the episode we have on his authority, the mythical and historical seem to have inextricably merged.

Five Tales

MIKE'S SHOT

As he was creeping along one morning, with the stealthy tread of a cat, his eye fell upon a beautiful buck, browsing on the edge of a barren spot, three hundred yards distant. The temptation was too strong for the woodsman, and he resolved to have a shot at every hazard. Re-priming his gun, and picking his flint, he made his approaches in the usual noiseless manner. At the moment he reached the spot, from which he meant to take his aim, he observed a large savage, intent upon the same object, advancing from a direction a little different from his own. Mike shrunk behind a tree, with the quickness of thought, and keeping his eye fixed on the hunter, waited the result with patience. In a few moments, the Indian halted within fifty paces, and levelled his piece at the deer. In the meanwhile, Mike presented his rifle at the body of the savage; and at the moment the smoke issued from the gun of the latter, the bullet of Fink passed through the red man's breast. He uttered a yell, and fell dead at the same instant with the deer. Mike re-loaded his rifle, and remained in his covert for some minutes, to ascertain whether there were more enemies at hand. He then stepped up to the prostrate savage, and having satisfied himself, that life was extinguished, turned his attention to the buck, and took from the carcase those pieces, suited to the process of jerking.

FINK'S BRAG

I'm a Salt River roarer! I'm a ring-tailed squealer! I'm a reg'lar screamer from the ol' Massassip'! WHOOP! I'm the very infant that refused his milk before its eyes were open, and called out for a bottle of old Rye! I love the women an' I'm chockful o' fight! I'm half wild horse and half cock-eyed alligator and the rest o' me is crooked snags an' red-hot snappin' turtle. I can hit like fourth-proof lightnin' an' every lick I make in the woods lets in an acre o' sunshine. I can out-run, out-jump, out-shoot, out-brag, out-drink, an' out-fight, rough-an'-tumble, no holts barred, ary man on both sides the river from Pittsburgh to New Orleans an' back ag'in to St. Louiee. Come on, you flatters, you bargers, you milk-white mechanics, an' see how tough I am to chaw! I ain't had a fight for two days an' I'm spilein' for exercise. Cock-a-doodle-do!

HURRAY FOR ME!

. . . "Hurray for me, you scapegoats! I'm a land-screamer—I'm a water-dog—I'm a snapping-turtle—I can lick five times my own weight in wild-cats. I can use up Injens by the cord. I can swallow niggers whole, raw or cooked. I can out-run, out-dance, out-jump, out-dive, out-drink, out-holler, and out-lick, any white thing in the shape o' human that's ever put foot within two thousand miles o' the big Massassip. Whoop! holler, you varmints! —holler fur the Snapping Turkle! or I'll jump right straight down yer throats, quicker nor a streak o' greased lightening can down a nigger's! . . . I'm in fur a fight, I'll go my death on- a fight, and a fight I must have, one that'll tar up the arth all round and look kankarifferous, or else I'll have to be salted down to save me from spiling, as sure nor Massassip alligators make fly traps o' thar infernal ugly jawrs."

DEATH OF MIKE FINK

"The Last of the Boatmen" has not become altogether a *mythic* personage. There be around us those who still remember him as one of flesh and blood, as well of proportions simply human, albeit he lacked not somewhat of the *heroic* in stature, as well as in being a "perfect terror" to people!

As regards Mike, it has not yet become that favourite question of doubt—"Did such a being really live?" Nor have we heard the skeptic inquiry—"Did such a being really die?" But his death in half a dozen different ways and places has been asserted, and this, we take it, is the first gathering of the *mythic* haze—that shadowy and indistinct enlargement of outline, which, deepening through long ages, invests distinguished mortality with the sublimer attributes of the hero and the demi-god. Had Mike lived in "early Greece," his flat-boat feats would, doubtless, in poetry, have rivalled those of Jason, in his ship; while in Scandinavian legends, he would have been a river-god, to a certainty! The Sea-Kings would have sacrificed to him every time they "crossed the bar," on their return; and as for Odin, himself, he would be duly advised, as far as any interference went, to "lay low and keep dark, or, *pre*-haps," &c.

The story of Mike Fink, including *a* death, has been beautifully told by the late Morgan Neville, of Cincinnati, a gentleman of the highest literary taste as well as the most amiable and polished manners. "The Last of the Boatmen," as his sketch is entitled, is unexceptionable in style, and, we believe, in *fact*, with one exception, and that is, the statement as to the manner and place of Fink's death. He did *not die* on the Arkansas, but at Fort Henry, near the mouth of the Yellow Stone. Our informant is Mr. Chas. Keemle of this paper [St. Louis *Reveille*], who held a command in the neighbourhood, at the time, and to whom every circumstance connected with the affair is most familiar. We give the story as it is told by himself.

In the year 1822, steamboats having left the "keels" and "broad-horns" entirely "out of sight," and Mike having, in consequence, fallen from his high estate—that of being "a little bit the almightiest man on the river, *any* how"—after a term of idleness, frolic and desperate rowdyism, along the different towns, he, at St. Louis, entered the service of the Mountain Fur Company, raised by our late fellow-citizen Gen. W. H. Ashley, as a trapper and hunter; and in that capacity was he employed by Major Henry, in command of the Fort at the mouth of Yellow Stone river, when the occurrence took place of which we write.

Mike, with many generous qualities, was always a reckless daredevil; but, at this time, advancing in years and decayed in influence, above all become a victim of whisky, he was morose and desperate in the extreme. There was a government regulation which forbade the free use of alcohol at the trading posts on the Missouri river, and this was a continual source of quarrel between the men and the commandant, Major Henry,—on the part of Fink, particularly. One of his freaks was to march with his rifle into the fort, and demand a supply of spirits. Argument was fruitless, force not to be thought of, and when, on being positively denied, Mike drew up his rifle and sent a ball through the cask, deliberately walked up and filled his can, while his particular "boys" followed his example, all that could be done was to look upon the matter as one of his "queer ways," and that was the end of it.

This state of things continued for some time; Mike's temper and exactions growing more unbearable every day, until, finally, a "split" took place, not only between himself and the commandant, but many others in the fort, and the unruly boatman swore he would not live among them. Followed only by a youth named Carpenter, whom he had brought up, and for whom he felt a rude but strong attachment, he prepared a sort of cave in the river's bank, furnished it with a supply of whisky, and, with his companion, *turned in* to pass the winter, which was then closing upon them. In this place he buried himself, sometimes unseen for weeks, his *protege* providing what else was *necessary* beyond the whisky. At length attempts were used, on the part of those in the fort, to withdraw Carpenter from Fink; foul insinuations were made as to the nature of their connection; the youth was twitted with being a mere slave, &c., all which (Fink heard of it in spite of his retirement) served to breed distrust between the two, and though they did not separate, much of their cordiality ceased.

The winter wore away in this sullen state of torpor; spring came with its reviving influences, and to celebrate the season, a supply of alcohol was procured, and a number of his acquaintances from the fort coming to "rouse out" Mike, a desperate "frolic," of course, ensued.

There were river yarns, and boatmen songs, and "nigger break-downs," interspersed with wrestling-matches, jumping, laugh, and yell, the can circulating freely, until Mike became somewhat mollified.

"I tell you what it is, boys," he cried, "the fort's a skunk-hole, and I rather live with the *bars* than stay in it. Some on ye's bin trying to part me and my boy, that I love like my own cub—but no matter. Maybe he's *pisoned* against me; but, Carpenter (striking the youth heavily on the shoulder), I took you by the hand when it had forgotten the touch of a father's or a mother's—you know me to be a man, and you ain't going to turn out a dog!"

Whether it was that the youth fancied something insulting in the manner of the appeal, or not, we can't say; but it was not responded to very warmly, and a reproach followed from Mike. However, they drank together, and the frolic went on, until Mike, filling his can, walked off some forty yards, placed it upon his head, and called to Carpenter to take his rifle.

This wild feat of shooting cans off each other's head was a favourite one with Mike—himself and "boy" generally winding up a hard frolic with this savage but deeply-meaning proof of continued confidence;—as for risk, their eagle eyes and iron nerves defied the might of whisky. After their recent alienation, a doubly generous impulse, without doubt, had induced Fink to propose and subject himself to the test.

Carpenter had been drinking wildly, and with a boisterous laugh snatched up his rifle. All present had seen the parties "shoot," and this desperate aim, instead of alarming, was merely made a matter of wild jest.

"Your grog is spilt, for ever, Mike!"

"Kill the old varmint, young 'un!"

"What'll his skin bring in St. Louis?" &c., &c.

Amid a loud laugh, Carpenter raised his piece—even the jesters remarked that he was unsteady,—crack!—the can fell,—a loud shout,—but, instead of a smile of pleasure, a dark frown settled upon the face of Fink! He made no motion except to clutch his rifle as though he would have crushed it, and there he stood, gazing at the youth strangely! Various shades of passion crossed his features—surprise, rage, suspicion—but at length they composed themselves into a sad expression; the ball had grazed the top of his head, cutting the scalp, and the thought of treachery had set his heart on fire.

There was a loud call upon Mike to know what he was waiting for, in which Carpenter joined, pointing to the can upon his head and bidding him fire, if he knew how!

"Carpenter, my son," said the boatman, "I taught you to shoot differently from that *last* shot! You've *missed* once, but you won't again."

He fired, and his ball, crashing through the forehead of the youth, laid him a corpse amid his as suddenly hushed companions!

Time wore on—many at the fort spoke darkly of the deed. Mike Fink had never been known to miss his aim—he had grown afraid of Carpenter—he had murdered him! While this feeling was gathering against him, the unhappy boatman lay in his cave, shunning both sympathy and sustenance. He spoke to none—when he did come forth, 'twas as a spectre, and only to haunt the grave of his "boy," or, if he did break silence, 'twas to burst into a paroxysm of rage against the enemies who had "turned his boy's heart from him!"

At the fort was a man by the name of Talbott, the gunsmith of the station: he was very loud and bitter in his denunciations of the "murderer," as he called Fink, which, finally, reaching the ears of latter, filled him with the most violent passion, and he swore that he would take the life of his defamer. This threat was almost forgotten, when one day, Talbott, who was at work in his shop, saw Fink enter the fort, his first visit since the death of Carpenter. Fink approached; he was care-

worn, sick, and wasted; there was no anger in his bearing, but he carried his rifle (had he ever gone without it?) and the gunsmith was not a coolly brave man; moreover, his life had been threatened.

"Fink," cried he, snatching up a pair of pistols from his bench, "don't approach me—if you do, you're a dead man!"

"Talbott," said the boatman, in a sad voice, "you needn't be afraid; you've done me wrong—I'm come to talk to you about—Carpenter—my boy!"

He continued to advance, and the gunsmith again called to him:

"Fink! I know you; if you come three steps nearer, I'll fire, by——!"

Mike carried his rifle across his arm, and made no hostile demonstration, except in gradually getting nearer—*if* hostile his aim was.

"Talbott, you've accused me of murdering—my boy—Carpenter—that I raised from a child—that I loved like a son—that I can't live without! I'm not mad with you *now*, but you must let me show you that I *couldn't* do it—that I'd rather died than done it—that you've wronged me——"

By this time he was within a few steps of the door, and Talbott's agitation became extreme. Both pistols were pointed at Fink's breast, in expectation of a spring from the latter.

"By the Almighty above us, Fink, I'll fire—I don't want to speak to you now—don't put your foot on that step—don't."

Fink did put his foot on the step, and the same moment fell heavily within it, receiving the contents of both barrels in his breast! His last and only words were,

"I didn't mean to kill my boy!"

Poor Mike! we are satisfied with our senior's conviction that you did *not* mean to kill him. Suspicion of treachery, doubtless, entered his mind, but cowardice and murder never dwelt there.

A few weeks after this event, Talbott himself perished in an attempt to cross the Missouri river in a skiff.

SAL FINK, THE MISSISSIPPI SCREAMER

I dar say you've all on you, if not more, frequently heerd this great she human crittur boasted of, an' pointed out as "*one o' the gals*"—but I tell you what, stranger, you have never really set your eyes on "*one of the gals*," till you have seen Sal Fink, the Mississippi screamer, whose miniature pictur I have here give, about as nat'ral as life, but not half as handsome—an' if thar ever was a gal that desarved to be christen—"*one o' the gals*," then this gal was that gal—and no mistake.

She fought a duel once with a thunderbolt, an' came off without a single scratch, while at the fust fire she split the thunderbolt all to flinders, an' gave the pieces to Uncle Sam's artillerymen, to touch off their canon with. When a gal about six years old, she used to play see-saw on the Mississippi snags, and arter she war done she would snap 'em off, an' so cleared a large district of the river. She used to ride down the river on an alligator's back, standen upright, an' dancing *Yankee Doodle*, and could leave all the steamers behind. But the greatest feat she ever did, positively outdid anything that ever was did.

One day when she war out in the forest, making a collection o' wild cat skins for her family's winter beddin, she war captered in the most all-sneaken manner by about fifty Injuns, an' carried by 'em to Roast Flesh Hollow, whar the blood drinkin' wild varmints detarmined to skin her alive, sprinkle a leetle salt over her, an' devour her before her own eyes; so they took an' tied her to a tree, to keep till mornin' should bring the rest o' thar ring-nosed sarpints to enjoy the fun. Arter that, they lit a large fire in the Holler, turned the bottom o' thar feet towards the blaze, Injun fashion, and went to sleep to dream o' thar mornin's feast; well, after the critturs got into a somniferous snore, Sal got into an all-lightnin' of a temper, and burst all the ropes about her like an apron-string! She then found a pile o' ropes, too, and tied all the Injun's heels together all round the fire,—then fixin' a cord to the shins of every two couple, she, with a suddenachous jerk, that made the intire woods tremble, pulled the intire lot o' sleepin' red-skins into that ar great fire, fast together, an' then sloped like a panther out of her pen, in the midst o' the tallest yellin', howlin', scramblin' and singin', that war ever seen or heerd on, since the great burnin' o' Buffalo prairie!

THOMAS B. THORPE (1815–1878)

Thomas B. Thorpe was one of the many New Englanders who emigrated to the South, in this instance, to Louisiana. Thorpe, like Longstreet, was a good example of the self-reliant American praised by Emerson, the man who could turn his hand to almost anything; he was a newspaper man, a writer, a soldier (a colonel in the Mexican War), and a painter (his portrait of General Zachary Taylor had honorable place in the legislative chamber of Arkansas). "The Big Bear of Arkansas," written in 1841, is his most famous piece of writing. It is a perfect example of the tall tale, here put in its setting and even given its appropriate audience, the tenderfoot. The "unhuntable bear" of the tale throws a long shadow forward to other such creatures in our literature, the last being the mythic quarry of the Big Woods, in *The Bear* by William Faulkner.

The Big Bear of Arkansas (1841)

A steamboat on the Mississippi frequently, in making her regular trips, carries between places varying from one to two thousand miles apart; and as these boats advertise to land passengers and freight at "all intermediate landings," the heterogeneous character of the passengers of one of these up-country boats can scarcely be imagined by one who has never seen it with his own eyes. Starting from New Orleans in one of these boats, you will find yourself associated with men from every state in the Union, and from every portion of the globe; and a man of observation need not lack for amusement or instruction in such a crowd, if he will take the trouble to read the great book of character so favourably opened before him. Here may be seen jostling together the wealthy Southern planter, and the pedlar of tin-ware from New England— the Northern merchant, and the Southern jockey —a venerable bishop, and a desperate gambler—the land speculator, and the honest farmer—professional men of all creeds and characters—Wolvereens, Suckers, Hoosiers, Buckeyes, and Corn-crackers, beside a "plentiful sprinkling" of the half-horse and half-alligator species of men, who are peculiar to "old Mississippi," and who appear to gain a livelihood simply by going up and down the river. In the pursuit of pleasure or business, I have frequently found myself in such a crowd.

On one occasion, when in New Orleans, I had occasion to take a trip of a few miles up the Mississippi, and I hurried on board the well-known "high-pressure-and-beat-everything" steamboat *Invincible*, just as the last note of the last bell was sounding; and when the confusion and bustle that is natural to a boat's getting under way had subsided, I discovered that I was associated in as heterogeneous a crowd as was ever got together. As my trip was to be of a few hours' duration only, I made no endeavours to become acquainted with my fellow passengers, most of whom would be together many days. Instead of this, I took out of my pocket the "latest paper," and more critically than usual examined its contents; my fellow passengers at the same time disposed themselves in little groups. While I was thus busily employed in reading, and my companions were more busily employed in discussing such subjects as suited their humours best, we were startled most unexpectedly by a loud Indian whoop, uttered in the "social hall," that part of the cabin fitted off for a bar; then was to be heard a loud crowing, which would not have continued to have interested us— such sounds being quite common in that place of spirits—had not the hero of these windy accomplishments stuck his head into the cabin and hallooed out, "Hurra for the Big Bar of Arkansaw!" and then might be heard a confused hum of voices, unintelligible, save in such broken sentences as "horse," "screamer," "lightning is slow," &c. As might have been expected, this continued interruption attracted the attention of every one in the cabin; all conversation dropped, and in the midst of this surprise the "Big Bar" walked into the cabin, took a chair, put his feet on the stove, and looking back over his shoulder, passed the general and familiar salute of "Strangers, how are you?" He then expressed himself as much at home as if

he had been at "the Forks of Cypress," and "perhaps a little more so." Some of the company at this familiarity looked a little angry, and some astonished; but in a moment every face was wreathed in a smile. There was something about the intruder that won the heart on sight. He appeared to be a man enjoying perfect health and contentment: his eyes were as sparkling as diamonds, and good-natured to simplicity. Then his perfect confidence in himself was irresistibly droll. "Perhaps," said he, "gentlemen," running on without a person speaking, "perhaps you have been to New Orleans often; I never made *the first visit before,* and I don't intend to make another in a crow's life. I am thrown away in that ar place, and useless, that ar a fact. Some of the gentlemen thar called me *green* —well, perhaps I am, said I, *but I arn't so at home;* and if I ain't off my trail much, the heads of them perlite chaps themselves weren't much the hardest; for according to my notion, they were real *know-nothings,* green as a pumpkin-vine—couldn't, in farming, I'll bet, raise a crop of turnips: and as for shooting, they'd miss a barn if the door was swinging, and that, too, with the best rifle in the country. And then they talked to me 'bout hunting, and laughed at my calling the principal game in Arkansaw poker, and high-low-jack. 'Perhaps,' said I, 'you prefer chickens and rolette'; at this they laughed harder than ever, and asked me if I lived in the woods, and didn't know what *game* was? At this I rather think I laughed. 'Yes,' I roared, and says, "Strangers, if you'd asked me *how we got our meat* in Arkansaw, I'd a told you at once, and given you a list of varmints that would make a caravan, beginning with the bar, and ending off with the cat; that's *meat* though, not game.' Game, indeed, that's what city folks call it; and with them it means chippen-birds and shite-pokes; maybe such trash live in my diggens, but I arn't noticed them yet: a bird any way is too trifling. I never did shoot at but one, and I'd never forgiven myself for that, had it weighed less than forty pounds. I wouldn't draw a rifle on any thing less than that; and when I meet with another wild turkey of the same weight I will drap him."

"A wild turkey weighing forty pounds!" exclaimed twenty voices in the cabin at once.

"Yes, strangers, and wasn't it a whopper? You see, the thing was so fat that it couldn't fly far; and when he fell out of the tree, after I shot him, on striking the ground he bust open behind, and the way the pound gobs of tallow rolled out of the opening was perfectly beautiful."

"Where did all that happen?" asked a cynical-looking Hoosier.

"Happen! happened in Arkansaw: where else could it have happened, but in the creation state, the finishing-up country—a state where the *sile* runs down to the centre of the 'arth, and government gives you a title to every inch of it? Then its airs—just breathe them, and they will make you snort like a horse. It's a state without a fault, it is."

"Excepting mosquitoes," cried the Hoosier.

"Well, stranger, except them; for it ar a fact that they are rather *enormous*, and do push themselves in somewhat troublesome. But, stranger, they never stick twice in the same place; and give them a fair chance for a few months, and you will get as much above noticing them as an alligator. They can't hurt my feelings, for they lay under the skin; and I never knew but one case of injury resulting from them, and that was to a Yankee: and they take worse to foreigners, any how, than they do to natives. But the way they used that fellow up! first they punched him until he swelled up and busted; then he su-per-a-ted, as the doctor called it, until he was as raw as beef; then he took the ager, owing to the warm weather, and finally he took a steamboat and left the country. He was the only man that ever took mosquitoes to heart that I know of. But mosquitoes is natur, and I never find fault with her. If they ar large, Arkansaw is large, her varmints ar large, her trees ar large, her rivers ar large, and a small mosquito would be of no more use in Arkansaw than preaching in a cane-brake."

This knock-down argument in favour of big mosquitoes used the Hoosier up, and the logician started on a new track, to explain how numerous bear were in his "diggins," where he represented them to be "about as plenty as blackberries, and a little plentifuler."

Upon the utterance of this assertion, a timid little man near me inquired if the bear in Arkansaw ever attacked the settlers in numbers.

"No," said our hero, warming with the subject, "no, stranger, for you see it ain't the natur of bar to go in droves; but the way they squander about in pairs and single ones is edifying. And then the way I hunt them the old black rascals know the crack of my gun as well as they know a pig's squealing. They grow thin in our parts, it frightens them so, and they do take the noise dreadfully, poor things. That gun of mine is perfect *epidemic among bar*; if not watched closely, it will go off as quick on a warm scent as my dog Bowie-knife will: and then that dog—whew! why the fellow thinks that the world is full of bar, he finds them so easy. It's lucky he don't talk as well as think; for with his natural modesty, if he should suddenly learn how much he is acknowledged to be ahead of all other dogs in the universe, he would be astonished to death in two minutes. Strangers, the dog knows a bar's way as well as a horse-jockey knows a woman's: he always barks at the right time, bites at the exact place, and whips without getting a scratch. I never could tell whether he was made expressly to hunt bar, or whether bar was made expressly for him to hunt: any way, I believe they were ordained to go together as naturally as Squire Jones says a man and woman is, when he moralizes in marrying a couple. In fact, Jones once said, said he, 'Marriage according to law is a civil contract of divine origin; it's common to all countries as well as Arkansaw, and people take to it as naturally as Jim Doggett's Bowie-knife takes to bar.'"

"What season of the year do your hunts take place?" inquired a gentlemanly foreigner, who, from some peculiarities of his baggage, I suspected to be an Englishman, on some hunting expedition, probably at the foot of the Rocky Mountains.

"The season for bar hunting, stranger," said the man of Arkansaw, "is generally all the year round, and the hunts take place about as regular. I read in history that varmints have their fat season, and their lean season. That is not the case in Arkansaw, feeding as they do upon the *spontenacious* production of the sile, they have one continuous fat season the year round: though in winter things in this way is rather more greasy than in summer, I must admit. For that reason bar with us run in warm weather, but in winter, they only waddle. Fat, fat! it's an enemy to speed! it tames everything that has plenty of it. I have seen wild turkeys, from its influence, as gentle as chickens. Run a bar in this fat condition, and the way it improves the critter for eating is amazing; it sort of mixes the ile up with the meat, until you can't tell t'other from which. I've done this often. I recollect one perty morning in particular, of putting an old fellow on the stretch, and considering the weight he carried, he run well. But the dogs soon tired him down, and when I came up with him wasn't he in a beautiful sweat—I might say fever; and then to see his tongue sticking out of his mouth a feet, and his sides sinking and opening like a bellows, and his cheeks so fat he couldn't look cross. In this fix I blazed at him, and pitch me naked into a briar patch if the steam didn't come out of the bullet-hole ten foot in a straight line. The fellow, I reckon, was made on the high-pressure system, and the lead sort of bust his biler."

"That column of steam was rather curious, or else the bear must have been *warm*," observed the foreigner, with a laugh.

"Stranger, as you observe, that bar was WARM, and the blowing off of the steam show'd it, and also how hard the varmint had been run. I have no doubt if he had kept on two miles farther his insides would have been stewed; and I expect to meet with a varmint yet of extra bottom, who will run himself into a skinfull of bar's grease: it is possible, much onlikelier things have happened."

"Whereabouts are these bears so abundant?" inquired the foreigner, with increasing interest.

"Why, stranger, they inhabit the neighbourhood of my settlement, one of the prettiest places on old Mississippi—a perfect location, and no mistake; a place that had some defects until the river made the 'cut-off' at 'Shirt-tail bend,' and that remedied the evil, as it brought my cabin on the edge of the river—a great advantage in wet weather, I assure you, as you can now row a barrel of whiskey into my yard in high water from a boat, as easy as falling off a log. It's a great improvement, as toting it by land in a jug, as I used to do, *evaporated* it too fast, and it became expensive. Just stop with me, stranger, a month or two, or a year if you like, and you will appreciate my place. I can give you plenty to eat; for beside hog and hominy, you can have bar-ham, and bar-sausages, and a mattrass of bar-skins to sleep on, and a wild-cat-skin, pulled off hull, stuffed with corn-shucks, for a pillow. That bed would put you to sleep if you had the rheumatics in every joint in your body. I call that ar bed a *quietus*. Then look at my land—the government ain' got another such a piece to dispose of. Such timber, and such a bottom land, why you can't preserve any thing natural you plant in it unless you pick it young, things thar will grow out of shape so quick. I once planted in those diggins a few potatoes and beets: they took a fine start, and after that an ox team couldn't have kept them from growing. About that time I went off to old Kentuck on bisiness, and did not hear from them things in three months, when I accidentally stumbled on a fellow who had stopped at my place, with an idea of buying me out. 'How did you like things?' said I. 'Pretty well,' said he; 'the cabin is convenient, and the timber land is good; but that bottom land ain't worth the first

red cent.' 'Why?' said I. ' 'Cause,' said he. ' 'Cause what?' said I. ' 'Cause it's full of cedar stumps and Indian mounds,' said he, *'and it can't be cleared.'* 'Lord,' said I, 'them ar "cedar stumps" is beets, and them ar "Indian mounds" ar tater hills.' As I expected, the crop was overgrown and useless: the sile is too rich, *and planting in Arkansaw is dangerous.* I had a good-sized sow killed in that same bottom land. The old thief stole an ear of corn, and took it down where she slept at night to eat. Well, she left a grain or two on the ground, and lay down on them: before morning the corn shot up, and the percussion killed her dead. I don't plant any more: natur intended Arkansaw for a hunting ground, and I go according to natur."

The questioner who thus elicited the description of our hero's settlement, seemed to be perfectly satisfied, and said no more; but the "Big Bar of Arkansaw" rambled on from one thing to another with a volubility perfectly astonishing, occasionally disputing with those around him, particularly with a "live Sucker" from Illinois, who had the daring to say that our Arkansaw friend's stories "smelt rather tall."

In this manner the evening was spent; but conscious that my own association with so singular a personage would probably end before morning, I asked him if he would not give me a description of some particular bear hunt; adding that I took great interest in such things, though I was no sportsman. The desire seemed to please him, and he squared himself round towards me, saying, that he could give me an idea of a bar hunt that was never beat in this world, or in any other. His manner was so singular, that half of his story consisted in his excellent way of telling it, the great peculiarity of which was, the happy manner he had of emphasizing the prominent parts of his conversation. As near as I can recollect, I have italicized them, and given the story in his own words.

"Stranger," said he, "in bar hunts *I am numerous*, and which particular one, as you say, I shall tell, puzzles me. There was the old she devil I shot at the Hurricane last fall—then there was the old hog thief I popped over at the Bloody Crossing, and then—Yes, I have it! I will give you an idea of a hunt, in which the greatest bar was killed that ever lived, *none excepted*; about an old fellow that I hunted, more or less, for two or three years; and if that ain't a particular bar hunt, I ain't got one to tell. But in the first place, stranger, let me say, I am pleased with you, because you ain't ashamed to gain information by asking, and listening, and that's what I say to Countess's pups every day when I'm home; and I have got great hopes of them ar pups, because they are continually *nosing* about; and though they stick it sometimes in the wrong place, they gain experience any how, and may learn something useful to boot. Well, as I was saying about this big bar, you see when I and some more first settled in our region, we were drivin to hunting naturally; we soon liked it, and after that we found it an easy matter to make the thing our business. One old chap who had pioneered 'afore us, gave us to understand that we had settled in the right place. He dwelt upon its merits until it was affecting, and showed us, to prove his assertions, more marks on the sassafras trees than I ever saw on a tavern door 'lection time. 'Who keeps that ar reckoning?' said I. 'The bar,' said he. 'What for?' said I. 'Can't tell,' said he; 'but so it is: the bar bite the bark and wood too, at the highest point from the ground they can reach, and you can tell, by the marks,' said he, 'the length of the bar to an inch.' 'Enough,' said I; 'I've learned something here a'ready, and I'll put it in practice.'

"Well, stranger, just one month from that time I killed a bar, and told its exact length before I measured it, by those very marks; and when I did that, I swelled up considerable—I've been a prouder man ever since. So I went on, larning something every day, until I was reckoned a buster, and allowed to be decidedly the best bar hunter in my district; and that is a reputation as much harder to earn than to be reckoned first man in Congress, as an iron ramrod is harder than a toadstool. Did the varmints grow over-cunning by being fooled with by green-horn hunters, and by this means get troublesome, they send for me as a matter of course; and thus I do my own hunting, and most of my neighbours'. I walk into the varmints though, and it has become about as much the same to me as drinking. It is told in two sentences—a bar is started, and he is killed. The thing is somewhat monotonous now—I know just how much they will run, where they will tire, how much they will growl, and what a thundering time I will have in getting them home. I could give you this history of the chase with all particulars at the commencement, I know the signs so well—*Stranger, I'm certain*. Once I met with a match though, and I will tell you about it; for a common hunt would not be worth relating.

"On a fine fall day, long time ago, I was trailing about for bar, and what should I see but fresh marks on the sassafras trees, about eight inches above any in the forests that I knew of. Says I, 'them marks is a hoax, or it indicates the d——t bar that was ever grown.' In fact, stranger, I couldn't believe it was real, and I went on. Again I saw the same marks, at the same height, and *I knew the thing lived.* That conviction came home to my soul like an earthquake. Says I, 'here is something a-purpose for me: that bar is mine, or I give up the hunting business.' The very next morning what should I see but a number of buzzards hovering over my cornfield. 'The rascal has been there,' said I, 'for that sign is certain:' and, sure enough, on examining, I found the bones of what had been as beautiful a hog the day before, as was ever raised by a Buckeye. Then I tracked the critter out of the field to the woods, and all the marks he left behind, showed me that he was *the bar.*

"Well, stranger, the first fair chase I ever had with that big critter, I saw him no less than three distinct times at a distance: the dogs run him over eighteen miles and broke down, my horse gave out; and I was as nearly used up as a man can be, made on *my* principle, *which is patent.* Before this adventure, such things were unknown to me as possible; but, strange as it was, that bar got me used to it before I was done with him; for he got so at last, that he would leave me on a long chase *quite easy.* How he did it, I never could understand. That a bar runs at all, is puzzling; but how this one could tire down and bust up a pack of hounds and a horse, that were used to overhauling everything they started after in no time, was past my understanding. Well, stranger, that bar finally got so sassy, that he used to help himself to a hog off my premises whenever he wanted one; the buzzards followed after what he left, and so between *bar and buzzard,* I rather think I was *out of pork.*

"Well, missing that bar so often took hold of my vitals, and I wasted away. The thing had been carried too far, and it reduced me in flesh faster than an ager. I would see that bar in every thing I did: *he hunted me,* and that, too, like a devil, which I began to think he was. While in this fix, I made preparations to give him a last brush, and be done with it. Having completed every thing to my satisfaction, I started at sunrise, and to my great joy, I discovered from the way the dogs run, that they were near him; finding his trail was nothing, for that had become as plain to the pack as a turnpike road. On we went, and coming to an open country, what should I see but the bar very leisurely ascending a hill, and the dogs close at his heels, either a match for him in speed, or else he did not care to get out of their way—I don't know which. But wasn't he a beauty, though? I loved him like a brother.

"On he went, until he came to a tree, the limbs of which formed a crotch about six feet from the ground. Into this crotch he got and seated himself, the dogs yelling all around it; and there he sat eyeing them as quiet as a pond in low water. A green-horn friend of mine, in company, reached shooting distance before me, and blazed away, hitting the critter in the centre of his forehead. The bar shook his head as the ball struck it, and then walked down from that tree as gently as a lady would from a carriage. 'Twas a beautiful sight to see him do that—he was in such a rage that he seemed to be as little afraid of the dogs as if they had been sucking pigs; and the dogs warn't slow in making a ring around him at a respectful distance, I tell you; even Bowie-knife, himself, stood off. Then the way his eyes flashed—why the fire of them would have singed a cat's hair; in fact that bar was in a *wrath all over*. Only one pup came near him, and he was brushed out so totally with the bar's left paw, that he entirely disappeared; and that made the old dogs more cautious still. In the mean time, I came up, and taking deliberate aim as a man should do, at his side, just back of his foreleg, *if my gun did not snap*, call me a coward, and I won't take it personal. Yes, stranger, *it snapped*, and I could not find a cap about my person. While in this predicament, I turned round to my fool friend—says I, 'Bill,' says I, 'you're an ass—you're a fool—you might as well have tried to kill that bar by barking the tree under his belly, as to have done it by hitting him in the head. Your shot has made a tiger of him, and blast me, if a dog gets killed or wounded when they come to blows, I will stick my knife into your liver, I will—' my wrath was up. I had lost my caps, my gun had snapped, the fellow with me had fired at the bar's head, and I expected every moment to see him close in with the dogs, and kill a dozen of them at least. In this thing I was mistaken, for the bar leaped over the ring formed by the dogs, and giving a fierce growl, was off—the pack, of course, in full cry after him. The run this time was short, for coming to the edge of a lake the varmint jumped in, and swam to a little island in the lake, which it reached just a moment before the dogs. 'I'll have him now,' said I, for I had found my caps in

the *lining of my coat*—so, rolling a log into the lake, I paddled myself across to the island, just as the dogs had cornered the bar in a thicket. I rushed up and fired—at the same time the critter leaped over the dogs and came within three feet of me, running like mad; he jumped into the lake, and tried to mount the log I had just deserted, but every time he got half his body on it, it would roll over and send him under; the dogs, too, got around him, and pulled him about, and finally Bowie-knife clenched with him, and they sunk into the lake together. Stranger, about this time, I was excited, and I stripped off my coat, drew my knife, and intended to have taken a part with Bowie-knife myself, when the bar rose to the surface. But the varmint staid under—Bowie-knife came up alone, more dead than alive, and with the pack came ashore. 'Thank God,' said I, 'the old villain has got his deserts at last.' Determined to have the body, I cut a grape-vine for a rope, and dove down where I could see the bar in the water, fastened my queer rope to his leg, and fished him, with great difficulty, ashore. Stranger, may I be chawed to death by young alligators, if the thing I looked at wasn't a *she bar, and not the old critter after all*. The way matters got mixed on that island was onaccountably curious, and thinking of it made me more than ever convinced that I was hunting the devil himself. I went home that night and took to my bed—the thing was killing me. The entire team of Arkansaw in bar-hunting, acknowledged himself used up, and the fact sunk into my feelings like a snagged boat will in the Mississippi. I grew as cross as a bar with two cubs and a sore tail. The thing got out 'mong my neighbours, and I was asked how come on that individu-al that never lost a bar when once started? and if that same individ-u-al didn't wear telescopes when he turned a she bar, of ordinary size, into an old he one, a little larger than a horse? 'Perhaps,' said I, 'friends'—getting wrathy—'perhaps you want to call somebody a liar.' 'Oh, no,' said they, 'we only heard such things as being *rather common* of late, but we don't believe one word of it; oh, no,'—and then they would ride off and laugh like so many hyenas over a dead nigger. It was too much, and I determined to catch that bar, go to Texas, or die, —and I made my preparations accordin'. I had the pack shut up and rested. I took my rifle to pieces and iled it. I put caps in every pocket about my person, *for fear of the lining*. I then told my neighbours, that on Monday morning—naming the day—I would start THAT BAR, and bring him home with me, or they might divide my settlement among them, the owner having disappeared. Well, stranger, on the morning previous to the great day of my hunting expedition, I went into the woods near my house, taking my gun and Bowie-knife along, just *from habit*, and there sitting down also from habit, what should I see, getting over my fence, but *the bar!* Yes, the old varmint was within a hundred yards of me, and the way he walked *over that fence*—stranger, he loomed up like a *black mist*, he seemed so large, and he walked right towards me. I raised myself, took deliberate aim, and fired. Instantly the varmint wheeled, gave a yell, and *walked through the fence* like a falling tree would through a cobweb. I started after, but was tripped up by my inexpressibles, which either from habit, or the excitement of the moment, were about my heels, and before I had really gathered myself up, I heard the old varmint groaning in a thicket near by, like a thousand sinners, and by the time I reached him he was a corpse. Stranger, it took five niggers and myself to put that carcase on a mule's back, and old long-ears waddled under the load, as if he was foundered in every leg of his body, and with a common whopper of a bar, he would have trotted off, and enjoyed himself. 'Twould astonish you to know how big he was: I made a *bed-spread of his skin*, and the way it used to cover my bar mattress, and leave several feet on each side to tuck up, would have delighted you. It was in fact a creation

bar, and if it had lived in Samson's time, and had met him, in a fair fight, it would have licked him in the twinkling of a dice-box. But, strangers, I never like the way I hunted, and *missed him*. There is something curious about it, I could never understand,—and I never was satisfied at his giving in so easy at last. Prehaps, he had heard of my preparations to hunt him the next day, so he jist come in, like Capt. Scott's coon, to save his wind to grunt with in dying; but that ain't likely. My private opinion is, that that bar was an *unhuntable bar, and died when his time come.*"

When the story was ended, our hero sat some minutes with his auditors in a grave silence; I saw there was a mystery to him connected with the bear whose death he had just related, that had evidently made a strong impression on his mind. It was also evident that there was some superstitious awe connected with the affair,—a feeling common with all "children of the wood," when they meet with any thing out of their everyday experience. He was the first one, however, to break the silence, and jumping up, he asked all present to "liquor" before going to bed,—a thing which he did, with a number of companions, evidently to his heart's content.

Long before day, I was put ashore at my place of destination, and I can only follow with the reader, in imagination, our Arkansas friend, in his adventures at the "Forks of Cypress" on the Mississippi.

GEORGE WASHINGTON HARRIS (1814–1869)

George Washington Harris came from the hill country of eastern Tennessee. He tried many occupations—inventor, journalist, silversmith and general worker in metals, farmer, steamboat captain, postmaster, railroad man, surveyor, writer—and in all of them except the last showed a genius for failure. In the writing he showed, however fitfully and on however limited a scale, simply genius.

Writing was not a profession or a career for Harris. He wrote out of his convivial and gusty appreciation of the life around him, a gay-hearted amateur finding refuge, in his created

world of amiable brutality, grotesque high jinks, and crazy poetry, from the practical world in which, over and over again, he failed. For years his sketches and stories were published in newspapers, even as far off as New York City, in the famous sporting weekly *Spirit of the Times*, where the character Sut Lovingood made his debut in 1854. Sut became, in 1867, a book, the only one Harris ever published.

The creature Sut is a type different from Jack Downing, as from Davy Crockett, Mike Fink, and the characters of *Georgia Scenes*. He is a grotesque projection, shorn of any of the dignity or courage with which that type is often endowed, of the southern hillbilly, the Appalachian mountaineer—the type of whom Li'l Abner of the comic strip is a projection, somewhat more amiable, in our time. Sut is the natural man unredeemed, a "nat'ral born durn'd fool" by his own admission, son of a "king fool" father, lecherous, cowardly, sadistic, lazy, drunken, with no ambition beyond that of taking another drag from the bottle and raising hell, raising hell being both a celebration of life and a vengeance on it. Sut knows himself for what he is, accepts himself, and can even laugh at himself, and this self-knowledge, set over against the pretensions of the world, is the fundamental source of his humor.

The saga of Sut gives a gallery of other characters drawn with verve and astuteness; around him there is a whole society, a world grotesque but humanly recognizable. And Harris caught, created even, a language for that world. It is a language of vital rhythms and vivid images. The reader can never forget the "Hard-Shell

preacher with his mouth mortised into his face in shape like a mule's shoe, heels down." Or the Sheriff's wife:

> There set the Sheriff's wife in a rocking chair. She were bony and pale. A drunk Indian could a-read a Dutch almanac thru her nose; and there were a new moon of indigo under her eyes. Away back into them, fifty foot or so, I seed her tear wells; their windlass were broke, the bucket in staves, and the waters all gone; and away still further two lights shined soft, like the stars above just afore their settin. Her waist was flat. And the finger cords on her hands were most as high, and looked as tight, and showed as clear thru the skin, as the strings of a fiddle. The hand itself were white, not like snow but like paint, and the forked blue veins made it look like a new map of the land of death.

It is a world and a language related, on the one hand, to the tall tale and, on the other, to Mark Twain and William Faulkner.

Mrs. Yardley's Quilting Party[1] (1867)

"That's been one durned nasty, muddy job, and I is just glad enough to take a horn or two on the strength of it."

"What have you been doing, Sut?"

"Helpin to salt ole Missis Yardley down."

"What do you mean by that?"

"Fixin her for rottin comfortably . . . coverin her up with soil to keep the buzzards from cheatin the worms."

"Oh, you have been helping to bury a woman."

"That's it, by golly! Now why the devil can't I explain myself like you? I ladles out my words at random like a calf kickin at yaller-jackets; you just rolls 'em out to the point like a feller a-layin bricks—every one fits. How is it that bricks fit so close't anyhow? Rocks won't nigh do it."

"Becaze they's all of a size," ventured a man with a wen over his eye.

"The devil you say, honey-head! Ain't reapinmachines of a size? I'd like to see two of 'em fit close't. You wait until you sprouts t'other horn afore you ventures to explain mixed questions. George, did you know ole Missis Yardley?"

"No."

"Well, she were a curious woman in her way, and she wore shiny specks. Now just listen: whenever you see a ole woman ahind a pair of *shiny* specks, you keep your eye skinned. They am dang'rous in the extreme. There is just no knowin what they can do. I had one a-straddle of me once't for kissin her gal. She went for my hair, and she went for my skin, until I thought she meant to kill me and woulda done it if my hollerin hadn't fetched ole Dave Jordan, a *bachelor*, to my aid. He, like a durned fool, ketched her by the leg and drug her back'ards offen me. She just covered him, and I run, by golly! The next time I seed him, he were bald-headed, and his face looked like he'd been a-fightin wildcats.

[1] The text here presented has been revised by Brom Weber, reducing somewhat Harris's use of dialect. The present editors have followed Weber's modifications, though a number of critics, Edmund Wilson among them, argue that some of the flavor of the story is thereby lost. Interested students are urged to see the original of the story.

"Ole Missis Yardley were a great noticer of little things that nobody else ever seed. She'd say, right in the middle of somebody's serious talk:

" 'Law sakes! Thar goes that yaller slut of a hen, a-flingin straws over her shoulder. She's arter settin now and hain't laid but seven aigs. I'll disappint her, see ef I don't. I'll put a punkin in her nest an' a feather in her nose. An' bless my soul! Jis' look at that cow wif the wilted horn, a-flingin up dirt and a-smellin the place whar it come from, wif the real, ginuine stillworm twist in her tail, too. What upon the face of the earth can she be arter now, the ole fool? Watch her, Sally. An' sakes alive, jis' look at that ole sow. She's a-gwine in a fast trot wif her empty bag a-flappin agin her sides. Thar, she hes stopped and's a-listenin! Mercy on us, what a long, earnest grunt she give. Hit come from way back of her kidneys. Thar she goes agin. She's arter no good; sich kerryin-on means no good.'

"And so she would gabble, no odds who were a-listenin. She looked like she might have been made at first 'bout four foot long and the common thickness of women when they's themselves . . . then had her hair tied to a stump, a pair of steers hitched to her heels, and then stretched out almost two foot more—most of the stretchin comin outen her legs and neck. Her stockins, a-hangin on the clothes-line to dry, looked like a pair of sabre-scabbards; and her neck looked like a dry beef shank smoked, and might been nigh onto as tough. I never felt it myself, I didn't; I just jedges by looks.

"Her daughter Sal were built at first 'bout the length of her mam, but were never stretched any by a pair of steers; and she were fat enough to kill: she were taller lying down than she were a-standin up. It were her who give me the 'hump shoulder.' Just look at me. Ain't I got a tetch of the dromedary back there bad? Ain't I humpy? Well, a-stoopin to kiss that squatty lard-stand of a gal is what done it to me. She were the fairest-lookin gal I ever seed. She allers wore thick woolen stockins 'bout six inches too long for her leg; they rolled down over her garters, lookin like a pair of life-preservers up there. I tell you she were a tearin gal anyhow. Loved kissin, wrasslin, and boiled cabbage; hated tight clothes, hot weather, and circuit riders. B'lieved strong in married folks' ways, cradles, and the remission of sins; didn't believe in corsets, fleas, pianos, nor the fashion plates."

"What caused the death of Mrs. Yardley, Sut?"

"Nothin, only her heart stopped beatin 'bout losin a nine-diamond quilt. True, she got a scared hoss to run over her, but she'd a-got over that if a quilt hadn't been mixed up in the catastrophe. You see, quilts were one of her special gifts; she run strong on the bed-cover question. Irish chain, Star of Texas, sunflower, nine-diamond, saw-teeth, checker-board, and shell quilts; blue and white, and yaller and black coverlets and calico-comforts reigned triumphant 'bout her house. They were packed in drawers; layin in shelves full; were hung four-double on lines in the loft; packed in chests; piled on chairs; and were everywhere, even onto the beds; and were changed every bed-makin.

"She told everybody she could git to listen to it that she meant to give every durned one of 'em to Sal when she got married. Oh, lordy! What as fat a gal as Sal Yardley could ever do with half of 'em, and sleepin with a husband at that, is more nor I ever could see through. Just think of her under twenty layers of quilts in July, and you in there too. Gee-whillikins, George! Look how I is sweatin now, and this is December. I'd 'bout as lief be shut up in a steam boiler with a three-hundred-pound bag of lard as to make a business of sleepin with that gal—it would kill a glass-blower.

"Well, to come to the serious part of this conversation: that is, how the old quilt-machine and coverlet-loom come to stop operations on this earth. She had narrated it through the neighborhood that next Saturday she'd give a quiltin—three quilts and one comfort to tie. 'Gobblers, fiddles, gals, and whiskey' were the words she sent to the men-folk, and more touchin or wakenin words never dropped offen a woman's tongue. She said to the gals: 'Sweet toddy, huggin, dancin, an' huggers in abundance.' Them words struck the gals right in the pit of the stomach and spread a ticklin sensation both ways, until they scratched their heads with one hand and their heels with t'other.

"Everybody—he and she—what were baptized believers in the righteousness of quiltins were there. It just so happened that everybody in them parts, from fifteen summers to fifty winters, were unanimous b'lievers. Strange, weren't it? It were the biggest quiltin ever Missis Yardley held, and she had held hundreds. Everybody were there except the constable and the circuit rider, two damn easily-spared persons. The numbers nigh onto even, too; just a few more boys nor gals. That made it more excitin, for it give the gals a chance to kick and squeal a little without runnin any risk of not gittin kissed at all; and it give reasonable grounds for a few scrimmages among the he's. Now as kissin and fightin am the pepper and salt of all social gatherings, so it were more especially with those of ours. As I swung my eyes over the crowd, George, I thought quiltins, managed in a moral and sensible way, truly am good things—good for free drinkin, good for free eatin, good for free huggin, good for free dancin, good for free fightin, and goodest of all for populatin a country fast.

"There am a far-seein wisdom in quiltins if they has proper trimmins: 'vittles, fiddles, and spirits in abundance.' One wholesome quiltin am worth three ole prayer-meetins on the population point, particularly if it's held in the dark of the moon and runs into the night a few hours, and April or May am the time chosen. The moon don't suit quiltins where everybody is well acquainted and already far along in courtin. She does help pow'ful to begin a courtin match underway, but when it draws nigh onto a head nobody wants a moon but the ole mammys.

"The mornin come: still, soft, sunshiny. Cocks crowin, hens singin, birds chirpin, turkeys gobblin —just the day to sun quilts, kick, kiss, squeal, and make love.

"All the plow-lines and clothes-lines were stretched to every post and tree. Quilts prevailed. Durn my gizzard if two acres round that-there house weren't just one solid quilt, all out a-sunnin and to be seed. They dazzled the eyes, scared the hosses, give women the heart-burn, and predominated.

"To'ards sundown, the he's begun to drop in. Earnest needle-drivin commenced to lose ground; threads broke often; thimbles got lost; and quilts needed another roll. Gigglin, winkin, whisperin, smoothin of hair, and gals a-ticklin one another were a-gainin every inch of ground what the needles lost.

"Did you ever notice, George, at all social gatherins, when the he's begin to gather, that the young she's begin to tickle one another and the ole maids swell their tails, roach up their backs, sharpen their nails onto the bed-posts and door-jambs, and spit and groan sorta like cats a-courtin? Does it mean *real* wrath, or is it a dare to the he's, sorta covered up with the outside signs of danger?

"I honestly b'lieve that the young shes' ticklin means: 'Come and take this job offen our hands.' But that swellin I just don't understand. Does you? It looks scary, and I never tetch one of 'em when they am in the swellin way.

"I may be mistakened 'bout the ticklin business too. It may be done like a feller chaws poplar bark when he ain't got any terbacker, a sorta better nor none make-shift. I does know one thing to a certainty: that is, when the he's take hold, the ticklin quits. And if you gits one of the ole maids out to herself, then she subsides and is the smoothest, sleekest, soft thing you ever seed, and damn if you can't hear her purr, just as plain!

"But then, George, gals and ole maids ain't the things to fool time away on. It's widders, by golly, what am the real sensible, steady-goin, never-scarin, never-kickin, willin, spirited, smooth pacers. They come close't up to the hoss-block, standin still with their purty, silky ears playin and the neck-veins a-throbbin, and waits for the word— which of course you gives after you finds your feet well in the stirrup—and away they moves like a cradle on cushioned rockers, or a spring buggy runnin in damp sand. A tetch of the bridle and they knows you want 'em to turn, and they does it as willin as if the idea were their own. I be dod-rabbitted if a man can't 'propriate happiness by the skinful if he is in contact with somebody's widder and is smart.

"Give me a willin widder the earth over: what they don't know ain't worth learnin. They has all been to Jamaicy and learnt how sugar's made, and knows how to sweeten with it. And, by golly, they is always ready to use it. All you has to do is to find the spoon, and then drink comfort till you're blind. Next to good spirits and my legs, I likes a twenty-five-year-old widder—with round ankles and bright eyes—honestly and squarely lookin into yourn, and sayin as plainly as a partridge says 'Bob White': 'Don't be afraid of me; I has been there; you know if you has any sense; and there's no use in any humbug, ole feller—come ahead!'

"If you understands widder nature, they can save you a power of trouble, uncertainty, and time; and if you is enterprisin, you gits monstrous well-paid for it. The very sound of their little shoe-heels speak full trainin and has a knowin click as they tap the floor. And the rustle of their dress says: 'I dare you to ask me.'

"When you has made up your mind to court one, just go at it like it were a job of rail-maulin. Wear yer workin clothes; use your common every-day motions and words; and, above all, fling away your cinnamon-oil vial and burn all your love songs. No use in tryin to fool 'em, for they sees plumb through you a durned sight plainer than they does through their veils. No use in a pasted shirt; she's been there. No use in borrowin a cavortin fat hoss; she's been there. No use in hair-dye; she's been there. No use in cloves to kill whis-key breath; she's been there. No use in buyin closed curtains for your bed, for she has been there. Widders am a special means, George, for ripenin green men, killin off weak ones, and makin 'ternally happy the sound ones.

"Well, as I said afore, I flew the track and got onto the widders. The fellers begun to ride up and walk up, sorta slow, like they weren't in a hurry—the durned 'ceitful rascals—hitchin their critters to anything they could find. One red-combed, long-spurred, Dominecker [Dominigue: a breed of black and white speckled chicken] feller from town—in a red and white gridiron jacket and patent-leather gaiters—hitched his hoss, a wild, scary, wall-eyed devil, inside the yard palings to a cherry-tree limb.

"Thinks I: 'That hoss has a scare into him big enough to run into town, and perhaps beyond it, if I kin only tetch it off.' So I set into thinkin.

"One end of a long clothes-line, with nine-diamond quilts onto it, were tied to the same cherry tree that the hoss were. I took my knife and socked it through every quilt, 'bout the middle and just below the rope, and tied them there with bark so they couldn't slip. Then I went to the back-end and untied the clothesline from the post, knottin in a hoe-handle by the middle to keep the quilts from slippin off if my bark strings failed, and laid it on the ground. Then I went to the t'other end; there were 'bout ten foot to spare a-lyin on the ground after tyin to the tree. I took it atwixt Wall-eye's hind legs and tied it fast to both stirrups; and then cut the cherry-tree limb betwixt his bridle and the tree almost off.

"Now, mind you, there were two or three other ropes full of quilts atween me and the house, so I were purty well hid from there. I just tore off a paling from the fence and took it in both hands; and, after raisin it way up yonder, I fetched it down as hard as I could flat-sided to'ard the ground, and it accidentally happened to hit Wall-eye 'bout nine inches ahead of the root of his tail. It landed so hard that it made my hands tingle, and then busted into splinters.

"The first thing I did were to feel of myself on the same spot where it had hit the hoss. I couldn't help doin it to save my life, and I swear I felt some of Wall-eye's sensation, just as plain. The first thing he did were to tear down the limb with a twenty-foot jump, his head to'ards the house. Thinks I: 'Now you have done it, you durned wall-eyed fool!' Tearin down that limb were the beginnin of all the trouble, and the hoss did it hisself. My conscience felt clear as a mountain spring, and I were in a frame of mind to observe things as

they happened. And they soon began to happen purty close't after one another right then and there and thereabouts clean onto town, through it, and still were a-happenin in the woods beyond there nigh onto eleven miles from ole man Yardley's gate, and four beyond town.

"The first line of quilts he tried to jump, but broke it down. The next one he ran under. The rope ketched onto the horn of the saddle, broke at both ends, and went along with the hoss, the cherry-tree limb, and the first line of quilts what I had providentially tied fast to the rope. That's what I calls foresight, George.

"Right fornent the front door he come in contact with ole Missis Yardley herself and another ole woman. They were a-holdin a nine-diamond quilt spread out, a-zaminin and a-praisin its perfections. The durned unmannerly, wall-eyed fool run plumb over Missis Yardley from ahind, stomped one hind foot through the quilt, takin it along and a'kickin until he made its corners snap like a whip. The gals screamed, the men hollered 'Whoa!', and the ole woman were toted into the house limber as a wet string. And every word she said were: 'Oh, my precious nine-diamond quilt!'

"Wall-eye busted through the palings and Dominecker seed him, made a mortal rush for his bits. Were too late for 'em, but in good time for the strings of flyin quilts, got tangled among 'em, and the gridiron jacket patron were lost to my sight among star and Irish chain quilts. He went from that quiltin at the rate of thirty miles to the hour. Nothin left on the lot of the whole concern but a nine-boiler hat, a pair of gloves, and the jack of hearts.

"What a unmannerly sudden way of leavin places some folks have got, anyhow.

"Thinks I: 'Well, that fool hoss tearin down that cherry-tree limb has done some good, anyhow. It has put the ole woman outen the way for the balance of the quiltin, and took Dominecker outen the way and outen danger, for that gridiron jacket would a-bred a scab on his nose afore midnight; it were morally bound to do it.'

"Two months after'ards, I tracked the route that hoss took in his calamitous scare by quilt rags, tufts of cotton, bunches of hair—human and hoss—and scraps of a gridiron jacket stickin onto the bushes. And plumb at the end of it, where all signs give out, I found a piece of watch chain and a hoss's head. The places what knowed Dominecker knowed him no more.

"Well, after they'd took the ole woman upstairs

and camphored her to sleep, things begun to work again. The widders broke the ice; and, after a little gigglin, gobblin, and gabblin, the kissin begun.

"*Smack!* 'Thar, now.' A widder said that.

"*Pop!* 'Oh, don't!'

"*Pfip!* 'Oh, you quit!'

"*Plosh!* 'Go 'way, you awk'ard critter, you kissed me in the eye!' Another widder said that.

"*Bop!* 'Now you are satisfied, I reckon, big mouth!'

"*Yip!* 'That ain't fair!'

"*Spat!* 'Oh, lordy! May, come pull Bill away. He's a-tanglin my hair.'

"*Thut!* 'I jist d-a-r-e you to do that agin!' A widder said that, too.

"It sounded all round that room like poppin corn in a hot skillet, and were pow'ful suggestive.

"It kept on until I be durned if *my* bristles didn't begin to rise, and somethin like a cold buck-shot would run down the marrow in my backbone 'bout every ten second, and then run up again tolerable hot. I kept a-swallerin with nothin to swaller, and my face felt swelled; and yet I were feared to make a bulge. Thinks I: 'I'll ketch one out to herself directly, and then I guess we'll rassle.'

"Purty soon Sal Yardley started for the smoke-house; so I just give my head a few short shakes, let down one of my wings a-trailin, and circled round her with a side-twist in my neck, steppin sidewise and a-fetchin up my hindmost foot with a sorta jerkin slide at every step.

"Says I: 'Too coo-took a-too.'

"She understood it and stopped, sorta spreadin her shoulders. And just as I had pouched out my mouth and were a-reachin for'ard with it for the article itself, somethin interfered with me, it did.

"George, were you ever onto your hands and knees, and let a hell-tearin, big, mad ram with a ten-yard run butt you earnestly—just once't—right square onto the point of your backbone?"

"No, you fool. Why do you ask?"

"Cause I wanted to know if you could have a realizin notion of my shock. It's scarcely worth-while to try to make you understand the case by words only, unless you have been tetched in that way. Great golly! The first thing I felt, I took it to be a back-action earthquake. And the first thing I seed were my chaw of terbacker a-flyin over Sal's head like a scared bat. My mouth were pouched out—ready for the article itself, you know—and it went outen the round hole like the wad outen a popgun—*thug!* And the first thing I knowed, I were a-flyin over Sal's head, too, and a-gainin on the chaw of terbacker fast. I were straightened out straight—toes hindmost, middle fingernails fore-most—and the first thing I heerd were: 'You damn Shanghai!'

"Great Jerus-a-lam! I lit onto my all-fours just in time to butt the yardgate offen its hinges and scare loose some more hosses—kept on in a four-footed gallop clean across't the lane afore I could straighten up, and here I ketched up with my chaw of terbacker stickin flat agin a fence-rail. I had got so good a start that I thought it a pity to spoil it, so I just jumped the fence and took through the orchard. I tell you I dusted these-here clothes, for I thought it were after me.

"After runnin a spell, I ventured to feel round back there for some signs of what had happened to me. George, after two pow'ful-hard tugs I pulled out the vamp and sole of one of ole man Yardley's big brogans, what he had lost among my coat-tails. Dreadful! Dreadful! After I got it away from there, my flesh went fast asleep from above my kidneys to my knees. About now, for the first time, the idea struck me what it were that had interfered with me and lost me the kiss. It were ole Yardley had kicked me. I walked for a month like I were straddlin a thorn hedge. Such a shock, at such a time and on such a place—just think of it! It am tremenjus, ain't it? The place feels numb right now."

"Well, Sut, how did the quilting come out?"

"How the hell do you expect me to know? I weren't there any more."

WILLIAM PENN BRANNAN (1825–1866)

Willian Penn Brannan was born in Ohio. He settled in Cincinnati about 1840 and became a portrait painter of ability. About 1860 he began to write for the daily press, using several names, most commonly Vandyke Brown. His only book is *Vagaries of Vandyke Brown* (1865), an auto-biography in verse. He died on August 9, 1866.

Where the Lion Roareth and the Wang-Doodle Mourneth (1858)

My beloved Brethering: I am a unlarnt Hard-Shell Baptist preacher, of whom you've no doubt hearn afore, and I now appear here to expound the scripters and pint out the narrow way which leads from a vain world to the streets of Jaroosalem; and my tex which I shall choose for the occasion is in the leds of the Bible, somewhar between the Second Chronik-ills and the last chapter of Timothy-titus; and when you find it, you'll find it in these words: "And they shall gnaw a file, and flee unto the mountains of Hepsidam, where the lion roareth and the wang-doodle mourneth for his first-born."

Now, my brethering, as I have before told you, I am an oneddicated man, and know nothing about grammer talk and collidge highfalutin, but I am a plane unlarnt preacher of the Gospil, what's been foreordaned and called to prepare a pervarse generashun for the day of wrath—ah! "For they shall gnaw a file, and flee unto the mountains of Hepsidam, whar the lion roareth and the wang-doodle mourneth for his first-born"—ah!

My beloved brethering, the tex says they shall gnaw a file. It does not say they *may*, but shall. Now, there is more than one kind of file. There's the hand-saw file, the rat-tail file, the single file, the double file, and profile; but the kind spoken of here isn't one of them kind nayther, bekaws it's a figger of speech, and means going it alone and getting ukered; "for they shall gnaw a file, and flee unto the mountains of Hepsidam, whar the lion roareth and the wang-doodle mourneth for its first-born"—ah!

And now there be some here with fine close on thar backs, brass rings on thar fingers, and lard on thar har, what goes it while they're yung; and thar be others here what, as long as thar constitooshins and forty-cent whiskey last, goes it blind. Thar be sisters here what, when they gets sixteen years old, cut their tiller-ropes and goes it with a rush. But I say, my dear brethering, take care you don't find, when Gabriel blows his last trump, your hand's played out, and you've got ukered—ah! "For they shall gnaw a file, and flee unto the mountains of Hepsidam, whar the lion roareth and the wang-doodle mourneth for his first-born."

Now, my brethering, "they shall flee unto the mountains of Hepsidam"; but thar's more dams than Hepsidam. Thar's Rotter-dam, Haddam, Amster-dam, and "Don't-care-a-dam"—the last of which, my brethering, is the worst of all, and reminds me of a sirkumstans I onst knowed in the state of Illenoy. There was a man what built him a mill on the north fork of Ager Crick, and it was a good mill and ground a sight of grain; but the man what built it was a miserable sinner, and never give anything to the church; and, my dear brethering, one night there came a dreadful storm of wind and rain, and the mountains of the great deep was broke up, and the waters rushed down and swept that man's mill-dam to kingdom cum, and when he woke up he found that he wasn't worth a dam—ah! "For they shall gnaw a file, and flee unto the mountains of Hepsidam, whar the lion roareth and the wang-doodle mourneth for his first-born"—ah!

I hope I don't hear any body larfin; do I?

Now, "whar the lion roareth and the wang-doodle mourneth for his first-born"—ah! This part of my tex, my beseaching brethering, is not to be taken as it says. It don't mean the howling wilderness, whar John the Hard-Shell Baptist fed on locusts and wild asses, but it means, my brethering, the city of New Y'Orleans, the mother of harlots and hard lots, whar corn is wuth six bits a bushel one day and nary a red the nex; whar niggers are as thick as black bugs in spiled bacon ham, and gamblers, thieves, and pickpockets goes skiting about the streets like weasels in a barn-yard; whar honest men are scarcer than hen's teeth; and whar a strange woman once took in your beluved teacher, and bamboozled him out of two hundred and twenty-seven dollars in the twinkling of a sheep's-tail; but she *can't* do it again! Hallelujah—ah! "For they shall gnaw a file, and flee unto the mountains of Hepsidam, whar the lion roareth and the wang-doodle mourneth for his first-born"—ah!

My brethering, I am the captain of that flat-boat you see tied up thar, and have got aboard of her flour, bacon, taters, and as good Monongahela whiskey as ever was drunk, and am mighty apt to get a big price for them all; but what, my dear brethering, would it all be wuth if I hadn't got religion? Thar's nothing like religion, my brethering: it's better nor silver or gold gimcracks; and you can no more get to heaven without it, than a jay-bird can fly without a tail—ah! Thank the Lord! I'm an oneddicated man, my brethering; but I've sarched the Scripters from Dan to Beersheba, and found Zion right side up, and hard-shell religion the best kind of religion—ah! 'Tis not like the Methodists, what specks to get to heaven by hollerin' hell-fire; nor like the Univarsalists, that get on the broad gage and goes the hull hog—ah!; nor like the Yewnited Brethering, that takes each other by the slack of thar breeches and hists themselves in; nor like the Katherliks, that buys threw tickets from their priests; but it may be likened unto a man what has to cross the river—ah!—and the ferry-boat was gone; so he tucked up his breeches and waded acrost—ah! "For they shall gnaw a file, and flee unto the mountains of Hepsidam, whar the lion roareth and the wang-doodle mourneth for his first-born!"

Pass the hat, Brother Flint, and let every Hard-Shell Baptist shell out.

The Literary Historians

The influential and progressive weekly the *Literary World* observed with some surprise in 1849 that "the movement on the part of American scholars and writers has of late been in a marked manner in the direction of history." The comment was accurate, but the surprise was understandable. The temper of the time, at least in those advanced intellectual circles to which the *Literary World* catered, was supposed to be unhistorical, even antihistorical— to be concerned with the stimulating present and with widening vistas of the future, and to regard the past as dead or otherwise irrelevant. The forward-looking *Democratic Review* had intoned characteristically in 1842 that "probably no other civilized nation has at any period . . . so completely thrown off its allegiance to the past as the American." Yet it was undoubtedly true that by 1849 some of the very best and most powerful writing of the day was being done in the field of history. The volumes of George Bancroft's celebrational *History of the United States* had been appearing periodically since 1834. William Hickling Prescott's *The Conquest of Mexico* had been published in 1843. John Lothrop Motley's panoramic *Rise of the Dutch Republic* (1856) was soon to come. And in the same year, 1849, there arrived the first book by the greatest of the nineteenth-century historians—Francis Parkman's *The Oregon Trail*. The writing of history in those years was indeed a main phenomenon in the developing literature of the country.[1]

Imaginative Americans, of course, had always been interested in the past in the limited sense of finding a fascination with ruins—especially those European ruins one visited faithfully and reported home about on the traditional grand tour after graduating from college. Ruins (say, the ruins of ancient Rome) fascinated the American because of the total absence of any

[1] It can be recalled that to some extent Washington Irving had led the way with his life of Christopher Columbus in 1828 and *The Conquest of Granada*—a book Prescott said he would like to have written—in 1829.

on the American scene. Ruins spoke of mystery and drama and vanished beauty; and by a certain cast of mind, they could be exploited as the setting for a dark romance—as Hawthorne did in *The Marble Faun,* after remarking in the preface that "romance and poetry . . . need ruin to make them grow." But that is not quite the same thing as having a sense of history, though it is not far from it. We can distinguish two contrary but not incompatible reasons for the rise of historical writing in the nineteenth century. One was the increasing awareness of the past in its pastness; the other was the awareness of the past in its evolutionary relation to the present.

It was the constant insistence on the supremacy of the present, on the novelty and originality of experience in the New World and its utter freedom from any ties with or inherited burden from the degenerate Old World, that helped isolate the past as a phenomenon, that made it visible suddenly as an object worth studying. Prescott said about the sixteenth-century world he explored in *The Conquest of Mexico* that it was precisely the "distance of the present age from the period of the narrative" that made possible a clarity of perspective; and Parkman seems at times to feel that the chief attraction of his major historical subject—the long conflict between French, English, and Indians in North America from about 1512 to the siege of Quebec in 1759—lay in the distance between that embattled and doom-laden age and the industrializing and democratic society in which he lived.

At the same time, the past was an indispensable vantage point from which to glorify the present, particularly the American present, by tracing the evolution of those qualities and conditions that came to full flower in America and were the defining features—so it was often argued—of her greatness. Put most simply, this involved the notion of history itself as the history of individual freedom—of actual history as the process (culminating in nineteenth-century America) whereby liberty was established among men and along with it political democracy, a sense of justice and decency, a devotion to the orderly in human affairs; and of the writing of history as the tracing of key moments in that process.

Motley, pitting William the Silent as the humane champion of freedom against Philip the Second of Spain as the Machiavellian oppressor in *The Rise of the Dutch Republic,* offered his narrative as an exemplary study of one nation's determination to gain and maintain its independence. Bancroft, not without cause, called his own *History* "an epic of liberty"; the American Revolution, he argued, had ushered in "a new and more glorious era," and it would be his purpose to describe the events leading up to that era, those by which Providence had "conducted the country to its present happiness and glory." Even Parkman, though in an incomparably subtler and more complex way, envisaged his story as bearing upon the eventual triumph of Anglo-American "civilization"; and Prescott, while urging that the conduct of his hero, Hernando Cortés (for example, in the appalling massacre in the Indian city of Cholula), be partly judged by the standards of the time, took occasion to reflect with some complacency on the great advance in humaneness accomplished in postrevolutionary America. History, in this view, was one important way (along with fiction and poetry and other literary forms) by which America sought to identify itself.

But what is equally to be stressed is the *literary* aspect of the historical writing in question—the aspect which justifies, and indeed demands, the inclusion of some of that writing in this volume. The historians we are mostly concerned with became known, in fact, as "literary historians"—sometimes, later, as "Romantic historians," with that capitalized adjective implying quite rightly an affinity with Romantic poetry and fiction, with the work of Byron and Scott. Parkman and the others were literary historians, first of all, in the fundamental sense that they were men of letters. David Levin (in *History as Romantic Art*, 1959) has pointed out that Bancroft wrote a book of poetry; that Prescott contributed literary criticism to the *North American Review*; that Motley published two novels (one of them, *Merry-Mount*, in 1849, dealing with the same group of anti-Puritan revelers to which Hawthorne once addressed himself); and that Parkman wrote a curiously revealing autobiographical romance called *Vassall Morton*.

These writers, however, were also literary *in* their histories, as well as apart from them. In composing their historical narratives, they drew—sometimes with consummate skill—upon the available resources of literature: of drama, the epic, the fictional romance. They wrote out of a cultivated consciousness of literary precedent, convention, and tradition; and they *saw* their subjects in literary terms—as human dramas with fully sketched individual characters engaged in heroic or terrible actions and presented with the handsomest narrative style at their command. "The true way of conceiving the subject," Prescott told himself in his notebook while preparing *The Conquest of Mexico*, "is, not as a philosophical theme, but as an epic in prose, a romance of chivalry," as something "borne onward on a tide of destiny, like that which broods over the fiction of the Grecian poets." As an apprentice historian, Parkman went to school to the epics of Milton, and even more to the tragedies of Shakespeare, and, closer to home, to the fictional excursions into the American wilderness of James Fenimore Cooper. In calling his history an "*epic* of liberty," Bancroft clearly had in mind (like certain of his Puritan predecessors) the Virgilian example; and his long list of actors play out their roles in a recognizable reenactment of the Trojan adventure, the departure from the Old World, the journey, the struggle to settle a new citadel with divine aid and comfort in the New World, and so on. Structure, theme, setting, characterization: all these are manipulated in these histories in the manner of uncommonly gifted literary artists.

This is not at all to say that Parkman and his colleagues were literary artists *rather than* true historians. They were prodigious, almost unbelievably energetic, researchers, with a fanatical devotion to fact. They never wittingly distorted a single detail for the sake of a poetic or dramatic pattern. It would be quite misleading to call them literary historians if that is to suggest that they were not what is rather tediously called "scientific historians."[2] They may have slighted the kind of economic and sociological inquiries that have since become fashionable; but the war goes on among professional historians about the place of human motivation and the "forces" at work in history, and in any case scholarly fashion is not necessarily to be equated with human truth. Howard Doughty, in his excellent critical biography of Parkman (1962), has put the matter well—speaking only of Parkman, but in language that to some real extent applies also to Prescott and Motley. Observing in Parkman the remarkable fusion of literary skills with the skills of the trained historical scholar, Doughty writes:

> To emphasize one set of elements at the expense of another . . . is inevitably to risk a degree of falsification. Even the lay reader is aware of how deeply the imaginative effect of Parkman's work is rooted in its impeccable factuality—in the minuteness and exhaustiveness of research, the perfect mastery of the historical *données*, the famous "methodology" which set a standard in these matters still unsuperseded. In short, whatever analogies his work suggests with other forms of literature, Parkman writing history is radically and quintessentially an historian, and not a poet or dramatist or novelist *manqué*.

As to whether Parkman was a scientific or a literary historian, Doughty argues correctly that "Parkman was, of course, conspicuously both, and here, as everywhere in his work, we have to do with an organic fusion of apparent opposites: scientific method and artistic sensibility; rational judgment and imaginative insight; factual realism and the evocativeness of poetry."

Two further points may be added. To the degree that these histories do display artistic sensibility, imaginative insight, and poetic evocation, they provide another measure of the nature and range of American literature. They provide other examples of those "original archetypes in literature" by which (according to Whitman) the American imagination tried to give shape and meaning to experience. Telling us about the Netherlands or Mexico or Canada in the sixteenth century, they tell us about the American

[2] Bancroft was the least interesting of the group as a writer and a historian, yet he was something of a pioneer in his scholarly handling of documents.

mind in the nineteenth century—what it honored and shunned, what it believed in and was suspicious of; where it thought it had come from, where it thought it was going. Secondly, and by something of the same token, the historians seized their materials with the hands of literary artists because they looked upon human life as having a story in it. This is obvious enough, but it will bear stressing. In a way not unlike that of the Puritans, but on a resolutely humanistic level, the literary historians were convinced that life made sense, and a sense altogether accessible to the human mind. They believed that experience—whether that of an individual or a nation, or even of mankind—was thick with discernible meaning, and not an affair of random accidents or of abstract and nearly incalculable forces. The meaning was not that moralistic kind (as of "lessons for the day") that was the hallmark of historical writing in the generation before them. It was rather a meaning to be disclosed by the arts of drama and narrative, and perhaps only by those arts.

Though Parkman has the strongest claim to our attention, there is much of interest in the lives and characters of the other three historians. George Bancroft (1800–1891), for example, had an influential career in politics and diplomacy, quite apart from his writing. He was Secretary of the Navy under Polk (and helped found the Naval Academy at Annapolis), and served as minister to Great Britain (1846–49) and to Germany (1867–74). He was an ardent, indeed an unrestrained, progressivist: "Every thing is in motion and for the better," he once declared. "The last system of philosophy is always the best. . . . The last political state of the world is likewise ever more excellent than the old." (One thinks irresistibly of the reply of Phoebe Pyncheon, in Hawthorne's *The House of the Seven Gables*, to a comparable outburst by Holgrave: "How you hate everything old! It makes me dizzy to think of such a shifting world!") The younger historians regarded Bancroft as their pioneer, and he was invariably kind and helpful to them: "I take delight in your honors," he wrote Parkman when *Montcalm and Wolfe* appeared, "as much or more than I should in my own." His honors had been immense; but he was swept away by his enthusiasms and his rhetoric, and his *History of the United States* now seems, ironically, no more than a historical curiosity. It was recognized even in its own time as a sort of long campaign speech for Andrew Jackson (Bancroft, unlike most Brahmins, was a Democrat), whose presidency, the work implied, represented the culmination of the American process. Today one is only conscious of the unmodulated glare of its optimistic idealism.

John Lothrop Motley (1814–1877) had a diplomatic career not unlike Bancroft's. He was Secretary of Legation at St. Petersburg, and then minister to Austria (1861–67) and to Great Britain (1869–70)—the latter two appointments being terminated as a result of political squabbles back home. After publishing two novels, he was seized (about 1846) with the large ambition of writing a history of Holland and spent five years in Europe sorting through archives. *The Rise of the Dutch Republic* appeared in 1856, and its four-volume successor, *The History of the United Netherlands*, in two installments in 1860 and 1868. He died before completing *The Life and Death of John of Barneveld*. Motley's subject never quite rises to the grandeur with which Prescott and Parkman invested their narratives, but it is a rich and lively story, and, as we have said, it takes the shape of a major episode in what the historians saw as the movement toward the realization of freedom.

FURTHER READINGS

George W. Curtis, ed., *The Writings of John Lothrop Motley* (1900; 14 vols.)

The Works of Francis Parkman (1907; 16 vols.) (no editor cited)

The Works of William H. Prescott (1863; 14 vols.) (no editor cited)

Howard Doughty, *Francis Parkman* (1962)

Oliver Wendell Holmes, *John Lothrop Motley: A Memoir* (1879)

David Levin, *History as Romantic Art: Bancroft, Prescott, Motley, and Parkman* (1967)

Samuel Eliot Morison, ed., *The Parkman Reader* (1955)

WILLIAM HICKLING PRESCOTT (1796–1859)

Prescott was born, like Bancroft, Motley, and Parkman, into the New England aristocracy and went to Harvard. Early on he abandoned the idea of a career in law and by 1826 had reached the decision "to embrace the gift of the Spanish subject"—essentially, the history of New Spain, the Spanish explorations and conquests in the New World. He had sufficient means to accumulate a huge number of manuscripts, many of them in Spain; he had cooperative friends and skilled assistants; and, as almost total blindness overtook him (he had lost the use of his left eye in an accident at Harvard), he so trained his memory as to be able to carry in his head scores of pages of manuscript. Working tirelessly in a darkened room, he completed *The Reign of Ferdinand and Isabella* by 1836 and *The Conquest of Mexico* (Irving, who had begun a similar history, withdrew in his favor) by 1843. *The Conquest of Peru* followed in 1846, and by the time he died three volumes of *The Reign of Philip the Second*.

Prescott's narrative is always on the move. The research had been impeccable, but sources and annotation are packed into footnotes, while in the text the action advances unimpeded. Everything belongs to that action; the minutest detail has been absorbed into the ongoing narration. The selection here offered can show as much; and one can observe that, for all the crowding detail and in the midst of the hideous carnage, the two main characters—Hernando Cortés and the Aztec emperor Guatemozin—grow steadily more visible *as* characters, and heroic ones; and the process by which they finally confront one another is handled as though by a master dramatist.

From The Conquest of Mexico (1843)

This is Prescott's account of the last stages of the Spanish triumph in Mexico, the capture of its capital (now Mexico City) and its courageous young emperor, Guatemozin. The latter was the son-in-law of the Emperor Montezuma, who had died a few years earlier from wounds received from his own people—who turned on him when he ordered them to surrender to Cortés. The century-long Aztec rule in Central America here comes to an end. For a long and confused period thereafter, New Spain would extend well into the southern and western portions of North America, until it lost the territories respectively to France and to England.

Note: all footnotes in this section, unless set off by brackets, are those of the historians.

CHAPTER 8

1521

There was no occasion to resort to artificial means to precipitate the ruin of the Aztecs. It was accelerated every hour by causes more potent than those arising from mere human agency. There they were, —pent up in their close and suffocating quarters, nobles, commoners, and slaves, men, women, and children, some in houses, more frequently in hovels, for this part of the city was not the best,—others in the open air in canoes, or in the streets, shivering in the cold rains of night, and scorched by the burning heat of day. An old chronicler mentions the fact of two women of rank remaining three days and nights up to their necks in the water among the reeds, with only a handful of maize for their support.[1] The ordinary means of sustaining life were long since gone. They wandered about in search of anything, however unwholesome or revolting, that might mitigate the fierce gnawings of hunger. Some hunted for insects and worms on the borders of the lake, or gathered the salt weeds and moss from its bottom, while at times they might be seen casting a wistful look at the green

hills beyond, which many of them had left to share the fate of their brethren in the capital.

To their credit, it is said by the Spanish writers, that they were not driven in their extremity to violate the laws of nature by feeding on one another.[2] But unhappily this is contradicted by the Indian authorities, who state that many a mother, in her agony, devoured the offspring which she had no longer the means of supporting. This is recorded of more than one siege in history; and it is the more probable here, where the sensibilities must have been blunted by familiarity with the brutal practices of the national superstition.[3]

But all was not sufficient, and hundreds of famished wretches died every day from extremity of suffering. Some dragged themselves into the houses, and drew their last breath alone, and in silence. Others sank down in the public streets. Wherever they died, there they were left. There was no one to bury or to remove them. Familiarity with the spectacle made men indifferent to it. They looked on in dumb despair, waiting for their own turn. There was no complaint, no lamentation, but deep, unutterable woe.

If in other quarters of the town the corpses might be seen scattered over the streets, here they were gathered in heaps. "They lay so thick," says Bernal Diaz, "that one could not tread except among the bodies." "A man could not set his foot down," says Cortés, yet more strongly, "unless on the corpse of an Indian!" They were piled one upon another, the living mingled with the dead. They stretched themselves on the bodies of their

---

[1] Torquemada had the anecdote from a nephew of one of the Indian matrons, then a very old man himself.—Monarch. Ind., lib. 4, cap. 102.

[2] Monarch. Ind., lib. 4, cap. 102—Bernal Diaz, Hist. de la Conquista, cap. 156.

[3] "De nos niños, no quedó nadie, que las mismas madres y padres los comian (que era gran lástima de ver, y mayormente de sufrir)." (Sahagun, Hist. de Nueva Esp., MS., lib. 12, cap. 39.) The historian derived his accounts from the Mexicans themselves, soon after the event.—One is reminded of the terrible denunciations of Moses: "The tender and delicate woman among you, which would not adventure to set the sole of her foot upon the ground for delicateness and tenderness, her eye shall be evil toward . . . her children which she shall bear; for she shall eat them for want of all things, secretly, in the siege and straitness wherewith thine enemy shall distress thee in thy gates."—Deuteronomy, chap. 28, verses 56, 57.

friends, and lay down to sleep there. Death was everywhere. The city was a vast charnel-house, in which all was hastening to decay and decomposition. A poisonous steam arose from the mass of putrefaction, under the action of alternate rain and heat, which so tainted the whole atmosphere, that the Spaniards, including the general himself, in their brief visits to the quarter, were made ill by it, and it bred a pestilence that swept off even greater numbers than the famine.

Men's minds were unsettled by these strange and accumulated horrors. They resorted to all the superstitious rites prescribed by their religion, to stay the pestilence. They called on their priests to invoke the gods in their behalf. But the oracles were dumb, or gave only gloomy responses. Their deities had deserted them, and in their place they saw signs of celestial wrath, telling of still greater woes in reserve. Many, after the siege, declared that, among other prodigies, they beheld a stream of light, of a blood-red colour, coming from the north in the direction of Tepejacac, with a rushing noise, like that of a whirlwind, which swept round the district of Tlatelolco, darting out sparkles and flakes of fire, till it shot far into the centre of the lake! In the disordered state of their nerves, a mysterious fear took possession of their senses. Prodigies were of familiar occurrence, and the most familiar phenomena of nature were converted into prodigies. Stunned by their calamities, reason was bewildered, and they became the sport of the wildest and most superstitious fancies.

In the midst of these awful scenes, the young emperor of the Aztecs remained, according to all accounts, calm and courageous. With his fair capital laid in ruins before his eyes, his nobles and faithful subjects dying around him, his territory rent away, foot by foot, till scarce enough remained for him to stand on, he rejected every invitation to capitulate, and showed the same indomitable spirit as at the commencement of the siege. When Cortés, in the hope that the extremities of the besieged would incline them to listen to an accommodation, persuaded a noble prisoner to bear to Guatemozin his proposals to that effect; the fierce young monarch, according to the general, ordered him at once to be sacrificed. It is a Spaniard, we must remember, who tells the story.

Cortés, who had suspended hostilities for several days, in the vain hope that the distresses of the Mexicans would bend them to submission, now determined to drive them to it by a general assault. Cooped up, as they were, within a narrow quarter of the city, their position favoured such an attempt. He commanded Alvarado to hold himself in readiness, and directed Sandoval—who, besides the causeway, had charge of the fleet, which lay off the Tlatelolcan district,—to support the attack by a cannonade on the houses near the water. He then led his forces into the city, or rather across the horrid waste that now encircled it.

On entering the Indian precincts, he was met by several of the chiefs, who, stretching forth their emaciated arms, exclaimed, "You are the children of the Sun. But the Sun is swift in his course. Why are you, then, so tardy? Why do you delay so long to put an end to our miseries? Rather kill us at once, that we may go to our god Huitzilopochtli, who waits for us in heaven to give us rest from our sufferings!"

Cortés was moved by their piteous appeal, and answered, that he desired not their death, but their submission. "Why does your master refuse to treat with me," he said, "when a single hour will suffice for me to crush him and all his people?" He then urged them to request Guatemozin to confer with him, with the assurance that he might do it in safety, as his person should not be molested.

The nobles, after some persuasion, undertook the mission; and it was received by the young monarch in a manner which showed—if the anecdote before related of him be true—that misfortune had, at length, asserted some power over his haughty spirit. He consented to the interview, though not to have it take place on that day, but the following, in the great square of Tlatelolco. Cortés, well satisfied, immediately withdrew from the city, and resumed his position on the causeway.

The next morning he presented himself at the place appointed, having previously stationed Alvarado there with a strong corps of infantry to guard against treachery. The stone platform in the centre of the square was covered with mats and carpets, and a banquet was prepared to refresh the famished monarch and his nobles. Having made these arrangements, he awaited the hour of the interview.

But Guatemozin, instead of appearing himself, sent his nobles, the same who had brought to him the general's invitation, and who now excused their master's absence on the plea of illness. Cortés, though disappointed, gave a courteous reception to the envoys, considering that it might still afford the means of opening a communication with the emperor. He persuaded them without much entreaty to partake of the good cheer spread before them, which they did with a voracity that told how severe had been their abstinence. He then dismissed them with a seasonable supply of provisions for their master, pressing him to consent to an interview, without which it was impossible their differences could be adjusted.

The Indian envoys returned in a short time, bearing with them a present of fine cotton fabrics, of no great value, from Guatemozin, who still declined to meet the Spanish general. Cortés, though deeply chagrined, was unwilling to give up the point. "He will surely come," he said to the envoys, "when he sees that I suffer you to go and come unharmed, you who have been my steady enemies, no less than himself, throughout the war. He has nothing to fear from me." He again parted with them, promising to receive their answer the following day.

On the next morning, the Aztec chiefs, entering the Christian quarters, announced to Cortés that Guatemozin would confer with him at noon in the market-place. The general was punctual at the hour; but without success. Neither monarch nor ministers appeared there. It was plain that the Indian prince did not care to trust the promises of his enemy. A thought of Montezuma may have passed across his mind. After he had waited three hours, the general's patience was exhausted, and, as he learned that the Mexicans were busy in preparations for defence, he made immediate dispositions for the assault.[4]

The confederates had been left without the walls, for he did not care to bring them in sight of the quarry, before he was ready to slip the leash. He now ordered them to join him; and, supported by Alvarado's division, marched at once into the enemy's quarters. He found them prepared to receive him. Their most able-bodied warriors were thrown into the van, covering their feeble and crippled comrades. Women were seen occasionally minging in the ranks, and, as well as children, thronged the *azoteas*, where, with famine-stricken visages and haggard eyes, they scowled defiance and hatred on their invaders.

As the Spaniards advanced, the Mexicans set up a fierce war-cry, and sent off clouds of arrows with their accustomed spirit, while the women and boys rained down darts and stones from their elevated position on the terraces. But the missiles were sent by hands too feeble to do much damage; and, when the squadrons closed, the loss of strength became still more sensible in the Aztecs. Their blows fell feebly and with doubtful aim; though some, it is true, of stronger constitution, or gathering strength from despair, maintained to the last a desperate fight.

The arquebusiers now poured in a deadly fire. The brigantines replied by successive volleys in the opposite quarter. The besieged, hemmed in, like deer surrounded by the huntsmen, were brought down on every side. The carnage was horrible. The ground was heaped up with slain, until the maddened combatants were obliged to climb over the human mounds to get at one another. The miry soil was saturated with blood, which ran off like water, and dyed the canals themselves with crimson. All was uproar and terrible confusion. The hideous yells of the barbarians; the oaths and execrations of the Spaniards; the cries of the wounded; the shrieks of women and children; the heavy blows of the Conquerors; the death-struggle of their victims; the rapid, reverberating echoes of musketry; the hissing of innumerable missiles; the crash and crackling of blazing buildings, crushing hundreds in their ruins; the blinding volumes of dust and sulphurous smoke shrouding all in their gloomy canopy,—made a scene appalling even to the soldiers of Cortés, steeled as they were by many a rough passage of war, and by long familiarity with blood and violence. "The piteous cries of the women and children, in particular," says the general, "were enough to break one's heart."[5] He commanded that they should be spared, and that all, who asked it, should receive quarter. He particularly urged this on to the confederates, and placed men among them to restrain their violence. But he had set an engine in motion too terrible to be controlled. It were as easy to curb the hurricane in its fury, as the passions of an infuriated horde of savages. "Never did I see so pitiless a race," he exclaims, "or any thing wearing the form of man so destitute of humanity." They made no

---

[4] The testimony is most emphatic and unequivocal to these repeated efforts on the part of Cortés to bring the Aztecs peaceably to terms. Besides his own Letter to the Emperor, see Bernal Diaz, cap. 155;—Herrera, Hist. General, lib. 2, cap. 6, 7;—Torquemada, Monarch. Ind., lib. 4, cap. 100;—Ixtlilxochitl, Venida de los Esp., pp. 44–48;—Oviedo, Hist. de las Ind., MS., lib. 33, cap. 29, 30.

[5] "Era tanta la grita y lloro de los Niños, y Mugeres, que no habia Persona, á quien no quebrantasse el corazon." (Rel. Terc. ap. Lorenzana, p. 296.) They were a rash and stiff-necked race, exclaims his reverend editor, the archbishop, with a charitable commentary! "*Gens duræ cervicis, gens absque consilio.*" Nota.

distinction of sex or age, and in this hour of vengeance seemed to be requiting the hoarded wrongs of a century. At length, sated with slaughter, the Spanish commander sounded a retreat. It was full time, if, according to his own statement,—we may hope it is an exaggeration,—forty thousand souls had perished! Yet their fate was to be envied, in comparison with that of those who survived.

Through the long night which followed, no movement was perceptible in the Aztec quarter. No light was seen there, no sound was heard, save the low moaning of some wounded or dying wretch, writhing in agony. All was dark and silent, —the darkness of the grave. The last blow seemed to have completely stunned them. They had parted with hope, and sat in sullen despair, like men waiting in silence the stroke of the executioner. Yet, for all this, they showed no disposition to submit. Every new injury had sunk deeper into their souls, and filled them with a deeper hatred of their enemy. Fortune, friends, kindred, home,—all were gone. They were content to throw away life itself, now that they had nothing more to live for.

Far different was the scene in the Christian camp, where, elated with their recent successes, all was alive with bustle, and preparation for the morrow. Bonfires were seen blazing along the causeways, lights gleamed from tents and barracks, and the sounds of music and merriment, borne over the waters, proclaimed the joy of the soldiers at the prospect of so soon terminating their wearisome campaign.

On the following morning the Spanish commander again mustered his forces, having decided to follow up the blow of the preceding day before the enemy should have time to rally, and at once to put an end to the war. He had arranged with Alvarado, on the evening previous, to occupy the market-place of Tlatelolco; and the discharge of an arquebuse was to be the signal for a simultaneous assault. Sandoval was to hold the northern causeway, and, with the fleet, to watch the movements of the Indian emperor, and to intercept the flight to the main land, which Cortés knew he meditated. To allow him to effect this, would be to leave a formidable enemy in his own neighbourhood, who might at any time kindle the flame of insurrection throughout the country. He ordered Sandoval, however, to do no harm to the royal person, and not to fire on the enemy at all, except in self-defence.

It was on the memorable 13th of August, 1521, the day of St. Hypolito,—from this circumstance selected as the patron saint of Modern Mexico,— that Cortés led his warlike array for the last time across the black and blasted environs which lay around the Indian capital. On entering the Aztec precincts, he paused, willing to afford its wretched inmates one more chance of escape, before striking the fatal blow. He obtained an interview with some of the principal chiefs, and expostulated with them on the conduct of their prince. "He surely will not," said the general, "see you all perish, when he can so easily save you." He then urged them to prevail on Guatemozin to hold a conference with him, repeating the assurances of his personal safety.

The messengers went on their mission, and soon returned with the *cihuacoatl* at their head, a magistrate of high authority among the Mexicans. He said, with a melancholy air, in which his own disappointment was visible, that "Guatemozin was ready to die where he was, but would hold no interview with the Spanish commander;" adding in a tone of resignation, "It is for you to work your pleasure." "Go, then," replied the stern Conqueror, "and prepare your countrymen for death. Their hour is come."

He still postponed the assault for several hours. But the impatience of his troops at this delay was heightened by the rumour that Guatemozin and his nobles were preparing to escape with their effects in the *piraguas* and canoes which were moored on the margin of the lake. Convinced of the fruitlessness and impolicy of further procrastination, Cortés made his final dispositions for the attack, and took his own station on an *azotea*, which commanded the theatre of operations.

When the assailants came into presence of the enemy, they found them huddled together in the utmost confusion, all ages and sexes, in masses so dense that they nearly forced one another over the brink of the causeways into the water below. Some had climbed on the terraces, others feebly supported themselves against the walls of the buildings. Their squalid and tattered garments gave a wildness to their appearance, which still further heightened the ferocity of their expression, as they glared on their enemy with eyes in which hate was mingled with despair. When the Spaniards had approached within bowshot, the Aztecs let off a flight of impotent missiles, showing to the last the resolute spirit, though they had lost the strength, of their better days. The fatal signal was then given by the discharge of an arquebuse,—speedily followed by peals of heavy ordnance, the rattle of fire-arms, and the hellish shouts of the confederates, as they sprang upon their victims. It is unnecessary to stain the page with a repetition of the horrors of the preceding day. Some of the wretched Aztecs threw themselves into the water, and were picked up by the canoes. Others sunk and were suffocated in the canals. The number of these became so great, that a bridge was made of their dead bodies, over which the assailants could climb to the opposite banks. Others again, especially the women, begged for mercy, which, as the chroniclers assure us, was everywhere granted by the Spaniards, and, contrary to the instructions and entreaties of Cortés, everywhere refused by the confederates.

While this work of butchery was going on, numbers were observed pushing off in the barks that lined the shore, and making the best of their way across the lake. They were constantly intercepted by the brigantines, which broke through the flimsy array of boats; sending off their volleys to the right and left, as the crews of the latter hotly assailed them. The battle raged as fiercely on the lake as on the land. Many of the Indian vessels were shattered and overturned. Some few, however, under cover of the smoke, which rolled darkly over the waters, succeeded in clearing themselves of the turmoil, and were fast nearing the opposite shore.

Sandoval had particularly charged his captains to keep an eye on the movements of any vessel in which it was at all probable that Guatemozin might be concealed. At this crisis, three or four of the largest *piraguas* were seen skimming over the water, and making their way rapidly across the lake. A captain named Garci Holguin, who had command of one of the best sailers in the fleet, instantly gave them chase. The wind was favourable, and every moment he gained on the fugitives, who pulled their oars with a vigour that despair alone could have given. But it was in vain; and, after a short race, Holguin, coming alongside of one of the *piraguas*, which, whether from its appearance, or from information he had received, he conjectured might bear the Indian emperor, ordered his men to level their crossbows at the boat. But, before they could discharge them, a cry arose from those in it, that their lord was on board. At the same moment, a young warrior, armed with buckler and *maquahuitl*, rose up, as if to beat off the assailants. But, as the Spanish captain ordered his men not to shoot, he dropped his weapons, and exclaimed, "I am Guatemozin; lead me to Malintzin, I am his prisoner; but let no harm come to my wife and my followers."

Holguin assured him that his wishes should be respected, and assisted him to get on board the brigantine, followed by his wife and attendants. These were twenty in number, consisting of Coanoca, the deposed lord of Tezcuco, the lord of Tlacopan, and several other caciques and dignitaries, whose rank, probably, had secured them some exemption from the general calamities of the siege. When the captives were seated on the deck of his vessel, Holguin requested the Aztec prince to put an end to the combat by commanding his people in the other canoes to surrender. But, with a dejected air, he replied, "It is not necessary. They will fight no longer, when they see that their prince is taken." He spoke truth. The news of Guatemozin's capture spread rapidly through the fleet, and on shore, where the Mexicans were still engaged in conflict with their enemies. It ceased, however, at once. They made no further resistance; and those on the water quickly followed the brigantines, which conveyed their captive monarch to land. It seemed as if the fight had been maintained thus long, the better to divert the enemy's attention, and cover their master's retreat.[6]

[6] For the preceding account of the capture of Guatemozin, told with little discrepancy, though with more or less minuteness by the different writers, see Bernal Diaz, Ibid., ubi supra,—Rel. Terc. de Cortés, p. 299,—Gonzalo de las Casas, Defensa, MS.,—Oviedo, Hist. de las Ind., MS., lib. 33, cap. 30,—Torquemada, Monarch. Ind., lib. 4, cap. 101.

FRANCIS PARKMAN (1823–1893)

Parkman, in the phrase of his sister Eliza, was a "reverent agnostic." He was so, it seems, in reaction to the large sprinkling of ministers in his family, in particular his father, the Reverend Francis Parkman of the New North Church in Boston—a somewhat self-important, affable, conventional, and (from the son's point of view) irritatingly imperturbable man. The quality of reverent disbelief, in any event, is what gives Parkman's history its dark and yet humane coloration. He hit upon the subject of that history while still at Harvard (where, incidentally, he was helped on his way by Jared Sparks, the first professor of history in any American university and the first to direct attention to the American past). There Parkman determined, as he said later, to write "the story of what was then known as the 'Old French War,' that is, the war that ended in the conquest of Canada." His plan soon enlarged "to include the whole course of the American conflict between France and England, or, in other words, the history of the American forest."

For Parkman, the American forest was first of all the New England wilderness stretching from Massachusetts to Canada which he explored with zest during his undergraduate summers—passing, as he recorded, "through the wild forest and among lakes and streams which have borne no bark but the canoe of the Indian or the hunter." Two other journeys went into the shaping of his history. The first was a trip to Europe in the fall of his senior year, after a partial breakdown—a trip which permitted his remarkably absorptive and responsive mind to take in the evidences of the past and present of Christian civilization in some depth. The second was his excursion to the Far West in 1846, with his cousin Quincy Shaw. He underwent every hardship; he observed; he hunted buffalo; and most important of all, through the chance of his guide's wife being a member of the tribe, he spent several weeks roving through the wilds with a band of Sioux Indians.

In his account of all this in *The Oregon Trail* (1849), it is Parkman's description of the Sioux that especially compels us. His final appraisal of them is strikingly similar to Melville's view of the Marquesan Islanders in *Typee*. They were magnificently handsome, and the males among them were altogether masculine; they were courageous and physically adept; they were completely free of Puritan shames and embarrassments ("Superb naked forms stood silently

gazing at us," Parkman recalled); they took a fierce joy in life. At the same time, they were amoral to an extreme; and worse, they were mindless and totally lacking in any sense of purpose ("they merely vegetate"). They possessed certain radical energies from which civilized man had long been shut off; but they were themselves bereft of civilized man's sometimes painful capacity to plan, to discriminate, to envisage. Parkman's reflections on the Sioux have a certain intensity, a sense of personal relevance, that compensates for their scientific inaccuracy. His examination of the Indians was an urgent inquiry into the recesses of human nature—into the uncivilized depths of his own self. What Howard Doughty says about *The Oregon Trail* brings it, with all accuracy, even closer to what we have said about *Typee*: "[Parkman's] journey backward in time was likewise a journey to the depths of the self, the exploration of a hinterland where Unitarianism preferred not to venture, which Transcendentalism mistook the nature of and which Utilitarianism simply ignored." (In this dimension *The Oregon Trail* also bears resemblance to Conrad's *Heart of Darkness*.)

Out of Parkman's visits to the New England wilderness and to Europe and the Far West, then, came a complex theme for his history: the experience of Europe in the American forest—specifically, to use Parkman's own collective title, *France and England in North America*. But that conjunction was further complicated, and the drama thickened, by the inclusion of the earlier inhabitants of the continent, the Indian tribes—while the grand historic conflict assumed the character on one level of a war between civilized and primitive peoples and on another of a struggle for supremacy between the warring elements of human nature.

Still another factor must be reckoned with, if we are to take the measure of Parkman's history. And that is the combination, or contradiction, in him of extraordinary energy and frequent, shattering illness. We have mentioned the breakdown in 1843. He suffered another after returning East from the Oregon Trail; and, indeed, he dictated that book to one of his sisters in the darkened attic of his father's house. In 1852, he virtually collapsed and remained incapacitated for several years. The diagnosis is still uncertain, but the symptoms included near-blindness, nervous indigestion, stoppage of circulation in fingers and toes, and, most terrible of all, the feeling of intolerable pressure inside his skull. The slightest effort at rational thought brought on the sensation of a weight of hundreds of pounds bearing down on his head.[1] There is considerable evidence, too, that Parkman had an unusually powerful sexual drive and that he repressed it at times—before his marriage and after his wife's death in 1857— with a kind of ferocity.[2] It was in the months following Mrs. Parkman's death that the historian genuinely feared for his sanity and went to Paris to consult, without much success, with a French specialist.

One way to combat "the enemy," as Parkman called his various ailments and harassments, was an active interest in horticulture; he won hundreds of awards from the Massachusetts Horticultural Society; a crab apple and a hybrid lily were named after him; and for a year, in 1871, he was professor of horticulture (his only teaching experience) at the Bussey Institute in Boston. Quite another way was simply to fight the enemy, so to speak, on its own terms. It was to show a masculine contempt for illness, to persist in physical activity (as he had on the Oregon Trail, where he often clung stubbornly to the saddle more dead than alive) and in the mental activity that went into his writing. Parkman made a sort of cult of masculine energy, of what was later known as "the strenuous life"

—especially the life whose strenuousness served to overcome physical limitations and difficulties; and indeed the author of that phrase, Theodore Roosevelt, dedicated to Parkman his book *The Winning of the West*. But Parkman's long battle with the enemy (which was more or less defeated by the mid-sixties) is reflected most significantly in the emphasis he places in his history on sheer endurance: in fact, on survival or extinction as the very issues at stake; on the capacity of his heroes La Salle and Pontiac, Montcalm and Wolfe to continue to their heroic deaths against enormous odds; and on the lesser figures—Jesuits and Indians—to make their way through torture and vilification to their chosen destinies.

France and England in North America consisted eventually of eight volumes. It begins with the "French Pioneers" in the New World, in the early sixteenth century; reaches one peak in the account of La Salle's "discovery of the great west" in the 1680's; comes to its climax in *Montcalm and Wolfe* and the British conquest of Canada in 1759; and ends with the narrative of the last, doomed uprising of the Indians and the conspiracy of Pontiac. One can debate at length, and fruitfully, which of these volumes taken individually is Parkman's masterpiece (*The Oregon Trail*, though by far Parkman's most popular work, is no more his greatest achievement than *Typee* was Melville's). *The Conspiracy of Pontiac*—the last in the series chronologically, but the first to be written and published—introduces perhaps the most appealing and certainly the most hopelessly outmatched of Parkman's heroes and carries him through a historic drama that verges on melodrama. As it traces what is in effect the final defeat of the Indian race in North America, it also discloses more clearly than any other volume Parkman's intricate conception of the conflict between the civilized and the primitive—a conception a good deal more artfully ambiguous and more charged with significant contradiction than the contrast recorded earlier in *The Oregon Trail*. Nature and its Indian inhabitants are at once fecund and destructive, beautiful and venomous. The western wilderness is in

---

[1] If we are to see *The Oregon Trail* as, on one level, an account of the descent into the unconscious self, and the Indians as the symbol of that unconscious self, it then becomes tempting to suggest that the wildly inaccurate description of the Indians as mindless and vegetative had its source in Parkman's psychic sense of his own deepest nature at the time. Further, Parkman's successful confrontation with his illness might explain his later ability to see more in the Indians' nature than mindlessness and amorality.

[2] Parkman's notebooks, his autobiographical novel *Vassall Morton*, and certain shadings in his description of the Sioux are among the sources for such speculation. See also Howard Doughty, *Francis Parkman* (1962).

one perspective the earthly paradise that the Romantic imagination had dreamed; and yet, Parkman writes, "this western paradise is not free from the primal curse"; it is a "land prodigal of good and evil." And if the urban civilization that conquers nature and destroys its inhabitants—the cities that rise over Pontiac's unmarked grave—exchanges primal forces, natural energies, and a harmony of flesh and spirit for industry, science, faceless crowds, and materialistic rationalism, it also brings blessings of mind and imagination, creative powers, and human safety and comfort. In the manner of Melville and to some degree Hawthorne, Parkman neither affirms the American pastoral myth nor repudiates it, but brings it within a larger vision where its attractions and dangers, its portion of enduring truth and its portion of perilous falsehood, show only the more clearly.

Parkman himself regarded *Montcalm and Wolfe* (1884) as his finest accomplishment, and many readers over the years have agreed with him. Henry Adams told Parkman that it was "a great work which puts you at the head of our living historians," and called the book "an event in our literary history." Henry James wrote from England describing "with what high appreciation and genuine gratitude I have been reading your *Wolfe and Montcalm*. (You see I am still so overturned by my emotion that I can't even write the name straight.)" He went on in the Jamesian way, speaking almost as one novelist to another: "The manner in which you have treated the prodigious theme is worthy of the theme itself, and that says everything. It is truly a noble book, my dear Parkman."

Indeed it is: not less in its brilliant slow massing and matching of forces—French and English, autocratic and independent, imperial and colonial—than in its uncommonly vivid battle scenes. Parkman, as he moves back and forth between the French and English governments at home and the local maneuvering in North America, displays as fully developed an awareness of political folly, contradiction and collision and shift of purpose, as Henry Adams would in his *Education*. And as he brings his two chief combatants ever nearer to the decisive

encounter on the Plains of Abraham, Parkman demonstrates a skill at thematic enlargement through action, character, and language not at all unworthy of Henry James. The theme is the historical, political, cultural, and even psychological fate of a continent; and as James remarked, Parkman's powers were altogether up to it.

Nevertheless, *La Salle and the Discovery of the Great West* is the book in which Parkman's dramatic genius is most vigorously manifested, and it is from this that we have taken the first of our selections. Parkman saw in the story of La Salle the outlines of a classic—or better, Shakespearean—tragic drama, and in its protagonist the figure of an unmistakably tragic hero. La Salle, in Parkman's treatment of him, reminds us at many turns of Melville's Ahab—the Frenchman too a monomaniac, driven by a fixed, unswerving purpose, pressing ever forward on his great quest; cold, strong, fatally proud; held in almost supernatural awe by his men, some of whom secretly (like Starbuck) long to destroy him and finally succeed in doing so.

Even Parkman's language, in his summary portrait of La Salle, seems to echo—though in simpler, sterner, and less poetic tonalities—Melville's first description of Ahab (as both writers are undoubtedly echoing the description of Satan in Milton's *Paradise Lost*): "He was the hero not of a principle nor of a faith, but simply of a fixed idea and a determined purpose. As often happens with concentrated and energetic natures, his purpose was to him a passion and an inspiration; and he clung to it with a certain fanaticism of devotion." And Melville: "There was an infinity of firmest fortitude, a determinate, unsurrenderable wilfulness, in the fixed and fearless forward dedication of that glance." La Salle, Parkman says, was "serious in all things, incapable of the lighter pleasures, incapable of repose, finding no joy but in the pursuit of great designs." Captain Ahab, communing with himself, declares that he is unable to rest and that the sunset soothes him no longer: "Gifted with the high perception, I lack the low, enjoying power."

There are moments, and we have selected

one, where Parkman's language, like Melville's, transforms the most scrupulously observed physical details into components of a mythic vision. It is just this myth-making capability that raises Parkman above any other American historian. His vision, at least in the passage following, is not dissimilar to the one arrived at (momentarily) by Ishmael in *Moby-Dick:* when the grandeur of the tragic quest and the mighty actions of the tragic hero are suddenly dwarfed by the immensities of nature, and all great human endeavor disappears, for an instant, behind the terrible blank of the fathomless universe.

From La Salle and the Discovery of the Great West (1869)

CHAPTER 20

1681-1682: Success of La Salle

This is the moment of La Salle's greatest achievement. After many extraordinary adventures and explorations, the French nobleman here arrives at the mouth of the Mississippi, and in the name of King Louis XIV takes possession of an enormous territory—"a stupendous accession," Parkman calls it in the last paragraph, from Texas to the Rocky Mountains.

———

The season was far advanced. On the bare limbs of the forest hung a few withered remnants of its gay autumnal livery; and the smoke crept upward through the sullen November air from the squalid wigwams of La Salle's Abenaki and Mohegan allies. These, his new friends, were savages whose midnight yells had startled the border hamlets of New England; who had danced around Puritan scalps, and whom Puritan imaginations painted as incarnate fiends. La Salle chose eighteen of them, whom he added to the twenty-three Frenchmen who remained with him, some of the rest having deserted and others lagged behind. The Indians insisted on taking their squaws with them. These were ten in number, besides three children; and thus the expedition included fifty-four persons, of whom some were useless, and others a burden.

On the 21st of December, Tonty and Membré set out from Fort Miami with some of the party in six canoes, and crossed to the little river Chicago.[1]

[1] La Salle, *Relation de la Découverte,* 1682, in Thomassy, *Géologie Pratique de la Louisiane,* 9; *Lettre du Père Zenobe Membré,* 3 *Juin,* 1682; *Ibid.,* 14 *Août,* 1682; Membré in Le Clerc, ii. 214; Tonty, 1684, 1693; *Procès Verbal de la Prise de Possession de la Louisiane,*

La Salle, with the rest of the men, joined them a few days later. It was the dead of winter, and the streams were frozen. They made sledges, placed on them the canoes, the baggage, and a disabled Frenchman; crossed from the Chicago to the northern branch of the Illinois, and filed in a long procession down its frozen course. They reached the site of the great Illinois village, found it tenantless, and continued their journey, still dragging their canoes, till at length they reached open water below Lake Peoria.

La Salle had abandoned for a time his original plan of building a vessel for the navigation of the Mississippi. Bitter experience had taught him the difficulty of the attempt, and he resolved to trust to his canoes alone. They embarked again, floating prosperously down between the leafless forests that flanked the tranquil river; till, on the sixth of February, they issued upon the majestic bosom of the Mississippi. Here, for the time, their progress was stopped; for the river was full of floating ice. La Salle's Indians, too, had lagged behind; but within a week all had arrived, the navigation was

———

Feuilles détachées d'une Lettre de La Salle (Margry, ii. 164); *Récit de Nicolas de la Salle* (Ibid., i. 547).

The narrative ascribed to Membré and published by Le Clerc is based on the document preserved in the Archives Scientifiques de la Marine, entitled *Relation de la Découverte de l'Embouchure de la Rivière Mississippi faite par le Sieur de la Salle, l'année passée,* 1682. The writer of the narrative has used it very freely, copying the greater part verbatim, with occasional additions of a kind which seem to indicate that he had taken part in the expedition. The *Relation de la Découverte,* though written in the third person, is the official report of the discovery made by La Salle, or perhaps for him by Membré.

once more free, and they resumed their course. Towards evening they saw on their right the mouth of a great river; and the clear current was invaded by the headlong torrent of the Missouri, opaque with mud. They built their camp-fires in the neighboring forest; and at daylight, embarking anew on the dark and mighty stream, drifted swiftly down towards unknown destinies. They passed a deserted town of the Tamaroas; saw, three days after, the mouth of the Ohio;[2] and, gliding by the wastes of bordering swamp, landed on the twenty-fourth of February near the Third Chickasaw Bluffs.[3] They encamped, and the hunters went out for game. All returned, excepting Pierre Prudhomme; and as the others had seen fresh tracks of Indians, La Salle feared that he was killed. While some of his followers built a small stockade fort on a high bluff[4] by the river, others ranged the woods in pursuit of the missing hunter. After six days of ceaseless and fruitless search, they met two Chickasaw Indians in the forest; and through them La Salle sent presents and peace-messages to that warlike people, whose villages were a few days' journey distant. Several days later Prudhomme was found, and brought into the camp, half-dead. He had lost his way while hunting; and to console him for his woes La Salle christened the newly built fort with his name, and left him, with a few others, in charge of it.

Again they embarked; and with every stage of their adventurous progress the mystery of this vast New World was more and more unveiled. More and more they entered the realms of spring. The hazy sunlight, the warm and drowsy air, the tender foliage, the opening flowers, betokened the reviving life of Nature. For several days more they followed the writhings of the great river on its tortuous course through wastes of swamp and canebrake, till on the thirteenth of March[5] they found themselves wrapped in a thick fog. Neither shore was visible; but they heard on the right the booming of an Indian drum and the shrill outcries of the war-dance. La Salle at once crossed to the opposite side, where, in less than an hour, his men threw up a rude fort of felled trees. Meanwhile the fog cleared; and from the farther bank the astonished Indians saw the strange visitors at their work. Some of the French advanced to the edge of the water, and beckoned them to come over. Several of them approached, in a wooden canoe, to within the distance of a gun-shot. La Salle displayed the calumet, and sent a Frenchman to meet them. He was well received; and the friendly mood of the Indians being now apparent, the whole party crossed the river.

On landing, they found themselves at a town of the Kappa band of the Arkansas, a people dwelling near the mouth of the river which bears their name. "The whole village," writes Membré to his superior, "came down to the shore to meet us, except the women, who had run off. I cannot tell you the civility and kindness we received from these barbarians, who brought us poles to make huts, supplied us with firewood during the three days we were among them, and took turns in feasting us. But, my Reverend Father, this gives no idea of the good qualities of these savages, who are gay, civil, and free-hearted. The young men, though the most alert and spirited we had seen, are nevertheless so modest that not one of them would take the liberty to enter our hut, but all stood quietly at the door. They are so well formed that we were in admiration at their beauty. We did not lose the value of a pin while we were among them."

Various were the dances and ceremonies with which they entertained the strangers, who, on their part, responded with a solemnity which their hosts would have liked less if they had understood it better. La Salle and Tonty, at the head of their followers, marched to the open area in the midst of the village. Here, to the admiration of the gazing crowd of warriors, women, and children, a cross was raised bearing the arms of France. Membré, in canonicals, sang a hymn; the men shouted *Vive le Roi*; and La Salle, in the King's name, took formal possession of the country.[6] The friar, not, he flatters himself, without success, labored to expound by signs the mysteries of the Faith; while La Salle, by methods equally satisfactory, drew from the chief an acknowledgment of fealty to Louis XIV.[7]

---

[2] Called by Membré the Ouabache (Wabash).

[3] La Salle, *Relation de la Découverte de l'Embouchure, etc.*; Thomassy, 10. Membré gives the same date; but the *Procès Verbal* makes it the twenty-sixth.

[4] Gravier, in his letter of 16 Feb., 1701, says that he encamped near a "great bluff of stone, called Fort Prudhomme, because M. de la Salle, going on his discovery, intrenched himself here with his party, fearing that Prudhomme, who had lost himself in the woods, had been killed by the Indians, and that he himself would be attacked."

[5] La Salle, *Relation*; Thomassy, 11.

[6] *Procès Verbal de la Prise de Possession du Pays des Arkansas, 14 Mars, 1682.*

[7] The nation of the Akanseas, Alkansas, or Arkansas, dwelt on the west bank of the Mississippi, near the

After touching at several other towns of this people, the voyagers resumed their course, guided by two of the Arkansas; passed the sites, since become historic, of Vicksburg and Grand Gulf; and, about three hundred miles below the Arkansas, stopped by the edge of a swamp on the western side of the river.[8] Here, as their two guides told them, was the path to the great town of the Taensas. Tonty and Membré were sent to visit it. They and their men shouldered their birch canoe through the swamp, and launched it on a lake which had once formed a portion of the channel of the river. In two hours, they reached the town; and Tonty gazed at it with astonishment. He had seen nothing like it in America,—large square dwellings, built of sun-baked mud mixed with straw, arched over with a dome-shaped roof of canes, and placed in regular order around an open area. Two of them were larger and better than the rest. One was the lodge of the chief; the other was the temple, or house of the Sun. They entered the former, and found a single room, forty feet square, where, in the dim light,—for there was no opening but the door,—the chief sat awaiting them on a sort of bedstead, three of his wives at his side; while sixty old men, wrapped in white cloaks woven of mulberry-bark, formed his divan. When he spoke, his wives howled to do him honor; and the assembled councillors listened with the reverence due to a potentate for whom, at his death, a hundred victims were to be sacrificed. He received the visitors graciously, and joyfully accepted the gifts which Tonty laid before him.[9] This interview over, the Frenchmen repaired to the temple,

wherein were kept the bones of the departed chiefs. In construction, it was much like the royal dwelling. Over it were rude wooden figures, representing three eagles turned towards the east. A strong mud wall surrounded it, planted with stakes, on which were stuck the skulls of enemies sacrificed to the Sun; while before the door was a block of wood, on which lay a large shell surrounded with the braided hair of the victims. The interior was rude as a barn, dimly lighted from the doorway, and full of smoke. There was a structure in the middle which Membré thinks was a kind of altar; and before it burned a perpetual fire, fed with three logs laid end to end, and watched by two old men devoted to this sacred office. There was a mysterious recess, too, which the strangers were forbidden to explore, but which, as Tonty was told, contained the riches of the nation, consisting of pearls from the Gulf, and trinkets obtained, probably through other tribes, from the Spaniards and other Europeans.

The chief condescended to visit La Salle at his camp,—a favor which he would by no means have granted, had the visitors been Indians. A master of ceremonies and six attendants preceded him, to clear the path and prepare the place of meeting. When all was ready, he was seen advancing, clothed in a white robe and preceded by two men bearing white fans, while a third displayed a disk of burnished copper,—doubtless to represent the Sun, his ancestor, or, as others will have it, his elder brother. His aspect was marvellously grave, and he and La Salle met with gestures of ceremonious courtesy. The interview was very friendly; and the chief returned well pleased with the gifts which his entertainer bestowed on him, and which, indeed, had been the principal motive of his visit.

On the next morning, as they descended the river, they saw a wooden canoe full of Indians; and Tonty gave chase. He had nearly overtaken it, when more than a hundred men appeared suddenly on the shore, with bows bent to defend their countrymen. La Salle called out to Tonty to withdraw. He obeyed; and the whole party encamped on the opposite bank. Tonty offered to cross the river with a peace-pipe, and set out accordingly with a small party of men. When he landed, the Indians made signs of friendship by joining their

---

mouth of the Arkansas. They were divided into four tribes, living for the most part in separate villages. Those first visited by La Salle were the Kappas, or Quapaws, a remnant of whom still subsists. The others were the Topingas, or Tongengas; the Torimans; and the Osotouoy, or Sauthouis. According to Charlevoix, who saw them in 1721, they were regarded as the tallest and best-formed Indians in America, and were known as *les Beaux Hommes.* Gravier says that they once lived on the Ohio.

[8] In Tensas County, Louisiana. Tonty's estimates of distance are here much too low. They seem to be founded on observations of latitude, without reckoning the windings of the river. It may interest sportsmen to know that the party killed several large alligators, on their way. Membré is much astonished that such monsters should be born of eggs like chickens.

[9] Tonty, 1684, 1693. In the spurious narrative, published in Tonty's name, the account is embellished and

---

exaggerated. Compare Membré in Le Clerc, ii. 227. La Salle's statements in the *Relation* of 1682 (Thomassy, 12) sustain those of Tonty.

hands,—a proceeding by which Tonty, having but one hand, was somewhat embarrassed; but he directed his men to respond in his stead. La Salle and Membré now joined him, and went with the Indians to their village, three leagues distant. Here they spent the night. "The Sieur de la Salle," writes Membré, "whose very air, engaging manners, tact, and address attract love and respect alike, produced such an effect on the hearts of these people that they did not know how to treat us well enough."[10]

The Indians of this village were the Natchez; and their chief was brother of the great chief, or Sun, of the whole nation. His town was several leagues distant, near the site of the city of Natchez; and thither the French repaired to visit him. They saw what they had already seen among the Taensas,—a religious and political despotism, a privileged caste descended from the sun, a temple, and a sacred fire.[11] La Salle planted a large cross, with the arms of France attached, in the midst of the town; while the inhabitants looked on with a satisfaction which they would hardly have displayed had they understood the meaning of the act.

The French next visited the Coroas, at their village two leagues below; and here they found a reception no less auspicious. On the thirty-first of March, as they approached Red River, they passed in the fog a town of the Oumas, and three days later discovered a party of fishermen, in wooden canoes, among the canes along the margin of the water. They fled at sight of the Frenchmen. La Salle sent men to reconnoitre, who, as they struggled through the marsh, were greeted with a shower of arrows; while from the neighboring village of the Quinipissas,[12] invisible behind the canebrake, they heard the sound of an Indian drum and the whoops of the mustering warriors. La Salle, anxious to keep the peace with all the tribes along the river, recalled his men, and pursued his voyage. A few leagues below they saw a cluster of Indian lodges on the left bank, apparently void of inhabitants. They landed, and found three of them filled with corpses. It was a village of the Tangibao, sacked by their enemies only a few days before.[13]

And now they neared their journey's end. On the sixth of April the river divided itself into three broad channels. La Salle followed that of the west, and Dautray that of the east; while Tonty took the middle passage. As he drifted down the turbid current, between the low and marshy shores, the brackish water changed to brine, and the breeze grew fresh with the salt breath of the sea. Then the broad bosom of the great Gulf opened on his sight, tossing its restless billows, limitless, voiceless, lonely as when born of chaos, without a sail, without a sign of life.

La Salle, in a canoe, coasted the marshy borders of the sea; and then the reunited parties assembled on a spot of dry ground, a short distance above the mouth of the river. Here a column was made ready, bearing the arms of France, and inscribed with the words, "Louis Le Grand, Roy de France et de Navarre, règne; le Neuvième Avril, 1682."

The Frenchmen were mustered under arms; and while the New England Indians and their squaws looked on in wondering silence, they chanted the *Te Deum*, the *Exaudiat*, and the *Domine salvum fac Regem*. Then, amid volleys of musketry and shouts of *Vive le Roi*, La Salle planted the column in its place, and, standing near it, proclaimed in a loud voice,—

---

[10] Membré in Le Clerc, ii. 232.

[11] The Natchez and the Taensas, whose habits and customs were similar, did not, in their social organization, differ radically from other Indians. The same principle of clanship, or *totemship*, so widely spread, existed in full force among them, combined with their religious ideas, and developed into forms of which no other example, equally distinct, is to be found. (For Indian clanship, see "The Jesuits in North America," *Introduction*.) Among the Natchez and Taensas, the principal clan formed a ruling caste; and its chiefs had the attributes of demi-gods. As descent was through the female, the chief's son never succeeded him, but the son of one of his sisters; and as she, by the usual totemic law, was forced to marry in another clan,—that is, to marry a common mortal,—her husband, though the destined father of a demi-god, was treated by her as little better than a slave. She might kill him, if he proved unfaithful; but he was forced to submit to her infidelities in silence.

The customs of the Natchez have been described by Du Pratz, Le Petit, Penecaut, and others. Charlevoix visited their temple in 1721, and found it in a somewhat shabby condition. At this time, the Taensas were extinct. In 1729 the Natchez, enraged by the arbitrary conduct of a French commandant, massacred the neighboring settlers, and were in consequence expelled from their country and nearly destroyed. A few still survive, incorporated with the Creeks; but they have lost their peculiar customs.

[12] In St. Charles County, on the left bank, not far above New Orleans.

[13] Hennepin uses this incident, as well as most of those which have preceded it, in making up the story of his pretended voyage to the Gulf.

"In the name of the most high, mighty, invincible, and victorious Prince, Louis the Great, by the grace of God King of France and of Navarre, Fourteenth of that name, I, this ninth day of April, one thousand six hundred and eighty-two, in virtue of the commission of his Majesty, which I hold in my hand, and which may be seen by all whom it may concern, have taken, and do now take, in the name of his Majesty and of his successors to the crown, possession of this country of Louisiana, the seas, harbors, ports, bays, adjacent straits and all the nations, peoples, provinces, cities, towns, villages, mines, minerals, fisheries, streams, and rivers, within the extent of the said Louisiana, from the mouth of the great river St. Louis, otherwise called the Ohio, . . . as also along the river Colbert, or Mississippi, and the rivers which discharge themselves thereinto, from its source beyond the country of the Nadouessioux . . . as far as its mouth at the sea, or Gulf of Mexico, and also to the mouth of the River of Palms, upon the assurance we have had from the natives of these countries that we are the first Europeans who have descended or ascended the said river Colbert; hereby protesting against all who may hereafter undertake to invade any or all of these aforesaid countries, peoples, or lands, to the prejudice of the rights of his Majesty, acquired by the consent of the nations dwelling herein. Of which, and of all else that is needful, I hereby take to witness those who hear me, and demand an act of the notary here present."[14]

Shouts of *Vive le Roi* and volleys of musketry responded to his words. Then a cross was planted

beside the column, and a leaden plate buried near it, bearing the arms of France, with a Latin inscription, *Ludovicus Magnus regnat*. The weather-beaten voyagers joined their voices in the grand hymn of the *Vexilla Regis:*—

> "The banners of Heaven's King advance,
> The mystery of the Cross shines forth;"

and renewed shouts of *Vive le Roi* closed the ceremony.

On that day, the realm of France received on parchment a stupendous accession. The fertile plains of Texas; the vast basin of the Mississippi, from its frozen northern springs to the sultry borders of the Gulf; from the woody ridges of the Alleghanies to the bare peaks of the Rocky Mountains,—a region of savannas and forests, sun-cracked deserts, and grassy prairies, watered by a thousand rivers, ranged by a thousand warlike tribes, passed beneath the sceptre of the Sultan of Versailles; and all by virtue of a feeble human voice, inaudible at half a mile.

CHAPTER 27

1687: Assassination of La Salle

The travellers were crossing a marshy prairie towards a distant belt of woods, that followed the course of a little river. They led with them their five horses, laden with their scanty baggage, and, with what was of no less importance, their stock of presents for Indians. Some wore the remains of the clothing they had worn from France, eked out with deer-skins, dressed in the Indian manner; and some had coats of old sail-cloth. Here was La Salle, in whom one would have known, at a glance, the chief of the party; and the priest, Cavelier, who seems to have shared not one of the high traits of his younger brother. Here, too, were their nephews, Moranget and the boy Cavelier, now about seventeen years old; the trusty soldier Joutel; and the friar Anastase Douay. Duhaut followed, a man of respectable birth and education; and Liotot, the surgeon of the party. At home, they might perhaps have lived and died with a fair repute; but the wilderness is a rude touchstone, which often reveals traits that would have lain buried and unsuspected in civilized life. The German Hiens, the ex-buccaneer, was also of the number. He had probably sailed with an English crew; for he was sometimes

---

[14] In the passages omitted above, for the sake of brevity, the Ohio is mentioned as being called also the *Olighin-* (Alleghany) *Sipou,* and *Chukagoua;* and La Salle declares that he takes possession of the country with the consent of the nations dwelling in it, of whom he names the Chaouanons (Shawanoes), Kious, or Nadouessious (Sioux), Chikachas (Chickasaws), Motantees (?), Illinois, Mitchigamias, Arkansas, Natchez, and Koroas. This alleged consent is, of course, mere farce. If there could be any doubt as to the meaning of the words of La Salle, as recorded in the *Procès Verbal de la Prise de Possession de la Louisiane,* it would be set at rest by Le Clerc, who says: "Le Sieur de la Salle prit au nom de sa Majesté possession de ce fleuve, *de toutes les rivières qui y entrent, et de tous les pays qu'elles arrosent.*" These words are borrowed from the report of La Salle (see Thomassy, 14). A copy of the original *Procès Verbal* is before me. It bears the name of Jacques de la Metairie, Notary of Fort Frontenac, who was one of the party.

known as *Gemme Anglais,* or "English Jem."[1] The Sieur de Marle; Teissier, a pilot; L'Archevêque, a servant of Duhaut; and others, to the number in all of seventeen,—made up the party; to which is to be added Nika, La Salle's Shawanoe hunter, who, as well as another Indian, had twice crossed the ocean with him, and still followed his fortunes with an admiring though undemonstrative fidelity.

They passed the prairie, and neared the forest. Here they saw buffalo; and the hunters approached, and killed several of them. Then they traversed the woods; found and forded the shallow and rushy stream, and pushed through the forest beyond, till they again reached the open prairie. Heavy clouds gathered over them, and it rained all night; but they sheltered themselves under the fresh hides of the buffalo they had killed.

. . .

Holding a northerly course, the travellers crossed the Brazos, and reached the waters of the Trinity. The weather was unfavorable, and on one occasion they encamped in the rain during four or five days together. It was not an harmonious company. La Salle's cold and haughty reserve had returned, at least for those of his followers to whom he was not partial. Duhaut and the surgeon Liotot, both of whom were men of some property, had a large pecuniary stake in the enterprise, and were disappointed and incensed at its ruinous result. They had a quarrel with young Moranget, whose hot and hasty temper was as little fitted to conciliate as was the harsh reserve of his uncle. Already at Fort St. Louis, Duhaut had intrigued among the men; and the mild admonition of Joutel had not, it seems, sufficed to divert him from his sinister purposes. Liotot, it is said, had secretly sworn vengeance against La Salle, whom he charged with having caused the death of his brother, or, as some will have it, his nephew. On one of the former journeys this young man's strength had failed; and, La Salle having ordered him to return to the fort, he had been killed by Indians on the way.

The party moved again as the weather improved, and on the fifteenth of March encamped within a few miles of a spot which La Salle had passed on his preceding journey, and where he had left a quantity of Indian corn and beans in *cache;* that is to say, hidden in the ground or in a hollow tree. As provisions were falling short, he sent a party from the camp to find it. These men were Duhaut, Liotot,[2] Hiens the buccaneer, Teissier, L'Archevêque, Nika the hunter, and La Salle's servant Saget. They opened the *cache,* and found the contents spoiled; but as they returned from their bootless errand they saw buffalo, and Nika shot two of them. They now encamped on the spot, and sent the servant to inform La Salle, in order that he might send horses to bring in the meat. Accordingly, on the next day, he directed Moranget and De Marle, with the necessary horses, to go with Saget to the hunters' camp. When they arrived, they found that Duhaut and his companions had already cut up the meat, and laid it upon scaffolds for smoking, though it was not yet so dry as, it seems, this process required. Duhaut and the others had also put by, for themselves, the marrow-bones and certain portions of the meat, to which, by woodland custom, they had a perfect right. Moranget, whose rashness and violence had once before caused a fatal catastrophe, fell into a most unreasonable fit of rage, berated and menaced Duhaut and his party, and ended by seizing upon the whole of the meat, including the reserved portion. This added fuel to the fire of Duhaut's old grudge against Moranget and his uncle. There is reason to think that he had harbored deadly designs, the execution of which was only hastened by the present outbreak. The surgeon also bore hatred against Moranget, whom he had nursed with constant attention when wounded by an Indian arrow, and who had since repaid him with abuse. These two now took counsel apart with Hiens, Teissier, and L'Archevêque; and it was resolved to kill Moranget that night. Nika, La Salle's devoted follower, and Saget, his faithful servant, must die with him. All of the five were of one mind except the pilot Teissier, who neither aided nor opposed the plot.

Night came; the woods grew dark; the evening meal was finished, and the evening pipes were smoked. The order of the guard was arranged; and, doubtless by design, the first hour of the night was assigned to Moranget, the second to Saget, and the third to Nika. Gun in hand, each stood watch in turn over the silent but not sleeping forms around him, till, his time expiring, he called the man who was to relieve him, wrapped himself in his blanket, and was soon buried in a slumber that was to be his last. Now the assassins rose. Duhaut and Hiens stood with their guns cocked, ready to shoot down any one of the destined victims who should resist

---

[1] Tonty also speaks of him as "un flibustier anglois." In another document, he is called "James."

[2] Called Lanquetot by Tonty.

or fly. The surgeon, with an axe, stole towards the three sleepers, and struck a rapid blow at each in turn. Saget and Nika died with little movement; but Moranget started spasmodically into a sitting posture, gasping and unable to speak; and the murderers compelled De Marle, who was not in their plot, to compromise himself by despatching him.

The floodgates of murder were open, and the torrent must have its way. Vengeance and safety alike demanded the death of La Salle. Hiens, or "English Jem," alone seems to have hesitated; for he was one of those to whom that stern commander had always been partial. Meanwhile, the intended victim was still at his camp, about six miles distant. It is easy to picture, with sufficient accuracy, the features of the scene,—the sheds of bark and branches, beneath which, among blankets and buffalo-robes, camp-utensils, pack-saddles, rude harness, guns, powder-horns, and bullet-pouches the men lounged away the hour, sleeping or smoking, or talking among themselves; the blackened kettles that hung from tripods of poles over the fires; the Indians strolling about the place or lying, like dogs in the sun, with eyes half-shut, yet all observant; and, in the neighboring meadow, the horses grazing under the eye of a watchman.

It was the eighteenth of March. Moranget and his companions had been expected to return the night before; but the whole day passed, and they did not appear. La Salle became very anxious. He resolved to go and look for them; but not well knowing the way, he told the Indians who were about the camp that he would give them a hatchet if they would guide him. One of them accepted the offer; and La Salle prepared to set out in the morning, at the same time directing Joutel to be ready to go with him. Joutel says: "That evening, while we were talking about what could have happened to the absent men, he seemed to have a presentiment of what was to take place. He asked me if I had heard of any machinations against them, or if I had noticed any bad design on the part of Duhaut and the rest. I answered that I had heard nothing, except that they sometimes complained of being found fault with so often; and that this was all I knew; besides which, as they were persuaded that I was in his interest, they would not have told me of any bad design they might have. We were very uneasy all the rest of the evening."

In the morning, La Salle set out with his Indian guide. He had changed his mind with regard to Joutel, whom he now directed to remain in charge of the camp and to keep a careful watch. He told the friar Anastase Douay to come with him instead of Joutel, whose gun, which was the best in the party, he borrowed for the occasion, as well as his pistol. The three proceeded on their way,—La Salle, the friar, and the Indian. "All the way," writes the friar, "he spoke to me of nothing but matters of piety, grace, and predestination; enlarging on the debt he owed to God, who had saved him from so many perils during more than twenty years of travel in America. Suddenly, I saw him overwhelmed with a profound sadness, for which he himself could not account. He was so much moved that I scarcely knew him." He soon recovered his usual calmness; and they walked on till they approached the camp of Duhaut, which was on the farther side of a small river. Looking about him with the eye of a woodsman, La Salle saw two eagles circling in the air nearly over him, as if attracted by carcasses of beasts or men. He fired his gun and his pistol, as a summons to any of his followers who might be within hearing. The shots reached the ears of the conspirators. Rightly conjecturing by whom they were fired, several of them, led by Duhaut, crossed the river at a little distance above, where trees or other intervening objects hid them from sight. Duhaut and the surgeon crouched like Indians in the long, dry, reed-like grass of the last summer's growth, while L'Archevêque stood in sight near the bank. La Salle, continuing to advance, soon saw him, and, calling to him, demanded where was Moranget. The man, without lifting his hat, or any show of respect, replied in an agitated and broken voice, but with a tone of studied insolence, that Moranget was strolling about somewhere. La Salle rebuked and menaced him. He rejoined with increased insolence, drawing back, as he spoke, towards the ambuscade, while the incensed commander advanced to chastise him. At that moment a shot was fired from the grass, instantly followed by another; and, pierced through the brain, La Salle dropped dead.

The friar at his side stood terror-stricken, unable to advance or to fly; when Duhaut, rising from the ambuscade, called out to him to take courage, for he had nothing to fear. The murderers now came forward, and with wild looks gathered about their victim. "There thou liest, great Bashaw! There thou liest!"[3] exclaimed the surgeon Liotot, in base exultation over the unconscious corpse. With mockery and insult, they stripped it naked, dragged

---

[3] "Te voilà, grand Bacha, te voilà!"—Joutel, *Journal Historique*, 203.

it into the bushes, and left it there, a prey to the buzzards and the wolves.

Thus in the vigor of his manhood, at the age of forty-three, died Robert Cavelier de la Salle, "one of the greatest men," writes Tonty, "of this age;" without question one of the most remarkable explorers whose names live in history. His faithful officer Joutel thus sketches his portrait: "His firmness, his courage, his great knowledge of the arts and sciences, which made him equal to every undertaking, and his untiring energy, which enabled him to surmount every obstacle, would have won at last a glorious success for his grand enterprise, had not all his fine qualities been counterbalanced by a haughtiness of manner which often made him insupportable, and by a harshness towards those under his command which drew upon him an implacable hatred, and was at last the cause of his death."[4]

The enthusiasm of the disinterested and chivalrous Champlain was not the enthusiasm of La Salle; nor had he any part in the self-devoted zeal of the early Jesuit explorers. He belonged not to the age of the knight-errant and the saint, but to the modern world of practical study and practical action. He was the hero not of a principle nor of a faith, but simply of a fixed idea and a determined purpose. As often happens with concentred and energetic natures, his purpose was to him a passion and an inspiration; and he clung to it with a certain fanaticism of devotion. It was the offspring of an ambition vast and comprehensive, yet acting in the interest both of France and of civilization.

Serious in all things, incapable of the lighter pleasures, incapable of repose, finding no joy but in the pursuit of great designs, too shy for society and too reserved for popularity, often unsympathetic and always seeming so, smothering emotions which he could not utter, schooled to universal distrust, stern to his followers and pitiless to himself, bearing the brunt of every hardship and every danger, demanding of others an equal constancy joined to an implicit deference, heeding no counsel but his own, attempting the impossible and grasping at what was too vast to hold,—he contained in his own complex and painful nature the chief springs of his triumphs, his failures, and his death.

It is easy to reckon up his defects, but it is not easy to hide from sight the Roman virtues that redeemed them. Beset by a throng of enemies, he stands, like the King of Israel, head and shoulders above them all. He was a tower of adamant, against whose impregnable front hardship and danger, the rage of man and of the elements, the southern sun, the northern blast, fatigue, famine, disease, delay, disappointment, and deferred hope emptied their quivers in vain. That very pride which, Coriolanus-like, declared itself most sternly in the thickest press of foes, has in it something to challenge admiration. Never, under the impenetrable mail of paladin or crusader, beat a heart of more intrepid mettle than within the stoic panoply that armed the breast of La Salle. To estimate aright the marvels of his patient fortitude, one must follow on his track through the vast scene of his interminable journeyings,—those thousands of weary miles of forest, marsh, and river, where, again and again, in the bitterness of baffled striving, the untiring pilgrim pushed onward towards the goal which he was never to attain. America owes him an enduring memory; for in this masculine figure she sees the pioneer who guided her to the possession of her richest heritage.[5]

---

[4] *Ibid.*

[5] On the assassination of La Salle, the evidence is fourfold: 1. The narrative of Douay, who was with him at the time. 2. That of Joutel, who learned the facts, immediately after they took place, from Douay and others, and who parted from La Salle an hour or more before his death. 3. A document preserved in the Archives de la Marine, entitled *Relation de la Mort du Sr. de la Salle, suivant le rapport d'un nommé Couture à qui M. Cavelier l'apprit en passant au pays des Akansa, avec toutes les circonstances que le dit Couture a apprises d'un François que M. Cavelier avoit laissé aux dits pays des Akansa, crainte qu'il ne gardât pas le secret.* 4. The authentic memoir of Tonty, of which a copy from the original is before me, and which has recently been printed by Margry.

The narrative of Cavelier unfortunately fails us several weeks before the death of his brother, the remainder being lost. On a study of these various documents, it is impossible to resist the conclusion that neither Cavelier nor Douay always wrote honestly. Joutel, on the contrary, gives the impression of sense, intelligence, and candor throughout. Charlevoix, who knew him long after, says that he was "un fort honnête homme, et le seul de la troupe de M. de la Salle, sur qui ce célèbre voyageur pût compter." Tonty derived his information from the survivors of La Salle's party. Couture, whose statements are embodied in the *Relation de la Mort de M. de la Salle*, was one of Tonty's men, who, as will be seen hereafter, were left by him at the mouth of the Arkansas, and to whom Cavelier told the story of his brother's death. Couture also repeats the statements of one of La Salle's followers, undoubtedly a Parisian boy, named Barthelemy, who was violently prejudiced against his

From The Oregon Trail (1849)

THE CHASE

The country before us was now thronged with buffalo, and a sketch of the manner of hunting them will not be out of place. There are two methods commonly practised, "running" and "approaching." The chase on horseback, which goes by the name of "running," is the more violent and dashing mode of the two, that is to say, when the buffalo are in one of their wild moods; for otherwise it is tame enough. A practised and skilful hunter, well mounted, will sometimes kill five or six cows in a single chase, loading his gun again and again as his horse rushes through the tumult. In attacking a small band of buffalo, or in separating a single animal from the herd and assailing it apart from the rest, there is less excitement and less danger. In fact, the animals are at times so stupid and lethargic that there is little sport in killing them. With a bold and well-trained horse the hunter may ride so close to the buffalo that as they gallop side by side he may touch him with his hand; nor is there much danger in this as long as the buffalo's strength and breath continue unabated; but when

he becomes tired and can no longer run with ease, when his tongue lolls out and the foam flies from his jaws, then the hunter had better keep a more respectful distance; the distressed brute may turn upon him at any instant; and especially at the moment when he fires his gun. The horse then leaps aside, and the hunter has need of a tenacious seat in the saddle, for if he is thrown to the ground there is no hope for him. When he sees his attack defeated, the buffalo resumes his flight, but if the shot is well directed he soon stops; for a few moments he stands still, then totters and falls heavily upon the prairie.

The chief difficulty in running buffalo, as it seems to me, is that of loading the gun or pistol at full gallop. Many hunters for convenience's sake carry three or four bullets in the mouth; the powder is poured down the muzzle of the piece, the bullet dropped in after it, the stock struck hard upon the pommel of the saddle, and the work is done. The danger of this is obvious. Should the blow on the pommel fail to send the bullet home,

---

chief, whom he slanders to the utmost of his skill, saying that he was so enraged at his failures that he did not approach the sacraments for two years; that he nearly starved his brother Cavelier, allowing him only a handful of meal a day; that he killed with his own hand "quantité de personnes," who did not work to his liking; and that he killed the sick in their beds, without mercy, under the pretence that they were counterfeiting sickness in order to escape work. These assertions certainly have no other foundation than the undeniable rigor of La Salle's command. Douay says that he confessed and made his devotions on the morning of his death, while Cavelier always speaks of him as the hope and the staff of the colony.

Douay declares that La Salle lived an hour after the fatal shot; that he gave him absolution, buried his body, and planted a cross on his grave. At the time, he told Joutel a different story; and the latter, with the best means of learning the facts, explicitly denies the friar's printed statement. Couture, on the authority of Cavelier himself, also says that neither he nor Douay was permitted to take any step for burying the body. Tonty says that Cavelier begged leave to do so, but was refused. Douay, unwilling to place upon record facts from which the inference might easily be drawn that he had been terrified from discharging his duty, no doubt invented

the story of the burial, as well as that of the edifying behavior of Moranget, after he had been struck in the head with an axe.

The locality of La Salle's assassination is sufficiently clear, from a comparison of the several narratives; and it is also indicated on a contemporary manuscript map, made on the return of the survivors of the party to France. The scene of the catastrophe is here placed on a southern branch of the Trinity.

La Salle's debts, at the time of his death, according to a schedule presented in 1701 to Champigny, intendant of Canada, amounted to 106,831 livres, without reckoning interest. This cannot be meant to include all, as items are given which raise the amount much higher. In 1678 and 1679 alone, he contracted debts to the amount of 97,184 livres, of which 46,000 were furnished by Branssac, fiscal attorney of the Seminary of Montreal. This was to be paid in beaver-skins. Frontenac, at the same time, became his surety for 13,623 livres. In 1684, he borrowed 34,825 livres from the Sieur Pen, at Paris. These sums do not include the losses incurred by his family, which, in the memorial presented by them to the King, are set down at 500,000 livres for the expeditions between 1678 and 1683, and 300,000 livres for the fatal Texan expedition of 1684. These last figures are certainly exaggerated.

or should the bullet, in the act of aiming, start from its place and roll towards the muzzle, the gun would probably burst in discharging. Many a shattered hand and worse casualties besides have been the result of such an accident. To obviate it, some hunters make use of a ramrod, usually hung by a string from the neck, but this materially increases the difficulty of loading. The bows and arrows which the Indians use in running buffalo have many advantages over firearms, and even white men occasionally employ them.

The danger of the chase arises not so much from the onset of the wounded animal as from the nature of the ground which the hunter must ride over. The prairie does not always present a smooth, level, and uniform surface; very often it is broken with hills and hollows, intersected by ravines, and in the remoter parts studded by the stiff wild-sage bushes. The most formidable obstructions, however, are the burrows of wild animals, wolves, badgers, and particularly prairie-dogs, with whose holes the ground for a very great extent is frequently honey-combed. In the blindness of the chase the hunter rushes over it unconscious of danger; his horse, at full career, thrusts his leg deep into one of the burrows, the bone snaps, the rider is hurled forward to the ground and probably killed. Yet accidents in buffalo running happen less frequently than one would suppose; in the recklessness of the chase, the hunter enjoys all the impunity of a drunken man, and may ride in safety over gullies and declivities, where, should he attempt to pass in his sober senses, he would infallibly break his neck.

The method of "approaching," being practised on foot, has many advantages over that of "running"; in the former, one neither breaks down his horse nor endangers his own life; he must be cool, collected, and watchful; must understand the buffalo, observe the features of the country and the course of the wind, and be well skilled in using the rifle. The buffalo are strange animals; sometimes they are so stupid and infatuated that a man may walk up to them in full sight on the open prairie, and even shoot several of their number before the rest will think it necessary to retreat. At another moment they will be so shy and wary that in order to approach them the utmost skill, experience, and judgment are necessary. Kit Carson, I believe, stands pre-eminent in running buffalo; in approaching, no man living can bear away the palm from Henry Chatillon.

After Tête Rouge had alarmed the camp, no further disturbance occurred during the night. The Arapahoes did not attempt mischief, or if they did the wakefulness of the party deterred them from effecting their purpose. The next day was one of activity and excitement, for about ten o'clock the man in advance shouted the gladdening cry of *buffalo, buffalo!* and in the hollow of the prairie just below us, a band of bulls was grazing. The temptation was irresistible, and Shaw and I rode down upon them. We were badly mounted on our travelling horses, but by hard lashing we overtook them, and Shaw, running alongside a bull, shot into him both balls of his doubled-barrelled gun. Looking round as I galloped by, I saw the bull in his mortal fury rushing again and again upon his antagonist, whose horse constantly leaped aside, and avoided the onset. My chase was more protracted, but at length I ran close to the bull and killed him with my pistols. Cutting off the tails of our victims by way of trophy, we rejoined the party in about a quarter of an hour after we had left it. Again and again that morning rang out the same welcome cry of *buffalo, buffalo!* Every few moments, in the broad meadows along the river, we saw bands of bulls, who, raising their shaggy heads, would gaze in stupid amazement at the approaching horsemen, and then breaking into a clumsy gallop, file off in a long line across the trail in front, towards the rising prairie on the left. At noon, the plain before us was alive with thousands of buffalo,—bulls, cows, and calves,—all moving rapidly as we drew near; and far off beyond the river the swelling prairie was darkened with them to the very horizon. The party was in gayer spirits than ever. We stopped for a nooning near a grove of trees by the river.

"Tongues and hump-ribs tomorrow," said Shaw, looking with contempt at the venison steaks which Deslauriers placed before us. Our meal finished, we lay down to sleep. A shout from Henry Chatillon aroused us, and we saw him standing on the cart-wheel, stretching his tall figure to its full height, while he looked towards the prairie beyond the river. Following the direction of his eyes, we could clearly distinguish a large, dark object, like the black shadow of a cloud, passing rapidly over swell after swell of the distant plain; behind it followed another of similar appearance, though smaller, moving more rapidly, and drawing closer and closer to the first. It was the hunters of the Arapahoe camp chasing a band of buffalo. Shaw and I caught and saddled our best horses, and went plunging through sand and water to the farther bank. We were too late. The hunters had already mingled with the herd, and the work of slaughter was nearly over. When we reached the ground we found it strewn far and near with numberless carcasses, while the remnants of the herd, scattered in all directions, were flying away in terror, and the Indians still rushing in pursuit. Many of the hunters, however, remained upon the spot, and among the rest was our yesterday's acquaintance, the chief of the village. He had alighted by the side of a cow, into which he had shot five or six arrows, and his squaw, who had followed him on horseback to the hunt, was giving him a draught of water from a canteen, purchased or plundered from some volunteer soldier. Recrossing the river, we overtook the party, who were already on their way.

We had gone scarcely a mile when we saw an imposing spectacle. From the river-bank on the right, away over the swelling prairie on the left, and in front as far as the eye could reach, was one vast host of buffalo. The outskirts of the herd were within a quarter of a mile. In many parts they were crowded so densely together that in the distance their rounded backs presented a surface of uniform blackness; but elsewhere they were more scattered, and from amid the multitude rose little columns of dust where some of them were rolling on the ground. Here and there a battle was going forward among the bulls. We could distinctly see them rushing against each other, and hear the clattering of their horns and their hoarse bellowing. Shaw was riding at some distance in advance, with Henry Chatillon; I saw him stop and draw the leather covering from his gun. With such a sight before us, but one thing could be thought of. That morning I had used pistols in the chase. I had now a mind to try the virtue of a gun. Deslauriers had one, and I rode up to the side of the cart; there he sat under the white covering, biting his pipe between his teeth and grinning with excitement.

"Lend me your gun, Deslauriers."

"*Oui, Monsieur, oui,*" said Deslauriers, tugging with might and main to stop the mule, which seemed obstinately bent on going forward. Then everything but his moccasons disappeared as he crawled into the cart and pulled at the gun to extricate it.

"Is it loaded?" I asked.

"*Oui, bien chargé;* you 'll kill, *mon bourgeois;* yes, you 'll kill—*c'est un bon fusil.*"

I handed him my rifle and rode forward to Shaw.

"Are you ready?" he asked.

"Come on," said I.

"Keep down that hollow," said Henry, "and then they won't see you till you get close to them."

The hollow was a kind of wide ravine; it ran obliquely towards the buffalo, and we rode at a canter along the bottom until it became too shallow; then we bent close to our horses' necks, and, at last, finding that it could no longer conceal us, came out of it and rode directly towards the herd. It was within gunshot; before its outskirts, numerous grizzly old bulls were scattered, holding guard over their females. They glared at us in anger and astonishment, walked towards us a few yards, and then turning slowly round, retreated at a trot which afterwards broke into a clumsy gallop. In an instant the main body caught the alarm. The buffalo began to crowd away from the point towards which we were approaching, and a gap was opened in the side of the herd. We entered it, still restraining our excited horses. Every instant the tumult was thickening. The buffalo, pressing together in large bodies, crowded away from us on every hand. In front and on either side we could see dark columns and masses, half hidden by clouds of dust, rushing along in terror and confusion, and hear the tramp and clattering of ten thousand hoofs. That countless multitude of powerful brutes, ignorant of their own strength, were flying in a panic from the approach of two feeble horsemen. To remain quiet longer was impossible.

"Take that band on the left," said Shaw; "I'll take these in front."

He sprang off, and I saw no more of him. A heavy Indian whip was fastened by a band to my wrist; I swung it into the air and lashed my horse's flank with all the strength of my arm. Away she darted, stretching close to the ground. I could see nothing but a cloud of dust before me, but I knew that it concealed a band of many hundreds of buffalo. In a moment I was in the midst of the cloud, half suffocated by the dust and stunned by the trampling of the flying herd; but I was drunk with the chase and cared for nothing but the buffalo. Very soon a long dark mass became visible, looming through the dust; then I could distinguish each bulky carcass, the hoofs flying out beneath, the short tails held rigidly erect. In a moment I was so close that I could have touched them with my gun. Suddenly, to my amazement, the hoofs were jerked upwards, the tails flourished in the air, and amid a cloud of dust the buffalo seemed to sink into the earth before me. One vivid impression of that instant remains upon my mind. I remember looking down upon the backs of several buffalo dimly visible through the dust. We had run unawares upon a ravine. At that moment I was not the most accurate judge of depth and width, but when I passed it on my return, I found it about twelve feet deep and not quite twice as wide at the bottom. It was impossible to stop; I would have done so gladly if I could; so, half sliding, half plunging, down went the little mare. She came down on her knees in the loose sand at the bottom; I was pitched forward against her neck and nearly thrown over her head among the buffalo, who amid dust and confusion came tumbling in all around. The mare was on her feet in an instant and scrambling like a cat up the opposite side. I thought for a moment that she would have fallen back and crushed me, but with a violent effort she clambered out and gained the hard prairie above. Glancing back, I saw the huge head of a bull clinging as it were by the forefeet at the edge of the dusty gulf. At length I was fairly among the buffalo. They were less densely crowded than before, and I could see nothing but bulls, who always run at the rear of a herd to protect their females. As I passed among them they would lower their heads, and turning as they ran, try to gore my horse; but as they were already at full speed there was no force in their onset, and as Pauline ran faster than they, they were always thrown behind her in the effort. I soon began to distinguish cows amid the throng. One just in front of me seemed to my liking, and I pushed close to her side. Dropping the reins, I fired, holding the muzzle of the gun within a foot of her shoulder. Quick as lightning she sprang at Pauline; the little mare dodged the attack, and I lost sight of the wounded animal amid the tumult. Immediately after, I selected another, and urging forward Pauline, shot into her both pistols in succession. For a while I kept her in view, but in attempting to load my gun, lost sight of her also in the confusion. Believing her to be mortally wounded and unable to keep up with the herd, I checked my horse. The crowd rushed onwards. The dust and tumult passed away, and on the prairie, far behind the rest, I saw a solitary buffalo galloping heavily. In a moment I and my victim were running side by side. My firearms were all empty, and I had in my pouch nothing but rifle bullets, too large for the pistols and too small for

the gun. I loaded the gun, however, but as often as I levelled it to fire, the bullets would roll out of the muzzle and the gun returned only a report like a squib, as the powder harmlessly exploded. I rode in front of the buffalo and tried to turn her back; but her eyes glared, her mane bristled, and lowering her head, she rushed at me with the utmost fierceness and activity. Again and again I rode before her, and again and again she repeated her furious charge. But little Pauline was in her element. She dodged her enemy at every rush, until at length the buffalo stood still, exhausted with her own efforts, her tongue lolling from her jaws.

Riding to a little distance, I dismounted, thinking to gather a handful of dry grass to serve the purpose of wadding, and load the gun at my leisure. No sooner were my feet on the ground than the buffalo came bounding in such a rage towards me that I jumped back again into the saddle and with all possible despatch. After waiting a few minutes more, I made an attempt to ride up and stab her with my knife; but Pauline was near being gored in the attempt. At length, bethinking me of the fringes at the seams of my buckskin trousers, I jerked off a few of them, and, reloading the gun, forced them down the barrel to keep the bullet in its place; then approaching, I shot the wounded buffalo through the heart. Sinking to her knees, she rolled over lifeless on the prairie. To my astonishment, I found that, instead of a cow, I had been slaughtering a stout yearling bull. No longer wondering at his fierceness, I opened his throat, and cutting out his tongue, tied it at the back of my saddle. My mistake was one which a more experienced eye than mine might easily make in the dust and confusion of such a chase.

Then for the first time I had leisure to look at the scene around me. The prairie in front was darkened with the retreating multitude, and on either hand the buffalo came filing up in endless columns from the low plains upon the river. The Arkansas was three or four miles distant. I turned and moved slowly towards it. A long time passed before, far in the distance, I distinguished the white covering of the cart and the little black specks of horsemen before and behind it. Drawing near, I recognized Shaw's elegant tunic, the red flannel shirt, conspicuous far off. I overtook the party, and asked him what success he had had. He had assailed a fat cow, shot her with two bullets, and mortally wounded her. But neither of us was prepared for the chase that afternoon, and Shaw, like myself, had no spare bullets in his pouch; so he abandoned the disabled animal to Henry Chatillon, who followed, despatched her with his rifle, and loaded his horse with meat.

We encamped close to the river. The night was dark, and as we lay down we could hear, mingled with the howling of wolves, the hoarse bellowing of the buffalo, like the ocean beating upon a distant coast.

Folk Songs of the White People

The various people who came to America brought their own folk music and folk songs with them. For instance, we know that the skippers of slavers, in an effort to keep a cargo healthy, would force their captives to dance and sing on deck, sometimes under the lash—though we do not know what songs they sang in this therapy. Nor do we know what songs Cotton Mather referred to, in his diary of 1713, when he complained that "the Minds and Manners of many people about the Countrey are much corrupted by foolish Songs and Ballads, which the Hawkers and Peddlars carry into all parts of the Countrey." It is not remarkable that we do not know what songs the hapless Africans sang, for in the slavery system deliberate efforts were made to sever connections with the tribal past; but even if we do not know what songs Cotton Mather complained of, there was a body of traditional white folk songs that survived in America, especially the English and Scottish ballads in the southern mountains.

It is in the very nature of folk song, depending on oral transmission, to be unstable. Lapses of memory and impulses to originality collaborate to bring changes. But the life of folk song demands not only the preservation of the traditional, but also the creation of the new; and since folk song, especially balladry, springs from the immediate texture of life, from what is generally interesting and moving, the new life in America would eventually lead not only to changes in the traditional songs, but to the creation of new ones. We can see the changes in the traditional ballads—for instance, in "Edward," "Barbara Allen," and "The Hangsman's Tree," which have come a long way from their original versions. But until the late eighteenth century we have little surviving of new creations. One of these surviving items, though not the earliest, is "Springfield Mountain," which commemorates a tragic event of 1761 and which charms us only by its touching ineptitude.

The greatest number of new folk songs among white people, which is our present topic, appeared after the Civil War, often the natural product of special ways of life, such as riding the range, lumbering, or railroading; but even in the earlier part of the century there had been an increasing number, from plantations, from the keelboats, from whalers, from the stage of minstrel shows, and from the battlefields of the Civil War.

The fact that some of the folk songs did come from the stage seems, at first glance, odd, but we should remember that the characteristic mark of folk song is not the origin but the way of survival of the work. The folk song is a composition that appeals to the folk, that enters the popular imagination and survives there, that is transmitted in oral tradition. The song "The Hunters of Kentucky," sung by an entertainer named Nook in a coonskin cap, before an audience in New Orleans, became part of the atmosphere of the Crockett legend; "The Ballad of Davy Crockett" is a song from black-face minstrel that entered folklore; "Dixie," to which many thousands of men marched to their death, was also composed by a professional songwriter for the minstrel stage and was first sung in New York City. One of the most durable and absurdly sentimental ballads of the period, "Young Charlotte," was written and printed by the same Seba Smith whom we already know as the father of Jack Downing.

The compositions just mentioned have rather sophisticated origins, but, of course, many folk songs do spring from authors who belong to, and are lost in, the simple world that adopts and transmits the song. But even here, no matter how much improvisation and tampering may change a composition, we are, in general, still indebted to some individual author or authors, and not to some mystical communal process among the "folk." For instance, in *Ballad Makin' in the Mountains of Kentucky*, the author, Jeannette Thomas, tells of a blind man named Jilson who made his living by composing ballads and quotes his account of how he attended a public hanging with his pockets full of copies of a new ballad devised for the occasion, much as Elizabethan makers of broadside ballads would have done under similar circumstances: "I had my pockets plum full of my song-ballet that I had made up about Bush (the condemned man) and that a printer had run off for me on a little hand press at the county seat. I sold every one I had." True, Jilson is of this century, and not every maker of ballads or songs carries his wares for sale, but the principle is the same for the past.

FURTHER READINGS

B. A. Botkin, *Treasury of American Folklore* (1944)

Theron Brown and Hezekiel Butterworth, *The Story of the Hymns* (1906)

Helen Flanders, *Ballads Migrant in New England* (1953)

H. H. Fuson, *Ballads of the Kentucky Highlands* (1931)

G. P. Jackson, *Spiritual Folk-Songs of Early America* (1937)

————, *White Spirituals in the Southern Uplands* (1937)

George S. Jackson, *Early Songs of Uncle Sam* (1933)

Eloise H. Linscott, *Folk Songs of Old New England* (1962)

Alan Lomax, *Folk Songs of North America* (1960)

John A. Lomax and Alan Lomax, *American Ballads and Folk Songs* (1934)

———, *Our Singing Country* (1941)
Frank Luther, *Americans and Their Songs* (1942)
Jeannette Robinson Murphy, *Southern Thoughts for Northern Thinkers*
Jean Ritchie, *Singing Family of the Cumberlands* (1955)
Carl Sandburg, *The American Songbag* (1927)

Dorothy Scarborough, *A Song Catcher in the Southern Mountains* (1937)
Cecil Sharp, *English Folk Songs from the Southern Appalachians* (1932)
Jeannette Thomas, *Ballad Makin' in the Mountains of Kentucky* (1939)

Bonny Barbara Allen

It was upon a high, high hill,
Two maidens chose their dwelling,
And one was known both far and wide,
Was known as Barb'ra Allen.

'Twas in the merry month of May,
All the flowers blooming,
A young man on his deathbed lay,
For the love of Barb'ra Allen.

He sent a servant unto her
In the town where she was dwelling.
"Come, Miss, O Miss to my master dying
If your name be Barb'ra Allen!"

Slowly, slowly she got up,
And to his bedside going;
She drew the curtain to one side
And said, "Young man you're dying."

He stretched one pale hand to her
As though he would to touch her.
She hopped and skipped across the floor.
"Young man," says, "I won't have you."

"Remember, 'member in the town,
'Twas in the tavern drinking,
You drank a health to the ladies all
But you slighted Barb'ra Allen."

He turned his face toward the wall,
His back upon his darling.

"I know I shall see you no more,
So goodbye, Barb'ra Allen."

As she was going to her home,
She heard the church bell tolling.
She looked to the east and looked to the west,
And saw the corpse a-coming.

"O hand me down that corpse of clay
That I may look upon it.
I might have saved that young man's life,
If I had done my duty.

"O mother, mother, make my bed;
O make it long and narrow.
Sweet William died for me today,
I shall die for him tomorrow."

Sweet William died on a Saturday night,
And Barb'ra Allen on a Sunday.
The old lady died for the love of them both,
She died on Easter morning.

Sweet William was buried in one graveyard,
Barb'ra Allen in another;
A rose grew on Sweet William's grave
And a brier on Barb'ra Allen's.

They grew and they grew to the steeple top,
And there they grew no higher;
And there they tied in a true-lover knot,
The rose clung 'round the brier.

The Hangsman's Tree

"Slack your rope, hangsaman,
O slack it for a while;
I think I see my father coming,
Riding many a mile.
O, father, have you brought me gold?
Or have you paid my fee?
Or have you come to see me hanging
On the gallows tree?"
"I have not brought you gold;
I have not paid your fee;

But I have come to see you hanging
On the gallows tree."

"Slack your hope, hangsaman,
O slack it for a while;
I think I see my mother[1] coming," etc.
"Slack your rope, hangsaman,
O slack it for a while;
I think I see my true love coming," etc.

[1] And other relatives for subsequent stanzas.

"Yes, I have brought you gold;
Yes, I have paid your fee;

Nor have I come to see you hanging
On the gallows tree."

The Cruel Mother

There was a lady near the town,
Low, so low and so lonely,
She walked all night and all around,
Down in the green woods of Iv'ry.

She had two pretty little babes,
Low, so low and so lonely,
She thought one day she'd take their lives,
Down in the green woods of Iv'ry.

She got a rope so long and neat,
And tied them down both hands and feet.

She got a knife so keen and sharp,

And pierced it through each tender heart.

Then she went out one moonlit night;
She saw two babes all dressed in white.

O babes, O babes, if you were mine,
I'd dress you up in silk so fine.

O mamma, O mamma, when we were yours,
You dressed us in our own heart's blood.

In seven years you'll hear a bell,
In seven years you'll land in hell.

Edward

How come that blood on the point of your knife?
My son, come tell to me.
It is the blood of my old coon dog
That chased the fox for me, me, me,
That chased the fox for me.

How come that blood, etc.
It is the blood of that old horse
That ploughed that field for me, etc.

How come that blood, etc.
It is the blood of one of my brothers
Which fell out with me, etc.

What did you fall out about?
We fell out about a holly-bush

That would have made a tree, etc.

What will you do when your father comes home?
I'll put my foot in a bunkum boat
And sail across the sea.

What will you do with your dear little wife?
I'll put her foot in a bunkum boat
And sail across the sea.

What will you do with your dear little babe?
I'll leave it here in this lone world
To dandle on your knee.

And what will you do with your old gobbler?
I'll leave it here with you when I'm gone
To gobble after me.

Black Is the Color

But black is the color of my true love's hair,
His face is like some rosy fair;
The prettiest face and neatest hands,
I love the ground whereon he stands.

I love my love and well he knows
I love the ground whereon he goes.
If you no more on earth I see,
I can't serve you as you have me.

The winter's passed and the leaves are green,
The time is passed that we have seen,

But still I hope the time will come
When you and I shall be as one.

I go to the Clyde for to mourn and weep,
But satisfied I never could sleep.
I'll write to you in a few short lines,
I'll suffer death ten thousand times.

So fare you well, my own true love,
The time has passed, but I wish you well;
But still I hope the time will come
When you and I will be as one.

I love my love and well he knows,
I love the ground whereon he goes;

The prettiest face, the neatest hands,
I love the ground whereon he stands.

The Ballad of Davy Crockett

"The Ballad of Davy Crockett" was originally a Negro minstrel song, "Pompey Smash," which entered into folk currency.

Now, don't you want to know something concernin'
Where it was I come from and where I got my learnin'?
Oh, the world is made of mud out o' the Mississippi River!
The sun's a ball of foxfire, as well you may disciver.

Chorus:
> Take the ladies out at night. They shine so bright
> They make the world light when the moon is out of sight.

And so one day as I was goin' a-spoonin'
I met Colonel Davy, and he was goin' a-coonin'.
Says I, "Where's your gun?" "I ain' got none."
"How you goin' kill a coon when you haven't got a gun?"

Says he, "Pompcalf, just follow after Davy,
And he'll soon show you how to grin a coon crazy."
I followed on a piece and thar sot a squirrel,
A-settin' on a log and a-eatin' sheep sorrel.

When Davy did that see, he looked around at me,
Saying, "All I want now is a brace agin your knee."
And thar I braced a great big sinner.

He grinned six times hard enough to git his dinner!

The critter on the log didn't seem to mind him—
Jest kep' a-settin' thar and wouldn't look behind him
Then it was he said, "The critter must be dead.
See the bark a-flyin' all around the critter's head?"

I walked right up the truth to disciver.
Drot! It was a pine knot so hard it made me shiver.
Says he, "Pompcalf, don't you begin to laugh—
I'll pin back your ears, and bite you half in half!"

I flung down my gun and all my ammunition.
Says I, "Davy Crockett, I can cool your ambition!"
He throwed back his head and he blowed like a steamer.
Says he, "Pompcalf, I'm a Tennessee screamer!"

Then we locked horns and we wallered in the thorns.
I never had such a fight since the hour I was born.
We fought a day and a night and then agreed to drop it.
I was purty badly whipped—and so was Davy Crockett.

I looked all around and found my head a-missin'—
He'd bit off my head and I had swallered his'n!
Then we did agree to let each other be;
I was too much for him, and he was too much for me.

The Hunters of Kentucky

On January 8, 1815, the deadly long rifle in the hands of the Kentucky militia slaughtered General Packenham's redcoats as they held ranks and marched, stolid and blunt-nosed, toward Andrew Jackson's cotton bales. None of them got there. Behind the cotton bales only eight men died.

Daniel Boone had elevated the Kentucky hunter to the level of legend, and the cold-blooded efficiency of the Kentuckians at the battle of New Orleans gave the legend confirmation. (See Audubon's "Kentucky Sports," p. 1066.) By 1822, appropriately in New Orleans,

the legend achieved literary form in the song that the entertainer Noah Ludlow sang to a rowdy and riffraff audience who knew what he was singing about.

Ye gentlemen and ladies fair
Who grace this famous city,
Just listen if you've time to spare,
While I rehearse a ditty;
And for the opportunity
Conceive yourselves quite lucky,
For 'tis not often that you see

A hunter from Kentucky.

Chorus:

Oh! Kentucky, the hunters of Kentucky,
Oh! Kentucky, the hunters of Kentucky.

We are a hardy, free-born race,
Each man to fear a stranger;
Whate'er the game we join in chase,
Despising time and danger;
And if a daring foe annoys,
Whate'er his strength and forces,
We'll show him that Kentucky boys
Are alligator horses.

You've heard, I s'pose, how New Orleans
Is fam'd for wealth and beauty—
There's girls of every hue it seems,
From snowy-white to sooty.
So Packenham he made his brags,
If he in fight was lucky,
He'd have their girls and cotton bags,
In spite of old Kentucky.

But Jackson he was wide awake
And was not scar'd at trifles;
For well he knew what aim we take
With our Kentucky rifles.
So he led us down to Cypress swamp—
The ground was low and mucky;

There stood John Bull in martial pomp
And here was old Kentucky!

A bank was rais'd to hide our breasts,
(Not that we thought of dying!)
But that we always like to rest
Unless the game is flying;
Behind it stood our little force—
None wished it to be greater;
For ev'ry man was half a horse,
And half an alligator.

They did not let our patience tire
Before they show'd their faces—
We did not choose to waste our fire,
So snugly kept our places;
But when so near we saw them wink,
We thought it time to stop 'em;
And 'twould have done you good I think
To see Kentuckians drop 'em.

They found, at last, 'twas vain to fight,
Where lead was all the booty;
And so they wisely took to flight,
And left us all our beauty.
And now, if danger e'er annoys,
Remember what our trade is;
Just send for us Kentucky boys,
And we'll protect you, ladies.

Sourwood Mountain

Chickens a-crowin' on Sourwood Mountain,
Chickens a-crowin' on Sourwood Mountain,
Call up yore dogs and let's go a-huntin',
Hey-ho, dee-iddle-um-day.

My true love lives over the river,
A few more jumps and I'll be with her.

My true love is a blue-eyed daisy,
Ef I don' git her, I'll go crazy.

My true love lives at the head of the holler,

She won't come and I won't foller.

My true love lives over the ocean,
I'll go to see her, if I take a notion.

Say, old man, I want yore daughter,
To wash my clothes and carry my water.

Fifteen cents, a dollar and a quarter,
Say, young man, take her if you want her.

Ducks in the pond, geese in the ocean,
Devil's in the women if they take a notion.

Oh, Lovely Appearance of Death

George Whitefield, who was a graduate of Cambridge University, one of the founders (with John and Charles Wesley) of Methodism, and the first circuit rider in the colonies, wrote

"Oh, Lovely Appearance of Death" to be sung at his own funeral. He died in 1770, but the song continued in use and in many communities it has passed into the realm of the folk. We may remark that Phillis Wheatley, the first black poet in America (see pp. 199–200), wrote an elegy on Whitefield.

Oh, lovely appearance of death,
What sight upon earth is so fair?
Not all the gay pageants that breathe
Can with a dead body compare.
In solemn delight I survey
A corpse when the spirit is fled,

In love with the beautiful clay,
And longing to lie in its stead.

Its languishing pain is at rest,
Its aching and aching are o'er;
The quiet immovable breast
Is pained by affliction no more.
The heart it no longer receives
Of trouble and torturing pain;
It ceases to flutter and beat,
It never shall flutter again.

Yankee Doodle

The origin of the song is uncertain but it probably dates to the French and Indian War and expresses the British regulars' contempt for the colonials. It appeared in print in Glasgow as early as 1782, but it had long since taken its place in American life and history. When, on the night of April 18, 1775, the British marched out from Boston on their unwitting way to their discomfiture at Concord Bridge, they stepped to this tune, but the colonials, ironically inverting the derision, sang it as they harried the redcoats on their return journey.

Father and I went down to camp,
Along with Captain Gooding;
And there we saw the men and boys,
As thick as hasty pudding.

Chorus:
> Yankee doodle, keep it up,
> Yankee doodle dandy;
> Mind the music and the step,
> And with the girls be handy.

There was Captain Washington
Upon a slapping stallion,
A-giving orders to his men,
I guess there was a million.

And then the feathers on his hat,
They looked so 'tarnal fin-a,
I wanted pockily to get
To give to my Jemima.

And then we saw a swamping gun,
Large as a log of maple;

Upon a deucèd little cart,
A load for father's cattle.

And every time they shoot it off,
It takes a horn of powder;
It makes a noise like father's gun,
Only a nation louder.

I went as nigh to one myself,
As 'Siah's underpinning;
And father went as nigh ag'in,
I thought the deuce was in him.

We saw a little barrel, too,
The heads were made of leather;
They knocked upon it with little clubs,
And called the folks together.

And there they'd fife away like fun,
And play on cornstalk fiddles,
And some had ribbons red as blood,
All bound around their middles.

The troopers, too, would gallop up
And fire right in our faces;
It scared me almost to death
To see them run such races.

Uncle Sam came there to change
Some pancakes and some onions,
For 'lasses cake to carry home
To give his wife and young ones.

But I can't tell half I see,
They kept up such a smother;
So I took my hat off, made a bow,
And scampered home to mother.

Cousin Simon grew so bold,
I thought he would have cocked it;
It scared me so I streaked it off,
And hung by father's pocket.

And there I saw a pumpkin shell,
As big as mother's basin;
And every time they touched it off,
They scampered like the nation.

Yankee doodle, keep it up,
Yankee doodle dandy;
Mind the music and the step,
And with the girls be handy.

John Brown's Body

John Brown's body lies a-mold'ring in the grave,
John Brown's body lies a-mold'ring in the grave,
John Brown's body lies a-mold'ring in the grave,
His soul is marching on.

Chorus:
> Glory, glory, hallelujah!
> Glory, glory, hallelujah!
> Glory, glory, hallelujah!
> His soul is marching on!

The stars of heaven are looking kindly down,
On the grave of old John Brown.

He's gone to be a soldier in the army of the Lord,
His soul is marching on.

John Brown died that the slave might be free,
But his soul goes marching on.

He captured Harper's Ferry with his nineteen men
    so true,
And he frightened old Virginia till she trembled
    through and through;
They hung him for a traitor, themselves the traitor
    crew,
But his soul goes marching on.

John Brown's knapsack is strapped to his back,
His soul is marching on.

His pet lambs will meet on the way,
And they'll go marching on.

They will hang Jeff Davis on a sour apple tree,
As they go marching on.

Now has come the glorious jubilee,
When all mankind are free.

I'm a Good Old Rebel

O I'm a good old rebel,
Now that's just what I am;
For the "fair land of freedom,"
I do not care a damn;
I'm glad I fit against it,
I only wish we'd won,
And I don't want no pardon,
For anything I done.

I hate the Constitution,
This great republic too;
I hate the freedman's buro,
In uniforms of blue.
I hate the nasty eagle,
With all his brags and fuss;
The lyin' thievin' Yankees,
I hate 'em wuss and wuss.

I hate the Yankee nation
And everything they do;
I hate the Declaration
Of Independence, too.
I hate the glorious Union,
'T is dripping with our blood;

I hate the striped banner,
I fit it all I could.

I followed old Marse Robert
For four years near about,
Got wounded in three places,
And starved on Point Lookout.
I cotch the roomatism
A-campin' in the snow,
But if I killed a chance of Yankees,
I'd like to kill some mo'.

Three hundred thousand Yankees
Is stiff in Southern dust;
We got three hundred thousand
Before they conquered us;
They died of Southern fever,
And Southern steel and shot,
I wish it was three million
Instead of what we got.

I can't take up my musket
And fight 'em now no more;

But I ain't a-goin' to love 'em,
Now that is certain sure.
And I don't want no pardon

For what I was and am;
I won't be reconstructed,
And I don't give a damn.

The Rebel Soldier, or The Poor Stranger

It's grape shot and musket, and the cannons lumber
    loud;
There's a many a mangled body, the blanket for
    their shroud,
There's a many a mangled body left on the fields
    alone,
I am a rebel soldier and far from my home.

O Polly, O Polly, it's for your sake alone
I've left my old father, my country and my home;
I've left my old mother to weep and to mourn,
I am a rebel soldier and far from my home.

I'll eat when I am hungry, I'll drink when I am dry,
If the Yankees don't kill me I'll live until I die;
If the Yankees don't kill me and cause me to
    mourn,

I am a rebel soldier and far from my home.

Here's a good old cup of brandy and a glass of nice
    wine,
You can drink to your true love and I will drink
    to mine;
And you can drink to your true love and I'll lament
    and mourn,
I am a rebel soldier and far from my home.

I'll build me a castle on the mountain, on some
    green mountain high,
Where I can see Polly as she is passing by;
Where I can see Polly and help her to mourn.
I am a rebel soldier and far from my home.

FRANCIS SCOTT KEY (1779–1843)

Francis Scott Key, born in Maryland to a family of cultivation, wealth, and influential connections, became, by the age of thirty, a successful lawyer in the raw new capital city of the nation. He was a versifier of sorts, as many young men of his time, class, and education were, but had no literary ambitions. He stumbled into immortality with "The Star-Spangled Banner," in a battle in a war of which he thoroughly disapproved and in which he did not serve until his native state was under immediate threat.

The War of 1812 was unpopular, with the country plagued by dissension, defeatism, and the fear that the young nation itself was about to crack up in its first major trial. New England, in fact, was on the verge of secession. The situation was aggravated by the fact that the war had gone badly from the first. Except for a few victories at sea, the military picture

was generally distressing, and when, in 1814, after a confused and pusillanimous defense, Washington fell and the Capitol was burned, all seemed over. The British fleet, transporting troops, moved on to occupy Baltimore, where Vice Admiral Cochrane had declared he would set up winter quarters. At this juncture, Key, with another officer, who had come out under a white flag to treat concerning the release of a certain Dr. Beane, was himself held on the frigate *Surprize* until the action should be over.

But Baltimore was not Washington. British attacks by land were frustrated, and Major Armistead, commander of Fort McHenry, acting against direct orders from Madison's administration to surrender the fort to save the city, undertook to hold off the fleet. On the morning of September 13, the British, with nearly forty vessels, began a massive bombardment that continued through the night. Key, on board the low cartel[1] boat in which he had come, now in tow to the *Surprize*, could not even see the fort, only the flag flying above it.

The climax came when, at dawn on September 14, an assault party was nearly annihilated. At this point, as the guns from the fort were wreaking destruction, Key began putting lines down on the back of an envelope. The battle was soon over, the British drew away, and on the cartel boat on the way to the shore Key finished the draft, making a final copy that night in a hotel in Baltimore. The next day, a friend carried it to the office of the Baltimore *American*, where a fourteen-year-old apprentice, Samuel Sands, ran off a handbill for general distribution. The poem appeared under the title "Defense of Fort McHenry," unsigned.

The form of the poem and the tune to which it was soon being sung were derived from "To Anacreon in Heaven," a drinking song with the refrain, "The myrtle of Venus with Bacchus' vine," which had been composed in 1778 for a club of gay blades in London, the Anacreontic Society. Some years later, Tom Paine had adapted the form and the tune for a patriotic composition; and Key had followed suit with another. So the speed with which Key composed the "Defense" was not altogether remarkable; the pattern was already in his head.

By 1815 the title as we now know it had

appeared on the first sheet-music form of the composition. But Key's name did not then appear and for half a century thereafter was generally omitted. It was not until the Civil War,[2] which gave the song a new popularity, that Key's name became firmly affixed, and the song itself began to be recognized as the national anthem. This recognition was, however, entirely unofficial; in 1916 it became semi-official, and in 1931 an act of Congress made it official.

The act, however, neglected to specify an official text, and a certain confusion has resulted, at least among those who do not make an automatic correlation between American foreign policy and abstract right. In Key's version, the fifth line of the last stanza runs: "Then conquer we must, when our cause it is just." Sometimes the word "for" takes the place of "when"—which is a way of saying that our "cause" is always and automatically "just."

Key had had, we may remember, some doubts about the justice of our "cause" in 1812.

The actual flag that Key saw was a new one, sewn especially for Fort McHenry in Baltimore, by Mrs. Mary Young Peckersgill, a professional flag-maker. The flag was enormous, thirty-six by twenty-nine feet, and to find space to assemble it Mrs. Peckersgill was compelled to work in Claggett's brewery.

[1] A cartel is a formal agreement signed by belligerents, ordinarily for negotiations concerning prisoners.

[2] In the South certain parodies appeared, and in answer to them Oliver Wendell Holmes wrote an additional stanza by way of patriotic rebuttal. That stanza has not stuck.

FURTHER READINGS

Edward S. Delaplaine, *Francis Scott Key: Life and Times* (1937)

Oscar George Theodore Sonneck, *The Star-Spangled Banner* (1914)

Victor Weybright, *Spangled Banner* (1935)

The Star-Spangled Banner (1814)

O say! can you see by the dawn's early light,
    What so proudly we hail'd at the twilight's last
      gleaming?
Whose broad stripes and bright stars, thro' the
      perilous fight,

    O'er the ramparts we watched were so gallantly
      streaming?
And the rocket's red glare, the bombs bursting in
      air,
Gave proof thro' the night that our flag was still

there.

> O say, does that star-spangled banner yet
> wave
> O'er the land of the free and the home of
> the brave?

On the shore, dimly seen thro' the mists of the
deep,
There the foe's haughty host in dread silence
reposes,
What is that which the breeze, o'er the towering
steep,
As it fitfully blows, half conceals, half discloses?
Now it catches the gleam of the morning's first
beam,
In full glory reflected now shines on the stream;
> 'Tis the star-spangled banner, O long may
> it wave
> O'er the land of the free and the home of
> the brave!

And where is that band who so vauntingly swore
> That the havoc of war and the battle's confusion,
A home and a country, shall leave us no more?

> Their blood has washed out their foul footsteps'
> pollution.
No refuge could save the hireling and slave,
From the terror of flight or the gloom of the grave,
> And the star-spangled banner in triumph
> doth wave
> O'er the land of the free and the home of
> the brave.

O! thus be it ever when free men shall stand
> Between their lov'd homes and the war's desola-
> tion!
Blest with vict'ry and peace, may the heav'n rescued
land
> Praise the Pow'r that hath made and preserved
> us a nation!
Then conquer we must, when our cause it is just,
And this be our motto, "In God is our trust!"
> And the star-spangled banner in triumph
> shall wave,
> O'er the land of the free and the home of
> the brave!

JULIA WARD HOWE (1819–1910)

In 1831, Samuel Ward, a banker, built the finest house on Bond Street, a new and very fashionable street south of Washington Square, and Julia Ward and her two sisters, who grew up there, were known in New York society as the Three Graces of Bond Street. They were, in fact, remarkable young ladies, carefully educated, talented, charming, and personable, and were heiresses to boot. The Wards were an old and distinguished New England family, but Julia also knew her Grandmother Cutler, whose eighteenth-century table manners and snuff-taking sometimes embarrassed the Wards, even if she had been a famous belle in her day, and who derived impeccably from the plantation aristocracy of South Carolina. Too, she was descended from the revolutionary hero General Francis Marion, the "Swamp Fox," about whom William Gilmore Simms had written a novel. From this grandmother, the future author of "The

Battle Hymn of the Republic" got her head full of southern lore.

Julia Ward was brilliant and ambitious and kicked against the pricks that then hemmed women in from public achievement; and when she married, her choice was expressive of her unconventional aspirations. Dr. Samuel Gridley Howe had an income of only three thousand dollars (a "mere pittance," said Sam Ward, Julia's brother, now head of the family), did not like social life, and was twenty years older than Julia; but he was an idealist and, in a way, a hero, having fought against the Turks for Greek liberty. He was also famous for his work with the blind and deaf, having performed the extraordinary feat of establishing communication with a child, Laura Bridgman, who had been blind and deaf from birth. Julia caught her first sight of Dr. Howe when, mounted on a beautiful black horse, he came galloping across a meadow; and he was, a few minutes later, introduced to her by Charles Sumner, then a rising young lawyer, and Henry Wadsworth Longfellow, then a rising young poet. History and literature presided, as it were, over the nuptials.

The marriage was a love match, and stormy. Freedom for Greece and for Negro slaves was fine, but Howe wanted to see women in their place, and that place was not in the limelight— which was precisely what Julia took to be her natural precinct. Her first book of poems, which appeared in 1853, did a good deal to put her there, for the title *Passion Flowers,* with its slightly improper connotations (not recognized by her or her adviser Longfellow), offset the dreariness of her small talent, and somewhat later, as a consequence, she was writing to one of her sisters:

Chev [Dr. Howe] was very angry about the book and I really thought at the time he would drive me to insanity, so horribly did he behave. . . . I try to please him as much as I can, but when he is angry he has no control over his own feelings and no consideration for those of others. . . . After three years of constantly increasing unkindness and estrangement, no alternative presented itself to me, but that of reconciliation or a final separation. The latter has been all along in Chev's mind. . . . His dream was to marry again—some young girl who would love him supremely.

Chev never got his dream. Julia's will was too strong for him, as it was for most people; she kept him—even if she could say to a sister just engaged: "Marriage, like death, is a debt we owe to nature." At the same time she went on to her public apotheosis.

Howe did, however, make a basic contribution to that apotheosis: he converted his wife to abolitionism. By the middle of the 1850's, he was active in the movement, actually leading one column of the New England emigrants to Kansas, where, after the Kansas-Nebraska Bill, a peculiarly savage state of guerrilla warfare and brigandage had broken out between Free Soil settlers and southern sympathizers.[1] It was here that John Brown made his reputation as a border leader, and by 1859 Howe, though perhaps unaware of the precise nature of the project, was ready to support Brown in the expedition that led to Harper's Ferry. By this time Mrs. Howe had met Brown and been greatly impressed by him, and so in the tangled skein of events leading up to "The Battle Hymn of the Republic," another strand was introduced.

Even as late as the summer of 1859, however, shortly before Harper's Ferry, Mrs. Howe, like so many northerners of antislavery convictions, had not wholly accepted the apocalyptic vision of the conflict which Brown embodied and which her "Hymn" was to express. After a visit to South Carolina (and here we may remember the plantation lore of Grandmother Cutler), she could write that the slaves were as "lazy as the laziest of brutes, chiefly ambitious to be of no use to anybody," and she could entertain "the unwelcome question whether compulsory labor be not better than none." She was even ready, she said, to dissent from "the habitual sneer, denunciation, and malediction, which have become consecrated forms of piety in speaking of the South."

But before long, the raid occurred, Howe fled to Canada to avoid being implicated, and apparently in a blue funk wrote a statement full of lies to save his hide. A little later Brown was hanged, war began, and by November, 1861, Mrs. Howe was in Washington, in a carriage, listening to troops sing "John Brown's Body." One of her companions, her favorite preacher James Freeman Clarke, said: "Why don't you write some good words for the stirring tune?" Here is the account as given in her *Reminiscences*:

I awoke in the gray of the morning twilight;

---

[1] Though Howe was not by nature or principle a quietist, he could recognize, as many northerners could not, the fact that some of the Free Soil leaders committed acts "fully as atrocious as those of the 'border ruffians' "—as the southern sympathizers were called. It is strange that he failed to put in this category the massacre carried out by John Brown at Pottawatomie. Or did he remain ignorant of the facts? See p. 1043.

and as I lay waiting for the dawn, the long lines of the desired poem began to twine themselves in my mind. Having thought out all the stanzas, I said to myself, "I must get up and write these verses down, lest I fall asleep again and forget them." So, with a sudden effort, I sprang out of bed, and found in the dimness an old stump of a pen which I remembered to have used the day before. I scrawled the verse almost without looking at the paper.

The sudden, dreamlike composition of the "Hymn" by a writer of such meager talent as Julia Ward Howe smacks of the miraculous—of automatic writing, literal inspiration, or divine guidance. Even she, in spite of her not inconsiderable vanity, was puzzled, even awestruck. But it is merely one more example of a not uncommon psychological situation, the moment in which deep and perhaps unsuspected elements in a writer's experience can, by some shock or a mere convergence of circumstances, be released and fused—as we have seen in the case of Whittier's *Snow-Bound*.[2]

Some of the elements that entered into the "Hymn" are fairly clear. For one thing, as critics have pointed out, there is the echo of Isaiah 63:1–4:

1. Who is this that cometh from Edom, with dyed garments from Bozrah? this that is glorious in his apparel, travelling in the greatness of his strength? I that speak in righteousness, mighty to save. 2. Wherefore art thou red in thine apparel, and thy garments like him that treadeth in the winevat? 3. I have trodden the winepress alone; and of the people there was none with me: for I will tread them in mine anger, and trample them in my fury; and their blood shall be sprinkled upon my garments, and I will stain all my raiment. 4. For the day of vengeance is in my heart, and the year of my redeemed is come.

This would focus all the echoes of the old Calvinistic sermons loaded with the ecstatic wrath of the Jew's *cherim* and the fury of damnation in which the early New England (and, one is tempted to say, American) sensibility, and that of Julia Ward Howe on Bond Street, had been steeped.

There is also the possible echo of Thomas Babington Macaulay's poem of the English Civil War, "The Battle of Naseby, by Obadiah Bind-Their-Kings-in-Chains . . . ," which celebrates the Puritan victory and which, in itself, is an echo of Isaiah. The first stanza runs:

Oh! wherefore come ye forth, in triumph from the North,
  With your hands, and your feet, and your raiment all red?
And wherefore doth your rout send forth a joyful shout?
  And whence be the grapes of the wine-press which ye tread?

Furthermore, as we know from Mrs. Howe's own account, the immediate stimulus was the singing of "John Brown's Body" by marching troops. That tune itself was from a hymn,[3] with all the apocalyptic associations; and to Mrs. Howe, as to others, John Brown himself had seemed the very incarnation of the old Puritanism—"a Puritan of the Puritans," as she wrote in recalling her first sight of him. Certainly, his imagination had been as blood-drenched as that of any Obadiah Bind-Their-Kings-in-Chains, and his favorite text from the Bible was "There is no remission of sins without the shedding of blood," from the Epistle to the Hebrews. By 1861 the authority generated by his Old Testament fury had been further, if somewhat paradoxically, affirmed by his new role as redemptive Christ-figure.[4]

---

[2] See pp. 549–50. Frost reports that his own best poems came effortlessly. The most famous instance of such dreamlike composition is, of course, Coleridge's "Kubla Khan."

[3] "Say, Brother, Will You Meet Us?" It was an old camp-meeting rouser from the South.

[4] The same paradox appears in the "Hymn" when Christ appears with the "beauty of the lilies" in the middle of exhortations to blood-letting. In this connection Edmund Wilson wrote in *Patriotic Gore*:

"This stanza is particularly interesting on account of the treatment of Jesus, so characteristic of Calvinism.

Add to all this the fever of a righteous war (before casualties had begun to mount and when victory still seemed not too difficult) and the excitement experienced by a gently bred lady on seeing, as Mrs. Howe just that afternoon had done, the federal cavalry galloping heroically to the rescue of a detachment about to be cut off by the Confederates, in the very shadow of Washington.

What other deeper, personal elements were drawn into that moment of dreamlike composition we do not know. In any case, after a few minor revisions of the poem—for it was at this stage only a poem—it was published in the *Atlantic Monthly*, in February, 1862. The fee was four dollars.

It was some time before the poem became a song and began to achieve folk acceptance. The process by which this occurred is not clear, but we do have some indication of it in the case of Charles McCabe, a Methodist chaplain, who saw the poem in the *Atlantic*, memorized it, and taught it to the Ohio regiment to which he was attached. Later, in Libby Prison in Richmond, he sang it to cheer his fellow inmates, and then sang it, in his fine baritone, to patriotic mass meetings of civilians. Soon it was universally sung, for it precisely phrased the mood of those who felt the war as a moral crusade, and the tune to which it was sung, long back a hymn and now a war song, fused the complex elements of that impulse.

The war was won, the Union was saved, the slaves were emancipated (to be reduced, a little later, to near-peonage), and the Gilded Age was ushered in, with Mrs. Howe's brother, Sam Ward, as one of its more glittering ornaments. Sam Ward, described by his nephew, the novelist F. Marion Crawford, as "full of thought and care for others, combined with vagueness concerning all points of morality," was treading out, in the corridors of the Capitol and in the more expensive suites of the more elegant hotels, a vintage not of wrath; he was known, in fact, as the "King of the Lobby," using his great personal charm, wit, aristocratic connections, and deep knowledge of food, wine, and other amenities to dazzle politicians who might be of service to the new breed of financiers.

As for Mrs. Howe, she lived on until 1910, a little old lady in black silk and a white lace cap, who, on the slightest provocation, or on none at all, would recite "The Battle Hymn of the Republic." She had long since fulfilled her wildest dreams of ambition: she was a public figure, a successful lecturer, a voluminous, if trivial, writer, the friend of the great, rich, and well-born, and, after death had removed the impediment of Dr. Howe, a doughty fighter for the rights of women. But her importance lay in the fact that she had become a national symbol.

She had also become a symbol for one strain in our national psychology. In 1899, a Civil War monument was being dedicated on Boston Common. On this occasion Julia Ward Howe was escorted by General Joseph Wheeler, once Lieutenant General C.S.A. and chief of Confederate cavalry, but more recently a hero of the Spanish-American War. At the dedication, Julia received her greatest ovation. The "Hymn" was rendered by a professional singer, and when he reached the line "As he died to make men holy, let us die to make men free," the whole vast audience rose, sobbing and singing together.

As is often the case with Calvinists, Mrs. Howe, though she feels she must bring Him in, gives Him a place which is merely peripheral. He is really irrelevant to her picture, for Christ died to make men holy; but this is not what God is having *us* do. He is a militant, a military God, and far from wanting us to love our enemies. He gives "the Hero" orders to "crush the serpent with his heel." The righteous object of this is to "make men [the Negroes] free," and we must die to accomplish this. Note that Christ is situated "across the sea"; he is not present on the battlefield with his Father, yet, intent on our grisly work, we somehow still share in his "glory." I have not been able to guess where Julia Ward Howe got these lilies in the beauty of which Jesus is supposed to have born. The only lilies mentioned in the gospel are those that toil not neither do they spin. Was she thinking of Easter lilies? But these are associated not with Christ's birth but with his resurrection. In any case, they serve to place him in a setting that is effeminate as well as remote. The gentle and no doubt very estimable Jesus is trampling no grapes of wrath. And now come on, New England boys, get in step with the marching God!"

A reporter from the Philadelphia *Press,* covering the occasion, described the moment and then added: "If volunteers were really needed for the Philippines,[5] McKinley could have had us all right there."

[5] Where American troops were fighting rebels who resisted annexation.

We do not know how much irony was in the reporter's nature; perhaps he did regard the Philippine operetta as a holy crusade. But we do know that the author of those lines that brought the audience sobbing to its feet ready to redeem the Philippines pasted the clipping in her journal. There was no irony in her nature.

FURTHER READINGS

Julia Ward Howe, *Reminiscences, 1819–1899* (1899)
———, *A Trip to Cuba* (1860)

Florence Marion Hall, *The Story of the Battle Hymn of the Republic* (1916)

Laura E. Richards and Maud Howe Elliott, *Julia Ward Howe* (1916)
Louise Tharp, *Three Saints and a Sinner* (1956)
Edmund Wilson, "The Battle Hymn of the Republic," in *Patriotic Gore* (1962)

The Battle Hymn of the Republic (1862)

Mine eyes have seen the glory of the coming of
 the Lord;
He is trampling out the vintage where the grapes
 of wrath are stored;
He hath loosed the fateful lightning of His terrible
 swift sword,
His truth is marching on.

Chorus:
 Glory! glory! Hallelujah!
 Glory! glory! Hallelujah!
 Glory! glory! Hallelujah!
 His truth is marching on.

I have seen Him in the watch-fires of a hundred
 circling camps;
They have builded Him an altar in the evening
 dews and damps;
I can read His righteous sentence by the dim and
 flaring lamps,
His day is marching on.

I have read a fiery gospel, writ in burnished rows
 of steel;

"As ye deal with my contemners, so with you my
 grace shall deal";
Let the Hero, born of woman, crush the serpent
 with His heel
Since God is marching on.

He has sounded forth the trumpet that shall never
 call retreat;
He is sifting out the hearts of men before His judgment seat;
Oh, be swift, my soul, to answer Him! be jubilant
 my feet!
Our God is marching on.

In the beauty of the lilies, Christ was born across
 the sea,
With a glory in His bosom that transfigures you
 and me;
As He died to make me holy, let us die to make
 men free,
While God is marching on.

DANIEL DECATUR EMMETT (1815–1904)

Daniel Decatur Emmett, descended from Virginia pioneers, was born in Ohio, son of a blacksmith. With little education, he became a drifter, working in newspaper offices, serving as a fifer in the army, traveling with a circus, and finally organizing the "Virginia Minstrels," and thus having a hand in the founding of the institution of black-face minstrel. In 1859, then a member of the "Bryant Minstrels," he was commissioned to compose a "hooray song," which he developed from the current minstrel phrase, "I wish I was in the land of Dixie." The song was first presented in Mechanics Hall in New York in 1859, but subsequently fired an audience in New Orleans, and gained status by being used at the inauguration of Jefferson Davis, on February 18, 1861.

The word "Dixie" is sometimes said to come from the name of a wealthy landowner and slave-holder on Manhattan Island in the period of the Revolution, who was so kind that his slaves— and other, as the fame spread—regarded his establishment as a place of bliss. But other explanations have been suggested, one being that a bank in New Orleans issued a ten-dollar note with the word "dix" on it, the note then getting the name "dixie."

Dixie (1859)

Dis world was made in jis' six days,
An' finished up in various ways.
Look away! look away! look away! Dixie land!
Dey den make Dixie trim and nice,
And Adam called it "Paradise."
Look away! look away! look away! Dixie land!

Chorus:

  Den I wish I was in Dixie; hooray, hooray!
  In Dixie land we'll take our stand,
  To lib and die in Dixie.
  Away, away, away down south in Dixie;
  Away, away, away down south in Dixie.

I wish I was in the land of cotton,
'Simmon seed and sandy bottom;
Look away, look away, look away, Dixie land.
In Dixie land, whar I was born in,
Early on a frosty mornin';
Look away, look away, look away, Dixie land.

Old missus marry "Will de Weaber";
William was a gay deceiber;
Look away, look away, look away, Dixie land.
When he put his arm around 'er
He smiled as fierce as a forty-pounder;
Look away, look away, look away, Dixie land.

His face was sharp as a butcher's cleaber,
But dat did not seem to grieb her;

Look away, look away, look away, Dixie land.
Old missus acted de foolish part,
And died fer de man dat broke her heart;
Look away, look away, look away, Dixie land.

Now here's a health to the nex' old missus
And all de gals dat want to kiss us;
Look away, look away, look away, Dixie land.
But if you want to drive away sorrow,
Come and hear dis song tomorrow;
Look away, look away, look away, Dixie land.

Dar's buckwheat cakes and Injun batter,
Makes you rat er a little fatter;
Look away, look away, look away, Dixie land.
Den hoe it down an' scratch your grabbel,
To Dixie's land I'm bound to trabbel;
Look away, look away, look away, Dixie land.

Added by Confederate soldiers:

Way down South in the fields of cotton,
Cinnamon seed and sandy bottom,
  Look away! look away!
Then way down in the fields of cotton,
Vinegar shoes and paper stockin's,
  Look away in Dixie land.

STEPHEN FOSTER (1826–1864)

Stephen Collins Foster, whose most famous songs are sentimental celebrations of the life of the pre-Civil War plantation of the South, was, ironically enough, born in Pittsburgh; and the songs found their way into the popular (white) heart through the black-face minstrel shows, chiefly in northern cities.

FURTHER READINGS

John T. Howard, *Stephen Foster* (1934)

Robert MacGowan, *The Significances of Stephen Collins Foster* (1932)

Old Folks at Home (1852)

Way down upon de Swanee ribber,
  Far, far away,
Dere's wha my heart is turning ebber,
  Dere's wha de old folks stay.
All up and down da whole creation,
  Sadly I roam,
Still longing for de old plantation,
  And for de old folks at home.

Chorus:
  All de world am sad and dreary,
    Ebrywhere I roam,
  Oh! darkeys, how my heart grows weary,
    Far from de old folks at home.

All round de little farm I wandered
  When I was young,

Den many happy days I squandered,
  Many the songs I sung
When I was playing wid my brudder,
  Happy was I.
Oh, take me to my kind ole mudder,
  Dere let me live and die.

One little hut among de bushes,
  One dat I love,
Still sadly to my mem'ry rushes,
  No matter where I rove.
When will I see de bees a-humming
  All round de comb?
When will I hear the banjo tumming
  Down in my good ole home.

My Old Kentucky Home, Good-Night! (1846)

The sun shines bright in the old Kentucky home,
'Tis summer, the darkeys are gay;
The corn top's ripe and the meadow's in the bloom,
While the birds make music all the day.
The young folks roll on the little cabin floor,
All merry, all happy and bright.
By'n by, hard times comes a knocking at the door,
Then my old Kentucky home, good-night!

Chorus:
  Weep no more, my lady,
  Oh! weep no more today!
  We will sing one song for the old Kentucky home,
  For the old Kentucky home far away.

They hunt no more for the possum and the coon,
On the meadow, the hill, and the shore,

They sing no more by the glimmer of the moon,
On the beach by the old cabin door.
The day goes by like a shadow o'er the heart,
With sorrow where all was delight;
The time has come when the darkeys have to part,
Then my old Kentucky home, good-night!

The head must bow and the back will have to bend,
Wherever the darkey may go;
A few more days, and the trouble all will end
In the field where the sugar canes grow;
A few more days for to tote the weary load,
No matter, 'twill never be light,
A few more days till we totter on the road,
Then, my old Kentucky home, good-night!

Massa's in the Cold, Cold Ground (1852)

Round de meadows am a-ringing,
  De darkey's mournful song,
While de mocking-bird am singing,
  Happy as de day am long.

Where de ivy am a-creeping,
  O'er de grassy mound,
Dere old massa am a-sleeping,
  Sleeping in de cold, cold ground.

Chorus:
> Down in de corn-field,
>> Hear dat mournful sound.
> All de darkeys am a-weeping,
>> Massa's in de cold, cold ground.

When de autumn leaves were falling,
> When de days were cold,
'T was hard to hear old massa calling,
> Cayse he was so weak and old.
Now de orange-tree am blooming
> On de sandy shore,

Now de summer days am coming,
> Massa nebber calls no more.

Massa make de darkeys love him,
> Cayse he was so kind;
Now, dey sadly weep above him,
> Mourning cayse he leave dem behind.
I cannot work before to-morrow,
> Cayse de tear-drop flow,
I try to drive away my sorrow,
> Pickin' on de old banjo.

Folk Songs of the Black People

The songs of the black Americans fall into two broad categories, religious and secular.[1] The greater number of songs, and the most famous ones, preserved from the period with which we are now concerned, are, of course, the religious songs known traditionally as spirituals—or, more precisely, "Negro spirituals," to distinguish them from the lesser known white spirituals. For many years there has been speculation and controversy about the origin of the black spirituals, and this involves, as we shall see, their relation to the white spirituals.

From 1619, when the Dutch ship set down twenty Africans at the colony of Jamestown,[2] on to 1863, when the last captain of an American slaver, a certain Maine man named Gordon, was hanged in New York, some 1.4 million unwilling black immigrants were landed on the shores of North America. How much African culture was retained by their descendants? How much, rather, of African cultures (for the Africans might be of different tribes and often could not even communicate with one another)?

Easy and full answers are not to be had to such questions, for in the slave

---

[1] The same could be said of the folk songs of the whites, but what are called white spirituals are generally so uninteresting from a literary point of view that this book does not represent them. The white spirituals developed in the wake of the revivalism that swept rural America after the Great Awakening of the eighteenth century and continued sporadically into the next century. The white spirituals often represented a wedding of religious verse, sometimes by earlier writers such as Isaac Watts, to traditional secular tunes, often of ballads. Sometimes, however, both the text and the music would be newly composed, and there were individuals, sometimes preachers, famous for their talent.

[2] Little is known of the precise status of the blacks in America for the early period, but they were not slaves; they were held, rather, under indenture. But between 1640 and 1660, the system of slavery began to harden, and in the 1660's the institution appears among the statutes of Virginia and other colonies. It became universally recognized.

system, sometimes by accident and sometimes by design, tribal groups were generally broken up and continuities severed. But researchers have more and more emphasized the idea that African elements did survive, in the spirituals as in other forms of black music in America. Some writers, to support this thesis, have used verbal parallels between the spirituals and African folk songs, as does James Weldon Johnson (see accompanying volume), the black poet, scholar, and anthologist of the spirituals, who in his introduction to *The Book of American Negro Spirituals* gives a song from a Bantu folk tale. The singer, an old woman with a child in her arms, sings to lure back the child's mother, who has been enchanted by the river.

> It is crying, it is crying
>   Sihamba Ngenyanga.
> The child of the walker by moonlight
>   Sihamba Ngenyanga.
> It was done intentionally by people, whose names cannot be mentioned,
>   Sihamba Ngenyanga.
> They sent her for water during the day,
>   Sihamba Ngenyanga.
> She tried to dip it with the milk basket, and then it sank,
>   Sihamba Ngenyanga.
> Tried to dip it with the ladle, and then it sank,
>   Sihamba Ngenyanga.
> Tried to dip it with the mantle, and then it sank,
>   Sihamba Ngenyanga.

Against this, Johnson places the spiritual "Oh, Wasn't Dat a Wide Ribber."

Such verbal parallels are generally taken to be less significant than the evidence of music itself, in rhythmic quality and intervallic structure.

Some years ago, Melville Herskovits, in *The Myth of the Negro Past*, insisted on a cultural continuity, and more recently additional data has been assembled to support his ideas. For instance, Alan Lomax, through a system that he calls cantometric analysis, arrives at the conclusion that, even though "European song style did influence African tradition in America in regard to melodic form and, of course, textual content," the "main traditions of Afro-American song, especially those of the old-time congregational spiritual—are derived from the main African song style model." But long before the invention of the cantometric system, about which there is some dispute among experts, many people were convinced of the black tradition solely on the grounds of experience—for instance, the poet and anthologist Louis Untermeyer, who says, "Only those who have heard the *cadences* can appreciate the originality of the Negro's contribution."

There has been, however, a considerable amount of work on musical and verbal parallels between the white spirituals, which still survive in the back country, and the black spirituals. For instance, there are such verbal parallels as the following, from *White Spirituals in the Southern Uplands,* by G. P. Jackson:

White	Black
Are there anybody here like Mary a-weeping?	If there's anybody here like weepin Mary,
Call to my Jesus and he'll draw nigh	Call upon yore Jesus and he'll draw nigh.
He gave his soul up to the stroke	An' he never said a mumbalin' word
Without a murmuring word	
They crucified my Savior and nailed him to the Cross.	They crucified my Savior and nailed him to de cross.
See Mary comes a-weeping to see where he was laid.	Oh, Mary come a-runnin' her Savior for to see.
He rose and ascended in a cloud.	He rose, he rose from de daid.
I'm travelling to my grave	I'm a travelin' to de grave
To lay this body down.	To lay dis body down.

Undoubtedly some of the hundreds of parallels are accidental or may be accounted for by a common source in the Bible, but some, such as those quoted above, would suggest that sometimes at least texts were drawn from the white spirituals. On this basis the originality of the black spirituals has erroneously been called into question. Such parallels, both musical and verbal, are important, but only insofar as they indicate the *context* in which the black spirituals originated.

There is, in fact, massive documentation of the presence of slaves at religious meetings of the whites and of their participation—sometimes singing all night, long after the whites had gone to bed.[3] They, too, knew the anguish of guilt and the terror of damnation, yearned for the bliss of redemption, and were subject to the same emotional excitement of the revivals as were the whites. In other words, the slaves were Christianized, sometimes because masters were pious and sometimes because masters cynically believed that religion would make slaves more docile. The slaves, usually long out of

[3] Illiterate, like many of the poor white countrymen, the slaves got the songs not from a book, but as "lined out" by a leader—a fact that some critics see as accounting, in part at least, for the loose and repetitive verbal structure of most Negro spirituals.

Africa and speaking only English, had developed their own new culture out of whatever had been preserved from racial past,[4] whatever might be called racial temperament and sensibility, and what had been assimilated from the surrounding white world. The spirituals were a great flowering of this complex process.

James Weldon Johnson has summarized the situation: "Why did he [the black American] not revive and continue the beating out of complex rhythms on tom toms and drums . . . ?[5] It was because at the precise and psychic moment there was blown through or fused into the vestiges of his African music the spirit of Christianity as he knew Christianity." And Johnson goes on to say that what the black man understood of the new religion was a "reversion to the simple principles of communal Christianity"—which was, in fact, what many white people also understood by the Great Awakening and subsequent manifestations of revivalism.

The religious context of the birth of the black spirituals suggests another controversy, that concerning their basic motive. One extreme view is that because the language and imagery found in the black spirituals have, for the whites, a purely religious reference (freedom, for instance, meaning relief from sin), it necessarily follows that the same was true for the black singer. The other extreme view is that the spirituals are to be taken primarily, or even exclusively, as a protest against slavery—that is, as a kind of allegory with, for example, "freedom" meaning emancipation, "Egypt land" the South, "Heb'n" or the "Promised Land" the North or the condition of freedom, and "burden" slavery. An early biographer of Harriet Tubman, a black woman who again and again risked her life in running slaves out of the South, reports that since slaves "must not be seen talking together . . . it comes about that their communication was often made by singing, and the words of their familiar hymns, telling of the heavenly journey, and the land of Canaan . . . conveyed to their brethren and sisters in bondage something more than met the ear." And Frederick Douglass, in his autobiography, confirms this practical aspect of the spirituals as songs of protest. And Douglass and the biographer of Harriet Tubman are not alone.

But such a use as Harriet Tubman made of the spirituals and Douglass reports would not necessarily imply that the songs originated purely in protest. The truth would likely lie somewhere between the two extreme positions and would emerge in a complex psychological situation. However devout a slave might be and however anxious for "freedom" from sin, and however

---

[4] Compare the report of the "ole shout song I'd heard 'em sing from Africa" in the quotation below from *Southern Thoughts for Northern Thinkers*.

[5] In Louisiana, there was such a continuity.

fatalistic about his earthly lot, the secondary meaning would inevitably inter-fuse with the first and official one. We have, in fact, contemporary records stating quite explicitly that slaves—at least, some slaves—did equate their lot with that of the Jews in Egypt.[6] At the same time that such a notion would not exclude the religious dimension, the religious dimension would not necessarily deny the element of protest, and by this token the spirituals would be, as the Negro writer and historian W. E. B. Du Bois has termed them, "sorrow songs" (see accompanying volume); the religious dimension might, in fact, deepen and fortify the more mundane meaning, and instead of mak-ing a slave more docile might make him look forward to "freedom" here and now as the will of God. For example, Nat Turner, the leader of the most nearly successful slave insurrection in the United States, was intensely religious.

The great power of the spirituals lies in the fact that they, like all effective art, drew on a complicated depth of experience and feeling in both those who molded and those who transmitted them and, by the same token, can draw on a complicated depth of quite different experience in the modern man, white or black.

But in this book, even though such a division does violence to the essential unity of the compositions, we are concerned with the poetic as distinguished from the musical quality of the Negro spirituals. And on this point we can paraphrase Lomax: no number of verbal parallels can ever make the poetry of the Negro spirituals feel like the poetry of the white spirituals. The white spirituals are, on this point, generally dull, but the Negro compositions, de-rived in whatever degree from them, are in a language marked by great originality and power. As James Weldon Johnson has pointed out, even the phrases that have come to be accepted as the titles are often of powerful suggestiveness and poetic beauty: "Go Down, Moses," "Joshua Fit de Battle ob Jerico," "Swing Low, Sweet Chariot," "All God's Chillen Got Wings," "Steal Away to Jesus," "Dere's No Hidin' Place Down Dere," "Gambler, Git Up Off Yo' Knees," "Some Times I Feel Lak a Motherless Chile," "Was You There When They Crucified Ma Lord?" "De Blood Come Twinklin' Down," and "Ride On, King Jesus."

Many of the spirituals—for instance "Swing Low, Sweet Chariot"—are, as literary compositions, highly organized, with dramatic and poetic quality, but many others which are, in general, verbally dull and lacking in structure and which depend almost exclusively on the music for effect, have fine poetic flashes. For instance, in "All My Sins Done Taken Away," we find the couplet:

[6] There is a latter-day parallel: sometimes now the blacks in the slums equate their situation with that of the Jews in Nazi Germany.

> My feet got wet in de midnight dew,
> An' de mornin' star was a witness, too,

and

> I gwine ter heaven on a eagle's wing,
> And all doan see me gwine ter hear me sing.

From "Come, Sinner, Come," there are also two memorable couplets:

> Ole Satan wears mighty loose ole shoe,
> Ef you doan min' gwine slip it on you,

and

> Up on de hillside King Jesus spoke,
> Outer his mouth come fire an' smoke.

Or take these examples from a number of spirituals:

> Gwine ter lay me on a coolin' board, one ob dese mornin's

> Run, sinner, run, yo' house on fire

> Dey nail his hands and rivet his feet,
> Dese bones gwine rise agin.
> De hammers was hear'd in Jerusalem street,
> Dese bones gwine rise agin.

> He sails in de light ob de Lamb

> Oh, dey spierced him in de side, an' de blood come twinklin' down[7]

> Death's gwine ter lay his cold icy hand on me

> Wheel, oh, wheel,
> Wheel in de middle ob a wheel!
> 'Zekiel saw de wheel ob time,
> Wheel in de middle ob a wheel,
> Every spoke was human kind,
> Wheel in de middle ob a wheel.

> I know moonrise, I know starrise,
> Lay dis body down.
> I walk in de moonlight, I walk in de starlight,
> To lay dis body down.

---

[7] "Twinklin'" here is said to be a corruption of "trinklin'," dialect for "trickling"; but however the word gets into the line, it is superlatively effective as an image.

The spirituals are, in general, suffused with poetry, and furthermore, in distinction from such suffusion, exhibit magnificent local and individual bursts of poetry. Without any disparagement of the poetic genius involved in the spirituals, we can distinguish the way in which it manifests itself from the way in which poetic genius manifests itself in more highly organized "literary" poems. The spirituals are, in fact, not poems; they are songs and the literary element operates primarily to support the song. What, from a strictly literary point of view, might seem, for instance, a loose and repetitive structure may often be perfectly adapted to the effect of song. We must understand the poetry in this context and remember, furthermore, that the spirituals are folk songs and that the process of their composition goes far to explain their structure.

As we have said in connection with the origin of folk ballads, the notion that a group—the "folk"—creates a ballad in some mystically unified act is scarcely acceptable; and the notion is equally inapplicable, in any strict sense, to spirituals. The actual process was complicated and variable. Many of the spirituals seem to have developed from the practice of a leader giving a line, or lines, and the congregation giving a response, a single line or, in more sophisticated instances, a chorus. Such a relationship would not be formal, but would allow for all sorts of improvisation and variation to fill in the gaps of memory on the part of the leader or to bring the song closer to the dominant mood of the occasion, with both the leader and the congregation caught up in a mounting urgency. We have accounts of such a process, or variations from it, as this passage quoted from an old Negro in *Southern Thoughts for Northern Thinkers*, by Jeannette Robinson Murphy:

We'd all be at de Prayers House de Lord's Day and de preacher he'd 'splain de word and read whar Ezekiel done say—

"Dry bones ter lib again."

And, honey, de Lord would come a-shinin' thoo dem pages and revive dis ole nigger's heart, and I'd jump up dar and den and holler and shout and sing and pat, and de would all catch de words and I'd sing it some ole shout song I'd heard 'em sing from Africa, and dey'd all take it up and keep at it, and keep a-addin' to it, and den it would be a speritulals.[8]

The leader might be a person with a recognized talent for composing songs, that is, a "songster." And such a songster might, of course, compose his

[8] There are also records of such improvisations and variations in white churches and camp meetings. For instance, see Theron Brown and Hezekiel Butterworth, *The Story of the Hymns* (1906). But in this quotation notice the significant reference to an African continuity.

songs in solitude and bring them ready in his head to present to the congregation. William H. Russell, an English correspondent during the Civil War, tells of encountering a songster:

> the oarsmen, as they bent to their task, beguiled the way by singing in unison a real negro melody which was as unlike the works of the Ethiopian Serenaders as anything in song could be unlike another. It was a barbaric sort of madrigal, in which one singer beginning was followed by the others in unison, repeating the refrain in chorus, and full of quaint expression and melancholy:—
> "Oh your soul! oh my soul! I'm going to the churchyard to lay my
>   body down;
> Oh my soul! oh your soul! we're going to the churchyard to lay this
>   nigger down."   (*My Diary North and South*, 1863)

After the war, when there was freedom of movement, such a songster might become a wandering bard carrying new songs, or new variations, from one county to another. But the habit of improvisation and variation was common, as was the urge to create, and probably as much is due to such random developments in the heat of an occasion as to the work of avowed and recognized songsters. When the work of a songster had caught on, it was, of course, always subjected to the fluid process of folk transmission, and this would account, of course, for the fact that spirituals do not have fixed and authorized forms, or even definite beginnings and endings. What we have in print are versions snatched at different moments from the folk process of transmission, and frozen in nonfolk performance or print, a process which began in 1867 with the publication of the first collection, *Slave Songs of the United States*, which was continued by the Fisk Jubilee Singers at Fisk University, in Nashville, Tennessee, and other such groups, and which is not yet ended.

The spirituals are so powerful that they tend to overwhelm the secular songs of the blacks in the period under discussion. As a matter of fact, the genius of the race did not fully show itself in secular composition until the later period. Even so, there is a rich body of early secular material. Certain of the traditional ballads were accepted and modified. There are a number of work songs, game songs, lullabies, and others like the famous "Jump, Jim Crow," which fits none of these categories:

> Thomas D. Rice, or Jim Crow Rice, as he was called, utilized an old Negro folk-song which he heard a slave sing in Louisville, Kentucky. William Winter relates the incident in his "Wallet of Time."

Jim Crow was old and had a deformity that caused him to limp peculiarly as he walked, and he would croon a queer old song, and "set his heel a-rocking" with the refrain,

> Wheel about, turn about, do jes' so,
> And ebery time I wheel about, I jump Jim Crow!

Rice wrote other words for the song and elaborated a make-up after that of the old darky, and created a sensation with it in a minstrel show.

The song attributed to Rice is as follows—though I do not know how much of it could be called a folk-song, or how much is Rice's composition. From various sections of the country I have received fragments of the song and the refrain, showing that it is a folk-song from usage, as well as in origin.

(Dorothy Scarborough, *On the Trail of Negro Folk Songs*, 1925, pp. 125–26)

The spirituals are often printed purged of dialect. James Weldon Johnson, however, says that an "understanding of the Spirituals" is "increased by a knowledge of the dialect in which the texts were composed." This is an understatement; to put the spirituals into standard American English is to do as great an act of violence to their nature as to put Robert Burns into standard British English. Even though the dialect of black southerners, like that of white southerners, is far from uniform, there is enough of a common denominator for all practical purposes.

The dialect of the spirituals deserves a further comment. It is not to be accounted for as simply a malformation or corruption of the pronunciation of standard English. As a matter of fact, it is a rather old-fashioned English, filled with seventeenth- and eighteenth-century standard forms that, with the passage of time, have become obsolete, along with generous borrowings from the local dialects of the southern and southwestern counties of England. Here, for example, are the first six verses of the Song of Solomon as transcribed into the dialect of Sussex in 1860.

1. De song of songs, dat is Solomon's. 2. Let him kiss me wud de kisses of his mouth; for yer love is better dan wine. 3. Cause of de smell of yer good intments, yer naüm is lik intment tipped out; derefore de maidens love ye. 4. Dråh me; we wull ran åhter ye: de king has brung me into his chåmbers: we wull be glad and be jobal in ye; we wull remember yer love more dan wine: de upright love ye. 5. I be black, but comely, O ye dåhters of Jerusalem; as de tents of Kedar, as de hangins of Solomon. 6. Look not upan me, cause I be black, cause de sun has shoun upan me; my mother's childun was mad wud me; day maüd me kipper of de vineyards; but my own vineyard I han't kipt.

If this was the speech of the folk as late as a century ago, how much more it must have varied from present-day standard in the 1620's and 1630's and 1640's, when the first great wave of English settlers came to the shores of North America. Moreover, one must remember that in an earlier day, the speech of even highly educated men reflected their local backgrounds. Sir Walter Raleigh spoke "broad Devon" to his dying day and Dr. Samuel Johnson in the eighteenth century betrayed his Lichfield origin in his pronunciation of certain words.

Instances of the retention of obsolete standard and provincial dialect forms could be multiplied almost *ad infinitum*. Here follow some examples from the texts of the spirituals printed below. "Fit" for "fought": a character in Congreve's *Way of the World* (1700) remarks of two quarreling men: "I thought once they wou'd have fitt." "Kase" for "[be]cause": in the seventeenth century John Aubrey noted that certain Oxford students from the southwest of England so pronounced "cause." "Cornfiel' " for "cornfield": the final *d* was regularly dropped from words like "field," "hand," "friend," and so on, in the southwestern (and other) counties. "Yaller" for "yellow": *r* spellings occur from a very early period and "yaller" (that is "yal-uh") is still found in the modern county dialects (including that of Sussex). "Year" for "hear": the addition of *y* in "here" as well as "hear" is attested in the dialects of some of the southern (and other) county dialects of England. "Gwine" for "going": "gwine" (or other forms with *gw*) occurs in the south midland, southern, and southwestern counties of England. As for the so-called dropping of the final *g* in words like "being," "doing," "thinking," such was standard English as late as the early nineteenth century as the rhymes of Wordsworth, Coleridge, Byron, Shelley, and Keats attest. The present pronunciation of *ing* was restored under the influence of spelling.

If the black man received such forms from the whites from whom he originally learned his English, why do we not find them now in the language spoken by the whites of the southern states? The answer is that some of them can still be found in white speech, and there is plenty of evidence that at an earlier period all of them could be found. The blacks have retained more of them because for a long time they had no schooling or less adequate schooling, for it was education and the printed word that tended to oust the obsolete standard forms and those derived from the provincial dialects.

For a more technical discussion of the pronunciation of English in the southern states, the reader is referred to Cleanth Brooks, *The Relation of the Alabama-Georgia Dialect to the Provincial Dialects of Great Britain* (1935; reprinted in 1972). This monograph makes special reference to the dialect spoken by "Uncle Remus." (See also Joel Chandler Harris in accompanying volume.)

FURTHER READINGS

W. F. Allen, C. P. Ware, and Lucy M. Garrison, *Slave Songs of the United States* (1867)

Theodore Canot, *Captain Canot, or Twenty Years of an African Slaver* (1854; 1969)

Maude Cuney-Hare, *Negro Musicians and Their Music* (1936)

Ralph Ellison, *The Shadow and the Act* (1964)

Olaudah Equiano, *The New Interesting Narrative of the Life of Olaudah Equiano, or Gustavus Vassa the African, Written by Himself* (1789; rev. ed. 1970)

Mary A. Grissom, *The Negro Sings a New Heaven* (1930)

M. J. Herskovits, *The Myth of the Negro Past* (1941)

James Weldon Johnson, *The Book of American Negro Spirituals* (1925)

LeRoi Jones, *Black Music* (1968)

———, *Blues People* (1963)

Bernard Katz, *The Second Book of Negro Spirituals* (1926)

———, ed., *The Social Implications of Early Negro Music in the United States* (1968)

Alan Lomax, "The Homogeneity of the African-Afro-American Musical Style," *Afro-American Anthropology*, N. E. Whitten, Jr., and John F. Szwed, eds. (1970)

John A. Lomax and Alan Lomax, *American Ballads and Folk Songs* (1934)

Alan Merriam, "African Music," *Continuity and Change*, W. R. Bascom and M. J. Herskovits, eds. (1959)

J. H. Kwabena Nketia, *African Music in Ghana* (1963)

———, *Folk Songs of Ghana* (1963)

Lydia Austin Parrish, *Slave Songs of the Georgia Sea Islands* (1942)

Dorothy Scarborough, *On the Trail of Negro Folk Songs* (1925)

Eileen Southern, *The Music of Black Americans* (1971)

Richard A. Waterman, "African Influences on the Music of the Americans," *Acculturation in the Americas*, Sol Tax, ed. (1952)

Never Said a Mumbalin' Word

Oh, dey whupped him up de hill, up de hill, up de hill,
Oh, dey whupped him up de hill, an' he never said a mumbalin' word,
Oh, dey whupped him up de hill, an' he never said a mumbalin' word,
He jes' hung down his head, an' he cried.

Oh, dey crowned him wid a thorny crown, thorny crown, thorny crown,
Oh, dey crowned him wid a thorny crown, an' he never said a mumbalin' word,
Oh, dey crowned him wid a thorny crown, an' he never said a mumbalin' word,
He jes' hung down his head, an' he cried.

Well, dey nailed him to de cross, to de cross, to de cross,
Well, dey nailed him to de cross, an' he never said a mumbalin' word,
Well, dey nailed him to de cross, an' he never said a mumbalin' word,
He jes' hung down his head, an' he cried.

Well, dey pierced him in de side, in de side, in de side,
Well, dey pierced him in de side, an' de blood come a-twinklin' down,
Well, dey pierced him in de side, an' de blood come a-twinklin' down,
Den he hung down his head, an' he died.

Dere's No Hidin' Place Down Dere

Dere's no hidin' place down dere,
Dere's no hidin' place down dere.
Oh I went to de rock to hide my face,
De rock cried out, "No hidin' place,
Dere's no hidin' place down dere."

Oh de rock cried, "I'm burnin' too."
Oh de rock cried, "I'm burnin' too."
Oh de rock cried, "I'm burnin' too,

I want to go to hebben as well as you,
Dere's no hidin' place down dere."

Oh de sinner man he gambled an' fell,
Oh de sinner man he gambled an' fell,
Oh de sinner man gambled, he gambled an' fell,
He wanted to go to hebben, but he had to go to hell,
Dere's no hidin' place down dere.

Joshua Fit de Battle ob Jerico

Joshua fit de battle ob Jerico,
Jerico, Jerico,
Joshua fit de battle ob Jerico,
An' de walls come tumblin' down.

You may talk about yo' king ob Gideon,
You may talk about yo' man ob Saul,
Dere's none like good ole Joshua!
At de battle ob Jerico.

Up to de walls ob Jerico
He marched with spear in han'.

"Go blow dem ram horns," Joshua cried,
"Kase de battle am in my han'."

Den de lam' ram sheep horns begin to blow,
Trumpets begin to soun',
Joshua commanded de chillen to shout,
An' de walls come tumblin' down.

Dat mornin', Joshua fit de battle ob Jerico,
Jerico, Jerico,
Joshua fit de battle ob Jerico,
An' de walls come tumblin' down.

Swing Low, Sweet Chariot

Swing low, sweet chariot, comin' fer to carry me
home.
Swing low, sweet chariot, comin' fer to carry me
home.

I looked over Jordan, an' what did I see,
Comin' fer to carry me home?
A band of angels comin' after me,

Comin' fer to carry me home.
Swing low, etc.

If you get-a dere befo' I do,
Comin' fer to carry me home,
Tell all my friends I'm comin' too,
Comin' fer to carry me home.

Swing low, etc.

Go Down, Moses

Go down, Moses, way down in Egypt land,
Tell ole Pharaoh, to let my people go.

When Israel was in Egypt's land:
Let my people go.
Oppressed so hard they could not stand,
Let my people go.

Go down, Moses, etc.

"Thus spoke the Lord," bold Moses said;
Let my people go.
If not I'll smite your first-born dead.
Let my people go.

Go down, Moses, etc.

I Know Moonrise

I know moonrise, I know starrise,
Lay dis body down.
I walk in de moonlight, I walk in de starlight,
To lay dis body down.

I walk in de graveyard, I walk through de graveyard,
To lay dis body down.

I'll lie in de grave and stretch out my arms;
Lay dis body down.
I go to de judgment in de evenin' of de day,
When I lay dis body down;
And my soul and yore soul will meet in de day
When I lay dis body down.

Run, Nigger, Run

Do, please, marster, don't ketch me,
Ketch dat nigger behin' dat tree;
He stole money en I stole none,
Put him in the calaboose des for fun!

Chorus:

Oh, run, nigger, run! de patter-roller[1] ketch you.
Run, nigger, run! hit's almos' day!
Oh, run, nigger, run! de patter-roller ketch you.
Run, nigger, run! hit's almos' day!

Some folks say dat a nigger won't steal,
But I kotch one in my corn-fiel';
He run ter de eas', he run ter de wes',
He run he head in a hornet nes'!

De sun am set, dis nigger am free;
De yaller gals he goes to see;
I heard a man cry, "Run, doggone you,"
Run, nigger, run, patter-roller ketch you.

Wid eyes wide open and head hangin' down,
Like de rabbit before de houn',
Dis nigger streak it for de pasture;

1 "Patter-roller" is dialect for "patrol"—the patrol of mounted men covering roads and lanes at night to pick up any slaves abroad without passes from the master.

Nigger run fast, white man run faster.

And ober de fence as slick as a eel
Dis nigger jumped all but his heel;
De white man ketch dat fast, you see,
And tied it tight aroun' de tree.

Dis nigger heard dat old whip crack,
But nebber stopped fur to look back;
I started home as straight as a bee
And left my heel tied aroun' de tree.

My ol' Miss, he prommus me
Dat when she die, she set me free;
But she done dead dis many year ago,
En yer I'm hoein' de same ol' row!

I'm a-hoein' across, I'm a-hoein' aroun',
I'm a-cleanin' up some mo' new groun'.
Whar I lif' so hard, I lif' so free,
Dat my sins rise up in front er me!

But some er dese days my time will come,
I'll year dat bugle, I'll year dat drum,
I'll see dem armies a-marchin' along,
I'll lif' my head en jine der song—
I'll dine no mo' behin' dat tree,
W'en de angels flock fer to wait on me!

Jump, Jim Crow

Come listen all you gals and boys,
Ise just from Tuckyhoe,
I'm goin' to sing a little song,
My name's Jim Crow.

Chorus:

Wheel about and turn about
And do jis' so
Ebry time I wheel about
I jump Jim Crow.

I went down to de river,
I didn't mean to stay,
But dere I saw so many gals
I couldn't get away.

And arter I been dere awhile
I t'ought I push my boat;

But I tumbled in de river
An' I find myself afloat.

I git upon a flat boat
I cotch de Uncle Sam;
Den I went to see de place where
Dey killed de Packenham.

An' den I go to Orleans
An' feel so full of fight;
Dey put me in de calaboose
An' keep me dere all night.

When I got out I hit a man.
His name I now forgot:
But dere was noting left of him
'Cept a little grease spot.

De Blue-Tail Fly

When Ah was young Ah use' to wait
On Massa an' hand him de plate,
An' pass de bottle when he git dry,
An' bresh away de blue-tail fly.

Chorus:
   Jimmy crack corn an' Ah don' care,
   Jimmy crack corn an' Ah don' care,
   Jimmy crack corn an' Ah don' care,
   Ol' Massa's gone away.

Den atter dinner Massa sleep.
He bid dis nigger vigil keep,
An' when he gwine to shut his eye
He tell me watch de blue-tail fly.

One day he ride aroun' de farm;
De flies so numerous dey did swarm.

One chance' to bite 'im on de thigh.
De Debble take dat blue-tail fly!

Dat pony run, he jump, he pitch,
He tumble Massa in de ditch.
He died, an' de jury wonder why;
De verdic' was de blue-tail fly.

Dey laid 'im under a 'simmon tree;
His epitaph am dar to see:
"Beneath dis stone Ah'm fo'ced to lie,
"All by de means ob de blue-tail fly."

Ol' Massa gone, now let 'im rest;
Dey say all t'ings am for de best.
Ah nebber forget till de day I die,
Ol' Massa an' dat blue-tail fly.

Indian Oratory

Within considerably less than a year after Custer's debacle at the Little Big Horn, the newly elected President Rutherford B. Hayes declared, in his first message to Congress, that "Many, if not most, of our Indian wars have had their origin in broken promises and acts of injustice on our part." From the seventeenth century, when King Philip of the Wampanoags of Massachusetts was drawn and quartered, his head set up on a gibbet at Plymouth to be exposed for twenty years, his right hand, preserved in rum, exhibited for a curiosity, and his wife and son sold into slavery in the Indies, on to the massacre at Wounded Knee, the story is of a piece: the Indian goaded, in the face of odds that he could scarcely fail to recognize, undertook a desperate resistance and met the inevitable fate.

Avarice, arrogance, and brutality collaborated over and over again, with the inevitability of natural law, to repeat the old pattern, and if there was a certain amount of moral outrage or sentimental guilt among the palefaces, the fact had little effect on the course of history. And the history is full of ironies. While the Civil War was in progress, for instance, a mass hanging[1] of Indians, tried and convicted without benefit of counsel, took place at

---

[1] In the trial, 303 of the Sioux had been sentenced to death, but President Lincoln intervened to save all but 39—probably the best deal he thought he could make under the circumstances. Two of the men hanged met their fate by accident or bureaucratic confusion. The names got mixed up.

Mankato, Minnesota. The state, in fact, was offering a bounty of twenty-five dollars for Sioux scalps, and the legislature was soon to vote a reward of one thousand dollars to a certain John McKenzie, who, in bald-faced defiance of international law, had kidnapped out of Canada, with the tools of bribery, laudanum, and dog sled, the chiefs Shakopee and Medicine Bottle, who were promptly hanged, even though, as the St. Paul *Pioneer* observed at the time, there was no "tangible evidence" of any guilt. The state of Minnesota—and the people of the then United States—knew what they wanted: the black man free and the red man penned up, or dead. In any case, the Minnesota Sioux were taken care of. Of the 1300 expelled in 1863 to an uninhabitable reservation on the Missouri River, more than 300 died the first winter.

Oratory was a highly respected art among the Indian tribes, and apart from hereditary and ritual considerations oratorical ability was considered the foremost attribute of a leader, exceeding even bravery in battle. What may explain this fact is that, with the notable exception of the Iroquois confederation, political organization was decentralized, and since all decisions had to be unanimous, leaders were those who possessed the ability to persuade the rest of the tribe of the rightness of their positions.

We know, then, of the importance of oratory to the Indians. Yet it is difficult to be certain how many of the speeches which have been recorded are legitimate examples of the Indians' art. Clearly Indians orating to other Indians in a tribal council spoke of different subjects in a different manner than when they were making their proud pleas to white soldiers and peace commissions, but it is this last type of speech that has been preserved. And these speeches in many instances were taken down by army officers whose credentials as translators were dubious, and who sometimes had literary pretensions of their own. This, combined with the fact that the translators were usually sympathetic to the Indians' cause, has led to the suspicion that they altered the words of the chiefs to more effectively plead their case, thus indicating their conviction, shared with less well-disposed whites, that they knew what was best for the red man. Fortunately, we have enough examples which have been proved to be accurate to show that the Indian verbal ability was highly effective in its intended purpose.

In this section the cut-off point is not, as is usual in this volume, 1861. For the continuing theme of the eloquence of the Indian orator, at least in the speeches recorded, was the ongoing ordeal of his people, and to make a division that was meaningless for the Indian would violate the unity of his story.

FURTHER READINGS

The United States Bureau of Ethnology Annual Reports (1879–1933) and Bulletins (1880–1965) contain the greatest concentration of American Indian material, not only poetry and prose of all kinds but entire religious rituals and a great deal of useful ethnographic background. Another useful source is the series published by the American Ethnological Society in the early part of this century.

John Bierhorst, ed., *In the Trail of the Wind: American Indian Poems and Ritual Orations* (1971)
Black Elk, *Sacred Pipe* (1953), Joseph E. Brown, ed.
William Brandon, ed., *The Magic Rainbow* (1971)

Dee Brown, *Bury My Heart at Wounded Knee* (1970)
Michael Coe, *The Maya* (1970)
Edward Dozier, *The Pueblo Indians* (1969)
Peter Farb, *Man's Rise to Civilization As Shown by the Indians of North America* (1968)
Alice Fletcher and Francis LaFlesche, *The Omaha Tribe* (1915; 1972)
Lewis H. Morgan, *The League of the Do-de-no-San-nee* (1851)
John Neihardt, ed., *Black Elk Speaks* (1932; 1967)
Gerardo Reichal-Dolmatoff, *Amazonian Cosmos* (1971)
Jerome Rothenberg, ed., *Shaking the Pumpkin* (1972)
John Stands in Timber and Margot Liberty, *Cheyenne Memories* (1965)

CHIEF LOGAN

The name Mingo was used sometimes to apply to the Six Nations of the Iroquois proper, and sometimes to an independent group of Iroquois in the region of the headwaters of the Ohio. Of the latter, the father of John Logan, reported to be of French blood, had been a chief.

The Pennsylvania-Ohio Mingos had generally been on good terms with the whites until 1774, when whites murdered a group of Mingos, including some members of Logan's family. After the war for revenge had broken out, Lord Dunmore, the colonial governor, summoned a council, at which Chief Logan delivered the speech so praised by Thomas Jefferson.

I appeal to any white man to say, if ever he entered Logan's cabin hungry, and he gave him not meat; if ever he came cold and naked, and he clothed him not. During the course of the last long and bloody war, Logan remained idle in his cabin, an advocate for peace. Such was my love for the whites that my countrymen pointed as they passed, and said, "Logan is the friend of the white man." I had even thought to have lived with you, but for the injuries of one man, Colonel Cressap, who last spring, in cold blood and unprovoked, murdered all the relations of Logan, not even sparing my women and children. There runs not a drop of my blood in the veins of any living creature. This called on me for revenge. I have sought it; I have killed many; I have fully glutted my vengeance. For my countrymen I rejoice at the beams of peace. But do not harbor a thought that mine is the joy of fear. Logan never felt fear! He will not turn on his heel to save his life. Who is there to mourn for Logan? Not one.

CHIEF SPECKLED SNAKE

Up until 1829 the United States government had regarded the individual Indian tribes as sovereign nations, but in 1829 the state of Georgia affirmed that the Cherokee and Creek nations (of the "Five Civilized Tribes") were subject to the laws of the state—an action provoked by greed for the rich lands occupied by these tribes that, adopting the white man's way of life, were now prospering. The Cherokees brought suit against Georgia, and the Supreme

Court sustained their position, but Andrew Jackson, now President, affirmed that he had no power to oppose states' rights and turned the Indians over to the tender mercies of Georgia and the eventual removal west, in 1839, known as the "Trail of Tears." The speech of the Creek chief Speckled Snake was in response to a public reading, in 1830, of a speech by Jackson urging the Indians to leave their holdings in South Carolina and Georgia and move further west.

———

Brothers: I have listened to many talks from our great father. When he first came over the wide waters, he was only a little man who wore a red coat. Our chiefs met him on the banks of the Savannah river, and they smoked the peace-pipe with him. He was very little then. His legs were cramped from sitting a long time in his big boat, and he begged us for a little land to light his fire on. He said he had come over the wide waters to teach the Indians new things, and to make them happy. He said he loved his red brothers. He was very kind.

Brothers: The Muskogees gave the white man land, and they made him a fire so he could warm himself. And when his enemies, the white men to the south [the Spaniards in Florida], made war on him, our young men drew the tomahawk and protected his head from the scalper's knife. But when the white man had warmed himself before the Indian's fire and filled himself with Indian corn, he became very big. He walked across the mountains at a single step, and his feet filled the plains and valleys. His hands reached out and held the seas to the east and the seas to the west, and his head rested on the moon. Then he became our Great Father. He loved his red children. And he said, "Move a little further on, so I don't step on you." With one foot he shoved the red man across the Oconee, and with the other he trampled down the graves of our fathers and the forest where we had so long hunted deer. But our Great Father still loved his red children. And soon he made us another talk. He said, "Move a little further on. You are too close to me." But there were some bad men among the Muskogees then, just as there are now. They stayed on, close to the graves of their fathers until they were crushed by the heavy feet of our Great Father. Their teeth bit his feet, and that made him angry. But he continued to love his red children. And when he found them too slow to move, he sent his big guns before him to sweep them out of his way.

Brothers: I have listened to a great many talks from our Great Father but they always begin and end the same way: "Move further on. You are too close to me."

Brothers: Our Great Father says "Where you are now, the white men have always claimed the land." He speaks with a straight tongue, and he cannot lie. But when he first came over the wide waters, while he was still a little man, and stood before the great chief at the council on Yamacraw Bluff, he said: "Give me a little land. You can spare it, and I will pay you for it."

Brothers: When our Great Father made us talk at an earlier time, he said, "Go a little further on. Go across the Oconee and the Okmulgee. There is good country there." He also said, "It will be yours forever." I have listened to his talk now. He says the land where you live is not yours. He says, "Move across the Mississippi. There is game there. You can stay there as long as the grass grows or the water runs."

Brothers: Won't our Great Father come there too? He loves his red children. He loves his red children, and his tongue is not forked.

Brothers: Our Great Father says that our bad men have made his heart bleed because they murdered one of his white children. But where are the red children he loves, who were once as many as the leaves of the forest? How many have been killed by his soldiers? How many have been crushed beneath his feet?

CHIEF BLACK HAWK

The Black Hawk War, in which both Abraham Lincoln and Jefferson Davis served, was provoked by the attempt, finally successful, of the whites to dispossess the Sauk and Fox tribes of their ancestral lands in Illinois and Wisconsin. The war was marked by the killing, by white militia, of the bearer of a flag of truce (an act that precipitated the actual fighting), a shameful rout of some 250 militia by some 40 Indians, and, at the so-called battle of Bad Axe, the massacre of a force of Indians trying to surrender.

After the battle of Bad Axe, Chief Black Hawk, a prisoner, addressed General Street, his captor. The date is August 27, 1832.

You have taken me prisoner with all my braves. My heart is sore because I hoped to defeat you or else to hold out longer and give you more trouble before I surrendered. I tried hard to lead you into an ambush, but your General Atkinson understood how Indians fight. I decided to rush you and fight you face to face. I fought hard, but your guns were well aimed. The bullets flew like birds in the air and whizzed by our ears like the wind through the trees in winter.

My braves fell around me. It began to look bad. I saw my evil day at hand. In the morning the sun rose bright. At night it went down in a dark cloud and looked like a ball of fire. This was the last sun to shine on Black Hawk. He is now the white man's prisoner. They will do with him what they want. But he can stand the torture. He is no coward.

Black Hawk is an Indian. He has done nothing an Indian should be ashamed of. He fought for his country against the white men. Year after year the white men came to cheat the Indians and steal their land. You know why we went to war. Every white man knows why. They should be ashamed of what they do. The white men hate the Indians and drive them from their homes. But the Indians do not deceive. The white men speak bad of the Indians, and look at them with spite. But Indians do not tell lies. Indians do not steal. An Indian who was as bad as a white man couldn't live among our people. He would be put to death and eaten by wolves.

The white men are bad teachers. Their looks are false, their actions are false. They smile in the face of the poor Indian to cheat him. They shake his hand to gain his trust, to get him drunk and then cheat him. We told them to let us alone and stay away from us. But they followed us. They hid themselves along our path and coiled among us like the snake. We were not safe. We lived in danger. We were becoming like the white men, hypocrites and liars, all talkers and no workers.

We looked up to the Great Spirit. We went to our Great Father in Washington. We were encouraged. His Great Council gave us fair words and big promises. But nothing was done for us. Things were getting worse. There were no deer in the forest. The possum and the beaver disappeared. The springs were drying up, and our people had no food to keep from starving. We called a great council and built a great fire. The spirits of our fathers rose and told us to avenge our wrongs or die. We raised the war cry and dug up the tomahawk. Our knives were ready, and Black Hawk's heart swelled in his chest as he led his braves to war. He is content. He will go to the world of the spirits contented. He has done what he had to do. His father will meet him and praise him. Black Hawk is a true Indian. He pities his wife, his children, and his friends, but he does not care about himself. He cares about his people and the Indians. They will suffer. He pities their fate.

The white men don't scalp heads. They do worse things. They poison the heart. It is not pure with them. Black Hawk's men will not be scalped. But in a few years they will become worse men. They will become like white men, so you cannot trust them. And then you cannot hurt them any more. And our villages will be like the white settlements, as many officers as men, to take care of them and keep them in order.

Farewell, my people. Black Hawk tried to save you and avenge your wrongs. He drank the blood of some of the whites. He has been taken prisoner, and his plans are stopped. He can do no more. He is near his end. His sun is setting and it will not rise again. Farewell to Black Hawk!

CHIEF COBB

After the Treaty of Dancing Rabbit Creek, in 1830, by which the Choctaws were led, by bribery and threat, to move to Oklahoma, certain Indians not party to the treaty were promised the right to continue to hold land in Mississippi —a promise never fulfilled. When, in 1843, the

Indian agent, one McRea, tried to persuade the remaining Choctaws to "take the hand of their great father, the president," to be led to their "Western homes," Chief Cobb responded.

Brother: We have heard your words as from the lips of our father, the great white chief at Washington, and my people have asked me to reply. The red man has no books, and when he wants to say what he thinks, he speaks from the mouth, like his fathers before him. He is afraid of *writing*. When he *speaks*, he knows what he says. The Great Spirit hears him. *Writing* is the invention of the palefaces. It gives birth to trouble and fighting. The Great Spirit *talks*. We hear him in the thunder, in the sound of the wind, and in the water. He never *writes*.

Brother: When you were young, we were strong. We fought at your side. But now our arms are broken. You have grown big. My people have grown little.

Brother: My voice is weak. You can scarcely hear me. It is not the shout of a warrior, but the cry of a baby. I have lost my voice mourning the sufferings of my people. These are their graves, and in those old pines you hear the ghosts of our dead. Their ashes are here, and we have been left behind to guard them. Our warriors have nearly all gone to the far country in the west. But our dead are *here*. Shall we go too and leave their bones to the wolves?

Brother: Two sleeps have passed since we heard you talk. We have thought about what you said. You ask us to leave our country, and you say it is our father's wish. We do not want to offend our father. We respect him and we respect you, his son. But the Choctaw always thinks. We want time to answer.

Brother: Our hearts are full. Twelve winters ago our chiefs sold our country. Every warrior you see here was opposed to that treaty. If the dead could have been counted, the treaty would never have been made. They were here, but they were not seen or heard. Their tears were in the rain, their voices were in the wind. But the palefaces did not know it, and our land was taken away.

Brother: We do not complain now. The Choctaw suffers, but he does not weep. You have the strong arm, and we cannot resist. But the white man worships the Great Spirit. The red man worships him too. The Great Spirit loves truth. When you took our country, you promised us land. There is your promise in the book. Twelve times the trees have dropped their leaves, but we have received no land. Our lodges have been taken from us. The white man's plough turns up the bones of our fathers. We dare not kindle our fires. And yet you told us we could stay here and you would give us land.

Brother: Is this *truth?* But we believe, now that our great father knows our condition, that he will hear us. We are like mourning orphans in our own country. But our father will take us by the hand. When he fulfills his promise, we will answer his talk. He means well. We know it. But we cannot think now. Suffering has made children of us. When our business is settled, we will be men again. Then we will talk to our great father about what he has proposed.

Brother: You stand in the moccasins of a great chief. You speak the words of a great nation, and your talk was long. My people are small. Their shadow barely reaches to your knee. They are scattered and gone. When I shout, I hear my own voice in the forest, but no shout answers back. This is why my words are few. I have nothing more to say, but to tell what I have said to the tall chief of the palefaces, whose brother[1] stands by your side.

[1] William Tyler, brother of President John Tyler (1841–45), who had recently been appointed one of the Choctaw commissioners.

CHIEF SEATTLE

Seattle (or Seathl) was chief of the tribes of the Puget Sound region, in Washington, born about 1790. By the time when he fatalistically signed the Port Elliott Treaty of 1855, he was an aging man and intelligent enough to know that resistance was useless. This is his speech concerning the treaty.

Brothers: That sky above us has pitied our fathers for many hundreds of years. To us it looks unchanging, but it may change. Today it is fair. Tomorrow it may be covered with cloud.

My words are like the stars. They do not set. What Seattle says, the great chief Washington[1] can count on as surely as our white brothers can count on the return of the seasons.

The White Chief's son[2] says his father sends us words of friendship and goodwill. This is kind. We know he has little need of our friendship in return. His people are many, like the grass that covers the plains. My people are few, like the trees scattered by the storms on the grasslands.

The great—and good, I believe—White Chief sends us word that he wants to buy our land. But he will reserve us enough so that we can live comfortably. This seems generous, since the red man no longer has rights he need respect. It may also be wise, since we no longer need a large country. Once my people covered this land like a flood-tide moving across the shell-covered flats. But that time is gone, and with it the greatness of tribes now almost forgotten.

But I will not mourn the passing of my people. And I do not blame our white brothers for causing it. We too were perhaps partly to blame. When our young men grow angry at some wrong, real or imagined, they make their faces ugly with black paint. Then their hearts are ugly and black. They are hard and their cruelty knows no limits. And our old men cannot restrain them.

Let us hope that the wars between the red man and his white brothers will never come again. We would have everything to lose and nothing to gain. Young men think revenge is gain, even when they lose their own lives. But the old men who stay behind in time of war, mothers with sons to lose—they know better.

Our great father Washington—for he must be our father now as well as yours, since George[3] has moved his boundary northward—our great and good father sends us word by his son, who is surely a great chief among his people, that he will protect us if we do what he wants. His brave soldiers will be a wall for my people, and his warships will fill our harbors. Then our ancient enemies to the north—the Haidas and Tsimshians—will no longer frighten our women and old men. Then he will be our father and we will be his children.

But can that ever be? Your God loves your people and hates mine. He puts his strong arm around the white man and leads him by the hand, as a father leads his little boy. He has abandoned his red children. He makes your people stronger every day. Soon they will flood all the land. But my people are an ebb-tide, we will never return. No, the white man's God cannot love his red children or he would protect them. Now we are orphans. There is no one to help us.

So how can we be brothers? How can your father be our father, and make us prosper and send us dreams of future greatness? Your God is prejudiced. He came to the white man. We never saw him, never even heard his voice. He gave the white man laws, but he had no word for his red children whose numbers once filled this land as the stars fill the sky.

No, we are two separate races, and we must stay separate. There is little in common between us.

To us the ashes of our fathers are sacred. Their graves are holy ground. But you white men are wanderers. You leave your fathers' graves behind you, and you do not care.

Your religion was written on tables of stone by the iron finger of an angry God, so you would not forget it. The red man could never understand it or remember it. Our religion is the ways of our forefathers, the dreams of our old men, sent them by the Great Spirit, and the visions of our sachems. And it is written in the hearts of our people.

Your dead forget you and the land where they were born as soon as they pass the grave and walk among the stars. They are soon forgotten and they never return. Our dead never forget this beautiful earth. It is their mother. They always love and remember her rivers, her great mountains, her valleys. They love and remember those they have left behind, and the living long for the dead. And the spirits of the dead often return to visit and console us.

No, day and night cannot live together.

The red man has always retreated before the advancing white man, as the mist on the mountain slopes runs before the morning sun.

So your offer seems fair, and I think my people

---

[1] The Indians of the mid-nineteenth century believed that Washington was still alive, perhaps because they confused the name of the city with the name of the "reigning chief." (All of the footnotes for this speech are from William Arrowsmith, the translator.)

[2] That is, the governor of Washington Territory, I. I. Stevens.

[3] The Indians believed King George III was still on the English throne, perhaps because the Hudson Bay traders referred to themselves as "King George men." In any case, the confusion was encouraged by the Hudson Bay Company in the belief that the Indians would not respect the subjects of a country ruled by a queen.

will accept it and go to the reservation you offer them. We will live apart, and in peace. The words of the Great White Chief are like the words of nature speaking to my people out of great darkness —a darkness that gathers around us like the night fog moving inland from the sea.

It does not matter much where we pass the rest of our days. They are not many. The Indians' night will be dark. No star shines on his horizons. The wind is sad. Death hunts the red man down. Wherever he goes, he will hear the steps of his destroyer approaching and prepare to die, like the wounded doe who hears the steps of the hunter.

A few more moons, a few more winters, and none of the children of the great tribes that once lived in this wide land or that roam in small bands in the forest will be left to mourn the graves of a people once as powerful and as hopeful as yours.

But why should I mourn the passing of my people? Tribes are made of men, nothing more. Men come and go, like the waves of the sea. A tear, a prayer to the Great Spirit, a dirge, and they are gone from our longing eyes forever. Even the white man, whose God walked and talked with him as friend to friend, cannot be exempt from the common doom.

We may be brothers after all. We shall see.

We will consider your offer. When we decide, we will let you know. If we accept, I here and now make this condition: we will always have the right to visit, at any time, the graves of our fathers and our friends.

Every part of this earth is sacred to my people. Every hillside, every valley, every clearing and wood, is holy in the memory and experience of my people. Those stones along the shore have no voices, but they are loved with events and memories in the life of my people. The ground where you stand responds more lovingly to our feet than yours, because it is the ashes of our grandfathers. Our bare feet know the kindred touch. The earth is rich with the lives of our kin.

The young men, the mothers, and girls, the little children who once lived and were happy here, still love these lonely places. And at night the forest is dark with the presence of the dead. When the red man has gone from this earth and is only a story among the whites, these shores will still swarm with the dead of my people. You will not see them. But when your children's children think they are alone, they will not be alone. There is no place in this country where a man can be alone. At night when the streets of your towns and cities are quiet, and you think they are empty, they will throng with the returning spirits who still love these places. The white man will never be alone.

So let him be just and deal kindly with my people. The dead have power too.

CHIEF COCHISE

Although the Apaches had been traditionally at peace with the Americans (though not with the Mexicans), hostilities broke out before the Civil War. After the war, Cochise, of the Chiricahua Apaches, began his long guerrilla struggle. The following speech was delivered at a conference where Cochise was informed that he and his tribe were to be sent to a reservation at Tularosa, New Mexico. As a matter of fact, the plan was not carried out. Cochise fled to the mountains, where, after a time, General Oliver Otis Howard personally hunted him out for a conference and spent some ten days with the tribe, becoming so impressed by the chief that he managed to persuade the government to settle him in his own region. After this, until his death, Cochise lived at peace with the whites.

The opening section of the speech by Chief Cochise is here omitted.

The white people have looked for me long. I am here. What do they want? They have looked for me long. Why am I worth so much? If I am worth so much, why not mark where I set my foot and where I spit?

The coyotes go around at night to rob and kill. I cannot see them. I am not God. I am no longer chief of the Apaches. I am no longer rich. I am only a poor man.

The world was not always this way. I cannot command the animals. If I did, they would not obey me. God made us different from you. We were born like the animals, in the dry grass, not on beds like you. That is why we do as the animals do, go around at night and rob and steal. If I had things like you, I would not do what I do. I would not need to.

There are Indians who go around killing and robbing. I do not command them. If I did, they would not do these things.

My warriors have been killed in Sonora. I came here because God told me to come. He said it was good to be at peace. So I came. I was going around the world with the clouds, and the air, when God spoke to my thought and told me to come in here and be at peace with all.

God said the world was for us all. How was it? When I was young I walked all over this country, east and west, and I saw no other people but Apaches. After many summers I walked again and found another race of people had come to take it. How is it? Why is it that the Apaches wait to die —that they carry their lives on their fingernails? They roam over the hills and plains and want the heavens to fall on them. The Apaches were once a great nation. They are now only a few. Because of this they want to die and so carry their lives on their fingernails. Many have been killed in war.

You must speak straight so your words will go like sunlight to our hearts.

Tell me, if the Virgin Mary has walked everywhere in the world, why has she never entered the wickiups of the Apache? Why have we never seen or heard her?

I have no father or mother. I am alone in the world. Nobody cares about Cochise. That is why I do not care to live and want the rocks to fall and cover me up. If I had a father and mother like you, I would be with them and they with me.

When I was going around the world, everybody was asking for Cochise. Now he is here. You see him and hear him. Are you glad? If so, say so. Speak, Americans and Mexicans. I do not want to hide anything from you nor have you hide anything from me. I will not lie to you. Do not lie to me.

I want to live in these mountains. I do not want to go to Tularosa. That is a long way off. The flies on those mountains eat out the eyes of the horses. The bad spirits live there. I have drunk of these waters, and they have cooled me. I do not want to leave this place.

CHIEF TEN BEARS

At the Council of Medicine Lodge Creek, in 1867, Chief Ten Bears of the Comanches, a fierce and intelligent nation fighting to hold their buffalo lands, stated the Indian position. The opening courtesies have been omitted here.

Two years ago, I came upon this road, following the buffalo, that my wives and children might have their cheeks plump and their bodies warm. But the soldiers fired on us. And since that time there has been a noise like thunder, and we have not known which way to go.

So it was on the Canadian River. Nor have we been made to cry only once. The blue-dressed soldiers and the Utes came from out of the night when it was dark and still. And for campfires they lit our lodges. Instead of hunting game they killed my braves, and the warriors of the tribe cut short their hair for the dead.

So it was in Texas. They made sorrow come in our camps, and we went out like the buffalo bulls when the cows are attacked. When we found them we killed them, and their scalps hang in our lodges. The Comanches are not weak and blind, like the pups of a dog when seven sleeps old. They are strong and they see far, like grown horses. We took their road and we went on it. The white women cried and our women laughed.

But there are things that you have said to me that I do not like. They were not sweet like sugar, but bitter like gourds. You said you wanted to put us on a reservation, to build us houses, and make us medicine lodges. I do not want them. I was born on the prairie, where the wind blew free and there was nothing to break the light of the sun. I was born where there were no fences and everything drew a free breath. I want to die there and not inside walls. I know every stream and every woods between the Rio Grande and the Arkansas. I have hunted and lived over that country. I live like my fathers before me and, like them, I live happily.

When I was at Washington the Great Father told me that all the Comanche land was ours, and that nobody should stop us from living on it. So why do you ask us to leave the rivers, and the sun, and the wind, and live in houses? Do not ask us

to give up the buffalo for the sheep. The young men have heard talk of this, and it has made them sad and angry. Do not speak of it any more.

. . .

Any good thing you say to me shall not be forgotten. I shall carry it as near to my heart as my children, and it shall be on my tongue as often as the name of the Great Spirit. I want no blood upon my land to stain the grass. I want it all clear and pure, and I want it so that all who go through among my people will find peace when they come in and leave it that way when they go out.

CHIEF JOSEPH

When, in 1805, the Lewis and Clark expedition came down from the Rockies into the valley of the Clearwater River, sick, starving, and exhausted, the Nez Percé tribe received them hospitably, fed them, and harbored them until strength returned. For more than half a century thereafter the boast of the tribe was that they had never harmed a white man. By that time the pressure of the whites in the Washington Territory was considerable, and the governor attempted to make a treaty limiting the Nez Percé lands. Old Chief Joseph refused to negotiate, saying that the earth could not be owned by men and that he had, therefore, no right to sell any part of it.[1] But some of the Nez Percés were persuaded to sign, and Old Joseph returned to his ancestral lands in the Wallowa Valley.

By 1873, after the death of Old Joseph, greater pressure was put on the recalcitrant group of Nez Percés, now under the leadership of Young Joseph, who directly petitioned President Grant for protection; Grant responded with an executive order barring white settlers

[1] See the same idea in Faulkner's *The Bear* uttered by Isaac McCaslin.

from the Wallowa lands; but the prize was too rich, and a few years later the order was revoked; by 1877 a military force was sent to clear the valley and put the Nez Percés on a reservation.

The officer entrusted with the mission was General Oliver Otis Howard, who had served with some distinction in the Civil War and lost an arm and after the war had served, with good intentions but little distinction, as head of the Freedman's Bureau in the South. After that fiasco, he was assigned to western duty, and in dealing with Chief Cochise and the Apaches had been decent and humane. He had, however, learned the score now, and his dealing with the Nez Percés exhibited little decency or humanity, and no tact. He wound up by flinging the official orator and prophet of the Nez Percés into the guardhouse and giving Joseph thirty days to clear the Wallowa Valley. When Joseph protested that thirty days was not enough to round up the herds and that the Snake River was now too high for fording, Howard would hear nothing from him and retorted that if they were not on reservation in thirty days all stock would be taken by the whites.

Joseph made the attempt to comply, abandoning some stock and managing to get his people across the flooded Snake, but while this dangerous business was in course, whites stole tribal cattle. In retaliation, a few days later a group of the young men slipped away and killed some whites, and the war was on. Howard pursued but was trapped and lost a third of a force that outnumbered the Nez Percés more than two to one. Thus began the great march of Joseph, heading for Canada. There was no other haven now.

Three armies were in pursuit of Joseph's force of 250 braves, burdened by more than 400 old men, women, and children, the tribal baggage, and 2000 horses. More than once it seemed that Joseph was caught in a pincers, but he fought himself free, always against heavy odds, and always inflicting heavy casualties. It was a military action often rated by historians with Xenophon's March to the Sea, but it had no such happy outcome. In the end, Joseph was worn down and accepted the terms of General Miles, to whom he surrendered, that the tribe would be sent back to the reservation to which they had been originally destined. Some young men, however, did manage to escape to Canada to join Sitting Bull, who had found refuge there.

As for Joseph, the terms promised were abrogated, and the entire tribe was shipped off to Fort Leavenworth, in Kansas, as prisoners of war, and there confined under intolerable conditions. Some hundred of the already dwindled tribe died in a short time, and when a transfer was made to the Indian Territory, the lethal conditions were scarcely improved. Joseph was finally allowed to go to Washington to plead the case for his people, and later, in the august pages of the *North American Review*, which Henry Adams had recently edited, a long account of the Nez Percé war, by Joseph, was published.

Nothing, however, interfered with the internal logic of the situation. In the end some of the tribe were allowed to go back to the reservation specified in the terms offered by General Miles, but Joseph, along with nearly a hundred others regarded as dangerous, was put on a reservation in the state of Washington, far from the home country. He died there in 1904, the cause of death, as reported by the post physician, being a "broken heart."

It should be added that it was in honor of General Howard, of Freedman's Bureau and Nez Percé fame, that the famous black university in Washington, D.C., is named.

I believe General Miles would have kept his word if he could have done so. I do not blame him for what we have suffered since the surrender. I do not know who is to blame. We gave up all our horses—over eleven hundred—and all our saddles—over one hundred—and we have not heard from them since. Somebody has got our horses.

General Miles turned my people over to another soldier, and we were taken to Bismarck. Captain Johnson, who now had charge of us, received an order to take us to Fort Leavenworth. At Leavenworth we were placed on a low river bottom, with no water except river-water to drink and cook with. We had always lived in a healthy country, where the mountains were high and the water was cold and clear. Many of my people sickened and died, and we buried them in this strange land. I can not tell how much my heart suffered for my people while at Leavenworth. The Great Spirit Chief who rules above seemed to be looking some other way, and did not see what was being done to my people.

During the hot days we received notice that we were to be moved farther away from our own country. We were not asked if we were willing to go. We were ordered to get into the railroad-cars. Three of my people died on the way to Baxter Springs. It was worse to die there than to die fighting in the mountains.

We were moved from Baxter Springs to the Indian Territory, and set down without our lodges. We had but little medicine, and we were nearly all sick. Seventy of my people have died since we moved there.

We have had a great many visitors who have talked many ways. Some of the chiefs from Washington came to see us, and selected land for us to live upon. We have not moved to that land, for it is not a good place to live.

The Commissioner Chief came to see us. I told him, as I told every one, that I expected General Miles's word would be carried out. He said it "could not be done; that white men now lived in my country and all the land was taken up; that, if I returned to Wallowa, I could not live in peace;

that law-papers were out against young men who began the war, and that the Government could not protect my people." This talk fell like a heavy stone upon my heart. I saw that I could not gain anything by talking to him. Other law chiefs [the congressional committee] came to see me and said they would help me to get a healthy country. I did not know who to believe. The white people have too many chiefs. They do not understand each other. They do not talk alike.

The Commissioner Chief invited me to go with him and hunt for a better home than we have now. I like the land we found (west of the Osage reservation) better than any place I have seen in that country; but it is not a healthy land. There are no mountains and rivers. The water is warm. It is not a good country for stock. I do not believe my people can live there. I am afraid they will all die. The Indians who occupy that country are dying off. I promised Chief Hayt to go there, and do the best I could until the Government got ready to make good General Miles's word. I was not satisfied, but I could not help myself.

Then the Inspector Chief came to my camp and we had a long talk. He said I ought to have a home in the mountain country north, and that he would write a letter to the Great Chief at Washington. Again the hope of seeing the mountains of Idaho and Oregon grew up in my heart.

At last I was granted permission to come to Washington and bring my friend Yellow Bull and our interpreter with me. I am glad we came. I have shaken hands with a great many friends, but there are some things I want to know which no one seems able to explain. I can not understand how the Government sends a man out to fight us, as it did General Miles, and then breaks his word. Such a Government has something wrong about it. I can not understand why so many chiefs are allowed to talk so many different ways, and promise so many different things. I have seen the Great Father Chief [the President], the next Great Chief [the Secretary of the Interior], the Commissioner Chief, the Law Chief [General Butler], and many other law chiefs [Congressmen], and they all say they are my friends, and that I shall have justice, but while their mouths all talk right I do not understand why nothing is done for my people. I have heard talk and talk, but nothing is done. Good words do not last long unless they amount to something. Words do not pay for my dead people. They do not pay for my country, now overrun by white men. They do not protect my father's grave. They do not pay for all my horses

and cattle. Good words will not give me back my children. Good words will not make good the promise of your War Chief General Miles. Good words will not give my people good health and stop them from dying. Good words will not get my people a home where they can live in peace and take care of themselves. I am tired of talk that comes to nothing. It makes my heart sick when I remember all the good words and all the broken promises. There has been too much talking by men who had no right to talk. Too many misrepresentations have been made, too many misunderstandings have come up between the white men about the Indians. If the white man wants to live in peace with the Indian he can live in peace. There need be no trouble. Treat all men alike. Give them all the same law. Give them all an even chance to live and grow. All men were made by the same Great Spirit Chief. They are all brothers. The earth is the mother of all people, and all people should have equal rights upon it. You might as well expect the rivers to run backward as that any man who was born a free man should be contented when penned up and denied liberty to go where he pleases. If you tie a horse to a stake, do you expect he will grow fat? If you pen an Indian up on a small spot of earth, and compel him to stay there, he will not be contented, nor will he grow and prosper. I have asked some of the great white chiefs where they get their authority to say to the Indian that he shall stay in one place, while he sees white men going where they please. They can not tell me.

I only ask of the Government to be treated as all other men are treated. If I can not go to my own home, let me have a home in some country where my people will not die so fast. I would like to go to Bitter Root Valley. There my people would be healthy; where they are now they are dying. Three have died since I left my camp to come to Washington.

When I think of our condition my heart is heavy. I see men of my race treated as outlaws and driven from country to country, or shot down like animals.

I know that my race must change. We can not hold our own with the white men as we are. We only ask an even chance to live as other men live. We ask to be recognized as men. We ask that the same law shall work alike on all men. If the Indian breaks the law, punish him by the law. If the white man breaks the law, punish him also.

Let me be a free man—free to travel, free to stop, free to work, free to trade where I choose, free to choose my own teachers, free to follow the religion of my fathers, free to think and talk and act for myself—and I will obey every law, or submit to the penalty.

Whenever the white man treats the Indian as they treat each other, then we will have no more wars. We shall all be alike—brothers of one father and one mother, with one sky above us and one country around us, and one government for all.

Then the Great Spirit Chief who rules above will smile upon this land, and send rain to wash out the bloody spots made by brothers' hands from the face of the earth. For this time the Indian race are waiting and praying. I hope that no more groans of wounded men and women will ever go to the ear of the Great Spirit Chief above, and that all people may be one people.

In-mut-too-yah-lat-lat has spoken for his people.

Indian Poetry

In almost every facet of Indian life, poetry, through song, chant, myth, and ritual, was an integral concern. Since religion dominated the lives of most tribes, the poetry appears in its context, entering into even the most mundane affairs, associated with the everyday awareness of the Indian of his intimate relation to supernatural beings and forces. The Cherokee hunter had to say a special prayer to a deer before killing him (lest the deer's spirit be angered and enter his own body to cause rheumatism), and a Navajo shaman had to chant for nine days as part of the ritual for healing the sick. Almost every activity of life was enriched by song and fantasy. As William Brandon says, in the introduction to *The Magic World*:

> If the Pawnees had operated a General Motors, each worker would have had his time-clock-punching song, his assembly-line song, and so on, and the management would have been at least as attentive to the songs as to the rate of production, probably more so.

A considerable body of such poetry has been preserved, but what does exist must be a very small fraction of what was current in the poetry-suffused world of the Indian.

Translation from one language to another is always difficult, for a language is the living embodiment of a special culture, but when the cultural differences are as great as those between the world of the first Americans and our latter-day breed, the problem is compounded many times over. All we can do is to try to achieve a certain degree of innocence, of submission to the specific and concrete elements to give us at least some sort of what we may call a "germ poem." As the poet Gary Snyder says of translation, "the problem, in a sense, is not one of 'writing' but of 'visualizing.' " He continues:

> I get the verbal meaning into mind as clear as I can, but then make an enormous effort of visualization, to "see" what the poem says, nonlinguistically, like a

movie in my mind: and to feel it. If I can do this (and much of the time the poem eludes this effort) then I write the scene down in English. It is not a translation of the words, it is the same poem in a different language, allowing for the peculiar distortions of my own vision—but keeping it as straight as possible. If I can do this to a poem the translation is uniformly successful, and is generally well received by scholars and critics. If I can't do this, I can still translate the words, and it may be well-received, but it doesn't feel like it should. (In Dell Hymes, "Some North Pacific Coast Poems: A Problem in Anthropological Philology," *American Anthropologist*, April, 1965)

The poem we get in any translation is always, at best, an approximation, and even if the "germ poem" we get here affects us as beautiful or moving we can be certain that the implications and resonances of the original poem for the red-skin auditor are missing. We can get some notion of what is missing only by anthropological, historical, and linguistic study. We may, for instance, be struck by a translation of Homer or Baudelaire, but only a knowledge of Greek life of the tenth century B.C. or of French life of the mid-nineteenth century can help us recover something of the force of the original works.

We should remind ourselves, too, that the Indians had no written language and that their poetry, like most of our own folk poetry, originated in an oral tradition, subject to a complex process of modification. The poems we have here are frozen moments of a living stream.

Three Songs of Mad Coyote

These are short songs of the Nez Percé tribe who lived in northern Idaho, eastern Washington, and western Montana until they were subjugated in 1880. The coyote is an important figure in American Indian mythology: a malicious and somewhat destructive character who often plays tricks on people.

1
Ravening Coyote comes
red hands, red mouth,

necklace of eyeballs

2
Mad Coyote
madly sings
then the west wind roars!

3
Daybreak finds me,
eastern daybreak finds me
the meaning of that song:
with blood-stained mouth
comes Mad Coyote!

Cherokee Love Magic

This poem is a Cherokee incantation for retaining affection. It is from the Oklahoma Cherokee, who were forced to migrate from their south-eastern homeland in 1837. There are hundreds of incantations such as this one, for attracting lovers, creating loneliness, abasing another, and separating from a lover. This particular incantation is taken from *Walk in Your Soul: Love Incantations of the Oklahoma Cherokees* by Jack and Anna Kilpatrick, who are both scholars and Cherokees.

I am red, as beautiful as the rainbow
Your heart has just been taken by me.

Your blood has been taken by me.
Your flesh has been taken by me.
Your eyes have been taken by me.
Your saliva has been taken by me.
Your saliva and mine are one forever
You are a wizard!

Prayer from Sioux Heyoka Ceremony

The Heyoka ceremony may only be performed by one who has received a vision from the thunder beings in the West. The purpose of the ceremony is to make people happier, to make them better appreciate the beauties of the world that they forget when they are sad. It involves the ritual killing of a dog, as offering to the Great Spirit along with prayers and joyful festivities.

This I burn as an offering.
Behold it!
A sacred praise I am making.
A sacred praise I am making.
My nation, behold it in kindness!
The day of the sun has been my strength.
The path of the moon shall be my robe.
A sacred praise I am making.
A sacred praise I am making.

A Vision of Handsome Lake

The Seneca are one of the Iroquoian tribes of upper New York state and lower Canada, who were very powerful in the Northeast until the late eighteenth century. Handsome Lake was the prophet of the new religion, which incorporated elements of ancient belief and ethics into new forms, with stress on principles of morality to offset the unhealthy trends of degeneration among the Iroquois as a result of their degradation at the hands of the whites.

The day was bright when I went into the planted field
Alone I wandered in the planted field

It was the time of the second hoeing

A maiden appeared and clasped me about the neck saying

When you leave this earth for the new world above
we want to follow you

I looked for the maiden
but saw only the long leaves of corn
twined round my shoulders

I understood it was the spirit of the corn   10
speaking
she the sustainer of life

I replied O spirit
follow me not

but remain here upon the earth
be strong and faithful to your purpose

Endure

Do not fail the children of women
It is not time for you to follow

The word I teach is only in the beginning   20

Zuñi Prayer

This poem is a prayer of the medicine cult of the Zuñi pueblo in New Mexico. It is a secret prayer said by a member of the cult.

My life-giving fathers,
At the place called since the first beginning Tcipia,
You dwell.

Where the deer stands,
At Dry place you dwell.
My fathers,
Life-giving priests, there you dwell.
This day,
Here at Itiwana,
Our daylight fathers,   10
Our mothers,
Our children,
In their inner rooms
For their fathers,
Life-giving priests,
Perpetuating the rite handed down since the first
    beginning,
Have spread out your cloud blanket,
Your life-giving road they have made.
Your spring they have made.
Perpetuating the rite handed down since the
    first beginning   20
You have sat down quietly before it;
At your back,
At your feet,
We shall sit down beside you.
Desiring your waters,

Your seeds,
Your riches,
Your long life,
Your old age,
Desiring these, I set you down quietly.   30
As you sit here quietly
As I wish, according to my words,
You will take us to be your children.
So that all my children
May be saved.
All will be happy.
Safely they will bring forth their young.
So that all my children may finish their roads,
So that they may grow old,
So that you may bless us with life,   40
So that none of my spring children
May be left standing outside.
So that you may protect us (I have done this).
May our roads be fulfilled;
May we grow old;
May our roads reach to dawn lake;
May we grow old;
May you bless us with life.

Osage Ritual

The Osage were a Scocian language tribe who lived on the edge of the plains in Missouri and Arkansas (who now reside in Oklahoma). One of the most important ceremonies an Osage child underwent was a ritual of child-naming. It was a long and involved ritual in which each child was given a ceremonial name that was referential to the mythology of the clan to which he belonged.

The ceremony chants were divided into sections called wigi-e, each one expressing a different tribal belief. The poem below is a section from the Life Symbol Taking Wigi-e, in which eight gods and goddesses are asked to give their bodies and strength to the children. It asks the evening star, who was considered to be a female deity, to give her body to the children of the Tsi-zhu Wanon war clan. The chief messenger in the poem is sent from the chief to each god and goddess with their pleas.

The ceremonies were originally transcribed and translated by Francis La Flesche, a member of the Osage tribe and an ethnologist for the USBAE.

The Chief Messenger
Hurried
to the star of Night (Evening Star), she
who sits in the heavens
and returned with her to our people
They spoke to her:
O grandmother
Our little ones have nothing
to make their bodies out of
so   10
The Star of Night said:
                    It is good
you sent for me
of all the groups of gods
I am a god by myself
The little ones shall make their bodies
from me
        and even the gods
won't be able to see the path
of their life's journey   20

Not even among the gods
is there anyone who has the power to cross my path
The little ones shall make their bodies
from my body
    and there will be no one
not even a god
who will be able to cross their path
in their life journey
For not even among the gods

is there one who can stand in front of me   30
and prevent me from going where I will
Let the little ones make their bodies
from my body
    and there will be no one
who can stop them from going where they will
And as I am not the only god
heed my words
and continue your search

Sioux Ghost Dance

The ghost dance was a late nineteenth-century
Indian millennarian movement, incorporating
elements of traditional religion and Christianity.
A Paiute, Wovoka, was its prophet; his vision
was of Christ, who told him that he had forsaken the whites for their cruelties and hypocri-
sies and that he had now become the messiah
of the Indians. The message for the Indians
was that if they lived morally, without whisky
and promiscuity, all the whites would die
through holocaust; America would return to the
state it had been in before the arrival of the
white men, and all Indians killed by them
would be resurrected.

Among many tribes, beaten, their old ways of
life no longer possible, the ghost dance was one
last hope that the whites could be destroyed
and harmony restored to the world. In the great
dances, many would fall down in a communal
vision of the new, redeemed earth sliding over
the present one of despair and sorrow, with
buffalo grazing and their dead standing there,
smiling and beckoning. Mothers who had
brought toys or tidbits to give children that
were dead would finally come to consciousness
and find the gifts still clutched in their hands.

The most recently subjugated tribes of the
Plains—Sioux, Cheyenne, and Arapaho—were
most excited by the new movement. Because
the Indians thought that the dance would make
them invulnerable to bullets and because the
whites feared the Sioux especially, the army
tried to ban the dance. The Sioux refusal to
stop precipitated the massacre at Wounded
Knee, in which some three hundred men,
women, and children died. This effectively dispelled Indian hopes for a miraculous victory
over the whites and the ghost dance died out
within ten years.

James Mooney, an ethnologist for the
USBAE, was sent out to investigate the ghost
dance among the various tribes that had adopted
it. He worked closely with the dancers and transcribed, translated, and described the songs and
philosophy of the movement.

The whole world is coming.
A nation is coming, a nation is coming,
The Eagle has brought the message to the tribe.
The father says so, the father says so.
Over the whole earth they are coming.
The buffalo are coming, the buffalo are coming,
The Crow has brought the message to the tribe,
The father says so, the father says so.

Two Arapaho Ghost Dances

These two Arapaho ghost dance songs show the
traditional elements that were present in the
new religion; an integral part of many Indian
religions, and especially Plains tribes like the
Arapaho, was the idea that men are pitiful and
completely helpless compared to God, the creator and spirit of all things.

This is one belief that was confirmed by the
realities of the lives of a subjugated peoples.
Songs such as these (there were many of them)

were sung to prepare the way for their redemption; in them was the hope for divine recognition and aid.

1

Father, have pity on me,
Father, have pity on me;
I am crying for thirst,
I am crying for thirst;
All is gone—I have nothing to eat,
All is gone—I have nothing to eat.

2

My children, my children,
It is I who wear the morning star on my head,
It is I who wear the morning star on my head;
I show it to my children,
I show it to my children,
Says the father,
Says the father.